THE INTERLINEAR
NASB⊢
NIV

PARALLEL
NEW TESTAMENT
IN GREEK
AND ENGLISH

THE INTERLINEAR
NASB⊨
NIV

PARALLEL
NEW TESTAMENT
IN GREEK
AND ENGLISH

INTERLINEAR TRANSLATION BY
ALFRED MARSHALL

ZondervanPublishingHouse
Grand Rapids, Michigan

A Division of HarperCollins*Publishers*

The Interlinear NASB/NIV Parallel New Testament in Greek and English
Copyright © 1993 by Zondervan Publishing House

Requests for information should be addressed to:
Zondervan Publishing House
Grand Rapids, Michigan 49530

Library of Congress Cataloging-in-Publication Data

Bible. N.T. English. New American Standard
The interlinear NASB–NIV parallel New Testament in Greek and English.
Includes Greek text and literal interlinear English translation of the New Testament.
1. Bible. N.T.—Interlinear translations, English. I. Marshall, Alfred. II. Bible. N.T.
English. New International. III. Bible. N.T. Greek.

ISBN 0-310-40170-4

Formerly published as The NASB-NIV Parallel New Testament in Greek and English, 1986.

Printed in the United States of America

05 06 07 08 /❖ DC/ 26 25 24 23 22 21

This edition is printed on acid-free paper and meets the American National Standards Institute
Z39.48 standard.

Introduction to the
Interlinear Greek Text and Translation

THE GREEK TEXT

THE text of the Greek New Testament has come down to us in various manuscripts, printing not being invented until the fifteenth century and Erasmus not publishing his Greek New Testament until 1516. Some of these manuscripts are more important than others (age not necessarily being indicative of importance). The study of the various manuscript copies, and the assessment of their individual value in attempting to reconstruct the original as nearly as possible, constitutes the science of textual criticism. For those who wish to study this seriously there are many books available; it is sufficient to say here that, after Erasmus, a great number of scholars have, over a long period, applied themselves to the task of constructing a reliable text out of the mass of various readings that have arisen from copying and making copies from copies of the old manuscripts (scholars such as Mill, Stephens, Griesbach, Lachmann, Tischendorf, Tregelles, and Alford).

The Greek text used in this book is that of the 21st edition of Eberhard Nestle's *Novum Testamentum Graece,* based on the study and critical research of generations of scholars, except that John 7:53–8:11 is not in that text but is relegated to the foot of the page as a critical note. It is here retained in the text. The critical notes of Nestle's work, which enable students to follow the reasons for variations in the text, have been omitted as being outside the scope of this publication. The student who requires these critical notes is referred to the Greek edition published in Great Britain by the British and Foreign Bible Society and in Germany (Stuttgart) by Privilegierte Württembergische Bibelanstalt, by whose permission this recension is used.

Square brackets are found in certain places in the Greek text.

These indicate only that, according to Nestle, some editors include and others omit the word or words so enclosed. Translation has been made here in the usual way.

Avoiding interpretation, then, we give some details of how we have proceeded in the matter of a literal translation. These should be studied and understood if proper use is to be made of this attempt to promote an intelligent reading of the Greek New Testament.

THE ENGLISH TRANSLATION

The Wording in General

The relationship between the Greek text and the interlinear English is as follows: Greek words not required in the translation into English are (a) represented by a short dash, as for example the definite article with proper names. Alternatively (b) italic type is used to show that words or even in some cases letters are not really needed for an idiomatic English rendering. For example, "man" is sometimes redundant (as in Matt. 20:1; Acts 2:22). On the other hand, words supplied in English for which there is no Greek equivalent are placed in square brackets [. . .]. Naturally, there will be differences of judgment as to this practice in the passages involved.

The modern form for the third person singular of verbs (present indicative) has been used (loves) in place of the now obsolete -(e)th (loveth); but the older "ye" has been retained for the nominative ("you" for the oblique cases) of the second person plural pronoun; and "thou" (thee), not "you," for the second person singular. It is a loss that in modern English these differences have disappeared; so unaccustomed are we now to them that even the average reader of the Authorized Version misses the point of Luke 22:31. The loss is even more to be regretted when God is addressed as "You."

Where some word other than the strictly literal one seems to be needed in the translation, the former is printed in parentheses immediately after the latter—e.g., Matthew 10:17, "beware from (of) men."

Occasionally it is not feasible to give a literal rendering without undue explanation; some idiomatic word or phrase has to be used. There are only a few of such passages, and they are indicated by the mark †.

There are a number of Greek phrases, other than where † is used, which are to be taken as a whole, not word for word:

ἐπὶ τὸ αὐτό = "on the same" = "together"
δια τοῦτο = "because-of this" = "therefore"
ἵνα μή = "in-order-that not" = "lest"
καθ' ὑπερβολήν = "by-way-of excess" = "excessively"

Εὐαγγελίζω. This and its cognate noun have been anglicized (evangelize, evangel). But while we can "evangelize" a city, we do not "evangelize" a person or a subject; so we must speak of "preaching (good tidings) to" a person or of "preaching" a subject. We can, of course, speak of "evangelizing" absolutely as in 1 Corinthians 1:17. Ellicott on 1 Thessalonians 3:6 has some useful information for the student.

Verbs

The ending of a Greek verb normally indicates the person (1st, 2nd, or 3rd, sing. or pl.). If the pronoun is separately expressed, this can be clearly seen in the interlinear translation.

Where there is more than one subject of a verb, Greek will often put the verb in the singular to agree with the nearest subject. This is not in accordance with English grammar, which requires a plural verb if there is more than one subject. In Revelation 9:2, "sun" and "air" call for the plural "were darkened," as in the Authorized Version. But the Greek verb is in the singular. It is sometimes typographically possible to indicate the difference of grammatical usage.

A peculiarity of Greek construction is that a neuter plural subject may take a singular verb; but this is by no means invariable, and there appears to be no rule to go by. In translating, the position is sometimes shown by the use of an italic letter for the ending of the verb ([they] commit*s*); at other times the alternative is given in parenthesis (is(are)). But there are places where neither course is possible without taking up too much space, and the matter is left to the intelligence of the reader.

The subjunctive mood is dying out in English, and no attempt has been made to represent consistently the Greek mood, except by the use of the analytic form "I may . . . ," with its related optative (of which latter there are only thirty-seven examples in the New Testament, fifteen of these being the familiar γένοιτο = "may it be"). But such words as ἵνα and compounds of ἄν (ὅταν, ἐάν), etc., introducing a subjective or hypothetical element into a verbal idea, must be followed by the subjunctive mood.

The Greek perfect can generally be taken as represented by an English present—a past action continuing in its effect down to the present, in contrast to an action wholly in the past. But in a literal translation the English perfect has been retained. In John 11:27, the Authorized Version is idiomatically correct, but the Revised Version is literally so (πεπίστευκα = "I have believed"); compare 2 Timothy 1:12, where the Authorized Version adopts the literal equivalent. So, for example, τετέλεσται = "it has been finished" = "it is finished." In participles, italics show that the auxiliary verbs may be dispensed with in English.   /

The interlinear translation has introduced a comma after "Behold" in a number of places. The reason for this is as follows. The Greek ἰδού (or other form), properly an imperative of the defective verb ὁράω, is used as an exclamation, as is its English equivalent. That is to say, it is not then an active verb taking a direct object in the accusative case; it is simply exclamatory and is followed by a noun in the nominative, with its predicate or complement understood. For example, in John 1:29, there is no command to behold the Lamb of God; instead, the idea is, "Look! [there goes]. . . ." The position is different in such passages as Matthew 28:6 and Romans 11:22, where there is a command.

Greek will often use a preposition in a compound verb and then repeat it (or use one similar) before a noun in the same sentence; in such passages the preposition would not be used twice in English. But in such a phrase as εἰσέρχεσθαι εἰς οἶκον we can say "to enter into a house" (the counterpart in French being *entrer dans une maison*). We can indeed say simply "to enter a house." Another exception would be ἀπέρχεσθαι ἀπό ("to go away from"). But διαφέρειν διὰ τοῦ ἱεροῦ means "to carry *through* through the temple" (e.g., Mark 11:16).

Necessity or compulsion is most frequently expressed by the use of an impersonal verb (or a verb used impersonally), with the person concerned in the accusative as the object of the verb (δεῖ με = "it behoves me" = "I must").

Participles

Greek is "a participle-loving language," said the late A. T. Robertson, and it uses this part of speech much more frequently than we do, and in different ways.

To begin with, it is absolutely essential to grasp the distinction between *continuous, momentary,* and *completed* action. The first is commonly, but wrongly, spoken of as a present participle, the second as an aorist (which does not mean "past"), and the third as a perfect. (There is a rare future participle—continuous in the future.)

1. A participle may be used as an adjective qualifying a noun,

just as in English (e.g., 1 Thess. 1:9—"a living God"; Heb. 7:8—"dying men"). This is so simple as not to need further remark.

2. A participle may be used, again as in English, as a verb to describe some action (e.g., Acts 9:39—"all the widows stood by . . . weeping and showing. . .").

3. A participle may be used, with the definite article, with, say, "one" understood, where we should use a noun or a relative phrase (e.g., frequently, ὁ πιστεύων = "the [one] believing" = "the believer" or "he who believes"). Here the participle is continuous; in Luke 1:45, it is momentary (and, naturally, feminine in gender, referring to Mary's one act of faith at the Annunciation). If two participles are used with but one definite article, as in John 5:24, the meaning is that one person is doubly described, not two persons doing two things. This feature has been preserved in our translation.

4. Very frequently indeed, where in English we use two or more finite verbs to describe associated actions, Greek will use participles and only one finite verb for the main action. But here judgment is necessary to distinguish two (or more) simultaneous actions from consecutive ones; and as we have no aorist participle in English the matter is not always free from difficulty. In Acts 10:34 ("Peter opening his mouth said") the two actions were obviously simultaneous! Likewise, Acts 1:24 ("Praying they said"). But sometimes one action must be completed before another could begin (e.g., Luke 22:17—"having given thanks, he said . . ."). Here the act of giving thanks to God would be complete before Jesus addressed His disciples; therefore the aorist participle must be represented in English by the analytic "having given thanks." That this is not unimportant is shown by Matthew 26:30 ("having sung a hymn they went out"). To translate the aorist participle here by "singing a hymn" would certainly convey the idea that the singing occurred as they went out. In Acts 21:14, it is not easy to see how the keeping silence and the saying could be contemporaneous ("Having said, The will of the Lord be done, we kept silence"). These few examples should, we think, suffice to show the principles involved.

Negatives

As the negatives οὐ(κ) (categorical) and μή (hypothetical) are easily recognizable, it has not been thought necessary always to render them separately, but they are included with any verb with which they may be used. But whereas in English the negative follows the verb, in Greek it precedes (e.g., Matt. 3:11). If such a phrase happens to be broken at the end of a line, this course has not been feasible.

The double negative οὐ μή has been consistently rendered "by no means."

Incidentally, though of importance, these two negative particles, or their compounds, when introducing questions, expect different answers. οὐ appeals to the fact, anticipating "Yes, it is so" (e.g., John 11:9, "Are there not twelve hours of the day?"). The answer would be "Yes, there are." On the contrary, μή denies the suggestion and expects the reply "No, it is not so"; or, if not so explicit as that, doubts whether it is so (e.g., John 18:35). The form of the question in the Authorized Version and the Revised Version indicates that Pilate was asking for information, whereas he was rejecting the idea with scorn and contempt—"I am not a Jew [am I]?" The answer, if any, would be—"No, certainly not." This distinction is largely overlooked in the English Versions. To assist to the correct nuance of thought, in such places the latter negative in the interlinear translation is italicized, and the reader must read into the original what is intended; the result is sometimes surprising. An article in *The Bible Translator* for January 1953 may be consulted.

While on the subject of negatives, Greek favors the use of two such, one strengthening the other. In such sentences the second negative has to be replaced in English by a positive (e.g., Matt. 22:46).

Nouns

In familiar proper names there will appear some inconsistency, a compromise between the actual spellings preferred by Nestle and the Authorized Version; but this is of no great importance.

In Greek, gender belongs to the word and not necessarily to what is indicated by the word; whereas, of course, in English we keep the ideas of masculine, feminine, and neuter to men, women, and inanimate things respectively—English, by the way, being the only great modern language to do so. Allowance must be made for this in translating; sometimes it is possible to transfer the idea from one language to another. The note to Revelation 13:1 may be consulted.

It has not been considered necessary always to indicate the order of a noun and its adjective; a knowledge of English is sufficient for this. But where there is any risk of ambiguity, small superior figures indicate the order in which the words should be read.

Adjectives

The construction of the demonstrative adjectives is peculiar in Greek. The definite article is used as well as the demonstrative adjective in one of two possible positions: either—

οὗτος ὁ οἶκος
this *the* house

or—

ὁ οἶκος οὗτος
the house this

The definite article is of course not wanted in English, and the proper translation of the phrase is obvious—"this house." Similarly ἐκεῖνος ("that"). It is sometimes possible typographically to treat the three-word phrase as a whole, with the idiomatic translation underneath.

There is no indefinite article in Greek. The use of it in translation is a matter of individual judgment. The numeral "one" is sometimes found; whether this means that just one, and no more, is to be understood is again open to argument (e.g., Matt. 21:19; 26:69). We have inserted "a" or "an" as a matter of course where it seems called for.

The definite article must sometimes be rendered by a pronoun or a possessive adjective. This is particularly so where parts of the body are indicated (e.g., Matt. 8:3). Sometimes it is used "pronominally"—that is, it must be rendered "he" (or otherwise according to the gender) or "they" (e.g., Mark 10:4).

Similarly, the definite article is used in Greek with a possessive adjective, as in Matthew 18:20—

εἰς τὸ ἐμὸν ὄνομα
in *the* my name

or, alternatively, the construction may be, say—

εἰς τὸ ὄνομα τὸ ἐμόν
in *the* name *the* my

This remark applies only to the first and second persons, singular and plural, not to the third, where the only possible construction in this respect would be "in the name of him/her/them." This has been followed literally, as the reader can always make the necessary English construction for himself. Occasionally such a construction as "in the name of me" will be found, meaning the same thing.

The neuter form of an adjective may be used as an adverb. In John 19:35, ἀληθῆ is the neuter of ἀληθής ("true") and must be rendered "truly." So πρῶτον ("firstly"), though "first" is quite often used in English as an adverb. Conversely, an adverb may be used as an adjective (e.g., νῦν, "now" = "present").

The word ταῦτα ("these things," neuter plural) might be rendered by the singular "this," as in the common phrase μετὰ ταῦτα ("after this"); but this liberty has not been taken in the present literal translation.

The gender of an adjective may demand "man," "woman," or "thing" to be supplied (e.g., Matt. 9:27—"two blind men").

There is the *genitive of quality,* of which there are many examples in the New Testament. If in English we say "a man of courage" or "an act of kindness," this is equivalent to "a courageous man" or "a kind act" respectively. We have translated literally, with an occasional footnote where this construction is not generally recognized.

As "first" is used as an adverb as well as "firstly," it has not been thought necessary always to print "first*ly*"; the matter is of no great importance.

Particles

A number of Greek particles are said to be "post-positive"— that is to say, they cannot stand as the first word in a sentence but are found in the second, third, or even the fourth place. Such words must of course be taken first in English; but it has not been thought necessary to show this, as the construction is sufficiently obvious. They include γάρ ("for"), δέ ("and, but, now"), οὖν ("therefore," which can be post-positive in English), τις (a certain), μέν (indeed), and γε ("really"—generally too subtle to be reproduced in English).

μέν . . . δέ. These two particles, in contrasted clauses, are not translatable literally, unless "indeed . . . but" be used, as we have done in some places. But by adopting the phrases "on the one hand . . . on the other" the contrast is brought out. These particles are, in fact, somewhat elusive as to their force. See John 19:24, 32, where μέν has been left untranslated—an example of the difficulty of rendering it satisfactorily in a literal translation.

The word ὅτι as a conjunction, when meaning "that," is used to introduce spoken words as recorded; it is then known as the "recitative ὅτι." In English the original present tense of any verb would in such a construction ("indirect speech") be changed to the past—e.g., "He said that the man was a liar." But Greek retains the original tense as actually used. What the speaker really said was "The man is a liar." The conjunction thus becomes superfluous and the reported words would in modern usage be put within quotation marks, as above. These, however, are not used in this translation (e.g., Matt. 21:3).

Strictly speaking, ἵνα is a "telic" particle—that is, it denotes purpose (τέλος, "an end"); hence a full translation is "in order that." But inasmuch as in New Testament times there was a tendency to use it where ὅτι would be expected, it sometimes means no more than the conjunction "that" (e.g., Matt. 5:29). Sometimes, then, where there may be room for difference of opinion as to its precise force, or even where there is none, "*in order* that" will be found in the literal translation.

Idiomatic constructions

There are five idiomatic Greek constructions that, being of frequent occurrence, call for explanation.

a. The *genitive absolute*. This is made up of a participle and a noun or pronoun, both in the genitive case and agreeing otherwise as well but having no grammatical relation to the context. It is used to indicate time during which, at which, or connected with which something takes place. The close of such a Greek phrase is shown by the superior letter ᵃ (e.g., Luke 3:1). There are variations of this. In Luke 12:36, two participles are used with no noun; it has to be supplied from the context. So also 2 Corinthians 7:15, and see the note on Romans 9:11 under "Notes on Particular Passages" below.

b. The *accusative* (or other case) *and infinitive*. Here what is in English the subject of the verb (the doer of the action) is put in the accusative (or other) case, and the verb itself is put in the infinitive. A superior letter ᵇ closes such a phrase (e.g., Luke 1:21).

c. The *dative of possession*. The possessor is put in the dative case. The idea may be grasped by comparing our English way of saying that a thing "belongs to so-and-so." The superior letter ᶜ shows this idiom (e.g., Luke 1:5, 7, 14).

d. The *genitive of purpose* or *result*. The infinitive of a verb is in the genitive case, as shown by the preceding definite article. The article itself can be ignored. Again the appropriate letter ᵈ shows the existence of the idiom (e.g., Matt. 2:13). The same idea can be shown without any article (e.g., Matt. 4:1).

e. The *dative of time*. This shows a point of time "in" or "at" which a thing happens (ἐν may or may not be used). The letter ᵉ indicates this (e.g., Luke 2:43; 18:35).

The constructions b and e can sometimes be combined (e.g., Luke 1:8).

NOTES ON PARTICULAR PASSAGES

Mark 10:11—An article by Dr. Nigel Turner in *The Bible Translator* for October 1956 gives good reasons for understanding the verse thus, αὐτήν referring to the last woman mentioned (ἄλλην).

Mark 14:6—The ἐν here is somewhat puzzling. The parallel in Matthew (26:10) has εἰς, which would mean "to," "toward," or "for"; and Mark's ἐν must then be taken as equivalent in meaning to εἰς. This may throw light on 1 John 4:16.

Luke 7:14—It does not seem right to insist here on the passive voice of ἐγέρθητι (cf. 8:54 and, in another connection, 11:8). But our Lord "was raised," as are the dead generally; they do not "rise"; (see 1 Cor. 15, etc.).

John 8:25—"The answer of Jesus is one of the most disputed passages in the Gospel" (Godet). Nestle punctuates as a question; hence we have given what appears to be a reasonable rendering interrogatively.

Acts 7:46—The word οἴκῳ is a manuscript variant for θεῷ. There is some uncertainty as to how this reading arose; see the Authorized Version. Has Psalm 24:6, text and margin, any bearing on the matter?

Acts 18:10—The words λαὸς πολύς must not be understood as meaning "many persons." λαός is the regular word for the chosen people, Israel (almost without exception). Here in Corinth was to be a new community, taking the place of the Jewish population. So translate it "a great people."

Romans 1:12—This refers to their faith (= "confidence") in one another—Paul and his readers. "Mutual" is correct in Authorized Version, but it is generally misunderstood as being equivalent to "common," which it is not.

Romans 9:11—There is no noun agreeing with the two participles. But it is nevertheless a "genitive absolute" construction. The Authorized Version supplies the subject.

2 Corinthians 11:28—There is another view of Paul's words here. The word ἐπίστασις occurs in the New Testament only here and in Acts 24:12. The related noun ἐπιστάτης ("one standing over,"

"superintendent," "master") is peculiar to Luke (six times in his Gospel). Then there is a variant reading in our verse, μου instead of μοι. So the meaning may be—"my daily superintendence *or* attention." This would bring it into line with the remainder of the verse.

Philippians 3:16—This is, according to Burton, the only certain use in the New Testament of the "imperatival infinitive," Romans 12:15 being a probable example. Moulton thinks it highly probable in Titus 2:1–10. The epistolary χαίρειν (Acts 15:23; 23:26; James 1:1) is said to be the same in origin, though a verb of bidding may be assumed, as in fact we do find in 2 John 10, 11. Compare the French warning in railway carriages—*Ne pas se pencher au dehors*. In English we have such a full expression as "You are 'to do' so and so" (e.g., 2 Thess. 3:14). If Nestle's text is accepted here, it is an additional instance to those given under Philippians 3:16 above, though with a negative as a prohibition. (Textus Receptus, etc., give a plain imperative.) But perhaps we may insert "so as" ("mark this man, so as not to mix with him").

2 Timothy 4:3—The construction of the last three words of this verse is difficult. "Having itching ears" may be a workable paraphrase, but it cannot be said to represent literally the actual Greek. There is no word for "having"; and there is nothing corresponding to "itching" as a participial adjective qualifying "ears." τὴν ἀκοήν is accusative singular, the object of a verb—and the only verb is the participle that precedes. This is masculine plural, agreeing with διδασκάλους, and, while this latter is accusative, whereas the participle is nominative, this must be taken as an example of rational rather than grammatical concord. It is the teachers who "tickle" the ears of those concerned.

Hebrews 2:10—That is, it is God who perfected Jesus Christ (the author, or captain, of our salvation) by means of sufferings, whose work it is to lead many sons to glory; ἀγαγόντα ("leading," referring to Jesus) agrees with ἀρχηγόν, not with αὐτῷ ("him," i.e., God). Besides, there is a parallel between Joshua and Jesus, as both leaders of their peoples. In fine, it is the function of a captain to lead, and Jesus is the leader here.

Hebrews 9:16–17—We are aware of the problem in regard to διαθήκη in this passage; but this translation is no place for purporting to settle a question that has divided commentators. It must suffice to say that we have translated the word consistently as "covenant"; the idea of a legatee receiving something on the death of a testator by reason of the latter's having made a "testament" or "will" is, so far as we can see, quite non-biblical. The covenant victim, then, is "the one making covenant," unless the person establishing the covenant is to be understood as identifying himself with it; and the covenant is in fact ratified over the dead body or bodies. But other views are taken of the matter.

James 2:1—This is an example of two genitives in apposition. There are other instances of such a construction. In Colossians 1:18, the meaning must be "of the body (,) *of* the church"—the body is the church, as verse 24 says. Colossians 2:2 has "of God, of Christ." For Romans 11:17, see the note at that place. Regarding John 8:44 ("of the father (,) *of* the devil"), their father was the Devil.

Revelation 16:14—The word "Almighty" is not an adjective but another noun in apposition.

NOTE on Matthew 16:3; 27:65; Luke 12:56; Acts 21:37; 1 Thessalonians 4:4; 1 Timothy 3:5; James 4:17; 2 Peter 2:9—As in French, so in the Greek of the New Testament, we have the idea of "to know (how) to do" a thing as being the same as "to be able to do" it. But while the French use only *savoir*, not *connaître*, in this way, both γινώσκω and οἶδα have this meaning in the New Testament. In fact, it is the former in Matthew 16:3 and the latter in the parallel in Luke (12:56). So, in French, *Savez-vous nager?* = Know you to swim? = Can you swim? In all the above passages this seems to be the meaning. It may be noted that the Authorized Version so renders the verbs in some passages, in others giving "know how." The instance in James 4:17 may be arguable. Philippians 4:12 also may be considered, and Matthew 7:11 = Luke 11:13.

The New American Standard Bible

SCRIPTURAL PROMISE

"The grass withers, the flower fades, but the word of our God stands forever." Isaiah 40:8

FOREWORD

The New American Standard Bible has been produced with the conviction that the words of Scripture as originally penned in the Hebrew, Aramaic, and Greek were inspired by God. Since they are the eternal Word of God, the Holy Scriptures speak with fresh power to each generation, to give wisdom that leads to salvation, that men may serve Christ to the glory of God.

The Editorial Board had a twofold purpose in making this translation: to adhere as closely as possible to the original languages of the Holy Scriptures, and to make the translation in a fluent and readable style according to current English usage.

THE FOURFOLD AIM
OF
THE LOCKMAN FOUNDATION

1. These publications shall be true to the original Hebrew, Aramaic, and Greek.
2. They shall be grammatically correct.
3. They shall be understandable to the masses.
4. They shall give the Lord Jesus Christ His proper place, the place which the Word gives Him; therefore, no work will ever be personalized.

PREFACE TO THE
NEW AMERICAN STANDARD BIBLE

In the history of English Bible translations, the King James Version is the most prestigious. This time-honored version of 1611, itself a revision of the Bishops' Bible of 1568, became the basis for the English Revised Version appearing in 1881 (New Testament) and 1885 (Old Testament). The American counterpart of this last work was published in 1901 as the American Standard Version. Recognizing the values of the American Standard Version, the Lockman Foundation felt an urgency to update it by incorporating recent discoveries of Hebrew and Greek textual sources and by rendering it into more current English. Therefore, in 1959 a new translation project was launched, based on the ASV. The result is the New American Standard Bible.

The American Standard Version (1901) has been highly regarded for its scholarship and accuracy. A product of both British and American scholarship, it has frequently been used as a standard for other translations. It is still recognized as a valuable tool for study of the Scriptures. The New American Standard Bible has sought to preserve these and other lasting values of the ASV.

Furthermore, in the preparation of this work numerous other translations have been consulted along with the linguistic tools and literature of biblical scholarship. Decisions about English renderings were made by consensus of a team composed of educators and pastors. Subsequently, review and evaluation by other Hebrew and Greek scholars outside the Editorial Board were sought and carefully considered.

The Editorial Board has continued to function since publication of the complete Bible in 1971. Minor revisions and refinements, recommended over the last several years, are presented in this edition.

PRINCIPLES OF TRANSLATION

MODERN ENGLISH USAGE: The attempt has been made to render the grammar and terminology in contemporary English. When it was felt that the word-for-word literalness was unacceptable to the modern reader, a change was made in the direction of a more current English idiom. In the instances where this has been done, the more literal rendering has been indicated in the notes.

ALTERNATIVE READINGS: In addition to the more literal renderings, notations have been made to include alternate translations, readings of variant manuscripts and explanatory equivalents of the text. Only such notations have been used as have been felt justified in assisting the reader's comprehension of the terms used by the original author.

GREEK TEXT: Consideration was given to the latest available manuscripts with a view to determining the best Greek text. In most instances the 23rd edition of Eberhard Nestle's NOVUM TESTAMENTUM GRAECE was followed.

GREEK TENSES: A careful distinction has been made in the treatment of the Greek aorist tense (usually translated as the English past, "He did") and the Greek imperfect tense (rendered either as English past progressive, "He was doing"; or, if inceptive, as "He *began* to do" or "He started to do"; or else if customary past, as "He used to do"). "Began" is italicized if it renders an imperfect tense, in order to distinguish it from the Greek verb for "begin."

On the other hand, not all aorists have been rendered as English pasts ("He did"), for some of them are clearly to be rendered as English perfects ("He has done"), or even as past perfects ("He had done"), judging from the context in which they occur. Such aorists have been rendered as perfects or past perfects in this translation.

As for the distinction between aorist and present imperatives, the translators have usually rendered these imperatives in the customary manner, rather than attempting any such fine distinction as "Begin to do!" (for the aorist imperative) or "Continually do!" (for the present imperative).

As for sequence of tenses, the translators took care to follow English rules rather than Greek in translating Greek presents, imperfects, and aorists. Thus, where English says, "We knew that he was doing," Greek puts it, "We knew that he does"; similarly, "We knew that he had done" is the Greek, "We knew that he did." Likewise, the English, "When he had come, they met him," is represented in Greek by: "When he came, they met him." In all cases a consistent transfer has been made from the Greek tense in the subordinate clause to the appropriate tense in English.

In the rendering of negative questions introduced by the particle **mē** (which always expects the answer "No") the wording has been altered from a mere, "Will he not do this?" to a more accurate, "He will not do this, will he?"

Explanation of
GENERAL FORMAT

FOOTNOTES are used only where the text especially requires them for clarification. Marginal notes and cross references have been deleted from this edition.

PARAGRAPHS are designated by bold face numbers or letters.

QUOTATION MARKS are used in the text in accordance with modern English usage.

"THOU," "THEE," and "THY" are not used in this translation except in the language of prayer when addressing Deity.

PERSONAL PRONOUNS are capitalized when pertaining to Deity.

ITALICS are used in the text to indicate words which are not found in the original Hebrew, Aramaic, or Greek but implied by it. Italics are used in the footnotes to signify alternate readings for the text.

SMALL CAPS in the New Testament are used in the text to indicate Old Testament quotations or obvious allusions to Old Testament texts. Variations of Old Testament wording are found in New Testament citations depending on whether the New Testament writer translated from a Hebrew text, used existing Greek or Aramaic translations, or paraphrased the material. It should be noted that modern rules for the indication of direct quotation were not used in biblical times, thus allowing freedom for omissions or insertions without specific indication of these.

ASTERISKS are used to mark verbs that are historical presents in the Greek which have been translated with an English past tense in order to conform to modern usage. The translators recognized that in some contexts the present tense seems more unexpected and unjustified to the English reader than a past tense would have been. But Greek authors frequently used the present tense for the sake of heightened vividness, thereby transporting their readers in imagination to the actual scene at the time of occurrence. However, the translators felt that it would be wise to change these historical presents to English past tenses.

ABBREVIATIONS AND SPECIAL MARKINGS

Aram. = Aramaic

Gr. = Greek translation of O.T. (Septuagint, or LXX) or Greek text of N.T.

Lit. = A literal translation

Or = An alternate translation justified by the Hebrew, Aramaic, or Greek

[ ] = In text, brackets indicate words probably not in the original writings

cf. = compare

ms., mss. = manuscript, manuscripts

v., vv. = verse, verses

The New International Version

The New International Version of the New Testament, first published in 1973, is a completely new translation made by many scholars working directly from the Greek. The Greek text used in the work of translation was an eclectic one. Where existing texts differ, the translators made their choice of readings in accord with sound principles of textual criticism. Footnotes call attention to places where there was uncertainty about what constituted the original text. These have been introduced by the phrase "Some MSS add (*or* omit *or* read)."

As in all translations of the Scriptures, the precise meaning of the original text could not in every case be determined. In important instances of this kind, footnotes introduced by "Or" suggest an alternate rendering of the text. In the translation itself, brackets were occasionally used to indicate words or phrases supplied for clarification.

Certain convictions and aims guided the translators. They were all committed to the full authority and complete trustworthiness of the Scriptures. Therefore, their first concern was the accuracy of the translation and its fidelity to the thought of the New Testament writers. While they weighed the significance of the lexical and grammatical details of the Greek text, they strove for more than a word-for-word translation. Because thought patterns and syntax differ from language to language, faithful communication of the meaning of the writers of the New Testament demanded frequent modifications in sentence structure and constant regard for the contextual meanings of words.

Concern for clarity of style—that it should be idiomatic without being idiosyncratic, contemporary without being dated—also motivated the translators and their consultants. They consistently aimed at simplicity of expression, with sensitive attention to the connotation and sound of the chosen word. At the same time, they endeavored to avoid a sameness of style in order to reflect the varied styles and moods of the New Testament writers.

As for the omission of the pronouns "thou," "thee," and

"thine" in reference to the Deity, the translators felt that to retain these archaisms (along with the strange verb forms, such as *doest, wouldest,* and *hadst*) would have violated their aim of faithful translation. The Greek text uses no special pronouns to express reverence for God and Christ. Scripture is not enhanced by keeping, as a special mode of addressing Deity, forms that in the day of the King James Bible were simply the regular pronouns and verbs used in everyday speech, whether referring to God or to man.

The Greek Alphabet

A	α	Alpha	a	
B	β	Beta	b	
Γ	γ	Gamma	g	hard, as in be*g*in[1]
Δ	δ	Delta	d	
E	ε	Epsilon	e	short, as in m*e*t
Z	ζ	Zeta	z	
H	η	Eta	e	long, as in sc*e*ne
Θ	θ	Theta	th	as in *th*in
I	ι	Iota	i	
K	κ	Kappa	k	
Λ	λ	Lambda	l	
M	μ	Mu	m	
N	ν	Nu	n	
Ξ	ξ	Xi	x	
O	o	Omicron	o	short, as in l*o*t
Π	π	Pi	p	
P	ρ	Rho	r	
Σ	σ, *final s*	Sigma	s[2]	
T	τ	Tau	t	
Υ	υ	Upsilon	u	
Φ	φ	Phi	ph	
X	χ	Chi	ch	hard, as in lo*ch*
Ψ	ψ	Psi	ps	
Ω	ω	Omega	o	long, as in thr*o*ne

[1]Except that before κ, χ or another γ, it is nasal—ng, as in a*n*chor.
[2]Sharp as in thi*s*, but flat before β or μ, as in a*s*bestos, di*s*mal.

The left-hand column contains the NASB text, the right-hand column, the NIV text.

Chapter 1

Genealogy of Jesus Christ

THE book of the genealogy of Jesus Christ, the son of David, the son of Abraham.

2To Abraham was born Isaac; and to Isaac, Jacob; and to Jacob, ᵃJudah and his brothers;

3and to Judah were born Perez and Zerah by Tamar; and to Perez was born Hezron; and to Hezron, Ram;

4and to Ram was born Amminadab; and to Amminadab, Nahshon; and to Nahshon, Salmon;

5and to Salmon was born Boaz by Rahab; and to Boaz was born Obed by Ruth; and to Obed, Jesse;

6and to Jesse was born David the king.

And to David was born Solomon by her *who had been the wife* of Uriah;

7and to Solomon was born Rehoboam; and to Rehoboam, Abijah; and to Abijah, Asa;

8and to Asa was born Jehoshaphat; and to Jehoshaphat, Joram; and to Joram, Uzziah;

9and to Uzziah was born Jotham; and to Jotham, Ahaz; and to Ahaz, Hezekiah;

10and to Hezekiah was born Manasseh; and to Manasseh, Amon; and to Amon, Josiah;

11and to Josiah were born Jeconiah and his brothers, at the time of the deportation to Babylon.

12And after the deportation to Babylon, to Jeconiah was born Shealtiel; and to Shealtiel, Zerubbabel;

13and to Zerubbabel was born Abiud; and to Abiud, Eliakim; and to Eliakim,

ᵃ Gr., *Judas*. Names of Old Testament characters will be given in their Old Testament form.

---

1 Βίβλος γενέσεως Ἰησοῦ Χριστοῦ
[The] book of [the] generation of Jesus Christ
υἱοῦ Δαυὶδ υἱοῦ Ἀβραάμ.
son of David son of Abraham.

2 Ἀβραὰμ ἐγέννησεν τὸν Ἰσαάκ, Ἰσαὰκ δὲ
Abraham begat - Isaac, and Isaac
ἐγέννησεν τὸν Ἰακώβ, Ἰακὼβ δὲ ἐγέννησεν τὸν
begat - Jacob, and Jacob begat -
Ἰούδαν καὶ τοὺς ἀδελφοὺς αὐτοῦ, 3 Ἰούδας δὲ
Judas and the brothers of him, and Judas
ἐγέννησεν τὸν Φάρες καὶ τὸν Ζάρα ἐκ τῆς
begat - Phares and - Zara out of the
Θαμάρ, Φάρες δὲ ἐγέννησεν τὸν Ἐσρώμ,
Thamar, and Phares begat - Esrom,
Ἐσρὼμ δὲ ἐγέννησεν τὸν Ἀράμ, 4 Ἀρὰμ δὲ
and Esrom begat - Aram, and Aram
ἐγέννησεν τὸν Ἀμιναδάβ, Ἀμιναδὰβ δὲ
begat - Aminadab, and Aminadab
ἐγέννησεν τὸν Ναασσών, Ναασσὼν δὲ ἐγέννησεν
begat - Naasson, and Naasson begat
τὸν Σαλμών, 5 Σαλμὼν δὲ ἐγέννησεν τὸν Βόες
- Salmon, and Salmon begat - Booz
ἐκ τῆς Ῥαχάβ, Βόες δὲ ἐγέννησεν τὸν Ἰωβὴδ
out of - Rachab, and Booz begat - Obed
ἐκ τῆς Ῥούθ, Ἰωβὴδ δὲ ἐγέννησεν τὸν Ἰεσσαί,
out of - Ruth, and Obed begat - Jesse,
6 Ἰεσσαὶ δὲ ἐγέννησεν τὸν Δαυὶδ τὸν βασιλέα.
and Jesse begat - David the king.
Δαυὶδ δὲ ἐγέννησεν τὸν Σολομῶνα ἐκ τῆς
And David begat - Solomon out of the
τοῦ Οὐρίου, 7 Σολομὼν δὲ ἐγέννησεν
[one who had been the wife]- of Uriah, and Solomon begat
τὸν Ῥοβοάμ, Ῥοβοὰμ δὲ ἐγέννησεν τὸν
- Roboam, and Roboam begat -
Ἀβιά, Ἀβιὰ δὲ ἐγέννησεν τὸν Ἀσάφ, 8 Ἀσὰφ
Abia, and Abia begat - Asaph, and Asaph
δὲ ἐγέννησεν τὸν Ἰωσαφάτ, Ἰωσαφὰτ δὲ
begat - Josaphat, and Josaphat
ἐγέννησεν τὸν Ἰωράμ, Ἰωρὰμ δὲ ἐγέννησεν τὸν
begat - Joram, and Joram begat -
Ὀζίαν, 9 Ὀζίας δὲ ἐγέννησεν τὸν Ἰωαθάμ,
Ozias, and Ozias begat - Joatham,
Ἰωαθὰμ δὲ ἐγέννησεν τὸν Ἀχάζ, Ἀχὰζ δὲ
and Joatham begat - Achaz, and Achaz
ἐγέννησεν τὸν Ἐζεκίαν, 10 Ἐζεκίας δὲ
begat - Hezekias, and Hezekias
ἐγέννησεν τὸν Μανασσῆ, Μανασσῆς δὲ ἐγέννησεν
begat - Manasses, and Manasses begat
τὸν Ἀμώς, Ἀμὼς δὲ ἐγέννησεν τὸν Ἰωσίαν,
- Amos, and Amos begat - Josias,
11 Ἰωσίας δὲ ἐγέννησεν τὸν Ἰεχονίαν καὶ
and Josias begat - Jechonias and
τοὺς ἀδελφοὺς αὐτοῦ ἐπὶ τῆς μετοικεσίας
the brothers of him at the deportation
Βαβυλῶνος. 12 Μετὰ δὲ τὴν μετοικεσίαν
of Babylon. And after the deportation
Βαβυλῶνος Ἰεχονίας ἐγέννησεν τὸν Σαλαθιήλ,
of Babylon Jechonias begat - Salathiel,
Σαλαθιὴλ δὲ ἐγέννησεν τὸν Ζοροβαβέλ,
and Salathiel begat - Zorobabel,
13 Ζοροβαβὲλ δὲ ἐγέννησεν τὸν Ἀβιούδ,
and Zorobabel begat - Abiud,
Ἀβιοὺδ δὲ ἐγέννησεν τὸν Ἐλιακίμ, Ἐλιακὶμ δὲ
and Abiud begat - Eliakim, and Eliakim

Chapter 1

The Genealogy of Jesus

A RECORD of the genealogy of Jesus Christ the son of David, the son of Abraham:

2Abraham was the father of Isaac,
Isaac the father of Jacob,
Jacob the father of Judah and his brothers,
3Judah the father of Perez and Zerah, whose mother was Tamar,
Perez the father of Hezron,
Hezron the father of Ram,
4Ram the father of Amminadab,
Amminadab the father of Nahshon,
Nahshon the father of Salmon,
5Salmon the father of Boaz, whose mother was Rahab,
Boaz the father of Obed, whose mother was Ruth,
Obed the father of Jesse,
6and Jesse the father of King David.

David was the father of Solomon, whose mother had been Uriah's wife,
7Solomon the father of Rehoboam,
Rehoboam the father of Abijah,
Abijah the father of Asa,
8Asa the father of Jehoshaphat,
Jehoshaphat the father of Jehoram,
Jehoram the father of Uzziah,
9Uzziah the father of Jotham,
Jotham the father of Ahaz,
Ahaz the father of Hezekiah,
10Hezekiah the father of Manasseh,
Manasseh the father of Amon,
Amon the father of Josiah,
11and Josiah the father of Jeconiahᵃ and his brothers at the time of the exile to Babylon.

12After the exile to Babylon:
Jeconiah was the father of Shealtiel,
Shealtiel the father of Zerubbabel,
13Zerubbabel the father of Abiud,
Abiud the father of Eliakim,
Eliakim the father of

ᵃ11 That is, Jehoiachin; also in verse 12

Azor;
14and to Azor was born Zadok; and to Zadok, Achim; and to Achim, Eliud;

15and to Eliud was born Eleazar; and to Eleazar, Matthan; and to Matthan, Jacob;

16and to Jacob was born Joseph the husband of Mary, by whom was born Jesus, who is called Christ.

17Therefore all the generations from Abraham to David are fourteen generations; and from David to the deportation to Babylon fourteen generations; and from the deportation to Babylon to *the time of* Christ fourteen generations.

Conception and Birth of Jesus

18Now the birth of Jesus Christ was as follows. When His mother Mary had been betrothed to Joseph, before they came together she was found to be with child by the Holy Spirit.

19And Joseph her husband, being a righteous man, and not wanting to disgrace her, desired *b*to put her away secretly.

20But when he had considered this, behold, an angel of the Lord appeared to him in a dream, saying, "Joseph, son of David, do not be afraid to take Mary as your wife; for that which has been cconceived in her is of the Holy Spirit.

21"And she will bear a Son; and you shall call His name Jesus, for it is He who will save His people from their sins."

22Now all this took place that what was spoken by the Lord through the prophet might be fulfilled, saying,

23"BEHOLD, THE VIRGIN SHALL BE WITH CHILD, AND SHALL BEAR A SON, AND

*b*Or, to divorce her
*c*Lit., begotten

ἐγέννησεν τὸν Ἀζώρ, 14 Ἀζὼρ δὲ ἐγέννησεν
begat   -   Azor,   and Azor   begat

τὸν Σαδώκ, Σαδὼκ δὲ ἐγέννησεν τὸν Ἀχίμ,
-   Sadoc,   and Sadoc   begat   -   Achim,

Ἀχὶμ δὲ ἐγέννησεν τὸν Ἐλιούδ, 15 Ἐλιοὺδ δὲ
and Achim   begat   -   Eliud,   and Eliud

ἐγέννησεν τὸν Ἐλεαζάρ, Ἐλεαζὰρ δὲ ἐγέννησεν
begat   -   Eleazar,   and Eleazar   begat

τὸν Ματθάν, Ματθὰν δὲ ἐγέννησεν τὸν Ἰακώβ,
-   Matthan,   and Matthan   begat   -   Jacob,

16 Ἰακὼβ δὲ ἐγέννησεν τὸν Ἰωσὴφ τὸν ἄνδρα
and Jacob   begat   -   Joseph   the husband

Μαρίας, ἐξ ἧς ἐγεννήθη Ἰησοῦς ὁ λεγόμενος
of Mary, of whom   was born   Jesus   the [one]   called

Χριστός.
Christ.

17 Πᾶσαι οὖν αἱ γενεαὶ ἀπὸ Ἀβραὰμ
Therefore all   the generations from   Abraham

ἕως Δαυὶδ γενεαὶ δεκατέσσαρες, καὶ ἀπὸ
until David generations   fourteen,   and   from

Δαυὶδ ἕως τῆς μετοικεσίας Βαβυλῶνος γενεαὶ
David until   the   deportation of Babylon generations

δεκατέσσαρες, καὶ ἀπὸ τῆς μετοικεσίας Βαβυ-
fourteen,   and from   the   deportation   of Baby-

λῶνος ἕως τοῦ Χριστοῦ γενεαὶ δεκατέσσαρες.
lon   until   the   Christ generations fourteen.

18 Τοῦ δὲ Ἰησοῦ Χριστοῦ ἡ γένεσις
- Now   ²of Jesus   ³Christ   ¹the   ⁵birth

οὕτως ἦν. μνηστευθείσης τῆς μητρὸς αὐτοῦ
⁴thus   ⁶was.   Being betrothed   the   mother   of him
=When his mother Mary was betrothed

Μαρίας τῷ Ἰωσήφ, πρὶν ἢ συνελθεῖν αὐτούς,
Mary*   -   to Joseph,   before to come together themᵇ
=before they came together

εὑρέθη ἐν γαστρὶ ἔχουσα ἐκ πνεύματος
¹she was found ³in   ⁴womb   ²having of(by)[the]   Spirit
= she was pregnant

ἁγίου. 19 Ἰωσὴφ δὲ ὁ ἀνὴρ αὐτῆς,
Holy.   Now Joseph   the   husband   of her,

δίκαιος ὢν καὶ μὴ θέλων αὐτὴν δειγμα-
¹just   ¹being and   not   wishing   her   to hold up as an

τίσαι, ἐβουλήθη λάθρα ἀπολῦσαι αὐτήν.
example,   resolved   secretly   to dismiss   her.

20 ταῦτα δὲ αὐτοῦ ἐνθυμηθέντος, ἰδοὺ
But these things   him   thinking on,*   behold
=while he thought on these things,

ἄγγελος κυρίου κατ᾽ ὄναρ ἐφάνη
an angel   of [the] Lord   by   a dream   appeared

αὐτῷ λέγων· Ἰωσὴφ υἱὸς Δαυίδ, μὴ
to him   saying: Joseph   son   of David,   ²not

φοβηθῇς παραλαβεῖν Μαρίαν τὴν
¹fear thou   to take   Mary   the

γυναῖκά σου· τὸ γὰρ ἐν αὐτῇ γεννηθὲν
wife   of thee: for the thing in   her   begotten

ἐκ πνεύματός ἐστιν ἁγίου. 21 τέξεται δὲ
²of ⁴[the] ⁵Spirit   ¹is   ⁶Holy.   And she will bear

υἱόν, καὶ καλέσεις τὸ ὄνομα αὐτοῦ
a son,   and   thou shalt call   the   name   of him

Ἰησοῦν· αὐτὸς γὰρ σώσει τὸν λαὸν
Jesus;   for he   will save   the   people

αὐτοῦ ἀπὸ τῶν ἁμαρτιῶν αὐτῶν. 22 Τοῦτο δὲ
of him from   the   sins   of them.   Now ²this

ὅλον γέγονεν ἵνα πληρωθῇ τὸ ῥηθὲν
¹all has occurred in order that might be fulfilled the [thing] spoken

ὑπὸ κυρίου διὰ τοῦ προφήτου λέγοντος·
by   [the] Lord through   the   prophet   saying:

23 ἰδοὺ ἡ παρθένος ἐν γαστρὶ ἕξει
Behold   the   virgin   ²in   ³womb ¹will have

Azor,
14Azor the father of Zadok,
Zadok the father of Akim,
Akim the father of Eliud,

15Eliud the father of Eleazar,
Eleazar the father of Matthan,
Matthan the father of Jacob,

16and Jacob the father of Joseph, the husband of Mary, of whom was born Jesus, who is called Christ.

17Thus there were fourteen generations in all from Abraham to David, fourteen from David to the exile to Babylon, and fourteen from the exile to the Christ. *b*

The Birth of Jesus Christ

18This is how the birth of Jesus Christ came about: His mother Mary was pledged to be married to Joseph, but before they came together, she was found to be with child through the Holy Spirit. 19Because Joseph her husband was a righteous man and did not want to expose her to public disgrace, he had in mind to divorce her quietly.

20But after he had considered this, an angel of the Lord appeared to him in a dream and said, "Joseph son of David, do not be afraid to take Mary home as your wife, because what is conceived in her is from the Holy Spirit. 21She will give birth to a son, and you are to give him the name Jesus, *c* because he will save his people from their sins."

22All this took place to fulfill what the Lord had said through the prophet: 23"The virgin will be with child and will give birth to a son, and they will call

b17 Or *Messiah*. "The Christ" (Greek) and "the Messiah" (Hebrew) both mean "the Anointed One."
c21 Jesus is the Greek form of *Joshua,* which means *the LORD saves.*

THEY SHALL CALL HIS NAME IMMANUEL,'' which translated means, ''GOD WITH US.''

24And Joseph arose from his sleep, and did as the angel of the Lord commanded him, and took *her* as his wife,

25and *d*kept her a virgin until she gave birth to a Son; and he called His name Jesus.

καὶ τέξεται υἱόν, καὶ καλέσουσιν τὸ
and will bear a son, and they will call the

ὄνομα αὐτοῦ 'Εμμανουήλ, ὅ ἐστιν
name of him Emmanuel, which is

μεθερμηνευόμενον μεθ' ἡμῶν ὁ θεός.
being interpreted with us - God.

24 ἐγερθεὶς δὲ [ὁ] 'Ιωσὴφ ἀπὸ τοῦ
Then ²being raised - ¹Joseph from the(his)

ὕπνου ἐποίησεν ὡς προσέταξεν αὐτῷ ὁ
sleep did as bade him the

ἄγγελος κυρίου, καὶ παρέλαβεν τὴν
angel of [the] Lord, and took the

γυναῖκα αὐτοῦ· 25 καὶ οὐκ ἐγίνωσκεν
wife of him; and knew not

αὐτὴν ἕως [οὗ] ἔτεκεν υἱόν· καὶ ἐκάλεσεν
her until she bore a son; and he called

τὸ ὄνομα αὐτοῦ 'Ιησοῦν.
the name of him Jesus.

---

him Immanuel''*d*—which means, ''God with us.''

24When Joseph woke up, he did what the angel of the Lord had commanded him and took Mary home as his wife. 25But he had no union with her until she gave birth to a son. And he gave him the name Jesus.

Chapter 2

Visit of the Wise Men

NOW after Jesus was born in Bethlehem of Judea in the days of Herod the king, behold, *e* magi from the east arrived in Jerusalem, saying,

2''Where is He who has been born King of the Jews? For we saw His star in the east, and have come to worship Him.''

3And when Herod the king heard it, he was troubled, and all Jerusalem with him.

4And gathering together all the chief priests and scribes of the people, he *began* to inquire of them where the Christ was to be born.

5And they said to him, ''In Bethlehem of Judea, for so it has been written by the prophet,

6 'AND YOU, BETH-LEHEM, LAND OF JUDAH,
ARE BY NO MEANS LEAST AMONG THE LEADERS OF JUDAH;
FOR OUT OF YOU SHALL COME FORTH A RULER,
WHO WILL SHEPHERD MY PEOPLE ISRAEL.' ''

7Then Herod secretly called the magi, and ascertained from them the time the star appeared.

8And he sent them to Bethlehem, and said, ''Go

---

2 Τοῦ δὲ 'Ιησοῦ γεννηθέντος ἐν Βηθλέεμ
- Now Jesus having been born* in Bethlehem
=when Jesus was born

τῆς 'Ιουδαίας ἐν ἡμέραις 'Ηρῴδου τοῦ
- of Judæa in [the] days of Herod the

βασιλέως, ἰδοὺ μάγοι ἀπὸ ἀνατολῶν
king, behold magi from [the] east

παρεγένοντο εἰς 'Ιεροσόλυμα 2 λέγοντες·
arrived in Jerusalem saying:

ποῦ ἐστιν ὁ τεχθεὶς βασιλεὺς τῶν
Where is the [one] born king of the

'Ιουδαίων; εἴδομεν γὰρ αὐτοῦ τὸν ἀστέρα
Jews? for we saw of him the star

ἐν τῇ ἀνατολῇ, καὶ ἤλθομεν προσκυνῆσαι
in the east, and came to worship

αὐτῷ. 3 ἀκούσας δὲ ὁ βασιλεὺς 'Ηρῴδης
him. Now hearing [this] the king Herod

ἐταράχθη, καὶ πᾶσα 'Ιεροσόλυμα μετ'
was troubled, and all Jerusalem with

αὐτοῦ, 4 καὶ συναγαγὼν πάντας τοὺς
him, and having assembled all the

ἀρχιερεῖς καὶ γραμματεῖς τοῦ λαοῦ
chief priests and scribes of the people

ἐπυνθάνετο παρ' αὐτῶν ποῦ ὁ χριστὸς
he inquired from them where the Christ

γεννᾶται. 5 οἱ δὲ εἶπαν αὐτῷ· ἐν
is being born. And they told him: In

Βηθλέεμ τῆς 'Ιουδαίας· οὕτως γὰρ
Bethlehem - of Judæa: for thus

γέγραπται διὰ τοῦ προφήτου· 6 καὶ
it has been written through the prophet: And

σὺ Βηθλέεμ, γῆ 'Ιούδα, οὐδαμῶς ἐλαχίστη
thou Bethlehem, land of Juda, ¹not at all ²least

εἶ ἐν τοῖς ἡγεμόσιν 'Ιούδα. ἐκ σοῦ γὰρ
¹art among the governors of Juda. For out of thee

ἐξελεύσεται ἡγούμενος, ὅστις ποιμανεῖ
will come forth a governor, who will shepherd

τὸν λαόν μου τὸν 'Ισραήλ.
the people of me - Israel.

7 Τότε 'Ηρῴδης λάθρα καλέσας τοὺς
Then Herod secretly calling the

μάγους ἠκρίβωσεν παρ' αὐτῶν. τὸν
magi inquired carefully from them the

χρόνον τοῦ φαινομένου ἀστέρος, 8 καὶ
time of the appearing star, and

πέμψας αὐτοὺς εἰς Βηθλέεμ εἶπεν·
sending them to Bethlehem said:

Chapter 2

The Visit of the Magi

AFTER Jesus was born in Bethlehem in Judea, during the time of King Herod, Magi*e* from the east came to Jerusalem 2and asked, ''Where is the one who has been born king of the Jews? We saw his star in the east*f* and have come to worship him.''

3When King Herod heard this he was disturbed, and all Jerusalem with him. 4When he had called together all the people's chief priests and teachers of the law, he asked them where the Christ*g* was to be born. 5''In Bethlehem in Judea,'' they replied, ''for this is what the prophet has written:

6'' 'But you, Bethlehem,
in the land of Judah,
are by no means least
among the rulers of Judah;
for out of you will come
a ruler
who will be the
shepherd of my
people Israel.' *h*''

7Then Herod called the Magi secretly and found out from them the exact time the star had appeared. 8He sent them to Bethlehem and said, ''Go and

---

d Lit., *was not knowing her*
e Pronounced may-ji, a caste of wise men specializing in astrology, medicine and natural science

*d*23 Isaiah 7:14
*e*1 Traditionally *Wise Men*
*f*2 Or *star when it rose*
*g*4 Or *Messiah*
*h*6 Micah 5:2

Left column (NASB):

and make careful search for the Child; and when you have found *Him*, report to me, that I too may come and worship Him."

9And having heard the king, they went their way; and lo, the star, which they had seen in the east, went on before them, until it came and stood over where the Child was.

10And when they saw the star, they rejoiced exceedingly with great joy.

11And they came into the house and saw the Child with Mary His mother; and they fell down and worshiped Him; and opening their treasures they presented to Him gifts of gold and frankincense and myrrh.

12And having been warned *by God* in a dream not to return to Herod, they departed for their own country by another way.

The Flight to Egypt

13Now when they had departed, behold, an angel of the Lord *appeared to Joseph in a dream, saying, "Arise and take the Child and His mother, and flee to Egypt, and remain there until I tell you; for Herod is going to search for the Child to destroy Him."

14And he arose and took the Child and His mother by night, and departed for Egypt;

15and was there until the death of Herod, that what was spoken by the Lord through the prophet might be fulfilled, saying, "OUT OF EGYPT DID I CALL MY SON."

Herod Slaughters Babies

16Then when Herod saw that he had been tricked by the magi, he became very enraged, and sent and slew all the male children who

πορευθέντες ἐξετάσατε ἀκριβῶς περὶ τοῦ
Going   question ye   carefully   concerning   the

παιδίου· ἐπὰν δὲ εὕρητε, ἀπαγγείλατέ
child;   and when   ye find,   report

μοι, ὅπως κἀγὼ ἐλθὼν προσκυνήσω αὐτῷ.
to me, so that   I also   coming   may worship   him.

9 οἱ δὲ ἀκούσαντες τοῦ βασιλέως ἐπορεύθησαν·
So they   hearing   the   king   went;

καὶ ἰδοὺ ὁ ἀστήρ, ὃν εἶδον ἐν τῇ
and behold   the   star,   which   they saw   in   the

ἀνατολῇ, προῆγεν αὐτοὺς ἕως ἐλθὼν
east,   went before   them   until   coming

ἐστάθη ἐπάνω οὗ ἦν τὸ παιδίον. **10** ἰδόντες
it stood   over   where was   the child.   ²seeing

δὲ τὸν ἀστέρα ἐχάρησαν χαρὰν μεγάλην
¹And the   star   they rejoiced   [with] a joy   great

σφόδρα. **11** καὶ ἐλθόντες εἰς τὴν οἰκίαν
exceedingly.   And   coming   into   the   house

εἶδον τὸ παιδίον μετὰ Μαρίας τῆς μητρὸς
they saw   the   child   with   Mary   the   mother

αὐτοῦ, καὶ πεσόντες προσεκύνησαν αὐτῷ,
of him,   and   falling   they worshipped   him,

καὶ ἀνοίξαντες τοὺς θησαυροὺς αὐτῶν
and   opening   the   treasures   of them

προσήνεγκαν αὐτῷ δῶρα, χρυσὸν καὶ
they offered   to him   gifts,   gold   and

λίβανον καὶ σμύρναν. **12** καὶ χρηματισθέντες
frankincense and   myrrh.   And having been warned

κατ' ὄναρ μὴ ἀνακάμψαι πρὸς Ἡρώδην,
by a dream   not   to return   to   Herod,

δι' ἄλλης ὁδοῦ ἀνεχώρησαν εἰς τὴν
by   another   way   they departed   to   the

χώραν αὐτῶν.
country   of them.

13 Ἀναχωρησάντων δὲ αὐτῶν, ἰδοὺ
Now having departed   them,ᵃ   behold
= when they had departed,

ἄγγελος κυρίου φαίνεται κατ' ὄναρ τῷ
an angel   of [the] Lord   appears   by   a dream   -

Ἰωσὴφ λέγων· ἐγερθεὶς παράλαβε τὸ
to Joseph   saying: Rising   take thou   the

παιδίον καὶ τὴν μητέρα αὐτοῦ, καὶ φεῦγε
child   and   the   mother   of him,   and   flee

εἰς Αἴγυπτον, καὶ ἴσθι ἐκεῖ ἕως ἂν εἴπω
into   Egypt,   and   be   there   until   I tell

σοι· μέλλει γὰρ Ἡρῴδης ζητεῖν τὸ παιδίον τοῦ
thee;   for ²is about   ¹Herod   to seek   the   child   -

ἀπολέσαι αὐτό. **14** ὁ δὲ ἐγερθεὶς παρέλαβεν
to destroyᵈ   him.   So he   rising   took

τὸ παιδίον καὶ τὴν μητέρα αὐτοῦ
the   child   and   the   mother   of him

νυκτὸς καὶ ἀνεχώρησεν εἰς Αἴγυπτον,
of(by) night   and   departed   to   Egypt,

15 καὶ ἦν ἐκεῖ ἕως τῆς τελευτῆς Ἡρῴδου·
and was   there   until   the   death   of Herod;

ἵνα πληρωθῇ τὸ ῥηθὲν ὑπὸ κυρίου
in order that might be fulfilled   the [thing]   spoken   by [the] Lord

διὰ τοῦ προφήτου λέγοντος· ἐξ
through   the   prophet   saying: Out of

Αἰγύπτου ἐκάλεσα τὸν υἱόν μου.
Egypt   I called   the   son   of me.

16 Τότε Ἡρῴδης ἰδὼν ὅτι ἐνεπαίχθη
Then   Herod   seeing   that   he was mocked

ὑπὸ τῶν μάγων ἐθυμώθη λίαν, καὶ
by   the   magi   was angered   exceedingly,   and

ἀποστείλας ἀνεῖλεν πάντας τοὺς παῖδας
sending   killed   all   the   boy-children

make a careful search for the child. As soon as you find him, report to me, so that I too may go and worship him."

9After they had heard the king, they went on their way, and the star they had seen in the eastⁱ went ahead of them until it stopped over the place where the child was.

10When they saw the star, they were overjoyed. 11On coming to the house, they saw the child with his mother Mary, and they bowed down and worshiped him. Then they opened their treasures and presented him with gifts of gold and of incense and of myrrh. 12And having been warned in a dream not to go back to Herod, they returned to their country by another route.

The Escape to Egypt

13When they had gone, an angel of the Lord appeared to Joseph in a dream. "Get up," he said, "take the child and his mother and escape to Egypt. Stay there until I tell you, for Herod is going to search for the child to kill him."

14So he got up, took the child and his mother during the night and left for Egypt, 15where he stayed until the death of Herod. And so was fulfilled what the Lord had said through the prophet: "Out of Egypt I called my son."ʲ

16When Herod realized that he had been outwitted by the Magi, he was furious, and he gave orders to kill all the boys in Bethle-

ⁱ9 Or *seen when it rose*
ʲ15 Hosea 11:1

were in Bethlehem and in all its environs, from two years old and under, according to the time which he had ascertained from the magi.

17Then that which was spoken through Jeremiah the prophet was fulfilled, saying,

18"A VOICE WAS HEARD IN RAMAH,
WEEPING AND GREAT MOURNING,
RACHEL WEEPING FOR HER CHILDREN;
AND SHE REFUSED TO BE COMFORTED,
BECAUSE THEY WERE NO MORE."

19But when Herod was dead, behold, an angel of the Lord *appeared in a dream to Joseph in Egypt, saying,

20"Arise and take the Child and His mother, and go into the land of Israel; for those who sought the Child's life are dead."

21And he arose and took the Child and His mother, and came into the land of Israel.

22But when he heard that Archelaus was reigning over Judea in place of his father Herod, he was afraid to go there. And being warned by God in a dream, he departed for the regions of Galilee,

23and came and resided in a city called Nazareth, that what was spoken through the prophets might be fulfilled, "He shall be called a Nazarene."

τοὺς ἐν Βηθλέεμ καὶ ἐν πᾶσι τοῖς
in Bethlehem and in all the
ὁρίοις αὐτῆς ἀπὸ διετοῦς καὶ κατωτέρω,
districts of it from two years and under,
κατὰ τὸν χρόνον ὃν ἠκρίβωσεν παρὰ τῶν
according to the time which he strictly inquired from the
μάγων. 17 τότε ἐπληρώθη τὸ ῥηθὲν διὰ
magi. Then was fulfilled the [thing] spoken through
Ἰερεμίου τοῦ προφήτου λέγοντος· 18 φωνὴ
Jeremiah the prophet saying: A voice
ἐν Ῥαμὰ ἠκούσθη, κλαυθμὸς καὶ ὀδυρμὸς
in Rama was heard, weeping and mourning
πολύς· Ῥαχὴλ κλαίουσα τὰ τέκνα αὐτῆς,
much; Rachel weeping for the children of her,
καὶ οὐκ ἤθελεν παρακληθῆναι, ὅτι
and would not to be comforted, because
οὐκ εἰσίν.
they are not.

19 Τελευτήσαντος δὲ τοῦ Ἡρῴδου, ἰδοὺ
But dying – Herod,ª behold
= Herod having died,
ἄγγελος κυρίου φαίνεται κατ' ὄναρ τῷ
an angel of [the] Lord appears by a dream
Ἰωσὴφ ἐν Αἰγύπτῳ 20 λέγων· ἐγερθεὶς
to Joseph in Egypt saying: Rising
παράλαβε τὸ παιδίον καὶ τὴν μητέρα
take thou the child and the mother
αὐτοῦ, καὶ πορεύου εἰς γῆν Ἰσραήλ·
of him, and go into [the] land of Israel;
τεθνήκασιν γὰρ οἱ ζητοῦντες τὴν ψυχὴν
for have died the [ones] seeking the life
τοῦ παιδίου. 21 ὁ δὲ ἐγερθεὶς παρέλαβεν
of the child. So he rising took
τὸ παιδίον καὶ τὴν μητέρα αὐτοῦ καὶ
the child and the mother of him and
εἰσῆλθεν εἰς γῆν Ἰσραήλ. 22 ἀκούσας δὲ
entered into [the] land of Israel. But hearing
ὅτι Ἀρχέλαος βασιλεύει τῆς Ἰουδαίας
that Archelaus reigns over – Judæa
ἀντὶ τοῦ πατρὸς αὐτοῦ Ἡρῴδου ἐφοβήθη
instead of the father of him Herod he feared
ἐκεῖ ἀπελθεῖν· χρηματισθεὶς δὲ κατ'
there to go; and being warned by
ὄναρ ἀνεχώρησεν εἰς τὰ μέρη τῆς
a dream he departed into the parts –
Γαλιλαίας, 23 καὶ ἐλθὼν κατῴκησεν εἰς
of Galilee, and coming dwelt in
πόλιν λεγομένην Ναζαρέθ· ὅπως πληρωθῇ
a city called Nazareth; so that was fulfilled
τὸ ῥηθὲν διὰ τῶν προφητῶν ὅτι
the [thing] spoken through the prophets[,] –
Ναζωραῖος κληθήσεται.
A Nazarene he shall be called.

---

hem and its vicinity who were two years old and under, in accordance with the time he had learned from the Magi. 17Then what was said through the prophet Jeremiah was fulfilled:

18"A voice is heard in Ramah,
weeping and great mourning,
Rachel weeping for her children
and refusing to be comforted,
because they are no more."k

The Return to Nazareth

19After Herod died, an angel of the Lord appeared in a dream to Joseph in Egypt 20and said, "Get up, take the child and his mother and go to the land of Israel, for those who were trying to take the child's life are dead."

21So he got up, took the child and his mother and went to the land of Israel. 22But when he heard that Archelaus was reigning in Judea in place of his father Herod, he was afraid to go there. Having been warned in a dream, he withdrew to the district of Galilee, 23and he went and lived in a town called Nazareth. So was fulfilled what was said through the prophets: "He will be called a Nazarene."

Chapter 3

John the Baptist Preaches

NOW in those days John the Baptist *came, preaching in the wilderness of Judea, saying,

2"Repent, for the kingdom of heaven is at hand."

3For this is the one referred to by Isaiah the prophet, saying,

"THE VOICE OF ONE CRY-

---

3 Ἐν δὲ ταῖς ἡμέραις ἐκείναις παραγίνεται
Now in – days those arrives
Ἰωάννης ὁ βαπτιστὴς κηρύσσων ἐν τῇ
John the Baptist proclaiming in the
ἐρήμῳ τῆς Ἰουδαίας, 2 λέγων· μετανοεῖτε·
wilderness of Judæa, saying: Repent ye;
ἤγγικεν γὰρ ἡ βασιλεία τῶν οὐρανῶν.
for has come near the kingdom of the heavens.
3 οὗτος γάρ ἐστιν ὁ ῥηθεὶς διὰ Ἡσαΐου
For this is the [one] spoken [of] through Isaiah
τοῦ προφήτου λέγοντος· φωνὴ βοῶντος
the prophet saying: A voice of [one] crying

Chapter 3

John the Baptist Prepares the Way

IN those days John the Baptist came, preaching in the Desert of Judea 2and saying, "Repent, for the kingdom of heaven is near." 3This is he who was spoken of through the prophet Isaiah:

"A voice of one calling

k18 Jer. 31:15

ING IN THE WILDER-
NESS,
'MAKE READY THE WAY
OF THE LORD,
MAKE HIS PATHS
STRAIGHT!' ''
4Now John himself had a
garment of camel's hair,
and a leather belt about his
waist; and his food was locusts and wild honey.
5Then Jerusalem was go-
ing out to him, and all
Judea, and all the district
around the Jordan;
6and they were being
baptized by him in the Jordan River, as they con-
fessed their sins.
7But when he saw many
of the Pharisees and Sad-
ducees coming for baptism,
he said to them, ''You
brood of vipers, who
warned you to flee from the
wrath to come?
8''Therefore bring forth
fruit in keeping with repentance;
9and do not suppose that
you can say to yourselves,
'We have Abraham for our
father'; for I say to you,
that God is able from these
stones to raise up children
to Abraham.
10''And the axe is already
laid at the root of the trees;
every tree therefore that
does not bear good fruit is
cut down and thrown into
the fire.
11''As for me, I baptize
you ⸍with water for repentance, but He who is com-
ing after me is mightier than
I, and I am not fit to remove
His sandals; He will bap-
tize you with the Holy
Spirit and fire.
12''And His winnowing
fork is in His hand, and He
will thoroughly clear His
threshing floor; and He will
gather His wheat into the
barn, but He will burn up

ἐν   τῇ   ἐρήμῳ·   ἑτοιμάσατε   τὴν   ὁδὸν
in   the   wilderness: Prepare ye   the   way

κυρίου,   εὐθείας   ποιεῖτε   τὰς   τρίβους
of [the] Lord, straight   make   the   paths

αὐτοῦ.   4 Αὐτὸς   δὲ   ὁ   ’Ιωάννης·   εἶχεν
of him.   Now ³himself   -   ¹John   had

τὸ   ἔνδυμα   αὐτοῦ   ἀπὸ   τριχῶν   καμήλου
the   raiment   of him   from   hairs   of a camel

καὶ   ζώνην   δερματίνην   περὶ   τὴν   ὀσφὺν
and   a girdle   leathern   round   the   loin[s]

αὐτοῦ·   ἡ   δὲ   τροφὴ   ἦν   αὐτοῦ   ἀκρίδες
of him;   and the   food   ²was   ¹of him   locusts

καὶ   μέλι   ἄγριον.   5 Τότε   ἐξεπορεύετο   πρὸς
and   honey   wild.   Then   went out   to

αὐτὸν   ’Ιεροσόλυμα   καὶ   πᾶσα   ἡ   ’Ιουδαία
him   Jerusalem   and   all   -   Judæa

καὶ   πᾶσα   ἡ   περίχωρος   τοῦ   ’Ιορδάνου,
and   all   the   neighbourhood of the   Jordan,

6 καὶ   ἐβαπτίζοντο   ἐν   τῷ   ’Ιορδάνῃ   ποταμῷ
and   were baptized   in   the   Jordan   river

ὑπ’   αὐτοῦ   ἐξομολογούμενοι   τὰς   ἁμαρτίας
by   him   confessing   the   sins

αὐτῶν.   7 ’Ιδὼν   δὲ   πολλοὺς   τῶν
of them.   And seeing   -   many   of the

Φαρισαίων   καὶ   Σαδδουκαίων   ἐρχομένους
Pharisees   and   Sadducees   coming

ἐπὶ   τὸ   βάπτισμα   εἶπεν   αὐτοῖς·   γεννήματα
to   the   baptism   he said   to them: Offspring

ἐχιδνῶν,   τίς   ὑπέδειξεν   ὑμῖν   φυγεῖν   ἀπὸ
of vipers,   who   warned   you   to flee   from

τῆς   μελλούσης   ὀργῆς;   8 ποιήσατε   οὖν
the   coming   wrath?   Produce   therefore

καρπὸν   ἄξιον   τῆς   μετανοίας·   9 καὶ
fruit   worthy   -   of repentance;   and

μὴ   δόξητε   λέγειν   ἐν   ἑαυτοῖς·   πατέρα
think not   to say   among   [your]selves: ³[as] father

ἔχομεν   τὸν   ’Αβραάμ·   λέγω   γὰρ   ὑμῖν   ὅτι
¹We have   -   ²Abraham;   for I tell   you   that

δύναται   ὁ   θεὸς   ἐκ   τῶν   λίθων   τούτων
²is able   ¹God   out of   -   stones   these

ἐγεῖραι   τέκνα   τῷ   ’Αβραάμ.   10 ἤδη   δὲ
to raise   children   -   to Abraham.   And already

ἡ   ἀξίνη   πρὸς   τὴν   ῥίζαν   τῶν   δένδρων
the   axe   at   the   root   of the   trees

κεῖται·   πᾶν   οὖν   δένδρον   μὴ   ποιοῦν
is laid;   therefore every   tree   not   producing

καρπὸν   καλὸν   ἐκκόπτεται   καὶ   εἰς   πῦρ
fruit   good   is cut down   and   into [the] fire

βάλλεται.   11 ἐγὼ   μὲν   ὑμᾶς   βαπτίζω
is cast.   I   indeed   you   baptize

ἐν   ὕδατι   εἰς   μετάνοιαν·   ὁ   δὲ
in   water   to   repentance;   but the [one]

ὀπίσω   μου   ἐρχόμενος   ἰσχυρότερός   μού
after   me   coming   ²stronger ³[than]   ⁴I

ἐστιν,   οὗ   οὐκ   εἰμὶ   ἱκανὸς   τὰ   ὑποδήματα
¹is,   of whom I am not   worthy   the   sandals

βαστάσαι·   αὐτὸς   ὑμᾶς   βαπτίσει   ἐν   πνεύματι
to bear;   he   ²you   ¹will baptize   in   [the] Spirit

ἁγίῳ   καὶ   πυρί·   12 οὗ   τὸ   πτύον   ἐν   τῇ
Holy   and   fire;   of whom the   fan [is]   in   the

χειρὶ   αὐτοῦ,   καὶ   διακαθαριεῖ   τὴν   ἅλωνα
hand   of him,   and he will thoroughly cleanse   the   threshing-floor

αὐτοῦ,   καὶ   συνάξει   τὸν   σῖτον   αὐτοῦ
of him,   and   will gather   the   wheat   of him

εἰς   τὴν   ἀποθήκην,   τὸ   δὲ   ἄχυρον   κατα-
into   the   barn,   but the   chaff   he will

in the desert,
'Prepare the way for the
Lord,
make straight paths for
him.' '' ⸍

4John's clothes were
made of camel's hair, and
he had a leather belt around
his waist. His food was locusts and wild honey. 5Peo-
ple went out to him from
Jerusalem and all Judea
and the whole region of the
Jordan. 6Confessing their
sins, they were baptized by
him in the Jordan River.
7But when he saw many
of the Pharisees and Sadducees coming to where he
was baptizing, he said to
them: ''You brood of vi-
pers! Who warned you to
flee from the coming
wrath? 8Produce fruit in
keeping with repentance.
9And do not think you can
say to yourselves, 'We
have Abraham as our fa-
ther.' I tell you that out of
these stones God can raise
up children for Abraham.
10The ax is already at the
root of the trees, and every
tree that does not produce
good fruit will be cut down
and thrown into the fire.
11''I baptize you with ᵐ
water for repentance. But
after me will come one who
is more powerful than I,
whose sandals I am not fit
to carry. He will baptize
you with the Holy Spirit
and with fire. 12His win-
nowing fork is in his hand,
and he will clear his threshing floor, gathering his
wheat into the barn and
burning up the chaff with

⸍The Gr. here can be translated *in,*
with or *by*

¹³ Isaiah 40:3
ᵐ11 Or *in*

the chaff with unquench-
able fire.''

The Baptism of Jesus

13Then Jesus *arrived
from Galilee at the Jordan
coming to John, to be baptized by him.

14But John tried to pre-
vent Him, saying, ''I have
need to be baptized by
You, and do You come to
me?''

15But Jesus answering
said to him, ''Permit it at
this time; for in this way it
is fitting for us to fulfill all
righteousness.'' Then he
*permitted Him.

16And after being bap-
tized, Jesus went up
immediately from the
water; and behold, the
heavens were opened, and
he saw the Spirit of God descending as a dove, and
coming upon Him,

17and behold, a voice out
of the heavens, saying,
''This is gMy beloved Son,
in whom I am well-
pleased.''

καύσει πυρὶ ἀσβέστῳ.
consume with fire unquenchable.

13 Τότε παραγίνεται ὁ Ἰησοῦς ἀπὸ τῆς
Then　arrives　-　Jesus　from　-

Γαλιλαίας ἐπὶ τὸν Ἰορδάνην πρὸς τὸν
Galilee　at　the　Jordan　to　-

Ἰωάννην τοῦ βαπτισθῆναι ὑπ᾽ αὐτοῦ.
John　-　to be baptizedd　by　him.

14 ὁ δὲ διεκώλυεν αὐτὸν λέγων· ἐγὼ
But he　forbade　him　saying:　I

χρείαν ἔχω ὑπὸ σοῦ βαπτισθῆναι, καὶ σὺ
1need　1have　4by　5thee　2to be baptized,　and　thou

ἔρχῃ πρὸς μέ; **15** ἀποκριθεὶς δὲ ὁ
comest　to　me?　But answering　-

Ἰησοῦς εἶπεν αὐτῷ· ἄφες ἄρτι· οὕτως γὰρ
Jesus　said　to him: Permit　now;　for thus

πρέπον ἐστὶν ἡμῖν πληρῶσαι πᾶσαν
2fitting　1it is　to us　to fulfil　all

δικαιοσύνην. τότε ἀφίησιν αὐτόν.
righteousness.　Then　he permits　him.

16 βαπτισθεὶς δὲ ὁ Ἰησοῦς εὐθὺς ἀνέβη
And having been baptized　-　Jesus immediately went up

ἀπὸ τοῦ ὕδατος· καὶ ἰδοὺ ἠνεῴχθησαν
from　the　water;　and　behold　1were opened

οἱ οὐρανοί, καὶ εἶδεν πνεῦμα θεοῦ
1the　2heavens,　and　he saw [the] Spirit　of God

καταβαίνον ὡσεὶ περιστεράν, ἐρχόμενον ἐπ᾽
coming down　as　a dove,　coming　upon

αὐτόν· **17** καὶ ἰδοὺ φωνὴ ἐκ τῶν
him;　and　behold　a voice out of　the

οὐρανῶν λέγουσα· οὗτός ἐστιν ὁ υἱός
heavens　saying:　This　is　the　son

μου ὁ ἀγαπητός, ἐν ᾧ εὐδόκησα.
of me the　beloved,　in　whom I was well pleased.

The Baptism of Jesus

13Then Jesus came from
Galilee to the Jordan to be
baptized by John. 14But
John tried to deter him,
saying, ''I need to be baptized by you, and do you
come to me?''

15Jesus replied, ''Let it be
so now; it is proper for us to
do this to fulfill all righteousness.'' Then John consented.

16As soon as Jesus was
baptized, he went up out of
the water. At that moment
heaven was opened, and he
saw the Spirit of God de-
scending like a dove and
lighting on him. 17And a
voice from heaven said,
''This is my Son, whom I
love; with him I am well
pleased.''

Chapter 4

Temptation of Jesus

THEN Jesus was led up
by the Spirit into the
wilderness to be tempted
by the devil.

2And after He had fasted
forty days and forty nights,
He hthen became hungry.

3And the tempter came
and said to Him, ''If You
are the Son of God, com-
mand that these stones
become bread.''

4But He answered and
said, ''It is written, 'MAN
SHALL NOT LIVE ON BREAD
ALONE, BUT ON EVERY WORD
THAT PROCEEDS OUT OF THE
MOUTH OF GOD.' ''

5Then the devil *took
Him into the holy city; and
he had Him stand on the
pinnacle of the temple,

6and *said to Him, ''If

4 Τότε ὁ Ἰησοῦς ἀνήχθη εἰς τὴν
Then　-　Jesus　was led up　into　the

ἔρημον ὑπὸ τοῦ πνεύματος πειρασθῆναι
wilderness　by　the　Spirit　to be tempted

ὑπὸ τοῦ διαβόλου. **2** καὶ νηστεύσας ἡμέρας
by　the　devil.　And having fasted　days

τεσσεράκοντα καὶ τεσσεράκοντα νύκτας
forty　and　forty　nights

ὕστερον ἐπείνασεν. **3** καὶ προσελθὼν ὁ
afterward　he hungered.　And　approaching　the

πειράζων εἶπεν αὐτῷ· εἰ υἱὸς εἶ τοῦ
tempting [one] said　to him:　If　Son　thou art　-

θεοῦ, εἰπὲ ἵνα οἱ λίθοι οὗτοι ἄρτοι
of God,　say in order that -　stones　these　3loaves

γένωνται. **4** ὁ δὲ ἀποκριθεὶς εἶπεν·
1may become.　But he　answering　said:

γέγραπται· οὐκ ἐπ᾽ ἄρτῳ μόνῳ ζήσεται
It has been written: Not　on　bread　only　shall live

ὁ ἄνθρωπος, ἀλλ᾽ ἐπὶ παντὶ ῥήματι
-　man,　but　on　every　word

ἐκπορευομένῳ διὰ στόματος θεοῦ. **5** Τότε
proceeding　through [the] mouth of God.　Then

παραλαμβάνει αὐτὸν ὁ διάβολος εἰς τὴν
takes　him　the　devil　into　the

ἁγίαν πόλιν, καὶ ἔστησεν αὐτὸν ἐπὶ τὸ
holy　city,　and　stood　him　on　the

πτερύγιον τοῦ ἱεροῦ, **6** καὶ λέγει αὐτῷ·
wing　of the temple,　and　says　to him:

The Temptation of Jesus

THEN Jesus was led by
the Spirit into the des-
ert to be tempted by the
devil. 2After fasting forty
days and forty nights, he
was hungry. 3The tempter
came to him and said, ''If
you are the Son of God, tell
these stones to become
bread.''

4Jesus answered, ''It is
written: 'Man does not live
on bread alone, but on every word that comes from
the mouth of God.' ''

5Then the devil took him
to the holy city and had him
stand on the highest point
of the temple. 6''If you are

---

g Lit., My Son, the Beloved
h Lit., later, afterward

n4 Deut. 8:3

You are the Son of God throw Yourself down; for it is written,
'HE WILL GIVE HIS ANGELS CHARGE CONCERNING YOU';
and
'ON *their* HANDS THEY WILL BEAR YOU UP, LEST YOU STRIKE YOUR FOOT AGAINST A STONE.' "

7Jesus said to him, "On the other hand, it is written, 'YOU SHALL NOT *i*PUT THE LORD YOUR GOD TO THE TEST.' "

8Again, the devil *took Him to a very high mountain, and *showed Him all the kingdoms of the world, and their glory;

9and he said to Him, "All these things will I give You, if You fall down and worship me."

10Then Jesus *said to him, "Begone, Satan! For it is written, 'YOU SHALL WORSHIP THE LORD YOUR GOD, AND SERVE HIM ONLY.' "

11Then the devil *left Him; and behold, angels came and *began to minister to Him.

Jesus Begins His Ministry

12Now when He heard that John had been taken into custody, He withdrew into Galilee;

13and leaving Nazareth, He came and settled in Capernaum, which is by the sea, in the region of Zebulun and Naphtali.

14*This was* to fulfill what was spoken through Isaiah the prophet, saying,
15"THE LAND OF ZEBULUN AND THE LAND OF NAPHTALI, BY THE WAY OF THE SEA, BEYOND THE JORDAN, GALILEE OF THE *j* GENTILES—
16"THE PEOPLE WHO WERE SITTING IN DARKNESS SAW A GREAT LIGHT, AND TO THOSE WHO WERE SITTING IN THE LAND AND SHADOW OF DEATH, UPON THEM A LIGHT DAWNED."

17From that time Jesus began to preach and say, "Repent, for the kingdom of heaven is at hand."

i Or, tempt . . . God
j Or, nations

εἰ   υἱὸς   εἶ   τοῦ   θεοῦ,   βάλε   σεαυτὸν
If   Son   thou art   -   of God,   cast   thyself

κάτω·   γέγραπται   γὰρ   ὅτι   τοῖς   ἀγγέλοις
down;   for it has been written[,]   -   To the   angels

αὐτοῦ   ἐντελεῖται   περὶ   σοῦ καὶ ἐπὶ χειρῶν
of him   he will give command   concerning   thee and on   hands

ἀροῦσίν   σε,   μήποτε   προσκόψῃς   πρὸς
they will bear   thee,   lest   thou strike   against

λίθον   τὸν   πόδα   σου.   7 ἔφη   αὐτῷ   ὁ
a stone   the   foot   of thee.   Said   to him   -

'Ιησοῦς·   πάλιν   γέγραπται·   οὐκ   ἐκπειράσεις
Jesus: Again it has been written: Not overtempt shalt thou

κύριον   τὸν   θεόν   σου.   8 Πάλιν   παρα-
[the] Lord   the   God   of thee.   Again

λαμβάνει   αὐτὸν   ὁ   διάβολος   εἰς   ὄρος
takes   him   the   devil   to   a mountain

ὑψηλὸν   λίαν,   καὶ   δείκνυσιν   αὐτῷ   πάσας
high   exceedingly,   and   shows   him   all

τὰς   βασιλείας   τοῦ   κόσμου   καὶ   τὴν
the   kingdoms   of the   world   and   the

δόξαν   αὐτῶν,   9 καὶ   εἶπεν   αὐτῷ·   ταῦτά
glory   of them,   and   said   to him: These things

σοι   πάντα   δώσω,   ἐὰν   πεσὼν   προσκυνήσῃς
to thee   all   I will give,   if   falling   thou wilt worship

μοι.   10 τότε   λέγει   αὐτῷ   ὁ   'Ιησοῦς·
me.   Then   says   to him   -   Jesus:

ὕπαγε,   σατανᾶ·   γέγραπται   γάρ·   κύριον
Go,   Satan;   for it has been written: [The] Lord

τὸν   θεόν   σου   προσκυνήσεις   καὶ   αὐτῷ
the   God   of thee   thou shalt worship   and   him

μόνῳ   λατρεύσεις.   11 Τότε   ἀφίησιν   αὐτὸν
only   thou shalt serve.   Then   leaves   him

ὁ   διάβολος,   καὶ   ἰδοὺ   ἄγγελοι   προσῆλθον
the   devil,   and   behold   angels   approached

καὶ   διηκόνουν   αὐτῷ.
and   ministered   to him.

12 'Ακούσας   δὲ   ὅτι   'Ιωάννης   παρεδόθη
Now hearing   that   John   was delivered up

ἀνεχώρησεν   εἰς   τὴν   Γαλιλαίαν.   13 καὶ
he departed   to   -   Galilee.   And

καταλιπὼν   τὴν   Ναζαρὰ   ἐλθὼν   κατῴκησεν
leaving   -   Nazareth   coming   he dwelt

εἰς   Καφαρναοὺμ   τὴν   παραθαλασσίαν   ἐν
in   Capernaum   -   beside the sea   in [the]

ὁρίοις   Ζαβουλὼν   καὶ   Νεφθαλίμ·   14 ἵνα
districts   of Zebulon   and   Naphtali;   in order that

πληρωθῇ   τὸ   ῥηθὲν   διὰ   'Ησαΐου
might be fulfilled   the [thing]   spoken   through   Isaiah

τοῦ   προφήτου   λέγοντος·   15 γῆ   Ζαβουλὼν
the   prophet   saying: Land   of Zebulon

καὶ   γῆ   Νεφθαλίμ,   ὁδὸν   θαλάσσης,
and   land   of Naphtali,   way   of [the] sea,

πέραν   τοῦ   'Ιορδάνου,   Γαλιλαία   τῶν   ἐθνῶν,
beyond   the   Jordan,   Galilee   of the   nations,

16 ὁ   λαὸς   ὁ   καθήμενος   ἐν   σκοτίᾳ   φῶς
the   people   -   sitting   in   darkness   *light

εἶδεν   μέγα,   καὶ   τοῖς   καθημένοις   ἐν
*saw   *a great,   and   to the [ones]   sitting   in

χώρᾳ   καὶ   σκιᾷ   θανάτου,   φῶς   ἀνέτειλεν
a land   and   shadow   of death,   light   sprang up

αὐτοῖς.
to them.

17 'Απὸ   τότε   ἤρξατο   ὁ   'Ιησοῦς   κηρύσσειν
From   then   began   -   Jesus   to proclaim

καὶ   λέγειν·   μετανοεῖτε·   ἤγγικεν   γὰρ
and   to say: Repent ye;   for has drawn near

---

the Son of God," he said, "throw yourself down. For it is written:

" 'He will command his angels concerning you, and they will lift you up in their hands, so that you will not strike your foot against a stone.' *o*"

7Jesus answered him, "It is also written: 'Do not put the Lord your God to the test.' *p*"

8Again, the devil took him to a very high mountain and showed him all the kingdoms of the world and their splendor. 9"All this I will give you," he said, "if you will bow down and worship me."

10Jesus said to him, "Away from me, Satan! For it is written: 'Worship the Lord your God, and serve him only.' *q*"

11Then the devil left him, and angels came and attended him.

Jesus Begins to Preach

12When Jesus heard that John had been put in prison, he returned to Galilee. 13Leaving Nazareth, he went and lived in Capernaum, which was by the lake in the area of Zebulun and Naphtali— 14to fulfill what was said through the prophet Isaiah:

15"Land of Zebulun and land of Naphtali, the way to the sea, along the Jordan, Galilee of the Gentiles— 16the people living in darkness have seen a great light; on those living in the land of the shadow of death a light has dawned." *r*

17From that time on Jesus began to preach, "Repent, for the kingdom of heaven is near."

*o*6 Psalm 91:11,12
*p*7 Deut. 6:16
*q*10 Deut. 6:13
*r*16 Isaiah 9:1,2

The First Disciples

18And walking by the Sea of Galilee, He saw two brothers, Simon who was called Peter, and Andrew his brother, casting a net into the sea; for they were fishermen.
19And He·*said to them, "Follow Me, and I will make you fishers of men."
20And they immediately left the nets, and followed Him.
21And going on from there He saw two other brothers, James the *son of* Zebedee, and John his brother, in the boat with Zebedee their father, mending their nets; and He called them.
22And they immediately left the boat and their father, and followed Him.

Ministry in Galilee

23And *Jesus* was going about in all Galilee, teaching in their synagogues, and proclaiming the gospel of the kingdom, and healing every kind of disease and every kind of sickness among the people.
24And the news about Him went out into all Syria; and they brought to Him all who were ill, taken with various diseases and pains, demoniacs, epileptics, paralytics; and He healed them.
25And great multitudes followed Him from Galilee and Decapolis and Jerusalem and Judea and *from* beyond the Jordan.

ἡ βασιλεία τῶν οὐρανῶν.
the kingdom of the heavens.

18 Περιπατῶν δὲ παρὰ τὴν θάλασσαν
And walking beside the sea

τῆς Γαλιλαίας εἶδεν δύο ἀδελφούς, Σίμωνα
- of Galilee he saw two brothers, Simon

τὸν λεγόμενον Πέτρον καὶ Ἀνδρέαν τὸν
- called Peter and Andrew the

ἀδελφὸν αὐτοῦ, βάλλοντας ἀμφίβληστρον εἰς
brother of him, casting a net into

τὴν θάλασσαν· ἦσαν γὰρ ἁλεεῖς. 19 καὶ
the sea; for they were fishers. And

λέγει αὐτοῖς· δεῦτε ὀπίσω μου, καὶ
he says to them: Come after me, and

ποιήσω ὑμᾶς ἁλεεῖς ἀνθρώπων. 20 οἱ
I will make you fishers of men. ¹they

δὲ εὐθέως ἀφέντες τὰ δίκτυα ἠκολούθη-
¹And immediately leaving the nets fol-

σαν αὐτῷ. 21 Καὶ προβὰς ἐκεῖθεν εἶδεν
lowed him. And going on thence he saw

ἄλλους δύο ἀδελφούς, Ἰάκωβον τὸν τοῦ
other two brothers, James the [son] -

Ζεβεδαίου καὶ Ἰωάννην τὸν ἀδελφὸν
of Zebedee and John the brother

αὐτοῦ, ἐν τῷ πλοίῳ μετὰ Ζεβεδαίου τοῦ
of him, in the boat with Zebedee the

πατρὸς αὐτῶν καταρτίζοντας τὰ δίκτυα
father of them mending the nets

αὐτῶν· καὶ ἐκάλεσεν αὐτούς. 22 οἱ δὲ
of them; and he called them. And they

εὐθέως ἀφέντες τὸ πλοῖον καὶ τὸν
immediately leaving the boat and the

πατέρα αὐτῶν ἠκολούθησαν αὐτῷ.
father of them followed him.

23 Καὶ περιῆγεν ἐν ὅλῃ τῇ Γαλιλαίᾳ,
And he went about in all - Galilee,

διδάσκων ἐν ταῖς συναγωγαῖς αὐτῶν
teaching in the synagogues of them

καὶ κηρύσσων τὸ εὐαγγέλιον τῆς βασιλείας
and proclaiming the gospel of the kingdom

καὶ θεραπεύων πᾶσαν νόσον καὶ πᾶσαν
and healing every disease and every

μαλακίαν ἐν τῷ λαῷ. 24 καὶ ἀπῆλθεν ἡ
illness among the people. And went the

ἀκοὴ αὐτοῦ εἰς ὅλην τὴν Συρίαν· καὶ
report of him into all - Syria; and

προσήνεγκαν αὐτῷ πάντας τοὺς κακῶς
they brought to him all the [ones] ²ill
=those who were ill

ἔχοντας ποικίλαις νόσοις καὶ βασάνοις
¹having ²various ³diseases ⁴and ⁵tortures

συνεχομένους, δαιμονιζομένους καὶ σεληνιαζ-
¹suffering from, demon-possessed and luna-

ομένους καὶ παραλυτικούς, καὶ ἐθεράπευσεν
tics and paralysed, and he healed

αὐτούς. 25 καὶ ἠκολούθησαν αὐτῷ ὄχλοι
them. And ³followed ⁴him ²crowds

πολλοὶ ἀπὸ τῆς Γαλιλαίας καὶ Δεκαπόλεως
¹many from - Galilee and Decapolis

καὶ Ἱεροσολύμων καὶ Ἰουδαίας καὶ πέραν
and Jerusalem and Judæa and beyond

τοῦ Ἰορδάνου.
the Jordan.

5 Ἰδὼν δὲ τοὺς ὄχλους ἀνέβη εἰς
And seeing the crowds he went up into

The Calling of the First Disciples

18As Jesus was walking beside the Sea of Galilee, he saw two brothers, Simon called Peter and his brother Andrew. They were casting a net into the lake, for they were fishermen. 19"Come, follow me," Jesus said, "and I will make you fishers of men." 20At once they left their nets and followed him.
21Going on from there, he saw two other brothers, James son of Zebedee and his brother John. They were in a boat with their father Zebedee, preparing their nets. Jesus called them, 22and immediately they left the boat and their father and followed him.

Jesus Heals the Sick

23Jesus went throughout Galilee, teaching in their synagogues, preaching the good news of the kingdom, and healing every disease and sickness among the people. 24News about him spread all over Syria, and people brought to him all who were ill with various diseases, those suffering severe pain, the demon-possessed, those having seizures, and the paralyzed, and he healed them. 25Large crowds from Galilee, the Decapolis,³ Jerusalem, Judea and the region across the Jordan followed him.

Chapter 5

The Sermon on the Mount
The Beatitudes

AND when He saw the multitudes, He went

Chapter 5

The Beatitudes

NOW when he saw the crowds, he went up

³25 That is, the Ten Cities

up on the mountain; and after He sat down, His disciples came to Him.

²And opening His mouth He *began* to teach them, saying,

³"Blessed are the poor in spirit, for theirs is the kingdom of heaven.

⁴"Blessed are those who mourn, for they shall be comforted.

⁵"Blessed are the ᵏ gentle, for they shall inherit the earth.

⁶"Blessed are those who hunger and thirst for righteousness, for they shall be satisfied.

⁷"Blessed are the merciful, for they shall receive mercy.

⁸"Blessed are the pure in heart, for they shall see God.

⁹"Blessed are the peacemakers, for they shall be called sons of God.

¹⁰"Blessed are those who have been persecuted for the sake of righteousness, for theirs is the kingdom of heaven.

¹¹"Blessed are you when *men* cast insults at you, and persecute you, and say all kinds of evil against you falsely, on account of Me.

¹²"Rejoice, and be glad, for your reward in heaven is great, for so they persecuted the prophets who were before you.

Disciples and the World

¹³"You are the salt of the earth; but if the salt has become tasteless, how will it be made salty *again*? It is good for nothing anymore, except to be thrown out and trampled under foot by men.

¹⁴"You are the light of the world. A city set on a hill cannot be hidden.

¹⁵"Nor do *men* light a lamp, and put it under the peck-measure, but on the lampstand; and it gives light to all who are in the

---

τὸ ὄρος· καὶ καθίσαντος αὐτοῦ προσῆλθαν
the mountain; and sitting = when he sat himᵃ ⁴approached

αὐτῷ οἱ μαθηταὶ αὐτοῦ· 2 καὶ ἀνοίξας τὸ
⁵to him ¹the ²disciples ³of him; and opening the

στόμα αὐτοῦ ἐδίδασκεν αὐτοὺς λέγων·
mouth of him he taught them saying:

3 Μακάριοι οἱ πτωχοὶ τῷ πνεύματι,
Blessed [are] the poor - in spirit,

ὅτι αὐτῶν ἐστιν ἡ βασιλεία τῶν οὐρανῶν.
for of them is the kingdom of the heavens.

4 μακάριοι οἱ πενθοῦντες, ὅτι αὐτοὶ
Blessed [are] the mourning [ones], for they

παρακληθήσονται. 5 μακάριοι οἱ πραεῖς,
shall be comforted. Blessed [are] the meek,

ὅτι αὐτοὶ κληρονομήσουσιν τὴν γῆν.
for they shall inherit the earth.

6 μακάριοι οἱ πεινῶντες καὶ διψῶντες
Blessed [are] the hungering and thirsting [ones] [after]

τὴν δικαιοσύνην, ὅτι αὐτοὶ χορτασ-
- righteousness, for they shall be

θήσονται. 7 μακάριοι οἱ ἐλεήμονες, ὅτι
satisfied. Blessed [are] the merciful, for

αὐτοὶ ἐλεηθήσονται. 8 μακάριοι οἱ καθαροὶ
they shall obtain mercy. Blessed [are] the clean

τῇ καρδίᾳ, ὅτι αὐτοὶ τὸν θεὸν ὄψονται.
- in heart, for they - ²God ¹shall see.

9 μακάριοι οἱ εἰρηνοποιοί, ὅτι [αὐτοὶ]
Blessed [are] the peacemakers, for they

υἱοὶ θεοῦ κληθήσονται. 10 μακάριοι οἱ
sons of God shall be called. Blessed [are] the [ones]

δεδιωγμένοι ἕνεκεν δικαιοσύνης, ὅτι αὐτῶν
having been persecuted for the sake of righteousness, for of them

ἐστιν ἡ βασιλεία τῶν οὐρανῶν. 11 μακάριοί
is the kingdom of the heavens. Blessed

ἐστε ὅταν ὀνειδίσωσιν ὑμᾶς καὶ διώξωσιν
are ye when they reproach you and persecute

καὶ εἴπωσιν πᾶν πονηρὸν καθ' ὑμῶν
and say all evil against you

ψευδόμενοι ἕνεκεν ἐμοῦ. 12 χαίρετε
lying for the sake of me. Rejoice

καὶ ἀγαλλιᾶσθε, ὅτι ὁ μισθὸς ὑμῶν
and be glad, because the reward of you [is]

πολὺς ἐν τοῖς οὐρανοῖς· οὕτως γὰρ
much in the heavens; for thus

ἐδίωξαν τοὺς προφήτας τοὺς πρὸ
they persecuted the prophets the before

ὑμῶν.
you.

13 Ὑμεῖς ἐστε τὸ ἅλας τῆς γῆς· ἐὰν δὲ
Ye are the salt of the earth; but if

τὸ ἅλας μωρανθῇ, ἐν τίνι ἁλισθήσεται;
the salt be tainted, by what shall it be salted?

εἰς οὐδὲν ἰσχύει ἔτι εἰ μὴ βληθὲν ἔξω
for nothing is it strong longer except being cast out

καταπατεῖσθαι ὑπὸ τῶν ἀνθρώπων. 14 Ὑμεῖς
to be trodden down by - men. Ye

ἐστε τὸ φῶς τοῦ κόσμου. οὐ δύναται
are the light of the world. ⁹Not ⁵can

πόλις κρυβῆναι ἐπάνω ὄρους κειμένη·
¹a city ⁷to be hid ⁶on ⁴a mountain ³set;

15 οὐδὲ καίουσιν λύχνον καὶ τιθέασιν
nor do they light a lamp and place

αὐτὸν ὑπὸ τὸν μόδιον, ἀλλ' ἐπὶ τὴν
it under the bushel, but on the

λυχνίαν, καὶ λάμπει πᾶσιν τοῖς ἐν τῇ
lampstand, and it lightens all the [ones] in the

---

on a mountainside and sat down. His disciples came to him, ²and he began to teach them, saying:

³"Blessed are the poor in spirit, for theirs is the kingdom of heaven.
⁴Blessed are those who mourn, for they will be comforted.
⁵Blessed are the meek, for they will inherit the earth.
⁶Blessed are those who hunger and thirst for righteousness, for they will be filled.
⁷Blessed are the merciful, for they will be shown mercy.
⁸Blessed are the pure in heart, for they will see God.
⁹Blessed are the peacemakers, for they will be called sons of God.
¹⁰Blessed are those who are persecuted because of righteousness, for theirs is the kingdom of heaven.

¹¹"Blessed are you when people insult you, persecute you and falsely say all kinds of evil against you because of me. ¹²Rejoice and be glad, because great is your reward in heaven, for in the same way they persecuted the prophets who were before you.

Salt and Light

¹³"You are the salt of the earth. But if the salt loses its saltiness, how can it be made salty again? It is no longer good for anything, except to be thrown out and trampled by men.

¹⁴"You are the light of the world. A city on a hill cannot be hidden. ¹⁵Neither do people light a lamp and put it under a bowl. Instead they put it on its stand, and it gives light to everyone in

---

ᵏ Or, *humble, meek*

house.
16"Let your light shine before men in such a way that they may see your good works, and glorify your Father who is in heaven.
17"Do not think that I came to abolish the Law or the Prophets; I did not come to abolish, but to fulfill.
18"For truly I say to you, until heaven and earth pass away, not the smallest letter or stroke shall pass away from the Law, until all is accomplished.
19"Whoever then annuls one of the least of these commandments, and so teaches others, shall be called least in the kingdom of heaven; but whoever keeps and teaches *them*, he shall be called great in the kingdom of heaven.
20"For I say to you, that unless your righteousness surpasses *that* of the scribes and Pharisees, you shall not enter the kingdom of heaven.

Personal Relationships
21"You have heard that the ancients were told, 'YOU SHALL NOT COMMIT MURDER' and 'Whoever commits murder shall be /liable to the court.'
22"But I say to you that everyone who is angry with his brother *m* shall be guilty before the court; and whoever shall say to his brother, '*n*Raca,' shall be guilty before *o*the supreme court; and whoever shall say, 'You fool,' shall be guilty *enough to go* into the *p*fiery hell.
23"If therefore you are presenting your offering at the altar, and there remember that your brother has something against you,

---

οἰκίᾳ. **16** οὕτως λαμψάτω τὸ φῶς ὑμῶν
house.   Thus   let shine   the   light   of you
ἔμπροσθεν τῶν ἀνθρώπων, ὅπως ἴδωσιν
before   —   men,   so that they may see
ὑμῶν τὰ καλὰ ἔργα καὶ δοξάσωσιν
of you the good works and   may glorify
τὸν πατέρα ὑμῶν τὸν ἐν τοῖς οὐρανοῖς.
the Father of you -   in the heavens.
17 Μὴ νομίσητε ὅτι ἦλθον καταλῦσαι
Think not   that I came to destroy
τὸν νόμον ἢ τοὺς προφήτας· οὐκ ἦλθον
the law   or the prophets;   I came not
καταλῦσαι ἀλλὰ πληρῶσαι. **18** ἀμὴν γὰρ
to destroy but   to fulfil.   For truly
λέγω ὑμῖν, ἕως ἂν παρέλθῃ ὁ οὐρανὸς
I say to you, until pass away the heaven
καὶ ἡ γῆ, ἰῶτα ἐν ἢ μία κεραία οὐ
and the earth, iota one or one point by no
μὴ παρέλθῃ ἀπὸ τοῦ νόμου, ἕως ἂν
means shall pass away from the law,   until
πάντα γένηται. **19** ὃς ἐὰν οὖν λύσῃ
all things come to pass.   *Whoever* *therefore* breaks
μίαν τῶν ἐντολῶν τούτων τῶν ἐλαχίστων
one   -   commandments of these the   least
καὶ διδάξῃ οὕτως τοὺς ἀνθρώπους, ἐλάχιστος
and teaches thus   -   men,   least
κληθήσεται ἐν τῇ βασιλείᾳ τῶν οὐρανῶν·
he shall be called in the kingdom of the heavens;
ὃς δ' ἂν ποιήσῃ καὶ διδάξῃ, οὗτος
but whoever   does   and teaches, this [one]
μέγας κληθήσεται ἐν τῇ βασιλεια τῶν
great shall be called in the kingdom of the
οὐρανῶν. **20** λέγω γὰρ ὑμῖν ὅτι ἐὰν μὴ
heavens.   For I tell   you   that   except
περισσεύσῃ ὑμῶν ἡ δικαιοσύνη πλεῖον
shall exceed of you the righteousness more [than] [that]
τῶν γραμματέων καὶ Φαρισαίων, οὐ μὴ
of the scribes   and Pharisees, by no means
εἰσέλθητε εἰς τὴν βασιλείαν τῶν οὐρανῶν.
shall ye enter into the kingdom of the heavens.
21 Ἠκούσατε ὅτι ἐρρέθη τοῖς ἀρχαίοις·
Ye heard   that it was said to the ancients:
οὐ φονεύσεις· ὃς δ' ἂν φονεύσῃ,
Thou shalt not kill;   and whoever   kills,
ἔνοχος ἔσται τῇ κρίσει. **22** ἐγὼ δὲ
liable shall be to the judgment.   But I
λέγω ὑμῖν ὅτι πᾶς ὁ ὀργιζόμενος τῷ
tell   you that everyone being angry with the
ἀδελφῷ αὐτοῦ ἔνοχος ἔσται τῇ κρίσει·
brother of him liable shall be to the judgment;
ὃς δ' ἂν εἴπῃ τῷ ἀδελφῷ αὐτοῦ ρακά,
and whoever says to the brother of him[,]   Raca,
ἔνοχος ἔσται τῷ συνεδρίῳ· ὃς δ' ἂν εἴπῃ
liable shall be to the council; and whoever says[,]
μωρέ, ἔνοχος ἔσται εἰς τὴν γέενναν
Fool, liable shall be to   the gehenna
τοῦ πυρός. **23** ἐὰν οὖν προσφέρῃς τὸ
 - of fire.   Therefore if thou bringest the
δῶρόν σου ἐπὶ τὸ θυσιαστήριον κἀκεῖ
gift of thee to the altar   and there
μνησθῇς ὅτι ὁ ἀδελφός σου ἔχει τι
rememberest that the brother of thee has something
κατὰ σοῦ, **24** ἄφες ἐκεῖ τὸ δῶρόν σου
against thee,   leave there the   gift   of thee
ἔμπροσθεν τοῦ θυσιαστηρίου, καὶ ὕπαγε
before   the   altar,   and   go

---

the house. 16In the same way, let your light shine before men, that they may see your good deeds and praise your Father in heaven.

The Fulfillment of the Law
17"Do not think that I have come to abolish the Law or the Prophets; I have not come to abolish them. 18I tell you the truth, until heaven and earth disappear, not the smallest letter, not the least stroke of a pen, will by any means disappear from the Law until everything is accomplished. 19Anyone who breaks one of the least of these commandments and teaches others to do the same will be called least in the kingdom of heaven, but whoever practices and teaches these commands will be called great in the kingdom of heaven. 20For I tell you that unless your righteousness surpasses that of the Pharisees and the teachers of the law, you will certainly not enter the kingdom of heaven.

Murder
21"You have heard that it was said to the people long ago, 'Do not murder,*t* and anyone who murders will be subject to judgment.' 22But I tell you that anyone who is angry with his brother*u* will be subject to judgment. Again, anyone who says to his brother, 'Raca,*v*' is answerable to the Sanhedrin. But anyone who says, 'You fool!' will be in danger of the fire of hell. 23"Therefore, if you are offering your gift at the altar and there remember that your brother has something against you, 24leave

---

*l*Or, *guilty before*
*m*Some mss. insert here: *without cause*
*n*Aramaic for *empty-head* or, *good for nothing*
*o*Lit., *the Sanhedrin*
*p*Lit., *Gehenna of fire*

*t*21 Exodus 20:13
*u*22 Some manuscripts *brother without cause*
*v*22 An Aramaic term of contempt

24leave your offering there before the altar, and go your way; first be reconciled to your brother, and then come and present your offering.
25"Make friends quickly with your opponent at law while you are with him on the way, in order that your opponent may not deliver you to the judge, and the judge to the officer, and you be thrown into prison.
26"Truly I say to you, you shall not come out of there, until you have paid up the last ᵃcent.
27"You have heard that it was said, 'YOU SHALL NOT COMMIT ADULTERY';
28but I say to you, that everyone who looks on a woman to lust for her has committed adultery with her already in his heart.
29"And if your right eye makes you stumble, tear it out, and throw it from you; for it is better for you that one of the parts of your body perish, than for your whole body to be thrown into hell.
30"And if your right hand makes you stumble, cut it off, and throw it from you; for it is better for you that one of the parts of your body perish, than for your whole body to go into hell.
31"And it was said, 'WHOEVER SENDS HIS WIFE AWAY, LET HIM GIVE HER A CERTIFICATE OF DIVORCE';
32but I say to you that everyone who divorces his wife, except for the cause of unchastity, makes her commit adultery; and whoever marries a divorced woman commits adultery.
33"Again, you have heard that the ancients were told, 'YOU SHALL NOT MAKE FALSE VOWS, BUT SHALL FULFILL YOUR VOWS TO THE LORD.'
34"But I say to you, make no oath at all, either by heaven, for it is the throne of God,

---

πρῶτον διαλλάγηθι τῷ ἀδελφῷ σου, καὶ
first be reconciled to the brother of thee, and
τότε ἐλθὼν πρόσφερε τὸ δῶρόν σου.
then coming offer the gift of thee.
25 ἴσθι εὐνοῶν τῷ ἀντιδίκῳ σου
Be well disposed to the opponent of thee
ταχὺ ἕως ὅτου εἶ μετ᾽ αὐτοῦ ἐν τῇ
quickly while thou art with him in the
ὁδῷ· μήποτέ σε παραδῷ ὁ ἀντίδικος τῷ
way; lest ⁴thee ³deliver ¹the ²opponent to the
κριτῇ καὶ ὁ κριτὴς τῷ ὑπηρέτῃ, καὶ
judge and the judge to the attendant, and
εἰς φυλακὴν βληθήσῃ· 26 ἀμὴν λέγω
into prison thou be cast; truly I say
σοι, οὐ μὴ ἐξέλθῃς ἐκεῖθεν ἕως ἂν
to thee, by no means shalt thou come out thence until
ἀποδῶς τὸν ἔσχατον κοδράντην.
thou repayest the last farthing.
27 Ἠκούσατε ὅτι ἐρρέθη· οὐ μοιχεύσεις.
Ye heard that it was said: Thou shalt not commit adultery.
28 ἐγὼ δὲ λέγω ὑμῖν ὅτι πᾶς ὁ βλέπων
But I tell you that everyone seeing
γυναῖκα πρὸς τὸ ἐπιθυμῆσαι [αὐτὴν]
a woman with a view – to desire her
ἤδη ἐμοίχευσεν αὐτὴν ἐν τῇ καρδίᾳ
already committed adultery with her in the heart
αὐτοῦ. 29 εἰ δὲ ὁ ὀφθαλμός σου ὁ δεξιὸς
of him. So if the ²eye ³of thee - ¹right
σκανδαλίζει σε, ἔξελε αὐτὸν καὶ βάλε
⁴causes ⁵to stumble ³thee, pluck out it and cast
ἀπὸ σοῦ· συμφέρει γάρ σοι ἵνα ἀπόληται·
from thee; for it is expedient for thee that ⁵perish
ἓν τῶν μελῶν σου καὶ μὴ ὅλον τὸ
¹one ²of the ³members ⁴of thee and not all the
σῶμά σου βληθῇ εἰς γέενναν. 30 καὶ
body of thee be cast into gehenna. And
εἰ ἡ δεξιά σου χείρ σκανδαλίζει σε, ἔκκοψον
if the ³right ²of thee ¹hand ⁴causes ⁵to stumble ³thee, cut out
αὐτὴν καὶ βάλε ἀπὸ σοῦ· συμφέρει γάρ
it and cast from thee; for it is expedient
σοι ἵνα ἀπόληται ἓν τῶν μελῶν σου
for thee that ⁵perish ¹one ²of the ³members ⁴of thee
καὶ μὴ ὅλον τὸ σῶμά σου εἰς γέενναν
and not all the body of thee into gehenna
ἀπέλθῃ. 31 Ἐρρέθη δέ· ὃς ἂν ἀπολύσῃ
go away. And it was said: Whoever dismisses
τὴν γυναῖκα αὐτοῦ, δότω αὐτῇ ἀποστάσιον.
the wife of him, let him give her a bill of divorce.
32 ἐγὼ δὲ λέγω ὑμῖν ὅτι πᾶς ὁ ἀπολύων
But I tell you that everyone dismissing
τὴν γυναῖκα αὐτοῦ παρεκτὸς λόγου
the wife of him apart from a matter
πορνείας ποιεῖ αὐτὴν μοιχευθῆναι,
of fornication makes her to commit adultery,
καὶ ὃς ἐὰν ἀπολελυμένην γαμήσῃ,
and whoever ²a dismissed [woman] ¹marries,
μοιχᾶται. 33 Πάλιν ἠκούσατε ὅτι ἐρρέθη
commits adultery. Again ye heard that it was said
τοῖς ἀρχαίοις· οὐκ ἐπιορκήσεις, ἀποδώσεις
to the ancients: Thou shalt not perjure, ²shalt repay
δὲ τῷ κυρίῳ τοὺς ὅρκους σου. 34 ἐγὼ δὲ
¹but to the Lord the oaths of thee. But I
λέγω ὑμῖν μὴ ὀμόσαι ὅλως· μήτε ἐν τῷ
tell you not to swear at all; neither by the
οὐρανῷ, ὅτι θρόνος ἐστὶν τοῦ θεοῦ·
heaven, because [the] throne it is - of God;

---

your gift there in front of the altar. First go and be reconciled to ỹour brother; then come and offer your gift.
25"Settle matters quickly with your adversary who is taking you to court. Do it while you are still with him on the way, or he may hand you over to the judge, and the judge may hand you over to the officer, and you may be thrown into prison. 26I tell you the truth, you will not get out until you have paid the last penny. ʷ

Adultery
27"You have heard that it was said, 'Do not commit adultery.'ˣ 28But I tell you that anyone who looks at a woman lustfully has already committed adultery with her in his heart. 29If your right eye causes you to sin, gouge it out and throw it away. It is better for you to lose one part of your body than for your whole body to be thrown into hell. 30And if your right hand causes you to sin, cut it off and throw it away. It is better for you to lose one part of your body than for your whole body to go into hell.

Divorce
31"It has been said, 'Anyone who divorces his wife must give her a certificate of divorce.'ʸ 32But I tell you that anyone who divorces his wife, except for marital unfaithfulness, causes her to become an adulteress, and anyone who marries the divorced woman commits adultery.

Oaths
33"Again, you have heard that it was said to the people long ago, 'Do not break your oath, but keep the oaths you have made to the Lord.' 34But I tell you, Do not swear at all: either by heaven, for it is God's throne; 35or by the earth,

---

ᵃ Lit., *quadrans* (equaling two lepta or mites), i.e., 1/64 of a denarius

ʷ26 Greek *kodrantes*
ˣ27 Exodus 20:14
ʸ31 Deut. 24:1

35or by the earth, for it is the footstool of His feet, or by Jerusalem, for it is THE CITY OF THE GREAT KING. 36"Nor shall you make an oath by your head, for you cannot make one hair white or black. 37"But let your statement be, 'Yes, yes' or 'No, no'; and anything beyond these is of evil. 38"You have heard that it was said, 'AN EYE FOR AN EYE, AND A TOOTH FOR A TOOTH.' 39"But I say to you, do not resist him who is evil; but whoever slaps you on your right cheek, turn to him the other also. 40"And if anyone wants to sue you, and take your rshirt, let him have your scoat also. 41"And whoever shall force you to go one mile, go with him two. 42"Give to him who asks of you, and do not turn away from him who wants to borrow from you. 43"You have heard that it was said, 'YOU SHALL LOVE YOUR NEIGHBOR, and hate your enemy.' 44"But I say to you, love your enemies, and pray for those who persecute you 45in order that you may be sons of your Father who is in heaven; for He causes His sun to rise on *the* evil and *the* good, and sends rain on *the* righteous and *the* unrighteous. 46"For if you love those who love you, what reward have you? Do not even the tax-gatherers do the same? 47"And if you greet your brothers only, what do you do more *than others*? Do

35 μήτε ἐν τῇ γῇ, ὅτι ὑποπόδιόν
nor by the earth, because footstool
ἐστιν τῶν ποδῶν αὐτοῦ· μήτε εἰς
it is of the feet of him; nor by
'Ιεροσόλυμα, ὅτι πόλις ἐστὶν τοῦ μεγάλου
Jerusalem, because city it is of the great
βασιλέως· 36 μήτε ἐν τῇ κεφαλῇ σου
King; nor by the head of thee
ὀμόσῃς, ὅτι οὐ δύνασαι μίαν τρίχα
swear, because thou canst not one hair
λευκὴν ποιῆσαι ἢ μέλαιναν. 37 ἔστω
white to make or black. ²let ⁴be
δὲ ὁ λόγος ὑμῶν ναὶ ναί, οὒ οὔ·
¹But ³the ⁴word ⁵of you Yes yes, No no;
τὸ δὲ περισσὸν τούτων ἐκ τοῦ πονηροῦ
for the excess of these of - evil
ἐστιν. 38 Ἠκούσατε ὅτι ἐρρέθη· ὀφθαλμὸν
is. Ye heard that it was said: An eye
ἀντὶ ὀφθαλμοῦ καὶ ὀδόντα ἀντὶ ὀδόντος.
instead of an eye and a tooth instead of a tooth.
39 ἐγὼ δὲ λέγω ὑμῖν μὴ ἀντιστῆναι
But I tell you not to oppose
τῷ πονηρῷ· ἀλλ' ὅστις σε ῥαπίζει εἰς
- evil; but who thee strikes on
τὴν δεξιὰν σιαγόνα [σου], στρέψον αὐτῷ
the right cheek of thee, turn to him
καὶ τὴν ἄλλην· 40 καὶ τῷ θέλοντί
also the other; and to the [one] wishing
σοι κριθῆναι καὶ τὸν χιτῶνά σου λαβεῖν,
thee to judge and the tunic of thee to take,
ἄφες αὐτῷ καὶ τὸ ἱμάτιον· 41 καὶ
allow him also the [outer] garment; and
ὅστις σε ἀγγαρεύσει μίλιον ἕν, ὕπαγε
who ⁴thee ¹shall impress ⁴mile ²one, go
μετ' αὐτοῦ δύο. 42 τῷ αἰτοῦντί
with him two. To the [one] asking
σε δός, καὶ τὸν θέλοντα ἀπὸ σοῦ
thee give, and the [one] wishing from thee
δανείσασθαι μὴ ἀποστραφῇς. 43 Ἠκούσατε
to borrow turn not away. Ye heard
ὅτι ἐρρέθη· ἀγαπήσεις τὸν πλησίον σου
that it was said: Thou shalt love the neighbour of thee
καὶ μισήσεις τὸν ἐχθρόν σου. 44 ἐγὼ
and thou shalt hate the enemy of thee. ²I
δὲ λέγω ὑμῖν· ἀγαπᾶτε τοὺς ἐχθροὺς
¹But tell you: Love ye the enemies
ὑμῶν καὶ προσεύχεσθε ὑπὲρ τῶν
of you and pray ye for the [ones]
διωκόντων ὑμᾶς· 45 ὅπως γένησθε υἱοὶ
persecuting you; so that ye may become sons
τοῦ πατρὸς ὑμῶν τοῦ ἐν οὐρανοῖς,
of the Father of you - in heavens,
ὅτι τὸν ἥλιον αὐτοῦ ἀνατέλλει ἐπὶ
because the sun of him he makes to rise on
πονηροὺς καὶ ἀγαθοὺς καὶ βρέχει ἐπὶ
evil men and good and rains on
δικαίους καὶ ἀδίκους. 46 ἐὰν γὰρ
just men and unjust. For if
ἀγαπήσητε τοὺς ἀγαπῶντας ὑμᾶς, τίνα
ye love the [ones] loving you, what
μισθὸν ἔχετε; οὐχὶ καὶ οἱ τελῶναι τὸ
reward have ye? ²not ³even ⁴the ⁶tax-collectors ⁶the
αὐτὸ ποιοῦσιν; 47 καὶ ἐὰν ἀσπάσησθε
⁷same ¹do? and if ye greet
τοὺς ἀδελφοὺς ὑμῶν μόνον, τί περισσὸν
the brothers of you only, what excess

for it is his footstool; or by Jerusalem, for it is the city of the Great King. 36And do not swear by your head, for you cannot make even one hair white or black. 37Simply let your 'Yes' be 'Yes,' and your 'No,' 'No'; anything beyond this comes from the evil one.

An Eye for an Eye

38"You have heard that it was said, 'Eye for eye, and tooth for tooth.'ᶜ 39But I tell you, Do not resist an evil person. If someone strikes you on the right cheek, turn to him the other also. 40And if someone wants to sue you and take your tunic, let him have your cloak as well. 41If someone forces you to go one mile, go with him two miles. 42Give to the one who asks you, and do not turn away from the one who wants to borrow from you.

Love for Enemies

43"You have heard that it was said, 'Love your neighborᵈ and hate your enemy.' 44But I tell you: Love your enemiesᵇ and pray for those who persecute you, 45that you may be sons of your Father in heaven. He causes his sun to rise on the evil and the good, and sends rain on the righteous and the unrighteous. 46If you love those who love you, what reward will you get? Are not even the tax collectors doing that? 47And if you greet only your brothers, what are you doing more than others? Do not even pagans

rOr, *tunic;* i.e., garment worn next to the body
sOr, *cloak;* i.e., outer garment

not even the Gentiles do
the same?
48"Therefore you are to
be perfect, as your heavenly Father is perfect.

ποιεῖτε; οὐχὶ καὶ οἱ ἐθνικοὶ τὸ αὐτὸ
do ye? ²not ³even ⁴the ⁵gentiles ⁶the ⁷same
ποιοῦσιν; **48** Ἔσεσθε οὖν ὑμεῖς τέλειοι
¹do? Be therefore ye perfect
ὡς ὁ πατὴρ ὑμῶν ὁ οὐράνιος τέλειός
as the ²Father ³of you - ¹heavenly perfect
ἐστιν.
is.

do that? 48Be perfect,
therefore, as your heavenly
Father is perfect.

Chapter 6

Concerning Alms and Prayer

"BEWARE of prac-
ticing your right-
eousness before men to be
noticed by them; otherwise
you have no reward with
your Father who is in
heaven.
2"When therefore you
give alms, do not sound a
trumpet before you, as the
hypocrites do in the synagogues and in the streets,
that they may be honored
by men. Truly I say to you,
they have their reward in
full.
3"But when you give
alms, do not let your left
hand know what your right
hand is doing
4that your alms may be
in secret; and your Father
who sees in secret will
repay you.
5"And when you pray,
you are not to be as the
hypocrites; for they love to
stand and pray in the synagogues and on the street
corners, in order to be seen
by men. Truly I say to you,
they have their reward in
full.
6"But you, when you
pray, go into your inner
room, and when you have
shut your door, pray to
your Father who is in se-
cret, and your Father who
sees in secret will repay
you.
7"And when you are
praying, do not use mean-
ingless repetition, as the
Gentiles do, for they suppose that they will be heard
for their many words.

6 Προσέχετε δὲ τὴν δικαιοσύνην ὑμῶν
And take ye heed the righteousness of you
μὴ ποιεῖν ἔμπροσθεν τῶν ἀνθρώπων πρὸς
not to do in front of - men with a view to
τὸ θεαθῆναι αὐτοῖς· εἰ δὲ μή γε, μισθὸν
- to be seen by them; otherwise, reward
οὐκ ἔχετε παρὰ τῷ πατρὶ ὑμῶν τῷ
ye have not with the Father of you -
ἐν τοῖς οὐρανοῖς. **2** Ὅταν οὖν ποιῇς
in the heavens. ²When ¹therefore thou doest
ἐλεημοσύνην, μὴ σαλπίσῃς ἔμπροσθέν σου,
alms, sound not a trumpet before thee,
ὥσπερ οἱ ὑποκριταὶ ποιοῦσιν ἐν ταῖς
as the hypocrites do in the
συναγωγαῖς καὶ ἐν ταῖς ῥύμαις, ὅπως
synagogues and in the streets, so that
δοξασθῶσιν ὑπὸ τῶν ἀνθρώπων· ἀμὴν
they may be glorified by - men; truly
λέγω ὑμῖν, ἀπέχουσιν τὸν μισθὸν αὐτῶν.
I tell you, they have the reward of them.
3 σοῦ δὲ ποιοῦντος ἐλεημοσύνην μὴ
But thee doing* alms not
= when thou doest
γνώτω ἡ ἀριστερά σου τί ποιεῖ ἡ
let know the left [hand] of thee what does the
δεξιά σου, **4** ὅπως ᾖ σου ἡ ἐλεημοσύνη
right of thee, so that ⁴may be ²of thee ¹the ³alms
ἐν τῷ κρυπτῷ· καὶ ὁ πατήρ σου
in - secret; and the Father of thee
ὁ βλέπων ἐν τῷ κρυπτῷ ἀποδώσει σοι.
the [one] seeing in - secret will repay thee.
5 Καὶ ὅταν προσεύχησθε, οὐκ ἔσεσθε
And when ye pray, be not ye
ὡς οἱ ὑποκριταί· ὅτι φιλοῦσιν ἐν ταῖς
as the hypocrites; because they love in the
συναγωγαῖς καὶ ἐν ταῖς γωνίαις τῶν
synagogues and in the corners of the
πλατειῶν ἑστῶτες προσεύχεσθαι, ὅπως
open streets standing to pray, so that
φανῶσιν τοῖς ἀνθρώποις· ἀμὴν λέγω
they may appear - to men; truly I tell
ὑμῖν, ἀπέχουσιν τὸν μισθὸν αὐτῶν. **6** σὺ
you, they have the reward of them. ²thou
δὲ ὅταν προσεύχῃ, εἴσελθε εἰς τὸ ταμιεῖον
¹But ²when ¹prayest, enter into the private room
σου καὶ κλείσας τὴν θύραν σου πρόσευξαι
of thee and having shut the door of thee pray
τῷ πατρί σου τῷ ἐν τῷ κρυπτῷ·
to the Father of thee the [one] in - secret;
καὶ ὁ πατήρ σου ὁ βλέπων ἐν τῷ
and the Father of thee the [one] seeing in -
κρυπτῷ ἀποδώσει σοι. **7** Προσευχόμενοι δὲ
secret will repay thee. But praying
μὴ βατταλογήσητε ὥσπερ οἱ ἐθνικοί·
do not utter empty words as the, gentiles;
δοκοῦσιν γὰρ ὅτι ἐν τῇ πολυλογίᾳ αὐτῶν
for they think that in the much speaking of them

Chapter 6

Giving to the Needy

"BE careful not to do
your 'acts of right-
eousness' before men, to
be seen by them. If you do,
you will have no reward
from your Father in heav-
en.
2"So when you give to
the needy, do not announce
it with trumpets, as the
hypocrites do in the synagogues and on the streets,
to be honored by men. I tell
you the truth, they have received their reward in full.
3But when you give to the
needy, do not let your left
hand know what your right
hand is doing, 4so that your
giving may be in secret.
Then your Father, who
sees what is done in secret,
will reward you.

Prayer

5"And when you pray, do
not be like the hypocrites,
for they love to pray standing in the synagogues and
on the street corners to be
seen by men. I tell you the
truth, they have received
their reward in full. 6But
when you pray, go into
your room, close the door
and pray to your Father,
who is unseen. Then your
Father, who sees what is
done in secret, will reward
you. 7And when you pray,
do not keep on babbling
like pagans, for they think
they will be heard because
of their many words. 8Do

8"Therefore do not be like them; for your Father knows what you need, before you ask Him.

9"Pray, then, in this way:

'Our Father who art in heaven,
Hallowed be Thy name.
10 Thy kingdom come.
Thy will be done,
On earth as it is in heaven.
11 'Give us this day our daily bread.
12 'And forgive us our debts, as we also have forgiven our debtors.
13 'And do not lead us into temptation, but deliver us from evil. [For Thine is the kingdom, and the power, and the glory, forever. Amen.]'

14"For if you forgive men for their transgressions, your heavenly Father will also forgive you.

15"But if you do not forgive men, then your Father will not forgive your transgressions.

Concerning Fasting
True Treasure Mammon

16"And whenever you fast, do not put on a gloomy face as the hypocrites do, for they neglect their appearance in order to be seen fasting by men. Truly I say to you, they have their reward in full.

17"But you, when you fast, anoint your head, and wash your face

18so that you may not be seen fasting by men, but by your Father who is in secret; and your Father who sees in secret will repay you.

19"Do not lay up for yourselves treasures upon earth, where moth and rust destroy, and where thieves break in and steal.

20"But lay up for your-

εἰσακουσθήσονται.   8 μὴ   οὖν   ὁμοιωθῆτε
they will be heard.   Not therefore   be ye like

αὐτοῖς·   οἶδεν   γὰρ   [ὁ   θεὸς]   ὁ   πατὴρ
them;   for ⁵knows   –   ¹God   ²the   ³Father

ὑμῶν   ὧν   χρείαν   ἔχετε   πρὸ   τοῦ   ὑμᾶς
⁴of you of what things   ⁶need   ⁷ye have before   –   you

αἰτῆσαι   αὐτόν.   9 οὕτως   οὖν   προσεύχεσθε
to ask[b]   him.   ²Thus ¹therefore   pray

ὑμεῖς·   Πάτερ   ἡμῶν   ὁ   ἐν   τοῖς   οὐρανοῖς·
ye: Father   of us   the [one]   in   the   heavens:

Ἁγιασθήτω   τὸ   ὄνομά   σου·   10 ἐλθάτω
Let it be hallowed   the   name   of thee;   let it come

ἡ   βασιλεία   σου·   γενηθήτω   τὸ   θέλημά   σου,
the   kingdom   of thee ; let it come about   the   will   of thee,

ὡς   ἐν   οὐρανῷ   καὶ   ἐπὶ   γῆς·   11 Τὸν
as   in   heaven   also   on   earth;   The

ἄρτον   ἡμῶν   τὸν   ἐπιούσιον   δὸς   ἡμῖν
²bread   ³of us   –   ¹daily   give   to us

σήμερον·   12 καὶ   ἄφες   ἡμῖν   τὰ   ὀφειλή-
to-day;   and   forgive   us   the   debts

ματα   ἡμῶν,   ὡς   καὶ   ἡμεῖς   ἀφήκαμεν
of us,   as   indeed   we   forgave

τοῖς   ὀφειλέταις   ἡμῶν·   13 καὶ   μὴ   εἰσενέγκῃς
the   debtors   of us;   and not   bring

ἡμᾶς   εἰς   πειρασμόν,   ἀλλὰ   ῥῦσαι   ἡμᾶς   ἀπὸ
us   into   temptation,   but   rescue   us   from

τοῦ   πονηροῦ.   14 Ἐὰν   γὰρ   ἀφῆτε   τοῖς
–   evil.   For if   ye forgive   –

ἀνθρώποις   τὰ   παραπτώματα   αὐτῶν,   ἀφήσει
men   the   trespasses   of them, will forgive

καὶ   ὑμῖν   ὁ   πατὴρ   ὑμῶν   ὁ   οὐράνιος·
also   you   the   ¹Father   ³of you   –   ¹heavenly;

15 ἐὰν   δὲ   μὴ   ἀφῆτε   τοῖς   ἀνθρώποις,
but if   ye forgive not   –   men,

οὐδὲ   ὁ   πατὴρ   ὑμῶν   ἀφήσει   τὰ   παραπτώ-
neither the   Father   of you   will forgive the   tres-

ματα   ὑμῶν.   16 Ὅταν   δὲ   νηστεύητε,
passes   of you.   And when   ye fast,

μὴ   γίνεσθε   ὡς   οἱ   ὑποκριταὶ   σκυθρωποί·
be not   as   the   hypocrites   gloomy;

ἀφανίζουσιν   γὰρ   τὰ   πρόσωπα   αὐτῶν
for they disfigure   the   faces   of them

ὅπως   φανῶσιν   τοῖς   ἀνθρώποις   νηστεύοντες·
so that they may appear   –   to men   fasting;

ἀμὴν   λέγω   ὑμῖν,   ἀπέχουσιν   τὸν   μισθὸν
truly   I tell   you,   they have   the   reward

αὐτῶν.   17 σὺ   δὲ   νηστεύων   ἄλειψαί   σου
of them.   But thou   fasting   anoint   of thee

τὴν   κεφαλὴν   καὶ   τὸ   πρόσωπόν   σου   νίψαι,
the   head   and the   face   of thee   wash,

18 ὅπως   μὴ   φανῇς   τοῖς   ἀνθρώποις   νηστεύων
so that thou appearest not   –   to men   fasting

ἀλλὰ   τῷ   πατρί   σου   τῷ   ἐν   τῷ   κρυφαίῳ·
but   to the   Father   of thee the [one] in   –   secret;

καὶ   ὁ   πατήρ   σου   ὁ   βλέπων   ἐν   τῷ
and   the   Father   of thee the [one] seeing   in   –

κρυφαίῳ   ἀποδώσει   σοι.
secret   will repay   thee.

19 Μὴ   θησαυρίζετε   ὑμῖν   θησαυροὺς
Do not lay up *treasure*   for you   treasures

ἐπὶ   τῆς   γῆς,   ὅπου   σὴς   καὶ   βρῶσις
on   the   earth,   where   moth   and   rust

ἀφανίζει,   καὶ   ὅπου   κλέπται   διορύσσουσιν
removes,   and   where   thieves   dig through

καὶ   κλέπτουσιν·   20 θησαυρίζετε   δὲ   ὑμῖν
and   steal;   but lay up *treasure*   for you

---

not be like them, for your Father knows what you need before you ask him.

9"This, then, is how you should pray:

" 'Our Father in heaven, hallowed be your name,
10your kingdom come, your will be done
on earth as it is in heaven.
11Give us today our daily bread.
12Forgive us our debts, as we also have forgiven our debtors.
13And lead us not into temptation, but deliver us from the evil one.[c]'

14For if you forgive men when they sin against you, your heavenly Father will also forgive you. 15But if you do not forgive men their sins, your Father will not forgive your sins.

Fasting

16"When you fast, do not look somber as the hypocrites do, for they disfigure their faces to show men they are fasting. I tell you the truth, they have received their reward in full. 17But when you fast, put oil on your head and wash your face, 18so that it will not be obvious to men that you are fasting, but only to your Father, who is unseen; and your Father, who sees what is done in secret, will reward you.

Treasures in Heaven

19"Do not store up for yourselves treasures on earth, where moth and rust destroy, and where thieves break in and steal. 20But store up for yourselves

---

c 13 Or *from evil;* some late manuscripts *one,* / *for yours is the kingdom and the power and the glory forever. Amen.*

selves treasures in heaven, where neither moth nor rust destroys, and where thieves do not break in or steal; 21for where your treasure is, there will your heart be also. 22"The lamp of the body is the eye; if therefore your eye is clear, your whole body will be full of light. 23"But if your eye is bad, your whole body will be full of darkness. If therefore the light that is in you is darkness, how great is the darkness! 24"No one can serve two masters; for either he will hate the one and love the other, or he will hold to one and despise the other. You cannot serve God and ¹ mammon.

The Cure for Anxiety

25"For this reason I say to you, do not be anxious for your life, *as to* what you shall eat, or what you shall drink; nor for your body, *as to* what you shall put on. Is not life more than food, and the body than clothing? 26"Look at the birds of the air, that they do not sow, neither do they reap, nor gather into barns, and *yet* your heavenly Father feeds them. Are you not worth much more than they? 27"And which of you by being anxious can add a *single* cubit to his life's span? 28"And why are you anxious about clothing? Observe how the lilies of the field grow; they do not toil nor do they spin, 29yet I say to you that even Solomon in all his glory did not clothe himself like one of these. 30"But if God so arrays

¹ Or, *riches*

θησαυροὺς ἐν οὐρανῷ, ὅπου οὔτε σὴς
treasures   in   heaven,   where   neither   moth

οὔτε βρῶσις ἀφανίζει, καὶ ὅπου κλέπται
nor   rust   removes,   and   where   thieves

οὐ διορύσσουσιν οὐδὲ κλέπτουσιν· 21 ὅπου
do not dig through   nor   steal;   ²where

γάρ ἐστιν ὁ θησαυρός σου, ἐκεῖ
¹for   is   the   treasure   of thee,   there

ἔσται καὶ ἡ καρδία σου. 22 Ὁ λύχνος
will be   also   the   heart   of thee.   The   lamp

τοῦ σώματός ἐστιν ὁ ὀφθαλμός. ἐὰν οὖν
of the   body   is   the   eye.   ²If ¹therefore

ᾖ ὁ ὀφθαλμός σου ἁπλοῦς, ὅλον τὸ σῶμά
²be ¹the   ²eye   ³of thee   single,   all   the   body

σου φωτεινὸν ἔσται· 23 ἐὰν δὲ ὁ
of thee   shining   will be;   but if   the

ὀφθαλμός σου πονηρὸς ᾖ, ὅλον τὸ σῶμά
eye   of thee   evil   be,   all   the   body

σου σκοτεινὸν ἔσται. εἰ οὖν τὸ φῶς
of thee   dark   will be.   ²If ¹therefore the   light

τὸ ἐν σοὶ σκότος ἐστιν, τὸ σκότος
–   in   thee   darkness   is,   the   darkness

πόσον. 24 Οὐδεὶς δύναται δυσὶ κυρίοις
how great.   No one   can   two   lords

δουλεύειν· ἢ γὰρ τὸν ἕνα μισήσει καὶ
to serve;   for either   the   one   he will hate   and

τὸν ἕτερον ἀγαπήσει, ἢ ἑνὸς ἀνθέξεται
the   other   he will love,   or   one   he will hold to

καὶ τοῦ ἑτέρου καταφρονήσει. οὐ δύνασθε
and   the   other   he will despise.   Ye cannot

θεῷ δουλεύειν καὶ μαμωνᾷ. 25 Διὰ
God   to serve   and   mammon.   There-

τοῦτο λέγω ὑμῖν· μὴ μεριμνᾶτε τῇ
fore   I say   to you: Be not anxious   for the

ψυχῇ ὑμῶν τί φάγητε [ἢ τί πίητε],
life   of you[,]   what ye may eat   or what ye may drink,

μηδὲ τῷ σώματι ὑμῶν τί ἐνδύσησθε.
nor   for the   body   of you[,]   what ye may put on.

οὐχὶ ἡ ψυχὴ πλεῖόν ἐστιν τῆς τροφῆς καὶ τὸ
²not ³the   ⁴life   ⁵more   ¹Is [than] the   food   and the

σῶμα τοῦ ἐνδύματος; 26 ἐμβλέψατε εἰς
body [than] the   raiment?   Look ye   at

τὰ πετεινὰ τοῦ οὐρανοῦ, ὅτι οὐ σπείρουσιν
the   birds   –   of heaven,   that   they sow not

οὐδὲ θερίζουσιν οὐδὲ συνάγουσιν εἰς
nor   reap   nor   gather   into

ἀποθήκας, καὶ ὁ πατὴρ ὑμῶν ὁ οὐράνιος
barns,   and the   ²Father   ³of you   –   ¹heavenly

τρέφει αὐτά· οὐχ ὑμεῖς μᾶλλον διαφέρετε
feeds   them;   do not ye   more   excel

αὐτῶν; 27 τίς δὲ ἐξ ὑμῶν μεριμνῶν
them?   But who   of   you   being anxious

δύναται προσθεῖναι ἐπὶ τὴν ἡλικίαν αὐτοῦ
can   to add   to   the   stature   of him

πῆχυν ἕνα; 28 καὶ περὶ ἐνδύματος τί
cubit   one?   and concerning   clothing   why

μεριμνᾶτε; καταμάθετε τὰ κρίνα τοῦ ἀγροῦ,
be ye anxious?   consider   the   lilies   of the field,

πῶς αὐξάνουσιν· οὐ κοπιῶσιν οὐδὲ
how   they grow;   they labour not   nor

νήθουσιν· 29 λέγω δὲ ὑμῖν ὅτι οὐδὲ Σολομὼν
spin;   but I tell   you   that   not   Solomon

ἐν πάσῃ τῇ δόξῃ αὐτοῦ περιεβάλετο ὡς
in   all   the   glory   of him   was clothed   as

ἐν τούτων. 30 εἰ δὲ τὸν χόρτον τοῦ
one   of these.   But if   the   grass   of the

---

treasures in heaven, where moth and rust do not destroy, and where thieves do not break in and steal. 21For where your treasure is, there your heart will be also. 22"The eye is the lamp of the body. If your eyes are good, your whole body will be full of light. 23But if your eyes are bad, your whole body will be full of darkness. If then the light within you is darkness, how great is that darkness! 24"No one can serve two masters. Either he will hate the one and love the other, or he will be devoted to the one and despise the other. You cannot serve both God and Money.

Do Not Worry

25"Therefore I tell you, do not worry about your life, what you will eat or drink; or about your body, what you will wear. Is not life more important than food, and the body more important than clothes? 26Look at the birds of the air; they do not sow or reap or store away in barns, and yet your heavenly Father feeds them. Are you not much more valuable than they? 27Who of you by worrying can add a single hour to his life ᵈ? 28"And why do you worry about clothes? See how the lilies of the field grow. They do not labor or spin. 29Yet I tell you that not even Solomon in all his splendor was dressed like one of these. 30If that is

ᵈ27 Or *single cubit to his height*

the grass of the field, which is alive today and tomorrow is thrown into the furnace, *will He* not much more *do so for* you, O men of little faith? 31"Do not be anxious then, saying, 'What shall we eat?' or 'What shall we drink?' or 'With what shall we clothe ourselves?' 32"For all these things the Gentiles eagerly seek; for your heavenly Father knows that you need all these things. 33"But seek first His kingdom and His righteousness; and all these things shall be added to you. 34"Therefore do not be anxious for tomorrow; for tomorrow will care for itself. *Each* day has enough trouble of its own.

ἀγροῦ	σήμερον	ὄντα	καὶ	αὔριον	εἰς
field	to-day	being	and	to-morrow	into

κλίβανον	βαλλόμενον	ὁ	θεὸς	οὕτως
an oven	being thrown	-	God	thus

ἀμφιέννυσιν,	οὐ	πολλῷ	μᾶλλον	ὑμᾶς,
clothes,	not	much	more	you,

ὀλιγόπιστοι;	**31** μὴ	οὖν	μεριμνήσητε
little-faiths?	Therefore be ye not anxious

λέγοντες·	τί	φάγωμεν;	ἤ·	τί
saying:	What	may we eat?	or:	What

πίωμεν;	ἤ·	τί	περιβαλώμεθα;	**32** πάντα
may we drink?	or:	What	may we put on?	¹all

γὰρ	ταῦτα	τὰ	ἔθνη	ἐπιζητοῦσιν·	οἶδεν
¹for	these things	the	nations	seek after;	⁶knows

γὰρ	ὁ	πατὴρ	ὑμῶν	ὁ	οὐράνιος	ὅτι
¹for	²the	⁴Father	⁵of you	-	³heavenly	that

χρῄζετε	τούτων	ἁπάντων.	**33** ζητεῖτε δὲ
ye need	these things	of all.	But seek ye

πρῶτον	τὴν	βασιλείαν	καὶ	τὴν	δικαιοσύνην
first	the	kingdom	and	the	righteousness

αὐτοῦ,	καὶ	ταῦτα	πάντα	προστεθήσεται
of him,	and	these things	all	shall be added

ὑμῖν.	**34** μὴ	οὖν	μεριμνήσητε	εἰς	τὴν
to you.	Therefore be ye not anxious	for	the

αὔριον,	ἡ	γὰρ	αὔριον	μεριμνήσει
morrow,	for the	morrow	will be anxious

ἑαυτῆς·	ἀρκετὸν	τῇ	ἡμέρᾳ	ἡ	κακία	αὐτῆς.
of itself;	sufficient	to the	day	the	evil	of it.

how God clothes the grass of the field, which is here today and tomorrow is thrown into the fire, will he not much more clothe you, O you of little faith? 31So do not worry, saying, 'What shall we eat?' or 'What shall we drink?' or 'What shall we wear?' 32For the pagans run after all these things, and your heavenly Father knows that you need them. 33But seek first his kingdom and his righteousness, and all these things will be given to you as well. 34Therefore do not worry about tomorrow, for tomorrow will worry about itself. Each day has enough trouble of its own.

Chapter 7

Concerning Judging Others

"DO not judge lest you be judged. 2"For in the way you judge, you will be judged; and by your standard of measure, it will be measured to you. 3"And why do you look at the speck that is in your brother's eye, but do not notice the log that is in your own eye? 4"Or how can you say to your brother, 'Let me take the speck out of your eye,' and behold, the log is in your own eye? 5"You hypocrite, first take the log out of your own eye, and then you will see clearly to take the speck out of your brother's eye. 6"Do not give what is holy to dogs, and do not throw your pearls before swine, lest they trample them under their feet, and turn and tear you to pieces.

Encouragement to Pray

7"Ask, and it shall be

7 Μὴ	κρίνετε,	ἵνα	μὴ	κριθῆτε·	**2** ἐν	ᾧ
Judge not,	lest	ye be judged;	²with	²what

γὰρ	κρίματι	κρίνετε	κριθήσεσθε,	καὶ
¹for	judgment	ye judge	ye shall be judged,	and

ἐν	ᾧ	μέτρῳ	μετρεῖτε	μετρηθήσεται	ὑμῖν.
with what	measure	ye measure	it shall be measured to you.

3 τί	δὲ	βλέπεις	τὸ	κάρφος	τὸ	ἐν
And why	seest thou	the	chip	the	in

τῷ	ὀφθαλμῷ	τοῦ	ἀδελφοῦ	σου,	τὴν
the	eye	of the	brother	of thee,	²the

δὲ	ἐν	τῷ	σῷ	ὀφθαλμῷ	δοκὸν	οὐ	κατα-
¹but	²in	³thine	⁴eye	³beam	thou consider-

νοεῖς;	**4** ἤ	πῶς	ἐρεῖς	τῷ	ἀδελφῷ	σου·
est not?	or	how	wilt thou say to the	brother	of thee:

ἄφες	ἐκβάλω	τὸ	κάρφος	ἐκ	τοῦ	ὀφθαλμοῦ
Allow [that] I may pluck *out*	the	chip	out of	the	eye

σου,	καὶ	ἰδοὺ	ἡ	δοκὸς	ἐν	τῷ	ὀφθαλμῷ
of thee,	and	behold	the	beam	in	the	eye

σου;	**5** ὑποκριτά,	ἔκβαλε	πρῶτον	ἐκ	τοῦ
of thee?	hypocrite,	pluck *out*	first	out of	the

ὀφθαλμοῦ	σου	τὴν	δοκόν,	καὶ	τότε
eye	of thee	the	beam,	and	then

διαβλέψεις	ἐκβαλεῖν	τὸ	κάρφος	ἐκ
thou wilt see clearly	to pluck *out*	the	chip	out of

τοῦ	ὀφθαλμοῦ	τοῦ	ἀδελφοῦ	σου.	**6** Μὴ
the	eye	of the	brother	of thee.	not

δῶτε	τὸ	ἅγιον	τοῖς	κυσίν,	μηδὲ	βάλητε
Give	the	holy	to the	dogs,	neither	cast

τοὺς	μαργαρίτας	ὑμῶν	ἔμπροσθεν	τῶν
the	pearls	of you	before	the

χοίρων,	μήποτε	καταπατήσουσιν	αὐτοὺς
pigs,	lest	they will trample	them

ἐν	τοῖς	ποσὶν	αὐτῶν	καὶ	στραφέντες
with	the	feet	of them	and	turning

ῥήξωσιν	ὑμᾶς.	**7** Αἰτεῖτε,	καὶ	δοθήσεται
may rend	you.	Ask,	and	it shall be given

Chapter 7

Judging Others

"DO not judge, or you too will be judged. 2For in the same way you judge others, you will be judged, and with the measure you use, it will be measured to you. 3"Why do you look at the speck of sawdust in your brother's eye and pay no attention to the plank in your own eye? 4How can you say to your brother, 'Let me take the speck out of your eye,' when all the time there is a plank in your own eye? 5You hypocrite, first take the plank out of your own eye, and then you will see clearly to remove the speck from your brother's eye. 6"Do not give dogs what is sacred; do not throw your pearls to pigs. If you do, they may trample them under their feet, and then turn and tear you to pieces.

Ask, Seek, Knock

7"Ask and it will be given

given to you; seek, and you shall find; knock, and it shall be opened to you.

8"For everyone who asks receives, and he who seeks finds, and to him who knocks it shall be opened.

9"Or what man is there among you, when his son shall ask him for a loaf, will give him a stone?

10"Or if he shall ask for a fish, he will not give him a snake, will he?

11"If you then, being evil, know how to give good gifts to your children, how much more shall your Father who is in heaven give what is good to those who ask Him!

12"Therefore, however you want people to treat you, so treat them, for this is the Law and the Prophets.

Ways Contrasted
Fruits Contrasted

13"Enter by the narrow gate; for the gate is wide, and the way is broad that leads to destruction, and many are those who enter by it.

14"For the gate is small, and the way is narrow that leads to life, and few are those who find it.

15"Beware of the false prophets, who come to you in sheep's clothing, but inwardly are ravenous wolves.

16"You will know them by their fruits. Grapes are not gathered from thorn bushes, nor figs from thistles, are they?

17"Even so, every good tree bears good fruit; but the bad tree bears bad fruit.

18"A good tree cannot produce bad fruit, nor can a bad tree produce good fruit.

ὑμῖν· ζητεῖτε, καὶ εὑρήσετε· κρούετε,
to you; seek, and ye shall find; knock,

καὶ ἀνοιγήσεται ὑμῖν. 8 πᾶς γὰρ ὁ αἰτῶν
and it shall be opened to you. For every asking [one]

λαμβάνει, καὶ ὁ ζητῶν εὑρίσκει, καὶ
receives, and the seeking [one] finds, and

τῷ κρούοντι ἀνοιγήσεται. 9 ἢ τίς ἐστιν
to the knocking [one] it shall be opened. Or ¹what ²is there

ἐξ ὑμῶν ἄνθρωπος, ὃν αἰτήσει ὁ υἱὸς
⁴of ⁵you ³man, whom ⁶will ask ⁷the ⁸son

αὐτοῦ ἄρτον, μὴ λίθον ἐπιδώσει αὐτῷ;
⁹of him ¹a loaf, *not* a stone he will give him?

10 ἢ καὶ ἰχθὺν αἰτήσει, μὴ ὄφιν ἐπιδώσει
or also a fish he will ask, *not* a serpent he will give

αὐτῷ; 11 εἰ οὖν ὑμεῖς πονηροὶ ὄντες
him? If therefore ye ²evil ¹being

οἴδατε· δόματα ἀγαθὰ διδόναι τοῖς τέκνοις
know ³gifts ²good ¹to give to the children

ὑμῶν, πόσῳ μᾶλλον ὁ πατὴρ ὑμῶν ὁ
of you, how much more the Father of you -

ἐν τοῖς οὐρανοῖς δώσει ἀγαθὰ τοῖς
in the heavens will give good things to the [ones]

αἰτοῦσιν αὐτόν. 12 Πάντα οὖν ὅσα ἐὰν
asking him. All things therefore as many soever as

θέλητε ἵνα ποιῶσιν ὑμῖν οἱ ἄνθρωποι,
ye wish that may do to you - men,

οὕτως καὶ ὑμεῖς ποιεῖτε αὐτοῖς· οὗτος
thus also ye do to them; ¹this

γάρ ἐστιν ὁ νόμος καὶ οἱ προφῆται.
²for is the law and the prophets.

13 Εἰσέλθατε διὰ τῆς στενῆς πύλης·
Enter ye in through the narrow gate;

ὅτι πλατεῖα [ἡ πύλη] καὶ εὐρύχωρος
because wide the gate and broad

ἡ ὁδὸς ἡ ἀπάγουσα εἰς τὴν ἀπώλειαν,
the way - leading away to - destruction,

καὶ πολλοί εἰσιν οἱ εἰσερχόμενοι δι'
and many are the [ones] going in through

αὐτῆς· 14 ὅτι στενὴ ἡ πύλη καὶ ·τεθλιμ-
it; because strait the gate and made

μένη ἡ ὁδὸς ἡ ἀπάγουσα εἰς τὴν ζωήν,
narrow the way - leading away to - life,

καὶ ὀλίγοι εἰσὶν οἱ εὑρίσκοντες αὐτήν.
and few are the [ones] finding it.

15 Προσέχετε ἀπὸ τῶν ψευδοπροφητῶν,
Beware from(of) - false prophets,

οἵτινες ἔρχονται πρὸς ὑμᾶς ἐν ἐνδύμασι
who come to you in clothes

προβάτων, ἔσωθεν δέ εἰσιν λύκοι ἄρπαγες.
of sheep, but within are wolves greedy.

16 ἀπὸ τῶν καρπῶν αὐτῶν ἐπιγνώσεσθε
From the fruits of them ye will know

αὐτούς. μήτι συλλέγουσιν ἀπὸ ἀκανθῶν σταφυλὰς
them. They do not gather from thorns grapes

ἢ ἀπὸ τριβόλων σῦκα; 17 οὕτως πᾶν
or from thistles figs? So ¹every

δένδρον ἀγαθὸν καρποὺς καλοὺς ποιεῖ,
³tree ²good ⁵fruits ⁴good ⁶produces,

τὸ δὲ σαπρὸν δένδρον καρποὺς πονηροὺς
but the corrupt tree fruits evil

ποιεῖ. 18 οὐ δύναται δένδρον ἀγαθὸν
produces. ²Cannot ¹tree ¹a good

καρποὺς πονηροὺς ἐνεγκεῖν, οὐδὲ δένδρον
⁴fruits ⁵evil ⁴to bear, nor ²tree

σαπρὸν καρποὺς καλοὺς ἐνεγκεῖν. 19 πᾶν
¹a corrupt ⁵fruits ⁴good ³to bear. Every

---

to you; seek and you will find; knock and the door will be opened to you. 8For everyone who asks receives; he who seeks finds; and to him who knocks, the door will be opened.

9"Which of you, if his son asks for bread, will give him a stone? 10Or if he asks for a fish, will give him a snake? 11If you, then, though you are evil, know how to give good gifts to your children, how much more will your Father in heaven give good gifts to those who ask him! 12So in everything, do to others what you would have them do to you, for this sums up the Law and the Prophets.

The Narrow and Wide Gates

13"Enter through the narrow gate. For wide is the gate and broad is the road that leads to destruction, and many enter through it. 14But small is the gate and narrow the road that leads to life, and only a few find it.

A Tree and Its Fruit

15"Watch out for false prophets. They come to you in sheep's clothing, but inwardly they are ferocious wolves. 16By their fruit you will recognize them. Do people pick grapes from thornbushes, or figs from thistles? 17Likewise every good tree bears good fruit, but a bad tree bears bad fruit. 18A good tree cannot bear bad fruit, and a bad tree cannot bear good fruit.

19"Every tree that does not bear good fruit is cut down and thrown into the fire.
20"So then, you will know them by their fruits.
21"Not everyone who says to Me, 'Lord, Lord,' will enter the kingdom of heaven; but he who does the will of My Father who is in heaven.
22"Many will say to Me on that day, 'Lord, Lord, did we not prophesy in Your name, and in Your name cast out demons, and in Your name perform many miracles?'
23"And then I will declare to them, 'I never knew you; DEPART FROM ME, YOU WHO PRACTICE LAWLESSNESS.'

The Two Foundations

24"Therefore everyone who hears these words of Mine, and acts upon them, may be compared to a wise man, who built his house upon the rock.
25"And the rain descended, and the floods came, and the winds blew, and burst against that house; and yet it did not fall, for it had been founded upon the rock.
26"And everyone who hears these words of Mine, and does not act upon them, will be like a foolish man, who built his house upon the sand.
27"And the rain descended, and the floods came, and the winds blew, and burst against that house; and it fell, and great was its fall."
28The result was that when Jesus had finished

δένδρον μὴ ποιοῦν καρπὸν καλὸν ἐκκόπτεται
tree not producing fruit good is cut down

καὶ εἰς πῦρ βάλλεται. 20 ἄρα γε ἀπὸ
and into fire is cast. Therefore from

τῶν καρπῶν αὐτῶν ἐπιγνώσεσθε αὐτούς.
the fruits of them ye will know them.

21 Οὐ πᾶς ὁ λέγων μοι κύριε κύριε,
Not everyone saying to me Lord[,] Lord,

εἰσελεύσεται εἰς τὴν βασιλείαν τῶν οὐρανῶν,
will enter into the kingdom of the heavens,

ἀλλ' ὁ ποιῶν τὸ θέλημα τοῦ πατρός
but the [one] doing the will of the Father

μου τοῦ ἐν τοῖς οὐρανοῖς. 22 πολλοὶ
of me - in the heavens. Many

ἐροῦσίν μοι ἐν ἐκείνῃ τῇ ἡμέρᾳ· κύριε
will say to me in that - day· Lord[,]

κύριε, οὐ τῷ σῷ ὀνόματι ἐπροφητεύσαμεν,
Lord, not - in thy name we prophesied,

καὶ τῷ σῷ ὀνόματι δαιμόνια ἐξεβάλομεν,
and - in thy name demons we expelled,

καὶ τῷ σῷ ὀνόματι δυνάμεις πολλὰς
and - in thy name mighty works many

ἐποιήσαμεν; 23 καὶ τότε ὁμολογήσω
did? and then I will declare

αὐτοῖς ὅτι οὐδέποτε ἔγνων ὑμᾶς· ἀπο-
to them[,] - Never I knew you; de-

χωρεῖτε ἀπ' ἐμοῦ οἱ ἐργαζόμενοι τὴν
part from me the [ones] working -

ἀνομίαν.
lawlessness.

24 Πᾶς οὖν ὅστις ἀκούει μου τοὺς
Everyone therefore who hears of me -

λόγους τούτους καὶ ποιεῖ αὐτούς,
words these and does them,

ὁμοιωθήσεται ἀνδρὶ φρονίμῳ, ὅστις ᾠκοδό-
shall be likened man to a prudent, who built

μησεν αὐτοῦ τὴν οἰκίαν ἐπὶ τὴν πέτραν.
of him the house on the rock.

25 καὶ κατέβη ἡ βροχὴ καὶ ἦλθον οἱ
And came down the rain and came the

ποταμοὶ καὶ ἔπνευσαν οἱ ἄνεμοι καὶ
rivers and blew the winds and

προσέπεσαν τῇ οἰκίᾳ ἐκείνῃ, καὶ οὐκ
fell against the house that, and not

ἔπεσεν· τεθεμελίωτο γὰρ ἐπὶ τὴν
it fell; for it had been founded on the

πέτραν. 26 καὶ πᾶς ὁ ἀκούων μου
rock. And everyone hearing of me

τοὺς λόγους τούτους καὶ μὴ ποιῶν
- words these and not doing

αὐτοὺς ὁμοιωθήσεται ἀνδρὶ μωρῷ, ὅστις
them shall be likened man to a foolish, who

ᾠκοδόμησεν αὐτοῦ τὴν οἰκίαν ἐπὶ τὴν
built of him the house on the

ἄμμον. 27 καὶ κατέβη ἡ βροχὴ καὶ
sand. And came down the rain and

ἦλθον οἱ ποταμοὶ καὶ ἔπνευσαν οἱ
came the rivers and blew the

ἄνεμοι καὶ προσέκοψαν τῇ οἰκίᾳ ἐκείνῃ,
winds and beat against the house that,

καὶ ἔπεσεν, καὶ ἦν ἡ πτῶσις αὐτῆς
and it fell, and was the fall of it

μεγάλη.
great.

28 Καὶ ἐγένετο ὅτε ἐτέλεσεν ὁ Ἰησοῦς
And it came to pass when finished - Jesus

19Every tree that does not bear good fruit is cut down and thrown into the fire.
20Thus, by their fruit you will recognize them.
21"Not everyone who says to me, 'Lord, Lord,' will enter the kingdom of heaven, but only he who does the will of my Father who is in heaven. 22Many will say to me on that day, 'Lord, Lord, did we not prophesy in your name, and in your name drive out demons and perform many miracles?' 23Then I will tell them plainly, 'I never knew you. Away from me, you evildoers!'

The Wise and Foolish Builders

24"Therefore everyone who hears these words of mine and puts them into practice is like a wise man who built his house on the rock. 25The rain came down, the streams rose, and the winds blew and beat against that house; yet it did not fall, because it had its foundation on the rock. 26But everyone who hears these words of mine and does not put them into practice is like a foolish man who built his house on sand. 27The rain came down, the streams rose, and the winds blew and beat against that house, and it fell with a great crash."

28When Jesus had finthese words, the multitudes were amazed at His teaching;

29for He was teaching them as *one* having authority, and not as their scribes.

Chapter 8

Jesus Cleanses a Leper
The Centurion's Faith

AND when He had come down from the mountain, great multitudes followed Him.

2And behold, a leper came to Him, and bowed down to Him, saying, "Lord, if You are willing, You can make me clean."

3And He stretched out His hand and touched him, saying, "I am willing; be cleansed." And immediately his leprosy was cleansed.

4And Jesus *said to him, "See that you tell no one; but go, show yourself to the priest, and present the offering that Moses commanded, for a testimony to them."

5And when He had entered Capernaum, a centurion came to Him, entreating Him,

6and saying, "Lord, my servant is lying paralyzed at home, suffering great pain."

7And He *said to him, "I will come and heal him."

8But the centurion answered and said, "Lord, I am not worthy for You to come under my roof, but just say the word, and my servant will be healed.

9"For I, too, am a man under authority, with soldiers under me; and I say to this one, 'Go!' and he goes, and to another, 'Come!' and he comes, and to my slave, 'Do this!' and he does *it*."

10Now when Jesus heard *this*, He marveled, and said to those who were following, "Truly I say to you, I

τοὺς λόγους τούτους, ἐξεπλήσσοντο οἱ
- words these, were astounded the

ὄχλοι ἐπὶ τῇ διδαχῇ αὐτοῦ· 29 ἦν γὰρ
crowds at the teaching of him; for he was

διδάσκων αὐτοὺς ὡς ἐξουσίαν ἔχων, καὶ
teaching them as authority having, and

οὐχ ὡς οἱ γραμματεῖς αὐτῶν.
not as the scribes of them.

8 Καταβάντος δὲ αὐτοῦ ἀπὸ τοῦ ὄρους
And coming down him[a] from the mountain
= as he came down

ἠκολούθησαν αὐτῷ ὄχλοι πολλοί. 2 καὶ
followed him crowds many. And

ἰδοὺ λεπρὸς προσελθὼν προσεκύνει αὐτῷ
behold a leper approaching worshipped him

λέγων· κύριε, ἐὰν θέλῃς, δύνασαί με
saying: Lord, if thou art willing, thou art able me

καθαρίσαι. 3 καὶ ἐκτείνας τὴν χεῖρα
to cleanse. And stretching out the(his) hand

ἥψατο αὐτοῦ λέγων· θέλω, καθαρίσθητι.
he touched him saying: I am willing, be thou cleansed.

καὶ εὐθέως ἐκαθαρίσθη αὐτοῦ ἡ λέπρα.
And immediately was cleansed of him the leprosy.

4 καὶ λέγει αὐτῷ ὁ Ἰησοῦς· ὅρα μηδενὶ
And says to him - Jesus: See to no one

εἴπῃς, ἀλλὰ ὕπαγε σεαυτὸν δεῖξον τῷ
thou tellest, but go thyself show to the

ἱερεῖ καὶ προσένεγκον τὸ δῶρον ὃ
priest and offer the gift which

προσέταξεν Μωϋσῆς, εἰς μαρτύριον αὐτοῖς.
commanded Moses, for a testimony to them.

5 Εἰσελθόντος δὲ αὐτοῦ εἰς Καφαρναοὺμ
And entering him[a] into Capernaum,
= as he entered

προσῆλθεν αὐτῷ ἑκατόνταρχος παρακαλῶν
approached to him a centurion beseeching

αὐτὸν 6 καὶ λέγων· κύριε, ὁ παῖς μου
him and saying: Lord, the boy of me

βέβληται ἐν τῇ οἰκίᾳ παραλυτικός,
has been laid [aside] in the house a paralytic,

δεινῶς βασανιζόμενος. 7 λέγει αὐτῷ·
terribly *being* tortured. He says to him:

ἐγὼ ἐλθὼν θεραπεύσω αὐτόν. 8 ἀποκριθεὶς
I coming will heal him. answering

δὲ ὁ ἑκατόνταρχος ἔφη· κύριε, οὐκ εἰμὶ
But the centurion said: Lord, I am not

ἱκανὸς ἵνα μου ὑπὸ τὴν στέγην εἰσέλθῃς·
worthy that of me under the roof thou mayest enter;

ἀλλὰ μόνον εἰπὲ λόγῳ, καὶ ἰαθήσεται ὁ παῖς
but only say in a word, and will be healed the boy

μου. 9 καὶ γὰρ ἐγὼ ἄνθρωπός εἰμι
of me. [a]also [i]For [b]I [a]a man [i]am

ὑπὸ ἐξουσίαν, ἔχων ὑπ᾽ ἐμαυτὸν στρατιώτας,
under authority, having under myself soldiers,

καὶ λέγω τούτῳ· πορεύθητι, καὶ πορεύεται,
and I say to this: Go, and he goes,

καὶ ἄλλῳ· ἔρχου, καὶ ἔρχεται, καὶ τῷ
and to another: Come, and he comes, and to the

δούλῳ μου· ποίησον τοῦτο, καὶ ποιεῖ.
slave of me: Do this, and he does [it].

10 ἀκούσας δὲ ὁ Ἰησοῦς ἐθαύμασεν
And hearing - Jesus marvelled

καὶ εἶπεν τοῖς ἀκολουθοῦσιν· ἀμὴν λέγω
and said to the [ones] following: Truly I tell

---

ished saying these things, the crowds were amazed at his teaching, 29because he taught as one who had authority, and not as their teachers of the law.

Chapter 8

The Man With Leprosy

WHEN he came down from the mountainside, large crowds followed him. 2A man with leprosy[e] came and knelt before him and said, "Lord, if you are willing, you can make me clean."

3Jesus reached out his hand and touched the man. "I am willing," he said. "Be clean!" Immediately he was cured[f] of his leprosy. 4Then Jesus said to him, "See that you don't tell anyone. But go, show yourself to the priest and offer the gift Moses commanded, as a testimony to them."

The Faith of the Centurion

5When Jesus had entered Capernaum, a centurion came to him, asking for help. 6"Lord," he said, "my servant lies at home paralyzed and in terrible suffering."

7Jesus said to him, "I will go and heal him."

8The centurion replied, "Lord, I do not deserve to have you come under my roof. But just say the word, and my servant will be healed. 9For I myself am a man under authority, with soldiers under me. I tell this one, 'Go,' and he goes; and that one, 'Come,' and he comes. I say to my servant, 'Do this,' and he does it."

10When Jesus heard this, he was astonished and said to those following him, "I tell you the truth, I have not

---

*e*2 The Greek word was used for various diseases affecting the skin—not necessarily leprosy.
*f*3 Greek *made clean*

have not found such great faith with anyone in Israel. 11"And I say to you, that many shall come from east and west, and "recline *at the table* with Abraham, and Isaac, and Jacob, in the kingdom of heaven; 12but the sons of the kingdom shall be cast out into the outer darkness; in that place there shall be weeping and gnashing of teeth." 13And Jesus said to the centurion, "Go your way; let it be done to you as you have believed." And the servant was healed that *very* hour.

Peter's Mother-in-law Healed
Many Healed
14And when Jesus had come to Peter's home, He saw his mother-in-law lying sick in bed with a fever. 15And He touched her hand, and the fever left her; and she arose, and waited on Him. 16And when evening had come, they brought to Him many who were demon-possessed; and He cast out the spirits with a word, and healed all who were ill 17in order that what was spoken through Isaiah the prophet might be fulfilled, saying, "HE HIMSELF TOOK OUR INFIRMITIES, AND CARRIED AWAY OUR DISEASES."

Discipleship Tested
18Now when Jesus saw a crowd around Him, He gave orders to depart to the other side. 19And a certain scribe came and said to Him, "Teacher, I will follow You wherever You go." 20And Jesus *said to him, "The foxes have holes, and the birds of the air *have* nests; but the Son of Man

ὑμῖν, παρ' οὐδενὶ τοσαύτην πίστιν ἐν τῷ
you, from no one such faith in -
'Ἰσραὴλ εὗρον. 11 λέγω δὲ ὑμῖν ὅτι
Israel I found. And I tell you that
πολλοὶ ἀπὸ ἀνατολῶν καὶ δυσμῶν ἥξουσιν
many from east and west will come
καὶ ἀνακλιθήσονται μετὰ 'Ἀβραάμ καὶ
and will recline with Abraham and
'Ἰσαὰκ καὶ 'Ἰακὼβ ἐν τῇ βασιλείᾳ τῶν
Isaac and Jacob in the kingdom of the
οὐρανῶν· 12 οἱ δὲ υἱοὶ τῆς βασιλείας
heavens; but the sons of the kingdom
ἐκβληθήσονται εἰς τὸ σκότος τὸ ἐξώτερον·
will be cast out into the darkness - outer;
ἐκεῖ ἔσται ὁ κλαυθμὸς καὶ ὁ βρυγμὸς
there will be the weeping and the gnashing
τῶν ὀδόντων. 13 καὶ εἶπεν ὁ 'Ἰησοῦς τῷ
of the teeth. And said - Jesus to the
ἑκατοντάρχῃ· ὕπαγε, ὡς ἐπίστευσας γενη-
centurion: Go, as thou believedst let it
θήτω σοι. καὶ ἰάθη ὁ παῖς ἐν τῇ
be to thee. And was healed the boy in -
ὥρᾳ ἐκείνῃ.
hour that.

14 Καὶ ἐλθὼν ὁ 'Ἰησοῦς εἰς τὴν οἰκίαν
And coming - Jesus into the house
Πέτρου εἶδεν τὴν πενθερὰν αὐτοῦ βεβλη-
of Peter he saw the mother-in-law of him *having been*
μένην καὶ πυρέσσουσαν· 15 καὶ ἥψατο
laid [aside] and fever-stricken; and he touched
τῆς χειρὸς αὐτῆς, καὶ ἀφῆκεν αὐτὴν ὁ
the hand of her, and left her the
πυρετός· καὶ ἡγέρθη, καὶ διηκόνει αὐτῷ.
fever; and she arose, and ministered to him.
16 'Ὀψίας δὲ γενομένης προσήνεγκαν
And evening coming² they brought
= when evening came
αὐτῷ δαιμονιζομένους πολλούς· καὶ ἐξέβαλεν
to him *being* demon-possessed many; and he expelled
τὰ πνεύματα λόγῳ, καὶ πάντας τοὺς
the spirits with a word, and all the [ones]
= those
κακῶς ἔχοντας ἐθεράπευσεν· 17 ὅπως
ill having he healed; so that
who were ill
πληρωθῇ τὸ ῥηθὲν διὰ 'Ἠσαΐου τοῦ
was fulfilled the [thing] spoken through Isaiah the
προφήτου λέγοντος· αὐτὸς τὰς ἀσθενείας
prophet saying: He the weaknesses
ἡμῶν ἔλαβεν καὶ τὰς νόσους ἐβάστασεν.
of us took and the diseases he bore.
18 'Ἰδὼν δὲ ὁ 'Ἰησοῦς ὄχλον περὶ
But ²seeing - ¹Jesus a crowd around
αὐτὸν ἐκέλευσεν ἀπελθεῖν εἰς τὸ πέραν.
him commanded to go away to the other side.
19 Καὶ προσελθὼν εἷς γραμματεὺς εἶπεν
And approaching one scribe said
αὐτῷ· διδάσκαλε, ἀκολουθήσω σοι
to him: Teacher, I will follow thee
ὅπου ἐὰν ἀπέρχῃ. 20 καὶ λέγει αὐτῷ
wherever thou mayest go. And says to him
ὁ 'Ἰησοῦς· αἱ ἀλώπεκες φωλεοὺς ἔχουσιν
- Jesus: The foxes holes have
καὶ τὰ πετεινὰ τοῦ οὐρανοῦ κατα-
and the birds of the heaven nests,
σκηνώσεις, ὁ δὲ υἱὸς τοῦ ἀνθρώπου
but the Son of man

found anyone in Israel with such great faith. 11I say to you that many will come from the east and the west, and will take their places at the feast with Abraham, Isaac and Jacob in the kingdom of heaven. 12But the subjects of the kingdom will be thrown outside, into the darkness, where there will be weeping and gnashing of teeth." 13Then Jesus said to the centurion, "Go! It will be done just as you believed it would." And his servant was healed at that very hour.

Jesus Heals Many
14When Jesus came into Peter's house, he saw Peter's mother-in-law lying in bed with a fever. 15He touched her hand and the fever left her, and she got up and began to wait on him. 16When evening came, many who were demon-possessed were brought to him, and he drove out the spirits with a word and healed all the sick. 17This was to fulfill what was spoken through the prophet Isaiah:

"He took up our
infirmities
and carried our
diseases."ᵍ

The Cost of Following Jesus
18When Jesus saw the crowd around him, he gave orders to cross to the other side of the lake. 19Then a teacher of the law came to him and said, "Teacher, I will follow you wherever you go." 20Jesus replied, "Foxes have holes and birds of the air have nests, but the Son of Man has no place to lay

"Or, *dine*

ᵍ17 Isaiah 53:4

has nowhere to lay His head."

21And another of the disciples said to Him, "Lord, permit me first to go and bury my father."

22But Jesus *said to him, "Follow Me; and allow the dead to bury their own dead."

23And when He got into the boat, His disciples followed Him.

24And behold, there arose a great storm in the sea, so that the boat was covered with the waves; but He Himself was asleep.

25And they came to *Him*, and awoke Him, saying, "Save *us*, Lord; we are perishing!"

26And He *said to them, "Why are you timid, you men of little faith?" Then He arose, and rebuked the winds and the sea; and it became perfectly calm.

27And the men marveled, saying, "What kind of a man is this, that even the winds and the sea obey Him?"

Jesus Casts Out Demons

28And when He had come to the other side into the country of the Gadarenes, two men who were demon-possessed met Him as they were coming out of the tombs; *they were* so exceedingly violent that no one could pass by that road.

29And behold, they cried out, saying, "What do we have to do with You, Son of God? Have You come here to torment us before the time?"

30Now there was at a distance from them a herd of many swine feeding.

31And the demons *began* to entreat Him, saying, "If You are *going to* cast us out, send us into the herd of

---

οὐκ   ἔχει   ποῦ   τὴν   κεφαλὴν   κλίνῃ.
has not   where   the(his)   head   he may lay.

21 ἕτερος   δὲ   τῶν   μαθητῶν   εἶπεν
And another   of the   disciples   said

αὐτῷ·   κύριε,   ἐπίτρεψόν   μοι   πρῶτον
to him: Lord,   allow   me   first

ἀπελθεῖν   καὶ   θάψαι   τὸν   πατέρα   μου.
to go away   and   bury   the   father   of me.

22 ὁ   δὲ   Ἰησοῦς   λέγει   αὐτῷ·   ἀκολούθει
-   But   Jesus   says   to him: Follow thou

μοι,   καὶ   ἄφες   τοὺς   νεκροὺς   θάψαι   τοὺς
me,   and   leave   the   dead   to bury   the

ἑαυτῶν   νεκρούς.
of themselves   dead.

23 Καὶ   ἐμβάντι   αὐτῷ   εἰς   τὸ   πλοῖον,
And   embarking   him⁰   in   the   ship,
   = as he embarked

ἠκολούθησαν   αὐτῷ   οἱ   μαθηταὶ   αὐτοῦ.
followed   him   the   disciples   of him.

24 καὶ   ἰδοὺ   σεισμὸς   μέγας   ἐγένετο   ἐν
And   behold   storm   a great   there was   in

τῇ   θαλάσσῃ,   ὥστε   τὸ   πλοῖον   καλύπτ-
the   sea,   so as   the   ship   to be en-

εσθαι   ὑπὸ   τῶν   κυμάτων·   αὐτὸς   δὲ   ἐκάθευδεν.
veloped   by   the   waves;   but he   was sleeping.

25 καὶ   προσελθόντες   ἤγειραν   αὐτὸν   λέγοντες·
And   approaching   they roused   him   saying:

κύριε,   σῶσον,   ἀπολλύμεθα.   **26** καὶ   λέγει
Lord,   save,   we are perishing.   And   he says

αὐτοῖς·   τί   δειλοί   ἐστε,   ὀλιγόπιστοι;
to them: Why   fearful   are ye,   little-faiths?

τότε   ἐγερθεὶς   ἐπετίμησεν   τοῖς   ἀνέμοις   καὶ
Then   rising   he rebuked   the   winds   and

τῇ   θαλάσσῃ,   καὶ   ἐγένετο   γαλήνη   μεγάλη.
the   sea,   and   there was   calm   a great.

27 οἱ   δὲ   ἄνθρωποι   ἐθαύμασαν   λέγοντες·
And the   men   marvelled   saying:

ποταπός   ἐστιν   οὗτος,   ὅτι   καὶ   οἱ   ἄνεμοι
Of what sort   is   this [man],   that   even   the   winds

καὶ   ἡ   θάλασσα   αὐτῷ   ὑπακούουσιν;
and   the   sea   him   obey?

28 Καὶ   ἐλθόντος   αὐτοῦ   εἰς   τὸ   πέραν   εἰς
And   coming   himᵃ   to   the   other side   into
   = when he came

τὴν   χώραν   τῶν   Γαδαρηνῶν   ὑπήντησαν
the   country   of the   Gadarenes   met

αὐτῷ   δύο   δαιμονιζόμενοι   ἐκ   τῶν   μνημείων
him   two   demon-possessed   out of the   tombs

ἐξερχόμενοι,   χαλεποὶ   λίαν,   ὥστε   μὴ
coming *out*,   dangerous   exceedingly,   so as   not

ἰσχύειν   τινὰ   παρελθεῖν   διὰ   τῆς   ὁδοῦ
to be able   anyoneᵇ   to pass   through   -   way

ἐκείνης.   **29** καὶ   ἰδοὺ   ἔκραξαν   λέγοντες·
that.   And   behold   they cried out   saying:

τί   ἡμῖν   καὶ   σοί,   υἱέ   τοῦ   θεοῦ;   ἦλθες
What to us   and   to thee,   Son   -   of God?   camest thou

ὧδε   πρὸ   καιροῦ   βασανίσαι   ἡμᾶς;   **30** ἦν
here   before [the]   time   to torture   us?   there was

δὲ   μακρὰν   ἀπ᾽   αὐτῶν   ἀγέλη   χοίρων
Now   far off   from   them   a herd   pigs

πολλῶν   βοσκομένη.   **31** οἱ   δὲ   δαίμονες
of many   feeding.   And the   demons

παρεκάλουν   αὐτὸν   λέγοντες·   εἰ   ἐκβάλλεις
besought   him   saying: If   thou expellest

ἡμᾶς,   ἀπόστειλον   ἡμᾶς   εἰς   τὴν   ἀγέλην
us,   send   us   into   the   herd

---

his head."

21Another disciple said to him, "Lord, first let me go and bury my father."

22But Jesus told him, "Follow me, and let the dead bury their own dead."

Jesus Calms the Storm

23Then he got into the boat and his disciples followed him. 24Without warning, a furious storm came up on the lake, so that the waves swept over the boat. But Jesus was sleeping. 25The disciples went and woke him, saying, "Lord, save us! We're going to drown!"

26He replied, "You of little faith, why are you so afraid?" Then he got up and rebuked the winds and the waves, and it was completely calm.

27The men were amazed and asked, "What kind of man is this? Even the winds and the waves obey him!"

The Healing of Two Demon-possessed Men

28When he arrived at the other side in the region of the Gadarenes,ʰ two demon-possessed men coming from the tombs met him. They were so violent that no one could pass that way. 29"What do you want with us, Son of God?" they shouted. "Have you come here to torture us before the appointed time?"

30Some distance from them a large herd of pigs was feeding. 31The demons begged Jesus, "If you drive us out, send us into the herd of pigs."

ʰ28 Some manuscripts *Gergesenes*; others *Gerasenes*

swine."
32And He said to them,
"Begone!" And they came
out, and went into the
swine, and behold, the
whole herd rushed down
the steep bank into the sea
and perished in the waters.
33And the herdsmen ran
away, and went to the city,
and reported everything,
including the *incident* of
the demoniacs.
34And behold, the whole
city came out to meet
Jesus; and when they saw
Him, they entreated *Him* to
depart from their region.

τῶν   χοίρων.   32 καὶ   εἶπεν   αὐτοῖς·
of the   pigs.   And   he said   to them:

ὑπάγετε.   οἱ   δὲ   ἐξελθόντες   ἀπῆλθον   εἰς
Go ye.   So the   coming out [ones]   went away   into

τοὺς   χοίρους·   καὶ   ἰδοὺ   ὥρμησεν   πᾶσα   ἡ
the   pigs;   and   behold   rushed   all   the

ἀγέλη   κατὰ   τοῦ   κρημνοῦ   εἰς   τὴν   θάλασσαν,
herd   down   the   precipice   into   the   sea,

καὶ   ἀπέθανον   ἐν   τοῖς   ὕδασιν.   33 οἱ
and   died   in   the   waters.   the

δὲ   βόσκοντες   ἔφυγον,   καὶ   ἀπελθόντες
But   feeding [ones]   fled,   and   going away

εἰς   τὴν   πόλιν   ἀπήγγειλαν   πάντα   καὶ
into   the   city   reported   all things   and

τὰ   τῶν   δαιμονιζομένων.   34 καὶ   ἰδοὺ
the [things] of the   demon-possessed [ones].   And   behold

πᾶσα ἡ πόλις ἐξῆλθεν   εἰς   ὑπάντησιν
all   the   city   came out   with a view to   a meeting [with]

τῷ   Ἰησοῦ,   καὶ   ἰδόντες   αὐτὸν   παρεκάλεσαν
-     Jesus,   and   seeing   2him   1besought

ὅπως   μεταβῇ   ἀπὸ   τῶν   ὁρίων   αὐτῶν.
so that   he might remove   from   the   borders   of them.

So they came out and went
into the pigs, and the whole
herd rushed down the steep
bank into the lake and died
in the water. 33Those tending the pigs ran off, went
into the town and reported
all this, including what had
happened to the demon-
possessed men. 34Then the
whole town went out to
meet Jesus. And when they
saw him, they pleaded with
him to leave their region.

Chapter 9

A Paralytic Cured

AND getting into a boat,
He crossed over, and
came to His own city.
2And behold, they were
bringing to Him a paralytic,
lying on a bed; and Jesus
seeing their faith said to the
paralytic, "Take courage,
My son, your sins are forgiven."
3And behold, some of
the scribes said to them-
selves, "This *fellow* blasphemes."
4And Jesus knowing
their thoughts said, "Why
are you thinking evil in
your hearts?
5"For which is easier, to
say, 'Your sins are for-
given,' or to say, 'Rise, and
walk'?
6"But in order that you
may know that the Son of
Man has authority on earth
to forgive sins"—then He
*said to the paralytic—
"Rise, take up your bed,
and go home."
7And he rose, and went
home.
8But when the multi-
tudes saw *this*, they were
filled with awe, and glorified God, who had given
such authority to men.

---

9 Καὶ   ἐμβὰς   εἰς   πλοῖον   διεπέρασεν,
And   embarking   in   a ship   he crossed over,

καὶ   ἦλθεν   εἰς   τὴν   ἰδίαν   πόλιν.   2 Καὶ
and   came   into   the(his)   own   city.   And

ἰδοὺ   προσέφερον   αὐτῷ   παραλυτικὸν   ἐπὶ
behold   they brought   to him   a paralytic   on

κλίνης   βεβλημένον.   καὶ   ἰδὼν   ὁ   Ἰησοῦς
a mattress   having been laid.   and   2seeing   -   1Jesus

τὴν   πίστιν   αὐτῶν   εἶπεν   τῷ   παραλυτικῷ·
the   faith   of them   said   to the   paralytic:

θάρσει,   τέκνον,   ἀφίενταί   σου   αἱ   ἁμαρτίαι.
Be of good cheer,   child,   are forgiven of thee the   sins.

3 καὶ   ἰδού   τινες   τῶν   γραμματέων   εἶπαν
And   behold   some   of the   scribes   said

ἐν   ἑαυτοῖς·   οὗτος   βλασφημεῖ.   4 καὶ
among themselves: This [man]   blasphemes.   And

εἰδὼς   ὁ   Ἰησοῦς   τὰς   ἐνθυμήσεις   αὐτῶν
1knowing   -   2Jesus   the   thoughts   of them

εἶπεν·   ἱνατί   ἐνθυμεῖσθε   πονηρὰ   ἐν   ταῖς
said: Why   think ye   evil things   in   the

καρδίαις   ὑμῶν;   5 τί   γάρ   ἐστιν   εὐκοπώ-
hearts   of you?   for which   is   easier,

τερον,   εἰπεῖν·   ἀφίενταί   σου   αἱ   ἁμαρτίαι,   ἢ
        to say: 2are forgiven   3of thee 1The   4sins,   or

εἰπεῖν·   ἔγειρε   καὶ   περιπάτει;   6 ἵνα   δὲ
to say: Rise   and   walk ?   But in order that

εἰδῆτε   ὅτι   ἐξουσίαν   ἔχει   ὁ   υἱὸς   τοῦ
ye may know that   authority   has   the   Son   -

ἀνθρώπου   ἐπὶ   τῆς   γῆς   ἀφιέναι   ἁμαρτίας—
of man   on   the   earth   to forgive   sins—

τότε   λέγει   τῷ   παραλυτικῷ·   ἔγειρε   ἆρόν
then   he says   to the   paralytic: Rise[,]   take

σου   τὴν   κλίνην   καὶ   ὕπαγε   εἰς   τὸν   οἶκόν
of thee   the   mattress   and   go   to   the   house

σου.   7 καὶ   ἐγερθεὶς   ἀπῆλθεν   εἰς   τὸν
of thee.   And   rising   he went away   to   the

οἶκον   αὐτοῦ.   8 ἰδόντες   δὲ   οἱ   ὄχλοι
house   of him.   But seeing   the   crowds

ἐφοβήθησαν   καὶ   ἐδόξασαν   τὸν   θεὸν   τὸν
feared   and   glorified   -   God the [one]

δόντα   ἐξουσίαν   τοιαύτην   τοῖς   ἀνθρώποις.
giving   2authority   1such   -   to men.

Chapter 9

Jesus Heals a Paralytic

JESUS stepped into a
boat, crossed over and
came to his own town.
2Some men brought to him
a paralytic, lying on a mat.
When Jesus saw their faith,
he said to the paralytic,
"Take heart, son; your sins
are forgiven."
3At this, some of the
teachers of the law said to
themselves, "This fellow is
blaspheming!"
4Knowing their thoughts,
Jesus said, "Why do you
entertain evil thoughts in
your hearts? 5Which is easier: to say, 'Your sins are
forgiven,' or to say, 'Get up
and walk'? 6But so that you
may know that the Son of
Man has authority on earth
to forgive sins. . . ." Then
he said to the paralytic,
"Get up, take your mat and
go home." 7And the man
got up and went home.
8When the crowd saw this,
they were filled with awe;
and they praised God, who
had given such authority to
men.

Matthew Called

9And as Jesus passed on from there, He saw a man, called Matthew, sitting in the tax office; and He *said to him, "Follow Me!" And he rose, and followed Him.

10And it happened that as He was reclining *at the table* in the house, behold many tax-gatherers and sinners came and were dining with Jesus and His disciples.

11And when the Pharisees saw *this*, they said to His disciples, "Why is your Teacher eating with the tax-gatherers and sinners?"

12But when He heard this, He said, "*It is* not those who are healthy who need a physician, but those who are sick.

13"But go and learn what *this* means, 'I DESIRE COMPASSION, 'AND NOT SACRIFICE,' for I did not come to call the righteous, but sinners."

14Then the disciples of John *came to Him, saying, "Why do we and the Pharisees fast, but Your disciples do not fast?"

15And Jesus said to them, "The attendants of the bridegroom cannot mourn as long as the bridegroom is with them, can they? But the days will come when the bridegroom is taken away from them, and then they will fast.

16"But no one puts a patch of unshrunk cloth on an old garment; for the patch pulls away from the garment, and a worse tear results.

17"Nor do *men* put new wine into old wineskins; otherwise the wineskins

---

9 Καὶ παράγων ὁ Ἰησοῦς ἐκεῖθεν εἶδεν
And ²passing by - ¹Jesus thence saw

ἄνθρωπον καθήμενον ἐπὶ τὸ τελώνιον,
a man sitting at the custom house,

Ματθαῖον λεγόμενον, καὶ λέγει αὐτῷ·
Matthew named, and says to him:

ἀκολούθει μοι. καὶ ἀναστὰς ἠκολούθησεν
Follow me. And rising up he followed

αὐτῷ. **10** Καὶ ἐγένετο αὐτοῦ ἀνακει-
him. And it came to pass him reclin-
                 =as he was reclining

μένου ἐν τῇ οἰκίᾳ, καὶ ἰδοὺ πολλοὶ
ing² in the house, and behold many

τελῶναι καὶ ἁμαρτωλοὶ ἐλθόντες συνανέκειντο
tax-collectors and sinners coming reclined at table with

τῷ Ἰησοῦ καὶ τοῖς μαθηταῖς αὐτοῦ.
- Jesus and the disciples of him.

11 καὶ ἰδόντες οἱ Φαρισαῖοι ἔλεγον τοῖς
And ²seeing ¹the ³Pharisees said to the

μαθηταῖς αὐτοῦ· διὰ τί μετὰ τῶν τελωνῶν
disciples of him: Why with - tax-collectors

καὶ ἁμαρτωλῶν ἐσθίει ὁ διδάσκαλος ὑμῶν;
and sinners eats the teacher of you?

12 ὁ δὲ ἀκούσας εἶπεν· οὐ χρείαν
But he hearing said: Not need

ἔχουσιν οἱ ἰσχύοντες ἰατροῦ ἀλλ' οἱ
have the [ones] being strong of a physician but the [ones]
                                         =those

κακῶς ἔχοντες. **13** πορευθέντες δὲ μάθετε
ill having. But going learn ye
who are ill.

τί ἐστιν· ἔλεος θέλω καὶ οὐ θυσίαν· οὐ
what it is: Mercy I desire and not sacrifice; not

γὰρ ἦλθον καλέσαι δικαίους ἀλλὰ
for I came to call righteous [people] but

ἁμαρτωλούς.
sinners.

14 Τότε προσέρχονται αὐτῷ οἱ μαθηταὶ
Then approach *to him* the disciples

Ἰωάννου λέγοντες· διὰ τί ἡμεῖς καὶ οἱ
of John saying: Why we and the

Φαρισαῖοι νηστεύομεν, οἱ δὲ μαθηταί
Pharisees fast, but the disciples

σου οὐ νηστεύουσιν; **15** καὶ εἶπεν
of thee fast not? And said

αὐτοῖς ὁ Ἰησοῦς· μὴ δύνανται οἱ
to them - Jesus: *not* Can the

υἱοὶ τοῦ νυμφῶνος πενθεῖν, ἐφ' ὅσον
sons of the bridechamber *to mourn,* so long as

μετ' αὐτῶν ἐστιν ὁ νυμφίος; ἐλεύσονται
with them is the bridegroom? ²will come

δὲ ἡμέραι ὅταν ἀπαρθῇ ἀπ' αὐτῶν ὁ
¹but ²days when is taken away from them the

νυμφίος, καὶ τότε νηστεύσουσιν. **16** οὐδεὶς
bridegroom, and then they will fast. no one

δὲ ἐπιβάλλει ἐπίβλημα ῥάκους ἀγνάφου
Now puts on a patch cloth of unfulled

ἐπὶ ἱματίῳ παλαιῷ· αἴρει γὰρ τὸ
on garment an old; for takes away the

πλήρωμα αὐτοῦ ἀπὸ τοῦ ἱματίου, καὶ
fullness of it from the garment, and

χεῖρον σχίσμα γίνεται. **17** οὐδὲ
a worse rent becomes. Neither

βάλλουσιν οἶνον νέον εἰς ἀσκοὺς
do they put wine new into wineskins

παλαιούς· εἰ δὲ μή γε, ῥήγνυνται
old; otherwise, are burst

The Calling of Matthew

9As Jesus went on from there, he saw a man named Matthew sitting at the tax collector's booth. "Follow me," he told him, and Matthew got up and followed him.

10While Jesus was having dinner at Matthew's house, many tax collectors and "sinners" came and ate with him and his disciples. 11When the Pharisees saw this, they asked his disciples, "Why does your teacher eat with tax collectors and 'sinners'?"

12On hearing this, Jesus said, "It is not the healthy who need a doctor, but the sick. 13But go and learn what this means: 'I desire mercy, not sacrifice.'ⁱ For I have not come to call the righteous, but sinners."

Jesus Questioned About Fasting

14Then John's disciples came and asked him, "How is it that we and the Pharisees fast, but your disciples do not fast?"

15Jesus answered, "How can the guests of the bridegroom mourn while he is with them? The time will come when the bridegroom will be taken from them; then they will fast.

16"No one sews a patch of unshrunk cloth on an old garment, for the patch will pull away from the garment, making the tear worse. 17Neither do men pour new wine into old wineskins. If they do, the skins will burst, the wine

---

ⁱ I.e., more than   ⁱ13 Hosea 6:6

burst, and the wine pours out, and the wineskins are ruined; but they put new wine into fresh wineskins, and both are preserved."

Miracles of Healing

18While He was saying these things to them, behold, there came a *synagogue* official, and bowed down before Him, saying, "My daughter has just died; but come and lay Your hand on her, and she will live."

19And Jesus rose and *began* to follow him, and *so did* His disciples.

20And behold, a woman who had been suffering from a hemorrhage for twelve years, came up behind Him and touched the fringe of His cloak;

21for she was saying to herself, "If I only touch His garment, I shall get well."

22But Jesus turning and seeing her said, "Daughter, take courage; your faith has made you well." And at once the woman was made well.

23And when Jesus came into the official's house, and saw the flute-players, and the crowd in noisy disorder,

24He *began* to say, "Depart; for the girl has not died, but is asleep." And they *began* laughing at Him.

25But when the crowd had been put out, He entered and took her by the hand; and the girl arose.

26And this news went out into all that land.

27And as Jesus passed on from there, two blind men followed Him, crying out, and saying, "Have mercy on us, Son of David!"

28And after He had come

οἱ ἀσκοί, καὶ ὁ οἶνος ἐκχεῖται καὶ
the wineskins, and the wine is poured out and

οἱ ἀσκοὶ ἀπόλλυνται. ἀλλὰ βάλλουσιν
the wineskins are destroyed. But they put

οἶνον νέον εἰς ἀσκοὺς καινούς, καὶ
wine new into wineskins fresh, and

ἀμφότεροι συντηροῦνται.
both are preserved.

18 Ταῦτα αὐτοῦ λαλοῦντος αὐτοῖς,
These things him speaking[a] to them,
= As he was speaking these things

ἰδοὺ ἄρχων [εἷς] προσελθὼν προσ-
behold ruler one approaching wor-

εκύνει αὐτῷ λέγων ὅτι ἡ θυγάτηρ
shipped him saying[,] – The daughter

μου ἄρτι ἐτελεύτησεν· ἀλλὰ ἐλθὼν
of me just now died; but coming

ἐπίθες τὴν χεῖρά σου ἐπ' αὐτήν,
lay on the hand of thee on her,

καὶ ζήσεται. **19** καὶ ἐγερθεὶς ὁ Ἰησοῦς
and she will live. And rising – Jesus

ἠκολούθει αὐτῷ καὶ οἱ μαθηταὶ αὐτοῦ.
followed him[,] also the disciples of him.

20 Καὶ ἰδοὺ γυνὴ αἱμορροοῦσα
And behold a woman suffering from a flow of blood

δώδεκα ἔτη προσελθοῦσα ὄπισθεν ἥψατο
twelve years approaching behind touched

τοῦ κρασπέδου τοῦ ἱματίου αὐτοῦ·
the fringe of the garment of him;

21 ἔλεγεν γὰρ ἐν ἑαυτῇ· ἐὰν μόνον
for she was saying in herself: If only

ἅψωμαι τοῦ ἱματίου αὐτοῦ, σωθήσομαι.
I may touch the garment of him, I shall be healed.

22 ὁ δὲ Ἰησοῦς στραφεὶς καὶ ἰδὼν
– And Jesus turning and seeing

αὐτὴν εἶπεν· θάρσει, θύγατερ· ἡ
her said: Be of good cheer, daughter; the

πίστις σου σέσωκέν σε. καὶ ἐσώθη
faith of thee has healed thee. And was healed

ἡ γυνὴ ἀπὸ τῆς ὥρας ἐκείνης. **23** Καὶ
the woman from – hour that. And

ἐλθὼν ὁ Ἰησοῦς εἰς τὴν οἰκίαν τοῦ ἄρχοντος
coming – Jesus into the house of the ruler

καὶ ἰδὼν τοὺς αὐλητὰς καὶ τὸν ὄχλον
and seeing the flute-players and the crowd

θορυβούμενον **24** ἔλεγεν· ἀναχωρεῖτε· οὐ
terrified he said: Depart ye; not

γὰρ ἀπέθανεν τὸ κοράσιον ἀλλὰ καθεύδει.
for died the girl but sleeps.

καὶ κατεγέλων αὐτοῦ. **25** ὅτε δὲ
And they ridiculed him. But when

ἐξεβλήθη ὁ ὄχλος, εἰσελθὼν ἐκράτησεν
was put out the crowd, entering he took hold of

τῆς χειρὸς αὐτῆς, καὶ ἠγέρθη τὸ κορά-
the hand of her, and was raised the girl.

σιον. **26** καὶ ἐξῆλθεν ἡ φήμη αὕτη
And went out the report this

εἰς ὅλην τὴν γῆν ἐκείνην. **27** Καὶ
into all – land that. And

παράγοντι ἐκεῖθεν τῷ Ἰησοῦ ἠκολούθησαν
passing by thence – Jesus[e] followed
= as Jesus passed by thence

δύο τυφλοὶ κράζοντες καὶ λέγοντες· ἐλέησον
two blind men crying out and saying: Pity

ἡμᾶς, υἱὸς Δαυίδ. **28** ἐλθόντι δὲ εἰς
us, son of David. And coming[e] into
= when he came

---

will run out and the wineskins will be ruined. No, they pour new wine into new wineskins, and both are preserved."

A Dead Girl and a Sick Woman

18While he was saying this, a ruler came and knelt before him and said, "My daughter has just died. But come and put your hand on her, and she will live." 19Jesus got up and went with him, and so did his disciples.

20Just then a woman who had been subject to bleeding for twelve years came up behind him and touched the edge of his cloak. 21She said to herself, "If I only touch his cloak, I will be healed."

22Jesus turned and saw her. "Take heart, daughter," he said, "your faith has healed you." And the woman was healed from that moment.

23When Jesus entered the ruler's house and saw the flute players and the noisy crowd, 24he said, "Go away. The girl is not dead but asleep." But they laughed at him. 25After the crowd had been put outside, he went in and took the girl by the hand, and she got up. 26News of this spread through all that region.

Jesus Heals the Blind and Mute

27As Jesus went on from there, two blind men followed him, calling out, "Have mercy on us, Son of David!"

28When he had gone indoors, the blind men came

into the house, the blind men came up to Him, and Jesus *said to them, "Do you believe that I am able to do this?" They *said to Him, "Yes, Lord." 29Then He touched their eyes, saying, "Be it done to you according to your faith." 30And their eyes were opened. And Jesus sternly warned them, saying, "See here, let no one know about this!" 31But they went out, and spread the news about Him in all that land. 32And as they were going out, behold, a dumb man, demon-possessed, was brought to Him. 33And after the demon was cast out, the dumb man spoke; and the multitudes marveled, saying, "Nothing like this was ever seen in Israel." 34But the Pharisees were saying, "He casts out the demons by the ruler of the demons." 35And Jesus was going about all the cities and the villages, teaching in their synagogues, and proclaiming the gospel of the kingdom, and healing every kind of disease and every kind of sickness. 36And seeing the multitudes, He felt compassion for them, because they were distressed and downcast like sheep without a shepherd. 37Then He *said to His disciples, "The harvest is plentiful, but the workers are few. 38Therefore beseech the Lord of the harvest to send out workers into His harvest."

τὴν   οἰκίαν   προσῆλθον   αὐτῷ   οἱ   τυφλοί,
the   house   approached   *to him*   the   blind men,

καὶ   λέγει   αὐτοῖς   ὁ   'Ιησοῦς·   πιστεύετε
and   says   to them   –   Jesus: Believe ye

ὅτι   δύναμαι   τοῦτο   ποιῆσαι;   λέγουσιν
that   I can   this   *to do?*   They say

αὐτῷ·   ναί,   κύριε.   29 τότε   ἥψατο   τῶν
to him: Yes,   Lord.   Then   he touched   the

ὀφθαλμῶν   αὐτῶν   λέγων·   κατὰ   τὴν
eyes   of them   saying: According to   the

πίστιν   ὑμῶν   γενηθήτω   ὑμῖν.   30 καὶ
faith   of you   let it be   to you.   And

ἠνεῴχθησαν   αὐτῶν   οἱ   ὀφθαλμοί.   καὶ
were opened   of them   the   eyes.   And

ἐνεβριμήθη   αὐτοῖς   ὁ   'Ιησοῦς   λέγων·
sternly admonished   them   –   Jesus   saying:

ὁρᾶτε   μηδεὶς   γινωσκέτω.   31 οἱ   δὲ
See   ²no one   ¹let ³know.   But they

ἐξελθόντες   διεφήμισαν   αὐτὸν   ἐν   ὅλῃ
going out   spread about   him   in   all

τῇ   γῇ   ἐκείνῃ.   32 Αὐτῶν   δὲ   ἐξερχομένων,
–   land   that.   And them   going out,ᵃ
= as they were going out,

ἰδοὺ   προσήνεγκαν   αὐτῷ   κωφὸν   δαι-
behold   they brought   to him   a dumb man   *being*

μονιζόμενον.   33 καὶ   ἐκβληθέντος   τοῦ
demon-possessed.   And   being expelled   the
= when the demon was expelled

δαιμονίου   ἐλάλησεν   ὁ   κωφός.   καὶ   ἐθαύμασαν
demonᵃ   spoke   the dumb man.   And   marvelled

οἱ   ὄχλοι   λέγοντες·   οὐδέποτε   ἐφάνη   οὕτως
the crowds   saying: Never   it appeared   thus

ἐν   τῷ   'Ισραήλ.   34 οἱ   δὲ   Φαρισαῖοι
in   –   Israel.   But the   Pharisees

ἔλεγον·   ἐν   τῷ   ἄρχοντι   τῶν   δαιμονίων
said: By   the   ruler   of the   demons

ἐκβάλλει   τὰ   δαιμόνια.
he expels   the   demons.

35 Καὶ   περιῆγεν   ὁ   'Ιησοῦς   τὰς
And   went about   –   Jesus   the

πόλεις   πάσας   καὶ   τὰς   κώμας,   διδάσκων
cities   all   and   the   villages,   teaching

ἐν   ταῖς   συναγωγαῖς   αὐτῶν   καὶ   κηρύσσων
in   the   synagogues   of them   and   proclaiming

τὸ   εὐαγγέλιον   τῆς   βασιλείας   καὶ   θεραπεύων
the   gospel   of the   kingdom   and   healing

πᾶσαν   νόσον   καὶ   πᾶσαν   μαλακίαν.
every   disease   and   every   illness.

36 'Ιδὼν   δὲ   τοὺς   ὄχλους   ἐσπλαγχνίσθη
And seeing   the   crowds   he was filled with tenderness

περὶ   αὐτῶν,   ὅτι   ἦσαν   ἐσκυλμένοι   καὶ
concerning them,   because   they were   distressed   and

ἐρριμμένοι   ὡσεὶ   πρόβατα   μὴ   ἔχοντα
prostrate   as   sheep   not   having

ποιμένα.   37 τότε   λέγει   τοῖς   μαθηταῖς
a shepherd.   Then   he says   to the   disciples

αὐτοῦ·   ὁ   μὲν   θερισμὸς   πολύς,   οἱ   δὲ
of him: Indeed the   harvest [is]   much,   but the

ἐργάται   ὀλίγοι·   38 δεήθητε   οὖν   τοῦ   κυρίου
workmen   few;   pray ye   therefore   the   Lord

τοῦ   θερισμοῦ   ὅπως   ἐκβάλῃ
of the   harvest   so that   he may thrust forth

ἐργάτας   εἰς   τὸν   θερισμὸν   αὐτοῦ.   10 Καὶ
workmen   into   the   harvest   of him.   And

to him, and he asked them, "Do you believe that I am able to do this?" "Yes, Lord," they replied. 29Then he touched their eyes and said, "According to your faith will it be done to you"; 30and their sight was restored. Jesus warned them sternly, "See that no one knows about this." 31But they went out and spread the news about him all over that region. 32While they were going out, a man who was demon-possessed and could not talk was brought to Jesus. 33And when the demon was driven out, the man who had been mute spoke. The crowd was amazed and said, "Nothing like this has ever been seen in Israel." 34But the Pharisees said, "It is by the prince of demons that he drives out demons."

The Workers Are Few

35Jesus went through all the towns and villages, teaching in their synagogues, preaching the good news of the kingdom and healing every disease and sickness. 36When he saw the crowds, he had compassion on them, because they were harassed and helpless, like sheep without a shepherd. 37Then he said to his disciples, "The harvest is plentiful but the workers are few. 38Ask the Lord of the harvest, therefore, to send out workers into his harvest field."

Chapter 10

The Twelve Disciples
Instructions for Service

AND having summoned His twelve disciples, He gave them authority over unclean spirits, to cast them out, and to heal every kind of disease and every kind of sickness.

2Now the names of the twelve apostles are these: The first, Simon, who is called Peter, and Andrew his brother; and James the *son* of Zebedee, and John his brother;

3Philip and Bartholomew; Thomas and Matthew the tax-gatherer; James the *son* of Alphaeus, and Thaddaeus;

4Simon the Zealot, and Judas Iscariot, the one who betrayed Him.

5These twelve Jesus sent out after instructing them, saying, "Do not go in *the* way of *the* Gentiles, and do not enter *any* city of the Samaritans;

6but rather go to the lost sheep of the house of Israel.

7"And as you go, preach, saying, 'The kingdom of heaven is at hand.'

8"Heal *the* sick, raise *the* dead, cleanse *the* lepers, cast out demons; freely you received, freely give.

9"Do not acquire gold, or silver, or copper for your money belts,

10or a bag for *your* journey, or even two tunics, or sandals, or a staff; for the worker is worthy of his support.

11"And into whatever city or village you enter, inquire who is worthy in it; and abide there until you go away.

προσκαλεσάμενος τοὺς δώδεκα μαθητὰς
calling forward the twelve disciples

αὐτοῦ ἔδωκεν αὐτοῖς ἐξουσίαν πνευμάτων
of him he gave to them authority of(over) spirits

ἀκαθάρτων ὥστε ἐκβάλλειν αὐτά, καὶ
unclean so as to expel them, and

θεραπεύειν πᾶσαν νόσον καὶ πᾶσαν μαλα-
to heal every disease and every ill-

κίαν. 2 Τῶν δὲ δώδεκα ἀποστόλων
ness. Now of the twelve apostles

τὰ ὀνόματά ἐστιν ταῦτα· πρῶτος Σίμων
the names is(are) these: first Simon

ὁ λεγόμενος Πέτρος καὶ 'Ανδρέας ὁ
the [one] named Peter and Andrew the

ἀδελφὸς αὐτοῦ, καὶ 'Ιάκωβος ὁ τοῦ
brother of him, and James the [son] –

Ζεβεδαίου καὶ 'Ιωάννης ὁ ἀδελφὸς αὐτοῦ,
of Zebedee and John the brother of him,

3 Φίλιππος καὶ Βαρθολομαῖος, Θωμᾶς
  Philip and Bartholomew, Thomas

καὶ Ματθαῖος ὁ τελώνης, 'Ιάκωβος
and Matthew the tax-collector, James

ὁ τοῦ 'Αλφαίου καὶ Θαδδαῖος, 4 Σίμων
the [son] – of Alphæus and Thaddæus, Simon

ὁ Καναναῖος καὶ 'Ιούδας ὁ 'Ισκαριώτης
the Cananæan and Judas the Iscariot

ὁ καὶ παραδοὺς αὐτόν. 5 Τούτους
the [one] also betraying him. These

τοὺς δώδεκα ἀπέστειλεν ὁ 'Ιησοῦς
– twelve sent forth – Jesus

παραγγείλας αὐτοῖς λέγων·
giving charge to them saying:

Εἰς ὁδὸν ἐθνῶν μὴ ἀπέλθητε, καὶ
Into [the] way of [the] nations go ye not, and

εἰς πόλιν Σαμαριτῶν μὴ εἰσέλθητε·
into a city of Samaritans not enter not;

6 πορεύεσθε δὲ μᾶλλον πρὸς τὰ πρόβατα
but go rather unto the sheep

τὰ ἀπολωλότα οἴκου 'Ισραήλ. 7 πορευ-
the lost of [the] house of Israel. And

όμενοι δὲ κηρύσσετε λέγοντες ὅτι ἤγγικεν
going proclaim ye saying[,] – has drawn near

ἡ βασιλεία τῶν οὐρανῶν. 8 ἀσθενοῦντας
The kingdom of the heavens. Ailing [ones]

θεραπεύετε, νεκροὺς ἐγείρετε, λεπροὺς
heal ye, dead [ones] raise, lepers

καθαρίζετε, δαιμόνια ἐκβάλλετε· δωρεὰν
cleanse, demons expel; freely

ἐλάβετε, δωρεὰν δότε. 9 Μὴ κτήσησθε
ye received, freely give. Do not provide

χρυσὸν μηδὲ ἄργυρον μηδὲ χαλκὸν εἰς
gold nor silver nor brass in

τὰς ζώνας ὑμῶν, 10 μὴ πήραν εἰς ὁδὸν
the girdles of you, not a wallet for [the] way

μηδὲ δύο χιτῶνας μηδὲ ὑποδήματα μηδὲ
nor two tunics nor sandals nor

ῥάβδον· ἄξιος γὰρ ὁ ἐργάτης τῆς
a staff; for worthy [is] the workman of the

τροφῆς αὐτοῦ. 11 εἰς ἣν δ' ἂν πόλιν
food of him. And into whatever city

ἢ κώμην εἰσέλθητε, ἐξετάσατε τίς ἐν
or village ye may enter, inquire who in

αὐτῇ ἄξιός ἐστιν· κἀκεῖ μείνατε ἕως ἂν
it worthy is; and there remain until

Chapter 10

Jesus Sends Out the Twelve

HE called his twelve disciples to him and gave them authority to drive out evil[j] spirits and to heal every disease and sickness.

2These are the names of the twelve apostles: first, Simon (who is called Peter) and his brother Andrew; James son of Zebedee, and his brother John; 3Philip and Bartholomew; Thomas and Matthew the tax collector; James son of Alphaeus, and Thaddaeus; 4Simon the Zealot and Judas Iscariot, who betrayed him.

5These twelve Jesus sent out with the following instructions: "Do not go among the Gentiles or enter any town of the Samaritans. 6Go rather to the lost sheep of Israel. 7As you go, preach this message: 'The kingdom of heaven is near.' 8Heal the sick, raise the dead, cleanse those who have leprosy,[k] drive out demons. Freely you have received, freely give. 9Do not take along any gold or silver or copper in your belts; 10take no bag for the journey, or extra tunic, or sandals or a staff; for the worker is worth his keep. 11Whatever town or village you enter, search for some worthy person there and stay at his house until

---

/1 Greek *unclean*
k 8 The Greek word was used for various diseases affecting the skin—not necessarily leprosy.

12"And as you enter the house, give it your greeting.

13"And if the house is worthy, let your *greeting of* peace come upon it; but if it is not worthy, let your *greeting of* peace return to you.

14"And whoever does not receive you, nor heed your words, as you go out of that house or that city, shake off the dust of your feet.

15"Truly I say to you, it will be more tolerable for *the* land of Sodom and Gomorrah in the day of judgment, than for that city.

A Hard Road before Them

16"Behold, I send you out as sheep in the midst of wolves; therefore be shrewd as serpents, and innocent as doves.

17"But beware of men; for they will deliver you up to *the* courts, and scourge you in their synagogues;

18and you shall even be brought before governors and kings for My sake, as a testimony to them and to the Gentiles.

19"But when they deliver you up, do not become anxious about how or what you will speak; for it shall be given you in that hour what you are to speak.

20"For it is not you who speak, but *it is* the Spirit of your Father who speaks in you.

21"And brother will deliver up brother to death, and a father *his* child; and children will rise up against parents, and cause them to be put to death.

22"And you will be hated by all on account of My name, but it is the one who has endured to the end who will be saved.

23"But whenever they

ἐξέλθητε. **12** εἰσερχόμενοι δὲ εἰς τὴν
ye may go out.   And entering   into   the

οἰκίαν ἀσπάσασθε αὐτήν· **13** καὶ ἐὰν μὲν
house   greet   it;   and   if   indeed

ᾖ ἡ οἰκία ἀξία, ἐλθάτω ἡ εἰρήνη ὑμῶν
be the house worthy, let come the peace of you

ἐπ’ αὐτήν· ἐὰν δὲ μὴ ᾖ ἀξία, ἡ εἰρήνη
on   it;   but if it be not worthy, the peace

ὑμῶν πρὸς ὑμᾶς ἐπιστραφήτω. **14** καὶ
of you unto you   let return.   And

ὃς ἂν μὴ δέξηται ὑμᾶς μηδὲ ἀκούσῃ
whoever may not receive you   nor   hear

τοὺς λόγους ὑμῶν, ἐξερχόμενοι ἔξω
the   words   of you, going out   outside

τῆς οἰκίας ἢ τῆς πόλεως ἐκείνης ἐκτινά-
- house or - city   that   shake

ξατε τὸν κονιορτὸν τῶν ποδῶν ὑμῶν.
off   the   dust   of the   feet   of you.

15 ἀμὴν λέγω ὑμῖν, ἀνεκτότερον ἔσται
Truly I tell you, more tolerable it will be [for]

γῇ Σοδόμων καὶ Γομόρρων ἐν ἡμέρᾳ κρίσεως
[the] land of Sodom and Gomorra in [the] day of judgment

ἢ τῇ πόλει ἐκείνῃ. **16** Ἰδοὺ ἐγὼ
than [for] - city   that.   Behold I

ἀποστέλλω ὑμᾶς ὡς πρόβατα ἐν μέσῳ
send forth   you as sheep in [the] midst

λύκων· γίνεσθε οὖν φρόνιμοι ὡς οἱ
of wolves; be ye therefore prudent as -

ὄφεις καὶ ἀκέραιοι ὡς αἱ περιστεραί.
serpents and harmless as - doves.

17 Προσέχετε δὲ ἀπὸ τῶν ἀνθρώπων·
And beware   from(of) -   men;

παραδώσουσιν γὰρ ὑμᾶς εἰς συνέδρια,
for they will deliver up you to councils,

καὶ ἐν ταῖς συναγωγαῖς αὐτῶν μαστιγώ-
and in the   synagogues of them they will

σουσιν ὑμᾶς· **18** καὶ ἐπὶ ἡγεμόνας δὲ καὶ
scourge you;   and before leaders and also

βασιλεῖς ἀχθήσεσθε ἕνεκεν ἐμοῦ, εἰς
kings ye will be led for the sake of me, for

μαρτύριον αὐτοῖς καὶ τοῖς ἔθνεσιν.
a testimony to them and to the nations.

19 ὅταν δὲ παραδῶσιν ὑμᾶς, μὴ μεριμνή-
But when they deliver up you,   do not be

σητε πῶς ἢ τί λαλήσητε· δοθήσεται
anxious how or what ye may say; ¹it will be given

γὰρ ὑμῖν ἐν ἐκείνῃ τῇ ὥρᾳ τί λαλήσητε·
¹for to you in that - hour what ye may say;

20 οὐ γὰρ ὑμεῖς ἐστε οἱ λαλοῦντες,
for not ye   are the [ones] speaking,

ἀλλὰ τὸ πνεῦμα τοῦ πατρὸς ὑμῶν τὸ
but the Spirit of the Father of you the [one]

λαλοῦν ἐν ὑμῖν. **21** παραδώσει δὲ
speaking in you.   And ²will deliver up

ἀδελφὸς ἀδελφὸν εἰς θάνατον καὶ πατὴρ
¹brother   brother to death   and father

τέκνον, καὶ ἐπαναστήσονται τέκνα ἐπὶ
child,   and will stand up   children against

γονεῖς καὶ θανατώσουσιν αὐτούς. **22** καὶ
parents and put to death   them.   And

ἔσεσθε μισούμενοι ὑπὸ πάντων διὰ
ye will be being hated by all men on account of

τὸ ὄνομά μου· ὁ δὲ ὑπομείνας εἰς
the name of me; but the [one] enduring to

τέλος, οὗτος σωθήσεται. **23** ὅταν δὲ
[the] end, this will be saved.   But when

---

you leave. 12As you enter the home, give it your greeting. 13If the home is deserving, let your peace rest on it; if it is not, let your peace return to you. 14If anyone will not welcome you or listen to your words, shake the dust off your feet when you leave that home or town. 15I tell you the truth, it will be more bearable for Sodom and Gomorrah on the day of judgment than for that town. 16I am sending you out like sheep among wolves. Therefore be as shrewd as snakes and as innocent as doves.

17"Be on your guard against men; they will hand you over to the local councils and flog you in their synagogues. 18On my account you will be brought before governors and kings as witnesses to them and to the Gentiles. 19But when they arrest you, do not worry about what to say or how to say it. At that time you will be given what to say, 20for it will not be you speaking, but the Spirit of your Father speaking through you.

21"Brother will betray brother to death, and a father his child; children will rebel against their parents and have them put to death. 22All men will hate you because of me, but he who stands firm to the end will be saved. 23When you are persecute you in this city, flee to the next; for truly I say to you, you shall not finish *going through* the cities of Israel, until the Son of Man comes.

The Meaning of Discipleship

24 "A disciple is not above his teacher, nor a slave above his master.
25 "It is enough for the disciple that he become as his teacher, and the slave as his master. If they have called the head of the house Beelzebul, how much more the members of his household!
26 "Therefore do not fear them, for there is nothing covered that will not be revealed, and hidden that will not be known.
27 "What I tell you in the darkness, speak in the light; and what you hear *whispered* in *your* ear, proclaim upon the housetops.
28 "And do not fear those who kill the body, but are unable to kill the soul; but rather fear Him who is able to destroy both soul and body in hell.
29 "Are not two sparrows sold for a "cent? And *yet* not one of them will fall to the ground apart from your Father.
30 "But the very hairs of your head are all numbered.
31 "Therefore do not fear; you are of more value than many sparrows.
32 "Everyone therefore who shall confess Me before men, I will also confess him before My Father who is in heaven.
33 "But whoever shall deny Me before men, I will also deny him before My

---

διώκωσιν ὑμᾶς ἐν τῇ πόλει ταύτῃ,
they persecute you in - city this,
φεύγετε εἰς τὴν ἑτέραν· ἀμὴν γὰρ
flee ye to - [an]other; for truly
λέγω ὑμῖν, οὐ μὴ τελέσητε τὰς πόλεις
I tell you, by no means ye will complete the cities
[τοῦ] Ἰσραὴλ ἕως ἔλθῃ ὁ υἱὸς τοῦ ἀν-
- of Israel until comes the Son - of
θρώπου. 24 Οὐκ ἔστιν μαθητὴς ὑπὲρ
man. not is A disciple above
τὸν διδάσκαλον οὐδὲ δοῦλος ὑπὲρ τὸν
the teacher nor a slave above the
κύριον αὐτοῦ. 25 ἀρκετὸν τῷ μαθητῇ
lord of him. Enough for the disciple
ἵνα .γένηται ὡς ὁ διδάσκαλος αὐτοῦ,
that he be as the teacher of him,
καὶ ὁ δοῦλος ὡς ὁ κύριος αὐτοῦ. εἰ
and the slave as the lord of him. If
τὸν οἰκοδεσπότην Βεελζεβοὺλ ἐπεκάλεσαν,
the housemaster Beelzebub they called,
πόσῳ μᾶλλον τοὺς οἰκιακοὺς αὐτοῦ.
how much more the members of [the] household of him.
26 μὴ οὖν φοβηθῆτε αὐτούς· οὐδὲν γάρ
Therefore fear ye not them; for nothing
ἐστιν κεκαλυμμένον ὃ οὐκ ἀποκαλυφ-
is having been veiled which will not be un-
θήσεται, καὶ κρυπτὸν ὃ οὐ γνωσθήσεται.
veiled, and hidden which will not be made known.
27 ὃ λέγω ὑμῖν ἐν τῇ σκοτίᾳ, εἴπατε
What I say to you in the darkness, say ye
ἐν τῷ φωτί· καὶ ὃ εἰς τὸ οὖς ἀκούετε,
in the light; and what in the ear ye hear,
κηρύξατε ἐπὶ τῶν δωμάτων. 28 καὶ
proclaim on the housetops. And
μὴ φοβεῖσθε ἀπὸ τῶν ἀποκτεννόντων
do not fear - the [ones] killing
τὸ σῶμα, τὴν δὲ ψυχὴν μὴ δυναμένων
the body, but the soul not being able
ἀποκτεῖναι· φοβεῖσθε δὲ μᾶλλον τὸν
to kill; but fear ye rather the [one]
δυνάμενον καὶ ψυχὴν καὶ σῶμα ἀπολέσαι
being able both soul and body to destroy
ἐν γεέννῃ. 29 οὐχὶ δύο στρουθία ἀσσα-
in gehenna. Not two sparrows of(for) a
ρίου πωλεῖται; καὶ ἓν ἐξ αὐτῶν οὐ
farthing are sold? and one of them not
πεσεῖται ἐπὶ τὴν γῆν ἄνευ τοῦ πατρὸς
will fall on the earth without the Father
ὑμῶν. 30 ὑμῶν δὲ καὶ αἱ τρίχες τῆς
of you. But of you even the hairs of the
κεφαλῆς πᾶσαι ἠριθμημέναι εἰσίν. 31 μὴ
head all having been numbered are. not
οὖν φοβεῖσθε· πολλῶν στρουθίων διαφέρετε
Therefore fear ye; ²many ¹sparrows ³excel
ὑμεῖς. 32 Πᾶς οὖν ὅστις ὁμολογήσει
¹ye. Everyone therefore who shall confess
ἐν ἐμοὶ ἔμπροσθεν τῶν ἀνθρώπων,
- me before - men,
ὁμολογήσω κἀγὼ ἐν αὐτῷ ἔμπροσθεν
will confess I also - him before
τοῦ πατρός μου τοῦ ἐν τοῖς οὐρανοῖς·
the Father of me - in the heavens;
33 ὅστις δ' ἂν ἀρνήσηται με ἔμπροσθεν
and whoever denies me before
τῶν ἀνθρώπων, ἀρνήσομαι κἀγὼ αὐτὸν
- men, will deny I also him

---

persecuted in one place, flee to another. I tell you the truth, you will not finish going through the cities of Israel before the Son of Man comes.
24 "A student is not above his teacher, nor a servant above his master. 25 It is enough for the student to be like his teacher, and the servant like his master. If the head of the house has been called Beelzebub,[l] how much more the members of his household!
26 "So do not be afraid of them. There is nothing concealed that will not be disclosed, or hidden that will not be made known. 27 What I tell you in the dark, speak in the daylight; what is whispered in your ear, proclaim from the roofs. 28 Do not be afraid of those who kill the body but cannot kill the soul. Rather, be afraid of the One who can destroy both soul and body in hell. 29 Are not two sparrows sold for a penny[m]? Yet not one of them will fall to the ground apart from the will of your Father. 30 And even the very hairs of your head are all numbered. 31 So don't be afraid; you are worth more than many sparrows.
32 "Whoever acknowledges me before men, I will also acknowledge him before my Father in heaven. 33 But whoever disowns me before men, I will disown

---

"Gr., *assarion*, the smallest copper coin

*l*25 Greek *Beezeboul* or *Beelzeboul*
*m*29 Greek *an assarion*

Father who is in heaven.
34"Do not think that I came to bring peace on the earth; I did not come to bring peace, but a sword.
35"For I came to SET A MAN AGAINST HIS FATHER, AND A DAUGHTER AGAINST HER MOTHER, AND A DAUGHTER-IN-LAW AGAINST HER MOTHER-IN-LAW;
36and A MAN'S ENEMIES WILL BE THE MEMBERS OF HIS HOUSEHOLD.
37"He who loves father or mother more than Me is not worthy of Me; and he who loves son or daughter more than Me is not worthy of Me.
38"And he who does not take his cross and follow after Me is not worthy of Me.
39"He who has found his life shall lose it, and he who has lost his life for My sake shall find it.
40"He who receives you receives Me, and he who receives Me receives Him who sent Me.
41"He who receives a prophet in *the* name of a prophet shall receive a prophet's reward; and he who receives a righteous man in the name of a righteous man shall receive a righteous man's reward.
42"And whoever in the name of a disciple gives to one of these little ones even a cup of cold water to drink, truly I say to you he shall not lose his reward."

ἔμπροσθεν τοῦ πατρός μου τοῦ ἐν	before the Father of me – in
τοῖς οὐρανοῖς. 34 Μὴ νομίσητε ὅτι	the heavens. Do not suppose that
ἦλθον βαλεῖν εἰρήνην ἐπὶ τὴν γῆν· οὐκ ἦλθον	I came to bring peace on the earth; I came not
βαλεῖν εἰρήνην ἀλλὰ μάχαιραν. 35 ἦλθον γὰρ	to bring peace but a sword. For I came
διχάσαι ἄνθρωπον κατὰ τοῦ πατρὸς	to make hostile a man against the father
αὐτοῦ καὶ θυγατέρα κατὰ τῆς μητρὸς	of him and a daughter against the mother
αὐτῆς καὶ νύμφην κατὰ τῆς πενθερᾶς	of her and a bride against the mother-in-law
αὐτῆς, 36 καὶ ἐχθροὶ τοῦ ἀνθρώπου οἱ	of her, and [the] enemies – of a man the
οἰκιακοὶ αὐτοῦ. 37 Ὁ φιλῶν πατέρα	members of [the] household of him. The [one] loving father
ἢ μητέρα ὑπὲρ ἐμὲ οὐκ ἔστιν μου ἄξιος·	or mother beyond me is not of me worthy;
καὶ ὁ φιλῶν υἱὸν ἢ θυγατέρα ὑπὲρ	and the [one] loving son or daughter beyond
ἐμὲ οὐκ ἔστιν μου ἄξιος·| 38 καὶ ὃς	me is not of me worthy; and [he] who
οὐ λαμβάνει τὸν σταυρὸν αὐτοῦ καὶ	takes not the cross of him and
ἀκολουθεῖ ὀπίσω μου, οὐκ ἔστιν μου	follows after me, is not of me
ἄξιος. 39 ὁ εὑρὼν τὴν ψυχὴν αὐτοῦ	worthy. The [one] finding the life of him
ἀπολέσει αὐτήν, καὶ ὁ ἀπολέσας τὴν	will lose it, and the [one] losing the
ψυχὴν αὐτοῦ ἕνεκεν ἐμοῦ εὑρήσει αὐτήν.	life of him for the sake of me will find it.
40 Ὁ δεχόμενος ὑμᾶς ἐμὲ δέχεται, καὶ	The [one] receiving you me receives, and
ὁ ἐμὲ δεχόμενος δέχεται τὸν	the [one] me receiving receives the [one]
ἀποστείλαντά με. 41 ὁ δεχόμενος προ-	having sent me. The [one] receiving a pro-
φήτην εἰς ὄνομα προφήτου μισθὸν	phet in [the] name of a prophet [the] reward
προφήτου λήμψεται, καὶ ὁ δεχόμενος	of a prophet will receive, and the [one] receiving
δίκαιον εἰς ὄνομα δικαίου μισθὸν	a righteous man in [the] name of a righteous man [the] reward
δικαίου λήμψεται. 42 καὶ ὃς ἐὰν ποτίσῃ	of a righteous man will receive. And whoever gives to drink
ἕνα τῶν μικρῶν τούτων ποτήριον ψυχροῦ	one – of these little [ones] a cup of cold water
μόνον εἰς ὄνομα μαθητοῦ, ἀμὴν λέγω ὑμῖν,	only in [the] name of a disciple, truly I tell you,
οὐ μὴ ἀπολέσῃ τὸν μισθὸν αὐτοῦ.	on no account will he lose the reward of him.

him before my Father in heaven.
34"Do not suppose that I have come to bring peace to the earth. I did not come to bring peace, but a sword. 35For I have come to turn

" 'a man against his father,
a daughter against her mother,
a daughter-in-law against her mother-in-law—
36 a man's enemies will be the members of his own household.' [n]

37"Anyone who loves his father or mother more than me is not worthy of me; anyone who loves his son or daughter more than me is not worthy of me; 38and anyone who does not take his cross and follow me is not worthy of me. 39Whoever finds his life will lose it, and whoever loses his life for my sake will find it.
40"He who receives you receives me, and he who receives me receives the one who sent me. 41Anyone who receives a prophet because he is a prophet will receive a prophet's reward, and anyone who receives a righteous man because he is a righteous man will receive a righteous man's reward. 42And if anyone gives even a cup of cold water to one of these little ones because he is my disciple, I tell you the truth, he will certainly not lose his reward."

Chapter 11

John's Questions

AND it came about that when Jesus had finished giving instructions to His twelve disciples, He departed from there to teach and preach in their cities.

11 Καὶ ἐγένετο ὅτε ἐτέλεσεν ὁ	And it came to pass when ended –
Ἰησοῦς διατάσσων τοῖς δώδεκα μαθηταῖς	Jesus giving charge to the twelve disciples
αὐτοῦ, μετέβη ἐκεῖθεν τοῦ διδάσκειν[d]	of him, he removed thence – to teach[d]
καὶ κηρύσσειν[d] ἐν ταῖς πόλεσιν αὐτῶν.	and to proclaim[d] in the cities of them.

Chapter 11

Jesus and John the Baptist

AFTER Jesus had finished instructing his twelve disciples, he went on from there to teach and preach in the towns of Galilee.[o]

[n]36 Micah 7:6
[o]1 Greek *in their towns*

2Now when John in prison heard of the works of Christ, he sent *word* by his disciples,

3and said to Him, "Are You the Expected One, or shall we look for someone else?"

4And Jesus answered and said to them, "Go and report to John what you hear and see:

5*the* BLIND RECEIVE SIGHT and *the* lame walk, *the* lepers are cleansed and *the* deaf hear, and *the* dead are raised up, and *the* POOR HAVE THE GOSPEL PREACHED TO THEM.

6"And blessed is he who keeps from stumbling over Me."

Jesus' Tribute to John

7And as these were going *away,* Jesus began to speak to the multitudes about John, "What did you go out into the wilderness to look at? A reed shaken by the wind?

8"But what did you go out to see? A man dressed in soft *clothing?* Behold, those who wear soft *clothing* are in kings' palaces.

9"But why did you go out? To see a prophet? Yes, I say to you, and one who is more than a prophet.

10"This is the one about whom it is written,

'BEHOLD, I SEND MY MESSENGER BEFORE YOUR FACE,
WHO WILL PREPARE YOUR WAY BEFORE YOU.'

11"Truly, I say to you, among those born of women there has not arisen *anyone* greater than John the Baptist; yet he who is least in the kingdom of heaven is greater than he.

12"And from the days of John the Baptist until now the kingdom of heaven suffers violence, and violent men take it by force.

13"For all the prophets and the Law prophesied

2 Ὁ δὲ Ἰωάννης ἀκούσας ἐν τῷ
- But John hearing in the
δεσμωτηρίῳ τὰ ἔργα τοῦ Χριστοῦ,
prison the works of Christ,
πέμψας διὰ τῶν μαθητῶν αὐτοῦ 3 εἶπεν
sending through the disciples of him said
αὐτῷ· σὺ εἶ ὁ ἐρχόμενος, ἢ ἕτερον
to him: Thou art the coming [one], or another
προσδοκῶμεν; 4 καὶ ἀποκριθεὶς ὁ
may we expect? And answering -
Ἰησοῦς εἶπεν αὐτοῖς· πορευθέντες ἀπαγ-
Jesus said to them: Going report
γείλατε Ἰωάννῃ ἃ ἀκούετε καὶ βλέπετε·
ye to John [the things] which ye hear and see:
5 τυφλοὶ ἀναβλέπουσιν καὶ χωλοὶ
blind men see again and lame men
περιπατοῦσιν, λεπροὶ καθαρίζονται καὶ κωφοὶ
walk, lepers are cleansed and deaf men
ἀκούουσιν, καὶ νεκροὶ ἐγείρονται καὶ
hear, and dead men are raised and
πτωχοὶ εὐαγγελίζονται· 6 καὶ μακάριός
poor men are evangelized; and blessed
ἐστιν ὃς ἐὰν μὴ σκανδαλισθῇ ἐν ἐμοί.
is whoever is not offended in me.
7 Τούτων δὲ πορευομένων ἤρξατο ὁ
And these going* began -
= as these were going
Ἰησοῦς λέγειν τοῖς ὄχλοις περὶ Ἰωάννου·
Jesus to say to the crowds concerning John:
τί ἐξήλθατε εἰς τὴν ἔρημον θεάσασθαι;
What went ye out into the wilderness to see?
κάλαμον ὑπὸ ἀνέμου σαλευόμενον; 8 ἀλλὰ
a reed by wind being shaken? But
τί ἐξήλθατε ἰδεῖν; ἄνθρωπον ἐν μαλακοῖς
what went ye out to see? a man in soft material
ἠμφιεσμένον; ἰδοὺ οἱ τὰ μαλακὰ
having been clothed? Behold[,] the [ones] - soft material
φοροῦντες ἐν τοῖς οἴκοις τῶν βασιλέων. 9 ἀλλὰ
wearing [are] in the houses - of kings. But
τί ἐξήλθατε; προφήτην ἰδεῖν; ναὶ λέγω
why went ye out? a prophet to see? Yes[,] I tell
ὑμῖν, καὶ περισσότερον προφήτου. 10 οὗτός
you, and more [than] a prophet. This
ἐστιν περὶ οὗ γέγραπται· ἰδοὺ ἐγὼ
is he concerning whom it has been written: Behold[,] I
ἀποστέλλω τὸν ἄγγελόν μου πρὸ προσώπου
send forth the messenger of me before [the] face
σου, ὃς κατασκευάσει τὴν ὁδόν σου
of thee, who will prepare the way of thee
ἔμπροσθέν σου. 11 ἀμὴν λέγω ὑμῖν,
before thee. Truly I tell you,
οὐκ ἐγήγερται ἐν γεννητοῖς γυναικῶν
there has not arisen among [those] born of women
μείζων Ἰωάννου τοῦ βαπτιστοῦ· ὁ δὲ
a greater [than] John the Baptist; but the
μικρότερος ἐν τῇ βασιλείᾳ τῶν οὐρανῶν
lesser in the kingdom of the heavens
μείζων αὐτοῦ ἐστιν. 12 ἀπὸ δὲ τῶν
greater [than] he is. And from the
ἡμερῶν Ἰωάννου τοῦ βαπτιστοῦ ἕως
days of John the Baptist until
ἄρτι ἡ βασιλεία τῶν οὐρανῶν βιάζεται,
now the kingdom of the heavens is forcibly treated,
καὶ βιασταὶ ἁρπάζουσιν αὐτήν. 13 πάντες γὰρ
and forceful men seize it. For all
οἱ προφῆται καὶ ὁ νόμος ἕως
the prophets and the law until

2When John heard in prison on what Christ was doing, he sent his disciples 3to ask him, "Are you the one who was to come, or should we expect someone else?"

4Jesus replied, "Go back and report to John what you hear and see: 5The blind receive sight, the lame walk, those who have leprosyᵖ are cured, the deaf hear, the dead are raised, and the good news is preached to the poor. 6Blessed is the man who does not fall away on account of me."

7As John's disciples were leaving, Jesus began to speak to the crowd about John: "What did you go out into the desert to see? A reed swayed by the wind? 8If not, what did you go out to see? A man dressed in fine clothes? No, those who wear fine clothes are in kings' palaces. 9Then what did you go out to see? A prophet? Yes, I tell you, and more than a prophet. 10This is the one about whom it is written:

" 'I will send my
    messenger ahead of
    you,
who will prepare your
    way before you.'�q

11I tell you the truth: Among those born of women there has not risen anyone greater than John the Baptist; yet he who is least in the kingdom of heaven is greater than he. 12From the days of John the Baptist until now, the kingdom of heaven has been forcefully advancing, and forceful men lay hold of it. 13For all the Prophets and the Law prophesied until John.

p5 The Greek word was used for various diseases affecting the skin—not necessarily leprosy.
q10 Mal. 3:1

until John.

14"And if you care to accept *it*, he himself is Elijah, who was to come.

15"He who has ears to hear, let him hear.

16"But to what shall I compare this generation? It is like children sitting in the market places, who call out to the other *children*,

17and say, 'We played the flute for you, and you did not dance; we sang a dirge, and you did not mourn.'

18"For John came neither eating nor drinking, and they say, 'He has a demon!'

19"The Son of Man came eating and drinking, and they say, 'Behold, a gluttonous man and a drunkard, a friend of tax-gatherers and sinners!' Yet wisdom is vindicated by her deeds."

The Unrepenting Cities

20Then He began to reproach the cities in which most of His miracles were done, because they did not repent.

21"Woe to you, Chorazin! Woe to you, Bethsaida! For if the miracles had occurred in Tyre and Sidon which occurred in you, they would have repented long ago in sackcloth and ashes.

22"Nevertheless I say to you, it shall be more tolerable for Tyre and Sidon in *the* day of judgment, than for you.

23"And you, Capernaum, will not be exalted to heaven, will you? You shall descend to Hades; for if the miracles had occurred in Sodom which occurred in you, it would have remained to this day.

24"Nevertheless I say to you that it shall be more tolerable for the land of Sodom in *the* day of judgment, than for you."

Come to Me

25At that time Jesus answered and said, "I praise

'Ιωάννου ἐπροφήτευσαν·
John   prophesied;

δέξασθαι, αὐτός ἐστιν 'Ηλίας ὁ μέλλων
to receive [it *or* him], he   is   Elias the [one] about

ἔρχεσθαι. 15 ὁ ἔχων ὦτα ἀκουέτω.
to come.   The [one] having ears let him hear.

16 Τίνι δὲ ὁμοιώσω τὴν γενεὰν ταύτην;
But to what shall I liken   –   generation this?

ὁμοία ἐστὶν παιδίοις καθημένοις ἐν ταῖς
Like it is   to children   sitting   in the

ἀγοραῖς ἃ προσφωνοῦντα τοῖς ἑτέροις
marketplaces who   calling to   the   others

17 λέγουσιν· ηὐλήσαμεν ὑμῖν καὶ οὐκ
say: We piped   to you   and   not

ὠρχήσασθε· ἐθρηνήσαμεν καὶ οὐκ ἐκόψασθε.
ye did dance;   we lamented   and   ye did not mourn.

18 ἦλθεν γὰρ 'Ιωάννης μήτε ἐσθίων μήτε
For came   John   neither   eating   nor

πίνων, καὶ λέγουσιν· δαιμόνιον ἔχει.
drinking, and   they say: a demon   He has.

19 ἦλθεν ὁ υἱὸς τοῦ ἀνθρώπου ἐσθίων καὶ
Came   the Son   –   of man   eating   and

πίνων, καὶ λέγουσιν· ἰδοὺ ἄνθρωπος
drinking, and   they say: Behold[,]   a man

φάγος καὶ οἰνοπότης, τελωνῶν φίλος καὶ
gluttonous and a wine-drinker, of tax-collectors a friend and

ἁμαρτωλῶν. καὶ ἐδικαιώθη ἡ σοφία ἀπὸ
of sinners.   And was(is) justified   –   wisdom from(by)

τῶν ἔργων αὐτῆς.
the   works   of her.

20 Τότε ἤρξατο ὀνειδίζειν τὰς πόλεις
Then   he began   to reproach   the   cities

ἐν αἷς ἐγένοντο αἱ πλεῖσται δυνάμεις
in which happened   the   very many powerful deeds

αὐτοῦ, ὅτι οὐ μετενόησαν· 21 οὐαί σοι,
of him, because they repented not: Woe to thee,

Χοραζίν· οὐαί σοι, Βηθσαϊδά· ὅτι εἰ
Chorazin;   woe to thee,   Bethsaida;   because   if

ἐν Τύρῳ καὶ Σιδῶνι ἐγένοντο αἱ δυνάμεις
in Tyre   and   Sidon   happened   the powerful deeds

αἱ γενόμεναι ἐν ὑμῖν, πάλαι ἂν
–   having happened   in   you,   long ago   –

ἐν σάκκῳ καὶ σποδῷ μετενόησαν.
in sackcloth   and   ashes they would have repented.

22 πλὴν λέγω ὑμῖν, Τύρῳ καὶ Σιδῶνι
However   I tell   you,   For Tyre   and   for Sidon

ἀνεκτότερον ἔσται ἐν ἡμέρᾳ κρίσεως ἢ
more tolerable   it will be in [the] day   of judgment than

ὑμῖν. 23 καὶ σύ, Καφαρναούμ, μὴ
for you.   And thou,   Capernaum,   not

ἕως οὐρανοῦ ὑψωθήσῃ; ἕως ᾅδου
as far as heaven   wast thou exalted? as far as   hades

καταβήσῃ· ὅτι εἰ ἐν Σοδόμοις ἐγενήθησαν
thou shalt descend; because if in Sodom   happened

αἱ δυνάμεις αἱ γενόμεναι ἐν σοί,
the powerful deeds   –   having happened   in   thee,

ἔμεινεν ἂν μέχρι τῆς σήμερον. 24 πλὴν
it would have remained until   –   to-day.   However

λέγω ὑμῖν ὅτι γῇ Σοδόμων ἀνεκτότερον
I tell   you that for [the] land of Sodom   more tolerable

ἔσται ἐν ἡμέρᾳ κρίσεως ἢ σοί.
it will be in [the] day   of judgment than for thee.

25 'Εν ἐκείνῳ τῷ καιρῷ ἀποκριθεὶς
At   that   –   time   answering

ὁ 'Ιησοῦς εἶπεν· ἐξομολογοῦμαί σοι,
–   Jesus   said: I give thanks   to thee,

14 καὶ εἰ θέλετε
and   if ye are willing

αὐτός ἐστιν 'Ηλίας ὁ μέλλων
he   is   Elias the [one] about

14And if you are willing to accept it, he is the Elijah who was to come. 15He who has ears, let him hear.

16"To what can I compare this generation? They are like children sitting in the marketplaces and calling out to others:

17 'We played the flute for you,
and you did not dance;
we sang a dirge,
and you did not mourn.'

18For John came neither eating nor drinking, and they say, 'He has a demon.' 19The Son of Man came eating and drinking, and they say, 'Here is a glutton and a drunkard, a friend of tax collectors and "sinners." ' But wisdom is proved right by her actions."

Woe on Unrepentant Cities

20Then Jesus began to denounce the cities in which most of his miracles had been performed, because they did not repent. 21"Woe to you, Korazin! Woe to you, Bethsaida! If the miracles that were performed in you had been performed in Tyre and Sidon, they would have repented long ago in sackcloth and ashes. 22But I tell you, it will be more bearable for Tyre and Sidon on the day of judgment than for you. 23And you, Capernaum, will you be lifted up to the skies? No, you will go down to the depths.' If the miracles that were performed in you had been performed in Sodom, it would have remained to this day. 24But I tell you that it will be more bearable for Sodom on the day of judgment than for you."

Rest for the Weary

25At that time Jesus said, "I praise you, Father, Lord

'23 Greek *Hades*

Thee, O Father, Lord of heaven and earth, that Thou didst hide these things from *the* wise and intelligent and didst reveal them to babes.
26"Yes, Father, for thus it was well-pleasing in Thy sight.
27"All things have been handed over to Me by My Father; and no one knows the Son, except the Father; nor does anyone know the Father, except the Son, and anyone to whom the Son wills to reveal *Him*.
28"Come to Me, all who are weary and heavy-laden, and I will give you rest.
29"Take My yoke upon you, and learn from Me, for I am gentle and humble in heart; and YOU SHALL FIND REST FOR YOUR SOULS.
30"For My yoke is easy, and My load is light."

πάτερ, κύριε τοῦ οὐρανοῦ καὶ τῆς γῆς,
Father, lord of the heaven and of the earth,

ὅτι ἔκρυψας ταῦτα ἀπὸ σοφῶν καὶ συνε-
because thou hiddest these things from wise and intel-

τῶν, καὶ ἀπεκάλυψας αὐτὰ νηπίοις·
ligent men, and didst reveal them to infants;

26 ναί, ὁ πατήρ, ὅτι οὕτως εὐδοκία
yes, - Father, because thus good pleasure

ἐγένετο ἔμπροσθέν σου. 27 Πάντα μοι
it was before thee. All things to me

παρεδόθη ὑπὸ τοῦ πατρός μου, καὶ
were delivered by the Father of me, and

οὐδεὶς ἐπιγινώσκει τὸν υἱὸν εἰ μὴ ὁ
no one fully knows the Son except the

πατήρ, οὐδὲ τὸν πατέρα τις ἐπιγινώσκει
Father, neither the Father anyone fully knows

εἰ μὴ ὁ υἱὸς καὶ ᾧ ἐὰν βούληται ὁ
except the Son and [he] to whom if wills the

υἱὸς ἀποκαλύψαι. 28 Δεῦτε πρός με
Son to reveal. Come unto me

πάντες οἱ κοπιῶντες καὶ πεφορτισμένοι,
all the[ones] labouring and *having been* burdened,

κἀγὼ ἀναπαύσω ὑμᾶς. 29 ἄρατε τὸν
and I will rest you. Take the

ζυγόν μου ἐφ᾿ ὑμᾶς καὶ μάθετε ἀπ᾿
yoke of me on you and learn from

ἐμοῦ, ὅτι πραΰς εἰμι καὶ ταπεινὸς τῇ
me, because meek I am and lowly -

καρδίᾳ, καὶ εὑρήσετε ἀνάπαυσιν ταῖς
in heart, and ye will find rest to the

ψυχαῖς ὑμῶν· 30 ὁ γὰρ ζυγός μου
souls of you; for the yoke of me

χρηστὸς καὶ τὸ φορτίον μου ἐλαφρόν
gentle and the burden of me light

ἐστιν.
is.

of heaven and earth, because you have hidden these things from the wise and learned, and revealed them to little children.
26Yes, Father, for this was your good pleasure.
27"All things have been committed to me by my Father. No one knows the Son except the Father, and no one knows the Father except the Son and those to whom the Son chooses to reveal him.
28"Come to me, all you who are weary and burdened, and I will give you rest. 29Take my yoke upon you and learn from me, for I am gentle and humble in heart, and you will find rest for your souls. 30For my yoke is easy and my burden is light."

Chapter 12

Sabbath Questions

AT that time Jesus went on the Sabbath through the grainfields, and His disciples became hungry and began to pick the heads *of grain* and eat.
2But when the Pharisees saw it, they said to Him, "Behold, Your disciples do what is not lawful to do on a Sabbath."
3But He said to them, "Have you not read what David did, when he became hungry, he and his companions;
4how he entered the house of God, and they ate the consecrated bread, which was not lawful for him to eat, nor for those with him, but for the priests alone?
5"Or have you not read

12 Ἐν ἐκείνῳ τῷ καιρῷ ἐπορεύθη ὁ
At that - time went -

Ἰησοῦς τοῖς σάββασιν διὰ τῶν σπορίμων·
Jesus on the sabbath through the cornfields;

οἱ δὲ μαθηταὶ αὐτοῦ ἐπείνασαν, καὶ
and the disciples of him hungered, and

ἤρξαντο τίλλειν στάχυας καὶ ἐσθίειν.
began to pluck ears [of corn] and to eat.

2 οἱ δὲ Φαρισαῖοι ἰδόντες εἶπαν αὐτῷ·
But the Pharisees seeing said to him:

ἰδοὺ οἱ μαθηταί σου ποιοῦσιν ὃ οὐκ
Behold[,] the disciples of thee are doing what not

ἔξεστιν ποιεῖν ἐν σαββάτῳ. 3 ὁ δὲ
it is lawful to do on a sabbath. And he

εἶπεν αὐτοῖς· οὐκ ἀνέγνωτε τί ἐποίησεν
said to them: Did ye not read what did

Δαυίδ, ὅτε ἐπείνασεν καὶ οἱ μετ᾿
David, when he hungered and the[ones] with

αὐτοῦ; 4 πῶς εἰσῆλθεν εἰς τὸν οἶκον
him? how he entered into the house

τοῦ θεοῦ καὶ τοὺς ἄρτους τῆς προ-
- of God and the loaves of the set-

θέσεως ἔφαγον, ὃ οὐκ ἐξὸν ἦν αὐτῷ
ting forth ate, which not lawful it was for him

φαγεῖν οὐδὲ τοῖς μετ᾿ αὐτοῦ, εἰ μὴ
to eat neither the[ones] with him, except

τοῖς ἱερεῦσιν μόνοις; 5 ἢ οὐκ ἀνέγνωτε
for the priests only? or did ye not read

Chapter 12

Lord of the Sabbath

AT that time Jesus went through the grainfields on the Sabbath. His disciples were hungry and began to pick some heads of grain and eat them.
2When the Pharisees saw this, they said to him, "Look! Your disciples are doing what is unlawful on the Sabbath."
3He answered, "Haven't you read what David did when he and his companions were hungry? 4He entered the house of God, and he and his companions ate the consecrated bread—which was not lawful for them to do, but only for the priests. 5Or haven't you

in the Law, that on the Sabbath the priests in the temple break the Sabbath, and are innocent?

6"But I say to you, that something greater than the temple is here.

7"But if you had known what this means, 'I DESIRE COMPASSION, AND NOT A SACRIFICE,' you would not have condemned the innocent.

Lord of the Sabbath

8"For the Son of Man is Lord of the Sabbath."

9And departing from there, He went into their synagogue.

10And behold, *there was* a man with a withered hand. And they questioned Him, saying, "Is it lawful to heal on the Sabbath?"—in order that they might accuse Him.

11And He said to them, "What man shall there be among you, who shall have one sheep, and if it falls into a pit on the Sabbath, will he not take hold of it, and lift it out?

12"Of how much more value then is a man than a sheep! So then, it is lawful to do good on the Sabbath."

13Then He *said to the man, "Stretch out your hand!" And he stretched it out, and it was restored to normal, like the other.

14But the Pharisees went out, and counseled together against Him, *as to* how they might destroy Him.

15But Jesus, aware of *this,* withdrew from there. And many followed Him, and He healed them all,

16and warned them not to make Him known,

17in order that what was spoken through Isaiah the prophet, might be fulfilled, saying,

18"BEHOLD, MY SERVANT
    WHOM I HAVE CHOSEN;
    MY BELOVED IN WHOM
    MY SOUL IS WELL-
    PLEASED;
    I WILL PUT MY SPIRIT
    UPON HIM,

ἐν   τῷ   νόμῳ   ὅτι   τοῖς   σάββασιν   οἱ
in   the   law   that   on the   sabbaths   the

ἱερεῖς   ἐν   τῷ   ἱερῷ   τὸ   σάββατον   βεβηλοῦ-
priests   in   the   temple   the   sabbath   pro-

σιν   καὶ   ἀναίτιοί   εἰσιν;   6 λέγω   δὲ
fane   and   guiltless   are?   And I tell

ὑμῖν   ὅτι   τοῦ   ἱεροῦ   μεῖζόν   ἐστιν   ὧδε.
you   that [than]   the   temple   a greater [thing] is   here.

7 εἰ   δὲ   ἐγνώκειτε   τί   ἐστιν·   ἔλεος
But if   ye had known   what   it is: Mercy

θέλω   καὶ   οὐ   θυσίαν,   οὐκ   ἂν   κατε-
I desire   and   not   sacrifice,   ye would not have

δικάσατε   τοὺς   ἀναιτίους.   8 κύριος   γάρ
condemned   the   guiltless.   For Lord

ἐστιν   τοῦ   σαββάτου   ὁ   υἱὸς   τοῦ   ἀνθρώπου.
is   of the   sabbath   the   Son   –   of man.

9 Καὶ   μεταβὰς   ἐκεῖθεν   ἦλθεν   εἰς   τὴν
And   removing   thence   he came   into   the

συναγωγὴν   αὐτῶν.   10 καὶ   ἰδοὺ   ἄνθρωπος
synagogue   of them.   And behold[,]   a man

χεῖρα   ἔχων   ξηράν·   καὶ   ἐπηρώτησαν   αὐτὸν
¹[this] hand   ¹having   ²withered;   and   they questioned   him

λέγοντες·   εἰ   ἔξεστιν   τοῖς   σάββασιν
saying: If   it is lawful   on the   sabbaths

θεραπεῦσαι;   ἵνα   κατηγορήσωσιν   αὐτοῦ.
to heal?   in order that   they might accuse   ⁺ him.

11 ὁ   δὲ   εἶπεν   αὐτοῖς·   τίς   ἔσται   ἐξ
So he   said   to them: ¹What   ²will there be   ⁶of

ὑμῶν   ἄνθρωπος   ὃς   ἕξει   πρόβατον   ἕν,
⁷you   ⁴man   who will have   sheep   one,

καὶ   ἐὰν   ἐμπέσῃ   τοῦτο   τοῖς   σάββασιν
and   if   ²fall in   ¹this   on the   sabbaths

εἰς   βόθυνον,   οὐχὶ   κρατήσει   αὐτὸ   καὶ
into   a ditch,   will he not lay hold of   it   and

ἐγερεῖ;   12 πόσῳ   οὖν   διαφέρει   ἄνθρωπος
raise?   By how much then   surpasses   a man

προβάτου.   ὥστε   ἔξεστιν   τοῖς   σάββασιν
a sheep.   So that   it is lawful   on the   sabbaths

καλῶς   ποιεῖν.   13 τότε   λέγει   τῷ   ἀνθρώπῳ·
well   to do.   Then   he says   to the   man:

ἔκτεινόν   σου   τὴν   χεῖρα.   καὶ   ἐξέτεινεν,
Stretch forth   of thee   the   hand.   And he stretched forth,

καὶ   ἀπεκατεστάθη   ὑγιὴς   ὡς   ἡ   ἄλλη.
and   it was restored   healthy   as   the   other.

14 ἐξελθόντες   δὲ   οἱ   Φαρισαῖοι   συμβούλιον
And going out   the   Pharisees   counsel

ἔλαβον   κατ'   αὐτοῦ,   ὅπως   αὐτὸν   ἀπολέ-
took   against   him,   so as   him   they might

σωσιν.   15 Ὁ   δὲ   Ἰησοῦς   γνοὺς   ἀνε-
destroy.   –   But   Jesus   knowing   de-

χώρησεν   ἐκεῖθεν.   καὶ   ἠκολούθησαν   αὐτῷ
parted   thence.   And   followed   him

πολλοί,   καὶ   ἐθεράπευσεν   αὐτοὺς   πάντας,
many,   and   he healed   them   all,

16 καὶ   ἐπετίμησεν   αὐτοῖς   ἵνα   μὴ   φανερὸν
and   warned   them   that   ²not   ¹manifest

αὐτὸν   ποιήσωσιν·   17 ἵνα   πληρωθῇ   τὸ
⁴him   ¹they ²should ³make;   that might be fulfilled the [thing]

ῥηθὲν   διὰ   Ἡσαΐου   τοῦ   προφήτου
spoken   through   Isaiah   the   prophet

λέγοντος·   18 ἰδοὺ   ὁ   παῖς   μου   ὃν
saying: Behold[,]   the   servant   of me   whom

ᾑρέτισα, ὁ ἀγαπητός μου   ὃν   εὐδόκησεν
I chose, the   beloved   of me [with] whom   was well pleased

ἡ   ψυχή   μου·   θήσω   τὸ   πνεῦμα   μου   ἐπ'
the   soul   of me;   I will put the   spirit   of me   on

---

read in the Law that on the Sabbath the priests in the temple desecrate the day and yet are innocent? 6I tell you that one⁵ greater than the temple is here. 7If you had known what these words mean, 'I desire mercy, not sacrifice,'ᶠ you would not have condemned the innocent. 8For the Son of Man is Lord of the Sabbath."

9Going on from that place, he went into their synagogue, 10and a man with a shriveled hand was there. Looking for a reason to accuse Jesus, they asked him, "Is it lawful to heal on the Sabbath?"

11He said to them, "If any of you has a sheep and it falls into a pit on the Sabbath, will you not take hold of it and lift it out? 12How much more valuable is a man than a sheep! Therefore it is lawful to do good on the Sabbath."

13Then he said to the man, "Stretch out your hand." So he stretched it out and it was completely restored, just as sound as the other. 14But the Pharisees went out and plotted how they might kill Jesus.

God's Chosen Servant

15Aware of this, Jesus withdrew from that place. Many followed him, and he healed all their sick, 16warning them not to tell who he was. 17This was to fulfill what was spoken through the prophet Isaiah:

18"Here is my servant
    whom I have
    chosen,
    the one I love, in
    whom I delight;
    I will put my Spirit on
    him,

AND HE SHALL PRO-
CLAIM JUSTICE TO THE
GENTILES.
19 "HE WILL NOT QUARREL,
NOR CRY OUT;
NOR WILL ANYONE
HEAR HIS VOICE IN
THE STREETS.
20 "A BATTERED REED HE
WILL NOT BREAK OFF,
AND A SMOLDERING
WICK HE WILL NOT
PUT OUT,
UNTIL HE LEADS JUS-
TICE TO VICTORY.
21 "AND IN HIS NAME
THE GENTILES WILL
HOPE."

The Pharisees Rebuked

22Then there was brought
to Him a demon-possessed
man *who was* blind and
dumb, and He healed him,
so that the dumb man
spoke and saw.
23And all the multitudes
were amazed, and *began to*
say, "This *man* cannot be
the Son of David, can he?"
24But when the Pharisees
heard it, they said, "This
man casts out demons only
by Beelzebul the ruler of
the demons."
25And knowing their
thoughts He said to them,
"Any kingdom divided
against itself is laid waste;
and any city or house di-
vided against itself shall not
stand.
26 "And if Satan casts out
Satan, he is divided against
himself; how then shall his
kingdom stand?
27 "And if I by Beelzebul
cast out demons, by whom
do your sons cast them out?
Consequently they shall be
your judges.
28 "But if I cast out de-
mons by the Spirit of God,
then the kingdom of God
has come upon you.
29 "Or how can anyone
enter the strong man's
house and carry off his

αὐτόν, καὶ κρίσιν τοῖς ἔθνεσιν ἀπαγγελεῖ.
him, and judgment to the nations he will announce.
19 οὐκ ἐρίσει οὐδὲ κραυγάσει, οὐδὲ
He will not strive nor will shout, nor
ἀκούσει τις ἐν ταῖς πλατείαις τὴν
will hear anyone in the streets the
φωνὴν αὐτοῦ. 20 κάλαμον συντετριμμένον
voice of him. A reed *having been* bruised
οὐ κατεάξει καὶ λίνον τυφόμενον οὐ
he will not break and flax smoking not
σβέσει, ἕως ἂν ἐκβάλῃ εἰς νῖκος τὴν
he will quench, until he put forth to victory –
κρίσιν. 21 καὶ τῷ ὀνόματι αὐτοῦ ἔθνη
judgment. And in the name of him nations
ἐλπιοῦσιν.
will hope.

22 Τότε προσηνέχθη αὐτῷ δαιμονιζ-
Then was brought to him a demon-
όμενος τυφλὸς καὶ κωφός· καὶ ἐθεράπευσεν
possessed man blind and dumb; and he healed
αὐτόν, ὥστε τὸν κωφὸν λαλεῖν καὶ
him, so as the dumb to speak and
βλέπειν. 23 καὶ ἐξίσταντο πάντες οἱ
to see[b]. And were astonished all the
ὄχλοι καὶ ἔλεγον· μήτι οὗτός ἐστιν ὁ
crowds and said: not This is the
υἱὸς Δαυίδ; 24 οἱ δὲ Φαρισαῖοι ἀκού-
son of David? But the Pharisees hear-
σαντες εἶπον· οὗτος οὐκ ἐκβάλλει τὰ
ing said: This man does not expel the
δαιμόνια εἰ μὴ ἐν τῷ Βεεζεβοὺλ ἄρχοντι
demons except by Beelzebul ruler
τῶν δαιμονίων. 25 εἰδὼς δὲ τὰς ἐνθυμήσεις
of the demons. But knowing the thoughts
αὐτῶν εἶπεν αὐτοῖς· πᾶσα βασιλεία
of them he said to them: Every kingdom
μερισθεῖσα καθ’ ἑαυτῆς ἐρημοῦται,
divided against itself is brought to desolation,
καὶ πᾶσα πόλις ἢ οἰκία μερισθεῖσα καθ’
and every city or house divided against
ἑαυτῆς οὐ σταθήσεται. 26 καὶ εἰ
itself will not stand. And if
ὁ σατανᾶς τὸν σατανᾶν ἐκβάλλει, ἐφ’
– Satan – [2]Satan [1]expels, against
ἑαυτὸν ἐμερίσθη· πῶς οὖν σταθή-
himself he was(is) divided; how therefore will
σεται ἡ βασιλεία αὐτοῦ; 27 καὶ εἰ
stand the kingdom of him? And if
ἐγὼ ἐν Βεεζεβοὺλ ἐκβάλλω τὰ δαιμόνια,
I by Beelzebub expel the demons,
οἱ υἱοὶ ὑμῶν ἐν τίνι ἐκβάλλουσιν;
the sons of you by what do they expel?
διὰ τοῦτο αὐτοὶ κριταὶ ἔσονται ὑμῶν.
therefore they judges shall be of you.
28 εἰ δὲ ἐν πνεύματι θεοῦ ἐγὼ
But if by [the] Spirit of God I
ἐκβάλλω τὰ δαιμόνια, ἄρα ἔφθασεν
expel the demons, then came
ἐφ’ ὑμᾶς ἡ βασιλεία τοῦ θεοῦ. 29 ἢ
upon you the kingdom – of God. Or
πῶς δύναταί τις εἰσελθεῖν εἰς τὴν
how can anyone *to* enter into the
οἰκίαν τοῦ ἰσχυροῦ καὶ τὰ σκεύη αὐτοῦ
house of the strong man and the vessels of him

and he will proclaim
justice to the
nations.
19He will not quarrel or
cry out;
no one will hear his
voice in the streets.
20A bruised reed he will
not break,
and a smoldering wick
he will not snuff out,
till he leads justice to
victory.
21 In his name the nations
will put their
hope." [u]

Jesus and Beelzebub

22Then they brought him
a demon-possessed man
who was blind and mute,
and Jesus healed him, so
that he could both talk and
see. 23All the people were
astonished and said,
"Could this be the Son of
David?"
24But when the Pharisees
heard this, they said, "It is
only by Beelzebub,[v] the
prince of demons, that this
fellow drives out demons."
25Jesus knew their
thoughts and said to them,
"Every kingdom divided
against itself will be ruined,
and every city or house-
hold divided against itself
will not stand. 26If Satan
drives out Satan, he is divided against himself. How
then can his kingdom
stand? 27And if I drive out
demons by Beelzebub, by
whom do your people drive
them out? So then, they
will be your judges. 28But if
I drive out demons by the
Spirit of God, then the
kingdom of God has come
upon you.
29 "Or again, how can
anyone enter a strong
man's house and carry off

[u]21 Isaiah 42:1-4
[v]24 Greek *Beezeboul* or
Beelzeboul; also in verse 27

property, unless he first binds the strong *man*? And then he will plunder his house.

The Unpardonable Sin

30"He who is not with Me is against Me; and he who does not gather with Me scatters.

31"Therefore I say to you, any sin and blasphemy shall be forgiven men, but blasphemy against the Spirit shall not be forgiven.

32"And whoever shall speak a word against the Son of Man, it shall be forgiven him; but whoever shall speak against the Holy Spirit, it shall not be forgiven him, either in this age, or in the *age* to come.

Words Reveal Character

33"Either make the tree good, and its fruit good; or make the tree bad, and its fruit bad; for the tree is known by its fruit.

34"You brood of vipers, how can you, being evil, speak what is good? For the mouth speaks out of that which fills the heart.

35"The good man out of *his* good treasure brings forth what is good; and the evil man out of *his* evil treasure brings forth what is evil.

36"And I say to you, that every careless word that men shall speak, they shall render account for it in the day of judgment.

37"For by your words you shall be justified, and by your words you shall be condemned."

The Desire for Signs

38Then some of the scribes and Pharisees answered Him, saying, "Teacher, we want to see a sign from You."

ἁρπάσαι,   ἐὰν   μὴ   πρῶτον   δήσῃ   τὸν
to seize,   if   not   first   he binds   the

ἰσχυρόν;   καὶ   τότε   τὴν   οἰκίαν   αὐτοῦ
strong man?   and   then   the   house   of him

διαρπάσει.   30 ὁ   μὴ   ὢν   μετ᾽   ἐμοῦ
he will plunder.   The [one] not   being   with   me

κατ᾽   ἐμοῦ   ἐστιν,   καὶ   ὁ   μὴ   συνάγων   μετ᾽
against   me   is,   and the [one] not   gathering   with

ἐμοῦ   σκορπίζει.   31 Διὰ   τοῦτο   λέγω
me   scatters.   Therefore   I tell

ὑμῖν,   πᾶσα   ἁμαρτία   καὶ   βλασφημία
you,   all   sin   and   blasphemy

ἀφεθήσεται   τοῖς   ἀνθρώποις,   ἡ   δὲ   τοῦ
will be forgiven   -   to men,   but the   of the

πνεύματος   βλασφημία   οὐκ   ἀφεθήσεται.
Spirit   blasphemy   will not be forgiven.

32 καὶ   ὃς   ἐὰν   εἴπῃ   λόγον   κατὰ   τοῦ
And   whoever   speaks   a word   against   the

υἱοῦ   τοῦ   ἀνθρώπου,   ἀφεθήσεται   αὐτῷ·
Son   -   of man,   it will be forgiven   to him;

ὃς   δ᾽   ἂν   εἴπῃ   κατὰ   τοῦ   πνεύματος
but whoever   speaks   against   the   Spirit

τοῦ   ἁγίου,   οὐκ   ἀφεθήσεται   αὐτῷ
-   Holy,   it will not be forgiven   to him

οὔτε   ἐν   τούτῳ   τῷ   αἰῶνι   οὔτε   ἐν   τῷ
neither   in   this   -   age   nor   in   the [one]

μέλλοντι.   33 Ἢ   ποιήσατε   τὸ   δένδρον
coming.   Either   make   the   tree

καλὸν   καὶ   τὸν   καρπὸν   αὐτοῦ   καλόν,
good   and   the   fruit   of it   good,

ἢ   ποιήσατε   τὸ   δένδρον   σαπρὸν   καὶ   τὸν
or   make   the   tree   bad   and   the

καρπὸν   αὐτοῦ   σαπρόν·   ἐκ   γὰρ   τοῦ
fruit   of it   bad;   for of (by)   the

καρποῦ   τὸ   δένδρον   γινώσκεται.   34 γεννή-
fruit   the   tree   is known.   Off-

ματα   ἐχιδνῶν,   πῶς   δύνασθε   ἀγαθὰ   λαλεῖν
spring   of vipers,   how   can ye   good things   to speak

πονηροὶ   ὄντες;   ἐκ   γὰρ   τοῦ   περισ-
³evil   ¹being?   for out of   the   abund-

σεύματος   τῆς   καρδίας   τὸ   στόμα   λαλεῖ.
ance   of the   heart   the   mouth   speaks.

35 ὁ   ἀγαθὸς   ἄνθρωπος   ἐκ   τοῦ   ἀγαθοῦ
The   good   man   out of   the   good

θησαυροῦ   ἐκβάλλει   ἀγαθά,   καὶ   ὁ   πονηρὸς
treasure   puts forth   good things, and   the   evil

ἄνθρωπος   ἐκ   τοῦ   πονηροῦ   θησαυροῦ
man   out of   the   evil   treasure

ἐκβάλλει   πονηρά.   36 λέγω   δὲ
puts forth   evil things.   But I tell

ὑμῖν   ὅτι   πᾶν   ῥῆμα   ἀργὸν   ὃ   λαλήσουσιν
you   that   every   word   idle   which   will speak

οἱ   ἄνθρωποι,   ἀποδώσουσιν   περὶ   αὐτοῦ
-   men,   they will render   concerning   it

λόγον   ἐν   ἡμέρᾳ   κρίσεως·   37 ἐκ   γὰρ
account   in [the] day   of judgment;   for of (by)

τῶν   λόγων   σου   δικαιωθήσῃ,   καὶ   ἐκ
the   words   of thee thou wilt be justified,   and of (by)

τῶν   λόγων   σου   καταδικασθήσῃ.
the   words   of thee thou wilt be condemned.

38 Τότε   ἀπεκρίθησαν   αὐτῷ   τινες   τῶν
Then   answered   him   some   of the

γραμματέων   καὶ   Φαρισαίων   λέγοντες·
scribes   and   Pharisees   saying:

διδάσκαλε,   θέλομεν   ἀπὸ   σοῦ   σημεῖον   ἰδεῖν.
Teacher,   we wish   from   thee   a sign   to see.

---

his possessions unless he first ties up the strong man? Then he can rob his house.

30"He who is not with me is against me, and he who does not gather with me scatters. 31And so I tell you, every sin and blasphemy will be forgiven men, but the blasphemy against the Spirit will not be forgiven. 32Anyone who speaks a word against the Son of Man will be forgiven, but anyone who speaks against the Holy Spirit will not be forgiven, either in this age or in the age to come.

33"Make a tree good and its fruit will be good, or make a tree bad and its fruit will be bad, for a tree is recognized by its fruit. 34You brood of vipers, how can you who are evil say anything good? For out of the overflow of the heart the mouth speaks. 35The good man brings good things out of the good stored up in him, and the evil man brings evil things out of the evil stored up in him. 36But I tell you that men will have to give account on the day of judgment for every careless word they have spoken. 37For by your words you will be acquitted, and by your words you will be condemned."

The Sign of Jonah

38Then some of the Pharisees and teachers of the law said to him, "Teacher, we want to see a miraculous sign from you."

³⁹But He answered and said to them, "An evil and adulterous generation craves for a sign; and *yet* no sign shall be given to it but the sign of Jonah the prophet;
⁴⁰for just as JONAH WAS THREE DAYS AND THREE NIGHTS IN THE BELLY OF THE SEA MONSTER, so shall the Son of Man be three days and three nights in the heart of the earth.
⁴¹"The men of Nineveh shall stand up with this generation at the judgment, and shall condemn it because they repented at the preaching of Jonah; and behold, something greater than Jonah is here.
⁴²"*The* Queen of *the* South shall rise up with this generation and shall condemn it, because she came from the ends of the earth to hear the wisdom of Solomon; and behold, something greater than Solomon is here.
⁴³"Now when the unclean spirit goes out of a man, it passes through waterless places, seeking rest, and does not find *it*.
⁴⁴"Then it says, 'I will return to my house from which I came'; and when it comes, it finds it unoccupied, swept, and put in order.
⁴⁵"Then it goes, and takes along with it seven other spirits more wicked than itself, and they go in and live there; and the last state of that man becomes worse than the first. That is the way it will also be with this evil generation."

Changed Relationships
⁴⁶While He was still speaking to the multitudes,

39 ὁ   δὲ   ἀποκριθεὶς   εἶπεν   αὐτοῖς·
But he   answering   said   to them:
γενεὰ   πονηρὰ   καὶ   μοιχαλὶς   σημεῖον
generation An evil   and   adulterous   a sign
ἐπιζητεῖ,   καὶ   σημεῖον   οὐ   δοθήσεται
seeks,   and   a sign   shall not be given
αὐτῇ   εἰ   μὴ   τὸ   σημεῖον   Ἰωνᾶ   τοῦ
to it except   the   sign   of Jonas   the
προφήτου.   **40** ὥσπερ   γὰρ   ἦν   Ἰωνᾶς
prophet.   For as   was   Jonas
ἐν   τῇ   κοιλίᾳ   τοῦ   κήτους   τρεῖς   ἡμέρας
in   the   belly   of the sea monster three   days
καὶ   τρεῖς   νύκτας,   οὕτως   ἔσται   ὁ   υἱὸς
and   three   nights,   so   will be   the   Son
τοῦ   ἀνθρώπου   ἐν   τῇ   καρδίᾳ   τῆς   γῆς
–   of man   in   the   heart   of the   earth
τρεῖς   ἡμέρας   καὶ   τρεῖς   νύκτας.   **41** ἄνδρες
three   days   and   three   nights.   Men
Νινευῖται   ἀναστήσονται   ἐν   τῇ   κρίσει
Ninevites   will stand up   in   the   judgment
μετὰ   τῆς   γενεᾶς   ταύτης   καὶ   κατα-
with   –   generation   this   and   will
κρινοῦσιν   αὐτήν·   ὅτι   μετενόησαν   εἰς   τὸ
condemn   it;   because   they repented   at   the
κήρυγμα   Ἰωνᾶ, καὶ ἰδοὺ   πλεῖον   Ἰωνᾶ
proclamation of Jonas, and behold a greater thing [than] Jonas
ὧδε.   **42** βασίλισσα   νότου   ἐγερθήσεται
[is] here.   [The] queen of [the] south   will be raised
ἐν   τῇ   κρίσει   μετὰ   τῆς   γενεᾶς   ταύτης
in   the   judgment   with   –   generation   this
καὶ   κατακρινεῖ   αὐτήν·   ὅτι   ἦλθεν   ἐκ
and   will condemn   it;   because she came out of
τῶν   περάτων   τῆς   γῆς   ἀκοῦσαι   τὴν   σοφίαν
the   limits   of the earth to hear   the   wisdom
Σολομῶνος,   καὶ ἰδοὺ   πλεῖον   Σολομῶνος
of Solomon,   and behold a greater thing [than] Solomon
ὧδε.   **43** Ὅταν   δὲ   τὸ   ἀκάθαρτον   πνεῦμα
[is] here.   Now when the   unclean   spirit
ἐξέλθῃ   ἀπὸ   τοῦ   ἀνθρώπου,   διέρχεται   δι'
goes out   from   –   a man,   he goes   through
ἀνύδρων   τόπων   ζητοῦν   ἀνάπαυσιν,   καὶ
dry   places   seeking   rest,   and
οὐχ   εὑρίσκει.   **44** τότε   λέγει·   εἰς   τὸν
finds not.   Then   he says: Into   the
οἶκόν   μου   ἐπιστρέψω   ὅθεν   ἐξῆλθον·
house   of me   I will return   whence   I came out;
καὶ   ἐλθὸν   εὑρίσκει   σχολάζοντα   [καὶ]
and   coming   he finds [it] standing empty   and
σεσαρωμένον   καὶ   κεκοσμημένον.   **45** τότε
having been swept and *having been* furnished.   Then
πορεύεται   καὶ   παραλαμβάνει   μεθ'   ἑαυτοῦ
he goes   and   takes   with   him*self*
ἑπτὰ   ἕτερα   πνεύματα   πονηρότερα   ἑαυτοῦ,
seven   other   spirits   more evil [than] himself,
καὶ   εἰσελθόντα   κατοικεῖ   ἐκεῖ·   καὶ
and   entering   dwells   there;   and
γίνεται   τὰ   ἔσχατα   τοῦ   ἀνθρώπου   ἐκείνου
becomes   the   last things   –   man   of that
χείρονα   τῶν   πρώτων.   οὕτως   ἔσται
worse [than] the   first.   Thus   it will be
καὶ   τῇ   γενεᾷ   ταύτῃ   τῇ   πονηρᾷ.
also   –   *generation ¹to this   –   *evil.
46 Ἔτι   αὐτοῦ   λαλοῦντος   τοῖς   ὄχλοις,
Yet   him   speaking*   to the   crowds,
=While he was still speaking

³⁹He answered, "A wicked and adulterous generation asks for a miraculous sign! But none will be given it except the sign of the prophet Jonah. ⁴⁰For as Jonah was three days and three nights in the belly of a huge fish, so the Son of Man will be three days and three nights in the heart of the earth. ⁴¹The men of Nineveh will stand up at the judgment with this generation and condemn it; for they repented at the preaching of Jonah, and now one ʷ greater than Jonah is here. ⁴²The Queen of the South will rise at the judgment with this generation and condemn it; for she came from the ends of the earth to listen to Solomon's wisdom, and now one greater than Solomon is here.

⁴³"When an evilˣ spirit comes out of a man, it goes through arid places seeking rest and does not find it. ⁴⁴Then it says, 'I will return to the house I left.' When it arrives, it finds the house unoccupied, swept clean and put in order. ⁴⁵Then it goes and takes with it seven other spirits more wicked than itself, and they go in and live there. And the final condition of that man is worse than the first. That is how it will be with this wicked generation."

Jesus' Mother and Brothers
⁴⁶While Jesus was still talking to the crowd, his

ʷ41 Or *something*; also in verse 42
ˣ43 Greek *unclean*

behold, His mother and brothers were standing outside, seeking to speak to Him. 47And someone said to Him, "Behold, Your mother and Your brothers are standing outside seeking to speak to You." 48But He answered the one who was telling Him and said, "Who is My mother and who are My brothers?" 49And stretching out His hand toward His disciples, He said, "Behold, My mother and My brothers! 50"For whoever does the will of My Father who is in heaven, he is My brother and sister and mother."

Greek	English
ἰδοὺ ἡ μήτηρ καὶ οἱ ἀδελφοὶ αὐτοῦ	behold the mother and the brothers of him
εἰστήκεισαν ἔξω ζητοῦντες αὐτῷ λαλῆσαι.	stood outside seeking to him to speak.
47 [εἶπεν δέ τις αὐτῷ· ἰδοὺ ἡ μήτηρ	And said someone to him: Behold[,] the mother
σου καὶ οἱ ἀδελφοί σου ἔξω ἑστήκασιν	of thee and the brothers of thee outside are standing
ζητοῦντές σοι λαλῆσαι.] **48** ὁ δὲ	seeking to thee to speak.] And he
ἀποκριθεὶς εἶπεν τῷ λέγοντι αὐτῷ· τίς	answering said to the [one] saying to him: Who
ἐστιν ἡ μήτηρ μου, καὶ τίνες εἰσὶν οἱ	is the mother of me, and who are the
ἀδελφοί μου; **49** καὶ ἐκτείνας τὴν	brothers of me? And stretching forth the
χεῖρα [αὐτοῦ] ἐπὶ τοὺς μαθητὰς αὐτοῦ	hand of him on the disciples of him
εἶπεν· ἰδοὺ ἡ μήτηρ μου καὶ οἱ ἀδελφοὶ	he said: Behold[,] the mother of me and the brothers
μου. **50** ὅστις γὰρ ἂν ποιήσῃ τὸ θέλημα	of me. For whoever does the will
τοῦ πατρός μου τοῦ ἐν οὐρανοῖς, αὐτός	of the Father of me in heavens, he
μου ἀδελφὸς καὶ ἀδελφὴ καὶ μήτηρ ἐστίν.	of me brother and sister and mother is.

mother and brothers stood outside, wanting to speak to him. 47Someone told him, "Your mother and brothers are standing outside, wanting to speak to you." ʸ 48He replied to him, "Who is my mother, and who are my brothers?" 49Pointing to his disciples, he said, "Here are my mother and my brothers. 50For whoever does the will of my Father in heaven is my brother and sister and mother."

Chapter 13

Jesus Teaches in Parables

ON that day Jesus went out of the house, and was sitting by the sea.
2And great multitudes gathered to Him, so that He got into a boat and sat down, and the whole multitude was standing on the beach.
3And He spoke many things to them in parables, saying, "Behold, the sower went out to sow;
4and as he sowed, some *seeds* fell beside the road, and the birds came and ate them up.
5"And others fell upon the rocky places, where they did not have much soil; and immediately they sprang up, because they had no depth of soil.
6"But when the sun had risen, they were scorched; and because they had no root, they withered away.
7"And others fell among the thorns, and the thorns

Greek	English
13 Ἐν τῇ ἡμέρᾳ ἐκείνῃ ἐξελθὼν ὁ	On — day that ᵍgoing out of —
Ἰησοῦς τῆς οἰκίας ἐκάθητο παρὰ τὴν	¹Jesus of the house sat beside the
θάλασσαν· **2** καὶ συνήχθησαν πρὸς αὐτὸν	sea; and were assembled to him
ὄχλοι πολλοί, ὥστε αὐτὸν εἰς πλοῖον	crowds many, so as him in a ship
ἐμβάντα καθῆσθαι, καὶ πᾶς ὁ ὄχλος	embarking to sitᵇ, and all the crowd
ἐπὶ τὸν αἰγιαλὸν εἰστήκει. **3** καὶ ἐλάλησεν	on the beach stood. And he spoke
αὐτοῖς πολλὰ ἐν παραβολαῖς λέγων·	to them many things in parables saying:
Ἰδοὺ ἐξῆλθεν ὁ σπείρων τοῦ σπείρειν.	Behold went out the [one] sowing — to sowᵈ.
4 καὶ ἐν τῷ σπείρειν αὐτὸν ἃ μὲν	And in the to sow himᵉ some indeed
=as he sowed	
ἔπεσεν παρὰ τὴν ὁδόν, καὶ ἐλθόντα τὰ	fell beside the way, and coming the
πετεινὰ κατέφαγεν αὐτά. **5** ἄλλα δὲ	birds devoured them. But others
ἔπεσεν ἐπὶ τὰ πετρώδη ὅπου οὐκ	fell on the rocky places where not
εἶχεν γῆν πολλήν, καὶ εὐθέως ἐξανέτειλεν	it had earth much, and immediately it sprang up
διὰ τὸ μὴ ἔχειν βάθος γῆς· **6** ἡλίου	on account of the not to have depth of earth; [the] sun
=because it had not	
δὲ ἀνατείλαντος ἐκαυματίσθη, καὶ διὰ	But having risenᵃ it was scorched, and on account of
=when the sun rose	=because
τὸ μὴ ἔχειν ῥίζαν ἐξηράνθη. **7** ἄλλα δὲ	the not to have root it was dried up. But others
it had not	
ἔπεσεν ἐπὶ τὰς ἀκάνθας, καὶ ἀνέβησαν	fell on the thorns, and came up

Chapter 13

The Parable of the Sower

THAT same day Jesus went out of the house and sat by the lake. 2Such large crowds gathered around him that he got into a boat and sat in it, while all the people stood on the shore. 3Then he told them many things in parables, saying: "A farmer went out to sow his seed. 4As he was scattering the seed, some fell along the path, and the birds came and ate it up. 5Some fell on rocky places, where it did not have much soil. It sprang up quickly, because the soil was shallow. 6But when the sun came up, the plants were scorched, and they withered because they had no root. 7Other seed fell among thorns, which grew came up and choked them out.

8"And others fell on the good soil, and *yielded a crop, some a hundredfold, some sixty, and some thirty.

9"He who has ears, let him hear."

An Explanation

10And the disciples came and said to Him, "Why do You speak to them in parables?"

11And He answered and said to them, "To you it has been granted to know the mysteries of the kingdom of heaven, but to them it has not been granted.

12"For whoever has, to him shall *more* be given, and he shall have an abundance; but whoever does not have, even what he has shall be taken away from him.

13"Therefore I speak to them in parables; because while seeing they do not see, and while hearing they do not hear, nor do they understand.

14"And in their case the prophecy of Isaiah is being fulfilled, which says,

'YOU WILL KEEP ON HEARING, BUT WILL NOT UNDERSTAND;
AND YOU WILL KEEP ON SEEING, BUT WILL NOT PERCEIVE;
15 FOR THE HEART OF THIS PEOPLE HAS BECOME DULL,
AND WITH THEIR EARS THEY SCARCELY HEAR,
AND THEY HAVE CLOSED THEIR EYES
LEST THEY SHOULD SEE WITH THEIR EYES,
AND HEAR WITH THEIR EARS,
AND UNDERSTAND WITH THEIR HEART AND RETURN,
AND I SHOULD HEAL THEM.'

16"But blessed are your eyes, because they see; and your ears, because they hear.

17"For truly I say to you, that many prophets and righteous men desired to see what you see, and did not see *it*; and to hear what you hear, and did not hear *it.*

αἱ ἄκανθαι καὶ ἀπέπνιξαν αὐτά. 8 ἄλλα δὲ
the thorns and choked them. And others

ἔπεσεν ἐπὶ τὴν γῆν τὴν καλὴν καὶ
fell on the earth - good and

ἐδίδου καρπόν, ὃ μὲν ἑκατόν, ὃ δὲ
gave fruit, the one a hundred, the other

ἐξήκοντα, ὃ δὲ τριάκοντα. 9 ὁ ἔχων
sixty, the other thirty. The [one] having

ὦτα ἀκουέτω. 10 Καὶ προσελθόντες οἱ
ears let him hear. And approaching the

μαθηταὶ εἶπαν αὐτῷ· διὰ τί ἐν παρα-
disciples said to him: Why in par-

βολαῖς λαλεῖς αὐτοῖς; 11 ὁ δὲ
ables speakest thou to them? And he

ἀποκριθεὶς εἶπεν· ὅτι ὑμῖν δέδοται
answering said: Because to you it has been given

γνῶναι τὰ μυστήρια τῆς βασιλείας τῶν
to know the mysteries of the kingdom of the

οὐρανῶν, ἐκείνοις δὲ οὐ δέδοται. 12 ὅστις
heavens, but to those it has not been given. [he] who

γὰρ ἔχει, δοθήσεται αὐτῷ καὶ περισ-
For has, it will be given to him and he will

σευθήσεται· ὅστις δὲ οὐκ ἔχει, καὶ
have abundance; but [he] who has not, even

ὃ ἔχει ἀρθήσεται ἀπ᾽ αὐτοῦ. 13 διὰ
what he has will be taken from him. There-

τοῦτο ἐν παραβολαῖς αὐτοῖς λαλῶ, ὅτι
fore in parables to them I speak, because

βλέποντες οὐ βλέπουσιν καὶ ἀκούοντες
seeing they see not and hearing

οὐκ ἀκούουσιν οὐδὲ συνιοῦσιν. 14 καὶ
they hear not neither understand. And

ἀναπληροῦται αὐτοῖς ἡ προφητεία Ἡσαΐου
is fulfilled in them the prophecy of Isaiah

ἡ λέγουσα· ἀκοῇ ἀκούσετε καὶ οὐ μὴ
- saying: In hearing ye will hear and by no means

συνῆτε, καὶ βλέποντες βλέψετε
understand, and seeing ye will see

καὶ οὐ μὴ ἴδητε. 15 ἐπαχύνθη γὰρ
and by no means perceive. For waxed gross

ἡ καρδία τοῦ λαοῦ τούτου, καὶ τοῖς
the heart - people of this, and with the

ὠσὶν βαρέως ἤκουσαν, καὶ τοὺς ὀφθαλμοὺς
ears heavily they heard, and the eyes

αὐτῶν ἐκάμμυσαν· μήποτε ἴδωσιν τοῖς
of them they closed; lest they see with the

ὀφθαλμοῖς καὶ τοῖς ὠσὶν ἀκούσωσιν
eyes and with the ears hear

καὶ τῇ καρδίᾳ συνῶσιν καὶ ἐπιστρέψωσιν,
and with the heart understand and turn back,

καὶ ἰάσομαι αὐτούς. 16 ὑμῶν δὲ μακάριοι
and I will heal them. But of you blessed

οἱ ὀφθαλμοὶ ὅτι βλέπουσιν, καὶ τὰ
the eyes because they see, and the

ὦτα [ὑμῶν] ὅτι ἀκούουσιν. 17 ἀμὴν
ears of you because they hear. truly

γὰρ λέγω ὑμῖν ὅτι πολλοὶ προφῆται καὶ
For I say to you that many prophets and

δίκαιοι ἐπεθύμησαν ἰδεῖν ἃ
righteous men desired to see [the things] which

βλέπετε καὶ οὐκ εἶδαν, καὶ ἀκοῦσαι
ye see and did not see, and to hear

ἃ ἀκούετε καὶ οὐκ ἤκουσαν.
[the things] which ye hear and did not hear.

---

up and choked the plants.

8Still other seed fell on good soil, where it produced a crop—a hundred, sixty or thirty times what was sown. 9He who has ears, let him hear."

10The disciples came to him and asked, "Why do you speak to the people in parables?"

11He replied, "The knowledge of the secrets of the kingdom of heaven has been given to you, but not to them. 12Whoever has will be given more, and he will have an abundance. Whoever does not have, even what he has will be taken from him. 13This is why I speak to them in parables:

"Though seeing, they do not see;
though hearing, they do not hear or understand.

14In them is fulfilled the prophecy of Isaiah:

"'You will be ever hearing but never understanding;
you will be ever seeing but never perceiving.
15For this people's heart has become calloused;
they hardly hear with their ears,
and they have closed their eyes.
Otherwise they might see with their eyes,
hear with their ears,
understand with their hearts
and turn, and I would heal them.'[z]

16But blessed are your eyes because they see, and your ears because they hear. 17For I tell you the truth, many prophets and righteous men longed to see what you see but did not see it, and to hear what you hear but did not hear it.

z15 Isaiah 6:9,10

The Sower Explained

18"Hear then the parable of the sower.

19"When anyone hears the word of the kingdom, and does not understand it, the evil *one* comes and snatches away what has been sown in his heart. This is the one on whom seed was sown beside the road.

20"And the one on whom seed was sown on the rocky places, this is the man who hears the word, and immediately receives it with joy;

21yet he has no *firm* root in himself, but is *only* temporary, and when affliction or persecution arises because of the word, immediately he falls away.

22"And the one on whom seed was sown among the thorns, this is the man who hears the word, and the worry of the world, and the deceitfulness of riches choke the word, and it becomes unfruitful.

23"And the one on whom seed was sown on the good soil, this is the man who hears the word and understands it; who indeed bears fruit, and brings forth, some a hundredfold, some sixty, and some thirty."

Tares among Wheat

24He presented another parable to them, saying, "The kingdom of heaven may be compared to a man who sowed good seed in his field.

25"But while men were sleeping, his enemy came and sowed ¹tares also among the wheat, and went away.

26"But when the wheat sprang up and bore grain, then the tares became evident also.

27"And the slaves of the landowner came and said

---

18 Ὑμεῖς οὖν ἀκούσατε τὴν παραβολὴν
¹Ye ²therefore ¹hear　the　parable

τοῦ σπείραντος. **19** Παντὸς ἀκούοντος
of the sowing [one].　Everyone hearing⁴
= When anyone hears

τὸν λόγον τῆς βασιλείας καὶ μὴ συνιέντος
the word of the kingdom and not understanding⁴
= does not understand

ἔρχεται ὁ πονηρὸς καὶ ἁρπάζει τὸ
comes the evil one and seizes the [thing]

ἐσπαρμένον ἐν τῇ καρδίᾳ αὐτοῦ· οὗτός
having been sown in the heart of him; this

ἐστιν ὁ παρὰ τὴν ὁδὸν σπαρείς. **20** ὁ
is the [word] by the way sown. the [word]

δὲ ἐπὶ τὰ πετρώδη σπαρείς, οὗτός ἐστιν
And on the rocky places sown, this is

ὁ τὸν λόγον ἀκούων καὶ εὐθὺς μετὰ
the [one] ²the ³word ¹hearing and immediately with

χαρᾶς λαμβάνων αὐτόν· **21** οὐκ ἔχει δὲ
joy receiving it; but he has not

ῥίζαν ἐν ἑαυτῷ ἀλλὰ πρόσκαιρός ἐστιν,
root in himself but short-lived is,

γενομένης δὲ θλίψεως ἢ διωγμοῦ
and occurring tribulation or persecution⁴
= when tribulation or persecution occurs

διὰ τὸν λόγον εὐθὺς σκανδαλίζεται.
on account of the word immediately he is offended.

22 ὁ δὲ εἰς τὰς ἀκάνθας σπαρείς, οὗτός
But the [word] in the thorns sown, this

ἐστιν ὁ τὸν λόγον ἀκούων, καὶ ἡ
is the [one] ²the ³word ¹hearing, and the

μέριμνα τοῦ αἰῶνος καὶ ἡ ἀπάτη
anxiety of the age and the deceit

τοῦ πλούτου συμπνίγει τὸν λόγον, καὶ
- of riches chokes the word, and

ἄκαρπος γίνεται. **23** ὁ δὲ ἐπὶ τὴν
unfruitful it becomes. And the [word] on the

καλὴν γῆν σπαρείς, οὗτός ἐστιν ὁ
good earth sown, this is the [one]

τὸν λόγον ἀκούων καὶ συνιείς, ὃς
²the ³word ¹hearing ²and ³understanding, who

δὴ καρποφορεῖ καὶ ποιεῖ ὃ μὲν ἑκατόν,
indeed bears fruit and produces one indeed a hundred,

ὃ δὲ ἑξήκοντα, ὃ δὲ τριάκοντα.
the other sixty, the other thirty.

24 Ἄλλην παραβολὴν παρέθηκεν αὐτοῖς
Another parable he set before them

λέγων· ὡμοιώθη ἡ βασιλεία τῶν
saying: was(is) likened The kingdom of the

οὐρανῶν ἀνθρώπῳ σπείραντι καλὸν σπέρμα
heavens to a man sowing good seed

ἐν τῷ ἀγρῷ αὐτοῦ. **25** ἐν δὲ τῷ
in the field of him. But in the
= while men slept

καθεύδειν τοὺς ἀνθρώπους ἦλθεν αὐτοῦ
to sleep - men⁴ came of him

ὁ ἐχθρὸς καὶ ἐπέσπειρεν ζιζάνια ἀνὰ μέσον
the enemy and oversowed tares in between

τοῦ σίτου καὶ ἀπῆλθεν. **26** ὅτε δὲ
the wheat and went away. But when

ἐβλάστησεν ὁ χόρτος καὶ καρπὸν
sprouted the grass and fruit

ἐποίησεν, τότε ἐφάνη καὶ τὰ ζιζάνια.
produced, then appeared also the tares.

27 προσελθόντες δὲ οἱ δοῦλοι τοῦ οἰκο-
So approaching the slaves of the house-

18"Listen then to what the parable of the sower means: 19When anyone hears the message about the kingdom and does not understand it, the evil one comes and snatches away what is sown in his heart. This is the seed sown along the path. 20The one who received the seed that fell on rocky places is the man who hears the word and at once receives it with joy. 21But since he has no root, he lasts only a short time. When trouble or persecution comes because of the word, he quickly falls away. 22The one who received the seed that fell among the thorns is the man who hears the word, but the worries of this life and the deceitfulness of wealth choke it, making it unfruitful. 23But the one who received the seed that fell on good soil is the man who hears the word and understands it. He produces a crop, yielding a hundred, sixty or thirty times what was sown."

The Parable of the Weeds

24Jesus told them another parable: "The kingdom of heaven is like a man who sowed good seed in his field. 25But while everyone was sleeping, his enemy came and sowed weeds among the wheat, and went away. 26When the wheat sprouted and formed heads, then the weeds also appeared.

27"The owner's servants came to him and said, 'Sir,

---

¹ Or, *darnel*, a weed resembling wheat

to him, 'Sir, did you not sow good seed in your field? How then does it have tares?'
28"And he said to them, 'An enemy has done this!' And the slaves *said to him, 'Do you want us, then, to go and gather them up?'
29"But he *said, 'No; lest while you are gathering up the tares, you may root up the wheat with them.
30"Allow both to grow together until the harvest; and in the time of the harvest I will say to the reapers, "First gather up the tares and bind them in bundles to burn them up; but gather the wheat into my barn." ' "

The Mustard Seed

31He presented another parable to them, saying, "The kingdom of heaven is like a mustard seed, which a man took and sowed in his field;
32and this is smaller than all *other* seeds; but when it is full grown, it is larger than the garden plants, and becomes a tree, so that THE BIRDS OF THE AIR come and NEST IN ITS BRANCHES."

The Leaven

33He spoke another parable to them, "The kingdom of heaven is like leaven, which a woman took, and hid in three pecks of meal, until it was all leavened."
34All these things Jesus spoke to the multitudes in parables, and He did not speak to them without a parable,
35so that what was spoken through the prophet might be fulfilled, saying,

"I WILL OPEN MY MOUTH
IN PARABLES;

δεσπότου εἶπον αὐτῷ· κύριε, οὐχὶ καλὸν
master said to him: Lord, not good

σπέρμα ἔσπειρας ἐν τῷ σῷ ἀγρῷ;
seed sowedst thou in - thy field?

πόθεν οὖν ἔχει ζιζάνια; 28 ὁ δὲ ἔφη
whence then has it tares? And he said

αὐτοῖς· ἐχθρὸς ἄνθρωπος τοῦτο ἐποίησεν.
to them: An enemy man this did.

οἱ δὲ δοῦλοι αὐτῷ λέγουσιν· θέλεις
So the slaves to him say: Willest thou

οὖν ἀπελθόντες συλλέξωμεν αὐτά; 29 ὁ
then going away we may collect them? he

δέ φησιν· οὔ, μήποτε συλλέγοντες τὰ
But says: No, lest collecting the

ζιζάνια ἐκριζώσητε ἅμα αὐτοῖς τὸν
tares ye should root up together with them the

σῖτον. 30 ἄφετε συναυξάνεσθαι ἀμφότερα
wheat. Leave to grow together both

ἕως τοῦ θερισμοῦ· καὶ ἐν καιρῷ τοῦ
until the harvest; and in time of the

θερισμοῦ ἐρῶ τοῖς θερισταῖς· συλλέξατε
harvest I will say to the reapers: Collect ye

πρῶτον τὰ ζιζάνια καὶ δήσατε αὐτὰ
first the tares and bind them

εἰς δέσμας πρὸς τὸ κατακαῦσαι αὐτά,
in bundles - to burn them,

τὸν δὲ σῖτον συναγάγετε εἰς τὴν ἀποθήκην
but the wheat gather ye into the barn

μου. 31 Ἄλλην παραβολὴν παρέθηκεν
of me. Another parable he set before

αὐτοῖς λέγων· ὁμοία ἐστὶν ἡ βασιλεία
them saying: Like is the kingdom

τῶν οὐρανῶν κόκκῳ σινάπεως, ὃν
of the heavens to a grain of mustard, which

λαβὼν ἄνθρωπος ἔσπειρεν ἐν τῷ ἀγρῷ
²taking ¹a man sowed in the field

αὐτοῦ· 32 ὃ μικρότερον μέν ἐστιν
of him; which less indeed is

πάντων τῶν σπερμάτων, ὅταν δὲ
[than] all the seeds, but when

αὐξηθῇ, μεῖζον τῶν λαχάνων ἐστὶν
it grows, greater [than] the herbs it is

καὶ γίνεται δένδρον, ὥστε ἐλθεῖν τὰ
and becomes a tree, so as to come the

πετεινὰ τοῦ οὐρανοῦ καὶ κατασκηνοῦν
birds of the heaven and dwell

ἐν τοῖς κλάδοις αὐτοῦ. 33 Ἄλλην
in the branches of it. Another

παραβολὴν ἐλάλησεν αὐτοῖς· ὁμοία
parable he spoke to them: Like

ἐστὶν ἡ βασιλεία τῶν οὐρανῶν ζύμῃ,
is the kingdom of the heavens to leaven,

ἣν λαβοῦσα γυνὴ ἐνέκρυψεν εἰς ἀλεύρου
which ²taking ¹a woman hid in ³of meal

σάτα τρία, ἕως οὗ ἐζυμώθη ὅλον.
²measures ¹three, until was leavened [the] whole.

34 Ταῦτα πάντα ἐλάλησεν ὁ Ἰησοῦς ἐν
These things all spoke - Jesus in

παραβολαῖς τοῖς ὄχλοις, καὶ χωρὶς παραβολῆς
parables to the crowds, and without a parable

οὐδὲν ἐλάλει αὐτοῖς· 35 ὅπως πληρωθῇ
nothing he spoke to them; so that was fulfilled

τὸ ῥηθὲν διὰ τοῦ προφήτου λέγοντος·
the [thing] spoken through the prophet saying:

ἀνοίξω ἐν παραβολαῖς τὸ στόμα μου,
I will open in parables the mouth of me,

---

didn't you sow good seed in your field? Where then did the weeds come from?'
28"An enemy did this,' he replied.
"The servants asked him, 'Do you want us to go and pull them up?'
29" 'No,' he answered, 'because while you are pulling the weeds, you may root up the wheat with them. 30Let both grow together until the harvest. At that time I will tell the harvesters: First collect the weeds and tie them in bundles to be burned; then gather the wheat and bring it into my barn.' "

The Parables of the Mustard Seed and the Yeast

31He told them another parable: "The kingdom of heaven is like a mustard seed, which a man took and planted in his field. 32Though it is the smallest of all your seeds, yet when it grows, it is the largest of garden plants and becomes a tree, so that the birds of the air come and perch in its branches."

33He told them still another parable: "The kingdom of heaven is like yeast that a woman took and mixed into a large amount[a] of flour until it worked all through the dough."
34Jesus spoke all these things to the crowd in parables; he did not say anything to them without using a parable. 35So was fulfilled what was spoken through the prophet:

"I will open my mouth
in parables,

---

*a33 Greek three satas (probably about 1/2 bushel or 22 liters)

I WILL UTTER THINGS HIDDEN SINCE THE FOUNDATION OF THE WORLD."

The Tares Explained

36Then He left the multitudes, and went into the house. And His disciples came to Him, saying, "Explain to us the parable of the tares of the field."

37And He answered and said, "The one who sows the good seed is the Son of Man,

38and the field is the world; and *as for* the good seed, these are the sons of the kingdom; and the tares are the sons of the evil *one;*

39and the enemy who sowed them is the devil, and the harvest is the end of the age; and the reapers are angels.

40"Therefore just as the tares are gathered up and burned with fire, so shall it be at the end of the age.

41"The Son of Man will send forth His angels, and they will gather out of His kingdom all stumbling blocks, and those who commit lawlessness,

42and will cast them into the furnace of fire; in that place there shall be weeping and gnashing of teeth.

43"Then THE RIGHTEOUS WILL SHINE FORTH AS THE SUN in the kingdom of their Father. He who has ears, let him hear.

Hidden Treasure

44"The kingdom of

ἐρεύξομαι κεκρυμμένα ἀπὸ καταβολῆς.
I will utter things having been hidden from [the] foundation.

36 Τότε ἀφεὶς τοὺς ὄχλους ἦλθεν
Then sending away the crowds he came

εἰς τὴν οἰκίαν. Καὶ προσῆλθον αὐτῷ
into the house. And approached to him

οἱ μαθηταὶ αὐτοῦ λέγοντες· διασάφησον
the disciples of him saying: Explain thou

ἡμῖν τὴν παραβολὴν τῶν ζιζανίων τοῦ
to us the parable of the tares of the

ἀγροῦ. **37** ὁ δὲ ἀποκριθεὶς εἶπεν· ὁ
field. And he answering said: The [one]

σπείρων τὸ καλὸν σπέρμα ἐστὶν ὁ
sowing the good seed is the

υἱὸς τοῦ ἀνθρώπου· **38** ὁ δὲ ἀγρός
Son - of man; and the field

ἐστιν ὁ κόσμος· τὸ δὲ καλὸν σπέρμα,
is the world; and the good seed,

οὗτοί εἰσιν οἱ υἱοὶ τῆς βασιλείας· τὰ δὲ
these are the sons of the kingdom; and the

ζιζάνιά εἰσιν οἱ υἱοὶ τοῦ πονηροῦ, **39** ὁ
tares are the sons of the evil [one], the

δὲ ἐχθρὸς ὁ σπείρας αὐτά ἐστιν ὁ
and enemy the [one] sowing them is the

διάβολος· ὁ δὲ θερισμὸς συντέλεια
devil; and the harvest [the] completion

αἰῶνός ἐστιν, οἱ δὲ θερισταὶ ἄγγελοί
of [the] age is, and the reapers angels

εἰσιν. **40** ὥσπερ οὖν συλλέγεται τὰ
are. As therefore are collected the

ζιζάνια καὶ πυρὶ κατακαίεται, οὕτως
tares and with fire are consumed, thus

ἔσται ἐν τῇ συντελείᾳ τοῦ αἰῶνος·
it will be at the completion of the age;

41 ἀποστελεῖ ὁ υἱὸς τοῦ ἀνθρώπου
will send forth the Son - of man

τοὺς ἀγγέλους αὐτοῦ, καὶ συλλέξουσιν
the angels of him, and they will collect

ἐκ τῆς βασιλείας αὐτοῦ πάντα
out of the kingdom of him all

τὰ σκάνδαλα καὶ τοὺς ποιοῦντας
the things leading to sin and the [ones] doing

τὴν ἀνομίαν, **42** καὶ βαλοῦσιν αὐτοὺς εἰς
- lawlessness, and will cast them into

τὴν κάμινον τοῦ πυρός· ἐκεῖ ἔσται ὁ
the furnace - of fire; there will be the

κλαυθμὸς καὶ ὁ βρυγμὸς τῶν ὀδόντων.
wailing and the gnashing of the teeth.

43 τότε οἱ δίκαιοι ἐκλάμψουσιν ὡς ὁ
Then the righteous will shine forth as the

ἥλιος ἐν τῇ βασιλείᾳ τοῦ πατρὸς
sun in the kingdom of the Father

αὐτῶν. ὁ ἔχων ὦτα ἀκουέτω.
of them. The [one] having ears let him hear.

44 Ὁμοία ἐστὶν ἡ βασιλεία τῶν
Like is the kingdom of the

οὐρανῶν θησαυρῷ κεκρυμμένῳ ἐν τῷ
heavens to treasure having been hidden in the

ἀγρῷ, ὃν εὑρὼν ἄνθρωπος ἔκρυψεν, καὶ
field, which ¹finding ¹a man hid, and

ἀπὸ τῆς χαρᾶς αὐτοῦ ὑπάγει καὶ πωλεῖ
from the joy of him goes and sells

ὅσα ἔχει καὶ ἀγοράζει τὸν ἀγρὸν
what things he has and buys - field

ἐκεῖνον. **45** Πάλιν ὁμοία ἐστὶν ἡ
that. Again like is the

I will utter things hidden since the creation of the world." [b]

The Parable of the Weeds Explained

36Then he left the crowd and went into the house. His disciples came to him and said, "Explain to us the parable of the weeds in the field."

37He answered, "The one who sowed the good seed is the Son of Man. **38**The field is the world, and the good seed stands for the sons of the kingdom. The weeds are the sons of the evil one, **39**and the enemy who sows them is the devil. The harvest is the end of the age, and the harvesters are angels.

40"As the weeds are pulled up and burned in the fire, so it will be at the end of the age. **41**The Son of Man will send out his angels, and they will weed out of his kingdom everything that causes sin and all who do evil. **42**They will throw them into the fiery furnace, where there will be weeping and gnashing of teeth. **43**Then the righteous will shine like the sun in the kingdom of their Father. He who has ears, let him hear.

The Parables of the Hidden Treasure and the Pearl

44"The kingdom of heav-

b35 Psalm 78:2

heaven is like a treasure hidden in the field, which a man found and hid; and from joy over it he goes and sells all that he has, and buys that field.

A Costly Pearl

45"Again, the kingdom of heaven is like a merchant seeking fine pearls,
46and upon finding one pearl of great value, he went and sold all that he had, and bought it.

A Dragnet

47"Again, the kingdom of heaven is like a dragnet cast into the sea, and gathering *fish* of every kind;
48and when it was filled, they drew it up on the beach; and they sat down, and gathered the good *fish* into containers, but the bad they threw away.

49"So it will be at the end of the age; the angels shall come forth, and take out the wicked from among the righteous,
50and will cast them into the furnace of fire; there shall be weeping and gnashing of teeth.

51"Have you understood all these things?" They *said to Him, "Yes."

52And He said to them, "Therefore every scribe who has become a disciple of the kingdom of heaven is like a head of a household, who brings forth out of his treasure things new and old."

Jesus Revisits Nazareth

53And it came about that when Jesus had finished these parables, He departed from there.

54And coming to His home town He *began* teaching them in their synagogue, so that they became astonished, and said, "Where *did* this man *get* this wisdom, and *these* miraculous powers?

55"Is not this the carpenter's son? Is not His mother called Mary, and His brothers, James and Joseph and

---

βασιλεία τῶν οὐρανῶν ἐμπόρῳ ζητοῦντι
kingdom of the heavens to a merchant seeking

καλοὺς μαργαρίτας· 46 εὑρὼν δὲ ἕνα πολύτιμον
beautiful pearls; and finding one valuable

μαργαρίτην ἀπελθὼν πέπρακεν πάντα
pearl going away sold all things

ὅσα εἶχεν καὶ ἠγόρασεν αὐτόν.
what he had and bought it.

47 Πάλιν ὁμοία ἐστὶν ἡ βασιλεία τῶν
Again like is the kingdom of the

οὐρανῶν σαγήνῃ βληθείσῃ εἰς τὴν θάλασσαν
heavens to a net cast into the sea

καὶ ἐκ παντὸς γένους συναγαγούσῃ·
and of every kind gathering;

48 ἣν ὅτε ἐπληρώθη ἀναβιβάσαντες ἐπὶ
which when it was filled bringing up onto

τὸν αἰγιαλὸν καὶ καθίσαντες συνέλεξαν
the shore and sitting collected

τὰ καλὰ εἰς ἄγγη, τὰ δὲ σαπρὰ ἔξω
the good into vessels, but the bad out

ἔβαλον. 49 οὕτως ἔσται ἐν τῇ συντελείᾳ
cast. Thus it will be at the completion

τοῦ αἰῶνος· ἐξελεύσονται οἱ ἄγγελοι καὶ
of the age; will go forth the angels and

ἀφοριοῦσιν τοὺς πονηροὺς ἐκ μέσου
will separate the evil men from [the] midst

τῶν δικαίων, 50 καὶ βαλοῦσιν αὐτοὺς
of the righteous, and will cast them

εἰς τὴν κάμινον τοῦ πυρός· ἐκεῖ
into the furnace - of fire; there

ἔσται ὁ κλαυθμὸς καὶ ὁ βρυγμὸς τῶν
will be the wailing and the gnashing of the

ὀδόντων. 51 Συνήκατε ταῦτα πάντα;
teeth. Did ye understand ¹these things ¹all?

λέγουσιν αὐτῷ· ναί. 52 ὁ δὲ εἶπεν
They say to him: Yes. So he said

αὐτοῖς· διὰ τοῦτο πᾶς γραμματεὺς
to them: Therefore every scribe

μαθητευθεὶς τῇ βασιλείᾳ τῶν οὐρανῶν
made a disciple to the kingdom of the heavens

ὅμοιός ἐστιν ἀνθρώπῳ οἰκοδεσπότῃ,
like is to a man a housemaster,

ὅστις ἐκβάλλει ἐκ τοῦ θησαυροῦ
who puts forth out of the treasure

αὐτοῦ καινὰ καὶ παλαιά.
of him new and old things.

53 Καὶ ἐγένετο ὅτε ἐτέλεσεν ὁ
And it came to pass when ended -

Ἰησοῦς τὰς παραβολὰς ταύτας, μετῆρεν
Jesus - parables these, he removed

ἐκεῖθεν. 54 καὶ ἐλθὼν εἰς τὴν πατρίδα
thence. And coming into the native town

αὐτοῦ ἐδίδασκεν αὐτοὺς ἐν τῇ συνα-
of him he taught them in the syna-

γωγῇ αὐτῶν, ὥστε ἐκπλήσσεσθαι αὐτοὺς
gogue of them, so as to be astounded them
=so that they were astounded

καὶ λέγειν· πόθεν τούτῳ ἡ σοφία αὕτη
and to say ᵇ: Whence to this man - wisdom this
and said:

καὶ αἱ δυνάμεις; 55 οὐχ οὗτός ἐστιν
and the powerful deeds? not this man is

ὁ τοῦ τέκτονος υἱός; οὐχ ἡ μήτηρ
the of the carpenter son? not the mother

αὐτοῦ λέγεται Μαριὰμ καὶ οἱ ἀδελφοὶ
of him called Mary and the brothers

αὐτοῦ Ἰάκωβος καὶ Ἰωσὴφ καὶ Σίμων
of him James and Joseph and Simon

---

en is like treasure hidden in a field. When a man found it, he hid it again, and then in his joy went and sold all he had and bought that field.

45"Again, the kingdom of heaven is like a merchant looking for fine pearls.
46When he found one of great value, he went away and sold everything he had and bought it.

The Parable of the Net

47"Once again, the kingdom of heaven is like a net that was let down into the lake and caught all kinds of fish. 48When it was full, the fishermen pulled it up on the shore. Then they sat down and collected the good fish in baskets, but threw the bad away. 49This is how it will be at the end of the age. The angels will come and separate the wicked from the righteous 50and throw them into the fiery furnace, where there will be weeping and gnashing of teeth.

51"Have you understood all these things?" Jesus asked.
"Yes," they replied.

52He said to them, "Therefore every teacher of the law who has been instructed about the kingdom of heaven is like the owner of a house who brings out of his storeroom new treasures as well as old."

A Prophet Without Honor

53When Jesus had finished these parables, he moved on from there. 54Coming to his hometown, he began teaching the people in their synagogue, and they were amazed. "Where did this man get this wisdom and these miraculous powers?" they asked. 55"Isn't this the carpenter's son? Isn't his mother's name Mary, and aren't his brothers James, Joseph,

Simon and Judas?
56"And His sisters, are they not all with us? Where then *did* this man *get* all these things?"
57And they took offense at Him. But Jesus said to them, "A prophet is not without honor except in his home town, and in his *own* household."
58And He did not do many miracles there because of their unbelief.

καὶ　'Ιούδας;　**56** καὶ　αἱ　ἀδελφαὶ　αὐτοῦ
and　Judas?　　and　the　sisters　of him
οὐχὶ　πᾶσαι　πρὸς　ἡμᾶς　εἰσιν;　πόθεν
not　all　with　us　are?　Whence
οὖν　τούτῳ　ταῦτα　πάντα;　**57** καὶ
then　to this man　these things　all?　　And
ἐσκανδαλίζοντο　ἐν　αὐτῷ.　ὁ δὲ　'Ιησοῦς
they were offended　in　him.　- But　Jesus
εἶπεν　αὐτοῖς·　οὐκ　ἔστιν　προφήτης
said　to them:　¹not　²is　¹A prophet
ἄτιμος　εἰ μὴ　ἐν　τῇ　πατρίδι　καὶ
unhonoured　except　in　the(his)　native town　and
ἐν τῇ οἰκίᾳ αὐτοῦ.　**58** καὶ οὐκ ἐποίησεν ἐκεῖ
in the house of him.　　And　not　he did　there
δυνάμεις　πολλὰς　διὰ　τὴν　ἀπιστίαν　αὐτῶν.
powerful deeds　many　because of the　unbelief　of them.

Simon and Judas? 56Aren't all his sisters with us? Where then did this man get all these things?" 57And they took offense at him.
But Jesus said to them, "Only in his hometown and in his own house is a prophet without honor."
58And he did not do many miracles there because of their lack of faith.

Chapter 14

John the Baptist Beheaded

AT that time Herod the tetrarch heard the news about Jesus,
2and said to his servants, "This is John the Baptist; he has risen from the dead; and that is why miraculous powers are at work in him."
3For when Herod had John arrested, he bound him, and put him in prison on account of Herodias, the wife of his brother Philip.
4For John had been saying to him, "It is not lawful for you to have her."
5And although he wanted to put him to death, he feared the multitude, because they regarded him as a prophet.
6But when Herod's birthday came, the daughter of Herodias danced before *them* and pleased Herod.
7Thereupon he promised with an oath to give her whatever she asked.
8And having been prompted by her mother, she *said, "Give me here on a platter the head of John the Baptist."
9And although he was grieved, the king commanded *it* to be given because of his oaths, and because of his dinner guests.
10And he sent and had

14 'Εν　ἐκείνῳ　τῷ　καιρῷ　ἤκουσεν
At　that　-　time　heard
'Ηρῴδης　ὁ　τετραάρχης　τὴν　ἀκοὴν　'Ιησοῦ,
Herod　the　tetrarch　the　report　of Jesus,
2 καὶ　εἶπεν　τοῖς　παισὶν　αὐτοῦ·　οὗτός
and　said　to the　servants　of him:　This
ἐστιν　'Ιωάννης　ὁ　βαπτιστής·　αὐτὸς
is　John　the　Baptist;　he
ἠγέρθη　ἀπὸ　τῶν　νεκρῶν,　καὶ　διὰ τοῦτο
was raised　from　the　dead,　and　therefore
αἱ　δυνάμεις　ἐνεργοῦσιν　ἐν　αὐτῷ.
the　powerful deeds　operate　in　him.
3 'Ο　γὰρ　'Ηρῴδης　κρατήσας　τὸν　'Ιωάννην
- For　Herod　seizing　-　John
ἔδησεν　καὶ　ἐν　φυλακῇ　ἀπέθετο　διὰ
bound　and　in　prison　put away on account of
'Ηρῳδιάδα　τὴν　γυναῖκα　Φιλίππου　τοῦ
Herodias　the　wife　of Philip　the
ἀδελφοῦ　αὐτοῦ·　**4** ἔλεγεν　γὰρ　ὁ　'Ιωάννης
brother　of him;　for said　-　John
αὐτῷ·　οὐκ　ἔξεστίν　σοι　ἔχειν　αὐτήν.
to him:　It is not lawful　for thee　to have　her.
5 καὶ　θέλων　αὐτὸν　ἀποκτεῖναι　ἐφοβήθη
And　wishing　him　to kill　he feared
τὸν　ὄχλον,　ὅτι　ὡς　προφήτην　αὐτὸν
the　crowd,　because　as　a prophet　him
εἶχον.　**6** γενεσίοις　δὲ　γενομένοις　τοῦ
they had.　Now on the birthday　occurring⁹　-
'Ηρῴδου　ὠρχήσατο　ἡ　θυγάτηρ　τῆς
of Herod　danced　the　daughter
'Ηρῳδιάδος　ἐν　τῷ　μέσῳ　καὶ　ἤρεσεν
of Herodias　in　the　midst　and　pleased
τῷ 'Ηρῴδῃ,　**7** ὅθεν　μεθ'　ὅρκου　ὡμολόγησεν
- Herod,　whence　with　an oath　he promised
αὐτῇ　δοῦναι　ὃ　ἐὰν　αἰτήσηται.　**8** ἡ δὲ
¹her　¹to give　whatever　she might ask.　So she
προβιβασθεῖσα　ὑπὸ　τῆς　μητρὸς　αὐτῆς·
being instructed　by　the　mother　of her:
δός　μοι,　φησίν,　ὧδε　ἐπὶ　πίνακι　τὴν
Give　me,　she says,　here　on　a platter　the
κεφαλὴν　'Ιωάννου　τοῦ　βαπτιστοῦ.　**9** καὶ
head　of John　the　Baptist.　And
λυπηθεὶς　ὁ　βασιλεὺς　διὰ　τοὺς
being grieved　the　king　on account of　the
ὅρκους　καὶ　τοὺς　συνανακειμένους
oaths　and　the [ones] reclining at table with [him]
ἐκέλευσεν　δοθῆναι,　**10** καὶ　πέμψας
he commanded　to be given,　　and　sending

Chapter 14

John the Baptist Beheaded

AT that time Herod the tetrarch heard the reports about Jesus, 2and he said to his attendants, "This is John the Baptist; he has risen from the dead! That is why miraculous powers are at work in him."
3Now Herod had arrested John and bound him and put him in prison because of Herodias, his brother Philip's wife, 4for John had been saying to him: "It is not lawful for you to have her." 5Herod wanted to kill John, but he was afraid of the people, because they considered him a prophet.
6On Herod's birthday the daughter of Herodias danced for them and pleased Herod so much 7that he promised with an oath to give her whatever she asked. 8Prompted by her mother, she said, "Give me here on a platter the head of John the Baptist." 9The king was distressed, but because of his oaths and his dinner guests, he ordered that her request be granted 10and had John

John beheaded in the prison.
11And his head was brought on a platter and given to the girl; and she brought *it* to her mother.
12And his disciples came and took away the body and buried it; and they went and reported to Jesus.

Five Thousand Fed
13Now when Jesus heard *it*, He withdrew from there in a boat, to a lonely place by Himself; and when the multitudes heard *of this*, they followed Him on foot from the cities.
14And when He went ashore, He saw a great multitude, and felt compassion for them, and healed their sick.
15And when it was evening, the disciples came to Him, saying, "The place is desolate, and the time is already past; so send the multitudes away, that they may go into the villages and buy food for themselves."
16But Jesus said to them, "They do not need to go away; you give them *something to eat*!"
17And they *said to Him, "We have here only five loaves and two fish."
18And He said, "Bring them here to Me."
19And ordering the multitudes to recline on the grass, He took the five loaves and the two fish, and looking up toward heaven, He blessed *the food*, and breaking the loaves He gave them to the disciples, and the disciples *gave* to the multitudes,
20and they all ate, and were satisfied. And they picked up what was left

---

ἀπεκεφάλισεν Ἰωάννην ἐν τῇ φυλακῇ.
beheaded John in the prison.
11 καὶ ἠνέχθη ἡ κεφαλὴ αὐτοῦ ἐπὶ
And was brought the head of him on
πίνακι καὶ ἐδόθη τῷ κορασίῳ, καὶ
a platter and was given to the maid, and
ἤνεγκεν τῇ μητρὶ αὐτῆς. 12 καὶ
she brought [it] to the mother of her. And
προσελθόντες οἱ μαθηταὶ αὐτοῦ ἦραν τὸ
⁴approaching ¹the ²disciples ³of him took the
πτῶμα καὶ ἔθαψαν αὐτόν, καὶ ἐλθόντες
corpse and buried him, and coming
ἀπήγγειλαν τῷ Ἰησοῦ. 13 Ἀκούσας δὲ
reported - to Jesus. And ²hearing
ὁ Ἰησοῦς ἀνεχώρησεν ἐκεῖθεν ἐν
- ¹Jesus departed thence in
πλοίῳ εἰς ἔρημον τόπον κατ᾽ ἰδίαν·
a ship to a desert place privately;
καὶ ἀκούσαντες οἱ ὄχλοι ἠκολούθησαν
and ²hearing ¹the ²crowds followed
αὐτῷ πεζῇ ἀπὸ τῶν πόλεων. 14 Καὶ
him afoot from the cities. And
ἐξελθὼν εἶδεν πολὺν ὄχλον, καὶ
going forth he saw a much crowd, and
ἐσπλαγχνίσθη ἐπ᾽ αὐτοῖς καὶ
was filled with tenderness over them and
ἐθεράπευσεν τοὺς ἀρρώστους αὐτῶν.
healed the sick of them.
15 ὀψίας δὲ γενομένης προσῆλθον αὐτῷ
Now evening coming on* approached to him
=when evening came on
οἱ μαθηταὶ λέγοντες· ἔρημός ἐστιν ὁ
the disciples saying: Desert is the
τόπος καὶ ἡ ὥρα ἤδη παρῆλθεν·
place and the hour already passed;
ἀπόλυσον οὖν τοὺς ὄχλους, ἵνα ἀπελθόντες
dismiss therefore the crowds, that going away
εἰς τὰς κώμας ἀγοράσωσιν ἑαυτοῖς
into the villages they may buy for themselves
βρώματα. 16 ὁ δὲ Ἰησοῦς εἶπεν αὐτοῖς·
foods. - But Jesus said to them:
οὐ χρείαν ἔχουσιν ἀπελθεῖν· δότε
Not need they have to go away; give
αὐτοῖς ὑμεῖς φαγεῖν. 17 οἱ δὲ λέγουσιν
them ye to eat. But they say
αὐτῷ· οὐκ ἔχομεν ὧδε εἰ μὴ πέντε
to him: We have not here except five
ἄρτους καὶ δύο ἰχθύας. 18 ὁ δὲ εἶπεν·
loaves and two fishes. And he said:
φέρετέ μοι ὧδε αὐτούς. 19 καὶ κελεύσας
Bring to me here them. And having commanded
τοὺς ὄχλους ἀνακλιθῆναι ἐπὶ τοῦ χόρτου,
the crowds to recline on the grass,
λαβὼν τοὺς πέντε ἄρτους καὶ τοὺς δύο
taking the five loaves and the two
ἰχθύας, ἀναβλέψας εἰς τὸν οὐρανὸν
fishes, looking up to - heaven
εὐλόγησεν, καὶ κλάσας ἔδωκεν τοῖς
he blessed, and breaking gave to the
μαθηταῖς τοὺς ἄρτους, οἱ δὲ μαθηταὶ
disciples the loaves, and the disciples
τοῖς ὄχλοις. 20 καὶ ἔφαγον πάντες καὶ
to the crowds, And ate all and
ἐχορτάσθησαν· καὶ ἦραν τὸ περισσεῦον
were satisfied; and they took the excess

---

beheaded in the prison.
11His head was brought in on a platter and given to the girl, who carried it to her mother. 12John's disciples came and took his body and buried it. Then they went and told Jesus.

Jesus Feeds the Five Thousand
13When Jesus heard what had happened, he withdrew by boat privately to a solitary place. Hearing of this, the crowds followed him on foot from the towns. 14When Jesus landed and saw a large crowd, he had compassion on them and healed their sick.
15As evening approached, the disciples came to him and said, "This is a remote place, and it's already getting late. Send the crowds away, so they can go to the villages and buy themselves some food."
16Jesus replied, "They do not need to go away. You give them something to eat."
17"We have here only five loaves of bread and two fish," they answered.
18"Bring them here to me," he said. 19And he directed the people to sit down on the grass. Taking the five loaves and the two fish and looking up to heaven, he gave thanks and broke the loaves. Then he gave them to the disciples, and the disciples gave them to the people. 20They all ate and were satisfied, and the disciples picked up twelve

over of the broken pieces, twelve full baskets.

21And there were about five thousand men who ate, aside from women and children.

Jesus Walks on the Water

22And immediately He made the disciples get into the boat, and go ahead of Him to the other side, while He sent the multitudes away.

23And after He had sent the multitudes away, He went up to the mountain by Himself to pray; and when it was evening, He was there alone.

24But the boat was already many ʸstadia away from the land, battered by the waves; for the wind was contrary.

25And in the ᶻfourth watch of the night He came to them, walking on the sea.

26And when the disciples saw Him walking on the sea, they were frightened, saying, "It is a ghost!" And they cried out for fear.

27But immediately Jesus spoke to them, saying, "Take courage, it is I; do not be afraid."

28And Peter answered Him and said, "Lord, if it is You, command me to come to You on the water."

29And He said, "Come!" And Peter got out of the boat, and walked on the water and came toward Jesus.

30But seeing the wind, he became afraid, and beginning to sink, he cried out, saying, "Lord, save me!"

31And immediately Jesus stretched out His hand and took hold of him, and *said to him, "O you of little

---

τῶν κλασμάτων, δώδεκα κοφίνους πλήρεις.
of the   fragments,   twelve   baskets   full.

21 οἱ δὲ ἐσθίοντες ἦσαν ἄνδρες ὡσεὶ
And the [ones] eating   were   men   about

πεντακισχίλιοι χωρὶς γυναικῶν καὶ
five thousand   apart from   women   and

παιδίων. 22 Καὶ [εὐθέως] ἠνάγκασεν
children.   And   immediately   he constrained

τοὺς μαθητὰς ἐμβῆναι εἰς τὸ πλοῖον
the   disciples   to embark   in   the   ship

καὶ προάγειν αὐτὸν εἰς τὸ πέραν,
and   to go before   him   to   the   other side,

ἕως οὗ ἀπολύσῃ τοὺς ὄχλους. 23 Καὶ
until   he should dismiss   the   crowds.   And

ἀπολύσας τοὺς ὄχλους ἀνέβη εἰς τὸ
having dismissed   the   crowds   he went up   into   the

ὄρος κατ' ἰδίαν προσεύξασθαι. ὀψίας
mountain   privately   to pray.   evening
                 = And when

δὲ γενομένης μόνος ἦν ἐκεῖ. 24 τὸ δὲ
And coming onᵃ   alone   he was there.   But the
evening came on

πλοῖον ἤδη σταδίους πολλοὺς ἀπὸ τῆς
ship   now   furlongs   many   from   the

γῆς ἀπεῖχεν, βασανιζόμενον ὑπὸ τῶν
land   was away,   being distressed   by   the

κυμάτων, ἦν γὰρ ἐναντίος ὁ ἄνεμος.
waves,   ⁴was   ¹for   ⁵contrary   ³the   ²wind.

25 τετάρτῃ δὲ φυλακῇ τῆς νυκτὸς
Now in [the] fourth   watch   of the   night

ἦλθεν πρὸς αὐτοὺς περιπατῶν ἐπὶ τὴν
he came   toward   them   walking   on   the

θάλασσαν. 26 οἱ δὲ μαθηταὶ ἰδόντες
sea.   And the   disciples   seeing

αὐτὸν ἐπὶ τῆς θαλάσσης περιπατοῦντα
him   on   the   sea   walking

ἐταράχθησαν λέγοντες ὅτι φάντασμά
were troubled   saying[,]   -   A phantasm

ἐστιν, καὶ ἀπὸ τοῦ φόβου ἔκραξαν.
it is,   and   from   the   fear   they cried out.

27 εὐθὺς δὲ ἐλάλησεν [ὁ Ἰησοῦς]
But immediately   spoke   -   Jesus

αὐτοῖς λέγων· θαρσεῖτε, ἐγώ εἰμι·
to them   saying: Be of good cheer,   I   am;

μὴ φοβεῖσθε. 28 ἀποκριθεὶς δὲ αὐτῷ ὁ
do not fear.   And answering   him   -

Πέτρος εἶπεν· κύριε, εἰ σὺ εἶ, κέλευσόν
Peter   said: Lord,   if   thou art,   command

με ἐλθεῖν πρὸς σὲ ἐπὶ τὰ ὕδατα. 29 ὁ
me   to come   to   thee   on   the   waters.   he

δὲ εἶπεν· ἐλθέ. καὶ καταβὰς ἀπὸ τοῦ
And said: Come.   And   going down   from   the

πλοίου Πέτρος περιπάτησεν ἐπὶ τὰ ὕδατα
ship   Peter   walked   on   the   waters

καὶ ἦλθεν πρὸς τὸν Ἰησοῦν. 30 βλέπων δὲ
and   came   toward   -   Jesus.   But seeing

τὸν ἄνεμον ἐφοβήθη, καὶ ἀρξάμενος
the   wind   he was afraid,   and   beginning

καταποντίζεσθαι ἔκραξεν λέγων·
to sink   he cried out   saying:

κύριε, σῶσόν με. 31 εὐθέως δὲ ὁ
Lord,   save   me.   And immediately   -

Ἰησοῦς ἐκτείνας τὴν χεῖρα ἐπελάβετο
Jesus   stretching out   the(his)   hand   took hold

αὐτοῦ, καὶ λέγει αὐτῷ· ὀλιγόπιστε,
of him,   and   says   to him: Little-faith,

---

basketfuls of broken pieces that were left over. 21The number of those who ate was about five thousand men, besides women and children.

Jesus Walks on the Water

22Immediately Jesus made the disciples get into the boat and go on ahead of him to the other side, while he dismissed the crowd. 23After he had dismissed them, he went up on a mountainside by himself to pray. When evening came, he was there alone, 24but the boat was already a considerable distanceᶜ from land, buffeted by the waves because the wind was against it.

25During the fourth watch of the night Jesus went out to them, walking on the lake. 26When the disciples saw him walking on the lake, they were terrified. "It's a ghost," they said, and cried out in fear.

27But Jesus immediately said to them: "Take courage! It is I. Don't be afraid."

28"Lord, if it's you," Peter replied, "tell me to come to you on the water."

29"Come," he said.

Then Peter got down out of the boat, walked on the water and came toward Jesus. 30But when he saw the wind, he was afraid and, beginning to sink, cried out, "Lord, save me!"

31Immediately Jesus reached out his hand and caught him. "You of little

---

ʸ A stadion was about 600 feet
ᶻ I.e., 3–6 a.m.

ᶜ24 Greek *many stadia*

faith, why did you doubt?"
³²And when they got into the boat, the wind stopped.
³³And those who were in the boat worshiped Him, saying, "You are certainly God's Son!"
³⁴And when they had crossed over, they came to land at Gennesaret.
³⁵And when the men of that place recognized Him, they sent into all that surrounding district and brought to Him all who were sick;
³⁶and they *began* to entreat Him that they might just touch the fringe of His cloak; and as many as touched *it* were cured.

εἰς τί ἐδίστασας;
why   didst thou doubt?
32 καὶ ἀναβάντων
And   going up
= as they went up
αὐτῶν εἰς τὸ πλοῖον ἐκόπασεν ὁ ἄνεμος.
them* into the ship   ceased   the wind.
33 οἱ δὲ ἐν τῷ πλοίῳ προσεκύνησαν αὐτῷ
And the [ones] in the ship   worshipped   him
λέγοντες· ἀληθῶς θεοῦ υἱὸς εἶ. **34** Καὶ
saying: Truly of God Son thou art.   And
διαπεράσαντες ἦλθον ἐπὶ τὴν γῆν εἰς
crossing over they came onto the land to
Γεννησαρέτ. **35** καὶ ἐπιγνόντες αὐτὸν
Gennesaret.   And recognizing   him
οἱ ἄνδρες τοῦ τόπου ἐκείνου ἀπέστειλαν
the men of that place of that   sent
εἰς ὅλην τὴν περίχωρον ἐκείνην, καὶ
into all - neighbourhood that,   and
προσήνεγκαν αὐτῷ πάντας τοὺς κακῶς
brought   tc him   all   the [ones] ill
= those who were ill,
ἔχοντας, **36** καὶ παρεκάλουν αὐτὸν ἵνα
having,   and   besought   him that
μόνον ἅψωνται τοῦ κρασπέδου τοῦ
only they might touch the fringe   of the
ἱματίου αὐτοῦ· καὶ ὅσοι ἥψαντο διεσώθησαν.
garment of him; and as many as touched were (the)ir completely healed.

faith," he said, "why did you doubt?"
³²And when they climbed into the boat, the wind died down. ³³Then those who were in the boat worshiped him, saying, "Truly you are the Son of God."
³⁴When they had crossed over, they landed at Gennesaret. ³⁵And when the men of that place recognized Jesus, they sent word to all the surrounding country. People brought all their sick to him ³⁶and begged him to let the sick just touch the edge of his cloak, and all who touched him were healed.

Chapter 15

Tradition and Commandment

THEN some Pharisees and scribes *came to Jesus from Jerusalem, saying,
²"Why do Your disciples transgress the tradition of the elders? For they do not wash their hands when they eat bread."
³And He answered and said to them, "And why do you yourselves transgress the commandment of God for the sake of your tradition?
⁴"For God said, 'HONOR YOUR FATHER AND MOTHER,' and, 'HE WHO SPEAKS EVIL OF FATHER OR MOTHER, LET HIM BE PUT TO DEATH.'
⁵"But you say, 'Whoever shall say to *his* father or mother, "Anything of mine you might have been helped by has been given *to God*,"
⁶he is not to honor his father ᵃor his mother ᵇ.' And *thus* you invalidated the word of God for the sake of your tradition.
⁷"You hypocrites, rightly did Isaiah prophesy of you, saying,
⁸'THIS PEOPLE HONORS

15 Τότε προσέρχονται τῷ Ἰησοῦ
Then   approach   -   to Jesus
ἀπὸ Ἱεροσολύμων Φαρισαῖοι καὶ γραμματεῖς
from Jerusalem   Pharisees and scribes
λέγοντες· **2** διὰ τί οἱ μαθηταί σου
saying: Why the disciples of thee
παραβαίνουσιν τὴν παράδοσιν τῶν
transgress   the tradition of the
πρεσβυτέρων; οὐ γὰρ νίπτονται τὰς χεῖρας
elders?   for not they wash the(ir) hands
ὅταν ἄρτον ἐσθίωσιν. **3** ὁ δὲ ἀπο-
whenever bread they eat.   And he answer-
κριθεὶς εἶπεν αὐτοῖς· διὰ τί καὶ ὑμεῖς
ing   said to them: Why indeed ye
παραβαίνετε τὴν ἐντολὴν τοῦ θεοῦ
transgress the commandment - of God
διὰ τὴν παράδοσιν ὑμῶν; **4** ὁ γὰρ
on account of the tradition of you? - For
θεὸς εἶπεν· τίμα τὸν πατέρα καὶ τὴν
God said: Honour the father and the
μητέρα, καί· ὁ κακολογῶν πατέρα
mother, and: The [one] speaking evil of father
ἢ μητέρα θανάτῳ τελευτάτω. **5** ὑμεῖς δὲ
or mother by death let him die.   But ye
λέγετε· ὃς ἂν εἴπῃ τῷ πατρὶ ἢ
say: Whoever says to the(his) father or
τῇ μητρί· δῶρον ὃ ἐὰν ἐξ ἐμοῦ
to the(his) mother: A gift whatever by me
ὠφελήθης, **6** οὐ μὴ τιμήσει τὸν
thou mightest be owed, by no means shall he honour the
πατέρα αὐτοῦ ἢ τὴν μητέρα αὐτοῦ·
father of him or the mother of him;
καὶ ἠκυρώσατε τὸν λόγον τοῦ θεοῦ
and ye annulled the word - of God
διὰ τὴν παράδοσιν ὑμῶν. **7** ὑποκρι-
on account of the tradition of you. Hypocrites,
ταί, καλῶς ἐπροφήτευσεν περὶ ὑμῶν
well prophesied concerning you
Ἡσαΐας λέγων· **8** ὁ λαὸς οὗτος τοῖς
Isaiah saying: This people with the

Chapter 15

Clean and Unclean

THEN some Pharisees and teachers of the law came to Jesus from Jerusalem and asked, ²"Why do your disciples break the tradition of the elders? They don't wash their hands before they eat!"
³Jesus replied, "And why do you break the command of God for the sake of your tradition? ⁴For God said, 'Honor your father and mother'ᵈ and 'Anyone who curses his father or mother must be put to death.'ᵉ ⁵But you say that if a man says to his father or mother, 'Whatever help you might otherwise have received from me is a gift devoted to God,' ⁶he is not to 'honor his father'ᶠ with it. Thus you nullify the word of God for the sake of your tradition. ⁷You hypocrites! Isaiah was right when he prophesied about you:

⁸"'These people honor

ᵃ Many mss. do not contain *or his mother*
ᵇ I.e., by supporting them with it

ᵈ4 Exodus 20:12; Deut. 5:16
ᵉ4 Exodus 21:17; Lev. 20:9
ᶠ6 Some manuscripts *father or his mother*

MATTHEW 15

48

ME WITH THEIR LIPS,
BUT THEIR HEART IS
FAR AWAY FROM ME.
9 'BUT IN VAIN DO THEY
WORSHIP ME,
TEACHING AS DOC-
TRINES THE PRECEPTS
OF MEN.' ''
10And after He called the
multitude to Him, He said
to them, ''Hear, and understand.
11''Not what enters into
the mouth defiles the man,
but what proceeds out of
the mouth, this defiles the
man.''
12Then the disciples
*came and *said to Him,
''Do You know that the
Pharisees were offended
when they heard this
statement?''
13But He answered and
said, ''Every plant which
My heavenly Father did
not plant shall be rooted
up.
14''Let them alone; they
are blind guides ᶜof the
blind. And if a blind man
guides a blind man, both
will fall into a pit.''

The Heart of Man

15And Peter answered
and said to Him, ''Explain
the parable to us.''
16And He said, ''Are you
still lacking in understanding also?
17''Do you not under-
stand that everything that
goes into the mouth passes
into the stomach, and is
eliminated?
18''But the things that
proceed out of the mouth
come from the heart, and
those defile the man.
19''For out of the heart
come evil thoughts, mur-
ders, adulteries, fornications, thefts, false witness,
slanders.
20''These are the things
which defile the man; but to
eat with unwashed hands
does not defile the man.''

*The Syrophoenician
Woman*

21And Jesus went away
from there, and withdrew

χείλεσίν με τιμᾷ, ἡ δὲ καρδία αὐτῶν
lips me honours, but the heart of them
πόρρω ἀπέχει ἀπ' ἐμοῦ· 9 μάτην δὲ
far is away from me; and vainly
σέβονται με, διδάσκοντες διδασκαλίας
they worship me, teaching teachings
ἐντάλματα ἀνθρώπων. 10 Καὶ προσκαλε-
ordinances of men. And calling
σάμενος τὸν ὄχλον εἶπεν αὐτοῖς·
forward the crowd he said to them:
ἀκούετε καὶ συνίετε· 11 οὐ τὸ εἰσερχ-
Hear ye and understand: Not the [thing] enter-
όμενον εἰς τὸ στόμα κοινοῖ τὸν ἄνθρωπον,
ing into the mouth defiles the man,
ἀλλὰ τὸ ἐκπορευόμενον ἐκ τοῦ στόματος,
but the [thing] coming forth out of the mouth,
τοῦτο κοινοῖ τὸν ἄνθρωπον. 12 Τότε
this defiles the man. Then
προσελθόντες οἱ μαθηταὶ λέγουσιν αὐτῷ·
approaching the disciples say to him:
οἶδες ὅτι οἱ Φαρισαῖοι ἀκούσαντες τὸν
Dost thou know that the Pharisees hearing the
λόγον ἐσκανδαλίσθησαν; 13 ὁ δὲ ἀπο-
saying were offended? And he answer-
κριθεὶς εἶπεν· πᾶσα φυτεία ἣν οὐκ
ing said: Every plant which not
ἐφύτευσεν ὁ πατήρ μου ὁ οὐράνιος ἐκριζω-
planted the Father of me – heavenly shall be
θήσεται. 14 ἄφετε αὐτούς· τυφλοί εἰσιν
uprooted. Leave them; blind they are
ὁδηγοὶ τυφλῶν· τυφλὸς δὲ τυφλὸν
leaders of blind; ᵃa blind man ᵃand ᵃa blind man
ἐὰν ὁδηγῇ, ἀμφότεροι εἰς βόθυνον πεσοῦνται.
ᵃif ᵃleads, both into a ditch will fall.
15 Ἀποκριθεὶς δὲ ὁ Πέτρος εἶπεν αὐτῷ·
And answering - Peter said to him:
φράσον ἡμῖν τὴν παραβολήν. 16 ὁ δὲ
Explain to us the parable. So he
εἶπεν· ἀκμὴν καὶ ὑμεῖς ἀσύνετοι
said: Thus also ye unintelligent
ἐστε; 17 οὐ νοεῖτε ὅτι πᾶν τὸ
are? Do ye not understand that everything the
εἰσπορευόμενον εἰς τὸ στόμα εἰς τὴν
entering into the mouth into the
κοιλίαν χωρεῖ καὶ εἰς ἀφεδρῶνα ἐκβάλλεται;
stomach goes and into a drain is cast out?
18 τὰ δὲ ἐκπορευόμενα ἐκ τοῦ
but the things coming forth out of the
στόματος ἐκ τῆς καρδίας ἐξέρχεται,
mouth out of the heart comes forth,
κἀκεῖνα κοινοῖ τὸν ἄνθρωπον. 19 ἐκ
and those defiles the man. out of
γὰρ τῆς καρδίας ἐξέρχονται διαλογισμοὶ
For the heart come forth thoughts
πονηροί, φόνοι, μοιχεῖαι, πορνεῖαι, κλοπαί,
evil, murders, adulteries, fornications, thefts,
ψευδομαρτυρίαι, βλασφημίαι. 20 ταῦτά
false witnessings, blasphemies. These things
ἐστιν τὰ κοινοῦντα τὸν ἄνθρωπον·
is(are) the [ones] defiling the man;
τὸ δὲ ἀνίπτοις χερσὶν φαγεῖν οὐ
– but with unwashed hands to eat not
κοινοῖ τὸν ἄνθρωπον.
defiles the man.
21 Καὶ ἐξελθὼν ἐκεῖθεν ὁ Ἰησοῦς
And going forth thence – Jesus

me with their lips,
but their hearts are far
from me.
9They worship me in
vain;
their teachings are but
rules taught by
men.' ᵍ''
10Jesus called the crowd
to him and said, ''Listen
and understand. 11What
goes into a man's mouth
does not make him 'un-
clean,' but what comes out
of his mouth, that is what
makes him 'unclean.' ''
12Then the disciples came
to him and asked, ''Do you
know that the Pharisees
were offended when they
heard this?''
13He replied, ''Every
plant that my heavenly Father has not planted will be
pulled up by the roots.
14Leave them; they are
blind guides. ʰ If a blind
man leads a blind man,
both will fall into a pit.''
15Peter said, ''Explain the
parable to us.''
16''Are you still so dull?''
Jesus asked them.
17''Don't you see that
whatever enters the mouth
goes into the stomach and
then out of the body? 18But
the things that come out of
the mouth come from the
heart, and these make a
man 'unclean.' 19For out of
the heart come evil
thoughts, murder, adul-
tery, sexual immorality,
theft, false testimony, slander. 20These are what make
a man 'unclean'; but eating
with unwashed hands does
not make him 'unclean.' ''

*The Faith of the
Canaanite Woman*

21Leaving that place,
Jesus withdrew to the re-

ᶜSome mss. do not contain *of the
blind*

ᵍ9 Isaiah 29:13
ʰ14 Some manuscripts *guides of
the blind*

into the district of Tyre and Sidon.
22And behold, a Canaanite woman came out from that region, and *began* to cry out, saying, "Have mercy on me, O Lord, Son of David; my daughter is cruelly demon-possessed."
23But He did not answer her a word. And His disciples came to *Him* and kept asking Him, saying, "Send her away, for she is shouting out after us."
24But He answered and said, "I was sent only to the lost sheep of the house of Israel."
25But she came and *began* to bow down before Him, saying, "Lord, help me!"
26And He answered and said, "It is not good to take the children's bread and throw it to the dogs."
27But she said, "Yes, Lord; but even the dogs feed on the crumbs which fall from their masters' table."
28Then Jesus answered and said to her, "O woman, your faith is great; be it done for you as you wish." And her daughter was healed at once.

Healing Multitudes

29And departing from there, Jesus went along by the Sea of Galilee, and having gone up to the mountain, He was sitting there.
30And great multitudes came to Him, bringing with them *those who were* lame, crippled, blind, dumb, and many others, and they laid them down at His feet; and He healed them,
31so that the multitude marveled as they saw the dumb speaking, the crip-

---

ἀνεχώρησεν εἰς τὰ μέρη Τύρου καὶ
departed into the parts of Tyre and

Σιδῶνος. 22 καὶ ἰδοὺ γυνὴ Χαναναία
Sidon. And behold woman a Canaanite

ἀπὸ τῶν ὁρίων ἐκείνων ἐξελθοῦσα
from – borders those coming forth

ἔκραζεν λέγουσα· ἐλέησόν με, κύριε
cried out saying: Pity me, Lord[,]

υἱὸς Δαυίδ· ἡ θυγάτηρ μου κακῶς
son of David; the daughter of me badly

δαιμονίζεται. 23 ὁ δὲ οὐκ ἀπεκρίθη
is demon-possessed. But he answered not

αὐτῇ λόγον. καὶ προσελθόντες οἱ μαθηταὶ
her a word. And approaching the disciples

αὐτοῦ ἠρώτων αὐτὸν λέγοντες· ἀπόλυσον
of him besought him saying: Dismiss

αὐτήν, ὅτι κράζει ὄπισθεν ἡμῶν. 24 ὁ
her, because she is crying out behind us. he

δὲ ἀποκριθεὶς εἶπεν· οὐκ ἀπεστάλην
But answering said: I was not sent

εἰ μὴ εἰς τὰ πρόβατα τὰ ἀπολωλότα
except to the sheep – lost

οἴκου Ἰσραήλ. 25 ἡ δὲ ἐλθοῦσα
of [the] house of Israel. But she coming

προσεκύνει αὐτῷ λέγουσα· κύριε, βοήθει
worshipped him saying: Lord, help

μοι. 26 ὁ δὲ ἀποκριθεὶς εἶπεν· οὐκ
me. But he answering said: not

ἔστιν καλὸν λαβεῖν τὸν ἄρτον τῶν τέκνων
It is good to take the bread of the children

καὶ βαλεῖν τοῖς κυναρίοις. 27 ἡ δὲ
and to throw to the dogs. And she

εἶπεν· ναί, κύριε· καὶ γὰρ τὰ κυνάρια
said: Yes, Lord; but even the dogs

ἐσθίει ἀπὸ τῶν ψιχίων τῶν πιπτόντων
eats from the crumbs – falling

ἀπὸ τῆς τραπέζης τῶν κυρίων αὐτῶν.
from the table of the masters of them.

28 τότε ἀποκριθεὶς ὁ Ἰησοῦς εἶπεν αὐτῇ·
Then answering – Jesus said to her:

ὦ γύναι, μεγάλη σου ἡ πίστις· γενηθήτω
O woman, great of thee the faith; let it be

σοι ὡς θέλεις. καὶ ἰάθη ἡ
to thee as thou desirest. And was healed the

θυγάτηρ αὐτῆς ἀπὸ τῆς ὥρας ἐκείνης.
daughter of her from the hour that.

29 Καὶ μεταβὰς ἐκεῖθεν ὁ Ἰησοῦς
And removing thence – Jesus

ἦλθεν παρὰ τὴν θάλασσαν τῆς Γαλιλαίας,
came by the sea of Galilee,

καὶ ἀναβὰς εἰς τὸ ὄρος ἐκάθητο ἐκεῖ.
and going up into the mountain he sat there.

30 καὶ προσῆλθον αὐτῷ ὄχλοι πολλοὶ ἔχοντες
And approached *to* him crowds many having

μεθ᾽ ἑαυτῶν χωλούς, κυλλούς, τυφλούς,
with them*selves* lame, maimed, blind,

κωφούς, καὶ ἑτέρους πολλούς, καὶ ἔρριψαν
dumb, and others many, and cast

αὐτοὺς παρὰ τοὺς πόδας αὐτοῦ· καὶ
them at the feet of him; and

ἐθεράπευσεν αὐτούς· 31 ὥστε τὸν ὄχλον
he healed them; so as the crowd
=so that the crowd marvelled

θαυμάσαι βλέποντας κωφοὺς λαλοῦντας,
to marvel[b] seeing dumb men speaking,

---

gion of Tyre and Sidon. 22A Canaanite woman from that vicinity came to him, crying out, "Lord, Son of David, have mercy on me! My daughter is suffering terribly from demon-possession."
23Jesus did not answer a word. So his disciples came to him and urged him, "Send her away, for she keeps crying out after us."
24He answered, "I was sent only to the lost sheep of Israel."
25The woman came and knelt before him. "Lord, help me!" she said.
26He replied, "It is not right to take the children's bread and toss it to their dogs."
27"Yes, Lord," she said, "but even the dogs eat the crumbs that fall from their masters' table."
28Then Jesus answered, "Woman, you have great faith! Your request is granted." And her daughter was healed from that very hour.

Jesus Feeds the Four Thousand

29Jesus left there and went along the Sea of Galilee. Then he went up on a mountainside and sat down. 30Great crowds came to him, bringing the lame, the blind, the crippled, the mute and many others, and laid them at his feet; and he healed them. 31The people were amazed when they saw the mute speaking, the crippled

pled restored, and the lame walking, and the blind seeing; and they glorified the God of Israel.

Four Thousand Fed

32And Jesus called His disciples to Him, and said, "I feel compassion for the multitude, because they have remained with Me now three days and have nothing to eat; and I do not wish to send them away hungry, lest they faint on the way."

33And the disciples *said to Him, "Where would we get so many loaves in a desolate place to satisfy such a great multitude?"

34And Jesus *said to them, "How many loaves do you have?" And they said, "Seven, and a few small fish."

35And He directed the multitude to sit down on the ground;

36and He took the seven loaves and the fish; and giving thanks, He broke them and started giving them to the disciples, and the disciples *in turn*, to the multitudes.

37And they all ate, and were satisfied, and they picked up what was left over of the broken pieces, seven large baskets full.

38And those who ate were four thousand men, besides women and children.

39And sending away the multitudes, He got into the boat, and came to the region of Magadan.

κυλλοὺς ὑγιεῖς καὶ χωλοὺς περιπατοῦντας
maimed　whole　and　lame　walking
καὶ τυφλοὺς βλέποντας· καὶ ἐδόξασαν
and　blind　seeing;　and　they glorified
τὸν θεὸν Ἰσραήλ. **32** Ὁ δὲ Ἰησοῦς
the　God　of Israel.　 － And　Jesus
προσκαλεσάμενος τοὺς μαθητὰς αὐτοῦ
calling forward　the　disciples　of him
εἶπεν· σπλαγχνίζομαι ἐπὶ τὸν ὄχλον,
said:　I am filled with tenderness　over　the　crowd,
ὅτι ἤδη ἡμέραι τρεῖς προσμένουσίν
because now　days　three　they remain
μοι καὶ οὐκ ἔχουσιν τί φάγωσιν·
with me and　have not　anything they may eat;
καὶ ἀπολῦσαι αὐτοὺς νήστεις οὐ θέλω,
and　to dismiss　them　without food I am not willing,
μήποτε ἐκλυθῶσιν ἐν τῇ ὁδῷ. **33** καὶ
lest　they fail　in　the　way.　　 And
λέγουσιν αὐτῷ οἱ μαθηταί· πόθεν
say　to him　the　disciples:　Whence
ἡμῖν ἐν ἐρημίᾳ ἄρτοι τοσοῦτοι ὥστε
to us　in　a desert　loaves　so many　so as
χορτάσαι ὄχλον τοσοῦτον; **34** καὶ λέγει
to satisfy　a crowd　so great?　　 And　says
αὐτοῖς ὁ Ἰησοῦς· πόσους ἄρτους ἔχετε;
to them　－　Jesus:　How many　loaves　have ye?
οἱ δὲ εἶπαν· ἑπτά, καὶ ὀλίγα ἰχθύδια.
And they　said:　Seven, and　a few　fishes.
35 καὶ παραγγείλας τῷ ὄχλῳ ἀναπεσεῖν
And　having enjoined　the　crowd　to recline
ἐπὶ τὴν γῆν **36** ἔλαβεν τοὺς ἑπτὰ
on　the　ground　　 he took　the　seven
ἄρτους καὶ τοὺς ἰχθύας καὶ εὐχαριστήσας
loaves　and　the　fishes　and　giving thanks
ἔκλασεν καὶ ἐδίδου τοῖς μαθηταῖς, οἱ δὲ
he broke　and　gave　to the　disciples,　and the
μαθηταὶ τοῖς ὄχλοις. **37** καὶ ἔφαγον πάντες
disciples　to the crowds.　　 And　ate　all
καὶ ἐχορτάσθησαν, καὶ τὸ περισσεῦον τῶν
and　were satisfied,　and　the　excess　of the
κλασμάτων ἦραν, ἑπτὰ σπυρίδας πλήρεις.
fragments　they took, seven　baskets　full.
38 οἱ δὲ ἐσθίοντες ἦσαν τετρακισχίλιοι
And the [ones]　eating　were　four thousand
ἄνδρες χωρὶς γυναικῶν καὶ παιδίων.
men　apart from　women　and　children.
39 Καὶ ἀπολύσας τοὺς ὄχλους ἐνέβη εἰς
And　having dismissed　the　crowds he embarked　in
τὸ πλοῖον, καὶ ἦλθεν εἰς τὰ ὅρια Μαγαδάν.
the　ship,　and　came　into the borders of Magadan.

---

made well, the lame walking and the blind seeing. And they praised the God of Israel.

32Jesus called his disciples to him and said, "I have compassion for these people; they have already been with me three days and have nothing to eat. I do not want to send them away hungry, or they may collapse on the way."

33His disciples answered, "Where could we get enough bread in this remote place to feed such a crowd?"

34"How many loaves do you have?" Jesus asked.

"Seven," they replied, "and a few small fish."

35He told the crowd to sit down on the ground. 36Then he took the seven loaves and the fish, and when he had given thanks, he broke them and gave them to the disciples, and they in turn to the people. 37They all ate and were satisfied. Afterward the disciples picked up seven basketfuls of broken pieces that were left over. 38The number of those who ate was four thousand, besides women and children. 39After Jesus had sent the crowd away, he got into the boat and went to the vicinity of Magadan.

Chapter 16

Pharisees Test Jesus

AND the Pharisees and Sadducees came up, and testing Him asked Him to show them a sign from heaven.

2But He answered and said to them, "When it is evening, you say, '*It will be* fair weather, for the sky is red.'

3"And in the morning, '*There will be* a storm today, for the sky is red and

---

16 Καὶ προσελθόντες οἱ Φαρισαῖοι καὶ
And　approaching　the　Pharisees　and
Σαδδουκαῖοι πειράζοντες ἐπηρώτησαν αὐτὸν
Sadducees　tempting　asked　him
σημεῖον ἐκ τοῦ οὐρανοῦ ἐπιδεῖξαι
a sign　out of　*the*　heaven　to show
αὐτοῖς. **2** ὁ δὲ ἀποκριθεὶς εἶπεν αὐτοῖς·
to them.　But he　answering　said　to them:
[ὀψίας γενομένης λέγετε· εὐδία,
Evening　coming on ͣ　ye say:　Fair weather,
＝When evening comes on
πυρράζει γὰρ ὁ οὐρανός· **3** καὶ πρωΐ·
for is red　the　heaven(sky);　and in the morning:
σήμερον χειμών, πυρράζει γὰρ στυγνάζων
To-day　stormy weather,　for is red　being overcast

Chapter 16

The Demand for a Sign

THE Pharisees and Sadducees came to Jesus and tested him by asking him to show them a sign from heaven.

2He replied, ͥ "When evening comes, you say, 'It will be fair weather, for the sky is red,' 3and in the

ͥ2 Some early manuscripts do not have the rest of verse 2 and all of verse 3.

threatening.' Do you know how to discern the appearance of the sky, but cannot *discern* the signs of the times?

4"An evil and adulterous generation seeks after a sign; and a sign will not be given it, except the sign of Jonah." And He left them, and went away.

5And the disciples came to the other side and had forgotten to take bread.

6And Jesus said to them, "Watch out and beware of the leaven of the Pharisees and Sadducees."

7And they began to discuss among themselves, saying, "*It is* because we took no bread."

8But Jesus, aware of this, said, "You men of little faith, why do you discuss among yourselves that you have no bread?

9"Do you not yet understand or remember the five loaves of the five thousand, and how many baskets you took up?

10"Or the seven loaves of the four thousand, and how many large baskets you took up?

11"How is it that you do not understand that I did not speak to you concerning bread? But beware of the leaven of the Pharisees and Sadducees."

12Then they understood that He did not say to beware of the leaven of bread, but of the teaching of the Pharisees and Sadducees.

Peter's Confession of Christ

13Now when Jesus came into the district of Caesarea Philippi, He *began* asking His disciples, saying, "Who do people say that the Son of Man is?"

14And they said, "Some *say* John the Baptist; and others, Elijah; but still others, Jeremiah, or one of the prophets."

ὁ οὐρανός. τὸ μὲν πρόσωπον τοῦ
the heaven(sky). The - face of the

οὐρανοῦ γινώσκετε διακρίνειν, τὰ δὲ
heaven(sky) ye know* to discern, but the

σημεῖα τῶν καιρῶν οὐ δύνασθε;] 4 γενεὰ
signs of the times can ye not? A generation

πονηρὰ καὶ μοιχαλὶς σημεῖον ἐπιζητεῖ,
evil and adulterous a sign seeks,

καὶ σημεῖον οὐ δοθήσεται αὐτῇ εἰ μὴ
and a sign shall not be given to it except

τὸ σημεῖον Ἰωνᾶ. καὶ καταλιπὼν αὐτοὺς
the sign of Jonah. And leaving them

ἀπῆλθεν. 5 Καὶ ἐλθόντες οἱ μαθηταὶ εἰς
he went away. And coming the disciples to

τὸ πέραν ἐπελάθοντο ἄρτους λαβεῖν.
the other side they forgot loaves to take.

ὁ δὲ Ἰησοῦς εἶπεν αὐτοῖς· 6 ὁρᾶτε καὶ
- And Jesus said to them: Beware and

προσέχετε ἀπὸ τῆς ζύμης τῶν Φαρισαίων
take heed from the leaven of the Pharisees

καὶ Σαδδουκαίων. 7 οἱ δὲ διελογίζοντο
and Sadducees. But they reasoned

ἐν ἑαυτοῖς λέγοντες ὅτι ἄρτους οὐκ
among themselves saying[:] - Loaves not

ἐλάβομεν. 8 γνοὺς δὲ ὁ Ἰησοῦς εἶπεν·
we took. But knowing - Jesus said:

τί διαλογίζεσθε ἐν ἑαυτοῖς, ὀλιγόπιστοι,
Why reason ye among yourselves, little-faiths,

ὅτι ἄρτους οὐκ ἔχετε; 9 οὔπω νοεῖτε,
because loaves ye have not? Do ye not yet understand,

οὐδὲ μνημονεύετε τοὺς πέντε ἄρτους τῶν
neither remember ye the five loaves of the

πεντακισχιλίων καὶ πόσους κοφίνους
five thousand and how many baskets

ἐλάβετε; 10 οὐδὲ τοὺς ἑπτὰ ἄρτους τῶν
ye took? Neither the seven loaves of the

τετρακισχιλίων καὶ πόσας σπυρίδας
four thousand and how many baskets

ἐλάβετε; 11 πῶς οὐ νοεῖτε ὅτι οὐ
ye took? How do ye not understand that not

περὶ ἄρτων εἶπον ὑμῖν; προσέχετε δὲ ἀπὸ
concerning loaves I said to you? But take heed from

τῆς ζύμης τῶν Φαρισαίων καὶ Σαδ-
the leaven of the Pharisees and Sad-

δουκαίων. 12 τότε συνῆκαν ὅτι οὐκ
ducees. Then they understood that not

εἶπεν προσέχειν ἀπὸ τῆς ζύμης [τῶν
he said to take heed from the leaven of the

ἄρτων], ἀλλὰ ἀπὸ τῆς διδαχῆς τῶν
loaves, but from the teaching of the

Φαρισαίων καὶ Σαδδουκαίων.
Pharisees and Sadducees.

13 Ἐλθὼν δὲ ὁ Ἰησοῦς εἰς τὰ μέρη
And coming - Jesus into the parts

Καισαρείας τῆς Φιλίππου ἠρώτα τοὺς
of Caesarea - of Philip he questioned the

μαθητὰς αὐτοῦ λέγων· τίνα λέγουσιν οἱ
disciples of him saying: Whom say -

ἄνθρωποι εἶναι τὸν υἱὸν τοῦ ἀνθρώπου;
men to be the Son - of man?

14 οἱ δὲ εἶπαν· οἱ μὲν Ἰωάννην τὸν
And they said: Some indeed John the

βαπτιστήν, ἄλλοι δὲ Ἠλίαν, ἕτεροι δὲ
Baptist, and others Elias, and others

Ἰερεμίαν ἢ ἕνα τῶν προφητῶν. 15 λέγει
Jeremias or one of the prophets. He says

---

morning, 'Today it will be stormy, for the sky is red and overcast.' You know how to interpret the appearance of the sky, but you cannot interpret the signs of the times. 4A wicked and adulterous generation looks for a miraculous sign, but none will be given it except the sign of Jonah." Jesus then left them and went away.

The Yeast of the Pharisees and Sadducees

5When they went across the lake, the disciples forgot to take bread. 6"Be careful," Jesus said to them. "Be on your guard against the yeast of the Pharisees and Sadducees."

7They discussed this among themselves and said, "It is because we didn't bring any bread."

8Aware of their discussion, Jesus asked, "You of little faith, why are you talking among yourselves about having no bread? 9Do you still not understand? Don't you remember the five loaves for the five thousand, and how many basketfuls you gathered? 10Or the seven loaves for the four thousand, and how many basketfuls you gathered? 11How is it you don't understand that I was not talking to you about bread? But be on your guard against the yeast of the Pharisees and Sadducees." 12Then they understood that he was not telling them to guard against the yeast used in bread, but against the teaching of the Pharisees and Sadducees.

Peter's Confession of Christ

13When Jesus came to the region of Caesarea Philippi, he asked his disciples, "Who do people say the Son of Man is?" 14They replied, "Some say John the Baptist; others say Elijah; and still others, Jeremiah or one of the prophets."

---

* See note on page xviii. Note the use in the next line of δύνασθε.

15He *said to them, "But who do you say that I am?"

16And Simon Peter answered and said, "Thou art the Christ, the Son of the living God."

17And Jesus answered and said to him, "Blessed are you, Simon Barjona, because flesh and blood did not reveal this to you, but My Father who is in heaven.

18"And I also say to you that you are Peter, and upon this rock I will build My church; and the gates of Hades shall not overpower it.

19"I will give you the keys of the kingdom of heaven; and whatever you shall bind on earth shall be bound in heaven, and whatever you shall loose on earth shall be loosed in heaven."

20Then He warned the disciples that they should tell no one that He was the Christ.

Jesus Foretells His Death

21From that time Jesus Christ began to show His disciples that He must go to Jerusalem, and suffer many things from the elders and chief priests and scribes, and be killed, and be raised up on the third day.

22And Peter took Him aside and began to rebuke Him, saying, "God forbid it, Lord! This shall never happen to You."

23But He turned and said to Peter, "Get behind Me, Satan! You are a stumbling block to Me; for you are not setting your mind on God's interests, but man's."

Discipleship Is Costly

24Then Jesus said to His disciples, "If anyone

αὐτοῖς· ὑμεῖς δὲ τίνα με λέγετε εἶναι;
to them: But ²ye ¹whom ⁴me ²say to be?

16 ἀποκριθεὶς δὲ Σίμων Πέτρος εἶπεν·
And answering Simon Peter said:

17 σὺ εἶ ὁ χριστὸς ὁ υἱὸς τοῦ θεοῦ
Thou art the Christ the Son - of God

τοῦ ζῶντος. ἀποκριθεὶς δὲ ὁ Ἰησοῦς
of the living. And answering - Jesus

εἶπεν αὐτῷ· μακάριος εἶ, Σίμων
said to him: Blessed art thou, Simon

Βαριωνᾶ, ὅτι σὰρξ καὶ αἷμα οὐκ ἀπεκά-
Barjonas, because flesh and blood did not

λυψέν σοι ἀλλ' ὁ πατήρ μου ὁ ἐν
reveal to thee but the Father of me - in

τοῖς οὐρανοῖς. 18 κἀγὼ δέ σοι λέγω
the heavens. And I also to thee say[,]

ὅτι σὺ εἶ Πέτρος, καὶ ἐπὶ ταύτῃ τῇ
- Thou art Peter, and on this the

πέτρᾳ οἰκοδομήσω μου τὴν ἐκκλησίαν,
rock I will build of me the church,

καὶ πύλαι ᾅδου οὐ κατισχύσουσιν
and [the] gates of hades will not prevail against

αὐτῆς. 19 δώσω σοι τὰς κλεῖδας τῆς
it. I will give thee the keys of the

βασιλείας τῶν οὐρανῶν, καὶ ὃ ἐὰν
kingdom of the heavens, and whatever

δήσῃς ἐπὶ τῆς γῆς ἔσται δεδεμένον ἐν τοῖς
thou bindest on the earth shall be having been bound in the

οὐρανοῖς, καὶ ὃ ἐὰν λύσῃς ἐπὶ τῆς
heavens, and whatever thou loosest on the

γῆς ἔσται λελυμένον ἐν τοῖς οὐρανοῖς.
earth shall be having been loosed in the heavens.

20 τότε ἐπετίμησεν τοῖς μαθηταῖς ἵνα
Then he warned the disciples that

μηδενὶ εἴπωσιν ὅτι αὐτός ἐστιν ὁ
to no one they should tell that he is the

χριστός.
Christ.

21 Ἀπὸ τότε ἤρξατο Ἰησοῦς Χριστὸς
From then began Jesus Christ

δεικνύειν τοῖς μαθηταῖς αὐτοῦ ὅτι δεῖ
to show to the disciples of him that it behoves

αὐτὸν εἰς Ἱεροσόλυμα ἀπελθεῖν καὶ
him to Jerusalem to go and

πολλὰ παθεῖν ἀπὸ τῶν πρεσβυτέρων καὶ
many things to suffer from the elders and

ἀρχιερέων καὶ γραμματέων καὶ ἀποκτανθῆναι
chief priests and scribes and to be killed

καὶ τῇ τρίτῃ ἡμέρᾳ ἐγερθῆναι. 22 καὶ
and on the third day to be raised. And

προσλαβόμενος αὐτὸν ὁ Πέτρος ἤρξατο
taking him - Peter began

ἐπιτιμᾶν αὐτῷ λέγων· ἵλεώς σοι,
to rebuke him saying: Propitious to thee, =May God help thee,

κύριε· οὐ μὴ ἔσται σοι τοῦτο. 23 ὁ δὲ
Lord: by no means shall be to thee this. But he

στραφεὶς εἶπεν τῷ Πέτρῳ· ὕπαγε ὀπίσω
turning said to Peter: Go behind

μου, σατανᾶ· σκάνδαλον εἶ ἐμοῦ,
me, Satan; an offence thou art of me,

ὅτι οὐ φρονεῖς τὰ τοῦ θεοῦ
because thou thinkest not the things - of God

ἀλλὰ τὰ τῶν ἀνθρώπων. 24 Τότε ὁ
but the things - of men. Then -

Ἰησοῦς εἶπεν τοῖς μαθηταῖς αὐτοῦ· εἰ
Jesus said to the disciples of him: If

15"But what about you?" he asked. "Who do you say I am?"

16Simon Peter answered, "You are the Christ,ʲ the Son of the living God."

17Jesus replied, "Blessed are you, Simon son of Jonah, for this was not revealed to you by man, but by my Father in heaven.

18And I tell you that you are Peter,ᵏ and on this rock I will build my church, and the gates of Hadesˡ will not overcome it.ᵐ 19I will give you the keys of the kingdom of heaven; whatever you bind on earth will beⁿ bound in heaven, and whatever you loose on earth will beⁿ loosed in heaven."

20Then he warned his disciples not to tell anyone that he was the Christ.

Jesus Predicts His Death

21From that time on Jesus began to explain to his disciples that he must go to Jerusalem and suffer many things at the hands of the elders, chief priests and teachers of the law, and that he must be killed and on the third day be raised to life.

22Peter took him aside and began to rebuke him. "Never, Lord!" he said. "This shall never happen to you!"

23Jesus turned and said to Peter, "Get behind me, Satan! You are a stumbling block to me; you do not have in mind the things of God, but the things of men."

24Then Jesus said to his disciples, "If anyone

ʲ16 Or Messiah; also in verse 20
ᵏ18 Peter means rock.
ˡ18 Or hell
ᵐ18 Or not prove stronger than it
ⁿ19 Or have been

wishes to come after Me, let him deny himself, and take up his cross, and follow Me.

25"For whoever wishes to save his life shall lose it; but whoever loses his life for My sake shall find it.

26"For what will a man be profited, if he gains the whole world, and forfeits his soul? Or what will a man give in exchange for his soul?

27"For the Son of Man is going to come in the glory of His Father with His angels; and WILL THEN RECOMPENSE EVERY MAN ACCORDING TO HIS DEEDS.

28"Truly I say to you, there are some of those who are standing here who shall not taste death until they see the Son of Man coming in His kingdom."

τις θέλει ὀπίσω μου ἐλθεῖν, ἀπαρνησάσθω
anyone wishes after me to come, let him deny

ἑαυτὸν καὶ ἀράτω τὸν σταυρὸν αὐτοῦ,
himself and let him take the cross of him,

καὶ ἀκολουθείτω μοι. 25 ὃς γὰρ ἐὰν
and let him follow me. For whoever

θέλῃ τὴν ψυχὴν αὐτοῦ σῶσαι, ἀπολέσει
wishes the life of him to save, he will lose

αὐτήν· ὃς δ' ἂν ἀπολέσῃ τὴν ψυχὴν
it; and whoever loses the life

αὐτοῦ ἕνεκεν ἐμοῦ, εὑρήσει αὐτήν. 26 τί
of him for the sake of me, he will find it. what

γὰρ ὠφεληθήσεται ἄνθρωπος, ἐὰν τὸν
For will be benefited a man, if the

κόσμον ὅλον κερδήσῃ, τὴν δὲ ψυχὴν
world whole he should gain, but the soul

αὐτοῦ ζημιωθῇ; ἢ τί δώσει ἄνθρωπος
of him loses? or what will give a man

ἀντάλλαγμα τῆς ψυχῆς αὐτοῦ; 27 μέλλει
an exchange of the soul of him? is about

γὰρ ὁ υἱὸς τοῦ ἀνθρώπου ἔρχεσθαι ἐν τῇ
For the Son - of man to come in the

δόξῃ τοῦ πατρὸς αὐτοῦ μετὰ τῶν ἀγγέλων
glory of the Father of him with the angels

αὐτοῦ, καὶ τότε ἀποδώσει ἑκάστῳ
of him, and then he will reward to each man

κατὰ τὴν πρᾶξιν αὐτοῦ. 28 ἀμὴν λέγω
according to the conduct of him. Truly I say

ὑμῖν ὅτι εἰσίν τινες τῶν ὧδε ἑστώτων
to you[,] - There are some of the [ones] here standing

οἵτινες οὐ μὴ γεύσωνται θανάτου ἕως ἂν
who by no means may taste of death until

ἴδωσιν τὸν υἱὸν τοῦ ἀνθρώπου ἐρχόμενον
they see the Son - of man coming

ἐν τῇ βασιλείᾳ αὐτοῦ.
in the kingdom of him.

would come after me, he must deny himself and take up his cross and follow me.

25For whoever wants to save his life* will lose it, but whoever loses his life for me will find it. 26What good will it be for a man if he gains the whole world, yet forfeits his soul? Or what can a man give in exchange for his soul? 27For the Son of Man is going to come in his Father's glory with his angels, and then he will reward each person according to what he has done. 28I tell you the truth, some who are standing here will not taste death before they see the Son of Man coming in his kingdom."

Chapter 17

The Transfiguration

AND six days later Jesus *took with Him Peter and James and John his brother, and *brought them up to a high mountain by themselves.

2And He was transfigured before them; and His face shone like the sun, and His garments became as white as light.

3And behold, Moses and Elijah appeared to them, talking with Him.

4And Peter answered and said to Jesus, "Lord, it is good for us to be here; if You wish, I will make three tabernacles here, one for You, and one for Moses, and one for Elijah."

5While he was still

17 Καὶ μεθ' ἡμέρας ἓξ παραλαμβάνει ὁ
And after days six takes -

Ἰησοῦς τὸν Πέτρον καὶ Ἰάκωβον καὶ
Jesus - Peter and James and

Ἰωάννην τὸν ἀδελφὸν αὐτοῦ, καὶ ἀναφέρει
John the brother of him, and leads up

αὐτοὺς εἰς ὄρος ὑψηλὸν κατ' ἰδίαν. 2 καὶ
them to mountain a high privately. And

μετεμορφώθη ἔμπροσθεν αὐτῶν, καὶ
he was transfigured before them, and

ἔλαμψεν τὸ πρόσωπον αὐτοῦ ὡς ὁ ἥλιος,
shone the face of him as the sun,

τὰ δὲ ἱμάτια αὐτοῦ ἐγένετο λευκὰ ὡς
and the garments of him became white as

τὸ φῶς. 3 καὶ ἰδοὺ ὤφθη αὐτοῖς Μωϋσῆς
the light. And behold was seen by them Moses

καὶ Ἠλίας συλλαλοῦντες μετ' αὐτοῦ.
and Elias conversing with him.

4 ἀποκριθεὶς δὲ ὁ Πέτρος εἶπεν τῷ
And answering - Peter said -

Ἰησοῦ· κύριε, καλόν ἐστιν ἡμᾶς ὧδε
to Jesus: Lord, good it is us here

εἶναι· εἰ θέλεις, ποιήσω ὧδε τρεῖς
to be; if thou willest, I will make here three

σκηνάς, σοὶ μίαν καὶ Μωϋσεῖ
tents, for thee one and for Moses

μίαν καὶ Ἠλίᾳ μίαν. 5 ἔτι αὐτοῦ
one and for Elias one. Yet him
= While he was yet

Chapter 17

The Transfiguration

AFTER six days Jesus took with him Peter, James and John the brother of James, and led them up a high mountain by themselves. 2There he was transfigured before them. His face shone like the sun, and his clothes became as white as the light. 3Just then there appeared before them Moses and Elijah, talking with Jesus.

4Peter said to Jesus, "Lord, it is good for us to be here. If you wish, I will put up three shelters—one for you, one for Moses and one for Elijah."

5While he was still speak-

speaking, behold, a bright cloud overshadowed them; and behold, a voice out of the cloud, saying, "This is My beloved Son, with whom I am well-pleased; listen to Him!"

6And when the disciples heard *this*, they fell on their faces and were much afraid.

7And Jesus came to *them* and touched them and said, "Arise, and do not be afraid."

8And lifting up their eyes, they saw no one, except Jesus Himself alone.

9And as they were coming down from the mountain, Jesus commanded them, saying, "Tell the vision to no one until the Son of Man has risen from the dead."

10And His disciples asked Him, saying, "Why then do the scribes say that Elijah must come first?"

11And He answered and said, "Elijah is coming and will restore all things;

12but I say to you, that Elijah already came, and they did not recognize him, but did to him whatever they wished. So also the Son of Man is going to suffer at their hands."

13Then the disciples understood that He had spoken to them about John the Baptist.

The Demoniac

14And when they came to the multitude, a man came up to Him, falling on his knees before Him, and saying,

15"Lord, have mercy on my son, for he is a lunatic, and is very ill; for he often falls into the fire, and often into the water.

16"And I brought him to Your disciples, and they

λαλοῦντος, ἰδοὺ νεφέλη φωτεινὴ ἐπεσκίασεν
speaking^a, behold cloud a bright overshadowed
speaking,

αὐτούς, καὶ ἰδοὺ φωνὴ ἐκ τῆς νεφέλης
them, and behold a voice out of the cloud

λέγουσα· οὗτός ἐστιν ὁ υἱός μου ὁ
saying: This is the son of me the

ἀγαπητός, ἐν ᾧ εὐδόκησα· ἀκούετε
beloved, in whom I was well pleased; hear ye

αὐτοῦ. 6 καὶ ἀκούσαντες οἱ μαθηταὶ
him. And hearing the disciples

ἔπεσαν ἐπὶ πρόσωπον αὐτῶν καὶ
fell on [the] face[s] of them and

ἐφοβήθησαν σφόδρα. 7 καὶ προσῆλθεν ὁ
feared exceedingly. And approached –

Ἰησοῦς καὶ ἁψάμενος αὐτῶν εἶπεν·
Jesus and touching them said:

ἐγέρθητε καὶ μὴ φοβεῖσθε. 8 ἐπάραντες δὲ
Rise and do not fear. And lifting up

τοὺς ὀφθαλμοὺς αὐτῶν οὐδένα εἶδον εἰ
the eyes of them no one they saw ex-

μὴ αὐτὸν Ἰησοῦν μόνον. 9 Καὶ κατα-
cept himself Jesus only. And com-
                                              =as

βαινόντων αὐτῶν ἐκ τοῦ ὄρους ἐνετείλατο
ing down them^a out of the mountain enjoined
they were coming down

αὐτοῖς ὁ Ἰησοῦς λέγων· μηδενὶ εἴπητε
them – Jesus saying: To no one tell

τὸ ὅραμα ἕως οὗ ὁ υἱὸς τοῦ ἀνθρώπου
the vision until the Son – of man

ἐκ νεκρῶν ἐγερθῇ. 10 Καὶ ἐπηρώτησαν
out of dead be raised. And questioned

αὐτὸν οἱ μαθηταὶ λέγοντες· τί οὖν
him the disciples saying: Why then

οἱ γραμματεῖς λέγουσιν ὅτι Ἠλίαν δεῖ
the scribes say that ^sElias ¹it behoves

ἐλθεῖν πρῶτον; 11 ὁ δὲ ἀποκριθεὶς εἶπεν·
to come first? And he answering said:

Ἠλίας μὲν ἔρχεται καὶ ἀποκαταστήσει
Elias indeed is coming and will restore

πάντα· 12 λέγω δὲ ὑμῖν ὅτι Ἠλίας
all things; but I tell you that Elias

ἤδη ἦλθεν, καὶ οὐκ ἐπέγνωσαν
already came, and they did not recognize

αὐτόν, ἀλλ' ἐποίησαν ἐν αὐτῷ ὅσα
him, but did by him whatever things

ἠθέλησαν· οὕτως καὶ ὁ υἱὸς τοῦ ἀνθρώπου
they wished; thus also the Son – of man

μέλλει πάσχειν ὑπ' αὐτῶν. 13 τότε
is about to suffer by them. Then

συνῆκαν οἱ μαθηταὶ ὅτι περὶ
understood the disciples that concerning

Ἰωάννου τοῦ βαπτιστοῦ εἶπεν αὐτοῖς.
John the Baptist he spoke to them.

14 Καὶ ἐλθόντων πρὸς τὸν ὄχλον προσ-
And [they] coming to the crowd ap-

ἦλθεν αὐτῷ ἄνθρωπος γονυπετῶν αὐτὸν
proached· to him a man falling on knees to him

15 καὶ λέγων· κύριε, ἐλέησόν μου τὸν
and saying: Lord, pity of me the

υἱόν, ὅτι σεληνιάζεται καὶ κακῶς ἔχει·
son, because he is moonstruck and ill has;
                                            =is ill;

πολλάκις γὰρ πίπτει εἰς τὸ πῦρ καὶ
for often he falls into the fire and

πολλάκις εἰς τὸ ὕδωρ. 16 καὶ προσήνεγκα
often into the water. And I brought

αὐτὸν τοῖς μαθηταῖς σου, καὶ οὐκ
him to the disciples of thee, and not

---

ing, a bright cloud enveloped them, and a voice from the cloud said, "This is my Son, whom I love; with him I am well pleased. Listen to him!"

6When the disciples heard this, they fell facedown to the ground, terrified. 7But Jesus came and touched them. "Get up," he said. "Don't be afraid." 8When they looked up, they saw no one except Jesus.

9As they were coming down the mountain, Jesus instructed them, "Don't tell anyone what you have seen, until the Son of Man has been raised from the dead."

10The disciples asked him, "Why then do the teachers of the law say that Elijah must come first?"

11Jesus replied, "To be sure, Elijah comes and will restore all things. 12But I tell you, Elijah has already come, and they did not recognize him, but have done to him everything they wished. In the same way the Son of Man is going to suffer at their hands." 13Then the disciples understood that he was talking to them about John the Baptist.

The Healing of a Boy With a Demon

14When they came to the crowd, a man approached Jesus and knelt before him. 15"Lord, have mercy on my son," he said. "He has seizures and is suffering greatly. He often falls into the fire or into the water. 16I brought him to your disciples, but they could not could not cure him.''

17And Jesus answered
and said, ''O unbelieving
and perverted generation,
how long shall I be with
you? How long shall I put
up with you? Bring him
here to Me.''

18And Jesus rebuked him,
and the demon came out of
him, and the boy was cured
at once.

19Then the disciples came
to Jesus privately and said,
''Why could we not cast it
out?''

20And He *said to them,
''Because of the littleness
of your faith; for truly I say
to you, if you have faith as
a mustard seed, you shall
say to this mountain,
'Move from here to there,'
and it shall move; and nothing shall be impossible to
you.

21[''dBut this kind does
not go out except by prayer
and fasting.'']

22And while they were
gathering together in Galilee, Jesus said to them,
''The Son of Man is going
to be delivered into the
hands of men;

23and they will kill Him,
and He will be raised on the
third day.'' And they were
deeply grieved.

The Tribute Money

24And when they had
come to Capernaum, those
who collected the ᵉtwo-
drachma *tax* came to Peter,
and said, ''Does your
teacher not pay the ᵉtwo-
drachma *tax*?''

25He *said, ''Yes.'' And
when he came into the
house, Jesus spoke to him
first, saying, ''What do you
think, Simon? From whom
do the kings of the earth
collect customs or poll-tax,
from their sons or from
strangers?''

ἠδυνήθησαν αὐτὸν θεραπεῦσαι.
they were able him to heal.

17 ἀπο-κριθεὶς δὲ ὁ Ἰησοῦς εἶπεν·
an-swering And - Jesus said:

ὦ γενεὰ ἄπιστος καὶ διεστραμμένη,
O generation unbelieving and having been perverted,

ἕως πότε μεθ’ ὑμῶν ἔσομαι;
until when with you shall I be?

ἕως πότε ἀνέξομαι ὑμῶν; φέρετέ μοι αὐτὸν ὧδε.
until when shall I endure you? bring to me him here.

18 καὶ ἐπετίμησεν αὐτῷ ὁ Ἰησοῦς,
And rebuked it - Jesus,

καὶ ἐξῆλθεν ἀπ’ αὐτοῦ τὸ δαιμόνιον,
and came out from him the demon,

καὶ ἐθεραπεύθη ὁ παῖς ἀπὸ τῆς ὥρας ἐκείνης.
and was healed the boy from - hour that.

19 Τότε προσελθόντες οἱ μαθηταὶ τῷ Ἰησοῦ κατ’ ἰδίαν εἶπον·
Then ᵃapproaching ¹the ²disciples - to Jesus privately said:

διὰ τί ἡμεῖς οὐκ ἠδυνήθημεν ἐκβαλεῖν αὐτό;
Why we were not able to expel it?

20 ὁ δὲ λέγει αὐτοῖς·
And he says to them:

διὰ τὴν ὀλιγο-πιστίαν ὑμῶν· ἀμὴν γὰρ λέγω ὑμῖν, ἐὰν
Because of the little faith of you; for truly I say to you, if

ἔχητε πίστιν ὡς κόκκον σινάπεως,
ye have faith as a grain of mustard,

ἐρεῖτε τῷ ὄρει τούτῳ· μετάβα
ye will say - mountain to this: Remove

ἔνθεν ἐκεῖ, καὶ μεταβήσεται, καὶ οὐδὲν
hence there, and it will be removed, and nothing

ἀδυνατήσει ὑμῖν. ‡
will be impossible to you.

22 Συστρεφομένων δὲ αὐτῶν ἐν τῇ
And strolling them in -
=as they were strolling

Γαλιλαίᾳ εἶπεν αὐτοῖς ὁ Ἰησοῦς· μέλλει
Galilee said to them - Jesus: is about

ὁ υἱὸς τοῦ ἀνθρώπου παραδίδοσθαι εἰς
The Son - of man to be delivered into

χεῖρας ἀνθρώπων, 23 καὶ ἀποκτενοῦσιν
[the] hands of men, and they will kill

αὐτόν, καὶ τῇ τρίτῃ ἡμέρᾳ ἐγερθήσεται.
him, and on the third day he will be raised.

καὶ ἐλυπήθησαν σφόδρα.
And they were grieved exceedingly.

24 Ἐλθόντων δὲ αὐτῶν εἰς Καφαρναοὺμ
And coming them to Capernaum
=when they came

προσῆλθον οἱ τὰ δίδραχμα λαμβάνοντες
approached the [ones] the didrachmæ receiving

τῷ Πέτρῳ καὶ εἶπαν· ὁ διδάσκαλος
- Peter and said: The teacher

ὑμῶν οὐ τελεῖ δίδραχμα; λέγει· ναί.
of you not pays drachmae? He says: Yes.

25 καὶ ἐλθόντα εἰς τὴν οἰκίαν προ-
And ⁴coming ⁵into ⁶the ⁷house ²pre-

έφθασεν αὐτὸν ὁ Ἰησοῦς λέγων· τί σοι
ceded ⁸him - ¹Jesus saying: What to thee

δοκεῖ, Σίμων; οἱ βασιλεῖς τῆς γῆς
seems it, Simon? the kings of the earth

ἀπὸ τίνων λαμβάνουσιν τέλη ἢ κῆνσον;
from whom do they take toll or poll-tax?

ἀπὸ τῶν υἱῶν αὐτῶν ἢ ἀπὸ τῶν ἀλλοτρίων;
from the sons of them or from - strangers?

---

heal him.''

17''O unbelieving and perverse generation,'' Jesus
replied, ''how long shall I
stay with you? How long
shall I put up with you?
Bring the boy here to me.''

18Jesus rebuked the de-
mon, and it came out of the
boy, and he was healed
from that moment.

19Then the disciples came
to Jesus in private and
asked, ''Why couldn't we
drive it out?''

20He replied, ''Because
you have so little faith. I tell
you the truth, if you have
faith as small as a mustard
seed, you can say to this
mountain, 'Move from here
to there' and it will move.
Nothing will be impossible
for you.ᵖ''

22When they came to-
gether in Galilee, he said to
them, ''The Son of Man is
going to be betrayed into
the hands of men. 23They
will kill him, and on the
third day he will be raised
to life.'' And the disciples
were filled with grief.

The Temple Tax

24After Jesus and his disciples arrived in Caperna_
um, the collectors of the
two-drachma tax came to
Peter and asked, ''Doesn't
your teacher pay the tem-
ple tax �q?''

25''Yes, he does,'' he replied.

When Peter came into the
house, Jesus was the first
to speak. ''What do you
think, Simon?'' he asked.
''From whom do the kings
of the earth collect duty
and taxes—from their own
sons or from others?''

ᵈMany mss. do not contain this
verse
ᵉEquivalent to two denarii or two
days' wages paid as a temple tax

‡ **Verse 21 omitted by Nestle;** *cf.* NIV

ᵖ20 Some manuscripts *you*. ²¹*But
this kind does not go out except by
prayer and fasting.*
�q24 Greek *the two drachmas*

26And upon his saying, "From strangers," Jesus said to him, "Consequently the sons are exempt.
27"But, lest we give them offense, go to the sea, and throw in a hook, and take the first fish that comes up; and when you open its mouth, you will find a /stater. Take that and give it to them for you and Me."

---

26 εἰπόντος   δέ·   ἀπὸ   τῶν   ἀλλο-
and [he] saying*:   From   -   strangers,
= when he said :

τρίων,   ἔφη   αὐτῷ   ὁ   Ἰησοῦς·   ἄρα   γε
   said   to him   -   Jesus: Then

ἐλεύθεροί   εἰσιν   οἱ   υἱοί.   **27** ἵνα   δὲ   μὴ
free   are   the   sons.   But lest

σκανδαλίσωμεν   αὐτούς,   πορευθεὶς   εἰς
we should offend   them,   going   to

θάλασσαν   βάλε   ἄγκιστρον   καὶ   τὸν
[the] sea   cast   a hook   and   the

ἀναβάντα   πρῶτον   ἰχθὺν   ἆρον,   καὶ   ἀνοίξας
²coming up   ³first   ¹fish   take,   and   opening

τὸ   στόμα   αὐτοῦ   εὑρήσεις   στατῆρα·
the   mouth   of it   thou wilt find   a stater;

ἐκεῖνον   λαβὼν   δὸς   αὐτοῖς   ἀντὶ   ἐμοῦ   καὶ
that   taking   give   them   for   me   and

σοῦ.
thee.

26"From others," Peter answered.
"Then the sons are exempt," Jesus said to him. 27"But so that we may not offend them, go to the lake and throw out your line. Take the first fish you catch; open its mouth and you will find a four-drachma coin. Take it and give it to them for my tax and yours."

Chapter 18

Rank in the Kingdom

AT that time the disciples came to Jesus, saying, "Who then is greatest in the kingdom of heaven?"
2And He called a child to Himself and set him before them,
3and said, "Truly I say to you, unless you are converted and become like children, you shall not enter the kingdom of heaven.
4"Whoever then humbles himself as this child, he is the greatest in the kingdom of heaven.
5"And whoever receives one such child in My name receives Me;
6but whoever causes one of these little ones who believe in Me to stumble, it is better for him that a heavy millstone be hung around his neck, and that he be drowned in the depth of the sea.

Stumbling Blocks

7"Woe to the world because of its stumbling blocks! For it is inevitable that stumbling blocks come; but woe to that man through whom the stumbling block comes!
8"And if your hand or your foot causes you to stumble, cut it off and

---

18 Ἐν   ἐκείνῃ   τῇ   ὥρᾳ   προσῆλθον   οἱ
   In   that   -   hour   approached   the

μαθηταὶ   τῷ   Ἰησοῦ   λέγοντες·   τίς   ἄρα
disciples   -   to Jesus   saying: Who   then

μείζων   ἐστὶν   ἐν   τῇ   βασιλείᾳ   τῶν   οὐρανῶν;
greater   is   in   the   kingdom   of the   heavens?

2 καὶ   προσκαλεσάμενος   παιδίον   ἔστησεν
And   calling forward   a child   he set

αὐτὸ   ἐν   μέσῳ   αὐτῶν   **3** καὶ   εἶπεν·   ἀμὴν
him   in [the] midst   of them   and   said: Truly

λέγω   ὑμῖν,   ἐὰν   μὴ   στραφῆτε   καὶ
I say   to you,   except   ye turn   and

γένησθε   ὡς   τὰ   παιδία,   οὐ   μὴ
become   as   -   children,   by no means

εἰσέλθητε   εἰς   τὴν   βασιλείαν   τῶν
may ye enter   into   the   kingdom   of the

οὐρανῶν.   **4** ὅστις   οὖν   ταπεινώσει   ἑαυτὸν
heavens.   ¹[he] who ²Therefore   will humble   himself

ὡς   τὸ   παιδίον   τοῦτο,   οὗτός   ἐστιν   ὁ
as   -   child   this,   this [one]   is   the

μείζων   ἐν   τῇ   βασιλείᾳ   τῶν   οὐρανῶν.
greater   in   the   kingdom   of the   heavens.

5 καὶ   ὃς   ἐὰν   δέξηται   ἓν   παιδίον
And   whoever   receives   one   child

τοιοῦτο   ἐπὶ   τῷ   ὀνόματί   μου,   ἐμὲ   δέχεται·
such   on(in)   the   name   of me,   me   receives;

6 ὃς   δ'   ἂν   σκανδαλίσῃ   ἕνα   τῶν
and whoever   offends   one   -

μικρῶν   τούτων   τῶν   πιστευόντων   εἰς   ἐμέ,
little [ones]   of these   -   believing   in   me,

συμφέρει   αὐτῷ   ἵνα   κρεμασθῇ   μύλος
it is expedient   for him   that   be hanged   an upper

ὀνικὸς   περὶ   τὸν   τράχηλον   αὐτοῦ   καὶ
millstone   round   the   neck   of him   and

καταποντισθῇ   ἐν   τῷ   πελάγει   τῆς   θαλάσσης.
he be drowned   in   the   depth   of the   sea.

7 Οὐαὶ   τῷ   κόσμῳ   ἀπὸ   τῶν   σκανδάλων·
Woe   to the   world   from   -   offences;

ἀνάγκη   γὰρ   ἐλθεῖν   τὰ   σκάνδαλα,   πλὴν
for [it is] a necessity   to come   -   offences,   but

οὐαὶ   τῷ   ἀνθρώπῳ   δι'   οὗ   τὸ   σκάνδαλον
woe   to the   man   through whom   the   offence

ἔρχεται.   **8** Εἰ   δὲ   ἡ   χείρ   σου   ἢ   ὁ
comes.   Now if   the   hand   of thee   or   the

πούς   σου   σκανδαλίζει   σε,   ἔκκοψον   αὐτὸν
foot   of thee   offends   thee,   cut off   it

Chapter 18

The Greatest in the Kingdom of Heaven

AT that time the disciples came to Jesus and asked, "Who is the greatest in the kingdom of heaven?"
2He called a little child and had him stand among them. 3And he said: "I tell you the truth, unless you change and become like little children, you will never enter the kingdom of heaven. 4Therefore, whoever humbles himself like this child is the greatest in the kingdom of heaven.
5"And whoever welcomes a little child like this in my name welcomes me.
6But if anyone causes one of these little ones who believe in me to sin, it would be better for him to have a large millstone hung around his neck and to be drowned in the depths of the sea.
7"Woe to the world because of the things that cause people to sin! Such things must come, but woe to the man through whom they come! 8If your hand or your foot causes you to sin, cut it off and throw it away.

/Or, shekel, worth four drachmas

throw it from you; it is better for you to enter life crippled or lame, than having two hands or two feet, to be cast into the eternal fire.

9"And if your eye causes you to stumble, pluck it out, and throw it from you. It is better for you to enter life with one eye, than having two eyes, to be cast into the fiery hell.

10"See that you do not despise one of these little ones, for I say to you, that their angels in heaven continually behold the face of My Father who is in heaven.

11["*gFor the Son of Man has come to save that which was lost.]

Ninety-nine Plus One

12"What do you think? If any man has a hundred sheep, and one of them has gone astray, does he not leave the ninety-nine on the mountains and go and search for the one that is straying?

13"And if it turns out that he finds it, truly I say to you, he rejoices over it more than over the ninety-nine which have not gone astray.

14"Thus it is not *the* will of your Father who is in heaven that one of these little ones perish.

Discipline and Prayer

15"And if your brother sins*h*, go and reprove him in private; if he listens to you, you have won your brother.

16"But if he does not listen *to you*, take one or two more with you, so that BY THE MOUTH OF TWO OR THREE WITNESSES EVERY FACT MAY BE CONFIRMED.

17"And if he refuses to listen to them, tell it to the

καὶ βάλε ἀπὸ σοῦ· καλόν σοί ἐστιν
and cast from thee; good for thee it is

εἰσελθεῖν εἰς τὴν ζωὴν κυλλὸν ἢ χωλόν,
to enter into - life maimed or lame,

ἢ δύο χεῖρας ἢ δύο πόδας ἔχοντα βληθῆναι
than two hands or two feet having to be cast

εἰς τὸ πῦρ τὸ αἰώνιον. 9 καὶ εἰ ὁ
into the fire - eternal. And if the

ὀφθαλμός σου σκανδαλίζει σε, ἔξελε αὐτὸν
eye of thee offends thee, pluck out it

καὶ βάλε ἀπὸ σοῦ· καλόν σοί ἐστιν
and cast from thee; good for thee it is

μονόφθαλμον εἰς τὴν ζωὴν εἰσελθεῖν, ἢ
one-eyed into the life to enter, than

δύο ὀφθαλμοὺς ἔχοντα βληθῆναι εἰς
two eyes having to be cast into

τὴν γέενναν τοῦ πυρός. 10 Ὁρᾶτε μὴ
the gehenna - of fire. See [that] not

καταφρονήσητε ἑνὸς τῶν μικρῶν τούτων·
ye despise one - little [ones] of these;

λέγω γὰρ ὑμῖν ὅτι οἱ ἄγγελοι αὐτῶν
for I tell you that the angels of them

ἐν οὐρανοῖς διὰ παντὸς βλέπουσι τὸ
in heavens always see the

πρόσωπον τοῦ πατρός μου τοῦ ἐν οὐρανοῖς.‡
face of the Father of me - in heavens.‡

12 Τί ὑμῖν δοκεῖ; ἐὰν γένηταί τινι
What to you seems it? if there be to any
= any man has

ἀνθρώπῳ ἑκατὸν πρόβατα καὶ πλανηθῇ
man*e* a hundred sheep and wanders

ἐν ἐξ αὐτῶν, οὐχὶ ἀφήσει τὰ ἐνενήκοντα
one of them, will he not leave the ninety-

ἐννέα ἐπὶ τὰ ὄρη καὶ πορευθεὶς ζητεῖ τὸ
nine on the mountains and going seeks the

πλανώμενον; 13 καὶ ἐὰν γένηται
wandering [one]? And if he happens

εὑρεῖν αὐτό, ἀμὴν λέγω ὑμῖν ὅτι
to find it, truly I say to you that

χαίρει ἐπ᾽ αὐτῷ μᾶλλον ἢ ἐπὶ τοῖς
he rejoices over it more than over the

ἐνενήκοντα ἐννέα τοῖς μὴ πεπλανημένοις.
ninety-nine - not having wandered.

14 οὕτως οὐκ ἔστιν θέλημα ἔμπροσθεν
So it is not [the] will before

τοῦ πατρὸς ὑμῶν τοῦ ἐν οὐρανοῖς ἵνα
the Father of you - in heavens that

ἀπόληται ἐν τῶν μικρῶν τούτων.
should perish one - little [ones] of these.

15 Ἐὰν δὲ ἁμαρτήσῃ ὁ ἀδελφός σου,
Now if sins the brother of thee,

ὕπαγε ἔλεγξον αὐτὸν μεταξὺ σοῦ καὶ
go reprove him between thee and

αὐτοῦ μόνου. ἐάν σου ἀκούσῃ, ἐκέρδησας
him alone. If thee he hears, thou gainedst

τὸν ἀδελφόν σου· 16 ἐὰν δὲ μὴ
the brother of thee; but if not

ἀκούσῃ, παράλαβε μετὰ σοῦ ἔτι ἕνα ἢ
he hears, take with thee more one or

δύο, ἵνα ἐπὶ στόματος δύο μαρτύρων
two, that on(by) [the] mouth of two witnesses

ἢ τριῶν σταθῇ πᾶν ῥῆμα· 17 ἐὰν δὲ
or three may be established every word; but if

παρακούσῃ αὐτῶν, εἰπὸν τῇ ἐκκλησίᾳ·
he refuses to hear them, tell *to* the church;

‡ Ver. 11 omitted by Nestle; *cf.* NIV note.

It is better for you to enter life maimed or crippled than to have two hands or two feet and be thrown into eternal fire. 9And if your eye causes you to sin, gouge it out and throw it away. It is better for you to enter life with one eye than to have two eyes and be thrown into the fire of hell.

The Parable of the Lost Sheep

10"See that you do not look down on one of these little ones. For I tell you that their angels in heaven always see the face of my Father in heaven.*r*

12"What do you think? If a man owns a hundred sheep, and one of them wanders away, will he not leave the ninety-nine on the hills and go to look for the one that wandered off? 13And if he finds it, I tell you the truth, he is happier about that one sheep than about the ninety-nine that did not wander off. 14In the same way your Father in heaven is not willing that any of these little ones should be lost.

A Brother Who Sins Against You

15"If your brother sins against you,*s* go and show him his fault, just between the two of you. If he listens to you, you have won your brother over. 16But if he will not listen, take one or two others along, so that 'every matter may be established by the testimony of two or three witnesses.'*t* 17If he refuses to listen to them, tell it to the

---

g Most ancient mss. do not contain this verse
h Many mss. add here: *against you*

r 10 Some manuscripts heaven.
11 The Son of Man came to save what was lost.
s 15 Some manuscripts do not have *against you.*
t 16 Deut. 19:15

church; and if he refuses to listen even to the church, let him be to you as a Gentile and a tax-gatherer.
18"Truly I say to you, whatever you shall bind on earth shall be bound in heaven; and whatever you loose on earth shall be loosed in heaven.
19"Again I say to you, that if two of you agree on earth about anything that they may ask, it shall be done for them by My Father who is in heaven.
20"For where two or three have gathered together in My name, there I am in their midst."

Forgiveness
21Then Peter came and said to Him, "Lord, how often shall my brother sin against me and I forgive him? Up to seven times?"
22Jesus *said to him, "I do not say to you, up to seven times, but up to seventy times seven.
23"For this reason the kingdom of heaven may be compared to a certain king who wished to settle accounts with his slaves.
24"And when he had begun to settle *them*, there was brought to him one who owed him *ten thousand talents.
25"But since he did not have *the means* to repay, his lord commanded him to be sold, along with his wife and children and all that he had, and repayment to be made.
26"The slave therefore falling down, prostrated himself before him, saying, 'Have patience with me, and I will repay you everything.'
27"And the lord of that slave felt compassion and released him and forgave

ἐὰν δὲ καὶ τῆς ἐκκλησίας παρακούσῃ,
and if even the church he refuses to hear,
ἔστω σοι ὥσπερ ὁ ἐθνικὸς καὶ
let him be to thee as the gentile and
ὁ τελώνης. 18 Ἀμὴν λέγω ὑμῖν,
the tax-collector. Truly I say to you,
ὅσα ἐὰν δήσητε ἐπὶ τῆς γῆς ἔσται
whatever things ye bind on the earth shall be
δεδεμένα ἐν οὐρανῷ, καὶ ὅσα ἐὰν
having been bound in heaven, and whatever things
λύσητε ἐπὶ τῆς γῆς ἔσται λελυμένα
ye loose on the earth shall be having been loosed
ἐν οὐρανῷ. 19 Πάλιν [ἀμὴν] λέγω
in heaven. Again truly I say
ὑμῖν ὅτι ἐὰν δύο συμφωνήσωσιν ἐξ
to you that if two agree of
ὑμῶν ἐπὶ τῆς γῆς περὶ παντὸς πράγ-
you on the earth concerning every thing
ματος οὗ ἐὰν αἰτήσωνται, γενήσεται
whatever they ask, it shall be
αὐτοῖς παρὰ τοῦ πατρός μου τοῦ ἐν
to them from the Father of me - in
οὐρανοῖς. 20 οὗ γάρ εἰσιν δύο ἢ τρεῖς
heavens. For where are two or three
συνηγμένοι εἰς τὸ ἐμὸν ὄνομα, ἐκεῖ εἰμι
having been assembled in - my name, there I am
ἐν μέσῳ αὐτῶν.
in [the] midst of them.
21 Τότε προσελθὼν ὁ Πέτρος εἶπεν
Then approaching - Peter said
αὐτῷ· κύριε, ποσάκις ἁμαρτήσει εἰς
to him: Lord, how often will sin against
ἐμὲ ὁ ἀδελφός μου καὶ ἀφήσω αὐτῷ;
me the brother of me and I will forgive him?
ἕως ἑπτάκις; 22 λέγει αὐτῷ ὁ Ἰησοῦς·
until seven times? says to him - Jesus:
οὐ λέγω σοι ἕως ἑπτάκις, ἀλλὰ
I tell not to thee until seven times, but
ἕως ἑβδομηκοντάκις ἑπτά. 23 Διὰ τοῦτο
until seventy times seven. Therefore
ὡμοιώθη ἡ βασιλεία τῶν οὐρανῶν
was(is) likened the kingdom of the heavens
ἀνθρώπῳ βασιλεῖ, ὃς ἠθέλησεν συνᾶραι
to a man a king, who wished to take
λόγον μετὰ τῶν δούλων αὐτοῦ. 24 ἀρξα-
account with the slaves of him. And
μένου δὲ αὐτοῦ συναίρειν, προσήχθη
beginning him to take, was brought forward
= as he began
εἷς αὐτῷ ὀφειλέτης μυρίων ταλάντων.
one to him debtor of ten thousand talents.
25 μὴ ἔχοντος δὲ αὐτοῦ ἀποδοῦναι, ἐκελευσεν
And not having him to repay, commanded
= as he had not
αὐτὸν ὁ κύριος πραθῆναι καὶ τὴν
him the lord to be sold and the(his)
γυναῖκα καὶ τὰ τέκνα καὶ πάντα ὅσα
wife and - children and all things whatever
ἔχει, καὶ ἀποδοθῆναι. 26 πεσὼν οὖν ὁ
he has, and to be repaid. Falling therefore the
δοῦλος προσεκύνει αὐτῷ λέγων· μακρο-
slave did obeisance to him saying: Defer
θύμησον ἐπ' ἐμοί, καὶ πάντα ἀποδώσω
anger over me, and all things I will repay
σοι. 27 σπλαγχνισθεὶς δὲ ὁ κύριος τοῦ
thee. And filled with tenderness the lord
δούλου ἐκείνου ἀπέλυσεν αὐτόν, καὶ τὸ
slave of that released him, and the

church; and if he refuses to listen even to the church, treat him as you would a pagan or a tax collector.
18"I tell you the truth, whatever you bind on earth will be" bound in heaven, and whatever you loose on earth will be" loosed in heaven.
19"Again, I tell you that if two of you on earth agree about anything you ask for, it will be done for you by my Father in heaven. 20For where two or three come together in my name, there am I with them."

The Parable of the Unmerciful Servant
21Then Peter came to Jesus and asked, "Lord, how many times shall I forgive my brother when he sins against me? Up to seven times?"
22Jesus answered, "I tell you, not seven times, but seventy-seven times. v
23"Therefore, the kingdom of heaven is like a king who wanted to settle accounts with his servants. 24As he began the settlement, a man who owed him ten thousand talents w was brought to him. 25Since he was not able to pay, the master ordered that he and his wife and his children and all that he had be sold to repay the debt.
26"The servant fell on his knees before him. 'Be patient with me,' he begged, 'and I will pay back everything.' 27The servant's master took pity on him,

*About $10,000,000 in silver content but worth much more in buying power

"18 Or *have been*
v22 Or *seventy times seven*
w24 That is, millions of dollars

him the debt.
28"But that slave went out and found one of his fellow slaves who owed him a hundred ʲdenarii; and he seized him and *began* to choke *him,* saying, 'Pay back what you owe.'
29"So his fellow slave fell down and *began* to entreat him, saying, 'Have patience with me and I will repay you.'
30"He was unwilling however, but went and threw him in prison until he should pay back what was owed.
31"So when his fellow slaves saw what had happened, they were deeply grieved and came and reported to their lord all that had happened.
32"Then summoning him, his lord *said to him, 'You wicked slave, I forgave you all that debt because you entreated me.
33"Should you not also have had mercy on your fellow slave, even as I had mercy on you?'
34"And his lord, moved with anger, handed him over to the torturers until he should repay all that was owed him.
35"So shall My heavenly Father also do to you, if each of you does not forgive his brother from your heart.''

δάνειον ἀφῆκεν αὐτῷ.   28 ἐξελθὼν δὲ
loan   forgave   him.   But going out
ὁ   δοῦλος   ἐκεῖνος   εὗρεν   ἕνα   τῶν
-    slave   that   found   one   of the
συνδούλων αὐτοῦ, ὃς ὤφειλεν αὐτὸν ἑκατὸν
fellow-slaves of him, who owed   him   a hundred
δηνάρια,   καὶ   κρατήσας   αὐτὸν   ἔπνιγεν
denarii,   and   seizing   him   throttled
λέγων·   ἀπόδος   εἴ   τι   ὀφείλεις.
saying: Repay   if   something thou owest.
29 πεσὼν   οὖν   ὁ   σύνδουλος   αὐτοῦ   παρε-
   Falling therefore the fellow-slave of him   be-
κάλει   αὐτὸν   λέγων·   μακροθύμησον   ἐπ’
sought him   saying: Defer anger   over
ἐμοί,   καὶ   ἀποδώσω   σοι.   30 ὁ   δὲ   οὐκ
me,   and   I will repay thee.   But he   not
ἤθελεν,   ἀλλὰ   ἀπελθὼν   ἔβαλεν   αὐτὸν   εἰς
wished,   but   going away threw   him   into
φυλακὴν   ἕως   ἀποδῷ   τὸ   ὀφειλόμενον.
prison   until he should repay the thing owing.
31 ἰδόντες   οὖν   οἱ   σύνδουλοι   αὐτοῦ   τὰ
   Seeing   therefore the fellow-slaves of him the things
γενόμενα   ἐλυπήθησαν   σφόδρα,   καὶ
having taken place they were grieved exceedingly, and
ἐλθόντες   διεσάφησαν   τῷ   κυρίῳ   ἑαυτῶν
coming   explained   to the lord   of themselves
πάντα   τὰ   γενόμενα.   32 τότε   προσ-
all   the things having taken place. Then   ¹call-
καλεσάμενος   αὐτὸν   ὁ   κύριος   αὐτοῦ   λέγει
ing ²forward   ²him   the lord   of him   says
αὐτῷ·   δοῦλε   πονηρέ,   πᾶσαν   τὴν   ὀφειλὴν
to him: ¹Slave ¹wicked, all   -   debt
ἐκείνην   ἀφῆκά   σοι,   ἐπεὶ   παρεκάλεσάς   με·
that   I forgave thee, since thou besoughtest me;
33 οὐκ   ἔδει   καὶ   σὲ   ἐλεῆσαι   τὸν
   did it not behove also thee to pity   the
σύνδουλόν   σου,   ὡς   κἀγὼ   σὲ   ἠλέησα;
fellow-slave of thee, as   I also   thee pitied?
34 καὶ   ὀργισθεὶς   ὁ   κύριος   αὐτοῦ
   And   being angry the lord   of him
παρέδωκεν   αὐτὸν   τοῖς   βασανισταῖς   ἕως   οὗ
delivered   him   to the tormentors   until
ἀποδῷ   πᾶν   τὸ   ὀφειλόμενον   αὐτῷ.
he should repay all   the thing owing   to him.
35 Οὕτως   καὶ   ὁ   πατήρ   μου   ὁ   οὐράνιος
   Thus   also the Father of me the heavenly
ποιήσει   ὑμῖν,   ἐὰν   μὴ   ἀφῆτε   ἕκαστος
will do   to you, unless ye forgive each one
τῷ   ἀδελφῷ   αὐτοῦ   ἀπὸ   τῶν   καρδιῶν
the brother   of him   from   the   hearts
ὑμῶν.
of you.

---

canceled the debt and let him go.
28"But when that servant went out, he found one of his fellow servants who owed him a hundred denarii. ˣ He grabbed him and began to choke him. 'Pay back what you owe me!' he demanded.
29"His fellow servant fell to his knees and begged him, 'Be patient with me, and I will pay you back.'
30"But he refused. Instead, he went off and had the man thrown into prison until he could pay the debt.
31When the other servants saw what had happened, they were greatly distressed and went and told their master everything that had happened.
32"Then the master called the servant in. 'You wicked servant,' he said, 'I canceled all that debt of yours because you begged me to.
33Shouldn't you have had mercy on your fellow servant just as I had on you?'
34In anger his master turned him over to the jailers to be tortured, until he should pay back all he owed.
35"This is how my heavenly Father will treat each of you unless you forgive your brother from your heart.''

Chapter 19

Concerning Divorce

AND it came about that when Jesus had finished these words, He departed from Galilee, and came into the region of Judea beyond the Jordan; ²and great multitudes followed Him, and He healed them there.

---

19 Καὶ   ἐγένετο   ὅτε   ἐτέλεσεν   ὁ
   And   it came to pass when ended   -
Ἰησοῦς   τοὺς   λόγους   τούτους,   μετῆρεν
Jesus   the   words   these,   he removed
ἀπὸ   τῆς   Γαλιλαίας   καὶ   ἦλθεν   εἰς   τὰ
from   -   Galilee   and   came   into the
ὅρια   τῆς   Ἰουδαίας   πέραν   τοῦ   Ἰορδάνου.
borders -   of Judæa   across   the   Jordan.
2 καὶ   ἠκολούθησαν   αὐτῷ   ὄχλοι   πολλοί,
  And   followed   him   crowds   many,
καὶ   ἐθεράπευσεν   αὐτοὺς   ἐκεῖ.
and   he healed   them   there.

Chapter 19

Divorce

WHEN Jesus had finished saying these things, he left Galilee and went into the region of Judea to the other side of the Jordan. ²Large crowds followed him, and he healed them there.

3And *some* Pharisees came to Him, testing Him, and saying, "Is it lawful *for a man* to divorce his wife for any cause at all?"
4And He answered and said, "Have you not read, that He who created *them* from the beginning MADE THEM MALE AND FEMALE,
5and said, 'FOR THIS CAUSE A MAN SHALL LEAVE HIS FATHER AND MOTHER, AND SHALL CLEAVE TO HIS WIFE; AND THE TWO SHALL BECOME ONE FLESH'?
6"Consequently they are no longer two, but one flesh. What therefore God has joined together, let no man separate."
7They *said to Him, "Why then did Moses command to GIVE HER A CERTIFICATE OF DIVORCE AND SEND *her* AWAY?"
8He *said to them, "Because of your hardness of heart, Moses permitted you to divorce your wives; but from the beginning it has not been this way.
9"And I say to you, whoever divorces his wife, except for immorality, and marries another woman commits adultery."
10The disciples *said to Him, "If the relationship of the man with his wife is like this, it is better not to marry."
11But He said to them, "Not all men *can* accept this statement, but *only* those to whom it has been given.
12"For there are eunuchs who were born that way from their mother's womb; and there are eunuchs who were made eunuchs by men; and there are *also* eunuchs who made themselves eunuchs for the sake of the kingdom of heaven. He who is able to accept *this*, let him accept *it*."

3 Καὶ προσῆλθον αὐτῷ Φαρισαῖοι
And approached to him Pharisees
πειράζοντες αὐτὸν καὶ λέγοντες· εἰ ἔξεστιν
tempting him and saying: If it is lawful
ἀπολῦσαι τὴν γυναῖκα αὐτοῦ κατὰ πᾶσαν
to dismiss the wife of him for every
αἰτίαν; **4** ὁ δὲ ἀποκριθεὶς εἶπεν· οὐκ
cause? And he answering said: not
ἀνέγνωτε ὅτι ὁ κτίσας ἀπ'
Did ye read that the [one] creating from
ἀρχῆς ἄρσεν καὶ θῆλυ ἐποίησεν αὐτούς;
[the] beginning male and female made them?
5 καὶ εἶπεν· ἕνεκα τούτου καταλείψει
And he said: For the sake of this shall leave
ἄνθρωπος τὸν πατέρα καὶ τὴν μητέρα
a man the(his) father and the(his) mother
καὶ κολληθήσεται τῇ γυναικὶ αὐτοῦ,
and shall cleave to the wife of him,
καὶ ἔσονται οἱ δύο εἰς σάρκα μίαν·
and ²shall be ¹the ²two ³in ⁴flesh ⁵one;
6 ὥστε οὐκέτι εἰσὶν δύο ἀλλὰ σὰρξ μία.
so as no longer are they two but flesh one.
ὃ οὖν ὁ θεὸς συνέζευξεν, ἄνθρωπος
What therefore – God yoked together, a man
μὴ χωριζέτω. **7** λέγουσιν αὐτῷ· τί οὖν
let not separate. They say to him: Why then
Μωϋσῆς ἐνετείλατο δοῦναι βιβλίον ἀπο-
²Moses ¹did ²enjoin to give a document of
στασίου καὶ ἀπολῦσαι; **8** λέγει αὐτοῖς·
divorce and to dismiss? He says to them:
ὅτι Μωϋσῆς πρὸς τὴν σκληροκαρδίαν
– Moses in view of the obduracy
ὑμῶν ἐπέτρεψεν ὑμῖν ἀπολῦσαι τὰς
of you allowed you to dismiss the
γυναῖκας ὑμῶν· ἀπ' ἀρχῆς δὲ οὐ
wives of you; but from [the] beginning not
γέγονεν οὕτως. **9** λέγω δὲ ὑμῖν ὅτι
it has been so. But I say to you that
ὃς ἂν ἀπολύσῃ τὴν γυναῖκα αὐτοῦ
whoever dismisses the wife of him
μὴ ἐπὶ πορνείᾳ καὶ γαμήσῃ ἄλλην,
not of(for) fornication and marries another,
μοιχᾶται. **10** λέγουσιν αὐτῷ οἱ μαθηταί·
commits adultery. Say to him the disciples:
εἰ οὕτως ἐστὶν ἡ αἰτία τοῦ ἀνθρώπου
If so is the cause of the man
μετὰ τῆς γυναικός, οὐ συμφέρει γαμῆσαι.
with the wife, it is not expedient to marry.
11 ὁ δὲ εἶπεν αὐτοῖς· οὐ πάντες χωροῦσιν
And he said to them: Not all men grasp
τὸν λόγον τοῦτον, ἀλλ' οἷς δέδοται.
– saying this, but [those] to whom it has been given.
12 εἰσὶν γὰρ εὐνοῦχοι οἵτινες ἐκ κοιλίας
For there are eunuchs who from [the] womb
μητρὸς ἐγεννήθησαν οὕτως, καὶ εἰσὶν
of a mother were born so, and there are
εὐνοῦχοι οἵτινες εὐνουχίσθησαν ὑπὸ τῶν
eunuchs who were made eunuchs by –
ἀνθρώπων, καὶ εἰσὶν εὐνοῦχοι οἵτινες
men, and there are eunuchs who
εὐνούχισαν ἑαυτοὺς διὰ τὴν
made eunuchs themselves on account of the
βασιλείαν τῶν οὐρανῶν. ὁ δυνάμενος
kingdom of the heavens. The [one] being able
χωρεῖν χωρείτω.
to grasp [it] let him grasp.

3Some Pharisees came to him to test him. They asked, "Is it lawful for a man to divorce his wife for any and every reason?"
4"Haven't you read," he replied, "that at the beginning the Creator 'made them male and female,'ʸ 5and said, 'For this reason a man will leave his father and mother and be united to his wife, and the two will become one flesh'ᶻ? 6So they are no longer two, but one. Therefore what God has joined together, let man not separate."
7"Why then," they asked, "did Moses command that a man give his wife a certificate of divorce and send her away?"
8Jesus replied, "Moses permitted you to divorce your wives because your hearts were hard. But it was not this way from the beginning. 9I tell you that anyone who divorces his wife, except for marital unfaithfulness, and marries another woman commits adultery."
10The disciples said to him, "If this is the situation between a husband and wife, it is better not to marry."
11Jesus replied, "Not everyone can accept this word, but only those to whom it has been given. 12For some are eunuchs because they were born that way; others were made that way by men; and others have renounced marriageᵃ because of the kingdom of heaven. The one who can accept this should accept it."

ʸ4 Gen. 1:27
ᶻ5 Gen. 2:24
ᵃ12 Or *have made themselves eunuchs*

Jesus Blesses Little Children

13Then *some* children were brought to Him so that He might lay His hands on them and pray; and the disciples rebuked them. 14But Jesus said, "Let the children alone, and do not hinder them from coming to Me; for the kingdom of heaven belongs to such as these." 15And after laying His hands on them, He departed from there.

The Rich Young Ruler

16And behold, one came to Him and said, "Teacher, what good thing shall I do that I may obtain eternal life?" 17And He said to him, "Why are you asking Me about what is good? There is *only* One who is good; but if you wish to enter into life, keep the commandments." 18He *said to Him, "Which ones?" And Jesus said, "YOU SHALL NOT COMMIT MURDER; YOU SHALL NOT COMMIT ADULTERY; YOU SHALL NOT STEAL; YOU SHALL NOT BEAR FALSE WITNESS; 19HONOR YOUR FATHER AND MOTHER; and YOU SHALL LOVE YOUR NEIGHBOR AS YOURSELF." 20The young man *said to Him, "All these things I have kept; what am I still lacking?" 21Jesus said to him, "If you wish to be complete, go *and* sell your possessions and give to *the* poor, and you shall have treasure in heaven; and come, follow Me." 22But when the young man heard this statement, he went away grieving; for he was one who owned much property. 23And Jesus said to His disciples, "Truly I say to you, it is hard for a rich man to enter the kingdom of heaven. 24And again I say to you, it is easier for a camel to go through the eye of a

---

13 Τότε προσηνέχθησαν αὐτῷ παιδία,
Then were brought to him children,

ἵνα τὰς χεῖρας ἐπιθῇ αὐτοῖς καὶ
that the(his) hands he should put on them and

προσεύξηται· οἱ δὲ μαθηταὶ ἐπετίμησαν
pray; but the disciples rebuked

αὐτοῖς. 14 ὁ δὲ Ἰησοῦς εἶπεν· ἄφετε
them. – But Jesus said: Permit

τὰ παιδία καὶ μὴ κωλύετε αὐτὰ ἐλθεῖν
the children and do not prevent them to come

πρός με· τῶν γὰρ τοιούτων ἐστὶν ἡ
unto me; – for of such is the

βασιλεία τῶν οὐρανῶν. 15 καὶ ἐπιθεὶς
kingdom of the heavens. And putting on

τὰς χεῖρας αὐτοῖς ἐπορεύθη ἐκεῖθεν.
the(his) hands on them he went thence.

16 Καὶ ἰδοὺ εἷς προσελθὼν αὐτῷ εἶπεν·
And behold one approaching to him said:

διδάσκαλε, τί ἀγαθὸν ποιήσω ἵνα
Teacher, what good thing may I do that

σχῶ ζωὴν αἰώνιον; ὁ δὲ εἶπεν αὐτῷ·
I may have life eternal? And he said to him:

17 τί με ἐρωτᾷς περὶ τοῦ ἀγαθοῦ;
Why me questionest thou concerning the good?

εἷς ἐστιν ὁ ἀγαθός· εἰ δὲ θέλεις εἰς
one is the good; but if thou wishest into

τὴν ζωὴν εἰσελθεῖν, τήρει τὰς ἐντολάς.
– life to enter, keep the commandments.

18 λέγει αὐτῷ· ποίας; ὁ δὲ Ἰησοῦς
He says to him: Which? – And Jesus

ἔφη· τὸ οὐ φονεύσεις, οὐ μοιχεύσεις,
said: – Thou shalt not kill, Thou shalt not commit adultery,

οὐ κλέψεις, οὐ ψευδομαρτυρήσεις,
Thou shalt not steal, Thou shalt not bear false witness,

19 τίμα τὸν πατέρα καὶ τὴν μητέρα,
Honour the(thy) father and the(thy) mother,

καὶ ἀγαπήσεις τὸν πλησίον σου ὡς
and Thou shalt love the neighbour of thee as

σεαυτόν. 20 λέγει αὐτῷ ὁ νεανίσκος·
thyself. Says to him the young man:

ταῦτα πάντα ἐφύλαξα· τί ἔτι ὑστερῶ;
These things all I kept; what yet do I lack?

21 ἔφη αὐτῷ ὁ Ἰησοῦς· εἰ θέλεις τέλειος
Said to him – Jesus: If thou wishest perfect

εἶναι, ὕπαγε πώλησόν σου τὰ ὑπάρχοντα
to be, go sell of thee the belongings

καὶ δὸς πτωχοῖς, καὶ ἕξεις
and give to [the] poor, and thou shalt have

θησαυρὸν ἐν οὐρανοῖς, καὶ δεῦρο ἀκολούθει
treasure in heavens, and come follow

μοι. 22 ἀκούσας δὲ ὁ νεανίσκος τὸν
me. But hearing the young man the

λόγον [τοῦτον] ἀπῆλθεν λυπούμενος·
word this went away grieving;

ἦν γὰρ ἔχων κτήματα πολλά. 23 Ὁ
for he was having possessions many.

δὲ Ἰησοῦς εἶπεν τοῖς μαθηταῖς αὐτοῦ·
So Jesus said to the disciples of him:

ἀμὴν λέγω ὑμῖν ὅτι πλούσιος δυσκόλως
Truly I tell you that a rich man hardly

εἰσελεύσεται εἰς τὴν βασιλείαν τῶν
will enter into the kingdom of the

οὐρανῶν. 24 πάλιν δὲ λέγω ὑμῖν,
heavens. And again I tell you,

εὐκοπώτερόν ἐστιν κάμηλον διὰ τρήματος
easier it is a camel through [the] eye

The Little Children and Jesus

13Then little children were brought to Jesus for him to place his hands on them and pray for them. But the disciples rebuked those who brought them. 14Jesus said, "Let the little children come to me, and do not hinder them, for the kingdom of heaven belongs to such as these." 15When he had placed his hands on them, he went on from there.

The Rich Young Man

16Now a man came up to Jesus and asked, "Teacher, what good thing must I do to get eternal life?" 17"Why do you ask me about what is good?" Jesus replied. "There is only One who is good. If you want to enter life, obey the commandments." 18"Which ones?" the man inquired. Jesus replied, " 'Do not murder, do not commit adultery, do not steal, do not give false testimony, 19honor your father and mother,'[b] and 'love your neighbor as yourself.'[c]" 20"All these I have kept," the young man said. "What do I still lack?" 21Jesus answered, "If you want to be perfect, go, sell your possessions and give to the poor, and you will have treasure in heaven. Then come, follow me." 22When the young man heard this, he went away sad, because he had great wealth. 23Then Jesus said to his disciples, "I tell you the truth, it is hard for a rich man to enter the kingdom of heaven. 24Again I tell you, it is easier for a camel to go through the eye of a

---

b19 Exodus 20:12-16; Deut. 5:16-20
c19 Lev. 19:18

needle, than for a rich man to enter the kingdom of God."

25And when the disciples heard *this*, they were very astonished and said, "Then who can be saved?"

26And looking upon *them* Jesus said to them, "With men this is impossible, but with God all things are possible."

The Disciples' Reward

27Then Peter answered and said to Him, "Behold, we have left everything and followed You; what then will there be for us?"

28And Jesus said to them, "Truly I say to you, that you who have followed Me, in the regeneration when the Son of Man will sit on His glorious throne, you also shall sit upon twelve thrones, judging the twelve tribes of Israel.

29"And everyone who has left houses or brothers or sisters or father or mother[k] or children or farms for My name's sake, shall receive many times as much, and shall inherit eternal life.

30"But many *who are* first will be last; and *the* last, first.

ῥαφίδος εἰσελθεῖν ἢ πλούσιον εἰς τὴν
of a needle to enter than a rich man into the

βασιλείαν τοῦ θεοῦ. 25 ἀκούσαντες δὲ
kingdom - of God.   And hearing

οἱ μαθηταὶ ἐξεπλήσσοντο σφόδρα
the disciples were astounded exceedingly

λέγοντες· τίς ἄρα δύναται σωθῆναι;
saying: Who then can *to* be saved?

26 ἐμβλέψας δὲ ὁ Ἰησοῦς εἶπεν
And looking upon - Jesus said

αὐτοῖς· παρὰ ἀνθρώποις τοῦτο ἀδύνατόν
to them: With men this impossible

ἐστιν, παρὰ δὲ θεῷ πάντα δυνατά.
is, but with God all things [are] possible.

27 Τότε ἀποκριθεὶς ὁ Πέτρος εἶπεν αὐτῷ·
Then answering - Peter said to him:

ἰδοὺ ἡμεῖς ἀφήκαμεν πάντα καὶ
Behold we left all things and

ἠκολουθήσαμέν σοι· τί ἄρα ἔσται
followed thee; what then shall be = shall we have?

ἡμῖν; 28 ὁ δὲ Ἰησοῦς εἶπεν αὐτοῖς·
to us? - And Jesus said to them:

ἀμὴν λέγω ὑμῖν ὅτι ὑμεῖς οἱ ἀκολουθή-
Truly I tell you that ye the [ones] having

σαντές μοι, ἐν τῇ παλιγγενεσίᾳ, ὅταν
followed me, in the regeneration, when

καθίσῃ ὁ υἱὸς τοῦ ἀνθρώπου ἐπὶ θρόνου
sits the Son - of man on [the] throne

δόξης αὐτοῦ, καθήσεσθε καὶ αὐτοὶ ἐπὶ
of glory of him, ye will sit also [your]selves on

δώδεκα θρόνους κρίνοντες τὰς δώδεκα
twelve thrones judging the twelve

φυλὰς τοῦ Ἰσραήλ. 29 καὶ πᾶς ὅστις
tribes - of Israel. And everyone who

ἀφῆκεν οἰκίας ἢ ἀδελφοὺς ἢ ἀδελφὰς ἢ
left houses or brothers or sisters or

πατέρα ἢ μητέρα ἢ τέκνα ἢ ἀγροὺς
father or mother or children or fields

ἕνεκεν τοῦ ἐμοῦ ὀνόματος, πολλαπλα-
for the sake of - my name,   mani-

σίονα λήμψεται καὶ ζωὴν αἰώνιον
fold will receive and life eternal

κληρονομήσει. 30 Πολλοὶ δὲ ἔσονται πρῶτοι
will inherit. But many ²will be ¹first

ἔσχατοι καὶ ἔσχατοι πρῶτοι.
¹last and last first.

---

needle than for a rich man to enter the kingdom of God."

25When the disciples heard this, they were greatly astonished and asked, "Who then can be saved?"

26Jesus looked at them and said, "With man this is impossible, but with God all things are possible."

27Peter answered him, "We have left everything to follow you! What then will there be for us?"

28Jesus said to them, "I tell you the truth, at the renewal of all things, when the Son of Man sits on his glorious throne, you who have followed me will also sit on twelve thrones, judging the twelve tribes of Israel. 29And everyone who has left houses or brothers or sisters or father or mother[d] or children or fields for my sake will receive a hundred times as much and will inherit eternal life. 30But many who are first will be last, and many who are last will be first.

Chapter 20

Laborers in the Vineyard

" FOR the kingdom of heaven is like a landowner who went out early in the morning to hire laborers for his vineyard.

2"And when he had agreed with the laborers for a *l*denarius for the day, he sent them into his vineyard.

3"And he went out about the *m*third hour and saw others standing idle in the market place;

4and to those he said,

---

20 Ὁμοία γάρ ἐστιν ἡ βασιλεία τῶν
   For like is the kingdom of the

οὐρανῶν ἀνθρώπῳ οἰκοδεσπότῃ, ὅστις
heavens to a man a housemaster, who

ἐξῆλθεν ἅμα πρωῒ μισθώσασθαι
went out early in the morning to hire

ἐργάτας εἰς τὸν ἀμπελῶνα αὐτοῦ. 2 συμ-
workmen in the vineyard of him. And

φωνήσας δὲ μετὰ τῶν ἐργατῶν ἐκ δηναρίου
agreeing with the workmen out of(for) a denarius

τὴν ἡμέραν ἀπέστειλεν αὐτοὺς εἰς τὸν
the day he sent them into the

ἀμπελῶνα αὐτοῦ. 3 καὶ ἐξελθὼν περὶ
vineyard of him. And going out about

τρίτην ὥραν εἶδεν ἄλλους ἑστῶτας
[the] third hour he saw others standing

ἐν τῇ ἀγορᾷ ἀργούς, 4 καὶ ἐκείνοις
in the marketplace idle, and to those

Chapter 20

The Parable of the Workers in the Vineyard

" FOR the kingdom of heaven is like a landowner who went out early in the morning to hire men to work in his vineyard. 2He agreed to pay them a denarius for the day and sent them into his vineyard.

3"About the third hour he went out and saw others standing in the marketplace doing nothing. 4He told them, 'You also go and

---

k Many mss. add here, *or wife*
l The denarius was equivalent to one day's wage
m I.e., 9 a.m.

d 29 Some manuscripts *mother or wife*

'You too go into the vineyard, and whatever is right I will give you.' And *so* they went.

5"Again he went out about the ⁿsixth and the ninth hour, and did the same thing.

6"And about the ᵒeleventh *hour* he went out, and found others standing; and he *said to them, 'Why have you been standing here idle all day long?'

7"They *said to him, 'Because no one hired us.' He *said to them, 'You too go into the vineyard.'

8"And when evening had come, the owner of the vineyard *said to his foreman, 'Call the laborers and pay them their wages, beginning with the last *group* to the first.'

9"And when those *hired* about the eleventh hour came, each one received a ᵖdenarius.

10"And when those *hired* first came, they thought that they would receive more; and they also received each one a ᵖdenarius.

11"And when they received it, they grumbled at the landowner,

12saying, 'These last men have worked *only* one hour, and you have made them equal to us who have borne the burden and the scorching heat of the day.'

13"But he answered and said to one of them, 'Friend, I am doing you no wrong; did you not agree with me for a ᵖdenarius?

14'Take what is yours and go your way, but I wish to give to this last man the same as to you.

15'Is it not lawful for me to do what I wish with what is my own? Or is your eye envious because I am generous?'

εἶπεν· ὑπάγετε καὶ ὑμεῖς εἰς τὸν
said: Go also ye into the

ἀμπελῶνα, καὶ ὃ ἐὰν ᾖ δίκαιον δώσω
vineyard, and whatever may be just I will give

ὑμῖν. οἱ δὲ ἀπῆλθον. 5 πάλιν [δὲ]
you. And they went. And again

ἐξελθὼν περὶ ἕκτην καὶ ἐνάτην ὥραν
going out about [the] sixth and [the] ninth hour

ἐποίησεν ὡσαύτως. 6 περὶ δὲ τὴν
he did similarly. And about the

ἑνδεκάτην ἐξελθὼν εὗρεν ἄλλους ἑστῶτας,
eleventh going out he found others standing,

καὶ λέγει αὐτοῖς· τί ὧδε ἑστήκατε
and says to them: Why here stand ye

ὅλην τὴν ἡμέραν ἀργοί; 7 λέγουσιν αὐτῷ·
all the day idle? They say to him:

ὅτι οὐδεὶς ἡμᾶς ἐμισθώσατο. λέγει αὐτοῖς·
Because no one us hired. He says to them:

ὑπάγετε καὶ ὑμεῖς εἰς τὸν ἀμπελῶνα.
Go also ye into the vineyard.

8 ὀψίας δὲ γενομένης λέγει ὁ κύριος
And evening having come* says the lord
= when evening had come

τοῦ ἀμπελῶνος τῷ ἐπιτρόπῳ αὐτοῦ·
of the vineyard to the steward of him:

κάλεσον τοὺς ἐργάτας καὶ ἀπόδος τὸν
Call the workmen and pay the

μισθόν, ἀρξάμενος ἀπὸ τῶν ἐσχάτων
wage, beginning from the last ones

ἕως τῶν πρώτων. 9 ἐλθόντες δὲ οἱ
until the first. And coming the [ones]

περὶ τὴν ἑνδεκάτην ὥραν ἔλαβον ἀνὰ
about the eleventh hour received each

δηνάριον. 10 καὶ ἐλθόντες οἱ πρῶτοι
a denarius. And coming the first

ἐνόμισαν ὅτι πλεῖον λήμψονται· καὶ
supposed that more they will receive; and

ἔλαβον τὸ ἀνὰ δηνάριον καὶ αὐτοί.
they received the ²each ¹denarius also [them]selves.

11 λαβόντες δὲ ἐγόγγυζον κατὰ τοῦ
And receiving they grumbled against the

οἰκοδεσπότου λέγοντες· 12 οὗτοι οἱ ἔσχατοι
housemaster saying: These - last

μίαν ὥραν ἐποίησαν, καὶ ἴσους αὐτοὺς
one hour wrought, and equal them

ἡμῖν ἐποίησας τοῖς βαστάσασι τὸ
to us thou madest the [ones] having borne the

βάρος τῆς ἡμέρας καὶ τὸν καύσωνα.
burden of the day and the heat.

13 ὁ δὲ ἀποκριθεὶς ἑνὶ αὐτῶν εἶπεν·
But he answering one of them said:

ἑταῖρε, οὐκ ἀδικῶ σε· οὐχὶ
Comrade, I do not injure thee; not

δηναρίου συνεφώνησάς μοι; 14 ἆρον
of(for) a denarius thou didst agree with me? take

τὸ σὸν καὶ ὕπαγε· θέλω δὲ
the thine and go; but I wish
= that which is thine

τούτῳ τῷ ἐσχάτῳ δοῦναι ὡς καὶ
to this - last man to give as also

σοί· 15 οὐκ ἔξεστίν μοι ὃ θέλω
to thee; is it not lawful to me what I wish

ποιῆσαι ἐν τοῖς ἐμοῖς; ἢ ὁ
to do among the my things? or the

ὀφθαλμός σου πονηρός ἐστιν ὅτι ἐγὼ
eye of thee evil is because I

---

work in my vineyard, and I will pay you whatever is right.' 5So they went.

"He went out again about the sixth hour and the ninth hour and did the same thing. 6About the eleventh hour he went out and found still others standing around. He asked them, 'Why have you been standing here all day long doing nothing?'

7"'Because no one has hired us,' they answered.

"He said to them, 'You also go and work in my vineyard.'

8"When evening came, the owner of the vineyard said to his foreman, 'Call the workers and pay them their wages, beginning with the last ones hired and going on to the first.'

9"The workers who were hired about the eleventh hour came and each received a denarius. 10So when those came who were hired first, they expected to receive more. But each one of them also received a denarius. 11When they received it, they began to grumble against the landowner. 12'These men who were hired last worked only one hour,' they said, 'and you have made them equal to us who have borne the burden of the work and the heat of the day.'

13"But he answered one of them, 'Friend, I am not being unfair to you. Didn't you agree to work for a denarius? 14Take your pay and go. I want to give the man who was hired last the same as I gave you. 15Don't I have the right to do what I want with my own money? Or are you envious because I am generous?'

ⁿ I.e., Noon and 3 p.m.
ᵒ I.e., 5 p.m.
ᵖ The denarius was equivalent to one day's wage

16"Thus the last shall be first, and the first last."

Death, Resurrection Foretold

17And as Jesus was about to go up to Jerusalem, He took the twelve *disciples* aside by themselves, and on the way He said to them, 18"Behold, we are going up to Jerusalem; and the Son of Man will be delivered to the chief priests and scribes, and they will condemn Him to death, 19and will deliver Him to the Gentiles to mock and scourge and crucify *Him,* and on the third day He will be raised up."

Preferment Asked

20Then the mother of the sons of Zebedee came to Him with her sons, bowing down, and making a request of Him. 21And He said to her, "What do you wish?" She *said to Him, "Command that in Your kingdom these two sons of mine may sit, one on Your right and one on Your left." 22But Jesus answered and said, "You do not know what you are asking for. Are you able to drink the cup that I am about to drink?" They *said to Him, "We are able." 23He *said to them, "My cup you shall drink; but to sit on My right and on *My left, this is not Mine to give, but it is for those for whom it has been prepared by My Father." 24And hearing *this,* the ten became indignant with the two brothers. 25But Jesus called them to Himself, and said, "You know that the rulers of the Gentiles lord it over them,

ἀγαθός	εἰμι;	**16** Οὕτως	ἔσονται οἱ ἔσχατοι
good	am?	Thus	will be the last [ones]

πρῶτοι	καὶ οἱ	πρῶτοι	ἔσχατοι.
first	and the	first	last.

17 Μέλλων δὲ ἀναβαίνειν Ἰησοῦς εἰς
And being about to go up Jesus to

Ἱεροσόλυμα παρέλαβεν τοὺς δώδεκα κατ'
Jerusalem he took the twelve private-

ἰδίαν, καὶ ἐν τῇ ὁδῷ εἶπεν αὐτοῖς·
ly, and in the way said to them:

18 ἰδοὺ ἀναβαίνομεν εἰς Ἱεροσόλυμα, καὶ
Behold we are going up to Jerusalem, and

ὁ υἱὸς τοῦ ἀνθρώπου παραδοθήσεται τοῖς
the Son - of man will be delivered to the

ἀρχιερεῦσιν καὶ γραμματεῦσιν, καὶ κατα-
chief priests and scribes, and they will

κρινοῦσιν αὐτὸν εἰς θάνατον, **19** καὶ
condemn him to death, and

παραδώσουσιν αὐτὸν τοῖς ἔθνεσιν εἰς
they will deliver him to the nations for

τὸ ἐμπαῖξαι καὶ μαστιγῶσαι καὶ
- to mock and to scourge and

σταυρῶσαι, καὶ τῇ τρίτῃ ἡμέρᾳ ἐγερθή-
to crucify, and on the third day he will be

σεται.
raised.

20 Τότε προσῆλθεν αὐτῷ ἡ μήτηρ τῶν
Then approached to him the mother of the

υἱῶν Ζεβεδαίου μετὰ τῶν υἱῶν αὐτῆς
sons of Zebedee with the sons of her

προσκυνοῦσα καὶ αἰτοῦσά τι ἀπ' αὐτοῦ.
doing obeisance and asking something from him.

21 ὁ δὲ εἶπεν αὐτῇ· τί θέλεις; λέγει
And he said to her: What wishest thou? She says

αὐτῷ· εἰπὲ ἵνα καθίσωσιν οὗτοι οἱ
to him: Say that may sit these the

δύο υἱοί μου εἷς ἐκ δεξιῶν καὶ εἷς
two sons of me one on [the] right and one

ἐξ εὐωνύμων σου ἐν τῇ βασιλείᾳ
on [the] left of thee in the kingdom

σου. **22** ἀποκριθεὶς δὲ ὁ Ἰησοῦς
of thee. And answering - Jesus

εἶπεν· οὐκ οἴδατε τί αἰτεῖσθε.
said: Ye know not what ye ask.

δύνασθε πιεῖν τὸ ποτήριον ὃ ἐγὼ
Can ye to drink the cup which I

μέλλω πίνειν; λέγουσιν αὐτῷ· δυνάμεθα.
am about to drink? They say to him: We can.

23 λέγει αὐτοῖς· τὸ μὲν ποτήριόν μου
He says to them: Indeed the cup of me

πίεσθε, τὸ δὲ καθίσαι ἐκ δεξιῶν
ye shall drink, - but to sit on [the] right

μου καὶ ἐξ εὐωνύμων οὐκ ἔστιν
of me and on [the] left is not

ἐμὸν τοῦτο δοῦναι, ἀλλ' οἷς ἡτοί-
mine this to give, but to whom it has

μασται ὑπὸ τοῦ πατρός μου. **24** καὶ
been prepared by the Father of me. And

ἀκούσαντες οἱ δέκα ἠγανάκτησαν περὶ
hearing the ten were incensed about

τῶν δύο ἀδελφῶν. **25** ὁ δὲ Ἰησοῦς
the two brothers. - So Jesus

προσκαλεσάμενος αὐτοῖς εἶπεν· οἴδατε
calling forward them said: Ye know

ὅτι οἱ ἄρχοντες τῶν ἐθνῶν κατακυριεύουσιν
that the rulers of the nations lord it over

16"So the last will be first, and the first will be last."

Jesus Again Predicts His Death

17Now as Jesus was going up to Jerusalem, he took the twelve disciples aside and said to them, 18"We are going up to Jerusalem, and the Son of Man will be betrayed to the chief priests and the teachers of the law. They will condemn him to death 19and will turn him over to the Gentiles to be mocked and flogged and crucified. On the third day he will be raised to life!"

A Mother's Request

20Then the mother of Zebedee's sons came to Jesus with her sons and, kneeling down, asked a favor of him.
21"What is it you want?" he asked.
She said, "Grant that one of these two sons of mine may sit at your right and the other at your left in your kingdom."
22"You don't know what you are asking," Jesus said to them. "Can you drink the cup I am going to drink?"
"We can," they answered.
23Jesus said to them, "You will indeed drink from my cup, but to sit at my right or left is not for me to grant. These places belong to those for whom they have been prepared by my Father."
24When the ten heard about this, they were indignant with the two brothers. 25Jesus called them together and said, "You know that the rulers of the Gentiles lord it over them, and

and *their* great men exercise authority over them.

26"It is not so among you, but whoever wishes to become great among you shall be your servant,

27and whoever wishes to be first among you shall be your slave;

28just as the Son of Man did not come to be served, but to serve, and to give His life a ransom for many."

Sight for the Blind

29And as they were going out from Jericho, a great multitude followed Him.

30And behold, two blind men sitting by the road, hearing that Jesus was passing by, cried out, saying, "Lord, have mercy on us, Son of David!"

31And the multitude sternly told them to be quiet; but they cried out all the more, saying, "Lord, have mercy on us, Son of David!"

32And Jesus stopped and called them, and said, "What do you want Me to do for you?"

33They *said to Him, "Lord, *we want* our eyes to be opened."

34And moved with compassion, Jesus touched their eyes; and immediately they regained their sight and followed Him.

αὐτῶν καὶ οἱ μεγάλοι κατεξουσιάζουσιν
them and the great ones have authority over

αὐτῶν. 26 οὐχ οὕτως ἐστὶν ἐν ὑμῖν·
them, Not thus is it among you;

ἀλλ' ὃς ἐὰν θέλῃ ἐν ὑμῖν μέγας γενέσθαι,
but whoever wishes among you great to become,

ἔσται ὑμῶν διάκονος, 27 καὶ ὃς ἂν
will be of you servant, and whoever

θέλῃ ἐν ὑμῖν εἶναι πρῶτος, ἔσται ὑμῶν
wishes among you to be first, shall be of you

δοῦλος· 28 ὥσπερ ὁ υἱὸς τοῦ ἀνθρώπου
slave; as the Son - of man

οὐκ ἦλθεν διακονηθῆναι, ἀλλὰ διακο-
came not to be served, but to

νῆσαι καὶ δοῦναι τὴν ψυχὴν αὐτοῦ
serve and to give the life of him

λύτρον ἀντὶ πολλῶν.
a ransom instead of many.

29 Καὶ ἐκπορευομένων αὐτῶν ἀπὸ Ἰεριχὼ
And going out them* from Jericho
= as they were going out

ἠκολούθησεν αὐτῷ ὄχλος πολύς. 30 καὶ
followed him crowd a much. And

ἰδοὺ δύο τυφλοὶ καθήμενοι παρὰ τὴν
behold two blind men sitting beside the

ὁδόν, ἀκούσαντες ὅτι Ἰησοῦς παράγει,
way, hearing that Jesus is passing by,

ἔκραξαν λέγοντες· κύριε, ἐλέησον ἡμᾶς,
cried out saying: Lord, pity us,

υἱὸς Δαυίδ. 31 ὁ δὲ ὄχλος ἐπετίμησεν
son of David. But the crowd rebuked

αὐτοῖς ἵνα σιωπήσωσιν· οἱ δὲ μεῖζον
them that they should be silent; but they more

ἔκραξαν λέγοντες· κύριε, ἐλέησον ἡμᾶς,
cried out saying: Lord, pity us,

υἱὸς Δαυίδ. 32 καὶ στὰς ὁ Ἰησοῦς
son of David. And standing - Jesus

ἐφώνησεν αὐτοὺς καὶ εἶπεν· τί θέλετε
called them and said: What wish ye

ποιήσω ὑμῖν; 33 λέγουσιν αὐτῷ· κύριε,
I may do to you? They say to him: Lord,

ἵνα ἀνοιγῶσιν οἱ ὀφθαλμοὶ ἡμῶν.
that may be opened the eyes of us.

34 σπλαγχνισθεὶς δὲ ὁ Ἰησοῦς ἥψατο
And being filled with tenderness - Jesus touched

τῶν ὀμμάτων αὐτῶν, καὶ εὐθέως ἀνέβλεψαν
the eyes of them, and immediately they saw again

καὶ ἠκολούθησαν αὐτῷ.
and followed him.

21 Καὶ ὅτε ἤγγισαν εἰς Ἱεροσόλυμα
And when they drew near to Jerusalem

καὶ ἦλθον εἰς Βηθφαγὴ εἰς τὸ ὄρος τῶν
and came to Bethphage to the mount of the

ἐλαιῶν, τότε Ἰησοῦς ἀπέστειλεν δύο
olives, then Jesus sent two

μαθητὰς 2 λέγων αὐτοῖς· πορεύεσθε εἰς
disciples telling them: Go ye into

τὴν κώμην τὴν κατέναντι ὑμῶν, καὶ εὐθὺς
the village - opposite you, and at once

εὑρήσετε ὄνον δεδεμένην καὶ πῶλον μετ'
ye will find an ass *having been* tied and a colt with

αὐτῆς· λύσαντες ἀγάγετέ μοι. 3 καὶ ἐάν
her/it; loosening bring to me. And if

τις ὑμῖν εἴπῃ τι, ἐρεῖτε ὅτι ὁ
anyone to you says anything, ye shall say[,] - The

---

their high officials exercise authority over them. 26Not so with you. Instead, whoever wants to become great among you must be your servant, 27and whoever wants to be first must .be your slave— 28just as the Son of Man did not come to be served, but to serve, and to give his life as a ransom for many."

Two Blind Men Receive Sight

29As Jesus and his disciples were leaving Jericho, a large crowd followed him. 30Two blind men were sitting by the roadside, and when they heard that Jesus was going by, they shouted, "Lord, Son of David, have mercy on us!" 31The crowd rebuked them and told them to be quiet, but they shouted all the louder, "Lord, Son of David, have mercy on us!" 32Jesus stopped and called them. "What do you want me to do for you?" he asked. 33"Lord," they answered, "we want our sight." 34Jesus had compassion on them and touched their eyes. Immediately they received their sight and followed him.

Chapter 21

The Triumphal Entry

AND when they had approached Jerusalem and had come to Bethphage, to the Mount of Olives, then Jesus sent two disciples,

2saying to them, "Go into the village opposite you, and immediately you will find a donkey tied *there* and a colt with her; untie *them*, and bring *them* to Me.

3"And if anyone says something to you, you shall

Chapter 21

The Triumphal Entry

AS they approached Jerusalem and came to Bethphage on the Mount of Olives, Jesus sent two disciples, 2saying to them, "Go to the village ahead of you, and at once you will find a donkey tied there, with her colt by her. Untie them and bring them to me. 3If anyone says anything to you, tell him that the Lord say, 'The Lord has need of them,' and immediately he will send them.''

4Now this took place that what was spoken through the prophet might be fulfilled, saying,

5"SAY TO THE DAUGHTER OF ZION,
'BEHOLD YOUR KING IS COMING TO YOU,
GENTLE, AND MOUNTED ON A DONKEY,
EVEN ON A COLT, THE FOAL OF A BEAST OF BURDEN.' ''

6And the disciples went and did just as Jesus had directed them,

7and brought the donkey and the colt, and laid on them their garments, on which He sat.

8And most of the multitude spread their garments in the road, and others were cutting branches from the trees, and spreading them in the road.

9And the multitudes going before Him, and those who followed after were crying out, saying,
"Hosanna to the Son of David;
BLESSED IS HE WHO COMES IN THE NAME OF THE LORD;
Hosanna in the highest!''

10And when He had entered Jerusalem, all the city was stirred, saying, "Who is this?"

11And the multitudes were saying, "This is the prophet Jesus, from Nazareth in Galilee.''

Cleansing the Temple

12And Jesus entered the temple and cast out all those who were buying and selling in the temple, and overturned the tables of the moneychangers and the seats of those who were selling doves.

13And He *said to them, "It is written, 'MY HOUSE SHALL BE CALLED A HOUSE OF PRAYER'; but you are making it a ROBBERS' DEN.''

14And *the* blind and *the* lame came to Him in the

κύριος αὐτῶν χρείαν ἔχει· εὐθὺς δὲ
Lord of them need has; and immediately

ἀποστελεῖ αὐτούς. 4 Τοῦτο δὲ γέγονεν
he will send them. Now this has happened

ἵνα πληρωθῇ τὸ ῥηθὲν διὰ τοῦ
that might be fulfilled the thing spoken through the

προφήτου λέγοντος· 5 εἴπατε τῇ θυγατρὶ
prophet saying: Tell ye the daughter

Σιών· ἰδοὺ ὁ βασιλεύς σου ἔρχεταί σοι
of Zion: Behold[,] the king of thee comes to thee

πραῢς καὶ ἐπιβεβηκὼς ἐπὶ ὄνον καὶ ἐπὶ
meek and having mounted on an ass and on

πῶλον υἱὸν ὑποζυγίου. 6 πορευθέντες δὲ
a colt son(foal) of an ass. And going

οἱ μαθηταὶ καὶ ποιήσαντες καθὼς συνέταξεν
the disciples and doing as directed

αὐτοῖς ὁ Ἰησοῦς 7 ἤγαγον τὴν ὄνον καὶ
them Jesus they brought the ass and

τὸν πῶλον, καὶ ἐπέθηκαν ἐπ' αὐτῶν
the colt, and put on on them

τὰ ἱμάτια, καὶ ἐπεκάθισεν ἐπάνω αὐτῶν.
the(ir) garments, and he sat on on them.

8 ὁ δὲ πλεῖστος ὄχλος ἔστρωσαν ἑαυτῶν
And the very large crowd strewed of themselves

τὰ ἱμάτια ἐν τῇ ὁδῷ, ἄλλοι δὲ ἔκοπτον
the garments in the way, and others cut

κλάδους ἀπὸ τῶν δένδρων καὶ ἐστρών-
branches from the trees and strewed

νυον ἐν τῇ ὁδῷ. 9 οἱ δὲ ὄχλοι οἱ
in the way. And the crowds the [ones]

προάγοντες αὐτὸν καὶ οἱ ἀκολουθοῦντες
going before him and the [ones] following

ἔκραζον λέγοντες· ὡσαννὰ τῷ υἱῷ Δαυίδ·
cried out saying: Hosanna to the son of David;

εὐλογημένος ὁ ἐρχόμενος ἐν ὀνόματι
blessed the [one] coming in [the] name

κυρίου· ὡσαννὰ ἐν τοῖς ὑψίστοις. 10 καὶ
of [the] Lord; hosanna in the highest [places]. And

εἰσελθόντος αὐτοῦ εἰς Ἱεροσόλυμα ἐσείσθη
entering him[a] into Jerusalem was shaken
=as he entered

πᾶσα ἡ πόλις λέγουσα· τίς ἐστιν οὗτος;
all the city saying: Who is this?

11 οἱ δὲ ὄχλοι ἔλεγον· οὗτός ἐστιν ὁ
And the crowds said: This is the

προφήτης Ἰησοῦς ὁ ἀπὸ Ναζαρὲθ τῆς
prophet Jesus the [one] from Nazareth –

Γαλιλαίας.
of Galilee.

12 Καὶ εἰσῆλθεν Ἰησοῦς εἰς τὸ ἱερὸν
And entered Jesus into the temple

καὶ ἐξέβαλεν πάντας τοὺς πωλοῦντας καὶ
and cast out all the [ones] selling and

ἀγοράζοντας ἐν τῷ ἱερῷ, καὶ τὰς τραπέζας
buying in the temple, and the tables

τῶν κολλυβιστῶν κατέστρεψεν καὶ τὰς
of the money-changers he overturned and the

καθέδρας τῶν πωλούντων τὰς περιστεράς,
seats of the [ones] selling the doves,

13 καὶ λέγει αὐτοῖς· γέγραπται· ὁ οἶκός
and says to them: It has been written: The house

μου οἶκος προσευχῆς κληθήσεται, ὑμεῖς
of me a house of prayer shall be called, [b]ye

δὲ αὐτὸν ποιεῖτε σπήλαιον λῃστῶν. 14 Καὶ
[1]but [4]it [a]are making a den of robbers. And

προσῆλθον αὐτῷ τυφλοὶ καὶ χωλοὶ ἐν τῷ
approached *to* him blind and lame [ones] in the

---

needs them, and he will send them right away.''

4This took place to fulfill what was spoken through the prophet:

5"Say to the Daughter of Zion,
'See, your king comes to you,
gentle and riding on a donkey,
on a colt, the foal of a donkey.' ''[e]

6The disciples went and did as Jesus had instructed them. 7They brought the donkey and the colt, placed their cloaks on them, and Jesus sat on them. 8A very large crowd spread their cloaks on the road, while others cut branches from the trees and spread them on the road. 9The crowds that went ahead of him and those that followed shouted,

"Hosanna[f] to the Son of David!"
"Blessed is he who comes in the name of the Lord!"[g]
"Hosanna[f] in the highest!"

10When Jesus entered Jerusalem, the whole city was stirred and asked, "Who is this?"

11The crowds answered, "This is Jesus, the prophet from Nazareth in Galilee.''

Jesus at the Temple

12Jesus entered the temple area and drove out all who were buying and selling there. He overturned the tables of the money changers and the benches of those selling doves. 13"It is written," he said to them, " 'My house will be called a house of prayer,'[h] but you are making it a 'den of robbers.'[i]''

14The blind and the lame came to him at the temple,

[e]5 Zech. 9:9
[f]9 A Hebrew expression meaning "Save!" which became an exclamation of praise; also in verse 15
[g]9 Psalm 118:26
[h]13 Isaiah 56:7
[i]13 Jer. 7:11

temple, and He healed them.

15But when the chief priests and the scribes saw the wonderful things that He had done, and the children who were crying out in the temple and saying, "Hosanna to the Son of David," they became indignant.

16and said to Him, "Do You hear what these are saying?" And Jesus *said to them, "Yes; have you never read, 'OUT OF THE MOUTH OF INFANTS AND NURSING BABES THOU HAST PREPARED PRAISE FOR THYSELF'?"

17And He left them and went out of the city to Bethany, and lodged there.

The Barren Fig Tree

18Now in the morning, when He returned to the city, He became hungry.

19And seeing a lone fig tree by the road, He came to it, and found nothing on it except leaves only; and He *said to it, "No longer shall there ever be *any* fruit from you." And at once the fig tree withered.

20And seeing *this*, the disciples marveled, saying, "How did the fig tree wither at once?"

21And Jesus answered and said to them, "Truly I say to you, if you have faith, and do not doubt, you shall not only do what was done to the fig tree, but even if you say to this mountain, 'Be taken up and cast into the sea,' it shall happen.

22"And all things you ask in prayer, believing, you shall receive."

Authority Challenged

23And when He had come into the temple, the chief priests and the elders of the people came to Him as He was teaching, and said, "By what authority are You doing these things, and who gave You this authority?"

ἱερῷ, καὶ ἐθεράπευσεν αὐτούς. 15 ἰδόντες
temple, and he healed them. 7seeing

δὲ οἱ ἀρχιερεῖς καὶ οἱ γραμματεῖς τὰ
1But 2the 3chief priests 4and 5the 6scribes the

θαυμάσια ἃ ἐποίησεν καὶ τοὺς παῖδας
marvels which he did and the children

τοὺς κράζοντας ἐν τῷ ἱερῷ καὶ λέγοντας·
- crying out in the temple and saying:

ὡσαννὰ τῷ υἱῷ Δαυίδ, ἠγανάκτησαν, 16 καὶ
Hosanna to the son of David, they were incensed, and

εἶπαν αὐτῷ· ἀκούεις τί οὗτοι λέγουσιν;
said to him: Hearest thou what these are saying?

ὁ δὲ Ἰησοῦς λέγει αὐτοῖς· ναί· οὐδέποτε
- And Jesus says to them: Yes; never

ἀνέγνωτε ὅτι ἐκ στόματος νηπίων καὶ
did ye read[,] - Out of [the] mouth of infants and

θηλαζόντων κατηρτίσω αἶνον; 17 Καὶ
sucking [ones] thou didst prepare praise? And

καταλιπὼν αὐτοὺς ἐξῆλθεν ἔξω τῆς
leaving them he went forth outside the

πόλεως εἰς Βηθανίαν, καὶ ηὐλίσθη ἐκεῖ.
city to Bethany, and lodged there.

18 Πρωὶ δὲ ἐπαναγαγὼν εἰς τὴν πόλιν
Now early going up to the city

ἐπείνασεν. 19 καὶ ἰδὼν συκῆν μίαν ἐπὶ τῆς
he hungered. And seeing fig-tree one on the

ὁδοῦ ἦλθεν ἐπ᾽ αὐτήν, καὶ οὐδὲν εὗρεν
way he went up(to) it, and nothing found

ἐν αὐτῇ εἰ μὴ φύλλα μόνον, καὶ λέγει
in it except leaves only, and says

αὐτῇ· οὐ μηκέτι ἐκ σοῦ καρπὸς γένηται
to it: Never of thee fruit may be

εἰς τὸν αἰῶνα. καὶ ἐξηράνθη παραχρῆμα
to the age. And was dried up instantly

ἡ συκῆ. 20 καὶ ἰδόντες οἱ μαθηταὶ
the fig-tree. And seeing the disciples

ἐθαύμασαν λέγοντες· πῶς παραχρῆμα
marvelled saying: How instantly

ἐξηράνθη ἡ συκῆ; 21 ἀποκριθεὶς δὲ ὁ
was withered the fig-tree? And answering -

Ἰησοῦς εἶπεν αὐτοῖς· ἀμὴν λέγω ὑμῖν,
Jesus said to them: Truly I say to you,

ἐὰν ἔχητε πίστιν καὶ μὴ διακριθῆτε,
If ye have faith and do not doubt,

οὐ μόνον τὸ τῆς συκῆς ποιήσετε, ἀλλὰ
not only the* of the fig-tree ye will do, but

κἂν τῷ ὄρει τούτῳ εἴπητε· ἄρθητι
also if - mountain to this ye say: Be thou taken

καὶ βλήθητι εἰς τὴν θάλασσαν, γενήσεται·
and cast into the sea, it shall be;

22 καὶ πάντα ὅσα ἂν αἰτήσητε ἐν τῇ
and all things whatever ye may ask in -

προσευχῇ πιστεύοντες λήμψεσθε.
prayer believing ye shall receive.

23 Καὶ ἐλθόντος αὐτοῦ εἰς τὸ ἱερὸν
And coming him* into the temple
=as he came

προσῆλθον αὐτῷ διδάσκοντι οἱ ἀρχιερεῖς
approached to him teaching* the chief priests
=while he taught

καὶ οἱ πρεσβύτεροι τοῦ λαοῦ λέγοντες·
and the elders of the people saying:

ἐν ποίᾳ ἐξουσίᾳ ταῦτα ποιεῖς; καὶ
By what authority these things doest thou? and

τίς σοι ἔδωκεν τὴν ἐξουσίαν ταύτην;
who thee gave - authority this?

---

and he healed them. 15But when the chief priests and the teachers of the law saw the wonderful things he did and the children shouting in the temple area, "Hosanna to the Son of David," they were indignant.

16"Do you hear what these children are saying?" they asked him.

"Yes," replied Jesus, "have you never read,

" 'From the lips of children and infants you have ordained praise'/?"

17And he left them and went out of the city to Bethany, where he spent the night.

The Fig Tree Withers

18Early in the morning, as he was on his way back to the city, he was hungry. 19Seeing a fig tree by the road, he went up to it but found nothing on it except leaves. Then he said to it, "May you never bear fruit again!" Immediately the tree withered.

20When the disciples saw this, they were amazed. "How did the fig tree wither so quickly?" they asked.

21Jesus replied, "I tell you the truth, if you have faith and do not doubt, not only can you do what was done to the fig tree, but also you can say to this mountain, 'Go, throw yourself into the sea,' and it will be done. 22If you believe, you will receive whatever you ask for in prayer."

The Authority of Jesus Questioned

23Jesus entered the temple courts, and, while he was teaching, the chief priests and the elders of the people came to him. "By what authority are you doing these things?" they asked. "And who gave you this authority?"

24And Jesus answered and said to them, "I will ask you one thing too, which if you tell Me, I will also tell you by what authority I do these things.

25"The baptism of John was from what *source,* from heaven or from men?" And they *began* reasoning among themselves, saying, "If we say, 'From heaven,' He will say to us, 'Then why did you not believe him?'

26"But if we say, 'From men,' we fear the multitude; for they all hold John to be a prophet."

27And answering Jesus, they said, "We do not know." He also said to them, "Neither will I tell you by what authority I do these things.

Parable of Two Sons

28"But what do you think? A man had two sons, and he came to the first and said, 'Son, go work today in the vineyard.'

29"And he answered and said, 'I will, sir'; and he did not go.

30"And he came to the second and said the same thing. But he answered and said, 'I will not'; *yet* he afterward regretted *it* and went.

31"Which of the two did the will of his father?" They *said, "The latter." Jesus *said to them, "Truly I say to you that the tax-gatherers and harlots will get into the kingdom of God before you.

32"For John came to you in the way of righteousness and you did not believe him; but the tax-gatherers and harlots did believe him; and you, seeing this, did not even feel remorse afterward so as to believe him.

Parable of the Landowner

33"Listen to another parable. There was a landown-

---

24 ἀποκριθεὶς δὲ ὁ Ἰησοῦς εἶπεν αὐτοῖς·
And answering - Jesus said to them:

ἐρωτήσω ὑμᾶς κἀγὼ λόγον ἕνα, ὃν
will question you I also word one, which

ἐὰν εἴπητέ μοι, κἀγὼ ὑμῖν ἐρῶ ἐν ποίᾳ
if ye tell me, I also you will tell by what

ἐξουσίᾳ ταῦτα ποιῶ· **25** τὸ βάπτισμα
authority these things I do: The baptism

τὸ Ἰωάννου πόθεν ἦν; ἐξ οὐρανοῦ ἢ
- of John whence was it? from heaven or

ἐξ ἀνθρώπων; οἱ δὲ διελογίζοντο ἐν
from men? And they reasoned among

ἑαυτοῖς λέγοντες· ἐὰν εἴπωμεν· ἐξ οὐρανοῦ,
themselves saying: If we say: From heaven,

ἐρεῖ ἡμῖν· διὰ τί οὖν οὐκ ἐπιστεύσατε
he will say to us: Why then believed ye not

αὐτῷ; **26** ἐὰν δὲ εἴπωμεν· ἐξ ἀνθρώπων,
him? But if we say: From men,

φοβούμεθα τὸν ὄχλον· πάντες γὰρ ὡς
we fear the crowd: for all as

προφήτην ἔχουσιν τὸν Ἰωάννην. **27** καὶ
a prophet have - John. And

ἀποκριθέντες τῷ Ἰησοῦ εἶπαν· οὐκ
answering - Jesus they said: We do

οἴδαμεν. ἔφη αὐτοῖς καὶ αὐτός· οὐδὲ
not know. said to them also He: Neither

ἐγὼ λέγω ὑμῖν ἐν ποίᾳ ἐξουσίᾳ ταῦτα
I tell you by what authority these things

ποιῶ. **28** Τί δὲ ὑμῖν δοκεῖ; ἄνθρωπος
I do. But what to you seems it? A man

εἶχεν τέκνα δύο· προσελθὼν τῷ πρώτῳ
had children two; approaching *to* the first

εἶπεν· τέκνον, ὕπαγε σήμερον ἐργάζου ἐν
he said: Child, go to-day work in

τῷ ἀμπελῶνι. **29** ὁ δὲ ἀποκριθεὶς εἶπεν·
the vineyard. But he answering said:

ἐγὼ κύριε, καὶ οὐκ ἀπῆλθεν. **30** προσ-
I [go], lord, and went not. And

ελθὼν δὲ τῷ δευτέρῳ εἶπεν ὡσαύτως.
approaching *to* the second he said similarly.

ὁ δὲ ἀποκριθεὶς εἶπεν· οὐ θέλω, ὕστερον
And he answering said: I will not, later

μεταμεληθεὶς ἀπῆλθεν. **31** τίς ἐκ τῶν δύο
repenting he went. Which of the two

ἐποίησεν τὸ θέλημα τοῦ πατρός; λέγουσιν·
did the will of the father? They say:

ὁ ὕστερος. λέγει αὐτοῖς ὁ Ἰησοῦς· ἀμὴν
The latter. Says to them - Jesus: Truly

λέγω ὑμῖν ὅτι οἱ τελῶναι καὶ αἱ πόρναι
I tell you[,] - The tax-collectors and the harlots

προάγουσιν ὑμᾶς εἰς τὴν βασιλείαν τοῦ
are going before you into the kingdom

θεοῦ. **32** ἦλθεν γὰρ Ἰωάννης πρὸς ὑμᾶς
of God. For came John to you

ἐν ὁδῷ δικαιοσύνης, καὶ οὐκ ἐπιστεύσατε
in a way of righteousness, and ye believed not

αὐτῷ· οἱ δὲ τελῶναι καὶ αἱ πόρναι
him; but the tax-collectors and the harlots

ἐπίστευσαν αὐτῷ· ὑμεῖς δὲ ἰδόντες οὐδὲ
believed him; but ye seeing not

μετεμελήθητε ὕστερον τοῦ πιστεῦσαι αὐτῷ.
repented[d] later - to believe him.
= so as to believe

33 Ἄλλην παραβολὴν ἀκούσατε. Ἄνθρωπος
Another parable hear ye. *A man*

24Jesus replied, "I will also ask you one question. If you answer me, I will tell you by what authority I am doing these things. 25John's baptism—where did it come from? Was it from heaven, or from men?"

They discussed it among themselves and said, "If we say, 'From heaven,' he will ask, 'Then why didn't you believe him?' 26But if we say, 'From men'—we are afraid of the people, for they all hold that John was a prophet."

27So they answered Jesus, "We don't know."

Then he said, "Neither will I tell you by what authority I am doing these things.

The Parable of the Two Sons

28"What do you think? There was a man who had two sons. He went to the first and said, 'Son, go and work today in the vineyard.'

29"'I will not,' he answered, but later he changed his mind and went.

30"Then the father went to the other son and said the same thing. He answered, 'I will, sir,' but he did not go.

31"Which of the two did what his father wanted?"

"The first," they answered.

Jesus said to them, "I tell you the truth, the tax collectors and the prostitutes are entering the kingdom of God ahead of you. 32For John came to you to show you the way of righteousness, and you did not believe him, but the tax collectors and the prostitutes did. And even after you saw this, you did not repent and believe him.

The Parable of the Tenants

33"Listen to another parable: There was a landown-

---

* Some such word as 'sign' must be supplied.

er who PLANTED A VINEYARD AND PUT A WALL AROUND IT AND DUG A WINE PRESS IN IT, AND BUILT A TOWER, and rented it out to vine-growers, and went on a journey. 34"And when the harvest time approached, he sent his slaves to the vine-growers to receive his produce. 35"And the vine-growers took his slaves and beat one, and killed another, and stoned a third. 36"Again he sent another group of slaves larger than the first; and they did the same thing to them. 37"But afterward he sent his son to them, saying, 'They will respect my son.' 38"But when the vine-growers saw the son, they said among themselves, 'This is the heir; come, let us kill him, and seize his inheritance.' 39"And they took him, and threw him out of the vineyard, and killed him. 40"Therefore when the owner of the vineyard comes, what will he do to those vine-growers?" 41They *said to Him, "He will bring those wretches to a wretched end, and will rent out the vineyard to other vine-growers, who will pay him the proceeds at the *proper seasons." 42Jesus said to them, "Did you never read in the Scriptures,

'THE STONE WHICH THE BUILDERS REJECTED, THIS BECAME THE CHIEF CORNER *stone;* THIS CAME ABOUT FROM THE LORD, AND IT IS MARVELOUS IN OUR EYES'?

43"Therefore I say to you, the kingdom of God will be taken away from you, and be given to a na-

ἦν οἰκοδεσπότης ὅστις ἐφύτευσεν ἀμπελῶνα,
there was a housemaster who planted a vineyard,

καὶ φραγμὸν αὐτῷ περιέθηκεν καὶ ὤρυξεν
and ²a hedge ²it ¹put round and dug

ἐν αὐτῷ ληνὸν καὶ ᾠκοδόμησεν πύργον,
in it a winepress and built a tower,

καὶ ἐξέδοτο αὐτὸν γεωργοῖς, καὶ ἀπεδή-
and let it to husbandmen, and departed.

μησεν. 34 ὅτε δὲ ἤγγισεν ὁ καιρὸς τῶν
And when drew near the time of the

καρπῶν, ἀπέστειλεν τοὺς δούλους αὐτοῦ
fruits, he sent the slaves of him

πρὸς τοὺς γεωργοὺς λαβεῖν τοὺς καρποὺς
to the husbandmen to receive the fruits

αὐτοῦ. 35 καὶ λαβόντες οἱ γεωργοὶ
of it. And ²taking ¹the ²husbandmen

τοὺς δούλους αὐτοῦ ὃν μὲν ἔδειραν, ὃν
the slaves of him this one they flogged, that

δὲ ἀπέκτειναν, ὃν δὲ ἐλιθοβόλησαν. 36 πάλιν
one they killed, another they stoned. Again

ἀπέστειλεν ἄλλους δούλους πλείονας τῶν
he sent other slaves more [than] the

πρώτων, καὶ ἐποίησαν αὐτοῖς ὡσαύτως.
first [ones], and they did to them similarly.

37 ὕστερον δὲ ἀπέστειλεν πρὸς αὐτοὺς
But later he sent to them

τὸν υἱὸν αὐτοῦ λέγων· ἐντραπήσονται
the son of him saying: They will reverence

τὸν υἱόν μου. 38 οἱ δὲ γεωργοὶ ἰδόντες
the son of me. But the husbandmen seeing

τὸν υἱὸν εἶπον ἐν ἑαυτοῖς· οὗτός ἐστιν
the son said among themselves: This is

ὁ κληρονόμος· δεῦτε ἀποκτείνωμεν αὐτὸν
the heir; come[,] let us kill him

καὶ σχῶμεν τὴν κληρονομίαν αὐτοῦ·
and let us possess the inheritance of him;

39 καὶ λαβόντες αὐτὸν ἐξέβαλον ἔξω τοῦ
and taking ²him ¹they cast out outside the

ἀμπελῶνος καὶ ἀπέκτειναν. 40 ὅταν οὖν
vineyard and killed. When therefore

ἔλθῃ ὁ κύριος τοῦ ἀμπελῶνος, τί ποιήσει
comes the lord of the vineyard, what will he do

τοῖς γεωργοῖς ἐκείνοις; 41 λέγουσιν αὐτῷ·
- husbandmen to those? They say to him:

κακοὺς κακῶς ἀπολέσει αὐτούς, καὶ τὸν
Bad men badly he will destroy them, and the

ἀμπελῶνα ἐκδώσεται ἄλλοις γεωργοῖς,
vineyard he will give out to other husbandmen,

οἵτινες ἀποδώσουσιν αὐτῷ τοὺς καοπούς
who will render to him the fruits

ἐν τοῖς καιροῖς αὐτῶν. 42 λέγει αὐτοῖς ὁ
in the seasons of them. Says to them the

Ἰησοῦς· οὐδέποτε ἀνέγνωτε ἐν ταῖς
Jesus: Did ye never read in the

γραφαῖς· λίθον ὃν ἀπεδοκίμασαν οἱ
scriptures; A stone which rejected the

οἰκοδομοῦντες, οὗτος ἐγενήθη εἰς κεφαλὴν
building [ones], this became - head

γωνίας· παρὰ κυρίου ἐγένετο αὕτη, καὶ
of [the] corner; from [the] Lord became this, and

ἔστιν θαυμαστὴ ἐν ὀφθαλμοῖς ἡμῶν; 43 διὰ
it is marvellous in [the] eyes of us? There-

τοῦτο λέγω ὑμῖν ὅτι ἀρθήσεται ἀφ' ὑμῶν
fore I tell you[,] - will be taken from you

ἡ βασιλεία τοῦ θεοῦ καὶ δοθήσεται
The kingdom - of God and will be given

er who planted a vineyard. He put a wall around it, dug a winepress in it and built a watchtower. Then he rented the vineyard to some farmers and went away on a journey. 34When the harvest time approached, he sent his servants to the tenants to collect his fruit. 35"The tenants seized his servants; they beat one, killed another, and stoned a third. 36Then he sent other servants to them, more than the first time, and the tenants treated them the same way. 37Last of all, he sent his son to them. 'They will respect my son,' he said. 38"But when the tenants saw the son, they said to each other, 'This is the heir. Come, let's kill him and take his inheritance.' 39So they took him and threw him out of the vineyard and killed him. 40"Therefore, when the owner of the vineyard comes, what will he do to those tenants?" 41"He will bring those wretches to a wretched end," they replied, "and he will rent the vineyard to other tenants, who will give him his share of the crop at harvest time." 42Jesus said to them, "Have you never read in the Scriptures:

" 'The stone the builders rejected has become the capstone*k*; the Lord has done this, and it is marvelous in our eyes'*l*?

43"Therefore I tell you that the kingdom of God will be taken away from you and given to a people

*k*42 Or *cornerstone*
*l*42 Psalm 118:22,23

tion producing the fruit of it.
44"And he who falls on this stone will be broken to pieces; but on whomever it falls, it will scatter him like dust."
45And when the chief priests and the Pharisees heard His parables, they understood that He was speaking about them.
46And when they sought to seize Him, they feared the multitudes, because they held Him to be a prophet.

Chapter 22

Parable of the Marriage Feast

AND Jesus answered and spoke to them again in parables, saying,
2"The kingdom of heaven may be compared to a king, who gave a wedding feast for his son.
3"And he sent out his slaves to call those who had been invited to the wedding feast, and they were unwilling to come.
4"Again he sent out other slaves saying, "Behold, I have prepared my dinner; my oxen and my fattened livestock are *all* butchered and everything is ready; come to the wedding feast."'
5"But they paid no attention and went their way, one to his own farm, another to his business,
6and the rest seized his slaves and mistreated them and killed them.
7"But the king was enraged and sent his armies, and destroyed those murderers, and set their city on fire.
8"Then he *said to his slaves, 'The wedding is ready, but those who were invited were not worthy.
9'Go therefore to the main highways, and as many as you find *there,* invite to the wedding feast.'

ἔθνει ποιοῦντι τοὺς καρποὺς αὐτῆς.
to a nation producing the fruits of it.
44 [καὶ ὁ πεσὼν ἐπὶ τὸν λίθον τοῦτον
And the[one] falling on - stone this
συνθλασθήσεται· ἐφ' ὃν δ' ἂν πέσῃ,
will be broken in pieces; but on whomever it falls,
λικμήσει αὐτόν.] **45** Καὶ ἀκούσαντες οἱ
it will crush to powder him. And hearing the
ἀρχιερεῖς καὶ οἱ Φαρισαῖοι τὰς παραβολὰς
chief priests and the Pharisees the parables
αὐτοῦ ἔγνωσαν ὅτι περὶ αὐτῶν λέγει·
of him they knew that concerning them he tells;
46 καὶ ζητοῦντες αὐτὸν κρατῆσαι ἐφοβήθησαν
and seeking him to seize they feared
τοὺς ὄχλους, ἐπεὶ εἰς προφήτην αὐτὸν εἶχον.
the crowds, since for a prophet him they had.

22 Καὶ ἀποκριθεὶς ὁ Ἰησοῦς πάλιν
And answering - Jesus again
εἶπεν ἐν παραβολαῖς αὐτοῖς λέγων·
spoke in parables to them saying:
2 ὡμοιώθη ἡ βασιλεία τῶν οὐρανῶν
Was(is) likened the kingdom of the heavens
ἀνθρώπῳ βασιλεῖ, ὅστις ἐποίησεν γάμους
to a man a king, who made a wedding feast
τῷ υἱῷ αὐτοῦ. **3** καὶ ἀπέστειλεν τοὺς
for the son of him. And he sent the
δούλους αὐτοῦ καλέσαι τοὺς κεκλημένους
slaves of him to call the[ones] having been invited
εἰς τοὺς γάμους, καὶ οὐκ ἤθελον ἐλθεῖν.
to the feast, and they wished not to come.
4 πάλιν ἀπέστειλεν ἄλλους δούλους λέγων·
Again he sent other slaves saying:
εἴπατε τοῖς κεκλημένοις· ἰδοὺ τὸ
Tell the[ones] having been invited: Behold[,] the
ἄριστόν μου ἡτοίμακα, οἱ ταῦροί μου
supper of me I have prepared, the oxen of me
καὶ τὰ σιτιστὰ τεθυμένα, καὶ πάντα
and the fatted beasts having been killed, and all things
ἕτοιμα· δεῦτε εἰς τοὺς γάμους. **5** οἱ δὲ
[are] ready; come to the feast. But they
ἀμελήσαντες ἀπῆλθον, ὃς μὲν εἰς τὸν
not caring went off, one to the(his)
ἴδιον ἀγρόν, ὃς δὲ ἐπὶ τὴν ἐμπορίαν
own field, another on the trading
αὐτοῦ· **6** οἱ δὲ λοιποὶ κρατήσαντες
of him; and the rest seizing
τοὺς δούλους αὐτοῦ ὕβρισαν καὶ ἀπέκτειναν.
the slaves of him insulted and killed.
7 ὁ δὲ βασιλεὺς ὠργίσθη, καὶ πέμψας
So the king became angry, and sending
τὰ στρατεύματα αὐτοῦ ἀπώλεσεν τοὺς
the armies of him destroyed -
φονεῖς ἐκείνους καὶ τὴν πόλιν αὐτῶν
murderers those and the city of them
ἐνέπρησεν. **8** τότε λέγει τοῖς δούλοις
burned. Then he says to the slaves
αὐτοῦ· ὁ μὲν γάμος ἕτοιμός ἐστιν, οἱ δὲ
of him: Indeed the feast ready is, but the[ones]
κεκλημένοι οὐκ ἦσαν ἄξιοι· **9** πορεύεσθε
having been invited were not worthy; go ye
οὖν ἐπὶ τὰς διεξόδους τῶν ὁδῶν, καὶ
therefore onto the partings of the ways, and
ὅσους ἐὰν εὕρητε καλέσατε εἰς τοὺς
as many as ye find call to the

---

who will produce its fruit.
44He who falls on this stone will be broken to pieces, but he on whom it falls will be crushed." *m*
45When the chief priests and the Pharisees heard Jesus' parables, they knew he was talking about them.
46They looked for a way to arrest him, but they were afraid of the crowd because the people held that he was a prophet.

Chapter 22

The Parable of the Wedding Banquet

JESUS spoke to them again in parables, saying: 2"The kingdom of heaven is like a king who prepared a wedding banquet for his son. 3He sent his servants to those who had been invited to the banquet to tell them to come, but they refused to come.
4"Then he sent some more servants and said, 'Tell those who have been invited that I have prepared my dinner: My oxen and fattened cattle have been butchered, and everything is ready. Come to the wedding banquet.'
5"But they paid no attention and went off—one to his field, another to his business. 6The rest seized his servants, mistreated them and killed them. 7The king was enraged. He sent his army and destroyed those murderers and burned their city.
8"Then he said to his servants, 'The wedding banquet is ready, but those I invited did not deserve to come. 9Go to the street corners and invite to the banquet anyone you find.' 10So

m44 Some manuscripts do not have verse 44.

10"And those slaves went out into the streets, and gathered together all they found, both evil and good; and the wedding hall was filled with dinner guests.

11"But when the king came in to look over the dinner guests, he saw there a man not dressed in wedding clothes,

12and he *said to him, 'Friend, how did you come in here without wedding clothes?' And he was speechless.

13"Then the king said to the servants, 'Bind him hand and foot, and cast him into the outer darkness; in that place there shall be weeping and gnashing of teeth.'

14"For many are called, but few *are* chosen."

Tribute to Caesar

15Then the Pharisees went and counseled together how they might trap Him in what He said.

16And they *sent their disciples to Him, along with the Herodians, saying, "Teacher, we know that You are truthful and teach the way of God in truth, and defer to no one; for You are not partial to any.

17"Tell us therefore, what do You think? Is it lawful to give a poll-tax to Caesar, or not?"

18But Jesus perceived their malice, and said, "Why are you testing Me, you hypocrites?

19"Show Me the coin *used* for the poll-tax." And they brought Him a denarius.

20And He *said to them, "Whose likeness and inscription is this?"

21They *said to Him, "Caesar's." Then He *said

γάμους. 10 καὶ ἐξελθόντες οἱ δοῦλοι
feast.   And going forth   -   slaves

ἐκεῖνοι εἰς τὰς ὁδοὺς συνήγαγον πάντας
those into the ways assembled all

οὓς εὗρον, πονηρούς τε καὶ ἀγαθούς·
whom they found, both bad and good;

καὶ ἐπλήσθη ὁ νυμφὼν ἀνακειμένων.
and was filled the wedding chamber of(with) reclining [ones].

11 εἰσελθὼν δὲ ὁ βασιλεὺς θεάσασθαι
But entering the king to behold

τοὺς ἀνακειμένους εἶδεν ἐκεῖ
the reclining [ones] he saw there

ἄνθρωπον οὐκ ἐνδεδυμένον ἔνδυμα γάμου·
a man not having been dressed[in] a dress of wedding;

12 καὶ λέγει αὐτῷ· ἑταῖρε, πῶς
and he says to him: Comrade, how

εἰσῆλθες ὧδε μὴ ἔχων ἔνδυμα γάμου;
enteredst thou here not having a dress of wedding?

ὁ δὲ ἐφιμώθη. 13 τότε ὁ βασιλεὺς
And he was silenced. Then the king

εἶπεν τοῖς διακόνοις· δήσαντες αὐτοῦ
said to the servants: Binding of him

πόδας καὶ χεῖρας ἐκβάλετε αὐτὸν
feet and hands throw out him

εἰς τὸ σκότος τὸ ἐξώτερον· ἐκεῖ ἔσται
into the darkness - outer; there will be

ὁ κλαυθμὸς καὶ ὁ βρυγμὸς τῶν
the wailing and the gnashing of the

ὀδόντων. 14 Πολλοὶ γάρ εἰσιν κλητοί,
teeth. For many are called,

ὀλίγοι δὲ ἐκλεκτοί.
but few chosen.

15 Τότε πορευθέντες οἱ Φαρισαῖοι συμ-
Then going the Pharisees coun-

βούλιον ἔλαβον ὅπως αὐτὸν παγιδεύσωσιν
sel took so as him they might ensnare

ἐν λόγῳ. 16 καὶ ἀποστέλλουσιν αὐτῷ
in a word. And they send to him

τοὺς μαθητὰς αὐτῶν μετὰ τῶν Ἡρω-
the disciples of them with the Hero-

διανῶν λέγοντας· διδάσκαλε, οἴδαμεν
dians saying: Teacher, we know

ὅτι ἀληθὴς εἶ καὶ τὴν ὁδὸν τοῦ
that truthful thou art and the way -

θεοῦ ἐν ἀληθείᾳ διδάσκεις, καὶ οὐ
of God in truth thou teachest, and not

μέλει σοι περὶ οὐδενός, οὐ γὰρ
it concerns to thee about no one(anyone), ²not ¹for

βλέπεις εἰς πρόσωπον ἀνθρώπων·
³thou lookest to face of men;

17 εἰπὸν οὖν ἡμῖν, τί σοι δοκεῖ;
tell therefore us, what to thee seems it?

ἔξεστιν δοῦναι κῆνσον Καίσαρι ἢ οὔ;
is it lawful to give tribute to Cæsar or no?

18 γνοὺς δὲ ὁ Ἰησοῦς τὴν πονηρίαν
But knowing - Jesus the wickedness

αὐτῶν εἶπεν· τί με πειράζετε, ὑποκριταί;
of them said: Why me tempt ye, hypocrites?

19 ἐπιδείξατέ μοι τὸ νόμισμα τοῦ κήνσου.
Show me the money of the tribute.

οἱ δὲ προσήνεγκαν αὐτῷ δηνάριον. 20 καὶ
And they brought to him a denarius. And

λέγει αὐτοῖς· τίνος ἡ εἰκὼν αὕτη
he says to them: Of whom - image this

καὶ ἡ ἐπιγραφή; 21 λέγουσιν· Καίσαρος.
and - superscription? They say: Of Cæsar.

---

the servants went out into the streets and gathered all the people they could find, both good and bad, and the wedding hall was filled with guests.

11"But when the king came in to see the guests, he noticed a man there who was not wearing wedding clothes. 12'Friend,' he asked, 'how did you get in here without wedding clothes?' The man was speechless.

13"Then the king told the attendants, 'Tie him hand and foot, and throw him outside, into the darkness, where there will be weeping and gnashing of teeth.'

14"For many are invited, but few are chosen."

Paying Taxes to Caesar

15Then the Pharisees went out and laid plans to trap him in his words. 16They sent their disciples to him along with the Herodians. "Teacher," they said, "we know you are a man of integrity and that you teach the way of God in accordance with the truth. You aren't swayed by men, because you pay no attention to who they are. 17Tell us then, what is your opinion? Is it right to pay taxes to Caesar or not?"

18But Jesus, knowing their evil intent, said, "You hypocrites, why are you trying to trap me? 19Show me the coin used for paying the tax." They brought him a denarius, 20and he asked them, "Whose portrait is this? And whose inscription?"

21"Caesar's," they replied.

Then he said to them,

to them, "Then render to Caesar the things that are Caesar's; and to God the things that are God's."

22And hearing *this*, they marveled, and leaving Him, they went away.

Jesus Answers the Sadducees

23On that day *some* Sadducees (who say there is no resurrection) came to Him and questioned Him,

24saying, "Teacher, Moses said, 'IF A MAN DIES, HAVING NO CHILDREN, HIS BROTHER AS NEXT OF KIN SHALL MARRY HIS WIFE, AND RAISE UP AN OFFSPRING TO HIS BROTHER.'

25"Now there were seven brothers with us; and the first married and died, and having no offspring left his wife to his brother;

26so also the second, and the third, down to the seventh.

27"And last of all, the woman died.

28"In the resurrection therefore whose wife of the seven shall she be? For they all had her."

29But Jesus answered and said to them, "You are mistaken, not understanding the Scriptures, or the power of God.

30"For in the resurrection they neither marry, nor are given in marriage, but are like angels in heaven.

31"But regarding the resurrection of the dead, have you not read that which was spoken to you by God, saying,

32'I AM THE GOD OF ABRAHAM, AND THE GOD OF ISAAC, AND THE GOD OF JACOB'? He is not the God of the dead but of the living."

33And when the multitudes heard *this*, they were astonished at His teaching.

34But when the Pharisees heard that He had put the

τότε λέγει αὐτοῖς· ἀπόδοτε οὖν τὰ
Then he says to them: Render then the things

Καίσαρος Καίσαρι καὶ τὰ τοῦ θεοῦ
of Caesar to Caesar and the things - of God

τῷ θεῷ. 22 καὶ ἀκούσαντες ἐθαύμασαν,
- to God. And hearing they marvelled,

καὶ ἀφέντες αὐτὸν ἀπῆλθαν.
and leaving him went away.

23 Ἐν ἐκείνῃ τῇ ἡμέρᾳ προσῆλθον
On that day approached

αὐτῷ Σαδδουκαῖοι, λέγοντες μὴ εἶναι
to him Sadducees, saying not to be

ἀνάστασιν, καὶ ἐπηρώτησαν αὐτὸν
a resurrection, and questioned him

24 λέγοντες· διδάσκαλε, Μωϋσῆς εἶπεν·
saying: Teacher, Moses said:

ἐάν τις ἀποθάνῃ μὴ ἔχων τέκνα,
If any man dies not having children,

ἐπιγαμβρεύσει ὁ ἀδελφὸς αὐτοῦ τὴν
shall take to wife after the brother of him the

γυναῖκα αὐτοῦ καὶ ἀναστήσει σπέρμα
wife of him and shall raise up seed

τῷ ἀδελφῷ αὐτοῦ. 25 ἦσαν δὲ παρ'
to the brother of him. Now there were with

ἡμῖν ἑπτὰ ἀδελφοί· καὶ ὁ πρῶτος
us seven brothers; and the first

γήμας ἐτελεύτησεν, καὶ μὴ ἔχων
having married died, and not having

σπέρμα ἀφῆκεν τὴν γυναῖκα αὐτοῦ τῷ
seed left the wife of him to the

ἀδελφῷ αὐτοῦ· 26 ὁμοίως καὶ ὁ δεύτερος
brother of him; likewise also the second

καὶ ὁ τρίτος, ἕως τῶν ἑπτά. 27 ὕστερον
and the third, until the seven. last

δὲ πάντων ἀπέθανεν ἡ γυνή. 28 ἐν τῇ
And of all died the woman. In the

ἀναστάσει οὖν τίνος τῶν ἑπτὰ ἔσται
resurrection then of which of the seven will she be

γυνή; πάντες γὰρ ἔσχον αὐτήν. 29 ἀπο-
wife? for all had her. an-

κριθεὶς δὲ ὁ Ἰησοῦς εἶπεν αὐτοῖς·
swering And - Jesus said to them:

πλανᾶσθε μὴ εἰδότες τὰς γραφὰς μηδὲ
Ye err not knowing the scriptures nor

τὴν δύναμιν τοῦ θεοῦ. 30 ἐν γὰρ τῇ
the power - of God. For in the

ἀναστάσει οὔτε γαμοῦσιν οὔτε γαμίζονται,
resurrection neither they marry nor are given in marriage,

ἀλλ' ὡς ἄγγελοι ἐν τῷ οὐρανῷ εἰσιν.
but as angels in *the* heaven are.

31 περὶ δὲ τῆς ἀναστάσεως τῶν νεκρῶν
But concerning the resurrection of the dead

οὐκ ἀνέγνωτε τὸ ῥηθὲν ὑμῖν ὑπὸ
did ye not read the thing said to you by

τοῦ θεοῦ λέγοντος· 32 ἐγώ εἰμι ὁ θεὸς
- God saying: I am the God

Ἀβραὰμ καὶ ὁ θεὸς Ἰσαὰκ καὶ ὁ θεὸς
of Abraham and the God of Isaac and the God

Ἰακώβ; οὐκ ἔστιν [ὁ] θεὸς νεκρῶν
of Jacob? He is not the God of dead men

ἀλλὰ ζώντων. 33 καὶ ἀκούσαντες οἱ ὄχλοι
but of living [ones]. And hearing the crowds

ἐξεπλήσσοντο ἐπὶ τῇ διδαχῇ αὐτοῦ.
were astounded over(at) the teaching of him.

34 Οἱ δὲ Φαρισαῖοι ἀκούσαντες ὅτι
But the Pharisees hearing that

"Give to Caesar what is Caesar's, and to God what is God's."

22When they heard this, they were amazed. So they left him and went away.

Marriage at the Resurrection

23That same day the Sadducees, who say there is no resurrection, came to him with a question. 24"Teacher," they said, "Moses told us that if a man dies without having children, his brother must marry the widow and have children for him. 25Now there were seven brothers among us. The first one married and died, and since he had no children, he left his wife to his brother. 26The same thing happened to the second and third brother, right on down to the seventh. 27Finally, the woman died. 28Now then, at the resurrection, whose wife will she be of the seven, since all of them were married to her?"

29Jesus replied, "You are in error because you do not know the Scriptures or the power of God. 30At the resurrection people will neither marry nor be given in marriage; they will be like the angels in heaven. 31But about the resurrection of the dead—have you not read what God said to you, 32'I am the God of Abraham, the God of Isaac, and the God of Jacob'*n*? He is not the God of the dead but of the living."

33When the crowds heard this, they were astonished at his teaching.

The Greatest Commandment

34Hearing that Jesus had silenced the Sadducees, the

n32 Exodus 3:6

Sadducees to silence, they gathered themselves together.

35And one of them, *a* a lawyer, asked Him *a question,* testing Him,

36"Teacher, which is the great commandment in the Law?"

37And He said to him, " 'YOU SHALL LOVE THE LORD YOUR GOD WITH ALL YOUR HEART, AND WITH ALL YOUR SOUL, AND WITH ALL YOUR MIND.'

38"This is the great and foremost commandment.

39"The second is like it, 'YOU SHALL LOVE YOUR NEIGHBOR AS YOURSELF.'

40"On these two commandments depend the whole Law and the Prophets."

41Now while the Pharisees were gathered together, Jesus asked them a question,

42saying, "What do you think about the Christ, whose son is He?" They *said to Him, "The son of David."

43He *said to them, "Then how does David in the Spirit call Him 'Lord,' saying,

44 'THE LORD SAID TO MY LORD,
"SIT AT MY RIGHT HAND,
UNTIL I PUT THINE ENEMIES BENEATH THY FEET" '?

45"If David then calls Him 'Lord,' how is He his son?"

46And no one was able to answer Him a word, nor did anyone dare from that day on to ask Him another question.

Chapter 23

Pharisaism Exposed

THEN Jesus spoke to the multitudes and to His disciples,

2saying, "The scribes and the Pharisees have seated themselves in the chair of Moses;

3therefore all that they tell you, do and observe, but do not do according to their deeds; for they say

a I.e., an expert in the Mosaic law

ἐφίμωσεν τοὺς Σαδδουκαίους, συνήχθησαν
he silenced the   Sadducees,   were assembled

ἐπὶ τὸ αὐτό, 35 καὶ ἐπηρώτησεν εἷς
together,   and *b*questioned *l*one

ἐξ αὐτῶν νομικὸς πειράζων αὐτόν· 36 δι-
*b*of *b*them *a*a lawyer *c*tempting him: Teach-

δάσκαλε, ποία ἐντολὴ μεγάλη ἐν τῷ
er,   what commandment [is] great in the

νόμῳ; 37 ὁ δὲ ἔφη αὐτῷ· ἀγαπήσεις
law? And he said to him: Thou shalt love

κύριον τὸν θεόν σου ἐν ὅλῃ τῇ καρδίᾳ
[the] Lord the God of thee with all the heart

σου καὶ ἐν ὅλῃ τῇ ψυχῇ σου καὶ ἐν
of thee and with all the soul of thee and with

ὅλῃ τῇ διανοίᾳ σου. 38 αὕτη ἐστὶν ἡ
all the understanding of thee. This is the

μεγάλη καὶ πρώτη ἐντολή. 39 δευτέρα
great   and first commandment.   [The] second

ὁμοία αὐτῇ· ἀγαπήσεις τὸν πλησίον σου
[is] like to it: Thou shalt love the neighbour of thee

ὡς σεαυτόν. 40 ἐν ταύταις ταῖς δυσὶν ἐντολαῖς
as thyself.   In(on) these —   two commandments

ὅλος ὁ νόμος κρέμαται καὶ οἱ προφῆται.
all the law hangs   and the prophets.

41 Συνηγμένων δὲ τῶν Φαρισαίων
And having assembled the Pharisees
= when the Pharisees were assembled

ἐπηρώτησεν αὐτοὺς ὁ Ἰησοῦς 42 λέγων· τι
questioned them — Jesus saying: What

ὑμῖν δοκεῖ περὶ τοῦ χριστοῦ; τίνος
to you seems it concerning the Christ? of whom

υἱός ἐστιν; λέγουσιν αὐτῷ· τοῦ Δαυίδ.
son is he? They say to him: — Of David.

43 λέγει αὐτοῖς· πῶς οὖν Δαυὶδ ἐν
He says to them: How then David in

πνεύματι καλεῖ αὐτὸν κύριον λέγων·
spirit calls him   Lord saying:

44 εἶπεν κύριος τῷ κυρίῳ μου·
Said [the] LORD to the Lord of me:

κάθου ἐκ δεξιῶν μου ἕως ἂν θῶ τοὺς
Sit on [the] right of me until I put the

ἐχθρούς σου ὑποκάτω τῶν ποδῶν σου;
enemies of thee underneath the feet of thee?

45 εἰ οὖν Δαυὶδ καλεῖ αὐτὸν κύριον, πῶς
If then David calls him   Lord, how

υἱὸς αὐτοῦ ἐστιν; 46 καὶ οὐδεὶς ἐδύνατο
son of him is he? And no one was able

ἀποκριθῆναι αὐτῷ λόγον οὐδὲ ἐτόλμησέν
to answer him a word nor dared

τις ἀπ᾽ ἐκείνης τῆς ἡμέρας ἐπερωτῆσαι
anyone from that — day *to* question

αὐτὸν οὐκέτι.
him no(any) more.

23 Τότε ὁ Ἰησοῦς ἐλάλησεν τοῖς ὄχλοις
Then — Jesus spoke to the crowds

καὶ τοῖς μαθηταῖς αὐτοῦ 2 λέγων· ἐπὶ
and to the disciples of him saying: On

τῆς Μωϋσέως καθέδρας ἐκάθισαν οἱ
the of Moses   seat   sat   the

γραμματεῖς καὶ οἱ Φαρισαῖοι. 3 πάντα
scribes   and the Pharisees. All things

οὖν ὅσα ἐὰν εἴπωσιν ὑμῖν ποιήσατε
therefore whatever they may tell you do ye

καὶ τηρεῖτε, κατὰ δὲ τὰ ἔργα αὐτῶν
and keep, but according to the works of them

Pharisees got together.

35One of them, an expert in the law, tested him with this question: 36"Teacher, which is the greatest commandment in the Law?"

37Jesus replied: " 'Love the Lord your God with all your heart and with all your soul and with all your mind.'*o* 38This is the first and greatest commandment. 39And the second is like it: 'Love your neighbor as yourself.'*p* 40All the Law and the Prophets hang on these two commandments."

Whose Son Is the Christ?

41While the Pharisees were gathered together, Jesus asked them, 42"What do you think about the Christ*q*? Whose son is he?"

"The son of David," they replied.

43He said to them, "How is it then that David, speaking by the Spirit, calls him 'Lord'? For he says,

44" 'The Lord said to my Lord:
"Sit at my right hand until I put your enemies under your feet." '*r*

45If then David calls him 'Lord,' how can he be his son?" 46No one could say a word in reply, and from that day on no one dared to ask him any more questions.

Chapter 23

Seven Woes

THEN Jesus said to the crowds and to his disciples: 2"The teachers of the law and the Pharisees sit in Moses' seat. 3So you must obey them and do everything they tell you. But do not do what they do, for

*o*37 Deut. 6:5
*p*39 Lev. 19:18
*q*42 Or Messiah
*r*44 Psalm 110:1

things, and do not do them.
4"And they tie up heavy loads, and lay them on men's shoulders; but they themselves are unwilling to move them with so much as a finger.
5"But they do all their deeds to be noticed by men; for they broaden their 'phylacteries, and lengthen the tassels of their garments.
6"And they love the place of honor at banquets, and the chief seats in the synagogues,
7and respectful greetings in the market places, and being called by men, Rabbi.
8"But do not be called Rabbi; for One is your Teacher, and you are all brothers.
9"And do not call anyone on earth your father; for One is your Father, He who is in heaven.
10"And do not be called leaders; for One is your Leader, that is, Christ.
11"But the greatest among you shall be your servant.
12"And whoever exalts himself shall be humbled; and whoever humbles himself shall be exalted.

Seven Woes

13"But woe to you, scribes and Pharisees, hypocrites, because you shut off the kingdom of heaven from men; for you do not enter in yourselves, nor do you allow those who are entering to go in.
14["²Woe to you, scribes and Pharisees, hypocrites, because you devour widows' houses, even while for a pretense you make long prayers; therefore you shall receive greater condemnation.]
15"Woe to you, scribes and Pharisees, hypocrites, because you travel about on sea and land to make one proselyte; and when he becomes one, you make him twice as much a son of hell as yourselves.
16"Woe to you, blind

μὴ ποιεῖτε· λέγουσιν γὰρ καὶ οὐ ποιοῦσιν.
do ye not; for they say and and do not.

4 δεσμεύουσιν δὲ φορτία βαρέα καὶ
And they bind burdens heavy and
ἐπιτιθέασιν ἐπὶ τοὺς ὤμους τῶν ἀνθρώπων,
put on on the shoulders - of men,
αὐτοὶ δὲ τῷ δακτύλῳ αὐτῶν οὐ
but they with the finger of them not
θέλουσιν κινῆσαι αὐτά. 5 πάντα δὲ
are willing to move them. But all
τὰ ἔργα αὐτῶν ποιοῦσιν πρὸς τὸ θεαθῆναι
the works of them they do for - to be seen
τοῖς ἀνθρώποις· πλατύνουσιν γὰρ τὰ
- by men; for they broaden the
φυλακτήρια αὐτῶν καὶ μεγαλύνουσιν τὰ
phylacteries of them and enlarge the
κράσπεδα, 6 φιλοῦσιν δὲ τὴν πρωτο-
fringes, and they like the chief
κλισίαν ἐν τοῖς δείπνοις καὶ τὰς πρωτο-
place in the suppers and the chief
καθεδρίας ἐν ταῖς συναγωγαῖς 7 καὶ τοὺς
seats in the synagogues . and the
ἀσπασμοὺς ἐν ταῖς ἀγοραῖς καὶ
greetings in the marketplaces and
καλεῖσθαι ὑπὸ τῶν ἀνθρώπων ραββί.
to be called by - men rabbi.
8 ὑμεῖς δὲ μὴ κληθῆτε ραββί· εἷς γὰρ
But ye be not called rabbi; for one
ἐστιν ὑμῶν ὁ διδάσκαλος, πάντες δὲ ὑμεῖς
is of you the teacher, and all ye
ἀδελφοί ἐστε. 9 καὶ πατέρα μὴ καλέσητε
brothers are. And father call ye not
ὑμῶν ἐπὶ τῆς γῆς· εἷς γάρ ἐστιν
of you on the earth; for one is
ὑμῶν ὁ πατὴρ ὁ οὐράνιος. 10 μηδὲ
of you the Father - heavenly. Neither
κληθῆτε καθηγηταί, ὅτι καθηγητὴς
be ye called leaders, because leader
ὑμῶν ἐστιν εἷς ὁ Χριστός. 11 ὁ δὲ
of you is one the Christ. And the
μείζων ὑμῶν ἔσται ὑμῶν διάκονος.
greater of you shall be of you servant.
12 Ὅστις δὲ ὑψώσει ἑαυτὸν ταπεινωθήσεται,
And [he] who will exalt himself shall be humbled,
καὶ ὅστις ταπεινώσει ἑαυτὸν ὑψωθήσεται.
and [he] who will humble himself shall be exalted.
13 Οὐαὶ δὲ ὑμῖν, γραμματεῖς καὶ Φαρισαῖοι
But woe to you, scribes and Pharisees
ὑποκριταί, ὅτι κλείετε τὴν βασιλείαν
hypocrites, because ye shut the kingdom
τῶν οὐρανῶν ἔμπροσθεν τῶν ἀνθρώπων·
of the heavens before - men;
ὑμεῖς γὰρ οὐκ εἰσέρχεσθε, οὐδὲ τοὺς
for ye do not enter, nor the [ones]
εἰσερχομένους ἀφίετε εἰσελθεῖν.‡ 15 Οὐαὶ
entering do ye allow to enter. Woe
ὑμῖν, γραμματεῖς καὶ Φαρισαῖοι ὑποκριταί,
to you, scribes and Pharisees hypocrites,
ὅτι περιάγετε τὴν θάλασσαν καὶ τὴν
because ye go about the sea and the
ξηρὰν ποιῆσαι ἕνα προσήλυτον, καὶ ὅταν
dry [land] to make one proselyte, and when
γένηται, ποιεῖτε αὐτὸν υἱὸν γεέννης διπλό-
he becomes, ye make him a son of gehenna twofold
τερον ὑμῶν. 16 Οὐαὶ ὑμῖν, ὁδηγοὶ τυφλοὶ
more [than] you. Woe to you, leaders blind

they do not practice what they preach. 4They tie up heavy loads and put them on men's shoulders, but they themselves are not willing to lift a finger to move them.
5"Everything they do is done for men to see: They make their phylacteries³ wide and the tassels on their garments long; 6they love the place of honor at banquets and the most important seats in the synagogues; 7they love to be greeted in the marketplaces and to have men call them 'Rabbi.'
8"But you are not to be called 'Rabbi,' for you have only one Master and you are all brothers. 9And do not call anyone on earth 'father,' for you have one Father, and he is in heaven. 10Nor are you to be called 'teacher,' for you have one Teacher, the Christ.¹ 11The greatest among you will be your servant. 12For whoever exalts himself will be humbled, and whoever humbles himself will be exalted.
13"Woe to you, teachers of the law and Pharisees, you hypocrites! You shut the kingdom of heaven in men's faces. You yourselves do not enter, nor will you let those enter who are trying to.ᵘ
15"Woe to you, teachers of the law and Pharisees, you hypocrites! You travel over land and sea to win a single convert, and when he becomes one, you make him twice as much a son of hell as you are.
16"Woe to you, blind

I.e., small boxes containing Scripture texts worn for religious purposes
³ This verse not found in the earliest mss.

³5 That is, boxes containing Scripture verses, worn on forehead and arm
¹10 Or Messiah
ᵘ13 Some manuscripts to. ¹⁴Woe to you, teachers of the law and Pharisees, you hypocrites! You devour widows' houses and for a show make lengthy prayers. Therefore you will be punished more severely.

guides, who say, 'Whoever swears by the temple, that is nothing; but whoever swears by the gold of the temple, he is obligated.' [17]"You fools and blind men; which is more important, the gold, or the temple that sanctified the gold? [18]"And, 'Whoever swears by the altar, *that* is nothing, but whoever swears by the offering upon it, he is obligated.' [19]"You blind men, which is more important, the offering or the altar that sanctifies the offering? [20]"Therefore he who swears, swears *both* by the altar and by everything on it. [21]"And he who swears by the temple, swears *both* by the temple and by Him who dwells within it. [22]"And he who swears by heaven, swears *both* by the throne of God and by Him who sits upon it. [23]"Woe to you, scribes and Pharisees, hypocrites! For you tithe mint and dill and cummin, and have neglected the weightier provisions of the law: justice and mercy and faithfulness; but these are the things you should have done without neglecting the others. [24]"You blind guides, who strain out a gnat and swallow a camel! [25]"Woe to you, scribes and Pharisees, hypocrites! For you clean the outside of the cup and of the dish, but inside they are full of robbery and self-indulgence. [26]"You blind Pharisee, first clean the inside of the cup and of the dish, so that the outside of it may become clean also. [27]"Woe to you, scribes and Pharisees! For you are like white-

οἱ λέγοντες· ὃς ἂν ὀμόσῃ ἐν τῷ ναῷ,
the [ones] saying: Whoever swears by the shrine,
οὐδέν ἐστιν· ὃς δ' ἂν ὀμόσῃ ἐν τῷ χρυσῷ
nothing it is; but whoever swears by the gold
τοῦ ναοῦ, ὀφείλει. 17 μωροὶ καὶ τυφλοί,
of the shrine, he owes. Fools and blind,
τίς γὰρ μείζων ἐστιν, ὁ χρυσὸς ἢ ὁ ναὸς
for which greater is, the gold or the shrine
ὁ ἁγιάσας τὸν χρυσόν; 18 καὶ· ὃς ἂν
- sanctifying the gold? And: whoever
ὀμόσῃ ἐν τῷ θυσιαστηρίῳ, οὐδέν ἐστιν·
swears by the altar, nothing it is;
ὃς δ' ἂν ὀμόσῃ ἐν τῷ δώρῳ τῷ ἐπάνω
but whoever swears by the gift - upon
αὐτοῦ, ὀφείλει. 19 τυφλοί, τί γὰρ μεῖζον,
it, he owes. Blind, for which [is] greater,
τὸ δῶρον ἢ τὸ θυσιαστήριον τὸ
the gift or the altar -
ἁγιάζον τὸ δῶρον; 20 ὁ οὖν ὀμόσας
sanctifying the gift? Therefore the [one] swearing
ἐν τῷ θυσιαστηρίῳ ὀμνύει ἐν αὐτῷ καὶ
by the altar swears by it and
ἐν πᾶσι τοῖς ἐπάνω αὐτοῦ· 21 καὶ ὁ
by all the things upon it; and the [one]
ὀμόσας ἐν τῷ ναῷ ὀμνύει ἐν αὐτῷ
swearing by the shrine swears by it
καὶ ἐν τῷ κατοικοῦντι αὐτόν· 22 καὶ
and by the [one] inhabiting it; and
ὁ ὀμόσας ἐν τῷ οὐρανῷ ὀμνύει ἐν τῷ
the [one] swearing by *the* heaven swears by the
θρόνῳ τοῦ θεοῦ καὶ ἐν τῷ καθημένῳ
throne - of God and by the [one] sitting
ἐπάνω αὐτοῦ. 23 Οὐαὶ ὑμῖν, γραμματεῖς
upon it. Woe to you, scribes
καὶ Φαρισαῖοι ὑποκριταί, ὅτι ἀποδεκατοῦτε
and Pharisees hypocrites, because ye tithe
τὸ ἡδύοσμον καὶ τὸ ἄνηθον καὶ τὸ
the mint and the dill and the
κύμινον, καὶ ἀφήκατε τὰ βαρύτερα
cummin, and ye [have] left the heavier things
τοῦ νόμου, τὴν κρίσιν καὶ τὸ ἔλεος
of the law, - judgment and - mercy
καὶ τὴν πίστιν· ταῦτα δὲ ἔδει ποιῆσαι
and - faith; but these things it behoved to do
κἀκεῖνα μὴ ἀφεῖναι. 24 ὁδηγοὶ τυφλοί,
and those not to leave. Leaders blind,
οἱ διϋλίζοντες τὸν κώνωπα, τὴν δὲ
the [ones] straining the gnat, but ²the
κάμηλον καταπίνοντες. 25 Οὐαὶ ὑμῖν,
²camel ¹swallowing. Woe to you,
γραμματεῖς καὶ Φαρισαῖοι ὑποκριταί, ὅτι
scribes and Pharisees hypocrites, because
καθαρίζετε τὸ ἔξωθεν τοῦ ποτηρίου καὶ
ye cleanse the outside of the cup and
τῆς παροψίδος, ἔσωθεν δὲ γέμουσιν ἐξ
the dish, but within they are full of
ἁρπαγῆς καὶ ἀκρασίας. 26 Φαρισαῖε τυφλέ,
robbery and intemperance. Pharisee blind,
καθάρισον πρῶτον τὸ ἐντὸς τοῦ ποτηρίου
cleanse thou first the inside of the cup
ἵνα γένηται καὶ τὸ ἐκτὸς αὐτοῦ καθαρόν.
that may be also the outside of it clean.
27 Οὐαὶ ὑμῖν, γραμματεῖς καὶ Φαρισαῖοι
Woe to you, scribes and Pharisees
ὑποκριταί, ὅτι παρομοιάζετε τάφοις κεκονια-
hypocrites, because ye resemble graves *having been*

‡ Ver. 14 omitted by Nestle; *cf.* NIV footnote.

guides! You say, 'If anyone swears by the temple, it means nothing; but if anyone swears by the gold of the temple, he is bound by his oath.' [17]You blind fools! Which is greater: the gold, or the temple that makes the gold sacred? [18]You also say, 'If anyone swears by the altar, it means nothing; but if anyone swears by the gift on it, he is bound by his oath.' [19]You blind men! Which is greater: the gift, or the altar that makes the gift sacred? [20]Therefore, he who swears by the altar swears by it and by everything on it. [21]And he who swears by the temple swears by it and by the one who dwells in it. [22]And he who swears by heaven swears by God's throne and by the one who sits on it. [23]"Woe to you, teachers of the law and Pharisees, you hypocrites! You give a tenth of your spices—mint, dill and cummin. But you have neglected the more important matters of the law—justice, mercy and faithfulness. You should have practiced the latter, without neglecting the former. [24]You blind guides! You strain out a gnat but swallow a camel. [25]"Woe to you, teachers of the law and Pharisees, you hypocrites! You clean the outside of the cup and dish, but inside they are full of greed and self-indulgence. [26]Blind Pharisee! First clean the inside of the cup and dish, and then the outside also will be clean. [27]"Woe to you, teachers of the law and Pharisees, you hypocrites! You are like whitewashed tombs, washed tombs which on the outside appear beautiful, but inside they are full of dead men's bones and all uncleanness.

28"Even so you too outwardly appear righteous to men, but inwardly you are full of hypocrisy and lawlessness.

29"Woe to you, scribes and Pharisees, hypocrites! For you build the tombs of the prophets and adorn the monuments of the righteous,

30and say, 'If we had been *living* in the days of our fathers, we would not have been partners with them in *shedding* the blood of the prophets.'

31"Consequently you bear witness against yourselves, that you are sons of those who murdered the prophets.

32"Fill up then the measure *of the guilt* of your fathers.

33"You serpents, you brood of vipers, how shall you escape the sentence of hell?

34"Therefore, behold, I am sending you prophets and wise men and scribes; some of them you will kill and crucify, and some of them you will scourge in your synagogues, and persecute from city to city,

35that upon you may fall *the guilt* of all the righteous blood shed on earth, from the blood of righteous Abel to the blood of Zechariah, the son of Berechiah, whom you murdered between the temple and the altar.

36"Truly I say to you, all these things shall come upon this generation.

Lament over Jerusalem

37"O Jerusalem, Jerusalem, who kills the prophets and stones those who are sent to her! How often I wanted to gather your chil-

---

μένοις,   οἵτινες   ἔξωθεν   μὲν   φαίνονται
whitewashed, who(which) outwardly   indeed   appear

ὡραῖοι,   ἔσωθεν   δὲ   γέμουσιν   ὀστέων
beautiful,   but within   they are full   of bones

νεκρῶν καὶ πάσης ἀκαθαρσίας.   28 οὕτως
of dead men and   of all   uncleanness.   Thus

καὶ ὑμεῖς ἔξωθεν μὲν φαίνεσθε τοῖς
also ye   outwardly   indeed   appear   -

ἀνθρώποις δίκαιοι, ἔσωθεν δέ ἐστε μεστοὶ
to men   righteous,   but within   ye are   full

ὑποκρίσεως καὶ ἀνομίας.   29 Οὐαὶ ὑμῖν,
of hypocrisy   and   of lawlessness.   Woe   to you

γραμματεῖς καὶ Φαρισαῖοι ὑποκριταί,
scribes   and   Pharisees   hypocrites,

ὅτι οἰκοδομεῖτε τοὺς τάφους τῶν προφητῶν
because ye build   the   graves   of the   prophets

καὶ κοσμεῖτε τὰ μνημεῖα τῶν δικαίων,
and   adorn   the   monuments   of the   righteous,

30 καὶ λέγετε· εἰ ἤμεθα ἐν ταῖς ἡμέραις
    and   say·   If   we were   in   the   days

τῶν πατέρων ἡμῶν, οὐκ ἂν ἤμεθα
of the   fathers   of us,   we would not have been

αὐτῶν κοινωνοὶ ἐν τῷ αἵματι τῶν προ-
of them   partakers   in   the   blood   of the   pro-

φητῶν.   31 ὥστε μαρτυρεῖτε ἑαυτοῖς ὅτι
phets.   So   ye witness   to [your]selves that

υἱοί ἐστε τῶν φονευσάντων τοὺς προφήτας.
sons ye are of the [ones] having killed   the   prophets.

32 καὶ ὑμεῖς πληρώσατε τὸ μέτρον τῶν
   And   ᵃye   ¹fulfil   the   measure   of the

πατέρων ὑμῶν. 33 ὄφεις, γεννήματα ἐχιδνῶν,
fathers   of you.   Serpents,   offspring   of vipers,

πῶς φύγητε ἀπὸ τῆς κρίσεως τῆς γεέννης;
how   escape ye from   the   judgment   -   of gehenna?

34 διὰ τοῦτο ἰδοὺ ἐγὼ ἀποστέλλω πρὸς
   Therefore   behold   I   send   to

ὑμᾶς προφήτας καὶ σοφοὺς καὶ γραμ-
you   prophets   and   wise men   and   scribes;

ματεῖς· ἐξ αὐτῶν ἀποκτενεῖτε καὶ
       of   them   ye will kill   and

σταυρώσετε, καὶ ἐξ αὐτῶν μαστιγώσετε
will crucify,   and   of   them   ye will scourge

ἐν ταῖς συναγωγαῖς ὑμῶν καὶ διώξετε
in   the   synagogues   of you   and will persecute

ἀπὸ πόλεως εἰς πόλιν· 35 ὅπως ἔλθῃ
from   city   to   city;   so   comes

ἐφ' ὑμᾶς πᾶν αἷμα δίκαιον ἐκχυννόμενον
on   you   all   blood   righteous   being shed

ἐπὶ τῆς γῆς ἀπὸ τοῦ αἵματος Ἄβελ τοῦ
on   the   earth from   the   blood   of Abel   the

δικαίου ἕως τοῦ αἵματος Ζαχαρίου υἱοῦ
righteous until   the   blood   of Zacharias   son

Βαραχίου, ὃν ἐφονεύσατε μεταξὺ τοῦ ναοῦ
Barachias, whom ye murdered   between   the   shrine

καὶ τοῦ θυσιαστηρίου.   36 ἀμὴν λέγω
and   the   altar.   Truly   I tell

ὑμῖν, ἥξει ταῦτα πάντα ἐπὶ τὴν
you,   will come all these things   on   -

γενεὰν ταύτην. 37 Ἰερουσαλὴμ Ἰερουσαλήμ,
generation this.   Jerusalem   Jerusalem,

ἡ ἀποκτείνουσα τοὺς προφήτας καὶ
the [one] killing   the   prophets   and

λιθοβολοῦσα τοὺς ἀπεσταλμένους πρὸς αὐτήν,
stoning   the [ones]   sent   to   her,

ποσάκις ἠθέλησα ἐπισυναγαγεῖν τὰ τέκνα
how often   I wished   to gather   the   children

---

which look beautiful on the outside but on the inside are full of dead men's bones and everything unclean. 28In the same way, on the outside you appear to people as righteous but on the inside you are full of hypocrisy and wickedness.

29"Woe to you, teachers of the law and Pharisees, you hypocrites! You build tombs for the prophets and decorate the graves of the righteous. 30And you say, 'If we had lived in the days of our forefathers, we would not have taken part with them in shedding the blood of the prophets.' 31So you testify against yourselves that you are the descendants of those who murdered the prophets. 32Fill up, then, the measure of the sin of your forefathers!

33"You snakes! You brood of vipers! How will you escape being condemned to hell? 34Therefore I am sending you prophets and wise men and teachers. Some of them you will kill and crucify; others you will flog in your synagogues and pursue from town to town. 35And so upon you will come all the righteous blood that has been shed on earth, from the blood of righteous Abel to the blood of Zechariah son of Berekiah, whom you murdered between the temple and the altar. 36I tell you the truth, all this will come upon this generation.

37"O Jerusalem, Jerusalem, you who kill the prophets and stone those sent to you, how often I have longed to gather your dren together, the way a hen gathers her chicks under her wings, and you were unwilling. 38"Behold, your house is being left to you desolate! 39"For I say to you, from now on you shall not see Me until you say, 'BLESSED IS HE WHO COMES IN THE NAME OF THE LORD!' ''

σου,	ὃν	τρόπον	ὄρνις	ἐπισυνάγει	τὰ
of thee,	as		a bird	gathers	the

νοσσία	[αὐτῆς]	ὑπὸ	τὰς	πτέρυγας,	καὶ
young	of her	under	the(her)	wings,	and

οὐκ	ἠθελήσατε.	38 ἰδοὺ	ἀφίεται	ὑμῖν	ὁ
ye wished not.		Behold	is left	to you	the

οἶκος	ὑμῶν.	39 λέγω	γὰρ	ὑμῖν,	οὐ μὴ
house	of you.	For I tell		you,	by no means

με	ἴδητε	ἀπ'	ἄρτι	ἕως	ἂν	εἴπητε·
me	ye see	from	now	until		ye say:

εὐλογημένος	ὁ	ἐρχόμενος	ἐν	ὀνόματι
Blessed	the [one]	coming	in	[the] name

κυρίου.
of [the] Lord.

children together, as a hen gathers her chicks under her wings, but you were not willing. 38Look, your house is left to you desolate. 39For I tell you, you will not see me again until you say, 'Blessed is he who comes in the name of the Lord.' [v] ''

Chapter 24

Signs of Christ's Return

AND Jesus came out from the temple and was going away when His disciples came up to point out the temple buildings to Him.

2And He answered and said to them, "Do you not see all these things? Truly I say to you, not one stone here shall be left upon another, which will not be torn down."

3And as He was sitting on the Mount of Olives, the disciples came to Him privately, saying, "Tell us, when will these things be, and what will be the sign of Your coming, and of the end of the age?"

4And Jesus answered and said to them, "See to it that no one misleads you. 5"For many will come in My name, saying, 'I am the Christ,' and will mislead many.

6"And you will be hearing of wars and rumors of wars; see that you are not frightened, for those things must take place, but that is not yet the end.

7"For nation will rise against nation, and kingdom against kingdom, and in various places there will be famines and earthquakes.

8"But all these things are merely the beginning of birth pangs.

9"Then they will deliver you to tribulation, and will kill you, and you will be

24 Καὶ	ἐξελθὼν	ὁ	Ἰησοῦς	ἀπὸ	τοῦ
And	going forth	–	Jesus	from	the

ἱεροῦ	ἐπορεύετο,	καὶ	προσῆλθον	οἱ	μαθηταὶ
temple	went,	and	[4]approached	[1]the	[2]disciples

αὐτοῦ	ἐπιδεῖξαι	αὐτῷ	τὰς	οἰκοδομὰς
[3]of him	to show	him	the	buildings

τοῦ	ἱεροῦ.	2 ὁ	δὲ	ἀποκριθεὶς	εἶπεν
of the	temple.	And he		answering	said

αὐτοῖς·	οὐ	βλέπετε	ταῦτα	πάντα;	ἀμὴν
to them:	See ye not		all these things?		Truly

λέγω	ὑμῖν,	οὐ μὴ	ἀφεθῇ	ὧδε	λίθος	ἐπὶ
I tell	you,	by no means	will be left	here	stone	on

λίθον	ὃς	οὐ	καταλυθήσεται.	3 Καθημένου
stone	which		shall not be overthrown.	sitting

δὲ	αὐτοῦ	ἐπὶ	τοῦ	ὄρους	τῶν	ἐλαιῶν
and	him[a]	on	the	mount	of the	olives

= And as he sat

προσῆλθον	αὐτῷ	οἱ	μαθηταὶ	κατ'	ἰδίαν
approached	to him	the	disciples		privately

λέγοντες·	εἰπὲ	ἡμῖν,	πότε	ταῦτα	ἔσται,
saying:	Tell	us,	when	these things	will be,

καὶ	τί	τὸ	σημεῖον	τῆς	σῆς	παρουσίας
and	what	the	sign		of thy	presence

καὶ	συντελείας	τοῦ	αἰῶνος;	4 καὶ	ἀπο-
and	of [the] completion of the		age?	And	answer-

κριθεὶς	ὁ	Ἰησοῦς	εἶπεν	αὐτοῖς·	βλέπετε
ing	–	Jesus	said	to them:	See ye

μή	τις	ὑμᾶς	πλανήσῃ.	5 πολλοὶ	γὰρ
not(lest) anyone	[2]you	[1]cause [3]to err.		For many	

ἐλεύσονται	ἐπὶ	τῷ	ὀνόματί	μου	λέγοντες·
will come	on(in)	the	name	of me	saying:

ἐγώ	εἰμι	ὁ	χριστός,	καὶ	πολλοὺς	πλανή-
I	am	the	Christ,	and	[2]many	[1]will cause

σουσιν.	6 μελλήσετε	δὲ	ἀκούειν	πολέ-
[3]to err.	But ye will be about		to hear	[of]

μους	καὶ	ἀκοὰς	πολέμων·	ὁρᾶτε	μὴ
wars	and	rumours	of wars;	see	not

θροεῖθε·	δεῖ	γὰρ	γενέσθαι,	ἀλλ'
ye are disturbed;	for it behoves		to happen,	but

οὔπω	ἐστὶν	τὸ	τέλος.	7 ἐγερθήσεται	γὰρ
not yet	is	the	end.	For will be raised	

ἔθνος	ἐπὶ	ἔθνος	καὶ	βασιλεία	ἐπὶ	βασιλείαν,
nation	against nation		and	kingdom	against	kingdom,

καὶ	ἔσονται	λιμοὶ	καὶ	σεισμοὶ
and	there will be	famines	and	earthquakes

κατὰ	τόπους·	8 πάντα	δὲ	ταῦτα	ἀρχὴ
throughout places;		but all these things [are]			beginning

ὠδίνων.	9 τότε	παραδώσουσιν	ὑμᾶς
of birth-pangs.	Then	they will deliver	you

εἰς	θλῖψιν	καὶ	ἀποκτενοῦσιν	ὑμᾶς,
to	affliction	and	will kill	you,

Chapter 24

Signs of the End of the Age

JESUS left the temple and was walking away when his disciples came up to him to call his attention to its buildings. 2"Do you see all these things?" he asked. "I tell you the truth, not one stone here will be left on another; every one will be thrown down."

3As Jesus was sitting on the Mount of Olives, the disciples came to him privately. "Tell us," they said, "when will this happen, and what will be the sign of your coming and of the end of the age?"

4Jesus answered: "Watch out that no one deceives you. 5For many will come in my name, claiming, 'I am the Christ,' [w] and will deceive many. 6You will hear of wars and rumors of wars, but see to it that you are not alarmed. Such things must happen, but the end is still to come. 7Nation will rise against nation, and kingdom against kingdom. There will be famines and earthquakes in various places. 8All these are the beginning of birth pains.

9"Then you will be handed over to be persecuted and put to death, and you

[v]39 Psalm 118:26
[w]5 Or Messiah; also in verse 23

hated by all nations on account of My name.
10"And at that time many will fall away and will deliver up one another and hate one another.
11"And many false prophets will arise, and will mislead many.
12"And because lawlessness is increased, most people's love will grow cold.
13"But the one who endures to the end, he shall be saved.
14"And this gospel of the kingdom shall be preached in the whole world for a witness to all the nations, and then the end shall come.

Perilous Times

15"Therefore when you see the ABOMINATION OF DESOLATION which was spoken of through Daniel the prophet, standing in the holy place (let the reader understand),
16then let those who are in Judea flee to the mountains;
17let him who is on the housetop not go down to get the things out that are in his house;
18and let him who is in the field not turn back to get his cloak.
19"But woe to those who are with child and to those who nurse babes in those days!
20"But pray that your flight may not be in the winter, or on a Sabbath;
21for then there will be a great tribulation, such as has not occurred since the beginning of the world until now, nor ever shall.
22"And unless those days had been cut short, no life would have been saved; but for the sake of the elect those days shall be cut short.
23"Then if anyone says to you, 'Behold, here is the

καὶ	ἔσεσθε	μισούμενοι	ὑπὸ	πάντων
and	ye will be	*being* hated	by	all

τῶν	ἐθνῶν	διὰ	τὸ	ὄνομά	μου.
the	nations	because of	the	name	of me.

10 καὶ τότε σκανδαλισθήσονται πολλοὶ καὶ
And then will be offended many and

ἀλλήλους παραδώσουσιν καὶ μισήσουσιν
one another will deliver and they will hate

ἀλλήλους· **11** καὶ πολλοὶ ψευδοπροφῆται
one another; and many false prophets

ἐγερθήσονται καὶ πλανήσουσιν πολλούς·
will be raised and will cause to err many;

12 καὶ διὰ τὸ πληθυνθῆναι τὴν
and because of - to be increased the

ἀνομίαν ψυγήσεται ἡ ἀγάπη τῶν
lawlessness will grow cold the love ,of the

πολλῶν. **13** ὁ δὲ ὑπομείνας εἰς τέλος,
many. But the [one] enduring to [the] end,

οὗτος σωθήσεται. **14** καὶ κηρυχθήσεται
this will be saved. And will be proclaimed

τοῦτο τὸ εὐαγγέλιον τῆς βασιλείας
this the gospel of the kingdom

ἐν ὅλῃ τῇ οἰκουμένῃ εἰς μαρτύριον
in all the inhabited earth for a testimony

πᾶσιν τοῖς ἔθνεσιν, καὶ τότε ἥξει τὸ
to all the nations, and then will come the

τέλος. **15** Ὅταν οὖν ἴδητε τὸ
end. When therefore ye see the

βδέλυγμα τῆς ἐρημώσεως τὸ ῥηθὲν διὰ
abomination - of desolation - spoken through

Δανιὴλ τοῦ προφήτου ἑστὸς ἐν τόπῳ
Daniel the prophet stand in place

ἁγίῳ, ὁ ἀναγινώσκων νοείτω,
holy, the [one] reading let him understand,

16 τότε οἱ ἐν τῇ Ἰουδαίᾳ φευγέτωσαν
then the [ones] in - Judæa let them flee

εἰς τὰ ὄρη, **17** ὁ ἐπὶ τοῦ δώματος μὴ
to the mountains, the [one] on the housetop let him

καταβάτω ἆραι τὰ ἐκ τῆς οἰκίας αὐτοῦ,
not come down to take the things out of the house of him,

18 καὶ ὁ ἐν τῷ ἀγρῷ μὴ ἐπιστρεψάτω
and the [one] in the field let him not turn back

ὀπίσω ἆραι τὸ ἱμάτιον αὐτοῦ. **19** οὐαὶ
behind to take the garment of him. woe

δὲ ταῖς ἐν γαστρὶ ἐχούσαις καὶ ταῖς
And to the women in womb having and to the [ones]
= the pregnant women

θηλαζούσαις ἐν ἐκείναις ταῖς ἡμέραις.
giving suck in those - days.

20 προσεύχεσθε δὲ ἵνα μὴ γένηται ἡ
And pray ye lest happen the

φυγὴ ὑμῶν χειμῶνος μηδὲ σαββάτῳ·
flight of you of(in) winter nor on a sabbath;

21 ἔσται γὰρ τότε θλῖψις μεγάλη, οἵα οὐ
for will be then affliction great, such as not

γέγονεν ἀπ' ἀρχῆς κόσμου ἕως
has happened from [the] beginning of [the] world until

τοῦ νῦν οὐδ' οὐ μὴ γένηται. **22** καὶ
- now neither by no means may happen. And

εἰ μὴ ἐκολοβώθησαν αἱ ἡμέραι ἐκεῖναι,
except were cut short - days those,

οὐκ ἂν ἐσώθη πᾶσα σάρξ· διὰ δὲ τοὺς
not - was saved all flesh; but on account of the
= no flesh would be saved;

ἐκλεκτοὺς κολοβωθήσονται αἱ ἡμέραι ἐκεῖναι.
chosen will be cut short - days those.

23 τότε ἐάν τις ὑμῖν εἴπῃ· ἰδοὺ ὧδε
Then if anyone to you says: Behold here

will be hated by all nations because of me. 10At that time many will turn away from the faith and will betray and hate each other, 11and many false prophets will appear and deceive many people. 12Because of the increase of wickedness, the love of most will grow cold, 13but he who stands firm to the end will be saved. 14And this gospel of the kingdom will be preached in the whole world as a testimony to all nations, and then the end will come.

15"So when you see standing in the holy place 'the abomination that causes desolation,'[x] spoken of through the prophet Daniel—let the reader understand—16then let those who are in Judea flee to the mountains. 17Let no one on the roof of his house go down to take anything out of the house. 18Let no one in the field go back to get his cloak. 19How dreadful it will be in those days for pregnant women and nursing mothers! 20Pray that your flight will not take place in winter or on the Sabbath. 21For then there will be great distress, unequaled from the beginning of the world until now—and never to be equaled again. 22If those days had not been cut short, no one would survive, but for the sake of the elect those days will be shortened. 23At that time if anyone says to you, 'Look, here is the Christ!'

ˣ*15* Daniel 9:27; 11:31; 12:11

Christ,' or 'There *He is*,' do not believe *him*.

24"For false Christs and false prophets will arise and will show great signs and wonders, so as to mislead, if possible, even the elect.

25"Behold, I have told you in advance.

26"If therefore they say to you, 'Behold, He is in the wilderness,' do not go forth, *or*, 'Behold, He is in the inner rooms,' do not believe *them*.

27"For just as the lightning comes from the east, and flashes even to the west, so shall the coming of the Son of Man be.

28"Wherever the corpse is, there the vultures will gather.

The Glorious Return

29"But immediately after the tribulation of those days THE SUN WILL BE DARKENED, AND THE MOON WILL NOT GIVE ITS LIGHT, AND THE STARS WILL FALL from the sky, and the powers of the heavens will be shaken,

30and then the sign of the Son of Man will appear in the sky, and then all the tribes of the earth will mourn, and they will see the SON OF MAN COMING ON THE CLOUDS OF THE SKY with power and great glory.

31"And He will send forth His angels with A GREAT TRUMPET and THEY WILL GATHER TOGETHER His elect from the four winds, from one end of the sky to the other.

Parable of the Fig Tree

32"Now learn the parable from the fig tree: when its branch has already become tender, and puts forth its leaves, you know that summer is near;

33even so you too, when

ὁ χριστός, ἤ· ὧδε, μὴ πιστεύσητε·
the Christ, or: Here, do not believe;

24 ἐγερθήσονται γὰρ ψευδόχριστοι καὶ
for will be raised false Christs and

ψευδοπροφῆται, καὶ δώσουσιν σημεῖα μεγάλα
false prophets, and they will give signs great

καὶ τέρατα, ὥστε πλανῆσαι, εἰ δυνατόν,
and marvels, so as to cause to err, if possible,

καὶ τοὺς ἐκλεκτούς. 25 ἰδοὺ προείρηκα
even the chosen. Behold I have before told

ὑμῖν. 26 ἐὰν οὖν εἴπωσιν ὑμῖν· ἰδοὺ
you. If therefore they say to you: Behold

ἐν τῇ ἐρήμῳ ἐστίν, μὴ ἐξέλθητε· ἰδοὺ
in the desert he is, go not ye forth; Behold

ἐν τοῖς ταμείοις, μὴ πιστεύσητε·
in the private rooms, do not ye believe;

27 ὥσπερ γὰρ ἡ ἀστραπὴ ἐξέρχεται ἀπὸ
for as the lightning comes forth from

ἀνατολῶν καὶ φαίνεται ἕως δυσμῶν,
[the] east and shines unto [the] west,

οὕτως ἔσται ἡ παρουσία τοῦ υἱοῦ
so will be the presence of the Son

τοῦ ἀνθρώπου· 28 ὅπου ἐὰν ᾖ τὸ
- of man; wherever may be the

πτῶμα, ἐκεῖ συναχθήσονται οἱ ἀετοί.
carcase, there will be assembled the eagles.

29 Εὐθέως δὲ μετὰ τὴν θλῖψιν τῶν
And immediately after the affliction -

ἡμερῶν ἐκείνων ὁ ἥλιος σκοτισθήσεται,
days of those the sun will be darkened,

καὶ ἡ σελήνη οὐ δώσει τὸ φέγγος
and the moon will not give the light

αὐτῆς, καὶ οἱ ἀστέρες πεσοῦνται ἀπὸ τοῦ
of her, and the stars will fall from -

οὐρανοῦ, καὶ αἱ δυνάμεις τῶν οὐρανῶν
heaven, and the powers of the heavens

σαλευθήσονται. 30 καὶ τότε φανήσεται
will be shaken. And then will appear

τὸ σημεῖον τοῦ υἱοῦ τοῦ ἀνθρώπου ἐν
the sign of the Son - of man in

οὐρανῷ, καὶ τότε κόψονται πᾶσαι αἱ
heaven, and then will bewail all the

φυλαὶ τῆς γῆς καὶ ὄψονται τὸν υἱὸν
tribes of the land and they will see the Son

τοῦ ἀνθρώπου ἐρχόμενον ἐπὶ τῶν
- of man coming on the

νεφελῶν τοῦ οὐρανοῦ μετὰ δυνάμεως καὶ
clouds - of heaven with power and

δόξης πολλῆς· 31 καὶ ἀποστελεῖ τοὺς
glory much; and he will send the

ἀγγέλους αὐτοῦ μετὰ σάλπιγγος μεγάλης,
angels of him with trumpet a great,

καὶ ἐπισυνάξουσιν τοὺς ἐκλεκτοὺς αὐτοῦ
and they will assemble the chosen of him

ἐκ τῶν τεσσάρων ἀνέμων ἀπ' ἄκρων
out of the four winds from [the] extremities

οὐρανῶν ἕως [τῶν] ἄκρων αὐτῶν. 32 Ἀπὸ
of [the] heavens unto the extremities of them. from

δὲ τῆς συκῆς μάθετε τὴν παραβολήν·
Now the fig-tree learn ye the parable:

ὅταν ἤδη ὁ κλάδος αὐτῆς γένηται ἀπαλὸς
When now the branch of it becomes tender

καὶ τὰ φύλλα ἐκφύῃ, γινώσκετε ὅτι
and the leaves it puts forth, ye know that

ἐγγὺς τὸ θέρος· 33 οὕτως καὶ ὑμεῖς
near [is] the summer; so also ye

---

or, 'There he is!' do not believe it. 24For false Christs and false prophets will appear and perform great signs and miracles to deceive even the elect—if that were possible. 25See, I have told you ahead of time.

26"So if anyone tells you, 'There he is, out in the desert,' do not go out; or, 'Here he is, in the inner rooms,' do not believe it. 27For as lightning that comes from the east is visible even in the west, so will be the coming of the Son of Man. 28Wherever there is a carcass, there the vultures will gather.

29"Immediately after the distress of those days

" 'the sun will be
    darkened,
  and the moon will not
    give its light;
  the stars will fall from
    the sky,
  and the heavenly
    bodies will be
    shaken.' [y]

30"At that time the sign of the Son of Man will appear in the sky, and all the nations of the earth will mourn. They will see the Son of Man coming on the clouds of the sky, with power and great glory. 31And he will send his angels with a loud trumpet call, and they will gather his elect from the four winds, from one end of the heavens to the other.

32"Now learn this lesson from the fig tree: As soon as its twigs get tender and its leaves come out, you know that summer is near. 33Even so, when you see all

[y]29 Isaiah 13:10; 34:4

you see all these things, recognize that He is near, *right* at the door.
34"Truly I say to you, this generation will not pass away until all these things take place.
35"Heaven and earth will pass away, but My words shall not pass away.
36"But of that day and hour no one knows, not even the angels of heaven, nor the Son, but the Father alone.
37"For the coming of the Son of Man will be just like the days of Noah.
38"For as in those days which were before the flood they were eating and drinking, they were marrying and giving in marriage, until the day that Noah entered the ark,
39and they did not understand until the flood came and took them all away; so shall the coming of the Son of Man be.
40"Then there shall be two men in the field; one will be taken, and one will be left.
41"Two women *will be* grinding at the mill; one will be taken, and one will be left.

Be Ready for His Coming
42"Therefore be on the alert, for you do not know which day your Lord is coming.
43"But be sure of this, that if the head of the house had known at what time of the night the thief was coming, he would have been on the alert and would not have allowed his house to be broken into.
44"For this reason you be ready too; for the Son of Man is coming at an hour when you do not think *He will.*
45"Who then is the faithful and sensible slave whom his master put in charge of his household to

ὅταν ἴδητε πάντα ταῦτα, γινώσκετε ὅτι
when ye see all these things, know that

ἐγγύς ἐστιν ἐπὶ θύραις. 34 ἀμὴν λέγω
near it is on(at) [the] doors. Truly I tell

ὑμῖν ὅτι οὐ μὴ παρέλθῃ ἡ γενεὰ
you that by no means passes away - generation

αὕτη ἕως ἂν πάντα ταῦτα γένηται.
this until all these things happens.

35 ὁ οὐρανὸς καὶ ἡ γῆ παρελεύσεται, οἱ
The heaven and the earth will pass away, ²the

δὲ λόγοι μου οὐ μὴ παρέλθωσιν. 36 Περὶ
¹but words of me by no means may pass away. concerning

δὲ τῆς ἡμέρας ἐκείνης καὶ ὥρας οὐδεὶς
But - day that and hour no one

οἶδεν, οὐδὲ οἱ ἄγγελοι τῶν οὐρανῶν
knows, neither the angels of *the* heavens

οὐδὲ ὁ υἱός, εἰ μὴ ὁ πατὴρ μόνος.
nor the Son, except the Father only.

37 ὥσπερ γὰρ αἱ ἡμέραι τοῦ Νῶε, οὕτως
For as the days - of Noah, so

ἔσται ἡ παρουσία τοῦ υἱοῦ τοῦ ἀνθρώπου.
will be the presence of the Son - of man.

38 ὡς γὰρ ἦσαν ἐν ταῖς ἡμέραις
For as they were in - days

[ἐκείναις] ταῖς πρὸ τοῦ κατακλυσμοῦ
those the [ones] before the flood

τρώγοντες καὶ πίνοντες, γαμοῦντες καὶ
eating and drinking, marrying and

γαμίζοντες, ἄχρι ἧς ἡμέρας εἰσῆλθεν
being given in marriage, until which day entered

Νῶε εἰς τὴν κιβωτόν, 39 καὶ οὐκ ἔγνωσαν
Noah into the ark, and knew not

ἕως ἦλθεν ὁ κατακλυσμὸς καὶ ἦρεν
until came the flood and took

ἅπαντας, οὕτως ἔσται καὶ ἡ παρουσία
all, so will be also the presence

τοῦ υἱοῦ τοῦ ἀνθρώπου 40 τότε ἔσονται
of the Son - of man. Then will be

δύο ἐν τῷ ἀγρῷ, εἷς παραλαμβάνεται
two men in the field, one is taken

καὶ εἷς ἀφίεται· 41 δύο ἀλήθουσαι
and one is left; two women grinding

ἐν τῷ μύλῳ, μία παραλαμβάνεται καὶ
in(at) the mill, one is taken and

μία ἀφίεται. 42 γρηγορεῖτε οὖν, ὅτι
one is left. Watch ye therefore, because

οὐκ οἴδατε ποίᾳ ἡμέρᾳ ὁ κύριος
ye know not on what day the lord

ὑμῶν ἔρχεται. 43 Ἐκεῖνο δὲ γινώσκετε
of you is coming. And that know ye

ὅτι εἰ ᾔδει ὁ οἰκοδεσπότης ποίᾳ
that if knew the housemaster in what

φυλακῇ ὁ κλέπτης ἔρχεται, ἐγρηγόρησεν
watch the thief is coming, he would have

ἂν καὶ οὐκ ἂν εἴασεν διορυχθῆναι
watched and would not have allowed to be dug through

τὴν οἰκίαν αὐτοῦ. 44 διὰ τοῦτο καὶ
the house of him. Therefore also

ὑμεῖς γίνεσθε ἕτοιμοι, ὅτι ᾗ οὐ δοκεῖτε
ye be ready, because ¹in which ²ye think not

ὥρᾳ ὁ υἱὸς τοῦ ἀνθρώπου ἔρχεται. 45 Τίς
²hour the Son - of man comes. Who

ἄρα ἐστὶν ὁ πιστὸς δοῦλος καὶ φρόνιμος
then is the faithful slave and prudent

ὃν κατέστησεν ὁ κύριος ἐπὶ τῆς οἰκετείας
whom appointed the lord over the household

these things, you know that it° is near, right at the door. 34I tell you the truth, this generation° will certainly not pass away until all these things have happened. 35Heaven and earth will pass away, but my words will never pass away.

The Day and Hour Unknown
36"No one knows about that day or hour, not even the angels in heaven, nor the Son,ᵇ but only the Father. 37As it was in the days of Noah, so it will be at the coming of the Son of Man. 38For in the days before the flood, people were eating and drinking, marrying and giving in marriage, up to the day Noah entered the ark; 39and they knew nothing about what would happen until the flood came and took them all away. That is how it will be at the coming of the Son of Man. 40Two men will be in the field; one will be taken and the other left. 41Two women will be grinding with a hand mill; one will be taken and the other left.

42"Therefore keep watch, because you do not know on what day your Lord will come. 43But understand this: If the owner of the house had known at what time of night the thief was coming, he would have kept watch and would not have let his house be broken into. 44So you also must be ready, because the Son of Man will come at an hour when you do not expect him.

45"Who then is the faithful and wise servant, whom the master has put in charge of the servants in his

ᶜ33 Or he
ᵃ34 Or race
ᵇ36 Some manuscripts do not have nor the Son.

give them their food at the proper time? 46"Blessed is that slave whom his master finds so doing when he comes. 47"Truly I say to you, that he will put him in charge of all his possessions. 48"But if that evil slave says in his heart, 'My master is not coming for a long time,' 49and shall begin to beat his fellow slaves and eat and drink with drunkards; 50the master of that slave will come on a day when he does not expect *him* and at an hour which he does not know, 51and shall cut him in pieces and assign him a place with the hypocrites; weeping shall be there and the gnashing of teeth.

αὐτοῦ	τοῦ	δοῦναι	αὐτοῖς	τὴν	τροφὴν	ἐν
of him	-	to give[d]	to them	the	food	in

καιρῷ;	46 μακάριος	ὁ	δοῦλος	ἐκεῖνος	ὃν
season?	blessed [is]	the	slave	that	whom

ἐλθὼν	ὁ	κύριος	αὐτοῦ	εὑρήσει	οὕτως
coming	the	lord	of him	will find	so

ποιοῦντα·	47 ἀμὴν	λέγω	ὑμῖν	ὅτι	ἐπὶ
doing;	truly	I tell	you	that	over

πᾶσιν	τοῖς	ὑπάρχουσιν	αὐτοῦ	καταστήσει
all	the	goods	of him	he will appoint

αὐτόν.	48 ἐὰν	δὲ	εἴπῃ	ὁ	κακὸς	δοῦλος
him.	But if		says	-	wicked	slave

ἐκεῖνος	ἐν	τῇ	καρδίᾳ	αὐτοῦ·	χρονίζει
that	in	the	heart	of him:	Delays

μου	ὁ	κύριος,	49 καὶ	ἄρξηται	τύπτειν
of me	the	lord,	and	begins	to strike

τοὺς	συνδούλους	αὐτοῦ,	ἐσθίῃ	δὲ	καὶ
the	fellow-slaves	of him,	and eats		and

πίνῃ	μετὰ	τῶν	μεθυόντων,	50 ἥξει	ὁ
drinks	with	the [ones]	being drunk,	will come	the

κύριος	τοῦ	δούλου	ἐκείνου	ἐν	ἡμέρᾳ	ᾗ
lord	-	slave	of that	on	a day	on which

οὐ	προσδοκᾷ	καὶ	ἐν	ὥρᾳ	ᾗ	οὐ
he does not expect		and	in	an hour	in which	not

γινώσκει,	51 καὶ	διχοτομήσει	αὐτόν,
he knows,	and	will cut asunder	him,

καὶ	τὸ	μέρος	αὐτοῦ	μετὰ	τῶν
and	the	portion	of him	with	the

ὑποκριτῶν	θήσει·	ἐκεῖ	ἔσταί	ὁ
hypocrites	will place;	there	will be	the

κλαυθμὸς	καὶ	ὁ	βρυγμὸς	τῶν	ὀδόντων.
wailing	and	the	gnashing	of the	teeth.

household to give them their food at the proper time? 46It will be good for that servant whose master finds him doing so when he returns. 47I tell you the truth, he will put him in charge of all his possessions. 48But suppose that servant is wicked and says to himself, 'My master is staying away a long time,' 49and he then begins to beat his fellow servants and to eat and drink with drunkards. 50The master of that servant will come on a day when he does not expect him and at an hour he is not aware of. 51He will cut him to pieces and assign him a place with the hypocrites, where there will be weeping and gnashing of teeth.

Chapter 25

Parable of Ten Virgins

" "THEN the kingdom of heaven will be comparable to ten virgins, who took their lamps, and went out to meet the bridegroom. 2"And five of them were foolish, and five were prudent. 3"For when the foolish took their lamps, they took no oil with them, 4but the prudent took oil in flasks along with their lamps. 5"Now while the bridegroom was delaying, they all got drowsy and *began* to sleep. 6"But at midnight there was a shout, 'Behold, the bridegroom! Come out to meet *him*.' 7"Then all those virgins

25 Τότε	ὁμοιωθήσεται	ἡ	βασιλεία
Then	shall be likened	the	kingdom

τῶν	οὐρανῶν	δέκα	παρθένοις,	αἵτινες
of the	heavens	to ten	virgins,	who

λαβοῦσαι	τὰς	λαμπάδας	ἑαυτῶν*	ἐξῆλθον
taking	the	lamps	of them*	went forth

εἰς	ὑπάντησιν	τοῦ	νυμφίου.	2 πέντε	δὲ
to	a meeting	of the	bridegroom.	Now five	

ἐξ	αὐτῶν	ἦσαν	μωραὶ	καὶ	πέντε	φρόνιμοι.
of	them	were	foolish	and	five	prudent.

3 αἱ	γὰρ	μωραὶ	λαβοῦσαι	τὰς	λαμπάδας
For the		foolish [ones]	taking	the	lamps

οὐκ	ἔλαβον	μεθ’	ἑαυτῶν	ἔλαιον.
did not take		with	them	oil.

4 αἱ	δὲ	φρόνιμοι	ἔλαβον	ἔλαιον	ἐν
But the		prudent [ones]	took	oil	in

τοῖς	ἀγγείοις	μετὰ	τῶν	λαμπάδων	ἑαυτῶν.
the	vessels	with	the	lamps	of them.

5 χρονίζοντος	δὲ	τοῦ	νυμφίου[a]	ἐνύσταξαν
But delaying		the	bridegroom[a]	slumbered

= while the bridegroom delayed

πᾶσαι	καὶ	ἐκάθευδον.	6 μέσης	δὲ
all	and	slept.	And of(in)	[the] middle

νυκτὸς	κραυγὴ	γέγονεν·	ἰδοὺ	ὁ
of [the] night	a cry	there has been:	Behold[,]	the

νυμφίος,	ἐξέρχεσθε	εἰς	ἀπάντησιν.	7 τότε
bridegroom,	go ye forth	to	a meeting.	Then

ἠγέρθησαν	πᾶσαι	αἱ	παρθένοι	ἐκεῖναι
were raised	all	-	virgins	those

Chapter 25

The Parable of the Ten Virgins

" "AT that time the kingdom of heaven will be like ten virgins who took their lamps and went out to meet the bridegroom. 2Five of them were foolish and five were wise. 3The foolish ones took their lamps but did not take any oil with them. 4The wise, however, took oil in jars along with their lamps. 5The bridegroom was a long time in coming, and they all became drowsy and fell asleep.
6"At midnight the cry rang out: 'Here's the bridegroom! Come out to meet him!'
7"Then all the virgins

*Here, and in the three following occurrences, as elsewhere, the strict meaning is emphatic or reflexive—'of themselves'; but this cannot be insisted on.

rose, and trimmed their lamps.

8 "And the foolish said to the prudent, 'Give us some of your oil, for our lamps are going out.'

9 "But the prudent answered, saying, 'No, there will not be enough for us and you *too*; go instead to the dealers and buy *some* for yourselves.'

10 "And while they were going away to make the purchase, the bridegroom came, and those who were ready went in with him to the wedding feast; and the door was shut.

11 "And later the other virgins also came, saying, 'Lord, lord, open up for us.'

12 "But he answered and said, 'Truly I say to you, I do not know you.'

13 "Be on the alert then, for you do not know the day nor the hour.

Parable of the Talents

14 "For *it is* just like a man *about* to go on a journey, who called his own slaves, and entrusted his possessions to them.

15 "And to one he gave five talents, to another, two, and to another, one, each according to his own ability; and he went on his journey.

16 "Immediately the one who had received the five talents went and traded with them, and gained five more talents.

17 "In the same manner the one who *had received* the two *talents* gained two more.

18 "But he who received the one *talent* went away and dug in the ground, and hid his master's money.

19 "Now after a long time the master of those slaves *came and *settled accounts with them.

καὶ ἐκόσμησαν τὰς λαμπάδας ἑαυτῶν.
and trimmed the lamps of them.

8 αἱ δὲ μωραὶ ταῖς φρονίμοις εἶπαν·
So the foolish [ones] to the prudent said:

δότε ἡμῖν ἐκ τοῦ ἐλαίου ὑμῶν, ὅτι
Give us of the oil of you, because

αἱ λαμπάδες ἡμῶν σβέννυνται. 9 ἀπεκρί-
the lamps of us are being quenched. But

θησαν δὲ αἱ φρόνιμοι λέγουσαι· μήποτε
answered the prudent saying: Lest

οὐ μὴ ἀρκέσῃ ἡμῖν καὶ ὑμῖν·
by no means it suffices to us and to you;

πορεύεσθε μᾶλλον πρὸς τοὺς πωλοῦντας
go ye rather to the [ones] selling

καὶ ἀγοράσατε ἑαυταῖς. 10 ἀπερχομένων
and buy for [your]selves. And going

δὲ αὐτῶν ἀγοράσαι ἦλθεν ὁ νυμφίος,
away them[a] to buy came the bridegroom,
were going away

καὶ αἱ ἕτοιμοι εἰσῆλθον μετ᾽ αὐτοῦ
and the ready [ones] went in with him

εἰς τοὺς γάμους, καὶ ἐκλείσθη ἡ
to the wedding festivities, and was shut the

θύρα. 11 ὕστερον δὲ ἔρχονται καὶ αἱ
door. Then later come also the

λοιπαὶ παρθένοι λέγουσαι· κύριε κύριε,
remaining virgins saying: Lord[,] Lord,

ἄνοιξον ἡμῖν. 12 ὁ δὲ ἀποκριθεὶς εἶπεν·
open to us. But he answering said:

ἀμὴν λέγω ὑμῖν, οὐκ οἶδα ὑμᾶς.
Truly I say to you, I know not you.

13 Γρηγορεῖτε οὖν, ὅτι οὐκ οἴδατε
Watch ye therefore, because ye know not

τὴν ἡμέραν οὐδὲ τὴν ὥραν. 14 Ὥσπερ
the day nor the hour. as

γὰρ ἄνθρωπος ἀποδημῶν ἐκάλεσεν
For a man going from home called

τοὺς ἰδίους δούλους καὶ παρέδωκεν αὐτοῖς
the(his) own slaves and delivered to them

τὰ ὑπάρχοντα αὐτοῦ, 15 καὶ ᾧ μὲν ἔδωκεν
the goods of him, and to one he gave

πέντε τάλαντα, ᾧ δὲ δύο, ᾧ δὲ
five talents, to another two, to another

ἕν, ἑκάστῳ κατὰ τὴν ἰδίαν δύναμιν,
one, to each according to the(his) own ability,

καὶ ἀπεδήμησεν. 16 εὐθέως πορευθεὶς
and went from home. Immediately going

ὁ τὰ πέντε τάλαντα λαβὼν ἠργάσατο
the [one] the five talents receiving traded

ἐν αὐτοῖς καὶ ἐκέρδησεν ἄλλα
in them and gained other

πέντε· 17 ὡσαύτως ὁ τὰ δύο ἐκέρδησεν
five; similarly the [one] the two gained
[receiving]

ἄλλα δύο. 18 ὁ δὲ τὸ ἓν λαβὼν
other two. But the [one] the one receiving

ἀπελθὼν ὤρυξεν γῆν καὶ ἔκρυψεν
going away dug earth and hid

τὸ ἀργύριον τοῦ κυρίου αὐτοῦ.
the silver of the lord of him.

19 μετὰ δὲ πολὺν χρόνον ἔρχεται ὁ
Then after much time comes the

κύριος τῶν δούλων ἐκείνων καὶ συναίρει
lord - slaves of those and takes

λόγον μετ᾽ αὐτῶν. 20 καὶ προσελθὼν
account with them. And approaching

---

woke up and trimmed their lamps. 8 The foolish ones said to the wise, 'Give us some of your oil; our lamps are going out.'

9 " 'No,' they replied, 'there may not be enough for both us and you. Instead, go to those who sell oil and buy some for yourselves.'

10 "But while they were on their way to buy the oil, the bridegroom arrived. The virgins who were ready went in with him to the wedding banquet. And the door was shut.

11 "Later the others also came. 'Sir! Sir!' they said. 'Open the door for us!'

12 "But he replied, 'I tell you the truth, I don't know you.'

13 "Therefore keep watch, because you do not know the day or the hour.

The Parable of the Talents

14 "Again, it will be like a man going on a journey, who called his servants and entrusted his property to them. 15 To one he gave five talents[c] of money, to another two talents, and to another one talent, each according to his ability. Then he went on his journey. 16 The man who had received the five talents went at once and put his money to work and gained five more. 17 So also, the one with the two talents gained two more. 18 But the man who had received the one talent went off, dug a hole in the ground and hid his master's money. 19 "After a long time the master of those servants returned and settled accounts

c 15 A talent was worth more than a thousand dollars.

20"And the one who had received the five talents came up and brought five more talents, saying, 'Master, you entrusted five talents to me; see, I have gained five more talents.'

21"His master said to him, 'Well done, good and faithful slave; you were faithful with a few things, I will put you in charge of many things, enter into the joy of your master.'

22"The one also who *had received* the two talents came up and said, 'Master, you entrusted to me two talents; see, I have gained two more talents.'

23"His master said to him, 'Well done, good and faithful slave; you were faithful with a few things, I will put you in charge of many things; enter into the joy of your master.'

24"And the one also who had received the one talent came up and said, 'Master, I knew you to be a hard man, reaping where you did not sow, and gathering where you scattered no *seed*.

25'And I was afraid, and went away and hid your talent in the ground; see, you have what is yours.'

26"But his master answered and said to him, 'You wicked, lazy slave, you knew that I reap where I did not sow, and gather where I scattered no *seed*.

27'Then you ought to have put my money in the bank, and on my arrival I would have received my *money* back with interest.

28'Therefore take away the talent from him, and give it to the one who has the ten talents.'

29"For to everyone who has shall *more* be given,

ὁ τὰ πέντε τάλαντα λαβὼν προσ-
the [one] the five talents receiving brought
ἤνεγκεν ἄλλα πέντε τάλαντα λέγων· κύριε,
other five talents saying: Lord,
πέντε τάλαντά μοι παρέδωκας· ἴδε ἄλλα
five talents to me thou deliveredst; behold other
πέντε τάλαντα ἐκέρδησα. 21 ἔφη αὐτῷ
five talents I gained. Said to him
ὁ κύριος αὐτοῦ· εὖ, δοῦλε ἀγαθὲ καὶ
the lord of him: Well, slave good and
πιστέ, ἐπὶ ὀλίγα ἦς πιστός,
faithful, over a few things thou wast faithful,
ἐπὶ πολλῶν σε καταστήσω· εἴσελθε
over many thee I will set; enter thou
εἰς τὴν χαρὰν τοῦ κυρίου σου. 22 προσ-
into the joy of the lord of thee. Ap-
ελθὼν καὶ ὁ τὰ δύο τάλαντα
proaching also the [one] the two talents
[having received]
εἶπεν· κύριε, δύο τάλαντά μοι
said: Lord, two talents to me
παρέδωκας· ἴδε ἄλλα δύο τάλαντα
thou deliveredst; behold other two talents
ἐκέρδησα. 23 ἔφη αὐτῷ ὁ κύριος αὐτοῦ·
I gained. Said to him the lord of him:
εὖ, δοῦλε ἀγαθὲ καὶ πιστέ, ἐπὶ
Well, slave good and faithful, over
ὀλίγα ἦς πιστός, ἐπὶ πολλῶν
a few things thou wast faithful, over many
σε καταστήσω· εἴσελθε εἰς τὴν
thee I will set; enter thou into the
χαρὰν τοῦ κυρίου σου. 24 προσ-
joy of the lord of thee. ap-
ελθὼν δὲ καὶ ὁ τὸ ἓν τάλαντον
proaching And also the [one] the one talent
εἰληφὼς εἶπεν· κύριε, ἔγνων σε
having received said: Lord, I knew thee
ὅτι σκληρὸς εἶ ἄνθρωπος, θερίζων
that ²a hard ¹thou art ³man, reaping
ὅπου οὐκ ἔσπειρας, καὶ συνάγων
where thou didst not sow, and gathering
ὅθεν οὐ διεσκόρπισας· 25 καὶ φοβηθεὶς
whence thou didst not scatter; and fearing
ἀπελθὼν ἔκρυψα τὸ τάλαντόν σου
going away I hid the talent of thee
ἐν τῇ γῇ· ἴδε ἔχεις τὸ σόν.
in the earth; behold thou hast the thine.
26 ἀποκριθεὶς δὲ ὁ κύριος αὐτοῦ εἶπεν
And answering the lord of him said
αὐτῷ· πονηρὲ δοῦλε καὶ ὀκνηρέ,
to him: Evil slave and slothful,
ᾔδεις ὅτι θερίζω ὅπου οὐκ ἔσπειρα,
thou knewest that I reap where I sowed not,
καὶ συνάγω ὅθεν οὐ διεσκόρπισα;
and I gather whence I did not scatter?
27 ἔδει σε οὖν βαλεῖν τὰ ἀργύριά
it behoved thee therefore to put the silver pieces
μου τοῖς τραπεζίταις, καὶ ἐλθὼν ἐγὼ
of me to the bankers, and coming I
ἐκομισάμην ἂν τὸ ἐμὸν σὺν τόκῳ.
would have received the mine with interest.
28 ἄρατε οὖν ἀπ' αὐτοῦ τὸ τάλαντον
Take therefore from him the talent
καὶ δότε τῷ ἔχοντι τὰ δέκα τάλαντα·
and give to the [one] having the ten talents;
29 τῷ γὰρ ἔχοντι παντὶ δοθήσεται καὶ
for to ²having ¹everyone will be given and

with them. 20The man who had received the five talents brought the other five. 'Master,' he said, 'you entrusted me with five talents. See, I have gained five more.'

21"His master replied, 'Well done, good and faithful servant! You have been faithful with a few things; I will put you in charge of many things. Come and share your master's happiness!'

22"The man with the two talents also came. 'Master,' he said, 'you entrusted me with two talents; see, I have gained two more.'

23"His master replied, 'Well done, good and faithful servant! You have been faithful with a few things; I will put you in charge of many things. Come and share your master's happiness!'

24"Then the man who had received the one talent came. 'Master,' he said, 'I knew that you are a hard man, harvesting where you have not sown and gathering where you have not scattered seed. 25So I was afraid and went out and hid your talent in the ground. See, here is what belongs to you.'

26"His master replied, 'You wicked, lazy servant! So you knew that I harvest where I have not sown and gather where I have not scattered seed? 27Well then, you should have put my money on deposit with the bankers, so that when I returned I would have received it back with interest. 28"Take the talent from him and give it to the one who has the ten talents. 29For everyone who has will be given more, and he and he shall have an abundance; but from the one who does not have, even what he does have shall be taken away.

30"And cast out the worthless slave into the outer darkness; in that place there shall be weeping and gnashing of teeth.

The Judgment

31"But when the Son of Man comes in His glory, and all the angels with Him, then He will sit on His glorious throne.

32"And all the nations will be gathered before Him; and He will separate them from one another, as the shepherd separates the sheep from the goats;

33and He will put the sheep on His right, and the goats on the left.

34"Then the King will say to those on His right, 'Come, you who are blessed of My Father, inherit the kingdom prepared for you from the foundation of the world.

35'For I was hungry, and you gave Me *something* to eat; I was thirsty, and you gave Me drink; I was a stranger, and you invited Me in;

36naked, and you clothed Me; I was sick, and you visited Me; I was in prison, and you came to Me.'

37"Then the righteous will answer Him, saying, 'Lord, when did we see You hungry, and feed You, or thirsty, and give You drink?

38'And when did we see You a stranger, and invite You in, or naked, and clothe You?

39'And when did we see You sick, or in prison, and come to You?'

40"And the King will answer and say to them, 'Truly I say to you, to the

---

περισσευθήσεται·
he will have abundance;
τοῦ δὲ μὴ ἔχοντος
but from the [one] not having
καὶ ὃ ἔχει ἀρθήσεται ἀπ᾽ αὐτοῦ.
even what he has will be taken from him.

30 καὶ τὸν ἀχρεῖον δοῦλον ἐκβάλετε εἰς
And the useless slave cast ye out into
τὸ σκότος τὸ ἐξώτερον· ἐκεῖ ἔσται ὁ
the darkness - outer; there will be the
κλαυθμὸς καὶ ὁ βρυγμὸς τῶν ὀδόντων
wailing and the gnashing of the teeth.

31 Ὅταν δὲ ἔλθῃ ὁ υἱὸς τοῦ ἀνθρώπου
And when comes the Son - of man
ἐν τῇ δόξῃ αὐτοῦ καὶ πάντες οἱ ἄγγελοι
in the glory of him and all the angels
μετ᾽ αὐτοῦ, τότε καθίσει ἐπὶ θρόνου
with him, then he will sit on a throne
δόξης αὐτοῦ· 32 καὶ συναχθήσονται
of glory of him; and will be assembled
ἔμπροσθεν αὐτοῦ πάντα τὰ ἔθνη, καὶ
before him all the nations, and
ἀφορίσει αὐτοὺς ἀπ᾽ ἀλλήλων, ὥσπερ
he will separate them from one another, as
ὁ ποιμὴν ἀφορίζει τὰ πρόβατα ἀπὸ
the shepherd separates the sheep from
τῶν ἐρίφων, 33 καὶ στήσει τὰ μὲν
the goats, and will set the -
πρόβατα ἐκ δεξιῶν αὐτοῦ, τὰ δὲ ἐρίφια
sheep on [the] right of him, but the goats
ἐξ εὐωνύμων. 34 τότε ἐρεῖ ὁ
on [the] left. Then will say the
βασιλεὺς τοῖς ἐκ δεξιῶν αὐτοῦ·
king to the [ones] on [the] right of him:
δεῦτε οἱ εὐλογημένοι τοῦ πατρός μου,
Come the [ones] blessed of the Father of me,
κληρονομήσατε τὴν ἡτοιμασμένην ὑμῖν
inherit ye the ³having been prepared ²for you
βασιλείαν ἀπὸ καταβολῆς κόσμου.
¹kingdom from [the] foundation of [the] world.
35 ἐπείνασα γὰρ καὶ ἐδώκατέ μοι
For I hungered and ye gave me
φαγεῖν, ἐδίψησα καὶ ἐποτίσατέ με,
to eat, I thirsted and ye gave ¹drink ²me,
ξένος ἤμην καὶ συνηγάγετέ με,
a stranger I was and ye entertained me,
36 γυμνὸς καὶ περιεβάλετέ με, ἠσθένησα
naked and ye clothed me, I ailed
καὶ ἐπεσκέψασθέ με, ἐν φυλακῇ ἤμην
and ye visited me, in prison I was
καὶ ἤλθατε πρός με. 37 τότε ἀποκριθή-
and ye came to me. Then will
σονται αὐτῷ οἱ δίκαιοι λέγοντες· κύριε,
answer him the righteous saying: Lord,
πότε σε εἴδομεν πεινῶντα καὶ ἐθρέψαμεν,
when thee saw we hungering and fed,
ἢ διψῶντα καὶ ἐποτίσαμεν; 38 πότε δέ
or thirsting and gave drink? and when
σε εἴδομεν ξένον καὶ συνηγάγομεν,
thee saw we a stranger and entertained,
ἢ γυμνὸν καὶ περιεβάλομεν; 39 πότε δέ
or naked and clothed? and when
σε εἴδομεν ἀσθενοῦντα ἢ ἐν φυλακῇ καὶ
thee saw we ailing or in prison and
ἤλθομεν πρὸς σέ; 40 καὶ ἀποκριθεὶς ὁ
came to thee? And answering the
βασιλεὺς ἐρεῖ αὐτοῖς· ἀμὴν λέγω
king will say to them: Truly I tell

---

will have an abundance. Whoever does not have, even what he has will be taken from him. 30And throw that worthless servant outside, into the darkness, where there will be weeping and gnashing of teeth.'

The Sheep and the Goats

31"When the Son of Man comes in his glory, and all the angels with him, he will sit on his throne in heavenly glory. 32All the nations will be gathered before him, and he will separate the people one from another as a shepherd separates the sheep from the goats. 33He will put the sheep on his right and the goats on his left.

34"Then the King will say to those on his right, 'Come, you who are blessed by my Father; take your inheritance, the kingdom prepared for you since the creation of the world. 35For I was hungry and you gave me something to eat, I was thirsty and you gave me something to drink, I was a stranger and you invited me in, 36I needed clothes and you clothed me, I was sick and you looked after me, I was in prison and you came to visit me.'

37"Then the righteous will answer him, 'Lord, when did we see you hungry and feed you, or thirsty and give you something to drink? 38When did we see you a stranger and invite you in, or needing clothes and clothe you? 39When did we see you sick or in prison and go to visit you?'

40"The King will reply, 'I tell you the truth, whatever

extent that you did it to one of these brothers of Mine, *even* the least *of them*, you did it to Me.'

41"Then He will also say to those on His left, 'Depart from Me, accursed ones, into the eternal fire which has been prepared for the devil and his angels.

42for I was hungry, and you gave Me *nothing* to eat; I was thirsty, and you gave Me nothing to drink;

43I was a stranger, and you did not invite Me in; naked, and you did not clothe Me; sick, and in prison, and you did not visit Me.'

44"Then they themselves also will answer, saying, 'Lord, when did we see You hungry, or thirsty, or a stranger, or naked, or sick, or in prison, and did not take care of You?'

45"Then He will answer them, saying, 'Truly I say to you, to the extent that you did not do it to one of the least of these, you did not do it to Me.'

46"And these will go away into eternal punishment, but the righteous into eternal life."

ὑμῖν, ἐφ' ὅσον ἐποιήσατε ἑνὶ τούτων
you, inasmuch as ye did to one of these

τῶν ἀδελφῶν μου τῶν ἐλαχίστων, ἐμοὶ
- brothers of me the least, to me

ἐποιήσατε. **41** τότε ἐρεῖ καὶ τοῖς ἐξ
ye did. Then he will say also to the [ones] on

εὐωνύμων· πορεύεσθε ἀπ' ἐμοῦ κατ-
[the] left: Go from me having been

ηραμένοι εἰς τὸ πῦρ τὸ αἰώνιον
cursed [ones] into the fire - eternal

τὸ ἡτοιμασμένον τῷ διαβόλῳ καὶ τοῖς
- having been prepared for the devil and the

ἀγγέλοις αὐτοῦ. **42** ἐπείνασα γὰρ καὶ
angels of him. For I hungered and

οὐκ ἐδώκατέ μοι φαγεῖν, ἐδίψησα
ye gave not me to eat, I thirsted

καὶ οὐκ ἐποτίσατέ με, **43** ξένος
and ye ¹gave ³not ⁴drink ²me, a stranger

ἤμην καὶ οὐ συνηγάγετέ με, γυμνὸς
I was and ye entertained not me, naked

καὶ οὐ περιεβάλετέ με, ἀσθενὴς καὶ ἐν
and ye clothed not me, ill and in

φυλακῇ καὶ οὐκ ἐπεσκέψασθέ με. **44** τότε
prison and ye visited not me. Then

ἀποκριθήσονται καὶ αὐτοὶ λέγοντες· κύριε,
will answer also they saying: Lord,

πότε σε εἴδομεν πεινῶντα ἢ διψῶντα ἢ
when thee saw we hungering or thirsting or

ξένον ἢ γυμνὸν ἢ ἀσθενῆ ἢ ἐν φυλακῇ
a stranger or naked or ill or in prison

καὶ οὐ διηκονήσαμέν σοι; **45** τότε
and did not minister to thee? Then

ἀποκριθήσεται αὐτοῖς λέγων· ἀμὴν λέγω
he will answer them saying: Truly I tell

ὑμῖν, ἐφ' ὅσον οὐκ ἐποιήσατε ἑνὶ
you, inasmuch as ye did not to one

τούτων τῶν ἐλαχίστων, οὐδὲ ἐμοὶ
of these - least [ones], neither to me

ἐποιήσατε. **46** καὶ ἀπελεύσονται οὗτοι εἰς
ye did. And will go away these into

κόλασιν αἰώνιον, οἱ δὲ δίκαιοι εἰς
punishment eternal, but the righteous into

ζωὴν αἰώνιον.
life eternal.

---

you did for one of the least of these brothers of mine, you did for me.'

41"Then he will say to those on his left, 'Depart from me, you who are cursed, into the eternal fire prepared for the devil and his angels. 42For I was hungry and you gave me nothing to eat, I was thirsty and you gave me nothing to drink, 43I was a stranger and you did not invite me in, I needed clothes and you did not clothe me, I was sick and in prison and you did not look after me.'

44"They also will answer, 'Lord, when did we see you hungry or thirsty or a stranger or needing clothes or sick or in prison, and did not help you?'

45"He will reply, 'I tell you the truth, whatever you did not do for one of the least of these, you did not do for me.'

46"Then they will go away to eternal punishment, but the righteous to eternal life."

The Plot to Kill Jesus

AND it came about that when Jesus had finished all these words, He said to His disciples,

2"You know that after two days the Passover is coming, and the Son of Man is *to be* delivered up for crucifixion."

3Then the chief priests and the elders of the people were gathered together in the court of the high priest, named Caiaphas;

4and they plotted together to seize Jesus by

---

26 Καὶ ἐγένετο ὅτε ἐτέλεσεν ὁ
And it came to pass when ended -

Ἰησοῦς πάντας τοὺς λόγους τούτους,
Jesus all the words these,

εἶπεν τοῖς μαθηταῖς αὐτοῦ· **2** οἴδατε
he said to the disciples of him: Ye know

ὅτι μετὰ δύο ἡμέρας τὸ πάσχα γίνεται,
that after two days the passover occurs,

καὶ ὁ υἱὸς τοῦ ἀνθρώπου παραδίδοται εἰς
and the Son of man is delivered

τὸ σταυρωθῆναι. **3** Τότε συνήχθησαν οἱ
- to be crucified. Then were assembled the

ἀρχιερεῖς καὶ οἱ πρεσβύτεροι τοῦ λαοῦ
chief priests and the elders of the people

εἰς τὴν αὐλὴν τοῦ ἀρχιερέως τοῦ
in the court of the high priest -

λεγομένον Καϊαφᾶ, **4** καὶ συνεβουλεύ-
named Caiaphas, and con-

σαντο ἵνα τὸν Ἰησοῦν δόλῳ κρατή-
sulted that - Jesus by guile they might

The Plot Against Jesus

WHEN Jesus had finished saying all these things, he said to his disciples, 2"As you know, the Passover is two days away —and the Son of Man will be handed over to be crucified."

3Then the chief priests and the elders of the people assembled in the palace of the high priest, whose name was Caiaphas, 4and they plotted to arrest Jesus stealth, and kill *Him*.

5But they were saying, "Not during the festival, lest a riot occur among the people."

The Precious Ointment

6Now when Jesus was in Bethany, at the home of Simon the leper,

7a woman came to Him with an alabaster vial of very costly perfume, and she poured it upon His head as He reclined *at the table.*

8But the disciples were indignant when they saw *this*, and said, "Why this waste?

9"For this *perfume* might have been sold for a high price and *the money* given to the poor."

10But Jesus, aware of this, said to them, "Why do you bother the woman? For she has done a good deed to Me.

11"For the poor you have with you always; but you do not always have Me.

12"For when she poured this perfume upon My body, she did it to prepare Me for burial.

13"Truly I say to you, wherever this gospel is preached in the whole world, what this woman has done shall also be spoken of in memory of her."

Judas' Bargain

14Then one of the twelve, named Judas Iscariot, went to the chief priests,

15and said, "What are you willing to give me to deliver Him up to you?" And they weighed out to him thirty pieces of silver.

16And from then on he *began* looking for a good opportunity to betray Him.

17Now on the first *day* of Unleavened Bread the disciples came to Jesus, saying, "Where do You want us to prepare for You to eat the Passover?"

σωσιν   καὶ   ἀποκτείνωσιν·   5 ἔλεγον   δέ·
seize   and   might kill;   but they said:

μὴ   ἐν   τῇ   ἑορτῇ,   ἵνα   μὴ   θόρυβος
Not   at   the   feast,   lest   a disturbance

γένηται   ἐν   τῷ   λαῷ.
occurs   among   the   people.

6 Τοῦ   δὲ   Ἰησοῦ   γενομένου   ἐν   Βηθανίᾳ
   -      And   Jesus   being[a]   in   Bethany
                              = when Jesus was

ἐν   οἰκίᾳ   Σίμωνος   τοῦ   λεπροῦ,
in [the] house   of Simon   the   leper,

7 προσῆλθεν   αὐτῷ   γυνὴ   ἔχουσα   ἀλάβαστρον
   approached   to him   a woman   having   an alabaster phial

μύρου   βαρυτίμου   καὶ   κατέχεεν   ἐπὶ
of ointment   very expensive   and   poured [it]   on

τῆς   κεφαλῆς   αὐτοῦ   ἀνακειμένου.   8 ἰδόντες
the   head   of him   reclining.   And seeing

δὲ   οἱ   μαθηταὶ   ἠγανάκτησαν   λέγοντες·
the   disciples   were angry   saying:

εἰς   τί   ἡ   ἀπώλεια   αὕτη;   9 ἐδύνατο   γὰρ
To what   -   waste   this?   for could

τοῦτο   πραθῆναι   πολλοῦ   καὶ   δοθῆναι
this   to be sold   of(for) much   and   to be given

πτωχοῖς.   10 γνοὺς   δὲ   ὁ   Ἰησοῦς   εἶπεν
to poor.   And knowing   -   Jesus   said

αὐτοῖς·   τί   κόπους   παρέχετε   τῇ   γυναικί;
to them: Why   trouble ye   the   woman?

ἔργον   γὰρ   καλὸν   ἠργάσατο   εἰς   ἐμέ·
for work   a good   she wrought   to   me:

11 πάντοτε   γὰρ   τοὺς   πτωχοὺς   ἔχετε   μεθ᾽
for always   the   poor   ye have   with

ἑαυτῶν,   ἐμὲ   δὲ   οὐ   πάντοτε   ἔχετε·
yourselves,   but me   not   always   ye have;

12 βαλοῦσα   γὰρ   αὕτη   τὸ   μύρον   τοῦτο
for [b]putting   [1]this woman   -   [4]ointment   [3]this

ἐπὶ   τοῦ   σώματός   μου   πρὸς   τὸ   ἐνταφιάσαι
on   the   body   of me   for   -   to bury

με   ἐποίησεν.   13 ἀμὴν   λέγω   ὑμῖν,   ὅπου
me   she did.   Truly   I tell   you,   wher-

ἐὰν   κηρυχθῇ   τὸ   εὐαγγέλιον   τοῦτο   ἐν
ever   is proclaimed   the   gospel   this   in

ὅλῳ   τῷ   κόσμῳ,   λαληθήσεται   καὶ   ὃ
all   the   world,   will be spoken   also   what

ἐποίησεν   αὕτη   εἰς   μνημόσυνον   αὐτῆς.
did   this woman   for   a memorial   of her.

14 Τότε   πορευθεὶς   εἷς   τῶν   δώδεκα,   ὁ
   Then   going   one   of the   twelve,   the [one]

λεγόμενος   Ἰούδας   Ἰσκαριώτης,   πρὸς
named   Judas   Iscariot,   to

τοὺς   ἀρχιερεῖς   15 εἶπεν·   τί   θέλετε   μοι
the   chief priests   he said: What are you willing   me

δοῦναι,   κἀγὼ   ὑμῖν   παραδώσω   αὐτόν;
to give,   and I   to you   will deliver   him?

οἱ   δὲ   ἔστησαν   αὐτῷ   τριάκοντα   ἀργύρια.
And they   weighed   him   thirty   pieces of silver.

16 καὶ   ἀπὸ   τότε   ἐζήτει   εὐκαιρίαν   ἵνα
   And   from   then   he sought   opportunity   that

αὐτὸν   παραδῷ.
him   he might deliver.

17 Τῇ   δὲ   πρώτῃ   τῶν   ἀζύμων
   Now on the   first [day]   - of unleavened bread

προσῆλθον   οἱ   μαθηταὶ   τῷ   Ἰησοῦ
approached   the   disciples   -   to Jesus

λέγοντες·   ποῦ   θέλεις   ἑτοιμάσωμέν
saying: Where   willest thou   we may prepare

σοι   φαγεῖν   τὸ   πάσχα;   18 ὁ   δὲ
for thee   to eat   the   passover?   So he

---

in some sly way and kill him. 5"But not during the Feast," they said, "or there may be a riot among the people."

Jesus Anointed at Bethany

6While Jesus was in Bethany in the home of a man known as Simon the Leper, 7a woman came to him with an alabaster jar of very expensive perfume, which she poured on his head as he was reclining at the table.

8When the disciples saw this, they were indignant. "Why this waste?" they asked. 9"This perfume could have been sold at a high price and the money given to the poor."

10Aware of this, Jesus said to them, "Why are you bothering this woman? She has done a beautiful thing to me. 11The poor you will always have with you, but you will not always have me. 12When she poured this perfume on my body, she did it to prepare me for burial. 13I tell you the truth, wherever this gospel is preached throughout the world, what she has done will also be told, in memory of her."

Judas Agrees to Betray Jesus

14Then one of the Twelve—the one called Judas Iscariot—went to the chief priests 15and asked, "What are you willing to give me if I hand him over to you?" So they counted out for him thirty silver coins. 16From then on Judas watched for an opportunity to hand him over.

The Lord's Supper

17On the first day of the Feast of Unleavened Bread, the disciples came to Jesus and asked, "Where do you want us to make preparations for you to eat the Passover?"

18And He said, "Go into the city to a certain man, and say to him, 'The Teacher says, "My time is at hand; I am to keep the Passover at your house with My disciples." ' "

19And the disciples did as Jesus had directed them; and they prepared the Passover.

The Last Passover

20Now when evening had come, He was reclining at the table with the twelve disciples.

21And as they were eating, He said, "Truly I say to you that one of you will betray Me."

22And being deeply grieved, they each one began to say to Him, "Surely not I, Lord?"

23And He answered and said, "He who dipped his hand with Me in the bowl is the one who will betray Me."

24"The Son of Man is to go, just as it is written of Him; but woe to that man by whom the Son of Man is betrayed! It would have been good for that man if he had not been born."

25And Judas, who was betraying Him, answered and said, "Surely it is not I, Rabbi?" He *said to him, "You have said it yourself."

The Lord's Supper Instituted

26And while they were eating, Jesus took some bread, and after a blessing, He broke it and gave it to the disciples, and said, "Take, eat; this is My body."

27And when He had taken a cup and given thanks, He gave it to them, saying, "Drink from it, all of you;

28for this is My blood of the covenant, which is poured out for many for forgiveness of sins.

εἶπεν· ὑπάγετε εἰς τὴν πόλιν πρὸς
said: Go ye into the city to

τὸν δεῖνα καὶ εἴπατε αὐτῷ· ὁ
such a one and say to him: The

διδάσκαλος λέγει· ὁ καιρός μου
teacher says: The time of me

ἐγγύς ἐστιν· πρὸς σὲ ποιῶ τὸ πάσχα
near is; with thee I make the passover

μετὰ τῶν μαθητῶν μου. 19 καὶ ἐποίησαν
with the disciples of me. And did

οἱ μαθηταὶ ὡς συνέταξεν αὐτοῖς ὁ
the disciples as enjoined them the

Ἰησοῦς, καὶ ἡτοίμασαν τὸ πάσχα. 20 Ὀψίας
Jesus, and prepared the passover. evening

δὲ γενομένης ἀνέκειτο μετὰ τῶν δώδεκα
And coming[a] he reclined with the twelve
= when evening came

[μαθητῶν]. 21 καὶ ἐσθιόντων αὐτῶν εἶπεν·
disciples. And eating them[a] he said:
= as they were eating

ἀμὴν λέγω ὑμῖν ὅτι εἷς ἐξ ὑμῶν παρα-
Truly I tell you that one of you will

δώσει με. 22 καὶ λυπούμενοι σφόδρα
betray me. And grieving exceedingly

ἤρξαντο λέγειν αὐτῷ εἷς ἕκαστος·
they began to say to him ªone ¹each:

μήτι ἐγώ εἰμι, κύριε; 23 ὁ δὲ ἀποκριθεὶς
Not I am, Lord? And he answering
= It is not I,

εἶπεν· ὁ ἐμβάψας μετ' ἐμοῦ τὴν
said: The [one] dipping with me the(his)

χεῖρα ἐν τῷ τρυβλίῳ, οὗτός με παρα-
hand in the dish, this man me will

δώσει. 24 ὁ μὲν υἱὸς τοῦ ἀνθρώπου
betray. Indeed the Son - of man

ὑπάγει καθὼς γέγραπται περὶ αὐτοῦ,
goes as it has been written concerning him,

οὐαὶ δὲ τῷ ἀνθρώπῳ ἐκείνῳ δι'
but woe to the man to that through

οὗ ὁ υἱὸς τοῦ ἀνθρώπου παραδίδοται·
whom the Son - of man is betrayed;

καλὸν ἦν αὐτῷ εἰ οὐκ ἐγεννήθη
good were it for him if was not born

ὁ ἄνθρωπος ἐκεῖνος. 25 ἀποκριθεὶς δὲ
- man that. And answering

Ἰούδας ὁ παραδιδοὺς αὐτὸν εἶπεν·
Judas the [one] betraying him said:

μήτι ἐγώ εἰμι, ῥαββί; λέγει αὐτῷ·
Not I am, rabbi? He says to him:
= It is not I,

σὺ εἶπας. 26 Ἐσθιόντων δὲ αὐτῶν
Thou saidst. And eating them[a]
= as they were eating

λαβὼν ὁ Ἰησοῦς ἄρτον καὶ εὐλογήσας
taking - Jesus a loaf and blessing

ἔκλασεν καὶ δοὺς τοῖς μαθηταῖς εἶπεν·
he broke and giving to the disciples said:

λάβετε φάγετε· τοῦτό ἐστιν τὸ σῶμά
Take ye[,] eat ye; this is the body

μου. 27 καὶ λαβὼν ποτήριον καὶ εὐχαρι-
of me. And taking a cup and giving

στήσας ἔδωκεν αὐτοῖς λέγων· πίετε ἐξ
thanks he gave to them saying: Drink ye of

αὐτοῦ πάντες· 28 τοῦτο γάρ ἐστιν τὸ
it all; for this is the

αἷμά μου τῆς διαθήκης τὸ περὶ πολλῶν
blood of me of the covenant the [blood] concerning many

ἐκχυννόμενον εἰς ἄφεσιν ἁμαρτιῶν. 29 λέγω
being shed for forgiveness of sins. I tell

18He replied, "Go into the city to a certain man and tell him, 'The Teacher says: My appointed time is near. I am going to celebrate the Passover with my disciples at your house.' "

19So the disciples did as Jesus had directed them and prepared the Passover.

20When evening came, Jesus was reclining at the table with the Twelve.

21And while they were eating, he said, "I tell you the truth, one of you will betray me."

22They were very sad and began to say to him one after the other, "Surely not I, Lord?"

23Jesus replied, "The one who has dipped his hand into the bowl with me will betray me. 24The Son of Man will go just as it is written about him. But woe to that man who betrays the Son of Man! It would be better for him if he had not been born."

25Then Judas, the one who would betray him, said, "Surely not I, Rabbi?"

Jesus answered, "Yes, it is you." d

26While they were eating, Jesus took bread, gave thanks and broke it, and gave it to his disciples, saying, "Take and eat; this is my body."

27Then he took the cup, gave thanks and offered it to them, saying, "Drink from it, all of you. 28This is my blood of the e covenant, which is poured out for many for the forgiveness of

---

5 Or "You yourself have said it"
8 Some manuscripts the new

29"But I say to you, I will not drink of this fruit of the vine from now on until that day when I drink it new with you in My Father's kingdom."

30And after singing a hymn, they went out to the Mount of Olives.

31Then Jesus *said to them, "You will all fall away because of Me this night, for it is written, 'I WILL STRIKE DOWN THE SHEPHERD, AND THE SHEEP OF THE FLOCK SHALL BE SCATTERED.'

32"But after I have been raised, I will go before you to Galilee."

33But Peter answered and said to Him, "Even though all may fall away because of You, I will never fall away."

34Jesus said to him, "Truly I say to you that this very night, before a cock crows, you shall deny Me three times."

35Peter *said to Him, "Even if I have to die with You, I will not deny You." All the disciples said the same thing too.

The Garden of Gethsemane

36Then Jesus *came with them to a place called Gethsemane, and *said to His disciples, "Sit here while I go over there and pray."

37And He took with Him Peter and the two sons of Zebedee, and began to be grieved and distressed.

38Then He *said to them, "My soul is deeply grieved, to the point of death; remain here and keep watch with Me."

39And He went a little beyond *them*, and fell on His face and prayed, saying, "My Father, if it is

---

δὲ ὑμῖν, οὐ μὴ πίω ἀπ' ἄρτι ἐκ
And you, by no means will I drink from now of

τούτου τοῦ γενήματος τῆς ἀμπέλου ἕως
this - fruit of the vine until

τῆς ἡμέρας ἐκείνης ὅταν αὐτὸ πίνω μεθ'
- day that when it I drink with

ὑμῶν καινὸν ἐν τῇ βασιλείᾳ τοῦ πατρός
you new in the kingdom of the Father

μου.
of me.

30 Καὶ ὑμνήσαντες ἐξῆλθον εἰς τὸ
And having sung a hymn they went forth to the

ὄρος τῶν ἐλαιῶν. 31 Τότε λέγει αὐτοῖς ὁ
mount of the olives. Then says to them -

Ἰησοῦς· πάντες ὑμεῖς σκανδαλισθήσεσθε
Jesus: All ye will be offended

ἐν ἐμοὶ ἐν τῇ νυκτὶ ταύτῃ· γέγραπται
in me in the to-night; it has been written

γάρ· πατάξω τὸν ποιμένα, καὶ δια-
for: I will strike the shepherd, and will

σκορπισθήσονται τὰ πρόβατα τῆς ποίμνης·
be scattered the sheep of the flock;

32 μετὰ δὲ τὸ ἐγερθῆναί με προάξω
but after the to be raised me[b] I will go before
=I am raised

ὑμᾶς εἰς τὴν Γαλιλαίαν. 33 ἀποκριθεὶς
you to - Galilee. answering

δὲ ὁ Πέτρος εἶπεν αὐτῷ· εἰ πάντες
And - Peter said to him: If all men

σκανδαλισθήσονται ἐν σοί, ἐγὼ οὐδέποτε
shall be offended in thee, I never

σκανδαλισθήσομαι. 34 ἔφη αὐτῷ ὁ Ἰησοῦς·
will be offended. Said to him - Jesus:

ἀμὴν λέγω σοι ὅτι ἐν ταύτῃ τῇ νυκτὶ
Truly I tell thee that in this to-night

πρὶν ἀλέκτορα φωνῆσαι τρὶς ἀπαρνήσῃ
before a cock to crow[b] three times thou wilt deny

με. 35 λέγει αὐτῷ ὁ Πέτρος· κἄν
me. Says to him - Peter: Even if

δέῃ με σὺν σοὶ ἀποθανεῖν, οὐ μή σε
it behoves me with thee to die, by no means thee
=I must die with thee.

ἀπαρνήσομαι. ὁμοίως καὶ πάντες οἱ
I will deny. Likewise also all the

μαθηταὶ εἶπαν.
disciples said.

36 Τότε ἔρχεται μετ' αὐτῶν ὁ Ἰησοῦς
Then comes with them - Jesus

εἰς χωρίον λεγόμενον Γεθσημανί, καὶ λέγει
to a piece of land called Gethsemane, and says

τοῖς μαθηταῖς· καθίσατε αὐτοῦ ἕως οὗ
to the disciples: Sit ye here until

ἀπελθὼν ἐκεῖ προσεύξωμαι. 37 καὶ παρα-
going away there I may pray. And tak-

λαβὼν τὸν Πέτρον καὶ τοὺς δύο υἱοὺς
ing Peter and the two sons

Ζεβεδαίου ἤρξατο λυπεῖσθαι καὶ ἀδημονεῖν.
of Zebedee he began to grieve and to be distressed.

38 τότε λέγει αὐτοῖς· περίλυπός ἐστιν
Then he says to them: Deeply grieved is

ἡ ψυχή μου ἕως θανάτου· μείνατε
the soul of me unto death; remain ye

ὧδε καὶ γρηγορεῖτε μετ' ἐμοῦ. 39 καὶ
here and watch ye with me. And

προελθὼν μικρὸν ἔπεσεν ἐπὶ πρόσωπον
going forward a little he fell on [the] face

αὐτοῦ προσευχόμενος καὶ λέγων· πάτερ
of him praying and saying: Father

---

sins. 29I tell you, I will not drink of this fruit of the vine from now on until that day when I drink it anew with you in my Father's kingdom."

30When they had sung a hymn, they went out to the Mount of Olives.

Jesus Predicts Peter's Denial

31Then Jesus told them, "This very night you will all fall away on account of me, for it is written:

" 'I will strike the shepherd,
and the sheep of the flock will be scattered.'[f]

32But after I have risen, I will go ahead of you into Galilee."

33Peter replied, "Even if all fall away on account of you, I never will."

34"I tell you the truth," Jesus answered, "this very night, before the rooster crows, you will disown me three times."

35But Peter declared, "Even if I have to die with you, I will never disown you." And all the other disciples said the same.

Gethsemane

36Then Jesus went with his disciples to a place called Gethsemane, and he said to them, "Sit here while I go over there and pray." 37He took Peter and the two sons of Zebedee along with him, and he began to be sorrowful and troubled. 38Then he said to them, "My soul is overwhelmed with sorrow to the point of death. Stay here and keep watch with me."

39Going a little farther, he fell with his face to the ground and prayed, "My

ech. 13:7

possible, let this cup pass from Me; yet not as I will, but as Thou wilt."
40And He *came to the disciples and *found them sleeping, and *said to Peter, "So, you men could not keep watch with Me for one hour?
41"Keep watching and praying, that you may not enter into temptation; the spirit is willing, but the flesh is weak."
42He went away again a second time and prayed, saying, "My Father, if this cannot pass away unless I drink it, Thy will be done."
43And again He came and found them sleeping, for their eyes were heavy.
44And He left them again, and went away and prayed a third time, saying the same thing once more.
45Then He *came to the disciples, and *said to them, "Are you still sleeping and taking your rest? Behold, the hour is at hand and the Son of Man is being betrayed into the hands of sinners.
46"Arise, let us be going; behold, the one who betrays Me is at hand!"

Jesus' Betrayal and Arrest

47And while He was still speaking, behold, Judas, one of the twelve, came up, accompanied by a great multitude with swords and clubs, from the chief priests and elders of the people.
48Now he who was betraying Him gave them a sign, saying, "Whomever I shall kiss, He is the one; seize Him."
49And immediately he went to Jesus and said, "Hail, Rabbi!" and kissed Him.

μου, εἰ δυνατόν ἐστιν, παρελθάτω ἀπ'
of me, if possible it is, let pass from
ἐμοῦ τὸ ποτήριον τοῦτο· πλὴν οὐχ
me - cup this; yet not
ὡς ἐγὼ θέλω ἀλλ' ὡς σύ. 40 καὶ
as I will but as thou. And
ἔρχεται πρὸς τοὺς μαθητὰς καὶ εὑρίσκει
he comes to the disciples and finds
αὐτοὺς καθεύδοντας, καὶ λέγει τῷ Πέτρῳ·
them sleeping, and says - to Peter:
οὕτως οὐκ ἰσχύσατε μίαν ὥραν
So were ye not able one hour
γρηγορῆσαι μετ' ἐμοῦ; 41 γρηγορεῖτε καὶ
to watch with me? Watch ye and
προσεύχεσθε, ἵνα μὴ εἰσέλθητε εἰς
pray, lest ye enter into
πειρασμόν· τὸ μὲν πνεῦμα πρόθυμον,
temptation; indeed the spirit [is] eager,
ἡ δὲ σὰρξ ἀσθενής. 42 πάλιν ἐκ
but the flesh weak. Again -
δευτέρου ἀπελθὼν προσηύξατο λέγων·
second [time] going away he prayed saying:
πάτερ μου, εἰ οὐ δύναται τοῦτο παρελθεῖν
Father of me, if cannot this to pass away
ἐὰν μὴ αὐτὸ πίω, γενηθήτω τὸ θέλημά
except it I drink, let be done the will
σου. 43 καὶ ἐλθὼν πάλιν εὗρεν αὐτοὺς
of thee. And coming again he found them
καθεύδοντας, ἦσαν γὰρ αὐτῶν οἱ ὀφθαλμοὶ
sleeping, for were of them the eyes
βεβαρημένοι. 44 καὶ ἀφεὶς αὐτοὺς πάλιν
having been burdened. And leaving them again
ἀπελθὼν προσηύξατο ἐκ τρίτου, τὸν
going away he prayed a third [time], the
αὐτὸν λόγον εἰπὼν πάλιν. 45 τότε ἔρχεται
same word saying again. Then he comes
πρὸς τοὺς μαθητὰς καὶ λέγει αὐτοῖς·
to the disciples and says to them:
καθεύδετε λοιπὸν καὶ ἀναπαύεσθε·
Sleep ye now and rest;
ἰδοὺ ἤγγικεν ἡ ὥρα καὶ ὁ υἱὸς τοῦ
behold has drawn near the hour and the Son -
ἀνθρώπου παραδίδοται εἰς χεῖρας
of man is betrayed into [the] hands
ἁμαρτωλῶν. 46 ἐγείρεσθε, ἄγωμεν· ἰδοὺ
of sinners. Rise ye, let us be going; behold
ἤγγικεν ὁ παραδιδούς με.
has drawn near the [one] betraying me.
47 Καὶ ἔτι αὐτοῦ λαλοῦντος, ἰδοὺ
And still him speaking,ᵃ behold
= while he was still speaking,
Ἰούδας εἷς τῶν δώδεκα ἦλθεν, καὶ μετ'
Judas one of the twelve came, and with
αὐτοῦ ὄχλος πολὺς μετὰ μαχαιρῶν καὶ
him crowd a much with swords and
ξύλων ἀπὸ τῶν ἀρχιερέων καὶ πρεσβυτέρων
clubs from the chief priests and elders
τοῦ λαοῦ. 48 ὁ δὲ παραδιδοὺς αὐτὸν ἔδωκεν
of the people. Now the [one] betraying him gave
αὐτοῖς σημεῖον λέγων· ὃν ἂν φιλήσω
them a sign saying: Whomever I may kiss
αὐτός ἐστιν· κρατήσατε αὐτόν. 49 καὶ
he it is; seize ye him. And
εὐθέως προσελθὼν τῷ Ἰησοῦ εἶπεν· χαῖρε,
immediately approaching - to Jesus he said: Hail,
ῥαββί, καὶ κατεφίλησεν αὐτόν. 50 ὁ
rabbi, and affectionately kissed him. -

Father, if it is possible, may this cup be taken from me. Yet not as I will, but as you will."
40Then he returned to his disciples and found them sleeping. "Could you men not keep watch with me for one hour?" he asked Peter.
41"Watch and pray so that you will not fall into temptation. The spirit is willing, but the body is weak."
42He went away a second time and prayed, "My Father, if it is not possible for this cup to be taken away unless I drink it, may your will be done."
43When he came back, he again found them sleeping, because their eyes were heavy. 44So he left them and went away once more and prayed the third time, saying the same thing.
45Then he returned to the disciples and said to them, "Are you still sleeping and resting? Look, the hour is near, and the Son of Man is betrayed into the hands of sinners. 46Rise, let us go! Here comes my betrayer!"

Jesus Arrested

47While he was still speaking, Judas, one of the Twelve, arrived. With him was a large crowd armed with swords and clubs, sent from the chief priests and the elders of the people. 48Now the betrayer had arranged a signal with them: "The one I kiss is the man; arrest him." 49Going at once to Jesus, Judas said, "Greetings, Rabbi!" and kissed him.

50And Jesus said to him, "Friend, *do* what you have come for." Then they came and laid hands on Jesus and seized Him.

51And behold, one of those who were with Jesus reached and drew out his sword, and struck the slave of the high priest, and cut off his ear.

52Then Jesus *said to him, "Put your sword back into its place; for all those who take up the sword shall perish by the sword.

53"Or do you think that I cannot appeal to My Father, and He will at once put at My disposal more than twelve ʲlegions of angels?

54"How then shall the Scriptures be fulfilled, that it must happen this way?"

55At that time Jesus said to the multitudes, "Have you come out with swords and clubs to arrest Me as against a robber? Every day I used to sit in the temple teaching and you did not seize Me.

56"But all this has taken place that the Scriptures of the prophets may be fulfilled." Then all the disciples left Him and fled.

Jesus before Caiaphas

57And those who had seized Jesus led Him away to Caiaphas, the high priest, where the scribes and the elders were gathered together.

58But Peter also was following Him at a distance as far as the courtyard of the high priest, and entered in, and sat down with the officers to see the outcome.

59Now the chief priests and the whole Council kept trying to obtain false testimony against Jesus, in or-

---

δὲ   'Ιησοῦς   εἶπεν   αὐτῷ·   ἑταῖρε,
But   Jesus   said   to him: Comrade, [do that]

ἐφ' ὃ   πάρει.   τότε   προσελθόντες ἐπέβαλον
on what thou art here. Then approaching   they laid on

τὰς χεῖρας ἐπὶ τὸν 'Ιησοῦν καὶ ἐκράτησαν
the(ir) hands on   -   Jesus   and seized

αὐτόν. 51 καὶ ἰδοὺ εἷς τῶν   μετὰ
him.   And behold one of the [ones] with

'Ιησοῦ ἐκτείνας τὴν χεῖρα ἀπέσπασεν
Jesus   stretching out the(his) hand   drew

τὴν μάχαιραν αὐτοῦ, καὶ πατάξας τὸν
the   sword   of him, and striking   the

δοῦλος τοῦ ἀρχιερέως ἀφεῖλεν αὐτοῦ τὸ
slave of the high priest cut off   of him   the

ὠτίον. 52 τότε λέγει αὐτῷ ὁ 'Ιησοῦς·
ear.   Then   says   to him   -   Jesus:

ἀπόστρεψον τὴν μάχαιράν σου εἰς τὸν
Put back   the   sword   of thee into the

τόπον αὐτῆς· πάντες γὰρ οἱ λαβόντες
place   of it;   for all the [ones] taking

μάχαιραν ἐν μαχαίρῃ ἀπολοῦνται. 53 ἢ
a sword   by   a sword   will perish.   Or

δοκεῖς ὅτι οὐ δύναμαι παρακαλέσαι
thinkest thou that I cannot   to ask

τὸν πατέρα μου, καὶ παραστήσει μοι
the   Father   of me,   and he will provide me

ἄρτι πλείω δώδεκα λεγιῶνας ἀγγέλων;
now more [than] twelve legions   of angels?

54 πῶς οὖν πληρωθῶσιν αἱ γραφαὶ ὅτι
   how   then may be fulfilled the scriptures that

οὕτως δεῖ γενέσθαι; 55 'Εν ἐκείνῃ τῇ ὥρᾳ
thus   it must be?   In   that   -   hour

εἶπεν ὁ 'Ιησοῦς τοῖς ὄχλοις· ὡς ἐπὶ
said   - Jesus   to the crowds: As against

λῃστὴν ἐξήλθατε μετὰ μαχαιρῶν καὶ
a robber came ye forth with   swords   and

ξύλων συλλαβεῖν με; καθ' ἡμέραν ἐν
clubs   to take   me? daily   in

τῷ ἱερῷ ἐκαθεζόμην διδάσκων, καὶ οὐκ
the temple I sat   teaching,   and not

ἐκρατήσατέ με. 56 τοῦτο δὲ ὅλον
ye seized   me.   But this   all

γέγονεν ἵνα πληρωθῶσιν αἱ γραφαὶ
has come to pass that may be fulfilled the scriptures

τῶν προφητῶν. Τότε οἱ μαθηταὶ πάντες
of the prophets.   Then the disciples all

ἀφέντες αὐτὸν ἔφυγον.
leaving   him   fled.

57 Οἱ δὲ κρατήσαντες τὸν 'Ιησοῦν
   But the [ones] having seized   -   Jesus

ἀπήγαγον πρὸς Καϊάφαν τὸν ἀρχιερέα,
led [him] away to   Caiaphas   the high priest,

ὅπου οἱ γραμματεῖς καὶ οἱ πρεσβύτεροι
where the scribes   and the elders

συνήχθησαν. 58 ὁ δὲ Πέτρος ἠκολούθει
were assembled.   -   And Peter   followed

αὐτῷ [ἀπὸ] μακρόθεν ἕως τῆς αὐλῆς
him   from   afar   up to the court

τοῦ ἀρχιερέως, καὶ εἰσελθὼν ἔσω ἐκάθητο
of the high priest, and entering   within sat

μετὰ τῶν ὑπηρετῶν ἰδεῖν τὸ τέλος.
with   the attendants to see the end.

59 Οἱ δὲ ἀρχιερεῖς καὶ τὸ συνέδριον
   And the chief priests and the council

ὅλον ἐζήτουν ψευδομαρτυρίαν κατὰ τοῦ
whole sought   false witness   against   -

50Jesus replied, "Friend, do what you came for."ᵍ
Then the men stepped forward, seized Jesus and arrested him. 51With that, one of Jesus' companions reached for his sword, drew it out and struck the servant of the high priest, cutting off his ear.

52"Put your sword back in its place," Jesus said to him, "for all who draw the sword will die by the sword. 53Do you think I cannot call on my Father, and he will at once put at my disposal more than twelve legions of angels? 54But how then would the Scriptures be fulfilled that say it must happen in this way?"

55At that time Jesus said to the crowd, "Am I leading a rebellion, that you have come out with swords and clubs to capture me? Every day I sat in the temple courts teaching, and you did not arrest me. 56But this has all taken place that the writings of the prophets might be fulfilled." Then all the disciples deserted him and fled.

Before the Sanhedrin

57Those who had arrested Jesus took him to Caiaphas, the high priest, where the teachers of the law and the elders had assembled. 58But Peter followed him at a distance, right up to the courtyard of the high priest. He entered and sat down with the guards to see the outcome.

59The chief priests and the whole Sanhedrin were looking for false evidence against Jesus so that they

---

ʲA legion equaled 6,000 troops

ᵍ50 Or *"Friend, why have you come?"*

der that they might put Him to death;

60and they did not find any, even though many false witnesses came forward. But later on two came forward,

61and said, "This man stated, 'I am able to destroy the temple of God and to rebuild it in three days.' "

62And the high priest stood up and said to Him, "Do You make no answer? What is it that these men are testifying against You?"

63But Jesus kept silent. And the high priest said to Him, "I adjure You by the living God, that You tell us whether You are the Christ, the Son of God."

64Jesus *said to him, "You have said it yourself; nevertheless I tell you, hereafter you shall see THE SON OF MAN SITTING AT THE RIGHT HAND OF POWER, and COMING ON THE CLOUDS OF HEAVEN."

65Then the high priest tore his robes, saying, "He has blasphemed! What further need do we have of witnesses? Behold, you have now heard the blasphemy;

66what do you think?" They answered and said, "He is deserving of death!"

67Then they spat in His face and beat Him with their fists; and others slapped Him,

68and said, "Prophesy to us, You Christ; who is the one who hit You?"

Peter's Denials

69Now Peter was sitting outside in the courtyard, and a certain servant-girl came to him and said, "You too were with Jesus the Galilean."

70But he denied *it* before them all, saying, "I do not know what you are talking about."

71And when he had gone out to the gateway, another *servant-girl* saw him and

---

'Ιησου ὅπως αὐτὸν θανατώσωσιν, 60 καὶ
Jesus so as him they might put to death, and

οὐχ εὗρον πολλῶν προσελθόντων
did not find[,] many approaching
=when many false witnesses approached.

ψευδομαρτύρων. ὕστερον δὲ προσελθόντες
false witnesses*. But later approaching

δύο 61 εἶπαν· οὗτος ἔφη· δύναμαι κατα-
two said: This man said: I can to de-

λῦσαι τὸν ναὸν τοῦ θεοῦ καὶ διὰ τριῶν
stroy the shrine - of God and through(after) three

ἡμερῶν οἰκοδομῆσαι. 62 καὶ ἀναστὰς
days to build. And standing up

ὁ ἀρχιερεὺς εἶπεν αὐτῷ· οὐδὲν
the high priest said to him: Nothing

ἀποκρίνῃ, τί οὗτοί σου κατα-
answerest thou, what these men thee give

μαρτυροῦσιν; 63 ὁ δὲ 'Ιησοῦς ἐσιώπα.
evidence against? - But Jesus remained silent.

καὶ ὁ ἀρχιερεὺς εἶπεν αὐτῷ· ἐξορκίζω
And the high priest said to him: I adjure

σε κατὰ τοῦ θεοῦ τοῦ ζῶντος ἵνα ἡμῖν
thee by - God the living that us

εἴπῃς εἰ σὺ εἶ ὁ χριστὸς ὁ υἱὸς τοῦ
thou tell if thou art the Christ the Son -

θεοῦ. 64 λέγει αὐτῷ ὁ 'Ιησοῦς· σὺ εἶπας·
of God. Says to him - Jesus: Thou saidst;

πλὴν λέγω ὑμῖν, ἀπ' ἄρτι ὄψεσθε τὸν
yet I tell you, from now ye will see the

υἱὸν τοῦ ἀνθρώπου καθήμενον ἐκ
Son - of man sitting on [the]

δεξιῶν τῆς δυνάμεως καὶ ἐρχόμενον
right [hand] of the power and coming

ἐπὶ τῶν νεφελῶν τοῦ οὐρανοῦ. 65 τότε
on the clouds - of heaven. Then

ὁ ἀρχιερεὺς διέρρηξεν τὰ ἱμάτια αὐτοῦ
the high priest rent the garments of him

λέγων· ἐβλασφήμησεν· τί ἔτι χρείαν ἔχομεν
saying: He blasphemed; what yet need have we

μαρτύρων; ἴδε νῦν ἠκούσατε τὴν βλασφη-
of witnesses? behold now ye heard the blas-

μίαν· 66 τί ὑμῖν δοκεῖ; οἱ δὲ ἀπο-
phemy; what to you seems it? And they answer-

κριθέντες εἶπαν· ἔνοχος θανάτου ἐστίν.
ing said: Liable of(to) death he is.

67 Τότε ἐνέπτυσαν εἰς τὸ πρόσωπον αὐτοῦ
Then they spat in the face of him

καὶ ἐκολάφισαν αὐτόν, οἱ δὲ
and violently maltreated him, and they

ἐρράπισαν 68 λέγοντες· προφήτευσον ἡμῖν,
slapped [him] saying: Prophesy thou to us,

χριστέ, τίς ἐστιν ὁ παίσας σε;
Christ, who is it the [one] having struck thee?

69 Ὁ δὲ Πέτρος ἐκάθητο ἔξω ἐν
- And Peter sat outside in

τῇ αὐλῇ· καὶ προσῆλθεν αὐτῷ μία
the court; and approached to him one

παιδίσκη λέγουσα· καὶ σὺ ἦσθα μετὰ
maidservant saying: Also thou wast with

'Ιησοῦ τοῦ Γαλιλαίου. 70 ὁ δὲ ἠρνήσατο
Jesus the Galilæan. But he denied

ἔμπροσθεν πάντων λέγων· οὐκ οἶδα
before all saying: I know not

τί λέγεις. 71 ἐξελθόντα δὲ εἰς τὸν
what thou sayest. And *going out ⁵into ᵗthe

πυλῶνα εἶδεν αὐτὸν ἄλλη καὶ λέγει
⁷porch ²saw ³him ¹another and says

---

could put him to death.

60But they did not find any, though many false witnesses came forward. Finally two came forward

61and declared, "This fellow said, 'I am able to destroy the temple of God and rebuild it in three days.' "

62Then the high priest stood up and said to Jesus, "Are you not going to answer? What is this testimony that these men are bringing against you?" 63But Jesus remained silent.

The high priest said to him, "I charge you under oath by the living God: Tell us if you are the Christ, [h] the Son of God."

64"Yes, it is as you say," Jesus replied. "But I say to all of you: In the future you will see the Son of Man sitting at the right hand of the Mighty One and coming on the clouds of heaven."

65Then the high priest tore his clothes and said, "He has spoken blasphemy! Why do we need any more witnesses? Look, now you have heard the blasphemy. 66What do you think?"

"He is worthy of death," they answered.

67Then they spit in his face and struck him with their fists. Others slapped him 68and said, "Prophesy to us, Christ. Who hit you?"

Peter Disowns Jesus

69Now Peter was sitting out in the courtyard, and a servant girl came to him. "You also were with Jesus of Galilee," she said.

70But he denied it before them all. "I don't know what you're talking about," he said.

71Then he went out to the gateway, where another girl saw him and said to the

---

h63 Or *Messiah*; also in verse 68

*said to those who were there, "This man was with Jesus of Nazareth."

72And again he denied it with an oath, "I do not know the man."

73And a little later the bystanders came up and said to Peter, "Surely you too are one of them; for the way you talk gives you away."

74Then he began to curse and swear, "I do not know the man!" And immediately a cock crowed.

75And Peter remembered the word which Jesus had said, "Before a cock crows, you will deny Me three times." And he went out and wept bitterly.

Chapter 27

Judas' Remorse

NOW when morning had come, all the chief priests and the elders of the people took counsel against Jesus to put Him to death;

2and they bound Him, and led Him away, and delivered Him up to Pilate the governor.

3Then when Judas, who had betrayed Him, saw that He had been condemned, he felt remorse and returned the thirty pieces of silver to the chief priests and elders,

4saying, "I have sinned by betraying innocent blood." But they said, "What is that to us? See to that yourself!"

5And he threw the pieces of silver into the sanctuary and departed; and he went away and hanged himself.

6And the chief priests took the pieces of silver and said, "It is not lawful to put them into the temple treasury, since it is the price of blood."

7And they counseled together and with the money bought the Potter's Field as a burial place for strangers.

τοῖς ἐκεῖ· οὗτος ἦν μετὰ Ἰησοῦ τοῦ
to the[ones] there: This man was with Jesus the

Ναζωραίου. 72 καὶ πάλιν ἠρνήσατο
Nazarene. And again he denied

μετὰ ὅρκου ὅτι οὐκ οἶδα τὸν ἄνθρωπον.
with an oath[,] - I know not the man.

73 μετὰ μικρὸν δὲ προσελθόντες οἱ
And after a little approaching the[ones]

ἑστῶτες εἶπον τῷ Πέτρῳ· ἀληθῶς καὶ
standing said - to Peter: Truly also

σὺ ἐξ αὐτῶν εἶ, καὶ γὰρ ἡ λαλιά σου
thou of them art, for indeed the speech of thee

δῆλόν σε ποιεῖ. 74 τότε ἤρξατο καταθε-
manifest thee makes. Then he began to

ματίζειν καὶ ὀμνύειν ὅτι οὐκ οἶδα τὸν
curse and to swear[,] - I know not the

ἄνθρωπον. καὶ εὐθὺς ἀλέκτωρ ἐφώνησεν
man. And immediately a cock crowed.

75 καὶ ἐμνήσθη ὁ Πέτρος τοῦ ῥήματος
And remembered - Peter the word

Ἰησοῦ εἰρηκότος ὅτι πρὶν ἀλέκτορα
of Jesus having said[,] - Before a cock

φωνῆσαι τρὶς ἀπαρνήσῃ με· καὶ
to crow[b] three times thou wilt deny me; and

ἐξελθὼν ἔξω ἔκλαυσεν πικρῶς.
going forth outside he wept bitterly.

27 Πρωΐας δὲ γενομένης συμβούλιον
And early morning coming[a] counsel
= when early morning came

ἔλαβον πάντες οἱ ἀρχιερεῖς καὶ οἱ
took all the chief priests and the

πρεσβύτεροι τοῦ λαοῦ κατὰ τοῦ
elders of the people against -

Ἰησοῦ ὥστε θανατῶσαι αὐτόν· 2 καὶ
Jesus so as to put to death him; and

δήσαντες αὐτὸν ἀπήγαγον καὶ παρ-
having bound him they led away and de-

έδωκαν Πιλάτῳ τῷ ἡγεμόνι. 3 Τότε
livered to Pilate the governor. Then

ἰδὼν Ἰούδας ὁ παραδοὺς αὐτὸν
[5]seeing [1]Judas [2]the [one] [3]having betrayed [4]him

ὅτι κατεκρίθη, μεταμεληθεὶς ἔστρεψεν τὰ
that he was condemned, repenting returned the

τριάκοντα ἀργύρια τοῖς ἀρχιερεῦσιν
thirty pieces of silver to the chief priests

καὶ πρεσβυτέροις 4 λέγων· ἥμαρτον
and elders saying: I sinned

παραδοὺς αἷμα ἀθῷον. οἱ δὲ εἶπαν·
betraying blood innocent. But they said:

τί πρὸς ἡμᾶς; σὺ ὄψῃ. 5 καὶ ῥίψας
What to us? thou shalt see [to it]. And tossing

τὰ ἀργύρια εἰς τὸν ναὸν ἀν-
the pieces of silver into the shrine he

εχώρησεν, καὶ ἀπελθὼν ἀπήγξατο. 6 οἱ
departed, and going away hanged himself. the

δὲ ἀρχιερεῖς λαβόντες τὰ ἀργύρια εἶπαν·
But chief priests taking the pieces of silver said:

οὐκ ἔξεστιν βαλεῖν αὐτὰ εἰς τὸν
It is not lawful to put them into the

κορβανᾶν, ἐπεὶ τιμὴ αἵματός ἐστιν.
treasury, since price of blood it is.

7 συμβούλιον δὲ λαβόντες ἠγόρασαν ἐξ
So counsel taking they bought of(with)

αὐτῶν τὸν ἀγρὸν τοῦ κεραμέως εἰς ταφὴν
them the field of the potter for burial

---

people there, "This fellow was with Jesus of Nazareth."

72He denied it again, with an oath: "I don't know the man!"

73After a little while, those standing there went up to Peter and said, "Surely you are one of them, for your accent gives you away."

74Then he began to call down curses on himself and he swore to them, "I don't know the man!" Immediately a rooster crowed. 75Then Peter remembered the word Jesus had spoken: "Before the rooster crows, you will disown me three times." And he went outside and wept bitterly.

Chapter 27

Judas Hangs Himself

EARLY in the morning, all the chief priests and the elders of the people came to the decision to put Jesus to death. 2They bound him, led him away and handed him over to Pilate, the governor.

3When Judas, who had betrayed him, saw that Jesus was condemned, he was seized with remorse and returned the thirty silver coins to the chief priests and the elders. 4"I have sinned," he said, "for I have betrayed innocent blood."

"What is that to us?" they replied. "That's your responsibility."

5So Judas threw the money into the temple and left. Then he went away and hanged himself.

6The chief priests picked up the coins and said, "It is against the law to put this into the treasury, since it is blood money." 7So they decided to use the money to buy the potter's field as a burial place for foreigners.

8For this reason that field has been called the Field of Blood to this day. 9Then that which was spoken through Jeremiah the prophet was fulfilled, saying, "AND THEY TOOK THE THIRTY PIECES OF SILVER, THE PRICE OF THE ONE WHOSE PRICE HAD BEEN SET by the sons of Israel; 10AND THEY GAVE THEM FOR THE POTTER'S FIELD, AS THE LORD DIRECTED ME."

Jesus before Pilate

11Now Jesus stood before the governor, and the governor questioned Him, saying, "Are You the King of the Jews?" And Jesus said to him, "*It is as* you say."
12And while He was being accused by the chief priests and elders, He made no answer. 13Then Pilate *said to Him, "Do You not hear how many things they testify against You?" 14And He did not answer him with regard to even a *single* charge, so that the governor was quite amazed.
15Now at *the* feast the governor was accustomed to release for the multitude *any* one prisoner whom they wanted. 16And they were holding at that time a notorious prisoner, called Barabbas.
17When therefore they were gathered together, Pilate said to them, "Whom do you want me to release for you? Barabbas, or Jesus who is called Christ?"
18For he knew that because of envy they had delivered Him up.
19And while he was sitting on the judgment seat, his wife sent to him, saying, "Have nothing to do with that righteous Man; for last night I suffered greatly in a

τοῖς ξένοις. 8 διὸ ἐκλήθη ὁ ἀγρὸς
for the strangers. Wherefore was called - field

ἐκεῖνος ἀγρὸς αἵματος ἕως τῆς σήμερον.
that Field of blood until - to-day.

9 τότε ἐπληρώθη τὸ ῥηθὲν διὰ
Then was fulfilled the[thing] spoken through

'Ιερεμίου τοῦ προφήτου λέγοντος· καὶ
Jeremiah the prophet saying: And

ἔλαβον τὰ τριάκοντα ἀργύρια, τὴν
they took the thirty pieces of silver, the

τιμὴν τοῦ τετιμημένου ὃν ἐτιμήσαντο
price of the [one] having been priced whom they priced

ἀπὸ υἱῶν 'Ισραήλ, 10 καὶ ἔδωκαν
from [the] sons of Israel, and gave

αὐτὰ εἰς τὸν ἀγρὸν τοῦ κεραμέως, καθὰ
them for the field of the potter, as

συνέταξέν μοι κύριος. 11 'Ο δὲ
directed me [the] Lord. - And

'Ιησοῦς ἐστάθη ἔμπροσθεν τοῦ ἡγεμόνος·
Jesus stood before the governor;

καὶ ἐπηρώτησεν αὐτὸν ὁ ἡγεμὼν λέγων·
and questioned him the governor saying:

σὺ εἶ ὁ βασιλεὺς τῶν 'Ιουδαίων; ὁ δὲ
Thou art the king of the Jews? - And

'Ιησοῦς ἔφη· σὺ λέγεις. 12 καὶ ἐν
Jesus said: Thou sayest. And in

τῷ κατηγορεῖσθαι αὐτὸν ὑπὸ τῶν
the to be accused him[e] by the
=as he was being accused

ἀρχιερέων καὶ πρεσβυτέρων οὐδὲν
chief priests and elders nothing

ἀπεκρίνατο. 13 τότε λέγει αὐτῷ ὁ Πιλᾶτος·
he answered. Then says to him - Pilate:

οὐκ ἀκούεις πόσα σου κατα-
Hearest thou not what things [a]thee [1]they

μαρτυροῦσιν; 14 καὶ οὐκ ἀπεκρίθη αὐτῷ
[2]give evidence against? And he answered not him

πρὸς οὐδὲ ἓν ῥῆμα, ὥστε θαυμάζειν
to not one word, so as to marvel
=so that the governor marvelled

τὸν ἡγεμόνα λίαν. 15 Κατὰ δὲ ἑορτὴν
the governor[b] exceedingly. Now at a feast

εἰώθει ὁ ἡγεμὼν ἀπολύειν ἕνα τῷ ὄχλῳ
was accustomed the governor to release [a]one [1]to the [2]crowd

δέσμιον ὃν· ἤθελον. 16 εἶχον δὲ τότε
[4]prisoner whom they wished. And they had then

δέσμιον ἐπίσημον λεγόμενον Βαραββᾶν
prisoner a notable named Barabbas.

17 συνηγμένων οὖν αὐτῶν εἶπεν αὐτοῖς
Therefore having assembled them[a] said to them
=when they were assembled

ὁ Πιλᾶτος· τίνα θέλετε ἀπολύσω
- Pilate: Whom do ye wish I may release

ὑμῖν, [τὸν] Βαραββᾶν ἢ 'Ιησοῦν τὸν
to you, - Barabbas or Jesus -

λεγόμενον χριστόν; 18 ᾔδει γὰρ ὅτι
called Christ? for he knew that

διὰ φθόνον παρέδωκαν αὐτόν. 19 Καθη-
because of envy they delivered him. sit-

μένου δὲ αὐτοῦ ἐπὶ τοῦ βήματος
ting Now him[a] on the tribunal
= Now as he sat

ἀπέστειλεν πρὸς αὐτὸν ἡ γυνὴ αὐτοῦ
sent to him the wife of him

λέγουσα· μηδὲν σοὶ καὶ τῷ δικαίῳ
saying: Nothing to thee and just man

ἐκείνῳ· πολλὰ γὰρ ἔπαθον σήμερον κατ'
to that; for many things I suffered to-day by

8That is why it has been called the Field of Blood to this day. 9Then what was spoken by Jeremiah the prophet was fulfilled: "They took the thirty silver coins, the price set on him by the people of Israel, 10and they used them to buy the potter's field, as the Lord commanded me."[i]

Jesus Before Pilate

11Meanwhile Jesus stood before the governor, and the governor asked him, "Are you the king of the Jews?"
"Yes, it is as you say," Jesus replied.
12When he was accused by the chief priests and the elders, he gave no answer. 13Then Pilate asked him, "Don't you hear the testimony they are bringing against you?" 14But Jesus made no reply, not even to a single charge—to the great amazement of the governor.
15Now it was the governor's custom at the Feast to release a prisoner chosen by the crowd. 16At that time they had a notorious prisoner, called Barabbas. 17So when the crowd had gathered, Pilate asked them, "Which one do you want me to release to you: Barabbas, or Jesus who is called Christ?" 18For he knew it was out of envy that they had handed Jesus over to him.
19While Pilate was sitting on the judge's seat, his wife sent him this message: "Don't have anything to do with that innocent man, for I have suffered a great deal

i10 See Zech. 11:12,13; Jer. 19:1-13; 32:6-9.

dream because of Him."

20But the chief priests and the elders persuaded the multitudes to ask for Barabbas, and to put Jesus to death.

21But the governor answered and said to them, "Which of the two do you want me to release for you?" And they said, "Barabbas."

22Pilate *said to them, "Then what shall I do with Jesus who is called Christ?" They all *said, "Let Him be crucified!"

23And he said, "Why, what evil has He done?" But they kept shouting all the more, saying, "Let Him be crucified!"

24And when Pilate saw that he was accomplishing nothing, but rather that a riot was starting, he took water and washed his hands in front of the multitude, saying, "I am innocent of this Man's blood; see to that yourselves."

25And all the people answered and said, "His blood be on us and on our children!"

26Then he released Barabbas for them; but after having Jesus scourged, he delivered Him to be crucified.

Jesus Is Mocked

27Then the soldiers of the governor took Jesus into the Praetorium and gathered the whole *Roman* cohort around Him.

28And they stripped Him, and put a scarlet robe on Him.

29And after weaving a crown of thorns, they put it on His head, and a reed in His right hand; and they kneeled down before Him and mocked Him, saying, "Hail, King of the Jews!"

30And they spat on Him, and took the reed and *began* to beat Him on the head.

31And after they had

ὄναρ δι’ αὐτόν. **20** Οἱ δὲ ἀρχιερεῖς
a dream because of him.   But the   chief priests

καὶ οἱ πρεσβύτεροι ἔπεισαν τοὺς
and the   elders   persuaded the

ὄχλους ἵνα αἰτήσωνται τὸν Βαραββᾶν,
crowds that they should ask - Barabbas,

τὸν δὲ Ἰησοῦν ἀπολέσωσιν. **21** ἀπο-
 - and Jesus should destroy.   So

κριθεὶς δὲ ὁ ἡγεμὼν εἶπεν αὐτοῖς·
answering the governor said to them:

τίνα θέλετε ἀπὸ τῶν δύο ἀπολύσω
Which do ye wish from the two I may release

ὑμῖν; οἱ δὲ εἶπαν· τὸν Βαραββᾶν.
to you? And they said: - Barabbas.

22 λέγει αὐτοῖς ὁ Πιλᾶτος· τί οὖν
Says to them - Pilate: What then

ποιήσω Ἰησοῦν τὸν λεγόμενον χριστόν;
may I do [to] Jesus - called Christ?

λέγουσιν πάντες· σταυρωθήτω. **23** ὁ δὲ
They say all: Let him be crucified. But he

ἔφη· τί γὰρ κακὸν ἐποίησεν; οἱ δὲ
said: Why what evil did he? But they

περισσῶς ἔκραζον λέγοντες· σταυρω-
more cried out saying: Let him be

θήτω. **24** ἰδὼν δὲ ὁ Πιλᾶτος ὅτι οὐδὲν
crucified. And seeing - Pilate that nothing

ὠφελεῖ ἀλλὰ μᾶλλον θόρυβος γίνεται,
is gained but rather an uproar occurs,

λαβὼν ὕδωρ ἀπενίψατο τὰς χεῖρας
taking water he washed the(his) hands

κατέναντι τοῦ ὄχλου λέγων· ἀθῷός
in front of the crowd saying: Innocent

εἰμι ἀπὸ τοῦ αἵματος τούτου· ὑμεῖς
I am from the blood of this man; ye

ὄψεσθε. **25** καὶ ἀποκριθεὶς πᾶς ὁ λαὸς
will see [to it]. And answering all the people

εἶπεν· τὸ αἷμα αὐτοῦ ἐφ’ ἡμᾶς καὶ
said: The blood of him on us and

ἐπὶ τὰ τέκνα ἡμῶν. **26** τότε ἀπέλυσεν
on the children of us. Then he released

αὐτοῖς τὸν Βαραββᾶν, τὸν δὲ Ἰησοῦν
to them - Barabbas, - but Jesus

φραγελλώσας παρέδωκεν ἵνα σταυρωθῇ.
having scourged he delivered that he might be crucified.

27 Τότε οἱ στρατιῶται τοῦ ἡγεμόνος
Then the soldiers of the governor

παραλαβόντες τὸν Ἰησοῦν εἰς τὸ πραιτώ-
having taken - Jesus into the præ-

ριον συνήγαγον ἐπ’ αὐτὸν ὅλην τὴν
torium assembled against him all the

σπεῖραν. **28** καὶ ἐκδύσαντες αὐτὸν χλαμύδα
band. And stripping him cloak

κοκκίνην περιέθηκαν αὐτῷ, **29** καὶ
a purple they placed round him, and

πλέξαντες στέφανον ἐξ ἀκανθῶν ἐπέθηκαν
having plaited a crown of thorns they placed [it] on

ἐπὶ τῆς κεφαλῆς αὐτοῦ καὶ κάλαμον
on the head of him and a reed

ἐν τῇ δεξιᾷ αὐτοῦ, καὶ γονυπετή-
in the right [hand] of him, and bowing

σαντες ἔμπροσθεν αὐτοῦ ἐνέπαιξαν αὐτῷ
the knee in front of him mocked at him

λέγοντες· χαῖρε, βασιλεῦ τῶν Ἰουδαίων,
saying: Hail, king of the Jews,

30 καὶ ἐμπτύσαντες εἰς αὐτὸν ἔλαβον
and spitting at him took

---

today in a dream because of him."

20But the chief priests and the elders persuaded the crowd to ask for Barabbas and to have Jesus executed.

21"Which of the two do you want me to release to you?" asked the governor.

"Barabbas," they answered.

22"What shall I do, then, with Jesus who is called Christ?" Pilate asked.

They all answered, "Crucify him!"

23"Why? What crime has he committed?" asked Pilate.

But they shouted all the louder, "Crucify him!"

24When Pilate saw that he was getting nowhere, but that instead an uproar was starting, he took water and washed his hands in front of the crowd. "I am innocent of this man's blood," he said. "It is your responsibility!"

25All the people answered, "Let his blood be on us and on our children!"

26Then he released Barabbas to them. But he had Jesus flogged, and handed him over to be crucified.

The Soldiers Mock Jesus

27Then the governor's soldiers took Jesus into the Praetorium and gathered the whole company of soldiers around him. 28They stripped him and put a scarlet robe on him, 29and then twisted together a crown of thorns and set it on his head. They put a staff in his right hand and knelt in front of him and mocked him. "Hail, king of the Jews!" they said. 30They spit on him, and took the staff and struck him on the head again and again. 31After they had mocked him, they mocked Him, they took His robe off and put His garments on Him, and led Him away to crucify Him.

32And as they were coming out, they found a man of Cyrene named Simon, whom they pressed into service to bear His cross.

The Crucifixion

33And when they had come to a place called Golgotha, which means Place of a Skull,

34they gave Him wine to drink mingled with gall; and after tasting *it*, He was unwilling to drink.

35And when they had crucified Him, they divided up His garments among themselves, casting lots;

36and sitting down, they *began* to keep watch over Him there.

37And they put up above His head the charge against Him which read, "THIS IS JESUS THE KING OF THE JEWS."

38At that time two robbers *were crucified with Him, one on the right and one on the left.

39And those passing by were hurling abuse at Him, wagging their heads,

40and saying, "You who *are going to* destroy the temple and rebuild it in three days, save Yourself! If You are the Son of God, come down from the cross."

41In the same way the chief priests also, along with the scribes and elders, were mocking *Him*, and saying,

42"He saved others; He cannot save Himself. He is the King of Israel; let Him now come down from the cross, and we shall believe in Him.

43"HE TRUSTS IN GOD; LET

τὸν κάλαμον καὶ ἔτυπτον εἰς τὴν κεφαλὴν
the reed and struck at the head

αὐτοῦ. 31 καὶ ὅτε ἐνέπαιξαν αὐτῷ,
of him. And when they mocked at him,

ἐξέδυσαν αὐτὸν τὴν χλαμύδα καὶ ἐνέδυσαν
they took off him the cloak and put on

αὐτὸν τὰ ἱμάτια αὐτοῦ, καὶ ἀπήγαγον
him the garments of him, and led away

αὐτὸν εἰς τὸ σταυρῶσαι. 32 Ἐξερχόμενοι
him -   - to crucify. going forth

δὲ εὗρον ἄνθρωπον Κυρηναῖον, ὀνό-
And they found a man a Cyrenian, by

ματι Σίμωνα· τοῦτον ἠγγάρευσαν ἵνα
name Simon; this man they impressed that

ἄρῃ τὸν σταυρὸν αὐτοῦ. 33 Καὶ
he should bear the cross of him. And

ἐλθόντες εἰς τόπον λεγόμενον Γολγοθά,
coming to a place called Golgotha,

ὅ ἐστιν κρανίου τόπος λεγόμενος,
which is ²of a skull ¹A place ¹called,

34 ἔδωκαν αὐτῷ πιεῖν οἶνον μετὰ
they gave him to drink wine with

χολῆς μεμιγμένον· καὶ γευσάμενος οὐκ
gall having been mixed; and tasting not

ἠθέλησεν πιεῖν. 35 σταυρώσαντες δὲ
he would to drink. And having crucified

αὐτὸν διεμερίσαντο τὰ ἱμάτια αὐτοῦ
him they divided the garments of him

βάλλοντες κλῆρον, 36 καὶ καθήμενοι ἐτήρουν
casting a lot, and sitting they guarded

αὐτὸν ἐκεῖ. 37 καὶ ἐπέθηκαν ἐπάνω
him there. And they placed *on* above

τῆς κεφαλῆς αὐτοῦ τὴν αἰτίαν αὐτοῦ
the head of him the charge of him

γεγραμμένην· ΟΥΤΟΣ ΕΣΤΙΝ ΙΗΣΟΥΣ
having been written: THIS IS JESUS

Ο ΒΑΣΙΛΕΥΣ ΤΩΝ ΙΟΥΔΑΙΩΝ. 38 Τότε
THE KING OF THE JEWS. Then

σταυροῦνται σὺν αὐτῷ δύο λῃσταί,
are crucified with him two robbers,

εἷς ἐκ δεξιῶν καὶ εἷς ἐξ εὐωνύμων.
one on [the] right and one on [the] left.

39 Οἱ δὲ παραπορευόμενοι ἐβλασφήμουν
And the [ones] passing by blasphemed

αὐτὸν κινοῦντες τὰς κεφαλὰς αὐτῶν
him wagging the heads of them

40 καὶ λέγοντες· ὁ καταλύων τὸν ναὸν
and saying: The [one] destroying the shrine

καὶ ἐν τρισὶν ἡμέραις οἰκοδομῶν,
and in three days building [it],

σῶσον σεαυτόν, εἰ υἱὸς εἶ τοῦ θεοῦ,
save thyself, if Son thou art - of God,

καὶ κατάβηθι ἀπὸ τοῦ σταυροῦ. 41 ὁμοίως
and come down from the cross. Likewise

[καὶ] οἱ ἀρχιερεῖς ἐμπαίζοντες μετὰ
also the chief priests mocking with

τῶν γραμματέων καὶ πρεσβυτέρων ἔλεγον
the scribes and elders said:

42 ἄλλους ἔσωσεν, ἑαυτὸν οὐ δύναται
Others he saved, himself he cannot

σῶσαι· βασιλεὺς Ἰσραήλ ἐστιν,
to save; King of Israel he is,

καταβάτω νῦν ἀπὸ τοῦ σταυροῦ καὶ
let him come down now from the cross and

πιστεύσομεν ἐπ' αὐτόν. 43 πέποιθεν
we will believe on him. He has trusted

---

took off the robe and put his own clothes on him. Then they led him away to crucify him.

The Crucifixion

32As they were going out, they met a man from Cyrene, named Simon, and they forced him to carry the cross. 33They came to a place called Golgotha (which means The Place of the Skull). 34There they offered Jesus wine to drink, mixed with gall; but after tasting it, he refused to drink it. 35When they had crucified him, they divided up his clothes by casting lots.ʲ 36And sitting down, they kept watch over him there. 37Above his head they placed the written charge against him: THIS IS JESUS, THE KING OF THE JEWS. 38Two robbers were crucified with him, one on his right and one on his left. 39Those who passed by hurled insults at him, shaking their heads 40and saying, "You who are going to destroy the temple and build it in three days, save yourself! Come down from the cross, if you are the Son of God!" 41In the same way the chief priests, the teachers of the law and the elders mocked him. 42"He saved others," they said, "but he can't save himself! He's the King of Israel! Let him come down now from the cross, and we will believe in him. 43He trusts in God.

ʲ35 A few late manuscripts *lots that the word spoken by the prophet might be fulfilled: "They divided my garments among themselves and cast lots for my clothing"* (Psalm 22:18)

HIM DELIVER *Him* now, IF HE TAKES PLEASURE IN HIM; for He said, 'I am the Son of God.'"

44And the robbers also who had been crucified with Him were casting the same insult at Him.

45Now from the ᵘsixth hour darkness fell upon all the land until the ᵛninth hour.

46And about the ninth hour Jesus cried out with a loud voice, saying, "ELI, ELI, LAMA SABACHTHANI?" that is, "MY GOD, MY GOD, WHY HAST THOU FORSAKEN ME?"

47And some of those who were standing there, when they heard it, *began* saying, "This man is calling for Elijah."

48And immediately one of them ran, and taking a sponge, he filled it with sour wine, and put it on a reed, and gave Him a drink.

49But the rest *of them* said, "Let us see whether Elijah will come to save Him.""

50And Jesus cried out again with a loud voice, and yielded up *His* spirit.

51And behold, the veil of the temple was torn in two from top to bottom, and the earth shook; and the rocks were split,

52and the tombs were opened; and many bodies of the saints who had fallen asleep were raised;

53and coming out of the tombs after His resurrection they entered the holy city and appeared to many.

54Now the centurion, and those who were with him keeping guard over Jesus, when they saw the earthquake and the things that were happening, became very frightened and said, "Truly this was the Son of God!"

55And many women were

ἐπὶ	τὸν	θεόν,	ῥυσάσθω νῦν εἰ θέλει
on	-	God,	let him rescue now if he wants

αὐτόν· εἶπεν γὰρ ὅτι θεοῦ εἰμι υἱός.
him; for he said[,] - of God I am Son.

44 τό δ' αὐτὸ καὶ οἱ λῃσταὶ οἱ συσταυρω-
And the same also the robbers - crucified-

θέντες σὺν αὐτῷ ὠνείδιζον αὐτόν. **45** Ἀπὸ
with with him reproached him. from

δὲ ἕκτης ὥρας σκότος ἐγένετο ἐπὶ
Now [the] sixth hour darkness occurred over

πᾶσαν τὴν γῆν ἕως ὥρας ἐνάτης.
all the land until hour [the] ninth.

46 περὶ δὲ τὴν ἐνάτην ὥραν ἀνεβόησεν ὁ
And about the ninth hour cried out -

Ἰησοῦς φωνῇ μεγάλῃ λέγων· ἠλὶ ἠλὶ
Jesus voice with a great saying; Eli Eli

λεμὰ σαβαχθάνι; τοῦτ' ἔστιν· θεέ μου
lema sabachthani? this is: God of me[,]

θεέ μου, ἱνατί με ἐγκατέλιπες; **47** τινὲς
God of me, why me didst thou forsake? some

δὲ τῶν ἐκεῖ ἑστηκότων ἀκούσαντες
And of the[ones] there standing hearing

ἔλεγον ὅτι Ἠλίαν φωνεῖ οὗτος.
said[,] ²Elias ²calls ¹this man.

48 καὶ εὐθέως δραμὼν εἷς ἐξ αὐτῶν καὶ
And immediately running one of them and

λαβὼν σπόγγον πλήσας τε ὄξους καὶ
taking a sponge and filling of(with) vinegar and

περιθεὶς καλάμῳ ἐπότιζεν αὐτόν.
putting [it] round a reed gave to drink him.

49 οἱ δὲ λοιποὶ εἶπαν· ἄφες ἴδωμεν
But the rest said: Leave[,] let us see

εἰ ἔρχεται Ἠλίας σώσων αὐτόν. **50** ὁ
if comes Elias saving him. -

δὲ Ἰησοῦς πάλιν κράξας φωνῇ
And Jesus again crying out voice

μεγάλῃ ἀφῆκεν τὸ πνεῦμα. **51** Καὶ
with a great released the(his) spirit. And

ἰδοὺ τὸ καταπέτασμα τοῦ ναοῦ ἐσχίσθη
behold the veil of the shrine was rent

[ἀπ'] ἄνωθεν ἕως κάτω εἰς δύο, καὶ ἡ
from above to below in two, and the

γῆ ἐσείσθη, καὶ αἱ πέτραι ἐσχίσ-
earth was shaken, and the rocks were

θησαν, **52** καὶ τὰ μνημεῖα ἀνεῴχθησαν
rent, and the tombs were opened

καὶ πολλὰ σώματα τῶν κεκοιμημένων
and many bodies of the having fallen asleep

ἁγίων ἠγέρθησαν· **53** καὶ ἐξελθόντες
saints were raised; and coming forth

ἐκ τῶν μνημείων μετὰ τὴν ἔγερσιν
out of the tombs after the rising

αὐτοῦ εἰσῆλθον εἰς τὴν ἁγίαν πόλιν καὶ
of him entered into the holy city and

ἐνεφανίσθησαν πολλοῖς. **54** Ὁ δὲ ἑκατόν-
appeared to many. And the centu-

ταρχος καὶ οἱ μετ' αὐτοῦ τηροῦντες
rion and the[ones] with him guarding

τὸν Ἰησοῦν ἰδόντες τὸν σεισμὸν καὶ
- Jesus seeing the earthquake and

τὰ γινόμενα ἐφοβήθησαν σφόδρα,
the things happening feared exceedingly,

λέγοντες· ἀληθῶς θεοῦ υἱὸς ἦν οὗτος.
saying: Truly ⁴of God ³Son ¹was ¹this man.

55 Ἦσαν δὲ ἐκεῖ γυναῖκες πολλαὶ
Now there were there women many

Let God rescue him now if he wants him, for he said, 'I am the Son of God.' " 44In the same way the robbers who were crucified with him also heaped insults on him.

The Death of Jesus

45From the sixth hour until the ninth hour darkness came over all the land. 46About the ninth hour Jesus cried out in a loud voice, "*Eloi, Eloi,*ᵏ *lama sabachthani?*"—which means, "My God, my God, why have you forsaken me?"ˡ 47When some of those standing there heard this, they said, "He's calling Elijah." 48Immediately one of them ran and got a sponge. He filled it with wine vinegar, put it on a stick, and offered it to Jesus to drink. 49The rest said, "Now leave him alone. Let's see if Elijah comes to save him." 50And when Jesus had cried out again in a loud voice, he gave up his spirit. 51At that moment the curtain of the temple was torn in two from top to bottom. The earth shook and the rocks split. 52The tombs broke open and the bodies of many holy people who had died were raised to life. 53They came out of the tombs, and after Jesus' resurrection they went into the holy city and appeared to many people. 54When the centurion and those with him who were guarding Jesus saw the earthquake and all that had happened, they were terrified, and exclaimed, "Surely he was the Sonᵐ of God!" 55Many women were

---

ᵘ I.e., noon
ᵛ I.e., 3 p.m.
ʷ Some early mss. add: *And another took a spear and pierced His side, and there came out water and blood.* (cf. John 19:34)

ᵏ46 Some manuscripts *Eli, Eli*
ˡ46 Psalm 22:1
ᵐ54 Or *a son*

there looking on from a distance, who had followed Jesus from Galilee, ministering to Him,

56among whom was Mary Magdalene, *along with* Mary the mother of James and Joseph, and the mother of the sons of Zebedee.

Jesus Is Buried

57And when it was evening, there came a rich man from Arimathea, named Joseph, who himself had also become a disciple of Jesus.

58This man went to Pilate and asked for the body of Jesus. Then Pilate ordered *it* to be given over *to him.*

59And Joseph took the body and wrapped it in a clean linen cloth,

60and laid it in his own new tomb, which he had hewn out in the rock; and he rolled a large stone against the entrance of the tomb and went away.

61And Mary Magdalene was there, and the other Mary, sitting opposite the grave.

62Now on the next day, which is *the one* after the preparation, the chief priests and the Pharisees gathered together with Pilate,

63and said, "Sir, we remember that when He was still alive that deceiver said, 'After three days I *am* to rise again.'

64"Therefore, give orders for the grave to be made secure until the third day, lest the disciples come and steal Him away and say to the people, 'He has risen from the dead,' and the last deception will be worse than the first."

65Pilate said to them, "You have a guard; go,

ἀπὸ μακρόθεν θεωροῦσαι, αἵτινες ἠκολού-
from afar   beholding,   who   followed

θησαν τῷ Ἰησοῦ ἀπὸ τῆς Γαλιλαίας
      the Jesus   from ᵗ   Galilee

διακονοῦσαι αὐτῷ· 56 ἐν αἷς ἦν
ministering   to him;   among whom was

Μαρία ἡ Μαγδαληνή, καὶ Μαρία ἡ
Mary the Magdalene,   and Mary the

τοῦ Ἰακώβου καὶ Ἰωσὴφ μήτηρ, καὶ ἡ
 - of James and of Joseph mother, and the

μήτηρ τῶν υἱῶν Ζεβεδαίου.
mother of the sons of Zebedee.

57 Ὀψίας δὲ γενομένης ἦλθεν ἄνθρωπος
   Now evening   having comeᵃ   came   man
   = when evening had come

πλούσιος ἀπὸ Ἀριμαθαίας, τοὔνομα Ἰωσήφ,
a rich   from Arimathæa,   the name Joseph,

ὃς καὶ αὐτὸς ἐμαθητεύθη τῷ Ἰησοῦ·
who also himself was discipled the to Jesus;

58 οὗτος προσελθὼν τῷ Πιλάτῳ ἠτήσατο
this man approaching   -   to Pilate   asked

τὸ σῶμα τοῦ Ἰησοῦ. τότε ὁ Πιλᾶτος
the body   - of Jesus. Then   -   Pilate

ἐκέλευσεν ἀποδοθῆναι. 59 καὶ λαβὼν
commanded [it] to be given [him].   And   taking

τὸ σῶμα ὁ Ἰωσὴφ ἐνετύλιξεν αὐτὸ [ἐν]
the body - Joseph   wrapped   it   in

σινδόνι καθαρᾷ, 60 καὶ ἔθηκεν αὐτὸ ἐν
sheet   a clean,   and placed   it   in

τῷ καινῷ αὐτοῦ μνημείῳ ὃ ἐλατό-
the new   of him   tomb   which he

μησεν ἐν τῇ πέτρᾳ, καὶ προσκυλίσας
hewed   in the rock,   and having rolled *to*

λίθον μέγαν τῇ θύρᾳ τοῦ μνημείου
stone a great to the door of the   tomb

ἀπῆλθεν. 61 Ἦν δὲ ἐκεῖ Μαριὰμ
went away.   And there was   there   Mary

ἡ Μαγδαληνὴ καὶ ἡ ἄλλη Μαρία,
the Magdalene   and the other Mary,

καθήμεναι ἀπέναντι τοῦ τάφου. 62 Τῇ
sitting   opposite   the   grave.   on the

δὲ ἐπαύριον, ἥτις ἐστὶν μετὰ τὴν παρα-
And morrow,   which is   after the   prepara-

σκευήν, συνήχθησαν οἱ ἀρχιερεῖς
tion,   were assembled the chief priests

καὶ οἱ Φαρισαῖοι πρὸς Πιλᾶτον 63 λέ-
and the Pharisees   to   Pilate   say-

γοντες· κύριε, ἐμνήσθημεν ὅτι ἐκεῖνος
ing: Sir,   we remembered that   that

ὁ πλάνος εἶπεν ἔτι ζῶν· μετὰ τρεῖς
- deceiver said yet living: After three

ἡμέρας ἐγείρομαι. 64 κέλευσον οὖν
days   I am raised.   Command   therefore

ἀσφαλισθῆναι τὸν τάφον ἕως τῆς
to be made fast   the   grave   until the

τρίτης ἡμέρας, μήποτε ἐλθόντες οἱ μαθηταὶ
third   day,   lest   coming   the disciples

κλέψωσιν αὐτὸν καὶ εἴπωσιν τῷ λαῷ·
may steal   him   and may say to the people:

ἠγέρθη ἀπὸ τῶν νεκρῶν, καὶ ἔσται
He was raised from the   dead,   and will be

ἡ ἐσχάτη πλάνη χείρων τῆς πρώτης.
the last   deceit worse [than] the   first.

65 ἔφη αὐτοῖς ὁ Πιλᾶτος· ἔχετε κου-
Said to them   -   Pilate: Ye have   a

---

there, watching from a distance. They had followed Jesus to care for his needs. 56Among them were Mary Magdalene, Mary the mother of James and Joses, and the mother of Zebedee's sons.

The Burial of Jesus

57As evening approached, there came a rich man from Arimathea, named Joseph, who had himself become a disciple of Jesus. 58Going to Pilate, he asked for Jesus' body, and Pilate ordered that it be given to him. 59Joseph took the body, wrapped it in a clean linen cloth, 60and placed it in his own new tomb that he had cut out of the rock. He rolled a big stone in front of the entrance to the tomb and went away. 61Mary Magdalene and the other Mary were sitting there opposite the tomb.

The Guard at the Tomb

62The next day, the one after Preparation Day, the chief priests and the Pharisees went to Pilate. 63"Sir," they said, "we remember that while he was still alive that deceiver said, 'After three days I will rise again.' 64So give the order for the tomb to be made secure until the third day. Otherwise, his disciples may come and steal the body and tell the people that he has been raised from the dead. This last deception will be worse than the first."

65"Take a guard," Pilate answered. "Go, make the

make it *as* secure as you know how."
66And they went and made the grave secure, and along with the guard they set a seal on the stone.

Chapter 28

Jesus Is Risen!

NOW after the Sabbath, as it began to dawn toward the first day of the week, Mary Magdalene and the other Mary came to look at the grave.
2And behold, a severe earthquake had occurred, for an angel of the Lord descended from heaven and came and rolled away the stone and sat upon it.
3And his appearance was like lightning, and his garment as white as snow;
4and the guards shook for fear of him, and became like dead men.
5And the angel answered and said to the women, "Do not be afraid; for I know that you are looking for Jesus who has been crucified.
6"He is not here, for He has risen, just as He said. Come, see the place where He was lying.
7"And go quickly and tell His disciples that He has risen from the dead; and behold, He is going before you into Galilee, there you will see Him; behold, I have told you."
8And they departed quickly from the tomb with fear and great joy and ran to report it to His disciples.
9And behold, Jesus met them and greeted them. And they came up and took hold of His feet and worshiped Him.

στωδίαν· ὑπάγετε ἀσφαλίσασθε ὡς οἴδατε.
guard; go ye make fast as ye know*.
66 οἱ δὲ πορευθέντες ἠσφαλίσαντο τὸν
And they going made fast the
τάφον σφραγίσαντες τὸν λίθον μετὰ τῆς
grave sealing the stone with the
κουστωδίας.
guard.

28 Ὀψὲ δὲ σαββάτων, τῇ ἐπιφωσκούσῃ
But late of [the] sabbaths, at the drawing on
εἰς μίαν σαββάτων, ἦλθεν Μαριὰμ ἡ
toward one of [the] sabbaths, came Mary the
= the first day of the week,
Μαγδαληνὴ καὶ ἡ ἄλλη Μαρία θεωρῆσαι
Magdalene and the other Mary to view
τὸν τάφον. 2 καὶ ἰδοὺ σεισμὸς ἐγένετο
the grave. And behold earthquake occurred
μέγας· ἄγγελος γὰρ κυρίου καταβὰς
a great; for an angel of [the] Lord descending
ἐξ οὐρανοῦ καὶ προσελθὼν ἀπεκύλισεν
out of heaven and approaching rolled away
τὸν λίθον καὶ ἐκάθητο ἐπάνω αὐτοῦ.
the stone and sat upon it.
3 ἦν δὲ ἡ εἰδέα αὐτοῦ ὡς ἀστραπή,
And was the appearance of him as lightning,
καὶ τὸ ἔνδυμα αὐτοῦ λευκὸν ὡς χιών.
and the dress of him white as snow.
4 ἀπὸ δὲ τοῦ φόβου αὐτοῦ ἐσείσθησαν
And from the fear of him were shaken
οἱ τηροῦντες καὶ ἐγενήθησαν ὡς
the [ones] guarding and they became as
νεκροί. 5 ἀποκριθεὶς δὲ ὁ ἄγγελος
dead. And answering the angel
εἶπεν ταῖς γυναιξίν· μὴ φοβεῖσθε ὑμεῖς·
said to the women: Fear not ye;
οἶδα γὰρ ὅτι Ἰησοῦν τὸν ἐσταυρω-
for I know that Jesus the [one] having been
μένον ζητεῖτε· 6 οὐκ ἔστιν ὧδε·
crucified ye seek; he is not here;
ἠγέρθη γὰρ καθὼς εἶπεν· δεῦτε ἴδετε τὸν
for he was raised as he said; come see ye the
τόπον ὅπου ἔκειτο. 7 καὶ ταχὺ πορευθεῖσαι
place where he lay. And quickly going
εἴπατε τοῖς μαθηταῖς ὅτι ἠγέρθη
tell the disciples of him that he was raised
ἀπὸ τῶν νεκρῶν, καὶ ἰδοὺ προάγει ὑμᾶς
from the dead, and behold he goes before you
εἰς τὴν Γαλιλαίαν, ἐκεῖ αὐτὸν ὄψεσθε.
to - Galilee, there him ye will see.
ἰδοὺ εἶπον ὑμῖν. 8 καὶ ἀπελθοῦσαι ταχὺ
Behold I told you. And going away quickly
ἀπὸ τοῦ μνημείου μετὰ φόβου καὶ χαρᾶς
from the tomb with fear and joy
μεγάλης ἔδραμον ἀπαγγεῖλαι τοῖς
great they ran to announce to the
μαθηταῖς αὐτοῦ. 9 καὶ ἰδοὺ Ἰησοῦς
disciples of him. And behold Jesus
ὑπήντησεν αὐταῖς λέγων· χαίρετε. αἱ δὲ
met them saying: Hail. And they
προσελθοῦσαι ἐκράτησαν αὐτοῦ τοὺς πόδας
approaching held of him the feet
καὶ προσεκύνησαν αὐτῷ. 10 τότε λέγει
and worshipped him. Then says

* can. See note on page xviii.

---

tomb as secure as you know how." 66So they went and made the tomb secure by putting a seal on the stone and posting the guard.

Chapter 28

The Resurrection

AFTER the Sabbath, at dawn on the first day of the week, Mary Magdalene and the other Mary went to look at the tomb.
2There was a violent earthquake, for an angel of the Lord came down from heaven and, going to the tomb, rolled back the stone and sat on it. 3His appearance was like lightning, and his clothes were white as snow. 4The guards were so afraid of him that they shook and became like dead men.
5The angel said to the women, "Do not be afraid, for I know that you are looking for Jesus, who was crucified. 6He is not here; he has risen, just as he said. Come and see the place where he lay. 7Then go quickly and tell his disciples: 'He has risen from the dead and is going ahead of you into Galilee. There you will see him.' Now I have told you."
8So the women hurried away from the tomb, afraid yet filled with joy, and ran to tell his disciples. 9Suddenly Jesus met them. "Greetings," he said. They came to him, clasped his feet and worshiped him.

10Then Jesus *said to them, "Do not be afraid; go and take word to My brethren to leave for Galilee, and there they shall see Me."

11Now while they were on their way, behold, some of the guard came into the city and reported to the chief priests all that had happened.

12And when they had assembled with the elders and counseled together, they gave a large sum of money to the soldiers,

13and said, "You are to say, 'His disciples came by night and stole Him away while we were asleep.'

14"And if this should come to the governor's ears, we will win him over and keep you out of trouble."

15And they took the money and did as they had been instructed; and this story was widely spread among the Jews, *and is to this day.*

The Great Commission

16But the eleven disciples proceeded to Galilee, to the mountain which Jesus had designated.

17And when they saw Him, they worshiped *Him*; but some were doubtful.

18And Jesus came up and spoke to them, saying, "All authority has been given to Me in heaven and on earth.

19"Go therefore and make disciples of all the nations, baptizing them in the name of the Father and the Son and the Holy Spirit,

20teaching them to observe all that I commanded you; and lo, I am with you always, even to the end of the age."

αὐταῖς ὁ Ἰησοῦς· μὴ φοβεῖσθε· ὑπάγετε
to them — Jesus: Fear ye not; go ye

ἀπαγγείλατε τοῖς ἀδελφοῖς μου ἵνα
announce to the brothers of me that

ἀπέλθωσιν εἰς τὴν Γαλιλαίαν, κἀκεῖ
they may go away into — Galilee, and there

με ὄψονται. 11 Πορευομένων δὲ αὐτῶν
me they will see. And going them[a]
= as they were going

ἰδοὺ τινες τῆς κουστωδίας ἐλθόντες εἰς
behold some of the guard coming into

τὴν πόλιν ἀπήγγειλαν τοῖς ἀρχιερεῦσιν
the city announced to the chief priests

ἅπαντα τὰ γενόμενα. 12 καὶ συν-
all the things having happened. And being

αχθέντες μετὰ τῶν πρεσβυτέρων συμβούλιόν
assembled with the elders [2]counsel

τε λαβόντες ἀργύρια ἱκανὰ ἔδωκαν τοῖς
[1]and [2]taking silver enough gave to the

στρατιώταις, 13 λέγοντες· εἴπατε ὅτι οἱ
soldiers, saying: Say ye that the

μαθηταὶ αὐτοῦ νυκτὸς ἐλθόντες ἔκλεψαν
disciples of him of(by) night coming stole

αὐτὸν ἡμῶν κοιμωμένων. 14 καὶ ἐὰν
him we sleeping.[a] And if
= while we slept.

ἀκουσθῇ τοῦτο ἐπὶ τοῦ ἡγεμόνος,
be heard this before the governor,

ἡμεῖς πείσομεν καὶ ὑμᾶς ἀμερίμνους
we will persuade and you free from anxiety

ποιήσομεν. 15 οἱ δὲ λαβόντες ἀργύρια
we will make. And they taking silver

ἐποίησαν ὡς ἐδιδάχθησαν. Καὶ διεφη-
did as they were taught. And was spread

μίσθη ὁ λόγος οὗτος παρὰ Ἰουδαίοις
about — saying this by Jews

μέχρι τῆς σήμερον [ἡμέρας]. 16 Οἱ δὲ
until to-day. So the

ἔνδεκα μαθηταὶ ἐπορεύθησαν εἰς τὴν
eleven disciples went to —

Γαλιλαίαν, εἰς τὸ ὄρος οὗ ἐτάξατο
Galilee, to the mountain where appointed

αὐτοῖς ὁ Ἰησοῦς, 17 καὶ ἰδόντες αὐτὸν
them — Jesus, and seeing him

προσεκύνησαν, οἱ δὲ ἐδίστασαν. 18 καὶ
they worshipped, but some doubted. And

προσελθὼν ὁ Ἰησοῦς ἐλάλησεν αὐτοῖς
approaching — Jesus talked with them

λέγων· ἐδόθη μοι πᾶσα ἐξουσία ἐν
saying: was given to me All authority in

οὐρανῷ καὶ ἐπὶ [τῆς] γῆς. 19 πορευθέντες
heaven and on the earth. Going

οὖν μαθητεύσατε πάντα τὰ ἔθνη, βαπτίζ-
therefore disciple ye all the nations, baptiz-

οντες αὐτοὺς εἰς τὸ ὄνομα τοῦ πατρὸς
ing them in the name of the Father

καὶ τοῦ υἱοῦ καὶ τοῦ ἁγίου πνεύματος,
and of the Son and of the Holy Spirit,

20 διδάσκοντες αὐτοὺς τηρεῖν πάντα
teaching them to observe all things

ὅσα ἐνετειλάμην ὑμῖν· καὶ ἰδοὺ ἐγὼ
whatever I gave command to you; and behold I

μεθ' ὑμῶν εἰμι πάσας τὰς ἡμέρας ἕως
with you am all the days until

τῆς συντελείας τοῦ αἰῶνος.
the completion of the age.

10Then Jesus said to them, "Do not be afraid. Go and tell my brothers to go to Galilee; there they will see me."

The Guards' Report

11While the women were on their way, some of the guards went into the city and reported to the chief priests everything that had happened. 12When the chief priests had met with the elders and devised a plan, they gave the soldiers a large sum of money, 13telling them, "You are to say, 'His disciples came during the night and stole him away while we were asleep.' 14If this report gets to the governor, we will satisfy him and keep you out of trouble." 15So the soldiers took the money and did as they were instructed. And this story has been widely circulated among the Jews to this very day.

The Great Commission

16Then the eleven disciples went to Galilee, to the mountain where Jesus had told them to go. 17When they saw him, they worshiped him; but some doubted. 18Then Jesus came to them and said, "All authority in heaven and on earth has been given to me. 19Therefore go and make disciples of all nations, baptizing them in[n] the name of the Father and of the Son and of the Holy Spirit, 20and teaching them to obey everything I have commanded you. And surely I am with you always, to the very end of the age."

---

n19 Or into; see Acts 8:16; 19:5; Romans 6:3; 1 Cor. 1:13; 10:2 and Gal. 3:27.

Chapter 1

Preaching of John the Baptist

THE beginning of the gospel of Jesus Christ, [a]the Son of God.

2As it is written in Isaiah the prophet,

"BEHOLD, I SEND MY MESSENGER BEFORE YOUR FACE, WHO WILL PREPARE YOUR WAY;

3 THE VOICE OF ONE CRYING IN THE WILDERNESS, 'MAKE READY THE WAY OF THE LORD, MAKE HIS PATHS STRAIGHT.'"

4John the Baptist appeared in the wilderness [b]preaching a baptism of repentance for the forgiveness of sins.

5And all the country of Judea was going out to him, and all the people of Jerusalem; and they were being baptized by him in the Jordan River, confessing their sins.

6And John was clothed with camel's hair and *wore* a leather belt around his waist, and his diet was locusts and wild honey.

7And he was preaching, and saying, "After me One is coming who is mightier than I, and I am not fit to stoop down and untie the thong of His sandals.

8"I baptized you [c]with water; but He will baptize you [c]with the Holy Spirit."

The Baptism of Jesus

9And it came about in those days that Jesus came from Nazareth in Galilee, and was baptized by John in the Jordan.

10And immediately coming up out of the water, He saw the heavens opening, and the Spirit like a dove descending upon Him;

11and a voice came out of the heavens: "Thou art My beloved Son, in Thee I am well-pleased."

12And immediately the Spirit *impelled Him to go* out into the wilderness.

13And He was in the wilderness forty days being tempted by Satan; and He was with the wild beasts, and the angels were minis-

---

1 Ἀρχὴ τοῦ εὐαγγελίου Ἰησοῦ Χριστοῦ.
[The] beginning of the   gospel   of Jesus   Christ.

2 Καθὼς γέγραπται ἐν τῷ Ἡσαΐᾳ τῷ
As   it has been written in   -   Isaiah   the

προφήτῃ· ἰδοὺ ἀποστέλλω τὸν ἄγγελόν μου
prophet: Behold[,] I send   the   messenger of me

πρὸ προσώπου σου, ὃς κατασκευάσει τὴν ὁδόν
before [the] face   of thee, who will prepare   the   way

σου. **3** φωνὴ βοῶντος ἐν τῇ ἐρήμῳ· ἑτοιμάσατε
of thee; a voice of [one] crying in the desert: Prepare ye

τὴν ὁδὸν κυρίου, εὐθείας ποιεῖτε τὰς τρίβους
the   way of [the] Lord, straight   make   the   paths

αὐτοῦ, **4** ἐγένετο Ἰωάννης ὁ βαπτίζων ἐν τῇ
of him,   came   John   the [one] baptizing in the

ἐρήμῳ κηρύσσων βάπτισμα μετανοίας εἰς
desert   proclaiming   a baptism   of repentance for

ἄφεσιν ἁμαρτιῶν. **5** καὶ ἐξεπορεύετο πρὸς
forgiveness of sins.   And   went out   to

αὐτὸν πᾶσα ἡ Ἰουδαία χώρα καὶ οἱ Ἱεροσο-
him   all the Judæan country and the   Jerusa-

λυμῖται πάντες, καὶ ἐβαπτίζοντο ὑπ' αὐτοῦ
lemites   all,   and   were baptized by   him

ἐν τῷ Ἰορδάνῃ ποταμῷ ἐξομολογούμενοι τὰς
in the Jordan   river   confessing   the

ἁμαρτίας αὐτῶν. **6** καὶ ἦν ὁ Ἰωάννης
sins   of them.   And was   -   John

ἐνδεδυμένος τρίχας καμήλου καὶ ζώνην
having been clothed [in] hairs of a camel   and   girdle

δερματίνην περὶ τὴν ὀσφὺν αὐτοῦ, καὶ ἔσθων
a leathern   round   the   loin[s]   of him,   and   eating

ἀκρίδας καὶ μέλι ἄγριον. **7** καὶ ἐκήρυσσεν
locusts   and honey   wild.   And he proclaimed

λέγων· ἔρχεται ὁ ἰσχυρότερός μου ὀπίσω
saying: Comes the [one] stronger   of me   after
                     =than I

[μου], οὗ οὐκ εἰμὶ ἱκανὸς κύψας λῦσαι
me, of whom I am not   competent stooping to loosen

τὸν ἱμάντα τῶν ὑποδημάτων αὐτοῦ. **8** ἐγὼ
the   thong   of the   sandals   of him.   I

ἐβάπτισα ὑμᾶς ὕδατι, αὐτὸς δὲ βαπτίσει ὑμᾶς
baptized   you in water, but he   will baptize   you

πνεύματι ἁγίῳ.
Spirit in [the] Holy.

9 Καὶ ἐγένετο ἐν ἐκείναις ταῖς ἡμέραις
And it came to pass in   those   -   days

ἦλθεν Ἰησοῦς ἀπὸ Ναζαρὲθ τῆς Γαλιλαίας
came   Jesus   from   Nazareth   -   of Galilee

καὶ ἐβαπτίσθη εἰς τὸν Ἰορδάνην ὑπὸ
and   was baptized   in   the   Jordan   by

Ἰωάννου. **10** καὶ εὐθὺς ἀναβαίνων ἐκ τοῦ
John.   And immediately going up   out of the

ὕδατος εἶδεν σχιζομένους τοὺς οὐρανοὺς
water   he saw   being rent   the   heavens

καὶ τὸ πνεῦμα ὡς περιστερὰν καταβαῖνον
and the   Spirit   as   a dove   coming down

εἰς αὐτόν· **11** καὶ φωνὴ [ἐγένετο] ἐκ τῶν
to   him.   and   a voice   there was   out of the

οὐρανῶν· σὺ εἶ ὁ υἱός μου ὁ ἀγαπητός,
heavens: Thou art the Son of me the   beloved,

ἐν σοὶ εὐδόκησα. **12** Καὶ εὐθὺς τὸ
in thee I was well pleased.   And immediately the

πνεῦμα αὐτὸν ἐκβάλλει εἰς τὴν ἔρημον.
Spirit   him   thrusts forth into   the   desert.

13 καὶ ἦν ἐν τῇ ἐρήμῳ τεσσεράκοντα
And he was in   the   desert   forty

ἡμέρας πειραζόμενος ὑπὸ τοῦ σατανᾶ, καὶ
days   being tempted   by   -   Satan,   and

ἦν μετὰ τῶν θηρίων, καὶ οἱ ἄγγελοι
was   with   the   wild beasts,   and   the   angels

Chapter 1

John the Baptist Prepares the Way

THE beginning of the gospel about Jesus Christ, the Son of God. [a]

2It is written in Isaiah the prophet:

"I will send my messenger ahead of you, who will prepare your way" [b]—

3"a voice of one calling in the desert, 'Prepare the way for the Lord, make straight paths for him.'" [c]

4And so John came, baptizing in the desert region and preaching a baptism of repentance for the forgiveness of sins. 5The whole Judean countryside and all the people of Jerusalem went out to him. Confessing their sins, they were baptized by him in the Jordan River. 6John wore clothing made of camel's hair, with a leather belt around his waist, and he ate locusts and wild honey. 7And this was his message: "After me will come one more powerful than I, the thongs of whose sandals I am not worthy to stoop down and untie. 8I baptize you [d] water, but he will baptize you with the Holy Spirit."

The Baptism and Temptation of Jesus

9At that time Jesus came from Nazareth in Galilee and was baptized by John in the Jordan. 10As Jesus was coming up out of the water, he saw heaven being torn open and the Spirit descending on him like a dove. 11And a voice came from heaven: "You are my Son, whom I love; with you I am well pleased."

12At once the Spirit sent him out into the desert, 13and he was in the desert forty days, being tempted by Satan. He was with the wild animals, and angels attended him.

---

[a] Many mss. do not contain *the Son of God*
[b] Or, *proclaiming*
[c] The Gr. here can be translated *in, with* or *by*

---

[a]1 Some manuscripts do not have *the Son of God.*
[b]2 Mal. 3:1
[c]3 Isaiah 40:3
[d]8 Or *in*

tering to Him.

Jesus Preaches in Galilee

14And after John had been taken into custody, Jesus came into Galilee, preaching the gospel of God,

15and saying, "The time is fulfilled, and the kingdom of God is at hand; repent and believe in the gospel."

16And as He was going along by the Sea of Galilee, He saw Simon and Andrew, the brother of Simon, casting a net in the sea; for they were fishermen.

17And Jesus said to them, "Follow Me, and I will make you become fishers of men."

18And they immediately left the nets and followed Him.

19And going on a little farther, He saw James the *son* of Zebedee, and John his brother, who were also in the boat mending the nets.

20And immediately He called them; and they left their father Zebedee in the boat with the hired servants, and went away to follow Him.

21And they *went into Capernaum; and immediately on the Sabbath He entered the synagogue and *began to teach.

22And they were amazed at His teaching; for He was teaching them as *one* having authority, and not as the scribes.

23And just then there was in their synagogue a man with an unclean spirit; and he cried out,

24saying, "What do we have to do with You, Jesus dof Nazareth? Have You come to destroy us? I know who You are—the Holy One of God!"

25And Jesus rebuked him,

Middle column (interlinear)

διηκόνουν αὐτῷ.
ministered to him.

14 Καὶ μετὰ τὸ παραδοθῆναι τὸν
And after the to be delivered -
= after John was delivered

Ἰωάννην ἦλθεν ὁ Ἰησοῦς εἰς τὴν Γαλιλαίαν
Johnb came - Jesus into - Galilee

κηρύσσων τὸ εὐαγγέλιον τοῦ θεοῦ **15** [καὶ
proclaiming the gospel - of God and

λέγων], ὅτι πεπλήρωται ὁ καιρὸς καὶ
saying, - Has been fulfilled the time and

ἤγγικεν ἡ βασιλεία τοῦ θεοῦ· μετανοεῖτε
has drawn near the kingdom - of God; repent ye

καὶ πιστεύετε ἐν τῷ εὐαγγελίῳ. **16** Καὶ
and believe in the gospel. And

παράγων παρὰ τὴν θάλασσαν τῆς Γαλιλαίας
passing along beside the sea - of Galilee

εἶδεν Σίμωνα καὶ Ἀνδρέαν τὸν ἀδελφὸν
he saw Simon and Andrew the brother

Σίμωνος ἀμφιβάλλοντας ἐν τῇ θαλάσσῃ
of Simon casting [a net] in the sea;

ἦσαν γὰρ ἁλεεῖς. **17** καὶ εἶπεν αὐτοῖς
for they were fishers. And said to them

ὁ Ἰησοῦς· δεῦτε ὀπίσω μου, καὶ ποιήσω
- Jesus: Come after me, and I will make

ὑμᾶς γενέσθαι ἁλεεῖς ἀνθρώπων. **18** καὶ
you to become fishers of men. And

εὐθὺς ἀφέντες τὰ δίκτυα ἠκολούθησαν
immediately leaving the nets they followed

αὐτῷ. **19** Καὶ προβὰς ὀλίγον εἶδεν
him. And going forward a little he saw

Ἰάκωβον τὸν τοῦ Ζεβεδαίου καὶ Ἰωάννην
James the [son] - of Zebedee and John

τὸν ἀδελφὸν αὐτοῦ καὶ αὐτοὺς ἐν τῷ
the brother of him even them in the

πλοίῳ καταρτίζοντας τὰ δίκτυα. **20** καὶ
ship mending the nets. And

εὐθὺς ἐκάλεσεν αὐτούς· καὶ ἀφέντες τὸν
immediately he called them; and leaving the

πατέρα αὐτῶν Ζεβεδαῖον ἐν τῷ πλοίῳ
father of them Zebedee in the ship

μετὰ τῶν μισθωτῶν ἀπῆλθον ὀπίσω αὐτοῦ.
with the hired servants they went after him.

21 Καὶ εἰσπορεύονται εἰς Καφαρναούμ·
And they enter into Capernaum;

καὶ εὐθὺς τοῖς σάββασιν εἰσελθὼν
and immediately on the sabbaths entering

εἰς τὴν συναγωγὴν ἐδίδασκεν. **22** καὶ
into the synagogue he taught. And

ἐξεπλήσσοντο ἐπὶ τῇ διδαχῇ αὐτοῦ· ἦν
they were astounded on(at) the teaching of him; aHe was

γὰρ διδάσκων αὐτοὺς ὡς ἐξουσίαν ἔχων,
1for teaching them as authority having,

καὶ οὐχ ὡς οἱ γραμματεῖς. **23** Καὶ εὐθὺς
and not as the scribes. And immediately

ἦν ἐν τῇ συναγωγῇ αὐτῶν ἄνθρωπος
there was in the synagogue of them a man

ἐν πνεύματι ἀκαθάρτῳ, καὶ ἀνέκραξεν
in spirit an unclean, and he cried out

24 λέγων· τί ἡμῖν καὶ σοί, Ἰησοῦ
saying: What to us and to thee, Jesus

Ναζαρηνέ; ἦλθες ἀπολέσαι ἡμᾶς; οἶδά
Nazarene? camest thou to destroy us? I know

σε τίς εἶ, ὁ ἅγιος τοῦ θεοῦ. **25** καὶ
thee who thou art, the holy [one] - of God. And

ἐπετίμησεν αὐτῷ ὁ Ἰησοῦς [λέγων]·
rebuked him - Jesus saying:

The Calling of the First Disciples

14After John was put in prison, Jesus went into Galilee, proclaiming the good news of God. 15"The time has come," he said. "The kingdom of God is near. Repent and believe the good news!"

16As Jesus walked beside the Sea of Galilee, he saw Simon and his brother Andrew casting a net into the lake, for they were fishermen. 17"Come, follow me," Jesus said, "and I will make you fishers of men." 18At once they left their nets and followed him.

19When he had gone a little farther, he saw James son of Zebedee and his brother John in a boat, preparing their nets. 20Without delay he called them, and they left their father Zebedee in the boat with the hired men and followed him.

Jesus Drives Out an Evil Spirit

21They went to Capernaum, and when the Sabbath came, Jesus went into the synagogue and began to teach. 22The people were amazed at his teaching, because he taught them as one who had authority, not as the teachers of the law. 23Just then a man in their synagogue who was possessed by an evilᵉ spirit cried out, 24"What do you want with us, Jesus of Nazareth? Have you come to destroy us? I know who you are—the Holy One of God!"

25"Be quiet!" said Jesus

---

d Lit., *the Nazarene*

e23 Greek *unclean*; also in verses 26 and 27

saying, "Be quiet, and come out of him!"

26And throwing him into convulsions, the unclean spirit cried out with a loud voice, and came out of him.

27And they were all amazed, so that they debated among themselves, saying, "What is this? A new teaching with authority! He commands even the unclean spirits, and they obey Him."

28And immediately the news about Him went out everywhere into all the surrounding district of Galilee.

Multitudes Healed

29And immediately after they had come out of the synagogue, they came into the house of Simon and Andrew, with James and John.

30Now Simon's mother-in-law was lying sick with a fever; and immediately they *spoke to Him about her.

31And He came to her and raised her up, taking her by the hand, and the fever left her, and she ʳwaited on them.

32And when evening had come, after the sun had set, they *began bringing to Him all who were ill and those who were demon-possessed.

33And the whole city had gathered at the door.

34And He healed many who were ill with various diseases, and cast out many demons; and He was not permitting the demons to speak, because they ᶠknew who He was.

35And in the early morning, while it was still dark, He arose and went out and departed to a lonely place, and was praying there.

36And Simon and his companions hunted for Him;

37and they found Him, and *said to Him, "Everyone is looking for You."

38And He *said to them, "Let us go somewhere else

φιμώθητι καὶ ἔξελθε [ἐξ αὐτοῦ]. 26 καὶ
Be quiet and come out out of him. And

σπαράξαν αὐτὸν τὸ πνεῦμα τὸ ἀκάθαρτον
throwing him the spirit the unclean

καὶ φωνῆσαν φωνῇ μεγάλῃ ἐξῆλθεν ἐξ
and shouting voice with a great he came out out of

αὐτοῦ. 27 καὶ ἐθαμβήθησαν ἅπαντες, ὥστε
him. And were astounded all, so as
= so that

συζητεῖν αὐτοὺς λέγοντας· τί ἐστιν τοῦτο;
to debate themᵇ saying: What is this?
they debated

διδαχὴ καινὴ κατ’ ἐξουσίαν· καὶ τοῖς
teaching a new by authority; and the

πνεύμασι τοῖς ἀκαθάρτοις ἐπιτάσσει, καὶ
spirits - unclean he commands, and

ὑπακούουσιν αὐτῷ. 28 καὶ ἐξῆλθεν ἡ
they obey him. And went forth the

ἀκοὴ αὐτοῦ εὐθὺς πανταχοῦ εἰς ὅλην
report of him immediately everywhere into all

τὴν περίχωρον τῆς Γαλιλαίας. 29 Καὶ
the neighbourhood - of Galilee. And

εὐθὺς ἐκ τῆς συναγωγῆς ἐξελθόντες ἦλθον
immediately out of the synagogue going forth came

εἰς τὴν οἰκίαν Σίμωνος καὶ Ἀνδρέου
into the house of Simon and Andrew

μετὰ Ἰακώβου καὶ Ἰωάννου. 30 ἡ δὲ
with James and John. Now the

πενθερὰ Σίμωνος κατέκειτο πυρέσσουσα,
mother-in-law of Simon was laid [aside] fever-stricken,

καὶ εὐθὺς λέγουσιν αὐτῷ περὶ αὐτῆς.
and immediately they tell him about her.

31 καὶ προσελθὼν ἤγειρεν αὐτὴν κρατήσας
And approaching he raised her holding

τῆς χειρός· καὶ ἀφῆκεν αὐτὴν ὁ πυρετός,
the(her) hand; and left her the fever,

καὶ διηκόνει αὐτοῖς. 32 Ὀψίας δὲ γενο-
and she served them. And evening com-
= when evening

μένης, ὅτε ἔδυσεν ὁ ἥλιος, ἔφερον πρὸς
ing,ᵃ when set the sun, they brought to
came,

αὐτὸν πάντας τοὺς κακῶς ἔχοντας καὶ
him all the [ones] ill having and
= those who were ill

τοὺς δαιμονιζομένους· 33 καὶ ἦν ὅλη ἡ
the being demon-possessed; and was all the

πόλις ἐπισυνηγμένη πρὸς τὴν θύραν.
city having been assembled at the door.

34 καὶ ἐθεράπευσεν πολλοὺς κακῶς ἔχοντας
And he healed many ill having
= who were ill

ποικίλαις νόσοις, καὶ δαιμόνια πολλὰ
with various diseases, and demons many

ἐξέβαλεν, καὶ οὐκ ἤφιεν λαλεῖν τὰ δαιμόνια,
he expelled, and did not allow to speak the demons,

ὅτι ᾔδεισαν αὐτόν. 35 Καὶ πρωΐ ἔννυχα
because they knew him. And ᵃearly ᵇin the night

λίαν ἀναστὰς ἐξῆλθεν καὶ ἀπῆλθεν εἰς
ᵇvery ¹rising up he went out and went away to

ἔρημον τόπον, κἀκεῖ προσηύχετο. 36 καὶ
a desert place, and there prayed. And

κατεδίωξεν αὐτὸν Σίμων καὶ οἱ μετ’
hunted down him Simon and the [ones] with

αὐτοῦ, καὶ εὗρον αὐτὸν καὶ λέγουσιν
him, and found him and say

αὐτῷ 37 ὅτι πάντες ζητοῦσίν σε. 38 καὶ
to him[,] - All are seeking thee. And

λέγει αὐτοῖς· ἄγωμεν ἀλλαχοῦ εἰς τὰς
he says to them: Let us go elsewhere into the

---

sternly. "Come out of him!" 26The evil spirit shook the man violently and came out of him with a shriek.

27The people were all so amazed that they asked each other, "What is this? A new teaching—and with authority! He even gives orders to evil spirits and they obey him." 28News about him spread quickly over the whole region of Galilee.

Jesus Heals Many

29As soon as they left the synagogue, they went with James and John to the home of Simon and Andrew. 30Simon's mother-in-law was in bed with a fever, and they told Jesus about her. 31So he went to her, took her hand and helped her up. The fever left her and she began to wait on them.

32That evening after sunset the people brought to Jesus all the sick and demon-possessed. 33The whole town gathered at the door, 34and Jesus healed many who had various diseases. He also drove out many demons, but he would not let the demons speak because they knew who he was.

Jesus Prays in a Solitary Place

35Very early in the morning, while it was still dark, Jesus got up, left the house and went off to a solitary place, where he prayed. 36Simon and his companions went to look for him, 37and when they found him, they exclaimed: "Everyone is looking for you!"

38Jesus replied, "Let us go somewhere else—to the

ᵉOr, *served*
ᶠSome mss. read: *knew Him to be Christ*

to the towns nearby, in order that I may preach there also; for that is what I came out for."

39And He went into their synagogues throughout all Galilee, preaching and casting out the demons.

40And a leper *came to Him, beseeching Him and falling on his knees before Him, and saying to Him, "If You are willing, You can make me clean."

41And moved with compassion, He stretched out His hand, and touched him, and *said to him, "I am willing; be cleansed."

42And immediately the leprosy left him and he was cleansed.

43And He sternly warned him and immediately sent him away,

44and He *said to him, "See that you say nothing to anyone; but go, show yourself to the priest and offer for your cleansing what Moses commanded, for a testimony to them."

45But he went out and began to proclaim it freely and to spread the news about, to such an extent that Jesus could no longer publicly enter a city, but *stayed out in unpopulated areas; and they were coming to Him from everywhere.

ἐχομένας κωμοπόλεις,˙ ἵνα καὶ ἐκεῖ
neighbouring　towns,　　that　also　there

κηρύξω˙ εἰς τοῦτο γὰρ ἐξῆλθον. 39 καὶ
I may proclaim; for for this [purpose]　I came forth.　And

ἦλθεν κηρύσσων εἰς τὰς συναγωγὰς αὐτῶν
he came proclaiming　in　the　synagogues　of them

εἰς ὅλην τὴν Γαλιλαίαν καὶ τὰ δαιμόνια
in　all　–　Galilee　and the　demons

ἐκβάλλων.
expelling.

40 Καὶ ἔρχεται πρὸς αὐτὸν λεπρὸς
　And　comes　to　him　a leper

παρακαλῶν αὐτὸν καὶ γονυπετῶν λέγων
beseeching　him　and　falling on [his] knees saying

αὐτῷ ὅτι ἐὰν θέλῃς δύνασαί με καθαρίσαι.
to him[,]　– If thou art willing thou art able me　to cleanse.

41 καὶ σπλαγχνισθεὶς ἐκτείνας τὴν
　And being filled with tenderness stretching forth the(his)

χεῖρα αὐτοῦ ἥψατο καὶ λέγει αὐτῷ· θέλω,
hand　ᵇhim ¹he touched and　says　to him: I am willing,

καθαρίσθητι. 42 καὶ εὐθὺς ἀπῆλθεν ἀπ'
be thou cleansed.　　And immediately departed from

αὐτοῦ ἡ λέπρα, καὶ ἐκαθαρίσθη. 43 καὶ
him　the leprosy,　and　he was cleansed.　　And

ἐμβριμησάμενος αὐτῷ εὐθὺς ἐξέβαλεν αὐτόν,
sternly admonishing　him immediately he put out　him,

44 καὶ λέγει αὐτῷ· ὅρα μηδενὶ μηδὲν
　and　says　to him:　See　no one no(any)thing

εἴπῃς, ἀλλὰ ὕπαγε σεαυτὸν δεῖξον τῷ
thou tellest, but　go　thyself　show　to the

ἱερεῖ καὶ προσένεγκε περὶ τοῦ καθαρισμοῦ σου
priest and　offer　concerning the　cleansing　of thee

ἃ προσέταξεν Μωϋσῆς, εἰς μαρτύριον
[the things] which commanded Moses,　for　a testimony

αὐτοῖς. 45 ὁ δὲ ἐξελθὼν ἤρξατο κηρύσσειν
to them.　　But he going out　began　to proclaim

πολλὰ καὶ διαφημίζειν τὸν λόγον, ὥστε
many things and　to spread about　the　matter,　so as
　　　　　　　　　　　　　　　　　　=, so that

μηκέτι αὐτὸν δύνασθαι φανερῶς εἰς πόλιν
no longer　him　to be ableᵇ　openly　into　a city
he was no longer able

εἰσελθεῖν, ἀλλ' ἔξω ἐπ' ἐρήμοις τόποις
to enter,　but　outside on(in)　desert　places

ἦν· καὶ ἤρχοντο πρὸς αὐτὸν πάντοθεν.
he was; and　they came　to　him from all directions.

---

nearby villages—so I can preach there also. That is why I have come." 39So he traveled throughout Galilee, preaching in their synagogues and driving out demons.

A Man With Leprosy

40A man with leprosyᶠ came to him and begged him on his knees, "If you are willing, you can make me clean."

41Filled with compassion, Jesus reached out his hand and touched the man. "I am willing," he said. "Be clean!" 42Immediately the leprosy left him and he was cured.

43Jesus sent him away at once with a strong warning: 44"See that you don't tell this to anyone. But go, show yourself to the priest and offer the sacrifices that Moses commanded for your cleansing, as a testimony to them." 45Instead he went out and began to talk freely, spreading the news. As a result, Jesus could no longer enter a town openly but stayed outside in lonely places. Yet the people still came to him from everywhere.

Chapter 2

The Paralytic Healed

AND when He had come back to Capernaum several days afterward, it was heard that He was at home.

2And many were gathered together, so that there was no longer room, even near the door; and He was speaking the word to them.

3And they *came, bringing to Him a paralytic, carried by four men.

4And being unable to get to Him because of the crowd, they removed the roof above Him; and when they had dug an opening, they let down the pallet on

---

2 Καὶ εἰσελθὼν πάλιν εἰς Καφαρναοὺμ
　And　entering　again　into　Capernaum

δι' ἡμερῶν ἠκούσθη ὅτι ἐν οἴκῳ ἐστίν.
through days　it was heard that　at home　he is(was).
= after [some] days

2 καὶ συνήχθησαν πολλοί, ὥστε μηκέτι
　And　were assembled　many,　so as　no longer

χωρεῖν μηδὲ τὰ πρὸς τὴν θύραν, καὶ
to have room not　–　at　the　door,　and

ἐλάλει αὐτοῖς τὸν λόγον. 3 καὶ ἔρχονται
he spoke to them　the　word.　And　they come

φέροντες πρὸς αὐτὸν παραλυτικὸν αἰρόμενον
carrying　to　him　a paralytic　being borne

ὑπὸ τεσσάρων. 4 καὶ μὴ δυνάμενοι
by　four [men].　　And　not　being able

προσενέγκαι αὐτῷ διὰ τὸν ὄχλον
to bring　to him because of　the　crowd

ἀπεστέγασαν τὴν στέγην ὅπου ἦν, καὶ
they unroofed　the　roof　where he was, and

ἐξορύξαντες χαλῶσι τὸν κράβατον ὅπου ὁ
having opened up they lower the　mattress　where the

Chapter 2

Jesus Heals a Paralytic

A FEW days later, when Jesus again entered Capernaum, the people heard that he had come home. 2So many gathered that there was no room left, not even outside the door, and he preached the word to them. 3Some men came, bringing to him a paralytic, carried by four of them. 4Since they could not get him to Jesus because of the crowd, they made an opening in the roof above Jesus and, after digging through it, lowered the mat the par-

---

ᶠ40 The Greek word was used for various diseases affecting the skin—not necessarily leprosy.

which the paralytic was lying.

5And Jesus seeing their faith *said to the paralytic, "My hson, your sins are forgiven."

6But there were some of the scribes sitting there and reasoning in their hearts,

7"Why does this man speak that way? He is blaspheming; who can forgive sins but God alone?"

8And immediately Jesus, aware in His spirit that they were reasoning that way within themselves, *said to them, "Why are you reasoning about these things in your hearts?

9"Which is easier, to say to the paralytic, 'Your sins are forgiven'; or to say, 'Arise, and take up your pallet and walk'?

10"But in order that you may know that the Son of Man has authority on earth to forgive sins"—He *said to the paralytic—

11"I say to you, rise, take up your pallet and go home."

12And he rose and immediately took up the pallet and went out in the sight of all; so that they were all amazed and were glorifying God, saying, "We have never seen anything like this."

13And He went out again by the seashore; and all the multitude were coming to Him, and He was teaching them.

Levi (Matthew) Called

14And as He passed by, He saw Levi the *son* of Alphaeus sitting in the tax office, and He *said to him, "Follow Me!" And he rose and followed Him.

15And it came about that He was reclining *at the table* in his house, and many tax-gatherers and sinners

---

παραλυτικὸς κατέκειτο. 5 καὶ ἰδὼν ὁ
paralytic was lying. And seeing -

'Ιησοῦς τὴν πίστιν αὐτῶν λέγει τῷ
Jesus the faith of them he says to the

παραλυτικῷ· τέκνον, ἀφίενταί σου αἱ
paralytic: Child, are forgiven of thee the

ἁμαρτίαι. 6 ἦσαν δέ τινες τῶν γραμματέων
sins. Now there were some of the scribes

ἐκεῖ καθήμενοι καὶ διαλογιζόμενοι ἐν ταῖς
there sitting and reasoning in the

καρδίαις αὐτῶν· 7 τί οὗτος οὕτως λαλεῖ;
hearts of them: Why this [man] thus speaks?

βλασφημεῖ· τίς δύναται ἀφιέναι ἁμαρτίας
he blasphemes; who can to forgive sins

εἰ μὴ εἷς ὁ θεός; 8 καὶ εὐθὺς ἐπιγνοὺς
except one[,] - God? And immediately knowing

ὁ 'Ιησοῦς τῷ πνεύματι αὐτοῦ ὅτι οὕτως
- Jesus in the spirit of him that thus

διαλογίζονται ἐν ἑαυτοῖς, λέγει αὐτοῖς·
they reason among themselves, he says to them:

τί ταῦτα διαλογίζεσθε ἐν ταῖς καρδίαις
Why these things reason ye in the hearts

ὑμῶν; 9 τί ἐστιν εὐκοπώτερον, εἰπεῖν
of you? What is easier, to say

τῷ παραλυτικῷ· ἀφίενταί σου αἱ ἁμαρτίαι,
to the paralytic: are forgiven of thee the sins,

ἢ εἰπεῖν· ἔγειρε καὶ ἆρον τὸν κράβατόν
or to say: Rise and take the mattress

σου καὶ περιπάτει; 10 ἵνα δὲ εἰδῆτε
of thee and walk? But that ye may know

ὅτι ἐξουσίαν ἔχει ὁ υἱὸς τοῦ ἀνθρώπου
that authority has the Son - of man

ἀφιέναι ἁμαρτίας ἐπὶ τῆς γῆς,—λέγει τῷ
to forgive sins on the earth,—he says to the

παραλυτικῷ· 11 σοὶ λέγω, ἔγειρε ἆρον
paralytic: To thee I say, rise[,] take

τὸν κράβατόν σου καὶ ὕπαγε εἰς τὸν
the mattress of thee and go to the

οἶκόν σου. 12 καὶ ἠγέρθη καὶ εὐθὺς
house of thee. And he arose and immediately

ἄρας τὸν κράβατον ἐξῆλθεν ἔμπροσθεν
taking the mattress he went forth before

πάντων, ὥστε ἐξίστασθαι πάντας καὶ
all, so as to be astonished all and
= so that they were all astonished and glorified

δοξάζειν τὸν θεὸν λέγοντας ὅτι οὕτως
to glorifyb - God saying[,] - Thus

οὐδέποτε εἴδαμεν.
never we saw.

13 Καὶ ἐξῆλθεν πάλιν παρὰ τὴν θάλασσαν·
And he went forth again by the sea;

καὶ πᾶς ὁ ὄχλος ἤρχετο πρὸς αὐτόν,
and all the crowd came to him,

καὶ ἐδίδασκεν αὐτούς. 14 Καὶ παράγων
and he taught them. And passing along

εἶδεν Λευὶν τὸν τοῦ 'Αλφαίου καθήμενον
he saw Levi the [son] - Alphæus sitting

ἐπὶ τὸ τελώνιον, καὶ λέγει αὐτῷ· ἀκολούθει
on(in or at) the custom house, and says to him: Follow

μοι. καὶ ἀναστὰς ἠκολούθησεν αὐτῷ.
me. And rising up he followed him.

15 Καὶ γίνεται κατακεῖσθαι αὐτὸν ἐν τῇ
And it comes to pass to recline himb in the
= he reclines

οἰκίᾳ αὐτοῦ, καὶ πολλοὶ τελῶναι καὶ
house of him, and many tax-collectors and

---

alyzed man was lying on.

5When Jesus saw their faith, he said to the paralytic, "Son, your sins are forgiven."

6Now some teachers of the law were sitting there, thinking to themselves, 7"Why does this fellow talk like that? He's blaspheming! Who can forgive sins but God alone?"

8Immediately Jesus knew in his spirit that this was what they were thinking in their hearts, and he said to them, "Why are you thinking these things? 9Which is easier: to say to the paralytic, 'Your sins are forgiven,' or to say, 'Get up, take your mat and walk'? 10But that you may know that the Son of Man has authority on earth to forgive sins . . . ." He said to the paralytic, 11"I tell you, get up, take your mat and go home." 12He got up, took his mat and walked out in full view of them all. This amazed everyone and they praised God, saying, "We have never seen anything like this!"

The Calling of Levi

13Once again Jesus went out beside the lake. A large crowd came to him, and he began to teach them. 14As he walked along, he saw Levi son of Alphaeus sitting at the tax collector's booth. "Follow me," Jesus told him, and Levi got up and followed him.

15While Jesus was having dinner at Levi's house, many tax collectors and

---

gLit., *was*
hLit., *child*

were dining with Jesus and His disciples; for there were many of them, and they were following Him. 16And when the scribes of the Pharisees saw that He was eating with the sinners and tax-gatherers, they *began saying to His disciples, "Why is He eating and drinking with tax-gatherers and sinners?" 17And hearing this, Jesus *said to them, "*It is not those who are healthy who need a physician, but those who are sick; I did not come to call the righteous, but sinners." 18And John's disciples and the Pharisees were fasting; and they *came and *said to Him, "Why do John's disciples and the disciples of the Pharisees fast, but Your disciples do not fast?" 19And Jesus said to them, "While the bridegroom is with them, the attendants of the bridegroom do not fast, do they? So long as they have the bridegroom with them, they cannot fast. 20"But the days will come when the bridegroom is taken away from them, and then they will fast in that day. 21"No one sews a patch of unshrunk cloth on an old garment; otherwise the patch pulls away from it, the new from the old, and a worse tear results. 22"And no one puts new wine into old wineskins; otherwise the wine will burst the skins, and the wine is lost, and the skins as well; but one puts new wine into fresh wineskins."

Question of the Sabbath
23And it came about that

ἁμαρτωλοὶ συνανέκειντο τῷ Ἰησοῦ καὶ
sinners   reclined with   -   Jesus   and
τοῖς μαθηταῖς αὐτοῦ· ἦσαν γὰρ πολλοί,
the   disciples   of him; for there were   many,
καὶ ἠκολούθουν αὐτῷ. 16 καὶ οἱ γραμματεῖς
and   they followed   him.   And the   scribes
τῶν Φαρισαίων ἰδόντες ὅτι ἐσθίει
of the   Pharisees   seeing   that   he eats(ate)
μετὰ τῶν ἁμαρτωλῶν καὶ τελωνῶν ἔλεγον
with - sinners   and tax-collectors   said
τοῖς μαθηταῖς αὐτοῦ· ὅτι μετὰ τῶν
to the   disciples   of him: With   -
τελωνῶν καὶ ἁμαρτωλῶν ἐσθίει; 17 καὶ
tax-collectors   and   sinners   does he eat ?   And
ἀκούσας ὁ Ἰησοῦς λέγει αὐτοῖς [ὅτι] οὐ
hearing - Jesus   says   to them[,] - Not
χρείαν ἔχουσιν οἱ ἰσχύοντες ἰατροῦ ἀλλ᾽
need   have the [ones] being strong of a physician   but
οἱ κακῶς ἔχοντες· οὐκ ἦλθον καλέσαι
the [ones] ill   having;   I came not   to call
= those who are ill;
δικαίους ἀλλὰ ἁμαρτωλούς. 18 Καὶ ἦσαν
righteous men   but   sinners.   And ⁷were
οἱ μαθηταὶ Ἰωάννου καὶ οἱ Φαρισαῖοι
¹the ²disciples ³of John ⁴and ⁵the ⁶Pharisees
νηστεύοντες. καὶ ἔρχονται καὶ λέγουσιν
⁸fasting.   And   they come   and   say
αὐτῷ· διὰ τί οἱ μαθηταὶ Ἰωάννου καὶ
to him: Why   the   disciples   of John   and
οἱ μαθηταὶ τῶν Φαρισαίων νηστεύουσιν,
the   disciples   of the   Pharisees   fast,
οἱ δὲ σοὶ μαθηταὶ οὐ νηστεύουσιν; 19 καὶ
-   but   thy   disciples   do not fast ?   And
εἶπεν αὐτοῖς ὁ Ἰησοῦς· μὴ δύνανται οἱ
said   to them - Jesus: not   can   the
υἱοὶ τοῦ νυμφῶνος, ἐν ᾧ ὁ νυμφίος
sons   of the   bridechamber,   while   the   bridegroom
μετ᾽ αὐτῶν ἐστιν, νηστεύειν; ὅσον χρόνον
with   them   is,   to fast ?   what   time
ἔχουσιν τὸν νυμφίον μετ᾽ αὐτῶν, οὐ
they have   the   bridegroom   with   them,   not
δύνανται νηστεύειν. 20 ἐλεύσονται δὲ ἡμέραι
they can   to fast.   But will come   days
ὅταν ἀπαρθῇ ἀπ᾽ αὐτῶν ὁ νυμφίος, καὶ
when   taken away   from   them   the   bridegroom,   and
τότε νηστεύσουσιν ἐν ἐκείνῃ τῇ ἡμέρᾳ.
then   they will fast   in   that   -   day.
21 Οὐδεὶς ἐπίβλημα ῥάκους ἀγνάφου ἐπιράπτει
No one   a patch   cloth   of unfulled   sews
ἐπὶ ἱμάτιον παλαιόν· εἰ δὲ μή, αἴρει
on   garment   an old;   otherwise,   ²takes
τὸ πλήρωμα ἀπ᾽ αὐτοῦ τὸ καινὸν τοῦ
⁴the ⁵fulness ⁶from ⁹itself ¹the ²new ³the
παλαιοῦ, καὶ χεῖρον σχίσμα γίνεται. 22 καὶ
⁸old,   and a worse   rent   occurs.   And
οὐδεὶς βάλλει οἶνον νέον εἰς ἀσκοὺς παλαιούς·
no one   puts   wine   new   into wineskins   old;
εἰ δὲ μή, ῥήξει ὁ οἶνος τοὺς ἀσκούς,
otherwise,   ²will burst ¹the ²wine   the   wineskins,
καὶ ὁ οἶνος ἀπόλλυται καὶ οἱ ἀσκοί.
and   the   wine   perishes   and   the wineskins.
[ἀλλὰ οἶνον νέον εἰς ἀσκοὺς καινούς.]
But   wine   new   into   wineskins   fresh.
23 Καὶ ἐγένετο αὐτὸν ἐν τοῖς σάββασιν
And it came to pass   him   on   the   sabbaths
= as he passed on the sabbath

"sinners" were eating with him and his disciples, for there were many who followed him. 16When the teachers of the law who were Pharisees saw him eating with the "sinners" and tax collectors, they asked his disciples: "Why does he eat with tax collectors and 'sinners'?" 17On hearing this, Jesus said to them, "It is not the healthy who need a doctor, but the sick. I have not come to call the righteous, but sinners."

Jesus Questioned About Fasting
18Now John's disciples and the Pharisees were fasting. Some people came and asked Jesus, "How is it that John's disciples and the disciples of the Pharisees are fasting, but yours are not?" 19Jesus answered, "How can the guests of the bridegroom fast while he is with them? They cannot, so long as they have him with them. 20But the time will come when the bridegroom will be taken from them, and on that day they will fast. 21"No one sews a patch of unshrunk cloth on an old garment. If he does, the new piece will pull away from the old, making the tear worse. 22And no one pours new wine into old wineskins. If he does, the wine will burst the skins, and both the wine and the wineskins will be ruined. No, he pours new wine into new wineskins."

Lord of the Sabbath
23One Sabbath Jesus was going through the grain-

He was passing through the grainfields on the Sabbath, and His disciples began to make their way along while picking the heads *of grain*.
24And the Pharisees were saying to Him, "See here, why are they doing what is not lawful on the Sabbath?"
25And He *said to them, "Have you never read what David did when he was in need and became hungry, he and his companions:
26how he entered the house of God in the time of Abiathar *the* high priest, and ate the consecrated bread, which is not lawful for *anyone* to eat except the priests, and he gave *it* also to those who were with him?"
27And He was saying to them, "The Sabbath was made for man, and not man for the Sabbath.
28"Consequently, the Son of Man is Lord even of the Sabbath."

παραπορεύεσθαι διὰ τῶν σπορίμων, καὶ
to pass[b] through the cornfields, and
οἱ μαθηταὶ αὐτοῦ ἤρξαντο ὁδὸν ποιεῖν
the disciples of him began way to make
τίλλοντες τοὺς στάχυας. 24 καὶ οἱ Φαρισαῖοι
plucking the ears of corn. And the Pharisees
ἔλεγον αὐτῷ· ἴδε τί ποιοῦσιν τοῖς σάββασιν
said to him: Behold[,] why do on the sabbaths
ὃ οὐκ ἔξεστιν; 25 καὶ λέγει αὐτοῖς·
what is not lawful? And he says to them:
οὐδέποτε ἀνέγνωτε τί ἐποίησεν Δαυίδ,
never read ye what did David,
ὅτε χρείαν ἔσχεν καὶ ἐπείνασεν αὐτὸς
when need he had and hungered he
καὶ οἱ μετ' αὐτοῦ; 26 [πῶς] εἰσῆλθεν
and the [ones] with him? how he entered
εἰς τὸν οἶκον τοῦ θεοῦ ἐπὶ 'Αβιαθὰρ
into the house – of God on(in the days of) Abiathar
ἀρχιερέως καὶ τοὺς ἄρτους τῆς προθέσεως
high priest and the loaves of the setting forth
ἔφαγεν, οὓς οὐκ ἔξεστιν φαγεῖν εἰ μὴ
ate, which it is not lawful to eat except
τοὺς ἱερεῖς, καὶ ἔδωκεν καὶ τοῖς σὺν
the priests, and gave also to the [ones] with
αὐτῷ οὖσιν; 27 καὶ ἔλεγεν αὐτοῖς·
him being? And he said to them:
τὸ σάββατον διὰ τὸν ἄνθρωπον ἐγένετο,
The sabbath on account of – man was,
καὶ οὐχ ὁ ἄνθρωπος διὰ τὸ σάββατον·
and not – man on account of the sabbath;
28 ὥστε κύριός ἐστιν ὁ υἱὸς τοῦ ἀνθρώπου
so as Lord is the Son – of man
καὶ τοῦ σαββάτου.
also of the sabbath.

fields, and as his disciples walked along, they began to pick some heads of grain. 24The Pharisees said to him, "Look, why are they doing what is unlawful on the Sabbath?"
25He answered, "Have you never read what David did when he and his companions were hungry and in need? 26In the days of Abiathar the high priest, he entered the house of God and ate the consecrated bread, which is lawful only for priests to eat. And he also gave some to his companions."
27Then he said to them, "The Sabbath was made for man, not man for the Sabbath. 28So the Son of Man is Lord even of the Sabbath."

Chapter 3

Jesus Heals on the Sabbath

AND He entered again into a synagogue; and a man was there with a withered hand.
2And they were watching Him *to see* if He would heal him on the Sabbath, in order that they might accuse Him.
3And He *said to the man with the withered hand, "Rise and *come* forward!"
4And He *said to them, "Is it lawful on the Sabbath to do good or to do harm, to save a life or to kill?" But they kept silent.
5And after looking around at them with anger, grieved at their hardness of heart, He *said to the man, "Stretch out your hand." And He stretched it out, and his hand was restored.
6And the Pharisees went out and immediately *began

3 Καὶ εἰσῆλθεν πάλιν εἰς συναγωγήν.
And he entered again into a synagogue.
καὶ ἦν ἐκεῖ ἄνθρωπος ἐξηραμμένην ἔχων
And there was there a man [4]having been withered [1]having
τὴν χεῖρα· 2 καὶ παρετήρουν αὐτὸν εἰ
[3]the [2]hand; and they watched carefully him if
τοῖς σάββασιν θεραπεύσει αὐτόν, ἵνα
on the sabbaths he will heal him, that
κατηγορήσωσιν αὐτοῦ. 3 καὶ λέγει τῷ
they might accuse him. And he says to the
ἀνθρώπῳ τῷ τὴν χεῖρα ἔχοντι ξηράν·
man – the hand having dry:
ἔγειρε εἰς τὸ μέσον. 4 καὶ λέγει αὐτοῖς·
Rise into the midst. And he says to them:
ἔξεστιν τοῖς σάββασιν ἀγαθὸν ποιῆσαι
Lawful on the sabbaths good to do
ἢ κακοποιῆσαι, ψυχὴν σῶσαι ἢ ἀποκτεῖναι;
or to do evil, life to save or to kill?
οἱ δὲ ἐσιώπων. 5 καὶ περιβλεψάμενος
But they were silent. And looking round
αὐτοὺς μετ' ὀργῆς, συλλυπούμενος ἐπὶ
[on] them with anger, being greatly grieved on(at)
τῇ πωρώσει τῆς καρδίας αὐτῶν, λέγει
the hardness of the heart of them, he says
τῷ ἀνθρώπῳ· ἔκτεινον τὴν χεῖρα. καὶ
to the man: Stretch forth the hand. And
ἐξέτεινεν, καὶ ἀπεκατεστάθη ἡ χεὶρ αὐτοῦ.
he stretched forth, and was restored the hand of him.
6 καὶ ἐξελθόντες οἱ Φαρισαῖοι εὐθὺς μετὰ
And going forth the Pharisees immediately with

Chapter 3

ANOTHER time he went into the synagogue, and a man with a shriveled hand was there. 2Some of them were looking for a reason to accuse Jesus, so they watched him closely to see if he would heal him on the Sabbath. 3Jesus said to the man with the shriveled hand, "Stand up in front of everyone."
4Then Jesus asked them, "Which is lawful on the Sabbath: to do good or to do evil, to save life or to kill?" But they remained silent.
5He looked around at them in anger and, deeply distressed at their stubborn hearts, said to the man, "Stretch out your hand." He stretched it out, and his hand was completely restored. 6Then the Pharisees went out and began to plot

taking counsel with the Herodians against Him, *as to* how they might destroy Him.

7And Jesus withdrew to the sea with His disciples; and a great multitude from Galilee followed; and *also* from Judea,

8and from Jerusalem, and from Idumea, and beyond the Jordan, and the vicinity of Tyre and Sidon, a great multitude heard of all that He was doing and came to Him.

9And He told His disciples that a boat should stand ready for Him because of the multitude, in order that they might not crowd Him;

10for He had healed many, with the result that all those who had afflictions pressed about Him in order to touch Him.

11And whenever the unclean spirits beheld Him, they would fall down before Him and cry out, saying, "You are the Son of God!"

12And He earnestly warned them not to make Him known.

The Twelve Are Chosen

13And He *went up to the mountain and *summoned those whom He Himself wanted, and they came to Him.

14And He appointed twelve*i*, that they might be with Him, and that He might send them out to preach,

15and to have authority to cast out the demons.

16And He appointed the twelve: Simon (to whom He gave the name Peter),

17and James, the *son of* Zebedee, and John the brother of James (to them He gave the name Boanerges, which means, "Sons of Thunder");

18and Andrew, and Philip, and Bartholomew, and Matthew, and Thomas, and James the *son of* Alphaeus, and Thaddaeus,

i Some early mss. add: *whom He named apostles*

Middle column (interlinear)

τῶν Ἡρῳδιανῶν συμβούλιον ἐδίδουν κατ'
the Herodians counsel gave against

αὐτοῦ, ὅπως αὐτὸν ἀπολέσωσιν.
him, that him they might destroy.

7 Καὶ ὁ Ἰησοῦς μετὰ τῶν μαθητῶν
And - Jesus with the disciples

αὐτοῦ ἀνεχώρησεν πρὸς τὴν θάλασσαν·
of him departed to the sea;

καὶ πολὺ πλῆθος ἀπὸ τῆς Γαλιλαίας
and a much(great) multitude from - Galilee

ἠκολούθησεν· καὶ ἀπὸ τῆς Ἰουδαίας **8** καὶ
followed; and from - Judæa and

ἀπὸ Ἱεροσολύμων καὶ ἀπὸ τῆς Ἰδουμαίας
from Jerusalem and from - Idumæa

καὶ πέραν τοῦ Ἰορδάνου καὶ περὶ Τύρον
and beyond the Jordan and round Tyre

καὶ Σιδῶνα, πλῆθος πολύ, ἀκούοντες ὅσα
and Sidon, multitude a much(great), hearing what things

ποιεῖ, ἦλθον πρὸς αὐτόν. **9** καὶ εἶπεν
he does, came to him. And he told

τοῖς μαθηταῖς αὐτοῦ ἵνα πλοιάριον προσκαρτέρῃ
the disciples of him that a boat should remain near

αὐτῷ διὰ τὸν ὄχλον, ἵνα μὴ θλίβωσιν
him because of the crowd, lest they should press upon

αὐτόν· **10** πολλοὺς γὰρ ἐθεράπευσεν, ὥστε
him; for many he healed, so as

ἐπιπίπτειν αὐτῷ ἵνα αὐτοῦ ἅψωνται
to fall upon him that him they might touch

ὅσοι εἶχον μάστιγας. **11** καὶ τὰ πνεύματα
as many as had plagues. And the spirits

τὰ ἀκάθαρτα, ὅταν αὐτὸν ἐθεώρουν, προσέπιπτον
- unclean, when him they saw, fell before

αὐτῷ καὶ ἔκραζον λέγοντα ὅτι σὺ εἶ ὁ
him and cried out saying[,] - Thou art the

υἱὸς τοῦ θεοῦ. **12** καὶ πολλὰ ἐπετίμα
Son - of God. And much he warned

αὐτοῖς ἵνα μὴ αὐτὸν φανερὸν ποιήσωσιν,
them that not him manifest they should make.

13 Καὶ ἀναβαίνει εἰς τὸ ὄρος, καὶ
And he goes up into the mountain, and

προσκαλεῖται οὓς ἤθελεν αὐτός, καὶ
calls to [him] [those] whom wished he, and

ἀπῆλθον πρὸς αὐτόν. **14** καὶ ἐποίησεν δώδεκα
they went to him. And he made twelve

ἵνα ὦσιν μετ' αὐτοῦ, καὶ ἵνα ἀποστέλλῃ
that they might be with him, and that he might send

αὐτοὺς κηρύσσειν **15** καὶ ἔχειν ἐξουσίαν
them to proclaim and to have authority

ἐκβάλλειν τὰ δαιμόνια· **16** καὶ ἐποίησεν
to expel the demons; and he made

τοὺς δώδεκα, καὶ ἐπέθηκεν ὄνομα τῷ
the twelve, and he added a name -

Σίμωνι Πέτρον· **17** καὶ Ἰάκωβον τὸν
to Simon[,] Peter; and James the [son] -

Ζεβεδαίου καὶ Ἰωάννην τὸν ἀδελφὸν τοῦ
of Zebedee and John the brother -

Ἰακώβου, καὶ ἐπέθηκεν αὐτοῖς ὄνομα
of James, and he added to them a name[,]

Βοανηργές, ὅ ἐστιν υἱοὶ βροντῆς· **18** καὶ
Boanerges, which is sons of thunder; and

Ἀνδρέαν καὶ Φίλιππον καὶ Βαρθολομαῖον
Andrew and Philip and Bartholomew

καὶ Ματθαῖον καὶ Θωμᾶν καὶ Ἰάκωβον
and Matthew and Thomas and James

τὸν τοῦ Ἁλφαίου καὶ Θαδδαῖον καὶ
the [son] - of Alphæus and Thaddæus and

with the Herodians how they might kill Jesus.

Crowds Follow Jesus

7Jesus withdrew with his disciples to the lake, and a large crowd from Galilee followed. 8When they heard all he was doing, many people came to him from Judea, Jerusalem, Idumea, and the regions across the Jordan and around Tyre and Sidon. 9Because of the crowd he told his disciples to have a small boat ready for him, to keep the people from crowding him. 10For he had healed many, so that those with diseases were pushing forward to touch him. 11Whenever the evilg spirits saw him, they fell down before him and cried out, "You are the Son of God." 12But he gave them strict orders not to tell who he was.

The Appointing of the Twelve Apostles

13Jesus went up on a mountainside and called to him those he wanted, and they came to him. 14He appointed twelve—designating them apostles*h*—that they might be with him and that he might send them out to preach 15and to have authority to drive out demons. 16These are the twelve he appointed: Simon (to whom he gave the name Peter); 17James son of Zebedee and his brother John (to them he gave the name Boanerges, which means Sons of Thunder); 18Andrew, Philip, Bartholomew, Matthew, Thomas, James son of Alphaeus, Thaddaeus, Simon the

g11 Greek *unclean*; also in verse 30
h14 Some manuscripts do not have *designating them apostles.*

and Simon the Zealot;
19and Judas Iscariot, who also betrayed Him.
20And He *came ʲ home, and the multitude *gathered again, to such an extent that they could not even eat a meal.
21And when His own ᵏpeople heard *of this*, they went out to take custody of Him; for they were saying, "He has lost His senses."
22And the scribes who came down from Jerusalem were saying, "He is possessed by Beelzebul," and "He casts out the demons by the ruler of the demons."
23And He called them to Himself and began speaking to them in parables, "How can Satan cast out Satan?
24"And if a kingdom is divided against itself, that kingdom cannot stand.
25"And if a house is divided against itself, that house will not be able to stand.
26"And if Satan has risen up against himself and is divided, he cannot stand, but he is finished!
27"But no one can enter the strong man's house and plunder his property unless he first binds the strong man, and then he will plunder his house.
28"Truly I say to you, all sins shall be forgiven the sons of men, and whatever blasphemies they utter;
29but whoever blasphemes against the Holy Spirit never has forgiveness, but is guilty of an eternal sin"—
30because they were saying, "He has an unclean spirit."
31And His mother and His brothers *arrived, and, standing outside they sent *word* to Him, and called Him.

Σίμωνα τὸν Καναναῖον 19 καὶ Ἰούδαν
Simon the Cananæan and Judas
Ἰσκαριώθ, ὃς καὶ παρέδωκεν αὐτόν.
Iscariot, who indeed betrayed him.
20 Καὶ ἔρχεται εἰς οἶκον· καὶ συνέρχεται
And he comes into a house; and comes together
πάλιν [ὁ] ὄχλος, ὥστε μὴ δύνασθαι
again the crowd, so as not to be able
= so that they were not able
αὐτοὺς μηδὲ ἄρτον φαγεῖν. 21 καὶ ἀκούσαντες
themᵇ not bread to eat. And hearing
οἱ παρ' αὐτοῦ ἐξῆλθον κρατῆσαι αὐτόν·
the[ones] with him went forth to seize him;
= his relations
ἔλεγον γὰρ ὅτι ἐξέστη. 22 καὶ οἱ
for they said[,] – He is beside himself. And the
γραμματεῖς οἱ ἀπὸ Ἱεροσολύμων καταβάντες
scribes from Jerusalem coming down
ἔλεγον ὅτι Βεελζεβοὺλ ἔχει, καὶ ὅτι ἐν
said[,] – Beelzebub he has, and[,] – By
τῷ ἄρχοντι τῶν δαιμονίων ἐκβάλλει τὰ
the ruler of the demons he expels the
δαιμόνια. 23 καὶ προσκαλεσάμενος αὐτοὺς
demons. And calling to [him] them
ἐν παραβολαῖς ἔλεγεν αὐτοῖς· πῶς δύναται
in parables he said to them: How can
σατανᾶς σατανᾶν ἐκβάλλειν; 24 καὶ ἐὰν
Satan ¹Satan ¹to expel? and if
βασιλεία ἐφ' ἑαυτὴν μερισθῇ, οὐ δύναται
a kingdom against itself be divided, cannot
σταθῆναι ἡ βασιλεία ἐκείνη· 25 καὶ ἐὰν
stand – kingdom that; and if
οἰκία ἐφ' ἑαυτὴν μερισθῇ, οὐ δυνήσεται
a house against itself be divided, will not be able
ἡ οἰκία ἐκείνη στῆναι. 26 καὶ εἰ ὁ
– house that to stand. And if –
σατανᾶς ἀνέστη ἐφ' ἑαυτὸν καὶ ἐμερίσθη,
Satan stood up against himself and was divided,
οὐ δύναται στῆναι ἀλλὰ τέλος ἔχει.
he cannot to stand but an end has.
27 ἀλλ' οὐ δύναται οὐδεὶς εἰς τὴν οἰκίαν
But cannot no(any)one into the house
τοῦ ἰσχυροῦ εἰσελθὼν τὰ σκεύη αὐτοῦ
of the strong man entering the goods of him
διαρπάσαι, ἐὰν μὴ πρῶτον τὸν ἰσχυρὸν
to plunder, unless first the strong man
δήσῃ, καὶ τότε τὴν οἰκίαν αὐτοῦ διαρπάσει.
he bind, and then the house of him he will plunder.
28 Ἀμὴν λέγω ὑμῖν ὅτι πάντα ἀφεθήσεται
Truly I say you that all will be forgiven
τοῖς υἱοῖς τῶν ἀνθρώπων τὰ ἁμαρτήματα
to the sons – of men the sins
καὶ αἱ βλασφημίαι, ὅσα ἐὰν βλασφημήσωσιν·
and the blasphemies, whatever they may blaspheme;
29 ὃς δ' ἂν βλασφημήσῃ εἰς τὸ πνεῦμα
but whoever blasphemes against the Spirit
τὸ ἅγιον, οὐκ ἔχει ἄφεσιν εἰς τὸν αἰῶνα,
– Holy, has not forgiveness unto the age,
ἀλλὰ ἔνοχός ἐστιν αἰωνίου ἁμαρτήματος.
but liable is of an eternal sin.
30 ὅτι ἔλεγον· πνεῦμα ἀκάθαρτον ἔχει.
Because they said: spirit an unclean he has.
31 Καὶ ἔρχονται ἡ μήτηρ αὐτοῦ καὶ οἱ
And come the mother of him and the
ἀδελφοὶ αὐτοῦ, καὶ ἔξω στήκοντες ἀπέστειλαν
brothers of him, and outside standing sent
πρὸς αὐτὸν καλοῦντες αὐτόν. 32 καὶ
to him calling him. And

Zealot 19and Judas Iscariot, who betrayed him.

Jesus and Beelzebub
20Then Jesus entered a house, and again a crowd gathered, so that he and his disciples were not even able to eat. 21When his family heard about this, they went to take charge of him, for they said, "He is out of his mind."
22And the teachers of the law who came down from Jerusalem said, "He is possessed by Beelzebub!ˡ By the prince of demons he is driving out demons."
23So Jesus called them and spoke to them in parables: "How can Satan drive out Satan? 24If a kingdom is divided against itself, that kingdom cannot stand. 25If a house is divided against itself, that house cannot stand. 26And if Satan opposes himself and is divided, he cannot stand; his end has come. 27In fact, no one can enter a strong man's house and carry off his possessions unless he first ties up the strong man. Then he can rob his house. 28I tell you the truth, all the sins and blasphemies of men will be forgiven them. 29But whoever blasphemes against the Holy Spirit will never be forgiven; he is guilty of an eternal sin."
30He said this because they were saying, "He has an evil spirit."

Jesus' Mother and Brothers
31Then Jesus' mother and brothers arrived. Standing outside, they sent someone in to call him. 32A crowd

ʲ Lit., *into a house*
ᵏ Or, *kinsmen*
ˡ22 Greek *Beezeboul* or *Beelzeboul*

32And a multitude was sitting around Him, and they *said to Him, "Behold, Your mother and Your brothers[i] are outside looking for You."
33And answering them, He *said, "Who are My mother and My brothers?"
34And looking about on those who were sitting around Him, He *said, "Behold, My mother and My brothers!
35"For whoever does the will of God, he is My brother and sister and mother."

ἐκάθητο περὶ αὐτὸν ὄχλος, καὶ λέγουσιν
sat   round   him   a crowd,   and   they say
αὐτῷ· ἰδοὺ ἡ μήτηρ σου καὶ οἱ ἀδελφοί
to him: Behold[,] the mother of thee and the   brothers
σου καὶ αἱ ἀδελφαί σου ἔξω ζητοῦσίν σε.
of thee and the   sisters   of thee outside seek   thee.
33 καὶ ἀποκριθεὶς αὐτοῖς λέγει· τίς ἐστιν
    And answering   them he says: Who is
ἡ μήτηρ μου καὶ οἱ ἀδελφοί; 34·καὶ
the mother of me and the brothers?   And
περιβλεψάμενος τοὺς περὶ αὐτὸν κύκλῳ
looking round [at] the [ones] round him in a circle
καθημένους λέγει· ἴδε ἡ μήτηρ μου
sitting   he says: Behold[,] the mother of me
καὶ οἱ ἀδελφοί μου. 35 ὃς ἂν ποιήσῃ τὸ
and the brothers of me. Whoever does the
θέλημα τοῦ θεοῦ, οὗτος ἀδελφός μου
will   -   of God, this one brother of me
καὶ ἀδελφὴ καὶ μήτηρ ἐστίν.
and sister and mother is.

Chapter 4

Parable of the Sower and Soils

AND He began to teach again by the sea. And such a very great multitude gathered to Him that He got into a boat in the sea and sat down; and the whole multitude was by the sea on the land.
2And He was teaching them many things in parables, and was saying to them in His teaching,
3"Listen *to this!* Behold, the sower went out to sow;
4and it came about that as he was sowing, some *seed* fell beside the road, and the birds came and ate it up.
5"And other *seed* fell on the rocky *ground* where it did not have much soil; and immediately it sprang up because it had no depth of soil.
6"And after the sun had risen, it was scorched; and because it had no root, it withered away.
7"And other *seed* fell among the thorns, and the thorns came up and choked it, and it yielded no crop.
8"And other *seeds* fell into the good soil and as

4 Καὶ πάλιν ἤρξατο διδάσκειν παρὰ τὴν
   And again he began   to teach   by   the
θάλασσαν· καὶ συνάγεται πρὸς αὐτὸν ὄχλος
sea;   and is assembled to   him   crowd
πλεῖστος, ὥστε αὐτὸν εἰς πλοῖον ἐμβάντα
a very large, so as him   in   a ship   embarking
                  = so that embarking in a ship he sat
καθῆσθαι ἐν τῇ θαλάσσῃ, καὶ πᾶς ὁ
to sit[b]   in the   sea,   and all the
ὄχλος πρὸς τὴν θάλασσαν ἐπὶ τῆς γῆς
crowd toward the   sea   on the land
ἦσαν. 2 καὶ ἐδίδασκεν αὐτοὺς ἐν παραβολαῖς
were.   And he taught   them   in   parables
πολλά, καὶ ἔλεγεν αὐτοῖς ἐν τῇ διδαχῇ
many things, and said to them in the teaching
αὐτοῦ· 3 ἀκούετε. ἰδοὺ ἐξῆλθεν ὁ σπείρων
of him: Hear ye. Behold[,] went out the [one] sowing
σπεῖραι. 4 καὶ ἐγένετο ἐν τῷ σπείρειν
to sow.   And it came to pass in the   to sow[e]
                              = as he sowed
ὃ μὲν ἔπεσεν παρὰ τὴν ὁδόν, καὶ ἦλθεν
some   fell   by   the   way,   and came
τὰ πετεινὰ καὶ κατέφαγεν αὐτό. 5 καὶ
the birds   and devoured   it.   And
ἄλλο ἔπεσεν ἐπὶ τὸ πετρῶδες ὅπου οὐκ
other fell   on the rocky place where not
εἶχεν γῆν πολλήν, καὶ εὐθὺς ἐξανέτειλεν
it had earth much,   and immediately it sprang up
διὰ τὸ μὴ ἔχειν βάθος γῆς·
on account of the not to have depth of earth;
= because it had no depth of earth;
6 καὶ ὅτε ἀνέτειλεν ὁ ἥλιος ἐκαυματίσθη, καὶ
  and when rose   the sun it was scorched, and
διὰ τὸ μὴ ἔχειν ῥίζαν ἐξηράνθη. 7 καὶ
on account of the not to have root it was withered. And
= because it had no root
ἄλλο ἔπεσεν εἰς τὰς ἀκάνθας, καὶ ἀνέβησαν
other fell among the thorns, and came up
αἱ ἄκανθαι καὶ συνέπνιξαν αὐτό, καὶ
the thorns   and   choked   it,   and
καρπὸν οὐκ ἔδωκεν. 8 καὶ ἄλλα ἔπεσεν
fruit   it gave not.   And others   fell
εἰς τὴν γῆν τὴν καλὴν καὶ ἐδίδου καρπὸν
into the earth -   good   and gave   fruit

was sitting around him, and they told him, "Your mother and brothers are outside looking for you."
33"Who are my mother and my brothers?" he asked.
34Then he looked at those seated in a circle around him and said, "Here are my mother and my brothers!
35Whoever does God's will is my brother and sister and mother."

Chapter 4

The Parable of the Sower

AGAIN Jesus began to teach by the lake. The crowd that gathered around him was so large that he got into a boat and sat in it out on the lake, while all the people were along the shore at the water's edge.
2He taught them many things by parables, and in his teaching said: 3"Listen! A farmer went out to sow his seed. 4As he was scattering the seed, some fell along the path, and the birds came and ate it up. 5Some fell on rocky places, where it did not have much soil. It sprang up quickly, because the soil was shallow. 6But when the sun came up, the plants were scorched, and they withered because they had no root. 7Other seed fell among the thorns, which grew up and choked the plants, so that they did not bear grain. 8Still other seed fell on good soil. It came up,

---

[i] Later mss. add: *and Your sisters*

they grew up and increased, they yielded a crop and produced thirty, sixty, and a hundredfold.''

9And He was saying, ''He who has ears to hear, let him hear.''

10And as soon as He was alone, His followers, along with the twelve, *began* asking Him *about* the parables.

11And He was saying to them, ''To you has been given the mystery of the kingdom of God; but those who are outside get everything in parables,

12in order that WHILE SEEING, THEY MAY SEE AND NOT PERCEIVE; AND WHILE HEARING, THEY MAY HEAR AND NOT UNDERSTAND LEST THEY RETURN AND BE FORGIVEN.''

Explanation

13And He *said to them, ''Do you not understand this parable? And how will you understand all the parables?

14''The sower sows the word.

15''And these are the ones who are beside the road where the word is sown; and when they hear, immediately Satan comes and takes away the word which has been sown in them.

16''And in a similar way these are the ones on whom seed was sown on the rocky *places*, who, when they hear the word, immediately receive it with joy;

17and they have no *firm* root in themselves, but are *only* temporary; then, when affliction or persecution arises because of the word, immediately they fall away.

18''And others are the ones on whom seed was sown among the thorns; these are the ones who have heard the word,

19and the worries of the ^mworld, and the deceitfulness of riches, and the desires for other things enter in and choke the word, and it becomes unfruitful.

20''And those are the

^m Or, *age*

ἀναβαίνοντα καὶ αὐξανόμενα καὶ ἔφερεν
coming up and growing and bore
εἰς τριάκοντα καὶ ἐν ἑξήκοντα καὶ ἐν
in thirty and in sixty and in
ἑκατόν. **9** καὶ ἔλεγεν· ὃς ἔχει ὦτα
a hundred. And he said: Who has ears
ἀκούειν ἀκουέτω. **10** Καὶ ὅτε ἐγένετο
to hear let him hear. And when he was
κατὰ μόνας, ἠρώτων αὐτὸν οἱ περὶ
alone,† asked him the [ones] round
αὐτὸν σὺν τοῖς δώδεκα τὰς παραβολάς.
him with the twelve the parables.
11 καὶ ἔλεγεν αὐτοῖς· ὑμῖν τὸ μυστήριον
And he said to them: To you the mystery
δέδοται τῆς βασιλείας τοῦ θεοῦ· ἐκείνοις δὲ
has been given of the kingdom – of God; but to those
τοῖς ἔξω ἐν παραβολαῖς τὰ πάντα
the [ones] outside in parables – all things
γίνεται, **12** ἵνα βλέποντες βλέπωσιν καὶ
is (are), that seeing they may see and
μὴ ἴδωσιν, καὶ ἀκούοντες ἀκούωσιν καὶ
not perceive, and hearing they may hear and
μὴ συνιῶσιν, μήποτε ἐπιστρέψωσιν καὶ
not understand, lest they should turn and
ἀφεθῇ αὐτοῖς. **13** καὶ λέγει αὐτοῖς·
it should be forgiven them. And he says to them:
οὐκ οἴδατε τὴν παραβολὴν ταύτην, καὶ πῶς
Know ye not – parable this, and how
πάσας τὰς παραβολὰς γνώσεσθε; **14** ὁ
all the parables will ye know? The [one]
σπείρων τὸν λόγον σπείρει. **15** οὗτοι δέ εἰσιν
sowing ²the ³word ¹sows. And these are
οἱ παρὰ τὴν ὁδόν, ὅπου σπείρεται ὁ
the [ones] by the way, where is sown the
λόγος, καὶ ὅταν ἀκούσωσιν, εὐθὺς ἔρχεται
word, and when they hear, immediately comes
ὁ σατανᾶς καὶ αἴρει τὸν λόγον τὸν
– Satan and takes the word –
ἐσπαρμένον εἰς αὐτούς. **16** καὶ οὗτοί εἰσιν
having been sown in them. And these are
ὁμοίως οἱ ἐπὶ τὰ πετρώδη σπειρόμενοι,
likewise the [ones] on the rocky places being sown,
οἳ ὅταν ἀκούσωσιν τὸν λόγον εὐθὺς
who when they hear the word immediately
μετὰ χαρᾶς λαμβάνουσιν αὐτόν, **17** καὶ
with joy receive it, and
οὐκ ἔχουσιν ῥίζαν ἐν ἑαυτοῖς ἀλλὰ
have not root in themselves but
πρόσκαιροί εἰσιν, εἶτα γενομένης θλίψεως
shortlived are, then happening affliction
= when affliction or persecution happens
ἢ διωγμοῦ διὰ τὸν λόγον εὐθὺς
or persecution^a on account of the word immediately
σκανδαλίζονται. **18** καὶ ἄλλοι εἰσὶν οἱ εἰς
they are offended. And others are the [ones] among
τὰς ἀκάνθας σπειρόμενοι· οὗτοί εἰσιν οἱ
the thorns being sown; these are the [ones]
τὸν λόγον ἀκούσαντες, **19** καὶ αἱ μέριμναι
the word hearing, and the cares
τοῦ αἰῶνος καὶ ἡ ἀπάτη τοῦ πλούτου
of the age and the deceitfulness – of riches
καὶ αἱ περὶ τὰ λοιπὰ ἐπιθυμίαι
and ¹the ³about ⁴the ⁵other things ²desires
εἰσπορευόμεναι συμπνίγουσιν τὸν λόγον, καὶ
coming in choke the word, and
ἄκαρπος γίνεται. **20** καὶ ἐκεῖνοί εἰσιν
unfruitful it becomes. And those are

---

grew and produced a crop, multiplying thirty, sixty, or even a hundred times.''

9Then Jesus said, ''He who has ears to hear, let him hear.''

10When he was alone, the Twelve and the others around him asked him about the parables. 11He told them, ''The secret of the kingdom of God has been given to you. But to those on the outside everything is said in parables 12so that,

'' 'they may be ever
  seeing but never
  perceiving,
and ever hearing but
  never
  understanding;
otherwise they might
  turn and be
  forgiven!' '^l''

13Then Jesus said to them, ''Don't you understand this parable? How then will you understand any parable? 14The farmer sows the word. 15Some people are like seed along the path, where the word is sown. As soon as they hear it, Satan comes and takes away the word that was sown in them. 16Others, like seed sown on rocky places, hear the word and at once receive it with joy. 17But since they have no root, they last only a short time. When trouble or persecution comes because of the word, they quickly fall away. 18Still others, like seed sown among thorns, hear the word; 19but the worries of this life, the deceitfulness of wealth and the desires for other things come in and choke the word, making it unfruitful. 20Others, like seed sown on

^l12 Isaiah 6:9,10

ones on whom seed was sown on the good soil; and they hear the word and accept it, and bear fruit, thirty, sixty, and a hundredfold.''

21And He was saying to them, ''A lamp is not brought to be put under a peck-measure, is it, or under a bed? Is it not *brought* to be put on the lampstand? 22''For nothing is hidden, except to be revealed; nor has *anything* been secret, but that it should come to light.

23''If any man has ears to hear, let him hear.''

24And He was saying to them, ''Take care what you listen to. By your standard of measure it shall be measured to you; and more shall be given you besides. 25''For whoever has, to him shall *more* be given; and whoever does not have, even what he has shall be taken away from him.''

Parable of the Seed

26And He was saying, ''The kingdom of God is like a man who casts seed upon the soil; 27and goes to bed at night and gets up by day, and the seed sprouts up and grows—how, he himself does not know. 28''The soil produces crops by itself; first the blade, then the head, then the mature grain in the head. 29''But when the crop permits, he immediately puts in the sickle, because the harvest has come.''

Parable of the Mustard Seed

30And He said, ''How shall we ⁿpicture the kingdom of God, or by what parable shall we present it? 31''*It is* like a mustard seed, which, when sown upon the soil, though it is smaller than all the seeds that are upon the soil, 32yet when it is sown, grows up and becomes larger than all the garden plants and forms large

ⁿ Lit., *compare*

οἱ　ἐπὶ　τὴν　γῆν　τὴν　καλὴν　σπαρέντες,
the [ones] on　the　earth　-　good　sown,

οἵτινες　ἀκούουσιν　τὸν　λόγον　καὶ　παραδέχονται
who　hear　the　word　and　welcome [it]

καὶ　καρποφοροῦσιν　ἐν　τριάκοντα　καὶ　ἐν
and　bear fruit　in　thirty　and　in

ἑξήκοντα　καὶ　ἐν　ἑκατόν.　21 Καὶ　ἔλεγεν
sixty　and　in　a hundred.　And　he said

αὐτοῖς　ὅτι　μήτι　ἔρχεται　ὁ　λύχνος　ἵνα
to them[,]　-　not　Comes　the　lamp　that

ὑπὸ　τὸν　μόδιον　τεθῇ　ἢ　ὑπὸ　τὴν
under　the　bushel　it may be placed　or　under　the

κλίνην;　οὐχ　ἵνα　ἐπὶ　τὴν　λυχνίαν
couch ?　not　that　on　the　lampstand

τεθῇ;　22 οὐ　γάρ　ἐστίν　τι　κρυπτόν,
it may be placed ?　For there is not　anything　hidden,

ἐὰν　μὴ　ἵνα　φανερωθῇ·　οὐδὲ　ἐγένετο
except　that it may be manifested;　nor　became

ἀπόκρυφον,　ἀλλ'　ἵνα　ἔλθῃ　εἰς　φανερόν.
covered,　but　that it may come into [the] open.

23 εἴ　τις　ἔχει　ὦτα　ἀκούειν　ἀκουέτω.
If　anyone　has　ears　to hear　let him hear.

24 Καὶ　ἔλεγεν　αὐτοῖς·　βλέπετε　τί
And　he said　to them:　Take heed　what

ἀκούετε.　ἐν　ᾧ　μέτρῳ　μετρεῖτε
ye hear.　With　what　measure　ye measure

μετρηθήσεται　ὑμῖν,　καὶ　προστεθήσεται　ὑμῖν.
it will be measured　to you,　and　it will be added　to you.

25 ὃς　γὰρ　ἔχει,　δοθήσεται　αὐτῷ·　καὶ　ὃς
For [he] who　has,　it will be given　to him;　and　who

οὐκ　ἔχει,　καὶ　ὃ　ἔχει　ἀρθήσεται　ἀπ'
has not,　even　what he has　will be taken　from

αὐτοῦ.　26 Καὶ　ἔλεγεν·　οὕτως　ἐστὶν　ἡ
him.　And　he said:　Thus　is　the

βασιλεία　τοῦ　θεοῦ,　ὡς　ἄνθρωπος　βάλῃ
kingdom　-　of God,　as　a man　might cast

τὸν　σπόρον　ἐπὶ　τῆς　γῆς,　27 καὶ　καθεύδῃ
the　seed　on　the　earth,　and　might sleep

καὶ　ἐγείρηται　νύκτα　καὶ　ἡμέραν,　καὶ　ὁ
and　rise　night　and　day,　and　the

σπόρος　βλαστᾷ　καὶ　μηκύνηται　ὡς　οὐκ
seed　sprouts　and　lengthens　as　not

οἶδεν　αὐτός.　28 αὐτομάτη　ἡ　γῆ　καρποφορεῖ,
knows　he.　Of its own accord　the earth　bears fruit,

πρῶτον　χόρτον,　εἶτεν　στάχυν,　εἶτεν　πλήρης
first　grass,　then　an ear,　then　full

σῖτος　ἐν　τῷ　στάχυϊ.　29 ὅταν　δὲ　παραδοῖ
corn　in　the　ear.　But when　permits

ὁ　καρπός,　εὐθὺς　ἀποστέλλει　τὸ　δρέπανον,
the　fruit,　immediately　he sends(puts) forth　the　sickle,

ὅτι　παρέστηκεν　ὁ　θερισμός.　30 Καὶ　ἔλεγεν·
because　has come　the　harvest.　And　he said:

πῶς　ὁμοιώσωμεν　τὴν　βασιλείαν　τοῦ　θεοῦ,
How　may we liken　the　kingdom　-　of God,

ἢ　ἐν　τίνι　αὐτὴν　παραβολῇ　θῶμεν;　31 ὡς
or by　¹what　⁴it　²parable　³may we place ?　As

κόκκῳ　σινάπεως,　ὃς　ὅταν　σπαρῇ　ἐπὶ　τῆς
a grain　of mustard,　which　when　it is sown　on　the

γῆς,　μικρότερον　ὂν　πάντων　τῶν　σπερμάτων
earth,　smaller　being [than]　all　the　seeds

τῶν　ἐπὶ　τῆς　γῆς,　32 καὶ　ὅταν　σπαρῇ,
-　on　the　earth,　and　when　it is sown,

ἀναβαίνει　καὶ　γίνεται　μεῖζον　πάντων　τῶν
comes up　and　becomes　greater [than]　all　the

λαχάνων,　καὶ　ποιεῖ　κλάδους　μεγάλους,
herbs,　and　makes　branches　great,

---

good soil, hear the word, accept it, and produce a crop—thirty, sixty or even a hundred times what was sown.''

A Lamp on a Stand

21He said to them, ''Do you bring in a lamp to put it under a bowl or a bed? Instead, don't you put it on its stand? 22For whatever is hidden is meant to be disclosed, and whatever is concealed is meant to be brought out into the open. 23If anyone has ears to hear, let him hear.''

24''Consider carefully what you hear,'' he continued. ''With the measure you use, it will be measured to you—and even more. 25Whoever has will be given more; whoever does not have, even what he has will be taken from him.''

The Parable of the Growing Seed

26He also said, ''This is what the kingdom of God is like. A man scatters seed on the ground. 27Night and day, whether he sleeps or gets up, the seed sprouts and grows, though he does not know how. 28All by itself the soil produces grain—first the stalk, then the head, then the full kernel in the head. 29As soon as the grain is ripe, he puts the sickle to it, because the harvest has come.''

The Parable of the Mustard Seed

30Again he said, ''What shall we say the kingdom of God is like, or what parable shall we use to describe it? 31It is like a mustard seed, which is the smallest seed you plant in the ground. 32Yet when planted, it grows and becomes the largest of all garden plants, branches; so that THE BIRDS OF THE °AIR can NEST UNDER ITS SHADE.''

33And with many such parables He was speaking the word to them as they were able to hear it;

34and He did not speak to them without a parable; but He was explaining everything privately to His own disciples.

Jesus Stills the Sea

35And on that day, when evening had come, He *said to them, ''Let us go over to the other side.''

36And leaving the multitude, they *took Him along with them, just as He was, in the boat; and other boats were with Him.

37And there *arose a fierce gale of wind, and the waves were breaking over the boat so much that the boat was already filling up.

38And He Himself was in the stern, asleep on the cushion; and they *awoke Him and *said to Him, ''Teacher, do You not care that we are perishing?''

39And being aroused, He rebuked the wind and said to the sea, ''Hush, be still.'' And the wind died down and it became perfectly calm.

40And He said to them, ''Why are you so timid? How is it that you have no faith?''

41And they became very much afraid and said to one another, ''Who then is this, that even the wind and the sea obey Him?''

Chapter 5

The Gerasene Demoniac

AND they came to the other side of the sea into the country of the Gerasenes.

2And when He had come out of the boat, immediately a man from the tomb

°Or, *sky*

ὥστε δύνασθαι ὑπὸ τὴν σκιὰν αὐτοῦ τὰ
so as to be able under the shade of it the
= so that the birds of heaven are able to dwell under its shade.

πετεινὰ τοῦ οὐρανοῦ κατασκηνοῦν. 33 Καὶ
birds – of heaven to dwell.ᵇ And

τοιαύταις παραβολαῖς πολλαῖς ἐλάλει αὐτοῖς
ˢsuch ᵃparables ¹in many he spoke to them

τὸν λόγον, καθὼς ἠδύναντο ἀκούειν·
the word, as they were able to hear;

34 χωρὶς δὲ παραβολῆς οὐκ ἐλάλει αὐτοῖς,
and without a parable he spoke not to them,

κατ’ ἰδίαν δὲ τοῖς ἰδίοις μαθηταῖς ἐπέλυεν
but privately to the(his) own disciples he explained

πάντα.
all things.

35 Καὶ λέγει αὐτοῖς ἐν ἐκείνῃ τῇ
And he says to them on that –

ἡμέρᾳ ὀψίας γενομένης· διέλθωμεν εἰς τὸ
day evening having come*: Let us pass over to the
= when evening had come:

πέραν. 36 καὶ ἀφέντες τὸν ὄχλον
other side. And leaving the crowd

παραλαμβάνουσιν αὐτὸν ὡς ἦν ἐν τῷ
they take him as he was in the

πλοίῳ, καὶ ἄλλα πλοῖα ἦν μετ’ αὐτοῦ.
ship, and other ships were with him.

37 καὶ γίνεται λαῖλαψ μεγάλη ἀνέμου,
And occurs storm a great of wind,

καὶ τὰ κύματα ἐπέβαλλεν εἰς τὸ πλοῖον,
and the waves struck into the ship,

ὥστε ἤδη γεμίζεσθαι τὸ πλοῖον. 38 καὶ
so as now to be filled the ship.ᵇ And

αὐτὸς ἦν ἐν τῇ πρύμνῃ ἐπὶ τὸ
he was in the stern on the

προσκεφάλαιον καθεύδων. καὶ ἐγείρουσιν
pillow sleeping. And they rouse

αὐτὸν καὶ λέγουσιν αὐτῷ· διδάσκαλε, οὐ μέλει
him and say to him: Teacher, matters it not

σοι ὅτι ἀπολλύμεθα; 39 καὶ διεγερθεὶς
to thee that we are perishing? And being roused

ἐπετίμησεν τῷ ἀνέμῳ καὶ εἶπεν τῇ
he rebuked the wind and said to the

θαλάσσῃ· σιώπα, πεφίμωσο. καὶ ἐκόπασεν
sea: Be quiet, be muzzled. And dropped

ὁ ἄνεμος, καὶ ἐγένετο γαλήνη μεγάλη.
the wind, and there was calm a great.

40 καὶ εἶπεν αὐτοῖς· τί δειλοί ἐστε
And he said to them: Why fearful are ye

οὕτως; πῶς οὐκ ἔχετε πίστιν; 41 καὶ
thus? how have ye not faith? And

ἐφοβήθησαν φόβον μέγαν, καὶ ἔλεγον πρὸς
they feared fear a great, and said to

ἀλλήλους· τίς ἄρα οὗτός ἐστιν, ὅτι καὶ
one another: Who then this man is, that both

ὁ ἄνεμος καὶ ἡ θάλασσα ὑπακούει αὐτῷ;
the wind and the sea obeys him?

5 Καὶ ἦλθον εἰς τὸ πέραν τῆς θαλάσσης
And they came to the other side of the sea

εἰς τὴν χώραν τῶν Γερασηνῶν. 2 καὶ
into the country of the Gerasenes. And

ἐξελθόντος αὐτοῦ ἐκ τοῦ πλοίου, [εὐθὺς]
coming out himˢ out of the ship, immediately
= as he came out

ὑπήντησεν αὐτῷ ἐκ τῶν μνημείων ἄνθρωπος
met him out of the tombs a man

---

with such big branches that the birds of the air can perch in its shade.''

33With many similar parables Jesus spoke the word to them, as much as they could understand. 34He did not say anything to them without using a parable. But when he was alone with his own disciples, he explained everything.

Jesus Calms the Storm

35That day when evening came, he said to his disciples, ''Let us go over to the other side.'' 36Leaving the crowd behind, they took him along, just as he was, in the boat. There were also other boats with him. 37A furious squall came up, and the waves broke over the boat, so that it was nearly swamped. 38Jesus was in the stern, sleeping on a cushion. The disciples woke him and said to him, ''Teacher, don't you care if we drown?''

39He got up, rebuked the wind and said to the waves, ''Quiet! Be still!'' Then the wind died down and it was completely calm.

40He said to his disciples, ''Why are you so afraid? Do you still have no faith?''

41They were terrified and asked each other, ''Who is this? Even the wind and the waves obey him!''

Chapter 5

The Healing of a Demon-possessed Man

THEY went across the lake to the region of the Gerasenes.ᵏ 2When Jesus got out of the boat, a man with an evilˡ spirit came from the tombs to

ᵏ1 Some manuscripts *Gadarenes*; other manuscripts *Gergesenes*
ˡ2 Greek *unclean*; also in verses 8 and 13

Left column (English)

with an unclean spirit met Him,

3and he had his dwelling among the tombs. And no one was able to bind him anymore, even with a chain;

4because he had often been bound with shackles and chains, and the chains had been torn apart by him, and the shackles broken in pieces, and no one was strong enough to subdue him.

5And constantly night and day, among the tombs and in the mountains, he was crying out and gashing himself with stones.

6And seeing Jesus from a distance, he ran up and bowed down before Him;

7and crying out with a loud voice, he *said, "What do I have to do with You, Jesus, Son of the Most High God? I implore You by God, do not torment me!"

8For He had been saying to him, "Come out of the man, you unclean spirit!"

9And He was asking him, "What is your name?" And he *said to Him, "My name is Legion; for we are many."

10And he *began* to entreat Him earnestly not to send them out of the country.

11Now there was a big herd of swine feeding there on the mountain.

12And *the demons* entreated Him, saying, "Send us into the swine so that we may enter them."

13And He gave them permission. And coming out, the unclean spirits entered the swine; and the herd rushed down the steep bank into the sea, about two thousand *of them;* and they were drowned in the sea.

14And their herdsmen ran away and reported it in the city and *out* in the country. And *the people* came to see

Middle column (Greek interlinear)

ἐν πνεύματι ἀκαθάρτῳ, 3 ὃς τὴν κατοίκησιν
in(with) spirit an unclean, who the(his) dwelling

εἶχεν ἐν τοῖς μνήμασιν, καὶ οὐδὲ ἁλύσει
had among the tombs, and not with a chain
=no one any more

οὐκέτι οὐδεὶς ἐδύνατο αὐτὸν δῆσαι, 4 διὰ
no longer no one was able him to bind, on account of
was able to bind him with a chain,   = because

τὸ αὐτὸν πολλάκις πέδαις καὶ ἁλύσεσιν
the him often with fetters and chains
he had often been bound with fetters and chains, and . . .

δεδέσθαι, καὶ διεσπάσθαι ὑπ' αὐτοῦ τὰς
to have been bound, and to be burst by him the

ἁλύσεις καὶ τὰς πέδας συντετρίφθαι, καὶ
chains and the fetters to have been broken, and

οὐδεὶς ἴσχυεν αὐτὸν δαμάσαι· 5 καὶ
no one was able him to subdue; and

διὰ παντὸς νυκτὸς καὶ ἡμέρας ἐν τοῖς μνήμασιν
always of(by) night and day among the tombs

καὶ ἐν τοῖς ὄρεσιν ἦν κράζων καὶ
and in the mountains he was crying out and

κατακόπτων ἑαυτὸν λίθοις. 6 καὶ ἰδὼν
cutting himself with stones. And seeing

τὸν Ἰησοῦν ἀπὸ μακρόθεν ἔδραμεν καὶ
- Jesus from afar he ran and

προσεκύνησεν αὐτόν, 7 καὶ κράξας φωνῇ
worshipped him, and crying out with a voice

μεγάλῃ λέγει· τί ἐμοὶ καὶ σοί, Ἰησοῦ
great(loud) he says: What to me and to thee, Jesus

υἱὲ τοῦ θεοῦ τοῦ ὑψίστου; ὁρκίζω σε
Son - of God the most high? I adjure thee

τὸν θεόν, μή με βασανίσῃς. 8 ἔλεγεν
- by God, not me thou mayest torment. he said

γὰρ αὐτῷ· ἔξελθε τὸ πνεῦμα τὸ ἀκάθαρτον
For to him: Come out the spirit - unclean

ἐκ τοῦ ἀνθρώπου. 9 καὶ ἐπηρώτα αὐτόν·
out of the man. And he questioned him:

τί ὄνομά σοι; καὶ λέγει αὐτῷ· λεγιὼν
What name to thee?ᵉ And he says to him: Legion
= What name hast thou ?   = My

ὄνομά μοι, ὅτι πολλοί ἐσμεν. 10 καὶ
name to me,ᵉ because many we are. And
name is Legion,

παρεκάλει αὐτὸν πολλὰ ἵνα μὴ αὐτὰ
he besought him much that not them

ἀποστείλῃ ἔξω τῆς χώρας. 11 ἦν δὲ
he would send outside the country. Now there was

ἐκεῖ πρὸς τῷ ὄρει ἀγέλη χοίρων μεγάλη
there near the mountain herd of pigs a great

βοσκομένη· 12 καὶ παρεκάλεσαν αὐτὸν
feeding; and they besought him

λέγοντες· πέμψον ἡμᾶς εἰς τοὺς χοίρους,
saying: Send us into the pigs,

ἵνα εἰς αὐτοὺς εἰσέλθωμεν. 13 καὶ ἐπέτρεψεν
that into them we may enter. And he allowed

αὐτοῖς. καὶ ἐξελθόντα τὰ πνεύματα τὰ
them. And coming out the spirits -

ἀκάθαρτα εἰσῆλθον εἰς τοὺς χοίρους, καὶ
unclean entered into the pigs, and

ὥρμησεν ἡ ἀγέλη κατὰ τοῦ κρημνοῦ εἰς
rushed the herd down the precipice into

τὴν θάλασσαν, ὡς δισχίλιοι, καὶ ἐπνίγοντο
the sea, about two thousand, and were choked

ἐν τῇ θαλάσσῃ. 14 καὶ οἱ βόσκοντες
in the sea. And the [ones] feeding

αὐτοὺς ἔφυγον καὶ ἀπήγγειλαν εἰς τὴν
them fled and reported in the

πόλιν καὶ εἰς τοὺς ἀγρούς· καὶ ἦλθον
city and in the fields; and they came

Right column (English)

meet him. 3This man lived in the tombs, and no one could bind him any more, not even with a chain. 4For he had often been chained hand and foot, but he tore the chains apart and broke the irons on his feet. No one was strong enough to subdue him. 5Night and day among the tombs and in the hills he would cry out and cut himself with stones.

6When he saw Jesus from a distance, he ran and fell on his knees in front of him. 7He shouted at the top of his voice, "What do you want with me, Jesus, Son of the Most High God? Swear to God that you won't torture me!" 8For Jesus had said to him, "Come out of this man, you evil spirit!"

9Then Jesus asked him, "What is your name?"

"My name is Legion," he replied, "for we are many." 10And he begged Jesus again and again not to send them out of the area.

11A large herd of pigs was feeding on the nearby hillside. 12The demons begged Jesus, "Send us among the pigs; allow us to go into them." 13He gave them permission, and the evil spirits came out and went into the pigs. The herd, about two thousand in number, rushed down the steep bank into the lake and were drowned.

14Those tending the pigs ran off and reported this in the town and countryside, and the people went out to what it was that had happened.

15And they *came to Jesus and *observed the man who had been demon-possessed sitting down, clothed and in his right mind, the very man who had had the "legion"; and they became frightened.

16And those who had seen it described to them how it had happened to the demon-possessed man, and *all* about the swine.

17And they began to entreat Him to depart from their region.

18And as He was getting into the boat, the man who had been demon-possessed was entreating Him that he might accompany Him.

19And He did not let him, but He *said to him, "Go home to your people and report to them *p*what great things the Lord has done for you, and *how* He had mercy on you."

20And he went away and began to proclaim in Decapolis what great things Jesus had done for him; and everyone marveled.

Miracles and Healing

21And when Jesus had crossed over again in the boat to the other side, a great multitude gathered about Him; and He stayed by the seashore.

22And one of the synagogue officials named Jairus *came up, and upon seeing Him, *fell at His feet,

23and *entreated Him earnestly, saying, "My little daughter is at the point of death; *please* come and lay Your hands on her, that she may get well and live."

24And He went off with him; and a great multitude was following Him and pressing in on Him.

25And a woman who had had a hemorrhage for twelve years,

26and had endured much at the hands of many physicians, and had spent all that she had and was not helped

---

ἰδεῖν   τί   ἐστιν   τὸ   γεγονός.   **15** καὶ
to see   what   is   the thing   having happened.   And

ἔρχονται   πρὸς   τὸν   Ἰησοῦν,   καὶ   θεωροῦσιν   τὸν
they come   to   –   Jesus,   and   see   the

δαιμονιζόμενον   καθήμενον   ἱματισμένον   καὶ
demon-possessed man   sitting   having been clothed   and

σωφρονοῦντα,   τὸν   ἐσχηκότα   τὸν   λεγιῶνα,
being in his senses,   the man   having had   the   legion,

καὶ   ἐφοβήθησαν.   **16** καὶ   διηγήσαντο   αὐτοῖς   οἱ
and they were afraid.   And   related   to them the [ones]

ἰδόντες   πῶς   ἐγένετο   τῷ   δαιμονιζομένῳ
seeing   how   it happened   to the demon-possessed man

καὶ   περὶ   τῶν   χοίρων.   **17** καὶ   ἤρξαντο
and   about   the   pigs.   And   they began

παρακαλεῖν   αὐτὸν   ἀπελθεῖν   ἀπὸ   τῶν   ὁρίων
to beseech   him   to depart   from   the   territory

αὐτῶν.   **18** καὶ   ἐμβαίνοντος   αὐτοῦ   εἰς   τὸ
of them.   And   embarking   him*   in   the
                                   = as he embarked

πλοῖον   παρεκάλει   αὐτὸν   ὁ   δαιμονισθεὶς
ship   besought   him   the [one]   demon-possessed

ἵνα   μετ'   αὐτοῦ   ᾖ.   **19** καὶ   οὐκ   ἀφῆκεν
that   with   him   he might be.   And   he permitted not

αὐτόν,   ἀλλὰ   λέγει   αὐτῷ·   ὕπαγε   εἰς   τὸν
him,   but   says   to him: Go   to   the

οἶκόν   σου   πρὸς   τοὺς   σούς,   καὶ   ἀπάγγειλον
house of thee   to   the   thine,   and   report
                                 = thy people,

αὐτοῖς   ὅσα   ὁ   κύριός   σοι   πεποίηκεν   καὶ
to them what things   the   Lord   to thee   has done   and

ἠλέησέν   σε.   **20** καὶ   ἀπῆλθεν   καὶ   ἤρξατο
pitied   thee.   And   he departed   and   began

κηρύσσειν   ἐν   τῇ   Δεκαπόλει   ὅσα   ἐποίησεν
to proclaim   in   the   Decapolis   what things   did

αὐτῷ   ὁ   Ἰησοῦς,   καὶ   πάντες   ἐθαύμαζον.
to him   the   Jesus,   and   all men   marvelled.

21 Καὶ   διαπεράσαντος   τοῦ   Ἰησοῦ   ἐν   τῷ
And   crossing over   –   Jesus*   in   the
      = when Jesus had crossed over

πλοίῳ   πάλιν   εἰς   τὸ   πέραν   συνήχθη   ὄχλος
ship   again   to   the   other side   was assembled   crowd

πολὺς   ἐπ'   αὐτόν, καὶ   ἦν   παρὰ   τὴν   θάλασσαν.
a much(great) to   him,   and he was   by   the   sea.

22 Καὶ   ἔρχεται   εἷς   τῶν   ἀρχισυναγώγων,
And   comes   one   of the   synagogue chiefs,

ὀνόματι   Ἰάϊρος,   καὶ   ἰδὼν   αὐτὸν   πίπτει
by name   Jairus,   and   seeing   him   falls

πρὸς   τοὺς   πόδας   αὐτοῦ,   **23** καὶ   παρακαλεῖ
at   the   feet   of him,   and   beseeches

αὐτὸν   πολλὰ   λέγων   ὅτι   τὸ   θυγάτριόν   μου
him   much   saying[,]   -   The   daughter   of me

ἐσχάτως   ἔχει,   ἵνα   ἐλθὼν   ἐπιθῇς
is at the point of death,†   that   coming   thou mayest lay *on*

τὰς   χεῖρας   αὐτῇ,   ἵνα   σωθῇ   καὶ   ζήσῃ.
the(thy) hands   on her,   that   she may be healed   and   may live.

24 καὶ   ἀπῆλθεν   μετ'   αὐτοῦ.   καὶ   ἠκολούθει   αὐτῷ
And   he went   with   him.   And   followed   him

ὄχλος   πολύς,   καὶ   συνέθλιβον   αὐτόν.   **25** Καὶ
crowd   a much(great),   and   pressed upon   him.   And

γυνὴ   οὖσα   ἐν   ῥύσει   αἵματος   δώδεκα
a woman   being   in   a flow   of blood   twelve
               = having

ἔτη,   **26** καὶ   πολλὰ   παθοῦσα   ὑπὸ   πολλῶν
years,   and   many things   suffering   by   many

ἰατρῶν   καὶ   δαπανήσασα   τὰ   παρ'   αὐτῆς
physicians   and   having spent   the   with   her

πάντα,   καὶ   μηδὲν   ὠφεληθεῖσα   ἀλλὰ   μᾶλλον
all things,   and   nothing having been profited   but   rather

---

see what had happened. 15When they came to Jesus, they saw the man who had been possessed by the legion of demons, sitting there, dressed and in his right mind; and they were afraid. 16Those who had seen it told the people what had happened to the demon-possessed man—and told about the pigs as well. 17Then the people began to plead with Jesus to leave their region.

18As Jesus was getting into the boat, the man who had been demon-possessed begged to go with him. 19Jesus did not let him, but said, "Go home to your family and tell them how much the Lord has done for you, and how he has had mercy on you." 20So the man went away and began to tell in the Decapolis *m* how much Jesus had done for him. And all the people were amazed.

A Dead Girl and a Sick Woman

21When Jesus had again crossed over by boat to the other side of the lake, a large crowd gathered around him while he was by the lake. 22Then one of the synagogue rulers, named Jairus, came there. Seeing Jesus, he fell at his feet 23and pleaded earnestly with him, "My little daughter is dying. Please come and put your hands on her so that she will be healed and live." 24So Jesus went with him.

A large crowd followed and pressed around him. 25And a woman was there who had been subject to bleeding for twelve years. 26She had suffered a great deal under the care of many doctors and had spent all

---

p Or, *everything that*

*m*20 That is, the Ten Cities

at all, but rather had grown worse,
27after hearing about Jesus, came up in the crowd behind *Him*, and touched His cloak.
28For she thought, "If I just touch His garments, I shall get well."
29And immediately the flow of her blood was dried up; and she felt in her body that she was healed of her affliction.
30And immediately Jesus, perceiving in Himself that the power *proceeding* from Him had gone forth, turned around in the crowd and said, "Who touched My garments?"
31And His disciples said to Him, "You see the multitude pressing in on You, and You say, 'Who touched Me?'"
32And He looked around to see the woman who had done this.
33But the woman fearing and trembling, aware of what had happened to her, came and fell down before Him, and told Him the whole truth.
34And He said to her, "Daughter, your faith has made you well; go in peace, and be healed of your affliction."
35While He was still speaking, they *came from the *house of* the synagogue official, saying, "Your daughter has died; why trouble the Teacher anymore?"
36But Jesus, overhearing what was being spoken, *said to the synagogue official, "Do not be afraid *any longer*, only believe."
37And He allowed no one to follow with Him, except Peter and James and John the brother of James.
38And they *came to the house of the synagogue official; and He *beheld a commotion, and *people loudly weeping and wailing.
39And entering in, He *said to them, "Why make a commotion and weep?

εἰς τὸ χεῖρον ἐλθοῦσα, 27 ἀκούσασα τὰ
to the worse having come, hearing the things
περὶ τοῦ Ἰησοῦ, ἐλθοῦσα ἐν τῷ ὄχλῳ
about – Jesus, coming in the crowd
ὄπισθεν ἥψατο τοῦ ἱματίου αὐτοῦ· 28 ἔλεγεν
behind touched the garment of him; she said[,]
γὰρ ὅτι ἐὰν ἅψωμαι κἂν τῶν ἱματίων
for – If I may touch even the garments
αὐτοῦ, σωθήσομαι. 29 καὶ εὐθὺς ἐξηράνθη
of him, I shall be healed. And immediately was dried up
ἡ πηγὴ τοῦ αἵματος αὐτῆς, καὶ ἔγνω
the fountain of the blood of her, and she knew
τῷ σώματι ὅτι ἴαται ἀπὸ τῆς
in the(her) body that she is(was) cured from the
μάστιγος. 30 καὶ εὐθὺς ὁ Ἰησοῦς ἐπιγνοὺς ἐν
plague. And immediately – Jesus knowing in
ἑαυτῷ τὴν ἐξ αὐτοῦ δύναμιν ἐξελθοῦσαν,
himself ¹the ⁴out of ⁵him ²power ³going forth,
ἐπιστραφεὶς ἐν τῷ ὄχλῳ ἔλεγεν· τίς μου ἥψατο τῶν
turning in the crowd said: Who of me touched the
ἱματίων; 31 καὶ ἔλεγον αὐτῷ οἱ μαθηταὶ
garments? And said to him the disciples
αὐτοῦ· βλέπεις τὸν ὄχλον συνθλίβοντά σε,
of him: Thou seest the crowd pressing upon thee,
καὶ λέγεις· τίς μου ἥψατο; 32 καὶ
and thou sayest: Who me touched? And
περιεβλέπετο ἰδεῖν τὴν τοῦτο ποιήσασαν.
he looked round to see the [one] this having done.
33 ἡ δὲ γυνὴ φοβηθεῖσα καὶ τρέμουσα,
And the woman fearing and trembling,
εἰδυῖα ὃ γέγονεν αὐτῇ, ἦλθεν καὶ προσέ-
knowing what has happened to her, came and fell
πεσεν αὐτῷ καὶ εἶπεν αὐτῷ πᾶσαν τὴν ἀλήθειαν.
before him and told him all the truth.
34 ὁ δὲ εἶπεν αὐτῇ· θυγάτηρ, ἡ πίστις
And he said to her: Daughter, the faith
σου σέσωκέν σε· ὕπαγε εἰς εἰρήνην, καὶ
of thee has healed thee; go in peace, and
ἴσθι ὑγιὴς ἀπὸ τῆς μάστιγός σου. 35 Ἔτι
be whole from the plague of thee. Still
                                          = While
αὐτοῦ λαλοῦντος ἔρχονται ἀπὸ τοῦ
him speakingᵃ they come from the
he was still speaking
ἀρχισυναγώγου λέγοντες ὅτι ἡ θυγάτηρ
synagogue chief saying[,] – The daughter
σου ἀπέθανεν· τί ἔτι σκύλλεις τὸν διδάσκαλον;
of thee died; why still troublest thou the teacher?
36 ὁ δὲ Ἰησοῦς παρακούσας τὸν λόγον
– But Jesus overhearing the word
λαλούμενον λέγει τῷ ἀρχισυναγώγῳ· μὴ
being spoken says to the synagogue chief: not
φοβοῦ, μόνον πίστευε. 37 καὶ οὐκ ἀφῆκεν
Fear, only believe. And he allowed not
οὐδένα μετ' αὐτοῦ συνακολουθῆσαι εἰ μὴ
no(any)one with him to accompany except
τὸν Πέτρον καὶ Ἰάκωβον καὶ Ἰωάννην
– Peter and James and John
τὸν ἀδελφὸν Ἰακώβου. 38 καὶ ἔρχονται
the brother of James. And they come
εἰς τὸν οἶκον τοῦ ἀρχισυναγώγου, καὶ
into the house of the synagogue chief, and
θεωρεῖ θόρυβον, καὶ κλαίοντάς καὶ
he sees an uproar, and [men] weeping and
ἀλαλάζοντας πολλά, 39 καὶ εἰσελθὼν λέγει
crying aloud much, and entering he says
αὐτοῖς· τί θορυβεῖσθε καὶ κλαίετε; τὸ
to them: Why make ye an uproar and weep? the

she had, yet instead of getting better she grew worse.
27When she heard about Jesus, she came up behind him in the crowd and touched his cloak, 28because she thought, "If I just touch his clothes, I will be healed." 29Immediately her bleeding stopped and she felt in her body that she was freed from her suffering.
30At once Jesus realized that power had gone out from him. He turned around in the crowd and asked, "Who touched my clothes?"
31"You see the people crowding against you," his disciples answered, "and yet you can ask, 'Who touched me?'"
32But Jesus kept looking around to see who had done it. 33Then the woman, knowing what had happened to her, came and fell at his feet and, trembling with fear, told him the whole truth. 34He said to her, "Daughter, your faith has healed you. Go in peace and be freed from your suffering."
35While Jesus was still speaking, some men came from the house of Jairus, the synagogue ruler. "Your daughter is dead," they said. "Why bother the teacher any more?"
36Ignoring what they said, Jesus told the synagogue ruler, "Don't be afraid; just believe."
37He did not let anyone follow him except Peter, James and John the brother of James. 38When they came to the home of the synagogue ruler, Jesus saw a commotion, with people crying and wailing loudly. 39He went in and said to them, "Why all this com-

The child has not died, but is asleep."

40And they *began* laughing at Him. But putting them all out, He *took along the child's father and mother and His own companions, and *entered *the room* where the child was.

41And taking the child by the hand, He *said to her, "Talitha kum!" (which translated means, "Little girl, I say to you, arise!").

42And immediately the girl rose and *began* to walk; for she was twelve years old. And immediately they were completely astounded.

43And He gave them strict orders that no one should know about this; and He said that *something* should be given her to eat.

παιδίον   οὐκ   ἀπέθανεν   ἀλλὰ   καθεύδει.
child   did not die   but   sleeps.

40 καὶ κατεγέλων   αὐτοῦ. αὐτὸς   δὲ   ἐκβαλὼν
And   they ridiculed   him.   But he   putting out

πάντας   παραλαμβάνει   τὸν   πατέρα   τοῦ
all   takes   the   father   of the

παιδίου   καὶ   τὴν   μητέρα   καὶ   τοὺς   μετ'
child   and   the   mother   and   the [ones]   with

αὐτοῦ,   καὶ   εἰσπορεύεται   ὅπου   ἦν   τὸ
him,   and   goes in   where   was   the

παιδίον.   **41** καὶ   κρατήσας   τῆς   χειρὸς
child.   And   taking hold of   the   hand

τοῦ   παιδίου   λέγει   αὐτῇ· ταλιθὰ κούμ,   ὅ
of the child   he says to her: Talitha   koum,   which

ἐστιν   μεθερμηνευόμενον· τὸ   κοράσιον,   σοὶ
is   being interpreted: -   Maid,   to thee

λέγω,   ἔγειρε. **42** καὶ   εὐθὺς   ἀνέστη   τὸ
I say,   arise.   And   immediately rose up   the

κοράσιον   καὶ   περιεπάτει·   ἦν   γὰρ
maid   and   walked;   for she was

ἐτῶν   δώδεκα.   καὶ   ἐξέστησαν   εὐθὺς
[of the age] twelve.   And   they were astonished immediately
of years   = immediately they were exceedingly astonished.

ἐκστάσει   μεγάλη.   **43** καὶ   διεστείλατο
astonishment   with a great.   And   he ordered

αὐτοῖς   πολλὰ   ἵνα   μηδεὶς   γνοῖ   τοῦτο,   καὶ
them   much   that   no one should know this,   and

εἶπεν   δοθῆναι   αὐτῇ   φαγεῖν.
told   to be given to her   to eat.
=[them] to give her [something] to eat.

---

motion and wailing? The child is not dead but asleep." 40But they laughed at him.

After he put them all out, he took the child's father and mother and the disciples who were with him, and went in where the child was. 41He took her by the hand and said to her, "Talitha koum!" (which means, "Little girl, I say to you, get up!"). 42Immediately the girl stood up and walked around (she was twelve years old). At this they were completely astonished. 43He gave strict orders not to let anyone know about this, and told them to give her something to eat.

Chapter 6

Teaching at Nazareth

AND He went out from there, and He *came into His home town; and His disciples *followed Him.

2And when the Sabbath had come, He began to teach in the synagogue; and the many listeners were astonished, saying, "Where did this man *get* these things, and what is *this* wisdom given to Him, and such miracles as these performed by His hands?

3"Is not this the carpenter, the son of Mary, and brother of James, and Joses, and Judas, and Simon? Are not His sisters here with us?" And they took offense at Him.

4And Jesus said to them, "A prophet is not without honor except in his home town and among his *own* relatives and in his *own* household."

---

6 Καὶ   ἐξῆλθεν   ἐκεῖθεν,   καὶ   ἔρχεται   εἰς
And   he went forth   thence,   and   comes   into

τὴν   πατρίδα   αὐτοῦ,   καὶ   ἀκολουθοῦσιν
the   native place   of him,   and   follow

αὐτῷ   οἱ   μαθηταὶ   αὐτοῦ.   **2** καὶ   γενομένου
him   the   disciples   of him.   And   coming
= when

σαββάτου   ἤρξατο   διδάσκειν   ἐν   τῇ   συναγωγῇ·
a sabbath[a] he began   to teach   in   the   synagogue;
a sabbath came

καὶ   οἱ   πολλοὶ   ἀκούοντες   ἐξεπλήσσοντο
and   the   many   hearing   were astonished

λέγοντες· πόθεν   τούτῳ   ταῦτα,   καὶ   τίς   ἡ
saying: Whence to this man these things, and   what the

σοφία   ἡ   δοθεῖσα   τούτῳ;   καὶ   αἱ   δυνάμεις
wisdom   -   given   to this(him)? And the powerful deeds

τοιαῦται   διὰ   τῶν   χειρῶν   αὐτοῦ   γινόμεναι;
such   through the   hands   of him   coming about?

3 οὐχ   οὗτός   ἐστιν   ὁ   τέκτων,   ὁ   υἱὸς
Not   this man   is   the carpenter,   the   son

τῆς   Μαρίας   καὶ   ἀδελφὸς   Ἰακώβου   καὶ
-        of Mary   and   brother   of James   and

Ἰωσῆτος   καὶ   Ἰούδα   καὶ   Σίμωνος;   καὶ
Joses   and   Judas   and   Simon?   and

οὐκ   εἰσὶν   αἱ   ἀδελφαὶ   αὐτοῦ   ὧδε   πρὸς
not   are   the sisters   of him   here   with

ἡμᾶς;   καὶ   ἐσκανδαλίζοντο   ἐν   αὐτῷ.   **4** καὶ
us?   And   they were offended   in(at)   him.   And

ἔλεγεν   αὐτοῖς   ὁ   Ἰησοῦς   ὅτι   οὐκ   ἔστιν
said   to them   -   Jesus[,]   that   not   is

προφήτης   ἄτιμος   εἰ   μὴ   ἐν   τῇ   πατρίδι
A prophet   unhonoured except in   the native place

αὐτοῦ   καὶ   ἐν   τοῖς   συγγενεῦσιν   αὐτοῦ
of him   and   in   the   relatives   of him

καὶ   ἐν   τῇ   οἰκίᾳ   αὐτοῦ.   **5** καὶ   οὐκ
and   in   the   house   of him.   And   not

Chapter 6

A Prophet Without Honor

JESUS left there and went to his hometown, accompanied by his disciples. 2When the Sabbath came, he began to teach in the synagogue, and many who heard him were amazed.

"Where did this man get these things?" they asked. "What's this wisdom that has been given him, that he even does miracles! 3Isn't this the carpenter? Isn't this Mary's son and the brother of James, Joseph,[n] Judas and Simon? Aren't his sisters here with us?" And they took offense at him.

4Jesus said to them, "Only in his hometown, among his relatives and in his own house is a prophet without honor." 5He could

n3 Greek *Joses*, a variant of *Joseph*

5And He could do no miracle there except that He laid His hands upon a few sick people and healed them.
6And He wondered at their unbelief.
And He was going around the villages teaching.

The Twelve Sent Out

7And He *summoned the twelve and began to send them out in pairs; and He was giving them authority over the unclean spirits;
8and He instructed them that they should take nothing for *their* journey, except a mere staff; no bread, no bag, no money in their belt;
9but *to* wear sandals; and He added, "Do not put on two ᵠtunics."
10And He said to them, "Wherever you enter a house, stay there until you leave town.
11"And any place that does not receive you or listen to you, as you go out from there, shake off the dust from the soles of your feet for a testimony against them."
12And they went out and preached that *men* should repent.
13And they were casting out many demons and were anointing with oil many sick people and healing them.

John's Fate Recalled

14And King Herod heard of it, for His name had become well known; and *people* were saying, "John the Baptist has risen from the dead, and that is why these miraculous powers are at work in Him."
15But others were saying, "He is Elijah." And others were saying, "*He is* a prophet, like one of the prophets *of old*."
16But when Herod heard of it, he kept saying, "John, whom I beheaded, has risen!"
17For Herod himself had sent and had John arrested

ᵠOr, *inner garments*

ἐδύνατο ἐκεῖ ποιῆσαι οὐδεμίαν δύναμιν,
he could there to do no(any) powerful deed,
εἰ μὴ ὀλίγοις ἀρρώστοις ἐπιθεὶς τὰς
except on a few sick [ones] laying on the(his)
χεῖρας ἐθεράπευσεν. 6 καὶ ἐθαύμασεν διὰ
hands he healed. And he marvelled because of
τὴν ἀπιστίαν αὐτῶν.
the unbelief of them.
Καὶ περιῆγεν τὰς κώμας κύκλῳ
And he went round the villages in circuit
διδάσκων. 7 Καὶ προσκαλεῖται τοὺς δώδεκα,
teaching. And he calls to [him] the twelve,
καὶ ἤρξατο αὐτοὺς ἀποστέλλειν δύο δύο,
and began them to send forth two [by] two,
καὶ ἐδίδου αὐτοῖς ἐξουσίαν τῶν πνευμάτων
and gave them authority the spirits
τῶν ἀκαθάρτων, 8 καὶ παρήγγειλεν αὐτοῖς
- of(over) unclean, and charged them
ἵνα μηδὲν αἴρωσιν εἰς ὁδὸν εἰ μὴ ῥάβδον
that nothing they should take in [the] way except a staff
μόνον, μὴ ἄρτον, μὴ πήραν, μὴ εἰς τὴν
only, not bread, not a wallet, not in the
ζώνην χαλκόν, 9 ἀλλὰ ὑποδεδεμένους σανδάλια,
girdle copper [money], but having had tied on sandals,
καὶ μὴ ἐνδύσησθε δύο χιτῶνας. 10 καὶ
and do not put on two tunics. And
ἔλεγεν αὐτοῖς· ὅπου ἐὰν εἰσέλθητε εἰς
he said to them: Wherever ye enter into
οἰκίαν, ἐκεῖ μένετε ἕως ἂν ἐξέλθητε
a house, there remain until ye go out
ἐκεῖθεν. 11 καὶ ὃς ἂν τόπος μὴ δέξηται
thence. And whatever place receives not
ὑμᾶς μηδὲ ἀκούσωσιν ὑμῶν, ἐκπορευόμενοι
you nor they hear you, going out
ἐκεῖθεν ἐκτινάξατε τὸν χοῦν τὸν ὑποκάτω
thence shake off the dust the under
τῶν ποδῶν ὑμῶν εἰς μαρτύριον αὐτοῖς.
the feet of you for a testimony to them.
12 Καὶ ἐξελθόντες ἐκήρυξαν ἵνα μετανοῶσιν,
And going forth they proclaimed that men should repent,
13 καὶ δαιμόνια πολλὰ ἐξέβαλλον, καὶ
and demons many they expelled, and
ἤλειφον ἐλαίῳ πολλοὺς ἀρρώστους καὶ
anointed with oil many sick [ones] and
ἐθεράπευον.
healed.
14 Καὶ ἤκουσεν ὁ βασιλεὺς Ἡρῴδης,
And heard the king Herod,
φανερὸν γὰρ ἐγένετο τὸ ὄνομα αὐτοῦ, καὶ
for manifest became the name of him, and
ἔλεγον ὅτι Ἰωάννης ὁ βαπτίζων ἐγήγερται
they said[,] - John the baptizing [one] has been raised
ἐκ νεκρῶν, καὶ διὰ τοῦτο ἐνεργοῦσιν αἱ
from [the] dead, and therefore operate the
δυνάμεις ἐν αὐτῷ. 15 ἄλλοι δὲ ἔλεγον
powerful deeds in him. But others said[,]
ὅτι Ἠλίας ἐστίν· ἄλλοι δὲ ἔλεγον ὅτι
- Elias it/he is; and [yet] others said[,] -
προφήτης ὡς εἷς τῶν προφητῶν. 16 ἀκούσας δὲ
A prophet as one of the prophets. But hearing
ὁ Ἡρῴδης ἔλεγεν· ὃν ἐγὼ ἀπεκεφάλισα
- Herod said: ²whom ³I ⁴beheaded
Ἰωάννην, οὗτος ἠγέρθη. 17 Αὐτὸς γὰρ ὁ
¹John, this was raised. For ³himself -
Ἡρῴδης ἀποστείλας ἐκράτησεν τὸν Ἰωάννην
¹Herod sending seized - John

not do any miracles there, except lay his hands on a few sick people and heal them. 6And he was amazed at their lack of faith.

Jesus Sends Out the Twelve

Then Jesus went around teaching from village to village. 7Calling the Twelve to him, he sent them out two by two and gave them authority over evilᵒ spirits.
8These were his instructions: "Take nothing for the journey except a staff —no bread, no bag, no money in your belts. 9Wear sandals but not an extra tunic. 10Whenever you enter a house, stay there until you leave that town. 11And if any place will not welcome you or listen to you, shake the dust off your feet when you leave, as a testimony against them."
12They went out and preached that people should repent. 13They drove out many demons and anointed many sick people with oil and healed them.

John the Baptist Beheaded

14King Herod heard about this, for Jesus' name had become well known. Some were saying,ᵖ "John the Baptist has been raised from the dead, and that is why miraculous powers are at work in him."
15Others said, "He is Elijah."
And still others claimed, "He is a prophet, like one of the prophets of long ago."
16But when Herod heard this, he said, "John, the man I beheaded, has been raised from the dead!"
17For Herod himself had given orders to have John

ᵒ7 Greek *unclean*
ᵖ14 Some early manuscripts *He was saying*

and bound in prison on account of Herodias, the wife of his brother Philip, because he had married her. 18For John had been saying to Herod, "It is not lawful for you to have your brother's wife." 19And Herodias had a grudge against him and wanted to put him to death and could not do so; 20for Herod was afraid of John, knowing that he was a righteous and holy man, and kept him safe. And when he heard him, he was very perplexed; but he used to enjoy listening to him. 21And a strategic day came when Herod on his birthday gave a banquet for his lords and military commanders and the leading men of Galilee; 22and when the daughter of Herodias herself came in and danced, she pleased Herod and his dinner guests; and the king said to the girl, "Ask me for whatever you want and I will give it to you." 23And he swore to her, "Whatever you ask of me, I will give it to you; up to half of my kingdom." 24And she went out and said to her mother, "What shall I ask for?" And she said, "The head of John the Baptist." 25And immediately she came in haste before the king and asked, saying, "I want you to give me right away the head of John the Baptist on a platter." 26And although the king was very sorry, yet because of his oaths and because of his dinner guests, he was unwilling to refuse her. 27And immediately the king sent an executioner

καὶ ἔδησεν αὐτὸν ἐν φυλακῇ διὰ Ἡρῳδιάδα
and bound him in prison because of Herodias
τὴν γυναῖκα Φιλίππου τοῦ ἀδελφοῦ αὐτοῦ,
the wife of Philip the brother of him,
ὅτι αὐτὴν ἐγάμησεν· 18 ἔλεγεν γὰρ ὁ
because her he married; for said the
Ἰωάννης τῷ Ἡρῴδῃ ὅτι οὐκ ἔξεστίν
John - to Herod[,] - It is not lawful
σοι ἔχειν τὴν γυναῖκα τοῦ ἀδελφοῦ σου.
for thee to have the wife of the brother of thee.
19 ἡ δὲ Ἡρῳδιὰς ἐνεῖχεν αὐτῷ καὶ
- Now Herodias had a grudge against him and
ἤθελεν αὐτὸν ἀποκτεῖναι, καὶ οὐκ ἠδύνατο
wished ²him ¹to kill, and could not;
20 ὁ γὰρ Ἡρῴδης ἐφοβεῖτο τὸν Ἰωάννην,
- for Herod feared - John.
εἰδὼς αὐτὸν ἄνδρα δίκαιον καὶ ἅγιον, καὶ
knowing him a man just and holy, and
συνετήρει αὐτόν, καὶ ἀκούσας αὐτοῦ πολλὰ
kept safe him, and hearing him much = was
ἠπόρει, καὶ ἡδέως αὐτοῦ ἤκουεν. 21 καὶ
was in difficulties, and gladly him heard. And
in great difficulties,
γενομένης ἡμέρας εὐκαίρου ὅτε Ἡρῴδης
coming day a suitable when Herod
= when a suitable day came
τοῖς γενεσίοις αὐτοῦ δεῖπνον ἐποίησεν τοῖς
on the birthday festivities of him a supper made for the
μεγιστᾶσιν αὐτοῦ καὶ τοῖς χιλιάρχοις καὶ
courtiers of him and the chiliarchs and
τοῖς πρώτοις τῆς Γαλιλαίας, 22 καὶ
the chief men - of Galilee, and
εἰσελθούσης τῆς θυγατρὸς αὐτῆς τῆς
entering the daughter ²of herself -
= when the daughter of Herodias herself entered and danced,
Ἡρῳδιάδος καὶ ὀρχησαμένης, ἤρεσεν τῷ
¹of Herodias and dancing, she pleased -
Ἡρῴδῃ καὶ τοῖς συνανακειμένοις. ὁ δὲ
Herod and the [ones] reclining with [him]. And the
βασιλεὺς εἶπεν τῷ κορασίῳ· αἴτησόν με
king said to the girl: Ask me
ὃ ἐὰν θέλῃς, καὶ δώσω σοι· 23 καὶ
whatever thou wishest, and I will give thee; and
ὤμοσεν αὐτῇ ὅτι ὃ ἐὰν αἰτήσῃς δώσω
he swore to her[,] - Whatever thou askest I will give
σοι ἕως ἡμίσους τῆς βασιλείας μου.
thee up to half of the kingdom of me.
24 καὶ ἐξελθοῦσα εἶπεν τῇ μητρὶ αὐτῆς·
And going out she said to the mother of her:
τί αἰτήσωμαι; ἡ δὲ εἶπεν· τὴν κεφαλὴν
What may I ask? And she said: The head
Ἰωάννου τοῦ βαπτίζοντος. 25 καὶ
of John the [one] baptizing. And
εἰσελθοῦσα εὐθὺς μετὰ σπουδῆς πρὸς τὸν
entering immediately with haste to the
βασιλέα ᾐτήσατο λέγουσα· θέλω ἵνα ἐξαυτῆς
king she asked saying: I wish that at once
δῷς μοι ἐπὶ πίνακι τὴν κεφαλὴν Ἰωάννου
thou mayest give me on a dish the head of John
τοῦ βαπτιστοῦ. 26 καὶ περίλυπος γενόμενος
the Baptist. And deeply grieved becoming
ὁ βασιλεὺς διὰ τοὺς ὅρκους καὶ τοὺς
the king because of the oaths and the [ones]
ἀνακειμένους οὐκ ἠθέλησεν ἀθετῆσαι αὐτήν.
reclining did not wish to reject her.
27 καὶ εὐθὺς ἀποστείλας ὁ βασιλεὺς
And immediately ³sending ¹the ²king

arrested, and he had him bound and put in prison. He did this because of Herodias, his brother Philip's wife, whom he had married. 18For John had been saying to Herod, "It is not lawful for you to have your brother's wife." 19So Herodias nursed a grudge against John and wanted to kill him. But she was not able to, 20because Herod feared John and protected him, knowing him to be a righteous and holy man. When Herod heard John, he was greatly puzzledᵠ; yet he liked to listen to him. 21Finally the opportune time came. On his birthday Herod gave a banquet for his high officials and military commanders and the leading men of Galilee. 22When the daughter of Herodias came in and danced, she pleased Herod and his dinner guests.
The king said to the girl, "Ask me for anything you want, and I'll give it to you." 23And he promised her with an oath, "Whatever you ask I will give you, up to half my kingdom." 24She went out and said to her mother, "What shall I ask for?"
"The head of John the Baptist," she answered. 25At once the girl hurried in to the king with the request: "I want you to give me right now the head of John the Baptist on a platter." 26The king was greatly distressed, but because of his oaths and his dinner guests, he did not want to refuse her. 27So he immediately sent an executioner

ᵠ20 Some early manuscripts he did many things

and commanded *him* to bring *back* his head. And he went and had him beheaded in the prison, 28and brought his head on a platter, and gave it to the girl; and the girl gave it to her mother. 29And when his disciples heard *about this*, they came and took away his body and laid it in a tomb. 30And the apostles *gathered together with Jesus; and they reported to Him all that they had done and taught. 31And He *said to them, "Come away by yourselves to a lonely place and rest a while." (For there were many *people* coming and going, and they did not even have time to eat.) 32And they went away in the boat to a lonely place by themselves.

Five Thousand Fed

33And *the people* saw them going, and many recognized *them,* and they ran there together on foot from all the cities, and got there ahead of them. 34And when He went ashore, He saw a great multitude, and He felt compassion for them because they were like sheep without a shepherd; and He began to teach them many things. 35And when it was already quite late, His disciples came up to Him and *began* saying, "The place is desolate and it is already quite late; 36send them away so that they may go into the surrounding countryside and villages and buy themselves something to eat." 37But He answered and said to them, "You give them *something* to eat!" And they *said to Him,

Middle column (interlinear)

σπεκουλάτορα ἐπέταξεν ἐνέγκαι τὴν κεφαλὴν
an executioner gave order to bring the head

αὐτοῦ. καὶ ἀπελθὼν ἀπεκεφάλισεν αὐτὸν
of him. And going he beheaded him

ἐν τῇ φυλακῇ, 28 καὶ ἤνεγκεν τὴν κεφαλὴν
in the prison, and brought the head

αὐτοῦ ἐπὶ πίνακι καὶ ἔδωκεν αὐτὴν τῷ
of him on a dish and gave it to the

κορασίῳ, καὶ τὸ κοράσιον ἔδωκεν αὐτὴν
girl, and the girl gave it

τῇ μητρὶ αὐτῆς. 29 καὶ ἀκούσαντες οἱ
to the mother of her. And hearing the

μαθηταὶ αὐτοῦ ἦλθαν καὶ ἦραν τὸ πτῶμα
disciples of him went and took the corpse

αὐτοῦ καὶ ἔθηκαν αὐτὸ ἐν μνημείῳ.
of him and put it in a tomb.

30 Καὶ συνάγονται οἱ ἀπόστολοι πρὸς
And assemble the apostles to

τὸν Ἰησοῦν, καὶ ἀπήγγειλαν αὐτῷ πάντα
- Jesus, and reported to him all things

ὅσα ἐποίησαν καὶ ὅσα ἐδίδαξαν. 31 καὶ
which they did and which they taught. And

λέγει αὐτοῖς· δεῦτε ὑμεῖς αὐτοὶ κατ'
he says to them: Come ye [your]selves pri-

ἰδίαν εἰς ἔρημον τόπον καὶ ἀναπαύσασθε ὀλίγον.
vately to a desert place and rest a little.

ἦσαν γὰρ οἱ ἐρχόμενοι καὶ οἱ
For ²were ³the [ones] ⁴coming ⁵and ⁶the [ones]

ὑπάγοντες πολλοί, καὶ οὐδὲ φαγεῖν
⁷going ¹many, and not to eat

εὐκαίρουν. 32 καὶ ἀπῆλθον ἐν τῷ πλοίῳ
they had opportunity. And they went away in the ship

εἰς ἔρημον τόπον κατ' ἰδίαν. 33 καὶ
to a desert place privately. And

εἶδον αὐτοὺς ὑπάγοντας καὶ ἐπέγνωσαν
²saw ³them ⁴going ⁵and ⁶knew

πολλοί, καὶ πεζῇ ἀπὸ πασῶν τῶν πόλεων
¹many, and on foot from all the cities

συνέδραμον ἐκεῖ καὶ προῆλθον αὐτούς.
ran together there and came before them.

34 Καὶ ἐξελθὼν εἶδεν πολὺν ὄχλον, καὶ
And going forth he saw a much(great) crowd, and

ἐσπλαγχνίσθη ἐπ' αὐτοὺς ὅτι ἦσαν ὡς
had compassion on them because they were as

πρόβατα μὴ ἔχοντα ποιμένα, καὶ ἤρξατο
sheep not having a shepherd, and he began

διδάσκειν αὐτοὺς πολλά. 35 Καὶ ἤδη ὥρας
to teach them many things. And now an hour
= it being

πολλῆς γενομένης προσελθόντες αὐτῷ οἱ
much coming* approaching to him the
late

μαθηταὶ αὐτοῦ ἔλεγον ὅτι ἔρημός ἐστιν
disciples of him said[,] - Desert is

ὁ τόπος καὶ ἤδη ὥρα πολλή· 36 ἀπόλυσον
the place and now hour a much; dismiss
= it is late;

αὐτούς, ἵνα ἀπελθόντες εἰς τοὺς κύκλῳ
them, that going away to the round about

ἀγροὺς καὶ κώμας ἀγοράσωσιν ἑαυτοῖς τί
fields and villages they may buy for themselves what

φάγωσιν. 37 ὁ δὲ ἀποκριθεὶς εἶπεν αὐτοῖς·
they may eat. But he answering said to them:

δότε αὐτοῖς ὑμεῖς φαγεῖν. καὶ λέγουσιν
Give them ye to eat. And they say

with orders to bring John's head. The man went, beheaded John in the prison, 28and brought back his head on a platter. He presented it to the girl, and she gave it to her mother. 29On hearing of this, John's disciples came and took his body and laid it in a tomb.

Jesus Feeds the Five Thousand

30The apostles gathered around Jesus and reported to him all they had done and taught. 31Then, because so many people were coming and going that they did not even have a chance to eat, he said to them, "Come with me by yourselves to a quiet place and get some rest." 32So they went away by themselves in a boat to a solitary place. 33But many who saw them leaving recognized them and ran on foot from all the towns and got there ahead of them. 34When Jesus landed and saw a large crowd, he had compassion on them, because they were like sheep without a shepherd. So he began teaching them many things.

35By this time it was late in the day, so his disciples came to him. "This is a remote place," they said, "and it's already very late. 36Send the people away so they can go to the surrounding countryside and villages and buy themselves something to eat." 37But he answered, "You give them something to eat."

They said to him, "That

"Shall we go and spend two hundred ᶠdenarii on bread and give them *something* to eat?"
38And He *said to them, "How many loaves do you have? Go look!" And when they found out, they *said, "Five and two fish."
39And He commanded them all to recline by groups on the green grass.
40And they reclined in companies of hundreds and of fifties.
41And He took the five loaves and the two fish, and looking up toward heaven, He blessed the *food* and broke the loaves and He kept giving *them* to the disciples to set before them; and He divided up the two fish among them all.
42And they all ate and were satisfied.
43And they picked up twelve full baskets of the broken pieces, and also of the fish.
44And there were five thousand men who ate the loaves.

Jesus Walks on the Water

45And immediately He made His disciples get into the boat and go ahead of *Him* to the other side to Bethsaida, while He Himself was sending the multitude away.
46And after bidding them farewell, He departed to the mountain to pray.
47And when it was evening, the boat was in the midst of the sea, and He *was* alone on the land.
48And seeing them straining at the oars, for the wind was against them, at about the fourth watch of the night, He *came to them, walking on the sea; and He intended to pass by them.
49But when they saw Him walking on the sea, they supposed that it was a ghost, and cried out;

αὐτῷ·   ἀπελθόντες   ἀγοράσωμεν   δηναρίων
to him: Going away   may we buy   ²of(for) ⁴denarii

διακοσίων   ἄρτους,   καὶ   δώσομεν   αὐτοῖς
³two hundred ¹loaves,   and   shall we give them

φαγεῖν;   38 ὁ   δὲ   λέγει   αὐτοῖς·   πόσους
to eat ?   And he   says   to them: How many

ἔχετε   ἄρτους;   ὑπάγετε   ἴδετε.   καὶ   γνόντες
have ye loaves ?   Go   see.   And   knowing

λέγουσιν·   πέντε,   καὶ   δύο   ἰχθύας.   39 καὶ
they say: Five,   and   two   fishes.   And

ἐπέταξεν   αὐτοῖς   ἀνακλιθῆναι   πάντας   συμπόσια
he instructed them   to recline   all   companies

συμπόσια   ἐπὶ   τῷ   χλωρῷ   χόρτῳ.   40 καὶ
companies   on   the   green   grass.   And

ἀνέπεσαν   πρασιαὶ   πρασιαὶ   κατὰ   ἑκατὸν
they reclined groups   groups   by   a hundred

καὶ   κατὰ   πεντήκοντα.   41 καὶ   λαβὼν   τοὺς
and   by   fifty.   And   taking   the

πέντε   ἄρτους   καὶ   τοὺς   δύο   ἰχθύας,
five   loaves   and   the   two   fishes,

ἀναβλέψας   εἰς   τὸν   οὐρανὸν   εὐλόγησεν   καὶ
looking up   to   -   heaven   he blessed   and

κατέκλασεν   τοὺς   ἄρτους   καὶ   ἐδίδου   τοῖς
broke   the   loaves   and   gave   to the

μαθηταῖς   ἵνα   παρατιθῶσιν   αὐτοῖς,   καὶ
disciples   that   they might set before them,   and

τοὺς   δύο   ἰχθύας   ἐμέρισεν   πᾶσιν.   42 καὶ
the   two   fishes   he divided   to all.   And

ἔφαγον   πάντες   καὶ   ἐχορτάσθησαν,   43 καὶ
they ate   all   and   were satisfied,   And

ἦραν   κλάσματα   δώδεκα   κοφίνων   πληρώματα
they took fragments   twelve   ²of baskets   ¹fullnesses

καὶ   ἀπὸ   τῶν   ἰχθύων   44 καὶ   ἦσαν   οἱ
and   from   the   fishes.   And   were   the

φαγόντες   τοὺς   ἄρτους   πεντακισχίλιοι   ἄνδρες.
[ones] eating the   loaves   five thousand   males.

45 Καὶ   εὐθὺς   ἠνάγκασεν   τοὺς   μαθητὰς
    And   immediately he constrained the   disciples

αὐτοῦ   ἐμβῆναι   εἰς   τὸ   πλοῖον   καὶ   προάγειν
of him   to embark   in   the   ship   and   to go before

εἰς   τὸ   πέραν   πρὸς   Βηθσαϊδάν,   ἕως   αὐτὸς
to   the   other side to   Bethsaida,   until   he

ἀπολύει   τὸν   ὄχλον.   46 καὶ   ἀποταξάμενος
dismisses   the   crowd.   And   having said farewell

αὐτοῖς   ἀπῆλθεν   εἰς   τὸ   ὄρος   προσεύξασθαι.
to them   he went away to   the   mountain to pray.

47 καὶ   ὀψίας   γενομένης   ἦν   τὸ   πλοῖον   ἐν
    And   evening   coming onᵃ   was   the   ship   in
= when evening came on

μέσῳ   τῆς   θαλάσσης,   καὶ   αὐτὸς   μόνος   ἐπὶ
[the] midst of the sea,   and   he   alone   on

τῆς   γῆς.   48 καὶ   ἰδὼν   αὐτοὺς   βασανιζομένους
the   land.   And   seeing   them   being distressed

ἐν   τῷ   ἐλαύνειν,   ἦν   γὰρ   ὁ   ἄνεμος   ἐναντίος
in   the   to row,   ⁴was   ¹for   ²the   ³wind   contrary
= rowing,

αὐτοῖς,   περὶ   τετάρτην   φυλακὴν   τῆς   νυκτὸς
to them,   about   [the] fourth   watch   of the night

ἔρχεται   πρὸς   αὐτοὺς   περιπατῶν   ἐπὶ   τῆς
he comes   toward   them   walking   on   the

θαλάσσης·   καὶ   ἤθελεν   παρελθεῖν   αὐτούς.
sea;   and   wished   to go by   them.

49 οἱ   δὲ   ἰδόντες   αὐτὸν   ἐπὶ   τῆς   θαλάσσης
    But they   seeing   him   on   the   sea

περιπατοῦντα   ἔδοξαν   ὅτι   φάντασμά   ἐστιν,
walking   thought   that   a phantasm   it is(was),

would take eight months of a man's wagesʳ! Are we to go and spend that much on bread and give it to them to eat?"
38"How many loaves do you have?" he asked. "Go and see."
When they found out, they said, "Five—and two fish."
39Then Jesus directed them to have all the people sit down in groups on the green grass. 40So they sat down in groups of hundreds and fifties. 41Taking the five loaves and the two fish and looking up to heaven, he gave thanks and broke the loaves. Then he gave them to his disciples to set before the people. He also divided the two fish among them all. 42They all ate and were satisfied, 43and the disciples picked up twelve basketfuls of broken pieces of bread and fish. 44The number of the men who had eaten was five thousand.

Jesus Walks on the Water

45Immediately Jesus made his disciples get into the boat and go on ahead of him to Bethsaida, while he dismissed the crowd. 46After leaving them, he went up on a mountainside to pray.
47When evening came, the boat was in the middle of the lake, and he was alone on land. 48He saw the disciples straining at the oars, because the wind was against them. About the fourth watch of the night he went out to them, walking on the lake. He was about to pass by them, 49but when they saw him walking on the lake, they thought he was a ghost. They cried

ᶠThe denarius was equivalent to one day's wage

ʳ37 Greek *take two hundred denarii*

50for they all saw Him and were frightened. But immediately He spoke with them and *said to them, "Take courage; it is I, do not be afraid."

51And He got into the boat with them, and the wind stopped; and they were greatly astonished,

52for they had not gained any insight from the *incident of the loaves, but their heart was hardened.

Healing at Gennesaret

53And when they had crossed over they came to land at Gennesaret, and moored to the shore.

54And when they had come out of the boat, immediately *the people recognized Him,

55and ran about that whole country and began to carry about on their pallets those who were sick, to the place they heard He was.

56And wherever He entered villages, or cities, or countryside, they were laying the sick in the market places, and entreating Him that they might just touch the fringe of His cloak; and as many as touched it were being cured.

καὶ ἀνέκραξαν· 50 πάντες γὰρ αὐτὸν εἶδαν
and cried out;   for all   him   saw

καὶ ἐταράχθησαν. ὁ δὲ εὐθὺς ἐλάλησεν
and were troubled. But he immediately talked

μετ' αὐτῶν, καὶ λέγει αὐτοῖς· θαρσεῖτε,
with them, and says to them: Be of good cheer,

ἐγώ εἰμι· μὴ φοβεῖσθε. 51 καὶ ἀνέβη
I   am; be ye not afraid.   And he went up

πρὸς αὐτοὺς εἰς τὸ πλοῖον, καὶ ἐκόπασεν
to   them   into the ship,   and ceased

ὁ ἄνεμος· καὶ λίαν ἐκ περισσοῦ ἐν ἑαυτοῖς
the wind; and very much exceedingly in themselves

ἐξίσταντο· 52 οὐ γὰρ συνῆκαν ἐπὶ
they were astonished ; for they did not understand concerning

τοῖς ἄρτοις ἀλλ' ἦν αὐτῶν ἡ καρδία
the loaves, but was of them the heart

πεπωρωμένη. 53 Καὶ διαπεράσαντες ἐπὶ
having been hardened. And crossing over ᵇonto

τὴν γῆν ἦλθον εἰς Γεννησαρὲτ καὶ
ᵃthe ⁴land ¹they came to Gennesaret   and

προσωρμίσθησαν. 54 καὶ ἐξελθόντων αὐτῶν
anchored.   And coming out   themᵃ
                       = as they came

ἐκ τοῦ πλοίου εὐθὺς ἐπιγνόντες αὐτὸν
out of the ship   immediately knowing   him

55 περιέδραμον ὅλην τὴν χώραν ἐκείνην
they ran round all -   country   that

καὶ ἤρξαντο ἐπὶ τοῖς κραβάτοις τοὺς
and began on the pallets   the [ones]
                                 = those

κακῶς ἔχοντας περιφέρειν, ὅπου ἤκουον
ill   having   to carry round, where they heard
who were ill

ὅτι ἐστίν. 56 καὶ ὅπου ἂν εἰσεπορεύετο
that he is(was). And wherever   he entered

εἰς κώμας ἢ εἰς πόλεις ἢ εἰς ἀγρούς,
into villages or into cities or into country,

ἐν ταῖς ἀγοραῖς ἐτίθεσαν τοὺς ἀσθενοῦντας,
in the marketplaces they put the ailing [ones],

καὶ παρεκάλουν αὐτὸν ἵνα κἂν τοῦ
and besought   him   that if even the

κρασπέδου τοῦ ἱματίου αὐτοῦ ἅψωνται·
fringe   of the garment of him they might touch;

καὶ ὅσοι ἂν ἥψαντο αὐτοῦ ἐσῴζοντο.
and as many as touched him   were healed.

---

out, 50because they all saw him and were terrified. Immediately he spoke to them and said, "Take courage! It is I. Don't be afraid." 51Then he climbed into the boat with them, and the wind died down. They were completely amazed, 52for they had not understood about the loaves; their hearts were hardened.

53When they had crossed over, they landed at Gennesaret and anchored there. 54As soon as they got out of the boat, people recognized Jesus. 55They ran throughout that whole region and carried the sick on mats to wherever they heard he was. 56And wherever he went—into villages, towns or countryside—they placed the sick in the marketplaces. They begged him to let them touch even the edge of his cloak, and all who touched him were healed.

Followers of Tradition

AND the Pharisees and some of the scribes gathered together around Him when they had come from Jerusalem,

2and had seen that some of His disciples were eating their bread with impure hands, that is, unwashed.

3(For the Pharisees and all the Jews do not eat unless they carefully wash their hands, *thus* observing the traditions of the elders;

4and *when they come* from the market place, they do not eat unless they cleanse themselves; and

---

7 Καὶ συνάγονται πρὸς αὐτὸν οἱ Φαρισαῖοι
And assemble   to   him   the Pharisees

καί τινες τῶν γραμματέων ἐλθόντες ἀπὸ
and some of the scribes   coming   from

Ἰεροσολύμων. 2 καὶ ἰδόντες τινὰς τῶν
Jerusalem.   And seeing   some of the

μαθητῶν αὐτοῦ ὅτι κοιναῖς χερσίν, τοῦτ'
disciples of him that with unclean hands, this

ἔστιν ἀνίπτοις, ἐσθίουσιν τοὺς ἄρτους,
is   unwashed, they eat   the   bread,

3 — οἱ γὰρ Φαρισαῖοι καὶ πάντες οἱ
— for the Pharisees   and all   the

Ἰουδαῖοι ἐὰν μὴ πυγμῇ νίψωνται τὰς
Jews   unless with [the] fist they wash the
                   = ? carefully

χεῖρας οὐκ ἐσθίουσιν, κρατοῦντες τὴν
hands   eat not,   holding   the

παράδοσιν τῶν πρεσβυτέρων, 4 καὶ ἀπ'
tradition of the elders,   and from

ἀγορᾶς ἐὰν μὴ ῥαντίσωνται οὐκ ἐσθίουσιν, καὶ
marketplaces unless they sprinkle they eat not, and

Clean and Unclean

THE Pharisees and some of the teachers of the law who had come from Jerusalem gathered around Jesus and 2saw some of his disciples eating food with hands that were "unclean," that is, unwashed. 3(The Pharisees and all the Jews do not eat unless they give their hands a ceremonial washing, holding to the tradition of the elders. 4When they come from the marketplace they do not eat unless they wash. And there are many other things which they have received in order to observe, such as the washing of cups and pitchers and copper pots.)

5And the Pharisees and the scribes *asked Him, "Why do Your disciples not walk according to the tradition of the elders, but eat their bread with impure hands?"

6And He said to them, "Rightly did Isaiah prophesy of you hypocrites, as it is written,

'THIS PEOPLE HONORS ME WITH THEIR LIPS, BUT THEIR HEART IS FAR AWAY FROM ME.
7 'BUT IN VAIN DO THEY WORSHIP ME, TEACHING AS DOCTRINES THE PRECEPTS OF MEN.'

8"Neglecting the commandment of God, you hold to the tradition of men."

9He was also saying to them, "You nicely set aside the commandment of God in order to keep your tradition.

10"For Moses said, 'HONOR YOUR FATHER AND YOUR MOTHER'; and, 'HE WHO SPEAKS EVIL OF FATHER OR MOTHER, LET HIM BE PUT TO DEATH';

11but you say, 'If a man says to his father or his mother, anything of mine you might have been helped by is Corban (that is to say, ²given to God),'

12you no longer permit him to do anything for his father or his mother;

13thus invalidating the word of God by your tradition which you have handed down; and you do many things such as that."

The Heart of Man

14And after He called the multitude to Him again, He began saying to them, "Listen to Me, all of you, and understand.

15there is nothing outside the man which going into him can defile him; but the things which proceed out of

¹ Or, a gift, an offering

ἄλλα πολλά ἐστιν ἃ παρέλαβον κρατεῖν,
other things many there are which they received to hold,

βαπτισμοὺς ποτηρίων καὶ ξεστῶν καὶ
washings of cups and of utensils and

χαλκίων, — 5 καὶ ἐπερωτῶσιν αὐτὸν οἱ
of bronze vessels, — and questioned him the

Φαρισαῖοι καὶ οἱ γραμματεῖς· διὰ τί
Pharisees and the scribes: Why

οὐ περιπατοῦσιν οἱ μαθηταί σου κατὰ τὴν
walk not the disciples of thee according to the

παράδοσιν τῶν πρεσβυτέρων, ἀλλὰ κοιναῖς
tradition of the elders, but with unclean

χερσὶν ἐσθίουσιν τὸν ἄρτον; 6 ὁ δὲ εἶπεν
hands eat the bread? And he said

αὐτοῖς· καλῶς ἐπροφήτευσεν Ἡσαΐας περὶ
to them: Well prophesied Esaias concerning

ὑμῶν τῶν ὑποκριτῶν, ὡς γέγραπται ὅτι
you the hypocrites, as it has been written[:] –

οὗτος ὁ λαὸς τοῖς χείλεσίν με τιμᾷ,
This – people with the lips me honours,

ἡ δὲ καρδία αὐτῶν πόρρω ἀπέχει ἀπ'
but the heart of them ²far ¹is ³away from

ἐμοῦ· 7 μάτην δὲ σέβονταί με, διδάσκοντες
me; and in vain they worship me, teaching

διδασκαλίας ἐντάλματα ἀνθρώπων. 8 ἀφέντες
teachings [which are] commands of men. Leaving

τὴν ἐντολὴν τοῦ θεοῦ κρατεῖτε τὴν
the commandment – of God ye hold the

παράδοσιν τῶν ἀνθρώπων. 9 καὶ ἔλεγεν
tradition – of men. And he said

αὐτοῖς· καλῶς ἀθετεῖτε τὴν ἐντολὴν τοῦ
to them: Well ye set aside the commandment –

θεοῦ, ἵνα τὴν παράδοσιν ὑμῶν τηρήσητε.
of God, that the tradition of you ye may keep.

10 Μωϋσῆς γὰρ εἶπεν· τίμα τὸν πατέρα σου
For Moses said: Honour the father of thee

καὶ τὴν μητέρα σου, καί· ὁ κακολογῶν
and the mother of thee, and: The [one] speaking evil of

πατέρα ἢ μητέρα θανάτῳ τελευτάτω. 11 ὑμεῖς
father or mother by death let him end(die). ye

δὲ λέγετε· ἐὰν εἴπῃ ἄνθρωπος τῷ πατρὶ
But say: If says a man to the(his) father

ἢ τῇ μητρί· κορβᾶν, ὅ ἐστιν δῶρον,
or to the mother: Korban, which is a gift,

ὃ ἐὰν ἐξ ἐμοῦ ὠφεληθῇς, 12 οὐκέτι ἀφίετε
whatever by me thou mightest profit, no longer ye allow

αὐτὸν οὐδὲν ποιῆσαι τῷ πατρὶ ἢ τῇ
him no(any)thing to do for the father or the

μητρί, 13 ἀκυροῦντες τὸν λόγον τοῦ θεοῦ
mother, annulling the word – of God

τῇ παραδόσει ὑμῶν ᾗ παρεδώκατε· καὶ
by the tradition of you which ye received; and

παρόμοια τοιαῦτα πολλὰ ποιεῖτε. 14 Καὶ
²similar things ²such ¹many ye do. And

προσκαλεσάμενος πάλιν τὸν ὄχλον ἔλεγεν
calling to [him] again the crowd he said

αὐτοῖς· ἀκούσατέ μου πάντες καὶ σύνετε.
to them: Hear ye me all and understand.

15 οὐδέν ἐστιν ἔξωθεν τοῦ ἀνθρώπου
Nothing there is from without – a man

εἰσπορευόμενον εἰς αὐτὸν ὃ δύναται κοινῶσαι
entering into him which can to defile

αὐτόν· ἀλλὰ τὰ ἐκ τοῦ ἀνθρώπου ἐκπο-
him; but the things out of – a man coming

---

they observe many other traditions, such as the washing of cups, pitchers and kettles. ⁵)

5So the Pharisees and teachers of the law asked Jesus, "Why don't your disciples live according to the tradition of the elders instead of eating their food with 'unclean' hands?"

6He replied, "Isaiah was right when he prophesied about you hypocrites; as it is written:

" 'These people honor me with their lips, but their hearts are far from me.
7They worship me in vain; their teachings are but rules taught by men.' ₜ

8You have let go of the commands of God and are holding on to the traditions of men."

9And he said to them: "You have a fine way of setting aside the commands of God in order to observe ᵘ your own traditions! 10For Moses said, 'Honor your father and your mother,' ᵛ and, 'Anyone who curses his father or mother must be put to death.' ʷ 11But you say that if a man says to his father or mother: 'Whatever help you might otherwise have received from me is Corban' (that is, a gift devoted to God), 12then you no longer let him do anything for his father or mother. 13Thus you nullify the word of God by your tradition that you have handed down. And you do many things like that."

14Again Jesus called the crowd to him and said, "Listen to me, everyone, and understand this. 15Nothing outside a man can make him 'unclean' by going into him. Rather, it is what comes out of a man

ₛ4 Some early manuscripts
pitchers, kettles and dining couches
ₜ6,7 Isaiah 29:13
ᵘ9 Some manuscripts set up
ᵛ10 Exodus 20:12; Deut. 5:16
ʷ10 Exodus 21:17; Lev. 20:9

the man are what defile the man.

16[‟*If any man has ears to hear, let him hear."]

17And when leaving the multitude, He had entered the house, His disciples questioned Him about the parable.

18And He *said to them, "Are you so lacking in understanding also? Do you not understand that whatever goes into the man from outside cannot defile him;

19because it does not go into his heart, but into his stomach, and is eliminated?" (Thus He declared all foods clean.)

20And He was saying, "That which proceeds out of the man, that is what defiles the man.

21"For from within, out of the heart of men, proceed the evil thoughts, fornications, thefts, murders, adulteries,

22deeds of coveting and wickedness, as well as deceit, sensuality, envy, slander, pride and foolishness.

23"All these evil things proceed from within and defile the man."

The Syrophoenician Woman

24And from there He arose and went away to the region of Tyre*. And when He had entered a house, He wanted no one to know *of it;* yet He could not escape notice.

25But after hearing of Him, a woman whose little daughter had an unclean spirit, immediately came and fell at His feet.

26Now the woman was a *Gentile, of the Syrophoenician race. And she kept asking Him to cast the demon out of her daughter.

27And He was saying to her, "Let the children be satisfied first, for it is not good to take the children's bread and throw it to the dogs."

*Many mss. do not contain this verse
*Some early mss. add: *and Sidon*
*Lit., *Greek*

ρευόμενά ἐστιν τὰ κοινοῦντα τὸν ἄνθρωπον. ‡
forth   are the [ones] defiling   -   a man.

17 Καὶ ὅτε εἰσῆλθεν εἰς οἶκον ἀπὸ τοῦ
And when he entered into a house from the

ὄχλου, ἐπηρώτων αὐτὸν οἱ μαθηταὶ αὐτοῦ
crowd, questioned him the disciples of him

τὴν παραβολήν. 18 καὶ λέγει αὐτοῖς·
the parable.   And he says to them:

οὕτως καὶ ὑμεῖς ἀσύνετοί ἐστε; οὐ
Thus also ye undiscerning are? do ye not

νοεῖτε ὅτι πᾶν τὸ ἔξωθεν εἰσπορευόμενον
understand that everything from without entering

εἰς τὸν ἄνθρωπον οὐ δύναται αὐτὸν
into a man cannot him

κοινῶσαι, 19 ὅτι οὐκ εἰσπορεύεται αὐτοῦ
to defile, because it enters not of him

εἰς τὴν καρδίαν ἀλλ' εἰς τὴν κοιλίαν,
into the heart but into the belly,

καὶ εἰς τὸν ἀφεδρῶνα ἐκπορεύεται, καθα-
and into the drain goes out, purg-

ρίζων πάντα τὰ βρώματα; 20 ἔλεγεν δὲ
ing all - foods? And he said[,]

ὅτι τὸ ἐκ τοῦ ἀνθρώπου ἐκπορευόμενον,
- The thing out of - a man coming forth,

ἐκεῖνο κοινοῖ τὸν ἄνθρωπον. 21 ἔσωθεν
that defiles - a man. from within

γὰρ ἐκ τῆς καρδίας τῶν ἀνθρώπων
For out of the heart of men

οἱ διαλογισμοὶ οἱ κακοὶ ἐκπορεύονται,
- thoughts evil come forth,

πορνεῖαι, κλοπαί, φόνοι, 22 μοιχεῖαι,
fornications, thefts, murders, adulteries,

πλεονεξίαι, πονηρίαι, δόλος, ἀσέλγεια, ὀφθαλμὸς
greedinesses, iniquities, deceit, lewdness, eye

πονηρός, βλασφημία, ὑπερηφανία, ἀφροσύνη·
an evil, blasphemy, arrogance, foolishness;

23 πάντα ταῦτα τὰ πονηρὰ ἔσωθεν ἐκπορεύεται
all these - evil things from within comes forth

καὶ κοινοῖ τὸν ἄνθρωπον.
and defile - a man.

24 Ἐκεῖθεν δὲ ἀναστὰς ἀπῆλθεν εἰς τὰ ὅρια
And thence rising up he went away into the district

Τύρου. Καὶ εἰσελθὼν εἰς οἰκίαν οὐδένα ἤθελεν
of Tyre. And entering into a house no one he wished

γνῶναι, καὶ οὐκ ἠδυνάσθη λαθεῖν· 25 ἀλλ'
to know, and could not *to* be hidden; but

εὐθὺς ἀκούσασα γυνὴ περὶ αὐτοῦ, ἧς
immediately *hearing ¹a woman about him, of whom
= whose

εἶχεν τὸ θυγάτριον αὐτῆς πνεῦμα ἀκάθαρτον,
had the daughter of her spirit an unclean,
daughter had

ἐλθοῦσα προσέπεσεν πρὸς τοὺς πόδας αὐτοῦ·
coming fell at the feet of him;

26 ἡ δὲ γυνὴ ἦν Ἑλληνίς, Συροφοινίκισσα
and the woman was a Greek, a Syrophenician

τῷ γένει· καὶ ἠρώτα αὐτὸν ἵνα τὸ
- by race; and she asked him that the

δαιμόνιον ἐκβάλῃ ἐκ τῆς θυγατρὸς αὐτῆς.
demon he would expel out of the daughter of her.

27 καὶ ἔλεγεν αὐτῇ· ἄφες πρῶτον
And he said to her: Permit first

χορτασθῆναι τὰ τέκνα· οὐ γάρ ἐστιν καλὸν
to be satisfied the children; for it is not good

λαβεῖν τὸν ἄρτον τῶν τέκνων καὶ τοῖς
to take the bread of the children and to the

‡ Verse 16 omitted by Nestle; *cf.* NIV footnote.

---

that makes him 'unclean.'*

17After he had left the crowd and entered the house, his disciples asked him about this parable.
18"Are you so dull?" he asked. "Don't you see that nothing that enters a man from the outside can make him 'unclean'? 19For it doesn't go into his heart but into his stomach, and then out of his body." (In saying this, Jesus declared all foods "clean.")

20He went on: "What comes out of a man is what makes him 'unclean.' 21For from within, out of men's hearts, come evil thoughts, sexual immorality, theft, murder, adultery, 22greed, malice, deceit, lewdness, envy, slander, arrogance and folly. 23All these evils come from inside and make a man 'unclean.'"

The Faith of a Syrophoenician Woman

24Jesus left that place and went to the vicinity of Tyre.y He entered a house and did not want anyone to know it; yet he could not keep his presence secret. 25In fact, as soon as she heard about him, a woman whose little daughter was possessed by an evil² spirit came and fell at his feet. 26The woman was a Greek, born in Syrian Phoenicia. She begged Jesus to drive the demon out of her daughter.

27"First let the children eat all they want," he told her, "for it is not right to take the children's bread and toss it to their dogs."

*15 Some early manuscripts 'unclean.' *16If anyone has ears to hear, let him hear.
y24 Many early manuscripts Tyre and Sidon
z25 Greek unclean

28But she answered and *said to Him, "Yes, Lord, *but* even the dogs under the table feed on the children's crumbs."

29And He said to her, "Because of this answer go your way; the demon has gone out of your daughter."

30And going back to her home, she found the child lying on the bed, the demon having departed.

31And again He went out from the region of Tyre, and came through Sidon to the Sea of Galilee, within the region of Decapolis.

32And they *brought to Him one who was deaf and spoke with difficulty, and they *entreated Him to lay His hand upon him.

33And He took him aside from the multitude by himself, and put His fingers into his ears, and after spitting, He touched his tongue *with the saliva;*

34and looking up to heaven with a deep sigh, He *said to him, "Ephphatha!" that is, "Be opened!"

35And his ears were opened, and the impediment of his tongue was removed, and he *began speaking plainly.

36And He gave them orders not to tell anyone; but the more He ordered them, the more widely they continued to proclaim it.

37And they were utterly astonished, saying, "He has done all things well; He makes even the deaf to hear, and the dumb to speak."

Chapter 8

Four Thousand Fed

IN those days again, when there was a great multitude and they had nothing to eat, He called His disciples and *said to them,

---

κυναρίοις βαλεῖν. **28** ἡ δὲ ἀπεκρίθη καὶ
dogs to throw [it]. And she answered and

λέγει αὐτῷ· ναί, κύριε· καὶ τὰ κυνάρια
says to him: Yes, Lord; and yet the dogs

ὑποκάτω τῆς τραπέζης ἐσθίουσιν ἀπὸ τῶν
under the table eat from the

ψιχίων τῶν παιδίων. **29** καὶ εἶπεν αὐτῇ·
crumbs of the children. And he said to her:

διὰ τοῦτον τὸν λόγον ὕπαγε, ἐξελήλυθεν
Because of this - word go, has gone forth

ἐκ τῆς θυγατρός σου τὸ δαιμόνιον. **30** καὶ
out of the daughter of thee the demon. And

ἀπελθοῦσα εἰς τὸν οἶκον αὐτῆς εὗρεν τὸ
going away to the house of her she found the

παιδίον βεβλημένον ἐπὶ τὴν κλίνην καὶ τὸ
child having been laid on the couch and the

δαιμόνιον ἐξεληλυθός. **31** Καὶ πάλιν ἐξελθὼν
demon having gone forth. And again going forth

ἐκ τῶν ὁρίων Τύρου ἦλθεν διὰ Σιδῶνος
out of the district of Tyre he came through Sidon

εἰς τὴν θάλασσαν τῆς Γαλιλαίας ἀνὰ
to the sea - of Galilee in the

μέσον τῶν ὁρίων Δεκαπόλεως. **32** Καὶ
midst of the district of Decapolis. And

φέρουσιν αὐτῷ κωφὸν καὶ μογιλάλον, καὶ
they bring to him a man deaf and speaking with difficulty, and

παρακαλοῦσιν αὐτὸν ἵνα ἐπιθῇ αὐτῷ τὴν
they beseech him that he would put on on him the(his)

χεῖρα. **33** καὶ ἀπολαβόμενος αὐτὸν ἀπὸ
hand. And taking away him from

τοῦ ὄχλου κατ᾽ ἰδίαν ἔβαλεν τοὺς δακτύλους
the crowd privately he put the fingers

αὐτοῦ εἰς τὰ ὦτα αὐτοῦ καὶ πτύσας
of him into the ears of him and spitting

ἥψατο τῆς γλώσσης αὐτοῦ, **34** καὶ
he touched the tongue of him, and

ἀναβλέψας εἰς τὸν οὐρανὸν ἐστέναξεν,
looking up to - heaven he groaned,

καὶ λέγει αὐτῷ· ἐφφαθά, ὅ ἐστιν διανοίχθητι.
and says to him: Ephphatha, which is Be thou opened.

35 καὶ ἠνοίγησαν αὐτοῦ αἱ ἀκοαί, καὶ
And were opened of him the ears, and

εὐθὺς ἐλύθη ὁ δεσμὸς τῆς γλώσσης αὐτοῦ,
immediately was loosened the bond of the tongue of him,

καὶ ἐλάλει ὀρθῶς. **36** καὶ διεστείλατο
and he spoke correctly. And he ordered

αὐτοῖς ἵνα μηδενὶ λέγωσιν· ὅσον δὲ
them that no one they should tell; but as much as

αὐτοῖς διεστέλλετο, αὐτοὶ μᾶλλον περισσότερον
them he ordered, they more exceedingly

ἐκήρυσσον. **37** καὶ ὑπερπερισσῶς ἐξεπλήσσοντο
proclaimed. And most exceedingly they were astounded

λέγοντες· καλῶς πάντα πεποίηκεν, καὶ
saying: Well all things he has done, both

τοὺς κωφοὺς ποιεῖ ἀκούειν καὶ ἀλάλους
the deaf he makes to hear and dumb

λαλεῖν.
to speak.

8 Ἐν ἐκείναις ταῖς ἡμέραις πάλιν πολλοῦ
In those - days again a much(great)
= there being

ὄχλου ὄντος καὶ μὴ ἐχόντων τί φάγωσιν,
crowd being* and not having* anything they might eat,
a great crowd

προσκαλεσάμενος τοὺς μαθητὰς λέγει αὐτοῖς·
calling to [him] the disciples he says to them:

28"Yes, Lord," she replied, "but even the dogs under the table eat the children's crumbs."

29Then he told her, "For such a reply, you may go; the demon has left your daughter."

30She went home and found her child lying on the bed, and the demon gone.

The Healing of a Deaf and Mute Man

31Then Jesus left the vicinity of Tyre and went through Sidon, down to the Sea of Galilee and into the region of the Decapolis.[a] 32There some people brought to him a man who was deaf and could hardly talk, and they begged him to place his hand on the man.

33After he took him aside, away from the crowd, Jesus put his fingers into the man's ears. Then he spit and touched the man's tongue. 34He looked up to heaven and with a deep sigh said to him, *"Ephphatha!"* (which means, "Be opened!"). 35At this, the man's ears were opened, his tongue was loosened and he began to speak plainly.

36Jesus commanded them not to tell anyone. But the more he did so, the more they kept talking about it. 37People were overwhelmed with amazement. "He has done everything well," they said. "He even makes the deaf hear and the mute speak."

Chapter 8

Jesus Feeds the Four Thousand

DURING those days another large crowd gathered. Since they had nothing to eat, Jesus called his disciples to him and

a31 That is, the Ten Cities

2"I feel compassion for the multitude because they have remained with Me now three days, and have nothing to eat;

3and if I send them away hungry to their home, they will faint on the way; and some of them have come from a distance."

4And His disciples answered Him, "Where will anyone be able to *find enough to* satisfy these men with bread here in a desolate place?"

5And He was asking them, "How many loaves do you have?" And they said, "Seven."

6And He *directed the multitude to sit down on the ground; and taking the seven loaves, He gave thanks and broke them, and started giving them to His disciples to serve to them, and they served them to the multitude.

7They also had a few small fish; and after He had blessed them, He ordered these to be served as well.

8And they ate and were satisfied; and they picked up seven large baskets full of what was left over of the broken pieces.

9And about four thousand were *there;* and He sent them away.

10And immediately He entered the boat with His disciples, and came to the district of Dalmanutha.

11And the Pharisees came out and began to argue with Him, seeking from Him a sign from heaven, to test Him.

12And sighing deeply in His spirit, He *said, "Why does this generation seek for a sign? Truly I say to you, no sign shall be given to this generation."

13And leaving them, He again embarked and went away to the other side.

14And they had forgotten to take bread; and did not have more than one loaf in the boat with them.

15And He was giving or-

---

2 σπλαγχνίζομαι ἐπὶ τὸν ὄχλον, ὅτι ἤδη
I have compassion on the crowd, because now

ἡμέραι τρεῖς προσμένουσίν μοι καὶ οὐκ
days three they remain with me and not

ἔχουσιν τί φάγωσιν· **3** καὶ ἐὰν ἀπολύσω
they have anything they may eat; and if I dismiss

αὐτοὺς νήστεις εἰς οἶκον αὐτῶν, ἐκλυθήσονται
them fasting to house of them, they will faint

ἐν τῇ ὁδῷ· καί τινες αὐτῶν ἀπὸ μακρόθεν
in the way; and some of them from afar

εἰσίν. **4** καὶ ἀπεκρίθησαν αὐτῷ οἱ μαθηταὶ
are. And answered him the disciples

αὐτοῦ ὅτι πόθεν τούτους δυνήσεταί τις
of him[,] — ¹Whence ²these people ²will ⁴be able ³anyone

ὧδε χορτάσαι ἄρτων ἐπ᾽ ἐρημίας; **5** καὶ
⁵here ⁶to satisfy ⁷of(with) loaves ⁸on(in) ⁹a desert ? And

ἠρώτα αὐτούς· πόσους ἔχετε ἄρτους;
he asked them: How many have ye loaves ?

οἱ δὲ εἶπαν· ἑπτά. **6** καὶ παραγγέλλει τῷ
And they said: Seven. And he commands the

ὄχλῳ ἀναπεσεῖν ἐπὶ τῆς γῆς· καὶ λαβὼν
crowd to recline on the ground; and taking

τοὺς ἑπτὰ ἄρτους εὐχαριστήσας ἔκλασεν
the seven loaves giving thanks he broke

καὶ ἐδίδου τοῖς μαθηταῖς αὐτοῦ ἵνα
and gave to the disciples of him that

παρατιθῶσιν, καὶ παρέθηκαν τῷ ὄχλῳ.
they might serve, and they served the crowd.

7 καὶ εἶχον ἰχθύδια ὀλίγα· καὶ εὐλογήσας
And they had fishes a few; and blessing

αὐτὰ εἶπεν καὶ ταῦτα παρατιθέναι. **8** καὶ
them he told also these to be served. And

ἔφαγον καὶ ἐχορτάσθησαν, καὶ ἦραν
they ate and were satisfied, and took

περισσεύματα κλασμάτων, ἑπτὰ σπυρίδας.
excesses of fragments, seven baskets.

9 ἦσαν δὲ ὡς τετρακισχίλιοι. καὶ ἀπέλυσεν
Now they were about four thousand. And he dismissed

αὐτούς. **10** Καὶ εὐθὺς ἐμβὰς εἰς τὸ
them. And immediately embarking in the

πλοῖον μετὰ τῶν μαθητῶν αὐτοῦ
ship with the disciples of him

ἦλθεν εἰς τὰ μέρη Δαλμανουθά.
he came into the region of Dalmanutha.

11 Καὶ ἐξῆλθον οἱ Φαρισαῖοι καὶ ἤρξαντο
And came forth the Pharisees and began

συζητεῖν αὐτῷ, ζητοῦντες παρ᾽ αὐτοῦ
to debate with him, seeking from him

σημεῖον ἀπὸ τοῦ οὐρανοῦ, πειράζοντες
a sign from — heaven, tempting

αὐτόν. **12** καὶ ἀναστενάξας τῷ πνεύματι
him. And groaning in the spirit

αὐτοῦ λέγει· τί ἡ γενεὰ αὕτη ζητεῖ
of him he says: Why — ²generation ³this ¹does ⁵seek

σημεῖον; ἀμὴν λέγω ὑμῖν, εἰ δοθήσεται
a sign ? Truly I tell you, if will be given

τῇ γενεᾷ ταύτῃ σημεῖον. **13** καὶ ἀφεὶς
— generation to this a sign. And leaving

αὐτοὺς πάλιν ἐμβὰς ἀπῆλθεν εἰς τὸ
them again embarking he went away to the

πέραν. **14** Καὶ ἐπελάθοντο λαβεῖν ἄρτους,
other side. And they forgot to take loaves,

καὶ εἰ μὴ ἕνα ἄρτον οὐκ εἶχον μεθ᾽
and except one loaf they had not with

ἑαυτῶν ἐν τῷ πλοίῳ. **15** καὶ διεστέλλετο
themselves in the ship. And he charged

---

said, 2"I have compassion for these people; they have already been with me three days and have nothing to eat. 3If I send them home hungry, they will collapse on the way, because some of them have come a long distance."

4His disciples answered, "But where in this remote place can anyone get enough bread to feed them?"

5"How many loaves do you have?" Jesus asked.

"Seven," they replied.

6He told the crowd to sit down on the ground. When he had taken the seven loaves and given thanks, he broke them and gave them to his disciples to set before the people, and they did so. 7They had a few small fish as well; he gave thanks for them also and told the disciples to distribute them. 8The people ate and were satisfied. Afterward the disciples picked up seven basketfuls of broken pieces that were left over. 9About four thousand men were present. And having sent them away, 10he got into the boat with his disciples and went to the region of Dalmanutha.

11The Pharisees came and began to question Jesus. To test him, they asked him for a sign from heaven. 12He sighed deeply and said, "Why does this generation ask for a miraculous sign? I tell you the truth, no sign will be given to it." 13Then he left them, got back into the boat and crossed to the other side.

The Yeast of the Pharisees and Herod

14The disciples had forgotten to bring bread, except for one loaf they had with them in the boat. 15"Be careful," Jesus ders to them, saying, "Watch out! Beware of the leaven of the Pharisees and the leaven of Herod."

16And they *began* to discuss with one another *the fact* that they had no bread.

17And Jesus, aware of this, *said to them, "Why do you discuss *the fact* that you have no bread? Do you not yet see or understand? Do you have a hardened heart?

18"HAVING EYES, DO YOU NOT SEE? AND HAVING EARS, DO YOU NOT HEAR? And do you not remember,

19when I broke the five loaves for the five thousand, how many baskets full of broken pieces you picked up?" They *said to Him, "Twelve."

20"And when *I broke* the seven for the four thousand, how many large baskets full of broken pieces did you pick up?" And they *said to Him, "Seven."

21And He was saying to them, "Do you not yet understand?"

22And they *came to Bethsaida. And they *brought a blind man to Him, and *entreated Him to touch him.

23And taking the blind man by the hand, He brought him out of the village; and after spitting on his eyes, and laying His hands upon him, He asked him, "Do you see anything?"

24And he looked up and said, "I see men, for I am seeing *them* like trees, walking about."

25Then again He laid His hands upon his eyes; and he looked intently and was restored, and *began* to see everything clearly.

26And He sent him to his home, saying, "Do not even enter the village."

Peter's Confession of Christ

27And Jesus went out, along with His disciples, to the villages of Caesarea

---

αὐτοῖς λέγων· ὁρᾶτε, βλέπετε ἀπὸ τῆς
them saying: See, look ye from the
=Beware of

ζύμης τῶν Φαρισαίων καὶ τῆς ζύμης
leaven of the Pharisees and of the leaven

Ἡρῴδου. 16 καὶ διελογίζοντο πρὸς ἀλλήλους
of Herod. And they reasoned with one another

ὅτι ἄρτους οὐκ ἔχουσιν. 17 καὶ γνοὺς
because loaves they have(had) not. And knowing

λέγει αὐτοῖς· τί διαλογίζεσθε ὅτι ἄρτους
he says to them: Why reason ye because loaves

οὐκ ἔχετε; οὔπω νοεῖτε οὐδὲ συνίετε;
ye have not? not yet understand ye nor realize?

πεπωρωμένην ἔχετε τὴν καρδίαν ὑμῶν;
having been hardened have ye the heart of you?

18 ὀφθαλμοὺς ἔχοντες οὐ βλέπετε, καὶ
eyes having see ye not, and

ὦτα ἔχοντες οὐκ ἀκούετε; καὶ
ears having hear ye not? and

οὐ μνημονεύετε, 19 ὅτε τοὺς πέντε ἄρτους
do ye not remember, when the five loaves

ἔκλασα εἰς τοὺς πεντακισχιλίους, πόσους
I broke to the five thousand, how many

κοφίνους κλασμάτων πλήρεις ἤρατε; λέγουσιν
baskets of fragments full ye took? They say

αὐτῷ· δώδεκα. 20 ὅτε τοὺς ἑπτὰ εἰς
to him: Twelve. When the seven to

τοὺς τετρακισχιλίους, πόσων σπυρίδων
the four thousand, ²of how many ³baskets

πληρώματα κλασμάτων ἤρατε; καὶ λέγουσιν·
¹fullnesses ⁴of fragments ye took? And they say:

ἑπτά. 21 καὶ ἔλεγεν αὐτοῖς· οὔπω συνίετε;
Seven. And he said to them: Not yet do ye realize?

22 Καὶ ἔρχονται εἰς Βηθσαϊδάν. Καὶ
And they come to Bethsaida. And

φέρουσιν αὐτῷ τυφλόν, καὶ παρακαλοῦσιν
they bring to him a blind man, and beseech

αὐτὸν ἵνα αὐτοῦ ἅψηται. 23 καὶ ἐπιλαβόμενος
him that him he would touch. And laying hold of

τῆς χειρὸς τοῦ τυφλοῦ ἐξήνεγκεν αὐτὸν
the hand of the blind man he led forth him

ἔξω τῆς κώμης, καὶ πτύσας εἰς τὰ
outside the village, and spitting in the

ὄμματα αὐτοῦ, ἐπιθεὶς τὰς χεῖρας αὐτῷ,
eyes of him, putting on the hands on him,

ἐπηρώτα αὐτόν· εἴ τι βλέπεις; 24 καὶ
questioned him: If anything thou seest? And

ἀναβλέψας ἔλεγεν· βλέπω τοὺς ἀνθρώπους,
looking up he said: I see - men,

ὅτι ὡς δένδρα ὁρῶ περιπατοῦντας.
that as trees I behold walking.

25 εἶτα πάλιν ἐπέθηκεν τὰς χεῖρας ἐπὶ
Then again he put on the hands on

τοὺς ὀφθαλμοὺς αὐτοῦ, καὶ διέβλεψεν καὶ
the eyes of him, and he looked steadily and

ἀπεκατέστη, καὶ ἐνέβλεπεν τηλαυγῶς ἅπαντα.
was restored, and saw clearly all things.

26 καὶ ἀπέστειλεν αὐτὸν εἰς οἶκον αὐτοῦ
And he sent him to house of him

λέγων· μηδὲ εἰς τὴν κώμην εἰσέλθῃς.
saying: Not into the village thou mayest enter.

27 Καὶ ἐξῆλθεν ὁ Ἰησοῦς καὶ οἱ μαθηταὶ
And went forth - Jesus and the disciples

αὐτοῦ εἰς τὰς κώμας Καισαρείας τῆς
of him to the villages of Cæsarea -

---

warned them. "Watch out for the yeast of the Pharisees and that of Herod."

16They discussed this with one another and said, "It is because we have no bread."

17Aware of their discussion, Jesus asked them: "Why are you talking about having no bread? Do you still not see or understand? Are your hearts hardened? 18Do you have eyes but fail to see, and ears but fail to hear? And don't you remember? 19When I broke the five loaves for the five thousand, how many basketfuls of pieces did you pick up?"

"Twelve," they replied.

20"And when I broke the seven loaves for the four thousand, how many basketfuls of pieces did you pick up?"

They answered, "Seven."

21He said to them, "Do you still not understand?"

The Healing of a Blind Man at Bethsaida

22They came to Bethsaida, and some people brought a blind man and begged Jesus to touch him. 23He took the blind man by the hand and led him outside the village. When he had spit on the man's eyes and put his hands on him, Jesus asked, "Do you see anything?"

24He looked up and said, "I see people; they look like trees walking around."

25Once more Jesus put his hands on the man's eyes. Then his eyes were opened, his sight was restored, and he saw everything clearly. 26Jesus sent him home, saying, "Don't go into the village.b"

Peter's Confession of Christ

27Jesus and his disciples went on to the villages around Caesarea Philippi.

b26 Some manuscripts *Don't go and tell anyone in the village*

Philippi; and on the way He questioned His disciples, saying to them, "Who do people say that I am?" 28And they told Him, saying, "John the Baptist; and others say Elijah; but others, one of the prophets." 29And He continued by questioning them, "But who do you say that I am?" Peter *answered and *said to Him, "Thou art the Christ." 30And He warned them to tell no one about Him.

31And He began to teach them that the Son of Man must suffer many things and be rejected by the elders and the chief priests and the scribes, and be killed, and after three days rise again. 32And He was stating the matter plainly. And Peter took Him aside and began to rebuke Him. 33But turning around and seeing His disciples, He rebuked Peter, and *said, "Get behind Me, Satan; for you are not setting your mind on *God's interests, but man's."

34And He summoned the multitude with His disciples, and said to them, "If anyone wishes to come after Me, let him deny himself, and take up his cross, and follow Me. 35"For whoever wishes to save his life shall lose it; but whoever loses his life for My sake and the gospel's shall save it. 36"For what does it profit a man to gain the whole world, and forfeit his soul? 37"For what shall a man give in exchange for his soul?

Φιλίππου· καὶ ἐν τῇ ὁδῷ ἐπηρώτα τοὺς
of Philip; and in the way he questioned the

μαθητὰς αὐτοῦ λέγων αὐτοῖς· τίνα με
disciples of him saying to them: Whom me

λέγουσιν οἱ ἄνθρωποι εἶναι; 28 οἱ δὲ
say - men to be? And they

εἶπαν αὐτῷ λέγοντες ὅτι Ἰωάννην τὸν
told him saying[,] - John the

βαπτιστήν, καὶ ἄλλοι Ἡλίαν, ἄλλοι δὲ
Baptist, and others Elias, but others[.]

ὅτι εἷς τῶν προφητῶν. 29 καὶ αὐτὸς
- one of the prophets. And he

ἐπηρώτα αὐτούς· ὑμεῖς δὲ τίνα με λέγετε
questioned them: But ye whom me say ye

εἶναι; ἀποκριθεὶς ὁ Πέτρος λέγει αὐτῷ·
to be? Answering - Peter says to him:

σὺ εἶ ὁ χριστός. 30 καὶ ἐπετίμησεν
Thou art the Christ. And he warned

αὐτοῖς ἵνα μηδενὶ λέγωσιν περὶ αὐτοῦ.
them that to no one they might tell about him.

31 Καὶ ἤρξατο διδάσκειν αὐτοὺς ὅτι δεῖ
And he began to teach them that it behoves

τὸν υἱὸν τοῦ ἀνθρώπου πολλὰ παθεῖν,
the Son of man many things to suffer,

καὶ ἀποδοκιμασθῆναι ὑπὸ τῶν πρεσβυτέρων
and to be rejected by the elders

καὶ τῶν ἀρχιερέων καὶ τῶν γραμματέων
and the chief priests and the scribes

καὶ ἀποκτανθῆναι καὶ μετὰ τρεῖς ἡμέρας
and to be killed and after three days

ἀναστῆναι· 32 καὶ παρρησίᾳ τὸν λόγον
to rise again; and openly the word

ἐλάλει. καὶ προσλαβόμενος ὁ Πέτρος
he spoke. And ¹taking ²aside - ¹Peter

αὐτὸν ἤρξατο ἐπιτιμᾶν αὐτῷ. 33 ὁ δὲ
³him began to rebuke him. But he

ἐπιστραφεὶς καὶ ἰδὼν τοὺς μαθητὰς αὐτοῦ
turning round and seeing the disciples of him

ἐπετίμησεν Πέτρῳ καὶ λέγει· ὕπαγε ὀπίσω
rebuked Peter and says: Go behind

μου, σατανᾶ, ὅτι οὐ φρονεῖς τὰ τοῦ
me, Satan, because thou mindest not the things -

θεοῦ ἀλλὰ τὰ τῶν ἀνθρώπων. 34 Καὶ
of God but the things - of men. And

προσκαλεσάμενος τὸν ὄχλον σὺν τοῖς μαθηταῖς
calling to [him] the crowd with the disciples

αὐτοῦ εἶπεν αὐτοῖς· εἴ τις θέλει ὀπίσω
of him he said to them: If anyone wishes after

μου ἐλθεῖν, ἀπαρνησάσθω ἑαυτὸν καὶ ἀράτω
me to come, let him deny himself and take

τὸν σταυρὸν αὐτοῦ, καὶ ἀκολουθείτω μοι.
the cross of him, and let him follow me.

35 ὃς γὰρ ἐὰν θέλῃ τὴν ψυχὴν αὐτοῦ σῶ-
For whoever wishes the life of him to

σαι, ἀπολέσει αὐτήν· ὃς δ' ἂν ἀπολέσει
save, will lose it; but whoever will lose

τὴν ψυχὴν αὐτοῦ ἕνεκεν ἐμοῦ καὶ τοῦ
the life of him for the sake of me and the

εὐαγγελίου, σώσει αὐτήν. 36 τί γὰρ ὠφελεῖ
gospel, will save it. For what profits

ἄνθρωπον κερδῆσαι τὸν κόσμον ὅλον καὶ
a man to gain the world whole and

ζημιωθῆναι τὴν ψυχὴν αὐτοῦ; 37 τί γὰρ
to be fined the soul of him? For what

δοῖ ἄνθρωπος ἀντάλλαγμα τῆς ψυχῆς αὐτοῦ;
might give a man an exchange of the soul of him?

On the way he asked them, "Who do people say I am?" 28They replied, "Some say John the Baptist; others say Elijah; and still others, one of the prophets." 29"But what about you?" he asked. "Who do you say I am?" Peter answered, "You are the Christ. ᶜ" 30Jesus warned them not to tell anyone about him.

Jesus Predicts His Death

31He then began to teach them that the Son of Man must suffer many things and be rejected by the elders, chief priests and teachers of the law, and that he must be killed and after three days rise again. 32He spoke plainly about this, and Peter took him aside and began to rebuke him. 33But when Jesus turned and looked at his disciples, he rebuked Peter. "Get behind me, Satan!" he said. "You do not have in mind the things of God, but the things of men."

34Then he called the crowd to him along with his disciples and said: "If anyone would come after me, he must deny himself and take up his cross and follow me. 35For whoever wants to save his lifeᵈ will lose it, but whoever loses his life for me and for the gospel will save it. 36What good is it for a man to gain the whole world, yet forfeit his soul? 37Or what can a man give in exchange for his soul? 38If anyone is

---

ᶜ29 Or Messiah. "The Christ" (Greek) and "the Messiah" (Hebrew) both mean "the Anointed One."

ᵈ35 The Greek word means either life or soul; also in verse 36.

ᵂ Lit., the things of God

38"For whoever is ashamed of Me and My words in this adulterous and sinful generation, the Son of Man will also be ashamed of him when He comes in the glory of His Father with the holy angels."

38 ὃς γὰρ ἐὰν ἐπαισχυνθῇ με καὶ
For whoever is ashamed of me and

τοὺς ἐμοὺς λόγους ἐν τῇ γενεᾷ ταύτῃ
- my words in - generation this

τῇ μοιχαλίδι καὶ ἁμαρτωλῷ, καὶ ὁ
- adulterous and sinful, also the

υἱὸς τοῦ ἀνθρώπου ἐπαισχυνθήσεται αὐτόν,
Son - of man will be ashamed of him,

ὅταν ἔλθῃ ἐν τῇ δόξῃ τοῦ πατρὸς
when he comes in the glory of the Father

αὐτοῦ μετὰ τῶν ἀγγέλων τῶν ἁγίων.
of him with the angels - holy.

ashamed of me and my words in this adulterous and sinful generation, the Son of Man will be ashamed of him when he comes in his Father's glory with the holy angels."

Chapter 9

The Transfiguration

AND He was saying to them, "Truly I say to you, there are some of those who are standing here who shall not taste death until they see the kingdom of God after it has come with power.

2And six days later, Jesus *took with Him Peter and James and John, and *brought them up to a high mountain by themselves. And He was transfigured before them;

3and His garments became radiant and exceedingly white, as no launderer on earth can whiten them.

4And Elijah appeared to them along with Moses; and they were talking with Jesus.

5And Peter answered and *said to Jesus, "Rabbi, it is good for us to be here; and let us make three tabernacles, one for You, and one for Moses, and one for Elijah."

6For he did not know what to answer; for they became terrified.

7Then a cloud formed, overshadowing them, and a voice came out of the cloud, "This is My beloved Son, listen to Him!"

8And all at once they looked around and saw no one with them anymore, except Jesus alone.

9And as they were coming down from the mountain, He gave them orders

9 καὶ ἔλεγεν αὐτοῖς· ἀμὴν λέγω ὑμῖν
And he said to them: Truly I tell you

ὅτι εἰσίν τινες ὧδε τῶν ἑστηκότων
that there are some here of the [ones] standing

οἵτινες οὐ μὴ γεύσωνται θανάτου ἕως ἂν
who by no means may taste of death until

ἴδωσιν τὴν βασιλείαν τοῦ θεοῦ ἐληλυθυῖαν
they see the kingdom - of God having come

ἐν δυνάμει.
in power.

2 Καὶ μετὰ ἡμέρας ἓξ παραλαμβάνει
And after days six takes

ὁ Ἰησοῦς τὸν Πέτρον καὶ τὸν Ἰάκωβον
- Jesus - Peter and - James

καὶ Ἰωάννην, καὶ ἀναφέρει αὐτοὺς εἰς
and John, and leads up them into

ὄρος ὑψηλὸν κατ' ἰδίαν μόνους. καὶ
mountain a high privately alone. And

μετεμορφώθη ἔμπροσθεν αὐτῶν, **3** καὶ τὰ
he was transfigured before them, and the

ἱμάτια αὐτοῦ ἐγένετο στίλβοντα λευκὰ λίαν,
garments of him became gleaming white exceedingly,

οἷα γναφεὺς ἐπὶ τῆς γῆς οὐ δύναται
such as fuller on the earth cannot

οὕτως λευκᾶναι. **4** καὶ ὤφθη αὐτοῖς Ἡλίας
so to whiten. And appeared to them Elias

σὺν Μωϋσεῖ, καὶ ἦσαν συλλαλοῦντες τῷ
with Moses, and they were conversing with -

Ἰησοῦ. **5** καὶ ἀποκριθεὶς ὁ Πέτρος λέγει
Jesus. And answering - Peter says

τῷ Ἰησοῦ· ῥαββί, καλόν ἐστιν ἡμᾶς ὧδε
- to Jesus: Rabbi, good it is us here

εἶναι, καὶ ποιήσωμεν τρεῖς σκηνάς, σοὶ
to be, and let us make three tents, for thee

μίαν καὶ Μωϋσεῖ μίαν καὶ Ἡλίᾳ μίαν.
one and for Moses one and for Elias one.

6 οὐ γὰρ ᾔδει τί ἀποκριθῇ· ἔκφοβοι γὰρ
For he knew not what he answered; for exceedingly afraid

ἐγένοντο. **7** καὶ ἐγένετο νεφέλη ἐπισκιάζουσα
they became. And there came a cloud overshadowing

αὐτοῖς, καὶ ἐγένετο φωνὴ ἐκ τῆς νεφέλης·
them, and there came a voice out of the cloud:

οὗτός ἐστιν ὁ υἱός μου ὁ ἀγαπητός,
This is the Son of me the beloved,

ἀκούετε αὐτοῦ. **8** καὶ ἐξάπινα περιβλεψάμενοι
hear ye him. And suddenly looking round

οὐκέτι οὐδένα εἶδον εἰ μὴ τὸν Ἰησοῦν
no longer no(any)one they saw except - Jesus

μόνον μεθ' ἑαυτῶν. **9** Καὶ καταβαινόντων
only with themselves. And coming down
= as they came down

αὐτῶν ἐκ τοῦ ὄρους διεστείλατο αὐτοῖς
them[a] out of the mountain he ordered them

Chapter 9

AND he said to them, "I tell you the truth, some who are standing here will not taste death before they see the kingdom of God come with power."

The Transfiguration

2After six days Jesus took Peter, James and John with him and led them up a high mountain, where they were all alone. There he was transfigured before them. 3His clothes became dazzling white, whiter than anyone in the world could bleach them. 4And there appeared before them Elijah and Moses, who were talking with Jesus.

5Peter said to Jesus, "Rabbi, it is good for us to be here. Let us put up three shelters—one for you, one for Moses and one for Elijah." 6(He did not know what to say, they were so frightened.)

7Then a cloud appeared and enveloped them, and a voice came from the cloud: "This is my Son, whom I love. Listen to him!"

8Suddenly, when they looked around, they no longer saw anyone with them except Jesus.

9As they were coming down the mountain, Jesus gave them orders not to tell not to relate to anyone what they had seen, until the Son of Man should rise from the dead.

10And they seized upon that statement, discussing with one another what rising from the dead might mean.

11And they asked Him, saying, *"Why is it* that the scribes say that Elijah must come first?"

12And He said to them, "Elijah does first come and restore all things. And *yet* how is it written of the Son of Man that He should suffer many things and be treated with contempt?

13"But I say to you, that Elijah has indeed come, and they did to him whatever they wished, just as it is written of him."

All Things Possible

14And when they came *back* to the disciples, they saw a large crowd around them, and *some* scribes arguing with them.

15And immediately, when the entire crowd saw Him, they were amazed, and *began* running up to greet Him.

16And He asked them, "What are you discussing with them?"

17And one of the crowd answered Him, "Teacher, I brought You my son, possessed with a spirit which makes him mute;

18and whenever it seizes him, it dashes him *to the ground* and he foams *at the mouth,* and grinds his teeth, and stiffens out. And I told Your disciples to cast it out, and they could not *do it.*"

19And He *answered them and *said, "O unbelieving generation, how long shall I be with you? How long shall I put up with you? Bring him to Me!"

20And they brought the boy to Him. And when he saw Him, immediately the spirit threw him into a con-

---

ἵνα   μηδενὶ   ἃ   εἶδον   διηγήσωνται,
that to no one [the] things which they saw they should relate,

εἰ μὴ   ὅταν   ὁ   υἱὸς   τοῦ   ἀνθρώπου   ἐκ   νεκρῶν
except   when   the   Son   -   of man   out of [the] dead

ἀναστῇ.   10 καὶ   τὸν   λόγον   ἐκράτησαν   πρὸς
should rise.   And   the   word   they held   to

ἑαυτοὺς   συζητοῦντες   τί   ἐστιν   τὸ   ἐκ
themselves   debating   what   is   the "out of

νεκρῶν   ἀναστῆναι.   11 Καὶ   ἐπηρώτων   αὐτὸν
[the] dead   to rise."   And   they questioned   him

λέγοντες·   ὅτι   λέγουσιν   οἱ   γραμματεῖς   ὅτι
saying·   Why   say   the   scribes   that

Ἡλίαν   δεῖ   ἐλθεῖν   πρῶτον;   12 ὁ   δὲ   ἔφη
Elias   it behoves to come   first?   And he   said

αὐτοῖς·   Ἡλίας   μὲν   ἐλθὼν   πρῶτον
to them: Elias   indeed   coming   first

ἀποκαθιστάνει   πάντα·   καὶ   πῶς   γέγραπται
restores   all things;   and   how   has it been written

ἐπὶ   τὸν   υἱὸν   τοῦ   ἀνθρώπου,   ἵνα   πολλὰ
on(concerning)   the   Son   -   of man,   that   many things

πάθῃ   καὶ   ἐξουδενηθῇ;   13 ἀλλὰ   λέγω   ὑμῖν
he should suffer   and   be set at naught?   But   I tell   you

ὅτι   καὶ   Ἡλίας   ἐλήλυθεν,   καὶ   ἐποίησαν
that   indeed   Elias   has come,   and   they did

αὐτῷ   ὅσα   ἤθελον,   καθὼς   γέγραπται
to him   what   they wished,   as   it has been written

ἐπ'   αὐτόν.
on(concerning)   him.

14 Καὶ   ἐλθόντες   πρὸς   τοὺς   μαθητὰς
And   coming   to   the   disciples

εἶδον   ὄχλον   πολὺν   περὶ   αὐτοὺς   καὶ
they saw   crowd   a much(great)   around   them   and

γραμματεῖς   συζητοῦντας   πρὸς   αὐτούς.
scribes   debating   with   them.

15 καὶ   εὐθὺς   πᾶς   ὁ   ὄχλος   ἰδόντες   αὐτὸν
And immediately   all   the   crowd   seeing   him

ἐξεθαμβήθησαν,   καὶ   προστρέχοντες   ἠσπάζοντο
were greatly astonished,   and   running up to   greeted

αὐτόν.   16 καὶ   ἐπηρώτησεν   αὐτούς·   τί
him.   And   he questioned   them·   What

συζητεῖτε   πρὸς   αὐτούς;   17 καὶ   ἀπεκρίθη
are ye debating   with   them?   And   answered

αὐτῷ   εἷς   ἐκ   τοῦ   ὄχλου·   διδάσκαλε,
him   one   of   the   crowd·   Teacher,

ἤνεγκα   τὸν   υἱόν   μου   πρὸς   σέ,   ἔχοντα
I brought   the   son   of me   to   thee,   having

πνεῦμα   ἄλαλον·   18 καὶ   ὅπου   ἐὰν   αὐτὸν
spirit   a dumb·   and   wherever   him

καταλάβῃ,   ῥήσσει   αὐτόν,   καὶ   ἀφρίζει   καὶ
it seizes,   it tears   him,   and   he foams   and

τρίζει   τοὺς   ὀδόντας   καὶ   ξηραίνεται·   καὶ
grinds   the(his)   teeth   and   he wastes away;   and

εἶπα   τοῖς   μαθηταῖς   σου   ἵνα   αὐτὸ
I told   the   disciples   of thee   that   it

ἐκβάλωσιν,   καὶ   οὐκ   ἴσχυσαν.   19 ὁ   δὲ
they might expel,   and   they were not able.   And he

ἀποκριθεὶς   αὐτοῖς   λέγει·   ὦ   γενεὰ   ἄπιστος,
answering   them   says: O   generation   unbelieving,

ἕως   πότε   πρὸς   ὑμᾶς   ἔσομαι;   ἕως   πότε
until   when   with   you   shall I be?   how long
= how long

ἀνέξομαι   ὑμῶν;   φέρετε   αὐτὸν   πρός   με.
shall I endure   you?   bring   him   to   me.

20 καὶ   ἤνεγκαν   αὐτὸν   πρὸς   αὐτόν.   καὶ
And   they brought   him   to   him.   And

ἰδὼν   αὐτὸν   τὸ   πνεῦμα   εὐθὺς   συνεσπάραξεν
seeing   him   the   spirit   immediately   violently threw

---

anyone what they had seen until the Son of Man had risen from the dead. 10They kept the matter to themselves, discussing what "rising from the dead" meant.

11And they asked him, "Why do the teachers of the law say that Elijah must come first?"

12Jesus replied, "To be sure, Elijah does come first, and restores all things. Why then is it written that the Son of Man must suffer much and be rejected? 13But I tell you, Elijah has come, and they have done to him everything they wished, just as it is written about him."

The Healing of a Boy With an Evil Spirit

14When they came to the other disciples, they saw a large crowd around them and the teachers of the law arguing with them. 15As soon as all the people saw Jesus, they were overwhelmed with wonder and ran to greet him.

16"What are you arguing with them about?" he asked.

17A man in the crowd answered, "Teacher, I brought you my son, who is possessed by a spirit that has robbed him of speech. 18Whenever it seizes him, it throws him to the ground. He foams at the mouth, gnashes his teeth and becomes rigid. I asked your disciples to drive out the spirit, but they could not."

19"O unbelieving generation," Jesus replied, "how long shall I stay with you? How long shall I put up with you? Bring the boy to me."

20So they brought him. When the spirit saw Jesus, it immediately threw the boy into a convulsion. He

vulsion, and falling to the ground, he *began* rolling about and foaming *at the mouth.*
21And He asked his father, "How long has this been happening to him?" And he said, "From childhood.
22"And it has often thrown him both into the fire and into the water to destroy him. But if You can do anything, take pity on us and help us!"
23And Jesus said to him, "'If You can!' All things are possible to him who believes."
24Immediately the boy's father cried out and *began* saying, "I do believe; help my unbelief."
25And when Jesus saw that a crowd was rapidly gathering, He rebuked the unclean spirit, saying to it, "You deaf and dumb spirit, I command you, come out of him and do not enter him again."
26And after crying out and throwing him into terrible convulsions, it came out; and *the boy* became so much like a corpse that most *of them* said, "He is dead!"
27But Jesus took him by the hand and raised him; and he got up.
28And when He had come into *the* house, His disciples *began* questioning Him privately, "Why could we not cast it out?"
29And He said to them, "This kind cannot come out by anything but prayerˣ."

Death and Resurrection Foretold

30And from there they went out and *began* to go through Galilee, and He was unwilling for anyone to know *about it.*
31For He was teaching His disciples and telling them, "The Son of Man is to be ʸdelivered into the hands of men, and they will kill Him; and when He has been killed, He will rise three days later."

αὐτόν, καὶ πεσὼν ἐπὶ τῆς γῆς ἐκυλίετο
him, and falling on the earth he wallowed
ἀφρίζων. 21 καὶ ἐπηρώτησεν τὸν πατέρα
foaming. And he questioned the father
αὐτοῦ· πόσος χρόνος ἐστὶν ὡς τοῦτο
of him: What time is it while this
γέγονεν αὐτῷ; ὁ δὲ εἶπεν· ἐκ παιδιόθεν·
has happened to him? And he said: From childhood;
22 καὶ πολλάκις καὶ εἰς πῦρ αὐτὸν
and often both into fire him
ἔβαλεν καὶ εἰς ὕδατα ἵνα ἀπολέσῃ αὐτόν· ἀλλ'
it threw and into waters that it may destroy him; but
εἴ τι δύνῃ, βοήθησον ἡμῖν σπλαγχνισθεὶς
if anything thou canst, help us having compassion
ἐφ' ἡμᾶς. 23 ὁ δὲ Ἰησοῦς εἶπεν αὐτῷ· τὸ εἰ
on us. And Jesus said to him: The "if
δύνῃ, πάντα δυνατὰ τῷ πιστεύοντι.
thou canst," all things possible to the [one] believing.
24 εὐθὺς κράξας ὁ πατὴρ τοῦ παιδίου
Immediately crying out the father of the child
ἔλεγεν· πιστεύω· βοήθει μου τῇ ἀπιστίᾳ.
said: I believe; help thou of me the unbelief.
25 ἰδὼν δὲ ὁ Ἰησοῦς ὅτι ἐπισυντρέχει
And ²seeing - ¹Jesus that is(was) running together
ὄχλος, ἐπετίμησεν τῷ πνεύματι τῷ ἀκαθάρτῳ
a crowd, rebuked the spirit - unclean
λέγων αὐτῷ· τὸ ἄλαλον καὶ κωφὸν
saying to it: - Dumb and deaf
πνεῦμα, ἐγὼ ἐπιτάσσω σοι, ἔξελθε ἐξ
spirit, I command thee, come forth out of
αὐτοῦ καὶ μηκέτι εἰσέλθῃς εἰς αὐτόν.
him and no more mayest thou enter into him.
26 καὶ κράξας καὶ πολλὰ σπαράξας
And crying out and much convulsing [him]
ἐξῆλθεν· καὶ ἐγένετο ὡσεὶ νεκρός, ὥστε
it came out; and he was as dead, so as
τοὺς πολλοὺς λέγειν ὅτι ἀπέθανεν. 27 ὁ
- many to sayᵇ that he died. -
= many said
δὲ Ἰησοῦς κρατήσας τῆς χειρὸς αὐτοῦ
But Jesus taking hold of the hand of him
ἤγειρεν αὐτόν, καὶ ἀνέστη. 28 καὶ
raised him, and he stood up. And
εἰσελθόντος αὐτοῦ εἰς οἶκον οἱ μαθηταὶ
entering himᵃ into a house the disciples
= when he entered
αὐτοῦ κατ' ἰδίαν ἐπηρώτων αὐτόν· ὅτι
of him privately questioned him: Why
ἡμεῖς οὐκ ἠδυνήθημεν ἐκβαλεῖν αὐτό;
we were not able to expel it?
29 καὶ εἶπεν αὐτοῖς· τοῦτο τὸ γένος ἐν
And he told them: This - kind by
οὐδενὶ δύναται ἐξελθεῖν εἰ μὴ ἐν προσευχῇ.
nothing can to come out except by prayer.
30 Κἀκεῖθεν ἐξελθόντες παρεπορεύοντο διὰ
And thence going forth they passed through
τῆς Γαλιλαίας, καὶ οὐκ ἤθελεν ἵνα
- Galilee, and he wished not that
τις γνοῖ· 31 ἐδίδασκεν γὰρ τοὺς μαθητὰς
anyone should know; for he was teaching the disciples
αὐτοῦ, καὶ ἔλεγεν αὐτοῖς ὅτι ὁ υἱὸς τοῦ
of him, and told them[,] - The Son
ἀνθρώπου παραδίδοται εἰς χεῖρας ἀνθρώπων,
of man is betrayed into [the] hands of men,
καὶ ἀποκτενοῦσιν αὐτόν, καὶ ἀποκτανθεὶς
and they will kill him, and being killed
μετὰ τρεῖς ἡμέρας ἀναστήσεται. 32 οἱ
after three days he will rise up. they

---

fell to the ground and rolled around, foaming at the mouth.
21Jesus asked the boy's father, "How long has he been like this?"
"From childhood," he answered. 22"It has often thrown him into fire or water to kill him. But if you can do anything, take pity on us and help us."
23"'If you can'?" said Jesus. "Everything is possible for him who believes."
24Immediately the boy's father exclaimed, "I do believe; help me overcome my unbelief!"
25When Jesus saw that a crowd was running to the scene, he rebuked the evil spirit. "You deaf and mute spirit," he said, "I command you, come out of him and never enter him again."
26The spirit shrieked, convulsed him violently and came out. The boy looked so much like a corpse that many said, "He's dead." 27But Jesus took him by the hand and lifted him to his feet, and he stood up.
28After Jesus had gone indoors, his disciples asked him privately, "Why couldn't we drive it out?"
29He replied, "This kind can come out only by prayer.ᶠ"
30They left that place and passed through Galilee. Jesus did not want anyone to know where they were, 31because he was teaching his disciples. He said to them, "The Son of Man is going to be betrayed into the hands of men. They will kill him, and after three days he will rise." 32But

---

ˣMany mss. add: *and fasting*
ʸOr, *betrayed*

ᵉ25 Greek *unclean*
ᶠ29 Some manuscripts *prayer and fasting*

32But they did not understand *this* statement, and they were afraid to ask Him.

33And they came to Capernaum; and when He was in the house, He began to question them, "What were you discussing on the way?"

34But they kept silent, for on the way they had discussed with one another which *of them was* the greatest.

35And sitting down, He called the twelve and *said to them, "If anyone wants to be first, he shall be last of all, and servant of all."

36And taking a child, He set him before them, and taking him in His arms, He said to them,

37"Whoever receives one child like this in My name receives Me; and whoever receives Me does not receive Me, but Him who sent Me."

Dire Warnings

38John said to Him, "Teacher, we saw someone casting out demons in Your name, and we tried to hinder him because he was not following us."

39But Jesus said, "Do not hinder him, for there is no one who shall perform a miracle in My name, and be able soon afterward to speak evil of Me.

40"For he who is not against us is ²for us.

41"For whoever gives you a cup of water to drink because of your name as *followers* of Christ, truly I say to you, he shall not lose his reward.

42"And whoever causes one of these little ones who believe to stumble, it would be better for him if, with a heavy millstone hung around his neck, he had been cast into the sea.

43"And if your hand causes you to stumble, cut

δὲ ἠγνόουν τὸ ῥῆμα, καὶ ἐφοβοῦντο
But did not know the word, and feared

αὐτὸν ἐπερωτῆσαι.
him to question.

33 Καὶ ἦλθον εἰς Καφαρναούμ. Καὶ
And they came to Capernaum. And

ἐν τῇ οἰκίᾳ γενόμενος ἐπηρώτα αὐτούς·
in the house being he questioned them:

τί ἐν τῇ ὁδῷ διελογίζεσθε; 34 οἱ δὲ
What in the way were ye debating? And they

ἐσιώπων· πρὸς ἀλλήλους γὰρ διελέχθησαν
were silent; ¹with ²one another ¹for they debated

ἐν τῇ ὁδῷ τίς μείζων. 35 καὶ καθίσας
in the way who [was] greater. And sitting

ἐφώνησεν τοὺς δώδεκα καὶ λέγει αὐτοῖς·
he called the twelve and says to them:

εἴ τις θέλει πρῶτος εἶναι, ἔσται πάντων
If anyone wishes first to be, he shall be of all

ἔσχατος καὶ πάντων διάκονος. 36 καὶ
last and of all servant. And

λαβὼν παιδίον ἔστησεν αὐτὸ ἐν μέσῳ
taking a child he set it(him) in [the] midst

αὐτῶν, καὶ ἐναγκαλισάμενος αὐτὸ εἶπεν
of them, and folding in [his] arms it he said

αὐτοῖς· 37 ὃς ἂν ἓν τῶν τοιούτων παιδίων
to them: Whoever one – of such children

δέξηται ἐπὶ τῷ ὀνόματί μου, ἐμὲ δέχεται·
receives on(in) the name of me, me receives;

καὶ ὃς ἂν ἐμὲ δέχηται, οὐχ ἐμὲ δέχεται
and whoever me receives, not me receives

ἀλλὰ τὸν ἀποστείλαντά με. 38 Ἔφη αὐτῷ
but the [one] having sent me. Said to him

ὁ Ἰωάννης· διδάσκαλε, εἴδομέν τινα ἐν
– John: Teacher, we saw someone in

τῷ ὀνόματί σου ἐκβάλλοντα δαιμόνια, ὃς
the name of thee expelling demons, who

οὐκ ἀκολουθεῖ ἡμῖν, καὶ ἐκωλύομεν αὐτόν,
does not follow us, and we forbade him,

ὅτι οὐκ ἠκολούθει ἡμῖν. 39 ὁ δὲ Ἰησοῦς
because he was not following us. – But Jesus

εἶπεν· μὴ κωλύετε αὐτόν· οὐδεὶς γὰρ
said: Do not forbid him: for no one

ἔστιν ὃς ποιήσει δύναμιν ἐπὶ τῷ ὀνόματί
there is who shall do a mighty work on(in) the name

μου καὶ δυνήσεται ταχὺ κακολογῆσαί με·
of me and will be able quickly to speak evil of me;

40 ὃς γὰρ οὐκ ἔστιν καθ' ἡμῶν, ὑπὲρ
for who is not against us, for

ἡμῶν ἐστιν. 41 Ὃς γὰρ ἂν ποτίσῃ
us is. For whoever ¹gives ³drink

ὑμᾶς ποτήριον ὕδατος ἐν ὀνόματι, ὅτι
²you a cup of water in [the] name, because

Χριστοῦ ἐστε, ἀμὴν λέγω ὑμῖν ὅτι
of Christ ye are, truly I tell you that

οὐ μὴ ἀπολέσῃ τὸν μισθὸν αὐτοῦ. 42 Καὶ
by no means he will lose the reward of him. And

ὃς ἂν σκανδαλίσῃ ἕνα τῶν μικρῶν τούτων
whoever offends one – ²little [ones] ¹of these

τῶν πιστευόντων, καλόν ἐστιν αὐτῷ μᾶλλον
– ¹believing, good is it for him rather

εἰ περίκειται μύλος ὀνικὸς περὶ τὸν
if be laid *round* a [heavy] millstone round the

τράχηλον αὐτοῦ καὶ βέβληται εἰς τὴν
neck of him and he be thrown into the

θάλασσαν. 43 Καὶ ἐὰν σκανδαλίσῃ σε ἡ
sea. And if offends thee the

---

they did not understand what he meant and were afraid to ask him about it.

Who Is the Greatest?

33They came to Capernaum. When he was in the house, he asked them, "What were you arguing about on the road?" 34But they kept quiet because on the way they had argued about who was the greatest.

35Sitting down, Jesus called the Twelve and said, "If anyone wants to be first, he must be the very last, and the servant of all."

36He took a little child and had him stand among them. Taking him in his arms, he said to them, 37"Whoever welcomes one of these little children in my name welcomes me; and whoever welcomes me does not welcome me but the one who sent me."

Whoever Is Not Against Us Is for Us

38"Teacher," said John, "we saw a man driving out demons in your name and we told him to stop, because he was not one of us."

39"Do not stop him," Jesus said. "No one who does a miracle in my name can in the next moment say anything bad about me, 40for whoever is not against us is for us. 41I tell you the truth, anyone who gives you a cup of water in my name because you belong to Christ will certainly not lose his reward.

Causing to Sin

42"And if anyone causes one of these little ones who believe in me to sin, it would be better for him to be thrown into the sea with a large millstone tied around his neck. 43If your hand causes you to sin, cut

---

²Or, *on our side*

it off; it is better for you to enter life crippled, than having your two hands, to go into hell, into the unquenchable fire, 44[*where THEIR WORM DOES NOT DIE, AND THE FIRE IS NOT QUENCHED.] 45"And if your foot causes you to stumble, cut it off; it is better for you to enter life lame, than having your two feet, to be cast into hell, 46[*where THEIR WORM DOES NOT DIE, AND THE FIRE IS NOT QUENCHED.] 47"And if your eye causes you to stumble, cast it out; it is better for you to enter the kingdom of God with one eye, than having two eyes, to be cast into hell, 48where THEIR WORM DOES NOT DIE, AND THE FIRE IS NOT QUENCHED. 49"For everyone will be salted with fire. 50"Salt is good; but if the salt becomes unsalty, with what will you make it salty again? Have salt in yourselves, and be at peace with one another."

Chapter 10

Jesus' Teaching about Divorce

AND rising up, He *went from there to the region of Judea, and beyond the Jordan; and crowds *gathered around Him again, and, according to His custom, He once more *began to teach them. 2And *some* Pharisees came up to Him, testing Him, and *began* to question Him whether it was lawful for a man to divorce a wife. 3And He answered and said to them, "What did Moses command you?" 4And they said, "Moses permitted *a man* TO WRITE A CERTIFICATE OF DIVORCE AND SEND *her* AWAY." 5But Jesus said to them, "Because of your hardness of heart he wrote you this commandment. 6"But from the beginning of creation, God MADE

χείρ σου, ἀπόκοψον αὐτήν· καλόν ἐστίν
hand of thee, cut off it; good is it

σε κυλλὸν εἰσελθεῖν εἰς τὴν ζωήν, ἢ τὰς
thee maimed to enter into – life, than the

δύο χεῖρας ἔχοντα ἀπελθεῖν εἰς τὴν
two hands having to go away into –

γέενναν, εἰς τὸ πῦρ τὸ ἄσβεστον.‡ 45 καὶ
gehenna, into the fire *the* unquenchable. And

ἐὰν ὁ πούς σου σκανδαλίζῃ σε, ἀπόκοψον
if the foot of thee offends thee, cut off

αὐτόν· καλόν ἐστίν σε εἰσελθεῖν εἰς τὴν
it; good is it thee to enter into –

ζωὴν χωλόν, ἢ τοὺς δύο πόδας ἔχοντα
life lame, than the two feet having

βληθῆναι εἰς τὴν γέενναν.‡ 47 καὶ ἐὰν ὁ
to be cast into – gehenna. And if the

ὀφθαλμός σου σκανδαλίζῃ σε, ἔκβαλε αὐτόν·
eye of thee offends thee, cast out it;

καλόν σέ ἐστιν μονόφθαλμον εἰσελθεῖν εἰς
good thee is it one-eyed to enter into

τὴν βασιλείαν τοῦ θεοῦ, ἢ δύο ὀφθαλμοὺς
the kingdom – .of God, than two eyes

ἔχοντα βληθῆναι εἰς τὴν γέενναν, 48 ὅπου
having to be cast into – gehenna, where

ὁ σκώληξ αὐτῶν οὐ τελευτᾷ καὶ τὸ
the worm of them dies not and the

πῦρ οὐ σβέννυται. 49 Πᾶς γὰρ πυρὶ
fire is not quenched. For everyone with fire

ἁλισθήσεται. 50 καλὸν τὸ ἅλας· ἐὰν δὲ
shall be salted. Good [is] – salt; but if

τὸ ἅλας ἄναλον γένηται, ἐν τίνι αὐτὸ
– salt saltless becomes, by what it

ἀρτύσετε; ἔχετε ἐν ἑαυτοῖς ἅλα καὶ
will ye season? Have in yourselves salt and

εἰρηνεύετε ἐν ἀλλήλοις.
be at peace among one another.

10 Καὶ ἐκεῖθεν ἀναστὰς ἔρχεται εἰς τὰ
And thence rising up he comes into the

ὅρια τῆς Ἰουδαίας καὶ πέραν τοῦ
territory – of Judæa and beyond the

Ἰορδάνου, καὶ συμπορεύονται πάλιν ὄχλοι
Jordan, and ²go with ¹again ³crowds

πρὸς αὐτόν, καὶ ὡς εἰώθει πάλιν ἐδίδασκεν
⁴with ⁵him, and as he was wont again he taught

αὐτούς. 2 Καὶ προσελθόντες Φαρισαῖοι
them. And ²approaching ¹Pharisees

ἐπηρώτων αὐτὸν εἰ ἔξεστιν ἀνδρὶ γυναῖκα
questioned him if it is(was) lawful for a man a wife

ἀπολῦσαι, πειράζοντες αὐτόν. 3 ὁ δὲ
to dismiss, testing him. And he

ἀποκριθεὶς εἶπεν αὐτοῖς· 4 τί ὑμῖν ἐνετείλατο
answering said to them: What you ordered

Μωϋσῆς; οἱ δὲ εἶπαν· ἐπέτρεψεν Μωϋσῆς
Moses? And they said: permitted Moses

βιβλίον ἀποστασίου γράψαι καὶ ἀπολῦσαι.
a roll of divorce to write and to dismiss.

5 ὁ δὲ Ἰησοῦς εἶπεν αὐτοῖς· πρὸς τὴν
– And Jesus said to them: For the

σκληροκαρδίαν ὑμῶν ἔγραψεν ὑμῖν τὴν
hardheartedness of you he wrote to you –

ἐντολὴν ταύτην. 6 ἀπὸ δὲ ἀρχῆς κτίσεως
this commandment. But from [the] beginning of creation

---

it off. It is better for you to enter life maimed than with two hands to go into hell, where the fire never goes out. *g* 45And if your foot causes you to sin, cut it off. It is better for you to enter life crippled than to have two feet and be thrown into hell. *h* 47And if your eye causes you to sin, pluck it out. It is better for you to enter the kingdom of God with one eye than to have two eyes and be thrown into hell, 48where

" 'their worm does not die,
and the fire is not quenched.' *i*

49Everyone will be salted with fire. 50"Salt is good, but if it loses its saltiness, how can you make it salty again? Have salt in yourselves, and be at peace with each other."

Chapter 10

Divorce

JESUS then left that place and went into the region of Judea and across the Jordan. Again crowds of people came to him, and as was his custom, he taught them. 2Some Pharisees came and tested him by asking, "Is it lawful for a man to divorce his wife?" 3"What did Moses command you?" he replied. 4They said, "Moses permitted a man to write a certificate of divorce and send her away." 5"It was because your hearts were hard that Moses wrote you this law," Jesus replied. 6"But at the beginning of creation God

---

*Vv. 44 and 46, which are identical with v. 48, are not found in the best ancient mss.

‡ Verse 44 omitted by Nestle; *cf.* NIV footnote.

‡ Verse 46 omitted by Nestle; *cf.* NIV footnote.

*g43 Some manuscripts out, 44where / " 'their worm does not die, / and the fire is not quenched.'
h45 Some manuscripts hell, 46where / " 'their worm does not die, / and the fire is not quenched.'
i48 Isaiah 66:24

THEM MALE AND FEMALE. 7"FOR THIS CAUSE A MAN SHALL LEAVE HIS FATHER AND MOTHER,[b] 8AND THE TWO SHALL BECOME ONE FLESH; consequently they are no longer two, but one flesh. 9"What therefore God has joined together, let no man separate."

10And in the house the disciples *began* questioning Him about this again. 11And He *said to them, "Whoever divorces his wife and marries another woman commits adultery against her; 12and if she herself divorces her husband and marries another man, she is committing adultery."

Jesus Blesses Little Children

13And they were bringing children to Him so that He might touch them; and the disciples rebuked them. 14But when Jesus saw this, He was indignant and said to them, "Permit the children to come to Me; do not hinder them; for the kingdom of God belongs to such as these. 15"Truly I say to you, whoever does not receive the kingdom of God like a child shall not enter it *at all*." 16And He took them in His arms and *began* blessing *them*, laying His hands upon them.

The Rich Young Ruler

17And as He was setting out on a journey, a man ran up to Him and knelt before Him, and *began* asking Him, "Good Teacher, what shall I do to inherit eternal life?" 18And Jesus said to him, "Why do you call Me good? No one is good except God alone. 19"You know the commandments, 'DO NOT MURDER, DO NOT COMMIT ADULTERY, DO NOT STEAL, DO NOT BEAR FALSE WITNESS, Do not defraud, HONOR YOUR FATHER AND MOTHER.'" 20And he said to Him, "Teacher, I have kept all

---

ἄρσεν καὶ θῆλυ ἐποίησεν αὐτούς· **7** ἕνεκεν
male and female he made them; for the sake of

τούτου καταλείψει ἄνθρωπος τὸν πατέρα
this shall leave a man the father

αὐτοῦ καὶ τὴν μητέρα, **8** καὶ ἔσονται
of him and the mother, and shall be

οἱ δύο εἰς σάρκα μίαν· ὥστε οὐκέτι
the two – flesh one; so as no longer

εἰσὶν δύο ἀλλὰ μία σάρξ. **9** ὃ οὖν ὁ
are they two but one flesh. What then –

θεὸς συνέζευξεν, ἄνθρωπος μὴ χωριζέτω.
God yoked together, ²man ¹not ¹let ²separate.

10 καὶ εἰς τὴν οἰκίαν πάλιν οἱ μαθηταὶ
And in the house again the disciples

περὶ τούτου ἐπηρώτων αὐτόν. **11** καὶ
about this questioned him. And

λέγει αὐτοῖς· ὃς ἂν ἀπολύσῃ τὴν γυναῖκα
he says to them: Whoever dismisses the wife

αὐτοῦ καὶ γαμήσῃ ἄλλην, μοιχᾶται ἐπ'
of him and marries another, commits adultery with

αὐτήν· **12** καὶ ἐὰν αὐτὴ ἀπολύσασα τὸν
her; and if she having dismissed the

ἄνδρα αὐτῆς γαμήσῃ ἄλλον, μοιχᾶται.
husband of her marries another, she commits adultery.

13 Καὶ προσέφερον αὐτῷ παιδία ἵνα
And they brought to him children that

αὐτῶν ἅψηται· οἱ δὲ μαθηταὶ ἐπετίμησαν
them he might touch; but the disciples rebuked

αὐτοῖς. **14** ἰδὼν δὲ ὁ Ἰησοῦς ἠγανάκτησεν
them. But ²seeing – ¹Jesus was angry

καὶ εἶπεν αὐτοῖς· ἄφετε τὰ παιδία
and said to them: Allow the children

ἔρχεσθαι πρός με, μὴ κωλύετε αὐτά·
to come to me, do not prevent them;

τῶν γὰρ τοιούτων ἐστὶν ἡ βασιλεία τοῦ
– for of such is the kingdom –

θεοῦ. **15** ἀμὴν λέγω ὑμῖν, ὃς ἂν
of God. Truly I tell you, whoever

μὴ δέξηται τὴν βασιλείαν τοῦ θεοῦ ὡς
receives not the kingdom of God as

παιδίον, οὐ μὴ εἰσέλθῃ εἰς αὐτήν. **16** καὶ
a child, by no means may enter into it. And

ἐναγκαλισάμενος αὐτὰ κατευλόγει τιθεὶς τὰς
folding in [his] arms them he blesses putting the(his)

χεῖρας ἐπ' αὐτά.
hands on them.

17 Καὶ ἐκπορευομένου αὐτοῦ εἰς ὁδὸν
And going forth him* into [the] way
= as he went forth

προσδραμὼν εἷς καὶ γονυπετήσας αὐτὸν
running to one and kneeling to him

ἐπηρώτα αὐτόν· διδάσκαλε ἀγαθέ, τί ποιήσω
questioned him: Teacher good, what may I do

ἵνα ζωὴν αἰώνιον κληρονομήσω; **18** ὁ δὲ
that life eternal I may inherit? – And

Ἰησοῦς εἶπεν αὐτῷ· τί με λέγεις ἀγαθόν;
Jesus said to him: Why me callest thou good?

οὐδεὶς ἀγαθὸς εἰ μὴ εἷς ὁ θεός. **19** τὰς ἐντολὰς
no one good except one – God. The commandments

οἶδας· μὴ φονεύσῃς, μὴ μοιχεύσῃς,
thou knowest: Do not kill, Do not commit adultery,

μὴ κλέψῃς, μὴ ψευδομαρτυρήσῃς, μὴ
Do not steal, Do not bear false witness, Do

ἀποστερήσῃς, τίμα τὸν πατέρα σου καὶ
not defraud, Honour the father of thee and

τὴν μητέρα. **20** ὁ δὲ ἔφη αὐτῷ· διδάσκαλε,
the mother. And he said to him: Teacher,

'made them male and female.'[j] 7"For this reason a man will leave his father and mother and be united to his wife,[k] 8and the two will become one flesh.'[l] So they are no longer two, but one. 9Therefore what God has joined together, let man not separate."

10When they were in the house again, the disciples asked Jesus about this. 11He answered, "Anyone who divorces his wife and marries another woman commits adultery against her. 12And if she divorces her husband and marries another man, she commits adultery."

The Little Children and Jesus

13People were bringing little children to Jesus to have him touch them, but the disciples rebuked them. 14When Jesus saw this, he was indignant. He said to them, "Let the little children come to me, and do not hinder them, for the kingdom of God belongs to such as these. 15I tell you the truth, anyone who will not receive the kingdom of God like a little child will never enter it." 16And he took the children in his arms, put his hands on them and blessed them.

The Rich Young Man

17As Jesus started on his way, a man ran up to him and fell on his knees before him. "Good teacher," he asked, "what must I do to inherit eternal life?"

18"Why do you call me good?" Jesus answered. "No one is good—except God alone. 19You know the commandments: 'Do not murder, do not commit adultery, do not steal, do not give false testimony, do not defraud, honor your father and mother.'[m]

20"Teacher," he declared, "all these I have

---

[b] Some mss. add: *and shall cleave to his wife*

[j] Gen. 1:27
[k] Some early manuscripts do not have *and be united to his wife*.
[l] Gen. 2:24
[m] 19 Exodus 20:12-16; Deut. 5:16-20

these things from my youth up."

21And looking at him, Jesus felt a love for him, and said to him, "One thing you lack: go and sell all you possess, and give to the poor, and you shall have treasure in heaven; and come, follow Me."

22But at these words his face fell, and he went away grieved, for he was one who owned much property.

23And Jesus, looking around, *said to His disciples, "How hard it will be for those who are wealthy to enter the kingdom of God!"

24And the disciples were amazed at His words. But Jesus *answered again and *said to them, "Children, how hard it is ᶜto enter the kingdom of God!

25"It is easier for a camel to go through the eye of a needle than for a rich man to enter the kingdom of God."

26And they were even more astonished and said to Him, "Then who can be saved?"

27Looking upon them, Jesus *said, "With men it is impossible, but not with God; for all things are possible with God."

28Peter began to say to Him, "Behold, we have left everything and followed You."

29Jesus said, "Truly I say to you, there is no one who has left house or brothers or sisters or mother or father or children or farms, for My sake and for the gospel's sake,

30but that he shall receive a hundred times as much now in the present age, houses and brothers and sisters and mothers and children and farms, along

---

ταῦτα πάντα ἐφυλαξάμην ἐκ νεότητός μου.
all these things I observed from youth of me.
21 ὁ δὲ Ἰησοῦς ἐμβλέψας αὐτῷ ἠγάπησεν
- But Jesus looking at him loved
αὐτὸν καὶ εἶπεν αὐτῷ· ἕν σε ὑστερεῖ·
him and said to him: One thing thee is wanting:
ὕπαγε, ὅσα ἔχεις πώλησον καὶ δὸς [τοῖς]
go, what things thou hast sell and give to the
πτωχοῖς, καὶ ἕξεις θησαυρὸν ἐν οὐρανῷ,
poor, and thou wilt have treasure in heaven,
καὶ δεῦρο ἀκολούθει μοι. 22 ὁ δὲ στυγνάσας
and come follow me. But he being sad
ἐπὶ τῷ λόγῳ ἀπῆλθεν λυπούμενος, ³he was
at the word went away grieving, ³he was
γὰρ ἔχων κτήματα πολλά. 23 Καὶ
¹for having possessions many. And
περιβλεψάμενος ὁ Ἰησοῦς λέγει τοῖς
looking round - Jesus says to the
μαθηταῖς αὐτοῦ· πῶς δυσκόλως οἱ τὰ
disciples of him: How hardly the [ones] the
χρήματα ἔχοντες εἰς τὴν βασιλείαν τοῦ
riches having into the kingdom -
θεοῦ εἰσελεύσονται. 24 οἱ δὲ μαθηταὶ
of God shall enter. And the disciples
ἐθαμβοῦντο ἐπὶ τοῖς λόγοις αὐτοῦ. ὁ δὲ
were amazed at the words of him. - And
Ἰησοῦς πάλιν ἀποκριθεὶς λέγει αὐτοῖς·
Jesus again answering says to them:
τέκνα, πῶς δύσκολόν ἐστιν εἰς τὴν
Children, how hard it is into the
βασιλείαν τοῦ θεοῦ εἰσελθεῖν· 25 εὐκοπώτερόν
kingdom - of God to enter; easier
ἐστιν κάμηλον διὰ τῆς τρυμαλιᾶς τῆς
it is a camel through the eye -
ῥαφίδος διελθεῖν ἢ πλούσιον εἰς τὴν
of a needle to go through than a rich man into the
βασιλείαν τοῦ θεοῦ εἰσελθεῖν. 26 οἱ δὲ
kingdom - of God to enter. But they
περισσῶς ἐξεπλήσσοντο λέγοντες πρὸς
exceedingly were astonished saying to
ἑαυτούς· καὶ τίς δύναται σωθῆναι;
themselves: And who can to be saved?
27 ἐμβλέψας αὐτοῖς ὁ Ἰησοῦς λέγει· παρὰ
Looking at them - Jesus says: With
ἀνθρώποις ἀδύνατον, ἀλλ᾽ οὐ παρὰ θεῷ·
men [it is] impossible, but not with God;
πάντα γὰρ δυνατὰ παρὰ τῷ θεῷ. 28 Ἤρξατο
for all things [are] possible with - God. Began
λέγειν ὁ Πέτρος αὐτῷ· ἰδοὺ ἡμεῖς ἀφήκαμεν
to say - Peter to him: Behold [,] we left
πάντα καὶ ἠκολουθήκαμέν σοι. 29 ἔφη ὁ
all things and have followed thee. Said -
Ἰησοῦς· ἀμὴν λέγω ὑμῖν, οὐδείς ἐστιν
Jesus: Truly I tell you, no one there is
ὃς ἀφῆκεν οἰκίαν ἢ ἀδελφοὺς ἢ ἀδελφὰς
who left house or · brothers or sisters
ἢ μητέρα ἢ πατέρα ἢ τέκνα ἢ ἀγροὺς
or mother or father or children or fields
ἕνεκεν ἐμοῦ καὶ ἕνεκεν τοῦ εὐαγγελίου,
for the sake of me and for the sake of the · gospel,
30 ἐὰν μὴ λάβῃ ἑκατονταπλασίονα νῦν
but he receives a hundredfold now
ἐν τῷ καιρῷ τούτῳ οἰκίας καὶ ἀδελφοὺς
in - time this houses and brothers
καὶ ἀδελφὰς καὶ μητέρας καὶ τέκνα καὶ
and sisters and mothers and children and

---

kept since I was a boy."

21Jesus looked at him and loved him. "One thing you lack," he said. "Go, sell everything you have and give to the poor, and you will have treasure in heaven. Then come, follow me."

22At this the man's face fell. He went away sad, because he had great wealth.

23Jesus looked around and said to his disciples, "How hard it is for the rich to enter the kingdom of God!"

24The disciples were amazed at his words. But Jesus said again, "Children, how hard it isⁿ to enter the kingdom of God! 25It is easier for a camel to go through the eye of a needle than for a rich man to enter the kingdom of God."

26The disciples were even more amazed, and said to each other, "Who then can be saved?"

27Jesus looked at them and said, "With man this is impossible, but not with God; all things are possible with God."

28Peter said to him, "We have left everything to follow you!"

29"I tell you the truth," Jesus replied, "no one who has left home or brothers or sisters or mother or father or children or fields for me and the gospel 30will fail to receive a hundred times as much in this present age (homes, brothers, sisters, mothers, children and

---

ᶜ Later mss. insert: for those who trust in wealth

ⁿ24 Some manuscripts is for those who trust in riches

with persecutions; and in the age to come, eternal life. ³¹"But many who are first, will be last; and the last, first."

Jesus' Sufferings Foretold

³²And they were on the road, going up to Jerusalem, and Jesus was walking on ahead of them; and they were amazed, and those who followed were fearful. And again He took the twelve aside and began to tell them what was going to happen to Him. ³³saying, "Behold, we are going up to Jerusalem, and the Son of Man is ᵈdelivered to the chief priests and the scribes; and they will condemn Him to death, and will deliver Him to the Gentiles. ³⁴"And they will mock Him and spit upon Him, and scourge Him, and kill Him, and three days later He will rise again."

³⁵And James and John, the two sons of Zebedee, *came to Him, saying to Him, "Teacher, we want You to do for us whatever we ask of You." ³⁶And He said to them, "What do you want Me to do for you?" ³⁷And they said to Him, "Grant that we may sit in Your glory, one on Your right, and one on Your left." ³⁸But Jesus said to them, "You do not know what you are asking for. Are you able to drink the cup that I drink, or to be baptized with the baptism with which I am baptized?" ³⁹And they said to Him, "We are able." And Jesus said to them, "The cup that I drink you shall drink; and you shall be baptized with the baptism with which I am baptized."

ἀγροὺς μετὰ διωγμῶν, καὶ ἐν τῷ αἰῶνι
fields with persecutions, and in the age
τῷ ἐρχομένῳ ζωὴν αἰώνιον. 31 πολλοὶ δὲ
- coming life eternal. And ¹many
ἔσονται πρῶτοι ἔσχατοι καὶ οἱ ἔσχατοι
²will be ³first ⁴last and the last
πρῶτοι.
first.
32 ᾿Ησαν δὲ ἐν τῇ ὁδῷ ἀναβαίνοντες
Now they were in the way going up
εἰς ᾿Ιεροσόλυμα, καὶ ἦν προάγων αὐτοὺς
to Jerusalem, and was going before them
ὁ ᾿Ιησοῦς, καὶ ἐθαμβοῦντο, οἱ δὲ
- Jesus, and they were astonished, and the
ἀκολουθοῦντες ἐφοβοῦντο. καὶ παραλαβὼν
[ones] following were afraid. And taking
πάλιν τοὺς δώδεκα ἤρξατο αὐτοῖς λέγειν
again the twelve he began them to tell
τὰ μέλλοντα αὐτῷ συμβαίνειν, 33 ὅτι ἰδοὺ
the things about to him to happen, - Behold
ἀναβαίνομεν εἰς ᾿Ιεροσόλυμα, καὶ ὁ υἱὸς
we are going up to Jerusalem, and the Son
τοῦ ἀνθρώπου παραδοθήσεται τοῖς
- of man will be betrayed to the
ἀρχιερεῦσιν καὶ τοῖς γραμματεῦσιν, καὶ
chief priests and to the scribes, and
κατακρινοῦσιν αὐτὸν θανάτῳ καὶ παραδώσουσιν
they will condemn him to death and will deliver
αὐτὸν τοῖς ἔθνεσιν 34 καὶ ἐμπαίξουσιν
him to the nations and they will mock
αὐτῷ καὶ ἐμπτύσουσιν αὐτῷ καὶ μαστι-
him and will spit at him and will
γώσουσιν αὐτὸν καὶ ἀποκτενοῦσιν, καὶ
scourge him and will kill, and
μετὰ τρεῖς ἡμέρας ἀναστήσεται.
after three days he will rise again.
35 Καὶ προσπορεύονται αὐτῷ ᾿Ιάκωβος
And approach to him James
καὶ ᾿Ιωάννης οἱ [δύο] υἱοὶ Ζεβεδαίου
and John the two sons of Zebedee
λέγοντες αὐτῷ· διδάσκαλε, θέλομεν ἵνα ὃ ἐὰν
saying to him: Teacher, we wish that whatever
αἰτήσωμέν σε ποιήσῃς ἡμῖν. 36 ὁ
we may ask thee thou mayest do for us. he
δὲ εἶπεν αὐτοῖς· τί θέλετέ με ποιήσω
And said to them: What wish ye me I may do
ὑμῖν; 37 οἱ δὲ εἶπαν αὐτῷ· δὸς ἡμῖν
for you? And they said to him: Give us
ἵνα εἷς σου ἐκ δεξιῶν καὶ εἷς ἐξ
that one of thee out of(on) [the] right and one on
= on thy right
ἀριστερῶν καθίσωμεν ἐν τῇ δόξῃ σου.
[thy] left we may sit in the glory of thee.
38 ὁ δὲ ᾿Ιησοῦς εἶπεν αὐτοῖς· οὐκ οἴδατε
- And Jesus said to them: Ye know not
τί αἰτεῖσθε. δύνασθε πιεῖν τὸ ποτήριον
what ye ask. Can ye to drink the cup
ὃ ἐγὼ πίνω, ἢ τὸ βάπτισμα ὃ ἐγὼ
which I drink, or the baptism which I
βαπτίζομαι βαπτισθῆναι; 39 οἱ δὲ εἶπαν
am baptized to be baptized [with]? And they said
αὐτῷ· δυνάμεθα. ὁ δὲ ᾿Ιησοῦς εἶπεν
to him: We can. - And Jesus said
αὐτοῖς· τὸ ποτήριον ὃ ἐγὼ πίνω πίεσθε,
to them: The cup which I drink shall ye drink,
καὶ τὸ βάπτισμα ὃ ἐγὼ βαπτίζομαι
and the baptism which I am baptized [with]

fields—and with them, persecutions) and in the age to come, eternal life. ³¹But many who are first will be last, and the last first."

Jesus Again Predicts His Death

³²They were on their way up to Jerusalem, with Jesus leading the way, and the disciples were astonished, while those who followed were afraid. Again he took the Twelve aside and told them what was going to happen to him. ³³"We are going up to Jerusalem," he said, "and the Son of Man will be betrayed to the chief priests and teachers of the law. They will condemn him to death and will hand him over to the Gentiles, ³⁴who will mock him and spit on him, flog him and kill him. Three days later he will rise."

The Request of James and John

³⁵Then James and John, the sons of Zebedee, came to him. "Teacher," they said, "we want you to do for us whatever we ask." ³⁶"What do you want me to do for you?" he asked. ³⁷They replied, "Let one of us sit at your right and the other at your left in your glory." ³⁸"You don't know what you are asking," Jesus said. "Can you drink the cup I drink or be baptized with the baptism I am baptized with?" ³⁹"We can," they answered. Jesus said to them, "You will drink the cup I drink and be baptized with the baptism I am baptized

ᵈOr, betrayed

40"But to sit on My right or on My left, this is not Mine to give; but it is for those for whom it has been prepared."

41And hearing this, the ten began to feel indignant with James and John.

42And calling them to Himself, Jesus *said to them, "You know that those who are recognized as rulers of the Gentiles lord it over them; and their great men exercise authority over them.

43"But it is not so among you, but whoever wishes to become great among you shall be your servant;

44and whoever wishes to be first among you shall be slave of all.

45"For even the Son of Man did not come to be served, but to serve, and to give His life a ransom for many."

Bartimaeus Receives His Sight

46And they *came to Jericho. And as He was going out from Jericho with His disciples and a great multitude, a blind beggar *named* Bartimaeus, the son of Timaeus, was sitting by the road.

47And when he heard that it was Jesus the Nazarene, he began to cry out and say, "Jesus, Son of David, have mercy on me!"

48And many were sternly telling him to be quiet, but he kept crying out all the more, "Son of David, have mercy on me!"

49And Jesus stopped and said, "Call him *here*." And they *called the blind man, saying to him, "Take courage, arise! He is calling for you."

50And casting aside his cloak, he jumped up, and came to Jesus.

51And answering him, Jesus said, "What do you want Me to do for you?"

βαπτισθήσεσθε· **40** τὸ δὲ καθίσαι ἐκ δεξιῶν
ye shall be baptized;   –   but   to sit   on   right

μου ἢ ἐξ εὐωνύμων οὐκ ἔστιν ἐμὸν
of me or on [my] left   is not   mine

δοῦναι, ἀλλ' οἷς ἡτοίμασται. **41** Καὶ
to give,   but   for whom it has been prepared.   And

ἀκούσαντες οἱ δέκα ἤρξαντο ἀγανακτεῖν
¹hearing   ¹the ²ten   began   to be incensed

περὶ Ἰακώβου καὶ Ἰωάννου. **42** καὶ
about   James   and   John.   And

προσκαλεσάμενος αὐτοὺς ὁ Ἰησοῦς λέγει
¹calling ³to ⁴[him]   ²them   –   Jesus   says

αὐτοῖς· οἴδατε ὅτι οἱ δοκοῦντες ἄρχειν
to them: Ye know that the [ones] thinking   to rule

τῶν ἐθνῶν κατακυριεύουσιν αὐτῶν καὶ
the nations   lord it over   them   and

οἱ μεγάλοι αὐτῶν κατεξουσιάζουσιν αὐτῶν.
the great [ones] of them   exercise authority over   them.

43 οὐχ οὕτως δέ ἐστιν ἐν ὑμῖν· ἀλλ'
   ²not   ³so   ¹But is it among you;   but

ὃς ἂν θέλῃ μέγας γενέσθαι ἐν ὑμῖν,
whoever wishes great to become among you,

ἔσται ὑμῶν διάκονος, **44** καὶ ὃς ἂν
shall be of you   servant,   and whoever

θέλῃ ἐν ὑμῖν εἶναι πρῶτος, ἔσται πάντων
wishes among you to be   first, shall be of all

δοῦλος· **45** καὶ γὰρ ὁ υἱὸς τοῦ ἀνθρώπου
slave;   for even the Son   –   of man

οὐκ ἦλθεν διακονηθῆναι ἀλλὰ διακονῆσαι
did not come   to be served   but   to serve

καὶ δοῦναι τὴν ψυχὴν αὐτοῦ λύτρον ἀντὶ
and to give the life of him a ransom instead of

πολλῶν.
many.

46 Καὶ ἔρχονται εἰς Ἰεριχώ. Καὶ
   And they come   to   Jericho.   And

ἐκπορευομένου αὐτοῦ ἀπὸ Ἰεριχὼ καὶ τῶν
going out   himᵃ from Jericho and the
= as he was going out

μαθητῶν αὐτοῦ καὶ ὄχλου ἱκανοῦ ὁ υἱὸς
disciplesᵃ of him and crowd a considerableᵃ the son

Τιμαίου Βαρτιμαῖος, τυφλὸς προσαίτης,
of Timæus Bartimæus,   a blind   beggar,

ἐκάθητο παρὰ τὴν ὁδόν. **47** καὶ ἀκούσας
sat   by   the way.   And hearing

ὅτι Ἰησοῦς ὁ Ναζαρηνός ἐστιν ἤρξατο
that Jesus the Nazarene   it is(was) he began

κράζειν καὶ λέγειν· υἱὲ Δαυὶδ Ἰησοῦ,
to cry out and to say: Son of David Jesus,

ἐλέησόν με. **48** καὶ ἐπετίμων αὐτῷ πολλοὶ
pity   me.   And   rebuked   him   many

ἵνα σιωπήσῃ· ὁ δὲ πολλῷ μᾶλλον ἔκραζεν·
that he should be quiet. But he much   more   cried out:

υἱὲ Δαυίδ, ἐλέησόν με. **49** καὶ στὰς
Son of David, pity   me.   And standing

ὁ Ἰησοῦς εἶπεν· φωνήσατε αὐτόν. καὶ
 – Jesus   said: Call   him.   And

φωνοῦσιν τὸν τυφλὸν λέγοντες αὐτῷ·
they call   the blind man   saying   to him:

θάρσει, ἔγειρε, φωνεῖ σε. **50** ὁ δὲ
Be of good courage, rise, he calls thee.   So he

ἀποβαλὼν τὸ ἱμάτιον αὐτοῦ ἀναπηδήσας ἦλθεν
throwing away the garment of him   leaping up   came

πρὸς τὸν Ἰησοῦν. **51** καὶ ἀποκριθεὶς αὐτῷ ὁ
to   –   Jesus.   And answering   him   –

Ἰησοῦς εἶπεν· τί σοι θέλεις ποιήσω;
Jesus   said: What for thee wishest thou I may do?

---

with, 40but to sit at my right or left is not for me to grant. These places belong to those for whom they have been prepared."

41When the ten heard about this, they became indignant with James and John. 42Jesus called them together and said, "You know that those who are regarded as rulers of the Gentiles lord it over them, and their high officials exercise authority over them. 43Not so with you. Instead, whoever wants to become great among you must be your servant, 44and whoever wants to be first must be slave of all. 45For even the Son of Man did not come to be served, but to serve, and to give his life as a ransom for many."

Blind Bartimaeus Receives His Sight

46Then they came to Jericho. As Jesus and his disciples, together with a large crowd, were leaving the city, a blind man, Bartimaeus (that is, the Son of Timaeus), was sitting by the roadside begging.

47When he heard that it was Jesus of Nazareth, he began to shout, "Jesus, Son of David, have mercy on me!"

48Many rebuked him and told him to be quiet, but he shouted all the more, "Son of David, have mercy on me!"

49Jesus stopped and said, "Call him."

So they called to the blind man, "Cheer up! On your feet! He's calling you." 50Throwing his cloak aside, he jumped to his feet and came to Jesus.

51"What do you want me to do for you?" Jesus asked him.

And the blind man said to Him, "*Rabboni, I want to regain my sight!*"
52And Jesus said to him, "Go your way; your faith has made you well." And immediately he regained his sight and *began* following Him on the road.

Chapter 11

The Triumphal Entry

AND as they *approached Jerusalem, at Bethphage and Bethany, near the Mount of Olives, He *sent two of His disciples,
2and *said to them, "Go into the village opposite you, and immediately as you enter it, you will find a colt tied *there*, on which no one yet has ever sat; untie it and bring it *here*.
3"And if anyone says to you, 'Why are you doing this?' you say, 'The Lord has need of it'; and immediately he will send it back here."
4And they went away and found a colt tied at the door outside in the street; and they *untied it.
5And some of the bystanders were saying to them, "What are you doing, untying the colt?"
6And they spoke to them just as Jesus had told *them*, and they gave them permission.
7And they *brought the colt to Jesus and put their garments on it; and He sat upon it.
8And many spread their garments in the road, and others spread leafy branches which they had cut from the fields.
9And those who went before, and those who followed after, were crying out,
"Hosanna!
BLESSED IS HE WHO COMES IN THE NAME OF THE LORD;
10 Blessed *is* the coming kingdom of our father David; Hosanna in the highest!"

*I.e., My Master

Middle column (Greek interlinear):

ὁ δὲ τυφλὸς εἶπεν αὐτῷ· ῥαββουνί, ἵνα
And the blind man said to him: Rabboni, that
ἀναβλέψω. 52 καὶ ὁ Ἰησοῦς εἶπεν αὐτῷ·
I may see again. And - Jesus said to him:
ὕπαγε, ἡ πίστις σου σέσωκέν σε. καὶ
Go, the faith of thee has healed thee. And
εὐθὺς ἀνέβλεψεν, καὶ ἠκολούθει αὐτῷ ἐν
immediately he saw again, and followed him in
τῇ ὁδῷ.
the way.

11 Καὶ ὅτε ἐγγίζουσιν εἰς Ἱεροσόλυμα
And when they draw near to Jerusalem
εἰς Βηθφαγὴ καὶ Βηθανίαν πρὸς τὸ
to Bethphage and Bethany at the
ὄρος τῶν ἐλαιῶν, ἀποστέλλει δύο τῶν
mount of the olives, he sends two of the
μαθητῶν αὐτοῦ 2 καὶ λέγει αὐτοῖς· ὑπάγετε
disciples of him and tells them: Go ye
εἰς τὴν κώμην τὴν κατέναντι ὑμῶν, καὶ
into the village - opposite you, and
εὐθὺς εἰσπορευόμενοι εἰς αὐτὴν εὑρήσετε
immediately entering into it ye will find
πῶλον δεδεμένον ἐφ᾽ ὃν οὐδεὶς οὔπω
a colt having been tied on which 'no one 'not yet
ἀνθρώπων ἐκάθισεν· λύσατε αὐτὸν καὶ
'of men 'sat; loosen it and
φέρετε. 3 καὶ ἐάν τις ὑμῖν εἴπῃ· τί
bring. And if anyone to you says: Why
ποιεῖτε τοῦτο; εἴπατε· ὁ κύριος αὐτοῦ
do ye this? say: The Lord of it
χρείαν ἔχει, καὶ εὐθὺς αὐτὸν ἀποστέλλει
need has, and immediately it he sends
πάλιν ὧδε. 4 καὶ ἀπῆλθον καὶ εὗρον
again here. And they went and found
πῶλον δεδεμένον πρὸς θύραν ἔξω ἐπὶ
a colt having been tied at a door outside on
τοῦ ἀμφόδου, καὶ λύουσιν αὐτόν. 5 καὶ
the open street, and they loosen it. And
τινες τῶν ἐκεῖ ἑστηκότων ἔλεγον αὐτοῖς·
some of the [ones] there standing said to them:
τί ποιεῖτε λύοντες τὸν πῶλον; 6 οἱ δὲ
What do ye loosening the colt? And they
εἶπαν αὐτοῖς καθὼς εἶπεν ὁ Ἰησοῦς·
said to them as said - Jesus;
καὶ ἀφῆκαν αὐτούς. 7 καὶ φέρουσιν τὸν
and they let go them. And they bring the
πῶλον πρὸς τὸν Ἰησοῦν, καὶ ἐπιβάλλουσιν
colt to - Jesus, and they throw on
αὐτῷ τὰ ἱμάτια αὐτῶν, καὶ ἐκάθισεν
it the garments of them, and he sat
ἐπ᾽ αὐτόν. 8 καὶ πολλοὶ τὰ ἱμάτια αὐτῶν
on it. And many the garments of them
ἔστρωσαν εἰς τὴν ὁδόν, ἄλλοι δὲ στιβάδας,
strewed in the way, and others wisps of twigs,
κόψαντες ἐκ τῶν ἀγρῶν. 9 καὶ οἱ
cutting out of the fields. And the [ones]
προάγοντες καὶ οἱ ἀκολουθοῦντες ἔκραζον·
going before and the [ones] following cried out:
ὡσαννά· εὐλογημένος ὁ ἐρχόμενος ἐν
Hosanna; blessed the [one] coming in
ὀνόματι κυρίου· 10 εὐλογημένη ἡ ἐρχομένη
[the] name of [the] Lord; blessed the coming
βασιλεία τοῦ πατρὸς ἡμῶν Δαυίδ· ὡσαννὰ
kingdom of the father of us David; Hosanna

The blind man said, "Rabbi, I want to see."
52"Go," said Jesus, "your faith has healed you." Immediately he received his sight and followed Jesus along the road.

Chapter 11

The Triumphal Entry

AS they approached Jerusalem and came to Bethphage and Bethany at the Mount of Olives, Jesus sent two of his disciples, 2saying to them, "Go to the village ahead of you, and just as you enter it, you will find a colt tied there, which no one has ever ridden. Untie it and bring it here. 3If anyone asks you, 'Why are you doing this?' tell him, 'The Lord needs it and will send it back here shortly.'"
4They went and found a colt outside in the street, tied at a doorway. As they untied it, 5some people standing there asked, "What are you doing, untying that colt?" 6They answered as Jesus had told them to, and the people let them go. 7When they brought the colt to Jesus and threw their cloaks over it, he sat on it. 8Many people spread their cloaks on the road, while others spread branches they had cut in the fields. 9Those who went ahead and those who followed shouted,

"Hosanna!⁰"

"Blessed is he who comes in the name of the Lord!"ᵖ

10"Blessed is the coming kingdom of our father David!"

"Hosanna in the highest!"

ᵒ9 A Hebrew expression meaning "Save!" which became an exclamation of praise; also in verse 10
ᵖ9 Psalm 118:25,26

11And He entered Jerusalem *and came* into the temple; and after looking all around, He departed for Bethany with the twelve, since it was already late.

12And on the next day, when they had departed from Bethany, He became hungry.

13And seeing at a distance a fig tree in leaf, He went *to see* if perhaps He would find anything on it; and when He came to it, He found nothing but leaves, for it was not the season for figs.

14And He answered and said to it, "May no one ever eat fruit from you again!" And His disciples were listening.

Jesus Drives Moneychangers from the Temple

15And they *came to Jerusalem. And He entered the temple and began to cast out those who were buying and selling in the temple, and overturned the tables of the moneychangers and the seats of those who were selling doves;

16and He would not permit anyone to carry goods through the temple.

17And He *began* to teach and say to them, "Is it not written, 'MY HOUSE SHALL BE CALLED A HOUSE OF PRAYER FOR ALL THE NATIONS'? But you have made it a ROBBERS' DEN."

18And the chief priests and the scribes heard *this*, and *began* seeking how to destroy Him; for they were afraid of Him, for all the multitude was astonished at His teaching.

19And whenever evening came, they would go out of the city.

20And as they were passing by in the morning, they saw the fig tree withered from the roots *up.*

21And being reminded, Peter *said to Him, "Rabbi, behold, the fig tree which You cursed has

---

ἐν τοῖς ὑψίστοις. 11 Καὶ εἰσῆλθεν εἰς
in the highest [places]. ,And he entered into

Ἱεροσόλυμα εἰς τὸ ἱερόν· καὶ περιβλεψάμενος
Jerusalem into the temple; and looking round at

πάντα, ὀψὲ ἤδη οὔσης τῆς ὥρας, ἐξῆλθεν
all things, ⁵late ⁴now ³being ¹the ²hour,ᵃ he went forth

εἰς Βηθανίαν μετὰ τῶν δώδεκα.
to Bethany with the twelve.

12 Καὶ τῇ ἐπαύριον ἐξελθόντων αὐτῶνᵃ
And on the morrow going forth them
= as they went forth

ἀπὸ Βηθανίας ἐπείνασεν. 13 καὶ ἰδὼν
from Bethany he hungered. And seeing

συκῆν ἀπὸ μακρόθεν ἔχουσαν φύλλα ἦλθεν
a fig-tree from afar having leaves he came

εἰ ἄρα τι εὑρήσει ἐν αὐτῇ, καὶ ἐλθὼν
if perhaps something he will find in it, and coming

ἐπ᾽ αὐτὴν οὐδὲν εὗρεν εἰ μὴ φύλλα·
upon it nothing he found except leaves;

ὁ γὰρ καιρὸς οὐκ ἦν σύκων. 14 καὶ
for the time was not of figs. And

ἀποκριθεὶς εἶπεν αὐτῇ· μηκέτι εἰς τὸν
answering he said to it: No more to the

αἰῶνα ἐκ σοῦ μηδεὶς καρπὸν φάγοι.
age of thee no one fruit may eat.
= May no one eat fruit of thee for ever.

καὶ ἤκουον οἱ μαθηταὶ αὐτοῦ. 15 Καὶ
And ⁴heard ¹the ²disciples ³of him. And

ἔρχονται εἰς Ἱεροσόλυμα. Καὶ εἰσελθὼν
they come to Jerusalem. And entering

εἰς τὸ ἱερὸν ἤρξατο ἐκβάλλειν τοὺς
into the temple he began to cast out the [ones]

πωλοῦντας καὶ τοὺς ἀγοράζοντας ἐν τῷ
selling and the [ones] buying in the

ἱερῷ, καὶ τὰς τραπέζας τῶν κολλυβιστῶν
temple, and the tables of the moneychangers

καὶ τὰς καθέδρας τῶν πωλούντων τὰς
and the seats of the [ones] selling the

περιστερὰς κατέστρεψεν, 16 καὶ οὐκ ἤφιεν
doves he overturned, and did not permit

ἵνα τις διενέγκῃ σκεῦος διὰ τοῦ
that anyone should carry *through* a vessel through the

ἱεροῦ, 17 καὶ ἐδίδασκεν καὶ ἔλεγεν αὐτοῖς· οὐ
temple, and taught and said to them: Not

γέγραπται ὅτι ὁ οἶκός μου οἶκος προσευχῆς
has it been written that the house of me a house of prayer

κληθήσεται πᾶσιν τοῖς ἔθνεσιν; ὑμεῖς δὲ
shall be called for all the nations? but ye

πεποιήκατε αὐτὸν σπήλαιον λῃστῶν. 18 καὶ
have made it a den of robbers. And

ἤκουσαν οἱ ἀρχιερεῖς καὶ οἱ γραμματεῖς,
⁴heard ¹the ²chief priests ³and ⁴the ⁵scribes,

καὶ ἐζήτουν πῶς αὐτὸν ἀπολέσωσιν·
and they sought how him they might destroy;

ἐφοβοῦντο γὰρ αὐτόν, πᾶς γὰρ ὁ ὄχλος
for they feared him, for all the crowd

ἐξεπλήσσετο ἐπὶ τῇ διδαχῇ αὐτοῦ. 19 Καὶ
was astounded at the teaching of him. And

ὅταν ὀψὲ ἐγένετο, ἐξεπορεύοντο ἔξω τῆς
when late it became, they went forth outside the

πόλεως. 20 Καὶ παραπορευόμενοι πρωὶ
city. And passing along early

εἶδον τὴν συκῆν ἐξηραμμένην ἐκ ῥιζῶν.
they saw the fig-tree *having been* withered from [the] roots.

21 καὶ ἀναμνησθεὶς ὁ Πέτρος λέγει αὐτῷ·
And ⁸remembering – ¹Peter says to him:

ῥαββί, ἴδε ἡ συκῆ ἣν κατηράσω
Rabbi, behold[,] the fig-tree which thou cursedst

11Jesus entered Jerusalem and went to the temple. He looked around at everything, but since it was already late, he went out to Bethany with the Twelve.

Jesus Clears the Temple

12The next day as they were leaving Bethany, Jesus was hungry. 13Seeing in the distance a fig tree in leaf, he went to find out if it had any fruit. When he reached it, he found nothing but leaves, because it was not the season for figs. 14Then he said to the tree, "May no one ever eat fruit from you again." And his disciples heard him say it.

15On reaching Jerusalem, Jesus entered the temple area and began driving out those who were buying and selling there. He overturned the tables of the money changers and the benches of those selling doves, 16and would not allow anyone to carry merchandise through the temple courts. 17And as he taught them, he said, "Is it not written:

" 'My house will be called a house of prayer for all nations'ᵠ?

But you have made it 'a den of robbers.'ʳ"

18The chief priests and the teachers of the law heard this and began looking for a way to kill him, for they feared him, because the whole crowd was amazed at his teaching.

19When evening came, theyˢ went out of the city.

The Withered Fig Tree

20In the morning, as they went along, they saw the fig tree withered from the roots. 21Peter remembered and said to Jesus, "Rabbi, look! The fig tree you cursed has withered!"

Left column (KJV)

withered.''
22And Jesus *answered saying to them, "Have faith in God.
23"Truly I say to you, whoever says to this mountain, 'Be taken up and cast into the sea,' and does not doubt in his heart, but believes that what he says is going to happen, it shall be *granted* him.
24"Therefore I say to you, all things for which you pray and ask, believe that you have received them, and they shall be *granted* you.
25"And whenever you stand praying, forgive, if you have anything against anyone; so that your Father also who is in heaven may forgive you your transgressions.
26["*f*But if you do not forgive, neither will your Father who is in heaven forgive your transgressions.''

Jesus' Authority Questioned
27And they *came again to Jerusalem. And as He was walking in the temple, the chief priests, and scribes, and elders *came to Him,
28and *began* saying to Him, "By what authority are You doing these things, or who gave You this authority to do these things?''
29And Jesus said to them, "I will ask you one question, and you answer Me, and *then* I will tell you by what authority I do these things.
30"Was the baptism of John from heaven, or from men? Answer Me.''
31And they *began* reasoning among themselves, saying, "If we say, 'From heaven,' He will say, 'Then why did you not believe him?'
32"But shall we say, 'From men'?''—they were afraid of the multitude, for all considered John to have been a prophet indeed.
33And answering Jesus, they *said, "We do not know.'' And Jesus *said to them, "Neither will I tell you by what authority I do these things.''

*f*Many mss. do not contain this verse

Center column (Greek interlinear)

ἐξήρανται.   **22** καὶ ἀποκριθεὶς ὁ Ἰησοῦς λέγει
has been withered.   And   answering   –   Jesus   says

αὐτοῖς· ἔχετε πίστιν θεοῦ.   **23** ἀμὴν λέγω ὑμῖν
to them: Have [the] faith of God.   Truly   I tell   you

ὅτι ὃς ἂν εἴπῃ τῷ ὄρει τούτῳ·   ἄρθητι
that whoever says   –   mountain to this: Be thou taken

καὶ βλήθητι εἰς τὴν θάλασσαν, καὶ μὴ
and   be thou cast into   the   sea,   and   not

διακριθῇ ἐν τῇ καρδίᾳ αὐτοῦ ἀλλὰ πιστεύῃ
doubts   in   the   heart   of him   but   believes

ὅτι ὃ λαλεῖ γίνεται, ἔσται αὐτῷ.   **24** διὰ
that what he says happens, it will be   to him.*c*   There-
= he will have it.

τοῦτο λέγω ὑμῖν, πάντα ὅσα προσεύχεσθε
fore   I tell   you,   all things   which   ye pray

καὶ αἰτεῖσθε, πιστεύετε ὅτι ἐλάβετε, καὶ
and   ask,   believe   that ye received,   and

ἔσται ὑμῖν,   **25** καὶ ὅταν στήκετε
it will be   to you.*e*   And   when   ye stand
= ye will have it.

προσευχόμενοι, ἀφίετε εἴ τι ἔχετε κατά
praying,   forgive   if anything ye have against

τινος, ἵνα καὶ ὁ πατὴρ ὑμῶν ὁ ἐν τοῖς
anyone, that also   the   Father   of you   –   in   the

οὐρανοῖς ἀφῇ ὑμῖν τὰ παραπτώματα ὑμῶν.‡
heavens   may forgive you the   trespasses   of you.

27 Καὶ ἔρχονται πάλιν εἰς Ἱεροσόλυμα.
And   they come   again   to   Jerusalem.

καὶ ἐν τῷ ἱερῷ περιπατοῦντος αὐτοῦ
And   in   the   temple   walking   him*a*
= as he walked

ἔρχονται πρὸς αὐτὸν οἱ ἀρχιερεῖς καὶ οἱ
come   to   him   the chief priests   and the

γραμματεῖς καὶ οἱ πρεσβύτεροι,   **28** καὶ
scribes   and   the   elders,   And

ἔλεγον αὐτῷ· ἐν ποίᾳ ἐξουσίᾳ ταῦτα
said   to him: By   what   authority these things

ποιεῖς; ἢ τίς σοι ἔδωκεν τὴν ἐξουσίαν
doest thou? or who thee   gave   –   authority

ταύτην ἵνα ταῦτα ποιῇς;   **29** ὁ δὲ Ἰησοῦς
this   that these things thou mayest do?   – And Jesus

εἶπεν αὐτοῖς· ἐπερωτήσω ὑμᾶς ἕνα λόγον,
said   to them: I will question   you   one word,

καὶ ἀποκρίθητέ μοι, καὶ ἐρῶ ὑμῖν ἐν
and   answer ye   me,   and I will tell   you   by

ποίᾳ ἐξουσίᾳ ταῦτα ποιῶ.   **30** τὸ βάπτισμα
what   authority these things I do.   The   baptism

τὸ Ἰωάννου ἐξ οὐρανοῦ ἦν ἢ ἐξ ἀνθρώπων;
–   of John   of   heaven   was it or of   men?

ἀποκρίθητέ μοι.   **31** καὶ διελογίζοντο πρὸς
answer ye   me.   And   they debated   with

ἑαυτοὺς λέγοντες· ἐὰν εἴπωμεν· ἐξ οὐρανοῦ,
themselves   saying: If   we say: Of   heaven,

ἐρεῖ· διὰ τί οὖν οὐκ ἐπιστεύσατε αὐτῷ;
he will say: Why   then   did ye not believe   him?

32 ἀλλὰ εἴπωμεν· ἐξ ἀνθρώπων;—ἐφοβοῦντο
But   may we say: Of   men?   — they feared

τὸν ὄχλον· ἅπαντες γὰρ εἶχον τὸν Ἰωάννην
the   crowd: for all men   held   –   John

ὄντως ὅτι προφήτης ἦν.   **33** καὶ
*a*really   *t*that   *a*a prophet   *the was.   And

ἀποκριθέντες τῷ Ἰησοῦ λέγουσιν· οὐκ
answering   –   Jesus   they say: not

οἴδαμεν. καὶ ὁ Ἰησοῦς λέγει αὐτοῖς·
We know.   And   –   Jesus   says   to them:

οὐδὲ ἐγὼ λέγω ὑμῖν ἐν ποίᾳ ἐξουσίᾳ
Neither   I   tell   you   by   what   authority

‡ Verse 26 omitted by Nestle; *cf*. NIV footnote.

Right column (NIV)

22"Have*i* faith in God," Jesus answered. 23"I tell you the truth, if anyone says to this mountain, 'Go, throw yourself into the sea,' and does not doubt in his heart but believes that what he says will happen, it will be done for him. 24Therefore I tell you, whatever you ask for in prayer, believe that you have received it, and it will be yours. 25And when you stand praying, if you hold anything against anyone, forgive him, so that your Father in heaven may forgive you your sins. *u*"

The Authority of Jesus Questioned

27They arrived again in Jerusalem, and while Jesus was walking in the temple courts, the chief priests, the teachers of the law and the elders came to him. 28"By what authority are you doing these things?" they asked. "And who gave you authority to do this?"

29Jesus replied, "I will ask you one question. Answer me, and I will tell you by what authority I am doing these things. 30John's baptism—was it from heaven, or from men? Tell me!"

31They discussed it among themselves and said, "If we say, 'From heaven,' he will ask, 'Then why didn't you believe him?' 32But if we say, 'From men' . . . ." (They feared the people, for everyone held that John really was a prophet.)

33So they answered Jesus, "We don't know."

Jesus said, "Neither will I tell you by what authority I am doing these things."

i22 Some early manuscripts *If you have*
u25 Some manuscripts *sins.* 26*But if you do not forgive, neither will your Father who is in heaven forgive your sins.*

Chapter 12

Parable of the Vine-growers

AND He began to speak to them in parables: "A man PLANTED A VINEYARD, AND PUT A WALL AROUND IT, AND DUG A VAT UNDER THE WINE PRESS, AND BUILT A TOWER, and rented it out to ᵍvine-growers and went on a journey.

2"And at the *harvest* time he sent a slave to the vine-growers, in order to receive *some* of the produce of the vineyard from the vine-growers.

3"And they took him, and beat him, and sent him away empty-handed.

4"And again he sent them another slave, and they wounded him in the head, and treated him shamefully.

5"And he sent another, and that one they killed; and *so with* many others, beating some, and killing others.

6"He had one more *to send*, a beloved son; he sent him last *of all* to them, saying, 'They will respect my son.'

7"But those vine-growers said to one another, 'This is the heir; come, let us kill him, and the inheritance will be ours!'

8"And they took him, and killed him, and threw him out of the vineyard.

9"What will the owner of the vineyard do? He will come and destroy the vine-growers, and will give the vineyard to others.

10"Have you not even read this Scripture:
'THE STONE WHICH THE BUILDERS REJECTED, THIS BECAME THE CHIEF CORNER *stone;*
11 THIS CAME ABOUT FROM THE LORD, AND IT IS MARVELOUS IN OUR EYES'?"

12And they were seeking to seize Him; and *yet* they feared the multitude; for they understood that He spoke the parable against

ᵍ Or, *tenant farmers,* also vv. 2, 7, 9

ταῦτα ποιῶ. **12** Καὶ ἤρξατο αὐτοῖς ἐν
these things I do. And he began to them in
παραβολαῖς λαλεῖν. ἀμπελῶνα ἄνθρωπος
parables to speak. ³a vineyard ¹A man
ἐφύτευσεν, καὶ περιέθηκεν φραγμὸν καὶ ὤρυξεν
²planted, and put round [it] a hedge and dug
ὑπολήνιον καὶ ᾠκοδόμησεν πύργον, καὶ
a winepress and built a tower, and
ἐξέδοτο αὐτὸν γεωργοῖς, καὶ ἀπεδήμησεν.
let out it to husbandmen, and went away.
2 καὶ ἀπέστειλεν πρὸς τοὺς γεωργοὺς τῷ
And he sent to the husbandmen at the
καιρῷ δοῦλον, ἵνα παρὰ τῶν γεωργῶν
time a slave, that from the husbandmen
λάβῃ ἀπὸ τῶν καρπῶν τοῦ ἀμπελῶνος·
he might from(of) the fruits of the vineyard;
receive
3 καὶ λαβόντες αὐτὸν ἔδειραν καὶ ἀπέστειλαν
And taking him they beat and sent away
κενόν. **4** καὶ πάλιν ἀπέστειλεν πρὸς αὐτοὺς
empty. And again he sent to them
ἄλλον δοῦλον· κἀκεῖνον ἐκεφαλαίωσαν καὶ
another slave; and that one they wounded in the head and
ἠτίμασαν. **5** καὶ ἄλλον ἀπέστειλεν· κἀκεῖνον
insulted. And another he sent; and that one
ἀπέκτειναν, καὶ πολλοὺς ἄλλους, οὓς μὲν
they killed, and many others, ²some
δέροντες, οὓς δὲ ἀποκτέννοντες. **6** ἔτι ἕνα
¹beating, ²others ¹killing. Still one
εἶχεν, υἱὸν ἀγαπητόν· ἀπέστειλεν αὐτὸν
he had, a son beloved; he sent him
ἔσχατον πρὸς αὐτοὺς λέγων ὅτι ἐντραπήσονται
last to them saying[,] – They will reverence
τὸν υἱόν μου. **7** ἐκεῖνοι δὲ οἱ γεωργοὶ
the son of me. But those – husbandmen
πρὸς ἑαυτοὺς εἶπαν ὅτι οὗτός ἐστιν ὁ
to themselves said[,] – This is the
κληρονόμος· δεῦτε ἀποκτείνωμεν αὐτόν, καὶ
heir; come[,] let us kill him, and
ἡμῶν ἔσται ἡ κληρονομία. **8** καὶ λαβόντες
of us will be the inheritance. And taking
ἀπέκτειναν αὐτόν, καὶ ἐξέβαλον αὐτὸν
they killed him, and cast *out* him
ἔξω τοῦ ἀμπελῶνος. **9** τί ποιήσει ὁ
outside the vineyard. What will do the
κύριος τοῦ ἀμπελῶνος; ἐλεύσεται καὶ
lord of the vineyard? he will come and
ἀπολέσει τοὺς γεωργούς, καὶ δώσει τὸν
will destroy the husbandmen, and will give the
ἀμπελῶνα ἄλλοις. **10** οὐδὲ τὴν γραφὴν
vineyard to others. ²not – ¹scripture
ταύτην ἀνέγνωτε· λίθον ὃν ἀπεδοκίμασαν
²this ¹Read ye: A stone which ³rejected
οἱ οἰκοδομοῦντες, οὗτος ἐγενήθη εἰς κεφαλὴν
¹the [ones] ²building, this became for head
γωνίας· **11** παρὰ κυρίου ἐγένετο αὕτη,
of corner; from [the] Lord was this,
καὶ ἔστιν θαυμαστὴ ἐν ὀφθαλμοῖς ἡμῶν;
and it is marvellous in eyes of us?
12 Καὶ ἐζήτουν αὐτὸν κρατῆσαι, καὶ
And they sought him to seize, and
ἐφοβήθησαν τὸν ὄχλον· ἔγνωσαν γὰρ
feared the crowd; for they knew
ὅτι πρὸς αὐτοὺς τὴν παραβολὴν
that to them the parable

The Parable of the Tenants

HE then began to speak to them in parables: "A man planted a vineyard. He put a wall around it, dug a pit for the winepress and built a watchtower. Then he rented the vineyard to some farmers and went away on a journey. 2At harvest time he sent a servant to the tenants to collect from them some of the fruit of the vineyard. 3But they seized him, beat him and sent him away empty-handed. 4Then he sent another servant to them; they struck this man on the head and treated him shamefully. 5He sent still another, and that one they killed. He sent many others; some of them they beat, others they killed.

6"He had one left to send, a son, whom he loved. He sent him last of all, saying, 'They will respect my son.'

7"But the tenants said to one another, 'This is the heir. Come, let's kill him, and the inheritance will be ours.' 8So they took him and killed him, and threw him out of the vineyard.

9"What then will the owner of the vineyard do? He will come and kill those tenants and give the vineyard to others. 10Haven't you read this scripture:

" 'The stone the builders rejected
has become the capstone ᵛ;
11the Lord has done this, and it is marvelous in our eyes' ʷ?"

12Then they looked for a way to arrest him because they knew he had spoken the parable against them.

ᵛ10 Or *cornerstone*
ʷ11 Psalm 118:22,23

them. And *so* they left Him, and went away.

Jesus Answers the Pharisees, Sadducees and Scribes

13And they *sent some of the Pharisees and Herodians to Him, in order to trap Him in a statement.
14And they *came and *said to Him, "Teacher, we know that You are truthful, and defer to no one; for You are not partial to any, but teach the way of God in truth. Is it lawful to pay a poll-tax to Caesar, or not?
15"Shall we pay, or shall we not pay?" But He, knowing their hypocrisy, said to them, "Why are you testing Me? Bring Me a *h*denarius to look at."
16And they brought *one.* And He *said to them, "Whose likeness and inscription is this?" And they said to Him, "Caesar's."
17And Jesus said to them, "Render to Caesar the things that are Caesar's, and to God the things that are God's." And they were amazed at Him.
18And *some* Sadducees (who say that there is no resurrection) *came to Him, and *began* questioning Him, saying,
19"Teacher, Moses wrote for us that IF A MAN'S BROTHER DIES, and leaves behind a wife, AND LEAVES NO CHILD, HIS BROTHER SHOULD TAKE THE WIFE, AND RAISE UP OFFSPRING TO HIS BROTHER.
20"There were seven brothers; and the first took a wife, and died, leaving no offspring.
21"And the second one took her, and died, leaving behind no offspring; and the third likewise;
22and *so* all seven left no offspring. Last of all the woman died also.
23"In the resurrection, *i*when they rise again,

εἶπεν. καὶ ἀφέντες αὐτὸν ἀπῆλθον.
he told. And leaving him they went away.

13 Καὶ ἀποστέλλουσιν πρὸς αὐτὸν τινας τῶν
And they send to him some of the

Φαρισαίων καὶ τῶν Ἡρωδιανῶν ἵνα αὐτὸν
Pharisees and of the Herodians that him

ἀγρεύσωσιν λόγῳ. 14 καὶ ἐλθόντες
they might catch in a word. And coming

λέγουσιν αὐτῷ· διδάσκαλε, οἴδαμεν ὅτι
they say to him: Teacher, we know that

ἀληθὴς εἶ καὶ οὐ μέλει σοι περὶ
true thou art and it matters not to thee about

οὐδενός· οὐ γὰρ βλέπεις εἰς πρόσωπον
no(any)one; for thou lookest not at [the] face

ἀνθρώπων, ἀλλ' ἐπ' ἀληθείας τὴν ὁδὸν
of men, but on(in) truth the way

τοῦ θεοῦ διδάσκεις· ἔξεστιν δοῦναι κῆνσον
- of God teachest; is it lawful to give tribute

Καίσαρι ἢ οὔ; δῶμεν ἢ μὴ δῶμεν;
to Cæsar or no? may we give or may we not give?

15 ὁ δὲ εἰδὼς αὐτῶν τὴν ὑπόκρισιν εἶπεν
But he knowing of them the hypocrisy said

αὐτοῖς· τί με πειράζετε; φέρετέ μοι
to them: Why me tempt ye? bring me

δηνάριον ἵνα ἴδω. 16 οἱ δὲ ἤνεγκαν. καὶ
a denarius that I may see. And they brought. And

λέγει αὐτοῖς· τίνος ἡ εἰκὼν αὕτη καὶ ἡ
he says to them: Of whom - image this and the

ἐπιγραφή; οἱ δὲ εἶπαν αὐτῷ· Καίσαρος.
superscription? And they tell him: Of Cæsar.

17 ὁ δὲ Ἰησοῦς εἶπεν αὐτοῖς· τὰ Καίσαρος
- So Jesus said to them: The things of Cæsar

ἀπόδοτε Καίσαρι καὶ τὰ τοῦ θεοῦ τῷ
render to Cæsar and the things - of God -

θεῷ. καὶ ἐξεθαύμαζον ἐπ' αὐτῷ.
to God. And they marvelled at him.

18 Καὶ ἔρχονται Σαδδουκαῖοι πρὸς αὐτόν,
And come Sadducees to him,

οἵτινες λέγουσιν ἀνάστασιν μὴ εἶναι, καὶ
who say resurrection not to be, and
= that there is no resurrection,

ἐπηρώτων αὐτὸν λέγοντες· 19 διδάσκαλε,
questioned him saying: Teacher,

Μωϋσῆς ἔγραψεν ἡμῖν ὅτι ἐάν τινος
Moses wrote to us that if of anyone

ἀδελφὸς ἀποθάνῃ καὶ καταλίπῃ γυναῖκα
a brother should die and leave behind a wife

καὶ μὴ ἀφῇ τέκνον, ἵνα λάβῃ ὁ ἀδελφὸς
and leave not a child. - ⁴may take ¹the ²brother

αὐτοῦ τὴν γυναῖκα καὶ ἐξαναστήσῃ σπέρμα
²of him the wife and may raise up seed

τῷ ἀδελφῷ αὐτοῦ. 20 ἑπτὰ ἀδελφοὶ ἦσαν·
to the brother of him. Seven brothers there were;

καὶ ὁ πρῶτος ἔλαβεν γυναῖκα, καὶ
and the first took a wife, and

ἀποθνῇσκων οὐκ ἀφῆκεν σπέρμα· 21 καὶ
dying left not seed; and

ὁ δεύτερος ἔλαβεν αὐτήν, καὶ ἀπέθανεν μὴ
the second took her, and died not

καταλιπὼν σπέρμα· καὶ ὁ τρίτος ὡσαύτως·
leaving behind seed; and the third similarly;

22 καὶ οἱ ἑπτὰ οὐκ ἀφῆκαν σπέρμα.
and the seven left not seed.

ἔσχατον πάντων καὶ ἡ γυνὴ ἀπέθανεν.
Last of all also the wife died.

23 ἐν τῇ ἀναστάσει, ὅταν ἀναστῶσιν,
In the resurrection, when they rise again,

But they were afraid of the crowd; so they left him and went away.

Paying Taxes to Caesar

13Later they sent some of the Pharisees and Herodians to Jesus to catch him in his words. 14They came to him and said, "Teacher, we know you are a man of integrity. You aren't swayed by men, because you pay no attention to who they are; but you teach the way of God in accordance with the truth. Is it right to pay taxes to Caesar or not? 15Should we pay or shouldn't we?"
But Jesus knew their hypocrisy. "Why are you trying to trap me?" he asked. "Bring me a denarius and let me look at it." 16They brought the coin, and he asked them, "Whose portrait is this? And whose inscription?"
"Caesar's," they replied.
17Then Jesus said to them, "Give to Caesar what is Caesar's and to God what is God's."
And they were amazed at him.

Marriage at the Resurrection

18Then the Sadducees, who say there is no resurrection, came to him with a question. 19"Teacher," they said, "Moses wrote for us that if a man's brother dies and leaves a wife but no children, the man must marry the widow and have children for his brother. 20Now there were seven brothers. The first one married and died without leaving any children. 21The second one married the widow, but he also died, leaving no child. It was the same with the third. 22In fact, none of the seven left any children. Last of all, the woman died too. 23At the resurrection*x* whose

---

h The denarius was equivalent to one day's wage

i Most ancient mss. do not contain *when they rise again*

x23 Some manuscripts *resurrection, when men rise from the dead.*

which one's wife will she be? For all seven had her as wife."

24Jesus said to them, "Is this not the reason you are mistaken, that you do not understand the Scriptures, or the power of God?

25"For when they rise from the dead, they neither marry, nor are given in marriage, but are like angels in heaven.

26"But regarding the fact that the dead rise again, have you not read in the book of Moses, in the *passage about the burning* bush, how God spoke to him, saying, 'I AM THE GOD OF ABRAHAM, AND THE GOD OF ISAAC, AND THE GOD OF JACOB'?

27"He is not the God of the dead, but of the living; you are greatly mistaken."

28And one of the scribes came and heard them arguing, and recognizing that He had answered them well, asked Him, "What commandment is the foremost of all?"

, 29Jesus answered, "The foremost is, 'HEAR, O ISRAEL! THE LORD OUR GOD IS ONE LORD;

30AND YOU SHALL LOVE THE LORD YOUR GOD WITH ALL YOUR HEART, AND WITH ALL YOUR SOUL, AND WITH ALL YOUR MIND, AND WITH ALL YOUR STRENGTH.'

31"The second is this, 'YOU SHALL LOVE YOUR NEIGHBOR AS YOURSELF.' There is no other commandment greater than these."

32And the scribe said to Him, "Right, Teacher, You have truly stated that HE IS ONE; AND THERE IS NO ONE ELSE BESIDES HIM;

33AND TO LOVE HIM WITH ALL THE HEART AND WITH ALL THE UNDERSTANDING AND WITH ALL THE STRENGTH, AND TO LOVE ONE'S NEIGHBOR AS HIMSELF,

τίνος αὐτῶν ἔσται γυνή; οἱ γὰρ ἑπτὰ
of which of them will she be wife? for the seven
ἔσχον αὐτὴν γυναῖκα. 24 ἔφη αὐτοῖς ὁ
had her [as] wife. Said to them -
'Ιησοῦς· οὐ διὰ τοῦτο πλανᾶσθε μὴ
Jesus: ³not ⁴therefore ¹Do ²ye ⁵err not
εἰδότες τὰς γραφὰς μηδὲ τὴν δύναμιν
knowing the scriptures nor the power
τοῦ θεοῦ; 25 ὅταν γὰρ ἐκ νεκρῶν
- of God? for when out of [the] dead
ἀναστῶσιν, οὔτε γαμοῦσιν οὔτε γαμίζονται,
they rise again, they neither marry nor are given in marriage,
ἀλλ' εἰσὶν ὡς ἄγγελοι ἐν τοῖς οὐρανοῖς.
but are as angels in the heavens.
26 περὶ δὲ τῶν νεκρῶν ὅτι ἐγείρονται,
But concerning the dead that they are raised,
οὐκ ἀνέγνωτε ἐν τῇ βίβλῳ Μωϋσέως ἐπὶ
did ye not read in the roll of Moses at
τοῦ βάτου πῶς εἶπεν αὐτῷ ὁ θεὸς λέγων·
the bush how said to him - God saying:
ἐγὼ ὁ θεὸς 'Αβραὰμ καὶ θεὸς 'Ισαὰκ
I [am] the God of Abraham and God of Isaac
καὶ θεὸς 'Ιακώβ; 27 οὐκ ἔστιν θεὸς
and God of Jacob? he is not God
νεκρῶν ἀλλὰ ζώντων. πολὺ πλανᾶσθε.
of dead [persons] but of living [ones]. Much ye err.
28 Καὶ προσελθὼν εἷς τῶν γραμματέων,
And ⁴approaching ¹one ²of the ³scribes,
ἀκούσας αὐτῶν συζητούντων, εἰδὼς ὅτι
hearing them debating, knowing that
καλῶς ἀπεκρίθη αὐτοῖς, ἐπηρώτησεν αὐτόν·
well he answered them, questioned him:
ποία ἐστὶν ἐντολὴ πρώτη πάντων;
What is [the] commandment first of all?
29 ἀπεκρίθη ὁ 'Ιησοῦς ὅτι πρώτη ἐστίν·
Answered - Jesus[,] - [The] first is:
ἄκουε, 'Ισραήλ, κύριος ὁ θεὸς ἡμῶν κύριος
Hear, Israel, Lord the God of us Lord
= The Lord our God is one Lord,
εἷς ἐστιν, 30 καὶ ἀγαπήσεις κύριον τὸν
one is, and thou shalt love Lord the
θεόν σου ἐξ ὅλης τῆς καρδίας σου καὶ
God of thee from(with) all the heart of thee and
ἐξ ὅλης τῆς ψυχῆς σου καὶ ἐξ ὅλης
with all the soul of thee and with all
τῆς διανοίας σου καὶ ἐξ ὅλης τῆς ἰσχύος
the mind of thee and with all the strength
σου. 31 δευτέρα αὕτη· ἀγαπήσεις τὸν
of thee. [The] second [is] this: Thou shalt love the
πλησίον σου ὡς σεαυτόν. μείζων τούτων
neighbour of thee as thyself. Greater [than] these
ἄλλη ἐντολὴ οὐκ ἔστιν. 32 καὶ εἶπεν
other commandment there is not. And said
αὐτῷ ὁ γραμματεύς· καλῶς, διδάσκαλε, ἐπ'
to him the scribe: Well, teacher, on(in)
ἀληθείας εἶπες ὅτι εἷς ἐστιν καὶ οὐκ
truth thou sayest that one there is and not
ἔστιν ἄλλος πλὴν αὐτοῦ· 33 καὶ τὸ
there is another besides him; and -
ἀγαπᾶν αὐτὸν ἐξ ὅλης τῆς καρδίας καὶ ἐξ
to love him with all the heart and with
ὅλης τῆς συνέσεως καὶ ἐξ ὅλης τῆς
all the understanding and with all the
ἰσχύος, καὶ τὸ ἀγαπᾶν τὸν πλησίον ὡς
strength, and - to love the(one's) neighbour as

wife will she be, since the seven were married to her?"

24Jesus replied, "Are you not in error because you do not know the Scriptures or the power of God? 25When the dead rise, they will neither marry nor be given in marriage; they will be like the angels in heaven. 26Now about the dead rising—have you not read in the book of Moses, in the account of the bush, how God said to him, 'I am the God of Abraham, the God of Isaac, and the God of Jacob'?[z] 27He is not the God of the dead, but of the living. You are badly mistaken!"

The Greatest Commandment

28One of the teachers of the law came and heard them debating. Noticing that Jesus had given them a good answer, he asked him, "Of all the commandments, which is the most important?"

29"The most important one," answered Jesus, "is this: 'Hear, O Israel, the Lord our God, the Lord is one.[z] 30Love the Lord your God with all your heart and with all your soul and with all your mind and with all your strength.'[a] 31The second is this: 'Love your neighbor as yourself.'[b] There is no commandment greater than these."

32"Well said, teacher," the man replied. "You are right in saying that God is one and there is no other but him. 33To love him with all your heart, with all your understanding and with all your strength, and to love your neighbor as yourself is

ʸ26 Exodus 3:6
ᶻ29 Or *the Lord our God is one Lord*
ᵃ30 Deut. 6:4,5
ᵇ31 Lev. 19:18

is much more than all burnt offerings and sacrifices."

34And when Jesus saw that he had answered intelligently, He said to him, "You are not far from the kingdom of God." And after that, no one would venture to ask Him any more questions.

35And Jesus answering began to say, as He taught in the temple, "How *is it that* the scribes say that the Christ is the son of David?

36"David himself said in the Holy Spirit,

'THE LORD SAID TO MY LORD,

"SIT AT MY RIGHT HAND,

UNTIL I PUT THINE ENEMIES BENEATH THY FEET." '

37"David himself calls Him 'Lord'; and *so* in what sense is He his son?" And the great crowd enjoyed listening to Him.

38And in His teaching He was saying: "Beware of the scribes who like to walk around in long robes, and *like* respectful greetings in the market places,

39and chief seats in the synagogues, and places of honor at banquets,

40who devour widows' houses, and for appearance's sake offer long prayers; these will receive greater condemnation."

The Widow's Mite

41And He sat down opposite the treasury, and *began* observing how the multitude were putting money into the treasury; and many rich people were putting in large sums.

42And a poor widow came and put in two small copper coins, which amount to a cent.

43And calling His disciples to Him, He said to them, "Truly I say to you, this poor widow put in

---

ἑαυτὸν περισσότερόν ἐστιν πάντων τῶν
himself   more   is [than] all   the
ὁλοκαυτωμάτων καὶ θυσιῶν. **34** καὶ ὁ
burnt offerings and sacrifices.   And -
'Ἰησοῦς, ἰδὼν αὐτὸν ὅτι νουνεχῶς ἀπεκρίθη,
Jesus, seeing him that sensibly he answered,
εἶπεν αὐτῷ· οὐ μακρὰν εἶ ἀπὸ τῆς
said to him: Not far   thou art from the
βασιλείας τοῦ θεοῦ. καὶ οὐδεὶς οὐκέτι
kingdom   - of God. And no one no(any) more
ἐτόλμα αὐτὸν ἐπερωτῆσαι.
dared   him   to question.

35 Καὶ ἀποκριθεὶς ὁ 'Ἰησοῦς ἔλεγεν
       And answering - Jesus said
διδάσκων ἐν τῷ ἱερῷ· πῶς λέγουσιν οἱ
teaching in the temple: How say   the
γραμματεῖς ὅτι ὁ χριστὸς υἱός Δαυὶδ
scribes   that - the Christ son of David
ἐστιν; **36** αὐτὸς Δαυὶδ εἶπεν ἐν τῷ πνεύματι
is?   himself David said   by the Spirit
τῷ ἁγίῳ· εἶπεν κύριος τῷ κυρίῳ μου·
- Holy: said [the] LORD to the Lord of me:
κάθου ἐκ δεξιῶν μου ἕως ἂν θῶ τοὺς
Sit at [the] right [hand] of me until I put the
ἐχθρούς σου ὑποκάτω τῶν ποδῶν σου.
enemies of thee under   the   feet of thee.
37 αὐτὸς Δαυὶδ λέγει αὐτὸν κύριον, καὶ
       himself David says(calls) him Lord, and
πόθεν αὐτοῦ ἐστιν υἱός;
whence of him is he son ?

Καὶ ὁ πολὺς ὄχλος ἤκουεν αὐτοῦ
And the much   crowd heard   him
ἡδέως. **38** Καὶ ἐν τῇ διδαχῇ αὐτοῦ
gladly.   And in the teaching of him
ἔλεγεν· βλέπετε ἀπὸ τῶν γραμματέων
he said: Beware from(of) the scribes
τῶν θελόντων ἐν στολαῖς περιπατεῖν καὶ
the [ones] wishing in robes to walk about and
ἀσπασμοὺς ἐν ταῖς ἀγοραῖς **39** καὶ
greetings in the marketplaces   and
πρωτοκαθεδρίας ἐν ταῖς συναγωγαῖς καὶ
chief seats   in the synagogues   and
πρωτοκλισίας ἐν τοῖς δείπνοις· **40** οἱ
chief places in the dinners;   the [ones]
κατέσθοντες τὰς οἰκίας τῶν χηρῶν καὶ
devouring the houses of the widows and
προφάσει μακρὰ προσευχόμενοι, οὗτοι
under pretence long praying,   these
λήμψονται περισσότερον κρίμα. **41** Καὶ
will receive greater   condemnation.   And
καθίσας κατέναντι τοῦ γαζοφυλακείου ἐθεώρει
sitting opposite the treasury he beheld
πῶς ὁ ὄχλος βάλλει χαλκὸν εἰς τὸ
how the crowd puts copper money into the
γαζοφυλακεῖον· καὶ πολλοὶ πλούσιοι ἔβαλλον
treasury;   and many rich men put
πολλά· **42** καὶ ἐλθοῦσα μία χήρα πτωχὴ
much;   and coming one widow poor
ἔβαλεν λεπτὰ δύο, ὅ ἐστιν κοδράντης.
put   lepta two, which is a quadrans.
43 καὶ προσκαλεσάμενος τοὺς μαθητὰς αὐτοῦ
     And calling to [him] the disciples of him
εἶπεν αὐτοῖς· ἀμὴν λέγω ὑμῖν ὅτι
he said to them: Truly I tell you that
ἡ χήρα αὕτη ἡ πτωχὴ πλεῖον πάντων
- ²widow ¹this - ²poor ⁴more [than] ⁶all

---

more important than all burnt offerings and sacrifices."

34When Jesus saw that he had answered wisely, he said to him, "You are not far from the kingdom of God." And from then on no one dared ask him any more questions.

Whose Son Is the Christ?

35While Jesus was teaching in the temple courts, he asked, "How is it that the teachers of the law say that the Christ[c] is the son of David? **36**David himself, speaking by the Holy Spirit, declared:

" 'The Lord said to my Lord:

"Sit at my right hand until I put your enemies under your feet." ' [d]

37David himself calls him 'Lord.' How then can he be his son?"

The large crowd listened to him with delight. **38**As he taught, Jesus said, "Watch out for the teachers of the law. They like to walk around in flowing robes and be greeted in the marketplaces, **39**and have the most important seats in the synagogues and the places of honor at banquets. **40**They devour widows' houses and for a show make lengthy prayers. Such men will be punished most severely."

The Widow's Offering

41Jesus sat down opposite the place where the offerings were put and watched the crowd putting their money into the temple treasury. Many rich people threw in large amounts. **42**But a poor widow came and put in two very small copper coins,[e] worth only a fraction of a penny.[f] **43**Calling his disciples to him, Jesus said, "I tell you the truth, this poor widow

---

c35 Or Messiah
d36 Psalm 110:1
e42 Greek two lepta
f42 Greek kodrantes

more than all the contributors to the treasury;

44for they all put in out of their surplus, but she, out of her poverty, put in all she owned, all she had to live on.''

ἔβαλεν τῶν βαλλόντων εἰς τὸ γαζοφυλακεῖον·
4put   the [ones] putting   into the   treasury;

44 πάντες γὰρ ἐκ τοῦ περισσεύοντος αὐτοῖς
for all   out of the   abounding   to them°
= their abundance

ἔβαλον, αὕτη δὲ ἐκ τῆς ὑστερήσεως αὐτῆς
put,   but this woman out of the   want   of her

πάντα ὅσα εἶχεν ἔβαλεν, ὅλον τὸν βίον
1all things 2how many 4she had   3put,   all   the   living

αὐτῆς.
of her.

has put more into the treasury than all the others.

44They all gave out of their wealth; but she, out of her poverty, put in everything —all she had to live on.''

Chapter 13

Things to Come

AND as He was going out of the temple, one of His disciples *said to Him, "Teacher, behold ⌐ what wonderful stones and what wonderful buildings!''

2And Jesus said to him, "Do you see these great buildings? Not one stone shall be left upon another which will not be torn down.''

3And as He was sitting on the Mount of Olives opposite the temple, Peter and James and John and Andrew were questioning Him privately,

4"Tell us, when will these things be, and what will be the sign when all these things are going to be fulfilled?''

5And Jesus began to say to them, "See to it that no one misleads you.

6"Many will come in My name, saying, 'I am He!' and will mislead many.

7"And when you hear of wars and rumors of wars, do not be frightened; those things must take place; but that is not yet the end.

8"For nation will arise against nation, and kingdom against kingdom; there will be earthquakes in various places; there will also be famines. These things are merely the beginning of birth pangs.

9"But be on your guard; for they will deliver you to the courts, and you will be flogged in the synagogues, and you will stand before governors and kings for My sake, as a testimony to

Chapter 13

Signs of the End of the Age

AS he was leaving the temple, one of his disciples said to him, "Look, Teacher! What massive stones! What magnificent buildings!''

2"Do you see all these great buildings?'' replied Jesus. "Not one stone here will be left on another; every one will be thrown down.''

3As Jesus was sitting on the Mount of Olives opposite the temple, Peter, James, John and Andrew asked him privately, 4"Tell us, when will these things happen? And what will be the sign that they are all about to be fulfilled?''

5Jesus said to them: "Watch out that no one deceives you. 6Many will come in my name, claiming, 'I am he,' and will deceive many. 7When you hear of wars and rumors of wars, do not be alarmed. Such things must happen, but the end is still to come. 8Nation will rise against nation, and kingdom against kingdom. There will be earthquakes in various places, and famines. These are the beginning of birth pains.

9"You must be on your guard. You will be handed over to the local councils and flogged in the synagogues. On account of me you will stand before governors and kings as wit-

13 Καὶ ἐκπορευομένου αὐτοῦ ἐκ τοῦ
And   going forth   hima   out of   the
= as he went forth

ἱεροῦ λέγει αὐτῷ εἷς τῶν μαθητῶν αὐτοῦ·
temple   says   to him   one   of the   disciples   of him:

διδάσκαλε, ἴδε ποταποὶ λίθοι καὶ ποταπαὶ
Teacher,   behold[,] what great   stones   and   what great

οἰκοδομαί. 2 καὶ ὁ Ἰησοῦς εἶπεν αὐτῷ·
buildings.   And -   Jesus   said   to him:

βλέπεις ταύτας τὰς μεγάλας οἰκοδομάς;
Seest thou   these   these -   great   buildings?

οὐ μὴ ἀφεθῇ λίθος ἐπὶ λίθον ὃς οὐ
by no means be left   stone   on   stone which by no
= there shall by no means be left stone on stone which will not

μὴ καταλυθῇ. 3 Καὶ καθημένου αὐτοῦ
means be overthrown.   And   sitting   hima
be overthrown.   = as he sat

εἰς τὸ ὄρος τῶν ἐλαιῶν κατέναντι τοῦ
in(on)   the   mount of the   olives   opposite   the

ἱεροῦ, ἐπηρώτα αὐτὸν κατ' ἰδίαν Πέτρος
temple,   questioned   him   privately   Peter

καὶ Ἰάκωβος καὶ Ἰωάννης καὶ Ἀνδρέας·
and   James   and   John   and   Andrew:

4 εἰπὸν ἡμῖν, πότε ταῦτα ἔσται, καὶ τί
Tell   us,   when   these things will be,   and   what

τὸ σημεῖον ὅταν μέλλῃ ταῦτα συντελεῖσθαι
the   sign   when   3are about 2these things 4to be completed

πάντα; 5 ὁ δὲ Ἰησοῦς ἤρξατο λέγειν
1all?   - And   Jesus   began   to say

αὐτοῖς· βλέπετε μή τις ὑμᾶς πλανήσῃ.
to them: See   lest anyone   you   lead astray.

6 πολλοὶ ἐλεύσονται ἐπὶ τῷ ὀνόματί μου
Many   will come   on(in)   the   name   of me

λέγοντες ὅτι ἐγώ εἰμι, καὶ πολλοὺς
saying[,]   that -   I   am,   and   many

πλανήσουσιν. 7 ὅταν δὲ ἀκούσητε πολέμους
they will lead astray.   But when   ye hear   [of] wars

καὶ ἀκοὰς πολέμων, μὴ θροεῖσθε· δεῖ
and   rumours   of wars,   be not disturbed; it behoves

γενέσθαι, ἀλλ' οὔπω τὸ τέλος. 8 ἐγερθήσεται
to happen,   but   not yet   the   end.   will be raised

γὰρ ἔθνος ἐπ' ἔθνος καὶ βασιλεία ἐπὶ
For   nation against   nation   and   kingdom against

βασιλείαν. ἔσονται σεισμοὶ κατὰ τόπους,
kingdom.   There will be earthquakes   in places,

ἔσονται λιμοί· ἀρχὴ ὠδίνων ταῦτα.
there will be famines; beginning of birth-pangs these things [are].

9 Βλέπετε δὲ ὑμεῖς ἑαυτούς· παραδώσουσιν
But see   ye   yourselves;   they will deliver

ὑμᾶς εἰς συνέδρια καὶ εἰς συναγωγὰς
you   to   councils   and   in   synagogues

δαρήσεσθε καὶ ἐπὶ ἡγεμόνων καὶ βασιλέων
ye will be beaten   and before   rulers   and   kings

σταθήσεσθε ἕνεκεν ἐμοῦ, εἰς μαρτύριον
ye will stand   for the sake   of me,   for   a testimony

ⅉLit., how great

them.
10"And the gospel must first be preached to all the nations.

11"And when they arrest you and deliver you up, do not be anxious beforehand about what you are to say, but say whatever is given you in that hour; for it is not you who speak, but *it is* the Holy Spirit.

12"And brother will deliver brother to death, and a father *his* child; and children will rise up against parents and have them put to death.

13"And you will be hated by all on account of My name, but the one who endures to the end, he shall be saved.

14"But when you see the ABOMINATION OF DESOLATION standing where it should not be (let the reader understand), then let those who are in Judea flee to the mountains.

15"And let him who is on the housetop not go down, or enter in, to get anything out of his house;

16and let him who is in the field not turn back to get his cloak.

17"But woe to those who are with child and to those who nurse babes in those days!

18"But pray that it may not happen in the winter.

19"For those days will be a *time of* tribulation such as has not occurred since the beginning of the creation which God created, until now, and never shall.

20"And unless the Lord had shortened *those* days, no life would have been saved; but for the sake of the elect whom He chose, He shortened the days.

21"And then if anyone says to you, 'Behold, here is the Christ'; or, 'Behold, *He is* there'; do not believe *him;*

αὐτοῖς. 10 καὶ εἰς πάντα τὰ ἔθνη πρῶτον
to them.   And to all the nations first

δεῖ κηρυχθῆναι τὸ εὐαγγέλιον. 11 καὶ ὅταν
it behoves to be proclaimed the gospel.   And when
= the gospel must be proclaimed.

ἄγωσιν ὑμᾶς παραδιδόντες, μὴ προμεριμνᾶτε
they lead you delivering, be not anxious beforehand

τί λαλήσητε, ἀλλ' ὃ ἐὰν δοθῇ ὑμῖν ἐν
what ye speak, but whatever is given you in

ἐκείνῃ τῇ ὥρᾳ, τοῦτο λαλεῖτε· οὐ γάρ
that hour. this speak ye; for not

ἐστε ὑμεῖς οἱ λαλοῦντες ἀλλὰ τὸ πνεῦμα
are - ye the [ones] speaking but the Spirit

τὸ ἅγιον. 12 καὶ παραδώσει ἀδελφὸς
- Holy. And ²will deliver ¹a brother

ἀδελφὸν εἰς θάνατον καὶ πατὴρ τέκνον, καὶ
a brother to death and a father a child, and

ἐπαναστήσονται τέκνα ἐπὶ γονεῖς καὶ
²will rise *against* ¹children against parents and

θανατώσουσιν αὐτούς· 13 καὶ ἔσεσθε
will put to death them; and ye will be

μισούμενοι ὑπὸ πάντων διὰ τὸ ὄνομά
being hated by all men on account of the name

μου· ὁ δὲ ὑπομείνας εἰς τέλος, οὗτος
of me; but the [one] enduring to [the] end, this

σωθήσεται. 14 Ὅταν δὲ ἴδητε τὸ βδέλυγμα
will be saved. But when ye see the abomination

τῆς ἐρημώσεως ἑστηκότα ὅπου οὐ δεῖ, ὁ
- of desolation stand where he (it) behoves not, the

ἀναγινώσκων νοείτω, τότε οἱ ἐν τῇ
[one] reading let him understand, then the [ones] in

Ἰουδαίᾳ φευγέτωσαν εἰς τὰ ὄρη, 15 ὁ ἐπὶ
Judæa let them flee to the mountains, the [one] on

τοῦ δώματος μὴ καταβάτω μηδὲ εἰσελθάτω
the roof let him not come down nor let him enter

τι ἆραι ἐκ τῆς οἰκίας αὐτοῦ, 16 καὶ ὁ
anything to take out of the house of him, and the [one]

εἰς τὸν ἀγρὸν μὴ ἐπιστρεψάτω εἰς τὰ
in the field let him not return to the things

ὀπίσω ἆραι τὸ ἱμάτιον αὐτοῦ. 17 οὐαὶ
behind to take the garment of him. woe

δὲ ταῖς ἐν γαστρὶ ἐχούσαις καὶ ταῖς
But to the women pregnant† and to the

θηλαζούσαις ἐν ἐκείναις ταῖς ἡμέραις.
[ones] giving suck in those - days.

18 προσεύχεσθε δὲ ἵνα μὴ γένηται χειμῶνος·
But pray ye that it may not happen of(in) winter;

19 ἔσονται γὰρ αἱ ἡμέραι ἐκεῖναι θλῖψις, οἷα
for ³will be - ²days ¹those ⁴affliction, of such a kind

οὐ γέγονεν τοιαύτη ἀπ' ἀρχῆς κτίσεως
²has not happened ¹as from [the] beginning of [the] creation

ἣν ἔκτισεν ὁ θεὸς ἕως τοῦ νῦν καὶ οὐ
which created - God until - now and by

μὴ γένηται. 20 καὶ εἰ μὴ ἐκολόβωσεν
no means may be. And unless ¹shortened

κύριος τὰς ἡμέρας, οὐκ ἂν ἐσώθη πᾶσα
¹[the] Lord the days, would not be saved all
= no flesh would be saved;

σάρξ· ἀλλὰ διὰ τοὺς ἐκλεκτοὺς οὓς
flesh; but on account of the chosen whom

ἐξελέξατο ἐκολόβωσεν τὰς ἡμέρας. 21 καὶ
he chose he shortened the days. And

τότε ἐάν τις ὑμῖν εἴπῃ· ἴδε ὧδε ὁ
then if anyone ²you ¹tells: Behold here [is] the

χριστός, ἴδε ἐκεῖ, μὴ πιστεύετε· 22 ἐγερθή-
Christ, behold there, believe ye not; ⁶will be

---

nesses to them. 10And the gospel must first be preached to all nations.

11Whenever you are arrested and brought to trial, do not worry beforehand about what to say. Just say whatever is given you at the time, for it is not you speaking, but the Holy Spirit.

12"Brother will betray brother to death, and a father his child. Children will rebel against their parents and have them put to death. 13All men will hate you because of me, but he who stands firm to the end will be saved.

14"When you see 'the abomination that causes desolation'[g] standing where it[h] does not belong —let the reader understand—then let those who are in Judea flee to the mountains. 15Let no one on the roof of his house go down or enter the house to take anything out. 16Let no one in the field go back to get his cloak. 17How dreadful it will be in those days for pregnant women and nursing mothers! 18Pray that this will not take place in winter, 19because those will be days of distress unequaled from the beginning, when God created the world, until now—and never to be equaled again. 20If the Lord had not cut short those days, no one would survive. But for the sake of the elect, whom he has chosen, he has shortened them. 21At that time if anyone says to you, 'Look, here is the Christ[i]!' or, 'Look, there he is!' do not believe it. 22For false

---

ᵍ14 Daniel 9:27; 11:31; 12:11
ʰ14 Or he; also in verse 29
ⁱ21 Or Messiah

22for false Christs and false prophets will arise, and will show signs and wonders, in order, if possible, to lead the elect astray.
23"But take heed; behold, I have told you everything in advance.

The Return of Christ

24"But in those days, after that tribulation, THE SUN WILL BE DARKENED, AND THE MOON WILL NOT GIVE ITS LIGHT,
25AND THE STARS WILL BE FALLING from heaven, and the powers that are in the heavens will be shaken.
26"And then they will see THE SON OF MAN COMING IN CLOUDS with great power and glory.
27"And then He will send forth the angels, and will gather together His elect from the four winds, from the farthest end of the earth, to the farthest end of heaven.
28"Now learn the parable from the fig tree: when its branch has already become tender, and puts forth its leaves, you know that summer is near.
29"Even so, you too, when you see these things happening, recognize that He is near, right at the door.
30"Truly I say to you, this *generation will not pass away until all these things take place.
31"Heaven and earth will pass away, but My words will not pass away.
32"But of that day or hour no one knows, not even the angels in heaven, nor the Son, but the Father *alone.
33"Take heed, keep on the alert; for you do not know when the *appointed time is.
34"*It is like a man, away on a journey, *who upon leaving his house and putting his slaves in charge, *assigning to each one his task, also commanded the

Middle column (interlinear)

σονται δὲ ψευδόχριστοι καὶ ψευδοπροφῆται
raised ²and ¹false Christs ³and ⁴false prophets

καὶ ποιήσουσιν σημεῖα καὶ τέρατα πρὸς
and they will do signs and wonders for

τὸ ἀποπλανᾶν, εἰ δυνατόν, τοὺς ἐκλεκτούς.
- to lead astray, if possible, the chosen.

23 ὑμεῖς δὲ βλέπετε· προείρηκα ὑμῖν πάντα.
But ²ye ¹see; ¹I have told ³before ²you ³all things.

24 Ἀλλὰ ἐν ἐκείναις ταῖς ἡμέραις μετὰ
But in those - days after

τὴν θλῖψιν ἐκείνην ὁ ἥλιος σκοτισθήσεται,
- affliction that the sun will be darkened,

καὶ ἡ σελήνη οὐ δώσει τὸ φέγγος αὐτῆς,
and the moon will not give the light of her,

25 καὶ οἱ ἀστέρες ἔσονται ἐκ τοῦ οὐρανοῦ
and the stars ¹will be ²out of - ⁴heaven

πίπτοντες, καὶ αἱ δυνάμεις αἱ ἐν τοῖς
³falling, and the powers - in the

οὐρανοῖς σαλευθήσονται. 26 καὶ τότε ὄψονται
heavens will be shaken. And then they will see

τὸν υἱὸν τοῦ ἀνθρώπου ἐρχόμενον ἐν
the Son - of man coming in

νεφέλαις μετὰ δυνάμεως πολλῆς καὶ δόξης.
clouds with power much and glory.

27 καὶ τότε ἀποστελεῖ τοὺς ἀγγέλους καὶ
And then he will send the angels and

ἐπισυνάξει τοὺς ἐκλεκτοὺς [αὐτοῦ] ἐκ τῶν
they will assemble the chosen of him out of the

τεσσάρων ἀνέμων ἀπ' ἄκρου γῆς ἕως
four winds from [the] extremity of earth to

ἄκρου οὐρανοῦ. 28 Ἀπὸ δὲ τῆς συκῆς
[the] extremity of heaven. Now from the fig-tree

μάθετε τὴν παραβολήν· ὅταν ἤδη ὁ
learn the parable; when now the

κλάδος αὐτῆς ἁπαλὸς γένηται καὶ ἐκφύῃ
branch of it tender becomes and puts forth

τὰ φύλλα, γινώσκετε ὅτι ἐγγὺς τὸ θέρος
the leaves, ye know that near the summer

ἐστίν· 29 οὕτως καὶ ὑμεῖς, ὅταν ἴδητε
is; so also ye, when ye see

ταῦτα γινόμενα, γινώσκετε ὅτι ἐγγύς ἐστιν
these things happening, know that near he/it is

ἐπὶ θύραις. 30 ἀμὴν λέγω ὑμῖν ὅτι οὐ
at [the] doors. Truly I tell you that by no

μὴ παρέλθῃ ἡ γενεὰ αὕτη μέχρις οὗ
means passes - generation this until

ταῦτα πάντα γένηται. 31 ὁ οὐρανὸς καὶ
these things all happen. The heaven and

ἡ γῆ παρελεύσονται, οἱ δὲ λόγοι μου
the earth will pass away, but the words of me

οὐ παρελεύσονται. 32 Περὶ δὲ τῆς ἡμέρας
will not pass away. But concerning - day

ἐκείνης ἢ τῆς ὥρας οὐδεὶς οἶδεν, οὐδὲ
that or hour no one knows, not

οἱ ἄγγελοι ἐν οὐρανῷ οὐδὲ ὁ υἱός, εἰ
the angels in heaven neither the Son, ex-

μὴ ὁ πατήρ. 33 Βλέπετε, ἀγρυπνεῖτε·
cept the Father. Look, be wakeful;

οὐκ οἴδατε γὰρ πότε ὁ καιρός ἐστιν.
for ye know not when the time is.

34 ὡς ἄνθρωπος ἀπόδημος ἀφεὶς τὴν οἰκίαν
As a man away from home leaving the house

αὐτοῦ καὶ δοὺς τοῖς δούλοις αὐτοῦ τὴν
of him and giving to the slaves of him -

ἐξουσίαν, ἑκάστῳ τὸ ἔργον αὐτοῦ, καὶ
authority, to each the work of him, and

Christs and false prophets will appear and perform signs and miracles to deceive the elect—if that were possible. 23So be on your guard; I have told you everything ahead of time.
24"But in those days, following that distress,

" 'the sun will be darkened,
and the moon will not give its light;
25the stars will fall from the sky,
and the heavenly bodies will be shaken.'ʲ

26"At that time men will see the Son of Man coming in clouds with great power and glory. 27And he will send his angels and gather his elect from the four winds, from the ends of the earth to the ends of the heavens.
28"Now learn this lesson from the fig tree: As soon as its twigs get tender and its leaves come out, you know that summer is near. 29Even so, when you see these things happening, you know that it is near, right at the door. 30I tell you the truth, this generationᵏ will certainly not pass away until all these things have happened. 31Heaven and earth will pass away, but my words will never pass away.

The Day and Hour Unknown

32"No one knows about that day or hour, not even the angels in heaven, nor the Son, but only the Father. 33Be on guard! Be alert!ˡ You do not know when that time will come. 34It's like a man going away: He leaves his house and puts his servants in charge, each with his assigned task, and tells the

---

ᵏ Or, race

ʲ25 Isaiah 13:10; 34:4
ᵏ30 Or race
ˡ33 Some manuscripts alert and pray

doorkeeper to stay on the alert.
35"Therefore, be on the alert—for you do not know when the master of the house is coming, whether in the evening, at midnight, at cockcrowing, or in the morning—
36lest he come suddenly and find you asleep.
37"And what I say to you I say to all, 'Be on the alert!' "

Chapter 14

Death Plot and Anointing

NOW the Passover and Unleavened Bread was two days off; and the chief priests and the scribes were seeking how to seize Him by stealth, and kill Him;
2for they were saying, "Not during the festival, lest there be a riot of the people."
3And while He was in Bethany at the home of Simon the leper, and reclining *at the table*, there came a woman with an alabaster vial of very costly perfume of pure nard; *and* she broke the vial and poured it over His head.
4But some were indignantly *remarking* to one another, "Why has this perfume been wasted?
5"For this perfume might have been sold for over three hundred *l* denarii, and *the money* given to the poor." And they were scolding her.
6But Jesus said, "Let her alone; why do you bother her? She has done a good deed to Me.
7"For the poor you always have with you, and whenever you wish, you can do them good; but you do not always have Me.
8"She has done what she could; she has anointed My body beforehand for the burial.

τῷ θυρωρῷ ἐνετείλατο ἵνα γρηγορῇ.
the doorkeeper he commanded that he should watch.
35 γρηγορεῖτε οὖν· οὐκ οἴδατε γὰρ πότε
Watch ye therefore; for ye know not when
ὁ κύριος τῆς οἰκίας ἔρχεται, ἢ ὀψὲ ἢ
the lord of the house comes, either late or
μεσονύκτιον ἢ ἀλεκτοροφωνίας ἢ πρωΐ·
at midnight or at cock-crowing or early;
36 μὴ ἐλθὼν ἐξαίφνης εὕρῃ ὑμᾶς καθεύδ-
lest coming suddenly he find you sleep-
οντας. **37** ὃ δὲ ὑμῖν λέγω, πᾶσιν λέγω,
ing. And what to you I say, to all I say,
γρηγορεῖτε.
watch ye.

14 *Ἦν* δὲ τὸ πάσχα καὶ τὰ ἄζυμα
Now it was the Passover and [the feast of] the
unleavened bread†
μετὰ δύο ἡμέρας. καὶ ἐζήτουν οἱ ἀρχιερεῖς
after two days. And sought the chief priests
καὶ οἱ γραμματεῖς πῶς αὐτὸν ἐν δόλῳ
and the scribes how ²him ³by ⁴guile
κρατήσαντες ἀποκτείνωσιν. **2** ἔλεγον γάρ·
¹seizing they might kill. For they said :
μὴ ἐν τῇ ἑορτῇ, μήποτε ἔσται θόρυβος
Not at the feast, lest there will be a disturbance
τοῦ λαοῦ.
of the people.
3 Καὶ ὄντος αὐτοῦ ἐν Βηθανίᾳ ἐν τῇ
And being himᵃ in Bethany in the
= when he was
οἰκίᾳ Σίμωνος τοῦ λεπροῦ, κατακειμένου
house of Simon the leper, reclining
= as he reclined
αὐτοῦ ἦλθεν γυνὴ ἔχουσα ἀλάβαστρον
himᵃ came a woman having an alabaster phial
μύρου νάρδου πιστικῆς πολυτελοῦς·
of ointment ¹of pure ¹nard ²costly;
συντρίψασα τὴν ἀλάβαστρον κατέχεεν αὐτοῦ
breaking the alabaster phial she poured over of him
τῆς κεφαλῆς. **4** ἦσαν δέ τινες ἀγανακτοῦντες
the head. Now there were some being angry
πρὸς ἑαυτούς· εἰς τί ἡ ἀπώλεια αὕτη
with themselves; Why waste this
τοῦ μύρου γέγονεν; **5** ἠδύνατο γὰρ τοῦτο
of the ointment has occurred ? for ³could ¹this
τὸ μύρον πραθῆναι ἐπάνω δηναρίων
- ²ointment to be sold [for] over denarii
τριακοσίων καὶ δοθῆναι τοῖς πτωχοῖς·
three hundred and to be given to the poor;
καὶ ἐνεβριμῶντο αὐτῇ. **6** ὁ δὲ 'Ἰησοῦς
and they were indignant with her. - But Jesus
εἶπεν· ἄφετε αὐτήν· τί αὐτῇ κόπους
said: Leave her; why ²to her ¹troubles
παρέχετε; καλὸν ἔργον ἠργάσατο ἐν ἐμοί.
¹cause ye ? a good work she wrought in me.
7 πάντοτε γὰρ τοὺς πτωχοὺς ἔχετε μεθ'
For always the poor ye have with
ἑαυτῶν, καὶ ὅταν θέλητε δύνασθε αὐτοῖς
yourselves, and whenever ye wish ye can to them
εὖ ποιῆσαι, ἐμὲ δὲ οὐ πάντοτε ἔχετε.
well to do, but me not always ye have.
8 ὃ ἔσχεν ἐποίησεν· προέλαβεν μυρίσαι τὸ
What she had she did; she was beforehand to anoint the
σῶμά μου εἰς τὸν ἐνταφιασμόν. **9** ἀμὴν
body of me for the burial. truly

Jesus Anointed at Bethany

NOW the Passover and the Feast of Unleavened Bread were only two days away, and the chief priests and the teachers of the law were looking for some sly way to arrest Jesus and kill him. 2"But not during the Feast," they said, "or the people may riot."
3While he was in Bethany, reclining at the table in the home of a man known as Simon the Leper, a woman came with an alabaster jar of very expensive perfume, made of pure nard. She broke the jar and poured the perfume on his head.
4Some of those present were saying indignantly to one another, "Why this waste of perfume? 5It could have been sold for more than a year's wages *m* and the money given to the poor." And they rebuked her harshly.
6"Leave her alone," said Jesus. "Why are you bothering her? She has done a beautiful thing to me. 7The poor you will always have with you, and you can help them any time you want. But you will not always have me. 8She did what she could. She poured perfume on my body beforehand to prepare for my burial. 9I

---

l The denarius was equivalent to one day's wage

*m*5 Greek *than three hundred denarii*

9"And truly I say to you, wherever the gospel is preached in the whole world, that also which this woman has done shall be spoken of in memory of her."

10And Judas Iscariot, who was one of the twelve, went off to the chief priests, in order to betray Him to them.

11And they were glad when they heard *this*, and promised to give him money. And he *began* seeking how to betray Him at an opportune time.

The Last Passover

12And on the first day of Unleavened Bread, when the Passover *lamb* was being sacrificed, His disciples *said to Him, "Where do You want us to go and prepare for You to eat the Passover?"

13And He *sent two of His disciples, and *said to them, "Go into the city, and a man will meet you carrying a pitcher of water; follow him;

14and wherever he enters, say to the owner of the house, 'The Teacher says, "Where is My guest room in which I may eat the Passover with My disciples?"'

15"And he himself will show you a large upper room furnished *and* ready; and prepare for us there."

16And the disciples went out, and came to the city, and found *it* just as He had told them; and they prepared the Passover.

17And when it was evening He *came with the twelve.

18And as they were reclining *at the table* and eating, Jesus said, "Truly I say to you that one of you will betray Me—one who is eating with Me."

19They began to be grieved and to say to Him one by one, "Surely not I?"

20And He said to them, "*It is* one of the twelve, one who dips with Me in the

δὲ λέγω ὑμῖν, ὅπου ἐὰν κηρυχθῇ τὸ
And I tell you, wherever is proclaimed the

εὐαγγέλιον εἰς ὅλον τὸν κόσμον, καὶ ὃ
gospel in all the world, also what

ἐποίησεν αὕτη λαληθήσεται εἰς μνημόσυνον
did this woman will be spoken for a memorial

αὐτῆς. 10 Καὶ Ἰούδας Ἰσκαριώθ, ὁ εἷς
of her. And Judas Iscariot, the one

τῶν δώδεκα, ἀπῆλθεν πρὸς τοὺς ἀρχιερεῖς
of the twelve, went to the chief priests

ἵνα αὐτὸν παραδοῖ αὐτοῖς. 11 οἱ δὲ
that him he might betray to them. And they

ἀκούσαντες ἐχάρησαν καὶ ἐπηγγείλαντο αὐτῷ
hearing rejoiced and promised him

ἀργύριον δοῦναι. καὶ ἐζήτει πῶς αὐτὸν
silver to give. And he sought how him

εὐκαίρως παραδοῖ.
opportunely he might betray.

12 Καὶ τῇ πρώτῃ ἡμέρᾳ τῶν ἀζύμων,
And on the first day of unleavened bread,†

ὅτε τὸ πάσχα ἔθυον, λέγουσιν αὐτῷ οἱ
when the passover they sacrificed, say to him the

μαθηταὶ αὐτοῦ· ποῦ θέλεις ἀπελθόντες
disciples of him: Where wishest thou ᵢ going

ἑτοιμάσωμεν ἵνα φάγῃς τὸ πάσχα; 13 καὶ
we may prepare that thou eatest the passover? And

ἀποστέλλει δύο τῶν μαθητῶν αὐτοῦ καὶ
he sends two of the disciples of him and

λέγει αὐτοῖς· ὑπάγετε εἰς τὴν πόλιν, καὶ
tells them: Go ye into the city, and

ἀπαντήσει ὑμῖν ἄνθρωπος κεράμιον ὕδατος
will meet you a man a pitcher of water

βαστάζων· ἀκολουθήσατε αὐτῷ, 14 καὶ ὅπου
carrying; follow him, and wher-

ἐὰν εἰσέλθῃ εἴπατε τῷ οἰκοδεσπότῃ ὅτι ὁ
ever he enters tell the housemaster[,] – The

διδάσκαλος λέγει· ποῦ ἐστιν τὸ κατάλυμά
teacher says: Where is the guest room

μου, ὅπου τὸ πάσχα μετὰ τῶν μαθητῶν
of me, where the passover with the disciples

μου φάγω; 15 καὶ αὐτὸς ὑμῖν δείξει
of me I may eat? And he you will show

ἀνάγαιον μέγα ἐστρωμένον ἕτοιμον· καὶ
upper room a large *having been* spread ready; and

ἐκεῖ ἑτοιμάσατε ἡμῖν. 16 καὶ ἐξῆλθον οἱ
there prepare ye for us. And went forth the

μαθηταὶ καὶ ἦλθον εἰς τὴν πόλιν καὶ
disciples and came into the city and

εὗρον καθὼς εἶπεν αὐτοῖς, καὶ ἡτοίμασαν
found as he told them, and they prepared

τὸ πάσχα. 17 Καὶ ὀψίας γενομένης ἔρχεται
the passover. And evening coming* he comes
= when evening came

μετὰ τῶν δώδεκα. 18 καὶ ἀνακειμένων
with the twelve. And reclining
= as they reclined and ate

αὐτῶν καὶ ἐσθιόντων ὁ Ἰησοῦς εἶπεν·
them and eating* – Jesus said:

ἀμὴν λέγω ὑμῖν ὅτι εἷς ἐξ ὑμῶν παραδώσει
Truly I tell you that one of you will betray

με, ὁ ἐσθίων μετ᾽ ἐμοῦ. 19 ἤρξαντο
me, the [one] eating with me. They began

λυπεῖσθαι καὶ λέγειν αὐτῷ εἷς κατὰ εἷς·
to grieve and to say to him one by one:

μήτι ἐγώ; 20 ὁ δὲ εἶπεν αὐτοῖς· εἷς τῶν
Not I? And he said to them: One of the

δώδεκα, ὁ ἐμβαπτόμενος μετ᾽ ἐμοῦ εἰς
twelve, the [one] dipping with me in

tell you the truth, wherever the gospel is preached throughout the world, what she has done will also be told, in memory of her."

10Then Judas Iscariot, one of the Twelve, went to the chief priests to betray Jesus to them. 11They were delighted to hear this and promised to give him money. So he watched for an opportunity to hand him over.

The Lord's Supper

12On the first day of the Feast of Unleavened Bread, when it was customary to sacrifice the Passover lamb, Jesus' disciples asked him, "Where do you want us to go and make preparations for you to eat the Passover?"

13So he sent two of his disciples, telling them, "Go into the city, and a man carrying a jar of water will meet you. Follow him. 14Say to the owner of the house he enters, 'The Teacher asks: Where is my guest room, where I may eat the Passover with my disciples?' 15He will show you a large upper room, furnished and ready. Make preparations for us there."

16The disciples left, went into the city and found things just as Jesus had told them. So they prepared the Passover.

17When evening came, Jesus arrived with the Twelve. 18While they were reclining at the table eating, he said, "I tell you the truth, one of you will betray me—one who is eating with me."

19They were saddened, and one by one they said to him, "Surely not I?"

20"It is one of the Twelve," he replied, "one who dips bread into the bowl.

21"For the Son of Man *is to go*, just as it is written of Him; but woe to that man by whom the Son of Man is betrayed! *It would have been* good for that man if he had not been born."

The Lord's Supper

22And while they were eating, He took *some* bread, and after a blessing He broke it; and gave *it* to them, and said, "Take *it;* this is My body."

23And when He had taken a cup, *and* given thanks, He gave *it* to them; and they all drank from it.

24And He said to them, "This is My blood of the covenant, which is poured out for many.

25"Truly I say to you, I shall never again drink of the fruit of the vine until that day when I drink it new in the kingdom of God."

26And after singing a hymn, they went out to the Mount of Olives.

27And Jesus *said to them, "You will all fall away, because it is written, 'I WILL STRIKE DOWN THE SHEPHERD, AND THE SHEEP SHALL BE SCATTERED.'

28"But after I have been raised, I will go before you to Galilee."

29But Peter said to Him, "*Even* though all may fall away, yet I will not."

30And Jesus *said to him, "Truly I say to you, that you yourself this very night, before a cock crows twice, shall three times deny Me."

31But *Peter* kept saying insistently, "*Even* if I have to die with You, I will not deny You!" And they all were saying the same thing, too.

Jesus in Gethsemane

32And they *came to a

τὸ [ἐν] τρύβλιον. 21 ὅτι ὁ μὲν υἱὸς τοῦ
the one dish. Because indeed the Son

ἀνθρώπου ὑπάγει καθὼς γέγραπται περὶ
of man is going as it has been written concerning

αὐτοῦ· οὐαὶ δε τῷ ἀνθρώπῳ ἐκείνῳ δι'
him; but woe - man to that through

οὗ ὁ υἱὸς τοῦ ἀνθρώπου παραδίδοται·
whom the Son - of man is betrayed;

καλὸν αὐτῷ εἰ οὐκ ἐγεννήθη ὁ ἄνθρωπος
good for him if was not born - man

ἐκεῖνος. 22 Καὶ ἐσθιόντων αὐτῶν λαβὼν
that. And eating them* taking
= as they were eating

ἄρτον εὐλογήσας ἔκλασεν καὶ ἔδωκεν αὐτοῖς
a loaf blessing he broke and gave to them

καὶ εἶπεν· λάβετε· τοῦτό ἐστιν τὸ σῶμά
and said: Take ye; this is the body

μου. 23 καὶ λαβὼν ποτήριον εὐχαριστήσας
of me. And taking a cup giving thanks

ἔδωκεν αὐτοῖς, καὶ ἔπιον ἐξ αὐτοῦ πάντες.
he gave to them, and drank of it all.

24 καὶ εἶπεν αὐτοῖς· τοῦτό ἐστιν τὸ αἷμά
And he said to them: This is the blood

μου τῆς διαθήκης τὸ ἐκχυννόμενον ὑπὲρ
of me of the covenant - being shed for

πολλῶν. 25 ἀμὴν λέγω ὑμῖν ὅτι οὐκέτι
many. Truly I tell you[,] - No more

οὐ μὴ πίω ἐκ τοῦ γενήματος τῆς ἀμπέλου
by no(any) will I drink of the fruit of the vine
means

ἕως τῆς ἡμέρας ἐκείνης ὅταν αὐτὸ πίνω
until - day that when it I drink

καινὸν ἐν τῇ βασιλείᾳ τοῦ θεοῦ.
new in the kingdom - of God.

26 Καὶ ὑμνήσαντες ἐξῆλθον εἰς τὸ
And having sung a hymn they went forth to the

ὄρος τῶν ἐλαιῶν. 27 Καὶ λέγει αὐτοῖς ὁ
mount of the olives. And says to them -

Ἰησοῦς ὅτι πάντες σκανδαλισθήσεσθε, ὅτι
Jesus[,] - *All ¹ye ²will ⁴be offended, because

γέγραπται· πατάξω τὸν ποιμένα, καὶ τὰ
it has been written: I will strike the shepherd, and the

πρόβατα διασκορπισθήσονται. 28 ἀλλὰ μετὰ
sheep will be scattered. But after

τὸ ἐγερθῆναί με προάξω ὑμᾶς εἰς τὴν
the to be raised me⁽ᵇ⁾ I will go before you to -
= I am raised

Γαλιλαίαν. 29 ὁ δὲ Πέτρος ἔφη αὐτῷ·
Galilee. - And Peter said to him:

εἰ καὶ πάντες σκανδαλισθήσονται, ἀλλ'
If even all men shall be offended, yet

οὐκ ἐγώ. 30 καὶ λέγει αὐτῷ ὁ Ἰησοῦς·
not I. And says to him - Jesus:

ἀμὴν λέγω σοι ὅτι σὺ σήμερον ταύτῃ τῇ
Truly I tell thee[,] - Thou to-day in this

νυκτὶ πρὶν ἢ δὶς ἀλέκτορα φωνῆσαι τρίς
night before twice a cock to sound⁽ᵇ⁾ thrice

με ἀπαρνήσῃ. 31 ὁ δὲ ἐκπερισσῶς ἐλάλει·
me thou wilt deny. But he more exceedingly said:

ἐὰν δέῃ με συναποθανεῖν σοι, οὐ μὴ
If it should behove me *to* die with thee, by no means
= I must

σε ἀπαρνήσομαι. ὡσαύτως [δὲ] καὶ πάντες
thee will I deny. And similarly also all

ἔλεγον.
said.

32 Καὶ ἔρχονται εἰς χωρίον οὗ τὸ
And they come to a piece of land of which the

---

bowl with me. 21The Son of Man will go just as it is written about him. But woe to that man who betrays the Son of Man! It would be better for him if he had not been born."

22While they were eating, Jesus took bread, gave thanks and broke it, and gave it to his disciples, saying, "Take it; this is my body."

23Then he took the cup, gave thanks and offered it to them, and they all drank from it.

24"This is my blood of the[n] covenant, which is poured out for many," he said to them. 25"I tell you the truth, I will not drink again of the fruit of the vine until that day when I drink it anew in the kingdom of God."

26When they had sung a hymn, they went out to the Mount of Olives.

Jesus Predicts Peter's Denial

27"You will all fall away," Jesus told them, "for it is written:

" 'I will strike the
shepherd,
and the sheep will be
scattered.'[o]

28But after I have risen, I will go ahead of you into Galilee."

29Peter declared, "Even if all fall away, I will not."

30"I tell you the truth," Jesus answered, "today— yes, tonight—before the rooster crows twice[p] you yourself will disown me three times."

31But Peter insisted emphatically, "Even if I have to die with you, I will never disown you." And all the others said the same.

Gethsemane

32They went to a place

ⁿ24 Some manuscripts *the new*
ᵒ27 Zech. 13:7
ᵖ30 Some early manuscripts do not have *twice.*

place named Gethsemane; and He *said to His disciples, "Sit here until I have prayed."
33And He *took with Him Peter and James and John, and began to be very distressed and troubled.
34And He *said to them, "My soul is deeply grieved to the point of death; remain here and keep watch."
35And He went a little beyond *them, and fell to the ground, and *began to pray that if it were possible, the hour might pass Him by.
36And He was saying, "Abba! Father! All things are possible for Thee; remove this cup from Me; yet not what I will, but what Thou wilt."
37And He *came and *found them sleeping, and *said to Peter, "Simon, are you asleep? Could you not keep watch for one hour?
38"Keep watching and praying, that you may not come into temptation; the spirit is willing, but the flesh is weak."
39And again He went away and prayed, saying the same words.
40And again He came and found them sleeping, for their eyes were very heavy; and they did not know what to answer Him.
41And He *came the third time, and *said to them, "Are you still sleeping and taking your rest? It is enough; the hour has come; behold, the Son of Man is being betrayed into the hands of sinners.
42"Arise, let us be going; behold, the one who betrays Me is at hand!"

Betrayal and Arrest

43And immediately while He was still speaking, Judas, one of the twelve, *came up, accompanied by a multitude with swords and clubs, from the chief

ὄνομα Γεθσημανί, καὶ λέγει τοῖς μαθηταῖς
name [was] Gethsemane, and he says to the disciples

αὐτοῦ· καθίσατε ὧδε ἕως προσεύξωμαι.
of him: Sit ye here while I pray.

33 καὶ παραλαμβάνει τὸν Πέτρον καὶ τὸν
And he takes — Peter and —

Ἰάκωβον καὶ τὸν Ἰωάννην μετ' αὐτοῦ,
James and — John with him,

καὶ ἤρξατο ἐκθαμβεῖσθαι καὶ ἀδημονεῖν,
and began to be greatly astonished and to be distressed,

34 καὶ λέγει αὐτοῖς· περίλυπός ἐστιν ἡ
and says to them: Deeply grieved is the

ψυχή μου ἕως θανάτου· μείνατε ὧδε καὶ
soul of me unto death; remain ye here and

γρηγορεῖτε. 35 καὶ προελθὼν μικρὸν ἔπιπτεν
watch. And going forward a little he fell

ἐπὶ τῆς γῆς, καὶ προσηύχετο ἵνα εἰ
on the ground, and prayed that if

δυνατόν ἐστιν παρέλθῃ ἀπ' αὐτοῦ ἡ ὥρα,
possible it is might pass away from him the hour,

36 καὶ ἔλεγεν· ἀββᾶ ὁ πατήρ, πάντα
and said: Abba — Father, all things

δυνατά σοι· παρένεγκε τὸ ποτήριον τοῦτο
[are] possible to thee; remove — cup this

ἀπ' ἐμοῦ· ἀλλ' οὐ τί ἐγὼ θέλω ἀλλὰ
from me; but not what I wish but

τί σύ. 37 καὶ ἔρχεται καὶ εὑρίσκει
what thou. And he comes and finds

αὐτοὺς καθεύδοντας, καὶ λέγει τῷ Πέτρῳ·
them sleeping, and says — to Peter:

Σίμων, καθεύδεις; οὐκ ἴσχυσας μίαν ὥραν
Simon, sleepest thou? couldest thou not one hour

γρηγορῆσαι; 38 γρηγορεῖτε καὶ προσεύχεσθε,
to watch? Watch ye and pray,

ἵνα μὴ ἔλθητε εἰς πειρασμόν· τὸ μὲν
lest ye come into temptation; indeed the

πνεῦμα πρόθυμον, ἡ δὲ σὰρξ ἀσθενής.
spirit [is] eager, but the flesh weak.

39 καὶ πάλιν ἀπελθὼν προσηύξατο τὸν
And again going away he prayed ¹the

αὐτὸν λόγον εἰπών. 40 καὶ πάλιν ἐλθὼν
³same ⁴word ¹saying. And again coming

εὗρεν αὐτοὺς καθεύδοντας, ἦσαν γὰρ αὐτῶν
he found them sleeping, for were of them

οἱ ὀφθαλμοὶ καταβαρυνόμενοι, καὶ οὐκ
the eyes becoming heavy, and not

ᾔδεισαν τί ἀποκριθῶσιν αὐτῷ. 41 καὶ
they knew what they might answer him. And

ἔρχεται τὸ τρίτον καὶ λέγει αὐτοῖς·
he comes the third [time] and says to them:

καθεύδετε τὸ λοιπὸν καὶ ἀναπαύεσθε·
Sleep ye now† and rest;

ἀπέχει· ἦλθεν ἡ ὥρα, ἰδοὺ παραδίδοται ὁ
it is enough; came the hour, behold is betrayed the

υἱὸς τοῦ ἀνθρώπου εἰς τὰς χεῖρας τῶν
Son — man into the hands —

ἁμαρτωλῶν. 42 ἐγείρεσθε, ἄγωμεν· ἰδοὺ ὁ
of sinners. Rise ye, let us go; behold the

παραδιδούς με ἤγγικεν. 43 Καὶ εὐθὺς ἔτι
[one] betraying me has drawn near. And immediately yet

αὐτοῦ λαλοῦντος παραγίνεται [ὁ] Ἰούδας
him speakingᵃ arrives — Judas
= while he was still speaking

εἷς τῶν δώδεκα, καὶ μετ' αὐτοῦ ὄχλος
one of the twelve, and with him a crowd

μετὰ μαχαιρῶν καὶ ξύλων παρὰ τῶν
with swords and clubs from the

called Gethsemane, and Jesus said to his disciples, "Sit here while I pray."
33He took Peter, James and John along with him, and he began to be deeply distressed and troubled.
34"My soul is overwhelmed with sorrow to the point of death," he said to them. "Stay here and keep watch."
35Going a little farther, he fell to the ground and prayed that if possible the hour might pass from him.
36"Abba,ᵃ Father," he said, "everything is possible for you. Take this cup from me. Yet not what I will, but what you will."
37Then he returned to his disciples and found them sleeping. "Simon," he said to Peter, "are you asleep? Could you not keep watch for one hour? 38Watch and pray so that you will not fall into temptation. The spirit is willing, but the body is weak."
39Once more he went away and prayed the same thing. 40When he came back, he again found them sleeping, because their eyes were heavy. They did not know what to say to him.
41Returning the third time, he said to them, "Are you still sleeping and resting? Enough! The hour has come. Look, the Son of Man is betrayed into the hands of sinners. 42Rise! Let us go! Here comes my betrayer!"

Jesus Arrested

43Just as he was speaking, Judas, one of the Twelve, appeared. With him was a crowd armed with swords and clubs, sent from the

ᵃ36 Aramaic for *Father*

priests and the scribes and the elders.
44Now he who was betraying Him had given them a signal, saying, "Whomever I shall kiss, He is the one; seize Him, and lead Him away under guard."
45And after coming, he immediately went to Him, saying, "Rabbi!" and kissed Him.
46And they laid hands on Him, and seized Him.
47But a certain one of those who stood by drew his sword, and struck the slave of the high priest, and cut off his ear.
48And Jesus answered and said to them, "Have you come out with swords and clubs to arrest Me, as against a robber?
49"Every day I was with you in the temple teaching, and you did not seize Me; but *this has happened* that the Scriptures might be fulfilled."
50And they all left Him and fled.
51And a certain young man was following Him, wearing *nothing but* a linen sheet over *his* naked *body;* and they *seized him.
52But he left the linen sheet behind, and escaped naked.

Jesus before His Accusers
53And they led Jesus away to the high priest; and all the chief priests and the elders and the scribes *gathered together.
54And Peter had followed Him at a distance, right into the courtyard of the high priest; and he was sitting with the officers, and warming himself at the fire.
55Now the chief priests and the whole ᵐCouncil kept trying to obtain testimony against Jesus to put Him to death; and they were not finding any.
56For many were giving false testimony against Him, and *yet* their testimony was not consistent.

ἀρχιερέων καὶ τῶν γραμματέων καὶ τῶν
chief priests and the scribes and the
πρεσβυτέρων. 44 δεδώκει δὲ ὁ παραδιδοὺς
elders. ¹Now ⁵had given ²the [one] ³betraying
αὐτὸν σύσσημον αὐτοῖς λέγων· ὃν ἂν
⁴him ⁷a signal ⁶them saying: Whomever
φιλήσω αὐτός ἐστιν· κρατήσατε αὐτὸν καὶ
I may kiss he is; seize ye him and
ἀπάγετε ἀσφαλῶς. 45 καὶ ἐλθὼν εὐθὺς
lead away securely. And coming immediately
προσελθὼν αὐτῷ λέγει· ῥαββί, καὶ
approaching to him he says: Rabbi, and
κατεφίλησεν αὐτόν· 46 οἱ δὲ ἐπέβαλαν τὰς
fervently kissed him; and they ¹laid ⁴on ²the(their)
χεῖρας αὐτῷ καὶ ἐκράτησαν αὐτόν. 47 εἰς
³hands him and seized him. ⁵one
δέ τις τῶν παρεστηκότων σπασάμενος
¹But ²a certain of the [ones] standing by drawing
τὴν μάχαιραν ἔπαισεν τὸν δοῦλον τοῦ ἀρχιερέως
the sword struck the slave of the high priest
καὶ ἀφεῖλεν αὐτοῦ τὸ ὠτάριον. 48 καὶ
and cut off of him the ear. And
ἀποκριθεὶς ὁ Ἰησοῦς εἶπεν αὐτοῖς· ὡς
answering - Jesus said to them: As
ἐπὶ λῃστὴν ἐξήλθατε μετὰ μαχαιρῶν καὶ
against a robber came ye forth with swords and
ξύλων συλλαβεῖν με; 49 καθ᾽ ἡμέραν ἤμην
clubs to arrest me? Daily I was
πρὸς ὑμᾶς ἐν τῷ ἱερῷ διδάσκων, καὶ οὐκ
with you in the temple teaching, and not
ἐκρατήσατέ με· ἀλλ᾽ ἵνα πληρωθῶσιν αἱ
ye did seize me; but that may be fulfilled the
γραφαί. 50 καὶ ἀφέντες αὐτὸν ἔφυγον
scriptures. And leaving him they fled
πάντες. 51 Καὶ νεανίσκος τις συνηκολούθει
all. And a certain young man accompanied
αὐτῷ περιβεβλημένος σινδόνα ἐπὶ γυμνοῦ,
him having been clothed [in] a nightgown over [his] naked [body],
καὶ κρατοῦσιν αὐτόν· 52 ὁ δὲ καταλιπὼν
and they seize him; and he leaving
τὴν σινδόνα γυμνὸς ἔφυγεν.
the nightgown naked fled.
53 Καὶ ἀπήγαγον τὸν Ἰησοῦν πρὸς τὸν
And they led away - Jesus to the
ἀρχιερέα, καὶ συνέρχονται πάντες οἱ
high priest, and come together all the
ἀρχιερεῖς καὶ οἱ πρεσβύτεροι καὶ οἱ
chief priests and the elders and the
γραμματεῖς. 54 καὶ ὁ Πέτρος ἀπὸ μακρόθεν
scribes. And - Peter from afar
ἠκολούθησεν αὐτῷ ἕως ἔσω εἰς τὴν αὐλὴν
followed him until within *in* the court
τοῦ ἀρχιερέως, καὶ ἦν συγκαθήμενος μετὰ
of the high priest, and was sitting *with* with
τῶν ὑπηρετῶν καὶ θερμαινόμενος πρὸς τὸ
the attendants and warming himself by the
φῶς. 55 Οἱ δὲ ἀρχιερεῖς καὶ ὅλον τὸ
bright fire. Now the chief priests and all the
συνέδριον ἐζήτουν κατὰ τοῦ Ἰησοῦ
council sought against - Jesus
μαρτυρίαν εἰς τὸ θανατῶσαι αὐτόν, καὶ
witness for the to put to death him, and
= so as
οὐχ ηὕρισκον· 56 πολλοὶ γὰρ ἐψευδομαρτύρουν
found not; for many falsely witnessed
κατ᾽ αὐτοῦ, καὶ ἴσαι αἱ μαρτυρίαι οὐκ
against him, and ⁵identical ¹the ²testimonies ⁴not

---

chief priests, the teachers of the law, and the elders.
44Now the betrayer had arranged a signal with them: "The one I kiss is the man; arrest him and lead him away under guard."
45Going at once to Jesus, Judas said, "Rabbi!" and kissed him. 46The men seized Jesus and arrested him. 47Then one of those standing near drew his sword and struck the servant of the high priest, cutting off his ear.
48"Am I leading a rebellion," said Jesus, "that you have come out with swords and clubs to capture me? 49Every day I was with you, teaching in the temple courts, and you did not arrest me. But the Scriptures must be fulfilled." 50Then everyone deserted him and fled.
51A young man, wearing nothing but a linen garment, was following Jesus. When they seized him, 52he fled naked, leaving his garment behind.

Before the Sanhedrin
53They took Jesus to the high priest, and all the chief priests, elders and teachers of the law came together. 54Peter followed him at a distance, right into the courtyard of the high priest. There he sat with the guards and warmed himself at the fire.
55The chief priests and the whole Sanhedrin were looking for evidence against Jesus so that they could put him to death, but they did not find any. 56Many testified falsely against him, but their statements did not agree.

ᵐOr, Sanhedrin

57And some stood up and *began* to give false testimony against Him, saying, 58"We heard Him say, 'I will destroy this temple made with hands, and in three days I will build another made without hands.' " 59And not even in this respect was their testimony consistent. 60And the high priest stood up *and came* forward and questioned Jesus, saying, "Do You make no answer? What is it that these men are testifying against You?" 61But He kept silent, and made no answer. Again the high priest was questioning Him, and saying to Him, "Are You the Christ, the Son of the Blessed *One?*" 62And Jesus said, "I am; and you shall see THE SON OF MAN SITTING AT THE RIGHT HAND OF POWER, and COMING WITH THE CLOUDS OF HEAVEN." 63And tearing his clothes, the high priest *said, "What further need do we have of witnesses? 64"You have heard the blasphemy; how does it seem to you?" And they all condemned Him to be deserving of death. 65And some began to spit at Him, and to blindfold Him, and to beat Him with their fists, and to say to Him, "Prophesy!" And the officers received Him with slaps *in the face.*

Peter's Denials

66And as Peter was below in the courtyard, one of the servant-girls of the high priest *came, 67and seeing Peter warming himself, she looked at him, and *said, "You, too, were with Jesus the Nazarene." 68But he denied *it,* saying, "I neither know nor understand what you are talking about." And he went out onto the porch. *n*

ἦσαν. 57 καὶ τινες ἀναστάντες ἐψευδομαρτύρουν
ᵃwere. And some standing up falsely witnessed

κατ' αὐτοῦ λέγοντες 58 ὅτι ἡμεῖς ἠκούσαμεν
against him saying[,] – We heard

αὐτοῦ λέγοντος ὅτι ἐγὼ καταλύσω τὸν
him saying[,] – I will overthrow –

ναὸν τοῦτον τὸν χειροποίητον καὶ διὰ
ᵃshrine ᵃthis – ᵃhandmade and through(after)

τριῶν ἡμερῶν ἄλλον ἀχειροποίητον οἰκο-
three days another not handmade I will

δομήσω. 59 καὶ οὐδὲ οὕτως ἴση ἦν ἡ
build. And not so identical was the

μαρτυρία αὐτῶν. 60 καὶ ἀναστὰς ὁ
witness of them. And standing up the

ἀρχιερεὺς εἰς μέσον ἐπηρώτησεν τὸν Ἰησοῦν
high priest in [the] midst questioned – Jesus

λέγων· οὐκ ἀποκρίνῃ οὐδὲν τί οὗτοί σου
saying: Answerest thou not no(any)thing what these men ᵃthee

καταμαρτυροῦσιν; 61 ὁ δὲ ἐσιώπα καὶ
¹testify against? But he was silent and

οὐκ ἀπεκρίνατο οὐδέν. πάλιν ὁ ἀρχιερεὺς
answered not no(any)thing. Again the high priest

ἐπηρώτα αὐτὸν καὶ λέγει αὐτῷ· σὺ εἶ ὁ
questioned him and says to him: Thou art the

χριστὸς ὁ υἱὸς τοῦ εὐλογητοῦ; 62 ὁ δὲ
Christ the Son of the Blessed [one]? – And

Ἰησοῦς εἶπεν· ἐγώ εἰμι, καὶ ὄψεσθε
Jesus said: I am, and ye will see

τὸν υἱὸν τοῦ ἀνθρώπου ἐκ δεξιῶν καθήμενον
the Son – of man ᵃat [the] right [hand] ¹sitting

τῆς δυνάμεως καὶ ἐρχόμενον μετὰ τῶν
of the Power and coming with the

νεφελῶν τοῦ οὐρανοῦ. 63 ὁ δὲ ἀρχιερεὺς
clouds – of heaven. And the high priest

διαρήξας τοὺς χιτῶνας αὐτοῦ λέγει· τί
rending the tunics of him says: What

ἔτι χρείαν ἔχομεν μαρτύρων; 64 ἠκούσατε
more need have we of witnesses? ye heard

τῆς βλασφημίας· τί ὑμῖν φαίνεται; οἱ δὲ
the blasphemy; what to you appears it? And they

πάντες κατέκριναν αὐτὸν ἔνοχον εἶναι
all condemned him liable to be

θανάτου. 65 Καὶ ἤρξαντό τινες ἐμπτύειν
of(to) death. And began some to spit at

αὐτῷ καὶ περικαλύπτειν αὐτοῦ τὸ πρόσωπον
him and to cover of him the face

καὶ κολαφίζειν αὐτὸν καὶ λέγειν αὐτῷ·
and to maltreat him and to say to him:

προφήτευσον, καὶ οἱ ὑπηρέται ῥαπίσμασιν
Prophesy, and the attendants with slaps

αὐτὸν ἔλαβον. 66 Καὶ ὄντος τοῦ Πέτρου
ᵃhim ¹took. And being – Peterᵃ
= as Peter was

κάτω ἐν τῇ αὐλῇ ἔρχεται μία τῶν
below in the court comes one of the

παιδισκῶν τοῦ ἀρχιερέως, 67 καὶ ἰδοῦσα
maidservants of the high priest, and seeing

τὸν Πέτρον θερμαινόμενον ἐμβλέψασα αὐτῷ
– Peter warming himself looking at him

λέγει· καὶ σὺ μετὰ τοῦ Ναζαρηνοῦ ἦσθα
says: And ¹thou ²with ⁴the ᵃNazarene ³wast

τοῦ Ἰησοῦ. 68 ὁ δὲ ἠρνήσατο λέγων· οὔτε
– ᵃJesus. But he denied saying: ᵃneither

οἶδα οὔτε ἐπίσταμαι σὺ τί λέγεις. καὶ
¹I ³know ⁴nor ⁵understand ⁷thou ⁶what ᵃsayest. And

ἐξῆλθεν ἔξω εἰς τὸ προαύλιον· 69 καὶ ἡ
he went forth outside into the forecourt; and the

57Then some stood up and gave this false testimony against him: 58"We heard him say, 'I will destroy this man-made temple and in three days will build another, not made by man.' " 59Yet even then their testimony did not agree.

60Then the high priest stood up before them and asked Jesus, "Are you not going to answer? What is this testimony that these men are bringing against you?" 61But Jesus remained silent and gave no answer.

Again the high priest asked him, "Are you the Christ,ʳ the Son of the Blessed One?"

62"I am," said Jesus. "And you will see the Son of Man sitting at the right hand of the Mighty One and coming on the clouds of heaven."

63The high priest tore his clothes. "Why do we need any more witnesses?" he asked. 64"You have heard the blasphemy. What do you think?"

They all condemned him as worthy of death. 65Then some began to spit at him; they blindfolded him, struck him with their fists, and said, "Prophesy!" And the guards took him and beat him.

Peter Disowns Jesus

66While Peter was below in the courtyard, one of the servant girls of the high priest came by. 67When she saw Peter warming himself, she looked closely at him.

"You also were with that Nazarene, Jesus," she said.

68But he denied it. "I don't know or understand what you're talking about," he said, and went out into the entryway.ˢ

---

n Later mss. add: *and a cock crowed*

*r*61 Or *Messiah*
*s*68 Some early manuscripts *entryway and the rooster crowed*

69And the maid saw him, and began once more to say to the bystanders, "This is one of them!"

70But again he was denying it. And after a little while the bystanders were again saying to Peter, "Surely you are one of them, for you are a Galilean too."

71But he began to curse and swear, "I do not know this man you are talking about!"

72And immediately a cock crowed a second time. And Peter remembered how Jesus had made the remark to him, "Before a cock crows twice, you will deny Me three times." And he began to weep.

παιδίσκη ἰδοῦσα αὐτὸν ἤρξατο πάλιν λέγειν
maidservant seeing   him   began   again   to say

τοῖς   παρεστῶσιν ὅτι οὗτος ἐξ αὐτῶν ἐστιν.
to the [ones] standing by[,] – This man of them   is.

70 ὁ   δὲ πάλιν ἠρνεῖτο. καὶ μετὰ μικρὸν
But he   again   denied.   And after   a little

πάλιν οἱ παρεστῶτες ἔλεγον τῷ Πέτρῳ·
again the [ones] standing by   said   to Peter:

ἀληθῶς ἐξ αὐτῶν εἶ· καὶ γὰρ Γαλιλαῖος
Truly   of   them thou art; 3indeed 1for   4a Galilæan

εἶ. 71 ὁ δὲ ἤρξατο ἀναθεματίζειν καὶ
3thou art. And he   began   to curse   and

ὀμνύναι ὅτι οὐκ οἶδα   τὸν ἄνθρωπον
to swear[,] – I know not –   man

τοῦτον ὃν λέγετε. 72 καὶ εὐθὺς ἐκ
this   whom ye say.   And immediately a

δευτέρου ἀλέκτωρ ἐφώνησεν. καὶ ἀνεμνήσθη
second time   a cock   crew.   And remembered

ὁ Πέτρος τὸ ῥῆμα ὡς εἶπεν αὐτῷ ὁ
– Peter   the word   as   said   to him –

Ἰησοῦς ὅτι πρὶν ἀλέκτορα δὶς φωνῆσαι
Jesus[,] – Before a cock   twice to crowb

τρίς με ἀπαρνήσῃ· καὶ ἐπιβαλὼν ἔκλαιεν.
thrice me thou wilt deny; and thinking thereon he wept.

69When the servant girl saw him there, she said again to those standing around, "This fellow is one of them." 70Again he denied it.

After a little while, those standing near said to Peter, "Surely you are one of them, for you are a Galilean."

71He began to call down curses on himself, and he swore to them, "I don't know this man you're talking about."

72Immediately the rooster crowed the second time.[I] Then Peter remembered the word Jesus had spoken to him: "Before the rooster crows twice[u] you will disown me three times." And he broke down and wept.

Chapter 15

Jesus before Pilate

AND early in the morning the chief priests with the elders and scribes, and the whole mCouncil, immediately held a consultation; and binding Jesus, they led Him away, and delivered Him up to Pilate.

2And Pilate questioned Him, "Are You the King of the Jews?" And answering He *said to him, "It is as you say."

3And the chief priests *began* to accuse Him harshly.

4And Pilate was questioning Him again, saying, "Do You make no answer? See how many charges they bring against You!"

5But Jesus made no further answer; so that Pilate was amazed.

6Now at *the* feast he used to release for them *any* one prisoner whom they requested.

7And the man named Barabbas had been imprisoned with the insurrectionists who had committed murder in the insurrection.

8And the multitude went up and began asking him *to do* as he had been accustomed to do for them.

9And Pilate answered them, saying, "Do you

---

15 Καὶ εὐθὺς πρωῒ συμβούλιον ἑτοιμάσαντες
And immediately early 3a council 1preparing

οἱ ἀρχιερεῖς μετὰ τῶν πρεσβυτέρων καὶ
the chief priests with the elders   and

γραμματέων καὶ ὅλον τὸ συνέδριον, δήσαντες
scribes   and all the council,   having bound

τὸν Ἰησοῦν ἀπήνεγκαν καὶ παρέδωκαν
– Jesus   led [him] away and delivered [him]

Πιλάτῳ. 2 καὶ ἐπηρώτησεν αὐτὸν ὁ
to Pilate. And questioned   him   –

Πιλᾶτος· σὺ εἶ ὁ βασιλεὺς τῶν Ἰουδαίων;
Pilate: Thou art the king   of the Jews?

ὁ δὲ ἀποκριθεὶς αὐτῷ λέγει· σὺ λέγεις.
And he answering   him   says: Thou sayest.

3 καὶ κατηγόρουν αὐτοῦ οἱ ἀρχιερεῖς πολλά.
And accused   him   the chief priests many things.

4 ὁ δὲ Πιλᾶτος πάλιν ἐπηρώτα αὐτόν [λέγων]·
– But Pilate   again   questioned him   saying:

οὐκ ἀποκρίνῃ οὐδέν; ἴδε πόσα
Answerest thou not no(any)thing? Behold how many things

σου κατηγοροῦσιν. 5 ὁ δὲ Ἰησοῦς οὐκ-
thee they accuse.   – But Jesus   no(any)

ἔτι οὐδὲν ἀπεκρίθη, ὥστε θαυμάζειν
more nothing answered,   so as   to marvel
                                = so that Pilate marvelled

τὸν Πιλᾶτον. 6 Κατὰ δὲ ἑορτὴν ἀπέλυεν
– Pilateb.   Now at   a feast   he released

αὐτοῖς ἕνα δέσμιον ὃν παρῃτοῦντο. 7 ἦν δὲ
to them one prisoner whom they begged.   There was

ὁ λεγόμενος Βαραββᾶς μετὰ τῶν
the [one] named   Barabbas   with the

στασιαστῶν δεδεμένος, οἵτινες ἐν τῇ στάσει
rebels   having been bound, who   in the rebellion

φόνον πεποιήκεισαν. 8 καὶ ἀναβὰς ὁ ὄχλος
murder   had done.   And going up the crowd

ἤρξατο αἰτεῖσθαι καθὼς ἐποίει αὐτοῖς.
began   to ask   as   he used to do for them.

9 ὁ δὲ Πιλᾶτος ἀπεκρίθη αὐτοῖς λέγων·
– But Pilate   answered   them   saying:

Chapter 15

Jesus Before Pilate

VERY early in the morning, the chief priests, with the elders, the teachers of the law and the whole Sanhedrin, reached a decision. They bound Jesus, led him away and handed him over to Pilate.

2"Are you the king of the Jews?" asked Pilate.

"Yes, it is as you say," Jesus replied.

3The chief priests accused him of many things. 4So again Pilate asked him, "Aren't you going to answer? See how many things they are accusing you of."

5But Jesus still made no reply, and Pilate was amazed.

6Now it was the custom at the Feast to release a prisoner whom the people requested. 7A man called Barabbas was in prison with the insurrectionists who had committed murder in the uprising. 8The crowd came up and asked Pilate to do for them what he usually did.

9"Do you want me to release to you the king of the

---

mOr, Sanhedrin

* Note the plural.

I72 Some early manuscripts do not have *the second time.*
u72 Some early manuscripts do not have *twice.*

want me to release for you the King of the Jews?''

10For he was aware that the chief priests had delivered Him up because of envy.

11But the chief priests stirred up the multitude *to ask* him to release Barabbas for them instead.

12And answering again, Pilate was saying to them, ''Then what shall I do with Him whom you call the King of the Jews?''

13And they shouted back, ''Crucify Him!''

14But Pilate was saying to them, ''Why, what evil has He done?'' But they shouted all the more, ''Crucify Him!''

15And wishing to satisfy the multitude, Pilate released Barabbas for them, and after having Jesus scourged, he delivered *Him* to be crucified.

Jesus Is Mocked

16And the soldiers took Him away into the palace (that is, the Praetorium), and they *called together the whole *Roman* °cohort.

17And they *dressed Him up in purple, and after weaving a crown of thorns, they put it on Him;

18and they began to acclaim Him, ''Hail, King of the Jews!''

19And they kept beating His head with a ᵖreed, and spitting at Him, and kneeling and bowing before Him.

20And after they had mocked Him, they took the purple off Him, and put His garments on Him. And they *led Him out to crucify Him.

21And they *pressed into service a passer-by coming from the country, Simon of Cyrene (the father of Alexander and Rufus), to bear His cross.

The Crucifixion

22And they *brought Him to the place Golgotha, which is translated, Place of a Skull.

θέλετε ἀπολύσω ὑμῖν τὸν βασιλέα τῶν
Do ye wish I may release to you the king of the

'Ιουδαίων; 10 ἐγίνωσκεν γὰρ ὅτι διὰ φθόνου
Jews? For he knew that on account of envy

παραδεδώκεισαν αὐτὸν οἱ ἀρχιερεῖς. 11 οἱ
had delivered him the chief priests. the

δὲ ἀρχιερεῖς ἀνέσεισαν τὸν ὄχλον ἵνα
But chief priests stirred up the crowd that

μᾶλλον τὸν Βαραββᾶν ἀπολύσῃ αὐτοῖς.
rather - Barabbas he should release to them.

12 ὁ δὲ Πιλᾶτος πάλιν ἀποκριθεὶς ἔλεγεν
- So Pilate again answering said

αὐτοῖς· τί οὖν ποιήσω [ὃν] λέγετε τὸν
to them: What then may I do [to him] whom ye call the

βασιλέα τῶν 'Ιουδαίων; 13 οἱ δὲ πάλιν
king of the Jews? And they again

ἔκραξαν· σταύρωσον αὐτόν. 14 ὁ δὲ
cried out: Crucify him. - But

Πιλᾶτος ἔλεγεν αὐτοῖς· τί γὰρ ἐποίησεν
Pilate said to them: Indeed what ²did he

κακόν; οἱ δὲ περισσῶς ἔκραξαν· σταύρωσον
¹evil? and they more cried out: Crucify

αὐτόν. 15 ὁ δὲ Πιλᾶτος βουλόμενος τῷ
him. - And Pilate resolving to the

ὄχλῳ τὸ ἱκανὸν ποιῆσαι ἀπέλυσεν αὐτοῖς
crowd to satisfy† released to them

τὸν Βαραββᾶν, καὶ παρέδωκεν τὸν 'Ιησοῦν
- Barabbas, and delivered - Jesus

φραγελλώσας ἵνα σταυρωθῇ.
having scourged [him] that he might be crucified.

16 Οἱ δὲ στρατιῶται ἀπήγαγον αὐτὸν
Then the soldiers led away him

ἔσω τῆς αὐλῆς, ὅ ἐστιν πραιτώριον, καὶ
inside the court, which is prætorium, and

συγκαλοῦσιν ὅλην τὴν σπεῖραν. 17 καὶ
they call together all the cohort. And

ἐνδιδύσκουσιν αὐτὸν πορφύραν καὶ περιτιθέασιν
they put on him a purple [robe] and place round

αὐτῷ πλέξαντες ἀκάνθινον στέφανον· 18 καὶ
him plaiting a thorny crown; and

ἤρξαντο ἀσπάζεσθαι αὐτόν· χαῖρε, βασιλεῦ
they began to salute him: Hail, king

τῶν 'Ιουδαίων· 19 καὶ ἔτυπτον αὐτοῦ τὴν
of the Jews; and they struck of him the

κεφαλὴν καλάμῳ καὶ ἐνέπτυον αὐτῷ, καὶ
head with a reed and spat at him, and

τιθέντες τὰ γόνατα προσεκύνουν αὐτῷ.
placing(bending) the(their) knees worshipped him.

20 καὶ ὅτε ἐνέπαιξαν αὐτῷ, ἐξέδυσαν
And when they mocked him, they took off

αὐτὸν τὴν πορφύραν καὶ ἐνέδυσαν αὐτὸν
him the purple [robe] and put on him

τὰ ἱμάτια αὐτοῦ. Καὶ ἐξάγουσιν αὐτὸν
the garments of him. And they lead forth him

ἵνα σταυρώσωσιν αὐτόν. 21 καὶ ἀγγαρεύουσιν
that they might crucify him. And they impress

παράγοντά τινα Σίμωνα Κυρηναῖον ἐρχόμενον
passing by a certain Simon a Cyrenian coming

ἀπ' ἀγροῦ, τὸν πατέρα 'Αλεξάνδρου καὶ
from [the] country, the father of Alexander and

'Ρούφου, ἵνα ἄρῃ τὸν σταυρὸν αὐτοῦ.
of Rufus, that he might bear the cross of him.

22 καὶ φέρουσιν αὐτὸν ἐπὶ τὸν Γολγοθὰν
And they bring him to the Golgotha

τόπον, ὅ ἐστιν μεθερμηνευόμενος κρανίου
place, which is being interpreted of a skull

Jews?'' asked Pilate, 10knowing it was out of envy that the chief priests had handed Jesus over to him. 11But the chief priests stirred up the crowd to have Pilate release Barabbas instead.

12''What shall I do, then, with the one you call the king of the Jews?'' Pilate asked them.

13''Crucify him!'' they shouted.

14''Why? What crime has he committed?'' asked Pilate.

But they shouted all the louder, ''Crucify him!''

15Wanting to satisfy the crowd, Pilate released Barabbas to them. He had Jesus flogged, and handed him over to be crucified.

The Soldiers Mock Jesus

16The soldiers led Jesus away into the palace (that is, the Praetorium) and called together the whole company of soldiers. 17They put a purple robe on him, then twisted together a crown of thorns and set it on him. 18And they began to call out to him, ''Hail, king of the Jews!'' 19Again and again they struck him on the head with a staff and spit on him. Falling on their knees, they paid homage to him. 20And when they had mocked him, they took off the purple robe and put his own clothes on him. Then they led him out to crucify him.

The Crucifixion

21A certain man from Cyrene, Simon, the father of Alexander and Rufus, was passing by on his way in from the country, and they forced him to carry the cross. 22They brought Jesus to the place called Golgotha (which means The Place of the Skull).

°Or, battalion
ᵖOr, staff (made of a reed)

23And they tried to give Him wine mixed with myrrh; but He did not take it.

24And they *crucified Him, and *divided up His garments among themselves, casting lots for them, to decide what each should take.

25And it was the ᵃthird hour when they crucified Him.

26And the inscription of the charge against Him read, "THE KING OF THE JEWS."

27And they *crucified two robbers with Him, one on His right and one on His left.

28[ᶠAnd the Scripture was fulfilled which says, "And He was numbered with transgressors."]

29And those passing by were hurling abuse at Him, wagging their heads, and saying, "Ha! You who are going to destroy the temple and rebuild it in three days,

30save Yourself, and come down from the cross!"

31In the same way the chief priests also, along with the scribes, were mocking Him among themselves and saying, "He saved others; He cannot save Himself.

32"Let this Christ, the King of Israel, now come down from the cross, so that we may see and believe!" And those who were crucified with Him were casting the same insult at Him.

33And when the ˢsixth hour had come, darkness fell over the whole land until the ᵗninth hour.

34And at the ninth hour Jesus cried out in a loud voice, "ELOI, ELOI, LAMA SABACHTHANI?" which is translated, "MY GOD, MY GOD, WHY HAST THOU FORSAKEN ME?"

35And when some of the bystanders heard it, they began saying, "Behold, He is calling for Elijah."

36And someone ran and filled a sponge with sour wine, put it on a reed, and gave Him a drink, saying, "Let us see whether Elijah will come to take Him down."

ᵃ I.e., 9 a.m.
ᶠ Many mss. do not contain this verse
ˢ I.e., noon
ᵗ I.e., 3 p.m.

τόπος.   23 καὶ   ἐδίδουν   αὐτῷ   ἐσμυρνισμένον
place.   And   they gave   him   ¹having been spiced
                                                    with myrrh

οἶνον·   ὃς δὲ   οὐκ ἔλαβεν.   24 καὶ   σταυροῦσιν
¹wine;   but who(he)   received not.   And   they crucify

αὐτόν, καὶ   διαμερίζονται   τὰ   ἱμάτια   αὐτοῦ,
him,   and   divide   the   garments   of him,

βάλλοντες   κλῆρον   ἐπ' αὐτὰ   τίς   τί   ἄρῃ.
casting   a lot   on   them   ²one   ¹what might take.

25 ἦν   δὲ   ὥρα   τρίτη   καὶ   ἐσταύρωσαν
Now it was   third   and   they crucified

αὐτόν. 26 καὶ   ἦν   ἡ   ἐπιγραφὴ   τῆς   αἰτίας
him.   And was the   superscription of the accusation

αὐτοῦ   ἐπιγεγραμμένη·   Ο ΒΑΣΙΛΕΥΣ ΤΩΝ
of him   having been written over: THE   KING   OF THE

ΙΟΥΔΑΙΩΝ. 27 Καὶ   σὺν   αὐτῷ   σταυροῦσιν
JEWS.   And   with   him   they crucify

δύο   λῃστάς,   ἕνα ἐκ δεξιῶν   καὶ   ἕνα ἐξ
two   robbers,   one on [the] right   and   one on

εὐωνύμων αὐτοῦ. ‡ 29 Καὶ   οἱ   παραπορευόμενοι
[the] left   of him.   And the [ones]   passing by

ἐβλασφήμουν   αὐτὸν   κινοῦντες   τὰς   κεφαλὰς
blasphemed   him   wagging   the   heads

αὐτῶν   καὶ   λέγοντες·   οὐὰ   ὁ   καταλύων
of them   and   saying: Ah the [one]   overthrowing

τὸν   ναὸν   καὶ   οἰκοδομῶν   [ἐν]   τρισὶν
the   shrine   and   building   in   three

ἡμέραις,   30 σῶσον   σεαυτὸν   καταβὰς   ἀπὸ
days,   save   thyself   coming down   from

τοῦ σταυροῦ.   31 ὁμοίως   καὶ   οἱ   ἀρχιερεῖς
the   cross.   Likewise   also   the   chief priests

ἐμπαίζοντες   πρὸς   ἀλλήλους   μετὰ   τῶν
mocking   to   one another   with   the

γραμματέων   ἔλεγον·   ἄλλους   ἔσωσεν,   ἑαυτὸν
scribes   said: Others   he saved,   himself

οὐ   δύναται   σῶσαι·   32 ὁ   χριστὸς   ὁ βασιλεὺς
he cannot   to save;   the   Christ   the   king

Ἰσραὴλ   καταβάτω   νῦν   ἀπὸ   τοῦ σταυροῦ,
of Israel   let come down   now   from   the   cross,

ἵνα   ἴδωμεν   καὶ   πιστεύσωμεν.   καὶ   οἱ
that   we may see   and   believe.   And the

συνεσταυρωμένοι   σὺν   αὐτῷ   ὠνείδιζον   αὐτόν.
[ones] crucified with   with   him   reproached   him.

33 Καὶ   γενομένης   ὥρας   ἕκτης   σκότος
And   becoming   hour   sixthᵃ   darkness
                        = when it was the sixth hour

ἐγένετο   ἐφ' ὅλην   τὴν   γῆν   ἕως   ὥρας
came   over all   the   land   until [the] hour

ἐνάτης.   34 καὶ   τῇ   ἐνάτῃ   ὥρᾳ   ἐβόησεν ὁ
ninth.   And at the ninth   hour   cried -

Ἰησοῦς   φωνῇ   μεγάλῃ·   ἐλωῒ   ἐλωῒ   λαμα
Jesus   with a voice   great(loud):   Eloi[,]   Eloi[,]   lama

σαβαχθάνι;   ὅ   ἐστιν   μεθερμηνευόμενον·   ὁ
sabachthani?   which   is   being interpreted: The

θεός   μου   ὁ θεός   μου,   εἰς τί   ἐγκατέλιπες
God of me[,]   the God   of me,   why   didst thou forsake

με;   35 καὶ   τινες   τῶν   παρεστηκότων
me?   And   some   of the [ones]   standing by

ἀκούσαντες   ἔλεγον·   ἴδε   Ἡλίαν   φωνεῖ.
hearing   said: Behold   Elias   he calls.

36 δραμὼν δέ τις   γεμίσας   σπόγγον   ὄξους
And running   one   having filled   a sponge of(with) vinegar

περιθεὶς   καλάμῳ   ἐπότιζεν   αὐτόν,   λέγων·
placing it round   a reed   ¹gave ²to drink   ³him,   saying:

ἄφετε   ἴδωμεν   εἰ   ἔρχεται   Ἡλίας   ·καθελεῖν
Leave[,]   let us see   if   comes   Elias   ¹to take ²down

‡ Verse 28 omitted by Nestle; cf. NIV footnote.

23Then they offered him wine mixed with myrrh, but he did not take it. 24And they crucified him. Dividing up his clothes, they cast lots to see what each would get.

25It was the third hour when they crucified him. 26The written notice of the charge against him read: THE KING OF THE JEWS. 27They crucified two robbers with him, one on his right and one on his left.ᵛ 29Those who passed by hurled insults at him, shaking their heads and saying, "So! You who are going to destroy the temple and build it in three days, 30come down from the cross and save yourself!" 31In the same way the chief priests and the teachers of the law mocked him among themselves. "He saved others," they said, "but he can't save himself! 32Let this Christ,ʷ this King of Israel, come down now from the cross, that we may see and believe." Those crucified with him also heaped insults on him.

The Death of Jesus

33At the sixth hour darkness came over the whole land until the ninth hour. 34And at the ninth hour Jesus cried out in a loud voice, *"Eloi, Eloi, lama sabachthani?"* — which means, "My God, my God, why have you forsaken me?"ˣ 35When some of those standing near heard this, they said, "Listen, he's calling Elijah." 36One man ran, filled a sponge with wine vinegar, put it on a stick, and offered it to Jesus to drink. "Now leave him alone. Let's see if Elijah comes to take him down," he said.

ᵛ27 Some manuscripts *left*, ²⁸*and the scripture was fulfilled which says, "He was counted with the lawless ones"* (Isaiah 53:12)
ʷ32 Or *Messiah*
ˣ34 Psalm 22:1

37And Jesus uttered a loud cry, and breathed His last.

38And the veil of the temple was torn in two from top to bottom.

39And when the centurion, who was standing right in front of Him, saw the way He breathed His last, he said, "Truly this man was the Son of God!"

40And there were also *some* women looking on from a distance, among whom *were* Mary Magdalene, and Mary the mother of James the Less and Joses, and Salome.

41And when He was in Galilee, they used to follow Him and minister to Him; and *there were* many other women who had come up with Him to Jerusalem.

Jesus Is Buried

42And when evening had already come, because it was the preparation day, that is, the day before the Sabbath,

43Joseph of Arimathea came, a prominent member of the Council, who himself was waiting for the kingdom of God; and he gathered up courage and went in before Pilate, and asked for the body of Jesus.

44And Pilate wondered if He was dead by this time, and summoning the centurion, he questioned him as to whether He was already dead.

45And ascertaining this from the centurion, he granted the body to Joseph.

46And *Joseph* bought a linen cloth, took Him down, wrapped Him in the linen cloth, and laid Him in a tomb which had been hewn out in the rock; and he rolled a stone against the entrance of the tomb.

47And Mary Magdalene and Mary the *mother* of Joses were looking on *to see* where He was laid.

αὐτόν. **37** ὁ δὲ Ἰησοῦς ἀφεὶς φωνὴν
⁵him.   - But Jesus letting go voice

μεγάλην ἐξέπνευσεν. **38** Καὶ τὸ καταπέτασμα
a great(loud) expired.   And the veil

τοῦ ναοῦ ἐσχίσθη εἰς δύο ἀπ' ἄνωθεν
of the shrine was rent in two from top

ἕως κάτω. **39** Ἰδὼν δὲ ὁ κεντυρίων ὁ
to bottom.   And ²seeing ¹the ³centurion

παρεστηκὼς ἐξ ἐναντίας αὐτοῦ ὅτι οὕτως
⁵standing by ⁴opposite ⁶him that thus

ἐξέπνευσεν, εἶπεν· ἀληθῶς οὗτος ὁ ἄνθρωπος
he expired, said: Truly this - man

υἱὸς θεοῦ ἦν. **40** ᾛσαν δὲ καὶ γυναῖκες
son of God was. Now there were also women

ἀπὸ μακρόθεν θεωροῦσαι, ἐν αἷς καὶ
from afar beholding, among whom both

Μαρία ἡ Μαγδαληνὴ καὶ Μαρία ἡ
Mary the Magdalene and Mary ¹the

Ἰακώβου τοῦ μικροῦ καὶ Ἰωσῆτος μήτηρ
²of James ⁴the ³little ⁵and ⁶of Joses ¹mother

καὶ Σαλώμη, **41** αἱ ὅτε ἦν ἐν τῇ Γαλιλαίᾳ
and Salome, who when he was in - Galilee

ἠκολούθουν αὐτῷ καὶ διηκόνουν αὐτῷ, καὶ
followed him and served him, and

ἄλλαι πολλαὶ αἱ συναναβᾶσαι αὐτῷ εἰς
others many - having come up with him to

Ἱεροσόλυμα.
Jerusalem.

42 Καὶ ἤδη ὀψίας γενομένης, ἐπεὶ ἦν
And now evening coming,ᵃ since it was
    = when it was evening,

παρασκευή, ὅ ἐστιν προσάββατον, **43** ἐλθὼν
[the] preparation, which is the day before the sabbath, coming

Ἰωσὴφ ὁ ἀπὸ Ἀριμαθαίας, εὐσχήμων
Joseph the[one] from Arimathæa, an honourable

βουλευτής, ὃς καὶ αὐτὸς ἦν προσδεχόμενος
councillor, who also [him]self was expecting

τὴν βασιλείαν τοῦ θεοῦ, τολμήσας εἰσῆλθεν
the kingdom - of God, taking courage went in

πρὸς τὸν Πιλᾶτον καὶ ᾐτήσατο τὸ σῶμα
to - Pilate and asked the body

τοῦ Ἰησοῦ. **44** ὁ δὲ Πιλᾶτος ἐθαύμασεν
- of Jesus. - And Pilate marvelled

εἰ ἤδη τέθνηκεν, καὶ προσκαλεσάμενος τὸν
if already he has died, and calling to [him] the

κεντυρίωνα ἐπηρώτησεν αὐτὸν εἰ πάλαι
centurion questioned him ⁱf long ago

ἀπέθανεν· **45** καὶ γνοὺς ἀπὸ τοῦ κεντυρίωνος
he died; and knowing from the centurion

ἐδωρήσατο τὸ πτῶμα τῷ Ἰωσήφ. **46** καὶ
he granted the corpse - to Joseph. And

ἀγοράσας σινδόνα καθελὼν αὐτὸν ἐνείλησεν
having bought a piece of taking down him he wrapped
   unused linen

τῇ σινδόνι καὶ κατέθηκεν αὐτὸν ἐν μνήματι
with the linen and deposited him in a tomb

ὃ ἦν λελατομημένον ἐκ πέτρας, καὶ
which was having been hewn out of rock, and

προσεκύλισεν λίθον ἐπὶ τὴν θύραν τοῦ
rolled a stone against the door of the

μνημείου. **47** ἡ δὲ Μαρία ἡ Μαγδαληνὴ
tomb. - And Mary the Magdalene

καὶ Μαρία ἡ Ἰωσῆτος ἐθεώρουν ποῦ
and Mary the [mother] of Joses beheld where

τέθειται.
he has been laid.

37With a loud cry, Jesus breathed his last.

38The curtain of the temple was torn in two from top to bottom. 39And when the centurion, who stood there in front of Jesus, heard his cry and ʸ saw how he died, he said, "Surely this man was the Son ᶻ of God!"

40Some women were watching from a distance. Among them were Mary Magdalene, Mary the mother of James the younger and of Joses, and Salome. 41In Galilee these women had followed him and cared for his needs. Many other women who had come up with him to Jerusalem were also there.

The Burial of Jesus

42It was Preparation Day (that is, the day before the Sabbath). So as evening approached, 43Joseph of Arimathea, a prominent member of the Council, who was himself waiting for the kingdom of God, went boldly to Pilate and asked for Jesus' body. 44Pilate was surprised to hear that he was already dead. Summoning the centurion, he asked him if Jesus had already died. 45When he learned from the centurion that it was so, he gave the body to Joseph. 46So Joseph bought some linen cloth, took down the body, wrapped it in the linen, and placed it in a tomb cut out of rock. Then he rolled a stone against the entrance of the tomb. 47Mary Magdalene and Mary the mother of Joses saw where he was laid.

ʸ39 Some manuscripts do not have *heard his cry and.*
ᶻ39 Or *a son*

Chapter 16

The Resurrection

AND when the Sabbath was over, Mary Magdalene, and Mary the *mother* of James, and Salome, bought spices, that they might come and anoint Him.

2And very early on the first day of the week, they *came to the tomb when the sun had risen.

3And they were saying to one another, "Who will roll away the stone for us from the entrance of the tomb?"

4And looking up, they *saw that the stone had been rolled away, although it was extremely large.

5And entering the tomb, they saw a young man sitting at the right, wearing a white robe; and they were amazed.

6And he *said to them, "Do not be amazed; you are looking for Jesus the Nazarene, who has been crucified. He is not here; behold, *here is* the place where they laid Him.

7"But go, tell His disciples and Peter, 'He is going before you into Galilee; there you will see Him, just as He said to you.' "

8And they went out and fled from the tomb, for trembling and astonishment had gripped them; and they said nothing to anyone, for they were afraid.

9["Now after He had risen early on the first day of the week, He first appeared to Mary Magdalene, from whom He had cast out seven demons.

10She went and reported to those who had been with Him, while they were mourning and weeping.

11And when they heard that He was alive, and had been seen by her, they refused to believe it.

12And after that, He appeared in a different form to two of them, while they were walking along on their way to the country.

---

16 Καὶ   διαγενομένου   τοῦ   σαββάτου   [ἡ]
And   passing   the   sabbath"   –
= when the sabbath was past

Μαρία   ἡ   Μαγδαληνὴ   καὶ   Μαρία   ἡ   [τοῦ]
Mary   the   Magdalene   and   Mary   the [mother] –

Ἰακώβου   καὶ   Σαλώμη   ἠγόρασαν   ἀρώματα
of James   and   Salome   bought   spices

ἵνα   ἐλθοῦσαι   ἀλείψωσιν   αὐτόν.   **2** καὶ   λίαν
that   coming   · they might anoint   him.   And   very

πρωΐ   [τῇ]   μιᾷ   τῶν   σαββάτων   ἔρχονται
early   on the   first day of the week†   they come

ἐπὶ   τὸ   μνῆμα,   ἀνατείλαντος   τοῦ   ἡλίου.
upon   the   tomb,   rising   the   sun."
= as the sun rose.

3 καὶ   ἔλεγον   πρὸς   ἑαυτάς·   τίς   ἀποκυλίσει
And   they said   to   themselves: Who   will roll away

ἡμῖν   τὸν   λίθον   ἐκ   τῆς   θύρας   τοῦ   μνημείου;
for us   the   stone   out of   the   door   of   the tomb ?

4 καὶ   ἀναβλέψασαι   θεωροῦσιν   ὅτι   ἀνακεκύλισται
And   looking up   they behold   that has been rolled back

ὁ   λίθος·   ἦν   γὰρ   μέγας   σφόδρα.   **5** καὶ
the   stone;   for it was   great   exceedingly.   And

εἰσελθοῦσαι   εἰς   τὸ   μνημεῖον   εἶδον   νεανίσκον
entering   into   the   tomb   they saw   a young man

καθήμενον   ἐν   τοῖς   δεξιοῖς   περιβεβλημένον
sitting   on   the   right   having been clothed

στολὴν   λευκήν,   καὶ   ἐξεθαμβήθησαν.   **6** ὁ   δὲ
robe   [in] a white,   and   they were greatly astonished.   But he

λέγει   αὐταῖς·   μὴ   ἐκθαμβεῖσθε·   Ἰησοῦν
says   to them: Be not greatly astonished;   Jesus

ζητεῖτε   τὸν   Ναζαρηνὸν   τὸν   ἐσταυρωμένον·
ye seek   the   Nazarene   –   having been crucified;

ἠγέρθη,   οὐκ   ἔστιν   ὧδε·   ἴδε   ὁ   τόπος
he was raised,   he is not   here; behold[,]   the   place

ὅπου   ἔθηκαν   αὐτόν.   **7** ἀλλὰ   ὑπάγετε   εἴπατε
where   they put   him.   But   go ye   tell

τοῖς   μαθηταῖς   αὐτοῦ   καὶ   τῷ   Πέτρῳ   ὅτι
the   disciples   of him   and   –   Peter   that

προάγει   ὑμᾶς   εἰς   τὴν   Γαλιλαίαν·   ἐκεῖ
he goes before you   to   –   Galilee;   there

αὐτὸν   ὄψεσθε,   καθὼς   εἶπεν   ὑμῖν.   **8** καὶ
him,   ye will see,   as   he told   you.   And

ἐξελθοῦσαι   ἔφυγον   ἀπὸ   τοῦ   μνημείου,   εἶχεν
going forth   they fled   from   the   tomb,   *had

γὰρ   αὐτὰς   τρόμος   καὶ   ἔκστασις·   καὶ
*for   *them   ²trembling   ³and   ⁴bewilderment;   and

οὐδενὶ   οὐδὲν   εἶπαν·   ἐφοβοῦντο   γάρ.
no one   no(any)thing   they told;   for they were afraid.

9 Ἀναστὰς   δὲ   πρωΐ   πρώτῃ   σαββάτου
And rising   early   on the first day of the week†

ἐφάνη   πρῶτον   Μαρίᾳ   τῇ   Μαγδαληνῇ,   παρ'
he appeared   first   to Mary   the   Magdalene,   from

ἧς   ἐκβεβλήκει   ἑπτὰ   δαιμόνια.   **10** ἐκείνη
whom he had expelled   seven   demons.   That [one]
= She

πορευθεῖσα   ἀπήγγειλεν   τοῖς   μετ'   αὐτοῦ
going   reported   to the [ones]   with   him
= those who had been with him

γενομένοις   πενθοῦσι   καὶ   κλαίουσιν·   **11** κἀκεῖνοι
having been   mourning   and   weeping;   and those

ἀκούσαντες   ὅτι   ζῇ   καὶ   ἐθεάθη   ὑπ'   αὐτῆς
hearing   that he lives and   was seen   by   her

ἠπίστησαν.   **12** Μετὰ   δὲ   ταῦτα   δυσὶν   ἐξ
disbelieved.   And after   these things to two   of

αὐτῶν   περιπατοῦσιν   ἐφανερώθη   ἐν   ἑτέρᾳ
them   walking   he was manifested   in a different

μορφῇ   πορευομένοις   εἰς   ἀγρόν·   **13** κἀκεῖνοι
form   going   into [the] country;   and those

Chapter 16

The Resurrection

WHEN the Sabbath was over, Mary Magdalene, Mary the mother of James, and Salome bought spices so that they might go to anoint Jesus' body. 2Very early on the first day of the week, just after sunrise, they were on their way to the tomb 3and they asked each other, "Who will roll the stone away from the entrance of the tomb?"

4But when they looked up, they saw that the stone, which was very large, had been rolled away. 5As they entered the tomb, they saw a young man dressed in a white robe sitting on the right side, and they were alarmed.

6"Don't be alarmed," he said. "You are looking for Jesus the Nazarene, who was crucified. He has risen! He is not here. See the place where they laid him. 7But go, tell his disciples and Peter, 'He is going ahead of you into Galilee. There you will see him, just as he told you.' "

8Trembling and bewildered, the women went out and fled from the tomb. They said nothing to anyone, because they were afraid.

[The most reliable early manuscripts and other ancient witnesses do not have Mark 16:9–20.]

9When Jesus rose early on the first day of the week, he appeared first to Mary Magdalene, out of whom he had driven seven demons. 10She went and told those who had been with him and who were mourning and weeping. 11When they heard that Jesus was alive and that she had seen him, they did not believe it. 12Afterward Jesus appeared in a different form to two of them while they were walking in the coun-

13And they went away and reported it to the others, but they did not believe them either.

The Disciples Commissioned

14And afterward He appeared to the eleven themselves as they were reclining *at the table;* and He reproached them for their unbelief and hardness of heart, because they had not believed those who had seen Him after He had risen.

15And He said to them, "Go into all the world and preach the gospel to all creation.

16"He who has believed and has been baptized shall be saved; but he who has disbelieved shall be condemned.

17"And these signs will accompany those who have believed: in My name they will cast out demons, they will speak with new tongues;

18they will pick up serpents, and if they drink any deadly *poison,* it shall not hurt them; they will lay hands on the sick, and they will recover."

19So then, when the Lord Jesus had spoken to them, He was received up into heaven, and sat down at the right hand of God.

20And they went out and preached everywhere, while the Lord worked with them, and confirmed the word by the signs that followed.][*v* *And they promptly reported all these instructions to Peter and his companions. And after that, Jesus Himself sent out through them from east to west the sacred and imperishable proclamation of eternal salvation.*]

ἀπελθόντες ἀπήγγειλαν τοῖς λοιποῖς· οὐδὲ
going   reported   to the rest;   neither
ἐκείνοις ἐπίστευσαν. 14 Ὕστερον [δὲ]
those   they believed.   And later
ἀνακειμένοις αὐτοῖς τοῖς ἔνδεκα ἐφανερώθη,
to the reclining them the eleven he was manifested,
= to the eleven as they reclined
καὶ ὠνείδισεν τὴν ἀπιστίαν αὐτῶν καὶ
and reproached the disbelief of them and
σκληροκαρδίαν ὅτι τοῖς θεασαμένοις αὐτὸν
hardness of heart because the [ones] beholding him
ἐγηγερμένον οὐκ ἐπίστευσαν. 15 καὶ εἶπεν
having been raised they did not believe.   And he said
αὐτοῖς· πορευθέντες εἰς τὸν κόσμον ἅπαντα
to them: Going   into ¹the ²world   ¹all
κηρύξατε τὸ εὐαγγέλιον πάσῃ τῇ κτίσει.
proclaim ye the gospel   to all the creation.
16 ὁ πιστεύσας καὶ βαπτισθεὶς σωθήσεται,
The [one] believing and being baptized will be saved,
ὁ δὲ ἀπιστήσας κατακριθήσεται. 17 σημεῖα
but the [one] disbelieving will be condemned.   ²signs
δὲ τοῖς πιστεύσασιν ταῦτα παρακολουθήσει·
¹And ⁵the [ones] ⁶believing ³these ⁴will follow:
ἐν τῷ ὀνόματί μου δαιμόνια ἐκβαλοῦσιν,
in the name of me demons   they will expel,
γλώσσαις λαλήσουσιν καιναῖς, 18 ὄφεις
²tongues ¹they will speak ¹with new,   serpents
ἀροῦσιν κἂν θανάσιμόν τι πίωσιν
they will take and if ²deadly ¹anything ¹they drink
οὐ μὴ αὐτοὺς βλάψῃ, ἐπὶ ἀρρώστους χεῖρας
by no means them it will hurt, on sick [ones] hands
ἐπιθήσουσιν καὶ καλῶς ἕξουσιν. 19 Ὁ μὲν
they will place on and well they will have. ¹The ⁴there-
= they will recover.
οὖν κύριος [Ἰησοῦς] μετὰ τὸ λαλῆσαι
fore ²Lord ³Jesus   after the to speak
= speaking
αὐτοῖς ἀνελήμφθη εἰς τὸν οὐρανὸν καὶ
to them was taken up into -   heaven   and
ἐκάθισεν ἐκ δεξιῶν τοῦ θεοῦ. 20 ἐκεῖνοι
sat   at [the] right [hand] - of God.   those
δὲ ἐξελθόντες ἐκήρυξαν πανταχοῦ, τοῦ
But going forth proclaimed everywhere, the
κυρίου συνεργοῦντος καὶ τὸν λόγον
Lord   working with   and the word
= while the Lord worked with [them] and confirmed the word
βεβαιοῦντος διὰ τῶν ἐπακολουθούντων
confirming* through the accompanying
σημείων.
signs.

try. 13These returned and reported it to the rest; but they did not believe them either.

14Later Jesus appeared to the Eleven as they were eating; he rebuked them for their lack of faith and their stubborn refusal to believe those who had seen him after he had risen.

15He said to them, "Go into all the world and preach the good news to all creation. 16Whoever believes and is baptized will be saved, but whoever does not believe will be condemned. 17And these signs will accompany those who believe: In my name they will drive out demons; they will speak in new tongues; 18they will pick up snakes with their hands; and when they drink deadly poison, it will not hurt them at all; they will place their hands on sick people, and they will get well."

19After the Lord Jesus had spoken to them, he was taken up into heaven and he sat at the right hand of God. 20Then the disciples went out and preached everywhere, and the Lord worked with them and confirmed his word by the signs that accompanied it.

v A few later mss. and versions contain this paragraph, usually after verse 8; a few have it at the end of chapter.

Chapter 1

Introduction

INASMUCH as many have undertaken to compile an account of the things accomplished among us,

2just as those who from the beginning were eyewitnesses and servants of the *a*word have handed them down to us,

3it seemed fitting for me as well, having investigated everything carefully from the beginning, to write *it* out for you in consecutive order, most excellent Theophilus;

4so that you might know the exact truth about the things you have been taught.

Birth of John the Baptist Foretold

5In the days of Herod, king of Judea, there was a certain priest named Zacharias, of the division of *b*Abijah; and he had a wife *c*from the daughters of Aaron, and her name was Elizabeth.

6And they were both righteous in the sight of God, walking blamelessly in all the commandments and requirements of the Lord.

7And they had no child, because Elizabeth was barren, and they were both advanced in years.

8Now it came about, while he was performing his priestly service before God in the *appointed* order of his division,

9according to the custom of the priestly office, he was chosen by lot to enter the temple of the Lord and burn incense.

10And the whole multitude of the people were in prayer outside at the hour of the incense offering.

11And an angel of the Lord appeared to him, standing to the right of the altar of incense.

12And Zacharias was troubled when he saw *him*, and fear gripped him.

13But the angel said to him, "Do not be afraid, Zacharias, for your petition has been heard, and your

---

1 Ἐπειδήπερ πολλοὶ ἐπεχείρησαν ἀνατάξασθαι
Since many took in hand to draw up

διήγησιν περὶ τῶν πεπληροφορημένων
a narrative concerning ¹the ²having been fullycarried out

ἐν ἡμῖν πραγμάτων, **2** καθὼς παρέδοσαν ἡμῖν
⁴among ³us, ²matters, as delivered to us

οἱ ἀπ' ἀρχῆς αὐτόπται καὶ ὑπηρέται
the [ones] from [the] beginning eyewitnesses and attendants

γενόμενοι τοῦ λόγου, **3** ἔδοξε κἀμοὶ
becoming of the Word, it seemed good to me also

παρηκολουθηκότι ἄνωθεν πᾶσιν ἀκριβῶς
having investigated from their source all things accurately

καθεξῆς σοι γράψαι, κράτιστε Θεόφιλε,
²in order ¹to thee ³to write, most excellent Theophilus,

4 ἵνα ἐπιγνῷς περὶ ὧν
that thou mightest know ⁴concerning ¹which

κατηχήθης λόγων τὴν ἀσφάλειαν.
⁵thou wast instructed ³of [the] things ¹the ²reliability.

5 Ἐγένετο ἐν ταῖς ἡμέραις
There was in the days

Ἡρῴδου βασιλέως τῆς Ἰουδαίας ἱερεύς
of Herod king – of Judæa ¹priest

τις ὀνόματι Ζαχαρίας ἐξ ἐφημερίας Ἀβιά,
¹a certain by name Zacharias of [the] course of Abia,

καὶ γυνὴ αὐτῷ ἐκ τῶν θυγατέρων Ἀαρών,
and wife to him⁰ of the daughters of Aaron,
=his wife

καὶ τὸ ὄνομα αὐτῆς Ἐλισάβετ. **6** ἦσαν δὲ
and the name of her Elisabeth. And they were

δίκαιοι ἀμφότεροι ἐναντίον τοῦ θεοῦ,
righteous both before – God,

πορευόμενοι ἐν πάσαις ταῖς ἐντολαῖς καὶ
going in all the commandments and

δικαιώμασιν τοῦ κυρίου ἄμεμπτοι. **7** καὶ
ordinances of the Lord blameless. And

οὐκ ἦν αὐτοῖς τέκνον, καθότι ἦν ἡ
there was not to them a child,⁰ because ²was –
=they had no child,

Ἐλισάβετ στεῖρα, καὶ ἀμφότεροι προβεβηκότες
¹Elisabeth barren, and both *having* advanced

ἐν ταῖς ἡμέραις αὐτῶν ἦσαν. **8** Ἐγένετο
in the days of them were. it came to pass

δὲ ἐν τῷ ἱερατεύειν αὐτὸν ἐν τῇ τάξει
Now in the to serve as priest him^be in the order
=while he served as priest

τῆς ἐφημερίας αὐτοῦ ἔναντι τοῦ θεοῦ,
of the course of him before – God,

9 κατὰ τὸ ἔθος τῆς ἱερατείας ἔλαχε τοῦ
according to the custom of the priesthood his lot was –

θυμιᾶσαι εἰσελθὼν εἰς τὸν ναὸν τοῦ κυρίου,
to burn incense^d entering into the shrine of the Lord,

10 καὶ πᾶν τὸ πλῆθος ἦν τοῦ λαοῦ
and all ¹the ²multitude ⁵was ³of the ⁴people

προσευχόμενον ἔξω τῇ ὥρᾳ τοῦ θυμιάματος.
praying outside at the hour – of incense.

11 ὤφθη δὲ αὐτῷ ἄγγελος κυρίου ἑστὼς
And there appeared to him an angel of [the] Lord standing

ἐκ δεξιῶν τοῦ θυσιαστηρίου τοῦ θυμιάματος.
on [the] right of the altar – of incense.

12 καὶ ἐταράχθη Ζαχαρίας ἰδών, καὶ φόβος
And was troubled Zacharias seeing, and fear

ἐπέπεσεν ἐπ' αὐτόν. **13** εἶπεν δὲ πρὸς
fell *on* upon him. But said to

αὐτὸν ὁ ἄγγελος· μὴ φοβοῦ, Ζαχαρία,
him the angel: Fear not, Zacharias,

διότι εἰσηκούσθη ἡ δέησίς σου, καὶ ἡ
because was heard the request of thee, and the

Chapter 1

Introduction

MANY have undertaken to draw up an account of the things that have been fulfilled *a* among us, 2just as they were handed down to us by those who from the first were eyewitnesses and servants of the word. 3Therefore, since I myself have carefully investigated everything from the beginning, it seemed good also to me to write an orderly account for you, most excellent Theophilus, 4so that you may know the certainty of the things you have been taught.

The Birth of John the Baptist Foretold

5In the time of Herod king of Judea there was a priest named Zechariah, who belonged to the priestly division of Abijah; his wife Elizabeth was also a descendant of Aaron. 6Both of them were upright in the sight of God, observing all the Lord's commandments and regulations blamelessly. 7But they had no children, because Elizabeth was barren; and they were both well along in years.

8Once when Zechariah's division was on duty and he was serving as priest before God, 9he was chosen by lot, according to the custom of the priesthood, to go into the temple of the Lord and burn incense. 10And when the time for the burning of incense came, all the assembled worshipers were praying outside.

11Then an angel of the Lord appeared to him, standing at the right side of the altar of incense. 12When Zechariah saw him, he was startled and was gripped with fear. 13But the angel said to him: "Do not be afraid, Zechariah; your prayer has been heard. Your wife Elizabeth

---

a I.e., gospel
b Gr., *Abia*
c I.e., of priestly descent

a 1 Or *been surely believed*

wife Elizabeth will bear you a son, and you will give him the name John.

14"And you will have joy and gladness, and many will rejoice at his birth.

15"For he will be great in the sight of the Lord, and he will drink no wine or liquor; and he will be filled with the Holy Spirit, while yet in his mother's womb.

16"And he will turn back many of the sons of Israel to the Lord their God.

17"And it is he who will go *as a forerunner* before Him in the spirit and power of Elijah, TO TURN THE HEARTS OF THE FATHERS BACK TO THE CHILDREN, and the disobedient to the attitude of the righteous; so as to make ready a people prepared for the Lord."

18And Zacharias said to the angel, "How shall I know this *for certain*? For I am an old man, and my wife is advanced in years."

19And the angel answered and said to him, "I am Gabriel, who stands in the presence of God; and I have been sent to speak to you, and to bring you this good news.

20"And behold, you shall be silent and unable to speak until the day when these things take place, because you did not believe my words, which shall be fulfilled in their proper time."

21And the people were waiting for Zacharias, and were wondering at his delay in the temple.

22But when he came out, he was unable to speak to them; and they realized that he had seen a vision in the temple; and he kept making signs to them, and remained mute.

γυνή σου Ἐλισάβετ γεννήσει υἱόν σοι,
wife of thee Elisabeth will bear a son to thee,

καὶ καλέσεις τὸ ὄνομα αὐτοῦ Ἰωάννην·
and thou shalt call the name of him John;

14 καὶ ἔσται χαρά σοι καὶ ἀγαλλίασις,ᶜ
and there shall be joy to thee and gladness,ᶜ
= thou shalt have joy and gladness,

καὶ πολλοὶ ἐπὶ τῇ γενέσει αὐτοῦ χαρή-
and many over the birth of him will

σονται. **15** ἔσται γὰρ μέγας ἐνώπιον
rejoice. For he will be great in the eyes of

κυρίου, καὶ οἶνον καὶ σίκερα οὐ μὴ
[the] Lord, and wine and strong drink by no means

πίῃ, καὶ πνεύματος ἁγίου πλησθήσεται
may he drink, and of(with) Spirit [the] Holy he will be filled

ἔτι ἐκ κοιλίας μητρὸς αὐτοῦ, **16** καὶ
even from [the] womb of [the] mother of him, and

πολλοὺς τῶν υἱῶν Ἰσραὴλ ἐπιστρέψει ἐπὶ κύριον
many of the sons of Israel he will turn to [the] Lord

τὸν θεὸν αὐτῶν· **17** καὶ αὐτὸς προελεύσεται
the God of them; and he will go before

ἐνώπιον αὐτοῦ ἐν πνεύματι καὶ δυνάμει
before him in [the] spirit and power

Ἠλίου, ἐπιστρέψαι καρδίας πατέρων ἐπὶ
of Elias, to turn [the] hearts of fathers to

τέκνα καὶ ἀπειθεῖς ἐν φρονήσει
children and disobedient [ones] to [the] understanding

δικαίων, ἑτοιμάσαι κυρίῳ λαὸν κατεσκευασ-
of [the] just, to prepare for [the] Lord a people having been

μένον. **18** καὶ εἶπεν Ζαχαρίας πρὸς τὸν ἄγγελον·
prepared. And said Zacharias to the angel:

κατὰ τί γνώσομαι τοῦτο; ἐγὼ γάρ εἰμι
By what shall I know this? for I am

πρεσβύτης καὶ ἡ γυνή μου προβεβηκυῖα
old and the wife of me having advanced

ἐν ταῖς ἡμέραις αὐτῆς. **19** καὶ ἀποκριθεὶς
in the days of her. And answering

ὁ ἄγγελος εἶπεν αὐτῷ· ἐγώ εἰμι Γαβριὴλ
the angel said to him: I am Gabriel

ὁ παρεστηκὼς ἐνώπιον τοῦ θεοῦ, καὶ
the [one] standing before - God, and

ἀπεστάλην λαλῆσαι πρὸς σὲ καὶ εὐαγ-
I was sent to speak to thee and to

γελίσασθαι σοι ταῦτα· **20** καὶ ἰδοὺ
announce to thee these things; and behold

ἔσῃ σιωπῶν καὶ μὴ δυνάμενος λαλῆσαι
thou shalt be being silent and not being able to speak

ἄχρι ἧς ἡμέρας γένηται ταῦτα, ἀνθ᾽ ὧν οὐκ
until which day happens these things, because not
= the day when these things happen,

ἐπίστευσας τοῖς λόγοις μου, οἵτινες πληρω-
thou believedst the words of me, which will be

θήσονται εἰς τὸν καιρὸν αὐτῶν. **21** καὶ ἦν
fulfilled in the time of them. And was

ὁ λαὸς προσδοκῶν τὸν Ζαχαρίαν, καὶ
the people expecting - Zacharias, and

ἐθαύμαζον ἐν τῷ χρονίζειν ἐν τῷ ναῷ
they marvelled in(at) the to delay in the shrine
= when he delayed in the shrine.

αὐτόν. **22** ἐξελθὼν δὲ οὐκ ἐδύνατο λαλῆσαι
him.ᵇᵉ And going out he was not able to speak

αὐτοῖς καὶ ἐπέγνωσαν ὅτι ὀπτασίαν ἑώρακεν
to them, and they knew that a vision he has(had) seen

ἐν τῷ ναῷ· καὶ αὐτὸς ἦν διανεύων
in the shrine; and he was beckoning

αὐτοῖς, καὶ διέμενεν κωφός. **23** καὶ
to them, and remained dumb. And

---

will bear you a son, and you are to give him the name John. 14He will be a joy and delight to you, and many will rejoice because of his birth, 15for he will be great in the sight of the Lord. He is never to take wine or other fermented drink, and he will be filled with the Holy Spirit even from birth.ᵇ 16Many of the people of Israel will he bring back to the Lord their God. 17And he will go on before the Lord, in the spirit and power of Elijah, to turn the hearts of the fathers to their children and the disobedient to the wisdom of the righteous—to make ready a people prepared for the Lord."

18Zechariah asked the angel, "How can I be sure of this? I am an old man and my wife is well along in years."

19The angel answered, "I am Gabriel. I stand in the presence of God, and I have been sent to speak to you and to tell you this good news. 20And now you will be silent and not able to speak until the day this happens, because you did not believe my words, which will come true at their proper time."

21Meanwhile, the people were waiting for Zechariah and wondering why he stayed so long in the temple. 22When he came out, he could not speak to them. They realized he had seen a vision in the temple, for he kept making signs to them but remained unable to speak.

ᵇ15 Or *from his mother's womb*

23And it came about, when the days of his priestly service were ended, that he went back home.
24And after these days Elizabeth his wife became pregnant; and she kept herself in seclusion for five months, saying,
25"This is the way the Lord has dealt with me in the days when He looked *with favor* upon *me,* to take away my disgrace among men."

Jesus' Birth Foretold

26Now in the sixth month the angel Gabriel was sent from God to a city in Galilee, called Nazareth,
27to a virgin engaged to a man whose name was Joseph, of the descendants of David; and the virgin's name was Mary.
28And coming in, he said to her, "Hail, favored one! The Lord *is* with you." *d*
29But she was greatly troubled at *this* statement, and kept pondering what kind of salutation this might be.
30And the angel said to her, "Do not be afraid, Mary; for you have found favor with God.
31"And behold, you will conceive in your womb, and bear a son, and you shall name Him Jesus.
32"He will be great, and will be called the Son of the Most High; and the Lord God will give Him the throne of His father David;
33and He will reign over the house of Jacob forever; and His kingdom will have no end."
34And Mary said to the angel, "How can this be, since I am a virgin?"
35And the angel answered and said to her, "The Holy Spirit will come upon you, and the power of the Most High will overshadow you; and for that reason the holy

ἐγένετο   ὡς   ἐπλήσθησαν   αἱ   ἡμέραι   τῆς
it came to pass when were fulfilled the days of the
λειτουργίας   αὐτοῦ,   ἀπῆλθεν   εἰς   τὸν   οἶκον
service   of him,   he went away to the   house
αὐτοῦ.   24 Μετὰ   δὲ   ταύτας   τὰς   ἡμέρας
of him.   And after   these   -   days
συνέλαβεν   'Ελισάβετ   ἡ   γυνὴ   αὐτοῦ,   καὶ
conceived   Elisabeth   the   wife of him,   and
περιέκρυβεν   ἑαυτὴν   μῆνας   πέντε,   λέγουσα
hid   herself   months   five,   saying[.]
25 ὅτι   οὕτως   μοι   πεποίηκεν   κύριος   ἐν
-    Thus   to me   has done   [the] Lord   in
ἡμέραις   αἷς   ἐπεῖδεν   ἀφελεῖν   ὄνειδός
days   in which he looked upon to take away reproach
μου   ἐν   ἀνθρώποις.
of me among   men.
26 'Εν   δὲ   τῷ   μηνὶ   τῷ   ἕκτῳ   ἀπεστάλη
Now in   the   month   -   sixth   was sent
ὁ   ἄγγελος   Γαβριὴλ   ἀπὸ   τοῦ   θεοῦ   εἰς
the   angel   Gabriel   from -   God   to
πόλιν   τῆς   Γαλιλαίας   ᾗ   ὄνομα   Ναζαρέθ,
a city   -   of Galilee to which name*   Nazareth,
                          = the name of which [was]
27 πρὸς   παρθένον   ἐμνηστευμένην   ἀνδρὶ   ᾧ   ὄνομα
to   a virgin   *having been*   to a man to whom name*
            betrothed
'Ιωσήφ,   ἐξ   οἴκου   Δαυίδ,   καὶ   τὸ   ὄνομα
Joseph, of [the] house of David, and the name
τῆς   παρθένου   Μαριάμ.   28 καὶ   εἰσελθὼν
of the   virgin   [was] Mary.   And   entering
πρὸς   αὐτὴν   εἶπεν·   χαῖρε,   κεχαριτωμένη,   ὁ
to   her   he said: Hail, *having been* favoured [one], the
κύριος   μετὰ   σοῦ.   29 ἡ   δὲ   ἐπὶ   τῷ   λόγῳ
Lord [is]   with thee.   And she at   the   saying
διεταράχθη,   καὶ   διελογίζετο   ποταπὸς   εἴη
was greatly disturbed, and considered of what sort *might be
ὁ   ἀσπασμὸς   οὗτος.   30 καὶ   εἶπεν   ὁ   ἄγγελος
-    *greeting   ¹this.   And   said   the   angel
αὐτῇ·   μὴ   φοβοῦ,   Μαριάμ·   εὗρες   γὰρ
to her :   Fear not,   Mary :   for thou didst find
χάριν παρὰ τῷ θεῷ.   31 καὶ   ἰδοὺ   συλλήμψῃ
favour with - God.   And behold thou wilt conceive
ἐν   γαστρὶ   καὶ   τέξῃ   υἱόν,   καὶ   καλέσεις   τὸ
in   womb   and bear a son, and thou shalt call the
ὄνομα   αὐτοῦ   'Ιησοῦν.   32 οὗτος   ἔσται   μέγας
name   of him   Jesus.   This   will be   great
καὶ   υἱὸς   ὑψίστου   κληθήσεται,   καὶ   δώσει
and Son   of [the] Most High will be called, and will give
αὐτῷ   κύριος   ὁ   θεὸς   τὸν   θρόνον   Δαυὶδ
him   [the] Lord - God the throne of David
τοῦ   πατρὸς   αὐτοῦ,   33 καὶ   βασιλεύσει   ἐπὶ
the   father   of him,   and he will reign over
τὸν   οἶκον   'Ιακὼβ   εἰς   τοὺς   αἰῶνας,   καὶ
the   house of Jacob unto the ages,   and
                                    =for ever,
τῆς   βασιλείας   αὐτοῦ   οὐκ   ἔσται   τέλος.
of the   kingdom   of him there will not be an end.
34 εἶπεν   δὲ   Μαριὰμ   πρὸς   τὸν   ἄγγελον·
And said   Mary   to   the   angel:
πῶς   ἔσται   τοῦτο,   ἐπεὶ   ἄνδρα   οὐ   γινώσκω;
How will be   this,   since a man   I know not?
35 καὶ   ἀποκριθεὶς   ὁ   ἄγγελος   εἶπεν   αὐτῇ·
And answering   the   angel   said   to her :
πνεῦμα   ἅγιον   ἐπελεύσεται   ἐπὶ   σέ,   καὶ
¹[The] ³Spirit ²Holy   will come *upon* upon thee, and
δύναμις   ὑψίστου   ἐπισκιάσει   σοι·   διὸ
[the] power of [the] Most High will overshadow thee; wherefore

23When his time of service was completed, he returned home. 24After this his wife Elizabeth became pregnant and for five months remained in seclusion. 25"The Lord has done this for me," she said. "In these days he has shown his favor and taken away my disgrace among people."

The Birth of Jesus Foretold

26In the sixth month, God sent the angel Gabriel to Nazareth, a town in Galilee, 27to a virgin pledged to be married to a man named Joseph, a descendant of David. The virgin's name was Mary. 28The angel went to her and said, "Greetings, you who are highly favored! The Lord is with you."
29Mary was greatly troubled at his words and wondered what kind of greeting this might be. 30But the angel said to her, "Do not be afraid, Mary, you have found favor with God. 31You will be with child and give birth to a son, and you are to give him the name Jesus. 32He will be great and will be called the Son of the Most High. The Lord God will give him the throne of his father David, 33and he will reign over the house of Jacob forever; his kingdom will never end."
34"How will this be," Mary asked the angel, "since I am a virgin?"
35The angel answered, "The Holy Spirit will come upon you, and the power of the Most High will overshadow you. So the holy

d Later mss. add: *you are blessed among women*

offspring shall be called the Son of God.

36"And behold, even your relative Elizabeth has also conceived a son in her old age; and she who was called barren is now in her sixth month.

37"For nothing will be impossible with God."

38And Mary said, "Behold, the ᶜbondslave of the Lord; be it done to me according to your word." And the angel departed from her.

Mary Visits Elizabeth

39Now at this time Mary arose and went with haste to the hill country, to a city of Judah,

40and entered the house of Zacharias and greeted Elizabeth.

41And it came about that when Elizabeth heard Mary's greeting, the baby leaped in her womb; and Elizabeth was filled with the Holy Spirit.

42And she cried out with a loud voice, and said, "Blessed among women *are* you, and blessed *is* the fruit of your womb!

43"And how has it *happened* to me, that the mother of my Lord should come to me?

44"For behold, when the sound of your greeting reached my ears, the baby leaped in my womb for joy.

45"And blessed *is* she who believed that there would be a fulfillment of what had been spoken to her by the Lord."

The Magnificat

46And Mary said:
"My soul exalts the Lord,

47"And my spirit has rejoiced in God my Savior.

48"For He has had regard for the humble state of His bondslave; For behold, from this time on all generations will count me blessed.

49"For the Mighty One has done great things for me;

καὶ τὸ γεννώμενον ἅγιον κληθήσεται υἱὸς θεοῦ.
also the thing being born   holy   will be called[,]   Son of God.

36 καὶ ἰδοὺ Ἐλισάβετ ἡ συγγενίς σου καὶ
And behold   Elisabeth   the   relative   of thee   also

αὐτὴ συνείληφεν υἱὸν ἐν γήρει αὐτῆς, καὶ
she   conceived   a son   in old age   of her,   and

οὗτος μὴν ἕκτος ἐστὶν αὐτῇ τῇ καλουμένῃ
this   month   sixth   is   with her the [one] being called

στείρα· 37 ὅτι οὐκ ἀδυνατήσει παρὰ τοῦ
barren;   because   will not be impossible   with

θεοῦ πᾶν ῥῆμα. 38 εἶπεν δὲ Μαριάμ· ἰδοὺ ἡ
God   every   word.   And said   Mary: Behold[,] the

δούλη κυρίου· γένοιτό μοι κατὰ
handmaid of [the]Lord;   may it be   to me according to

τὸ ῥῆμά σου. καὶ ἀπῆλθεν ἀπ᾽ αὐτῆς
the   word   of thee.   And   went away   from   her

ὁ ἄγγελος. 39 Ἀναστᾶσα δὲ Μαριὰμ ἐν
the   angel.   And rising up   Mary   in

ταῖς ἡμέραις ταύταις ἐπορεύθη εἰς τὴν
-   days   these   she went   to   the

ὀρεινὴν μετὰ σπουδῆς εἰς πόλιν Ἰούδα,
mountain country with   haste   to   a city   of Juda,

40 καὶ εἰσῆλθεν εἰς τὸν οἶκον Ζαχαρίου
and   entered   into   the   house   of Zacharias

καὶ ἠσπάσατο τὴν Ἐλισάβετ. 41 καὶ
and   greeted   the   -   Elisabeth.   And

ἐγένετο ὡς ἤκουσεν τὸν ἀσπασμὸν τῆς
it came to pass when ²heard   ³the   ⁴greeting   -

Μαρίας ἡ Ἐλισάβετ, ἐσκίρτησεν τὸ βρέφος
⁵of Mary   -   ¹Elisabeth,   leaped   the   babe

ἐν τῇ κοιλίᾳ αὐτῆς, καὶ ἐπλήσθη πνεύματος
in   the   womb   of her,   and ²was filled ³of(with) ⁵Spirit

ἁγίου ἡ Ἐλισάβετ, 42 καὶ ἀνεφώνησεν
⁴[the] Holy   -   ¹Elisabeth,   and   she called out

κραυγῇ μεγάλῃ καὶ εἶπεν· εὐλογημένη
cry   with a great   and   said :   Blessed [art]

σὺ ἐν γυναιξίν, καὶ εὐλογημένος ὁ καρπὸς
thou among women,   and   blessed [is]   the   fruit

τῆς κοιλίας σου. 43 καὶ πόθεν μοι τοῦτο
of the   womb   of thee.   And   whence   to me   this

ἵνα ἔλθῃ ἡ μήτηρ τοῦ κυρίου μου πρὸς
that comes   the   mother   of the   Lord   of me   to

ἐμέ; 44 ἰδοὺ γὰρ ὡς ἐγένετο ἡ φωνὴ τοῦ
me ?   For behold   when   came   the sound   of the

ἀσπασμοῦ σου εἰς τὰ ὦτά μου, ἐσκίρτησεν
greeting   of thee   in   the   ears   of me,   leaped

ἐν ἀγαλλιάσει τὸ βρέφος ἐν τῇ κοιλίᾳ
in   gladness   the   babe   in   the   womb

μου. 45 καὶ μακαρία ἡ πιστεύσασα ὅτι
of me.   And   blessed the [one]   believing   because

ἔσται τελείωσις τοῖς λελαλημένοις αὐτῇ
there shall be a completion to the things *having been*   to her
                                    spoken

παρὰ κυρίου. 46 Καὶ εἶπεν Μαριάμ·
from   [the] Lord.   And   said   Mary :

Μεγαλύνει ἡ ψυχή μου τὸν κύριον, 47 καὶ
Magnifies   the   soul   of me   the   Lord,   and

ἠγαλλίασεν τὸ πνεῦμά μου ἐπὶ τῷ θεῷ
exulted   the   spirit   of me   in   -   God

τῷ σωτῆρί μου· 48 ὅτι ἐπέβλεψεν ἐπὶ τὴν
the   saviour   of me;   because   he looked *on*   upon   the

ταπείνωσιν τῆς δούλης αὐτοῦ. ἰδοὺ γὰρ
humiliation   of the   handmaid   of him.   For behold

ἀπὸ τοῦ νῦν μακαριοῦσίν με πᾶσαι αἱ
from   -   now   ⁴will ⁵deem ⁷blessed ⁶me   ²all   ³the

γενεαί· 49 ὅτι ἐποίησέν μοι μεγάλα ὁ
³generations;   because   did   to me   great things   the

---

one to be born will be calledᶜ the Son of God.

36Even Elizabeth your relative is going to have a child in her old age, and she who was said to be barren is in her sixth month. 37For nothing is impossible with God."

38"I am the Lord's servant," Mary answered. "May it be to me as you have said." Then the angel left her.

Mary Visits Elizabeth

39At that time Mary got ready and hurried to a town in the hill country of Judea, 40where she entered Zechariah's home and greeted Elizabeth. 41When Elizabeth heard Mary's greeting, the baby leaped in her womb, and Elizabeth was filled with the Holy Spirit. 42In a loud voice she exclaimed: "Blessed are you among women, and blessed is the child you will bear! 43But why am I so favored, that the mother of my Lord should come to me? 44As soon as the sound of your greeting reached my ears, the baby in my womb leaped for joy. 45Blessed is she who has believed that what the Lord has said to her will be accomplished!"

Mary's Song

46And Mary said:
"My soul glorifies the Lord
47 and my spirit rejoices in God my Savior,
48for he has been mindful of the humble state of his servant.
From now on all generations will call me blessed,
49 for the Mighty One has done great things for me—

ᶜ I.e., female slave

ᶜ35 Or *So the child to be born will be called holy.*

And holy is His name.
50 "AND HIS MERCY IS UPON GENERATION AFTER GENERATION TOWARD THOSE WHO FEAR HIM.
51 "He has done mighty deeds with His arm; He has scattered *those who were* proud in the thoughts of their heart.
52 "He has brought down rulers from *their* thrones, And has exalted those who were humble.
53 "HE HAS FILLED THE HUNGRY WITH GOOD THINGS; And sent away the rich empty-handed.
54 "He has given help to Israel His servant, In remembrance of His mercy,
55 As He spoke to our fathers, To Abraham and his offspring forever."
56 And Mary stayed with her about three months, and *then* returned to her home.

John Is Born

57 Now the time had come for Elizabeth to give birth, and she brought forth a son.
58 And her neighbors and her relatives heard that the Lord had displayed His great mercy toward her; and they were rejoicing with her.
59 And it came about that on the eighth day they came to circumcise the child, and they were going to call him Zacharias, after his father.
60 And his mother answered and said, "No indeed; but he shall be called John."
61 And they said to her, "There is no one among your relatives who is called by that name."
62 And they made signs to his father, as to what he wanted him called.
63 And he asked for a tablet, and wrote as follows, "His name is John." And they were all astonished.
64 And at once his mouth was opened and his tongue

δυνατός. καὶ ἄγιον τὸ ὄνομα αὐτοῦ,
Mighty [one]. And holy the name of him,

50 καὶ τὸ ἔλεος αὐτοῦ εἰς γενεὰς καὶ
and the mercy of him to generations and

γενεὰς τοῖς φοβουμένοις αὐτόν. 51 Ἐποίησεν
generations to the [ones] fearing him. He did

κράτος ἐν βραχίονι αὐτοῦ, διεσκόρπισεν
might with [the] arm of him, he scattered

ὑπερηφάνους διανοίᾳ καρδίας αὐτῶν·
haughty [ones] in [the] understanding of [the] heart of them;

52 καθεῖλεν δυνάστας ἀπὸ θρόνων καὶ ὕψω-
he pulled down potentates from thrones and exalt-

σεν ταπεινούς, 53 πεινῶντας ἐνέπλησεν
ed humble [ones], hungering [ones] he filled

ἀγαθῶν καὶ πλουτοῦντας ἐξαπέστειλεν
of(with) good things and rich [ones] he sent away

κενούς. 54 ἀντελάβετο Ἰσραὴλ παιδὸς αὐτοῦ,
empty. He succoured Israel servant of him,

μνησθῆναι ἐλέους, 55 καθὼς ἐλάλησεν
to remember mercy, as he spoke

πρὸς τοὺς πατέρας ἡμῶν, τῷ Ἀβραὰμ
to the fathers of us, – to Abraham

καὶ τῷ σπέρματι αὐτοῦ εἰς τὸν αἰῶνα.
and to the seed of him to the age. =for ever.

56 Ἔμεινεν δὲ Μαριὰμ σὺν αὐτῇ ὡς
And remained Mary with her about

μῆνας τρεῖς, καὶ ὑπέστρεψεν εἰς τὸν
months three, and returned to the

οἶκον αὐτῆς.
house of her.

57 Τῇ δὲ Ἐλισάβετ ἐπλήσθη ὁ χρόνος
– Now ᵃto Elisabeth ᵃwas fulfilled ¹the ¹time

τοῦ τεκεῖν αὐτήν,ᵇᵈ καὶ ἐγέννησεν υἱόν.
– to bear her,ᵇᵈ and she brought forth a son.
=that she should bear,

58 καὶ ἤκουσαν οἱ περίοικοι καὶ οἱ
And heard the neighbours and the

συγγενεῖς αὐτῆς ὅτι ἐμεγάλυνεν κύριος τὸ
relatives of her that magnified [the] Lord the

ἔλεος αὐτοῦ μετ᾽ αὐτῆς, καὶ συνέχαιρον
mercy of him with her, and they rejoiced with

αὐτῇ. 59 Καὶ ἐγένετο ἐν τῇ ἡμέρᾳ τῇ
her. And it came to pass on the day –

ὀγδόῃ ἦλθον περιτεμεῖν τὸ παιδίον, καὶ
eighth they came to circumcise the child, and

ἐκάλουν αὐτὸ ἐπὶ τῷ ὀνόματι τοῦ πατρὸς
were calling it(him) by the name of the father

αὐτοῦ Ζαχαρίαν. 60 καὶ ἀποκριθεῖσα ἡ
of him Zacharias. And answering the

μήτηρ αὐτοῦ εἶπεν· οὐχί, ἀλλὰ κληθήσεται
mother of him said: No, but he shall be called

Ἰωάννης. 61 καὶ εἶπαν πρὸς αὐτὴν ὅτι
John. And they said to her[.] –

οὐδεὶς ἐστιν ἐκ τῆς συγγενείας σου ὃς
No one there is of the kindred of thee who

καλεῖται τῷ ὀνόματι τούτῳ. 62 ἐνένευον
is called – name by this. they nodded

δὲ τῷ πατρὶ αὐτοῦ τὸ τί ἂν θέλοι
And to the father of him – what he might wish

καλεῖσθαι αὐτό. 63 καὶ αἰτήσας πινακίδιον
ᵃto be called ¹him. And asking for a tablet

ἔγραψεν λέγων· Ἰωάννης ἐστιν ὄνομα
he wrote saying : John is name

αὐτοῦ. καὶ ἐθαύμασαν πάντες. 64 ἀνεῴχθη δὲ
of him. And they marvelled all. And was opened

τὸ στόμα αὐτοῦ παραχρῆμα καὶ ἡ
the mouth of him instantly and the

holy is his name.
50 His mercy extends to those who fear him, from generation to generation.
51 He has performed mighty deeds with his arm;
he has scattered those who are proud in their inmost thoughts.
52 He has brought down rulers from their thrones but has lifted up the humble.
53 He has filled the hungry with good things but has sent the rich away empty.
54 He has helped his servant Israel, remembering to be merciful
55 to Abraham and his descendants forever, even as he said to our fathers."
56 Mary stayed with Elizabeth for about three months and then returned home.

The Birth of John the Baptist

57 When it was time for Elizabeth to have her baby, she gave birth to a son.
58 Her neighbors and relatives heard that the Lord had shown her great mercy, and they shared her joy.
59 On the eighth day they came to circumcise the child, 'and they were going to name him after his father Zechariah, 60 but his mother spoke up and said, "No! He is to be called John."
61 They said to her, "There is no one among your relatives who has that name."
62 Then they made signs to his father, to find out what he would like to name the child. 63 He asked for a writing tablet, and to everyone's astonishment he wrote, "His name is John." 64 Immediately his mouth was opened and his

loosed, and he *began* to speak in praise of God.
65And fear came on all those living around them; and all these matters were being talked about in all the hill country of Judea.
66And all who heard them kept them in mind, saying, "What then will this child *turn out to* be?" For the hand of the Lord was certainly with him.

Zacharias' Prophecy

67And his father Zacharias was filled with the Holy Spirit, and prophesied, saying:
68"Blessed *be* the Lord God of Israel,
    For He has visited us and accomplished redemption for His people,
69 And has raised up a horn of salvation for us
    In the house of David His servant—
70 As He spoke by the mouth of His holy prophets from of old—
71 Salvation FROM OUR ENEMIES,
    And FROM THE HAND OF ALL WHO HATE US;
72 To show mercy toward our fathers,
    And to remember His holy covenant,
73 The oath which He swore to Abraham our father,
74 To grant us that we, being delivered from the hand of our enemies,
    Might serve Him without fear,
75 In holiness and righteousness before Him all our days.
76"And you, child, will be called the prophet of the Most High;
    For you will go on BEFORE THE LORD TO PREPARE HIS WAYS;
77 To give to His people *the* knowledge of salvation
    By the forgiveness of their sins,
78 Because of the tender mercy of our God,
    With which the Sunrise from on high shall visit us,
79 TO SHINE UPON THOSE WHO SIT IN DARKNESS AND THE SHADOW OF DEATH,

---

γλῶσσα αὐτοῦ, καὶ ἐλάλει εὐλογῶν τὸν
tongue of him, and he spoke blessing   –
θεόν. 65 Καὶ ἐγένετο ἐπὶ πάντας φόβος
God.   And ²came ³on ⁴all ¹fear
τοὺς περιοικοῦντας αὐτούς, καὶ ἐν ὅλῃ τῇ
the [ones] dwelling round them, and in all the
ὀρεινῇ τῆς Ἰουδαίας διελαλεῖτο πάντα
mountain country – of Judæa ⁴were talked over ¹all
τὰ ῥήματα ταῦτα, 66 καὶ ἔθεντο πάντες
– ²facts ³these, and ⁴put ¹all
οἱ ἀκούσαντες ἐν τῇ καρδίᾳ αὐτῶν,
²the [ones] ³hearing in the heart of them,
λέγοντες· τί ἄρα τὸ παιδίον τοῦτο ἔσται;
saying : What then – child this will be ?
καὶ γὰρ χεὶρ κυρίου ἦν μετ' αὐτοῦ.
for indeed [the] hand of [the] Lord was with him.
67 Καὶ Ζαχαρίας ὁ πατὴρ αὐτοῦ ἐπλήσθη
And Zacharias the father of him was filled
πνεύματος ἁγίου καὶ ἐπροφήτευσεν λέγων·
of(with) Spirit ¹Holy and prophesied saying :
68 Εὐλογητὸς κύριος ὁ θεὸς τοῦ Ἰσραήλ,
Blessed [be] [the] Lord the God – of Israel,
ὅτι ἐπεσκέψατο καὶ ἐποίησεν λύτρωσιν τῷ
because he visited and wrought redemption for the
λαῷ αὐτοῦ, 69 καὶ ἤγειρεν κέρας σωτηρίας
people of him, and raised a horn of salvation
ἡμῖν ἐν οἴκῳ Δαυίδ παιδὸς αὐτοῦ, 70 καθὼς
for us in [the] house of David servant of him, as
ἐλάλησεν διὰ στόματος τῶν ἁγίων ἀπ'
he spoke through [the] mouth of the ¹holy ⁴from
αἰῶνος προφητῶν αὐτοῦ, 71 σωτηρίαν ἐξ
²[the] age ¹prophets ³of him, salvation out of
ἐχθρῶν ἡμῶν καὶ ἐκ χειρὸς πάντων τῶν
[the] enemies of us and out of [the] hand of all the [ones]
μισούντων ἡμᾶς, 72 ποιῆσαι ἔλεος μετὰ
hating us, to perform mercy with
τῶν πατέρων ἡμῶν καὶ μνησθῆναι διαθήκης
the fathers of us and to remember [the] covenant
ἁγίας αὐτοῦ, 73 ὅρκον ὃν ὤμοσεν πρὸς Ἀβραὰμ
holy of him, [the] oath which he swore to Abraham
τὸν πατέρα ἡμῶν, 74 τοῦ δοῦναι ἡμῖν
the father of us, – to give[d] us
ἀφόβως ἐκ χειρὸς ἐχθρῶν ῥυσθέντας
⁵fearlessly ²out of ³[the] hand ⁴of [our] enemies ¹having been delivered
λατρεύειν αὐτῷ 75 ἐν ὁσιότητι καὶ δικαιοσύνῃ
⁶to serve him in holiness and righteousness
ἐνώπιον αὐτοῦ πάσαις ταῖς ἡμέραις ἡμῶν.
before him all the days• of us.
76 Καὶ σὺ δέ, παιδίον, προφήτης ὑψίστου
And thou also, child, a prophet of [the] Most High
κληθήσῃ· προπορεύσῃ γὰρ ἐνώπιον κυρίου
wilt be called; for thou wilt go *before* before [the] Lord
ἑτοιμάσαι ὁδοὺς αὐτοῦ, 77 τοῦ δοῦναι
to prepare [the] ways of him, – to give[d]
γνῶσιν σωτηρίας τῷ λαῷ αὐτοῦ ἐν
a knowledge of salvation to the people of him by
ἀφέσει ἁμαρτιῶν αὐτῶν, 78 διὰ σπλάγχνα·
forgiveness of sins of them, because of [the] bowels
ἐλέους θεοῦ ἡμῶν, ἐν οἷς ἐπισκέψεται
of mercy of God of us, whereby will visit
ἡμᾶς ἀνατολὴ ἐξ ὕψους, 79 ἐπιφᾶναι τοῖς
us a [sun]rising from [the] height, to appear ¹to the [ones]
ἐν σκότει καὶ σκιᾷ θανάτου καθημένοις,
²in ⁴darkness ³and ⁵in a shadow ⁷of death ⁶sitting,

---

tongue was loosed, and he began to speak, praising God. 65The neighbors were all filled with awe, and throughout the hill country of Judea people were talking about all these things. 66Everyone who heard this wondered about it, asking, "What then is this child going to be?" For the Lord's hand was with him.

Zechariah's Song

67His father Zechariah was filled with the Holy Spirit and prophesied:
68"Praise be to the Lord, the God of Israel, because he has come and has redeemed his people.
69He has raised up a horn[d] of salvation for us in the house of his servant David
70(as he said through his holy prophets of long ago),
71salvation from our enemies and from the hand of all who hate us—
72to show mercy to our fathers and to remember his holy covenant,
73 the oath he swore to our father Abraham:
74to rescue us from the hand of our enemies, and to enable us to serve him without fear
75 in holiness and righteousness before him all our days.
76And you, my child, will be called a prophet of the Most High; for you will go on before the Lord to prepare the way for him,
77to give his people the knowledge of salvation through the forgiveness of their sins,
78because of the tender mercy of our God, by which the rising sun will come to us from heaven
79to shine on those living in darkness and in the shadow of death,

---

d69 *Horn* here symbolizes strength.

To guide our feet into the way of peace.''
80And the child continued to grow, and to become strong in spirit, and he lived in the deserts until the day of his public appearance to Israel.

τοῦ   κατευθῦναι   τοὺς   πόδας   ἡμῶν   εἰς   ὁδὸν
-     to guided   the   feet   of us   into a way
εἰρήνης.
of peace.
80 Τὸ   δὲ   παιδίον   ηὔξανεν   καὶ   ἐκραταιοῦτο
And the   child   grew   and   became strong
πνεύματι,   καὶ   ἦν   ἐν   ταῖς   ἐρήμοις   ἕως
in spirit,   and   was iᵤ   the   deserts   until
ἡμέρας   ἀναδείξεως   αὐτοῦ   πρὸς   τὸν   Ἰσραήλ.
[the] days of showing   of him   to   -   Israel.

to guide our feet into the path of peace.''
80And the child grew and became strong in spirit; and he lived in the desert until he appeared publicly to Israel.

Chapter 2

Jesus' Birth in Bethlehem

NOW it came about in those days that a decree went out from Caesar Augustus, that a census be taken of all ᶠthe inhabited earth.
2This was the first census taken while ᵍQuirinius was governor of Syria.
3And all were proceeding to register for the census, everyone to his own city.
4And Joseph also went up from Galilee, from the city of Nazareth, to Judea, to the city of David, which is called Bethlehem, because he was of the house and family of David,
5in order to register, along with Mary, who was engaged to him, and was with child.
6And it came about that while they were there, the days were completed for her to give birth.
7And she gave birth to her first-born son; and she wrapped Him in cloths, and laid Him in a manger, because there was no room for them in the inn.
8And in the same region there were some shepherds staying out in the fields, and keeping watch over their flock by night.
9And an angel of the Lord suddenly stood before them, and the glory of the Lord shone around them; and they were terribly frightened.
10And the angel said to them, ''Do not be afraid; for behold, I bring you

2 Ἐγένετο   δὲ   ἐν   ταῖς   ἡμέραις   ἐκείναις
Now it came to pass in   -   days   those
ἐξῆλθεν   δόγμα   παρὰ   Καίσαρος   Αὐγούστου
went out   a decree from   Cæsar   Augustus
ἀπογράφεσθαι   πᾶσαν   τὴν   οἰκουμένην.   2 αὕτη
to be enrolled   all   the   inhabited earth.   This
ἀπογραφὴ   πρώτη   ἐγένετο   ἡγεμονεύοντος   τῆς
ᵃenrolment   ¹first   was   governing   -
                                              = when Cyrenius governed Syria.
Συρίας   Κυρηνίου.   3 καὶ   ἐπορεύοντο   πάντες
Syria   Cyrenius.ᵃ   And   went   all
ἀπογράφεσθαι,   ἕκαστος   εἰς   τὴν   ἑαυτοῦ
to be enrolled,   each man   to   the   of himself
πόλιν.   4 Ἀνέβη   δὲ   καὶ   Ἰωσὴφ   ἀπὸ   τῆς
city.   So went up   also   Joseph   from   -
Γαλιλαίας   ἐκ   πόλεως   Ναζαρὲθ   εἰς   τὴν
Galilee   out of a city   Nazareth   to   -
Ἰουδαίαν   εἰς   πόλιν   Δαυὶδ   ἥτις   καλεῖται   Βηθλέεμ,
Judæa   to   a city of David which is called   Bethlehem,
διὰ   τὸ   εἶναι   αὐτὸν   ἐξ   οἴκου   καὶ
because of the to be   himᵇ   out of [the] house   and
= because he was
πατριᾶς   Δαυίδ,   5 ἀπογράψασθαι   σὺν   Μαριὰμ
family   of David,   to be enrolled   with   Mary
τῇ   ἐμνηστευμένῃ   αὐτῷ,   οὔσῃ   ἐγκύῳ.
the[one] having been betrothed to him,   being pregnant.
6 Ἐγένετο   δὲ   ἐν   τῷ   εἶναι   αὐτοὺς   ἐκεῖ
And it came to pass in   the   to be   themᵇᵉ   there
                                  = while they were
ἐπλήσθησαν   αἱ   ἡμέραι   τοῦ   τεκεῖν   αὐτήν,
were fulfilled   the   days   -   to bear   her,ᵇᵈ
                                                 = for her to bear,
7 καὶ   ἔτεκεν   τὸν   υἱὸν   αὐτῆς   τὸν   πρωτότοκον,
and   she bore   the   son   of her   the   firstborn,
καὶ   ἐσπαργάνωσεν   αὐτὸν   καὶ   ἀνέκλινεν
and   she swathed   him   and   laid
αὐτὸν   ἐν   φάτνῃ,   διότι   οὐκ   ἦν   αὐτοῖς
him   in   a manger, because there was not for them
τόπος   ἐν   τῷ   καταλύματι.   8 Καὶ   ποιμένες
place   in   the   inn.   And   shepherds
ἦσαν   ἐν   τῇ   χώρᾳ   τῇ   αὐτῇ   ἀγραυλοῦντες
there were in   the country the   same   living in the fields
καὶ   φυλάσσοντες   φυλακὰς   τῆς   νυκτὸς   ἐπὶ
and   keeping   guard   of(in) the   night   over
τὴν   ποίμνην   αὐτῶν.   9 καὶ   ἄγγελος   κυρίου
the   flock   of them.   And   an angel   of [the] Lord
ἐπέστη   αὐτοῖς   καὶ   δόξα   κυρίου   περιέλαμψεν
came upon them   and   [the] glory of [the]Lord shone around
αὐτούς,   καὶ   ἐφοβήθησαν   φόβον   μέγαν.
them,   and   they feared   fear   a great.
                                                    = exceedingly.
10 καὶ   εἶπεν   αὐτοῖς   ὁ   ἄγγελος·   μὴ
And   said   to them   the   angel :   not
φοβεῖσθε·   ἰδοὺ   γὰρ   εὐαγγελίζομαι   ὑμῖν
Fear ye;   for behold   I announce   to you

Chapter 2

The Birth of Jesus

IN those days Caesar Augustus issued a decree that a census should be taken of the entire Roman world. 2(This was the first census that took place while Quirinius was governor of Syria.) 3And everyone went to his own town to register.
4So Joseph also went up from the town of Nazareth in Galilee to Judea, to Bethlehem the town of David, because he belonged to the house and line of David. 5He went there to register with Mary, who was pledged to be married to him and was expecting a child. 6While they were there, the time came for the baby to be born, 7and she gave birth to her firstborn, a son. She wrapped him in cloths and placed him in a manger, because there was no room for them in the inn.

The Shepherds and the Angels

8And there were shepherds living out in the fields nearby, keeping watch over their flocks at night. 9An angel of the Lord appeared to them, and the glory of the Lord shone around them, and they were terrified. 10But the angel said to them, ''Do not be afraid. I bring you good

ᶠI.e., the Roman empire
ᵍGr., Kyrenios

good news of a great joy which shall be for all the people;

11for today in the city of David there has been born for you a Savior, who is hChrist the Lord.

12"And this will be a sign for you: you will find a baby wrapped in cloths, and lying in a manger."

13And suddenly there appeared with the angel a multitude of the heavenly host praising God, and saying,

14"Glory to God in the highest,
And on earth peace among men i with whom He is pleased."

15And it came about when the angels had gone away from them into heaven, that the shepherds began saying to one another, "Let us go straight to Bethlehem then, and see this thing that has happened which the Lord has made known to us."

16And they came in haste and found their way to Mary and Joseph, and the baby as He lay in the manger.

17And when they had seen this, they made known the statement which had been told them about this Child.

18And all‾ who heard it wondered at the things which were told them by the shepherds.

19But Mary treasured up all these things, pondering them in her heart.

20And the shepherds went back, glorifying and praising God for all that they had heard and seen, just as had been told them.

Jesus Presented at the Temple

21And when eight days were completed before His circumcision, His name was then called Jesus, the name given by the angel before He was conceived in the womb.

22And when the days for

Middle column (Greek interlinear)

χαρὰν μεγάλην, ἥτις ἔσται παντὶ τῷ λαῷ,
joy a great, which will be to all the people,

11 ὅτι ἐτέχθη ὑμῖν σήμερον σωτήρ, ὅς
because was born to you to-day a Saviour, who

ἐστιν χριστὸς κύριος, ἐν πόλει Δαυίδ.
is Christ [the] Lord, in a city of David.

12 καὶ τοῦτο ὑμῖν σημεῖον, εὑρήσετε βρέφος
And this to you a sign, ye will find a babe

ἐσπαργανωμένον καὶ κείμενον ἐν φάτνῃ.
having been swathed and lying in a manger.

13 καὶ ἐξαίφνης ἐγένετο σὺν τῷ ἀγγέλῳ
And suddenly there was with the angel

πλῆθος στρατιᾶς οὐρανίου αἰνούντων τὸν
a multitude army of a heavenly praising –

θεὸν καὶ λεγόντων· 14 δόξα ἐν ὑψίστοις
God and saying : Glory in highest [places]

θεῷ καὶ ἐπὶ γῆς εἰρήνη ἐν ἀνθρώποις
to God and on earth peace among men

εὐδοκίας. 15 Καὶ ἐγένετο ὡς ἀπῆλθον
of goodwill. And it came to pass when went away

ἀπ᾽ αὐτῶν εἰς τὸν οὐρανὸν οἱ ἄγγελοι,
from them to – heaven the angels,

οἱ ποιμένες ἐλάλουν πρὸς ἀλλήλους·
the shepherds said to one another :

διέλθωμεν δὴ ἕως Βηθλέεμ καὶ ἴδωμεν
Let us go then unto Bethlehem and let us see

τὸ ῥῆμα τοῦτο τὸ γεγονὸς ὃ ὁ κύριος
– thing this – having happened which the Lord

ἐγνώρισεν ἡμῖν. 16 καὶ ἦλθαν σπεύσαντες,
made known to us. And they came hastening,

καὶ ἀνεῦραν τήν τε Μαριὰμ καὶ τὸν
and found – both Mary and –

Ἰωσὴφ καὶ τὸ βρέφος κείμενον ἐν τῇ
Joseph and the babe lying in the

φάτνῃ 17 ἰδόντες δὲ ἐγνώρισαν περὶ τοῦ
manger; and seeing they made known concerning the

ῥήματος τοῦ λαληθέντος αὐτοῖς περὶ τοῦ
word – spoken to them concerning –

παιδίου τούτου. 18 καὶ πάντες οἱ ἀκούσαντες
child this. And all the [ones] hearing

ἐθαύμασαν περὶ τῶν λαληθέντων ὑπὸ τῶν
marvelled concerning the things spoken by the

ποιμένων πρὸς αὐτούς· 19 ἡ δὲ Μαρία
shepherds to them; but Mary

πάντα συνετήρει τὰ ῥήματα ταῦτα συμβάλλουσα
²all ¹kept – ⁴things ³these pondering

ἐν τῇ καρδίᾳ αὐτῆς. 20 καὶ ὑπέστρεψαν
in the heart of her. And returned

οἱ ποιμένες δοξάζοντες καὶ αἰνοῦντες τὸν
the shepherds glorifying and praising –

θεὸν ἐπὶ πᾶσιν οἷς ἤκουσαν καὶ εἶδον
God at all things which they heard and saw

καθὼς ἐλαλήθη πρὸς αὐτούς.
as was spoken to them.

21 Καὶ ὅτε ἐπλήσθησαν ἡμέραι ὀκτὼ
And when were completed days eight

τοῦ περιτεμεῖν αὐτόν, καὶ ἐκλήθη τὸ
– to circumcise himd, and was called the

ὄνομα αὐτοῦ Ἰησοῦς, τὸ κληθὲν ὑπὸ τοῦ
name of him Jesus, the [name] called by the

ἀγγέλου πρὸ τοῦ συλλημφθῆναι αὐτὸν ἐν
angel before the to be conceived himb in
=he was conceived

τῇ κοιλίᾳ.
the womb.

22 Καὶ ὅτε ἐπλήσθησαν αἱ ἡμέραι τοῦ
And when were completed the days of the

news of great joy that will be for all the people. 11Today in the town of David a Savior has been born to you; he is Christe the Lord. 12This will be a sign to you: You will find a baby wrapped in cloths and lying in a manger."

13Suddenly a great company of the heavenly host appeared with the angel, praising God and saying,

14"Glory to God in the highest,
and on earth peace to men on whom his favor rests."

15When the angels had left them and gone into heaven, the shepherds said to one another, "Let's go to Bethlehem and see this thing that has happened, which the Lord has told us about."

16So they hurried off and found Mary and Joseph, and the baby, who was lying in the manger. 17When they had seen him, they spread the word concerning what had been told them about this child, 18and all who heard it were amazed at what the shepherds said to them. 19But Mary treasured up all these things and pondered them in her heart. 20The shepherds returned, glorifying and praising God for all the things they had heard and seen, which were just as they had been told.

Jesus Presented in the Temple

21On the eighth day, when it was time to circumcise him, he was named Jesus, the name the angel had given him before he had been conceived.

22When the time of their

hI.e., Messiah
iLit., of good pleasure; or possibly, of good will

e11 Or Messiah. "The Christ" (Greek) and "the Messiah" (Hebrew) both mean "the Anointed One"; also in verse 26.

their purification according to the law of Moses were completed, they brought Him up to Jerusalem to present Him to the Lord ²³(as it is written in the Law of the Lord, "EVERY *first-born* MALE THAT OPENS THE WOMB SHALL BE CALLED HOLY TO THE LORD"), ²⁴and to offer a sacrifice according to what was said in the Law of the Lord, "A PAIR OF TURTLEDOVES, OR TWO YOUNG PIGEONS."

²⁵And behold, there was a man in Jerusalem whose name was Simeon; and this man was righteous and devout, looking for the consolation of Israel; and the Holy Spirit was upon him. ²⁶And it had been revealed to him by the Holy Spirit that he would not see death before he had seen the Lord's Christ. ²⁷And he came in the Spirit into the temple; and when the parents brought in the child Jesus, to carry out for Him the custom of the Law, ²⁸then he took Him into his arms, and blessed God, and said,

²⁹"Now Lord, Thou dost let Thy bond-servant depart
In peace, according to Thy word;
³⁰ For my eyes have seen Thy salvation,
³¹ Which Thou hast prepared in the presence of all peoples,
³² A LIGHT OF REVELATION TO THE GENTILES,

And the glory of Thy people Israel."

³³And His father and mother were amazed at the things which were being said about Him. ³⁴And Simeon blessed them, and said to Mary His mother, "Behold, this *Child* is appointed for the fall and rise of many in Is-

καθαρισμοῦ αὐτῶν κατὰ τὸν νόμον
cleansing of them according to the law
Μωϋσέως, ἀνήγαγον αὐτὸν εἰς Ἰεροσόλυμα
of Moses, they took up him to Jerusalem
παραστῆσαι τῷ κυρίῳ, 23 καθὼς γέγραπται
to present to the Lord, as it has been written
ἐν νόμῳ κυρίου ὅτι πᾶν ἄρσεν διανοῖγον
in [the] law of the Lord[,] – Every male opening
μήτραν ἅγιον τῷ κυρίῳ κληθήσεται, 24 καὶ
a womb holy to the Lord shall be called, and
τοῦ δοῦναι θυσίαν κατὰ τὸ εἰρημένον ἐν
– to give[d] a sacrifice according to the thing said in
τῷ νόμῳ κυρίου, ζεῦγος τρυγόνων ἢ δύο
the law of [the] Lord, a pair of turtledoves or two
νοσσοὺς περιστερῶν. 25 Καὶ ἰδοὺ ἄνθρωπος
nestlings of doves. And behold[,] a man
ἦν ἐν Ἰερουσαλὴμ ᾧ ὄνομα Συμεών, καὶ
was in Jerusalem to whom name[c] Simeon, and
=whose name was
ὁ ἄνθρωπος οὗτος δίκαιος καὶ εὐλαβής,
– man this [was] just and devout,
προσδεχόμενος παράκλησιν τοῦ Ἰσραήλ, καὶ
expecting [the] consolation – of Israel, and
πνεῦμα ἦν ἅγιον ἐπ᾽ αὐτόν· 26 καὶ ἦν
¹[the] ³Spirit ⁴was ²Holy upon him; and it was
αὐτῷ κεχρηματισμένον ὑπὸ τοῦ πνεύματος
to him *having been* communicated by the Spirit
τοῦ ἁγίου μὴ ἰδεῖν θάνατον πρὶν ἢ ἂν
– Holy not to see death before
ἴδῃ τὸν χριστὸν κυρίου. 27 καὶ ἦλθεν
he should see the Christ of [the] Lord. And he came
ἐν τῷ πνεύματι εἰς τὸ ἱερόν· καὶ ἐν τῷ
by the Spirit into the temple; and in the
=as the(his) parents brought in
εἰσαγαγεῖν τοὺς γονεῖς τὸ παιδίον Ἰησοῦν
to bring in the parents[be] the child Jesus
τοῦ ποιῆσαι αὐτοὺς κατὰ τὸ εἰθισμένον
– to do them[bd] according to the custom
=for them to do
τοῦ νόμου περὶ αὐτοῦ, 28 καὶ αὐτὸς
of the law concerning him, and he
ἐδέξατο αὐτὸ εἰς τὰς ἀγκάλας καὶ
received him in the(his) arms and
εὐλόγησεν τὸν θεὸν καὶ εἶπεν· 29 νῦν
blessed – God and said : Now
ἀπολύεις τὸν δοῦλόν σου, δέσποτα, κατὰ
thou releasest the slave of thee, Master, according to
τὸ ῥῆμά σου ἐν εἰρήνῃ· 30 ὅτι εἶδον οἱ
the word of thee in peace; because saw the
ὀφθαλμοί μου τὸ σωτήριόν σου, 31 ὃ
eyes of me the salvation of thee, which
ἡτοίμασας κατὰ πρόσωπον πάντων τῶν
thou didst prepare before [the] face of all the
λαῶν, 32 φῶς εἰς ἀποκάλυψιν ἐθνῶν καὶ
peoples, a light for a revelation of [the] nations and
δόξαν λαοῦ σου Ἰσραήλ. 33 καὶ ἦν
a glory of [the] people of thee Israel. And ᵗwas(were)
ὁ πατὴρ αὐτοῦ καὶ ἡ μήτηρ θαυμάζοντες
¹the ²father ³of him ⁴and ⁵the ⁶mother ⁸marvelling
ἐπὶ τοῖς λαλουμένοις περὶ αὐτοῦ. 34 καὶ
at the things being said concerning him. And
εὐλόγησεν αὐτοὺς Συμεὼν καὶ εἶπεν πρὸς
blessed them Simeon and said to
Μαριὰμ τὴν μητέρα αὐτοῦ· ἰδοὺ οὗτος
Mary the mother of him : Behold[,] this
κεῖται εἰς πτῶσιν καὶ ἀνάστασιν πολλῶν
is set for fall and rising again of many

purification according to the Law of Moses had been completed, Joseph and Mary took him to Jerusalem to present him to the Lord ²³(as it is written in the Law of the Lord, "Every firstborn male is to be consecrated to the Lord"ᶠ), ²⁴and to offer a sacrifice in keeping with what is said in the Law of the Lord: "a pair of doves or two young pigeons."ᵍ

²⁵Now there was a man in Jerusalem called Simeon, who was righteous and devout. He was waiting for the consolation of Israel, and the Holy Spirit was upon him. ²⁶It had been revealed to him by the Holy Spirit that he would not die before he had seen the Lord's Christ. ²⁷Moved by the Spirit, he went into the temple courts. When the parents brought in the child Jesus to do for him what the custom of the Law required, ²⁸Simeon took him in his arms and praised God, saying:

²⁹"Sovereign Lord, as you have promised,
you now dismissʰ your servant in peace.
³⁰For my eyes have seen your salvation,
³¹ which you have prepared in the sight of all people,
³²a light for revelation to the Gentiles
and for glory to your people Israel."

³³The child's father and mother marveled at what was said about him. ³⁴Then Simeon blessed them and said to Mary, his mother: "This child is destined to cause the falling and rising of many in Israel, and to be

ᶠ23 Exodus 13:2,12
ᵍ24 Lev. 12:8
ʰ29 Or *promised,* / *now dismiss*

rael, and for a sign to be opposed—

35and a sword will pierce even your own soul—to the end that thoughts from many hearts may be revealed."

36And there was a prophetess, Anna the daughter of Phanuel, of the tribe of Asher. She was advanced in years, having lived with a husband seven years after her marriage,

37and then as a widow to the age of eighty-four. And she never left the temple, serving night and day with fastings and prayers.

38And at that very moment she came up and *began* giving thanks to God, and continued to speak of Him to all those who were looking for the redemption of Jerusalem.

Return to Nazareth

39And when they had performed everything according to the Law of the Lord, they returned to Galilee, to their own city of Nazareth.

40And the Child continued to grow and become strong, increasing in wisdom; and the grace of God was upon Him.

Visit to Jerusalem

41And His parents used to go to Jerusalem every year at the Feast of the Passover.

42And when He became twelve, they went up *there* according to the custom of the Feast;

43and as they were returning, after spending the full number of days, the boy Jesus stayed behind in Jerusalem. And His parents were unaware of it,

44but supposed Him to be in the caravan, and went a day's journey; and they *began* looking for Him among their relatives and acquaintances.

45And when they did not find Him, they returned to

ἐν τῷ Ἰσραὴλ καὶ εἰς σημεῖον ἀντιλεγ-
in   -   Israel   and   for   a sign   spoken

όμενον — 35 καὶ σοῦ δὲ αὐτῆς τὴν ψυχὴν
against   —   and ⁵of thee ⁷also ⁸[thy]self ³the   ⁴soul

διελεύσεται ρομφαία—, ὅπως ἂν ἀποκαλυφθῶσιν
²will go through ¹a sword —, so as   — may be revealed

ἐκ πολλῶν καρδιῶν διαλογισμοί. 36 Καὶ
of   many   hearts   [the] thoughts.   And

ἦν Ἅννα προφῆτις, θυγάτηρ Φανουήλ, ἐκ
there was Anna   a prophetess,   a daughter   of Phanuel,   of

φυλῆς Ἀσήρ· αὕτη προβεβηκυῖα ἐν ἡμέραις
[the] tribe of Asher;   this   having advanced   in   days

πολλαῖς, ζήσασα μετὰ ἀνδρὸς ἔτη ἑπτὰ
many,   having lived   with   a husband   years   seven

ἀπὸ τῆς παρθενίας αὐτῆς, 37 καὶ αὐτὴ
from   the   virginity   of her,   and she [was]

χήρα ἕως ἐτῶν ὀγδοήκοντα τεσσάρων, ἣ
a widow until   years   eighty-four,   who

οὐκ ἀφίστατο τοῦ ἱεροῦ νηστείαις καὶ
withdrew not from   the   temple   with fastings   and

δεήσεσιν λατρεύουσα νύκτα καὶ ἡμέραν.
petitionings   serving   night   and   day.

38 καὶ αὐτῇ τῇ ὥρᾳ ἐπιστᾶσα ἀνθωμολογεῖτο
And   at the very hour*   coming upon   she gave thanks

τῷ θεῷ καὶ ἐλάλει περὶ αὐτοῦ πᾶσιν τοῖς
- to God and   spoke   about   him   to all the [ones]

προσδεχομένοις λύτρωσιν Ἰερουσαλήμ. 39 Καὶ
expecting   redemption   in Jerusalem.   And

ὡς ἐτέλεσαν πάντα τὰ κατὰ τὸν νόμον
when they finished   all things   - according to the   law

κυρίου, ἐπέστρεψαν εἰς τὴν Γαλιλαίαν εἰς
of [the] Lord, they returned   to   -   Galilee   to

πόλιν ἑαυτῶν Ναζαρέθ.
a city   of them*selves*   Nazareth.

40 Τὸ δὲ παιδίον ηὔξανεν καὶ ἐκραταιοῦτο
And the   child   grew   and   became strong

πληρούμενον σοφίᾳ, καὶ χάρις θεοῦ ἦν ἐπ᾽
being filled   with wisdom, and [the] grace of God was upon

αὐτό.
him.

41 Καὶ ἐπορεύοντο οἱ γονεῖς αὐτοῦ κατ᾽
And   went   the   parents   of him   year

ἔτος εἰς Ἰερουσαλὴμ τῇ ἑορτῇ τοῦ πάσχα.
by year† to   Jerusalem   at the   feast   of the Passover.

42 Καὶ ὅτε ἐγένετο ἐτῶν δώδεκα, ἀναβαινόντων
And when   he became of years   twelve,   going up
                                     = as they went up

αὐτῶν κατὰ τὸ ἔθος τῆς ἑορτῆς, 43 καὶ
them* according to the custom of the   feast,   and

τελειωσάντων τὰς ἡμέρας, ἐν τῷ ὑποστρέφειν
fulfilling*   the   days,   in the   to return
                                 = when they returned

αὐτοὺς ὑπέμεινεν Ἰησοῦς ὁ παῖς ἐν
them*be*   ⁴remained   ²Jesus   ¹the   ³boy   in

Ἰερουσαλήμ, καὶ οὐκ ἔγνωσαν οἱ γονεῖς
Jerusalem,   and   ⁴knew not   ¹the   ²parents

αὐτοῦ. 44 νομίσαντες δὲ αὐτὸν εἶναι ἐν
³of him.   But supposing   him   to be   in

τῇ συνοδίᾳ ἦλθον ἡμέρας ὁδὸν καὶ ἀνεζήτουν
the company   they went of a day a journey and   sought

αὐτὸν ἐν τοῖς συγγενεῦσιν καὶ τοῖς
him   among   the(ir)   relatives   and   the(ir)

γνωστοῖς, 45 καὶ μὴ εὑρόντες ὑπέστρεψαν
acquaintances,   and   not   finding   returned

* Strictly, this construction should mean " the hour itself "; but the context demands " the same hour ". See 10. 7, 21; 12. 12; 13. 1, 31; 20. 19; 23. 12; 24. 13. " Luke seems to be the only N.T. writer who affects the construction " (C. F. D. Moule). See also Acts 16. 18; 22. 13. Of course there is not a great difference between " the hour itself ", " the very hour ", and " the same hour ".

---

a sign that will be spoken against, 35so that the thoughts of many hearts will be revealed. And a sword will pierce your own soul too."

36There was also a prophetess, Anna, the daughter of Phanuel, of the tribe of Asher. She was very old; she had lived with her husband seven years after her marriage, 37and then was a widow until she was eighty-four.*i* She never left the temple but worshiped night and day, fasting and praying. 38Coming up to them at that very moment, she gave thanks to God and spoke about the child to all who were looking forward to the redemption of Jerusalem.

39When Joseph and Mary had done everything required by the Law of the Lord, they returned to Galilee to their own town of Nazareth. 40And the child grew and became strong; he was filled with wisdom, and the grace of God was upon him.

The Boy Jesus at the Temple

41Every year his parents went to Jerusalem for the Feast of the Passover. 42When he was twelve years old, they went up to the Feast, according to the custom. 43After the Feast was over, while his parents were returning home, the boy Jesus stayed behind in Jerusalem, but they were unaware of it. 44Thinking he was in their company, they traveled on for a day. Then they began looking for him among their relatives and friends. 45When they did not find him, they

Jerusalem, looking for Him.
46And it came about that after three days they found Him in the temple, sitting in the midst of the teachers, both listening to them, and asking them questions.
47And all who heard Him were amazed at His understanding and His answers.
48And when they saw Him, they were astonished; and His mother said to Him, "Son, why have You treated us this way? Behold, Your father and I have been anxiously looking for You."
49And He said to them, "Why is it that you were looking for Me? Did you not know that I had to be in My Father's *house*?"
50And they did not understand the statement which He had made to them.
51And He went down with them, and came to Nazareth; and He continued in subjection to them; and His mother treasured all *these* things in her heart.
52And Jesus kept increasing in wisdom and stature, and in favor with God and men.

εἰς Ἰερουσαλὴμ ἀναζητοῦντες αὐτόν. **46** καὶ
to   Jerusalem   seeking   him.   And

ἐγένετο μετὰ ἡμέρας τρεῖς εὗρον αὐτὸν
it came to pass after days   three they found him

ἐν τῷ ἱερῷ καθεζόμενον ἐν μέσῳ τῶν
in the temple sitting   in [the] midst of the

διδασκάλων καὶ ἀκούοντα αὐτῶν καὶ
teachers   both hearing   them   and

ἐπερωτῶντα αὐτούς· **47** ἐξίσταντο δὲ πάντες
questioning   them;   and were astonished all

οἱ ἀκούοντες αὐτοῦ ἐπὶ τῇ συνέσει καὶ
the [ones] hearing   him   at the intelligence and

ταῖς ἀποκρίσεσιν αὐτοῦ. **48** καὶ ἰδόντες
the   answers   of him.   And   seeing

αὐτὸν ἐξεπλάγησαν, καὶ εἶπεν πρὸς αὐτὸν
him   they were astounded, and said   to   him

ἡ μήτηρ αὐτοῦ· τέκνον, τί ἐποίησας ἡμῖν
the mother of him : Child, why didst thou to us

οὕτως; ἰδοὺ ὁ πατήρ σου κἀγὼ ὀδυνώμενοι
thus? behold[,] the father of thee and I greatly distressed

ζητοῦμέν σε. **49** καὶ εἶπεν πρὸς αὐτούς·
are seeking thee.   And he said   to   them :

τί ὅτι ἐζητεῖτέ με; οὐκ ᾔδειτε ὅτι ἐν
Why [is it] that ye sought me? did ye not know that in
                                                    =I

τοῖς τοῦ πατρός μου δεῖ εἶναί με;
the [affairs] of the Father of me it behoves to be me?
must be about my Father's business?

50 καὶ αὐτοὶ οὐ συνῆκαν τὸ ῥῆμα ὃ
    And   they   did not understand the word   which

ἐλάλησεν αὐτοῖς. **51** καὶ κατέβη μετ'
he spoke   to them.   And he went down with

αὐτῶν καὶ ἦλθεν εἰς Ναζαρέθ, καὶ ἦν
them   and came   to Nazareth,   and was

ὑποτασσόμενος αὐτοῖς. καὶ ἡ μήτηρ
being subject   to them.   And the mother

αὐτοῦ διετήρει πάντα τὰ ῥήματα ἐν τῇ
of him carefully kept all   the matters   in the

καρδίᾳ αὐτῆς. **52** Καὶ Ἰησοῦς προέκοπτεν
heart   of her.   And Jesus   progressed

ἐν τῇ σοφίᾳ καὶ ἡλικίᾳ καὶ χάριτι παρὰ
in - wisdom and age   and favour   before

θεῷ καὶ ἀνθρώποις.
God and   men.

Chapter 3

John the Baptist Preaches

3 Ἐν ἔτει δὲ πεντεκαιδεκάτῳ τῆς
Now in [the] year   fifteenth   of the

ἡγεμονίας Τιβερίου Καίσαρος, ἡγεμονεύοντος
government of Tiberius   Cæsar,   governing
                                    = while Pontius Pilate

Ποντίου Πιλάτου τῆς Ἰουδαίας, καὶ
Pontius   Pilate*   -   of Judæa,   and
was governing

τετρααρχοῦντος τῆς Γαλιλαίας Ἡρώδου,
ruling as tetrarch   -   of Galilee   Herod,*
= while Herod was ruling as tetrarch of Galilee,

Φιλίππου δὲ τοῦ ἀδελφοῦ αὐτοῦ τετρα-
and Philip   the   brother   of him   ruling

αρχοῦντος τῆς Ἰτουραίας καὶ Τραχωνίτιδος
as tetrarch*   ¹of the ²of Ituræa ⁴and ⁵of Trachonitis

χώρας, καὶ Λυσανίου τῆς Ἀβιληνῆς
³country, and Lysanias   -   of Abilene

τετρααρχοῦντος, **2** ἐπὶ ἀρχιερέως Ἄννα
ruling as tetrarch*,   in the time of [the] high priest Anna

καὶ Καϊαφᾶ, ἐγένετο ῥῆμα θεοῦ ἐπὶ Ἰωάννην
and Caiaphas,   came   a word of God to   John

τὸν Ζαχαρίου υἱὸν ἐν τῇ ἐρήμῳ. **3** καὶ
the of Zacharias son in the desert.   And

---

went back to Jerusalem to look for him. 46After three days they found him in the temple courts, sitting among the teachers, listening to them and asking them questions. 47Everyone who heard him was amazed at his understanding and his answers. 48When his parents saw him, they were astonished. His mother said to him, "Son, why have you treated us like this? Your father and I have been anxiously searching for you."
49"Why were you searching for me?" he asked. "Didn't you know I had to be in my Father's house?" 50But they did not understand what he was saying to them.
51Then he went down to Nazareth with them and was obedient to them. But his mother treasured all these things in her heart. 52And Jesus grew in wisdom and stature, and in favor with God and men.

Chapter 3

John the Baptist Prepares the Way

IN the fifteenth year of the reign of Tiberius Caesar—when Pontius Pilate was governor of Judea, Herod tetrarch of Galilee, his brother Philip tetrarch of Iturea and Traconitis, and Lysanias tetrarch of Abilene—2during the high priesthood of Annas and Caiaphas, the word of God came to John son of Zechariah in the desert. 3He went

3And he came into all the district around the Jordan, preaching a baptism of repentance for the forgiveness of sins;

4as it is written in the book of the words of Isaiah the prophet,
"THE VOICE OF ONE CRYING IN THE WILDERNESS,
'MAKE READY THE WAY OF THE LORD,
MAKE HIS PATHS STRAIGHT.
5 'EVERY RAVINE SHALL BE FILLED UP,
AND EVERY MOUNTAIN AND HILL SHALL BE BROUGHT LOW;
AND THE CROOKED SHALL BECOME STRAIGHT,
AND THE ROUGH ROADS SMOOTH;
6 AND ALL FLESH SHALL SEE THE SALVATION OF GOD.' ''

7He therefore *began* saying to the multitudes who were going out to be baptized by him, "You brood of vipers, who warned you to flee from the wrath to come?

8"Therefore bring forth fruits in keeping with repentance, and do not begin to say to yourselves, 'We have Abraham for our father,' for I say to you that God is able from these stones to raise up children to Abraham.

9"And also the axe is already laid at the root of the trees; every tree therefore that does not bear good fruit is cut down and thrown into the fire."

10And the multitudes were questioning him, saying, "Then what shall we do?"

11And he would answer and say to them, "Let the man who has two tunics share with him who has none; and let him who has food do likewise."

12And *some* *j* tax-gatherers also came to be baptized, and they said to him, "Teacher, what shall we do?"

13And he said to them, "Collect no more than what you have been ordered to."

14And *some* *k* soldiers were questioning him, saying, "And *what about* us,

---

ἦλθεν εἰς πᾶσαν τὴν περίχωρον τοῦ
he came into all the neighbourhood of the

Ἰορδάνου κηρύσσων βάπτισμα μετανοίας
Jordan proclaiming a baptism of repentance

εἰς ἄφεσιν ἁμαρτιῶν, 4 ὡς γέγραπται ἐν
for forgiveness of sins, as it has been written in

βίβλῳ λόγων Ἡσαΐου τοῦ προφήτου·
[the] roll of [the] words of Esaias the prophet :

φωνὴ βοῶντος ἐν τῇ ἐρήμῳ· ἑτοιμάσατε
Voice of [one] crying in the desert : Prepare ye

τὴν ὁδὸν κυρίου, εὐθείας ποιεῖτε τὰς
the way of [the] Lord, straight make the

τρίβους αὐτοῦ· 5 πᾶσα φάραγξ πληρωθήσεται
paths of him; every valley shall be filled up

καὶ πᾶν ὄρος καὶ βουνὸς ταπεινωθήσεται,
and every mountain and hill shall be laid low,

καὶ ἔσται τὰ σκολιὰ εἰς εὐθείας καὶ αἱ
and shall be the crooked [places] into straight [ones] and the

τραχεῖαι εἰς ὁδοὺς λείας· 6 καὶ ὄψεται
rough [places] into ways smooth; and ²shall see

πᾶσα σὰρξ τὸ σωτήριον τοῦ θεοῦ.
¹all ²flesh the salvation − of God.

7 Ἔλεγεν οὖν τοῖς ἐκπορευομένοις ὄχλοις
He said therefore to the ²going out ¹crowds

βαπτισθῆναι ὑπ' αὐτοῦ· γεννήματα ἐχιδνῶν,
to be baptized by him : Offspring of vipers,

τίς ὑπέδειξεν ὑμῖν φυγεῖν ἀπὸ τῆς
who warned you to flee from the

μελλούσης ὀργῆς; 8 ποιήσατε οὖν καρποὺς
coming wrath? Produce therefore fruits

ἀξίους τῆς μετανοίας· καὶ μὴ ἄρξησθε
worthy − of repentance; and do not begin

λέγειν ἐν ἑαυτοῖς· πατέρα ἔχομεν τὸν
to say among yourselves : Father we have the

Ἀβραάμ· λέγω γὰρ ὑμῖν ὅτι δύναται ὁ
Abraham; for I tell you that ²can the

θεὸς ἐκ τῶν λίθων τούτων ἐγεῖραι τέκνα
¹God out of − stones these to raise children

τῷ Ἀβραάμ. 9 ἤδη δὲ καὶ ἡ ἀξίνη πρὸς
− to Abraham. And ²already ¹even the axe at

τὴν ῥίζαν τῶν δένδρων κεῖται· πᾶν οὖν
the root of the trees is laid; ²every ¹therefore

δένδρον μὴ ποιοῦν καρπὸν καλὸν
tree not producing fruit good

ἐκκόπτεται καὶ εἰς πῦρ βάλλεται. 10 Καὶ
is being cut down and into fire is being cast. And

ἐπηρώτων αὐτὸν οἱ ὄχλοι λέγοντες· τί
asked him the crowds saying : What

οὖν ποιήσωμεν; 11 ἀποκριθεὶς δὲ ἔλεγεν
then may we do? And answering he told

αὐτοῖς· ὁ ἔχων δύο χιτῶνας μεταδότω
them : The [one] having two tunics let him impart

τῷ μὴ ἔχοντι, καὶ ὁ ἔχων βρώματα
to the [one] not having, and the [one] having foods

ὁμοίως ποιείτω. 12 ἦλθον δὲ καὶ τελῶναι
likewise let him do. And there came also tax-collectors

βαπτισθῆναι καὶ εἶπαν πρὸς αὐτόν·
to be baptized and they said to him :

διδάσκαλε, τί ποιήσωμεν; 13 ὁ δὲ εἶπεν
Teacher, what may we do? And he said

πρὸς αὐτούς· μηδὲν πλέον παρὰ τὸ
to them : Nothing more besides the [thing]

διατεταγμένον ὑμῖν πράσσετε. 14 ἐπηρώτων δὲ
having been commanded you do ye. And asked

αὐτὸν καὶ στρατευόμενοι λέγοντες· τί
him also men serving in the army saying : What

---

into all the country around the Jordan, preaching a baptism of repentance for the forgiveness of sins. 4As is written in the book of the words of Isaiah the prophet:

"A voice of one calling in the desert,
'Prepare the way for the Lord,
make straight paths for him.
5Every valley shall be filled in,
every mountain and hill made low.
The crooked roads shall become straight,
the rough ways smooth.
6And all mankind will see God's salvation.' ''[j]

7John said to the crowds coming out to be baptized by him, "You brood of vipers! Who warned you to flee from the coming wrath? 8Produce fruit in keeping with repentance. And do not begin to say to yourselves, 'We have Abraham as our father.' For I tell you that out of these stones God can raise up children for Abraham. 9The ax is already at the root of the trees, and every tree that does not produce good fruit will be cut down and thrown into the fire.''

10"What should we do then?" the crowd asked.

11John answered, "The man with two tunics should share with him who has none, and the one who has food should do the same.''

12Tax collectors also came to be baptized. "Teacher,'' they asked, "what should we do?"

---

j I.e., Collectors of Roman taxes for profit

k I.e., men in active military service

j 6 Isaiah 40:3-5

what shall we do?'' And he said to them, ''Do not take money from anyone by force, or accuse *anyone* falsely, and be content with your wages.''

15Now while the people were in a state of expectation and all were wondering in their hearts about John, as to whether he might be the Christ,

16John answered and said to them all, ''As for me, I baptize you with water; but One is coming who is mightier than I, and I am not fit to untie the thong of His sandals; He will baptize you with the Holy Spirit and fire.

17''And His winnowing fork is in His hand to thoroughly clear His threshing floor, and to gather the wheat into His barn; but He will burn up the chaff with unquenchable fire.''

18So with many other exhortations also he preached the gospel to the people.

19But when Herod the tetrarch was reproved by him on account of Herodias, his brother's wife, and on account of all the wicked things which Herod had done,

20he added this also to them all, that he locked John up in prison.

Jesus Is Baptized

21Now it came about when all the people were baptized, that Jesus also was baptized, and while He was praying, heaven was opened,

22and the Holy Spirit descended upon Him in bodily form like a dove, and a voice came out of heaven, ''Thou art My beloved Son, in Thee I am well-pleased.''

Genealogy of Jesus

23And when He began His ministry, Jesus Himself was about thirty years of

---

ποιήσωμεν καὶ ἡμεῖς; καὶ εἶπεν αὐτοῖς·
may do also we? And he told them:

μηδένα διασείσητε μηδὲ συκοφαντήσητε,
No one intimidate nor accuse falsely,

καὶ ἀρκεῖσθε τοῖς ὀψωνίοις ὑμῶν.
and be satisfied with the pay of you.

15 Προσδοκῶντος δὲ τοῦ λαοῦ[a] καὶ
Now expecting the people and
= while the people were expecting and all were debating

διαλογιζομένων πάντων[a] ἐν ταῖς καρδίαις
debating all in the hearts

αὐτῶν περὶ τοῦ Ἰωάννου, μήποτε αὐτὸς
of them concerning John, perhaps he

εἴη ὁ χριστός, 16 ἀπεκρίνατο λέγων πᾶσιν
might be the Christ, [2]answered [3]saying [4]to all

ὁ Ἰωάννης· ἐγὼ μὲν ὕδατι βαπτίζω ὑμᾶς·
- [1]John: I indeed with water baptize you;

ἔρχεται δὲ ὁ ἰσχυρότερός μου, οὗ οὐκ
but there comes the [one] stronger of me, of whom not
= than I,

εἰμὶ ἱκανὸς λῦσαι τὸν ἱμάντα τῶν ὑποδημά-
I am competent to loosen the thong of the san-

των αὐτοῦ· αὐτὸς ὑμᾶς βαπτίσει ἐν
dals of him; he you will baptize with

πνεύματι ἁγίῳ καὶ πυρί· 17 οὗ τὸ πτύον
Spirit [the] Holy and fire; of whom the fan [is]

ἐν τῇ χειρὶ αὐτοῦ διακαθάραι τὴν ἅλωνα
in the hand of him thoroughly to cleanse the threshing-floor

αὐτοῦ καὶ συναγαγεῖν τὸν σῖτον εἰς τὴν
of him and to gather the wheat into the

ἀποθήκην αὐτοῦ, τὸ δὲ ἄχυρον κατακαύσει
barn of him, but the chaff he will burn up

πυρὶ ἀσβέστῳ. 18 Πολλὰ μὲν οὖν καὶ
with fire unquenchable. Many things indeed therefore and

ἕτερα παρακαλῶν εὐηγγελίζετο τὸν λαόν·
different exhorting he evangelized the people;

19 ὁ δὲ Ἡρῴδης ὁ τετραάρχης, ἐλεγχόμενος
- but Herod the tetrarch, being reproved

ὑπ᾽ αὐτοῦ περὶ Ἡρῳδιάδος τῆς γυναικὸς
by him concerning Herodias the wife

τοῦ ἀδελφοῦ αὐτοῦ καὶ περὶ πάντων ὧν
of the brother of him and concerning [1]all [2]things [4]which

ἐποίησεν πονηρῶν ὁ Ἡρῴδης, 20 προσέθηκεν
[5]did [3]evil - [1]Herod, added

καὶ τοῦτο ἐπὶ πᾶσιν, κατέκλεισεν τὸν
also this above all, he shut up

Ἰωάννην ἐν φυλακῇ.
John in prison.

21 Ἐγένετο δὲ ἐν τῷ βαπτισθῆναι ἅπαντα
Now it came to pass in the to be baptized all
= when all the people were baptized

τὸν λαὸν[b] καὶ Ἰησοῦ βαπτισθέντος καὶ
the people and Jesus being baptized and
= as Jesus had been baptized and was praying

προσευχομένου ἀνεῳχθῆναι τὸν οὐρανὸν 22 καὶ
praying to be opened the heaven and
= the heaven was opened and the Holy Spirit came down

καταβῆναι τὸ πνεῦμα τὸ ἅγιον σωματικῷ
to come down the Spirit the Holy[b] in a bodily

εἴδει ὡς περιστερὰν ἐπ᾽ αὐτόν, καὶ φωνὴν
form as a dove upon him, and a voice

ἐξ οὐρανοῦ γενέσθαι· σὺ εἶ ὁ υἱός μου
out of heaven to come[b]: Thou art the Son of me

ὁ ἀγαπητός, ἐν σοὶ εὐδόκησα. 23 Καὶ
- beloved, in thee I was well pleased. And

αὐτὸς ἦν Ἰησοῦς ἀρχόμενος ὡσεὶ ἐτῶν
[3]himself [2]was [1]Jesus [4]beginning about years

13''Don't collect any more than you are required to,'' he told them.

14Then some soldiers asked him, ''And what should we do?''

He replied, ''Don't extort money and don't accuse people falsely—be content with your pay.''

15The people were waiting expectantly and were all wondering in their hearts if John might possibly be the Christ.[k] 16John answered them all, ''I baptize you with[l] water. But one more powerful than I will come, the thongs of whose sandals I am not worthy to untie. He will baptize you with the Holy Spirit and with fire. 17His winnowing fork is in his hand to clear his threshing floor and to gather the wheat into his barn, but he will burn up the chaff with unquenchable fire.'' 18And with many other words John exhorted the people and preached the good news to them.

19But when John rebuked Herod the tetrarch because of Herodias, his brother's wife, and all the other evil things he had done, 20Herod added this to them all: He locked John up in prison.

The Baptism and Genealogy of Jesus

21When all the people were being baptized, Jesus was baptized too. And as he was praying, heaven was opened 22and the Holy Spirit descended on him in bodily form like a dove. And a voice came from heaven: ''You are my Son, whom I love; with you I am well pleased.''

23Now Jesus himself was about thirty years old when he began his ministry. He

---

*k*15 Or *Messiah*
*l*16 Or *in*

age, being supposedly *the* son of Joseph, the *son* of Eli,

24the *son* of Matthat, the *son* of Levi, the *son* of Melchi, the *son* of Jannai, the *son* of Joseph,

25the *son* of Mattathias, the *son* of Amos, the *son* of Nahum, the *son* of Hesli, the *son* of Naggai,

26the *son* of Maath, the *son* of Mattathias, the *son* of Semein, the *son* of Josech, the *son* of Joda,

27the *son* of Joanan, the *son* of Rhesa, the *son* of Zerubbabel, the *son* of Shealtiel, the *son* of Neri,

28the *son* of Melchi, the *son* of Addi, the *son* of Cosam, the *son* of Elmadam, the *son* of Er,

29the *son* of Joshua, the *son* of Eliezer, the *son* of Jorim, the *son* of Matthat, the *son* of Levi,

30the *son* of Simeon, the *son* of Judah, the *son* of Joseph, the *son* of Jonam, the *son* of Eliakim,

31the *son* of Melea, the *son* of Menna, the *son* of Mattatha, the *son* of Nathan, the *son* of David,

32the *son* of Jesse, the *son* of Obed, the *son* of Boaz, the *son* of Salmon, the *son* of Nahshon,

33the *son* of Amminadab, the *son* of Admin, the *son* of Ram, the *son* of Hezron, the *son* of Perez, the *son* of Judah,

34the *son* of Jacob, the *son* of Isaac, the *son* of Abraham, the *son* of Terah, the *son* of Nahor,

35the *son* of Serug, the *son* of Reu, the *son* of Peleg, the *son* of Heber, the *son* of Shelah,

36the *son* of Cainan, the *son* of Arphaxad, the *son* of Shem, the *son* of Noah, the *son* of Lamech,

37the *son* of Methuselah, the *son* of Enoch, the *son* of Jared, the *son* of Mahalaleel, the *son* of Cainan,

38the *son* of Enosh, the *son* of Seth, the *son* of Adam, the *son* of God.

Greek					
τριάκοντα, thirty,	ὢν being	υἱός, son,	ὡς as	ἐνομίζετο, was supposed,	Ἰωσήφ, of Joseph,
τοῦ –	Ἠλὶ of Eli	24 τοῦ –	Ματθὰτ of Matthat	τοῦ –	Λευὶ of Levi τοῦ –
Μελχὶ of Melchi	τοῦ –	Ἰανναὶ of Jannai	τοῦ –	Ἰωσὴφ of Joseph	25 τοῦ –
Ματταθίου of Mattathias	τοῦ –	Ἀμὼς of Amos	τοῦ –	Ναοὺμ of Naum	τοῦ –
Ἐσλὶ of Hesli	τοῦ –	Ναγγαὶ of Naggai	26 τοῦ –	Μάαθ of Maath	τοῦ –
Ματταθίου of Mattathias	τοῦ –	Σεμεΐν of Semein	τοῦ –	Ἰωσὴχ of Josech	τοῦ –
Ἰωδὰ of Jodah	27 τοῦ –	Ἰωανὰν of Joanan	τοῦ –	Ῥησὰ of Rhesa	τοῦ –
Ζοροβαβὲλ of Zorobabel	τοῦ –	Σαλαθιὴλ of Salathiel	τοῦ –	Νηρὶ of Neri	28 τοῦ –
Μελχὶ of Melchi	τοῦ –	Ἀδδὶ of Addi	τοῦ –	Κωσὰμ of Kosam	τοῦ –
Ἐλμαδὰμ of Elmadam	τοῦ –	Ἢρ of Er	29 τοῦ –	Ἰησοῦ of Jesus	τοῦ –
Ἐλιέζερ of Eliezer	τοῦ –	Ἰωρὶμ of Jorim	τοῦ –	Ματθὰτ of Matthat	τοῦ –
Λευὶ of Levi	30 τοῦ –	Συμεὼν of Simeon	τοῦ –	Ἰούδα of Juda	τοῦ –
Ἰωσὴφ of Joseph	τοῦ –	Ἰωνὰμ of Jonam	τοῦ –	Ἐλιακίμ of Eliakim	31 τοῦ –
Μελεὰ of Melea	τοῦ –	Μεννὰ of Menna	τοῦ –	Ματταθὰ of Mattatha	τοῦ –
Ναθὰμ of Natham	τοῦ –	Δαυὶδ of David	32 τοῦ –	Ἰεσσαὶ of Jesse	τοῦ –
Ἰωβὴδ of Jobed	τοῦ –	Βόος of Boos	τοῦ –	Σάλα of Sala	τοῦ Ναασσὼν of Naasson
33 τοῦ –	Ἀμιναδὰβ of Aminadab	τοῦ –	Ἀδμὶν of Admin	τοῦ –	Ἀρνὶ of Arni
τοῦ –	Ἑσρὼμ of Hesrom	τοῦ –	Φάρες of Phares	τοῦ –	Ἰούδα of Juda
34 τοῦ –	Ἰακὼβ of Jacob	τοῦ –	Ἰσαὰκ of Isaac	τοῦ –	Ἀβραὰμ of Abraham
τοῦ –	Θάρα of Thara	τοῦ –	Ναχὼρ of Nachor	35 τοῦ –	Σερούχ of Seruch
τοῦ –	Ῥαγαὺ of Rhagau	τοῦ –	Φάλεκ of Phalek	τοῦ –	Ἔβερ of Eber τοῦ –
Σάλα of Sala	36 τοῦ –	Καϊνὰμ of Cainam	τοῦ –	Ἀρφαξὰδ of Arphaxad	τοῦ –
Σὴμ of Sem	τοῦ Νῶε – of Noe	τοῦ Λάμεχ – of Lamech	37 τοῦ –	Μαθουσάλα of Mathusala	
τοῦ –	Ἑνὼχ of Henoch	τοῦ –	Ἰάρετ of Jaret	τοῦ –	Μαλελεὴλ of Maleleel
τοῦ –	Καϊνὰμ of Cainam	38 τοῦ –	Ἐνὼς of Enos	τοῦ –	Σὴθ of Seth τοῦ –
Ἀδὰμ of Adam	τοῦ –	θεοῦ. of God.			

was the son, so it was thought, of Joseph,

the son of Heli, 24the son of Matthat, the son of Levi, the son of Melki,

the son of Jannai, the son of Joseph, 25the son of Mattathias, the son of Amos,

the son of Nahum, the son of Esli, the son of Naggai, 26the son of Maath,

the son of Mattathias, the son of Semein, the son of Josech, the son of Joda,

27the son of Joanan, the son of Rhesa, the son of Zerubbabel, the son of Shealtiel,

the son of Neri, 28the son of Melki, the son of Addi, the son of Cosam,

the son of Elmadam, the son of Er, 29the son of Joshua, the son of Eliezer,

the son of Jorim, the son of Matthat, the son of Levi, 30the son of Simeon,

the son of Judah, the son of Joseph, the son of Jonam, the son of Eliakim,

31the son of Melea, the son of Menna, the son of Mattatha, the son of Nathan,

the son of David, 32the son of Jesse, the son of Obed, the son of Boaz,

the son of Salmon, [m] the son of Nahshon, 33the son of Amminadab,

the son of Ram, [n] the son of Hezron, the son of Perez, the son of Judah, 34the son of Jacob,

the son of Isaac, the son of Abraham, the son of Terah, the son of Nahor,

35the son of Serug, the son of Reu, the son of Peleg, the son of Eber,

the son of Shelah, 36the son of Cainan, the son of Arphaxad, the son of Shem,

the son of Noah, the son of Lamech, 37the son of Methuselah, the son of Enoch,

the son of Jared, the son of Mahalalel, the son of Kenan, 38the son of Enosh,

the son of Seth, the son of Adam, the son of God.

Chapter 4

The Temptation of Jesus

AND Jesus, full of the Holy Spirit, returned from the Jordan and was led about by the Spirit in the wilderness

2for forty days, being tempted by the devil. And

Greek				
4 Ἰησοῦς And Jesus	δὲ	πλήρης full	πνεύματος of ¹[the] ²Spirit	ἁγίου ¹Holy
ὑπέστρεψεν returned	ἀπὸ from	τοῦ the	Ἰορδάνου, Jordan,	καὶ ἤγετο and was led
ἐν by	τῷ the	πνεύματι Spirit	ἐν τῇ in the	ἐρήμῳ 2 ἡμέρας desert days
τεσσεράκοντα forty	πειραζόμενος being tempted	ὑπὸ by	τοῦ the	διαβόλου. devil.

m32 Some early manuscripts *Sala*
n33 Some manuscripts *Amminadab, the son of Admin, the son of Arni*; other manuscripts vary widely.

He ate nothing during those days; and when they had ended, He became hungry.

3And the devil said to Him, "If You are the Son of God, tell this stone to become bread."

4And Jesus answered him, "It is written, 'MAN SHALL NOT LIVE ON BREAD ALONE.' "

5And he led Him up and showed Him all the kingdoms of the world in a moment of time.

6And the devil said to Him, "I will give You all this domain and its glory; for it has been handed over to me, and I give it to whomever I wish.

7"Therefore if You worship before me, it shall all be Yours."

8And Jesus answered and said to him, "It is written, 'YOU SHALL WORSHIP THE LORD YOUR GOD AND SERVE HIM ONLY.' "

9And he led Him to Jerusalem and had Him stand on the pinnacle of the temple, and said to Him, "If You are the Son of God, throw Yourself down from here;

10for it is written,

'HE WILL GIVE HIS ANGELS CHARGE CONCERNING YOU TO GUARD YOU,'

11 and,

'ON their HANDS THEY WILL BEAR YOU UP, LEST YOU STRIKE YOUR FOOT AGAINST A STONE.' "

12And Jesus answered and said to him, "It is said, 'YOU SHALL NOT *PUT THE LORD YOUR GOD TO THE TEST.' "

13And when the devil had finished every temptation, he departed from Him until an opportune time.

Jesus' Public Ministry

14And Jesus returned to Galilee in the power of the Spirit; and news about Him spread through all the surrounding district.

15And He *began teaching

Καὶ οὐκ ἔφαγεν οὐδὲν ἐν ταῖς ἡμέραις
And he ate not no(any)thing in — days

ἐκείναις, καὶ συντελεσθεισῶν αὐτῶν ἐπεί-
those, and being ended them   he
= when they were ended

νασεν. 3 εἶπεν δὲ αὐτῷ ὁ διάβολος·
hungered.   And said   to him the   devil :

εἰ υἱὸς εἶ τοῦ θεοῦ, εἰπὲ τῷ λίθῳ
If Son thou art — of God, tell — stone

τούτῳ ἵνα γένηται ἄρτος. 4 καὶ ἀπεκρίθη
this that it become a loaf. And made answer

πρὸς αὐτὸν ὁ Ἰησοῦς· γέγραπται ὅτι
to him — Jesus : It has been written[,] —

οὐκ ἐπ' ἄρτῳ μόνῳ ζήσεται ὁ ἄνθρωπος.
Not on bread only shall live — man.

5 Καὶ ἀναγαγὼν αὐτὸν ἔδειξεν αὐτῷ πάσας
And leading up him he showed him all

τὰς βασιλείας τῆς οἰκουμένης ἐν στιγμῇ
the kingdoms of the inhabited earth in a moment

χρόνου. 6 καὶ εἶπεν αὐτῷ ὁ διάβολος·
of time. And said to him the devil :

σοὶ δώσω τὴν ἐξουσίαν ταύτην ἅπασαν καὶ
To thee I will give — authority this all and

τὴν δόξαν αὐτῶν, ὅτι ἐμοὶ παραδέδοται
the glory of them, because to me it has been delivered

καὶ ᾧ ἐὰν θέλω δίδωμι αὐτήν· 7 σὺ οὖν
and to whomever I wish I give it; thou therefore

ἐὰν προσκυνήσῃς ἐνώπιον ἐμοῦ, ἔσται σοῦ
if worship before me, will be of thee

πᾶσα. 8 καὶ ἀποκριθεὶς ὁ Ἰησοῦς εἶπεν
all. And answering — Jesus said

αὐτῷ· γέγραπται· προσκυνήσεις κύριον τὸν
to him : It has been written: Thou shalt worship [the] Lord the

θεόν σου καὶ αὐτῷ μόνῳ λατρεύσεις.
God of thee and him only shalt thou serve.

9 Ἤγαγεν δὲ αὐτὸν εἰς Ἰερουσαλὴμ καὶ
And he led him to Jerusalem and

ἔστησεν ἐπὶ τὸ πτερύγιον τοῦ ἱεροῦ, καὶ
set on the gable of the temple, and

εἶπεν αὐτῷ· εἰ υἱὸς εἶ τοῦ θεοῦ, βάλε
said to him : If Son thou art — of God, throw

σεαυτὸν ἐντεῦθεν κάτω· 10 γέγραπται γὰρ ὅτι
thyself hence down; for it has been written[,] —

τοῖς ἀγγέλοις αὐτοῦ ἐντελεῖται περὶ
The angels of him he will command concerning

σοῦ τοῦ διαφυλάξαι σε, 11 καὶ ὅτι ἐπὶ
thee — to preserve thee, and — on

χειρῶν ἀροῦσίν σε, μήποτε προσκόψῃς
[their] hands they will bear thee, lest thou dash

πρὸς λίθον τὸν πόδα σου. 12 καὶ
against a stone the foot of thee. And

ἀποκριθεὶς εἶπεν αὐτῷ ὁ Ἰησοῦς ὅτι
answering said to him — Jesus[,] —

εἴρηται· οὐκ ἐκπειράσεις κύριον τὸν
It has been said : Thou shalt not overtempt [the] Lord the

θεόν σου. 13 Καὶ συντελέσας πάντα πειρασμὸν
God of thee. And having finished every temptation

ὁ διάβολος ἀπέστη ἀπ' αὐτοῦ ἄχρι καιροῦ.
the devil went away from him until a season.

14 Καὶ ὑπέστρεψεν ὁ Ἰησοῦς ἐν τῇ
And returned — Jesus in the

δυνάμει τοῦ πνεύματος εἰς τὴν Γαλιλαίαν·
power of the Spirit to — Galilee;

καὶ φήμη ἐξῆλθεν καθ' ὅλης τῆς περιχώρου
and a rumour went forth throughout all the neighbourhood

περὶ αὐτοῦ. 15 καὶ αὐτὸς ἐδίδασκεν ἐν
concerning him. And he taught in

Chapter 4

The Temptation of Jesus

JESUS, full of the Holy Spirit, returned from the Jordan and was led by the Spirit in the desert, 2where for forty days he was tempted by the devil. He ate nothing during those days, and at the end of them he was hungry.

3The devil said to him, "If you are the Son of God, tell this stone to become bread."

4Jesus answered, "It is written: 'Man does not live on bread alone.'°"

5The devil led him up to a high place and showed him in an instant all the kingdoms of the world. 6And he said to him, "I will give you all their authority and splendor, for it has been given to me, and I can give it to anyone I want to. 7So if you worship me, it will all be yours."

8Jesus answered, "It is written: 'Worship the Lord your God and serve him only.'ᵖ"

9The devil led him to Jerusalem and had him stand on the highest point of the temple. "If you are the Son of God," he said, "throw yourself down from here.
10For it is written:

" 'He will command his angels concerning you
to guard you carefully;

11they will lift you up in their hands,
so that you will not strike your foot
against a stone.'ᵠ"

12Jesus answered, "It says: 'Do not put the Lord your God to the test.'ʳ"

13When the devil had finished all this tempting, he left him until an opportune time.

Jesus Rejected at Nazareth

14Jesus returned to Galilee in the power of the Spirit, and news about him spread through the whole countryside. 15He taught in

---

°4 Deut. 8:3
ᵖ8 Deut. 6:13
ᵠ11 Psalm 91:11,12
ʳ12 Deut. 6:16

1Or, tempt . . . God

in their synagogues and was praised by all.

16And He came to Nazareth, where He had been brought up; and, as was His custom, He entered the synagogue on the Sabbath, and stood up to read.

17And the book of the prophet Isaiah was handed to Him. And He opened the book, and found the place where it was written,

18"THE SPIRIT OF THE LORD IS UPON ME, BECAUSE HE ANOINTED ME TO PREACH THE GOSPEL TO THE POOR. HE HAS SENT ME TO PROCLAIM RELEASE TO THE CAPTIVES, AND RECOVERY OF SIGHT TO THE BLIND, TO SET FREE THOSE WHO ARE DOWNTRODDEN,

19 TO PROCLAIM THE FAVORABLE YEAR OF THE LORD."

20And He closed the book, and gave it back to the attendant, and sat down; and the eyes of all in the synagogue were fixed upon Him.

21And He began to say to them, "Today this Scripture has been fulfilled in your hearing."

22And all were speaking well of Him, and wondering at the gracious words which were falling f- ...n His lips; and they were saying, "Is this not Joseph's son?"

23And He said to them, "No doubt you will quote this proverb to Me, 'Physician, heal yourself! Whatever we heard was done at Capernaum, do here in your home town as well.'"

24And He said, "Truly I say to you, no prophet is welcome in his home town.

25"But I say to you in truth, there were many widows in Israel in the days of Elijah, when the sky was shut up for three years and

ταῖς συναγωγαῖς αὐτῶν, δοξαζόμενος ὑπὸ
the synagogues of them, being glorified by
πάντων.
all.

16 Καὶ ἦλθεν εἰς Ναζαρά, οὗ ἦν
And he came to Nazareth, where he was
τεθραμμένος, καὶ εἰσῆλθεν κατὰ τὸ εἰωθὸς
having been and entered accord- the custom
brought up, ing to =his custom
αὐτῷ ἐν τῇ ἡμέρᾳ τῶν σαββάτων εἰς τὴν
to himᵉ on the day of the sabbaths into the
συναγωγήν, καὶ ἀνέστη ἀναγνῶναι. 17 καὶ
synagogue, and stood up to read. And
ἐπεδόθη αὐτῷ βιβλίον τοῦ προφήτου
was handed to him a roll of the prophet
Ἡσαΐου, καὶ ἀνοίξας τὸ βιβλίον εὗρεν
Esaias, and having opened the roll he found
[τὸν] τόπον οὗ ἦν γεγραμμένον· 18 πνεῦμα
the place where it was having been written: [The] Spirit
κυρίου ἐπ᾽ ἐμέ, οὗ εἵνεκεν ἔχρισέν με
of [the] Lord [is] upon me, wherefore he anointed me
εὐαγγελίσασθαι πτωχοῖς, ἀπέσταλκέν με
to evangelize [the] poor, he has sent me
κηρῦξαι αἰχμαλώτοις ἄφεσιν καὶ τυφλοῖς
to proclaim to captives release and to blind [ones]
ἀνάβλεψιν, ἀποστεῖλαι τεθραυσμένους ἐν
sight, to send away having been crushed [ones] in
ἀφέσει, 19 κηρῦξαι ἐνιαυτὸν κυρίου δεκτόν.
release, to proclaim a year of [the] Lord acceptable.
20 καὶ πτύξας τὸ βιβλίον ἀποδοὺς τῷ
And having closed the roll returning [it] to the
ὑπηρέτῃ ἐκάθισεν· καὶ πάντων οἱ ὀφθαλμοὶ
attendant he sat; and of all the eyes
ἐν τῇ συναγωγῇ ἦσαν ἀτενίζοντες αὐτῷ.
in the synagogue were gazing at him.
21 ἤρξατο δὲ λέγειν πρὸς αὐτοὺς ὅτι
And he began to say to them[,] –
σήμερον πεπλήρωται ἡ γραφὴ αὕτη ἐν
To-day has been fulfilled – scripture this in
τοῖς ὠσὶν ὑμῶν. 22 καὶ πάντες ἐμαρτύρουν
the ears of you. And all bore witness
αὐτῷ καὶ ἐθαύμαζον ἐπὶ τοῖς λόγοις τῆς
to him and marvelled at the words –
χάριτος τοῖς ἐκπορευομένοις ἐκ τοῦ στόματος
of grace – proceeding out of the mouth
αὐτοῦ, καὶ ἔλεγον· οὐχὶ υἱός ἐστιν Ἰωσὴφ
of him, and they said: ²not ⁴son ¹Is ⁵of Joseph
οὗτος; 23 καὶ εἶπεν πρὸς αὐτούς· πάντως
³this man? And he said to them: To be sure
ἐρεῖτέ μοι τὴν παραβολὴν ταύτην· ἰατρέ,
ye will say to me the parable this: Physician,
θεράπευσον σεαυτόν· ὅσα ἠκούσαμεν γεν-
heal thyself; what things we heard hap-
όμενα εἰς τὴν Καφαρναούμ, ποίησον καὶ
pening in – Capernaum, do also
ὧδε ἐν τῇ πατρίδι σου. 24 εἶπεν δέ·
here in the native place of thee. And he said:
ἀμὴν λέγω ὑμῖν ὅτι οὐδεὶς προφήτης
Truly I tell you that no prophet
δεκτός ἐστιν ἐν τῇ πατρίδι αὐτοῦ. 25 ἐπ᾽
acceptable is in the native place of him. ²on(in)
ἀληθείας δὲ λέγω ὑμῖν, πολλαὶ χῆραι ἦσαν
³truth ¹But I tell you, many widows were
ἐν ταῖς ἡμέραις Ἠλίου ἐν τῷ Ἰσραήλ,
in the days of Elias in – Israel,
ὅτε ἐκλείσθη ὁ οὐρανὸς ἐπὶ ἔτη τρία καὶ
when was shut up the heaven over years three and

their synagogues, and everyone praised him.

16He went to Nazareth, where he had been brought up, and on the Sabbath day he went into the synagogue, as was his custom. And he stood up to read. 17The scroll of the prophet Isaiah was handed to him. Unrolling it, he found the place where it is written:

18"The Spirit of the Lord is on me, because he has anointed me to preach good news to the poor. He has sent me to proclaim freedom for the prisoners and recovery of sight for the blind, to release the oppressed, 19 to proclaim the year of the Lord's favor.'"ˢ

20Then he rolled up the scroll, gave it back to the attendant and sat down. The eyes of everyone in the synagogue were fastened on him, 21and he began by saying to them, "Today this scripture is fulfilled in your hearing."

22All spoke well of him and were amazed at the gracious words that came from his lips. "Isn't this Joseph's son?" they asked.

23Jesus said to them, "Surely you will quote this proverb to me: 'Physician, heal yourself! Do here in your hometown what we have heard that you did in Capernaum.'"

24"I tell you the truth," he continued, "no prophet is accepted in his hometown. 25I assure you that there were many widows in Israel in Elijah's time, when the sky was shut for three and a half years and

ˢ19 Isaiah 61:1,2

Left column (English)

six months, when a great famine came over all the land;

26and yet Elijah was sent to none of them, but only to Zarephath, *in the land* of Sidon, to a woman who was a widow.

27"And there were many lepers in Israel in the time of Elisha the prophet; and none of them was cleansed, but only Naaman the Syrian."

28And all in the synagogue were filled with rage as they heard these things;

29and they rose up and cast Him out of the city, and led Him to the brow of the hill on which their city had been built, in order to throw Him down the cliff.

30But passing through their midst, He went His way.

31And He came down to Capernaum, a city of Galilee. And He was teaching them on the Sabbath;

32and they were amazed at His teaching, for His message was with authority.

33And there was a man in the synagogue possessed by the spirit of an unclean demon, and he cried out with a loud voice,

34"Ha! What do we have to do with You, Jesus of Nazareth? Have You come to destroy us? I know who You are—the Holy One of God!"

35And Jesus rebuked him, saying, "Be quiet and come out of him!" And when the demon had thrown Him down in *their* midst, he came out of him without doing him any harm.

36And amazement came upon them all, and they *began* discussing with one another saying, "What is this message? For with authority and power He commands the unclean spirits, and they come out."

37And the report about Him was getting out into

Middle column (Greek interlinear)

μῆνας ἕξ, ὡς ἐγένετο λιμὸς μέγας ἐπὶ
months six, when came famine a great over

πᾶσαν τὴν γῆν, 26 καὶ πρὸς οὐδεμίαν
all the land, and to not one

αὐτῶν ἐπέμφθη Ἡλίας εἰ μὴ εἰς Σάρεπτα
of them was sent Elias except to Sarepta

τῆς Σιδωνίας πρὸς γυναῖκα χήραν. 27 καὶ
- of Sidon to a woman a widow. And

πολλοὶ λεπροὶ ἦσαν ἐν τῷ Ἰσραὴλ ἐπὶ
many lepers were in - Israel during

Ἐλισαίου τοῦ προφήτου, καὶ οὐδεὶς αὐτῶν
Elisæus the prophet, and not one of them

ἐκαθαρίσθη εἰ μὴ Ναιμὰν ὁ Σύρος.
was cleansed except Naaman the Syrian.

28 καὶ ἐπλήσθησαν πάντες θυμοῦ ἐν τῇ
And ²were filled ¹all of(with) anger in the

συναγωγῇ ἀκούοντες ταῦτα, 29 καὶ ἀναστάντες
synagogue hearing these things, and rising up

ἐξέβαλον αὐτὸν ἔξω τῆς πόλεως, καὶ
they cast *out* him outside the city, and

ἤγαγον αὐτὸν ἕως ὀφρύος τοῦ ὄρους ἐφ'
led him to a brow of the hill on

οὗ ἡ πόλις ᾠκοδόμητο αὐτῶν, ὥστε
which the city was built of them, so as

κατακρημνίσαι αὐτόν· 30 αὐτὸς δὲ διελθὼν
to throw down him; but he passing *through*

διὰ μέσου αὐτῶν ἐπορεύετο.
through [the] midst of them went.

31 Καὶ κατῆλθεν εἰς Καφαρναοὺμ πόλιν
And he went down to Capernaum a city

τῆς Γαλιλαίας. καὶ ἦν διδάσκων αὐτοὺς
- of Galilee. And he was teaching them

ἐν τοῖς σάββασιν· 32 καὶ ἐξεπλήσσοντο
on the sabbaths; and they were astounded

ἐπὶ τῇ διδαχῇ αὐτοῦ, ὅτι ἐν ἐξουσίᾳ
at the teaching of him, because with authority

ἦν ὁ λόγος αὐτοῦ. 33 καὶ ἐν τῇ συναγωγῇ
was the word of him. And in the synagogue

ἦν ἄνθρωπος ἔχων πνεῦμα δαιμονίου
there was a man having a spirit ²demon

ἀκαθάρτου, καὶ ἀνέκραξεν φωνῇ μεγάλῃ·
¹of an unclean, and he shouted voice with a great:

34 ἔα, τί ἡμῖν καὶ σοί, Ἰησοῦ Ναζαρηνέ;
Ah, what to us and to thee, Jesus Nazarene?

ἦλθες ἀπολέσαι ἡμᾶς; οἶδά σε τίς εἶ,
Camest thou to destroy us? I know thee who thou art,

ὁ ἅγιος τοῦ θεοῦ. 35 καὶ ἐπετίμησεν αὐτῷ
the holy one - of God. And rebuked him

ὁ Ἰησοῦς λέγων· φιμώθητι καὶ ἔξελθε
- Jesus saying: Be muzzled and come out

ἀπ' αὐτοῦ. καὶ ῥῖψαν αὐτὸν τὸ δαιμόνιον
from him. And ³throwing ⁴him ¹the ²demon

εἰς τὸ μέσον ἐξῆλθεν ἀπ' αὐτοῦ μηδὲν
in the midst came out from him nothing

βλάψαν αὐτόν. 36 καὶ ἐγένετο θάμβος
injuring him. And came astonishment

ἐπὶ πάντας, καὶ συνελάλουν πρὸς ἀλλήλους
on all, and they spoke to one another

λέγοντες· τίς ὁ λόγος οὗτος, ὅτι ἐν
saying: What [is] - word this, because with

ἐξουσίᾳ καὶ δυνάμει ἐπιτάσσει τοῖς
authority and power he commands the

ἀκαθάρτοις πνεύμασιν καὶ ἐξέρχονται; 37 καὶ
unclean spirits and they come out? And

ἐξεπορεύετο ἦχος περὶ αὐτοῦ εἰς πάντα
went forth a rumour concerning him into every

Right column (English)

there was a severe famine throughout the land. 26Yet Elijah was not sent to any of them, but to a widow in Zarephath in the region of Sidon. 27And there were many in Israel with leprosy[f] in the time of Elisha the prophet, yet not one of them was cleansed—only Naaman the Syrian."

28All the people in the synagogue were furious when they heard this. 29They got up, drove him out of the town, and took him to the brow of the hill on which the town was built, in order to throw him down the cliff. 30But he walked right through the crowd and went on his way.

Jesus Drives Out an Evil Spirit

31Then he went down to Capernaum, a town in Galilee, and on the Sabbath began to teach the people. 32They were amazed at his teaching, because his message had authority.

33In the synagogue there was a man possessed by a demon, an evil[u] spirit. He cried out at the top of his voice, 34"Ha! What do you want with us, Jesus of Nazareth? Have you come to destroy us? I know who you are—the Holy One of God!"

35"Be quiet!" Jesus said sternly. "Come out of him!" Then the demon threw the man down before them all and came out without injuring him.

36All the people were amazed and said to each other, "What is this teaching? With authority and power he gives orders to evil spirits and they come out!" 37And the news about

ᶠ27 The Greek word was used for various diseases affecting the skin—not necessarily leprosy.
ᵘ33 Greek *unclean*; also in verse 36

every locality in the surrounding district.

Many Are Healed

38And He arose and *left*
the synagogue, and entered
Simon's home. Now Si-
mon's mother-in-law was
suffering from a high fever;
and they made request of
Him on her behalf.

39And standing over her,
He rebuked the fever, and
it left her; and she immediately arose and waited on
them.

40And while the sun was
setting, all who had any
sick with various diseases
brought them to Him; and
laying His hands on every
one of them, He was heal-
ing them.

41And demons also were
coming out of many, crying
out and saying, "You are
the Son of God!" And
rebuking them, He would
not allow them to speak,
because they knew Him to
be the Christ.

42And when day came,
He departed and went to a
lonely place; and the multitudes were searching for
Him, and came to Him, and
tried to keep Him from going away from them.

43But He said to them, "I
must preach the kingdom
of God to the other cities
also, for I was sent for this
purpose."

44And He kept on preaching in the synagogues of
ᵐJudea.

τόπον   τῆς   περιχώρου.   **38** Ἀναστὰς   δὲ
place   of the   neighbourhood.   And rising up

ἀπὸ   τῆς   συναγωγῆς   εἰσῆλθεν   εἰς   τὴν
from   the   synagogue   he entered   into   the

οἰκίαν   Σίμωνος.   πενθερὰ   δὲ   τοῦ   Σίμωνος
house   of Simon.   And [the] mother-in-law – of Simon

ἦν   συνεχομένη   πυρετῷ   μεγάλῳ,   καὶ
was   being seized   fever   with a great,   and

ἠρώτησαν   αὐτὸν   περὶ   αὐτῆς.   **39** καὶ
they ask   ₚhim   about   her.   And

ἐπιστὰς   ἐπάνω   αὐτῆς   ἐπετίμησεν   τῷ   πυρετῷ,
standing   over   her   he rebuked   the   fever,

καὶ   ἀφῆκεν   αὐτήν·   παραχρῆμα   δὲ   ἀναστᾶσα
and   it left   her;   and at once   rising up

διηκόνει   αὐτοῖς.   **40** Δύνοντος   δὲ   τοῦ
she served   them.   And setting   the
                              = as the sun was setting

ἡλίου   ἅπαντες   ὅσοι   εἶχον   ἀσθενοῦντας
sunᵃ   all   as many as   had   ailing [ones]

νόσοις   ποικίλαις   ἤγαγον   αὐτοὺς   πρὸς   αὐτόν·
diseases   with various   brought   them   to   him;

ὁ   δὲ   ἑνὶ   ἑκάστῳ   αὐτῶν   τὰς   χεῖρας
and he   ⁵one   ⁶on each   ⁷of them   ¹the(his)   ³hands

ἐπιτιθεὶς   ἐθεράπευεν   αὐτούς.   **41** ἐξήρχετο
¹putting *on*   healed   them.   came out

δὲ   καὶ   δαιμόνια   ἀπὸ   πολλῶν,   κραυγάζοντα
And also   demons   from   many,   crying out

καὶ   λέγοντα   ὅτι   σὺ   εἶ   ὁ   υἱὸς   τοῦ   θεοῦ.
and   saying[,]   –   Thou   art   the   Son   –   of God.

καὶ   ἐπιτιμῶν   οὐκ   εἴα   αὐτὰ   λαλεῖν,   ὅτι
And   rebuking   he allowed not   them   to speak,   because

ᾔδεισαν   τὸν   χριστὸν   αὐτὸν   εἶναι.   **42** Γενομένης
they knew ³the   ⁴Christ   ¹him   ²to be.   coming
                                                       = And when

δὲ   ἡμέρας   ἐξελθὼν   ἐπορεύθη   εἰς   ἔρημον
And   dayᵃ   going forth   he went   to   a desert
day came

τόπον·   καὶ   οἱ   ὄχλοι   ἐπεζήτουν   αὐτόν,   καὶ
place;   and   the   crowds   sought   him,   and

ἦλθον   ἕως   αὐτοῦ,   καὶ   κατεῖχον   αὐτὸν
₂came   up to   him,   and   detained   him

τοῦ   μὴ   πορεύεσθαι   ἀπ’   αὐτῶν.   **43** ὁ   δὲ
–   not   to goᵈ   from   them.   And he
= so that he should not go

εἶπεν   πρὸς   αὐτοὺς   ὅτι   καὶ   ταῖς   ἑτέραις
said   to   them[,]   –   Also to the   other

πόλεσιν   εὐαγγελίσασθαί   με   δεῖ   τὴν
cities   ³to preach   ²me   ¹it behoves   the

βασιλείαν   τοῦ   θεοῦ,   ὅτι   ἐπὶ   τοῦτο   ἀπεστάλην.
kingdom   – of God, because on   this   I was sent.

44 καὶ   ἦν   κηρύσσων   εἰς   τὰς   συναγωγὰς
And   he was   proclaiming   in   the   synagogues

τῆς   Ἰουδαίας.
–   of Judæa.

---

him spread throughout the
surrounding area.

Jesus Heals Many

38Jesus left the synagogue
and went to the home of Simon. Now Simon's moth-
er-in-law was suffering
from a high fever, and they
asked Jesus to help her.
39So he bent over her and
rebuked the fever, and it
left her. She got up at once
and began to wait on them.

40When the sun was setting, the people brought to
Jesus all who had various
kinds of sickness, and laying his hands on each one,
he healed them. **41**Moreover, demons came out of
many people, shouting,
"You are the Son of God!"
But he rebuked them and
would not allow them to
speak, because they knew
he was the Christ.

42At daybreak Jesus went
out to a solitary place. The
people were looking for
him and when they came to
where he was, they tried to
keep him from leaving
them. **43**But he said, "I
must preach the good news
of the kingdom of God to
the other towns also, be-
cause that is why I was
sent." **44**And he kept on
preaching in the syna-
gogues of Judea.ʷ

Chapter 5

The First Disciples

NOW it came about that
while the multitude
were pressing around Him
and listening to the word of
God, He was standing by
the lake of Gennesaret;
²and He saw two boats
lying at the edge of the lake;
but the fishermen had got-
ten out of them, and were
washing their nets.

ᵐI.e., the country of the Jews
(including Galilee); some mss. read
Galilee

---

5 Ἐγένετο   δὲ   ἐν   τῷ   τὸν   ὄχλον   ἐπικεῖσθαι
Now it came to pass   in   the   the   crowd   to press upon
= as the crowd pressed upon him and heard

αὐτῷ   καὶ   ἀκούειν   τὸν   λόγον   τοῦ   θεοῦ,
him   and   to hearᵇᵉ   the   word   –   of God,

καὶ   αὐτὸς   ἦν   ἑστὼς   παρὰ   τὴν   λίμνην
and   he   was   standing   by   the   lake

Γεννησαρέτ,   **2** καὶ   εἶδεν   δύο   πλοιάρια
Gennesaret,   and   saw   two   boats

ἑστῶτα   παρὰ   τὴν   λίμνην·   οἱ   δὲ   ἁλεεῖς
standing   by   the   lake;   but the   fishermen

ἀπ’   αὐτῶν   ἀποβάντες   ἔπλυνον   τὰ   δίκτυα.
from   them   having gone away   were washing   the   nets.

Chapter 5

*The Calling of the First
Disciples*

ONE day as Jesus was
standing by the Lake
of Gennesaret,ˣ with the
people crowding around
him and listening to the
word of God, ²he saw at the
water's edge two boats, left
there by the fishermen,
who were washing their

ᵛ*41 Or Messiah*
ʷ*44 Or the land of the Jews; some
manuscripts Galilee*
ˣ*1 That is, Sea of Galilee*

3And He got into one of the boats, which was Simon's, and asked him to put out a little way from the land. And He sat down and *began* teaching the multitudes from the boat.

4And when He had finished speaking, He said to Simon, "Put out into the deep water and let down your nets for a catch."

5And Simon answered and said, "Master, we worked hard all night and caught nothing, but at Your bidding I will let down the nets."

6And when they had done this, they enclosed a great quantity of fish; and their nets *began* to break;

7and they signaled to their partners in the other boat, for them to come and help them. And they came, and filled both of the boats, so that they began to sink.

8But when Simon Peter saw *that*, he fell down at Jesus' feet, saying, "Depart from me, for I am a sinful man, O Lord!"

9For amazement had seized him and all his companions because of the catch of fish which they had taken;

10and so also James and John, sons of Zebedee, who were partners with Simon. And Jesus said to Simon, "Do not fear, from now on you will be catching men."

11And when they had brought their boats to land, they left everything and followed Him.

The Leper and the Paralytic

12And it came about that while He was in one of the cities, behold, *there was* a man full of leprosy; and when he saw Jesus, he fell on his face and implored Him, saying, "Lord, if You

---

3 ἐμβὰς δὲ εἰς ἓν τῶν πλοίων, ὃ ἦν
And embarking in one of the boats, which was
Σίμωνος, ἠρώτησεν αὐτὸν ἀπὸ τῆς γῆς
of Simon, he asked him from the land
ἐπαναγαγεῖν ὀλίγον· καθίσας δὲ ἐκ τοῦ
to put out a little; and sitting ⁴out of ⁵the
πλοίου ἐδίδασκεν τοὺς ὄχλους. 4 ὡς δὲ
⁶boat ¹he taught ²the ³crowds. And when
ἐπαύσατο λαλῶν, εἶπεν πρὸς τὸν Σίμωνα·
he ceased speaking, he said to - Simon:
ἐπανάγαγε εἰς τὸ βάθος, καὶ χαλάσατε
Put out into the deep, and let down
τὰ δίκτυα ὑμῶν εἰς ἄγραν. 5 καὶ
the nets of you for a draught. And
ἀποκριθεὶς Σίμων εἶπεν· ἐπιστάτα, δι'
answering Simon said: Master, through
ὅλης νυκτὸς κοπιάσαντες οὐδὲν ἐλάβομεν·
[the] whole night labouring nothing we took;
ἐπὶ δὲ τῷ ῥήματί σου χαλάσω τὰ δίκτυα.
but at the word of thee I will let down the nets.
6 καὶ τοῦτο ποιήσαντες συνέκλεισαν πλῆθος
And this doing they enclosed multitude
ἰχθύων πολύ· διερρήσσετο δὲ τὰ δίκτυα
of fishes a much; and were being torn the nets
αὐτῶν. 7 καὶ κατένευσαν τοῖς μετόχοις
of them. And they nodded to the(ir) partners
ἐν τῷ ἑτέρῳ πλοίῳ τοῦ ἐλθόντας
in the other boat - coming
= that they should come
συλλαβέσθαι αὐτοῖς· καὶ ἦλθαν, καὶ ἔπλησαν
to help[d] them; and they came, and filled
ἀμφότερα τὰ πλοῖα ὥστε βυθίζεσθαι αὐτά.
both the boats so as to be sinking them.[b]
= so that they were sinking.
8 ἰδὼν δὲ Σίμων Πέτρος προσέπεσεν τοῖς
And seeing Simon Peter fell at the
γόνασιν Ἰησοῦ λέγων· ἔξελθε ἀπ' ἐμοῦ,
knees of Jesus saying: Depart from me,
ὅτι ἀνὴρ ἁμαρτωλός εἰμι, κύριε. 9 θάμβος
because man a sinful I am, Lord. astonishment
γὰρ περιέσχεν αὐτὸν καὶ πάντας τοὺς
For seized him and all the [ones]
σὺν αὐτῷ ἐπὶ τῇ ἄγρᾳ τῶν ἰχθύων ᾗ
with him at the draught of the fishes which
συνέλαβον, 10 ὁμοίως δὲ καὶ Ἰάκωβον καὶ
they took, and likewise both James and
Ἰωάννην υἱοὺς Ζεβεδαίου, οἳ ἦσαν κοινωνοὶ
John sons of Zebedee, who were sharers
τῷ Σίμωνι. καὶ εἶπεν πρὸς τὸν Σίμωνα
- with Simon. And said to - Simon
ὁ Ἰησοῦς· μὴ φοβοῦ· ἀπὸ τοῦ νῦν
- Jesus: Fear thou not; from - now
ἀνθρώπους ἔσῃ ζωγρῶν. 11 καὶ καταγαγόντες
men thou wilt be taking alive. And bringing down
τὰ πλοῖα ἐπὶ τὴν γῆν, ἀφέντες πάντα
the boats onto the land, leaving all things
ἠκολούθησαν αὐτῷ.
they followed him.
12 Καὶ ἐγένετο ἐν τῷ εἶναι αὐτὸν ἐν
And it came to pass in the to be him[be] in
= as he was
μιᾷ τῶν πόλεων καὶ ἰδοὺ ἀνὴρ πλήρης
one of the cities and behold[,] a man full
λέπρας· ἰδὼν δὲ τὸν Ἰησοῦν, πεσὼν ἐπὶ
of leprosy; and seeing — Jesus, falling on
πρόσωπον ἐδεήθη αὐτοῦ λέγων· κύριε,
[his] face he begged him saying: Lord,

---

nets. 3He got into one of the boats, the one belonging to Simon, and asked him to put out a little from shore. Then he sat down and taught the people from the boat.

4When he had finished speaking, he said to Simon, "Put out into deep water, and let down the nets for a catch."

5Simon answered, "Master, we've worked hard all night and haven't caught anything. But because you say so, I will let down the nets."

6When they had done so, they caught such a large number of fish that their nets began to break. 7So they signaled their partners in the other boat to come and help them, and they came and filled both boats so full that they began to sink.

8When Simon Peter saw this, he fell at Jesus' knees and said, "Go away from me, Lord; I am a sinful man!" 9For he and all his companions were astonished at the catch of fish they had taken, 10and so were James and John, the sons of Zebedee, Simon's partners.

Then Jesus said to Simon, "Don't be afraid; from now on you will catch men." 11So they pulled their boats up on shore, left everything and followed him.

The Man With Leprosy

12While Jesus was in one of the towns, a man came along who was covered with leprosy.[z] When he saw Jesus, he fell with his face to the ground and begged him, "Lord, if you

---

*y*4 The Greek verb is plural.
*z*12 The Greek word was used for various diseases affecting the skin—not necessarily leprosy.

are willing, You can make me clean.''

13And He stretched out His hand, and touched him, saying, ''I am willing; be cleansed.'' And immediately the leprosy left him.

14And He ordered him to tell no one, ''But go and show yourself to the priest, and make an offering for your cleansing, just as Moses commanded, for a testimony to them.''

15But the news about Him was spreading even farther, and great multitudes were gathering to hear *Him* and to be healed of their sicknesses.

16But He Himself would *often* slip away to the wilderness and pray.

17And it came about one day that He was teaching; and there were *some* Pharisees and teachers of the law sitting *there*, who had come from every village of Galilee and Judea and *from* Jerusalem; and the power of the Lord was *present* for Him to perform healing.

18And behold, *some* men *were* carrying on a bed a man who was paralyzed; and they were trying to bring him in, and to set him down in front of Him.

19And not finding any *way* to bring him in because of the crowd, they went up on the roof and let him down through the tiles with his stretcher, right in the center, in front of Jesus.

20And seeing their faith, He said, ''Friend, your sins are forgiven you.''

21And the scribes and the Pharisees began to reason, saying, ''Who is this *man* who speaks blasphemies? Who can forgive sins, but God alone?''

22But Jesus, aware of

ἐὰν θέλῃς, δύνασαί με καθαρίσαι. 13 καὶ
if thou wilt, thou canst me to cleanse. And

ἐκτείνας τὴν χεῖρα ἥψατο αὐτοῦ λέγων·
stretching out the(his) hand he touched him saying :

θέλω, καθαρίσθητι· καὶ εὐθέως ἡ λέπρα
I am willing, be thou cleansed; and immediately the leprosy

ἀπῆλθεν ἀπ᾽ αὐτοῦ. 14 καὶ αὐτὸς παρήγγειλεν
departed from him. And he charged

αὐτῷ μηδενὶ εἰπεῖν, ἀλλὰ ἀπελθὼν δεῖξον
him no one to tell, but going away show

σεαυτὸν τῷ ἱερεῖ, καὶ προσένεγκε περὶ
thyself to the priest, and offer concerning

τοῦ καθαρισμοῦ σου καθὼς προσέταξεν
the cleansing of thee as commanded

Μωϋσῆς, εἰς μαρτύριον αὐτοῖς. 15 διήρχετο
Moses, for a testimony to them. went

δὲ μᾶλλον ὁ λόγος περὶ αὐτοῦ, καὶ
But rather the word concerning him, and

συνήρχοντο ὄχλοι πολλοὶ ἀκούειν καὶ
³accompanied ²crowds ¹many to hear and

θεραπεύεσθαι ἀπὸ τῶν ἀσθενειῶν αὐτῶν·
to be healed from the infirmities of them;

16 αὐτὸς δὲ ἦν ὑποχωρῶν ἐν ταῖς ἐρήμοις
but he was withdrawing in the deserts

καὶ προσευχόμενος.
and praying.

17 Καὶ ἐγένετο ἐν μιᾷ τῶν ἡμερῶν καὶ
And it came to pass on one of the days *and*

αὐτὸς ἦν διδάσκων, καὶ ἦσαν καθήμενοι
he was teaching, and were sitting

Φαρισαῖοι καὶ νομοδιδάσκαλοι οἳ ἦσαν
Pharisees and law-teachers who were

ἐληλυθότες ἐκ πάσης κώμης τῆς Γαλιλαίας
having come out of every village - of Galilee

καὶ Ἰουδαίας καὶ Ἰερουσαλήμ· καὶ δύναμις
and Judaea and Jerusalem; and [the] power

κυρίου ἦν εἰς τὸ ἰᾶσθαι αὐτόν. 18 καὶ
of [the] Lord was ¹in - ³to cure ²him. And

ἰδοὺ ἄνδρες φέροντες ἐπὶ κλίνης ἄνθρωπον
behold[,] men bearing on a couch a man

ὃς ἦν παραλελυμένος, καὶ ἐζήτουν αὐτὸν
who was *having been* paralysed, and they sought ²him

εἰσενεγκεῖν καὶ θεῖναι [αὐτὸν] ἐνώπιον
¹to carry in and to lay him before

αὐτοῦ. 19 καὶ μὴ εὑρόντες ποίας εἰσ-
him. And not finding how† they

ενέγκωσιν αὐτὸν διὰ τὸν ὄχλον, ἀναβάντες
might carry in him because of the crowd, going up

ἐπὶ τὸ δῶμα διὰ τῶν κεράμων καθῆκαν
onto the roof through the tiles they let down

αὐτὸν σὺν τῷ κλινιδίῳ εἰς τὸ μέσον
him with the couch into the midst

ἔμπροσθεν τοῦ Ἰησοῦ. 20 καὶ ἰδὼν τὴν
in front of - Jesus. And seeing the

πίστιν αὐτῶν εἶπεν· ἄνθρωπε, ἀφέωνταί
faith of them he said : Man, have been forgiven

σοι αἱ ἁμαρτίαι σου. 21 καὶ ἤρξαντο
thee the sins of thee. And began

διαλογίζεσθαι οἱ γραμματεῖς καὶ οἱ Φαρισαῖοι
to reason the scribes and the Pharisees

λέγοντες· τίς ἐστιν οὗτος ὃς λαλεῖ
saying : Who is this man who speaks

βλασφημίας; τίς δύναται ἁμαρτίας ἀφεῖναι
blasphemies? Who can sins to forgive

εἰ μὴ μόνος ὁ θεός; 22 ἐπιγνοὺς δὲ ὁ
except only - God? But knowing -

are willing, you can make me clean.''

13Jesus reached out his hand and touched the man. ''I am willing,'' he said. ''Be clean!'' And immediately the leprosy left him.

14Then Jesus ordered him, ''Don't tell anyone, but go, show yourself to the priest and offer the sacrifices that Moses commanded for your cleansing, as a testimony to them.''

15Yet the news about him spread all the more, so that crowds of people came to hear him and to be healed of their sicknesses. 16But Jesus often withdrew to lonely places and prayed.

Jesus Heals a Paralytic

17One day as he was teaching, Pharisees and teachers of the law, who had come from every village of Galilee and from Judea and Jerusalem, were sitting there. And the power of the Lord was present for him to heal the sick. 18Some men came carrying a paralytic on a mat and tried to take him into the house to lay him before Jesus. 19When they could not find a way to do this because of the crowd, they went up on the roof and lowered him on his mat through the tiles into the middle of the crowd, right in front of Jesus.

20When Jesus saw their faith, he said, ''Friend, your sins are forgiven.''

21The Pharisees and the teachers of the law began thinking to themselves, ''Who is this fellow who speaks blasphemy? Who can forgive sins but God alone?''

22Jesus knew what they

their reasonings, answered and said to them, "Why are you reasoning in your hearts?
23"Which is easier, to say, 'Your sins have been forgiven you,' or to say, 'Rise and walk'?
24"But in order that you may know that the Son of Man has authority on earth to forgive sins,"—He said to the paralytic—"I say to you, rise, and take up your stretcher and go home."
25And at once he rose up before them, and took up what he had been lying on, and went home, glorifying God.
26And they were all seized with astonishment and began glorifying God; and they were filled with fear, saying, "We have seen remarkable things to-day."

Call of Levi (Matthew)

27And after that He went out, and noticed a ⁿtax-gatherer named Levi, sitting in the tax office, and He said to him, "Follow Me."
28And he left everything behind, and rose and began to follow Him.
29And Levi gave 'a big reception for Him in his house; and there was a great crowd of tax-gatherers and other *people* who were reclining *at the table* with them.
30And the Pharisees and their scribes *began* grumbling at His disciples, saying, "Why do you eat and drink with the tax-gatherers and sinners?"
31And Jesus answered and said to them, "*It is* not those who are well who need a physician, but those who are sick.
32"I have not come to call the righteous but sinners to repentance."
33And they said to Him, "The disciples of John often fast and offer prayers;

Ἰησοῦς τοὺς διαλογισμοὺς αὐτῶν, ἀποκριθεὶς
Jesus the reasonings of them, answering
εἶπεν πρὸς αὐτούς· τί διαλογίζεσθε ἐν
said to them : Why reason ye in
ταῖς καρδίαις ὑμῶν; 23 τί ἐστιν εὐκοπώτερον,
the hearts of you? What is easier,
εἰπεῖν· ἀφέωνταί σοι αἱ ἁμαρτίαι σου, ἢ
to say : Have been forgiven thee the sins of thee, or
εἰπεῖν· ἔγειρε καὶ περιπάτει; 24 ἵνα δὲ
to say : Rise and walk? but that
εἰδῆτε ὅτι ὁ υἱὸς τοῦ ἀνθρώπου ἐξουσίαν
ye may know that the Son - of man authority
ἔχει ἐπὶ τῆς γῆς ἀφιέναι ἁμαρτίας, —
has on the earth to forgive sins, —
εἶπεν τῷ παραλελυμένῳ· σοὶ λέγω, ἔγειρε
he said to the paralysed [one] : To thee I say, rise
καὶ ἄρας τὸ κλινίδιόν σου πορεύου εἰς
and taking the pallet of thee go to
τὸν οἶκόν σου. 25 καὶ παραχρῆμα ἀναστὰς
the house of thee. And at once rising up
ἐνώπιον αὐτῶν, ἄρας ἐφ' ὃ κατέκειτο,
before them, taking [that] on which he was lying,
ἀπῆλθεν εἰς τὸν οἶκον αὐτοῦ δοξάζων τὸν
he went away to the house of him glorifying -
θεόν. 26 καὶ ἔκστασις ἔλαβεν ἅπαντας, καὶ
God. And bewilderment took all, and
ἐδόξαζον τὸν θεόν, καὶ ἐπλήσθησαν φόβου
they glorified - God, and were filled of(with) fear
λέγοντες ὅτι εἴδομεν παράδοξα σήμερον.
saying[,] - We saw wonderful things to-day.
27 Καὶ μετὰ ταῦτα ἐξῆλθεν, καὶ ἐθεάσατο
And after these things he went forth, and saw
τελώνην ὀνόματι Λευὶν καθήμενον ἐπὶ τὸ
a tax-collector by name Levi sitting on(in) the
τελώνιον, καὶ εἶπεν αὐτῷ· ἀκολούθει μοι.
custom house, and said to him : Follow me.
28 καὶ καταλιπὼν πάντα ἀναστὰς ἠκολούθει
And abandoning all things rising up he followed
αὐτῷ. 29 Καὶ ἐποίησεν δοχὴν μεγάλην
him. And ³made ⁴feast ³a great
Λευὶς αὐτῷ ἐν τῇ οἰκίᾳ αὐτοῦ· καὶ ἦν
¹Levi for him in the house of him; and there was
ὄχλος πολὺς τελωνῶν καὶ ἄλλων οἳ ἦσαν
crowd a much of tax-collectors and of others who were
μετ' αὐτῶν κατακείμενοι. 30 καὶ ἐγόγγυζον
⁶with ⁵them ¹reclining. And grumbled
οἱ Φαρισαῖοι καὶ οἱ γραμματεῖς αὐτῶν
the Pharisees and the scribes of them
πρὸς τοὺς μαθητὰς αὐτοῦ λέγοντες· διὰ
at the disciples of him saying : Why
τί μετὰ τῶν τελωνῶν καὶ ἁμαρτωλῶν
with the tax-collectors and sinners
ἐσθίετε καὶ πίνετε; 31 καὶ ἀποκριθεὶς ὁ
eat ye and drink ye? And answering -
Ἰησοῦς εἶπεν πρὸς αὐτούς· οὐ χρείαν
Jesus said to them : not need
ἔχουσιν οἱ ὑγιαίνοντες ἰατροῦ ἀλλὰ οἱ
have the [ones] being healthy of a physician but the =those who are ill;
κακῶς ἔχοντες· 32 οὐκ ἐλήλυθα καλέσαι
[ones] ill having; I have not come to call
δικαίους ἀλλὰ ἁμαρτωλοὺς εἰς μετάνοιαν.
righteous persons but sinners to repentance.
33 Οἱ δὲ εἶπαν πρὸς αὐτόν· οἱ μαθηταὶ
And they said to him : The disciples
Ἰωάννου νηστεύουσιν πυκνὰ καὶ δεήσεις
of John fast often and prayers

---

were thinking and asked, "Why are you thinking these things in your hearts? 23Which is easier: to say, 'Your sins are forgiven,' or to say, 'Get up and walk'? 24But that you may know that the Son of Man has authority on earth to forgive sins...." He said to the paralyzed man, "I tell you, get up, take your mat and go home." 25Immediately he stood up in front of them, took what he had been lying on and went home praising God. 26Everyone was amazed and gave praise to God. They were filled with awe and said, "We have seen remarkable things today."

The Calling of Levi

27After this, Jesus went out and saw a tax collector by the name of Levi sitting at his tax booth. "Follow me," Jesus said to him, 28and Levi got up, left everything and followed him.
29Then Levi held a great banquet for Jesus at his house, and a large crowd of tax collectors and others were eating with them. 30But the Pharisees and the teachers of the law who belonged to their sect complained to his disciples, "Why do you eat and drink with tax collectors and 'sinners'?"
31Jesus answered them, "It is not the healthy who need a doctor, but the sick. 32I have not come to call the righteous, but sinners to repentance."

Jesus Questioned About Fasting

33They said to him, "John's disciples often fast and pray, and so do the dis-

---

ⁿ I.e., Collector of Roman taxes for profit

the *disciples* of the Pharisees also do the same; but Yours eat and drink."

34And Jesus said to them, "You cannot make the attendants of the bridegroom fast while the bridegroom is with them, can you?

35"But *the* days will come; and when the bridegroom is taken away from them, then they will fast in those days."

36And He was also telling them a parable: "No one tears a piece from a new garment and puts it on an old garment; otherwise he will both tear the new, and the piece from the new will not match the old.

37"And no one puts new wine into old wineskins; otherwise the new wine will burst the skins, and it will be spilled out, and the skins will be ruined.

38"But new wine must be put into fresh wineskins.

39"And no one, after drinking old *wine* wishes for new; for he says, 'The old is good *enough.*'"

ποιοῦνται, ὁμοίως καὶ οἱ τῶν Φαρισαίων,
make, likewise also those of the Pharisees,

οἱ δὲ σοὶ ἐσθίουσιν καὶ πίνουσιν. 34 ὁ
but those to thee° eat and drink. -
=but thine

δὲ Ἰησοῦς εἶπεν πρὸς αὐτούς· μὴ δύνασθε
And Jesus said to them: not ¹Can ye

τοὺς υἱοὺς τοῦ νυμφῶνος, ἐν ᾧ ὁ νυμφίος
³the ⁴sons ⁵of the ⁶bride-chamber, ⁸while ⁹the ¹⁰bridegroom

μετ᾽ αὐτῶν ἐστιν, ποιῆσαι νηστεῦσαι;
¹¹with ¹²them ¹¹is, ²to make ⁷to fast?

35 ἐλεύσονται δὲ ἡμέραι, καὶ ὅταν ἀπαρθῇ
but will come days, and when is taken away

ἀπ᾽ αὐτῶν ὁ νυμφίος, τότε νηστεύσουσιν
from them the bridegroom, then they will fast

ἐν ἐκείναις ταῖς ἡμέραις. 36 Ἔλεγεν δὲ
in those - days. And he told

καὶ παραβολὴν πρὸς αὐτοὺς ὅτι οὐδεὶς
also a parable to them[:] - No one

ἐπίβλημα ἀπὸ ἱματίου καινοῦ σχίσας
²a patch ³from ⁴garment ⁴a new ¹tearing

ἐπιβάλλει ἐπὶ ἱμάτιον παλαιόν· εἰ δὲ μή γε,
⁵puts [it] ⁶on ⁷a garment ⁸an old; otherwise,

καὶ τὸ καινὸν σχίσει καὶ τῷ παλαιῷ
both the new will tear and ⁷with the ⁸old

οὐ συμφωνήσει τὸ ἐπίβλημα τὸ ἀπὸ τοῦ
⁶will not agree ¹the ²patch - ³from ⁴the

καινοῦ. 37 καὶ οὐδεὶς βάλλει οἶνον νέον
⁵new. And no one puts wine new

εἰς ἀσκοὺς παλαιούς· εἰ δὲ μή γε, ῥήξει
into wineskins old; otherwise, ⁴will burst

ὁ οἶνος ὁ νέος τοὺς ἀσκούς, καὶ αὐτὸς
¹the ²wine - ³new ⁵the ⁶wineskins, and it

ἐκχυθήσεται καὶ οἱ ἀσκοὶ ἀπολοῦνται.
will be poured out and the wineskins will perish.

38 ἀλλὰ οἶνον νέον εἰς ἀσκοὺς καινοὺς
But wine new into wineskins new

βλητέον. 39 καὶ οὐδεὶς πιὼν παλαιὸν
one must put. And no one having drunk old

θέλει νέον· λέγει γάρ· ὁ παλαιὸς χρηστός
desires new; for he says: The old good

ἐστιν.
is.

---

ciples of the Pharisees, but yours go on eating and drinking."

34Jesus answered, "Can you make the guests of the bridegroom fast while he is with them? 35But the time will come when the bridegroom will be taken from them; in those days they will fast."

36He told them this parable: "No one tears a patch from a new garment and sews it on an old one. If he does, he will have torn the new garment, and the patch from the new will not match the old. 37And no one pours new wine into old wineskins. If he does, the new wine will burst the skins, the wine will run out and the wineskins will be ruined. 38No, new wine must be poured into new wineskins. 39And no one after drinking old wine wants the new, for he says, 'The old is better.'"

Chapter 6

Jesus Is Lord of the Sabbath

NOW it came about that on a *certain* Sabbath He was passing through *some* grainfields; and His disciples were picking and eating the heads *of grain*, rubbing them in their hands.

2But some of the Pharisees said, "Why do you do what is not lawful on the Sabbath?"

3And Jesus answering them said, "Have you not even read what David did when he was hungry, he and those who were with him,

4how he entered the house of God, and took and ate the °consecrated bread which is not lawful for any to eat except the priests

° Or, *showbread*, lit., *loaves of presentation*

---

6 Ἐγένετο δὲ ἐν σαββάτῳ διαπορεύεσθαι
And it came to pass on a sabbath to go through
=he went through

αὐτὸν διὰ σπορίμων, καὶ ἔτιλλον οἱ
him ᵇ through cornfields, and ⁴plucked ¹the

μαθηταὶ αὐτοῦ καὶ ἤσθιον τοὺς στάχυας
²disciples ³of him and ate the ears

ψώχοντες ταῖς χερσίν. 2 τινὲς δὲ τῶν
rubbing with the(ir) hands. And some of the

Φαρισαίων εἶπαν· τί ποιεῖτε ὃ οὐκ ἔξεστιν
Pharisees said: Why do ye what is not lawful

τοῖς σάββασιν; 3 καὶ ἀποκριθεὶς πρὸς
on the sabbaths? And replying to

αὐτοὺς εἶπεν ὁ Ἰησοῦς· οὐδὲ τοῦτο ἀνέγνωτε
them said - Jesus: ²not ³this ¹read ye

ὃ ἐποίησεν Δαυίδ, ὁπότε ἐπείνασεν αὐτὸς
which did David, when hungered he

καὶ οἱ μετ᾽ αὐτοῦ ὄντες; 4 ὡς εἰσῆλθεν
and the [ones] with him being? how he entered

εἰς τὸν οἶκον τοῦ θεοῦ καὶ τοὺς ἄρτους
into the house - of God and the loaves

τῆς προθέσεως λαβὼν ἔφαγεν καὶ ἔδωκεν
of the setting forth taking he ate and gave

Chapter 6

Lord of the Sabbath

ONE Sabbath Jesus was going through the grainfields, and his disciples began to pick some heads of grain, rub them in their hands and eat the kernels. 2Some of the Pharisees asked, "Why are you doing what is unlawful on the Sabbath?"

3Jesus answered them, "Have you never read what David did when he and his companions were hungry? 4He entered the house of God, and taking the consecrated bread, he ate what is lawful only for alone, and gave it to his companions?''

5And He was saying to them, ''The Son of Man is Lord of the Sabbath.''

6And it came about on another Sabbath, that He entered the synagogue and was teaching; and there was a man there whose right hand was withered.

7And the scribes and the Pharisees were watching Him closely, *to see* if He healed on the Sabbath, in order that they might find *reason* to accuse Him.

8But He knew what they were thinking, and He said to the man with the withered hand, ''Rise and come forward!'' And he rose and came forward.

9And Jesus said to them, ''I ask you, is it lawful on the Sabbath to do good, or to do harm, to save a life, or to destroy it?''

10And after looking around at them all, He said to him, ''Stretch out your hand!'' And he did *so;* and his hand was restored.

11But they themselves were filled with rage, and discussed together what they might do to Jesus.

Choosing the Twelve

12And it was at this time that He went off to the mountain to pray, and He spent the whole night in prayer to God.

13And when day came, He called His disciples to Him; and chose twelve of them, whom He also named as apostles:

14Simon, whom He also named Peter, and Andrew his brother; and James and John; and Philip and Bartholomew;

15and Matthew and Thomas; James *the son* of

τοῖς   μετ' αὐτοῦ,   οὓς   οὐκ ἔξεστιν φαγεῖν
to the [ones] with   him,   which it is not lawful   to eat

εἰ μὴ   μόνους   τοὺς   ἱερεῖς;   5 καὶ   ἔλεγεν
except   only   the   priests?   And   he said

αὐτοῖς·   κύριός   ἐστιν   τοῦ   σαββάτου   ὁ
to them :   Lord   is   of the   sabbath   the

υἱὸς   τοῦ   ἀνθρώπου.   6 Ἐγένετο   δὲ   ἐν
Son   -   of man.   And it came to pass on

ἑτέρῳ   σαββάτῳ   εἰσελθεῖν   αὐτὸν   εἰς   τὴν
another   sabbath   to enter   him   into   the
=he entered into the synagogue and

συναγωγὴν καὶ   διδάσκειν·   καὶ   ἦν   ἄνθρωπος
synagogue   and   to teach[b];   and there was   a man
taught;

ἐκεῖ καὶ   ἡ   χεὶρ   αὐτοῦ   ἡ   δεξιὰ   ἦν   ξηρά·
there   and   the   ⁸hand   ⁹of him   -   ¹right   was withered;

7 παρετηροῦντο   δὲ   αὐτὸν   οἱ   γραμματεῖς
and carefully watched   him   the   scribes

καὶ   οἱ   Φαρισαῖοι   εἰ   ἐν   τῷ   σαββάτῳ
and   the   Pharisees   if   on   the   sabbath

θεραπεύει,   ἵνα   εὕρωσιν   κατηγορεῖν   αὐτοῦ.
he heals,   that   they might find   to accuse   him.

8 αὐτὸς   δὲ   ᾔδει   τοὺς   διαλογισμοὺς   αὐτῶν,
But he   knew   the   reasonings   of them,

εἶπεν   δὲ   τῷ   ἀνδρὶ   τῷ   ξηρὰν   ἔχοντι   τὴν
and said   to the   man   -   ⁵withered   ¹having   ²the

χεῖρα·   ἔγειρε   καὶ   στῆθι   εἰς   τὸ   μέσον·
⁴hand :   Rise   and   stand   in   the   midst;

καὶ   ἀναστὰς   ἔστη.   9 εἶπεν   δὲ   ὁ   Ἰησοῦς
and   rising up   he stood.   And said   -   Jesus

πρὸς   αὐτούς·   ἐπερωτῶ   ὑμᾶς   εἰ   ἔξεστιν
to   them: I ask   you   if   it is lawful

τῷ   σαββάτῳ   ἀγαθοποιῆσαι   ἢ   κακοποιῆσαι,
on the   sabbath   to do good   or   to do evil,

ψυχὴν   σῶσαι   ἢ   ἀπολέσαι;   10 καὶ   περι-
life   to save   or   to destroy?   And looking

βλεψάμενος   πάντας   αὐτοὺς   εἶπεν   αὐτῷ·
round at   all   them   he said   to him :

ἔκτεινον   τὴν   χεῖρά   σου.   ὁ   δὲ   ἐποίησεν,
Stretch out   the   hand   of thee.   And he   did,

καὶ   ἀπεκατεστάθη   ἡ   χεὶρ   αὐτοῦ.   11 αὐτοὶ
and   was restored   the   hand   of him.   they

δὲ   ἐπλήσθησαν   ἀνοίας,   καὶ   διελάλουν   πρὸς
But   were filled of(with) madness,   and   talked   to

ἀλλήλους   τί   ἂν   ποιήσαιεν   τῷ   Ἰησοῦ.
one another   what   they might do   -   to Jesus.

12 Ἐγένετο   δὲ   ἐν   ταῖς   ἡμέραις   ταύταις
Now it came to pass in   -   days   these

ἐξελθεῖν   αὐτὸν   εἰς   τὸ   ὄρος   προσεύξασθαι,
to go forth   him[b]   to   the   mountain   to pray,
=he went forth

καὶ   ἦν   διανυκτερεύων   ἐν   τῇ   προσευχῇ   τοῦ
and   was spending the whole   in   the   prayer   -
night

θεοῦ.   13 καὶ   ὅτε   ἐγένετο   ἡμέρα, προσεφώνησεν
of God.   And when it became   day,   he called to [him]

τοὺς   μαθητὰς   αὐτοῦ,   καὶ   ἐκλεξάμενος   ἀπ'
the   disciples   of him,   and   choosing   from

αὐτῶν   δώδεκα,   οὓς   καὶ   ἀποστόλους   ὠνόμασεν,
them   twelve,   whom also   apostles   he named,

14 Σίμωνα,   ὃν   καὶ   ὠνόμασεν   Πέτρον,   καὶ
Simon,   whom also   he named   Peter,   and

Ἀνδρέαν   τὸν   ἀδελφὸν   αὐτοῦ,   καὶ   Ἰάκωβον
Andrew   the   brother   of him,   and   James

καὶ   Ἰωάννην,   καὶ   Φίλιππον   καὶ   Βαρθο-
and   John,   and   Philip   and   Bartho-

λομαῖον,   15 καὶ   Μαθθαῖον   καὶ   Θωμᾶν,
lomew,   and   Matthew   and   Thomas,

priests to eat. And he also gave some to his companions.'' 5Then Jesus said to them, ''The Son of Man is Lord of the Sabbath.''

6On another Sabbath he went into the synagogue and was teaching, and a man was there whose right hand was shriveled. 7The Pharisees and the teachers of the law were looking for a reason to accuse Jesus, so they watched him closely to see if he would heal on the Sabbath. 8But Jesus knew what they were thinking and said to the man with the shriveled hand, ''Get up and stand in front of everyone.'' So he got up and stood there.

9Then Jesus said to them, ''I ask you, which is lawful on the Sabbath: to do good or to do evil, to save life or to destroy it?''

10He looked around at them all, and then said to the man, ''Stretch out your hand.'' He did so, and his hand was completely restored. 11But they were furious and began to discuss with one another what they might do to Jesus.

The Twelve Apostles

12One of those days Jesus went out to a mountainside to pray, and spent the night praying to God. 13When morning came, he called his disciples to him and chose twelve of them, whom he also designated apostles: 14Simon (whom he named Peter), his brother Andrew, James, John, Philip, Bartholomew, 15Matthew, Thomas, James son of Alphaeus, Si-

Alphaeus, and Simon who was called the Zealot;

16Judas the son of James, and Judas Iscariot, who became a traitor.

17And He descended with them, and stood on a level place; and there was a great multitude of His disciples, and a great throng of people from all Judea and Jerusalem and the coastal region of Tyre and Sidon,

18who had come to hear Him, and to be healed of their diseases; and those who were troubled with unclean spirits were being cured.

19And all the multitude were trying to touch Him, for power was coming from Him and healing them all.

The Beatitudes

20And turning His gaze on His disciples, He began to say, "Blessed are you who are poor, for yours is the kingdom of God.

21"Blessed are you who hunger now, for you shall be satisfied. Blessed are you who weep now, for you shall laugh.

22"Blessed are you when men hate you, and ostracize you, and cast insults at you, and spurn your name as evil, for the sake of the Son of Man.

23"Be glad in that day, and leap for joy, for behold, your reward is great in heaven; for in the same way their fathers used to treat the prophets.

24"But woe to you who are rich, for you are receiving your comfort in full.

25"Woe to you who are well-fed now, for you shall be hungry. Woe to you who laugh now, for you shall mourn and weep.

26"Woe to you when all

[καὶ] Ἰάκωβον Ἀλφαίου καὶ Σίμωνα τὸν
and   James [son] of Alphæus   and   Simon   the [one]

καλούμενον ζηλωτήν, 16 καὶ Ἰούδαν Ἰακώβου,
being called   a Zealot,   and   Judas   of James,

καὶ Ἰούδαν Ἰσκαριώθ, ὃς ἐγένετο προδότης,
and   Judas   Iscariot,   who   became   betrayer,

17 καὶ καταβὰς μετ' αὐτῶν ἔστη ἐπὶ
  and   coming down   with   them   he stood   on

τόπου πεδινοῦ, καὶ ὄχλος πολὺς μαθητῶν
place   a level,   and   crowd   a much   of disciples

αὐτοῦ, καὶ πλῆθος πολὺ τοῦ λαοῦ ἀπὸ
of him,   and   multitude   a much   of the   people   from

πάσης τῆς Ἰουδαίας καὶ Ἱερουσαλὴμ καὶ
all   Judæa   and   Jerusalem   and

τῆς παραλίου Τύρου καὶ Σιδῶνος, 18 οἳ
the   coast country   of Tyre   and   Sidon,   who

ἦλθον ἀκοῦσαι αὐτοῦ καὶ ἰαθῆναι ἀπὸ
came   to hear   him   and   to be cured   from

τῶν νόσων αὐτῶν, καὶ οἱ ἐνοχλούμενοι
the   diseases   of them,   and the [ones]   being tormented

ἀπὸ πνευμάτων ἀκαθάρτων ἐθεραπεύοντο.
from   spirits   unclean   were healed.

19 καὶ πᾶς ὁ ὄχλος ἐζήτουν ἅπτεσθαι
  And   all   the   crowd   sought   to touch

αὐτοῦ, ὅτι δύναμις παρ' αὐτοῦ ἐξήρχετο
him,   because   power   from   him   went forth

καὶ ἰᾶτο πάντας. 20 Καὶ αὐτὸς ἐπάρας
and   cured   all.   And   he   lifting up

τοὺς ὀφθαλμοὺς αὐτοῦ εἰς τοὺς μαθητὰς
the   eyes   of him   to   the   disciples

αὐτοῦ ἔλεγεν·
of him   said :

Μακάριοι οἱ πτωχοί, ὅτι ὑμετέρα ἐστὶν
Blessed [are] the   poor,   because   yours   is

ἡ βασιλεία τοῦ θεοῦ. 21 μακάριοι οἱ
the   kingdom   -   of God.   Blessed [are] the [ones]

πεινῶντες νῦν, ὅτι χορτασθήσεσθε. μακάριοι
hungering   now, because   ye will be satisfied.   Blessed [are]

οἱ κλαίοντες νῦν, ὅτι γελάσετε. 22 μακάριοί
the [ones] weeping   now, because ye will laugh.   Blessed

ἐστε ὅταν μισήσωσιν ὑμᾶς οἱ ἄνθρωποι,
are ye   when   ¹hate   ²you   -   ¹men,

καὶ ὅταν ἀφορίσωσιν ὑμᾶς καὶ ὀνειδίσωσιν
and   when   they separate   you   and   reproach

καὶ ἐκβάλωσιν τὸ ὄνομα ὑμῶν ὡς πονηρὸν
and   cast out   the   name   of you   as   evil

ἕνεκα τοῦ υἱοῦ τοῦ ἀνθρώπου. 23 χάρητε
for the sake of the   Son   -   of man.   Rejoice

ἐν ἐκείνῃ τῇ ἡμέρᾳ καὶ σκιρτήσατε·
in   that   -   day   and   leap for joy;

ἰδοὺ γὰρ ὁ μισθὸς ὑμῶν πολὺς ἐν τῷ
for behold[,] the   reward   of you   much   in   -

οὐρανῷ· κατὰ τὰ αὐτὰ γὰρ ἐποίουν τοῖς
heaven;   for according to the same things   ⁴did   ⁵to the
      =in the same way

προφήταις οἱ πατέρες αὐτῶν.
⁶prophets   ¹the   ²fathers   ³of them.

24 Πλὴν οὐαὶ ὑμῖν τοῖς πλουσίοις, ὅτι
   But   woe   to you   the   rich [ones], because

ἀπέχετε τὴν παράκλησιν ὑμῶν. 25 οὐαὶ ὑμῖν,
ye have   the   consolation   of you.   Woe to you,

οἱ ἐμπεπλησμένοι νῦν, ὅτι πεινάσετε.
the [ones] having been filled up   now,   because   ye will hunger.

οὐαί, οἱ γελῶντες νῦν, ὅτι πενθήσετε
Woe,   the [ones]   laughing   now,   because   ye will mourn

καὶ κλαύσετε. 26 οὐαὶ ὅταν καλῶς ὑμᾶς
and   lament.   Woe   when   well   [of] you

---

mon who was called the Zealot, 16Judas son of James, and Judas Iscariot, who became a traitor.

Blessings and Woes

17He went down with them and stood on a level place. A large crowd of his disciples was there and a great number of people from all over Judea, from Jerusalem, and from the coast of Tyre and Sidon, 18who had come to hear him and to be healed of their diseases. Those troubled by evil[a] spirits were cured, 19and the people all tried to touch him, because power was coming from him and healing them all.

20Looking at his disciples, he said:

"Blessed are you who
    are poor,
  for yours is the
    kingdom of God.
21Blessed are you who
    hunger now,
  for you will be
    satisfied.
Blessed are you who
    weep now,
  for you will laugh.
22Blessed are you when
    men hate you,
  when they exclude you
    and insult you
  and reject your name
    as evil,
    because of the Son of
    Man.

23"Rejoice in that day and leap for joy, because great is your reward in heaven. For that is how their fathers treated the prophets.

24"But woe to you who
    are rich,
  for you have already
    received your
    comfort.
25Woe to you who are well
    fed now,
  for you will go hungry.
Woe to you who laugh
    now,
  for you will mourn and
    weep.
26Woe to you when all

---

a18 Greek *unclean*

men speak well of you, for in the same way their fathers used to treat the false prophets.
27"But I say to you who hear, love your enemies, do good to those who hate you,
28bless those who curse you, pray for those who mistreat you.
29"Whoever hits you on the cheek, offer him the other also; and whoever takes away your coat, do not withhold your shirt from him either.
30"Give to everyone who asks of you, and whoever takes away what is yours, do not demand it back.
31"And just as you want people to treat you, treat them in the same way.
32"And if you love those who love you, what credit is *that* to you? For even sinners love those who love them.
33"And if you do good to those who do good to you, what credit is *that* to you? For even sinners do the same.
34"And if you lend to those from whom you expect to receive, what credit is *that* to you? Even sinners lend to sinners, in order to receive back the same *amount*.
35"But love your enemies, and do good, and lend, expecting nothing in return; and your reward will be great, and you will be sons of the Most High; for He Himself is kind to ungrateful and evil *men*.
36"Be merciful, just as your Father is merciful.
37"And do not judge and you will not be judged; and

εἴπωσιν πάντες οἱ ἄνθρωποι· κατὰ τὰ
say all - men; for according to
=in the same way

αὐτὰ γὰρ ἐποίουν τοῖς ψευδοπροφήταις οἱ
the same things did to the false prophets the

πατέρες αὐτῶν. 27 Ἀλλὰ ὑμῖν λέγω
fathers of them. But you I tell

τοῖς ἀκούουσιν· ἀγαπᾶτε τοὺς ἐχθροὺς
the [ones] hearing : Love ye the enemies

ὑμῶν, καλῶς ποιεῖτε τοῖς μισοῦσιν ὑμᾶς,
of you, ²well ¹do to the [ones] hating you,

28 εὐλογεῖτε τοὺς καταρωμένους ὑμᾶς,
bless the [ones] cursing you,

προσεύχεσθε περὶ τῶν ἐπηρεαζόντων ὑμᾶς.
pray about the [ones] insulting you.

29 τῷ τύπτοντί σε ἐπὶ τὴν σιαγόνα
To the [one] striking thee on the cheek

πάρεχε καὶ τὴν ἄλλην, καὶ ἀπὸ τοῦ
turn also the other, and from the [one]

αἴροντός σου τὸ ἱμάτιον καὶ τὸν χιτῶνα
taking of thee the garment also the tunic

μὴ κωλύσῃς. 30 παντὶ αἰτοῦντί σε δίδου,
do not prevent. To everyone asking thee give,

καὶ ἀπὸ τοῦ αἴροντος τὰ σὰ μὴ ἀπαίτει.
and from the [one] taking thy things do not ask back.

31 καὶ καθὼς θέλετε ἵνα ποιῶσιν ὑμῖν
And as ye wish that may do to you

οἱ ἄνθρωποι, ποιεῖτε αὐτοῖς ὁμοίως. 32 καὶ
- men, do ye to them likewise. And

εἰ ἀγαπᾶτε τοὺς ἀγαπῶντας ὑμᾶς, ποία
if ye love the [ones] loving you, what

ὑμῖν χάρις ἐστίν; καὶ γὰρ οἱ ἁμαρτωλοὶ
to you thanks is there?c for even - sinners
=thanks have ye?

τοὺς ἀγαπῶντας αὐτοὺς ἀγαπῶσιν. 33 καὶ
²the [ones] ³loving ⁴them ¹love. And

γὰρ ἐὰν ἀγαθοποιῆτε τοὺς ἀγαθοποιοῦντας
For if ye do good to the [ones] doing good to

ὑμᾶς, ποία ὑμῖν χάρις ἐστίν; καὶ οἱ
you, what to you thanks is there?c even -
=thanks have ye?

ἁμαρτωλοὶ τὸ αὐτὸ ποιοῦσιν. 34 καὶ ἐὰν
sinners the same thing do. And if

δανείσητε παρ᾽ ὧν ἐλπίζετε λαβεῖν, ποία
ye lend from whom ye hope to receive, what

ὑμῖν χάρις [ἐστίν]; καὶ ἁμαρτωλοὶ
to you thanks is there?c even sinners
=thanks have ye?

ἁμαρτωλοῖς δανείζουσιν ἵνα ἀπολάβωσιν τὰ
to sinners lend that they may receive back the

ἴσα. 35 πλὴν ἀγαπᾶτε τοὺς ἐχθροὺς ὑμῶν
equal things. But love ye the enemies of you

καὶ ἀγαθοποιεῖτε καὶ δανείζετε μηδὲν
and do good and lend nothing

ἀπελπίζοντες· καὶ ἔσται ὁ μισθὸς ὑμῶν
despairing; and will be the reward of you
=despairing not at all;

πολύς, καὶ ἔσεσθε υἱοὶ ὑψίστου, ὅτι
much, and ye will be sons of [the] Most High, because

αὐτὸς χρηστός ἐστιν ἐπὶ τοὺς ἀχαρίστους
he kind is to the unthankful

καὶ πονηρούς. 36 Γίνεσθε οἰκτίρμονες,
and evil. Be ye compassionate,

καθὼς ὁ πατὴρ ὑμῶν οἰκτίρμων ἐστίν.
as the Father of you compassionate is.

37 καὶ μὴ κρίνετε, καὶ οὐ μὴ κριθῆτε· καὶ
And do not judge, and by no means ye may be and
judged;

---

men speak well of you,
for that is how their fathers treated the false prophets.

Love for Enemies

27"But I tell you who hear me: Love your enemies, do good to those who hate you, 28bless those who curse you, pray for those who mistreat you. 29If someone strikes you on one cheek, turn to him the other also. If someone takes your cloak, do not stop him from taking your tunic. 30Give to everyone who asks of you, and if anyone takes what belongs to you, do not demand it back. 31Do to others as you would have them do to you.

32"If you love those who love you, what credit is that to you? Even 'sinners' love those who love them. 33And if you do good to those who are good to you, what credit is that to you? Even 'sinners' do that. 34And if you lend to those from whom you expect repayment, what credit is that to you? Even 'sinners' lend to 'sinners,' expecting to be repaid in full. 35But love your enemies, do good to them, and lend to them without expecting to get anything back. Then your reward will be great, and you will be sons of the Most High, because he is kind to the ungrateful and wicked. 36Be merciful, just as your Father is merciful.

Judging Others

37"Do not judge, and you will not be judged. Do not

do not condemn, and you will not be condemned; pardon, and you will be pardoned.
38"Give, and it will be given to you; good measure, pressed down, shaken together, running over, they will pour into your lap. For by your standard of measure it will be measured to you in return."
39And He also spoke a parable to them: "A blind man cannot guide a blind man, can he? Will they not both fall into a pit?
40"A pupil is not above his teacher; but everyone, after he has been fully trained, will be like his teacher.
41"And why do you look at the speck that is in your brother's eye, but do not notice the log that is in your own eye?
42"Or how can you say to your brother, 'Brother, let me take out the speck that is in your eye,' when you yourself do not see the log that is in your own eye? You hypocrite, first take the log out of your own eye, and then you will see clearly to take out the speck that is in your brother's eye.
43"For there is no good tree which produces bad fruit; nor, on the other hand, a bad tree which produces good fruit.
44"For each tree is known by its own fruit. For men do not gather figs from thorns, nor do they pick grapes from a briar bush.
45"The good man out of the good treasure of his heart brings forth what is good; and the evil *man* out of the evil *treasure* brings forth what is evil; for his mouth speaks from that which fills his heart.

μὴ καταδικάζετε, καὶ οὐ μὴ καταδικασθῆτε.
do not condemn, and by no means ye may be condemned.

ἀπολύετε, καὶ ἀπολυθήσεσθε· 38 δίδοτε, καὶ
Forgive, and ye will be forgiven; give, and

δοθήσεται ὑμῖν· μέτρον καλὸν πεπιεσμένον
it will be given to you; measure good *having been* pressed down

σεσαλευμένον ὑπερεκχυννόμενον δώσουσιν εἰς
having been shaken running over they will give into

τὸν κόλπον ὑμῶν· ᾧ γὰρ μέτρῳ μετρεῖτε
the bosom of you; for in what measure ye measure

ἀντιμετρηθήσεται ὑμῖν. 39 Εἶπεν δὲ καὶ
it will be measured in return to you. And he told also

παραβολὴν αὐτοῖς· μήτι δύναται τυφλὸς
a parable to them : Not can a blind man

τυφλὸν ὁδηγεῖν; οὐχὶ ἀμφότεροι εἰς βόθυνον
a blind man *guide?* not both into a ditch

ἐμπεσοῦνται; 40 οὐκ ἔστιν μαθητὴς ὑπὲρ
will fall in? *not* *is* *A disciple* above

τὸν . διδάσκαλον· κατηρτισμένος δὲ πᾶς
the teacher; *but* *having been* perfected *everyone*

ἔσται ὡς ὁ διδάσκαλος αὐτοῦ. 41 Τί δὲ
will be as the teacher of him. And why

βλέπεις τὸ κάρφος τὸ ἐν τῷ ὀφθαλμῷ
seest thou the mote the - in the eye

τοῦ ἀδελφοῦ σου, τὴν δὲ δοκὸν τὴν ἐν
of the brother of thee, but the beam - in

τῷ ἰδίῳ ὀφθαλμῷ οὐ κατανοεῖς; 42 πῶς
thine own eye thou considerest not? how

δύνασαι λέγειν τῷ ἀδελφῷ σου· ἀδελφέ,
canst thou *to* say to the brother of thee : Brother,

ἄφες ἐκβάλω τὸ κάρφος τὸ ἐν τῷ
allow I may take out the mote the - in the
= allow me to take out

ὀφθαλμῷ σου, αὐτὸς τὴν ἐν τῷ ὀφθαλμῷ
eye of thee, ¹[thy]self ⁴the ⁶in ⁷the ⁸eye

σου δοκὸν οὐ βλέπων; ὑποκριτά, ἔκβαλε
⁵of thee ³beam ²not ³seeing? hypocrite, take *out*

πρῶτον τὴν δοκὸν ἐκ τοῦ ὀφθαλμοῦ σου,
first the beam out of the eye of thee,

καὶ τότε διαβλέψεις τὸ κάρφος τὸ ἐν τῷ
and then thou wilt see clearly the mote - in the

ὀφθαλμῷ τοῦ ἀδελφοῦ σου ἐκβαλεῖν. 43 Οὐ
eye of the brother of thee to take out. ³no

γάρ ἐστιν δένδρον καλὸν ποιοῦν καρπὸν
¹For ²there is ⁵tree ⁴good producing fruit

σαπρόν, οὐδὲ πάλιν δένδρον σαπρὸν ποιοῦν
bad, nor again tree a bad producing

καρπὸν καλόν. 44 ἕκαστον γὰρ δένδρον
fruit good. For each tree

ἐκ τοῦ ἰδίου καρποῦ γινώσκεται· οὐ γὰρ
by the(its) own fruit is known; for not

ἐξ ἀκανθῶν συλλέγουσιν σῦκα, οὐδὲ ἐκ
of thorns do they gather figs, nor of

βάτου σταφυλὴν τρυγῶσιν. 45 ὁ ἀγαθὸς
a thorn bush a grape do they pick. The good

ἄνθρωπος ἐκ τοῦ ἀγαθοῦ θησαυροῦ τῆς
man out of the good treasure of the(his)

καρδίας προφέρει τὸ ἀγαθόν, καὶ ὁ
heart brings forth the good, and the
          = that which is good,

πονηρὸς ἐκ τοῦ πονηροῦ προφέρει τὸ
evil man out of the evil brings forth the

πονηρόν· ἐκ γὰρ περισσεύματος καρδίας
evil; for out of [the] abundance of [his] heart
= that which is evil;

condemn, and you will not be condemned. Forgive, and you will be forgiven.
38Give, and it will be given to you. A good measure, pressed down, shaken together and running over, will be poured into your lap. For with the measure you use, it will be measured to you."
39He also told them this parable: "Can a blind man lead a blind man? Will they not both fall into a pit? 40A student is not above his teacher, but everyone who is fully trained will be like his teacher.
41"Why do you look at the speck of sawdust in your brother's eye and pay no attention to the plank in your own eye? 42How can you say to your brother, 'Brother, let me take the speck out of your eye,' when you yourself fail to see the plank in your own eye? You hypocrite, first take the plank out of your eye, and then you will see clearly to remove the speck from your brother's eye.

A Tree and Its Fruit

43"No good tree bears bad fruit, nor does a bad tree bear good fruit. 44Each tree is recognized by its own fruit. People do not pick figs from thornbushes, or grapes from briers. 45The good man brings good things out of the good stored up in his heart, and the evil man brings evil things out of the evil stored up in his heart. For out of the overflow of his heart his mouth speaks.

Builders and Foundations

46"And why do you call Me, 'Lord, Lord,' and do not do what I say?

47"Everyone who comes to Me, and hears My words, and acts upon them, I will show you whom he is like:

48he is like a man building a house, who dug deep and laid a foundation upon the rock; and when a flood rose, the torrent burst against that house and could not shake it, because it had been well built.

49"But the one who has heard, and has not acted *accordingly*, is like a man who built a house upon the ground without any foundation; and the torrent burst against it and immediately it collapsed, and the ruin of that house was great."

Chapter 7

Jesus Heals a Centurion's Servant

WHEN He had completed all His discourse in the hearing of the people, He went to Capernaum.

2And a certain centurion's slave, who was highly regarded by him, was sick and about to die.

3And when he heard about Jesus, he sent some Jewish elders asking Him to come and save the life of his slave.

4And when they had come to Jesus, they earnestly entreated Him, saying, "He is worthy for You to grant this to him;

5for he loves our nation, and it was he who built us our synagogue."

6Now Jesus *started* on His way with them; and when He was already not far from the house, the cen-

---

λαλεῖ τὸ στόμα αὐτοῦ. **46** Τί δέ με καλεῖτε·
speaks the mouth of him. And why me call ye :

κύριε κύριε, καὶ οὐ ποιεῖτε ἃ
Lord[,] Lord, and do not [the things] which

λέγω; **47** Πᾶς ὁ ἐρχόμενος πρός με καὶ
I say? Everyone coming to me and

ἀκούων μου τῶν λόγων καὶ ποιῶν αὐτούς,
hearing of me the words and doing them,

ὑποδείξω ὑμῖν τίνι ἐστὶν ὅμοιος. **48** ὅμοιός
I will show you to whom he is like. Like

ἐστιν ἀνθρώπῳ οἰκοδομοῦντι οἰκίαν, ὃς
he is to a man building a house, who

ἔσκαψεν καὶ ἐβάθυνεν καὶ ἔθηκεν θεμέλιον
dug and deepened and laid a foundation

ἐπὶ τὴν πέτραν· πλημμύρης δὲ γενομένης
on the rock; and a flood occurring[a]
= when a flood occurred

προσέρρηξεν ὁ ποταμὸς τῇ οἰκίᾳ ἐκείνῃ,
[a]dashed against [1]the [a]river – house that,

καὶ οὐκ ἴσχυσεν σαλεῦσαι αὐτὴν διὰ
and was not able to shake it because of

τὸ καλῶς οἰκοδομῆσθαι αὐτήν. **49** ὁ δὲ
the well to be built it.[b] But the [one]
= because it was well built.

ἀκούσας καὶ μὴ ποιήσας ὅμοιός ἐστιν
hearing and not doing [a]like [1]is

ἀνθρώπῳ οἰκοδομήσαντι οἰκίαν ἐπὶ τὴν
a man having built a house on the

γῆν χωρὶς θεμελίου, ᾗ προσέρρηξεν ὁ
earth without a foundation, [a]which [a]dashed [1]against [a]the

ποταμός, καὶ εὐθὺς συνέπεσεν, καὶ ἐγένετο
[a]river, and immediately it collapsed, and [a]was

τὸ ῥῆγμα τῆς οἰκίας ἐκείνης μέγα.
[1]the [a]ruin – [4]house [a]of that [a]great.

7 Ἐπειδὴ ἐπλήρωσεν πάντα τὰ ῥήματα
When he completed all the words

αὐτοῦ εἰς τὰς ἀκοὰς τοῦ λαοῦ, εἰσῆλθεν
of him in the ears of the people, he entered

εἰς Καφαρναούμ. **2** Ἑκατοντάρχου δέ
into Capernaum. Now [1]of [a]a [a]centurion

τινος δοῦλος κακῶς ἔχων ἤμελλεν τελευτᾶν,
[a]certain [1]a slave [2]ill [a]having(being) [1a]was about [1b]to die,

ὃς ἦν αὐτῷ ἔντιμος. **3** ἀκούσας δὲ περὶ
[1]who [1]was [1]to him [1]dear. And hearing about

τοῦ Ἰησοῦ ἀπέστειλεν πρὸς αὐτὸν πρε-
– Jesus he sent to him eld-

σβυτέρους τῶν Ἰουδαίων, ἐρωτῶν αὐτὸν
ers of the Jews, asking him

ὅπως ἐλθὼν διασώσῃ τὸν δοῦλον αὐτοῦ.
that coming he might recover the slave of him.

4 οἱ δὲ παραγενόμενοι πρὸς τὸν Ἰησοῦν
And they coming to – Jesus

παρεκάλουν αὐτὸν σπουδαίως, λέγοντες ὅτι ἄξιός
besought him earnestly, saying[,] – Worthy

ἐστιν ᾧ παρέξῃ τοῦτο· **5** ἀγαπᾷ γὰρ
he is for whom thou shouldest grant this; for he loves

τὸ ἔθνος ἡμῶν καὶ τὴν συναγωγὴν
the nation of us and the synagogue

αὐτὸς ᾠκοδόμησεν ἡμῖν. **6** ὁ δὲ Ἰησοῦς
he built for us. – And Jesus

ἐπορεύετο σὺν αὐτοῖς. ἤδη δὲ αὐτοῦ οὐ
went with them. And yet him not
= while he was yet

μακρὰν ἀπέχοντος ἀπὸ τῆς οἰκίας, ἔπεμψεν
far being away[a] from the house, sent
not far away

The Wise and Foolish Builders

46"Why do you call me, 'Lord, Lord,' and do not do what I say? 47I will show you what he is like who comes to me and hears my words and puts them into practice. 48He is like a man building a house, who dug down deep and laid the foundation on rock. When a flood came, the torrent struck that house but could not shake it, because it was well built. 49But the one who hears my words and does not put them into practice is like a man who built a house on the ground without a foundation. The moment the torrent struck that house, it collapsed and its destruction was complete."

Chapter 7

The Faith of the Centurion

WHEN Jesus had finished saying all this in the hearing of the people, he entered Capernaum. 2There a centurion's servant, whom his master valued highly, was sick and about to die. 3The centurion heard of Jesus and sent some elders of the Jews to him, asking him to come and heal his servant. 4When they came to Jesus, they pleaded earnestly with him, "This man deserves to have you do this, 5because he loves our nation and has built our synagogue." 6So Jesus went with them.

He was not far from the house when the centurion

turion sent friends, saying to Him, "Lord, do not trouble Yourself further, for I am not worthy for You to come under my roof;

7for this reason I did not even consider myself worthy to come to You, but *just* say the word, and my servant will be healed.

8"For I, too, am a man under authority, with soldiers under me; and I say to this one, 'Go!' and he goes; and to another, 'Come!' and he comes; and to my slave, 'Do this!' and he does it."

9Now when Jesus heard this, He marveled at him, and turned and said to the multitude that was following Him, "I say to you, not even in Israel have I found such great faith."

10And when those who had been sent returned to the house, they found the slave in good health.

11And it came about soon afterwards, that He went to a city called Nain; and His disciples were going along with Him, accompanied by a large multitude.

12Now as He approached the gate of the city, behold, a dead man was being carried out, the only son of his mother, and she was a widow; and a sizeable crowd from the city was with her.

13And when the Lord saw her, He felt compassion for her, and said to her, "Do not weep."

14And He came up and touched the coffin; and the bearers came to a halt. And He said, "Young man, I say to you, arise!"

15And the dead man sat up, and began to speak. And *Jesus* gave him back to his mother.

16And fear gripped them all, and they *began* glorifying God, saying, "A great prophet has arisen among us!" and, "God has visited

---

φίλους ὁ ἑκατοντάρχης λέγων αὐτῷ· κύριε,
friends the centurion saying to him : Lord,

μὴ σκύλλου· οὐ γὰρ ἱκανός εἰμι ἵνα ὑπὸ
do not trouble; for not worthy am I that under

τὴν στέγην μου εἰσέλθῃς· 7 διὸ οὐδὲ
the roof of me thou shouldest enter; wherefore not

ἐμαυτὸν ἠξίωσα πρὸς σὲ ἐλθεῖν· ἀλλὰ εἰπὲ
myself I accounted worthy to thee to come; but say

λόγῳ, καὶ ἰαθήτω ὁ παῖς μου. 8 καὶ
in a word, and let be cured the servant of me. *also

γὰρ ἐγὼ ἄνθρωπός εἰμι ὑπὸ ἐξουσίαν
¹For ¹I *a man *am ⁷under *authority

τασσόμενος, ἔχων ὑπ' ἐμαυτὸν στρατιώτας,
*being set, having under myself soldiers,

καὶ λέγω τούτῳ· πορεύθητι, καὶ πορεύεται,
and I tell this one : Go, and he goes,

καὶ ἄλλῳ· ἔρχου, καὶ ἔρχεται, καὶ τῷ
and another : Come, and he comes, and the

δούλῳ μου· ποίησον τοῦτο, καὶ ποιεῖ.
slave of me : Do this, and he does.

9 ἀκούσας δὲ ταῦτα ὁ Ἰησοῦς ἐθαύμασεν
And hearing these [words] - Jesus marvelled at

αὐτόν, καὶ στραφεὶς τῷ ἀκολουθοῦντι αὐτῷ
him, and turning to the *following *him

ὄχλῳ εἶπεν· λέγω ὑμῖν, οὐδὲ ἐν τῷ
¹crowd said : I tell you, not in -

Ἰσραὴλ τοσαύτην πίστιν εὗρον. 10 καὶ
Israel such faith I found. And

ὑποστρέψαντες εἰς τὸν οἶκον οἱ πεμφθέντες
returning to the house the [ones] sent

εὗρον τὸν δοῦλον ὑγιαίνοντα. 11 Καὶ
found the slave well. And

ἐγένετο ἐν τῷ ἑξῆς ἐπορεύθη εἰς πόλιν
it came to pass on the next day he went into a city

καλουμένην Ναΐν, καὶ συνεπορεύοντο αὐτῷ
being called Nain, and went with him

οἱ μαθηταὶ αὐτοῦ καὶ ὄχλος πολύς.
the disciples of him and crowd a much.

12 ὡς δὲ ἤγγισεν τῇ πύλῃ τῆς πόλεως, καὶ
And as he drew near to the gate of the city, and

ἰδοὺ ἐξεκομίζετο τεθνηκὼς μονογενὴς
behold was being carried out having died an only born
[for burial]

υἱὸς τῇ μητρὶ αὐτοῦ, καὶ αὕτη ἦν χήρα,
son to the mother of him, and this was a widow,

καὶ ὄχλος τῆς πόλεως ἱκανὸς ἦν σὺν
and a *crowd *of the ⁴city ¹considerable was with

αὐτῇ. 13 καὶ ἰδὼν αὐτὴν ὁ κύριος
her. And seeing her the Lord

ἐσπλαγχνίσθη ἐπ' αὐτῇ καὶ εἶπεν αὐτῇ·
felt compassion over her and said to her :

μὴ κλαῖε. 14 καὶ προσελθὼν ἥψατο τῆς
Do not weep. And approaching he touched the

σοροῦ, οἱ δὲ βαστάζοντες ἔστησαν, καὶ
bier, and the [ones] bearing stood, and

εἶπεν· νεανίσκε, σοὶ λέγω, ἐγέρθητι. 15 καὶ
he said : Young man, to thee I say, Arise. And

ἀνεκάθισεν ὁ νεκρὸς καὶ ἤρξατο λαλεῖν,
sat up the dead man and began to speak,

καὶ ἔδωκεν αὐτὸν τῇ μητρὶ αὐτοῦ.
and he gave him to the mother of him.

16 ἔλαβεν δὲ φόβος πάντας, καὶ ἐδόξαζον
And *took ¹fear *all, and they glorified

τὸν θεὸν λέγοντες ὅτι προφήτης μέγας
- God saying[,] - prophet A great

ἠγέρθη ἐν ἡμῖν, καὶ ὅτι ἐπεσκέψατο ὁ
was raised among us, and[,] - *visited -

---

sent friends to say to him: "Lord, don't trouble yourself, for I do not deserve to have you come under my roof. 7That is why I did not even consider myself worthy to come to you. But say the word, and my servant will be healed. 8For I myself am a man under authority, with soldiers under me. I tell this one, 'Go,' and he goes; and that one, 'Come,' and he comes. I say to my servant, 'Do this,' and he does it."

9When Jesus heard this, he was amazed at him, and turning to the crowd following him, he said, "I tell you, I have not found such great faith even in Israel." 10Then the men who had been sent returned to the house and found the servant well.

Jesus Raises a Widow's Son

11Soon afterward, Jesus went to a town called Nain, and his disciples and a large crowd went along with him. 12As he approached the town gate, a dead person was being carried out—the only son of his mother, and she was a widow. And a large crowd from the town was with her. 13When the Lord saw her, his heart went out to her and he said, "Don't cry."

14Then he went up and touched the coffin, and those carrying it stood still. He said, "Young man, I say to you, get up!" 15The dead man sat up and began to talk, and Jesus gave him back to his mother.

16They were all filled with awe and praised God. "A great prophet has appeared among us," they said.

His people!"

17And this report concerning Him went out all over Judea, and in all the surrounding district.

A Deputation from John

18And the disciples of John reported to him about all these things.

19And summoning two of his disciples, John sent them to the Lord, saying, "Are You the Expected One, or do we look for someone else?"

20And when the men had come to Him, they said, "John the Baptist has sent us to You, saying, 'Are You the Expected One, or do we look for someone else?'"

21At that very time He cured many *people* of diseases and afflictions and evil spirits; and He granted sight to many *who were* blind.

22And He answered and said to them, "Go and report to John what you have seen and heard: *the* BLIND RECEIVE SIGHT, *the* lame walk, *the* lepers are cleansed, and *the* deaf hear, *the* dead are raised up, *the* POOR HAVE THE GOSPEL PREACHED TO THEM.

23"And blessed is he who keeps from stumbling over Me."

24And when the messengers of John had left, He began to speak to the multitudes about John, "What did you go out into the wilderness to look at? A reed shaken by the wind?

25"But what did you go out to see? A man dressed in soft clothing? Behold, those who are splendidly clothed and live in luxury are *found* in royal palaces.

26"But what did you go out to see? A prophet? Yes, I say to you, and one who is more than a prophet.

27"This is the one about whom it is written,

θεὸς τὸν λαὸν αὐτοῦ.
¹God the people of him.

17 καὶ ἐξῆλθεν ὁ
And went forth the

λόγος οὗτος ἐν ὅλῃ τῇ Ἰουδαίᾳ περὶ
word this in all - Judæa ²concerning

αὐτοῦ καὶ πάσῃ τῇ περιχώρῳ.
⁶him ¹and ³all ³the ⁴neighbourhood.

18 Καὶ ἀπήγγειλαν Ἰωάννῃ οἱ μαθηταὶ
And reported to John the disciples

αὐτοῦ περὶ πάντων τούτων. καὶ
of him about all these things. And

προσκαλεσάμενος δύο τινὰς τῶν μαθητῶν
calling to [him] ¹two ¹a certain of the disciples

αὐτοῦ ὁ Ἰωάννης 19 ἔπεμψεν πρὸς τὸν
of him - John sent to the

κύριον λέγων· σὺ εἶ ὁ ἐρχόμενος, ἢ ἄλλον
Lord saying: Thou art the coming [one], or another

προσδοκῶμεν; 20 παραγενόμενοι δὲ πρὸς
may we expect? And coming to

αὐτὸν οἱ ἄνδρες εἶπαν· Ἰωάννης ὁ βαπτιστὴς
him the men said: John the Baptist

ἀπέστειλεν ἡμᾶς πρὸς σὲ λέγων· σὺ εἶ ὁ
sent us to thee saying: Thou art the

ἐρχόμενος, ἢ ἄλλον προσδοκῶμεν; 21 ἐν
coming [one], or another may we expect? In

ἐκείνῃ τῇ ὥρᾳ ἐθεράπευσεν πολλοὺς ἀπὸ
that - hour he healed many from(of)

νόσων καὶ μαστίγων καὶ πνευμάτων πονηρῶν,
diseases and plagues and spirits evil,

καὶ τυφλοῖς πολλοῖς ἐχαρίσατο βλέπειν.
and blind persons to many he gave to see.

22 καὶ ἀποκριθεὶς εἶπεν αὐτοῖς· πορευθέντες
And answering he said to them: Going

ἀπαγγείλατε Ἰωάννῃ ἃ εἴδετε καὶ
report to John [the things] which ye saw and

ἠκούσατε· τυφλοὶ ἀναβλέπουσιν, χωλοὶ
heard: blind men see again, lame men

περιπατοῦσιν, λεπροὶ καθαρίζονται, καὶ κωφοὶ
walk, lepers are being cleansed, and deaf men

ἀκούουσιν, νεκροὶ ἐγείρονται, πτωχοὶ
hear, dead men are raised, poor people

εὐαγγελίζονται· 23 καὶ μακάριός ἐστιν ὃς ἐὰν
are evangelized; and blessed is whoever

μὴ σκανδαλισθῇ ἐν ἐμοί. 24 Ἀπελθόντων δὲ
is not offended in me. And going away =as the

τῶν ἀγγέλων Ἰωάννου ἤρξατο λέγειν πρὸς
the messengers of John* he began to say to
messengers of John went away

τοὺς ὄχλους περὶ Ἰωάννου· τί ἐξήλθατε
the crowds concerning John: What went ye forth

εἰς τὴν ἔρημον θεάσασθαι; κάλαμον ὑπὸ
into the desert to see? a reed by

ἀνέμου σαλευόμενον; 25 ἀλλὰ τί ἐξήλθατε
wind being shaken? But what went ye forth

ἰδεῖν; ἄνθρωπον ἐν μαλακοῖς ἱματίοις
to see? a man in soft garments

ἠμφιεσμένον; ἰδοὺ οἱ ἐν ἱματισμῷ ἐνδόξῳ
having been behold[,] the ¹in ²raiment ²splendid
clothed? [ones]

καὶ τρυφῇ ὑπάρχοντες ἐν τοῖς βασιλείοις
⁶and ⁶in luxury ⁴being ³in - ¹royal palaces

εἰσίν. 26 ἀλλὰ τί ἐξήλθατε ἰδεῖν; προφήτην;
²are. But what went ye forth to see? a prophet?

ναὶ λέγω ὑμῖν, καὶ περισσότερον προφήτου.
yes I tell you, and more [than] a prophet.

27 οὗτός ἐστιν περὶ οὗ γέγραπται· ἰδοὺ
This is he concerning whom it has been written: Behold

"God has come to help his people." 17This news about Jesus spread throughout Judea[b] and the surrounding country.

Jesus and John the Baptist

18John's disciples told him about all these things. Calling two of them, he sent them to the Lord to ask, "Are you the one who was to come, or should we expect someone else?"

20When the men came to Jesus, they said, "John the Baptist sent us to you to ask, 'Are you the one who was to come, or should we expect someone else?'"

21At that very time Jesus cured many who had diseases, sicknesses and evil spirits, and gave sight to many who were blind. 22So he replied to the messengers, "Go back and report to John what you have seen and heard: The blind receive sight, the lame walk, those who have leprosy[c] are cured, the deaf hear, the dead are raised, and the good news is preached to the poor. 23Blessed is the man who does not fall away on account of me."

24After John's messengers left, Jesus began to speak to the crowd about John: "What did you go out into the desert to see? A reed swayed by the wind? 25If not, what did you go out to see? A man dressed in fine clothes? No, those who wear expensive clothes and indulge in luxury are in palaces. 26But what did you go out to see? A prophet? Yes, I tell you, and more than a prophet. 27This is the one about whom it is written:

'Behold, I send My
Messenger before
Your face,
Who will prepare
Your way before
You.'
28"I say to you, among
those born of women, there
is no one greater than John;
yet he who is least in the
kingdom of God is greater
than he."
29And when all the people
and the p tax-gatherers
heard this, they acknowl-
edged God's justice, having
been baptized with the
baptism of John.
30But the Pharisees and
the qlawyers rejected
God's purpose for them-
selves, not having been
baptized by John.
31"To what then shall I
compare the men of this
generation, and what are
they like?
32"They are like children
who sit in the market place
and call to one another; and
they say, 'We played the
flute for you, and you did
not dance; we sang a dirge,
and you did not weep.'
33"For John the Baptist
has come eating no bread
and drinking no wine; and
you say, 'He has a demon!'
34"The Son of Man has
come eating and drinking;
and you say, 'Behold, a
gluttonous man, and a
drunkard, a friend of tax-
gatherers and sinners!'
35"Yet wisdom is vin-
dicated by all her chil-
dren."
36Now one of the Phari-
sees was requesting Him to
dine with him. And He en-
tered the Pharisee's house,
and reclined at the table.
37And behold, there was a
woman in the city who was
a sinner; and when she
learned that He was reclining at the table in the Pharisee's house, she brought an
alabaster vial of perfume,
38and standing behind
Him at His feet, weeping,
she began to wet His feet
with her tears, and kept

p I.e., Collectors of Roman taxes
for profit
q I.e., experts in the Mosaic law

Middle column (interlinear)

ἀποστέλλω τὸν ἄγγελόν μου πρὸ προσώπου
I send　　the　messenger　of me　before　[the] face

σου, ὃς κατασκευάσει τὴν ὁδόν σου.
of thee, who　will prepare　the　way　of thee

ἔμπροσθέν σου. 28 λέγω ὑμῖν, μείζων
before　thee.　　I tell　you,　ʰgreater

ἐν γεννητοῖς γυναικῶν Ἰωάννου οὐδείς
¹among ²[those] born ³of women [⁴than] ⁵John ⁴no one

ἐστιν· ὁ δὲ μικρότερος ἐν τῇ βασιλείᾳ τοῦ
⁵is;　but the　less　in　the　kingdom　-

θεοῦ μείζων αὐτοῦ ἐστιν. 29 καὶ πᾶς ὁ
of God greater [than] he　is.　　And all the

λαὸς ἀκούσας καὶ οἱ τελῶναι ἐδικαίωσαν
people hearing and the tax-collectors justified

τὸν θεόν, βαπτισθέντες τὸ βάπτισμα
-　God, being baptized [with] the　baptism

Ἰωάννου· 30 οἱ δὲ Φαρισαῖοι καὶ οἱ
of John;　but the　Pharisees　and the

νομικοὶ τὴν βουλὴν τοῦ θεοῦ ἠθέτησαν εἰς
lawyers ⁴the ³counsel - ²of God ¹rejected ⁵for

ἑαυτούς, μὴ βαπτισθέντες ὑπ' αὐτοῦ. 31 Τίνι
⁵themselves, not being baptized by him.　To what

οὖν ὁμοιώσω τοὺς ἀνθρώπους τῆς γενεᾶς
then may I liken the　men　- generation

ταύτης, καὶ τίνι εἰσὶν ὅμοιοι; 32 ὅμοιοί εἰσιν
of this, and to what are they like? Like are they

παιδίοις τοῖς ἐν ἀγορᾷ καθημένοις καὶ
to children - in a marketplace sitting and

προσφωνοῦσιν ἀλλήλοις ἃ λέγει· ηὐλήσαμεν
calling　to one another who says : We piped

ὑμῖν καὶ οὐκ ὠρχήσασθε· ἐθρηνήσαμεν καὶ
to you and ye did not dance; we mourned and

οὐκ ἐκλαύσατε. 33 ἐλήλυθεν γὰρ Ἰωάννης
ye did not weep.　For has come　John

ὁ βαπτιστὴς μὴ ἐσθίων ἄρτον μήτε πίνων
the Baptist not eating bread nor drinking

οἶνον, καὶ λέγετε· δαιμόνιον ἔχει.
wine,　and　ye say :　A demon　he has.

34 ἐλήλυθεν ὁ υἱὸς τοῦ ἀνθρώπου ἐσθίων
Has come the Son - of man eating

καὶ πίνων, καὶ λέγετε· ἰδοὺ ἄνθρωπος
and drinking, and ye say : Behold[,]　a man

φάγος καὶ οἰνοπότης, φίλος τελωνῶν καὶ
a glutton and a winebibber, a friend of tax-collectors and

ἁμαρτωλῶν. 35 καὶ ἐδικαιώθη ἡ σοφία
of sinners.　And　was(is) justified - wisdom

ἀπὸ πάντων τῶν τέκνων αὐτῆς.
from(by) all the children of her.

36 Ἠρώτα δέ τις αὐτὸν τῶν Φαρισαίων
And ⁴asked ¹a certain one ⁵him ²of the ³Pharisees

ἵνα φάγῃ μετ' αὐτοῦ· καὶ εἰσελθὼν εἰς
that he would eat with him; and entering into

τὸν οἶκον τοῦ Φαρισαίου κατεκλίθη. 37 καὶ
the house of the Pharisee he reclined. And[,]

ἰδοὺ γυνὴ ἥτις ἦν ἐν τῇ πόλει ἁμαρτωλός,
behold[,] a woman who was in the city　a sinner,

καὶ ἐπιγνοῦσα ὅτι κατάκειται ἐν τῇ
and knowing that he reclines in the

οἰκίᾳ τοῦ Φαρισαίου, κομίσασα ἀλάβαστρον
house of the Pharisee, bringing an alabaster box

μύρου 38 καὶ στᾶσα ὀπίσω παρὰ τοὺς
of ointment and standing behind at the

πόδας αὐτοῦ κλαίουσα, τοῖς δάκρυσιν
feet of him weeping, with the(her) tears

ἤρξατο βρέχειν τοὺς πόδας αὐτοῦ, καὶ
began to wet the feet of him, and

" 'I will send my
messenger ahead of
you,
who will prepare your
way before you.' d
28I tell you, among those
born of women there is no
one greater than John; yet
the one who is least in the
kingdom of God is greater
than he."
29(All the people, even
the tax collectors, when
they heard Jesus' words,
acknowledged that God's
way was right, because
they had been baptized by
John. 30But the Pharisees
and experts in the law rejected God's purpose for
themselves, because they
had not been baptized by
John.)
31"To what, then, can I
compare the people of this
generation? What are they
like? 32They are like children sitting in the marketplace and calling out to
each other:

" 'We played the flute
for you,
and you did not dance;
we sang a dirge,
and you did not cry.'

33For John the Baptist
came neither eating bread
nor drinking wine, and you
say, 'He has a demon.'
34The Son of Man came
eating and drinking, and
you say, 'Here is a glutton
and a drunkard, a friend of
tax collectors and "sin-
ners." ' 35But wisdom is
proved right by all her children."

*Jesus Anointed by a Sinful
Woman*

36Now one of the Phari-
sees invited Jesus to have
dinner with him, so he went
to the Pharisee's house and
reclined at the table.
37When a woman who had
lived a sinful life in that
town learned that Jesus
was eating at the Pharisee's
house, she brought an alabaster jar of perfume, 38and
as she stood behind him at
his feet weeping, she began
to wet his feet with her

wiping them with the hair of her head, and kissing His feet, and anointing them with the perfume.

39Now when the Pharisee who had invited Him saw this, he said to himself, "If this man were a prophet He would know who and what sort of person this woman is who is touching Him, that she is a sinner."

Parable of Two Debtors

40And Jesus answered and said to him, "Simon, I have something to say to you." And he replied, "Say it, Teacher."

41"A certain moneylender had two debtors: one owed five hundred ʳ denarii, and the other fifty.

42"When they were unable to repay, he graciously forgave them both. Which of them therefore will love him more?"

43Simon answered and said, "I suppose the one whom he forgave more." And He said to him, "You have judged correctly."

44And turning toward the woman, He said to Simon, "Do you see this woman? I entered your house; you gave Me no water for My feet, but she has wet My feet with her tears, and wiped them with her hair.

45"You gave Me no kiss; but she, since the time I came in, has not ceased to kiss My feet.

46"You did not anoint My head with oil, but she anointed My feet with perfume.

47"For this reason I say to you, her sins, which are many, have been forgiven, for she loved much; but he who is forgiven little, loves little."

48And He said to her, "Your sins have been forgiven."

49And those who were reclining *at the table* with Him began to say to them-

ʳThe denarius was equivalent to one day's wage

ταῖς θριξὶν τῆς κεφαλῆς αὐτῆς ἐξέμασσεν,
with the hairs of the head of her wiped off,
καὶ κατεφίλει τοὺς πόδας αὐτοῦ καὶ
and fervently kissed the feet of him and
ἤλειφεν τῷ μύρῳ. 39 ἰδὼν δὲ ὁ Φαρισαῖος
anointed with the ointment. But ²seeing ¹the ²Pharisee
ὁ καλέσας αὐτὸν εἶπεν ἐν ἑαυτῷ λέγων·
- ³having invited ⁴him spoke within himself saying :
οὗτος εἰ ἦν [ὁ] προφήτης, ἐγίνωσκεν ἂν
This man if he was the prophet, would have known
τίς καὶ ποταπὴ ἡ γυνὴ ἥτις ἅπτεται
who and what sort the woman who is touching
αὐτοῦ, ὅτι ἁμαρτωλός ἐστιν. 40 καὶ
him, because a sinner she is. And
ἀποκριθεὶς ὁ Ἰησοῦς εἶπεν πρὸς αὐτόν·
answering - Jesus said to him :
Σίμων, ἔχω σοί τι εἰπεῖν. ὁ δέ· διδάσκαλε,
Simon, I have to thee something to say. And he : Teacher,
εἰπέ, φησίν. 41 δύο χρεοφειλέται ἦσαν
say, says. Two debtors were
= A certain creditor had two debtors;
δανειστῇ τινι· ὁ εἷς ὤφειλεν δηνάρια
creditor to a certain;ᵉ the one owed denarii
πεντακόσια, ὁ δὲ ἕτερος πεντήκοντα. 42 μὴ
five hundred, and the other fifty. Not
= As they had no[thing]
ἐχόντων αὐτῶν ἀποδοῦναι ἀμφοτέροις
having themᵃ to repay ²both
ἐχαρίσατο. τίς οὖν αὐτῶν πλεῖον ἀγαπήσει
¹he freely forgave. Who then of them more will love
αὐτόν; 43 ἀποκριθεὶς Σίμων εἶπεν·
him? Answering Simon said :
ὑπολαμβάνω ὅτι ᾧ τὸ πλεῖον ἐχαρίσατο.
I suppose[,] - to whom the more he freely forgave.
ὁ δὲ εἶπεν αὐτῷ· ὀρθῶς ἔκρινας. 44 καὶ
And he said to him : Rightly thou didst judge. And
στραφεὶς πρὸς τὴν γυναῖκα τῷ Σίμωνι
turning to the woman - to Simon
ἔφη· βλέπεις ταύτην τὴν γυναῖκα; εἰσῆλθόν
he said : Seest thou this - woman? I entered
σου εἰς τὴν οἰκίαν, ὕδωρ μοι ἐπὶ πόδας
of thee into the house, water to me on(for) [my] feet
οὐκ ἔδωκας· αὕτη δὲ τοῖς δάκρυσιν
thou gavest not; but this woman with the(her) tears
ἔβρεξέν μου τοὺς πόδας καὶ ταῖς θριξὶν
wet of me the feet and with the hairs
αὐτῆς ἐξέμαξεν. 45 φίλημά μοι οὐκ ἔδωκας·
of her wiped off. A kiss to me thou gavest not;
αὕτη δὲ ἀφ' ἧς εἰσῆλθον οὐ διέλειπεν
but this woman from [the time] I entered ceased not
    which
καταφιλοῦσά μου τοὺς πόδας. 46 ἐλαίῳ
fervently kissing of me the feet. With oil
τὴν κεφαλήν μου οὐκ ἤλειψας· αὕτη δὲ
the head of me thou didst not anoint; but this woman
μύρῳ ἤλειψεν τοὺς πόδας μου. 47 οὗ
with ointment anointed the feet of me. Of which
    = Wherefore
χάριν λέγω σοι, ἀφέωνται αἱ ἁμαρτίαι
for the sake of I tell thee, ¹have been forgiven ¹the ²sins
αὐτῆς αἱ πολλαί, ὅτι ἠγάπησεν πολύ·
⁴of her - ³many, because she loved much;
ᾧ δὲ ὀλίγον ἀφίεται, ὀλίγον ἀγαπᾷ.
but to whom little is forgiven, little he loves.
48 εἶπεν δὲ αὐτῇ· ἀφέωνταί σου αἱ
And he said to her : Have been forgiven of thee the
ἁμαρτίαι. 49 καὶ ἤρξαντο οἱ συνανακείμενοι
sins. And began the [ones] reclining with [him]

tears. Then she wiped them with her hair, kissed them and poured perfume on them.

39When the Pharisee who had invited him saw this, he said to himself, "If this man were a prophet, he would know who is touching him and what kind of woman she is—that she is a sinner."

40Jesus answered him, "Simon, I have something to tell you."

"Tell me, teacher," he said.

41"Two men owed money to a certain moneylender. One owed him five hundred denarii,ᵉ and the other fifty. 42Neither of them had the money to pay him back, so he canceled the debts of both. Now which of them will love him more?"

43Simon replied, "I suppose the one who had the bigger debt canceled."

"You have judged correctly," Jesus said.

44Then he turned toward the woman and said to Simon, "Do you see this woman? I came into your house. You did not give me any water for my feet, but she wet my feet with her tears and wiped them with her hair. 45You did not give me a kiss, but this woman, from the time I entered, has not stopped kissing my feet. 46You did not put oil on my head, but she has poured perfume on my feet. 47Therefore, I tell you, her many sins have been forgiven—for she loved much. But he who has been forgiven little loves little."

48Then Jesus said to her, "Your sins are forgiven."

49The other guests began to say among themselves,

ᵉ41 A denarius was a coin worth about a day's wages.

selves, "Who is this *man* who even forgives sins?"

⁵⁰And He said to the woman, "Your faith has saved you; go in peace."

Chapter 8

Ministering Women

AND it came about soon afterwards, that He *began* going about from one city and village to another, proclaiming and preaching the kingdom of God; and the twelve were with Him,

²and *also* some women who had been healed of evil spirits and sicknesses: Mary who was called Magdalene, from whom seven demons had gone out,

³and Joanna the wife of Chuza, Herod's steward, and Susanna, and many others who were contributing to their support out of their private means.

Parable of the Sower

⁴And when a great multitude were coming together, and those from the various cities were journeying to Him, He spoke by way of a parable:

⁵"The sower went out to sow his seed; and as he sowed, some fell beside the road; and it was trampled under foot, and the birds of the air ate it up.

⁶"And other *seed* fell on rocky *soil*, and as soon as it grew up, it withered away, because it had no moisture.

⁷"And other *seed* fell among the thorns; and the thorns grew up with it, and choked it out.

⁸"And other *seed* fell into the good soil, and grew up, and produced a crop a hundred times as great." As He said these things, He would call out, "He who has ears to hear, let him hear."

λέγειν ἐν ἑαυτοῖς· τίς οὗτός ἐστιν, ὃς καὶ
to say among themselves : Who this is, who even

ἁμαρτίας ἀφίησιν; 50 εἶπεν δὲ πρὸς τὴν
sins forgives? But he said to the

γυναῖκα· ἡ πίστις σου σέσωκέν σε·
woman : The faith of thee has saved thee;

πορεύου εἰς εἰρήνην.
go in peace.

8 Καὶ ἐγένετο ἐν τῷ καθεξῆς καὶ αὐτὸς
And it came to pass afterwards *and* he

διώδευεν κατὰ πόλιν καὶ κώμην κηρύσσων
journeyed through every† city and village proclaiming

καὶ εὐαγγελιζόμενος τὴν βασιλείαν τοῦ
and preaching the kingdom -

θεοῦ, καὶ οἱ δώδεκα σὺν αὐτῷ, 2 καὶ
of God, and the twelve with him, and

γυναῖκές τινες αἳ ἦσαν τεθεραπευμέναι ἀπὸ
women certain who having been healed from

πνευμάτων πονηρῶν καὶ ἀσθενειῶν, Μαρία
spirits evil and infirmities, Mary

ἡ καλουμένη Μαγδαληνή, ἀφ' ἧς δαιμόνια
- being called Magdalene, from whom demons

ἑπτὰ ἐξεληλύθει, 3 καὶ Ἰωάννα γυνὴ Χουζᾶ
seven had gone out, and Joanna wife of Chuza

ἐπιτρόπου Ἡρῴδου καὶ Σουσάννα καὶ
steward of Herod and Susanna and

ἕτεραι πολλαί, αἵτινες διηκόνουν αὐτοῖς
others many, who ministered to them

ἐκ τῶν ὑπαρχόντων αὐταῖς.ᶜ
out of the possessions to them.

4 Συνιόντος δὲ ὄχλου πολλοῦ καὶ τῶν
And coming together crowd a much and the [ones]
=when a great crowd came together and people in each city

κατὰ πόλιν ἐπιπορευομένων πρὸς αὐτὸν
in each city† resortingᵃ to him
resorted

εἶπεν διὰ παραβολῆς· 5 ἐξῆλθεν ὁ σπείρων
he said by a parable : Went forth the [one] sowing

τοῦ σπεῖραι τὸν σπόρον αὐτοῦ. καὶ ἐν τῷ
- to sowᵈ the seed of him. And in the

σπείρειν αὐτὸν ὃ μὲν ἔπεσεν παρὰ τὴν
to sow himᵇᵉ this fell by the
=as he sowed

ὁδὸν καὶ κατεπατήθη, καὶ τὰ πετεινὰ τοῦ
way and was trodden down, and the birds of the

οὐρανοῦ κατέφαγεν αὐτό. 6 καὶ ἕτερον
heaven(air) devoured it. And other [seed]

κατέπεσεν ἐπὶ τὴν πέτραν, καὶ φυὲν
fell on the rock, and grown

ἐξηράνθη διὰ τὸ μὴ ἔχειν ἰκμάδα.
it was withered because of the not to have moisture.
=because it had no moisture.

7 καὶ ἕτερον ἔπεσεν ἐν μέσῳ τῶν ἀκανθῶν, καὶ
And other fell in [the] of the thorns, and
midst

συμφυεῖσαι αἱ ἄκανθαι ἀπέπνιξαν αὐτό.
growing up with [it] the thorns choked it.

8 καὶ ἕτερον ἔπεσεν εἰς τὴν γῆν τὴν
And other fell in the soil -

ἀγαθὴν καὶ φυὲν ἐποίησεν καρπὸν
good and grown it produced fruit

ἑκατονταπλασίονα. ταῦτα λέγων ἐφώνει· ὁ
a hundredfold. These things saying he called: The [one]

ἔχων ὦτα ἀκούειν ἀκουέτω. 9 Ἐπηρώτων δὲ
having ears to hear let him hear. And questioned

"Who is this who even forgives sins?"

⁵⁰Jesus said to the woman, "Your faith has saved you; go in peace."

Chapter 8

The Parable of the Sower

AFTER this, Jesus traveled about from one town and village to another, proclaiming the good news of the kingdom of God. The Twelve were with him, ²and also some women who had been cured of evil spirits and diseases: Mary (called Magdalene) from whom seven demons had come out; ³Joanna the wife of Cuza, the manager of Herod's household; Susanna; and many others. These women were helping to support them out of their own means.

⁴While a large crowd was gathering and people were coming to Jesus from town after town, he told this parable: ⁵"A farmer went out to sow his seed. As he was scattering the seed, some fell along the path; it was trampled on, and the birds of the air ate it up. ⁶Some fell on rock, and when it came up, the plants withered because they had no moisture. ⁷Other seed fell among thorns, which grew up with it and choked the plants. ⁸Still other seed fell on good soil. It came up and yielded a crop, a hundred times more than was sown."

When he said this, he called out, "He who has ears to hear, let him hear."

9And His disciples *began* questioning Him as to what this parable might be.

10And He said, "To you it has been granted to know the mysteries of the kingdom of God, but to the rest *it is* in parables, in order that SEEING THEY MAY NOT SEE, AND HEARING THEY MAY NOT UNDERSTAND.

11"Now the parable is this: the seed is the word of God.

12"And those beside the road are those who have heard; then the devil comes and takes away the word from their heart, so that they may not believe and be saved.

13"And those on the rocky *soil are* those who, when they hear, receive the word with joy; and these have no *firm* root; they believe for a while, and in time of temptation fall away.

14"And the *seed* which fell among the thorns, these are the ones who have heard, and as they go on their way are choked with worries and riches and pleasures of *this* life, and bring no fruit to maturity.

15"And the *seed* in the good soil, these are the ones who have heard the word in an honest and good heart, and hold it fast, and bear fruit with perseverance.

Parable of the Lamp

16"Now no one after lighting a lamp covers it over with a container, or puts it under a bed; but he puts it on a lampstand, in order that those who come in may see the light.

17"For nothing is hidden that shall not become evident, nor *anything* secret that shall not be known and come to light.

18"Therefore take care how you listen; for whoever has, to him shall *more* be given; and whoever does not have, even what he thinks he has shall be taken away from him."

19And His mother and brothers came to Him, and

αὐτὸν οἱ μαθηταὶ αὐτοῦ τίς αὕτη εἴη ἡ
him the disciples of him what ¹this ²might be -

παραβολή. 10 ὁ δὲ εἶπεν· ὑμῖν δέδοται
²parable. And he said: To you it has been given

γνῶναι τὰ μυστήρια τῆς βασιλείας τοῦ
to know the mysteries of the kingdom -

θεοῦ, τοῖς δὲ λοιποῖς ἐν παραβολαῖς, ἵνα
of God, but to the rest in parables, that

βλέποντες μὴ βλέπωσιν καὶ ἀκούοντες μὴ
seeing they may not see and hearing not

συνιῶσιν. 11 ἔστιν δὲ αὕτη ἡ παραβολή.
they may understand. ²is ¹Now ³this - ⁴parable.

ὁ σπόρος ἐστὶν ὁ λόγος τοῦ θεοῦ.
The seed is the word - of God.

12 οἱ δὲ παρὰ τὴν ὁδόν εἰσιν οἱ ἀκούσαντες,
And the [ones] by the way are the [ones] hearing,

εἶτα ἔρχεται ὁ διάβολος καὶ αἴρει τὸν
then comes the devil and takes the

λόγον ἀπὸ τῆς καρδίας αὐτῶν, ἵνα μὴ
word from the heart of them, lest

πιστεύσαντες σωθῶσιν. 13 οἱ δὲ ἐπὶ τῆς
believing they may be saved. And the [ones] on the

πέτρας οἳ ὅταν ἀκούσωσιν μετὰ χαρᾶς
rock who when they hear with joy

δέχονται τὸν λόγον· καὶ οὗτοι ῥίζαν
receive the word; and these root

οὐκ ἔχουσιν, οἳ πρὸς καιρὸν πιστεύουσιν
have not, who for a time believe

καὶ ἐν καιρῷ πειρασμοῦ ἀφίστανται. 14 τὸ
and in time of trial withdraw. the [one]

δὲ εἰς τὰς ἀκάνθας πεσόν, οὗτοί εἰσιν
And in the thorns falling, these are

οἱ ἀκούσαντες, καὶ ὑπὸ μεριμνῶν καὶ
the [ones] hearing, ¹and ⁴by ⁵cares ⁶and

πλούτου καὶ ἡδονῶν τοῦ βίου πορευόμενοι
⁷riches ⁸and ⁹pleasures - ¹⁰of life ³going

συμπνίγονται καὶ οὐ τελεσφοροῦσιν. 15 τὸ
²are choked and do not bear [fruit] to maturity. the [one]

δὲ ἐν τῇ καλῇ γῇ, οὗτοί εἰσιν οἵτινες ἐν
And in the good soil, these are [those] who in

καρδίᾳ καλῇ καὶ ἀγαθῇ ἀκούσαντες τὸν
heart a worthy and good hearing the

λόγον κατέχουσιν καὶ καρποφοροῦσιν ἐν
word hold fast and bear fruit in

ὑπομονῇ. 16 Οὐδεὶς δὲ λύχνον ἅψας
patience. No one a lamp having lit

καλύπτει αὐτὸν σκεύει ἢ ὑποκάτω κλίνης
hides it with a vessel or underneath a couch

τίθησιν, ἀλλ' ἐπὶ λυχνίας τίθησιν, ἵνα οἱ
puts, but on a lampstand puts, that the

εἰσπορευόμενοι βλέπωσιν τὸ φῶς. 17 οὐ
[ones] coming in may see the light. not

γάρ ἐστιν κρυπτὸν ὃ οὐ φανερὸν
For [anything] is hidden which ²not ⁴manifest

γενήσεται, οὐδὲ ἀπόκρυφον ὃ οὐ μὴ
¹will ³become, nor secret which by no means

γνωσθῇ καὶ εἰς φανερὸν ἔλθη. 18 βλέπετε
will be known and to [be] manifest come. See

οὖν πῶς ἀκούετε· ὃς ἂν γὰρ ἔχῃ,
therefore how ye hear; for whoever has,

δοθήσεται αὐτῷ· καὶ ὃς ἂν μὴ ἔχῃ,
it will be given to him; and whoever has not,

καὶ ὃ δοκεῖ ἔχειν ἀρθήσεται ἀπ' αὐτοῦ.
even what he seems to have will be taken from him.

19 Παρεγένετο δὲ πρὸς αὐτὸν ἡ μήτηρ
And came to him the mother

9His disciples asked him what this parable meant.

10He said, "The knowledge of the secrets of the kingdom of God has been given to you, but to others I speak in parables, so that,

" 'though seeing, they
may not see;
though hearing, they
may not
understand.'*f*

11"This is the meaning of the parable: The seed is the word of God. 12Those along the path are the ones who hear, and then the devil comes and takes away the word from their hearts, so that they may not believe and be saved. 13Those on the rock are the ones who receive the word with joy when they hear it, but they have no root. They believe for a while, but in the time of testing they fall away. 14The seed that fell among thorns stands for those who hear, but as they go on their way they are choked by life's worries, riches and pleasures, and they do not mature. 15But the seed on good soil stands for those with a noble and good heart, who hear the word, retain it, and by persevering produce a crop.

A Lamp on a Stand

16"No one lights a lamp and hides it in a jar or puts it under a bed. Instead, he puts it on a stand, so that those who come in can see the light. 17For there is nothing hidden that will not be disclosed, and nothing concealed that will not be known or brought out into the open. 18Therefore consider carefully how you listen. Whoever has will be given more; whoever does not have, even what he thinks he has will be taken from him."

Jesus' Mother and Brothers

19Now Jesus' mother and brothers came to see him,

*f*10 Isaiah 6:9

they were unable to get to Him because of the crowd. 20And it was reported to Him, "Your mother and Your brothers are standing outside, wishing to see You."

21But He answered and said to them, "My mother and My brothers are these who hear the word of God and do it."

Jesus Stills the Sea

22Now it came about on one of *those* days, that He and His disciples got into a boat, and He said to them, "Let us go over to the other side of the lake." And they launched out.

23But as they were sailing along He fell asleep; and a fierce gale of wind descended upon the lake, and they *began* to be swamped and to be in danger.

24And they came to Him and woke Him up, saying, "Master, Master, we are perishing!" And being aroused, He rebuked the wind and the surging waves, and they stopped, and it became calm.

25And He said to them, "Where is your faith?" And they were fearful and amazed, saying to one another, "Who then is this, that He commands even the winds and the water, and they obey Him?"

The Demoniac Cured

26And they sailed to the country of the Gerasenes, which is opposite Galilee.

27And when He had come out onto the land, He was met by a certain man from the city who was possessed with demons; and who had not put on any clothing for a long time, and was not living in a house, but in the tombs.

28And seeing Jesus, he cried out and fell before Him, and said in a loud voice, "What do I have to do with You, Jesus, Son of the Most High God? I beg

καὶ οἱ ἀδελφοὶ αὐτοῦ, καὶ οὐκ ἠδύναντο
and the brothers of him, and were not able

συντυχεῖν αὐτῷ διὰ τὸν ὄχλον. 20 ἀπηγγέλη δὲ
to come up with him be- the crowd. And it was reported
cause of

αὐτῷ· ἡ μήτηρ σου καὶ οἱ ἀδελφοί σου
to him : The mother of thee and the brothers of thee

ἑστήκασιν ἔξω ἰδεῖν θέλοντές σε. 21 ὁ δὲ
are standing outside ³to see ¹wishing thee. But he

ἀποκριθεὶς εἶπεν πρὸς αὐτούς· μήτηρ μου
answering said to them : Mother of me

καὶ ἀδελφοί μου οὗτοί εἰσιν οἱ τὸν λόγον
and brothers of me ¹these ¹are ²the [ones] ³the ⁴word

τοῦ θεοῦ ἀκούοντες καὶ ποιοῦντες.
- ⁵of God ⁶hearing ⁷and ⁸doing.

22 Ἐγένετο δὲ ἐν μιᾷ τῶν ἡμερῶν καὶ
And it came to pass on one of the days *and*

αὐτὸς ἐνέβη εἰς πλοῖον καὶ οἱ μαθηταὶ
he embarked in a boat and the disciples

αὐτοῦ, καὶ εἶπεν πρὸς αὐτούς· διέλθωμεν
of him, and he said to them; Let us go over

εἰς τὸ πέραν τῆς λίμνης· καὶ ἀνήχθησαν.
to the other side of the lake; and they put to sea.

23 πλεόντων δὲ αὐτῶν ἀφύπνωσεν. καὶ
And sailing them* he fell asleep. And
=as they sailed

κατέβη λαῖλαψ ἀνέμου εἰς τὴν λίμνην, καὶ
came down a storm of wind to the lake, and

συνεπληροῦντο καὶ ἐκινδύνευον. 24 προσ-
they were filling up and were in danger. ap-

ελθόντες δὲ διήγειραν αὐτὸν λέγοντες·
proaching And they awoke him saying :

ἐπιστάτα ἐπιστάτα, ἀπολλύμεθα. ὁ δὲ
Master[,] Master, we are perishing. But he

διεγερθεὶς ἐπετίμησεν τῷ ἀνέμῳ καὶ τῷ
being awakened rebuked the wind and the

κλύδωνι τοῦ ὕδατος· καὶ ἐπαύσαντο, καὶ ἐγένετο
roughness of the water; and they ceased, and there was

γαλήνη. 25 εἶπεν δὲ αὐτοῖς· ποῦ ἡ πίστις ὑμῶν;
a calm. Then he said to them: Where the faith of you?

φοβηθέντες δὲ ἐθαύμασαν, λέγοντες πρὸς
And fearing they marvelled, saying to

ἀλλήλους· τίς ἄρα οὗτός ἐστιν, ὅτι καὶ
one another : Who then ²this man ¹is, that ²even

τοῖς ἀνέμοις ἐπιτάσσει καὶ τῷ ὕδατι, καὶ
²the ⁴winds ¹he commands and the water, and

ὑπακούουσιν αὐτῷ; 26 Καὶ κατέπλευσαν εἰς
they obey him? And they sailed down to

τὴν χώραν τῶν Γερασηνῶν, ἥτις ἐστὶν
the country of the Gerasenes, which is

ἀντιπέρα τῆς Γαλιλαίας. 27 ἐξελθόντι δὲ
opposite - Galilee. And going out
=as he went out

αὐτῷ* ἐπὶ τὴν γῆν ὑπήντησεν ἀνήρ τις
him* onto the land met [him] man a certain

ἐκ τῆς πόλεως ἔχων δαιμόνια, καὶ χρόνῳ
out of the city having demons, and ²time

ἱκανῷ οὐκ ἐνεδύσατο ἱμάτιον, καὶ ἐν οἰκίᾳ
¹for a con- put not on a garment, and in a house
siderable

οὐκ ἔμενεν ἀλλ' ἐν τοῖς μνήμασιν. 28 ἰδὼν
remained not but among the tombs. seeing

δὲ τὸν Ἰησοῦν ἀνακράξας προσέπεσεν αὐτῷ
And - Jesus crying out he fell prostrate before him

καὶ φωνῇ μεγάλῃ εἶπεν· τί ἐμοὶ καὶ σοί,
and voice in a great(loud) said : What to me and to thee,

Ἰησοῦ υἱὲ τοῦ θεοῦ τοῦ ὑψίστου; δέομαί
Jesus Son - of God - most high? I beg

but they were not able to get near him because of the crowd. 20Someone told him, "Your mother and brothers are standing outside, wanting to see you."

21He replied, "My mother and brothers are those who hear God's word and put it into practice."

Jesus Calms the Storm

22One day Jesus said to his disciples, "Let's go over to the other side of the lake." So they got into a boat and set out. 23As they sailed, he fell asleep. A squall came down on the lake, so that the boat was being swamped, and they were in great danger.

24The disciples went and woke him, saying, "Master, Master, we're going to drown!"

He got up and rebuked the wind and the raging waters; the storm subsided, and all was calm. 25"Where is your faith?" he asked his disciples.

In fear and amazement they asked one another, "Who is this? He commands even the winds and the water, and they obey him."

The Healing of a Demon-possessed Man

26They sailed to the region of the Gerasenes,ᵍ which is across the lake from Galilee. 27When Jesus stepped ashore, he was met by a demon-possessed man from the town. For a long time this man had not worn clothes or lived in a house, but had lived in the tombs. 28When he saw Jesus, he cried out and fell at his feet, shouting at the top of his voice, "What do you want with me, Jesus, Son of the Most High God? I beg you,

You, do not torment me."
²⁹For He had been commanding the unclean spirit to come out of the man. For it had seized him many times; and he was bound with chains and shackles and kept under guard; but *yet* he would burst his fetters and be driven by the demon into the desert.
³⁰And Jesus asked him, "What is your name?" And he said, "Legion"; for many demons had entered him.
³¹And they were entreating Him not to command them to depart into the abyss.
³²Now there was a herd of many swine feeding there on the mountain; and *the demons* entreated Him to permit them to enter the swine. And He gave them permission.
³³And the demons came out from the man and entered the swine; and the herd rushed down the steep bank into the lake, and were drowned.
³⁴And when the herdsmen saw what had happened, they ran away and reported it in the city and *out* in the country.
³⁵And *the people* went out to see what had happened; and they came to Jesus, and found the man from whom the demons had gone out, sitting down at the feet of Jesus, clothed and in his right mind; and they became frightened.
³⁶And those who had seen it reported to them how the man who was demon-possessed had been made well.
³⁷And all the people of the country of the Gerasenes and the surrounding district asked Him to depart from them; for they were gripped with great fear; and He got into a boat, and returned.

σου, μή με βασανίσῃς. 29 παρήγγελλεν
of thee, do not me torment.   he charged
γὰρ τῷ πνεύματι τῷ ἀκαθάρτῳ ἐξελθεῖν
For the spirit – unclean to come out
ἀπὸ τοῦ ἀνθρώπου. πολλοῖς γὰρ χρόνοις
from the man. For many times
συνηρπάκει αὐτόν, καὶ ἐδεσμεύετο ἁλύσεσιν
it had seized him, and he was bound with chains
καὶ πέδαις φυλασσόμενος, καὶ διαρρήσσων
and fetters being guarded, and tearing asunder
τὰ δεσμὰ ἠλαύνετο ἀπὸ τοῦ δαιμονίου εἰς
the bonds he was driven from(by) the demon into
τὰς ἐρήμους. 30 ἐπηρώτησεν δὲ αὐτὸν ὁ
the deserts.   And questioned him . –
Ἰησοῦς· τί σοι ὄνομά ἐστιν; ὁ δὲ εἶπεν·
Jesus : What to thee name is?ᶜ And he said :
λεγιών, ὅτι εἰσῆλθεν δαιμόνια πολλὰ εἰς
Legion, because ³entered ²demons ¹many into
αὐτόν. 31 καὶ παρεκάλουν αὐτὸν ἵνα μὴ
him. And they besought him that not
ἐπιτάξῃ αὐτοῖς εἰς τὴν ἄβυσσον ἀπελθεῖν.
he would order them into the abyss to go away.
32 ἦν δὲ ἐκεῖ ἀγέλη χοίρων ἱκανῶν
Now there was there a herd pigs of many
βοσκομένη ἐν τῷ ὄρει· καὶ παρεκάλεσαν
feeding in the mountain; and they besought
αὐτὸν ἵνα ἐπιτρέψῃ αὐτοῖς εἰς ἐκείνους
him that he would allow them into those
εἰσελθεῖν· καὶ ἐπέτρεψεν αὐτοῖς. 33 ἐξελθόντα
to enter; and he allowed them. ⁴coming out
δὲ τὰ δαιμόνια ἀπὸ τοῦ ἀνθρώπου εἰσῆλθον
¹So ²the ³demons from the man entered
εἰς τοὺς χοίρους, καὶ ὥρμησεν ἡ ἀγέλη
into the pigs, and rushed the herd
κατὰ τοῦ κρημνοῦ εἰς τὴν λίμνην καὶ
down the precipice into the lake and
ἀπεπνίγη. 34 ἰδόντες δὲ οἱ βόσκοντες
was choked. And ³seeing ¹the [ones] ²feeding
τὸ γεγονὸς ἔφυγον καὶ ἀπήγγειλαν εἰς
⁴the thing ³having fled and reported · in
     happened
=what had happened
τὴν πόλιν καὶ εἰς τοὺς ἀγρούς. 35 ἐξῆλθον
the city and in the farms. they went out
δὲ ἰδεῖν τὸ γεγονός, καὶ ἦλθον πρὸς τὸν
And to see the thing having and came to –
     happened,
=what had happened,
Ἰησοῦν, καὶ εὗρον καθήμενον τὸν ἄνθρωπον
Jesus, and found sitting the man
ἀφ᾽ οὗ τὰ δαιμόνια ἐξῆλθεν ἱματισμένον
from whom the demons went out *having been* clothed
καὶ σωφρονοῦντα παρὰ τοὺς πόδας τοῦ
and being in his senses by the feet –
Ἰησοῦ, καὶ ἐφοβήθησαν. 36 ἀπήγγειλαν δὲ
of Jesus, and they were afraid. And ²reported
αὐτοῖς οἱ ἰδόντες πῶς ἐσώθη ὁ δαιμο-
⁴to them ¹the [ones] ³seeing ⁵how ⁶was healed ⁷the ⁸demon-
νισθείς. 37 καὶ ἠρώτησεν αὐτὸν ἅπαν τὸ
possessed. And asked him all the
πλῆθος τῆς περιχώρου τῶν Γερασηνῶν
multitude of the neighbourhood of the Gerasenes
ἀπελθεῖν ἀπ᾽ αὐτῶν, ὅτι φόβῳ μεγάλῳ
to go away from them, because fear with a great
συνείχοντο· αὐτὸς δὲ ἐμβὰς εἰς πλοῖον
they were seized; so he embarking in a boat

don't torture me!" ²⁹For Jesus had commanded the evilʰ spirit to come out of the man. Many times it had seized him, and though he was chained hand and foot and kept under guard, he had broken his chains and had been driven by the demon into solitary places.
³⁰Jesus asked him, "What is your name?"
"Legion," he replied, because many demons had gone into him. ³¹And they begged him repeatedly not to order them to go into the Abyss.
³²A large herd of pigs was feeding there on the hillside. The demons begged Jesus to let them go into them, and he gave them permission. ³³When the demons came out of the man, they went into the pigs, and the herd rushed down the steep bank into the lake and was drowned.
³⁴When those tending the pigs saw what had happened, they ran off and reported this in the town and countryside, ³⁵and the people went out to see what had happened. When they came to Jesus, they found the man from whom the demons had gone out, sitting at Jesus' feet, dressed and in his right mind; and they were afraid. ³⁶Those who had seen it told the people how the demon-possessed man had been cured. ³⁷Then all the people of the region of the Gerasenes asked Jesus to leave them, because they were overcome with fear. So he got into the boat and left.

ʰ29 Greek *unclean*

38But the man from whom the demons had gone out was begging Him that he might accompany Him; but He sent him away, saying, 39"Return to your house and describe what great things God has done for you." And he went away, proclaiming throughout the whole city what great things Jesus had done for him.

Miracles of Healing

40And as Jesus returned, the multitude welcomed Him, for they had all been waiting for Him. 41And behold, there came a man named Jairus, and he was an official of the synagogue; and he fell at Jesus' feet, and *began* to entreat Him to come to his house; 42for he had an only daughter, about twelve years old, and she was dying. But as He went, the multitudes were pressing against Him.

43And a woman who had a hemorrhage for twelve years, ˢand could not be healed by anyone, 44came up behind Him, and touched the fringe of His cloak; and immediately her hemorrhage stopped. 45And Jesus said, "Who is the one who touched Me?" And while they were all denying it, Peter said, "Master, the multitudes are crowding and pressing upon You." 46But Jesus said, "Someone did touch Me, for I was aware that power had gone out of Me." 47And when the woman saw that she had not escaped notice, she came trembling and fell down before Him, and declared in the presence of all the people the reason why she had touched Him, and how

ˢ Some mss. add *who had spent all her living upon physicians*

ὑπέστρεψεν. 38 ἐδεῖτο δὲ αὐτοῦ ὁ ἀνὴρ
returned.   And begged   of him   the man
ἀφ' οὗ ἐξεληλύθει τὰ δαιμόνια εἶναι σὺν
from whom had gone out the demons   to be   with
αὐτῷ· ἀπέλυσεν δὲ αὐτὸν λέγων· 39 ὑπόστρεφε
him; but he dismissed him saying :   Return
εἰς τὸν οἶκόν σου, καὶ διηγοῦ ὅσα σοι
to the house of thee, and relate what ²to thee things
ἐποίησεν ὁ θεός. καὶ ἀπῆλθεν καθ' ὅλην
¹did   - ¹God.   And he went away throughout all
τὴν πόλιν κηρύσσων ὅσα ἐποίησεν αὐτῷ
the city proclaiming what things ²did ²to him
ὁ Ἰησοῦς.
- ¹Jesus.
40 Ἐν δὲ τῷ ὑποστρέφειν τὸν Ἰησοῦν
Now in the   to return   -   Jesus
=when Jesus returned
ἀπεδέξατο αὐτὸν ὁ ὄχλος· ἦσαν γὰρ
welcomed him   the crowd; for they were
πάντες προσδοκῶντες αὐτόν. 41 καὶ ἰδοὺ
all   expecting   him.   And behold
ἦλθεν ἀνὴρ ᾧ ὄνομα Ἰάϊρος, καὶ οὗτος
came a man to whom name Jairus, and this man
ἄρχων τῆς συναγωγῆς ὑπῆρχεν· καὶ πεσὼν
a ruler of the synagogue was;   and falling
παρὰ τοὺς πόδας Ἰησοῦ παρεκάλει αὐτὸν
at   the   feet of Jesus he besought him
εἰσελθεῖν εἰς τὸν οἶκον αὐτοῦ, 42 ὅτι
to enter into the house of him,   because
θυγάτηρ μονογενὴς ἦν αὐτῷ ὡς ἐτῶν
daughter an only born was to him about of years
=he had an only daughter
δώδεκα καὶ αὕτη ἀπέθνησκεν. Ἐν δὲ τῷ
twelve and this(she) was dying. Now in the
=as he went
ὑπάγειν αὐτὸν οἱ ὄχλοι συνέπνιγον αὐτόν.
to go   him   the crowds pressed upon him.
43 καὶ γυνὴ οὖσα ἐν ῥύσει αἵματος ἀπὸ
And a woman being in a flow of blood from
=having
ἐτῶν δώδεκα, ἥτις οὐκ ἴσχυσεν ἀπ'
years twelve, who was not able   from
οὐδενὸς θεραπευθῆναι, 44 προσελθοῦσα ὄπισθεν
no(any)one to be healed, approaching behind
ἥψατο τοῦ κρασπέδου τοῦ ἱματίου αὐτοῦ,
touched the fringe   of the garment of him,
καὶ παραχρῆμα ἔστη ἡ ῥύσις τοῦ αἵματος
and at once stood the flow of the blood
αὐτῆς. 45 καὶ εἶπεν ὁ Ἰησοῦς· τίς ὁ
of her. And said - Jesus :   Who the
ἁψάμενός μου; ἀρνουμένων δὲ πάντων
[one] touching me? And denying   all
=when all denied
εἶπεν ὁ Πέτρος· ἐπιστάτα, οἱ ὄχλοι
said - Peter :   Master,   the crowds
συνέχουσίν σε καὶ ἀποθλίβουσιν. 46 ὁ δὲ
press upon thee and jostle.   - But
Ἰησοῦς εἶπεν· ἥψατό μού τις· ἐγὼ γὰρ
Jesus said : Touched me someone; for I
ἔγνων δύναμιν ἐξεληλυθυῖαν ἀπ' ἐμοῦ.
knew power   having gone forth from me.
47 ἰδοῦσα δὲ ἡ γυνὴ ὅτι οὐκ ἔλαθεν,
And ²seeing ¹the ²woman that she was not hidden,
τρέμουσα ἦλθεν καὶ προσπεσοῦσα αὐτῷ δι'
trembling came and prostrating before him ⁶for
ἦν αἰτίαν ἥψατο αὐτοῦ ἀπήγγειλεν ἐνώπιον
⁷what ⁸cause ⁹she touched ¹⁰him ¹declared ³before

38The man from whom the demons had gone out begged to go with him, but Jesus sent him away, saying, 39"Return home and tell how much God has done for you." So the man went away and told all over town how much Jesus had done for him.

A Dead Girl and a Sick Woman

40Now when Jesus returned, a crowd welcomed him, for they were all expecting him. 41Then a man named Jairus, a ruler of the synagogue, came and fell at Jesus' feet, pleading with him to come to his house 42because his only daughter, a girl of about twelve, was dying.

As Jesus was on his way, the crowds almost crushed him. 43And a woman was there who had been subject to bleeding for twelve years,ⁱ but no one could heal her. 44She came up behind him and touched the edge of his cloak, and immediately her bleeding stopped.
45"Who touched me?" Jesus asked.
When they all denied it, Peter said, "Master, the people are crowding and pressing against you."
46But Jesus said, "Someone touched me; I know that power has gone out from me."
47Then the woman, seeing that she could not go unnoticed, came trembling and fell at his feet. In the presence of all the people, she told why she had touched him and how she

ⁱ43 Many manuscripts *years, and she had spent all she had on doctors* she had been immediately healed.

48And He said to her, "Daughter, your faith has made you well; go in peace."

49While He was still speaking, someone *came from *the house of* the synagogue official, saying, "Your daughter has died; do not trouble the Teacher anymore."

50But when Jesus heard this, He answered him, "Do not be afraid any longer; only believe, and she shall be made well."

51And when He had come to the house, He did not allow anyone to enter with Him, except Peter and John and James, and the girl's father and mother.

52Now they were all weeping and lamenting for her; but He said, "Stop weeping, for she has not died, but is asleep."

53And they began laughing at Him, knowing that she had died.

54He, however, took her by the hand and called, saying, "Child, arise!"

55And her spirit returned, and she rose immediately; and He gave orders for something to be given her to eat.

56And her parents were amazed; but He instructed them to tell no one what had happened.

παντὸς τοῦ λαοῦ, καὶ ὡς ἰάθη παραχρῆμα.
ᵃall ⁴the ⁵people, and how she was cured at once.

48 ὁ δὲ εἶπεν αὐτῇ· θυγάτηρ, ἡ πίστις
And he said to her: Daughter, the faith

σου σέσωκέν σε· πορεύου εἰς εἰρήνην.
of thee has healed thee; go in peace.

49 Ἔτι αὐτοῦ λαλοῦντος ἔρχεταί τις παρὰ
Yet him speakingᵃ comes someone from
=While he was yet speaking

τοῦ ἀρχισυναγώγου λέγων ὅτι τέθνηκεν
the synagogue ruler saying[,] - Has died

ἡ θυγάτηρ σου· μηκέτι σκύλλε τὸν
the daughter of thee; no more trouble the

διδάσκαλον. 50 ὁ δὲ Ἰησοῦς ἀκούσας
teacher. - But Jesus hearing

ἀπεκρίθη αὐτῷ· μὴ φοβοῦ· μόνον πίστευσον,
answered him: Fear not; only believe,

καὶ σωθήσεται. 51 ἐλθὼν δὲ εἰς τὴν
and she will be healed. And coming into the

οἰκίαν οὐκ ἀφῆκεν εἰσελθεῖν τινα σὺν
house he allowed not to enter anyone with

αὐτῷ εἰ μὴ Πέτρον καὶ Ἰωάννην καὶ
him except Peter and John and

Ἰάκωβον καὶ τὸν πατέρα τῆς παιδὸς καὶ
James and the father of the maid and

τὴν μητέρα. 52 ἔκλαιον δὲ πάντες καὶ
the mother. And were weeping all and

ἐκόπτοντο αὐτήν. ὁ δὲ εἶπεν· μὴ κλαίετε·
bewailing her. But he said: Weep ye not;

οὐκ ἀπέθανεν ἀλλὰ καθεύδει. 53 καὶ
she did not die but sleeps. And

κατεγέλων αὐτοῦ, εἰδότες ὅτι ἀπέθανεν.
they ridiculed him, knowing that she died.

54 αὐτὸς δὲ κρατήσας τῆς χειρὸς αὐτῆς
But he holding the hand of her

ἐφώνησεν λέγων· ἡ παῖς, ἔγειρε. 55 καὶ
called saying: - Maid, arise. And

ἐπέστρεψεν τὸ πνεῦμα αὐτῆς, καὶ ἀνέστη
returned the spirit of her, and she rose up

παραχρῆμα, καὶ διέταξεν αὐτῇ δοθῆναι
at once, and he commanded ¹to her ¹to be given

φαγεῖν. 56 καὶ ἐξέστησαν οἱ γονεῖς
to eat. And were amazed the parents

αὐτῆς· ὁ δὲ παρήγγειλεν αὐτοῖς μηδενὶ
of her; but he enjoined them ²no one

εἰπεῖν τὸ γεγονός.
¹to tell the thing having happened.
=what had happened.

---

had been instantly healed.
48Then he said to her, "Daughter, your faith has healed you. Go in peace."

49While Jesus was still speaking, someone came from the house of Jairus, the synagogue ruler. "Your daughter is dead," he said. "Don't bother the teacher any more."

50Hearing this, Jesus said to Jairus, "Don't be afraid; just believe, and she will be healed."

51When he arrived at the house of Jairus, he did not let anyone go in with him except Peter, John and James, and the child's father and mother. 52Meanwhile, all the people were wailing and mourning for her. "Stop wailing," Jesus said. "She is not dead but asleep."

53They laughed at him, knowing that she was dead. 54But he took her by the hand and said, "My child, get up!" 55Her spirit returned, and at once she stood up. Then Jesus told them to give her something to eat. 56Her parents were astonished, but he ordered them not to tell anyone what had happened.

Chapter 9

Ministry of the Twelve

AND He called the twelve together, and gave them power and authority over all the demons, and to heal diseases.

2And He sent them out to proclaim the kingdom of God, and to perform healing.

3And He said to them, "Take nothing for your journey, neither a staff, nor a bag, nor bread, nor money; and do not even have two tunics apiece.

---

9 Συγκαλεσάμενος δὲ τοὺς δώδεκα ἔδωκεν
And having called together the twelve he gave

αὐτοῖς δύναμιν καὶ ἐξουσίαν ἐπὶ πάντα τὰ
them power and authority over all the

δαιμόνια καὶ νόσους θεραπεύειν· 2 καὶ
demons and diseases to heal; and

ἀπέστειλεν αὐτοὺς κηρύσσειν τὴν βασιλείαν
sent them to proclaim the kingdom

τοῦ θεοῦ καὶ ἰᾶσθαι, 3 καὶ εἶπεν πρὸς
- of God and to cure, and said to

αὐτούς· μηδὲν αἴρετε εἰς τὴν ὁδόν, μήτε
them: Nothing take ye for the way, neither

ῥάβδον μήτε πήραν μήτε ἄρτον μήτε
staff nor wallet nor bread nor

ἀργύριον μήτε ἀνὰ δύο χιτῶνας ἔχειν.
silver nor each two tunics to have.

Chapter 9

Jesus Sends Out the Twelve

WHEN Jesus had called the Twelve together, he gave them power and authority to drive out all demons and to cure diseases, 2and he sent them out to preach the kingdom of God and to heal the sick. 3He told them: "Take nothing for the journey—no staff, no bag, no bread, no money, no extra tunic.

4"And whatever house you enter, stay there, and take your leave from there.

5"And as for those who do not receive you, as you go out from that city, shake off the dust from your feet as a testimony against them."

6And departing, they *began* going about among the villages, preaching the gospel, and healing everywhere.

7Now Herod the tetrarch heard of all that was happening; and he was greatly perplexed, because it was said by some that John had risen from the dead,

8and by some that Elijah had appeared, and by others, that one of the prophets of old had risen again.

9And Herod said, "I myself had John beheaded; but who is this man about whom I hear such things?" And he kept trying to see Him.

10And when the apostles returned, they gave an account to Him of all that they had done. And taking them with Him, He withdrew by Himself to a city called Bethsaida.

11But the multitudes were aware of this and followed Him; and welcoming them, He *began* speaking to them about the kingdom of God and curing those who had need of healing.

Five Thousand Fed

12And the day began to decline, and the twelve came and said to Him, "Send the multitude away, that they may go into the surrounding villages and countryside and find lodging and get something to eat; for here we are in a desolate place."

13But He said to them, "You give them *something* to eat!" And they said, "We have no more than five loaves and two fish,

---

4 καὶ εἰς ἣν ἂν οἰκίαν εἰσέλθητε, ἐκεῖ
And into whatever house ye may enter, there

μένετε καὶ ἐκεῖθεν ἐξέρχεσθε. 5 καὶ
remain and thence go forth. And

ὅσοι ἂν μὴ δέχωνται ὑμᾶς, ἐξερχόμενοι
as many as may not receive you, going forth

ἀπὸ τῆς πόλεως ἐκείνης τὸν κονιορτὸν
from — city that the dust

ἀπὸ τῶν ποδῶν ὑμῶν ἀποτινάσσετε εἰς
from the feet of you shake off for

μαρτύριον ἐπ' αὐτούς. 6 ἐξερχόμενοι δὲ
a testimony against them. And going forth

διήρχοντο κατὰ τὰς κώμας εὐαγγελιζόμενοι
they went throughout the villages evangelizing
through

καὶ θεραπεύοντες πανταχοῦ. 7 ῞Ηκουσεν
and healing everywhere. ¹heard

δὲ ῾Ηρῴδης ὁ τετραάρχης τὰ γινόμενα
¹And ²Herod ³the ⁴tetrarch the things happening

πάντα, καὶ διηπόρει διὰ τὸ λέγεσθαι
all, and was in perplexity because of the to be said
=because it was said

ὑπό τινων ὅτι ᾽Ιωάννης ἠγέρθη ἐκ νεκρῶν,
by some that John was raised from [the] dead,

8 ὑπό τινων δὲ ὅτι ᾽Ηλίας ἐφάνη, ἄλλων
and by some that Elias appeared, ²others

δὲ ὅτι προφήτης τις τῶν ἀρχαίων ἀνέστη.
¹but that prophet a certain of the ancients rose again.

9 εἶπεν δὲ [ὁ] ῾Ηρῴδης· ᾽Ιωάννην ἐγὼ
But said - Herod : John I

ἀπεκεφάλισα· τίς δέ ἐστιν οὗτος περὶ οὗ
beheaded; but who is this about whom

ἀκούω τοιαῦτα; καὶ ἐζήτει ἰδεῖν αὐτόν.
I hear such things? And he sought to see him.

10 Καὶ ὑποστρέψαντες οἱ ἀπόστολοι
And having returned the apostles

διηγήσαντο αὐτῷ ὅσα ἐποίησαν. Καὶ
narrated to him what things they did. And

παραλαβὼν αὐτοὺς ὑπεχώρησεν κατ' ἰδίαν
taking them he departed privately

εἰς πόλιν καλουμένην Βηθσαϊδά. 11 οἱ δὲ
to a city being called Bethsaida. But the

ὄχλοι γνόντες ἠκολούθησαν αὐτῷ· καὶ
crowds knowing followed him; and

ἀποδεξάμενος αὐτοὺς ἐλάλει αὐτοῖς περὶ
welcoming them he spoke to them about

τῆς βασιλείας τοῦ θεοῦ, καὶ τοὺς χρείαν
the kingdom - of God, and the [ones] ²need

ἔχοντας θεραπείας ἰᾶτο. 12 ῾Η δὲ ἡμέρα
¹having of healing he cured. But the day

ἤρξατο κλίνειν· προσελθόντες δὲ οἱ δώδεκα
began to decline; and approaching the twelve

εἶπαν αὐτῷ· ἀπόλυσον τὸν ὄχλον, ἵνα
said to him : Dismiss the crowd, that

πορευθέντες εἰς τὰς κύκλῳ κώμας καὶ
going to ¹the ²around ³villages ²and

ἀγροὺς καταλύσωσιν καὶ εὕρωσιν ἐπισιτισμόν,
⁴farms they may lodge and may find provisions,

ὅτι ὧδε ἐν ἐρήμῳ τόπῳ ἐσμέν. 13 εἶπεν
because here in a desert place we are. he said

δὲ πρὸς αὐτούς· δότε αὐτοῖς φαγεῖν
And to them : ¹Give ²them ⁴to eat

ὑμεῖς. οἱ δὲ εἶπαν· οὐκ εἰσὶν ἡμῖν
³ye. But they said : There are not to us⁵
=We have not

πλεῖον ἢ ἄρτοι πέντε καὶ ἰχθύες δύο, εἰ
more than loaves five and fishes two, un-

4Whatever house you enter, stay there until you leave that town. 5If people do not welcome you, shake the dust off your feet when you leave their town, as a testimony against them." 6So they set out and went from village to village, preaching the gospel and healing people everywhere.

7Now Herod the tetrarch heard about all that was going on. And he was perplexed, because some were saying that John had been raised from the dead, 8others that Elijah had appeared, and still others that one of the prophets of long ago had come back to life. 9But Herod said, "I beheaded John. Who, then, is this I hear such things about?" And he tried to see him.

Jesus Feeds the Five Thousand

10When the apostles returned, they reported to Jesus what they had done. Then he took them with him and they withdrew by themselves to a town called Bethsaida, 11but the crowds learned about it and followed him. He welcomed them and spoke to them about the kingdom of God, and healed those who needed healing.

12Late in the afternoon the Twelve came to him and said, "Send the crowd away so they can go to the surrounding villages and countryside and find food and lodging, because we are in a remote place here."

13He replied, "You give them something to eat."

They answered, "We have only five loaves of bread and two fish—unless

unless perhaps we go and buy food for all these people."

14(For there were about five thousand men.) And He said to His disciples, "Have them recline *to eat* in groups of about fifty each."

15And they did so, and had them all recline.

16And He took the five loaves and the two fish, and looking up to heaven, He blessed them, and broke *them*, and kept giving *them* to the disciples to set before the multitude.

17And they all ate and were satisfied; and the broken pieces which they had left over were picked up, twelve baskets *full*.

18And it came about that while He was praying alone, the disciples were with Him, and He questioned them, saying, "Who do the multitudes say that I am?"

19And they answered and said, "John the Baptist, and others *say* Elijah; but others, that one of the prophets of old has risen again."

20And He said to them, "But who do you say that I am?" And Peter answered and said, "The Christ of God."

21But He warned them, and instructed *them* not to tell this to anyone,

22saying, "The Son of Man must suffer many things, and be rejected by the elders and chief priests and scribes, and be killed, and be raised up on the third day."

23And He was saying to *them* all, "If anyone wishes to come after Me, let him deny himself, and take up his cross daily, and follow Me."

μήτι πορευθέντες ἡμεῖς ἀγοράσωμεν εἰς
less going we may buy for
πάντα τὸν λαὸν τοῦτον βρώματα. 14 ἦσαν
all - people this foods. there were
γὰρ ὡσεὶ ἄνδρες πεντακισχίλιοι. εἶπεν δὲ
For about men five thousand. And he said
πρὸς τοὺς μαθητὰς αὐτοῦ· κατακλίνατε
to the disciples of him : ¹Make ²to recline
αὐτοὺς κλισίας ὡσεὶ ἀνὰ πεντήκοντα.
³them [in] groups ¹about ²each ³fifty.
15 καὶ ἐποίησαν οὕτως καὶ κατέκλιναν
And they did so and made to recline
ἅπαντας. 16 λαβὼν δὲ τοὺς πέντε ἄρτους
all. And taking the five loaves
καὶ τοὺς δύο ἰχθύας, ἀναβλέψας εἰς τὸν
and the two fishes, looking up to -
οὐρανὸν εὐλόγησεν αὐτοὺς καὶ κατέκλασεν,
heaven he blessed them and broke,
καὶ ἐδίδου τοῖς μαθηταῖς παραθεῖναι τῷ
and gave to the disciples to set before the
ὄχλῳ. 17 καὶ ἔφαγον καὶ ἐχορτάσθησαν
crowd. And they ate and were satisfied
πάντες· καὶ ἤρθη τὸ περισσεῦσαν αὐτοῖς
all; and were taken the excess to them
κλασμάτων κόφινοι δώδεκα.
of fragments baskets twelve.
18 Καὶ ἐγένετο ἐν τῷ εἶναι αὐτὸν
And it came to pass in the to be him ᵇᵉ
=as he was
προσευχόμενον κατὰ μόνας συνῆσαν αὐτῷ
praying alone were with him
οἱ μαθηταί, καὶ ἐπηρώτησεν αὐτοὺς λέγων·
the disciples, and he questioned them saying :
τίνα με οἱ ὄχλοι λέγουσιν εἶναι; 19 οἱ δὲ
Whom me the crowds say to be? And they
=Whom do the crowds say that I am?
ἀποκριθέντες εἶπαν· Ἰωάννην τὸν βαπτιστήν,
answering said : John the Baptist,
ἄλλοι δὲ Ἡλίαν, ἄλλοι δὲ ὅτι προφήτης
but others Elias, and others that prophet
τις τῶν ἀρχαίων ἀνέστη. 20 εἶπεν . δὲ
a certain of the ancients rose again. And he said
αὐτοῖς· ὑμεῖς δὲ τίνα με λέγετε εἶναι;
to them : But ye whom me say to be?
=whom say ye that I am?
Πέτρος δὲ ἀποκριθεὶς εἶπεν· τὸν χριστὸν
And Peter answering said: The Christ
τοῦ θεοῦ. 21 ὁ δὲ ἐπιτιμήσας αὐτοῖς
- of God. But he warning ²them
παρήγγειλεν μηδενὶ λέγειν τοῦτο, 22 εἰπὼν
¹charged ⁴no one ³to tell ⁵this, saying
ὅτι δεῖ τὸν υἱὸν τοῦ ἀνθρώπου πολλὰ
that it behoves the Son - of man many things
παθεῖν καὶ ἀποδοκιμασθῆναι ἀπὸ τῶν
to suffer and to be rejected from(by) the
πρεσβυτέρων καὶ ἀρχιερέων καὶ γραμματέων
elders and chief priests and scribes
καὶ ἀποκτανθῆναι καὶ τῇ τρίτῃ ἡμέρᾳ
and to be killed and on the third day
ἐγερθῆναι. 23 Ἔλεγεν δὲ πρὸς πάντας·
to be raised. And he said to all :
εἴ τις θέλει ὀπίσω μου ἔρχεσθαι, ἀρνησάσθω
If anyone wishes after me to come, let him deny
ἑαυτὸν καὶ ἀράτω τὸν σταυρὸν
himself and take the cross
αὐτοῦ καθ' ἡμέραν, καὶ ἀκολουθείτω μοι.
of him daily, and let him follow me.

---

we go and buy food for all this crowd." 14(About five thousand men were there.)

But he said to his disciples, "Have them sit down in groups of about fifty each." 15The disciples did so, and everybody sat down. 16Taking the five loaves and the two fish and looking up to heaven, he gave thanks and broke them. Then he gave them to the disciples to set before the people. 17They all ate and were satisfied, and the disciples picked up twelve basketfuls of broken pieces that were left over.

Peter's Confession of Christ

18Once when Jesus was praying in private and his disciples were with him, he asked them, "Who do the crowds say I am?"

19They replied, "Some say John the Baptist; others say Elijah; and still others, that one of the prophets of long ago has come back to life."

20"But what about you?" he asked. "Who do you say I am?"

Peter answered, "The Christ ʲ of God."

21Jesus strictly warned them not to tell this to anyone. 22And he said, "The Son of Man must suffer many things and be rejected by the elders, chief priests and teachers of the law, and he must be killed and on the third day be raised to life."

23Then he said to them all: "If anyone would come after me, he must deny himself and take up his cross daily and follow me. 24For

ʲ20 Or *Messiah*

24"For whoever wishes to save his life shall lose it, but whoever loses his life for My sake, he is the one who will save it.

25"For what is a man profited if he gains the whole world, and loses or forfeits himself?

26"For whoever is ashamed of Me and My words, of him will the Son of Man be ashamed when He comes in His glory, and *the glory* of the Father and of the holy angels.

27"But I say to you truthfully, there are some of those standing here who shall not taste death until they see the kingdom of God."

The Transfiguration

28And some eight days after these sayings, it came about that He took along Peter and John and James, and went up to the mountain to pray.

29And while He was praying, the appearance of His face became different, and His clothing *became* white *and* gleaming.

30And behold, two men were talking with Him; and they were Moses and Elijah,

31who, appearing in glory, were speaking of His departure which He was about to accomplish at Jerusalem.

32Now Peter and his companions had been overcome with sleep; but when they were fully awake, they saw His glory and the two men standing with Him.

33And it came about, as these were parting from Him, Peter said to Jesus, "Master, it is good for us to be here; and let us make three tabernacles: one for

---

24 ὃς γὰρ ἐὰν θέλῃ τὴν ψυχὴν αὐτοῦ
For whoever wishes the life of him

σῶσαι, ἀπολέσει αὐτήν· ὃς δ' ἂν ἀπολέσῃ
to save, he will lose it; but whoever loses

τὴν ψυχὴν αὐτοῦ ἕνεκεν ἐμοῦ, οὗτος
the life of him for the sake of me, this [one]

σώσει αὐτήν. **25** τί γὰρ ὠφελεῖται
will save it. For what is profited

ἄνθρωπος κερδήσας τὸν κόσμον ὅλον ἑαυτὸν
a man gaining the world whole ²himself

δὲ ἀπολέσας ἢ ζημιωθείς; **26** ὃς γὰρ ἂν
¹but ²losing or suffering loss? For whoever

ἐπαισχυνθῇ με καὶ τοὺς ἐμοὺς λόγους,
is ashamed of me and   -   my words,

τοῦτον ὁ υἱὸς τοῦ ἀνθρώπου ἐπαι-
this [one] the Son   -   of man will be

σχυνθήσεται, ὅταν ἔλθῃ ἐν τῇ δόξῃ
ashamed of, when he comes in the glory

αὐτοῦ καὶ τοῦ πατρὸς καὶ τῶν ἁγίων
of him and of the Father and of the holy

ἀγγέλων. **27** λέγω δὲ ὑμῖν ἀληθῶς,
angels.   But I tell you truly,

εἰσίν τινες τῶν αὐτοῦ ἑστηκότων οἳ
there are some of the [ones] here standing who

οὐ μὴ γεύσωνται θανάτου ἕως ἂν ἴδωσιν
by no means may taste of death until they see

τὴν βασιλείαν τοῦ θεοῦ.
the kingdom   -   of God.

28 Ἐγένετο δὲ μετὰ τοὺς λόγους τούτους
And it came to pass ⁴after   -   ⁵sayings ⁵these

ὡσεὶ ἡμέραι ὀκτώ, καὶ παραλαβὼν Πέτρον
¹about ²days ³eight, *and* taking Peter

καὶ Ἰωάννην καὶ Ἰάκωβον ἀνέβη εἰς τὸ
and John and James he went up into the

ὄρος προσεύξασθαι. **29** καὶ ἐγένετο ἐν τῷ
mountain to pray. And ⁹became in the
                                   =¹as ¹he ²prayed

προσεύχεσθαι αὐτὸν τὸ εἶδος τοῦ προσώπου
to pray himbe ⁴the ⁵appearance ⁶of the ⁷face

αὐτοῦ ἕτερον καὶ ὁ ἱματισμὸς αὐτοῦ
⁸of him ¹⁰different and the raiment of him

λευκὸς ἐξαστράπτων. **30** καὶ ἰδοὺ ἄνδρες
⁹white ¹gleaming.   And[,] behold[,] men

δύο συνελάλουν αὐτῷ, οἵτινες ἦσαν Μωϋσῆς
two conversed with him, who were Moses

καὶ Ἡλίας, **31** οἳ ὀφθέντες ἐν δόξῃ ἔλεγον
and Elias, who appearing in glory spoke of

τὴν ἔξοδον αὐτοῦ, ἣν ἤμελλεν πληροῦν
the exodus of him, which he was about to accomplish

ἐν Ἰερουσαλήμ. **32** ὁ δὲ Πέτρος καὶ οἱ
in Jerusalem.   - But Peter and the [ones]

σὺν αὐτῷ ἦσαν βεβαρημένοι ὕπνῳ· δια-
with him were *having been* burdened with sleep; ²wak-

γρηγορήσαντες δὲ εἶδαν τὴν δόξαν αὐτοῦ
ing thoroughly ¹but they saw the glory of him

καὶ τοὺς δύο ἄνδρας τοὺς συνεστῶτας
and the two men   -   standing with

αὐτῷ. **33** καὶ ἐγένετο ἐν τῷ διαχωρίζεσθαι
him.   And it came to pass in the to part
                                   =when they parted

αὐτοὺς ἀπ' αὐτοῦ εἶπεν ὁ Πέτρος πρὸς
thembe from him said   -   Peter to

τὸν Ἰησοῦν· ἐπιστάτα, καλόν ἐστιν ἡμᾶς
   -    Jesus: Master, good it is [for] us

ὧδε εἶναι, καὶ ποιήσωμεν σκηνὰς τρεῖς,
here to be, and let us make tents three,

---

whoever wants to save his life will lose it, but whoever loses his life for me will save it. 25What good is it for a man to gain the whole world, and yet lose or forfeit his very self? 26If anyone is ashamed of me and my words, the Son of Man will be ashamed of him when he comes in his glory and in the glory of the Father and of the holy angels. 27I tell you the truth, some who are standing here will not taste death before they see the kingdom of God."

The Transfiguration

28About eight days after Jesus said this, he took Peter, John and James with him and went up onto a mountain to pray. 29As he was praying, the appearance of his face changed, and his clothes became as bright as a flash of lightning. 30Two men, Moses and Elijah, 31appeared in glorious splendor, talking with Jesus. They spoke about his departure, which he was about to bring to fulfillment at Jerusalem. 32Peter and his companions were very sleepy, but when they became fully awake, they saw his glory and the two men standing with him. 33As the men were leaving Jesus, Peter said to him, "Master, it is good for us to be here. Let us put up three shelters—one for you, one

You, and one for Moses, and one for Elijah"—not realizing what he was saying.

34And while he was saying this, a cloud formed and *began* to overshadow them; and they were afraid as they entered the cloud.

35And a voice came out of the cloud, saying, "This is My Son, *My* Chosen One; listen to Him!"

36And when the voice had spoken, Jesus was found alone. And they kept silent, and reported to no one in those days any of the things which they had seen.

37And it came about on the next day, that when they had come down from the mountain, a great multitude met Him.

38And behold, a man from the multitude shouted out, saying, "Teacher, I beg You to look at my son, for he is my only *boy,*

39and behold, a spirit seizes him, and he suddenly screams, and it throws him into a convulsion with foaming *at the mouth,* and as it mauls him, it scarcely leaves him.

40"And I begged Your disciples to cast it out, and they could not."

41And Jesus answered and said, "O unbelieving and perverted generation, how long shall I be with you, and put up with you? Bring your son here."

42And while he was still approaching, the demon dashed him *to the ground,* and threw him into a convulsion. But Jesus rebuked the unclean spirit, and healed the boy, and gave him back to his father.

43And they were all

μίαν σοὶ καὶ μίαν Μωϋσεῖ καὶ μίαν
one for thee and one for Moses and one

'Ηλίᾳ, μὴ εἰδὼς ὃ λέγει. 34 ταῦτα δὲ
for Elias, not knowing what he says. And these things

αὐτοῦ λέγοντος ἐγένετο νεφέλη καὶ
him saying[a] came a cloud and
= while he said these things

ἐπεσκίαζεν αὐτούς· ἐφοβήθησαν δὲ ἐν τῷ
overshadowed them; and they feared in the
= as they entered

εἰσελθεῖν αὐτοὺς εἰς τὴν νεφέλην. 35 καὶ
to enter them[be] into the cloud. And

φωνὴ ἐγένετο ἐκ τῆς νεφέλης λέγουσα·
a voice came out of the cloud saying :

οὗτός ἐστιν ὁ υἱός μου ὁ ἐκλελεγμένος,
This is the Son of me - having been chosen,

αὐτοῦ ἀκούετε, 36 καὶ ἐν τῷ γενέσθαι
him hear ye, and in the to become
= when the voice came

τὴν φωνὴν εὑρέθη 'Ιησοῦς μόνος. καὶ
the voice[be] was found Jesus alone. And

αὐτοὶ ἐσίγησαν καὶ οὐδενὶ ἀπήγγειλαν ἐν ἐκείναις
they were silent and to no one reported in those

ταῖς ἡμέραις οὐδὲν ὧν ἑώρακαν.
- days no(any) of [the things] which they have
thing (had) seen.

37 'Εγένετο δὲ τῇ ἑξῆς ἡμέρᾳ κατελ-
And it came to pass on the following day coming

θόντων αὐτῶν ἀπὸ τοῦ ὄρους συνήντησεν
down them[a] from the mountain met
= as they came down

αὐτῷ ὄχλος πολύς. 38 καὶ ἰδοὺ ἀνὴρ
him crowd a much. And[,] behold[,] a man

ἀπὸ τοῦ ὄχλου ἐβόησεν λέγων· διδάσκαλε,
from the crowd called aloud saying : Teacher,

δέομαί σου ἐπιβλέψαι ἐπὶ τὸν υἱόν μου,
I beg of thee to look at at the son of me,

ὅτι μονογενής μοί ἐστιν, 39 καὶ ἰδοὺ
because only born to me he is, and[,] behold[,]

πνεῦμα λαμβάνει αὐτόν, καὶ ἐξαίφνης
a spirit takes him, and suddenly

κράζει καὶ σπαράσσει αὐτὸν μετὰ ἀφροῦ,
cries out and throws him with foam,

καὶ μόλις ἀποχωρεῖ ἀπ' αὐτοῦ συντρίβον
and scarcely departs from him bruising

αὐτόν· 40 καὶ ἐδεήθην τῶν μαθητῶν σου
him; and I begged of the disciples of thee

ἵνα ἐκβάλωσιν αὐτό, καὶ οὐκ ἠδυνήθησαν.
that they would expel it, and they were not able.

41 ἀποκριθεὶς δὲ ὁ 'Ιησοῦς εἶπεν· ὦ
And answering - Jesus said : O

γενεὰ ἄπιστος καὶ διεστραμμένη, ἕως πότε
generation unbelieving and *having been* perverted, until when

ἔσομαι πρὸς ὑμᾶς καὶ ἀνέξομαι ὑμῶν;
shall I be with you and endure you?

προσάγαγε ὧδε τὸν υἱόν σου. 42 ἔτι
Bring here the son of thee. yet

δὲ προσερχομένου αὐτοῦ ἔρρηξεν αὐτὸν τὸ
But approaching him[a] tore him the
= But while he was yet approaching

δαιμόνιον καὶ συνεσπάραξεν· ἐπετίμησεν δὲ
demon and threw violently; but [r]rebuked

ὁ 'Ιησοῦς τῷ πνεύματι τῷ ἀκαθάρτῳ, καὶ
- [1]Jesus [3]the [5]spirit, [4]unclean, and

ἰάσατο τὸν παῖδα καὶ ἀπέδωκεν αὐτὸν τῷ
cured the boy and restored him to the

πατρὶ αὐτοῦ. 43 ἐξεπλήσσοντο δὲ πάντες
father of him. And were astounded all

---

for Moses and one for Elijah." (He did not know what he was saying.)

34While he was speaking, a cloud appeared and enveloped them, and they were afraid as they entered the cloud. 35A voice came from the cloud, saying, "This is my Son, whom I have chosen; listen to him." 36When the voice had spoken, they found that Jesus was alone. The disciples kept this to themselves, and told no one at that time what they had seen.

The Healing of a Boy With an Evil Spirit

37The next day, when they came down from the mountain, a large crowd met him. 38A man in the crowd called out, "Teacher, I beg you to look at my son, for he is my only child. 39A spirit seizes him and he suddenly screams; it throws him into convulsions so that he foams at the mouth. It scarcely ever leaves him and is destroying him. 40I begged your disciples to drive it out, but they could not."

41"O unbelieving and perverse generation," Jesus replied, "how long shall I stay with you and put up with you? Bring your son here."

42Even while the boy was coming, the demon threw him to the ground in a convulsion. But Jesus rebuked the evil[k] spirit, healed the boy and gave him back to his father. 43And they were

---

[k]42 Greek *unclean*

amazed at the greatness of God.

But while everyone was marveling at all that He was doing, He said to His disciples,

44"Let these words sink into your ears; for the Son of Man is going to be delivered into the hands of men."

45But they did not understand this statement, and it was concealed from them so that they might not perceive it; and they were afraid to ask Him about this statement.

The Test of Greatness

46And an argument arose among them as to which of them might be the greatest.

47But Jesus, knowing what they were thinking in their heart, took a child and stood him by His side,

48and said to them, "Whoever receives this child in My name receives Me; and whoever receives Me receives Him who sent Me; for he who is least among you, this is the one who is great."

49And John answered and said, "Master, we saw someone casting out demons in Your name; and we tried to hinder him because he does not follow along with us."

50But Jesus said to him, "Do not hinder *him;* for he who is not against you is for you."

51And it came about, when the days were approaching for His ascension, that He resolutely set His face to go to Jerusalem;

52and He sent messengers on ahead of Him. And they went, and entered a village of the Samaritans, to make arrangements for Him.

53And they did not re-

ἐπὶ τῇ μεγαλειότητι τοῦ θεοῦ.
at the majesty - of God.

Πάντων δὲ θαυμαζόντων ἐπὶ πᾶσιν οἶς
And all marvelling[a] at all things which
=while all marvelled

ἐποίει εἶπεν πρὸς τοὺς μαθητὰς αὐτοῦ·
he did he said to the disciples of him:

44 θέσθε ὑμεῖς εἰς τὰ ὦτα ὑμῶν τοὺς
Lay ye in the ears of you -

λόγους τούτους· ὁ γὰρ υἱὸς τοῦ ἀνθρώπου
sayings these; for the Son - of man

μέλλει παραδίδοσθαι εἰς χεῖρας ἀνθρώπων.
is about to be betrayed into [the] hands of men.

45 οἱ δὲ ἠγνόουν τὸ ῥῆμα τοῦτο, καὶ ἦν
But they knew not - word this, and it was

παρακεκαλυμμένον ἀπ' αὐτῶν ἵνα μὴ
having been veiled from them lest

αἴσθωνται αὐτό, καὶ ἐφοβοῦντο ἐρωτῆσαι
they should perceive it, and they feared to ask

αὐτὸν περὶ τοῦ ῥήματος τούτου. 46 Εἰσῆλθεν
him about - word this. entered

δὲ διαλογισμὸς ἐν αὐτοῖς, τὸ τίς ἂν εἴη
And a debate among them, - who might be
=a debate arose

μείζων αὐτῶν. 47 ὁ δὲ Ἰησοῦς εἰδὼς τὸν
greater(est) of them. - And Jesus knowing the

διαλογισμὸν τῆς καρδίας αὐτῶν, ἐπιλαβόμενος
debate of the heart of them, taking

παιδίον ἔστησεν αὐτὸ παρ' ἑαυτῷ, 48 καὶ
a child stood it(him) beside himself, and

εἶπεν αὐτοῖς· ὃς ἐὰν δέξηται τοῦτο τὸ
said to them: Whoever receives this -

παιδίον ἐπὶ τῷ ὀνόματί μου, ἐμὲ δέχεται·
child on(in) the name of me, me receives;

καὶ ὃς ἂν ἐμὲ δέξηται, δέχεται τὸν
and whoever me receives, receives the [one]

ἀποστείλαντά με· ὁ γὰρ μικρότερος ἐν
having sent me; for [1]the [one] [3]lesser [4]among

πᾶσιν ὑμῖν ὑπάρχων, οὗτός ἐστιν μέγας.
[5]all [2]you [2]being, this [one] is great.

49 Ἀποκριθεὶς δὲ ὁ Ἰωάννης εἶπεν· ἐπιστάτα,
And answering - John said: Master,

εἴδομέν τινα ἐν τῷ ὀνόματί σου ἐκβάλλοντα
we saw someone in the name of thee expelling

δαιμόνια, καὶ ἐκωλύομεν αὐτόν, ὅτι
demons, and we prevented him, because

οὐκ ἀκολουθεῖ μεθ' ἡμῶν. 50 εἶπεν δὲ πρὸς
he does not follow with us. And said to

αὐτὸν Ἰησοῦς· μὴ κωλύετε· ὃς γὰρ οὐκ
him Jesus: Do not prevent; for [he] who not

ἔστιν καθ' ὑμῶν, ὑπὲρ ὑμῶν ἐστιν.
is against you, for you is.

51 Ἐγένετο δὲ ἐν τῷ συμπληροῦσθαι
And it came to pass in the to be fulfilled

τὰς ἡμέρας τῆς ἀναλήμψεως αὐτοῦ καὶ
the days of the assumption of him[be] and
=as the days of his assumption were fulfilled

αὐτὸς τὸ πρόσωπον ἐστήρισεν τοῦ
he the(his) face set -

πορεύεσθαι εἰς Ἰερουσαλήμ, 52 καὶ ἀπέστειλεν
to go[d] to Jerusalem, and sent

ἀγγέλους πρὸ προσώπου αὐτοῦ. καὶ
messengers before face of him. And

πορευθέντες εἰσῆλθον εἰς κώμην Σαμαριτῶν,
going they entered into a village of Samaritans,

ὥστε ἑτοιμάσαι αὐτῷ· 53 καὶ οὐκ ἐδέξαντο
so as to prepare for him; and they did not receive

---

all amazed at the greatness of God.

While everyone was marveling at all that Jesus did, he said to his disciples, 44"Listen carefully to what I am about to tell you: The Son of Man is going to be betrayed into the hands of men." 45But they did not understand what this meant. It was hidden from them, so that they did not grasp it, and they were afraid to ask him about it.

Who Will Be the Greatest?

46An argument started among the disciples as to which of them would be the greatest. 47Jesus, knowing their thoughts, took a little child and had him stand beside him. 48Then he said to them, "Whoever welcomes this little child in my name welcomes me; and whoever welcomes me welcomes the one who sent me. For he who is least among you all—he is the greatest."

49"Master," said John, "we saw a man driving out demons in your name and we tried to stop him, because he is not one of us."

50"Do not stop him," Jesus said, "for whoever is not against you is for you."

Samaritan Opposition

51As the time approached for him to be taken up to heaven, Jesus resolutely set out for Jerusalem. 52And he sent messengers on ahead, who went into a Samaritan village to get things ready for him; 53but the people there did not ceive Him, because He was journeying with His face toward Jerusalem.

54And when His disciples James and John saw *this*, they said, "Lord, do You want us to command fire to come down from heaven and consume them?"

55But He turned and rebuked them, [and said, "You do not know what kind of spirit you are of;

56for the Son of Man did not come to destroy men's lives, but to save them."]
And they went on to another village.

Exacting Discipleship

57And as they were going along the road, someone said to Him, "I will follow You wherever You go."

58And Jesus said to him, "The foxes have holes, and the birds of the air *have* nests, but the Son of Man has nowhere to lay His head."

59And He said to another, "Follow Me." But he said, "Permit me first to go and bury my father."

60But He said to him, "Allow the dead to bury their own dead; but as for you, go and proclaim everywhere the kingdom of God."

61And another also said, "I will follow You, Lord; but first permit me to say good-bye to those at home."

62But Jesus said to him, "No one, after putting his hand to the plow and looking back, is fit for the kingdom of God."

Chapter 10

The Seventy Sent Out

NOW after this the Lord appointed seventy others, and sent them two and two ahead of Him to every city and place where He Himself was about to come.

2And He was saying to them, "The harvest is plentiful, but the laborers are

t Some mss. add Lord

αὐτόν, ὅτι τὸ πρόσωπον αὐτοῦ ἦν
him, because the face of him was

πορευόμενον εἰς Ἰερουσαλήμ. 54 ἰδόντες
going to Jerusalem. ⁶seeing

δὲ οἱ μαθηταὶ Ἰάκωβος καὶ Ἰωάννης
And ¹the ²disciples ³James ⁴and ⁵John

εἶπαν· κύριε, θέλεις εἴπωμεν πῦρ κατα-
⁷said: Lord, wilt thou we may tell fire to come

βῆναι ἀπὸ τοῦ οὐρανοῦ καὶ ἀναλῶσαι
down from – heaven and to destroy

αὐτούς; 55 στραφεὶς δὲ ἐπετίμησεν αὐτοῖς.
them? But turning he rebuked them.

56 καὶ ἐπορεύθησαν εἰς ἑτέραν κώμην.
And they went to another village.

57 Καὶ πορευομένων αὐτῶν ἐν τῇ ὁδῷ
And going them* in the way
=as they went

εἶπέν τις πρὸς αὐτόν· ἀκολουθήσω σοι
said one to him: I will follow thee

ὅπου ἐὰν ἀπέρχῃ. 58 καὶ εἶπεν αὐτῷ ὁ
wherever thou goest. And said to him –

Ἰησοῦς· αἱ ἀλώπεκες φωλεοὺς ἔχουσιν καὶ
Jesus: The foxes holes have and

τὰ πετεινὰ τοῦ οὐρανοῦ κατασκηνώσεις, ὁ
the birds – of heaven nests, ²the

δὲ υἱὸς τοῦ ἀνθρώπου οὐκ ἔχει ποῦ τὴν
¹but Son – of man has not where the(his)

κεφαλὴν κλίνῃ. 59 Εἶπεν δὲ πρὸς ἕτερον·
head he may lay. And he said to another:

ἀκολούθει μοι. ὁ δὲ εἶπεν· ἐπίτρεψόν μοι
Follow me. But he said: Allow me

πρῶτον ἀπελθόντι θάψαι τὸν πατέρα μου.
first going to bury the father of me.

60 εἶπεν δὲ αὐτῷ· ἄφες τοὺς νεκροὺς
But he said to him: Leave the dead

θάψαι τοὺς ἑαυτῶν νεκρούς, σὺ δὲ ἀπελθὼν
to bury the of themselves dead, but thou going
=their own dead,

διάγγελλε τὴν βασιλείαν τοῦ θεοῦ. 61 Εἶπεν
announce the kingdom – of God. said

δὲ καὶ ἕτερος· ἀκολουθήσω σοι, κύριε·
And also another: I will follow thee, Lord;

πρῶτον δὲ ἐπίτρεψόν μοι ἀποτάξασθαι τοῖς
but first allow me to say farewell to the [ones]

εἰς τὸν οἶκόν μου. 62 εἶπεν δὲ [πρὸς
in the house of me. But said to

αὐτόν] ὁ Ἰησοῦς· οὐδεὶς ἐπιβαλὼν τὴν
him – Jesus: No one putting on the(his)

χεῖρα ἐπ' ἄροτρον καὶ βλέπων εἰς τὰ
hand on a plough and looking at the things

ὀπίσω εὔθετός ἐστιν τῇ βασιλείᾳ τοῦ θεοῦ.
behind fit is for the kingdom – of God.

10 Μετὰ δὲ ταῦτα ἀνέδειξεν ὁ κύριος
Now after these things appointed the Lord

ἑτέρους ἑβδομήκοντα [δύο], καὶ ἀπέστειλεν
others seventy-two, and sent

αὐτοὺς ἀνὰ δύο πρὸ προσώπου αὐτοῦ εἰς
them two by two† before face of him into

πᾶσαν πόλιν καὶ τόπον οὗ ἤμελλεν αὐτὸς
every city and place where ²was about ¹he

ἔρχεσθαι. 2 ἔλεγεν δὲ πρὸς αὐτούς· ὁ
to come. And he said to them: the

μὲν θερισμὸς πολύς, οἱ δὲ ἐργάται ὀλίγοι·
Indeed harvest much, but the workmen few;

---

welcome him, because he was heading for Jerusalem.

54When the disciples James and John saw this, they asked, "Lord, do you want us to call fire down from heaven to destroy them *l* ?"

55But Jesus turned and rebuked them, 56and *m* they went to another village.

The Cost of Following Jesus

57As they were walking along the road, a man said to him, "I will follow you wherever you go."

58Jesus replied, "Foxes have holes and birds of the air have nests, but the Son of Man has no place to lay his head."

59He said to another man, "Follow me."
But the man replied, "Lord, first let me go and bury my father."

60Jesus said to him, "Let the dead bury their own dead, but you go and proclaim the kingdom of God."

61Still another said, "I will follow you, Lord; but first let me go back and say good-by to my family."

62Jesus replied, "No one who puts his hand to the plow and looks back is fit for service in the kingdom of God."

Chapter 10

Jesus Sends Out the Seventy-two

AFTER this the Lord appointed seventy-two *n* others and sent them two by two ahead of him to every town and place where he was about to go. 2He told them, "The harvest is plentiful, but the workers

l54 Some manuscripts them, even as Elijah did
m55,56 Some manuscripts them. And he said, "You do not know what kind of spirit you are of, for the Son of Man did not come to destroy men's lives, but to save them." 56And
n1 Some manuscripts seventy; also in verse 17

few; therefore beseech the Lord of the harvest to send out laborers into His harvest.

3"Go your ways; behold, I send you out as lambs in the midst of wolves.

4"Carry no purse, no bag, no shoes; and greet no one on the way.

5"And whatever house you enter, first say, 'Peace *be* to this house.'

6"And if a man of peace is there, your peace will rest upon him; but if not, it will return to you.

7"And stay in that house, eating and drinking what they give you; for the laborer is worthy of his wages. Do not keep moving from house to house.

8"And whatever city you enter, and they receive you, eat what is set before you;

9and heal those in it who are sick, and say to them, 'The kingdom of God has come near to you.'

10"But whatever city you enter and they do not receive you, go out into its streets and say,

11"Even the dust of your city which clings to our feet, we wipe off *in protest* against you; yet be sure of this, that the kingdom of God has come near.'

12"I say to you, it will be more tolerable in that day for Sodom, than for that city.

13"Woe to you, Chorazin! Woe to you, Bethsaida! For if the miracles had been performed in Tyre and Sidon which occurred in you, they would have repented long ago, sitting in sackcloth and ashes.

δεήθητε οὖν τοῦ κυρίου τοῦ θερισμοῦ
beg ye therefore of the Lord of the harvest
ὅπως ἐργάτας ἐκβάλῃ εἰς τὸν θερισμὸν
that workmen he would thrust forth into the harvest
αὐτοῦ. 3 ὑπάγετε· ἰδοὺ ἀποστέλλω ὑμᾶς
of him. Go ye; behold I send you
ὡς ἄρνας ἐν μέσῳ λύκων. 4 μὴ βαστάζετε
as lambs in [the] midst of wolves. Do not carry
βαλλάντιον, μὴ πήραν, μὴ ὑποδήματα· καὶ
a purse, nor a wallet, nor sandals; and
μηδένα κατὰ τὴν ὁδὸν ἀσπάσησθε. 5 εἰς
no one by the way greet. ¹into
ἣν δ' ἂν εἰσέλθητε οἰκίαν, πρῶτον λέγετε·
¹And ³whatever ⁵ye enter ⁴house, first say:
εἰρήνη τῷ οἴκῳ τούτῳ. 6 καὶ ἐὰν ἐκεῖ
Peace - house to this. And if there
ᾖ υἱὸς εἰρήνης, ἐπαναπαήσεται ἐπ' αὐτὸν
there is a son of peace, shall rest on it(?him)
ἡ εἰρήνη ὑμῶν· εἰ δὲ μή γε, ἐφ' ὑμᾶς
the peace of you; otherwise, on you
ἀνακάμψει. 7 ἐν αὐτῇ δὲ τῇ οἰκίᾳ μένετε,
it shall return. ²in ⁴same ¹And ³the house* remain,
ἔσθοντες καὶ πίνοντες τὰ παρ' αὐτῶν·
eating and drinking the things with them;
ἄξιος γὰρ ὁ ἐργάτης τοῦ μισθοῦ αὐτοῦ.
for worthy [is] the workman of the pay of him.
μὴ μεταβαίνετε ἐξ οἰκίας εἰς οἰκίαν.
Do not remove from house to house.
8 καὶ εἰς ἣν ἂν πόλιν εἰσέρχησθε καὶ
And into whatever city ye enter and
δέχωνται ὑμᾶς, ἐσθίετε τὰ παρατιθέμενα
they receive you, eat the things being set before
ὑμῖν, 9 καὶ θεραπεύετε τοὺς ἐν αὐτῇ
you, and heal the ²in ³it
ἀσθενεῖς, καὶ λέγετε αὐτοῖς· ἤγγικεν ἐφ'
¹sick, and tell them: Has drawn near on(to)
ὑμᾶς ἡ βασιλεία τοῦ θεοῦ. 10 εἰς ἣν δ'
you the kingdom - of God. And into what-
ἂν πόλιν εἰσέλθητε καὶ μὴ δέχωνται ὑμᾶς,
ever city ye enter and they do not receive you,
ἐξελθόντες εἰς τὰς πλατείας αὐτῆς εἴπατε·
going forth into the streets of it say:
11 καὶ τὸν κονιορτὸν τὸν κολληθέντα ἡμῖν
Even the dust - adhering to us
=the dust of your city adhering to us, on our feet,
ἐκ τῆς πόλεως ὑμῶν εἰς τοὺς πόδας
of the city of you on the(our) feet
ἀπομασσόμεθα ὑμῖν· πλὴν τοῦτο γινώσκετε,
we shake off to you; nevertheless this know ye,
ὅτι ἤγγικεν ἡ βασιλεία τοῦ θεοῦ. 12 λέγω
that has drawn near the kingdom - of God. I tell
ὑμῖν ὅτι Σοδόμοις ἐν τῇ ἡμέρᾳ ἐκείνῃ
you that for Sodom in - day that
ἀνεκτότερον ἔσται ἢ τῇ πόλει ἐκείνῃ.
more endurable it will be for that - city for that.
13 Οὐαί σοι, Χοραζίν, οὐαί σοι, Βηθσαϊδά·
Woe to thee, Chorazin, woe to thee, Bethsaida:
ὅτι εἰ ἐν Τύρῳ καὶ Σιδῶνι ἐγενήθησαν αἱ
because if in Tyre and Sidon happened the
δυνάμεις αἱ γενόμεναι ἐν ὑμῖν, πάλαι ἂν ἐν
powerful deeds - happening in you, long ago - in
σάκκῳ καὶ σποδῷ καθήμενοι μετενόησαν.
sackcloth and ashes sitting they would have repented.

---

are few. Ask the Lord of the harvest, therefore, to send out workers into his harvest field. ³Go! I am sending you out like lambs among wolves. ⁴Do not take a purse or bag or sandals; and do not greet anyone on the road.

⁵"When you enter a house, first say, 'Peace to this house.' ⁶If a man of peace is there, your peace will rest on him; if not, it will return to you. ⁷Stay in that house, eating and drinking whatever they give you, for the worker deserves his wages. Do not move around from house to house.

⁸"When you enter a town and are welcomed, eat what is set before you. ⁹Heal the sick who are there and tell them, 'The kingdom of God is near you.' ¹⁰But when you enter a town and are not welcomed, go into its streets and say, ¹¹'Even the dust of your town that sticks to our feet we wipe off against you. Yet be sure of this: The kingdom of God is near.' ¹²I tell you, it will be more bearable on that day for Sodom than for that town.

¹³"Woe to you, Korazin! Woe to you, Bethsaida! For if the miracles that were performed in you had been performed in Tyre and Sidon, they would have repented long ago, sitting in sackcloth and ashes.

---

* Luke here, and in 2. 38; 10. 21; 12. 12; 13. 31; 24. 13, as well as in Acts 16. 18; 22. 13, ignores the strict idiomatic construction of αὐτός when in apposition. The words here should mean " in the house itself " but obviously do mean " in the same house ". So elsewhere. See note on Luke 2. 38.

14"But it will be more tolerable for Tyre and Sidon in the judgment, than for you.

15"And you, Capernaum, will not be exalted to heaven, will you? You will be brought down to Hades!

16"The one who listens to you listens to Me, and the one who rejects you rejects Me; and he who rejects Me rejects the One who sent Me."

The Happy Results

17And the seventy returned with joy, saying, "Lord, even the demons are subject to us in Your name."

18And He said to them, "I was watching Satan fall from heaven like lightning.

19"Behold, I have given you authority to tread upon serpents and scorpions, and over all the power of the enemy, and nothing shall injure you.

20"Nevertheless do not rejoice in this, that the spirits are subject to you, but rejoice that your names are recorded in heaven."

21At that very time He rejoiced greatly in the Holy Spirit, and said, "I praise Thee, O Father, Lord of heaven and earth, that Thou didst hide these things from *the* wise and intelligent and didst reveal them to babes. Yes, Father, for thus it was well-pleasing in Thy sight.

22"All things have been handed over to Me by My Father, and no one knows who the Son is except the Father, and who the Father is except the Son, and anyone to whom the Son wills to reveal *Him*."

23And turning to the disciples, He said privately, "Blessed *are* the eyes which see the things you see,

24for I say to you, that

---

14 πλὴν Τύρῳ καὶ Σιδῶνι ἀνεκτότερον
Nevertheless for Tyre and Sidon more endurable

ἔσται ἐν τῇ κρίσει ἢ ὑμῖν. **15** καὶ σύ,
it will be in the judgment than for you. And thou,

Καφαρναούμ, μὴ ἕως οὐρανοῦ ὑψωθήσῃ;
Capernaum, not to heaven wast thou lifted?

ἕως τοῦ ᾅδου καταβήσῃ. **16** Ὁ ἀκούων
to - hades thou shalt come down. The [one] hearing

ὑμῶν ἐμοῦ ἀκούει, καὶ ὁ ἀθετῶν ὑμᾶς
you me hears, and the [one] rejecting you

ἐμὲ ἀθετεῖ· ὁ δὲ ἐμὲ ἀθετῶν ἀθετεῖ τὸν
me rejects; and the [one] me rejecting rejects the [one]

ἀποστείλαντά με. **17** Ὑπέστρεψαν δὲ οἱ
having sent me. And returned the

ἑβδομήκοντα [δύο] μετὰ χαρᾶς λέγοντες·
seventy-two with joy saying :

κύριε, καὶ τὰ δαιμόνια ὑποτάσσεται ἡμῖν
Lord, even the demons submits to us

ἐν τῷ ὀνόματί σου. **18** εἶπεν δὲ αὐτοῖς·
in the name of thee. And he said to them :

ἐθεώρουν τὸν σατανᾶν ὡς ἀστραπὴν ἐκ
I beheld - Satan as lightning out of

τοῦ οὐρανοῦ πεσόντα. **19** ἰδοὺ δέδωκα
- heaven fall. Behold I have given

ὑμῖν τὴν ἐξουσίαν τοῦ πατεῖν ἐπάνω
you the authority - to tread on

ὄφεων καὶ σκορπίων, καὶ ἐπὶ πᾶσαν τὴν
serpents and scorpions, and on all the

δύναμιν τοῦ ἐχθροῦ, καὶ οὐδὲν ὑμᾶς οὐ μὴ
power of the enemy, and nothing you by no(any) means

ἀδικήσει. **20** πλὴν ἐν τούτῳ μὴ χαίρετε
shall hurt. Nevertheless in this rejoice not

ὅτι τὰ πνεύματα ὑμῖν ὑποτάσσεται, χαίρετε
that the spirits to you submits, ¹rejoice

δὲ ὅτι τὰ ὀνόματα ὑμῶν ἐγγέγραπται ἐν
¹but that the names of you have been enrolled in

τοῖς οὐρανοῖς. **21** Ἐν αὐτῇ τῇ ὥρᾳ
the heavens. In ¹same ¹the hour

ἠγαλλιάσατο τῷ πνεύματι τῷ ἁγίῳ καὶ
he exulted in(?by) the Spirit - Holy and

εἶπεν· ἐξομολογοῦμαί σοι, πάτερ, κύριε
said : I praise thee, Father, Lord

τοῦ οὐρανοῦ καὶ τῆς γῆς, ὅτι ἀπέκρυψας
- of heaven and - of earth, because thou didst hide

ταῦτα ἀπὸ σοφῶν καὶ συνετῶν, καὶ
these things from wise and intelligent [ones], and

ἀπεκάλυψας αὐτὰ νηπίοις· ναί, ὁ πατήρ,
didst reveal them to infants; yes - Father,

ὅτι οὕτως εὐδοκία ἐγένετο ἔμπροσθέν σου.
because thus good pleasure it was before thee.

22 πάντα μοι παρεδόθη ὑπὸ τοῦ πατρός
All things to me were delivered by the Father

μου, καὶ οὐδεὶς γινώσκει τίς ἐστιν ὁ
of me, and no one knows who is the

υἱὸς εἰ μὴ ὁ πατήρ, καὶ τίς ἐστιν ὁ πατὴρ
Son except the Father, and who is the Father

εἰ μὴ ὁ υἱὸς καὶ ᾧ ἐὰν βούληται
except the Son and [he] to whomever wills

ὁ υἱὸς ἀποκαλύψαι. **23** Καὶ στραφεὶς
the Son to reveal [him]. And turning

πρὸς τοὺς μαθητὰς κατ' ἰδίαν εἶπεν·
to the disciples privately he said :

μακάριοι οἱ ὀφθαλμοὶ οἱ βλέποντες ἃ
Blessed the eyes - seeing the things which

βλέπετε. **24** λέγω γὰρ ὑμῖν ὅτι πολλοὶ
ye see. For I tell you that many

14But it will be more bearable for Tyre and Sidon at the judgment than for you. 15And you, Capernaum, will you be lifted up to the skies? No, you will go down to the depths. *o*

16"He who listens to you listens to me; he who rejects you rejects me; but he who rejects me rejects him who sent me."

17The seventy-two returned with joy and said, "Lord, even the demons submit to us in your name."

18He replied, "I saw Satan fall like lightning from heaven. 19I have given you authority to trample on snakes and scorpions and to overcome all the power of the enemy; nothing will harm you. 20However, do not rejoice that the spirits submit to you, but rejoice that your names are written in heaven."

21At that time Jesus, full of joy through the Holy Spirit, said, "I praise you, Father, Lord of heaven and earth, because you have hidden these things from the wise and learned, and revealed them to little children. Yes, Father, for this was your good pleasure.

22"All things have been committed to me by my Father. No one knows who the Son is except the Father, and no one knows who the Father is except the Son and those to whom the Son chooses to reveal him."

23Then he turned to his disciples and said privately, "Blessed are the eyes that see what you see. 24For I tell you that many

---

o15 Greek Hades

many prophets and kings wished to see the things which you see, and did not see *them*, and to hear the things which you hear, and did not hear *them*.

25And behold, a certain lawyer stood up and put Him to the test, saying, "Teacher, what shall I do to inherit eternal life?" 26And He said to him, "What is written in the Law? How does it read to you?" 27And he answered and said, "YOU SHALL LOVE THE LORD YOUR GOD WITH ALL YOUR HEART, AND WITH ALL YOUR SOUL, AND WITH ALL YOUR STRENGTH, AND WITH ALL YOUR MIND, AND YOUR NEIGHBOR AS YOURSELF." 28And He said to him, "You have answered correctly; DO THIS, AND YOU WILL LIVE." 29But wishing to justify himself, he said to Jesus, "And who is my neighbor?"

The Good Samaritan

30Jesus replied and said, "A certain man was going down from Jerusalem to Jericho; and he fell among robbers, and they stripped him and beat him, and went off leaving him half dead. 31And by chance a certain priest was going down on that road, and when he saw him, he passed by on the other side. 32And likewise a Levite also, when he came to the place and saw him, passed by on the other side. 33"But a certain Samaritan, who was on a journey, came upon him; and when he saw him, he felt compassion, 34and came to him, and bandaged up his wounds, pouring oil and wine on *them;* and he put him on his own beast, and brought him to an inn, and took care of him. 35"And on the next day he took out two *a*denarii and gave them to the innkeeper and said, 'Take care

a The denarius was equivalent to one day's wage

προφῆται καὶ βασιλεῖς ἠθέλησαν ἰδεῖν   ἃ
prophets and kings desired to see the things which
ὑμεῖς βλέπετε καὶ οὐκ εἶδαν, καὶ ἀκοῦσαι
ye see and did not see, and to hear
ἃ   ἀκούετε καὶ οὐκ ἤκουσαν.
the things which ye hear and did not hear.

25 Καὶ ἰδοὺ νομικός τις ἀνέστη
And[,] behold[,] lawyer a certain stood up
ἐκπειράζων αὐτὸν λέγων· διδάσκαλε, τί
tempting him saying: Teacher, what
ποιήσας ζωὴν αἰώνιον κληρονομήσω; 26 ὁ
doing ²life ¹eternal ³I ¹may ³inherit he
δὲ εἶπεν πρὸς αὐτόν· ἐν τῷ νόμῳ τί
And said to him: In the law what
γέγραπται; πῶς ἀναγινώσκεις; 27 ὁ δὲ
has been written? how readest thou? And he
ἀποκριθεὶς εἶπεν· ἀγαπήσεις κύριον τὸν
answering said: Thou shalt love [the] Lord the
θεόν σου ἐξ ὅλης τῆς καρδίας σου καὶ
God of thee from all the heart of thee and
ἐν ὅλῃ τῇ ψυχῇ σου καὶ ἐν ὅλῃ τῇ
with all the soul of thee and with all the
ἰσχύϊ σου καὶ ἐν ὅλῃ τῇ διανοίᾳ σου,
strength of thee and with all the mind of thee,
καὶ τὸν πλησίον σου ὡς σεαυτόν. 28 εἶπεν
and the neighbour of thee as thyself. he said
δὲ αὐτῷ· ὀρθῶς ἀπεκρίθης· τοῦτο ποίει
And to him: Rightly thou didst answer; this do
καὶ ζήσῃ. 29 ὁ δὲ θέλων δικαιῶσαι ἑαυτὸν
and thou shalt live. But he wishing to justify himself
εἶπεν πρὸς τὸν Ἰησοῦν· καὶ τίς ἐστίν
said to Jesus: And who is
μου πλησίον; 30 ὑπολαβὼν ὁ Ἰησοῦς
of me neighbour? Taking [him] up Jesus
εἶπεν· ἄνθρωπός τις κατέβαινεν ἀπὸ
said: A certain man was going down from
Ἰερουσαλὴμ εἰς Ἰεριχώ, καὶ λῃσταῖς
Jerusalem to Jericho, and ²robbers
περιέπεσεν, οἳ καὶ ἐκδύσαντες αὐτὸν καὶ
¹fell in with, who both stripping him and
πληγὰς ἐπιθέντες ἀπῆλθον ἀφέντες ἡμιθανῆ.
²blows ¹laying ³on ⁴[him] went away leaving [him] half dead.

31 κατὰ συγκυρίαν δὲ ἱερεύς τις κατέβαινεν
And by a coincidence a certain priest was going down
ἐν τῇ ὁδῷ ἐκείνῃ, καὶ ἰδὼν αὐτὸν
in - way that, and seeing him
ἀντιπαρῆλθεν. 32 ὁμοίως δὲ καὶ Λευίτης
passed by opposite. And likewise also a Levite
κατὰ τὸν τόπον ἐλθὼν καὶ ἰδὼν
upon the place coming and seeing
ἀντιπαρῆλθεν. 33 Σαμαρίτης δέ τις ὁδεύων
passed by opposite. And a certain Samaritan journeying
ἦλθεν κατ' αὐτὸν καὶ ἰδὼν ἐσπλαγχνίσθη,
came upon him and seeing was filled with pity,
34 καὶ προσελθὼν κατέδησεν τὰ τραύματα
and approaching bound up the wounds
αὐτοῦ ἐπιχέων ἔλαιον καὶ οἶνον, ἐπιβιβάσας
of him pouring on oil and wine, ²placing
δὲ αὐτὸν ἐπὶ τὸ ἴδιον κτῆνος ἤγαγεν
¹and him on the(his) own beast brought
αὐτὸν εἰς πανδοχεῖον καὶ ἐπεμελήθη αὐτοῦ.
him to an inn and cared for him.
35 καὶ ἐπὶ τὴν αὔριον ἐκβαλὼν δύο
And on the morrow taking out two
δηνάρια ἔδωκεν τῷ πανδοχεῖ καὶ εἶπεν·
denarii he gave to the innkeeper and said:

---

prophets and kings wanted to see what you see but did not see it, and to hear what you hear but did not hear it."

The Parable of the Good Samaritan

25On one occasion an expert in the law stood up to test Jesus. "Teacher," he asked, "what must I do to inherit eternal life?" 26"What is written in the Law?" he replied. "How do you read it?" 27He answered: " 'Love the Lord your God with all your heart and with all your soul and with all your strength and with all your mind'*p*; and, 'Love your neighbor as yourself.'*q*" 28"You have answered correctly," Jesus replied. "Do this and you will live." 29But he wanted to justify himself, so he asked Jesus, "And who is my neighbor?" 30In reply Jesus said: "A man was going down from Jerusalem to Jericho, when he fell into the hands of robbers. They stripped him of his clothes, beat him and went away, leaving him half dead. 31A priest happened to be going down the same road, and when he saw the man, he passed by on the other side. 32So too, a Levite, when he came to the place and saw him, passed by on the other side. 33But a Samaritan, as he traveled, came where the man was; and when he saw him, he took pity on him. 34He went to him and bandaged his wounds, pouring on oil and wine. Then he put the man on his own donkey, took him to an inn and took care of him. 35The next day he took out two silver coins*r* and gave them to the innkeeper. 'Look after him,' he said,

p27 Deut. 6:5
q27 Lev. 19:18
r35 Greek two denarii

of him; and whatever more you spend, when I return, I will repay you.'

36"Which of these three do you think proved to be a neighbor to the man who fell into the robbers' hands?"

37And he said, "The one who showed mercy toward him." And Jesus said to him, "Go and do the same."

Martha and Mary

38Now as they were traveling along, He entered a certain village; and a woman named Martha welcomed Him into her home.

39And she had a sister called Mary, who moreover was listening to the Lord's word, seated at His feet.

40But Martha was distracted with all her preparations; and she came up *to Him*, and said, "Lord, do You not care that my sister has left me to do all the serving alone? Then tell her to help me."

41But the Lord answered and said to her, "Martha, Martha, you are worried and bothered about so many things;

42but *only* a few things are necessary, really *only* one, for Mary has chosen the good part, which shall not be taken away from her."

ἐπιμελήθητι αὐτοῦ, καὶ ὅ τι ἂν προσδα-
Care thou for   him,   and   whatever thou spendest

πανήσης ἐγὼ ἐν τῷ ἐπανέρχεσθαί με
in addition I   in   the   to return   me[be]
                            =when I return

ἀποδώσω σοι. 36 τίς τούτων τῶν τριῶν πλησίον
will repay thee. Who of these – three ⁴neighbour

δοκεῖ σοι γεγονέναι τοῦ ἐμπεσόντος
¹seems it ²to thee ³to have become of the [one] falling *into*

εἰς τοὺς λῃστάς; 37 ὁ δὲ εἶπεν· ὁ ποιήσας
among the robbers?   And he said : The [one] doing

τὸ ἔλεος μετ᾽ αὐτοῦ. εἶπεν δὲ αὐτῷ ὁ
the mercy with him.   And said   to him

Ἰησοῦς· πορεύου καὶ σὺ ποίει ὁμοίως.
Jesus :   Go   and thou   do   likewise.

38 Ἐν δὲ τῷ πορεύεσθαι αὐτοὺς αὐτὸς
And in the   to go   them[be]   he
     =as they went

εἰσῆλθεν εἰς κώμην τινά· γυνὴ δέ τις
entered   into a certain village; and a certain woman

ὀνόματι Μάρθα ὑπεδέξατο αὐτὸν εἰς τὴν
by name Martha received   him   into the

οἰκίαν. 39 καὶ τῇδε ἦν ἀδελφὴ καλουμένη
house.   And to this was a sister° *being* called
                                      =she had a sister

Μαριάμ, ἣ καὶ παρακαθεσθεῖσα πρὸς τοὺς
Mary, who also sitting beside   at   the

πόδας τοῦ κυρίου ἤκουεν τὸν λόγον αὐτοῦ.
feet of the Lord   heard the word of him.

40 ἡ δὲ Μάρθα περιεσπᾶτο περὶ πολλὴν
– But Martha was distracted about much

διακονίαν· ἐπιστᾶσα δὲ εἶπεν· κύριε, οὐ
serving; and coming upon [him] she said : Lord, not

μέλει σοι ὅτι ἡ ἀδελφή μου μόνην με
matters it to thee that the sister of me ³alone ¹me

κατέλειπεν διακονεῖν; εἰπὸν οὖν αὐτῇ ἵνα
¹left   to serve? tell therefore her   that

μοι συναντιλάβηται. 41 ἀποκριθεὶς δὲ εἶπεν
²me ¹she may help.   And answering   said

αὐτῇ ὁ κύριος· Μάρθα Μάρθα, μεριμνᾷς
to her the Lord : Martha[,] Martha, thou art anxious

καὶ θορυβάζῃ περὶ πολλά, 42 ὀλίγων δέ
and disturbed about many things, but of few things

ἐστιν χρεία ἢ ἑνός· Μαριὰμ γὰρ τὴν
there is need or of one; for Mary the

ἀγαθὴν μερίδα ἐξελέξατο, ἥτις οὐκ
good   part   chose,   which not

ἀφαιρεθήσεται αὐτῆς.
shall be taken from her.

'and when I return, I will reimburse you for any extra expense you may have.'

36"Which of these three do you think was a neighbor to the man who fell into the hands of robbers?"

37The expert in the law replied, "The one who had mercy on him."

Jesus told him, "Go and do likewise."

At the Home of Martha and Mary

38As Jesus and his disciples were on their way, he came to a village where a woman named Martha opened her home to him.

39She had a sister called Mary, who sat at the Lord's feet listening to what he said. 40But Martha was distracted by all the preparations that had to be made. She came to him and asked, "Lord, don't you care that my sister has left me to do the work by myself? Tell her to help me!"

41"Martha, Martha," the Lord answered, "you are worried and upset about many things, 42but only one thing is needed.ʲ Mary has chosen what is better, and it will not be taken away from her."

Chapter 11

Instruction about Prayer

AND it came about that while He was praying in a certain place, after He had finished, one of His disciples said to Him, "Lord, teach us to pray just as John also taught his disciples."

2And He said to them, "When you pray, say:

'Father, hallowed be

---

11 Καὶ ἐγένετο ἐν τῷ εἶναι αὐτὸν ἐν
And it came to pass in the to be   him[be] in
                            =when he was

τόπῳ τινὶ προσευχόμενον, ὡς ἐπαύσατο,
a certain place praying,   as he ceased,

εἶπέν τις τῶν μαθητῶν αὐτοῦ πρὸς
said a certain one of the disciples of him   to

αὐτόν· κύριε, δίδαξον ἡμᾶς προσεύχεσθαι,
him : Lord, teach   us   to pray,

καθὼς καὶ Ἰωάννης ἐδίδαξεν τοὺς μαθητὰς
even as also John   taught   the disciples

αὐτοῦ. 2 εἶπεν δὲ αὐτοῖς· ὅταν
of him.   And he said   to them :   When

προσεύχησθε, λέγετε· Πάτερ, ἁγιασθήτω τὸ
ye pray,   say : Father, let be hallowed the

Chapter 11

Jesus' Teaching on Prayer

ONE day Jesus was praying in a certain place. When he finished, one of his disciples said to him, "Lord, teach us to pray, just as John taught his disciples."

2He said to them, "When you pray, say:

" 'Father,ˡ
hallowed be your name,

ʲ42 Some manuscripts *but few things are needed—or only one*
ˡ2 Some manuscripts *Our Father in heaven*

Left column (English)

Thy name.
Thy kingdom come.
3 'Give us each day our daily bread.
4 'And forgive us our sins,
For we ourselves also forgive everyone who is indebted to us.
And lead us not into temptation.' "

5And He said to them, "Suppose one of you shall have a friend, and shall go to him at midnight, and say to him, 'Friend, lend me three loaves';

6for a friend of mine has come to me from a journey, and I have nothing to set before him';

7and from inside he shall answer and say, 'Do not bother me; the door has already been shut and my children and I are in bed; I cannot get up and give you *anything*.'

8"I tell you, even though he will not get up and give him *anything* because he is his friend, yet because of his persistence he will get up and give him as much as he needs.

9"And I say to you, ask, and it shall be given to you; seek, and you shall find; knock, and it shall be opened to you.

10"For everyone who asks, receives; and he who seeks, finds; and to him who knocks, it shall be opened.

11"Now suppose one of you fathers is asked by his son for a fish; he will not give him a snake instead of a fish, will he?

12"Or *if* he is asked for an egg, he will not give him a scorpion, will he?

13"If you then, being evil, know how to give good gifts to your children, how much more shall *your* heavenly Father give the Holy Spirit to those who ask Him?"

Pharisees' Blasphemy

14And He was casting out a demon, and it was dumb; and it came about that when the demon had gone

Center column (Greek interlinear)

ὄνομά σου· ἐλθάτω ἡ βασιλεία σου·
name of thee; let come the kingdom of thee;

3 τὸν ἄρτον ἡμῶν τὸν ἐπιούσιον δίδου
the bread of us – belonging to the morrow give

ἡμῖν τὸ καθ' ἡμέραν· 4 καὶ ἄφες ἡμῖν τὰς
us each day†; and forgive us the

ἁμαρτίας ἡμῶν, καὶ γὰρ αὐτοὶ ἀφίομεν
sins of us, for indeed [our]selves we forgive

παντὶ ὀφείλοντι ἡμῖν· καὶ μὴ εἰσενέγκῃς
everyone owing to us; and lead not

ἡμᾶς εἰς πειρασμόν. 5 Καὶ εἶπεν πρὸς
us into temptation. And he said to

αὐτούς· τίς ἐξ ὑμῶν ἕξει φίλον, καὶ
them: Who of you shall have a friend, and

πορεύσεται πρὸς αὐτὸν μεσονυκτίου καὶ
will come to him at midnight and

εἴπῃ αὐτῷ· φίλε, χρῆσόν μοι τρεῖς ἄρτους,
say to him: Friend, lend me three loaves,

6 ἐπειδὴ φίλος μου παρεγένετο ἐξ ὁδοῦ
since a friend of me arrived off a journey

πρός με καὶ οὐκ ἔχω ὃ παραθήσω αὐτῷ·
to me and I have not what I may set before him;

7 κἀκεῖνος ἔσωθεν ἀποκριθεὶς εἴπῃ· μή
and that one within answering may say: Not

μοι κόπους πάρεχε· ἤδη ἡ θύρα κέκλεισται,
me troubles cause; now the door has been shut,

καὶ τὰ παιδία μου μετ' ἐμοῦ εἰς τὴν
and the children of me with me in the

κοίτην εἰσίν· οὐ δύναμαι ἀναστὰς δοῦναί
bed are; I cannot rising up to give

σοι. 8 λέγω ὑμῖν, εἰ καὶ οὐ δώσει
thee. I tell you, if even he will not give

αὐτῷ ἀναστὰς διὰ τὸ εἶναι φίλον αὐτοῦ,
him rising up on account of the to be friend of him,
                                    = because he is his friend,

διά γε τὴν ἀναίδειαν αὐτοῦ ἐγερθεὶς
yet on account of the importunity of him rising

δώσει αὐτῷ ὅσων χρῄζει. 9 Κἀγὼ ὑμῖν
he will give him as many as he needs. And I ¹you

λέγω, αἰτεῖτε, καὶ δοθήσεται ὑμῖν· ζητεῖτε,
¹tell, ask, and it will be given you; seek,

καὶ εὑρήσετε· κρούετε, καὶ ἀνοιγήσεται
and ye will find; knock, and it will be opened

ὑμῖν. 10 πᾶς γὰρ ὁ αἰτῶν λαμβάνει, καὶ
to you. For everyone asking receives, and

ὁ ζητῶν εὑρίσκει, καὶ τῷ κρούοντι
the [one] seeking finds, and to the [one] knocking

ἀνοιγήσεται. 11 τίνα δὲ ἐξ ὑμῶν τὸν
it will be opened. And ¹what ⁴of ⁵you –

πατέρα αἰτήσει ὁ υἱὸς ἰχθύν, μὴ
¹father ²[is there] ⁶[of whom] will ask ⁵the ⁴son ¹⁰a fish, not

ἀντὶ ἰχθύος ὄφιν αὐτῷ ἐπιδώσει; 12 ἢ
instead of a fish ²a serpent ⁸to him ¹will hand? or

καὶ αἰτήσει ᾠόν, ἐπιδώσει αὐτῷ σκορπίον;
even he will ask an egg, will hand to him a scorpion?

13 εἰ οὖν ὑμεῖς πονηροὶ ὑπάρχοντες οἴδατε δόματα
If therefore ye ²evil ¹being know gifts

ἀγαθὰ διδόναι τοῖς τέκνοις ὑμῶν, πόσῳ
good to give to the children of you, how much

μᾶλλον ὁ πατὴρ ὁ ἐξ οὐρανοῦ δώσει
more the Father – of heaven will give

πνεῦμα ἅγιον τοῖς αἰτοῦσιν αὐτόν.
Spirit [the] Holy to the [ones] asking him.

14 Καὶ ἦν ἐκβάλλων δαιμόνιον, καὶ αὐτὸ
And he was expelling a demon, and it

ἦν κωφόν· ἐγένετο δὲ τοῦ δαιμονίου
was dumb; and it came to pass the demon
                                    = as the demon went out

Right column (English)

your kingdom come. ᵘ
3Give us each day our daily bread.
4Forgive us our sins, for we also forgive everyone who sins against us. ᵛ
And lead us not into temptation. ʷᵛ "

5Then he said to them, "Suppose one of you has a friend, and he goes to him at midnight and says, 'Friend, lend me three loaves of bread, 6because a friend of mine on a journey has come to me, and I have nothing to set before him.'

7"Then the one inside answers, 'Don't bother me. The door is already locked, and my children are with me in bed. I can't get up and give you anything.' 8I tell you, though he will not get up and give him the bread because he is his friend, yet because of the man's boldnessˣ he will get up and give him as much as he needs.

9"So I say to you: Ask and it will be given to you; seek and you will find; knock and the door will be opened to you. 10For everyone who asks receives; he who seeks finds; and to him who knocks, the door will be opened.

11"Which of you fathers, if your son asks forʸ a fish, will give him a snake instead? 12Or if he asks for an egg, will give him a scorpion? 13If you then, though you are evil, know how to give good gifts to your children, how much more will your Father in heaven give the Holy Spirit to those who ask him!"

Jesus and Beelzebub

14Jesus was driving out a demon that was mute. When the demon left, the

ᵛ Some mss. insert phrases from Matt. 6:9–13 to make the two passages closely similar

ᵘ2 Some manuscripts *come. May your will be done on earth as it is in heaven.*
ᵛ4 Greek *everyone who is indebted to us*
ʷ4 Some manuscripts *temptation but deliver us from the evil one*
ˣ8 Or *persistence*
ʸ11 Some manuscripts *for bread, will give him a stone; or if he asks for*

out, the dumb man spoke; and the multitudes marveled.

15But some of them said, "He casts out demons by Beelzebul, the ruler of the demons."

16And others, to test *Him*, were demanding of Him a sign from heaven.

17But He knew their thoughts, and said to them, "Any kingdom divided against itself is laid waste; and a house *divided* against itself falls.

18"And if Satan also is divided against himself, how shall his kingdom stand? For you say that I cast out demons by Beelzebul.

19"And if I by Beelzebul cast out demons, by whom do your sons cast them out? Consequently they shall be your judges.

20"But if I cast out demons by the finger of God, then the kingdom of God has come upon you.

21"When a strong *man*, fully armed, guards his own homestead, his possessions are undisturbed;

22but when someone stronger than he attacks him and overpowers him, he takes away from him all his armor on which he had relied, and distributes his plunder.

23"He who is not with Me is against Me; and he who does not gather with Me, scatters.

24"When the unclean spirit goes out of a man, it passes through waterless places seeking rest, and not finding any, it says, 'I will return to my house from which I came.'

25"And when it comes, it finds it swept and put in order.

26"Then it goes and takes *along* seven other spirits more evil than itself, and

---

ἐξελθόντος ἐλάλησεν ὁ κωφός· καὶ
going out* spoke the dumb man; and

ἐθαύμασαν οἱ ὄχλοι· 15 τινὲς δὲ ἐξ
marvelled the crowds; but some of

αὐτῶν εἶπαν· ἐν Βεεζεβοὺλ τῷ ἄρχοντι
them said: By Beelzebub the chief

τῶν δαιμονίων ἐκβάλλει τὰ δαιμόνια·
of the demons he expels the demons;

16 ἕτεροι δὲ πειράζοντες σημεῖον ἐξ οὐρανοῦ
and others tempting a sign out of heaven

ἐζήτουν παρ' αὐτοῦ. 17 αὐτὸς δὲ εἰδὼς
sought from him. But he knowing

αὐτῶν τὰ διανοήματα εἶπεν αὐτοῖς· πᾶσα
of them the thoughts said to them : Every

βασιλεία ἐφ' ἑαυτὴν διαμερισθεῖσα ἐρημοῦται,
kingdom against itself divided is made desolate,

καὶ οἶκος ἐπὶ οἶκον πίπτει. 18 εἰ δὲ
and a house against a house falls. And if

καὶ ὁ σατανᾶς ἐφ' ἑαυτὸν διεμερίσθη,
also - Satan against himself was divided,

πῶς σταθήσεται ἡ βασιλεία αὐτοῦ; ὅτι
how will stand the kingdom of him? because

λέγετε ἐν Βεεζεβοὺλ ἐκβάλλειν με τὰ
ye say by Beelzebub to expel me[b] the
=[that] by Beelzebub I expel

δαιμόνια. 19 εἰ δὲ ἐγὼ ἐν Βεεζεβοὺλ
demons. But if I by Beelzebub

ἐκβάλλω τὰ δαιμόνια, οἱ υἱοὶ ὑμῶν ἐν
expel the demons, the sons of you by

τίνι ἐκβάλλουσιν; διὰ τοῦτο αὐτοὶ ὑμῶν
what do they expel? therefore they of you

κριταὶ ἔσονται. 20 εἰ δὲ ἐν δακτύλῳ
judges shall be. But if by [the] finger

θεοῦ [ἐγὼ] ἐκβάλλω τὰ δαιμόνια, ἄρα
of God I expel the demons, then

ἔφθασεν ἐφ' ὑμᾶς ἡ βασιλεία τοῦ θεοῦ.
came upon you the kingdom - of God.

21 ὅταν ὁ ἰσχυρὸς καθωπλισμένος φυλάσσῃ
When the strong man *having been* well armed guards

τὴν ἑαυτοῦ αὐλήν, ἐν εἰρήνῃ ἐστὶν τὰ
the of him*self* palace, in peace is(are) the

ὑπάρχοντα αὐτοῦ· 22 ἐπὰν δὲ ἰσχυρότερος
goods of him; but when a stronger

αὐτοῦ ἐπελθὼν νικήσῃ αὐτόν, τὴν πανοπλίαν
[than] him coming upon overcomes him, the armour

αὐτοῦ αἴρει, ἐφ' ᾗ ἐπεποίθει, καὶ τὰ
of him he takes, on which he had relied, and the

σκῦλα αὐτοῦ διαδίδωσιν. 23 Ὁ μὴ ὢν
arms of him distributes. The [one] not being

μετ' ἐμοῦ κατ' ἐμοῦ ἐστιν, καὶ ὁ μὴ
with me against me is, and the [one] not

συνάγων μετ' ἐμοῦ σκορπίζει. 24 Ὅταν
gathering with me scatters. When

τὸ ἀκάθαρτον πνεῦμα ἐξέλθῃ ἀπὸ τοῦ
the unclean spirit goes out from the

ἀνθρώπου, διέρχεται δι' ἀνύδρων τόπων
man, he goes *through* through dry places

ζητοῦν ἀνάπαυσιν, καὶ μὴ εὑρίσκον λέγει·
seeking rest, and not finding says :

ὑποστρέψω εἰς τὸν οἶκόν μου ὅθεν ἐξῆλθον·
I will return to the house of me whence I came out;

25 καὶ ἐλθὸν εὑρίσκει σεσαρωμένον καὶ
and coming he finds [it] *having been* swept and

κεκοσμημένον. 26 τότε πορεύεται καὶ
having been furnished. Then he goes and

παραλαμβάνει ἕτερα πνεύματα πονηρότερα
takes other spirits more wicked

---

man who had been mute spoke, and the crowd was amazed. 15But some of them said, "By Beelzebub,[z] the prince of demons, he is driving out demons." 16Others tested him by asking for a sign from heaven.

17Jesus knew their thoughts and said to them: "Any kingdom divided against itself will be ruined, and a house divided against itself will fall. 18If Satan is divided against himself, how can his kingdom stand? I say this because you claim that I drive out demons by Beelzebub. 19Now if I drive out demons by Beelzebub, by whom do your followers drive them out? So then, they will be your judges. 20But if I drive out demons by the finger of God, then the kingdom of God has come to you.

21"When a strong man, fully armed, guards his own house, his possessions are safe. 22But when someone stronger attacks and overpowers him, he takes away the armor in which the man trusted and divides up the spoils.

23"He who is not with me is against me, and he who does not gather with me, scatters.

24"When an evil[a] spirit comes out of a man, it goes through arid places seeking rest and does not find it. Then it says, 'I will return to the house I left.' 25When it arrives, it finds the house swept clean and put in order. 26Then it goes and takes seven other spirits more wicked than itself,

they go in and live there; and the last state of that man becomes worse than the first.''

27And it came about while He said these things, one of the women in the crowd raised her voice, and said to Him, ''Blessed is the womb that bore You, and the breasts at which You nursed.''

28But He said, ''On the contrary, blessed are those who hear the word of God, and observe it.''

The Sign of Jonah

29And as the crowds were increasing, He began to say, ''This generation is a wicked generation; it seeks for a sign, and *yet* no sign shall be given to it but the sign of Jonah.

30''For just as Jonah became a sign to the Ninevites, so shall the Son of Man be to this generation.

31''The Queen of the South shall rise up with the men of this generation at the judgment and condemn them, because she came from the ends of the earth to hear the wisdom of Solomon; and behold, something greater than Solomon is here.

32''The men of Nineveh shall stand up with this generation at the judgment and condemn it, because they repented at the preaching of Jonah; and behold, something greater than Jonah is here.

33''No one, after lighting a lamp, puts it away in a cellar, nor under a peckmeasure, but on the lampstand, in order that those who enter may see the light.

34''The lamp of your body is your eye; when your eye is clear, your whole body also is full of light; but when it is bad, your body also is full of darkness.

ἑαυτοῦ ἑπτά, καὶ εἰσελθόντα κατοικεῖ
[than] himself seven, and entering he dwells

ἐκεῖ· καὶ γίνεται τὰ ἔσχατα τοῦ ἀνθρώπου
there; and becomes the last things – man

ἐκείνου χείρονα τῶν πρώτων. 27 Ἐγένετο
of that worse [than] the first. it came to pass

δὲ ἐν τῷ λέγειν αὐτὸν ταῦτα ἐπάρασά τις
And in the to say him‑ᵇᵉ these things ⁹lifting up ¹a certain
— as he said

φωνὴν γυνὴ ἐκ τοῦ ὄχλου εἶπεν αὐτῷ·
⁷[her] ⁸voice ²woman ³of ⁴the ⁵crowd said to him :

μακαρία ἡ κοιλία ἡ βαστάσασά σε καὶ
Blessed the womb – having borne thee and

μαστοὶ οὓς ἐθήλασας. 28 αὐτὸς δὲ εἶπεν·
[the] breasts which thou didst suck. But he said :

μενοῦν μακάριοι οἱ ἀκούοντες τὸν λόγον
Nay rather blessed the [ones] hearing the word

τοῦ θεοῦ καὶ φυλάσσοντες.
– of God and keeping.

29 Τῶν δὲ ὄχλων ἐπαθροιζομένων ἤρξατο
And the crowds pressing upon⁸ he began
= as the crowds pressed upon [him]

λέγειν· ἡ γενεὰ αὕτη γενεὰ πονηρά ἐστιν·
to say : – ²generation ¹This ³generation ⁴an evil ⁵is;

σημεῖον ζητεῖ, καὶ σημεῖον οὐ δοθήσεται
a sign it seeks, and a sign will not be given

αὐτῇ εἰ μὴ τὸ σημεῖον Ἰωνᾶ. 30 καθὼς
to it except the sign of Jonas. even as

γὰρ ἐγένετο [ὁ] Ἰωνᾶς τοῖς Νινευΐταις
For ²became ¹Jonas ⁴to the ⁵Ninevites

σημεῖον, οὕτως ἔσται καὶ ὁ υἱὸς τοῦ
³a sign, so will be also the Son of

ἀνθρώπου τῇ γενεᾷ ταύτῃ. 31 βασίλισσα
of man – generation to this. [The] queen

νότου ἐγερθήσεται ἐν τῇ κρίσει μετὰ τῶν
of [the] south will be raised in the judgment with the

ἀνδρῶν τῆς γενεᾶς ταύτης καὶ κατακρινεῖ
men – generation of this and will condemn

αὐτούς· ὅτι ἦλθεν ἐκ τῶν περάτων τῆς
them; because she came from the extremities of the

γῆς ἀκοῦσαι τὴν σοφίαν Σολομῶνος, καὶ
earth to hear the wisdom of Solomon, and

ἰδοὺ πλεῖον Σολομῶνος ὧδε. 32 ἄνδρες
behold a greater [than] Solomon [is] here. Men

Νινευῖται ἀναστήσονται ἐν τῇ κρίσει μετὰ
Ninevites will rise up in the judgment

τῆς γενεᾶς ταύτης καὶ κατακρινοῦσιν αὐτήν·
– generation this and will condemn it;

ὅτι μετενόησαν εἰς τὸ κήρυγμα Ἰωνᾶ, καὶ
because they repented at the proclamation of Jonas, and

ἰδοὺ πλεῖον Ἰωνᾶ ὧδε. 33 Οὐδεὶς λύχνον
behold a greater [than] Jonas [is] here. No one ²a lamp

ἅψας εἰς κρύπτην τίθησιν οὐδὲ ὑπὸ τὸν
¹having lit ⁴in ⁵secret ³places [it] nor under the

μόδιον, ἀλλ' ἐπὶ τὴν λυχνίαν, ἵνα οἱ
bushel, but on the lampstand, that the

εἰσπορευόμενοι τὸ φέγγος βλέπωσιν. 34 ὁ
ones] entering the light may see. The

λύχνος τοῦ σώματός ἐστιν ὁ ὀφθαλμός σου.
lamp of the body is the eye of thee.

ὅταν ὁ ὀφθαλμός σου ἁπλοῦς ᾖ, καὶ
When the eye of thee single is, also

ὅλον τὸ σῶμά σου φωτεινόν ἐστιν· ἐπὰν
all the body of thee bright is; ²when

δὲ πονηρὸς ᾖ, καὶ τὸ σῶμά σου σκοτεινόν.
¹but evil it is, also the body of thee [is] dark.

and they go in and live there. And the final condition of that man is worse than the first.''

27As Jesus was saying these things, a woman in the crowd called out, ''Blessed is the mother who gave you birth and nursed you.''

28He replied, ''Blessed rather are those who hear the word of God and obey it.''

The Sign of Jonah

29As the crowds increased, Jesus said, ''This is a wicked generation. It asks for a miraculous sign, but none will be given it except the sign of Jonah. 30For as Jonah was a sign to the Ninevites, so also will the Son of Man be to this generation. 31The Queen of the South will rise at the judgment with the men of this generation and condemn them; for she came from the ends of the earth to listen to Solomon's wisdom, and now oneᵇ greater than Solomon is here. 32The men of Nineveh will stand up at the judgment with this generation and condemn it; for they repented at the preaching of Jonah, and now one greater than Jonah is here.

The Lamp of the Body

33''No one lights a lamp and puts it in a place where it will be hidden, or under a bowl. Instead he puts it on its stand, so that those who come in may see the light. 34Your eye is the lamp of your body. When your eyes are good, your whole body also is full of light. But when they are bad, your body also is full of

ᵇ31 Or *something*; also in verse 32

35"Then watch out that the light in you may not be darkness.

36"If therefore your whole body is full of light, with no dark part in it, it shall be wholly illumined, as when the lamp illumines you with its rays."

Woes upon the Pharisees

37Now when He had spoken, a Pharisee *asked Him to have lunch with him; and He went in, and reclined *at the table.*

38And when the Pharisee saw it, he was surprised that He had not first ceremonially washed before the meal.

39But the Lord said to him, "Now you Pharisees clean the outside of the cup and of the platter; but inside of you, you are full of robbery and wickedness.

40"You foolish ones, did not He who made the outside make the inside also?

41"But give that which is within as charity, and then all things are clean for you.

42"But woe to you Pharisees! For you pay tithe of mint and rue and every *kind of* garden herb, and *yet* disregard justice and the love of God; but these are the things you should have done without neglecting the others.

43"Woe to you Pharisees! For you love the front seats in the synagogues, and the respectful greetings in the market places.

44"Woe to you! For you are like concealed tombs, and the people who walk over *them* are unaware *of* it."

45And one of the ʷlawyers *said to Him in reply, "Teacher, when You say this, You insult us too."

46But He said, "Woe to you lawyers as well! For you weigh men down with burdens hard to bear, while you yourselves will not

---

35 σκόπει οὖν μὴ τὸ φῶς τὸ ἐν σοὶ
Watch therefore lest the light – in thee

σκότος ἐστίν. **36** εἰ οὖν τὸ σῶμά σου
darkness is. If therefore ¹the ²body ⁴of thee

ὅλον φωτεινόν, μὴ ἔχον μέρος τι σκοτεινόν,
³whole [is] bright, not having ²part ¹any dark,

ἔσται φωτεινὸν ὅλον ὡς ὅταν ὁ λύχνος
⁴will be ²bright ¹all as when the lamp

τῇ ἀστραπῇ φωτίζῃ σε.
with the(its) shining enlightens thee.

37 Ἐν δὲ τῷ λαλῆσαι ἐρωτᾷ αὐτὸν
Now in the to speakᵉ asks him
=as [he] spoke

Φαρισαῖος ὅπως ἀριστήσῃ παρ' αὐτῷ·
a Pharisee that he would dine with him;

εἰσελθὼν δὲ ἀνέπεσεν. **38** ὁ δὲ Φαρισαῖος
and entering he reclined. But the Pharisee

ἰδὼν ἐθαύμασεν ὅτι οὐ πρῶτον ἐβαπτίσθη
seeing marvelled that not first he washed

πρὸ τοῦ ἀρίστου. **39** εἶπεν δὲ ὁ κύριος
before the dinner. But said the Lord

πρὸς αὐτόν· νῦν ὑμεῖς οἱ Φαρισαῖοι τὸ
to him: Now ye the Pharisees the

ἔξωθεν τοῦ ποτηρίου καὶ τοῦ πίνακος
outside of the cup and of the dish

καθαρίζετε, τὸ δὲ ἔσωθεν ὑμῶν γέμει
cleanse, but the inside of you is full

ἁρπαγῆς καὶ πονηρίας. **40** ἄφρονες, οὐχ
of robbery and wickedness. Foolish men, not

ὁ ποιήσας τὸ ἔξωθεν καὶ τὸ ἔσωθεν
the [one] making the outside also the inside

ἐποίησεν; **41** πλὴν τὰ ἐνόντα δότε
made? Nevertheless the things being within give

ἐλεημοσύνην, καὶ ἰδοὺ πάντα καθαρὰ ὑμῖν
alms, and behold all things clean to you

ἐστιν. **42** ἀλλὰ οὐαὶ ὑμῖν τοῖς Φαρισαίοις,
is(are). But woe to you Pharisees,

ὅτι ἀποδεκατοῦτε τὸ ἡδύοσμον καὶ τὸ
because ye tithe the mint and the

πήγανον καὶ πᾶν λάχανον, καὶ παρέρχεσθε
rue and every herb, and pass by

τὴν κρίσιν καὶ τὴν ἀγάπην τοῦ θεοῦ·
the judgment and the love of God;

ταῦτα δὲ ἔδει ποιῆσαι κἀκεῖνα μὴ
but these things it behoved to do and those not

παρεῖναι. **43** οὐαὶ ὑμῖν τοῖς Φαρισαίοις,
to pass by. Woe to you Pharisees,

ὅτι ἀγαπᾶτε τὴν πρωτοκαθεδρίαν ἐν ταῖς
because ye love the chief seat in the

συναγωγαῖς καὶ τοὺς ἀσπασμοὺς ἐν ταῖς
synagogues and the greetings in the

ἀγοραῖς. **44** οὐαὶ ὑμῖν, ὅτι ἐστὲ ὡς τὰ
marketplaces. Woe to you, because ye are as the

μνημεῖα τὰ ἄδηλα, καὶ οἱ ἄνθρωποι οἱ
tombs – unseen, and the men –

περιπατοῦντες ἐπάνω οὐκ οἴδασιν.
walking over do not know.

45 Ἀποκριθεὶς δέ τις τῶν νομικῶν λέγει
And answering one of the lawyers says

αὐτῷ· διδάσκαλε, ταῦτα λέγων καὶ ἡμᾶς
to him: Teacher, these things saying also us

ὑβρίζεις. **46** ὁ δὲ εἶπεν· καὶ ὑμῖν τοῖς
thou insultest. And he said: Also to you

νομικοῖς οὐαί, ὅτι φορτίζετε τοὺς ἀνθρώπους
lawyers woe, because ye burden – men

φορτία δυσβάστακτα, καὶ αὐτοὶ ἑνὶ τῶν
[with] burdens difficult to carry, and [your]selves with one of the

---

darkness. 35See to it, then, that the light within you is not darkness. 36Therefore, if your whole body is full of light, and no part of it dark, it will be completely lighted, as when the light of a lamp shines on you."

Six Woes

37When Jesus had finished speaking, a Pharisee invited him to eat with him; so he went in and reclined at the table. 38But the Pharisee, noticing that Jesus did not first wash before the meal, was surprised.

39Then the Lord said to him, "Now then, you Pharisees clean the outside of the cup and dish, but inside you are full of greed and wickedness. 40You foolish people! Did not the one who made the outside make the inside also? 41But give what is inside ᵗhe dishᶜ to the poor, and everything will be clean for you.

42"Woe to you Pharisees, because you give God a tenth of your mint, rue and all other kinds of garden herbs, but you neglect justice and the love of God. You should have practiced the latter without leaving the former undone.

43"Woe to you Pharisees, because you love the most important seats in the synagogues and greetings in the marketplaces.

44"Woe to you, because you are like unmarked graves, which men walk over without knowing it."

45One of the experts in the law answered him, "Teacher, when you say these things, you insult us also."

46Jesus replied, "And you experts in the law, woe to you, because you load people down with burdens they can hardly carry, and you yourselves will not lift

---

ʷ I.e., experts in the Mosaic law   [with] burdens difficult to carry, and [your]selves with one of the   ᶜ41 Or *what you have* even touch the burdens with one of your fingers.

47"Woe to you! For you build the tombs of the prophets, and *it was* your fathers *who* killed them.

48"Consequently, you are witnesses and approve the deeds of your fathers; because it was they who killed them, and you build *their tombs.*

49"For this reason also the wisdom of God said, 'I will send to them prophets and apostles, and *some* of them they will kill and *some* they will persecute,

50in order that the blood of all the prophets, shed since the foundation of the world, may be charged against this generation,

51from the blood of Abel to the blood of Zechariah, who perished between the altar and the house *of God;* yes, I tell you, it shall be charged against this generation.'

52"Woe to you lawyers! For you have taken away the key of knowledge; you did not enter in yourselves, and those who were entering in you hindered."

53And when He left there, the scribes and the Pharisees began to be very hostile and to question Him closely on many subjects,

54plotting against Him, to catch *Him* in something He might say.

δακτύλων ὑμῶν οὐ προσψαύετε τοῖς φορτίοις.
fingers   of you   ye do not touch   the   burdens.

47 οὐαὶ ὑμῖν, ὅτι οἰκοδομεῖτε τὰ μνημεῖα
Woe to you, because   ye build   the   tombs

τῶν προφητῶν, οἱ δὲ πατέρες ὑμῶν
of the prophets,   and the fathers   of you

ἀπέκτειναν αὐτούς. **48** ἄρα μάρτυρές ἐστε
killed   them.   Therefore witnesses ye are

καὶ συνευδοκεῖτε τοῖς ἔργοις τῶν πατέρων
and ye entirely approve the works of the fathers

ὑμῶν, ὅτι αὐτοὶ μὲν ἀπέκτειναν αὐτούς,
of you, because they on one hand killed   them,

ὑμεῖς δὲ οἰκοδομεῖτε. **49** διὰ τοῦτο καὶ
ye on the other hand build.   Therefore also

ἡ σοφία τοῦ θεοῦ εἶπεν· ἀποστελῶ εἰς
the Wisdom - of God said :   I will send   to

αὐτοὺς προφήτας καὶ ἀποστόλους, καὶ ἐξ
them   prophets and apostles,   and of

αὐτῶν ἀποκτενοῦσιν καὶ διώξουσιν, **50** ἵνα
them   they will kill and persecute,   that

ἐκζητηθῇ τὸ αἷμα πάντων τῶν προφητῶν
¹¹may be required ¹the ²blood ³of all ⁴the ⁵prophets

τὸ ἐκκεχυμένον ἀπὸ καταβολῆς κόσμου
- ⁶having been shed ⁷from ⁸[the] ⁹foundation ¹⁰of [the] world

ἀπὸ τῆς γενεᾶς ταύτης, **51** ἀπὸ αἵματος
¹¹from   -   generation   this,   from [the] blood

Ἀβελ ἕως αἵματος Ζαχαρίου τοῦ
of Abel to [the] blood of Zacharias -

ἀπολομένου μεταξὺ τοῦ θυσιαστηρίου καὶ
destroyed   between the altar   and

τοῦ οἴκου· ναὶ λέγω ὑμῖν, ἐκζητηθήσεται
the house; yes I tell you,   it will be required

ἀπὸ τῆς γενεᾶς ταύτης. **52** οὐαὶ ὑμῖν τοῖς
from   -   generation   this.   Woe to you   -

νομικοῖς, ὅτι ἤρατε τὴν κλεῖδα τῆς
lawyers, because ye took the   key   -

γνώσεως· αὐτοὶ οὐκ εἰσήλθατε καὶ τοὺς
of knowledge; [your]selves ye did not enter and the

εἰσερχομένους ἐκωλύσατε. **53** Κἀκεῖθεν ἐξελ-
[ones] entering ye prevented.   And thence going
= as he went forth thence

θόντος αὐτοῦ ἤρξαντο οἱ γραμματεῖς καὶ
forth him²   began the   scribes   and

οἱ Φαρισαῖοι δεινῶς ἐνέχειν καὶ ἀποστοματίζειν
the Pharisees ¹terribly ¹to be ²angry and to ¹draw ²out

αὐτὸν περὶ πλειόνων, **54** ἐνεδρεύοντες
²him concerning a great number of things, lying in wait for

αὐτὸν θηρεῦσαί τι ἐκ τοῦ στόματος αὐτοῦ.
him to catch something out of the mouth   of him.

one finger to help them.

47"Woe to you, because you build tombs for the prophets, and it was your forefathers who killed them. 48So you testify that you approve of what your forefathers did; they killed the prophets, and you build their tombs. 49Because of this, God in his wisdom said, 'I will send them prophets and apostles, some of whom they will kill and others they will persecute.' 50Therefore this generation will be held responsible for the blood of all the prophets that has been shed since the beginning of the world, 51from the blood of Abel to the blood of Zechariah, who was killed between the altar and the sanctuary. Yes, I tell you, this generation will be held responsible for it all.

52"Woe to you experts in the law, because you have taken away the key to knowledge. You yourselves have not entered, and you have hindered those who were entering."

53When Jesus left there, the Pharisees and the teachers of the law began to oppose him fiercely and to besiege him with questions, 54waiting to catch him in something he might say.

Chapter 12

God Knows and Cares

UNDER these circumstances, after so many thousands of the multitude had gathered together that they were stepping on one another, He began saying to His disciples first of all, "Beware of the leaven of the Pharisees, which is hypocrisy.

2"But there is nothing covered up that will not be revealed, and hidden that will not be known.

12 Ἐν οἷς ἐπισυναχθεισῶν τῶν μυριάδων
In which things being assembled the thousands
= Meanwhile as the thousands of the crowd were assembled,

τοῦ ὄχλου, ὥστε καταπατεῖν ἀλλήλους,
of the crowd,³   so as to tread on   one another,

ἤρξατο λέγειν πρὸς τοὺς μαθητὰς αὐτοῦ
he began to say   to   the   disciples   of him

πρῶτον· προσέχετε ἑαυτοῖς ἀπὸ τῆς ζύμης,
first :   Take heed to yourselves from the   leaven,

ἥτις ἐστὶν ὑπόκρισις, τῶν Φαρισαίων.
which is   hypocrisy, of the Pharisees.

2 οὐδὲν δὲ συγκεκαλυμμένον ἐστὶν ὃ οὐκ
And ²nothing   ³having been   ¹there is which not
                completely covered

ἀποκαλυφθήσεται, καὶ κρυπτὸν ὃ οὐ γνωσθήσεται.
will be uncovered,   and hidden which will not be known.

Chapter 12

Warnings and Encouragements

MEANWHILE, when a crowd of many thousands had gathered, so that they were trampling on one another, Jesus began to speak first to his disciples, saying: "Be on your guard against the yeast of the Pharisees, which is hypocrisy. 2There is nothing concealed that will not be disclosed, or hidden that will not be made known. 3What

LUKE 12

211

3"Accordingly, whatever you have said in the dark shall be heard in the light, and what you have whispered in the inner rooms shall be proclaimed upon the housetops.

4"And I say to you, My friends, do not be afraid of those who kill the body, and after that have no more that they can do.

5"But I will warn you whom to fear: fear the One who after He has killed has authority to cast into hell; yes, I tell you, fear Him!

6"Are not five sparrows sold for two cents? And yet not one of them is forgotten before God.

7"Indeed, the very hairs of your head are all numbered. Do not fear; you are of more value than many sparrows.

8"And I say to you, everyone who confesses Me before men, the Son of Man shall confess him also before the angels of God;

9but he who denies Me before men shall be denied before the angels of God.

10"And everyone who will speak a word against the Son of Man, it shall be forgiven him; but he who blasphemes against the Holy Spirit, it shall not be forgiven him.

11"And when they bring you before the synagogues and the rulers and the authorities, do not become anxious about how or what you should speak in your defense, or what you should say;

12for the Holy Spirit will teach you in that very hour what you ought to say."

Covetousness Denounced

13And someone in the crowd said to Him, "Teacher, tell my brother to divide the *family* inheritance with me."

3 ἀνθ’ ὧν ὅσα ἐν τῇ σκοτίᾳ εἴπατε ἐν
Therefore what things in the darkness ye said in
τῷ φωτὶ ἀκουσθήσεται, καὶ ὃ πρὸς τὸ
the light will be heard, and what to the
οὖς ἐλαλήσατε ἐν τοῖς ταμείοις κηρυχθήσεται
ear ye spoke in the private rooms will be proclaimed
ἐπὶ τῶν δωμάτων. 4 Λέγω δὲ ὑμῖν τοῖς
on the roofs. And I say to you the
φίλοις μου, μὴ φοβηθῆτε ἀπὸ τῶν
friends of me, do not be afraid from(of) the [ones]
ἀποκτεννόντων τὸ σῶμα καὶ μετὰ ταῦτα
killing the body and after these things
μὴ ἐχόντων περισσότερόν τι ποιῆσαι.
no' having anything more to do.
5 ὑποδείξω δὲ ὑμῖν τίνα φοβηθῆτε·
But I will warn you whom ye may fear :
φοβήθητε τὸν μετὰ τὸ ἀποκτεῖναι ἔχοντα
¹fear ³the [one] ⁵after the ⁶to kill(killing) ³having
ἐξουσίαν ἐμβαλεῖν εἰς τὴν γέενναν. ναὶ
⁴authority ⁷to cast in into - gehenna. Yes[,]
λέγω ὑμῖν, τοῦτον φοβήθητε. 6 οὐχὶ
I say to you, this one fear ye. Not
πέντε στρουθία πωλοῦνται ἀσσαρίων δύο;
five sparrows are sold of(for) farthings two?
καὶ ἓν ἐξ αὐτῶν οὐκ ἔστιν ἐπιλελησμένον
and one of them is not having been forgotten
ἐνώπιον τοῦ θεοῦ. 7 ἀλλὰ καὶ αἱ τρίχες
before - God. But even the hairs
τῆς κεφαλῆς ὑμῶν πᾶσαι ἠρίθμηνται.
of the head of you all have been numbered.
μὴ φοβεῖσθε· πολλῶν στρουθίων διαφέρετε.
Fear ye not; from many sparrows ye differ.
8 λέγω δὲ ὑμῖν, πᾶς ὃς ἂν ὁμολογήσῃ
But I tell you, everyone whoever confesses
ἐν ἐμοὶ ἔμπροσθεν τῶν ἀνθρώπων, καὶ ὁ
- me before - men, also the
υἱὸς τοῦ ἀνθρώπου ὁμολογήσει ἐν αὐτῷ
Son - of man will confess - him'
ἔμπροσθεν τῶν ἀγγέλων τοῦ θεοῦ· 9 ὁ δὲ
before the angels - of God; and the
ἀρνησάμενός με ἐνώπιον τῶν ἀνθρώπων
[one] denying me before - men
ἀπαρνηθήσεται ἐνώπιον τῶν ἀγγέλων τοῦ
will be denied before the angels -
θεοῦ. 10 καὶ πᾶς ὃς ἐρεῖ λόγον εἰς τὸν
of God. And everyone who shall say a word against the
υἱὸν τοῦ ἀνθρώπου, ἀφεθήσεται αὐτῷ· τῷ
Son - of man, it will be forgiven him; ²the [one]
δὲ εἰς τὸ ἅγιον πνεῦμα βλασφημήσαντι
¹but against the Holy Spirit blaspheming
οὐκ ἀφεθήσεται. 11 ὅταν δὲ εἰσφέρωσιν
will not be forgiven. And when they bring in
ὑμᾶς ἐπὶ τὰς συναγωγὰς καὶ τὰς ἀρχὰς
you before - synagogues and - rulers
καὶ τὰς ἐξουσίας, μὴ μεριμνήσητε πῶς ἢ
and - authorities, do not be anxious how or
τί ἀπολογήσησθε ἢ τί εἴπητε· 12 τὸ γὰρ
what ye may answer or what ye may say; for the
ἅγιον πνεῦμα διδάξει ὑμᾶς ἐν αὐτῇ τῇ
Holy Spirit will teach you in ¹same ³the
ὥρᾳ ἃ δεῖ εἰπεῖν. 13 Εἶπεν δέ τις
hour what things it behoves [you] to say. And said someone
ἐκ τοῦ ὄχλου αὐτῷ· διδάσκαλε, εἰπὲ τῷ
out of the crowd to him : Teacher, tell the
ἀδελφῷ μου μερίσασθαι μετ’ ἐμοῦ τὴν
brother of me to divide with me the

you have said in the dark will be heard in the daylight, and what you have whispered in the ear will be proclaimed from the roofs.

4"I tell you, my friends, do not be afraid of those who kill the body and after that can do no more. 5But I will show you whom you should fear: Fear him who, after the killing of the body, has power to throw you into hell. Yes, I tell you, fear him. 6Are not five sparrows sold for two pennies*d*? Yet not one of them is forgotten by God. 7Indeed, the very hairs of your head are all numbered. Don't be afraid; you are worth more than many sparrows.

8"I tell you, whoever acknowledges me before men, the Son of Man will also acknowledge him before the angels of God. 9But he who disowns me before men will be disowned before the angels of God. 10And everyone who speaks a word against the Son of Man will be forgiven, but anyone who blasphemes against the Holy Spirit will not be forgiven.

11"When you are brought before synagogues, rulers and authorities, do not worry about how you will defend yourselves or what you will say, 12for the Holy Spirit will teach you at that time what you should say."

The Parable of the Rich Fool

13Someone in the crowd said to him, "Teacher, tell my brother to divide the inheritance with me."

*d*6 Greek *two assaria*

14But He said to him, "Man, who appointed Me a judge or arbiter over you?"
15And He said to them, "Beware, and be on your guard against every form of greed; for not *even* when one has an abundance does his life consist of his possessions."
16And He told them a parable, saying, "The land of a certain rich man was very productive.
17"And he began reasoning to himself, saying, 'What shall I do, since I have no place to store my crops?'
18"And he said, 'This is what I will do: I will tear down my barns and build larger ones, and there I will store all my grain and my goods.
19'And I will say to my soul, "Soul, you have many goods laid up for many years *to come;* take your ease, eat, drink *and be* merry."
20"But God said to him, 'You fool! This *very* night your soul is required of you; and *now* who will own what you have prepared?'
21"So is the man who lays up treasure for himself, and is not rich toward God."
22And He said to His disciples, "For this reason I say to you, do not be anxious for *your* life, *as to* what you shall eat; nor for your body, *as to* what you shall put on.
23"For life is more than food, and the body than clothing.
24"Consider the ravens, for they neither sow nor reap; and they have no storeroom nor barn; and *yet* God feeds them; how much more valuable you are than the birds!
25"And which of you by being anxious can add a *single* ˣcubit to his ʸlife's span?

κληρονομίαν. 14 ὁ δὲ εἶπεν αὐτῷ· ἄνθρωπε,
inheritance   But he said to him: Man,
τίς με κατέστησεν κριτὴν ἢ μεριστὴν ἐφ'
who me appointed a judge or a divider over
ὑμᾶς; 15 εἶπεν δὲ πρὸς αὐτούς· ὁρᾶτε
you?   And he said to   them: Beware
καὶ φυλάσσεσθε ἀπὸ πάσης πλεονεξίας,
and guard   from(against) all covetousness,
ὅτι οὐκ ἐν τῷ περισσεύειν τινὶ ἡ ζωὴ
because ⁶not ⁷in ⁷the ⁸to abound ⁹to anyone ¹the ²life
αὐτοῦ ἐστιν ἐκ τῶν ὑπαρχόντων αὐτῷ.
³of him ⁴is ¹⁰of   the things existing to him.ᶜ
=¹¹his ¹²possessions.

16 Εἶπεν δὲ παραβολὴν πρὸς αὐτοὺς λέγων·
   And he told a parable   to   them saying:
ἀνθρώπου τινὸς πλουσίου εὐφόρησεν ἡ
³of a certain ⁵man ⁴rich ⁶bore well ¹The
χώρα. 17 καὶ διελογίζετο ἐν ἑαυτῷ λέγων·
²land. And he reasoned in himself saying:
τί ποιήσω, ὅτι οὐκ ἔχω ποῦ συνάξω τοὺς
What may I do, because I have not where I may gather the
καρπούς μου; 18 καὶ εἶπεν· τοῦτο ποιήσω·
fruits of me? And he said: This will I do:
καθελῶ μου τὰς ἀποθήκας καὶ μείζονας
I will pull down of me the barns   and larger ones
οἰκοδομήσω, καὶ συνάξω ἐκεῖ πάντα τὸν
I will build, and I will gather there all the
σῖτον καὶ τὰ ἀγαθά μου, 19 καὶ ἐρῶ τῇ
wheat and the goods of me, and I will say to the
ψυχῇ μου· ψυχή, ἔχεις πολλὰ ἀγαθὰ
soul of me: Soul, thou hast many goods
κείμενα εἰς ἔτη πολλά· ἀναπαύου, φάγε,
laid [up] for years many· take rest, eat,
πίε, εὐφραίνου. 20 εἶπεν δὲ αὐτῷ ὁ
drink, be glad.   But said to him —
θεός· ἄφρων, ταύτῃ τῇ νυκτὶ τὴν ψυχήν
God: Foolish man, in this the night the soul
σου ἀπαιτοῦσιν ἀπὸ σοῦ· ἃ δὲ
of thee they demand from thee; then [the] things which
ἡτοίμασας, τίνι ἔσται; 21 οὕτως ὁ
thou preparedst, to whom will they be?ᵉ So the [one]
=whose will they be?
θησαυρίζων αὐτῷ καὶ μὴ εἰς θεὸν πλουτῶν.
treasuring to himself and not toward God being rich.

22 Εἶπεν δὲ πρὸς τοὺς μαθητὰς [αὐτοῦ]· διὰ τοῦτο
   And he said to the disciples of him: Therefore
λέγω ὑμῖν· μὴ μεριμνᾶτε τῇ ψυχῇ τί
I tell you: Do not be anxious for the life what
φάγητε, μηδὲ τῷ σώματι [ὑμῶν] τί
ye may eat, nor for the body of you what
ἐνδύσησθε. 23 ἡ γὰρ ψυχὴ πλεῖόν ἐστιν
ye may put on. For the life more is
τῆς τροφῆς καὶ τὸ σῶμα τοῦ ἐνδύματος.
[than] the food and the body [than] the clothing.
24 κατανοήσατε τοὺς κόρακας, ὅτι οὔτε
   Consider ye the ravens, that neither
σπείρουσιν οὔτε θερίζουσιν, οἷς οὐκ ἔστινᶜ
they sow   nor reap,   to which is notᶜ
=which have not
ταμιεῖον οὐδὲ ἀποθήκη, καὶ ὁ θεὸς τρέφει
storehouse nor barn,   and — God feeds
αὐτούς· πόσῳ μᾶλλον ὑμεῖς διαφέρετε τῶν
them; by how much rather ye   differ from the
πετεινῶν. 25 τίς δὲ ἐξ ὑμῶν μεριμνῶν
birds.   And who of you being anxious
δύναται ἐπὶ τὴν ἡλικίαν αὐτοῦ προσθεῖναι
can   on the stature of him to add

14Jesus replied, "Man, who appointed me a judge or an arbiter between you?" 15Then he said to them, "Watch out! Be on your guard against all kinds of greed; a man's life does not consist in the abundance of his possessions."
16And he told them this parable: "The ground of a certain rich man produced a good crop. 17He thought to himself, 'What shall I do? I have no place to store my crops.'
18"Then he said, 'This is what I'll do. I will tear down my barns and build bigger ones, and there I will store all my grain and my goods. 19And I'll say to myself, "You have plenty of good things laid up for many years. Take life easy; eat, drink and be merry." '
20"But God said to him, 'You fool! This very night your life will be demanded from you. Then who will get what you have prepared for yourself?'
21"This is how it will be with anyone who stores up things for himself but is not rich toward God."

Do Not Worry

22Then Jesus said to his disciples: "Therefore I tell you, do not worry about your life, what you will eat; or about your body, what you will wear. 23Life is more than food, and the body more than clothes. 24Consider the ravens: They do not sow or reap, they have no storeroom or barn; yet God feeds them. And how much more valuable you are than birds! 25Who of you by worrying can add a single hour to his

26"If then you cannot do even a very little thing, why are you anxious about other matters?

27"Consider the lilies, how they grow; they neither toil nor spin; but I tell you, even Solomon in all his glory did not clothe himself like one of these.

28"But if God so arrays the grass in the field, which is alive today and tomorrow is thrown into the furnace, how much more will He clothe you, O men of little faith!

29"And do not seek what you shall eat, and what you shall drink, and do not keep worrying.

30"For all these things the nations of the world eagerly seek; but your Father knows that you need these things.

31"But seek for His kingdom, and these things shall be added to you.

32"Do not be afraid, little flock, for your Father has chosen gladly to give you the kingdom.

33"Sell your possessions and give to charity; make yourselves purses which do not wear out, an unfailing treasure in heaven, where no thief comes near, nor moth destroys.

34"For where your treasure is, there will your heart be also.

Be in Readiness

35"Be dressed in readiness, and *keep* your lamps alight.

36"And be like men who are waiting for their master when he returns from the wedding feast, so that they may immediately open *the door* to him when he comes and knocks.

37"Blessed are those slaves whom the master shall find on the alert when he comes; truly I say to you, that he will gird himself *to serve,* and have them recline *at the table,* and will come up and wait on them.

πῆχυν; **26** εἰ οὖν οὐδὲ ἐλάχιστον δύνασθε,
a cubit?　If therefore not [the] least　ye can,

τί περὶ τῶν λοιπῶν μεριμνᾶτε; **27** κατα-
why concerning the other things are ye anxious?　Con-

νοήσατε τὰ κρίνα, πῶς οὔτε νήθει οὔτε
sider ye　the lilies,　how　neither they spin　nor

ὑφαίνει· λέγω δὲ ὑμῖν, οὐδὲ Σολομὼν ἐν
weave;　but I tell　you,　not　Solomon　in

πάσῃ τῇ δόξῃ αὐτοῦ περιεβάλετο ὡς ἐν
all　the　glory　of him　was arrayed　as　one

τούτων. **28** εἰ δὲ ἐν ἀγρῷ τὸν χόρτον
of these.　¹And ²if　³in　¹⁰a field　⁴the　⁷grass

ὄντα σήμερον καὶ αὔριον εἰς κλίβανον
⁸being　¹¹to-day　¹²and　¹³tomorrow　¹⁵into　¹⁴an oven

βαλλόμενον ὁ θεὸς οὕτως ἀμφιάζει, πόσῳ
¹⁴being thrown　–　⁹God　⁵so　⁵clothes,　by how much

μᾶλλον ὑμᾶς, ὀλιγόπιστοι. **29** καὶ ὑμεῖς
rather　you,　little-faiths.　And　ye

μὴ ζητεῖτε τί φάγητε καὶ τί πίητε, καὶ
do not seek what ye may eat　and what ye may drink, and

μὴ μετεωρίζεσθε· **30** ταῦτα γὰρ πάντα τὰ
do not be in suspense;　for these things　all　the

ἔθνη τοῦ κόσμου ἐπιζητοῦσιν· ὑμῶν δὲ
nations of the　world　seek after;　but of you

ὁ πατὴρ οἶδεν ὅτι χρήζετε τούτων·
the　Father　knows　that　ye have need　of them;

31 πλὴν ζητεῖτε τὴν βασιλείαν αὐτοῦ, καὶ
but　seek ye　the　kingdom　of him,　and

ταῦτα προστεθήσεται ὑμῖν. **32** Μὴ φοβοῦ,
these things　will be added　to you.　Fear not,

τὸ μικρὸν ποίμνιον· ὅτι εὐδόκησεν ὁ
–　little　flock;　because was well pleased the

πατὴρ ὑμῶν δοῦναι ὑμῖν τὴν βασιλείαν.
Father　of you　to give　you　the　kingdom.

33 Πωλήσατε τὰ ὑπάρχοντα ὑμῶν καὶ
Sell　the　possessions　of you　and

δότε ἐλεημοσύνην· ποιήσατε ἑαυτοῖς βαλ-
give　alms;　make　for yourselves

λάντια μὴ παλαιούμενα, θησαυρὸν ἀνέκλειπτον
purses　not　becoming old,　a treasure　unfailing

ἐν τοῖς οὐρανοῖς, ὅπου κλέπτης οὐκ
in　the　heavens,　where　a thief　not

ἐγγίζει οὐδὲ σὴς διαφθείρει· **34** ὅπου γάρ
comes near nor　moth　corrupts;　for where

ἐστιν ὁ θησαυρὸς ὑμῶν, ἐκεῖ καὶ ἡ
is　the　treasure　of you,　there　also　the

καρδία ὑμῶν ἔσται. **35** Ἔστωσαν ὑμῶν αἱ
heart　of you　will be.　Let be　of you　the

ὀσφύες περιεζωσμέναι καὶ οἱ λύχνοι
loins　*having been* girded　and　the　lamps

καιόμενοι· **36** καὶ ὑμεῖς ὅμοιοι ἀνθρώποις
burning;　and　ye　like　men

προσδεχομένοις τὸν κύριον ἑαυτῶν, πότε
awaiting　the　lord　of them*selves,*　when

ἀναλύσῃ ἐκ τῶν γάμων, ἵνα ἐλθόντος
he returns from　the wedding festivities, that　coming³

καὶ κρούσαντος εὐθέως ἀνοίξωσιν αὐτῷ.
and　knocking³　immediately they may open　to him.

37 μακάριοι οἱ δοῦλοι ἐκεῖνοι, οὓς ἐλθὼν
Blessed　–　slaves　those,　whom　coming

ὁ κύριος εὑρήσει γρηγοροῦντας· ἀμὴν λέγω
the lord　will find　watching;　truly　I tell

ὑμῖν ὅτι περιζώσεται καὶ ἀνακλινεῖ αὐτοὺς
you　that he will gird himself　and　¹make ²to recline ³them

καὶ παρελθὼν διακονήσει αὐτοῖς. **38** κἂν
and　coming up to　will serve　them.　And if

---

life ᵉ? 26Since you cannot do this very little thing, why do you worry about the rest?

27"Consider how the lilies grow. They do not labor or spin. Yet I tell you, not even Solomon in all his splendor was dressed like one of these. 28If that is how God clothes the grass of the field, which is here today, and tomorrow is thrown into the fire, how much more will he clothe you, O you of little faith! 29And do not set your heart on what you will eat or drink; do not worry about it. 30For the pagan world runs after all such things, and your Father knows that you need them. 31But seek his kingdom, and these things will be given to you as well.

32"Do not be afraid, little flock, for your Father has been pleased to give you the kingdom. 33Sell your possessions and give to the poor. Provide purses for yourselves that will not wear out, a treasure in heaven that will not be exhausted, where no thief comes near and no moth destroys. 34For where your treasure is, there your heart will be also.

Watchfulness

35"Be dressed ready for service and keep your lamps burning, 36like men waiting for their master to return from a wedding banquet, so that when he comes and knocks they can immediately open the door for him. 37It will be good for those servants whose master finds them watching when he comes. I tell you the truth, he will dress himself to serve, will have them recline at the table and will come and wait on

---

ᵉ25 *Or* single cubit to his height

38"Whether he comes in the ²second watch, or even in the ᵃthird, and finds *them* so, blessed are those slaves.

39"And be sure of this, that if the head of the house had known at what hour the thief was coming, he would not have allowed his house to be broken into.

40"You too, be ready; for the Son of Man is coming at an hour that you do not expect."

41And Peter said, "Lord, are You addressing this parable to us, or to everyone *else* as well?"

42And the Lord said, "Who then is the faithful and sensible steward, whom his master will put in charge of his servants, to give them their rations at the proper time?

43"Blessed is that slave whom his master finds so doing when he comes.

44"Truly I say to you, that he will put him in charge of all his possessions.

45"But if that slave says in his heart, 'My master will be a long time in coming,' and begins to beat the slaves, *both* men and women, and to eat and drink and get drunk;

46the master of that slave will come on a day when he does not expect *him*, and at an hour he does not know, and will cut him in pieces, and assign him a place with the unbelievers.

47"And that slave who knew his master's will and did not get ready or act in accord with his will, shall receive many lashes;

48but the one who did not know *it*, and committed deeds worthy of a flogging, will receive but few. And from everyone who has been given much shall much be required; and to

ἐν τῇ δευτέρᾳ κἂν ἐν τῇ τρίτῃ φυλακῇ
in the second and if in the third watch
ἔλθῃ καὶ εὕρῃ οὕτως, μακάριοί εἰσιν
he comes and finds so, blessed are
ἐκεῖνοι. 39 τοῦτο δὲ γινώσκετε, ὅτι εἰ
those [slaves]. But this know ye, that if
ᾔδει ὁ οἰκοδεσπότης ποίᾳ ὥρᾳ ὁ κλέπτης
knew the house-master in what hour the thief
ἔρχεται, οὐκ ἂν ἀφῆκεν διορυχθῆναι τὸν
comes, he would not have allowed to be dug through the
οἶκον αὐτοῦ. 40 καὶ ὑμεῖς γίνεσθε ἕτοιμοι,
house of him. And ¹ye ¹be prepared.
ὅτι ᾗ ὥρᾳ οὐ δοκεῖτε ὁ υἱὸς τοῦ
because in what hour ye think not the Son –
ἀνθρώπου ἔρχεται. 41 Εἶπεν δὲ ὁ Πέτρος·
of man comes. And said – Peter:
κύριε, πρὸς ἡμᾶς τὴν παραβολὴν ταύτην
Lord, to us – parable this
λέγεις ἢ καὶ πρὸς πάντας; 42 καὶ εἶπεν
sayest thou or also to all? And said
ὁ κύριος· τίς ἄρα ἐστὶν ὁ πιστὸς
the Lord: Who then is the faithful
οἰκονόμος ὁ φρόνιμος, ὃν καταστήσει ὁ
steward the prudent, whom will appoint the
κύριος ἐπὶ τῆς θεραπείας αὐτοῦ τοῦ
lord over the household attendants of him –
διδόναι ἐν καιρῷ [τὸ] σιτομέτριον;
to giveᵈ in season the portion of food?
43 μακάριος ὁ δοῦλος ἐκεῖνος, ὃν ἐλθὼν
Blessed – slave that, whom coming
ὁ κύριος αὐτοῦ εὑρήσει ποιοῦντα οὕτως.
the lord of him will find doing so.
44 ἀληθῶς λέγω ὑμῖν ὅτι ἐπὶ πᾶσιν τοῖς
Truly I tell you that over all the
ὑπάρχουσιν αὐτοῦ καταστήσει αὐτόν. 45 ἐὰν
possessions of him he will appoint him. if
δὲ εἴπῃ ὁ δοῦλος ἐκεῖνος ἐν τῇ καρδίᾳ
But says – slave that in the heart
αὐτοῦ· χρονίζει ὁ κύριός μου ἔρχεσθαι,
of him: Delays the lord of me to come,
καὶ ἄρξηται τύπτειν τοὺς παῖδας καὶ τὰς
and begins to strike the menservants and the
παιδίσκας, ἐσθίειν τε καὶ πίνειν καὶ
maidservants, ¹to eat ¹both and to drink and
μεθύσκεσθαι, 46 ἥξει ὁ κύριος τοῦ δούλου
to become drunk, will come the lord – slave
ἐκείνου ἐν ἡμέρᾳ ᾗ οὐ προσδοκᾷ καὶ ἐν
of that in a day in which he does not expect and in
ὥρᾳ ᾗ οὐ γινώσκει, καὶ διχοτομήσει
an hour *in* which he knows not, and will cut asunder
αὐτόν, καὶ τὸ μέρος αὐτοῦ μετὰ τῶν
him, and the portion of him with the
ἀπίστων θήσει. 47 ἐκεῖνος δὲ ὁ δοῦλος
unbelievers will place. But that – slave
ὁ γνοὺς τὸ θέλημα τοῦ κυρίου αὐτοῦ
– having known the will of the lord of him
καὶ μὴ ἑτοιμάσας ἢ ποιήσας πρὸς τὸ θέλημα
and not having prepared or done according to the will
ᵃαὐτοῦ δαρήσεται πολλάς· 48 ὁ δὲ
of him will be beaten [with] many [stripes]; but the [one]
μὴ γνούς, ποιήσας δὲ ἄξια πληγῶν,
not having known, but having done things worthy of stripes,
δαρήσεται ὀλίγας. παντὶ δὲ ᾧ
will be beaten [with] few [stripes]. But to everyone to whom
ἐδόθη πολύ, πολὺ ζητηθήσεται παρ' αὐτοῦ, καὶ
was given much, much will be demanded from him, and

them. 38It will be good for those servants whose master finds them ready, even if he comes in the second or third watch of the night. 39But understand this: If the owner of the house had known at what hour the thief was coming, he would not have let his house be broken into. 40You also must be ready, because the Son of Man will come at an hour when you do not expect him."

41Peter asked, "Lord, are you telling this parable to us, or to everyone?"

42The Lord answered, "Who then is the faithful and wise manager, whom the master puts in charge of his servants to give them their food allowance at the proper time? 43It will be good for that servant whom the master finds doing so when he returns. 44I tell you the truth, he will put him in charge of all his possessions. 45But suppose the servant says to himself, 'My master is taking a long time in coming,' and he then begins to beat the menservants and maidservants and to eat and drink and get drunk. 46The master of that servant will come on a day when he does not expect him and at an hour he is not aware of. He will cut him to pieces and assign him a place with the unbelievers.

47"That servant who knows his master's will and does not get ready or does not do what his master wants will be beaten with many blows. 48But the one who does not know and does things deserving punishment will be beaten with few blows. From everyone who has been given much, much will be demanded;

---

²I.e., 9 p.m. to midnight
ᵃI.e., midnight to 3 a.m.

whom they entrusted much, of him they will ask all the more.

Christit Divides Men

49"I have come to cast fire upon the earth; and how I wish it were already kindled!

50"But I have a baptism to undergo, and how distressed I am until it is accomplished!

51"Do you suppose that I came to grant peace on earth? I tell you, no, but rather division;

52for from now on five *members* in one household will be divided, three against two, and two against three.

53"They will be divided, father against son, and son against father; mother against daughter, and daughter against mother; mother-in-law against daughter-in-law, and daughter-in-law against mother-in-law."

54And He was also saying to the multitudes, "When you see a cloud rising in the west, immediately you say, 'A shower is coming,' and so it turns out.

55"And when *you see* a south wind blowing, you say, 'It will be a hot day,' and it turns out *that way.*

56"You hypocrites! You know how to analyze the appearance of the earth and the sky, but why do you not analyze this present time?

57"And why do you not even on your own initiative judge what is right?

58"For while you are going with your opponent to appear before the magistrate, on *your* way *there* make an effort to settle with him, in order that he may not drag you before the judge, and the judge turn you over to the constable, and the constable throw you into prison.

59"I say to you, you shall not get out of there until you have paid the very last cent."

Chapter 13

Call to Repent

NOW on the same occasion there were some present who reported to Him about the Galileans,

---

ᾧ   παρέθεντο πολύ, περισσότερον αἰτήσουσιν
with whom was deposited much, more exceedingly they will ask

αὐτόν. 49 Πῦρ ἦλθον βαλεῖν ἐπὶ τὴν γῆν,
him.   Fire I came to cast on the earth,

καὶ τί θέλω εἰ ἤδη ἀνήφθη. 50 βάπτισμα
and what will I if already it was kindled. ᵃa baptism

δὲ ἔχω βαπτισθῆναι, καὶ πῶς συνέχομαι
¹And ᵃI have to be baptized [with], and how am I pressed

ἕως ὅτου τελεσθῇ. 51 δοκεῖτε ὅτι εἰρήνην
until it is accomplished. Think ye that peace

παρεγενόμην δοῦναι ἐν τῇ γῇ; οὐχί, λέγω
I came   to give in the earth? No, I tell

ὑμῖν, ἀλλ᾽ ἢ διαμερισμόν. 52 ἔσονται γὰρ
you, but rather division.   For there will be

ἀπὸ τοῦ νῦν πέντε ἐν ἑνὶ οἴκω διαμεμε-
from - now five in one house having been

ρισμένοι, τρεῖς ἐπὶ δυσὶν καὶ δύο ἐπὶ
divided,   three against two and two against

τρισὶν 53 διαμερισθήσονται, πατὴρ ἐπὶ υἱῷ
three   will be divided,   father against son

καὶ υἱὸς ἐπὶ πατρί, μήτηρ ἐπὶ θυγατέρα
and son against father, mother against daughter

καὶ θυγάτηρ ἐπὶ τὴν μητέρα, πενθερὰ
and daughter against the mother, mother-in-law

ἐπὶ τὴν νύμφην αὐτῆς καὶ νύμφη ἐπὶ
against the daughter-in-law of her and daughter-in-law against

τὴν πενθεράν. 54 Ἔλεγεν δὲ καὶ τοῖς
the mother-in-law.   And he said also to the

ὄχλοις· ὅταν ἴδητε νεφέλην ἀνατέλλουσαν
crowds: When ye see a cloud rising

ἐπὶ δυσμῶν, εὐθέως λέγετε ὅτι ὄμβρος
over [the] west, immediately ye say that a storm

ἔρχεται, καὶ γίνεται οὕτως· 55 καὶ ὅταν
is coming, and it becomes so;   and when

νότον πνέοντα, λέγετε ὅτι καύσων ἔσται,
a south wind blowing, ye say that heat there will be,

καὶ γίνεται. 56 ὑποκριταί, τὸ πρόσωπον
and it becomes. Hypocrites, the face

τῆς γῆς καὶ τοῦ οὐρανοῦ οἴδατε δοκιμάζειν,
of the earth and of the heaven ye know* to discern,

τὸν καιρὸν δὲ τοῦτον πῶς οὐ δοκιμάζετε;
- ᵃtime ¹but ²this how do ye not discern?

57 Τί δὲ καὶ ἀφ᾽ ἑαυτῶν οὐ κρίνετε
And why even from yourselves do ye not judge

τὸ δίκαιον; 58 ὡς γὰρ ὑπάγεις μετὰ τοῦ
the righteous thing? For as thou goest with the

ἀντιδίκου σου ἐπ᾽ ἄρχοντα, ἐν τῇ ὁδῷ
adversary of thee to a ruler, in the way

δὸς ἐργασίαν ἀπηλλάχθαι ἀπ᾽ αὐτοῦ, μήποτε
give(take) pains to be rid from(of) him, lest

κατασύρη σε πρὸς τὸν κριτήν, καὶ ὁ
he drag thee to the judge, and the

κριτής σε παραδώσει τῷ πράκτορι, καὶ ὁ
judge thee will deliver to the usher, and the

πράκτωρ σε βαλεῖ εἰς φυλακήν. 59 λέγω
usher thee will cast into prison. I tell

σοι, οὐ μὴ ἐξέλθῃς ἐκεῖθεν ἕως
thee, by no means mayest thou come out thence until

καὶ τὸ ἔσχατον λεπτὸν ἀποδῷς.
even the last lepton thou payest.

13 Παρῆσαν δέ τινες ἐν αὐτῷ τῷ
And there were present some at ²same ¹the

καιρῷ ἀπαγγέλλοντες αὐτῷ περὶ τῶν
time reporting to him about the

* can, as Mat. 16. 3.

---

and from the one who has been entrusted with much, much more will be asked.

Not Peace but Division

49"I have come to bring fire on the earth, and how I wish it were already kindled! 50But I have a baptism to undergo, and how distressed I am until it is completed! 51Do you think I came to bring peace on earth? No, I tell you, but division. 52From now on there will be five in one family divided against each other, three against two and two against three. 53They will be divided, father against son and son against father, mother against daughter and daughter against mother, mother-in-law against daughter-in-law and daughter-in-law against mother-in-law."

Interpreting the Times

54He said to the crowd: "When you see a cloud rising in the west, immediately you say, 'It's going to rain,' and it does. 55And when the south wind blows, you say, 'It's going to be hot,' and it is. 56Hypocrites! You know how to interpret the appearance of the earth and the sky. How is it that you don't know how to interpret this present time? 57"Why don't you judge for yourselves what is right? 58As you are going with your adversary to the magistrate, try hard to be reconciled to him on the way, or he may drag you off to the judge, and the judge turn you over to the officer, and the officer throw you into prison. 59I tell you, you will not get out until you have paid the last penny.ᶠ"

Chapter 13

Repent or Perish

NOW there were some present at that time who told Jesus about the

ᶠ59 Greek lepton

whose blood Pilate had mingled with their sacrifices.

²And He answered and said to them, "Do you suppose that these Galileans were *greater* sinners than all *other* Galileans, because they suffered this *fate?*

³"I tell you, no, but, unless you repent, you will all likewise perish.

⁴"Or do you suppose that those eighteen on whom the tower in Siloam fell and killed them, were *worse* culprits than all the men who live in Jerusalem?

⁵"I tell you, no, but unless you repent, you will all likewise perish."

⁶And He *began* telling this parable: "A certain man had a fig tree which had been planted in his vineyard; and he came looking for fruit on it, and did not find any.

⁷"And he said to the vineyard-keeper, 'Behold, for three years I have come looking for fruit on this fig tree without finding any. Cut it down! Why does it even use up the ground?'

⁸"And he answered and said to him, 'Let it alone, sir, for this year too, until I dig around it and put in fertilizer;

⁹and if it bears fruit next year, *fine;* but if not, cut it down.' "

Healing on the Sabbath

¹⁰And He was teaching in one of the synagogues on the Sabbath.

¹¹And behold, there was a woman who for eighteen years had had a sickness caused by a spirit; and she was bent double, and could not straighten up at all.

¹²And when Jesus saw her, He called her over and said to her, "Woman, you are freed from your sickness."

Γαλιλαίων ὦν τὸ αἷμα Πιλᾶτος ἔμιξεν
Galilæans of whom the blood Pilate mixed

μετὰ τῶν θυσιῶν αὐτῶν. 2 καὶ ἀποκριθεὶς
with the sacrifices of them. And answering

εἶπεν αὐτοῖς· δοκεῖτε ὅτι οἱ Γαλιλαῖοι
he said to them : Think ye that – Galilæans

οὗτοι ἁμαρτωλοὶ παρὰ πάντας τοὺς Γαλι-
these sinners above all †he Gali-

λαίους ἐγένοντο, ὅτι ταῦτα πεπόνθασιν;
læans were, because these things they have suffered?

3 οὐχί, λέγω ὑμῖν, ἀλλ᾽ ἐὰν μὴ μετανοῆτε,
No, I tell you, but unless ye repent,

πάντες ὁμοίως ἀπολεῖσθε. 4 ἢ ἐκεῖνοι οἱ
all likewise ye will perish. Or those –

δεκαοκτὼ ἐφ᾽ οὓς ἔπεσεν ὁ πύργος ἐν
eighteen on whom fell the tower in

τῷ Σιλωὰμ καὶ ἀπέκτεινεν αὐτούς, δοκεῖτε
– Siloam and killed them, think ye

ὅτι αὐτοὶ ὀφειλέται ἐγένοντο παρὰ πάντας
that they debtors were above all

τοὺς ἀνθρώπους τοὺς κατοικοῦντας ᾽Ιερου-
the men – dwelling in Jeru-

σαλήμ; 5 οὐχί, λέγω ὑμῖν, ἀλλ᾽ ἐὰν μὴ
salem? No, I tell you, but unless

μετανοήσητε, πάντες ὡσαύτως ἀπολεῖσθε.
ye repent, all similarly ye will perish.

6 Ἔλεγεν δὲ ταύτην τὴν παραβολήν. συκῆν
And he told this – parable. ²A fig-tree

εἶχέν τις πεφυτευμένην ἐν τῷ ἀμπελῶνι
¹had ¹a certain man *having been* planted in the vineyard

αὐτοῦ, καὶ ἦλθεν ζητῶν καρπὸν ἐν αὐτῇ
of him, and came seeking fruit in it

καὶ οὐχ εὗρεν. 7 εἶπεν δὲ πρὸς τὸν
and found not. And he said to the

ἀμπελουργόν· ἰδοὺ τρία ἔτη ἀφ᾽ οὗ
vinedresser : Behold[,] three years [it is] since

ἔρχομαι ζητῶν καρπὸν ἐν τῇ συκῇ ταύτῃ
I come seeking fruit in – fig-tree this

καὶ οὐχ εὑρίσκω· ἔκκοψον αὐτήν· ἱνατί
and find not; cut down it; why

καὶ τὴν γῆν καταργεῖ; 8 ὁ δὲ ἀποκριθεὶς
even the ground it spoils? But he answering

λέγει αὐτῷ· κύριε, ἄφες αὐτὴν καὶ τοῦτο
says to him : Lord, leave it also this

τὸ ἔτος, ἕως ὅτου σκάψω περὶ αὐτὴν καὶ
– year, until I may dig round it and

βάλω κόπρια, 9 κἂν μὲν ποιήσῃ καρπὸν
may throw dung, and if indeed it makes fruit

εἰς τὸ μέλλον· εἰ δὲ μή γε, ἐκκόψεις
in the future; otherwise, thou shalt cut down

αὐτήν.
it.

10 Ἦν δὲ διδάσκων ἐν μιᾷ τῶν συναγωγῶν
And he was teaching in one of the synagogues

ἐν τοῖς σάββασιν. 11 καὶ ἰδοὺ γυνὴ
on the sabbaths. And[,] behold[,] a woman

πνεῦμα ἔχουσα ἀσθενείας ἔτη δεκαοκτώ,
²a spirit ¹having of infirmity years eighteen,

καὶ ἦν συγκύπτουσα καὶ μὴ δυναμένη
and was bending double and, not being able

ἀνακύψαι εἰς τὸ παντελές. 12 ἰδὼν δὲ
to become erect entirely.† And seeing

αὐτὴν ὁ ᾽Ιησοῦς προσεφώνησεν καὶ εἶπεν
her – Jesus called to [him] and said

αὐτῇ· γύναι, ἀπολέλυσαι τῆς ἀσθενείας
to her : Woman, thou hast been loosed from the infirmity

Galileans whose blood Pilate had mixed with their sacrifices. ²Jesus answered, "Do you think that these Galileans were worse sinners than all the other Galileans because they suffered this way? ³I tell you, no! But unless you repent, you too will all perish. ⁴Or those eighteen who died when the tower in Siloam fell on them—do you think they were more guilty than all the others living in Jerusalem? ⁵I tell you, no! But unless you repent, you too will all perish."

⁶Then he told this parable: "A man had a fig tree, planted in his vineyard, and he went to look for fruit on it, but did not find any. ⁷So he said to the man who took care of the vineyard, 'For three years now I've been coming to look for fruit on this fig tree and haven't found any. Cut it down! Why should it use up the soil?'

⁸" 'Sir,' the man replied, 'leave it alone for one more year, and I'll dig around it and fertilize it. ⁹If it bears fruit next year, fine! If not, then cut it down.' "

A Crippled Woman Healed on the Sabbath

¹⁰On a Sabbath Jesus was teaching in one of the synagogues, ¹¹and a woman was there who had been crippled by a spirit for eighteen years. She was bent over and could not straighten up at all. ¹²When Jesus saw her, he called her forward and said to her, "Woman, you are set free from your

13And He laid His hands upon her; and immediately she was made erect again, and *began* glorifying God.
14And the synagogue official, indignant because Jesus had healed on the Sabbath, *began* saying to the multitude in response, "There are six days in which work should be done; therefore come during them and get healed, and not on the Sabbath day."
15But the Lord answered him and said, "You hypocrites, does not each of you on the Sabbath untie his ox or his donkey from the stall, and lead him away to water *him?*
16"And this woman, a daughter of Abraham as she is, whom Satan has bound for eighteen long years, should she not have been released from this bond on the Sabbath day?"
17And as He said this, all His opponents were being humiliated; and the entire multitude was rejoicing over all the glorious things being done by Him.

Parables of Mustard Seed and Leaven
18Therefore He was saying, "What is the kingdom of God like, and to what shall I compare it?
19"It is like a mustard seed, which a man took and threw into his own garden; and it grew and became a tree; and THE BIRDS OF THE AIR NESTED IN ITS BRANCHES."
20And again He said, "To what shall I compare the kingdom of God?
21"It is like leaven, which a woman took and hid in three pecks of meal, until it was all leavened."

Teaching in the Villages
22And He was passing through from one city and village to another, teaching, and proceeding on His way to Jerusalem.
23And someone said to

σου, **13** καὶ ἐπέθηκεν αὐτῇ τὰς χεῖρας·
of thee, and he put on her the(his) hands;
καὶ παραχρῆμα ἀνωρθώθη, καὶ ἐδόξαζεν
and at once she was straightened, and glorified
τὸν θεόν. **14** ἀποκριθεὶς δὲ ὁ ἀρχι-
- God. But answering the syn-
συνάγωγος, ἀγανακτῶν ὅτι τῷ σαββάτῳ
agogue ruler, being angry that [1]on the [2]sabbath
ἐθεράπευσεν ὁ Ἰησοῦς, ἔλεγεν τῷ ὄχλῳ
[1]healed - [1]Jesus, said to the crowd[,]
ὅτι ἐξ ἡμέραι εἰσὶν ἐν αἷς δεῖ ἐργάζεσθαι·
- six days there are on which it behoves to work;
ἐν αὐταῖς οὖν ἐρχόμενοι θεραπεύεσθε καὶ
on them therefore coming be ye healed and
μὴ τῇ ἡμέρᾳ τοῦ σαββάτου. **15** ἀπεκρίθη δὲ
not on the day of the sabbath. But answered
αὐτῷ ὁ κύριος καὶ εἶπεν· ὑποκριταί,
him the Lord and said : Hypocrites,
ἕκαστος ὑμῶν τῷ σαββάτῳ οὐ λύει τὸν
each one of you on the sabbath does he not loosen the
βοῦν αὐτοῦ ἢ τὸν ὄνον ἀπὸ τῆς φάτνης
ox of him or the ass from the manger
καὶ ἀπαγαγὼν ποτίζει; **16** ταύτην δὲ
and leading [it] away give drink? And this woman
θυγατέρα Ἀβραὰμ οὖσαν, ἣν ἔδησεν ὁ
a daughter of Abraham being, whom bound -
σατανᾶς ἰδοὺ δέκα καὶ ὀκτὼ ἔτη, οὐκ ἔδει
Satan behold ten and eight years, behoved it not
λυθῆναι ἀπὸ τοῦ δεσμοῦ τούτου τῇ
to be loosened from - bond this on the
ἡμέρᾳ τοῦ σαββάτου; **17** καὶ ταῦτα λέγοντος
day of the sabbath? And these things saying
=when he said these things
αὐτοῦ κατῃσχύνοντο πάντες οἱ ἀντικείμενοι
him[a] were put to shame all the [ones] opposing
αὐτῷ, καὶ πᾶς ὁ ὄχλος ἔχαιρεν ἐπὶ
him, and all the crowd rejoiced over
πᾶσιν τοῖς ἐνδόξοις τοῖς γινομένοις ὑπ᾽
all the glorious things - happening by
αὐτοῦ. **18** Ἔλεγεν οὖν· τίνι ὁμοία ἐστὶν ἡ
him. He said therefore: To what like is the
βασιλεία τοῦ θεοῦ, καὶ τίνι ὁμοιώσω
kingdom - of God, and to what may I liken
αὐτήν; **19** ὁμοία ἐστὶν κόκκῳ σινάπεως, ὃν
it? Like it is to a grain of mustard, which
λαβὼν ἄνθρωπος ἔβαλεν εἰς κῆπον ἑαυτοῦ,
[1]taking [1]a man cast into a garden of him*self*,
καὶ ηὔξησεν καὶ ἐγένετο εἰς δένδρον, καὶ
and it grew and became into a tree, and
τὰ πετεινὰ τοῦ οὐρανοῦ κατεσκήνωσεν
the birds of the heaven(air) lodged
ἐν τοῖς κλάδοις αὐτοῦ. **20** Καὶ πάλιν
in the branches of it. And again
εἶπεν· τίνι ὁμοιώσω τὴν βασιλείαν τοῦ
he said : To what may I liken the kingdom -
θεοῦ; **21** ὁμοία ἐστὶν ζύμῃ, ἣν λαβοῦσα
of God? Like it is to leaven, which [1]taking
γυνὴ ἔκρυψεν εἰς ἀλεύρου σάτα τρία,
[1]a woman hid in of meal measures three,
ἕως οὗ ἐζυμώθη ὅλον.
until was leavened all.
22 Καὶ διεπορεύετο κατὰ πόλεις καὶ
And he journeyed *through* throughout cities and
κώμας διδάσκων καὶ πορείαν ποιούμενος
villages teaching and journey making
εἰς Ἱεροσόλυμα. **23** Εἶπεν δέ τις αὐτῷ·
to Jerusalem. And said someone to him :

infirmity." 13Then he put his hands on her, and immediately she straightened up and praised God.
14Indignant because Jesus had healed on the Sabbath, the synagogue ruler said to the people, "There are six days for work. So come and be healed on those days, not on the Sabbath."
15The Lord answered him, "You hypocrites! Doesn't each of you on the Sabbath untie his ox or donkey from the stall and lead it out to give it water?
16Then should not this woman, a daughter of Abraham, whom Satan has kept bound for eighteen long years, be set free on the Sabbath day from what bound her?"
17When he said this, all his opponents were humiliated, but the people were delighted with all the wonderful things he was doing.

The Parables of the Mustard Seed and the Yeast
18Then Jesus asked, "What is the kingdom of God like? What shall I compare it to? 19It is like a mustard seed, which a man took and planted in his garden. It grew and became a tree, and the birds of the air perched in its branches."
20Again he asked, "What shall I compare the kingdom of God to? 21It is like yeast that a woman took and mixed into a large amount[#] of flour until it worked all through the dough."

The Narrow Door
22Then Jesus went through the towns and villages, teaching as he made his way to Jerusalem. 23Someone asked him,

#21 Greek *three satas* (probably about 1/2 bushel or 22 liters)

Him, "Lord, are there *just a few who are being saved*?" And He said to them,
24"Strive to enter by the narrow door; for many, I tell you, will seek to enter and will not be able.
25"Once the head of the house gets up and shuts the door, and you begin to stand outside and knock on the door, saying, 'Lord, open up to us!' then He will answer and say to you, 'I do not know where you are from.'
26"Then you will begin to say, 'We ate and drank in Your presence, and You taught in our streets';
27and He will say, 'I tell you, I do not know where you are from; DEPART FROM ME, ALL YOU EVILDOERS.'
28"There will be weeping and gnashing of teeth there when you see Abraham and Isaac and Jacob and all the prophets in the kingdom of God, but yourselves being cast out.
29"And they will come from east and west, and from north and south, and will recline *at the table* in the kingdom of God.
30"And behold, *some* are last who will be first and *some* are first who will be last."
31Just at that time some Pharisees came up, saying to Him, "Go away and depart from here, for Herod wants to kill You."
32And He said to them, "Go and tell that fox, 'Behold, I cast out demons and perform cures today and tomorrow, and the third *day* I reach My goal.'
33"Nevertheless I must journey on today and tomorrow and the next *day;* for it cannot be that a prophet should perish outside of Jerusalem.
34"O Jerusalem, Jerusa-

κύριε, εἰ ὀλίγοι οἱ σωζόμενοι; ὁ δὲ εἶπεν
Lord,   if   few   the [ones] being saved?   And he   said
πρὸς αὐτούς· 24 ἀγωνίζεσθε εἰσελθεῖν διὰ
to   them :   Struggle   to enter through
τῆς στενῆς θύρας, ὅτι πολλοί, λέγω ὑμῖν,
the   strait   door,   because   many,   I tell   you,
ζητήσουσιν εἰσελθεῖν καὶ οὐκ ἰσχύσουσιν.
will seek   to enter   and   will not be able.
25 ἀφ' οὗ ἂν ἐγερθῇ ὁ οἰκοδεσπότης καὶ
From [the time] when is risen the   house-master   and
ἀποκλείσῃ τὴν θύραν, καὶ ἄρξησθε ἔξω
he shuts   the   door,   and   ye begin   outside
ἑστάναι καὶ κρούειν τὴν θύραν λέγοντες·
to stand   and   to knock   the   door   saying :
κύριε, ἄνοιξον ἡμῖν, καὶ ἀποκριθεὶς ἐρεῖ
Lord,   open   to us,   and   answering   he will say
ὑμῖν· οὐκ οἶδα ὑμᾶς πόθεν ἐστέ. 26 τότε
to you :   I know not   you   whence ye are.   Then
ἄρξεσθε λέγειν· ἐφάγομεν ἐνώπιόν σου καὶ
ye will begin to say :   We ate   before   thee   and
ἐπίομεν, καὶ ἐν ταῖς πλατείαις ἡμῶν
drank,   and   in   the   streets   of us
ἐδίδαξας· 27 καὶ ἐρεῖ λέγων ὑμῖν· οὐκ
thou didst teach;   and he will say telling   you :   not
οἶδα πόθεν ἐστέ· ἀπόστητε ἀπ' ἐμοῦ
I know   whence ye are;   stand away   from   me
πάντες ἐργάται ἀδικίας. 28 ἐκεῖ ἔσται ὁ
all   workers of unrighteousness.   There   will be the
κλαυθμὸς καὶ ὁ βρυγμὸς τῶν ὀδόντων,
weeping   and   the   gnashing   of the   teeth,
ὅταν ὄψησθε Ἀβραὰμ καὶ Ἰσαὰκ καὶ
when   ye see   Abraham   and   Isaac   and
Ἰακὼβ καὶ πάντας τοὺς προφήτας ἐν τῇ
Jacob   and   all   the   prophets   in the
βασιλείᾳ τοῦ θεοῦ, ὑμᾶς δὲ ἐκβαλλομένους
kingdom   -   of God,   but you   being thrust out
ἔξω. 29 καὶ ἥξουσιν ἀπὸ ἀνατολῶν καὶ
outside.   And they will come from   east   and
δυσμῶν καὶ ἀπὸ βορρᾶ καὶ νότου, καὶ
west   and   from   north   and   south,   and
ἀνακλιθήσονται ἐν τῇ βασιλείᾳ τοῦ θεοῦ.
will recline   in   the   kingdom   - of God.
30 καὶ ἰδοὺ εἰσὶν ἔσχατοι οἳ ἔσονται
And   behold there are   last [ones]   who   will be
πρῶτοι, καὶ εἰσὶν πρῶτοι οἳ ἔσονται
first,   and   there are   first [ones]   who   will be
ἔσχατοι. 31 Ἐν αὐτῇ τῇ ὥρᾳ προσῆλθάν
last.   In   ¹same   ¹the hour   approached
τινες Φαρισαῖοι λέγοντες αὐτῷ· ἔξελθε καὶ
some   Pharisees   saying   to him :   Depart   and
πορεύου ἐντεῦθεν, ὅτι Ἡρῴδης θέλει σε
go   hence,   because   Herod   wishes   thee
ἀποκτεῖναι. 32 καὶ εἶπεν αὐτοῖς· πορευθέντες
to kill.   And   he said   to them :   Going
εἴπατε τῇ ἀλώπεκι ταύτῃ· ἰδοὺ ἐκβάλλω
tell   -   fox   this :   Behold   I expel
δαιμόνια καὶ ἰάσεις ἀποτελῶ σήμερον καὶ
demons   and   ²cures   ¹accomplish   to-day   and
αὔριον, καὶ τῇ τρίτῃ τελειοῦμαι. 33 πλὴν
to-morrow, and on the third [day] I am perfected.   Nevertheless
δεῖ με σήμερον καὶ αὔριον καὶ τῇ ἐχομένῃ
it be- me   to-day   and   to-   and on the following
hoves   morrow   [day]
πορεύεσθαι, ὅτι οὐκ ἐνδέχεται προφήτην
to journey,   because   it is not possible   a prophet
ἀπολέσθαι ἔξω Ἱερουσαλήμ. 34 Ἱερουσαλὴμ
to perish   outside   Jerusalem.   Jerusalem[,]

"Lord, are only a few people going to be saved?"
He said to them, 24"Make every effort to enter through the narrow door, because many, I tell you, will try to enter and will not be able to. 25Once the owner of the house gets up and closes the door, you will stand outside knocking and pleading, 'Sir, open the door for us.'
"But he will answer, 'I don't know you or where you come from.'
26"Then you will say, 'We ate and drank with you, and you taught in our streets.'
27"But he will reply, 'I don't know you or where you come from. Away from me, all you evildoers!'
28"There will be weeping there, and gnashing of teeth, when you see Abraham, Isaac and Jacob and all the prophets in the kingdom of God, but you yourselves thrown out. 29People will come from east and west and north and south, and will take their places at the feast in the kingdom of God. 30Indeed there are those who are last who will be first, and first who will be last."

Jesus' Sorrow for Jerusalem
31At that time some Pharisees came to Jesus and said to him, "Leave this place and go somewhere else. Herod wants to kill you."
32He replied, "Go tell that fox, 'I will drive out demons and heal people today and tomorrow, and on the third day I will reach my goal.' 33In any case, I must keep going today and tomorrow and the next day —for surely no prophet can die outside Jerusalem!
34"O Jerusalem, Jerusa-

lem, *the city* that kills the prophets and stones those sent to her! How often I wanted to gather your children together, as a hen *gathers* her brood under her wings, and you would not *have it!*

35"Behold, your house is left to you *desolate;* and I say to you, you shall not see Me until *the time* comes when you say, 'BLESSED IS HE WHO COMES IN THE NAME OF THE LORD!' "

Ἰερουσαλήμ, ἡ ἀποκτείνουσα τοὺς προφήτας
Jerusalem, the [one]   killing   the   prophets

καὶ λιθοβολοῦσα τοὺς ἀπεσταλμένους πρὸς
and   stoning   the [ones] *having been* sent   to

αὐτήν, ποσάκις ἠθέλησα ἐπισυνάξαι τὰ
her,   how often   I wished   to gather   the

τέκνα σου ὃν τρόπον ὄρνις τὴν ἑαυτῆς
children of thee   as †   a bird   the   of herself

νοσσιὰν ὑπὸ τὰς πτέρυγας, καὶ οὐκ
brood   under   the(her)   wings,   and   not

ἠθελήσατε. 35 ἰδοὺ ἀφίεται ὑμῖν ὁ οἶκος
ye wished.   Behold   is left   to you   the   house

ὑμῶν. λέγω [δὲ] ὑμῖν, οὐ μὴ ἴδητέ με
of you.   And I tell   you,   by no means ye may see   me

ἕως ἥξει ὅτε εἴπητε· εὐλογημένος ὁ
until shall come [the   ye say   Blessed   the
                 time] when

ἐρχόμενος ἐν ὀνόματι κυρίου.
[one] coming   in   [the] name of [the] Lord.

---

lem, you who kill the prophets and stone those sent to you, how often I have longed to gather your children together, as a hen gathers her chicks under her wings, but you were not willing! 35Look, your house is left to you desolate. I tell you, you will not see me again until you say, 'Blessed is he who comes in the name of the Lord.' [h] "

Chapter 14

Jesus Heals on the Sabbath

AND it came about when He went into the house of one of the leaders of the Pharisees on *the* Sabbath to eat bread, that they were watching Him closely.

2And there, in front of Him was a certain man suffering from dropsy.

3And Jesus answered and spoke to the lawyers and Pharisees, saying, "Is it lawful to heal on the Sabbath, or not?"

4But they kept silent. And He took hold of him, and healed him, and sent him away.

5And He said to them, "Which one of you shall have a son or an ox fall into a well, and will not immediately pull him out on a Sabbath day?"

6And they could make no reply to this.

Parable of the Guests

7And He *began* speaking a parable to the invited guests when He noticed how they had been picking out the places of honor *at the table;* saying to them,

8"When you are invited by someone to a wedding feast, do not take the place of honor, lest someone more distinguished than you may have been invited by him,

9and he who invited you both shall come and say to you, 'Give place to this man,' and then in disgrace you proceed to occupy the last place.

---

14 Καὶ ἐγένετο ἐν τῷ ἐλθεῖν αὐτὸν εἰς
And it came to pass in the to go him[be] into
                            =as he went,

οἶκόν τινος τῶν ἀρχόντων τῶν Φαρισαίων
a house of one of the   leaders   of the   Pharisees

σαββάτῳ φαγεῖν ἄρτον, καὶ αὐτοὶ ἦσαν
on a sabbath to eat   bread,   *and*   they   were

παρατηρούμενοι αὐτόν. 2 καὶ ἰδοὺ ἄνθρωπός
carefully watching   him.   And[,] behold[,]   man

τις ἦν ὑδρωπικὸς ἔμπροσθεν αὐτοῦ. 3 καὶ
a certain was   dropsical   before   him.   And

ἀποκριθεὶς ὁ Ἰησοῦς εἶπεν πρὸς τοὺς
answering   -   Jesus   spoke   to   the

νομικοὺς καὶ Φαρισαίους λέγων· ἔξεστιν
lawyers   and   Pharisees   saying :   Is it lawful

τῷ σαββάτῳ θεραπεῦσαι ἢ οὔ; 4 οἱ δὲ
on the sabbath   to heal   or   not?   And they

ἡσύχασαν. καὶ ἐπιλαβόμενος ἰάσατο αὐτὸν
were silent.   And   taking   he cured   him

καὶ ἀπέλυσεν. 5 καὶ πρὸς αὐτοὺς εἶπεν·
and   dismissed.   And   to   them   he said :

τίνος ὑμῶν υἱὸς ἢ βοῦς εἰς φρέαρ πεσεῖται,
Of whom of you a son or an ox into a pit   shall fall,

καὶ οὐκ εὐθέως ἀνασπάσει αὐτὸν ἐν
and   not immediately he will pull up   it   on

ἡμέρᾳ τοῦ σαββάτου; 6 καὶ οὐκ ἴσχυσαν
a day   of the   sabbath?   And   they were not able

ἀνταποκριθῆναι πρὸς ταῦτα. 7 Ἔλεγεν δὲ
to reply   against these things.   And he said

πρὸς τοὺς κεκλημένους παραβολήν, ἐπέχων
to the [ones] *having been* invited   a parable,   noting

πῶς τὰς πρωτοκλισίας ἐξελέγοντο, λέγων
how ²the   ³chief seats   ¹they were choosing,   saying

πρὸς αὐτούς· 8 ὅταν κληθῇς ὑπό τινος εἰς
to   them :   When thou art invited by   anyone   to

γάμους, μὴ κατακλιθῇς εἰς τὴν πρωτοκλισίαν,
wedding festivities, do not recline   in   the   chief seat,

μήποτε ἐντιμότερός σου ᾖ κεκλημένος ὑπ'
lest   a more honour-   thou   be *having been* invited   by
       able [than]

αὐτοῦ, 9 καὶ ἐλθὼν ὁ σὲ καὶ αὐτὸν καλέσας
him,   and coming ¹the [one] ³thee ⁴and   ⁵him   ²inviting

ἐρεῖ σοι· δὸς τούτῳ τόπον, καὶ τότε
will say to thee : Give this man place,   and   then

ἄρξῃ μετὰ αἰσχύνης τὸν ἔσχατον τόπον
thou wilt begin with   shame   the   last   place

Chapter 14

Jesus at a Pharisee's House

ONE Sabbath, when Jesus went to eat in the house of a prominent Pharisee, he was being carefully watched. 2There in front of him was a man suffering from dropsy. 3Jesus asked the Pharisees and experts in the law, "Is it lawful to heal on the Sabbath or not?" 4But they remained silent. So taking hold of the man, he healed him and sent him away.

5Then he asked them, "If one of you has a son[i] or an ox that falls into a well on the Sabbath day, will you not immediately pull him out?" 6And they had nothing to say.

7When he noticed how the guests picked the places of honor at the table, he told them this parable: 8"When someone invites you to a wedding feast, do not take the place of honor, for a person more distinguished than you may have been invited. 9If so, the host who invited both of you will come and say to you, 'Give this man your seat.' Then, humiliated, you will have to take the least important place. 10But

---

h35 Psalm 118:26
i5 Some manuscripts donkey

10"But when you are invited, go and recline at the last place, so that when the one who has invited you comes, he may say to you, 'Friend, move up higher'; then you will have honor in the sight of all who are at the table with you.

11"For everyone who exalts himself shall be humbled, and he who humbles himself shall be exalted."

12And He also went on to say to the one who had invited Him, "When you give a luncheon or a dinner, do not invite your friends or your brothers or your relatives or rich neighbors, lest they also invite you in return, and repayment come to you.

13"But when you give a reception, invite the poor, *the* crippled, *the* lame, *the* blind,

14and you will be blessed, since they do not have *the means* to repay you; for you will be repaid at the resurrection of the righteous."

15And when one of those who were reclining *at the table* with Him heard this, he said to Him, "Blessed is everyone who shall eat bread in the kingdom of God!"

Parable of the Dinner

16But He said to him, "A certain man was giving a big dinner, and he invited many;

17and at the dinner hour he sent his slave to say to those who had been invited, 'Come; for everything is ready now.'

18"But they all alike began to make excuses. The first one said to him, 'I have bought a piece of land and I need to go out and look at it; please consider me excused.'

19"And another one said, 'I have bought five yoke of oxen, and I am going to try them out; please consider me excused.'

20"And another one said, 'I have married a wife, and

κατέχειν. **10** ἀλλ' ὅταν κληθῇς, πορευθεὶς
to take.　　　But　when thou art invited,　going

ἀνάπεσε εἰς τὸν ἔσχατον τόπον, ἵνα ὅταν ἔλθῃ
recline in the last place, that when ⁴comes

ὁ　　κεκληκώς σε　ἐρεῖ σοι· φίλε,
¹the [one] ²having invited ³thee he will say to thee : Friend,

προσανάβηθι ἀνώτερον· τότε ἔσται σοι δόξα
go up　　higher;　then there will be to thee° glory

ἐνώπιον πάντων τῶν συνανακειμένων σοι.
before　all the [ones] reclining with　thee.

11 ὅτι πᾶς ὁ ὑψῶν ἑαυτὸν ταπεινωθήσεται,
Because everyone exalting himself will be humbled,

καὶ ὁ ταπεινῶν ἑαυτὸν ὑψωθήσεται.
and the [one] humbling himself will be exalted.

12 Ἔλεγεν δὲ καὶ τῷ κεκληκότι αὐτόν·
And he said also to the [one] having invited him :

ὅταν ποιῇς ἄριστον ἢ δεῖπνον, μὴ φώνει
When thou makest a dinner or a supper, do not call

τοὺς φίλους σου μηδὲ τοὺς ἀδελφούς
the friends of thee nor the brothers

σου μηδὲ τοὺς συγγενεῖς σου μηδὲ
of thee nor the relatives of thee nor

γείτονας πλουσίους, μήποτε καὶ αὐτοὶ
neighbours rich, lest also they

ἀντικαλέσωσίν σε καὶ γένηται ἀνταπόδομά
¹invite ²in ⁴return ³thee and it becomes a recompence

σοι. **13** ἀλλ' ὅταν δοχὴν ποιῇς, κάλει
to thee. But when a party thou makest, invite

πτωχούς, ἀναπήρους, χωλούς, τυφλούς·
poor [persons], maimed, lame, blind;

14 καὶ μακάριος ἔσῃ, ὅτι οὐκ ἔχουσιν
and blessed thou shalt be, because they have not

ἀνταποδοῦναί σοι· ἀνταποδοθήσεται γάρ σοι
to recompense thee; for it will be recompensed to thee

ἐν τῇ ἀναστάσει τῶν δικαίων. **15** Ἀκούσας
in the resurrection of the just. ²hearing

δέ τις τῶν συνανακειμένων ταῦτα εἶπεν
¹And ⁴one ⁵of the [ones] ⁶reclining with ³these things said

αὐτῷ· μακάριος ὅστις φάγεται ἄρτον ἐν
to him : Blessed [is he] who shall eat bread in

τῇ βασιλείᾳ τοῦ θεοῦ. **16** ὁ δὲ εἶπεν
the kingdom － of God. And he said

αὐτῷ· ἄνθρωπός τις ἐποίει δεῖπνον μέγα,
to him : A certain man made supper a great,

καὶ ἐκάλεσεν πολλούς, **17** καὶ ἀπέστειλεν
and invited many, and sent

τὸν δοῦλον αὐτοῦ τῇ ὥρᾳ τοῦ δείπνου
the slave of him at the hour of the supper

εἰπεῖν τοῖς κεκλημένοις· ἔρχεσθε, ὅτι ἤδη
to say to the [ones] having been invited : Come, because ¹now

ἕτοιμά ἐστιν. **18** καὶ ἤρξαντο ἀπὸ μιᾶς
²prepared ¹it is. And they began from one [mind]

πάντες παραιτεῖσθαι. ὁ πρῶτος εἶπεν
all to beg off. The first said

αὐτῷ· ἀγρὸν ἠγόρασα, καὶ ἔχω ἀνάγκην
to him : ¹A farm ¹I bought, and I am obliged†

ἐξελθὼν ἰδεῖν αὐτόν· ἐρωτῶ σε, ἔχε με
going out to see it; I ask thee, have me

παρῃτημένον. **19** καὶ ἕτερος εἶπεν· ζεύγη
begged off. And another said : ¹Yoke

βοῶν ἠγόρασα πέντε, καὶ πορεύομαι
⁴of oxen ¹I bought ³five, and I am going

δοκιμάσαι αὐτά· ἐρωτῶ σε, ἔχε με
to prove them; I ask thee, have me

παρῃτημένον. **20** καὶ ἕτερος εἶπεν· γυναῖκα
begged off. And another said : ¹A wife

when you are invited, take the lowest place, so that when your host comes, he will say to you, 'Friend, move up to a better place.' Then you will be honored in the presence of all your fellow guests. 11For everyone who exalts himself will be humbled, and he who humbles himself will be exalted."

12Then Jesus said to his host, "When you give a luncheon or dinner, do not invite your friends, your brothers or relatives, or your rich neighbors; if you do, they may invite you back and so you will be repaid. 13But when you give a banquet, invite the poor, the crippled, the lame, the blind, 14and you will be blessed. Although they cannot repay you, you will be repaid at the resurrection of the righteous."

The Parable of the Great Banquet

15When one of those at the table with him heard this, he said to Jesus, "Blessed is the man who will eat at the feast in the kingdom of God."

16Jesus replied: "A certain man was preparing a great banquet and invited many guests. 17At the time of the banquet he sent his servant to tell those who had been invited, 'Come, for everything is now ready.'

18"But they all alike began to make excuses. The first said, 'I have just bought a field, and I must go and see it. Please excuse me.'

19"Another said, 'I have just bought five yoke of oxen, and I'm on my way to try them out. Please excuse me.'

20"Still another said, 'I

for that reason I cannot come.'

21"And the slave came *back* and reported this to his master. Then the head of the household became angry and said to his slave, 'Go out at once into the streets and lanes of the city and bring in here the poor and crippled and blind and lame.'

22"And the slave said, 'Master, what you commanded has been done, and still there is room.'

23"And the master said to the slave, 'Go out into the highways and along the hedges, and compel *them* to come in, that my house may be filled.

24'For I tell you, none of those men who were invited shall taste of my dinner.' ''

Discipleship Tested

25Now great multitudes were going along with Him; and He turned and said to them,

26"If anyone comes to Me, and does not *b*hate his own father and mother and wife and children and brothers and sisters, yes, and even his own life, he cannot be My disciple.

27"Whoever does not carry his own cross and come after Me cannot be My disciple.

28"For which one of you, when he wants to build a tower, does not first sit down and calculate the cost, to see if he has enough to complete it?

29"Otherwise, when he has laid a foundation, and is not able to finish, all who observe it begin to ridicule him,

30saying, 'This man began to build and was not able to finish.'

31"Or what king, when he sets out to meet another

ἔγημα, καὶ διὰ τοῦτο οὐ δύναμαι ἐλθεῖν.
I married, and   therefore   I cannot   *to* come.

21 καὶ παραγενόμενος ὁ δοῦλος ἀπήγγειλεν
And   coming up   the   slave   reported

τῷ κυρίῳ αὐτοῦ ταῦτα. τότε ὀργισθεὶς ὁ
to the lord   of him   these things.   Then   being angry   the

οἰκοδεσπότης εἶπεν τῷ δούλῳ αὐτοῦ· ἔξελθε
house-master   told   the   slave   of him: Go out

ταχέως εἰς τὰς πλατείας καὶ ῥύμας τῆς
quickly   into the   streets   and   lanes   of the

πόλεως, καὶ τοὺς πτωχοὺς καὶ ἀναπήρους
city,   and   the   poor   and   maimed

καὶ τυφλοὺς καὶ χωλοὺς εἰσάγαγε ὧδε.
and   blind   and   lame   bring in   here.

22 καὶ εἶπεν ὁ δοῦλος· κύριε, γέγονεν ὃ
And   said   the   slave: Lord,   has happened   what

ἐπέταξας, καὶ ἔτι τόπος ἐστίν. 23 καὶ
thou didst command, and   yet   room   there is.   And

εἶπεν ὁ κύριος πρὸς τὸν δοῦλον· ἔξελθε εἰς
said   the   lord   to   the   slave: Go out   into

τὰς ὁδοὺς καὶ φραγμοὺς καὶ ἀνάγκασον
the   ways   and   hedges   and   compel

εἰσελθεῖν, ἵνα γεμισθῇ μου ὁ οἶκος·
to come in,   that   may be filled   of me   the   house;

24 λέγω γὰρ ὑμῖν ὅτι οὐδεὶς τῶν ἀνδρῶν
for I tell   you   that   not one   —   men

ἐκείνων τῶν κεκλημένων γεύσεταί μου
of those   —   having been invited   shall taste   of me

τοῦ δείπνου.
the   supper.

25 Συνεπορεύοντο δὲ αὐτῷ ὄχλοι πολλοί,
And came together   to him   crowds   many,

καὶ στραφεὶς εἶπεν πρὸς αὐτούς· 26 εἴ τις
and   turning   he said   to   them: If anyone

ἔρχεται πρός με καὶ οὐ μισεῖ τὸν πατέρα
comes   to   me   and   hates not   the   father

αὐτοῦ καὶ τὴν μητέρα καὶ τὴν γυναῖκα
of him   and   the   mother   and   the   wife

καὶ τὰ τέκνα καὶ τοὺς ἀδελφοὺς καὶ τὰς
and   the   children   and   the   brothers   and   the

ἀδελφάς, ἔτι τε καὶ τὴν ψυχὴν ἑαυτοῦ,
sisters,   and besides   also   the   life   of himself,

οὐ δύναται εἶναί μου μαθητής. 27 ὅστις
he cannot   *to* be   of me   a disciple.   Who

οὐ βαστάζει τὸν σταυρὸν ἑαυτοῦ καὶ
bears not   the   cross   of himself   and

ἔρχεται ὀπίσω μου, οὐ δύναται εἶναί μου
comes   after   me,   he cannot   *to* be   of me

μαθητής. 28 Τίς γὰρ ἐξ ὑμῶν θέλων
a disciple.   For who   of   you   wishing

πύργον οἰκοδομῆσαι οὐχὶ πρῶτον καθίσας
a tower   to build   not   first   sitting

ψηφίζει τὴν δαπάνην, εἰ ἔχει εἰς ἀπαρ-
counts   the   cost,   if   he has   for   com-

τισμόν; 29 ἵνα μή ποτε θέντος αὐτοῦ*
pletion?   Lest   when   laying   him*
=he has laid

θεμέλιον καὶ μὴ ἰσχύοντος ἐκτελέσαι πάντες
a foundation and not   being able*   to finish   all

οἱ θεωροῦντες ἄρξωνται αὐτῷ ἐμπαίζειν
the [ones]   seeing   begin   him   to mock

30 λέγοντες ὅτι οὗτος ὁ ἄνθρωπος ἤρξατο
saying[,]   that   This   man   began

οἰκοδομεῖν καὶ οὐκ ἴσχυσεν ἐκτελέσαι.
to build   and   was not able   to finish.

31 Ἢ τίς βασιλεὺς πορευόμενος ἑτέρῳ βασιλεῖ
Or what   king   ¹going   ²another   ⁴king

---

just got married, so I can't come.'

21"The servant came back and reported this to his master. Then the owner of the house became angry and ordered his servant, 'Go out quickly into the streets and alleys of the town and bring in the poor, the crippled, the blind and the lame.'

22"'Sir,' the servant said, 'what you ordered has been done, but there is still room.'

23"Then the master told his servant, 'Go out to the roads and country lanes and make them come in, so that my house will be full.

24I tell you, not one of those men who were invited will get a taste of my banquet.' ''

The Cost of Being a Disciple

25Large crowds were traveling with Jesus, and turning to them he said:

26"If anyone comes to me and does not hate his father and mother, his wife and children, his brothers and sisters—yes, even his own life—he cannot be my disciple. 27And anyone who does not carry his cross and follow me cannot be my disciple.

28"Suppose one of you wants to build a tower. Will he not first sit down and estimate the cost to see if he has enough money to complete it? 29For if he lays the foundation and is not able to finish it, everyone who sees it will ridicule him, 30saying, 'This fellow began to build and was not able to finish.'

31"Or suppose a king is about to go to war against

---

b I.e., by comparison of his love for Me

king in battle, will not first sit down and take counsel whether he is strong enough with ten thousand *men* to encounter the one coming against him with twenty thousand?

32"Or else, while the other is still far away, he sends a delegation and asks terms of peace.

33"So therefore, no one of you can be My disciple who does not give up all his own possessions.

34"Therefore, salt is good; but if even salt has become tasteless, with what will it be seasoned?

35"It is useless either for the soil or for the manure pile; it is thrown out. He who has ears to hear, let him hear."

συμβαλεῖν εἰς πόλεμον οὐχὶ καθίσας πρῶτον
²to attack ³in ⁴war not sitting first

βουλεύσεται εἰ δυνατός ἐστιν ἐν δέκα
will deliberate if able he is with ten

χιλιάσιν ὑπαντῆσαι τῷ μετὰ εἴκοσι χιλιάδων
thousands to meet ¹the [one] ⁵with ⁶twenty ⁷thousands

ἐρχομένῳ ἐπ᾽ αὐτόν; 32 εἰ δὲ μή γε, ἔτι
²coming ³upon ⁴him? 32 Otherwise, yet
=while

αὐτοῦ πόρρω ὄντος πρεσβείαν ἀποστείλας
him afar being° a delegation sending
he is yet at a distance

ἐρωτᾷ τὰ πρὸς εἰρήνην. 33 οὕτως οὖν
he asks the things for peace. So therefore

πᾶς ἐξ ὑμῶν ὃς οὐκ ἀποτάσσεται πᾶσιν
everyone of you who does not say farewell to all

τοῖς ἑαυτοῦ ὑπάρχουσιν οὐ δύναται εἶναί
¹the ²of himself ²possessions cannot to be

μου μαθητής. 34 Καλὸν οὖν τὸ ἅλας·
of me a disciple. Good therefore the salt;

ἐὰν δὲ καὶ τὸ ἅλας μωρανθῇ, ἐν τίνι
but if even the salt becomes useless, with what

ἀρτυθήσεται; 35 οὔτε εἰς γῆν οὔτε εἰς
will it be seasoned? neither for soil nor for

κοπρίαν εὔθετόν ἐστιν· ἔξω βάλλουσιν
manure suitable is it; outside they cast

αὐτό. ὁ ἔχων ὦτα ἀκούειν ἀκουέτω.
it. The [one] having ears to hear let him hear.

---

another king. Will he not first sit down and consider whether he is able with ten thousand men to oppose the one coming against him with twenty thousand? 32If he is not able, he will send a delegation while the other is still a long way off and will ask for terms of peace. 33In the same way, any of you who does not give up everything he has cannot be my disciple.

34"Salt is good, but if it loses its saltiness, how can it be made salty again? 35It is fit neither for the soil nor for the manure pile; it is thrown out.

"He who has ears to hear, let him hear."

Chapter 15

The Lost Sheep

NOW all the tax-gatherers and the sinners were coming near Him to listen to Him.

2And both the Pharisees and the scribes *began* to grumble, saying, "This man receives sinners and eats with them."

3And He told them this parable, saying,

4"What man among you, if he has a hundred sheep and has lost one of them, does not leave the ninety-nine in the open pasture, and go after the one which is lost, until he finds it?

5"And when he has found it, he lays it on his shoulders, rejoicing.

6"And when he comes home, he calls together his friends and his neighbors, saying to them, 'Rejoice with me, for I have found my sheep which was lost!'

7"I tell you that in the same way, there will be *more* joy in heaven over one sinner who repents, than over ninety-nine right-

---

15 Ἦσαν δὲ αὐτῷ ἐγγίζοντες πάντες
Now there were to him drawing near all

οἱ τελῶναι καὶ οἱ ἁμαρτωλοὶ ἀκούειν
the tax-collectors and the sinners to hear

αὐτοῦ. 2 καὶ διεγόγγυζον οἵ τε Φαρισαῖοι
him. And greatly murmured both the Pharisees

καὶ οἱ γραμματεῖς λέγοντες ὅτι οὗτος
and the scribes saying[,] — This man

ἁμαρτωλοὺς προσδέχεται καὶ συνεσθίει αὐ-
sinners receives and eats with them.

τοῖς. 3 εἶπεν δὲ πρὸς αὐτοὺς τὴν παρα-
And he spoke to them — para-

βολὴν ταύτην λέγων· 4 τίς ἄνθρωπος ἐξ
ble this saying : What man of

ὑμῶν ἔχων ἑκατὸν πρόβατα καὶ ἀπολέσας
you having a hundred sheep and losing

ἐξ αὐτῶν ἓν οὐ καταλείπει τὰ ἐνενήκοντα
of them one does not leave the ninety-

ἐννέα ἐν τῇ ἐρήμῳ καὶ πορεύεται ἐπὶ
nine in the desert and goes after

τὸ ἀπολωλὸς ἕως εὕρη αὐτό; 5 καὶ
the [one] having been lost until he finds it? and

εὑρὼν ἐπιτίθησιν ἐπὶ τοὺς ὤμους αὐτοῦ
finding places on [it] on the shoulders of him

χαίρων, 6 καὶ ἐλθὼν εἰς τὸν οἶκον
rejoicing, and coming into the house

συγκαλεῖ τοὺς φίλους καὶ τοὺς γείτονας,
he calls together the friends and the neighbours,

λέγων αὐτοῖς· συγχάρητέ μοι, ὅτι εὗρον
saying to them : Rejoice with me, because I found

τὸ πρόβατόν μου τὸ ἀπολωλός. 7 λέγω
the sheep of me — having been lost. I tell

ὑμῖν ὅτι οὕτως χαρὰ ἐν τῷ οὐρανῷ
you that thus joy in heaven

ἔσται ἐπὶ ἑνὶ ἁμαρτωλῷ μετανοοῦντι ἢ
will be over one sinner repenting than

ἐπὶ ἐνενήκοντα ἐννέα δικαίοις οἵτινες οὐ
over ninety-nine just men who no

Chapter 15

The Parable of the Lost Sheep

NOW the tax collectors and "sinners" were all gathering around to hear him. 2But the Pharisees and the teachers of the law muttered, "This man welcomes sinners and eats with them."

3Then Jesus told them this parable: 4"Suppose one of you has a hundred sheep and loses one of them. Does he not leave the ninety-nine in the open country and go after the lost sheep until he finds it? 5And when he finds it, he joyfully puts it on his shoulders 6and goes home. Then he calls his friends and neighbors together and says, 'Rejoice with me; I have found my lost sheep.' 7I tell you that in the same way there will be more rejoicing in heaven over one sinner who repents than over ninety-nine righteous

eous persons who need no repentance.

The Lost Coin

8"Or what woman, if she has ten silver coins and loses one coin, does not light a lamp and sweep the house and search carefully until she finds it?

9"And when she has found it, she calls together her friends and neighbors, saying, 'Rejoice with me, for I have found the coin which I had lost!'

10"In the same way, I tell you, there is joy in the presence of the angels of God over one sinner who repents."

The Prodigal Son

11And He said, "A certain man had two sons;

12and the younger of them said to his father, 'Father, give me the share of the estate that falls to me.' And he divided his wealth between them.

13"And not many days later, the younger son gathered everything up and went on a journey into a distant country, and there he squandered his estate with loose living.

14"Now when he had spent everything, a severe famine occurred in that country, and he began to be in need.

15"And he went and attached himself to one of the citizens of that country, and he sent him into his fields to feed swine.

16"And he was longing to fill his stomach with the pods that the swine were eating, and no one was giving *anything* to him.

17"But when he came to his senses, he said, 'How many of my father's hired men have more than enough bread, but I am dying here with hunger!

18'I will get up and go to my father, and will say to him, "Father, I have sinned against heaven, and in your sight;

19I am no longer worthy to be called your son; make

χρείαν ἔχουσιν μετανοίας. 8 Ἢ τίς γυνὴ
need   have   of repentance.   Or what woman

δραχμὰς ἔχουσα δέκα, ἐὰν ἀπολέσῃ
²drachmae ¹having ³ten, if   she loses

δραχμὴν μίαν, οὐχὶ ἅπτει λύχνον καὶ
drachma one, does not light a lamp   and

σαροῖ τὴν οἰκίαν καὶ ζητεῖ ἐπιμελῶς
sweep the house   and seek   carefully

ἕως οὗ εὕρῃ; 9 καὶ εὑροῦσα συγκαλεῖ
until she finds? and finding she calls together

τὰς φίλας καὶ γείτονας λέγουσα· συγχάρητέ
the friends and neighbours saying: Rejoice with

μοι, ὅτι εὗρον τὴν δραχμὴν ἣν ἀπώλεσα.
me, because I found the drachma which I lost.

10 οὕτως, λέγω ὑμῖν, γίνεται χαρὰ ἐνώπιον
So,   I tell   you, there is joy   before

τῶν ἀγγέλων τοῦ θεοῦ ἐπὶ ἑνὶ ἁμαρτωλῷ
the angels   of God over one sinner

μετανοοῦντι. 11 Εἶπεν δέ· ἄνθρωπός τις
repenting.   And he said: A certain man

εἶχεν δύο υἱούς. 12 καὶ εἶπεν ὁ νεώτερος
had   two sons.   And said the younger

αὐτῶν τῷ πατρί· πάτερ, δός μοι τὸ
of them to the father: Father, give me   the

ἐπιβάλλον μέρος τῆς οὐσίας. ὁ δὲ διεῖλεν
falling upon share of the property. And he divided
=share of the property falling to [me].

αὐτοῖς τὸν βίον. 13 καὶ μετ' οὐ πολλὰς
to them the living.   And after not many

ἡμέρας συναγαγὼν πάντα ὁ νεώτερος υἱὸς
days   having gathered all things the younger   son

ἀπεδήμησεν εἰς χώραν μακράν, καὶ ἐκεῖ
departed   to country a far,   and there

διεσκόρπισεν τὴν οὐσίαν αὐτοῦ ζῶν ἀσώτως.
scattered   the property of him living prodigally.

14 δαπανήσαντος δὲ αὐτοῦ πάντα ἐγένετο
   But having spent   him* all things there came
   =when he had spent

λιμὸς ἰσχυρὰ κατὰ τὴν χώραν ἐκείνην,
famine a severe throughout the country   that,

καὶ αὐτὸς ἤρξατο ὑστερεῖσθαι. 15 καὶ
and he   began   to be in want.   And

πορευθεὶς ἐκολλήθη ἑνὶ τῶν πολιτῶν τῆς
going   he was joined to one of the citizens   –

χώρας ἐκείνης, καὶ ἔπεμψεν αὐτὸν εἰς
country of that, and he sent   him   into

τοὺς ἀγροὺς αὐτοῦ βόσκειν χοίρους· 16 καὶ
the fields   of him to feed   pigs;   and

ἐπεθύμει γεμίσαι τὴν κοιλίαν αὐτοῦ ἐκ
he longed to fill   the stomach of him out of(with)

τῶν κερατίων ὧν ἤσθιον οἱ χοῖροι, καὶ
the husks   which ²ate ¹the ²pigs,   and

οὐδεὶς ἐδίδου αὐτῷ. 17 εἰς ἑαυτὸν δὲ
no one gave   to him.   ²to ⁴himself ¹But

ἐλθὼν ἔφη· πόσοι μίσθιοι τοῦ πατρός μου
²coming ³he said: How many hired servants of the father of me

περισσεύονται ἄρτων, ἐγὼ δὲ λιμῷ ὧδε
abound   of loaves, but I   with famine here
=have abundance of bread,

ἀπόλλυμαι. 18 ἀναστὰς πορεύσομαι πρὸς
am perishing.   Rising up I will go   to

τὸν πατέρα μου καὶ ἐρῶ αὐτῷ· πάτερ,
the father of me and I will say to him: Father,

ἥμαρτον εἰς τὸν οὐρανὸν καὶ ἐνώπιόν σου,
I sinned against – the heaven and before thee,

19 οὐκέτι εἰμὶ ἄξιος κληθῆναι υἱός σου·
   no longer am I worthy to be called a son of thee;

---

persons who do not need to repent.

The Parable of the Lost Coin

8"Or suppose a woman has ten silver coins[j] and loses one. Does she not light a lamp, sweep the house and search carefully until she finds it? 9And when she finds it, she calls her friends and neighbors together and says, 'Rejoice with me; I have found my lost coin.' 10In the same way, I tell you, there is rejoicing in the presence of the angels of God over one sinner who repents."

The Parable of the Lost Son

11Jesus   continued: "There was a man who had two sons. 12The younger one said to his father, 'Father, give me my share of the estate.' So he divided his property between them.

13"Not long after that, the younger son got together all he had, set off for a distant country and there squandered his wealth in wild living. 14After he had spent everything, there was a severe famine in that whole country, and he began to be in need. 15So he went and hired himself out to a citizen of that country, who sent him to his fields to feed pigs. 16He longed to fill his stomach with the pods that the pigs were eating, but no one gave him anything.

17"When he came to his senses, he said, 'How many of my father's hired men have food to spare, and here I am starving to death! 18I will set out and go back to my father and say to him: Father, I have sinned against heaven and against you. 19I am no longer worthy to be called

---

j8 Greek ten drachmas, each worth about a day's wages

me as one of your hired men.'"

20"And he got up and came to his father. But while he was still a long way off, his father saw him, and felt compassion *for him*, and ran and embraced him, and kissed him.

21"And the son said to him, 'Father, I have sinned against heaven and in your sight; I am no longer worthy to be called your son.'

22"But the father said to his slaves, 'Quickly bring out the best robe and put it on him, and put a ring on his hand and sandals on his feet;

23and bring the fattened calf, kill it, and let us eat and be merry;

24for this son of mine was dead, and has come to life again; he was lost, and has been found.' And they began to be merry.

25"Now his older son was in the field, and when he came and approached the house, he heard music and dancing.

26"And he summoned one of the servants and *began* inquiring what these things might be.

27"And he said to him, 'Your brother has come, and your father has killed the fattened calf, because he has received him back safe and sound.'

28"But he became angry, and was not willing to go in; and his father came out and *began* entreating him.

29"But he answered and said to his father, 'Look! For so many years I have been serving you, and I have never neglected a command of yours; and *yet* you have never given me a kid, that I might be merry with my friends;

30but when this son of yours came, who has devoured your wealth with

---

ποίησόν με ὡς ἕνα τῶν μισθίων σου.
make me as one of the hired servants of thee.

20 καὶ ἀναστὰς ἦλθεν πρὸς τὸν πατέρα
And rising up he came to the father

ἑαυτοῦ. ἔτι δὲ αὐτοῦ μακρὰν ἀπέχοντος*
of himself. But yet him afar being away*
=while he was yet far away

εἶδεν αὐτὸν ὁ πατὴρ αὐτοῦ καὶ ἐσπλαγχνίσθη,
saw him the father of him and was moved with pity,

καὶ δραμὼν ἐπέπεσεν ἐπὶ τὸν τράχηλον
and running fell on the neck

αὐτοῦ καὶ κατεφίλησεν αὐτόν. 21 εἶπεν δὲ
of him and fervently kissed him. And said

ὁ υἱὸς αὐτῷ· πάτερ, ἥμαρτον εἰς τὸν
the son to him: Father, I sinned against –

οὐρανὸν καὶ ἐνώπιόν σου, οὐκέτι εἰμὶ
heaven and before thee, no longer am I

ἄξιος κληθῆναι υἱός σου. 22 εἶπεν δὲ
worthy to be called a son of thee. But said

ὁ πατὴρ πρὸς τοὺς δούλους αὐτοῦ· ταχὺ
the father to the slaves of him : Quickly

ἐξενέγκατε στολὴν τὴν πρώτην καὶ ἐνδύσατε
bring ye out a robe the first and clothe

αὐτόν, καὶ δότε δακτύλιον εἰς τὴν χεῖρα
him, and give(put) a ring to the hand

αὐτοῦ καὶ ὑποδήματα εἰς τοὺς πόδας,
of him and sandals to the feet,

23 καὶ φέρετε τὸν μόσχον τὸν σιτευτόν,
and bring the calf – fattened,

θύσατε, καὶ φαγόντες εὐφρανθῶμεν, 24 ὅτι
kill, and eating let us be merry, because

οὗτος ὁ υἱός μου νεκρὸς ἦν καὶ ἀνέζησεν,
this – son of me dead was and lived again,

ἦν ἀπολωλὼς καὶ εὑρέθη. καὶ ἤρξαντο
was *having been* lost and was found. And they began

εὐφραίνεσθαι. 25 ἦν δὲ ὁ υἱὸς αὐτοῦ
to be merry. But was the son of him

ὁ πρεσβύτερος ἐν ἀγρῷ· καὶ ὡς ἐρχόμενος
– older in a field; and as coming

ἤγγισεν τῇ οἰκίᾳ, ἤκουσεν συμφωνίας καὶ
he drew near to the house, he heard music and

χορῶν, 26 καὶ προσκαλεσάμενος ἕνα τῶν
dances, and calling to [him] one of the

παίδων ἐπυνθάνετο τί ἂν εἴη ταῦτα.
lads he inquired what might be these things.

27 ὁ δὲ εἶπεν αὐτῷ ὅτι ὁ ἀδελφός σου
And he said to him[,] – The brother of thee

ἥκει, καὶ ἔθυσεν ὁ πατήρ σου τὸν μόσχον τὸν
has come, and *killed ¹the ²father ²of thee ⁴the ⁷calf

σιτευτόν, ὅτι ὑγιαίνοντα αὐτὸν ἀπέλαβεν.
⁶fattened, because ⁶being in health ²him ¹he ⁷received ⁴back.

28 ὠργίσθη δὲ καὶ οὐκ ἤθελεν εἰσελθεῖν·
But he was angry and did not wish to enter;

ὁ δὲ πατὴρ αὐτοῦ ἐξελθὼν παρεκάλει
so the father of him coming out besought

αὐτόν. 29 ὁ δὲ ἀποκριθεὶς εἶπεν τῷ
him. But he answering said to the

πατρί· ἰδοὺ τοσαῦτα ἔτη δουλεύω σοι καὶ
father: Behold[,] so many years I serve thee and

οὐδέποτε ἐντολήν σου παρῆλθον, καὶ ἐμοὶ
never a command of thee I transgressed, and to me

οὐδέποτε ἔδωκας ἔριφον ἵνα μετὰ τῶν
never thou gavest a goat that with the

φίλων μου εὐφρανθῶ· 30 ὅτε δὲ ὁ υἱός
friends of me I might be merry; but when – ¹son

σου οὗτος ὁ καταφαγών σου τὸν βίον
²of thee ¹this – having devoured of thee the living

---

your son; make me like one of your hired men.' 20So he got up and went to his father.

"But while he was still a long way off, his father saw him and was filled with compassion for him; he ran to his son, threw his arms around him and kissed him.

21"The son said to him, 'Father, I have sinned against heaven and against you. I am no longer worthy to be called your son.*'

22"But the father said to his servants, 'Quick! Bring the best robe and put it on him. Put a ring on his finger and sandals on his feet. 23Bring the fattened calf and kill it. Let's have a feast and celebrate. 24For this son of mine was dead and is alive again; he was lost and is found.' So they began to celebrate.

25"Meanwhile, the older son was in the field. When he came near the house, he heard music and dancing. 26So he called one of the servants and asked him what was going on. 27'Your brother has come,' he replied, 'and your father has killed the fattened calf because he has him back safe and sound.'

28"The older brother became angry and refused to go in. So his father went out and pleaded with him. 29But he answered his father, 'Look! All these years I've been slaving for you and never disobeyed your orders. Yet you never gave me even a young goat so I could celebrate with my friends. 30But when this son of yours who has squandered your property

*21 Some early manuscripts son. Make me like one of your hired men.

harlots, you killed the fattened calf for him.'
31"And he said to him, 'My child, you have always been with me, and all that is mine is yours.
32"But we had to be merry and rejoice, for this brother of yours was dead and *has begun* to live, and *was* lost and has been found.' "

μετὰ πορνῶν ἦλθεν, ἔθυσας αὐτῷ τὸν
with   harlots   came,   thou killedst for him   the

σιτευτὸν μόσχον. 31 ὁ δὲ εἶπεν αὐτῷ·
fattened   calf.   And he   said   to him:

τέκνον, σὺ πάντοτε μετ' ἐμοῦ εἶ, καὶ
Child,   thou   always   with   me   art,   and

πάντα τὰ ἐμὰ σά ἐστιν· 32 εὐφρανθῆναι
¹all ²things -   ³my   ²thine ¹is(are);   ³to be merry

δὲ καὶ χαρῆναι ἔδει, ὅτι ὁ ἀδελφός
¹And ⁴and   ⁵to rejoice   ²it be-   because -   ²brother
hoved [us],

σου οὗτος νεκρὸς ἦν καὶ ἔζησεν, καὶ ἀπο-
²of thee ¹this   ⁵dead   ⁴was and came to life, and   having

λωλὼς καὶ εὑρέθη.
been lost   also   was found.

with prostitutes comes home, you kill the fattened calf for him!'
31" 'My son,' the father said, 'you are always with me, and everything I have is yours. 32But we had to celebrate and be glad, because this brother of yours was dead and is alive again; he was lost and is found.' "

Chapter 16

The Unrighteous Steward

NOW He was also saying to the disciples, "There was a certain rich man who had a steward, and this *steward* was reported to him as squandering his possessions.
2"And he called him and said to him, 'What is this I hear about you? Give an account of your stewardship, for you can no longer be steward.'
3"And the steward said to himself, 'What shall I do, since my master is taking the stewardship away from me? I am not strong enough to dig; I am ashamed to beg.
4'I know what I shall do, so that when I am removed from the stewardship, they will receive me into their homes.'
5"And he summoned each one of his master's debtors, and he *began* saying to the first, 'How much do you owe my master?'
6"And he said, 'A hundred measures of oil.' And he said to him, 'Take your bill, and sit down quickly and write fifty.'
7"Then he said to another, 'And how much do you owe?' And he said, 'A hundred measures of wheat.' He *said to him, 'Take your bill, and write eighty.'
8"And his master praised the unrighteous steward because he had acted shrewdly; for the sons of this age are more

Chapter 16

16 Ἔλεγεν δὲ καὶ πρὸς τοὺς μαθητάς·
And he said   also   to   the   disciples :

ἄνθρωπός τις ἦν πλούσιος ὃς εἶχεν
²A certain ⁴man ¹there was ³rich   who   had

οἰκονόμον, καὶ οὗτος διεβλήθη αὐτῷ ὡς
a steward,   and   this   was complained of to him   as

διασκορπίζων τὰ ὑπάρχοντα αὐτοῦ. 2 καὶ
wasting   the   possessions   of him.   And

φωνήσας αὐτὸν εἶπεν αὐτῷ· τί τοῦτο
calling   him   he said   to him : What [is]   this

ἀκούω περὶ σοῦ; ἀπόδος τὸν λόγον τῆς
I hear   about   thee?   render   the   account of the

οἰκονομίας σου· οὐ γὰρ δύνῃ ἔτι οἰκονομεῖν.
stewardship of thee;   for thou canst not longer   to be steward.

3 εἶπεν δὲ ἐν ἑαυτῷ ὁ οἰκονόμος· τί
And said   in   himself   the   steward :   What

ποιήσω, ὅτι ὁ κύριός μου ἀφαιρεῖται τὴν
may I do, because the   lord   of me   takes away   the

οἰκονομίαν ἀπ' ἐμοῦ; σκάπτειν οὐκ ἰσχύω,
stewardship   from   me?   to dig   I am not able,

ἐπαιτεῖν αἰσχύνομαι. 4 ἔγνων τί ποιήσω,
to beg   I am ashamed.   I knew(know) what I may do,

ἵνα ὅταν μετασταθῶ ἐκ τῆς οἰκονομίας
that   when   I am removed out of   the   stewardship

δέξωνταί με εἰς τοὺς οἴκους ἑαυτῶν.
they may receive me   into   the   houses   of them*selves*.

5 καὶ προσκαλεσάμενος ἕνα ἕκαστον τῶν
And   calling to [him]   ¹one   ¹each   of the

χρεοφειλετῶν τοῦ κυρίου ἑαυτοῦ ἔλεγεν τῷ
debtors   of the   lord   of him*self* he said to the

πρώτῳ· πόσον ὀφείλεις τῷ κυρίῳ μου;
first :   How much   owest thou to the   lord   of me?

6 ὁ δὲ εἶπεν· ἑκατὸν βάτους ἐλαίου. ὁ δὲ
And he   said :   A hundred   baths   of oil.   And he

εἶπεν αὐτῷ· δέξαι σου τὰ γράμματα καὶ
told   him :   Take   of thee the   letters(bill)   and

καθίσας ταχέως γράψον πεντήκοντα. 7 ἔπειτα
sitting   quickly   write   fifty.   Then

ἑτέρῳ εἶπεν· σὺ δὲ πόσον ὀφείλεις; ὁ δὲ
to another he said : ¹thou ¹And   ²how much   ²owest? And he

εἶπεν· ἑκατὸν κόρους σίτου. λέγει αὐτῷ·
said :   A hundred   cors   of wheat.   He tells   him :

δέξαι σου τὰ γράμματα καὶ γράψον
Take   of thee   the   bill   and   write

ὀγδοήκοντα. 8 καὶ ἐπήνεσεν ὁ κύριος τὸν
eighty.   And   ²praised   ¹the   ²lord   the

οἰκονόμον τῆς ἀδικίας ὅτι φρονίμως
steward   -   of unrighteousness   because   prudently

ἐποίησεν· ὅτι οἱ υἱοὶ τοῦ αἰῶνος τούτου
he acted;   because   the   sons   -   age   of this

The Parable of the Shrewd Manager

JESUS told his disciples: "There was a rich man whose manager was accused of wasting his possessions. 2So he called him in and asked him, 'What is this I hear about you? Give an account of your management, because you cannot be manager any longer.'
3"The manager said to himself, 'What shall I do now? My master is taking away my job. I'm not strong enough to dig, and I'm ashamed to beg— 4I know what I'll do so that, when I lose my job here, people will welcome me into their houses.'
5"So he called in each one of his master's debtors. He asked the first, 'How much do you owe my master?'
6" 'Eight hundred gallons[i] of olive oil,' he replied.
"The manager told him, 'Take your bill, sit down quickly, and make it four hundred.'
7"Then he asked the second, 'And how much do you owe?'
" 'A thousand bushels[m] of wheat,' he replied.
"He told him, 'Take your bill and make it eight hundred.'
8"The master commended the dishonest manager because he had acted shrewdly. For the people of

[i]6 Greek *one hundred batous* (probably about 3 kiloliters)
[m]7 Greek *one hundred korous* (probably about 35 kiloliters)

shrewd in relation to their own kind than the sons of light.

9"And I say to you, make friends for yourselves by means of the ᶜmammon of unrighteousness; that when it fails, they may receive you into the eternal dwellings.

10"He who is faithful in a very little thing is faithful also in much; and he who is unrighteous in a very little thing is unrighteous also in much.

11"If therefore you have not been faithful in the *use of* unrighteous mammon, who will entrust the true *riches* to you?

12"And if you have not been faithful in *the use of* that which is another's, who will give you that which is your own?

13"No servant can serve two masters; for either he will hate the one, and love the other, or else he will hold to one, and despise the other. You cannot serve God and mammon."

14Now the Pharisees, who were lovers of money, were listening to all these things, and they were scoffing at Him.

15And He said to them, "You are those who justify yourselves in the sight of men, but God knows your hearts; for that which is highly esteemed among men is detestable in the sight of God.

16"The Law and the Prophets *were proclaimed* until John; since then the gospel of the kingdom of God is preached, and everyone is forcing his way into it.

17"But it is easier for heaven and earth to pass away than for one stroke of a letter of the Law to fail.

18"Everyone who divorces his wife and marries another commits adultery; and he who marries one

---

φρονιμώτεροι ὑπὲρ τοὺς υἱοὺς τοῦ φωτὸς
more prudent than the sons of the light

εἰς τὴν γενεὰν τὴν ἑαυτῶν εἰσιν. 9 Καὶ
in the generation – of themselves are. And

ἐγὼ ὑμῖν λέγω, ἑαυτοῖς ποιήσατε φίλους
I ²you ¹tell, To yourselves make friends

ἐκ τοῦ μαμωνᾶ τῆς ἀδικίας, ἵνα ὅταν
by the mammon – of unrighteousness, that when

ἐκλίπῃ δέξωνται ὑμᾶς εἰς τὰς αἰωνίους
it fails they may receive you into the eternal

σκηνάς. 10 ὁ πιστὸς ἐν ἐλαχίστῳ καὶ ἐν
tabernacles. The man faithful in least also in

πολλῷ πιστός ἐστιν, καὶ ὁ ἐν ἐλαχίστῳ
much faithful is, and the man in least

ἄδικος καὶ ἐν πολλῷ ἄδικός ἐστιν. 11 εἰ
unrighteous also in much unrighteous is. If

οὖν ἐν τῷ ἀδίκῳ μαμωνᾶ πιστοὶ οὐκ
therefore in the unrighteous mammon faithful not

ἐγένεσθε, τὸ ἀληθινὸν τίς ὑμῖν πιστεύσει;
ye were, the true who to you will entrust?

12 καὶ εἰ ἐν τῷ ἀλλοτρίῳ πιστοὶ οὐκ
And if in the thing belonging to another faithful not

ἐγένεσθε, τὸ ἡμέτερον τίς δώσει ὑμῖν;
ye were, the ours who will give you?
= that which is ours

13 Οὐδεὶς οἰκέτης δύναται δυσὶ κυρίοις
No household slave can two lords

δουλεύειν· ἢ γὰρ τὸν ἕνα μισήσει καὶ τὸν
to serve; for either the one he will hate and the

ἕτερον ἀγαπήσει, ἢ ἑνὸς ἀνθέξεται καὶ
other he will love, or one he will hold fast to and

τοῦ ἑτέρου καταφρονήσει. οὐ δύνασθε
the other he will despise. Ye cannot

θεῷ δουλεύειν καὶ μαμωνᾷ. 14 Ἤκουον
God to serve and mammon. ᵉheard

δὲ ταῦτα πάντα οἱ Φαρισαῖοι φιλάργυροι
¹Now ²these things ⁷all ³the ³Pharisees ⁶moneylovers

ὑπάρχοντες, καὶ ἐξεμυκτήριζον αὐτόν. 15 καὶ
⁶being, and they scoffed at him. And

εἶπεν αὐτοῖς· ὑμεῖς ἐστε οἱ δικαιοῦντες
he said to them: Ye are the [ones] justifying

ἑαυτοὺς ἐνώπιον τῶν ἀνθρώπων, ὁ δὲ
yourselves before – men, – but

θεὸς γινώσκει τὰς καρδίας ὑμῶν· ὅτι τὸ
God knows the hearts of you; because the thing

ἐν ἀνθρώποις ὑψηλὸν βδέλυγμα ἐνώπιον
¹among ²men ¹lofty [is] an abomination before

τοῦ θεοῦ. 16 Ὁ νόμος καὶ οἱ προφῆται
– God. The law and the prophets

μέχρι Ἰωάννου· ἀπὸ τότε ἡ βασιλεία τοῦ
[were] until John; from then the kingdom –

θεοῦ εὐαγγελίζεται καὶ πᾶς εἰς αὐτὴν
of God is being preached and everyone into it

βιάζεται. 17 εὐκοπώτερον δέ ἐστιν τὸν οὐρανὸν
is pressing. But easier it is the heaven

καὶ τὴν γῆν παρελθεῖν ἢ τοῦ νόμου μίαν
and the earth to pass away than of the law one

κεραίαν πεσεῖν. 18 Πᾶς ὁ ἀπολύων τὴν
little horn* to fall. Everyone dismissing the

γυναῖκα αὐτοῦ καὶ γαμῶν ἑτέραν μοιχεύει,
wife of him and marrying another commits adultery,

καὶ ὁ ἀπολελυμένην ἀπὸ
and ¹the [one] ²a woman having been dismissed ⁴from

---

this world are more shrewd in dealing with their own kind than are the people of the light. 9I tell you, use worldly wealth to gain friends for yourselves, so that when it is gone, you will be welcomed into eternal dwellings.

10"Whoever can be trusted with very little can also be trusted with much, and whoever is dishonest with very little will also be dishonest with much. 11So if you have not been trustworthy in handling worldly wealth, who will trust you with true riches? 12And if you have not been trustworthy with someone else's property, who will give you property of your own?

13"No servant can serve two masters. Either he will hate the one and love the other, or he will be devoted to the one and despise the other. You cannot serve both God and Money."

14The Pharisees, who loved money, heard all this and were sneering at Jesus. 15He said to them, "You are the ones who justify yourselves in the eyes of men, but God knows your hearts. What is highly valued among men is detestable in God's sight.

Additional Teachings

16"The Law and the Prophets were proclaimed until John. Since that time, the good news of the kingdom of God is being preached, and everyone is forcing his way into it. 17It is easier for heaven and earth to disappear than for the least stroke of a pen to drop out of the Law.

18"Anyone who divorces his wife and marries another woman commits adultery, and the man who marries a divorced woman commits adultery.

ᶜOr, *riches*

* The little projection which distinguishes some Hebrew letters from those otherwise similar.

who is divorced from a husband commits adultery.

The Rich Man and Lazarus

19"Now there was a certain rich man, and he habitually dressed in purple and fine linen, gaily living in splendor every day.

20"And a certain poor man named Lazarus was laid at his gate, covered with sores,

21and longing to be fed with the *crumbs* which were falling from the rich man's table; besides, even the dogs were coming and licking his sores.

22"Now it came about that the poor man died and he was carried away by the angels to Abraham's bosom; and the rich man also died and was buried.

23"And in Hades he lifted up his eyes, being in torment, and *saw Abraham far away, and Lazarus in his bosom.

24"And he cried out and said, 'Father Abraham, have mercy on me, and send Lazarus, that he may dip the tip of his finger in water and cool off my tongue; for I am in agony in this flame.'

25"But Abraham said, 'Child, remember that during your life you received your good things, and likewise Lazarus bad things; but now he is being comforted here, and you are in agony.

26'And besides all this, between us and you there is a great chasm fixed, in order that those who wish to come over from here to you may not be able, and *that* none may cross over from there to us.'

27"And he said, 'Then I beg you, Father, that you send him to my father's house—

28for I have five brothers—that he may warn them, lest they also come

---

ἀνδρὸς   γαμῶν   μοιχεύει.   19 Ἄνθρωπος   δέ
ᵃa husband ᵇmarrying ᶜcommits adultery.   Now a certain

τις   ἦν   πλούσιος,   καὶ   ἐνεδιδύσκετο   πορφύραν
man was   rich,   and   used to put on   a purple robe

καὶ   βύσσον   εὐφραινόμενος   καθ'   ἡμέραν
and   fine linen   being merry   every day†

λαμπρῶς.   20 πτωχὸς   δέ   τις   ὀνόματι
splendidly.   And a certain poor man   by name

Λάζαρος   ἐβέβλητο   πρὸς   τὸν   πυλῶνα   αὐτοῦ
Lazarus   had been placed   at   the   gate   of him

εἱλκωμένος   21 καὶ   ἐπιθυμῶν   χορτασθῆναι
being covered with sores   and   desiring   to be satisfied

ἀπὸ   τῶν   πιπτόντων   ἀπὸ   τῆς   τραπέζης
from the things   falling   from   the   table

τοῦ   πλουσίου·,   ἀλλὰ   καὶ   οἱ   κύνες   ἐρχόμενοι
of the   rich man;   but   even the   dogs   coming

ἐπέλειχον   τὰ   ἕλκη   αὐτοῦ.   22 ἐγένετο   δὲ
licked   the   sores   of him.   And it came to pass

ἀποθανεῖν   τὸν   πτωχὸν   καὶ   ἀπενεχθῆναι
to die   the   poor man   and   to be carried away
=that the poor man died and he was carried away

αὐτὸν   ὑπὸ   τῶν   ἀγγέλων   εἰς   τὸν   κόλπον
himᵇ   by the   angels   into   the   bosom

Ἀβραάμ·   ἀπέθανεν   δὲ   καὶ   ὁ   πλούσιος   καὶ
of Abraham;   and died   also   the   rich man   and

ἐτάφη.   23 καὶ   ἐν   τῷ   ᾅδῃ   ἐπάρας   τοὺς
was buried.   And   in   -   hades   lifting up   the

ὀφθαλμοὺς   αὐτοῦ,   ὑπάρχων   ἐν   βασάνοις,
eyes   of him,   being   in   torments,

ὁρᾷ   Ἀβραὰμ   ἀπὸ   μακρόθεν   καὶ   Λάζαρον
he sees   Abraham   from   afar   and   Lazarus

ἐν   τοῖς   κόλποις   αὐτοῦ.   24 καὶ   αὐτὸς
in   the   bosoms   of him.   And   he

φωνήσας   εἶπεν·   πάτερ   Ἀβραάμ,   ἐλέησόν
calling   said :   Father   Abraham,   pity

με   καὶ   πέμψον   Λάζαρον   ἵνα   βάψῃ   τὸ
me   and   send   Lazarus   that he may dip   the

ἄκρον   τοῦ   δακτύλου   αὐτοῦ   ὕδατος   καὶ
tip   of the   finger   of him   of(in) water   and

καταψύξῃ.   τὴν   γλῶσσάν   μου,   ὅτι   ὀδυνῶμαι
may cool   the   tongue   of me, because I am suffering

ἐν   τῇ   φλογὶ   ταύτῃ.   25 εἶπεν   δὲ   Ἀβραάμ·
in   -   flame   this.   But said   Abraham :

τέκνον,   μνήσθητι   ὅτι   ἀπέλαβες   τὰ   ἀγαθά
Child,   remember   that thou didst receive   the good things

σου   ἐν   τῇ   ζωῇ   σου,   καὶ   Λάζαρος   ὁμοίως
of thee in   the   life   of thee, and   Lazarus   likewise

τὰ   κακά·   νῦν   δὲ   ὧδε   παρακαλεῖται,   σὺ   δὲ
the   bad;   but now   here   he is comforted,   but thou

ὀδυνᾶσαι.   26 καὶ   ἐν   πᾶσι   τούτοις   μεταξὺ
art suffering.   And among   all   these things   between

ἡμῶν   καὶ   ὑμῶν   χάσμα   μέγα   ἐστήρικται,
us   and   you   chasm   a great has been firmly fixed,

ὅπως   οἱ   θέλοντες   διαβῆναι   ἔνθεν   πρὸς
so that the [ones]   wishing   to pass   hence   to

ὑμᾶς   μὴ   δύνωνται,   μηδὲ   ἐκεῖθεν   πρὸς
you   cannot,   neither   thence   to

ἡμᾶς   διαπερῶσιν.   27 εἶπεν   δέ·   ἐρωτῶ
us   may they cross over.   And he said :   I ask

σε   οὖν,   πάτερ,   ἵνα   πέμψῃς   αὐτὸν   εἰς
thee therefore,   father,   that thou mayest send   him   to

τὸν   οἶκον   τοῦ   πατρός   μου·   28 ἔχω   γὰρ
the   house   of the   father   of me;   for I have

πέντε   ἀδελφούς·   ὅπως   διαμαρτύρηται   αὐτοῖς,
five   brothers;   so that   he may witness   to them,

ἵνα   μὴ   καὶ   αὐτοὶ   ἔλθωσιν   εἰς   τὸν   τόπον
lest   also   they   come   to   -   place   ⁿ23 Greek Hades

The Rich Man and Lazarus

19"There was a rich man who was dressed in purple and fine linen and lived in luxury every day. 20At his gate was laid a beggar named Lazarus, covered with sores 21and longing to eat what fell from the rich man's table. Even the dogs came and licked his sores.

22"The time came when the beggar died and the angels carried him to Abraham's side. The rich man also died and was buried. 23In hell, ⁿ where he was in torment, he looked up and saw Abraham far away, with Lazarus by his side. 24So he called to him, 'Father Abraham, have pity on me and send Lazarus to dip the tip of his finger in water and cool my tongue, because I am in agony in this fire.'

25"But Abraham replied, 'Son, remember that in your lifetime you received your good things, while Lazarus received bad things, but now he is comforted here and you are in agony. 26And besides all this, between us and you a great chasm has been fixed, so that those who want to go from here to you cannot, nor can anyone cross over from there to us.'

27"He answered, 'Then I beg you, father, send Lazarus to my father's house, 28for I have five brothers. Let him warn them, so that they will not also come to to this place of torment.'

29"But Abraham *said, 'They have Moses and the Prophets; let them hear them.'

30"But he said, 'No, Father Abraham, but if someone goes to them from the dead, they will repent!'

31"But he said to him, 'If they do not listen to Moses and the Prophets, neither will they be persuaded if someone rises from the dead.' "

τοῦτον τῆς βασάνου. 29 λέγει δὲ Ἀβραάμ·
this — of torment. But says Abraham :

ἔχουσι Μωϋσέα καὶ τοὺς προφήτας·
They have Moses and the prophets;

ἀκουσάτωσαν αὐτῶν. 30 ὁ δὲ εἶπεν·
let them hear them. But he said :

οὐχί, πάτερ Ἀβραάμ, ἀλλ᾽ ἐάν τις ἀπὸ
No, father Abraham, but if someone from

νεκρῶν πορευθῇ πρὸς αὐτούς, μετανοήσουσιν.
[the] dead should go to them, they will repent.

31 εἶπεν δὲ αὐτῷ· εἰ Μωϋσέως καὶ τῶν
But he said to him : If Moses and the

προφητῶν οὐκ ἀκούουσιν, οὐδὲ ἐάν τις
prophets they do not hear, neither if someone

ἐκ νεκρῶν ἀναστῇ πεισθήσονται.
out of [the] dead should rise again will they be persuaded.

this place of torment.'

29"Abraham replied, 'They have Moses and the Prophets; let them listen to them.'

30"'No, father Abraham,' he said, 'but if someone from the dead goes to them, they will repent.'

31"He said to him, 'If they do not listen to Moses and the Prophets, they will not be convinced even if someone rises from the dead.' "

Chapter 17

Instructions

AND He said to His disciples, "It is inevitable that stumbling blocks should come, but woe to him through whom they come!

2"It would be better for him if a millstone were hung around his neck and he were thrown into the sea, than that he should cause one of these little ones to stumble.

3"Be on your guard! If your brother sins, rebuke him; and if he repents, forgive him.

4"And if he sins against you seven times a day, and returns to you seven times, saying, 'I repent,' forgive him."

5And the apostles said to the Lord, "Increase our faith!"

6And the Lord said, "If you had faith like a mustard seed, you would say to this mulberry tree, 'Be uprooted and be planted in the sea'; and it would obey you.

7"But which of you, having a slave plowing or tending sheep, will say to him when he has come in from the field, 'Come immediately and sit down to eat'?

8"But will he not say to him, 'Prepare something for me to eat, and properly clothe yourself and serve me until I have eaten and drunk; and afterward you will eat and drink'?

9"He does not thank the

17 Εἶπεν δὲ πρὸς τοὺς μαθητὰς αὐτοῦ·
And he said to the disciples of him :

ἀνένδεκτόν ἐστιν τοῦ τὰ σκάνδαλα μὴ ἐλθεῖν,ᵈ
Impossible it is — the offences not to come,ᵈ

οὐαὶ δὲ δι᾽ οὗ ἔρχεται· 2 λυσιτελεῖ
but woe [to him] through whom they come; it profits

αὐτῷ εἰ λίθος μυλικὸς περίκειται περὶ
him if a millstone is put round round

τὸν τράχηλον αὐτοῦ καὶ ἔρριπται εἰς τὴν
the neck of him and he has been thrown into the

θάλασσαν, ἢ ἵνα σκανδαλίσῃ τῶν μικρῶν
sea, than that he should offend — ²little ones

τούτων ἕνα. 3 προσέχετε ἑαυτοῖς. ἐὰν
²of these ¹one. Take heed to yourselves. If

ἁμάρτῃ ὁ ἀδελφός σου, ἐπιτίμησον αὐτῷ,
sins the brother of thee, rebuke him,

καὶ ἐὰν μετανοήσῃ, ἄφες αὐτῷ. 4 καὶ
and if he repents, forgive him. And

ἐὰν ἑπτάκις τῆς ἡμέρας ἁμαρτήσῃ εἰς σὲ
if seven times of(in) the day he sins against thee

καὶ ἑπτάκις ἐπιστρέψῃ πρὸς σὲ λέγων·
and seven times turns to thee saying :

μετανοῶ, ἀφήσεις αὐτῷ. 5 Καὶ εἶπαν οἱ
I repent, thou shalt forgive him. And said the

ἀπόστολοι τῷ κυρίῳ· πρόσθες ἡμῖν πίστιν.
apostles to the Lord : Add to us faith.

6 εἶπεν δὲ ὁ κύριος· εἰ ἔχετε πίστιν ὡς
And said the Lord : If ye have faith as

κόκκον σινάπεως, ἐλέγετε ἂν τῇ συκαμίνῳ
a grain of mustard, ye would have said — sycamine-tree

ταύτῃ· ἐκριζώθητι καὶ φυτεύθητι ἐν τῇ
to this : Be thou uprooted and be thou planted in the

θαλάσσῃ· καὶ ὑπήκουσεν ἂν ὑμῖν. 7 Τίς
sea; and it would have obeyed you. who

δὲ ἐξ ὑμῶν δοῦλον ἔχων ἀροτριῶντα ἢ
But of you ²a slave ¹having ploughing or

ποιμαίνοντα, ὃς εἰσελθόντι ἐκ τοῦ ἀγροῦ
herding, who on [his] coming in⁰ out of the farm

ἐρεῖ αὐτῷ· εὐθέως παρελθὼν ἀνάπεσε,
will say to him : Immediately coming up recline,

8 ἀλλ᾽ οὐχὶ ἐρεῖ αὐτῷ· ἑτοίμασον τί
but will not say to him : Prepare something

δειπνήσω, καὶ περιζωσάμενος διακόνει μοι
I may dine, and having girded thyself serve me

ἕως φάγω καὶ πίω, καὶ μετὰ ταῦτα
until I eat and drink, and after these things

φάγεσαι καὶ πίεσαι σύ; 9 μὴ ἔχει χάριν
eat and drink thou? Not he has thanks

Chapter 17

Sin, Faith, Duty

JESUS said to his disciples: "Things that cause people to sin are bound to come, but woe to that person through whom they come. 2It would be better for him to be thrown into the sea with a millstone tied around his neck than for him to cause one of these little ones to sin. 3So watch yourselves.

"If your brother sins, rebuke him, and if he repents, forgive him. 4If he sins against you seven times in a day, and seven times comes back to you and says, 'I repent,' forgive him."

5The apostles said to the Lord, "Increase our faith!"

6He replied, "If you have faith as small as a mustard seed, you can say to this mulberry tree, 'Be uprooted and planted in the sea,' and it will obey you.

7"Suppose one of you had a servant plowing or looking after the sheep. Would he say to the servant when he comes in from the field, 'Come along now and sit down to eat'? 8Would he not rather say, 'Prepare my supper, get yourself ready and wait on me while I eat and drink; after that you may eat and drink'? 9Would he thank the serslave because he did the things which were commanded, does he?

10"So you too, when you do all the things which are commanded you, say, 'We are unworthy slaves; we have done *only* that which we ought to have done.' "

Ten Lepers Cleansed

11And it came about while He was on the way to Jerusalem, that He was passing between Samaria and Galilee.

12And as He entered a certain village, ten leprous men who stood at a distance met Him;

13and they raised their voices, saying, "Jesus, Master, have mercy on us!"

14And when He saw them, He said to them, "Go and show yourselves to the priests." And it came about that as they were going, they were cleansed.

15Now one of them, when he saw that he had been healed, turned back, glorifying God with a loud voice,

16and he fell on his face at His feet, giving thanks to Him. And he was a Samaritan.

17And Jesus answered and said, "Were there not ten cleansed? But the nine—where are they?

18"Was no one found who turned back to give glory to God, except this foreigner?"

19And He said to him, "Rise, and go your way; your faith *d*has made you well."

20Now having been questioned by the Pharisees as to when the kingdom of God was coming, He answered them and said, "The kingdom of God is not coming with signs to be observed;

21nor will they say, 'Look, here *it is!*' or, 'There *it is!*' For behold, the kingdom of God is in your midst."

Second Coming Foretold

22And He said to the dis-

τῷ δούλῳ ὅτι ἐποίησεν τὰ διαταχθέντα;
to the slave because he did the things commanded?

10 οὕτως καὶ ὑμεῖς, ὅταν ποιήσητε πάντα
So also ye, when ye do all

τὰ διαταχθέντα ὑμῖν, λέγετε ὅτι δοῦλοι
the things commanded you, say[,] - Slaves

ἀχρεῖοί ἐσμεν, ὃ ὠφείλομεν ποιῆσαι
unprofitable we are, what we ought to do

πεποιήκαμεν.
we have done.

11 Καὶ ἐγένετο ἐν τῷ πορεύεσθαι εἰς
And it came to pass in the to go* to
= [he] went

Ἰερουσαλήμ, καὶ αὐτὸς διήρχετο διὰ μέσον
Jerusalem, *and* he passed through [the]
through midst

Σαμαρείας καὶ Γαλιλαίας. 12 καὶ εἰσερχομένου
of Samaria and Galilee. And entering
=as he entered

αὐτοῦ εἰς τινα κώμην ἀπήντησαν δέκα
him* into a certain village met [him] ten

λεπροὶ ἄνδρες, οἳ ἔστησαν πόρρωθεν, 13 καὶ
leprous men, who stood afar off, and

αὐτοὶ ἦραν φωνὴν λέγοντες· Ἰησοῦ
they lifted voice saying : Jesus

ἐπιστάτα, ἐλέησον ἡμᾶς. 14 καὶ ἰδὼν εἶπεν
Master, pity us. And seeing he said

αὐτοῖς· πορευθέντες ἐπιδείξατε ἑαυτοὺς τοῖς
to them : Going show yourselves to the

ἱερεῦσιν. καὶ ἐγένετο ἐν τῷ ὑπάγειν
priests. And it came to pass in the to go
= as they went

αὐτοὺς ἐκαθαρίσθησαν. 15 εἷς δὲ ἐξ
them*ᵇᵉ they were cleansed. But one of

αὐτῶν, ἰδὼν ὅτι ἰάθη, ὑπέστρεψεν μετὰ
them, seeing that he was cured, returned with

φωνῆς μεγάλης δοξάζων τὸν θεόν, 16 καὶ
voice a great glorifying - God, and

ἔπεσεν ἐπὶ πρόσωπον παρὰ τοὺς πόδας
fell on [his] face at the feet

αὐτοῦ εὐχαριστῶν αὐτῷ· καὶ αὐτὸς ἦν
of him thanking him; and he was

Σαμαρίτης. 17 ἀποκριθεὶς δὲ ὁ Ἰησοῦς
a Samaritan. And answering - Jesus

εἶπεν· οὐχ οἱ δέκα ἐκαθαρίσθησαν; οἱ [δὲ]
said : Not the ten were cleansed? but the

ἐννέα ποῦ; 18 οὐχ εὑρέθησαν ὑποστρέψαντες
nine where? were there not found returning

δοῦναι δόξαν τῷ θεῷ εἰ μὴ ὁ ἀλλογενὴς
to give glory - to God only - stranger

οὗτος; 19 καὶ εἶπεν αὐτῷ· ἀναστὰς πορεύου·
this ? And he said to him : Rising up go;

ἡ πίστις σου σέσωκέν σε.
the faith of thee has healed thee.

20 Ἐπερωτηθεὶς δὲ ὑπὸ τῶν Φαρισαίων
And being questioned by the Pharisees

πότε ἔρχεται ἡ βασιλεία τοῦ θεοῦ,
when comes the kingdom - of God,

ἀπεκρίθη αὐτοῖς καὶ εἶπεν· οὐκ ἔρχεται
he answered them and said : Comes not

ἡ βασιλεία τοῦ θεοῦ μετὰ παρατηρήσεως,
the kingdom - of God with observation,

21 οὐδὲ ἐροῦσιν· ἰδοὺ ὧδε ἤ· ἐκεῖ· ἰδοὺ
nor will they say : Behold[,] here or there; ᵇbehold

γὰρ ἡ βασιλεία τοῦ θεοῦ ἐντὸς ὑμῶν
ᶠfor the kingdom - of God within you

ἐστιν. 22 Εἶπεν δὲ πρὸς τοὺς μαθητάς·
is. And he said to the disciples :

---

vant because he did what he was told to do? 10So you also, when you have done everything you were told to do, should say, 'We are unworthy servants; we have only done our duty.' "

Ten Healed of Leprosy

11Now on his way to Jerusalem, Jesus traveled along the border between Samaria and Galilee. 12As he was going into a village, ten men who had leprosy*ᵒ* met him. They stood at a distance 13and called out in a loud voice, "Jesus, Master, have pity on us!"

14When he saw them, he said, "Go, show yourselves to the priests." And as they went, they were cleansed.

15One of them, when he saw he was healed, came back, praising God in a loud voice. 16He threw himself at Jesus' feet and thanked him—and he was a Samaritan.

17Jesus asked, "Were not all ten cleansed? Where are the other nine? 18Was no one found to return and give praise to God except this foreigner?" 19Then he said to him, "Rise and go; your faith has made you well."

The Coming of the Kingdom of God

20Once, having been asked by the Pharisees when the kingdom of God would come, Jesus replied, "The kingdom of God does not come with your careful observation, 21nor will people say, 'Here it is,' or 'There it is,' because the kingdom of God is within*ᵖ* you."

22Then he said to his dis-

---

d Or, *has saved you*

o 12 The Greek word was used for various diseases affecting the skin—not necessarily leprosy.
p 21 Or *among*

ciples, "The days shall come when you will long to see one of the days of the Son of Man, and you will not see it.
23"And they will say to you, 'Look there! Look here!' Do not go away, and do not run after *them*.
24"For just as the lightning, when it flashes out of one part of the sky, shines to the other part of the sky, so will the Son of Man be in His day.
25"But first He must suffer many things and be rejected by this generation.
26"And just as it happened in the days of Noah, so it shall be also in the days of the Son of Man:
27they were eating, they were drinking, they were marrying, they were being given in marriage, until the day that Noah entered the ark, and the flood came and destroyed them all.
28"It was the same as happened in the days of Lot: they were eating, they were drinking, they were buying, they were selling, they were planting, they were building;
29but on the day that Lot went out from Sodom it rained fire and brimstone from heaven and destroyed them all.
30"It will be just the same on the day that the Son of Man is revealed.
31"On that day, let not the one who is on the housetop and whose goods are in the house go down to take them away; and likewise let not the one who is in the field turn back.
32"Remember Lot's wife.
33"Whoever seeks to keep his life shall lose it, and whoever loses *his life* shall preserve it.
34"I tell you, on that night there will be two men in one bed; one will be taken, and the other will be left.

ἐλεύσονται ἡμέραι ὅτε ἐπιθυμήσετε μίαν
Will come days when ye will long one
τῶν ἡμερῶν τοῦ υἱοῦ τοῦ ἀνθρώπου ἰδεῖν
of the days of the Son - of man to see
καὶ οὐκ ὄψεσθε. 23 καὶ ἐροῦσιν ὑμῖν·
and will not see. And they will say to you :
ἰδοὺ ἐκεῖ, ἰδοὺ ὧδε· μὴ ἀπέλθητε μηδὲ
Behold there, behold here; do not go away nor
διώξητε. 24 ὥσπερ γὰρ ἡ ἀστραπὴ
follow. For as the lightning
ἀστράπτουσα ἐκ τῆς ὑπὸ τὸν οὐρανὸν
flashing out of the [one part] under - heaven
εἰς τὴν ὑπ' οὐρανὸν λάμπει, οὕτως ἔσται
to the [other part] under heaven shines, so will be
ὁ υἱὸς τοῦ ἀνθρώπου ἐν τῇ ἡμέρᾳ αὐτοῦ.
the Son - of man in the day of him.
25 πρῶτον δὲ δεῖ αὐτὸν πολλὰ παθεῖν καὶ
But first it behoves him many things to suffer and
ἀποδοκιμασθῆναι ἀπὸ τῆς γενεᾶς ταύτης.
to be rejected from - generation this.
26 καὶ καθὼς ἐγένετο ἐν ταῖς ἡμέραις
And as it was in the days
Νῶε, οὕτως ἔσται καὶ ἐν ταῖς ἡμέραις
of Noah, so it will be also in the days
τοῦ υἱοῦ τοῦ ἀνθρώπου· 27 ἤσθιον, ἔπινον,
of the Son - of man; they were eating, drinking,
ἐγάμουν, ἐγαμίζοντο, ἄχρι ἧς ἡμέρας
marrying, giving in marriage, until which day
= the day when
εἰσῆλθεν Νῶε εἰς τὴν κιβωτόν, καὶ
entered Noah into the ark, and
ἦλθεν ὁ κατακλυσμὸς καὶ ἀπώλεσεν πάντας.
came the flood and destroyed all.
28 ὁμοίως καθὼς ἐγένετο ἐν ταῖς ἡμέραις
Likewise as it was in the days
Λώτ· ἤσθιον, ἔπινον, ἠγόραζον, ἐπώλουν,
of Lot; they were eating, drinking, buying, selling,
ἐφύτευον, ᾠκοδόμουν· 29 ᾗ δὲ ἡμέρᾳ ἐξῆλθεν
planting, building; but on which day went forth
Λώτ ἀπὸ Σοδόμων, ἔβρεξεν πῦρ καὶ
Lot from Sodom, it rained fire and
θεῖον ἀπ' οὐρανοῦ καὶ ἀπώλεσεν πάντας.
brimstone from heaven and destroyed all.
30 κατὰ τὰ αὐτὰ ἔσται ᾗ ἡμέρᾳ ὁ υἱὸς
According to the same things it will be in which day the Son
= In the same way = on the day when
τοῦ ἀνθρώπου ἀποκαλύπτεται. 31 ἐν ἐκείνῃ
- of man is revealed. In that
τῇ ἡμέρᾳ ὃς ἔσται ἐπὶ τοῦ δώματος καὶ
- day who will be on the roof and
τὰ σκεύη αὐτοῦ ἐν τῇ οἰκίᾳ, μὴ καταβάτω
the goods of him in the house, let him not come down
ἆραι αὐτά, καὶ ὁ ἐν ἀγρῷ ὁμοίως μὴ
to take them, and the [one] in a field likewise not
ἐπιστρεψάτω εἰς τὰ ὀπίσω. 32 μνημονεύετε
let him turn back to the things behind. Remember
τῆς γυναικὸς Λώτ. 33 ὃς ἐὰν ζητήσῃ
the wife of Lot. Whoever seeks
τὴν ψυχὴν αὐτοῦ περιποιήσασθαι, ἀπολέσει
the life of him to preserve, he will lose
αὐτήν, καὶ ὃς ἂν ἀπολέσει, ζῳογονήσει
it, and whoever will lose, will preserve
αὐτήν. 34 λέγω ὑμῖν, ταύτῃ τῇ νυκτὶ
it. I tell you, in this - night
ἔσονται δύο ἐπὶ κλίνης μιᾶς, ὁ εἷς
there will be two men on couch one, the one
παραλημφθήσεται καὶ ὁ ἕτερος ἀφεθήσεται·
will be taken and the other will be left;

ciples, "The time is coming when you will long to see one of the days of the Son of Man, but you will not see it. 23Men will tell you, 'There he is!' or 'Here he is!' Do not go running off after them. 24For the Son of Man in his day*ᵃ* will be like the lightning, which flashes and lights up the sky from one end to the other. 25But first he must suffer many things and be rejected by this generation.
26"Just as it was in the days of Noah, so also will it be in the days of the Son of Man. 27People were eating, drinking, marrying and being given in marriage up to the day Noah entered the ark. Then the flood came and destroyed them all.
28"It was the same in the days of Lot. People were eating and drinking, buying and selling, planting and building. 29But the day Lot left Sodom, fire and sulfur rained down from heaven and destroyed them all.
30"It will be just like this on the day the Son of Man is revealed. 31On that day no one who is on the roof of his house, with his goods inside, should go down to get them. Likewise, no one in the field should go back for anything. 32Remember Lot's wife. 33Whoever tries to keep his life will lose it, and whoever loses his life will preserve it. 34I tell you, on that night two people will be in one bed; one will be taken and the other left.

ᵃ24 Some manuscripts do not have *in his day.*

35"There will be two women grinding at the same place; one will be taken, and the other will be left.

36["'Two men will be in the field; one will be taken and the other will be left."]

37And answering they *said to Him, "Where, Lord?" And He said to them, "Where the body *is*, there also will the vultures be gathered."

Chapter 18

Parables on Prayer

NOW He was telling them a parable to show that at all times they ought to pray and not to lose heart,

2saying, "There was in a certain city a judge who did not fear God, and did not respect man.

3"And there was a widow in that city, and she kept coming to him, saying, 'Give me legal protection from my opponent.'

4"And for a while he was unwilling; but afterward he said to himself, 'Even though I do not fear God nor respect man,

5yet because this widow bothers me, I will give her legal protection, lest by continually coming she wear me out.'"

6And the Lord said, "Hear what the unrighteous judge *said;

7now shall not God bring about justice for His elect, who cry to Him day and night, and will He delay long over them?

8"I tell you that He will bring about justice for them speedily. However, when the Son of Man comes, will He find faith on the earth?"

The Pharisee and the Publican

9And He also told this parable to certain ones who trusted in themselves that they were righteous, and viewed others with contempt:

---

35 ἔσονται δύο ἀλήθουσαι ἐπὶ τὸ αὐτό, ἡ
there will be two women grinding together,† the

μία παραλημφθήσεται ἡ δὲ ἐτέρα ἀφεθήσεται.‡
one will be taken but the other will be left.

37 καὶ ἀποκριθέντες λέγουσιν αὐτῷ· ποῦ,
And answering they say to him : Where,

κύριε; ὁ δὲ εἶπεν αὐτοῖς· ὅπου τὸ σῶμα,
Lord? And he said to them : Where the body,

ἐκεῖ καὶ οἱ ἀετοὶ ἐπισυναχθήσονται.
there also the eagles will be gathered together.

18 Ἔλεγεν δὲ παραβολὴν αὐτοῖς πρὸς
And he told ²a parable ¹them to
=that

τὸ δεῖν πάντοτε προσεύχεσθαι αὐτοὺς καὶ
the ¹to behove ²always ³to pray ⁴them and
they must always pray and not faint,

μὴ ἐγκακεῖν, 2 λέγων· κριτής τις ἦν ἐν
not to faint, saying : ²judge ¹a certain ¹There ⁴in
was

τινι πόλει τὸν θεὸν μὴ φοβούμενος καὶ
²a certain ⁶city – ³God ¹not ²fearing and

ἄνθρωπον μὴ ἐντρεπόμενος. 3 χήρα δὲ ἦν
³man ¹not ³regarding. And ²a widow ¹there was

ἐν τῇ πόλει ἐκείνῃ, καὶ ἤρχετο πρὸς
in – city that, and she came to

αὐτὸν λέγουσα· ἐκδίκησόν με ἀπὸ τοῦ
him saying : Vindicate me from the

ἀντιδίκου μου. 4 καὶ οὐκ ἤθελεν ἐπὶ
opponent of me. And he would not for

χρόνον· μετὰ ταῦτα δὲ εἶπεν ἐν ἑαυτῷ·
a time; but after these things he said in himself :

εἰ καὶ τὸν θεὸν οὐ φοβοῦμαι οὐδὲ ἄνθρωπον
If indeed – God I fear not nor man

ἐντρέπομαι, 5 διὰ γε τὸ παρέχειν
regard, at least because of – to cause
=because this widow causes me trouble

μοι κόπον τὴν χήραν ταύτην ἐκδικήσω αὐτήν,
me trouble – widow this[b] I will vindicate her,

ἵνα μὴ εἰς τέλος ἐρχομένη ὑπωπιάζῃ με.
lest in [the] end coming she exhausts me.

6 Εἶπεν δὲ ὁ κύριος· ἀκούσατε τί ὁ κριτὴς
And said the Lord : Hear ye what the judge

τῆς ἀδικίας λέγει· 7 ὁ δὲ θεὸς οὐ μὴ
– of unrighteousness says; – and God by no means

ποιήσῃ τὴν ἐκδίκησιν τῶν ἐκλεκτῶν
will he make the vindication of the chosen [ones]

αὐτοῦ τῶν βοώντων αὐτῷ ἡμέρας καὶ
of him – crying to him day and

νυκτός, καὶ μακροθυμεῖ ἐπ’ αὐτοῖς; 8 λέγω
night, and be patient over them? I tell

ὑμῖν ὅτι ποιήσει τὴν ἐκδίκησιν αὐτῶν
you that he will make the vindication of them

ἐν τάχει. πλὴν ὁ υἱὸς τοῦ ἀνθρώπου ἐλθὼν
quickly. Nevertheless the Son – of man coming

ἆρα εὑρήσει τὴν πίστιν ἐπὶ τῆς γῆς;
then will he find the faith on the earth?

9 Εἶπεν δὲ καὶ πρός τινας τοὺς
And he said also to some the [ones]

πεποιθότας ἐφ’ ἑαυτοῖς ὅτι εἰσὶν
relying on themselves that they are

δίκαιοι καὶ ἐξουθενοῦντας τοὺς λοιποὺς
righteous and despising the rest

τὴν παραβολὴν ταύτην. 10 Ἄνθρωποι δύο
– parable this. Men two

35Two women will be grinding grain together; one will be taken and the other left.'"

37"Where, Lord?" they asked.

He replied, "Where there is a dead body, there the vultures will gather."

Chapter 18

The Parable of the Persistent Widow

THEN Jesus told his disciples a parable to show them that they should always pray and not give up. 2He said: "In a certain town there was a judge who neither feared God nor cared about men. 3And there was a widow in that town who kept coming to him with the plea, 'Grant me justice against my adversary.'

4"For some time he refused. But finally he said to himself, 'Even though I don't fear God or care about men, 5yet because this widow keeps bothering me, I will see that she gets justice, so that she won't eventually wear me out with her coming!'"

6And the Lord said, "Listen to what the unjust judge says. 7And will not God bring about justice for his chosen ones, who cry out to him day and night? Will he keep putting them off? 8I tell you, he will see that they get justice, and quickly. However, when the Son of Man comes, will he find faith on the earth?"

The Parable of the Pharisee and the Tax Collector

9To some who were confident of their own righteousness and looked down on everybody else, Jesus told this parable: 10"Two

---

*Many mss. do not contain this verse

‡ Verse 36 omitted by Nestle; *cf.* NIV footnote.

*35 Some manuscripts left. ³⁶Two men will be in the field; one will be taken and the other left.

10"Two men went up into the temple to pray, one a Pharisee, and the other a tax-gatherer.

11"The Pharisee stood and was praying thus to himself, 'God, I thank Thee that I am not like other people: swindlers, unjust, adulterers, or even like this tax-gatherer.

12'I fast twice a week; I pay tithes of all that I get.'

13"But the tax-gatherer, standing some distance away, was even unwilling but was beating his breast, saying, 'God, be merciful to me, the sinner!'

14"I tell you, this man went down to his house justified rather than the other; for everyone who exalts himself shall be humbled, but he who humbles himself shall be exalted."

15And they were bringing even their babies to Him so that He might touch them, but when the disciples saw it, they *began* rebuking them.

16But Jesus called for them, saying, "Permit the children to come to Me, and do not hinder them, for the kingdom of God belongs to such as these.

17"Truly I say to you, whoever does not receive the kingdom of God like a child shall not enter it *at all*."

The Rich Young Ruler

18And a certain ruler questioned Him, saying, "Good Teacher, what shall I do to inherit eternal life?"

19And Jesus said to him, "Why do you call Me good? No one is good except God alone.

20'You know the commandments, 'Do not commit adultery, Do not murder, Do not steal, Do not bear false witness, Honor

---

ἀνέβησαν εἰς τὸ ἱερὸν προσεύξασθαι, ὁ εἷς
went up   to   the   temple   to pray,   the one

Φαρισαῖος καὶ ὁ ἕτερος τελώνης. 11 ὁ
a Pharisee   and the   other   a tax-collector.

Φαρισαῖος σταθεὶς ταῦτα πρὸς ἑαυτὸν
Pharisee   standing   these things   to   himself

προσηύχετο· ὁ θεός, εὐχαριστῶ σοι ὅτι
prayed :   -   God,   I thank   thee   that

οὐκ εἰμὶ ὥσπερ οἱ λοιποὶ τῶν ἀνθρώπων,
I am not   as   the   rest   -   of men,

ἅρπαγες, ἄδικοι, μοιχοί, ἢ καὶ ὡς οὗτος
rapacious,   unjust,   adulterers,   or   even   as   this

ὁ τελώνης· 12 νηστεύω δὶς τοῦ σαββάτου,
- tax-collector;   I fast   twice of(in) the   week,

ἀποδεκατεύω πάντα ὅσα κτῶμαι. 13 ὁ δὲ
I tithe   all things how many I get.   But the

τελώνης μακρόθεν ἑστὼς οὐκ ἤθελεν οὐδὲ
tax-collector   far off   standing   would not   not even

τοὺς ὀφθαλμοὺς ἐπᾶραι εἰς τὸν οὐρανόν,
the(his)   eyes   *to* lift up   to   -   heaven,

ἀλλ' ἔτυπτεν τὸ στῆθος αὐτοῦ λέγων· ὁ
but   smote   the   breast   of him   saying : -

θεός, ἱλάσθητί μοι τῷ ἁμαρτωλῷ. 14 λέγω
God,   be propitious to me the   sinner.   I tell

ὑμῖν, κατέβη οὗτος δεδικαιωμένος εἰς τὸν
you,   went down this man   having been justified   to   the

οἶκον αὐτοῦ παρ' ἐκεῖνον· ὅτι πᾶς ὁ
house   of him [rather] than   that one;   because   everyone

ὑψῶν ἑαυτὸν ταπεινωθήσεται, ὁ δὲ ταπεινῶν
exalting himself   will be humbled,   and the [one] humbling

ἑαυτὸν ὑψωθήσεται.
himself   will be exalted.

15 Προσέφερον δὲ αὐτῷ καὶ τὰ βρέφη
And they brought   to him   also   the   babes

ἵνα αὐτῶν ἅπτηται· ἰδόντες δὲ οἱ μαθηταὶ
that   them he might touch;   but ²seeing   ¹the   ³disciples

ἐπετίμων αὐτοῖς. 16 ὁ δὲ Ἰησοῦς
rebuked   them.   -   But   Jesus

προσεκαλέσατο αὐτὰ λέγων· ἄφετε τὰ
called to [him]   them*   saying :   Allow   the

παιδία ἔρχεσθαι πρός με καὶ μὴ κωλύετε
children   to come   to   me   and   do not prevent

αὐτά· τῶν γὰρ τοιούτων ἐστὶν ἡ βασιλεία
them;   -   for   of such   is   the   kingdom

τοῦ θεοῦ. 17 ἀμὴν λέγω ὑμῖν, ὃς ἂν
- of God.   Truly   I tell   you,   whoever

μὴ δέξηται τὴν βασιλείαν τοῦ θεοῦ ὡς
does not receive   the   kingdom   -   of God as

παιδίον, οὐ μὴ εἰσέλθῃ εἰς αὐτήν.
a child,   by no means enters   into   it.

18 Καὶ ἐπηρώτησέν τις αὐτὸν ἄρχων
And   ³questioned ¹a certain ⁴him   ²ruler

λέγων· διδάσκαλε ἀγαθέ, τί ποιήσας ζωὴν
saying :   Teacher   good,   what   doing   life

αἰώνιον κληρονομήσω; 19 εἶπεν δὲ αὐτῷ
eternal   may I inherit?   And said   to him

ὁ Ἰησοῦς· τί με λέγεις ἀγαθόν; οὐδεὶς
- Jesus : Why   me sayest thou   good?   no one

ἀγαθὸς εἰ μὴ εἷς [ὁ] θεός. 20 τὰς ἐντολὰς
[is] good   except one[,]   -   God.   The commandments

οἶδας· μὴ μοιχεύσῃς, μὴ φονεύσῃς,
thou knowest : Do not commit adultery,   Do not kill,

μὴ κλέψῃς, μὴ ψευδομαρτυρήσῃς, τίμα
Do not steal,   Do not bear false witness,   Honour

---

men went up to the temple to pray, one a Pharisee and the other a tax collector.

11The Pharisee stood and prayed about¹ himself: 'God, I thank you that I am not like other men—robbers, evildoers, adulterers —or even like this tax collector. 12I fast twice a week and give a tenth of all I get.'

13"But the tax collector stood at a distance. He would not even look up to heaven, but beat his breast and said, 'God, have mercy on me, a sinner.'

14"I tell you that this man, rather than the other, went home justified before God. For everyone who exalts himself will be humbled, and he who humbles himself will be exalted."

The Little Children and Jesus

15People were also bringing babies to Jesus to have him touch them. When the disciples saw this, they rebuked them. 16But Jesus called the children to him and said, "Let the little children come to me, and do not hinder them, for the kingdom of God belongs to such as these. 17I tell you the truth, anyone who will not receive the kingdom of God like a little child will never enter it."

The Rich Ruler

18A certain ruler asked him, "Good teacher, what must I do to inherit eternal life?"

19"Why do you call me good?" Jesus answered. "No one is good—except God alone. 20You know the commandments: 'Do not commit adultery, do not murder, do not steal, do not give false testimony, honor

---

* That is, "the babes" (τὰ βρέφη in ver. 15).

YOUR FATHER AND MOTHER.' ''
21And he said, "All these things I have kept from *my* youth."
22And when Jesus heard *this*, He said to him, "One thing you still lack; sell all that you possess, and distribute it to the poor, and you shall have treasure in heaven; and come, follow Me."
23But when he had heard these things, he became very sad; for he was extremely rich.
24And Jesus looked at him and said, "How hard it is for those who are wealthy to enter the kingdom of God!
25"For it is easier for a camel to go through the eye of a needle, than for a rich man to enter the kingdom of God.'
26And they who heard it said, "Then who can be saved?"
27But He said, "The things impossible with men are possible with God."
28And Peter said, "Behold, we have left our own *homes*, and followed You."
29And He said to them, "Truly I say to you, there is no one who has left house or wife or brothers or parents or children, for the sake of the kingdom of God,
30who shall not receive many times as much at this time and in the age to come, eternal life."
31And He took the twelve aside and said to them, "Behold, we are going up to Jerusalem, and all things which are written through the prophets about the Son of Man will be accomplished.
32"For He will be delivered to the Gentiles, and will be mocked and mistreated and spit upon,
33and after they have scourged Him, they will kill Him; and the third day He

---

τὸν πατέρα σου καὶ τὴν μητέρα. 21 ὁ δὲ
the father of thee and the mother. And he

εἶπεν· ταῦτα πάντα ἐφύλαξα ἐκ νεότητος.
said: All these things I kept from youth.

22 ἀκούσας δὲ ὁ Ἰησοῦς εἶπεν αὐτῷ· ἔτι
But hearing - Jesus said to him: Yet

ἕν σοι λείπει· πάντα ὅσα ἔχεις
one thing to thee is lacking; all things how many thou hast

πώλησον καὶ διάδος πτωχοῖς, καὶ ἕξεις
sell and distribute to poor people, and thou wilt have

θησαυρὸν ἐν [τοῖς] οὐρανοῖς, καὶ δεῦρο
treasure in heavens, and come

ἀκολούθει μοι. 23 ὁ δὲ ἀκούσας ταῦτα
follow me. But he hearing these things

περίλυπος ἐγενήθη, ἦν γὰρ πλούσιος σφόδρα.
very grieved became, for he was rich exceedingly.

24 ἰδὼν δὲ αὐτὸν ὁ Ἰησοῦς εἶπεν· πῶς
And seeing him - Jesus said: How

δυσκόλως οἱ τὰ χρήματα ἔχοντες εἰς τὴν
hardly ¹the [ones] ²property ³having into the

βασιλείαν τοῦ θεοῦ εἰσπορεύονται· 25 εὐκο-
kingdom - of God go in; ¹easi-

πώτερον γάρ ἐστιν κάμηλον διὰ τρήματος
er ¹for it is [for] a camel through [the] eye

βελόνης εἰσελθεῖν ἢ πλούσιον εἰς τὴν
of a needle to enter than a rich man into the

βασιλείαν τοῦ θεοῦ εἰσελθεῖν. 26 εἶπαν
kingdom - of God to enter. said

δὲ οἱ ἀκούσαντες· καὶ τίς δύναται
And the [ones] hearing: and who can

σωθῆναι; 27 ὁ δὲ εἶπεν· τὰ ἀδύνατα παρὰ
to be saved? And he said: The things impossible with

ἀνθρώποις δυνατὰ παρὰ τῷ θεῷ ἐστιν.
men possible with - God is(are).

28 Εἶπεν δὲ ὁ Πέτρος· ἰδοὺ ἡμεῖς ἀφέντες
And said - Peter: Behold[,] we leaving

τὰ ἴδια ἠκολουθήσαμέν σοι. 29 ὁ δὲ
our own things followed thee. And he

εἶπεν αὐτοῖς· ἀμὴν λέγω ὑμῖν ὅτι οὐδείς
said to them: Truly I tell you that no one

ἐστιν ὃς ἀφῆκεν οἰκίαν ἢ γυναῖκα ἢ
there is who left house or wife or

ἀδελφοὺς ἢ γονεῖς ἢ τέκνα εἵνεκεν τῆς
brothers or parents or children for the sake of the

βασιλείας τοῦ θεοῦ, 30 ὃς οὐχὶ μὴ λάβῃ
kingdom - of God, who by no means receives

πολλαπλασίονα ἐν τῷ καιρῷ τούτῳ καὶ ἐν
many times over in - time this and in

τῷ αἰῶνι τῷ ἐρχομένῳ ζωὴν αἰώνιον.
the age the coming life eternal.

31 Παραλαβὼν δὲ τοὺς δώδεκα εἶπεν πρὸς
And taking the twelve he said to

αὐτούς· ἰδοὺ ἀναβαίνομεν εἰς Ἰερουσαλήμ,
them: Behold we are going up to Jerusalem,

καὶ τελεσθήσεται πάντα τὰ γεγραμ-
and will be accomplished all things - having been

μένα διὰ τῶν προφητῶν τῷ υἱῷ τοῦ
written through the prophets to the Son -

ἀνθρώπου· 32 παραδοθήσεται γὰρ τοῖς ἔθνεσιν
of man; for he will be delivered to the nations

καὶ ἐμπαιχθήσεται καὶ ὑβρισθήσεται καὶ
and will be mocked and *will be* insulted and

ἐμπτυσθήσεται, 33 καὶ μαστιγώσαντες
will be spit at, and having scourged

ἀποκτενοῦσιν αὐτόν, καὶ τῇ ἡμέρᾳ τῇ
they will kill him, and on the day -

---

your father and mother.'¹ ''
21"All these I have kept since I was a boy," he said.
22When Jesus heard this, he said to him, "You still lack one thing. Sell everything you have and give to the poor, and you will have treasure in heaven. Then come, follow me."
23When he heard this, he became very sad, because he was a man of great wealth. 24Jesus looked at him and said, "How hard it is for the rich to enter the kingdom of God! 25Indeed, it is easier for a camel to go through the eye of a needle than for a rich man to enter the kingdom of God.''
26Those who heard this asked, "Who then can be saved?"
27Jesus replied, "What is impossible with men is possible with God.''
28Peter said to him, "We have left all we had to follow you!"
29"I tell you the truth," Jesus said to them, "no one who has left home or wife or brothers or parents or children for the sake of the kingdom of God 30will fail to receive many times as much in this age and, in the age to come, eternal life.''

Jesus Again Predicts His Death
31Jesus took the Twelve aside and told them, "We are going up to Jerusalem, and everything that is written by the prophets about the Son of Man will be fulfilled. 32He will be handed over to the Gentiles. They will mock him, insult him, spit on him, flog him and

will rise again."
34And they understood none of these things, and this saying was hidden from them, and they did not comprehend the things that were said.

Bartimaeus Receives Sight

35And it came about that as He was approaching Jericho, a certain blind man was sitting by the road, begging.
36Now hearing a multitude going by, he *began* to inquire what this might be.
37And they told him that Jesus of Nazareth was passing by.
38And he called out, saying, "Jesus, Son of David, have mercy on me!"
39And those who led the way were sternly telling him to be quiet; but he kept crying out all the more, "Son of David, have mercy on me!"
40And Jesus stopped and commanded that he be brought to Him; and when he had come near, He questioned him,
41"What do you want Me to do for you?" And he said, "Lord, *I want* to regain my sight!"
42And Jesus said to him, "Receive your sight; your faith has made you well."
43And immediately he regained his sight, and *began* following Him, glorifying God; and when all the people saw it, they gave praise to God.

τρίτῃ   ἀναστήσεται.   34 καὶ   αὐτοὶ   οὐδὲν
third   he will rise again.   And   they   none
τούτων   συνῆκαν,   καὶ ἦν τὸ ῥῆμα τοῦτο
of these things understood,   and ²was - ²utterance ¹this
κεκρυμμένον ἀπ' αὐτῶν, καὶ οὐκ ἐγίνωσκον
⁴having been hidden from   them,   and   they knew not
τὰ   λεγόμενα.
the things being said.

35 Ἐγένετο   δὲ ἐν τῷ ἐγγίζειν αὐτὸν εἰς
And it came to pass in   the to draw near him^{be}   to
                                                        =as he drew near
Ἰεριχὼ τυφλός τις ἐκάθητο παρὰ τὴν ὁδὸν
Jericho a certain blind man sat   by   the   way
ἐπαιτῶν. 36 ἀκούσας δὲ ὄχλου διαπορευομένου
begging.   And hearing a crowd   passing through
ἐπυνθάνετο τί εἴη τοῦτο. 37 ἀπήγγειλαν
he inquired what ²might be ¹this.   And they re-
δὲ   αὐτῷ ὅτι Ἰησοῦς ὁ Ναζωραῖος
ported to him[,]   -   Jesus   the   Nazarene
παρέρχεται. 38 καὶ ἐβόησεν λέγων· Ἰησοῦ
is passing by.   And he cried saying: Jesus
υἱὲ Δαυίδ, ἐλέησόν με. 39 καὶ οἱ
son of David,   pity   me.   And the [ones]
προάγοντες ἐπετίμων αὐτῷ ἵνα σιγήσῃ.
going before   rebuked   him that he should be quiet;
αὐτὸς δὲ πολλῷ μᾶλλον ἔκραζεν· υἱὲ
but he   by much   more   cried out :   Son
Δαυίδ, ἐλέησόν με. 40 σταθεὶς δὲ ὁ
of David,   pity   me.   And standing
Ἰησοῦς ἐκέλευσεν αὐτὸν ἀχθῆναι πρὸς
Jesus   commanded   him to be brought   to
αὐτόν. ἐγγίσαντος δὲ αὐτοῦ ἐπηρώτησεν
him.   And drawing near   him^a   he questioned
                              =as he drew near
αὐτόν· 41 τί σοι θέλεις ποιήσω; ὁ δὲ
him :   What for thee wishest thou I may do? And he
εἶπεν· κύριε, ἵνα ἀναβλέψω. 42 καὶ ὁ Ἰησοῦς
said :   Lord, that I may see again.   And -   Jesus
εἶπεν αὐτῷ· ἀνάβλεψον· ἡ πίστις σου
said   to him :   See again;   the   faith   of thee
σέσωκέν σε. 43 καὶ παραχρῆμα ἀνέβλεψεν,
has healed thee.   And   at once   he saw again,
καὶ ἠκολούθει αὐτῷ δοξάζων τὸν θεόν.
and   followed   him   glorifying   -   God.
καὶ πᾶς ὁ λαὸς ἰδὼν ἔδωκεν αἶνον τῷ
And all the people seeing gave   praise   -
θεῷ.
to God.

A Blind Beggar Receives His Sight

35As Jesus approached Jericho, a blind man was sitting by the roadside begging. 36When he heard the crowd going by, he asked what was happening. 37They told him, "Jesus of Nazareth is passing by."
38He called out, "Jesus, Son of David, have mercy on me!"
39Those who led the way rebuked him and told him to be quiet, but he shouted all the more, "Son of David, have mercy on me!"
40Jesus stopped and ordered the man to be brought to him. When he came near, Jesus asked him, 41"What do you want me to do for you?"
"Lord, I want to see," he replied.
42Jesus said to him, "Receive your sight; your faith has healed you." 43Immediately he received his sight and followed Jesus, praising God. When all the people saw it, they also praised God.

Chapter 19

Zaccheus Converted

AND He entered and was passing through Jericho.
2And behold, there was a man called by the name of Zaccheus; and he was a chief tax-gatherer, and he was rich.
3And he was trying to see who Jesus was, and he was unable because of the crowd, for he was small in stature.
4And he ran on ahead and climbed up into a sycamore tree in order to see Him, for He was about to pass through that way.

---

19 Καὶ εἰσελθὼν   διήρχετο τὴν Ἰεριχώ.
And having entered he passed through -   Jericho.
2 Καὶ ἰδοὺ ἀνὴρ ὀνόματι καλούμενος
And behold[,]   a man   by name   being called
Ζακχαῖος, καὶ αὐτὸς ἦν ἀρχιτελώνης, καὶ
Zacchæus,   and   he   was a chief tax-collector, and
αὐτὸς πλούσιος· 3 καὶ ἐζήτει ἰδεῖν τὸν
he [was] rich·   and   he sought to see   -
Ἰησοῦν τίς ἐστιν, καὶ οὐκ ἠδύνατο ἀπὸ
Jesus   who he is(was), and   was not able   from
τοῦ ὄχλου, ὅτι τῇ ἡλικίᾳ μικρὸς ἦν.
the   crowd,   because -   ²in stature   ³little ¹he was.
4 καὶ προδραμὼν εἰς τὸ ἔμπροσθεν ἀνέβη
And having run forward to   the   front   he went up
ἐπὶ συκομορέαν, ἵνα ἴδῃ αὐτόν, ὅτι
onto   a sycamore-tree,   that he might see him,   because
ἐκείνης ἤμελλεν διέρχεσθαι. 5 καὶ ὡς
²that [way] ¹he was about ³to pass along.   And   as

Chapter 19

Zacchaeus the Tax Collector

JESUS entered Jericho and was passing through. 2A man was there by the name of Zacchaeus; he was a chief tax collector and was wealthy. 3He wanted to see who Jesus was, but being a short man he could not, because of the crowd. 4So he ran ahead and climbed a sycamore-fig tree to see him, since Jesus was coming that way.

5And when Jesus came to the place, He looked up and said to him, "Zaccheus, hurry and come down, for today I must stay at your house."

6And he hurried and came down, and received Him gladly.

7And when they saw it, they all *began* to grumble, saying, "He has gone to be the guest of a man who is a sinner."

8And Zaccheus stopped and said to the Lord, "Behold, Lord, half of my possessions I will give to the poor, and if I have defrauded anyone of anything, I will give back four times as much."

9And Jesus said to him, "Today salvation has come to this house, because he, too, is a son of Abraham.

10"For the Son of Man has come to seek and to save that which was lost."

Parable of Money Usage

11And while they were listening to these things, He went on to tell a parable, because He was near Jerusalem, and they supposed that the kingdom of God was going to appear immediately.

12He said therefore, "A certain nobleman went to a distant country to receive a kingdom for himself, and *then* return.

13"And he called ten of his slaves, and gave them ten /minas, and said to them, 'Do business *with this* until I come *back.*'

14"But his citizens hated him, and sent a delegation after him, saying, 'We do not want this man to reign over us.'

15"And it came about that

ἦλθεν ἐπὶ τὸν τόπον, ἀναβλέψας ὁ Ἰησοῦς
he came upon the place, looking up - Jesus

εἶπεν πρὸς αὐτόν· Ζακχαῖε, σπεύσας
said to him : Zacchæus, making haste

κατάβηθι· σήμερον γὰρ ἐν τῷ οἴκῳ σου
come down; for to-day in the house of thee

δεῖ με μεῖναι. 6 καὶ σπεύσας κατέβη,
it behoves me to remain. And making haste he came down,

καὶ ὑπεδέξατο αὐτὸν χαίρων. 7 καὶ
and welcomed him rejoicing. And

ἰδόντες πάντες διεγόγγυζον λέγοντες ὅτι
seeing all murmured saying[,] -

παρὰ ἁμαρτωλῷ ἀνδρὶ εἰσῆλθεν καταλῦσαι.
With a sinful man he entered to lodge.

8 σταθεὶς δὲ Ζακχαῖος εἶπεν πρὸς τὸν
And standing Zacchæus said to the

κύριον· ἰδοὺ τὰ ἡμίση μου τῶν ὑπαρχόντων,
Lord : Behold[,] the half of me of the possessions,

κύριε, τοῖς πτωχοῖς δίδωμι, καὶ εἴ τινός
Lord, to the poor I give, and if anyone

τι ἐσυκοφάντησα, ἀποδίδωμι τετραπλοῦν.
anything I accused falsely, I restore fourfold.

9 εἶπεν δὲ πρὸς αὐτὸν ὁ Ἰησοῦς ὅτι
And said to him - Jesus[,] -

σήμερον σωτηρία τῷ οἴκῳ τούτῳ ἐγένετο,
To-day salvation to the house to this came,

καθότι καὶ αὐτὸς υἱὸς Ἀβραάμ [ἐστιν]·
because even he a son of Abraham is;

10 ἦλθεν γὰρ ὁ υἱὸς τοῦ ἀνθρώπου ζητῆσαι
for came the Son of man to seek

καὶ σῶσαι τὸ ἀπολωλός.
and to save the thing having been lost.

11 Ἀκουόντων δὲ αὐτῶν ταῦτα προσθεὶς
And hearing them[a] these things adding
= as they heard

εἶπεν παραβολήν, διὰ τὸ ἐγγὺς εἶναι
he told a parable, because of the near to be
= because he was near to Jerusalem and they thought

Ἰερουσαλὴμ αὐτὸν καὶ δοκεῖν αὐτοὺς ὅτι
Jerusalem him and to think them[b] that

παραχρῆμα μέλλει ἡ βασιλεία τοῦ θεοῦ
at once is(was) about the kingdom - of God

ἀναφαίνεσθαι. 12 εἶπεν οὖν· ἄνθρωπός τις
to appear; he said therefore : A certain man

εὐγενὴς ἐπορεύθη εἰς χώραν μακρὰν λαβεῖν
well born went to country a far to receive

ἑαυτῷ βασιλείαν καὶ ὑποστρέψαι. 13 καλέσας
for himself a kingdom and to return. having called

δὲ δέκα δούλους ἑαυτοῦ ἔδωκεν αὐτοῖς
And ten slaves of himself he gave them

δέκα μνᾶς, καὶ εἶπεν πρὸς αὐτούς·
ten minas, and said to them :

πραγματεύσασθε ἐν ᾧ ἔρχομαι. 14 οἱ δὲ
Trade ye while I am coming.* But the

πολῖται αὐτοῦ ἐμίσουν αὐτόν, καὶ ἀπέστειλαν
citizens of him hated him, and sent

πρεσβείαν ὀπίσω αὐτοῦ λέγοντες· οὐ θέλομεν
a delegation after him saying : We do not wish

τοῦτον βασιλεῦσαι ἐφ' ἡμᾶς. 15 καὶ
this man to reign over us. And

ἐγένετο ἐν τῷ ἐπανελθεῖν αὐτὸν λαβόντα
it came to pass in the to return him[be] having received
= when he returned

5When Jesus reached the spot, he looked up and said to him, "Zacchaeus, come down immediately. I must stay at your house today."

6So he came down at once and welcomed him gladly.

7All the people saw this and began to mutter, "He has gone to be the guest of a 'sinner.'"

8But Zacchaeus stood up and said to the Lord, "Look, Lord! Here and now I give half of my possessions to the poor, and if I have cheated anybody out of anything, I will pay back four times the amount."

9Jesus said to him, "Today salvation has come to this house, because this man, too, is a son of Abraham. 10For the Son of Man came to seek and to save what was lost."

The Parable of the Ten Minas

11While they were listening to this, he went on to tell them a parable, because he was near Jerusalem and the people thought that the kingdom of God was going to appear at once. 12He said: "A man of noble birth went to a distant country to have himself appointed king and then to return. 13So he called ten of his servants and gave them ten minas.[u] 'Put this money to work,' he said, 'until I come back.'

14"But his subjects hated him and sent a delegation after him to say, 'We don't want this man to be our king.'

15"He was made king,

/A mina is equal to about 100 days' wages or nearly $20

*That is, " again." The present of this verb often has a futurist significance; cf. John 14. 3.

[u]13 A mina was about three months' wages.

when he returned, after receiving the kingdom, he ordered that these slaves, to whom he had given the money, be called to him in order that he might know what business they had done.

16"And the first appeared, saying, 'Master, your mina has made ten minas more.'

17"And he said to him, 'Well done, good slave, because you have been faithful in a very little thing, be in authority over ten cities.'

18"And the second came, saying, 'Your mina, master, has made five minas.'

19"And he said to him also, 'And you are to be over five cities.'

20"And another came, saying, 'Master, behold your mina, which I kept put away in a handkerchief;

21for I was afraid of you, because you are an exacting man; you take up what you did not lay down, and reap what you did not sow.'

22"He *said to him, 'By your own words I will judge you, you worthless slave. Did you know that I am an exacting man, taking up what I did not lay down, and reaping what I did not sow?

23'Then why did you not put the money in the bank, and having come, I would have collected it with interest?'

24"And he said to the bystanders, 'Take the mina away from him, and give it to the one who has the ten minas.'

25"And they said to him, 'Master, he has ten minas already.'

26"I tell you, that to everyone who has shall more be given, but from the one who does not have, even what he does have shall be taken away.

27"But these enemies of mine, who did not want me to reign over them, bring them here and slay them in my presence."

Triumphal Entry

28And after He had said these things, He was going

τὴν βασιλείαν καὶ εἶπεν φωνηθῆναι αὐτῷ
the kingdom and he said to be called to him

τοὺς δούλους τούτους οἷς δεδώκει τὸ
- slaves these to whom he had given the

ἀργύριον, ἵνα γνοῖ τίς τί
money, that he might know ²anyone ¹what

διεπραγματεύσατο. 16 παρεγένετο δὲ ὁ πρῶτος
gained by trading. And came the first

λέγων· κύριε, ἡ μνᾶ σου δέκα προσηργάσατο
saying: Lord, the mina of thee ²ten ¹gained

μνᾶς. 17 καὶ εἶπεν αὐτῷ· εὖ γε, ἀγαθὲ δοῦλε,
¹minas. And he said to him: Well, good slave,

ὅτι ἐν ἐλαχίστῳ πιστὸς ἐγένου, ἴσθι
because in a least thing faithful thou wast, be thou

ἐξουσίαν ἔχων ἐπάνω δέκα πόλεων. 18 καὶ
²authority ¹having over ten cities. And

ἦλθεν ὁ δεύτερος λέγων· ἡ μνᾶ σου,
came the second saying: The mina of thee,

κύριε, ἐποίησεν πέντε μνᾶς. 19 εἶπεν δὲ
lord, made five minas. And he said

καὶ τούτῳ· καὶ σὺ ἐπάνω γίνου πέντε
also to this one: And ²thou ³over ¹be five

πόλεων. 20 καὶ ὁ ἕτερος ἦλθεν λέγων·
cities. And the other came saying:

κύριε, ἰδοὺ ἡ μνᾶ σου, ἣν εἶχον
Lord, behold[,] the mina of thee, which I had

ἀποκειμένην ἐν σουδαρίῳ· 21 ἐφοβούμην γάρ
being put away in a napkin· for I feared

σε, ὅτι ἄνθρωπος αὐστηρὸς εἶ, αἴρεις ὃ
thee, because man an exacting thou art, thou takest what

οὐκ ἔθηκας, καὶ θερίζεις ὃ οὐκ ἔσπειρας.
thou didst not lay, and thou reapest what thou didst not sow.

22 λέγει αὐτῷ· ἐκ τοῦ στόματός σου
He says to him: Out of the mouth of thee

κρινῶ σε, πονηρὲ δοῦλε. ᾔδεις ὅτι ἐγὼ
I will judge thee, wicked slave. Knewest thou that I

ἄνθρωπος αὐστηρός εἰμι, αἴρων ὃ οὐκ
man an exacting am, taking what not

ἔθηκα, καὶ θερίζων ὃ οὐκ ἔσπειρα; 23 καὶ
I laid, and reaping what I sowed not? And

διὰ τί οὐκ ἔδωκάς μου τὸ ἀργύριον ἐπὶ
why didst thou not give of me the money on

τράπεζαν; κἀγὼ ἐλθὼν σὺν τόκῳ ἂν
a table?* And I coming with interest -

αὐτὸ ἔπραξα. 24 καὶ τοῖς παρεστῶσιν
it would have exacted. And to the [ones] standing by

εἶπεν· ἄρατε ἀπ᾽ αὐτοῦ τὴν μνᾶν καὶ
he said: Take from him the mina and

δότε τῷ τὰς δέκα μνᾶς ἔχοντι. 25 καὶ
give ¹to the [one] ²the ⁴ten ⁵minas ³having. And

εἶπαν αὐτῷ· κύριε, ἔχει δέκα μνᾶς.
they said to him: Lord, he has ten minas.

26 λέγω ὑμῖν ὅτι παντὶ τῷ ἔχοντι
I tell you that to everyone having

δοθήσεται, ἀπὸ δὲ τοῦ μὴ ἔχοντος καὶ
it will be given, and from the [one] not having even

ὃ ἔχει ἀρθήσεται. 27 πλὴν τοὺς ἐχθρούς
what he has will be taken. Nevertheless - enemies

μου τούτους τοὺς μὴ θελήσαντάς με
of me these the [ones] not wishing me

βασιλεῦσαι ἐπ᾽ αὐτοὺς ἀγάγετε ὧδε καὶ
to reign over them bring ye here and

κατασφάξατε αὐτοὺς ἔμπροσθέν μου.
slay them before me.

28 Καὶ εἰπὼν ταῦτα ἐπορεύετο ἔμπροσθεν
And having said these things he went in front

* That is, a moneychanger's or banker's table.

---

however, and returned home. Then he sent for the servants to whom he had given the money, in order to find out what they had gained with it.

16"The first one came and said, 'Sir, your mina has earned ten more.'

17" 'Well done, my good servant!' his master replied. 'Because you have been trustworthy in a very small matter, take charge of ten cities.'

18"The second came and said, 'Sir, your mina has earned five more.'

19"His master answered, 'You take charge of five cities.'

20"Then another servant came and said, 'Sir, here is your mina; I have kept it laid away in a piece of cloth. 21I was afraid of you, because you are a hard man. You take out what you did not put in and reap what you did not sow.'

22"His master replied, 'I will judge you by your own words, you wicked servant! You knew, did you, that I am a hard man, taking out what I did not put in, and reaping what I did not sow? 23Why then didn't you put my money on deposit, so that when I came back, I could have collected it with interest?'

24"Then he said to those standing by, 'Take his mina away from him and give it to the one who has ten minas.'

25" 'Sir,' they said, 'he already has ten!'

26"He replied, 'I tell you that to everyone who has, more will be given, but as for the one who has nothing, even what he has will be taken away. 27But those enemies of mine who did not want me to be king over them—bring them here and kill them in front of me.' "

The Triumphal Entry

28After Jesus had said this, he went on ahead, go-on ahead, ascending to Jerusalem.

29And it came about that when He approached Bethphage and Bethany, near the mount that is called Olivet, He sent two of the disciples,

30saying, "Go into the village opposite *you*, in which as you enter you will find a colt tied, on which no one yet has ever sat; untie it, and bring it *here*.

31"And if anyone asks you, 'Why are you untying it?' thus shall you speak, 'The Lord has need of it.' "

32And those who were sent went away and found it just as He had told them.

33And as they were untying the colt, its owners said to them, "Why are you untying the colt?"

34And they said, "The Lord has need of it."

35And they brought it to Jesus, and they threw their garments on the colt, and put Jesus *on it.*

36And as He was going, they were spreading their garments in the road.

37And as He was now approaching, near the descent of the Mount of Olives, the whole multitude of the disciples began to praise God joyfully with a loud voice for all the miracles which they had seen,

38saying,

"Blessed is the King who comes in the name of the Lord;
Peace in heaven and glory in the highest!"

39And some of the Pharisees in the multitude said to Him, "Teacher, rebuke Your disciples."

40And He answered and said, "I tell you, if these become silent, the stones

---

ἀναβαίνων εἰς Ἱεροσόλυμα. 29 Καὶ ἐγένετο
going up to Jerusalem. And it came to pass

ὡς ἤγγισεν εἰς Βηθφαγὴ καὶ Βηθανίαν
as he drew near to Bethphage and Bethany

πρὸς τὸ ὄρος τὸ καλούμενον ἐλαιών,
toward the mount - being called of olives,

ἀπέστειλεν δύο τῶν μαθητῶν λέγων·
he sent two of the disciples saying :

30 ὑπάγετε εἰς τὴν κατέναντι κώμην, ἐν ᾗ
Go ye into the opposite village, in which

εἰσπορευόμενοι εὑρήσετε πῶλον δεδεμένον,
entering ye will find a colt having been tied,

ἐφ' ὃν οὐδεὶς πώποτε ἀνθρώπων ἐκάθισεν,
on which no one ever yet of men sat,

καὶ λύσαντες αὐτὸν ἀγάγετε. 31 καὶ ἐάν
and loosening it bring. And if

τις ὑμᾶς ἐρωτᾷ· διὰ τί λύετε; οὕτως
anyone you asks : Why loosen ye? thus

ἐρεῖτε· ὅτι ὁ κύριος αὐτοῦ χρείαν ἔχει.
shall ye say : Because the Lord of it need has.

32 ἀπελθόντες δὲ οἱ ἀπεσταλμένοι εὗρον
And going the [ones] having been sent found

καθὼς εἶπεν αὐτοῖς. 33 λυόντων δὲ
as he told them. And loosening
= as they were

αὐτῶν τὸν πῶλον εἶπαν οἱ κύριοι αὐτοῦ
them[a] the colt said the owners of it
loosening

πρὸς αὐτούς· τί λύετε τὸν πῶλον; 34 οἱ
to them : Why loosen ye the colt? [a]they

δὲ εἶπαν· ὅτι ὁ κύριος αὐτοῦ χρείαν ἔχει.
[a]And said : Because the Lord of it need has.

35 καὶ ἤγαγον αὐτὸν πρὸς τὸν Ἰησοῦν,
And they led it to - Jesus,

καὶ ἐπιρίψαντες αὐτῶν τὰ ἱμάτια ἐπὶ τὸν
and throwing on of them the garments on the

πῶλον ἐπεβίβασαν τὸν Ἰησοῦν. 36 πορευ-
colt they put on [it] - Jesus. And

ομένου δὲ αὐτοῦ ὑπεστρώννυον τὰ ἱμάτια
going him[a] they strewed the garments
= as he went

ἑαυτῶν ἐν τῇ ὁδῷ. 37 ἐγγίζοντος δὲ
of themselves in the way. And drawing near
= as he drew near

αὐτοῦ ἤδη πρὸς τῇ καταβάσει τοῦ ὄρους
him[a] now to the descent of the mount

τῶν ἐλαιῶν ἤρξαντο ἅπαν τὸ πλῆθος τῶν
of the olives began all the multitude of the

μαθητῶν χαίροντες αἰνεῖν τὸν θεὸν φωνῇ
disciples rejoicing to praise - God voice

μεγάλῃ περὶ πασῶν ὧν εἶδον δυνάμεων,
with a about [a]all [a]which [a]they saw [a][the] powerful
great deeds,

38 λέγοντες· εὐλογημένος ὁ ἐρχόμενος, ὁ
saying : Blessed the coming [one], the

βασιλεὺς ἐν ὀνόματι κυρίου· ἐν οὐρανῷ
king in [the] name of [the] Lord; in heaven

εἰρήνη καὶ δόξα ἐν ὑψίστοις. 39 καὶ
peace and glory in highest places. And

τινες τῶν Φαρισαίων ἀπὸ τοῦ ὄχλου
some of the Pharisees from the crowd

εἶπαν πρὸς αὐτόν· διδάσκαλε, ἐπιτίμησον
said to him : Teacher, rebuke

τοῖς μαθηταῖς σου. 40 καὶ ἀποκριθεὶς
the disciples of thee. And answering

εἶπεν· λέγω ὑμῖν, ἐὰν οὗτοι σιωπήσουσιν,
he said : I tell you, if these shall(should) be silent,

---

ing up to Jerusalem. 29As he approached Bethphage and Bethany at the hill called the Mount of Olives, he sent two of his disciples, saying to them, 30"Go to the village ahead of you, and as you enter it, you will find a colt tied there, which no one has ever ridden. Untie it and bring it here. 31If anyone asks you, 'Why are you untying it?' tell him, 'The Lord needs it.' "

32Those who were sent ahead went and found it just as he had told them. 33As they were untying the colt, its owners asked them, "Why are you untying the colt?"

34They replied, "The Lord needs it."

35They brought it to Jesus, threw their cloaks on the colt and put Jesus on it. 36As he went along, people spread their cloaks on the road.

37When he came near the place where the road goes down the Mount of Olives, the whole crowd of disciples began joyfully to praise God in loud voices for all the miracles they had seen:

38"Blessed is the king who comes in the name of the Lord!"[v]

"Peace in heaven and glory in the highest!"

39Some of the Pharisees in the crowd said to Jesus, "Teacher, rebuke your disciples!"

40"I tell you," he replied, "if they keep quiet, the

v38 Psalm 118:26

will cry out!''

41And when He approached, He saw the city and wept over it,

42saying, ''If you had known in this day, even you, the things which make for peace! But now they have been hidden from your eyes.

43''For the days shall come upon you when your enemies will throw up a bank before you, and surround you, and hem you in on every side,

44and will level you to the ground and your children within you, and they will not leave in you one stone upon another, because you did not recognize the time of your visitation.''

Traders Driven from the Temple

45And He entered the temple and began to cast out those who were selling,

46saying to them, ''It is written, 'AND MY HOUSE SHALL BE A HOUSE OF PRAYER,' but you have made it a ROBBERS' DEN.''

47And He was teaching daily in the temple; but the chief priests and the scribes and the leading men among the people were trying to destroy Him,

48and they could not find anything that they might do, for all the people were hanging upon His words.

Chapter 20

Jesus' Authority Questioned

AND it came about on one of the days while He was teaching the people in the temple and preaching the gospel, that the chief priests and the scribes with the elders confronted *Him*,

2and they spoke, saying to Him, ''Tell us by what authority You are doing these things, or who is the one who gave You this authority?''

3And He answered and said to them, ''I shall also ask you a question, and you tell Me:

4''Was the baptism of John from heaven or from men?''

οἱ λίθοι κράξουσιν. 41 Καὶ ὡς ἤγγισεν,
the stones will cry out. And as he drew near,

ἰδὼν τὴν πόλιν ἔκλαυσεν ἐπ᾽ αὐτήν,
seeing the city he wept over it,

42 λέγων ὅτι εἰ ἔγνως ἐν τῇ ἡμέρᾳ
saying[,] - If thou knewest in - day

ταύτῃ καὶ σὺ τὰ πρὸς εἰρήνην· νῦν δὲ
this even thou the things for peace; but now

ἐκρύβη ἀπὸ ὀφθαλμῶν σου. 43 ὅτι ἥξουσιν
they were hidden from eyes of thee. Because will come

ἡμέραι ἐπὶ σὲ καὶ παρεμβαλοῦσιν οἱ
days upon thee and ⁴will raise up ¹the

ἐχθροί σου χάρακά σοι καὶ περικυκλώσουσίν
²enemies ³of thee ⁵a rampart to thee and will surround

σε καὶ συνέξουσίν σε πάντοθεν, 44 καὶ
thee and will press thee on all sides, and

ἐδαφιοῦσίν σε καὶ τὰ τέκνα σου ἐν σοί,
dash to the ground thee and the children of thee in thee,

καὶ οὐκ ἀφήσουσιν λίθον ἐπὶ λίθον ἐν σοί,
and will not leave stone upon stone in thee,

ἀνθ᾽ ὧν οὐκ ἔγνως τὸν καιρὸν τῆς
because† thou knewest not the time of the

ἐπισκοπῆς σου. 45 Καὶ εἰσελθὼν εἰς τὸ
visitation of thee. And entering into the

ἱερὸν ἤρξατο ἐκβάλλειν τοὺς πωλοῦντας,
temple he began to expel the [ones] selling,

46 λέγων αὐτοῖς· γέγραπται· καὶ ἔσται ὁ
telling them : It has been written : And shall be the

οἶκός μου οἶκος προσευχῆς· ὑμεῖς δὲ
house of me a house of prayer; but ye

αὐτὸν ἐποιήσατε σπήλαιον λῃστῶν.
it made a den of robbers.

47 Καὶ ἦν διδάσκων τὸ καθ᾽ ἡμέραν ἐν
And he was teaching - daily† in

τῷ ἱερῷ· οἱ δὲ ἀρχιερεῖς καὶ οἱ
the temple; but the chief priests and the

γραμματεῖς ἐζήτουν αὐτὸν ἀπολέσαι καὶ οἱ
scribes sought ³him ⁷to destroy ¹and ²the

πρῶτοι τοῦ λαοῦ, 48 καὶ οὐχ εὕρισκον
⁵chief men ⁶of the ⁶people, and did not find

τὸ τί ποιήσωσιν· ὁ λαὸς γὰρ ἅπας
- what they might do; ⁴the ³people ¹for ²all

ἐξεκρέματο αὐτοῦ ἀκούων.
hung upon him hearing.

20 Καὶ ἐγένετο ἐν μιᾷ τῶν ἡμερῶν
And it came to pass on one of the days

διδάσκοντος αὐτοῦ τὸν λαὸν ἐν τῷ ἱερῷ
teaching himᵃ the people in the temple
= as he was teaching

καὶ εὐαγγελιζομένου ἐπέστησαν οἱ ἀρχιερεῖς
and preaching good newsᵃ came upon [him] the chief priests

καὶ οἱ γραμματεῖς σὺν τοῖς πρεσβυτέροις,
and the scribes with the elders,

2 καὶ εἶπαν λέγοντες πρὸς αὐτόν· εἰπὸν
and spoke, saying to him : Tell

ἡμῖν ἐν ποίᾳ ἐξουσίᾳ ταῦτα ποιεῖς, ἢ τίς
us by what authority these things thou doest, or who

ἐστιν ὁ δούς σοι τὴν ἐξουσίαν ταύτην;
is the [one] having given thee - authority this?

3 ἀποκριθεὶς δὲ εἶπεν πρὸς αὐτούς·
And answering he said to them :

ἐρωτήσω ὑμᾶς κἀγὼ λόγον, καὶ εἴπατέ
Will ask you I also a word, and tell ye

μοι· 4 τὸ βάπτισμα Ἰωάννου ἐξ οὐρανοῦ
me : The baptism of John from heaven

---

stones will cry out.''

41As he approached Jerusalem and saw the city, he wept over it 42and said, ''If you, even you, had only known on this day what would bring you peace—but now it is hidden from your eyes. 43The days will come upon you when your enemies will build an embankment against you and encircle you and hem you in on every side. 44They will dash you to the ground, you and the children within your walls. They will not leave one stone on another, because you did not recognize the time of God's coming to you.''

Jesus at the Temple

45Then he entered the temple area and began driving out those who were selling. 46''It is written,'' he said to them, '' 'My house will be a house of prayer'ʷ; but you have made it 'a den of robbers.' ˣ''

47Every day he was teaching at the temple. But the chief priests, the teachers of the law and the leaders among the people were trying to kill him. 48Yet they could not find any way to do it, because all the people hung on his words.

Chapter 20

The Authority of Jesus Questioned

ONE day as he was teaching the people in the temple courts and preaching the gospel, the chief priests and the teachers of the law, together with the elders, came up to him. 2''Tell us by what authority you are doing these things,'' they said. ''Who gave you this authority?'' 3He replied, ''I will also ask you a question. Tell me, 4John's baptism—was it from heaven, or from men?''

ʷ46 Isaiah 56:7
ˣ46 Jer. 7:11

⁵And they reasoned among themselves, saying, "If we say, 'From heaven,' He will say, 'Why did you not believe him?'"

⁶"But if we say, 'From men,' all the people will stone us to death, for they are convinced that John was a prophet."

⁷And they answered that they did not know where *it* came from.

⁸And Jesus said to them, "Neither will I tell you by what authority I do these things."

Parable of the Vine-growers

⁹And He began to tell the people this parable: "A man planted a vineyard and rented it out to vine-growers, and went on a journey for a long time.

¹⁰"And at the *harvest* time he sent a slave to the vine-growers, in order that they might give him *some* of the produce of the vineyard; but the vine-growers beat him and sent him away empty-handed.

¹¹"And he proceeded to send another slave; and they beat him also and treated him shamefully, and sent him away empty-handed.

¹²"And he proceeded to send a third; and this one also they wounded and cast out.

¹³"And the owner of the vineyard said, 'What shall I do? I will send my beloved son; perhaps they will respect him.'

¹⁴"But when the vine-growers saw him, they reasoned with one another, saying, 'This is the heir; let us kill him that the inheritance may be ours.'

¹⁵"And they threw him out of the vineyard and killed him. What, therefore, will the owner of the vineyard do to them?

¹⁶"He will come and destroy these vine-growers and will give the vineyard to others." And when they

---

ἦν ἢ ἐξ ἀνθρώπων; 5 οἱ δὲ συνελογίσαντο
was it or from men? And they debated

πρὸς ἑαυτοὺς λέγοντες ὅτι ἐὰν εἴπωμεν·
with themselves saying[,] – If we say :

ἐξ οὐρανοῦ, ἐρεῖ· διὰ τί οὐκ ἐπιστεύσατε
From heaven, he will say: Why did ye not believe

αὐτῷ; 6 ἐὰν δὲ εἴπωμεν· ἐξ ἀνθρώπων, ὁ
him? And if we say : From men, the

λαὸς ἅπας καταλιθάσει ἡμᾶς· πεπεισμένος
people all will stone us; for having been per-

γάρ ἐστιν Ἰωάννην προφήτην εἶναι. 7 καὶ
suaded it is* John a prophet to be. And

ἀπεκρίθησαν μὴ εἰδέναι πόθεν. 8 καὶ ὁ
they answered not to know whence. And –

Ἰησοῦς εἶπεν αὐτοῖς· οὐδὲ ἐγὼ λέγω
Jesus said to them : Neither I tell

ὑμῖν ἐν ποίᾳ ἐξουσίᾳ ταῦτα ποιῶ. 9 Ἤρξατο
you by what authority these things I do. He began

δὲ πρὸς τὸν λαὸν λέγειν τὴν παραβολὴν
And to the people to tell – parable

ταύτην. ἄνθρωπος ἐφύτευσεν ἀμπελῶνα,
this. A man planted a vineyard,

καὶ ἐξέδοτο αὐτὸν γεωργοῖς, καὶ ἀπεδή-
and let out it to husbandmen, and went

μησεν χρόνους ἱκανούς. 10 καὶ καιρῷ
away periods for considerable. And in time
                                        = a long time.

ἀπέστειλεν πρὸς τοὺς γεωργοὺς δοῦλον,
he sent to the husbandmen a slave,

ἵνα ἀπὸ τοῦ καρποῦ τοῦ ἀμπελῶνος
that from the fruit of the vineyard

δώσουσιν αὐτῷ· οἱ δὲ γεωργοὶ ἐξαπέστειλαν
they will give him; but the husbandmen ³sent ⁴away out

αὐτὸν δείραντες κενόν. 11 καὶ προσέθετο
³him ¹beating ²empty. And he added

ἕτερον πέμψαι δοῦλον· οἱ δὲ κἀκεῖνον
²another ¹to send slave; but they that one also
= he sent another slave in addition;

δείραντες καὶ ἀτιμάσαντες ἐξαπέστειλαν
beating and insulting sent away out

κενόν. 12 καὶ προσέθετο τρίτον πέμψαι·
empty. And he added a third to send;

οἱ δὲ καὶ τοῦτον τραυματίσαντες ἐξέβαλον.
but they also this one wounding threw out.

13 εἶπεν δὲ ὁ κύριος τοῦ ἀμπελῶνος· τί
And said the owner of the vineyard : What

ποιήσω; πέμψω τὸν υἱόν μου τὸν ἀγαπητόν·
may I do? I will send the son of me – beloved;

ἴσως τοῦτον ἐντραπήσονται. 14 ἰδόντες δὲ
perhaps this one they will regard. But seeing

αὐτὸν οἱ γεωργοὶ διελογίζοντο πρὸς
him the husbandmen debated with

ἀλλήλους λέγοντες· οὗτός ἐστιν ὁ κληρονόμος·
one another saying : This is the heir;

ἀποκτείνωμεν αὐτόν, ἵνα ἡμῶν γένηται
let us kill him, that of us may become

ἡ κληρονομία. 15 καὶ ἐκβαλόντες αὐτὸν
the inheritance. And throwing out him

ἔξω τοῦ ἀμπελῶνος ἀπέκτειναν. τί οὖν
outside the vineyard they killed. What therefore

ποιήσει αὐτοῖς ὁ κύριος τοῦ ἀμπελῶνος;
will do to them the owner of the vineyard?

16 ἐλεύσεται καὶ ἀπολέσει τοὺς γεωργοὺς
he will come and *will* destroy – husbandmen

τούτους, καὶ δώσει τὸν ἀμπελῶνα ἄλλοις.
these, and will give the vineyard to others.

* That is, the people (a collective singular) have been (=are) persuaded.

---

⁵They discussed it among themselves and said, "If we say, 'From heaven,' he will ask, 'Why didn't you believe him?' ⁶But if we say, 'From men,' all the people will stone us, because they are persuaded that John was a prophet."

⁷So they answered, "We don't know where it was from."

⁸Jesus said, "Neither will I tell you by what authority I am doing these things."

The Parable of the Tenants

⁹He went on to tell the people this parable: "A man planted a vineyard, rented it to some farmers and went away for a long time. ¹⁰At harvest time he sent a servant to the tenants so they would give him some of the fruit of the vineyard. But the tenants beat him and sent him away empty-handed. ¹¹He sent another servant, but that one also they beat and treated shamefully and sent away empty-handed. ¹²He sent still a third, and they wounded him and threw him out.

¹³"Then the owner of the vineyard said, 'What shall I do? I will send my son, whom I love; perhaps they will respect him.'

¹⁴"But when the tenants saw him, they talked the matter over. 'This is the heir,' they said. 'Let's kill him, and the inheritance will be ours.' ¹⁵So they threw him out of the vineyard and killed him.

"What then will the owner of the vineyard do to them? ¹⁶He will come and kill those tenants and give the vineyard to others."

When the people heard

heard it, they said, "May it never be!"

17But He looked at them and said, "What then is this that is written,

'THE STONE WHICH THE BUILDERS REJECTED, THIS BECAME THE CHIEF CORNER *stone*'?

18"Everyone who falls on that stone will be broken to pieces; but on whomever it falls, it will scatter him like dust."

Tribute to Caesar

19And the scribes and the chief priests tried to lay hands on Him at that very hour, and they feared the people; for they understood that He spoke this parable against them.

20And they watched Him, and sent spies who pretended to be righteous, in order that they might catch Him in some statement, so as to deliver Him up to the rule and the authority of the governor.

21And they questioned Him, saying, "Teacher, we know that You speak and teach correctly, and You are not partial to any, but teach the way of God in truth.

22"Is it lawful for us to pay taxes to Caesar, or not?"

23But He detected their trickery and said to them,

24"Show Me a *ᵍ*denarius. Whose likeness and inscription does it have?" And they said, "Caesar's."

25And He said to them, "Then render to Caesar the things that are Caesar's, and to God the things that are God's."

26And they were unable to catch Him in a saying in the presence of the people; and marveling at His answer, they became silent.

Is There a Resurrection?

27Now there came to Him some of the Sadducees (who say that there is no resurrection),

---

ἀκούσαντες δὲ εἶπαν· μὴ γένοιτο. 17 ὁ δὲ
And hearing   they said :   May it not be.   And he

ἐμβλέψας αὐτοῖς εἶπεν· τί οὖν ἐστιν τὸ
looking at them   said : What therefore is —

γεγραμμένον τοῦτο· λίθον ὃν ἀπεδοκίμασαν
having been written this : [The] stone which ²rejected

οἱ οἰκοδομοῦντες, οὗτος ἐγενήθη εἰς κεφαλὴν
¹the [ones] ³building, this came to be for [the] head

γωνίας; 18 πᾶς ὁ πεσὼν ἐπ' ἐκεῖνον τὸν
of [the] corner? Everyone falling on that —

λίθον συνθλασθήσεται· ἐφ' ὃν δ' ἂν πέσῃ,
stone will be broken in pieces; but on whomever it falls,

λικμήσει   αὐτόν. 19 Καὶ ἐζήτησαν οἱ
it will crush to powder him.   And sought the

γραμματεῖς καὶ οἱ ἀρχιερεῖς ἐπιβαλεῖν ἐπ'
scribes   and the chief priests to lay on   on

αὐτὸν τὰς χεῖρας ἐν αὐτῇ τῇ ὥρᾳ, καὶ
him the(ir) hands in ²same ¹the hour,   and

ἐφοβήθησαν τὸν λαόν· ἔγνωσαν γὰρ ὅτι
feared   the people; for they knew that

πρὸς αὐτοὺς εἶπεν τὴν παραβολὴν ταύτην.
at them he told — parable   this.

20 Καὶ παρατηρήσαντες ἀπέστειλαν ἐγκαθέτους
And watching carefully they sent   spies

ὑποκρινομένους ἑαυτοὺς δικαίους εἶναι, ἵνα
pretending   themselves righteous to be, that

ἐπιλάβωνται αὐτοῦ λόγου, ὥστε παραδοῦναι
they might seize of him a word, so as to deliver

αὐτὸν τῇ ἀρχῇ καὶ τῇ ἐξουσίᾳ τοῦ
him to the rule and to the authority of the

ἡγεμόνος. 21 καὶ ἐπηρώτησαν αὐτὸν
governor.   And they questioned him

λέγοντες· διδάσκαλε, οἴδαμεν ὅτι ὀρθῶς
saying : Teacher, we know that ²rightly

λέγεις καὶ διδάσκεις καὶ οὐ λαμβάνεις
¹thou speakest ²and ³teachest and receivest not

πρόσωπον, ἀλλ' ἐπ' ἀληθείας τὴν ὁδὸν τοῦ
a face, but on [the basis of] truth the way —

θεοῦ διδάσκεις· 22 ἔξεστιν ἡμᾶς Καίσαρι
of God teachest; is it lawful for us to Cæsar

φόρον δοῦναι ἢ οὔ; 23 κατανοήσας δὲ
tribute to give or not? And perceiving

αὐτῶν τὴν πανουργίαν εἶπεν πρὸς αὐτούς·
of them the cleverness he said to them :

24 δείξατέ μοι δηνάριον· τίνος ἔχει εἰκόνα
Show me a denarius; of whom has it an image

καὶ ἐπιγραφήν; οἱ δὲ εἶπαν· Καίσαρος.
and superscription? And they said : Of Cæsar.

25 ὁ δὲ εἶπεν πρὸς αὐτούς· τοίνυν ἀπόδοτε
And he said to them : So render

τὰ Καίσαρος Καίσαρι καὶ τὰ τοῦ θεοῦ
the things of Cæsar to Cæsar and the things — of God

τῷ θεῷ. 26 καὶ οὐκ ἴσχυσαν ἐπιλαβέσθαι
— to God.   And they were not able to seize

αὐτοῦ ῥήματος ἐναντίον τοῦ λαοῦ, καὶ
of him a word in the presence of the people, and

θαυμάσαντες ἐπὶ τῇ ἀποκρίσει αὐτοῦ
marvelling at the   answer   of him

ἐσίγησαν.
they were silent.

27 Προσελθόντες δὲ τινες τῶν Σαδ-
And ⁴approaching ¹some ²of the ³Sad-

δουκαίων, οἱ ἀντιλέγοντες ἀνάστασιν μὴ
ducees, the [ones] saying in opposition* a resurrection not

---

this, they said, "May this never be!"

17Jesus looked directly at them and asked, "Then what is the meaning of that which is written:

" 'The stone the builders rejected has become the capstone *ʸ* *ᶻ*?

18Everyone who falls on that stone will be broken to pieces, but he on whom it falls will be crushed."

19The teachers of the law and the chief priests looked for a way to arrest him immediately, because they knew he had spoken this parable against them. But they were afraid of the people.

Paying Taxes to Caesar

20Keeping a close watch on him, they sent spies, who pretended to be honest. They hoped to catch Jesus in something he said so that they might hand him over to the power and authority of the governor. 21So the spies questioned him: "Teacher, we know that you speak and teach what is right, and that you do not show partiality but teach the way of God in accordance with the truth. 22Is it right for us to pay taxes to Caesar or not?"

23He saw through their duplicity and said to them, 24"Show me a denarius. Whose portrait and inscription are on it?"

25"Caesar's," they replied.

He said to them, "Then give to Caesar what is Caesar's, and to God what is God's."

26They were unable to trap him in what he had said there in public. And astonished by his answer, they became silent.

The Resurrection and Marriage

27Some of the Sadducees, who say there is no resurrection, came to Jesus with

---

ᵍThe denarius was equivalent to one day's wage

*That is, to the Pharisees and to the generally held opinion.

ʸ17 Or *cornerstone*
ᶻ17 Psalm 118:22

28and they questioned Him, saying, "Teacher, Moses wrote for us that IF A MAN'S BROTHER DIES, having a wife, AND HE IS CHILDLESS, HIS BROTHER SHOULD TAKE THE WIFE AND RAISE UP OFFSPRING TO HIS BROTHER.
29"Now there were seven brothers; and the first took a wife, and died childless;
30and the second
31and the third took her; and in the same way all seven died, leaving no children.
32"Finally, the woman died also.
33"In the resurrection therefore, which one's wife will she be? For all seven had her as wife."
34And Jesus said to them, "The sons of this age marry and are given in marriage,
35but those who are considered worthy to attain to that age and the resurrection from the dead, neither marry, nor are given in marriage;
36for neither can they die anymore, for they are like angels, and are sons of God, being sons of the resurrection.
37"But that the dead are raised, even Moses showed, in the *passage about the burning* bush, where he calls the Lord THE GOD OF ABRAHAM, AND THE GOD OF ISAAC, AND THE GOD OF JACOB.
38"Now He is not the God of the dead, but of the living; for all live to Him."
39And some of the scribes answered and said "Teacher, You have spoken well."
40For they did not have courage to question Him any longer about anything.
41And He said to them, "How *is it that* they say *h*the Christ is David's son?
42"For David himself says in the book of Psalms,

*h*I.e., the Messiah

εἶναι, ἐπηρώτησαν αὐτὸν 28 λέγοντες·
to be, they questioned him saying :
διδάσκαλε, Μωϋσῆς ἔγραψεν ἡμῖν, ἐάν
Teacher, Moses wrote to us, If
τινος ἀδελφὸς ἀποθάνῃ ἔχων γυναῖκα, καὶ
of anyone a brother dies having a wife, and
οὗτος ἄτεκνος ᾖ, ἵνα λάβῃ ὁ ⁴ἀδελφὸς
this man childless is, that ⁴should take ¹the ²brother
αὐτοῦ τὴν γυναῖκα καὶ ἐξαναστήσῃ σπέρμα
³of him ⁵the ⁶wife and raise up seed
τῷ ἀδελφῷ αὐτοῦ. 29 ἑπτὰ οὖν ἀδελφοὶ
to the brother of him. Seven therefore brothers
ἦσαν· καὶ ὁ πρῶτος λαβὼν γυναῖκα
there were; and the first having taken a wife
ἀπέθανεν ἄτεκνος· 30 καὶ ὁ δεύτερος 31 καὶ
died childless; and the second and
ὁ τρίτος ἔλαβεν αὐτήν, ὡσαύτως δὲ καὶ
the third took her, and similarly also
οἱ ἑπτὰ οὐ κατέλιπον τέκνα καὶ ἀπέθανον.
the seven did not leave children and died.
32 ὕστερον καὶ ἡ γυνὴ ἀπέθανεν. 33 ἡ
Lastly also the woman died. The
γυνὴ οὖν ἐν τῇ ἀναστάσει τίνος αὐτῶν
woman therefore in the resurrection of which of them
γίνεται γυνή; οἱ γὰρ ἑπτὰ ἔσχον αὐτὴν
becomes she wife? for the seven had her
γυναῖκα. 34 καὶ εἶπεν αὐτοῖς ὁ Ἰησοῦς·
[as] wife. And said to them - Jesus :
οἱ υἱοὶ τοῦ αἰῶνος τούτου γαμοῦσιν καὶ
The sons - age of this marry and
γαμίσκονται, 35 οἱ δὲ καταξιωθέντες τοῦ
are given in marriage, but the [ones] counted worthy -
αἰῶνος ἐκείνου τυχεῖν καὶ τῆς ἀναστάσεως
²age ³of that ¹to obtain and of the resurrection
τῆς ἐκ νεκρῶν οὔτε γαμοῦσιν οὔτε
- out of [the] dead neither marry nor
γαμίζονται· 36 οὐδὲ γὰρ ἀποθανεῖν ἔτι
are given in marriage; for not even to die more
δύνανται, ἰσάγγελοι γάρ εἰσιν, καὶ υἱοί
can they, for equal to angels they are, and ²sons
εἰσιν θεοῦ τῆς ἀναστάσεως υἱοὶ ὄντες.
¹they are ³of God ⁵of the ⁷resurrection ⁴sons ⁶being.
37 ὅτι δὲ ἐγείρονται οἱ νεκροί, καὶ
But that are raised the dead, even
Μωϋσῆς ἐμήνυσεν ἐπὶ τῆς βάτου, ὡς
Moses pointed out at the bush, as
λέγει κύριον τὸν θεὸν Ἀβραὰμ καὶ θεὸν
he calls [the] Lord the God of Abraham and God
Ἰσαὰκ καὶ θεὸν Ἰακώβ· 38 θεὸς δὲ οὐκ
of Isaac and God of Jacob; but God not
ἔστιν νεκρῶν ἀλλὰ ζώντων· πάντες γὰρ
he is of dead persons but of living; for all
αὐτῷ ζῶσιν. 39 ἀποκριθέντες δέ τινες
to him live. And answering some
τῶν γραμματέων εἶπαν· διδάσκαλε, καλῶς
of the scribes said : Teacher, well
εἶπας. 40 οὐκέτι γὰρ ἐτόλμων ἐπερωτᾶν
thou sayest. For no more dared they to question
αὐτὸν οὐδέν.
him no(any)thing.
41 Εἶπεν δὲ πρὸς αὐτούς· πῶς λέγουσιν
And he said to them : How say they
τὸν χριστὸν εἶναι Δαυὶδ υἱόν; 42 αὐτὸς
the Christ to be of David son? himself
γὰρ Δαυὶδ λέγει ἐν βίβλῳ ψαλμῶν·
For David says in [the] roll of psalms :

---

a question. 28"Teacher," they said, "Moses wrote for us that if a man's brother dies and leaves a wife but no children, the man must marry the widow and have children for his brother. 29Now there were seven brothers. The first one married a woman and died childless. 30The second 31and then the third married her, and in the same way the seven died, leaving no children. 32Finally, the woman died too. 33Now then, at the resurrection whose wife will she be, since the seven were married to her?"
34Jesus replied, "The people of this age marry and are given in marriage. 35But those who are considered worthy of taking part in that age and in the resurrection from the dead will neither marry nor be given in marriage, 36and they can no longer die; for they are like the angels. They are God's children, since they are children of the resurrection. 37But in the account of the bush, even Moses showed that the dead rise, for he calls the Lord 'the God of Abraham, and the God of Isaac, and the God of Jacob.'*a* 38He is not the God of the dead, but of the living, for to him all are alive."
39Some of the teachers of the law responded, "Well said, teacher!" 40And no one dared to ask him any more questions.

Whose Son Is the Christ?

41Then Jesus said to them, "How is it that they say the Christ*b* is the Son of David? 42David himself declares in the Book of

*a*37 Exodus 3:6
*b*41 Or *Messiah*

'THE LORD SAID TO MY LORD,
"SIT AT MY RIGHT HAND,
43 UNTIL I MAKE THINE ENEMIES A FOOTSTOOL FOR THY FEET.'' '

44"David therefore calls Him 'Lord,' and how is He his son?''

45And while all the people were listening, He said to the disciples,

46"Beware of the scribes, who like to walk around in long robes, and love respectful greetings in the market places, and chief seats in the synagogues, and places of honor at banquets,

47who devour widows' houses, and for appearance's sake offer long prayers; these will receive greater condemnation.''

εἶπεν κύριος τῷ κυρίῳ μου· κάθου ἐκ
Said [the] LORD to the Lord of me : Sit thou at

δεξιῶν μου 43 ἕως ἂν θῶ τοὺς ἐχθρούς σου
[the] right of me until I put the enemies of thee

ὑποπόδιον τῶν ποδῶν σου. 44 Δαυὶδ
a footstool of the feet of thee. David

οὖν αὐτὸν κύριον καλεῖ, καὶ πῶς αὐτοῦ
therefore him Lord calls, and how of him

υἱός ἐστιν;
son is he?

45 Ἀκούοντος δὲ παντὸς τοῦ λαοῦ εἶπεν
And hearing all the people* he said
=as all the people heard

τοῖς μαθηταῖς· 46 προσέχετε ἀπὸ τῶν
to the disciples : Beware from(of) the

γραμματέων τῶν θελόντων περιπατεῖν ἐν
scribes - wishing to walk about in

στολαῖς καὶ φιλούντων ἀσπασμοὺς ἐν ταῖς
robes and liking greetings in the

ἀγοραῖς καὶ πρωτοκαθεδρίας ἐν ταῖς
marketplaces and chief seats in the

συναγωγαῖς καὶ πρωτοκλισίας ἐν τοῖς
synagogues and chief couches in the

δείπνοις, 47 οἱ κατεσθίουσιν τὰς οἰκίας
suppers, who devour the houses

τῶν χηρῶν καὶ προφάσει μακρὰ προσεύχονται·
of the widows and under pretence long pray;

οὗτοι λήμψονται περισσότερον κρίμα.
these will receive severer judgment.

Psalms:

" 'The Lord said to my Lord:
"Sit at my right hand
43until I make your enemies
a footstool for your feet.'' 'c

44David calls him 'Lord.' How then can he be his son?''

45While all the people were listening, Jesus said to his disciples, 46"Beware of the teachers of the law. They like to walk around in flowing robes and love to be greeted in the marketplaces and have the most important seats in the synagogues and the places of honor at banquets. 47They devour widows' houses and for a show make lengthy prayers. Such men will be punished most severely.''

Chapter 21

The Widow's Gift

AND He looked up and saw the rich putting their gifts into the treasury.

2And He saw a certain poor widow putting in two small copper coins.

3And He said, "Truly I say to you, this poor widow put in more than all of them;

4for they all out of their surplus put into the offering; but she out of her poverty put in all that she had to live on.''

5And while some were talking about the temple, that it was adorned with beautiful stones and votive gifts, He said,

6"As for these things which you are looking at, the days will come in which there will not be left one stone upon another which will not be torn down.''

7And they questioned Him, saying, "Teacher, when therefore will these things be? And what will be the sign when these things

---

21 Ἀναβλέψας δὲ εἶδεν τοὺς βάλλοντας
And looking up he saw ¹the ²putting

εἰς τὸ γαζοφυλακεῖον τὰ δῶρα αὐτῶν
⁴into ⁵the ⁶treasury ⁷the ⁸gifts ⁹of them

πλουσίους. 2 εἶδεν δέ τινα χήραν πενιχρὰν
³rich [ones]. And he saw a certain widow poor

βάλλουσαν ἐκεῖ λεπτὰ δύο, 3 καὶ εἶπεν·
putting there lepta two, and he said :

ἀληθῶς λέγω ὑμῖν ὅτι ἡ χήρα αὕτη ἡ
Truly I tell you that ¹the ²widow ³this the

πτωχὴ πλεῖον πάντων ἔβαλεν· 4 πάντες
³poor more [than] all put; ²all

γὰρ οὗτοι ἐκ τοῦ περισσεύοντος αὐτοῖς
¹for these out of the abounding to them⁶
=their abundance

ἔβαλον εἰς τὰ δῶρα, αὕτη δὲ ἐκ τοῦ
put into the gifts, but this woman out of the

ὑστερήματος αὐτῆς πάντα τὸν βίον ὃν
want of her ²all ³the ⁴living ⁵which

εἶχεν ἔβαλεν.
⁶she had ¹put.

5 Καὶ τινων λεγόντων περὶ τοῦ ἱεροῦ, ὅτι
And some speaking* about the temple, that
=as some spoke

λίθοις καλοῖς καὶ ἀναθήμασιν κεκόσμηται,
with stones beautiful and gifts it has(had) been adorned,

εἶπεν· 6 ταῦτα ἃ θεωρεῖτε, ἐλεύσονται
he said : These things which ye behold, will come

ἡμέραι ἐν αἷς οὐκ ἀφεθήσεται λίθος ἐπὶ
days in which there will not be left stone on

λίθῳ ὃς οὐ καταλυθήσεται. 7 ἐπηρώτησαν δὲ
stone which will not be overthrown. And they questioned

αὐτὸν λέγοντες· διδάσκαλε, πότε οὖν
him saying : Teacher, when therefore

ταῦτα ἔσται; καὶ τί τὸ σημεῖον ὅταν
these things will be? And what [will be] the sign when

Chapter 21

The Widow's Offering

AS he looked up, Jesus saw the rich putting their gifts into the temple treasury. 2He also saw a poor widow put in two very small copper coins.d 3"I tell you the truth,'' he said, "this poor widow has put in more than all the others. 4All these people gave their gifts out of their wealth; but she out of her poverty put in all she had to live on.''

Signs of the End of the Age

5Some of his disciples were remarking about how the temple was adorned with beautiful stones and with gifts dedicated to God. But Jesus said, 6"As for what you see here, the time will come when not one stone will be left on another; every one of them will be thrown down.''

7"Teacher,'' they asked, "when will these things happen? And what will be the sign that they are about

c43 Psalm 110:1
d2 Greek two lepta

are about to take place?''
8And He said, "See to it that you be not misled; for many will come in My name, saying, 'I am He,' and, 'The time is at hand'; do not go after them.
9"And when you hear of wars and disturbances, do not be terrified; for these things must take place first, but the end *does* not *follow* immediately "

Things to Come

10Then He continued by saying to them, "Nation will rise against nation, and kingdom against kingdom,
11and there will be great earthquakes, and in various places plagues and famines; and there will be terrors and great signs from heaven.
12"But before all these things, they will lay their hands on you and will persecute you, delivering you to the synagogues and prisons, bringing you before kings and governors for My name's sake.
13"It will lead to an opportunity for your testimony.
14"So make up your minds not to prepare beforehand to defend yourselves;
15for I will give you utterance and wisdom which none of your opponents will be able to resist or refute.
16"But you will be delivered up even by parents and brothers and relatives and friends, and they will put *some* of you to death,
17and you will be hated by all on account of My name.
18"Yet not a hair of your head will perish.
19"By your endurance you will gain your lives.
20"But when you see Jerusalem surrounded by armies, then recognize that her desolation is at hand.
21"Then let those who are in Judea flee to the mountains, and let those who are

μέλλη   ταῦτα   γίνεσθαι;   8 ὁ   δὲ   εἶπεν·
¹are about ¹these things ²to happen?   And he   said :

βλέπετε   μὴ   πλανηθῆτε·   πολλοὶ   γὰρ
Beware   lest   ye be led astray;   for many

ἐλεύσονται   ἐπὶ   τῷ   ὀνόματί   μου   λέγοντες·
will come   on(in)   the   name   of me   saying :

ἐγώ   εἰμι,   καὶ·   ὁ   καιρὸς   ἤγγικεν·   μὴ
I   am,   and :   The   time   has drawn near;   not

πορευθῆτε   ὀπίσω   αὐτῶν.   9 ὅταν   δὲ
go ye   after   them.   And when

ἀκούσητε   πολέμους   καὶ   ἀκαταστασίας,   μὴ
ye hear [of]   wars   and   commotions,   not

πτοηθῆτε·   δεῖ   γὰρ   ταῦτα   γενέσθαι
be ye scared;   for it behoves   these things   to happen

πρῶτον,   ἀλλ'   οὐκ   εὐθέως   τὸ   τέλος.   10 Τότε
first,   but   not immediately   the   end.   Then

ἔλεγεν   αὐτοῖς·   ἐγερθήσεται   ἔθνος   ἐπ'   ἔθνος
he said   to them :   Will be raised   nation   against nation

καὶ   βασιλεία   ἐπὶ   βασιλείαν,   11 σεισμοί   τε
and   kingdom   against   kingdom,   and earthquakes

μεγάλοι   καὶ   κατὰ   τόπους   λοιμοὶ   καὶ   λιμοὶ
great   and   from place to place† pestilences and famines

ἔσονται,   φόβητρά   τε   καὶ   ἀπ'   οὐρανοῦ
there will be,   and terrors   and   ⁴from   ⁴heaven

σημεῖα   μεγάλα   ἔσται.   12 πρὸ   δὲ   τούτων
¹signs   ¹great   there will be.   But before these things

πάντων   ἐπιβαλοῦσιν   ἐφ'   ὑμᾶς   τὰς   χεῖρας
all   they will lay *on*   on   you   the   hands

αὐτῶν   καὶ   διώξουσιν,   παραδιδόντες   εἰς   τὰς
of them   and   will persecute,   delivering   to   the

συναγωγὰς   καὶ   φυλακάς,   ἀπαγομένους   ἐπὶ
synagogues   and   prisons,   being led away   on(before)

βασιλεῖς   καὶ   ἡγεμόνας   ἔνεκεν   τοῦ   ὀνόματός
kings   and   governors   for the sake of the   name

μου·   13 ἀποβήσεται   ὑμῖν   εἰς   μαρτύριον.
of me;   it will turn out   to you   for   a testimony.

14 θέτε   οὖν   ἐν   ταῖς   καρδίαις   ὑμῶν   μὴ
Put   therefore   in   the   hearts   of you   not

προμελετᾶν   ἀπολογηθῆναι·   15 ἐγώ   γὰρ
to practise beforehand   to defend [yourselves];   for I

δώσω   ὑμῖν   στόμα   καὶ   σοφίαν,   ᾗ   οὐ
will give   you   a mouth   and   wisdom,   which   not

δυνήσονται   ἀντιστῆναι   ἢ   ἀντειπεῖν   ἅπαντες   οἱ
will be able   to withstand   or   to contradict   all   the

ἀντικείμενοι   ὑμῖν.   16 παραδοθήσεσθε   δὲ   καὶ
[ones] opposing   you.   And ye will be betrayed   also

ὑπὸ   γονέων   καὶ   ἀδελφῶν   καὶ   συγγενῶν
by   parents   and   brothers   and   relatives

καὶ   φίλων,   καὶ   θανατώσουσιν   ἐξ   ὑμῶν,
and   friends,   and they will put to death [some] of you,

17 καὶ   ἔσεσθε   μισούμενοι   ὑπὸ   πάντων   διὰ
and   ye will be   *being* hated   by   all men because of

τὸ   ὄνομά   μου.   18 καὶ   θρὶξ   ἐκ   τῆς
the   name   of me.   And   a hair   of   the

κεφαλῆς   ὑμῶν   οὐ   μὴ   ἀπόληται·   19 ἐν   τῇ
head   of you   by no means   will perish;   in   the

ὑπομονῇ   ὑμῶν   κτήσεσθε   τὰς   ψυχὰς   ὑμῶν.
endurance   of you   ye will gain   the   souls   of you.

20 Ὅταν   δὲ   ἴδητε   κυκλουμένην   ὑπὸ
But when   ye see   ²being surrounded   ³by

στρατοπέδων   Ἰερουσαλήμ,   τότε   γνῶτε   ὅτι
⁴camps   ¹Jerusalem,   then   know ye   that

ἤγγικεν   ἡ   ἐρήμωσις   αὐτῆς.   21 τότε   οἱ   ἐν
has drawn near   the   desolation   of it.   Then the [ones] in

τῇ   Ἰουδαίᾳ   φευγέτωσαν   εἰς   τὰ   ὄρη,   καὶ
-    Judæa   let them flee   to   the mountains, and

to take place?''
8He replied: "Watch out that you are not deceived. For many will come in my name, claiming, 'I am he,' and, 'The time is near.' Do not follow them. 9When you hear of wars and revolutions, do not be frightened. These things must happen first, but the end will not come right away."
10Then he said to them: "Nation will rise against nation, and kingdom against kingdom. 11There will be great earthquakes, famines and pestilences in various places, and fearful events and great signs from heaven.
12"But before all this, they will lay hands on you and persecute you. They will deliver you to synagogues and prisons, and you will be brought before kings and governors, and all on account of my name. 13This will result in your being witnesses to them. 14But make up your mind not to worry beforehand how you will defend yourselves. 15For I will give you words and wisdom that none of your adversaries will be able to resist or contradict. 16You will be betrayed even by parents, brothers, relatives and friends, and they will put some of you to death. 17All men will hate you because of me. 18But not a hair of your head will perish. 19By standing firm you will gain life.
20"When you see Jerusalem being surrounded by armies, you will know that its desolation is near. 21Then let those who are in Judea flee to the mountains, let those in the city

in the midst of the city depart, and let not those who are in the country enter the city;

22because these are days of vengeance, in order that all things which are written may be fulfilled.

23"Woe to those who are with child and to those who nurse babes in those days; for there will be great distress upon the land, and wrath to this people,

24and they will fall by the edge of the sword, and will be led captive into all the nations; and Jerusalem will be trampled under foot by the Gentiles until the times of the Gentiles be fulfilled.

The Return of Christ

25"And there will be signs in sun and moon and stars, and upon the earth dismay among nations, in perplexity at the roaring of the sea and the waves,

26men fainting from fear and the expectation of the things which are coming upon the world; for the powers of the heavens will be shaken.

27"And then they will see THE SON OF MAN COMING IN A CLOUD with power and great glory.

28"But when these things begin to take place, straighten up and lift up your heads, because your redemption is drawing near."

29And He told them a parable: "Behold the fig tree and all the trees;

30as soon as they put forth *leaves*, you see it and know for yourselves that summer is now near.

31"Even so you, too, when you see these things happening, recognize that the kingdom of God is now near.

32"Truly I say to you, this generation will not pass away until all things take place.

33"Heaven and earth will pass away, but My words will not pass away.

οἱ ἐν μέσῳ αὐτῆς ἐκχωρείτωσαν, καὶ
the [ones] in [the] midst of it let them depart out, and

οἱ ἐν ταῖς χώραις μὴ εἰσερχέσθωσαν εἰς
the [ones] in the districts let them not enter into

αὐτήν, 22 ὅτι ἡμέραι ἐκδικήσεως αὗταί
it, because days of vengeance these

εἰσιν τοῦ πλησθῆναι πάντα τὰ γεγραμμένα.
are - to be fulfilled[d] all the things having been written.

23 οὐαὶ ταῖς ἐν γαστρὶ ἐχούσαις καὶ ταῖς
Woe to the pregnant woment and to the

θηλαζούσαις ἐν ἐκείναις ταῖς ἡμέραις·
[ones] giving suck in those - days;

ἔσται γὰρ ἀνάγκη μεγάλη ἐπὶ τῆς γῆς
for there will be distress great on the land

καὶ ὀργὴ τῷ λαῷ τούτῳ, 24 καὶ πεσοῦνται
and wrath - people to this, and they will fall

στόματι μαχαίρης καὶ αἰχμαλωτισθή-
by [the] mouth(edge) of [the] sword and will be led

σονται εἰς τὰ ἔθνη πάντα, καὶ Ἰερουσαλὴμ
captive to the nations all, and Jerusalem

ἔσται πατουμένη ὑπὸ ἐθνῶν, ἄχρι οὗ
will be *being* trodden down by nations, until

πληρωθῶσιν καιροὶ ἐθνῶν. 25 Καὶ ἔσονται
are accomplished [the] times of [the] nations. And there will be

σημεῖα ἐν ἡλίῳ καὶ σελήνῃ καὶ ἄστροις,
signs in sun and moon and stars,

καὶ ἐπὶ τῆς γῆς συνοχὴ ἐθνῶν ἐν ἀπορίᾳ
and on the earth anxiety of nations in perplexity

ἤχους θαλάσσης καὶ σάλου, 26 ἀποψυχόντων
of [the] sound of [the] sea and surf, fainting
=while men faint

ἀνθρώπων ἀπὸ φόβου καὶ προσδοκίας τῶν
men[a] from fear and expectation of the

ἐπερχομένων τῇ οἰκουμένῃ· αἱ γὰρ δυνάμεις
things coming on the inhabited earth; for the powers

τῶν οὐρανῶν σαλευθήσονται. 27 καὶ τότε
of the heavens will be shaken. And then

ὄψονται τὸν υἱὸν τοῦ ἀνθρώπου ἐρχόμενον
they will see the Son - of man coming

ἐν νεφέλῃ μετὰ δυνάμεως καὶ δόξης
in a cloud with power and glory

πολλῆς. 28 ἀρχομένων δὲ τούτων γίνεσθαι
much(great). And beginning these things[a] to happen
=when these things begin

ἀνακύψατε καὶ ἐπάρατε τὰς κεφαλὰς ὑμῶν,
stand erect and lift up the heads of you,

διότι ἐγγίζει ἡ ἀπολύτρωσις ὑμῶν. 29 Καὶ
because draws near the redemption of you. And

εἶπεν παραβολὴν αὐτοῖς· ἴδετε τὴν συκῆν
he told [a] parable [a]them : Ye see the fig-tree

καὶ πάντα τὰ δένδρα· 30 ὅταν προβάλωσιν
and all the trees; when [a]they burst into leaf

ἤδη, βλέποντες ἀφ' ἑαυτῶν γινώσκετε ὅτι
now, seeing from(of) yourselves ye know that

ἤδη ἐγγὺς τὸ θέρος ἐστίν· 31 οὕτως καὶ
now near the summer is; so also

ὑμεῖς, ὅταν ἴδητε ταῦτα γινόμενα,
ye, when ye see these things happening,

γινώσκετε ὅτι ἐγγύς ἐστιν ἡ βασιλεία
know that near is the kingdom

τοῦ θεοῦ. 32 ἀμὴν λέγω ὑμῖν ὅτι οὐ μὴ
- of God. Truly I tell you that by no means

παρέλθῃ ἡ γενεὰ αὕτη ἕως ἂν πάντα
will pass away - generation this until all things

γένηται. 33 ὁ οὐρανὸς καὶ ἡ γῆ παρ-
happens. The heaven and the earth will

ελεύσονται, οἱ δὲ λόγοι μου οὐ μὴ παρελεύ-
pass away, but the words of me by no means will pass

---

get out, and let those in the country not enter the city. 22For this is the time of punishment in fulfillment of all that has been written. 23How dreadful it will be in those days for pregnant women and nursing mothers! There will be great distress in the land and wrath against this people. 24They will fall by the sword and will be taken as prisoners to all the nations. Jerusalem will be trampled on by the Gentiles until the times of the Gentiles are fulfilled.

25"There will be signs in the sun, moon and stars. On the earth, nations will be in anguish and perplexity at the roaring and tossing of the sea. 26Men will faint from terror, apprehensive of what is coming on the world, for the heavenly bodies will be shaken. 27At that time they will see the Son of Man coming in a cloud with power and great glory. 28When these things begin to take place, stand up and lift up your heads, because your redemption is drawing near."

29He told them this parable: "Look at the fig tree and all the trees. 30When they sprout leaves, you can see for yourselves and know that summer is near. 31Even so, when you see these things happening, you know that the kingdom of God is near.

32"I tell you the truth, this generation[e] will certainly not pass away until all these things have happened. 33Heaven and earth will pass away, but my words will never pass away."

e32 Or race

34"Be on guard, that your hearts may not be weighted down with dissipation and drunkenness and the worries of life, and that day come on you suddenly like a trap;

35for it will come upon all those who dwell on the face of all the earth.

36"But keep on the alert at all times, praying in order that you may have strength to escape all these things that are about to take place, and to stand before the Son of Man."

37Now during the day He was teaching in the temple, but at evening He would go out and spend the night on the mount that is called Olivet.

38And all the people would get up early in the morning *to come* to Him in the temple to listen to Him.

σονται.　34 Προσέχετε δὲ ἑαυτοῖς μήποτε
away.　　And take heed　to　to yourselves　lest
βαρηθῶσιν ὑμῶν αἱ καρδίαι ἐν κραιπάλῃ
become burdened of you　the　hearts　with　surfeiting
καὶ μέθῃ καὶ μερίμναις βιωτικαῖς, καὶ
and deep drinking and anxieties　of life,†　and
ἐπιστῇ ἐφ' ὑμᾶς αἰφνίδιος ἡ ἡμέρα ἐκείνη
come on　on　you　suddenly　-　day　that
35 ὡς παγίς· ἐπεισελεύσεται γὰρ ἐπὶ πάντας
as　a snare;　for it will come in *on*　on　all
τοὺς καθημένους ἐπὶ πρόσωπον πάσης τῆς
the [ones]　sitting　on　[the] face　of all　the
γῆς. 36 ἀγρυπνεῖτε δὲ ἐν παντὶ καιρῷ
earth.　But be ye watchful　at　every　time
δεόμενοι ἵνα κατισχύσητε ἐκφυγεῖν ταῦτα
begging　that　ye may be able　to escape these things
πάντα τὰ μέλλοντα γίνεσθαι, καὶ σταθῆναι
all　the　being about　to happen,　and　to stand
ἔμπροσθεν τοῦ υἱοῦ τοῦ ἀνθρώπου.
before　the　Son　-　of man.
37 Ἦν δὲ τὰς ἡμέρας ἐν τῷ ἱερῷ
Now he was [in] the　days　in　the　temple
διδάσκων, τὰς δὲ νύκτας ἐξερχόμενος
teaching,　and [in] the　nights　going forth
ηὐλίζετο εἰς τὸ ὄρος τὸ καλούμενον
he lodged　in　the　mountain　-　*being* called
ἐλαιών. 38 καὶ πᾶς ὁ λαὸς ὤρθριζεν
of olives.　And　all the　people came in the morning
πρὸς αὐτὸν ἐν τῷ ἱερῷ ἀκούειν αὐτοῦ.
to　him　in　the　temple　to hear　him.

34"Be careful, or your hearts will be weighed down with dissipation, drunkenness and the anxieties of life, and that day will close on you unexpectedly like a trap. 35For it will come upon all those who live on the face of the whole earth. 36Be always on the watch, and pray that you may be able to escape all that is about to happen, and that you may be able to stand before the Son of Man."

37Each day Jesus was teaching at the temple, and each evening he went out to spend the night on the hill called the Mount of Olives, 38and all the people came early in the morning to hear him at the temple.

Chapter 22

Preparing the Passover

NOW the Feast of Unleavened Bread, which is called the Passover, was approaching.

2And the chief priests and the scribes were seeking how they might put Him to death; for they were afraid of the people.

3And Satan entered into Judas who was called Iscariot, belonging to the number of the twelve.

4And he went away and discussed with the chief priests and officers how he might betray Him to them.

5And they were glad, and agreed to give him money.

6And he consented, and *began* seeking a good opportunity to betray Him to them apart from the multitude.

7Then came the *first* day of Unleavened Bread on which the Passover *lamb* had to be sacrificed.

8And He sent Peter and John, saying, "Go and prepare the Passover for us, that we may eat it."

9And they said to Him, "Where do You want us to prepare it?"

---

22 Ἤγγιζεν δὲ ἡ ἑορτὴ τῶν ἀζύμων ἡ
Now drew near　the　feast　of unleavened bread　-
λεγομένη πάσχα. 2 καὶ ἐζήτουν οἱ ἀρχιερεῖς
being called Passover.　And　*sought* ¹the ²chief priests
καὶ οἱ γραμματεῖς τὸ πῶς ἀνέλωσιν
²and ³the ⁴scribes　-　how　they might destroy
αὐτόν· ἐφοβοῦντο γὰρ τὸν λαόν. 3 Εἰσῆλθεν δὲ
him;　for they feared　the people.　And entered
σατανᾶς εἰς Ἰούδαν τὸν καλούμενον
Satan　into　Judas　-　*being* called
Ἰσκαριώτην, ὄντα ἐκ τοῦ ἀριθμοῦ τῶν
Iscariot,　being　of　the　number　of the
δώδεκα· 4 καὶ ἀπελθὼν συνελάλησεν τοῖς
twelve;　and　going　he conversed with　the
ἀρχιερεῦσιν καὶ στρατηγοῖς τὸ πῶς αὐτοῖς
chief priests　and　captains　-　how　to them
παραδῷ αὐτόν. 5 καὶ ἐχάρησαν, καὶ
he might betray him.　And　they rejoiced,　and
συνέθεντο αὐτῷ ἀργύριον δοῦναι. 6 καὶ
they agreed　¹him　²money　¹to give.　And
ἐξωμολόγησεν, καὶ ἐζήτει εὐκαιρίαν τοῦ
he fully consented,　and　sought　opportunity　-
παραδοῦναι αὐτὸν ἄτερ ὄχλου αὐτοῖς.
to betray\ᵈ　him　apart from　a crowd　to them.
7 Ἦλθεν δὲ ἡ ἡμέρα τῶν ἀζύμων, ᾗ
And came　the　day　of unleavened bread, on which
ἔδει θύεσθαι τὸ πάσχα· 8 καὶ ἀπέστειλεν
it behoved　to kill　the　passover [lamb];　and　he sent
Πέτρον καὶ Ἰωάννην εἰπών· πορευθέντες
Peter　and　John　saying·　Going
ἑτοιμάσατε ἡμῖν τὸ πάσχα, ἵνα φάγωμεν. 9 οἱ
prepare ye　for us the passover, that we may eat.　they
δὲ εἶπαν αὐτῷ· ποῦ θέλεις ἑτοιμάσωμεν;
And said　to him : Where wishest thou [that] we may prepare?

Chapter 22

Judas Agrees to Betray Jesus

NOW the Feast of Unleavened Bread, called the Passover, was approaching, 2and the chief priests and the teachers of the law were looking for some way to get rid of Jesus, for they were afraid of the people. 3Then Satan entered Judas, called Iscariot, one of the Twelve. 4And Judas went to the chief priests and the officers of the temple guard and discussed with them how he might betray Jesus. 5They were delighted and agreed to give him money. 6He consented, and watched for an opportunity to hand Jesus over to them when no crowd was present.

The Last Supper

7Then came the day of Unleavened Bread on which the Passover lamb had to be sacrificed. 8Jesus sent Peter and John, saying, "Go and make preparations for us to eat the Passover."

9"Where do you want us to prepare for it?" they asked.

10And He said to them,
"Behold, when you have
entered the city, a man will
meet you carrying a pitcher
of water; follow him into
the house that he enters.
11"And you shall say to
the owner of the house,
'The Teacher says to you,
"Where is the guest room
in which I may eat the Passover with My disciples?" '
12"And he will show you
a large, furnished, upper
room; prepare it there."
13And they departed and
found everything just as He
had told them; and they
prepared the Passover.

The Lord's Supper

14And when the hour had
come He reclined *at the table,* and the apostles with
Him.
15And He said to them, "I
have earnestly desired to
eat this Passover with you
before I suffer;
16for I say to you, I shall
never again eat it until it is
fulfilled in the kingdom of
God."
17And when He had taken
a cup *and* given thanks, He
said, "Take this and share
it among yourselves;
18for I say to you, I will
not drink of the fruit of the
vine from now on until the
kingdom of God comes."
19And when He had taken
some bread *and* given
thanks, He broke *it,* and
gave *it* to them, saying,
"This is My body 'which is
given for you; do this in
remembrance of Me."
20And in the same way *He
took* the cup after they had
eaten, saying, "This cup
which is poured out for you
is the new covenant in My
blood.
21"But behold, the hand
of the one betraying Me is

---

10 ὁ δὲ εἶπεν αὐτοῖς· ἰδοὺ εἰσελθόντων
   And he told them: Behold[,] entering
                            =as ye enter
ὑμῶν εἰς τὴν πόλιν συναντήσει ὑμῖν
youᵃ into the city will meet you
ἄνθρωπος κεράμιον ὕδατος βαστάζων·
a man a pitcher of water bearing;
ἀκολουθήσατε αὐτῷ εἰς τὴν οἰκίαν εἰς ἣν
follow him into the house into which
εἰσπορεύεται· 11 καὶ ἐρεῖτε τῷ οἰκοδεσπότῃ
he enters; and ye will say to the *house*-master
τῆς οἰκίας· λέγει σοι ὁ διδάσκαλος·
of the house: Says to thee the teacher:
ποῦ ἐστιν τὸ κατάλυμα ὅπου τὸ πάσχα
Where is the guest room where the passover
μετὰ τῶν μαθητῶν μου φάγω; 12 κἀκεῖνος
with the disciples of me I may eat? And that man
ὑμῖν δείξει ἀνάγαιον μέγα ἐστρωμένον·
you will show upper room a large *having been* spread;ᵃ
ἐκεῖ ἑτοιμάσατε. 13 ἀπελθόντες δὲ εὗρον
there prepare ye. And going they found
καθὼς εἰρήκει αὐτοῖς, καὶ ἡτοίμασαν τὸ
as he had told them, and they prepared the
πάσχα. 14 Καὶ ὅτε ἐγένετο ἡ ὥρα,
passover. And, when came the hour,
ἀνέπεσεν, καὶ οἱ ἀπόστολοι σὺν αὐτῷ.
he reclined, and the apostles with him.
15 καὶ εἶπεν πρὸς αὐτούς· ἐπιθυμίᾳ
And he said to them: With desire
ἐπεθύμησα τοῦτο τὸ πάσχα φαγεῖν μεθ᾽
I desired this the passover to eat with
ὑμῶν πρὸ τοῦ με παθεῖν· 16 λέγω γὰρ
you before the me to suffer;ᵇ for I tell
             =I suffer;
ὑμῖν ὅτι οὐκέτι οὐ μὴ φάγω αὐτὸ
you that no more by no(any) means I eat it
ἕως ὅτου πληρωθῇ ἐν τῇ βασιλείᾳ τοῦ θεοῦ.
until it is fulfilled in the kingdom - of God.
17 καὶ δεξάμενος ποτήριον εὐχαριστήσας
And taking a cup having given thanks
εἶπεν· λάβετε τοῦτο καὶ διαμερίσατε εἰς
he said: Take this and divide among
ἑαυτούς· 18 λέγω γὰρ ὑμῖν, οὐ μὴ πίω
yourselves; for I tell you, by no means I drink
ἀπὸ τοῦ νῦν ἀπὸ τοῦ γενήματος τῆς
from - now [on] from the produce of the
ἀμπέλου ἕως οὗ ἡ βασιλεία τοῦ θεοῦ
vine until the kingdom - of God
ἔλθῃ. 19 καὶ λαβὼν ἄρτον εὐχαριστήσας
comes. And taking a loaf having given thanks
ἔκλασεν καὶ ἔδωκεν αὐτοῖς λέγων· τοῦτό
he broke and gave to them saying: This
ἐστιν τὸ σῶμά μου [τὸ ὑπὲρ ὑμῶν
is the body of me - for you
διδόμενον· τοῦτο ποιεῖτε εἰς τὴν ἐμὴν
being given; this do ye for - my
ἀνάμνησιν. 20 καὶ τὸ ποτήριον ὡσαύτως
memorial. And the cup similarly
μετὰ τὸ δειπνῆσαι, λέγων· τοῦτο τὸ
after the to sup, saying: This -
ποτήριον ἡ καινὴ διαθήκη ἐν τῷ αἵματί
cup [is] the new covenant in the blood
μου, τὸ ὑπὲρ ὑμῶν ἐκχυννόμενον.] 21 πλὴν
of me, - for you being shed. However
ἰδοὺ ἡ χεὶρ τοῦ παραδιδόντος με μετ᾽
behold[,] the hand of the [one] betraying me with

10He replied, "As you en-
ter the city, a man carrying
a jar of water will meet you.
Follow him to the house
that he enters, 11and say to
the owner of the house,
'The Teacher asks: Where
is the guest room, where I
may eat the Passover with
my disciples?' 12He will
show you a large upper
room, all furnished. Make
preparations there."
13They left and found
things just as Jesus had told
them. So they prepared the
Passover.
14When the hour came,
Jesus and his apostles reclined at the table. 15And
he said to them, "I have eagerly desired to eat this
Passover with you before I
suffer. 16For I tell you, I
will not eat it again until it
finds fulfillment in the kingdom of God."
17After taking the cup, he
gave thanks and said,
"Take this and divide it
among you. 18For I tell you
I will not drink again of the
fruit of the vine until the
kingdom of God comes."
19And he took bread,
gave thanks and broke it,
and gave it to them, saying,
"This is my body given for
you; do this in remem-
brance of me."
20In the same way, after
the supper he took the cup,
saying, "This cup is the
new covenant in my blood,
which is poured out for
you. 21But the hand of him
who is going to betray me is

'Some ancient mss. do not contain
the remainder of v. 19 nor any of
v. 20

ᵃ That is, with carpets, and the dining couches supplied with
cushions.

with Me on the table.
22"For indeed, the Son of Man is going as it has been determined; but woe to that man by whom He is betrayed!"

23And they began to discuss among themselves which one of them it might be who was going to do this thing.

Who Is Greatest

24And there arose also a dispute among them *as to* which one of them was regarded to be greatest.

25And He said to them, "The kings of the Gentiles lord it over them; and those who have authority over them are called 'Benefactors.'

26"But not so with you, but let him who is the greatest among you become as the youngest, and the leader as the servant.

27"For who is greater, the one who reclines *at the table,* or the one who serves? Is it not the one who reclines *at the table?* But I am among you as the one who serves.

28"And you are those who have stood by Me in My trials;

29and just as My Father has granted Me a kingdom, I grant you

30that you may eat and drink at My table in My kingdom, and you will sit on thrones judging the twelve tribes of Israel.

31"Simon, Simon, behold, Satan has demanded permission to sift you like wheat;

32but I have prayed for you, that your faith may not fail; and you, when once you have turned again, strengthen your brothers."

33And he said to Him, "Lord, with You I am ready to go both to prison and to death!"

34And He said, "I say to you, Peter, the cock will not crow today until you have denied three times that you know Me."

ἐμοῦ ἐπὶ τῆς τραπέζης. 22 ὅτι ὁ υἱὸς μὲν
me on the table. Because *the *Son ¹indeed
τοῦ ἀνθρώπου κατὰ τὸ ὡρισμένον
- of man according to the [thing] having been determined
πορεύεται, πλὴν οὐαὶ τῷ ἀνθρώπῳ ἐκείνῳ
goes, nevertheless woe - man to that
δι' οὗ παραδίδοται. 23 καὶ αὐτοὶ ἤρξαντο
through whom he is betrayed. And they began
συζητεῖν πρὸς ἑαυτοὺς τὸ τίς ἄρα εἴη
to debate with themselves - who then it might be
ἐξ αὐτῶν ὁ τοῦτο μέλλων πράσσειν.
of them the [one] *this ¹being about *to do.
24 Ἐγένετο δὲ καὶ φιλονεικία ἐν αὐτοῖς,
And there was also a rivalry among them,
τὸ τίς αὐτῶν δοκεῖ εἶναι μείζων. 25 ὁ δὲ
- who of them seems to be greater. So he
εἶπεν αὐτοῖς· οἱ βασιλεῖς τῶν ἐθνῶν
said to them: The kings of the nations
κυριεύουσιν αὐτῶν, καὶ οἱ ἐξουσιάζοντες
lord it over them, and the [ones] having authority over
αὐτῶν εὐεργέται καλοῦνται. 26 ὑμεῖς δὲ
them benefactors are called. But ye
οὐχ οὕτως, ἀλλ' ὁ μείζων ἐν ὑμῖν
not so, but the greater among you
γινέσθω ὡς ὁ νεώτερος, καὶ ὁ ἡγούμενος
let him become as the younger, and the [one] governing
ὡς ὁ διακονῶν. 27 τίς γὰρ μείζων, ὁ
as the [one] serving. For who [is] greater, the
ἀνακείμενος ἢ ὁ διακονῶν; οὐχὶ ὁ
[one] reclining or the [one] serving? not the
ἀνακείμενος; ἐγὼ δὲ ἐν μέσῳ ὑμῶν εἰμι
[one] reclining? But I in [the] midst of you am
ὡς ὁ διακονῶν. 28 ὑμεῖς δέ ἐστε οἱ
as the [one] serving. But ye are the [ones]
διαμεμενηκότες μετ' ἐμοῦ ἐν τοῖς πειρα-
having remained throughout with me in the tempta-
σμοῖς μου· 29 κἀγὼ διατίθεμαι ὑμῖν καθὼς
tions of me; and I appoint to you as
διέθετό μοι ὁ πατήρ μου βασιλείαν,
appointed to me the Father of me a kingdom,
30 ἵνα ἔσθητε καὶ πίνητε ἐπὶ τῆς τραπέζης
that ye may eat and drink at the table
μου ἐν τῇ βασιλείᾳ μου, καὶ καθήσεσθε
of me in the kingdom of me, and ye will sit
ἐπὶ θρόνων τὰς δώδεκα φυλὰς κρίνοντες
on thrones *the *twelve *tribes ¹judging
τοῦ Ἰσραήλ. 31 Σίμων Σίμων, ἰδοὺ ὁ
- of Israel. Simon[,] Simon, behold[,] -
σατανᾶς ἐξητήσατο ὑμᾶς τοῦ σινιάσαι ὡς
Satan begged earnestly for you to sift^d as
τὸν σῖτον· 32 ἐγὼ δὲ ἐδεήθην περὶ σοῦ
the wheat; but I requested concerning thee
ἵνα μὴ ἐκλίπῃ ἡ πίστις σου· καὶ σύ
that might not fail the faith of thee; and thou
ποτε ἐπιστρέψας στήρισον τοὺς ἀδελφούς
when having turned support the brothers
σου. 33 ὁ δὲ εἶπεν αὐτῷ· κύριε, μετὰ
of thee. And he said to him: Lord, with
σοῦ ἕτοιμός εἰμι καὶ εἰς φυλακὴν καὶ εἰς
thee prepared I am both to prison and to
θάνατον πορεύεσθαι. 34 ὁ δὲ εἶπεν· λέγω
death to go. But he said: I tell
σοι, Πέτρε, οὐ φωνήσει σήμερον ἀλέκτωρ
thee, Peter, will not sound to-day a cock
ἕως τρίς με ἀπαρνήσῃ μὴ εἰδέναι. 35 Καὶ
until thrice me thou wilt deny not to know. And

---

with mine on the table. 22The Son of Man will go as it has been decreed, but woe to that man who betrays him." 23They began to question among themselves which of them it might be who would do this.

24Also a dispute arose among them as to which of them was considered to be greatest. 25Jesus said to them, "The kings of the Gentiles lord it over them; and those who exercise authority over them call themselves Benefactors. 26But you are not to be like that. Instead, the greatest among you should be like the youngest, and the one who rules like the one who serves. 27For who is greater, the one who is at the table or the one who serves? Is it not the one who is at the table? But I am among you as one who serves. 28You are those who have stood by me in my trials. 29And I confer on you a kingdom, just as my Father conferred one on me, 30so that you may eat and drink at my table in my kingdom and sit on thrones, judging the twelve tribes of Israel. 31"Simon, Simon, Satan has asked to sift you^f as wheat. 32But I have prayed for you, Simon, that your faith may not fail. And when you have turned back, strengthen your brothers."

33But he replied, "Lord, I am ready to go with you to prison and to death."

34Jesus answered, "I tell you, Peter, before the rooster crows today, you will deny three times that you know me."

35And He said to them, "When I sent you out without purse and bag and sandals, you did not lack anything, did you?" And they said, "*No*, nothing."

36And He said to them, "But now, let him who has a purse take it along, likewise also a bag, and let him who has no sword sell his robe and buy one.

37"For I tell you, that this which is written must be fulfilled in Me, 'AND HE WAS NUMBERED WITH TRANSGRESSORS'; for that which refers to Me has *its* fulfillment."

38And they said, "Lord, look, here are two swords." And He said to them, "It is enough."

The Garden of Gethsemane

39And He came out and proceeded as was His custom to the Mount of Olives; and the disciples also followed Him.

40And when He arrived at the place, He said to them, "Pray that you may not enter into temptation."

41And He withdrew from them about a stone's throw, and He knelt down and *began* to pray,

42saying, "Father, if Thou art willing, remove this cup from Me; yet not My will, but Thine be done."

43Now an angel from heaven appeared to Him, strengthening Him.

44And being in agony He was praying very fervently; and His sweat became like drops of blood, falling down upon the ground.

45And when He rose from prayer, He came to the disciples and found them sleeping from sorrow,

46and said to them, "Why are you sleeping? Rise and pray that you may not enter into temptation."

Jesus Betrayed by Judas

47While He was still speaking, behold, a multitude *came*, and the one called Judas, one of the

---

εἶπεν αὐτοῖς· ὅτε ἀπέστειλα ὑμᾶς ἄτερ
he said to them : When I sent you without

βαλλαντίου καὶ πήρας καὶ ὑποδημάτων, μή
a purse and a wallet and sandals, not

τινος ὑστερήσατε; οἱ δὲ εἶπαν· οὐθενός.
of anything were ye short? And they said : Of nothing.

36 εἶπεν δὲ αὐτοῖς· ἀλλὰ νῦν ὁ ἔχων
And he said to them : But now the [one] having

βαλλάντιον ἀράτω, ὁμοίως καὶ πήραν, καὶ
a purse let him take [it], likewise also a wallet, and

ὁ μὴ ἔχων πωλησάτω τὸ ἱμάτιον αὐτοῦ
the [one] not having let him sell the garment of him

καὶ ἀγορασάτω μάχαιραν. 37 λέγω γὰρ
and let him buy a sword. For I tell

ὑμῖν ὅτι τοῦτο τὸ γεγραμμένον δεῖ
you that this — having been written it behoves

τελεσθῆναι ἐν ἐμοί, τό· καὶ μετὰ ἀνόμων
to be finished in me, — And with lawless men

ἐλογίσθη· καὶ γὰρ τὸ περὶ ἐμοῦ τέλος
he was reckoned; for indeed the thing concerning me an end

ἔχει. 38 οἱ δὲ εἶπαν· κύριε, ἰδοὺ μάχαιραι
has. And they said : Lord, behold[,] swords

ὧδε δύο. ὁ δὲ εἶπεν αὐτοῖς· ἱκανόν ἐστιν.
here two. And he said to them : Enough it is.

39 Καὶ ἐξελθὼν ἐπορεύθη κατὰ τὸ ἔθος
And going forth he went according to the(his) habit

εἰς τὸ ὄρος τῶν ἐλαιῶν· ἠκολούθησαν δὲ
to the mountain of the olives; and ⁴followed

αὐτῷ καὶ οἱ μαθηταί. 40 γενόμενος δὲ
³him ²also ¹the ⁴disciples. And coming

ἐπὶ τοῦ τόπου εἶπεν αὐτοῖς· προσεύχεσθε
upon the place he said to them : Pray ye

μὴ εἰσελθεῖν εἰς πειρασμόν. 41 καὶ αὐτὸς
not to enter into temptation. And he

ἀπεσπάσθη ἀπ᾽ αὐτῶν ὡσεὶ λίθου βολήν,
was withdrawn from them about of a stone a throw,

καὶ θεὶς τὰ γόνατα προσηύχετο 42 λέγων·
and placing the knees he prayed saying :

πάτερ, εἰ βούλει παρένεγκε τοῦτο τὸ
Father, if thou wilt take away this —

ποτήριον ἀπ᾽ ἐμοῦ· πλὴν μὴ τὸ θέλημά
cup from me; nevertheless not the will

μου ἀλλὰ τὸ σὸν γινέσθω. 43 [ὤφθη δὲ
of me but — thine let be. And appeared

αὐτῷ ἄγγελος ἀπ᾽ οὐρανοῦ ἐνισχύων αὐτόν.
to him an angel from heaven strengthening him.

44 καὶ γενόμενος ἐν ἀγωνίᾳ ἐκτενέστερον
And becoming in an agony more earnestly

προσηύχετο· καὶ ἐγένετο ὁ ἱδρὼς αὐτοῦ
he prayed; and became the sweat of him

ὡσεὶ θρόμβοι αἵματος καταβαίνοντες ἐπὶ
as drops of blood falling down onto

τὴν γῆν.] 45 καὶ ἀναστὰς ἀπὸ τῆς
the earth. And rising up from the

προσευχῆς, ἐλθὼν πρὸς τοὺς μαθητὰς
prayer, coming to the disciples

εὗρεν κοιμωμένους αὐτοὺς ἀπὸ τῆς λύπης,
he found ¹sleeping ²them from the grief,

46 καὶ εἶπεν αὐτοῖς· τί καθεύδετε;
and said to them : Why sleep ye?

ἀναστάντες προσεύχεσθε, ἵνα μὴ εἰσέλθητε
rising up pray ye, lest ye enter

εἰς πειρασμόν. 47 Ἔτι αὐτοῦ λαλοῦντος
into temptation. Yet him speaking⁼
= While he was yet speaking

ἰδοὺ ὄχλος, καὶ ὁ λεγόμενος Ἰούδας εἷς
behold[,] a crowd, and the [one] being named Judas one

35Then Jesus asked them, "When I sent you without purse, bag or sandals, did you lack anything?"

"Nothing," they answered.

36He said to them, "But now if you have a purse, take it, and also a bag; and if you don't have a sword, sell your cloak and buy one. 37It is written: 'And he was numbered with the transgressors[g]; and I tell you that this must be fulfilled in me. Yes, what is written about me is reaching its fulfillment."

38The disciples said, "See, Lord, here are two swords."

"That is enough," he replied.

Jesus Prays on the Mount of Olives

39Jesus went out as usual to the Mount of Olives, and his disciples followed him. 40On reaching the place, he said to them, "Pray that you will not fall into temptation." 41He withdrew about a stone's throw beyond them, knelt down and prayed, 42"Father, if you are willing, take this cup from me; yet not my will, but yours be done." 43An angel from heaven appeared to him and strengthened him. 44And being in anguish, he prayed more earnestly, and his sweat was like drops of blood falling to the ground.[h]

45When he rose from prayer and went back to the disciples, he found them asleep, exhausted from sorrow. 46"Why are you sleeping?" he asked them. "Get up and pray so that you will not fall into temptation."

Jesus Arrested

47While he was still speaking a crowd came up, and the man who was called Judas, one of the

---

twelve, was preceding them; and he approached Jesus to kiss Him.

[48]But Jesus said to him, "Judas, are you betraying the Son of Man with a kiss?"

[49]And when those who were around Him saw what was going to happen, they said, "Lord, shall we strike with the sword?"

[50]And a certain one of them struck the slave of the high priest and cut off his right ear.

[51]But Jesus answered and said, "Stop! No more of this." And He touched his ear and healed him.

[52]And Jesus said to the chief priests and officers of the temple and elders who had come against Him, "Have you come out with swords and clubs as against a robber?

[53]"While I was with you daily in the temple, you did not lay hands on Me; but this hour and the power of darkness are yours."

Jesus' Arrest

[54]And having arrested Him, they led Him *away*, and brought Him to the house of the high priest; but Peter was following at a distance.

[55]And after they had kindled a fire in the middle of the courtyard and had sat down together, Peter was sitting among them.

[56]And a certain servant-girl, seeing him as he sat in the firelight, and looking intently at him, said, "This man was with Him too."

[57]But he denied *it*, saying, "Woman, I do not know Him."

[58]And a little later, another saw him and said, "You are *one* of them too!" But Peter said, "Man, I am not!"

[59]And after about an hour had passed, another man

τῶν δώδεκα προήρχετο αὐτούς, καὶ ἤγγισεν
of the twelve came before them, and drew near

τῷ Ἰησοῦ φιλῆσαι αὐτόν. 48 Ἰησοῦς δὲ
- to Jesus to kiss him. But Jesus

εἶπεν αὐτῷ· Ἰούδα, φιλήματι τὸν υἱὸν
said to him: Judas, with a kiss the Son

τοῦ ἀνθρώπου παραδίδως; 49 ἰδόντες δὲ
of man betrayest thou? And ⁴seeing

οἱ περὶ αὐτὸν τὸ ἐσόμενον εἶπαν·κύριε,
¹the [ones] ²round ³him the thing going to be said: Lord,

εἰ πατάξομεν ἐν μαχαίρῃ; 50 καὶ ἐπάταξεν
if we shall strike with a sword? And ⁴struck

εἷς τις ἐξ αὐτῶν τοῦ ἀρχιερέως τὸν
¹a certain one ²of ³them ⁷of the ⁸high priest ⁸the

δοῦλον καὶ ἀφεῖλεν τὸ οὖς αὐτοῦ τὸ
⁸slave and cut off ¹the ²ear ⁴of him

δεξιόν. 51 ἀποκριθεὶς δὲ ὁ Ἰησοῦς εἶπεν·
⁵right. And answering — Jesus said:

ἐᾶτε ἕως τούτου· καὶ ἁψάμενος τοῦ
Permit ye until this; and touching the

ὠτίου ἰάσατο αὐτόν. 52 Εἶπεν δὲ Ἰησοῦς
ear he cured him. And said Jesus

πρὸς τοὺς παραγενομένους ἐπ' αὐτὸν
to ¹the ²coming ¹⁰upon ¹¹him

ἀρχιερεῖς καὶ στρατηγοὺς τοῦ ἱεροῦ καὶ
²chief priests ¹and ²captains ⁵of the ⁶temple ⁷and

πρεσβυτέρους· ὡς ἐπὶ λῃστὴν ἐξήλθατε
⁸elders: As against a robber came ye out

μετὰ μαχαιρῶν καὶ ξύλων; 53 καθ' ἡμέραν
with swords and clubs? daily

ὄντος μου μεθ' ὑμῶν ἐν τῷ ἱερῷ οὐκ
being me³ with you in the temple not
=while I was

ἐξετείνατε τὰς χεῖρας ἐπ' ἐμέ· ἀλλ' αὕτη
ye stretched out the(your) hands against me; but this

ἐστὶν ὑμῶν ἡ ὥρα καὶ ἡ ἐξουσία τοῦ
is of you the hour and the authority of the

σκότους.
darkness.

54 Συλλαβόντες δὲ αὐτὸν ἤγαγον καὶ
And having arrested him they led and

εἰσήγαγον εἰς τὴν οἰκίαν τοῦ ἀρχιερέως·
brought *in* into the house of the high priest;

ὁ δὲ Πέτρος ἠκολούθει μακρόθεν. 55 περι-
- and Peter followed afar off. light-

αψάντων δὲ πῦρ ἐν μέσῳ τῆς αὐλῆς καὶ
ing And a fire in [the] centre of the court and
=when they had lit a fire . . . and had sat down together

συγκαθισάντων ἐκάθητο ὁ Πέτρος μέσος
sitting down together³ sat — Peter among

αὐτῶν. 56 ἰδοῦσα δὲ αὐτὸν παιδίσκη τις
them. And ²seeing ³him ¹a certain maidservant

καθήμενον πρὸς τὸ φῶς καὶ ἀτενίσασα
sitting near the light and gazing at

αὐτῷ εἶπεν· καὶ οὗτος σὺν αὐτῷ ἦν. 57 ὁ
him said: And this man with him was. he

δὲ ἠρνήσατο λέγων· οὐκ οἶδα αὐτόν,
But denied saying: I know not him,

γύναι. 58 καὶ μετὰ βραχὺ ἕτερος ἰδὼν
woman. And after a short while another seeing

αὐτὸν ἔφη· καὶ σὺ ἐξ αὐτῶν εἶ. ὁ
him said: And thou of them art.

δὲ Πέτρος ἔφη· ἄνθρωπε, οὐκ εἰμί.
But Peter said: Man, I am not.

59 καὶ διαστάσης ὡσεὶ ὥρας μιᾶς ἄλλος
And intervening about hour one³ ¹other man
=when about an hour had intervened

Twelve, was leading them. He approached Jesus to kiss him, [48]but Jesus asked him, "Judas, are you betraying the Son of Man with a kiss?"

[49]When Jesus' followers saw what was going to happen, they said, "Lord, should we strike with our swords?" [50]And one of them struck the servant of the high priest, cutting off his right ear.

[51]But Jesus answered, "No more of this!" And he touched the man's ear and healed him.

[52]Then Jesus said to the chief priests, the officers of the temple guard, and the elders, who had come for him, "Am I leading a rebellion, that you have come with swords and clubs? [53]Every day I was with you in the temple courts, and you did not lay a hand on me. But this is your hour— when darkness reigns."

Peter Disowns Jesus

[54]Then seizing him, they led him away and took him into the house of the high priest. Peter followed at a distance. [55]But when they had kindled a fire in the middle of the courtyard and had sat down together, Peter sat down with them. [56]A servant girl saw him seated there in the firelight. She looked closely at him and said, "This man was with him."

[57]But he denied it. "Woman, I don't know him," he said.

[58]A little later someone else saw him and said, "You also are one of them."

"Man, I am not!" Peter replied.

[59]About an hour later another asserted, "Certainly

began to insist, saying, "Certainly this man also was with Him, for he is a Galilean too."

60But Peter said, "Man, I do not know what you are talking about." And immediately, while he was still speaking, a cock crowed.

61And the Lord turned and looked at Peter. And Peter remembered the word of the Lord, how He had told him, "Before a cock crows today, you will deny Me three times."

62And he went out and wept bitterly.

63And the men who were holding Jesus in custody were mocking Him, and beating Him,

64and they blindfolded Him and were asking Him, saying, "Prophesy, who is the one who hit You?"

65And they were saying many other things against Him, blaspheming.

Jesus before the Sanhedrin

66And when it was day, the ᴶCouncil of elders of the people assembled, both chief priests and scribes, and they led Him away to their council *chamber*, saying,

67"If You are the Christ, tell us." But He said to them, "If I tell you, you will not believe;

68and if I ask a question, you will not answer.

69"But from now on THE SON OF MAN WILL BE SEATED AT THE RIGHT HAND of the power of GOD."

70And they all said, "Are You the Son of God, then?" And He said to them, "Yes, I am."

71And they said, "What further need do we have of testimony? For we have heard it ourselves from His own mouth."

τις διϊσχυρίζετο λέγων· ἐπ' ἀληθείας καὶ
ᴬa cer- emphatically saying: Of a truth also
tain asserted

οὗτος μετ' αὐτοῦ ἦν, καὶ γὰρ Γαλιλαῖός
this man with him was, for indeed a Galilæan

ἐστιν. 60 εἶπεν δὲ ὁ Πέτρος· ἄνθρωπε,
he is. But said - Peter: Man,

οὐκ οἶδα ὃ λέγεις. καὶ παραχρῆμα ἔτι
I know not what thou sayest. And at once yet

λαλοῦντος αὐτοῦ ἐφώνησεν ἀλέκτωρ. 61 καὶ
speaking himᵃ sounded a cock. And
=while he was yet speaking

στραφεὶς ὁ κύριος ἐνέβλεψεν τῷ Πέτρῳ,
turning the Lord looked at - Peter,

καὶ ὑπεμνήσθη ὁ Πέτρος τοῦ λόγου τοῦ
and remembered - Peter the word of the

κυρίου, ὡς εἶπεν αὐτῷ ὅτι πρὶν ἀλέκτορα
Lord, as he told him that before a cock

φωνῆσαι σήμερον ἀπαρνήσῃ με τρίς. 62 καὶ
to soundᵇ to-day thou wilt deny me thrice. And

ἐξελθὼν ἔξω ἔκλαυσεν πικρῶς. 63 Καὶ οἱ
going out outside he wept bitterly. And the

ἄνδρες οἱ συνέχοντες αὐτὸν ἐνέπαιζον αὐτῷ
men - having in charge him* mocked him

δέροντες, 64 καὶ περικαλύψαντες αὐτὸν
beating, and covering over him

ἐπηρώτων λέγοντες· προφήτευσον, τίς ἐστιν
questioned saying: Prophesy, who is

ὁ παίσας σε; 65 καὶ ἕτερα πολλὰ
the [one] playing thee? And other things many

βλασφημοῦντες ἔλεγον εἰς αὐτόν.
blaspheming they said against him.

66 Καὶ ὡς ἐγένετο ἡμέρα, συνήχθη τὸ
And when came day, was assembled the

πρεσβυτέριον τοῦ λαοῦ, ἀρχιερεῖς τε καὶ
body of elders of the people, both chief priests and

γραμματεῖς, καὶ ἀπήγαγον αὐτὸν εἰς τὸ
scribes, and led away him to the

συνέδριον αὐτῶν, 67 λέγοντες· εἰ σὺ εἶ ὁ
council of them, saying: If thou art the

χριστός, εἰπὸν ἡμῖν. εἶπεν δὲ αὐτοῖς·
Christ, tell us. And he said to them:

ἐὰν ὑμῖν εἴπω, οὐ μὴ πιστεύσητε· 68 ἐὰν
If you I tell, by no means will ye believe; ᵃif

δὲ ἐρωτήσω, οὐ μὴ ἀποκριθῆτε. 69 ἀπὸ
ᴵand I question, by no means will ye answer. ⁹from

τοῦ νῦν δὲ ἔσται ὁ υἱὸς τοῦ ἀνθρώπου
- ⁹now ¹But ⁷will be ⁴the ⁶Son - ⁸of man

καθήμενος ἐκ δεξιῶν τῆς δυνάμεως τοῦ
⁵sitting at [the] right of the power -

θεοῦ. 70 εἶπαν δὲ πάντες· σὺ οὖν εἶ ὁ
of God. And they said all: Thou therefore art the

υἱὸς τοῦ θεοῦ; ὁ δὲ πρὸς αὐτοὺς ἔφη·
Son - of God? And he to them said:

ὑμεῖς λέγετε ὅτι ἐγώ εἰμι. 71 οἱ δὲ
Ye say that I am. And they

εἶπαν· τί ἔτι ἔχομεν μαρτυρίας χρείαν;
said: Why yet have we of witness need?

αὐτοὶ γὰρ ἠκούσαμεν ἀπὸ τοῦ στόματος
for [our]selves we heard from the mouth

αὐτοῦ.
of him.

---

this fellow was with him, for he is a Galilean."

60Peter replied, "Man, I don't know what you're talking about!" Just as he was speaking, the rooster crowed. 61The Lord turned and looked straight at Peter. Then Peter remembered the word the Lord had spoken to him: "Before the rooster crows today, you will disown me three times." 62And he went outside and wept bitterly.

The Soldiers Mock Jesus

63The men who were guarding Jesus began mocking and beating him. 64They blindfolded him and demanded, "Prophesy! Who hit you?" 65And they said many other insulting things to him.

Jesus Before Pilate and Herod

66At daybreak the council of the elders of the people, both the chief priests and teachers of the law, met together, and Jesus was led before them. 67"If you are the Christ,ᶦ" they said, "tell us."

Jesus answered, "If I tell you, you will not believe me, 68and if I asked you, you would not answer. 69But from now on, the Son of Man will be seated at the right hand of the mighty God."

70They all asked, "Are you then the Son of God?"

He replied, "You are right in saying I am."

71Then they said, "Why do we need any more testimony? We have heard it from his own lips."

Chapter 23

Jesus before Pilate

THEN the whole body of them arose and brought Him before Pilate. ²And they began to accuse Him, saying, "We found this man misleading our nation and forbidding to pay taxes to Caesar, and saying that He Himself is Christ, a King."

³And Pilate asked Him, saying, "Are You the King of the Jews?" And He answered him and said, "*It is as* you say."

⁴And Pilate said to the chief priests and the multitudes, "I find no guilt in this man."

⁵But they kept on insisting, saying, "He stirs up the people, teaching all over Judea, starting from Galilee, even as far as this place."

⁶But when Pilate heard it, he asked whether the man was a Galilean.

⁷And when he learned that He belonged to Herod's jurisdiction, he sent Him to Herod, who himself also was in Jerusalem at that time.

Jesus before Herod

⁸Now Herod was very glad when he saw Jesus; for he had wanted to see Him for a long time, because he had been hearing about Him and was hoping to see some sign performed by Him.

⁹And he questioned Him at some length; but He answered him nothing.

¹⁰And the chief priests and the scribes were standing there, accusing Him vehemently.

¹¹And Herod with his soldiers, after treating Him with contempt and mocking Him, dressed Him in a gorgeous robe and sent Him back to Pilate.

---

23 Καὶ ἀναστὰν ἅπαν τὸ πλῆθος αὐτῶν
And rising up all the multitude of them

ἤγαγον αὐτὸν ἐπὶ τὸν Πιλᾶτον. **2** ἤρξαντο
led him before - Pilate. they began

δὲ κατηγορεῖν αὐτοῦ λέγοντες· τοῦτον
And to accuse him saying : This man

εὕραμεν διαστρέφοντα τὸ ἔθνος ἡμῶν καὶ
we found perverting the nation of us and

κωλύοντα φόρους Καίσαρι διδόναι, καὶ
forbidding tribute to Cæsar to give, and

λέγοντα ἑαυτὸν χριστὸν βασιλέα εἶναι.
saying himself Christ a king to be.

3 ὁ δὲ Πιλᾶτος ἠρώτησεν αὐτὸν λέγων·
- And Pilate questioned him saying :

σὺ εἶ ὁ βασιλεὺς τῶν Ἰουδαίων; ὁ δὲ
Thou art the king of the Jews? And he

ἀποκριθεὶς αὐτῷ ἔφη· σὺ λέγεις. **4** ὁ δὲ
answering him said : Thou sayest. - And

Πιλᾶτος εἶπεν πρὸς τοὺς ἀρχιερεῖς καὶ
Pilate said to the chief priests and

τοὺς ὄχλους· ⁹No ¹I find °crime in
the crowds :

τῷ ἀνθρώπῳ τούτῳ. **5** οἱ δὲ ἐπίσχυον λέγοντες
- man this. But they insisted saying[,]

ὅτι ἀνασείει τὸν λαόν, διδάσκων καθ'
- He excites the people, teaching throughout

ὅλης τῆς Ἰουδαίας, καὶ ἀρξάμενος ἀπὸ
all the Judæa, even beginning from

τῆς Γαλιλαίας ἕως ὧδε. **6** Πιλᾶτος δὲ
- Galilee to here. And Pilate

ἀκούσας ἐπηρώτησεν εἰ ὁ ἄνθρωπος
hearing questioned if the man

Γαλιλαῖός ἐστιν, **7** καὶ ἐπιγνοὺς ὅτι ἐκ
a Galilæan is(was), and perceiving that of

τῆς ἐξουσίας Ἡρώδου ἐστίν, ἀνέπεμψεν
the authority of Herod he is(was), he sent up

αὐτὸν πρὸς Ἡρώδην, ὄντα καὶ αὐτὸν ἐν
him to Herod, being also him(he) in

Ἰεροσολύμοις ἐν ταύταις ταῖς ἡμέραις.
Jerusalem in these the days.

8 ὁ δὲ Ἡρώδης ἰδὼν τὸν Ἰησοῦν ἐχάρη
- And Herod seeing - Jesus rejoiced

λίαν· ἦν γὰρ ἐξ ἱκανῶν χρόνων θέλων
greatly; for he was of a long times wishing

ἰδεῖν αὐτὸν διὰ τὸ ἀκούειν περὶ αὐτοῦ,
to see him because of the to hearᵇ about him,
=because he had heard

καὶ ἤλπιζέν τι σημεῖον ἰδεῖν ὑπ' αὐτοῦ
and he hoped some sign to see by him

γινόμενον. **9** ἐπηρώτα δὲ αὐτὸν ἐν λόγοις
brought about. And he questioned him in words

ἱκανοῖς· αὐτὸς δὲ οὐδὲν ἀπεκρίνατο αὐτῷ.
many; but he nothing answered him.

10 εἱστήκεισαν δὲ οἱ ἀρχιερεῖς καὶ οἱ
And stood the chief priests and the

γραμματεῖς εὐτόνως κατηγοροῦντες αὐτοῦ.
scribes vehemently accusing him.

11 ἐξουθενήσας δὲ αὐτὸν ὁ Ἡρώδης σὺν
And despising him - Herod with

τοῖς στρατεύμασιν αὐτοῦ καὶ ἐμπαίξας,
the soldiery of him and mocking,

περιβαλὼν ἐσθῆτα λαμπρὰν ἀνέπεμψεν αὐτὸν
throwing round clothing splendid sent back him

τῷ Πιλᾶτῳ. **12** ἐγένοντο δὲ φίλοι ὅ τε
- to Pilate. And became friends - both

Chapter 23

THEN the whole assembly rose and led him off to Pilate. ²And they began to accuse him, saying, "We have found this man subverting our nation. He opposes payment of taxes to Caesar and claims to be Christ,ʲ a king."

³So Pilate asked Jesus, "Are you the king of the Jews?"

"Yes, it is as you say," Jesus replied.

⁴Then Pilate announced to the chief priests and the crowd, "I find no basis for a charge against this man."

⁵But they insisted, "He stirs up the people all over Judeaᵏ by his teaching. He started in Galilee and has come all the way here."

⁶On hearing this, Pilate asked if the man was a Galilean. ⁷When he learned that Jesus was under Herod's jurisdiction, he sent him to Herod, who was also in Jerusalem at that time.

⁸When Herod saw Jesus, he was greatly pleased, because for a long time he had been wanting to see him. From what he had heard about him, he hoped to see him perform some miracle. ⁹He plied him with many questions, but Jesus gave him no answer. ¹⁰The chief priests and the teachers of the law were standing there, vehemently accusing him. ¹¹Then Herod and his soldiers ridiculed and mocked him. Dressing him in an elegant robe, they sent him back to Pilate.

ʲ2 Or *Messiah*; also in verses 35 and 39
ᵏ5 Or *over the land of the Jews*

12Now Herod and Pilate became friends with one another that very day; for before they had been at enmity with each other.

Pilate Seeks Jesus' Release

13And Pilate summoned the chief priests and the rulers and the people,

14and said to them, "You brought this man to me as one who incites the people to rebellion, and behold, having examined Him before you, I have found no guilt in this man regarding the charges which you make against Him.

15"No, nor has Herod, for he sent Him back to us; and behold, nothing deserving death has been done by Him.

16"I will therefore punish Him and release Him."

17[*k*Now he was obliged to release to them at the feast one prisoner.]

18But they cried out all together, saying, "Away with this man, and release for us Barabbas!"

19(He was one who had been thrown into prison for a certain insurrection made in the city, and for murder.)

20And Pilate, wanting to release Jesus, addressed them again,

21but they kept on calling out, saying, "Crucify, crucify Him!"

22And he said to them the third time, "Why, what evil has this man done? I have found in Him no guilt demanding death; I will therefore punish Him and release Him."

23But they were insistent, with loud voices asking that He be crucified. And their voices *began* to prevail.

24And Pilate pronounced sentence that their demand should be granted.

25And he released the man they were asking for who had been thrown into prison for insurrection and murder, but he delivered Jesus to their will.

'Ηρώδης καὶ ὁ Πιλᾶτος ἐν αὐτῇ τῇ
Herod and - Pilate on ²same ¹the

ἡμέρᾳ μετ' ἀλλήλων· προϋπῆρχον γὰρ ἐν
day with each other; for they were previously in

ἔχθρα ὄντες πρὸς αὑτούς. 13 Πιλᾶτος δὲ
enmity being with themselves. And Pilate

συγκαλεσάμενος τοὺς ἀρχιερεῖς καὶ τοὺς
calling together the chief priests and the

ἄρχοντας καὶ τὸν λαὸν 14 εἶπεν πρὸς
leaders and the people said to

αὐτούς· προσηνέγκατέ μοι τὸν ἄνθρωπον
them: Ye brought to me - man

τοῦτον ὡς ἀποστρέφοντα τὸν λαόν, καὶ
this as perverting the people, and

ἰδοὺ ἐγὼ ἐνώπιον ὑμῶν ἀνακρίνας οὐθὲν
behold I ²before ³you ¹examining ⁵nothing

εὗρον ἐν τῷ ἀνθρώπῳ τούτῳ αἴτιον ὧν
⁴found ⁷in - ⁶man ⁸this ⁹crime of the [things] which

κατηγορεῖτε κατ' αὐτοῦ. 15 ἀλλ' οὐδὲ
ye bring accusation against him. But neither

'Ηρώδης· ἀνέπεμψεν γὰρ αὐτὸν πρὸς ἡμᾶς·
Herod: for he sent back him to us;

καὶ ἰδοὺ οὐδὲν ἄξιον θανάτου ἐστὶν
and behold nothing worthy of death is

πεπραγμένον αὐτῷ· 16 παιδεύσας οὖν αὐτὸν
having been done by him; chastising therefore him

ἀπολύσω.‡ 18 ἀνέκραγον δὲ παμπληθεὶ
I will release. But they shouted with the whole multitude

λέγοντες· αἶρε τοῦτον, ἀπόλυσον δὲ ἡμῖν
saying: Take this man, and release to us

τὸν Βαραββᾶν· 19 ὅστις ἦν διὰ στάσιν
- Barabbas; who was because ²insurrection

τινὰ γενομένην ἐν τῇ πόλει καὶ φόνον
¹some happening in the city and murder

βληθεὶς ἐν τῇ φυλακῇ. 20 πάλιν δὲ
thrown in the prison. But again

ὁ Πιλᾶτος προσεφώνησεν αὐτοῖς, θέλων
- Pilate called to them, wishing

ἀπολῦσαι τὸν 'Ιησοῦν. 21 οἱ δὲ ἐπεφώνουν
to release - Jesus. But they shouted

λέγοντες· σταύρου σταύρου αὐτόν. 22 ὁ δὲ
saying: Crucify[,] crucify thou him. But he

τρίτον εἶπεν πρὸς αὐτούς· τί γὰρ κακὸν
a third time said to them: But what evil

ἐποίησεν οὗτος; οὐδὲν αἴτιον θανάτου
did this man? nothing cause of death

εὗρον ἐν αὐτῷ· παιδεύσας οὖν αὐτὸν
I found in him; chastising therefore him

ἀπολύσω. 23 οἱ δὲ ἐπέκειντο φωναῖς
I will release. But they insisted voices

μεγάλαις αἰτούμενοι αὐτὸν σταυρωθῆναι,
with great asking him to be crucified,

καὶ κατίσχυον αἱ φωναὶ αὐτῶν. 24 κλὶ
and prevailed the voices of them. And

Πιλᾶτος ἐπέκρινεν γενέσθαι τὸ αἴτημα
Pilate decided to be [carried out] the request

αὐτῶν· 25 ἀπέλυσεν δὲ τὸν διὰ στάσιν
of them; and he released the [one] because of insurrection

καὶ φόνον βεβλημένον εἰς φυλακήν, ὃν
and murder having been thrown into prison, whom

ἠτοῦντο, τὸν δὲ 'Ιησοῦν παρέδωκεν τῷ
they asked, - but Jesus he delivered to the

θελήματι αὐτῶν.
will of them.

12That day Herod and Pilate became friends—before this they had been enemies.

13Pilate called together the chief priests, the rulers and the people, 14and said to them, "You brought me this man as one who was inciting the people to rebellion. I have examined him in your presence and have found no basis for your charges against him. 15Neither has Herod, for he sent him back to us; as you can see, he has done nothing to deserve death. 16Therefore, I will punish him and then release him.¹"

18With one voice they cried out, "Away with this man! Release Barabbas to us!" 19(Barabbas had been thrown into prison for an insurrection in the city, and for murder.)

20Wanting to release Jesus, Pilate appealed to them again. 21But they kept shouting, "Crucify him! Crucify him!"

22For the third time he spoke to them: "Why? What crime has this man committed? I have found in him no grounds for the death penalty. Therefore I will have him punished and then release him."

23But with loud shouts they insistently demanded that he be crucified, and their shouts prevailed. 24So Pilate decided to grant their demand. 25He released the man who had been thrown into prison for insurrection and murder, the one they asked for, and surrendered Jesus to their will.

---

*k*Many mss. do not contain this verse

‡ Ver. 17 omitted by Nestle; *cf.* NIV footnote.

¹16 Some manuscripts him."
¹7Now he was obliged to release one man to them at the Feast.

Simon Bears the Cross

26And when they led Him away, they laid hold of one Simon of Cyrene, coming in from the country, and placed on him the cross to carry behind Jesus.

27And there were following Him a great multitude of the people, and of women who were mourning and lamenting Him.

28But Jesus turning to them said, "Daughters of Jerusalem, stop weeping for Me, but weep for yourselves and for your children.

29"For behold, the days are coming when they will say, 'Blessed are the barren, and the wombs that never bore, and the breasts that never nursed.'

30"Then they will begin TO SAY TO THE MOUNTAINS, 'FALL ON US,' AND TO THE HILLS, 'COVER US.'

31"For if they do these things in the green tree, what will happen in the dry?"

32And two others also, who were criminals, were being led away to be put to death with Him.

The Crucifixion

33And when they came to the place called The Skull, there they crucified Him and the criminals, one on the right and the other on the left.

34But Jesus was saying, "Father, forgive them; for they do not know what they are doing." And they cast lots, dividing up His garments among themselves.

35And the people stood by, looking on. And even the rulers were sneering at Him, saying, "He saved others; let Him save Himself if this is the Christ of God, His Chosen One."

36And the soldiers also mocked Him, coming up to Him, offering Him sour wine,

---

26 Καὶ ὡς ἀπήγαγον αὐτόν, ἐπιλαβόμενοι
And as they led away him, seizing

Σίμωνά τινα Κυρηναῖον ἐρχόμενον ἀπ'
Simon a certain Cyrenian coming from

ἀγροῦ ἐπέθηκαν αὐτῷ τὸν σταυρὸν φέρειν
[the] country they placed on him the cross to carry

ὄπισθεν τοῦ Ἰησοῦ. 27 Ἠκολούθει δὲ
behind - Jesus. And followed

αὐτῷ πολὺ πλῆθος τοῦ λαοῦ καὶ γυναικῶν
him a much multitude of the people and of women

αἳ ἐκόπτοντο καὶ ἐθρήνουν αὐτόν. 28 στρα-
who mourned and lamented him. turn

φεὶς δὲ πρὸς αὐτὰς Ἰησοῦς εἶπεν·
ing And to them Jesus said:

θυγατέρες Ἰερουσαλήμ, μὴ κλαίετε ἐπ'
Daughters of Jerusalem, do not weep over

ἐμέ· πλὴν ἐφ' ἑαυτὰς κλαίετε καὶ ἐπὶ
me; but over yourselves weep and over

τὰ τέκνα ὑμῶν, 29 ὅτι ἰδοὺ ἔρχονται
the children of you, because behold come

ἡμέραι ἐν αἷς ἐροῦσιν· μακάριαι αἱ
days in which they will say: Blessed the

στεῖραι, καὶ αἱ κοιλίαι αἳ οὐκ ἐγέννησαν,
barren, and the wombs which bare not,

καὶ μαστοὶ οἳ οὐκ ἔθρεψαν. 30 τότε
and breasts which gave not suck. Then

ἄρξονται λέγειν τοῖς ὄρεσιν· πέσατε ἐφ'
they will begin to say to the mountains: Fall on

ἡμᾶς, καὶ τοῖς βουνοῖς· καλύψατε ἡμᾶς·
us, and to the hills: Cover us;

31 ὅτι εἰ ἐν ὑγρῷ ξύλῳ ταῦτα ποιοῦσιν,
because if in *full of sap ¹a tree these things they do,

ἐν τῷ ξηρῷ τί γένηται; 32 Ἤγοντο δὲ
in the dry what may happen? And were led

καὶ ἕτεροι κακοῦργοι δύο σὺν αὐτῷ
also others* criminals two with him

ἀναιρεθῆναι. 33 Καὶ ὅτε ἦλθον ἐπὶ τὸν
to be killed. And when they came upon the

τόπον τὸν καλούμενον Κρανίον, ἐκεῖ ἐσταύ-
place - being called Skull, there they

ρωσαν αὐτὸν καὶ τοὺς κακούργους, ὃν μὲν
crucified him and the criminals, one†

ἐκ δεξιῶν ὃν δὲ ἐξ ἀριστερῶν. 34 [ὁ δὲ
on [the] right and one† on [the] left. - And

Ἰησοῦς ἔλεγεν· πάτερ, ἄφες αὐτοῖς· οὐ
Jesus said: Father, forgive them; *not

γὰρ οἴδασιν τί ποιοῦσιν.] διαμεριζόμενοι
¹for *they know what they are doing.] dividing

δὲ τὰ ἱμάτια αὐτοῦ ἔβαλον κλήρους.
And the garments of him they cast lots.

35 καὶ εἱστήκει ὁ λαὸς θεωρῶν. ἐξεμυκ-
And stood the people beholding. scoff-

τήριζον δὲ καὶ οἱ ἄρχοντες λέγοντες·
ed And also the rulers saying:

ἄλλους ἔσωσεν, σωσάτω ἑαυτόν, εἰ οὗτός
Others he saved, let him save himself, if this man

ἐστιν ὁ χριστὸς τοῦ θεοῦ ὁ ἐκλεκτός.
is the Christ of God the chosen [one].

36 ἐνέπαιξαν δὲ αὐτῷ καὶ οἱ στρατιῶται
And mocked him also the soldiers

προσερχόμενοι, ὄξος προσφέροντες αὐτῷ
approaching, vinegar offering to him

The Crucifixion

26As they led him away, they seized Simon from Cyrene, who was on his way in from the country, and put the cross on him and made him carry it behind Jesus. 27A large number of people followed him, including women who mourned and wailed for him. 28Jesus turned and said to them, "Daughters of Jerusalem, do not weep for me; weep for yourselves and for your children. 29For the time will come when you will say, 'Blessed are the barren women, the wombs that never bore and the breasts that never nursed!' 30Then

" 'they will say to the mountains, "Fall on us!"
and to the hills,
"Cover us!" ' " [m]

31For if men do these things when the tree is green, what will happen when it is dry?"

32Two other men, both criminals, were also led out with him to be executed. 33When they came to the place called the Skull, there they crucified him, along with the criminals—one on his right, the other on his left. 34Jesus said, "Father, forgive them, for they do not know what they are doing." [n] And they divided up his clothes by casting lots.

35The people stood watching, and the rulers even sneered at him. They said, "He saved others; let him save himself if he is the Christ of God, the Chosen One."

36The soldiers also came up and mocked him. They offered him wine vinegar

---

* Luke uses ἕτεροι here with strict accuracy = "different." Jesus was not himself a criminal. Note punctuation of A.V. Cf. Acts 28. 1.

[m]30 Hosea 10:8

[n]34 Some early manuscripts do not have this sentence.

37and saying, "If You are the King of the Jews, save Yourself!"

38Now there was also an inscription above Him, "THIS IS THE KING OF THE JEWS."

39And one of the criminals who were hanged *there* was hurling abuse at Him, saying, "Are You not the Christ? Save Yourself and us!"

40But the other answered, and rebuking him said, "Do you not even fear God, since you are under the same sentence of condemnation?

41"And we indeed justly, for we are receiving what we deserve for our deeds; but this man has done nothing wrong."

42And he was saying, "Jesus, remember me when You come in Your kingdom!"

43And He said to him, "Truly I say to you, today you shall be with Me in Paradise."

44And it was now about *l*the sixth hour, and darkness fell over the whole land until *m*the ninth hour,

45the sun being obscured; and the veil of the temple was torn in two.

46And Jesus, crying out with a loud voice, said, "Father, INTO THY HANDS I COMMIT MY SPIRIT." And having said this, He breathed His last.

47Now when the centurion saw what had happened, he *began* praising God, saying, "Certainly this man was innocent."

48And all the multitudes who came together for this spectacle, when they observed what had happened, *began* to return, beating their breasts.

49And all His acquaintances and the women who accompanied Him from Galilee, were standing at a distance, seeing these things.

Jesus Is Buried

50And behold, a man named Joseph, who was a

---

37 καὶ λέγοντες· εἰ σὺ εἶ ὁ βασιλεὺς
and   saying :   If thou art the   king

τῶν Ἰουδαίων, σῶσον σεαυτόν. **38** ἦν δὲ
of the   Jews,   save   thyself.   And there was

καὶ ἐπιγραφὴ ἐπ᾽ αὐτῷ Ο ΒΑΣΙΛΕΥΣ
also a superscription over   him :   THE   KING

ΤΩΝ ΙΟΥΔΑΙΩΝ ΟΥΤΟΣ. **39** Εἷς δὲ
OF THE   JEWS   THIS.   And one

τῶν κρεμασθέντων κακούργων ἐβλασφήμει
of the   hanged   criminals   blasphemed

αὐτόν· οὐχὶ σὺ εἶ ὁ χριστός; σῶσον
him : Not thou art the Christ?   save

σεαυτὸν καὶ ἡμᾶς **40** ἀποκριθεὶς δὲ ὁ
thyself   and   us.   But answering

ἕτερος ἐπιτιμῶν αὐτῷ ἔφη· οὐδὲ φοβῇ σὺ
other   rebuking   him   said :   Not fearest thou

τὸν θεόν, ὅτι ἐν τῷ αὐτῷ κρίματι εἶ;
-    God, because in the   same   judgment thou art?

41 καὶ ἡμεῖς μὲν δικαίως, ἄξια γὰρ ὧν
And we   indeed justly, for things worthy of what

ἐπράξαμεν ἀπολαμβάνομεν· οὗτος δὲ οὐδὲν
we did   we receive back;   but this man   nothing

ἄτοπον ἔπραξεν. **42** καὶ ἔλεγεν Ἰησοῦ,
amiss   did.   And he said :   Jesus,

μνήσθητί μου ὅταν ἔλθῃς εἰς τὴν βασιλείαν
remember me when thou comest into the   kingdom

σου. **43** καὶ εἶπεν αὐτῷ· ἀμήν σοι λέγω,
of thee.   And he said to him. Truly thee   I tell,

σήμερον μετ᾽ ἐμοῦ ἔσῃ ἐν τῷ παραδείσῳ.
to-day   with me thou wilt be in the   paradise.

44 Καὶ ἦν ἤδη ὡσεὶ ὥρα ἕκτη καὶ
And it was now about hour sixth and

σκότος ἐγένετο ἐφ᾽ ὅλην τὴν γῆν ἕως
darkness came   over all the land   until

ὥρας ἐνάτης **45** τοῦ ἡλίου ἐκλιπόντος·ᵃ
hour ninth   the   sun   failing;
                                     = as the sun failed;

ἐσχίσθη δὲ τὸ καταπέτασμα τοῦ ναοῦ
and was torn   the   veil   of the shrine

μέσον. **46** καὶ φωνήσας φωνῇ μεγάλῃ ὁ
in the middle. And crying   voice with a great -

Ἰησοῦς εἶπεν· πάτερ, εἰς χεῖράς σου
Jesus   said : Father, into hands of thee

παρατίθεμαι τὸ πνεῦμά μου. τοῦτο δὲ
I commit   the   spirit   of me.   And this

εἰπὼν ἐξέπνευσεν. **47** ἰδὼν δὲ ὁ ἑκατον-
saying he expired.   And ²seeing ¹the ²cen-

τάρχης τὸ γενόμενον ἐδόξαζεν τὸν θεὸν
turion the thing happening glorified   -   God

λέγων· ὄντως ὁ ἄνθρωπος οὗτος δίκαιος
saying : Really - man this righteous

ἦν. **48** καὶ πάντες οἱ συμπαραγενόμενοι
was.   And all   ¹the   ²arriving together

ὄχλοι ἐπὶ τὴν θεωρίαν ταύτην, θεωρήσαντες τὰ
²crowds at - sight this, beholding the things

γενόμενα, τύπτοντες τὰ στήθη ὑπέστρεφον.
happening, smiting   the(ir) breasts returned.

49 εἰστήκεισαν δὲ πάντες οἱ γνωστοὶ αὐτῷ
And ²stood   ¹all ²the [ones] ³known ⁴to him

ἀπὸ μακρόθεν, καὶ γυναῖκες αἱ συνακο-
²afar off,   and   women the [ones] accom-

λουθοῦσαι αὐτῷ ἀπὸ τῆς Γαλιλαίας, ὁρῶσαι
panying   him from -   Galilee,   seeing

ταῦτα.
these things.

50 Καὶ ἰδοὺ ἀνὴρ ὀνόματι Ἰωσὴφ
And behold[,] a man by name Joseph

37and said, "If you are the king of the Jews, save yourself."

38There was a written notice above him, which read: THIS IS THE KING OF THE JEWS.

39One of the criminals who hung there hurled insults at him: "Aren't you the Christ? Save yourself and us!"

40But the other criminal rebuked him. "Don't you fear God," he said, "since you are under the same sentence? 41We are punished justly, for we are getting what our deeds deserve. But this man has done nothing wrong."

42Then he said, "Jesus, remember me when you come into your kingdom.ᵒ"

43Jesus answered him, "I tell you the truth, today you will be with me in paradise."

Jesus' Death

44It was now about the sixth hour, and darkness came over the whole land until the ninth hour, 45for the sun stopped shining. And the curtain of the temple was torn in two. 46Jesus called out with a loud voice, "Father, into your hands I commit my spirit." When he had said this, he breathed his last.

47The centurion, seeing what had happened, praised God and said, "Surely this was a righteous man." 48When all the people who had gathered to witness this sight saw what took place, they beat their breasts and went away. 49But all those who knew him, including the women who had followed him from Galilee, stood at a distance, watching these things.

Jesus' Burial

50Now there was a man named Joseph, a member

---

*l*I.e., 12 noon
*m*I.e., 3 p.m.

ᵒ42 Some manuscripts *come with your kingly power*

member of the Council, a good and righteous man ⁵¹(he had not consented to their plan and action), *a man* from Arimathea, a city of the Jews, who was waiting for the kingdom of God; ⁵²this man went to Pilate and asked for the body of Jesus. ⁵³And he took it down and wrapped it in a linen cloth, and laid Him in a tomb cut into the rock, where no one had ever lain. ⁵⁴And it was the preparation day, and the Sabbath was about to begin. ⁵⁵Now the women who had come with Him out of Galilee followed after, and saw the tomb and how His body was laid. ⁵⁶And they returned and prepared spices and perfumes.

And on the Sabbath they rested according to the commandment.

Chapter 24

The Resurrection

BUT on the first day of the week, at early dawn, they came to the tomb, bringing the spices which they had prepared. ²And they found the stone rolled away from the tomb, ³but when they entered, they did not find the body of the Lord Jesus. ⁴And it happened that while they were perplexed about this, behold, two men suddenly stood near them in dazzling apparel; ⁵and as *the women* were terrified and bowed their faces to the ground, *the men* said to them, "Why do you seek the living One among the dead? ⁶"He is not here, but He has risen. Remember how He spoke to you while He was still in Galilee, ⁷saying that the Son of Man must be delivered into the hands of sinful men,

---

βουλευτὴς ὑπάρχων, ἀνὴρ ἀγαθὸς καὶ
a councillor   being,   a man   good   and
δίκαιος, — 51 οὗτος οὐκ ἦν συγκατατεθειμένος
righteous, —   this man was not   agreeing with
τῇ βουλῇ καὶ τῇ πράξει αὐτῶν, — ἀπὸ
the counsel and the action of them, — from
'Αριμαθαίας πόλεως τῶν 'Ιουδαίων, ὃς
Arimathæa   a city of the Jews,   who
προσεδέχετο τὴν βασιλείαν τοῦ θεοῦ,
was awaiting the   kingdom   -   of God,
52 οὗτος προσελθὼν τῷ Πιλάτῳ ἠτήσατο
this man approaching - to Pilate   asked
τὸ σῶμα τοῦ 'Ιησοῦ, 53 καὶ καθελὼν
the body of the Jesus,   and taking down
ἐνετύλιξεν αὐτὸ σινδόνι, καὶ ἔθηκεν αὐτὸν
wrapped   it   in linen, and placed him
ἐν μνήματι λαξευτῷ, οὗ οὐκ ἦν οὐδεὶς
in tomb   a hewn, where was not no(any)one
οὔπω κείμενος. 54 καὶ ἡμέρα ἦν παρασκευῆς,
not yet laid. And day it was of preparation,
καὶ σάββατον ἐπέφωσκεν. 55 Κατακολουθήσασαι
and a sabbath was coming on.   ⁴following after
δὲ αἱ γυναῖκες, αἵτινες ἦσαν συνεληλυθυῖαι
¹And ²the ³women,   who   were ¹having come *with*
ἐκ τῆς Γαλιλαίας αὐτῷ, ἐθεάσαντο τὸ
²out of - ⁴Galilee ³with him, beheld   the
μνημεῖον καὶ ὡς ἐτέθη τὸ σῶμα αὐτοῦ,
tomb and how was placed the body of him,
56 ὑποστρέψασαι δὲ ἡτοίμασαν ἀρώματα καὶ
and returning   prepared   spices and
μύρα.
ointment.

Καὶ τὸ μὲν σάββατον ἡσύχασαν κατὰ
And [on] the ²indeed ¹sabbath they rested according to
τὴν ἐντολήν. 24 τῇ δὲ μιᾷ τῶν σαββάτων
the commandment. But on the one of the week
ὄρθρου βαθέως ἐπὶ τὸ μνῆμα ἦλθον φέρουσαι
while still very early† upon the tomb they came carrying
ἃ ἡτοίμασαν ἀρώματα. 2 εὗρον δὲ τὸν
²which ³they prepared ¹spices. And they found the
λίθον ἀποκεκυλισμένον ἀπὸ τοῦ μνημείου,
stone *having been* rolled away from the   tomb,
3 εἰσελθοῦσαι δὲ οὐχ εὗρον τὸ σῶμα
and entering   did they found not the body
τοῦ κυρίου 'Ιησοῦ. 4 καὶ ἐγένετο ἐν τῷ
of the Lord Jesus. And it was in the
= as they were perplexed
ἀπορεῖσθαι αὐτὰς περὶ τούτου καὶ ἰδοὺ
to be perplexed them^be about this *and* behold[,]
ἄνδρες δύο ἐπέστησαν αὐταῖς ἐν ἐσθῆτι
men   two   stood by   them   in clothing
ἀστραπτούσῃ· 5 ἐμφόβων δὲ γενομένων
shining;   and terrified   becoming
= as they became terrified and bent their faces
αὐτῶν καὶ κλινουσῶν τὰ πρόσωπα εἰς τὴν
them and bending the(ir) faces^a to the
γῆν, εἶπαν πρὸς αὐτάς· τί ζητεῖτε τὸν
earth, they said to   them : Why seek ye the
ζῶντα μετὰ τῶν νεκρῶν; 6 [οὐκ ἔστιν
living [one] with the dead [ones]? He is not
ὧδε, ἀλλὰ ἠγέρθη.] μνήσθητε ὡς ἐλάλησεν
here, but was raised.] Remember how he spoke
ὑμῖν ἔτι ὢν ἐν τῇ Γαλιλαίᾳ, 7 λέγων
to you yet being in - Galilee,   saying[,]
τὸν υἱὸν τοῦ ἀνθρώπου ὅτι δεῖ παραδο-
The Son   of man   that - it behoves to be de-
θῆναι εἰς χεῖρας ἀνθρώπων ἁμαρτωλῶν καὶ
livered into hands   men   of sinful   and

---

of the Council, a good and upright man, ⁵¹who had not consented to their decision and action. He came from the Judean town of Arimathea and he was waiting for the kingdom of God. ⁵²Going to Pilate, he asked for Jesus' body. ⁵³Then he took it down, wrapped it in linen cloth and placed it in a tomb cut in the rock, one in which no one had yet been laid. ⁵⁴It was Preparation Day, and the Sabbath was about to begin.

⁵⁵The women who had come with Jesus from Galilee followed Joseph and saw the tomb and how his body was laid in it. ⁵⁶Then they went home and prepared spices and perfumes. But they rested on the Sabbath in obedience to the commandment.

Chapter 24

The Resurrection

ON the first day of the week, very early in the morning, the women took the spices they had prepared and went to the tomb. ²They found the stone rolled away from the tomb, ³but when they entered, they did not find the body of the Lord Jesus. ⁴While they were wondering about this, suddenly two men in clothes that gleamed like lightning stood beside them. ⁵In their fright the women bowed down with their faces to the ground, but the men said to them, "Why do you look for the living among the dead? ⁶He is not here; he has risen! Remember how he told you, while he was still with you in Galilee: ⁷'The Son of Man must be delivered into the hands of and be crucified, and the third day rise again.''

8And they remembered His words,

9and returned from the tomb and reported all these things to the eleven and to all the rest.

10Now they were Mary Magdalene and Joanna and Mary the *mother* of James; also the other women with them were telling these things to the apostles.

11And these words appeared to them as nonsense, and they would not believe them.

12[ⁿBut Peter arose and ran to the tomb; stooping and looking in, he *saw the linen wrappings only; and he went away to his home, marveling at that which had happened.]

The Road to Emmaus

13And behold, two of them were going that very day to a village named Emmaus, which was ᵒabout seven miles from Jerusalem.

14And they were conversing with each other about all these things which had taken place.

15And it came about that while they were conversing and discussing, Jesus Himself approached, and *began* traveling with them.

16But their eyes were prevented from recognizing Him.

17And He said to them, ''What are these words that you are exchanging with one another as you are walking?'' And they stood still, looking sad.

18And one of them, named Cleopas, answered and said to Him, ''Are You the only one visiting Jerusalem and unaware of the things which have happened here in these days?''

19And He said to them, ''What things?'' And they said to Him, ''The things about Jesus the Nazarene, who was a prophet mighty in deed and word in the sight of God and all the people,

20and how the chief priests and our rulers delivered Him up to the sen-

---

σταυρωθῆναι καὶ τῇ τρίτῃ ἡμέρᾳ ἀναστῆναι.
to be crucified   and on the third   day   to rise again.

8 καὶ ἐμνήσθησαν τῶν ῥημάτων αὐτοῦ,
And   they remembered   the   words   of him,

9 καὶ ὑποστρέψασαι ἀπὸ τοῦ μνημείου
and   returning   from   the   tomb

ἀπήγγειλαν ταῦτα πάντα τοῖς ἕνδεκα καὶ
reported   these things   all   to the   eleven   and

πᾶσιν τοῖς λοιποῖς. 10 ἦσαν δὲ ἡ
to all   the   rest.   Now they were   the

Μαγδαληνὴ Μαρία καὶ Ἰωάννα καὶ Μαρία
Magdalene   Mary   and   Joanna   and   Mary

ἡ Ἰακώβου· καὶ αἱ λοιπαὶ* σὺν αὐταῖς*
the [mother] of James; and   the   rest   with   them

ἔλεγον πρὸς τοὺς ἀποστόλους ταῦτα. 11 καὶ
told   to   the   apostles   these things.   And

ἐφάνησαν ἐνώπιον αὐτῶν ὡσεὶ λῆρος
seemed   before   them   as   folly

τὰ ῥήματα ταῦτα, καὶ ἠπίστουν αὐταῖς.* ‡
–   words   these,   and they disbelieved   them.

13 Καὶ ἰδοὺ δύο ἐξ αὐτῶν ἐν αὐτῇ τῇ
And   behold[,]   two   of   them   on   same   the

ἡμέρᾳ ἦσαν πορευόμενοι εἰς κώμην ἀπέχουσαν
day   were   journeying   to   a village   being distant

σταδίους ἑξήκοντα ἀπὸ Ἰερουσαλήμ, ᾗ
furlongs   sixty   from   Jerusalem, to which

ὄνομα Ἐμμαοῦς, 14 καὶ αὐτοὶ ὡμίλουν
name   Emmaus,   and   they   talked

πρὸς ἀλλήλους περὶ πάντων τῶν συμβεβηκότων
to   each other   about   all   –   ²having occurred

τούτων. 15 καὶ ἐγένετο ἐν τῷ ὁμιλεῖν
¹these things.   And it came to pass in   the   to talk

αὐτοὺς καὶ συζητεῖν, καὶ αὐτὸς Ἰησοῦς
them   and   to discussᵇᵉ,   *and*   [him]self   Jesus
=as they talked and discussed,

ἐγγίσας συνεπορεύετο αὐτοῖς· 16 οἱ δὲ
drawing near   journeyed with   them;   but the

ὀφθαλμοὶ αὐτῶν ἐκρατοῦντο τοῦ μὴ
eyes   of them   were held   –   not

ἐπιγνῶναι αὐτόν. 17 εἶπεν δὲ πρὸς αὐτούς·
to recognizeᵈ   him.   And he said   to   them :

τίνες οἱ λόγοι οὗτοι οὓς ἀντιβάλλετε
What   –   words   these   which   ye exchange

πρὸς ἀλλήλους περιπατοῦντες; καὶ ἐστάθησαν
with   each other   walking?   And   they stood

σκυθρωποί. 18 ἀποκριθεὶς δὲ εἷς ὀνόματι
sad-faced.   And answering   one   by name

Κλεοπᾶς εἶπεν πρὸς αὐτόν· σὺ μόνος
Cleopas   said   to   him :   Thou   only

παροικεῖς Ἰερουσαλὴμ καὶ οὐκ ἔγνως τὰ
a stranger   in Jerusalem   and   knewest not the things

γενόμενα ἐν αὐτῇ ἐν ταῖς ἡμέραις ταύταις;
happening   in   it   in   –   days   these ?

19 καὶ εἶπεν αὐτοῖς· ποῖα; οἱ δὲ εἶπαν
And   he said   to them : What things? And they   said

αὐτῷ· τὰ περὶ Ἰησοῦ τοῦ Ναζαρηνοῦ, ὃς
to him : The things about Jesus   the   Nazarene,   who

ἐγένετο ἀνὴρ προφήτης δυνατὸς ἐν ἔργῳ
was   a *man*   prophet   powerful   in   work

καὶ λόγῳ ἐναντίον τοῦ θεοῦ καὶ παντὸς
and   word   before   –   God   and   all

τοῦ λαοῦ, 20 ὅπως τε παρέδωκαν αὐτὸν οἱ
the   people,   how   both   ⁷delivered   ⁸him   ¹the

ἀρχιερεῖς καὶ οἱ ἄρχοντες ἡμῶν εἰς
³chief priests   ²and   ⁴the   ⁵rulers   ⁶of us   to

---

sinful men, be crucified and on the third day be raised again.' '' 8Then they remembered his words.

9When they came back from the tomb, they told all these things to the Eleven and to all the others. 10It was Mary Magdalene, Joanna, Mary the mother of James, and the others with them who told this to the apostles. 11But they did not believe the women, because their words seemed to them like nonsense. 12Peter, however, got up and ran to the tomb. Bending over, he saw the strips of linen lying by themselves, and he went away, wondering to himself what had happened.

On the Road to Emmaus

13Now that same day two of them were going to a village called Emmaus, about seven milesᵖ from Jerusalem. 14They were talking with each other about everything that had happened. 15As they talked and discussed these things with each other, Jesus himself came up and walked along with them; 16but they were kept from recognizing him.

17He asked them, ''What are you discussing together as you walk along?''

They stood still, their faces downcast. 18One of them, named Cleopas, asked him, ''Are you only a visitor to Jerusalem and do not know the things that have happened there in these days?''

19''What things?'' he asked.

''About Jesus of Nazareth,'' they replied. ''He was a prophet, powerful in word and deed before God and all the people. 20The chief priests and our rulers handed him over to be sen-

---

ⁿ Some ancient mss. do not contain v. 12

ᵒ I.e., 60 stadia, one stadion was about 600 feet

* Note the feminines.

‡ Verse 12 omitted by Nestle.

ᵖ13 Greek *sixty stadia* (about 11 kilometers)

tence of death, and crucified Him.
21"But we were hoping
that it was He who was going to redeem Israel. In-
deed, besides all this, it is
the third day since these
things happened.
22"But also some women
among us amazed us.
When they were at the
tomb early in the morning,
23and did not find His
body, they came, saying
that they had also seen a
vision of angels, who said
that He was alive.
24"And some of those
who were with us went to
the tomb and found it just
exactly as the women also
had said; but Him they did
not see."
25And He said to them,
"O foolish men and slow of
heart to believe in all that
the prophets have spoken!
26"Was it not necessary
for the Christ to suffer
these things and to enter
into His glory?"
27And beginning with
Moses and with all the
prophets, He explained to
them the things concerning
Himself in all the Scrip-
tures.
28And they approached
the village where they were
going, and He acted as
though He would go far-
ther.
29And they urged Him,
saying, "Stay with us, for it
is getting toward evening,
and the day is now nearly
over." And He went in to
stay with them.
30And it came about that
when He had reclined at
the table with them, He
took the bread and blessed
it, and breaking it, He began giving it to them.
31And their eyes were
opened and they recog-
nized Him; and He van-
ished from their sight.
32And they said to one another, "Were not our

κρίμα θανάτου καὶ ἐσταύρωσαν αὐτόν.
[the] judgment of death and crucified him.
21 ἡμεῖς δὲ ἠλπίζομεν ὅτι αὐτός ἐστιν
But we were hoping that he it is(was)
ὁ μέλλων λυτροῦσθαι τὸν Ἰσραήλ· ἀλλά
the [one] being about to redeem - Israel; but
γε καὶ σὺν πᾶσιν τούτοις τρίτην ταύτην
- also with all these things third this
=this is the third day
ἡμέραν ἄγει ἀφ' οὗ ταῦτα ἐγένετο.
day it leads since these things happened.
22 ἀλλὰ καὶ γυναῖκές τινες ἐξ ἡμῶν
But also ²women ¹some of us
ἐξέστησαν ἡμᾶς, γενόμεναι ὀρθριναὶ ἐπὶ τὸ
astonished us, being early at the
μνημεῖον, 23 καὶ μὴ εὑροῦσαι τὸ σῶμα
tomb, and not finding the body
αὐτοῦ ἦλθον λέγουσαι καὶ ὀπτασίαν ἀγγέλων
of him came saying also a vision of angels
ἑωρακέναι, οἳ λέγουσιν αὐτὸν ζῆν. 24 καὶ
to have seen, who say him to live. And
=that he lives.
ἀπῆλθόν τινες τῶν σὺν ἡμῖν ἐπὶ τὸ
²went ¹some ³of the [ones] ⁴with ⁵us to the
μνημεῖον, καὶ εὗρον οὕτως καθὼς καὶ αἱ
tomb, and found so as indeed the
γυναῖκες εἶπον, αὐτὸν δὲ οὐκ εἶδον.
women said, but him they saw not.
25 καὶ αὐτὸς εἶπεν πρὸς αὐτούς· ὦ
And he said to them· O
ἀνόητοι καὶ βραδεῖς τῇ καρδίᾳ τοῦ πιστεύειν
foolish [ones] and slow - in heart - to believe
ἐπὶ πᾶσιν οἷς ἐλάλησαν οἱ προφῆται·
on(in) all things which spoke the prophets·
26 οὐχὶ ταῦτα ἔδει παθεῖν τὸν χριστὸν καὶ
²not ³these things ¹behoved it ⁴to suffer ⁵the ⁶Christ and
εἰσελθεῖν εἰς τὴν δόξαν αὐτοῦ; 27 καὶ
to enter into the glory of him? And
ἀρξάμενος ἀπὸ Μωϋσέως καὶ ἀπὸ πάντων
beginning from Moses and from all
τῶν προφητῶν διηρμήνευσεν αὐτοῖς ἐν
the prophets he explained to them in
πάσαις ταῖς γραφαῖς τὰ περὶ ἑαυτοῦ.
all the scriptures the things concerning himself.
28 Καὶ ἤγγισαν εἰς τὴν κώμην οὗ
And they drew near to the village whither
ἐπορεύοντο, καὶ αὐτὸς προσεποιήσατο
they were journeying, and he pretended
πορρώτερον πορεύεσθαι. 29 καὶ παρε-
farther to journey. And they
βιάσαντο αὐτὸν λέγοντες· μεῖνον μεθ'
urged him saying· Remain with
ἡμῶν, ὅτι πρὸς ἑσπέραν ἐστὶν καὶ κέκλικεν
us, because toward evening it is and has declined
ἤδη ἡ ἡμέρα. καὶ εἰσῆλθεν τοῦ μεῖναι
now the day. And he went in - to remain
σὺν αὐτοῖς. 30 καὶ ἐγένετο ἐν τῷ
with them. And it came to pass in the
=as he reclined
κατακλιθῆναι αὐτὸν μετ' αὐτῶν λαβὼν τὸν
to recline him with them taking the
ἄρτον εὐλόγησεν καὶ κλάσας ἐπεδίδου
loaf he blessed and having broken he handed
αὐτοῖς· 31 αὐτῶν δὲ διηνοίχθησαν οἱ
to them; and of them were opened up the
ὀφθαλμοί, καὶ ἐπέγνωσαν αὐτόν· καὶ αὐτὸς
eyes, and they recognized him; and he
ἄφαντος ἐγένετο ἀπ' αὐτῶν. 32 καὶ
invisible became from them. And

tenced to death, and they
crucified him; 21but we had
hoped that he was the one
who was going to redeem
Israel. And what is more, it
is the third day since all this
took place. 22In addition,
some of our women
amazed us. They went to
the tomb early this morning
23but didn't find his body.
They came and told us that
they had seen a vision of
angels, who said he was
alive. 24Then some of our
companions went to the
tomb and found it just as
the women had said, but
him they did not see."
25He said to them, "How
foolish you are, and how
slow of heart to believe all
that the prophets have spoken! 26Did not the Christ[a]
have to suffer these things
and then enter into his glory?"
27And beginning with Mo-
ses and all the Prophets, he
explained to them what
was said in all the Scriptures concerning himself.
28As they approached the
village to which they were
going, Jesus acted as if he
were going farther. 29But
they urged him strongly,
"Stay with us, for it is nearly evening, the day is almost over." So he went in
to stay with them.
30When he was at the ta-
ble with them, he took
bread, gave thanks, broke
it and began to give it to
them. 31Then their eyes
were opened and they rec-
ognized him, and he disappeared from their sight.
32They asked each other,

a26 Or Messiah; also in verse 46

hearts burning within us while He was speaking to us on the road, while He was explaining the Scriptures to us?"

33And they arose that very hour and returned to Jerusalem, and found gathered together the eleven and those who were with them,

34saying, "The Lord has really risen, and has appeared to Simon."

35And they began to relate their experiences on the road and how He was recognized by them in the breaking of the bread.

Other Appearances

36And while they were telling these things, He Himself stood in their midst. p

37But they were startled and frightened and thought that they were seeing a spirit.

38And He said to them, "Why are you troubled, and why do doubts arise in your hearts?

39"See My hands and My feet, that it is I Myself; touch Me and see, for a spirit does not have flesh and bones as you see that I have."

40[qAnd when He had said this, He showed them His hands and His feet.]

41And while they still could not believe it for joy and were marveling, He said to them, "Have you anything here to eat?"

42And they gave Him a piece of a broiled fish;

43and He took it and ate it before them.

44Now He said to them, "These are My words which I spoke to you while I was still with you, that all things which are written about Me in the Law of Moses and the Prophets and the Psalms must be fulfilled."

45Then He opened their minds to understand the Scriptures,

46and He said to them, "Thus it is written, that the Christ should suffer and

εἶπαν πρὸς ἀλλήλους· οὐχὶ ἡ καρδία
they said   to each other :   Not the   heart
ἡμῶν καιομένη ἦν ἐν ἡμῖν, ὡς ἐλάλει
of us burning was in   us,   as he spoke
ἡμῖν ἐν τῇ ὁδῷ, ὡς διήνοιγεν ἡμῖν τὰς
to us in the way,   as he opened up to us the
γραφάς; 33 Καὶ ἀναστάντες αὐτῇ τῇ ὥρᾳ
scriptures? And rising up   ²same ¹in the hour
ὑπέστρεψαν εἰς Ἰερουσαλήμ, καὶ εὗρον
they returned to Jerusalem,   and found
ἠθροισμένους τοὺς ἕνδεκα καὶ τοὺς σὺν
having been collected the eleven and the [ones] with
αὐτοῖς, 34 λέγοντας ὅτι ὄντως ἠγέρθη ὁ
them,   saying[,]   - Really was raised the
κύριος καὶ ὤφθη Σίμωνι. 35 καὶ αὐτοὶ ἐξηγοῦντο
Lord and appeared to Simon. And they   related
τὰ ἐν τῇ ὁδῷ καὶ ὡς ἐγνώσθη
the things in the   way   and how he was known
αὐτοῖς ἐν τῇ κλάσει τοῦ ἄρτου. 36 Ταῦτα
by them in the breaking of the loaf.   these things
δὲ αὐτῶν λαλούντων αὐτὸς ἔστη ἐν
And them saying²   he   stood in
=as they said these things
μέσῳ αὐτῶν. 37 πτοηθέντες δὲ καὶ
[the] midst of them.   But scared   and
ἔμφοβοι γενόμενοι ἐδόκουν πνεῦμα θεωρεῖν.
terrified becoming they thought a spirit to behold.
38 καὶ εἶπεν αὐτοῖς· τί τεταραγμένοι ἐστέ,
And he said to them : Why having been troubled are ye,
καὶ διὰ τί διαλογισμοὶ ἀναβαίνουσιν ἐν
and why   thoughts   come up   in
τῇ καρδίᾳ ὑμῶν; 39 ἴδετε τὰς χεῖρας
the heart of you? See the   hands
μου καὶ τοὺς πόδας μου, ὅτι ἐγώ εἰμι
of me and the   feet of me, that I   am
αὐτός· ψηλαφήσατέ με καὶ ἴδετε, ὅτι
[my]self;   feel   me and see, because
πνεῦμα σάρκα καὶ ὀστέα οὐκ ἔχει καθὼς
a spirit flesh and bones has not as
ἐμὲ θεωρεῖτε ἔχοντα. ‡ 41 ἔτι δὲ ἀπιστούντων
me ye behold having.   And yet disbelieving
=while they yet disbelieved
αὐτῶν ἀπὸ τῆς χαρᾶς καὶ θαυμαζόντων,
them²   from the   joy   and marvelling³,
εἶπεν αὐτοῖς· ἔχετέ τι βρώσιμον ἐνθάδε;
he said to them : Have ye any food   here?
42 οἱ δὲ ἐπέδωκαν αὐτῷ ἰχθύος ὀπτοῦ
And they handed   to him ²fish ³of a broiled
μέρος· 43 καὶ λαβὼν ἐνώπιον αὐτῶν ἔφαγεν.
¹part;   and taking before   them   he ate.
44 Εἶπεν δὲ πρὸς αὐτούς· οὗτοι οἱ λόγοι
And he said to   them : These - words
μου οὓς ἐλάλησα πρὸς ὑμᾶς ἔτι ὢν σὺν
of me which I spoke to   you yet being with
ὑμῖν, ὅτι δεῖ πληρωθῆναι πάντα τὰ
you, that it behoves to be fulfilled all the things
γεγραμμένα ἐν τῷ νόμῳ Μωϋσέως καὶ
having been written in the law of Moses and
τοῖς προφήταις καὶ ψαλμοῖς περὶ ἐμοῦ.
the prophets and psalms concerning me.
45 τότε διήνοιξεν αὐτῶν τὸν νοῦν τοῦ
Then he opened up of them the mind   -
συνιέναι τὰς γραφάς· 46 καὶ εἶπεν αὐτοῖς
to understand⁴ the scriptures; and said to them[,]
ὅτι οὕτως γέγραπται παθεῖν τὸν χριστὸν
- Thus it has been written ²to suffer ¹the ²Christ

"Were not our hearts burning within us while He talked with us on the road and opened the Scriptures to us?"

33They got up and returned at once to Jerusalem. There they found the Eleven and those with them, assembled together

34and saying, "It is true! The Lord has risen and has appeared to Simon."

35Then the two told what had happened on the way, and how Jesus was recognized by them when he broke the bread.

Jesus Appears to the Disciples

36While they were still talking about this, Jesus himself stood among them and said to them, "Peace be with you."

37They were startled and frightened, thinking they saw a ghost. 38He said to them, "Why are you troubled, and why do doubts rise in your minds? 39Look at my hands and my feet. It is I myself! Touch me and see; a ghost does not have flesh and bones, as you see I have."

40When he had said this, he showed them his hands and feet. 41And while they still did not believe it because of joy and amazement, he asked them, "Do you have anything to eat?" 42They gave him a piece of broiled fish, 43and he took it and ate it in their presence.

44He said to them, "This is what I told you while I was still with you: Everything must be fulfilled that is written about me in the Law of Moses, the Prophets and the Psalms."

45Then he opened their minds so they could understand the Scriptures. 46He told them, "This is what is written: The Christ will suf-

p Some ancient mss. insert And He says to them, "Peace be to you."
q Many mss. do not contain this verse

‡ Verse 40 omitted by Nestle.

rise again from the dead the third day;

47and that repentance for forgiveness of sins should be proclaimed in His name to all the nations, beginning from Jerusalem.

48"You are witnesses of these things.

49"And behold, I am sending forth the promise of My Father upon you; but you are to stay in the city until you are clothed with power from on high.''

The Ascension

50And He led them out as far as Bethany, and He lifted up His hands and blessed them.

51And it came about that while He was blessing them, He parted from them.ʳ

52And theyˢ returned to Jerusalem with great joy,

53and were continually in the temple, praising God.

καὶ ἀναστῆναι ἐκ νεκρῶν τῇ τρίτῃ ἡμέρᾳ,
and   to rise again out of [the] dead on the third   day,

47 καὶ κηρυχθῆναι ἐπὶ τῷ ὀνόματι αὐτοῦ
and to be proclaimed on(in) the   name   of him

μετάνοιαν εἰς ἄφεσιν ἁμαρτιῶν εἰς πάντα
repentance unto forgiveness of sins   to   all

τὰ ἔθνη, — ἀρξάμενοι ἀπὸ 'Ιερουσαλήμ.
the nations, — beginning from Jerusalem.

48 ὑμεῖς μάρτυρες τούτων.   49 καὶ ἰδοὺ
Ye [are] witnesses of these things.   And behold

ἐγὼ ἐξαποστέλλω τὴν ἐπαγγελίαν τοῦ
I   send forth   the   promise   of the

πατρός μου ἐφ' ὑμᾶς· ὑμεῖς δὲ καθίσατε
Father of me on you;   but ye   sit

ἐν τῇ πόλει ἕως οὗ ἐνδύσησθε ἐξ ὕψους
in the city until ¹ye are clothed[with]²out of ⁴height

δύναμιν.
¹power.

50 Ἐξήγαγεν δὲ αὐτοὺς ἕως πρὸς
And he led out   them   until toward

Βηθανίαν, καὶ ἐπάρας τὰς χεῖρας αὐτοῦ
Bethany,   and lifting up the   hands of him

εὐλόγησεν αὐτούς. 51 καὶ ἐγένετο ἐν τῷ
he blessed   them.   And it came to pass in the

εὐλογεῖν αὐτὸν αὐτοὺς διέστη ἀπ' αὐτῶν.
to bless   himᵇᵉ   them   he withdrew from them.
=while he blessed

52 καὶ αὐτοὶ ὑπέστρεψαν εἰς 'Ιερουσαλὴμ
And they   returned   to   Jerusalem

μετὰ χαρᾶς μεγάλης, 53 καὶ ἦσαν διὰ παντὸς
with   joy   great,   and were   continually

ἐν τῷ ἱερῷ εὐλογοῦντες τὸν θεόν.
in the temple blessing   -   God.

fer and rise from the dead on the third day, 47and repentance and forgiveness of sins will be preached in his name to all nations, beginning at Jerusalem. 48You are witnesses of these things. 49I am going to send you what my Father has promised; but stay in the city until you have been clothed with power from on high.''

The Ascension

50When he had led them out to the vicinity of Bethany, he lifted up his hands and blessed them. 51While he was blessing them, he left them and was taken up into heaven. 52Then they worshiped him and returned to Jerusalem with great joy. 53And they stayed continually at the temple, praising God.

ʳ Some mss. add *and was carried up into heaven*
ˢ Some mss. insert *worshiped Him, and*

Chapter 1 (left)

The Deity of Jesus Christ

IN the beginning was the Word, and the Word was with God, and the Word was God. 2He was in the beginning with God.

3All things came into being by Him, and apart from Him nothing came into being that has come into being. 4In Him was life, and the life was the light of men. 5And the light shines in the darkness, and the darkness did not *a*comprehend it.

The Witness of John

6There *b*came a man, sent from God, whose name was John. 7He came for a witness, that he might bear witness of the light, that all might believe through him. 8He was not the light, but *came* that he might bear witness of the light. 9There was the true light *c*which, coming into the world, enlightens every man.

10He was in the world, and the world was made through Him, and the world did not know Him. 11He came to His *d*own, and those who were His own did not receive Him. 12But as many as received Him, to them He gave the right to become children of God, *even* to those who believe in His name, 13who were born not of blood, nor of the will of the flesh, nor of the will of man, but of God.

The Word Made Flesh

14And the Word became flesh, and dwelt among us, and we beheld His glory, glory as of the only begotten from the Father, full of grace and truth. 15John *bore witness of Him, and cried out, saying, "This was He of whom I said, 'He who comes after

Greek interlinear (center)

1 Ἐν ἀρχῇ ἦν ὁ λόγος, καὶ ὁ λόγος
In [the] beginning was the Word, and the Word

ἦν πρὸς τὸν θεόν, καὶ θεὸς ἦν ὁ λόγος.*
was with - God, and God was the Word.*

2 οὗτος ἦν ἐν ἀρχῇ πρὸς τὸν θεόν.
This one was in [the] beginning with - God.

3 πάντα δι᾿ αὐτοῦ ἐγένετο, καὶ χωρὶς
All things through him became, and without

αὐτοῦ ἐγένετο οὐδὲ ἕν ὃ γέγονεν. **4** ἐν
him became not one thing which has become. In

αὐτῷ ζωὴ ἦν, καὶ ἡ ζωὴ ἦν τὸ φῶς
him life was, and the life was the light

τῶν ἀνθρώπων· **5** καὶ τὸ φῶς ἐν τῇ
- of men; and the light in the

σκοτίᾳ φαίνει, καὶ ἡ σκοτία αὐτὸ οὐ
darkness shines, and the darkness it not

κατέλαβεν. **6** Ἐγένετο ἄνθρωπος, ἀπεσταλμένος
overtook. There was a man, *having been* sent

παρὰ θεοῦ, ὄνομα αὐτῷ Ἰωάννης· **7** οὗτος
from God, name to him[e] John; this man

ἦλθεν εἰς μαρτυρίαν, ἵνα μαρτυρήσῃ περὶ
came for witness, that he might witness concerning

τοῦ φωτός, ἵνα πάντες πιστεύσωσιν δι᾿
the light, that all men might believe through

αὐτοῦ. **8** οὐκ ἦν ἐκεῖνος τὸ φῶς, ἀλλ᾿ ἵνα
him. He was not - light, but that

μαρτυρήσῃ περὶ τοῦ φωτός. **9** Ἦν τὸ φῶς
he might witness concerning the light. It was the light

τὸ ἀληθινόν, ὃ φωτίζει πάντα ἄνθρωπον,
- true, which enlightens every man,

ἐρχόμενον εἰς τὸν κόσμον. **10** ἐν τῷ
coming into the world. In the

κόσμῳ ἦν, καὶ ὁ κόσμος δι᾿ αὐτοῦ
world he was, and the world through him

ἐγένετο, καὶ ὁ κόσμος αὐτὸν οὐκ ἔγνω.
became, and the world him knew not.

11 εἰς τὰ ἴδια ἦλθεν, καὶ οἱ ἴδιοι αὐτὸν
To his own things he came, and his own people him

οὐ παρέλαβον. **12** ὅσοι δὲ ἔλαβον αὐτόν,
received not. But as many as received him,

ἔδωκεν αὐτοῖς ἐξουσίαν τέκνα θεοῦ γεν-
he gave to them right children of God to be-

έσθαι, τοῖς πιστεύουσιν εἰς τὸ ὄνομα αὐτοῦ,
come, to the [ones] believing in the name of him,

13 οἳ οὐκ ἐξ αἱμάτων οὐδὲ ἐκ θελήματος
who not of bloods nor of [the] will

σαρκὸς οὐδὲ ἐκ θελήματος ἀνδρὸς ἀλλ᾿
of [the] flesh nor of [the] will of a man but

ἐκ θεοῦ ἐγεννήθησαν. **14** Καὶ ὁ λόγος
of God were born. And the Word

σὰρξ ἐγένετο καὶ ἐσκήνωσεν ἐν ἡμῖν,
flesh became and tabernacled among us,

καὶ ἐθεασάμεθα τὴν δόξαν αὐτοῦ, δόξαν
and we beheld the glory of him, glory

ὡς μονογενοῦς παρὰ πατρός, πλήρης χάριτος
as of an only begotten from a father, full of grace

καὶ ἀληθείας. **15** Ἰωάννης μαρτυρεῖ περὶ
and of truth. John witnesses concerning

αὐτοῦ καὶ κέκραγεν λέγων· οὗτος ἦν ὃν
him and has cried out saying: This man was he whom

εἶπον· ὁ ὀπίσω μου ἐρχόμενος ἔμπροσθέν
I said: The [one] after me coming before

Chapter 1 (right)

The Word Became Flesh

IN the beginning was the Word, and the Word was with God, and the Word was God. 2He was with God in the beginning.

3Through him all things were made; without him nothing was made that has been made. 4In him was life, and that life was the light of men. 5The light shines in the darkness, but the darkness has not understood *a* it.

6There came a man who was sent from God; his name was John. 7He came as a witness to testify concerning that light, so that through him all men might believe. 8He himself was not the light; he came only as a witness to the light. 9The true light that gives light to every man was coming into the world. *b*

10He was in the world, and though the world was made through him, the world did not recognize him. 11He came to that which was his own, but his own did not receive him. 12Yet to all who received him, to those who believed in his name, he gave the right to become children of God— 13children born not of natural descent, *c* nor of human decision or a husband's will, but born of God.

14The Word became flesh and made his dwelling among us. We have seen his glory, the glory of the One and Only, *d* who came from the Father, full of grace and truth.

15John testifies concerning him. He cries out, saying, "This was he of whom I said, 'He who comes after

---

a Or, overpower
b Or, came into being
c Or, which enlightens every man coming into the world
d Or, own things, possessions, domain

* But note that the subject has the article and the predicate has it not; hence translate—"the Word was God."

*a*5 Or *darkness, and the darkness has not overcome*
*b*9 Or *This was the true light that gives light to every man who comes into the world*
*c*13 Greek *of bloods*
*d*14,18 Or *the Only Begotten*

me has a higher rank than I, for He existed before me.' "

16For of His fulness we have all received, and grace upon grace.

17For the Law was given through Moses; grace and truth were realized through Jesus Christ.

18No man has seen God at any time; the only begotten ^eGod, who is in the bosom of the Father, He has explained *Him*.

The Testimony of John

19And this is the witness of John, when the Jews sent to him priests and Levites from Jerusalem to ask him, "Who are you?"

20And he confessed, and did not deny, and he confessed, "I am not the Christ."

21And they asked him, "What then? Are you Elijah?" And he *said, "I am not." "Are you the Prophet?" And he answered, "No."

22They said then to him, "Who are you, so that we may give an answer to those who sent us? What do you say about yourself?"

23He said, "I am a VOICE OF ONE CRYING IN THE WILDERNESS, 'MAKE STRAIGHT THE WAY OF THE LORD,' as Isaiah the prophet said."

24Now they had been sent from the Pharisees.

25And they asked him, and said to him, "Why then are you baptizing, if you are not the Christ, nor Elijah, nor the Prophet?"

26John answered them saying, "I baptize ^f in water, *but* among you stands One whom you do not know.

27"*It is* He who comes after me, the thong of whose sandal I am not worthy to untie."

28These things took place in Bethany beyond the Jordan, where John was baptizing.

29The next day he *saw

μου γέγονεν, ὅτι πρῶτός μου ἦν. **16** ὅτι
me has become, because first of me he was. Because

ἐκ τοῦ πληρώματος αὐτοῦ ἡμεῖς πάντες
of the fulness of him we all

ἐλάβομεν, καὶ χάριν ἀντὶ χάριτος· **17** ὅτι
received, and grace instead of grace; because

ὁ νόμος διὰ Μωϋσέως ἐδόθη, ἡ χάρις καὶ
the law through Moses was given, the grace and

ἡ ἀλήθεια διὰ Ἰησοῦ Χριστοῦ ἐγένετο.
the truth through Jesus Christ became.

18 Θεὸν οὐδεὶς ἑώρακεν πώποτε· μονογενὴς
God no man has seen never; [the] only begotten

θεὸς ὁ ὢν εἰς τὸν κόλπον τοῦ πατρός,
God the [one] being in the bosom of the Father,

ἐκεῖνος ἐξηγήσατο.
that one declared [?him].

19 Καὶ αὕτη ἐστὶν ἡ μαρτυρία τοῦ
And this is the witness -

Ἰωάννου, ὅτε ἀπέστειλαν πρὸς αὐτὸν οἱ
of John, when ³sent ⁴to ¹him ¹the

Ἰουδαῖοι ἐξ Ἱεροσολύμων ἱερεῖς καὶ Λευίτας
²Jews ⁹from ¹⁰Jerusalem ⁶priests ⁷and ⁸Levites

ἵνα ἐρωτήσωσιν αὐτόν· σὺ τίς εἶ; **20** καὶ
that they might ask him: Thou who art? And

ὡμολόγησεν καὶ οὐκ ἠρνήσατο, καὶ
he confessed and denied not, and

ὡμολόγησεν ὅτι ἐγὼ οὐκ εἰμὶ ὁ χριστός.
he confessed[,] - I am not the Christ.

21 καὶ ἠρώτησαν αὐτόν· τί οὖν; Ἡλίας εἶ
And they asked him: ^r What then? Elias art

σύ; καὶ λέγει· οὐκ εἰμί. ὁ προφήτης εἶ σύ;
thou? And he says: I am not. The prophet art thou?

καὶ ἀπεκρίθη· οὔ. **22** εἶπαν οὖν αὐτῷ·
And he answered: No. They said therefore to him:

τίς εἶ; ἵνα ἀπόκρισιν δῶμεν τοῖς
Who art thou? that an answer we may give to the [ones]

πέμψασιν ἡμᾶς· τί λέγεις περὶ σεαυτοῦ;
having sent us; What sayest thou concerning thyself?

23 ἔφη· ἐγὼ φωνὴ βοῶντος ἐν τῇ ἐρήμῳ·
He said: I [am] a voice of [one] crying in the desert:

εὐθύνατε τὴν ὁδὸν κυρίου, καθὼς εἶπεν
Make straight the way of [the] Lord, as said

Ἡσαΐας ὁ προφήτης. **24** Καὶ ἀπεσταλμένοι
Esaias the prophet. And [the ones] *having been sent*

ἦσαν ἐκ τῶν Φαρισαίων. **25** καὶ ἠρώτησαν
were of the Pharisees. And they asked

αὐτὸν καὶ εἶπαν αὐτῷ· τι οὖν βαπτίζεις
him and said to him: Why then baptizest thou

εἰ σὺ οὐκ εἶ ὁ χριστὸς οὐδὲ Ἡλίας
if thou art not the Christ nor Elias

οὐδὲ ὁ προφήτης; **26** ἀπεκρίθη αὐτοῖς ὁ
nor the prophet? Answered them -

Ἰωάννης λέγων· ἐγὼ βαπτίζω ἐν ὕδατι·
John saying: I baptize in water;

μέσος ὑμῶν στήκει ὃν ὑμεῖς οὐκ οἴδατε,
among you stands [one] whom ye know not,

27 ὁ ὀπίσω μου ἐρχόμενος, οὗ οὐκ εἰμὶ
the [one] after me coming, of whom am not

ἐγὼ ἄξιος ἵνα λύσω αὐτοῦ τὸν ἱμάντα
I worthy that I should loosen of him the thong

τοῦ ὑποδήματος. **28** Ταῦτα ἐν Βηθανίᾳ
of the sandal. These things in Bethany

ἐγένετο πέραν τοῦ Ἰορδάνου, ὅπου ἦν ὁ
happened beyond the Jordan, where was -

Ἰωάννης βαπτίζων. **29** Τῇ ἐπαύριον βλέπει
John baptizing. On the morrow he sees

---

me has surpassed me because he was before me.' "

16From the fullness of his grace we have all received one blessing after another.

17For the law was given through Moses; grace and truth came through Jesus Christ. 18No one has ever seen God, but God the One and Only,^d ^ewho is at the Father's side, has made him known.

John the Baptist Denies Being the Christ

19Now this was John's testimony when the Jews of Jerusalem sent priests and Levites to ask him who he was. 20He did not fail to confess, but confessed freely, "I am not the Christ.^f"

21They asked him, "Then who are you? Are you Elijah?"

He said, "I am not."

"Are you the Prophet?"

He answered, "No."

22Finally they said, "Who are you? Give us an answer to take back to those who sent us. What do you say about yourself?"

23John replied in the words of Isaiah the prophet, "I am the voice of one calling in the desert, 'Make straight the way for the Lord.' "^g

24Now some Pharisees who had been sent 25questioned him, "Why then do you baptize if you are not the Christ, nor Elijah, nor the Prophet?"

26"I baptize with^h water," John replied, "but among you stands one you do not know. 27He is the one who comes after me, the thongs of whose sandals I am not worthy to untie."

28This all happened at Bethany on the other side of the Jordan, where John was baptizing.

Jesus the Lamb of God

29The next day John saw

---

^eSome later mss. read *Son*
^fThe Gr. here can be translated *in*, *with* or *by*

^d18 Some manuscripts *but the only* (or *only begotten*) *Son*
^f20 Or *Messiah*. "The Christ" (Greek) and "the Messiah" (Hebrew) both mean "the Anointed One"; also in verse 25.
^g23 Isaiah 40:3
^h26 Or *in*; also in verses 31 and 33

Jesus coming to him, and *said, "Behold, the Lamb of God who takes away the sin of the world!

30"This is He on behalf of whom I said, 'After me comes a Man who has a higher rank than I, for He existed before me.'

31"And I did not recognize Him, but in order that He might be manifested to Israel, I came baptizing *in water."

32And John bore witness saying, "I have beheld the Spirit descending as a dove out of heaven, and He remained upon Him.

33"And I did not recognize Him, but He who sent me to baptize *in water said to me, 'He upon whom you see the Spirit descending and remaining upon Him, this is the one who baptizes in the Holy Spirit.'

34"And I have seen, and have borne witness that this is the Son of God."

Jesus' Public Ministry, First Converts

35Again the next day John was standing with two of his disciples,

36and he looked upon Jesus as He walked, and *said, "Behold, the Lamb of God!"

37And the two disciples heard him speak, and they followed Jesus.

38And Jesus turned, and beheld them following, and *said to them, "What do you seek?" And they said to Him, "Rabbi (which translated means Teacher), where are You staying?"

39He *said to them, "Come, and you will see." They came therefore and

τὸν Ἰησοῦν ἐρχόμενον πρὸς αὐτόν, καὶ
- Jesus coming toward him, and

λέγει· ἴδε ὁ ἀμνὸς τοῦ θεοῦ ὁ αἴρων
says : Behold[,] the Lamb - of God - taking

τὴν ἁμαρτίαν τοῦ κόσμου. 30 οὗτός ἐστιν
the sin of the world. This is he

ὑπὲρ οὗ ἐγὼ εἶπον· ὀπίσω μου ἔρχεται
as to whom I said : After me comes

ἀνὴρ ὃς ἔμπροσθέν μου γέγονεν, ὅτι
a man who before me has become, because

πρῶτός μου ἦν. 31 κἀγὼ οὐκ ᾔδειν
first of me he was. And I knew not

αὐτόν, ἀλλ' ἵνα φανερωθῇ τῷ Ἰσραήλ,
him, but that he might be manifested - to Israel,

διὰ τοῦτο ἦλθον ἐγὼ ἐν ὕδατι βαπτίζων.
therefore came I in water baptizing.

32 Καὶ ἐμαρτύρησεν Ἰωάννης λέγων ὅτι
And witnessed John saying[,] -

τεθέαμαι τὸ πνεῦμα καταβαῖνον ὡς
I have beheld the Spirit coming down as

περιστερὰν ἐξ οὐρανοῦ, καὶ ἔμεινεν ἐπ'
a dove out of heaven, and he remained on

αὐτόν. 33 κἀγὼ οὐκ ᾔδειν αὐτόν, ἀλλ'
him. And I knew not him, but

ὁ πέμψας με βαπτίζειν ἐν ὕδατι, ἐκεῖνός
the [one] having sent me to baptize in water, that [one]

μοι εἶπεν· ἐφ' ὃν ἂν ἴδῃς τὸ πνεῦμα
to me said : On whomever thou seest the Spirit

καταβαῖνον καὶ μένον ἐπ' αὐτόν, οὗτός
coming down and remaining on him, this

ἐστιν ὁ βαπτίζων ἐν πνεύματι ἁγίῳ.
is the [one] baptizing in Spirit Holy.

34 κἀγὼ ἑώρακα, καὶ μεμαρτύρηκα ὅτι
And I have seen, and have witnessed that

οὗτός ἐστιν ὁ υἱὸς τοῦ θεοῦ.
this [one] is the Son - of God.

35 Τῇ ἐπαύριον πάλιν εἱστήκει ὁ Ἰωάννης
On the morrow again stood - John

καὶ ἐκ τῶν μαθητῶν αὐτοῦ δύο, 36 καὶ
and of the disciples of him two, and

ἐμβλέψας τῷ Ἰησοῦ περιπατοῦντι λέγει·
looking at - Jesus walking he says :

ἴδε ὁ ἀμνὸς τοῦ θεοῦ. 37 καὶ ἤκουσαν
Behold[,] the Lamb - of God. And ⁴heard

οἱ δύο μαθηταὶ αὐτοῦ λαλοῦντος καὶ
¹the ²two ³disciples ⁵him ⁶speaking and

ἠκολούθησαν τῷ Ἰησοῦ. 38 στραφεὶς δὲ
they followed - Jesus. And ²turning

ὁ Ἰησοῦς καὶ θεασάμενος αὐτοὺς ἀκολουθοῦντας
- ¹Jesus and beholding them following

λέγει αὐτοῖς· τί ζητεῖτε; οἱ δὲ εἶπαν
says to them : What seek ye? And they said

αὐτῷ· ῥαββί (ὃ λέγεται μεθερμηνευόμενον
to him : Rabbi (which is called being translated

διδάσκαλε), ποῦ μένεις; 39 λέγει αὐτοῖς·
Teacher), where remainest thou? He says to them :

ἔρχεσθε καὶ ὄψεσθε. ἦλθαν οὖν καὶ εἶδαν
Come and ye will see. They went therefore and saw

ποῦ μένει, καὶ παρ' αὐτῷ ἔμειναν τὴν
where he remains(ed), and with him remained the

ἡμέραν ἐκείνην· ὥρα ἦν ὡς δεκάτη.
day that; hour was about tenth.

40 Ἦν Ἀνδρέας ὁ ἀδελφὸς Σίμωνος Πέτρου
It was Andrew the brother of Simon Peter

εἷς ἐκ τῶν δύο τῶν ἀκουσάντων παρὰ
one of the two - hearing from

Jesus coming toward him and said, "Look, the Lamb of God, who takes away the sin of the world! 30This is the one I meant when I said, 'A man who comes after me has surpassed me because he was before me.' 31I myself did not know him, but the reason I came baptizing with water was that he might be revealed to Israel."

32Then John gave this testimony: "I saw the Spirit come down from heaven as a dove and remain on him. 33I would not have known him, except that the one who sent me to baptize with water told me, 'The man on whom you see the Spirit come down and remain is he who will baptize with the Holy Spirit.' 34I have seen and I testify that this is the Son of God."

Jesus' First Disciples

35The next day John was there again with two of his disciples. 36When he saw Jesus passing by, he said, "Look, the Lamb of God!"

37When the two disciples heard him say this, they followed Jesus. 38Turning around, Jesus saw them following and asked, "What do you want?"

They said, "Rabbi" (which means Teacher), "where are you staying?"

39"Come," he replied, "and you will see."

So they went and saw

*The Gr. here can be translated in, with or by

saw where He was staying; and they stayed with Him that day, for it was about the [h]tenth hour.

40One of the two who heard John *speak*, and followed Him, was Andrew, Simon Peter's brother.

41He *found first his own brother Simon, and *said to him, "We have found the Messiah" (which translated means Christ).

42He brought him to Jesus. Jesus looked at him, and said, "You are Simon the son of John; you shall be called Cephas" (which is translated Peter).

43The next day He purposed to go forth into Galilee, and He *found Philip. And Jesus *said to him, "Follow Me."

44Now Philip was from Bethsaida, of the city of Andrew and Peter.

45Philip *found Nathanael and *said to him, "We have found Him of whom Moses in the Law and *also the Prophets wrote, Jesus of Nazareth, the son of Joseph."

46And Nathanael *said to him, "Can any good thing come out of Nazareth?" Philip *said to him, "Come and see."

47Jesus saw Nathanael coming to Him, and *said of him, "Behold, an Israelite indeed, in whom is no guile!"

48Nathanael *said to Him, "How do You know me?" Jesus answered and said to him, "Before Philip called you, when you were under the fig tree, I saw you."

49Nathanael answered Him, "Rabbi, You are the Son of God; You are the King of Israel."

50Jesus answered and said to him, "Because I said to you that I saw you under the fig tree, do you believe? You shall see greater things than these."

51And He *said to him, "Truly, truly, I say to you, you shall see the heavens

Middle column (interlinear)

Ἰωάννου καὶ ἀκολουθησάντων αὐτῷ·
John and following him;

41 εὑρίσκει οὗτος πρῶτον τὸν ἀδελφὸν τὸν
³finds ¹this one ²first ⁴the(his) ⁵brother –

ἴδιον Σίμωνα καὶ λέγει αὐτῷ· εὑρήκαμεν
⁶own Simon and tells him: We have found

τὸν Μεσσίαν (ὅ ἐστιν μεθερμηνευόμενον
the Messiah (which is being translated

χριστός). 42 ἤγαγεν αὐτὸν πρὸς τὸν
Christ). He led him to –

Ἰησοῦν. ἐμβλέψας αὐτῷ ὁ Ἰησοῦς εἶπεν·
Jesus. Looking at him – Jesus said:

σὺ εἶ Σίμων ὁ υἱὸς Ἰωάννου, σὺ κληθήσῃ
Thou art Simon the son of John, thou shalt be called

Κηφᾶς (ὃ ἑρμηνεύεται Πέτρος). 43 Τῇ
Cephas (which is translated Peter). On the

ἐπαύριον ἠθέλησεν ἐξελθεῖν εἰς τὴν Γαλιλαίαν,
morrow he wished to go forth into – Galilee,

καὶ εὑρίσκει Φίλιππον. καὶ λέγει αὐτῷ ὁ
and finds Philip. And says to him –

Ἰησοῦς· ἀκολούθει μοι. 44 ἦν δὲ ὁ
Jesus: Follow me. Now was –

Φίλιππος ἀπὸ Βηθσαϊδά, ἐκ τῆς πόλεως
Philip from Bethsaida, of the city

Ἀνδρέου καὶ Πέτρου. 45 εὑρίσκει Φίλιππος
of Andrew and of Peter. ²Finds ¹Philip

τὸν Ναθαναὴλ καὶ λέγει αὐτῷ· ὃν ἔγραψεν
– ³Nathanael and tells him: [He] whom wrote

Μωϋσῆς ἐν τῷ νόμῳ καὶ οἱ προφῆται
Moses in the law and the prophets

εὑρήκαμεν, Ἰησοῦν υἱὸν τοῦ Ἰωσὴφ τὸν
we have found, Jesus son of Joseph –

ἀπὸ Ναζαρέθ. 46 καὶ εἶπεν αὐτῷ
from Nazareth. And said to him

Ναθαναήλ· ἐκ Ναζαρὲθ δύναταί τι ἀγαθὸν
Nathanael: Out of Nazareth can anything good

εἶναι; λέγει αὐτῷ ὁ Φίλιππος· ἔρχου καὶ
to be? Says to him – Philip: Come and

ἴδε. 47 εἶδεν Ἰησοῦς τὸν Ναθαναὴλ
see. ²Saw ¹Jesus – ³Nathanael

ἐρχόμενον πρὸς αὐτὸν καὶ λέγει περὶ
coming toward him and says concerning

αὐτοῦ· ἴδε ἀληθῶς Ἰσραηλίτης, ἐν ᾧ
him: Behold[,] truly an Israelite, in whom

δόλος οὐκ ἔστιν. 48 λέγει αὐτῷ Ναθαναήλ·
guile is not. Says to him Nathanael:

πόθεν με γινώσκεις; ἀπεκρίθη Ἰησοῦς καὶ
Whence me knowest thou? Answered Jesus and

εἶπεν αὐτῷ· πρὸ τοῦ σε Φίλιππον φωνῆσαι
said to him: Before the thee Philip to call[b]
                                  = Philip called thee

ὄντα ὑπὸ τὴν συκῆν εἶδόν σε. 49 ἀπεκρίθη
being under the fig-tree I saw thee. Answered

αὐτῷ Ναθαναήλ· ῥαββί, σὺ εἶ ὁ υἱὸς τοῦ
him Nathanael: Rabbi, thou art the Son

θεοῦ, σὺ βασιλεὺς εἶ τοῦ Ἰσραήλ.
of God, thou king art of Israel.

50 ἀπεκρίθη Ἰησοῦς καὶ εἶπεν αὐτῷ·
Answered Jesus and said to him:

ὅτι εἶπόν σοι ὅτι εἶδόν σε ὑποκάτω τῆς
Because I told thee that I saw thee underneath the

συκῆς, πιστεύεις; μείζω τούτων ὄψῃ.
fig-tree, believest thou? greater [than] these things thou shalt see.

51 καὶ λέγει αὐτῷ· ἀμὴν ἀμὴν λέγω
And he says to him: Truly truly I tell

ὑμῖν, ὄψεσθε τὸν οὐρανὸν ἀνεῳγότα καὶ
you, ye shall see the heaven *having been* opened and

where he was staying, and spent that day with him. It was about the tenth hour.

40Andrew, Simon Peter's brother, was one of the two who heard what John had said and who had followed Jesus. 41The first thing Andrew did was to find his brother Simon and tell him, "We have found the Messiah" (that is, the Christ). 42And he brought him to Jesus.

Jesus looked at him and said, "You are Simon son of John. You will be called Cephas" (which, when translated, is Peter[i]).

Jesus Calls Philip and Nathanael

43The next day Jesus decided to leave for Galilee. Finding Philip, he said to him, "Follow me."

44Philip, like Andrew and Peter, was from the town of Bethsaida. 45Philip found Nathanael and told him, "We have found the one Moses wrote about in the Law, and about whom the prophets also wrote— Jesus of Nazareth, the son of Joseph."

46"Nazareth! Can anything good come from there?" Nathanael asked.

"Come and see," said Philip.

47When Jesus saw Nathanael approaching, he said of him, "Here is a true Israelite, in whom there is nothing false."

48"How do you know me?" Nathanael asked.

Jesus answered, "I saw you while you were still under the fig tree before Philip called you."

49Then Nathanael declared, "Rabbi, you are the Son of God; you are the King of Israel."

50Jesus said, "You believe[j] because I told you I saw you under the fig tree. You shall see greater things than that." 51He then added, "I tell you[k] the truth, you[k] shall see heaven

[h] Perhaps 10 a.m. (Roman time)

[i]42 Both *Cephas* (Aramaic) and *Peter* (Greek) mean *rock*.
[j]50 Or *Do you believe . . . ?*
[k]51 The Greek is plural.

opened, and the angels of God ascending and descending on the Son of Man.''

Chapter 2

Miracle at Cana

AND on the third day there was a wedding in Cana of Galilee, and the mother of Jesus was there; 2and Jesus also was invited, and His disciples, to the wedding.

3And when the wine gave out, the mother of Jesus *said to Him, ''They have no wine.''

4And Jesus *said to her, ''Woman, what do I have to do with you? My hour has not yet come.''

5His mother *said to the servants, ''Whatever He says to you, do it.''

6Now there were six stone waterpots set there for the Jewish custom of purification, containing twenty or thirty gallons each.

7Jesus *said to them, ''Fill the waterpots with water.'' And they filled them up to the brim.

8And He *said to them, ''Draw some out now, and take it to the headwaiter.'' And they took it to him.

9And when the headwaiter tasted the water which had become wine, and did not know where it came from (but the servants who had drawn the water knew), the headwaiter *called the bridegroom,

10and *said to him, ''Every man serves the good wine first, and when men have drunk freely, then that which is poorer; you have kept the good wine until now.''

11This beginning of His signs Jesus did in Cana of Galilee, and manifested His glory, and His disciples believed in Him.

12After this He went down to Capernaum, He

ⁱOr, steward

τοὺς ἀγγέλους τοῦ θεοῦ ἀναβαίνοντας καὶ
the   angels   -   of God   going up   and
καταβαίνοντας ἐπὶ τὸν υἱὸν τοῦ ἀνθρώπου.
coming down   on   the   Son   -   of man.

2 Καὶ τῇ ἡμέρᾳ τῇ τρίτῃ γάμος ἐγένετο
And on the day   the   third   a wedding there was
ἐν Κανὰ τῆς Γαλιλαίας, καὶ ἦν ἡ μήτηρ
in   Cana   -   of Galilee,   and   was the mother
τοῦ Ἰησοῦ ἐκεῖ· **2** ἐκλήθη δὲ καὶ ὁ
-   of Jesus   there;   and was invited both   -
Ἰησοῦς καὶ οἱ μαθηταὶ αὐτοῦ εἰς τὸν
Jesus   and   the   disciples   of him   to   the
γάμον. **3** καὶ ὑστερήσαντος οἴνου λέγει ἡ
wedding.   And   lacking   wine^a   says   the
                 = when wine was lacking
μήτηρ τοῦ Ἰησοῦ πρὸς αὐτόν· οἶνον
mother   -   of Jesus   to   him :   wine
οὐκ ἔχουσιν. **4** καὶ λέγει αὐτῇ ὁ Ἰησοῦς·
they have not.   And   says   to her   -   Jesus :
τί ἐμοὶ καὶ σοί, γύναι; οὔπω ἥκει ἡ
What to me   and   to thee,   woman?   not yet is come the
ὥρα μου. **5** λέγει ἡ μήτηρ αὐτοῦ τοῖς
hour   of me.   Says   the   mother   of him   to the
διακόνοις· ὅ τι ἂν λέγῃ ὑμῖν, ποιήσατε.
servants: Whatever   he tells   you,   do ye.
6 ἦσαν δὲ ἐκεῖ λίθιναι ὑδρίαι ἓξ κατὰ
Now there were there   stone   water-pots   six   according to
τὸν καθαρισμὸν τῶν Ἰουδαίων κείμεναι,
the   purifying   of the   Jews   lying,
χωροῦσαι ἀνὰ μετρητὰς δύο ἢ τρεῖς.
containing   each†   measures   two   or   three.
7 λέγει αὐτοῖς ὁ Ἰησοῦς· γεμίσατε τὰς
Tells   them   -   Jesus :   Fill ye   the
ὑδρίας ὕδατος. καὶ ἐγέμισαν αὐτὰς ἕως
water-pots of(with) water.   And   they filled   them   up to
ἄνω. **8** καὶ λέγει αὐτοῖς· ἀντλήσατε νῦν
[the] top.   And   he tells   them :   Draw   now
καὶ φέρετε τῷ ἀρχιτρικλίνῳ. οἱ δὲ
and   carry   to the master of the feast.   And they
ἤνεγκαν. **9** ὡς δὲ ἐγεύσατο ὁ ἀρχιτρίκλινος
carried.   But when   tasted   the master of the feast
τὸ ὕδωρ οἶνον γεγενημένον, καὶ οὐκ ᾔδει
the   water   ²wine   ¹having become,   and   did not know
πόθεν ἐστίν, οἱ δὲ διάκονοι ᾔδεισαν οἱ
whence   it is(was),   but the   servants   knew the [ones]
ἠντληκότες τὸ ὕδωρ, φωνεῖ τὸν νυμφίον
having drawn   the   water,   ³calls   ⁴the   ⁵bridegroom
ὁ ἀρχιτρίκλινος **10** καὶ λέγει αὐτῷ· πᾶς
¹the   ²master of the feast   and   says   to him :   Every
ἄνθρωπος πρῶτον τὸν καλὸν οἶνον τίθησιν,
man   first   the   good   wine   sets forth,
καὶ ὅταν μεθυσθῶσιν τὸν ἐλάσσω· σὺ
and   when   they become drunk the   worse;   thou
τετήρηκας τὸν καλὸν οἶνον ἕως ἄρτι.
hast kept   the   good   wine   until   now.
11 Ταύτην ἐποίησεν ἀρχὴν τῶν σημείων ὁ
¹This   ⁵did   ²beginning ³of the   ⁴signs   -
Ἰησοῦς ἐν Κανὰ τῆς Γαλιλαίας καὶ
Jesus   in   Cana   -   of Galilee   and
ἐφανέρωσεν τὴν δόξαν αὐτοῦ, καὶ ἐπίστευσαν
manifested   the   glory   of him,   and   believed
εἰς αὐτὸν οἱ μαθηταὶ αὐτοῦ.
in   him   the   disciples   of him.
12 Μετὰ τοῦτο κατέβη εἰς Καφαρναοὺμ
After   this   went down   to   Capernaum

---

open, and the angels of God ascending and descending on the Son of Man.''

Chapter 2

Jesus Changes Water to Wine

ON the third day a wedding took place at Cana in Galilee. Jesus' mother was there, 2and Jesus and his disciples had also been invited to the wedding. 3When the wine was gone, Jesus' mother said to him, ''They have no more wine.''

4''Dear woman, why do you involve me?'' Jesus replied. ''My time has not yet come.''

5His mother said to the servants, ''Do whatever he tells you.''

6Nearby stood six stone water jars, the kind used by the Jews for ceremonial washing, each holding from twenty to thirty gallons.ⁱ

7Jesus said to the servants, ''Fill the jars with water''; so they filled them to the brim.

8Then he told them, ''Now draw some out and take it to the master of the banquet.''

They did so, 9and the master of the banquet tasted the water that had been turned into wine. He did not realize where it had come from, though the servants who had drawn the water knew. Then he called the bridegroom aside 10and said, ''Everyone brings out the choice wine first and then the cheaper wine after the guests have had too much to drink; but you have saved the best till now.''

11This, the first of his miraculous signs, Jesus performed in Cana of Galilee. He thus revealed his glory, and his disciples put their faith in him.

Jesus Clears the Temple

12After this he went down to Capernaum with his

ⁱ6 Greek two to three metretes (probably about 75 to 115 liters)

and His mother, and *His* brothers, and His disciples; and there they stayed a few days.

First Passover—Cleansing the Temple

13And the Passover of the Jews was at hand, and Jesus went up to Jerusalem.

14And He found in the temple those who were selling oxen and sheep and doves, and the money-changers seated.

15And He made a scourge of cords, and drove *them* all out of the temple, with the sheep and the oxen; and He poured out the coins of the moneychangers, and overturned their tables;

16and to those who were selling the doves He said, "Take these things away; stop making My Father's house a house of merchandise."

17His disciples remembered that it was written, "ZEAL FOR THY HOUSE WILL CONSUME ME."

18The Jews therefore answered and said to Him, "What sign do You show to us, seeing that You do these things?"

19Jesus answered and said to them, "Destroy this temple, and in three days I will raise it up."

20The Jews therefore said, "It took forty-six years to build this temple, and will You raise it up in three days?"

21But He was speaking of the temple of His body.

22When therefore He was raised from the dead, His disciples remembered that He said this; and they believed the Scripture, and the word which Jesus had spoken.

23Now when He was in Jerusalem at the Passover, during the feast, many believed in His name, behold-

αὐτὸς καὶ ἡ μήτηρ αὐτοῦ καὶ
he and the mother of him and

οἱ ἀδελφοὶ καὶ οἱ μαθηταὶ αὐτοῦ, καὶ
the brothers and the disciples of him, and

ἐκεῖ ἔμειναν οὐ πολλὰς ἡμέρας.
there remained not many days.

13 Καὶ ἐγγὺς ἦν τὸ πάσχα τῶν Ἰουδαίων,
And near was the Passover of the Jews,

καὶ ἀνέβη εἰς Ἱεροσόλυμα ὁ Ἰησοῦς.
and went up to Jerusalem - Jesus.

14 καὶ εὗρεν ἐν τῷ ἱερῷ τοὺς πωλοῦντας
And he found in the temple the [ones] selling

βόας καὶ πρόβατα καὶ περιστερὰς καὶ τοὺς
oxen and sheep and doves and the

κερματιστὰς καθημένους, **15** καὶ ποιήσας
coindealers sitting, and having made

φραγέλλιον ἐκ σχοινίων πάντας ἐξέβαλεν
a lash out of ropes ²all ¹he expelled

ἐκ τοῦ ἱεροῦ, τά τε πρόβατα καὶ τοὺς
out of the temple, both the sheep and the

βόας, καὶ τῶν κολλυβιστῶν ἐξέχεεν τὰ
oxen, and ⁴of the ¹moneychangers ²poured out ³the

κέρματα καὶ τὰς τραπέζας ἀνέτρεψεν,
⁵coins ⁶and ⁸the ⁹tables ⁷overturned,

16 καὶ τοῖς τὰς περιστερὰς πωλοῦσιν
and ¹to the [ones] ⁴the ⁵doves ²selling

εἶπεν· ἄρατε ταῦτα ἐντεῦθεν, μὴ ποιεῖτε
¹said: Take these things hence, do not make

τὸν οἶκον τοῦ πατρός μου οἶκον ἐμπορίου.
the house of the Father of me a house of merchandise.

17 ἐμνήσθησαν οἱ μαθηταὶ αὐτοῦ ὅτι
Remembered the disciples of him that

γεγραμμένον ἐστίν· ὁ ζῆλος τοῦ οἴκου
having been written it is: The zeal of the house

σου καταφάγεταί με. **18** ἀπεκρίθησαν οὖν
of thee will consume me. Answered therefore

οἱ Ἰουδαῖοι καὶ εἶπαν αὐτῷ· τί σημεῖον
the Jews and said to him: What sign

δεικνύεις ἡμῖν, ὅτι ταῦτα ποιεῖς;
showest thou to us, because these things thou doest?

19 ἀπεκρίθη Ἰησοῦς καὶ εἶπεν αὐτοῖς· λύσατε τὸν
Answered Jesus and said to them: Destroy -

ναὸν τοῦτον, καὶ ἐν τρισὶν ἡμέραις ἐγερῶ αὐτόν.
shrine this, and in three days I will raise it.

20 εἶπαν οὖν οἱ Ἰουδαῖοι· τεσσεράκοντα
Said therefore the Jews: In forty

καὶ ἓξ ἔτεσιν οἰκοδομήθη ὁ ναὸς οὗτος,
and six years was built - shrine this,

καὶ σὺ ἐν τρισὶν ἡμέραις ἐγερεῖς αὐτόν;
and thou in three days wilt raise it?

21 ἐκεῖνος δὲ ἔλεγεν περὶ τοῦ ναοῦ τοῦ
But that [one]* spoke about the shrine of the

σώματος αὐτοῦ. **22** ὅτε οὖν ἠγέρθη ἐκ
body of him. When therefore he was raised from

νεκρῶν, ἐμνήσθησαν οἱ μαθηταὶ αὐτοῦ
[the] dead, remembered the disciples of him

ὅτι τοῦτο ἔλεγεν, καὶ ἐπίστευσαν τῇ
that this he said, and they believed the

γραφῇ καὶ τῷ λόγῳ ὃν εἶπεν ὁ Ἰησοῦς.
scripture and the word which said - Jesus.

23 Ὡς δὲ ἦν ἐν τοῖς Ἱεροσολύμοις ἐν
And when he was in - Jerusalem at

τῷ πάσχα ἐν τῇ ἑορτῇ, πολλοὶ ἐπίστευσαν
the Passover at the feast, many believed

εἰς τὸ ὄνομα αὐτοῦ, θεωροῦντες αὐτοῦ τὰ
in the name of him, beholding of him the

mother and brothers and his disciples. There they stayed for a few days.

13When it was almost time for the Jewish Passover, Jesus went up to Jerusalem. 14In the temple courts he found men selling cattle, sheep and doves, and others sitting at tables exchanging money. 15So he made a whip out of cords, and drove all from the temple area, both sheep and cattle; he scattered the coins of the money changers and overturned their tables. 16To those who sold doves he said, "Get these out of here! How dare you turn my Father's house into a market!"

17His disciples remembered that it is written: "Zeal for your house will consume me." *m*

18Then the Jews demanded of him, "What miraculous sign can you show us to prove your authority to do all this?"

19Jesus answered them, "Destroy this temple, and I will raise it again in three days."

20The Jews replied, "It has taken forty-six years to build this temple, and you are going to raise it in three days?" 21But the temple he had spoken of was his body. 22After he was raised from the dead, his disciples recalled what he had said. Then they believed the Scripture and the words that Jesus had spoken.

23Now while he was in Jerusalem at the Passover Feast, many people saw

---

* John repeatedly uses the demonstrative adjective ἐκεῖνος in the sense of "he," referring to Christ.

m 17 Psalm 69:9

ing His signs which He was doing.

24But Jesus, on His part, was not entrusting Himself to them, for He knew all men,

25and because He did not need anyone to bear witness concerning man for He Himself knew what was in man.

Chapter 3

The New Birth

NOW there was a man of the Pharisees, named Nicodemus, a ruler of the Jews;

2this man came to Him by night, and said to Him, "Rabbi, we know that You have come from God *as* a teacher; for no one can do these signs that You do unless God is with him."

3Jesus answered and said to him, "Truly, truly, I say to you, unless one is born again, he cannot see the kingdom of God."

4Nicodemus *said to Him, "How can a man be born when he is old? He cannot enter a second time into his mother's womb and be born, can he?"

5Jesus answered, "Truly, truly, I say to you, unless one is born of water and the Spirit, he cannot enter into the kingdom of God.

6"That which is born of the flesh is flesh, and that which is born of the Spirit is spirit.

7"Do not marvel that I said to you, 'You must be born again.'

8"The wind blows where it wishes and you hear the sound of it, but do not know where it comes from and where it is going; so is everyone who is born of the Spirit."

9Nicodemus answered and said to Him, "How can these things be?"

σημεῖα ἃ ἐποίει· 24 αὐτὸς δὲ Ἰησοῦς
signs which he was doing; [1]but [3][him]self, [2]Jesus

οὐκ ἐπίστευεν αὐτὸν αὐτοῖς διὰ τὸ αὐτὸν
did not commit himself to them because of the him
= because he knew

γινώσκειν πάντας, 25 καὶ ὅτι οὐ χρείαν εἶχεν
to know[b] all men, and because no need he had

ἵνα τις μαρτυρήσῃ περὶ τοῦ ἀνθρώπου·
that anyone should witness concerning - man;

αὐτὸς γὰρ ἐγίνωσκεν τί ἦν ἐν τῷ ἀνθρώπῳ.
for he knew what was in - man.

3 Ἦν δὲ ἄνθρωπος ἐκ τῶν Φαρισαίων,
Now there was a man of the Pharisees,

Νικόδημος ὄνομα αὐτῷ, ἄρχων τῶν
Nicodemus name to him[e], a ruler of the
= his name,

Ἰουδαίων· 2 οὗτος ἦλθεν πρὸς αὐτὸν νυκτὸς
Jews; this man came to him of(by) night

καὶ εἶπεν αὐτῷ· ῥαββί, οἴδαμεν ὅτι ἀπὸ
and said to him : Rabbi, we know that from

θεοῦ ἐλήλυθας διδάσκαλος· οὐδεὶς γὰρ
God thou hast come a teacher; for no one

δύναται ταῦτα τὰ σημεῖα ποιεῖν ἃ σὺ
can these - signs *to* do which thou

ποιεῖς, ἐὰν μὴ ᾖ ὁ θεὸς μετ' αὐτοῦ.
doest, except [3]is - [1]God with him.

3 ἀπεκρίθη Ἰησοῦς καὶ εἶπεν αὐτῷ· ἀμὴν
Answered Jesus and said to him : Truly

ἀμὴν λέγω σοι, ἐὰν μή τις γεννηθῇ
truly I tell thee, except anyone is born

ἄνωθεν, οὐ δύναται ἰδεῖν τὴν βασιλείαν
from above, he cannot *to* see the kingdom

τοῦ θεοῦ. 4 λέγει πρὸς αὐτὸν ὁ Νικόδημος·
- of God. Says to him - Nicodemus :

πῶς δύναται ἄνθρωπος γεννηθῆναι γέρων ὤν;
How can a man *to* be born old being?

μὴ δύναται εἰς τὴν κοιλίαν τῆς μητρὸς
not can he into the womb of the mother

αὐτοῦ δεύτερον εἰσελθεῖν καὶ γεννηθῆναι;
of him secondly *to* enter and *to* be born?

5 ἀπεκρίθη Ἰησοῦς· ἀμὴν ἀμὴν λέγω σοι,
Answered Jesus : Truly truly I tell thee,

ἐὰν μή τις γεννηθῇ ἐξ ὕδατος καὶ
except anyone is born of water and

πνεύματος, οὐ δύναται εἰσελθεῖν εἰς τὴν
spirit, he cannot *to* enter into the

βασιλείαν τοῦ θεοῦ. 6 τὸ γεγεννημένον ἐκ
kingdom - of God. The thing *having been* born of

τῆς σαρκὸς σάρξ ἐστιν, καὶ τὸ γεγεννημένον
the flesh flesh is, and the thing *having been* born

ἐκ τοῦ πνεύματος πνεῦμά ἐστιν. 7 μὴ
of the Spirit spirit is. not

θαυμάσῃς ὅτι εἶπόν σοι· δεῖ ὑμᾶς
Marvel because I told thee : It behoves you

γεννηθῆναι ἄνωθεν. 8 τὸ πνεῦμα ὅπου θέλει
to be born from above. The spirit(?wind) where it wishes

πνεῖ, καὶ τὴν φωνὴν αὐτοῦ ἀκούεις, ἀλλ'
blows, and the sound of it thou hearest, but

οὐκ οἶδας πόθεν ἔρχεται καὶ ποῦ ὑπάγει·
thou knowest not whence it comes and whither it goes;

οὕτως ἐστὶν πᾶς ὁ γεγεννημένος ἐκ τοῦ
so is everyone *having been* born of the

πνεύματος. 9 ἀπεκρίθη Νικόδημος καὶ
Spirit. Answered Nicodemus and

εἶπεν αὐτῷ· πῶς δύναται ταῦτα γενέσθαι;
said to him : How can these things *to* come about?

---

the miraculous signs he was doing and believed in his name.[n] 24But Jesus would not entrust himself to them, for he knew all men. 25He did not need man's testimony about man, for he knew what was in a man.

Chapter 3

Jesus Teaches Nicodemus

NOW there was a man of the Pharisees named Nicodemus, a member of the Jewish ruling council. 2He came to Jesus at night and said, "Rabbi, we know you are a teacher who has come from God. For no one could perform the miraculous signs you are doing if God were not with him."

3In reply Jesus declared, "I tell you the truth, no one can see the kingdom of God unless he is born again.[o]"

4"How can a man be born when he is old?" Nicodemus asked. "Surely he cannot enter a second time into his mother's womb to be born!"

5Jesus answered, "I tell you the truth, no one can enter the kingdom of God unless he is born of water and the Spirit. 6Flesh gives birth to flesh, but the Spirit[p] gives birth to spirit. 7You should not be surprised at my saying, 'You[q] must be born again.' 8The wind blows wherever it pleases. You hear its sound, but you cannot tell where it comes from or where it is going. So it is with everyone born of the Spirit."

9"How can this be?" Nicodemus asked.

*n*23 Or *and believed in him*
*o*3 Or *born from above;* also in verse 7
*p*6 Or *but spirit*
*q*7 The Greek is plural.

¹⁰Jesus answered and said to him, "Are you the teacher of Israel, and do not understand these things?

¹¹"Truly, truly, I say to you, we speak that which we know, and bear witness of that which we have seen; and you do not receive our witness.

¹²"If I told you earthly things and you do not believe, how shall you believe if I tell you heavenly things?

¹³"And no one has ascended into heaven, but He who descended from heaven, *even* the Son of Man.

¹⁴"And as Moses lifted up the serpent in the wilderness, even so must the Son of Man be lifted up;

¹⁵that whoever *ʲ* believes may in Him have eternal life.

¹⁶"For God so loved the world, that He gave His only begotten Son, that whoever believes in Him should not perish, but have eternal life.

¹⁷"For God did not send the Son into the world to judge the world, but that the world should be saved through Him.

¹⁸"He who believes in Him is not judged; he who does not believe has been judged already, because he has not believed in the name of the only begotten Son of God.

¹⁹"And this is the judgment, that the light is come into the world, and men loved the darkness rather than the light; for their deeds were evil.

²⁰"For everyone who does evil hates the light, and does not come to the light, lest his deeds should be exposed.

²¹"But he who practices the truth comes to the light, that his deeds may be mani-

---

10 ἀπεκρίθη Ἰησοῦς καὶ εἶπεν αὐτῷ· σὺ
Answered Jesus and said to him : Thou

εἶ ὁ διδάσκαλος τοῦ Ἰσραὴλ καὶ ταῦτα
art the teacher - of Israel and these things

οὐ γινώσκεις; **11** ἀμὴν ἀμὴν λέγω σοι ὅτι
knowest not? Truly truly I tell thee[,]

ὃ οἴδαμεν λαλοῦμεν καὶ ὃ ἑωράκαμεν
What we know we speak and what we have seen

μαρτυροῦμεν, καὶ τὴν μαρτυρίαν ἡμῶν
we witness, and the witness of us

οὐ λαμβάνετε. **12** εἰ τὰ ἐπίγεια εἶπον
ye receive not. If the earthly things I told

ὑμῖν καὶ οὐ πιστεύετε, πῶς ἐὰν εἴπω
you and ye believe not, how if I tell

ὑμῖν τὰ ἐπουράνια πιστεύσετε; **13** καὶ
you the heavenly things will ye believe? And

οὐδεὶς ἀναβέβηκεν εἰς τὸν οὐρανὸν εἰ μὴ
no man has gone up into - heaven except

ὁ ἐκ τοῦ οὐρανοῦ καταβάς, ὁ υἱὸς
the [one] out of - heaven having come down, the Son

τοῦ ἀνθρώπου. **14** Καὶ καθὼς Μωϋσῆς ὕψωσεν
- of man. And as Moses lifted up

τὸν ὄφιν ἐν τῇ ἐρήμῳ, οὕτως ὑψωθῆναι
the serpent in the desert, so to be lifted up

δεῖ τὸν υἱὸν τοῦ ἀνθρώπου, **15** ἵνα πᾶς ὁ
it behoves the Son - of man, that everyone

πιστεύων ἐν αὐτῷ ἔχῃ ζωὴν αἰώνιον.
believing in him may have life eternal.

16 οὕτως γὰρ ἠγάπησεν ὁ θεὸς τὸν
For thus ²loved - ¹God the

κόσμον, ὥστε τὸν υἱὸν τὸν μονογενῆ
world, so as the Son the only begotten

ἔδωκεν, ἵνα πᾶς ὁ πιστεύων εἰς αὐτὸν
he gave, that everyone believing in him

μὴ ἀπόληται ἀλλ' ἔχῃ ζωὴν αἰώνιον.
may not perish but may have life eternal.

17 οὐ γὰρ ἀπέστειλεν ὁ θεὸς τὸν υἱὸν
For ²not ¹sent - ¹God the Son

εἰς τὸν κόσμον ἵνα κρίνῃ τὸν κόσμον,
into the world that he might judge the world,

ἀλλ' ἵνα σωθῇ ὁ κόσμος δι' αὐτοῦ.
but that ³might be saved ¹the ²world through him.

18 ὁ πιστεύων εἰς αὐτὸν οὐ κρίνεται·
The [one] believing in him is not judged;

ὁ μὴ πιστεύων ἤδη κέκριται, ὅτι
the [one] not believing already has been judged, because

μὴ πεπίστευκεν εἰς τὸ ὄνομα τοῦ μονογενοῦς
he has not believed in the name of the only begotten

υἱοῦ τοῦ θεοῦ. **19** αὕτη δέ ἐστιν ἡ
Son - of God. And this is the

κρίσις, ὅτι τὸ φῶς ἐλήλυθεν εἰς τὸν
judgment, that the light has come into the

κόσμον καὶ ἠγάπησαν οἱ ἄνθρωποι μᾶλλον
world and ²loved - ¹men ⁵rather

τὸ σκότος ἢ τὸ φῶς· ἦν γὰρ αὐτῶν
³the ⁴darkness ⁶than the light; for was(were) of them

πονηρὰ τὰ ἔργα. **20** πᾶς γὰρ ὁ φαῦλα
evil the works. For everyone evil things

πράσσων μισεῖ τὸ φῶς καὶ οὐκ ἔρχεται
doing hates the light and does not come

πρὸς τὸ φῶς, ἵνα μὴ ἐλεγχθῇ τὰ ἔργα
to the light, lest is(are) reproved the works

αὐτοῦ· **21** ὁ δὲ ποιῶν τὴν ἀλήθειαν ἔρχεται
of him; but the [one] doing the truth comes

πρὸς τὸ φῶς, ἵνα φανερωθῇ αὐτοῦ τὰ
to the light, that may be manifested of him the

---

¹⁰"You are Israel's teacher," said Jesus, "and do you not understand these things? ¹¹I tell you the truth, we speak of what we know, and we testify to what we have seen, but still you people do not accept our testimony. ¹²I have spoken to you of earthly things and you do not believe if I speak of heavenly things? ¹³No one has ever gone into heaven except the one who came from heaven—the Son of Man. *ʳ* ¹⁴Just as Moses lifted up the snake in the desert, so the Son of Man must be lifted up, ¹⁵that everyone who believes in him may have eternal life. *ˢ*

¹⁶"For God so loved the world that he gave his one and only Son, *ᵗ* that whoever believes in him shall not perish but have eternal life. ¹⁷For God did not send his Son into the world to condemn the world, but to save the world through him. ¹⁸Whoever believes in him is not condemned, but whoever does not believe stands condemned already because he has not believed in the name of God's one and only Son. *ᵘ* ¹⁹This is the verdict: Light has come into the world, but men loved darkness instead of light because their deeds were evil. ²⁰Everyone who does evil hates the light, and will not come into the light for fear that his deeds will be exposed. ²¹But whoever lives by the truth comes into the light, so that it may be seen plainly that

---

*ʲ*Some mss. read *believes in Him may have eternal life*

*ʳ*13 Some manuscripts *Man, who is in heaven*
*ˢ*15 Or *believes may have eternal life in him*
*ᵗ*16 Or *his only begotten Son*
*ᵘ*18 Or *God's only begotten Son*

fested as having been wrought in God.''

John's Last Testimony

22After these things Jesus and His disciples came into the land of Judea, and there He was spending time with them and baptizing.

23And John also was baptizing in Aenon near Salim, because there was much water there; and they were coming and were being baptized.

24For John had not yet been thrown into prison.

25There arose therefore a discussion on the part of John's disciples with a Jew about purification.

26And they came to John and said to him, ''Rabbi, He who was with you beyond the Jordan, to whom you have borne witness, behold, He is baptizing, and all are coming to Him.''

27John answered and said, ''A man can receive nothing, unless it has been given him from heaven.

28''You yourselves bear me witness, that I said, 'I am not the Christ,' but, 'I have been sent before Him.'

29''He who has the bride is the bridegroom; but the friend of the bridegroom, who stands and hears him, rejoices greatly because of the bridegroom's voice. And so this joy of mine has been made full.

30''He must increase, but I must decrease.

31''He who comes from above is above all, he who is of the earth is from the earth and speaks of the earth. He who comes from heaven is above all.

32''What He has seen and heard, of that He bears witness; and no man receives His witness.

33''He who has received

ἔργα ὅτι ἐν θεῷ ἐστιν εἰργασμένα.
works that in God is are *having been* wrought.

22 Μετὰ ταῦτα ἦλθεν ὁ Ἰησοῦς καὶ οἱ
After these things came - Jesus and the

μαθηταὶ αὐτοῦ εἰς τὴν Ἰουδαίαν γῆν, καὶ
disciples of him into *the* Judæan land, and

ἐκεῖ διέτριβεν μετ' αὐτῶν καὶ ἐβάπτιζεν.
there continued with them and baptized.

23 ἦν δὲ καὶ Ἰωάννης βαπτίζων ἐν
And was also John baptizing in

Αἰνὼν ἐγγὺς τοῦ Σαλίμ, ὅτι ὕδατα
Ainon near - Salim, because waters

πολλὰ ἦν ἐκεῖ, καὶ παρεγίνοντο καὶ
many was(were) there, and they came and

ἐβαπτίζοντο· **24** οὔπω γὰρ ἦν βεβλημένος
were baptized; for ³not yet ¹was ²*having been* cast

εἰς τὴν φυλακὴν Ἰωάννης. **25** Ἐγένετο
⁵into ⁶the ⁷prison ¹John. There was

οὖν ζήτησις ἐκ τῶν μαθητῶν Ἰωάννου
therefore a questioning of the disciples of John

μετὰ Ἰουδαίου περὶ καθαρισμοῦ. **26** καὶ
with a Jew about purifying. And

ἦλθον πρὸς τὸν Ἰωάννην καὶ εἶπαν αὐτῷ·
they came to - John and said to him:

ῥαββί, ὃς ἦν μετὰ σοῦ πέραν τοῦ
Rabbi, [he] who was with thee beyond the

Ἰορδάνου, ᾧ σὺ μεμαρτύρηκας, ἴδε
Jordan, to whom thou hast borne witness, behold[,]

οὗτος βαπτίζει καὶ πάντες ἔρχονται πρὸς
this man baptizes and all men are coming to

αὐτόν. **27** ἀπεκρίθη Ἰωάννης καὶ εἶπεν·
him. Answered John and said:

οὐ δύναται ἄνθρωπος λαμβάνειν οὐδὲν ἐὰν μὴ
Cannot a man *to* receive no(any)thing unless

ᾖ δεδομένον αὐτῷ ἐκ τοῦ οὐρανοῦ.
it is *having been* given to him out of - heaven.

28 αὐτοὶ ὑμεῖς μοι μαρτυρεῖτε ὅτι εἶπον·
[Your]selves ye to me bear witness that I said:

οὐκ εἰμὶ ἐγὼ ὁ χριστός, ἀλλ' ὅτι
³not ²am ¹I the Christ, but that

ἀπεσταλμένος εἰμὶ ἔμπροσθεν ἐκείνου. **29** ὁ
having been sent I am before that one.* The [one]

ἔχων τὴν νύμφην νυμφίος ἐστίν· ὁ δὲ
having the bride a bridegroom is; but the

φίλος τοῦ νυμφίου, ὁ ἑστηκὼς καὶ ἀκούων
friend of the bridegroom, - standing and hearing

αὐτοῦ, χαρᾷ χαίρει διὰ τὴν φωνὴν τοῦ
him, with joy rejoices because of the voice of the

νυμφίου. αὕτη οὖν ἡ χαρὰ ἡ ἐμὴ
bridegroom. ²This ¹therefore - ⁴joy - ³my

πεπλήρωται. **30** ἐκεῖνον δεῖ αὐξάνειν, ἐμὲ
has been fulfilled. That one it behoves to increase, ¹me

δὲ ἐλαττοῦσθαι. **31** Ὁ ἄνωθεν ἐρχόμενος
²but to decrease. The [one] from above coming

ἐπάνω πάντων ἐστίν· ὁ ὢν ἐκ τῆς γῆς
over all is; the [one] being of the earth

ἐκ τῆς γῆς ἐστιν καὶ ἐκ τῆς γῆς λαλεῖ.
of the earth is and of the earth speaks.

ὁ ἐκ τοῦ οὐρανοῦ ἐρχόμενος ἐπάνω
The [one] of - heaven coming over

πάντων ἐστίν· **32** ὃ ἑώρακεν καὶ ἤκουσεν,
all is; what he has seen and heard,

τοῦτο μαρτυρεῖ, καὶ τὴν μαρτυρίαν αὐτοῦ
this he witnesses [to], and the witness of him

οὐδεὶς λαμβάνει. **33** ὁ λαβὼν αὐτοῦ τὴν
no man receives. The [one] receiving of him the

* See note to 2. 21.

what he has done has been done through God.'' v

John the Baptist's Testimony About Jesus

22After this, Jesus and his disciples went out into the Judean countryside, where he spent some time with them, and baptized. 23Now John also was baptizing at Aenon near Salim, because there was plenty of water, and people were constantly coming to be baptized. 24(This was before John was put in prison.) 25An argument developed between some of John's disciples and a certain Jew w over the matter of ceremonial washing. 26They came to John and said to him, ''Rabbi, that man who was with you on the other side of the Jordan—the one you testified about—well, he is baptizing, and everyone is going to him.''

27To this John replied, ''A man can receive only what is given him from heaven. 28You yourselves can testify that I said, 'I am not the Christ x but am sent ahead of him.' 29The bride belongs to the bridegroom. The friend who attends the bridegroom waits and listens for him, and is full of joy when he hears the bridegroom's voice. That joy is mine, and it is now complete. 30He must become greater; I must become less.

31''The one who comes from above is above all; the one who is from the earth belongs to the earth, and speaks as one from the earth. The one who comes from heaven is above all. 32He testifies to what he has seen and heard, but no one accepts his testimony. 33The man who has accept-

v21 Some interpreters end the quotation after verse 15.
w25 Some manuscripts *and certain Jews*
x28 Or *Messiah*

His witness has set his seal to *this*, that God is true. 34"For He whom God has sent speaks the words of God; for He gives the Spirit without measure. 35"The Father loves the Son, and has given all things into His hand. 36"He who believes in the Son has eternal life; but he who does not obey the Son shall not see life, but the wrath of God abides on him."

μαρτυρίαν ἐσφράγισεν ὅτι ὁ θεὸς ἀληθής
witness   sealed   that – God   true

ἐστιν. 34 ὃν γὰρ ἀπέστειλεν ὁ θεὸς τὰ
is.   For [he] whom ²sent   – ¹God the

ῥήματα τοῦ θεοῦ λαλεῖ· οὐ γὰρ ἐκ
words   – of God speaks; for not by

μέτρου δίδωσιν τὸ πνεῦμα. 35 ὁ πατὴρ
measure he gives the Spirit.   The Father

ἀγαπᾷ τὸν υἱόν, καὶ πάντα δέδωκεν ἐν
loves   the Son, and all things has given in[to]

τῇ χειρὶ αὐτοῦ. 36 ὁ πιστεύων εἰς τὸν
the hand of him.   The [one] believing in   the

υἱὸν ἔχει ζωὴν αἰώνιον· ὁ δὲ ἀπειθῶν
Son has life eternal; but the [one] disobeying

τῷ υἱῷ οὐκ ὄψεται ζωήν, ἀλλ' ἡ ὀργὴ
the Son will not see life,   but the wrath

τοῦ θεοῦ μένει ἐπ' αὐτόν.
– of God remains on   him.

ed it has certified that God is truthful. 34For the one whom God has sent speaks the words of God, for God[y] gives the Spirit without limit. 35The Father loves the Son and has placed everything in his hands. 36Whoever believes in the Son has eternal life, but whoever rejects the Son will not see life, for God's wrath remains on him."[z]

Chapter 4

Jesus Goes to Galilee

WHEN therefore the Lord knew that the Pharisees had heard that Jesus was making and baptizing more disciples than John

2(although Jesus Himself was not baptizing, but His disciples were),

3He left Judea, and departed again into Galilee.

4And He had to pass through Samaria.

5So He *came to a city of Samaria, called Sychar, near the parcel of ground that Jacob gave to his son Joseph;

6and Jacob's well was there. Jesus therefore, being wearied from His journey, was sitting thus by the well. It was about [k] the sixth hour.

The Woman of Samaria

7There *came a woman of Samaria to draw water. Jesus *said to her, "Give Me a drink."

8For His disciples had gone away into the city to buy food.

9The Samaritan woman therefore *said to Him, "How is it that You, being a Jew, ask me for a drink since I am a Samaritan woman?" (For Jews have no dealings with Samaritans.)

10Jesus answered and said to her, "If you knew

4 Ὡς οὖν ἔγνω ὁ κύριος ὅτι ἤκουσαν
When ¹therefore ²knew ³the ⁴Lord ⁵that ⁶heard

οἱ Φαρισαῖοι ὅτι Ἰησοῦς πλείονας μαθητὰς
⁷the ⁸Pharisees that Jesus   more   disciples

ποιεῖ καὶ βαπτίζει ἢ Ἰωάννης, — 2 καίτοι γε
makes and baptizes than John,   —   though

Ἰησοῦς αὐτὸς οὐκ ἐβάπτιζεν ἀλλ' οἱ
Jesus [him]self baptized not   but the

μαθηταὶ αὐτοῦ, — 3 ἀφῆκεν τὴν Ἰουδαίαν
disciples of him, —   he left – Judæa

καὶ ἀπῆλθεν πάλιν εἰς τὴν Γαλιλαίαν.
and went away again into –   Galilee.

4 Ἔδει δὲ αὐτὸν διέρχεσθαι διὰ τῆς
And it behoved him to pass through *through* –

Σαμαρείας. 5 ἔρχεται οὖν εἰς πόλιν τῆς
Samaria.   He comes therefore to a city –

Σαμαρείας λεγομένην Σύχαρ, πλησίον τοῦ
of Samaria *being* called Sychar, near   –

χωρίου ὃ ἔδωκεν Ἰακὼβ [τῷ] Ἰωσὴφ
piece of land which ²gave ¹Jacob – to Joseph

τῷ υἱῷ αὐτοῦ· 6 ἦν δὲ ἐκεῖ πηγὴ τοῦ
the son of him; and was there a fountain –

Ἰακώβ. – οὖν Ἰησοῦς κεκοπιακὼς ἐκ
of Jacob. – Therefore Jesus having become wearied from

τῆς ὁδοιπορίας ἐκαθέζετο οὕτως ἐπὶ τῇ
the   journey   sat   thus   at   the

πηγῇ· ὥρα ἦν ὡς ἕκτη. 7 ἔρχεται γυνὴ
fountain; [the] hour was about sixth. Comes a woman

ἐκ τῆς Σαμαρείας ἀντλῆσαι ὕδωρ. λέγει
of – Samaria   to draw   water. Says

αὐτῇ ὁ Ἰησοῦς· δός μοι πεῖν. 8 οἱ γὰρ
to her – Jesus : Give me to drink. For the

μαθηταὶ αὐτοῦ ἀπεληλύθεισαν εἰς τὴν
disciples of him had gone away into the

πόλιν, ἵνα τροφὰς ἀγοράσωσιν. 9 λέγει
city, that foods they might buy. Says

οὖν αὐτῷ ἡ γυνὴ ἡ Σαμαρῖτις· πῶς
therefore to him the woman the Samaritan : How

σὺ Ἰουδαῖος ὢν παρ' ἐμοῦ πεῖν
thou ²a Jew ¹being ⁵from ⁶me ⁴to drink

αἰτεῖς γυναικὸς Σαμαρίτιδος οὔσης;
³askest ⁸woman   ⁹a Samaritan ⁷being?

[οὐ γὰρ συγχρῶνται Ἰουδαῖοι Σαμαρίταις.]
¹For ⁴not ³associate   ²Jews   ⁵with Samaritans.

10 ἀπεκρίθη Ἰησοῦς καὶ εἶπεν αὐτῇ· εἰ ᾔδεις
Answered Jesus and said to her : If thou knewest

Chapter 4

Jesus Talks With a Samaritan Woman

THE Pharisees heard that Jesus was gaining and baptizing more disciples than John, 2although in fact it was not Jesus who baptized, but his disciples. 3When the Lord learned of this, he left Judea and went back once more to Galilee. 4Now he had to go through Samaria. 5So he came to a town in Samaria called Sychar, near the plot of ground Jacob had given to his son Joseph. 6Jacob's well was there, and Jesus, tired as he was from the journey, sat down by the well. It was about the sixth hour.

7When a Samaritan woman came to draw water, Jesus said to her, "Will you give me a drink?" 8(His disciples had gone into the town to buy food.)

9The Samaritan woman said to him, "You are a Jew and I am a Samaritan woman. How can you ask me for a drink?" (For Jews do not associate with Samaritans.[a])

10Jesus answered her, "If you knew the gift of God

[k] Perhaps 6 p.m. (Roman time)

[y]34 Greek *he*
[z]36 Some interpreters end the quotation after verse 30.
[a]9 Or *do not use dishes Samaritans have used*

the gift of God, and who it is who says to you, 'Give Me a drink,' you would have asked Him, and He would have given you living water.''
¹¹She *said to Him, ''Sir, You have nothing to draw with and the well is deep; where then do You get that living water?
¹²You are not greater than our father Jacob, are You, who gave us the well, and drank of it himself, and his sons, and his cattle?''
¹³Jesus answered and said to her, ''Everyone who drinks of this water shall thirst again;
¹⁴but whoever drinks of the water that I shall give him shall never thirst; but the water that I shall give him shall become in him a well of water springing up to eternal life.''
¹⁵The woman *said to Him, ''Sir, give me this water, so I will not be thirsty, nor come all the way here to draw.''
¹⁶He *said to her, ''Go, call your husband, and come here.''
¹⁷The woman answered and said, ''I have no husband.'' Jesus *said to her, ''You have well said, 'I have no husband';
¹⁸for you have had five husbands, and the one whom you now have is not your husband; this you have said truly.''
¹⁹The woman *said to Him, ''Sir, I perceive that You are a prophet.
²⁰''Our fathers worshiped in this mountain, and you *people* say that in Jerusalem is the place where men ought to worship.''
²¹Jesus *said to her, ''Woman, believe Me, an hour is coming when neither in this mountain, nor in Jerusalem, shall you

τὴν δωρεὰν τοῦ θεοῦ, καὶ τίς ἐστιν ὁ
the gift - of God, and who is the [one]
λέγων σοι· δός μοι πεῖν, σὺ ἂν ἤτησας
saying to thee: Give me to drink, thou wouldest have asked
αὐτὸν καὶ ἔδωκεν ἄν σοι ὕδωρ ζῶν.
him and he would have given thee water living.
11 λέγει αὐτῷ· κύριε, οὔτε ἄντλημα ἔχεις
She says to him: Sir, no pail thou hast
καὶ τὸ φρέαρ ἐστὶν βαθύ· πόθεν οὖν
and the well is deep; whence then
ἔχεις τὸ ὕδωρ τὸ ζῶν; 12 μὴ σὺ μείζων
hast thou the water - living? not thou greater
εἶ τοῦ πατρὸς ἡμῶν Ἰακώβ, ὃς ἔδωκεν
art [than] the father of us Jacob, who gave
ἡμῖν τὸ φρέαρ, καὶ αὐτὸς ἐξ αὐτοῦ
us the well, and [him]self of it
ἔπιεν καὶ οἱ υἱοὶ αὐτοῦ καὶ τὰ θρέμματα
drank and the sons of him and the cattle
αὐτοῦ; 13 ἀπεκρίθη Ἰησοῦς καὶ εἶπεν αὐτῇ·
of him? Answered Jesus and said to her:
πᾶς ὁ πίνων ἐκ τοῦ ὕδατος τούτου
Everyone drinking of - water this
διψήσει πάλιν· 14 ὃς δ᾽ ἂν πίῃ ἐκ τοῦ
will thirst again; but whoever drinks of the
ὕδατος οὗ ἐγὼ δώσω αὐτῷ, οὐ μὴ
water which I will give him, by no means
διψήσει εἰς τὸν αἰῶνα, ἀλλὰ τὸ ὕδωρ ὃ
will thirst unto the age, but the water which
δώσω αὐτῷ γενήσεται ἐν αὐτῷ πηγὴ
I will give him will become in him a fountain
ὕδατος ἁλλομένου εἰς ζωὴν αἰώνιον. 15 λέγει
of water springing to life eternal. Says
πρὸς αὐτὸν ἡ γυνή· κύριε, δός μοι
to him the woman: Sir, give me
τοῦτο τὸ ὕδωρ, ἵνα μὴ διψῶ μηδὲ
this - water, that I thirst not nor
διέρχωμαι ἐνθάδε ἀντλεῖν. 16 λέγει αὐτῇ·
come through hither to draw. He says to her:
ὕπαγε φώνησον τὸν ἄνδρα σου καὶ ἐλθὲ
Go call the husband of thee and come
ἐνθάδε. 17 ἀπεκρίθη ἡ γυνὴ καὶ εἶπεν·
hither. Answered the woman and said:
οὐκ ἔχω ἄνδρα. λέγει αὐτῇ ὁ Ἰησοῦς·
I have not a husband. Says to her - Jesus:
καλῶς εἶπες ὅτι ἄνδρα οὐκ ἔχω· 18 πέντε
Well sayest thou[,] - A husband I have not; ²five
γὰρ ἄνδρας ἔσχες, καὶ νῦν ὃν ἔχεις
¹for husbands thou hadst, and now [he] whom thou hast
οὐκ ἔστιν σου ἀνήρ· τοῦτο ἀληθὲς εἴρηκας.
is not of thee husband; this truly thou hast said.
19 λέγει αὐτῷ ἡ γυνή· κύριε, θεωρῶ
Says to him the woman: Sir, I perceive
ὅτι προφήτης εἶ σύ. 20 οἱ πατέρες
that a prophet art thou. The fathers
ἡμῶν ἐν τῷ ὄρει τούτῳ προσεκύνησαν·
of us in - mountain this worshipped;
καὶ ὑμεῖς λέγετε ὅτι ἐν Ἱεροσολύμοις
and ye say that in Jerusalem
ἐστὶν ὁ τόπος ὅπου προσκυνεῖν δεῖ.
is the place where to worship it behoves.
21 λέγει αὐτῇ ὁ Ἰησοῦς· πίστευέ μοι,
Says to her - Jesus: Believe me,
γύναι, ὅτι ἔρχεται ὥρα ὅτε οὔτε ἐν
woman, that is coming an hour when neither in
τῷ ὄρει τούτῳ οὔτε ἐν Ἱεροσολύμοις
- mountain this nor in Jerusalem

and who it is that asks you for a drink, you would have asked him and he would have given you living water.''
¹¹''Sir,'' the woman said, ''you have nothing to draw with and the well is deep. Where can you get this living water? ¹²Are you greater than our father Jacob, who gave us the well and drank from it himself, as did also his sons and his flocks and herds?''
¹³Jesus answered, ''Everyone who drinks this water will be thirsty again, ¹⁴but whoever drinks the water I give him will never thirst. Indeed, the water I give him will become in him a spring of water welling up to eternal life.''
¹⁵The woman said to him, ''Sir, give me this water so that I won't get thirsty and have to keep coming here to draw water.''
¹⁶He told her, ''Go, call your husband and come back.''
¹⁷''I have no husband,'' she replied.
Jesus said to her, ''You are right when you say you have no husband. ¹⁸The fact is, you have had five husbands, and the man you now have is not your husband. What you have just said is quite true.''
¹⁹''Sir,'' the woman said, ''I can see that you are a prophet. ²⁰Our fathers worshiped on this mountain, but you Jews claim that the place where we must worship is in Jerusalem.''
²¹Jesus declared, ''Believe me, woman, a time is coming when you will worship the Father neither on

worship the Father.
22"You worship that which you do not know; we worship that which we know, for salvation is from the Jews.

23"But an hour is coming, and now is, when the true worshipers shall worship the Father in spirit and truth; for such people the Father seeks to be His worshipers.

24"God is spirit, and those who worship Him must worship in spirit and truth."

25The woman *said to Him, "I know that Messiah is coming (He who is called Christ); when that One comes, He will declare all things to us."

26Jesus *said to her, "I who speak to you am *He.*"

27And at this point His disciples came, and they marveled that He had been speaking with a woman; yet no one said, "What do You seek?" or, "Why do You speak with her?"

28So the woman left her waterpot, and went into the city, and *said to the men

29"Come, see a man who told me all the things that I *have* done; this is not the Christ, is it?"

30They went out of the city, and were coming to Him.

31In the meanwhile the disciples were requesting Him, saying, "Rabbi, eat."

32But He said to them, "I have food to eat that you do not know about."

33The disciples therefore were saying to one another, "No one brought Him *anything* to eat, did he?"

34Jesus *said to them, "My food is to do the will of Him who sent Me, and to accomplish His work.

35"Do you not say,

προσκυνήσετε τῷ πατρί. 22 ὑμεῖς προσκυ-
will ye worship　the　Father.　Ye　wor-
νεῖτε ὃ οὐκ οἴδατε, ἡμεῖς προσκυνοῦμεν ὃ
ship　what ye know not,　we　worship　what
οἴδαμεν, ὅτι ἡ σωτηρία ἐκ τῶν Ἰουδαίων
we know, because –　salvation　of　the　Jews
ἐστίν· 23 ἀλλὰ ἔρχεται ὥρα καὶ νῦν
is;　　but　is coming　an hour　and　now
ἐστιν, ὅτε οἱ ἀληθινοὶ προσκυνηταὶ προσκυνή-
is,　when the　true　　worshippers　will
σουσιν τῷ πατρὶ ἐν πνεύματι καὶ ἀληθείᾳ·
worship　the　Father　in　spirit　and　truth;
καὶ γὰρ ὁ πατὴρ τοιούτους ζητεῖ τοὺς
for indeed　the　Father　²such　²seeks　the [ones]
προσκυνοῦντας αὐτόν· 24 πνεῦμα ὁ θεός,
worshipping　him;　　God [is] spirit,*
καὶ τοὺς προσκυνοῦντας ἐν πνεύματι καὶ
and　¹the [ones]　²worshipping　⁴in　⁵spirit　⁷and
ἀληθείᾳ δεῖ προσκυνεῖν. 25 λέγει αὐτῷ
⁶truth　¹it behoves　⁴to worship.　Says　to him
ἡ γυνή· οἶδα ὅτι Μεσσίας ἔρχεται, ὁ
the woman : I know　that　Messiah　is coming, the [one]
λεγόμενος χριστός· ὅταν ἔλθῃ ἐκεῖνος,
being called　Christ;　when　comes　that one,
ἀναγγελεῖ ἡμῖν ἅπαντα. 26 λέγει αὐτῇ
he will announce　to us　all things.　Says　to her
ὁ Ἰησοῦς· ἐγώ εἰμι, ὁ λαλῶν σοι.
–　Jesus :　I　am,　the [one] speaking to thee.
27 Καὶ ἐπὶ τούτῳ ἦλθαν οἱ μαθηταὶ
And　on　this　came　the　disciples
αὐτοῦ, καὶ ἐθαύμαζον ὅτι μετὰ γυναικὸς
of him,　and　marvelled　that　with　a woman
ἐλάλει· οὐδεὶς μέντοι εἶπεν· τί ζητεῖς
he was speaking; no one however said :　What seekest thou
ἢ τί λαλεῖς μετ' αὐτῆς; 28 ἀφῆκεν οὖν
or　why speakest thou with　her?　⁴Left ³therefore
τὴν ὑδρίαν αὐτῆς ἡ γυνὴ καὶ ἀπῆλθεν
³the　⁵waterpot　⁷of her　¹the　²woman　and　went away
εἰς τὴν πόλιν, καὶ λέγει τοῖς ἀνθρώποις·
into　the　city,　and　says　to the　men :
29 δεῦτε ἴδετε ἄνθρωπον ὃς εἶπέν μοι
Come　see　a man　who　told　me
πάντα ἃ ἐποίησα· μήτι οὗτός ἐστιν ὁ
all things which　I did;　not　this　is　the
χριστός; 30 ἐξῆλθον ἐκ τῆς πόλεως καὶ
Christ?　They went forth out of　the　city　and
ἤρχοντο πρὸς αὐτόν. 31 Ἐν τῷ μεταξὺ
came　to　him.　　In　the　meantime
ἠρώτων αὐτὸν οἱ μαθηταὶ λέγοντες· ῥαββί,
asked　him　the　disciples　saying :　Rabbi,
φάγε. 32 ὁ δὲ εἶπεν αὐτοῖς· ἐγὼ βρῶσιν
eat.　But he　said　to them :　I　food
ἔχω φαγεῖν ἣν ὑμεῖς οὐκ οἴδατε. 33 ἔλεγον
have　to eat which ye　do not know.　Said
οὖν οἱ μαθηταὶ πρὸς ἀλλήλους· μή τις
therefore the　disciples　to　one another :　Not anyone
ἤνεγκεν αὐτῷ φαγεῖν; 34 λέγει αὐτοῖς ὁ
brought　him　to eat?　Says　to them　–
Ἰησοῦς· ἐμὸν βρῶμά ἐστιν ἵνα ποιῶ τὸ
Jesus :　My　food　is　that I may do the
θέλημα τοῦ πέμψαντός με καὶ τελειώσω
will　of the [one] having sent　me　and　may finish
αὐτοῦ τὸ ἔργον. 35 οὐχ ὑμεῖς λέγετε ὅτι
of him　the　work.　²Not　²ye　¹say　that

this mountain nor in Jerusalem. 22You Samaritans worship what you do not know; we worship what we do know, for salvation is from the Jews. 23Yet a time is coming and has now come when the true worshipers will worship the Father in spirit and truth, for they are the kind of worshipers the Father seeks. 24God is spirit, and his worshipers must worship in spirit and in truth."

25The woman said, "I know that Messiah" (called Christ) "is coming. When he comes, he will explain everything to us."

26Then Jesus declared, "I who speak to you am he."

The Disciples Rejoin Jesus

27Just then his disciples returned and were surprised to find him talking with a woman. But no one asked, "What do you want?" or "Why are you talking with her?"

28Then, leaving her water jar, the woman went back to the town and said to the people, 29"Come, see a man who told me everything I ever did. Could this be the Christ*ᵇ*?" 30They came out of the town and made their way toward him.

31Meanwhile his disciples urged him, "Rabbi, eat something."

32But he said to them, "I have food to eat that you know nothing about."

33Then his disciples said to each other, "Could someone have brought him food?"

34"My food," said Jesus, "is to do the will of him who sent me and to finish his work. 35Do you not say,

---

* See note on 1. 1.

'There are yet four months, and *then* comes the harvest'? Behold, I say to you, lift up your eyes, and look on the fields, that they are white for harvest.
36"Already he who reaps is receiving wages, and is gathering fruit for life eternal; that he who sows and he who reaps may rejoice together.
37"For in this *case* the saying is true, 'One sows, and another reaps.'
38"I sent you to reap that for which you have not labored; others have labored, and you have entered into their labor."

The Samaritans

39And from that city many of the Samaritans believed in Him because of the word of the woman who testified, "He told me all the things that I *have* done."
40So when the Samaritans came to Him, they were asking Him to stay with them; and He stayed there two days.
41And many more believed because of His word;
42and they were saying to the woman, "It is no longer because of what you said that we believe, for we have heard for ourselves and know that this One is indeed the Savior of the world."
43And after the two days He went forth from there into Galilee.
44For Jesus Himself testified that a prophet has no honor in his own country.
45So when He came to Galilee, the Galileans received Him, having seen all the things that He did in Jerusalem at the feast; for they themselves also went to the feast.

Healing a Nobleman's Son

46He came therefore again to Cana of Galilee

ἔτι τετράμηνός ἐστιν καὶ ὁ θερισμὸς
yet   four months   it is   and   the   harvest

ἔρχεται; ἰδοὺ λέγω ὑμῖν, ἐπάρατε τοὺς
comes?   Behold   I tell   you,   lift up   the

ὀφθαλμοὺς ὑμῶν καὶ θεάσασθε τὰς χώρας,
eyes   of you   and   behold   the   fields,

ὅτι λευκαί εἰσιν πρὸς θερισμόν. ἤδη
because   white   they are   to   harvest.   Already

36 ὁ θερίζων μισθὸν λαμβάνει καὶ συνάγει
the [one] reaping   wages   receives   and   gathers

καρπὸν εἰς ζωὴν αἰώνιον, ἵνα ὁ σπείρων
fruit   to   life   eternal,   that   ¹the [one] ²sowing

ὁμοῦ χαίρῃ καὶ ὁ θερίζων. 37 ἐν γὰρ
⁷together ⁶may rejoice ³and ⁴the [one] ⁵reaping.   For in

τούτῳ ὁ λόγος ἐστὶν ἀληθινὸς ὅτι ἄλλος
this   the word   is   true   that another(one)

ἐστὶν ὁ σπείρων καὶ ἄλλος ὁ θερίζων.
is   the [one] sowing   and another the [one] reaping.

38 ἐγὼ ἀπέστειλα ὑμᾶς θερίζειν ὃ οὐχ
I   sent   you   to reap   what   not

ὑμεῖς κεκοπιάκατε· ἄλλοι κεκοπιάκασιν, καὶ
ye   have laboured;   others   have laboured,   and

ὑμεῖς εἰς τὸν κόπον αὐ ῶν εἰσεληλύθατε.
ye   into   the   labour   of them   have entered.

39 Ἐκ δὲ τῆς πόλεως ἐκείνης πολλοὶ
And out of   -   city   that   many

ἐπίστευσαν εἰς αὐτὸν τῶν Σαμαριτῶν διὰ
believed   in   him   of the   Samaritans   because of

τὸν λόγον τῆς γυναικὸς μαρτυρούσης ὅτι
the   word   of the   woman   witnessing[,]   that

εἶπέν μοι πάντα ἃ ἐποίησα. 40 ὡς
He told   me   all things   which   I did.   When

οὖν ἦλθον πρὸς αὐτὸν οἱ Σαμαρῖται,
therefore   came   to   him   the   Samaritans,

ἠρώτων αὐτὸν μεῖναι παρ' αὐτοῖς· καὶ
they asked   him   to remain   with   them;   and

ἔμεινεν ἐκεῖ δύο ἡμέρας. 41 καὶ πολλῷ
he remained   there   two   days.   And   ²more

πλείους ἐπίστευσαν διὰ τὸν λόγον αὐτοῦ,
¹many   believed   because of   the   word   of him,

42 τῇ τε γυναικὶ ἔλεγον ὅτι οὐκέτι διὰ
and to the   woman   they said[,]   - No longer because of

τὴν σὴν λαλιὰν πιστεύομεν· αὐτοὶ γὰρ
-   thy   talk   we believe;   for [our]selves

ἀκηκόαμεν, καὶ οἴδαμεν ὅτι οὗτός ἐστιν
we have heard,   and   we know   that   this man   is

ἀληθῶς ὁ σωτὴρ τοῦ κόσμου.
truly   the   Saviour   of the   world.

43 Μετὰ δὲ τὰς δύο ἡμέρας ἐξῆλθεν
And after   the   two   days   he went forth

ἐκεῖθεν εἰς τὴν Γαλιλαίαν. 44 αὐτὸς γὰρ
thence   into   -   Galilee.   For ²[him]self

Ἰησοῦς ἐμαρτύρησεν ὅτι προφήτης ἐν
¹Jesus   witnessed   that   a prophet   in

τῇ ἰδίᾳ πατρίδι τιμὴν οὐκ ἔχει. 45 ὅτε
the(his) own   native place   honour   has not.   When

οὖν ἦλθεν εἰς τὴν Γαλιλαίαν, ἐδέξαντο
therefore   he came   into   -   Galilee,   received

αὐτὸν οἱ Γαλιλαῖοι, πάντα ἑωρακότες
him   the   Galilæans,   all things   having seen

ὅσα ἐποίησεν ἐν Ἱεροσολύμοις ἐν τῇ
which   he did   in   Jerusalem   at   the

ἑορτῇ· καὶ αὐτοὶ γὰρ ἦλθον εἰς τὴν
feast;   ²also   ³they   ¹for   went   to   the

ἑορτήν. 46 *Ἦλθεν οὖν πάλιν εἰς τὴν
feast.   He came   therefore   again   to   -

'Four months more and then the harvest'? I tell you, open your eyes and look at the fields! They are ripe for harvest. 36Even now the reaper draws his wages, even now he harvests the crop for eternal life, so that the sower and the reaper may be glad together. 37Thus the saying 'One sows and another reaps' is true. 38I sent you to reap what you have not worked for. Others have done the hard work, and you have reaped the benefits of their labor."

Many Samaritans Believe

39Many of the Samaritans from that town believed in him because of the woman's testimony, "He told me everything I ever did." 40So when the Samaritans came to him, they urged him to stay with them, and he stayed two days. 41And because of his words many more became believers.
42They said to the woman, "We no longer believe just because of what you said; now we have heard for ourselves, and we know that this man really is the Savior of the world."

Jesus Heals the Official's Son

43After the two days he left for Galilee. 44(Now Jesus himself had pointed out that a prophet has no honor in his own country.) 45When he arrived in Galilee, the Galileans welcomed him. They had seen all that he had done in Jerusalem at the Passover Feast, for they also had been there.
46Once more he visited Cana in Galilee, where he

where He had made the water wine. And there was a certain royal official, whose son was sick at Capernaum.

47When he heard that Jesus had come out of Judea into Galilee, he went to Him, and was requesting Him to come down and heal his son; for he was at the point of death.

48Jesus therefore said to him, "Unless you *people* see signs and wonders, you *simply* will not believe."

49The royal official *said to Him, "Sir, come down before my child dies."

50Jesus *said to him, "Go your way; your son lives." The man believed the word that Jesus spoke to him, and he started off.

51And as he was now going down, *his* slaves met him, saying that his son was living.

52So he inquired of them the hour when he began to get better. They said therefore to him, "Yesterday at the *seventh hour the fever left him."

53So the father knew that *it was* at that hour in which Jesus said to him, "Your son lives"; and he himself believed, and his whole household.

54This is again a second sign that Jesus performed, when He had come out of Judea into Galilee.

*l*Perhaps 7 p.m. (Roman time)
*m*Many mss. read *the feast*, i.e., the Passover

Κανὰ τῆς Γαλιλαίας, ὅπου ἐποίησεν τὸ
Cana - of Galilee, where he made the
ὕδωρ οἶνον. καὶ ἦν τις βασιλικὸς
water wine. And there was a certain courtier
οὗ ὁ υἱὸς ἠσθένει ἐν Καφαρναούμ· 47 οὗτος
of whom the son ailed in Capernaum; this man
ἀκούσας ὅτι Ἰησοῦς ἥκει ἐκ τῆς Ἰουδαίας
hearing that Jesus comes(came) out of - Judæa
εἰς τὴν Γαλιλαίαν, ἀπῆλθεν πρὸς αὐτὸν καὶ
into the Galilee, went to him and
ἠρώτα ἵνα καταβῇ καὶ ἰάσηται αὐτοῦ
asked that he would come down and would cure of him
τὸν υἱόν· ἤμελλεν γὰρ ἀποθνῄσκειν. 48 εἶπεν
the son; for he was about to die. Said
οὖν ὁ Ἰησοῦς πρὸς αὐτόν· ἐὰν μὴ σημεῖα
therefore - Jesus to him: Except signs
καὶ τέρατα ἴδητε, οὐ μὴ πιστεύσητε.
and prodigies ye see, by no means ye believe.
49 λέγει πρὸς αὐτὸν ὁ βασιλικός· κύριε,
Says to him the courtier: Sir,
κατάβηθι πρὶν ἀποθανεῖν τὸ παιδίον μου.
come down before to die the child of me.
50 λέγει αὐτῷ ὁ Ἰησοῦς· πορεύου, ὁ
Tells him - Jesus: Go, the
υἱός σου ζῇ. ἐπίστευσεν ὁ ἄνθρωπος τῷ
son of thee lives. ³Believed ¹the ²man ⁴the
λόγῳ ὃν εἶπεν αὐτῷ ὁ Ἰησοῦς, καὶ
⁵word ⁸which ⁷said ⁶to him - ⁷Jesus, and
ἐπορεύετο. 51 ἤδη δὲ αὐτοῦ καταβαίνοντος
went. And already him going down
=while he was going down
οἱ δοῦλοι ὑπήντησαν αὐτῷ λέγοντες ὅτι
the slaves met him saying that
ὁ παῖς αὐτοῦ ζῇ. 52 ἐπύθετο οὖν τὴν
the boy of him lives. He inquired therefore the
ὥραν παρ' αὐτῶν ἐν ᾗ κομψότερον ἔσχεν·
hour from them in which better he had;
=he got better;
εἶπαν οὖν αὐτῷ ὅτι ἐχθὲς ὥραν ἑβδόμην
they said therefore to him[,] Yesterday [at] hour seventh
ἀφῆκεν αὐτὸν ὁ πυρετός. 53 ἔγνω οὖν
left him the fever. Knew therefore
ὁ πατὴρ ὅτι ἐκείνῃ τῇ ὥρᾳ ἐν ᾗ εἶπεν
the father that in that - hour in which told
αὐτῷ ὁ Ἰησοῦς· ὁ υἱός σου ζῇ· καὶ
him - Jesus: The son of thee lives; and
ἐπίστευσεν αὐτὸς καὶ ἡ οἰκία αὐτοῦ ὅλη.
believed he and the household of him whole.
54 Τοῦτο [δὲ] πάλιν δεύτερον σημεῖον
And this again a second sign
ἐποίησεν ὁ Ἰησοῦς ἐλθὼν ἐκ τῆς Ἰουδαίας
did - Jesus having come out of - Judæa
εἰς τὴν Γαλιλαίαν.
into - Galilee.

---

had turned the water into wine. And there was a certain royal official whose son lay sick at Capernaum.

47When this man heard that Jesus had arrived in Galilee from Judea, he went to him and begged him to come and heal his son, who was close to death.

48"Unless you people see miraculous signs and wonders," Jesus told him, "you will never believe."

49The royal official said, "Sir, come down before my child dies."

50Jesus replied, "You may go. Your son will live."

The man took Jesus at his word and departed. 51While he was still on the way, his servants met him with the news that his boy was living. 52When he inquired as to the time when his son got better, they said to him, "The fever left him yesterday at the seventh hour."

53Then the father realized that this was the exact time at which Jesus had said to him, "Your son will live." So he and all his household believed.

54This was the second miraculous sign that Jesus performed, having come from Judea to Galilee.

Chapter 5

The Healing at Bethesda

AFTER these things there was a *m*a feast of the Jews, and Jesus went up to Jerusalem.

2Now there is in Jerusalem by the sheep *gate* a pool, which is called in He-

---

5 Μετὰ ταῦτα ἦν ἑορτὴ τῶν Ἰουδαίων,
After these things there was a feast of the Jews,
καὶ ἀνέβη Ἰησοῦς εἰς Ἱεροσόλυμα. 2 ἔστιν
and went up Jesus to Jerusalem. there is
δὲ ἐν τοῖς Ἱεροσολύμοις ἐπὶ τῇ προβατικῇ
Now in - Jerusalem at the sheepgate
κολυμβήθρα, ἡ ἐπιλεγομένη Ἑβραϊστὶ
a pool, the [one] being called in Hebrew

Chapter 5

The Healing at the Pool

SOME time later, Jesus went up to Jerusalem for a feast of the Jews. 2Now there is in Jerusalem near the Sheep Gate a pool, which in Aramaic is called brew Bethesda, having five porticoes.

3In these lay a multitude of those who were sick, blind, lame, and withered, [nwaiting for the moving of the waters;

4for an angel of the Lord went down at certain seasons into the pool, and stirred up the water; whoever then first, after the stirring up of the water, stepped in was made well from whatever disease with which he was afflicted.]

5And a certain man was there, who had been thirty-eight years in his sickness.

6When Jesus saw him lying there, and knew that he had already been a long time in that condition, He *said to him, "Do you wish to get well?"

7The sick man answered Him, "Sir, I have no man to put me into the pool when the water is stirred up, but while I am coming, another steps down before me."

8Jesus *said to him, "Arise, take up your pallet, and walk."

9And immediately the man became well, and took up his pallet and began to walk.

Now it was the Sabbath on that day.

10Therefore the Jews were saying to him who was cured, "It is the Sabbath, and it is not permissible for you to carry your pallet."

11But he answered them, "He who made me well was the one who said to me, 'Take up your pallet and walk.'"

12They asked him, "Who is the man who said to you, 'Take up your pallet, and walk'?"

13But he who was healed did not know who it was; for Jesus had slipped away while there was a crowd in that place.

14Afterward Jesus *found him in the temple, and said to him, "Behold, you have become well; do not sin anymore, so that nothing worse may befall you."

15The man went away, and told the Jews that it was Jesus who had made him well.

Βηθζαθά, πέντε στοὰς ἔχουσα. 3 ἐν
Bethzatha, five porches having. In

ταύταις κατέκειτο πλῆθος τῶν ἀσθενούντων,
these lay a multitude of the ailing [ones],

τυφλῶν, χωλῶν, ξηρῶν. ‡ 5 ἦν δέ τις
blind, lame, withered. And there was a

ἄνθρωπος ἐκεῖ τριάκοντα καὶ ὀκτὼ ἔτη
certain man there thirty-eight years

ἔχων ἐν τῇ ἀσθενείᾳ αὐτοῦ· 6 τοῦτον
having in the ailment of him; ³this man

ἰδὼν ὁ Ἰησοῦς κατακείμενον, καὶ γνοὺς
²seeing - ¹Jesus ⁴lying, and knowing

ὅτι πολὺν ἤδη χρόνον ἔχει, λέγει αὐτῷ·
that ²much ³already ¹time ¹he has, says to him :

θέλεις ὑγιὴς γενέσθαι; 7 ἀπεκρίθη αὐτῷ
Wishest thou whole to become? Answered him

ὁ ἀσθενῶν· κύριε, ἄνθρωπον οὐκ ἔχω,
the ailing [one] : Sir, a man I have not,

ἵνα ὅταν ταραχθῇ τὸ ὕδωρ βάλῃ με εἰς
that when is troubled the water he may put me into

τὴν κολυμβήθραν· ἐν ᾧ δὲ ἔρχομαι ἐγώ,
the pool; but while am coming I,

ἄλλος πρὸ ἐμοῦ καταβαίνει. 8 λέγει αὐτῷ
another before me goes down. Says to him

ὁ Ἰησοῦς· ἔγειρε ἆρον τὸν κράβατόν
- Jesus : Rise[,] take the mattress

σου καὶ περιπάτει. 9 καὶ εὐθέως ἐγένετο
of thee and walk. And immediately became

ὑγιὴς ὁ ἄνθρωπος, καὶ ἦρεν τὸν κράβατον
whole the man, and took the mattress

αὐτοῦ καὶ περιεπάτει. Ἦν δὲ σάββατον
of him and walked. And it was a sabbath

ἐν ἐκείνῃ τῇ ἡμέρᾳ. 10 ἔλεγον οὖν οἱ
on that - day. Said therefore the

Ἰουδαῖοι τῷ τεθεραπευμένῳ· σάββατόν ἐστιν,
Jews to the [one] having been healed : A sabbath it is,

καὶ οὐκ ἔξεστίν σοι ἆραι τὸν κράβατον.
and it is not lawful for thee to take the mattress.

11 ὃς δὲ ἀπεκρίθη αὐτοῖς· ὁ ποιήσας
But who(he) answered them : The [one] making

με ὑγιῆ, ἐκεῖνός μοι εἶπεν· ἆρον τὸν
me whole, that one me told : Take the

κράβατόν σου καὶ περιπάτει. 12 ἠρώτησαν
mattress of thee and walk. They asked

αὐτόν· τίς ἐστιν ὁ ἄνθρωπος ὁ εἰπών
him : Who is the man - telling

σοι· ἆρον καὶ περιπάτει; 13 ὁ δὲ ἰαθεὶς
thee : Take and walk? But the [one] cured

οὐκ ᾔδει τίς ἐστιν· ὁ γὰρ Ἰησοῦς
did not know who it is(was); - for Jesus

ἐξένευσεν ὄχλου ὄντος ἐν τῷ τόπῳ.
withdrew a crowd being⁼ in the place.
⁼as there was a crowd

14 μετὰ ταῦτα εὑρίσκει αὐτὸν ὁ Ἰησοῦς
After these things finds him - Jesus

ἐν τῷ ἱερῷ καὶ εἶπεν αὐτῷ· ἴδε ὑγιὴς
in the temple and said to him : Behold[,] whole

γέγονας· μηκέτι ἁμάρτανε, ἵνα μὴ χεῖρόν
thou hast become; no longer sin, lest ²worse

σοί τι γένηται. 15 ἀπῆλθεν ὁ ἄνθρωπος
⁴to thee ¹something ³happens. Went away the man

καὶ εἶπεν τοῖς Ἰουδαίοις ὅτι Ἰησοῦς
and told the Jews that Jesus

ἐστιν ὁ ποιήσας αὐτὸν ὑγιῆ. 16 καὶ διὰ
it is(was) the [one] having made him whole. And there-

Bethesdac and which is surrounded by five covered colonnades. 3Here a great number of disabled people used to lie—the blind, the lame, the paralyzed. d 5One who was there had been an invalid for thirty-eight years. 6When Jesus saw him lying there and learned that he had been in this condition for a long time, he asked him, "Do you want to get well?"

7"Sir," the invalid replied, "I have no one to help me into the pool when the water is stirred. While I am trying to get in, someone else goes down ahead of me."

8Then Jesus said to him, "Get up! Pick up your mat and walk." 9At once the man was cured; he picked up his mat and walked.

The day on which this took place was a Sabbath, 10and so the Jews said to the man who had been healed, "It is the Sabbath; the law forbids you to carry your mat."

11But he replied, "The man who made me well said to me, 'Pick up your mat and walk.'"

12So they asked him, "Who is this fellow who told you to pick it up and walk?"

13The man who was healed had no idea who it was, for Jesus had slipped away into the crowd that was there.

14Later Jesus found him at the temple and said to him, "See, you are well again. Stop sinning or something worse may happen to you." 15The man went away and told the Jews that it was Jesus who had made him well.

---

c2 Some manuscripts Bethzatha; other manuscripts Bethsaida
d3 Some less important manuscripts paralyzed—and they waited for the moving of the waters. 4From time to time an angel of the Lord would come down and stir up the waters. The first one into the pool after each such disturbance would be cured of whatever disease he had.

n Many mss. do not contain the remainder of v. 3 nor v. 4

‡ End of ver. 3 and ver. 4 omitted by Nestle; cf. NIV footnote.

16And for this reason the Jews were persecuting Jesus, because He was doing these things on the Sabbath.

17But He answered them, "My Father is working until now, and I Myself am working."

Jesus' Equality with God

18For this cause therefore the Jews were seeking all the more to kill Him, because He not only was breaking the Sabbath, but also was calling God His own Father, making Himself equal with God.

19Jesus therefore answered and was saying to them, "Truly, truly, I say to you, the Son can do nothing of Himself, unless *it is* something that He sees the Father doing; for whatever *the Father* does, these things the Son also does in like manner.

20"For the Father loves the Son, and shows Him all things that He Himself is doing; and greater works than these will He show Him, that you may marvel.

21"For just as the Father raises the dead and gives them life, even so the Son also gives life to whom He wishes.

22"For not even the Father judges anyone, but He has given all judgment to the Son,

23in order that all may honor the Son, even as they honor the Father. He who does not honor the Son does not honor the Father who sent Him.

24"Truly, truly, I say to you, he who hears My word, and believes Him who sent Me, has eternal life, and does not come into judgment, but has passed out of death into life.

τοῦτο ἐδίωκον οἱ Ἰουδαῖοι τὸν Ἰησοῦν,
fore ³persecuted ¹the ²Jews – ⁴Jesus,

ὅτι ταῦτα ἐποίει ἐν σαββάτῳ. 17 ὁ δὲ
because these things he did on a sabbath. But he

ἀπεκρίνατο αὐτοῖς· ὁ πατήρ μου ἕως
answered them: The Father of me until

ἄρτι ἐργάζεται, κἀγὼ ἐργάζομαι· 18 διὰ
now works, and I work; because of

τοῦτο οὖν μᾶλλον ἐζήτουν αὐτὸν οἱ
this therefore ⁴the more ³sought ⁵him ¹the

Ἰουδαῖοι ἀποκτεῖναι, ὅτι οὐ μόνον ἔλυεν
²Jews ⁶to kill, because not only he broke

τὸ σάββατον, ἀλλὰ καὶ πατέρα ἴδιον
the sabbath, but also Father [his] own

ἔλεγεν τὸν θεόν, ἴσον ἑαυτὸν ποιῶν τῷ
said – God [to be], equal himself making –

θεῷ. 19 Ἀπεκρίνατο οὖν ὁ Ἰησοῦς καὶ
to God. Answered therefore – Jesus and

ἔλεγεν αὐτοῖς· ἀμὴν ἀμὴν λέγω ὑμῖν,
said to them: Truly truly I say to you,

οὐ δύναται ὁ υἱὸς ποιεῖν ἀφ᾽ ἑαυτοῦ
cannot the Son to do from himself

οὐδέν, ἂν μή τι βλέπῃ τὸν πατέρα
no(any)thing, except what he sees the Father

ποιοῦντα· ἃ γὰρ ἂν ἐκεῖνος ποιῇ, ταῦτα
doing; for whatever things that one does, these

καὶ ὁ υἱὸς ὁμοίως ποιεῖ. 20 ὁ γὰρ
also the Son likewise does. For the

πατὴρ φιλεῖ τὸν υἱὸν καὶ πάντα δείκνυσιν
Father loves the Son and all things shows

αὐτῷ ἃ αὐτὸς ποιεῖ, καὶ μείζονα τούτων
him which he does, and ¹greater ²[than] ⁴these

δείξει αὐτῷ ἔργα, ἵνα ὑμεῖς θαυμάζητε.
⁵he will show ⁶him ³works, that ye may marvel.

21 ὥσπερ γὰρ ὁ πατὴρ ἐγείρει τοὺς
For as the Father raises the

νεκροὺς καὶ ζωοποιεῖ, οὕτως καὶ ὁ υἱὸς
dead and quickens, so also the Son

οὓς θέλει ζωοποιεῖ. 22 οὐδὲ γὰρ ὁ
whom he wills quickens. For not the

πατὴρ κρίνει οὐδένα, ἀλλὰ τὴν κρίσιν
Father judges no(any) one, but – judgment

πᾶσαν δέδωκεν τῷ υἱῷ, 23 ἵνα πάντες
all he has given to the Son, that all men

τιμῶσι τὸν υἱὸν καθὼς τιμῶσι τὸν πατέρα.
may honour the Son as they honour the Father.

ὁ μὴ τιμῶν τὸν υἱὸν οὐ τιμᾷ τὸν πατέρα
The [one] not honouring the Son honours not the Father

τὸν πέμψαντα αὐτόν. 24 Ἀμὴν ἀμὴν
– having sent him. Truly truly

λέγω ὑμῖν ὅτι ὁ τὸν λόγον μου ἀκούων
I say to you[,] – The [one] the word of me hearing

καὶ πιστεύων τῷ πέμψαντί με ἔχει
and believing the [one] having sent me has

ζωὴν αἰώνιον, καὶ εἰς κρίσιν οὐκ ἔρχεται
life eternal, and into judgment comes not

ἀλλὰ μεταβέβηκεν ἐκ τοῦ θανάτου εἰς
but has passed over out of – death into

τὴν ζωήν. 25 ἀμὴν ἀμὴν λέγω ὑμῖν ὅτι
– life. Truly truly I say to you[,] –

ἔρχεται ὥρα καὶ νῦν ἐστιν ὅτε οἱ νεκροὶ
Comes an hour and now is when the dead

ἀκούσουσιν τῆς φωνῆς τοῦ υἱοῦ τοῦ
will hear the voice of the Son –

θεοῦ καὶ οἱ ἀκούσαντες ζήσουσιν. 26 ὥσπερ
of God and the [ones] hearing will live. as

Life Through the Son

16So, because Jesus was doing these things on the Sabbath, the Jews persecuted him. 17Jesus said to them, "My Father is always at his work to this very day, and I, too, am working." 18For this reason the Jews tried all the harder to kill him; not only was he breaking the Sabbath, but he was even calling God his own Father, making himself equal with God.

19Jesus gave them this answer: "I tell you the truth, the Son can do nothing by himself; he can do only what he sees his Father doing, because whatever the Father does the Son also does. 20For the Father loves the Son and shows him all he does. Yes, to your amazement he will show him even greater things than these. 21For just as the Father raises the dead and gives them life, even so the Son gives life to whom he is pleased to give it. 22Moreover, the Father judges no one, but has entrusted all judgment to the Son, 23that all may honor the Son just as they honor the Father. He who does not honor the Son does not honor the Father, who sent him.

24"I tell you the truth, whoever hears my word and believes him who sent me has eternal life and will not be condemned; he has crossed over from death to

Two Resurrections

25"Truly, truly, I say to you, an hour is coming and now is, when the dead shall hear the voice of the Son of God; and those who hear shall live.

26"For just as the Father has life in Himself, even so He gave to the Son also to have life in Himself;

27and He gave Him authority to execute judgment, because He is *the* Son of Man.

28"Do not marvel at this; for an hour is coming, in which all who are in the tombs shall hear His voice,

29and shall come forth; those who did the good *deeds* to a resurrection of life, those who committed the evil *deeds* to a resurrection of judgment.

30"I can do nothing on My own initiative. As I hear, I judge; and My judgment is just, because I do not seek My own will, but the will of Him who sent Me.

31"If I *alone* bear witness of Myself, My testimony is not true.

32"There is another who bears witness of Me, and I know that the testimony which He bears of Me is true.

Witness of John

33"You have sent to John, and he has borne witness to the truth.

34"But the witness which I receive is not from man, but I say these things that you may be saved.

35"He was the lamp that was burning and was shining, and you were willing to rejoice for a while in his light.

Witness of Works

36"But the witness which I have is greater than *that of* John; for the works which the Father has given Me to accomplish, the very works that I do, bear witness of Me, that the Father has sent Me.

Witness of the Father

37"And the Father who sent Me, He has borne witness of Me. You have neither heard His voice at any time, nor seen His form.

γὰρ ὁ πατὴρ ἔχει ζωὴν ἐν ἑαυτῷ, οὕτως
For the Father has life in himself, so

καὶ τῷ υἱῷ ἔδωκεν ζωὴν ἔχειν ἐν ἑαυτῷ.
also to the Son he gave life to have in himself.

27 καὶ ἐξουσίαν ἔδωκεν αὐτῷ κρίσιν ποιεῖν,
And authority he gave him judgment to do,

ὅτι υἱὸς ἀνθρώπου ἐστίν. 28 μὴ θαυμάζετε
because son of man* he is. Marvel not [at]

τοῦτο, ὅτι ἔρχεται ὥρα ἐν ᾗ πάντες οἱ
this, because comes an hour in which all the [ones]

ἐν τοῖς μνημείοις ἀκούσουσιν τῆς φωνῆς
in the tombs will hear the voice

αὐτοῦ 29 καὶ ἐκπορεύσονται οἱ τὰ ἀγαθὰ
of him and will come forth the [ones] the good things

ποιήσαντες εἰς ἀνάστασιν ζωῆς, οἱ τὰ
having done to a resurrection of life, the [ones] the

φαῦλα πράξαντες εἰς ἀνάστασιν κρίσεως.
evil things having done to a resurrection of judgment.

30 Οὐ δύναμαι ἐγὼ ποιεῖν ἀπ’ ἐμαυτοῦ
Cannot I to do from myself

οὐδέν· καθὼς ἀκούω κρίνω, καὶ ἡ κρίσις
no(any)thing; as I hear I judge, and judgment

ἡ ἐμὴ δικαία ἐστίν, ὅτι οὐ ζητῶ τὸ
— my just is, because I seek not —

θέλημα τὸ ἐμὸν ἀλλὰ τὸ θέλημα τοῦ
will — my but the will of the [one]

πέμψαντός με. 31 Ἐὰν ἐγὼ μαρτυρῶ
having sent me. If I witness

περὶ ἐμαυτοῦ, ἡ μαρτυρία μου οὐκ ἔστιν
concerning myself, the witness of me is not

ἀληθής· 32 ἄλλος ἐστιν ὁ μαρτυρῶν περὶ
true; another there is the [one] witnessing concerning

ἐμοῦ, καὶ οἶδα ὅτι ἀληθής ἐστιν ἡ
me, and I know that true is the

μαρτυρία ἣν μαρτυρεῖ περὶ ἐμοῦ. 33 ὑμεῖς
witness which he witnesses concerning me. Ye

ἀπεστάλκατε πρὸς Ἰωάννην, καὶ μεμαρ-
have sent to John, and he has

τύρηκεν τῇ ἀληθείᾳ· 34 ἐγὼ δὲ οὐ παρὰ
witnessed to the truth; but I not from

ἀνθρώπου τὴν μαρτυρίαν λαμβάνω, ἀλλὰ
man the witness receive, but

ταῦτα λέγω ἵνα ὑμεῖς σωθῆτε. 35 ἐκεῖνος
these things I say that ye may be saved. That man

ἦν ὁ λύχνος ὁ καιόμενος καὶ φαίνων,
was the lamp — burning and shining,

ὑμεῖς δὲ ἠθελήσατε ἀγαλλιαθῆναι πρὸς
and ye were willing to exult for

ὥραν ἐν τῷ φωτὶ αὐτοῦ. 36 Ἐγὼ δὲ
an hour in the light of him. But I

ἔχω τὴν μαρτυρίαν μείζω τοῦ Ἰωάννου·
have the witness greater [than] — of John;

τὰ γὰρ ἔργα ἃ δέδωκέν μοι ὁ πατὴρ ἵνα
for the works which has given me the Father that

τελειώσω αὐτά, αὐτὰ τὰ ἔργα ἃ ποιῶ,
I may finish them, ³[them]selves ¹the ²works which I do,

μαρτυρεῖ περὶ ἐμοῦ ὅτι ὁ πατήρ με
witnesses concerning me that the Father me

ἀπέσταλκεν. 37 καὶ ὁ πέμψας με πατήρ,
has sent. And ¹the ³having sent ⁴me ¹Father,

ἐκεῖνος μεμαρτύρηκεν περὶ ἐμοῦ. οὔτε
that [one] has witnessed concerning me. Neither

φωνὴν αὐτοῦ πώποτε ἀκηκόατε οὔτε εἶδος
voice of him never ye have heard nor form

* Note the absence of the definite article here. See also Rev. 1. 13 and 14. 14.

life. 25I tell you the truth, a time is coming and has now come when the dead will hear the voice of the Son of God and those who hear will live. 26For as the Father has life in himself, so he has granted the Son to have life in himself. 27And he has given him authority to judge because he is the Son of Man.

28"Do not be amazed at this, for a time is coming when all who are in their graves will hear his voice 29and come out—those who have done good will rise to live, and those who have done evil will rise to be condemned. 30By myself I can do nothing; I judge only as I hear, and my judgment is just, for I seek not to please myself but him who sent me.

Testimonies About Jesus

31"If I testify about myself, my testimony is not valid. 32There is another who testifies in my favor, and I know that his testimony about me is valid.

33"You have sent to John and he has testified to the truth. 34Not that I accept human testimony; but I mention it that you may be saved. 35John was a lamp that burned and gave light, and you chose for a time to enjoy his light.

36"I have testimony weightier than that of John. For the very work that the Father has given me to finish, and which I am doing, testifies that the Father has sent me. 37And the Father who sent me has himself testified concerning me. You have never heard his voice nor seen his form,

38"And you do not have His word abiding in you, for you do not believe Him whom He sent.

Witness of the Scripture

39"ᵒYou search the Scriptures, because you think that in them you have eternal life; and it is these that bear witness of Me;

40and you are unwilling to come to Me, that you may have life.

41"I do not receive glory from men;

42but I know you, that you do not have the love of God in yourselves.

43"I have come in My Father's name, and you do not receive Me; if another shall come in his own name, you will receive him.

44"How can you believe, when you receive glory from one another, and you do not seek the glory that is from the *one and* only God?

45"Do not think that I will accuse you before the Father; the one who accuses you is Moses, in whom you have set your hope.

46"For if you believed Moses, you would believe Me; for he wrote of Me.

47"But if you do not believe his writings, how will you believe My words?''

αὐτοῦ ἑωράκατε, **38** καὶ τὸν λόγον αὐτοῦ
of him ye have seen,   and   the   word   of him

οὐκ ἔχετε ἐν ὑμῖν μένοντα, ὅτι ὃν
ye have not in   you remaining, because [he] whom

ἀπέστειλεν ἐκεῖνος, τούτῳ ὑμεῖς οὐ πιστεύετε.
²sent   ¹that [one], this [one] ye   do not believe.

39 ἐρευνᾶτε τὰς γραφάς, ὅτι ὑμεῖς δοκεῖτε
Ye search   the scriptures, because ye   think

ἐν αὐταῖς ζωὴν αἰώνιον ἔχειν· καὶ ἐκεῖναί
in   them   life   eternal to have; and   those

εἰσιν αἱ μαρτυροῦσαι περὶ ἐμοῦ· **40** καὶ
are the [ones] witnessing concerning me ;   and

οὐ θέλετε ἐλθεῖν πρός με ἵνα ζωὴν
ye wish not to come   to me that life

ἔχητε. **41** Δόξαν παρὰ ἀνθρώπων οὐ
ye may have.   Glory   from   men   not

λαμβάνω, **42** ἀλλὰ ἔγνωκα ὑμᾶς ὅτι τὴν
I receive,   but I have known you   that the

ἀγάπην τοῦ θεοῦ οὐκ ἔχετε ἐν ἑαυτοῖς.
love   – of God ye have not in your*selves*.

43 ἐγὼ ἐλήλυθα ἐν τῷ ὀνόματι τοῦ πατρός
I   have come   in the   name   of the Father

μου, καὶ οὐ λαμβάνετέ με· ἐὰν ἄλλος
of me, and ye receive not me;   if   another

ἔλθῃ ἐν τῷ ὀνόματι τῷ ἰδίῳ, ἐκεῖνον
comes in –   name the(his) own,   that [one]

λήμψεσθε. **44** πῶς δύνασθε ὑμεῖς πιστεῦσαι,
ye will receive.   How   can   ye   *to* believe,

δόξαν παρὰ ἀλλήλων λαμβάνοντες, καὶ
glory   from one another   receiving,   and

τὴν δόξαν τὴν παρὰ τοῦ μόνου θεοῦ
the   glory   –   from the   only   God

οὐ ζητεῖτε; **45** μὴ δοκεῖτε ὅτι ἐγὼ κατηγορήσω
ye seek not?   Do not think that I   will accuse

ὑμῶν πρὸς τὸν πατέρα· ἐστιν ὁ κατηγορῶν
you   to   the Father; there is the [one] accusing

ὑμῶν Μωϋσῆς, εἰς ὃν ὑμεῖς ἠλπίκατε. **46** εἰ
you[,] Moses,   in whom ye   have hoped.   if

γὰρ ἐπιστεύετε Μωϋσεῖ, ἐπιστεύετε ἂν
For   ye believed   Moses,   ye would have believed

ἐμοί· περὶ γὰρ ἐμοῦ ἐκεῖνος ἔγραψεν.
me;   for concerning me   that [one] wrote.

47 εἰ δὲ τοῖς ἐκείνου γράμμασιν οὐ
But ¹if ⁴the ⁵of that [one] ⁶letters   ²not

πιστεύετε, πῶς τοῖς ἐμοῖς ῥήμασιν
³ye believe, how   –   my   words

πιστεύσετε;
will ye believe?

Chapter 6

Five Thousand Fed

AFTER these things Jesus went away to the other side of the Sea of Galilee (or Tiberias).

2And a great multitude was following Him, because they were seeing the signs which He was performing on those who were sick.

3And Jesus went up on the mountain, and there He sat with His disciples.

4Now the Passover, the feast of the Jews, was at hand.

5Jesus therefore lifting

ᵒOr, (a command) *Search the Scriptures!*

---

6 Μετὰ ταῦτα ἀπῆλθεν ὁ Ἰησοῦς πέραν
After these things went away   –   Jesus   across

τῆς θαλάσσης τῆς Γαλιλαίας τῆς Τιβεριάδος.
the   sea   – of Galilee[,] –   of Tiberias.

2 ἠκολούθει δὲ αὐτῷ ὄχλος πολύς, ὅτι
And followed   him   crowd a much, because

ἑώρων τὰ σημεῖα ἃ ἐποίει ἐπὶ τῶν
they saw the signs which he did   on   the

ἀσθενούντων. **3** ἀνῆλθεν δὲ εἰς τὸ ὄρος
ailing [ones].   And went up   to   the mountain

Ἰησοῦς, καὶ ἐκεῖ ἐκάθητο μετὰ τῶν
Jesus,   and there   sat   with   the

μαθητῶν αὐτοῦ. **4** ἦν δὲ ἐγγὺς τὸ πάσχα,
disciples of him.   And was near the Passover,

ἡ ἑορτὴ τῶν Ἰουδαίων. **5** ἐπάρας οὖν
the feast of the Jews.   Lifting up therefore

38nor does his word dwell in you, for you do not believe the one he sent. 39You diligently study ᵉ the Scriptures because you think that by them you possess eternal life. These are the Scriptures that testify about me, 40yet you refuse to come to me to have life.

41"I do not accept praise from men, 42but I know you. I know that you do not have the love of God in your hearts. 43I have come in my Father's name, and you do not accept me; but if someone else comes in his own name, you will accept him. 44How can you believe if you accept praise from one another, yet make no effort to obtain the praise that comes from the only God ᶠ?

45"But do not think I will accuse you before the Father. Your accuser is Moses, on whom your hopes are set. 46If you believed Moses, you would believe me, for he wrote about me. 47But since you do not believe what he wrote, how are you going to believe what I say?''

Chapter 6

Jesus Feeds the Five Thousand

SOME time after this, Jesus crossed to the far shore of the Sea of Galilee (that is, the Sea of Tiberias), 2and a great crowd of people followed him because they saw the miraculous signs he had performed on the sick. 3Then Jesus went up on a mountainside and sat down with his disciples. 4The Jewish Passover Feast was near. 5When Jesus looked up

ᵉ39 Or *Study diligently* (the imperative)
ᶠ44 Some early manuscripts *the Only One*

up His eyes, and seeing that a great multitude was coming to Him, *said to Philip, "Where are we to buy bread, that these may eat?"

6And this He was saying to test him; for He Himself knew what He was intending to do.

7Philip answered Him, "Two hundred ᵖdenarii worth of bread is not sufficient for them, for every-one to receive a little."

8One of His disciples, Andrew, Simon Peter's brother, *said to Him,

9"There is a lad here who has five barley loaves and two fish, but what are these for so many people?"

10Jesus said, "Have the people sit down." Now there was much grass in the place. So the men sat down, in number about five thousand.

11Jesus therefore took the loaves; and having given thanks, He distributed to those who were seated; likewise also of the fish as much as they wanted.

12And when they were filled, He *said to His disciples, "Gather up the left-over fragments that nothing may be lost."

13And so they gathered them up, and filled twelve baskets with fragments from the five barley loaves, which were left over by those who had eaten.

14When therefore the people saw the sign which He had performed, they said, "This is of a truth the Prophet who is to come into the world."

Jesus Walks on the Water

15Jesus therefore perceiving that they were intending to come and take Him by force, to make Him king, withdrew again to the mountain by Himself alone.

τοὺς ὀφθαλμοὺς ὁ Ἰησοῦς καὶ θεασάμενος
the(his) eyes – Jesus and beholding

ὅτι πολὺς ὄχλος ἔρχεται πρὸς αὐτόν,
that a much crowd is(was) coming toward him,

λέγει πρὸς Φίλιππον· πόθεν ἀγοράσωμεν
he says to Philip : Whence may we buy

ἄρτους ἵνα φάγωσιν οὗτοι; 6 τοῦτο δὲ
loaves that may eat these? And this

ἔλεγεν πειράζων αὐτόν· αὐτὸς γὰρ ᾔδει
he said testing him; for he knew

τί ἔμελλεν ποιεῖν. 7 ἀπεκρίθη αὐτῷ ὁ
what he was about to do. Answered him –

Φίλιππος· διακοσίων δηναρίων ἄρτοι οὐκ
Philip : ⁹Of two hundred ³denarii ¹loaves not

ἀρκοῦσιν αὐτοῖς, ἵνα ἕκαστος βραχύ τι
are enough for them, that each a little

λάβῃ. 8 λέγει αὐτῷ εἷς ἐκ τῶν μαθητῶν
may take. Says to him one of the disciples

αὐτοῦ, Ἀνδρέας ὁ ἀδελφὸς Σίμωνος
of him, Andrew the brother of Simon

Πέτρου· 9 ἔστιν παιδάριον ὧδε ὃς ἔχει
Peter : There is a lad here who has

πέντε ἄρτους κριθίνους καὶ δύο ὀψάρια·
five loaves barley and two fishes;

ἀλλὰ ταῦτα τί ἐστιν εἰς τοσούτους;
but ²these ¹what ²is(are) among so many?

10 εἶπεν ὁ Ἰησοῦς· ποιήσατε τοὺς ἀνθρώπους
Said – Jesus : Make the men*

ἀναπεσεῖν. ἦν δὲ χόρτος πολὺς ἐν τῷ
to recline. Now there was grass much in the

τόπῳ. ἀνέπεσαν οὖν οἱ ἄνδρες τὸν ἀριθμὸν
place. Reclined therefore the men the number

ὡς πεντακισχίλιοι. 11 ἔλαβεν οὖν τοὺς
about five thousand. Took therefore the

ἄρτους ὁ Ἰησοῦς καὶ εὐχαριστήσας
loaves – Jesus and having given thanks

διέδωκεν τοῖς ἀνακειμένοις, ὁμοίως καὶ
distributed to the [ones] lying down, likewise also

ἐκ τῶν ὀψαρίων ὅσον ἤθελον. 12 ὡς δὲ
of the fishes as much as they wished. Now when

ἐνεπλήσθησαν, λέγει τοῖς μαθηταῖς αὐτοῦ·
they were filled, he tells the disciples of him:

συναγάγετε τὰ περισσεύσαντα κλάσματα, ἵνα
Gather ye the left over fragments, that

μή τι ἀπόληται. 13 συνήγαγον οὖν, καὶ
not anything is lost. They gathered therefore, and

ἐγέμισαν δώδεκα κοφίνους κλασμάτων ἐκ
filled twelve baskets of fragments of

τῶν πέντε ἄρτων τῶν κριθίνων ἃ ἐπερίσσευσαν
the five loaves – barley which were left over

τοῖς βεβρωκόσιν. 14 Οἱ οὖν ἄνθρωποι
to the [ones] having eaten. Therefore the men*

ἰδόντες ὃ ἐποίησεν σημεῖον ἔλεγον ὅτι
seeing ¹what ³he did ²sign said[,] –

οὗτός ἐστιν ἀληθῶς ὁ προφήτης ὁ
This is truly the prophet –

ἐρχόμενος εἰς τὸν κόσμον. 15 Ἰησοῦς
coming into the world. Jesus

οὖν γνοὺς ὅτι μέλλουσιν ἔρχεσθαι καὶ
therefore knowing that they are(were) about to come and

ἁρπάζειν αὐτὸν ἵνα ποιήσωσιν βασιλέα,
seize him that they might make a king,

ἀνεχώρησεν πάλιν εἰς τὸ ὄρος αὐτὸς
departed again to the mountain [him]self

---

and saw a great crowd coming toward him, he said to Philip, "Where shall we buy bread for these people to eat?" 6He asked this only to test him, for he already had in mind what he was going to do.

7Philip answered him, "Eight months' wages ᵍ would not buy enough bread for each one to have a bite!"

8Another of his disciples, Andrew, Simon Peter's brother, spoke up, 9"Here is a boy with five small barley loaves and two small fish, but how far will they go among so many?"

10Jesus said, "Have the people sit down." There was plenty of grass in that place, and the men sat down, about five thousand of them. 11Jesus then took the loaves, gave thanks, and distributed to those who were seated as much as they wanted. He did the same with the fish.

12When they had all had enough to eat, he said to his disciples, "Gather the pieces that are left over. Let nothing be wasted." 13So they gathered them and filled twelve baskets with the pieces of the five barley loaves left over by those who had eaten.

14After the people saw the miraculous sign that Jesus did, they began to say, "Surely this is the Prophet who is to come into the world." 15Jesus, knowing that they intended to come and make him king by force, withdrew again to a mountain by himself.

---

* That is, people. Compare ἄνδρες in ver. 10.

ᵍ7 Greek *two hundred denarii*

16Now when evening came, His disciples went down to the sea, 17and after getting into a boat, they *started* to cross the sea to Capernaum. And it had already become dark, and Jesus had not yet come to them. 18And the sea *began* to be stirred up because a strong wind was blowing. 19When therefore they had rowed about three or four miles, they *beheld Jesus walking on the sea and drawing near to the boat; and they were frightened. 20But He *said to them, "It is I; do not be afraid." 21They were willing therefore to receive Him into the boat; and immediately the boat was at the land to which they were going. 22The next day the multitude that stood on the other side of the sea saw that there was no other small boat there, except one, and that Jesus had not entered with His disciples into the boat, but *that* His disciples had gone away alone. 23There came other small boats from Tiberias near to the place where they ate the bread after the Lord had given thanks. 24When the multitude therefore saw that Jesus was not there, nor His disciples, they themselves got into the small boats, and came to Capernaum, seeking Jesus. 25And when they found Him on the other side of the sea, they said to Him, "Rabbi, when did You get here?"

Words to the People

26Jesus answered them and said, "Truly, truly, I say to you, you seek Me, not because you saw

---

μόνος. **16** Ὡς δὲ ὀψία ἐγένετο, κατέβησαν
alone.　　And when evening came,　went down

οἱ μαθηταὶ αὐτοῦ ἐπὶ τὴν θάλασσαν,
the disciples of him to the sea,

17 καὶ ἐμβάντες εἰς πλοῖον ἤρχοντο πέραν
and embarking in a boat came across

τῆς θαλάσσης εἰς Καφαρναούμ. καὶ
the sea to Capernaum. and

σκοτία ἤδη ἐγεγόνει καὶ οὔπω ἐληλύθει
darkness now had come and not yet had come

πρὸς αὐτοὺς ὁ Ἰησοῦς, **18** ἥ τε θάλασσα
to them - Jesus, and the sea

ἀνέμου μεγάλου πνέοντος διηγείρετο.
wind a great blowing[a] was roused.
=as a great wind blew

19 ἐληλακότες οὖν ὡς σταδίους εἴκοσι
Having rowed therefore about furlongs twenty-

πέντε ἢ τριάκοντα θεωροῦσιν τὸν Ἰησοῦν
five or thirty they behold - Jesus

περιπατοῦντα ἐπὶ τῆς θαλάσσης καὶ ἐγγὺς
walking on the sea and near

τοῦ πλοίου γινόμενον, καὶ ἐφοβήθησαν.
the boat becoming, and they feared.

20 ὁ δὲ λέγει αὐτοῖς· ἐγώ εἰμι· μὴ
But he says to them: I am; not

φοβεῖσθε. **21** ἤθελον οὖν λαβεῖν αὐτὸν εἰς
fear ye. They wished therefore to take him into

τὸ πλοῖον, καὶ εὐθέως ἐγένετο τὸ πλοῖον
the boat, and immediately was the boat

ἐπὶ τῆς γῆς εἰς ἣν ὑπῆγον.
at the land to which they were going.

22 Τῇ ἐπαύριον ὄχλος ὁ ἑστηκὼς
On the morrow the crowd - standing

πέραν τῆς θαλάσσης εἶδον ὅτι πλοιάριον
across the sea saw that boat

ἄλλο οὐκ ἦν ἐκεῖ εἰ μὴ ἕν, καὶ ὅτι
other was not there except one, and that

οὐ συνεισῆλθεν τοῖς μαθηταῖς αὐτοῦ ὁ
[a]did not come in with [a]the [a]disciples [a]of him -

Ἰησοῦς εἰς τὸ πλοῖον ἀλλὰ μόνοι οἱ
[a]Jesus in the boat but alone the

μαθηταὶ αὐτοῦ ἀπῆλθον· **23** ἄλλα ἦλθεν
disciples of him went away; [a]other [a]came

πλοιάρια ἐκ Τιβεριάδος ἐγγὺς τοῦ τόπου
[a]boats from Tiberias near the place

ὅπου ἔφαγον τὸν ἄρτον εὐχαριστήσαντος
where they ate the bread having given thanks

τοῦ κυρίου. **24** ὅτε οὖν εἶδεν ὁ ὄχλος
the Lord.[a] When therefore saw the crowd
=when the Lord had given thanks.

ὅτι Ἰησοῦς οὐκ ἔστιν ἐκεῖ οὐδὲ οἱ
that Jesus is(was) not there nor the

μαθηταὶ αὐτοῦ, ἐνέβησαν αὐτοὶ εἰς τὰ
disciples of him, embarked they in the

πλοιάρια καὶ ἦλθον εἰς Καφαρναοὺμ
boats and came to Capernaum

ζητοῦντες τὸν Ἰησοῦν. **25** καὶ εὑρόντες
seeking - Jesus. And finding

αὐτὸν πέραν τῆς θαλάσσης εἶπον αὐτῷ·
him across the sea they said to him:

ῥαββί, πότε ὧδε γέγονας; **26** ἀπεκρίθη
Rabbi, when here hast thou come? Answered

αὐτοῖς ὁ Ἰησοῦς καὶ εἶπεν· ἀμὴν ἀμὴν
them - Jesus and said: Truly truly

λέγω ὑμῖν, ζητεῖτέ με οὐχ ὅτι εἴδετε
I say to you, ye seek me not because ye saw

Jesus Walks on the Water

16When evening came, his disciples went down to the lake, 17where they got into a boat and set off across the lake for Capernaum. By now it was dark, and Jesus had not yet joined them. 18A strong wind was blowing and the waters grew rough. 19When they had rowed three or three and a half miles,[h] they saw Jesus approaching the boat, walking on the water; and they were terrified. 20But he said to them, "It is I; don't be afraid." 21Then they were willing to take him into the boat, and immediately the boat reached the shore where they were heading. 22The next day the crowd that had stayed on the opposite shore of the lake realized that only one boat had been there, and that Jesus had not entered it with his disciples, but that they had gone away alone. 23Then some boats from Tiberias landed near the place where the people had eaten the bread after the Lord had given thanks. 24Once the crowd realized that neither Jesus nor his disciples were there, they got into the boats and went to Capernaum in search of Jesus.

Jesus the Bread of Life

25When they found him on the other side of the lake, they asked him, "Rabbi, when did you get here?"

26Jesus answered, "I tell you the truth, you are looking for me, not because you

---

h19 Greek rowed twenty-five or thirty stadia (about 5 or 6 kilometers) signs, but because you ate of the loaves, and were filled.

27"Do not work for the food which perishes, but for the food which endures to eternal life, which the Son of Man shall give to you, for on Him the Father, *even* God, has set His seal."

28They said therefore to Him, "What shall we do, that we may work the works of God?"

29Jesus answered and said to them, "This is the work of God, that you believe in Him whom He has sent."

30They said therefore to Him, "What then do You do for a sign, that we may see, and believe You? What work do You perform?

31"Our fathers ate the manna in the wilderness; as it is written, 'HE GAVE THEM BREAD OUT OF HEAVEN TO EAT.'"

32Jesus therefore said to them, "Truly, truly, I say to you, it is not Moses who has given you the bread out of heaven, but it is My Father who gives you the true bread out of heaven.

33"For the bread of God is ᵃthat which comes down out of heaven, and gives life to the world."

34They said therefore to Him, "Lord, evermore give us this bread.' "

35Jesus said to them, "I am the bread of life; he who comes to Me shall not hunger, and he who believes in Me shall never thirst.

36"But I said to you, that you have seen Me, and yet do not believe.

37"All that the Father gives Me shall come to Me, and the one who comes to Me I will certainly not cast out.

38"For I have come down

σημεῖα, ἀλλ' ὅτι ἐφάγετε ἐκ τῶν ἄρτων
signs, but because ye ate of the loaves

καὶ ἐχορτάσθητε. 27 ἐργάζεσθε μὴ τὴν
and were satisfied. Work not [for] the

βρῶσιν τὴν ἀπολλυμένην, ἀλλὰ τὴν βρῶσιν
food – perishing, but [for] the food

τὴν μένουσαν εἰς ζωὴν αἰώνιον, ἢν ὁ
– remaining to life eternal, which the

υἱὸς τοῦ ἀνθρώπου ὑμῖν δώσει· τοῦτον γὰρ
Son – of man you will give; for this [one]

ὁ πατὴρ ἐσφράγισεν ὁ θεός. 28 εἶπον
¹the ³Father ²sealed – ¹God. They said

οὖν πρὸς αὐτόν· τί ποιῶμεν ἵνα ἐργαζ-
therefore to him: What may we do that we may

ώμεθα τὰ ἔργα τοῦ θεοῦ; 29 ἀπεκρίθη
work the works – of God? Answered

Ἰησοῦς καὶ εἶπεν αὐτοῖς· τοῦτό ἐστιν τὸ
Jesus and said to them: This is the

ἔργον τοῦ θεοῦ, ἵνα πιστεύητε εἰς ὃν
work – of God, that ye believe in [him] whom

ἀπέσταλκεν ἐκεῖνος. 30 εἶπον οὖν αὐτῷ·
sent that [one]. They said therefore to him:

τί οὖν ποιεῖς σὺ σημεῖον, ἵνα ἴδωμεν
¹What ²then ³doest ⁴thou ⁵sign, that we may see

καὶ πιστεύσωμέν σοι; τί ἐργάζῃ; 31 οἱ
and believe thee? what workest thou? The

πατέρες ἡμῶν τὸ μάννα ἔφαγον ἐν τῇ
fathers of us the manna ate in the

ἐρήμῳ, καθώς ἐστιν γεγραμμένον· ἄρτον
desert, as it is *having been* written: Bread

ἐκ τοῦ οὐρανοῦ ἔδωκεν αὐτοῖς φαγεῖν.
out of – heaven he gave them to eat.

32 Εἶπεν οὖν αὐτοῖς ὁ Ἰησοῦς· ἀμὴν
Said therefore to them – Jesus: Truly

ἀμὴν λέγω ὑμῖν, οὐ Μωϋσῆς δέδωκεν
truly I say to you, not Moses has given

ὑμῖν τὸν ἄρτον ἐκ τοῦ οὐρανοῦ, ἀλλ' ὁ
you the bread out of – heaven, but the

πατήρ μου δίδωσιν ὑμῖν τὸν ἄρτον ἐκ
Father of me gives you ¹the ³bread ⁴out of

τοῦ οὐρανοῦ τὸν ἀληθινόν· 33 ὁ γὰρ ἄρτος
– ⁵heaven *the* ²true; for the bread

τοῦ θεοῦ ἐστιν ὁ καταβαίνων ἐκ τοῦ
– of God is the [one] coming down out of –

οὐρανοῦ καὶ ζωὴν διδοὺς τῷ κόσμῳ.
heaven and life giving to the world.

34 εἶπον οὖν πρὸς αὐτόν· κύριε, πάντοτε
They said therefore to him: Lord, always

δὸς ἡμῖν τὸν ἄρτον τοῦτον. 35 εἶπεν
give us – bread this. Said

αὐτοῖς ὁ Ἰησοῦς· ἐγώ εἰμι ὁ ἄρτος τῆς
to them – Jesus: I am the bread –

ζωῆς· ὁ ἐρχόμενος πρὸς ἐμὲ οὐ μὴ
of life; the [one] coming to me by no means

πεινάσῃ, καὶ ὁ πιστεύων εἰς ἐμὲ οὐ μὴ
hungers, and the [one] believing in me by no means

διψήσει πώποτε. 36 Ἀλλ' εἶπον ὑμῖν ὅτι
will thirst never. But I told you that

καὶ ἑωράκατέ [με] καὶ οὐ πιστεύετε.
both ye have seen me and do not believe.

37 πᾶν ὃ δίδωσίν μοι ὁ πατὴρ πρὸς
All which gives to me the Father to

ἐμὲ ἥξει, καὶ τὸν ἐρχόμενον πρός με
me will come, and the [one] coming to me

οὐ μὴ ἐκβάλω ἔξω, 38 ὅτι καταβέβηκα
by no means I will cast *out* outside, because I have come down

---

saw miraculous signs but because you ate the loaves and had your fill. 27Do not work for food that spoils, but for food that endures to eternal life, which the Son of Man will give you. On him God the Father has placed his seal of approval."

28Then they asked him, "What must we do to do the works God requires?"

29Jesus answered, "The work of God is this: to believe in the one he has sent."

30So they asked him, "What miraculous sign then will you give that we may see it and believe you? What will you do? 31Our forefathers ate the manna in the desert; as it is written: 'He gave them bread from heaven to eat.'ⁱ"

32Jesus said to them, "I tell you the truth, it is not Moses who has given you the bread from heaven, but it is my Father who gives you the true bread from heaven. 33For the bread of God is he who comes down from heaven and gives life to the world."

34"Sir," they said, "from now on give us this bread."

35Then Jesus declared, "I am the bread of life. He who comes to me will never go hungry, and he who believes in me will never be thirsty. 36But as I told you, you have seen me and still you do not believe. 37All that the Father gives me will come to me, and whoever comes to me I will never drive away. 38For I have come down from

---

ᵃ Or, *He who comes*

ⁱ31 Exodus 16:4; Neh. 9:15; Psalm 78:24,25

from heaven, not to do My own will, but the will of Him who sent Me.

39"And this is the will of Him who sent Me, that of all that He has given Me I lose nothing, but raise it up on the last day.

40"For this is the will of My Father, that everyone who beholds the Son and believes in Him, may have eternal life; and I Myself will raise him up on the last day."

Words to the Jews

41The Jews therefore were grumbling about Him, because He said, "I am the bread that came down out of heaven."

42And they were saying, "Is not this Jesus, the son of Joseph, whose father and mother we know? How does He now say, 'I have come down out of heaven'?"

43Jesus answered and said to them, "Do not grumble among yourselves.

44"No one can come to Me, unless the Father who sent Me draws him; and I will raise him up on the last day.

45"It is written in the prophets, 'AND THEY SHALL ALL BE TAUGHT OF GOD.' Everyone who has heard and learned from the Father, comes to Me.

46"Not that any man has seen the Father, except the One who is from God; He has seen the Father.

47"Truly, truly, I say to you, he who believes has eternal life.

48"I am the bread of life.

49"Your fathers ate the manna in the wilderness, and they died.

50"This is the bread which comes down out of heaven, so that one may eat

ἀπὸ τοῦ οὐρανοῦ οὐχ ἵνα ποιῶ τὸ θέλημα
from — heaven not that I may do *the* ²will
τὸ ἐμὸν ἀλλὰ τὸ θέλημα τοῦ πέμψαντός
- ¹my but the will of the [one] having sent
με. 39 τοῦτο δέ ἐστιν τὸ θέλημα τοῦ
me. And this is the will of the [one]
πέμψαντός με, ἵνα πᾶν ὃ δέδωκέν μοι
having sent me, that all which he has given me
μὴ ἀπολέσω ἐξ αὐτοῦ, ἀλλὰ ἀναστήσω
I shall not lose of it, but shall raise up
αὐτὸ ἐν τῇ ἐσχάτῃ ἡμέρᾳ. 40 τοῦτο
it in the last day. this
γάρ ἐστιν τὸ θέλημα τοῦ πατρός μου,
For is the will of the Father of me,
ἵνα πᾶς ὁ θεωρῶν τὸν υἱὸν καὶ πιστεύων
that everyone beholding the Son and believing
εἰς αὐτὸν ἔχῃ ζωὴν αἰώνιον, καὶ ἀναστήσω
in him may have life eternal, and will raise up
αὐτὸν ἐγὼ ἐν τῇ ἐσχάτῃ ἡμέρᾳ. 41 Ἐγόγ-
him I in the last day. Mur-
γυζον οὖν οἱ Ἰουδαῖοι περὶ αὐτοῦ ὅτι
mured therefore the Jews about him because
εἶπεν· ἐγώ εἰμι ὁ ἄρτος ὁ καταβὰς ἐκ
he said : I am the bread - having come down out
τοῦ οὐρανοῦ, 42 καὶ ἔλεγον· οὐχ οὗτός
- of heaven, and they said: Not this man
ἐστιν Ἰησοῦς ὁ υἱὸς Ἰωσήφ, οὗ ἡμεῖς
is Jesus the son of Joseph, of whom we
οἴδαμεν τὸν πατέρα καὶ τὴν μητέρα;
know the father and the mother?
πῶς νῦν λέγει ὅτι ἐκ τοῦ οὐρανοῦ
how now says he[,] - Out of - heaven
καταβέβηκα; 43 ἀπεκρίθη Ἰησοῦς καὶ εἶπεν
I have come down? Answered Jesus and said
αὐτοῖς· μὴ γογγύζετε μετ' ἀλλήλων.
to them: Do not murmur with one another.
44 Οὐδεὶς δύναται ἐλθεῖν πρός με ἐὰν μὴ
No one can *to* come to me unless
ὁ πατὴρ ὁ πέμψας με ἑλκύσῃ αὐτόν,
the Father the [one] having sent me should draw him,
κἀγὼ ἀναστήσω αὐτὸν ἐν τῇ ἐσχάτῃ
and I will raise up him in the last
ἡμέρᾳ. 45 ἔστιν γεγραμμένον ἐν τοῖς
day. It is *having been* written in the
προφήταις· καὶ ἔσονται πάντες διδακτοὶ
prophets : And they shall be all taught
θεοῦ· πᾶς ὁ ἀκούσας παρὰ τοῦ πατρὸς
of God; everyone hearing from the Father
καὶ μαθὼν ἔρχεται πρὸς ἐμέ. 46 οὐχ
and learning comes to me. Not
ὅτι τὸν πατέρα ἑώρακέν τις, εἰ μὴ ὁ
that ³the ⁴Father ⁵has seen ¹anyone, except the [one]
ὢν παρὰ τοῦ θεοῦ, οὗτος ἑώρακεν τὸν
being from - God, this [one] has seen the
πατέρα. 47 ἀμὴν ἀμὴν λέγω ὑμῖν, ὁ
Father. Truly truly I say to you, the
πιστεύων ἔχει ζωὴν αἰώνιον. 48 Ἐγώ
[one] believing has life eternal. I
εἰμι ὁ ἄρτος τῆς ζωῆς. 49 οἱ πατέρες
am the bread - of life. The fathers
ὑμῶν ἔφαγον ἐν τῇ ἐρήμῳ τὸ μάννα καὶ
of you ate in the desert the manna and
ἀπέθανον· 50 οὗτός ἐστιν ὁ ἄρτος ὁ ἐκ
died ; this is the bread - out of
τοῦ οὐρανοῦ καταβαίνων, ἵνα τις ἐξ
- heaven coming down, that anyone of

heaven not to do my will but to do the will of him who sent me. 39And this is the will of him who sent me, that I shall lose none of all that he has given me, but raise them up at the last day. 40For my Father's will is that everyone who looks to the Son and believes in him shall have eternal life, and I will raise him up at the last day."

41At this the Jews began to grumble about him because he said, "I am the bread that came down from heaven." 42They said, "Is this not Jesus, the son of Joseph, whose father and mother we know? How can he now say, 'I came down from heaven'?"

43"Stop grumbling among yourselves," Jesus answered. 44"No one can come to me unless the Father who sent me draws him, and I will raise him up at the last day. 45It is written in the Prophets: 'They will all be taught by God.'ʲ Everyone who listens to the Father and learns from him comes to me. 46No one has seen the Father except the one who is from God; only he has seen the Father. 47I tell you the truth, he who believes has everlasting life. 48I am the bread of life. 49Your forefathers ate the manna in the desert, yet they died. 50But here is the bread that comes down from heaven, which a man may eat and not die. 51I am

ʲ45 Isaiah 54:13

of it and not die.
51"I am the living bread that came down out of heaven; if anyone eats of this bread, he shall live forever; and the bread also which I shall give for the life of the world is My flesh."
52The Jews therefore *began* to argue with one another, saying, "How can this man give us *His* flesh to eat?"
53Jesus therefore said to them, "Truly, truly, I say to you, unless you eat the flesh of the Son of Man and drink His blood, you have no life in yourselves.
54"He who eats My flesh and drinks My blood has eternal life, and I will raise him up on the last day.
55"For My flesh is true food, and My blood is true drink.
56"He who eats My flesh and drinks My blood abides in Me, and I in him.
57"As the living Father sent Me, and I live because of the Father, so he who eats Me, he also shall live because of Me.
58"This is the bread which came down out of heaven; not as the fathers ate, and died, he who eats this bread shall live forever."

Words to the Disciples
59These things He said in the synagogue, as He taught in Capernaum.
60Many therefore of His disciples, when they heard *this* said, "This is a difficult statement; who can listen to it?"
61But Jesus, conscious that His disciples grumbled at this, said to them, "Does this cause you to stumble?

αὐτοῦ φάγῃ καὶ μὴ ἀποθάνῃ. 51 ἐγώ
it may eat and may not die. I

εἰμι ὁ ἄρτος ὁ ζῶν ὁ ἐκ τοῦ οὐρανοῦ
am the bread - living the [one] out of - heaven

καταβάς· ἐάν τις φάγῃ ἐκ τούτου τοῦ
having come down; if anyone eats of this

ἄρτου, ζήσει εἰς τὸν αἰῶνα· ¹indeed ³the ⁴bread
bread, he will live to the age;

δὲ ὃν ἐγὼ δώσω ἡ σάρξ μού ἐστιν
¹and which I will give the flesh of me is

ὑπὲρ τῆς τοῦ κόσμου ζωῆς. 52 Ἐμάχοντο
for ¹the ²of the ⁴world ³life. Fought

οὖν πρὸς ἀλλήλους οἱ Ἰουδαῖοι λέγοντες·
therefore with one another the Jews saying:

πῶς δύναται οὗτος ἡμῖν δοῦναι τὴν
How can this man us to give the(his)

σάρκα φαγεῖν; 53 εἶπεν οὖν αὐτοῖς ὁ
flesh to eat? Said therefore to them -

Ἰησοῦς· ἀμὴν ἀμὴν λέγω ὑμῖν, ἐὰν μὴ
Jesus: Truly truly I say to you, unless

φάγητε τὴν σάρκα τοῦ υἱοῦ τοῦ ἀνθρώπου
ye eat the flesh of the Son - of man

καὶ πίητε αὐτοῦ τὸ αἷμα, οὐκ ἔχετε
and drink of him the blood, ye have not

ζωὴν ἐν ἑαυτοῖς. 54 ὁ τρώγων μου τὴν
life in yourselves. The [one] eating of me the

σάρκα καὶ πίνων μου τὸ αἷμα ἔχει ζωὴν
flesh and drinking of me the blood has life

αἰώνιον, κἀγὼ ἀναστήσω αὐτὸν τῇ ἐσχάτῃ
eternal, and I will raise up him in the last

ἡμέρα. 55 ἡ γὰρ σάρξ μου ἀληθής
day. For the flesh of me ²true

ἐστιν βρῶσις, καὶ τὸ αἷμά μου ἀληθής
¹is ⁴food, and the blood of me ²true

ἐστιν πόσις. 56 ὁ τρώγων μου τὴν
¹is ³drink. The [one] eating of me the

σάρκα καὶ πίνων μου τὸ αἷμα ἐν ἐμοὶ
flesh and drinking of me the blood in me

μένει κἀγὼ ἐν αὐτῷ. 57 καθὼς ἀπέστειλέν
remains and I in him. As sent

με ὁ ζῶν πατὴρ κἀγὼ ζῶ διὰ τὸν
me the living Father and I live because of the

πατέρα, καὶ ὁ τρώγων με κἀκεῖνος
Father, also the [one] eating me even that one

ζήσει δι᾽ ἐμέ. 58 οὗτός ἐστιν ὁ ἄρτος ὁ
will live because of me. This is the bread -

ἐξ οὐρανοῦ καταβάς, οὐ καθὼς ἔφαγον
out of heaven having come down, not as ate

οἱ πατέρες καὶ ἀπέθανον· ὁ τρώγων
the fathers and died; the [one] eating

τοῦτον τὸν ἄρτον ζήσει εἰς τὸν αἰῶνα.
this - bread will live unto the age.

59 Ταῦτα εἶπεν ἐν συναγωγῇ διδάσκων ἐν
These things he said in a synagogue teaching in

Καφαρναούμ. 60 Πολλοὶ οὖν ἀκούσαντες
Capernaum. ²Many ¹therefore ⁷hearing

ἐκ τῶν μαθητῶν αὐτοῦ εἶπαν· σκληρός
³of ⁴the ⁵disciples ⁶of him said: Hard

ἐστιν ὁ λόγος οὗτος· τίς δύναται αὐτοῦ
is - word this; who can it

ἀκούειν; 61 εἰδὼς δὲ ὁ Ἰησοῦς ἐν ἑαυτῷ
to hear? But knowing - Jesus in himself

ὅτι γογγύζουσιν περὶ τούτου οἱ μαθηταὶ
that ⁴are murmuring ⁵about ⁶this ¹the ²disciples

αὐτοῦ, εἶπεν αὐτοῖς· τοῦτο ὑμᾶς σκανδαλίζει;
³of him, said to them: This you offends?

---

the living bread that came down from heaven. If anyone eats of this bread, he will live forever. This bread is my flesh, which I will give for the life of the world."
52Then the Jews began to argue sharply among themselves, "How can this man give us his flesh to eat?"
53Jesus said to them, "I tell you the truth, unless you eat the flesh of the Son of Man and drink his blood, you have no life in you. 54Whoever eats my flesh and drinks my blood has eternal life, and I will raise him up at the last day. 55For my flesh is real food and my blood is real drink. 56Whoever eats my flesh and drinks my blood remains in me, and I in him. 57Just as the living Father sent me and I live because of the Father, so the one who feeds on me will live because of me. 58This is the bread that came down from heaven. Your forefathers ate manna and died, but he who feeds on this bread will live forever." 59He said this while teaching in the synagogue in Capernaum.

Many Disciples Desert Jesus

60On hearing it, many of his disciples said, "This is a hard teaching. Who can accept it?"
61Aware that his disciples were grumbling about this, Jesus said to them, "Does this offend you? 62What if

Left column (English)

62"What then if you should behold the Son of Man ascending where He was before?

63"It is the Spirit who gives life; the flesh profits nothing; the words that I have spoken to you are spirit and are life.

64"But there are some of you who do not believe." For Jesus knew from the beginning who they were who did not believe, and who it was that would betray Him.

65And He was saying, "For this reason I have said to you, that no one can come to Me, unless it has been granted him from the Father."

Peter's Confession of Faith

66As a result of this many of His disciples withdrew, and were not walking with Him anymore.

67Jesus said therefore to the twelve, "You do not want to go away also, do you?"

68Simon Peter answered Him, "Lord, to whom shall we go? You have words of eternal life.

69"And we have believed and have come to know that You are the Holy One of God."

70Jesus answered them, "Did I Myself not choose you, the twelve, and *yet* one of you is a devil?"

71Now He meant Judas *the son* of Simon Iscariot, for he, one of the twelve, was going to betray Him.

Chapter 7

Jesus Teaches at the Feast

AND after these things Jesus was walking in Galilee; for He was unwilling to walk in Judea, because the Jews were seeking to kill Him.

2Now the feast of the Jews, the Feast of Booths, was at hand.

3His brothers therefore said to Him, "Depart from

Middle column (Greek interlinear)

62 ἐὰν οὖν θεωρῆτε τὸν υἱὸν τοῦ ἀνθρώπου
If then ye behold the Son - of man

ἀναβαίνοντα ὅπου ἦν τὸ πρότερον; **63** τὸ
ascending where he was at first? † The

πνεῦμά ἐστιν τὸ ζωοποιοῦν, ἡ σὰρξ οὐκ
spirit is the [thing] quickening, the flesh not

ὠφελεῖ οὐδέν· τὰ ῥήματα ἃ ἐγὼ λελάληκα
profits no(any)thing; the words which I have spoken

ὑμῖν πνεῦμά ἐστιν καὶ ζωή ἐστιν. **64** ἀλλ᾽
to you spirit is(are) and life is(are). But

εἰσὶν ἐξ ὑμῶν τινες οἳ οὐ πιστεύουσιν. ἤδει
there are of you some who do not believe. knew

γὰρ ἐξ ἀρχῆς ὁ Ἰησοῦς τίνες εἰσὶν
For from [the] beginning - Jesus who are(were)

οἱ μὴ πιστεύοντες καὶ τίς ἐστιν ὁ
the [ones] not believing and who is(was) the

παραδώσων αὐτόν. **65** καὶ ἔλεγεν·
[one] betraying him. And he said :

διὰ τοῦτο εἴρηκα ὑμῖν ὅτι οὐδεὶς δύναται
Therefore I have told you that no one can

ἐλθεῖν πρός με ἐὰν μὴ ᾖ δεδομένον
to come to me unless it is *having been* given

αὐτῷ ἐκ τοῦ πατρός.
to him of the Father.

66 Ἐκ τούτου πολλοὶ τῶν μαθητῶν
From this many of the disciples

αὐτοῦ ἀπῆλθον εἰς τὰ ὀπίσω καὶ οὐκέτι
of him went away back† and no longer

μετ᾽ αὐτοῦ περιεπάτουν. **67** εἶπεν οὖν ὁ
with him walked. Said therefore -

Ἰησοῦς τοῖς δώδεκα· μὴ καὶ ὑμεῖς
Jesus to the twelve : Not also ye

θέλετε ὑπάγειν; **68** ἀπεκρίθη αὐτῷ Σίμων
wish to go? Answered him Simon

Πέτρος· κύριε, πρὸς τίνα ἀπελευσόμεθα;
Peter : Lord, to whom shall we go away?

ῥήματα ζωῆς αἰωνίου ἔχεις· **69** καὶ ἡμεῖς
words of life eternal thou hast; and we

πεπιστεύκαμεν καὶ ἐγνώκαμεν ὅτι σὺ εἶ
have believed and have known that thou art

ὁ ἅγιος τοῦ θεοῦ. **70** ἀπεκρίθη αὐτοῖς ὁ
the holy one - of God. Answered them -

Ἰησοῦς· οὐκ ἐγὼ ὑμᾶς τοὺς δώδεκα
Jesus : ³Not ²I ⁴you ⁵the ⁶twelve

ἐξελεξάμην; καὶ ἐξ ὑμῶν εἷς διάβολός
¹chose? and of you one a devil

ἐστιν. **71** ἔλεγεν δὲ τὸν Ἰούδαν Σίμωνος
is. Now he spoke [of] - Judas [son] of Simon

Ἰσκαριώτου· οὗτος γὰρ ἔμελλεν παραδιδόναι
Iscariot; for this one was about to betray

αὐτόν, εἷς ἐκ τῶν δώδεκα.
him, one of the twelve.

7 Καὶ μετὰ ταῦτα περιεπάτει ὁ Ἰησοῦς
And after these things walked - Jesus

ἐν τῇ Γαλιλαίᾳ· οὐ γὰρ ἤθελεν ἐν τῇ
in - Galilee; for he did not wish in -

Ἰουδαίᾳ περιπατεῖν, ὅτι ἐζήτουν αὐτὸν οἱ
Judæa to walk, because ²were seeking ³him ¹the

Ἰουδαῖοι ἀποκτεῖναι. **2** ἦν δὲ ἐγγὺς ἡ
³Jews ⁴to kill. Now was near the

ἑορτὴ τῶν Ἰουδαίων ἡ σκηνοπηγία. **3** εἶπον
feast of the Jews the Tabernacles. Said

οὖν πρὸς αὐτὸν οἱ ἀδελφοὶ αὐτοῦ·
therefore to him the brothers of him :

Right column (English)

you see the Son of Man ascend to where he was before! 63The Spirit gives life; the flesh counts for nothing. The words I have spoken to you are spirit*k* and they are life. 64Yet there are some of you who do not believe." For Jesus had known from the beginning which of them did not believe and who would betray him. 65He went on to say, "This is why I told you that no one can come to me unless the Father has enabled him."

66From this time many of his disciples turned back and no longer followed him.

67"You do not want to leave too, do you?" Jesus asked the Twelve.

68Simon Peter answered him, "Lord, to whom shall we go? You have the words of eternal life. 69We believe and know that you are the Holy One of God."

70Then Jesus replied, "Have I not chosen you, the Twelve? Yet one of you is a devil!" 71(He meant Judas, the son of Simon Iscariot, who, though one of the Twelve, was later to betray him.)

Chapter 7

Jesus Goes to the Feast of Tabernacles

AFTER this, Jesus went around in Galilee, purposely staying away from Judea because the Jews there were waiting to take his life. 2But when the Jewish Feast of Tabernacles was near, 3Jesus' brothers said to him, "You

k63 Or Spirit

here, and go into Judea, that Your disciples also may behold Your works which You are doing.
4"For no one does anything in secret, when he himself seeks to be *known* publicly. If You do these things, show Yourself to the world."
5For not even His brothers were believing in Him.
6Jesus therefore *said to them, "My time is not yet at hand, but your time is always opportune.
7"The world cannot hate you; but it hates Me because I testify of it, that its deeds are evil.
8"Go up to the feast yourselves; I do not go up to this feast because My time has not yet fully come."
9And having said these things to them, He stayed in Galilee.
10But when His brothers had gone up to the feast, then He Himself also went up, not publicly, but as it were, in secret.
11The Jews therefore were seeking Him at the feast, and were saying, "Where is He?"
12And there was much grumbling among the multitudes concerning Him; some were saying, "He is a good man"; others were saying, "No, on the contrary, He leads the multitude astray."
13Yet no one was speaking openly of Him for fear of the Jews.
14But when it was now the midst of the feast Jesus went up into the temple, and *began to* teach.
15The Jews therefore were marveling, saying, "How has this man become learned, having never been educated?"
16Jesus therefore answered them, and said,

μετάβηθι ἐντεῦθεν καὶ ὕπαγε εἰς τὴν Ἰουδαίαν,
Depart hence and go into - Judaea,

ἵνα καὶ οἱ μαθηταί σου θεωρήσουσιν τὰ
that also the disciples of thee will behold the

ἔργα σου ἃ ποιεῖς· 4 οὐδεὶς γάρ τι ἐν
works of thee which thou doest; for no one anything in

κρυπτῷ ποιεῖ καὶ ζητεῖ αὐτὸς ἐν παρρησίᾳ
secret does and seeks [him]self in [the] open

εἶναι. εἰ ταῦτα ποιεῖς, φανέρωσον σεαυτὸν
to be. If these things thou doest, manifest thyself

τῷ κόσμῳ. 5 οὐδὲ γὰρ οἱ ἀδελφοὶ
to the world. For not the brothers

αὐτοῦ ἐπίστευον εἰς αὐτόν. 6 λέγει οὖν
of him believed in him. Says therefore

αὐτοῖς ὁ Ἰησοῦς· ὁ καιρὸς ὁ ἐμὸς
to them - Jesus: The - time - ¹my

οὔπω πάρεστιν, ὁ δὲ καιρὸς ὁ ὑμέτερος
not yet is arrived, but the ²time - ¹your

πάντοτέ ἐστιν ἕτοιμος. 7 οὐ δύναται ὁ
always is ready. Cannot the

κόσμος μισεῖν ὑμᾶς, ἐμὲ δὲ μισεῖ, ὅτι
world to hate you, but me it hates, because

ἐγὼ μαρτυρῶ περὶ αὐτοῦ ὅτι τὰ ἔργα
I witness about it that the works

αὐτοῦ πονηρά ἐστιν. 8 ὑμεῖς ἀνάβητε εἰς
of it evil is(are). ¹Ye ²go ³up to

τὴν ἑορτήν· ἐγὼ οὐκ ἀναβαίνω εἰς τὴν
the feast; I am not going up to -

ἑορτὴν ταύτην, ὅτι ὁ ἐμὸς καιρὸς οὔπω
feast this, because the my time not yet

πεπλήρωται. 9 ταῦτα δὲ εἰπὼν αὐτοῖς
has been fulfilled. And these things saying to them

ἔμεινεν ἐν τῇ Γαλιλαίᾳ. 10 Ὡς δὲ
he remained in - Galilee. But when

ἀνέβησαν οἱ ἀδελφοὶ αὐτοῦ εἰς τὴν ἑορτήν,
went up the brothers of him to the feast,

τότε καὶ αὐτὸς ἀνέβη, οὐ φανερῶς ἀλλὰ
then also he went up, not manifestly but

ὡς ἐν κρυπτῷ. 11 οἱ οὖν Ἰουδαῖοι
as in secret. Therefore the Jews

ἐζήτουν αὐτὸν ἐν τῇ ἑορτῇ καὶ ἔλεγον·
sought him at the feast and said :

ποῦ ἐστιν ἐκεῖνος; 12 καὶ γογγυσμὸς περὶ
Where is that man? And ²murmuring ⁴about

αὐτοῦ ἦν πολὺς ἐν τοῖς ὄχλοις· οἱ μὲν
⁵him ¹there was ³much in the crowds; some

ἔλεγον ὅτι ἀγαθός ἐστιν· ἄλλοι [δὲ]
said[,] - A good man he is; but others

ἔλεγον· οὔ, ἀλλὰ πλανᾷ τὸν ὄχλον.
said : No, but he deceives the crowd.

13 οὐδεὶς μέντοι παρρησίᾳ ἐλάλει περὶ
No one however openly spoke about

αὐτοῦ διὰ τὸν φόβον τῶν Ἰουδαίων.
him because of the fear of the Jews.

14 Ἤδη δὲ τῆς ἑορτῆς μεσούσης ἀνέβη
But now the feast being in [its] middle⁸ went up
= in the middle of the feast

Ἰησοῦς εἰς τὸ ἱερὸν καὶ ἐδίδασκεν.
Jesus to the temple and taught.

15 ἐθαύμαζον οὖν οἱ Ἰουδαῖοι λέγοντες·
Marvelled therefore the Jews saying :

πῶς οὗτος γράμματα οἶδεν μὴ μεμαθηκώς;
How this man letters knows not having learned?

16 ἀπεκρίθη οὖν αὐτοῖς Ἰησοῦς καὶ εἶπεν·
Answered therefore them Jesus and said :

ought to leave here and go to Judea, so that your disciples may see the miracles you do. 4No one who wants to become a public figure acts in secret. Since you are doing these things, show yourself to the world." 5For even his own brothers did not believe in him.
6Therefore Jesus told them, "The right time for me has not yet come; for you any time is right. 7The world cannot hate you, but it hates me because I testify that what it does is evil. 8You go to the Feast. I am not yet[ʲ] going up to this Feast, because for me the right time has not yet come." 9Having said this, he stayed in Galilee.
10However, after his brothers had left for the Feast, he went also, not publicly, but in secret. 11Now at the Feast the Jews were watching for him and asking, "Where is that man?"
12Among the crowds there was widespread whispering about him. Some said, "He is a good man." Others replied, "No, he deceives the people." 13But no one would say anything publicly about him for fear of the Jews.

Jesus Teaches at the Feast
14Not until halfway through the Feast did Jesus go up to the temple courts and begin to teach. 15The Jews were amazed and asked, "How did this man get such learning without having studied?"
16Jesus answered, "My

ʲ8 Some early manuscripts do not have yet.

"My teaching is not Mine, but His who sent Me.

17"If any man is willing to do His will, he shall know of the teaching, whether it is of God, or *whether* I speak from Myself.

18"He who speaks from himself seeks his own glory; but He who is seeking the glory of the one who sent Him, He is true, and there is no unrighteousness in Him.

19"Did not Moses give you the Law, and *yet* none of you carries out the Law? Why do you seek to kill Me?"

20The multitude answered, "You have a demon! Who seeks to kill You?"

21Jesus answered and said to them, "I did one deed, and you all marvel.

22"On this account Moses has given you circumcision (not because it is from Moses, but from the fathers), and on *the* Sabbath you circumcise a man.

23"If a man receives circumcision on *the* Sabbath that the Law of Moses may not be broken, are you angry with Me because I made an entire man well on *the* Sabbath?

24"Do not judge according to appearance, but judge with righteous judgment."

25Therefore some of the people of Jerusalem were saying, "Is this not the man whom they are seeking to kill?

26"And look, He is speaking publicly, and they are saying nothing to Him. The rulers do not really know that this is the Christ, do they?

27"However, we know where this man is from; but whenever the Christ may come, no one knows where He is from."

28Jesus therefore cried out in the temple, teaching

ἡ ἐμὴ διδαχὴ οὐκ ἔστιν ἐμὴ ἀλλὰ τοῦ
The my teaching is not mine but of the
πέμψαντός με· **17** ἐάν τις θέλῃ τὸ θέλημα
[one] having sent me; if anyone wishes the will
αὐτοῦ ποιεῖν, γνώσεται περὶ τῆς διδαχῆς,
of him to do, he will know concerning the teaching,
πότερον ἐκ τοῦ θεοῦ ἐστιν ἢ ἐγὼ ἀπ'
whether of - God it is or I from
ἐμαυτοῦ λαλῶ. **18** ὁ ἀφ' ἑαυτοῦ λαλῶν
myself speak. The [one] from himself speaking
τὴν δόξαν τὴν ἰδίαν ζητεῖ· ὁ δὲ ζητῶν
his own glory seeks; but the [one] seeking
τὴν δόξαν τοῦ πέμψαντος αὐτόν, οὗτος
the glory of the [one] having sent him, this man
ἀληθής ἐστιν καὶ ἀδικία ἐν αὐτῷ οὐκ
true is and unrighteousness in him not
ἔστιν. **19** οὐ Μωϋσῆς ἔδωκεν ὑμῖν τὸν
is. Not Moses gave you the
νόμον; καὶ οὐδεὶς ἐξ ὑμῶν ποιεῖ τὸν
law? and no one of you does the
νόμον. τί με ζητεῖτε ἀποκτεῖναι;
law. Why me seek ye to kill?
20 ἀπεκρίθη ὁ ὄχλος· δαιμόνιον ἔχεις·
Answered the crowd : A demon thou hast;
τίς σε ζητεῖ ἀποκτεῖναι; **21** ἀπεκρίθη
who thee seeks to kill? Answered
Ἰησοῦς καὶ εἶπεν αὐτοῖς· ἓν ἔργον ἐποίησα
Jesus and said to them : One work I did
καὶ πάντες θαυμάζετε. **22** διὰ τοῦτο
and all ye marvel. Because of this
Μωϋσῆς δέδωκεν ὑμῖν τὴν περιτομήν, —
Moses has given you - circumcision, —
οὐχ ὅτι ἐκ τοῦ Μωϋσέως ἐστὶν ἀλλ' ἐκ
not that of - Moses it is but of
τῶν πατέρων, — καὶ ἐν σαββάτῳ
the fathers, — and on a sabbath
περιτέμνετε ἄνθρωπον **23** εἰ περιτομὴν
ye circumcise a man. If ªcircumcision
λαμβάνει [ὁ] ἄνθρωπος ἐν σαββάτῳ ἵνα
²receives - ¹a man on a sabbath in
μὴ λυθῇ ὁ νόμος Μωϋσέως, ἐμοὶ χολᾶτε,
is not broken the law of Moses, with me are ye angry
ὅτι ὅλον ἄνθρωπον ὑγιῆ ἐποίησα ἐν
because a whole man healthy I made on
σαββάτῳ; **24** μὴ κρίνετε κατ' ὄψιν, ἀλλὰ
a sabbath? Judge not according to face, but
τὴν δικαίαν κρίσιν κρίνατε. **25** Ἔλεγον
- righteous judgment judge. Said
οὖν τινες ἐκ τῶν Ἱεροσολυμιτῶν· οὐχ
therefore some of the Jerusalemites : ²Not
οὗτός ἐστιν ὃν ζητοῦσιν ἀποκτεῖναι; **26** καὶ
³this man ¹is it whom they are seeking to kill? and
ἴδε παρρησίᾳ λαλεῖ, καὶ οὐδὲν αὐτῷ
behold openly he speaks, and nothing to him
λέγουσιν. μήποτε ἀληθῶς ἔγνωσαν οἱ
they say. Perhaps indeed knew the
ἄρχοντες ὅτι οὗτός ἐστιν ὁ χριστός; *
rulers that this is the Christ? *
27 ἀλλὰ τοῦτον οἴδαμεν πόθεν ἐστίν· ὁ δὲ
But this man we know whence he is; but ²the
χριστὸς ὅταν ἔρχηται, οὐδεὶς γινώσκει
³Christ ¹when comes, no one knows
πόθεν ἐστίν. **28** ἔκραξεν οὖν ἐν τῷ ἱερῷ
whence he is. ³Cried out ²therefore ⁴in ⁵the ⁶temple

teaching is not my own. It comes from him who sent me. 17If anyone chooses to do God's will, he will find out whether my teaching comes from God or whether I speak on my own. 18He who speaks on his own does so to gain honor for himself, but he who works for the honor of the one who sent him is a man of truth; there is nothing false about him. 19Has not Moses given you the law? Yet not one of you keeps the law. Why are you trying to kill me?"

20"You are demon-possessed," the crowd answered. "Who is trying to kill you?"

21Jesus said to them, "I did one miracle, and you are all astonished. 22Yet, because Moses gave you circumcision (though actually it did not come from Moses, but from the patriarchs), you circumcise a child on the Sabbath. 23Now if a child can be circumcised on the Sabbath so that the law of Moses may not be broken, why are you angry with me for healing the whole man on the Sabbath? 24Stop judging by mere appearances, and make a right judgment."

Is Jesus the Christ?

25At that point some of the people of Jerusalem began to ask, "Isn't this the man they are trying to kill? 26Here he is, speaking publicly, and they are not saying a word to him. Have the authorities really concluded that he is the Christ*m*? 27But we know where this man is from; when the Christ comes, no one will know where he is from."

28Then Jesus, still teaching in the temple courts,

---

* As this question is introduced by μήποτε, a negative answer is expected; see page xiii, and note ver. 31 below.

*m*26 Or *Messiah*; also in verses 27, 31, 41 and 42

and saying, "You both know Me and know where I am from; and I have not come of Myself, but He who sent Me is true, whom you do not know.
29"I know Him; because I am from Him, and He sent Me."
30They were seeking therefore to seize Him; and no man laid his hand on Him, because His hour had not yet come.
31But many of the multitude believed in Him; and they were saying, "When the Christ shall come, He will not perform more signs than those which this man has, will He?"
32The Pharisees heard the multitude muttering these things about Him; and the chief priests and the Pharisees sent officers to seize Him.
33Jesus therefore said, "For a little while longer I am with you, then I go to Him who sent Me.
34"You shall seek Me, and shall not find Me; and where I am, you cannot come."
35The Jews therefore said to one another, "Where does this man intend to go that we shall not find Him? He is not intending to go to the Dispersion among the Greeks, and teach the Greeks, is He?
36"What is this statement that He said, 'You will seek Me, and will not find Me; and where I am, you cannot come'?"
37Now on the last day, the great *day* of the feast, Jesus stood and cried out, saying, "If any man is thirsty, let him come to Me and drink.
38"He who believes in Me, as the Scripture said, 'From his innermost being

διδάσκων ὁ Ἰησοῦς καὶ λέγων· κἀμὲ
teaching - ¹Jesus ²and ³saying : Both me
οἴδατε καὶ οἴδατε πόθεν εἰμί· καὶ ἀπ'
ye know and ye know whence I am; and from
ἐμαυτοῦ οὐκ ἐλήλυθα, ἀλλ' ἔστιν ἀληθινὸς
myself I have not come, but he is true
ὁ πέμψας με, ὃν ὑμεῖς οὐκ οἴδατε·
the [one] having sent me, whom ye know not;
29 ἐγὼ οἶδα αὐτόν, ὅτι παρ' αὐτοῦ εἰμι
I know him, because ²from ³him ¹I am
κἀκεῖνός με ἀπέστειλεν. 30 Ἐζήτουν οὖν
⁴and that one ⁵me ⁶sent. They sought therefore
αὐτὸν πιάσαι, καὶ οὐδεὶς ἐπέβαλεν ἐπ'
him to arrest, and no one laid *on* on
αὐτὸν τὴν χεῖρα, ὅτι οὔπω ἐληλύθει ἡ
him the hand, because not yet had come the
ὥρα αὐτοῦ. 31 Ἐκ τοῦ ὄχλου δὲ πολλοὶ
hour of him. ³of ⁴the ⁵crowd ¹But ²many
ἐπίστευσαν εἰς αὐτόν, καὶ ἔλεγον· ὁ
believed in him, and said : ²The
χριστὸς ὅταν ἔλθῃ, μὴ πλείονα σημεῖα
³Christ ¹when ⁴comes, *not* more signs
ποιήσει ὧν οὗτος ἐποίησεν; 32 ἤκουσαν
will he do [than] which this man did? ³Heard
οἱ Φαρισαῖοι τοῦ ὄχλου γογγύζοντος περὶ
¹the ²Pharisees ⁴the ⁵crowd ⁶murmuring ⁷about
αὐτοῦ ταῦτα, καὶ ἀπέστειλαν οἱ ἀρχιερεῖς
⁹him ⁷these things, and ⁸sent ¹the ²chief priests
καὶ οἱ Φαρισαῖοι ὑπηρέτας ἵνα πιάσωσιν
³and ⁴the ⁵Pharisees ⁶attendants that they might arrest
αὐτόν. 33 εἶπεν οὖν ὁ Ἰησοῦς· ἔτι
him. Said therefore - Jesus : Yet
χρόνον μικρὸν μεθ' ὑμῶν εἰμι καὶ ὑπάγω
time a little with you I am and I go
πρὸς τὸν πέμψαντά με. 34 ζητήσετέ με
to the [one] having sent me. Ye will seek me
καὶ οὐχ εὑρήσετε, καὶ ὅπου εἰμὶ ἐγὼ
and will not find, and where am I
ὑμεῖς οὐ δύνασθε ἐλθεῖν. 35 εἶπον οὖν
ye cannot *to* come. Said therefore
οἱ Ἰουδαῖοι πρὸς ἑαυτούς· ποῦ οὗτος
the Jews to themselves : Where this man
μέλλει πορεύεσθαι, ὅτι ἡμεῖς οὐχ εὑρήσομεν
is about to go, that we will not find
αὐτόν; μὴ εἰς τὴν διασπορὰν τῶν Ἑλλήνων
him? *not* to the dispersion of the Greeks
μέλλει πορεύεσθαι καὶ διδάσκειν τοὺς
is he about to go and to teach the
Ἕλληνας; 36 τίς ἐστιν ὁ λόγος οὗτος
Greeks? What is - word this
ὃν εἶπεν· ζητήσετέ με καὶ οὐχ εὑρήσετε,
which he said : Ye will seek me and will not find,
καὶ ὅπου εἰμὶ ἐγὼ ὑμεῖς οὐ δύνασθε
and where am I ye cannot
ἐλθεῖν;
to come?
37 Ἐν δὲ τῇ ἐσχάτῃ ἡμέρᾳ τῇ μεγάλῃ
Now in the last day the great [day]
τῆς ἑορτῆς εἱστήκει ὁ Ἰησοῦς καὶ ἔκραξεν
of the feast stood - Jesus and cried out
λέγων· ἐάν τις διψᾷ, ἐρχέσθω πρός με
saying : If anyone thirsts, let him come to me
καὶ πινέτω. 38 ὁ πιστεύων εἰς ἐμέ,
and drink. The [one] believing in me,
καθὼς εἶπεν ἡ γραφή, ποταμοὶ ἐκ τῆς
as said the scripture, ¹rivers ⁵out of ⁶the

cried out, "Yes, you know me, and you know where I am from. I am not here on my own, but he who sent me is true. You do not know him, 29but I know him because I am from him and he sent me."
30At this they tried to seize him, but no one laid a hand on him, because his time had not yet come.
31Still, many in the crowd put their faith in him. They said, "When the Christ comes, will he do more miraculous signs than this man?"
32The Pharisees heard the crowd whispering such things about him. Then the chief priests and the Pharisees sent temple guards to arrest him.
33Jesus said, "I am with you for only a short time, and then I go to the one who sent me. 34You will look for me, but you will not find me; and where I am, you cannot come."
35The Jews said to one another, "Where does this man intend to go that we cannot find him? Will he go where our people live scattered among the Greeks, and teach the Greeks? 36What did he mean when he said, 'You will look for me, but you will not find me,' and 'Where I am, you cannot come'?"
37On the last and greatest day of the Feast, Jesus stood and said in a loud voice, "If anyone is thirsty, let him come to me and drink. 38Whoever believes in me, as [n] the Scripture has said, streams of

[n] 37,38 Or / If anyone is thirsty, let him come to me. / And let him drink. 38who believes in me. / As

shall flow rivers of living water.' "

39But this He spoke of the Spirit, whom those who believed in Him were to receive; for the Spirit was not yet *given,* because Jesus was not yet glorified.

Division of People over Jesus

40*Some* of the multitude therefore, when they heard these words, were saying, "This certainly is the Prophet."

41Others were saying, "This is the Christ." Still others were saying, "Surely the Christ is not going to come from Galilee, is He?

42"Has not the Scripture said that the Christ comes from the offspring of David, and from Bethlehem, the village where David was?"

43So there arose a division in the multitude because of Him.

44And some of them wanted to seize Him, but no one laid hands on Him.

45The officers therefore came to the chief priests and Pharisees, and they said to them, "Why did you not bring Him?"

46The officers answered, "Never did a man speak the way this man speaks."

47The Pharisees therefore answered them, "You have not also been led astray, have you?

48"No one of the rulers or Pharisees has believed in Him, has he?

49"But this multitude which does not know the Law is accursed."

50Nicodemus *said to them (he who came to Him before, being one of them),

51"Our Law does not judge a man, unless it first hears from him and knows what he is doing, does it?"

52They answered and said to him, "You are not also from Galilee, are you? Search, and see that no

---

κοιλίας αὐτοῦ ῥεύσουσιν ὕδατος ζῶντος.
[7]belly [8]of him [4]will flow [5]water [6]of living.

39 τοῦτο δὲ εἶπεν περὶ τοῦ πνεύματος
But this he said concerning the Spirit

οὗ ἔμελλον λαμβάνειν οἱ πιστεύσαντες
whom were about to receive the [ones] believing

εἰς αὐτόν· οὔπω γὰρ ἦν πνεῦμα, ὅτι
in him; for not yet was [?the] Spirit, because

Ἰησοῦς οὐδέπω ἐδοξάσθη. 40 Ἐκ τοῦ
Jesus not yet was glorified. [Some] of the

ὄχλου οὖν ἀκούσαντες τῶν λόγων τούτων
crowd therefore hearing – words these

ἔλεγον [ὅτι]· οὗτός ἐστιν ἀληθῶς ὁ
said – : This man is truly the

προφήτης· 41 ἄλλοι ἔλεγον· οὗτός ἐστιν ὁ
prophet; Others said : This man is the

χριστός· οἱ δὲ ἔλεγον· μὴ γὰρ ἐκ τῆς
Christ; But others† said : Not then out of –

Γαλιλαίας ὁ χριστὸς ἔρχεται; 42 οὐχ ἡ
Galilee the Christ comes? not the

γραφὴ εἶπεν ὅτι ἐκ τοῦ σπέρματος Δαυίδ,
scripture said that of the seed of David,

καὶ ἀπὸ Βηθλέεμ τῆς κώμης ὅπου ἦν
and from Bethlehem the village where was

Δαυίδ, ἔρχεται ὁ χριστός; 43 σχίσμα
David, comes the Christ? A division

οὖν ἐγένετο ἐν τῷ ὄχλῳ δι᾽ αὐτόν·
therefore became in the crowd because of him;

44 τινὲς δὲ ἤθελον ἐξ αὐτῶν πιάσαι αὐτόν,
and [1]some [4]wished [2]of [3]them to arrest him,

ἀλλ᾽ οὐδεὶς ἐπέβαλεν ἐπ᾽ αὐτὸν τὰς χεῖρας.
but no one laid on on him the(his) hands.

45 Ἦλθον οὖν οἱ ὑπηρέται πρὸς τοὺς
Came therefore the attendants to the

ἀρχιερεῖς καὶ Φαρισαίους, καὶ εἶπον αὐτοῖς
chief priests and Pharisees, and [2]said [3]to them

ἐκεῖνοι· διὰ τί οὐκ ἠγάγετε αὐτόν;
[1]those: Why did ye not bring him?

46 ἀπεκρίθησαν οἱ ὑπηρέται· οὐδέποτε
Answered the attendants : Never

ἐλάλησεν οὕτως ἄνθρωπος, ὡς οὗτος λαλεῖ
spoke so a man, as [1]this [2]speaks

ὁ ἄνθρωπος. 47 ἀπεκρίθησαν οὖν αὐτοῖς
– [2]man. Answered therefore them

οἱ Φαρισαῖοι· μὴ καὶ ὑμεῖς πεπλάνησθε;
the Pharisees : Not also ye have been deceived?

48 μή τις ἐκ τῶν ἀρχόντων ἐπίστευσεν
not anyone of the rulers believed

εἰς αὐτὸν ἢ ἐκ τῶν Φαρισαίων; 49 ἀλλὰ
in him or of the Pharisees? But

ὁ ὄχλος οὗτος ὁ μὴ γινώσκων τὸν
– crowd this – not knowing the

νόμον ἐπάρατοί εἰσιν. 50 λέγει Νικόδημος
law cursed are. Says Nicodemus

πρὸς αὐτούς, ὁ ἐλθὼν πρὸς αὐτὸν πρότερον,
to them, the [one] having come to him firstly,

εἷς ὢν ἐξ αὐτῶν· 51 μὴ ὁ νόμος ἡμῶν
[2]one [1]being of them : Not the law of us

κρίνει τὸν ἄνθρωπον ἐὰν μὴ ἀκούσῃ
judges the man unless it hears

πρῶτον παρ᾽ αὐτοῦ καὶ γνῷ τί ποιεῖ;
first from him and knows what he does?

52 ἀπεκρίθησαν καὶ εἶπαν αὐτῷ· μὴ καὶ
They answered and said to him : Not also

σὺ ἐκ τῆς Γαλιλαίας εἶ; ἐρεύνησον καὶ
thou of – Galilee art? search and

---

living water will flow from within him." 39By this he meant the Spirit, whom those who believed in him were later to receive. Up to that time the Spirit had not been given, since Jesus had not yet been glorified.

40On hearing his words, some of the people said, "Surely this man is the Prophet."

41Others said, "He is the Christ."

Still others asked, "How can the Christ come from Galilee? 42Does not the Scripture say that the Christ will come from David's family*o* and from Bethlehem, the town where David lived?" 43Thus the people were divided because of Jesus. 44Some wanted to seize him, but no one laid a hand on him.

Unbelief of the Jewish Leaders

45Finally the temple guards went back to the chief priests and Pharisees, who asked them, "Why didn't you bring him in?"

46"No one ever spoke the way this man does," the guards declared.

47"You mean he has deceived you also?" the Pharisees retorted. 48"Has any of the rulers or of the Pharisees believed in him? 49No! But this mob that knows nothing of the law—there is a curse on them."

50Nicodemus, who had gone to Jesus earlier and who was one of their own number, asked, 51"Does our law condemn anyone without first hearing him to find out what he is doing?"

52They replied, "Are you from Galilee, too? Look

*o*42 Greek *seed*

prophet arises out of Galilee."
53['And everyone went to his home.

Chapter 8

The Adulterous Woman

B UT Jesus went to the Mount of Olives.
2And early in the morning He came again into the temple, and all the people were coming to Him; and He sat down and *began* to teach them.
3And the scribes and the Pharisees *brought a woman caught in adultery, and having set her in the midst,
4they *said to Him, "Teacher, this woman has been caught in adultery, in the very act.
5"Now in the Law Moses commanded us to stone such women; what then do You say?"
6And they were saying this, testing Him, in order that they might have grounds for accusing Him. But Jesus stooped down, and with His finger wrote on the ground.
7But when they persisted in asking Him, He straightened up, and said to them, "He who is without sin among you, let him *be the first to throw a stone at her.*
8And again He stooped down, and wrote on the ground.
9And when they heard it, they *began* to go out one by one, beginning with the older ones, and He was left alone, and the woman, where she was, in the midst.
10And straightening up, Jesus said to her, "Woman, where are they? Did no one condemn you?"
11And she said, "No one, Lord." And Jesus said, "Neither do I condemn you; go your way. From now on sin no more."]

Jesus Is the Light of the World

12Again therefore Jesus spoke to them, saying, "I am the light of the world; he who follows Me shall not walk in the darkness, but

ἴδε ὅτι ἐκ τῆς Γαλιλαίας προφήτης οὐκ
see that out of – Galilee a prophet not
ἐγείρεται.
is raised.

53 Καὶ ἐπορεύθησαν ἔκαστος εἰς τὸν οἶκον
And they went each one to the house
αὐτοῦ, **8** Ἰησοῦς δὲ ἐπορεύθη εἰς τὸ
of him, but Jesus went to the
Ὄρος τῶν Ἐλαιῶν. **2** Ὄρθρου δὲ πάλιν
Mount of the Olives. And at dawn again
παρεγένετο εἰς τὸ ἱερόν [, καὶ πᾶς ὁ
he arrived in the temple, and all the
λαὸς ἤρχετο πρὸς αὐτόν, καὶ καθίσας
people came to him, and sitting
ἐδίδασκεν αὐτούς]. **3** Ἄγουσιν δὲ οἱ
he taught them. And lead the
γραμματεῖς καὶ οἱ Φαρισαῖοι γυναῖκα ἐπὶ
scribes and the Pharisees a woman in
μοιχείᾳ κατειλημμένην, καὶ στήσαντες αὐτὴν
adultery having been caught, and standing her
ἐν μέσῳ **4** λέγουσιν αὐτῷ Διδάσκαλε,
in [the] midst they say to him[,] Teacher,
αὕτη ἡ γυνὴ κατείληπται ἐπ᾽ αὐτοφώρῳ
this – woman has been caught in the act
μοιχευομένη· **5** ἐν δὲ τῷ νόμῳ [ἡμῖν]
committing adultery; now in the law to us
Μωυσῆς ἐνετείλατο τὰς τοιαύτας λιθάζειν·
Moses enjoined – ³such ¹to stone;
σὺ οὖν τί λέγεις; **6** [τοῦτο δὲ ἔλεγον
thou therefore what sayest thou? But this they said
πειράζοντες αὐτόν, ἵνα ἔχωσιν κατηγορεῖν
tempting him, that they might have to accuse
αὐτοῦ.] ὁ δὲ Ἰησοῦς κάτω κύψας τῷ
him. – But Jesus down stooping with the
δακτύλῳ κατέγραφεν εἰς τὴν γῆν. **7** ὡς δὲ
finger wrote in the earth. But as
ἐπέμενον ἐρωτῶντες [αὐτόν], ἀνέκυψεν καὶ
they remained questioning him, he stood erect and
εἶπεν [αὐτοῖς] Ὁ ἀναμάρτητος ὑμῶν
said to them[.] The [one] sinless of you
πρῶτος ἐπ᾽ αὐτὴν βαλέτω λίθον. **8** καὶ
first on her let him cast a stone. And
πάλιν κατακύψας ἔγραφεν εἰς τὴν γῆν.
again stooping down he wrote in the earth.
9 οἱ δὲ ἀκούσαντες ἐξήρχοντο εἷς καθ᾽
And they hearing went out one by
εἷς ἀρξάμενοι ἀπὸ τῶν πρεσβυτέρων, καὶ
one beginning from the older ones, and
κατελείφθη μόνος, καὶ ἡ γυνὴ ἐν μέσῳ
he was left alone, and the woman in [the] midst
οὖσα. **10** ἀνακύψας δὲ ὁ Ἰησοῦς εἶπεν
being. And standing erect – Jesus said
αὐτῇ Γύναι, ποῦ εἰσιν; οὐδείς σε κατέκρινεν;
to her[,] Woman, where are they? no one thee condemned?
11 ἡ δὲ εἶπεν Οὐδείς, κύριε. εἶπεν δὲ
And she said[,] No one, sir. So said
ὁ Ἰησοῦς Οὐδὲ ἐγώ σε κατακρίνω·
– Jesus[,] Neither I thee condemn;
πορεύου, ἀπὸ τοῦ νῦν μηκέτι ἁμάρτανε.
go, from – now no longer sin.
12 Πάλιν οὖν αὐτοῖς ἐλάλησεν ὁ Ἰησοῦς
Again therefore to them spoke – Jesus
λέγων· ἐγώ εἰμι τὸ φῶς τοῦ κόσμου·
saying; I am the light of the world;
ὁ ἀκολουθῶν μοι οὐ μὴ περιπατήσῃ ἐν
the [one] following me by no means will walk in

into it, and you will find that a prophet[p] does not come out of Galilee."

[The earliest and most reliable manuscripts and other ancient witnesses do not have John 7:53–8:11.]

53Then each went to his own home.

Chapter 8

B UT Jesus went to the Mount of Olives. 2At dawn he appeared again in the temple courts, where all the people gathered around him, and he sat down to teach them. 3The teachers of the law and the Pharisees brought in a woman caught in adultery. They made her stand before the group 4and said to Jesus, "Teacher, this woman was caught in the act of adultery. 5In the Law Moses commanded us to stone such women. Now what do you say?" 6They were using this question as a trap, in order to have a basis for accusing him.
But Jesus bent down and started to write on the ground with his finger. 7When they kept on questioning him, he straightened up and said to them, "If any one of you is without sin, let him be the first to throw a stone at her." 8Again he stooped down and wrote on the ground.
9At this, those who heard began to go away one at a time, the older ones first, until only Jesus was left, with the woman still standing there. 10Jesus straightened up and asked her, "Woman, where are they? Has no one condemned you?"
11"No one, sir," she said.
"Then neither do I condemn you," Jesus declared. "Go now and leave your life of sin."

The Validity of Jesus' Testimony

12When Jesus spoke again to the people, he said, "I am the light of the world. Whoever follows me will never walk in darkness, but

---

ʳ John 7:53–8:11 is not found in most of the old mss.

ᵖ52 Two early manuscripts *the Prophet*

shall have the light of life."
13The Pharisees therefore said to Him, "You are bearing witness of Yourself; Your witness is not true."
14Jesus answered and said to them, "Even if I bear witness of Myself, My witness is true; for I know where I came from, and where I am going; but you do not know where I come from, or where I am going.
15"You people judge according to the flesh; I am not judging anyone.
16"But even if I do judge, My judgment is true; for I am not alone *in it*, but I and [1]He who sent Me.
17"Even in your law it has been written, that the testimony of two men is true.
18"I am He who bears witness of Myself, and the Father who sent Me bears witness of Me."
19And so they were saying to Him, "Where is Your Father?" Jesus answered, "You know neither Me, nor My Father; if you knew Me, you would know My Father also."
20These words He spoke in the treasury, as He taught in the temple; and no one seized Him, because His hour had not yet come.
21He said therefore again to them, "I go away, and you shall seek Me, and shall die in your sin; where I am going, you cannot come."
22Therefore the Jews were saying, "Surely He will not kill Himself, will He, since He says, 'Where I am going, you cannot come'?"
23And He was saying to them, "You are from below, I am from above;

τῇ σκοτίᾳ, ἀλλ' ἕξει τὸ φῶς τῆς ζωῆς.
the darkness, but will have the light – of life.

13 εἶπον οὖν αὐτῷ οἱ Φαρισαῖοι· σὺ περὶ
Said therefore to him the Pharisees; Thou concerning

σεαυτοῦ μαρτυρεῖς· ἡ μαρτυρία σου οὐκ
thyself witnessest; the witness of thee not

ἔστιν ἀληθής. 14 ἀπεκρίθη Ἰησοῦς καὶ
is true. Answered Jesus and

εἶπεν αὐτοῖς· κἂν ἐγὼ μαρτυρῶ περὶ
said to them: Even if I witness concerning

ἐμαυτοῦ, ἀληθής ἐστιν ἡ μαρτυρία μου,
myself, true is the witness of me,

ὅτι οἶδα πόθεν ἦλθον καὶ ποῦ ὑπάγω·
because I know whence I came and where I go;

ὑμεῖς δὲ οὐκ οἴδατε πόθεν ἔρχομαι ἢ
but ye know not whence I come or

ποῦ ὑπάγω. 15 ὑμεῖς κατὰ τὴν σάρκα
where I go. Ye according to the flesh

κρίνετε, ἐγὼ οὐ κρίνω οὐδένα. 16 καὶ
judge, I judge not no(any)one. [2]even

ἐὰν κρίνω δὲ ἐγώ, ἡ κρίσις ἡ ἐμὴ
[1]if [3]judge [1]But [4]I, the [2]judgment – [1]my

ἀληθινή ἐστιν, ὅτι μόνος οὐκ εἰμί, ἀλλ'
true is, because alone I am not, but

ἐγὼ καὶ ὁ πέμψας με. 17 καὶ ἐν τῷ
I and the [one] having sent me. [2]even [3]in the

νόμῳ δὲ τῷ ὑμετέρῳ γέγραπται ὅτι δύο
[1]law [1]And – [4]your it has been written that of two

ἀνθρώπων ἡ μαρτυρία ἀληθής ἐστιν.
men the witness true is.

18 ἐγώ εἰμι ὁ μαρτυρῶν περὶ ἐμαυτοῦ,
I am the [one] witnessing concerning myself,

καὶ μαρτυρεῖ περὶ ἐμοῦ ὁ πέμψας με
and witnesses concerning me [1]the [2]having sent [4]me

πατήρ. 19 ἔλεγον οὖν αὐτῷ· ποῦ ἐστιν ὁ
[3]Father. They said therefore to him: Where is the

πατήρ σου; ἀπεκρίθη Ἰησοῦς· οὔτε ἐμὲ
Father of thee? Answered Jesus: Neither me

οἴδατε οὔτε τὸν πατέρα μου· εἰ ἐμὲ
ye know nor the Father of me; if me

ᾔδειτε, καὶ τὸν πατέρα μου ἂν ᾔδειτε.
ye knew, also the Father of me ye would have known.

20 Ταῦτα τὰ ῥήματα ἐλάλησεν ἐν τῷ
These – words he spoke in the

γαζοφυλακείῳ διδάσκων ἐν τῷ ἱερῷ· καὶ
treasury teaching in the temple; and

οὐδεὶς ἐπίασεν αὐτόν, ὅτι οὔπω ἐληλύθει
no one seized him, because not yet had come

ἡ ὥρα αὐτοῦ.
the hour of him.

21 Εἶπεν οὖν πάλιν αὐτοῖς· ἐγὼ ὑπάγω
He said therefore again to them: I go

καὶ ζητήσετέ με, καὶ ἐν τῇ ἁμαρτίᾳ
and ye will seek me, and in the sin

ὑμῶν ἀποθανεῖσθε· ὅπου ἐγὼ ὑπάγω ὑμεῖς
of you ye will die; where I go ye

οὐ δύνασθε ἐλθεῖν. 22 ἔλεγον οὖν οἱ
cannot to come. Said therefore the

Ἰουδαῖοι· μήτι ἀποκτενεῖ ἑαυτόν, ὅτι
Jews: Not will he kill himself, because

λέγει· ὅπου ἐγὼ ὑπάγω ὑμεῖς οὐ δύνασθε
he says: Where I go ye cannot

ἐλθεῖν; 23 καὶ ἔλεγεν αὐτοῖς· ὑμεῖς ἐκ
to come? And he said to them: Ye of

τῶν κάτω ἐστέ, ἐγὼ ἐκ τῶν ἄνω εἰμί·
the things below are, I of the things above am;

will have the light of life."
13The Pharisees challenged him, "Here you are, appearing as your own witness; your testimony is not valid."
14Jesus answered, "Even if I testify on my own behalf, my testimony is valid, for I know where I came from and where I am going. But you have no idea where I come from or where I am going. 15You judge by human standards; I pass judgment on no one. 16But if I do judge, my decisions are right, because I am not alone. I stand with the Father, who sent me. 17In your own Law it is written that the testimony of two men is valid. 18I am one who testifies for myself; my other witness is the Father, who sent me."
19Then they asked him, "Where is your father?"
"You do not know me or my Father," Jesus replied. "If you knew me, you would know my Father also." 20He spoke these words while teaching in the temple area near the place where the offerings were put. Yet no one seized him, because his time had not yet come.
21Once more Jesus said to them, "I am going away, and you will look for me, and you will die in your sin. Where I go, you cannot come."
22This made the Jews ask, "Will he kill himself? Is that why he says, 'Where I go, you cannot come'?"
23But he continued, "You are from below; I am from above. You are of this

[1] Many ancient mss. read *the Father who sent Me*

you are of this world, I am not of this world. 24"I said therefore to you, that you shall die in your sins; for unless you believe that I am *He*, you shall die in your sins." 25And so they were saying to Him, "Who are You?" Jesus said to them, "What have I been saying to you *from* the beginning? 26"I have many things to speak and to judge concerning you, but He who sent Me is true; and the things which I heard from Him, these I speak to the world." 27They did not realize that He had been speaking to them about the Father. 28Jesus therefore said, "When you lift up the Son of Man, then you will know that I am *He*, and I do nothing on My own initiative, but I speak these things as the Father taught Me. 29"And He who sent Me is with Me; He has not left Me alone, for I always do the things that are pleasing to Him." 30As He spoke these things, many came to believe in Him.

The Truth Shall Make You Free

31Jesus therefore was saying to those Jews who had believed Him, "If you abide in My word, *then* you are truly disciples of Mine; 32and you shall know the truth, and the truth shall make you free." 33They answered Him, "We are Abraham's offspring, and have never yet been enslaved to anyone; how is it that You say, 'You shall become free'?" 34Jesus answered them, "Truly, truly, I say to you, everyone who commits sin is the slave of sin. 35"And the slave does not remain in the house for-

---

ὑμεῖς ἐκ τούτου τοῦ κόσμου ἐστέ, ἐγὼ
ye of this - world are, I

οὐκ εἰμὶ ἐκ τοῦ κόσμου τούτου. 24 εἶπον
am not of - world this. I said

οὖν ὑμῖν ὅτι ἀποθανεῖσθε ἐν ταῖς ἁμαρτίαις
therefore to you that ye will die in the sins

ὑμῶν· ἐὰν γὰρ μὴ πιστεύσητε ὅτι ἐγώ
of you ; for if ye believe not that I

εἰμι, ἀποθανεῖσθε ἐν ταῖς ἁμαρτίαις ὑμῶν.
am, ye will die in the sins of you.

25 ἔλεγον οὖν αὐτῷ· σὺ τίς εἶ; εἶπεν
They said therefore to him : ⁹Thou ¹who ²art? Said

αὐτοῖς ὁ Ἰησοῦς· τὴν ἀρχὴν ὅ τι καὶ
to them - Jesus : ⁵at all † ¹Why ²indeed

λαλῶ ὑμῖν; 26 πολλὰ ἔχω περὶ ὑμῶν
³speak I ⁴to you? Many things I have about you

λαλεῖν καὶ κρίνειν· ἀλλ' ὁ πέμψας με
to speak and to judge; but the [one] having sent me

ἀληθής ἐστιν, κἀγὼ ἃ ἤκουσα παρ'
true is, and I what I heard from

αὐτοῦ, ταῦτα λαλῶ εἰς τὸν κόσμον.
him, these things I speak in the world.

27 οὐκ ἔγνωσαν ὅτι τὸν πατέρα αὐτοῖς
They did not know that ⁸the ²Father ⁴to them

ἔλεγεν. 28 εἶπεν οὖν ὁ Ἰησοῦς· ὅταν
¹he spoke [of]. Said therefore - Jesus : When

ὑψώσητε τὸν υἱὸν τοῦ ἀνθρώπου, τότε
ye lift up the Son - of man, then

γνώσεσθε ὅτι ἐγώ εἰμι, καὶ ἀπ' ἐμαυτοῦ
ye will know that I am, and from myself

ποιῶ οὐδέν, ἀλλὰ καθὼς ἐδίδαξέν με ὁ
I do nothing, but as taught me the

πατήρ, ταῦτα λαλῶ. 29 καὶ ὁ πέμψας
Father, these things I speak. And the [one] having sent

με μετ' ἐμοῦ ἐστιν· οὐκ ἀφῆκέν με
me with me is; he did not leave me

μόνον, ὅτι ἐγὼ τὰ ἀρεστὰ αὐτῷ ποιῶ
alone, because I the things pleasing to him do

πάντοτε.
always.

30 Ταῦτα αὐτοῦ λαλοῦντος πολλοὶ ἐπίσ-
These things him saying⁹ many be-
= As he said these things

τευσαν εἰς αὐτόν. 31 ἔλεγεν οὖν ὁ Ἰησοῦς
lieved - in him. Said therefore - Jesus

πρὸς τοὺς πεπιστευκότας αὐτῷ Ἰουδαίους·
to ¹the ²having believed ⁴him ³Jews :

ἐὰν ὑμεῖς μείνητε ἐν τῷ λόγῳ τῷ ἐμῷ,
If ye continue in *the* ²word - ¹my,

ἀληθῶς μαθηταί μού ἐστε, 32 καὶ γνώσεσθε
truly disciples of me ye are, and ye will know

τὴν ἀλήθειαν, καὶ ἡ ἀλήθεια ἐλευθερώσει
the truth, and the truth will free

ὑμᾶς. 33 ἀπεκρίθησαν πρὸς αὐτόν· σπέρμα
you. They answered *to* him : Seed

Ἀβραάμ ἐσμεν, καὶ οὐδενὶ δεδουλεύκαμεν
of Abraham we are, and to no one have we been enslaved

πώποτε· πῶς σὺ λέγεις ὅτι ἐλεύθεροι
never; how thou sayest that free

γενήσεσθε; 34 ἀπεκρίθη αὐτοῖς ὁ Ἰησοῦς·
ye will become? Answered them - Jesus :

ἀμὴν ἀμὴν λέγω ὑμῖν ὅτι πᾶς ὁ ποιῶν
Truly truly I tell you that everyone doing

τὴν ἁμαρτίαν δοῦλός ἐστιν τῆς ἁμαρτίας.
- sin a slave is - of sin.

35 ὁ δὲ δοῦλος οὐ μένει ἐν τῇ οἰκίᾳ
But the slave does not remain in the house

---

world; I am not of this world. 24I told you that you would die in your sins; if you do not believe that I am the one I claim to be[j],[q] you will indeed die in your sins."

25"Who are you?" they asked.

"Just what I have been claiming all along," Jesus replied. 26"I have much to say in judgment of you. But he who sent me is reliable, and what I have heard from him I tell the world."

27They did not understand that he was telling them about his Father. 28So Jesus said, "When you have lifted up the Son of Man, then you will know that I am the one I claim to be, and that I do nothing on my own but speak just what the Father has taught me. 29The one who sent me is with me; he has not left me alone, for I always do what pleases him." 30Even as he spoke, many put their faith in him.

The Children of Abraham

31To the Jews who had believed him, Jesus said, "If you hold to my teaching, you are really my disciples. 32Then you will know the truth, and the truth will set you free."

33They answered him, "We are Abraham's descendants[r] and have never been slaves of anyone. How can you say that we shall be set free?"

34Jesus replied, "I tell you the truth, everyone who sins is a slave to sin. 35Now a slave has no permanent place in the family,

---

[q]24 Or *I am he*; also in verse 28
[r]33 Greek *seed*; also in verse 37

ever; the son does remain forever.

36 "If therefore the Son shall make you free, you shall be free indeed.

37 "I know that you are Abraham's offspring; yet you seek to kill Me, because My word has no place in you.

38 "I speak the things which I have seen with My Father; therefore you also do the things which you heard from *your* father."

39 They answered and said to Him, "Abraham is our father." Jesus *said to them, "If you are Abraham's children, do the deeds of Abraham.

40 "But as it is, you are seeking to kill Me, a man who has told you the truth, which I heard from God; this Abraham did not do.

41 "You are doing the deeds of *your* father." They said to Him, "We were not born of fornication; we have one Father, *even* God."

42 Jesus said to them, "If God were your Father, you would love Me; for I proceeded forth and have come from God, for I have not even come on My own initiative, but He sent Me.

43 "Why do you not understand what I am saying? *It is* because you cannot hear My word.

44 "You are of *your* father the devil, and you want to do the desires of your father. He was a murderer from the beginning, and does not stand in the truth, because there is no truth in him. Whenever he speaks a lie, he speaks from his own *nature*; for he is a liar, and the father of lies.

45 "But because I speak the truth, you do not believe Me.

εἰς τὸν αἰῶνα· ὁ υἱὸς μένει εἰς τὸν
unto the age; the son remains unto the

αἰῶνα. 36 ἐὰν οὖν ὁ υἱὸς ὑμᾶς ἐλευθερώσῃ,
age. If therefore the Son you frees,

ὄντως ἐλεύθεροι ἔσεσθε. 37 Οἶδα ὅτι
really free ye will be. I know that

σπέρμα 'Αβραάμ ἐστε· ἀλλὰ ζητεῖτέ με
seed of Abraham ye are; but ye seek me

ἀποκτεῖναι, ὅτι ὁ λόγος ὁ ἐμὸς οὐ χωρεῖ
to kill, because the ¹word – ¹my finds no room

ἐν ὑμῖν. 38 ἃ ἐγὼ ἑώρακα παρὰ τῷ
in you. What I have seen with the

πατρὶ λαλῶ· καὶ ὑμεῖς οὖν ἃ ἠκού-
Father I speak; and ye therefore what ye

σατε παρὰ τοῦ πατρὸς ποιεῖτε. 39 ἀπεκρί-
heard from the father ye do. They

θησαν καὶ εἶπαν αὐτῷ· ὁ πατὴρ ἡμῶν 'Αβραάμ
answered and said to him: The father of us Abraham

ἐστιν. λέγει αὐτοῖς ὁ 'Ιησοῦς· εἰ τέκνα
is. Says to them – Jesus: If children

τοῦ 'Αβραάμ ἐστε, τὰ ἔργα τοῦ 'Αβραὰμ
– of Abraham ye are, the works – of Abraham

ποιεῖτε· 40 νῦν δὲ ζητεῖτέ με ἀποκτεῖναι,
ye do; but now ye seek me to kill,

ἄνθρωπον ὃς τὴν ἀλήθειαν ὑμῖν λελάληκα,
a man who the truth to you has spoken,

ἣν ἤκουσα παρὰ τοῦ θεοῦ· τοῦτο 'Αβραὰμ
which I heard from – God; this Abraham

οὐκ ἐποίησεν. 41 ὑμεῖς ποιεῖτε τὰ ἔργα
did not. Ye do the works

τοῦ πατρὸς ὑμῶν. εἶπαν αὐτῷ· ἡμεῖς ἐκ
of the father of you. They said to him: We of

πορνείας οὐκ ἐγεννήθημεν, ἕνα πατέρα
fornication were not born, one father

ἔχομεν τὸν θεόν. 42 εἶπεν αὐτοῖς ὁ
we have[,] – God. Said to them –

'Ιησοῦς· εἰ ὁ θεὸς πατὴρ ὑμῶν ἦν,
Jesus: If – God father of you was,

ἠγαπᾶτε ἂν ἐμέ· ἐγὼ γὰρ ἐκ τοῦ θεοῦ
ye would have loved me; for I of – God

ἐξῆλθον καὶ ἥκω· οὐδὲ γὰρ ἀπ' ἐμαυτοῦ
came forth and have come; for not from myself

ἐλήλυθα, ἀλλ' ἐκεῖνός με ἀπέστειλεν. 43 διὰ τί
I have come, but that one me sent. Why

τὴν λαλιὰν τὴν ἐμὴν οὐ γινώσκετε;
the ¹speech – ¹my know ye not?

ὅτι οὐ δύνασθε ἀκούειν τὸν λόγον τὸν
because ye cannot *to* hear the ¹word –

ἐμόν. 44 ὑμεῖς ἐκ τοῦ πατρὸς τοῦ
¹my. Ye of the father of the

διαβόλου ἐστὲ καὶ τὰς ἐπιθυμίας τοῦ
devil are and the desires of the

πατρὸς ὑμῶν θέλετε ποιεῖν. ἐκεῖνος
father of you ye wish to do. That one

ἀνθρωποκτόνος ἦν ἀπ' ἀρχῆς, καὶ ἐν
a murderer was from [the] beginning, and in

τῇ ἀληθείᾳ οὐκ ἔστηκεν, ὅτι οὐκ ἔστιν
the truth stood not, because not is

ἀλήθεια ἐν αὐτῷ. ὅταν λαλῇ τὸ ψεῦδος,
truth in him. When he speaks the lie,

ἐκ τῶν ἰδίων λαλεῖ, ὅτι ψεύστης ἐστὶν
out of his own things he speaks, because a liar he is

καὶ ὁ πατὴρ αὐτοῦ. 45 ἐγὼ δὲ ὅτι τὴν
and the father of it. But ²I ¹because ⁴the

ἀλήθειαν λέγω, οὐ πιστεύετέ μοι. 46 τίς
⁵truth ³say, ye do not believe me. Who

---

but a son belongs to it forever. 36 So if the Son sets you free, you will be free indeed. 37 I know you are Abraham's descendants. Yet you are ready to kill me, because you have no room for my word. 38 I am telling you what I have seen in the Father's presence, and you do what you have heard from your father.ˢ "

39 "Abraham is our father," they answered.

"If you were Abraham's children," said Jesus, "then you wouldᵗ do the things Abraham did. 40 As it is, you are determined to kill me, a man who has told you the truth that I heard from God. Abraham did not do such things. 41 You are doing the things your own father does."

"We are not illegitimate children," they protested. "The only Father we have is God himself."

The Children of the Devil

42 Jesus said to them, "If God were your Father, you would love me, for I came from God and now am here. I have not come on my own; but he sent me. 43 Why is my language not clear to you? Because you are unable to hear what I say. 44 You belong to your father, the devil, and you want to carry out your father's desire. He was a murderer from the beginning, not holding to the truth, for there is no truth in him. When he lies, he speaks his native language, for he is a liar and the father of lies. 45 Yet because I tell the truth, you do not be-

---

ˢ38 Or presence. Therefore do what you have heard from the Father.
ᵗ39 Some early manuscripts "If you are Abraham's children," said Jesus, "then

46"Which one of you convicts Me of sin? If I speak truth, why do you not believe Me?

47"He who is of God hears the words of God; for this reason you do not hear *them*, because you are not of God."

48The Jews answered and said to Him, "Do we not say rightly that You are a Samaritan and have a demon?"

49Jesus answered, "I do not have a demon; but I honor My Father, and you dishonor Me.

50"But I do not seek My glory; there is One who seeks and judges.

51"Truly, truly, I say to you, if anyone keeps My word he shall never see death."

52The Jews said to Him, "Now we know that You have a demon. Abraham died, and the prophets *also;* and You say, 'If anyone keeps My word, he shall never taste of death.'

53"Surely You are not greater than our father Abraham, who died? The prophets died too; whom do You make Yourself out *to be?*"

54Jesus answered, "If I glorify Myself, My glory is nothing; it is My Father who glorifies Me, of whom you say, 'He is our God';

55and you have not come to know Him, but I know Him; and if I say that I do not know Him, I shall be a liar like you, but I do know Him, and keep His word.

56"Your father Abraham rejoiced to see My day, and he saw *it* and was glad."

57The Jews therefore said

ἐξ ὑμῶν ἐλέγχει με περὶ ἁμαρτίας; εἰ
of you reproves me concerning sin? If

ἀλήθειαν λέγω, διὰ τί ὑμεῖς οὐ πιστεύετέ
truth I say, why ²ye ¹do not believe

μοι; 47 ὁ ὢν ἐκ τοῦ θεοῦ τὰ ῥήματα
me? The [one] being of - God the words

τοῦ θεοῦ ἀκούει· διὰ τοῦτο ὑμεῖς οὐκ
- of God hears; therefore ye not

ἀκούετε, ὅτι ἐκ τοῦ θεοῦ οὐκ ἐστέ.
hear, because of - God ye are not.

48 Ἀπεκρίθησαν οἱ Ἰουδαῖοι καὶ εἶπαν
Answered the Jews and said

αὐτῷ· οὐ καλῶς λέγομεν ἡμεῖς ὅτι
to him: ³Not ⁴well ¹say ²we ⁵that

Σαμαρίτης εἶ σὺ καὶ δαιμόνιον ἔχεις;
⁸a Samaritan ⁷art ⁶thou ⁹and ¹¹a demon ¹⁰hast?

49 ἀπεκρίθη Ἰησοῦς· ἐγὼ δαιμόνιον οὐκ
Answered Jesus: I a demon not

ἔχω, ἀλλὰ τιμῶ τὸν πατέρα μου, καὶ
have, but I honour the Father of me, and

ὑμεῖς ἀτιμάζετέ με. 50 ἐγὼ δὲ οὐ ζητῶ
ye dishonour me. But I seek not

τὴν δόξαν μου· ἔστιν ὁ ζητῶν καὶ
the glory of me; there is the [one] seeking and

κρίνων. 51 ἀμὴν ἀμὴν λέγω ὑμῖν, ἐάν
judging. Truly truly I tell you, if

τις τὸν ἐμὸν λόγον τηρήσῃ, θάνατον
anyone - my word keeps, death

οὐ μὴ θεωρήσῃ εἰς τὸν αἰῶνα. 52 εἶπαν
by no means will he behold unto the age. Said

αὐτῷ οἱ Ἰουδαῖοι· νῦν ἐγνώκαμεν ὅτι
to him the Jews: Now we have known that

δαιμόνιον ἔχεις. Ἀβραὰμ ἀπέθανεν καὶ οἱ
a demon thou hast. Abraham died and the

προφῆται, καὶ σὺ λέγεις· ἐάν τις τὸν
prophets, and thou sayest: If anyone the

λόγον μου τηρήσῃ, οὐ μὴ γεύσηται
word of me keeps, by no means will he taste

θανάτου εἰς τὸν αἰῶνα. 53 μὴ σὺ μείζων
of death unto the age. Not thou greater

εἶ τοῦ πατρὸς ἡμῶν Ἀβραάμ, ὅστις
art [than] the father of us Abraham, who

ἀπέθανεν; καὶ οἱ προφῆται ἀπέθανον· τίνα
died? and the prophets died;- whom

σεαυτὸν ποιεῖς; 54 ἀπεκρίθη Ἰησοῦς· ἐὰν
thyself makest thou? Answered Jesus: If

ἐγὼ δοξάσω ἐμαυτόν, ἡ δόξα μου οὐδέν
I glorify myself, the glory of me nothing

ἐστιν· ἔστιν ὁ πατήρ μου ὁ δοξάζων με,
is; ⁴is ¹the ²Father ³of me the [one] glorifying me,

ὃν ὑμεῖς λέγετε ὅτι θεὸς ἡμῶν ἐστιν,
whom ye say[,] - God of us he is,

55 καὶ οὐκ ἐγνώκατε αὐτόν, ἐγὼ δὲ
and ye have not known him, but I

οἶδα αὐτόν. κἂν εἴπω ὅτι οὐκ οἶδα
know him. Even if I say that I know not

αὐτόν, ἔσομαι ὅμοιος ὑμῖν ψεύστης· ἀλλὰ
him, I shall be like you a liar; but

οἶδα αὐτὸν καὶ τὸν λόγον αὐτοῦ τηρῶ.
I know him and the word of him I keep.

56 Ἀβραὰμ ὁ πατὴρ ὑμῶν ἠγαλλιάσατο
Abraham the father of you was glad

ἵνα ἴδῃ τὴν ἡμέραν τὴν ἐμήν, καὶ εἶδεν
that he should see *the* ²day - ¹my, and he saw

καὶ ἐχάρη. 57 εἶπαν οὖν οἱ Ἰουδαῖοι
and rejoiced. Said therefore the Jews

---

lieve me! 46Can any of you prove me guilty of sin? If I am telling the truth, why don't you believe me? 47He who belongs to God hears what God says. The reason you do not hear is that you do not belong to God."

The Claims of Jesus About Himself

48The Jews answered him, "Aren't we right in saying that you are a Samaritan and demon-possessed?"

49"I am not possessed by a demon," said Jesus, "but I honor my Father and you dishonor me. 50I am not seeking glory for myself; but there is one who seeks it, and he is the judge. 51I tell you the truth, if anyone keeps my word, he will never see death."

52At this the Jews exclaimed, "Now we know that you are demon-possessed! Abraham died and so did the prophets, yet you say that if anyone keeps your word, he will never taste death. 53Are you greater than our father Abraham? He died, and so did the prophets. Who do you think you are?"

54Jesus replied, "If I glorify myself, my glory means nothing. My Father, whom you claim as your God, is the one who glorifies me. 55Though you do not know him, I know him. If I said I did not, I would be a liar like you, but I do know him and keep his word. 56Your father Abraham rejoiced at the thought of seeing my day; he saw it and was glad."

57"You are not yet fifty

to Him, "You are not yet fifty years old, and have You seen Abraham?"

⁵⁸Jesus said to them, "Truly, truly, I say to you, before Abraham was born, I am."

⁵⁹Therefore they picked up stones to throw at Him; but Jesus hid Himself, and went out of the temple.

Chapter 9

Healing the Man Born Blind

AND as He passed by, He saw a man blind from birth.

²And His disciples asked Him, saying, "Rabbi, who sinned, this man or his parents, that he should be born blind?"

³Jesus answered, "It was neither that this man sinned, nor his parents; but it was in order that the works of God might be displayed in him.

⁴"We must work the works of Him who sent Me, as long as it is day; night is coming, when no man can work.

⁵"While I am in the world, I am the light of the world."

⁶When He had said this, He spat on the ground, and made clay of the spittle, and applied the clay to his eyes,

⁷and said to him, "Go, wash in the pool of Siloam" (which is translated, Sent). And so he went away and washed, and came back seeing.

⁸The neighbors therefore, and those who previously saw him as a beggar, were saying, "Is not this the one who used to sit and beg?"

⁹Others were saying, "This is he," still others were saying, "No, but he is like him." He kept saying, "I am the one."

¹⁰Therefore they were saying to him, "How then were your eyes opened?"

πρὸς αὐτόν· πεντήκοντα ἔτη οὔπω ἔχεις
to him: Fifty years not yet thou hast

καὶ Ἀβραὰμ ἑώρακας; 58 εἶπεν αὐτοῖς
and Abraham hast thou seen? Said to them

Ἰησοῦς· ἀμὴν ἀμὴν λέγω ὑμῖν, πρὶν
Jesus: Truly truly I tell you, before

Ἀβραὰμ γενέσθαι ἐγὼ εἰμί. 59 ἦραν
Abraham to become[b] I am. They took
=became

οὖν λίθους ἵνα βάλωσιν ἐπ' αὐτόν·
therefore stones that they might cast on him;

Ἰησοῦς δὲ ἐκρύβη καὶ ἐξῆλθεν ἐκ τοῦ
but Jesus was hidden and went forth out of the

ἱεροῦ.
temple.

9 Καὶ παράγων εἶδεν ἄνθρωπον τυφλὸν
And passing along he saw a man blind

ἐκ γενετῆς. 2 καὶ ἠρώτησαν αὐτὸν οἱ
from birth. And asked him the

μαθηταὶ αὐτοῦ λέγοντες· ῥαββί, τίς ἥμαρτεν,
disciples of him saying: Rabbi, who sinned,

οὗτος ἢ οἱ γονεῖς αὐτοῦ, ἵνα τυφλὸς
this man or the parents of him, that blind

γεννηθῇ; 3 ἀπεκρίθη Ἰησοῦς· οὔτε οὗτος
he was born? Answered Jesus: Neither this man

ἥμαρτεν οὔτε οἱ γονεῖς αὐτοῦ, ἀλλ' ἵνα
sinned nor the parents of him, but that

φανερωθῇ τὰ ἔργα τοῦ θεοῦ ἐν αὐτῷ.
might be manifested the works - of God in him.

4 ἡμᾶς δεῖ ἐργάζεσθαι τὰ ἔργα τοῦ
Us it behoves to work the works of the

πέμψαντός με ἕως ἡμέρα ἐστίν· ἔρχεται
[one] having sent me while day it is; comes

νὺξ ὅτε οὐδεὶς δύναται ἐργάζεσθαι. 5 ὅταν
night when no one can to work. When

ἐν τῷ κόσμῳ ὦ, φῶς εἰμι τοῦ κόσμου.
in the world I am, light I am of the world.

6 ταῦτα εἰπὼν ἔπτυσεν χαμαὶ καὶ ἐποίησεν
These things having said he spat on the ground and made

πηλὸν ἐκ τοῦ πτύσματος, καὶ ἐπέθηκεν
clay out of the spittle, and ¹put on

αὐτοῦ τὸν πηλὸν ἐπὶ τοὺς ὀφθαλμούς,
⁷of him ²the ³clay ⁴on ⁵the ⁶eyes,

7 καὶ εἶπεν αὐτῷ· ὕπαγε νίψαι εἰς τὴν
and said to him: Go wash in the

κολυμβήθραν τοῦ Σιλωάμ (ὃ ἑρμηνεύεται
pool - of Siloam (which is translated

ἀπεσταλμένος). ἀπῆλθεν οὖν καὶ ἐνίψατο,
having been sent). He went therefore and washed,

καὶ ἦλθεν βλέπων. 8 Οἱ οὖν γείτονες
and came seeing. Therefore the neighbours

καὶ οἱ θεωροῦντες αὐτὸν τὸ πρότερον,
and the [ones] beholding him formerly, †

ὅτι προσαίτης ἦν, ἔλεγον· οὐχ οὗτός
that a beggar he was, said: ²Not ³this man

ἐστιν ὁ καθήμενος καὶ προσαιτῶν; 9 ἄλλοι
¹is the [one] sitting and begging? Some

ἔλεγον ὅτι οὗτός ἐστιν· ἄλλοι ἔλεγον·
said[,] - This is he; others said :

οὐχί, ἀλλὰ ὅμοιος αὐτῷ ἐστιν. ἐκεῖνος
No, but like to him he is. That [one]

ἔλεγεν ὅτι ἐγώ εἰμι. 10 ἔλεγον οὖν
said[,] - I am. They said therefore

αὐτῷ· πῶς [οὖν] ἠνεῴχθησάν σου οἱ
to him : How then were opened of thee the

---

years old," the Jews said to him, "and you have seen Abraham!"

⁵⁸"I tell you the truth," Jesus answered, "before Abraham was born, I am!"

⁵⁹At this, they picked up stones to stone him, but Jesus hid himself, slipping away from the temple grounds.

Chapter 9

Jesus Heals a Man Born Blind

AS he went along, he saw a man blind from birth. ²His disciples asked him, "Rabbi, who sinned, this man or his parents, that he was born blind?"

³"Neither this man nor his parents sinned," said Jesus, "but this happened so that the work of God might be displayed in his life. ⁴As long as it is day, we must do the work of him who sent me. Night is coming, when no one can work. ⁵While I am in the world, I am the light of the world."

⁶Having said this, he spit on the ground, made some mud with the saliva, and put it on the man's eyes. ⁷"Go," he told him, "wash in the Pool of Siloam" (this word means Sent). So the man went and washed, and came home seeing.

⁸His neighbors and those who had formerly seen him begging asked, "Isn't this the same man who used to sit and beg?" ⁹Some claimed that he was.

Others said, "No, he only looks like him."

But he himself insisted, "I am the man."

¹⁰"How then were your eyes opened?" they demanded.

11 He answered, "The man who is called Jesus made clay, and anointed my eyes, and said to me, 'Go to Siloam, and wash'; so I went away and washed, and I received sight."
12 And they said to him, "Where is He?" He *said, "I do not know."

Controversy over the Man

13 They *brought to the Pharisees him who was formerly blind.
14 Now it was a Sabbath on the day when Jesus made the clay, and opened his eyes.
15 Again, therefore, the Pharisees also were asking him how he received his sight. And he said to them, "He applied clay to my eyes, and I washed, and I see."
16 Therefore some of the Pharisees were saying, "This man is not from God, because He does not keep the Sabbath." But others were saying, "How can a man who is a sinner perform such signs?" And there was a division among them.
17 They *said therefore to the blind man again, "What do you say about Him, since He opened your eyes?" And he said, "He is a prophet."
18 The Jews therefore did not believe *it* of him, that he had been blind, and had received sight, until they called the parents of the very one who had received his sight,
19 and questioned them, saying, "Is this your son, who you say was born blind? Then how does he now see?"
20 His parents answered them and said, "We know that this is our son, and that he was born blind;
21 but how he now sees,

ὀφθαλμοί; 11 ἀπεκρίθη ἐκεῖνος· ὁ ἄνθρωπος
eyes? Answered that [one] : The man

ὁ λεγόμενος Ἰησοῦς πηλὸν ἐποίησεν καὶ
- being named Jesus clay made and

ἐπέχρισέν μου τοὺς ὀφθαλμοὺς καὶ εἶπέν
anointed of me the eyes and told

μοι ὅτι ὕπαγε εἰς τὸν Σιλωὰμ καὶ
me[,] - Go to - Siloam and

νίψαι· ἀπελθὼν οὖν καὶ νιψάμενος ἀνέβλεψα.
wash; going therefore and washing I saw.

12 καὶ εἶπαν αὐτῷ· ποῦ ἐστιν ἐκεῖνος;
And they said to him : Where is that [one]?

λέγει· οὐκ οἶδα. 13 Ἄγουσιν αὐτὸν
He says: I do not know. They lead him

πρὸς τοὺς Φαρισαίους, τόν ποτε τυφλόν.
to the Pharisees, the at one time blind.

14 ἦν δὲ σάββατον ἐν ᾗ ἡμέρᾳ τὸν
Now it was a sabbath on which day the

πηλὸν ἐποίησεν ὁ Ἰησοῦς καὶ ἀνέῳξεν
clay made - Jesus and opened

αὐτοῦ τοὺς ὀφθαλμούς. 15 πάλιν οὖν
of him the eyes. Again therefore

ἠρώτων αὐτὸν καὶ οἱ Φαρισαῖοι πῶς
asked him also the Pharisees how

ἀνέβλεψεν. ὁ δὲ εἶπεν αὐτοῖς· πηλὸν
he saw. And he said to them : Clay

ἐπέθηκέν μου ἐπὶ τοὺς ὀφθαλμούς, καὶ
he put on of me on the eyes, and

ἐνιψάμην, καὶ βλέπω. 16 ἔλεγον οὖν ἐκ
I washed, and I see. Said therefore of

τῶν Φαρισαίων τινές· οὐκ ἔστιν οὗτος
the Pharisees some : not is This

παρὰ θεοῦ ὁ ἄνθρωπος, ὅτι τὸ σάββατον
from God the man, because the sabbath

οὐ τηρεῖ. ἄλλοι [δὲ] ἔλεγον· πῶς δύναται
he keeps not. But others said : How can

ἄνθρωπος ἁμαρτωλὸς τοιαῦτα σημεῖα ποιεῖν;
man a sinful such signs to do?

καὶ σχίσμα ἦν ἐν αὐτοῖς. 17 λέγουσιν
And a division there was among them. They say

οὖν τῷ τυφλῷ πάλιν· τί σὺ λέγεις
therefore to the blind man again : What thou sayest

περὶ αὐτοῦ, ὅτι ἠνέῳξέν σου τοὺς
about him, because he opened of thee the

ὀφθαλμούς; ὁ δὲ εἶπεν ὅτι προφήτης ἐστίν.
eyes? And he said[,] - A prophet he is.

18 οὐκ ἐπίστευσαν οὖν οἱ Ἰουδαῖοι περὶ
Did not believe therefore the Jews about

αὐτοῦ ὅτι ἦν τυφλὸς καὶ ἀνέβλεψεν,
him that he was blind and saw,

ἕως ὅτου ἐφώνησαν τοὺς γονεῖς αὐτοῦ
until they called the parents of him

τοῦ ἀναβλέψαντος 19 καὶ ἠρώτησαν αὐτοὺς
of the [one] having seen and asked them

λέγοντες· οὗτός ἐστιν ὁ υἱὸς ὑμῶν, ὃν
saying : This is the son of you, whom

ὑμεῖς λέγετε ὅτι τυφλὸς ἐγεννήθη; πῶς
ye say that blind he was born? how

οὖν βλέπει ἄρτι; 20 ἀπεκρίθησαν οὖν οἱ
then sees he now? Answered therefore the

γονεῖς αὐτοῦ καὶ εἶπαν· οἴδαμεν ὅτι
parents of him and said : We know that

οὗτός ἐστιν ὁ υἱὸς ἡμῶν καὶ ὅτι τυφλὸς
this is the son of us and that blind

ἐγεννήθη· 21 πῶς δὲ νῦν βλέπει οὐκ
he was born; but how now he sees not

---

11 He replied, "The man they call Jesus made some mud and put it on my eyes. He told me to go to Siloam and wash. So I went and washed, and then I could see."
12 "Where is this man?" they asked him.
"I don't know," he said.

The Pharisees Investigate the Healing

13 They brought to the Pharisees the man who had been blind. 14 Now the day on which Jesus had made the mud and opened the man's eyes was a Sabbath. 15 Therefore the Pharisees also asked him how he had received his sight. "He put mud on my eyes," the man replied, "and I washed, and now I see."
16 Some of the Pharisees said, "This man is not from God, for he does not keep the Sabbath."
But others asked, "How can a sinner do such miraculous signs?" So they were divided.
17 Finally they turned again to the blind man, "What have you to say about him? It was your eyes he opened."
The man replied, "He is a prophet."
18 The Jews still did not believe that he had been blind and had received his sight until they sent for the man's parents. 19 "Is this your son?" they asked. "Is this the one you say was born blind? How is it that now he can see?"
20 "We know he is our son," the parents answered, "and we know he was born blind. 21 But how

we do not know; or who opened his eyes, we do not know. Ask him; he is of age, he shall speak for himself."

22His parents said this because they were afraid of the Jews; for the Jews had already agreed, that if anyone should confess Him to be Christ, he should be put out of the synagogue.

23For this reason his parents said, "He is of age; ask him."

24So a second time they called the man who had been blind, and said to him, "Give glory to God; we know that this man is a sinner."

25He therefore answered, "Whether He is a sinner, I do not know; one thing I do know, that, whereas I was blind, now I see."

26They said therefore to him, "What did He do to you? How did He open your eyes?"

27He answered them, "I told you already, and you did not listen; why do you want to hear it again? You do not want to become His disciples too, do you?"

28And they reviled him, and said, "You are His disciple, but we are disciples of Moses.

29We know that God has spoken to Moses; but as for this man, we do not know where He is from."

30The man answered and said to them, "Well, here is an amazing thing, that you do not know where He is from, and yet He opened my eyes.

31We know that God does not hear sinners; but if anyone is God-fearing, and does His will, He hears him.

32Since the beginning of time it has never been heard that anyone opened the eyes of a person born blind.

οἴδαμεν, ἢ τίς ἤνοιξεν αὐτοῦ τοὺς ὀφθαλμοὺς
we know, or who opened of him the eyes

ἡμεῖς οὐκ οἴδαμεν· αὐτὸν ἐρωτήσατε,
we know not; him ask ye,

ἡλικίαν ἔχει, αὐτὸς περὶ ἑαυτοῦ λαλήσει.
age he has, he about himself will speak.

22 ταῦτα εἶπαν οἱ γονεῖς αὐτοῦ ὅτι ἐφο-
These things said the parents of him because they

βοῦντο τοὺς Ἰουδαίους· ἤδη γὰρ συνετέθειντο
feared the Jews; for already had agreed

οἱ Ἰουδαῖοι ἵνα ἐάν τις αὐτὸν ὁμολογήσῃ
the Jews that if anyone him should acknowledge

χριστόν, ἀποσυνάγωγος γένηται.
[to be] Christ, put away from [the] synagogue he would be.

23 διὰ τοῦτο οἱ γονεῖς αὐτοῦ εἶπαν ὅτι
Therefore the parents of him said[,] –

ἡλικίαν ἔχει, αὐτὸν ἐπερωτήσατε. 24 Ἐφώνησαν
Age he has, him question ye. They called

οὖν τὸν ἄνθρωπον ἐκ δευτέρου ὃς ἦν
therefore the man a second time who was

τυφλός, καὶ εἶπαν αὐτῷ· δὸς δόξαν τῷ
blind, and said to him : Give glory –

θεῷ· ἡμεῖς οἴδαμεν ὅτι οὗτος ὁ ἄνθρωπος
to God; we know that this – man

ἁμαρτωλός ἐστιν. 25 ἀπεκρίθη οὖν ἐκεῖνος·
sinful is. Answered therefore that [one]:

εἰ ἁμαρτωλός ἐστιν οὐκ οἶδα· ἓν οἶδα,
If sinful he is I know not; one thing I know,

ὅτι τυφλὸς ὢν ἄρτι βλέπω. 26 εἶπαν
that blind being now I see. They said

οὖν αὐτῷ· τί ἐποίησέν σοι; πῶς ἤνοιξέν
therefore to him : What did he to thee? how opened

σου τοὺς ὀφθαλμούς; 27 ἀπεκρίθη αὐτοῖς·
of thee the eyes? He answered them :

εἶπον ὑμῖν ἤδη καὶ οὐκ ἠκούσατε· τί
I told you already and ye heard not; why

πάλιν θέλετε ἀκούειν; μὴ καὶ ὑμεῖς
again wish ye to hear? not also ye

θέλετε αὐτοῦ μαθηταὶ γενέσθαι; 28 καὶ
wish of him disciples to become? And

ἐλοιδόρησαν αὐτὸν καὶ εἶπαν· σὺ μαθητὴς
they reviled him and said : Thou a disciple

εἶ ἐκείνου, ἡμεῖς δὲ τοῦ Μωϋσέως ἐσμὲν
art of that man, but we – of Moses are

μαθηταί· 29 ἡμεῖς οἴδαμεν ὅτι Μωϋσεῖ
disciples; we know that by Moses

λελάληκεν ὁ θεός, τοῦτον δὲ οὐκ οἴδαμεν
has spoken – God, but this man we know not

πόθεν ἐστίν. 30 ἀπεκρίθη ὁ ἄνθρωπος
whence he is. Answered the man

καὶ εἶπεν αὐτοῖς· ἐν τούτῳ γὰρ τὸ
and said to them : In this then the

θαυμαστόν ἐστιν, ὅτι ὑμεῖς οὐκ οἴδατε
marvellous thing is, that ye do not know

πόθεν ἐστίν, καὶ ἤνοιξέν μου τοὺς
whence he is, and he opened of me the

ὀφθαλμούς. 31 οἴδαμεν ὅτι ὁ θεὸς
eyes. We know that – God

ἁμαρτωλῶν οὐκ ἀκούει, ἀλλ' ἐάν τις
sinful men does not hear, but if anyone

θεοσεβὴς ᾖ καὶ τὸ θέλημα αὐτοῦ ποιῇ,
godfearing is and the will of him does,

τούτου ἀκούει. 32 ἐκ τοῦ αἰῶνος οὐκ
this man he hears. From the age not

ἠκούσθη ὅτι ἠνέῳξέν τις ὀφθαλμοὺς τυφλοῦ
it was heard that ²opened ¹anyone eyes of a blind man

---

he can see now, or who opened his eyes, we don't know. Ask him. He is of age; he will speak for himself." 22His parents said this because they were afraid of the Jews, for already the Jews had decided that anyone who acknowledged that Jesus was the Christ*u* would be put out of the synagogue. 23That was why his parents said, "He is of age; ask him."

24A second time they summoned the man who had been blind. "Give glory to God,"*v* they said. "We know this man is a sinner."

25He replied, "Whether he is a sinner or not, I don't know. One thing I do know. I was blind but now I see!"

26Then they asked him, "What did he do to you? How did he open your eyes?"

27He answered, "I have told you already and you did not listen. Why do you want to hear it again? Do you want to become his disciples, too?"

28Then they hurled insults at him and said, "You are this fellow's disciple! We are disciples of Moses! 29We know that God spoke to Moses, but as for this fellow, we don't even know where he comes from."

30The man answered, "Now that is remarkable! You don't know where he comes from, yet he opened my eyes. 31We know that God does not listen to sinners. He listens to the godly man who does his will. 32Nobody has ever heard of opening the eyes of a man born blind. 33If this man

---

*u*22 Or *Messiah*
*v*24 A solemn charge to tell the truth (see Joshua 7:19)

33"If this man were not from God, He could do nothing."

34They answered and said to him, "You were born entirely in sins, and are you teaching us?" And they put him out.

Jesus Affirms His Deity

35Jesus heard that they had put him out; and finding him, He said, "Do you believe in the Son of Man?"

36He answered and said, "And who is He, Lord, that I may believe in Him?"

37Jesus said to him, "You have both seen Him, and He is the one who is talking with you."

38And he said, "Lord, I believe." And he worshiped Him.

39And Jesus said, "For judgment I came into this world, that those who do not see may see; and that those who see may become blind."

40Those of the Pharisees who were with Him heard these things, and said to Him, "We are not blind too, are we?"

41Jesus said to them, "If you were blind, you would have no sin; but since you say, 'We see,' your sin remains.

γεγεννημένου· **33** εἰ μὴ ἦν οὗτος παρὰ
having been born;　　　if　'not　²was　¹this man　from

θεοῦ, οὐκ ἠδύνατο ποιεῖν οὐδέν. **34** ἀπεκρίθησαν
God,　he could not　*to* do no(any)thing.　　They answered

καὶ εἶπαν αὐτῷ· ἐν ἁμαρτίαις σὺ ἐγεννήθης
and　said　to him :　In　sins　thou　wast born

ὅλος, καὶ σὺ διδάσκεις ἡμᾶς; καὶ ἐξέβαλον
wholly,　and　thou　teachest　us?　and they cast out

αὐτὸν ἔξω. **35** Ἤκουσεν Ἰησοῦς ὅτι
him　outside.　　Heard　　Jesus　that

ἐξέβαλον αὐτὸν ἔξω, καὶ εὑρὼν αὐτὸν
they cast out　him　outside,　and　finding　him

εἶπεν· σὺ πιστεύεις εἰς τὸν υἱὸν τοῦ
said :　Thou　believest　in　the　Son　–

ἀνθρώπου; **36** ἀπεκρίθη ἐκεῖνος καὶ εἶπεν·
of man?　　Answered　that [one]　and　said :

καὶ τίς ἐστιν, κύριε, ἵνα πιστεύσω εἰς
And who　is he,　sir,　that　I may believe　in

αὐτόν; **37** εἶπεν αὐτῷ ὁ Ἰησοῦς· καὶ
him?　　Said　to him　–　Jesus :　Both

ἑώρακας αὐτὸν καὶ ὁ λαλῶν μετὰ σοῦ
thou hast seen　him　and the [one] speaking with　thee

ἐκεῖνός ἐστιν. **38** ὁ δὲ ἔφη· πιστεύω, κύριε·
that [one]　is.　　And he said :　I believe,　sir;

καὶ προσεκύνησεν αὐτῷ. **39** καὶ εἶπεν ὁ
and　he worshipped　him.　　And　said　–

Ἰησοῦς· εἰς κρίμα ἐγὼ εἰς τὸν κόσμον
Jesus :　For　judgment　I　into　–　world

τοῦτον ἦλθον, ἵνα οἱ μὴ βλέποντες
this　came,　that the [ones]　not　seeing

βλέπωσιν καὶ οἱ βλέποντες· τυφλοὶ γένωνται.
may see　and　the [ones] seeing　blind　may become.

40 Ἤκουσαν ἐκ τῶν Φαρισαίων ταῦτα
heard　¹[Some]　²of　³the　⁴Pharisees　⁵these things

οἱ μετ' αὐτοῦ ὄντες, καὶ εἶπαν αὐτῷ·
–　⁶with　⁷him　⁸being,　and　they said　to him :

μὴ καὶ ἡμεῖς τυφλοί ἐσμεν; **41** εἶπεν
Not　also　we　blind　are?　　Said

αὐτοῖς ὁ Ἰησοῦς· εἰ τυφλοὶ ἦτε, οὐκ
to them　–　Jesus :　If　blind　ye were,　not

ἂν εἴχετε ἁμαρτίαν· νῦν δὲ λέγετε ὅτι
ye would have had　sin;　but now　ye say[,]　–

βλέπομεν· ἡ ἁμαρτία ὑμῶν μένει.
We see;　the　sin　of you　remains.

---

were not from God, he could do nothing."

34To this they replied, "You were steeped in sin at birth; how dare you lecture us!" And they threw him out.

Spiritual Blindness

35Jesus heard that they had thrown him out, and when he found him, he said, "Do you believe in the Son of Man?"

36"Who is he, sir?" the man asked. "Tell me so that I may believe in him."

37Jesus said, "You have now seen him; in fact, he is the one speaking with you."

38Then the man said, "Lord, I believe," and he worshiped him.

39Jesus said, "For judgment I have come into this world, so that the blind will see and those who see will become blind."

40Some Pharisees who were with him heard him say this and asked, "What? Are we blind too?"

41Jesus said, "If you were blind, you would not be guilty of sin; but now that you claim you can see, your guilt remains.

Chapter 10

Parable of the Good Shepherd

"TRULY, truly, I say to you, he who does not enter by the door into the fold of the sheep, but climbs up some other way, he is a thief and a robber.

2"But he who enters by the door is a shepherd of the sheep.

3"To him the doorkeeper opens, and the sheep hear his voice, and he calls his own sheep by name, and leads them out.

4"When he puts forth all

---

10 Ἀμὴν ἀμὴν λέγω ὑμῖν, ὁ μὴ
Truly　truly　I say　to you,　the [one] not

εἰσερχόμενος διὰ τῆς θύρας εἰς τὴν
entering　through　the　door　into　the

αὐλὴν τῶν προβάτων ἀλλὰ ἀναβαίνων
fold　of the　sheep　but　going up

ἀλλαχόθεν, ἐκεῖνος κλέπτης ἐστὶν καὶ
by another way,　that [one]　a thief　is　and

λῃστής· **2** ὁ δὲ εἰσερχόμενος διὰ τῆς
a robber;　but the [one]　entering　through　the

θύρας ποιμήν ἐστιν τῶν προβάτων. **3** τούτῳ
door　shepherd　is　of the　sheep.　To this [one]

ὁ θυρωρὸς ἀνοίγει, καὶ τὰ πρόβατα τῆς
the doorkeeper　opens,　and the　sheep　the

φωνῆς αὐτοῦ ἀκούει, καὶ τὰ ἴδια πρόβατα
voice　of him　hears,　and the(his) own　sheep

φωνεῖ κατ' ὄνομα καὶ ἐξάγει αὐτά.
he calls　by　name　and　leads out　them.

4 ὅταν τὰ ἴδια πάντα ἐκβάλῃ, ἔμπροσθεν
When　the(his) own　all　he puts forth,　in front of

Chapter 10

The Shepherd and His Flock

"I TELL you the truth, the man who does not enter the sheep pen by the gate, but climbs in by some other way, is a thief and a robber. 2The man who enters by the gate is the shepherd of his sheep. 3The watchman opens the gate for him, and the sheep listen to his voice. He calls his own sheep by name and leads them out. 4When he has his own, he goes before them, and the sheep follow him because they know his voice.

5"And a stranger they simply will not follow, but will flee from him, because they do not know the voice of strangers."

6This figure of speech Jesus spoke to them, but they did not understand what those things were which He had been saying to them.

7Jesus therefore said to them again, "Truly, truly, I say to you, I am the door of the sheep.

8"All who came before Me are thieves and robbers, but the sheep did not hear them.

9"I am the door; if anyone enters through Me, he shall be saved, and shall go in and out, and find pasture.

10"The thief comes only to steal, and kill, and destroy; I came that they might have life, and might have it abundantly.

11"I am the good shepherd; the good shepherd lays down His life for the sheep.

12"He who is a hireling, and not a shepherd, who is not the owner of the sheep, beholds the wolf coming, and leaves the sheep, and flees, and the wolf snatches them, and scatters them.

13"He flees because he is a hireling, and is not concerned about the sheep.

14"I am the good shepherd; and I know My own, and My own know Me,

15even as the Father knows Me and I know the Father; and I lay down My life for the sheep.

16"And I have other sheep, which are not of this

αὐτῶν πορεύεται, καὶ τὰ πρόβατα αὐτῷ
them he goes, and the sheep him

ἀκολουθεῖ, ὅτι οἴδασιν τὴν φωνὴν αὐτοῦ·
follows, because they know the voice of him;

5 ἀλλοτρίῳ δὲ οὐ μὴ ἀκολουθήσουσιν,
but a stranger by no means will they follow,

ἀλλὰ φεύξονται ἀπ' αὐτοῦ, ὅτι οὐκ
but will flee from him, because not

οἴδασιν τῶν ἀλλοτρίων τὴν φωνήν.
they know of the strangers the voice.

6 Ταύτην τὴν παροιμίαν εἶπεν αὐτοῖς ὁ
This — allegory told them —

Ἰησοῦς· ἐκεῖνοι δὲ οὐκ ἔγνωσαν τίνα
Jesus; but those men knew not what things

ἦν ἃ ἐλάλει αὐτοῖς. 7 Εἶπεν οὖν πάλιν
they were which he spoke to them. Said therefore again

ὁ Ἰησοῦς· ἀμὴν ἀμὴν λέγω ὑμῖν ὅτι
— Jesus: Truly truly I say to you that

ἐγώ εἰμι ἡ θύρα τῶν προβάτων. 8 πάντες
I am the door of the sheep. All

ὅσοι ἦλθον πρὸ ἐμοῦ κλέπται εἰσὶν καὶ
who came before me thieves are and

λησταί· ἀλλ' οὐκ ἤκουσαν αὐτῶν τὰ
robbers; but did not hear them the

πρόβατα. 9 ἐγώ εἰμι ἡ θύρα· δι' ἐμοῦ
sheep. I am the door; through me

ἐάν τις εἰσέλθῃ, σωθήσεται, καὶ εἰσελεύ-
if anyone enters, he will be saved, and will go

σεται καὶ ἐξελεύσεται καὶ νομὴν εὑρήσει.
in and will go out and pasture will find.

10 ὁ κλέπτης οὐκ ἔρχεται εἰ μὴ ἵνα
The thief comes not except that

κλέψῃ καὶ θύσῃ καὶ ἀπολέσῃ· ἐγὼ ἦλθον
he may steal and kill and destroy; I came

ἵνα ζωὴν ἔχωσιν καὶ περισσὸν ἔχωσιν.
that life they may have and abundantly they may have.

11 Ἐγώ εἰμι ὁ ποιμὴν ὁ καλός. ὁ
I am the shepherd — good. The

ποιμὴν ὁ καλὸς τὴν ψυχὴν αὐτοῦ τίθησιν
shepherd — good the life of him lays down

ὑπὲρ τῶν προβάτων· 12 ὁ μισθωτὸς καὶ
for the sheep; the hireling and

οὐκ ὢν ποιμήν, οὗ οὐκ ἔστιν τὰ πρόβατα
not being a shepherd, of whom is(are) not the sheep

ἴδια, θεωρεῖ τὸν λύκον ἐρχόμενον καὶ
[his] own, beholds the wolf coming and

ἀφίησιν τὰ πρόβατα καὶ φεύγει, — καὶ
leaves the sheep and flees, — and

ὁ λύκος ἁρπάζει αὐτὰ καὶ σκορπίζει· —
the wolf seizes them and scatters; —

13 ὅτι μισθωτός ἐστιν καὶ οὐ μέλει
because a hireling he is and it matters not

αὐτῷ περὶ τῶν προβάτων. 14 ἐγώ εἰμι
to him about the sheep. I am

ὁ ποιμὴν ὁ καλός, καὶ γινώσκω τὰ
the shepherd — good, and I know the

ἐμὰ καὶ γινώσκουσί με τὰ ἐμά, 15 καθὼς
mine and ²know ³me — ¹mine, as

γινώσκει με ὁ πατὴρ κἀγὼ γινώσκω τὸν
³knows ⁴me ¹the ²Father and I know the

πατέρα, καὶ τὴν ψυχήν μου τίθημι ὑπὲρ
Father, and the life of me I lay down for

τῶν προβάτων. 16 καὶ ἄλλα πρόβατα
the sheep. And other sheep

ἔχω ἃ οὐκ ἔστιν ἐκ τῆς αὐλῆς ταύτης·
I have which is(are) not of — fold this;

---

brought out all his own, he goes on ahead of them, and his sheep follow him because they know his voice. 5But they will never follow a stranger; in fact, they will run away from him because they do not recognize a stranger's voice." 6Jesus used this figure of speech, but they did not understand what he was telling them.

7Therefore Jesus said again, "I tell you the truth, I am the gate for the sheep. 8All who ever came before me were thieves and robbers, but the sheep did not listen to them. 9I am the gate; whoever enters through me will be saved.ʷ He will come in and go out, and find pasture. 10The thief comes only to steal and kill and destroy; I have come that they may have life, and have it to the full. 11"I am the good shepherd. The good shepherd lays down his life for the sheep. 12The hired hand is not the shepherd who owns the sheep. So when he sees the wolf coming, he abandons the sheep and runs away. Then the wolf attacks the flock and scatters it. 13The man runs away because he is a hired hand and cares nothing for the sheep. 14"I am the good shepherd; I know my sheep and my sheep know me— 15just as the Father knows me and I know the Father— and I lay down my life for the sheep. 16I have other sheep that are not of this

w 9 Or kept safe

fold; I must bring them also, and they shall hear My voice; and they shall become one flock *with* one shepherd. [17]"For this reason the Father loves Me, because I lay down My life that I may take it again. [18]"No one 'has taken it away from Me, but I lay it down on My own initiative. I have authority to lay it down, and I have authority to take it up again. This commandment I received from My Father." [19]There arose a division again among the Jews because of these words. [20]And many of them were saying, "He has a demon and is insane. Why do you listen to Him?" [21]Others were saying, "These are not the sayings of one demon-possessed. A demon cannot open the eyes of the blind, can he?"

Jesus Asserts His Deity

[22]At that time the Feast of the Dedication took place at Jerusalem; [23]it was winter, and Jesus was walking in the temple in the portico of Solomon. [24]The Jews therefore gathered around Him, and were saying to Him, "How long will You keep us in suspense? If You are the Christ, tell us plainly." [25]Jesus answered them, "I told you, and you do not believe; the works that I do in My Father's name, these bear witness of Me. [26]"But you do not believe, because you are not of My sheep. [27]"My sheep hear My voice, and I know them, and they follow Me; [28]and I give eternal life to them, and they shall never

κἀκεῖνα δεῖ με ἀγαγεῖν, καὶ τῆς φωνῆς
those also it behoves me to bring, and the voice
μου ἀκούσουσιν, καὶ γενήσεται μία ποίμνη,
of me they will hear, and there will become one flock,
εἰς ποιμήν. **17** διὰ τοῦτό με ὁ πατὴρ
one shepherd. Therefore me the Father
ἀγαπᾷ ὅτι ἐγὼ τίθημι τὴν ψυχήν μου,
loves because I lay down the life of me,
ἵνα πάλιν λάβω αὐτήν. **18** οὐδεὶς ἦρεν
that again I may take it. No one took
αὐτὴν ἀπ᾽ ἐμοῦ, ἀλλ᾽ ἐγὼ τίθημι αὐτὴν
it from me, but I lay down it
ἀπ᾽ ἐμαυτοῦ. ἐξουσίαν ἔχω θεῖναι αὐτήν,
from myself. Authority I have to lay down it,
καὶ ἐξουσίαν ἔχω πάλιν λαβεῖν αὐτήν·
and authority I have again to take it;
ταύτην τὴν ἐντολὴν ἔλαβον παρὰ τοῦ
this - commandment I received from the
πατρός μου. **19** Σχίσμα πάλιν ἐγένετο ἐν
Father of me. A division again there was among
τοῖς Ἰουδαίοις διὰ τοὺς λόγους τούτους.
the Jews because of - words these.
20 ἔλεγον δὲ πολλοὶ ἐξ αὐτῶν· δαιμόνιον
And said many of them: A demon
ἔχει καὶ μαίνεται· τί αὐτοῦ ἀκούετε;
he has and raves; why him hear ye?
21 ἄλλοι ἔλεγον· ταῦτα τὰ ῥήματα οὐκ
Others said: These - words not
ἔστιν δαιμονιζομένου· μὴ δαιμόνιον δύναται
is(are) of one demon-possessed; *not* a demon can
τυφλῶν ὀφθαλμοὺς ἀνοῖξαι;
of blind men eyes *to* open?
22 Ἐγένετο τότε τὰ ἐγκαίνια ἐν τοῖς
There was then the Dedication in -
Ἰεροσολύμοις· χειμὼν ἦν· **23** καὶ περιεπάτει
Jerusalem; winter it was; and walked
ὁ Ἰησοῦς ἐν τῷ ἱερῷ ἐν τῇ στοᾷ τοῦ
- Jesus in the temple in the porch -
Σολομῶνος. **24** ἐκύκλωσαν οὖν αὐτὸν οἱ
of Solomon. Surrounded therefore him the
Ἰουδαῖοι καὶ ἔλεγον αὐτῷ· ἕως πότε
Jews and said to him: Until when
τὴν ψυχὴν ἡμῶν αἴρεις; εἰ σὺ εἶ
the life(soul) of us holdest thou * ? if thou art
ὁ χριστός, εἰπὸν ἡμῖν παρρησίᾳ. **25** ἀπεκρίθη
the Christ, tell us plainly. Answered
αὐτοῖς ὁ Ἰησοῦς· εἶπον ὑμῖν, καὶ
them - Jesus: I told you, and
οὐ πιστεύετε· τὰ ἔργα ἃ ἐγὼ ποιῶ ἐν τῷ
ye do not believe; the works which I do in the
ὀνόματι τοῦ πατρός μου, ταῦτα μαρτυρεῖ
name of the Father of me, these witnesses
περὶ ἐμοῦ· **26** ἀλλὰ ὑμεῖς οὐ πιστεύετε,
concerning me; but ye do not believe,
ὅτι οὐκ ἐστὲ ἐκ τῶν προβάτων τῶν
because ye are not of *the* 'sheep -
ἐμῶν. **27** τὰ πρόβατα τὰ ἐμὰ τῆς φωνῆς
'my. the sheep - My the voice
μου ἀκούουσιν, κἀγὼ γινώσκω αὐτά, καὶ
of me hear, and I know them, and
ἀκολουθοῦσίν μοι, **28** κἀγὼ δίδωμι αὐτοῖς
they follow me, and I give to them
ζωὴν αἰώνιον, καὶ οὐ μὴ ἀπόλωνται εἰς
life eternal, and by no means they perish unto

sheep pen. I must bring them also. They too will listen to my voice, and there shall be one flock and one shepherd. [17]The reason my Father loves me is that I lay down my life—only to take it up again. [18]No one takes it from me, but I lay it down of my own accord. I have authority to lay it down and authority to take it up again. This command I received from my Father."

[19]At these words the Jews were again divided. [20]Many of them said, "He is demon-possessed and raving mad. Why listen to him?" [21]But others said, "These are not the sayings of a man possessed by a demon. Can a demon open the eyes of the blind?"

The Unbelief of the Jews

[22]Then came the Feast of Dedication[x] at Jerusalem. It was winter, [23]and Jesus was in the temple area walking in Solomon's Colonnade. [24]The Jews gathered around him, saying, "How long will you keep us in suspense? If you are the Christ,[y] tell us plainly."

[25]Jesus answered, "I did tell you, but you do not believe. The miracles I do in my Father's name speak for me, [26]but you do not believe because you are not my sheep. [27]My sheep listen to my voice; I know them, and they follow me. [28]I give them eternal life, and they shall never perish;

'Many Gr. mss. read *takes*

* That is, in suspense.

perish; and no one shall snatch them out of My hand.
29"My Father, who has given *them* to Me, is greater than all; and no one is able to snatch *them* out of the Father's hand.
30"I and the Father are one."
31The Jews took up stones again to stone Him.
32Jesus answered them, "I showed you many good works from the Father; for which of them are you stoning Me?"
33The Jews answered Him, "For a good work we do not stone You, but for blasphemy; and because You, being a man, make Yourself out *to be* God."
34Jesus answered them, "Has it not been written in your Law, 'I SAID, YOU ARE GODS'?
35"If he called them gods, to whom the word of God came (and the Scripture cannot be broken),
36do you say of Him, whom the Father sanctified and sent into the world, 'You are blaspheming,' because I said, 'I am the Son of God'?
37"If I do not do the works of My Father, do not believe Me;
38but if I do them, though you do not believe Me, believe the works, that you may know and understand that the Father is in Me, and I in the Father."
39Therefore they were seeking again to seize Him, and He eluded their grasp.
40And He went away again beyond the Jordan to the place where John was first baptizing, and He was staying there.
41And many came to Him

τὸν αἰῶνα, καὶ οὐχ ἁρπάσει τις αὐτὰ
the age, and ⁴shall not seize ¹anyone them

ἐκ τῆς χειρός μου. 29 ὁ πατήρ μου ὃ
out of the hand of me. The Father of me who

δέδωκέν μοι πάντων μεῖζόν ἐστιν, καὶ
has given to me [than] all greater is, and

οὐδεὶς δύναται ἁρπάζειν ἐκ τῆς χειρὸς
no one can to seize out of the hand

τοῦ πατρός. 30 ἐγὼ καὶ ὁ πατὴρ ἕν
of the Father. I and the Father one

ἐσμεν. 31 Ἐβάστασαν πάλιν λίθους οἱ
we are. Lifted again stones the

Ἰουδαῖοι ἵνα λιθάσωσιν αὐτόν. 32 ἀπ-
Jews that they might stone him. An-

εκρίθη αὐτοῖς ὁ Ἰησοῦς· πολλὰ ἔργα
swered them - Jesus: Many ⁹works

ἔδειξα ὑμῖν καλὰ ἐκ τοῦ πατρός· διὰ
¹I showed ⁴you ⁵good of the Father; because of

ποῖον αὐτῶν ἔργον ἐμὲ λιθάζετε;
which ⁵of them ¹work ⁴me ⁸stone ye?

33 ἀπεκρίθησαν αὐτῷ οἱ Ἰουδαῖοι· περὶ
Answered him the Jews : Concerning

καλοῦ ἔργου οὐ λιθάζομέν σε ἀλλὰ περὶ
a good work we do not stone thee but concerning

βλασφημίας, καὶ ὅτι σὺ ἄνθρωπος ὢν
blasphemy, and because thou a man being

ποιεῖς σεαυτὸν θεόν. 34 ἀπεκρίθη αὐτοῖς
makest thyself God. Answered them

ὁ Ἰησοῦς· οὐκ ἔστιν γεγραμμένον ἐν τῷ
- Jesus : Is it not *having been* written in the

νόμῳ ὑμῶν ὅτι ἐγὼ εἶπα· θεοί ἐστε;
law of you[,] - I said : Gods ye are?

35 εἰ ἐκείνους εἶπεν θεοὺς πρὸς οὓς ὁ
¹if ⁵those ⁴he called ⁶gods with whom the

λόγος τοῦ θεοῦ ἐγένετο, καὶ οὐ δύναται
word - of God was, and cannot

λυθῆναι ἡ γραφή, 36 ὃν ὁ πατὴρ
to be broken the scripture, ⁸[him] whom ⁴the ⁵Father

ἡγίασεν καὶ ἀπέστειλεν εἰς τὸν κόσμον
⁶sanctified ⁷and ⁸sent ⁹into ¹⁰the ¹¹world

ὑμεῖς λέγετε ὅτι βλασφημεῖς, ὅτι εἶπον·
¹ye ²tell[,] - Thou blasphemest, because I said :

υἱὸς τοῦ θεοῦ εἰμι; 37 εἰ οὐ ποιῶ τὰ ἔργα
Son - of God I am? If I do not the works

τοῦ πατρός μου, μὴ πιστεύετέ μοι· 38 εἰ δὲ
of the Father of me, do not believe me; but if

ποιῶ, κἂν ἐμοὶ μὴ πιστεύητε, τοῖς ἔργοις
I do, even if me ye do not believe, the works

πιστεύετε, ἵνα γνῶτε καὶ γινώσκητε
believe, that ye may know* and continue to know*

ὅτι ἐν ἐμοὶ ὁ πατὴρ κἀγὼ ἐν τῷ πατρί.
that in me the Father [is] and I in the Father.

39 Ἐζήτουν οὖν αὐτὸν πάλιν πιάσαι· καὶ
They sought therefore him again to arrest; and

ἐξῆλθεν ἐκ τῆς χειρὸς αὐτῶν.
he went forth out of the hand of them.

40 Καὶ ἀπῆλθεν πάλιν πέραν τοῦ
And he went away again across the

Ἰορδάνου εἰς τὸν τόπον ὅπου ἦν Ἰωάννης
Jordan to the place where was John

τὸ πρῶτον βαπτίζων, καὶ ἔμενεν ἐκεῖ.
at first baptizing, and remained there.

41 καὶ πολλοὶ ἦλθον πρὸς αὐτὸν καὶ
And · many came to him and

---

no one can snatch them out of my hand. 29My Father, who has given them to me, is greater than all[z]; no one can snatch them out of my Father's hand. 30I and the Father are one."
31Again the Jews picked up stones to stone him, 32but Jesus said to them, "I have shown you many great miracles from the Father. For which of these do you stone me?"
33"We are not stoning you for any of these," replied the Jews, "but for blasphemy, because you, a mere man, claim to be God."
34Jesus answered them, "Is it not written in your Law, 'I have said you are gods'[a]? 35If he called them 'gods,' to whom the word of God came—and the Scripture cannot be broken—36what about the one whom the Father set apart as his very own and sent into the world? Why then do you accuse me of blasphemy because I said, 'I am God's Son'? 37Do not believe me unless I do what my Father does. 38But if I do it, even though you do not believe me, believe the miracles, that you may know and understand that the Father is in me, and I in the Father." 39Again they tried to seize him, but he escaped their grasp.
40Then Jesus went back across the Jordan to the place where John had been baptizing in the early days. Here he stayed 41and many people came to him. They

---

u Some early mss. read *What My Father has given Me is greater than all*

* Different tenses (aorist and present) of the same verb.

*z*29 Many early manuscripts *What my Father has given me is greater than all*
*a*34 Psalm 82:6

and were saying, "While John performed no sign, yet everything John said about this man was true."
42And many believed in Him there.

Chapter 11

The Death and Resurrection of Lazarus

NOW a certain man was sick, Lazarus of Bethany, the village of Mary and her sister Martha.
2And it was the Mary who anointed the Lord with ointment, and wiped His feet with her hair, whose brother Lazarus was sick.
3The sisters therefore sent to Him, saying, "Lord, behold, he whom You love is sick."
4But when Jesus heard it, He said, "This sickness is not unto death, but for the glory of God, that the Son of God may be glorified by it."
5Now Jesus loved Martha, and her sister, and Lazarus.
6When therefore He heard that he was sick, He stayed then two days *longer* in the place where He was.
7Then after this He *said to the disciples, "Let us go to Judea again."
8The disciples *said to Him, "Rabbi, the Jews were just now seeking to stone You, and are You going there again?"
9Jesus answered, "Are there not twelve hours in the day? If anyone walks in the day, he does not stumble, because he sees the light of this world.
10But if anyone walks in the night, he stumbles, because the light is not in him."
11This He said, and after that He *said to them, "Our friend Lazarus has

---

ἔλεγον ὅτι Ἰωάννης μὲν σημεῖον ἐποίησεν
said[,] – John indeed sign did
οὐδέν, πάντα δὲ ὅσα εἶπεν Ἰωάννης περὶ
none, but all things how many said John about
τούτου ἀληθῆ ἦν. 42 καὶ πολλοὶ ἐπίστευσαν
this man true was(were). And many believed
εἰς αὐτὸν ἐκεῖ.
in him there.

11 Ἦν δέ τις ἀσθενῶν, Λάζαρος ἀπὸ
Now there was a certain [man] ailing, Lazarus from
Βηθανίας, ἐκ τῆς κώμης Μαρίας καὶ
Bethany, of the village of Mary and
Μάρθας τῆς ἀδελφῆς αὐτῆς. 2 ἦν δὲ
Martha the sister of her. And it was
Μαριὰμ ἡ ἀλείψασα τὸν κύριον μύρῳ
Mary the [one] anointing the Lord with ointment
καὶ ἐκμάξασα τοὺς πόδας αὐτοῦ ταῖς
and wiping off the feet of him with the
θριξὶν αὐτῆς, ἧς ὁ ἀδελφὸς Λάζαρος
hairs of her, of whom the brother Lazarus
ἠσθένει. 3 ἀπέστειλαν οὖν αἱ ἀδελφαὶ
ailed. Sent therefore the sisters
πρὸς αὐτὸν λέγουσαι· κύριε, ἴδε ὃν
to him saying : Lord, behold[,] [he] whom
φιλεῖς ἀσθενεῖ. 4 ἀκούσας δὲ ὁ Ἰησοῦς
thou lovest ails. And hearing – Jesus
εἶπεν· αὕτη ἡ ἀσθένεια οὐκ ἔστιν πρὸς
said: This – ailment is not to
θάνατον ἀλλ' ὑπὲρ τῆς δόξης τοῦ θεοῦ,
death but for the glory – of God,
ἵνα δοξασθῇ ὁ υἱὸς τοῦ θεοῦ δι' αὐτῆς.
that may be glorified the Son – of God through it.
5 ἠγάπα δὲ ὁ Ἰησοῦς τὴν Μάρθαν καὶ
Now ²loved – ¹Jesus – Martha and
τὴν ἀδελφὴν αὐτῆς καὶ τὸν Λάζαρον.
the sister of her and – Lazarus.
6 ὡς οὖν ἤκουσεν ὅτι ἀσθενεῖ, τότε μὲν
When therefore he heard that he ails(ed), then –
ἔμεινεν ἐν ᾧ ἦν τόπῳ δύο ἡμέρας·
he remained ¹in ³which ⁴he was ²place two days;
7 ἔπειτα μετὰ τοῦτο λέγει τοῖς μαθηταῖς·
then after this he says to the disciples :
ἄγωμεν εἰς τὴν Ἰουδαίαν πάλιν. 8 λέγουσιν
Let us go into – Judæa again. Say
αὐτῷ οἱ μαθηταί· ῥαββί, νῦν ἐζήτουν
to him the disciples : Rabbi, ⁴now ²were ³seeking
σε λιθάσαι οἱ Ἰουδαῖοι, καὶ πάλιν ὑπάγεις
¹thee ⁵to stone ¹the ²Jews, and again goest thou
ἐκεῖ; 9 ἀπεκρίθη Ἰησοῦς· οὐχὶ δώδεκα
there? Answered Jesus : Not twelve
ὧραί εἰσιν τῆς ἡμέρας; ἐάν τις περιπατῇ
hours are there of the day? if anyone walks
ἐν τῇ ἡμέρᾳ, οὐ προσκόπτει, ὅτι τὸ φῶς
in the day, he does not stumble, because the light
τοῦ κόσμου τούτου βλέπει· 10 ἐὰν δέ
– world of this he sees; but if
τις περιπατῇ ἐν τῇ νυκτί, προσκόπτει,
anyone walks in the night, he stumbles,
ὅτι τὸ φῶς οὐκ ἔστιν ἐν αὐτῷ. 11 ταῦτα
because the light is not in him. These things
εἶπεν, καὶ μετὰ τοῦτο λέγει αὐτοῖς·
he said, and after this he says to them :
Λάζαρος ὁ φίλος ἡμῶν κεκοίμηται· ἀλλὰ
Lazarus the friend of us has fallen asleep; but

Chapter 11

The Death of Lazarus

NOW a man named Lazarus was sick. He was from Bethany, the village of Mary and her sister Martha. 2This Mary, whose brother Lazarus now lay sick, was the same one who poured perfume on the Lord and wiped his feet with her hair. 3So the sisters sent word to Jesus, "Lord, the one you love is sick."
4When he heard this, Jesus said, "This sickness will not end in death. No, it is for God's glory so that God's Son may be glorified through it." 5Jesus loved Martha and her sister and Lazarus. 6Yet when he heard that Lazarus was sick, he stayed where he was two more days.
7Then he said to his disciples, "Let us go back to Judea."
8"But Rabbi," they said, "a short while ago the Jews tried to stone you, and yet you are going back there?"
9Jesus answered, "Are there not twelve hours of daylight? A man who walks by day will not stumble, for he sees by this world's light. 10It is when he walks by night that he stumbles, for he has no light."
11After he had said this, he went on to tell them, "Our friend Lazarus has

---

said, "Though John never performed a miraculous sign, all that John said about this man was true."
42And in that place many believed in Jesus.

fallen asleep; but I go, that I may awaken him out of sleep."

12The disciples therefore said to Him, "Lord, if he has fallen asleep, he will recover."

13Now Jesus had spoken of his death, but they thought that He was speaking of literal sleep.

14Then Jesus therefore said to them plainly, "Lazarus is dead,

15and I am glad for your sakes that I was not there, so that you may believe; but let us go to him."

16Thomas therefore, who is called Didymus, said to *his* fellow disciples, "Let us also go, that we may die with Him."

17So when Jesus came, He found that he had already been in the tomb four days.

18Now Bethany was near Jerusalem, about two miles off;

19and many of the Jews had come to Martha and Mary, to console them concerning *their* brother.

20Martha therefore, when she heard that Jesus was coming, went to meet Him; but Mary still sat in the house.

21Martha therefore said to Jesus, "Lord, if You had been here, my brother would not have died.

22"Even now I know that whatever You ask of God, God will give You."

23Jesus *said to her, "Your brother shall rise again."

24Martha *said to Him, "I know that he will rise again in the resurrection on the last day."

25Jesus said to her, "I am the resurrection and the life; he who believes in Me shall live even if he dies,

26and everyone who lives and believes in Me shall never die. Do you believe

---

πορεύομαι ἵνα ἐξυπνίσω αὐτόν. 12 εἶπαν
I am going that I may awaken him. Said

οὖν οἱ μαθηταὶ αὐτῷ· κύριε, εἰ κεκοίμηται,
there- the disciples to him: Lord, if he has fallen asleep,
fore

σωθήσεται. 13 εἰρήκει δὲ ὁ Ἰησοῦς περὶ
he will be healed. Now had spoken - Jesus concerning

τοῦ θανάτου αὐτοῦ· ἐκεῖνοι δὲ ἔδοξαν ὅτι
the death of him; but those men thought that

περὶ τῆς κοιμήσεως τοῦ ὕπνου λέγει.
concerning the sleep - of slumber he says.

14 τότε οὖν εἶπεν αὐτοῖς ὁ Ἰησοῦς
Then therefore told them - Jesus

παρρησίᾳ· Λάζαρος ἀπέθανεν, 15 καὶ χαίρω
plainly : Lazarus died, and I rejoice

δι' ὑμᾶς, ἵνα πιστεύσητε, ὅτι οὐκ ἤμην
because of you, that ye may believe, that I was not

ἐκεῖ· ἀλλὰ ἄγωμεν πρὸς αὐτόν. 16 εἶπεν
there; but let us go to him. Said

οὖν Θωμᾶς ὁ λεγόμενος Δίδυμος τοῖς
therefore Thomas - being called Twin to the(his)

συμμαθηταῖς· ἄγωμεν καὶ ἡμεῖς ἵνα
fellow-disciples : Let go also we(us) that

ἀποθάνωμεν μετ' αὐτοῦ. 17 Ἐλθὼν οὖν
we may die with him. Coming therefore

ὁ Ἰησοῦς εὗρεν αὐτὸν τέσσαρας ἤδη
- Jesus found him ²four ¹already

ἡμέρας ἔχοντα ἐν τῷ μνημείῳ. 18 ἦν δὲ
²days having(being) in the tomb. Now was

Βηθανία ἐγγὺς τῶν Ἰεροσολύμων ὡς ἀπὸ
Bethany near Jerusalem about ²away

σταδίων δεκαπέντε. 19 πολλοὶ δὲ ἐκ τῶν
²furlongs ¹fifteen. And many of the

Ἰουδαίων ἐληλύθεισαν πρὸς τὴν Μάρθαν
Jews had come to - Martha

καὶ Μαριάμ, ἵνα παραμυθήσωνται αὐτὰς
and Mary, that they might console them

περὶ τοῦ ἀδελφοῦ. 20 ἡ οὖν Μάρθα ὡς
concerning the(ir) brother. - Therefore Martha when

ἤκουσεν ὅτι Ἰησοῦς ἔρχεται, ὑπήντησεν
she heard that Jesus is(was) coming, met

αὐτῷ· Μαριὰμ δὲ ἐν τῷ οἴκῳ ἐκαθέζετο.
him; but Mary in the house sat.

21 εἶπεν οὖν ἡ Μάρθα πρὸς Ἰησοῦν·
Said therefore - Martha to Jesus :

κύριε, εἰ ἦς ὧδε, οὐκ ἂν ἀπέθανεν ὁ
Lord, if thou wast here, would not have died the

ἀδελφός μου. 22 καὶ νῦν οἶδα ὅτι ὅσα ἂν
brother of me. And now I know that whatever things

αἰτήσῃ τὸν θεὸν δώσει σοι ὁ θεός.
thou askest - God ²will give ³thee - ¹God.

23 λέγει αὐτῇ ὁ Ἰησοῦς· ἀναστήσεται ὁ
Says to her - Jesus : Will rise again the

ἀδελφός σου. 24 λέγει αὐτῷ ἡ Μάρθα·
brother of thee. Says to him - Martha :

οἶδα ὅτι ἀναστήσεται ἐν τῇ ἀναστάσει
I know that he will rise again in the resurrection

ἐν τῇ ἐσχάτῃ ἡμέρᾳ. 25 εἶπεν αὐτῇ ὁ
in the last day. Said to her -

Ἰησοῦς· ἐγώ εἰμι ἡ ἀνάστασις καὶ ἡ
Jesus : I am the resurrection and the

ζωή· ὁ πιστεύων εἰς ἐμὲ κἂν ἀποθάνῃ
life; the [one] believing in me even if he should die

ζήσεται, 26 καὶ πᾶς ὁ ζῶν καὶ πιστεύων
will live, and everyone living and believing

εἰς ἐμὲ οὐ μὴ ἀποθάνῃ εἰς τὸν αἰῶνα·
in me by no means dies unto the age :

---

fallen asleep; but I am going there to wake him up."

12His disciples replied, "Lord, if he sleeps, he will get better." 13Jesus had been speaking of his death, but his disciples thought he meant natural sleep.

14So then he told them plainly, "Lazarus is dead, 15and for your sake I am glad I was not there, so that you may believe. But let us go to him."

16Then Thomas (called Didymus) said to the rest of the disciples, "Let us also go, that we may die with him."

Jesus Comforts the Sisters

17On his arrival, Jesus found that Lazarus had already been in the tomb for four days. 18Bethany was less than two miles[b] from Jerusalem, 19and many Jews had come to Martha and Mary to comfort them in the loss of their brother. 20When Martha heard that Jesus was coming, she went out to meet him, but Mary stayed at home.

21"Lord," Martha said to Jesus, "if you had been here, my brother would not have died. 22But I know that even now God will give you whatever you ask." 23Jesus said to her, "Your brother will rise again."

24Martha answered, "I know he will rise again in the resurrection at the last day."

25Jesus said to her, "I am the resurrection and the life. He who believes in me will live, even though he dies; 26and whoever lives and believes in me will never die. Do you believe this?"

---

b18 Greek *fifteen stadia* (about 3 kilometers)

this?"
27She *said to Him, "Yes, Lord; I have believed that You are the Christ, the Son of God, even He who comes into the world."

28And when she had said this, she went away, and called Mary her sister, saying secretly, "The Teacher is here, and is calling for you."

29And when she heard it, she *arose quickly, and was coming to Him.

30Now Jesus had not yet come into the village, but was still in the place where Martha met Him.

31The Jews then who were with her in the house, and consoling her, when they saw that Mary rose up quickly and went out, followed her, supposing that she was going to the tomb to weep there.

32Therefore, when Mary came where Jesus was, she saw Him, and fell at His feet, saying to Him, "Lord, if You had been here, my brother would not have died."

33When Jesus therefore saw her weeping, and the Jews who came with her, also weeping, He was deeply moved in spirit, and was troubled,

34and said, "Where have you laid him?" They *said to Him, "Lord, come and see."

35Jesus wept.

36And so the Jews were saying, "Behold how He loved him!"

37But some of them said, "Could not this man, who opened the eyes of him who was blind, have kept this man also from dying?"

38Jesus therefore again being deeply moved within, *came to the tomb. Now it was a cave, and a stone was

---

πιστεύεις τοῦτο; 27 λέγει αὐτῷ· ναί, κύριε·
believest thou this? She says to him : Yes, Lord;

ἐγὼ πεπίστευκα ὅτι σὺ εἶ ὁ χριστὸς ὁ
I have believed that thou art the Christ the

υἱὸς τοῦ θεοῦ ὁ εἰς τὸν κόσμον ἐρχόμενος.
Son - of God ¹the ²into ⁴the ⁵world ²[one] coming.

28 καὶ τοῦτο εἰποῦσα ἀπῆλθεν καὶ ἐφώνησεν
And this saying she went away and called

Μαριὰμ τὴν ἀδελφὴν αὐτῆς λάθρα εἰποῦσα·
Mary the sister of her secretly saying :

ὁ διδάσκαλος πάρεστιν καὶ φωνεῖ σε.
The Teacher is here and calls thee.

29 ἐκείνη δὲ ὡς ἤκουσεν, ἐγείρεται ταχὺ
And that [one] when she heard, ^ rose quickly

καὶ ἤρχετο πρὸς αὐτόν· 30 οὔπω δὲ
and came to him; now not yet

ἐληλύθει ὁ Ἰησοῦς εἰς τὴν κώμην, ἀλλ'
had come - Jesus into the village, but

ἦν ἔτι ἐν τῷ τόπῳ ὅπου ὑπήντησεν
was still in the place where met

αὐτῷ ἡ Μάρθα. 31 οἱ οὖν Ἰουδαῖοι
him - Martha. Therefore the Jews

οἱ ὄντες μετ' αὐτῆς ἐν τῇ οἰκίᾳ καὶ
the [ones] being with her in the house and

παραμυθούμενοι αὐτήν, ἰδόντες τὴν Μαριὰμ
consoling her, seeing - Mary

ὅτι ταχέως ἀνέστη καὶ ἐξῆλθεν,
that quickly she rose up and went out,

ἠκολούθησαν αὐτῇ, δόξαντες ὅτι ὑπάγει
followed her, thinking[,] - She is going

εἰς τὸ μνημεῖον ἵνα κλαύσῃ ἐκεῖ. 32 ἡ
to the tomb that she may weep there. -

οὖν Μαριὰμ ὡς ἦλθεν ὅπου ἦν Ἰησοῦς,
Therefore Mary when she came where was Jesus,

ἰδοῦσα αὐτὸν ἔπεσεν αὐτοῦ πρὸς τοὺς
seeing him fell of him at the

πόδας, λέγουσα αὐτῷ· κύριε, εἰ ἧς ὧδε,
feet, saying to him : Lord, if thou wast here,

οὐκ ἄν μου ἀπέθανεν ὁ ἀδελφός.
⁴would not ³of me ⁵have died ¹the ²brother.

33 Ἰησοῦς οὖν ὡς εἶδεν αὐτὴν κλαίουσαν
Jesus therefore when he saw her weeping

καὶ τοὺς συνελθόντας αὐτῇ Ἰουδαίους
and ¹the ²coming with ⁴her ³Jews

κλαίοντας, ἐνεβριμήσατο τῷ πνεύματι καὶ
weeping, groaned in the(his) spirit and

ἐτάραξεν ἑαυτόν, 34 καὶ εἶπεν· ποῦ
troubled himself, and said : Where

τεθείκατε αὐτόν; λέγουσιν αὐτῷ· κύριε,
have ye put him? They say to him : Lord,

ἔρχου καὶ ἴδε. 35 ἐδάκρυσεν ὁ Ἰησοῦς.
come and see. Shed tears - Jesus.

36 ἔλεγον οὖν οἱ Ἰουδαῖοι· ἴδε πῶς
Said therefore the Jews : See how

ἐφίλει αὐτόν. 37 τινὲς δὲ ἐξ αὐτῶν
he loved him. But some of them

εἶπαν· οὐκ ἐδύνατο οὗτος ὁ ἀνοίξας
said : Could not this man the [one] opening

τοὺς ὀφθαλμοὺς τοῦ τυφλοῦ ποιῆσαι ἵνα
the eyes of the blind man to cause that

καὶ οὗτος μὴ ἀποθάνῃ; 38 Ἰησοῦς οὖν
even this man should not die ? Jesus therefore

πάλιν ἐμβριμώμενος ἐν ἑαυτῷ ἔρχεται
again groaning in himself comes

εἰς τὸ μνημεῖον· ἦν δὲ σπήλαιον, καὶ
to the tomb; now it was a cave, and

27"Yes, Lord," she told him, "I believe that you are the Christ,ᶜ the Son of God, who was to come into the world."

28And after she had said this, she went back and called her sister Mary aside. "The Teacher is here," she said, "and is asking for you." 29When Mary heard this, she got up quickly and went to him. 30Now Jesus had not yet entered the village, but was still at the place where Martha had met him. 31When the Jews who had been with Mary in the house, comforting her, noticed how quickly she got up and went out, they followed her, supposing she was going to the tomb to mourn there.

32When Mary reached the place where Jesus was and saw him, she fell at his feet and said, "Lord, if you had been here, my brother would not have died."

33When Jesus saw her weeping, and the Jews who had come along with her also weeping, he was deeply moved in spirit and troubled. 34"Where have you laid him?" he asked.

"Come and see, Lord," they replied.

35Jesus wept.

36Then the Jews said, "See how he loved him!"

37But some of them said, "Could not he who opened the eyes of the blind man have kept this man from dying?"

Jesus Raises Lazarus From the Dead

38Jesus, once more deeply moved, came to the tomb. It was a cave with a stone laid across the en-

ᶜ27 Or *Messiah*

JOHN 11

303

lying against it.
39Jesus *said, "Remove the stone." Martha, the sister of the deceased, *said to Him, "Lord, by this time there will be a stench, for he has been *dead* four days."
40Jesus *said to her, "Did I not say to you, if you believe, you will see the glory of God?"
41And so they removed the stone. And Jesus raised His eyes, and said, "Father, I thank Thee that Thou heardest Me.
42"And I knew that Thou hearest Me always; but because of the people standing around I said it, that they may believe that Thou didst send Me."
43And when He had said these things, He cried out with a loud voice, "Lazarus, come forth."
44He who had died came forth, bound hand and foot with wrappings; and his face was wrapped around with a cloth. Jesus *said to them, "Unbind him, and let him go."
45Many therefore of the Jews, who had come to Mary and beheld what He had done, believed in Him.
46But some of them went away to the Pharisees, and told them the things which Jesus had done.

Conspiracy to Kill Jesus

47Therefore the chief priests and the Pharisees convened a council, and were saying, "What are we doing? For this man is performing many signs.
48"If we let Him *go on* like this, all men will believe in Him, and the Romans will come and take away both our place and our nation."
49But a certain one of them, Caiaphas, who was high priest that year, said to

λίθος ἐπέκειτο ἐπ' αὐτῷ. 39 λέγει ὁ
a stone was lying on on it. Says –
Ἰησοῦς· ἄρατε τὸν λίθον. λέγει αὐτῷ
Jesus: Lift ye the stone. Says to him
ἡ ἀδελφὴ τοῦ τετελευτηκότος Μάρθα·
the sister of the [one] having died Martha:
κύριε, ἤδη ὄζει· τεταρταῖος γάρ ἐστιν.
Lord, now he smells; for fourth [day] it is.
40 λέγει αὐτῇ ὁ Ἰησοῦς· οὐκ εἶπόν
Says to her – Jesus: Not I told
σοι ὅτι ἐὰν πιστεύσῃς ὄψῃ τὴν δόξαν
thee that if thou believest thou wilt see the glory
τοῦ θεοῦ; 41 ἦραν οὖν τὸν λίθον. ὁ
– of God? They lifted therefore the stone. –
δὲ Ἰησοῦς ἦρεν τοὺς ὀφθαλμοὺς ἄνω
And Jesus lifted the(his) eyes up
καὶ εἶπεν· πάτερ, εὐχαριστῶ σοι ὅτι
and said: Father, I thank thee that
ἤκουσάς μου. 42 ἐγὼ δὲ ᾔδειν ὅτι
thou didst hear me. And I knew that
πάντοτέ μου ἀκούεις· ἀλλὰ διὰ τὸν
always me thou hearest; but because of the
ὄχλον τὸν περιεστῶτα εἶπον, ἵνα
crowd – standing round I said, that
πιστεύσωσιν ὅτι σύ με ἀπέστειλας.
they may believe that thou me didst send.
43 καὶ ταῦτα εἰπὼν φωνῇ μεγάλῃ
And these things saying voice with a great
ἐκραύγασεν· Λάζαρε, δεῦρο ἔξω. 44 ἐξῆλθεν
he cried out: Lazarus, come out. Came out
ὁ τεθνηκὼς δεδεμένος τοὺς πόδας καὶ
the [one] having died *having been* bound the feet and
τὰς χεῖρας κειρίαις, καὶ ἡ ὄψις αὐτοῦ
the hands with bandages, and the face of him
σουδαρίῳ περιεδέδετο. λέγει αὐτοῖς ὁ
with a napkin had been bound round. Says to them –
Ἰησοῦς· λύσατε αὐτὸν καὶ ἄφετε αὐτὸν ὑπάγειν.
Jesus: Loosen him and let him *to go.*
45 Πολλοὶ οὖν ἐκ τῶν Ἰουδαίων, οἱ
Many therefore of the Jews, the [ones]
ἐλθόντες πρὸς τὴν Μαριὰμ καὶ θεασάμενοι
having come to – Mary and having beheld
ὃ ἐποίησεν, ἐπίστευσαν εἰς αὐτόν· 46 τινὲς δὲ
what he did, believed in him; but some
ἐξ αὐτῶν ἀπῆλθον πρὸς τοὺς Φαρισαίους
of them went away to the Pharisees
καὶ εἶπαν αὐτοῖς ἃ ἐποίησεν Ἰησοῦς.
and told them what things did Jesus.
47 συνήγαγον οὖν οἱ ἀρχιερεῖς καὶ οἱ
Assembled therefore the chief priests and the
Φαρισαῖοι συνέδριον, καὶ ἔλεγον· τί
Pharisees a council, and said: What
ποιοῦμεν, ὅτι οὗτος ὁ ἄνθρωπος πολλὰ
are we doing, because this – man ¹many
ποιεῖ σημεῖα; 48 ἐὰν ἀφῶμεν αὐτὸν οὕτως,
¹does ³signs? If we leave him thus,
πάντες πιστεύσουσιν εἰς αὐτόν, καὶ
all men will believe in him, and
ἐλεύσονται οἱ Ῥωμαῖοι καὶ ἀροῦσιν ἡμῶν
will come the Romans and will take of us
καὶ τὸν τόπον καὶ τὸ ἔθνος. 49 εἰς
both the place and the nation. ²one
δέ τις ἐξ αὐτῶν Καϊάφας, ἀρχιερεὺς
¹But ²a certain of them[,] Caiaphas, high priest
ὢν τοῦ ἐνιαυτοῦ ἐκείνου, εἶπεν αὐτοῖς·
being – year of that, said to them:

trance. 39"Take away the stone," he said.
"But, Lord," said Martha, the sister of the dead man, "by this time there is a bad odor, for he has been there four days."
40Then Jesus said, "Did I not tell you that if you believed, you would see the glory of God?"
41So they took away the stone. Then Jesus looked up and said, "Father, I thank you that you have heard me. 42I knew that you always hear me, but I said this for the benefit of the people standing here, that they may believe that you sent me."
43When he had said this, Jesus called in a loud voice, "Lazarus, come out!" 44The dead man came out, his hands and feet wrapped with strips of linen, and a cloth around his face.
Jesus said to them, "Take off the grave clothes and let him go."

The Plot to Kill Jesus

45Therefore many of the Jews who had come to visit Mary, and had seen what Jesus did, put their faith in him. 46But some of them went to the Pharisees and told them what Jesus had done. 47Then the chief priests and the Pharisees called a meeting of the Sanhedrin.
"What are we accomplishing?" they asked. "Here is this man performing many miraculous signs. 48If we let him go on like this, everyone will believe in him, and then the Romans will come and take away both our place*d* and our nation."
49Then one of them, named Caiaphas, who was high priest that year, spoke

d48 Or temple

them, "You know nothing at all,
50nor do you take into account that it is expedient for you that one man should die for the people, and that the whole nation should not perish."
51Now this he did not say on his own initiative; but being high priest that year, he prophesied that Jesus was going to die for the nation,
52and not for the nation only, but that He might also gather together into one the children of God who are scattered abroad.
53So from that day on they planned together to kill Him.
54Jesus therefore no longer continued to walk publicly among the Jews, but went away from there to the country near the wilderness, into a city called Ephraim; and there He stayed with the disciples.
55Now the Passover of the Jews was at hand, and many went up to Jerusalem out of the country before the Passover, to purify themselves.
56Therefore they were seeking for Jesus, and were saying to one another, as they stood in the temple, "What do you think; that He will not come to the feast at all?"
57Now the chief priests and the Pharisees had given orders ..at if anyone knew where He was, he should report it, that they might seize Him.

Chapter 12

Mary Anoints Jesus

JESUS, therefore, six days before the Passover, came to Bethany where Lazarus was, whom Jesus had raised from the dead.
2So they made Him a supper there, and Martha was serving; but Lazarus was one of those reclining *at the table* with Him.

ὑμεῖς οὐκ οἴδατε οὐδέν, 50 οὐδὲ λογίζεσθε
Ye　　know not　no(any)thing,　　nor　　reckon
ὅτι συμφέρει ὑμῖν ἵνα εἷς ἄνθρωπος
that it is expedient for us that one man
ἀποθάνῃ ὑπὲρ τοῦ λαοῦ καὶ μὴ ὅλον
should die for the people and not all
τὸ ἔθνος ἀπόληται. 51 τοῦτο δὲ ἀφ'
the nation perish. But this from
ἑαυτοῦ οὐκ εἶπεν, ἀλλὰ ἀρχιερεὺς ὢν
himself he said not, but high priest being
τοῦ ἐνιαυτοῦ ἐκείνου ἐπροφήτευσεν ὅτι
- year of that he prophesied that
ἔμελλεν Ἰησοῦς ἀποθνήσκειν ὑπὲρ τοῦ
was about Jesus to die for the
ἔθνους, 52 καὶ οὐχ ὑπὲρ τοῦ ἔθνους
nation, and not for the nation
μόνον, ἀλλ' ἵνα καὶ τὰ τέκνα τοῦ θεοῦ
only, but that also the children - of God
τὰ διεσκορπισμένα συναγάγῃ εἰς ἕν.
- *having been* scattered he might gather into one.
53 ἀπ' ἐκείνης οὖν τῆς ἡμέρας ἐβουλεύσαντο
From ¹that ³therefore - ²day they took counsel
ἵνα ἀποκτείνωσιν αὐτόν. 54 Ὁ οὖν
that they might kill him. - Therefore
Ἰησοῦς οὐκέτι παρρησίᾳ περιεπάτει ἐν
Jesus no longer openly walked among
τοῖς Ἰουδαίοις, ἀλλὰ ἀπῆλθεν ἐκεῖθεν εἰς
the Jews, but went away thence into
τὴν χώραν ἐγγὺς τῆς ἐρήμου, εἰς Ἐφράϊμ
the country near the desert, to ²Ephraim
λεγομένην πόλιν, κἀκεῖ ἔμεινεν μετὰ τῶν
³being called ¹a city, and there remained with the
μαθητῶν.
disciples.

55 Ἦν δὲ ἐγγὺς τὸ πάσχα τῶν
Now was near the Passover of the
Ἰουδαίων, καὶ ἀνέβησαν πολλοὶ εἰς
Jews, and went up many to
Ἱεροσόλυμα ἐκ τῆς χώρας πρὸ τοῦ
Jerusalem out of the country before the
πάσχα, ἵνα ἁγνίσωσιν ἑαυτούς.
Passover, that they might purify themselves.
56 ἐζήτουν οὖν τὸν Ἰησοῦν καὶ ἔλεγον
They sought therefore - Jesus and said
μετ' ἀλλήλων ἐν τῷ ἱερῷ ἑστηκότες·
with one another in the temple standing :
τί δοκεῖ ὑμῖν; ὅτι οὐ μὴ ἔλθῃ εἰς
What seems it to you? that by no means he comes to
τὴν ἑορτήν; 57 δεδώκεισαν δὲ οἱ ἀρχιερεῖς
the feast? Now had given the chief priests
καὶ οἱ Φαρισαῖοι ἐντολὰς ἵνα ἐάν τις
and the Pharisees commands that if anyone
γνῷ ποῦ ἐστιν μηνύσῃ, ὅπως πιάσωσιν
knew where he is (was) he should inform, so as they might arrest
αὐτόν. 12 Ὁ οὖν Ἰησοῦς πρὸ ἓξ ἡμερῶν
him. - Therefore Jesus ²before ¹six ³days
τοῦ πάσχα ἦλθεν εἰς Βηθανίαν, ὅπου
the Passover came to Bethany, where
ἦν Λάζαρος, ὃν ἤγειρεν ἐκ νεκρῶν
was Lazarus, whom ²raised ³out of [the] ⁴dead
Ἰησοῦς. 2 ἐποίησαν οὖν αὐτῷ δεῖπνον ἐκεῖ,
¹Jesus. They made therefore for him a supper there,
καὶ ἡ Μάρθα διηκόνει, ὁ δὲ Λάζαρος εἷς
and - Martha served, - but Lazarus one
ἦν ἐκ τῶν ἀνακειμένων σὺν αὐτῷ· 3 ἡ
was of the [ones] reclining with him;　-

up, "You know nothing at all! 50You do not realize that it is better for you that one man die for the people than that the whole nation perish."
51He did not say this on his own, but as high priest that year he prophesied that Jesus would die for the Jewish nation, 52and not only for that nation but also for the scattered children of God, to bring them together and make them one. 53So from that day on they plotted to take his life.
54Therefore Jesus no longer moved about publicly among the Jews. Instead he withdrew to a region near the desert, to a village called Ephraim, where he stayed with his disciples.
55When it was almost time for the Jewish Passover, many went up from the country to Jerusalem for their ceremonial cleansing before the Passover.
56They kept looking for Jesus, and as they stood in the temple area they asked one another, "What do you think? Isn't he coming to the Feast at all?" 57But the chief priests and Pharisees had given orders that if anyone found out where Jesus was, he should report it so that they might arrest him.

Chapter 12

Jesus Anointed at Bethany

SIX days before the Passover, Jesus arrived at Bethany, where Lazarus lived, whom Jesus had raised from the dead. 2Here a dinner was given in Jesus' honor. Martha served, while Lazarus was among those reclining at the table with him. 3Then

3Mary therefore took a pound of very costly perfume of pure nard, and anointed the feet of Jesus, and wiped His feet with her hair; and the house was filled with the fragrance of the perfume.

4But Judas Iscariot, one of His disciples, who was intending to betray Him, *said,

5"Why was this perfume not sold for ᵛthree hundred denarii, and given to poor people?''

6Now he said this, not because he was concerned about the poor, but because he was a thief, and as he had the money box, he used to pilfer what was put into it.

7Jesus therefore said, "Let her alone, in order that she may keep ʷit for the day of My burial.

8"For the poor you always have with you, but you do not always have Me.''

9The great multitude therefore of the Jews learned that He was there; and they came, not for Jesus' sake only, but that they might also see Lazarus, whom He raised from the dead.

10But the chief priests took counsel that they might put Lazarus to death also;

11because on account of him many of the Jews were going away, and were believing in Jesus.

Jesus Enters Jerusalem

12On the next day the great multitude who had come to the feast, when they heard that Jesus was coming to Jerusalem,

13took the branches of the palm trees, and went out to meet Him, and *began* to cry out, "Hosanna! BLESSED IS HE WHO COMES IN THE NAME OF THE LORD,

---

οὖν   Μαριὰμ   λαβοῦσα   λίτραν   μύρου
therefore   Mary   taking   a pound   ⁸ointment

νάρδου   πιστικῆς   πολυτίμου   ἤλειψεν   τοὺς
⁴of spikenard   ³of pure   ⁵costly   anointed   the

πόδας   τοῦ   Ἰησοῦ   καὶ   ἐξέμαξεν   ταῖς
feet   -   of Jesus   and   wiped off   with the

θριξὶν   αὐτῆς   τοὺς   πόδας   αὐτοῦ·   ἡ   δὲ
hairs   of her   the   feet   of him;   and the

οἰκία   ἐπληρώθη   ἐκ   τῆς   ὀσμῆς   τοῦ
house   was filled   of(with)   the   odour   of the

μύρου.   4 λέγει   δὲ   Ἰούδας   ὁ   Ἰσκαριώτης
ointment.   And says   Judas   the   Iscariot

εἷς   τῶν   μαθητῶν   αὐτοῦ,   ὁ   μέλλων
one   of the   disciples   of him, the [one] being about

αὐτὸν   παραδιδόναι·   5 διὰ   τί   τοῦτο   τὸ
him   to betray :   Why   this   -

μύρον   οὐκ   ἐπράθη   τριακοσίων   δηναρίων
ointment   not   was sold of(for) three hundred   denarii

καὶ   ἐδόθη   πτωχοῖς;   6 εἶπεν   δὲ   τοῦτο
and   given   to [the] poor?   But he said   this

οὐχ   ὅτι   περὶ   τῶν   πτωχῶν   ἔμελεν   αὐτῷ,
not because   about   the   poor   it mattered to him,

ἀλλ'   ὅτι   κλέπτης   ἦν   καὶ   τὸ   ⁸τhε   ⁸bag
but because   a thief   he was and   ⁸the   ⁶bag

ἔχων   τὰ   βαλλόμενα   ἐβάσταζεν.
¹having   ⁵the things   ⁶being put [in]   ⁴carried. *

7 εἶπεν   οὖν   ὁ   Ἰησοῦς·   ἄφες   αὐτήν,
Said   therefore   -   Jesus :   Leave   her,

ἵνα   εἰς   τὴν   ἡμέραν   τοῦ   ἐνταφιασμοῦ
that   to   the   day   of the   burial

μου   τηρήσῃ   αὐτό·   8 τοὺς   πτωχοὺς   γὰρ
of me   she may keep   it;   ²the   ³poor   ¹for

πάντοτε   ἔχετε   μεθ'   ἑαυτῶν,   ἐμὲ   δὲ
always   ye have   with   yourselves,   but me

οὐ   πάντοτε   ἔχετε.   9 Ἔγνω   οὖν   ὁ   ὄχλος
not   always   ye have.   Knew   therefore   the   crowd

πολὺς   ἐκ   τῶν   Ἰουδαίων   ὅτι   ἐκεῖ   ἐστιν,
great   of   the   Jews   that   there   he is(was),

καὶ   ἦλθον   οὐ   διὰ   τὸν   Ἰησοῦν   μόνον,
and   they came   not because of   -   Jesus   only,

ἀλλ'   ἵνα   καὶ   τὸν   Λάζαρον   ἴδωσιν   ὃν
but   that   also   -   Lazarus   they might see whom

ἤγειρεν   ἐκ   νεκρῶν.   10 ἐβουλεύσαντο   δὲ
he raised   out of [the] dead.   But took counsel

οἱ   ἀρχιερεῖς   ἵνα   καὶ   τὸν   Λάζαρον
the   chief priests   that   also   -   Lazarus

ἀποκτείνωσιν,   11 ὅτι   πολλοὶ   δι'   αὐτὸν
they might kill,   because   ¹many   ⁴because of   ⁵him

ὑπῆγον   τῶν   Ἰουδαίων   καὶ   ἐπίστευον   εἰς
⁶went   ²of the   ³Jews   and   believed   in

τὸν   Ἰησοῦς.
-    Jesus.

12 Τῇ   ἐπαύριον   ὁ   ὄχλος   πολὺς   ὁ
On the   morrow   the   crowd   much   the

ἐλθὼν   εἰς   τὴν   ἑορτήν,   ἀκούσαντες   ὅτι
coming   to   the   feast,   hearing   that

ἔρχεται   Ἰησοῦς   εἰς   Ἱεροσόλυμα, 13 ἔλαβον
is(was) coming   Jesus   to   Jerusalem,   took

τὰ   βαῖα   τῶν   φοινίκων   καὶ   ἐξῆλθον   εἰς
the branches   of the   palm-trees   and   went out   to

ὑπάντησιν   αὐτῷ,   καὶ   ἐκραύγαζον·   ὡσαννά,
a meeting   with him, and   cried out :   Hosanna,

εὐλογημένος   ὁ   ἐρχόμενος   ἐν   ὀνόματι
being blessed   the [one] coming   in [the]   name

* This may mean " stole "; *cf.* our euphemism for " steal "—to " lift " a thing.

Mary took about a pintᵉ of pure nard, an expensive perfume; she poured it on Jesus' feet and wiped his feet with her hair. And the house was filled with the fragrance of the perfume.

4But one of his disciples, Judas Iscariot, who was later to betray him, objected, 5"Why wasn't this perfume sold and the money given to the poor? It was worth a year's wages.ᶠ''

6He did not say this because he cared about the poor but because he was a thief; as keeper of the money bag, he used to help himself to what was put into it.

7"Leave her alone,'' Jesus replied. "It was intended that she should save this perfume for the day of my burial. 8You will always have the poor among you, but you will not always have me.''

9Meanwhile a large crowd of Jews found out that Jesus was there and came, not only because of him but also to see Lazarus, whom he had raised from the dead. 10So the chief priests made plans to kill Lazarus as well, 11for on account of him many of the Jews were going over to Jesus and putting their faith in him.

The Triumphal Entry

12The next day the great crowd that had come for the Feast heard that Jesus was on his way to Jerusalem. 13They took palm branches and went out to meet him, shouting,

"Hosanna!ᵍ''

"Blessed is he who comes in the name of the Lord!'' ʰ

ᵛ Equivalent to 11 months' wages
ʷ I.e., The custom of anointing for burial

ᵉ3 Greek *a litra* (probably about 0.5 liter)
ᶠ5 Greek *three hundred denarii*
ᵍ13 A Hebrew expression meaning "Save!'' which became an exclamation of praise
ʰ13 Psalm 118:25, 26

even the King of Israel."
14And Jesus, finding a young donkey, sat on it; as it is written,
15"FEAR NOT, DAUGHTER OF ZION; BEHOLD, YOUR KING IS COMING, SEATED ON A DONKEY'S COLT."
16These things His disciples did not understand at the first; but when Jesus was glorified, then they remembered that these things were written of Him, and that they had done these things to Him.
17And so the multitude who were with Him when He called Lazarus out of the tomb, and raised him from the dead, were bearing Him witness.
18For this cause also the multitude went and met Him, because they heard that He had performed this sign.
19The Pharisees therefore said to one another, "You see that you are not doing any good; look, the world has gone after Him."

Greeks Seek Jesus

20Now there were certain Greeks among those who were going up to worship at the feast;
21these therefore came to Philip, who was from Bethsaida of Galilee, and *began to* ask him, saying, "Sir, we wish to see Jesus."
22Philip *came and *told Andrew; Andrew and Philip *came, and they *told Jesus.
23And Jesus *answered them, saying, "The hour has come for the Son of Man to be glorified.
24"Truly, truly, I say to you, unless a grain of wheat falls into the earth and dies, it remains by itself alone; but if it dies, it bears much fruit.
25"He who loves his life

κυρίου, καὶ ὁ βασιλεὺς τοῦ Ἰσραήλ.
of [the] Lord, even the king - of Israel.

14 εὑρὼν δὲ ὁ Ἰησοῦς ὀνάριον ἐκάθισεν
And ᵇhaving found - ¹Jesus a young ass sat

ἐπ' αὐτό, καθὼς ἐστιν γεγραμμένον·
on it, as it is *having been* written :

15 μὴ φοβοῦ, θυγάτηρ Σιών· ἰδοὺ ὁ
Fear not, daughter of Sion : behold[,] the

βασιλεύς σου ἔρχεται, καθήμενος ἐπὶ
king of thee comes, sitting on

πῶλον ὄνου. 16 ταῦτα οὐκ ἔγνωσαν
a foal of an ass. These things knew not

αὐτοῦ οἱ μαθηταὶ τὸ πρῶτον, ἀλλ' ὅτε
of him the disciples at first, but when

ἐδοξάσθη Ἰησοῦς, τότε ἐμνήσθησαν ὅτι
was glorified Jesus, then they remembered that

ταῦτα ἦν ἐπ' αὐτῷ γεγραμμένα καὶ
these things were on him *having been* written and

ταῦτα ἐποίησαν αὐτῷ. 17 ἐμαρτύρει οὖν
these things they did to him. Witnessed therefore

ὁ ὄχλος ὁ ὢν μετ' αὐτοῦ ὅτε τὸν
the crowd - being with him when -

Λάζαρον ἐφώνησεν ἐκ τοῦ μνημείου καὶ
Lazarus he called out of the tomb and

ἤγειρεν αὐτὸν ἐκ νεκρῶν. 18 διὰ τοῦτο
raised him out of [the] dead. Therefore

καὶ ὑπήντησεν αὐτῷ ὁ ὄχλος, ὅτι
also met him the crowd, because

ἤκουσαν τοῦτο αὐτὸν πεποιηκέναι τὸ
¹they heard ⁴this ³him ²to have done^b -

σημεῖον. 19 οἱ οὖν Φαρισαῖοι εἶπαν
⁵sign. Therefore the Pharisees said

πρὸς ἑαυτούς· θεωρεῖτε ὅτι οὐκ ὠφελεῖτε
to themselves : Behold ye that ye profit not

οὐδέν· ἴδε ὁ κόσμος ὀπίσω αὐτοῦ ἀπῆλθεν.
no(any)thing; see[,] the world after him went(is gone).

20 Ἦσαν δὲ Ἕλληνές τινες ἐκ τῶν
Now there were ²Greeks ¹some of the

ἀναβαινόντων ἵνα προσκυνήσωσιν ἐν τῇ
[ones] going up that they might worship at the

ἑορτῇ. 21 οὗτοι οὖν προσῆλθον Φιλίππῳ
feast; these therefore approached to Philip

τῷ ἀπὸ Βηθσαϊδὰ τῆς Γαλιλαίας. καὶ
the [one] from Bethsaida - of Galilee, and

ἠρώτων αὐτὸν λέγοντες· κύριε, θέλομεν
asked him saying : Sir, we wish

τὸν Ἰησοῦν ἰδεῖν. 22 ἔρχεται ὁ Φίλιππος
- Jesus to see. Comes - Philip

καὶ λέγει τῷ Ἀνδρέᾳ· ἔρχεται Ἀνδρέας
and tells - Andrew; comes Andrew

καὶ Φίλιππος καὶ λέγουσιν τῷ Ἰησοῦ.
and Philip and tell - Jesus.

23 ὁ δὲ Ἰησοῦς ἀποκρίνεται αὐτοῖς λέγων·
- And Jesus answers them saying:

ἐλήλυθεν ἡ ὥρα ἵνα δοξασθῇ ὁ υἱὸς τοῦ
Has come the hour that is glorified the Son -

ἀνθρώπου. 24 ἀμὴν ἀμὴν λέγω ὑμῖν,
of man. Truly truly I say to you,

ἐὰν μὴ ὁ κόκκος τοῦ σίτου πεσὼν εἰς
unless the grain - of wheat falling into

τὴν γῆν ἀποθάνῃ, αὐτὸς μόνος μένει·
the ground dies, it alone remains;

ἐὰν δὲ ἀποθάνῃ, πολὺν καρπὸν φέρει.
but if it dies, much fruit it bears.

25 ὁ φιλῶν τὴν ψυχὴν αὐτοῦ ἀπολλύει
The [one] loving the life of him loses

"Blessed is the King of Israel!"
14Jesus found a young donkey and sat upon it, as it is written,
15"Do not be afraid, O Daughter of Zion;
see, your king is coming,
seated on a donkey's colt."^i
16At first his disciples did not understand all this. Only after Jesus was glorified did they realize that these things had been written about him and that they had done these things to him.
17Now the crowd that was with him when he called Lazarus from the tomb and raised him from the dead continued to spread the word. 18Many people, because they had heard that he had given this miraculous sign, went out to meet him. 19So the Pharisees said to one another, "See, this is getting us nowhere. Look how the whole world has gone after him!"

Jesus Predicts His Death

20Now there were some Greeks among those who went up to worship at the Feast. 21They came to Philip, who was from Bethsaida in Galilee, with a request. "Sir," they said, "we would like to see Jesus." 22Philip went to tell Andrew; Andrew and Philip in turn told Jesus.
23Jesus replied, "The hour has come for the Son of Man to be glorified. 24I tell you the truth, unless a kernel of wheat falls to the ground and dies, it remains only a single seed. But if it dies, it produces many seeds. 25The man who loves his life will lose it,

^i15 Zech. 9:9

loses it; and he who hates his life in this world shall keep it to life eternal.

26"If anyone serves Me, let him follow Me; and where I am, there shall My servant also be; if anyone serves Me, the Father will honor him.

Jesus Foretells His Death

27"Now My soul has become troubled; and what shall I say, 'Father, save Me from this hour'? But for this purpose I came to this hour.

28"Father, glorify Thy name." There came therefore a voice out of heaven: "I have both glorified it, and will glorify it again."

29The multitude therefore, who stood by and heard it, were saying that it had thundered; others were saying, "An angel has spoken to Him."

30Jesus answered and said, "This voice has not come for My sake, but for your sakes.

31"Now judgment is upon this world; now the ruler of this world shall be cast out.

32"And I, if I be lifted up from the earth, will draw all men to Myself."

33But He was saying this to indicate the kind of death by which He was to die.

34The multitude therefore answered Him, "We have heard out of the Law that the Christ is to remain forever; and how can You say, 'The Son of Man must be lifted up'? Who is this Son of Man?"

35Jesus therefore said to them, "For a little while longer the light is among you. Walk while you have the light, that darkness may not overtake you; he who walks in the darkness does not know where he goes.

αὐτήν, καὶ ὁ μισῶν τὴν ψυχὴν αὐτοῦ
it, and the [one] hating the life of him

ἐν τῷ κόσμῳ τούτῳ εἰς ζωὴν αἰώνιον
in - world this unto life eternal

φυλάξει αὐτήν. 26 ἐὰν ἐμοί τις διακονῇ,
will keep it. If me anyone serves,

ἐμοὶ ἀκολουθείτω, καὶ ὅπου εἰμὶ ἐγώ,
me let him follow, and where am I,

ἐκεῖ καὶ ὁ διάκονος ὁ ἐμὸς ἔσται·
there also *the* 'servant - 'my will be;

ἐάν τις ἐμοὶ διακονῇ, τιμήσει αὐτὸν
if anyone me serves, will honour him

ὁ πατήρ. 27 νῦν ἡ ψυχή μου τετάρακται,
the Father. Now the soul of me has been troubled,

καὶ τί εἴπω; πάτερ, σῶσόν με ἐκ
and what may I say? Father, save me out of

τῆς ὥρας ταύτης. ἀλλὰ διὰ τοῦτο ἦλθον
- hour this. But therefore I came

εἰς τὴν ὥραν ταύτην. 28 πάτερ, δόξασόν
to the hour this. Father, glorify

σου τὸ ὄνομα. ἦλθεν οὖν φωνὴ ἐκ
of thee the name. Came therefore a voice out of

τοῦ οὐρανοῦ· καὶ ἐδόξασα καὶ πάλιν
- heaven: Both I glorified and again

δοξάσω. 29 ὁ οὖν ὄχλος ὁ ἑστὼς καὶ
I will glorify. Therefore the crowd - standing and

ἀκούσας ἔλεγεν βροντὴν γεγονέναι· ἄλλοι
hearing said thunder to have happened; others

ἔλεγον· ἄγγελος αὐτῷ λελάληκεν.
said : An angel to him has spoken.

30 ἀπεκρίθη Ἰησοῦς καὶ εἶπεν· οὐ δι᾽ ἐμὲ
Answered Jesus and said : Not because of me

ἡ φωνὴ αὕτη γέγονεν ἀλλὰ δι᾽ ὑμᾶς.
- voice this has happened but because of you.

31 νῦν κρίσις ἐστὶν τοῦ κόσμου τούτου·
Now judgment is - world of this ;

νῦν ὁ ἄρχων τοῦ κόσμου τούτου
now the ruler - world of this

ἐκβληθήσεται ἔξω· 32 κἀγὼ ἐὰν ὑψωθῶ
shall be cast *out* outside; and I if I am lifted up

ἐκ τῆς γῆς, πάντας ἑλκύσω πρὸς
out of the earth, all men will draw to

ἐμαυτόν. 33 τοῦτο δὲ ἔλεγεν σημαίνων
myself. And this he said signifying

ποίῳ θανάτῳ ἤμελλεν ἀποθνῄσκειν.
by what kind of death he was about to die.

34 ἀπεκρίθη οὖν αὐτῷ ὁ ὄχλος· ἡμεῖς
Answered therefore him the crowd : We

ἠκούσαμεν ἐκ τοῦ νόμου ὅτι ὁ χριστὸς
heard out of the law that the Christ

μένει εἰς τὸν αἰῶνα, καὶ πῶς λέγεις
remains unto the age, and how sayest

σὺ ὅτι δεῖ ὑψωθῆναι τὸν υἱὸν τοῦ
thou that it behoves to be lifted up the Son -

ἀνθρώπου; τίς ἐστιν οὗτος ὁ υἱὸς τοῦ
of man? who is this - Son -

ἀνθρώπου; 35 εἶπεν οὖν αὐτοῖς ὁ Ἰησοῦς·
of man? Said therefore to them - Jesus :

ἔτι μικρὸν χρόνον τὸ φῶς ἐν ὑμῖν
Yet a little time the light among you

ἐστιν. περιπατεῖτε ὡς τὸ φῶς ἔχετε,
is. Walk while the light ye have,

ἵνα μὴ σκοτία ὑμᾶς καταλάβῃ· καὶ
lest darkness you overtakes; and

ὁ περιπατῶν ἐν τῇ σκοτίᾳ οὐκ οἶδεν
the [one] walking in the darkness knows not

while the man who hates his life in this world will keep it for eternal life. 26Whoever serves me must follow me; and where I am, my servant also will be. My Father will honor the one who serves me.

27"Now my heart is troubled, and what shall I say? 'Father, save me from this hour'? No, it was for this very reason I came to this hour. 28Father, glorify your name!"

Then a voice came from heaven, "I have glorified it, and will glorify it again." 29The crowd that was there and heard it said it had thundered; others said an angel had spoken to him.

30Jesus said, "This voice was for your benefit, not mine. 31Now is the time for judgment on this world; now the prince of this world will be driven out. 32But I, when I am lifted up from the earth, will draw all men to myself." 33He said this to show the kind of death he was going to die.

34The crowd spoke up, "We have heard from the Law that the Christ[/] will remain forever, so how can you say, 'The Son of Man must be lifted up'? Who is this 'Son of Man'?"

35Then Jesus told them, "You are going to have the light just a little while longer. Walk while you have the light, before darkness overtakes you. The man who walks in the dark does not know where he is go-

/34 Or Messiah

36"While you have the light, believe in the light, in order that you may become sons of light."
These things Jesus spoke, and He departed and hid Himself from them.
37But though He had performed so many signs before them, yet they were not believing in Him;
38that the word of Isaiah the prophet might be fulfilled, which he spoke, "LORD, WHO HAS BELIEVED OUR REPORT? AND TO WHOM HAS THE ARM OF THE LORD BEEN REVEALED?"
39For this cause they could not believe, for Isaiah said again,
40"HE HAS BLINDED THEIR EYES, AND HE HARDENED THEIR HEART; LEST THEY SEE WITH THEIR EYES, AND PERCEIVE WITH THEIR HEART, AND BE CONVERTED, AND I HEAL THEM."
41These things Isaiah said, because he saw His glory, and he spoke of Him.
42Nevertheless many even of the rulers believed in Him, but because of the Pharisees they were not confessing Him, lest they should be put out of the synagogue;
43for they loved the approval of men rather than the approval of God.
44And Jesus cried out and said, "He who believes in Me does not believe in Me, but in Him who sent Me.
45"And he who beholds Me beholds the One who sent Me.
46"I have come as light into the world, that everyone who believes in Me may not remain in darkness.
47"And if anyone hears My sayings, and does not keep them, I do not judge him; for I did not come to

---

ποῦ ὑπάγει. **36** ὡς τὸ φῶς ἔχετε,
where he is going.　　While the light ye have,
πιστεύετε εἰς τὸ φῶς, ἵνα υἱοὶ φωτὸς
believe in the light, that sons of light
γένησθε.
ye may become.

Ταῦτα ἐλάλησεν Ἰησοῦς, καὶ ἀπελθὼν
These things spoke Jesus, and going away
ἐκρύβη ἀπ' αὐτῶν. **37** Τοσαῦτα δὲ αὐτοῦ
was hidden from them.　　But so many him
σημεῖα πεποιηκότος ἔμπροσθεν αὐτῶν οὐκ
signs having done before them not
=But while he did so many signs
ἐπίστευον εἰς αὐτόν, **38** ἵνα ὁ λόγος
they believed in him, that the word
Ἡσαΐου τοῦ προφήτου πληρωθῇ ὃν
of Esaias the prophet might be fulfilled which
εἶπεν· κύριε, τίς ἐπίστευσεν τῇ ἀκοῇ
he said : Lord, who believed the report
ἡμῶν; καὶ ὁ βραχίων κυρίου τίνι
of us? and the arm of [the] Lord to whom
ἀπεκαλύφθη, **39** διὰ τοῦτο οὐκ ἠδύναντο
was it revealed?　　Therefore they could not
πιστεύειν, ὅτι πάλιν εἶπεν Ἡσαΐας·
to believe, because again said Esaias :
40 τετύφλωκεν αὐτῶν τοὺς ὀφθαλμοὺς καὶ
He has blinded of them the eyes and
ἐπώρωσεν αὐτῶν τὴν καρδίαν, ἵνα
hardened of them the heart, that
μὴ ἴδωσιν τοῖς ὀφθαλμοῖς καὶ νοήσωσιν
they might not see with the eyes and understand
τῇ καρδίᾳ καὶ στραφῶσιν, καὶ ἰάσομαι
with the heart and might turn, and I will cure
αὐτούς. **41** ταῦτα εἶπεν Ἡσαΐας ὅτι
them.　　These things said Esaias because
εἶδεν τὴν δόξαν αὐτοῦ, καὶ ἐλάλησεν
he saw the glory of him, and spoke
περὶ αὐτοῦ. **42** ὅμως μέντοι καὶ ἐκ
about him.　　Nevertheless however even of
τῶν ἀρχόντων πολλοὶ ἐπίστευσαν εἰς αὐτόν,
the rulers many believed in him,
ἀλλὰ διὰ τοὺς Φαρισαίους οὐχ ὡμολόγουν,
but because of the Pharisees did not confess,
ἵνα μὴ ἀποσυνάγωγοι γένωνται·
lest put out of [the] synagogue they should become;
43 ἠγάπησαν γὰρ τὴν δόξαν τῶν ἀνθρώπων
for they loved the glory - of men
μᾶλλον ἤπερ τὴν δόξαν τοῦ θεοῦ.
more than the glory - of God.
44 Ἰησοῦς δὲ ἔκραξεν καὶ εἶπεν· ὁ
But Jesus cried out and said : The
πιστεύων εἰς ἐμὲ οὐ πιστεύει εἰς ἐμὲ
[one] believing in me believes not in me
ἀλλὰ εἰς τὸν πέμψαντά με, **45** καὶ ὁ
but in the [one] having sent me, and the
θεωρῶν ἐμὲ θεωρεῖ τὸν πέμψαντά με.
[one] beholding me beholds the [one] having sent me.
46 ἐγὼ φῶς εἰς τὸν κόσμον ἐλήλυθα,
I a light into the world have come,
ἵνα πᾶς ὁ πιστεύων εἰς ἐμὲ ἐν τῇ
that everyone believing in me in the
σκοτίᾳ μὴ μείνῃ. **47** καὶ ἐάν τίς μου
darkness may not remain.　　And if anyone of me
ἀκούσῃ τῶν ῥημάτων καὶ μὴ φυλάξῃ,
hears the words and keeps not,
ἐγὼ οὐ κρίνω αὐτόν· οὐ γὰρ ἦλθον
I do not judge him;　　for I came not

---

ing. 36Put your trust in the light while you have it, so that you may become sons of light." When he had finished speaking, Jesus left and hid himself from them.

The Jews Continue in Their Unbelief

37Even after Jesus had done all these miraculous signs in their presence, they still would not believe in him. 38This was to fulfill the word of Isaiah the prophet:

"Lord, who has believed
　our message
and to whom has the
　arm of the Lord
been revealed?" [k]

39For this reason they could not believe, because, as Isaiah says elsewhere:

40"He has blinded their
　eyes
and deadened their
　hearts,
so they can neither see
　with their eyes,
nor understand with
　their hearts,
nor turn—and I would
　heal them." [l]

41Isaiah said this because he saw Jesus' glory and spoke about him.
42Yet at the same time many even among the leaders believed in him. But because of the Pharisees they would not confess their faith for fear they would be put out of the synagogue;
43for they loved praise from men more than praise from God.
44Then Jesus cried out, "When a man believes in me, he does not believe in me only, but in the one who sent me. 45When he looks at me, he sees the one who sent me. 46I have come into the world as a light, so that no one who believes in me should stay in darkness.
47"As for the person who hears my words but does not keep them, I do not judge him. For I did not

---

k38 Isaiah 53:1
l40 Isaiah 6:10

judge the world, but to save the world.

48"He who rejects Me, and does not receive My sayings, has one who judges him; the word I spoke is what will judge him at the last day.

49"For I did not speak on My own initiative, but the Father Himself who sent Me has given Me commandment, what to say, and what to speak.

50"And I know that His commandment is eternal life; therefore the things I speak, I speak just as the Father has told Me."

ἵνα κρίνω τὸν κόσμον, ἀλλ' ἵνα σώσω
that I might judge the world, but that I might save

τὸν κόσμον. **48** ὁ ἀθετῶν ἐμὲ καὶ μὴ
the world. The [one] rejecting me and not

λαμβάνων τὰ ῥήματά μου ἔχει τὸν
receiving the words of me has the

κρίνοντα αὐτόν· ὁ λόγος ὃν ἐλάλησα,
[one] judging him; the word which I spoke,

ἐκεῖνος κρινεῖ αὐτὸν ἐν τῇ ἐσχάτῃ ἡμέρᾳ.
that will judge him in the last day.

49 ὅτι ἐγὼ ἐξ ἐμαυτοῦ οὐκ ἐλάλησα,
Because I of myself did not speak,

ἀλλ' ὁ πέμψας με πατὴρ αὐτός μοι
but ¹the ²having sent ⁴me ³Father ⁵he ⁷me

ἐντολὴν δέδωκεν τί εἴπω καὶ τί
⁶commandment ⁶has given what I may say and what

λαλήσω. **50** καὶ οἶδα ὅτι ἡ ἐντολὴ
I may speak. And I know that the commandment

αὐτοῦ ζωὴ αἰώνιός ἐστιν. ἃ οὖν ἐγὼ
of him life eternal is. What things therefore I

λαλῶ, καθὼς εἴρηκέν μοι ὁ πατήρ,
speak, as has said to me the Father,

οὕτως λαλῶ.
so I speak.

---

come to judge the world, but to save it. 48There is a judge for the one who rejects me and does not accept my words; that very word which I spoke will condemn him at the last day. 49For I did not speak of my own accord, but the Father who sent me commanded me what to say and how to say it. 50I know that his command leads to eternal life. So whatever I say is just what the Father has told me to say."

Chapter 13

The Lord's Supper

NOW before the Feast of the Passover, Jesus knowing that His hour had come that He should depart out of this world to the Father, having loved His own who were in the world, He loved them to the end.

2And during supper, the devil having already put into the heart of Judas Iscariot, *the son* of Simon, to betray Him,

3*Jesus*, knowing that the Father had given all things into His hands, and that He had come forth from God, and was going back to God,

4*rose from supper, and *laid aside His garments; and taking a towel, He girded Himself about.

Jesus Washes the Disciples' Feet

5Then He *poured water into the basin, and began to wash the disciples' feet, and to wipe them with the towel with which He was girded.

6And so He *came to Simon Peter. He *said to Him, "Lord, do You wash my feet?"

---

13 Πρὸ δὲ τῆς ἑορτῆς τοῦ πάσχα
Now before the feast of the Passover

εἰδὼς ὁ Ἰησοῦς ὅτι ἦλθεν αὐτοῦ ἡ
¹knowing - ¹Jesus that came of him the

ὥρα ἵνα μεταβῇ ἐκ τοῦ κόσμου τούτου
hour that he should remove out of - world this

πρὸς τὸν πατέρα, ἀγαπήσας τοὺς ἰδίους
to the Father, having loved the(his) own

τοὺς ἐν τῷ κόσμῳ, εἰς τέλος ἠγάπησεν
- in the world, to [the] end he loved

αὐτούς. **2** καὶ δείπνου γινομένου, τοῦ
them. And supper taking place,ᵃ the
    =during supper,

διαβόλου ἤδη βεβληκότος εἰς τὴν καρδίαν
devil now having putᵃ into the heart
= as the devil had now put

ἵνα παραδοῖ αὐτὸν Ἰούδας Σίμωνος
that ⁴should betray ⁵him ¹Judas ²[son] of Simon

Ἰσκαριώτης, **3** εἰδὼς ὅτι πάντα ἔδωκεν
³Iscariot, knowing* that all things gave

αὐτῷ ὁ πατὴρ εἰς τὰς χεῖρας, καὶ
him the Father into the(his) hands, and

ὅτι ἀπὸ θεοῦ ἐξῆλθεν καὶ πρὸς τὸν
that from God he came forth and to -

θεὸν ὑπάγει, **4** ἐγείρεται ἐκ τοῦ δείπνου
God goes, he rises out of(from) the supper

καὶ τίθησιν τὰ ἱμάτια, καὶ λαβὼν
and places [aside] the(his) garments, and taking

λέντιον διέζωσεν ἑαυτόν· **5** εἶτα βάλλει
a towel he girded himself; then he puts

ὕδωρ εἰς τὸν νιπτῆρα, καὶ ἤρξατο νίπτειν
water into the basin, and began to wash

τοὺς πόδας τῶν μαθητῶν καὶ ἐκμάσσειν
the feet of the disciples and to wipe off

τῷ λεντίῳ ᾧ ἦν διεζωσμένος.
with the towel with which he was *having been* girded.

6 ἔρχεται οὖν πρὸς Σίμωνα Πέτρον·
He comes therefore to Simon Peter;

λέγει αὐτῷ· κύριε, σύ μου νίπτεις τοὺς
he says to him: Lord, thou of me washest the

Chapter 13

Jesus Washes His Disciples' Feet

IT was just before the Passover Feast. Jesus knew that the time had come for him to leave this world and go to the Father. Having loved his own who were in the world, he now showed them the full extent of his love. *m*

2The evening meal was being served, and the devil had already prompted Judas Iscariot, son of Simon, to betray Jesus. 3Jesus knew that the Father had put all things under his power, and that he had come from God and was returning to God; 4so he got up from the meal, took off his outer clothing, and wrapped a towel around his waist. 5After that, he poured water into a basin and began to wash his disciples' feet, drying them with the towel that was wrapped around him.

6He came to Simon Peter, who said to him, "Lord, are you going to wash my feet?"

---

* Repeated from ver. 1; the subject is therefore again "Jesus".   *m* 1 Or *he loved them to the last*

7Jesus answered and said to him, "What I do you do not realize now, but you shall understand hereafter."

8Peter *said to Him, "Never shall You wash my feet!" Jesus answered him, "If I do not wash you, you have no part with Me."

9Simon Peter *said to Him, "Lord, not my feet only, but also my hands and my head."

10Jesus *said to him, "He who has bathed needs only to wash his feet, but is completely clean; and you are clean, but not all of you."

11For He knew the one who was betraying Him; for this reason He said, "Not all of you are clean."

12And so when He had washed their feet, and taken His garments, and reclined *at the table* again, He said to them, "Do you know what I have done to you?

13"You call Me Teacher and Lord; and you are right, for *so* I am.

14"If I then, the Lord and the Teacher, washed your feet, you also ought to wash one another's feet.

15"For I gave you an example that you also should do as I did to you.

16"Truly, truly, I say to you, a slave is not greater than his master; neither *is* one who is sent greater than the one who sent him.

17"If you know these things, you are blessed *if* you do them.

18"I do not speak of all of you. I know the ones I have chosen; but *it is* that the Scripture may be fulfilled, 'HE WHO EATS MY BREAD

πόδας; **7** ἀπεκρίθη Ἰησοῦς καὶ εἶπεν αὐτῷ·
feet? Answered Jesus and said to him :

ὃ ἐγὼ ποιῶ σὺ οὐκ οἶδας ἄρτι,
What I am doing thou knowest not yet,

γνώσῃ δὲ μετὰ ταῦτα. **8** λέγει αὐτῷ
but thou wilt know after these things. Says to him

Πέτρος· οὐ μὴ νίψῃς μου τοὺς πόδας
Peter : By no means shalt thou wash of me the feet

εἰς τὸν αἰῶνα. ἀπεκρίθη Ἰησοῦς αὐτῷ·
unto the age. ¹Answered ¹Jesus ³him :

ἐὰν μὴ νίψω σε, οὐκ ἔχεις μέρος μετ'
Unless I wash thee, thou hast no part with

ἐμοῦ. **9** λέγει αὐτῷ Σίμων Πέτρος·
me. Says to him Simon Peter :

κύριε, μὴ τοὺς πόδας μου μόνον ἀλλὰ
Lord, not the feet of me only but

καὶ τὰς χεῖρας καὶ τὴν κεφαλήν. **10** λέγει
also the hands and the head. Says

αὐτῷ Ἰησοῦς· ὁ λελουμένος οὐκ ἔχει
to him Jesus : The [one] having been bathed has not

χρείαν [εἰ μὴ τοὺς πόδας] νίψασθαι,
need except the feet to wash,

ἀλλ' ἔστιν καθαρὸς ὅλος· καὶ ὑμεῖς
but is clean wholly; and ye

καθαροί ἐστε, ἀλλ' οὐχὶ πάντες. **11** ᾔδει
clean are, but not all. he knew

γὰρ τὸν παραδιδόντα αὐτόν· διὰ τοῦτο
For the [one] betraying him; therefore

εἶπεν ὅτι οὐχὶ πάντες καθαροί ἐστε.
he said[,] – Not all clean ye are.

12 Ὅτε οὖν ἔνιψεν τοὺς πόδας αὐτῶν
When therefore he washed the feet of them

καὶ ἔλαβεν τὰ ἱμάτια αὐτοῦ καὶ ἀνέπεσεν
and took the garments of him and reclined

πάλιν, εἶπεν αὐτοῖς· γινώσκετε τί πε-
again, he said to them : Do ye know what I

ποίηκα ὑμῖν; **13** ὑμεῖς φωνεῖτέ με· ὁ
have done to you? Ye call me : The

διδάσκαλος καὶ ὁ κύριος, καὶ καλῶς
Teacher and the Lord, and well

λέγετε· εἰμὶ γάρ. **14** εἰ οὖν ἐγὼ ἔνιψα
ye say; for I am. If therefore I washed

ὑμῶν τοὺς πόδας ὁ κύριος καὶ ὁ
of you the feet the Lord and the

διδάσκαλος, καὶ ὑμεῖς ὀφείλετε ἀλλήλων
Teacher, also ye ought of one another

νίπτειν τοὺς πόδας· **15** ὑπόδειγμα γὰρ
to wash the feet; for an example

ἔδωκα ὑμῖν ἵνα καθὼς ἐγὼ ἐποίησα
I gave you that as I did

ὑμῖν καὶ ὑμεῖς ποιῆτε. **16** ἀμὴν ἀμὴν
to you also ye may do. Truly truly

λέγω ὑμῖν, οὐκ ἔστιν δοῦλος μείζων
I tell you, is not a slave greater [than]

τοῦ κυρίου αὐτοῦ, οὐδὲ ἀπόστολος μείζων
the lord of him, nor a sent one greater [than]

τοῦ πέμψαντος αὐτόν. **17** εἰ ταῦτα
the [one] sending him. If these things

οἴδατε, μακάριοί ἐστε ἐὰν ποιῆτε αὐτά.
ye know, blessed are ye if ye do them.

18 Οὐ περὶ πάντων ὑμῶν λέγω· ἐγὼ
Not concerning ¹all ¹you I speak; I

οἶδα τίνας ἐξελεξάμην· ἀλλ' ἵνα ἡ
know whom I chose; but that the

γραφὴ πληρωθῇ· ὁ τρώγων μου τὸν
scripture may be fulfilled : The [one] eating of me the

7Jesus replied, "You do not realize now what I am doing, but later you will understand."

8"No," said Peter, "you shall never wash my feet." Jesus answered, "Unless I wash you, you have no part with me."

9"Then, Lord," Simon Peter replied, "not just my feet but my hands and my head as well!"

10Jesus answered, "A person who has had a bath needs only to wash his feet; his whole body is clean. And you are clean, though not every one of you." 11For he knew who was going to betray him, and that was why he said not every one was clean.

12When he had finished washing their feet, he put on his clothes and returned to his place. "Do you understand what I have done for you?" he asked them. 13"You call me 'Teacher' and 'Lord,' and rightly so, for that is what I am. 14Now that I, your Lord and Teacher, have washed your feet, you also should wash one another's feet. 15I have set you an example that you should do as I have done for you. 16I tell you the truth, no servant is greater than his master, nor is a messenger greater than the one who sent him. 17Now that you know these things, you will be blessed if you do them.

Jesus Predicts His Betrayal

18"I am not referring to all of you; I know those I have chosen. But this is to fulfill the scripture: 'He who shares my bread has

HAS LIFTED UP HIS HEEL AGAINST ME.'

19"From now on I am telling you before it comes to pass, so that when it does occur, you may believe that I am He.

20"Truly, truly, I say to you, he who receives whomever I send receives Me; and he who receives Me receives Him who sent Me."

Jesus Predicts His Betrayal

21When Jesus had said this, He became troubled in spirit, and testified, and said, "Truly, truly, I say to you, that one of you will betray Me."

22The disciples *began* looking at one another, at a loss *to know* of which one He was speaking.

23There was reclining on Jesus' breast one of His disciples, whom Jesus loved.

24Simon Peter therefore *gestured to him, and *said to him, "Tell *us* who it is of whom He is speaking."

25He, leaning back thus on Jesus' breast, *said to Him, "Lord, who is it?"

26Jesus therefore *answered, "That is the one for whom I shall dip the morsel and give it to him." So when He had dipped the morsel, He *took and *gave it to Judas, *the son* of Simon Iscariot.

27And after the morsel, Satan then entered into him. Jesus therefore *said to him, "What you do, do quickly."

28Now no one of those reclining *at the table* knew for what purpose He had said this to him.

29For some were supposing, because Judas had the money box, that Jesus was saying to him, "Buy the things we have need of for the feast"; or else, that he should give something to the poor.

30And so after receiving

ἄρτον ἐπῆρεν ἐπ' ἐμὲ τὴν πτέρναν αὐτοῦ.
bread lifted up against me the heel of him.

19 ἀπ' ἄρτι λέγω ὑμῖν πρὸ τοῦ γενέσθαι,
From now I tell you before the to happen, =it happens,

ἵνα πιστεύητε ὅταν γένηται ὅτι ἐγώ
that ye may believe when it happens that I

εἰμι. 20 ἀμὴν ἀμὴν λέγω ὑμῖν, ὁ
am. Truly truly I say to you, the

λαμβάνων ἄν τινα πέμψω ἐμὲ λαμβάνει,
[one] receiving whomever I may send me receives,

ὁ δὲ ἐμὲ λαμβάνων λαμβάνει τὸν
and the [one] me receiving receives the [one]

πέμψαντά με. 21 ταῦτα εἰπὼν Ἰησοῦς
having sent me. These things saying Jesus

ἐταράχθη τῷ πνεύματι καὶ ἐμαρτύρησεν
was troubled in the(his) spirit and witnessed

καὶ εἶπεν· ἀμὴν ἀμὴν λέγω ὑμῖν ὅτι
and said : Truly truly I tell you that

εἷς ἐξ ὑμῶν παραδώσει με. 22 ἔβλεπον
one of you will betray me. Looked

εἰς ἀλλήλους οἱ μαθηταὶ ἀπορούμενοι περὶ
at one another the disciples being perplexed about

τίνος λέγει. 23 ἦν ἀνακείμενος εἷς ἐκ
whom he speaks. Was reclining one of

τῶν μαθητῶν αὐτοῦ ἐν τῷ κόλπῳ τοῦ
the disciples of him in the bosom

Ἰησοῦ, ὃν ἠγάπα ὁ Ἰησοῦς· 24 νεύει
of Jesus, whom loved the Jesus; nods

οὖν τούτῳ Σίμων Πέτρος καὶ λέγει
therefore to this one Simon Peter and says

αὐτῷ· εἰπὲ τίς ἐστιν περὶ οὗ λέγει.
to him : Say who it is about whom he speaks.

25 ἀναπεσὼν ἐκεῖνος οὕτως ἐπὶ τὸ
Falling back that one thus on the

στῆθος τοῦ Ἰησοῦ λέγει αὐτῷ· κύριε,
breast - of Jesus he says to him : Lord,

τίς ἐστιν, 26 ἀποκρίνεται οὖν ὁ Ἰησοῦς·
who is it? Answers therefore - Jesus :

ἐκεῖνός ἐστιν ᾧ ἐγὼ βάψω τὸ ψωμίον
That one it is to whom I shall dip the morsel

καὶ δώσω αὐτῷ. βάψας οὖν [τὸ]
and shall give him. Dipping therefore the

ψωμίον λαμβάνει καὶ δίδωσιν Ἰούδᾳ
morsel he takes and gives to Judas

Σίμωνος Ἰσκαριώτου. 27 καὶ μετὰ τὸ
[son] of Simon Iscariot. And after the

ψωμίον τότε εἰσῆλθεν εἰς ἐκεῖνον ὁ
morsel then entered into that one

σατανᾶς. λέγει οὖν αὐτῷ Ἰησοῦς· ὁ
Satan. Says therefore to him Jesus : What

ποιεῖς ποίησον τάχιον. 28 τοῦτο [δὲ]
thou doest do quickly. But this

οὐδεὶς ἔγνω τῶν ἀνακειμένων πρὸς τί
no one knew of the [ones] reclining for what

εἶπεν αὐτῷ· 29 τινὲς γὰρ ἐδόκουν, ἐπεὶ
he told him; for some thought, since

τὸ γλωσσόκομον εἶχεν Ἰούδας, ὅτι λέγει
the bag had Judas, that tells

αὐτῷ Ἰησοῦς· ἀγόρασον ὧν χρείαν
him Jesus : Buy [the] things of which need

ἔχομεν εἰς τὴν ἑορτήν, ἢ τοῖς πτωχοῖς
we have for the feast, or to the poor

ἵνα τι δῷ. 30 λαβὼν οὖν τὸ
that something he should give. Having taken therefore the

---

lifted up his heel against me.'[n]

19"I am telling you now before it happens, so that when it does happen you will believe that I am He. 20I tell you the truth, whoever accepts anyone I send accepts me; and whoever accepts me accepts the one who sent me."

21After he had said this, Jesus was troubled in spirit and testified, "I tell you the truth, one of you is going to betray me."

22His disciples stared at one another, at a loss to know which of them he meant. 23One of them, the disciple whom Jesus loved, was reclining next to him. 24Simon Peter motioned to this disciple and said, "Ask him which one he means."

25Leaning back against Jesus, he asked him, "Lord, who is it?"

26Jesus answered, "It is the one to whom I will give this piece of bread when I have dipped it in the dish." Then, dipping the piece of bread, he gave it to Judas Iscariot, son of Simon. 27As soon as Judas took the bread, Satan entered into him.

"What you are about to do, do quickly," Jesus told him, 28but no one at the meal understood why Jesus said this to him. 29Since Judas had charge of the money, some thought Jesus was telling him to buy what was needed for the Feast, or to give something to the poor. 30As soon as Judas had tak-

[n]18 Psalm 41:9

the morsel he went out immediately; and it was night.

31When therefore he had gone out, Jesus *said, "Now is the Son of Man glorified, and God is glorified in Him;

32if God is glorified in Him, God will also glorify Him in Himself, and will glorify Him immediately.

33"Little children, I am with you a little while longer. You shall seek Me; and as I said to the Jews, I now say to you also, 'Where I am going, you cannot come.'

34"A new commandment I give to you, that you love one another, even as I have loved you, that you also love one another.

35"By this all men will know that you are My disciples, if you have love for one another."

36Simon Peter *said to Him, "Lord, where are You going?" Jesus answered, "Where I go, you cannot follow Me now; but you shall follow later."

37Peter *said to Him, "Lord, why can I not follow You right now? I will lay down my life for You."

38Jesus *answered, "Will you lay down your life for Me? Truly, truly, I say to you, a cock shall not crow, until you deny Me three times.

Chapter 14

Jesus Comforts His Disciples

"LET not your heart be troubled; *x*believe in God, believe also in Me.

2"In My Father's house are many dwelling places; if it were not so, I would have told you; for I go to prepare a place for you.

3"And if I go and pre-

x Or, *you believe in God*

Middle column (interlinear)

ψωμίον   ἐκεῖνος   ἐξῆλθεν   εὐθύς·   ἦν   δὲ
morsel   that one   went out   immediately;   and   it was

νύξ.
night.

31 Ὅτε   οὖν   ἐξῆλθεν,   λέγει   Ἰησοῦς·
When   therefore   he went out,   says   Jesus :

νῦν   ἐδοξάσθη   ὁ   υἱὸς   τοῦ   ἀνθρώπου,
Now   was(is) glorified   the   Son   -   of man,

καὶ   ὁ   θεὸς   ἐδοξάσθη   ἐν   αὐτῷ·   **32** εἰ
and   -   God   was(is) glorified   in   him;   if

ὁ   θεὸς   ἐδοξάσθη   ἐν   αὐτῷ,   καὶ   ὁ   θεὸς
-    God   was(is) glorified   in   him,   both   -   God

δοξάσει   αὐτὸν   ἐν   αὐτῷ,   καὶ   εὐθὺς
will glorify   him   in   him,   and immediately

δοξάσει   αὐτόν.   **33** τεκνία,   ἔτι   μικρὸν
will glorify   him.   Children,   yet   a little while

μεθ'   ὑμῶν   εἰμι·   ζητήσετέ   με,   καὶ   καθὼς
with   you   I am;   ye will seek   me,   and   as

εἶπον   τοῖς   Ἰουδαίοις   ὅτι   ὅπου   ἐγὼ
I said   to the   Jews   that   where   I

ὑπάγω   ὑμεῖς   οὐ   δύνασθε   ἐλθεῖν,   καὶ
go   ye   cannot   to come,   also

ὑμῖν   λέγω   ἄρτι.   **34** Ἐντολὴν   καινὴν
to you   I say   now.   commandment   A new

δίδωμι   ὑμῖν,   ἵνα   ἀγαπᾶτε   ἀλλήλους,
I give   you,   that   ye love   one another,

καθὼς   ἠγάπησα   ὑμᾶς   ἵνα   καὶ   ὑμεῖς
as   I loved   you   that   also   ye

ἀγαπᾶτε   ἀλλήλους.   **35** ἐν   τούτῳ   γνώσονται
love   one another.   By   this   will know

πάντες   ὅτι   ἐμοὶ   μαθηταί   ἐστε,   ἐὰν
all men   that   to me   disciples   ye are,   if

ἀγάπην   ἔχητε   ἐν   ἀλλήλοις.   **36** Λέγει
love   ye have   among   one another.   Says

αὐτῷ   Σίμων   Πέτρος·   κύριε,   ποῦ   ὑπάγεις;
to him   Simon   Peter :   Lord,   where   goest thou?

ἀπεκρίθη   Ἰησοῦς·   ὅπου   ὑπάγω   οὐ   δύνασαί
Answered   Jesus :   Where   I go   thou canst not

μοι   νῦν   ἀκολουθῆσαι,   ἀκολουθήσεις   δὲ
me   now   to follow,   but thou wilt follow

ὕστερον.   **37** λέγει   αὐτῷ   [ὁ]   Πέτρος·
later.   Says   to him   -   Peter :

κύριε,   διὰ   τί   οὐ   δύναμαί   σοι   ἀκολουθῆσαι
Lord,   why   can I not   thee   to follow

ἄρτι;   τὴν   ψυχήν   μου   ὑπὲρ   σοῦ   θήσω.
yet?   the   life   of me   for   thee I will lay down.

38 ἀποκρίνεται   Ἰησοῦς·   τὴν   ψυχήν   σου
Answers   Jesus :   The   life   of thee

ὑπὲρ   ἐμοῦ   θήσεις;   ἀμὴν   ἀμὴν   λέγω
for   me   wilt thou lay down?   truly   truly   I tell

σοι,   οὐ   μὴ   ἀλέκτωρ   φωνήσῃ   ἕως   οὗ
thee,   by no means   a cock   crows   until

ἀρνήσῃ   με   τρίς.   **14** Μὴ   ταρασσέσθω
thou deniest   me   thrice.   Let not be troubled

ὑμῶν   ἡ   καρδία·   πιστεύετε   εἰς   τὸν   θεόν,   καὶ
of you   the   heart;   believe   in   -   God,   also

εἰς   ἐμὲ   πιστεύετε.   **2** ἐν   τῇ   οἰκίᾳ   τοῦ
in   me   believe.   In   the   house of the

πατρός   μου   μοναὶ   πολλαί   εἰσιν·   εἰ   δὲ   μή,
Father   of me   abodes   many   there are;   otherwise,

εἶπον   ἂν   ὑμῖν·   ὅτι   πορεύομαι   ἑτοιμάσαι
I would have told   you;   because   I go   to prepare

τόπον   ὑμῖν·   **3** καὶ   ἐὰν   πορευθῶ   καὶ
a place   for you;   and   if   I go   and

en the bread, he went out. And it was night.

Jesus Predicts Peter's Denial

31When he was gone, Jesus said, "Now is the Son of Man glorified and God is glorified in him. 32If God is glorified in him,*o* God will glorify the Son in himself, and will glorify him at once.

33"My children, I will be with you only a little longer. You will look for me, and just as I told the Jews, so I tell you now: Where I am going, you cannot come.

34"A new command I give you: Love one another. As I have loved you, so you must love one another. 35By this all men will know that you are my disciples, if you love one another."

36Simon Peter asked him, "Lord, where are you going?"

Jesus replied, "Where I am going, you cannot follow now, but you will follow later."

37Peter asked, "Lord, why can't I follow you now? I will lay down my life for you."

38Then Jesus answered, "Will you really lay down your life for me? I tell you the truth, before the rooster crows, you will disown me three times!

Chapter 14

Jesus Comforts His Disciples

"DO not let your hearts be troubled. Trust in God;*p* trust also in me. 2In my Father's house are many rooms; if it were not so, I would have told you. I am going there to prepare a place for you. 3And if I go and prepare a

*o*32 Many early manuscripts do not have *If God is glorified in him.*
*p*1 Or *You trust in God*

pare a place for you, I will come again, and receive you to Myself; that where I am, *there* you may be also. 4''yAnd you know the way where I am going.''

5Thomas *said to Him, ''Lord, we do not know where You are going, how do we know the way?''

6Jesus *said to him, ''I am the way, and the truth, and the life; no one comes to the Father, but through Me.

Oneness with the Father

7''If you had known Me, you would have known My Father also; from now on you know Him, and have seen Him.''

8Philip *said to Him, ''Lord, show us the Father, and it is enough for us.''

9Jesus *said to him, ''Have I been so long with you, and *yet* you have not come to know Me, Philip? He who has seen Me has seen the Father; how do you say, 'Show us the Father'?

10''Do you not believe that I am in the Father, and the Father is in Me? The words that I say to you I do not speak on My own initiative, but the Father abiding in Me does His works.

11''Believe Me that I am in the Father, and the Father in Me; otherwise believe on account of the works themselves.

12''Truly, truly, I say to you, he who believes in Me, the works that I do shall he do also; and greater *works* than these shall he do; because I go to the Father.

13''And whatever you ask in My name, that will I do, that the Father may be glorified in the Son.

14''If you ask Me anything in My name, I will do it.

y Many ancient authorities read *And where I go you know, and the way you know*

Middle column (Greek interlinear)

ἐτοιμάσω τόπον ὑμῖν, πάλιν ἔρχομαι καὶ
prepare a place for you, again I come and

παραλήμψομαι ὑμᾶς πρὸς ἐμαυτόν, ἵνα
will receive you to myself, that

ὅπου εἰμὶ ἐγὼ καὶ ὑμεῖς ἦτε. 4 Καὶ
where am I also ye may be. And

ὅπου ἐγὼ ὑπάγω οἴδατε τὴν ὁδόν.
where I go ye know the way.

5 λέγει αὐτῷ Θωμᾶς· κύριε, οὐκ οἴδαμεν
Says to him Thomas: Lord, we know not

ποῦ ὑπάγεις· πῶς οἴδαμεν τὴν ὁδόν;
where thou goest; how do we know the way?

6 λέγει αὐτῷ Ἰησοῦς· ἐγώ εἰμι ἡ ὁδὸς
Says to him Jesus: I am the way

καὶ ἡ ἀλήθεια καὶ ἡ ζωή· οὐδεὶς ἔρχεται
and the truth and the life; no one comes

πρὸς τὸν πατέρα εἰ μὴ δι᾽ ἐμοῦ. 7 εἰ
to the Father except through me. If

ἐγνώκειτέ με, καὶ τὸν πατέρα μου
ye had known me, also the Father of me

ἂν ᾔδειτε. ἀπ᾽ ἄρτι γινώσκετε αὐτὸν
ye would have known. From now ye know him

καὶ ἑωράκατε. 8 Λέγει αὐτῷ Φίλιππος·
and have seen. Says to him Philip:

κύριε, δεῖξον ἡμῖν τὸν πατέρα, καὶ
Lord, show us the Father, and

ἀρκεῖ ἡμῖν. 9 λέγει αὐτῷ ὁ Ἰησοῦς·
it suffices for us. Says to him – Jesus:

τοσοῦτον χρόνον μεθ᾽ ὑμῶν εἰμι καὶ
So long time with you I am and

οὐκ ἔγνωκάς με, Φίλιππε; ὁ ἑωρακὼς
thou hast not known me, Philip? The [one] having seen

ἐμὲ ἑώρακεν τὸν πατέρα· πῶς σὺ λέγεις·
me has seen the Father; how thou sayest:

δεῖξον ἡμῖν τὸν πατέρα; 10 οὐ πιστεύεις
Show us the Father? believest thou not

ὅτι ἐγὼ ἐν τῷ πατρὶ καὶ ὁ πατὴρ
that I in the Father and the Father

ἐν ἐμοί ἐστιν; τὰ ῥήματα ἃ ἐγὼ λέγω
in me is? the words which I say

ὑμῖν ἀπ᾽ ἐμαυτοῦ οὐ λαλῶ· ὁ δὲ πατὴρ
to you from myself I speak not; but the Father

ἐν ἐμοὶ μένων ποιεῖ τὰ ἔργα αὐτοῦ.
in me remaining does the works of him.

11 πιστεύετέ μοι ὅτι ἐγὼ ἐν τῷ πατρὶ
Believe ye me that I in the Father

καὶ ὁ πατὴρ ἐν ἐμοί· εἰ δὲ μή, διὰ
and the Father in me; otherwise, because of

τὰ ἔργα αὐτὰ πιστεύετε. 12 ἀμὴν ἀμὴν
the works [them]selves believe ye. Truly truly

λέγω ὑμῖν, ὁ πιστεύων εἰς ἐμὲ τὰ
I tell you, the [one] believing in me the

ἔργα ἃ ἐγὼ ποιῶ κἀκεῖνος ποιήσει,
works which I do that one also will do,

καὶ μείζονα τούτων ποιήσει, ὅτι ἐγὼ
and greater [than] these he will do, because I

πρὸς τὸν πατέρα πορεύομαι· 13 καὶ ὅ τι
to the Father am going; and what-

ἂν αἰτήσητε ἐν τῷ ὀνόματί μου, τοῦτο
ever ye ask in the name of me, this

ποιήσω, ἵνα δοξασθῇ ὁ πατὴρ ἐν τῷ
I will do, that may be glorified the Father in the

υἱῷ. 14 ἐάν τι αἰτήσητέ με ἐν τῷ
Son. If anything ye ask me in the

ὀνόματί μου, ἐγὼ ποιήσω. 15 Ἐὰν
name of me, I will do. If

place for you, I will come back and take you to be with me that you also may be where I am. 4You know the way to the place where I am going.''

Jesus the Way to the Father

5Thomas said to him, ''Lord, we don't know where you are going, so how can we know the way?''

6Jesus answered, ''I am the way and the truth and the life. No one comes to the Father except through me. 7If you really knew me, you would knowᑫ my Father as well. From now on, you do know him and have seen him.''

8Philip said, ''Lord, show us the Father and that will be enough for us.''

9Jesus answered: ''Don't you know me, Philip, even after I have been among you such a long time? Anyone who has seen me has seen the Father. How can you say, 'Show us the Father'? 10Don't you believe that I am in the Father, and that the Father is in me? The words I say to you are not just my own. Rather, it is the Father, living in me, who is doing his work. 11Believe me when I say that I am in the Father and the Father is in me; or at least believe on the evidence of the miracles themselves. 12I tell you the truth, anyone who has faith in me will do what I have been doing. He will do even greater things than these, because I am going to the Father. 13And I will do whatever you ask in my name, so that the Son may bring glory to the Father. 14You may ask me for anything in my name, and I will do it.

q7 Some early manuscripts *If you really have known me, you will know*

15"If you love Me, you will keep My commandments.

Role of the Spirit

16"And I will ask the Father, and He will give you another Helper, that He may be with you forever; 17that is the Spirit of truth, whom the world cannot receive, because it does not behold Him or know Him, *but* you know Him because He abides with you, and will be in you. 18"I will not leave you as orphans; I will come to you. 19"After a little while the world will behold Me no more; but you *will* behold Me; because I live, you shall live also. 20"In that day you shall know that I am in My Father, and you in Me, and I in you. 21"He who has My commandments and keeps them, he it is who loves Me; and he who loves Me shall be loved by My Father, and I will love him, and will disclose Myself to him." 22Judas (not Iscariot) *said to Him, "Lord, what then has happened that You are going to disclose Yourself to us, and not to the world?" 23Jesus answered and said to him, "If anyone loves Me, he will keep My word; and My Father will love him, and We will come to him, and make Our abode with him. 24"He who does not love Me does not keep My words; and the word which you hear is not Mine, but the Father's who sent Me. 25"These things I have

---

ἀγαπᾶτέ   με,   τὰς   ἐντολὰς   τὰς   ἐμὰς
ye love   me,   the   ²commandments -   ¹my
τηρήσετε.   16 κἀγὼ   ἐρωτήσω   τὸν   πατέρα
ye will keep.   And I   will request   the   Father
καὶ   ἄλλον   παράκλητον   δώσει   ὑμῖν,   ἵνα
and   another   Comforter   he will give   you,   that
ᾖ   μεθ'   ὑμῶν   εἰς   τὸν   αἰῶνα,   17 τὸ
he may be with   you   unto   the   age,   the
πνεῦμα   τῆς   ἀληθείας,   ὃ   ὁ   κόσμος
Spirit   -   of truth,   which*   the   world
οὐ   δύναται   λαβεῖν,   ὅτι   οὐ   θεωρεῖ   αὐτό
cannot   to receive, because   it beholds not   it*
οὐδὲ   γινώσκει·   ὑμεῖς   γινώσκετε   αὐτό,
nor   knows;   ye   know   it,*
ὅτι   παρ'   ὑμῖν   μένει   καὶ   ἐν   ὑμῖν   ἔσται.
because with   you   he remains and   in   you   will be.
18 Οὐκ   ἀφήσω   ὑμᾶς   ὀρφανούς,   ἔρχομαι
I will not leave   you   orphans,   I am coming
πρὸς   ὑμᾶς.   19 ἔτι   μικρὸν   καὶ   ὁ   κόσμος
to   you.   Yet   a little   and   the   world
με   οὐκέτι   θεωρεῖ,   ὑμεῖς   δὲ   θεωρεῖτέ
me   no longer   beholds,   but ye   behold
με,   ὅτι   ἐγὼ   ζῶ   καὶ   ὑμεῖς   ζήσετε.
me, because   I   live   also   ye   will live.
20 ἐν   ἐκείνῃ   τῇ   ἡμέρᾳ   γνώσεσθε   ὑμεῖς
In   that   -   day   will know   ye
ὅτι   ἐγὼ   ἐν   τῷ   πατρί   μου   καὶ   ὑμεῖς
that   I   in   the   Father   of me   and   ye
ἐν   ἐμοὶ   κἀγὼ   ἐν   ὑμῖν.   21 Ὁ   ἔχων
in   me   and I   in   you.   The [one] having
τὰς   ἐντολάς   μου   καὶ   τηρῶν   αὐτάς,
the   commandments   of me   and   keeping   them,
ἐκεῖνός   ἐστιν   ὁ   ἀγαπῶν   με·   ὁ   δὲ   ἀγαπῶν
that   is   the [one] loving   me;   and the [one] loving
με   ἀγαπηθήσεται   ὑπὸ   τοῦ   πατρός   μου,
me   will be loved   by   the   Father   of me,
κἀγὼ   ἀγαπήσω   αὐτὸν   καὶ   ἐμφανίσω   αὐτῷ
and I   will love   him   and   will manifest   to him
ἐμαυτόν.   22 λέγει   αὐτῷ   Ἰούδας,   οὐχ
myself.   Says   to him   Judas,   not
ὁ   Ἰσκαριώτης·   κύριε,   καὶ   τί   γέγονεν
the   Iscariot :   Lord,   and   what has happened
ὅτι   ἡμῖν   μέλλεις   ἐμφανίζειν   σεαυτὸν   καὶ
that   to us   thou art about   to manifest   thyself   and
οὐχὶ   τῷ   κόσμῳ;   23 ἀπεκρίθη   Ἰησοῦς
not   to the   world?   Answered   Jesus
καὶ   εἶπεν   αὐτῷ·   ἐάν   τις   ἀγαπᾷ   με,
and   said   to him :   If   anyone   loves   me,
τὸν   λόγον   μου   τηρήσει,   καὶ   ὁ   πατήρ
the   word   of me   he will keep,   and   the   Father
μου   ἀγαπήσει   αὐτόν,   καὶ   πρὸς   αὐτὸν
of me   will love   him,   and   to   him
ἐλευσόμεθα   καὶ   μονὴν   παρ'   αὐτῷ
we will come   and   abode   with   him
ποιησόμεθα.   24 ὁ   μὴ   ἀγαπῶν   με   τοὺς
we will make.   The [one] not   loving   me   the
λόγους   μου   οὐ   τηρεῖ·   καὶ   ὁ   λόγος   ὃν
words   of me   keeps not ;   and   the   word   which
ἀκούετε   οὐκ   ἔστιν   ἐμὸς   ἀλλὰ   τοῦ
ye hear   is not   mine   but   ¹of the
πέμψαντός   με   πατρός.   25 Ταῦτα   λελάληκα
²having sent   ⁴me   ³Father.   These things   I have spoken

Jesus Promises the Holy Spirit

15"If you love me, you will obey what I command. 16And I will ask the Father, and he will give you another Counselor to be with you forever— 17the Spirit of truth. The world cannot accept him, because it neither sees him nor knows him. But you know him, for he lives with you and will beʳ in you. 18I will not leave you as orphans; I will come to you. 19Before long, the world will not see me anymore, but you will see me. Because I live, you also will live. 20On that day you will realize that I am in my Father, and you are in me, and I am in you. 21Whoever has my commands and obeys them, he is the one who loves me. He who loves me will be loved by my Father, and I too will love him and show myself to him."

22Then Judas (not Judas Iscariot) said, "But, Lord, why do you intend to show yourself to us and not to the world?"

23Jesus replied, "If anyone loves me, he will obey my teaching. My Father will love him, and we will come to him and make our home with him. 24He who does not love me will not obey my teaching. These words you hear are not my own; they belong to the Father who sent me.

25"All this I have spoken

---

* The gender of these pronouns agrees, of course, with the antecedent πνεῦμα (neuter); and this has been kept though the personal Spirit of God is meant. Elsewhere, masculine pronouns are in fact used.

ʳ17 Some early manuscripts *and is*

spoken to you, while abiding with you.

26"But the Helper, the Holy Spirit, whom the Father will send in My name, He will teach you all things, and bring to your remembrance all that I said to you.

27"Peace I leave with you; My peace I give to you; not as the world gives, do I give to you. Let not your heart be troubled, nor let it be fearful.

28"You heard that I said to you, 'I go away, and I will come to you.' If you loved Me, you would have rejoiced, because I go to the Father; for the Father is greater than I.

29"And now I have told you before it comes to pass, that when it comes to pass, you may believe.

30"I will not speak much more with you, for the ruler of the world is coming, and he has nothing in Me;

31but that the world may know that I love the Father, and as the Father gave Me commandment, even so I do. Arise, let us go from here.

ὑμῖν παρ᾽ ὑμῖν μένων·
to you with you remaining;

26 ὁ δὲ παρά-
but the Com-

κλητος, τὸ πνεῦμα τὸ ἅγιον ὃ πέμψει ὁ
forter, the Spirit - Holy which will send the

πατὴρ ἐν τῷ ὀνόματί μου, ἐκεῖνος ὑμᾶς
Father in the name of me, that one you

διδάξει πάντα καὶ ὑπομνήσει ὑμᾶς πάντα
will teach all things and remind you [of] all things

ἃ εἶπον ὑμῖν ἐγώ. 27 Εἰρήνην ἀφίημι
which ²told ³you ¹I. Peace I leave

ὑμῖν, εἰρήνην τὴν ἐμὴν δίδωμι ὑμῖν·
to you, ²peace ¹my I give you;

οὐ καθὼς ὁ κόσμος δίδωσιν ἐγὼ δίδωμι
not as the world gives I give

ὑμῖν. μὴ ταρασσέσθω ὑμῶν ἡ καρδία
you. Let not be troubled of you the heart

μηδὲ δειλιάτω. 28 ἠκούσατε ὅτι ἐγὼ
nor let it be fearful. Ye heard that I

εἶπον ὑμῖν· ὑπάγω καὶ ἔρχομαι πρὸς
told you: I go and come to

ὑμᾶς. εἰ ἠγαπᾶτέ με, ἐχάρητε ἂν ὅτι
you. If ye loved me, ye would have rejoiced that

πορεύομαι πρὸς τὸν πατέρα, ὅτι ὁ πατὴρ
I am going to the Father, because the Father

μείζων μού ἐστιν. 29 καὶ νῦν εἴρηκα
greater [than] me(I) is. And now I have told

ὑμῖν πρὶν γενέσθαι, ἵνα ὅταν γένηται
you before to happen, that when it happens
　　　　　=it happens,

πιστεύσητε. 30 οὐκέτι πολλὰ λαλήσω μεθ᾽
ye may believe. No longer many things I will speak with

ὑμῶν, ἔρχεται γὰρ ὁ τοῦ κόσμου ἄρχων·
you, for ⁵is coming ¹the ²of the ⁴world ³ruler;

καὶ ἐν ἐμοὶ οὐκ ἔχει οὐδέν, 31 ἀλλ᾽
and in me he has not no(any)thing, but

ἵνα γνῷ ὁ κόσμος ὅτι ἀγαπῶ τὸν
that may know the world that I love the

πατέρα, καὶ καθὼς ἐνετείλατό μοι ὁ
Father, and as commanded me the

πατήρ, οὕτως ποιῶ. Ἐγείρεσθε, ἄγωμεν
Father, so I do. Rise, let us go

ἐντεῦθεν.
hence.

---

while still with you. 26But the Counselor, the Holy Spirit, whom the Father will send in my name, will teach you all things and will remind you of everything I have said to you. 27Peace I leave with you; my peace I give you. I do not give to you as the world gives. Do not let your hearts be troubled and do not be afraid.

28"You heard me say, 'I am going away and I am coming back to you.' If you loved me, you would be glad that I am going to the Father, for the Father is greater than I. 29I have told you now before it happens, so that when it does happen you will believe. 30I will not speak with you much longer, for the prince of this world is coming. He has no hold on me, 31but the world must learn that I love the Father and that I do exactly what my Father has commanded me.

"Come now; let us leave."

Chapter 15

Jesus Is the Vine—Followers Are Branches

" I am the true vine, and My Father is the vinedresser.

2"Every branch in Me that does not bear fruit, He takes away; and every *branch* that bears fruit, He ²prunes it, that it may bear more fruit.

3"You are already clean because of the word which I have spoken to you.

4"Abide in Me, and I in you. As the branch cannot bear fruit of itself, unless it abides in the vine, so neither *can* you, unless you abide in Me.

---

15 Ἐγώ εἰμι ἡ ἄμπελος ἡ ἀληθινή,
I am the vine - true,

καὶ ὁ πατήρ μου ὁ γεωργός ἐστιν.
and the Father of me the husbandman is.

2 πᾶν κλῆμα ἐν ἐμοὶ μὴ φέρον καρπόν,
Every branch in me not bearing fruit,

αἴρει αὐτό, καὶ πᾶν τὸ καρπὸν φέρον,
he takes it, and every [branch] the fruit bearing,

καθαίρει αὐτὸ ἵνα καρπὸν πλείονα φέρῃ.
he prunes it that fruit more it may bear.

3 ἤδη ὑμεῖς καθαροί ἐστε διὰ τὸν λόγον
Now ye clean are because of the word

ὃν λελάληκα ὑμῖν· 4 μείνατε ἐν ἐμοί,
which I have spoken to you; remain in me,

κἀγὼ ἐν ὑμῖν. καθὼς τὸ κλῆμα
and I in you. As the branch

οὐ δύναται καρπὸν φέρειν ἀφ᾽ ἑαυτοῦ ἐὰν μὴ
cannot fruit to bear from itself unless

μένῃ ἐν τῇ ἀμπέλῳ, οὕτως οὐδὲ ὑμεῖς
it remains in the vine, so not ye

ἐὰν μὴ ἐν ἐμοὶ μένητε. 5 ἐγώ εἰμι
unless in me ye remain. I am

Chapter 15

The Vine and the Branches

" I AM the true vine, and my Father is the gardener. 2He cuts off every branch in me that bears no fruit, while every branch that does bear fruit he prunes ˢ so that it will be even more fruitful. 3You are already clean because of the word I have spoken to you. 4Remain in me, and I will remain in you. No branch can bear fruit by itself; it must remain in the vine. Neither can you bear fruit unless you remain in me.

ᶻLit., *cleanses*

ˢ2 The Greek for *prunes* also means *cleans.*

5"I am the vine, you are the branches; he who abides in Me, and I in him, he bears much fruit; for apart from Me you can do nothing.

6"If anyone does not abide in Me, he is thrown away as a branch, and dries up; and they gather them, and cast them into the fire, and they are burned.

7"If you abide in Me, and My words abide in you, ask whatever you wish, and it shall be done for you.

8"By this is My Father glorified, that you bear much fruit, and so prove to be My disciples.

9"Just as the Father has loved Me, I have also loved you; abide in My love.

10"If you keep My commandments, you will abide in My love; just as I have kept My Father's commandments, and abide in His love.

11"These things I have spoken to you, that My joy may be in you, and that your joy may be made full.

Disciples' Relation to Each Other

12"This is My commandment, that you love one another, just as I have loved you.

13"Greater love has no one than this, that one lay down his life for his friends.

14"You are My friends, if you do what I command you.

15"No longer do I call you slaves, for the slave does not know what his master is doing; but I have called you friends, for all things that I have heard from My Father I have made known to you.

16"You did not choose Me, but I chose you, and appointed you, that you should go and bear fruit,

---

ἡ ἄμπελος, ὑμεῖς τὰ κλήματα. ὁ μένων
the   vine,   ye   the   branches. The [one] remaining

ἐν ἐμοὶ κἀγὼ ἐν αὐτῷ, οὗτος φέρει
in   me   and I   in   him,   this one   bears

καρπὸν πολύν, ὅτι χωρὶς ἐμοῦ οὐ δύνασθε
fruit   much, because apart from me   ye cannot

ποιεῖν οὐδέν. 6 ἐὰν μή τις μένῃ ἐν
to do no(any)thing.   Unless   anyone remains   in

ἐμοί, ἐβλήθη ἔξω ὡς τὸ κλῆμα καὶ
me,   he was(is) cast outside as   the   branch   and

ἐξηράνθη, καὶ συνάγουσιν αὐτὰ καὶ εἰς
was(is) dried,   and   they gather   them   and into

τὸ πῦρ βάλλουσιν, καὶ καίεται. 7 ἐὰν
the   fire   they cast,   and they are burned.   If

μείνητε ἐν ἐμοὶ καὶ τὰ ῥήματά μου
ye remain   in   me   and   the   words   of me

ἐν ὑμῖν μείνῃ, ὃ ἐὰν θέλητε αἰτήσασθε,
in   you   remains, whatever ye wish   ask,

καὶ γενήσεται ὑμῖν. 8 ἐν τούτῳ ἐδοξάσθη
and it shall happen to you.   By   this   was glorified

ὁ πατήρ μου, ἵνα καρπὸν πολὺν φέρητε
the Father of me, that   fruit   much   ye bear

καὶ γενήσεσθε ἐμοὶ μαθηταί. 9 καθὼς
and   ye will be   to me° disciples.   As

ἠγάπησέν με ὁ πατήρ, κἀγὼ ὑμᾶς
loved   me the Father,   I also   you

ἠγάπησα· μείνατε ἐν τῇ ἀγάπῃ τῇ ἐμῇ.
loved;   remain ye in   the   ¹love   -   ¹my.

10 ἐὰν τὰς ἐντολάς μου τηρήσητε, μενεῖτε
If   the commandments of me ye keep, ye will remain

ἐν τῇ ἀγάπῃ μου, καθὼς ἐγὼ τοῦ πατρός
in the   love   of me,   as   I   of the   Father

μου τὰς ἐντολὰς τετήρηκα καὶ μένω
of me   the   commandments have kept   and   remain

αὐτοῦ ἐν τῇ ἀγάπῃ. 11 Ταῦτα λελάληκα
of him   in   the   love.   These things I have spoken

ὑμῖν ἵνα ἡ χαρὰ ἡ ἐμὴ ἐν ὑμῖν ᾖ
to you that   the   ²joy   -   ¹my   in   you may be

καὶ ἡ χαρὰ ὑμῶν πληρωθῇ. 12 αὕτη
and the   joy   of you   may be filled.   This

ἐστὶν ἡ ἐντολὴ ἡ ἐμή, ἵνα ἀγαπᾶτε
is   the ²commandment -   ¹my,   that   ye love

ἀλλήλους καθὼς ἠγάπησα ὑμᾶς. 13 μείζονα
one another   as   I loved   you.   ¹Greater

ταύτης ἀγάπην οὐδεὶς ἔχει, ἵνα τις
[³than] ⁴this   ²love   no one   has,   that anyone

τὴν ψυχὴν αὐτοῦ θῇ ὑπὲρ τῶν φίλων
the   life   of him should lay down for   the   friends

αὐτοῦ. 14 ὑμεῖς φίλοι μού ἐστε, ἐὰν
of him.   Ye   friends   of me   are,   if

ποιῆτε ὃ ἐγὼ ἐντέλλομαι ὑμῖν. 15 οὐκέτι
ye do what I   command   you.   No longer

λέγω ὑμᾶς δούλους, ὅτι ὁ δοῦλος οὐκ οἶδεν
I call   you   slaves, because the   slave   knows not

τί ποιεῖ αὐτοῦ ὁ κύριος· ὑμᾶς δὲ
what does   of him   the   lord;   but you

εἴρηκα φίλους, ὅτι πάντα ἃ ἤκουσα
I have called friends, because all things which   I heard

παρὰ τοῦ πατρός μου ἐγνώρισα ὑμῖν.
from   the   Father of me I made known   to you.

16 οὐχ ὑμεῖς με ἐξελέξασθε, ἀλλ' ἐγὼ
Not   ye   me   chose,   but   I

ἐξελεξάμην ὑμᾶς, καὶ ἔθηκα ὑμᾶς ἵνα
chose   you,   and appointed   you   that

ὑμεῖς ὑπάγητε καὶ καρπὸν φέρητε καὶ
ye   should go   and   fruit   should bear   and

5"I am the vine; you are the branches. If a man remains in me and I in him, he will bear much fruit; apart from me you can do nothing. 6If anyone does not remain in me, he is like a branch that is thrown away and withers; such branches are picked up, thrown into the fire and burned. 7If you remain in me and my words remain in you, ask whatever you wish, and it will be given you. 8This is to my Father's glory, that you bear much fruit, showing yourselves to be my disciples.

9"As the Father has loved me, so have I loved you. Now remain in my love. 10If you obey my commands, you will remain in my love, just as I have obeyed my Father's commands and remain in his love. 11I have told you this so that my joy may be in you and that your joy may be complete. 12My command is this: Love each other as I have loved you. 13Greater love has no one than this, that he lay down his life for his friends. 14You are my friends if you do what I command. 15I no longer call you servants, because a servant does not know his master's business. Instead, I have called you friends, for everything that I learned from my Father I have made known to you. 16You did not choose me, but I chose you and appointed you to go and bear and *that* your fruit should remain, that whatever you ask of the Father in My name, He may give to you. 17"This I command you, that you love one another.

Disciples' Relation to the World

18"If the world hates you, you know that it has hated Me before *it hated* you.

19"If you were of the world, the world would love its own; but because you are not of the world, but I chose you out of the world, therefore the world hates you.

20"Remember the word that I said to you, 'A slave is not greater than his master.' If they persecuted Me, they will also persecute you; if they kept My word, they will keep yours also.

21"But all these things they will do to you for My name's sake, because they do not know the One who sent Me.

22"If I had not come and spoken to them, they would not have sin, but now they have no excuse for their sin.

23"He who hates Me hates My Father also.

24"If I had not done among them the works which no one else did, they would not have sin; but now they have both seen and hated Me and My Father also.

25"But *they have done this* in order that the word may be fulfilled that is written in their Law, 'THEY HATED ME WITHOUT A CAUSE.'

26"When the Helper comes, whom I will send to you from the Father, *that is* the Spirit of truth, who proceeds from the Father, He will bear witness of Me,

27and you *will* bear witness also, because you have been with Me from the beginning.

ὁ καρπὸς ὑμῶν μένῃ, ἵνα ὅ τι ἂν
the fruit of you should remain, that whatever

αἰτήσητε τὸν πατέρα ἐν τῷ ὀνόματί
ye may ask the Father in the name

μου δῷ ὑμῖν. 17 ταῦτα ἐντέλλομαι ὑμῖν,
of me he may give you. These things I command you,

ἵνα ἀγαπᾶτε ἀλλήλους. 18 Εἰ ὁ κόσμος
that ye love one another. If the world

ὑμᾶς μισεῖ, γινώσκετε ὅτι ἐμὲ πρῶτον
you hates, ye know that me before

ὑμῶν μεμίσηκεν. 19 εἰ ἐκ τοῦ κόσμου ἦτε,
you it has hated. If of the world ye were,

ὁ κόσμος ἂν τὸ ἴδιον ἐφίλει· ὅτι δὲ
the world ¹would ⁸the(its) ⁴own ³have loved; but because

ἐκ τοῦ κόσμου οὐκ ἐστέ, ἀλλ' ἐγὼ
of the world ye are not, but I

ἐξελεξάμην ὑμᾶς ἐκ τοῦ κόσμου, διὰ τοῦτο
chose you out of the world, therefore

μισεῖ ὑμᾶς ὁ κόσμος. 20 μνημονεύετε
hates you the world. Remember ye

τοῦ λόγου οὗ ἐγὼ εἶπον ὑμῖν· οὐκ
the word which I said to you: Not

ἔστιν δοῦλος μείζων τοῦ κυρίου αὐτοῦ.
is a slave greater [than] the lord of him.

εἰ ἐμὲ ἐδίωξαν, καὶ ὑμᾶς διώξουσιν·
If me they persecuted, also you they will persecute;

εἰ τὸν λόγον μου ἐτήρησαν, καὶ τὸν
if the word of me they kept, also the –

ὑμέτερον τηρήσουσιν. 21 ἀλλὰ ταῦτα πάντα
yours they will keep. But these things all

ποιήσουσιν εἰς ὑμᾶς διὰ τὸ ὄνομά μου,
they will do to you because of the name of me,

ὅτι οὐκ οἴδασιν τὸν πέμψαντά με.
because they know not the [one] having sent me.

22 εἰ μὴ ἦλθον καὶ ἐλάλησα αὐτοῖς, ἁμαρτίαν
Unless I came and spoke to them, sin

οὐκ εἴχοσαν· νῦν δὲ πρόφασιν οὐκ ἔχουσιν
they had not had; but now cloak they have not

περὶ τῆς ἁμαρτίας αὐτῶν. 23 ὁ ἐμὲ
concerning the sin of them. The [one] me

μισῶν καὶ τὸν πατέρα μου μισεῖ. 24 εἰ
hating also the Father of me hates. If

τὰ ἔργα μὴ ἐποίησα ἐν αὐτοῖς ἃ οὐδεὶς
the works I did not among them which no man

ἄλλος ἐποίησεν, ἁμαρτίαν οὐκ εἴχοσαν
other did, sin they had not had;

νῦν δὲ καὶ ἑωράκασιν καὶ μεμισήκασιν
but now both they have seen and have hated

καὶ ἐμὲ καὶ τὸν πατέρα μου. 25 ἀλλ'
both me and the Father of me. But

ἵνα πληρωθῇ ὁ λόγος ὁ ἐν τῷ νόμῳ
that may be fulfilled the word – in the law

αὐτῶν γεγραμμένος ὅτι ἐμίσησάν με
of them *having been* written[,] – They hated me

δωρεάν. 26 Ὅταν ἔλθῃ ὁ παράκλητος
freely. When comes the Comforter

ὃν ἐγὼ πέμψω ὑμῖν παρὰ τοῦ πατρός,
whom I will send to you from the Father,

τὸ πνεῦμα τῆς ἀληθείας ὃ παρὰ τοῦ
the Spirit – of truth which from the

πατρὸς ἐκπορεύεται, ἐκεῖνος μαρτυρήσει
Father proceeds, that one will witness

περὶ ἐμοῦ· 27 καὶ ὑμεῖς δὲ μαρτυρεῖτε,
concerning me; ¹also ¹ye ¹and witness,

ὅτι ἀπ' ἀρχῆς μετ' ἐμοῦ ἐστε.
because from [the] beginning with me ye are.

---

fruit—fruit that will last. Then the Father will give you whatever you ask in my name. 17This is my command: Love each other.

The World Hates the Disciples

18"If the world hates you, keep in mind that it hated me first. 19If you belonged to the world, it would love you as its own. As it is, you do not belong to the world, but I have chosen you out of the world. That is why the world hates you. 20Remember the words I spoke to you: 'No servant is greater than his master.'ᵗ If they persecuted me, they will persecute you also. If they obeyed my teaching, they will obey yours also. 21They will treat you this way because of my name, for they do not know the One who sent me. 22If I had not come and spoken to them, they would not be guilty of sin. Now, however, they have no excuse for their sin. 23He who hates me hates my Father as well. 24If I had not done among them what no one else did, they would not be guilty of sin. But now they have seen these miracles, and yet they have hated both me and my Father. 25But this is to fulfill what is written in their Law: 'They hated me without reason.'ᵘ

26"When the Counselor comes, whom I will send to you from the Father, the Spirit of truth who goes out from the Father, he will testify about me. 27And you also must testify, for you have been with me from the beginning.

ᵗ20 John 13:16
ᵘ25 Psalms 35:19; 69:4

Chapter 16

Jesus' Warning

"THESE things I have spoken to you, that you may be kept from stumbling.

2"They will make you outcasts from the synagogue, but an hour is coming for everyone who kills you to think that he is offering service to God.

3"And these things they will do, because they have not known the Father, or Me.

4"But these things I have spoken to you, that when their hour comes, you may remember that I told you of them. And these things I did not say to you at the beginning, because I was with you.

The Holy Spirit Promised

5"But now I am going to Him who sent Me; and none of you asks Me, 'Where are You going?'

6"But because I have said these things to you, sorrow has filled your heart.

7"But I tell you the truth, it is to your advantage that I go away; for if I do not go away, the Helper shall not come to you; but if I go, I will send Him to you.

8"And He, when He comes, will convict the world concerning sin, and righteousness, and judgment;

9concerning sin, because they do not believe in Me;

10and concerning righteousness, because I go to the Father, and you no longer behold Me;

11and concerning judgment, because the ruler of this world has been judged.

12"I have many more things to say to you, but you cannot bear *them* now.

13"But when He, the Spirit of truth, comes, He will guide you into all the truth; for He will not speak on His own initiative, but whatever He hears, He will speak; and He will disclose to you what is to come.

14"He shall glorify Me;

---

16 Ταῦτα λελάληκα ὑμῖν ἵνα μὴ
These things I have spoken to you that not
σκανδαλισθῆτε. 2 ἀποσυναγώγους ποιή-
ye be offended. Put away from [the] synagogue they
σουσιν ὑμᾶς· ἀλλ' ἔρχεται ὥρα ἵνα πᾶς ὁ
will make you; but comes an hour that everyone
ἀποκτείνας ὑμᾶς δόξῃ λατρείαν προσφέρειν
killing you thinks service to offer
τῷ θεῷ. 3 καὶ ταῦτα ποιήσουσιν ὅτι
- to God. And these things they will do because
οὐκ ἔγνωσαν τὸν πατέρα οὐδὲ ἐμέ.
they knew not the Father nor me.
4 ἀλλὰ ταῦτα λελάληκα ὑμῖν ἵνα ὅταν
But these things I have spoken to you that when
ἔλθῃ ἡ ὥρα αὐτῶν μνημονεύητε αὐτῶν,
comes the hour of them ye may remember them,
ὅτι ἐγὼ εἶπον ὑμῖν. Ταῦτα δὲ ὑμῖν
that I told you. And these things to you
ἐξ ἀρχῆς οὐκ εἶπον, ὅτι μεθ' ὑμῶν
from [the] beginning I said not, because with you
ἤμην. 5 νῦν δὲ ὑπάγω πρὸς τὸν πέμψαντά
I was. But now I am going to the [one] having sent
με, καὶ οὐδεὶς ἐξ ὑμῶν ἐρωτᾷ με·
me, and not one of you asks me:
ποῦ ὑπάγεις; 6 ἀλλ' ὅτι ταῦτα λελάληκα
Where goest thou? but because these things I have spoken
ὑμῖν, ἡ λύπη πεπλήρωκεν ὑμῶν τὴν
to you, - grief has filled of you the
καρδίαν. 7 ἀλλ' ἐγὼ τὴν ἀλήθειαν λέγω
heart. But I the truth tell
ὑμῖν, συμφέρει ὑμῖν ἵνα ἐγὼ ἀπέλθω.
you, it is expedient for you that I should go away.
ἐὰν γὰρ μὴ ἀπέλθω, ὁ παράκλητος
For if I go not away, the Comforter
οὐ μὴ ἔλθῃ πρὸς ὑμᾶς· ἐὰν δὲ πορευθῶ,
by no means comes to you; but if I go,
πέμψω αὐτὸν πρὸς ὑμᾶς. 8 καὶ ἐλθὼν
I will send him to you. And coming
ἐκεῖνος ἐλέγξει τὸν κόσμον περὶ ἁμαρτίας
that one will reprove the world concerning sin
καὶ περὶ δικαιοσύνης καὶ περὶ κρίσεως·
and concerning righteousness and concerning judgment;
9 περὶ ἁμαρτίας μέν, ὅτι οὐ πιστεύουσιν
concerning sin, - because they believe not
εἰς ἐμέ· 10 περὶ δικαιοσύνης δέ, ὅτι
in me; concerning righteousness, - because
πρὸς τὸν πατέρα ὑπάγω καὶ οὐκέτι
to the Father I am going and no longer
θεωρεῖτέ με· 11 περὶ δὲ κρίσεως, ὅτι
ye behold me; concerning - judgment, because
ὁ ἄρχων τοῦ κόσμου τούτου κέκριται.
the ruler - world of this has been judged.
12 Ἔτι πολλὰ ἔχω ὑμῖν λέγειν, ἀλλ'
Yet many things I have you to tell, but
οὐ δύνασθε βαστάζειν ἄρτι· 13 ὅταν δὲ
ye cannot to bear now; but when
ἔλθῃ ἐκεῖνος, τὸ πνεῦμα τῆς ἀληθείας,
comes that one, the Spirit - of truth,
ὁδηγήσει ὑμᾶς εἰς τὴν ἀλήθειαν πᾶσαν·
he will guide you into the truth all;
οὐ γὰρ λαλήσει ἀφ' ἑαυτοῦ, ἀλλ' ὅσα
for not will he speak from himself, but what things
ἀκούει λαλήσει, καὶ τὰ ἐρχόμενα
he hears he will speak, and the coming things
ἀναγγελεῖ ὑμῖν. 14 ἐκεῖνος ἐμὲ δοξάσει,
he will announce to you. That one me will glorify,

Chapter 16

"ALL this I have told you so that you will not go astray. 2They will put you out of the synagogue; in fact, a time is coming when anyone who kills you will think he is offering a service to God. 3They will do such things because they have not known the Father or me. 4I have told you this, so that when the time comes you will remember that I warned you. I did not tell you this at first because I was with you.

The Work of the Holy Spirit

5"Now I am going to him who sent me, yet none of you asks me, 'Where are you going?' 6Because I have said these things, you are filled with grief. 7But I tell you the truth: It is for your good that I am going away. Unless I go away, the Counselor will not come to you; but if I go, I will send him to you. 8When he comes, he will convict the world of guilt[v] in regard to sin and righteousness and judgment: 9in regard to sin, because men do not believe in me; 10in regard to righteousness, because I am going to the Father, where you can see me no longer; 11and in regard to judgment, because the prince of this world now stands condemned.

12"I have much more to say to you, more than you can now bear. 13But when he, the Spirit of truth, comes, he will guide you into all truth. He will not speak on his own; he will speak only what he hears, and he will tell you what is

[v]8 Or *will expose the guilt of the world*

for He shall take of Mine, and shall disclose *it* to you.

15"All things that the Father has are Mine; therefore I said, that He takes of Mine, and will disclose *it* to you.

Jesus' Death and Resurrection Foretold

16"A little while, and you will no longer behold Me; and again a little while, and you will see Me."

17*Some* of His disciples therefore said to one another, "What is this thing He is telling us, 'A little while, and you will not behold Me; and again a little while, and you will see Me'; and, 'because I go to the Father'?"

18And so they were saying, "What is this that He says, 'A little while'? We do not know what He is talking about."

19Jesus knew that they wished to question Him, and He said to them, "Are you deliberating together about this, that I said, 'A little while, and you will not behold Me, and again a little while, and you will see Me'?

20"Truly, truly, I say to you, that you will weep and lament, but the world will rejoice; you will be sorrowful, but your sorrow will be turned to joy.

21"Whenever a woman is in travail she has sorrow, because her hour has come; but when she gives birth to the child, she remembers the anguish no more, for joy that a child has been born into the world.

22"Therefore you too now have sorrow; but I will see you again, and your heart will rejoice, and no one takes your joy away from you.

Prayer Promises

23"And in that day you will ask Me no question. Truly, truly, I say to you, if you shall ask the Father for anything, He will give *it* to you in My name.

ὅτι ἐκ τοῦ ἐμοῦ λήμψεται καὶ ἀναγγελεῖ
because of the of me* he will receive and will announce

ὑμῖν. 15 πάντα ὅσα ἔχει ὁ πατὴρ ἐμά
to you.   All things which has the Father mine

ἐστιν· διὰ τοῦτο εἶπον ὅτι ἐκ τοῦ ἐμοῦ
is(are);   therefore   I said that of the of me*

λαμβάνει καὶ ἀναγγελεῖ ὑμῖν. 16 Μικρὸν
he receives and will announce to you.   A little while

καὶ οὐκέτι θεωρεῖτέ με, καὶ πάλιν
and no longer ye behold me, and again

μικρὸν καὶ ὄψεσθέ με. 17 εἶπαν οὖν
a little while and ye will see me.   Said therefore

ἐκ τῶν μαθητῶν αὐτοῦ πρὸς ἀλλήλους·
[some] of the disciples of him to one another:

τί ἐστιν τοῦτο ὃ λέγει ἡμῖν· μικρὸν
What is this which he tells us: A little while

καὶ οὐ θεωρεῖτέ με, καὶ πάλιν μικρὸν
and ye behold not me, and again a little while

καὶ ὄψεσθέ με; καί· ὅτι ὑπάγω
and ye will see me? and: Because I am going

πρὸς τὸν πατέρα; 18 ἔλεγον οὖν· τοῦτο
to the Father?   They said therefore : *This

τί ἐστιν ὃ λέγει τὸ μικρόν; οὐκ οἴδαμεν
¹what ²is which he says[,] the "little while"? We do not know

τί λαλεῖ. 19 ἔγνω Ἰησοῦς ὅτι ἤθελον
what he speaks.   Knew Jesus that they wished

αὐτὸν ἐρωτᾶν, καὶ εἶπεν αὐτοῖς· περὶ
him to question, and said to them : Concerning

τούτου ζητεῖτε μετ᾽ ἀλλήλων ὅτι εἶπον·
this seek ye with one another because I said :

μικρὸν καὶ οὐ θεωρεῖτέ με, καὶ πάλιν
A little while and ye behold not me, and again

μικρὸν καὶ ὄψεσθέ με; 20 ἀμὴν ἀμὴν
a little while and ye will see me?   Truly truly

λέγω ὑμῖν ὅτι κλαύσετε καὶ θρηνήσετε
I tell you that will weep and will lament

ὑμεῖς, ὁ δὲ κόσμος χαρήσεται· ὑμεῖς
ye, and the world will rejoice; ye

λυπηθήσεσθε, ἀλλ᾽ ἡ λύπη ὑμῶν εἰς
will be grieved, but the grief of you into

χαρὰν γενήσεται. 21 ἡ γυνὴ ὅταν τίκτῃ
joy will become.   The woman when she gives birth

λύπην ἔχει, ὅτι ἦλθεν ἡ ὥρα αὐτῆς·
grief has, because came the hour of her;

ὅταν δὲ γεννήσῃ τὸ παιδίον, οὐκέτι
but when she brings forth the child, no longer

μνημονεύει τῆς θλίψεως διὰ τὴν χαρὰν
she remembers the distress because of the joy

ὅτι ἐγεννήθη ἄνθρωπος εἰς τὸν κόσμον.
that was born a man into the world.

22 καὶ ὑμεῖς οὖν νῦν μὲν λύπην ἔχετε·
And ye therefore now indeed grief have;

πάλιν δὲ ὄψομαι ὑμᾶς, καὶ χαρήσεται
but again I will see you, and ²will rejoice

ὑμῶν ἡ καρδία, καὶ τὴν χαρὰν ὑμῶν
³of you ¹the ³heart, and the joy of you

οὐδεὶς αἴρει ἀφ᾽ ὑμῶν. 23 καὶ ἐν ἐκείνῃ τῇ
no one takes from you.   And in that —

ἡμέρᾳ ἐμὲ οὐκ ἐρωτήσετε οὐδέν.
day me ye will not question no(any)thing.

ἀμὴν ἀμὴν λέγω ὑμῖν, ἄν τι αἰτήσητε
Truly truly I tell you, whatever ye ask

τὸν πατέρα δώσει ὑμῖν ἐν τῷ ὀνόματί
the Father he will give you in the name

---

yet to come. 14He will bring glory to me by taking from what is mine and making it known to you. 15All that belongs to the Father is mine. That is why I said the Spirit will take from what is mine and make it known to you.

16"In a little while you will see me no more, and then after a little while you will see me."

The Disciples' Grief Will Turn to Joy

17Some of his disciples said to one another, "What does he mean by saying, 'In a little while you will see me no more, and then after a little while you will see me,' and 'Because I am going to the Father'?" 18They kept asking, "What does he mean by 'a little while'? We don't understand what he is saying."

19Jesus saw that they wanted to ask him about this, so he said to them, "Are you asking one another what I meant when I said, 'In a little while you will see me no more, and then after a little while you will see me'? 20I tell you the truth, you will weep and mourn while the world rejoices. You will grieve, but your grief will turn to joy. 21A woman giving birth to a child has pain because her time has come; but when her baby is born she forgets the anguish because of her joy that a child is born into the world. 22So with you: Now is your time of grief, but I will see you again and you will rejoice, and no one will take away your joy. 23In that day you will no longer ask me anything. I tell you the truth, my Father will give you whatever you ask in my name. 24Un-

---

* Understand "that which is mine".

24"Until now you have asked for nothing in My name; ask, and you will receive, that your joy may be made full.

25"These things I have spoken to you in figurative language; an hour is coming when I will speak no more to you in figurative language, but will tell you plainly of the Father.

26"In that day you will ask in My name, and I do not say to you that I will request the Father on your behalf;

27for the Father Himself loves you, because you have loved Me, and have believed that I came forth from the Father.

28"I came forth from the Father, and have come into the world; I am leaving the world again, and going to the Father."

29His disciples *said, "Lo, now You are speaking plainly, and are not using a figure of speech.

30"Now we know that You know all things, and have no need for anyone to question You; by this we believe that You came from God."

31Jesus answered them, "Do you now believe?

32"Behold, an hour is coming, and has *already* come, for you to be scattered, each to his own *home*, and to leave Me alone; and *yet* I am not alone, because the Father is with Me.

33"These things I have spoken to you, that in Me you may have peace. In the world you have tribulation, but take courage; I have overcome the world."

Chapter 17

The High Priestly Prayer

THESE things Jesus spoke; and lifting up His eyes to heaven, He said, "Father, the hour has come; glorify Thy Son, that

---

μου. **24** ἕως ἄρτι οὐκ ἠτήσατε οὐδὲν
of me. Until now ye asked not no(any)thing

ἐν τῷ ὀνόματί μου· αἰτεῖτε, καὶ λήμψεσθε,
in the name of me; ask, and ye will receive,

ἵνα ἡ χαρὰ ὑμῶν ᾖ πεπληρωμένη.
that the joy of you may be having been filled.

25 Ταῦτα ἐν παροιμίαις λελάληκα ὑμῖν·
These things in allegories I have spoken to you;

ἔρχεται ὥρα ὅτε οὐκέτι ἐν παροιμίαις
comes an hour when no longer in allegories

λαλήσω ὑμῖν, ἀλλὰ παρρησίᾳ περὶ τοῦ
I will speak to you, but plainly concerning the

πατρὸς ἀπαγγελῶ ὑμῖν. **26** ἐν ἐκείνῃ τῇ
Father will declare to you. In that —

ἡμέρᾳ ἐν τῷ ὀνόματί μου αἰτήσεσθε,
day in the name of me ye will ask,

καὶ οὐ λέγω ὑμῖν ὅτι ἐγὼ ἐρωτήσω
and I tell not you that I will request

τὸν πατέρα περὶ ὑμῶν· **27** αὐτὸς γὰρ
the Father concerning you; for [him]self

ὁ πατὴρ φιλεῖ ὑμᾶς, ὅτι ὑμεῖς ἐμὲ
the Father loves you, because ye me

πεφιλήκατε καὶ πεπιστεύκατε ὅτι ἐγὼ
have loved and have believed that I

παρὰ τοῦ θεοῦ ἐξῆλθον. **28** ἐξῆλθον
from — God came forth. I came forth

ἐκ τοῦ πατρὸς καὶ ἐλήλυθα εἰς τὸν
out of the Father and have come into the

κόσμον· πάλιν ἀφίημι τὸν κόσμον καὶ
world; again I leave the world and

πορεύομαι πρὸς τὸν πατέρα. **29** Λέγουσιν
go to the Father. Say

οἱ μαθηταὶ αὐτοῦ· ἴδε νῦν ἐν παρρησίᾳ
the disciples of him: Behold[,] now in plainness

λαλεῖς, καὶ παροιμίαν οὐδεμίαν λέγεις.
thou speakest, and ¹allegory ¹no thou sayest.

30 νῦν οἴδαμεν ὅτι οἶδας πάντα καὶ
Now we know that thou knowest all things and

οὐ χρείαν ἔχεις ἵνα τίς σε ἐρωτᾷ· ἐν
no need hast that anyone thee should question; by

τούτῳ πιστεύομεν ὅτι ἀπὸ θεοῦ ἐξῆλθες.
this we believe that from God thou camest forth.

31 ἀπεκρίθη αὐτοῖς Ἰησοῦς· ἄρτι πιστεύετε;
Answered them Jesus: Now believe ye?

32 ἰδοὺ ἔρχεται ὥρα καὶ ἐλήλυθεν ἵνα
behold[,] comes an hour and has come that

σκορπισθῆτε ἕκαστος εἰς τὰ ἴδια κἀμὲ
ye are scattered each one to the(his) own and me

μόνον ἀφῆτε· καὶ οὐκ εἰμὶ μόνος, ὅτι
alone ye leave; and I am not alone, because

ὁ πατὴρ μετ᾽ ἐμοῦ ἐστιν. **33** ταῦτα
the Father with me is. These things

λελάληκα ὑμῖν ἵνα ἐν ἐμοὶ εἰρήνην
I have spoken to you that in me peace

ἔχητε. ἐν τῷ κόσμῳ θλῖψιν ἔχετε·
ye may have. In the world distress ye have;

ἀλλὰ θαρσεῖτε, ἐγὼ νενίκηκα τὸν κόσμον.
but cheer ye up, I have overcome the world.

17 Ταῦτα ἐλάλησεν Ἰησοῦς, καὶ ἐπάρας
These things spoke Jesus, and lifting up

τοὺς ὀφθαλμοὺς αὐτοῦ εἰς τὸν οὐρανὸν
the eyes of him to — heaven

εἶπεν· πάτερ, ἐλήλυθεν ἡ ὥρα· δόξασόν
said : Father, has come the hour; glorify

---

til now you have not asked for anything in my name. Ask and you will receive, and your joy will be complete.

25"Though I have been speaking figuratively, a time is coming when I will no longer use this kind of language but will tell you plainly about my Father. 26In that day you will ask in my name. I am not saying that I will ask the Father on your behalf. 27No, the Father himself loves you because you have loved me and have believed that I came from God. 28I came from the Father and entered the world; now I am leaving the world and going back to the Father."

29Then Jesus' disciples said, "Now you are speaking clearly and without figures of speech. 30Now we can see that you know all things and that you do not even need to have anyone ask you questions. This makes us believe that you came from God."

31"You believe at last!" ʷ Jesus answered. 32"But a time is coming, and has come, when you will be scattered, each to his own home. You will leave me all alone. Yet I am not alone, for my Father is with me.

33"I have told you these things, so that in me you may have peace. In this world you will have trouble. But take heart! I have overcome the world."

Chapter 17

Jesus Prays for Himself

AFTER Jesus said this, he looked toward heaven and prayed:

"Father, the time has come. Glorify your

ʷ31 Or "Do you now believe?"

the Son may glorify Thee, ²even as Thou gavest Him authority over all mankind, that to all whom Thou hast given Him, He may give eternal life.

³"And this is eternal life, that they may know Thee, the only true God, and Jesus Christ whom Thou hast sent.

⁴"I glorified Thee on the earth, having accomplished the work which Thou hast given Me to do.

⁵"And now, glorify Thou Me together with Thyself, Father, with the glory which I had with Thee before the world was.

⁶"I manifested Thy name to the men whom Thou gavest Me out of the world; Thine they were, and Thou gavest them to Me, and they have kept Thy word.

⁷"Now they have come to know that everything Thou hast given Me is from Thee;

⁸for the words which Thou gavest Me I have given to them; and they received *them*, and truly understood that I came forth from Thee, and they believed that Thou didst send Me.

⁹"I ask on their behalf; I do not ask on behalf of the world, but of those whom Thou hast given Me; for they are Thine;

¹⁰and all things that are Mine are Thine, and Thine are Mine; and I have been glorified in them.

¹¹"And I am no more in the world; and *yet* they themselves are in the world, and I come to Thee. Holy Father, keep them in Thy name, *the name* which Thou hast given Me, that they may be one, even as We *are*.

¹²"While I was with them, I was keeping them in Thy name which Thou hast given Me; and I guard-

σου τὸν υἱόν, ἵνα ὁ υἱὸς δοξάσῃ σέ,
of thee the Son, that the Son may glorify thee,

2 καθὼς ἔδωκας αὐτῷ ἐξουσίαν πάσης
as thou gavest him authority of(over) all

σαρκός, ἵνα πᾶν ὃ δέδωκας αὐτῷ δώσῃ
flesh, that all which thou hast given him he may give

αὐτοῖς ζωὴν αἰώνιον. 3 αὕτη δέ ἐστιν
to them life eternal. And this is

ἡ αἰώνιος ζωή, ἵνα γινώσκωσιν σὲ τὸν
- eternal life, that they may know thee the

μόνον ἀληθινὸν θεὸν καὶ ὃν ἀπέστειλας
only true God and [he] whom thou didst send

Ἰησοῦν Χριστόν. 4 ἐγώ σε ἐδόξασα
Jesus Christ. I thee glorified

ἐπὶ τῆς γῆς, τὸ ἔργον τελειώσας ὃ
on the earth, the work finishing which

δέδωκάς μοι ἵνα ποιήσω· 5 καὶ νῦν
thou hast given to me that I should do; and now

δόξασόν με σύ, πάτερ, παρὰ σεαυτῷ
glorify me thou, Father, with thyself

τῇ δόξῃ ᾗ εἶχον πρὸ τοῦ τὸν κόσμον
with the glory which I had before the the world
= before the world was

εἶναι παρὰ σοί. 6 Ἐφανέρωσά σου τὸ
to be^b with thee. I manifested of thee the

ὄνομα τοῖς ἀνθρώποις οὓς ἔδωκάς μοι
name to the men whom thou gavest to me

ἐκ τοῦ κόσμου. σοὶ ἦσαν κἀμοὶ αὐτοὺς
out of the world. To thee^c they were and to me them
=Thine

ἔδωκας, καὶ τὸν λόγον σου τετήρηκαν.
thou gavest, and the word of thee they have kept.

7 νῦν ἔγνωκαν ὅτι πάντα ὅσα δέδωκάς
Now they have known that all things as many as thou hast given

μοι παρὰ σοῦ εἰσιν· 8 ὅτι τὰ ῥήματα
to me from thee are; because the words

ἃ ἔδωκάς μοι δέδωκα αὐτοῖς, καὶ αὐτοὶ
which thou gavest to me I have given to them, and they

ἔλαβον, καὶ ἔγνωσαν ἀληθῶς ὅτι παρὰ
received, and knew truly that from

σοῦ ἐξῆλθον, καὶ ἐπίστευσαν ὅτι σύ
thee I came forth, and they believed that thou

με ἀπέστειλας. 9 ἐγὼ περὶ αὐτῶν ἐρωτῶ·
me didst send. I concerning them make request;

οὐ περὶ τοῦ κόσμου ἐρωτῶ, ἀλλὰ περὶ
not concerning the world do I make request, but concerning

ὧν δέδωκάς μοι, ὅτι σοί εἰσιν,
[those] whom thou hast given to me, because to thee^d they are,
=thine

10 καὶ τὰ ἐμὰ πάντα σά ἐστιν καὶ
and ¹the ³my things ¹all ⁵thine ⁴is(are) and

τὰ σὰ ἐμά, καὶ δεδόξασμαι ἐν αὐτοῖς.
the thy things mine, and I have been glorified in them.

11 καὶ οὐκέτι εἰμὶ ἐν τῷ κόσμῳ, καὶ
And no longer am I in the world, and

αὐτοὶ ἐν τῷ κόσμῳ εἰσίν, κἀγὼ πρὸς
they in the world are, and I to

σὲ ἔρχομαι. πάτερ ἅγιε, τήρησον αὐτοὺς
thee come. Father holy, keep them

ἐν τῷ ὀνόματί σου ᾧ δέδωκάς μοι,
in the name of thee which thou hast given to me,

ἵνα ὦσιν ἓν καθὼς ἡμεῖς. 12 ὅτε ἤμην
that they may be one as we. When I was

μετ' αὐτῶν, ἐγὼ ἐτήρουν αὐτοὺς ἐν
with them, I kept them in

τῷ ὀνόματί σου ᾧ δέδωκάς μοι, καὶ
the name of thee which thou hast given to me, and

Son, that your Son may glorify you. ²For you granted him authority over all people that he might give eternal life to all those you have given him. ³Now this is eternal life: that they may know you, the only true God, and Jesus Christ. whom you have sent. ⁴I have brought you glory on earth by completing the work you gave me to do. ⁵And now, Father, glorify me in your presence with the glory I had with you before the world began.

Jesus Prays for His Disciples

⁶"I have revealed you˟ to those whom you gave me out of the world. They were yours; you gave them to me and they have obeyed your word. ⁷Now they know that everything you have given me comes from you. ⁸For I gave them the words you gave me and they accepted them. They knew with certainty that I came from you, and they believed that you sent me. ⁹I pray for them. I am not praying for the world, but for those you have given me, for they are yours. ¹⁰All I have is yours, and all you have is mine. And glory has come to me through them. ¹¹I will remain in the world no longer, but they are still in the world, and I am coming to you. Holy Father, protect them by the power of your name— the name you gave me —so that they may be one as we are one. ¹²While I was with them, I protected them and kept them safe by

˟6 Greek *your name*; also in verse 26

ed them, and not one of them perished but the son of perdition, that the Scripture might be fulfilled.

The Disciples in the World

13"But now I come to Thee; and these things I speak in the world, that they may have My joy made full in themselves.
14"I have given them Thy word; and the world has hated them, because they are not of the world, even as I am not of the world.
15"I do not ask Thee to take them out of the world, but to keep them from the evil one.
16"They are not of the world, even as I am not of the world.
17"Sanctify them in the truth; Thy word is truth.
18"As Thou didst send Me into the world, I also have sent them into the world.
19"And for their sakes I sanctify Myself, that they themselves also may be sanctified in truth.
20"I do not ask in behalf of these alone, but for those also who believe in Me through their word;
21that they may all be one; even as Thou, Father, *art* in Me, and I in Thee, that they also may be in Us, that the world may believe that Thou didst send Me.

Their Future Glory

22"And the glory which Thou hast given Me I have given to them; that they may be one, just as We are one;
23I in them, and Thou in Me, that they may be perfected in unity, that the world may know that Thou didst send Me, and didst love them, even as Thou didst love Me.
24"Father, I desire that they also, whom Thou hast given Me, be with Me

ἐφύλαξα, καὶ οὐδεὶς ἐξ αὐτῶν ἀπώλετο
I guarded, and not one of them perished
εἰ μὴ ὁ υἱὸς τῆς ἀπωλείας, ἵνα ἡ
except the son - perdition, that the
γραφὴ πληρωθῇ. 13 νῦν δὲ πρὸς σὲ
scripture might be fulfilled. But now to thee
ἔρχομαι, καὶ ταῦτα λαλῶ ἐν τῷ κόσμῳ
I come, and these things I speak in the world
ἵνα ἔχωσιν τὴν χαρὰν τὴν ἐμὴν
that they may have *the* ²joy - ¹my
πεπληρωμένην ἐν ἑαυτοῖς. 14 ἐγὼ δέδωκα
having been fulfilled in themselves. I have given
αὐτοῖς τὸν λόγον σου, καὶ ὁ κόσμος
to them the word of thee, and the world
ἐμίσησεν αὐτούς, ὅτι οὐκ εἰσὶν ἐκ τοῦ
hated them, because they are not of the
κόσμου καθὼς ἐγὼ οὐκ εἰμὶ ἐκ τοῦ
world as I am not of the
κόσμου. 15 οὐκ ἐρωτῶ ἵνα ἄρῃς αὐτοὺς
world. I do not request that thou shouldest take them
ἐκ τοῦ κόσμου, ἀλλ' ἵνα τηρήσῃς αὐτοὺς
out of the world, but that thou shouldest keep them
ἐκ τοῦ πονηροῦ. 16 ἐκ τοῦ κόσμου
out of the evil [?one]. Of the world
οὐκ εἰσὶν καθὼς ἐγὼ οὐκ εἰμὶ ἐκ τοῦ
they are not as I am not of the
κόσμου. 17 ἁγίασον αὐτοὺς ἐν τῇ
world. Sanctify them in(?by) the
ἀληθείᾳ· ὁ λόγος ὁ σὸς ἀλήθειά ἐστιν.
truth; the ²word - ¹thy truth is.
18 καθὼς ἐμὲ ἀπέστειλας εἰς τὸν κόσμον,
As me thou didst send into the world,
κἀγὼ ἀπέστειλα αὐτοὺς εἰς τὸν κόσμον·
I also sent them into the world;
19 καὶ ὑπὲρ αὐτῶν [ἐγὼ] ἁγιάζω ἐμαυτόν,
and on behalf of them [I] sanctify myself,
ἵνα ὦσιν καὶ αὐτοὶ ἡγιασμένοι ἐν ἀληθείᾳ.
that ²may be ³also ¹they *having been* sanctified in truth.
20 Οὐ περὶ τούτων δὲ ἐρωτῶ μόνον,
²Not ³concerning ⁴these ¹but I make request only,
ἀλλὰ καὶ περὶ τῶν πιστευόντων διὰ
but also concerning the [ones] believing through
τοῦ λόγου αὐτῶν εἰς ἐμέ, 21 ἵνα πάντες
the word of them in me, that all
ἓν ὦσιν, καθὼς σύ, πατήρ, ἐν ἐμοὶ
one may be, as thou, Father, in me
κἀγὼ ἐν σοί, ἵνα καὶ αὐτοὶ ἐν ἡμῖν
and I in thee, that also they in us
ὦσιν, ἵνα ὁ κόσμος πιστεύῃ ὅτι σύ
may be, that the world may believe that thou
με ἀπέστειλας. 22 κἀγὼ τὴν δόξαν ἣν
me didst send. And I the glory which
δέδωκάς μοι δέδωκα αὐτοῖς, ἵνα ὦσιν
thou hast given to me have given to them, that they may be
ἓν καθὼς ἡμεῖς ἕν· 23 ἐγὼ ἐν αὐτοῖς
one as we [are] one; I in them
καὶ σὺ ἐν ἐμοί, ἵνα ὦσιν τετελειωμένοι
and thou in me, that they may be *having been* perfected
εἰς ἕν, ἵνα γινώσκῃ ὁ κόσμος ὅτι σύ
in one, that may know the world that thou
με ἀπέστειλας καὶ ἠγάπησας αὐτοὺς
me didst send and didst love them
καθὼς ἐμὲ ἠγάπησας. 24 Πατήρ, ὃ
as me thou didst love. Father, what
δέδωκάς μοι, θέλω ἵνα ὅπου εἰμὶ ἐγὼ
thou hast given to me, I wish that where am I

that name you gave me. None has been lost except the one doomed to destruction so that Scripture would be fulfilled.
13"I am coming to you now, but I say these things while I am still in the world, so that they may have the full measure of my joy within them. 14I have given them your word and the world has hated them, for they are not of the world any more than I am of the world. 15My prayer is not that you take them out of the world but that you protect them from the evil one. 16They are not of the world, even as I am not of it. 17Sanctify ⁽ʸ⁾ them by the truth; your word is truth. 18As you sent me into the world, I have sent them into the world. 19For them I sanctify myself, that they too may be truly sanctified.

Jesus Prays for All Believers

20"My prayer is not for them alone. I pray also for those who will believe in me through their message, 21that all of them may be one, Father, just as you are in me and I am in you. May they also be in us so that the world may believe that you have sent me. 22I have given them the glory that you gave me, that they may be one as we are one: 23I in them and you in me. May they be brought to complete unity to let the world know that you sent me and have loved them even as you have loved me.
24"Father, I want those you have given me to be with me where

where I am, in order that they may behold My glory, which Thou hast given Me; for Thou didst love Me before the foundation of the world.

25 "O righteous Father, although the world has not known Thee, yet I have known Thee; and these have known that Thou didst send Me;

26 and I have made Thy name known to them, and will make it known; that the love wherewith Thou didst love Me may be in them, and I in them.''

κἀκεῖνοι ὦσιν μετ᾽ ἐμοῦ, ἵνα θεωρῶσιν
those also may be with me, that they may behold

τὴν δόξαν τὴν ἐμήν, ἣν δέδωκάς μοι
the ²glory - ¹my, which thou hast given to me

ὅτι ἠγάπησάς με πρὸ καταβολῆς κόσμου.
because thou didst love me before [the] foundation of [the] world.

25 πατὴρ δίκαιε, καὶ ὁ κόσμος σε
Father righteous, indeed the world thee

οὐκ ἔγνω, ἐγὼ δέ σε ἔγνων, καὶ οὗτοι
knew not, but I thee knew, and these

ἔγνωσαν ὅτι σύ με ἀπέστειλας· 26 καὶ
knew that thou me didst send; and

ἐγνώρισα αὐτοῖς τὸ ὄνομά σου καὶ
I made known to them the name of thee and

γνωρίσω, ἵνα ἡ ἀγάπη ἣν ἠγάπησάς
will make known, that the love [with] which thou lovedst

με ἐν αὐτοῖς ᾖ κἀγὼ ἐν αὐτοῖς.
me in them may be and I in them.

I am, and to see my glory, the glory you have given me because you loved me before the creation of the world.

25 "Righteous Father, though the world does not know you, I know you, and they know that you have sent me. 26 I have made you known to them, and will continue to make you known in order that the love you have for me may be in them and that I myself may be in them.''

Chapter 18

Judas Betrays Jesus

WHEN Jesus had spoken these words, He went forth with His disciples over the ravine of the Kidron, where there was a garden, into which He Himself entered, and His disciples.

2 Now Judas also, who was betraying Him, knew the place; for Jesus had often met there with His disciples.

3 Judas then, having received the Roman cohort, and officers from the chief priests and the Pharisees, *came there with lanterns and torches and weapons.

4 Jesus therefore, knowing all the things that were coming upon Him, went forth, and *said to them, "Whom do you seek?"

5 They answered Him, "Jesus the Nazarene." He *said to them, "I am He." And Judas also who was betraying Him, was standing with them.

6 When therefore He said to them, "I am He," they drew back, and fell to the ground.

7 Again therefore He asked them, "Whom do you seek?" And they said, "Jesus the Nazarene."

8 Jesus answered, "I told you that I am He; if therefore you seek Me, let these go their way,"

Chapter 18

18 Ταῦτα εἰπὼν Ἰησοῦς ἐξῆλθεν σὺν
These things having said Jesus went forth with

τοῖς μαθηταῖς αὐτοῦ πέραν τοῦ χειμάρρου
the disciples of him across the torrent

τοῦ Κεδρών, ὅπου ἦν κῆπος, εἰς ὃν
- Kedron, where there was a garden, into which

εἰσῆλθεν αὐτὸς καὶ οἱ μαθηταὶ αὐτοῦ.
entered he and the disciples of him.

2 ᾔδει δὲ καὶ Ἰούδας ὁ παραδιδοὺς
¹Now ⁷knew ²also ³Judas ⁴the [one] ⁶betraying

αὐτὸν τὸν τόπον, ὅτι πολλάκις συνήχθη
⁵him ⁵the ⁹place, because often assembled

Ἰησοῦς ἐκεῖ μετὰ τῶν μαθητῶν αὐτου.
Jesus there with the disciples of him.

3 ὁ οὖν Ἰούδας λαβὼν τὴν σπεῖραν
- Therefore Judas taking the band

καὶ ἐκ τῶν ἀρχιερέων καὶ [ἐκ] τῶν
and ⁵from ⁶the ⁴chief priests ⁵and ⁶from ⁷the

Φαρισαίων ὑπηρέτας ἔρχεται ἐκεῖ μετὰ
⁸Pharisees ¹attendants comes there with

φανῶν καὶ λαμπάδων καὶ ὅπλων. 4 Ἰησοῦς
lanterns and lamps and weapons. Jesus

οὖν εἰδὼς πάντα τὰ ἐρχόμενα ἐπ᾽ αὐτὸν
therefore knowing all the things coming on him

ἐξῆλθεν καὶ λέγει αὐτοῖς· τίνα ζητεῖτε;
went forth and says to them: Whom seek ye?

5 ἀπεκρίθησαν αὐτῷ· Ἰησοῦν τὸν
They answered him: Jesus the

Ναζωραῖον. λέγει αὐτοῖς· ἐγώ εἰμι.
Nazarene. He tells them: I am.

εἱστήκει δὲ καὶ Ἰούδας ὁ παραδιδοὺς
Now stood also Judas the [one] betraying

αὐτὸν μετ᾽ αὐτῶν. 6 ὡς οὖν εἶπεν
him with them. When therefore he told

αὐτοῖς· ἐγώ εἰμι, ἀπῆλθαν εἰς τὰ ὀπίσω
them: I am, they went away back †

καὶ ἔπεσαν χαμαί. 7 πάλιν οὖν
and fell on the ground. Again therefore

ἐπηρώτησεν αὐτούς· τίνα ζητεῖτε; οἱ δὲ
he questioned them: Whom seek ye? And they

εἶπαν· Ἰησοῦν τὸν Ναζωραῖον. 8 ἀπεκρίθη
said: Jesus the Nazarene. Answered

Ἰησοῦς· εἶπον ὑμῖν ὅτι ἐγώ εἰμι· εἰ
Jesus: I told you that I am; if

οὖν ἐμὲ ζητεῖτε, ἄφετε τούτους ὑπάγειν·
therefore me ye seek, allow these to go;

Jesus Arrested

WHEN he had finished praying, Jesus left with his disciples and crossed the Kidron Valley. On the other side there was an olive grove, and he and his disciples went into it.

2 Now Judas, who betrayed him, knew the place, because Jesus had often met there with his disciples. 3 So Judas came to the grove, guiding a detachment of soldiers and some officials from the chief priests and Pharisees. They were carrying torches, lanterns and weapons.

4 Jesus, knowing all that was going to happen to him, went out and asked them, "Who is it you want?"

5 "Jesus of Nazareth," they replied.

"I am he," Jesus said. (And Judas the traitor was standing there with them.) 6 When Jesus said, "I am he," they drew back and fell to the ground.

7 Again he asked them, "Who is it you want?"

And they said, "Jesus of Nazareth."

8 "I told you that I am he," Jesus answered. "If you are looking for me, then let these men go."

9that the word might be fulfilled which He spoke, "Of those whom Thou hast given Me I lost not one."

10Simon Peter therefore having a sword, drew it, and struck the high priest's slave, and cut off his right ear; and the slave's name was Malchus.

11Jesus therefore said to Peter, "Put the sword into the sheath; the cup which the Father has given Me, shall I not drink it?"

Jesus before the Priests

12So the Roman cohort and the commander, and the officers of the Jews, arrested Jesus and bound Him,

13and led Him to Annas first; for he was father-in-law of Caiaphas, who was high priest that year.

14Now Caiaphas was the one who had advised the Jews that it was expedient for one man to die on behalf of the people.

15And Simon Peter was following Jesus, and so was another disciple. Now that disciple was known to the high priest, and entered with Jesus into the court of the high priest,

16but Peter was standing at the door outside. So the other disciple, who was known to the high priest, went out and spoke to the doorkeeper, and brought in Peter.

17The slave-girl therefore who kept the door *said to Peter, "You are not also one of this man's disciples, are you?" He *said, "I am not."

18Now the slaves and the officers were standing there, having made a charcoal fire, for it was cold and they were warming themselves; and Peter also was

---

9 ἵνα πληρωθῇ ὁ λόγος ὃν εἶπεν, ὅτι
that might be fulfilled the word which he said, –

οὓς δέδωκάς μοι, οὐκ ἀπώλεσα ἐξ
[Those] whom thou hast given to me, I lost not of

αὐτῶν οὐδένα. 10 Σίμων οὖν Πέτρος
them no(any)one. ¹Simon ³therefore ²Peter

ἔχων μάχαιραν εἵλκυσεν αὐτὴν καὶ ἔπαισεν
having a sword drew it and smote

τὸν τοῦ ἀρχιερέως δοῦλον καὶ ἀπέκοψεν
¹the ²of the ³high priest ⁴slave and cut off

αὐτοῦ τὸ ὠτάριον τὸ δεξιόν· ἦν δὲ
of him the ²ear – ¹right; and was

ὄνομα τῷ δούλῳ Μάλχος. 11 εἶπεν οὖν
name to the slave° Malchus. Said therefore

ὁ Ἰησοῦς τῷ Πέτρῳ· βάλε τὴν μάχαιραν
– Jesus – to Peter : Put the sword

εἰς τὴν θήκην· τὸ ποτήριον ὃ δέδωκέν
into the sheath; the cup which has given

μοι ὁ πατήρ, οὐ μὴ πίω αὐτό;
to me the Father, by no means shall I drink it?

12 Ἡ οὖν σπεῖρα καὶ ὁ χιλίαρχος
Therefore the band and the chiliarch

καὶ οἱ ὑπηρέται τῶν Ἰουδαίων συνέλαβον
and the attendants of the Jews took

τὸν Ἰησοῦν καὶ ἔδησαν αὐτόν, 13 καὶ
– Jesus and bound him, and

ἤγαγον πρὸς Ἄνναν πρῶτον· ἦν γὰρ
led to Annas first; for he was

πενθερὸς τοῦ Καϊάφα, ὃς ἦν ἀρχιερεὺς
father-in-law – of Caiaphas, who was high priest

τοῦ ἐνιαυτοῦ ἐκείνου· 14 ἦν δὲ Καϊάφας
year of that; now it was Caiaphas

ὁ συμβουλεύσας τοῖς Ἰουδαίοις ὅτι
the [one] having advised the Jews that

συμφέρει ἕνα ἄνθρωπον ἀποθανεῖν ὑπὲρ
it is(was) expedient one man to die on behalf of

τοῦ λαοῦ. 15 Ἠκολούθει δὲ τῷ Ἰησοῦ
the people. And followed – Jesus

Σίμων Πέτρος καὶ ἄλλος μαθητής. ὁ δὲ
Simon Peter and another disciple. – And

μαθητὴς ἐκεῖνος ἦν γνωστὸς τῷ ἀρχιερεῖ,
disciple that was known to the high priest,

καὶ συνεισῆλθεν τῷ Ἰησοῦ εἰς τὴν αὐλὴν
and entered with – Jesus into the court

τοῦ ἀρχιερέως, 16 ὁ δὲ Πέτρος εἱστήκει
of the high priest, – but Peter stood

πρὸς τῇ θύρᾳ ἔξω. ἐξῆλθεν οὖν ὁ
at the door outside. Went out therefore the

μαθητὴς ὁ ἄλλος ὁ γνωστὸς τοῦ ἀρχιερέως
²disciple – ¹other – known of(to) the high priest

καὶ εἶπεν τῇ θυρωρῷ, καὶ εἰσήγαγεν
and told the portress, and brought in

τὸν Πέτρον. 17 λέγει οὖν τῷ Πέτρῳ ἡ
– Peter. Says therefore – to Peter the

παιδίσκη ἡ θυρωρός· μὴ καὶ σὺ ἐκ
maidservant the portress : Not also thou of

τῶν μαθητῶν εἶ τοῦ ἀνθρώπου τούτου;
the disciples art – of the man of this?

λέγει ἐκεῖνος· οὐκ εἰμί. 18 εἱστήκεισαν δὲ
Says that one : I am not. And stood

οἱ δοῦλοι καὶ οἱ ὑπηρέται ἀνθρακιὰν
the slaves and the attendants a fire

πεποιηκότες, ὅτι ψῦχος ἦν, καὶ
having made, because cold it was, and

ἐθερμαίνοντο· ἦν δὲ καὶ ὁ Πέτρος μετ᾽
were warming themselves; and was also – Peter with

9This happened so that the words he had spoken would be fulfilled: "I have not lost one of those you gave me."ᶻ

10Then Simon Peter, who had a sword, drew it and struck the high priest's servant, cutting off his right ear. (The servant's name was Malchus.)

11Jesus commanded Peter, "Put your sword away! Shall I not drink the cup the Father has given me?"

Jesus Taken to Annas

12Then the detachment of soldiers with its commander and the Jewish officials arrested Jesus. They bound him 13and brought him first to Annas, who was the father-in-law of Caiaphas, the high priest that year.

14Caiaphas was the one who had advised the Jews that it would be good if one man died for the people.

Peter's First Denial

15Simon Peter and another disciple were following Jesus. Because this disciple was known to the high priest, he went with Jesus into the high priest's courtyard, 16but Peter had to wait outside at the door. The other disciple, who was known to the high priest, came back, spoke to the girl on duty there and brought Peter in.

17"You are not one of his disciples, are you?" the girl at the door asked Peter.

He replied, "I am not."

18It was cold, and the servants and officials stood around a fire they had made to keep warm. Peter also with them, standing and warming himself.

19The high priest therefore questioned Jesus about His disciples, and about His teaching.

20Jesus answered him, "I have spoken openly to the world; I always taught in synagogues, and in the temple, where all the Jews come together; and I spoke nothing in secret.

21"Why do you question Me? Question those who have heard what I spoke to them; behold, these know what I said."

22And when He had said this, one of the officers standing by gave Jesus a blow, saying, "Is that the way You answer the high priest?"

23Jesus answered him, "If I have spoken wrongly, bear witness of the wrong; but if rightly, why do you strike Me?"

24Annas therefore sent Him bound to Caiaphas the high priest.

Peter's Denial of Jesus

25Now Simon Peter was standing and warming himself. They said therefore to him, "You are not also one of His disciples, are you?" He denied it, and said, "I am not."

26One of the slaves of the high priest, being a relative of the one whose ear Peter cut off, *said, "Did I not see you in the garden with Him?"

27Peter therefore denied it again; and immediately a cock crowed.

Jesus before Pilate

28They *led Jesus therefore from Caiaphas into the aPraetorium, and it was early; and they themselves did not enter into the Praetorium in order that they might not be defiled, but might eat the Passover.

29Pilate therefore went out to them, and *said, "What accusation do you bring against this Man?"

30They answered and said to him, "If this Man were not an evildoer, we would not have delivered Him up to you."

31Pilate therefore said to

aI.e., governor's official residence

αὐτῶν ἑστὼς καὶ θερμαινόμενος. 19 Ὁ
them standing and warming himself. - 1The

οὖν ἀρχιερεὺς ἠρώτησεν τὸν Ἰησοῦν
2therefore 3high priest questioned - Jesus

περὶ τῶν μαθητῶν αὐτοῦ καὶ περὶ τῆς
about the disciples of him and about the

διδαχῆς αὐτοῦ. 20 ἀπεκρίθη αὐτῷ Ἰησοῦς·
teaching of him. Answered him Jesus:

ἐγὼ παρρησίᾳ λελάληκα τῷ κόσμῳ· ἐγὼ
I with plainness have spoken to the world; I

πάντοτε ἐδίδαξα ἐν συναγωγῇ καὶ ἐν
always taught in a synagogue and in

τῷ ἱερῷ, ὅπου πάντες οἱ Ἰουδαῖοι
the temple, where all the Jews

συνέρχονται, καὶ ἐν κρυπτῷ ἐλάλησα
come together, and in secret I spoke

οὐδέν. 21 τί με ἐρωτᾷς; ἐρώτησον
nothing. Why me questionest thou? question

τοὺς ἀκηκοότας τί ἐλάλησα αὐτοῖς· ἴδε
the [ones] having heard what I spoke to them; behold[,]

οὗτοι οἴδασιν ἃ εἶπον ἐγώ. 22 ταῦτα
these know what things said I. These things

δὲ αὐτοῦ εἰπόντος εἷς παρεστηκὼς τῶν
and him sayinga one standing by of the
=And as he said this

ὑπηρετῶν ἔδωκεν ῥάπισμα τῷ Ἰησοῦ
attendants gave a blow - to Jesus

εἰπών· οὕτως ἀποκρίνῃ τῷ ἀρχιερεῖ;
saying: Thus answerest thou the high priest?

23 ἀπεκρίθη αὐτῷ Ἰησοῦς· εἰ κακῶς
Answered him Jesus: If ill

ἐλάλησα, μαρτύρησον περὶ τοῦ κακοῦ·
I spoke, witness concerning the evil;

εἰ δὲ καλῶς, τί με δέρεις; 24 ἀπέστειλεν
but if well, why me beatest thou? 3Sent

οὖν αὐτὸν ὁ Ἄννας δεδεμένον πρὸς
2therefore 4him - 1Annas having been bound to

Καϊάφαν τὸν ἀρχιερέα. 25 Ἦν δὲ Σίμων
Caiaphas the high priest. Now was Simon

Πέτρος ἑστὼς καὶ θερμαινόμενος. εἶπον
Peter standing and warming himself. They said

οὖν αὐτῷ· μὴ καὶ σὺ ἐκ τῶν μαθητῶν
therefore to him: Not also thou of the disciples

αὐτοῦ εἶ; ἠρνήσατο ἐκεῖνος καὶ εἶπεν·
of him art? Denied that one and said:

οὐκ εἰμί. 26 λέγει εἷς ἐκ τῶν δούλων τοῦ
I am not. Says one of the slaves of the

ἀρχιερέως, συγγενὴς ὢν οὗ ἀπέκοψεν
high priest, 2a relative 1being 3[of him] of whom 5cut off

Πέτρος τὸ ὠτίον· οὐκ ἐγώ σε εἶδον
4Peter 6the 7ear: 8Not 9I 10thee 11saw

ἐν τῷ κήπῳ μετ' αὐτοῦ; 27 πάλιν οὖν
in the garden with him? Again therefore

ἠρνήσατο Πέτρος, καὶ εὐθέως ἀλέκτωρ
denied Peter, and immediately a cock

ἐφώνησεν.
sounded(crew).

28 Ἄγουσιν οὖν τὸν Ἰησοῦν ἀπὸ τοῦ
They lead therefore - Jesus from -

Καϊάφα εἰς τὸ πραιτώριον· ἦν δὲ πρωΐ·
Caiaphas to the prætorium; and it was early;

καὶ αὐτοὶ οὐκ εἰσῆλθον εἰς τὸ πραιτώριον,
and they entered not into the prætorium,

ἵνα μὴ μιανθῶσιν ἀλλὰ φάγωσιν τὸ
lest they should be defiled but might eat the

πάσχα. 29 ἐξῆλθεν οὖν ὁ Πιλᾶτος ἔξω
passover. Went forth therefore - Pilate outside

---

was standing with them, warming himself.

The High Priest Questions Jesus

19Meanwhile, the high priest questioned Jesus about his disciples and his teaching.

20"I have spoken openly to the world," Jesus replied. "I always taught in synagogues or at the temple, where all the Jews come together. I said nothing in secret. 21Why question me? Ask those who heard me. Surely they know what I said."

22When Jesus said this, one of the officials nearby struck him in the face. "Is this the way you answer the high priest?" he demanded.

23"If I said something wrong," Jesus replied, "testify as to what is wrong. But if I spoke the truth, why did you strike me?" 24Then Annas sent him, still bound, to Caiaphas the high priest.a

Peter's Second and Third Denials

25As Simon Peter stood warming himself, he was asked, "You are not one of his disciples, are you?"

He denied it, saying, "I am not."

26One of the high priest's servants, a relative of the man whose ear Peter had cut off, challenged him, "Didn't I see you with him in the olive grove?"

27Again Peter denied it, and at that moment a rooster began to crow.

Jesus Before Pilate

28Then the Jews led Jesus from Caiaphas to the palace of the Roman governor. By now it was early morning, and to avoid ceremonial uncleanness the Jews did not enter the palace; they wanted to be able to eat the Passover. 29So Pilate came out to them and asked, "What charges are you bringing against this man?"

30"If he were not a criminal," they replied, "we would not have handed him over to you."

31Pilate said, "Take him

a24 Or (Now Annas had sent him, still bound, to Caiaphas the high priest.)

them, "Take Him yourselves, and judge Him according to your law." The Jews said to him, "We are not permitted to put anyone to death,"

32that the word of Jesus might be fulfilled, which He spoke, signifying by what kind of death He was about to die.

33Pilate therefore entered again into the *a*Praetorium, and summoned Jesus, and said to Him, "Are You the King of the Jews?"

34Jesus answered, "Are you saying this on your own initiative, or did others tell you about Me?"

35Pilate answered, "I am not a Jew, am I? Your own nation and the chief priests delivered You up to me; what have You done?"

36Jesus answered, "My kingdom is not of this world. If My kingdom were of this world, then My servants would be fighting, that I might not be delivered up to the Jews; but as it is, My kingdom is not *b*of this realm."

37Pilate therefore said to Him, "So You are a king?" Jesus answered, "You say *correctly* that I am a king. For this I have been born, and for this I have come into the world, to bear witness to the truth. Everyone who is of the truth hears My voice."

38Pilate *said to Him, "What is truth?"

πρὸς αὐτοὺς καὶ φησίν· τίνα κατηγορίαν
to them and says· What accusation

φέρετε τοῦ ἀνθρώπου τούτου; 30 ἀπεκρίθησαν
bring ye - man of this? They answered

καὶ εἶπαν αὐτῷ· εἰ μὴ ἦν
and said to him: Unless was

οὗτος κακὸν ποιῶν, οὐκ ἄν σοι
this man evil doing, *would *not *to thee

παρεδώκαμεν αὐτόν. 31 εἶπεν οὖν αὐτοῖς
¹we *have *delivered *him. Said therefore to them

ὁ Πιλᾶτος· λάβετε αὐτὸν ὑμεῖς, καὶ
- Pilate: Take him ye, and

κατὰ τὸν νόμον ὑμῶν κρίνατε αὐτόν.
according to the law of you judge ye him.

εἶπον αὐτῷ οἱ Ἰουδαῖοι· ἡμῖν οὐκ ἔξεστιν
Said· to him the Jews: For us it is not lawful

ἀποκτεῖναι οὐδένα· 32 ἵνα ὁ λόγος τοῦ
to kill no(any)one; that the word

Ἰησοῦ πληρωθῇ ὃν εἶπεν σημαίνων ποίῳ
of Jesus might be fulfilled which he said signifying by what

θανάτῳ ἤμελλεν ἀποθνῄσκειν. 33 Εἰσῆλθεν
death he was about to die. Entered

οὖν πάλιν εἰς τὸ πραιτώριον ὁ Πιλᾶτος
therefore again into the prætorium - Pilate

καὶ ἐφώνησεν τὸν Ἰησοῦν καὶ εἶπεν
and called - Jesus and said

αὐτῷ· σὺ εἶ ὁ βασιλεὺς τῶν Ἰουδαίων;
to him: Thou art the king of the Jews?

34 ἀπεκρίθη Ἰησοῦς· ἀφ᾽ ἑαυτοῦ σὺ τοῦτο
Answered Jesus: From [thy]self *thou *this

λέγεις, ἢ ἄλλοι εἶπόν σοι περὶ ἐμοῦ;
¹sayest, or others told thee about me?

35 ἀπεκρίθη ὁ Πιλᾶτος· μήτι ἐγὼ
Answered - Pilate: not I

Ἰουδαῖός εἰμι; τὸ ἔθνος τὸ σὸν καὶ
a Jew am? *the *nation - ¹thy and

οἱ ἀρχιερεῖς παρέδωκάν σε ἐμοί· τί
the chief priests delivered thee to me; what

ἐποίησας; 36 ἀπεκρίθη Ἰησοῦς· ἡ βασιλεία
didst thou? Answered Jesus: The ¹kingdom

ἡ ἐμὴ οὐκ ἔστιν ἐκ τοῦ κόσμου τούτου·
- ¹my is not of - world this;

εἰ ἐκ τοῦ κόσμου τούτου ἦν ἡ βασιλεία
if of - world this was the ¹kingdom

ἡ ἐμή, οἱ ὑπηρέται ἂν οἱ ἐμοὶ ἠγωνίζοντο,
- ¹my, the *attendants *would - ¹my *have struggled,

ἵνα μὴ παραδοθῶ τοῖς Ἰουδαίοις· νῦν
that I should not be delivered to the Jews; *now

δὲ ἡ βασιλεία ἡ ἐμὴ οὐκ ἔστιν ἐντεῦθεν.
¹but the ¹kingdom - ¹my is not hence.

37 εἶπεν οὖν αὐτῷ ὁ Πιλᾶτος· οὐκοῦν
Said therefore to him - Pilate: Not really

βασιλεὺς εἶ σύ; ἀπεκρίθη [ὁ] Ἰησοῦς·
a king art thou? Answered - Jesus:

σὺ λέγεις ὅτι βασιλεύς εἰμι. ἐγὼ εἰς
Thou sayest that a king I am. I for

τοῦτο γεγέννημαι καὶ εἰς τοῦτο ἐλήλυθα
this have been born and for this I have come

εἰς τὸν κόσμον, ἵνα μαρτυρήσω τῇ
into the world, that I might witness to the

ἀληθείᾳ· πᾶς ὁ ὢν ἐκ τῆς ἀληθείας
truth; everyone being of the truth

ἀκούει μου τῆς φωνῆς. 38 λέγει αὐτῷ
hears of me the voice. Says to him

ὁ Πιλᾶτος· τί ἐστιν ἀλήθεια; Καὶ
- Pilate: What is truth? And

---

yourselves and judge him by your own law."

"But we have no right to execute anyone," the Jews objected. 32This happened so that the words Jesus had spoken indicating the kind of death he was going to die would be fulfilled.

33Pilate then went back inside the palace, summoned Jesus and asked him, "Are you the king of the Jews?"

34"Is that your own idea," Jesus asked, "or did others talk to you about me?"

35"Am I a Jew?" Pilate replied. "It was your people and your chief priests who handed you over to me. What is it you have done?"

36Jesus said, "My kingdom is not of this world. If it were, my servants would fight to prevent my arrest by the Jews. But now my kingdom is from another place."

37"You are a king, then!" said Pilate.

Jesus answered, "You are right in saying I am a king. In fact, for this reason I was born, and for this I came into the world, to testify to the truth. Everyone on the side of truth listens to me."

38"What is truth?" Pilate asked. With this he went

---

b Lit., *from here*

And when he had said this, he went out again to the Jews, and *said to them, "I find no guilt in Him.
39"But you have a custom, that I should release someone for you at the Passover; do you wish then that I release for you the King of the Jews?"
40Therefore they cried out again, saying, "Not this Man, but Barabbas." Now Barabbas was a robber.

Chapter 19

The Crown of Thorns

THEN Pilate therefore took Jesus, and scourged Him.
2And the soldiers wove a crown of thorns and put it on His head, and arrayed Him in a purple robe;
3and they began to come up to Him, and say, "Hail, King of the Jews!" and to give Him blows in the face.
4And Pilate came out again, and *said to them, "Behold, I am bringing Him out to you, that you may know that I find no guilt in Him."
5Jesus therefore came out, wearing the crown of thorns and the purple robe. And Pilate *said to them, "Behold, the Man!"
6When therefore the chief priests and the officers saw Him, they cried out, saying, "Crucify, crucify!" Pilate *said to them, "Take Him yourselves, and crucify Him, for I find no guilt in Him."
7The Jews answered him, "We have a law, and by that law He ought to die because He made Himself out to be the Son of God."
8When Pilate therefore heard this statement, he was the more afraid;

τοῦτο εἰπὼν πάλιν ἐξῆλθεν πρὸς τοὺς
this having said again he went forth to the

'Ιουδαίους, καὶ λέγει αὐτοῖς· ἐγὼ οὐδεμίαν
Jews, and tells them: ¹I ²no

εὑρίσκω ἐν αὐτῷ αἰτίαν. 39 ἔστιν δὲ
³find ³in ⁶him ⁴crime. But there is

συνήθεια ὑμῖν ἵνα ἕνα ἀπολύσω ὑμῖν
a custom to you⁵ that one I should release to you

ἐν τῷ πάσχα· βούλεσθε οὖν ἀπολύσω
at the Passover; will ye therefore [that] I release

ὑμῖν τὸν βασιλέα τῶν 'Ιουδαίων; 40 ἐκραύ-
to you the king of the Jews? They cried

γασαν οὖν πάλιν λέγοντες· μὴ τοῦτον,
out therefore again saying: Not this man,

ἀλλὰ τὸν Βαραββᾶν. ἦν δὲ ὁ Βαραββᾶς
but — Barabbas. ¹But ²was — ³Barabbas

λῃστής. 19 Τότε οὖν ἔλαβεν ὁ Πιλᾶτος
⁴a robber. Then therefore ²took — ¹Pilate

τὸν 'Ιησοῦν καὶ ἐμαστίγωσεν. 2 καὶ οἱ
³Jesus and scourged [him]. And the

στρατιῶται πλέξαντες στέφανον ἐξ ἀκανθῶν
soldiers having plaited a wreath out of thorns

ἐπέθηκαν αὐτοῦ τῇ κεφαλῇ, καὶ ἱμάτιον
put [it] on of him the head, and ⁴garment

πορφυροῦν περιέβαλον αὐτόν, 3 καὶ ἤρχοντο
²a purple ¹threw round ³him, and came

πρὸς αὐτὸν καὶ ἔλεγον· χαῖρε ὁ βασιλεὺς
to him and said: Hail[,] — king

τῶν 'Ιουδαίων· καὶ ἐδίδοσαν αὐτῷ
of the Jews; and they gave him

ῥαπίσματα. 4 Καὶ ἐξῆλθεν πάλιν ἔξω
blows. And went forth again outside

ὁ Πιλᾶτος καὶ λέγει αὐτοῖς· ἴδε ἄγω
— Pilate and says to them: Behold ¹I bring

ὑμῖν αὐτὸν ἔξω, ἵνα γνῶτε ὅτι οὐδεμίαν
⁴to you ²him ³out, that ye may know that no

αἰτίαν εὑρίσκω ἐν αὐτῷ. 5 ἐξῆλθεν
crime I find in him. Came forth

οὖν ὁ 'Ιησοῦς ἔξω, φορῶν τὸν ἀκάνθινον
therefore — Jesus outside, wearing the thorny

στέφανον καὶ τὸ πορφυροῦν ἱμάτιον. καὶ
wreath and the purple garment. And

λέγει αὐτοῖς· ἰδοὺ ὁ ἄνθρωπος. 6 ὅτε
he says to them: Behold[,] the man. When

οὖν εἶδον αὐτὸν οἱ ἀρχιερεῖς καὶ οἱ
therefore saw him the chief priests and the

ὑπηρέται, ἐκραύγασαν λέγοντες· σταύρωσον
attendants, they shouted saying: Crucify[,]

σταύρωσον. λέγει αὐτοῖς ὁ Πιλᾶτος·
crucify. Says to them — Pilate:

λάβετε αὐτὸν ὑμεῖς καὶ σταυρώσατε·
¹Take ²him ²ye and crucify;

ἐγὼ γὰρ οὐχ εὑρίσκω ἐν αὐτῷ αἰτίαν.
for I find not in him crime.

7 ἀπεκρίθησαν αὐτῷ οἱ 'Ιουδαῖοι· ἡμεῖς
Answered him the Jews: We

νόμον ἔχομεν, καὶ κατὰ τὸν νόμον
a law have, and according to the law

ὀφείλει ἀποθανεῖν, ὅτι υἱὸν θεοῦ ἑαυτὸν
he ought to die, because Son of God himself

ἐποίησεν. 8 Ὅτε οὖν ἤκουσεν ὁ Πιλᾶτος
he made. When therefore heard — Pilate

τοῦτον τὸν λόγον, μᾶλλον ἐφοβήθη, 9 καὶ
this — word, more he was afraid, and

---

out again to the Jews and said, "I find no basis for a charge against him. 39But it is your custom for me to release to you one prisoner at the time of the Passover. Do you want me to release 'the king of the Jews'?"
40They shouted back, "No, not him! Give us Barabbas!" Now Barabbas had taken part in a rebellion.

Chapter 19

Jesus Sentenced to be Crucified

THEN Pilate took Jesus and had him flogged.
2The soldiers twisted together a crown of thorns and put it on his head. They clothed him in a purple robe 3and went up to him again and again, saying, "Hail, king of the Jews!" And they struck him in the face.
4Once more Pilate came out and said to the Jews, "Look, I am bringing him out to you to let you know that I find no basis for a charge against him."
5When Jesus came out wearing the crown of thorns and the purple robe, Pilate said to them, "Here is the man!"
6As soon as the chief priests and their officials saw him, they shouted, "Crucify! Crucify!"
But Pilate answered, "You take him and crucify him. As for me, I find no basis for a charge against him."
7The Jews insisted, "We have a law, and according to that law he must die, because he claimed to be the Son of God."
8When Pilate heard this, he was even more afraid,

9and he entered into the
cPraetorium again, and
*said to Jesus, "Where are
You from?" But Jesus gave
him no answer.

10Pilate therefore *said to
Him, "You do not speak to
me? Do You not know that
I have authority to release
You, and I have authority
to crucify You?"

11Jesus answered, "You
would have no authority
over Me, unless it had been
given you from above; for
this reason he who de-
livered Me to you has
the greater sin."

12As a result of this Pilate
made efforts to release
Him, but the Jews cried
out, saying, "If you release
this Man, you are no friend
of Caesar; everyone who
makes himself out *to be* a
king opposes Caesar."

13When Pilate therefore
heard these words, he
brought Jesus out, and sat
down on the judgment seat
at a place called The Pavement, but in Hebrew, Gab-
batha.

14Now it was the day of
preparation for the Pass-
over; it was about the
dsixth hour. And he *said
to the Jews, "Behold, your
King!"

15They therefore cried
out, "Away with *Him*,
away with *Him*, crucify
Him!" Pilate *said to them,
"Shall I crucify your
King?" The chief priests
answered, "We have no
king but Caesar."

The Crucifixion

16So he then delivered
Him to them to be cruci-
fied.

17They took Jesus there-
fore, and He went out,
bearing His own cross, to
the place called the Place of
a Skull, which is called in
Hebrew, Golgotha.

18There they crucified
Him, and with Him two
other men, one on either
side, and Jesus in between.

εἰσῆλθεν εἰς τὸ πραιτώριον πάλιν καὶ
entered into the prætorium again and
λέγει τῷ Ἰησοῦ· πόθεν εἶ σύ; ὁ δὲ
says - to Jesus : Whence art thou? - But
Ἰησοῦς ἀπόκρισιν οὐκ ἔδωκεν αὐτῷ.
Jesus answer did not give him.
10 λέγει οὖν αὐτῷ ὁ Πιλᾶτος· ἐμοὶ
Says therefore to him - Pilate : To me
οὐ λαλεῖς; οὐκ οἶδας ὅτι ἐξουσίαν ἔχω
speakest thou not? knowest thou not that authority I have
ἀπολῦσαί σε καὶ ἐξουσίαν ἔχω σταυρῶσαί
to release thee and authority I have to crucify
σε; 11 ἀπεκρίθη Ἰησοῦς· οὐκ εἶχες
thee? Answered Jesus : Thou hadst not
ἐξουσίαν κατ' ἐμοῦ οὐδεμίαν εἰ μὴ ἦν
authority against me no(any) unless it was
δεδομένον σοι ἄνωθεν· διὰ τοῦτο ὁ
having been given thee from above; therefore the [one]
παραδούς μέ σοι μείζονα ἁμαρτίαν ἔχει.
having delivered me to thee a greater sin has.
12 ἐκ τούτου ὁ Πιλᾶτος ἐζήτει ἀπολῦσαι
From this - Pilate sought to release
αὐτόν· οἱ δὲ Ἰουδαῖοι ἐκραύγασαν λέγοντες·
him; but the Jews shouted saying :
ἐὰν τοῦτον ἀπολύσῃς, οὐκ εἶ φίλος τοῦ
If this man thou releasest, thou art not a friend -
Καίσαρος· πᾶς ὁ βασιλέα ἑαυτὸν ποιῶν
of Caesar; everyone a king himself making
ἀντιλέγει τῷ Καίσαρι. 13 Ὁ οὖν Πιλᾶτος
speaks against - Caesar. - Therefore Pilate
ἀκούσας τῶν λόγων τούτων ἤγαγεν ἔξω
hearing words these brought outside
τὸν Ἰησοῦν, καὶ ἐκάθισεν ἐπὶ βήματος
- Jesus, and sat on a tribunal
εἰς τόπον λεγόμενον Λιθόστρωτον, Ἑβραϊστὶ δὲ
in a place being called Pavement, but in Hebrew
Γαββαθά. 14 ἦν δὲ παρασκευὴ τοῦ
Gabbatha. Now it was preparation of the
πάσχα, ὥρα ἦν ὡς ἕκτη· καὶ λέγει
Passover, hour it was about sixth; and he says
τοῖς Ἰουδαίοις· ἴδε ὁ βασιλεὺς ὑμῶν.
to the Jews; Behold[,] the king of you.
15 ἐκραύγασαν οὖν ἐκεῖνοι· ἆρον ἆρον,
Shouted therefore those : Take[,] take,
σταύρωσον αὐτόν. λέγει αὐτοῖς ὁ Πιλᾶτος·
crucify him. Says to them - Pilate :
τὸν βασιλέα ὑμῶν σταυρώσω; ἀπεκρίθησαν
The king of you shall I crucify? Answered
οἱ ἀρχιερεῖς· οὐκ ἔχομεν βασιλέα εἰ
the chief priests : We have not a king ex-
μὴ Καίσαρα. 16 τότε οὖν παρέδωκεν
cept Caesar. Then therefore he delivered
αὐτὸν αὐτοῖς ἵνα σταυρωθῇ.
him to them that he should be crucified.
Παρέλαβον οὖν τὸν Ἰησοῦν· 17 καὶ
They took therefore - Jesus; and
βαστάζων ἑαυτῷ τὸν σταυρὸν ἐξῆλθεν
carrying to himself the cross he went forth
εἰς τὸν λεγόμενον κρανίου τόπον, ὃ
to the being called of a skull place, which
λέγεται Ἑβραϊστὶ Γολγοθά, 18 ὅπου αὐτὸν
is called in Hebrew Golgotha, where him
ἐσταύρωσαν, καὶ μετ' αὐτοῦ ἄλλους δύο
they crucified, and with him others two
ἐντεῦθεν καὶ ἐντεῦθεν, μέσον δὲ τὸν
on this side and on that, † and in the middle -

9and he went back inside
the palace. "Where do you
come from?" he asked
Jesus, but Jesus gave him
no answer. 10"Do you re-
fuse to speak to me?" Pi-
late said. "Don't you realize I have power either to
free you or to crucify
you?"

11Jesus answered, "You
would have no power over
me if it were not given to
you from above. Therefore
the one who handed me
over to you is guilty of a
greater sin."

12From then on, Pilate
tried to set Jesus free, but
the Jews kept shouting, "If
you let this man go, you are
no friend of Caesar. Any-
one who claims to be a king
opposes Caesar."

13When Pilate heard this,
he brought Jesus out and
sat down on the judge's
seat at a place known as the
Stone Pavement (which in
Aramaic is Gabbatha). 14It
was the day of Preparation
of Passover Week, about
the sixth hour.

"Here is your king," Pi-
late said to the Jews.

15But they shouted,
"Take him away! Take him
away! Crucify him!"

"Shall I crucify your
king?" Pilate asked.

"We have no king but
Caesar," the chief priests
answered.

16Finally Pilate handed
him over to them to be crucified.

The Crucifixion

So the soldiers took
charge of Jesus. 17Carrying
his own cross, he went out
to the place of the Skull
(which in Aramaic is called
Golgotha). 18Here they crucified him, and with him
two others—one on each
side and Jesus in the middle.

cI.e., governor's official residence
dPerhaps 6 a.m. (Roman time)

19And Pilate wrote an inscription also, and put it on the cross. And it was written, "JESUS THE NAZARENE, THE KING OF THE JEWS."

20Therefore this inscription many of the Jews read, for the place where Jesus was crucified was near the city; and it was written in Hebrew, Latin, *and* in Greek.

21And so the chief priests of the Jews were saying to Pilate, "Do not write, 'The King of the Jews'; but that He said, 'I am King of the Jews.' "

22Pilate answered, "What I have written I have written."

23The soldiers therefore, when they had crucified Jesus, took His outer garments and made four parts, a part to every soldier and *also* the ʳtunic; now the tunic was seamless, woven in one piece.

24They said therefore to one another, "Let us not tear it, but cast lots for it, *to decide* whose it shall be"; that the Scripture might be fulfilled, "THEY DIVIDED MY OUTER GARMENTS AMONG THEM, AND FOR MY CLOTHING THEY CAST LOTS."

25Therefore the soldiers did these things. But there were standing by the cross of Jesus His mother, and His mother's sister, Mary the *wife* of Clopas, and Mary Magdalene.

26When Jesus therefore saw His mother, and the disciple whom He loved standing nearby, He *said to His mother, "Woman, behold, your son!"

27Then He *said to the disciple, "Behold, your mother!" And from that

---

'Ιησοῦν.　**19** ἔγραψεν δὲ καὶ τίτλον ὁ
Jesus.　　　And wrote also a title -

Πιλᾶτος καὶ ἔθηκεν ἐπὶ τοῦ σταυροῦ·
Pilate and put [it] on the cross;

ἦν δὲ γεγραμμένον· ΙΗΣΟΥΣ Ο
and it was *having been* written: JESUS THE

ΝΑΖΩΡΑΙΟΣ Ο ΒΑΣΙΛΕΥΣ ΤΩΝ
NAZARENE THE KING OF THE

ΙΟΥΔΑΙΩΝ.　**20** τοῦτον οὖν τὸν τίτλον
JEWS.　　　¹This ²therefore - ⁴title

πολλοὶ ἀνέγνωσαν τῶν 'Ιουδαίων, ὅτι
¹many ⁴read ²of the ³Jews, because

ἐγγὺς ἦν ὁ τόπος τῆς πόλεως ὅπου
⁷near ⁶was ¹the ²place ³the ⁴city ⁵where

ἐσταυρώθη ὁ 'Ιησοῦς· καὶ ἦν γεγραμμένον
⁸was crucified - ⁵Jesus; and it was *having been* written

'Εβραϊστί, 'Ρωμαϊστί, 'Ελληνιστί.　**21** ἔλεγον
in Hebrew, in Latin, in Greek.　　Said

οὖν τῷ Πιλάτῳ οἱ ἀρχιερεῖς τῶν 'Ιουδαίων·
therefore - to Pilate the chief priests of the Jews:

μὴ γράφε· ὁ βασιλεὺς τῶν 'Ιουδαίων,
Write not: The king of the Jews,

ἀλλ' ὅτι ἐκεῖνος εἶπεν· βασιλεύς εἰμι
but that that man said: King I am

τῶν 'Ιουδαίων.　**22** ἀπεκρίθη ὁ Πιλᾶτος·
of the Jews.　　Answered - Pilate:

ὁ γέγραφα, γέγραφα.　**23** Οἱ οὖν
What I have written, I have written.　Therefore the

στρατιῶται, ὅτε ἐσταύρωσαν τὸν 'Ιησοῦν,
soldiers, when they crucified - Jesus,

ἔλαβον τὰ ἱμάτια αὐτοῦ καὶ ἐποίησαν
took the garments of him and made

τέσσερα μέρη, ἑκάστῳ στρατιώτῃ μέρος,
four parts, to each soldier a part,

καὶ τὸν χιτῶνα. ἦν δὲ ὁ χιτὼν ἄρραφος,
and the tunic. Now was the tunic seamless,

ἐκ τῶν ἄνωθεν ὑφαντὸς δι' ὅλου.　**24** εἶπαν
from the top woven throughout.　They said

οὖν πρὸς ἀλλήλους· μὴ σχίσωμεν αὐτόν,
therefore to one another: Let us not tear it,

ἀλλὰ λάχωμεν περὶ αὐτοῦ τίνος ἔσται·
but let us cast lots about it of whom it shall be;

ἵνα ἡ γραφὴ πληρωθῇ· διεμερίσαντο τὰ
that the scripture might be fulfilled: They parted the

ἱμάτιά μου ἑαυτοῖς καὶ ἐπὶ τὸν ἱματισμόν
garments of me to themselves and over the raiment

μου ἔβαλον κλῆρον. Οἱ μὲν οὖν στρατιῶται
of me they cast a lot. ²The -ᵃtherefore ²soldiers

ταῦτα ἐποίησαν.　**25** εἱστήκεισαν δὲ παρὰ
¹these things did.　　²there stood ¹But by

τῷ σταυρῷ τοῦ 'Ιησοῦ ἡ μήτηρ αὐτοῦ
the cross of Jesus the mother of him

καὶ ἡ ἀδελφὴ τῆς μητρὸς αὐτοῦ, Μαρία
and the sister of the mother of him, Mary

ἡ τοῦ Κλωπᾶ καὶ Μαρία ἡ Μαγδαληνή.
the [?wife] - of Clopas and Mary the Magdalene.

26 'Ιησοῦς οὖν ἰδὼν τὴν μητέρα καὶ
Jesus therefore seeing the(his) mother and

τὸν μαθητὴν παρεστῶτα ὃν ἠγάπα, λέγει
the disciple standing by whom he loved, says

τῇ μητρί· γύναι, ἴδε ὁ υἱός σου.
to the(his) mother: Woman, behold[,] the son of thee.

27 εἶτα λέγει τῷ μαθητῇ· ἴδε ἡ μήτηρ
Then he says to the disciple: Behold[,] the mother

19Pilate had a notice prepared and fastened to the cross. It read: JESUS OF NAZARETH, THE KING OF THE JEWS. 20Many of the Jews read this sign, for the place where Jesus was crucified was near the city, and the sign was written in Aramaic, Latin and Greek. 21The chief priests of the Jews protested to Pilate, "Do not write 'The King of the Jews,' but that this man claimed to be king of the Jews."

22Pilate answered, "What I have written, I have written."

23When the soldiers crucified Jesus, they took his clothes, dividing them into four shares, one for each of them, with the undergarment remaining. This garment was seamless, woven in one piece from top to bottom.

24"Let's not tear it," they said to one another. "Let's decide by lot who will get it."

This happened that the scripture might be fulfilled which said,

"They divided my garments among them
and cast lots for my clothing." ᵇ

So this is what the soldiers did.

25Near the cross of Jesus stood his mother, his mother's sister, Mary the wife of Clopas, and Mary Magdalene. 26When Jesus saw his mother there, and the disciple whom he loved standing nearby, he said to his mother, "Dear woman, here is your son," 27and to the disciple, "Here is your mother." From that time

---

ʳ Gr., *khiton*, the garment worn next to the skin

* μέν is scarcely translatable. But note the δέ in ver. 25: John contrasts two groups—the soldiers and the women.

ᵇ24 Psalm 22:18

hour the disciple took her into his own *household*.

28After this, Jesus, knowing that all things had already been accomplished, in order that the Scripture might be fulfilled, *said, "I am thirsty."

29A jar full of sour wine was standing there; so they put a sponge full of the sour wine upon *a branch of* hyssop, and brought it up to His mouth.

30When Jesus therefore had received the sour wine, He said, "It is finished!" And He bowed His head, and gave up His spirit.

Care of the Body of Jesus

31The Jews therefore, because it was the day of preparation, so that the bodies should not remain on the cross on the Sabbath (for that Sabbath was a high *day*), asked Pilate that their legs might be broken, and *that* they might be taken away.

32The soldiers therefore came, and broke the legs of the first man, and of the other man who was crucified with Him;

33but coming to Jesus, when they saw that He was already dead, they did not break His legs;

34but one of the soldiers pierced His side with a spear, and immediately there came out blood and water.

35And he who has seen has borne witness, and his witness is true; and he knows that he is telling the truth, so that you also may believe.

36For these things came to pass, that the Scripture might be fulfilled, "Not a bone of Him shall be broken."

37And again another Scripture says, "They shall look on Him whom they pierced."

38And after these things Joseph of Arimathea, being

Middle column (interlinear)

σου. καὶ ἀπ' ἐκείνης τῆς ὥρας ἔλαβεν
of thee. And from that hour took
ὁ μαθητὴς αὐτὴν εἰς τὰ ἴδια. 28 Μετὰ
the disciple her to his own [home]. † After
τοῦτο εἰδὼς ὁ Ἰησοῦς ὅτι ἤδη πάντα
this knowing Jesus that now all things
τετέλεσται, ἵνα τελειωθῇ ἡ γραφή, λέγει·
have been finished, that might be fulfilled the scripture, says:
διψῶ. 29 σκεῦος ἔκειτο ὄξους μεστόν·
I thirst. A vessel was set of vinegar full;
σπόγγον οὖν μεστὸν τοῦ ὄξους ὑσσώπῳ
a sponge therefore full of the vinegar a hyssop §
περιθέντες προσήνεγκαν αὐτοῦ τῷ · στόματι.
putting round they brought [it] to of him the mouth.
30 ὅτε οὖν ἔλαβεν τὸ ὄξος [ὁ] Ἰησοῦς
When therefore took the vinegar Jesus
εἶπεν· τετέλεσται, καὶ κλίνας τὴν κεφαλὴν
he said: It has been finished, and inclining the(his) head
παρέδωκεν τὸ πνεῦμα.
delivered up the(his) spirit.
31 Οἱ οὖν Ἰουδαῖοι, ἐπεὶ παρασκευὴ
The therefore Jews, since preparation
ἦν, ἵνα μὴ μείνῃ ἐπὶ τοῦ σταυροῦ τὰ
it was, that might not remain on the cross the
σώματα ἐν τῷ σαββάτῳ, ἦν γὰρ μεγάλη
bodies on the sabbath, for was great
ἡ ἡμέρα ἐκείνου τοῦ σαββάτου, ἠρώτησαν
the day of that sabbath, they asked
τὸν Πιλᾶτον ἵνα κατεαγῶσιν αὐτῶν τὰ
Pilate that might be broken of them the
σκέλη καὶ ἀρθῶσιν. 32 ἦλθον οὖν οἱ
legs and they might be taken. Came therefore the
στρατιῶται, καὶ τοῦ μὲν πρώτου κατέαξαν
soldiers, and of the first broke
τὰ σκέλη καὶ τοῦ ἄλλου τοῦ
the legs and of the other
συσταυρωθέντος αὐτῷ· 33 ἐπὶ δὲ τὸν
crucified with him; on but the
Ἰησοῦν ἐλθόντες, ὡς εἶδον ἤδη αὐτὸν
Jesus coming, when they saw already him
τεθνηκότα, οὐ κατέαξαν αὐτοῦ τὰ σκέλη,
to have died, they did not break of him the legs,
34 ἀλλ' εἷς τῶν στρατιωτῶν λόγχῃ αὐτοῦ
but one of the soldiers with a lance of him
τὴν πλευρὰν ἔνυξεν, καὶ ἐξῆλθεν εὐθὺς αἷμα
the side pricked, and there came immediately blood
καὶ ὕδωρ. 35 καὶ ὁ ἑωρακὼς μεμαρτύρηκεν,
and water. And the [one] having seen has witnessed,
καὶ ἀληθινὴ αὐτοῦ ἐστιν ἡ μαρτυρία,
and true of him is the witness,
καὶ ἐκεῖνος οἶδεν ὅτι ἀληθῆ λέγει, ἵνα
and that one knows that truly he says, that
καὶ ὑμεῖς πιστεύητε. 36 ἐγένετο γὰρ
also ye may believe. For happened
ταῦτα ἵνα ἡ γραφὴ πληρωθῇ· ὀστοῦν
these things that the scripture might be fulfilled: A bone
οὐ συντριβήσεται αὐτοῦ. 37 καὶ πάλιν
shall not be broken of him. And again
ἑτέρα γραφὴ λέγει· ὄψονται εἰς ὃν
another scripture says: They shall look at [him] whom
ἐξεκέντησαν. 38 Μετὰ δὲ ταῦτα ἠρώτησεν
they pierced. Now after these things asked
τὸν Πιλᾶτον Ἰωσὴφ ἀπὸ Ἀριμαθαίας,
Pilate Joseph from Arimathæa,

§ It has been suggested that ὑσσώπῳ is a graphic error for ὑσσῷ (*pilum*), pike; but *cf.* Mat. 27. 48.

* See note on 19. 24. Here see ver. 33—two actions contrasted.

The Death of Jesus

on, this disciple took her into his home.

28Later, knowing that all was now completed, and so that the Scripture would be fulfilled, Jesus said, "I thirst." 29A jar of wine vinegar was there, so they soaked a sponge in it, put the sponge on a stalk of the hyssop plant, and lifted it to Jesus' lips. 30When he had received the drink, Jesus said, "It is finished." With that, he bowed his head and gave up his spirit.

31Now it was the day of Preparation, and the next day was to be a special Sabbath. Because the Jews did not want the bodies left on the crosses during the Sabbath, they asked Pilate to have the legs broken and the bodies taken down. 32The soldiers therefore came and broke the legs of the first man who had been crucified with Jesus, and then those of the other. 33But when they came to Jesus and found that he was already dead, they did not break his legs. 34Instead, one of the soldiers pierced Jesus' side with a spear, bringing a sudden flow of blood and water. 35The man who saw it has given testimony, and his testimony is true. He knows that he tells the truth, and he testifies so that you also may believe. 36These things happened so that the scripture would be fulfilled: "Not one of his bones will be broken,"[c] 37and, as another scripture says, "They will look on the one they have pierced."[d]

The Burial of Jesus

38Later, Joseph of Arimathea asked Pilate for the

c36 Exodus 12:46; Num. 9:12; Psalm 34:20
d37 Zech. 12:10

a disciple of Jesus, but a secret *one*, for fear of the Jews, asked Pilate that he might take away the body of Jesus; and Pilate granted permission. He came therefore, and took away His body.

39And Nicodemus came also, who had first come to Him by night; bringing a mixture of myrrh and aloes, about a hundred pounds *weight*.

40And so they took the body of Jesus, and bound it in linen wrappings with the spices, as is the burial custom of the Jews.

41Now in the place where He was crucified there was a garden; and in the garden a new tomb, in which no one had yet been laid.

42Therefore on account of the Jewish day of preparation, because the tomb was nearby, they laid Jesus there.

ὢν   μαθητὴς   [τοῦ]   Ἰησοῦ   κεκρυμμένος
⁴being ⁵a disciple –   ⁶of Jesus ⁸having been hidden

δὲ   διὰ   τὸν   φόβον   τῶν   Ἰουδαίων,   ἵνα
⁷but ⁹because ¹⁰the ¹¹fear ¹²of the ¹³Jews,   that

ἄρῃ   τὸ   σῶμα   τοῦ   Ἰησοῦ·   καὶ
he might take the body   –   of Jesus; and

ἐπέτρεψεν   ὁ   Πιλᾶτος.   ἦλθεν   οὖν   καὶ   ἦρεν
allowed   –   Pilate.   He came there- and took
                                fore

τὸ   σῶμα   αὐτοῦ.   39 ἦλθεν   δὲ   καὶ   Νικόδημος,
the body   of him.   And came also   Nicodemus,

ὁ   ἐλθὼν   πρὸς   αὐτὸν   νυκτὸς   τὸ   πρῶτον,
the [one] having come to   him of (by) night at first,†

φέρων   μίγμα   σμύρνης   καὶ   ἀλόης   ὡς
bearing a mixture of myrrh and   aloes   about

λίτρας   ἑκατόν.   40 ἔλαβον   οὖν   τὸ   σῶμα
pounds   a hundred.   They took there- the body
                                  fore

τοῦ   Ἰησοῦ   καὶ   ἔδησαν   αὐτὸ   ὀθονίοις
 –   of Jesus and   bound   it   in sheets

μετὰ   τῶν   ἀρωμάτων,   καθὼς   ἔθος   ἐστὶν
with   the   spices,   as   custom   is

τοῖς   Ἰουδαίοις   ἐνταφιάζειν.   41 ἦν   δὲ
with the Jews   to bury.   Now there was

ἐν   τῷ   τόπῳ   ὅπου   ἐσταυρώθη   κῆπος,
in   the place   where   he was crucified a garden,

καὶ   ἐν   τῷ   κήπῳ   μνημεῖον   καινόν,   ἐν
and   in the garden   tomb   a new,   in

ᾧ   οὐδέπω   οὐδεὶς   ἦν   τεθειμένος·   42 ἐκεῖ
which never yet no(any) was having been put;   there
                 one

οὖν   διὰ   τὴν   παρασκευὴν   τῶν   Ἰουδαίων,
therefore because of the preparation   of the Jews,

ὅτι   ἐγγὺς   ἦν   τὸ   μνημεῖον,   ἔθηκαν   τὸν
because   near   was the   tomb,   they put   –

Ἰησοῦν.
Jesus.

---

body of Jesus. Now Joseph was a disciple of Jesus, but secretly because he feared the Jews. With Pilate's permission, he came and took the body away. 39He was accompanied by Nicodemus, the man who earlier had visited Jesus at night. Nicodemus brought a mixture of myrrh and aloes, about seventy-five pounds.ᵉ 40Taking Jesus' body, the two of them wrapped it, with the spices, in strips of linen. This was in accordance with Jewish burial customs. 41At the place where Jesus was crucified, there was a garden, and in the garden a new tomb, in which no one had ever been laid. 42Because it was the Jewish day of Preparation and since the tomb was nearby, they laid Jesus there.

Chapter 20   *Chapter 20*

The Empty Tomb   *The Empty Tomb*

NOW on the first *day* of the week Mary Magdalene *came early to the tomb, while it *was still dark, and *saw the stone *already* taken away from the tomb.

2And so she *ran and *came to Simon Peter, and to the other disciple whom Jesus loved, and *said to them, "They have taken away the Lord out of the tomb, and we do not know where they have laid Him."

3Peter therefore went forth, and the other disciple, and they were going to the tomb.

4And the two were running together; and the other disciple ran ahead faster than Peter, and came to the tomb first;

5and stooping and look-

---

20 Τῇ   δὲ   μιᾷ   τῶν   σαββάτων   Μαρία
   Now on the one(first) [day] of the week   Mary

ἡ   Μαγδαληνὴ   ἔρχεται   πρωῒ   σκοτίας   ἔτι
the Magdalene   comes   early darkness   yet
                                   =while it was yet dark,

οὔσης   εἰς   τὸ   μνημεῖον,   καὶ   βλέπει   τὸν
beingᵃ   to   the   tomb,   and   sees   the

λίθον   ἠρμένον   ἐκ   τοῦ   μνημείου.
stone   having been taken out of the   tomb.

2 τρέχει   οὖν   καὶ   ἔρχεται   πρὸς   Σίμωνα
  She runs therefore and comes   to   Simon

Πέτρον   καὶ   πρὸς   τὸν   ἄλλον   μαθητὴν   ὃν
Peter   and   to   the   other   disciple   whom

ἐφίλει   ὁ   Ἰησοῦς,   καὶ   λέγει   αὐτοῖς·   ἦραν
ᵇloved   –   ¹Jesus,   and   says   to them: They
                                                took

τὸν   κύριον   ἐκ   τοῦ   μνημείου,   καὶ   οὐκ   οἴδαμεν
the   Lord   out of the tomb,   and   we do not know

ποῦ   ἔθηκαν   αὐτόν.   3 Ἐξῆλθεν   οὖν   ὁ
where they put him.   Went forth therefore –

Πέτρος   καὶ   ὁ   ἄλλος   μαθητής,   καὶ   ἤρχοντο
Peter   and   the other   disciple,   and   came

εἰς   τὸ   μνημεῖον.   4 ἔτρεχον   δὲ   οἱ   δύο
to   the   tomb.   And ran   the   two

ὁμοῦ·   καὶ   ὁ   ἄλλος   μαθητὴς   προέδραμεν
together; and   the other   disciple   ran before

τάχιον   τοῦ   Πέτρου   καὶ   ἦλθεν   πρῶτος
more quickly [than] –   Peter   and   came   first

εἰς   τὸ   μνημεῖον,   5 καὶ   παρακύψας   βλέπει
to   the   tomb,   and   stooping   sees

EARLY on the first day of the week, while it was still dark, Mary Magdalene went to the tomb and saw that the stone had been removed from the entrance. 2So she came running to Simon Peter and the other disciple, the one Jesus loved, and said, "They have taken the Lord out of the tomb, and we don't know where they have put him!"

3So Peter and the other disciple started for the tomb. 4Both were running, but the other disciple outran Peter and reached the tomb first. 5He bent over and looked in at the strips

ᵉ39 Greek *a hundred litrai* (about 34 kilograms)

ing in, he *saw the linen wrappings lying *there;* but he did not go in.
6Simon Peter therefore also *came, following him, and entered the tomb; and he *beheld the linen wrappings lying *there,*
7and the face-cloth, which had been on His head, not lying with the linen wrappings, but rolled up in a place by itself.
8So the other disciple who had first come to the tomb entered then also, and he saw and believed.
9For as yet they did not understand the Scripture, that He must rise again from the dead.
10So the disciples went away again to their own homes.
11But Mary was standing outside the tomb weeping; and so, as she wept, she stooped and looked into the tomb;
12and she *beheld two angels in white sitting, one at the head, and one at the feet, where the body of Jesus had been lying.
13And they *said to her, "Woman, why are you weeping?" She *said to them, "Because they have taken away my Lord, and I do not know where they have laid Him."
14When she had said this, she turned around, and *beheld Jesus standing *there,* and did not know that it was Jesus.
15Jesus *said to her, "Woman, why are you weeping? Whom are you seeking?" Supposing Him to be the gardener, she *said to Him, "Sir, if you have carried Him away, tell me where you have laid Him, and I will take Him away."
16Jesus *said to her, "Mary!" She *turned and *said to Him in Hebrew, "Rabboni!" (which means, Teacher).
17Jesus *said to her,

κείμενα τὰ ὀθόνια, οὐ μέντοι εἰσῆλθεν.
lying the sheets, not however he entered.
6 ἔρχεται οὖν καὶ Σίμων Πέτρος ἀκο-
Comes therefore also Simon Peter follow-
λουθῶν αὐτῷ, καὶ εἰσῆλθεν εἰς τὸ
ing him, and entered into the
μνημεῖον· καὶ θεωρεῖ τὰ ὀθόνια κείμενα,
tomb; and he beholds the sheets lying,
7 καὶ τὸ σουδάριον, ὃ ἦν ἐπὶ τῆς
and the kerchief, which was on the
κεφαλῆς αὐτοῦ, οὐ μετὰ τῶν ὀθονίων
head of him, not with the sheets
κείμενον ἀλλὰ χωρὶς ἐντετυλιγμένον εἰς
lying but apart having been wrapped up in
ἕνα τόπον. 8 τότε οὖν εἰσῆλθεν καὶ
one place. Then therefore entered also
ὁ ἄλλος μαθητὴς ὁ ἐλθὼν πρῶτος εἰς
the other disciple having come first to
τὸ μνημεῖον, καὶ εἶδεν καὶ ἐπίστευσεν·
the tomb, and he saw and believed;
9 οὐδέπω γὰρ ᾔδεισαν τὴν γραφήν, ὅτι
for not yet they knew the scripture, that
δεῖ αὐτὸν ἐκ νεκρῶν ἀναστῆναι.
it behoves him from [the] dead to rise again.
10 ἀπῆλθον οὖν πάλιν πρὸς αὐτοὺς οἱ
Went away therefore again to themselves* the
μαθηταί. 11 Μαρία δὲ εἰστήκει πρὸς
disciples. But Mary stood at
τῷ μνημείῳ ἔξω κλαίουσα. ὡς οὖν
the tomb outside weeping. As therefore
ἔκλαιεν, παρέκυψεν εἰς τὸ μνημεῖον,
she was weeping, she stooped into the tomb,
12 καὶ θεωρεῖ δύο ἀγγέλους ἐν λευκοῖς
and beholds two angels in white
καθεζομένους, ἕνα πρὸς τῇ κεφαλῇ καὶ
sitting, one at the head and
ἕνα πρὸς τοῖς ποσίν, ὅπου ἔκειτο τὸ
one at the feet, where lay the
σῶμα τοῦ Ἰησοῦ. 13 καὶ λέγουσιν αὐτῇ
body - of Jesus. And say to her
ἐκεῖνοι· γύναι, τί κλαίεις; λέγει αὐτοῖς
those: Woman, why weepest thou? She says to them[,]
ὅτι ἦραν τὸν κύριόν μου, καὶ οὐκ οἶδα
- They took the Lord of me, and I know not
ποῦ ἔθηκαν αὐτόν. 14 ταῦτα εἰποῦσα
where they put him. These things saying
ἐστράφη εἰς τὰ ὀπίσω, καὶ θεωρεῖ τὸν
she turned back,† and beholds -
Ἰησοῦν ἑστῶτα, καὶ οὐκ ᾔδει ὅτι Ἰησοῦς
Jesus standing, and knew not that Jesus
ἐστιν. 15 λέγει αὐτῇ Ἰησοῦς· γύναι,
it is(was). Says to her Jesus: Woman,
τί κλαίεις; τίνα ζητεῖς; ἐκείνη δοκοῦσα
why weepest thou? whom seekest thou? That one thinking
ὅτι ὁ κηπουρός ἐστιν, λέγει αὐτῷ· κύριε,
that the gardener it is(was), says to him: Sir,
εἰ σὺ ἐβάστασας αὐτόν, εἰπέ μοι ποῦ
if thou didst carry him, tell me where
ἔθηκας αὐτόν, κἀγὼ αὐτὸν ἀρῶ. 16 λέγει
thou didst put him, and I him will take. Says
αὐτῇ Ἰησοῦς· Μαριάμ. στραφεῖσα ἐκείνη
to her Jesus: Mary. Turning that one
λέγει αὐτῷ Ἑβραϊστί· ῥαββουνί (ὃ λέγεται
says to him in Hebrew: Rabboni (which is said
διδάσκαλε). 17 λέγει αὐτῇ Ἰησοῦς· μή
Teacher). Says to her Jesus: Not

* That is, to their own home; cf. 19. 27.

of linen lying there but did not go in. 6Then Simon Peter, who was behind him, arrived and went into the tomb. He saw the strips of linen lying there, 7as well as the burial cloth that had been around Jesus' head. The cloth was folded up by itself, separate from the linen. 8Finally the other disciple, who had reached the tomb first, also went inside. He saw and believed. 9(They still did not understand from Scripture that Jesus had to rise from the dead.)

Jesus Appears to Mary Magdalene

10Then the disciples went back to their homes, 11but Mary stood outside the tomb crying. As she wept, she bent over to look into the tomb 12and saw two angels in white, seated where Jesus' body had been, one at the head and the other at the foot.
13They asked her, "Woman, why are you crying?"
"They have taken my Lord away," she said, "and I don't know where they have put him." 14At this, she turned around and saw Jesus standing there, but she did not realize that it was Jesus.
15"Woman," he said, "why are you crying? Who is it you are looking for?"
Thinking he was the gardener, she said, "Sir, if you have carried him away, tell me where you have put him, and I will get him."
16Jesus said to her, "Mary."
She turned toward him and cried out in Aramaic, "Rabboni!" (which means Teacher).
17Jesus said, "Do not

"Stop clinging to Me, for I have not yet ascended to the Father; but go to My brethren, and say to them, 'I ascend to My Father and your Father, and My God and your God.' "
18Mary Magdalene *came, announcing to the disciples, "I have seen the Lord," and *that* He had said these things to her.

Jesus among His Disciples

19When therefore it was evening, on that day, the first *day* of the week, and when the doors were shut where the disciples were, for fear of the Jews, Jesus came and stood in their midst, "Peace *be* with you."
20And when He had said this, He showed them both His hands and His side. The disciples therefore rejoiced when they saw the Lord.
21Jesus therefore said to them again, "Peace *be* with you; as the Father has sent Me, I also send you."
22And when He had said this, He breathed on them, and *said to them, "Receive the Holy Spirit.
23"If you forgive the sins of any, *their sins* have been forgiven them; if you retain the *sins* of any, they have been retained."
24But Thomas, one of the twelve, called Didymus, was not with them when Jesus came.
25The other disciples therefore were saying to him, "We have seen the Lord!" But he said to them, "Unless I shall see in His hands the imprint of the nails, and put my finger into the place of the nails, and put my hand into His side, I will not believe."

μου ἅπτου, οὔπω γὰρ ἀναβέβηκα πρὸς
me touch, for not yet have I ascended to
τὸν πατέρα· πορεύου δὲ πρὸς τοὺς
the Father; but go thou to the
ἀδελφούς μου καὶ εἰπὲ αὐτοῖς· ἀναβαίνω
brothers of me and tell them: I ascend
πρὸς τὸν πατέρα μου καὶ πατέρα ὑμῶν
to the Father of me and Father of you
καὶ θεόν μου καὶ θεὸν ὑμῶν. 18 ἔρχεται
and God of me and God of you. Comes
Μαριὰμ ἡ Μαγδαληνὴ ἀγγέλλουσα τοῖς
Mary the Magdalene announcing to the
μαθηταῖς ὅτι ἑώρακα τὸν κύριον, καὶ
disciples[,] - I have seen the Lord, and
ταῦτα εἶπεν αὐτῇ.
these things he said to her.

19 Οὔσης οὖν ὀψίας τῇ ἡμέρᾳ ἐκείνῃ
Being therefore early evening* - day on that
=Therefore when it was early evening
τῇ μιᾷ σαββάτων, καὶ τῶν θυρῶν
the one(first) of the week, and the doors
κεκλεισμένων ὅπου ἦσαν οἱ μαθηταὶ διὰ
having been shut* where were the disciples because of
τὸν φόβον τῶν Ἰουδαίων, ἦλθεν ὁ Ἰησοῦς
the fear of the Jews, came - Jesus
καὶ ἔστη εἰς τὸ μέσον, καὶ λέγει αὐτοῖς·
and stood in the midst, and says to them:
εἰρήνη ὑμῖν. 20 καὶ τοῦτο εἰπὼν ἔδειξεν
Peace to you. And this saying he showed
καὶ τὰς χεῖρας καὶ τὴν πλευρὰν αὐτοῖς.
both the(his) hands and the(his) side to them.
ἐχάρησαν οὖν οἱ μαθηταὶ ἰδόντες τὸν
Rejoiced therefore the disciples seeing the
κύριον. 21 εἶπεν οὖν αὐτοῖς [ὁ Ἰησοῦς]
Lord. Said therefore to them [- Jesus]
πάλιν· εἰρήνη ὑμῖν· καθὼς ἀπέσταλκέν
again: Peace to you; as has sent
με ὁ πατήρ, κἀγὼ πέμπω ὑμᾶς. 22 καὶ
me the Father, I also send you. And
τοῦτο εἰπὼν ἐνεφύσησεν καὶ λέγει αὐτοῖς·
this saying he breathed in and says to them:
λάβετε πνεῦμα ἅγιον. 23 ἄν τινων
Receive ye Spirit Holy. Of whomever
ἀφῆτε τὰς ἁμαρτίας, ἀφέωνται αὐτοῖς·
ye forgive the sins, they have been to them;
forgiven
ἄν τινων κρατῆτε, κεκράτηνται.
of whomever ye hold, they have been held.

24 Θωμᾶς δὲ εἷς ἐκ τῶν δώδεκα,
But Thomas one of the twelve,
ὁ λεγόμενος Δίδυμος, οὐκ ἦν μετ᾿ αὐτῶν
- being called Twin, was not with them
ὅτε ἦλθεν Ἰησοῦς. 25 ἔλεγον οὖν αὐτῷ
when came Jesus. Said therefore to him
οἱ ἄλλοι μαθηταί· ἑωράκαμεν τὸν κύριον.
the other disciples: We have seen the Lord.
ὁ δὲ εἶπεν αὐτοῖς· ἐὰν μὴ ἴδω ἐν
But he said to them: Unless I see in
ταῖς χερσὶν αὐτοῦ τὸν τύπον τῶν ἥλων
the hands of him the mark of the nails
καὶ βάλω τὸν δάκτυλόν μου εἰς τὸν
and put the finger of me into the
τόπον τῶν ἥλων καὶ βάλω μου τὴν
place of the nails and put of me the
χεῖρα εἰς τὴν πλευρὰν αὐτοῦ, οὐ μὴ
hand into the side of him, by no means

hold on to me, for I have not yet returned to the Father. Go instead to my brothers and tell them, 'I am returning to my Father and your Father, to my God and your God.' "
18Mary Magdalene went to the disciples with the news: "I have seen the Lord!" And she told them that he had said these things to her.

Jesus Appears to His Disciples

19On the evening of that first day of the week, when the disciples were together, with the doors locked for fear of the Jews, Jesus came and stood among them and said, "Peace be with you!" 20After he said this, he showed them his hands and side. The disciples were overjoyed when they saw the Lord.
21Again Jesus said, "Peace be with you! As the Father has sent me, I am sending you." 22And with that he breathed on them and said, "Receive the Holy Spirit. 23If you forgive anyone his sins, they are forgiven; if you do not forgive them, they are not forgiven."

Jesus Appears to Thomas

24Now Thomas (called Didymus), one of the Twelve, was not with the disciples when Jesus came. 25So the other disciples told him, "We have seen the Lord!"
But he said to them, "Unless I see the nail marks in his hands and put my finger where the nails were, and put my hand into his side, I will not believe it."

26And after eight days again His disciples were inside, and Thomas with them. Jesus *came, the doors having been shut, and stood in their midst, and said, "Peace be with you."

27Then He *said to Thomas, "Reach here your finger, and see My hands; and reach here your hand, and put it into My side; and be not unbelieving, but believing."

28Thomas answered and said to Him, "My Lord and my God!"

29Jesus *said to him, "Because you have seen Me, have you believed? Blessed are they who did not see, and yet believed."

Why This Gospel Was Written

30Many other signs therefore Jesus also performed in the presence of the disciples, which are not written in this book;

31but these have been written that you may believe that Jesus is the Christ, the Son of God; and that believing you may have life in His name.

πιστεύσω.   26 Καὶ   μεθ'   ἡμέρας   ὀκτὼ
will I believe.   And   after   days   eight
πάλιν   ἦσαν   ἔσω   οἱ   μαθηταὶ   αὐτοῦ,   καὶ
again   were   within   the   disciples   of him,   and
Θωμᾶς   μετ'   αὐτῶν.   ἔρχεται   ὁ   ᾿Ιησοῦς
Thomas   with   them.   Comes   –   Jesus
τῶν   θυρῶν   κεκλεισμένων,   καὶ   ἔστη   εἰς
the   doors   having been shut[a],   and   stood   in
τὸ   μέσον   καὶ   εἶπεν·   εἰρήνη   ὑμῖν.   27 εἶτα
the   midst   and   said :   Peace   to you.   Then
λέγει   τῷ   Θωμᾷ·   φέρε   τὸν   δάκτυλόν
he says   –   to Thomas :   Bring   the   finger
σου   ὧδε   καὶ   ἴδε   τὰς   χεῖράς   μου,   καὶ
of thee   here   and   see   the   hands   of me,   and
φέρε   τὴν   χεῖρά   σου   καὶ   βάλε   εἰς   τὴν
bring   the   hand   of thee   and   put   into   the
πλευράν   μου,   καὶ   μὴ   γίνου   ἄπιστος
side   of me,   and   be not   faithless
ἀλλὰ   πιστός.   28 ἀπεκρίθη   Θωμᾶς   καὶ
but   faithful.   Answered   Thomas   and
εἶπεν   αὐτῷ·   ὁ   κύριός   μου   καὶ   ὁ   θεός
said   to him :   The   Lord   of me   and   the   God
μου.   29 λέγει   αὐτῷ   ὁ   ᾿Ιησοῦς·   ὅτι
of me.   Says   to him   –   Jesus :   Because
ἑώρακάς   με,   πεπίστευκας;   μακάριοι   οἱ
thou hast seen me,   hast thou believed?   blessed the [ones]
μὴ   ἰδόντες   καὶ   πιστεύσαντες.
not   seeing   and §   believing.
30   Πολλὰ   μὲν   οὖν   καὶ   ἄλλα   σημεῖα
Many   –*   therefore   and   other   signs
ἐποίησεν   ὁ   ᾿Ιησοῦς   ἐνώπιον   τῶν   μαθητῶν,
did   –   Jesus   before   the   disciples,
ἃ   οὐκ   ἔστιν   γεγραμμένα   ἐν   τῷ   βιβλίῳ
which is(are) not   *having been* written   in   –   roll
τούτῳ·   31 ταῦτα   δὲ   γέγραπται   ἵνα
this;   but these*   has(ve) been written   that
πιστεύητε   ὅτι   ᾿Ιησοῦς   ἐστιν   ὁ   χριστὸς   ὁ
ye may believe   that   Jesus   is   the   Christ   the
υἱὸς   τοῦ   θεοῦ,   καὶ   ἵνα   πιστεύοντες   ζωὴν
Son   –   of God,   and   that   believing   life
ἔχητε   ἐν   τῷ   ὀνόματι   αὐτοῦ.
ye may have in   the   name   of him.

♠ 26A week later his disciples were in the house again, and Thomas was with them. Though the doors were locked, Jesus came and stood among them and said, "Peace be with you!" 27Then he said to Thomas, "Put your finger here; see my hands. Reach out your hand and put it into my side. Stop doubting and believe."

28Thomas said to him, "My Lord and my God!"

29Then Jesus told him, "Because you have seen me, you have believed; blessed are those who have not seen and yet have believed."

30Jesus did many other miraculous signs in the presence of his disciples, which are not recorded in this book. 31But these are written that you may[f] believe that Jesus is the Christ, the Son of God, and that by believing you may have life in his name.

Chapter 21

Jesus Appears at the Sea of Galilee

AFTER these things Jesus manifested Himself again to the disciples at the Sea of Tiberias, and He manifested *Himself* in this way.

2There were together Simon Peter, and Thomas called Didymus, and Nathanael of Cana in Galilee, and the *sons* of Zebedee, and two others of His disciples.

3Simon Peter *said to them, "I am going fishing." They *said to him, "We will also come with you." They went out, and got into the boat; and that

---

21 Μετὰ   ταῦτα   ἐφανέρωσεν   ἑαυτὸν   πάλιν
After   these things   manifested   himself   again
᾿Ιησοῦς   τοῖς   μαθηταῖς   ἐπὶ   τῆς   θαλάσσης
Jesus   to the   disciples   on   the   sea
τῆς   Τιβεριάδος·   ἐφανέρωσεν   δὲ   οὕτως.
–   of Tiberias;   and he manifested [himself]   thus.
2   ἦσαν   ὁμοῦ   Σίμων   Πέτρος   καὶ   Θωμᾶς
There were together   Simon   Peter   and   Thomas
ὁ   λεγόμενος   Δίδυμος   καὶ   Ναθαναὴλ   ὁ
–   *being* called   Twin   and   Nathanael   –
ἀπὸ   Κανὰ   τῆς   Γαλιλαίας   καὶ   οἱ   τοῦ
from   Cana   –   of Galilee   and   the [sons] –
Ζεβεδαίου   καὶ   ἄλλοι   ἐκ   τῶν   μαθητῶν
of Zebedee   and   others   of   the   disciples
αὐτοῦ   δύο.   3 λέγει   αὐτοῖς   Σίμων   Πέτρος·
of him   two.   Says   to them   Simon   Peter :
ὑπάγω   ἁλιεύειν.   λέγουσιν   αὐτῷ·   ἐρχόμεθα
I am going   to fish.   They say   to him :   Are coming
καὶ   ἡμεῖς   σὺν   σοί.   ἐξῆλθον   καὶ   ἐνέβησαν
also   we   with thee.   They went forth and   embarked
εἰς   τὸ   πλοῖον,   καὶ   ἐν   ἐκείνῃ   τῇ   νυκτὶ
in   the   boat,   and   in   that   –   night

* See note on 19. 24 and 32.

§ καὶ sometimes = and yet ; see 5. 40 ; 8. 55 ; 9. 30 ; 16. 32 ; 17. 11.

Chapter 21

Jesus and the Miraculous Catch of Fish

AFTERWARD Jesus appeared again to his disciples, by the Sea of Tiberias.[g] It happened this way: 2Simon Peter, Thomas (called Didymus), Nathanael from Cana in Galilee, the sons of Zebedee, and two other disciples were together. 3"I'm going out to fish," Simon Peter told them, and they said, "We'll go with you." So they went out and got into the boat, but that night they

night they caught nothing.
⁴But when the day was now breaking, Jesus stood on the beach; yet the disciples did not know that it was Jesus.
⁵Jesus therefore *said to them, "Children, you do not have any fish, do you?" They answered Him, "No."
⁶And He said to them, "Cast the net on the right-hand side of the boat, and you will find *a catch.*" They cast therefore, and then they were not able to haul it in because of the great number of fish.
⁷That disciple therefore whom Jesus loved *said to Peter, "It is the Lord." And so when Simon Peter heard that it was the Lord, he put his outer garment on (for he was stripped *for work*), and threw himself into the sea.
⁸But the other disciples came in the little boat, for they were not far from the land, but about one hundred yards away, dragging the net *full* of fish.
⁹And so when they got out upon the land, they *saw a charcoal fire *already* laid, and fish placed on it, and bread.
¹⁰Jesus *said to them, "Bring some of the fish which you have now caught."
¹¹Simon Peter went up, and drew the net to land, full of large fish, a hundred and fifty-three; and although there were so many, the net was not torn.

Jesus Provides

¹²Jesus *said to them, "Come *and* have breakfast." None of the disciples ventured to question Him, "Who are You?" knowing that it was the Lord.
¹³Jesus *came and *took the bread, and *gave them, and the fish likewise.
¹⁴This is now the third time that Jesus was manifested to the disciples, after He was raised from the

---

ἐπίασαν οὐδέν. 4 πρωΐας δὲ ἤδη γινομένης
they caught nothing.   Early morning but now   becomingᵃ
= But when it became early morning

ἔστη Ἰησοῦς εἰς τὸν αἰγιαλόν· οὐ μέντοι
stood Jesus in(on) the   shore;   not however

ᾔδεισαν οἱ μαθηταὶ ὅτι Ἰησοῦς ἐστιν.
knew   the disciples that Jesus it is(was).

5 λέγει οὖν αὐτοῖς Ἰησοῦς· παιδία, μή
Says therefore to them Jesus: Children, not

τι προσφάγιον ἔχετε; ἀπεκρίθησαν αὐτῷ·
any   fish   have ye? They answered   him:

οὔ. 6 ὁ δὲ εἶπεν αὐτοῖς· βάλετε εἰς τὰ
No.   So he   said to them: Cast   in the

δεξιὰ μέρη τοῦ πλοίου τὸ δίκτυον, καὶ
right parts of the boat   the   net,   and

εὑρήσετε. ἔβαλον οὖν, καὶ οὐκέτι αὐτὸ
ye will find. They cast therefore, and ¹no longer ⁴it

ἑλκύσαι ἴσχυον ἀπὸ τοῦ πλήθους τῶν
²to drag ²were they able from the   multitude of the

ἰχθύων. 7 λέγει οὖν ὁ μαθητὴς ἐκεῖνος
fishes.   Says therefore - disciple   that

ὃν ἠγάπα ὁ Ἰησοῦς τῷ Πέτρῳ· ὁ κύριός
whom ²loved - ¹Jesus - to Peter: The Lord

ἐστιν. Σίμων οὖν Πέτρος, ἀκούσας ὅτι
it is. ³Simon ¹therefore ²Peter,   hearing that

ὁ κύριός ἐστιν, τὸν ἐπενδύτην διεζώσατο,
the Lord it is(was),³[with]the ²coat ¹girded himself,

ἦν γὰρ γυμνός, καὶ ἔβαλεν ἑαυτὸν εἰς
for he was naked, and   threw himself into

τὴν θάλασσαν· 8 οἱ δὲ ἄλλοι μαθηταὶ
the   sea;   but the other disciples

τῷ πλοιαρίῳ ἦλθον, οὐ γὰρ ἦσαν μακρὰν
in the little boat came, for not they were far

ἀπὸ τῆς γῆς ἀλλὰ ὡς ἀπὸ πηχῶν
from the land but about from cubits

διακοσίων, σύροντες τὸ δίκτυον τῶν ἰχθύων.
two hundred, dragging the net of the fishes.

9 ὡς οὖν ἀπέβησαν εἰς τὴν γῆν, βλέπουσιν
When therefore they disembarked onto the land, they see

ἀνθρακιὰν κειμένην καὶ ὀψάριον ἐπικείμενον
a coal fire lying and a fish lying on

καὶ ἄρτον. 10 λέγει αὐτοῖς ὁ Ἰησοῦς·
and bread.   Says to them - Jesus:

ἐνέγκατε ἀπὸ τῶν ὀψαρίων ὧν ἐπιάσατε
Bring from the fishes which ye caught

νῦν. 11 ἀνέβη Σίμων Πέτρος καὶ εἵλκυσεν
now.   Went up Simon Peter and dragged

τὸ δίκτυον εἰς τὴν γῆν μεστὸν ἰχθύων
the net to the land full fishes

μεγάλων ἑκατὸν πεντήκοντα τριῶν· καὶ
of great a hundred fifty   three; and

τοσούτων ὄντων οὐκ ἐσχίσθη τὸ δίκτυον.
so many beingᵃ was not torn the net.

12 λέγει αὐτοῖς ὁ Ἰησοῦς· δεῦτε ἀριστήσατε.
Says to them - Jesus: Come breakfast ye.

οὐδεὶς ἐτόλμα τῶν μαθητῶν ἐξετάσαι
No one dared of the disciples to question

αὐτόν· σὺ τίς εἶ; εἰδότες ὅτι ὁ κύριός
him: Thou who art? knowing that the Lord

ἐστιν. 13 ἔρχεται Ἰησοῦς καὶ λαμβάνει
it is(was).   Comes Jesus and takes

τὸν ἄρτον καὶ δίδωσιν αὐτοῖς, καὶ τὸ
the bread and gives to them, and the

ὀψάριον ὁμοίως. 14 τοῦτο ἤδη τρίτον
fish likewise.   This [was] now [the] third [time]
[that]

ἐφανερώθη Ἰησοῦς τοῖς μαθηταῖς ἐγερθεὶς
¹was manifested ¹Jesus to the disciples raised

---

caught nothing.
⁴Early in the morning, Jesus stood on the shore, but the disciples did not realize that it was Jesus.
⁵He called out to them, "Friends, haven't you any fish?"
"No," they answered.
⁶He said, "Throw your net on the right side of the boat and you will find some." When they did, they were unable to haul the net in because of the large number of fish.
⁷Then the disciple whom Jesus loved said to Peter, "It is the Lord!" As soon as Simon Peter heard him say, "It is the Lord," he wrapped his outer garment around him (for he had taken it off) and jumped into the water. ⁸The other disciples followed in the boat, towing the net full of fish, for they were not far from shore, about a hundred yards.ʰ ⁹When they landed, they saw a fire of burning coals there with fish on it, and some bread.
¹⁰Jesus said to them, "Bring some of the fish you have just caught."
¹¹Simon Peter climbed aboard and dragged the net ashore. It was full of large fish, 153, but even with so many the net was not torn. ¹²Jesus said to them, "Come and have breakfast." None of the disciples dared ask him, "Who are you?" They knew it was the Lord. ¹³Jesus came, took the bread and gave it to them, and did the same with the fish. ¹⁴This was now the third time Jesus appeared to his disciples after he was raised from the dead.

ʰ8 Greek *about two hundred cubits* (about 90 meters)

The Love Motivation

15So when they had finished breakfast, Jesus *said to Simon Peter, "Simon, *son* of John, do you love Me more than these?" He *said to Him, "Yes, Lord; You know that I love You." He *said to him, "Tend My lambs."

16He *said to him again a second time, "Simon, *son* of John, do you love Me?" He *said to Him, "Yes, Lord; You know that I love You." He *said to him, "Shepherd My sheep."

17He *said to him the third time, "Simon, *son* of John, do you love Me?" Peter was grieved because He said to him the third time, "Do you love Me?" And he said to Him, "Lord, You know all things; You know that I love You." Jesus *said to him, "Tend My sheep."

Our Times Are in His Hand

18"Truly, truly, I say to you, when you were younger, you used to gird yourself, and walk wherever you wished; but when you grow old, you will stretch out your hands, and someone else will gird you, and bring you where you do not wish to *go*."

19Now this He said, signifying by what kind of death he would glorify God. And when He had spoken this, He *said to him, "Follow Me!"

20Peter, turning around, *saw the disciple whom Jesus loved following *them*; the one who also had leaned back on His breast at the supper, and said, "Lord, who is the one who betrays You?"

21Peter therefore seeing him *said to Jesus, "Lord, and what about this man?"

22Jesus *said to him, "If I want him to remain until I come, what *is that* to you? You follow Me!"

23This saying therefore went out among the brethren that that disciple would

---

ἐκ νεκρῶν.
from [the] dead.

15 Ὅτε οὖν ἠρίστησαν, λέγει τῷ
When therefore they breakfasted, says —

Σίμωνι Πέτρῳ ὁ Ἰησοῦς· Σίμων Ἰωάννου,
to Simon Peter — Jesus: Simon [son] of John,

ἀγαπᾷς με πλέον τούτων; λέγει αὐτῷ·
lovest thou me more [than] these? He says to him:

ναί, κύριε, σὺ οἶδας ὅτι φιλῶ σε. λέγει
Yes, Lord, thou knowest that I love thee. He says

αὐτῷ· βόσκε τὰ ἀρνία μου. 16 λέγει
to him: Feed the lambs of me. He says

αὐτῷ πάλιν δεύτερον· Σίμων Ἰωάννου,
to him again secondly: Simon [son] of John,

ἀγαπᾷς με; λέγει αὐτῷ· ναί, κύριε,
lovest thou me? He says to him: Yes, Lord,

σὺ οἶδας ὅτι φιλῶ σε. λέγει αὐτῷ·
thou knowest that I love thee. He says to him:

ποίμαινε τὰ προβάτιά μου. 17 λέγει
Shepherd the little sheep of me. He says

αὐτῷ τὸ τρίτον· Σίμων Ἰωάννου, φιλεῖς
to him the third [time]: Simon [son] of John, lovest thou

με; ἐλυπήθη ὁ Πέτρος ὅτι εἶπεν αὐτῷ
me? Was grieved — Peter that he said to him

τὸ τρίτον· φιλεῖς με; καὶ εἶπεν αὐτῷ·
the third [time]: Lovest thou me? and said to him:

κύριε, πάντα σὺ οἶδας, σὺ γινώσκεις
Lord, all things thou knowest, thou knowest

ὅτι φιλῶ σε· λέγει αὐτῷ Ἰησοῦς· βόσκε
that I love thee; says to him Jesus: Feed

τὰ προβάτιά μου. 18 ἀμὴν ἀμὴν λέγω
the little sheep of me. Truly truly I tell

σοι, ὅτε ἦς νεώτερος, ἐζώννυες σεαυτὸν
thee, when thou wast younger, thou girdedst thyself

καὶ περιεπάτεις ὅπου ἤθελες· ὅταν δὲ
and walkedst where thou wishedst; but when

γηράσῃς, ἐκτενεῖς τὰς χεῖράς σου, καὶ
thou growest thou wilt the hands of thee, and
old, stretch out

ἄλλος ζώσει σε καὶ οἴσει ὅπου οὐ θέλεις.
another will gird thee and will carry where thou wishest not.

19 τοῦτο δὲ εἶπεν σημαίνων ποίῳ θανάτῳ
And this he said signifying by what death

δοξάσει τὸν θεόν. καὶ τοῦτο εἰπὼν λέγει
he will glorify — God. And this saying he tells

αὐτῷ· ἀκολούθει μοι. 20 ἐπιστραφεὶς ὁ
him: Follow me. Turning —

Πέτρος βλέπει τὸν μαθητὴν ὃν ἠγάπα ὁ
Peter sees the disciple whom ¹loved —

Ἰησοῦς ἀκολουθοῦντα, ὃς καὶ ἀνέπεσεν
¹Jesus following, who also leaned

ἐν τῷ δείπνῳ ἐπὶ τὸ στῆθος αὐτοῦ καὶ
at the supper on the breast of him and

εἶπεν· κύριε, τίς ἐστιν ὁ παραδιδούς σε;
said: Lord, who is the[one] betraying thee?

21 τοῦτον οὖν ἰδὼν ὁ Πέτρος λέγει τῷ
⁴This one ²therefore ³seeing — ¹Peter says —

Ἰησοῦ· κύριε, οὗτος δὲ τί; 22 λέγει
to Jesus: Lord, and this one what? Says

αὐτῷ ὁ Ἰησοῦς· ἐὰν αὐτὸν θέλω μένειν
to him — Jesus: If him I wish to remain

ἕως ἔρχομαι, τί πρὸς σέ; σύ μοι
until I come, what to thee? ²thou ³me

ἀκολούθει. 23 ἐξῆλθεν οὖν οὗτος ὁ λόγος
¹follow. Went forth therefore this — word

εἰς τοὺς ἀδελφοὺς ὅτι ὁ μαθητὴς ἐκεῖνος
to the brothers that — disciple that

Jesus Reinstates Peter

15When they had finished eating, Jesus said to Simon Peter, "Simon son of John, do you truly love me more than these?"

"Yes, Lord," he said, "you know that I love you."

Jesus said, "Feed my lambs."

16Again Jesus said, "Simon son of John, do you truly love me?"

He answered, "Yes, Lord, you know that I love you."

Jesus said, "Take care of my sheep."

17The third time he said to him, "Simon son of John, do you love me?"

Peter was hurt because Jesus asked him the third time, "Do you love me?" He said, "Lord, you know all things; you know that I love you."

Jesus said, "Feed my sheep. 18I tell you the truth, when you were younger you dressed yourself and went where you wanted; but when you are old you will stretch out your hands, and someone else will dress you and lead you where you do not want to go." 19Jesus said this to indicate the kind of death by which Peter would glorify God. Then he said to him, "Follow me!"

20Peter turned and saw that the disciple whom Jesus loved was following them. (This was the one who had leaned back against Jesus at the supper and had said, "Lord, who is going to betray you?") 21When Peter saw him, he asked, "Lord, what about him?"

22Jesus answered, "If I want him to remain alive until I return, what is that to you? You must follow me." 23Because of this, the rumor spread among the brothers that this disciple not die; yet Jesus did not say to him that he would not die, but *only*, "If I want him to remain until I come, what *is that* to you?''

24This is the disciple who bears witness of these things, and wrote these things; and we know that his witness is true.

25And there are also many other things which Jesus did, which if they *were written in detail, I suppose that even the world itself *would not contain the books which *were written.

οὐκ	ἀποθνήσκει·	οὐκ	εἶπεν	δὲ	αὐτῷ	ὁ
does not die;		but	said not		to him	-

'Ιησοῦς	ὅτι	οὐκ	ἀποθνήσκει,	ἀλλ'·	ἐὰν
Jesus	that		he does not die,	but :	If

αὐτὸν	θέλω	μένειν	ἕως	ἔρχομαι,	τί	πρὸς
him	I wish	to remain	until	I come,	what	to

σέ;
thee?

24 Οὗτός ἐστιν ὁ μαθητὴς ὁ μαρτυρῶν
　　 This　 is 　the　 disciple 　-　 witnessing

περὶ	τούτων	καὶ	ὁ	γράψας	ταῦτα,
concerning	these things	and	-	having written	these things,

καὶ	οἴδαμεν	ὅτι	ἀληθὴς	αὐτοῦ	ἡ	μαρτυρία
and	we know	that	true	of him	the	witness

ἐστίν.　**25** "Εστιν δὲ καὶ ἄλλα πολλὰ ἃ
is.　　　 And there are 　also　 other 　many which
　　　　　　　　　　　　　 things

ἐποίησεν	ὁ	'Ιησοῦς,	ἅτινα	ἐὰν	γράφηται
did	-	Jesus,	which	if	they were written

καθ'	ἕν,	οὐδ'	αὐτὸν	οἶμαι	τὸν	κόσμον
singly,†		³not	⁴[it]self	¹I think	³the	⁵world

χωρήσειν	τὰ	γραφόμενα	βιβλία.
⁶to contain	⁷the	⁸being written	⁹rolls.

would not die. But Jesus did not say that he would not die; he only said, "If I want him to remain alive until I return, what is that to you?''

24This is the disciple who testifies to these things and who wrote them down. We know that his testimony is true.

25Jesus did many other things as well. If every one of them were written down, I suppose that even the whole world would not have room for the books that would be written.

Chapter 1

Introduction

THE first account I composed, Theophilus, about all that Jesus began to do and to teach,

2until the day when He was taken up, after He had by the Holy Spirit given orders to the apostles whom He had chosen.

3To these He also presented Himself alive, after His suffering, by many convincing proofs, appearing to them over *a period of* forty days, and speaking of the things concerning the kingdom of God.

4And gathering them together, He commanded them not to leave Jerusalem, but to wait for what the Father had promised, "Which," *He said,* "you heard of from Me;

5for John baptized with water, but you shall be baptized with the Holy Spirit not many days from now."

6And so when they had come together, they were asking Him, saying, "Lord, is it at this time You are restoring the kingdom to Israel?"

7He said to them, "It is not for you to know times or epochs which the Father has fixed by His own authority;

8but you shall receive power when the Holy Spirit has come upon you; and you shall be My witnesses both in Jerusalem, and in all Judea and Samaria, and even to the remotest part of the earth."

The Ascension

9And after He had said these things, He was lifted up while they were looking on, and a cloud received Him out of their sight.

10And as they were gazing intently into the sky while He was departing, behold, two men in white clothing stood beside them;

---

1 Τὸν μὲν πρῶτον λόγον ἐποιησάμην
The - first account I made

περὶ πάντων, ὦ Θεόφιλε, ὧν ἤρξατο
concerning all things, O Theophilus, which began

ὁ Ἰησοῦς ποιεῖν τε καὶ διδάσκειν,
- Jesus both to do and to teach,

2 ἄχρι ἧς ἡμέρας ἐντειλάμενος τοῖς
until which day [5]having given injunctions [6]to the
=the day on which

ἀποστόλοις διὰ πνεύματος ἁγίου οὓς
[1]apostles [2]through [3]Spirit [4]Holy [7]whom

ἐξελέξατο ἀνελήμφθη· **3** οἷς καὶ παρέστησεν
[8]he chose [1]he was taken up; to whom also he presented

ἑαυτὸν ζῶντα μετὰ τὸ παθεῖν αὐτὸν ἐν
himself living after the to suffer him[b] by
=he suffered

πολλοῖς τεκμηρίοις, δι' ἡμερῶν τεσσεράκοντα
many infallible proofs, through days forty

ὀπτανόμενος αὐτοῖς καὶ λέγων τὰ περὶ
being seen by them and speaking the things concerning

τῆς βασιλείας τοῦ θεοῦ· **4** καὶ συναλιζόμενος
the kingdom - of God; and meeting with [them]

παρήγγειλεν αὐτοῖς ἀπὸ Ἱεροσολύμων μὴ
he charged them from Jerusalem not

χωρίζεσθαι, ἀλλὰ περιμένειν τὴν ἐπαγγελίαν
to depart, but to await the promise

τοῦ πατρὸς ἣν ἠκούσατέ μου· **5** ὅτι
of the Father which ye heard of me: because

Ἰωάννης μὲν ἐβάπτισεν ὕδατι, ὑμεῖς δὲ
John indeed baptized in water, but ye

ἐν πνεύματι βαπτισθήσεσθε ἁγίῳ οὐ μετὰ
in [3]Spirit [2]will be baptized [1]Holy not after

πολλὰς ταύτας ἡμέρας. **6** Οἱ μὲν οὖν
many these days. [2]the [ones] [1]So then

συνελθόντες ἠρώτων αὐτὸν λέγοντες· κύριε,
[3]coming together questioned him saying: Lord,

εἰ ἐν τῷ χρόνῳ τούτῳ ἀποκαθιστάνεις
if at this time restorest thou

τὴν βασιλείαν τῷ Ἰσραήλ; **7** εἶπεν πρὸς
the kingdom - to Israel? He said to

αὐτούς· οὐχ ὑμῶν ἐστιν γνῶναι χρόνους
them: Not of you it is to know times

ἢ καιροὺς οὓς ὁ πατὴρ ἔθετο ἐν τῇ
or seasons which the Father placed in the(his)

ἰδίᾳ ἐξουσίᾳ, **8** ἀλλὰ λήμψεσθε δύναμιν
own authority, but ye will receive power

ἐπελθόντος τοῦ ἁγίου πνεύματος ἐφ' ὑμᾶς,
coming *upon* the Holy Spirit[a] upon you,
=when the Holy Spirit comes

καὶ ἔσεσθέ μου μάρτυρες ἔν τε Ἰερουσαλὴμ
and ye will be of me witnesses both in Jerusalem

καὶ ἐν πάσῃ τῇ Ἰουδαίᾳ καὶ Σαμαρείᾳ
and in all - Judæa and Samaria

καὶ ἕως ἐσχάτου τῆς γῆς. **9** καὶ ταῦτα
and unto [the] extremity of the earth. And these things

εἰπὼν βλεπόντων αὐτῶν ἐπήρθη, καὶ
saying looking them[a] he was taken up, and
=as they looked

νεφέλη ὑπέλαβεν αὐτὸν ἀπὸ τῶν ὀφθαλμῶν
a cloud received him from the eyes

αὐτῶν. **10** καὶ ὡς ἀτενίζοντες ἦσαν εἰς
of them. And as gazing they were to

τὸν οὐρανὸν πορευομένου αὐτοῦ, καὶ ἰδού
- heaven going him,[a] - behold[,]
=as he went,

ἄνδρες δύο παρειστήκεισαν αὐτοῖς ἐν ἐσθήσεσι
men two stood by them in garments

Jesus Taken Up Into Heaven

IN my former book, Theophilus, I wrote about all that Jesus began to do and to teach 2until the day he was taken up to heaven, after giving instructions through the Holy Spirit to the apostles he had chosen. 3After his suffering, he showed himself to these men and gave many convincing proofs that he was alive. He appeared to them over a period of forty days and spoke about the kingdom of God. 4On one occasion, while he was eating with them, he gave them this command: "Do not leave Jerusalem, but wait for the gift my Father promised, which you have heard me speak about. 5For John baptized with[a] water, but in a few days you will be baptized with the Holy Spirit."

6So when they met together, they asked him, "Lord, are you at this time going to restore the kingdom to Israel?"

7He said to them: "It is not for you to know the times or dates the Father has set by his own authority. 8But you will receive power when the Holy Spirit comes on you; and you will be my witnesses in Jerusalem, and in all Judea and Samaria, and to the ends of the earth."

9After he said this, he was taken up before their very eyes, and a cloud hid him from their sight.

10They were looking intently up into the sky as he was going, when suddenly two men dressed in white stood beside them. 11"Men

---

[a]5 Or *in*

11and they also said, "Men of Galilee, why do you stand looking into the sky? This Jesus, who has been taken up from you into heaven, will come in just the same way as you have watched Him go into heaven."

The Upper Room

12Then they returned to Jerusalem from the mount called Olivet, which is near Jerusalem, a Sabbath day's journey away.

13And when they had entered, they went up to the upper room, where they were staying; that is, Peter and John and James and Andrew, Philip and Thomas, Bartholomew and Matthew, James *the son* of Alphaeus, and Simon the Zealot, and Judas *the son* of James.

14These all with one mind were continually devoting themselves to prayer, along with *the* women, and Mary the mother of Jesus, and with His brothers.

15And at this time Peter stood up in the midst of the brethren (a gathering of about one hundred and twenty persons was there together), and said,

16"Brethren, the Scripture had to be fulfilled, which the Holy Spirit foretold by the mouth of David concerning Judas, who became a guide to those who arrested Jesus.

17"For he was counted among us, and received his portion in this ministry."

18(Now this man acquired a field with the price of his wickedness; and falling headlong, he burst open in the middle and all his bowels gushed out.

λευκαῖς, **11** οἳ καὶ εἶπαν· ἄνδρες Γαλιλαῖοι,
white,   who also said :   Men   Galilæans,

τί ἑστήκατε βλέποντες εἰς τὸν οὐρανόν;
why stand ye looking   to -   heaven?

οὗτος ὁ 'Ιησοῦς ὁ ἀναλημφθεὶς
This - Jesus the [one] having been taken up

ἀφ' ὑμῶν εἰς τὸν οὐρανὸν οὕτως ἐλεύσεται
from you to   -   heaven   thus   will come

ὃν τρόπον ἐθεάσασθε αὐτὸν πορευόμενον
in the way† ye beheld   him   going

εἰς τὸν οὐρανόν. **12** Τότε ὑπέστρεψαν
to   - heaven.   Then they returned

εἰς 'Ιερουσαλὴμ ἀπὸ ὄρους τοῦ καλου-
to Jerusalem   from [the] mount the [one]

μένου ἐλαιῶνος, ὅ ἐστιν ἐγγὺς 'Ιερουσαλὴμ
called of [the] olive grove, which is near Jerusalem

σαββάτου ἔχον ὁδόν. **13** καὶ ὅτε εἰσῆλθον,
of a sabbath having a way.   And when they entered,
=a sabbath's journey off.

εἰς τὸ ὑπερῷον ἀνέβησαν οὗ ἦσαν
into the upper room they went up where they were

καταμένοντες, ὅ τε Πέτρος καὶ 'Ιωάννης
waiting,   - both Peter and   John

καὶ 'Ιάκωβος καὶ 'Ανδρέας, Φίλιππος καὶ
and James   and Andrew,   Philip   and

Θωμᾶς, Βαρθολομαῖος καὶ Μαθθαῖος,
Thomas, Bartholomew   and   Matthew,

'Ιάκωβος 'Αλφαίου καὶ Σίμων ὁ ζηλωτὴς
James [son] of Alphæus and Simon the zealot

καὶ 'Ιούδας 'Ιακώβου. **14** οὗτοι πάντες
and Judas [brother] of James.   These   all

ἦσαν προσκαρτεροῦντες ὁμοθυμαδὸν τῇ
were continuing steadfastly   with one mind   -

προσευχῇ σὺν γυναιξὶν καὶ Μαριὰμ τῇ
in prayer with [the] women and Mary   the

μητρὶ [τοῦ] 'Ιησοῦ καὶ σὺν τοῖς ἀδελφοῖς
mother   - of Jesus and with the   brothers

αὐτοῦ.
of him.

15 Καὶ ἐν ταῖς ἡμέραις ταύταις ἀναστὰς
And in the   days   these   standing up

Πέτρος ἐν μέσῳ τῶν ἀδελφῶν εἶπεν·
Peter   in [the] midst of the brothers   said :

ἦν τε ὄχλος ὀνομάτων ἐπὶ τὸ αὐτὸ
⁶was ¹and ²[the] ³crowd ⁴of names   ⁵together

ὡσεὶ ἑκατὸν εἴκοσι· **16** ἄνδρες ἀδελφοί,
about a hundred twenty :   Men   brothers,

ἔδει πληρωθῆναι τὴν γραφὴν ἣν
it behoved to be fulfilled the scripture which

προεῖπεν τὸ πνεῦμα τὸ ἅγιον διὰ στόματος
spoke before the Spirit - Holy through [the] mouth

Δαυὶδ περὶ 'Ιούδα τοῦ γενομένου ὁδηγοῦ
of David concerning Judas the [one] having become guide

τοῖς συλλαβοῦσιν 'Ιησοῦν, **17** ὅτι κατ-
to the [ones] taking   Jesus,   because having

ηριθμημένος ἦν ἐν ἡμῖν καὶ ἔλαχεν τὸν
been numbered he was among us and obtained the

κλῆρον τῆς διακονίας ταύτης. **18** οὗτος μὲν οὖν
portion of this ministry.   This one therefore

ἐκτήσατο χωρίον ἐκ μισθοῦ τῆς
bought   a field out of [the] reward   of

ἀδικίας, καὶ πρηνὴς γενόμενος ἐλάκησεν
of unrighteousness, and swollen up having become he burst asunder

μέσος, καὶ ἐξεχύθη πάντα τὰ σπλάγχνα
in the middle, and were poured out all the bowels

of Galilee," they said, "why do you stand here looking into the sky? This same Jesus, who has been taken from you into heaven, will come back in the same way you have seen him go into heaven."

Matthias Chosen to Replace Judas

12Then they returned to Jerusalem from the hill called the Mount of Olives, a Sabbath day's walk[b] from the city. 13When they arrived, they went upstairs to the room where they were staying. Those present were Peter, John, James and Andrew; Philip and Thomas, Bartholomew and Matthew; James son of Alphaeus and Simon the Zealot, and Judas son of James. 14They all joined together constantly in prayer, along with the women and Mary the mother of Jesus, and with his brothers.

15In those days Peter stood up among the believers[c] (a group numbering about a hundred and twenty) 16and said, "Brothers, the Scripture had to be fulfilled which the Holy Spirit spoke long ago through the mouth of David concerning Judas, who served as guide for those who arrested Jesus—17he was one of our number and shared in this ministry."

18(With the reward he got for his wickedness, Judas bought a field; there he fell headlong, his body burst open and all his intestines

b12 That is, about 3/4 mile (about 1,100 meters)
c15 Greek brothers

19And it became known to all who were living in Jerusalem; so that in their own language that field was called Hakeldama, that is, Field of Blood.)

20"For it is written in the book of Psalms,

'LET HIS HOMESTEAD BE MADE DESOLATE,

AND LET NO MAN DWELL IN IT';

and,

'HIS OFFICE LET ANOTHER MAN TAKE.'

21"It is therefore necessary that of the men who have accompanied us all the time that the Lord Jesus went in and out among us—

22beginning with the baptism of John, until the day that He was taken up from us—one of these should become a witness with us of His resurrection."

23And they put forward two men, Joseph called Barsabbas (who was also called Justus), and Matthias.

24And they prayed, and said, "Thou, Lord, who knowest the hearts of all men, show which one of these two Thou hast chosen

25to occupy this ministry and apostleship from which Judas turned aside to go to his own place."

26And they drew lots for them, and the lot fell to Matthias; and he was numbered with the eleven apostles.

αὐτοῦ· **19** καὶ γνωστὸν ἐγένετο πᾶσι τοῖς
of him;   and known   it became to all the

κατοικοῦσιν Ἰερουσαλήμ, ὥστε κληθῆναι
[ones] inhabiting Jerusalem, so as to be called

τὸ χωρίον ἐκεῖνο τῇ ἰδίᾳ διαλέκτῳ αὐτῶν
that field   in their own language

Ἀκελδαμάχ, τοῦτ' ἔστιν χωρίον
Aceldamach, this   is   Field

αἵματος. **20** γέγραπται γὰρ ἐν βίβλῳ
of blood.   For it has been written in [the] roll

ψαλμῶν· γενηθήτω ἡ ἔπαυλις αὐτοῦ ἔρημος
of Psalms: Let become the estate of him deserted

καὶ μὴ ἔστω ὁ κατοικῶν ἐν αὐτῇ, καὶ·
and let not be the [one] dwelling in it, and:

τὴν ἐπισκοπὴν αὐτοῦ λαβέτω ἕτερος.
The office   of him let take another.

21 δεῖ οὖν τῶν συνελθόντων ἡμῖν ἀνδρῶν
It behoves therefore ¹of the ²accompanying ⁴us ³men

ἐν παντὶ χρόνῳ ᾧ εἰσῆλθεν καὶ
in all [the] time in which went in and

ἐξῆλθεν ἐφ' ἡμᾶς ὁ κύριος Ἰησοῦς,
went out among us   the Lord   Jesus,

22 ἀρξάμενος ἀπὸ τοῦ βαπτίσματος
beginning from the baptism

Ἰωάννου ἕως τῆς ἡμέρας ἧς ἀνελήμφθη
of John until the day   when he was taken up

ἀφ' ἡμῶν, μάρτυρα τῆς ἀναστάσεως
from us, ⁴a witness⁵ ⁷of the ⁸resurrection

αὐτοῦ σὺν ἡμῖν γενέσθαι ἕνα τούτων.
⁶of him ³with ²us ¹to become ¹one⁴ ³of these.

23 Καὶ ἔστησαν δύο, Ἰωσὴφ τὸν καλού-
And they set two, Joseph the [one] being

μενον Βαρσαββᾶν, ὃς ἐπεκλήθη Ἰοῦστος,
called Barsabbas, who was surnamed Justus,

καὶ Μαθθίαν. **24** καὶ προσευξάμενοι εἶπαν·
and Matthias.   and praying   they said :

σὺ κύριε καρδιογνῶστα πάντων, ἀνάδειξον
Thou Lord Heart-knower of all men, show

ὃν ἐξελέξω ἐκ τούτων τῶν δύο ἕνα
whom thou didst choose of these the two one

25 λαβεῖν τὸν τόπον τῆς διακονίας ταύτης
to take the place of this ministry

καὶ ἀποστολῆς, ἀφ' ἧς παρέβη Ἰούδας
and apostleship, from which fell Judas

πορευθῆναι εἰς τὸν τόπον τὸν ἴδιον.
to go   to the(his) place   own.

26 καὶ ἔδωκαν κλήρους αὐτοῖς, καὶ ἔπεσεν
And they gave lots   for them, and fell

ὁ κλῆρος ἐπὶ Μαθθίαν, καὶ συγκατεψηφίσθη
the lot on Matthias, and he was reckoned along with

μετὰ τῶν ἕνδεκα ἀποστόλων.
with the eleven apostles.

---

spilled out. 19Everyone in Jerusalem heard about this, so they called that field in their language Akeldama, that is, Field of Blood.)

20"For," said Peter, "it is written in the book of Psalms,

" 'May his place be deserted;

let there be no one to dwell in it,' ᵈ

and,

" 'May another take his place of leadership.' ᵉ

21Therefore it is necessary to choose one of the men who have been with us the whole time the Lord Jesus went in and out among us, 22beginning from John's baptism to the time when Jesus was taken up from us. For one of these must become a witness with us of his resurrection."

23So they proposed two men: Joseph called Barsabbas (also known as Justus) and Matthias. 24Then they prayed, "Lord, you know everyone's heart. Show us which of these two you have chosen 25to take over this apostolic ministry, which Judas left to go where he belongs." 26Then they cast lots, and the lot fell to Matthias; so he was added to the eleven apostles.

Chapter 2

The Day of Pentecost

AND when the day of Pentecost had come, they were all together in one place.

2And suddenly there came from heaven a noise like a violent, rushing

---

2 Καὶ ἐν τῷ συμπληροῦσθαι τὴν ἡμέραν
And in the to be completed the day
= when the day of Pentecost was completed

τῆς πεντηκοστῆς ἦσαν πάντες ὁμοῦ ἐπὶ
- of Pentecostᵉ they were all together to-

τὸ αὐτό· **2** καὶ ἐγένετο ἄφνω ἐκ τοῦ
gether;† and there was suddenly out of -

οὐρανοῦ ἦχος ὥσπερ φερομένης πνοῆς
heaven a sound as ⁵being borne ¹of³a ⁴wind

Chapter 2

The Holy Spirit Comes at Pentecost

WHEN the day of Pentecost came, they were all together in one place. 2Suddenly a sound like the blowing of a violent

---

* The object (according to the Greek construction) of the verb δεῖ is ἕνα, with μάρτυρα as its complement after γενέσθαι.

ᵈ20 Psalm 69:25
ᵉ20 Psalm 109:8

wind, and it filled the whole house where they were sitting.

3And there appeared to them tongues of fire distributing themselves, and they rested on each one of them.

4And they were all filled with the Holy Spirit and began to speak with other tongues, as the Spirit was giving them utterance.

5Now there were Jews living in Jerusalem, devout men, from every nation under heaven.

6And when this sound occurred, the multitude came together, and were bewildered, because they were each one hearing them speak in his own language.

7And they were amazed and marveled, saying, "Why, are not all these who are speaking Galileans?

8"And how is it that we each hear *them* in our own language to which we were born?

9"Parthians and Medes and Elamites, and residents of Mesopotamia, Judea and Cappadocia, Pontus and Asia,

10Phrygia and Pamphylia, Egypt and the districts of Libya around Cyrene, and visitors from Rome, both Jews and *a* proselytes,

11Cretans and Arabs—we hear them in our *own* tongues speaking of the mighty deeds of God."

12And they all continued in amazement and great perplexity, saying to one another, "What does this mean?"

13But others were mocking and saying, "They are full of sweet wine."

Peter's Sermon

14But Peter, taking his stand with the eleven, raised his voice and de-

---

βιαίας καὶ ἐπλήρωσεν ὅλον τὸν οἶκον
3violent and it filled all the house

οὗ ἦσαν καθήμενοι, 3 καὶ ὤφθησαν αὐτοῖς
where they were sitting, and there appeared to them

διαμεριζόμεναι γλῶσσαι ὡσεὶ πυρός, καὶ
being distributed tongues as of fire, and

ἐκάθισεν ἐφ᾽ ἕνα ἕκαστον αὐτῶν, 4 καὶ
it sat on 2one 1each of them, and

ἐπλήσθησαν πάντες πνεύματος ἁγίου, καὶ
they were filled all of(with) Spirit Holy, and

ἤρξαντο λαλεῖν ἑτέραις γλώσσαις καθὼς
began to speak in other tongues as

τὸ πνεῦμα ἐδίδου ἀποφθέγγεσθαι αὐτοῖς.
the Spirit gave 2to speak out 1them.

5 Ἦσαν δὲ εἰς Ἰερουσαλὴμ κατοικοῦντες
Now there were in Jerusalem dwelling

Ἰουδαῖοι, ἄνδρες εὐλαβεῖς ἀπὸ παντὸς ἔθνους
Jews, men devout from every nation

τῶν ὑπὸ τὸν οὐρανόν· 6 γενομένης
of the [ones] under – heaven; happening

δὲ τῆς φωνῆς ταύτης συνῆλθεν τὸ πλῆθος
and this sound*a* came together the multitude
=when this sound happened

καὶ συνεχύθη, ὅτι ἤκουον εἷς ἕκαστος
and were confounded, because they heard 4one 3each

τῇ ἰδίᾳ διαλέκτῳ λαλούντων αὐτῶν.
5in his own language 2speaking 1them.

7 ἐξίσταντο δὲ καὶ ἐθαύμαζον λέγοντες·
And they were amazed and marvelled saying:

οὐχὶ ἰδοὺ πάντες οὗτοί εἰσιν οἱ λαλοῦντες
3not 1behold 2all 5these 4are 6the [ones] 7speaking

Γαλιλαῖοι; 8 καὶ πῶς ἡμεῖς ἀκούομεν
8Galilæans? and how 2we 1hear

ἕκαστος τῇ ἰδίᾳ διαλέκτῳ ἡμῶν ἐν ᾗ
3each 4in his own language 5of us in which

ἐγεννήθημεν, 9 Πάρθοι καὶ Μῆδοι καὶ
we were born, Parthians and Medes and

Ἐλαμῖται, καὶ οἱ κατοικοῦντες τὴν
Elamites, and the [ones] inhabiting –

Μεσοποταμίαν, Ἰουδαίαν τε καὶ Καππα-
Mesopotamia, both Judæa and Cappa-

δοκίαν, Πόντον καὶ τὴν Ἀσίαν, 10 Φρυγίαν
docia, Pontus and – Asia, Phrygia

τε καὶ Παμφυλίαν, Αἴγυπτον καὶ τὰ
both and Pamphylia, Egypt and the

μέρη τῆς Λιβύης τῆς κατὰ Κυρήνην,
regions – of Libya – over against Cyrene,

καὶ οἱ ἐπιδημοῦντες Ῥωμαῖοι, 11 Ἰουδαῖοί
and the temporarily residing Romans, 2Jews

τε καὶ προσήλυτοι, Κρῆτες καὶ Ἄραβες,
1both and proselytes, Cretans and Arabians,

ἀκούομεν λαλούντων αὐτῶν ταῖς ἡμετέραις
we hear 2speaking 1them in the our

γλώσσαις τὰ μεγαλεῖα τοῦ θεοῦ;
tongues the great deeds – of God?

12 ἐξίσταντο δὲ πάντες καὶ διηπόρουντο,
And were amazed all and were troubled,

ἄλλος πρὸς ἄλλον λέγοντες· τί θέλει
other to other saying: What wishes·

τοῦτο εἶναι; 13 ἕτεροι δὲ διαχλευάζοντες
this to be? But others mocking

ἔλεγον ὅτι γλεύκους μεμεστωμένοι εἰσίν.
said[,] – Of(with) sweet wine *having been* filled they are.

14 Σταθεὶς δὲ ὁ Πέτρος σὺν τοῖς ἕνδεκα
But standing – Peter with the eleven

ἐπῆρεν τὴν φωνὴν αὐτοῦ καὶ ἀπεφθέγξατο
lifted up the voice of him and spoke out

---

wind came from heaven and filled the whole house where they were sitting.
3They saw what seemed to be tongues of fire that separated and came to rest on each of them. 4All of them were filled with the Holy Spirit and began to speak in other tongues*f* as the Spirit enabled them.

5Now there were staying in Jerusalem God-fearing Jews from every nation under heaven. 6When they heard this sound, a crowd came together in bewilderment, because each one heard them speaking in his own language. 7Utterly amazed, they asked: "Are not all these men who are speaking Galileans? 8Then how is it that each of us hears them in his own native language? 9Parthians, Medes and Elamites; residents of Mesopotamia, Judea and Cappadocia, Pontus and Asia, 10Phrygia and Pamphylia, Egypt and the parts of Libya near Cyrene; visitors from Rome 11(both Jews and converts to Judaism); Cretans and Arabs—we hear them declaring the wonders of God in our own tongues!" 12Amazed and perplexed, they asked one another, "What does this mean?"

13Some, however, made fun of them and said, "They have had too much wine.*g*"

Peter Addresses the Crowd

14Then Peter stood up with the Eleven, raised his voice and addressed the

---

a I.e., Gentile converts to Judaism

f 4 Or *languages*; also in verse 11
g 13 Or *sweet wine*

clared to them: "Men of Judea, and all you who live in Jerusalem, let this be known to you, and give heed to my words.

15"For these men are not drunk, as you suppose, for it is *only* the [b]third hour of the day;

16but this is what was spoken of through the prophet Joel:

17 'AND IT SHALL BE IN THE LAST DAYS,' God says,
'THAT I WILL POUR FORTH OF MY SPIRIT UPON ALL MANKIND;
AND YOUR SONS AND YOUR DAUGHTERS SHALL PROPHESY,
AND YOUR YOUNG MEN SHALL SEE VISIONS,
AND YOUR OLD MEN SHALL DREAM DREAMS;

18 EVEN UPON MY BOND-SLAVES, BOTH MEN AND WOMEN,
I WILL IN THOSE DAYS POUR FORTH OF MY SPIRIT
And they shall prophesy.

19 'AND I WILL GRANT WONDERS IN THE SKY ABOVE,
AND SIGNS ON THE EARTH BENEATH,
BLOOD, AND FIRE, AND VAPOR OF SMOKE.

20 'THE SUN SHALL BE TURNED INTO DARK-NESS,
AND THE MOON INTO BLOOD,
BEFORE THE GREAT AND GLORIOUS DAY OF THE LORD SHALL COME.

21 'AND IT SHALL BE, THAT EVERYONE WHO CALLS ON THE NAME OF THE LORD SHALL BE SAVED.'

22"Men of Israel, listen to these words: Jesus the Nazarene, a man attested to you by God with miracles and wonders and signs which God performed through Him in your midst, just as you yourselves know—

23this *Man*, delivered up by the predetermined plan and foreknowledge of God, you nailed to a cross by the

---

αὐτοῖς·
to them :

Ἄνδρες Ἰουδαῖοι καὶ οἱ κατοικοῦντες
Men   Jews   and the [ones] inhabiting

Ἰερουσαλὴμ πάντες, τοῦτο ὑμῖν γνωστὸν
Jerusalem   all,   this to you known

ἔστω, καὶ ἐνωτίσασθε τὰ ῥήματά μου.
let be, and give ear to the words of me.

15 οὐ γὰρ ὡς ὑμεῖς ὑπολαμβάνετε οὗτοι
For not as ye   imagine   these men

μεθύουσιν, ἔστιν γὰρ ὥρα τρίτη τῆς
are drunk, for it is hour third of the

ἡμέρας, 16 ἀλλὰ τοῦτό ἐστιν τὸ εἰρημένον
day,   but this is the thing having been spoken

διὰ τοῦ προφήτου Ἰωήλ· 17 καὶ ἔσται
through the prophet Joel :   And it shall be

ἐν ταῖς ἐσχάταις ἡμέραις, λέγει ὁ θεός,
in the last   days, says - God,

ἐκχεῶ ἀπὸ τοῦ πνεύματός μου ἐπὶ
I will pour out from the Spirit of me on

πᾶσαν σάρκα, καὶ προφητεύσουσιν οἱ υἱοὶ
all   flesh, and will prophesy the sons

ὑμῶν καὶ αἱ θυγατέρες ὑμῶν, καὶ οἱ
of you and the daughters of you, and the

νεανίσκοι ὑμῶν ὁράσεις ὄψονται, καὶ οἱ
young men of you visions will see, and the

πρεσβύτεροι ὑμῶν ἐνυπνίοις ἐνυπνιασθήσονται·
old men of you dreams will dream;

18 καὶ γε ἐπὶ τοὺς δούλους μου καὶ ἐπὶ
and - on the male slaves of me and on

τὰς δούλας μου ἐν ταῖς ἡμέραις ἐκείναις
the female slaves of me in those days

ἐκχεῶ ἀπὸ τοῦ πνεύματός μου, καὶ
I will pour out from the Spirit of me, and

προφητεύσουσιν. 19 καὶ δώσω τέρατα ἐν
they will prophesy.   And I will give wonders in

τῷ οὐρανῷ ἄνω καὶ σημεῖα ἐπὶ τῆς
the heaven above and signs on the

γῆς κάτω, αἷμα καὶ πῦρ καὶ ἀτμίδα
earth below, blood and fire and vapour

καπνοῦ. 20 ὁ ἥλιος μεταστραφήσεται εἰς
of smoke.   The sun will be turned into

σκότος καὶ ἡ σελήνη εἰς αἷμα, πρὶν
darkness and the moon into blood, before

ἐλθεῖν ἡμέραν κυρίου τὴν μεγάλην καὶ
[7]to come(comes) [8]day [9]of [the] Lord [1]the [2]great [3]and

ἐπιφανῆ. 21 καὶ ἔσται πᾶς ὃς ἐὰν
[4]notable.[b] And it will be everyone whoever

ἐπικαλέσηται τὸ ὄνομα κυρίου σωθήσεται.
invokes   the name of [the] Lord will be saved.

22 Ἄνδρες Ἰσραηλῖται, ἀκούσατε τοὺς
Men   Israelites, hear ye the

λόγους τούτους· Ἰησοῦν τὸν Ναζωραῖον,
words these: Jesus the Nazarene,

ἄνδρα ἀποδεδειγμένον ἀπὸ τοῦ θεοῦ εἰς
a man having been approved from - God among

ὑμᾶς δυνάμεσι καὶ τέρασι καὶ σημείοις,
you by powerful deeds and wonders and signs,

οἷς ἐποίησεν δι' αὐτοῦ ὁ θεὸς ἐν μέσῳ
which did through him - God in [the] midst

ὑμῶν, καθὼς αὐτοὶ οἴδατε, 23 τοῦτον
of you, as [your]selves ye know, this man

τῇ ὡρισμένῃ βουλῇ καὶ προγνώσει τοῦ
[5]by the [6]having been fixed [4]counsel [3]and [2]foreknowledge -

θεοῦ ἔκδοτον διὰ χειρὸς ἀνόμων
[1]of God [5]given up [6]through [10][the] hand [11]of lawless men

---

crowd: "Fellow Jews and all of you who live in Jerusalem, let me explain this to you; listen carefully to what I say. 15These men are not drunk, as you suppose. It's only nine in the morning! 16No, this is what was spoken by the prophet Joel:

17" 'In the last days, God says,
I will pour out my Spirit on all people.
Your sons and daughters will prophesy,
your young men will see visions,
your old men will dream dreams.

18Even on my servants, both men and women,
I will pour out my Spirit in those days, and they will prophesy.

19I will show wonders in the heaven above and signs on the earth below,
blood and fire and billows of smoke.

20The sun will be turned to darkness and the moon to blood before the coming of the great and glorious day of the Lord.

21And everyone who calls on the name of the Lord will be saved.' [h]

22"Men of Israel, listen to this: Jesus of Nazareth was a man accredited by God to you by miracles, wonders and signs, which God did among you through him, as you yourselves know. 23This man was handed over to you by God's set purpose and foreknowledge; and you, with the help of wicked men, [i] put him to death by nailing him hands of godless men and put *Him* to death.

24"And God raised Him up again, putting an end to the agony of death, since it was impossible for Him to be held in its power.

25"For David says of Him,

'I WAS ALWAYS BEHOLD-
ING THE LORD IN MY
PRESENCE;
FOR HE IS AT MY RIGHT
HAND, THAT I MAY
NOT BE SHAKEN.
26 'THEREFORE MY HEART
WAS GLAD AND MY
TONGUE EXULTED;
MOREOVER MY FLESH
ALSO WILL ABIDE IN
HOPE;
27 BECAUSE THOU WILT
NOT ABANDON MY
SOUL TO HADES,
NOR ALLOW THY HOLY
ONE TO UNDERGO
DECAY.
28 'THOU HAST MADE
KNOWN TO ME THE
WAYS OF LIFE;
THOU WILT MAKE ME
FULL OF GLADNESS
WITH THY PRESENCE.'

29"Brethren, I may confi-
dently say to you regarding
the patriarch David that he
both died and was buried,
and his tomb is with us to
this day.

30"And so, because he
was a prophet, and knew
that GOD HAD SWORN TO HIM
WITH AN OATH TO SEAT *one*
OF HIS DESCENDANTS UPON
HIS THRONE,

31he looked ahead and
spoke of the resurrection of
ᶜthe Christ, that HE WAS
NEITHER ABANDONED TO
HADES, NOR DID His flesh
SUFFER DECAY.

32"This Jesus God raised
up again, to which we are
all witnesses.

33"Therefore having been
exalted to the right hand of
God, and having received
from the Father the prom-
ise of the Holy Spirit, He
has poured forth this which
you both see and hear.

34"For it was not David

προσπήξαντες ἀνείλατε, 24 ὃν ὁ θεὸς
ᵇ"fastening"　¹²ye killed,　　whom　－　God
ἀνέστησεν λύσας τὰς ὠδῖνας τοῦ θανάτου,
raised up loosening the pangs　－　of death,
καθότι οὐκ ἦν δυνατὸν κρατεῖσθαι αὐτὸν
because it was not possible ᵇto be held ¹him
ὑπ' αὐτοῦ. 25 Δαυὶδ γὰρ λέγει εἰς
by it.　　For David says [as] to
αὐτόν· προορώμην τὸν κύριον ἐνώπιόν
him :　I foresaw　the　Lord　before
μου διὰ παντός, ὅτι ἐκ δεξιῶν μού
me always,　because on right of me
ἐστιν, ἵνα μὴ σαλευθῶ. 26 διὰ τοῦτο
he is,　lest I be moved.　　Therefore
ηὐφράνθη μου ἡ καρδία καὶ ἠγαλλιάσατο
was glad of me the heart and exulted
ἡ γλῶσσά μου, ἔτι δὲ καὶ ἡ σάρξ
the tongue of me, and now also the flesh
μου κατασκηνώσει ἐπ' ἐλπίδι, 27 ὅτι οὐκ
of me will dwell on(in) hope, because not
ἐγκαταλείψεις τὴν ψυχήν μου εἰς ἅδην
thou wilt abandon the soul of me in hades
οὐδὲ δώσεις τὸν ὅσιόν σου ἰδεῖν
nor wilt thou give the holy one of thee to see
διαφθοράν. 28 ἐγνώρισάς μοι ὁδοὺς ζωῆς,
corruption. Thou madest known to me ways of life,
πληρώσεις με εὐφροσύνης μετὰ τοῦ προσώ-
thou wilt fill me of(with) gladness with the pres-
που σου. 29 Ἄνδρες ἀδελφοί, ἐξὸν εἰπεῖν
ence of thee. Men brothers, it is permitted to speak
μετὰ παρρησίας πρὸς ὑμᾶς περὶ τοῦ
with plainness to you concerning the
πατριάρχου Δαυὶδ, ὅτι καὶ ἐτελεύτησεν
patriarch David, that both he died
καὶ ἐτάφη, καὶ τὸ μνῆμα αὐτοῦ ἔστιν
and was buried, and the tomb of him is
ἐν ἡμῖν ἄχρι τῆς ἡμέρας ταύτης.
among us until this day.
30 προφήτης οὖν ὑπάρχων καὶ εἰδὼς ὅτι
A prophet therefore being and knowing that
ὅρκῳ ὤμοσεν αὐτῷ ὁ θεὸς ἐκ καρποῦ
with an oath swore to him － God of [the] fruit
τῆς ὀσφύος αὐτοῦ καθίσαι ἐπὶ τὸν θρόνον
of the loin[s] of him to sit on the throne
αὐτοῦ, 31 προϊδὼν ἐλάλησεν περὶ τῆς
of him, foreseeing he spoke concerning the
ἀναστάσεως τοῦ Χριστοῦ, ὅτι οὔτε
resurrection of the Christ, that neither
ἐγκατελείφθη εἰς ἅδην οὔτε ἡ σὰρξ
he was abandoned in hades nor the flesh
αὐτοῦ εἶδεν διαφθοράν. 32 τοῦτον τὸν
of him saw corruption. This －
Ἰησοῦν ἀνέστησεν ὁ θεός, οὗ πάντες
Jesus ᵇraised up － ¹God, of which all
ἡμεῖς ἐσμεν μάρτυρες· 33 τῇ δεξιᾷ οὖν
we are witnesses; to the right [hand] therefore
τοῦ θεοῦ ὑψωθεὶς τήν τε ἐπαγγελίαν
－ of God having been exalted ⁸the ¹and ⁷promise
τοῦ πνεύματος τοῦ ἁγίου λαβὼν παρὰ
⁹of the ¹⁰Spirit － ⁹Holy ⁶receiving ⁵from
τοῦ πατρὸς ἐξέχεεν τοῦτο ὃ ὑμεῖς καὶ
⁴the ⁵Father he poured out this which ye both
βλέπετε καὶ ἀκούετε. 34 οὐ γὰρ Δαυὶδ
see and hear.　　For not David

---

to the cross. 24But God
raised him from the dead,
freeing him from the agony
of death, because it was impossible for death to keep
its hold on him. 25David
said about him:

"'I saw the Lord always
before me.
Because he is at my
right hand,
I will not be shaken.
26Therefore my heart is
glad and my tongue
rejoices;
my body also will live
in hope,
27because you will not
abandon me to the
grave,
nor will you let your
Holy One see
decay.
28You have made known
to me the paths of
life;
you will fill me with joy
in your presence.'ʲ

29"Brothers, I can tell
you confidently that the patriarch David died and was
buried, and his tomb is here
to this day. 30But he was a
prophet and knew that God
had promised him on oath
that he would place one of
his descendants on his
throne. 31Seeing what was
ahead, he spoke of the resurrection of the Christ,ᵏ
that he was not abandoned
to the grave, nor did his
body see decay. 32God has
raised this Jesus to life, and
we are all witnesses of the
fact. 33Exalted to the right
hand of God, he has re-
ceived from the Father the
promised Holy Spirit and
has poured out what you
now see and hear. 34For
David did not ascend to

ᶜ I.e., the Messiah

ᵇ That is, to a tree; see ch. 5. 30.

ʲ28 Psalm 16:8-11
ᵏ31 Or *Messiah*. "The Christ"
(Greek) and "the Messiah"
(Hebrew) both mean "the Anointed
One"; also in verse 36.

who ascended into heaven, but he himself says:
'THE LORD SAID TO MY LORD,
"SIT AT MY RIGHT HAND,
35 UNTIL I MAKE THINE ENEMIES A FOOTSTOOL FOR THY FEET."''

36"Therefore let all the house of Israel know for certain that God has made Him both Lord and Christ—this Jesus whom you crucified."

The Ingathering

37Now when they heard *this*, they were pierced to the heart, and said to Peter and the rest of the apostles, "Brethren, what shall we do?"

38And Peter *said* to them, "Repent, and let each of you be baptized in the name of Jesus Christ for the forgiveness of your sins; and you shall receive the gift of the Holy Spirit.

39"For the promise is for you and your children, and for all who are far off, as many as the Lord our God shall call to Himself."

40And with many other words he solemnly testified and kept on exhorting them, saying, "Be saved from this perverse generation!"

41So then, those who had received his word were baptized; and there were added that day about three thousand *d* souls.

42And they were continually devoting themselves to the apostles' teaching and to fellowship, to the breaking of bread and to prayer.

43And everyone kept feeling a sense of awe; and many wonders and signs were taking place through the apostles *e*.

44And all those who had believed *f* were together, and had all things in common;

45and they *began* selling their property and posses-

d I.e., persons
e Some ancient mss. add in Jerusalem; and great fear was upon all
f Some ancient mss. do not contain were

ἀνέβη εἰς τοὺς οὐρανούς, λέγει δὲ αὐτός·
ascended to the heavens, but says he:

εἶπεν κύριος τῷ κυρίῳ μου· κάθου ἐκ
Said [the] LORD to the Lord of me: Sit at

δεξιῶν μου, 35 ἕως ἂν θῶ τοὺς ἐχθρούς
right of me, until I put the enemies

σου ὑποπόδιον τῶν ποδῶν σου. 36 ἀσφαλῶς
of thee a footstool of the feet of thee. Assuredly

οὖν γινωσκέτω πᾶς οἶκος Ἰσραὴλ ὅτι
therefore ¹let ³know ²all ³[the] ⁴house ⁵of Israel that

καὶ κύριον αὐτὸν καὶ χριστὸν ἐποίησεν
⁴both ⁵Lord ³him ⁶and ⁷Christ ²made

ὁ θεός, τοῦτον τὸν Ἰησοῦν ὃν ὑμεῖς
- ¹God, this - Jesus whom ye

ἐσταυρώσατε. 37 Ἀκούσαντες δὲ κατενύγ-
crucified. And hearing they were

ησαν τὴν καρδίαν, εἶπόν τε πρὸς τὸν
stung [in] the heart, and said to -

Πέτρον καὶ τοὺς λοιποὺς ἀποστόλους·
Peter and the remaining apostles:

τί ποιήσωμεν, ἄνδρες ἀδελφοί; 38 Πέτρος
What may we do, men brothers? Peter

δὲ πρὸς αὐτούς· μετανοήσατε, καὶ
And to them: Repent ye, and

βαπτισθήτω ἕκαστος ὑμῶν ἐπὶ τῷ ὀνόματι
let be baptized each of you on the name

Ἰησοῦ Χριστοῦ εἰς ἄφεσιν τῶν
of Jesus Christ [with a view] to forgiveness of the

ἁμαρτιῶν ὑμῶν, καὶ λήμψεσθε τὴν δωρεὰν
sins of you, and ye will receive the gift

τοῦ ἁγίου πνεύματος. 39 ὑμῖν γάρ ἐστιν
of the Holy Spirit. For to you is

ἡ ἐπαγγελία καὶ τοῖς τέκνοις ὑμῶν καὶ
the promise and to the children of you and

πᾶσιν τοῖς εἰς μακράν, ὅσους ἂν
to all the [ones] far away, as many as

προσκαλέσηται κύριος ὁ θεὸς ἡμῶν.
may call to [him] [the] Lord the God of us.

40 ἑτέροις τε λόγοις πλείοσιν διεμαρτύρατο,
And with other words many he solemnly witnessed,

καὶ παρεκάλει αὐτοὺς λέγων· σώθητε
and exhorted them saying: Be ye saved

ἀπὸ τῆς γενεᾶς τῆς σκολιᾶς ταύτης. 41 οἱ
from - ³generation - ²perverse ¹this. The [ones]

μὲν οὖν ἀποδεξάμενοι τὸν λόγον αὐτοῦ
- therefore welcoming the word of him

ἐβαπτίσθησαν, καὶ προσετέθησαν ἐν
were baptized, and there were added in

τῇ ἡμέρᾳ ἐκείνῃ ψυχαὶ ὡσεὶ τρισχίλιαι·
that day souls about three thousand;

42 ἦσαν δὲ προσκαρτεροῦντες τῇ διδαχῇ
and they were continuing steadfastly in the teaching

τῶν ἀποστόλων καὶ τῇ κοινωνίᾳ, τῇ
of the apostles and in the fellowship, in the

κλάσει τοῦ ἄρτου καὶ ταῖς προσευχαῖς.
breaking of the foaf and in the prayers.

43 Ἐγίνετο δὲ πάσῃ ψυχῇ φόβος· πολλὰ δὲ
And came to every soul fear; and many

τέρατα καὶ σημεῖα διὰ τῶν ἀποστόλων
wonders and signs through the apostles

ἐγίνετο. 44 πάντες δὲ οἱ πιστεύσαντες
happened. And all the believing [ones]

ἐπὶ τὸ αὐτὸ εἶχον ἅπαντα κοινά, 45 καὶ
together had all things common, and

τὰ κτήματα καὶ τὰς ὑπάρξεις ἐπίπρασκον
the properties and the possessions they sold

heaven, and yet he said,
" 'The Lord said to my Lord:
"Sit at my right hand,
35until I make your enemies a footstool for your feet." '*¹*

36"Therefore let all Israel be assured of this: God has made this Jesus, whom you crucified, both Lord and Christ."

37When the people heard this, they were cut to the heart and said to Peter and the other apostles, "Brothers, what shall we do?"

38Peter replied, "Repent and be baptized, every one of you, in the name of Jesus Christ for the forgiveness of your sins. And you will receive the gift of the Holy Spirit. 39The promise is for you and your children and for all who are far off—for all whom the Lord our God will call."

40With many other words he warned them; and he pleaded with them, "Save yourselves from this corrupt generation." 41Those who accepted his message were baptized, and about three thousand were added to their number that day.

The Fellowship of the Believers

42They devoted themselves to the apostles' teaching and to the fellowship, to the breaking of bread and to prayer. 43Everyone was filled with awe, and many wonders and miraculous signs were done by the apostles. 44All the believers were together and had everything in common. 45Selling their possessions

¹35 Psalm 110:1

sions, and were sharing them with all, as anyone might have need.

46And day by day continuing with one mind in the temple, and breaking bread from house to house, they were taking their meals together with gladness and sincerity of heart,

47praising God, and having favor with all the people. And the Lord was adding to their number day by day those who were being saved.

Chapter 3

Healing the Lame Beggar

NOW Peter and John were going up to the temple at the ᵍninth *hour*, the hour of prayer.

2And a certain man who had been lame from his mother's womb was being carried along, whom they used to set down every day at the gate of the temple which is called Beautiful, in order to beg ʰalms of those who were entering the temple.

3And when he saw Peter and John about to go into the temple, he *began* asking to receive alms.

4And Peter, along with John, fixed his gaze upon him and said, "Look at us!"

5And he *began* to give them his attention, expecting to receive something from them.

6But Peter said, "I do not possess silver and gold, but what I do have I give to you: In the name of Jesus Christ the Nazarene— walk!"

7And seizing him by the right hand, he raised him up; and immediately his feet and his ankles were strengthened.

8And with a leap, he stood upright and *began* to walk; and he entered the temple with them, walking and leaping and praising

---

καὶ διεμέριζον αὐτὰ πᾶσιν, καθότι ἄν
and distributed them to all, according as

τις χρείαν εἶχεν. **46** καθ’ ἡμέραν τε
anyone need had. And from day to day†

προσκαρτεροῦντες ὁμοθυμαδὸν ἐν τῷ ἱερῷ,
continuing steadfastly with one mind in the temple,

κλῶντές τε κατ’ οἶκον ἄρτον, μετε-
and ¹breaking ²from house to house† ³bread, they

λάμβανον τροφῆς ἐν ἀγαλλιάσει καὶ
shared food in gladness and

ἀφελότητι καρδίας, **47** αἰνοῦντες τὸν θεὸν
simplicity of heart, praising - God

καὶ ἔχοντες χάριν πρὸς ὅλον τὸν λαόν.
and having favour with all the people.

ὁ δὲ κύριος προσετίθει τοὺς σῳζομένους
And the Lord added the [ones] being saved

καθ’ ἡμέραν ἐπὶ τὸ αὐτό.
from day to day† together.†

---

3 Πέτρος δὲ καὶ Ἰωάννης ἀνέβαινον
Now Peter and John were going up

εἰς τὸ ἱερὸν ἐπὶ τὴν ὥραν τῆς προσευχῆς
to the temple at the hour of the prayer

τὴν ἐνάτην. **2** καί τις ἀνὴρ χωλὸς ἐκ
the ninth. And a certain man ²lame ³from

κοιλίας μητρὸς αὐτοῦ ὑπάρχων ἐβαστάζετο,
⁴[the] ⁵of [the] ⁶of him ¹being was being carried,

ὃν ἐτίθουν καθ’ ἡμέραν πρὸς τὴν θύραν
whom they used from day to day† at the door
to put

τοῦ ἱεροῦ τὴν λεγομένην ὡραίαν τοῦ
of the temple - being called Beautiful of the

αἰτεῖν ἐλεημοσύνην παρὰ τῶν εἰσπορευομέ-
to askᵈ alms from the [ones] enter-

νων εἰς τὸ ἱερόν· **3** ὃς ἰδὼν Πέτρον καὶ
ing into the temple; who seeing Peter and

Ἰωάννην μέλλοντας εἰσιέναι εἰς τὸ ἱερὸν
John being about to go *in* into the temple

ἠρώτα ἐλεημοσύνην λαβεῖν. **4** ἀτενίσας δὲ
asked alms to receive. And ²gazing

Πέτρος εἰς αὐτὸν σὺν τῷ Ἰωάννῃ εἶπεν·
¹Peter at him with - John said:

βλέψον εἰς ἡμᾶς. **5** ὁ δὲ ἐπεῖχεν αὐτοῖς
Look at us. And he paid heed to them

προσδοκῶν τι παρ’ αὐτῶν λαβεῖν. **6** εἶπεν
expecting something from them to receive. said

δὲ Πέτρος· ἀργύριον καὶ χρυσίον οὐχ
And Peter: Silver and gold not

ὑπάρχει μοι· ὃ δὲ ἔχω, τοῦτό σοι δίδωμι·
is to meᵉ; but what I have, this to thee I give;
=I have not;

ἐν τῷ ὀνόματι Ἰησοῦ Χριστοῦ τοῦ
in the name of Jesus Christ the

Ναζωραίου περιπάτει. **7** καὶ πιάσας αὐτὸν τῆς
Nazarene walk. And seizing him of(by)

δεξιᾶς χειρὸς ἤγειρεν αὐτόν· παραχρῆμα
the right hand he raised him; ¹at once

δὲ ἐστερεώθησαν αἱ βάσεις αὐτοῦ καὶ τὰ
¹and were made firm the feet of him and the

σφυδρά, **8** καὶ ἐξαλλόμενος ἔστη, καὶ
ankle-bones, and leaping up he stood, and

περιεπάτει, καὶ εἰσῆλθεν σὺν αὐτοῖς εἰς
walked, and entered with them into

τὸ ἱερὸν περιπατῶν καὶ ἁλλόμενος καὶ
the temple walking and leaping and

---

and goods, they gave to anyone as he had need.

46Every day they continued to meet together in the temple courts. They broke bread in their homes and ate together with glad and sincere hearts, 47praising God and enjoying the favor of all the people. And the Lord added to their number daily those who were being saved.

Chapter 3

Peter Heals the Crippled Beggar

ONE day Peter and John were going up to the temple at the time of prayer —at three in the afternoon. 2Now a man crippled from birth was being carried to the temple gate called Beautiful, where he was put every day to beg from those going into the temple courts. 3When he saw Peter and John about to enter, he asked them for money. 4Peter looked straight at him, as did John. Then Peter said, "Look at us!" 5So the man gave them his attention, expecting to get something from them.

6Then Peter said, "Silver or gold I do not have, but what I have I give you. In the name of Jesus Christ of Nazareth, walk." 7Taking him by the right hand, he helped him up, and instantly the man's feet and ankles became strong. 8He jumped to his feet and began to walk. Then he went with them into the temple courts, walking and jump-

---

ᵍ I.e., 3 p.m.

ʰ Or, *a gift of charity*

God.

9And all the people saw him walking and praising God;

10and they were taking note of him as being the one who used to sit at the Beautiful Gate of the temple, to beg alms, and they were filled with wonder and amazement at what had happened to him.

Peter's Second Sermon

11And while he was clinging to Peter and John, all the people ran together to them at the so-called portico of Solomon, full of amazement.

12But when Peter saw *this*, he replied to the people, "Men of Israel, why do you marvel at this, or why do you gaze at us, as if by our own power or piety we had made him walk?

13"The God of Abraham, Isaac, and Jacob, the God of our fathers, has glorified His servant Jesus, *the one* whom you delivered up, and disowned in the presence of Pilate, when he had decided to release Him.

14"But you disowned the Holy and Righteous One, and asked for a murderer to be granted to you,

15but put to death the Prince of life, *the one* whom God raised from the dead, *a fact* to which we are witnesses.

16"And on the basis of faith in His name, *it is* the name of Jesus which has strengthened this man whom you see and know; and the faith which *comes* through Him has given him this perfect health in the presence of you all.

17"And now, brethren, I know that you acted in ignorance, just as your rulers

---

αἰώνων τὸν θεόν.   9 καὶ εἶδεν πᾶς ὁ
praising   -   God.   And   ⁴saw   ¹all   ²the

λαὸς αὐτὸν περιπατοῦντα καὶ αἰνοῦντα
²people   him   walking   and   praising

τὸν θεόν·   10 ἐπεγίνωσκον δὲ αὐτόν, ὅτι
-    God;   and they recognized   him,   that

οὗτος ἦν ὁ πρὸς τὴν ἐλεημοσύνην
this   was   the [one]   for   alms

καθήμενος ἐπὶ τῇ ὡραίᾳ πύλῃ τοῦ ἱεροῦ,
sitting   at   the   Beautiful   gate   of the   temple,

καὶ ἐπλήσθησαν θάμβους καὶ ἐκστάσεως
and   they were filled   of(with)   and   bewilderment
                   amazement

ἐπὶ τῷ συμβεβηκότι αὐτῷ. 11 Κρατοῦντος δὲ
at   the thing having happened to him.   And holding
                            = as he held

αὐτοῦ τὸν Πέτρον καὶ τὸν Ἰωάννην
himᵃ   -   Peter   and   -   John

συνέδραμεν πᾶς ὁ λαὸς πρὸς αὐτοὺς
ran together   all   the   people   to   them

ἐπὶ τῇ στοᾷ τῇ καλουμένῃ Σολομῶντος
-   the   porch   -   being called   of Solomon

ἔκθαμβοι. 12 ἰδὼν δὲ ὁ Πέτρος ἀπεκρίνατο
greatly amazed.   And ²seeing -   ¹Peter   answered

πρὸς τὸν λαόν· ἄνδρες Ἰσραηλῖται, τί
to   the   people :   Men   Israelites,   why

θαυμάζετε ἐπὶ τούτῳ, ἢ ἡμῖν τί ἀτενίζετε
marvel ye   at   this man,   or   at us   why   gaze ye

ὡς ἰδίᾳ δυνάμει ἢ εὐσεβείᾳ πεποιηκόσιν
as   by [our] own   power   or   piety   having made

τοῦ περιπατεῖν αὐτόν; 13 ὁ θεὸς Ἀβραὰμ
-   to walkᵈ   him?   The God of Abraham

καὶ Ἰσαὰκ καὶ Ἰακώβ, ὁ θεὸς τῶν
and   Isaac   and   Jacob,   the   God   of the

πατέρων ἡμῶν, ἐδόξασεν τὸν παῖδα αὐτοῦ
fathers   of us,   glorified   the   servant   of him

Ἰησοῦν, ὃν ὑμεῖς μὲν παρεδώκατε καὶ
Jesus,   whom   ye   -   delivered   and

ἠρνήσασθε κατὰ πρόσωπον Πιλάτου,
denied   in   [the] presence   of Pilate,

κρίναντος ἐκείνου ἀπολύειν· 14 ὑμεῖς δὲ
having decided that oneᵃ to release [him];   but ye
= when he had decided

τὸν ἅγιον καὶ δίκαιον ἠρνήσασθε, καὶ
the   holy   and   just one   denied,   and

ᾐτήσασθε ἄνδρα φονέα χαρισθῆναι ὑμῖν,
asked   a man   a murderer   to be granted   you,

15 τὸν δὲ ἀρχηγὸν τῆς ζωῆς ἀπεκτείνατε,
and the   Author   -   of life   ye killed,

ὃν ὁ θεὸς ἤγειρεν ἐκ νεκρῶν, οὗ ἡμεῖς
whom -   God   raised   from [the] dead, of which   we

μάρτυρές ἐσμεν. 16 καὶ ἐπὶ τῇ πίστει
witnesses   are.   And   on   the   faith

τοῦ ὀνόματος αὐτοῦ τοῦτον, ὃν θεωρεῖτε
of(in)   name*   of him   ⁵this man,   ⁶whom   ⁷ye behold
the

καὶ οἴδατε, ἐστερέωσεν τὸ ὄνομα αὐτοῦ,
³and   ⁹know,   ⁴made firm   ¹the   ²name   ³of him,

καὶ ἡ πίστις ἡ δι' αὐτοῦ ἔδωκεν αὐτῷ
and   the   faith   - through   him   gave   him

τὴν ὁλοκληρίαν ταύτην ἀπέναντι πάντων
this   soundness   before   all

ὑμῶν. 17 καὶ νῦν, ἀδελφοί, οἶδα ὅτι
you.   And   now,   brothers,   I know   that

κατὰ ἄγνοιαν ἐπράξατε, ὥσπερ καὶ οἱ
by way of ignorance   ye acted,   as   also   the

---

ing, and praising God.

9When all the people saw him walking and praising God, 10they recognized him as the same man who used to sit begging at the temple gate called Beautiful, and they were filled with wonder and amazement at what had happened to him.

Peter Speaks to the Onlookers

11While the beggar held on to Peter and John, all the people were astonished and came running to them in the place called Solomon's Colonnade. 12When Peter saw this, he said to them: "Men of Israel, why does this surprise you? Why do you stare at us as if by our own power or godliness we had made this man walk? 13The God of Abraham, Isaac and Jacob, the God of our fathers, has glorified his servant Jesus. You handed him over to be killed, and you disowned him before Pilate, though he had decided to let him go. 14You disowned the Holy and Righteous One and asked that a murderer be released to you. 15You killed the author of life, but God raised him from the dead. We are witnesses of this. 16By faith in the name of Jesus, this man whom you see and know was made strong. It is Jesus' name and the faith that comes through him that has given this complete healing to him, as you can all see.

17"Now, brothers, I know that you acted in ignorance, as did your lead-

---

* Objective genitive; *cf.* "the fear of God" = the fear which has God for its object; and see Gal. 2. 20, etc.

did also.

18"But the things which God announced beforehand by the mouth of all the prophets, that His Christ should suffer, He has thus fulfilled.

19"Repent therefore and return, that your sins may be wiped away, in order that times of refreshing may come from the presence of the Lord;

20and that He may send Jesus, the Christ appointed for you,

21whom heaven must receive until *the* period of restoration of all things about which God spoke by the mouth of His holy prophets from ancient time.

22"Moses said, 'THE LORD GOD SHALL RAISE UP FOR YOU A PROPHET LIKE ME FROM YOUR BRETHREN; TO HIM YOU SHALL GIVE HEED IN everything He says to you.

23'And it shall be that every soul that does not heed that prophet shall be utterly destroyed from among the people.'

24"And likewise, all the prophets who have spoken, from Samuel and *his* successors onward, also announced these days.

25"It is you who are the sons of the prophets, and of the covenant which God made with your fathers, saying to Abraham, 'AND IN YOUR SEED ALL THE FAMILIES OF THE EARTH SHALL BE BLESSED.'

26"For you first, God raised up His Servant, and sent Him to bless you by turning every one *of you* from your wicked ways."

Chapter 4

Peter and John Arrested

AND as they were speaking to the people, the priests and the captain of the temple *guard,* and the

---

ἄρχοντες ὑμῶν· **18** ὁ δὲ θεὸς ἃ
rulers of you; but God the things which

προκατήγγειλεν διὰ στόματος πάντων
he foreannounced through [the] mouth of all

τῶν προφητῶν, παθεῖν τὸν χριστὸν αὐτοῦ,
the prophets, to suffer the Christ of him[b],
=that his Christ was to suffer,

ἐπλήρωσεν οὕτως. **19** μετανοήσατε οὖν
fulfilled thus. Repent ye therefore

καὶ ἐπιστρέψατε πρὸς τὸ ἐξαλειφθῆναι
and turn for the to be wiped away
=that your sins may be wiped away,

ὑμῶν τὰς ἁμαρτίας, **20** ὅπως ἂν ἔλθωσιν
of you the sins, so as may come

καιροὶ ἀναψύξεως ἀπὸ προσώπου τοῦ
times of refreshing from [the] presence of the

κυρίου καὶ ἀποστείλῃ τὸν προκεχειρισμένον
Lord and he may send [1]the [3]having been foreappointed

ὑμῖν χριστὸν Ἰησοῦν, **21** ὃν δεῖ οὐρανὸν
[4]for you [2]Christ [5]Jesus, whom it behoves heaven

μὲν δέξασθαι ἄχρι χρόνων ἀποκαταστάσεως
- to receive until [the] times of restitution

πάντων ὧν ἐλάλησεν ὁ θεὸς διὰ στόματος
of all things which [8]spoke - [7]God [9]through [9][the] mouth

τῶν ἁγίων ἀπ' αἰῶνος αὐτοῦ προφητῶν.
[5]of the [6]holy [8]from [10][the] age [6]of him [7]prophets.

22 Μωϋσῆς μὲν εἶπεν ὅτι προφήτην ὑμῖν
Moses indeed said[,] - [4]A prophet [5]for you

ἀναστήσει κύριος ὁ θεὸς ἐκ τῶν ἀδελφῶν
[1]will raise up [1](the) Lord - [1]God of the brothers

ὑμῶν ὡς ἐμέ· αὐτοῦ ἀκούσεσθε κατὰ
of you as me; him shall ye hear according to

πάντα ὅσα ἂν λαλήσῃ πρὸς ὑμᾶς.
all things whatever he may speak to you.

23 ἔσται δὲ πᾶσα ψυχὴ ἥτις ἐὰν μὴ ἀκούσῃ
And it shall be every soul whoever hears not

τοῦ προφήτου ἐκείνου ἐξολεθρευθήσεται
that prophet will be utterly destroyed

ἐκ τοῦ λαοῦ. **24** καὶ πάντες δὲ οἱ
out of the people. [2]also [1]all [1]And the

προφῆται ἀπὸ Σαμουὴλ καὶ τῶν καθεξῆς
prophets from Samuel and the [ones] in order

ὅσοι ἐλάλησαν καὶ κατήγγειλαν τὰς ἡμέρας
as many as spoke also announced - days

ταύτας. **25** ὑμεῖς ἐστε οἱ υἱοὶ τῶν
these. Ye are the sons of the

προφητῶν καὶ τῆς διαθήκης ἧς ὁ θεὸς
prophets and of the covenant which - God

διέθετο πρὸς τοὺς πατέρας ὑμῶν, λέγων
made with the fathers of us, saying

πρὸς Ἀβραάμ· καὶ ἐν τῷ σπέρματί
to Abraham: And in the seed

σου ἐνευλογηθήσονται πᾶσαι αἱ πατριαὶ
of thee shall be blessed all the families

τῆς γῆς. **26** ὑμῖν πρῶτον ἀναστήσας ὁ
of the earth. To you first [1]having raised up -

θεὸς τὸν παῖδα αὐτοῦ ἀπέστειλεν αὐτὸν
[1]God the servant of him sent him

εὐλογοῦντα ὑμᾶς ἐν τῷ ἀποστρέφειν
blessing you in the to turn away
=in turning away

ἕκαστον ἀπὸ τῶν πονηριῶν ὑμῶν.
each one from the iniquities of you.

4 Λαλούντων δὲ αὐτῶν πρὸς τὸν λαόν,
And speaking them[a] to the people,
=while they were speaking

ἐπέστησαν αὐτοῖς οἱ ἱερεῖς καὶ ὁ στρατηγὸς
came upon them the priests and the commandant

---

ers. 18But this is how God fulfilled what he had foretold through all the prophets, saying that his Christ[m] would suffer. 19Repent, then, and turn to God, so that your sins may be wiped out, that times of refreshing may come from the Lord, 20and that he may send the Christ, who has been appointed for you—even Jesus. 21He must remain in heaven until the time comes for God to restore everything, as he promised long ago through his holy prophets. 22For Moses said, 'The Lord your God will raise up for you a prophet like me from among your own people; you must listen to everything he tells you. 23Anyone who does not listen to him will be completely cut off from among his people.'[n] 24"Indeed, all the prophets from Samuel on, as many as have spoken, have foretold these days. 25And you are heirs of the prophets and of the covenant God made with your fathers. He said to Abraham, 'Through your offspring all peoples on earth will be blessed.'[o] 26When God raised up his servant, he sent him first to you to bless you by turning each of you from your wicked ways."

Chapter 4

Peter and John Before the Sanhedrin

THE priests and the captain of the temple guard and the Sadducees

Sadducees, came upon them,

2being greatly disturbed because they were teaching the people and proclaiming in Jesus the resurrection from the dead.

3And they laid hands on them, and put them in jail until the next day, for it was already evening.

4But many of those who had heard the message believed; and the number of the men came to be about five thousand.

5And it came about on the next day, that their rulers and elders and scribes were gathered together in Jerusalem;

6and Annas the high priest was there, and Caiaphas and John and Alexander, and all who were of high-priestly descent.

7And when they had placed them in the center, they began to inquire, "By what power, or in what name, have you done this?"

8Then Peter, filled with the Holy Spirit, said to them, "Rulers and elders of the people,

9if we are on trial today for a benefit done to a sick man, as to how this man has been made well,

10let it be known to all of you, and to all the people of Israel, that by the name of Jesus Christ the Nazarene, whom you crucified, whom God raised from the dead— by this name this man stands here before you in good health.

11"He is the STONE WHICH WAS REJECTED by you, THE BUILDERS, but WHICH BECAME THE VERY CORNER stone.

12"And there is salvation in no one else; for there is no other name under

τοῦ ἱεροῦ καὶ οἱ Σαδδουκαῖοι, 2 διαπονούμενοι
of the . temple and the Sadducees, being greatly troubled

διὰ τὸ διδάσκειν αὐτοὺς τὸν λαὸν καὶ
because of the to teach them(b) the people and
=because they taught . . . announced

καταγγέλλειν ἐν τῷ Ἰησοῦ τὴν ἀνάστασιν
to announce(b) by - Jesus the resurrection

τὴν ἐκ νεκρῶν, 3 καὶ ἐπέβαλον αὐτοῖς
- from [the] dead, and laid on them

τὰς χεῖρας καὶ ἔθεντο εἰς τήρησιν εἰς
the(ir) hands and put in guard till

τὴν αὔριον· ἦν γὰρ ἑσπέρα ἤδη. 4 πολλοὶ
the morrow; for it was evening now. many

δὲ τῶν ἀκουσάντων τὸν λόγον ἐπίστευσαν,
But of the [ones] hearing the word believed,

καὶ ἐγενήθη ἀριθμὸς τῶν ἀνδρῶν ὡς
and became [the] number of the men about

χιλιάδες πέντε.
thousands five.

5 Ἐγένετο δὲ ἐπὶ τὴν αὔριον
Now it came to pass on the morrow

συναχθῆναι αὐτῶν τοὺς ἄρχοντας καὶ τοὺς
to be assembled of them the rulers and the

πρεσβυτέρους καὶ τοὺς γραμματεῖς ἐν
elders and the scribes in

Ἰερουσαλήμ, 6 καὶ Ἅννας ὁ ἀρχιερεὺς
Jerusalem, and Annas the high priest

καὶ Καϊάφας καὶ Ἰωάννης καὶ Ἀλέξανδρος
and Caiaphas and John and Alexander

καὶ ὅσοι ἦσαν ἐκ γένους ἀρχιερατικοῦ,
and as many as were of [the] race high-priestly,

7 καὶ στήσαντες αὐτοὺς ἐν τῷ μέσῳ
and having stood them in the midst

ἐπυνθάνοντο· ἐν ποίᾳ δυνάμει ἢ ἐν ποίῳ
inquired : By what power or in what

ὀνόματι ἐποιήσατε τοῦτο ὑμεῖς; 8 τότε
name did this ye? Then

Πέτρος πλησθεὶς πνεύματος ἁγίου εἶπεν
Peter filled of(with) [the] Spirit Holy said

πρὸς αὐτούς· ἄρχοντες τοῦ λαοῦ καὶ
to them : Rulers of the people and

πρεσβύτεροι, 9 εἰ ἡμεῖς σήμερον ἀνα-
elders, if we to-day are be-

κρινόμεθα ἐπὶ εὐεργεσίᾳ ἀνθρώπου ἀσθενοῦς,
ing examined on a good deed man of an infirm,
=[done to] an infirm man,

ἐν τίνι οὗτος σέσωσται, 10 γνωστὸν ἔστω
by what this man has been healed, known let it be

πᾶσιν ὑμῖν καὶ παντὶ τῷ λαῷ Ἰσραήλ,
to all you and to all the people of Israel,

ὅτι ἐν τῷ ὀνόματι Ἰησοῦ Χριστοῦ τοῦ
that in the name of Jesus Christ the

Ναζωραίου, ὃν ὑμεῖς ἐσταυρώσατε, ὃν ὁ
Nazarene, whom ye crucified, whom -

θεὸς ἤγειρεν ἐκ νεκρῶν, ἐν τούτῳ οὗτος
God raised from [the] dead, in this [name] this man

παρέστηκεν ἐνώπιον ὑμῶν ὑγιής. 11 οὗτός
stands before you whole. This

ἐστιν ὁ λίθος ὁ ἐξουθενηθεὶς ὑφ' ὑμῶν
is the stone - despised by you

τῶν οἰκοδόμων, ὁ γενόμενος εἰς κεφαλὴν
the [ones] building, the [one] become to head

γωνίας. 12 καὶ οὐκ ἔστιν ἐν ἄλλῳ οὐδενὶ
of [the] corner. And there is not ¹in ²other ³no(any)

ἡ σωτηρία· οὐδὲ γὰρ ὄνομά ἐστιν ἕτερον
the salvation: for neither ²name ¹is there ³other

* The rough breathing in the Greek is ignored in the transliteration of some familiar proper names.

came up to Peter and John while they were speaking to the people. 2They were greatly disturbed because the apostles were teaching the people and proclaiming in Jesus the resurrection of the dead. 3They seized Peter and John, and because it was evening, they put them in jail until the next day. 4But many who heard the message believed, and the number of men grew to about five thousand.

5The next day the rulers, elders and teachers of the law met in Jerusalem. 6Annas the high priest was there, and so were Caiaphas, John, Alexander and the other men of the high priest's family. 7They had Peter and John brought before them and began to question them: "By what power or what name did you do this?"

8Then Peter, filled with the Holy Spirit, said to them: "Rulers and elders of the people! 9If we are being called to account today for an act of kindness shown to a cripple and are asked how he was healed, 10then know this, you and all the people of Israel: It is by the name of Jesus Christ of Nazareth, whom you crucified but whom God raised from the dead, that this man stands before you healed. 11He is

" 'the stone you builders rejected,
which has become the capstone.'p q

12Salvation is found in no one else, for there is no other name under heaven giv-

p11 Or cornerstone
q11 Psalm 118:22

heaven that has been given among men, by which we must be saved.''

Threat and Release

13Now as they observed the confidence of Peter and John, and understood that they were uneducated and untrained men, they were marveling, and *began* to recognize them as having been with Jesus.

14And seeing the man who had been healed standing with them, they had nothing to say in reply.

15But when they had ordered them to go aside out of the Council, they *began* to confer with one another,

16saying, ''What shall we do with these men? For the fact that a noteworthy miracle has taken place through them is apparent to all who live in Jerusalem, and we cannot deny it.

17''But in order that it may not spread any further among the people, let us warn them to speak no more to any man in this name.''

18And when they had summoned them, they commanded them not to speak or teach at all in the name of Jesus.

19But Peter and John answered and said to them, ''Whether it is right in the sight of God to give heed to you rather than to God, you be the judge;

20for we cannot stop speaking what we have seen and heard.''

21And when they had threatened them further, they let them go (finding no basis on which they might punish them) on account of the people, because they were all glorifying God for what had happened;

22for the man was more than forty years old on whom this miracle of healing had been performed.

ὑπὸ τὸν οὐρανὸν τὸ δεδομένον ἐν
under - heaven - having been given among

ἀνθρώποις ἐν ᾧ δεῖ σωθῆναι ἡμᾶς.
men by which it behoves ²to be saved ¹us.

13 Θεωροῦντες δὲ τὴν τοῦ Πέτρου
And beholding the - of Peter

παρρησίαν καὶ Ἰωάννου, καὶ καταλαβόμενοι
boldness and of John, and perceiving

ὅτι ἄνθρωποι ἀγράμματοί εἰσιν καὶ
that men unlettered they are(were) and

ἰδιῶται, ἐθαύμαζον, ἐπεγίνωσκόν τε αὐτοὺς
laymen, they marvelled, and recognized them

ὅτι σὺν τῷ Ἰησοῦ ἦσαν, 14 τόν τε
that with - Jesus they were(had been), ³the ¹and

ἄνθρωπον βλέποντες σὺν αὐτοῖς ἑστῶτα τὸν
⁴man ²seeing ⁷with ⁸them ⁵standing -

τεθεραπευμένον, οὐδὲν εἶχον ἀντειπεῖν.
⁶having been healed, nothing they had to say against.

15 κελεύσαντες δὲ αὐτοὺς ἔξω τοῦ συνεδρίου
So having commanded them outside the council

ἀπελθεῖν, συνέβαλλον πρὸς ἀλλήλους
to go, they discussed with with one another

16 λέγοντες· τί ποιήσωμεν τοῖς ἀνθρώποις
saying: What may we do - men

τούτοις; ὅτι μὲν γὰρ γνωστὸν σημεῖον
to these? for that indeed a notable sign

γέγονεν δι' αὐτῶν, πᾶσιν τοῖς κατοικοῦσιν
has happened through them, to all the [ones] inhabiting

Ἰερουσαλὴμ φανερόν, καὶ οὐ δυνάμεθα
Jerusalem [is] manifest, and we cannot

ἀρνεῖσθαι· 17 ἀλλ' ἵνα μὴ ἐπὶ πλεῖον
to deny [it]; but ¹lest ²more†

διανεμηθῇ εἰς τὸν λαόν, ἀπειλησώμεθα
³it is spread abroad ⁴to the people, let us threaten

αὐτοῖς μηκέτι λαλεῖν ἐπὶ τῷ ὀνόματι
them no longer to speak on - name

τούτῳ μηδενὶ ἀνθρώπων. 18 καὶ καλέσαντες
this to no(any)one of men. And calling

αὐτοὺς παρήγγειλαν καθόλου μὴ φθέγγεσθαι
them they charged at all not to utter

μηδὲ διδάσκειν ἐπὶ τῷ ὀνόματι τοῦ
nor to teach on the name -

Ἰησοῦ. 19 ὁ δὲ Πέτρος καὶ Ἰωάννης
of Jesus. - But Peter and John

ἀποκριθέντες εἶπον πρὸς αὐτούς· εἰ
answering said to them: If

δίκαιόν ἐστιν ἐνώπιον τοῦ θεοῦ, ὑμῶν
right it is before - God, you

ἀκούειν μᾶλλον ἢ τοῦ θεοῦ, κρίνατε·
to hear rather than - God, decide ye;

20 οὐ δυνάμεθα γὰρ ἡμεῖς ἃ εἴδαμεν
for cannot we [the] things which we saw

καὶ ἠκούσαμεν μὴ λαλεῖν. 21 οἱ δὲ
and heard not to speak. And they

προσαπειλησάμενοι ἀπέλυσαν αὐτούς, μηδὲν
having added threats released them, nothing

εὑρίσκοντες τὸ πῶς κολάσωνται αὐτούς,
finding - how they might punish them,

διὰ τὸν λαόν, ὅτι πάντες ἐδόξαζον τὸν
because of the people, because all men glorified -

θεὸν ἐπὶ τῷ γεγονότι· 22 ἐτῶν γὰρ
God on the thing having happened; for of years

ἦν πλειόνων τεσσεράκοντα ὁ ἄνθρωπος
was more [than] forty the man

ἐφ' ὃν γεγόνει τὸ σημεῖον τοῦτο τῆς
on whom had happened this sign -

---

en to men by which we must be saved.''

13When they saw the courage of Peter and John and realized that they were unschooled, ordinary men, they were astonished and they took note that these men had been with Jesus.

14But since they could see the man who had been healed standing there with them, there was nothing they could say. 15So they ordered them to withdraw from the Sanhedrin and then conferred together. 16''What are we going to do with these men?'' they asked. ''Everybody living in Jerusalem knows they have done an outstanding miracle, and we cannot deny it. 17But to stop this thing from spreading any further among the people, we must warn these men to speak no longer to anyone in this name.''

18Then they called them in again and commanded them not to speak or teach at all in the name of Jesus. 19But Peter and John replied, ''Judge for yourselves whether it is right in God's sight to obey you rather than God. 20For we cannot help speaking about what we have seen and heard.''

21After further threats they let them go. They could not decide how to punish them, because all the people were praising God for what had happened. 22For the man who was miraculously healed was over forty years old.

23And when they had been released, they went to their own *companions*, and reported all that the chief priests and the elders had said to them.
24And when they heard *this*, they lifted their voices to God with one accord and said, "O Lord, it is Thou who DIDST MAKE THE HEAVEN AND THE EARTH AND THE SEA, AND ALL THAT IS IN THEM,
25who by the Holy Spirit, *through* the mouth of our father David Thy servant, didst say,

'WHY DID THE / GEN-
TILES RAGE,
AND THE PEOPLES DE-
VISE FUTILE THINGS?
26 'THE KINGS OF THE
EARTH TOOK THEIR
STAND,
AND THE RULERS WERE
GATHERED TOGETHER
AGAINST THE LORD,
AND AGAINST HIS
CHRIST.'

27"For truly in this city there were gathered together against Thy holy servant Jesus, whom Thou didst anoint, both Herod and Pontius Pilate, along with the Gentiles and the peoples of Israel,
28to do whatever Thy hand and Thy purpose predestined to occur.
29"And now, Lord, take note of their threats, and grant that Thy bond-servants may speak Thy word with all confidence,
30while Thou dost extend Thy hand to heal, and signs and wonders take place through the name of Thy holy servant Jesus."
31And when they had prayed, the place where they had gathered together was shaken, and they were all filled with the Holy Spirit, and *began* to speak the word of God with boldness.

Sharing among Believers

32And the congregation of those who believed were of

ἰάσεως.   23 Ἀπολυθέντες δὲ   ἦλθον πρὸς
of cure.   And being released   they went   to

τοὺς   ἰδίους   καὶ   ἀπήγγειλαν   ὅσα   πρὸς
the(ir) own [people]   and   reported   what things   to

αὐτοὺς   οἱ   ἀρχιερεῖς   καὶ   οἱ   πρεσβύτεροι
them   the   chief priests   and   the   elders

εἶπαν.   24 οἱ   δὲ   ἀκούσαντες   ὁμοθυμαδὸν
said.   And they   having heard   with one mind

ἦραν   φωνὴν   πρὸς   τὸν   θεὸν   καὶ   εἶπαν·
lifted   voice   to   -   God   and   said :

δέσποτα,   σὺ   ὁ   ποιήσας   τὸν   οὐρανὸν   καὶ
Master,   thou   the [one]   having made   the   heaven   and

τὴν   γῆν   καὶ   τὴν   θάλασσαν   καὶ   πάντα
the   earth   and   the   sea   and   all things

τὰ   ἐν   αὐτοῖς,   25 ὁ   τοῦ   πατρὸς   ἡμῶν
-   in   them,   ¹the   ⁸the   ⁹father   ¹⁰of us
[one]

διὰ   πνεύματος   ἁγίου   στόματος   Δαυὶδ
³through   ⁵[the] Spirit   ⁴Holy   ⁶[by] mouth   ⁷of David

παιδός   σου   εἰπών·   ἱνατί   ἐφρύαξαν   ἔθνη
¹¹servant   ¹²of thee   ²saying :*   Why   raged   nations

καὶ   λαοὶ   ἐμελέτησαν   κενά;   26 παρέστησαν
and   peoples   devised   vain things?   came

οἱ   βασιλεῖς   τῆς   γῆς   καὶ   οἱ   ἄρχοντες
the   kings   of the   earth   and   the   rulers

συνήχθησαν   ἐπὶ   τὸ   αὐτὸ   κατὰ   τοῦ   κυρίου
assembled   together   against   the   Lord

καὶ   κατὰ   τοῦ   χριστοῦ   αὐτοῦ.
and   against   the   Christ   of him.

27 συνήχθησαν   γὰρ   ἐπ'   ἀληθείας   ἐν   τῇ
For assembled   in   truth   in   -

πόλει   ταύτῃ   ἐπὶ   τὸν   ἅγιον   παῖδά   σου
city   this   against   the   holy   servant of thee

Ἰησοῦν,   ὃν   ἔχρισας,   Ἡρῴδης   τε   καὶ
Jesus,   whom thou didst anoint,   both Herod   and

Πόντιος   Πιλᾶτος   σὺν   ἔθνεσιν   καὶ   λαοῖς
Pontius   Pilate   with   nations   and   peoples

Ἰσραήλ,   28 ποιῆσαι   ὅσα   ἡ   χείρ   σου   καὶ
of Israel,   to do   what   the   hand   of thee   and
things

ἡ   βουλὴ   προώρισεν   γενέσθαι.   29 καὶ   τὰ
the   counsel   foreordained   to happen.   And   -

νῦν,   κύριε,   ἔπιδε   ἐπὶ   τὰς   ἀπειλὰς   αὐτῶν,
now,   Lord,   look *on*   on   the   threatenings   of them,

καὶ   δὸς   τοῖς   δούλοις   σου   μετὰ   παρρησίας
and   give   to the   slaves   of thee   with   ²boldness

πάσης   λαλεῖν   τὸν   λόγον   σου,   30 ἐν   τῷ
¹all   to speak   the   word   of thee,   by   the

τὴν   χεῖρα   ἐκτείνειν   σε   εἰς   ἴασιν   καὶ
the   hand   to stretch forth   thee[b]   for   cure   and
=by stretching forth thy hand

σημεῖα   καὶ   τέρατα   γίνεσθαι   διὰ   τοῦ
signs   and   wonders   to happen   through   the

ὀνόματος   τοῦ   ἁγίου   παιδός   σου   Ἰησοῦ.
name   of the   holy   servant   of thee   Jesus.

31 καὶ   δεηθέντων   αὐτῶν   ἐσαλεύθη   ὁ   τόπος
And   requesting   them*   was shaken   the   place
=as they were making request

ἐν   ᾧ   ἦσαν   συνηγμένοι,   καὶ   ἐπλήσθησαν
in   which they were   *having been*   and   they were filled
assembled,

ἅπαντες   τοῦ   ἁγίου   πνεύματος,   καὶ   ἐλάλουν
all   of(with) the   Holy   Spirit,   and   spoke

τὸν   λόγον   τοῦ   θεοῦ   μετὰ   παρρησίας.
the   word   -   of God   with   boldness.

32 Τοῦ   δὲ   πλήθους   τῶν   πιστευσάντων
⁴Now   ⁶of   ⁷the   ⁵multitude   ⁸of the [ones]   ¹⁰having believed

* It is recognized that there is a primitive error in the text in the first half of ver. 25; it is impossible to construe it as it stands. See ch. 1. 16.

The Believers' Prayer

23On their release, Peter and John went back to their own people and reported all that the chief priests and elders had said to them. 24When they heard this, they raised their voices together in prayer to God. "Sovereign Lord," they said, "you made the heaven and the earth and the sea, and everything in them. 25You spoke by the Holy Spirit through the mouth of your servant, our father David:

"'Why do the nations
rage
and the peoples plot in
vain?
26The kings of the earth
take their stand
and the rulers gather
together
against the Lord
and against his
Anointed One.'[rs]

27Indeed Herod and Pontius Pilate met together with the Gentiles and the people[t] of Israel in this city to conspire against your holy servant Jesus, whom you anointed. 28They did what your power and will had decided beforehand should happen. 29Now, Lord, consider their threats and enable your servants to speak your word with great boldness. 30Stretch out your hand to heal and perform miraculous signs and wonders through the name of your holy servant Jesus." 31After they prayed, the place where they were meeting was shaken. And they were all filled with the Holy Spirit and spoke the word of God boldly.

The Believers Share Their Possessions

32All the believers were one in heart and mind. No

Or, nations

[r]26 That is, Christ or Messiah
[s]26 Psalm 2:1,2
[t]27 The Greek is plural.

one heart and soul; and not one *of them* claimed that anything belonging to him was his own; but all things were common property to them.

³³And with great power the apostles were giving witness to the resurrection of the Lord Jesus, and abundant grace was upon them all.

³⁴For there was not a needy person among them, for all who were owners of land or houses would sell them and bring the proceeds of the sales,

³⁵and lay them at the apostles' feet; and they would be distributed to each, as any had need.

³⁶And Joseph, a Levite of Cyprian birth, who was also called Barnabas by the apostles (which translated means, Son of Encouragement),

³⁷and who owned a tract of land, sold it and brought the money and laid it at the apostles' feet.

Chapter 5

Fate of Ananias and Sapphira

BUT a certain man named Ananias, with his wife Sapphira, sold a piece of property,

²and kept back *some* of the price for himself, with his wife's full knowledge, and bringing a portion of it, he laid it at the apostles' feet.

³But Peter said, "Ananias, why has Satan filled your heart to lie to the Holy Spirit, and to keep back *some* of the price of the land?

⁴"While it remained *unsold*, did it not remain your own? And after it was sold, was it not under your control? Why is it that you have conceived this deed in

---

ἦν καρδία καὶ ψυχὴ μία, καὶ οὐδὲ
¹¹was ²[the] ³heart ⁴and ⁵soul ¹²one, and ¹not

εἷς τι τῶν ὑπαρχόντων αὐτῷ ἔλεγεν
⁵one ⁶any-thing ⁵of the ⁶possessions [belonging] to him⁶ ⁵said

ἴδιον εἶναι, ἀλλ' ἦν αὐτοῖς πάντα κοινά.
⁵[his] own ⁶to be, but were to them⁶ all things common.

33 καὶ δυνάμει μεγάλῃ ἀπεδίδουν τὸ
And ¹with ²power ²great ¹gave ⁷the

μαρτύριον οἱ ἀπόστολοι τοῦ κυρίου Ἰησοῦ
⁸testimony ⁴the ⁵apostles ¹⁰of the ¹²Lord ¹³Jesus

τῆς ἀναστάσεως, χάρις τε μεγάλη ἦν
⁹of the ¹⁰resurrection, and ²grace ¹great was

ἐπὶ πάντας αὐτούς. 34 οὐδὲ γὰρ ἐνδεής
upon all them. ¹For ²neither ⁶needy

τις ἦν ἐν αὐτοῖς· ὅσοι γὰρ κτήτορες
⁴anyone ⁵was among them; for as many as owners

χωρίων ἢ οἰκιῶν ὑπῆρχον, πωλοῦντες
of lands or of houses were, selling

ἔφερον τὰς τιμὰς τῶν πιπρασκομένων
brought the prices of the things being sold

35 καὶ ἐτίθουν παρὰ τοὺς πόδας τῶν
and placed at the feet of the

ἀποστόλων· διεδίδοτο δὲ ἑκάστῳ καθότι ἄν
apostles; and it was distributed to each according as

τις χρείαν εἶχεν. 36 Ἰωσὴφ δὲ ὁ
anyone need had. And Joseph the [one]

ἐπικληθεὶς Βαρναβᾶς ἀπὸ τῶν ἀποστόλων,
surnamed Barnabas from(by) the apostles,

ὅ ἐστιν μεθερμηνευόμενον υἱὸς παρακλήσεως,
which is being translated Son of consolation,

Λευίτης, Κύπριος τῷ γένει, 37 ὑπάρχοντος
a Levite, a Cypriote by race, being

αὐτῷ ἀγροῦ, πωλήσας ἤνεγκεν τὸ χρῆμα
to him⁶ a field,ª having sold [it] brought the proceeds
=as he had a field,

καὶ ἔθηκεν πρὸς τοὺς πόδας τῶν ἀποστόλων.
and placed at the feet of the apostles.

5 Ἀνὴρ δέ τις Ἁνανίας ὀνόματι σὺν
And a certain man Ananias* by name with

Σαπφίρῃ τῇ γυναικὶ αὐτοῦ ἐπώλησεν
Sapphira the wife of him sold

κτῆμα, 2 καὶ ἐνοσφίσατο ἀπὸ τῆς τιμῆς,
a property, and appropriated from the price,

συνειδυίης καὶ τῆς γυναικός, καὶ ἐνέγκας
aware of [it] also the(his) wife,ª and bringing
=his wife also being aware of it,

μέρος τι παρὰ τοὺς πόδας τῶν ἀποστόλων
a certain part at the feet of the apostles

ἔθηκεν. 3 εἶπεν δὲ ὁ Πέτρος· Ἁνανία,
placed [it]. But said — Peter: Ananias,

διὰ τί ἐπλήρωσεν ὁ σατανᾶς τὴν καρδίαν
why filled — Satan the heart

σου, ψεύσασθαί σε τὸ πνεῦμα τὸ ἅγιον
of thee, to deceive theeᵇ the Spirit — Holy
=that thou shouldest deceive

καὶ νοσφίσασθαι ἀπὸ τῆς τιμῆς τοῦ
and to appropriate from the price of the

χωρίου; 4 οὐχὶ μένον σοὶ ἔμενεν καὶ
land? Not remaining to thee it remained and

πραθὲν ἐν τῇ σῇ ἐξουσίᾳ ὑπῆρχεν; τί ὅτι
sold in thy authority it was? Why

ἔθου ἐν τῇ καρδίᾳ σου τὸ πρᾶγμα
was put in the heart of thee — action

* See note to 4. 6.

---

one claimed that any of his possessions was his own, but they shared everything they had. ³³With great power the apostles continued to testify to the resurrection of the Lord Jesus, and much grace was upon them all. ³⁴There were no needy persons among them. For from time to time those who owned lands or houses sold them, brought the money from the sales ³⁵and put it at the apostles' feet, and it was distributed to anyone as he had need.

³⁶Joseph, a Levite from Cyprus, whom the apostles called Barnabas (which means Son of Encouragement), ³⁷sold a field he owned and brought the money and put it at the apostles' feet.

Chapter 5

Ananias and Sapphira

NOW a man named Ananias, together with his wife Sapphira, also sold a piece of property. ²With his wife's full knowledge he kept back part of the money for himself, but brought the rest and put it at the apostles' feet.

³Then Peter said, "Ananias, how is it that Satan has so filled your heart that you have lied to the Holy Spirit and have kept for yourself some of the money you received for the land? ⁴Didn't it belong to you before it was sold? And after it was sold, wasn't the money at your disposal? What made you think of doing such a thing? You have

your heart? You have not lied to men, but to God."

5And as he heard these words, Ananias fell down and breathed his last; and great fear came upon all who heard of it.

6And the young men arose and covered him up, and after carrying him out, they buried him.

7Now there elapsed an interval of about three hours, and his wife came in, not knowing what had happened.

8And Peter responded to her, "Tell me whether you sold the land for such and such a price?" And she said, "Yes, that was the price."

9Then Peter said to her, "Why is it that you have agreed together to put the Spirit of the Lord to the test? Behold, the feet of those who have buried your husband are at the door, and they shall carry you out as well."

10And she fell immediately at his feet, and breathed her last; and the young men came in and found her dead, and they carried her out and buried her beside her husband.

11And great fear came upon the whole church, and upon all who heard of these things.

12And at the hands of the apostles many signs and wonders were taking place among the people; and they were all with one accord in Solomon's portico.

13But none of the rest dared to associate with them; however, the people held them in high esteem.

14And all the more believers in the Lord, multitudes of men and women, were constantly added to their number;

15to such an extent that they even carried the sick out into the streets, and laid them on cots and pallets, so

τοῦτο; οὐκ ἐψεύσω ἀνθρώποις ἀλλὰ
this? thou didst not lie to men but

τῷ θεῷ. 5 ἀκούων δὲ ὁ Ἀνανίας
− to God. And hearing − Ananias

τοὺς λόγους τούτους πεσὼν ἐξέψυξεν· καὶ
these words falling expired; and

ἐγένετο φόβος μέγας ἐπὶ πάντας τοὺς
came fear great on all the [ones]

ἀκούοντας. 6 ἀναστάντες δὲ οἱ νεώτεροι
hearing. And rising up the young men

συνέστειλαν αὐτὸν καὶ ἐξενέγκαντες ἔθαψαν.
wrapped him and carrying out buried [him].

7 Ἐγένετο δὲ ὡς ὡρῶν τριῶν διάστημα
¹And there was ³of about ²hours ⁴three ⁵an interval

καὶ ἡ γυνὴ αὐτοῦ μὴ εἰδυῖα τὸ γεγονὸς
and the wife of him not knowing the thing having happened

εἰσῆλθεν. 8 ἀπεκρίθη δὲ πρὸς αὐτὴν
entered. And answered to her

Πέτρος· εἰπέ μοι, εἰ τοσούτου τὸ χωρίον
Peter: Tell me, if of(for) so much the land

ἀπέδοσθε; ἡ δὲ εἶπεν· ναί, τοσούτου.
ye sold? And she said: Yes, of(for) so much.

9 ὁ δὲ Πέτρος πρὸς αὐτήν· τί ὅτι
− And Peter to her: Why

συνεφωνήθη ὑμῖν πειράσαι τὸ πνεῦμα
was it agreed with you to tempt the Spirit

κυρίου; ἰδοὺ οἱ πόδες τῶν θαψάντων τὸν
of [the] Lord? behold[,] the feet of the [ones] having buried the

ἄνδρα σου ἐπὶ τῇ θύρᾳ καὶ ἐξοίσουσίν
husband of thee at the door and they will carry out

σε. 10 ἔπεσεν δὲ παραχρῆμα πρὸς τοὺς
thee. And she fell at once at the

πόδας αὐτοῦ καὶ ἐξέψυξεν· εἰσελθόντες δὲ
feet of him and expired; and entering

οἱ νεανίσκοι εὗρον αὐτὴν νεκράν, καὶ
the young men found her dead, and

ἐξενέγκαντες ἔθαψαν πρὸς τὸν ἄνδρα
carrying out buried [her] beside the husband

αὐτῆς. 11 Καὶ ἐγένετο φόβος μέγας
of her. And came fear great

ἐφ’ ὅλην τὴν ἐκκλησίαν καὶ ἐπὶ πάντας
on all the church and on all

τοὺς ἀκούοντας ταῦτα.
the [ones] hearing these things.

12 Διὰ δὲ τῶν χειρῶν τῶν ἀποστόλων
And through the hands of the apostles

ἐγίνετο σημεῖα καὶ τέρατα πολλὰ ἐν
⁶happened ²signs ³and ⁴wonders ¹many among

τῷ λαῷ· καὶ ἦσαν ὁμοθυμαδὸν πάντες
the people; and were with one mind all

ἐν τῇ στοᾷ Σολομῶντος· 13 τῶν δὲ
in the porch of Solomon; and of the

λοιπῶν οὐδεὶς ἐτόλμα κολλᾶσθαι αὐτοῖς,
rest no one dared to be joined to them,

ἀλλ’ ἐμεγάλυνεν αὐτοὺς ὁ λαός· 14 μᾶλλον
but magnified them the people; ²more

δὲ προσετίθεντο πιστεύοντες τῷ κυρίῳ,
¹and were added believing [ones] to the Lord,

πλήθη ἀνδρῶν τε καὶ γυναικῶν· 15 ὥστε
multitudes both of men and of women; so as

καὶ εἰς τὰς πλατείας ἐκφέρειν τοὺς
even into the streets to bring out the
=they brought out

ἀσθενεῖς καὶ τιθέναι ἐπὶ κλιναρίων καὶ
ailing and to place on pallets and

not lied to men but to God."

5When Ananias heard this, he fell down and died. And great fear seized all who heard what had happened. 6Then the young men came forward, wrapped up his body, and carried him out and buried him.

7About three hours later his wife came in, not knowing what had happened. 8Peter asked her, "Tell me, is this the price you and Ananias got for the land?"

"Yes," she said, "that is the price."

9Peter said to her, "How could you agree to test the Spirit of the Lord? Look! The feet of the men who buried your husband are at the door, and they will carry you out also."

10At that moment she fell down at his feet and died. Then the young men came in and, finding her dead, carried her out and buried her beside her husband. 11Great fear seized the whole church and all who heard about these events.

The Apostles Heal Many

12The apostles performed many miraculous signs and wonders among the people. And all the believers used to meet together in Solomon's Colonnade. 13No one else dared join them, even though they were highly regarded by the people. 14Nevertheless, more and more men and women believed in the Lord and were added to their number. 15As a result, people brought the sick into the streets and laid them on beds and mats so that at that when Peter came by, at least his shadow might fall on any one of them.

16And also the people from the cities in the vicinity of Jerusalem were coming together, bringing people who were sick *j* or afflicted with unclean spirits; and they were all being healed.

Imprisonment and Release

17But the high priest rose up, along with all his associates (that is the sect of the Sadducees), and they were filled with jealousy;

18and they laid hands on the apostles, and put them in a public jail.

19But an angel of the Lord during the night opened the gates of the prison, and taking them out he said,

20"Go your way, stand and speak to the people in the temple the whole message of this Life."

21And upon hearing *this,* they entered into the temple about daybreak, and *began* to teach. Now when the high priest and his associates had come, they called the Council together, even all the Senate of the sons of Israel, and sent *orders* to the prison house for them to be brought.

22But the officers who came did not find them in the prison; and they returned and reported back,

23saying, "We found the prison house locked quite securely and the guards standing at the doors; but when we had opened up, we found no one inside."

24Now when the captain of the temple *guard* and the chief priests heard these words, they were greatly perplexed about them as to what would come of this.

25But someone came and reported to them, "Behold, the men whom you put in

---

κραβάτων, ἵνα ἐρχομένου Πέτρου κἂν ἡ σκιὰ
mattresses, that ⁶coming ⁴of Peter ²if even ²the ³shadow

ἐπισκιάσῃ τινὶ αὐτῶν. 16 συνήρχετο δὲ
might overshadow some one of them. And came together

καὶ τὸ πλῆθος τῶν πέριξ πόλεων
also the multitude of the ²round about ¹cities

Ἰερουσαλήμ, φέροντες ἀσθενεῖς καὶ
Jerusalem, carrying ailing [ones] and

ὀχλουμένους ὑπὸ πνευμάτων ἀκαθάρτων,
being tormented by spirits unclean,

οἵτινες ἐθεραπεύοντο ἅπαντες.
who were healed all.

17 Ἀναστὰς δὲ ὁ ἀρχιερεὺς καὶ πάντες
And rising up the high priest and all

οἱ σὺν αὐτῷ, ἡ οὖσα αἵρεσις τῶν
the[ones] with him, the existing sect of the

Σαδδουκαίων, ἐπλήσθησαν ζήλου 18 καὶ
Sadducees, were filled of(with) jealousy and

ἐπέβαλον τὰς χεῖρας ἐπὶ τοὺς ἀποστόλους
laid *on* the(ir) hands on the apostles

καὶ ἔθεντο αὐτοὺς ἐν τηρήσει δημοσίᾳ.
and put them in custody publicly.

19 Ἄγγελος δὲ κυρίου διὰ νυκτὸς
But an angel of [the] Lord through(during) [the] night

ἤνοιξε τὰς θύρας τῆς φυλακῆς ἐξαγαγών τε
opened the doors of the prison and leading out

αὐτοὺς εἶπεν· 20 πορεύεσθε καὶ σταθέντες
them said : Go ye and standing

λαλεῖτε ἐν τῷ ἱερῷ τῷ λαῷ πάντα
speak in the temple to the people all

τὰ ῥήματα τῆς ζωῆς ταύτης.
the words of this life.

21 ἀκούσαντες δὲ εἰσῆλθον ὑπὸ τὸν ὄρθρον
And having heard they entered about the dawn

εἰς τὸ ἱερὸν καὶ ἐδίδασκον. Παραγενόμενος δὲ
into the temple and taught. And having come

ὁ ἀρχιερεὺς καὶ οἱ σὺν αὐτῷ
the high priest and the [ones] with him

συνεκάλεσαν τὸ συνέδριον καὶ πᾶσαν τὴν
called together the council and all the

γερουσίαν τῶν υἱῶν Ἰσραήλ, καὶ ἀπέστειλαν
senate of the sons of Israel, and sent

εἰς τὸ δεσμωτήριον ἀχθῆναι αὐτούς.
to the jail to be brought them.ᵇ

22 οἱ δὲ παραγενόμενοι ὑπηρέται οὐχ εὗρον
¹But ²the ⁴having come ³attendants found not

αὐτοὺς ἐν τῇ φυλακῇ· ἀναστρέψαντες δὲ
them in the prison; and having returned

ἀπήγγειλαν 23 λέγοντες ὅτι τὸ δεσμωτήριον
they reported saying[,] - The jail

εὕρομεν κεκλεισμένον ἐν πάσῃ ἀσφαλείᾳ
we found *having been shut* in all security

καὶ τοὺς φύλακας ἑστῶτας ἐπὶ τῶν
and the guards standing at the

θυρῶν, ἀνοίξαντες δὲ ἔσω οὐδένα εὕρομεν.
doors, but having opened ³inside ²no one ¹we found.

24 ὡς δὲ ἤκουσαν τοὺς λόγους τούτους
And as ⁵heard ¹⁰these ¹¹words

ὅ τε στρατηγὸς τοῦ ἱεροῦ καὶ οἱ ἀρχιερεῖς,
²the ¹both ³commandant ⁴of the ⁵temple ⁶and ⁷the ⁸chief priests,

διηπόρουν περὶ αὐτῶν τί ἂν γένοιτο
they were in doubt about them what ²might become

τοῦτο. 25 παραγενόμενος δέ τις ἀπήγγειλεν
¹this thing. And having come someone reported

αὐτοῖς ὅτι ἰδοὺ οἱ ἄνδρες, οὓς
to them[,] - Behold[,] the men, whom

---

least Peter's shadow might fall on some of them as he passed by. 16Crowds gathered also from the towns around Jerusalem, bringing their sick and those tormented by evil*u* spirits, and all of them were healed.

The Apostles Persecuted

17Then the high priest and all his associates, who were members of the party of the Sadducees, were filled with jealousy. 18They arrested the apostles and put them in the public jail. 19But during the night an angel of the Lord opened the doors of the jail and brought them out. 20"Go, stand in the temple courts," he said, "and tell the people the full message of this new life."

21At daybreak they entered the temple courts, as they had been told, and began to teach the people.

When the high priest and his associates arrived, they called together the Sanhedrin—the full assembly of the elders of Israel—and sent to the jail for the apostles. 22But on arriving at the jail, the officers did not find them there. So they went back and reported, 23"We found the jail securely locked, with the guards standing at the doors; but when we opened them, we found no one inside." 24On hearing this report, the captain of the temple guard and the chief priests were puzzled, wondering what would come of this.

25Then someone came and said, "Look! The men you put in jail are standing

---

j Lit., *and*   *u* 16 Greek *unclean*

prison are standing in the temple and teaching the people.''

26Then the captain went along with the officers and *proceeded* to bring them *back* without violence (for they were afraid of the people, lest they should be stoned).

27And when they had brought them, they stood them before the Council. And the high priest questioned them,

28saying, "We gave you strict orders not to continue teaching in this name, and behold, you have filled Jerusalem with your teaching, and intend to bring this man's blood upon us.''

29But Peter and the apostles answered and said, "We must obey God rather than men.

30"The God of our fathers raised up Jesus, whom you had put to death by hanging Him on a cross.

31"He is the one whom God exalted to His right hand as a Prince and a Savior, to grant repentance to Israel, and forgiveness of sins.

32"And we are witnesses[k] of these things; and *so is* the Holy Spirit, whom God has given to those who obey Him.''

Gamaliel's Counsel

33But when they heard this, they were cut to the quick and were intending to slay them.

34But a certain Pharisee named Gamaliel, a teacher of the Law, respected by all the people, stood up in the Council and gave orders to put the men outside for a short time.

35And he said to them, "Men of Israel, take care what you propose to do

---

ἔθεσθε ἐν τῇ φυλακῇ, εἰσὶν ἐν τῷ ἱερῷ
ye put in the prison, are in the temple

ἑστῶτες καὶ διδάσκοντες τὸν λαόν.
standing and teaching the people.

26 Τότε ἀπελθὼν ὁ στρατηγὸς σὺν τοῖς
Then going the commandant with the

ὑπηρέταις ἦγεν αὐτούς, οὐ μετὰ βίας,
attendants brought them, not with force,

ἐφοβοῦντο γὰρ τὸν λαόν, μὴ λιθασθῶσιν·
for they feared the people, lest they should be stoned;

27 ἀγαγόντες δὲ αὐτοὺς ἔστησαν ἐν τῷ
and bringing them they stood in the

συνεδρίῳ. καὶ ἐπηρώτησεν αὐτοὺς ὁ
council. And questioned them the

ἀρχιερεὺς **28** λέγων· παραγγελίᾳ παρηγ-
high priest saying : With charge we
          =We strictly

γείλαμεν ὑμῖν μὴ διδάσκειν ἐπὶ
charged you not to teach on(in)

τῷ ὀνόματι τούτῳ, καὶ ἰδοὺ πεπληρώκατε
this name, and behold ye have filled

τὴν Ἰερουσαλὴμ τῆς διδαχῆς ὑμῶν, καὶ
- Jerusalem of(with) the teaching of you and

βούλεσθε ἐπαγαγεῖν ἐφ' ἡμᾶς τὸ αἷμα
intend to bring *on* on us the blood

τοῦ ἀνθρώπου τούτου. **29** ἀποκριθεὶς δὲ
of this man. And answering

Πέτρος καὶ οἱ ἀπόστολοι εἶπαν· πειθαρχεῖν
Peter and the apostles said : ¹to obey

δεῖ θεῷ μᾶλλον ἢ ἀνθρώποις. **30** ὁ
¹It behoves God rather than men. The

θεὸς τῶν πατέρων ἡμῶν ἤγειρεν Ἰησοῦν,
God of the fathers of us raised Jesus,

ὃν ὑμεῖς διεχειρίσασθε κρεμάσαντες ἐπὶ
whom ye killed hanging on

ξύλου. **31** τοῦτον ὁ θεὸς ἀρχηγὸν καὶ
a tree; this man - God a Ruler and

σωτῆρα ὕψωσεν τῇ δεξιᾷ αὐτοῦ τοῦ
a Saviour exalted to the right [hand] of him -

δοῦναι μετάνοιαν τῷ Ἰσραὴλ καὶ ἄφεσιν
to give[d] repentance - to Israel and forgiveness

ἁμαρτιῶν. **32** καὶ ἡμεῖς ἐσμεν μάρτυρες
of sins. And we are witnesses

τῶν ῥημάτων τούτων, καὶ τὸ πνεῦμα
of these words(things), and the Spirit

τὸ ἅγιον ὃ ἔδωκεν ὁ θεὸς τοῖς
- Holy which ²gave ¹God to the

πειθαρχοῦσιν αὐτῷ. **33** οἱ δὲ ἀκούσαντες
[ones] obeying him. And the [ones] hearing

διεπρίοντο καὶ ἐβούλοντο ἀνελεῖν αὐτούς.
were cut* and intended to kill them.

34 Ἀναστὰς δέ τις ἐν τῷ συνεδρίῳ
¹But ⁴standing up ²a certain ⁵in ⁶the ⁷council

Φαρισαῖος ὀνόματι Γαμαλιήλ, νομοδιδάσκαλος
³Pharisee by name Gamaliel, a teacher of the law

τίμιος παντὶ τῷ λαῷ, ἐκέλευσεν ἔξω
honoured by all the people, commanded ⁴outside

βραχὺ τοὺς ἀνθρώπους ποιῆσαι, **35** εἶπέν
⁵a little ³the ²men ¹to make(put), ⁶said

τε πρὸς αὐτούς· ἄνδρες Ἰσραηλῖται,
¹and to them : Men Israelites,

προσέχετε ἑαυτοῖς ἐπὶ τοῖς ἀνθρώποις τούτοις
take heed to yourselves ⁴on(to) ⁵these ⁶men

---

in the temple courts teaching the people.'' 26At that, the captain went with his officers and brought the apostles. They did not use force, because they feared that the people would stone them.

27Having brought the apostles, they made them appear before the Sanhedrin to be questioned by the high priest. 28"We gave you strict orders not to teach in this name," he said. "Yet you have filled Jerusalem with your teaching and are determined to make us guilty of this man's blood.''

29Peter and the other apostles replied: "We must obey God rather than men! 30The God of our fathers raised Jesus from the dead —whom you had killed by hanging him on a tree. 31God exalted him to his own right hand as Prince and Savior that he might give repentance and forgiveness of sins to Israel. 32We are witnesses of these things, and so is the Holy Spirit, whom God has given to those who obey him.''

33When they heard this, they were furious and wanted to put them to death. 34But a Pharisee named Gamaliel, a teacher of the law, who was honored by all the people, stood up in the Sanhedrin and ordered that the men be put outside for a little while. 35Then he addressed them: "Men of Israel, consider carefully what you in-

---

* That is, to the heart; *cf.* 7. 54.

with these men.
36"For some time ago Theudas rose up, claiming to be somebody; and a group of about four hundred men joined up with him. And he was slain; and all who followed him were dispersed and came to nothing.

37"After this man Judas of Galilee rose up in the days of the census, and drew away *some* people after him, he too perished, and all those who followed him were scattered.

38"And so in the present case, I say to you, stay away from these men and let them alone, for if this plan or action should be of men, it will be overthrown;

39but if it is of God, you will not be able to overthrow them; or else you may even be found fighting against God."

40And they took his advice; and after calling the apostles in, they flogged them and ordered them to speak no more in the name of Jesus, and *then* released them.

41So they went on their way from the presence of the Council, rejoicing that they had been considered worthy to suffer shame for *His* name.

42And every day, in the temple and from house to house, they kept right on teaching and preaching Jesus *as* the Christ.

τί   μέλλετε   πράσσειν.   **36** πρὸ   γὰρ
¹what   ²ye intend   ³to do.   For before

τούτων   τῶν   ἡμερῶν   ἀνέστη   Θευδᾶς,   λέγων
these   the   days   stood up   Theudas,   saying

εἶναί   τινα   ἑαυτόν,   ᾧ   προσεκλίθη   ἀνδρῶν
to be   someone himself, ¹to whom ²were attached ³of men

ἀριθμὸς   ὡς   τετρακοσίων·   ὃς   ἀνῃρέθη,   καὶ
²a number ⁴about ⁵four hundreds; who   was killed, and

πάντες   ὅσοι   ἐπείθοντο   αὐτῷ   διελύθησαν
all   as many as obeyed   him   were dispersed

καὶ   ἐγένοντο   εἰς   οὐδέν.   **37** μετὰ   τοῦτον
and   came   to   nothing.   After   this

ἀνέστη   Ἰούδας   ὁ   Γαλιλαῖος   ἐν   ταῖς
stood up Judas   the Galilæan   in   the

ἡμέραις   τῆς   ἀπογραφῆς   καὶ   ἀπέστησεν
days   of the enrolment   and   drew away

λαὸν   ὀπίσω   αὐτοῦ·   κἀκεῖνος   ἀπώλετο,
people after   him;   and that man perished,

καὶ   πάντες   ὅσοι   ἐπείθοντο   αὐτῷ
and   all   as many as obeyed   him

διεσκορπίσθησαν.   **38** καὶ   τὰ   νῦν   λέγω
were scattered.   And   –   now   I say

ὑμῖν,   ἀπόστητε   ἀπὸ   τῶν   ἀνθρώπων   τούτων
to you, stand away from   the   men   these

καὶ   ἄφετε   αὐτούς·   ὅτι   ἐὰν   ᾖ   ἐξ   ἀνθρώπων
and   leave   them;   because if   be   of   men

ἡ   βουλὴ   αὕτη   ἢ   τὸ   ἔργον   τοῦτο,
this counsel   or   this work,

καταλυθήσεται·   **39** εἰ   δὲ   ἐκ   θεοῦ   ἐστιν,
it will be destroyed;   but if   of   God   it is,

οὐ   δυνήσεσθε   καταλῦσαι   αὐτούς,   μήποτε
ye will not be able to destroy   them,   lest

καὶ   θεομάχοι   εὑρεθῆτε.   ἐπείσθησαν   δὲ
even fighters against God ye be found.   And they obeyed

αὐτῷ,   **40** καὶ   προσκαλεσάμενοι   τοὺς
him,   and   having called to [them]   the

ἀποστόλους   δείραντες   παρήγγειλαν   μὴ
apostles   beating   charged   not

λαλεῖν   ἐπὶ   τῷ   ὀνόματι   τοῦ   Ἰησοῦ   καὶ
to speak on(in) the name   –   of Jesus and

ἀπέλυσαν.   **41** Οἱ   μὲν   οὖν   ἐπορεύοντο
released [them].   They   –   therefore went

χαίροντες   ἀπὸ   προσώπου   τοῦ   συνεδρίου,
rejoicing   from [the] presence   of the council,

ὅτι   κατηξιώθησαν   ὑπὲρ   τοῦ   ὀνόματος
because they were deemed worthy on behalf of the name

ἀτιμασθῆναι·   **42** πᾶσάν   τε   ἡμέραν   ἐν   τῷ
to be dishonoured;   and every   day   in   the

ἱερῷ   καὶ   κατ'   οἶκον   οὐκ   ἐπαύοντο
temple and   from house to house† they ceased not

διδάσκοντες   καὶ   εὐαγγελιζόμενοι   τὸν   χριστὸν
teaching   and   preaching   the   Christ

Ἰησοῦν.
Jesus.

---

tend to do to these men. 36Some time ago Theudas appeared, claiming to be somebody, and about four hundred men rallied to him. He was killed, all his followers were dispersed, and it all came to nothing. 37After him, Judas the Galilean appeared in the days of the census and led a band of people in revolt. He too was killed, and all his followers were scattered. 38Therefore, in the present case I advise you: Leave these men alone! Let them go! For if their purpose or activity is of human origin, it will fail. 39But if it is from God, you will not be able to stop these men; you will only find yourselves fighting against God."

40His speech persuaded them. They called the apostles in and had them flogged. Then they ordered them not to speak in the name of Jesus, and let them go.

41The apostles left the Sanhedrin, rejoicing because they had been counted worthy of suffering disgrace for the Name. 42Day after day, in the temple courts and from house to house, they never stopped teaching and proclaiming the good news that Jesus is the Christ.ᵛ

Chapter 6

Choosing of the Seven

NOW at this time while the disciples were increasing *in number,* a complaint arose on the part of the ᴵHellenistic *Jews* against the *native* Hebrews, because their widows were being overlooked in the daily serving *of food.*

ᴵI.e., non-Palestinian Jews who normally spoke Greek

---

6 Ἐν   δὲ   ταῖς   ἡμέραις   ταύταις
Now in   these days

πληθυνόντων   τῶν   μαθητῶν   ἐγένετο
being multiplied the disciplesᵃ   there was
=as the disciples were multiplied

γογγυσμὸς   τῶν   Ἑλληνιστῶν   πρὸς   τοὺς
a murmuring of the Hellenists   against the

Ἑβραίους,   ὅτι   παρεθεωροῦντο   ἐν   τῇ
Hebrews,   because ⁴were overlooked ⁵in   ⁶the

διακονία   τῇ   καθημερινῇ   αἱ   χῆραι   αὐτῶν.
⁸service   –   ⁷daily   ¹the ²widows ³of them.

Chapter 6

The Choosing of the Seven

IN those days when the number of disciples was increasing, the Grecian Jews among them complained against the Hebraic Jews because their widows were being overlooked in the daily distribution of

ᵛ42 Or *Messiah*

2And the twelve summoned the congregation of the disciples and said, "It is not desirable for us to neglect the word of God in order to serve tables.
3"But select from among you, brethren, seven men of good reputation, full of the Spirit and of wisdom, whom we may put in charge of this task.
4"But we will devote ourselves to prayer, and to the ministry of the word."
5And the statement found approval with the whole congregation; and they chose Stephen, a man full of faith and of the Holy Spirit, and Philip, Prochorus, Nicanor, Timon, Parmenas and Nicolas, a *m*proselyte from Antioch.
6And these they brought before the apostles; and after praying, they laid their hands on them.
7And the word of God kept on spreading; and the number of the disciples continued to increase greatly in Jerusalem, and a great many of the priests were becoming obedient to the faith.
8And Stephen, full of grace and power, was performing great wonders and signs among the people.
9But some men from what was called the Synagogue of the Freedmen, *including* both Cyrenians and Alexandrians, and some from Cilicia and Asia, rose up and argued with Stephen.
10And *yet* they were unable to cope with the wisdom and the Spirit with which he was speaking.
11Then they secretly induced men to say, "We have heard him speak blasphemous words against Moses and *against* God."
12And they stirred up the

---

2 προσκαλεσάμενοι δὲ οἱ δώδεκα τὸ
⁴having called to [them] ¹And ²the ³twelve the
πλῆθος τῶν μαθητῶν εἶπαν· οὐκ ἀρεστόν
multitude of the disciples said: not pleasing
ἐστιν ἡμᾶς καταλείψαντας τὸν λόγον τοῦ
It is us leaving the word –
θεοῦ διακονεῖν τραπέζαις. 3 ἐπισκέψασθε
of God to serve tables. look ye out
δέ, ἀδελφοί, ἄνδρας ἐξ ὑμῶν μαρτυρουμένους
But, brothers, ³men ²of ⁴you ¹being witnessed to
ἑπτὰ πλήρεις πνεύματος καὶ σοφίας, οὓς
¹seven [as] full of Spirit and of wisdom, whom
καταστήσομεν ἐπὶ τῆς χρείας ταύτης·
we will appoint over this office;
4 ἡμεῖς δὲ τῇ προσευχῇ καὶ τῇ διακονίᾳ
but we to the prayer and to the service
τοῦ λόγου προσκαρτερήσομεν. 5 καὶ ἤρεσεν
of the word will keep. And ³pleased
ὁ λόγος ἐνώπιον παντὸς τοῦ πλήθους,
¹the ²word before all the multitude,
καὶ ἐξελέξαντο Στέφανον, ἄνδρα πλήρη
and they chose Stephen, a man full
πίστεως καὶ πνεύματος ἁγίου, καὶ Φίλιππον
of faith and Spirit of Holy, and Philip
καὶ Πρόχορον καὶ Νικάνορα καὶ Τίμωνα
and Prochorus and Nicanor and Timon
καὶ Παρμενᾶν καὶ Νικόλαον προσήλυτον
and Parmenas and Nicolaus a proselyte
Ἀντιοχέα, 6 οὓς ἔστησαν ἐνώπιον τῶν
of Antioch, whom they set before the
ἀποστόλων, καὶ προσευξάμενοι ἐπέθηκαν
apostles, and having prayed they placed on
αὐτοῖς τὰς χεῖρας.
them the(ir) hands.
7 Καὶ ὁ λόγος τοῦ θεοῦ ηὔξανεν, καὶ
And the word – of God grew, and
ἐπληθύνετο ὁ ἀριθμὸς τῶν μαθητῶν ἐν
was multiplied the number of the disciples in
Ἰερουσαλὴμ σφόδρα, πολύς τε ὄχλος τῶν
Jerusalem greatly, and a much(great) crowd of the
ἱερέων ὑπήκουον τῇ πίστει.
priests obeyed the faith.
8 Στέφανος δὲ πλήρης χάριτος καὶ
And Stephen full of grace and
δυνάμεως ἐποίει τέρατα καὶ σημεῖα μεγάλα
of power did wonders and signs great
ἐν τῷ λαῷ. 9 ἀνέστησαν δέ τινες τῶν
among the people. But rose up some of the
[ones]
ἐκ τῆς συναγωγῆς τῆς λεγομένης
of the synagogue – being called
Λιβερτίνων καὶ Κυρηναίων καὶ Ἀλεξ-
of Freedmen and of Cyrenians and of
ανδρέων καὶ τῶν ἀπὸ Κιλικίας καὶ
Alexandrians and of the [ones] from Cilicia and
Ἀσίας συζητοῦντες τῷ Στεφάνῳ, 10 καὶ
Asia discussing – with Stephen, and
οὐκ ἴσχυον ἀντιστῆναι τῇ σοφίᾳ καὶ
were not able to withstand the wisdom and
τῷ πνεύματι ᾧ ἐλάλει. 11 τότε ὑπέβαλον
the spirit with which he spoke. Then they suborned
ἄνδρας λέγοντας ὅτι ἀκηκόαμεν αὐτοῦ
men saying[,] – We have heard him
λαλοῦντος ῥήματα βλάσφημα εἰς Μωϋσῆν
speaking words blasphemous against Moses
καὶ τὸν θεόν· 12 συνεκίνησάν τε τὸν
and – God; and they stirred up the

---

food. 2So the Twelve gathered all the disciples together and said, "It would not be right for us to neglect the ministry of the word of God in order to wait on tables. 3Brothers, choose seven men from among you who are known to be full of the Spirit and of the Holy wisdom. We will turn this responsibility over to them 4and will give our attention to prayer and the ministry of the word."
5This proposal pleased the whole group. They chose Stephen, a man full of faith and of the Holy Spirit; also Philip, Procorus, Nicanor, Timon, Parmenas, and Nicolas from Antioch, a convert to Judaism. 6They presented these men to the apostles, who prayed and laid their hands on them.
7So the word of God spread. The number of disciples in Jerusalem increased rapidly, and a large number of priests became obedient to the faith.

Stephen Seized

8Now Stephen, a man full of God's grace and power, did great wonders and miraculous signs among the people. 9Opposition arose, however, from members of the Synagogue of the Freedmen (as it was called)—Jews of Cyrene and Alexandria as well as the provinces of Cilicia and Asia. These men began to argue with Stephen, 10but they could not stand up against his wisdom or the Spirit by whom he spoke. 11Then they secretly persuaded some men to say, "We have heard Stephen speak words of blasphemy against Moses and against God."
12So they stirred up the

---

people, the elders and the scribes, and they came upon him and dragged him away, and brought him before the Council.

13And they put forward false witnesses who said, "This man incessantly speaks against this holy place, and the Law;

14for we have heard him say that this Nazarene, Jesus, will destroy this place and alter the customs which Moses handed down to us."

15And fixing their gaze on him, all who were sitting in the Council saw his face like the face of an angel.

λαὸν	καὶ	τοὺς	πρεσβυτέρους	καὶ	τοὺς
people	and	the	elders	and	the

γραμματεῖς,	καὶ	ἐπιστάντες	συνήρπασαν
scribes,	and	coming on	they seized

αὐτὸν	καὶ	ἤγαγον	εἰς	τὸ	συνέδριον,
him	and	led	to	the	council,

13 | ἔστησάν | τε | μάρτυρας | ψευδεῖς | λέγοντας· |
|---|---|---|---|---|
| and stood | | witnesses | false | saying : |

ὁ	ἄνθρωπος	οὗτος	οὐ	παύεται	λαλῶν
	This man			ceases	not	speaking

ῥήματα	κατὰ	τοῦ	τόπου	τοῦ	ἁγίου	[τούτου]
words	against	-	³place	-	²holy	¹this

καὶ	τοῦ	νόμου·	14 ἀκηκόαμεν	γὰρ	αὐτοῦ
and	the	law;	for we have heard		him

λέγοντος	ὅτι	Ἰησοῦς	ὁ	Ναζωραῖος	οὗτος
saying	that	²Jesus	³the	⁴Nazarene	¹this

καταλύσει	τὸν	τόπον	τοῦτον	καὶ	ἀλλάξει
will destroy		this place		and	will change

τὰ	ἔθη	ἃ	παρέδωκεν	ἡμῖν	Μωϋσῆς.
the	customs which		delivered	to us	Moses.

15 | καὶ | ἀτενίσαντες | εἰς | αὐτὸν | πάντες | οἱ |
|---|---|---|---|---|---|
| And | gazing | at | him | all | the |

καθεζόμενοι	ἐν	τῷ	συνεδρίῳ	εἶδον	τὸ
[ones] sitting	in	the	council	saw	the

πρόσωπον	αὐτοῦ	ὡσεὶ	πρόσωπον	ἀγγέλου.
face	of him	as	a face	of an angel.

people and the elders and the teachers of the law. They seized Stephen and brought him before the Sanhedrin. 13They produced false witnesses, who testified, "This fellow never stops speaking against this holy place and against the law. 14For we have heard him say that this Jesus of Nazareth will destroy this place and change the customs Moses handed down to us."

15All who were sitting in the Sanhedrin looked intently at Stephen, and they saw that his face was like the face of an angel.

Chapter 7

Stephen's Defense

AND the high priest said, "Are these things so?"

2And he said, "Hear me, brethren and fathers! The God of glory appeared to our father Abraham when he was in Mesopotamia, before he lived in Haran,

3and said to him, 'DEPART FROM YOUR COUNTRY AND YOUR RELATIVES, AND COME INTO THE LAND THAT I WILL SHOW YOU.'

4"Then he departed from the land of the Chaldeans, and settled in Haran. And from there, after his father died, God removed him into this country in which you are now living.

5"And He gave him no inheritance in it, not even a foot of ground; and yet, even when he had no child, He promised that HE WOULD GIVE IT TO HIM AS A POSSESSION, AND TO HIS OFFSPRING AFTER HIM.

7 | Εἶπεν | δὲ | ὁ | ἀρχιερεύς· | εἰ | ταῦτα |
|---|---|---|---|---|---|
| And said | | the | high priest : | If | these things |

οὕτως	ἔχει;	2 ὁ	δὲ	ἔφη·
thus	have(are)?	And he		said:

Ἄνδρες	ἀδελφοὶ	καὶ	πατέρες,	ἀκούσατε.
Men	brothers	and	fathers,	hear ye.

Ὁ	θεὸς	τῆς	δόξης	ὤφθη	τῷ	πατρὶ
The	God	-	of glory	appeared	to the	father

ἡμῶν	Ἀβραὰμ	ὄντι	ἐν	τῇ	Μεσοποταμίᾳ
of us	Abraham	being	in	-	Mesopotamia

πρὶν	ἢ	κατοικῆσαι	αὐτὸν	ἐν	Χαρράν,
before		to dwell	him^b	in	Charran,
		=he dwelt			

3 | καὶ | εἶπεν | πρὸς | αὐτόν· | ἔξελθε | ἐκ | τῆς |
|---|---|---|---|---|---|---|
| and | said | to | him : | Go forth | out of | the |

γῆς	σου	καὶ	τῆς	συγγενείας	σου,	καὶ
land	of thee	and	the	kindred	of thee,	and

δεῦρο	εἰς	τὴν	γῆν	ἣν	ἄν	σοι	δείξω.
come	into	the	land	whichever		to thee	I may show.

4 | τότε | ἐξελθὼν | ἐκ | γῆς | Χαλδαίων |
|---|---|---|---|---|
| Then | going forth | out of [the] land of [the] | Chaldæans |

κατῴκησεν	ἐν	Χαρράν.	κἀκεῖθεν	μετὰ
he dwelt	in	Charran.	And thence	after

τὸ	ἀποθανεῖν	τὸν	πατέρα	αὐτοῦ	μετῴκισεν
the	to die	the	father	of him^b	[God] removed
=his father died					

αὐτὸν	εἰς	τὴν	γῆν	ταύτην	εἰς	ἣν	ὑμεῖς
him	into	the	this land		in	which	ye

νῦν	κατοικεῖτε,	5 καὶ	οὐκ	ἔδωκεν	αὐτῷ
now	dwell,	and	gave not		to him

κληρονομίαν	ἐν	αὐτῇ	οὐδὲ	βῆμα	ποδός,
an inheritance	in	it	nor	a foot's space,

καὶ	ἐπηγγείλατο	δοῦναι	αὐτῷ	εἰς
and	promised	to give	him	for

κατάσχεσιν	αὐτὴν	καὶ	τῷ	σπέρματι	αὐτοῦ
a possession	it	and to the		seed	of him

μετ᾽	αὐτόν,	οὐκ	ὄντος	αὐτῷ	τέκνου.
after	him,	not	being	to him^c	a child.^a
		=while he had no child.			

Chapter 7

Stephen's Speech to the Sanhedrin

THEN the high priest asked him, "Are these charges true?"

2To this he replied: "Brothers and fathers, listen to me! The God of glory appeared to our father Abraham while he was still in Mesopotamia, before he lived in Haran. 3'Leave your country and your people,' God said, 'and go to the land I will show you.'ʷ

4"So he left the land of the Chaldeans and settled in Haran. After the death of his father, God sent him to this land where you are now living. 5He gave him no inheritance here, not even a foot of ground. But God promised him that he and his descendants after him would possess the land, even though at that time Abraham had no

ʷ3 Gen. 12:1

6"But God spoke to this effect, that his OFFSPRING WOULD BE ALIENS IN A FOREIGN LAND, AND THAT THEY WOULD BE ENSLAVED AND MISTREATED FOR FOUR HUNDRED YEARS.

7"'AND WHATEVER NATION TO WHICH THEY SHALL BE IN BONDAGE I MYSELF WILL JUDGE,' said God, 'AND AFTER THAT THEY WILL COME OUT AND ⁿSERVE ME IN THIS PLACE.'

8"And He gave him the covenant of circumcision; and so *Abraham* became the father of Isaac, and circumcised him on the eighth day; and Isaac *became the father of* Jacob, and Jacob *of* the twelve patriarchs.

9"And the patriarchs became jealous of Joseph and sold him into Egypt. And *yet* God was with him, ¹⁰and rescued him from all his afflictions, and granted him favor and wisdom in the sight of Pharaoh, king of Egypt; and he made him governor over Egypt and all his household.

11"Now a famine came over all Egypt and Canaan, and great affliction *with it;* and our fathers could find no food.

12"But when Jacob heard that there was grain in Egypt, he sent our fathers *there* the first time.

13"And on the second *visit* Joseph made himself known to his brothers, and Joseph's family was disclosed to Pharaoh.

14"And Joseph sent *word* and invited Jacob his father and all his relatives to come to him, seventy-five persons *in all.*

15"And Jacob went down to Egypt and *there* passed away, he and our fathers.

---

6 ἐλάλησεν δὲ οὕτως ὁ θεός, ὅτι ἔσται
And spoke thus – God, that will be

τὸ σπέρμα αὐτοῦ πάροικον ἐν γῇ ἀλλοτρίᾳ,
the seed of him a sojourner in a land belonging to others,

καὶ δουλώσουσιν αὐτὸ καὶ κακώσουσιν
and they will enslave it and will ill-treat

ἔτη τετρακόσια· 7 καὶ τὸ ἔθνος ᾧ ἐὰν
years four hundred; and the nation whichever

δουλεύσουσιν κρινῶ ἐγώ, ὁ θεὸς εἶπεν,
they will serve will judge I, – God said,

καὶ μετὰ ταῦτα ἐξελεύσονται καὶ
and after these things they will come forth and

λατρεύσουσίν μοι ἐν τῷ τόπῳ τούτῳ.
will worship me in this place.

8 καὶ ἔδωκεν αὐτῷ διαθήκην περιτομῆς·
And he gave him a covenant of circumcision;

καὶ οὕτως ἐγέννησεν τὸν Ἰσαὰκ καὶ
and thus he begat – Isaac and

περιέτεμεν αὐτὸν τῇ ἡμέρᾳ τῇ ὀγδόῃ,
circumcised him on the day – eighth,

καὶ Ἰσαὰκ τὸν Ἰακώβ, καὶ Ἰακὼβ
and Isaac [begat] – Jacob, and Jacob [begat]

τοὺς δώδεκα πατριάρχας. 9 Καὶ οἱ
the twelve patriarchs. And the

πατριάρχαι ζηλώσαντες τὸν Ἰωσὴφ
patriarchs becoming jealous – ³Joseph

ἀπέδοντο εἰς Αἴγυπτον· καὶ ἦν ὁ θεὸς
¹sold into Egypt; and was – God

μετ' αὐτοῦ, 10 καὶ ἐξείλατο αὐτὸν ἐκ
with him, and rescued him out of

πασῶν τῶν θλίψεων αὐτοῦ, καὶ ἔδωκεν
all the afflictions of him, and gave

αὐτῷ χάριν καὶ σοφίαν ἐναντίον Φαραὼ
him favour and wisdom before Pharaoh

βασιλέως Αἰγύπτου, καὶ κατέστησεν αὐτὸν
king of Egypt, and he appointed him

ἡγούμενον ἐπ' Αἴγυπτον καὶ ὅλον τὸν
governor over Egypt and all the

οἶκον αὐτοῦ. 11 ἦλθεν δὲ λιμὸς ἐφ'
household of him. But came a famine over

ὅλην τὴν Αἴγυπτον καὶ Χανάαν καὶ
all – Egypt and Canaan and

θλῖψις μεγάλη, καὶ οὐχ ηὕρισκον
affliction great, and found not

χορτάσματα οἱ πατέρες ἡμῶν. 12 ἀκούσας
sustenance the fathers of us. ³having heard

δὲ Ἰακὼβ ὄντα σιτία εἰς Αἴγυπτον
¹But ²Jacob ⁵being ⁴corn in Egypt

ἐξαπέστειλεν τοὺς πατέρας ἡμῶν πρῶτον·
sent forth the fathers of us first;

13 καὶ ἐν τῷ δευτέρῳ ἐγνωρίσθη Ἰωσὴφ
and at the second [time] was made known Joseph

τοῖς ἀδελφοῖς αὐτοῦ, καὶ φανερὸν ἐγένετο τῷ
to the brothers of him, and ⁵manifest ⁴became –

Φαραὼ τὸ γένος Ἰωσήφ. 14 ἀποστείλας δὲ
⁶to Pharaoh ¹the ²race ³of Joseph. And sending

Ἰωσὴφ μετεκαλέσατο Ἰακὼβ τὸν πατέρα
Joseph called Jacob the father

αὐτοῦ καὶ πᾶσαν τὴν συγγένειαν ἐν
of him and all the(his) kindred in

ψυχαῖς ἑβδομήκοντα πέντε. 15 καὶ κατέβη
souls seventy-five. And went down

Ἰακὼβ εἰς Αἴγυπτον, καὶ ἐτελεύτησεν
Jacob to Egypt, and died

αὐτὸς καὶ οἱ πατέρες ἡμῶν, 16 καὶ
he and the fathers of us, and

---

child. 6God spoke to him in this way: 'Your descendants will be strangers in a country not their own, and they will be enslaved and mistreated four hundred years. 7But I will punish the nation they serve as slaves,' God said, 'and afterward they will come out of that country and worship me in this place.'ˣ 8Then he gave Abraham the covenant of circumcision. And Abraham became the father of Isaac and circumcised him eight days after his birth. Later Isaac became the father of Jacob, and Jacob became the father of the twelve patriarchs.

9"Because the patriarchs were jealous of Joseph, they sold him as a slave into Egypt. But God was with him 10and rescued him from all his troubles. He gave Joseph wisdom and enabled him to gain the goodwill of Pharaoh king of Egypt; so he made him ruler over Egypt and all his palace.

11"Then a famine struck all Egypt and Canaan, bringing great suffering, and our fathers could not find food. 12When Jacob heard that there was grain in Egypt, he sent our fathers on their first visit. 13On their second visit, Joseph told his brothers who he was, and Pharaoh learned about Joseph's family. 14After this, Joseph sent for his father Jacob and his whole family, seventy-five in all. 15Then Jacob went down to Egypt, where he and our fathers

---

ⁿOr, *worship*

ˣ7 Gen. 15:13,14

16"And *from there* they were removed to Shechem, and laid in the tomb which Abraham had purchased for a sum of money from the sons of Hamor in Shechem.

17"But as the time of the promise was approaching which God had assured to Abraham, the people increased and multiplied in Egypt,

18until THERE AROSE ANOTHER KING OVER EGYPT WHO KNEW NOTHING ABOUT JOSEPH.

19"It was he who took shrewd advantage of our race, and mistreated our fathers so that they would expose their infants and they would not survive.

20"And it was at this time that Moses was born; and he was lovely in the sight of God; and he was nurtured three months in his father's home.

21"And after he had been exposed, Pharaoh's daughter took him away, and nurtured him as her own son.

22"And Moses was educated in all the learning of the Egyptians, and he was a man of power in words and deeds.

23"But when he was approaching the age of forty, it entered his mind to visit his brethren, the sons of Israel.

24"And when he saw one *of them* being treated unjustly, he defended him and took vengeance for the oppressed by striking down the Egyptian.

25"And he supposed that his brethren understood that God was granting them deliverance through him; but they did not understand.

26"And on the following day he appeared to them as they were fighting together, and he tried to reconcile them in peace, saying, 'Men, you are brethren, why do you injure one another?'

μετετέθησαν εἰς Συχὲμ καὶ ἐτέθησαν ἐν
were transferred to Sychem and were put in

τῷ μνήματι ᾧ ὠνήσατο Ἀβραὰμ τιμῆς
the tomb which ²bought ¹Abraham of(for) a price

ἀργυρίου παρὰ τῶν υἱῶν Ἐμμὼρ ἐν
of silver from the sons of Emmor in

Συχέμ. 17 Καθὼς δὲ ἤγγιζεν ὁ χρόνος
Sychem. And as drew near the time

τῆς ἐπαγγελίας ἧς ὡμολόγησεν ὁ θεὸς
of the promise which ²declared - ¹God

τῷ Ἀβραάμ, ηὔξησεν ὁ λαὸς καὶ
to Abraham, ³grew ¹the ²people and

ἐπληθύνθη ἐν Αἰγύπτῳ, 18 ἄχρι οὗ ἀνέστη
were multiplied in Egypt, until ²rose up

βασιλεὺς ἕτερος ἐπ' Αἴγυπτον, ὃς οὐκ ᾔδει
²king ¹another over Egypt, who did not know

τὸν Ἰωσήφ. 19 οὗτος κατασοφισάμενος
- Joseph. This man dealing craftily with

τὸ γένος ἡμῶν ἐκάκωσεν τοὺς πατέρας
the race of us ill-treated the fathers

τοῦ ποιεῖν τὰ βρέφη ἔκθετα αὐτῶν
to makeᵈ ¹the ²babes ⁴exposed ³of them

εἰς τὸ μὴ ζωογονεῖσθαι. 20 Ἐν ᾧ
to the not to be preserved alive. At which
=so that they should not be . . .

καιρῷ ἐγεννήθη Μωϋσῆς, καὶ ἦν ἀστεῖος
time was born Moses, and was fair

τῷ θεῷ· ὃς ἀνετράφη μῆνας τρεῖς ἐν
- to God; who was reared months three in

τῷ οἴκῳ τοῦ πατρός· 21 ἐκτεθέντος δὲ
the house of the(his) father; being exposed and
=and when he was exposed

αὐτοῦ ἀνείλατο αὐτὸν ἡ θυγάτηρ Φαραὼ
himᵃ took up him the daughter of Pharaoh

καὶ ἀνεθρέψατο αὐτὸν ἑαυτῇ εἰς υἱόν.
and reared him to herself for a son.
=as her own son.

22 καὶ ἐπαιδεύθη Μωϋσῆς πάσῃ σοφίᾳ
And was trained Moses in all [the] wisdom

Αἰγυπτίων, ἦν δὲ δυνατὸς ἐν λόγοις
of [the] Egyptians, and was powerful in words

καὶ ἔργοις αὐτοῦ. 23 Ὡς δὲ ἐπληροῦτο
and works of him. But when ³was fulfilled

αὐτῷ τεσσερακονταέτης χρόνος, ἀνέβη ἐπὶ
⁴to him ²of forty years ¹a time, it came up upon

τὴν καρδίαν αὐτοῦ ἐπισκέψασθαι τοὺς
the heart of him to visit the

ἀδελφοὺς αὐτοῦ τοὺς υἱοὺς Ἰσραήλ. 24 καὶ
brothers of him the sons of Israel. And

ἰδών τινα ἀδικούμενον ἠμύνατο, καὶ
seeing one being injured he defended [him], and

ἐποίησεν ἐκδίκησιν τῷ καταπονουμένῳ
he wrought vengeance for the [one] getting the worse

πατάξας τὸν Αἰγύπτιον. 25 ἐνόμιζεν δὲ
striking the Egyptian. Now he supposed

συνιέναι τοὺς ἀδελφοὺς ὅτι ὁ θεὸς διὰ
to understand the(his) brothersᵇ that - God through
=that his brothers would understand

χειρὸς αὐτοῦ δίδωσιν σωτηρίαν αὐτοῖς·
hand of him would give salvation to them;

οἱ δὲ οὐ συνῆκαν. 26 τῇ τε ἐπιούσῃ
but they understood not. And on the coming

ἡμέρᾳ ὤφθη αὐτοῖς μαχομένοις, καὶ
day he appeared to them fighting, and

συνήλλασσεν αὐτοὺς εἰς εἰρήνην εἰπών·
attempted to reconcile them in peace saying:

ἄνδρες, ἀδελφοί ἐστε· ἱνατί ἀδικεῖτε
Men, brothers ye are; why injure ye

---

died. 16Their bodies were brought back to Shechem and placed in the tomb that Abraham had bought from the sons of Hamor at Shechem for a certain sum of money.

17"As the time drew near for God to fulfill his promise to Abraham, the number of our people in Egypt greatly increased. 18Then another king, who knew nothing about Joseph, became ruler of Egypt. 19He dealt treacherously with our people and oppressed our forefathers by forcing them to throw out their newborn babies so that they would die.

20"At that time Moses was born, and he was no ordinary child.ʸ For three months he was cared for in his father's house. 21When he was placed outside, Pharaoh's daughter took him and brought him up as her own son. 22Moses was educated in all the wisdom of the Egyptians and was powerful in speech and action.

23"When Moses was forty years old, he decided to visit his fellow Israelites. 24He saw one of them being mistreated by an Egyptian, so he went to his defense and avenged him by killing the Egyptian. 25Moses thought that his own people would realize that God was using him to rescue them, but they did not. 26The next day Moses came upon two Israelites who were fighting. He tried to reconcile them by saying, 'Men, you are brothers; why do you want to hurt each other?'

ʸ20 Or *was fair in the sight of God*

27"But the one who was injuring his neighbor pushed him away, saying, 'WHO MADE YOU A RULER AND JUDGE OVER US?

28'YOU DO NOT MEAN TO KILL ME AS YOU KILLED THE EGYPTIAN YESTERDAY, DO YOU?'

29"And at this remark MOSES FLED, AND BECAME AN ALIEN IN THE LAND OF MIDIAN, where he became the father of two sons.

30"And after forty years had passed, AN ANGEL APPEARED TO HIM IN THE WILDERNESS OF MOUNT SINAI, IN THE FLAME OF A BURNING THORN BUSH.

31"And when Moses saw it, he *began* to marvel at the sight; and as he approached to look *more* closely, there came the voice of the Lord:

32'I AM THE GOD OF YOUR FATHERS, THE GOD OF ABRAHAM AND ISAAC AND JACOB.' And Moses shook with fear and would not venture to look.

33"BUT THE LORD SAID TO HIM, 'TAKE OFF THE SANDALS FROM YOUR FEET, FOR THE PLACE ON WHICH YOU ARE STANDING IS HOLY GROUND.

34'I HAVE CERTAINLY SEEN THE OPPRESSION OF MY PEOPLE IN EGYPT, AND HAVE HEARD THEIR GROANS, AND I HAVE COME DOWN TO DELIVER THEM; COME NOW, AND I WILL SEND YOU TO EGYPT.'

35"This Moses whom they disowned, saying, 'WHO MADE YOU A RULER AND A JUDGE?' is the one whom God sent *to be* both a ruler and a deliverer with the help of the angel who appeared to him in the thorn bush.

36"This man led them out, performing wonders and signs in the land of Egypt and in the Red Sea and in the wilderness for forty years.

37"This is the Moses who

ἀλλήλους; 27 ὁ δὲ ἀδικῶν τὸν πλησίον
each other? But the [one] injuring the(his) neighbour

ἀπώσατο αὐτὸν εἰπών· τίς σε κατέστησεν
thrust away him saying: Who thee appointed

ἄρχοντα καὶ δικαστὴν ἐφ' ἡμῶν; 28 μὴ
a ruler and a judge over us? not

ἀνελεῖν με σὺ θέλεις ὃν τρόπον ἀνεῖλες
to kill me thou wishest in the same way as† thou killedst

ἐχθὲς τὸν Αἰγύπτιον; 29 ἔφυγεν δὲ
yesterday the Egyptian? So fled

Μωϋσῆς ἐν τῷ λόγῳ τούτῳ, καὶ ἐγένετο
Moses at this word, and became

πάροικος ἐν γῇ Μαδιάμ, οὗ ἐγέννησεν
a sojourner in [the] land Midian, where he begat

υἱοὺς δύο. 30 Καὶ πληρωθέντων ἐτῶν
sons two. And being fulfilled years
                         = when forty years were fulfilled

τεσσεράκοντα ὤφθη αὐτῷ ἐν τῇ ἐρήμῳ
forty[a] appeared to him in the desert

τοῦ ὄρους Σινὰ ἄγγελος ἐν φλογὶ πυρὸς
of the mount Sinai an angel in a flame of fire

βάτου. 31 ὁ δὲ Μωϋσῆς ἰδὼν ἐθαύμαζεν
of a thorn bush. - And Moses seeing marvelled at

τὸ ὅραμα· προσερχομένου δὲ αὐτοῦ κατα-
the vision; and approaching him[a] to take
                       = as he approached

νοῆσαι ἐγένετο φωνὴ κυρίου· 32 ἐγὼ ὁ
notice there was a voice of [the] Lord: I the

θεὸς τῶν πατέρων σου, ὁ θεὸς Ἀβραὰμ
God of the fathers of thee, the God of Abraham

καὶ Ἰσαὰκ καὶ Ἰακώβ. ἔντρομος δὲ
and of Isaac and of Jacob. But trembling

γενόμενος Μωϋσῆς οὐκ ἐτόλμα κατανοῆσαι.
becoming Moses dared not to take notice.

33 εἶπεν δὲ αὐτῷ ὁ κύριος· λῦσον τὸ
And said to him the Lord: Loosen the

ὑπόδημα τῶν ποδῶν σου· ὁ γὰρ τόπος
sandal of the feet of thee; for the place

ἐφ' ᾧ ἕστηκας γῆ ἁγία ἐστίν. 34 ἰδὼν
on which thou standest ground holy is. Seeing

εἶδον τὴν κάκωσιν τοῦ λαοῦ μου τοῦ
I saw the ill-treatment of the people of me --

ἐν Αἰγύπτῳ, καὶ τοῦ στεναγμοῦ αὐτοῦ
in Egypt, and the groan of it

ἤκουσα, καὶ κατέβην ἐξελέσθαι αὐτούς·
I heard, and I came down to rescue them;

καὶ νῦν δεῦρο ἀποστείλω σε εἰς Αἴγυπτον.
and now come I will send thee to Egypt.

35 Τοῦτον τὸν Μωϋσῆν, ὃν ἠρνήσαντο
This - Moses, whom they denied

εἰπόντες· τίς σε κατέστησεν ἄρχοντα καὶ
saying: Who thee appointed a ruler and

δικαστήν; τοῦτον ὁ θεὸς καὶ ἄρχοντα
a judge? this man God both a ruler

καὶ λυτρωτὴν ἀπέσταλκεν σὺν χειρὶ
and a redeemer has sent with [the] hand

ἀγγέλου τοῦ ὀφθέντος αὐτῷ ἐν τῇ βάτῳ.
of [the] angel - appearing to him in the bush.

36 οὗτος ἐξήγαγεν αὐτοὺς ποιήσας τέρατα
This man led forth them doing wonders

καὶ σημεῖα ἐν γῇ Αἰγύπτῳ καὶ ἐν
and signs in [the] land Egypt and in

ἐρυθρᾷ θαλάσσῃ καὶ ἐν τῇ ἐρήμῳ ἔτη
[the] Red Sea and in the desert years

τεσσεράκοντα. 37 οὗτός ἐστιν ὁ Μωϋσῆς
forty. This is the Moses

27"But the man who was mistreating the other pushed Moses aside and said, 'Who made you ruler and judge over us? 28Do you want to kill me as you killed the Egyptian yesterday?'[z] 29When Moses heard this, he fled to Midian, where he settled as a foreigner and had two sons.

30"After forty years had passed, an angel appeared to Moses in the flames of a burning bush in the desert near Mount Sinai. 31When he saw this, he was amazed at the sight. As he went over to look more closely, he heard the Lord's voice: 32'I am the God of your fathers, the God of Abraham, Isaac and Jacob.'[a] Moses trembled with fear and did not dare to look.

33"Then the Lord said to him, 'Take off your sandals; the place where you are standing is holy ground. 34I have indeed seen the oppression of my people in Egypt. I have heard their groaning and have come down to set them free. Now come, I will send you back to Egypt.'[b]

35"This is the same Moses whom they had rejected with the words, 'Who made you ruler and judge?' He was sent to be their ruler and deliverer by God himself, through the angel who appeared to him in the bush. 36He led them out of Egypt and did wonders and miraculous signs in Egypt, at the Red Sea[c] and for forty years in the desert.

37"This is that Moses

---

z 28 Exodus 2:14
a 32 Exodus 3:6
b 34 Exodus 3:5,7,8,10
c 36 That is, Sea of Reeds

said to the sons of Israel, 'GOD SHALL RAISE UP FOR YOU A PROPHET LIKE ME FROM YOUR BRETHREN.'
38"This is the one who was in the congregation in the wilderness together with the angel who was speaking to him on Mount Sinai, and who was with our fathers; and he received living oracles to pass on to you.
39"And our fathers were unwilling to be obedient to him, but repudiated him and in their hearts turned back to Egypt,
40SAYING TO AARON, 'MAKE FOR US GODS WHO WILL GO BEFORE US; FOR THIS MOSES WHO LED US OUT OF THE LAND OF EGYPT—WE DO NOT KNOW WHAT HAPPENED TO HIM.'
41"And at that time they made a calf and brought a sacrifice to the idol, and were rejoicing in the works of their hands.
42"But God turned away and delivered them up to serve the host of heaven; as it is written in the book of the prophets, 'IT WAS NOT TO ME THAT YOU OFFERED VICTIMS AND SACRIFICES FORTY YEARS IN THE WILDERNESS, WAS IT, O HOUSE OF ISRAEL?
43'YOU ALSO TOOK ALONG THE TABERNACLE OF MOLOCH AND THE STAR OF THE GOD ROMPHA, THE IMAGES WHICH YOU MADE TO WORSHIP THEM. I ALSO WILL REMOVE YOU BEYOND BABYLON.'
44"Our fathers had the tabernacle of testimony in the wilderness, just as He who spoke to Moses directed him to make it according to the pattern which he had seen.
45"And having received it in their turn, our fathers brought it in with Joshua upon dispossessing the nations whom God drove out

---

ὁ　εἴπας　τοῖς　υἱοῖς　Ἰσραήλ·　προφήτην
-　saying　to the　sons　of Israel :　A prophet

ὑμῖν　ἀναστήσει　ὁ　θεὸς　ἐκ　τῶν　ἀδελφῶν
for you　will raise up　-　God　of　the　brothers

ὑμῶν　ὡς　ἐμέ.　**38** οὗτός　ἐστιν　ὁ　γενόμενος
of you　as　me.　This　is　the [one] having been

ἐν　τῇ　ἐκκλησίᾳ　ἐν　τῇ　ἐρήμῳ　μετὰ　τοῦ
in　the　church　in　the　desert　with　the

ἀγγέλου　τοῦ　λαλοῦντος　αὐτῷ　ἐν　τῷ
angel　-　speaking　to him　in　the

ὄρει　Σινὰ　καὶ　τῶν　πατέρων　ἡμῶν,　ὃς
mount　Sinai　and　[with] the　fathers　of us,　who

ἐδέξατο　λόγια　ζῶντα　δοῦναι　ὑμῖν,　**39** ᾧ
received　oracles　living　to give　to you,　¹to whom

οὐκ　ἠθέλησαν　ὑπήκοοι　γενέσθαι　οἱ　πατέρες
⁴wished ⁵not　⁶obedient　⁷to become　²the　³fathers

ἡμῶν,　ἀλλὰ　ἀπώσαντο　καὶ　ἐστράφησαν
¹of us,　but　thrust away　and　turned

ἐν　ταῖς　καρδίαις　αὐτῶν　εἰς　Αἴγυπτον,
in　the　hearts　of them　to　Egypt,

40 εἰπόντες　τῷ　Ἀαρών·　ποίησον　ἡμῖν
saying　-　to Aaron :　Make　for us

θεοὺς　οἳ　προπορεύσονται　ἡμῶν·　ὁ　γὰρ
gods　which　will go before　us;　-　for

Μωϋσῆς　οὗτος,　ὃς　ἐξήγαγεν　ἡμᾶς　ἐκ
this Moses,　who　led forth　us　out of

γῆς　Αἰγύπτου,　οὐκ　οἴδαμεν　τί　ἐγένετο
[the] land　Egypt,　we know not　what　happened

αὐτῷ.　**41** καὶ　ἐμοσχοποίησαν　ἐν
to him.　And　they made [a model of] a calf　in

ταῖς　ἡμέραις　ἐκείναις　καὶ　ἀνήγαγον　θυσίαν　τῷ
those days　and　brought up　a sacrifice to the

εἰδώλῳ,　καὶ　εὐφραίνοντο　ἐν　τοῖς　ἔργοις
idol,　and　made merry　in　the　works

τῶν　χειρῶν　αὐτῶν.　**42** ἔστρεψεν　δὲ　ὁ
of the　hands　of them.　And ²turned　-

θεὸς　καὶ　παρέδωκεν　αὐτοὺς　λατρεύειν
¹God　and　delivered　them　to worship

τῇ　στρατιᾷ　τοῦ　οὐρανοῦ,　καθὼς　γέγραπται
the　host　-　of heaven,　as　it has been written

ἐν　βίβλῳ　τῶν　προφητῶν·　μὴ　σφάγια
in　[the] roll　of the　prophets :　Not　victims

καὶ　θυσίας　προσηνέγκατέ　μοι　ἔτη
and　sacrifices　ye offered　to me　years

τεσσεράκοντα　ἐν　τῇ　ἐρήμῳ,　οἶκος　Ἰσραήλ,
forty　in　the　desert,　[O] house　of Israel,

43 καὶ　ἀνελάβετε　τὴν　σκηνὴν　τοῦ　Μόλοχ
and　ye took up　the　tent　- of Moloch

καὶ　τὸ　ἄστρον　τοῦ　θεοῦ　Ῥομφά,　τοὺς
and　the　star　of the　god　Rompha,　the

τύπους　οὓς　ἐποιήσατε　προσκυνεῖν　αὐτοῖς;
models　which　ye made　to worship　them?

καὶ　μετοικιῶ　ὑμᾶς　ἐπέκεινα　Βαβυλῶνος.
and　I will deport　you　beyond　Babylon.

44 Ἡ　σκηνὴ　τοῦ　μαρτυρίου　ἦν　τοῖς
The　tent　-　of witness　was　to the
=Our fathers had the tent of witness

πατράσιν　ἡμῶν　ἐν　τῇ　ἐρήμῳ,　καθὼς
fathers　of us°　in　the　desert,　as

διετάξατο　ὁ　λαλῶν　τῷ　Μωϋσῆ　ποιῆσαι
commanded the [one]　speaking　-　to Moses　to make

αὐτὴν　κατὰ　τὸν　τύπον　ὃν　ἑωράκει·
it　according to　the　model　which　he had seen;

45 ἣν　καὶ　εἰσήγαγον　διαδεξάμενοι　οἱ
which　also　⁵brought in　⁴having received　¹the

πατέρες　ἡμῶν　μετὰ　Ἰησοῦ　ἐν　τῇ　κατα-
²fathers　³of us　with　Jesus　in　the　pos-

---

who told the Israelites, 'God will send you a prophet like me from your own people.'d 38He was in the assembly, with the angel who spoke to him on Mount Sinai, and with our fathers; and he received living words to pass on to us.
39"But our fathers refused to obey him. Instead, they rejected him and in their hearts turned back to Egypt. They told Aaron, 'Make us gods who will go before us. As for this fellow Moses who led us out of Egypt—we don't know what has happened to him!'e 41That was the time they made an idol in the form of a calf. They brought sacrifices to it and held a celebration in honor of what their hands had made. 42But God turned away and gave them over to the worship of the heavenly bodies. This agrees with what is written in the book of the prophets:

" 'Did you bring me
sacrifices and
offerings
forty years in the
desert, O house of
Israel?
43You have lifted up the
shrine of Molech
and the star of your
god Rephan,
the idols you made to
worship.
Therefore I will send you
into exile'/ beyond
Babylon.

44"Our forefathers had the tabernacle of the Testimony with them in the desert. It had been made as God directed Moses, according to the pattern he had seen. 45Having received the tabernacle, our fathers under Joshua brought it with them when they took the land from the nations God drove out before them. It remained in

d37 Deut. 18:15
e40 Exodus 32:1
f43 Amos 5:25-27

before our fathers, until the time of David. ⁴⁶"And *David* found favor in God's sight, and asked that he might find a dwelling place for the ᵒGod of Jacob. ⁴⁷"But it was Solomon who built a house for Him. ⁴⁸"However, the Most High does not dwell in *houses* made by *human* hands; as the prophet says: ⁴⁹ 'HEAVEN IS MY THRONE, AND EARTH IS THE FOOTSTOOL OF MY FEET; WHAT KIND OF HOUSE WILL YOU BUILD FOR ME?' says the Lord; 'OR WHAT PLACE IS THERE FOR MY REPOSE? ⁵⁰ 'WAS IT NOT MY HAND WHICH MADE ALL THESE THINGS?' ⁵¹"You men who are stiff-necked and uncircumcised in heart and ears are always resisting the Holy Spirit; you are doing just as your fathers did. ⁵²"Which one of the prophets did your fathers not persecute? And they killed those who had previously announced the coming of the Righteous One, whose betrayers and murderers you have now become; ⁵³you who received the law as ordained by angels, and *yet* did not keep it."

Stephen Put to Death

⁵⁴Now when they heard this, they were cut to the quick, and they *began* gnashing their teeth at him. ⁵⁵But being full of the Holy Spirit, he gazed intently into heaven and saw the glory of God, and Jesus standing at the right hand of God; ⁵⁶and he said, "Behold, I see the heavens opened up and the Son of Man standing at the right hand of God." ⁵⁷But they cried out with a loud voice, and covered their ears, and they rushed upon him with one impulse. ⁵⁸And when they had

---

σχέσει	τῶν	ἐθνῶν,	ὧν	ἐξῶσεν ὁ θεὸς
session	of the	nations,	whom	you put out - God

ἀπὸ προσώπου τῶν πατέρων ἡμῶν, ἕως
from [the] face of the fathers of us, until

τῶν ἡμερῶν Δαυίδ· **46** ὃς εὗρεν χάριν
the days of David; who found favour

ἐνώπιον τοῦ θεοῦ καὶ ᾐτήσατο εὑρεῖν
before - God and asked to find

σκήνωμα τῷ οἴκῳ Ἰακώβ. **47** Σολομὼν δὲ
a tent for the house of Jacob. But Solomon

οἰκοδόμησεν αὐτῷ οἶκον. **48** ἀλλ'
built for him a house. But

οὐχ ὁ ὕψιστος ἐν χειροποιήτοις κατοικεῖ·
⁴not ¹the ²Most High ⁵in ⁶[places] made by hand ³dwells;

καθὼς ὁ προφήτης λέγει· **49** ὁ οὐρανός
as the prophet says : The heaven

μοι θρόνος, ἡ δὲ γῆ ὑποπόδιον τῶν
to me a throne, and the earth a footstool of the

ποδῶν μου· ποῖον οἶκον οἰκοδομήσετέ μοι,
feet of me; what house will ye build for me,

λέγει κύριος, ἢ τίς τόπος τῆς καταπαύσεώς
says [the] Lord, or what place of the rest

μου; **50** οὐχὶ ἡ χείρ μου ἐποίησεν ταῦτα
of me? not the hand of me made these things

πάντα; **51** Σκληροτράχηλοι καὶ ἀπερίτμητοι
all? Hard-necked and uncircumcised

καρδίαις καὶ τοῖς ὠσίν, ὑμεῖς ἀεὶ τῷ
in hearts and - ears, ye always the

πνεύματι τῷ ἁγίῳ ἀντιπίπτετε, ὡς οἱ
Spirit - Holy oppose, as the

πατέρες ὑμῶν καὶ ὑμεῖς. **52** τίνα τῶν
fathers of you also ye. Which of the

προφητῶν οὐκ ἐδίωξαν οἱ πατέρες ὑμῶν;
prophets persecuted not the fathers of you?

καὶ ἀπέκτειναν τοὺς προκαταγγείλαντας
and they killed the [ones] announcing beforehand

περὶ τῆς ἐλεύσεως τοῦ δικαίου, οὗ
concerning the coming of the righteous one, of whom

νῦν ὑμεῖς προδόται καὶ φονεῖς ἐγένεσθε,
now ye betrayers and murderers became,

53 οἵτινες ἐλάβετε τὸν νόμον εἰς διαταγὰς
who received the law in(by) dispositions

ἀγγέλων, καὶ οὐκ ἐφυλάξατε.
of angels, and did not keep [it].

54 Ἀκούοντες δὲ ταῦτα διεπρίοντο ταῖς
And hearing these things they were cut to the

καρδίαις αὐτῶν καὶ ἔβρυχον τοὺς ὀδόντας
hearts of them and gnashed the teeth

ἐπ' αὐτόν. **55** ὑπάρχων δὲ πλήρης
at him. But being full

πνεύματος ἁγίου ἀτενίσας εἰς τὸν οὐρανὸν
of [the] Spirit Holy gazing into - heaven

εἶδεν δόξαν θεοῦ καὶ Ἰησοῦν ἑστῶτα ἐκ
he saw [the] glory of God and Jesus standing at

δεξιῶν τοῦ θεοῦ, **56** καὶ εἶπεν· ἰδοὺ
[the] right [hand] - of God, and said : Behold

θεωρῶ τοὺς οὐρανοὺς διηνοιγμένους καὶ
I see the heavens having been opened up and

τὸν υἱὸν τοῦ ἀνθρώπου ἐκ δεξιῶν ἑστῶτα
the Son - of man at [the] right [hand] standing

τοῦ θεοῦ. **57** κράξαντες δὲ φωνῇ μεγάλῃ
- of God. And crying out voice with a great

συνέσχον τὰ ὦτα αὐτῶν, καὶ ὥρμησαν
they closed the ears of them, and rushed

ὁμοθυμαδὸν ἐπ' αὐτόν, **58** καὶ ἐκβαλόντες
with one mind on him, and casting out

---

the land until the time of David, ⁴⁶who enjoyed God's favor and asked that he might provide a dwelling place for the God of Jacob. ᵍ ⁴⁷But it was Solomon who built the house for him. ⁴⁸"However, the Most High does not live in houses made by men. As the prophet says:

⁴⁹" 'Heaven is my throne, and the earth is my footstool. What kind of house will you build for me? says the Lord. Or where will my resting place be? ⁵⁰Has not my hand made all these things?' ʰ

⁵¹"You stiff-necked people, with uncircumcised hearts and ears! You are just like your fathers: You always resist the Holy Spirit! ⁵²Was there ever a prophet your fathers did not persecute? They even killed those who predicted the coming of the Righteous One. And now you have betrayed and murdered him— ⁵³you who have received the law that was put into effect through angels but have not obeyed it."

The Stoning of Stephen

⁵⁴When they heard this, they were furious and gnashed their teeth at him. ⁵⁵But Stephen, full of the Holy Spirit, looked up to heaven and saw the glory of God, and Jesus standing at the right hand of God. ⁵⁶"Look," he said, "I see heaven open and the Son of Man standing at the right hand of God."

⁵⁷At this they covered

ᵒ The earliest mss. read *house* instead of *God*; the Septuagint reads *God*

ᵍ46 Some early manuscripts *the house of Jacob*
ʰ50 Isaiah 66:1,2

driven him out of the city, they *began* stoning *him*, and the witnesses laid aside their robes at the feet of a young man named Saul.

59And they went on stoning Stephen as he called upon *the* Lord and said, "Lord Jesus, receive my spirit!"

60And falling on his knees, he cried out with a loud voice, "Lord, do not hold this sin against them!" And having said this, he fell asleep.

Chapter 8

Saul Persecutes the Church

AND Saul was in hearty agreement with putting him to death.

And on that day a great persecution arose against the church in Jerusalem; and they were all scattered throughout the regions of Judea and Samaria, except the apostles.

2And *some* devout men buried Stephen, and made loud lamentation over him.

3But Saul *began* ravaging the church, entering house after house; and dragging off men and women, he would put them in prison.

Philip in Samaria

4Therefore, those who had been scattered went about preaching the word.

5And Philip went down to the city of Samaria and *began* proclaiming Christ to them.

6And the multitudes with one accord were giving attention to what was said by Philip, as they heard and saw the signs which he was performing.

7For *in the case of* many who had unclean spirits, they were coming out *of them* shouting with a loud voice; and many who had been paralyzed and lame were healed.

8And there was much re-

ἔξω τῆς πόλεως ἐλιθοβόλουν. καὶ οἱ
outside the city they stoned [him]. And the

μάρτυρες ἀπέθεντο τὰ ἱμάτια αὐτῶν παρὰ
witnesses put off the garments of them at

τοὺς πόδας νεανίου καλουμένου Σαύλου.
the feet of a young man *being* called Saul.

59 καὶ ἐλιθοβόλουν τὸν Στέφανον, ἐπικαλ-
And they stoned – Stephen, invok-

ούμενον καὶ λέγοντα· κύριε Ἰησοῦ, δέξαι
ing [God] and saying : Lord Jesus, receive

τὸ πνεῦμά μου. 60 θεὶς δὲ τὰ γόνατα
the spirit of me. And placing the knees
= kneeling down

ἔκραξεν φωνῇ μεγάλῃ· κύριε, μὴ στήσῃς
he cried voice with a great : Lord, place not

αὐτοῖς ταύτην τὴν ἁμαρτίαν. καὶ τοῦτο
to them this – sin. And ²this

εἰπὼν ἐκοιμήθη. 8 Σαῦλος δὲ ἦν συνευδοκῶν
¹saying he fell asleep. And Saul was consenting

τῇ ἀναιρέσει αὐτοῦ.
to the killing of him.

Ἐγένετο δὲ ἐν ἐκείνῃ τῇ ἡμέρᾳ
And there was in that the day

διωγμὸς μέγας ἐπὶ τὴν ἐκκλησίαν τὴν
persecution a great on(against) the church –

ἐν Ἰεροσολύμοις· πάντες [δὲ] διεσπάρησαν
in Jerusalem; and all were scattered

κατὰ τὰς χώρας τῆς Ἰουδαίας καὶ
throughout the countries of the of Judæa and

Σαμαρείας πλὴν τῶν ἀποστόλων.
Samaria except the apostles.

2 συνεκόμισαν δὲ τὸν Στέφανον ἄνδρες
And ²recovered – ⁴Stephen ²men

εὐλαβεῖς καὶ ἐποίησαν κοπετὸν μέγαν
¹devout and made lamentation great

ἐπ᾽ αὐτῷ. 3 Σαῦλος δὲ ἐλυμαίνετο τὴν
over him. But Saul ravaged the

ἐκκλησίαν κατὰ τοὺς οἴκους εἰσπορευόμενος,
church house by house† entering,

σύρων τε ἄνδρας καὶ γυναῖκας παρεδίδου
dragging both men and women delivered

εἰς φυλακήν.
to prison.

4 Οἱ μὲν οὖν διασπαρέντες διῆλθον
The [ones] –* therefore being scattered passed through

εὐαγγελιζόμενοι τὸν λόγον. 5 Φίλιππος δὲ
preaching the word. But Philip

κατελθὼν εἰς τὴν πόλιν τῆς
going down to the city –

Σαμαρείας ἐκήρυσσεν αὐτοῖς τὸν Χριστόν.
of Samaria proclaimed to them the Christ.

6 προσεῖχον δὲ οἱ ὄχλοι τοῖς
And gave heed the crowds to the things

λεγομένοις ὑπὸ τοῦ Φιλίππου ὁμοθυμαδὸν
being said by – Philip with one mind

ἐν τῷ ἀκούειν αὐτοὺς καὶ βλέπειν τὰ
in the to hear them and to see^be the
= as they heard and saw

σημεῖα ἃ ἐποίει. 7 πολλοὶ γὰρ τῶν
signs which he was doing. For many of the

ἐχόντων πνεύματα ἀκάθαρτα βοῶντα φωνῇ
[ones] having spirits unclean crying voice

μεγάλῃ ἐξήρχοντο· πολλοὶ δὲ παραλελυμένοι
¹with a great came out; and many *having been* paralysed

καὶ χωλοὶ ἐθεραπεύθησαν· 8 ἐγένετο δὲ
and lame were healed; and there was

* See note on John 19. 24.

---

their ears and, yelling at the top of their voices, they all rushed at him, 58dragged him out of the city and began to stone him. Meanwhile, the witnesses laid their clothes at the feet of a young man named Saul.

59While they were stoning him, Stephen prayed, "Lord Jesus, receive my spirit." 60Then he fell on his knees and cried out, "Lord, do not hold this sin against them." When he had said this, he fell asleep.

Chapter 8

AND Saul was there, giving approval to his death.

The Church Persecuted and Scattered

On that day a great persecution broke out against the church at Jerusalem, and all except the apostles were scattered throughout Judea and Samaria. 2Godly men buried Stephen and mourned deeply for him. 3But Saul began to destroy the church. Going from house to house, he dragged off men and women and put them in prison.

Philip in Samaria

4Those who had been scattered preached the word wherever they went. 5Philip went down to a city in Samaria and proclaimed the Christ^*i* there. 6When the crowds heard Philip and saw the miraculous signs he did, they all paid close attention to what he said. 7With shrieks, evil^*j* spirits came out of many, and many paralytics and cripples were healed. 8So

---

joicing in that city.

9Now there was a certain man named Simon, who formerly was practicing magic in the city, and astonishing the people of Samaria, claiming to be someone great;

10and they all, from smallest to greatest, were giving attention to him, saying, "This man is what is called the Great Power of God."

11And they were giving him attention because he had for a long time astonished them with his magic arts.

12But when they believed Philip preaching the good news about the kingdom of God and the name of Jesus Christ, they were being baptized, men and women alike.

13And even Simon himself believed; and after being baptized, he continued on with Philip; and as he observed signs and great miracles taking place, he was constantly amazed.

14Now when the apostles in Jerusalem heard that Samaria had received the word of God, they sent them Peter and John,

15who came down and prayed for them, that they might receive the Holy Spirit.

16For He had not yet fallen upon any of them; they had simply been baptized in the name of the Lord Jesus.

17Then they *began* laying their hands on them, and they were receiving the Holy Spirit.

18Now when Simon saw that the Spirit was bestowed through the laying on of the apostles' hands, he offered them money,

19saying, "Give this authority to me as well, so that everyone on whom I lay my hands may receive

---

πολλὴ χαρὰ ἐν τῇ πόλει ἐκείνῃ. 9 Ἀνὴρ δέ τις
much   joy in the city   that.   And a certain man

ὀνόματι   Σίμων   προϋπῆρχεν   ἐν   τῇ
by name   Simon   was previously in   the

πόλει   μαγεύων   καὶ   ἐξιστάνων   τὸ
city   practising sorcery and   astonishing   the

ἔθνος   τῆς   Σαμαρείας,   λέγων   εἶναί   τινα
nation   -   of Samaria,   saying ³to be ²someone

ἑαυτὸν   μέγαν, 10 ᾧ   προσεῖχον   πάντες
¹himself   ⁴great,   to whom gave heed   all

ἀπὸ   μικροῦ   ἕως   μεγάλου   λέγοντες·   οὗτός
from   small   to   great   saying :   This man

ἐστιν   ἡ   δύναμις   τοῦ   θεοῦ   ἡ   καλουμένη
is   the   power   -   of God   -   being called

μεγάλη. 11   προσεῖχον   δὲ   αὐτῷ   διὰ   τὸ
great.   And they gave heed to him because of the

ἱκανῷ   χρόνῳ   ταῖς   μαγείαις   ἐξεστακέναι
for a considerable time by the sorceries to have astonished
=because for a considerable time he had astonished them by his
sorceries.

αὐτούς. 12 ὅτε   δὲ   ἐπίστευσαν   τῷ   Φιλίππῳ
them.   But when   they believed   -   Philip

εὐαγγελιζομένῳ   περὶ   τῆς   βασιλείας   τοῦ
preaching   about   the   kingdom

θεοῦ   καὶ   τοῦ   ὀνόματος   Ἰησοῦ   Χριστοῦ,
of God and   the   name   of Jesus   Christ,

ἐβαπτίζοντο   ἄνδρες   τε   καὶ   γυναῖκες.
they were baptized both men   and   women.

13 ὁ   δὲ   Σίμων   καὶ   αὐτὸς   ἐπίστευσεν,
   -   And   Simon   also   [him]self   believed,

καὶ   βαπτισθεὶς   ἦν   προσκαρτερῶν   τῷ
and   having been baptized was attaching himself

Φιλίππῳ,   θεωρῶν   τε   σημεῖα   καὶ   δυνάμεις
to Philip,   and beholding signs and   powerful deeds

μεγάλας   γινομένας   ἐξίστατο. 14 Ἀκούσαντες
great   happening   he was amazed.   ³hearing

δὲ   οἱ   ἐν   Ἱεροσολύμοις   ἀπόστολοι   ὅτι
¹And ²the   ⁴in   ⁵Jerusalem   ²apostles   that

δέδεκται   ἡ   Σαμάρεια   τὸν   λόγον   τοῦ
¹has received -   ¹Samaria   the   word   -

θεοῦ,   ἀπέστειλαν   πρὸς   αὐτοὺς   Πέτρον
of God,   they sent   to   them   Peter

καὶ   Ἰωάννην,   15 οἵτινες   καταβάντες
and   John,   who   going down

προσηύξαντο   περὶ   αὐτῶν   ὅπως   λάβωσιν
prayed   concerning them   so as they might receive

πνεῦμα   ἅγιον· 16 οὐδέπω   γὰρ   ἦν   ἐπ'
Spirit   Holy;   for ²not yet ¹he was ⁴on

οὐδενὶ   αὐτῶν   ἐπιπεπτωκός,   μόνον   δὲ
⁵no(any)one ⁶of them ³having fallen on,   but only

βεβαπτισμένοι   ὑπῆρχον   εἰς   τὸ   ὄνομα   τοῦ
having been baptized they were in the   name   of the

κυρίου   Ἰησοῦ.   17 τότε   ἐπετίθεσαν   τὰς
Lord   Jesus.   Then   they laid on   the(ir)

χεῖρας   ἐπ'   αὐτούς,   καὶ   ἐλάμβανον   πνεῦμα
hands   on   them,   and   they received   ²Spirit

ἅγιον. 18 ἰδὼν   δὲ   ὁ   Σίμων   ὅτι   διὰ
¹Holy.   And ²seeing -   ¹Simon   that through

τῆς   ἐπιθέσεως   τῶν   χειρῶν   τῶν   ἀποστόλων
the   laying on   of the hands   of the   apostles

δίδοται   τὸ   πνεῦμα,   προσήνεγκεν   αὐτοῖς
is(was) given the Spirit,   he offered   them

χρήματα   λέγων· 19 δότε   κἀμοὶ   τὴν
money   saying :   Give   me also   -

ἐξουσίαν   ταύτην   ἵνα   ᾧ   ἐὰν   ἐπιθῶ   τὰς
authority   this   that whomever I lay on the(my)

---

there was great joy in that city.

Simon the Sorcerer

9Now for some time a man named Simon had practiced sorcery in the city and amazed all the people of Samaria. He boasted that he was someone great, 10and all the people, both high and low, gave him their attention and exclaimed, "This man is the divine power known as the Great Power." 11They followed him because he had amazed them for a long time with his magic. 12But when they believed Philip as he preached the good news of the kingdom of God and the name of Jesus Christ, they were baptized, both men and women. 13Simon himself believed and was baptized. And he followed Philip everywhere, astonished by the great signs and miracles he saw.

14When the apostles in Jerusalem heard that Samaria had accepted the word of God, they sent Peter and John to them. 15When they arrived, they prayed for them that they might receive the Holy Spirit, 16because the Holy Spirit had not yet come upon any of them; they had simply been baptized into*ᵏ* the name of the Lord Jesus. 17Then Peter and John placed their hands on them, and they received the Holy Spirit.

18When Simon saw that the Spirit was given at the laying on of the apostles' hands, he offered them money 19and said, "Give me also this ability so that everyone on whom I lay my hands may receive the Holy Spirit."

ᵏ16 Or in

the Holy Spirit.''
20But Peter said to him, ''May your silver perish with you, because you thought you could obtain the gift of God with money!
21''You have no part or portion in this matter, for your heart is not right before God.
22''Therefore repent of this wickedness of yours, and pray the Lord that if possible, the intention of your heart may be forgiven you.
23''For I see that you are in the gall of bitterness and in the bondage of iniquity.''
24But Simon answered and said, ''Pray to the Lord for me yourselves, so that nothing of what you have said may come upon me.''

An Ethiopian Receives Christ

25And so, when they had solemnly testified and spoken the word of the Lord, they started back to Jerusalem, and were preaching the gospel to many villages of the Samaritans.
26But an angel of the Lord spoke to Philip saying, ''Arise and go south to the road that descends from Jerusalem to Gaza.'' (This is a desert *road*.)
27And he arose and went; and behold, there was an Ethiopian eunuch, a court official of Candace, queen of the Ethiopians, who was in charge of all her treasure; and he had come to Jerusalem to worship.
28And he was returning and sitting in his chariot, and was reading the prophet Isaiah.
29And the Spirit said to Philip, ''Go up and join this

χεῖρας λαμβάνῃ πνεῦμα ἅγιον. 20 Πέτρος δὲ
hands he may receive Spirit Holy. But Peter

εἶπεν πρὸς αὐτόν· τὸ ἀργύριόν σου
said to him: The silver of thee

σὺν σοὶ εἴη εἰς ἀπώλειαν, ὅτι τὴν δωρεὰν
with thee may it be into perdition, because the gift

τοῦ θεοῦ ἐνόμισας διὰ χρημάτων κτᾶσθαι.
- of God thou didst suppose through money to get.

21 οὐκ ἔστιν σοι μερὶς οὐδὲ κλῆρος
There is not to thee⁰ part nor lot
=Thou hast no

ἐν τῷ λόγῳ τούτῳ· ἡ γὰρ καρδία σου
in this matter; for the heart of thee

οὐκ ἔστιν εὐθεῖα ἔναντι τοῦ θεοῦ.
is not right before - God.

22 μετανόησον οὖν ἀπὸ τῆς κακίας σου
Repent thou therefore from - ²wickedness ³of thee

ταύτης, καὶ δεήθητι τοῦ κυρίου εἰ ἄρα
¹this, and petition the Lord if perhaps

ἀφεθήσεταί σοι ἡ ἐπίνοια τῆς καρδίας
will be forgiven thee the thought of the heart

σου· 23 εἰς γὰρ χολὴν πικρίας καὶ
of thee; for in gall of bitterness and

σύνδεσμον ἀδικίας ὁρῶ σε ὄντα.
bond of unrighteousness I see thee being.

24 ἀποκριθεὶς δὲ ὁ Σίμων εἶπεν· δεήθητε
And answering - Simon said: Petition

ὑμεῖς ὑπὲρ ἐμοῦ πρὸς τὸν κύριον, ὅπως
ye for me to the Lord, so as

μηδὲν ἐπέλθῃ ἐπ᾽ ἐμὲ ὧν εἰρήκατε.
¹not one ⁴may come on ⁵on ⁶me ²of the ³ye have
things which spoken.

25 Οἱ μὲν οὖν διαμαρτυράμενοι καὶ λαλή-
They - therefore having solemnly witnessed and having

σαντες τὸν λόγον τοῦ κυρίου ὑπέστρεφον
spoken the word of the Lord returned

εἰς Ἱεροσόλυμα, πολλάς τε κώμας τῶν
to Jerusalem, and ²many ³villages ⁴of the

Σαμαριτῶν εὐηγγελίζοντο.
⁵Samaritans ¹evangelized.

26 Ἄγγελος δὲ κυρίου ἐλάλησεν πρὸς
But an angel of [the] Lord spoke to

Φίλιππον λέγων· ἀνάστηθι καὶ πορεύου
Philip saying: Rise up and go

κατὰ μεσημβρίαν ἐπὶ τὴν ὁδὸν τὴν
along south on the way -

καταβαίνουσαν ἀπὸ Ἱερουσαλὴμ εἰς Γάζαν·
going down from Jerusalem to Gaza;

αὕτη ἐστὶν ἔρημος. 27 καὶ ἀναστὰς
this is desert. And rising up

ἐπορεύθη. καὶ ἰδοὺ ἀνὴρ Αἰθίοψ εὐνοῦχος
he went. And behold[,] *a man* Ethiopian a eunuch

δυνάστης Κανδάκης βασιλίσσης Αἰθιόπων,
a courtier of Candace queen of [the] Ethiopians,

ὃς ἦν ἐπὶ πάσης τῆς γάζης αὐτῆς,
who was over all the treasure of her,

[ὃς] ἐληλύθει προσκυνήσων εἰς Ἱερουσαλήμ,
who had come worshipping in Jerusalem,

28 ἦν δὲ ὑποστρέφων καὶ καθήμενος ἐπὶ
and was returning and sitting on

τοῦ ἅρματος αὐτοῦ καὶ ἀνεγίνωσκεν τὸν
the chariot of him and was reading the

προφήτην Ἠσαΐαν. 29 εἶπεν δὲ τὸ πνεῦμα
prophet Esaias. And said the Spirit

τῷ Φιλίππῳ· πρόσελθε καὶ κολλήθητι
- to Philip: Approach and keep company with

20Peter answered: ''May your money perish with you, because you thought you could buy the gift of God with money! 21You have no part or share in this ministry, because your heart is not right before God. 22Repent of this wickedness and pray to the Lord. Perhaps he will forgive you for having such a thought in your heart. 23For I see that you are full of bitterness and captive to sin.''
24Then Simon answered, ''Pray to the Lord for me so that nothing you have said may happen to me.''
25When they had testified and proclaimed the word of the Lord, Peter and John returned to Jerusalem, preaching the gospel in many Samaritan villages.

Philip and the Ethiopian

26Now an angel of the Lord said to Philip, ''Go south to the road—the desert road—that goes down from Jerusalem to Gaza.'' 27So he started out, and on his way he met an Ethiopian/ eunuch, an important official in charge of all the treasury of Candace, queen of the Ethiopians. This man had gone to Jerusalem to worship, 28and on his way home was sitting in his chariot reading the book of Isaiah the prophet. 29The Spirit told Philip, ''Go to

/27 That is, from the upper Nile region

chariot.''

30And when Philip had run up, he heard him reading Isaiah the prophet, and said, ''Do you understand what you are reading?''

31And he said, ''Well, how could I, unless someone guides me?'' And he invited Philip to come up and sit with him.

32Now the passage of Scripture which he was reading was this:

"HE WAS LED AS A SHEEP
TO SLAUGHTER;
AND AS A LAMB BEFORE
ITS SHEARER IS SILENT,
SO HE DOES NOT OPEN
HIS MOUTH.

33 "IN HUMILIATION HIS
JUDGMENT WAS TAKEN
AWAY;
WHO SHALL RELATE
HIS GENERATION?
FOR HIS LIFE IS RE-
MOVED FROM THE
EARTH."

34And the eunuch answered Philip and said, ''Please *tell me*, of whom does the prophet say this? Of himself, or of someone else?''

35And Philip opened his mouth, and beginning from this Scripture he preached Jesus to him.

36And as they went along the road they came to some water; and the eunuch *said, ''Look! Water! What prevents me from being baptized?''

37[pAnd Philip said, ''If you believe with all your heart, you may.'' And he answered and said, ''I believe that Jesus Christ is the Son of God.'']

38And he ordered the chariot to stop; and they both went down into the water, Philip as well as the eunuch; and he baptized him.

39And when they came up out of the water, the Spirit of the Lord snatched Philip away; and the eunuch saw him no more, but went on his way rejoicing.

40But Philip found himself at Azotus; and as he passed

τῷ   ἅρματι   τούτῳ.
         this chariot.

30 προσδραμὼν   δὲ
And running up

ὁ   Φίλιππος   ἤκουσεν   αὐτοῦ   ἀναγινώσκοντος
-    Philip   heard   him   reading

'Ησαΐαν   τὸν   προφήτην,   καὶ   εἶπεν·   ἆρά   γε
Esaias   the   prophet,   and   said :   Then

γινώσκεις   ἃ   ἀναγινώσκεις;   31 ὁ   δὲ
knowest thou   what things   thou art reading?   And he

εἶπεν·   πῶς   γὰρ   ἂν   δυναίμην   ἐὰν   μή
said :   How   indeed   should I be able   unless

τις   ὁδηγήσει   με;   παρεκάλεσέν   τε   τὸν
someone   shall guide   me?   And he besought   -

Φίλιππον   ἀναβάντα   καθίσαι   σὺν   αὐτῷ.
Philip   coming up   to sit   with   him.

32 ἡ   δὲ   περιοχὴ   τῆς   γραφῆς   ἣν   ἀνεγίνω-
Now the   passage   of the scripture   which   he was

σκεν   ἦν   αὕτη·   ὡς   πρόβατον   ἐπὶ   σφαγὴν
reading was   this :   As   a sheep   to   slaughter

ἤχθη,   καὶ ὡς   ἀμνὸς   ἐναντίον   τοῦ   κείροντος
he was led,   and as   a lamb   before   the [one]   shearing

αὐτὸν   ἄφωνος,   οὕτως   οὐκ   ἀνοίγει   τὸ
it   [is] dumb,   so   he opens not   the

στόμα   αὐτοῦ.   33 'Εν   τῇ   ταπεινώσει
mouth   of him.   In   the   humiliation

ἡ   κρίσις   αὐτοῦ   ἤρθη·   τὴν   γενεὰν   αὐτοῦ
the judgment   of him   was taken away;   the   generation of him

τίς   διηγήσεται;   ὅτι   αἴρεται   ἀπὸ   τῆς
who   will relate?   because   is taken   from   the

γῆς   ἡ   ζωὴ   αὐτοῦ.   34 ἀποκριθεὶς   δὲ   ὁ
earth   the   life   of him.   And answering   the

εὐνοῦχος   τῷ   Φιλίππῳ   εἶπεν·   δέομαί   σου,
eunuch   -   to Philip   said :   I ask   thee,

περὶ   τίνος   ὁ   προφήτης   λέγει   τοῦτο;
about   whom   the   prophet   says   this?

περὶ   ἑαυτοῦ   ἢ   περὶ   ἑτέρου   τινός;
about   himself   or   about   other   someone?

35 ἀνοίξας   δὲ   ὁ   Φίλιππος   τὸ   στόμα
And opening   -   Philip   the   mouth

αὐτοῦ   καὶ   ἀρξάμενος   ἀπὸ   τῆς   γραφῆς   ταύτης
of him   and   beginning   from   this scripture

εὐηγγελίσατο   αὐτῷ   τὸν   'Ιησοῦν.
preached   to him   -   Jesus.

36 ὡς   δὲ   ἐπορεύοντο   κατὰ   τὴν   ὁδόν,
And as   they were going   along   the   way,

ἦλθον   ἐπί   τι   ὕδωρ,   καί φησιν ὁ   εὐνοῦχος·
they came   upon certain   water,   and   says   the   eunuch :

ἰδοὺ   ὕδωρ·   τί   κωλύει   με   βαπτισθῆναι;‡
Behold[,]   water;   what   prevents   me   to be baptized?

38 καὶ   ἐκέλευσεν   στῆναι   τὸ   ἅρμα,   καὶ
And   he commanded   to stand   the   chariot,   and

κατέβησαν   ἀμφότεροι   εἰς   τὸ   ὕδωρ,   ὅ
went down   both   into   the   water,   -

τε   Φίλιππος   καὶ   ὁ   εὐνοῦχος,   καὶ   ἐβάπτισεν
both   Philip   and the   eunuch,   and   he baptized

αὐτόν.   39 ὅτε   δὲ   ἀνέβησαν   ἐκ   τοῦ   ὕδατος,
him.   And when   they came up out of the   water,

πνεῦμα   κυρίου   ἥρπασεν   τὸν   Φίλιππον,
[the] Spirit   of [the] Lord   seized   -   Philip,

καὶ   οὐκ   εἶδεν   αὐτὸν   οὐκέτι   ὁ   εὐνοῦχος,
and   saw not   him   no(any) more   the   eunuch,

ἐπορεύετο   γὰρ   τὴν   ὁδὸν   αὐτοῦ   χαίρων.
for he went   the   way   of him   rejoicing.

40 Φίλιππος   δὲ   εὑρέθη   εἰς   "Αζωτον,   καὶ
But Philip   was found   in   Azotus,   and

---

that chariot and stay near it.''

30Then Philip ran up to the chariot and heard the man reading Isaiah the prophet. ''Do you understand what you are reading?'' Philip asked.

31''How can I,'' he said, ''unless someone explains it to me?'' So he invited Philip to come up and sit with him.

32The eunuch was reading this passage of Scripture:

''He was led like a sheep
to the slaughter,
and as a lamb before
the shearer is silent,
so he did not open his
mouth.

33In his humiliation he was
deprived of justice.
Who can speak of his
descendants?
For his life was taken
from the earth.''m

34The eunuch asked Philip, ''Tell me, please, who is the prophet talking about, himself or someone else?'' 35Then Philip began with that very passage of Scripture and told him the good news about Jesus.

36As they traveled along the road, they came to some water and the eunuch said, ''Look, here is water. Why shouldn't I be baptized?''n 38And he gave orders to stop the chariot. Then both Philip and the eunuch went down into the water and Philip baptized him. 39When they came up out of the water, the Spirit of the Lord suddenly took Philip away, and the eunuch did not see him again, but went on his way rejoicing. 40Philip, however, appeared at Azotus and trav-

---

m33 Isaiah 53:7,8
n36 Some late manuscripts
baptized?'' 37Philip said, ''If you
believe with all your heart, you
may.'' The eunuch answered, ''I
believe that Jesus Christ is the Son
of God.''

---

p Many mss. do not contain this verse

‡ Verse 37 omitted by Nestle; cf. NIV footnote.

through he kept preaching the gospel to all the cities, until he came to Caesarea.

Chapter 9

The Conversion of Saul

NOW Saul, still breathing threats and murder against the disciples of the Lord, went to the high priest, ²and asked for letters from him to the synagogues at Damascus, so that if he found any belonging to the Way, both men and women, he might bring them bound to Jerusalem. ³And it came about that as he journeyed, he was approaching Damascus, and suddenly a light from heaven flashed around him; ⁴and he fell to the ground, and heard a voice saying to him, "Saul, Saul, why are you persecuting Me?"

⁵And he said, "Who art Thou, Lord?" And He said, "I am Jesus whom you are persecuting, ⁶but rise, and enter the city, and it shall be told you what you must do."

⁷And the men who traveled with him stood speechless, hearing the voice, but seeing no one. ⁸And Saul got up from the ground, and though his eyes were open, he could see nothing; and leading him by the hand, they brought him into Damascus. ⁹And he was three days without sight, and neither ate nor drank.

¹⁰Now there was a certain disciple at Damascus, named Ananias; and the Lord said to him in a vision, "Ananias." And he said, "Behold, *here am* I, Lord."

¹¹And the Lord *said* to him, "Arise and go to the

διερχόμενος εὐηγγελίζετο τὰς πόλεις πάσας
passing through he evangelized the cities all

ἕως τοῦ ἐλθεῖν αὐτὸν εἰς Καισάρειαν.
until the to come himᵇ to Cæsarea.
=he came

9 Ὁ δὲ Σαῦλος ἔτι ἐμπνέων ἀπειλῆς
— But Saul still breathing threatening

καὶ φόνου εἰς τοὺς μαθητὰς τοῦ κυρίου,
and murder against the disciples of the Lord,

προσελθὼν τῷ ἀρχιερεῖ **2** ᾐτήσατο παρ'
approaching *to* the high priest asked from

αὐτοῦ ἐπιστολὰς εἰς Δαμασκὸν πρὸς τὰς
him letters to Damascus for the

συναγωγάς, ὅπως ἐάν τινας εὕρῃ τῆς
synagogues, so as if ¹any ¹he found ⁴of the

ὁδοῦ ὄντας, ἄνδρας τε καὶ γυναῖκας, δεδεμένους
⁵way ³being, both men and women, ⁶having been bound

ἀγάγῃ εἰς Ἰερουσαλήμ. **3** Ἐν
¹he might bring [them] to Jerusalem. In

δὲ τῷ πορεύεσθαι ἐγένετο αὐτὸν ἐγγίζειν
Now the to goᵉ it came to pass him to draw nearᵇ
=as he went =he drew near

τῇ Δαμασκῷ, ἐξαίφνης τε αὐτὸν περιήστ-
— to Damascus, and suddenly ⁵him ⁴shone

ραψεν φῶς ἐκ τοῦ οὐρανοῦ, **4** καὶ πεσὼν
round ¹a light ²out of — ³heaven, and falling

ἐπὶ τὴν γῆν ἤκουσεν φωνὴν λέγουσαν
on the earth he heard a voice saying

αὐτῷ· Σαοὺλ Σαούλ, τί με διώκεις;
to him: Saul[,] Saul, why me persecutest thou?

5 εἶπεν δέ· τίς εἶ, κύριε; ὁ δέ· ἐγὼ
And he said: Who art thou, Lord? And he [said]: I

εἰμι Ἰησοῦς ὃν σὺ διώκεις· **6** ἀλλὰ
am Jesus whom thou persecutest; but

ἀνάστηθι καὶ εἴσελθε εἰς τὴν πόλιν,
rise thou up, and enter into the city,

καὶ λαληθήσεταί σοι ὅ τί σε δεῖ ποιεῖν.
and it shall be told thee what thee it behoves to do.

7 οἱ δὲ ἄνδρες οἱ συνοδεύοντες αὐτῷ
Now the men — journeying with him

εἱστήκεισαν ἐνεοί, ἀκούοντες μὲν τῆς
stood speechless, hearing indeed the

φωνῆς, μηδένα δὲ θεωροῦντες. **8** ἠγέρθη δὲ
sound, but no man beholding. And was raised

Σαῦλος ἀπὸ τῆς γῆς, ἀνεῳγμένων δὲ
Saul from the ground, and having been opened
=when his eyes were opened

τῶν ὀφθαλμῶν αὐτοῦ οὐδὲν ἔβλεπεν·
the eyes of himᵃ nothing he saw;

χειραγωγοῦντες δὲ αὐτὸν εἰσήγαγον εἰς
and leading by the hand him they brought *in* into

Δαμασκόν. **9** καὶ ἦν ἡμέρας τρεῖς μὴ
Damascus. And he was days three not

βλέπων, καὶ οὐκ ἔφαγεν οὐδὲ ἔπιεν.
seeing, and ate not nor drank.

10 Ἦν δέ τις μαθητὴς ἐν Δαμασκῷ
Now there was a certain disciple in Damascus

ὀνόματι Ἀνανίας, καὶ εἶπεν πρὸς αὐτὸν
by name Ananias, and said to him

ἐν ὁράματι ὁ κύριος· Ἀνανία. ὁ δὲ
in a vision the Lord: Ananias. And he

εἶπεν· ἰδοὺ ἐγώ, κύριε. **11** ὁ δὲ κύριος
said: Behold[,] I, Lord. And the Lord

πρὸς αὐτόν· ἀναστὰς πορεύθητι ἐπὶ τὴν
[said] to him: Rising up go thou to the

eled about, preaching the gospel in all the towns until he reached Caesarea.

Chapter 9

Saul's Conversion

MEANWHILE, Saul was still breathing out murderous threats against the Lord's disciples. He went to the high priest ²and asked him for letters to the synagogues in Damascus, so that if he found any there who belonged to the Way, whether men or women, he might take them as prisoners to Jerusalem. ³As he neared Damascus on his journey, suddenly a light from heaven flashed around him. ⁴He fell to the ground and heard a voice say to him, "Saul, Saul, why do you persecute me?"

⁵"Who are you, Lord?" Saul asked.

"I am Jesus, whom you are persecuting," he replied. ⁶"Now get up and go into the city, and you will be told what you must do."

⁷The men traveling with Saul stood there speechless; they heard the sound but did not see anyone. ⁸Saul got up from the ground, but when he opened his eyes he could see nothing. So they led him by the hand into Damascus. ⁹For three days he was blind, and did not eat or drink anything.

¹⁰In Damascus there was a disciple named Ananias. The Lord called to him in a vision, "Ananias!"

"Yes, Lord," he answered.

¹¹The Lord told him, "Go to the house of Judas on

street called Straight, and inquire at the house of Judas for a man from Tarsus named Saul, for behold, he is praying,

12and he has seen ⁹in a vision a man named Ananias come in and lay his hands on him, so that he might regain his sight."

13But Ananias answered, "Lord, I have heard from many about this man, how much harm he did to Thy saints at Jerusalem;

14and here he has authority from the chief priests to bind all who call upon Thy name."

15But the Lord said to him, "Go, for he is a chosen ʳinstrument of Mine, to bear My name before the Gentiles and kings and the sons of Israel;

16for I will show him how much he must suffer for My name's sake."

17And Ananias departed and entered the house, and after laying his hands on him said, "Brother Saul, the Lord Jesus, who appeared to you on the road by which you were coming, has sent me so that you may regain your sight, and be filled with the Holy Spirit."

18And immediately there fell from his eyes something like scales, and he regained his sight, and he arose and was baptized;

19and he took food and was strengthened.

Saul Begins to Preach Christ

Now for several days he was with the disciples who were at Damascus,

20and immediately he *began* to proclaim Jesus in the synagogues, saying, "He is the Son of God."

21And all those hearing him continued to be amazed, and were saying, "Is this not he who in Jerusalem destroyed those who called on this name,

---

ῥύμην τὴν καλουμένην εὐθεῖαν καὶ ζήτησον
street   -   *being* called   Straight   and   seek

ἐν οἰκίᾳ ᾽Ιούδα Σαῦλον ὀνόματι Ταρσέα·
in [the] house of Judas ²Saul ³by name ¹a Tarsian;

ἰδοὺ γὰρ προσεύχεται, 12 καὶ εἶδεν ἄνδρα
for behold he is praying, and saw ³a man

[ἐν ὁράματι] ᾽Ανανίαν ὀνόματι εἰσελθόντα
¹in ²a vision Ananias by name coming in

καὶ ἐπιθέντα αὐτῷ χεῖρας, ὅπως ἀναβλέψῃ.
and putting on him hands, so as he may see again.

13 ἀπεκρίθη δὲ ᾽Ανανίας· κύριε, ἤκουσα
And answered   Ananias :   Lord,   I heard

ἀπὸ πολλῶν περὶ τοῦ ἀνδρὸς τούτου,
from many about this man,

ὅσα κακὰ τοῖς ἁγίοις σου ἐποίησεν
how many evil things to the saints of thee he did

ἐν ᾽Ιερουσαλήμ· 14 καὶ ὧδε ἔχει ἐξουσίαν
in Jerusalem·   and here he has authority

παρὰ τῶν ἀρχιερέων δῆσαι πάντας τοὺς
from the chief priests to bind all the

ἐπικαλουμένους τὸ ὄνομά σου. 15 εἶπεν
[ones] invoking the name of thee.   said

δὲ πρὸς αὐτὸν ὁ κύριος· πορεύου, ὅτι
But to him the Lord : Go thou, because

σκεῦος ἐκλογῆς ἐστίν μοι οὗτος τοῦ
³a vessel ⁴of choice ²is ¹to me ¹this man -

βαστάσαι τὸ ὄνομά μου ἐνώπιον [τῶν]
to bearᵈ the name of me ²before ³the

ἐθνῶν τε καὶ βασιλέων υἱῶν τε ᾽Ισραήλ·
⁴nations ¹both ⁵and ⁵kings ⁶sons ⁷and ⁶of Israel;

16 ἐγὼ γὰρ ὑποδείξω αὐτῷ ὅσα δεῖ
for I will show him how many things it behoves

αὐτὸν ὑπὲρ τοῦ ὀνόματός μου παθεῖν.
him on behalf of the name of me to suffer.

17 ᾽Απῆλθεν δὲ ᾽Ανανίας καὶ εἰσῆλθεν
And went away   Ananias and entered

εἰς τὴν οἰκίαν, καὶ ἐπιθεὶς ἐπ᾽ αὐτὸν
into the house, and putting *on* on him

τὰς χεῖρας εἶπεν· Σαοὺλ ἀδελφέ, ὁ
the(his) hands said : Saul brother, the

κύριος ἀπέσταλκέν με, ᾽Ιησοῦς ὁ ὀφθείς σοι
Lord has sent me, Jesus the [one] appear- to
ing thee

ἐν τῇ ὁδῷ ᾗ ἤρχου, ὅπως ἀναβλέψῃς
in the way which thou camest, so as thou mayest see again

καὶ πλησθῇς πνεύματος ἁγίου. 18 καὶ
and be filled of(with) Spirit Holy.   And

εὐθέως ἀπέπεσαν αὐτοῦ ἀπὸ τῶν ὀφθαλμῶν
immediately fell away of him from the eyes

ὡς λεπίδες, ἀνέβλεψέν τε, καὶ ἀναστὰς
as scales, and he saw again, and rising up

ἐβαπτίσθη, 19 καὶ λαβὼν τροφὴν ἐνίσχυσεν.
was baptized, and taking food was strengthened.

᾽Εγένετο δὲ μετὰ τῶν ἐν Δαμασκῷ
Now he was with the in Damascus

μαθητῶν ἡμέρας τινάς, 20 καὶ εὐθέως
disciples days some, and immediately

ἐν ταῖς συναγωγαῖς ἐκήρυσσεν τὸν ᾽Ιησοῦν,
in the synagogues he proclaimed - Jesus,

ὅτι οὗτός ἐστιν ὁ υἱὸς τοῦ θεοῦ.
that this one is the Son - of God.

21 ἐξίσταντο δὲ πάντες οἱ ἀκούοντες καὶ
And were amazed all the [ones] hearing and

ἔλεγον· οὐχ οὗτός ἐστιν ὁ πορθήσας
said : Not this man is the [one] having destroyed

εἰς ᾽Ιερουσαλὴμ τοὺς ἐπικαλουμένους
in Jerusalem the [ones] invoking

Straight Street and ask for a man from Tarsus named Saul, for he is praying. 12In a vision he has seen a man named Ananias come and place his hands on him to restore his sight."

13"Lord," Ananias answered, "I have heard many reports about this man and all the harm he has done to your saints in Jerusalem. 14And he has come here with authority from the chief priests to arrest all who call on your name."

15But the Lord said to Ananias, "Go! This man is my chosen instrument to carry my name before the Gentiles and their kings and before the people of Israel. 16I will show him how much he must suffer for my name."

17Then Ananias went to the house and entered it. Placing his hands on Saul, he said, "Brother Saul, the Lord—Jesus, who appeared to you on the road as you were coming here—has sent me so that you may see again and be filled with the Holy Spirit." 18Immediately, something like scales fell from Saul's eyes, and he could see again. He got up and was baptized, 19and after taking some food, he regained his strength.

Saul in Damascus and Jerusalem

Saul spent several days with the disciples in Damascus. 20At once he began to preach in the synagogues that Jesus is the Son of God. 21All those who heard him were astonished and asked, "Isn't he the man who raised havoc in Jerusalem among those who call on this name? And hasn't

---

ᵃ Some mss. do not contain *in a vision*
ʳ Or, *vessel*

and *who* had come here for the purpose of bringing them bound before the chief priests?''

22But Saul kept increasing in strength and confounding the Jews who lived at Damascus by proving that this *Jesus* is the Christ.

23And when many days had elapsed, the Jews plotted together to do away with him,

24but their plot became known to Saul. And they were also watching the gates day and night so that they might put him to death;

25but his disciples took him by night, and let him down through *an opening in* the wall, lowering him in a large basket.

26And when he had come to Jerusalem, he was trying to associate with the disciples; and they were all afraid of him, not believing that he was a disciple.

27But Barnabas took hold of him and brought him to the apostles and described to them how he had seen the Lord on the road, and that He had talked to him, and how at Damascus he had spoken out boldly in the name of Jesus.

28And he was with them moving about freely in Jerusalem, speaking out boldly in the name of the Lord.

29And he was talking and arguing with the Hellenistic Jews; but they were attempting to put him to death.

30But when the brethren learned *of it,* they brought him down to Caesarea and sent him away to Tarsus.

31So the church throughout all Judea and Galilee and Samaria enjoyed peace, being built up; and,

---

τὸ ὄνομα τοῦτο, καὶ ὧδε εἰς τοῦτο ἐληλύθει,
this name, and here for this he had come,

ἵνα δεδεμένους αὐτοὺς ἀγάγῃ ἐπὶ τοὺς
that *having been* bound them he might bring before the

ἀρχιερεῖς; 22 Σαῦλος δὲ μᾶλλον ἐνε-
chief priests? But Saul more was filled

δυναμοῦτο καὶ συνέχυννεν Ἰουδαίους τοὺς κατ-
with power and confounded Jews the [ones]

οἰκοῦντας ἐν Δαμασκῷ, συμβιβάζων ὅτι οὗτός
dwelling in Damascus, proving that this one

ἐστιν ὁ χριστός. 23 Ὡς δὲ ἐπληροῦντο
is the Christ. And when were fulfilled

ἡμέραι ἱκαναί, 24 συνεβουλεύσαντο
days considerable(many), consulted together

οἱ Ἰουδαῖοι ἀνελεῖν αὐτόν· ἐγνώσθη δὲ
the Jews to kill him; but was known

τῷ Σαύλῳ ἡ ἐπιβουλὴ αὐτῶν. παρετη-
- to Saul the plot of them. And they

ροῦντο δὲ καὶ τὰς πύλας ἡμέρας τε καὶ
carefully watched also the gates both by day and

νυκτὸς ὅπως αὐτὸν ἀνέλωσιν· 25 λαβόντες δὲ
by night so as him they might destroy; but ⁴taking

οἱ μαθηταὶ αὐτοῦ νυκτὸς διὰ τοῦ
¹the ²disciples ³of him by night through the

τείχους καθῆκαν αὐτὸν χαλάσαντες ἐν
wall let down him lowering in

σπυρίδι. 26 Παραγενόμενος δὲ εἰς
a basket. And arriving at

Ἰερουσαλὴμ ἐπείραζεν κολλᾶσθαι τοῖς
Jerusalem he tried to be joined to the

μαθηταῖς· καὶ πάντες ἐφοβοῦντο αὐτόν,
disciples; and all feared him,

μὴ πιστεύοντες ὅτι ἐστὶν μαθητής.
not believing that he is(was) a disciple.

27 Βαρνάβας δὲ ἐπιλαβόμενος αὐτὸν ἤγαγεν
But Barnabas taking hold of him led

πρὸς τοὺς ἀποστόλους, καὶ διηγήσατο
to the apostles, and narrated

αὐτοῖς πῶς ἐν τῇ ὁδῷ εἶδεν τὸν κύριον
to them how in the way he saw the Lord

καὶ ὅτι ἐλάλησεν αὐτῷ, καὶ πῶς ἐν
and that he spoke to him, and how in

Δαμασκῷ ἐπαρρησιάσατο ἐν τῷ ὀνόματι
Damascus he spoke boldly in the name

Ἰησοῦ. 28 καὶ ἦν μετ' αὐτῶν εἰσπορευόμενος
of Jesus. And he was with them going in

καὶ ἐκπορευόμενος εἰς Ἰερουσαλήμ,
and going out in Jerusalem,

παρρησιαζόμενος ἐν τῷ ὀνόματι τοῦ
speaking boldly in the name of the

κυρίου, 29 ἐλάλει τε καὶ συνεζήτει πρὸς
Lord, ³spoke ¹both ²and ⁴discussed with

τοὺς Ἑλληνιστάς· οἱ δὲ ἐπεχείρουν ἀνελεῖν
the Hellenists; and they attempted to kill

αὐτόν. 30 ἐπιγνόντες δὲ οἱ ἀδελφοὶ
him. But ²knowing ¹the ³brothers

κατήγαγον αὐτὸν εἰς Καισάρειαν καὶ
brought down him to Cæsarea and

ἐξαπέστειλαν αὐτὸν εἰς Ταρσόν.
sent forth him to Tarsus.

31 Ἡ μὲν οὖν ἐκκλησία καθ' ὅλης
²The - ¹therefore ³church throughout all

τῆς Ἰουδαίας καὶ Γαλιλαίας καὶ Σαμαρείας
- Judæa and Galilee and Samaria

εἶχεν εἰρήνην οἰκοδομουμένη καὶ πορευομένη
had peace being built and going

---

he come here to take them as prisoners to the chief priests?'' 22Yet Saul grew more and more powerful and baffled the Jews living in Damascus by proving that Jesus is the Christ. ⁰

23After many days had gone by, the Jews conspired to kill him, 24but Saul learned of their plan. Day and night they kept close watch on the city gates in order to kill him. 25But his followers took him by night and lowered him in a basket through an opening in the wall.

26When he came to Jerusalem, he tried to join the disciples, but they were all afraid of him, not believing that he really was a disciple. 27But Barnabas took him and brought him to the apostles. He told them how Saul on his journey had seen the Lord and that the Lord had spoken to him, and how in Damascus he had preached fearlessly in the name of Jesus. 28So Saul stayed with them and moved about freely in Jerusalem, speaking boldly in the name of the Lord. 29He talked and debated with the Grecian Jews, but they tried to kill him. 30When the brothers learned of this, they took him down to Caesarea and sent him off to Tarsus.

31Then the church throughout Judea, Galilee and Samaria enjoyed a time of peace. It was strengthened; and encouraged by

°22 Or Messiah

going on in the fear of the Lord and in the comfort of the Holy Spirit, it continued to increase.

Peter's Ministry

32Now it came about that as Peter was traveling through all *those parts*, he came down also to the saints who lived at Lydda. 33And there he found a certain man named Aeneas, who had been bedridden eight years, for he was paralyzed. 34And Peter said to him, "Aeneas, Jesus Christ heals you; arise, and make your bed." And immediately he arose. 35And all who lived at Lydda and Sharon saw him, and they turned to the Lord.

36Now in Joppa there was a certain disciple named Tabitha (which translated *in Greek* is called Dorcas); this woman was abounding with deeds of kindness and charity, which she continually did. 37And it came about at that time that she fell sick and died; and when they had washed her body, they laid it in an upper room. 38And since Lydda was near Joppa, the disciples, having heard that Peter was there, sent two men to him, entreating him, "Do not delay to come to us." 39And Peter arose and went with them. And when he had come, they brought him into the upper room; and all the widows stood beside him weeping, and showing all the ³tunics and garments that Dorcas used to make while she was with them. 40But Peter sent them all out and knelt down and prayed, and turning to the body, he said, "Tabitha,

---

τῷ φόβῳ τοῦ κυρίου, καὶ τῇ παρακλήσει
in the fear of the Lord, and in the comfort

τοῦ ἁγίου πνεύματος ἐπληθύνετο.
of the Holy Spirit was multiplied.

32 Ἐγένετο δὲ Πέτρον διερχόμενον διὰ
Now it came to pass Peter passing *through* through

πάντων κατελθεῖν καὶ πρὸς τοὺς ἁγίους
all [quarters] to come downᵇ also to the saints

τοὺς κατοικοῦντας Λύδδα. 33 εὗρεν δὲ
- inhabiting Lydda. And he found

ἐκεῖ ἄνθρωπόν τινα ὀνόματι Αἰνέαν ἐξ
there a certain man by name Aeneas of

ἐτῶν ὀκτὼ κατακείμενον ἐπὶ κραβάτου,
years eight lying on a mattress,

ὃς ἦν παραλελυμένος. 34 καὶ εἶπεν αὐτῷ
who was *having been* paralysed. And said to him

ὁ Πέτρος· Αἰνέα, ἰᾶταί σε Ἰησοῦς Χριστός·
- Peter: Aeneas, cures thee Jesus Christ;

ἀνάστηθι καὶ στρῶσον σεαυτῷ. καὶ
rise up and gird thyself. And

εὐθέως ἀνέστη. 35 καὶ εἶδαν αὐτὸν
immediately he rose up. And saw him

πάντες οἱ κατοικοῦντες Λύδδα καὶ τὸν
all the [ones] inhabiting Lydda and -

Σαρῶνα, οἵτινες ἐπέστρεψαν ἐπὶ τὸν κύριον.
Saron, who turned to the Lord.

Ἐν Ἰόππῃ δέ τις ἦν μαθήτρια ὀνόματι
¹in ¹Joppa ¹Now ³a certain ⁴was ²disciple by name

Ταβιθά, 36 ἣ διερμηνευομένη λέγεται
Tabitha, who being translated is called

Δορκάς· αὕτη ἦν πλήρης ἔργων ἀγαθῶν
Dorcas; this woman was full works of good

καὶ ἐλεημοσυνῶν ὧν ἐποίει. 37 ἐγένετο δὲ
and of alms which she did. And it happened

ἐν ταῖς ἡμέραις ἐκείναις ἀσθενήσασαν
in those days ailing

αὐτὴν ἀποθανεῖν· λούσαντες δὲ ἔθηκαν
she to dieᵇ; and having washed they put [her]
=being ill she died;

ἐν ὑπερῴῳ. 38 ἐγγὺς δὲ οὔσης Λύδδας
in an upper room. Now ²near ³being ¹Lyddaᵃ

τῇ Ἰόππῃ οἱ μαθηταὶ ἀκούσαντες ὅτι
- to Joppa the disciples having heard that

Πέτρος ἐστὶν ἐν αὐτῇ ἀπέστειλαν δύο
Peter is(was) in it sent two

ἄνδρας πρὸς αὐτὸν παρακαλοῦντες· μὴ
men to him beseeching: ⁵not

ὀκνήσῃς διελθεῖν ἕως ἡμῶν. 39 ἀναστὰς δὲ
¹hesitate to come to us. And rising up

Πέτρος συνῆλθεν αὐτοῖς· ὃν παραγενόμενον
Peter went with them; whom arriving

ἀνήγαγον εἰς τὸ ὑπερῷον, καὶ παρέστησαν
they led up into the upper room, and stood by

αὐτῷ πᾶσαι αἱ χῆραι κλαίουσαι καὶ
him all the widows weeping and

ἐπιδεικνύμεναι χιτῶνας καὶ ἱμάτια, ὅσα
showing tunics and garments, which

ἐποίει μετ' αὐτῶν οὖσα ἡ Δορκάς.
¹made ⁴with ⁵them ²being ¹Dorcas.

40 ἐκβαλὼν δὲ ἔξω πάντας ὁ Πέτρος
And ²putting *out* ⁴outside ³all - ¹Peter

καὶ θεὶς τὰ γόνατα προσηύξατο, καὶ
and placing the knees he prayed, and
=kneeling down

ἐπιστρέψας πρὸς τὸ σῶμα εἶπεν· Ταβιθά,
turning to the body said: Tabitha,

---

the Holy Spirit, it grew in numbers, living in the fear of the Lord.

Aeneas and Dorcas

32As Peter traveled about the country, he went to visit the saints in Lydda. 33There he found a man named Aeneas, a paralytic who had been bedridden for eight years. 34"Aeneas," Peter said to him, "Jesus Christ heals you. Get up and take care of your mat." Immediately Aeneas got up. 35All those who lived in Lydda and Sharon saw him and turned to the Lord.

36In Joppa there was a disciple named Tabitha (which, when translated, is Dorcasᵖ), who was always doing good and helping the poor. 37About that time she became sick and died, and her body was washed and placed in an upstairs room. 38Lydda was near Joppa; so when the disciples heard that Peter was in Lydda, they sent two men to him and urged him, "Please come at once!"

39Peter went with them, and when he arrived he was taken upstairs to the room. All the widows stood around him, crying and showing him the robes and other clothing that Dorcas had made while she was still with them. 40Peter sent them all out of the room; then he got down on his knees and prayed. Turning toward the dead woman, he said,

---

³ Or, *inner garments*

ᵖ36 Both *Tabitha* (Aramaic) and *Dorcas* (Greek) mean *gazelle*.

arise.'' And she opened her eyes, and when she saw Peter, she sat up.

41And he gave her his hand and raised her up; and calling the saints and widows, he presented her alive.

42And it became known all over Joppa, and many believed in the Lord.

43And it came about that he stayed many days in Joppa with a certain tanner, Simon.

Chapter 10

Cornelius' Vision

NOW there was a certain man at Caesarea named Cornelius, a centurion of what was called the Italian [t] cohort,

2a devout man, and one who feared God with all his household, and gave many ᵘalms to the Jewish people, and prayed to God continually.

3About the ᵛninth hour of the day he clearly saw in a vision an angel of God who had *just* come in to him, and said to him, ''Cornelius!''

4And fixing his gaze upon him and being much alarmed, he said, ''What is it, Lord?'' And he said to him, ''Your prayers and ʷalms have ascended as a memorial before God.

5''And now dispatch *some* men to Joppa, and send for a man *named* Simon, who is also called Peter;

6he is staying with a certain tanner *named* Simon, whose house is by the sea.''

7And when the angel who was speaking to him had departed, he summoned two of his servants and a devout soldier of those who were in constant attendance upon him,

8and after he had explained everything to them,

ἀνάστηθι. ἡ δὲ ἤνοιξεν τοὺς ὀφθαλμοὺς
rise up.   And she opened   the   eyes

αὐτῆς, καὶ ἰδοῦσα τὸν Πέτρον ἀνεκάθισεν.
of her, and seeing   -   Peter   sat up.

41 δοὺς δὲ αὐτῇ χεῖρα ἀνέστησεν αὐτήν·
   And giving her a hand he raised up   her;

φωνήσας δὲ τοὺς ἁγίους καὶ τὰς χήρας
and calling   the   saints   and the widows

παρέστησεν αὐτὴν ζῶσαν. **42** γνωστὸν δὲ
he presented   her   living.   And known

ἐγένετο καθ' ὅλης τῆς Ἰόππης, καὶ
it became throughout all   -   Joppa,   and

ἐπίστευσαν πολλοὶ ἐπὶ τὸν κύριον.
believed   many   on   the   Lord.

43 Ἐγένετο δὲ ἡμέρας ἱκανὰς μεῖναι ἐν
And it came to pass days   several to remain in
= he remained many days

Ἰόππῃ παρά τινι Σίμωνι βυρσεῖ.
Joppa with one   Simon   a tanner.

10 Ἀνὴρ δέ τις ἐν Καισαρείᾳ ὀνόματι
Now a certain man in Caesarea   by name

Κορνήλιος, ἑκατοντάρχης ἐκ σπείρης τῆς
Cornelius,   a centurion   of a cohort   -

καλουμένης Ἰταλικῆς, **2** εὐσεβὴς καὶ
being called   Italian,   devout   and

φοβούμενος τὸν θεὸν σὺν παντὶ τῷ οἴκῳ
fearing   -   God with all   the household

αὐτοῦ, ποιῶν ἐλεημοσύνας πολλὰς τῷ
of him, doing   alms   many   to the

λαῷ καὶ δεόμενος τοῦ θεοῦ διὰ παντός,
people and petitioning -   God   continually,

3 εἶδεν ἐν ὁράματι φανερῶς, ὡσεὶ περὶ
saw   in a vision   clearly,   as it were around

ὥραν ἐνάτην τῆς ἡμέρας, ἄγγελον τοῦ
hour ninth   of the   day,   an angel   -

θεοῦ εἰσελθόντα πρὸς αὐτὸν καὶ εἰπόντα
of God entering   to   him   and saying

αὐτῷ· Κορνήλιε. **4** ὁ δὲ ἀτενίσας αὐτῷ
to him: Cornelius.   And he gazing   at him

καὶ ἔμφοβος γενόμενος εἶπεν· τί ἐστιν,
and terrified becoming   said : What is it,

κύριε; εἶπεν δὲ αὐτῷ· αἱ προσευχαί
lord?   And he said to him: The   prayers

σου καὶ αἱ ἐλεημοσύναι σου ἀνέβησαν
of thee and the   alms   of thee went up

εἰς μνημόσυνον ἔμπροσθεν τοῦ θεοῦ. **5** καὶ
for a memorial   before   -   God.   And

νῦν πέμψον ἄνδρας εἰς Ἰόππην καὶ
now   send   men   to   Joppa   and

μετάπεμψαι Σίμωνά τινα ὃς ἐπικαλεῖται
[summon   ²Simon ¹one who is surnamed

Πέτρος· **6** οὗτος ξενίζεται παρά τινι
Peter;   this man is lodged   with   one

Σίμωνι βυρσεῖ, ᾧ ἐστιν οἰκία παρὰ
Simon   a tanner, to whom is a house[e] by
= who has a house

θάλασσαν. **7** ὡς δὲ ἀπῆλθεν ὁ ἄγγελος ὁ
[the] sea.   And as went away the angel   the

λαλῶν αὐτῷ, φωνήσας δύο τῶν οἰκετῶν
speaking to him, calling   two   of the household
slaves

καὶ στρατιώτην εὐσεβῆ τῶν προσκαρτερού-
and soldier   a devout of the [ones]   waiting

των αὐτῷ, **8** καὶ ἐξηγησάμενος ἅπαντα
on   him,   and   explaining   all things

''Tabitha, get up.'' She opened her eyes, and seeing Peter she sat up. 41He took her by the hand and helped her to her feet. Then he called the believers and the widows and presented her to them alive. 42This became known all over Joppa, and many people believed in the Lord. 43Peter stayed in Joppa for some time with a tanner named Simon.

Chapter 10

Cornelius Calls for Peter

AT Caesarea there was a man named Cornelius, a centurion in what was known as the Italian Regiment. 2He and all his family were devout and God-fearing; he gave generously to those in need and prayed to God regularly. 3One day at about three in the afternoon he had a vision. He distinctly saw an angel of God, who came to him and said, ''Cornelius!''

4Cornelius stared at him in fear. ''What is it, Lord?'' he asked.

The angel answered, ''Your prayers and gifts to the poor have come up as a memorial offering before God. 5Now send men to Joppa to bring back a man named Simon who is called Peter. 6He is staying with Simon the tanner, whose house is by the sea.''

7When the angel who spoke to him had gone, Cornelius called two of his servants and a devout soldier who was one of his attendants. 8He told them ev-

---

ᵗ Or, *battalion*
ᵘ Or, *gifts of charity*
ᵛ I.e., 3 p.m.
ʷ Or, *deeds of charity*

he sent them to Joppa.

9And on the next day, as they were on their way, and approaching the city, Peter went up on the housetop about the ˣsixth hour to pray.

10And he became hungry, and was desiring to eat; but while they were making preparations, he fell into a trance;

11and he *beheld the sky opened up, and a certain ʸobject like a great sheet coming down, lowered by four corners to the ground,

12and there were in it all kinds of four-footed animals and ᶻcrawling creatures of the earth and birds of the air.

13And a voice came to him, "Arise, Peter, kill and eat!"

14But Peter said, "By no means, Lord, for I have never eaten anything unholy and unclean."

15And again a voice came to him a second time, "What God has cleansed, no longer consider unholy."

16And this happened three times; and immediately the object was taken up into the sky.

17Now while Peter was greatly perplexed in mind as to what the vision which he had seen might be, behold, the men who had been sent by Cornelius, having asked directions for Simon's house, appeared at the gate;

18and calling out, they were asking whether Simon, who was also called Peter, was staying there.

19And while Peter was reflecting on the vision, the Spirit said to him, "Behold, three men are looking for you.

20"But arise, go downstairs, and accompany them without misgivings; for I have sent them Myself."

αὐτοῖς ἀπέστειλεν αὐτοὺς εἰς τὴν Ἰόππην.
to them sent them to – Joppa.

9 Τῇ δὲ ἐπαύριον ὁδοιπορούντων ἐκείνων
And on the morrow journeying those

καὶ τῇ πόλει ἐγγιζόντων ἀνέβη Πέτρος
and to the city drawing nearᵃ went up Peter
=as they journeyed and drew near to the city

ἐπὶ τὸ δῶμα προσεύξασθαι περὶ ὥραν
onto the roof to pray about hour

ἕκτην. 10 ἐγένετο δὲ πρόσπεινος καὶ
sixth. And he became hungry and

ἤθελεν γεύσασθαι· παρασκευαζόντων δὲ
wished to taste(eat); and preparing
=while they prepared

αὐτῶν ἐγένετο ἐπ᾽ αὐτὸν ἔκστασις, 11 καὶ
themᵃ there came on him an ecstasy, and

θεωρεῖ τὸν οὐρανὸν ἀνεῳγμένον καὶ
he beholds the heaven having been opened and

καταβαῖνον σκεῦός τι ὡς ὀθόνην μεγάλην,
coming down a certain vessel like sheet a great,

τέσσαρσιν ἀρχαῖς καθιέμενον ἐπὶ τῆς γῆς,
by four corners being let down onto the earth,

12 ἐν ᾧ ὑπῆρχεν πάντα τὰ τετράποδα
in which were all the quadrupeds

καὶ ἑρπετὰ τῆς γῆς καὶ πετεινὰ τοῦ
and reptiles of the earth and birds of the

οὐρανοῦ. 13 καὶ ἐγένετο φωνὴ πρὸς
heaven(air). And there came a voice to

αὐτόν· ἀναστάς, Πέτρε, θῦσον καὶ φάγε.
him: Rise up, Peter, slay and eat.

14 ὁ δὲ Πέτρος εἶπεν· μηδαμῶς, κύριε,
– But Peter said: Not at all, Lord,

ὅτι οὐδέποτε ἔφαγον πᾶν κοινὸν καὶ
because never did I eat every(any)thing common and

ἀκάθαρτον. 15 καὶ φωνὴ πάλιν ἐκ δευτέρου
unclean. And a voice again a second [time]

πρὸς αὐτόν· ἃ ὁ θεὸς ἐκαθάρισεν σὺ
[came] to him: What things – God cleansed ᵃthou

μὴ κοίνου. 16 τοῦτο δὲ ἐγένετο ἐπὶ
¹not ¹treat ⁴as ⁵unclean. And this occurred on

τρίς, καὶ εὐθὺς ἀνελήμφθη τὸ σκεῦος
three [occasions], and immediately was taken up the vessel

εἰς τὸν οὐρανόν. 17 Ὡς δὲ ἐν ἑαυτῷ
into – heaven. Now as in himself

διηπόρει ὁ Πέτρος τί ἂν εἴη τὸ ὅραμα
was doubting – Peter what might be the vision

ὃ εἶδεν, ἰδοὺ οἱ ἄνδρες οἱ ἀπεσταλμένοι
which he saw, behold[,] the men having been sent

ὑπὸ τοῦ Κορνηλίου διερωτήσαντες τὴν
by – Cornelius asking for the

οἰκίαν τοῦ Σίμωνος ἐπέστησαν ἐπὶ τὸν
house – of Simon stood at at the

πυλῶνα, 18 καὶ φωνήσαντες ἐπυνθάνοντο
porch, and calling inquired

εἰ Σίμων ὁ ἐπικαλούμενος Πέτρος ἐνθάδε
if Simon – being surnamed Peter here

ξενίζεται. 19 Τοῦ δὲ Πέτρου διενθυμουμένου
is lodged. – And Peter ponderingᵃ
=while Peter pondered

περὶ τοῦ ὁράματος εἶπεν τὸ πνεῦμα·
about the vision ²said ¹the ³Spirit:

ἰδοὺ ἄνδρες δύο ζητοῦντές σε· 20 ἀλλὰ
Behold[,] men two seeking thee; but

ἀναστὰς κατάβηθι, καὶ πορεύου σὺν αὐτοῖς
rising up go down, and go with them

μηδὲν διακρινόμενος, ὅτι ἐγὼ ἀπέσταλκα
nothing doubting, because I have sent

---

erything that had happened and sent them to Joppa.

Peter's Vision

9About noon the following day as they were on their journey and approaching the city, Peter went up on the roof to pray. 10He became hungry and wanted something to eat, and while the meal was being prepared, he fell into a trance. 11He saw heaven opened and something like a large sheet being let down to earth by its four corners. 12It contained all kinds of four-footed animals, as well as reptiles of the earth and birds of the air. 13Then a voice told him, "Get up, Peter. Kill and eat."

14"Surely not, Lord!" Peter replied. "I have never eaten anything impure or unclean."

15The voice spoke to him a second time, "Do not call anything impure that God has made clean."

16This happened three times, and immediately the sheet was taken back to heaven.

17While Peter was wondering about the meaning of the vision, the men sent by Cornelius found out where Simon's house was and stopped at the gate. 18They called out, asking if Simon who was known as Peter was staying there.

19While Peter was still thinking about the vision, the Spirit said to him, "Simon, threeᵈ men are looking for you. 20So get up and go downstairs. Do not hesitate to go with them, for I have sent them."

ˣ I.e., noon
ʸ Or, vessel
ᶻ Or possibly, reptiles

ᵈ19 One early manuscript two; other manuscripts do not have the number.

21And Peter went down to the men and said, "Behold, I am the one you are looking for; what is the reason for which you have come?"

22And they said, "Cornelius, a centurion, a righteous and God-fearing man well spoken of by the entire nation of the Jews, divinely directed by a holy angel to send for you to come to his house and hear a message from you."

23And so he invited them in and gave them lodging.

Peter at Caesarea

And on the next day he arose, and went away with them, and some of the brethren from Joppa accompanied him.

24And on the following day he entered Caesarea. Now Cornelius was waiting for them, and had called together his relatives and close friends.

25And when it came about that Peter entered, Cornelius met him, and fell at his feet and worshiped *him*.

26But Peter raised him up, saying, "Stand up; I too am *just* a man."

27And as he talked with him, he entered, and found many people assembled.

28And he said to them, "You yourselves know how unlawful it is for a man who is a Jew to associate with a foreigner or to visit him; and *yet* God has shown me that I should not call any man unholy or unclean.

29"That is why I came without even raising any objection when I was sent for. And so I ask for what reason you have sent for me."

30And Cornelius said, "Four days ago to this hour, I was praying in my house during the ᵃninth

---

αὐτούς. **21** καταβὰς δὲ Πέτρος πρὸς
them. And going down Peter to

τοὺς ἄνδρας εἶπεν· ἰδοὺ ἐγώ εἰμι ὃν
the men said: Behold[,] I am [he] whom

ζητεῖτε· τίς ἡ αἰτία δι' ἣν πάρεστε;
ye seek; what [is] the cause for which ye are here?

22 οἱ δὲ εἶπαν· Κορνήλιος ἑκατοντάρχης,
And they said: Cornelius a centurion,

ἀνὴρ δίκαιος καὶ φοβούμενος τὸν θεόν,
a man just and fearing – God,

μαρτυρούμενός τε ὑπὸ ὅλου τοῦ ἔθνους
and being witnessed to by all the nation

τῶν Ἰουδαίων, ἐχρηματίσθη ὑπὸ ἀγγέλου
of the Jews, was warned by angel

ἁγίου μεταπέμψασθαί σε εἰς τὸν οἶκον
a holy to summon thee to the house

αὐτοῦ καὶ ἀκοῦσαι ῥήματα παρὰ σοῦ.
of him and to hear words from thee.

23 εἰσκαλεσάμενος οὖν αὐτοὺς ἐξένισεν.
Calling in therefore them he lodged.

Τῇ δὲ ἐπαύριον ἀναστὰς ἐξῆλθεν σὺν
And on the morrow rising up he went forth with

αὐτοῖς, καί τινες τῶν ἀδελφῶν τῶν
them, and some of the brothers –

ἀπὸ Ἰόππης συνῆλθον αὐτῷ. **24** τῇ δὲ
from Joppa accompanied him. And on the

ἐπαύριον εἰσῆλθεν εἰς τὴν Καισάρειαν·
morrow he entered into – Caesarea;

ὁ δὲ Κορνήλιος ἦν προσδοκῶν αὐτούς,
– and Cornelius was awaiting them,

συγκαλεσάμενος τοὺς συγγενεῖς αὐτοῦ καὶ
having called together the relatives of him and

τοὺς ἀναγκαίους φίλους. **25** Ὡς δὲ
the intimate friends. Now when

ἐγένετο τοῦ εἰσελθεῖν τὸν Πέτρον,ᵇ
it came to pass the to enter – Peter,
= Now it came to pass when Peter entered,

συναντήσας αὐτῷ ὁ Κορνήλιος πεσὼν
²meeting ³him ¹Cornelius falling

ἐπὶ τοὺς πόδας προσεκύνησεν. **26** ὁ δὲ
at the(his) feet worshipped. – But

Πέτρος ἤγειρεν αὐτὸν λέγων· ἀνάστηθι·
Peter raised him saying: Stand up;

καὶ ἐγὼ αὐτὸς ἄνθρωπός εἰμι. **27** καὶ
also I [my]self a man am. And

συνομιλῶν αὐτῷ εἰσῆλθεν, καὶ εὑρίσκει
talking with him he entered, and finds

συνεληλυθότας πολλούς, **28** ἔφη τε πρὸς
having come together many, and said to

αὐτούς· ὑμεῖς ἐπίστασθε ὡς ἀθέμιτόν ἐστιν
them: Ye understand how unlawful it is

ἀνδρὶ Ἰουδαίῳ κολλᾶσθαι ἢ προσέρχεσθαι
for a man a Jew to adhere or to approach

ἀλλοφύλῳ· κἀμοὶ ὁ θεὸς ἔδειξεν μηδένα
a foreigner; and to me – God showed ²not any

κοινὸν ἢ ἀκάθαρτον λέγειν ἄνθρωπον·
⁴common ⁵or ⁶unclean ¹to call ³man;

29 διὸ καὶ ἀναντιρρήτως ἦλθον μετα-
wherefore indeed ²unquestioningly ¹I came ¹being

πεμφθείς. πυνθάνομαι οὖν, τίνι λόγῳ
summoned. I inquire therefore, for what reason

μετεπέμψασθέ με; **30** καὶ ὁ Κορνήλιος
ye summoned me? And – Cornelius

ἔφη· ἀπὸ τετάρτης ἡμέρας μέχρι ταύτης τῆς
said: From fourth day until this –
= Four days ago

ὥρας ἤμην τὴν ἐνάτην προσευχόμενος
hour I was [at] the ninth praying

21Peter went down and said to the men, "I'm the one you're looking for. Why have you come?"

22The men replied, "We have come from Cornelius the centurion. He is a righteous and God-fearing man, who is respected by all the Jewish people. A holy angel told him to have you come to his house so that he could hear what you have to say." 23Then Peter invited the men into the house to be his guests.

Peter at Cornelius' House

The next day Peter started out with them, and some of the brothers from Joppa went along. 24The following day he arrived in Caesarea. Cornelius was expecting them and had called together his relatives and close friends. 25As Peter entered the house, Cornelius met him and fell at his feet in reverence. 26But Peter made him get up. "Stand up," he said, "I am only a man myself."

27Talking with him, Peter went inside and found a large gathering of people. 28He said to them: "You are well aware that it is against our law for a Jew to associate with a Gentile or visit him. But God has shown me that I should not call any man impure or unclean. 29So when I was sent for, I came without raising any objection. May I ask why you sent for me?"

30Cornelius answered: "Four days ago I was in my house praying at this hour, at three in the afternoon.

ᵃ I.e., 3 to 4 p.m.

hour; and behold, a man stood before me in shining garments,
31and he *said, 'Cornelius, your prayer has been heard and your alms have been remembered before God.
32'Send therefore to Joppa and invite Simon, who is also called Peter, to come to you; he is staying at the house of Simon the tanner by the sea.'
33"And so I sent to you immediately, and you have been kind enough to come. Now then, we are all here present before God to hear all that you have been commanded by the Lord."

Gentiles Hear Good News
34And opening his mouth, Peter said:
"I most certainly understand *now* that God is not one to show partiality,
35but in every nation the man who fears Him and does what is right, is welcome to Him.
36"The word which He sent to the sons of Israel, preaching peace through Jesus Christ (He is Lord of all)—
37you yourselves know the thing which took place throughout all Judea, starting from Galilee, after the baptism which John proclaimed.
38"*You know of* Jesus of Nazareth, how God anointed Him with the Holy Spirit and with power, and *how* He went about doing good, and healing all who were oppressed by the devil; for God was with Him.
39"And we are witnesses of all the things He did both in the land of the Jews and in Jerusalem. And they also put Him to death by hanging Him on a cross.
40"God raised Him up on the third day, and granted

ἐν   τῷ   οἴκῳ   μου,   καὶ   ἰδοὺ   ἀνὴρ   ἔστη
in   the   house   of me,   and   behold[,]   a man   stood
ἐνώπιόν   μου   ἐν   ἐσθῆτι   λαμπρᾷ,   31 καὶ
before   me   in   clothing   bright,   and
φησίν·   Κορνήλιε,   εἰσηκούσθη   σου   ἡ
says: Cornelius,   was heard   of thee   the
προσευχὴ   καὶ   αἱ   ἐλεημοσύναι   σου   ἐμνήσθησαν
prayer   and the   alms   of thee   were remembered
ἐνώπιον   τοῦ   θεοῦ.   32 πέμψον   οὖν   εἰς
before   -   God.   Send thou   therefore   to
Ἰόππην   καὶ   μετακάλεσαι   Σίμωνα   ὃς   ἐπι-
Joppa   and   send for   Simon   who   is
καλεῖται   Πέτρος·   οὗτος   ξενίζεται   ἐν   οἰκίᾳ
surnamed   Peter: this man   is lodged   in [the]   house
Σίμωνος   βυρσέως   παρὰ   θάλασσαν.   33 ἐξαυτῆς
of Simon   a tanner   by   [the] sea.   At once
οὖν   ἔπεμψα   πρὸς   σέ,   σύ   τε   καλῶς
therefore   I sent   to   thee,   and thou   well
ἐποίησας   παραγενόμενος.   νῦν   οὖν   πάντες
didst   arriving.   Now   therefore   all
ἡμεῖς   ἐνώπιον   τοῦ   θεοῦ   πάρεσμεν   ἀκοῦσαι
we   before   -   God   are present   to hear
πάντα   τὰ   προστεταγμένα   σοι   ὑπὸ   τοῦ
all   the things   having been commanded   thee   by   the
κυρίου.   34 Ἀνοίξας   δὲ   Πέτρος   τὸ   στόμα
Lord.   And opening   Peter   the(his)   mouth
εἶπεν·   ἐπ'   ἀληθείας   καταλαμβάνομαι   ὅτι
said: On(in)   truth   I perceive   that
οὐκ   ἔστιν   προσωπολήμπτης   ὁ   θεός,   35 ἀλλ'
³not   ²is   ⁴a respecter of persons   -   ¹God,   but
ἐν   παντὶ   ἔθνει   ὁ   φοβούμενος   αὐτὸν   καὶ
in   every   nation   the [one]   fearing   him   and
ἐργαζόμενος   δικαιοσύνην   δεκτὸς   αὐτῷ   ἐστιν·
working   righteousness   acceptable   to him   is;
36 τὸν   λόγον   ὃν   ἀπέστειλεν   τοῖς   υἱοῖς
the   word   which   he sent   to the   sons
Ἰσραὴλ   εὐαγγελιζόμενος   εἰρήνην   διὰ   Ἰησοῦ
of Israel   preaching   peace   through   Jesus
Χριστοῦ·   οὗτός   ἐστιν   πάντων   κύριος.
Christ: this one   is   of all   Lord.
37 ὑμεῖς   οἴδατε   τὸ   γενόμενον   ῥῆμα   καθ'
Ye   know   the   having become   thing   throughout   = that which took place
ὅλης   τῆς   Ἰουδαίας,   ἀρξάμενος   ἀπὸ   τῆς
all   -   Judæa,   beginning   from   -
Γαλιλαίας   μετὰ   τὸ   βάπτισμα   ὃ   ἐκήρυξεν
Galilee   after   the   baptism   which   ²proclaimed
Ἰωάννης,   38 Ἰησοῦν   τὸν   ἀπὸ   Ναζαρέθ,
¹John,   Jesus   the one   from   Nazareth,
ὡς   ἔχρισεν   αὐτὸν   ὁ   θεὸς   πνεύματι   ἁγίῳ
how   anointed   him   -   God   with Spirit   Holy
καὶ   δυνάμει,   ὃς   διῆλθεν   εὐεργετῶν   καὶ
and   power,   who   went about   doing good   and
ἰώμενος   πάντας   τοὺς   καταδυναστευομένους
curing   all   the [ones]   being oppressed
ὑπὸ   τοῦ   διαβόλου,   ὅτι   ὁ   θεὸς   ἦν   μετ'
by   the   devil,   because   -   God   was   with
αὐτοῦ·   39 καὶ   ἡμεῖς   μάρτυρες   πάντων
him;   and   we [are]   witnesses   of all things
ὧν   ἐποίησεν   ἔν   τε   τῇ   χώρᾳ   τῶν   Ἰουδαίων
which   he did   both in   the   country   of the   Jews
καὶ   Ἰερουσαλήμ·   ὃν   καὶ   ἀνεῖλαν
and   Jerusalem;   whom   indeed   they killed
κρεμάσαντες   ἐπὶ   ξύλου.   40 τοῦτον   ὁ
hanging   on   a tree.   This one   -
θεὸς   ἤγειρεν   ἐν   τῇ   τρίτῃ   ἡμέρᾳ   καὶ
God   raised   on   the   third   day   and

Suddenly a man in shining clothes stood before me 31and said, 'Cornelius, God has heard your prayer and remembered your gifts to the poor. 32Send to Joppa for Simon who is called Peter. He is a guest in the home of Simon the tanner, who lives by the sea.' 33So I sent for you immediately, and it was good of you to come. Now we are all here in the presence of God to listen to everything the Lord has commanded you to tell us."
34Then Peter began to speak: "I now realize how true it is that God does not show favoritism 35but accepts men from every nation who fear him and do what is right. 36You know the message God sent to the people of Israel, telling the good news of peace through Jesus Christ, who is Lord of all. 37You know what has happened throughout Judea, beginning in Galilee after the baptism that John preached —38how God anointed Jesus of Nazareth with the Holy Spirit and power, and how he went around doing good and healing all who were under the power of the devil, because God was with him.
39"We are witnesses of everything he did in the country of the Jews and in Jerusalem. They killed him by hanging him on a tree, 40but God raised him from the dead on the third day

that He should become visible,

41not to all the people, but to witnesses who were chosen beforehand by God, that is, to us, who ate and drank with Him after He arose from the dead.

42"And He ordered us to preach to the people, and solemnly to testify that this is the One who has been appointed by God as Judge of the living and the dead.

43"Of Him all the prophets bear witness that through His name everyone who believes in Him receives forgiveness of sins."

44While Peter was still speaking these words, the Holy Spirit fell upon all those who were listening to the message.

45And all the circumcised believers who had come with Peter were amazed, because the gift of the Holy Spirit had been poured out upon the Gentiles also.

46For they were hearing them speaking with tongues and exalting God. Then Peter answered,

47"Surely no one can refuse the water for these to be baptized who have received the Holy Spirit just as we did, can he?"

48And he ordered them to be baptized in the name of Jesus Christ. Then they asked him to stay on for a few days.

ἔδωκεν   αὐτὸν   ἐμφανῆ   γενέσθαι,   **41** οὐ
gave   him   visible   to become,   not

παντὶ   τῷ   λαῷ,   ἀλλὰ   μάρτυσιν   τοῖς
to all the people, but   to witnesses

προκεχειροτονημένοις   ὑπὸ   τοῦ   θεοῦ,   ἡμῖν,
having been previously appointed by - God, to us,

οἵτινες   συνεφάγομεν   καὶ   συνεπίομεν   αὐτῷ
who   ate with   and   drank with   him

μετὰ   τὸ   ἀναστῆναι   αὐτὸν   ἐκ   νεκρῶν·
after the to rise again him[b] out of [the] dead;
                        =he rose again

42 καὶ   παρήγγειλεν   ἡμῖν   κηρύξαι   τῷ   λαῷ
      and   he commanded   us   to proclaim to the people

καὶ   διαμαρτύρασθαι   ὅτι   οὗτός   ἐστιν   ὁ
and   solemnly to witness that this man is the[one]

ὡρισμένος   ὑπὸ   τοῦ   θεοῦ   κριτὴς   ζώντων
having been by   -   God   judge   of living
designated

καὶ   νεκρῶν.   **43** τούτῳ   πάντες   οἱ   προφῆται
and   of dead. To this man all   the   prophets

μαρτυροῦσιν,   ἄφεσιν   ⁶ἁμαρτιῶν   λαβεῖν   διὰ
witness, ⁵forgiveness ⁷of sins ⁵to receive ⁸through

τοῦ   ὀνόματος   αὐτοῦ   πάντα   τὸν   πιστεύοντα
⁹the ¹⁰name   ¹¹of him ¹everyone ²believing

εἰς   αὐτόν.   **44** Ἔτι   λαλοῦντος   τοῦ   Πέτρου
³in   ⁴him.   Yet   speaking   -   Peter[a]
                  =While Peter was still speaking

τὰ   ῥήματα   ταῦτα   ἐπέπεσεν   τὸ   πνεῦμα
these words   ⁴fell on   ¹the   ³Spirit

τὸ   ἅγιον   ἐπὶ   πάντας   τοὺς   ἀκούοντας
-   ²Holy   on   all   the [ones] hearing

τὸν   λόγον.   **45** καὶ   ἐξέστησαν   οἱ   ἐκ
the   discourse.   And   ⁵were amazed ¹the ³of [the]

περιτομῆς   πιστοὶ   ὅσοι   συνῆλθαν   τῷ   Πέτρῳ,
⁴circumcision faithful as many as accompanied - Peter,

ὅτι   καὶ   ἐπὶ   τὰ   ἔθνη   ἡ   δωρεὰ   τοῦ   ἁγίου
because also on the nations the gift of the Holy

πνεύματος   ἐκκέχυται·   **46** ἤκουον   γὰρ
Spirit   has been poured out;   for they heard

αὐτῶν   λαλούντων   γλώσσαις   καὶ   μεγαλυνόν-
them   speaking   in tongues and   magnify-

των   τὸν   θεόν.   τότε   ἀπεκρίθη   Πέτρος·
ing   -   God.   Then   answered   Peter:

47 μήτι   τὸ   ὕδωρ   δύναται   κωλῦσαί   τις
      Not   ⁴the ⁵water ¹can ³to forbid ²anyone

τοῦ   μὴ   βαπτισθῆναι   τούτους,   οἵτινες   τὸ
-    ⁷not ⁸to be baptized[d] ⁶these,   who   the

πνεῦμα   τὸ   ἅγιον   ἔλαβον   ὡς   καὶ   ἡμεῖς;
Spirit   -   Holy   received   as   also   we?

48 προσέταξεν   δὲ   αὐτοὺς   ἐν   τῷ   ὀνόματι
And he commanded   them   in   the   name

Ἰησοῦ   Χριστοῦ   βαπτισθῆναι.   τότε   ἠρώτησαν
of Jesus Christ   to be baptized.   Then   they asked

αὐτὸν   ἐπιμεῖναι   ἡμέρας   τινάς.
him   to remain   days   some.

Chapter 11

Peter Reports at Jerusalem

11 Ἤκουσαν   δὲ   οἱ   ἀπόστολοι   καὶ   οἱ
      Now heard   the   apostles   and   the

ἀδελφοὶ   οἱ   ὄντες   κατὰ   τὴν   Ἰουδαίαν
brothers   -   being throughout - Judæa

ὅτι   καὶ   τὰ   ἔθνη   ἐδέξαντο   τὸν   λόγον
that   also   the   nations   received   the   word

τοῦ   θεοῦ.   **2** Ὅτε   δὲ   ἀνέβη   Πέτρος   εἰς
-   of God.   And when   went up   Peter   to

Ἰερουσαλήμ,   διεκρίνοντο   πρὸς   αὐτὸν   οἱ
Jerusalem,   disputed   with   him   the [ones]

---

and caused him to be seen.

41He was not seen by all the people, but by witnesses whom God had already chosen—by us who ate and drank with him after he rose from the dead. 42He commanded us to preach to the people and to testify that he is the one whom God appointed as judge of the living and the dead. 43All the prophets testify about him that everyone who believes in him receives forgiveness of sins through his name."

44While Peter was still speaking these words, the Holy Spirit came on all who heard the message. 45The circumcised believers who had come with Peter were astonished that the gift of the Holy Spirit had been poured out even on the Gentiles. 46For they heard them speaking in tongues[r] and praising God.

Then Peter said, 47"Can anyone keep these people from being baptized with water? They have received the Holy Spirit just as we have." 48So he ordered that they be baptized in the name of Jesus Christ. Then they asked Peter to stay with them for a few days.

Chapter 11

Peter Explains His Actions

THE apostles and the brothers throughout Judea heard that the Gentiles also had received the word of God. 2So when Peter went up to Jerusalem,

were circumcised took issue with him,
³saying, "You went to uncircumcised men and ate with them."
⁴But Peter began *speaking* and *proceeded* to explain to them in orderly sequence, saying,
⁵"I was in the city of Joppa praying; and in a trance I saw a vision, a certain object coming down like a great sheet lowered by four corners from the sky; and it came right down to me,
⁶and when I had fixed my gaze upon it and was observing it I saw the four-footed animals of the earth and the wild beasts and the ᵇcrawling creatures and the birds of the air.
⁷"And I also heard a voice saying to me, 'Arise, Peter; kill and eat.'
⁸"But I said, 'By no means, Lord, for nothing unholy or unclean has ever entered my mouth.'
⁹"But a voice from heaven answered a second time, 'What God has cleansed, no longer consider unholy.'
¹⁰"And this happened three times, and everything was drawn back up into the sky.
¹¹"And behold, at that moment three men appeared before the house in which we were *staying*, having been sent to me from Caesarea.
¹²"And the Spirit told me to go with them without misgivings. And these six brethren also went with me, and we entered the man's house.
¹³"And he reported to us how he had seen the angel standing in his house, and saying, 'Send to Joppa, and have Simon, who is also called Peter, brought here;
¹⁴and he shall speak words to you by which you will be saved, you and all your household.'

ἐκ περιτομῆς 3 λέγοντες ὅτι εἰσῆλθες
of [the] circumcision   saying[.]   – Thou enteredst
πρὸς ἄνδρας ἀκροβυστίαν ἔχοντας καὶ
to   men   uncircumcision   having   and
συνέφαγες αὐτοῖς. 4 ἀρξάμενος δὲ Πέτρος
didst eat with   them.   And beginning   Peter
ἐξετίθετο αὐτοῖς καθεξῆς λέγων· 5 ἐγὼ
explained   to them   in order   saying: I
ἤμην ἐν πόλει Ἰόππῃ προσευχόμενος, καὶ
was   in [the] city   Joppa   praying,   and
εἶδον ἐν ἐκστάσει ὅραμα, καταβαῖνον
I saw   in   an ecstasy   a vision,   coming down
σκεῦός τι ὡς ὀθόνην μεγάλην τέσσαρσιν
a certain vessel   as   sheet   a great   by four
ἀρχαῖς καθιεμένην ἐκ τοῦ οὐρανοῦ, καὶ
corners   having been let down out of   –   heaven,   and
ἦλθεν ἄχρι ἐμοῦ· 6 εἰς ἣν ἀτενίσας
it came   up to   me;   into   which   gazing
κατενόουν, καὶ εἶδον τὰ τετράποδα τῆς
I perceived,   and   I saw   the   quadrupeds   of the
γῆς καὶ τὰ θηρία καὶ τὰ ἑρπετὰ καὶ τὰ
earth   and   the wild beasts   and   the   reptiles   and   the
πετεινὰ τοῦ οὐρανοῦ. 7 ἤκουσα δὲ καὶ
birds   of the heaven(air).   And I heard   also
φωνῆς λεγούσης μοι· ἀναστάς, Πέτρε,
a voice   saying   to me: Rise up,   Peter,
θῦσον καὶ φάγε. 8 εἶπον δέ· μηδαμῶς,
slay   and   eat.   And I said: Not at all,
κύριε, ὅτι κοινὸν ἢ ἀκάθαρτον οὐδέποτε
Lord,   because a common   or   unclean thing   never
εἰσῆλθεν εἰς τὸ στόμα μου. 9 ἀπεκρίθη δὲ
entered   into   the mouth   of me.   And answered
ἐκ δευτέρου φωνὴ ἐκ τοῦ οὐρανοῦ·
a second [time]   a voice   out of   –   heaven:
ἃ ὁ θεὸς ἐκαθάρισεν σὺ μὴ κοίνου.
What   –   God   cleansed   thou regard not common.
things
10 τοῦτο δὲ ἐγένετο ἐπὶ τρίς, καὶ
And this   happened   on three [occasions],   and
ἀνεσπάσθη πάλιν ἅπαντα εἰς τὸν οὐρανόν.
was pulled up   again   all things   to   –   ʰheaven.
11 καὶ ἰδοὺ ἐξαυτῆς τρεῖς ἄνδρες ἐπέστησαν
And behold   at once   three   men   stood *at*
ἐπὶ τὴν οἰκίαν ἐν ᾗ ἦμεν, ἀπεσταλμένοι
at   the   house   in which   I was,   having been sent
ἀπὸ Καισαρείας πρός με. 12 εἶπεν δὲ
from   Caesarea   to   me.   And ʰtold
τὸ πνεῦμά μοι συνελθεῖν αὐτοῖς μηδὲν
¹the   ²Spirit   ⁴me   to go with   them   nothing
διακρίναντα. ἦλθον δὲ σὺν ἐμοὶ καὶ
doubting.   And came   with   me   also
οἱ ἓξ ἀδελφοὶ οὗτοι, καὶ εἰσήλθομεν εἰς
–   six   brothers   these,   and   we entered   into
τὸν οἶκον τοῦ ἀνδρός. 13 ἀπήγγειλεν δὲ
the   house   of the   man.   And he reported
ἡμῖν πῶς εἶδεν τὸν ἄγγελον ἐν τῷ
to us   how   he saw   the   angel   in   the
οἴκῳ αὐτοῦ σταθέντα καὶ εἰπόντα·
house   of him   standing   and   saying:
ἀπόστειλον εἰς Ἰόππην καὶ μετάπεμψαι
Send   to   Joppa   and   summon
Σίμωνα τὸν ἐπικαλούμενον Πέτρον, 14 ὃς
Simon   –   *being* surnamed   Peter,   who
λαλήσει ῥήματα πρὸς σὲ ἐν οἷς σωθήσῃ
will speak   words   to   thee   by   which   mayest be saved
σὺ καὶ πᾶς ὁ οἶκός σου. 15 ἐν δὲ
thou   and   all   the household   of thee.   And in

the circumcised believers criticized him ³and said, "You went into the house of uncircumcised men and ate with them."
⁴Peter began and explained everything to them precisely as it had happened: ⁵"I was in the city of Joppa praying, and in a trance I saw a vision. I saw something like a large sheet being let down from heaven by its four corners, and it came down to where I was.
⁶I looked into it and saw four-footed animals of the earth, wild beasts, reptiles, and birds of the air. ⁷Then I heard a voice telling me, 'Get up, Peter. Kill and eat.'
⁸"I replied, 'Surely not, Lord! Nothing impure or unclean has ever entered my mouth.'
⁹"The voice spoke from heaven a second time, 'Do not call anything impure that God has made clean.'
¹⁰This happened three times, and then it was all pulled up to heaven again.
¹¹"Right then three men who had been sent to me from Caesarea stopped at the house where I was staying. ¹²The Spirit told me to have no hesitation about going with them. These six brothers also went with me, and we entered the man's house. ¹³He told us how he had seen an angel appear in his house and say, 'Send to Joppa for Simon who is called Peter. ¹⁴He will bring you a message through which you and all your household will be saved.'

ᵇ Or possibly, *reptiles*

15"And as I began to speak, the Holy Spirit fell upon them, just as *He did* upon us at the beginning.

16"And I remembered the word of the Lord, how He used to say, 'John baptized with water, but you shall be baptized with the Holy Spirit.'

17"If God therefore gave to them the same gift as *He gave* to us also after believing in the Lord Jesus Christ, who was I that I could stand in God's way?"

18And when they heard this, they quieted down, and glorified God, saying, "Well then, God has granted to the Gentiles also the repentance *that leads* to life."

The Church at Antioch

19So then those who were scattered because of the persecution that arose in connection with Stephen made their way to Phoenicia and Cyprus and Antioch, speaking the word to no one except to Jews alone.

20But there were some of them, men of Cyprus and Cyrene, who came to Antioch and *began* speaking to the ᶜGreeks also, preaching the Lord Jesus.

21And the hand of the Lord was with them, and a large number who believed turned to the Lord.

22And the news about them reached the ears of the church at Jerusalem, and they sent Barnabas off to Antioch.

23Then when he had come and witnessed the grace of God, he rejoiced and *began* to encourage them all with resolute heart to remain *true* to the Lord;

24for he was a good man, and full of the Holy Spirit and of faith. And consider-

---

Greek	English
τῷ ἄρξασθαί με λαλεῖν ἐπέπεσεν τὸ	the to begin me^be to speak ⁴fell on ¹the
= as I began	
πνεῦμα τὸ ἅγιον ἐπ' αὐτοὺς ὥσπερ καὶ	²Spirit - ³Holy on them as also
ἐφ' ἡμᾶς ἐν ἀρχῇ. 16 ἐμνήσθην δὲ τοῦ	on us at [the] beginning. And I remembered the
ῥήματος τοῦ κυρίου, ὡς ἔλεγεν· Ἰωάννης	word of the Lord, how he saіᵈ: John
μὲν ἐβάπτισεν ὕδατι, ὑμεῖς δὲ βαπτισθήσεσθε	indeed baptized with water, but ye will be baptized
ἐν πνεύματι ἁγίῳ. 17 εἰ οὖν τὴν ἴσην	in Spirit Holy. If therefore ⁴the ⁵equal
δωρεὰν ἔδωκεν αὐτοῖς ὁ θεὸς ὡς καὶ	⁶gift ³gave ⁶them - ¹God as also
ἡμῖν, πιστεύσασιν ἐπὶ τὸν κύριον Ἰησοῦν	to us, having believed on the Lord Jesus
Χριστόν, ἐγὼ τίς ἤμην δυνατὸς κωλῦσαι	Christ, ³I ¹who ²was [to be] able to hinder
τὸν θεόν; 18 ἀκούσαντες δὲ ταῦτα ἡσύχασαν,	- God? And hearing these things they kept silence
καὶ ἐδόξασαν τὸν θεὸν λέγοντες· ἄρα καὶ	and glorified - God saying: Then also
τοῖς ἔθνεσιν ὁ θεὸς τὴν μετάνοιαν εἰς	to the nations - God - repentance to
ζωὴν ἔδωκεν.	life gave.
19 Οἱ μὲν οὖν διασπαρέντες ἀπὸ τῆς	The [ones] - therefore being scattered from the
θλίψεως τῆς γενομένης ἐπὶ Στεφάνῳ	affliction - occurring over Stephen
διῆλθον ἕως Φοινίκης καὶ Κύπρου καὶ	passed through to Phœnicia and Cyprus and
Ἀντιοχείας, μηδενὶ λαλοῦντες τὸν λόγον	Antioch, to no one speaking the word
εἰ μὴ μόνον Ἰουδαίοις. 20 Ἦσαν δὲ	except only to Jews. But ⁴were
τινες ἐξ αὐτῶν ἄνδρες Κύπριοι καὶ	¹some ³of ²them men Cypriotes and
Κυρηναῖοι, οἵτινες ἐλθόντες εἰς Ἀντιόχειαν	Cyrenians, who coming to Antioch
ἐλάλουν καὶ πρὸς τοὺς Ἕλληνας,	spoke also to the Greeks,
εὐαγγελιζόμενοι τὸν κύριον Ἰησοῦν. 21 καὶ ἦν	preaching the Lord Jesus. And was
χεὶρ κυρίου μετ' αὐτῶν, πολύς τε	[the] hand of [the] Lord with them, and a much(great)
ἀριθμὸς ὁ πιστεύσας ἐπέστρεψεν ἐπὶ τὸν	number - believing turned to the
κύριον. 22 Ἠκούσθη δὲ ὁ λόγος εἰς	Lord. And was heard the account in
τὰ ὦτα τῆς ἐκκλησίας τῆς οὔσης ἐν	the ears of the church - being in
Ἰερουσαλὴμ περὶ αὐτῶν, καὶ ἐξαπέστειλαν	Jerusalem about them, and they sent out
Βαρναβᾶν ἕως Ἀντιοχείας· 23 ὃς παραγεν-	Barnabas to Antioch; who arriv-
όμενος καὶ ἰδὼν τὴν χάριν τὴν τοῦ	ing and seeing the grace the -
θεοῦ ἐχάρη, καὶ παρεκάλει πάντας τῇ	of God rejoiced, and exhorted all -
προθέσει τῆς καρδίας προσμένειν τῷ	with purpose - of heart to remain with the
κυρίῳ, 24 ὅτι ἦν ἀνὴρ ἀγαθὸς καὶ	Lord, because he was man a good and
πλήρης πνεύματος ἁγίου καὶ πίστεως.	full of [the] Spirit Holy and of faith.

15"As I began to speak, the Holy Spirit came on them as he had come on us at the beginning. 16Then I remembered what the Lord had said: 'John baptized withʲ water, but you will be baptized with the Holy Spirit.' 17So if God gave them the same gift as he gave us, who believed in the Lord Jesus Christ, who was I to think that I could oppose God?"

18When they heard this, they had no further objections and praised God, saying, "So then, God has granted even the Gentiles repentance unto life."

The Church in Antioch

19Now those who had been scattered in connection with the persecution in connection with Stephen traveled as far as Phoenicia, Cyprus and Antioch, telling the message only to Jews. 20Some of them, however, men from Cyprus and Cyrene, went to Antioch and began to speak to Greeks also, telling them the good news about the Lord Jesus. 21The Lord's hand was with them, and a great number of people believed and turned to the Lord.

22News of this reached the ears of the church at Jerusalem, and they sent Barnabas to Antioch. 23When he arrived and saw the evidence of the grace of God, he was glad and encouraged them all to remain true to the Lord with all their hearts. 24He was a good man, full of the Holy Spirit and faith, and a great num-

---

ᶜ Some mss. read *Greek-speaking Jews*   ʲ16 Or *in*

able numbers were brought to the Lord.

25And he left for Tarsus to look for Saul;

26and when he had found him, he brought him to Antioch. And it came about that for an entire year they met with the church, and taught considerable numbers; and the disciples were first called Christians in Antioch.

27Now at this time some prophets came down from Jerusalem to Antioch.

28And one of them named Agabus stood up and *began* to indicate by the Spirit that there would certainly be a great famine all over the world. And this took place in the *reign* of Claudius.

29And in the proportion that any of the disciples had means, each of them determined to send *a contribution* for the relief of the brethren living in Judea.

30And this they did, sending it in charge of Barnabas and Saul to the elders.

καὶ προσετέθη ὄχλος ἱκανὸς τῷ κυρίῳ.
And was added a crowd considerable to the Lord.

25 ἐξῆλθεν δὲ εἰς Ταρσὸν ἀναζητῆσαι
And he went forth to Tarsus to seek

Σαῦλον, **26** καὶ εὑρὼν ἤγαγεν εἰς Ἀντιόχειαν.
Saul, and finding brought to Antioch.

ἐγένετο δὲ αὐτοῖς καὶ ἐνιαυτὸν ὅλον
And it happened to them also year a whole

συναχθῆναι ἐν τῇ ἐκκλησίᾳ καὶ διδάξαι
to be assembled in the church and to teach

ὄχλον ἱκανόν, χρηματίσαι τε πρώτως ἐν
a crowd considerable, and to call firstly in

Ἀντιοχείᾳ τοὺς μαθητὰς Χριστιανούς.
Antioch the disciples Christians.

27 Ἐν ταύταις δὲ ταῖς ἡμέραις κατῆλθον
And in these – days came down

ἀπὸ Ἱεροσολύμων προφῆται εἰς Ἀντιόχειαν·
from Jerusalem prophets to Antioch;

28 ἀναστὰς δὲ εἷς ἐξ αὐτῶν ὀνόματι
and rising up one of them by name

Ἄγαβος ἐσήμαινεν διὰ τοῦ πνεύματος
Agabus signified through the Spirit

λιμὸν μεγάλην μέλλειν ἔσεσθαι ἐφ᾽ ὅλην τὴν
famine a great to be about to be over all the

οἰκουμένην· ἥτις ἐγένετο ἐπὶ Κλαυδίου.
inhabited earth; which happened in the time of Claudius.

29 τῶν δὲ μαθητῶν καθὼς εὐπορεῖτό
So ³of the ⁴disciples ¹as ⁶was prosperous

τις, ὥρισαν ἕκαστος αὐτῶν εἰς διακονίαν
⁵anyone, they determined each of them for ministration

πέμψαι τοῖς κατοικοῦσιν ἐν τῇ Ἰουδαίᾳ
to send ¹to the ³dwelling ⁴in – ⁵Judæa

ἀδελφοῖς· **30** ὃ καὶ ἐποίησαν ἀποστείλαντες
²brothers; which indeed they did sending

πρὸς τοὺς πρεσβυτέρους διὰ χειρὸς
to the elders through [the] hand

Βαρναβᾶ καὶ Σαύλου.
of Barnabas and of Saul.

---

ber of people were brought to the Lord.

25Then Barnabas went to Tarsus to look for Saul, 26and when he found him, he brought him to Antioch. So for a whole year Barnabas and Saul met with the church and taught great numbers of people. The disciples were called Christians first at Antioch.

27During this time some prophets came down from Jerusalem to Antioch. 28One of them, named Agabus, stood up and through the Spirit predicted that a severe famine would spread over the entire Roman world. (This happened during the reign of Claudius.) 29The disciples, each according to his ability, decided to provide help for the brothers living in Judea. 30This they did, sending their gift to the elders by Barnabas and Saul.

Chapter 12

Peter's Arrest and Deliverance

NOW about that time Herod the king laid hands on some who belonged to the church, in order to mistreat them.

2And he had James the brother of John put to death with a sword.

3And when he saw that it pleased the Jews, he proceeded to arrest Peter also. Now it was during the days of Unleavened Bread.

4And when he had seized him, he put him in prison, delivering him to four squads of soldiers to guard him, intending after the Passover to bring him out before the people.

5So Peter was kept in the prison, but prayer for him

---

12 Κατ᾽ ἐκεῖνον δὲ τὸν καιρὸν ἐπέβαλεν
Now at that – time laid on

Ἡρῴδης ὁ βασιλεὺς τὰς χεῖρας κακῶσαί
Herod the king the(his) hands to ill-treat

τινας τῶν ἀπὸ τῆς ἐκκλησίας. **2** ἀνεῖλεν δὲ
some of the [ones] from the church. And he killed

Ἰάκωβον τὸν ἀδελφὸν Ἰωάννου μαχαίρῃ.
James the brother of John with a sword.

3 ἰδὼν δὲ ὅτι ἀρεστόν ἐστιν τοῖς Ἰουδαίοις
And seeing that pleasing it is(was) to the Jews

προσέθετο συλλαβεῖν καὶ Πέτρον, ἦσαν δὲ
he added to arrest also Peter, and they were

ἡμέραι τῶν ἀζύμων, **4** ὃν καὶ πιάσας
days – of unleavened bread, whom also seizing

ἔθετο εἰς φυλακήν, παραδοὺς τέσσαρσιν
he put in prison, delivering to four

τετραδίοις στρατιωτῶν φυλάσσειν αὐτόν,
quaternions of soldiers to guard him,

βουλόμενος μετὰ τὸ πάσχα ἀναγαγεῖν
intending after the Passover to bring up

αὐτὸν τῷ λαῷ. **5** ὁ μὲν οὖν Πέτρος
him to the people. – –* therefore Peter

ἐτηρεῖτο ἐν τῇ φυλακῇ· προσευχὴ δὲ ἦν
was kept in the prison; but prayer was

* μέν and δέ are in contrast : " on one hand . . ."—" on the other . . ."

Chapter 12

Peter's Miraculous Escape From Prison

IT was about this time that King Herod arrested some who belonged to the church, intending to persecute them. 2He had James, the brother of John, put to death with the sword. 3When he saw that this pleased the Jews, he proceeded to seize Peter also. This happened during the Feast of Unleavened Bread. 4After arresting him, he put him in prison, handing him over to be guarded by four squads of four soldiers each. Herod intended to bring him out for public trial after the Passover.

5So Peter was kept in prison, but the church was

was being made fervently by the church to God.

6And on the very night when Herod was about to bring him forward, Peter was sleeping between two soldiers, bound with two chains; and guards in front of the door were watching over the prison.

7And behold, an angel of the Lord suddenly appeared, and a light shone in the cell; and he struck Peter's side and roused him, saying, "Get up quickly." And his chains fell off his hands.

8And the angel said to him, "Gird yourself and put on your sandals." And he did so. And he *said to him, "Wrap your cloak around you and follow me."

9And he went out and continued to follow, and he did not know that what was being done by the angel was real, but thought he was seeing a vision.

10And when they had passed the first and second guard, they came to the iron gate that leads into the city, which opened for them by itself; and they went out and went along one street; and immediately the angel departed from him.

11And when Peter came to himself, he said, "Now I know for sure that the Lord has sent forth His angel and rescued me from the hand of Herod and from all that the Jewish people were expecting."

12And when he realized this, he went to the house of Mary, the mother of John who was also called Mark, where many were gathered together and were praying.

ἐκτενῶς γινομένη ὑπὸ τῆς ἐκκλησίας πρὸς
earnestly   being made   by   the   church   to
τὸν θεὸν περὶ αὐτοῦ. 6 Ὅτε δὲ ἤμελλεν
-   God concerning him.   And when ¹was about
προαγαγεῖν αὐτὸν ὁ Ἡρώδης, τῇ νυκτὶ
³to bring forward ⁴him   -   ¹Herod,   -   ²night
ἐκείνη ἦν ὁ Πέτρος κοιμώμενος μεταξὺ
¹in that was   -   Peter   sleeping   between
δύο στρατιωτῶν δεδεμένος ἁλύσεσιν δυσίν,
two   soldiers   having been bound with chains two,
φύλακές τε πρὸ τῆς θύρας ἐτήρουν τὴν
and guards   before the   door   were keeping the
φυλακήν. 7 καὶ ἰδοὺ ἄγγελος κυρίου
prison.   And behold[,]   an angel of[the] Lord
ἐπέστη, καὶ φῶς ἔλαμψεν ἐν τῷ οἰκήματι·
came upon, and a light shone in the building;
πατάξας δὲ τὴν πλευρὰν τοῦ Πέτρου
and striking the   side   - of Peter
ἤγειρεν αὐτὸν λέγων· ἀνάστα ἐν τάχει.
he raised him saying: Rise up in haste.
καὶ ἐξέπεσαν αὐτοῦ αἱ ἁλύσεις ἐκ τῶν
And fell off of him the chains off the(his)
χειρῶν. 8 εἶπεν δὲ ὁ ἄγγελος πρὸς
hands.   And said the   angel   to
αὐτόν· ζῶσαι καὶ ὑπόδησαι τὰ σανδάλιά
him: Gird thyself and put on   the sandals
σου. ἐποίησεν δὲ οὕτως. καὶ λέγει
of thee. And he did so.   And he tells
αὐτῷ· περιβαλοῦ τὸ ἱμάτιόν σου καὶ
him: Cast round the garment of thee and
ἀκολούθει μοι. 9 καὶ ἐξελθὼν ἠκολούθει,
follow me.   And going forth he followed,
καὶ οὐκ ᾔδει ὅτι ἀληθές ἐστιν τὸ
and knew not that ³true ²is(was) ¹the thing
γινόμενον διὰ τοῦ ἀγγέλου, ἐδόκει δὲ
happening through the angel, but he thought
ὅραμα βλέπειν. 10 διελθόντες δὲ πρώτην
a vision to see.   And going through [the] first
φυλακὴν καὶ δευτέραν ἦλθαν ἐπὶ τὴν
prison and [the] second they came on   the
πύλην τὴν σιδηρᾶν τὴν φέρουσαν εἰς τὴν
gate   -   iron   -   leading   to   the
πόλιν, ἥτις αὐτομάτη ἠνοίγη αὐτοῖς, καὶ
city, which of itself was opened to them, and
ἐξελθόντες προῆλθον ῥύμην μίαν, καὶ
going out they went forward street one, and
εὐθέως ἀπέστη ὁ ἄγγελος ἀπ' αὐτοῦ.
immediately departed the angel from him.
11 καὶ ὁ Πέτρος ἐν ἑαυτῷ γενόμενος
And   -   Peter in himself having become
εἶπεν· νῦν οἶδα ἀληθῶς ὅτι ἐξαπέστειλεν
said: Now I know truly that   sent forth
ὁ κύριος τὸν ἄγγελον αὐτοῦ καὶ ἐξείλατό
the Lord the   angel   of him and delivered
με ἐκ χειρὸς Ἡρώδου καὶ πάσης τῆς
me out of [the] hand of Herod and of all the
προσδοκίας τοῦ λαοῦ τῶν Ἰουδαίων.
expectation of the people of the Jews.
12 συνιδών τε ἦλθεν ἐπὶ τὴν οἰκίαν τῆς
And realizing he came on the house   -
Μαρίας τῆς μητρὸς Ἰωάννου τοῦ
of Mary the   mother of John
ἐπικαλουμένου Μάρκου, οὗ ἦσαν ἱκανοὶ
being surnamed Mark, where were many
συνηθροισμένοι καὶ προσευχόμενοι. 13 κρού-
having been assembled and   praying.   And

earnestly praying to God for him.

6The night before Herod was to bring him to trial, Peter was sleeping between two soldiers, bound with two chains, and sentries stood guard at the entrance. 7Suddenly an angel of the Lord appeared and a light shone in the cell. He struck Peter on the side and woke him up. "Quick, get up!" he said, and the chains fell off Peter's wrists.

8Then the angel said to him, "Put on your clothes and sandals." And Peter did so. "Wrap your cloak around you and follow me," the angel told him. 9Peter followed him out of the prison, but he had no idea that what the angel was doing was really happening; he thought he was seeing a vision. 10They passed the first and second guards and came to the iron gate leading to the city. It opened for them by itself, and they went through it. When they had walked the length of one street, suddenly the angel left him.

11Then Peter came to himself and said, "Now I know without a doubt that the Lord sent his angel and rescued me from Herod's clutches and from everything the Jewish people were anticipating."

12When this had dawned on him, he went to the house of Mary the mother of John, also called Mark, where many people had gathered and were praying.

13And when he knocked at the door of the gate, a servant-girl named Rhoda came to answer.

14And when she recognized Peter's voice, because of her joy she did not open the gate, but ran in and announced that Peter was standing in front of the gate.

15And they said to her, "You are out of your mind!" But she kept insisting that it was so. And they kept saying, "It is his angel."

16But Peter continued knocking; and when they had opened *the door*, they saw him and were amazed.

17But motioning to them with his hand to be silent, he described to them how the Lord had led him out of the prison. And he said, "Report these things to James and the brethren." And he departed and went to another place.

18Now when day came, there was no small disturbance among the soldiers *as to* what could have become of Peter.

19And when Herod had searched for him and had not found him, he examined the guards and ordered that they be led away *to execution*. And he went down from Judea to Caesarea and was spending time there.

Death of Herod

20Now he was very angry with the people of Tyre and Sidon; and with one accord they came to him, and having won over Blastus the king's chamberlain, they were asking for peace, because their country was fed by the king's country.

21And on an appointed day Herod, having put on his royal apparel, took his seat on the rostrum and *began* delivering an address to them.

22And the people kept crying out, "The voice of a

σαντος δὲ αὐτοῦ τὴν θύραν τοῦ πυλῶνος
knocking him   the door of the porch
=as he knocked

προσῆλθεν παιδίσκη ὑπακοῦσαι ὀνόματι
approached a maidservant to listen by name

'Ρόδη, 14 καὶ ἐπιγνοῦσα τὴν φωνὴν τοῦ
Rhoda, and recognizing the voice –

Πέτρου ἀπὸ τῆς χαρᾶς οὐκ ἤνοιξεν τὸν
of Peter from – joy she did not open the

πυλῶνα, εἰσδραμοῦσα δὲ ἀπήγγειλεν ἑστάναι
porch, but running in announced ²to stand

τὸν Πέτρον πρὸ τοῦ πυλῶνος. 15 οἱ δὲ
– ¹Peter before the porch. But they

πρὸς αὐτὴν εἶπαν· μαίνῃ. ἡ δὲ διϊσχυρίζετο
to her said: Thou ravest. But she emphatically asserted

οὕτως ἔχειν. οἱ δὲ ἔλεγον· ὁ ἄγγελός
so to have(be). So they said: The angel

ἐστιν αὐτοῦ. 16 ὁ δὲ Πέτρος ἐπέμενεν
it is of him. – But Peter continued

κρούων· ἀνοίξαντες δὲ εἶδαν αὐτὸν καὶ
knocking; and having opened they saw him and

ἐξέστησαν. 17 κατασείσας δὲ αὐτοῖς τῇ
were amazed. And beckoning to them with the

χειρὶ σιγᾶν διηγήσατο αὐτοῖς πῶς ὁ
hand to be quiet he related to them how the

κύριος αὐτὸν ἐξήγαγεν ἐκ τῆς φυλακῆς,
Lord him led *out* out of the prison,

εἶπέν τε· ἀπαγγείλατε 'Ιακώβῳ καὶ τοῖς
and said: Report to James and to the

ἀδελφοῖς ταῦτα. καὶ ἐξελθὼν ἐπορεύθη εἰς
brothers these things. And going out he went to

ἕτερον τόπον. 18 Γενομένης δὲ ἡμέρας ἦν
another place. And becoming day there was
=when it became day

τάραχος οὐκ ὀλίγος ἐν τοῖς στρατιώταις,
disturbance not a little among the soldiers,

τί ἄρα ὁ Πέτρος ἐγένετο. 19 'Ηρῴδης δὲ
what then [of] Peter became. And Herod

ἐπιζητήσας αὐτὸν καὶ μὴ εὑρών,
searching for him and not finding,

ἀνακρίνας τοὺς φύλακας ἐκέλευσεν ἀπ-
examining the guards commanded to

αχθῆναι, καὶ κατελθὼν ἀπὸ τῆς 'Ιουδαίας
be led away,* and going down from – Judæa

εἰς Καισάρειαν διέτριβεν. 20 Ἦν δὲ
to Cæsarea stayed. Now he was

θυμομαχῶν Τυρίοις καὶ Σιδωνίοις·
being furiously angry with Tyrians and Sidonians·

ὁμοθυμαδὸν δὲ παρῆσαν πρὸς αὐτόν, καὶ
and with one mind they came to him, and

πείσαντες Βλάστον τὸν ἐπὶ τοῦ κοιτῶνος
having persuaded Blastus the one over the bedchamber

τοῦ βασιλέως ἠτοῦντο εἰρήνην, διὰ τὸ
of the king they asked peace, because the

τρέφεσθαι αὐτῶν τὴν χώραν ἀπὸ τῆς
to be fed of them the country from the
=their country was fed

βασιλικῆς. 21 τακτῇ δὲ ἡμέρᾳ ὁ 'Ηρῴδης
royal. And on an appointed day – Herod

ἐνδυσάμενος ἐσθῆτα βασιλικὴν καθίσας ἐπὶ
having been arrayed with clothing regal sitting on

τοῦ βήματος ἐδημηγόρει πρὸς αὐτούς·
the tribunal made a public speech to them;

22 ὁ δὲ δῆμος ἐπεφώνει· θεοῦ φωνὴ
and the mob cried out: Of a god a voice

13Peter knocked at the outer entrance, and a servant girl named Rhoda came to answer the door. 14When she recognized Peter's voice, she was so overjoyed she ran back without opening it and exclaimed, "Peter is at the door!"

15"You're out of your mind," they told her. When she kept insisting that it was so, they said, "It must be his angel."

16But Peter kept on knocking, and when they opened the door and saw him, they were astonished. 17Peter motioned with his hand for them to be quiet and described how the Lord had brought him out of prison. "Tell James and the brothers about this," he said, and then he left for another place.

18In the morning, there was no small commotion among the soldiers as to what had become of Peter. 19After Herod had a thorough search made for him and did not find him, he cross-examined the guards and ordered that they be executed.

Herod's Death

Then Herod went from Judea to Caesarea and stayed there a while. 20He had been quarreling with the people of Tyre and Sidon; they now joined together and sought an audience with him. Having secured the support of Blastus, a trusted personal servant of the king, they asked for peace, because they depended on the king's country for their food supply.

21On the appointed day Herod, wearing his royal robes, sat on his throne and delivered a public address to the people. 22They shouted, "This is the voice

---

* That is, to execution.

god and not of a man!''

23And immediately an angel of the Lord struck him because he did not give God the glory, and he was eaten by worms and died.

24But the word of the Lord continued to grow and to be multiplied.

25And Barnabas and Saul returned from Jerusalem when they had fulfilled their mission, taking along with *them* John, who was also called Mark.

καὶ οὐκ ἀνθρώπου. **23** παραχρῆμα δὲ
and not of a man.   And at once

ἐπάταξεν αὐτὸν ἄγγελος κυρίου ἀνθ᾽ ὧν
smote him an angel of [the] Lord because

οὐκ ἔδωκεν τὴν δόξαν τῷ θεῷ, καὶ
he gave not the glory - to God, and

γενόμενος σκωληκόβρωτος ἐξέψυξεν.
becoming eaten by worms he expired.

24 Ὁ δὲ λόγος τοῦ κυρίου ηὔξανεν
But the word of the Lord grew

καὶ ἐπληθύνετο. **25** Βαρναβᾶς δὲ καὶ
and increased.   And Barnabas and

Σαῦλος ὑπέστρεψαν ἐξ Ἰερουσαλήμ,
Saul returned out of Jerusalem,

πληρώσαντες τὴν διακονίαν, συμπαρα-
having completed the ministration, taking

λαβόντες Ἰωάννην τὸν ἐπικληθέντα Μᾶρκον.
with [them] John - surnamed Mark.

---

of a god, not of a man.''

23Immediately, because Herod did not give praise to God, an angel of the Lord struck him down, and he was eaten by worms and died.

24But the word of God continued to increase and spread.

25When Barnabas and Saul had finished their mission, they returned from[1] Jerusalem, taking with them John, also called Mark.

Chapter 13

First Missionary Journey

NOW there were at Antioch, in the church that was *there*, prophets and teachers: Barnabas, and Simeon who was called Niger, and Lucius of Cyrene, and Manaen who had been brought up with Herod the tetrarch, and Saul.

2And while they were ministering to the Lord and fasting, the Holy Spirit said, "Set apart for Me Barnabas and Saul for the work to which I have called them."

3Then, when they had fasted and prayed and laid their hands on them, they sent them away.

4So, being sent out by the Holy Spirit, they went down to Seleucia and from there they sailed to Cyprus.

5And when they reached Salamis, they *began* to proclaim the word of God in the synagogues of the Jews; and they also had John as their helper.

6And when they had gone through the whole island as far as Paphos, they found a certain magician, a Jewish false prophet whose name was Bar-Jesus,

7who was with the proconsul, Sergius Paulus, a

---

13 Ἦσαν δὲ ἐν Ἀντιοχείᾳ κατὰ τὴν
Now there were in Antioch among the

οὖσαν ἐκκλησίαν προφῆται καὶ διδάσκαλοι
existing church prophets and teachers

ὅ τε Βαρναβᾶς καὶ Συμεὼν ὁ καλούμενος
- both Barnabas and Simeon - *being* called

Νίγερ, καὶ Λούκιος ὁ Κυρηναῖος, Μαναήν τε
Niger, and Lucius the Cyrenian, and Manaen

Ἡρώδου τοῦ τετραάρχου σύντροφος
[2]of Herod [3]the [4]tetrarch [1]foster brother

καὶ Σαῦλος. **2** Λειτουργούντων δὲ αὐτῶν
and Saul.   And ministering them[a]
      =as they ministered

τῷ κυρίῳ καὶ νηστευόντων εἶπεν τὸ
to the Lord and fasting[a] said the

πνεῦμα τὸ ἅγιον· ἀφορίσατε δή μοι
Spirit the Holy: [2]Separate ye [1]so then [3]to me

τὸν Βαρναβᾶν καὶ Σαῦλον εἰς τὸ ἔργον
- Barnabas and Saul for the work

ὃ προσκέκλημαι αὐτούς· **3** τότε νηστεύ-
[to] which I have called them; then having

σαντες καὶ προσευξάμενοι καὶ ἐπιθέντες
fasted and *having* prayed and [1]laying [4]on

τὰς χεῖρας αὐτοῖς ἀπέλυσαν.
[2]the(ir) [3]hands [4]them they dismissed [them].

4 Αὐτοὶ μὲν οὖν ἐκπεμφθέντες ὑπὸ τοῦ
They - therefore sent out by the

ἁγίου πνεύματος κατῆλθον εἰς Σελεύκειαν,
Holy Spirit went down to Seleucia,

ἐκεῖθέν τε ἀπέπλευσαν εἰς Κύπρον, **5** καὶ
and thence sailed away to Cyprus, and

γενόμενοι ἐν Σαλαμῖνι κατήγγελλον τὸν
being in Salamis they announced the

λόγον τοῦ θεοῦ ἐν ταῖς συναγωγαῖς τῶν
word - of God in the synagogues of the

Ἰουδαίων· εἶχον δὲ καὶ Ἰωάννην ὑπηρέτην.
Jews; and they had also John [as] attendant.

6 Διελθόντες δὲ ὅλην τὴν νῆσον ἄχρι
And passing through all the island unto

Πάφου εὗρον ἄνδρα τινὰ μάγον ψευδο-
Paphos they found a certain man a sorcerer a [2]false

προφήτην Ἰουδαῖον, ᾧ ὄνομα᾽ Βαριησοῦς,
[3]prophet [1]Jewish, to whom name[c] Barjesus,
      =whose name was

7 ὃς ἦν σὺν τῷ ἀνθυπάτῳ Σεργίῳ
who was with the proconsul Sergius

Chapter 13

Barnabas and Saul Sent Off

IN the church at Antioch there were prophets and teachers: Barnabas, Simeon called Niger, Lucius of Cyrene, Manaen (who had been brought up with Herod the tetrarch) and Saul. 2While they were worshiping the Lord and fasting, the Holy Spirit said, "Set apart for me Barnabas and Saul for the work to which I have called them." 3So after they had fasted and prayed, they placed their hands on them and sent them off.

On Cyprus

4The two of them, sent on their way by the Holy Spirit, went down to Seleucia and sailed from there to Cyprus. 5When they arrived at Salamis, they proclaimed the word of God in the Jewish synagogues. John was with them as their helper. 6They traveled through the whole island until they came to Paphos. There they met a Jewish sorcerer and false prophet named Bar-Jesus, 7who was an attendant of the proconsul,

---

*25 Some manuscripts *to*

man of intelligence. This man summoned Barnabas and Saul and sought to hear the word of God.

8But Elymas the magician (for thus his name is translated) was opposing them, seeking to turn the proconsul away from the faith.

9But Saul, who was also *known as* Paul, filled with the Holy Spirit, fixed his gaze upon him,

10and said, "You who are full of all deceit and fraud, you son of the devil, you enemy of all righteousness, will you not cease to make crooked the straight ways of the Lord?

11"And now, behold, the hand of the Lord is upon you, and you will be blind and not see the sun for a time." And immediately a mist and a darkness fell upon him, and he went about seeking those who would lead him by the hand.

12Then the proconsul believed when he saw what had happened, being amazed at the teaching of the Lord.

13Now Paul and his companions put out to sea from Paphos and came to Perga in Pamphylia; and John left them and returned to Jerusalem.

14But going on from Perga, they arrived at Pisidian Antioch, and on the Sabbath day they went into the synagogue and sat down.

15And after the reading of the Law and the Prophets the synagogue officials sent to them, saying, "Brethren, if you have any word of exhortation for the people, say it."

16And Paul stood up, and

Παύλῳ, ἀνδρὶ συνετῷ.
Paulus, man an intelligent.

καλεσάμενος Βαρναβᾶν καὶ Σαῦλον ἐπεζήτησεν
to [him] calling Barnabas and Saul sought

ἀκοῦσαι τὸν λόγον τοῦ θεοῦ·
to hear the word of God;

αὐτοῖς Ἐλύμας ὁ μάγος,
them Elymas the sorcerer,

μεθερμηνεύεται τὸ ὄνομα αὐτοῦ, ζητῶν
is translated the name of him, seeking

διαστρέψαι τὸν ἀνθύπατον ἀπὸ τῆς
to divert the proconsul from the

πίστεως. 9 Σαῦλος δέ, ὁ καὶ Παῦλος,
faith. But Saul, the [one] also Paul,

πληθεὶς πνεύματος ἁγίου ἀτενίσας εἰς
filled of(with) Spirit Holy gazing at

αὐτὸν εἶπεν· 10 ὦ πλήρης παντὸς δόλου
him said: O full of all deceit

καὶ πάσης ῥᾳδιουργίας, υἱὲ διαβόλου,
and of all fraud, son of [the] devil,

ἐχθρὲ πάσης δικαιοσύνης, οὐ παύσῃ
enemy of all righteousness, wilt thou not cease

διαστρέφων τὰς ὁδοὺς τοῦ κυρίου τὰς
perverting the ways of the Lord –

εὐθείας; 11 καὶ νῦν ἰδοὺ χεὶρ κυρίου
right? And now behold[,] [the] hand of [the] Lord

ἐπὶ σέ, καὶ ἔσῃ τυφλὸς μὴ βλέπων
[is] on thee, and thou wilt be blind not seeing

τὸν ἥλιον ἄχρι καιροῦ. παραχρῆμα δὲ
the sun until [such] a time. And at once

ἔπεσεν ἐπ' αὐτὸν ἀχλὺς καὶ σκότος, καὶ
fell on him a mist and darkness, and

περιάγων ἐζήτει χειραγωγούς. 12 τότε
going about he sought leaders by the hand. Then

ἰδὼν ὁ ἀνθύπατος τὸ γεγονὸς
²seeing ¹the ²proconsul the thing having occurred

ἐπίστευσεν, ἐκπλησσόμενος ἐπὶ τῇ διδαχῇ
believed, being astounded at the teaching

τοῦ κυρίου.
of the Lord.

13 Ἀναχθέντες δὲ ἀπὸ τῆς Πάφου οἱ
And setting sail from – Paphos the ones

περὶ Παῦλον ἦλθον εἰς Πέργην τῆς
around(with) Paul came to Perga of

Παμφυλίας· Ἰωάννης δὲ ἀποχωρήσας ἀπ'
of Pamphylia; and John departing from

αὐτῶν ὑπέστρεψεν εἰς Ἰεροσόλυμα.
them returned to Jerusalem.

14 Αὐτοὶ δὲ διελθόντες ἀπὸ τῆς Πέργης
And they going through from – Perga

παρεγένοντο εἰς Ἀντιόχειαν τὴν Πισιδίαν,
arrived in Antioch the Pisidian,

καὶ ἐλθόντες εἰς τὴν συναγωγὴν τῇ
and going into the synagogue on the

ἡμέρᾳ τῶν σαββάτων ἐκάθισαν. 15 μετὰ δὲ
day of the sabbaths sat down. And after

τὴν ἀνάγνωσιν τοῦ νόμου καὶ τῶν
the reading of the law and of the

προφητῶν ἀπέστειλαν οἱ ἀρχισυνάγωγοι
prophets sent the synagogue rulers

πρὸς αὐτοὺς λέγοντες· ἄνδρες ἀδελφοί,
to them saying: Men brothers,

εἴ τίς ἐστιν ἐν ὑμῖν λόγος παρακλήσεως
¹if ²any ³there is ²among ⁴you ⁵word of exhortation

πρὸς τὸν λαόν, λέγετε. 16 ἀναστὰς δὲ
to the people, say ye. And ¹rising up

Sergius Paulus. The proconsul, an intelligent man, sent for Barnabas and Saul because he wanted to hear the word of God. 8But Elymas the sorcerer (for that is what his name means) opposed them and tried to turn the proconsul from the faith. 9Then Saul, who was also called Paul, filled with the Holy Spirit, looked straight at Elymas and said, 10"You are a child of the devil and an enemy of everything that is right! You are full of all kinds of deceit and trickery. Will you never stop perverting the right ways of the Lord? 11Now the hand of the Lord is against you. You are going to be blind, and for a time you will be unable to see the light of the sun."

Immediately mist and darkness came over him, and he groped about, seeking someone to lead him by the hand. 12When the proconsul saw what had happened, he believed, for he was amazed at the teaching about the Lord.

In Pisidian Antioch

13From Paphos, Paul and his companions sailed to Perga in Pamphylia, where John left them to return to Jerusalem. 14From Perga they went on to Pisidian Antioch. On the Sabbath they entered the synagogue and sat down. 15After the reading from the Law and the Prophets, the synagogue rulers sent word to them, saying, "Brothers, if you have a message of encouragement for the people, please speak."

16Standing up, Paul mo-

motioning with his hand, he said,

"Men of Israel, and you who fear God, listen:

17"The God of this people Israel chose our fathers, and made the people great during their stay in the land of Egypt, and with an uplifted arm He led them out from it.

18"And for a period of about forty years He put up with them in the wilderness.

19"And when He had destroyed seven nations in the land of Canaan, He distributed their land as an inheritance—*all of which took* about four hundred and fifty years.

20"And after these things He gave *them* judges until Samuel the prophet.

21"And then they asked for a king, and God gave them Saul the son of Kish, a man of the tribe of Benjamin, for forty years.

22"And after He had removed him, He raised up David to be their king, concerning whom He also testified and said, 'I HAVE FOUND DAVID the son of Jesse, A MAN AFTER MY HEART, who will do all My will.'

23"From the offspring of this man, according to promise, God has brought to Israel a Savior, Jesus,

24after John had proclaimed before His coming a baptism of repentance to all the people of Israel.

25"And while John was completing his course, he kept saying, 'What do you suppose that I am? I am not *He*. But behold, one is coming after me the sandals of whose feet I am not worthy to untie.'

26"Brethren, sons of Abraham's family, and those among you who fear

---

Παῦλος   καὶ   κατασείσας   τῇ   χειρὶ   εἶπεν·
⁶Paul   ²and   ³beckoning   ⁴with the(his)   ³hand   said:

ἄνδρες   Ἰσραηλῖται   καὶ   οἱ   φοβούμενοι   τὸν
Men   Israelites   and   the [ones] fearing   –

θεόν,   ἀκούσατε.   17 ὁ   θεὸς   τοῦ   λαοῦ
God,   hear ye.   The   God   –   people

τούτου   Ἰσραὴλ   ἐξελέξατο   τοὺς   πατέρας
of this   Israel   chose   the   fathers

ἡμῶν,   καὶ   τὸν   λαὸν   ὕψωσεν   ἐν   τῇ
of us,   and   ²the   ³people   ¹exalted   in   the

παροικίᾳ   ἐν   γῇ   Αἰγύπτου,   καὶ   μετὰ
sojourn   in [the] land   of Egypt,   and   with

βραχίονος   ὑψηλοῦ   ἐξήγαγεν   αὐτοὺς   ἐξ
arm   a high   he led forth   them   out of

αὐτῆς,   18 καὶ   ὡς   τεσσερακονταέτη   χρόνον
it,   and   about   forty years   time

ἐτροποφόρησεν   αὐτοὺς   ἐν   τῇ   ἐρήμῳ,   19 καὶ
endured   them   in   the   desert,   and

καθελὼν   ἔθνη   ἑπτὰ   ἐν   γῇ   Χανάαν
having destroyed   nations   seven   in   [the] land   Canaan

κατεκληρονόμησεν   τὴν   γῆν   αὐτῶν   20 ὡς
gave as an inheritance   the   land   of them   about

ἔτεσιν   τετρακοσίοις   καὶ   πεντήκοντα.   καὶ
years   four hundreds   and   fifty.   And

μετὰ   ταῦτα   ἔδωκεν   κριτὰς   ἕως   Σαμουὴλ
after   these things   he gave   judges   until   Samuel

προφήτου.   21 κἀκεῖθεν   ᾐτήσαντο   βασιλέα,
a prophet.   And thence   they asked   a king,

καὶ   ἔδωκεν   αὐτοῖς   ὁ   θεὸς   τὸν   Σαοὺλ
and   gave   them   –   God   –   Saul

υἱὸν   Κίς,   ἄνδρα   ἐκ   φυλῆς   Βενιαμίν,
son   of Cis,   a man   of [the]   tribe   of Benjamin,

ἔτη   τεσσεράκοντα·   22 καὶ   μεταστήσας
years   forty;   and   removing

αὐτὸν   ἤγειρεν   τὸν   Δαυὶδ   αὐτοῖς   εἰς
him   he raised   –   David   to them   for

βασιλέα,   ᾧ   καὶ   εἶπεν   μαρτυρήσας·
a king,   to whom   also   he said   giving witness:

εὗρον   Δαυὶδ   τὸν   τοῦ   Ἰεσσαί,   ἄνδρα
I found   David   the [son] –   of Jesse,   a man

κατὰ   τὴν   καρδίαν   μου,   ὃς   ποιήσει   πάντα
according to   the   heart   of me,   who   will do   all

τὰ   θελήματά   μου.   23 τούτου   ὁ   θεὸς
the   wishes   of me.   ⁶Of this man   –   ⁵God

ἀπὸ   τοῦ   σπέρματος   κατ'   ἐπαγγελίαν
¹from   ³the   ⁴seed   according to   promise

ἤγαγεν   τῷ   Ἰσραὴλ   σωτῆρα   Ἰησοῦν,
brought   to Israel   a Saviour   Jesus,

24 προκηρύξαντος   Ἰωάννου   πρὸ   προσώπου
previously proclaiming   Johnᵃ   before   face
=when John had previously proclaimed

τῆς   εἰσόδου   αὐτοῦ   βάπτισμα   μετανοίας
of the   entrance   of him   a baptism   of repentance

παντὶ   τῷ   λαῷ   Ἰσραήλ.   25 ὡς   δὲ
to all   the   people   of Israel.   Now as

ἐπλήρου   Ἰωάννης   τὸν   δρόμον,   ἔλεγεν·
completed   John   the(his)   course,   he said:

τί   ἐμὲ   ὑπονοεῖτε   εἶναι;   οὐκ   εἰμὶ   ἐγώ·
What   me   suppose ye   to be?   ³Not   ²am   ¹I;

ἀλλ'   ἰδοὺ   ἔρχεται   μετ'   ἐμὲ   οὗ   οὐκ   εἰμὶ
but   behold   he comes   after   me   of whom   I am not

ἄξιος   τὸ   ὑπόδημα   τῶν   ποδῶν   λῦσαι.
worthy   the   sandal   of the   feet   to loosen.

26 Ἄνδρες   ἀδελφοί,   υἱοὶ   γένους   Ἀβραὰμ
Men   brothers,   sons   of [the] race   of Abraham

καὶ   οἱ   ἐν   ὑμῖν   φοβούμενοι   τὸν   θεόν,
and   the [ones]   among   you   fearing   –   God,

---

tioned with his hand and said: "Men of Israel and you Gentiles who worship God, listen to me! 17The God of the people of Israel chose our fathers; he made the people prosper during their stay in Egypt, with mighty power he led them out of that country, 18he endured their conductᵘ for about forty years in the desert, 19he overthrew seven nations in Canaan and gave their land to his people as their inheritance. 20All this took about 450 years.

"After this, God gave them judges until the time of Samuel the prophet. 21Then the people asked for a king, and he gave them Saul son of Kish, of the tribe of Benjamin, who ruled forty years. 22After removing Saul, he made David their king. He testified concerning him: 'I have found David son of Jesse a man after my own heart; he will do everything I want him to do.'

23"From this man's descendants God has brought to Israel the Savior Jesus, as he promised. 24Before the coming of Jesus, John preached repentance and baptism to all the people of Israel. 25As John was completing his work, he said: 'Who do you think I am? I am not that one. No, but he is coming after me, whose sandals I am not worthy to untie.'

26"Brothers, children of Abraham, and you God-fearing Gentiles, it is to us

---

ᵘ18 Some manuscripts *and cared for them*

God, to us the word of this salvation is sent out.

27"For those who live in Jerusalem, and their rulers, recognizing neither Him nor the utterances of the prophets which are read every Sabbath, fulfilled *these* by condemning *Him*.

28"And though they found no ground for *putting Him to* death, they asked Pilate that He be executed.

29"And when they had carried out all that was written concerning Him, they took Him down from the cross and laid Him in a tomb.

30"But God raised Him from the dead;

31and for many days He appeared to those who came up with Him from Galilee to Jerusalem, the very ones who are now His witnesses to the people.

32"And we preach to you the good news of the promise made to the fathers,

33that God has fulfilled this *promise* to our children in that He raised up Jesus, as it is also written in the second Psalm, 'THOU ART MY SON; TODAY I HAVE BEGOTTEN THEE.'

34"And as for the fact that He raised Him up from the dead, no more to return to decay, He has spoken in this way: 'I WILL GIVE YOU THE HOLY and SURE blessings OF DAVID.'

35"Therefore He also says in another *Psalm*, 'THOU WILT NOT ALLOW THY HOLY ONE TO UNDERGO DECAY.'

36"For David, after he had served the purpose of God in his own generation, fell asleep, and was laid among his fathers, and underwent decay;

37but He whom God raised did not undergo decay.

38"Therefore let it be known to you, brethren, that through Him forgive-

---

ἡμῖν   ὁ   λόγος   τῆς   σω:ηρίας   ταύτης
to us   the   word   of this salvation

ἐξαπεστάλη.   27 οἱ   γὰρ   κατοικοῦντες   ἐν
was sent forth.   For the [ones]   dwelling   in

Ἰερουσαλὴμ   καὶ   οἱ   ἄρχοντες   αὐτῶν   τοῦτον
Jerusalem   and   the   rulers   of them   ²this man

ἀγνοήσαντες   καὶ   τὰς   φωνὰς   τῶν   προφητῶν   τὰς
¹not knowing   and   the   voices   of the   prophets   -

κατὰ   πᾶν   σάββατον   ἀναγινωσκομένας
¹throughout(on)   ³every   ⁴sabbath   ¹being read

κρίναντες   ἐπλήρωσαν,   28 καὶ   μηδεμίαν
judging   they fulfilled,   and   no

αἰτίαν   θανάτου   εὑρόντες   ᾐτήσαντο   Πιλᾶτον
cause   of death   finding   they asked   Pilate

ἀναιρεθῆναι   αὐτόν·   29 ὡς   δὲ   ἐτέλεσαν   πάντα
to be destroyed   him;   and when they finished   all

τὰ   περὶ   αὐτοῦ   γεγραμμένα,   καθελόντες
the things concerning him having been written, taking down

ἀπὸ   τοῦ   ξύλου   ἔθηκαν   εἰς   μνημεῖον.
from   the   tree   they laid   in   a tomb.

30 ὁ   δὲ   θεὸς   ἤγειρεν   αὐτὸν   ἐκ   νεκρῶν·
- But   God   raised   him   out of [the] dead;

31 ὃς   ὤφθη   ἐπὶ   ἡμέρας   πλείους   τοῖς
who   appeared   over   days   many   to the [ones]

συναναβᾶσιν   αὐτῷ   ἀπὸ   τῆς   Γαλιλαίας   εἰς
having come up with him   from   -   Galilee   to

Ἰερουσαλήμ,   οἵτινες   [νῦν]   εἰσιν   μάρτυρες
Jerusalem,   who   now   are   witnesses

αὐτοῦ   πρὸς   τὸν   λαόν.   32 καὶ   ἡμεῖς
of him   to   the   people.   And   we

ὑμᾶς   εὐαγγελιζόμεθα   τὴν   πρὸς   τοὺς
[to] you   preach   ¹the   ⁴to   ⁵the

πατέρας   ἐπαγγελίαν   γενομένην,   33 ὅτι
⁶fathers   ²promise   ³having come,   that

ταύτην   ὁ   θεὸς   ἐκπεπλήρωκεν   τοῖς   τέκνοις
this [promise] -   God   has fulfilled   ²to the   ³children

ἡμῖν   ἀναστήσας   Ἰησοῦν,   ὡς   καὶ   ἐν   τῷ
¹to us   raising up   Jesus,   as   also   in   the

ψαλμῷ   γέγραπται   τῷ   δευτέρῳ·   υἱός   μου
²psalm   ³it has been written -   ¹second ·   Son   of me

εἶ   σύ,   ἐγὼ   σήμερον   γεγέννηκά   σε.   34 ὅτι   δὲ
art thou,   I   to-day   have begotten   thee.   And that

ἀνέστησεν   αὐτὸν   ἐκ   νεκρῶν   μηκέτι
he raised up   him   out of   [the] dead   no more

μέλλοντα   ὑποστρέφειν   εἰς   διαφθοράν,   οὕτως
being about   to return   to   corruption,   thus

εἴρηκεν   ὅτι   δώσω   ὑμῖν   τὰ   ὅσια   Δαυὶδ   τὰ
he has said[,]   - I will give   you   the   ²holy things   ³of David   the

πιστά.   35 διότι   καὶ   ἐν   ἑτέρῳ   λέγει·
¹faithful.   Wherefore   also   in another [psalm]   he says:

οὐ   δώσεις   τὸν   ὅσιόν   σου   ἰδεῖν   διαφθοράν.
Thou wilt not give   the   holy one   of thee   to see   corruption.

36 Δαυὶδ   μὲν   γὰρ   ἰδίᾳ   γενεᾷ   ὑπηρετήσας
For David indeed   [his] own   generation   having served

τῇ   τοῦ   θεοῦ   βουλῇ   ἐκοιμήθη   καὶ   προσετέθη
by the   -   of God   counsel   fell asleep   and   was added

πρὸς   τοὺς   πατέρας   αὐτοῦ   καὶ   εἶδεν
to   the   fathers   of him   and   saw

διαφθοράν·   37 ὃν   δὲ   ὁ   θεὸς   ἤγειρεν,
corruption;   but [he] whom   -   God   raised,

οὐκ   εἶδεν   διαφθοράν.   38 γνωστὸν   οὖν
did not see   corruption.   Known   therefore

ἔστω   ὑμῖν,   ἄνδρες   ἀδελφοί,   ὅτι   διὰ
let it be   to you,   *men*   brothers,   that   through

---

that this message of salvation has been sent. 27The people of Jerusalem and their rulers did not recognize Jesus, yet in condemning him they fulfilled the words of the prophets that are read every Sabbath. 28Though they found no proper ground for a death sentence, they asked Pilate to have him executed. 29When they had carried out all that was written about him, they took him down from the tree and laid him in a tomb. 30But God raised him from the dead, 31and for many days he was seen by those who had traveled with him from Galilee to Jerusalem. They are now his witnesses to our people.

32"We tell you the good news: What God promised our fathers 33he has fulfilled for us, their children, by raising up Jesus. As it is written in the second Psalm:

" 'You are my Son;
today I have become
your Father.'ᵛ ʷ

34The fact that God raised him from the dead, never to decay, is stated in these words:

" 'I will give you the
holy and sure
blessings promised
to David.'ˣ

35So it is stated elsewhere:

" 'You will not let your
Holy One see
decay.'ʸ

36"For when David had served God's purpose in his own generation, he fell asleep; he was buried with his fathers and his body decayed. 37But the one whom God raised from the dead did not see decay.

38"Therefore, my brothers, I want you to know that through Jesus the for-

---

ᵛ33 Or *have begotten you*
ʷ33 Psalm 2:7
ˣ34 Isaiah 55:3
ʸ35 Psalm 16:10

ness of sins is proclaimed to you,

39and through Him everyone who believes is freed from all things, from which you could not be freed through the Law of Moses.

40"Take heed therefore, so that the thing spoken of in the Prophets may not come upon *you*:

41 'BEHOLD, YOU SCOFFERS, AND MARVEL, AND PERISH;
FOR I AM ACCOMPLISHING A WORK IN YOUR DAYS,
A WORK WHICH YOU WILL NEVER BELIEVE, THOUGH SOMEONE SHOULD DESCRIBE IT TO YOU.' "

42And as Paul and Barnabas were going out, the people kept begging that these things might be spoken to them the next Sabbath.

43Now when *the meeting of* the synagogue had broken up, many of the Jews and of the God-fearing proselytes followed Paul and Barnabas, who, speaking to them, were urging them to continue in the grace of God.

Paul Turns to the Gentiles

44And the next Sabbath nearly the whole city assembled to hear the word of God.

45But when the Jews saw the crowds, they were filled with jealousy, and *began* contradicting the things spoken by Paul, and were blaspheming.

46And Paul and Barnabas spoke out boldly and said, "It was necessary that the word of God should be spoken to you first; since you repudiate it, and judge yourselves unworthy of eternal life, behold, we are turning to the Gentiles.

47"For thus the Lord has commanded us,

'I HAVE PLACED YOU AS A LIGHT FOR THE GENTILES,
THAT YOU SHOULD BRING SALVATION TO THE END OF THE EARTH.' "

48And when the Gentiles heard this, they *began* rejoicing and glorifying the word of the Lord; and as

---

τούτου ὑμῖν ἄφεσις ἁμαρτιῶν καταγγέλ-
this man to you forgiveness of sins is an-

λεται, καὶ ἀπὸ πάντων ὧν οὐκ ἠδυνήθητε
nounced, and from all things from which ye could not

ἐν νόμῳ Μωϋσέως δικαιωθῆναι, 39 ἐν
by [the] law of Moses *to* be justified, by

τούτῳ πᾶς ὁ πιστεύων δικαιοῦται. 40 βλέπετε
this man everyone believing is justified. Look ye

οὖν μὴ ἐπέλθῃ τὸ εἰρημένον
therefore lest come on [you] the thing having been said

ἐν τοῖς προφήταις· 41 ἴδετε, οἱ κατα-
in the prophets: See, the des-

φρονηταί, καὶ θαυμάσατε καὶ ἀφανίσθητε,
pisers, and marvel ye and perish,

ὅτι ἔργον ἐργάζομαι ἐγὼ ἐν ταῖς ἡμέραις
because a work work I in the days

ὑμῶν, ἔργον ὃ οὐ μὴ πιστεύσητε ἐάν
of you, a work which by no means ye believe if

τις ἐκδιηγῆται ὑμῖν. 42 Ἐξιόντων δὲ
anyone declares to you. And going out =as they went out

αὐτῶν παρεκάλουν εἰς τὸ μεταξὺ σάββατον
them[a] they besought in the intervening sabbath(week)

λαληθῆναι αὐτοῖς τὰ ῥήματα ταῦτα.
to be spoken to them the words these words.

43 λυθείσης δὲ τῆς συναγωγῆς ἠκολούθησαν
And being broken up the assembly[a] [b]followed
=when the assembly was broken up

πολλοὶ τῶν Ἰουδαίων καὶ τῶν σεβομένων
[1]many [2]of the [3]Jews [4]and [5]of the [6]worshipping

προσηλύτων τῷ Παύλῳ καὶ τῷ Βαρναβᾷ,
[7]proselytes – [8]Paul and – Barnabas,

οἵτινες προσλαλοῦντες αὐτοῖς ἔπειθον αὐτοὺς
who speaking to them persuaded them

προσμένειν τῇ χάριτι τοῦ θεοῦ. 44 Τῷ δὲ
to continue in the grace – of God. And on the

ἐρχομένῳ σαββάτῳ σχεδὸν πᾶσα ἡ
coming sabbath almost all the

πόλις συνήχθη ἀκοῦσαι τὸν λόγον τοῦ
city was assembled to hear the word –

θεοῦ. 45 ἰδόντες δὲ οἱ Ἰουδαῖοι τοὺς
of God. But [1]seeing [2]the [3]Jews the

ὄχλους ἐπλήσθησαν ζήλου, καὶ ἀντέλεγον
crowds were filled of(with) jealousy, and contradicted

τοῖς ὑπὸ Παύλου λαλουμένοις βλασφημοῦντες.
the things by Paul being spoken blaspheming.

46 παρρησιασάμενοί τε ὁ Παῦλος καὶ ὁ
And speaking boldly – Paul and –

Βαρναβᾶς εἶπαν· ὑμῖν ἦν ἀναγκαῖον πρῶτον
Barnabas said: To you it was necessary firstly

λαληθῆναι τὸν λόγον τοῦ θεοῦ· ἐπειδὴ
to be spoken the word – of God; since

ἀπωθεῖσθε αὐτὸν καὶ οὐκ ἀξίους κρίνετε
ye put away it and not worthy judge

ἑαυτοὺς τῆς αἰωνίου ζωῆς, ἰδοὺ στρεφόμεθα
yourselves of the eternal life, behold we turn

εἰς τὰ ἔθνη. 47 οὕτως γὰρ ἐντέταλται
to the nations. For thus has commanded

ἡμῖν ὁ κύριος· τέθεικά σε εἰς φῶς
us the Lord: I have set thee for a light

ἐθνῶν τοῦ εἶναί σε εἰς σωτηρίαν ἕως
of nations – to be thee[b] for salvation to

ἐσχάτου τῆς γῆς. 48 ἀκούοντα δὲ τὰ ἔθνη
[the] end of the earth. And [2]hearing [1]the [3]nations

ἔχαιρον καὶ ἐδόξαζον τὸν λόγον τοῦ κυρίου, καὶ
rejoiced and glorified the word of the Lord, and

---

giveness of sins is proclaimed to you. 39Through him everyone who believes is justified from everything you could not be justified from by the law of Moses.

40Take care that what the prophets have said does not happen to you:

41" 'Look, you scoffers, wonder and perish,
for I am going to do something in your days
that you would never believe,
even if someone told you.'[z]"

42As Paul and Barnabas were leaving the synagogue, the people invited them to speak further about these things on the next Sabbath. 43When the congregation was dismissed, many of the Jews and devout converts to Judaism followed Paul and Barnabas, who talked with them and urged them to continue in the grace of God.

44On the next Sabbath almost the whole city gathered to hear the word of the Lord. 45When the Jews saw the crowds, they were filled with jealousy and talked abusively against what Paul was saying.

46Then Paul and Barnabas answered them boldly: "We had to speak the word of God to you first. Since you reject it and do not consider yourselves worthy of eternal life, we now turn to the Gentiles. 47For this is what the Lord has commanded us:

" 'I have made you[a] a light for the Gentiles,
that you[a] may bring salvation to the ends of the earth.'[b]"

48When the Gentiles heard this, they were glad and honored the word of

---

many as had been appointed to eternal life believed.
49And the word of the Lord was being spread through the whole region.
50But the Jews aroused the devout women of prominence and the leading men of the city, and instigated a persecution against Paul and Barnabas, and drove them out of their district.
51But they shook off the dust of their feet in protest against them and went to Iconium.
52And the disciples were continually filled with joy and with the Holy Spirit.

Chapter 14

Acceptance and Opposition

AND it came about that in Iconium they entered the synagogue of the Jews together, and spoke in such a manner that a great multitude believed, both of Jews and of Greeks.
2But the Jews who disbelieved stirred up the minds of the Gentiles, and embittered them against the brethren.
3Therefore they spent a long time *there* speaking boldly *with reliance* upon the Lord, who was bearing witness to the word of His grace, granting that signs and wonders be done by their hands.
4But the multitude of the city was divided; and some sided with the Jews, and some with the apostles.
5And when an attempt was made by both the Gentiles and the Jews with their rulers, to mistreat and to stone them,
6they became aware of it and fled to the cities of Lycaonia, Lystra and Derbe, and the surrounding region;
7and there they continued to preach the gospel.
8And at Lystra there was sitting a certain man, with-

ἐπίστευσαν ὅσοι ἦσαν τεταγμένοι εἰς
7believed ¹as many as ²were ³having been disposed ⁴to

ζωὴν αἰώνιον· 49 διεφέρετο δὲ ὁ λόγος τοῦ
⁴life ⁵eternal; and was carried *through* the word of the

κυρίου δι᾽ ὅλης τῆς χώρας. 50 οἱ δὲ
Lord through all the country. But the

᾽Ιουδαῖοι παρώτρυναν τὰς σεβομένας γυναῖκας
Jews urged on the ²worshipping ³women

τὰς εὐσχήμονας καὶ τοὺς πρώτους τῆς
- ¹honourable and the chief men of the

πόλεως, καὶ ἐπήγειραν διωγμὸν ἐπὶ τὸν
city, and raised up persecution against -

Παῦλον καὶ Βαρναβᾶν, καὶ ἐξέβαλον αὐτοὺς
Paul and Barnabas, and expelled them

ἀπὸ τῶν ὁρίων αὐτῶν. 51 οἱ δὲ ἐκτιναξάμενοι
from the borders of them. But they shaking off

τὸν κονιορτὸν τῶν ποδῶν ἐπ᾽ αὐτοὺς ἦλθον
the dust of the(ir) feet on them came

εἰς ᾽Ικόνιον, 52 οἵ τε μαθηταὶ ἐπλη-
to Iconium, and the disciples were

ροῦντο χαρᾶς καὶ πνεύματος ἁγίου.
filled of(with) joy and of(with) Spirit Holy.

14 ᾽Εγένετο δὲ ἐν ᾽Ικονίῳ κατὰ τὸ αὐτὸ
Now it happened in Iconium ²together†

εἰσελθεῖν αὐτοὺς εἰς τὴν συναγωγὴν
¹to enter them to ᵇ into the synagogue
=they entered

τῶν ᾽Ιουδαίων καὶ λαλῆσαι οὕτως ὥστε
of the Jews and to speakᵇ so so

πιστεῦσαι ᾽Ιουδαίων τε καὶ ᾽Ελλήνων
to believe both of Jews and of Greeks

πολὺ πλῆθος. 2 οἱ δὲ ἀπειθήσαντες
a much(great) multitude. But the disobeying

᾽Ιουδαῖοι ἐπήγειραν καὶ ἐκάκωσαν τὰς
Jews excited and embittered the

ψυχὰς τῶν ἐθνῶν κατὰ τῶν ἀδελφῶν.
minds of the nations against the brothers.

3 ἱκανὸν μὲν οὖν χρόνον διέτριψαν
A considerable - ²therefore ¹time they continued

παρρησιαζόμενοι ἐπὶ τῷ κυρίῳ τῷ μαρ-
speaking boldly on the Lord - wit-

τυροῦντι ἐπὶ τῷ λόγῳ τῆς χάριτος αὐτοῦ,
nessing to the word of the grace of him,

διδόντι σημεῖα καὶ τέρατα γίνεσθαι διὰ
giving signs and wonders to happen through

τῶν χειρῶν αὐτῶν. 4 ἐσχίσθη δὲ τὸ
the hands of them. But was divided the

πλῆθος τῆς πόλεως, καὶ οἱ μὲν ἦσαν
multitude of the city, and some were

σὺν τοῖς ᾽Ιουδαίοις, οἱ δὲ σὺν τοῖς
with the Jews, but others with the

ἀποστόλοις. 5 ὡς δὲ ἐγένετο ὁρμὴ τῶν
apostles. And when there was a rush ²of the

ἐθνῶν τε καὶ ᾽Ιουδαίων σὺν τοῖς ἄρχουσιν
¹nations ¹both ⁴and of Jews with the rulers

αὐτῶν ὑβρίσαι καὶ λιθοβολῆσαι αὐτούς,
of them to insult and to stone them,

6 συνιδόντες κατέφυγον εἰς τὰς πόλεις
perceiving they escaped to the cities

τῆς Λυκαονίας Λύστραν καὶ Δέρβην καὶ
- of Lycaonia Lystra and Derbe and

τὴν περίχωρον· 7 κἀκεῖ εὐαγγελιζόμενοι
the neighbourhood; and there evangelizing

ἦσαν. 8 Καὶ τις ἀνὴρ ἀδύνατος ἐν
they were. And a certain man impotent in

---

the Lord; and all who were appointed for eternal life believed.
49The word of the Lord spread through the whole region. 50But the Jews incited the God-fearing women of high standing and the leading men of the city. They stirred up persecution against Paul and Barnabas, and expelled them from their region. 51So they shook the dust from their feet in protest against them and went to Iconium. 52And the disciples were filled with joy and with the Holy Spirit.

Chapter 14

In Iconium

AT Iconium Paul and Barnabas went as usual into the Jewish synagogue. There they spoke so effectively that a great number of Jews and Gentiles believed. 2But the Jews who refused to believe stirred up the Gentiles and poisoned their minds against the brothers. 3So Paul and Barnabas spent considerable time there, speaking boldly for the Lord, who confirmed the message of his grace by enabling them to do miraculous signs and wonders. 4The people of the city were divided; some sided with the Jews, others with the apostles. 5There was a plot afoot among the Gentiles and Jews, together with their leaders, to mistreat them and stone them. 6But they found out about it and fled to the Lycaonian cities of Lystra and Derbe and to the surrounding country, 7where they continued to preach the good news.

In Lystra and Derbe

8In Lystra there sat a man crippled in his feet, who

out strength in his feet, lame from his mother's womb, who had never walked.

9This man was listening to Paul as he spoke, who, when he had fixed his gaze upon him, and had seen that he had faith to be made well,

10said with a loud voice, "Stand upright on your feet." And he leaped up and *began* to walk.

11And when the multitudes saw what Paul had done, they raised their voice, saying in the Lycaonian language, "The gods have become like men and have come down to us."

12And they *began* calling Barnabas, Zeus, and Paul, Hermes, because he was the chief speaker.

13And the priest of Zeus, whose *temple* was just outside the city, brought oxen and garlands to the gates, and wanted to offer sacrifice with the crowds.

14But when the apostles, Barnabas and Paul, heard of it, they tore their robes and rushed out into the crowd, crying out

15and saying, "Men, why are you doing these things? We are also men of the same nature as you, and preach the gospel to you in order that you should turn from these dvain things to a living God, WHO MADE THE HEAVEN AND THE EARTH AND THE SEA, AND ALL THAT IS IN THEM.

16"And in the generations gone by He permitted all the nations to go their own ways;

17and yet He did not leave Himself without witness, in that He did good and gave you rains from heaven and fruitful seasons, satisfying your hearts with food and gladness."

Λύστροις τοῖς ποσὶν ἐκάθητο, χωλὸς ἐκ
Lystra in the feet sat, lame from

κοιλίας μητρὸς αὐτοῦ ὃς οὐδέποτε
[the] womb of [the] mother of him who never

περιεπάτησεν. 9 οὗτος ἤκουεν τοῦ Παύλου
walked. This man heard - Paul

λαλοῦντος· ὃς ἀτενίσας αὐτῷ καὶ ἰδὼν
speaking; who gazing at him and seeing

ὅτι ἔχει πίστιν τοῦ σωθῆναι, 10 εἶπεν
that he has(had) faith - to be healed,d said

μεγάλῃ φωνῇ· ἀνάστηθι ἐπὶ τοὺς πόδας
with a voice: Stand up on the feet
great(loud)

σου ὀρθός. καὶ ἥλατο καὶ περιεπάτει.
of thee erect. And he leaped up and walked.

11 οἵ τε ὄχλοι ἰδόντες ὃ ἐποίησεν Παῦλος
And the crowds seeing what did Paul

ἐπῆραν τὴν φωνὴν αὐτῶν Λυκαονιστὶ
lifted up the voice of them in Lycaonian

λέγοντες· οἱ θεοὶ ὁμοιωθέντες ἀνθρώποις
saying: The gods made like men

κατέβησαν πρὸς ἡμᾶς, 12 ἐκάλουν τε τὸν
came down to us, and they called -

Βαρναβᾶν Δία, τὸν δὲ Παῦλον Ἑρμῆν,
Barnabas Zeus, - and Paul Hermes,

ἐπειδὴ αὐτὸς ἦν ὁ ἡγούμενος τοῦ λόγου.
since he was the leader of the discourse.

13 ὅ τε ἱερεὺς τοῦ Διὸς τοῦ ὄντος πρὸ
And the priest - of Zeus - being before

τῆς πόλεως, ταύρους καὶ στέμματα ἐπὶ
the city, bulls and garlands to

τοὺς πυλῶνας ἐνέγκας, σὺν τοῖς ὄχλοις
the gates bringing, with the crowds

ἤθελεν θύειν. 14 ἀκούσαντες δὲ οἱ
wished to sacrifice. But ehearing 1the

ἀπόστολοι Βαρναβᾶς καὶ Παῦλος, διαρ-
2apostles 3Barnabas 4and 5Paul, rend-

ρήξαντες τὰ ἱμάτια ἑαυτῶν ἐξεπήδησαν εἰς
ing the garments of themselves rushed out into

τὸν ὄχλον, κράζοντες 15 καὶ λέγοντες·
the crowd, crying out and saying:

ἄνδρες, τί ταῦτα ποιεῖτε; καὶ ἡμεῖς
Men, why these things do ye? 2also 1we

ὁμοιοπαθεῖς ἐσμεν ὑμῖν ἄνθρωποι, εὐαγ-
6of like nature 5are 6to you 4men, preach-

γελιζόμενοι ὑμᾶς ἀπὸ τούτων τῶν ματαίων
ing [to] you from these - vanities

ἐπιστρέφειν ἐπὶ θεὸν ζῶντα, ὃς ἐποίησεν
to turn to God a living, who made

τὸν οὐρανὸν καὶ τὴν γῆν καὶ τὴν
the heaven and the earth and the

θάλασσαν καὶ πάντα τὰ ἐν αὐτοῖς· 16 ὃς
sea and all the things in them; who

ἐν ταῖς παρῳχημέναις γενεαῖς εἴασεν πάντα
in the having passed generations allowed all

τὰ ἔθνη πορεύεσθαι ταῖς ὁδοῖς αὐτῶν·
the nations to go in the ways of them;

17 καίτοι οὐκ ἀμάρτυρον αὐτὸν ἀφῆκεν
and yet 2not 4unwitnessed 3himself 1left

ἀγαθουργῶν, οὐρανόθεν ὑμῖν ὑετοὺς διδοὺς
doing good, 4from heaven 5us 3rain 1giving

καὶ καιροὺς καρποφόρους, ἐμπιπλῶν τροφῆς
and times fruit-bearing, filling of(with) food

καὶ εὐφροσύνης τὰς καρδίας ὑμῶν. 18 καὶ
and of(with) gladness the hearts of us. And

---

was lame from birth and had never walked. 9He listened to Paul as he was speaking. Paul looked directly at him, saw that he had faith to be healed 10and called out, "Stand up on your feet!" At that, the man jumped up and began to walk.

11When the crowd saw what Paul had done, they shouted in the Lycaonian language, "The gods have come down to us in human form!" 12Barnabas they called Zeus, and Paul they called Hermes because he was the chief speaker. 13The priest of Zeus, whose temple was just outside the city, brought bulls and wreaths to the city gates because he and the crowd wanted to offer sacrifices to them.

14But when the apostles Barnabas and Paul heard of this, they tore their clothes and rushed out into the crowd, shouting: 15"Men, why are you doing this? We too are only men, human like you. We are bringing you good news, telling you to turn from these worthless things to the living God, who made heaven and earth and sea and everything in them. 16In the past, he let all nations go their own way. 17Yet he has not left himself without testimony: He has shown kindness by giving you rain from heaven and crops in their seasons; he provides you with plenty of food and fills your hearts with joy."

---

d I.e., idols

18And *even* saying these things, they with difficulty restrained the crowds from offering sacrifice to them. 19But Jews came from Antioch and Iconium, and having won over the multitudes, they stoned Paul and dragged him out of the city, supposing him to be dead. 20But while the disciples stood around him, he arose and entered the city. And the next day he went away with Barnabas to Derbe. 21And after they had preached the gospel to that city and had made many disciples, they returned to Lystra and to Iconium and to Antioch, 22strengthening the souls of the disciples, encouraging them to continue in the faith, and *saying*, "Through many tribulations we must enter the kingdom of God." 23And when they had appointed elders for them in every church, having prayed with fasting, they commended them to the Lord in whom they had believed. 24And they passed through Pisidia and came into Pamphylia. 25And when they had spoken the word in Perga, they went down to Attalia. 26and from there they sailed to Antioch, from which they had been commended to the grace of God for the work that they had accomplished. 27And when they had arrived and gathered the church together, they *began* to report all things that God had done with them and how He had opened a door of faith to the Gentiles. 28And they spent a long time with the disciples.

ταῦτα λέγοντες μόλις κατέπαυσαν τοὺς
these things saying scarcely they restrained the
ὄχλους τοῦ μὴ θύειν αὐτοῖς. 19 Ἐπῆλθαν
crowds - not to sacrifice[d] to them. [e]came upon [the scene]
δὲ ἀπὸ Ἀντιοχείας καὶ Ἰκονίου Ἰουδαῖοι,
And [a]from [a]Antioch [a]and [a]Iconium [a]Jews,
καὶ πείσαντες τοὺς ὄχλους καὶ λιθάσαντες
and persuading the crowds and stoning
τὸν Παῦλον ἔσυρον ἔξω τῆς πόλεως,
- Paul dragged outside the city,
νομίζοντες αὐτὸν τεθνηκέναι. 20 κυκλω-
supposing him to have died. But sur-
σάντων δὲ τῶν μαθητῶν αὐτὸν ἀναστὰς
rounding the disciples[a] him rising up
— as the disciples surrounded
εἰσῆλθεν εἰς τὴν πόλιν. Καὶ τῇ ἐπαύριον
he entered into the city. And on the morrow
ἐξῆλθεν σὺν τῷ Βαρναβᾷ εἰς Δέρβην.
he went forth with - Barnabas to Derbe.
21 εὐαγγελιζόμενοί τε τὴν πόλιν ἐκείνην
And evangelizing that city
καὶ μαθητεύσαντες ἱκανοὺς ὑπέστρεψαν εἰς
and having made disciples many they returned to
τὴν Λύστραν καὶ εἰς Ἰκόνιον καὶ [εἰς]
- Lystra and to Iconium and to
Ἀντιόχειαν, 22 ἐπιστηρίζοντες τὰς ψυχὰς
Antioch, confirming the minds
τῶν μαθητῶν, παρακαλοῦντες ἐμμένειν τῇ
of the disciples, exhorting to continue in the
πίστει, καὶ ὅτι διὰ πολλῶν θλίψεων
faith, and that through many afflictions
δεῖ ἡμᾶς εἰσελθεῖν εἰς τὴν βασιλείαν τοῦ
it behoves us to enter into the kingdom -
θεοῦ. 23 χειροτονήσαντες δὲ αὐτοῖς κατ᾽
of God. And having appointed for them in
ἐκκλησίαν πρεσβυτέρους, προσευξάμενοι
every church elders, praying
μετὰ νηστειῶν παρέθεντο αὐτοὺς τῷ κυρίῳ
with fastings they committed them to the Lord
εἰς ὃν πεπιστεύκεισαν. 24 καὶ διελθόντες
in whom they had believed. And passing through
τὴν Πισιδίαν ἦλθον εἰς τὴν Παμφυλίαν,
- Pisidia they came to - Pamphylia,
25 καὶ λαλήσαντες εἰς τὴν Πέργην τὸν
and speaking in - Perga the
λόγον κατέβησαν εἰς Ἀττάλειαν, κἀκεῖθεν
word they came down to Attalia, and thence
ἀπέπλευσαν εἰς Ἀντιόχειαν, 26 ὅθεν ἦσαν
sailed away to Antioch, whence they were
παραδεδομένοι τῇ χάριτι τοῦ θεοῦ εἰς
having been commended to the grace - of God for
τὸ ἔργον ὃ ἐπλήρωσαν. 27 Παραγεν-
the work which they accomplished. And having
όμενοι δὲ καὶ συναγαγόντες τὴν ἐκκλησίαν,
arrived and assembling the church,
ἀνήγγελλον ὅσα ἐποίησεν ὁ θεὸς μετ᾽
they reported what things did - God with
αὐτῶν, καὶ ὅτι ἤνοιξεν τοῖς ἔθνεσιν
them, and that he opened to the nations
θύραν πίστεως. 28 διέτριβον δὲ χρόνον
a door of faith. And they continued time
οὐκ ὀλίγον σὺν τοῖς μαθηταῖς.
not a little with the disciples.

18Even with these words, they had difficulty keeping the crowd from sacrificing to them. 19Then some Jews came from Antioch and Iconium and won the crowd over. They stoned Paul and dragged him outside the city, thinking he was dead. 20But after the disciples had gathered around him, he got up and went back into the city. The next day he and Barnabas left for Derbe.

The Return to Antioch in Syria

21They preached the good news in that city and won a large number of disciples. Then they returned to Lystra, Iconium and Antioch, 22strengthening the disciples and encouraging them to remain true to the faith. "We must go through many hardships to enter the kingdom of God," they said. 23Paul and Barnabas appointed elders[c] for them in each church and, with prayer and fasting, committed them to the Lord, in whom they had put their trust. 24After going through Pisidia, they came into Pamphylia, 25and when they had preached the word in Perga, they went down to Attalia. 26From Attalia they sailed back to Antioch, where they had been committed to the grace of God for the work they had now completed. 27On arriving there, they gathered the church together and reported all that God had done through them and how he had opened the door of faith to the Gentiles. 28And they stayed there a long time with the disciples.

c23 Or *Barnabas ordained elders;* or *Barnabas had elders elected*

Chapter 15

The Council at Jerusalem

AND some men came down from Judea and *began* teaching the brethren, "Unless you are circumcised according to the custom of Moses, you cannot be saved."

2And when Paul and Barnabas had great dissension and debate with them, *the brethren* determined that Paul and Barnabas and certain others of them should go up to Jerusalem to the apostles and elders concerning this issue.

3Therefore, being sent on their way by the church, they were passing through both Phoenicia and Samaria, describing in detail the conversion of the Gentiles, and were bringing great joy to all the brethren.

4And when they arrived at Jerusalem, they were received by the church and the apostles and the elders, and they reported all that God had done with them.

5But certain ones of the sect of the Pharisees who had believed, stood up, saying, "It is necessary to circumcise them, and to direct them to observe the Law of Moses."

6And the apostles and the elders came together to look into this matter.

7And after there had been much debate, Peter stood up and said to them, "Brethren, you know that in the early days God made a choice among you, that by my mouth the Gentiles should hear the word of the gospel and believe.

8"And God, who knows the heart, bore witness to

---

15 Καί τινες κατελθόντες ἀπὸ τῆς
And some going down from

'Ιουδαίας ἐδίδασκον τοὺς ἀδελφοὺς ὅτι
Judæa taught the brothers[,] –

ἐὰν μὴ περιτμηθῆτε τῷ ἔθει τῷ Μωϋσέως,
Unless ye are circumcised by the custom – of Moses,

οὐ δύνασθε σωθῆναι. **2** γενομένης δὲ
ye cannot to be saved. And taking place

στάσεως καὶ ζητήσεως οὐκ ὀλίγης τῷ
discord and questioning not a little[a] –
= when there took place not a little . . .

Παύλῳ καὶ τῷ Βαρναβᾷ πρὸς αὐτούς,
by Paul and – Barnabas with them,

ἔταξαν ἀναβαίνειν Παῦλον καὶ Βαρναβᾶν
they assigned to go up Paul and Barnabas

καὶ τινας ἄλλους ἐξ αὐτῶν πρὸς τοὺς
and some others of them to the

ἀποστόλους καὶ πρεσβυτέρους εἰς 'Ιερουσαλὴμ
apostles and elders in Jerusalem

περὶ τοῦ ζητήματος τούτου. **3** Οἱ μὲν
about this question. They –

οὖν προπεμφθέντες ὑπὸ τῆς ἐκκλησίας
therefore being set forward by the church

διήρχοντο τήν τε Φοινίκην καὶ Σαμάρειαν
passed through – both Phœnicia and Samaria

ἐκδιηγούμενοι τὴν ἐπιστροφὴν τῶν ἐθνῶν,
telling in detail the conversion of the nations,

καὶ ἐποίουν χαρὰν μεγάλην πᾶσιν τοῖς
and caused joy great to all the

ἀδελφοῖς. **4** παραγενόμενοι δὲ εἰς 'Ιεροσόλυμα
brothers. And having arrived in Jerusalem

παρεδέχθησαν ἀπὸ τῆς ἐκκλησίας καὶ τῶν
they were welcomed from the church and the

ἀποστόλων καὶ τῶν πρεσβυτερων, ἀνήγ-
apostles and the elders, and

γειλάν τε ὅσα ὁ θεὸς ἐποίησεν μετ'
reported what things – God did with

αὐτῶν. **5** 'Εξανέστησαν δέ τινες τῶν
them. But stood forth some of the [ones]

ἀπὸ τῆς αἱρέσεως τῶν Φαρισαίων
from the sect of the Pharisees

πεπιστευκότες, λέγοντες ὅτι δεῖ περιτέμνειν
having believed, saying[,] – It be- to circumcise
hoves

αὐτοὺς παραγγέλλειν τε τηρεῖν τὸν νόμον
them and to charge to keep the law

Μωϋσέως.
of Moses.

6 Συνήχθησάν τε οἱ ἀπόστολοι καὶ οἱ
And were assembled the apostles and the

πρεσβύτεροι ἰδεῖν περὶ τοῦ λόγου τούτου.
elders to see about this matter.

7 Πολλῆς δὲ ζητήσεως γενομένης ἀναστὰς
And much questioning having taken place[a] rising up
= When much questioning had . . .

Πέτρος εἶπεν πρὸς αὐτούς· ἄνδρες ἀδελφοί,
Peter said to them: Men brothers,

ὑμεῖς ἐπίστασθε ὅτι ἀφ' ἡμερῶν ἀρχαίων
ye understand that from days olden

ἐν ὑμῖν ἐξελέξατο ὁ θεὸς διὰ τοῦ στόματός
[a]among [4]you [3]chose – [1]God through the mouth

μου ἀκοῦσαι τὰ ἔθνη τὸν λόγον τοῦ
of me [2]to hear [1]the [2]nations the word of the

εὐαγγελίου καὶ πιστεῦσαι. **8** καὶ ὁ
gospel and to believe. And [1]the

καρδιογνώστης θεὸς ἐμαρτύρησεν αὐτοῖς
[2]Heart-knower [1]God witnessed to them

Chapter 15

The Council at Jerusalem

SOME men came down from Judea to Antioch and were teaching the brothers: "Unless you are circumcised, according to the custom taught by Moses, you cannot be saved."

2This brought Paul and Barnabas into sharp dispute and debate with them. So Paul and Barnabas were appointed, along with some other believers, to go up to Jerusalem to see the apostles and elders about this question. 3The church sent them on their way, and as they traveled through Phoenicia and Samaria, they told how the Gentiles had been converted. This news made all the brothers very glad. 4When they came to Jerusalem, they were welcomed by the church and the apostles and elders, to whom they reported everything God had done through them.

5Then some of the believers who belonged to the party of the Pharisees stood up and said, "The Gentiles must be circumcised and required to obey the law of Moses."

6The apostles and elders met to consider this question. 7After much discussion, Peter got up and addressed them: "Brothers, you know that some time ago God made a choice among you that the Gentiles might hear from my lips the message of the gospel and believe. 8God, who knows the heart, showed them, giving them the Holy Spirit, just as He also did to us;

9and He made no distinction between us and them, cleansing their hearts by faith.

10"Now therefore why do you put God to the test by placing upon the neck of the disciples a yoke which neither our fathers nor we have been able to bear?

11"But we believe that we are saved through the grace of the Lord Jesus, in the same way as they also are."

12And all the multitude kept silent, and they were listening to Barnabas and Paul as they were relating what signs and wonders God had done through them among the Gentiles.

James' Judgment

13And after they had stopped speaking, James answered, saying, "Brethren, listen to me.

14"Simeon has related how God first concerned Himself about taking from among the Gentiles a people for His name.

15"And with this the words of the Prophets agree, just as it is written,

16 'AFTER THESE THINGS I will return,
AND I WILL REBUILD THE TABERNACLE OF DAVID WHICH HAS FALLEN,
AND I WILL REBUILD ITS RUINS,
AND I WILL RESTORE IT,
17 IN ORDER THAT THE REST OF MANKIND MAY SEEK THE LORD,
AND ALL THE GENTILES WHO ARE CALLED BY MY NAME,'
18 SAYS THE LORD, WHO MAKES THESE THINGS KNOWN FROM OF OLD.

19"Therefore it is my judgment that we do not trouble those who are turning to God from among the Gentiles,

20but that we write to

δοὺς   τὸ   πνεῦμα   τὸ   ἅγιον   καθὼς   καὶ
giving   the   Spirit   -   Holy   as   also

ἡμῖν,   9 καὶ   οὐδὲν   διέκρινεν   μεταξὺ   ἡμῶν
to us,   and   nothing   distinguished   between   ³us

τε   καὶ   αὐτῶν,   τῇ   πίστει   καθαρίσας   τὰς
¹both and   them,   -   by faith   cleansing   the

καρδίας   αὐτῶν.   10 νῦν   οὖν   τί   πειράζετε
hearts   of them.   Now   therefore why   test ye

τὸν   θεόν,   ἐπιθεῖναι   ζυγὸν   ἐπὶ   τὸν
-      God,   to put on   a yoke   on   the

τράχηλον   τῶν   μαθητῶν,   ὃν   οὔτε   οἱ
neck   of the   disciples,   which neither   the

πατέρες   ἡμῶν   οὔτε   ἡμεῖς   ἰσχύσαμεν
fathers   of us   nor   we   were able

βαστάσαι;   11 ἀλλὰ   διὰ   τῆς   χάριτος   τοῦ
to bear?   but   through the   grace   of the

κυρίου.   Ἰησοῦ   πιστεύομεν   σωθῆναι   καθ'
Lord   Jesus   we believe   to be saved   in

ὃν   τρόπον   κἀκεῖνοι.   12 Ἐσίγησεν   δὲ
the same way as†   those also.   And was silent

πᾶν   τὸ   πλῆθος,   καὶ   ἤκουον   Βαρναβᾶ
all   the   multitude,   and   heard   Barnabas

καὶ   Παύλου   ἐξηγουμένων   ὅσα   ἐποίησεν
and   Paul   relating   ¹what   ⁴did

ὁ   θεὸς   σημεῖα   καὶ   τέρατα   ἐν   τοῖς
-    ²God   ³signs   ⁴and   ⁴wonders among   the

ἔθνεσιν   δι'   αὐτῶν.   13 Μετὰ   δὲ   τὸ   σιγῆσαι
nations   through   them.   And after   the to keep silence
                                                  =they kept silence

αὐτοὺς   ἀπεκρίθη   Ἰάκωβος   λέγων·   14 ἄνδρες
them⁵   answered   James   saying: Men

ἀδελφοί,   ἀκούσατέ   μου.   Συμεὼν   ἐξηγήσατο
brothers,   hear ye   me.   Simeon   declared

καθὼς   πρῶτον   ὁ   θεὸς   ἐπεσκέψατο   λαβεῖν   ἐξ
even as   firstly   -   God   visited   to take   out of

ἐθνῶν   λαὸν   τῷ   ὀνόματι   αὐτοῦ.   15 καὶ
[the] nations a people for the   name   of him.   And

τούτῳ   συμφωνοῦσιν   οἱ   λόγοι   τῶν   προφητῶν,
to this   agree   the   words   of the   prophets,

καθὼς   γέγραπται·   16 μετὰ   ταῦτα
even as   it has been written: After   these things

ἀναστρέψω   καὶ   ἀνοικοδομήσω   τὴν   σκηνὴν
I will return   and   I will rebuild   the   tent

Δαυὶδ   τὴν   πεπτωκυῖαν,   καὶ   τὰ   κατεστραμ-
of David   -   having fallen,   and   the   having been
                                                   things

μένα   αὐτῆς   ἀνοικοδομήσω   καὶ   ἀνορθώσω
overturned of it   I will rebuild   and   I will rear again
=its ruins

αὐτήν,   17 ὅπως   ἂν   ἐκζητήσωσιν   οἱ
it,   so as   -   ⁴may seek   ¹the

κατάλοιποι   τῶν   ἀνθρώπων   τὸν   κύριον,
²rest   -   ³of men   ⁵the   ⁶Lord,

καὶ   πάντα   τὰ   ἔθνη   ἐφ'   οὓς   ἐπικέκληται
even   all   the   nations   on   whom   has been invoked

τὸ   ὄνομά   μου   ἐπ'   αὐτούς,   λέγει   κύριος
the   name   of me   on   them,   says   [the] Lord

ποιῶν   ταῦτα   18 γνωστὰ   ἀπ'   αἰῶνος.
doing   these things   known   from   [the] age.

19 διὸ   ἐγὼ   κρίνω   μὴ   παρενοχλεῖν   τοῖς
Wherefore   I   decide   not   to trouble   the [ones]

ἀπὸ   τῶν   ἐθνῶν   ἐπιστρέφουσιν   ἐπὶ   τὸν
from   the   nations   turning   to   -

θεόν,   20 ἀλλὰ   ἐπιστεῖλαι   αὐτοῖς   τοῦ
God,   but   to write word   to them   -

---

that he accepted them by giving the Holy Spirit to them, just as he did to us. 9He made no distinction between us and them, for he purified their hearts by faith. 10Now then, why do you try to test God by putting on the necks of the disciples a yoke that neither we nor our fathers have been able to bear? 11No! We believe it is through the grace of our Lord Jesus that we are saved, just as they are."

12The whole assembly became silent as they listened to Barnabas and Paul telling about the miraculous signs and wonders God had done among the Gentiles through them. 13When they finished, James spoke up: "Brothers, listen to me. 14Simon*d* has described to us how God at first showed his concern by taking from the Gentiles a people for himself. 15The words of the prophets are in agreement with this, as it is written:

16" 'After this I will return and rebuild David's fallen tent.
Its ruins I will rebuild, and I will restore it,
17that the remnant of men may seek the Lord,
and all the Gentiles who bear my name,
says the Lord, who does these things'*e*
18 that have been known for ages.*f*

19"It is my judgment, therefore, that we should not make it difficult for the Gentiles who are turning to God. 20Instead we should write to them, telling them

---

*d*14 Greek *Simeon*, a variant of *Simon*; that is, Peter
*e*17 Amos 9:11,12
*f*17,18 Some manuscripts *things*— / 18*known to the Lord for ages is his work*

them that they abstain from things contaminated by idols and from fornication and from what is strangled and from blood.

21"For Moses from ancient generations has in every city those who preach him, since he is read in the synagogues every Sabbath."

22Then it seemed good to the apostles and the elders, with the whole church, to choose men from among them to send to Antioch with Paul and Barnabas— Judas called Barsabbas, and Silas, leading men among the brethren,

23and they sent this letter by them,

"The apostles and the brethren who are elders, to the brethren in Antioch and Syria and Cilicia who are from the Gentiles, greetings.

24"Since we have heard that some of our number to whom we gave no instruction have disturbed you with *their* words, unsettling your souls,

25 it seemed good to us, having become of one mind, to select men to send to you with our beloved Barnabas and Paul,

26 men who have risked their lives for the name of our Lord Jesus Christ.

27"Therefore we have sent Judas and Silas, who themselves will also report the same things by word *of mouth.*

28"For it seemed good to the Holy Spirit and to us to lay upon you no greater burden than these essentials:

29 that you abstain from things sacrificed to idols and from blood and from things strangled and from fornication; if you keep yourselves free from such

ἀπέχεσθαι τῶν ἀλισγημάτων τῶν εἰδώλων
to abstain from[d] the pollutions − of idols

καὶ τῆς πορνείας καὶ πνικτοῦ καὶ τοῦ
and − fornication and a thing strangled and −

αἵματος. 21 Μωϋσῆς γὰρ ἐκ γενεῶν
blood. For [1]Moses [2]from [4]generations

ἀρχαίων κατὰ πόλιν τοὺς κηρύσσοντας
[3]ancient [6]in every city [7]the [ones] [8]proclaiming

αὐτὸν ἔχει ἐν ταῖς συναγωγαῖς κατὰ
[9]him [5]has [11]in [12]the [13]synagogues [14]on

πᾶν σάββατον ἀναγινωσκόμενος. 22 Τότε
[15]every [16]sabbath [10]being read. Then

ἔδοξε τοῖς ἀποστόλοις καὶ τοῖς πρεσ-
it seemed [good] to the apostles and to the el-

βυτέροις σὺν ὅλῃ τῇ ἐκκλησίᾳ ἐκλεξαμένους
ders with all the church chosen

ἄνδρας ἐξ αὐτῶν πέμψαι εἰς Ἀντιόχειαν
men of them to send to Antioch

σὺν τῷ Παύλῳ καὶ Βαρναβᾷ, Ἰούδαν
with − Paul and Barnabas, Judas

τὸν καλούμενον Βαρσαββᾶν καὶ Σιλᾶν,
− being called Barsabbas and Silas,

ἄνδρας ἡγουμένους ἐν τοῖς ἀδελφοῖς,
men leading among the brothers,

23 γράψαντες διὰ χειρὸς αὐτῶν· Οἱ
writing through [the] hand of them: The

ἀπόστολοι καὶ οἱ πρεσβύτεροι ἀδελφοὶ
apostles and the elder brothers

τοῖς κατὰ τὴν Ἀντιόχειαν καὶ Συρίαν
[1]to the [2]throughout − [4]Antioch [5]and [6]Syria

καὶ Κιλικίαν ἀδελφοῖς τοῖς ἐξ ἐθνῶν
[8]and [10]Cilicia [3]brothers − [9]of [the] [4]nations

χαίρειν. 24 Ἐπειδὴ ἠκούσαμεν ὅτι τινὲς
[11]greeting. Since we heard that some

ἐξ ἡμῶν ἐτάραξαν ὑμᾶς λόγοις ἀνασκευάζ-
of us troubled you with words unsettl-

οντες τὰς ψυχὰς ὑμῶν, οἷς οὐ διεστειλάμεθα,
ing the minds of you, to whom we did not give commission,

25 ἔδοξεν ἡμῖν γενομένοις ὁμοθυμαδόν,
it seemed [good] to us becoming of one mind,

ἐκλεξαμένους ἄνδρας πέμψαι πρὸς ὑμᾶς
chosen men to send to you

σὺν τοῖς ἀγαπητοῖς ἡμῶν Βαρναβᾷ καὶ
with the beloved of us Barnabas and

Παύλῳ, 26 ἀνθρώποις παραδεδωκόσι τὰς
Paul, men having given up the

ψυχὰς αὐτῶν ὑπὲρ τοῦ ὀνόματος τοῦ
lives of them on behalf of the name of the

κυρίου ἡμῶν Ἰησοῦ Χριστοῦ. 27 ἀπεστάλ-
Lord of us Jesus Christ. We have

καμεν οὖν Ἰούδαν καὶ Σιλᾶν, καὶ αὐτοὺς
sent therefore Judas and Silas, and they

διὰ λόγου ἀπαγγέλλοντας τὰ αὐτά.
through speech announcing the same
(by) things.

28 ἔδοξεν γὰρ τῷ πνεύματι τῷ ἁγίῳ
For it seemed [good] to the Spirit − Holy

καὶ ἡμῖν μηδὲν πλέον ἐπιτίθεσθαι ὑμῖν
and to us [2]nothing [3]more [1]to be put on [4]you

βάρος πλὴν τούτων τῶν ἐπάναγκες,
[4]burden than these − necessary things,

29 ἀπέχεσθαι εἰδωλοθύτων καὶ αἵματος καὶ
to abstain from idol sacrifices and blood and

πνικτῶν καὶ πορνείας· ἐξ ὧν διατηροῦντες
things and fornication; from which keeping
strangled

to abstain from food polluted by idols, from sexual immorality, from the meat of strangled animals and from blood. 21For Moses has been preached in every city from the earliest times and is read in the synagogues on every Sabbath."

The Council's Letter to Gentile Believers

22Then the apostles and elders, with the whole church, decided to choose some of their own men and send them to Antioch with Paul and Barnabas. They chose Judas (called Barsabbas) and Silas, two men who were leaders among the brothers. 23With them they sent the following letter:

The apostles and elders, your brothers,

To the Gentile believers in Antioch, Syria and Cilicia:

Greetings.

24We have heard that some went out from us without our authorization and disturbed you, troubling your minds by what they said. 25So we all agreed to choose some men and send them to you with our dear friends Barnabas and Paul— 26men who have risked their lives for the name of our Lord Jesus Christ. 27Therefore we are sending Judas and Silas to confirm by word of mouth what we are writing. 28It seemed good to the Holy Spirit and to us not to burden you with anything beyond the following requirements: 29You are to abstain from food sacrificed to idols, from blood, from the meat of strangled animals and from sexual immorality.

things, you will do well. Farewell."

30So, . when they were sent away, they went down to Antioch; and having gathered the congregation together, they delivered the letter.

31And when they had read it, they rejoiced because of its encouragement.

32And Judas and Silas, also being prophets themselves, encouraged and strengthened the brethren with a lengthy message.

33And after they had spent time *there*, they were sent away from the brethren in peace to those who had sent them out.

34[ᵉBut it seemed good to Silas to remain there.]

35But Paul and Barnabas stayed in Antioch, teaching and preaching, with many others also, the word of the Lord.

Second Missionary Journey

36And after some days Paul said to Barnabas, "Let us return and visit the brethren in every city in which we proclaimed the word of the Lord, *and see how they are.*"

37And Barnabas was desirous of taking John, called Mark, along with them also.

38But Paul kept insisting that they should not take him along who had deserted them in Pamphylia and had not gone with them to the work.

39And there arose such a sharp disagreement that they separated from one another, and Barnabas took Mark with him and sailed away to Cyprus.

40But Paul chose Silas and departed, being committed by the brethren to the grace of the Lord.

41And he was traveling through Syria and Cilicia, strengthening the churches.

ἑαυτοὺς   εὖ   πράξετε.   Ἔρρωσθε.
yourselves   well   ye will do.   Farewell.

30 Οἱ   μὲν   οὖν   ἀπολυθέντες   κατῆλθον   εἰς
They   -   therefore   being dismissed   went down   to

Ἀντιόχειαν,   καὶ   συναγαγόντες   τὸ   πλῆθος
Antioch,   and   assembling   the   multitude

ἐπέδωκαν   τὴν   ἐπιστολήν.   31 ἀναγνόντες   δὲ
handed in   the   letter.   And having read

ἐχάρησαν   ἐπὶ   τῇ   παρακλήσει.   32 Ἰούδας   τε
they rejoiced   at   the   exhortation.   And Judas

καὶ   Σιλᾶς,   καὶ   αὐτοὶ   προφῆται   ὄντες,
and   Silas,   also   [them]selves   prophets   being,

διὰ   λόγου   πολλοῦ   παρεκάλεσαν   τοὺς
through   speech   much   exhorted   the
(by)

ἀδελφοὺς   καὶ   ἐπεστήριξαν·   33 ποιήσαντες   δὲ
brothers   and   confirmed;   and having continued

χρόνον   ἀπελύθησαν   μετ'   εἰρήνης   ἀπὸ
a time   they were dismissed   with   peace   from

τῶν   ἀδελφῶν   πρὸς   τοὺς   ἀποστείλαντας
the   brothers   to   the [ones]   having sent

αὐτούς.   ‡ 35 Παῦλος   δὲ   καὶ   Βαρναβᾶς
them.   But Paul   and   Barnabas

διέτριβον   ἐν   Ἀντιοχείᾳ,   διδάσκοντες   καὶ
stayed   in   Antioch,   teaching   and

εὐαγγελιζόμενοι   μετὰ   καὶ   ἑτέρων   πολλῶν
preaching   ¹with   ⁴also   ³others   ²many

τὸν   λόγον   τοῦ   κυρίου.
the   word   of the   Lord.

36 Μετὰ   δέ   τινας   ἡμέρας   εἶπεν   πρὸς
Now after   some   days   ²said   ¹to

Βαρναβᾶν   Παῦλος·   ἐπιστρέψαντες   δὴ
⁴Barnabas   ¹Paul: Returning   then

ἐπισκεψώμεθα   τοὺς   ἀδελφοὺς   κατὰ   πόλιν
let us visit   the   brothers   throughout   ²city

πᾶσαν   ἐν   αἷς   κατηγγείλαμεν   τὸν   λόγον
¹every   in   which   we announced   the   word

τοῦ   κυρίου,   πῶς   ἔχουσιν.   37 Βαρναβᾶς
of the   Lord,   how   they have(are).   Barnabas

δὲ   ἐβούλετο   συμπαραλαβεῖν   καὶ   τὸν
And   wished   to take with [them]   also   -

Ἰωάννην   τὸν   καλούμενον   Μᾶρκον·   38 Παῦλος
John   -   *being* called   Mark;   ²Paul

δὲ   ἠξίου,   τὸν   ἀποστάντα   ἀπ'   αὐτῶν
¹but   ³thought fit,   -   ⁷withdrawing   ⁸from   ⁹them

ἀπὸ   Παμφυλίας   καὶ   μὴ   συνελθόντα   αὐτοῖς
¹⁰from   ¹¹Pamphylia   ¹²and   ¹³not   ¹⁴going with   ¹⁵them

εἰς   τὸ   ἔργον,   μὴ   συμπαραλαμβάνειν   τοῦτον.
¹⁶to   ¹⁷the   ¹⁸work,   ⁴not   ⁵to take with [them]   ⁶this one.

39 ἐγένετο   δὲ   παροξυσμός,   ὥστε   ἀποχωρισ-
And there was   sharp feeling,   so as   to separ-

θῆναι   αὐτοὺς   ἀπ'   ἀλλήλων,   τόν   τε
ate   them   from   each other,   -   and

Βαρναβᾶν   παραλαβόντα   τὸν   Μᾶρκον
Barnabas   taking   -   Mark

ἐκπλεῦσαι   εἰς   Κύπρον.   40 Παῦλος   δὲ
to sail away   to   Cyprus.   But Paul

ἐπιλεξάμενος   Σιλᾶν   ἐξῆλθεν,   παραδοθεὶς
having chosen   Silas   went forth,   being commended

τῇ   χάριτι   τοῦ   κυρίου   ὑπὸ   τῶν
to the   grace   of the   Lord   by   the

ἀδελφῶν·   41 διήρχετο   δὲ   τὴν   Συρίαν
brothers;   and he went through   -   Syria

καὶ   Κιλικίαν   ἐπιστηρίζων   τὰς   ἐκκλησίας.
and   Cilicia   confirming   the   churches.

You will do well to avoid these things.

Farewell.

30The men were sent off and went down to Antioch, where they gathered the church together and delivered the letter. 31The people read it and were glad for its encouraging message. 32Judas and Silas, who themselves were prophets, said much to encourage and strengthen the brothers. 33After spending some time there, they were sent off by the brothers with the blessing of peace to return to those who had sent them. ᵍ 35But Paul and Barnabas remained in Antioch, where they and many others taught and preached the word of the Lord.

Disagreement Between Paul and Barnabas

36Some time later Paul said to Barnabas, "Let us go back and visit the brothers in all the towns where we preached the word of the Lord and see how they are doing." 37Barnabas wanted to take John, also called Mark, with them, 38but Paul did not think it wise to take him, because he had deserted them in Pamphylia and had not continued with them in the work. 39They had such a sharp disagreement that they parted company. Barnabas took Mark and sailed for Cyprus, 40but Paul chose Silas and left, commended by the brothers to the grace of the Lord. 41He went through Syria and Cilicia, strengthening the churches.

ᵉMany mss. do not contain this verse

‡ Verse 34 omitted by Nestle; *cf.* NIV

ᵍ33 Some manuscripts *them,* 34*but Silas decided to remain there*

Chapter 16

The Macedonian Vision

AND he came also to Derbe and to Lystra. And behold, a certain disciple was there, named Timothy, the son of a Jewish woman who was a believer, but his father was a Greek, 2and he was well spoken of by the brethren who were in Lystra and Iconium.

3Paul wanted this man to go with him; and he took him and circumcised him because of the Jews who were in those parts, for they all knew that his father was a Greek. 4Now while they were passing through the cities, they were delivering the decrees, which had been decided upon by the apostles and elders who were in Jerusalem, for them to observe. 5So the churches were being strengthened in the faith, and were increasing in number daily.

6And they passed through the Phrygian and Galatian region, having been forbidden by the Holy Spirit to speak the word in Asia; 7and when they had come to Mysia, they were trying to go into Bithynia, and the Spirit of Jesus did not permit them; 8and passing by Mysia, they came down to Troas. 9And a vision appeared to Paul in the night: a certain man of Macedonia was standing and appealing to him, and saying, "Come over to Macedonia and help us."

10And when he had seen the vision, immediately we sought to go into Macedonia, concluding that God had called us to preach the

---

16 Κατήντησεν δὲ καὶ εἰς Δέρβην καὶ
And he came down also to Derbe and
εἰς Λύστραν. καὶ ἰδοὺ μαθητής τις ἦν
to Lystra. And behold[,] a certain disciple was
ἐκεῖ ὀνόματι Τιμόθεος, υἱὸς γυναικὸς
there by name Timothy, son ²woman
Ἰουδαίας πιστῆς πατρὸς δὲ Ἕλληνος,
¹Jewish ¹of a faithful ⁴but ⁵father ⁶of a Greek,
2 ὃς ἐμαρτυρεῖτο ὑπὸ τῶν ἐν Λύστροις
who was witnessed to by ¹the ²in ⁴Lystra
καὶ Ἰκονίῳ ἀδελφῶν. 3 τοῦτον ἠθέλησεν
⁵and ⁶Iconium ³brothers. ²This one ¹wished
ὁ Παῦλος σὺν αὐτῷ ἐξελθεῖν, καὶ λαβὼν
- ¹Paul with him to go forth, and taking
περιέτεμεν αὐτὸν διὰ τοὺς Ἰουδαίους τοὺς
circumcised him on account the Jews -
of
ὄντας ἐν τοῖς τόποις ἐκείνοις· ᾔδεισαν
being in those places; ²they knew
γὰρ ἅπαντες ὅτι Ἕλλην ὁ πατὴρ αὐτοῦ
¹for all that a Greek the father of him
ὑπῆρχεν. 4 Ὡς δὲ διεπορεύοντο τὰς
was. Now as they went through the
πόλεις, παρεδίδοσαν αὐτοῖς φυλάσσειν τὰ
cities, they delivered to them* to keep the
δόγματα τὰ κεκριμένα ὑπὸ τῶν ἀποστόλων
decrees - having been by the apostles
decided [on]
καὶ πρεσβυτέρων τῶν ἐν Ἱεροσολύμοις.
and elders - in Jerusalem.
5 Αἱ μὲν οὖν ἐκκλησίαι ἐστερεοῦντο
¹The - ¹therefore ³churches were strengthened
τῇ πίστει καὶ ἐπερίσσευον τῷ ἀριθμῷ
in the faith and increased - in number
καθ' ἡμέραν.
daily.
6 Διῆλθον δὲ τὴν Φρυγίαν καὶ Γαλατικὴν
And they went through the Phrygian and Galatian
χώραν, κωλυθέντες ὑπὸ τοῦ ἁγίου
country, being prevented by the Holy
πνεύματος λαλῆσαι τὸν λόγον ἐν τῇ
Spirit to 'speak the word in the
=from speaking
Ἀσίᾳ· 7 ἐλθόντες δὲ κατὰ τὴν Μυσίαν
Asia; but coming against - Mysia
ἐπείραζον εἰς τὴν Βιθυνίαν πορευθῆναι,
they attempted into - Bithynia to go,
καὶ οὐκ εἴασεν αὐτοὺς τὸ πνεῦμα Ἰησοῦ·
and ⁵not ⁴allowed ⁶them ¹the ²Spirit ³of Jesus;
8 παρελθόντες δὲ τὴν Μυσίαν κατέβησαν
so passing by - Mysia they came down
εἰς Τρῳάδα. 9 καὶ ὅραμα διὰ νυκτὸς
to Troas. And a vision through [the]
(during) night
τῷ Παύλῳ ὤφθη, ἀνὴρ Μακεδών τις
- to Paul appeared, a man Macedonian certain
ἦν ἑστὼς καὶ παρακαλῶν αὐτὸν καὶ
was standing and beseeching him and
λέγων· διαβὰς εἰς Μακεδονίαν βοήθησον
saying: Crossing into Macedonia help
ἡμῖν. 10 ὡς δὲ τὸ ὅραμα εἶδεν, εὐθέως
us. So when the vision he saw, immediately
ἐζητήσαμεν ἐξελθεῖν εἰς Μακεδονίαν,
we sought to go forth to Macedonia,
συμβιβάζοντες ὅτι προσκέκληται ἡμᾶς ὁ
concluding that ³has(had) called ²us -

* Note the gender: πόλις is feminine.

Chapter 16

Timothy Joins Paul and Silas

HE came to Derbe and then to Lystra, where a disciple named Timothy lived, whose mother was a Jewess and a believer, but whose father was a Greek. 2The brothers at Lystra and Iconium spoke well of him. 3Paul wanted to take him along on the journey, so he circumcised him because of the Jews who lived in that area, for they all knew that his father was a Greek. 4As they traveled from town to town, they delivered the decisions reached by the apostles and elders in Jerusalem for the people to obey. 5So the churches were strengthened in the faith and grew daily in numbers.

Paul's Vision of the Man of Macedonia

6Paul and his companions traveled throughout the region of Phrygia and Galatia, having been kept by the Holy Spirit from preaching the word in the province of Asia. 7When they came to the border of Mysia, they tried to enter Bithynia, but the Spirit of Jesus would not allow them to. 8So they passed by Mysia and went down to Troas. 9During the night Paul had a vision of a man of Macedonia standing and begging him, "Come over to Macedonia and help us." 10After Paul had seen the vision, we got ready at once to leave for Macedonia, concluding that God had called us to

gospel to them.
11Therefore putting out to sea from Troas, we ran a straight course to Samothrace, and on the day following to Neapolis;
12and from there to Philippi, which is a leading city of the district of Macedonia, a *Roman* colony; and we were staying in this city for some days.
13And on the Sabbath day we went outside the gate to a riverside, where we were supposing that there would be a place of prayer; and we sat down and began speaking to the women who had assembled.

First Convert in Europe

14And a certain woman named Lydia, from the city of Thyatira, a seller of purple fabrics, a worshiper of God, was listening; and the Lord opened her heart to respond to the things spoken by Paul.
15And when she and her household had been baptized, she urged us, saying, "If you have judged me to be faithful to the Lord, come into my house and stay." And she prevailed upon us.
16And it happened that as we were going to the place of prayer, a certain slave-girl having a spirit of divination met us, who was bringing her masters much profit by fortunetelling.
17Following after Paul and us, she kept crying out, saying, "These men are bond-servants of the Most High God, who are proclaiming to you the way of salvation."
18And she continued doing this for many days. But Paul was greatly annoyed, and turned and said to the spirit, "I command you in the name of Jesus Christ to come out of her!" And it came out at that very moment.

θεὸς   εὐαγγελίσασθαι   αὐτούς.
¹God   to evangelize   them.

11 Ἀναχθέντες   δὲ   ἀπὸ   Τρῳάδος   εὐθυδρο-
And setting sail   from   Troas   we ran a

μήσαμεν   εἰς   Σαμοθρᾴκην,   τῇ   δὲ   ἐπιούσῃ
straight course to   Samothracia,   and on the   next day

εἰς   Νέαν   πόλιν,   12 κἀκεῖθεν   εἰς   Φιλίππους,
to   Neapolis,   and thence to   Philippi,

ἥτις   ἐστὶν   πρώτη   τῆς   μερίδος   Μακεδονίας
which   is   ¹[the] ⁴first   ⁴of the   ⁵part   ⁶of Macedonia

πόλις,   κολωνία.   Ἦμεν   δὲ   ἐν   ταύτῃ   τῇ
²city,   a colony.   And we were   in   this   —

πόλει   διατρίβοντες   ἡμέρας   τινάς.   13 τῇ   τε
city   staying   days   some.   And on the

ἡμέρᾳ   τῶν   σαββάτων   ἐξήλθομεν   ἔξω   τῆς
day   of the   sabbaths   we went forth   outside   the

πύλης   παρὰ   ποταμὸν   οὗ   ἐνομίζομεν
gate   by   a river   where   we supposed

προσευχὴν   εἶναι,   καὶ   καθίσαντες   ἐλαλοῦμεν
a place of prayer to be,   and   sitting   we spoke

ταῖς   συνελθούσαις   γυναιξίν.   14 καί   τις
to the   ²coming together   ¹women.   And a certain

γυνὴ   ὀνόματι   Λυδία,   πορφυρόπωλις
woman   by name   Lydia,   a dealer in purple-dyed [garments]

πόλεως   Θυατίρων,   σεβομένη   τὸν   θεόν,
of [the] city   of Thyatira,   worshipping   —   God,

ἤκουεν,   ἧς   ὁ   κύριος   διήνοιξεν   τὴν   καρδίαν
heard,   of whom   the   Lord   opened up   the   heart

προσέχειν   τοῖς   λαλουμένοις   ὑπὸ   Παύλου.
to take heed to the things   being spoken   by   Paul.

15 ὡς   δὲ   ἐβαπτίσθη   καὶ   ὁ   οἶκος   αὐτῆς,
And when   she was baptized   and   the   household   of her,

παρεκάλεσεν   λέγουσα·   εἰ   κεκρίκατέ   με
she besought   saying: If   ye have decided   me

πιστὴν   τῷ   κυρίῳ   εἶναι,   εἰσελθόντες   εἰς
faithful   to the   Lord   to be,   entering   into

τὸν   οἶκόν   μου   μένετε·   καὶ   παρεβιάσατο
the   house   of me   remain;   and   she urged

ἡμᾶς.   16 Ἐγένετο   δὲ   πορευομένων   ἡμῶν
us.   And it happened   going   us⁴
   =as we went

εἰς   τὴν   προσευχήν,   παιδίσκην   τινὰ   ἔχουσαν
to   the   place of prayer,   a certain maid   having

πνεῦμα   πύθωνα   ὑπαντῆσαι   ἡμῖν,   ἥτις
a spirit   of a python   to meet   us,   who

ἐργασίαν   πολλὴν   παρεῖχεν   τοῖς   κυρίοις
²gain   ¹much   ¹brought   to the   masters

αὐτῆς   μαντευομένη.   17 αὕτη   κατακολουθοῦσα
of her   practising soothsaying.   This one   following after

τῷ   Παύλῳ   καὶ   ἡμῖν   ἔκραζεν   λέγουσα·
—   Paul   and   us   cried out   saying:

οὗτοι   οἱ   ἄνθρωποι   δοῦλοι   τοῦ   θεοῦ   τοῦ
These   —   men   slaves   of the   God   —

ὑψίστου   εἰσίν,   οἵτινες   καταγγέλλουσιν   ὑμῖν
most high   are,   who   announce   to you

ὁδὸν   σωτηρίας.   18 τοῦτο   δὲ   ἐποίει   ἐπὶ
a way   of salvation.   And this   she did   over

πολλὰς   ἡμέρας.   διαπονηθεὶς   δὲ   Παῦλος
many   days.   But becoming greatly troubled   Paul

καὶ   ἐπιστρέψας   τῷ   πνεύματι   εἶπεν·   παραγ-
and   turning   ²to the   ⁸spirit   ¹he said: I

γέλλω   σοι   ἐν   ὀνόματι   Ἰησοῦ   Χριστοῦ
charge   thee   in   [the] name   of Jesus   Christ

ἐξελθεῖν   ἀπ’   αὐτῆς·   καὶ   ἐξῆλθεν   αὐτῇ
to come out   from   her;   and   it came out   in the

---

preach the gospel to them.

Lydia's Conversion in Philippi

11From Troas we put out to sea and sailed straight for Samothrace, and the next day on to Neapolis.
12From there we traveled to Philippi, a Roman colony and the leading city of that district of Macedonia. And we stayed there several days.
13On the Sabbath we went outside the city gate to the river, where we expected to find a place of prayer. We sat down and began to speak to the women who had gathered there.
14One of those listening was a woman named Lydia, a dealer in purple cloth from the city of Thyatira, who was a worshiper of God. The Lord opened her heart to respond to Paul's message. 15When she and the members of her household were baptized, she invited us to her home. "If you consider me a believer in the Lord," she said, "come and stay at my house." And she persuaded us.

Paul and Silas in Prison

16Once when we were going to the place of prayer, we were met by a slave girl who had a spirit by which she predicted the future. She earned a great deal of money for her owners by fortune-telling. 17This girl followed Paul and the rest of us, shouting, "These men are servants of the Most High God, who are telling you the way to be saved." 18She kept this up for many days. Finally Paul became so troubled that he turned around and said to the spirit, "In the name of Jesus Christ I command you to come out of her!" At that moment the spirit left her.

19But when her masters saw that their hope of profit was gone, they seized Paul and Silas and dragged them into the market place before the authorities,

20and when they had brought them to the chief magistrates, they said, "These men are throwing our city into confusion, being Jews,

21and are proclaiming customs which it is not lawful for us to accept or to observe, being Romans."

Paul and Silas Imprisoned

22And the crowd rose up together against them, and the chief magistrates tore their robes off them, and proceeded to order *them* to be beaten with rods.

23And when they had inflicted many blows upon them, they threw them into prison, commanding the jailer to guard them securely;

24and he, having received such a command, threw them into the inner prison, and fastened their feet in the stocks.

25But about midnight Paul and Silas were praying and singing hymns of praise to God, and the prisoners were listening to them;

26and suddenly there came a great earthquake, so that the foundations of the prison house were shaken; and immediately all the doors were opened, and everyone's chains were unfastened.

27And when the jailer had been roused out of sleep and had seen the prison doors opened, he drew his sword and was about to kill himself, supposing that the prisoners had escaped.

28But Paul cried out with a loud voice, saying, "Do yourself no harm, for we are all here!"

29And he called for lights

τῇ ὥρᾳ. 19 Ἰδόντες δὲ οἱ κύριοι αὐτῆς
same hour.* And ⁶seeing ¹the ²masters ³of her
ὅτι ἐξῆλθεν ἡ ἐλπὶς τῆς ἐργασίας αὐτῶν,
⁴that ¹¹went out ⁶the ⁷hope ⁸of the ⁹gain ¹⁰of them,
ἐπιλαβόμενοι τὸν Παῦλον καὶ τὸν Σιλᾶν
having seized – Paul and – Silas
εἵλκυσαν εἰς τὴν ἀγορὰν ἐπὶ τοὺς ἄρχοντας,
dragged to the marketplace before the rulers,
20 καὶ προσαγαγόντες αὐτοὺς τοῖς στρατηγοῖς
and ¹bringing ²to ³them the prætors
εἶπαν· οὗτοι οἱ ἄνθρωποι ἐκταράσσουσιν
said: These – men are greatly troubling
ἡμῶν τὴν πόλιν, Ἰουδαῖοι ὑπάρχοντες,
of us the city, ²Jews ¹being,
21 καὶ καταγγέλλουσιν ἔθη ἃ οὐκ ἔξεστιν
and they announce customs which it is not lawful
ἡμῖν παραδέχεσθαι οὐδὲ ποιεῖν Ῥωμαίοις
for us to receive nor to do ¹Romans
οὖσιν. 22 καὶ συνεπέστη ὁ ὄχλος κατ'
¹being. And rose up together the crowd against
αὐτῶν, καὶ οἱ στρατηγοὶ περιρήξαντες
them, and the prætors tearing off
αὐτῶν τὰ ἱμάτια ἐκέλευον ῥαβδίζειν,
of them the garments commanded to flog,
23 πολλὰς δὲ ἐπιθέντες αὐτοῖς πληγὰς
and ²many ¹laying on ³them ⁴stripes
ἔβαλον εἰς φυλακήν, παραγγείλαντες τῷ
threw into prison, charging the
δεσμοφύλακι ἀσφαλῶς τηρεῖν αὐτούς· 24 ὃς
jailer securely to keep them; who
παραγγελίαν τοιαύτην λαβὼν ἔβαλεν αὐτοὺς
²a charge ²such ¹having received threw them
εἰς τὴν ἐσωτέραν φυλακὴν καὶ τοὺς
into the inner prison and ⁵the
πόδας ἠσφαλίσατο αὐτῶν εἰς τὸ ξύλον.
³feet ¹secured ⁴of them in the stocks.
25 Κατὰ δὲ τὸ μεσονύκτιον Παῦλος καὶ
And about – midnight Paul and
Σιλᾶς προσευχόμενοι ὕμνουν τὸν θεόν,
Silas praying ³praised ²in a hymn – ¹God,
ἐπηκροῶντο δὲ αὐτῶν οἱ δέσμιοι· 26 ἄφνω δὲ
and ³listened to ⁴them ¹the ²prisoners; and suddenly
σεισμὸς ἐγένετο μέγας, ὥστε σαλευ-
³earthquake ¹there was ²a great, so as to be
θῆναι τὰ θεμέλια τοῦ δεσμωτηρίου·
shaken the foundations of the jail;
ἠνεῴχθησαν δὲ παραχρῆμα αἱ θύραι πᾶσαι,
and ⁵were opened ¹at once ²the ⁴doors ³all,
καὶ πάντων τὰ δεσμὰ ἀνέθη. 27 ἔξυπνος δὲ
and ²of all ¹the ³bonds were And ⁴awake
loosened.
γενόμενος ὁ δεσμοφύλαξ καὶ ἰδὼν
³having become ¹the ²jailer and seeing
ἀνεῳγμένας τὰς θύρας τῆς φυλακῆς,
having been opened the doors of the prison,
σπασάμενος τὴν μάχαιραν ἤμελλεν ἑαυτὸν
having drawn the sword was about himself
ἀναιρεῖν, νομίζων ἐκπεφευγέναι τοὺς
to kill, supposing to have escaped the
δεσμίους. 28 ἐφώνησεν δὲ Παῦλος μεγάλῃ
prisoners. But called – Paul with a
great(loud)
φωνῇ λέγων· μηδὲν πράξῃς σεαυτῷ κακόν,
voice saying: ¹Nothing ²do ⁴thyself ³harm,
ἅπαντες γάρ ἐσμεν ἐνθάδε. 29 αἰτήσας
for ²all ¹we are ³here. asking

* See Luke 2. 38.

19When the owners of the slave girl realized that their hope of making money was gone, they seized Paul and Silas and dragged them into the marketplace to face the authorities. 20They brought them before the magistrates and said, "These men are Jews, and are throwing our city into an uproar 21by advocating customs unlawful for us Romans to accept or practice."

22The crowd joined in the attack against Paul and Silas, and the magistrates ordered them to be stripped and beaten. 23After they had been severely flogged, they were thrown into prison, and the jailer was commanded to guard them carefully. 24Upon receiving such orders, he put them in the inner cell and fastened their feet in the stocks.

25About midnight Paul and Silas were praying and singing hymns to God, and the other prisoners were listening to them. 26Suddenly there was such a violent earthquake that the foundations of the prison were shaken. At once all the prison doors flew open, and everybody's chains came loose. 27The jailer woke up, and when he saw the prison doors open, he drew his sword and was about to kill himself because he thought the prisoners had escaped. 28But Paul shouted, "Don't harm yourself! We are all here!"

29The jailer called for

and rushed in and, trembling with fear, he fell down before Paul and Silas,

³⁰and after he brought them out, he said, "Sirs, what must I do to be saved?"

The Jailer Converted

³¹And they said, "Believe in the Lord Jesus, and you shall be saved, you and your household."

³²And they spoke the word of the Lord to him together with all who were in his house.

³³And he took them that *very* hour of the night and washed their wounds, and immediately he was baptized, he and all his *household.*

³⁴And he brought them into his house and set food before them, and rejoiced greatly, having believed in God with his whole household.

³⁵Now when day came, the chief magistrates sent their policemen, saying, "Release those men."

³⁶And the jailer reported these words to Paul, *saying,* "The chief magistrates have sent to release you. Now therefore, come out and go in peace."

³⁷But Paul said to them, "They have beaten us in public without trial, men who are Romans, and have thrown us into prison; and now are they sending us away secretly? No indeed! But let them come themselves and bring us out."

³⁸And the policemen reported these words to the chief magistrates. And they were afraid when they heard that they were Romans,

³⁹and they came and appealed to them, and when they had brought them out, they kept begging them to

δὲ φῶτα εἰσεπήδησεν, καὶ ἔντρομος
And lights he rushed in, and trembling

γενόμενος προσέπεσεν τῷ Παύλῳ καὶ
becoming he fell before — Paul and

Σιλᾷ, 30 καὶ προαγαγὼν αὐτοὺς ἔξω ἔφη·
Silas, and ¹leading ³forward ²them outside said :

κύριοι, τί με δεῖ ποιεῖν ἵνα σωθῶ;
Sirs, what ²me ¹behoves it to do that I may be saved?

31 οἱ δὲ εἶπαν· πίστευσον ἐπὶ τὸν κύριον
And they said: Believe on the Lord

'Ιησοῦν, καὶ σωθήσῃ σὺ καὶ ὁ οἶκός
Jesus, and shalt be saved thou and the household

σου. 32 καὶ ἐλάλησαν αὐτῷ τὸν λόγον
of thee. And they spoke to him the word

τοῦ θεοῦ σὺν πᾶσιν τοῖς ἐν τῇ οἰκίᾳ
— of God with all the [ones] in the house

αὐτοῦ. 33 καὶ παραλαβὼν αὐτοὺς ἐν
of him. And taking them in

ἐκείνῃ τῇ ὥρᾳ τῆς νυκτὸς ἔλουσεν ἀπὸ
that hour of the night he washed from

τῶν πληγῶν, καὶ ἐβαπτίσθη αὐτὸς καὶ
the stripes, and was baptized he and

οἱ αὐτοῦ ἅπαντες παραχρῆμα, 34 ἀναγαγών
the of him all at once, ²bringing up

τε αὐτοὺς εἰς τὸν οἶκον παρέθηκεν
¹and them to the house he set [them]
= all his before [them]

τράπεζαν, καὶ ἠγαλλιάσατο πανοικεὶ πεπι-
a table, and exulted with all the having
household

στευκὼς τῷ θεῷ. 35 'Ημέρας δὲ γενομένης
believed — God. And day coming
= when day came

ἀπέστειλαν οἱ στρατηγοὶ τοὺς ῥαβδούχους
²sent ¹the ²prætors the tipstaffs

λέγοντες· ἀπόλυσον τοὺς ἀνθρώπους
saying: Release — men

ἐκείνους. 36 ἀπήγγειλεν δὲ ὁ δεσμοφύλαξ
those. And announced the jailer

τοὺς λόγους τούτους πρὸς τὸν Παῦλον,
these words to — Paul,

ὅτι ἀπέσταλκαν οἱ στρατηγοὶ ἵνα ἀπολυθῆτε.
— ²have sent ¹The ²prætors that ye may be
released.

νῦν οὖν ἐξελθόντες πορεύεσθε ἐν εἰρήνῃ.
Now therefore going forth proceed in peace.

37 ὁ δὲ Παῦλος ἔφη πρὸς αὐτούς·
— But Paul said to them:

δείραντες ἡμᾶς δημοσίᾳ ἀκατακρίτους,
Having beaten us publicly uncondemned,

ἀνθρώπους 'Ρωμαίους ὑπάρχοντας, ἔβαλαν
men ²Romans ¹being, they threw [us]

εἰς φυλακήν· καὶ νῦν λάθρα ἡμᾶς ἐκβάλ-
into prison; and now secretly us they

λουσιν; οὐ γάρ, ἀλλὰ ἐλθόντες αὐτοὶ
expel? No indeed, but coming [them]selves

ἡμᾶς ἐξαγαγέτωσαν. 38 ἀπήγγειλαν δὲ τοῖς
us let them bring out. And ²reported ⁴to the

στρατηγοῖς οἱ ῥαβδοῦχοι τὰ ῥήματα ταῦτα.
³prætors ¹the ²tipstaffs these words.

ἐφοβήθησαν δὲ ἀκούσαντες ὅτι 'Ρωμαῖοί
And they were afraid hearing that Romans

εἰσιν, 39 καὶ ἐλθόντες παρεκάλεσαν
they are(were), and coming besought

αὐτούς, καὶ ἐξαγαγόντες ἠρώτων ἀπελθεῖν
them, and bringing out asked to go away

lights, rushed in and fell trembling before Paul and Silas. ³⁰He then brought them out and asked, "Sirs, what must I do to be saved?"

³¹They replied, "Believe in the Lord Jesus, and you will be saved—you and your household." ³²Then they spoke the word of the Lord to him and to all the others in his house. ³³At that hour of the night the jailer took them and washed their wounds; then immediately he and all his family were baptized. ³⁴The jailer brought them into his house and set a meal before them; he was filled with joy because he had come to believe in God —he and his whole family.

³⁵When it was daylight, the magistrates sent their officers to the jailer with the order: "Release those men." ³⁶The jailer told Paul, "The magistrates have ordered that you and Silas be released. Now you can leave. Go in peace."

³⁷But Paul said to the officers: "They beat us publicly without a trial, even though we are Roman citizens, and threw us into prison. And now do they want to get rid of us quietly? No! Let them come themselves and escort us out."

³⁸The officers reported this to the magistrates, and when they heard that Paul and Silas were Roman citizens, they were alarmed. ³⁹They came to appease them and escorted them from the prison, requesting

leave the city.
40And they went out of the prison and entered *the house* of Lydia, and when they saw the brethren, they encouraged them and departed.

Chapter 17

Paul at Thessalonica

NOW when they had traveled through Amphipolis and Apollonia, they came to Thessalonica, where there was a synagogue of the Jews.
2And according to Paul's custom, he went to them, and for three Sabbaths reasoned with them from the Scriptures,
3explaining and giving evidence that the Christ had to suffer and rise again from the dead, and *saying,* "This Jesus whom I am proclaiming to you is the Christ."
4And some of them were persuaded and joined Paul and Silas, along with a great multitude of the God-fearing Greeks and a number of the leading women.
5But the Jews, becoming jealous and taking along some wicked men from the market place, formed a mob and set the city in an uproar; and coming upon the house of Jason, they were seeking to bring them out to the people.
6And when they did not find them, they *began* dragging Jason and some brethren before the city authorities, shouting, "These men who have upset *f* the world have come here also;
7and Jason has welcomed them, and they all act contrary to the decrees of Caesar, saying that there is another king, Jesus."
8And they stirred up the crowd and the city authori-

ἀπὸ τῆς πόλεως. 40 ἐξελθόντες δὲ ἀπὸ
from the city. And going out from

τῆς φυλακῆς εἰσῆλθον πρὸς τὴν Λυδίαν,
the prison they entered to [the - Lydia,
house of]

καὶ ἰδόντες παρεκάλεσαν τοὺς ἀδελφοὺς
and seeing they exhorted the brothers

καὶ ἐξῆλθαν.
and went forth.

17 Διοδεύσαντες δὲ τὴν Ἀμφίπολιν καὶ
And travelling through - Amphipolis and

τὴν Ἀπολλωνίαν ἦλθον εἰς Θεσσαλονίκην,
- Apollonia they came to Thessalonica,

ὅπου ἦν συναγωγὴ τῶν Ἰουδαίων. 2 κατὰ
where was a synagogue of the Jews. according
ing to

δὲ τὸ εἰωθὸς τῷ Παύλῳ εἰσῆλθεν πρὸς
And the custom - with Paul*e* he entered to

αὐτούς, καὶ ἐπὶ σάββατα τρία διελέξατο
them, and on sabbaths three lectured

αὐτοῖς ἀπὸ τῶν γραφῶν, 3 διανοίγων
to them from the scriptures, opening up

καὶ παρατιθέμενος ὅτι τὸν χριστὸν ἔδει
and setting before [them] that *the* *1*the behoved

παθεῖν καὶ ἀναστῆναι ἐκ νεκρῶν, καὶ
to suffer and to rise again out of [the] dead, and

ὅτι οὗτός ἐστιν ὁ χριστός, ὁ Ἰησοῦς,
that this is(was) the Christ, - Jesus,

ὃν ἐγὼ καταγγέλλω ὑμῖν. 4 καί τινες
whom I announce to you. And some

ἐξ αὐτῶν ἐπείσθησαν καὶ προσεκληρώθησαν
of them were persuaded and threw in their lot

τῷ Παύλῳ καὶ τῷ Σιλᾷ, τῶν τε
- with Paul and - Silas, both of the

σεβομένων Ἑλλήνων πλῆθος πολύ, γυναικῶν τε
worshipping Greeks *3*multitude *1*a much and of*2*women
(great),

τῶν πρώτων οὐκ ὀλίγαι. 5 Ζηλώσαντες δὲ
*1*the *2*chief not a few. But becoming jealous

οἱ Ἰουδαῖοι καὶ προσλαβόμενοι τῶν
the Jews and taking aside of the

ἀγοραίων ἄνδρας τινὰς πονηροὺς καὶ
loungers in the men some wicked and
marketplace

ὀχλοποιήσαντες ἐθορύβουν τὴν πόλιν, καὶ
having gathered a disturbed the city, and
crowd

ἐπιστάντες τῇ οἰκίᾳ Ἰάσονος ἐζήτουν
coming on the house of Jason sought

αὐτοὺς προαγαγεῖν εἰς τὸν δῆμον· 6 μὴ
them to bring forward to the mob; *2*not

εὑρόντες δὲ αὐτοὺς ἔσυρον Ἰάσονα καὶ
*3*finding *1*but them they dragged Jason and

τινας ἀδελφοὺς ἐπὶ τοὺς πολιτάρχας,
some brothers to the politarchs,

βοῶντες ὅτι οἱ τὴν οἰκουμένην ἀναστατώ-
crying[,] - *2*the *4*the *3*inhabited *5*having turned
[ones] earth

σαντες οὗτοι καὶ ἐνθάδε πάρεισιν, 7 οὓς
upside *1*these also here have arrived, whom
down men

ὑποδέδεκται Ἰάσων· καὶ οὗτοι πάντες
*2*has received *1*Jason; and these all

ἀπέναντι τῶν δογμάτων Καίσαρος
*2*contrary to *1*the *3*decrees *4*of Cæsar

πράσσουσιν, βασιλέα ἕτερον λέγοντες εἶναι
*1*act, *4*king *3*another *2*saying *5*to be

Ἰησοῦν. 8 ἐτάραξαν δὲ τὸν ὄχλον καὶ
*6*Jesus. And they troubled the crowd and

---

them to leave the city. 40After Paul and Silas came out of the prison, they went to Lydia's house, where they met with the brothers and encouraged them. Then they left.

Chapter 17

In Thessalonica

WHEN they had passed through Amphipolis and Apollonia, they came to Thessalonica, where there was a Jewish synagogue. 2As his custom was, Paul went into the synagogue, and on three Sabbath days he reasoned with them from the Scriptures, 3explaining and proving that the Christ*h* had to suffer and rise from the dead. "This Jesus I am proclaiming to you is the Christ,*h*" he said. 4Some of the Jews were persuaded and joined Paul and Silas, as did a large number of God-fearing Greeks and not a few prominent women.

5But the Jews were jealous; so they rounded up some bad characters from the marketplace, formed a mob and started a riot in the city. They rushed to Jason's house in search of Paul and Silas in order to bring them out to the crowd.*i* 6But when they did not find them, they dragged Jason and some other brothers before the city officials, shouting: "These men who have caused trouble all over the world have now come here, 7and Jason has welcomed them into his house. They are all defying Caesar's decrees, saying that there is another king, one called Jesus." 8When they heard this, the crowd and the city

---

f Lit., *the inhabited earth*

h3 Or *Messiah*
i5 Or *the assembly of the people*

ties who heard these things.

9And when they had received a pledge from Jason and the others, they released them.

Paul at Berea

10And the brethren immediately sent Paul and Silas away by night to Berea; and when they arrived, they went into the synagogue of the Jews. 11Now these were more noble-minded than those in Thessalonica, for they received the word with great eagerness, examining the Scriptures daily, *to see* whether these things were so. 12Many of them therefore believed, along with a number of prominent Greek women and men. 13But when the Jews of Thessalonica found out that the word of God had been proclaimed by Paul in Berea also, they came there likewise, agitating and stirring up the crowds. 14And then immediately the brethren sent Paul out to go as far as the sea; and Silas and Timothy remained there. 15Now those who conducted Paul brought him as far as Athens; and receiving a command for Silas and Timothy to come to him as soon as possible, they departed.

Paul at Athens

16Now while Paul was waiting for them at Athens, his spirit was being provoked within him as he was beholding the city full of idols. 17So he was reasoning in the synagogue with the Jews and the God-fearing

---

τοὺς πολιτάρχας ἀκούοντας ταῦτα, 9 καὶ
the politarchs hearing these things, and

λαβόντες τὸ ἱκανὸν παρὰ τοῦ ᾽Ιάσονος
taking the surety from – Jason

καὶ τῶν λοιπῶν ἀπέλυσαν αὐτούς. 10 Οἱ δὲ
and the rest released them. And the

ἀδελφοὶ εὐθέως διὰ νυκτὸς ἐξεπεμψαν
brothers immediately through [the] night sent forth
           (during)

τόν τε Παῦλον καὶ τὸν Σιλᾶν εἰς Βέροιαν,
– both Paul and – Silas to Berœa,

οἵτινες παραγενόμενοι εἰς τὴν συναγωγὴν
who having arrived ²into ³the synagogue

τῶν ᾽Ιουδαίων ἀπῄεσαν· 11 οὗτοι δὲ ἦσαν
⁴of the ⁵Jews ¹went; and these were

εὐγενέστεροι τῶν ἐν Θεσσαλονίκῃ, οἵτινες
more noble [than] the [ones] in Thessalonica, who

ἐδέξαντο τὸν λόγον μετὰ πάσης προθυμίας,
received the word with all eagerness,

[τὸ] καθ᾽ ἡμέραν ἀνακρίνοντες τὰς γραφὰς
– daily examining the scriptures

εἰ ἔχοι ταῦτα οὕτως. 12 πολλοὶ μὲν
if ²have(are) ¹these things ²so. Many –

οὖν ἐξ αὐτῶν ἐπίστευσαν, καὶ τῶν
therefore of them believed, and of the

῾Ελληνίδων γυναικῶν τῶν εὐσχημόνων καὶ
²Greek ³women – ¹honourable and

ἀνδρῶν οὐκ ὀλίγοι. 13 ῾Ως δὲ ἔγνωσαν
of men not a few. But when ⁵knew

οἱ ἀπὸ τῆς Θεσσαλονίκης ᾽Ιουδαῖοι ὅτι
¹the ²from – ³Thessalonica ⁴Jews that

καὶ ἐν τῇ Βεροίᾳ κατηγγέλη ὑπὸ τοῦ
also in – Berœa was announced by –

Παύλου ὁ λόγος τοῦ θεοῦ, ἦλθον κἀκεῖ
Paul the word – of God, they came there also

σαλεύοντες καὶ ταράσσοντες τοὺς ὄχλους.
shaking and troubling the crowds.

14 εὐθέως δὲ τότε τὸν Παῦλον ἐξαπέστειλαν
So immediately then – ⁴Paul ⁵sent away

οἱ ἀδελφοὶ πορεύεσθαι ἕως ἐπὶ τὴν
¹the ²brothers to go as far as to the

θάλασσαν· ὑπέμεινάν τε ὅ τε Σιλᾶς καὶ
sea; ¹but ⁶remained – ²both ³Silas ⁴and

ὁ Τιμόθεος ἐκεῖ. 15 οἱ δὲ καθιστάνοντες
– ⁵Timothy ⁷there. And the [ones] conducting

τὸν Παῦλον ἤγαγον ἕως ᾽Αθηνῶν, καὶ
– Paul brought [him] as far as Athens, and

λαβόντες ἐντολὴν πρὸς τὸν Σιλᾶν καὶ τὸν
receiving a command to – Silas and –

Τιμόθεον ἵνα ὡς τάχιστα ἔλθωσιν πρὸς
Timothy that as quickly they should to
         [as possible] come

αὐτὸν ἐξῄεσαν.
him they departed.

16 ᾽Εν δὲ ταῖς ᾽Αθήναις ἐκδεχομένου
And in – Athens awaiting
          = while Paul awaited them,

αὐτοὺς τοῦ Παύλου, παρωξύνετο τὸ πνεῦμα
them – Paul,ᵃ ⁴was provoked ¹the ²spirit

αὐτοῦ ἐν αὐτῷ θεωροῦντος κατείδωλον
³of him in him beholding ⁴full of images

οὖσαν τὴν πόλιν. 17 διελέγετο μὲν οὖν
³being ¹the ²city. He addressed –* therefore

ἐν τῇ συναγωγῇ τοῖς ᾽Ιουδαίοις καὶ
in the synagogue the Jews and

* See note on ch. 12. 5.

---

officials were thrown into turmoil. 9Then they made Jason and the others post bond and let them go.

In Berea

10As soon as it was night, the brothers sent Paul and Silas away to Berea. On arriving there, they went to the Jewish synagogue. 11Now the Bereans were of more noble character than the Thessalonians, for they received the message with great eagerness and examined the Scriptures every day to see if what Paul said was true. 12Many of the Jews believed, as did also a number of prominent Greek women and many Greek men.

13When the Jews in Thessalonica learned that Paul was preaching the word of God at Berea, they went there too, agitating the crowds and stirring them up. 14The brothers immediately sent Paul to the coast, but Silas and Timothy stayed at Berea. 15The men who escorted Paul brought him to Athens and then left with instructions for Silas and Timothy to join him as soon as possible.

In Athens

16While Paul was waiting for them in Athens, he was greatly distressed to see that the city was full of idols. 17So he reasoned in the synagogue with the Jews and the God-fearing

Gentiles, and in the market place every day with those who happened to be present.

18And also some of the Epicurean and Stoic philosophers were conversing with him. And some were saying, "What would this idle babbler wish to say?" Others, "He seems to be a proclaimer of strange deities,"—because he was preaching Jesus and the resurrection.

19And they took him and brought him to the Areopagus, saying, "May we know what this new teaching is which you are proclaiming?

20"For you are bringing some strange things to our ears; we want to know therefore what these things mean."

21(Now all the Athenians and the strangers visiting there used to spend their time in nothing other than telling or hearing something new.)

Sermon on Mars Hill

22And Paul stood in the midst of the Areopagus and said, "Men of Athens, I observe that you are very religious in all respects.

23"For while I was passing through and examining the objects of your worship, I also found an altar with this inscription, 'TO AN UNKNOWN GOD.' What therefore you worship in ignorance, this I proclaim to you.

24"The God who made the world and all things in it, since He is Lord of heaven and earth, does not dwell in temples made with hands;

25neither is He served by human hands, as though He needed anything, since He Himself gives to all life and breath and all things;

26and He made from *g*one, every nation of mankind to live on all the face of the earth, having determined *their* appointed

---

τοῖς σεβομένοις καὶ ἐν τῇ ἀγορᾷ κατὰ
the [ones] worshipping and in the marketplace –

πᾶσαν ἡμέραν πρὸς τοὺς παρατυγχάνοντας.
every day to the [ones] chancing to be [there].

18 τινὲς δὲ καὶ τῶν Ἐπικουρείων καὶ
But some also of the Epicurean and

Στωϊκῶν φιλοσόφων συνέβαλλον αὐτῷ, καὶ
Stoic philosophers fell in with him, and

τινες ἔλεγον· τί ἂν θέλοι ὁ σπερμολόγος
some said: What may wish – ²ignorant plagiarist

οὗτος λέγειν; οἱ δέ· ξένων δαιμονίων
¹this to say? And others [said]: Of foreign demons

δοκεῖ καταγγελεὺς εἶναι· ὅτι τὸν Ἰησοῦν
he seems an announcer to be; because – Jesus

καὶ τὴν ἀνάστασιν εὐηγγελίζετο. 19 ἐπιλα-
and the resurrection he preached. taking

βόμενοι δὲ αὐτοῦ ἐπὶ τὸν Ἄρειον πάγον
hold And of him to the Areopagus

ἤγαγον, λέγοντες· δυνάμεθα γνῶναι τίς
they led [him], saying: Can we to know what

ἡ καινὴ αὕτη ἡ ὑπὸ σοῦ λαλουμένη
¹this ²new – ⁵by ⁶thee ⁴being spoken

διδαχή; 20 ξενίζοντα γάρ τινα εἰσφέρεις
³teaching [is]? for ²startling things ¹some thou bringest *in*

εἰς τὰς ἀκοὰς ἡμῶν· βουλόμεθα οὖν
to the ears of us; we are minded therefore

γνῶναι τίνα θέλει ταῦτα εἶναι. 21 Ἀθηναῖοι
to know what wishes these things to be. ²Athenians

δὲ πάντες καὶ οἱ ἐπιδημοῦντες ξένοι εἰς
Now ¹all ³and ⁴the ⁵dwelling ⁶strangers ⁷for

οὐδὲν ἕτερον ηὐκαίρουν ἢ λέγειν τι ἢ
⁸nothing ¹⁰different ⁷have leisure either to say something or

ἀκούειν τι καινότερον. 22 Σταθεὶς δὲ
to hear something newer. And standing

Παῦλος ἐν μέσῳ τοῦ Ἀρείου πάγου
⁵Paul ¹in ²[the] midst ³of the ⁴Areopagus

ἔφη· ἄνδρες Ἀθηναῖοι, κατὰ πάντα ὡς
said: Men Athenians, in everything how

δεισιδαιμονεστέρους ὑμᾶς θεωρῶ. 23 διερχόμενος
very religious ²you ¹I behold. passing along

γὰρ καὶ ἀναθεωρῶν τὰ σεβάσματα ὑμῶν
For and looking up at the objects of worship of you

εὗρον καὶ βωμὸν ἐν ᾧ ἐπεγέγραπτο·
I found also an altar in which had been inscribed:

ΑΓΝΩΣΤΩ ΘΕΩ. ὃ οὖν ἀγνοοῦντες
TO AN UNKNOWN GOD. What therefore being ignorant

εὐσεβεῖτε, τοῦτο ἐγὼ καταγγέλλω ὑμῖν.
ye reverence, this I announce to you.

24 ὁ θεὸς ὁ ποιήσας τὸν κόσμον καὶ
The God the [one] having made the world and

πάντα τὰ ἐν αὐτῷ, οὗτος οὐρανοῦ καὶ
all the things in it, this one ³of heaven ⁴and

γῆς ὑπάρχων κύριος οὐκ ἐν χειροποιήτοις
⁵of earth ¹being ²lord ²not ³in ⁴hand-made

ναοῖς κατοικεῖ, 25 οὐδὲ ὑπὸ χειρῶν
⁵shrines ¹dwells, nor ²by ³hands

ἀνθρωπίνων θεραπεύεται προσδεόμενός
²human ¹is served having need

τινος, αὐτὸς διδοὺς πᾶσι ζωὴν καὶ πνοὴν
of anything, he giving to all life and breath

καὶ τὰ πάντα· 26 ἐποίησέν τε ἐξ ἑνὸς
and – all things; and he made of one

πᾶν ἔθνος ἀνθρώπων κατοικεῖν ἐπὶ παντὸς
every nation of men to dwell on all

προσώπου τῆς γῆς, ὁρίσας προστεταγμένους
[the] face of the earth, fixing *having been* appointed

Greeks, as well as in the marketplace day by day with those who happened to be there. 18A group of Epicurean and Stoic philosophers began to dispute with him. Some of them asked, "What is this babbler trying to say?" Others remarked, "He seems to be advocating foreign gods." They said this because Paul was preaching the good news about Jesus and the resurrection. 19Then they took him and brought him to a meeting of the Areopagus, where they said to him, "May we know what this new teaching is that you are presenting? 20You are bringing some strange ideas to our ears, and we want to know what they mean." 21(All the Athenians and the foreigners who lived there spent their time doing nothing but talking about and listening to the latest ideas.)

22Paul then stood up in the meeting of the Areopagus and said: "Men of Athens! I see that in every way you are very religious. 23For as I walked around and looked carefully at your objects of worship, I even found an altar with this inscription: TO AN UNKNOWN GOD. Now what you worship as something unknown I am going to proclaim to you.

24"The God who made the world and everything in it is the Lord of heaven and earth and does not live in temples built by hands. 25And he is not served by human hands, as if he needed anything, because he himself gives all men life and breath and everything else. 26From one man he made every nation of men, that they should inhabit the whole earth; and he determined the times set for

---

times, and the boundaries of their habitation,

27that they should seek God, if perhaps they might grope for Him and find Him, though He is not far from each one of us;

28for in Him we live and move and exist, as even some of your own poets have said, 'For we also are His offspring.'

29"Being then the offspring of God, we ought not to think that the Divine Nature is like gold or silver or stone, an image formed by the art and thought of man.

30"Therefore having overlooked the times of ignorance, God is now declaring to men that all everywhere should repent,

31because He has fixed a day in which He will judge the world in righteousness through a Man whom He has appointed, having furnished proof to all men by raising Him from the dead."

32Now when they heard of the resurrection of the dead, some *began* to sneer, but others said, "We shall hear you again concerning this."

33So Paul went out of their midst.

34But some men joined him and believed, among whom also were Dionysius the Areopagite and a woman named Damaris and others with them.

καιροὺς   καὶ   τὰς   ὁροθεσίας   τῆς   κατοικίας
seasons   and   the   boundaries   of the   dwelling

αὐτῶν,   27 ζητεῖν   τὸν   θεόν,   εἰ   ἄρα   γε
of them,   to seek   -   God,   if   perchance

ψηλαφήσειαν   αὐτὸν   καὶ   εὕροιεν,   καὶ   γε
they might feel after   him   and   might find,   though

οὐ   μακρὰν   ἀπὸ   ἑνὸς   ἑκάστου   ἡμῶν
³not   ⁵far   ⁴from   ⁶one   ⁷each   ⁷of us

ὑπάρχοντα.   28 ἐν   αὐτῷ   γὰρ   ζῶμεν   καὶ
¹being.   ²in   ³him   ¹For   we live   and

κινούμεθα   καὶ   ἐσμέν,   ὡς   καί   τινες   τῶν
move   and   are,   as   indeed   some   of the

καθ'   ὑμᾶς   ποιητῶν   εἰρήκασιν·   τοῦ   γὰρ
²among   ³you   ¹poets   have said: ²of him   ¹For

καὶ   γένος   ἐσμέν.   29 γένος   οὖν   ὑπάρχοντες
²also   ⁵offspring   ⁴we are.   Offspring   therefore   being

τοῦ   θεοῦ   οὐκ   ὀφείλομεν   νομίζειν,   χρυσῷ
-   of God   we ought not   to suppose,   ⁵to gold

ἢ   ἀργύρῳ   ἢ   λίθῳ,   χαράγματι   τέχνης
⁶or   ⁷to silver   ⁸or   ⁹to stone,   ¹⁰to an   ¹¹of art
                                                engraved work

καὶ   ἐνθυμήσεως   ἀνθρώπου,   τὸ   θεῖον   εἶναι
¹²and   ¹³of meditation   ¹⁴of man,   ¹the   ²divine   ³to be
                                                              nature

ὅμοιον.   30 τοὺς   μὲν   οὖν   χρόνους   τῆς
⁴like.   ⁵The   ¹so   ²then   ³times   -

ἀγνοίας   ὑπεριδὼν   ὁ   θεὸς   τὰ   νῦν
⁷of ignorance   ⁴having   -   ⁵God   -   now
                  overlooked

ἀπαγγέλλει   τοῖς   ἀνθρώποις   πάντας   πανταχοῦ
declares   -   to men   all men   everywhere

μετανοεῖν,   31 καθότι   ἔστησεν   ἡμέραν   ἐν
to repent,   because   he set   a day   in

ᾗ   μέλλει   κρίνειν   τὴν   οἰκουμένην   ἐν
which he is about   to judge   the   inhabited earth   in

δικαιοσύνῃ,   ἐν   ἀνδρὶ   ᾧ   ὥρισεν,   πίστιν
righteousness,   by   a man   whom   he desig-   ²a
                                        nated,   guarantee

παρασχὼν   πᾶσιν   ἀναστήσας   αὐτὸν   ἐκ
¹offering   to all   having raised up   him   out of

νεκρῶν.   32 ἀκούσαντες   δὲ   ἀνάστασιν
[the] dead.   And hearing [of]   a resurrection

νεκρῶν,   οἱ   μὲν   ἐχλεύαζον,   οἱ   δὲ   εἶπαν·
of dead   some   scoffed,   others   said:
persons,

ἀκουσόμεθά   σου   περὶ   τούτου   καὶ   πάλιν.
We will hear   thee   concerning   this   also   again.

33 οὕτως   ὁ   Παῦλος   ἐξῆλθεν   ἐκ   μέσου
Thus   -   Paul   went forth   from [the] midst

αὐτῶν.   34 τινὲς   δὲ   ἄνδρες   κολληθέντες
of them.   But some   -   men   adhering

αὐτῷ   ἐπίστευσαν,   ἐν   οἷς   καὶ   Διονύσιος
to him   believed,   among whom   both   Dionysius

ὁ   Ἀρεοπαγίτης   καὶ   γυνὴ   ὀνόματι   Δαμαρὶς
the   Areopagite   and a woman   by name   Damaris

καὶ   ἕτεροι   σὺν   αὐτοῖς.
and   others   with   them.

---

them and the exact places where they should live.

27God did this so that men would seek him and perhaps reach out for him and find him, though he is not far from each one of us.

28'For in him we live and move and have our being.' As some of your own poets have said, 'We are his offspring.'

29"Therefore since we are God's offspring, we should not think that the divine being is like gold or silver or stone—an image made by man's design and skill. 30In the past God overlooked such ignorance, but now he commands all people everywhere to repent. 31For he has set a day when he will judge the world with justice by the man he has appointed. He has given proof of this to all men by raising him from the dead."

32When they heard about the resurrection of the dead, some of them sneered, but others said, "We want to hear you again on this subject." 33At that, Paul left the Council. 34A few men became followers of Paul and believed. Among them was Dionysius, a member of the Areopagus, also a woman named Damaris, and a number of others.

Chapter 18

Paul at Corinth

AFTER these things he left Athens and went to Corinth.

2And he found a certain Jew named Aquila, a native of Pontus, having recently come from Italy with his wife Priscilla, because

---

18 Μετὰ   ταῦτα   χωρισθεὶς   ἐκ   τῶν
After   these things   departing   out of   -

Ἀθηνῶν   ἦλθεν   εἰς   Κόρινθον.   2 καὶ
Athens   he came   to   Corinth.   And

εὑρών   τινα   Ἰουδαῖον   ὀνόματι   Ἀκύλαν,
finding   a certain   Jew   by name   Aquila,

Ποντικὸν   τῷ   γένει,   προσφάτως   ἐληλυθότα
belonging to   -   by race,   recently   having come
Pontus

ἀπὸ   τῆς   Ἰταλίας,   καὶ   Πρίσκιλλαν   γυναῖκα
from   -   Italy,   and   Priscilla   wife

Chapter 18

In Corinth

AFTER this, Paul left Athens and went to Corinth. 2There he met a Jew named Aquila, a native of Pontus, who had recently come from Italy with his wife Priscilla, because

Claudius had commanded all the Jews to leave Rome. He came to them, 3and because he was of the same trade, he stayed with them and they were working; for by trade they were tent-makers.

4And he was reasoning in the synagogue every Sabbath and trying to persuade Jews and Greeks.

5But when Silas and Timothy came down from Macedonia, Paul *began* devoting himself completely to the word, solemnly testifying to the Jews that Jesus was the Christ.

6And when they resisted and blasphemed, he shook out his garments and said to them, "Your blood *be* upon your own heads! I am clean. From now on I shall go to the Gentiles."

7And he departed from there and went to the house of a certain man named Titius Justus, a worshiper of God, whose house was next to the synagogue.

8And Crispus, the leader of the synagogue, believed in the Lord with all his household, and many of the Corinthians when they heard were believing and being baptized.

9And the Lord said to Paul in the night by a vision, "Do not be afraid *any longer*, but go on speaking and do not be silent;

10for I am with you, and no man will attack you in order to harm you, for I have many people in this city."

11And he settled *there* a year and six months, teaching the word of God among them.

12But while Gallio was

αὐτοῦ,   διὰ   τὸ   διατεταχέναι   Κλαύδιον
of him,   because of   the   to have commanded   Claudius[b]
= because Claudius had commanded

χωρίζεσθαι   πάντας   τοὺς   'Ιουδαίους   ἀπὸ
to depart   all   the   Jews   from

τῆς   'Ρώμης,   προσῆλθεν   αὐτοῖς,   3 καὶ
-    Rome,   he came to   them,   and

διὰ   τὸ   ὁμότεχνον   εἶναι   ἔμενεν   παρ'
because of   the   of the same trade   to be[b] he remained   with
= because [he] was of the same trade

αὐτοῖς,   καὶ   ἠργάζοντο· ἦσαν   γὰρ   σκηνοποιοὶ
them,   and   they wrought;   for they were   tentmakers

τῇ   τέχνῃ.   4 διελέγετο   δὲ   ἐν   τῇ   συναγωγῇ
-    by trade.   And he lectured   in   the   synagogue

κατὰ   πᾶν   σάββατον,   ἔπειθέν   τε   'Ιουδαίους
on   every   sabbath,   he persuaded both   Jews

καὶ   "Ελληνας.   5 'Ως   δὲ   κατῆλθον   ἀπὸ
and   Greeks.   And when   came down   from

τῆς   Μακεδονίας   ὅ   τε   Σιλᾶς   καὶ   ὁ
-    Macedonia   both   Silas   and   -

Τιμόθεος,   συνείχετο   τῷ   λόγῳ   ὁ   Παῦλος,
Timothy,   was pressed   by the   word   -   Paul,

διαμαρτυρόμενος   τοῖς   'Ιουδαίοις   εἶναι   τὸν
solemnly witnessing   to the   Jews   to be   the
= that Jesus was the Christ.

χριστὸν   'Ιησοῦν.   6 ἀντιτασσομένων   δὲ   αὐτῶν
Christ   Jesus.   But resisting   them
= when they resisted and blasphemed

καὶ   βλασφημούντων   ἐκτιναξάμενος   τὰ   ἱμάτια
and   blaspheming[a]   shaking off   the(his) garments

εἶπεν   πρὸς   αὐτούς·   τὸ   αἷμα   ὑμῶν   ἐπὶ
he said   to   them: The   blood   of you   on

τὴν   κεφαλὴν   ὑμῶν·   καθαρὸς   ἐγὼ   ἀπὸ
the   head   of you;   clean   I   from

τοῦ   νῦν   εἰς   τὰ   ἔθνη   πορεύσομαι.   7 καὶ
-    now   to   the   nations   will go.   And

μεταβὰς   ἐκεῖθεν   ἦλθεν   εἰς   οἰκίαν   τινὸς
removing   thence   he went   into [the] house   of one

ὀνόματι   Τιτίου   'Ιούστου   σεβομένου   τὸν
by name   Titius   Justus   worshipping   -

θεόν,   οὗ   ἡ   οἰκία   ἦν   συνομοροῦσα   τῇ
God,   of whom the   house   was   being next door   to the

συναγωγῇ.   8 Κρῖσπος   δὲ   ὁ   ἀρχισυνάγωγος
synagogue.   Now Crispus   the   synagogue ruler

ἐπίστευσεν   τῷ   κυρίῳ   σὺν   ὅλῳ   τῷ   οἴκῳ
believed   the   Lord   with   all   the household

αὐτοῦ,   καὶ   πολλοὶ   τῶν   Κορινθίων   ἀκούοντες
of him,   and   many   of the   Corinthians   hearing

ἐπίστευον   καὶ   ἐβαπτίζοντο.   9 Εἶπεν   δὲ
believed   and   were baptized.   And said

ὁ   κύριος   ἐν   νυκτὶ   δι'   ὁράματος   τῷ
the   Lord   in   [the] night through   a vision   -

Παύλῳ·   μὴ   φοβοῦ,   ἀλλὰ   λάλει   καὶ
to Paul: Do not fear,   but   speak   and

μὴ   σιωπήσῃς,   10 διότι   ἐγώ   εἰμι   μετὰ   σοῦ
keep not silence,   because   I   am   with   thee

καὶ   οὐδεὶς   ἐπιθήσεταί   σοι   τοῦ   κακῶσαί
and   no one   shall set on   thee   -   to illtreat[d]

σε,   διότι   λαός   ἐστί   μοι   πολὺς   ἐν
thee,   because   people   is   to me   much[e]   in
= I have a great people

τῇ   πόλει   ταύτῃ.   11 'Εκάθισεν   δὲ   ἐνιαυτὸν
this city.   And he sat   a year

καὶ   μῆνας   ἓξ   διδάσκων   ἐν   αὐτοῖς   τὸν
and   months   six   teaching   among   them   the

λόγον   τοῦ   θεοῦ.   12 Γαλλίωνος   δὲ
word   -   of God.   And Gallio
= when Gallio

Claudius had ordered all the Jews to leave Rome. Paul went to see them, 3and because he was a tentmaker as they were, he stayed and worked with them. 4Every Sabbath he reasoned in the synagogue, trying to persuade Jews and Greeks.

5When Silas and Timothy came from Macedonia, Paul devoted himself exclusively to preaching, testifying to the Jews that Jesus was the Christ.*j* 6But when the Jews opposed Paul and became abusive, he shook out his clothes in protest and said to them, "Your blood be on your own heads! I am clear of my responsibility. From now on I will go to the Gentiles."

7Then Paul left the synagogue and went next door to the house of Titius Justus, a worshiper of God. 8Crispus, the synagogue ruler, and his entire household believed in the Lord; and many of the Corinthians who heard him believed and were baptized.

9One night the Lord spoke to Paul in a vision: "Do not be afraid; keep on speaking, do not be silent. 10For I am with you, and no one is going to attack and harm you, because I have many people in this city." 11So Paul stayed for a year and a half, teaching them the word of God.

12While Gallio was pro-

Or *Messiah;* also in verse 28

proconsul of Achaia, the Jews with one accord rose up against Paul and brought him before the judgment seat,

13saying, "This man persuades men to worship God contrary to the law."

14But when Paul was about to open his mouth, Gallio said to the Jews, "If it were a matter of wrong or of vicious crime, O Jews, it would be reasonable for me to put up with you;

15but if there are questions about words and names and your own law, look after it yourselves; I am unwilling to be a judge of these matters."

16And he drove them away from the judgment seat.

17And they all took hold of Sosthenes, the leader of the synagogue, and *began* beating him in front of the judgment seat. And Gallio was not concerned about any of these things.

18And Paul, having remained many days longer, took leave of the brethren and put out to sea for Syria, and with him were Priscilla and Aquila. In Cenchrea he had his hair cut, for he was keeping a vow.

19And they came to Ephesus, and he left them there. Now he himself entered the synagogue and reasoned with the Jews.

20And when they asked him to stay for a longer time, he did not consent,

21but taking leave of them and saying, "I will return to you again if God wills," he set sail from Ephesus.

22And when he had landed at Caesarea, he went up and greeted the church,

---

ἀνθυπάτου ὄντος τῆς Ἀχαΐας κατεπέστησαν
proconsul being^a – of Achaia ⁶set on
was proconsul

ὁμοθυμαδὸν οἱ Ἰουδαῖοι τῷ Παύλῳ καὶ
³with one mind ¹the ²Jews – Paul and

ἤγαγον αὐτὸν ἐπὶ τὸ βῆμα, 13 λέγοντες
brought him to the tribunal, saying[,]

ὅτι παρὰ τὸν νόμον ἀναπείθει οὗτος
– ⁵[differently] from ⁷the ⁸law ³urges ¹This man

τοὺς ἀνθρώπους σέβεσθαι τὸν θεόν.
– ²men ⁴to worship – ⁶God.

14 μέλλοντος δὲ τοῦ Παύλου ἀνοίγειν τὸ
And being about – Paul^a to open the(his)
=when Paul was about

στόμα εἶπεν ὁ Γαλλίων πρὸς τοὺς
mouth said – Gallio to the

Ἰουδαίους· εἰ μὲν ἦν ἀδίκημά τι
Jews: If indeed it was crime some

ἢ ῥᾳδιούργημα πονηρόν, ὦ Ἰουδαῖοι,
or villainy evil, O Jews,

κατὰ λόγον ἂν ἀνεσχόμην ὑμῶν· 15 εἰ δὲ ζητή-
rightly I would endure you; but if ques-

ματά ἐστιν περὶ λόγου καὶ ὀνομάτων καὶ
tions it is concerning a word and names and

νόμου τοῦ καθ' ὑμᾶς, ὄψεσθε αὐτοί·
law the according to you, ye will see [your]selves;
=your law,

κριτὴς ἐγὼ τούτων οὐ βούλομαι εἶναι.
a judge ¹I ³of these things ²do not intend ⁴to be.

16 καὶ ἀπήλασεν αὐτοὺς ἀπὸ τοῦ βήματος.
And he drove away them from the tribunal.

17 ἐπιλαβόμενοι δὲ πάντες Σωσθένην τὸν
But ²seizing ¹all Sosthenes the

ἀρχισυνάγωγον ἔτυπτον ἔμπροσθεν τοῦ
synagogue ruler they struck [him] in front of the

βήματος· καὶ οὐδὲν τούτων τῷ Γαλλίωνι
tribunal; and not one of these things – ²to Gallio

ἔμελεν. 18 Ὁ δὲ Παῦλος ἔτι προσμείνας
¹mattered. – But Paul yet having remained

ἡμέρας ἱκανάς, τοῖς ἀδελφοῖς ἀποταξάμενος
days many, to the brothers bidding farewell

ἐξέπλει εἰς τὴν Συρίαν, καὶ σὺν αὐτῷ
he sailed away to – Syria, and with him

Πρίσκιλλα καὶ Ἀκύλας, κειράμενος ἐν
Priscilla and Aquila, having shorn in

Κεγχρεαῖς τὴν κεφαλήν· εἶχεν γὰρ εὐχήν.
Cenchrea the(his) head; for he had a vow.

19 κατήντησαν δὲ εἰς Ἔφεσον, κἀκείνους
And they came down to Ephesus, and those

κατέλιπεν αὐτοῦ, αὐτὸς δὲ εἰσελθὼν εἰς
he left there, but he entering into

τὴν συναγωγὴν διελέξατο τοῖς Ἰουδαίοις.
the synagogue lectured to the Jews.

20 ἐρωτώντων δὲ αὐτῶν ἐπὶ πλείονα
And asking them^a over a more(longer)
=as they asked

χρόνον μεῖναι οὐκ ἐπένευσεν, 21 ἀλλὰ
time to remain he consented not, but

ἀποταξάμενος καὶ εἰπών· πάλιν ἀνακάμψω
bidding farewell and saying: Again I will return

πρὸς ὑμᾶς τοῦ θεοῦ θέλοντος, ἀνήχθη
to you – God willing,^a he set sail
=if God wills,

ἀπὸ τῆς Ἐφέσου, 22 καὶ κατελθὼν εἰς
from – Ephesus, and coming down to

Καισάρειαν, ἀναβὰς καὶ ἀσπασάμενος τὴν
Caesarea, going up and greeting the

---

consul of Achaia, the Jews made a united attack on Paul and brought him into court. 13"This man," they charged, "is persuading the people to worship God in ways contrary to the law."

14Just as Paul was about to speak, Gallio said to the Jews, "If you Jews were making a complaint about some misdemeanor or serious crime, it would be reasonable for me to listen to you. 15But since it involves questions about words and names and your own law— settle the matter yourselves. I will not be a judge of such things." 16So he had them ejected from the court. 17Then they all turned on Sosthenes the synagogue ruler and beat him in front of the court. But Gallio showed no concern whatever.

Priscilla, Aquila and Apollos

18Paul stayed on in Corinth for some time. Then he left the brothers and sailed for Syria, accompanied by Priscilla and Aquila. Before he sailed, he had his hair cut off at Cenchrea because of a vow he had taken. 19They arrived at Ephesus, where Paul left Priscilla and Aquila. He himself went into the synagogue and reasoned with the Jews. 20When they asked him to spend more time with them, he declined. 21But as he left, he promised, "I will come back if it is God's will." Then he set sail from Ephesus. 22When he landed at Caesarea, he went up and greeted the and went down to Antioch.

Third Missionary Journey

23And having spent some time *there*, he departed and passed successively through the Galatian region and Phrygia, strengthening all the disciples.

24Now a certain Jew named Apollos, an Alexandrian by birth, an eloquent man, came to Ephesus; and he was mighty in the Scriptures.

25This man had been instructed in the way of the Lord; and being fervent in spirit, he was speaking and teaching accurately the things concerning Jesus, being acquainted only with the baptism of John;

26and he began to speak out boldly in the synagogue. But when Priscilla and Aquila heard him, they took him aside and explained to him the way of God more accurately.

27And when he wanted to go across to Achaia, the brethren encouraged him and wrote to the disciples to welcome him; and when he had arrived, he helped greatly those who had believed through grace;

28for he powerfully refuted the Jews in public, demonstrating by the Scriptures that Jesus was the Christ.

ἐκκλησίαν, κατέβη εἰς Ἀντιόχειαν, **23** καὶ
church, he went down to Antioch, and

ποιήσας χρόνον τινὰ ἐξῆλθεν, διερχόμενος
having spent time some he went forth, passing through

καθεξῆς τὴν Γαλατικὴν χώραν καὶ Φρυγίαν,
in order the Galatian country and Phrygia,

στηρίζων πάντας τοὺς μαθητάς.
confirming all the disciples.

24 Ἰουδαῖος δέ τις Ἀπολλῶς ὀνόματι,
And a certain Jew Apollos by name,

Ἀλεξανδρεὺς τῷ γένει, ἀνὴρ λόγιος,
an Alexandrian – by race, a man eloquent,

κατήντησεν εἰς Ἔφεσον, δυνατὸς ὢν ἐν
came to Ephesus, powerful being in

ταῖς γραφαῖς. **25** οὗτος ἦν κατηχημένος
the scriptures. This man was orally instructed [in]

τὴν ὁδὸν τοῦ κυρίου, καὶ ζέων τῷ
the way of the Lord, and burning –

πνεύματι ἐλάλει καὶ ἐδίδασκεν ἀκριβῶς
in spirit he spoke and taught accurately

τὰ περὶ τοῦ Ἰησοῦ, ἐπιστάμενος
the things concerning – Jesus, understanding

μόνον τὸ βάπτισμα Ἰωάννου· **26** οὗτός τε
only the baptism of John; and this man

ἤρξατο παρρησιάζεσθαι ἐν τῇ συναγωγῇ.
began to speak boldly in the synagogue.

ἀκούσαντες δὲ αὐτοῦ Πρίσκιλλα καὶ
And hearing him Priscilla and

Ἀκύλας προσελάβοντο αὐτὸν καὶ ἀκριβέστε-
Aquila took him and more accurate-

ρον αὐτῷ ἐξέθεντο τὴν ὁδὸν τοῦ θεοῦ.
ly to him explained the way of God.

27 βουλομένου δὲ αὐτοῦ διελθεῖν εἰς τὴν
And intending himᵃ to go through into –
= when he intended

Ἀχαΐαν, προτρεψάμενοι οἱ ἀδελφοὶ ἔγραψαν
Achaia, being encouraged the brothers wrote

τοῖς μαθηταῖς ἀποδέξασθαι αὐτόν· ὃς
to the disciples to welcome him; who

παραγενόμενος συνεβάλετο πολὺ τοῖς
arriving contributed much to the [ones]

πεπιστευκόσιν διὰ τῆς χάριτος· **28** εὐτόνως
having believed through – grace; ¹vehemently

γὰρ τοῖς Ἰουδαίοις διακατηλέγχετο δημοσίᾳ
¹for ⁴the ⁵Jews ³he confuted publicly

ἐπιδεικνὺς διὰ τῶν γραφῶν εἶναι τὸν
proving through the scriptures ⁷to be ⁸the

χριστὸν Ἰησοῦν.
⁶Christ ⁹Jesus.

Chapter 19

Paul at Ephesus

AND it came about that while Apollos was at Corinth, Paul having passed through the upper country came to Ephesus and found some disciples.

2and he said to them, "Did you receive the Holy Spirit when you believed?" And they *said* to him, "No, we have not even heard whether there is a Holy Spirit."

3And he said, "Into what

---

19 Ἐγένετο δὲ ἐν τῷ τὸν Ἀπολλῶ
Now it came to pass in the – Apollos
= while Apollos was

εἶναι ἐν Κορίνθῳ Παῦλον διελθόντα τὰ
to beᵇᵉ in Corinth Paul having passed through the

ἀνωτερικὰ μέρη ἐλθεῖν εἰς Ἔφεσον καὶ
higher parts to comeᵇ to Ephesus and

εὑρεῖν τινας μαθητάς, **2** εἶπέν τε πρὸς
to findᵇ some disciples, and said to

αὐτούς· εἰ πνεῦμα ἅγιον ἐλάβετε πιστεύσαν-
them: If Spirit Holy ye received believ-

τες; οἱ δὲ πρὸς αὐτόν· ἀλλ᾽ οὐδ᾽ εἰ
ing? And they [said] to him: But ²not ³if

πνεῦμα ἅγιον ἔστιν ἠκούσαμεν. **3** εἶπέν τε·
⁶Spirit ⁵Holy ⁴there is ¹we heard. And he said:

---

church and then went down to Antioch.

23After spending some time in Antioch, Paul set out from there and traveled from place to place throughout the region of Galatia and Phrygia, strengthening all the disciples.

24Meanwhile a Jew named Apollos, a native of Alexandria, came to Ephesus. He was a learned man, with a thorough knowledge of the Scriptures. 25He had been instructed in the way of the Lord, and he spoke with great fervorᵏ and taught about Jesus accurately, though he knew only the baptism of John. 26He began to speak boldly in the synagogue. When Priscilla and Aquila heard him, they invited him to their home and explained to him the way of God more adequately.

27When Apollos wanted to go to Achaia, the brothers encouraged him and wrote to the disciples there to welcome him. On arriving, he was a great help to those who by grace had believed. 28For he vigorously refuted the Jews in public debate, proving from the Scriptures that Jesus was the Christ.

Chapter 19

Paul in Ephesus

WHILE Apollos was at Corinth, Paul took the road through the interior and arrived at Ephesus. There he found some disciples 2and asked them, "Did you receive the Holy Spirit when ˡ you believed?"

They answered, "No, we have not even heard that there is a Holy Spirit."

3So Paul asked, "Then

ᵏ25 Or *with fervor in the Spirit*
ˡ2 Or *after*

then were you baptized?''
And they said, "Into
John's baptism.''

4And Paul said, "John
baptized with the baptism
of repentance, telling the
people to believe in Him
who was coming after him,
that is, in Jesus.''

5And when they heard
this, they were baptized in
the name of the Lord Jesus.

6And when Paul had laid
his hands upon them, the
Holy Spirit came on them,
and they *began* speaking
with tongues and prophesying.

7And there were in all
about twelve men.

8And he entered the
synagogue and continued
speaking out boldly for
three months, reasoning
and persuading *them* about
the kingdom of God.

9But when some were
becoming hardened and
disobedient, speaking evil
of the Way before the multitude, he withdrew from
them and took away the
disciples, reasoning daily in
the school of Tyrannus.

10And this took place for
two years, so that all who
lived in Asia heard the
word of the Lord, both
Jews and Greeks.

Miracles at Ephesus

11And God was perform-
ing extraordinary miracles
by the hands of Paul,
12so that handkerchiefs or
aprons were even carried
from his body to the sick,
and the diseases left them
and the evil spirits went
out.

13But also some of the
Jewish exorcists, who went
from place to place, at-
tempted to name over
those who had the evil

εἰς τί οὖν ἐβαπτίσθητε; οἱ δὲ εἶπαν·
To what therefore were ye baptized? And they said:
εἰς τὸ Ἰωάννου βάπτισμα. 4 εἶπεν δὲ
To the of John baptism. And said
Παῦλος· Ἰωάννης ἐβάπτισεν βάπτισμα μετα-
Paul: John baptized [with] a baptism of repent-
νοίας, τῷ λαῷ λέγων εἰς τὸν ἐρχόμενον
ance, ²to the ³people ¹saying ⁴in ⁷the [one] ⁶coming
μετ' αὐτὸν ἵνα πιστεύσωσιν, τοῦτ' ἔστιν
⁸after ¹⁰him ⁹that ⁵they should believe, this is
εἰς τὸν Ἰησοῦν. 5 ἀκούσαντες δὲ ἐβαπτίσ-
in Jesus. And hearing they were
θησαν εἰς τὸ ὄνομα τοῦ κυρίου Ἰησοῦ.
baptized in the name of the Lord Jesus.
6 καὶ ἐπιθέντος αὐτοῖς τοῦ Παύλου χεῖρας
And laying on them - Paul hands*
=as Paul laid [his] hands on them
ἦλθε τὸ πνεῦμα τὸ ἅγιον ἐπ' αὐτούς,
came the Spirit - Holy on them,
ἐλάλουν τε γλώσσαις καὶ ἐπροφήτευον.
and they spoke in tongues and prophesied.
7 ἦσαν δὲ οἱ πάντες ἄνδρες ὡσεὶ δώδεκα.
And ⁴were ²the ¹all ³men about twelve.
8 Εἰσελθὼν δὲ εἰς τὴν συναγωγὴν
And entering into the synagogue
ἐπαρρησιάζετο ἐπὶ μῆνας τρεῖς διαλεγόμενος
he spoke boldly over months three lecturing
καὶ πείθων περὶ τῆς βασιλείας τοῦ θεοῦ.
and persuading concerning the kingdom - of God.
9 ὡς δέ τινες ἐσκληρύνοντο καὶ ἠπείθουν
But as some were hardened and disobeyed
κακολογοῦντες τὴν ὁδὸν ἐνώπιον τοῦ
speaking ill [of] the way before the
πλήθους, ἀποστὰς ἀπ' αὐτῶν ἀφώρισεν
multitude, withdrawing from them he separated
τοὺς μαθητάς, καθ' ἡμέραν διαλεγόμενος
the disciples, daily lecturing
ἐν τῇ σχολῇ Τυράννου. 10 τοῦτο δὲ
in the school of Tyrannus. And this
ἐγένετο ἐπὶ ἔτη δύο, ὥστε πάντας τοὺς
happened over years two, so as all the
=so that all who inhabited
κατοικοῦντας τὴν Ἀσίαν ἀκοῦσαι τὸν
[ones] inhabiting - Asia to hear[b] the
Asia heard
λόγον τοῦ κυρίου, Ἰουδαίους τε καὶ
word of the Lord, ²Jews ¹both and
Ἕλληνας. 11 Δυνάμεις τε οὐ τὰς τυχούσας
Greeks. And powerful deeds not the ordinary
ὁ θεὸς ἐποίει διὰ τῶν χειρῶν Παύλου,
- God did through the hands of Paul,
12 ὥστε καὶ ἐπὶ τοὺς ἀσθενοῦντας
so as even onto the [ones] ailing
=so that there were even brought away from his skin hand-
ἀποφέρεσθαι ἀπὸ τοῦ χρωτὸς αὐτοῦ
to be brought away from the skin of him
kerchiefs or aprons onto those who ailed and the diseases were rid
σουδάρια ἢ σιμικίνθια καὶ ἀπαλλάσσεσθαι
handkerchiefs or aprons and to be rid
from them, and the evil spirits went out.
ἀπ' αὐτῶν τὰς νόσους, τά τε πνεύματα
from them the diseases, and the spirits
τὰ πονηρὰ ἐκπορεύεσθαι. 13 Ἐπεχείρησαν δέ
evil to go out. But ⁷attempted
τινες καὶ τῶν περιερχομένων Ἰουδαίων
¹some ²also ³of the ⁴strolling ⁵Jews
ἐξορκιστῶν ὀνομάζειν ἐπὶ τοὺς ἔχοντας
⁶exorcists to name over the [ones] having

---

what baptism did you re-
ceive?''

"John's baptism," they
replied.

4Paul said, "John's bap-
tism was a baptism of re-
pentance. He told the people to believe in the one
coming after him, that is, in
Jesus." 5On hearing this,
they were baptized into[m]
the name of the Lord Jesus.
6When Paul placed his
hands on them, the Holy
Spirit came on them, and
they spoke in tongues[n] and
prophesied. 7There were
about twelve men in all.

8Paul entered the syna-
gogue and spoke boldly
there for three months, arguing persuasively about
the kingdom of God. 9But
some of them became ob-
stinate; they refused to believe and publicly maligned
the Way. So Paul left them.
He took the disciples with
him and had discussions
daily in the lecture hall of
Tyrannus. 10This went on
for two years, so that all the
Jews and Greeks who lived
in the province of Asia
heard the word of the Lord.

11God did extraordinary
miracles through Paul, 12so
that even handkerchiefs
and aprons that had
touched him were taken to
the sick, and their illnesses
were cured and the evil
spirits left them.

13Some Jews who went
around driving out evil
spirits tried to invoke the
name of the Lord Jesus
over those who were de-

m5 Or in
n6 Or other languages

spirits the name of the Lord Jesus, saying, "I adjure you by Jesus whom Paul preaches."

14And seven sons of one Sceva, a Jewish chief priest, were doing this.

15And the evil spirit answered and said to them, "I recognize Jesus, and I know about Paul, but who are you?"

16And the man, in whom was the evil spirit, leaped on them and subdued all of them and overpowered them, so that they fled out of that house naked and wounded.

17And this became known to all, both Jews and Greeks, who lived in Ephesus; and fear fell upon them all and the name of the Lord Jesus was being magnified.

18Many also of those who had believed kept coming, confessing and disclosing their practices.

19And many of those who practiced magic brought their books together and began burning them in the sight of all; and they counted up the price of them and found it fifty thousand pieces of silver.

20So the word of the Lord was growing mightily and prevailing.

21Now after these things were finished, Paul purposed in the spirit to go to Jerusalem after he had passed through Macedonia and Achaia, saying, "After I have been there, I must also see Rome."

22And having sent into Macedonia two of those

τὰ πνεύματα τὰ πονηρὰ τὸ ὄνομα τοῦ
the spirits - evil the name of the

κυρίου Ἰησοῦ λέγοντες· ὁρκίζω ὑμᾶς τὸν
Lord Jesus saying: I exorcise you [by] -

Ἰησοῦν ὃν Παῦλος κηρύσσει. 14 ἦσαν δέ
Jesus whom Paul proclaims. And there were

τινος Σκευᾶ Ἰουδαίου ἀρχιερέως ἑπτὰ
²of one ⁴Sceva ³a Jewish ⁵chief priest ¹seven

υἱοὶ τοῦτο ποιοῦντες. 15 ἀποκριθὲν δὲ
⁸sons ⁶this ⁷doing. And answering

τὸ πνεῦμα τὸ πονηρὸν εἶπεν αὐτοῖς·
the spirit - evil said to them:

τὸν [μὲν] Ἰησοῦν γινώσκω καὶ -
- ¹indeed ²Jesus I know and -

Παῦλον ἐπίσταμαι· ὑμεῖς δὲ τίνες ἐστέ;
Paul I understand; but ye who are?

16 καὶ ἐφαλόμενος ὁ ἄνθρωπος ἐπ᾽ αὐτούς,
And ³leaping on ¹the ²man ⁴on them,

ἐν ᾧ ἦν τὸ πνεῦμα τὸ πονηρόν,
³in ¹whom ²was ⁴the ⁵spirit - ⁷evil,

κατακυριεύσας ἀμφοτέρων ἴσχυσεν κατ᾽
overmastering both was strong against

αὐτῶν, ὥστε γυμνοὺς καὶ τετραυματισμένους
them, so as naked and having been wounded
=so that they escaped out of that house naked and

ἐκφυγεῖν ἐκ τοῦ οἴκου ἐκείνου. 17 τοῦτο
to escape out of that house. this
wounded.

δὲ ἐγένετο γνωστὸν πᾶσιν Ἰουδαίοις τε
And became known to all ¹Jews ²both

καὶ Ἕλλησιν τοῖς κατοικοῦσιν τὴν Ἔφεσον,
and Greeks - inhabiting - Ephesus,

καὶ ἐπέπεσεν φόβος ἐπὶ πάντας αὐτούς,
and ²fell on ¹fear ³on ⁴all ⁵them,

καὶ ἐμεγαλύνετο τὸ ὄνομα τοῦ κυρίου
and was magnified the name of the Lord

Ἰησοῦ· 18 πολλοί τε τῶν πεπιστευκότων
Jesus; and many of the [ones] having believed

ἤρχοντο ἐξομολογούμενοι καὶ ἀναγγέλλοντες
came confessing and telling

τὰς πράξεις αὐτῶν. 19 ἱκανοὶ δὲ τῶν τὰ
the doings of them. And a consider- of the the
able number [ones]

περίεργα πραξάντων συνενέγκαντες τὰς βίβλους
curious things doing bringing together the rolls

κατέκαιον ἐνώπιον πάντων· καὶ συνεψήφισαν
burnt before all; and they reckoned up

τὰς τιμὰς αὐτῶν καὶ εὗρον ἀργυρίου μυριάδας
the prices of them and found [pieces] ²thousand
³of silver

πέντε. 20 Οὕτως κατὰ κράτος τοῦ κυρίου
¹five. Thus by might ³of the ⁴Lord

ὁ λόγος ηὔξανεν καὶ ἴσχυεν.
¹the ²word increased and was strong.

21 Ὡς δὲ ἐπληρώθη ταῦτα, ἔθετο ὁ
And when were fulfilled these things, purposed -

Παῦλος ἐν τῷ πνεύματι διελθὼν τὴν
Paul in the(his) spirit passing through -

Μακεδονίαν καὶ Ἀχαΐαν πορεύεσθαι εἰς
Macedonia and Achaia to go to

Ἱεροσόλυμα, εἰπὼν ὅτι μετὰ τὸ γενέσθαι
Jerusalem, saying[,] - After the to become
=After I am

με ἐκεῖ δεῖ με καὶ Ῥώμην ἰδεῖν.
meᵇ there it behoves me ²also ¹Rome ¹to see.

22 ἀποστείλας δὲ εἰς Μακεδονίαν δύο
And sending into Macedonia two

---

mon-possessed. They would say, "In the name of Jesus, whom Paul preaches, I command you to come out." 14Seven sons of Sceva, a Jewish chief priest, were doing this. 15One day the evil spirit answered them, "Jesus I know, and I know about Paul, but who are you?" 16Then the man who had the evil spirit jumped on them and overpowered them all. He gave them such a beating that they ran out of the house naked and bleeding.

17When this became known to the Jews and Greeks living in Ephesus, they were all seized with fear, and the name of the Lord Jesus was held in high honor. 18Many of those who believed now came and openly confessed their evil deeds. 19A number who had practiced sorcery brought their scrolls together and burned them publicly. When they calculated the value of the scrolls, the total came to fifty thousand drachmas.ᵒ 20In this way the word of the Lord spread widely and grew in power.

21After all this had happened, Paul decided to go to Jerusalem, passing through Macedonia and Achaia. "After I have been there," he said, "I must visit Rome also." 22He sent two of his helpers, Timothy

ᵒ19 A drachma was a silver coin worth about a day's wages.

who ministered to him, Timothy and Erastus, he himself stayed in Asia for a while.

23And about that time there arose no small disturbance concerning the Way.

24For a certain man named Demetrius, a silversmith, who made silver shrines of Artemis, was bringing no little business to the craftsmen;

25these he gathered together with the workmen of similar *trades,* and said, "Men, you know that our prosperity depends upon this business.

26"And you see and hear that not only in Ephesus, but in almost all of Asia, this Paul has persuaded and turned away a considerable number of people, saying that gods made with hands are no gods *at all.*

27"And not only is there danger that this trade of ours fall into disrepute, but also that the temple of the great goddess Artemis be regarded as worthless and that she whom all of Asia and the world worship should even be dethroned from her magnificence."

28And when they heard *this* and were filled with rage, they *began* crying out, saying, "Great is Artemis of the Ephesians!"

29And the city was filled with the confusion, and they rushed with one accord into the theater, dragging along Gaius and Aristarchus, Paul's traveling companions from Macedonia.

30And when Paul wanted to go into the assembly, the disciples would not let him.

31And also some of the [h]Asiarchs who were

τῶν διακονούντων αὐτῷ, Τιμόθεον καὶ
of the [ones] ministering to him, Timothy and

Ἔραστον, αὐτὸς ἐπέσχεν χρόνον εἰς τὴν
Erastus, he delayed a time in -

Ἀσίαν. 23 Ἐγένετο δὲ κατὰ τὸν καιρὸν
Asia. Now there was about - time

ἐκεῖνον τάραχος οὐκ ὀλίγος περὶ τῆς
that ²trouble ¹no ³little concerning the

ὁδοῦ. 24 Δημήτριος γάρ τις ὀνόματι,
way. For ¹Demetrius ²one by name,

ἀργυροκόπος, ποιῶν ναοὺς ἀργυροῦς
a silversmith, making shrines silver

Ἀρτέμιδος παρείχετο τοῖς τεχνίταις οὐκ
of Artemis provided the artisans no

ὀλίγην ἐργασίαν, 25 οὓς συναθροίσας καὶ
little trade, ¹whom ²assembling also

τοὺς περὶ τὰ τοιαῦτα ἐργάτας εἶπεν·
¹the ²about(in) - ⁴such things ³workmen said:

ἄνδρες, ἐπίστασθε ὅτι ἐκ ταύτης τῆς
Men, ye understand that from this -

ἐργασίας ἡ εὐπορία ἡμῖν ἐστιν, 26 καὶ
trade the gain to us is,° and
=we have [our] gain,

θεωρεῖτε καὶ ἀκούετε ὅτι οὐ μόνον
ye behold and hear that ²not ¹only

Ἐφέσου ἀλλὰ σχεδὸν πάσης τῆς Ἀσίας
of Ephesus ¹⁰but ¹¹almost ¹²of all - ¹³Asia

ὁ Παῦλος οὗτος πείσας μετέστησεν ἱκανὸν
- ²Paul ¹this ³having ⁴perverted ⁵a considerable
persuaded

ὄχλον, λέγων ὅτι οὐκ εἰσὶν θεοὶ οἱ διὰ
⁶crowd, saying that they are not gods ¹the ²through
[ones]

χειρῶν γινόμενοι. 27 οὐ μόνον δὲ τοῦτο
³hands ⁴coming into being. ²not ¹only - ³Now ¹this

κινδυνεύει ἡμῖν τὸ μέρος εἰς ἀπελεγμὸν
²is in danger to us the share° ²into ³disrepute
=⁴our share

ἐλθεῖν, ἀλλὰ καὶ τὸ τῆς μεγάλης θεᾶς
¹to come, but also ¹the ²of the ⁴great ⁵goddess

Ἀρτέμιδος ἱερὸν εἰς οὐθὲν λογισθῆναι,
³Artemis ⁶temple ⁸for(as) ⁷nothing ⁷to be reckoned,

μέλλειν τε καὶ καθαιρεῖσθαι τῆς μεγα-
²to be about ¹and ³also ⁴to be diminished the great-

λειότητος αὐτῆς, ἣν ὅλη ἡ Ἀσία καὶ
ness of her, whom all - Asia and

ἡ οἰκουμένη σέβεται. 28 ἀκούσαντες δὲ
the inhabited earth worships. And hearing

καὶ γενόμενοι πλήρεις θυμοῦ ἔκραζον
and becoming full of anger they cried out

λέγοντες· μεγάλη ἡ Ἄρτεμις Ἐφεσίων.
saying: Great [is] - Artemis of [the] Ephesians.

29 καὶ ἐπλήσθη ἡ πόλις τῆς συγχύσεως,
And was filled the city of(with) the confusion,

ὥρμησάν τε ὁμοθυμαδὸν εἰς τὸ θέατρον,
and they rushed with one mind into the theatre,

συναρπάσαντες Γάϊον καὶ Ἀρίσταρχον
keeping a firm grip on Gaius and Aristarchus[,]

Μακεδόνας, συνεκδήμους Παύλου. 30 Παύλου
Macedonians, travelling companions of Paul. Paul

δὲ βουλομένου εἰσελθεῖν εἰς τὸν δῆμον
And intending* to enter into the mob
=as Paul intended

οὐκ εἴων αὐτὸν οἱ μαθηταί· 31 τινὲς
⁵not ²allowed ⁴him ¹the ³disciples; some

δὲ καὶ τῶν Ἀσιαρχῶν, ὄντες αὐτῷ
and also of the Asiarchs, being to him

---

and Erastus, to Macedonia, while he stayed in the province of Asia a little longer.

The Riot in Ephesus

23About that time there arose a great disturbance about the Way. 24A silversmith named Demetrius, who made silver shrines of Artemis, brought in no little business for the craftsmen. 25He called them together, along with the workmen in related trades, and said: "Men, you know we receive a good income from this business. 26And you see and hear how this fellow Paul has convinced and led astray large numbers of people here in Ephesus and in practically the whole province of Asia. He says that man-made gods are no gods at all. 27There is danger not only that our trade will lose its good name, but also that the temple of the great goddess Artemis will be discredited, and the goddess herself, who is worshiped throughout the province of Asia and the world, will be robbed of her divine majesty."

28When they heard this, they were furious and began shouting: "Great is Artemis of the Ephesians!" 29Soon the whole city was in an uproar. The people seized Gaius and Aristarchus, Paul's traveling companions from Macedonia, and rushed as one man into the theater. 30Paul wanted to appear before the crowd, but the disciples would not let him. 31Even some of the officials of the province,

---

[h] I.e., political or religious officials of the province of Asia

friends of his sent to him and repeatedly urged him not to venture into the theater.

32So then, some were shouting one thing and some another, for the assembly was in confusion, and the majority did not know for what cause they had come together.

33And some of the crowd concluded it was Alexander, since the Jews had put him forward; and having motioned with his hand, Alexander was intending to make a defense to the assembly.

34But when they recognized that he was a Jew, a *single* outcry arose from them all as they shouted for about two hours, "Great is Artemis of the Ephesians!"

35And after quieting the multitude, the town clerk *said, "Men of Ephesus, what man is there after all who does not know that the city of the Ephesians is guardian of the temple of the great Artemis, and of the *image* which fell down from heaven?

36"Since then these are undeniable facts, you ought to keep calm and to do nothing rash.

37"For you have brought these men *here* who are neither robbers of temples nor blasphemers of our goddess.

38"So then, if Demetrius and the craftsmen who are with him have a complaint against any man, the courts are in session and proconsuls are *available*; let them bring charges against one another.

39"But if you want anything beyond this, it shall be settled in the lawful assembly.

40"For indeed we are in danger of being accused of a riot in connection with today's affair, since there is no *real* cause *for it*; and in this connection we shall be unable to account for this disorderly gathering."

φίλοι,   πέμψαντες   πρὸς   αὐτὸν   παρεκάλουν
friends,   sending   to   him   besought

μὴ   δοῦναι   ἑαυτὸν   εἰς   τὸ   θέατρον.   32 ἄλλοι
not   to give   himself   in   the   theatre.   Others

μὲν   οὖν   ἄλλο   τι   ἔκραζον·   ἦν   γὰρ
indeed therefore ²different ¹something cried out;   for ²was

ἡ   ἐκκλησία   συγκεχυμένη,   καὶ   οἱ   πλείους
¹the ²assembly *having been* confounded, and the majority

οὐκ   ᾔδεισαν   τίνος   ἕνεκα   συνεληλύθεισαν.
knew not   ¹of what ¹on account   they had come together.

33 ἐκ   δὲ   τοῦ   ὄχλου   συνεβίβασαν   Ἀλέξανδρον,
But [some] of the crowd   instructed   Alexander,

προβαλόντων   αὐτὸν   τῶν   Ἰουδαίων·   ὁ   δὲ
putting forward   him   the   Jews[a];   -   and
= as the Jews put him forward;

Ἀλέξανδρος   κατασείσας   τὴν   χεῖρα   ἤθελεν
Alexander   waving   the(his) hand   wished

ἀπολογεῖσθαι   τῷ   δήμῳ.   34 ἐπιγνόντες   δὲ
to defend himself   to the   mob.   But knowing

ὅτι   Ἰουδαῖός   ἐστιν,   φωνὴ   ἐγένετο   μία
that   a Jew   he is(was),   ¹voice ²there was   ²one

ἐκ   πάντων,   ὡς   ἐπὶ   ὥρας   δύο   κράζοντες·
from   all,   about over   hours   two   crying out:

μεγάλη   ἡ   Ἄρτεμις   Ἐφεσίων.   35 κατα-
Great [is]   -   Artemis   of [the] Ephesians.   ²having

στείλας   δὲ   ὁ   γραμματεὺς   τὸν   ὄχλον
quietened ¹And ¹the ²town clerk   the   crowd

φησίν·   ἄνδρες   Ἐφέσιοι,   τίς   γάρ   ἐστιν
says: Men   Ephesians,   who indeed is there

ἀνθρώπων   ὃς   οὐ   γινώσκει   τὴν   Ἐφεσίων
of men   who does not know   ¹the ²of [the] Ephesians

πόλιν   νεωκόρον   οὖσαν   τῆς   μεγάλης
²city   ³temple warden   ⁴being   of the   great

Ἀρτέμιδος   καὶ   τοῦ   διοπετοῦς;   36 ἀναντιρ-
Artemis   and of the   fallen from   undeni-
            [image]   the sky?

ρήτων   οὖν   ὄντων   τούτων   δέον   ἐστὶν
able   therefore being   these things[a] necessary   it is
= as these things are undeniable

ὑμᾶς   κατεσταλμένους   ὑπάρχειν   καὶ   μηδὲν
you   ²having been quietened   ¹to be   and   ³nothing

προπετὲς   πράσσειν.   37 ἠγάγετε   γὰρ   τοὺς
²rash   ¹to do.   For ye brought   for   these

ἄνδρας   τούτους   οὔτε   ἱεροσύλους   οὔτε
men   these   neither   temple robbers   nor

βλασφημοῦντας   τὴν   θεὸν   ἡμῶν.   38 εἰ
blaspheming   the   goddess   of you.   If

μὲν   οὖν   Δημήτριος   καὶ   οἱ   σὺν   αὐτῷ
indeed therefore Demetrius   and   ¹the ²with ⁴him

τεχνῖται   ἔχουσι   πρός   τινα   λόγον,   ἀγοραῖοι
³artisans   have   against anyone an account,   assizes

ἄγονται   καὶ   ἀνθύπατοί   εἰσιν,   ἐγκαλείτωσαν
are   and   proconsuls   there are,   let them bring a
being(held)   charge against

ἀλλήλοις.   39 εἰ   δέ   τι   περαιτέρω   ἐπιζητεῖτε,
one another.   But if ²anything   ²further   ¹ye seek,

ἐν   τῇ   ἐννόμῳ   ἐκκλησίᾳ   ἐπιλυθήσεται.
in   the   lawful   assembly   it will be settled.

40 καὶ   γὰρ   κινδυνεύομεν   ἐγκαλεῖσθαι
For indeed   we are in danger   to be charged with

στάσεως   περὶ   τῆς   σήμερον,   μηδενὸς
insurrection concerning   the   to-day,   nothing

αἰτίου   ὑπάρχοντος,   περὶ   οὗ   οὐ   δυνησόμεθα
cause   being*,   concerning which   we shall *not* be able
= there being no cause,

ἀποδοῦναι   λόγον   περὶ   τῆς   συστροφῆς
to give   account concerning   -   ²crowding together

---

friends of Paul, sent him a message begging him not to venture into the theater.

32The assembly was in confusion: Some were shouting one thing, some another. Most of the people did not even know why they were there. 33The Jews pushed Alexander to the front, and some of the crowd shouted instructions to him. He motioned for silence in order to make a defense before the people. 34But when they realized he was a Jew, they all shouted in unison for about two hours: "Great is Artemis of the Ephesians!"

35The city clerk quieted the crowd and said: "Men of Ephesus, doesn't all the world know that the city of Ephesus is the guardian of the temple of the great Artemis and of her image, which fell from heaven? 36Therefore, since these facts are undeniable, you ought to be quiet and not do anything rash. 37You have brought these men here, though they have neither robbed temples nor blasphemed our goddess. 38If, then, Demetrius and his fellow craftsmen have a grievance against anybody, the courts are open and there are proconsuls. They can press charges. 39If there is anything further you want to bring up, it must be settled in a legal assembly. 40As it is, we are in danger of being charged with rioting because of today's events. In that case we would not be able to account for this commotion, since there is no reason for

41And after saying this he dismissed the assembly.

Chapter 20

Paul in Macedonia and Greece

AND after the uproar had ceased, Paul sent for the disciples and when he had exhorted them and taken his leave of them, he departed to go to Macedonia.

2And when he had gone through those districts and had given them much exhortation, he came to Greece.

3And *there* he spent three months, and when a plot was formed against him by the Jews as he was about to set sail for Syria, he determined to return through Macedonia.

4And he was accompanied by Sopater of Berea, *the son* of Pyrrhus; and by Aristarchus and Secundus of the Thessalonians; and Gaius of Derbe, and Timothy; and Tychicus and Trophimus of Asia.

5But these had gone on ahead and were waiting for us at Troas.

6And we sailed from Philippi after the days of Unleavened Bread, and came to them at Troas within five days; and there we stayed seven days.

7And on the first day of the week, when we were gathered together to break bread, Paul *began* talking to them, intending to depart the next day, and he prolonged his message until midnight.

8And there were many lamps in the upper room where we were gathered together.

9And there was a certain young man named Eutychus sitting on the window sill, sinking into a deep sleep; and as Paul kept on

---

ταύτης. **41** καὶ ταῦτα εἰπὼν ἀπέλυσεν τὴν
¹this.   And these things saying   he dismissed   the

ἐκκλησίαν.
assembly.

20 Μετὰ δὲ τὸ παύσασθαι τὸν θόρυβονᵇ
And after   the   to cease   the   uproarᵇ
=after the uproar ceased

μεταπεμψάμενος ὁ Παῦλος τοὺς μαθητὰς
²summoning   –   ¹Paul   ⁵the   ⁶disciples

καὶ παρακαλέσας, ἀσπασάμενος ἐξῆλθεν
³and   ⁴exhorting,   taking leave   he went forth

πορεύεσθαι εἰς Μακεδονίαν. **2** διελθὼν δὲ
to go   to   Macedonia.   And having gone through

τὰ μέρη ἐκεῖνα καὶ παρακαλέσας αὐτοὺς
those parts   and   having exhorted   them

λόγῳ πολλῷ ἦλθεν εἰς τὴν Ἑλλάδα,
¹with ³speech ²much   he came   into   –   Greece,

3 ποιήσας τε μῆνας τρεῖς, γενομένης
and spending   months   three,   there being

ἐπιβουλῆς αὐτῷ ὑπὸ τῶν Ἰουδαίων
a plotᵃ   [against] him   by   the   Jews

μέλλοντι ἀνάγεσθαι εἰς τὴν Συρίαν, ἐγένετο
being about to set sail   to(for)   –   Syria,   he was
=as he was about

γνώμης τοῦ ὑποστρέφειν διὰ Μακεδονίας.
of a mind   –   to returnᵈ   through   Macedonia.

4 συνείπετο δὲ αὐτῷ Σώπατρος Πύρρου
And there accompanied   him   Sopater [son] of Pyrrhus

Βεροιαῖος, Θεσσαλονικέων δὲ Ἀρίσταρχος
a Berœan,   and of Thessalonians   Aristarchus

καὶ Σέκουνδος, καὶ Γάϊος Δερβαῖος καὶ
and   Secundus,   and   Gaius   a Derbæan   and

Τιμόθεος, Ἀσιανοὶ δὲ Τύχικος καὶ
Timothy,   and Asians   Tychicus   and

Τρόφιμος. **5** οὗτοι δὲ προελθόντες ἔμενον
Trophimus.   And these men   going forward   awaited

ἡμᾶς ἐν Τρῳάδι· **6** ἡμεῖς δὲ ἐξεπλεύσαμεν
us   in   Troas;   and we   sailed away

μετὰ τὰς ἡμέρας τῶν ἀζύμων ἀπὸ
after   the   days   – of unleavened bread from

Φιλίππων, καὶ ἤλθομεν πρὸς αὐτοὺς εἰς
Philippi,   and –   came   to   them   in

τὴν Τρῳάδα ἄχρι ἡμερῶν πέντε, ὅπου
–   Troas   until   days   five,   where

διετρίψαμεν ἡμέρας ἑπτά. **7** Ἐν δὲ τῇ
we stayed   days   seven.   And on   the

μιᾷ τῶν σαββάτων συνηγμένων ἡμῶν
one(first) of the   sabbaths(week)   having been   usᵃ
[day]   assembled
         =as we were assembled

κλάσαι ἄρτον ὁ Παῦλος διελέγετο αὐτοῖς,
to break   bread   –   Paul   lectured   to them,

μέλλων ἐξιέναι τῇ ἐπαύριον, παρέτεινέν τε
being about to depart on the   morrow,   and continued

τὸν λόγον μέχρι μεσονυκτίου. **8** ἦσαν δὲ
the   speech   until   midnight.   Now there were

λαμπάδες ἱκαναὶ ἐν τῷ ὑπερῴῳ οὗ
lamps   a considerable in   the   upper room where
    number of

ἦμεν συνηγμένοι. **9** καθεζόμενος δέ τις
we were *having been* assembled.   And sitting   a certain

νεανίας ὀνόματι Εὔτυχος ἐπὶ τῆς θυρίδος,
young man by name   Eutychus   on   the window sill,

καταφερόμενος ὕπνῳ βαθεῖ, διαλεγομένου
being overborne   sleep   by a deep,   lecturing

---

it.'' 41After he had said this, he dismissed the assembly.

Chapter 20

Through Macedonia and Greece

WHEN the uproar had ended, Paul sent for the disciples and, after encouraging them, said good-by and set out for Macedonia. 2He traveled through that area, speaking many words of encouragement to the people, and finally arrived in Greece, 3where he stayed three months. Because the Jews made a plot against him just as he was about to sail for Syria, he decided to go back through Macedonia. 4He was accompanied by Sopater son of Pyrrhus from Berea, Aristarchus and Secundus from Thessalonica, Gaius from Derbe, Timothy also, and Tychicus and Trophimus from the province of Asia. 5These men went on ahead and waited for us at Troas. 6But we sailed from Philippi after the Feast of Unleavened Bread, and five days later joined the others at Troas, where we stayed seven days.

Eutychus Raised From the Dead at Troas

7On the first day of the week we came together to break bread. Paul spoke to the people and, because he intended to leave the next day, kept on talking until midnight. 8There were many lamps in the upstairs room where we were meeting. 9Seated in a window was a young man named Eutychus, who was sinking into a deep sleep as Paul talked on and on. When he talking, he was overcome by sleep and fell down from the third floor, and was picked up dead. 10But Paul went down and fell upon him and after embracing him, he said, "Do not be troubled, for his life is in him."

11And when he had gone *back* up, and had broken the bread and eaten, he talked with them a long while, until daybreak, and so departed.

12And they took away the boy alive, and were greatly comforted.

Troas to Miletus

13But we, going ahead to the ship, set sail for Assos, intending from there to take Paul on board; for thus he had arranged it, intending himself to go by land. 14And when he met us at Assos, we took him on board and came to Mitylene. 15And sailing from there, we arrived the following day opposite Chios; and the next day we crossed over to Samos; and the day following we came to Miletus. 16For Paul had decided to sail past Ephesus in order that he might not have to spend time in Asia; for he was hurrying to be in Jerusalem, if possible, on the day of Pentecost.

Farewell to Ephesus

17And from Miletus he sent to Ephesus and called to him the elders of the church. 18And when they had come to him, he said to them, "You yourselves know, from the first day that I set

τοῦ Παύλου ἐπὶ πλεῖον, κατενεχθεὶς ἀπὸ
– Paul^a for a longer time, having been from
=while Paul lectured overborne

τοῦ ὕπνου ἔπεσεν ἀπὸ τοῦ τριστέγου
the sleep he fell from the third floor[•]

κάτω καὶ ἤρθη νεκρός. 10 καταβὰς δὲ
down and was taken up dead. But going down

ὁ Παῦλος ἐπέπεσεν αὐτῷ καὶ συμπεριλαβὼν
– Paul fell on him and closely embracing
[him]

εἶπεν· μὴ θορυβεῖσθε· ἡ γὰρ ψυχὴ αὐτοῦ
said: Be ye not terrified; for the life of him

ἐν αὐτῷ ἐστιν. 11 ἀναβὰς δὲ καὶ κλάσας
in him is. And going up and breaking

τὸν ἄρτον καὶ γευσάμενος, ἐφ᾽ ἱκανόν τε
the bread and tasting, and over a considerable
[time]

ὁμιλήσας ἄχρι αὐγῆς, οὕτως ἐξῆλθεν.
conversing until light [of day], thus he went forth.

12 ἤγαγον δὲ τὸν παῖδα ζῶντα, καὶ
And they brought the lad living, and

παρεκλήθησαν οὐ μετρίως. 13 Ἡμεῖς δὲ
were comforted not moderately. And we

προελθόντες ἐπὶ τὸ πλοῖον ἀνήχθημεν
going before onto the ship set sail

ἐπὶ τὴν Ἄσσον, ἐκεῖθεν μέλλοντες ἀνα-
to(for) – Assos, thence intending to

λαμβάνειν τὸν Παῦλον· οὕτως γὰρ
take up – Paul; for thus

διατεταγμένος ἦν, μέλλων αὐτὸς πεζεύειν.
having been arranged it was, ²intending ¹he to go afoot.

14 ὡς δὲ συνέβαλλεν ἡμῖν εἰς τὴν Ἄσσον,
Now when he met with us in – Assos,

ἀναλαβόντες αὐτὸν ἤλθομεν εἰς Μιτυλήνην·
taking up him we came to Mitylene;

15 κἀκεῖθεν ἀποπλεύσαντες τῇ ἐπιούσῃ
and thence sailing away on the next [day]

κατηντήσαμεν ἄντικρυς Χίου, τῇ δὲ ἑτέρᾳ
we arrived off Chios, and on the other(next)

παρεβάλομεν εἰς Σάμον, τῇ δὲ ἐχομένῃ
we crossed over to Samos, and on the next

ἤλθομεν εἰς Μίλητον. 16 κεκρίκει γὰρ ὁ
we came to Miletus. For had decided –

Παῦλος παραπλεῦσαι τὴν Ἔφεσον, ὅπως
Paul to sail past – Ephesus, so as

μὴ γένηται αὐτῷ χρονοτριβῆσαι ἐν τῇ
not be to him to spend time in the
=so that he should not . . .

Ἀσίᾳ· ἔσπευδεν γάρ, εἰ δυνατὸν εἴη
Asia; for he hasted, if possible it might be

αὐτῷ, τὴν ἡμέραν τῆς πεντηκοστῆς
to him, the day – of Pentecost

γενέσθαι εἰς Ἱεροσόλυμα.
to be in Jerusalem.

17 Ἀπὸ δὲ τῆς Μιλήτου πέμψας εἰς
And from – Miletus sending to

Ἔφεσον μετεκαλέσατο τοὺς πρεσβυτέρους
Ephesus he summoned the elders

τῆς ἐκκλησίας. 18 ὡς δὲ παρεγένοντο
of the church. And when they came

πρὸς αὐτόν, εἶπεν αὐτοῖς· ὑμεῖς ἐπίστασθε,
to him, he said to them: Ye understand,

ἀπὸ πρώτης ἡμέρας ἀφ᾽ ἧς ἐπέβην εἰς
from [the] first day from which I set foot on in

was sound asleep, he fell to the ground from the third story and was picked up dead. 10Paul went down, threw himself on the young man and put his arms around him. "Don't be alarmed," he said. "He's alive!" 11Then he went upstairs again and broke bread and ate. After talking until daylight, he left. 12The people took the young man home alive and were greatly comforted.

Paul's Farewell to the Ephesian Elders

13We went on ahead to the ship and sailed for Assos, where we were going to take Paul aboard. He had made this arrangement because he was going there on foot. 14When he met us at Assos, we took him aboard and went on to Mitylene. 15The next day we set sail from there and arrived off Kios. The day after that we crossed over to Samos, and on the following day arrived at Miletus. 16Paul had decided to sail past Ephesus to avoid spending time in the province of Asia, for he was in a hurry to reach Jerusalem, if possible, by the day of Pentecost.

17From Miletus, Paul sent to Ephesus for the elders of the church. 18When they arrived, he said to them: "You know how I lived the whole time I was with you,

---

* Souter remarks that it is uncertain whether the ground floor was counted or not in the enunciation; " if so, we should have to translate ' the second floor '."

foot in Asia, how I was with you the whole time, ¹⁹serving the Lord with all humility and with tears and with trials which came upon me through the plots of the Jews; ²⁰how I did not shrink from declaring to you anything that was profitable, and teaching you publicly and from house to house, ²¹solemnly testifying to both Jews and Greeks of repentance toward God and faith in our Lord Jesus Christ. ²²"And now, behold, bound in spirit, I am on my way to Jerusalem, not knowing what will happen to me there, ²³except that the Holy Spirit solemnly testifies to me in every city, saying that bonds and afflictions await me. ²⁴"But I do not consider my life of any account as dear to myself, in order that I may finish my course, and the ministry which I received from the Lord Jesus, to testify solemnly of the gospel of the grace of God. ²⁵"And now, behold, I know that all of you, among whom I went about preaching the kingdom, will see my face no more. ²⁶"Therefore I testify to you this day, that I am innocent of the blood of all men. ²⁷"For I did not shrink from declaring to you the whole purpose of God. ²⁸"Be on guard for yourselves and for all the flock, among which the Holy Spirit has made you overseers, to shepherd the church of God which He purchased with His own blood.

τὴν Ἀσίαν, πῶς μεθ' ὑμῶν τὸν πάντα
- Asia, how with you the whole
χρόνον ἐγενόμην, 19 δουλεύων τῷ κυρίῳ
time I was, serving the Lord
μετὰ πάσης ταπεινοφροσύνης καὶ δακρύων
with all humility and tears
καὶ πειρασμῶν τῶν συμβάντων μοι ἐν
and trials - happening to me by
ταῖς ἐπιβουλαῖς τῶν Ἰουδαίων, 20 ὡς
the plots of the Jews, as
οὐδὲν ὑπεστειλάμην τῶν συμφερόντων τοῦ
¹nothing ¹I kept back of the things beneficial -
μὴ ἀναγγεῖλαι ὑμῖν καὶ διδάξαι ὑμᾶς
not to declareᵈ to you and to teachᵈ you
δημοσίᾳ καὶ κατ' οἴκους, 21 διαμαρτυρόμενος
publicly and from house to house,† solemnly witnessing
Ἰουδαίοις τε καὶ Ἕλλησιν τὴν εἰς θεὸν
²to Jews ¹both and to Greeks - toward God
μετάνοιαν καὶ πίστιν εἰς τὸν κύριον
repentance and faith toward(?in) the Lord
ἡμῶν Ἰησοῦν. 22 καὶ νῦν ἰδοὺ δεδεμένος
of us Jesus. And now behold having been bound
ἐγὼ τῷ πνεύματι πορεύομαι εἰς Ἰερου-
I by the Spirit am going to Jeru-
σαλήμ, ³τὰ ἐν αὐτῇ συναντήσοντα ἐμοὶ
salem, ³the things ⁵in ⁴it ⁴going to meet ⁶me
μὴ εἰδώς, 23 πλὴν ὅτι τὸ πνεῦμα τὸ
¹not ²knowing, except that the Spirit -
ἅγιον κατὰ πόλιν διαμαρτύρεταί μοι λέγον
Holy in every city† solemnly witnesses to me saying
ὅτι δεσμὰ καὶ θλίψεις με μένουσιν.
that bonds and afflictions me await.
24 ἀλλ' οὐδενὸς λόγου ποιοῦμαι τὴν ψυχὴν
But ⁴of nothing ⁵account ¹I make ²the(my) ³life
τιμίαν ἐμαυτῷ ὡς τελειώσω τὸν δρόμον
precious to myself so as I may finish the course
μου καὶ τὴν διακονίαν ἣν ἔλαβον παρὰ
of me and the ministry which I received from
τοῦ κυρίου Ἰησοῦ, διαμαρτύρασθαι τὸ
the Lord Jesus, to witness solemnly the
εὐαγγέλιον τῆς χάριτος τοῦ θεοῦ. 25 καὶ
gospel of the grace - of God. And
νῦν ἰδοὺ ἐγὼ οἶδα ὅτι οὐκέτι ὄψεσθε
now behold I know that ⁴no more ²will see
τὸ πρόσωπόν μου ὑμεῖς πάντες ἐν οἷς
⁵the ⁶face ⁷of me ¹ye ³all among whom
διῆλθον κηρύσσων τὴν βασιλείαν. 26 διότι
I went about proclaiming the kingdom. Wherefore
μαρτύρομαι ὑμῖν ἐν τῇ σήμερον ἡμέρᾳ
I witness to you on this day
ὅτι καθαρός εἰμι ἀπὸ τοῦ αἵματος πάντων·
that clean I am from the blood of all men;
27 οὐ γὰρ ὑπεστειλάμην τοῦ μὴ ἀναγγεῖλαι
for I kept not back - not to declareᵈ
πᾶσαν τὴν βουλὴν τοῦ θεοῦ ὑμῖν.
all the counsel - of God to you.
28 προσέχετε ἑαυτοῖς καὶ παντὶ τῷ
Take heed to yourselves and to all the
ποιμνίῳ, ἐν ᾧ ὑμᾶς τὸ πνεῦμα τὸ
flock, in which ⁶you ¹the ²Spirit -
ἅγιον ἔθετο ἐπισκόπους, ποιμαίνειν τὴν
³Holy ⁴placed overseers, to shepherd the
ἐκκλησίαν τοῦ θεοῦ, ἣν περιεποιήσατο
church - of God, which he acquired
διὰ τοῦ αἵματος τοῦ ἰδίου. 29 ἐγὼ
through the blood of the(his) own.* I

* This = his own blood or the blood of his own [?Son].

from the first day I came into the province of Asia. ¹⁹I served the Lord with great humility and with tears, although I was severely tested by the plots of the Jews. ²⁰You know that I have not hesitated to preach anything that would be helpful to you but have taught you publicly and from house to house. ²¹I have declared to both Jews and Greeks that they must turn to God in repentance and have faith in our Lord Jesus.
²²"And now, compelled by the Spirit, I am going to Jerusalem, not knowing what will happen to me there. ²³I only know that in every city the Holy Spirit warns me that prison and hardships are facing me. ²⁴However, I consider my life worth nothing to me, if only I may finish the race and complete the task the Lord Jesus has given me— the task of testifying to the gospel of God's grace.
²⁵"Now I know that none of you among whom I have gone about preaching the kingdom will ever see me again. ²⁶Therefore, I declare to you today that I am innocent of the blood of all men. ²⁷For I have not hesitated to proclaim to you the whole will of God. ²⁸Keep watch over yourselves and all the flock of which the Holy Spirit has made you overseers.ᵖ Be shepherds of the church of God,ᑫ which he bought with his own blood. ²⁹I know that

29"I know that after my departure savage wolves will come in among you, not sparing the flock;

30and from among your own selves men will arise, speaking perverse things, to draw away the disciples after them.

31"Therefore be on the alert, remembering that night and day for a period of three years I did not cease to admonish each one with tears.

32"And now I commend you to God and to the word of His grace, which is able to build *you* up and to give *you* the inheritance among all those who are sanctified.

33"I have coveted no one's silver or gold or clothes.

34"You yourselves know that these hands ministered to my *own* needs and to the men who were with me.

35"In everything I showed you that by working hard in this manner you must help the weak and remember the words of the Lord Jesus, that He Himself said, 'It is more blessed to give than to receive.' "

36And when he had said these things, he knelt down and prayed with them all.

37And they *began* to weep aloud and embraced Paul, and repeatedly kissed him,

38grieving especially over the word which he had spoken, that they should see his face no more. And they were accompanying him to the ship.

Chapter 21

Paul Sails from Miletus

AND when it came about that we had parted from them and had set sail, we ran a straight course to Cos and the next day to

---

οἶδα ὅτι εἰσελεύσονται μετὰ τὴν ἄφιξίν
know that ⁷will come in ¹after ⁸the ⁹departure

μου λύκοι βαρεῖς εἰς ὑμᾶς μὴ φειδόμενοι
⁴of me ⁵wolves ⁶grievous ⁸into you not sparing

τοῦ ποιμνίου, 30 καὶ ἐξ ὑμῶν αὐτῶν
the flock, and of you [your]selves

ἀναστήσονται ἄνδρες λαλοῦντες διεστραμμένα
will rise up men speaking *having been*
perverted things

τοῦ ἀποσπᾶν τοὺς μαθητὰς ὀπίσω ἑαυτῶν.
- to drag away⁴ the disciples after themselves.

31 διὸ γρηγορεῖτε, μνημονεύοντες ὅτι
Wherefore watch ye, remembering that

τριετίαν νύκτα καὶ ἡμέραν οὐκ ἐπαυσάμην
for three years night and day I ceased not

μετὰ δακρύων νουθετῶν ἕνα ἕκαστον.
with tears admonishing ²one ¹each.

32 καὶ τὰ νῦν παρατίθεμαι ὑμᾶς τῷ
And - now I commend you to the

κυρίῳ καὶ τῷ λόγῳ τῆς χάριτος αὐτοῦ
Lord and to the word of the grace of him

τῷ δυναμένῳ οἰκοδομῆσαι καὶ δοῦναι τὴν
- being able to build and to give the

κληρονομίαν ἐν τοῖς ἡγιασμένοις πᾶσιν.
inheritance among ²the [ones] ³having been ¹all.
sanctified

33 ἀργυρίου ἢ χρυσίου ἢ ἱματισμοῦ οὐδενὸς
Silver or gold or raiment of no one

ἐπεθύμησα· 34 αὐτοὶ γινώσκετε ὅτι ταῖς
I coveted; [your]selves ye know that ⁴to the

χρείαις μου καὶ τοῖς οὖσιν μετ᾽ ἐμοῦ
⁵needs ⁶of me ⁷and ⁸to the [ones] being ¹⁰with ¹¹me

ὑπηρέτησαν αἱ χεῖρες αὗται. 35 πάντα
²ministered ¹these ²hands. All things

ὑπέδειξα ὑμῖν, ὅτι οὕτως κοπιῶντας δεῖ
I showed you, that thus labouring it behoves

ἀντιλαμβάνεσθαι τῶν ἀσθενούντων, μνημονεύειν
to succour the ailing [ones], ²to remember

τε τῶν λόγων τοῦ κυρίου Ἰησοῦ, ὅτι
¹and the words of the Lord Jesus, that

αὐτὸς εἶπεν· μακάριόν ἐστιν μᾶλλον διδόναι
he said: Blessed it is rather to give

ἢ λαμβάνειν. 36 καὶ ταῦτα εἰπών,
than to receive. And ²these things ¹having said,

θεὶς τὰ γόνατα αὐτοῦ σὺν πᾶσιν αὐτοῖς
placing the knees of him with ²all ¹them
= kneeling down

προσηύξατο. 37 ἱκανὸς δὲ κλαυθμὸς ἐγένετο
he prayed. And ²considerable ³weeping ¹there was

πάντων, καὶ ἐπιπεσόντες ἐπὶ τὸν τράχηλον
of all, and falling *on* on the neck

τοῦ Παύλου κατεφίλουν αὐτόν, 38 ὀδυνώ-
- of Paul they kissed fervently him, suffer-

μενοι μάλιστα ἐπὶ τῷ λόγῳ ᾧ εἰρήκει,
ing most over the word which he had said,

ὅτι οὐκέτι μέλλουσιν τὸ πρόσωπον αὐτοῦ
that no more they are(were) the face of him

θεωρεῖν. προέπεμπον δὲ αὐτὸν εἰς τὸ
to behold. And they escorted him to the

πλοῖον.
ship.

21 Ὡς δὲ ἐγένετο ἀναχθῆναι ἡμᾶς
Now when it came to pass to set sail we

ἀποσπασθέντας ἀπ᾽ αὐτῶν, εὐθυδρομήσαντες
having been withdrawn from them, taking a straight course

ἤλθομεν εἰς τὴν Κῶ, τῇ δὲ ἑξῆς εἰς
we came to - Cos, and on the next [day] to

---

after I leave, savage wolves will come in among you and will not spare the flock.

30Even from your own number men will arise and distort the truth in order to draw away disciples after them. 31So be on your guard! Remember that for three years I never stopped warning each of you night and day with tears.

32"Now I commit you to God and to the word of his grace, which can build you up and give you an inheritance among all those who are sanctified. 33I have not coveted anyone's silver or gold or clothing. 34You yourselves know that these hands of mine have supplied my own needs and the needs of my companions. 35In everything I did, I showed you that by this kind of hard work we must help the weak, remembering the words the Lord Jesus himself said: 'It is more blessed to give than to receive.' "

36When he had said this, he knelt down with all of them and prayed. 37They all wept as they embraced him and kissed him. 38What grieved them most was his statement that they would never see his face again. Then they accompanied him to the ship.

Chapter 21

On to Jerusalem

AFTER we had torn ourselves away from them, we put out to sea and sailed straight to Cos. The

Rhodes, and from there to Patara;

²and having found a ship crossing over to Phoenicia, we went aboard and set sail.

³And when we had come in sight of Cyprus, leaving it on the left, we kept sailing to Syria and landed at Tyre; for there the ship was to unload its cargo.

⁴And after looking up the disciples, we stayed there seven days; and they kept telling Paul through the Spirit not to set foot in Jerusalem.

⁵And when it came about that our days there were ended, we departed and started on our journey, while they all, with wives and children, escorted us until *we were* out of the city. And after kneeling down on the beach and praying, we said farewell to one another.

⁶Then we went on board the ship, and they returned home again.

⁷And when we had finished the voyage from Tyre, we arrived at Ptolemais; and after greeting the brethren, we stayed with them for a day.

⁸And on the next day we departed and came to Caesarea; and entering the house of Philip the evangelist, who was one of the seven, we stayed with him.

⁹Now this man had four virgin daughters who were prophetesses.

¹⁰And as we were staying there for some days, a certain prophet named Agabus came down from Judea.

¹¹And coming to us, he took Paul's belt and bound

τὴν Ῥόδον κἀκεῖθεν εἰς Πάταρα· 2 καὶ
- Rhodes and thence to Patara; and

εὑρόντες πλοῖον διαπερῶν εἰς Φοινίκην,
having found a ship crossing over to Phœnice,

ἐπιβάντες ἀνήχθημεν. 3 ἀναφάναντες δὲ
embarking we set sail. And sighting

τὴν Κύπρον καὶ καταλιπόντες αὐτὴν
- Cyprus and leaving it

εὐώνυμον ἐπλέομεν εἰς Συρίαν, καὶ κατήλ-
on the left we sailed to Syria, and came

θομεν εἰς Τύρον· ἐκεῖσε γὰρ τὸ πλοῖον
down to Tyre; for there the ship

ἦν ἀποφορτιζόμενον τὸν γόμον. 4 ἀνευρ-
was unloading the cargo. find-

όντες δὲ τοὺς μαθητὰς ἐπεμείναμεν αὐτοῦ
ing And the disciples we remained there

ἡμέρας ἑπτά· οἵτινες τῷ Παύλῳ ἔλεγον
days seven; who - ¹Paul ¹told

διὰ τοῦ πνεύματος μὴ ἐπιβαίνειν εἰς
through the Spirit not to go up to

Ἱεροσόλυμα. 5 ὅτε δὲ ἐγένετο ἐξαρτίσαι
Jerusalem. But when it came to pass to accomplish
= we accomplished

ἡμᾶς τὰς ἡμέρας, ἐξελθόντες ἐπορευόμεθα
us[b] the days, going forth we journeyed

προπεμπόντων ἡμᾶς πάντων σὺν γυναιξὶ
¹escorting ²us ¹all[a] with women

καὶ τέκνοις ἕως ἔξω τῆς πόλεως, καὶ
and children as far as outside the city, and

θέντες τὰ γόνατα ἐπὶ τὸν αἰγιαλὸν
placing the knees on the shore
= kneeling

προσευξάμενοι 6 ἀπησπασάμεθα ἀλλήλους,
praying we gave parting greetings to one another,

καὶ ἐνέβημεν εἰς τὸ πλοῖον, ἐκεῖνοι δὲ
and embarked in the ship, and those

ὑπέστρεψαν εἰς τὰ ἴδια. 7 Ἡμεῖς δὲ
returned to ¹the(ir) ²things ³own. But we
= home.

τὸν πλοῦν διανύσαντες ἀπὸ Τύρου κατηντή-
²the ³voyage ¹finishing from Tyre ar-

σαμεν εἰς Πτολεμαΐδα, καὶ ἀσπασάμενοι
rived at Ptolemais, and greeting

τοὺς ἀδελφοὺς ἐμείναμεν ἡμέραν μίαν
the brothers we remained day one

παρ' αὐτοῖς. 8 τῇ δὲ ἐπαύριον ἐξελθόντες
with them. And on the morrow going forth

ἤλθομεν εἰς Καισάρειαν, καὶ εἰσελθόντες
we came to Cæsarea, and entering

εἰς τὸν οἶκον Φιλίππου τοῦ εὐαγγελιστοῦ
into the house of Philip the evangelist

ὄντος ἐκ τῶν ἑπτά, ἐμείναμεν παρ'
being of the seven, we remained with

αὐτῷ. 9 τούτῳ δὲ ἦσαν θυγατέρες
him. Now to this man were daughters
= this man had four daughters

τέσσαρες παρθένοι προφητεύουσαι. 10 Ἐπιμεν-
four[c] virgins prophesying. remain-

όντων δὲ ἡμέρας πλείους κατῆλθέν τις
ing[a] And days more(many) ²came down ¹a certain

ἀπὸ τῆς Ἰουδαίας προφήτης ὀνόματι
⁴from - ⁷Judæa ²prophet ³by name

Ἄγαβος, 11 καὶ ἐλθὼν πρὸς ἡμᾶς καὶ
¹Agabus, and coming to us and

ἄρας τὴν ζώνην τοῦ Παύλου, δήσας
taking the girdle - of Paul, having bound

---

next day we went to Rhodes and from there to Patara. ²We found a ship crossing over to Phoenicia, went on board and set sail. ³After sighting Cyprus and passing to the south of it, we sailed on to Syria. We landed at Tyre, where our ship was to unload its cargo. ⁴Finding the disciples there, we stayed with them seven days. Through the Spirit they urged Paul not to go on to Jerusalem. ⁵But when our time was up, we left and continued on our way. All the disciples and their wives and children accompanied us out of the city, and there on the beach we knelt to pray. ⁶After saying good-by to each other, we went aboard the ship, and they returned home.

⁷We continued our voyage from Tyre and landed at Ptolemais, where we greeted the brothers and stayed with them for a day. ⁸Leaving the next day, we reached Caesarea and stayed at the house of Philip the evangelist, one of the Seven. ⁹He had four unmarried daughters who prophesied.

¹⁰After we had been there a number of days, a prophet named Agabus came down from Judea. ¹¹Coming over to us, he took Paul's belt, tied his own

his own feet and hands, and said, "This is what the Holy Spirit says: 'In this way the Jews at Jerusalem will bind the man who owns this belt and deliver him into the hands of the Gentiles.' "

12And when we had heard this, we as well as the local residents *began* begging him not to go up to Jerusalem.

13Then Paul answered, "What are you doing, weeping and breaking my heart? For I am ready not only to be bound, but even to die at Jerusalem for the name of the Lord Jesus."

14And since he would not be persuaded, we fell silent, remarking, "The will of the Lord be done!"

Paul at Jerusalem

15And after these days we got ready and started on our way up to Jerusalem.

16And *some* of the disciples from Caesarea also came with us, taking us to Mnason of Cyprus, a disciple of long standing with whom we were to stay.

17And when we had come to Jerusalem, the brethren received us gladly.

18And now the following day Paul went in with us to James, and all the elders were present.

19And after he had greeted them, he *began* to relate one by one the things which God had done among the Gentiles through his ministry.

20And when they heard it they *began* glorifying God; and they said to him, "You see, brother, how many thousands there are among the Jews of those who have

---

ἑαυτοῦ τοὺς πόδας καὶ τὰς χεῖρας εἶπεν·
of himself the feet and the hands said:

τάδε λέγει τὸ πνεῦμα τὸ ἅγιον· τὸν
These things says the Spirit - Holy: ⁷The

ἄνδρα οὗ ἐστιν ἡ ζώνη αὕτη οὕτως
⁸man ⁹of whom ¹⁰is ¹¹this ¹²girdle ¹thus

δήσουσιν ἐν Ἰερουσαλὴμ οἱ Ἰουδαῖοι καὶ
⁴will bind ⁵in ⁶Jerusalem ²the ³Jews and

παραδώσουσιν εἰς χεῖρας ἐθνῶν. 12 ὡς
will deliver into [the] hands of [the] nations. when

δὲ ἠκούσαμεν ταῦτα, παρεκαλοῦμεν ἡμεῖς
And we heard these things, ⁵besought ⁴we

τε καὶ οἱ ἐντόπιοι τοῦ μὴ ἀναβαίνειν
¹both ²and ³the ³residents - ⁶not ⁷to go up⁴

αὐτὸν εἰς Ἰερουσαλήμ. 13 τότε ἀπεκρίθη
⁷him to Jerusalem. Then answered

ὁ Παῦλος τί ποιεῖτε κλαίοντες καὶ
- Paul: What are ye doing weeping and

συνθρύπτοντές μου τὴν καρδίαν; ἐγὼ γὰρ
weakening of me the heart? For I

οὐ μόνον δεθῆναι ἀλλὰ καὶ ἀποθανεῖν
not only to be bound but also to die

εἰς Ἰερουσαλὴμ ἑτοίμως ἔχω ὑπὲρ τοῦ
in Jerusalem readily have on behalf of the
= am ready

ὀνόματος τοῦ κυρίου Ἰησοῦ. 14 μὴ
name of the Lord Jesus. Not

πειθομένου δὲ αὐτοῦ ἡσυχάσαμεν εἰπόντες·
being persuaded and him= we kept silence having said:
= And when he was not persuaded

τοῦ κυρίου τὸ θέλημα γινέσθω.
⁴Of the ¹Lord ²the ³will ⁵let ⁶be [done].

15 Μετὰ δὲ τὰς ἡμέρας ταύτας
And after these days

ἐπισκευασάμενοι ἀνεβαίνομεν εἰς Ἰεροσόλυμα·
having made ready we went up to Jerusalem;

16 συνῆλθον δὲ καὶ τῶν μαθητῶν ἀπὸ
and went with also [some] of the disciples from

Καισαρείας σὺν ἡμῖν, ἄγοντες παρ' ᾧ
Caesarea with us, bringing [one] with whom

ξενισθῶμεν Μνάσωνί τινι Κυπρίῳ,
we might be lodged Mnason a certain Cypriote,

ἀρχαίῳ μαθητῇ. 17 Γενομένων δὲ ἡμῶν εἰς
an ancient disciple. And being us* in
(early) = when we were

Ἰεροσόλυμα ἀσμένως ἀπεδέξαντο ἡμᾶς οἱ
Jerusalem ³joyfully ²received ⁴us ¹the

ἀδελφοί. 18 τῇ δὲ ἐπιούσῃ εἰσῄει ὁ
²brothers. And on the next day went in -

Παῦλος σὺν ἡμῖν πρὸς Ἰάκωβον, πάντες
Paul with us to James, ²all

τε παρεγένοντο οἱ πρεσβύτεροι. 19 καὶ
¹and ⁵came ³the ⁴elders. And

ἀσπασάμενος αὐτοὺς ἐξηγεῖτο καθ' ἓν
having greeted them he related according to one
= singly

ἕκαστον ὧν ἐποίησεν ὁ θεὸς ἐν τοῖς
each of [the] did - God among the
things] which

ἔθνεσιν διὰ τῆς διακονίας αὐτοῦ. 20 οἱ
nations through the ministry of him. they

δὲ ἀκούσαντες ἐδόξαζον τὸν θεόν, εἶπάν τε
And hearing glorified - God, and said

αὐτῷ· θεωρεῖς, ἀδελφέ, πόσαι μυριάδες
to him: Thou beholdest, brother, how many *ten* thousands

εἰσὶν ἐν τοῖς Ἰουδαίοις τῶν πεπιστευκότων,
there are among the Jews - having believed,

---

hands and feet with it and said, "The Holy Spirit says, 'In this way the Jews of Jerusalem will bind the owner of this belt and will hand him over to the Gentiles.' "

12When we heard this, we and the people there pleaded with Paul not to go up to Jerusalem. 13Then Paul answered, "Why are you weeping and breaking my heart? I am ready not only to be bound, but also to die in Jerusalem for the name of the Lord Jesus." 14When he would not be dissuaded, we gave up and said, "The Lord's will be done."

15After this, we got ready and went up to Jerusalem. 16Some of the disciples from Caesarea accompanied us and brought us to the home of Mnason, where we were to stay. He was a man from Cyprus and one of the early disciples.

Paul's Arrival at Jerusalem

17When we arrived at Jerusalem, the brothers received us warmly. 18The next day Paul and the rest of us went to see James, and all the elders were present. 19Paul greeted them and reported in detail what God had done among the Gentiles through his ministry.

20When they heard this, they praised God. Then they said to Paul: "You see, brother, how many thousands of Jews have be-

believed, and they are all zealous for the Law;

21and they have been told about you, that you are teaching all the Jews who are among the Gentiles to forsake Moses, telling them not to circumcise their children nor to walk according to the customs.

22"What, then, is *to be done*? They will certainly hear that you have come.

23"Therefore do this that we tell you. We have four men who are under a vow;

24take them and purify yourself along with them, and pay their expenses in order that they may shave their heads; and all will know that there is nothing to the things which they have been told about you, but that you yourself also walk orderly, keeping the Law.

25"But concerning the Gentiles who have believed, we wrote, having decided that they should abstain from meat sacrificed to idols and from blood and from what is strangled and from fornication."

26Then Paul took the men, and the next day, purifying himself along with them, went into the temple, giving notice of the completion of the days of purification, until the sacrifice was offered for each one of them.

Paul Seized in the Temple

27And when the seven days were almost over, the Jews from Asia, upon seeing him in the temple, *began* to stir up all the multitude and laid hands on him,

28crying out, "Men of Israel, come to our aid! This is the man who preaches to all men everywhere against

καὶ πάντες ζηλωταὶ τοῦ νόμου ὑπάρχουσιν·
and all zealots of the law are;

21 κατηχήθησαν δὲ περὶ σοῦ, ὅτι ἀποστα-
and they were informed about thee that ᵃapo-

σίαν διδάσκεις ἀπὸ Μωϋσέως τοὺς κατὰ
stasy ¹thou teachest ²from ¹⁰Moses ³the ⁵throughout

τὰ ἔθνη πάντας Ἰουδαίους, λέγων μὴ
⁴the ⁷nations ²all ⁴Jews, ¹telling ²not

περιτέμνειν αὐτοὺς τὰ τέκνα μηδὲ τοῖς
⁴to circumcise ²them the children nor in the

ἔθεσιν περιπατεῖν. 22 τί οὖν ἐστιν·
customs to walk. What therefore is it?

πάντως ἀκούσονται ὅτι ἐλήλυθας. 23 τοῦτο
At all events they will hear that thou hast come. This

οὖν ποίησον ὅ σοι λέγομεν· εἰσὶν ἡμῖν
therefore do thou which thee we tell; There are to usᵉ
=We have

ἄνδρες τέσσαρες εὐχὴν ἔχοντες ἐφ' ἑαυτῶν·
men four a vow having on themselves;

24 τούτους παραλαβὼν ἁγνίσθητι σὺν αὐτοῖς,
these taking be thou purified with them,

καὶ δαπάνησον ἐπ' αὐτοῖς ἵνα ξυρήσονται
and spend on them that they will shave

τὴν κεφαλήν, καὶ γνώσονται πάντες ὅτι
the head, and will know all men that

ὧν κατήχηνται περὶ σοῦ οὐδέν
²[of the things] ⁴they have been ⁵about ⁶thee ¹nothing
of which informed

ἐστιν, ἀλλὰ στοιχεῖς καὶ αὐτὸς φυλάσσων τὸν
¹there is, but thou walkest also [thy]self keeping the

νόμον. 25 περὶ δὲ τῶν πεπιστευκότων
law. And concerning ¹the ²having believed

ἐθνῶν ἡμεῖς ἐπεστείλαμεν κρίναντες φυλάσ-
²nations we joined in writing ¹judging ¹to keep

σεσθαι αὐτοὺς τό τε εἰδωλόθυτον καὶ
themselves ³them ⁴[from] ²the ⁵both idol sacrifice and

αἷμα καὶ πνικτὸν καὶ πορνείαν. 26 τότε
blood and a thing strangled and fornication. Then

ὁ Παῦλος παραλαβὼν τοὺς ἄνδρας τῇ
- Paul taking the men on the

ἐχομένη ἡμέρα σὺν αὐτοῖς ἁγνισθεὶς εἰσῄει
next day with them having been purified went in

εἰς τὸ ἱερόν, διαγγέλλων τὴν ἐκπλήρωσιν
to the temple, announcing the completion

τῶν ἡμερῶν τοῦ ἁγνισμοῦ, ἕως οὗ
of the days of the purification, until

προσηνέχθη ὑπὲρ ἑνὸς ἑκάστου αὐτῶν ἡ
should be offered on behalf of ²one ¹each of them the

προσφορά.
offering.

27 Ὡς δὲ ἔμελλον αἱ ἑπτὰ ἡμέραι
Now when were about the seven days

συντελεῖσθαι, οἱ ἀπὸ τῆς Ἀσίας Ἰουδαῖοι
to be fulfilled, ¹the ²from - ⁴Asia ³Jews

θεασάμενοι αὐτὸν ἐν τῷ ἱερῷ συνέχεον
seeing him in the temple stirred up

πάντα τὸν ὄχλον, καὶ ἐπέβαλαν ἐπ'
all the crowd, and laid on on

αὐτὸν τὰς χεῖρας, 28 κράζοντες· ἄνδρες
him the(ir) hands, crying out: Men

Ἰσραηλῖται, βοηθεῖτε· οὗτός ἐστιν ὁ
Israelites, help: this is the

ἄνθρωπος ὁ κατὰ τοῦ λαοῦ καὶ τοῦ
man ¹the [one] ⁵against ⁶the ⁷people ⁸and ⁹the

νόμου καὶ τοῦ τόπου τούτου πάντας
¹⁰law ¹¹and ¹²the ¹³this ¹⁴place ³all men

lieved, and all of them are zealous for the law. 21They have been informed that you teach all the Jews who live among the Gentiles to turn away from Moses, telling them not to circumcise their children or live according to our customs. 22What shall we do? They will certainly hear that you have come, 23so do what we tell you. There are four men with us who have made a vow. 24Take these men, join in their purification rites and pay their expenses, so that they can have their heads shaved. Then everybody will know there is no truth in these reports about you, but that you yourself are living in obedience to the law. 25As for the Gentile believers, we have written to them our decision that they should abstain from food sacrificed to idols, from blood, from the meat of strangled animals and from sexual immorality."

26The next day Paul took the men and purified himself along with them. Then he went to the temple to give notice of the date when the days of purification would end and the offering would be made for each of them.

Paul Arrested

27When the seven days were nearly over, some Jews from the province of Asia saw Paul at the temple. They stirred up the whole crowd and seized him, 28shouting, "Men of Israel, help us! This is the man who teaches all men everywhere against our

our people, and the Law, and this place; and besides he has even brought Greeks into the temple and has defiled this holy place.''

29For they had previously seen Trophimus the Ephesian in the city with him, and they supposed that Paul had brought him into the temple.

30And all the city was aroused, and the people rushed together; and taking hold of Paul, they dragged him out of the temple; and immediately the doors were shut.

31And while they were seeking to kill him, a report came up to the [i] commander of the *Roman* cohort that all Jerusalem was in confusion.

32And at once he took along *some* soldiers and centurions, and ran down to them; and when they saw the commander and the soldiers, they stopped beating Paul.

33Then the commander came up and took hold of him, and ordered him to be bound with two chains; and he *began* asking who he was and what he had done.

34But among the crowd some were shouting one thing *and* some another, and when he could not find out the facts on account of the uproar, he ordered him to be brought into the barracks.

35And when he got to the stairs, it so happened that he was carried by the soldiers because of the violence of the mob;

36for the multitude of the people kept following behind, crying out, ''Away with him!''

37And as Paul was about to be brought into the barracks, he said to the commander, ''May I say something to you?'' And he

---

πανταχῇ διδάσκων, ἔτι τε καὶ ῞Ελληνας
everywhere **teaching,** **and even** **also** **Greeks**

εἰσήγαγεν εἰς τὸ ἱερὸν καὶ κεκοίνωκεν
brought in **into** **the** **temple** **and** **has profaned**

τὸν ἅγιον τόπον τοῦτον. 29 ἦσαν γὰρ
- **⁵holy** **⁶place** **¹this.** **For they were**

προεωρακότες Τρόφιμον τὸν ᾿Εφέσιον ἐν
having previously seen **Trophimus** **the** **Ephesian** **in**

τῇ πόλει σὺν αὐτῷ, ὃν ἐνόμιζον ὅτι
the **city** **with** **him,** **whom they supposed** **that**

εἰς τὸ ἱερὸν εἰσήγαγεν ὁ Παῦλος. 30 ἐκινήθη
³into **⁴the** **⁵temple** **⁶brought in** **-** **¹Paul.** **²was moved**

τε ἡ πόλις ὅλη καὶ ἐγένετο συνδρομὴ
¹And **³the** **⁴city** **²whole** **and** **there was a running together**

τοῦ λαοῦ, καὶ ἐπιλαβόμενοι τοῦ Παύλου
of the **people,** **and** **laying hold** **-** **of Paul**

εἷλκον αὐτὸν ἔξω τοῦ ἱεροῦ, καὶ εὐθέως
they dragged **him** **outside** **the** **temple,** **and immediately**

ἐκλείσθησαν αἱ θύραι. 31 Ζητούντων τε
were shut **the** **doors.** **And [while they were] seeking⁴**

αὐτὸν ἀποκτεῖναι ἀνέβη φάσις τῷ
³him **¹to kill** **⁴came up** **³information** **to the**

χιλιάρχῳ τῆς σπείρης ὅτι ὅλη συγχύν-
chiliarch **of the** **cohort** **that** **¹all** **²is(was) in**

νεται ᾿Ιερουσαλήμ· 32 ὃς ἐξαυτῆς παρα-
confusion **²Jerusalem;** **who** **at once** **tak-**

λαβὼν στρατιώτας καὶ ἑκατοντάρχας
ing **soldiers** **and** **centurions**

κατέδραμεν ἐπ᾿ αὐτούς· οἱ δὲ ἰδόντες
ran down **on** **them;** **and they** **seeing**

τὸν χιλίαρχον καὶ τοὺς στρατιώτας
the **chiliarch** **and** **the** **soldiers**

ἐπαύσαντο τύπτοντες τὸν Παῦλον. 33 τότε
ceased **beating** **-** **Paul.** **Then**

ἐγγίσας ὁ χιλίαρχος ἐπελάβετο αὐτοῦ
drawing near **the** **chiliarch** **laid hold** **of him**

καὶ ἐκέλευσεν δεθῆναι ἁλύσεσι δυσί, καὶ
and **commanded** **to be bound** **chains** **with two,** **and**

ἐπυνθάνετο τίς εἴη καὶ τί ἐστιν πεποιηκώς.
inquired **who he** **might be** **and what he is** **having done.**

34 ἄλλοι δὲ ἄλλο τι ἐπεφώνουν ἐν τῷ
And ¹others **⁷different** **⁶some- thing** **⁵called out** **²among** **³the**

ὄχλῳ· μὴ δυναμένου δὲ αὐτοῦ γνῶναι
⁴crowd; **and not being able** **himᵃ** **to know**
=as he was not able

τὸ ἀσφαλὲς διὰ τὸν θόρυβον, ἐκέλευσεν
the certain thing **because of the** **uproar,** **he commanded**

ἄγεσθαι αὐτὸν εἰς τὴν παρεμβολήν. 35 ὅτε
to be brought him **into** **the** **fort.** **when**

δὲ ἐγένετο ἐπὶ τοὺς ἀναβαθμούς, συνέβη
And **he was** **on** **the** **steps,** **it happened**

βαστάζεσθαι αὐτὸν ὑπὸ τῶν στρατιωτῶν
to be carried **himᵇ** **by** **the** **soldiers**
=he was carried

διὰ τὴν βίαν τοῦ ὄχλου· 36 ἠκολούθει
because of the **violence** **of the** **crowd;** **⁵followed**

γὰρ τὸ πλῆθος τοῦ λαοῦ κράζοντες·
¹for **²the** **³multitude** **⁴of the** **⁵people** **crying out:**

αἶρε αὐτόν. 37 Μέλλων τε εἰσάγεσθαι
Take away **him.** **And being about** **to be brought in**

εἰς τὴν παρεμβολὴν ὁ Παῦλος λέγει τῷ
into **the** **fort** **-** **Paul** **says** **to the**

χιλιάρχῳ· εἰ ἔξεστίν μοι εἰπεῖν τι πρὸς
chiliarch: **If** **it is lawful** **for me** **to say** **something** **to**

---

people and our law and this place. And besides, he has brought Greeks into the temple area and defiled this holy place.'' 29(They had previously seen Trophimus the Ephesian in the city with Paul and assumed that Paul had brought him into the temple area.)

30The whole city was aroused, and the people came running from all directions. Seizing Paul, they dragged him from the temple, and immediately the gates were shut. 31While they were trying to kill him, news reached the commander of the Roman troops that the whole city of Jerusalem was in an uproar. 32He at once took some officers and soldiers and ran down to the crowd. When the rioters saw the commander and his soldiers, they stopped beating Paul.

33The commander came up and arrested him and ordered him to be bound with two chains. Then he asked who he was and what he had done. 34Some in the crowd shouted one thing and some another, and since the commander could not get at the truth because of the uproar, he ordered that Paul be taken into the barracks. 35When Paul reached the steps, the violence of the mob was so great he had to be carried by the soldiers. 36The crowd that followed kept shouting, ''Away with him!''

Paul Speaks to the Crowd

37As the soldiers were about to take Paul into the barracks, he asked the commander, ''May I say something to you?''

---

[i] I.e., chiliarch, in command of one thousand troops

*said, "Do you know Greek?

38"Then you are not the Egyptian who some time ago stirred up a revolt and led the four thousand men of the Assassins out into the wilderness?"

39But Paul said, "I am a Jew of Tarsus in Cilicia, a citizen of no insignificant city; and I beg you, allow me to speak to the people."

40And when he had given him permission, Paul, standing on the stairs, motioned to the people with his hand; and when there was a great hush, he spoke to them in the Hebrew dialect, saying,

Chapter 22

Paul's Defense before the Jews

" BRETHREN and fathers, hear my defense which I now *offer* to you."

2And when they heard that he was addressing them in the Hebrew dialect, they became even more quiet; and he *said,

3"I am a Jew, born in Tarsus of Cilicia, but brought up in this city, educated under Gamaliel, strictly according to the law of our fathers, being zealous for God, just as you all are today.

4"And I persecuted this Way to the death, binding and putting both men and women into prisons,

5as also the high priest and all the Council of the elders can testify. From them I also received letters to the brethren, and started off for Damascus in order

---

σέ; ὁ δὲ ἔφη· Ἑλληνιστὶ γινώσκεις;
thee? And he said: in Greek Knowest thou
[to speak]?*

38 οὐκ ἄρα σὺ εἶ ὁ Αἰγύπτιος ὁ πρὸ
²Not ³then ³thou ¹art the Egyptian the [one] before

τούτων τῶν ἡμερῶν ἀναστατώσας καὶ
these days unsettling and

ἐξαγαγὼν εἰς τὴν ἔρημον τοὺς τετρα-
leading out into the desert the four

κισχιλίους ἄνδρας τῶν σικαρίων; **39** εἶπεν
thousand men of the Sicarii? said

δὲ ὁ Παῦλος· ἐγὼ ἄνθρωπος μέν εἰμι
And Paul: I a man indeed am

Ἰουδαῖος, Ταρσεύς, τῆς Κιλικίας οὐκ
a Jew, a Tarsian, of Cilicia not

ἀσήμου πόλεως πολίτης· δέομαι δέ σου,
of a mean city a citizen; and I beg of thee,

ἐπίτρεψόν μοι λαλῆσαι πρὸς τὸν λαόν.
permit me to speak to the people.

40 ἐπιτρέψαντος δὲ αὐτοῦ ὁ Παῦλος ἑστὼς
And permitting him⁸ - Paul standing
=when he gave permission

ἐπὶ τῶν ἀναβαθμῶν κατέσεισεν τῇ χειρὶ
on the steps beckoned with the(his) hand

τῷ λαῷ· πολλῆς δὲ σιγῆς γενομένης
to the people; and much silence becoming⁸
=when there was great silence

προσεφώνησεν τῇ Ἑβραΐδι διαλέκτῳ λέγων·
he addressed in the Hebrew language saying:

22 Ἄνδρες ἀδελφοὶ καὶ πατέρες, ἀκούσατέ
Men brothers and fathers, hear ye

μου τῆς πρὸς ὑμᾶς νυνὶ ἀπολογίας.
²of me ¹the ³to ⁵you ⁴now ²defence.

— **2** ἀκούσαντες δὲ ὅτι τῇ Ἑβραΐδι
(And hearing that in the Hebrew

διαλέκτῳ προσεφώνει αὐτοῖς μᾶλλον
language he addressed them more

παρέσχον ἡσυχίαν. καὶ φησίν· **3** ἐγώ εἰμι
they showed quietness. And he says:) I am

ἀνὴρ Ἰουδαῖος, γεγεννημένος ἐν Ταρσῷ
a man a Jew, having been born in Tarsus

τῆς Κιλικίας, ἀνατεθραμμένος δὲ ἐν τῇ
- of Cilicia, and having been brought up in -

πόλει ταύτῃ, παρὰ τοὺς πόδας Γαμαλιὴλ
city this, at the feet of Gamaliel

πεπαιδευμένος κατὰ ἀκρίβειαν τοῦ πατρῴου
having been trained according exactness of the ancestral
to [the]

νόμου, ζηλωτὴς ὑπάρχων τοῦ θεοῦ καθὼς
law, a zealot being - of God even as

πάντες ὑμεῖς ἐστε σήμερον· **4** ὃς ταύτην
all ye are to-day; who this

τὴν ὁδὸν ἐδίωξα ἄχρι θανάτου, δεσμεύων
- way persecuted as far as to death, binding

καὶ παραδιδοὺς εἰς φυλακὰς ἄνδρας τε
and delivering to prisons both men

καὶ γυναῖκας. **5** ὡς καὶ ὁ ἀρχιερεὺς
and women. As even the high priest

μαρτυρεῖ μοι καὶ πᾶν τὸ πρεσβυτέριον·
witnesses to me and all the senate;

παρ’ ὧν καὶ ἐπιστολὰς δεξάμενος πρὸς
from whom also letters having received to

τοὺς ἀδελφοὺς εἰς Δαμασκὸν ἐπορευόμην,
the brothers in Damascus I journeyed,

* See note on page xviii.

"Do you speak Greek?" he replied. 38"Aren't you the Egyptian who started a revolt and led four thousand terrorists out into the desert some time ago?"

39Paul answered, "I am a Jew, from Tarsus in Cilicia, a citizen of no ordinary city. Please let me speak to the people."

40Having received the commander's permission, Paul stood on the steps and motioned to the crowd. When they were all silent, he said to them in Aramaic: 1"Brothers and fathers, listen now to my defense."

2When they heard him speak to them in Aramaic, they became very quiet.

Then Paul said: 3"I am a Jew, born in Tarsus of Cilicia, but brought up in this city. Under Gamaliel I was thoroughly trained in the law of our fathers and was just as zealous for God as any of you are today. 4I persecuted the followers of this Way to their death, arresting both men and women and throwing them into prison, 5as also the high priest and all the Council can testify. I even obtained letters from them to their brothers in Damascus, and to bring even those who were there to Jerusalem as prisoners to be punished.

6"And it came about that as I was on my way, approaching Damascus about noontime, a very bright light suddenly flashed from heaven all around me,

7and I fell to the ground and heard a voice saying to me, 'Saul, Saul, why are you persecuting Me?'

8"And I answered, 'Who art Thou, Lord?' And He said to me, 'I am Jesus the Nazarene, whom you are persecuting.'

9"And those who were with me beheld the light, to be sure, but did not understand the voice of the One who was speaking to me.

10"And I said, 'What shall I do, Lord?' And the Lord said to me, 'Arise and go on into Damascus; and there you will be told of all that has been appointed for you to do.'

11"But since I could not see because of the brightness of that light, I was led by the hand by those who were with me, and came into Damascus.

12"And a certain Ananias, a man who was devout by the standard of the Law, and well spoken of by all the Jews who lived there,

13came to me, and standing near said to me, 'Brother Saul, receive your sight!' And at that very time I looked up at him.

14"And he said, 'The God of our fathers has appointed you to know His will, and to see the Righteous One, and to hear an utterance from His mouth.

15'For you will be a witness for Him to all men of what you have seen and heard.

16'And now why do you delay? Arise, and be baptized, and wash away your

---

ἄξων καὶ τοὺς ἐκεῖσε ὄντας δεδεμένους
leading also the [ones] ⁵there ¹being *having been* bound

εἰς Ἰερουσαλὴμ ἵνα τιμωρηθῶσιν.
to Jerusalem that they might be punished.

6 Ἐγένετο δέ μοι πορευομένῳ καὶ ἐγγίζοντι
Now it happened to me journeying and drawing near

τῇ Δαμασκῷ περὶ μεσημβρίαν ἐξαίφνης ἐκ
- to Damascus about midday suddenly out of

τοῦ οὐρανοῦ περιαστράψαι φῶς ἱκανὸν
- heaven ⁴to shine round ¹a ³light ²considerable

περὶ ἐμέ, 7 ἔπεσά τε εἰς τὸ ἔδαφος
round me, and I fell to the ground

καὶ ἤκουσα φωνῆς λεγούσης μοι· Σαοὺλ
and heard a voice saying to me: Saul[,]

Σαούλ, τί με διώκεις; 8 ἐγὼ δὲ ἀπεκρίθην·
Saul, why me persecutest thou? And I answered:

τίς εἶ, κύριε; εἶπέν τε πρὸς ἐμέ· ἐγώ
Who art thou, Lord? And he said to me: I

εἰμι Ἰησοῦς ὁ Ναζωραῖος, ὃν σὺ διώκεις.
am Jesus the Nazarene, whom thou persecutest.

9 οἱ δὲ σὺν ἐμοὶ ὄντες τὸ μὲν φῶς
Now ¹the [ones] ⁵with ⁶me ²being ⁷the ⁴indeed ³light

ἐθεάσαντο, τὴν δὲ φωνὴν οὐκ ἤκουσαν
⁸beheld, but the voice they heard not

τοῦ λαλοῦντός μοι. 10 εἶπον δέ· τί
of the [one] speaking to me. And I said: What

ποιήσω, κύριε; ὁ δὲ κύριος εἶπεν πρός
may I do, Lord? And the Lord said to

με· ἀναστὰς πορεύου εἰς Δαμασκόν, κἀκεῖ σοι
me: Rising up go into Damascus, and there to thee

λαληθήσεται περὶ πάντων ὧν τέτακταί
it will be told concerning all things which has(ve) been

σοι ποιῆσαι. 11 ὡς δὲ οὐκ ἐνέβλεπον
for thee to do. And as I saw not   arranged

ἀπὸ τῆς δόξης τοῦ φωτὸς ἐκείνου,
from the glory of that light,

χειραγωγούμενος ὑπὸ τῶν συνόντων μοι
being led by the hand by the [ones] being with me

ἦλθον εἰς Δαμασκόν. 12 Ἁνανίας δέ τις,
I went into Damascus. And a certain Ananias,

ἀνὴρ εὐλαβὴς κατὰ τὸν νόμον, μαρτυρού-
a man devout according to the law, being witnessed

μενος ὑπὸ πάντων τῶν κατοικούντων
[to] by all ¹the ²dwelling ⁴[there]

Ἰουδαίων, 13 ἐλθὼν πρὸς ἐμὲ καὶ ἐπιστὰς
³Jews, coming to me and standing by

εἶπέν μοι· Σαοὺλ ἀδελφέ, ἀνάβλεψον.
said to me: Saul brother, look up.

κἀγὼ αὐτῇ τῇ ὥρᾳ ἀνέβλεψα εἰς αὐτόν.
And I in that hour* looked up at him.

14 ὁ δὲ εἶπεν· ὁ θεὸς τῶν πατέρων
And he said: The God of the fathers

ἡμῶν προεχειρίσατό σε γνῶναι τὸ θέλημα
of us previously appointed thee to know the will

αὐτοῦ καὶ ἰδεῖν τὸν δίκαιον καὶ ἀκοῦσαι
of him and to see the Just One and to hear

φωνὴν ἐκ τοῦ στόματος αὐτοῦ, 15 ὅτι
a voice out of the mouth of him, because

ἔσῃ μάρτυς αὐτῷ πρὸς πάντας ἀνθρώπους
thou wilt be a witness to him° to all men

ὧν ἑώρακας καὶ ἤκουσας. 16 καὶ νῦν
of things which thou hast seen and didst hear. And now

τί μέλλεις; ἀναστὰς βάπτισαι καὶ ἀπόλου-
what intendest thou? Rising up be baptized and wash

* See Luke 2. 38.

---

went there to bring these people as prisoners to Jerusalem to be punished.

6"About noon as I came near Damascus, suddenly a bright light from heaven flashed around me. 7I fell to the ground and heard a voice say to me, 'Saul! Saul! Why do you persecute me?'

8" 'Who are you, Lord?' I asked.

" 'I am Jesus of Nazareth, whom you are persecuting,' he replied. 9My companions saw the light, but they did not understand the voice of him who was speaking to me.

10" 'What shall I do, Lord?' I asked.

" 'Get up,' the Lord said, 'and go into Damascus. There you will be told all that you have been assigned to do.' 11My companions led me by the hand into Damascus, because the brilliance of the light had blinded me.

12"A man named Ananias came to see me. He was a devout observer of the law and highly respected by all the Jews living there. 13He stood beside me and said, 'Brother Saul, receive your sight!' And at that very moment I was able to see him.

14"Then he said: 'The God of our fathers has chosen you to know his will and to see the Righteous One and to hear words from his mouth. 15You will be his witness to all men of what you have seen and heard. 16And now what are you waiting for? Get up, be baptized and wash your

sins, calling on His name.'
17"And it came about when I returned to Jerusalem and was praying in the temple, that I fell into a trance,
18and I saw Him saying to me, 'Make haste, and get out of Jerusalem quickly, because they will not accept your testimony about Me.'
19"And I said, 'Lord, they themselves understand that in one synagogue after another I used to imprison and beat those who believed in Thee.
20'And when the blood of Thy witness Stephen was being shed, I also was standing by approving, and watching out for the cloaks of those who were slaying him.'
21"And He said to me, 'Go! For I will send you far away to the Gentiles.' "
22And they listened to him up to this statement, and *then* they raised their voices and said, "Away with such a fellow from the earth, for he should not be allowed to live!"
23And as they were crying out and throwing off their cloaks and tossing dust into the air,
24the *j*commander ordered him to be brought into the barracks, stating that he should be examined by scourging so that he might find out the reason why they were shouting against him that way.
25And when they stretched him out with thongs, Paul said to the centurion who was standing by, "Is it lawful for you to scourge a man who is a Roman and uncondemned?"
26And when the centurion heard *this*, he went to the commander and told him,

---

σαι τὰς ἁμαρτίας σου, ἐπικαλεσάμενος τὸ
away the sins of thee, invoking the
ὄνομα αὐτοῦ. 17 Ἐγένετο δέ μοι ὑποστρέ-
name of him. And it happened. to me having
ψαντι εἰς Ἰερουσαλὴμ καὶ προσευχομένου
returned to Jerusalem and praying
                                              = as I was praying
μου ἐν τῷ ἱερῷ γενέσθαι με ἐν ἐκστάσει,
me*a* in the temple to become me*b* in an ecstasy,
                                              = I became
18 καὶ ἰδεῖν*b* αὐτὸν λέγοντά μοι· σπεῦσον
and to see him saying to me; Haste
   = I saw
καὶ ἔξελθε ἐν τάχει ἐξ Ἰερουσαλήμ,
and go forth quickly out of Jerusalem,
διότι οὐ παραδέξονταί σου μαρτυρίαν
because they will not receive of thee witness
περὶ ἐμοῦ. 19 κἀγὼ εἶπον· κύριε, αὐτοὶ
concerning me. And I said: Lord, they
ἐπίστανται ὅτι ἐγὼ ἤμην φυλακίζων καὶ
understand that I was imprisoning and
δέρων κατὰ τὰς συναγωγὰς τοὺς πιστεύον-
beating throughout the synagogues the [ones] believ-
τας ἐπὶ σέ· 20 καὶ ὅτε ἐξεχύννετο τὸ αἷμα
ing on thee; and when was being shed the blood
Στεφάνου τοῦ μάρτυρός σου, καὶ αὐτὸς
of Stephen the witness of thee, even [my]self
ἤμην ἐφεστὼς καὶ συνευδοκῶν καὶ
I was standing by and consenting and
φυλάσσων τὰ ἱμάτια τῶν ἀναιρούντων
keeping the garments of the [ones] killing
αὐτόν. 21 καὶ εἶπεν πρός με· πορεύου,
him. And he said to me: Go,
ὅτι ἐγὼ εἰς ἔθνη μακρὰν ἐξαποστελῶ σε.
because I to nations afar will send forth thee.
22 Ἤκουον δὲ αὐτοῦ ἄχρι τούτου τοῦ
And they heard him as far as to this —
λόγου, καὶ ἐπῆραν τὴν φωνὴν αὐτῶν
word, and lifted up the voice of them
λέγοντες· αἶρε ἀπὸ τῆς γῆς τὸν τοιοῦτον·
saying: Take from the earth such a man;
οὐ γὰρ καθῆκεν αὐτὸν ζῆν. 23 κραυγαζόν-
for not it is fitting him to live. And shout-
των τε αὐτῶν καὶ ῥιπτούντων τὰ ἱμάτια
ing and and tearing*a* the(ir) garments
   = as they shouted and tore . . .
καὶ κονιορτὸν βαλλόντων εἰς τὸν ἀέρα,
and *2*dust *1*throwing*a* in the air,
                   = threw dust
24 ἐκέλευσεν ὁ χιλίαρχος εἰσάγεσθαι αὐτὸν
commanded the chiliarch to be brought *in* him
εἰς τὴν παρεμβολήν, εἴπας μάστιξιν
into the fort, bidding *2*with scourges
ἀνετάζεσθαι αὐτόν, ἵνα ἐπιγνῷ δι' ἣν
*1*to be examined *1*him, that he might fully know for what
αἰτίαν οὕτως ἐπεφώνουν αὐτῷ. 25 ὡς δὲ
crime thus they were calling against him. But as
προέτειναν αὐτὸν τοῖς ἱμᾶσιν, εἶπεν πρὸς
they stretched him with the thongs, *3*said *3*to
forward
τὸν ἑστῶτα ἑκατόνταρχον ὁ Παῦλος· εἰ
*4*the *5*standing [by] *6*centurion - *1*Paul: *1*If
ἄνθρωπον Ῥωμαῖον καὶ ἀκατάκριτον ἔξεστιν
a man *6*a Roman *8*and *7*uncondemned *2*it is lawful
ὑμῖν μαστίζειν; 26 ἀκούσας δὲ ὁ ἑκατον-
*1*for you *4*to scourge? And *3*hearing *1*the *2*cen-
τάρχης προσελθὼν τῷ χιλιάρχῳ ἀπήγγειλεν
turion approaching *to* the chiliarch reported

---

sins away, calling on his name.'
17"When I returned to Jerusalem and was praying at the temple, I fell into a trance 18and saw the Lord speaking. 'Quick!' he said to me. 'Leave Jerusalem immediately, because they will not accept your testimony about me.'
19" 'Lord,' I replied, 'these men know that I went from one synagogue to another to imprison and beat those who believe in you. 20And when the blood of your martyr*s* Stephen was shed, I stood there giving my approval and guarding the clothes of those who were killing him.'
21"Then the Lord said to me, 'Go; I will send you far away to the Gentiles.' "

Paul the Roman Citizen
22The crowd listened to Paul until he said this. Then they raised their voices and shouted, "Rid the earth of him! He's not fit to live!"
23As they were shouting and throwing off their cloaks and flinging dust into the air, 24the commander ordered Paul to be taken into the barracks. He directed that he be flogged and questioned in order to find out why the people were shouting at him like this. 25As they stretched him out to flog him, Paul said to the centurion standing there, "Is it legal for you to flog a Roman citizen who hasn't even been found guilty?"
26When the centurion heard this, he went to the commander and reported

---

*j*I.e., chiliarch, in command of one thousand troops

*s*20 Or *witness*

saying, "What are you about to do? For this man is a Roman."

27And the commander came and said to him, "Tell me, are you a Roman?" And he said, "Yes."

28And the commander answered, "I acquired this citizenship with a large sum of money." And Paul said, "But I was actually born *a citizen*."

29Therefore those who were about to examine him immediately let go of him; and the commander also was afraid when he found out that he was a Roman, and because he had put him in chains.

30But on the next day, wishing to know for certain why he had been accused by the Jews, he released him and ordered the chief priests and all the Council to assemble, and brought Paul down and set him before them.

Chapter 23

Paul before the Council

AND Paul, looking intently at the Council, said, "Brethren, I have lived my life with a perfectly good conscience before God up to this day."

2And the high priest Ananias commanded those standing beside him to strike him on the mouth.

3Then Paul said to him, "God is going to strike you, you whitewashed wall! And do you sit to try me according to the Law, and in violation of the Law order me to be struck?"

4But the bystanders said, "Do you revile God's high priest?"

5And Paul said, "I was not aware, brethren, that he was high priest; for it is written, 'YOU SHALL NOT SPEAK EVIL OF A RULER OF YOUR PEOPLE.'"

6But perceiving that one part were Sadducees and

λέγων· τί μέλλεις ποιεῖν; ὁ γὰρ ἄνθρωπος
saying: What art thou about to do? - for ¹man

οὗτος Ῥωμαῖός ἐστιν. 27 προσελθὼν δὲ
¹this ⁴a Roman ³is. And approaching

ὁ χιλίαρχος εἶπεν αὐτῷ· λέγε μοι, σὺ
the chiliarch said to him: Tell me, thou

Ῥωμαῖος εἶ; ὁ δὲ ἔφη· ναί. 28 ἀπεκρίθη
a Roman art? And he said: Yes. answered

δὲ ὁ χιλίαρχος· ἐγὼ πολλοῦ κεφαλαίου
And the chiliarch: ¹I ⁵of(for) ⁶sum [of money] much(great)

τὴν πολιτείαν ταύτην ἐκτησάμην. ὁ δὲ
²this ⁴citizenship ³acquired. - So

Παῦλος ἔφη· ἐγὼ δὲ καὶ γεγέννημαι.
Paul said: But I indeed have been born.

29 εὐθέως οὖν ἀπέστησαν ἀπ' αὐτοῦ οἱ
Immediately therefore ⁵stood away ⁶from ⁷him ¹the [ones]

μέλλοντες αὐτὸν ἀνετάζειν· καὶ ὁ χιλίαρχος
²being about ⁴him ³to examine; ⁸also ¹the ⁹chiliarch

δὲ ἐφοβήθη ἐπιγνοὺς ὅτι Ῥωμαῖός ἐστιν
¹and ⁴feared ⁵fully knowing that a Roman he is(was)

καὶ ὅτι αὐτὸν ἦν δεδεκώς.
and that ³him ¹he was ²having bound.

30 Τῇ δὲ ἐπαύριον βουλόμενος γνῶναι τὸ
And on the morrow being minded to know the

ἀσφαλές, τὸ τί κατηγορεῖται ὑπὸ τῶν
certain thing, - why he was accused by the

Ἰουδαίων, ἔλυσεν αὐτόν, καὶ ἐκέλευσεν
Jews, he released him, and commanded

συνελθεῖν τοὺς ἀρχιερεῖς καὶ πᾶν τὸ
to come together the chief priests and all the

συνέδριον, καὶ καταγαγὼν τὸν Παῦλον
council, and having brought down - Paul

ἔστησεν εἰς αὐτούς. 23 ἀτενίσας δὲ
set [him] among them. And ²gazing

ὁ Παῦλος τῷ συνεδρίῳ εἶπεν· ἄνδρες
- ¹Paul at the council said: Men

ἀδελφοί, ἐγὼ πάσῃ συνειδήσει ἀγαθῇ
brothers, I in all conscience good

πεπολίτευμαι τῷ θεῷ ἄχρι ταύτης τῆς
have lived - to God until this -

ἡμέρας. 2 ὁ δὲ ἀρχιερεὺς Ἀνανίας
day. And the high priest Ananias

ἐπέταξεν τοῖς παρεστῶσιν αὐτῷ τύπτειν
gave order to the [ones] standing by him to strike

αὐτοῦ τὸ στόμα. 3 τότε ὁ Παῦλος πρὸς
of him the mouth. Then - Paul to

αὐτὸν εἶπεν· τύπτειν σε μέλλει ὁ θεός,
him said: ³To strike ⁴thee ²is about ¹God,

τοῖχε κεκονιαμένε· καὶ σὺ κάθῃ κρίνων
wall *having been* whitened; and thou sittest judging

με κατὰ τὸν νόμον, καὶ παρανομῶν
me according to the law, and contravening law

κελεύεις με τύπτεσθαι; 4 οἱ δὲ παρεστῶτες
commandest me to be struck? And the [ones] standing by

εἶπαν· τὸν ἀρχιερέα τοῦ θεοῦ λοιδορεῖς;
said: The high priest - of God revilest thou?

5 ἔφη τε ὁ Παῦλος· οὐκ ᾔδειν, ἀδελφοί,
And said - Paul: I did not know, brothers,

ὅτι ἐστὶν ἀρχιερεύς· γέγραπται γὰρ ὅτι
that he is high priest; for it has been written[,] -

ἄρχοντα τοῦ λαοῦ σου οὐκ ἐρεῖς κακῶς.
A ruler of the people of thee thou shalt not speak evilly.

6 γνοὺς δὲ ὁ Παῦλος ὅτι τὸ ἓν μέρος
And knowing - Paul that the one part

---

it. "What are you going to do?" he asked. "This man is a Roman citizen."

27The commander went to Paul and asked, "Tell me, are you a Roman citizen?"

"Yes, I am," he answered.

28Then the commander said, "I had to pay a big price for my citizenship."

"But I was born a citizen," Paul replied.

29Those who were about to question him withdrew immediately. The commander himself was alarmed when he realized that he had put Paul, a Roman citizen, in chains.

Before the Sanhedrin

30The next day, since the commander wanted to find out exactly why Paul was being accused by the Jews, he released him and ordered the chief priests and all the Sanhedrin to assemble. Then he brought Paul and had him stand before them.

Chapter 23

PAUL looked straight at the Sanhedrin and said, "My brothers, I have fulfilled my duty to God in all good conscience to this day." 2At this the high priest Ananias ordered those standing near Paul to strike him on the mouth. 3Then Paul said to him, "God will strike you, you whitewashed wall! You sit there to judge me according to the law, yet you yourself violate the law by commanding that I be struck!"

4Those who were standing near Paul said, "You dare to insult God's high priest?"

5Paul replied, "Brothers, I did not realize that he was the high priest; for it is written: 'Do not speak evil about the ruler of your people.'*'*

6Then Paul, knowing that some of them were Saddu-

⁵⁵ Exodus 22:28

the other Pharisees, Paul *began* crying out in the Council, "Brethren, I am a Pharisee, a son of Pharisees; I am on trial for the hope and resurrection of the dead!"

7And as he said this, there arose a dissension between the Pharisees and Sadducees; and the assembly was divided.

8For the Sadducees say that there is no resurrection, nor an angel, nor a spirit; but the Pharisees acknowledge them all.

9And there arose a great uproar; and some of the scribes of the Pharisaic party stood up and *began* to argue heatedly, saying, "We find nothing wrong with this man; suppose a spirit or an angel has spoken to him?"

10And as a great dissension was developing, the *k*commander was afraid Paul would be torn to pieces by them and ordered the troops to go down and take him away from them by force, and bring him into the barracks.

11But on the night *immediately* following, the Lord stood at his side and said, "Take courage; for as you have solemnly witnessed to My cause at Jerusalem, so you must witness at Rome also."

A Conspiracy to Kill Paul

12And when it was day, the Jews formed a conspiracy and bound themselves under an oath, saying that they would neither eat nor drink until they had killed Paul.

13And there were more than forty who formed this plot.

14And they came to the chief priests and the elders, and said, "We have bound ourselves under a solemn

---

ἐστὶν Σαδδουκαίων τὸ δὲ ἕτερον Φαρισαίων
is(was) of Sadducees but the other of Pharisees

ἔκραζεν ἐν τῷ συνεδρίῳ· ἄνδρες ἀδελφοί,
cried out in the council: Men brothers,

ἐγὼ Φαρισαῖός εἰμι, υἱὸς Φαρισαίων· περὶ
I a Pharisee am, a son of Pharisees; concerning

ἐλπίδος καὶ ἀναστάσεως νεκρῶν κρίνομαι.
hope and resurrection of dead ones I am being
judged.

7 τοῦτο δὲ αὐτοῦ λαλοῦντος ἐγένετο
And this him saying* there was
=as he said this

στάσις τῶν Φαρισαίων καὶ Σαδδουκαίων,
a discord of the Pharisees and Sadducees,

καὶ ἐσχίσθη τὸ πλῆθος. **8** Σαδδουκαῖοι
and was divided the multitude. Sadducees

γὰρ λέγουσιν μὴ εἶναι ἀνάστασιν μήτε
For say not to be a resurrection nor

ἄγγελον μήτε πνεῦμα, Φαρισαῖοι δὲ
angel nor spirit, but Pharisees

ὁμολογοῦσιν τὰ ἀμφότερα. **9** ἐγένετο δὲ
confess both. And there was

κραυγὴ μεγάλη, καὶ ἀναστάντες τινὲς
cry a great, and rising up some

τῶν γραμματέων τοῦ μέρους τῶν Φαρισαίων
of the scribes of the part of the Pharisees

διεμάχοντο λέγοντες· οὐδὲν κακὸν εὑρίσκομεν
strove saying: Nothing evil we find

ἐν τῷ ἀνθρώπῳ τούτῳ· εἰ δὲ πνεῦμα
in this man; and if ¹a spirit

ἐλάλησεν αὐτῷ ἢ ἄγγελος —. **10** Πολλῆς δὲ
¹spoke ²to him ³or ⁴an angel —. And much

γινομένης στάσεως φοβηθεὶς ὁ χιλίαρχος
arising discord* ²fearing ¹the ³chiliarch
=when much discord arose

μὴ διασπασθῇ ὁ Παῦλος ὑπ᾽ αὐτῶν,
⁴lest ⁵should be — ⁶Paul by them,
torn asunder

ἐκέλευσεν τὸ στράτευμα καταβὰν ἁρπάσαι
commanded the soldiery coming down to seize

αὐτὸν ἐκ μέσου αὐτῶν ἄγειν τε εἰς
him out of [the] midst of them and to bring [him] into

τὴν παρεμβολήν. **11** Τῇ δὲ ἐπιούσῃ
the fort. And in the following

νυκτὶ ἐπιστὰς αὐτῷ ὁ κύριος εἶπεν·
night ²coming *on* ⁴to him ¹the ³Lord said:

θάρσει· ὡς γὰρ διεμαρτύρω τὰ περὶ
Be of good for as thou didst the concerning
courage; solemnly witness things

ἐμοῦ εἰς Ἰερουσαλήμ, οὕτω σε· δεῖ καὶ
me in Jerusalem, so thee it behoves also

εἰς Ῥώμην μαρτυρῆσαι. **12** Γενομένης δὲ
in Rome to witness. And becoming

ἡμέρας ποιήσαντες συστροφὴν οἱ Ἰουδαῖοι
day* ²making ⁴a conspiracy ¹the ³Jews
=when it became day

ἀνεθεμάτισαν ἑαυτούς, λέγοντες μήτε φαγεῖν
cursed themselves, saying neither to eat

μήτε πεῖν ἕως οὗ ἀποκτείνωσιν τὸν
nor to drink until they should kill —

Παῦλον. **13** ἦσαν δὲ πλείους τεσσεράκοντα
Paul. And there were more [than] forty

οἱ ταύτην τὴν συνωμοσίαν ποιησάμενοι·
the [ones] this — plot making;

14 οἵτινες προσελθόντες τοῖς ἀρχιερεῦσιν
who approaching *to* the chief priests

καὶ τοῖς πρεσβυτέροις εἶπαν· ἀναθέματι
and *to* the elders said: With a curse

---

cees and the others Pharisees, called out in the Sanhedrin, "My brothers, I am a Pharisee, the son of a Pharisee. I stand on trial because of my hope in the resurrection of the dead."

7When he said this, a dispute broke out between the Pharisees and the Sadducees, and the assembly was divided. 8(The Sadducees say that there is no resurrection, and that there are neither angels nor spirits, but the Pharisees acknowledge them all.)

9There was a great uproar, and some of the teachers of the law who were Pharisees stood up and argued vigorously. "We find nothing wrong with this man," they said. "What if a spirit or an angel has spoken to him?" 10The dispute became so violent that the commander was afraid Paul would be torn to pieces by them. He ordered the troops to go down and take him away from them by force and bring him into the barracks.

11The following night the Lord stood near Paul and said, "Take courage! As you have testified about me in Jerusalem, so you must also testify in Rome."

The Plot to Kill Paul

12The next morning the Jews formed a conspiracy and bound themselves with an oath not to eat or drink until they had killed Paul. 13More than forty men were involved in this plot. 14They went to the chief priests and elders and said, "We have taken a solemn oath not to eat anything un-

---

k I.e., chiliarch, in command of one thousand troops

oath to taste nothing until we have killed Paul. ¹⁵"Now, therefore, you and the Council notify the commander to bring him down to you, as though you were going to determine his case by a more thorough investigation; and we for our part are ready to slay him before he comes near *the place*." ¹⁶But the son of Paul's sister heard of their ambush, and he came and entered the barracks and told Paul. ¹⁷And Paul called one of the centurions to him and said, "Lead this young man to the commander, for he has something to report to him." ¹⁸So he took him and led him to the commander and *said, "Paul the prisoner called me to him and asked me to lead this young man to you since he has something to tell you." ¹⁹And the commander took him by the hand and stepping aside, *began* to inquire of him privately, "What is it that you have to report to me?" ²⁰And he said, "The Jews have agreed to ask you to bring Paul down tomorrow to the Council, as though they were going to inquire somewhat more thoroughly about him. ²¹"So do not listen to them, for more than forty of them are lying in wait for him who have bound themselves under a curse not to eat or drink until they slay him; and now they are ready and waiting for the promise from you." ²²Therefore the com-

ἀνεθεματίσαμεν ἑαυτοὺς μηδενὸς γεύσασθαι
we cursed   ourselves   of nothing   to taste
ἕως οὗ ἀποκτείνωμεν τὸν Παῦλον. 15 νῦν
until   we may kill   -   Paul.   Now
οὖν ὑμεῖς ἐμφανίσατε τῷ χιλιάρχῳ σὺν
therefore ²ye ¹inform   the   chiliarch   with
τῷ συνεδρίῳ ὅπως καταγάγῃ αὐτὸι εἰς
the   council   so as he may bring down him to
ὑμᾶς ὡς μέλλοντας διαγινώσκειν ἀκριβέστε-
you   as intending   to ascertain *exactly* more accurate-
ρον τὰ περὶ αὐτοῦ· ἡμεῖς δὲ πρὸ τοῦ
ly the things concerning him;   and we   before   -
ἐγγίσαι αὐτὸν ἕτοιμοί ἐσμεν τοῦ ἀνελεῖν
to draw near himᵇ ready are   -   to killᵈ
= he draws near
αὐτόν. 16 Ἀκούσας δὲ ὁ υἱὸς τῆς ἀδελφῆς
him.   And ⁴hearing ¹the ²son ³of the ⁵sister
Παύλου τὴν ἐνέδραν, παραγενόμενος καὶ
⁶of Paul   the   treachery,   coming   and
εἰσελθὼν εἰς τὴν παρεμβολὴν ἀπήγγειλεν
entering   into   the   fort   reported
τῷ Παύλῳ. 17 προσκαλεσάμενος δὲ ὁ
-   to Paul.   And ²calling to [him]   δὲ   ὁ
Παῦλος ἕνα τῶν ἑκατονταρχῶν ἔφη· τὸν
¹Paul   one of the   centurions   said: -
νεανίαν τοῦτον ἄπαγε πρὸς τὸν χιλίαρχον,
³youth   ²this   ¹Bring up   to   the   chiliarch,
ἔχει γὰρ ἀπαγγειλαί τι αὐτῷ. 18 ὁ
for ¹he has ³to report ²something ⁴to him.   He
μὲν οὖν παραλαβὼν αὐτὸν ἤγαγεν πρὸς
- therefore taking   ²him   ¹brought   to
τὸν χιλίαρχον καὶ φησίν· ὁ δέσμιος
the   chiliarch   and   says: The   prisoner
Παῦλος προσκαλεσάμενός με ἠρώτησεν
Paul   calling to [him]   me   asked
τοῦτον τὸν νεανίσκον ἀγαγεῖν πρὸς σέ,
²this   -   ³young man   ¹to bring   to   thee,
ἔχοντά τι λαλῆσαί σοι. 19 ἐπιλαβόμενος
having something to tell   thee.   ²laying hold
δὲ τῆς χειρὸς αὐτοῦ ὁ χιλίαρχος καὶ
And ⁴of the ⁵hand ⁶of him ¹the ³chiliarch and
ἀναχωρήσας κατ' ἰδίαν ἐπυνθάνετο· τί
retiring   ²privately   ¹inquired: What
ἐστιν ὃ ἔχεις ἀπαγγειλαί μοι; 20 εἶπεν
is it   which thou hast to report   to me?   he said[,]
δὲ ὅτι οἱ Ἰουδαῖοι συνέθεντο τοῦ ἐρωτῆσαί
And   -   The   Jews   agreed   -   to askᵈ
σε ὅπως αὔριον τὸν Παῦλον καταγάγῃς
thee so as to-morrow   -   ²Paul   ¹thou shouldest bring down
εἰς τὸ συνέδριον ὡς μέλλον τι ἀκριβέστερον
to the council   as intending some- more accurately thing
πυνθάνεσθαι περὶ αὐτοῦ. 21 σὺ οὖν μὴ
to inquire concerning him.   Thou therefore not
πεισθῇς αὐτοῖς· ἐνεδρεύουσιν γὰρ αὐτὸν
be persuaded by them;   for there lie in wait for   him
ἐξ αὐτῶν ἄνδρες πλείους τεσσεράκοντα,
of them ⁴men ¹more ²[than]   ³forty,
οἵτινες ἀνεθεμάτισαν ἑαυτοὺς μήτε φαγεῖν
who   cursed   themselves neither to eat
μήτε πεῖν ἕως οὗ ἀνέλωσιν αὐτόν, καὶ νῦν
nor to drink until   they kill   him,   and now
εἰσιν ἕτοιμοι προσδεχόμενοι τὴν ἀπὸ σοῦ
they are • ready   awaiting   ¹the ³from ⁴thee
ἐπαγγελίαν. 22 ὁ μὲν οὖν χιλίαρχος
²promise.   the   -   Therefore chiliarch

til we have killed Paul. ¹⁵Now then, you and the Sanhedrin petition the commander to bring him before you on the pretext of wanting more accurate information about his case. We are ready to kill him before he gets here." ¹⁶But when the son of Paul's sister heard of this plot, he went into the barracks and told Paul. ¹⁷Then Paul called one of the centurions and said, "Take this young man to the commander; he has something to tell him." ¹⁸So he took him to the commander. The centurion said, "Paul, the prisoner, sent for me and asked me to bring this young man to you because he has something to tell you." ¹⁹The commander took the young man by the hand, drew him aside and asked, "What is it you want to tell me?" ²⁰He said: "The Jews have agreed to ask you to bring Paul before the Sanhedrin tomorrow on the pretext of wanting more accurate information about him. ²¹Don't give in to them, because more than forty of them are waiting in ambush for him. They have taken an oath not to eat or drink until they have killed him. They are ready now, waiting for your consent to their request." ²²The commander dismander let the young man go, instructing him, "Tell no one that you have notified me of these things."

Paul Moved to Caesarea

23And he called to him two of the centurions, and said, "Get two hundred soldiers ready by *the third hour of the night to proceed to Caesarea, with seventy horsemen and two hundred spearmen."

24*They were* also to provide mounts to put Paul on and bring him safely to Felix the governor.

25And he wrote a letter having this form:

26"Claudius Lysias, to the most excellent governor Felix, greetings.

27"When this man was arrested by the Jews and was about to be slain by them, I came upon them with the troops and rescued him, having learned that he was a Roman.

28"And wanting to ascertain the charge for which they were accusing him, I brought him down to their Council;

29 and I found him to be accused over questions about their Law, but under no accusation deserving death or imprisonment.

30"And when I was informed that there would be a plot against the man, I sent him to you at once, also instructing his accusers to bring charges against him before you."

31So the soldiers, in accordance with their orders, took Paul and brought him by night to Antipatris.

32But the next day, leaving the horsemen to go on with him, they returned to the barracks.

33And when these had come to Caesarea and de-

I.e., 9 p.m.

ἀπέλυσε τὸν νεανίσκον, παραγγείλας μηδενὶ
dismissed the young man, charging [him] to no one
ἐκλαλῆσαι ὅτι ταῦτα ἐνεφάνισας πρὸς ἐμέ.
to divulge that these things thou reportedst to me.

23 Καὶ προσκαλεσάμενός τινας δύο τῶν
And calling to [him] a certain two of the
ἑκατονταρχῶν εἶπεν· ἑτοιμάσατε στρατιώτας
centurions he said: Prepare ye soldiers
διακοσίους ὅπως πορευθῶσιν ἕως Καισαρείας,
two hundred so as they may go as far as Caesarea,
καὶ ἱππεῖς ἑβδομήκοντα καὶ δεξιολάβους
and horsemen seventy and spearmen
διακοσίους, ἀπὸ τρίτης ὥρας τῆς νυκτός,
two hundred, from third hour of the night,
24 κτήνη τε παραστῆσαι, ἵνα ἐπιβιβάσαντες
and beasts to stand by, that putting on
τὸν Παῦλον διασώσωσι πρὸς Φήλικα τὸν
- Paul they may bring safely to Felix the
ἡγεμόνα, **25** γράψας ἐπιστολὴν ἔχουσαν
governor, writing a letter having
τὸν τύπον τοῦτον· **26** Κλαύδιος Λυσίας τῷ
this pattern: Claudius Lysias to the
κρατίστῳ ἡγεμόνι Φήλικι χαίρειν. **27** Τὸν
most excellent governor Felix greeting. -
ἄνδρα τοῦτον συλλημφθέντα ὑπὸ τῶν
man This having been arrested by the
Ἰουδαίων καὶ μέλλοντα ἀναιρεῖσθαι ὑπ'
Jews and being about to be killed by
αὐτῶν ἐπιστὰς σὺν τῷ στρατεύματι
them coming on with the soldiery
[the scene]
ἐξειλάμην, μαθὼν ὅτι Ῥωμαῖός ἐστιν·
I rescued, having learned that a Roman he is;
28 βουλόμενός τε ἐπιγνῶναι τὴν αἰτίαν
and being minded to know fully the cause
δι' ἣν ἐνεκάλουν αὐτῷ, κατήγαγον εἰς
on ac- which they were him, I brought to
count of accusing [him] down
τὸ συνέδριον αὐτῶν· **29** ὃν εὗρον ἐγκαλούμενον
the council of them; whom I found being accused
περὶ ζητημάτων τοῦ νόμου αὐτῶν, μηδὲν
about questions of the law of them, ²nothing
δὲ ἄξιον θανάτου ἢ δεσμῶν ἔχοντα
¹but ⁵worthy ⁶of death ⁷or ⁸of bonds ⁴having
ἔγκλημα. **30** μηνυθείσης δέ μοι ἐπιβουλῆς
⁴charge. And being revealed to me a plotᵃ
=when it was revealed to me that there was a plot
εἰς τὸν ἄνδρα ἔσεσθαι, ἐξαυτῆς ἔπεμψα
against the man to be, at once I sent
πρὸς σέ, παραγγείλας καὶ τοῖς κατηγόροις
to thee, commanding also the accusers
λέγειν πρὸς αὐτὸν ἐπὶ σοῦ. **31** Οἱ μὲν
to say to him before thee. the -
οὖν στρατιῶται κατὰ τὸ διατεταγμένον
Therefore soldiers according the *having been*
to thing appointed
αὐτοῖς ἀναλαβόντες τὸν Παῦλον ἤγαγον
them taking up - Paul brought
διὰ νυκτὸς εἰς τὴν Ἀντιπατρίδα· **32** τῇ δὲ
through [the] night to - Antipatris; and on the
(during)
ἐπαύριον ἐάσαντες τοὺς ἱππεῖς ἀπέρχεσθαι
morrow allowing the horsemen to depart
σὺν αὐτῷ, ὑπέστρεψαν εἰς τὴν παρεμβολήν·
with him, they returned to the fort;
33 οἵτινες εἰσελθόντες εἰς τὴν Καισάρειαν
who entering into - Caesarea

---

missed the young man and cautioned him, "Don't tell anyone that you have reported this to me."

Paul Transferred to Caesarea

23Then he called two of his centurions and ordered them, "Get ready a detachment of two hundred soldiers, seventy horsemen and two hundred spearmenᵃ to go to Caesarea at nine tonight. 24Provide mounts for Paul so that he may be taken safely to Governor Felix."

25He wrote a letter as follows:

26Claudius Lysias,

To His Excellency, Governor Felix:

Greetings.

27This man was seized by the Jews and they were about to kill him, but I came with my troops and rescued him, for I had learned that he is a Roman citizen. 28I wanted to know why they were accusing him, so I brought him to their Sanhedrin. 29I found that the accusation had to do with questions about their law, but there was no charge against him that deserved death or imprisonment. 30When I was informed of a plot to be carried out against the man, I sent him to you at once. I also ordered his accusers to present to you their case against him.

31So the soldiers, carrying out their orders, took Paul with them during the night and brought him as far as Antipatris. 32The next day they let the cavalry go on with him, while they returned to the barracks. 33When the cavalry arrived in Caesarea, they

ᵃ23 The meaning of the Greek for this word is uncertain.

livered the letter to the governor, they also presented Paul to him. 34And when he had read it, he asked from what province he was; and when he learned that he was from Cilicia, 35he said, "I will give you a hearing after your accusers arrive also," giving orders for him to be kept in Herod's mPraetorium.

καὶ ἀναδόντες τὴν ἐπιστολὴν τῷ ἡγεμόνι,
and handing over the letter to the governor,

παρέστησαν καὶ τὸν Παῦλον αὐτῷ.
presented also – Paul to him.

34 ἀναγνοὺς δὲ καὶ ἐπερωτήσας ἐκ ποίας
And having read and asking of what

ἐπαρχείας ἐστίν, καὶ πυθόμενος ὅτι ἀπὸ
province he is(was), and learning[,] – From

Κιλικίας, 35 διακούσομαί σου, ἔφη, ὅταν
Cilicia, I will hear thee, he said, when

καὶ οἱ κατήγοροί σου παραγένωνται·
also the accusers of thee arrive;

κελεύσας ἐν τῷ πραιτωρίῳ τοῦ Ἡρώδου
commanding in the prætorium of Herod
= that he be kept in Herod's prætorium.

φυλάσσεσθαι αὐτόν.
to be kept him.

delivered the letter to the governor and handed Paul over to him. 34The governor read the letter and asked what province he was from. Learning that he was from Cilicia, 35he said, "I will hear your case when your accusers get here." Then he ordered that Paul be kept under guard in Herod's palace.

Chapter 24

Paul before Felix

AND after five days the high priest Ananias came down with some elders, with a certain attorney named Tertullus; and they brought charges against Paul.

2And after Paul had been summoned, Tertullus began to accuse him, saying to the governor,

"Since we have through you attained much peace, and since by your providence reforms are being carried out for this nation, 3we acknowledge this in every way and everywhere, most excellent Felix, with all thankfulness.

4"But, that I may not weary you any further, I beg you to grant us, by your kindness, a brief hearing.

5"For we have found this man a real pest and a fellow who stirs up dissension among all the Jews throughout nthe world, and a ringleader of the sect of the Nazarenes.

6"And he even tried to desecrate the temple; and then we arrested him. [oAnd we wanted to judge him according to our own Law.

7"But Lysias the commander came along, and with much violence took him out of our hands,

8ordering his accusers to come before you.] And by examining him yourself concerning all these matters, you will be able to ascertain the things of which we accuse him."

9And the Jews also joined in the attack, asserting that these things were so.

24 Μετὰ δὲ πέντε ἡμέρας κατέβη ὁ
And after five days came down the

ἀρχιερεὺς Ἁνανίας μετὰ πρεσβυτέρων τινῶν
high priest Ananias with elders some

καὶ ῥήτορος Τερτύλλου τινός, οἵτινες
and an orator Tertullus one, who

ἐνεφάνισαν τῷ ἡγεμόνι κατὰ τοῦ Παύλου.
informed the governor against – Paul.

2 κληθέντος δὲ [αὐτοῦ] ἤρξατο κατηγορεῖν
And being called hima 1began 2to accuse
= when he was called

ὁ Τέρτυλλος λέγων· πολλῆς εἰρήνης
– 1Tertullus saying: Much peace

τυγχάνοντες διὰ σοῦ καὶ διορθωμάτων
obtaining through thee and reforms

γινομένων τῷ ἔθνει τούτῳ διὰ τῆς σῆς
coming to this nation through thy

προνοίας, 3 πάντῃ τε καὶ πανταχοῦ
forethought, both in everything and everywhere

ἀποδεχόμεθα, κράτιστε Φῆλιξ, μετὰ πάσης
we welcome, most excellent Felix, with all

εὐχαριστίας. 4 ἵνα δὲ μὴ ἐπὶ πλεῖόν
thankfulness. But that 1not 4more

σε ἐγκόπτω, παρακαλῶ ἀκοῦσαί σε ἡμῶν
3thee 1I hinder, I beseech 2to hear 3thee us

συντόμως τῇ σῇ ἐπιεικείᾳ. 5 εὑρόντες γὰρ
briefly – in thy forbearance. For having found

τὸν ἄνδρα τοῦτον λοιμὸν καὶ κινοῦντα
this man pestilent and moving

στάσεις πᾶσιν τοῖς Ἰουδαίοις τοῖς κατὰ
seditions [among] all the Jews – throughout

τὴν οἰκουμένην πρωτοστάτην τε τῆς τῶν
the inhabited [earth] and a ringleader of the 1of the

Ναζωραίων αἱρέσεως, 6 ὃς καὶ τὸ ἱερὸν
1Nazarenes 1sect, who also 3the 4temple

ἐπείρασεν βεβηλῶσαι, ὃν καὶ ἐκρατήσαμεν,
1attempted 2to profane, whom also we laid hold of,‡

8 παρ' οὗ δυνήσῃ αὐτὸς ἀνακρίνας
from whom thou wilt be able [thy]self 1having examined

περὶ πάντων τούτων ἐπιγνῶναι ὧν ἡμεῖς
2concerning 4all 5these things 1to know fully 3of which we

κατηγοροῦμεν αὐτοῦ. 9 συνεπέθεντο δὲ
accuse him. And 6joined in

καὶ οἱ Ἰουδαῖοι φάσκοντες ταῦτα οὕτως
2also 1the 3Jews alleging these things thus

Chapter 24

The Trial Before Felix

FIVE days later the high priest Ananias went down to Caesarea with some of the elders and a lawyer named Tertullus, and they brought their charges against Paul before the governor. 2When Paul was called in, Tertullus presented his case before Felix: "We have enjoyed a long period of peace under you, and your foresight has brought about reforms in this nation. 3Everywhere and in every way, most excellent Felix, we acknowledge this with profound gratitude. 4But in order not to weary you further, I would request that you be kind enough to hear us briefly.

5"We have found this man to be a troublemaker, stirring up riots among the Jews all over the world. He is a ringleader of the Nazarene sect 6and even tried to desecrate the temple; so we seized him. 8Byv examining him yourself you will be able to learn the truth about all these charges we are bringing against him."

9The Jews joined in the accusation, asserting that these things were true.

---

m I.e., governor's official residence
n Lit., the inhabited earth
o Many mss. do not contain the remainder of v. 6, v. 7, nor the first part of v. 8

‡ Verse 7 omitted by Nestle; cf. NIV footnote.

v 6-8 Some manuscripts him and wanted to judge him according to our law. 7But the commander, Lysias, came and with the use of much force snatched him from our hands 8and ordered his accusers to come before you. By

10And when the governor had nodded for him to speak, Paul responded:

"Knowing that for many years you have been a judge to this nation, I cheerfully make my defense,

11since you can take note of the fact that no more than twelve days ago I went up to Jerusalem to worship.

12"And neither in the temple, nor in the synagogues, nor in the city *itself* did they find me carrying on a discussion with anyone or causing a riot.

13"Nor can they prove to you *the charges* of which they now accuse me.

14"But this I admit to you, that according to the Way which they call a sect I do serve the God of our fathers, believing everything that is in accordance with the Law, and that is written in the Prophets;

15having a hope in God, which these men cherish themselves, that there shall certainly be a resurrection of both the righteous and the wicked.

16"In view of this, I also do my best to maintain always a blameless conscience *both* before God and before men.

17"Now after several years I came to bring *p* alms to my nation and to present offerings;

18in which they found me *occupied* in the temple, having been purified, without *any* crowd or uproar. But *there were* certain Jews from Asia—

19who ought to have been present before you, and to make accusation, if they should have anything against me.

20"Or else let these men

p Or, gifts to charity

ἔχειν.   10 Ἀπεκρίθη   τε   ὁ   Παῦλος,
to have(be).   And answered   -   Paul,

νεύσαντος   αὐτῷ   τοῦ   ἡγεμόνος   λέγειν· ἐκ
³having   ⁴to him   ¹the   ²governor³   to speak: ⁴of
beckoned   (for)

πολλῶν ἐτῶν ὄντα σε κριτὴν τῷ ἔθνει τούτῳ
⁵many ⁶years ²being ¹thee ⁷a judge ⁸to ⁹this ¹⁰nation
(to be)

ἐπιστάμενος   εὐθύμως   τὰ   περὶ
¹understanding   ¹²cheerfully   ¹³[as to]   ¹⁴the things   ¹⁵concerning

ἐμαυτοῦ   ἀπολογοῦμαι,   11 δυναμένου   σου
¹⁶myself   ¹¹I defend myself,   being able   thee³
                                               =as thou art able

ἐπιγνῶναι   ὅτι   οὐ   πλείους   εἰσίν   μοι   ἡμέραι
to know fully   that   ²not   ⁴more   ¹there   ²to ⁵[than] ⁷days
                                            are   me

δώδεκα   ἀφ'   ἧς   ἀνέβην   προσκυνήσων   εἰς
⁶twelve   from   which   I went up   worshipping   in
           =since

Ἰερουσαλήμ.   12 καὶ   οὔτε   ἐν   τῷ   ἱερῷ
Jerusalem.   And   neither   in   the   temple

εὑρόν   με   πρός   τινα   διαλεγόμενον   ἢ
they found me   ²with   ³anyone   ¹discoursing   or

ἐπίστασιν   ποιοῦντα   ὄχλου,   οὔτε   ἐν   ταῖς
²collection   ¹making   of a crowd,   neither   in   the

συναγωγαῖς   οὔτε   κατὰ   τὴν   πόλιν,   13 οὐδὲ
synagogues   nor   throughout   the   city,   nor

παραστῆσαι   δύνανταί   σοι   περὶ   ὧν   νυνὶ
²to prove   ¹are they able to thee   con-   [the] things now
                                         cerning of which

κατηγοροῦσίν   μου.   14 ὁμολογῶ   δὲ   τοῦτό
they accuse   me.   But I confess   this

σοι,   ὅτι   κατὰ   τὴν   ὁδὸν   ἣν   λέγουσιν
to thee,   that   according to the   way   which they say(call)

αἵρεσιν   οὕτως   λατρεύω   τῷ   πατρῴῳ   θεῷ,
a sect   thus   I worship   the   ancestral   God,

πιστεύων   πᾶσι   τοῖς   κατὰ   τὸν   νόμον   καὶ
believing   all   the   according the   law   and
                things to

τοῖς   ἐν   τοῖς   προφήταις   γεγραμμένοις,
the things in   the   prophets   *having been* written,

15 ἐλπίδα   ἔχων   εἰς   τὸν   θεόν,   ἣν   καὶ
hope   having   toward   -   God,   which   ²also

αὐτοὶ   οὗτοι   προσδέχονται,   ἀνάστασιν   μέλ-
²[them]selves ¹these   expect,   a resurrection   to be

λειν   ἔσεσθαι   δικαίων   τε   καὶ   ἀδίκων.
about   to be   both of just   and   of unjust.

16 ἐν   τούτῳ   καὶ   αὐτὸς   ἀσκῶ   ἀπρόσκοπον
By   this   also   ²[my]self   ¹I exercise   ⁴a blameless

συνείδησιν   ἔχειν   πρὸς   τὸν   θεὸν   καὶ   τοὺς
⁵conscience   ³to have   toward   -   God   and   -

ἀνθρώπους   διὰ   παντός.   17 δι'   ἐτῶν   δὲ
men   always.   And after years

πλειόνων   ἐλεημοσύνας   ποιήσων   εἰς   τὸ
many   ²alms   ¹making(bringing)   ³to   ⁴the

ἔθνος   μου   παρεγενόμην   καὶ   προσφοράς,
⁵nation   ⁶of me   ¹I arrived   ⁷and   ⁸offerings,

18 ἐν   αἷς   εὑρόν   με   ἡγνισμένον   ἐν   τῷ
among   which   they found   me   *having been* purified in   the

ἱερῷ,   οὐ   μετὰ   ὄχλου   οὐδὲ   μετὰ   θορύβου,
temple,   not   with   a crowd   nor   with   uproar,

19 τινὲς   δὲ   ἀπὸ   τῆς   Ἀσίας   Ἰουδαῖοι,
but some   ²from   -   ³Asia   ¹Jews,

οὓς   ἔδει   ἐπὶ   σοῦ   παρεῖναι   καὶ   κατηγορεῖν
whom   it be-   before   thee   to be present   and   to accuse
      hoved

εἴ   τι   ἔχοιεν   πρὸς   ἐμέ.   20 ἢ   αὐτοὶ
if anything they have   against   me.   Or   ²[them]selves

10When the governor motioned for him to speak, Paul replied: "I know that for a number of years you have been a judge over this nation; so I gladly make my defense. 11You can easily verify that no more than twelve days ago I went up to Jerusalem to worship. 12My accusers did not find me arguing with anyone at the temple, or stirring up a crowd in the synagogues or anywhere else in the city. 13And they cannot prove to you the charges they are now making against me. 14However, I admit that I worship the God of our fathers as a follower of the Way, which they call a sect. I believe everything that agrees with the Law and that is written in the Prophets, 15and I have the same hope in God as these men, that there will be a resurrection of both the righteous and the wicked. 16So I strive always to keep my conscience clear before God and man.

17"After an absence of several years, I came to Jerusalem to bring my people gifts for the poor and to present offerings. 18I was ceremonially clean when they found me in the temple courts doing this. There was no crowd with me, nor was I involved in any disturbance. 19But there are some Jews from the province of Asia, who ought to be here before you and bring charges if they have anything against me. 20Or these who are here should themselves tell what misdeed they found when I stood before the Council,

21other than for this one statement which I shouted out while standing among them, 'For the resurrection of the dead I am on trial before you today.' "

22But Felix, having a more exact knowledge about the Way, put them off, saying, "When Lysias the [a]commander comes down, I will decide your case."

23And he gave orders to the centurion for him to be kept in custody and yet have some freedom, and not to prevent any of his friends from ministering to him.

24But some days later, Felix arrived with Drusilla, his wife who was a Jewess, and sent for Paul, and heard him speak about faith in Christ Jesus.

25And as he was discussing righteousness, self-control and the judgment to come, Felix became frightened and said, "Go away for the present, and when I find time, I will summon you."

26At the same time too, he was hoping that money would be given him by Paul; therefore he also used to send for him quite often and converse with him.

27But after two years had passed, Felix was succeeded by Porcius Festus; and wishing to do the Jews a favor, Felix left Paul imprisoned.

Chapter 25

Paul before Festus

FESTUS therefore, having arrived in the province, three days later went up to Jerusalem from Caesarea.

[a] I.e., chiliarch, in command of one thousand troops

οὗτοι εἰπάτωσαν τί εὗρον ἀδίκημα στάντος
[1]these [1]let [4]say [1]what [3]they found [2]misdeed standing

μου ἐπὶ τοῦ συνεδρίου, 21 ἢ περὶ μιᾶς
me[2] before the council, unless concerning [2]one
= while I stood

ταύτης φωνῆς ἧς ἐκέκραξα ἐν αὐτοῖς
[1]this voice which I have cried out [2]among [1]them

ἑστὼς ὅτι περὶ ἀναστάσεως νεκρῶν ἐγὼ
[1]standing[,] – Concerning a resurrection of dead persons I

κρίνομαι σήμερον ἐφ' ὑμῶν. 22 Ἀνεβάλετο
am being judged to-day before you. [2]postponed

δὲ αὐτοὺς ὁ Φῆλιξ, ἀκριβέστερον εἰδὼς
And [3]them – [1]Felix, more exactly knowing

τὰ περὶ τῆς ὁδοῦ, εἴπας· ὅταν Λυσίας ὁ
the con- the way, saying· When Lysias the
things cerning

χιλίαρχος καταβῇ, διαγνώσομαι τὰ καθ'
chiliarch comes down, I will determine the things as to

ὑμᾶς· 23 διαταξάμενος τῷ ἑκατοντάρχῃ
you; commanding the centurion

τηρεῖσθαι αὐτὸν ἔχειν τε ἄνεσιν καὶ
to keep him and to have indulgence and

μηδένα κωλύειν τῶν ἰδίων αὐτοῦ ὑπηρετεῖν
[2]no one [1]to forbid of his own [people] to attend

αὐτῷ. 24 Μετὰ δὲ ἡμέρας τινὰς παραγενό-
him. And after days some [2]arriv-

μενος ὁ Φῆλιξ σὺν Δρουσίλλῃ τῇ ἰδίᾳ
ing – [1]Felix with Drusilla the(his) own

γυναικὶ οὔσῃ Ἰουδαίᾳ μετεπέμψατο τὸν
wife being a Jewess he sent for –

Παῦλον, καὶ ἤκουσεν αὐτοῦ περὶ τῆς
Paul, and heard him about [1]the(?his)

εἰς Χριστὸν Ἰησοῦν πίστεως. 25 διαλεγομέ-
[3]in [4]Christ [5]Jesus [2]faith. discours-
= And as he discoursed

νου δὲ αὐτοῦ περὶ δικαιοσύνης καὶ
ing And him[2] concerning righteousness and

ἐγκρατείας καὶ τοῦ κρίματος τοῦ μέλλοντος
self-control and the [2]judgment – [1]coming

ἔμφοβος γενόμενος ὁ Φῆλιξ ἀπεκρίθη·
afraid becoming – Felix answered:

τὸ νῦν ἔχον πορεύου, καιρὸν δὲ μεταλαβὼν
For the present† go thou, but [2]time [1]taking [3]later

μετακαλέσομαί σε· 26 ἅμα καὶ ἐλπίζων
I will send for thee; at the also hoping
same time

ὅτι χρήματα δοθήσεται αὐτῷ ὑπὸ τοῦ
that money will be given him by –

Παύλου· διὸ καὶ πυκνότερον αὐτὸν
Paul: wherefore also more frequently him

μεταπεμπόμενος ὡμίλει αὐτῷ. 27 Διετίας δὲ
sending for he conversed with him. And two years
with

πληρωθείσης ἔλαβεν διάδοχον ὁ Φῆλιξ
being completed[2] [2]received [3]a successor – [1]Felix

Πόρκιον Φῆστον· θέλων τε χάριτα κατα-
Porcius Festus; and wishing a favour to

θέσθαι τοῖς Ἰουδαίοις ὁ Φῆλιξ κατέλιπε
show to the Jews – Felix left

τὸν Παῦλον δεδεμένον.
– Paul *having been* bound.

25 Φῆστος οὖν ἐπιβὰς τῇ ἐπαρχείῳ
Festus therefore having entered the province

μετὰ τρεῖς ἡμέρας ἀνέβη εἰς Ἱεροσόλυμα
after three days went up to Jerusalem

---

state what crime they found in me when I stood before the Sanhedrin—

21unless it was this one thing I shouted as I stood in their presence: 'It is concerning the resurrection of the dead that I am on trial before you today.' "

22Then Felix, who was well acquainted with the Way, adjourned the proceedings. "When Lysias the commander comes," he said, "I will decide your case." 23He ordered the centurion to keep Paul under guard but to give him some freedom and permit his friends to take care of his needs.

24Several days later Felix came with his wife Drusilla, who was a Jewess. He sent for Paul and listened to him as he spoke about faith in Christ Jesus. 25As Paul discoursed on righteousness, self-control and the judgment to come, Felix was afraid and said, "That's enough for now! You may leave. When I find it convenient, I will send for you." 26At the same time he was hoping that Paul would offer him a bribe, so he sent for him frequently and talked with him.

27When two years had passed, Felix was succeeded by Porcius Festus, but because Felix wanted to grant a favor to the Jews, he left Paul in prison.

Chapter 25

The Trial Before Festus

THREE days after arriving in the province, Festus went up from Caesarea to Jerusalem, 2where

²And the chief priests and the leading men of the Jews brought charges against Paul; and they were urging him,

³requesting a concession against Paul, that he might have him brought to Jerusalem (*at the same time,* setting an ambush to kill him on the way).

⁴Festus then answered that Paul was being kept in custody at Caesarea and that he himself was about to leave shortly.

⁵"Therefore," he *said, "let the influential men among you go there with me, and if there is anything wrong about the man, let them prosecute him."

⁶And after he had spent not more than eight or ten days among them, he went down to Caesarea; and on the next day he took his seat on the tribunal and ordered Paul to be brought.

⁷And after he had arrived, the Jews who had come down from Jerusalem stood around him, bringing many and serious charges against him which they could not prove;

⁸while Paul said in his own defense, "I have committed no offense either against the Law of the Jews or against the temple or against Caesar."

⁹But Festus, wishing to do the Jews a favor, answered Paul and said, "Are you willing to go up to Jerusalem and stand trial before me on these *charges?*"

¹⁰But Paul said, "I am standing before Caesar's tribunal, where I ought to be tried. I have done no wrong to *the* Jews, as you also very well know.

¹¹"If then I am a wrongdoer, and have committed anything worthy of death, I do not refuse to die; but if

---

ἐν ὑμῖν, φησίν, δυνατοὶ συγκαταβάντες,
⁴among ⁵you, ⁶he says, ³able men going down with [me],

ἀπὸ Καισαρείας, 2 ἐνεφάνισάν τε αὐτῷ
from Caesarea, and ⁴informed ⁵him

οἱ ἀρχιερεῖς καὶ οἱ πρῶτοι τῶν Ἰουδαίων
¹the ²chief priests ³and ⁴the ⁵chiefs ⁶of the ⁷Jews

κατὰ τοῦ Παύλου, καὶ παρεκάλουν αὐτὸν
against - Paul, and they besought him

3 αἰτούμενοι χάριν κατ' αὐτοῦ, ὅπως μετα-
asking a favour against him, so as he might

πέμψηται αὐτὸν εἰς Ἰερουσαλήμ, ἐνέδραν
summon him to Jerusalem, a plot

ποιοῦντες ἀνελεῖν αὐτὸν κατὰ τὴν ὁδόν.
making to kill him by the way.

4 ὁ μὲν οὖν Φῆστος ἀπεκρίθη τηρεῖσθαι
- Therefore Festus answered ¹to be kept

τὸν Παῦλον εἰς Καισάρειαν, ἑαυτὸν δὲ
- ¹Paul in Caesarea, and ²himself

μέλλειν ἐν τάχει ἐκπορεύεσθαι· 5 οἱ οὖν
¹to intend shortly to go forth; ²the ¹therefore

εἴ τί ἐστιν ἐν τῷ ἀνδρὶ ἄτοπον,
if anything there is in the man amiss,

κατηγορείτωσαν αὐτοῦ. 6 Διατρίψας δὲ ἐν
let them accuse him. And having stayed among

αὐτοῖς ἡμέρας οὐ πλείους ὀκτὼ ἢ δέκα,
them days not more [than] eight or ten,

καταβὰς εἰς Καισάρειαν, τῇ ἐπαύριον
going down to Caesarea, on the morrow

καθίσας ἐπὶ τοῦ βήματος ἐκέλευσεν τὸν
sitting on the tribunal he commanded -

Παῦλον ἀχθῆναι. 7 παραγενομένου δὲ
Paul to be brought. And arriving
= when he arrived

αὐτοῦ περιέστησαν αὐτὸν οἱ ἀπὸ Ἰεροσο-
him⁶ ⁵stood round ⁷him the ⁴from ⁵Jeru-

λύμων καταβεβηκότες Ἰουδαῖοι, πολλὰ καὶ
salem ⁶having come down ²Jews, many and

βαρέα αἰτιώματα καταφέροντες, ἃ οὐκ
heavy charges bringing against [him], which not

ἴσχυον ἀποδεῖξαι, 8 τοῦ Παύλου ἀπολογου-
they were able to prove, - Paul defending him-

μένου ὅτι οὔτε εἰς τὸν νόμον τῶν
self[,]ᵃ - Neither against the law of the
= while Paul defended himself,

Ἰουδαίων οὔτε εἰς τὸ ἱερὸν οὔτε εἰς
Jews nor against the temple nor against

Καίσαρά τι ἥμαρτον. 9 ὁ Φῆστος δὲ,
Caesar anything I sinned. - But Festus,

θέλων τοῖς Ἰουδαίοις χάριν καταθέσθαι,
wishing the Jews a favour to show,

ἀποκριθεὶς τῷ Παύλῳ εἶπεν· θέλεις εἰς
answering - Paul said: Dost thou wish ²to

Ἰεροσόλυμα ἀναβὰς ἐκεῖ περὶ τούτων
³Jerusalem ¹going up ⁴there ⁵concerning ⁶these things

κριθῆναι ἐπ' ἐμοῦ; 10 εἶπεν δὲ ὁ Παῦλος·
¹to be judged ⁶before ⁷me? And said - Paul:

ἑστὼς ἐπὶ τοῦ βήματος Καίσαρός εἰμι,
Standing before the tribunal of Caesar I am,

οὗ με δεῖ κρίνεσθαι. Ἰουδαίους οὐδὲν
where me it behoves to be judged. Jews nothing

ἠδίκηκα, ὡς καὶ σὺ κάλλιον ἐπιγινώσκεις.
I have wronged, as indeed thou very well knowest.

11 εἰ μὲν οὖν ἀδικῶ καὶ ἄξιον θανάτου
If - therefore I do wrong and worthy of death

πέπραχά τι, οὐ παραιτοῦμαι τὸ ἀποθανεῖν·
I have done anything, I do not refuse *the* to die;

---

the chief priests and Jewish leaders appeared before him and presented the charges against Paul. ³They urgently requested Festus, as a favor to them, to have Paul transferred to Jerusalem, for they were preparing an ambush to kill him along the way. ⁴Festus answered, "Paul is being held at Caesarea, and I myself am going there soon. ⁵Let some of your leaders come with me and press charges against the man there, if he has done anything wrong."

⁶After spending eight or ten days with them, he went down to Caesarea, and the next day he convened the court and ordered that Paul be brought before him. ⁷When Paul appeared, the Jews who had come down from Jerusalem stood around him, bringing many serious charges against him, which they could not prove.

⁸Then Paul made his defense: "I have done nothing wrong against the law of the Jews or against the temple or against Caesar."

⁹Festus, wishing to do the Jews a favor, said to Paul, "Are you willing to go up to Jerusalem and stand trial before me there on these charges?"

¹⁰Paul answered: "I am now standing before Caesar's court, where I ought to be tried. I have not done any wrong to the Jews, as you yourself know very well. ¹¹If, however, I am guilty of doing anything deserving death, I do not refuse to die. But if the

none of those things is *true* of which these men accuse me, no one can hand me over to them. I appeal to Caesar."

12Then when Festus had conferred with his council, he answered, "You have appealed to Caesar, to Caesar you shall go."

13Now when several days had elapsed, King Agrippa and Bernice arrived at Caesarea, and paid their respects to Festus.

14And while they were spending many days there, Festus laid Paul's case before the king, saying, "There is a certain man left a prisoner by Felix;

15and when I was at Jerusalem, the chief priests and the elders of the Jews brought charges against him, asking for a sentence of condemnation upon him.

16"And I answered them that it is not the custom of the Romans to hand over any man before the accused meets his accusers face to face, and has an opportunity to make his defense against the charges.

17"And so after they had assembled here, I made no delay, but on the next day took my seat on the tribunal, and ordered the man to be brought.

18"And when the accusers stood up, they *began* bringing charges against him not of such crimes as I was expecting;

19but they *simply* had some points of disagreement with him about their own religion and about a certain dead man, Jesus, whom Paul asserted to be alive.

20"And being at a loss how to investigate such matters, I asked whether he was willing to go to

---

εἰ   δὲ   οὐδέν   ἐστιν   ὧν   οὗτοι   κατηγοροῦσίν
but if   not one   there is   of [the   these   accuse
                              things] which

μου,   οὐδείς   με   δύναται   αὐτοῖς   χαρίσασθαι·
me,   no one   ¹me   ²can   ⁴to them   ³to grant;

Καίσαρα   ἐπικαλοῦμαι.   12 τότε   ὁ   Φῆστος
²Cæsar   ¹I appeal to.   Then   -   Festus

συλλαλήσας   μετὰ   τοῦ   συμβουλίου   ἀπεκρίθη·
having talked *with* with   the   council   answered:

Καίσαρα   ἐπικέκλησαι,   ἐπὶ   Καίσαρα   πορεύσῃ.
²Cæsar   ¹thou hast appealed to,   before   Cæsar   thou shalt go.

13 Ἡμερῶν   δὲ   διαγενομένων   τινῶν
And days   passing   someª
= when some days had passed

Ἀγρίππας   ὁ   βασιλεὺς   καὶ   Βερνίκη
Agrippa   the   king   and   Bernice

κατήντησαν   εἰς   Καισάρειαν   ἀσπασάμενοι
arrived   at   Cæsarea   greeting

τὸν   Φῆστον.   14 ὡς   δὲ   πλείους   ἡμέρας
-   Festus.   And as   more   days

διέτριβον   ἐκεῖ,   ὁ   Φῆστος   τῷ   βασιλεῖ
they stayed   there,   -   Festus   ²to the   ³king

ἀνέθετο   τὰ   κατὰ   τὸν   Παῦλον   λέγων·
¹set forth the matters regarding   -   Paul   saying:

ἀνήρ   τίς   ἐστιν   καταλελειμμένος   ὑπὸ
A certain man   there is   having been left behind   by

Φήλικος   δέσμιος,   15 περὶ   οὗ   γενομένου
Felix   prisoner,   about whom   being
= when I was

μου   εἰς   Ἱεροσόλυμα   ἐνεφάνισαν   οἱ   ἀρχιερεῖς
meª   in   Jerusalem   ³informed   ¹the   ²chief priests

καὶ   οἱ   πρεσβύτεροι   τῶν   Ἰουδαίων,
²and   ⁴the   ⁵elders   ⁶of the   ⁷Jews,

αἰτούμενοι   κατ᾽   αὐτοῦ   καταδίκην·   16 πρὸς
asking   against   him   sentence;   to

οὓς   ἀπεκρίθην   ὅτι   οὐκ   ἔστιν   ἔθος   Ῥωμαίοις
whom   I answered   that   it is not   a custom with Romans

χαρίζεσθαί   τινα   ἄνθρωπον   πρὶν   ἢ   ὁ
to grant   any   man   before   the

κατηγορούμενος   κατὰ   πρόσωπον   ἔχοι   τοὺς
[one] being accused   face to face†   should have the

κατηγόρους   τόπον   τε   ἀπολογίας   λάβοι
accusers   ³place*   ¹and   ⁴of defence   ²receive

περὶ   τοῦ   ἐγκλήματος.   17 συνελθόντων
concerning the   charge.   Coming togetherª

οὖν   ἐνθάδε   ἀναβολὴν   μηδεμίαν   ποιησάμενος
therefore thither   ³delay   ²no   ¹making

τῇ   ἑξῆς   καθίσας   ἐπὶ   τοῦ   βήματος   ἐκέλευσα
on the next [day] sitting   on   the   tribunal   I commanded

ἀχθῆναι   τὸν   ἄνδρα·   18 περὶ   οὗ   σταθέντες
to be brought the   man;   concerning whom   standing

οἱ   κατήγοροι   οὐδεμίαν   αἰτίαν   ἔφερον   ὧν
the   accusers   ²no   ³charge   ¹brought   ⁴of   ⁵things
                                                   ⁷which

ἐγὼ   ὑπενόουν   πονηρῶν,   19 ζητήματα   δέ
⁶I   ⁸suspected   ⁵evil,   but   ²questions

τινα   περὶ   τῆς   ἰδίας   δεισιδαιμονίας   εἶχον
³certain   ⁴about   ⁵the(ir)   own   ⁶religion   ¹they had

πρὸς   αὐτὸν   καὶ   περὶ   τινος   Ἰησοῦ
with   him   and   about   one   Jesus

τεθνηκότος,   ὃν   ἔφασκεν   ὁ   Παῦλος   ζῆν.
having died,   whom   ²asserted   -   ¹Paul   to live.

20 ἀπορούμενος   δὲ   ἐγὼ   τὴν   περὶ   τούτων
And ⁵being perplexed at   ¹I   ²the   ³about   ⁴these things

ζήτησιν   ἔλεγον   εἰ   βούλοιτο   πορεύεσθαι   εἰς
⁶debate   said   if   he wished   to go   to

---

charges brought against me by these Jews are not true, no one has the right to hand me over to them. I appeal to Caesar!"

12After Festus had conferred with his council, he declared: "You have appealed to Caesar. To Caesar you will go!"

Festus Consults King Agrippa

13A few days later King Agrippa and Bernice arrived at Caesarea to pay their respects to Festus. 14Since they were spending many days there, Festus discussed Paul's case with the king. He said: "There is a man here whom Felix left as a prisoner. 15When I went to Jerusalem, the chief priests and elders of the Jews brought charges against him and asked that he be condemned.

16"I told them that it is not the Roman custom to hand over any man before he has faced his accusers and has had an opportunity to defend himself against their charges. 17When they came here with me, I did not delay the case, but convened the court the next day and ordered the man to be brought in. 18When his accusers got up to speak, they did not charge him with any of the crimes I had expected. 19Instead, they had some points of dispute with him about their own religion and about a dead man named Jesus who Paul claimed was alive. 20I was at a loss how to investigate such matters; so I asked if he would be willing to go to

---

* That is, opportunity.

Jerusalem and there stand trial on these matters.
21"But when Paul appealed to be held in custody for 'the Emperor's decision, I ordered him to be kept in custody until I send him to Caesar."
22And Agrippa *said* to Festus, "I also would like to hear the man myself." "Tomorrow," he *said, "you shall hear him."

Paul before Agrippa
23And so, on the next day when Agrippa had come together with Bernice, amid great pomp, and had entered the auditorium *s* accompanied by the commanders and the prominent men of the city, at the command of Festus, Paul was brought in.
24And Festus *said, "King Agrippa, and all you gentlemen here present with us, you behold this man about whom all the people of the Jews appealed to me, both at Jerusalem and here, loudly declaring that he ought not to live any longer.
25"But I found that he had committed nothing worthy of death; and since he himself appealed to the Emperor, I decided to send him.
26"Yet I have nothing definite about him to write to my lord. Therefore I have brought him before you *all* and especially before you, King Agrippa, so that after the investigation has taken place, I may have something to write.
27"For it seems absurd to me in sending a prisoner, not to indicate also the charges against him."

Chapter 26

Paul's Defense before Agrippa

AND Agrippa said to Paul, "You are permitted to speak for your-

r Lit., *the Augustus'* (in this case Nero)
s Lit., *and with*

Ἰεροσόλυμα κἀκεῖ κρίνεσθαι περὶ τούτων.
Jerusalem   and there   to be judged   about   these things.

21 τοῦ δὲ Παύλου ἐπικαλεσαμένου τηρηθῆναι
   – But   Paul   having appealed*   to be kept
            =when Paul appealed

αὐτὸν εἰς τὴν τοῦ Σεβαστοῦ διάγνωσιν,
him   to   the   –   *of Augustus   ¹decision,

ἐκέλευσα τηρεῖσθαι αὐτὸν ἕως οὗ ἀναπέμψω
I commanded   to be kept   him   until   I may send up

αὐτὸν πρὸς Καίσαρα. 22 Ἀγρίππας δὲ
him   to   Cæsar.   And Agrippa

πρὸς τὸν Φῆστον· ἐβουλόμην καὶ αὐτὸς
[said] to – Festus· I was minded   also   [my]self

τοῦ ἀνθρώπου ἀκοῦσαι. αὔριον, φησίν,
the   man   to hear.   Tomorrow,   he says,

ἀκούσῃ αὐτοῦ. 23 Τῇ οὖν ἐπαύριον
thou shalt hear   him.   *On the   ¹therefore   *morrow

ἐλθόντος τοῦ Ἀγρίππα καὶ τῆς Βερνίκης
coming   –   Agrippa   and   –   Bernice*
          =when Agrippa and Bernice came

μετὰ πολλῆς φαντασίας καὶ εἰσελθόντων
with   much   display   and   entering*

εἰς τὸ ἀκροατήριον σύν τε χιλιάρχοις
into   the   place of audience   with   both   chiliarchs

καὶ ἀνδράσιν τοῖς κατ᾽ ἐξοχὴν τῆς πόλεως,
and   *men   ¹the   *chief †   of   the   city,

καὶ κελεύσαντος τοῦ Φῆστου ἤχθη ὁ
and   having commanded   –   Festus*   *was brought –
      =when Festus commanded

Παῦλος. 24 καὶ φησὶν ὁ Φῆστος· Ἀγρίππα
¹Paul.   And   says   –   Festus: Agrippa

βασιλεῦ καὶ πάντες οἱ συμπαρόντες ἡμῖν
king   and   all   the   *present together with   *us

ἄνδρες, θεωρεῖτε τοῦτον περὶ οὗ ἅπαν
¹men,   ye behold   this man   about whom   all   the

πλῆθος τῶν Ἰουδαίων ἐνέτυχόν μοι ἔν τε
multitude   of the   Jews   petitioned   me   *in ¹both

Ἰεροσολύμοις καὶ ἐνθάδε, βοῶντες μὴ
Jerusalem   and   here,   crying   not

δεῖν αὐτὸν ζῆν μηκέτι. 25 ἐγὼ δὲ κατε-
ought   him   to live   *no* longer.   But I   dis-
=that he ought not to live any longer.

λαβόμην μηδὲν ἄξιον αὐτὸν θανάτου
covered   *nothing   *worthy   ¹him   *of death

πεπραχέναι, αὐτοῦ δὲ τούτου ἐπικαλεσαμένου
to have done,   but [him]self   this man   appealing to
                 =when he himself appealed to

τὸν Σεβαστὸν ἔκρινα πέμπειν. 26 περὶ
 –   Augustus   I decided   to send.   Concerning

οὗ ἀσφαλές τι γράψαι τῷ κυρίῳ οὐκ
whom   *certain   *anything   *to write   *to the   *lord   *not

ἔχω· διὸ προήγαγον αὐτὸν ἐφ᾽ ὑμῶν καὶ
¹I have; where-   I brought   him   before   you   and
fore   forth

μάλιστα ἐπὶ σοῦ, βασιλεῦ Ἀγρίππα, ὅπως
most of all   before thee,   king   Agrippa,   so as
                                                = when

τῆς ἀνακρίσεως γενομένης σχῶ τί γράψω·
the   examination   being*   I may have what   I may
there has been an examination   have   write;

27 ἄλογον γάρ μοι δοκεῖ πέμποντα δέσμιον
for *unreasonable   *to me   ¹it seems   sending   a prisoner

μὴ καὶ τας κατ᾽ αὐτοῦ αἰτίας σημᾶναι.
not   also   *the   *against   *him   *charges   ¹to signify.

26 Ἀγρίππας δὲ πρὸς τὸν Παῦλον ἔφη·
   And Agrippa   to   –   Paul   said:

ἐπιτρέπεταί σοι ὑπὲρ σεαυτοῦ λέγειν.
It is permitted   to thee   on behalf of   thyself   to speak.

Jerusalem and stand trial there on these charges.
21When Paul made his appeal to be held over for the Emperor's decision, I ordered him held until I could send him to Caesar."
22Then Agrippa said to Festus, "I would like to hear this man myself."
He replied, "Tomorrow you will hear him."

Paul Before Agrippa
23The next day Agrippa and Bernice came with great pomp and entered the audience room with the high ranking officers and the leading men of the city. At the command of Festus, Paul was brought in. 24Festus said: "King Agrippa, and all who are present with us, you see this man! The whole Jewish community has petitioned me about him in Jerusalem and here in Caesarea, shouting that he ought not to live any longer. 25I found he had done nothing deserving of death, but because he made his appeal to the Emperor I decided to send him to Rome. 26But I have nothing definite to write to His Majesty about him. Therefore I have brought him before all of you, and especially before you, King Agrippa, so that as a result of this investigation I may have something to write. 27For I think it is unreasonable to send on a prisoner without specifying the charges against him."

Chapter 26

THEN Agrippa said to Paul, "You have permission to speak for yourself."

self." Then Paul stretched out his hand and *proceeded* to make his defense:

2"In regard to all the things of which I am accused by the Jews, I consider myself fortunate, King Agrippa, that I am about to make my defense before you today;

3especially because you are an expert in all customs and questions among *the* Jews; therefore I beg you to listen to me patiently.

4"So then, all Jews know my manner of life from my youth up, which from the beginning was spent among my *own* nation and at Jerusalem;

5since they have known about me for a long time previously, if they are willing to testify, that I lived *as* a Pharisee according to the strictest sect of our religion.

6"And now I am standing trial for the hope of the promise made by God to our fathers;

7*the promise* to which our twelve tribes hope to attain, as they earnestly serve *God* night and day. And for this hope, O King, I am being accused by Jews.

8"Why is it considered incredible among you *people* if God does raise the dead?

9"So then, I thought to myself that I had to do many things hostile to the name of Jesus of Nazareth.

10"And this is just what I did in Jerusalem; not only did I lock up many of the saints in prisons, having received authority from the chief priests, but also when they were being put to death I cast my vote against them.

11"And as I punished them often in all the synagogues, I tried to force them to blaspheme; and being furiously enraged at them, I kept pursuing them

---

τότε   ὁ   Παῦλος   ἐκτείνας   τὴν   χεῖρα
Then   -   Paul   stretching out   the(his)   hand

ἀπελογεῖτο·   2 Περὶ   πάντων   ὧν   ἐγκαλοῦμαι
defended himself: Concerning   all things   of which   I am being accused

ὑπὸ   'Ιουδαίων,   βασιλεῦ   'Αγρίππα,   ἥγημαι
by   Jews,   king   Agrippa,   I consider

ἐμαυτὸν   μακάριον   ἐπὶ   σοῦ   μέλλων   σήμερον
myself   happy   ²before   ³thee   ¹being about   ⁴to-day

ἀπολογεῖσθαι,   3 μάλιστα   γνώστην   ὄντα   σε
¹to defend myself,   most of all   ¹an expert   ²being   ³thee

πάντων   τῶν   κατὰ   'Ιουδαίους   ἐθῶν   τε
⁶of all   ⁴the   ⁵among   ⁵Jews   ⁷customs   ⁸both

καὶ   ζητημάτων·   διὸ   δέομαι   μακροθύμως
¹⁰and   ¹¹questions;   wherefore   I beg   patiently

ἀκοῦσαί   μου.   4 Τὴν   μὲν   οὖν   βίωσίν
to hear   me.   ²the   ¹So   ³then   ⁴manner of life

μου   ἐκ   νεότητος   τὴν   ἀπ'   ἀρχῆς   γενομένην
of me   from   youth   -   ²from   ⁴beginning   ¹having been
³[the]

ἐν   τῷ   ἔθνει   μου   ἔν   τε   'Ιεροσολύμοις
in   the   nation   of me   ²in   ¹and   Jerusalem

ἴσασι   πάντες   'Ιουδαῖοι,   5 προγινώσκοντές
know   all   Jews,   previously knowing

με   ἄνωθεν,   ἐὰν   θέλωσι   μαρτυρεῖν,   ὅτι
me   from the first,   if   they are willing   to testify,   that

κατὰ   τὴν   ἀκριβεστάτην   αἵρεσιν   τῆς
according to the   most exact   sect   -

ἡμετέρας   θρησκείας   ἔζησα   Φαρισαῖος.   6 καὶ
of our   religion   I lived   a Pharisee.   And

νῦν   ἐπ'   ἐλπίδι   τῆς   εἰς   τοὺς   πατέρας
now   on(in)   hope   of the   ⁵to   ⁶the   ⁷fathers

ἡμῶν   ἐπαγγελίας   γενομένης   ὑπὸ   τοῦ   θεοῦ
⁸of us   ¹promise   ²having been [made]   ³by   -   ⁴God

ἔστηκα   κρινόμενος,   7 εἰς   ἣν   τὸ   δωδεκά-
I stand   being judged,   to   which   the   twelve

φυλον   ἡμῶν   ἐν   ἐκτενείᾳ   νύκτα   καὶ
tribes   of us   with   earnestness   night   and

ἡμέραν   λατρεῦον   ἐλπίζει   καταντῆσαι·   περὶ
day   worshipping   hopes   to arrive;   concerning

ἧς   ἐλπίδος   ἐγκαλοῦμαι   ὑπὸ   'Ιουδαίων,
which   hope   I am accused   by   Jews,

βασιλεῦ.   8 τί   ἄπιστον   κρίνεται   παρ'
[O] king.   Why   incredible   is it judged   by

ὑμῖν   εἰ   ὁ   θεὸς   νεκροὺς   ἐγείρει;   9 ἐγὼ
you   if   -   God   ²dead persons   ¹raises?   ³I

μὲν   οὖν   ἔδοξα   ἐμαυτῷ   πρὸς   τὸ   ὄνομα
¹indeed   ²then   ⁴thought   ⁵to myself   ¹⁰to   ¹¹the   ¹²name

'Ιησοῦ   τοῦ   Ναζωραίου   δεῖν   πολλὰ   ἐναντία
¹³of Jesus   ¹⁴the   ¹⁵Nazarene   ⁶ought   ⁸many   ⁹contrary
things

πρᾶξαι·   10 ὃ   καὶ   ἐποίησα   ἐν   'Ιεροσολύμοις,
⁷to do;   which indeed   I did   in   Jerusalem,

καὶ   πολλούς   τε   τῶν   ἁγίων   ἐγὼ   ἐν
and   many   -   of the   saints   ¹I   ³in

φυλακαῖς   κατέκλεισα   τὴν   παρὰ   τῶν
⁴prisons   ²shut up   ⁶the   ⁸from   ⁹the

ἀρχιερέων   ἐξουσίαν   λαβών,   ἀναιρουμένων   τε
¹⁰chief priests   ⁷authority   ⁵having received,   being killed   and
= and when they were killed

αὐτῶν   κατήνεγκα   ψῆφον,   11 καὶ   κατὰ
them   I cast   a vote,   and throughout

πάσας   τὰς   συναγωγὰς   πολλάκις   τιμωρῶν
all   the   synagogues   often   punishing

αὐτοὺς   ἠνάγκαζον   βλασφημεῖν,   περισσῶς   τε
them   I compelled [them]   to blaspheme,   and excessively

ἐμμαινόμενος   αὐτοῖς   ἐδίωκον   ἕως   καὶ   εἰς
raging against   them   I persecuted   as far as   even   to

So Paul motioned with his hand and began his defense: 2"King Agrippa, I consider myself fortunate to stand before you today as I make my defense against all the accusations of the Jews, 3and especially so because you are well acquainted with all the Jewish customs and controversies. Therefore, I beg you to listen to me patiently.

4"The Jews all know the way I have lived ever since I was a child, from the beginning of my life in my own country, and also in Jerusalem. 5They have known me for a long time and can testify, if they are willing, that according to the strictest sect of our religion, I lived as a Pharisee. 6And now it is because of my hope in what God has promised our fathers that I am on trial today. 7This is the promise our twelve tribes are hoping to see fulfilled as they earnestly serve God day and night. O king, it is because of this hope that the Jews are accusing me. 8Why should any of you consider it incredible that God raises the dead?

9"I too was convinced that I ought to do all that was possible to oppose the name of Jesus of Nazareth. 10And that is just what I did in Jerusalem. On the authority of the chief priests I put many of the saints in prison, and when they were put to death, I cast my vote against them. 11Many a time I went from one synagogue to another to have them punished, and I tried to force them to blaspheme. In my obsession against them, I even went

even to foreign cities.
12"While thus engaged as I was journeying to Damascus with the authority and commission of the chief priests,
13at midday, O King, I saw on the way a light from heaven, brighter than the sun, shining all around me and those who were journeying with me.
14"And when we had all fallen to the ground, I heard a voice saying to me in the Hebrew dialect, 'Saul, Saul, why are you persecuting Me? It is hard for you to kick against the goads.'
15"And I said, 'Who art Thou, Lord?' And the Lord said, 'I am Jesus whom you are persecuting.
16'But arise, and stand on your feet; for this purpose I have appeared to you, to appoint you a minister and a witness not only to the things which you have seen, but also to the things in which I will appear to you;
17delivering you from the *Jewish* people and from the Gentiles, to whom I am sending you,
18to open their eyes so that they may turn from darkness to light and from the dominion of Satan to God, in order that they may receive forgiveness of sins and an inheritance among those who have been sanctified by faith in Me.'
19"Consequently, King Agrippa, I did not prove disobedient to the heavenly vision,
20but *kept* declaring both to those of Damascus first, and *also* at Jerusalem and *then* throughout all the region of Judea, and *even* to the Gentiles, that they should repent and turn to God, performing deeds appropriate to repentance.
21"For this reason *some* Jews seized me in the tem-

τὰς ἔξω πόλεις. 12 Ἐν οἷς πορευόμενος
the outside cities. In which journeying
εἰς τὴν Δαμασκὸν μετ' ἐξουσίας καὶ
to - Damascus with authority and
ἐπιτροπῆς τῆς τῶν ἀρχιερέων, 13 ἡμέρας
power to decide - of the chief priests, at ⁴day
μέσης κατὰ τὴν ὁδὸν εἶδον, βασιλεῦ,
¹mid along the way I saw, [O] king,
οὐρανόθεν ὑπὲρ τὴν λαμπρότητα τοῦ ἡλίου
⁷from heaven ³above ⁴the ⁵brightness ⁶of the ⁷sun
περιλάμψαν με φῶς καὶ τοὺς σὺν ἐμοὶ
⁸shining round ⁹me ¹a light ¹⁰and ¹¹the [ones] ¹²with ¹³me
πορευομένους· 14 πάντων τε καταπεσόντων
¹³journeying; and all having fallen down
= when we had all fallen
ἡμῶν εἰς τὴν γῆν ἤκουσα φωνὴν λέγουσαν
us² to the earth I heard a voice saying
πρός με τῇ Ἑβραΐδι διαλέκτῳ· Σαοὺλ
to me in the Hebrew language: Saul[,]
Σαούλ, τί με διώκεις; σκληρόν σοι
Saul, why me persecutest thou? hard for thee
πρὸς κέντρα λακτίζειν. 15 ἐγὼ δὲ εἶπα·
against goads to kick. And I said:
τίς εἶ, κύριε; ὁ δὲ κύριος εἶπεν· ἐγώ
Who art thou, Lord? And the Lord said: I
εἰμι Ἰησοῦς ὃν σὺ διώκεις. 16 ἀλλὰ
am Jesus whom thou persecutest. But
ἀνάστηθι καὶ στῆθι ἐπὶ τοὺς πόδας σου·
rise thou up and stand on the feet of thee;
εἰς τοῦτο γὰρ ὤφθην σοι, προχειρίσασθαί
²for ³this [purpose] ¹for I appeared to thee, to appoint
σε ὑπηρέτην καὶ μάρτυρα ὧν τε
thee an attendant and a witness ²of the things ³both
which
εἶδές με ὧν τε ὀφθήσομαί σοι,
³thou sawest ⁴me ⁶of the things ⁵and I will appear to thee,
which
17 ἐξαιρούμενός σε ἐκ τοῦ λαοῦ καὶ ἐκ
delivering thee from the people and from
τῶν ἐθνῶν, εἰς οὓς ἐγὼ ἀποστέλλω σε,
the nations, to whom I send thee,
18 ἀνοῖξαι ὀφθαλμοὺς αὐτῶν, τοῦ ἐπιστρέψαι
to open eyes of them, - to turnᵇ
ἀπὸ σκότους εἰς φῶς καὶ τῆς ἐξουσίας
from darkness to light and [from] the authority
τοῦ σατανᾶ ἐπὶ τὸν θεόν, τοῦ λαβεῖν
- of Satan to - God, - to receive
= that they may receive
αὐτοὺς ἄφεσιν ἁμαρτιῶν καὶ κλῆρον ἐν
themᵇᵈ forgiveness of sins and a lot among
τοῖς ἡγιασμένοις πίστει τῇ εἰς ἐμέ.
the [ones] having been sanctified by faith - in me.
19 Ὅθεν, βασιλεῦ Ἀγρίππα, οὐκ ἐγενόμην
Whence, king Agrippa, I was not
ἀπειθὴς τῇ οὐρανίῳ ὀπτασίᾳ, 20 ἀλλὰ
disobedient to the heavenly vision, but
τοῖς ἐν Δαμασκῷ πρῶτόν τε καὶ
to the [ones] in Damascus firstly and also
Ἱεροσολύμοις, πᾶσάν τε τὴν χώραν τῆς
[in] Jerusalem, and all the country -
Ἰουδαίας καὶ τοῖς ἔθνεσιν ἀπήγγελλον
of Judæa and to the nations I announced
μετανοεῖν καὶ ἐπιστρέφειν ἐπὶ τὸν θεόν,
to repent and to turn to - God,
ἄξια τῆς μετανοίας ἔργα πράσσοντας.
³worthy ⁴of the ⁵repentance ²works ¹doing.
21 ἕνεκα τούτων με Ἰουδαῖοι συλλαβόμενοι
On these things ²me ¹Jews ³having seized
account of

to foreign cities to persecute them.
12"On one of these journeys I was going to Damascus with the authority and commission of the chief priests. 13About noon, O king, as I was on the road, I saw a light from heaven, brighter than the sun, blazing around me and my companions. 14We all fell to the ground, and I heard a voice saying to me in Aramaic, ʷ 'Saul, Saul, why do you persecute me? It is hard for you to kick against the goads.'
15"Then I asked, 'Who are you, Lord?'
" 'I am Jesus, whom you are persecuting,' the Lord replied. 16'Now get up and stand on your feet. I have appeared to you to appoint you as a servant and as a witness of what you have seen of me and what I will show you. 17I will rescue you from your own people and from the Gentiles. I am sending you to them 18to open their eyes and turn them from darkness to light, and from the power of Satan to God, so that they may receive forgiveness of sins and a place among those who are sanctified by faith in me.'
19"So then, King Agrippa, I was not disobedient to the vision from heaven. 20First to those in Damascus, then to those in Jerusalem and in all Judea, and to the Gentiles also, I preached that they should repent and turn to God and prove their repentance by their deeds. 21That is why the Jews seized me in the

ple and tried to put me to death.

22"And so, having obtained help from God, I stand to this day testifying both to small and great, stating nothing but what the Prophets and Moses said was going to take place;

23that the Christ was to suffer, and that by reason of His resurrection from the dead He should be the first to proclaim light both to the Jewish people and to the Gentiles."

24And while Paul was saying this in his defense, Festus *said in a loud voice, "Paul, you are out of your mind! Your great learning is driving you mad."

25But Paul *said, "I am not out of my mind, most excellent Festus, but I utter words of sober truth.

26"For the king knows about these matters, and I speak to him also with confidence, since I am persuaded that none of these things escape his notice; for this has not been done in a corner.

27"King Agrippa, do you believe the Prophets? I know that you do."

28And Agrippa replied to Paul, "In a short time you will persuade me to become a Christian."

29And Paul said, "I would to God, that whether in a short or long time, not only you, but also all who hear me this day, might become such as I am, except for these chains."

30And the king arose and the governor and Bernice, and those who were sitting with them,

31and when they had drawn aside, they began talking to one another, saying, "This man is not doing

---

ἐν τῷ ἱερῷ ἐπειρῶντο διαχειρίσασθαι.
in the temple tried to kill [me].

22 ἐπικουρίας οὖν τυχὼν τῆς ἀπὸ τοῦ
Succour therefore having obtained - from -

θεοῦ ἄχρι τῆς ἡμέρας ταύτης ἕστηκα
God until this day I stand

μαρτυρόμενος μικρῷ τε καὶ μεγάλῳ, οὐδὲν
witnessing to small both and to great, nothing

ἐκτὸς λέγων ὧν τε οἱ προφῆται
apart from saying the things which both the prophets

ἐλάλησαν μελλόντων γίνεσθαι καὶ Μωϋσῆς,
said being about to happen and Moses,

23 εἰ παθητὸς ὁ χριστός, εἰ πρῶτος
if subject to suffering the Christ, if first

ἐξ ἀναστάσεως νεκρῶν φῶς μέλλει
by a resurrection of dead persons a light he is about

καταγγέλλειν τῷ τε λαῷ καὶ τοῖς ἔθνεσιν.
to announce to the both people and to the nations.

24 Ταῦτα δὲ αὐτοῦ ἀπολογουμένου ὁ Φῆστος
And these things him defending himself - Festus
=as he defended himself with these things

μεγάλῃ τῇ φωνῇ φησιν· μαίνῃ, Παῦλε·
great with the(his) voice says: Thou ravest, Paul:

τὰ πολλά σε γράμματα εἰς μανίαν
the many thee letters to madness

περιτρέπει. 25 ὁ δὲ Παῦλος· οὐ μαίνομαι,
turn[s]. - But Paul: I do not rave,

φησίν, κράτιστε Φῆστε, ἀλλὰ ἀληθείας
he says, most excellent Festus, but of truth

καὶ σωφροσύνης ῥήματα ἀποφθέγγομαι.
and of good sense words I speak forth.

26 ἐπίσταται γὰρ περὶ τούτων ὁ βασιλεύς,
For understands about these things the king,

πρὸς ὃν καὶ παρρησιαζόμενος λαλῶ·
to whom indeed being bold of speech I speak;

λανθάνειν γὰρ αὐτὸν τούτων οὐ πείθομαι
for to be hidden [from] him of these things not I am persuaded

οὐθέν· οὐ γάρ ἐστιν ἐν γωνίᾳ πεπραγμένον
nothing; for not is in a corner having been done

τοῦτο. 27 πιστεύεις, βασιλεῦ Ἀγρίππα,
this. Believest thou, king Agrippa,

τοῖς προφήταις; οἶδα ὅτι πιστεύεις. 28 ὁ
the prophets? I know that thou believest. -

δὲ Ἀγρίππας πρὸς τὸν Παῦλον· ἐν
And Agrippa to - Paul: In

ὀλίγῳ με πείθεις Χριστιανὸν ποιῆσαι.
a little me thou persuadest a Christian to make(act).

29 ὁ δὲ Παῦλος· εὐξαίμην ἂν τῷ θεῷ
- And Paul [said]: I would pray - God

καὶ ἐν ὀλίγῳ καὶ ἐν μεγάλῳ οὐ μόνον
both in a little and in great not only

σὲ ἀλλὰ καὶ πάντας τοὺς ἀκούοντάς
thee but also all the [ones] hearing

μου σήμερον γενέσθαι τοιούτους ὁποῖος
me to-day to become such of what kind

καὶ ἐγώ εἰμι, παρεκτὸς τῶν δεσμῶν
indeed I am, except - bonds

τούτων. 30 Ἀνέστη τε ὁ βασιλεὺς καὶ
these. Rose up both the king and

ὁ ἡγεμὼν ἥ τε Βερνίκη καὶ οἱ συγ-
the governor - and Bernice and the [ones] sit-

καθήμενοι αὐτοῖς, 31 καὶ ἀναχωρήσαντες
ting with them, and having left

ἐλάλουν πρὸς ἀλλήλους λέγοντες ὅτι οὐδὲν
spoke to one another saying [,] - nothing

---

temple courts and tried to kill me. 22But I have had God's help to this very day, and so I stand here and testify to small and great alike. I am saying nothing beyond what the prophets and Moses said would happen— 23that the Christ[x] would suffer and, as the first to rise from the dead, would proclaim light to his own people and to the Gentiles."

24At this point Festus interrupted Paul's defense. "You are out of your mind, Paul!" he shouted. "Your great learning is driving you insane."

25"I am not insane, most excellent Festus," Paul replied. "What I am saying is true and reasonable. 26The king is familiar with these things, and I can speak freely to him. I am convinced that none of this has escaped his notice, because it was not done in a corner. 27King Agrippa, do you believe the prophets? I know you do."

28Then Agrippa said to Paul, "Do you think that in such a short time you can persuade me to be a Christian?"

29Paul replied, "Short time or long—I pray God that not only you but all who are listening to me today may become what I am, except for these chains."

30The king rose, and with him the governor and Bernice and those sitting with them. 31They left the room, and while talking with one another, they said, "This

[x]23 Or Messiah

anything worthy of death or imprisonment."

32And Agrippa said to Festus, "This man might have been set free if he had not appealed to Caesar."

Chapter 27

Paul Is Sent to Rome

AND when it was decided that we should sail for Italy, they proceeded to deliver Paul and some other prisoners to a centurion of the Augustan ¹ cohort named Julius.

2And embarking in an Adramyttian ship, which was about to sail to the regions along the coast of Asia, we put out to sea, accompanied by Aristarchus, a Macedonian of Thessalonica.

3And the next day we put in at Sidon; and Julius treated Paul with consideration and allowed him to go to his friends and receive care.

4And from there we put out to sea and sailed under the shelter of Cyprus because the winds were contrary.

5And when we had sailed through the sea along the coast of Cilicia and Pamphylia, we landed at Myra in Lycia.

6And there the centurion found an Alexandrian ship sailing for Italy, and he put us aboard it.

7And when we had sailed slowly for a good many days, and with difficulty had arrived off Cnidus, since the wind did not permit us *to go* farther, we sailed under the shelter of Crete, off Salmone;

8and with difficulty sailing past it we came to a certain place called Fair Havens, near which was the city of Lasea.

9And when considerable

θανάτου ἢ δεσμῶν ἄξιον πράσσει ὁ
⁶of death ⁷or ⁵of bonds ⁴worthy ³does -

ἄνθρωπος οὗτος. 32 Ἀγρίππας δὲ τῷ
¹man ¹This.   32 And Agrippa -

Φήστῳ ἔφη· ἀπολελύσθαι ἐδύνατο
to Festus said: ³to have been released ¹was able(could)

ὁ ἄνθρωπος οὗτος εἰ μὴ ἐπεκέκλητο Καίσαρα.
¹This man if he had not appealed to Cæsar.

27 Ὡς δὲ ἐκρίθη τοῦ ἀποπλεῖν ἡμᾶς
And when it was decided - to sail -
                         =that we should sail

εἰς τὴν Ἰταλίαν, παρεδίδουν τόν τε
to - Italy, they delivered - both

Παῦλον καί τινας ἑτέρους δεσμώτας
Paul and some other prisoners

ἑκατοντάρχῃ ὀνόματι Ἰουλίῳ σπείρης
to a centurion by name Julius of a cohort

Σεβαστῆς. 2 ἐπιβάντες δὲ πλοίῳ Ἀδρα-
Augustan.   And embarking in a ship belonging to

μυττηνῷ μέλλοντι πλεῖν εἰς τοὺς κατὰ
Adramyttium being about to sail ¹for ³the ⁴along [the coast of]

τὴν Ἀσίαν τόπους ἀνήχθημεν, ὄντος σὺν
- ⁵Asia ³places we set sail, being with

ἡμῖν Ἀριστάρχου Μακεδόνος Θεσσαλονικέως·
us Aristarchus a Macedonianᵃ of Thessalonica;

3 τῇ τε ἑτέρᾳ κατήχθημεν εἰς Σιδῶνα,
and on the next [day] we were brought at Sidon,
                      to land

φιλανθρώπως τε ὁ Ἰούλιος τῷ Παύλῳ
²and ³kindly - ¹Julius ⁴the ⁵Paul

χρησάμενος ἐπέτρεψεν πρὸς τοὺς φίλους
²treating [him] ⁴allowed ⁷to ⁸the ⁹friends

πορευθέντι ἐπιμελείας τυχεῖν. 4 κἀκεῖθεν
⁶going ¹¹attention ¹⁰to obtain.   And thence

ἀναχθέντες ὑπεπλεύσαμεν τὴν Κύπρον διὰ
putting to sea we sailed close to - Cyprus because of

τὸ τοὺς ἀνέμους εἶναι ἐναντίους, 5 τό τε
- the winds to be(being) contrary,   and ²the

πέλαγος τὸ κατὰ τὴν Κιλικίαν καὶ
³sea - ⁴against - ⁵Cilicia ⁶and

Παμφυλίαν διαπλεύσαντες κατήλθαμεν εἰς
⁷Pamphylia ¹sailing over we came down to

Μύρα τῆς Λυκίας. 6 Κἀκεῖ εὑρὼν ὁ
Myra of Lycia.   And there ²having found ¹the

ἑκατοντάρχης πλοῖον Ἀλεξανδρῖνον πλέον
²centurion ship an Alexandrian sailing

εἰς τὴν Ἰταλίαν ἐνεβίβασεν ἡμᾶς εἰς
to - Italy he embarked us in

αὐτό. 7 ἐν ἱκαναῖς δὲ ἡμέραις βραδυπλο-
it.   And in a number of days sailing

οῦντες καὶ μόλις γενόμενοι κατὰ τὴν
slowly and hardly coming against -

Κνίδον, μὴ προσεῶντος ἡμᾶς τοῦ ἀνέμου,ᵃ
Cnidus, not allowing us the wind,
            =as the wind did not allow us,

ὑπεπλεύσαμεν τὴν Κρήτην κατὰ Σαλμώνην,
we sailed close to - Crete against Salmone,

8 μόλις τε παραλεγόμενοι αὐτὴν ἤλθομεν
and hardly sailing along it we came

εἰς τόπον τινὰ καλούμενον Καλοὺς λιμένας,
to place a certain *being* called Fair Havens,

ᾧ ἐγγὺς ἦν πόλις Λασαία. 9 Ἱκανοῦ δὲ
²to which ¹near was a city Lasæa.   And much
                            =when

¹Or, *battalion*

---

man is not doing anything that deserves death or imprisonment."

32Agrippa said to Festus, "This man could have been set free if he had not appealed to Caesar."

Chapter 27

Paul Sails for Rome

WHEN it was decided that we would sail for Italy, Paul and some other prisoners were handed over to a centurion named Julius, who belonged to the Imperial Regiment. 2We boarded a ship from Adramyttium about to sail for ports along the coast of the province of Asia, and we put out to sea. Aristarchus, a Macedonian from Thessalonica, was with us.

3The next day we landed at Sidon; and Julius, in kindness to Paul, allowed him to go to his friends so they might provide for his needs. 4From there we put out to sea again and passed to the lee of Cyprus because the winds were against us. 5When we had sailed across the open sea off the coast of Cilicia and Pamphylia, we landed at Myra in Lycia. 6There the centurion found an Alexandrian ship sailing for Italy and put us on board. 7We made slow headway for many days and had difficulty arriving off Cnidus. When the wind did not allow us to hold our course, we sailed to the lee of Crete, opposite Salmone. 8We moved along the coast with difficulty and came to a place called Fair Havens, near the town of Lasea.

9Much time had been

time had passed and the voyage was now dangerous, since even the "fast was already over, Paul *began* to admonish them,

10and said to them, "Men, I perceive that the voyage will certainly be *attended* with damage and great loss, not only of the cargo and the ship, but also of our lives."

11Men the centurion was more persuaded by the pilot and the captain of the ship, than by what was being said by Paul.

12And because the harbor was not suitable for wintering, the majority reached a decision to put out to sea from there, if somehow they could reach Phoenix, a harbor of Crete, facing southwest and northwest, and spend the winter *there.*

13And when a moderate south wind came up, supposing that they had gained their purpose, they weighed anchor and *began* sailing along Crete, close *inshore.*

Shipwreck

14But before very long there rushed down from the land a violent wind, called ᵛEuraquilo;

15and when the ship was caught *in it,* and could not face the wind, we gave way *to it,* and let ourselves be driven along.

16And running under the shelter of a small island called Clauda, we were scarcely able to get the *ship's* boat under control.

17And after they had hoisted it up, they used supporting cables in undergirding the ship; and fearing that they might run aground on *the shallows* of Syrtis, they let down the sea anchor, and so let

---

χρόνου διαγενομένου καὶ ὄντος ἤδη
time having passed* and being now
much time had passed = as the voyage

ἐπισφαλοῦς τοῦ πλοὸς διὰ τὸ καὶ τὴν
dangerous the voyage* on account of - also the
was now dangerous = because also the fast had now

νηστείαν ἤδη παρεληλυθέναι, παρήνει ὁ
fast now to have gone by, ²advised -
gone by,

Παῦλος 10 λέγων αὐτοῖς· ἄνδρες, θεωρῶ
¹Paul saying to them: Men, I see

ὅτι μετὰ ὕβρεως καὶ πολλῆς ζημίας οὐ
that with injury and much loss not

μόνον τοῦ φορτίου καὶ τοῦ πλοίου ἀλλὰ
only of the cargo and of the ship but

καὶ τῶν ψυχῶν ἡμῶν μέλλειν ἔσεσθαι
also of the lives of us ³to be about ⁴to be
= will be

τὸν πλοῦν. 11 ὁ δὲ ἑκατοντάρχης τῷ
¹the ²voyage. But the centurion ²the

κυβερνήτῃ καὶ τῷ ναυκλήρῳ μᾶλλον
³steersman ⁴and ⁵the ⁶shipmaster ⁷rather

ἐπείθετο ἢ τοῖς ὑπὸ Παύλου λεγομένοις.
¹was persuaded by ⁸than ⁹the ¹¹by ¹²Paul ¹⁰things said.

12 ἀνευθέτου δὲ τοῦ λιμένος ὑπάρχοντος
But unsuitable the port being*
= as the port was unsuitable

πρὸς παραχειμασίαν οἱ πλείονες ἔθεντο
for wintering the majority placed
= decided

βουλὴν ἀναχθῆναι ἐκεῖθεν, εἴ πως δύναιντο
counsel to set sail thence, if some- they might
how be able

καταντήσαντες εἰς Φοίνικα παραχειμάσαι,
having arrived at Phœnix to pass the winter,

λιμένα τῆς Κρήτης βλέποντα κατὰ λίβα
a port of Crete looking toward southwest

καὶ κατὰ χῶρον. 13 Ὑποπνεύσαντος δὲ
and toward north-west. And blowing gently
= when a south wind

νότου δόξαντες τῆς προθέσεως κεκρατηκέναι,
a south wind* thinking ²the(ir) ³purpose ¹to have obtained,
blew gently

ἄραντες ἆσσον παρελέγοντο τὴν Κρήτην.
raising ³close in- ¹they coasted by - ²Crete.
[anchor] shore

14 μετ' οὐ πολὺ δὲ ἔβαλεν κατ' αὐτῆς
And after not much there beat down it

ἄνεμος τυφωνικὸς ὁ καλούμενος εὐρακύλων·
wind a tempestuous - being called Euraquilo;

15 συναρπασθέντος δὲ τοῦ πλοίου καὶ μὴ
and ³being seized ¹the ²ship* and not

δυναμένου ἀντοφθαλμεῖν τῷ ἀνέμῳ ἐπιδόντες
being able* to beat up against the wind giving way

ἐφερόμεθα. 16 νησίον δέ τι ὑποδραμόντες
we were borne. And ³islet ²a certain ¹running under
the lee of

καλούμενον Κλαῦδα ἰσχύσαμεν μόλις
being called Clauda we were able hardly

περικρατεῖς γενέσθαι τῆς σκάφης, 17 ἦν
control to get of the boat, which

ἄραντες βοηθείαις ἐχρῶντο, ὑποζωννύντες
taking ²helps ¹they used, undergirding

τὸ πλοῖον· φοβούμενοί τε μὴ εἰς τὴν
the ship; and fearing lest into -

Σύρτιν ἐκπέσωσιν, χαλάσαντες τὸ σκεῦος,
Syrtis they might fall off,* lowering the tackle,

---

lost, and sailing had already become dangerous because by now it was after the Fast. ʸ So Paul warned them, 10"Men, I can see that our voyage is going to be disastrous and bring great loss to ship and cargo, and to our own lives also."

11But the centurion, instead of listening to what Paul said, followed the advice of the pilot and of the owner of the ship. 12Since the harbor was unsuitable to winter in, the majority decided that we should sail on, hoping to reach Phoenix and winter there. This was a harbor in Crete, facing both southwest and northwest.

The Storm

13When a gentle south wind began to blow, they thought they had obtained what they wanted; so they weighed anchor and sailed along the shore of Crete. 14Before very long, a wind of hurricane force, called the "northeaster," swept down from the island. 15The ship was caught by the storm and could not head into the wind; so we gave way to it and were driven along. 16As we passed to the lee of a small island called Cauda, we were hardly able to make the lifeboat secure. 17When the men had hoisted it aboard, they passed ropes under the ship itself to hold it together. Fearing that they would run aground on the sandbars of Syrtis, they lowered the sea anchor and

---

ᵘ I.e., Day of Atonement in September or October
ᵛ I.e., a northeaster

* This is the classical Greek word for a ship being driven out of her course on to shoals, rocks, etc. (Page). See also vers 26 and 29.

ʸ9 That is, the Day of Atonement (Yom Kippur)

themselves be driven along.

18 The next day as we were being violently storm-tossed, they began to jettison the cargo;

19 and on the third day they threw the ship's tackle overboard with their own hands.

20 And since neither sun nor stars appeared for many days, and no small storm was assailing *us,* from then on all hope of our being saved was gradually abandoned.

21 And when they had gone a long time without food, then Paul stood up in their midst and said, "Men, you ought to have followed my advice and not to have set sail from Crete, and incurred this damage and loss.

22 "And *yet* now I urge you to keep up your courage, for there shall be no loss of life among you, but *only* of the ship.

23 "For this very night an angel of the God to whom I belong and whom I serve stood before me,

24 saying, 'Do not be afraid, Paul; you must stand before Caesar; and behold, God has granted you all those who are sailing with you.'

25 "Therefore, keep up your courage, men, for I believe God, that it will turn out exactly as I have been told.

26 "But we must run aground on a certain island."

27 But when the fourteenth night had come, as we were being driven about in the Adriatic Sea, about midnight the sailors *began* to surmise that they were approaching some land.

28 And they took soundings, and found *it to be* twenty fathoms; and a little

---

οὕτως ἐφέροντο. 18 σφοδρῶς δὲ χειμαζ-
thus · they were borne. · But exceedingly · being in
= as we were exceedingly in . . .

ομένων ἡμῶν τῇ ἑξῆς ἐκβολὴν ἐποιοῦντο,
the grip · us° · on the next · a jettisoning · they made,
of a storm · [day]

19 καὶ τῇ τρίτῃ αὐτόχειρες τὴν σκευὴν
and · on the third · with their · the · tackle
[day] · own hands

τοῦ πλοίου ἔρριψαν. 20 μήτε δὲ ἡλίου
of the · ship · they threw [out]. · And neither · sun
= when neither . . .

μήτε ἄστρων ἐπιφαινόντων ἐπὶ πλείονας
nor · stars · appearing° · over · many

ἡμέρας, χειμῶνός τε οὐκ ὀλίγου ἐπικειμένου,
days, · and stormy weather · no · little · pressing hard,°

λοιπὸν περιῃρεῖτο ἐλπὶς πᾶσα τοῦ σῴζεσθαι
now · was taken away · ²hope · ¹all · - · to be saved
= that we might

ἡμᾶς. 21 Πολλῆς τε ἀσιτίας ὑπαρχούσης
us.^bd · And much · abstinence · being°
be saved. · = when there was long abstinence

τότε σταθεὶς ὁ Παῦλος ἐν μέσῳ αὐτῶν εἶπεν·
then · ²standing · - · ¹Paul · in [the] midst · of them · said:

ἔδει μέν, ὦ ἄνδρες, πειθαρχήσαντάς
It behoved · - · O · men, · obeying
[you],

μοι μὴ ἀνάγεσθαι ἀπὸ τῆς Κρήτης
me · not · to set sail · from · - · Crete

κερδῆσαί τε τὴν ὕβριν ταύτην καὶ τὴν
and to come by · - · injury · this · and · the

ζημίαν. 22 καὶ τὰ νῦν παραινῶ ὑμᾶς
loss. · And · - · now · I advise · you

εὐθυμεῖν· ἀποβολὴ γὰρ ψυχῆς οὐδεμία
to be of good · ³throwing away · for · ⁴of life · ¹no
cheer;

ἔσται ἐξ ὑμῶν πλὴν τοῦ πλοίου.
¹there will be · of · you · but · of the · ship.

23 παρέστη γάρ μοι ταύτῃ τῇ νυκτὶ
For there stood by · me · *in* this · - · night

τοῦ θεοῦ οὗ εἰμι, ᾧ καὶ λατρεύω,
- · ²of God · ³of whom · ⁴I am, · ⁵whom · ⁶also · ⁷I serve,

ἄγγελος 24 λέγων· μὴ φοβοῦ, Παῦλε·
¹an angel · saying: · Fear not, · Paul;

Καίσαρί σε δεῖ παραστῆναι, καὶ ἰδοὺ
⁴Cæsar · ²thee · ¹it behoves · ³to stand before, · and · behold

κεχάρισταί σοι ὁ θεὸς πάντας τοὺς
²has given · ³thee · - · ¹God · all · the [ones]

πλέοντας μετὰ σοῦ. 25 διὸ εὐθυμεῖτε,
sailing · with · thee. · Wherefore · be ye of
good cheer,

ἄνδρες· πιστεύω γὰρ τῷ θεῷ ὅτι οὕτως
men; · for I believe · - · God · that · thus

ἔσται καθ' ὃν τρόπον λελάληταί μοι.
it will be · in the way in which† · it has been spoken · to me.

26 εἰς νῆσον δέ τινα δεῖ ἡμᾶς ἐκπεσεῖν.
⁵Onto · ⁷island · ¹but · ⁶a · ²it · ³us · ⁴to fall off.
certain · behoves

27 Ὡς δὲ τεσσαρεσκαιδεκάτη νὺξ ἐγένετο
Now when · [the] fourteenth · night · came

διαφερομένων ἡμῶν ἐν τῷ Ἀδρίᾳ, κατὰ
being carried about · us° · in · the · Adria, · about
= while we were being carried about

μέσον τῆς νυκτὸς ὑπενόουν οἱ ναῦται
[the] middle · of the · night · ²supposed · ¹the · ²sailors

προσάγειν τινὰ αὐτοῖς χώραν. 28 καὶ
⁴to approach · ⁶some · ⁵to them · ⁷country. · And

βολίσαντες εὗρον ὀργυιὰς εἴκοσι, βραχὺ δὲ
sounding · they found · fathoms · twenty, · and ²a little

---

let the ship be driven along.

18 We took such a violent battering from the storm that the next day they began to throw the cargo overboard. 19 On the third day, they threw the ship's tackle overboard with their own hands. 20 When neither sun nor stars appeared for many days and the storm continued raging, we finally gave up all hope of being saved.

21 After the men had gone a long time without food, Paul stood up before them and said: "Men, you should have taken my advice not to sail from Crete; then you would have spared yourselves this damage and loss. 22 But now I urge you to keep up your courage, because not one of you will be lost; only the ship will be destroyed. 23 Last night an angel of the God whose I am and whom I serve stood beside me 24 and said, 'Do not be afraid, Paul. You must stand trial before Caesar; and God has graciously given you the lives of all who sail with you.' 25 So keep up your courage, men, for I have faith in God that it will happen just as he told me. 26 Nevertheless, we must run aground on some island."

The Shipwreck

27 On the fourteenth night we were still being driven across the Adriatic[z] Sea, when about midnight the sailors sensed they were approaching land. 28 They took soundings and found that the water was a hundred and twenty feet[a] deep. A short time later

---

[z]27 In ancient times the name referred to an area extending well south of Italy.

[a]28 Greek *twenty orguias* (about 37 meters)

farther on they took another sounding and found *it to be* fifteen fathoms. 29And fearing that we might run aground somewhere on the rocks, they cast four anchors from the stern and wished for daybreak. 30And as the sailors were trying to escape from the ship, and had let down the *ship's* boat into the sea, on the pretense of intending to lay out anchors from the bow, 31Paul said to the centurion and to the soldiers, "Unless these men remain in the ship, you yourselves cannot be saved." 32Then the soldiers cut away the ropes of the *ship's* boat, and let it fall away. 33And until the day was about to dawn, Paul was encouraging them all to take some food, saying, "Today is the fourteenth day that you have been constantly watching and going without eating, having taken nothing. 34"Therefore I encourage you to take some food, for this is for your preservation; for not a hair from the head of any of you shall perish." 35And having said this, he took bread and gave thanks to God in the presence of all; and he broke it and began to eat. 36And all of them were encouraged, and they themselves also took food. 37And all of us in the ship were two hundred and seventy-six persons. 38And when they had eaten enough, they *began* to lighten the ship by throwing out the wheat into the sea. 39And when day came, they could not recognize the land; but they did ob-

διαστήσαντες καὶ πάλιν βολίσαντες εὗρον
¹having moved   also again   sounding   they found

ὀργυιὰς δεκαπέντε· 29 φοβούμενοί τε μὴ
fathoms   fifteen;   and fearing   lest

που κατὰ τραχεῖς τόπους ἐκπέσωμεν,
²somewhere ³against ⁴rough ⁵places ¹we might fall off,

ἐκ πρύμνης ῥίψαντες ἀγκύρας τέσσαρας
out of [the] stern throwing anchors four

ηὔχοντο ἡμέραν γενέσθαι. 30 Τῶν δὲ
they prayed day   to become.   And the

ναυτῶν ζητούντων φυγεῖν ἐκ τοῦ πλοίου
sailors seeking² to flee out of the ship
= when the sailors sought

καὶ χαλασάντων τὴν σκάφην εἰς τὴν
and lowering²   the   boat into the
=lowered

θάλασσαν προφάσει ὡς ἐκ πρῴρης ἀγκύρας
sea under pretence as ⁴out of ⁵[the] prow ³anchors

μελλόντων ἐκτείνειν, 31 εἶπεν ὁ Παῦλος
¹intending ²to cast out,   said   -   Paul

τῷ ἑκατοντάρχη καὶ τοῖς στρατιώταις·
to the centurion and to the soldiers:

ἐὰν μὴ οὗτοι μείνωσιν ἐν τῷ πλοίῳ,
Unless these remain in the ship,

ὑμεῖς σωθῆναι οὐ δύνασθε. 32 τότε
ye   ²to be saved ¹cannot.   Then

ἀπέκοψαν οἱ στρατιῶται τὰ σχοινία τῆς
cut away the soldiers the ropes of the

σκάφης καὶ εἴασαν αὐτὴν ἐκπεσεῖν.
boat   and let   it   to fall off.

33 Ἄχρι δὲ οὗ ἡμέρα ἤμελλεν γίνεσθαι,
And until   day   was about to come,

παρεκάλει ὁ Παῦλος ἅπαντας μεταλαβεῖν
besought - Paul   all   to partake

τροφῆς λέγων· τεσσαρεσκαιδεκάτην σήμερον
of food saying: ²[the] fourteenth   ¹To-day [is]

ἡμέραν προσδοκῶντες ἄσιτοι διατελεῖτε,
²day   ⁵waiting ⁴without food ⁴ye continued,

μηθὲν προσλαβόμενοι. 34 διὸ παρακαλῶ
nothing taking.   Wherefore I beseech

ὑμᾶς μεταλαβεῖν τροφῆς· τοῦτο γὰρ πρὸς
you   to partake of food; for this to

τῆς ὑμετέρας σωτηρίας ὑπάρχει· οὐδενὸς
-    your   salvation   is;   ²of no one

γὰρ ὑμῶν θρὶξ ἀπὸ τῆς κεφαλῆς ἀπολεῖται.
¹for of you a hair from the head shall perish.

35 εἴπας δὲ ταῦτα καὶ λαβὼν ἄρτον
And saying these things and taking bread

εὐχαρίστησεν τῷ θεῷ ἐνώπιον πάντων
he gave thanks - to God before   all

καὶ κλάσας ἤρξατο ἐσθίειν. 36 εὔθυμοι δὲ
and breaking began to eat.   And ⁴in good spirits

γενόμενοι πάντες καὶ αὐτοὶ προσελάβοντο
³becoming ¹all   ²also they took

τροφῆς. 37 ἤμεθα δὲ αἱ πᾶσαι ψυχαὶ
food.   Now we were ²the ¹all souls

ἐν τῷ πλοίῳ διακόσιαι ἑβδομήκοντα ἕξ.
in the ship two hundreds [and] seventy six.

38 κορεσθέντες δὲ τροφῆς ἐκούφιζον τὸ
And having been satisfied of(with) food they lightened

πλοῖον ἐκβαλλόμενοι τὸν σῖτον εἰς τὴν
ship   ⁴throwing out   the wheat into the

θάλασσαν. 39 Ὅτε δὲ ἡμέρα ἐγένετο,
sea.   And when day   came,

τὴν γῆν οὐκ ἐπεγίνωσκον, κόλπον δέ
²the ³land ¹they did not recognize, but ²bay

they took soundings again and found it was ninety feet[b] deep. 29Fearing that we would be dashed against the rocks, they dropped four anchors from the stern and prayed for daylight. 30In an attempt to escape from the ship, the sailors let the lifeboat down into the sea, pretending they were going to lower some anchors from the bow. 31Then Paul said to the centurion and the soldiers, "Unless these men stay with the ship, you cannot be saved." 32So the soldiers cut the ropes that held the lifeboat and let it fall away.

33Just before dawn Paul urged them all to eat. "For the last fourteen days," he said, "you have been in constant suspense and have gone without food—you haven't eaten anything. 34Now I urge you to take some food. You need it to survive. Not one of you will lose a single hair from his head." 35After he said this, he took some bread and gave thanks to God in front of them all. Then he broke it and began to eat. 36They were all encouraged and ate some food themselves. 37Altogether there were 276 of us on board. 38When they had eaten as much as they wanted, they lightened the ship by throwing the grain into the sea.

39When daylight came, they did not recognize the land, but they saw a bay

b28 Greek fifteen orguias (about 27 meters)

serve a certain bay with a beach, and they resolved to ʷdrive the ship onto it if they could.

40And casting off the anchors, they left them in the sea while at the same time they were loosening the ropes of the rudders, and hoisting the foresail to the wind, they were heading for the beach.

41But striking a reef where two seas met, they ran the vessel aground; and the prow stuck fast and remained immovable, but the stern *began* to be broken up by the force *of the waves*.

42And the soldiers' plan was to kill the prisoners, that none *of them* should swim away and escape;

43but the centurion, wanting to bring Paul safely through, kept them from their intention, and commanded that those who could swim should jump overboard first and get to land,

44and the rest *should follow*, some on planks, and others on various things from the ship. And thus it happened that they all were brought safely to land.

τινα κατενόουν ἔχοντα αἰγιαλόν, εἰς ὃν
¹a certain ¹they noticed   having   a shore,   into which

ἐβουλεύοντο εἰ δύναιντο ἐξῶσαι τὸ πλοῖον.
they were minded if they were able to drive the ship.

40 καὶ τὰς ἀγκύρας περιελόντες εἴων
And ²the ²anchors ¹having cast off they left [them]

εἰς τὴν θάλασσαν, ἅμα ἀνέντες τὰς
in the   sea,   at the same time loosening the

ζευκτηρίας τῶν πηδαλίων, καὶ ἐπάραντες
fastenings of the rudders,   and   raising

τὸν ἀρτέμωνα τῇ πνεούσῃ κατεῖχον εἰς
the foresail to the breeze they held [the ship] to

τὸν αἰγιαλόν. 41 περιπεσόντες δὲ εἰς
the shore.   And coming upon   to

τόπον διθάλασσον ἐπέκειλαν τὴν ναῦν,
a place between two seas they drove the vessel,

καὶ ἡ μὲν πρῷρα ἐρείσασα ἔμεινεν
and ²the ¹while prow having run aground remained

ἀσάλευτος, ἡ δὲ πρύμνα ἐλύετο ὑπὸ
immovable, ²the ¹yet stern was broken by

τῆς βίας. 42 Τῶν δὲ στρατιωτῶν βουλὴ
the force.*   Now ²of the ³soldiers ¹[the] mind

ἐγένετο ἵνα τοὺς δεσμώτας ἀποκτείνωσιν,
was   that ²the ²prisoners ¹they should kill,

μή τις ἐκκολυμβήσας διαφύγῃ· 43 ὁ δὲ
lest anyone swimming out should escape; but the

ἑκατοντάρχης βουλόμενος διασῶσαι τὸν
centurion   being minded to save   –

Παῦλον ἐκώλυσεν αὐτοὺς τοῦ βουλήματος,
Paul   forbade   them   the(ir) intention,

ἐκέλευσέν τε τοὺς δυναμένους κολυμβᾶν
and commanded the [ones] being able to swim

ἀπορίψαντας πρώτους ἐπὶ τὴν γῆν
casting [themselves] first onto the land
overboard

ἐξιέναι, 44 καὶ τοὺς λοιποὺς οὓς μὲν ἐπὶ
to go out, and the rest some on

σανίσιν, οὓς δὲ ἐπί τινων τῶν ἀπὸ τοῦ
planks, others on some of the things from the

πλοίου. καὶ οὕτως ἐγένετο πάντας
ship.   And thus it came to pass all

διασωθῆναι ἐπὶ τὴν γῆν.
to be saved on the land.

---

with a sandy beach, where they decided to run the ship aground if they could.

40Cutting loose the anchors, they left them in the sea and at the same time untied the ropes that held the rudders. Then they hoisted the foresail to the wind and made for the beach. 41But the ship struck a sandbar and ran aground. The bow stuck fast and would not move, and the stern was broken to pieces by the pounding of the surf.

42The soldiers planned to kill the prisoners to prevent any of them from swimming away and escaping. 43But the centurion wanted to spare Paul's life and welcomed them from carrying out their plan. He ordered those who could swim to jump overboard first and get to land. 44The rest were to get there on planks or on pieces of the ship. In this way everyone reached land in safety.

Chapter 28

Safe at Malta

AND when they had been brought safely through, then we found out that the island was called Malta.

2And the natives showed us extraordinary kindness; for because of the rain that had set in and because of the cold, they kindled a fire and received us all.

3But when Paul gathered a bundle of sticks and laid them on the fire, a viper came out because of the heat, and fastened on his hand.

4And when the natives

---

28 Καὶ διασωθέντες τότε ἐπέγνωμεν ὅτι
And having been saved then we found out that

Μελίτη ἡ νῆσος καλεῖται. 2 οἵ τε
Melita the island is(was) called.   And the

βάρβαροι παρεῖχον οὐ τὴν τυχοῦσαν
foreigners ¹showed ³not ⁴the ⁵ordinary

φιλανθρωπίαν ἡμῖν· ἅψαντες γὰρ πυρὰν
²kindness ¹us; for having lit a fire

προσελάβοντο πάντας ἡμᾶς διὰ τὸν ὑετὸν
they welcomed ²all ¹us because of the rain

τὸν ἐφεστῶτα καὶ διὰ τὸ ψῦχος. 3 συστρέ-
– coming on and because of the cold.   col-

ψαντος δὲ τοῦ Παύλου φρυγάνων τι
lecting And – Paulᵃ ³of sticks ¹a
=when Paul collected

πλῆθος καὶ ἐπιθέντος ἐπὶ τὴν πυράν,
²quantity and putting onᵃ on the fire,
=put them

ἔχιδνα ἀπὸ τῆς θέρμης ἐξελθοῦσα καθῆψεν
a snake from the heat coming out fastened on

τῆς χειρὸς αὐτοῦ. 4 ὡς δὲ εἶδον οἱ
the hand of him.   And when ²saw ¹the

Chapter 28

Ashore on Malta

ONCE safely on shore, we found out that the island was called Malta. 2The islanders showed us unusual kindness. They built a fire and welcomed us all because it was raining and cold. 3Paul gathered a pile of brushwood and, as he put it on the fire, a viper, driven out by the heat, fastened itself on his hand. 4When the islanders saw

---

ʷ Some ancient mss. read *bring the ship safely ashore*

* That is, of the waves, as indeed some MSS have.

saw the creature hanging from his hand, they *began* saying to one another, "Undoubtedly this man is a murderer, and though he has been saved from the sea, justice has not allowed him to live."

5However he shook the creature off into the fire and suffered no harm.

6But they were expecting that he was about to swell up or suddenly fall down dead. But after they had waited a long time and had seen nothing unusual happen to him, they changed their minds and *began* to say that he was a god.

7Now in the neighborhood of that place were lands belonging to the leading man of the island, named Publius, who welcomed us and entertained us courteously three days.

8And it came about that the father of Publius was lying *in bed* afflicted with *recurrent* fever and dysentery; and Paul went in *to see* him and after he had prayed, he laid his hands on him and healed him.

9And after this had happened, the rest of the people on the island who had diseases were coming to him and getting cured.

10And they also honored us with many marks of respect; and when we were setting sail, they supplied *us* with all we needed.

Paul Arrives at Rome

11And at the end of three months we set sail on an Alexandrian ship which had wintered at the island, and which had had the Twin Brothers for its figurehead.

12And after we put in at Syracuse, we stayed there for three days.

13And from there we sailed around and arrived at Rhegium, and a day later

---

βάρβαροι κρεμάμενον τὸ θηρίον ἐκ τῆς
²foreigners ⁶hanging ⁴the ⁵beast from the

χειρὸς αὐτοῦ, πρὸς ἀλλήλους ἔλεγον·
hand of him, to one another they said:

πάντως φονεύς ἐστιν ὁ ἄνθρωπος οὗτος,
To be sure ⁴a murderer ³is ¹this man,

ὃν διασωθέντα ἐκ τῆς θαλάσσης ἡ δίκη
whom having been out of the sea - justice
saved

ζῆν οὐκ εἴασεν. 5 ὁ μὲν οὖν ἀποτινάξας
²to live ¹did not allow. He - then shaking off

τὸ θηρίον εἰς τὸ πῦρ ἔπαθεν οὐδὲν
the beast into the fire suffered no

κακόν· 6 οἱ δὲ προσεδόκων αὐτὸν μέλλειν
harm; but they expected him to be about

πίμπρασθαι ἢ καταπίπτειν ἄφνω νεκρόν.
to swell or to fall down suddenly dead.

ἐπὶ πολὺ δὲ αὐτῶν προσδοκώντων καὶ
But over much [time] they expecting and
= while they expected and beheld

θεωρούντων μηδὲν ἄτοπον εἰς αὐτὸν
beholdingᵃ nothing amiss ²to ³him

γινόμενον, μεταβαλόμενοι ἔλεγον αὐτὸν εἶναι
¹happening, changing their minds they said him to be

θεόν. 7 Ἐν δὲ τοῖς περὶ τὸν τόπον
a god. Now in the [parts] about - place

ἐκεῖνον ὑπῆρχεν χωρία τῷ πρώτῳ τῆς
that were lands to the chief manᵉ of the
= the chief man . . . had lands

νήσου ὀνόματι Ποπλίῳ, ὃς ἀναδεξάμενος
island by name Publius, who welcoming

ἡμᾶς ἡμέρας τρεῖς φιλοφρόνως ἐξένισεν.
us ⁴days ³three ²friendlily ¹lodged [us].

8 ἐγένετο δὲ τὸν πατέρα τοῦ Ποπλίου
Now it happened the father - of Publius

πυρετοῖς καὶ δυσεντερίῳ συνεχόμενον
³feverish attacks ⁴and ⁵dysentery ²suffering from

κατακεῖσθαι, πρὸς ὃν ὁ Παῦλος εἰσελθὼν
¹to be lying down, to whom - Paul entering

καὶ προσευξάμενος, ἐπιθεὶς τὰς χεῖρας
and praying, ¹putting ²on ²the(his) ³hands

αὐτῷ ἰάσατο αὐτόν. 9 τούτου δὲ γενομένου
⁵him cured him. And this happeningᵃ
= when this happened

καὶ οἱ λοιποὶ οἱ ἐν τῇ νήσῳ ἔχοντες
³also ¹the ²rest - in the island having

ἀσθενείας προσήρχοντο καὶ ἐθεραπεύοντο,
ailments came up and were healed,

10 οἳ καὶ πολλαῖς τιμαῖς ἐτίμησαν ἡμᾶς
who also with many honours honoured us

καὶ ἀναγομένοις ἐπέθεντο τὰ πρὸς τὰς
and on our putting to sea placed on [us] the things for the(our)

χρείας.
needs.

11 Μετὰ δὲ τρεῖς μῆνας ἀνήχθημεν ἐν
And after three months we embarked in

πλοίῳ παρακεχειμακότι ἐν τῇ νήσῳ,
a ship having passed the winter in the island,

Ἀλεξανδρίνῳ, παρασήμῳ Διοσκούροις. 12 καὶ
an Alexandrian, with a sign Dioscuri. And

καταχθέντες εἰς Συρακούσας ἐπεμείναμεν
being brought to land to(at) Syracuse we remained

ἡμέρας τρεῖς, 13 ὅθεν περιελθόντες κατην-
days three, whence tacking we ar-

τήσαμεν εἰς Ῥήγιον. καὶ μετὰ μίαν
rived at Rhegium. And after one

---

the snake hanging from his hand, they said to each other, "This man must be a murderer; for though he escaped from the sea, Justice has not allowed him to live." 5But Paul shook the snake off into the fire and suffered no ill effects. 6The people expected him to swell up or suddenly fall dead, but after waiting a long time and seeing nothing unusual happen to him, they changed their minds and said he was a god.

7There was an estate nearby that belonged to Publius, the chief official of the island. He welcomed us to his home and for three days entertained us hospitably. 8His father was sick in bed, suffering from fever and dysentery. Paul went in to see him and, after prayer, placed his hands on him and healed him. 9When this had happened, the rest of the sick on the island came and were cured. 10They honored us in many ways and when we were ready to sail, they furnished us with the supplies we needed.

Arrival at Rome

11After three months we put out to sea in a ship that had wintered in the island. It was an Alexandrian ship with the figurehead of the twin gods Castor and Pollux. 12We put in at Syracuse and stayed there three days. 13From there we set sail and arrived at Rhegia south wind sprang up, and on the second day we came to Puteoli. 14There we found *some* brethren, and were invited to stay with them for seven days; and thus we came to Rome. 15And the brethren, when they heard about us, came from there as far as the Market of Appius and Three Inns to meet us; and when Paul saw them, he thanked God and took courage. 16And when we entered Rome, Paul was allowed to stay by himself, with the soldier who was guarding him. 17And it happened that after three days he called together those who were the leading men of the Jews, and when they had come together, he *began* saying to them, "Brethren, though I had done nothing against our people, or the customs of our fathers, yet I was delivered prisoner from Jerusalem into the hands of the Romans. 18"And when they had examined me, they were willing to release me because there was no ground for putting me to death. 19"But when the Jews objected, I was forced to appeal to Caesar; not that I had any accusation against my nation. 20"For this reason therefore, I requested to see you and to speak with you, for I am wearing this chain for the sake of the hope of Israel." 21And they said to him, "We have neither received letters from Judea concern-

---

ἡμέραν ἐπιγενομένου νότου δευτεραῖοι
day / coming on = as a south wind came on / a south wind[a] / on the second day

ἤλθομεν εἰς Ποτιόλους, 14 οὗ εὑρόντες
we came / to / Puteoli, / where / having found

ἀδελφοὺς παρεκλήθημεν παρ' αὐτοῖς ἐπιμεῖναι
brothers / we were besought / with them / to remain

ἡμέρας ἑπτά· καὶ οὕτως εἰς τὴν Ῥώμην
days / seven; / and / thus / to / - / Rome

ἤλθαμεν. 15 κἀκεῖθεν οἱ ἀδελφοὶ ἀκούσαντες
we went. / And thence / the / brothers / having heard

τὰ περὶ ἡμῶν ἦλθαν εἰς ἀπάντησιν ἡμῖν
the con- concerning / us / came / to / a meeting / with us
things

ἄχρι Ἀππίου φόρου καὶ Τριῶν ταβερνῶν,
as far as / Appii / Forum / and / Three / Taverns,

οὓς ἰδὼν ὁ Παῦλος εὐχαριστήσας τῷ
whom / seeing / - / Paul / thanking / -

θεῷ ἔλαβε θάρσος. 16 Ὅτε δὲ εἰσήλθομεν
God / he took / courage. / And when / we entered

εἰς Ῥώμην, ἐπετράπη τῷ Παύλῳ μένειν
into / Rome, / he* permitted / - / Paul / to remain

καθ' ἑαυτὸν σὺν τῷ φυλάσσοντι αὐτὸν
by / himself / with / ¹the / ³guarding / ⁴him

στρατιώτῃ.
²soldier.

17 Ἐγένετο δὲ μετὰ ἡμέρας τρεῖς
And it came to pass / after / days / three

συγκαλέσασθαι αὐτὸν τοὺς ὄντας τῶν
to call together / him[b] / the [ones] / being / of the
= he called together

Ἰουδαίων πρώτους· συνελθόντων δὲ αὐτῶν
Jews / first(chief); / and coming together / them[a]
= and when they came together

ἔλεγεν πρὸς αὐτούς· ἐγώ, ἄνδρες ἀδελφοί,
he said / to / them: / I, / men / brothers,

οὐδὲν ἐναντίον ποιήσας τῷ λαῷ ἢ τοῖς
²nothing / ³contrary / ¹having done / to the / people / or / to the

ἔθεσι τοῖς πατρῴοις, δέσμιος ἐξ Ἱεροσο-
customs / - / ancestral, / a prisoner / from / Jeru-

λύμων παρεδόθην εἰς τὰς χεῖρας τῶν
salem / I was delivered / into / the / hands / of the

Ῥωμαίων, 18 οἵτινες ἀνακρίναντές με ἐβούλοντο
Romans, / who / having examined me / were minded

ἀπολῦσαι διὰ τὸ μηδεμίαν αἰτίαν θανάτου
to release / on account of / - / no / cause / of death

ὑπάρχειν ἐν ἐμοί· 19 ἀντιλεγόντων δὲ
to be / in / me; / but speaking against [this]
= when the Jews spoke

τῶν Ἰουδαίων ἠναγκάσθην ἐπικαλέσασθαι
the / Jews[a] / I was compelled / to appeal to
against this

Καίσαρα, οὐχ ὡς τοῦ ἔθνους μου ἔχων
Caesar, / not / as / ⁴the / ⁵nation / ⁶of me / ¹having

τι κατηγορεῖν. 20 διὰ ταύτην οὖν τὴν
²anything / ³to accuse. / ¹On account of ²this / ⁴therefore / -

αἰτίαν παρεκάλεσα ὑμᾶς ἰδεῖν καὶ προσ-
³cause / I called / you / to see / and / to

λαλῆσαι· εἵνεκεν γὰρ τῆς ἐλπίδος τοῦ
speak to; / for for the sake of / the / hope / -

Ἰσραὴλ τὴν ἅλυσιν ταύτην περίκειμαι.
of Israel / ²this ³chain / ¹I have round [me].

21 οἱ δὲ πρὸς αὐτὸν εἶπαν· ἡμεῖς οὔτε
And they / to / him / said: / We / neither

γράμματα περὶ σοῦ ἐδεξάμεθα ἀπὸ τῆς
³letters / ²about / ⁴thee / ¹received / from / -

* That is, the officer to whom Paul was handed over by the centurion Julius.

---

um. The next day the south wind came up, and on the following day we reached Puteoli. 14There we found some brothers who invited us to spend a week with them. And so we came to Rome. 15The brothers there had heard that we were coming, and they traveled as far as the Forum of Appius and the Three Taverns to meet us. At the sight of these men Paul thanked God and was encouraged. 16When we got to Rome, Paul was allowed to live by himself, with a soldier to guard him.

Paul Preaches at Rome Under Guard

17Three days later he called together the leaders of the Jews. When they had assembled, Paul said to them: "My brothers, although I have done nothing against our people or against the customs of our ancestors, I was arrested in Jerusalem and handed over to the Romans. 18They examined me and wanted to release me, because I was not guilty of any crime deserving death. 19But when the Jews objected, I was compelled to appeal to Caesar—not that I had any charge to bring against my own people. 20For this reason I have asked to see you and talk with you. It is because of the hope of Israel that I am bound with this chain." 21They replied, "We have not received any letters from Judea concerning

ing you, nor have any of the brethren come here and reported or spoken anything bad about you.

22 "But we desire to hear from you what your views are; for concerning this sect, it is known to us that it is spoken against everywhere."

23 And when they had set a day for him, they came to him at his lodging in large numbers; and he was explaining to them by solemnly testifying about the kingdom of God, and trying to persuade them concerning Jesus, from both the Law of Moses and from the Prophets, from morning until evening.

24 And some were being persuaded by the things spoken, but others would not believe.

25 And when they did not agree with one another, they *began* leaving after Paul had spoken one *parting* word, "The Holy Spirit rightly spoke through Isaiah the prophet to your fathers,

26 saying,

'GO TO THIS PEOPLE AND SAY,
"YOU WILL KEEP ON HEARING, BUT WILL NOT UNDERSTAND;
AND YOU WILL KEEP ON SEEING, BUT WILL NOT PERCEIVE;

27 FOR THE HEART OF THIS PEOPLE HAS BECOME DULL,
AND WITH THEIR EARS THEY SCARCELY HEAR,
AND THEY HAVE CLOSED THEIR EYES;
LEST THEY SHOULD SEE WITH THEIR EYES,
AND HEAR WITH THEIR EARS,
AND UNDERSTAND WITH THEIR HEART AND RETURN,
AND I SHOULD HEAL THEM." '

28 "Let it be known to you therefore, that this salvation of God has been sent to the Gentiles; they will also listen."

29 [ˣAnd when he had spoken these words, the Jews departed, having a great dispute among themselves.]

30 And he stayed two full years in his own rented quarters, and was welcom-

---

'Ιουδαίας,   οὔτε   παραγενόμενός   τις   τῶν
Judæa,   nor   arriving   anyone of the

ἀδελφῶν   ἀπήγγειλεν ἢ   ἐλάλησέν   τι   περὶ
brothers told   or   spoke   anything ᵃabout

σοῦ   πονηρόν.   22 ἀξιοῦμεν δὲ   παρὰ σοῦ
²thee ¹evil.   But we think fit from thee

ἀκοῦσαι ἃ   φρονεῖς· περὶ μὲν γὰρ τῆς
to hear what thou ²concerning ³indeed ¹for –
         things thinkest;

αἱρέσεως ταύτης γνωστὸν ἡμῖν ἐστιν ὅτι
⁵sect   ⁴this   ⁷known   ⁸to us ⁶it is that

πανταχοῦ ἀντιλέγεται.   23 Ταξάμενοι δὲ
everywhere it is spoken against.   And arranging

αὐτῷ ἡμέραν ἦλθον πρὸς αὐτὸν εἰς τὴν
with him a day ²came   ³to   ⁴him   ⁵in ⁶the(his)

ξενίαν πλείονες, οἷς ἐξετίθετο διαμαρτυρ-
⁷lodging ¹more,   to whom he set forth   solemnly

όμενος τὴν βασιλείαν τοῦ θεοῦ, πείθων
witnessing the kingdom   –   of God, ²persuading

τε αὐτοὺς περὶ τοῦ Ἰησοῦ ἀπό τε τοῦ
¹and them concerning – Jesus from both the

νόμου Μωϋσέως καὶ τῶν προφητῶν, ἀπὸ
law   of Moses and the prophets,   from

πρωῒ ἕως ἑσπέρας.   24 καὶ οἱ μὲν
morning until evening.   And some

ἐπείθοντο τοῖς λεγομένοις, 25 οἱ δὲ
were persuaded by the things being said, others

ἠπίστουν· ἀσύμφωνοι δὲ ὄντες πρὸς ἀλλή-
disbelieved; and ²disagreed ¹being with one an-

λους ἀπελύοντο, εἰπόντος τοῦ Παύλου
other they were dismissed, having said – Paulᵃ
                            ᵃafter Paul had said

ῥῆμα ἕν, ὅτι καλῶς τὸ πνεῦμα τὸ ἅγιον
word one, – Well the Spirit – Holy

ἐλάλησεν διὰ Ἡσαΐου τοῦ προφήτου πρὸς
spoke   through Esaias the prophet to

τοὺς πατέρας ὑμῶν 26 λέγων· πορεύθητι
the fathers of you saying: Go thou

πρὸς τὸν λαὸν τοῦτον καὶ εἰπόν· ἀκοῇ
to this people and say: In hearing

ἀκούσετε καὶ οὐ μὴ συνῆτε, καὶ βλέποντες
ye will hear and by no means understand, and looking

βλέψετε καὶ οὐ μὴ ἴδητε· 27 ἐπαχύνθη
ye will look and by no means see; ¹was thickened

γὰρ ἡ καρδία τοῦ λαοῦ τούτου, καὶ
¹for the heart of this people, and

τοῖς ὠσὶν βαρέως ἤκουσαν, καὶ τοὺς
with the(ir) ears heavily they heard, and the

ὀφθαλμοὺς αὐτῶν ἐκάμμυσαν· μήποτε ἴδωσιν
eyes of them they closed; lest at any time they see

τοῖς ὀφθαλμοῖς καὶ τοῖς ὠσὶν ἀκούσωσιν
with the eyes and with the ears hear

καὶ τῇ καρδίᾳ συνῶσιν καὶ ἐπιστρέψωσιν,
and with the heart understand and turn,

καὶ ἰάσομαι αὐτούς.   28 γνωστὸν οὖν
and I shall cure them.   Known therefore

ἔστω ὑμῖν ὅτι τοῖς ἔθνεσιν ἀπεστάλη
let it be to you that to the nations was sent

τοῦτο τὸ σωτήριον τοῦ θεοῦ· αὐτοὶ καὶ
this – salvation – of God; and they

ἀκούσονται.‡
will hear.

30 Ἐνέμεινεν δὲ διετίαν ὅλην ἐν ἰδίῳ
And he remained a whole two years in [his] own

μισθώματι, καὶ ἀπεδέχετο πάντας τοὺς
hired apartment, and welcomed all the

---

you, and none of the brothers who have come from there have reported or said anything bad about you. 22 But we want to hear what your views are, for we know that people everywhere are talking against this sect."

23 They arranged to meet Paul on a certain day, and came in even larger numbers to the place where he was staying. From morning till evening he explained and declared to them the kingdom of God and tried to convince them about Jesus from the Law of Moses and from the Prophets. 24 Some were convinced by what he said, but others would not believe. 25 They disagreed among themselves and began to leave after Paul had made this final statement: "The Holy Spirit spoke the truth to your forefathers when he said through Isaiah the prophet:

26 " 'Go to this people and say,
"You will be ever hearing but never understanding;
you will be ever seeing but never perceiving."

27 For this people's heart has become calloused;
they hardly hear with their ears,
and they have closed their eyes.
Otherwise they might see with their eyes,
hear with their ears,
understand with their hearts
and turn, and I would heal them.'ᶜ

28 "Therefore I want you to know that God's salvation has been sent to the Gentiles, and they will listen!"ᵈ

30 For two whole years Paul stayed there in his own rented house and wel-

ᶜ27 Isaiah 6:9,10
ᵈ28 Some manuscripts listen!"
²⁹After he said this, the Jews left, arguing vigorously among themselves.

ˣMany mss. do not contain this verse

‡ Verse 29 omitted by Nestle; cf. NIV footnote.

ing all who came to him,
31preaching the kingdom
of God, and teaching con-
cerning the Lord Jesus
Christ with all openness,
unhindered.

εἰσπορευομένους	πρὸς	αὐτόν,	31	κηρύσσων
[ones] coming in	to	him,		proclaiming

τὴν	βασιλείαν	τοῦ	θεοῦ	καὶ	διδάσκων
the	kingdom	–	of God	and	teaching

τὰ	περὶ	τοῦ	κυρίου	Ἰησοῦ	Χριστοῦ
the things	concerning	the	Lord	Jesus	Christ

μετὰ	πάσης	παρρησίας	ἀκωλύτως.
with	all	boldness	unhinderedly.

comed all who came to see
him. 31Boldly and without
hindrance he preached the
kingdom of God and taught
about the Lord Jesus
Christ.

Chapter 1

The Gospel Exalted

PAUL, a bond-servant of Christ Jesus, called *as* an apostle, set apart for the gospel of God,

2which He promised beforehand through His prophets in the holy Scriptures,

3concerning His Son, who was born of a descendant of David according to the flesh,

4who was declared the Son of God with power *a* by the resurrection from the dead, according to the spirit of holiness, Jesus Christ our Lord,

5through whom we have received grace and apostleship to bring about *the* obedience of faith among all the Gentiles, for His name's sake,

6among whom you also are the called of Jesus Christ;

7to all who are beloved of God in Rome, called *as* saints: Grace to you and peace from God our Father and the Lord Jesus Christ.

8First, I thank my God through Jesus Christ for you all, because your faith is being proclaimed throughout the whole world.

9For God, whom I serve in my spirit in the *preaching of the* gospel of His Son, is my witness *as to* how unceasingly I make mention of you,

10always in my prayers making request, if perhaps now at last by the will of God I may succeed in coming to you.

11For I long to see you in order that I may impart some spiritual gift to you, that you may be established;

12that is, that I may be encouraged together with you *while* among you, each of us by the other's faith, both yours and mine.

---

1 Παῦλος δοῦλος Χριστοῦ 'Ιησοῦ, κλητὸς
Paul a slave of Christ Jesus, called

ἀπόστολος ἀφωρισμένος εἰς εὐαγγέλιον
an apostle *having been* separated to [the] gospel

θεοῦ, **2** ὃ προεπηγγείλατο διὰ τῶν
of God, which he promised beforehand through the

προφητῶν αὐτοῦ ἐν γραφαῖς ἁγίαις **3** περὶ
prophets of him in writings holy concerning

τοῦ υἱοῦ αὐτοῦ τοῦ γενομένου ἐκ
the Son of him – come of

σπέρματος Δαυὶδ κατὰ σάρκα, **4** τοῦ
[the] seed of David according to [the] flesh, –

ὁρισθέντος υἱοῦ θεοῦ ἐν δυνάμει
designated Son of God in power

κατὰ πνεῦμα ἁγιωσύνης ἐξ ἀναστάσεως
according to [the] Spirit of holiness by a resurrection

νεκρῶν, 'Ιησοῦ Χριστοῦ τοῦ κυρίου ἡμῶν,
of dead persons, Jesus Christ the Lord of us.

5 δι' οὗ ἐλάβομεν χάριν καὶ ἀποστολὴν
through whom we received grace and apostleship

εἰς ὑπακοὴν πίστεως ἐν πᾶσιν τοῖς
for obedience of faith among all the

ἔθνεσιν ὑπὲρ τοῦ ὀνόματος αὐτοῦ, **6** ἐν
nations on behalf of the name of him, among

οἷς ἐστε καὶ ὑμεῖς κλητοὶ 'Ιησοῦ Χριστοῦ,
whom are also ye called of Jesus Christ,

7 πᾶσιν τοῖς οὖσιν ἐν 'Ρώμῃ ἀγαπητοῖς
to all the [ones] being in Rome beloved

θεοῦ, κλητοῖς ἁγίοις· χάρις ὑμῖν καὶ
of God, called holy· Grace to you and

εἰρήνη ἀπὸ θεοῦ πατρὸς ἡμῶν καὶ κυρίου
peace from God [the] Father of us and Lord

'Ιησοῦ Χριστοῦ.
Jesus Christ.

8 Πρῶτον μὲν εὐχαριστῶ τῷ θεῷ μου
Firstly – I thank the God of me

διὰ 'Ιησοῦ Χριστοῦ περὶ πάντων ὑμῶν,
through Jesus Christ concerning all you,

ὅτι ἡ πίστις ὑμῶν καταγγέλλεται ἐν
because the faith of you is being announced in

ὅλῳ τῷ κόσμῳ. **9** μάρτυς γάρ μού
all the world. For witness of me

ἐστιν ὁ θεός, ᾧ λατρεύω ἐν τῷ πνεύματί
is – God, whom I serve in the spirit

μου ἐν τῷ εὐαγγελίῳ τοῦ υἱοῦ αὐτοῦ,
of me in the gospel of the Son of him,

ὡς ἀδιαλείπτως μνείαν ὑμῶν ποιοῦμαι
how unceasingly mention of you I make

10 πάντοτε ἐπὶ τῶν προσευχῶν μου,
always on(in) the prayers of me,

δεόμενος εἴ πως ἤδη ποτὲ εὐοδω-
requesting if somehow now at some time I shall have

θήσομαι ἐν τῷ θελήματι τοῦ θεοῦ ἐλθεῖν
a happy journey in the will – of God to come

πρὸς ὑμᾶς. **11** ἐπιποθῶ γὰρ ἰδεῖν ὑμᾶς,
unto you. For I long to see you,

ἵνα τι μεταδῶ χάρισμα ὑμῖν πνευματικὸν
that ²some ¹I may impart ⁴gift ³to you ³spiritual

εἰς τὸ στηριχθῆναι ὑμᾶς, **12** τοῦτο δέ
for the to be established you,*b* and this
=that ye may be established,

ἐστιν συμπαρακληθῆναι ἐν ὑμῖν διὰ τῆς
is to be encouraged *with* among you through ¹the

ἐν ἀλλήλοις πίστεως ὑμῶν τε καὶ ἐμοῦ.
²in ⁴one another ²faith ⁶of you ⁵both ⁷and ⁸of me.

Chapter 1

PAUL, a servant of Christ Jesus, called to be an apostle and set apart for the gospel of God—

2the gospel he promised beforehand through his prophets in the Holy Scriptures

3regarding his Son, who as to his human nature was a descendant of David,

4and who through the Spirit *a* of holiness was declared with power to be the Son of God*b* by his resurrection from the dead: Jesus Christ our Lord.

5Through him and for his name's sake, we received grace and apostleship to call people from among all the Gentiles to the obedience that comes from faith.

6And you also are among those who are called to belong to Jesus Christ.

7To all in Rome who are loved by God and called to be saints:

Grace and peace to you from God our Father and from the Lord Jesus Christ.

Paul's Longing to Visit Rome

8First, I thank my God through Jesus Christ for all of you, because your faith is being reported all over the world.

9God, whom I serve with my whole heart in preaching the gospel of his Son, is my witness how constantly I remember you

10in my prayers at all times; and I pray that now at last by God's will the way may be opened for me to come to you.

11I long to see you so that I may impart to you some spiritual gift to make you strong—

12that is, that you and I may be mutually encouraged by each other's

---

a Or, as a result of

*a*4 Or who as to his spirit
*b*4 Or was appointed to be the Son of God with power

13And I do not want you to be unaware, brethren, that often I have planned to come to you (and have been prevented thus far) in order that I might obtain some fruit among you also, even as among the rest of the Gentiles.

14I am [b]under obligation both to Greeks and to barbarians, both to the wise and to the foolish.

15Thus, for my part, I am eager to preach the gospel to you also who are in Rome.

16For I am not ashamed of the gospel, for it is the power of God for salvation to everyone who believes, to the Jew first and also to the Greek.

17For in it *the* righteousness of God is revealed from faith to faith; as it is written, "BUT THE RIGHTEOUS *man* SHALL LIVE BY FAITH."

Unbelief and Its Consequences

18For the wrath of God is revealed from heaven against all ungodliness and unrighteousness of men, who suppress the truth in unrighteousness,

19because that which is known about God is evident within them; for God made it evident to them.

20For since the creation of the world His invisible attributes, His eternal power and divine nature, have been clearly seen, being understood through what has been made, so that they are without excuse.

21For even though they knew God, they did not [c]honor Him as God, or give thanks; but they became futile in their speculations, and their foolish heart was darkened.

22Professing to be fools, they became fools,

23and exchanged the glory of the incorruptible God for an image in the form of corruptible man and of birds and four-footed animals and [d]crawling creatures.

---

13 οὐ θέλω δὲ ὑμᾶς ἀγνοεῖν, ἀδελφοί,
[3]not [1]I wish [1]But you to be ignorant, brothers,

ὅτι πολλάκις προεθέμην ἐλθεῖν πρὸς ὑμᾶς,
that often I purposed to come unto you,

καὶ ἐκωλύθην ἄχρι τοῦ δεῦρο, ἵνα τινὰ
and was hindered until the present, that some

καρπὸν σχῶ καὶ ἐν ὑμῖν καθὼς καὶ
fruit I may have also among you as indeed

ἐν τοῖς λοιποῖς ἔθνεσιν. 14 Ἕλλησίν
among the remaining nations. [2]to Greeks

τε καὶ βαρβάροις, σοφοῖς τε καὶ ἀνοήτοις
[1]Both [3]and [4]to foreigners, [5]to wise men [6]both [7]and [8]to foolish

ὀφειλέτης εἰμί· 15 οὕτως τὸ κατ᾽ ἐμὲ
[1,9]a debtor [9]I am; so as far as in me lies†

πρόθυμον καὶ ὑμῖν τοῖς ἐν Ῥώμῃ
[I am] eager [2]also [3]to you [4]the [ones] [5]in [6]Rome

εὐαγγελίσασθαι. 16 οὐ γὰρ ἐπαισχύνομαι
[1]to preach. For I am not ashamed of

τὸ εὐαγγέλιον· δύναμις γὰρ θεοῦ ἐστιν
the gospel; [2]power [1]for of God it is

εἰς σωτηρίαν παντὶ τῷ πιστεύοντι, Ἰουδαίῳ
to salvation to everyone believing, [1]to Jew

τε πρῶτον καὶ Ἕλληνι. 17 δικαιοσύνη
[1]both firstly and to Greek. a righteousness

γὰρ θεοῦ ἐν αὐτῷ ἀποκαλύπτεται ἐκ
For of God in it is revealed from

πίστεως εἰς πίστιν, καθὼς γέγραπται·
faith to faith, as it has been written:

ὁ δὲ δίκαιος ἐκ πίστεως ζήσεται.
Now the just man by faith will live.

18 Ἀποκαλύπτεται γὰρ ὀργὴ θεοῦ ἀπ᾽
For [4]is revealed [1][the] [2]wrath [3]of God from

οὐρανοῦ ἐπὶ πᾶσαν ἀσέβειαν καὶ ἀδικίαν
heaven against all impiety and unrighteousness

ἀνθρώπων τῶν τὴν ἀλήθειαν ἐν ἀδικίᾳ
of men – [3]the [2]truth [4]in [5]unrighteousness

κατεχόντων, 19 διότι τὸ γνωστὸν τοῦ θεοῦ
[1]holding fast, because the thing known – of God

φανερόν ἐστιν ἐν αὐτοῖς· ὁ θεὸς γὰρ αὐτοῖς
manifest is among them; – for God to them

ἐφανέρωσεν. 20 τὰ γὰρ ἀόρατα αὐτοῦ
manifested [it]. For the invisible things of him

ἀπὸ κτίσεως κόσμου τοῖς ποιήμασιν
[2]from [3][the] [4]creation [5]of [the] world [6]by the [8]things made

νοούμενα καθορᾶται, ἥ τε
[6]being understood [1]is(are) clearly seen, [10]the [9]both

ἀΐδιος αὐτοῦ δύναμις καὶ θειότης, εἰς
[11]everlasting [15]of him [12]power [13]and [14]divinity, for

τὸ εἶναι αὐτοὺς ἀναπολογήτους, 21 διότι
the to be them[b] without excuse, because
=so that they are

γνόντες τὸν θεὸν οὐχ ὡς θεὸν ἐδόξασαν
knowing – God [1]not [2]as [4]God [1]they glorified [him]

ἢ ηὐχαρίστησαν, ἀλλὰ ἐματαιώθησαν ἐν
[1]or [2]thanked [him], but became vain in

τοῖς διαλογισμοῖς αὐτῶν, καὶ ἐσκοτίσθη
the reasonings of them, and [5]was darkened

ἡ ἀσύνετος αὐτῶν καρδία. 22 φάσκοντες
[1]the [2]undiscerning [4]of them [3]heart. Asserting

εἶναι σοφοὶ ἐμωράνθησαν, 23 καὶ ἤλλαξαν
to be wise they became foolish, and changed

τὴν δόξαν τοῦ ἀφθάρτου θεοῦ ἐν ὁμοιώματι
the glory of the incorruptible God in[to] a likeness

εἰκόνος φθαρτοῦ ἀνθρώπου καὶ πετεινῶν
of an image of corruptible man and birds

καὶ τετραπόδων καὶ ἑρπετῶν· 24 διὸ
and quadrupeds and reptiles; wherefore

---

faith. 13I do not want you to be unaware, brothers, that I planned many times to come to you (but have been prevented from doing so until now) in order that I might have a harvest among you, just as I have had among the other Gentiles.

14I am obligated both to Greeks and non-Greeks, both to the wise and the foolish. 15That is why I am so eager to preach the gospel also to you who are at Rome.

16I am not ashamed of the gospel, because it is the power of God for the salvation of everyone who believes: first for the Jew, then for the Gentile. 17For in the gospel a righteousness from God is revealed, a righteousness that is by faith from first to last, [c] just as it is written: "The righteous will live by faith." [d]

God's Wrath Against Mankind

18The wrath of God is being revealed from heaven against all the godlessness and wickedness of men who suppress the truth by their wickedness, 19since what may be known about God is plain to them, because God has made it plain to them. 20For since the creation of the world God's invisible qualities—his eternal power and divine nature—have been clearly seen, being understood from what has been made, so that men are without excuse.

21For although they knew God, they neither glorified him as God nor gave thanks to him, but their thinking became futile and their foolish hearts were darkened. 22Although they claimed to be wise, they became fools 23and exchanged the glory of the immortal God for images made to look like mortal man and birds and animals and reptiles.

---

[b] Lit., *debtor*
[c] Lit., *glorify*
[d] Or possibly, *reptiles*

[c]17 Or *is from faith to faith*
[d]17 Hab. 2:4

24Therefore God gave them over in the lusts of their hearts to impurity, that their bodies might be dishonored among them.

25For they exchanged the truth of God for a lie, and worshiped and served the creature rather than the Creator, who is blessed forever. Amen.

26For this reason God gave them over to degrading passions; for their women exchanged the natural function for that which is unnatural,

27and in the same way also the men abandoned the natural function of the woman and burned in their desire toward one another, men with men committing indecent acts and receiving in their own persons the due penalty of their error.

28And just as they did not see fit to acknowledge God any longer, God gave them over to a depraved mind, to do those things which are not proper,

29being filled with all unrighteousness, wickedness, greed, evil; full of envy, murder, strife, deceit, malice; they are gossips,

30slanderers, haters of God, insolent, arrogant, boastful, inventors of evil, disobedient to parents,

31without understanding, untrustworthy, unloving, unmerciful;

32and, although they know the ordinance of God, that those who practice such things are worthy of death, they not only do the same, but also give hearty approval to those who practice them.

παρέδωκεν αὐτοὺς ὁ θεὸς ἐν ταῖς
²gave up ³them - ¹God in the

ἐπιθυμίαις τῶν καρδιῶν αὐτῶν εἰς ἀκαθαρ-
desires of the hearts of them to unclean-

σίαν τοῦ ἀτιμάζεσθαι τὰ σώματα αὐτῶν
ness - to be dishonoured⁴ the bodies of them

ἐν αὐτοῖς. 25 Οἴτινες μετήλλαξαν τὴν
among them[selves]. Who changed the

ἀλήθειαν τοῦ θεοῦ ἐν τῷ ψεύδει, καὶ
truth - of God in[to] the lie, and

ἐσεβάσθησαν καὶ ἐλάτρευσαν τῇ κτίσει
worshipped and served the creature

παρὰ τὸν κτίσαντα, ὅς ἐστιν εὐλογητὸς
rather the [one] having created, who is blessed
than

εἰς τοὺς αἰῶνας· ἀμήν. 26 διὰ τοῦτο
unto the ages: Amen. Therefore

παρέδωκεν αὐτοὺς ὁ θεὸς εἰς πάθη
²gave up ³them - ¹God to passions

ἀτιμίας· αἵ τε γὰρ θήλειαι αὐτῶν
of dishonour; ⁴the ²even . ¹for females of them

μετήλλαξαν τὴν φυσικὴν χρῆσιν εἰς τὴν
changed the natural use to the [use]

παρὰ φύσιν, 27 ὁμοίως τε καὶ οἱ ἄρσενες
against nature, likewise and also the males

ἀφέντες τὴν φυσικὴν χρῆσιν τῆς θηλείας
leaving the natural use of the female

ἐξεκαύθησαν ἐν τῇ ὀρέξει αὐτῶν εἰς
burned in the desire of them toward

ἀλλήλους, ἄρσενες ἐν ἄρσεσιν τὴν
one another, males among males ³the

ἀσχημοσύνην κατεργαζόμενοι καὶ τὴν
²unseemliness ¹working and ⁴the

ἀντιμισθίαν ἣν ἔδει τῆς πλάνης αὐτῶν
⁵requital ⁶which ¹⁰behoved ⁸of the ⁷error ⁹of them

ἐν ἑαυτοῖς ἀπολαμβάνοντες. 28 Καὶ
¹in ³themselves ¹receiving back. And

καθὼς οὐκ ἐδοκίμασαν τὸν θεὸν ἔχειν
as they thought not fit - God to have

ἐν ἐπιγνώσει, παρέδωκεν αὐτοὺς ὁ θεὸς
in knowledge, ²gave up ³them - ¹God

εἰς ἀδόκιμον νοῦν, ποιεῖν τὰ μὴ καθήκοντα,
to a reprobate mind, to do the not being proper,
things

29 πεπληρωμένους πάσῃ ἀδικίᾳ πονηρίᾳ
having been filled with all unrighteousness wickedness

πλεονεξίᾳ κακίᾳ, μεστοὺς φθόνου φόνου
covetousness evil, full of envy of murder

ἔριδος δόλου κακοηθείας, ψιθυριστάς,
of strife of guile of malignity, whisperers,*

30 καταλάλους, θεοστυγεῖς, ὑβριστάς, ὑπερ-
railers, God-haters, insolent, arro-

ηφάνους, ἀλαζόνας, ἐφευρετὰς κακῶν,
gant, boasters, inventors of evil things,

γονεῦσιν ἀπειθεῖς, 31 ἀσυνέτους, ἀσυνθέτους,
to parents disobedient, undiscerning, faithless,

ἀστόργους, ἀνελεήμονας· 32 οἴτινες τὸ
without unmerciful; who ²the
natural affection,

δικαίωμα τοῦ θεοῦ ἐπιγνόντες, ὅτι οἱ
³ordinance - ⁴of God ¹knowing, that the

τὰ τοιαῦτα πράσσοντες ἄξιοι θανάτου
the ²such things ¹[ones] practising worthy of death

εἰσίν, οὐ μόνον αὐτὰ ποιοῦσιν, ἀλλὰ
are, not only them do, but

καὶ συνευδοκοῦσιν τοῖς πράσσουσιν.
also consent to the [ones] practising.

* " In a bad sense " (Abbott-Smith).

24Therefore God gave them over in the sinful desires of their hearts to sexual impurity for the degrading of their bodies with one another. 25They exchanged the truth of God for a lie, and worshiped and served created things rather than the Creator—who is forever praised. Amen.

26Because of this, God gave them over to shameful lusts. Even their women exchanged natural relations for unnatural ones. 27In the same way the men also abandoned natural relations with women and were inflamed with lust for one another. Men committed indecent acts with other men, and received in themselves the due penalty for their perversion.

28Furthermore, since they did not think it worthwhile to retain the knowledge of God, he gave them over to a depraved mind, to do what ought not to be done. 29They have become filled with every kind of wickedness, evil, greed and depravity. They are full of envy, murder, strife, deceit and malice. They are gossips, 30slanderers, God-haters, insolent, arrogant and boastful; they invent ways of doing evil; they disobey their parents; 31they are senseless, faithless, heartless, ruthless. 32Although they know God's righteous decree that those who do such things deserve death, they not only continue to do these very things but also approve of those who practice them.

Chapter 2

The Impartiality of God

THEREFORE you are without excuse, every man *of you* who passes judgment, for in that you judge another, you condemn yourself; for you who judge practice the same things.

2And we know that the judgment of God rightly falls upon those who practice such things.

3And do you suppose this, O man, when you pass judgment upon those who practice such things and do the same *yourself*, that you will escape the judgment of God?

4Or do you think lightly of the riches of His kindness and forbearance and patience, not knowing that the kindness of God leads you to repentance?

5But because of your stubbornness and unrepentant heart you are storing up wrath for yourself in the day of wrath and revelation of the righteous judgment of God,

6who WILL RENDER TO EVERY MAN ACCORDING TO HIS DEEDS:

7to those who by perseverance in doing good seek for glory and honor and immortality, eternal life;

8but to those who are selfishly ambitious and do not obey the truth, but obey unrighteousness, wrath and indignation.

9*There will be* tribulation and distress for every soul of man who does evil, of the Jew first and also of the Greek,

10but glory and honor and peace to every man who does good, to the Jew first and also to the Greek.

11For there is no partiality with God.

12For all who have sinned without the Law will also

Chapter 2

2 Διὸ ἀναπολόγητος εἶ, ὦ ἄνθρωπε
Wherefore inexcusable thou art, O man

πᾶς ὁ κρίνων· ἐν ᾧ γὰρ κρίνεις τὸν
everyone judging; ²in ²what ¹for thou judgest the

ἕτερον, σεαυτὸν κατακρίνεις· τὰ γὰρ αὐτὰ
other, thyself thou for the same
condemnest; things

πράσσεις ὁ κρίνων. **2** οἴδαμεν δὲ ὅτι τὸ
thou the judging. But we know that the
practisest [one]

κρίμα τοῦ θεοῦ ἐστιν κατὰ ἀλήθειαν ἐπὶ
judg- - of is accord- truth on
ment God ing to

τοὺς τὰ τοιαῦτα πράσσοντας. **3** λογίζῃ
the the ²such things ¹[ones] practising. reckonest thou

δὲ τοῦτο, ὦ ἄνθρωπε ὁ κρίνων τοὺς
And this, O man the judging the
[one] [ones]

τὰ τοιαῦτα πράσσοντας καὶ ποιῶν αὐτά,
the such things practising and doing them,

ὅτι σὺ ἐκφεύξῃ τὸ κρίμα τοῦ θεοῦ;
that thou wilt escape the judgment - of God?

4 ἢ τοῦ πλούτου τῆς χρηστότητος αὐτοῦ
or the riches of the kindness of him

καὶ τῆς ἀνοχῆς καὶ τῆς μακροθυμίας
and the forbearance and the longsuffering

καταφρονεῖς, ἀγνοῶν ὅτι τὸ χρηστὸν τοῦ
despisest thou, not knowing that the kindness -

θεοῦ εἰς μετάνοιάν σε ἄγει; **5** κατὰ δὲ
of God to repentance thee leads? but according to

τὴν σκληρότητά σου καὶ ἀμετανόητον
the hardness of thee and impenitent

καρδίαν θησαυρίζεις σεαυτῷ ὀργὴν ἐν
heart treasurest for thyself wrath in

ἡμέρᾳ ὀργῆς καὶ ἀποκαλύψεως δικαιοκρισίας
a day of wrath and *of* revelation of a righteous
judgment

τοῦ θεοῦ, **6** ὃς ἀποδώσει ἑκάστῳ κατὰ τὰ
- of God, who will requite to each man accord- the
ing to

ἔργα αὐτοῦ· **7** τοῖς μὲν καθ' ὑπομονὴν
works of him : to the on ²by ¹endurance
[ones] one hand

ἔργου ἀγαθοῦ δόξαν καὶ τιμὴν καὶ
³work ⁴of(in) good ⁵glory ⁷and ⁸honour ⁹and

ἀφθαρσίαν ζητοῦσιν ζωὴν αἰώνιον·
¹⁰incorruption ¹seeking ¹¹life ¹¹eternal;

8 τοῖς δὲ ἐξ ἐριθείας καὶ ἀπειθοῦσι τῇ
to the [ones] of self-seeking and disobeying the
on the other

ἀληθείᾳ πειθομένοις δὲ τῇ ἀδικίᾳ, ὀργὴ
truth ²obeying ¹but - unrighteousness, wrath

καὶ θυμός. **9** θλῖψις καὶ στενοχωρία ἐπὶ
and anger. Affliction and anguish on

πᾶσαν ψυχὴν ἀνθρώπου τοῦ κατεργαζομένου
every soul of man - working

τὸ κακόν, Ἰουδαίου τε πρῶτον καὶ
the evil, both of Jew firstly and

Ἕλληνος· **10** δόξα δὲ καὶ τιμὴ καὶ
of Greek; but glory and honour and

εἰρήνη παντὶ τῷ ἐργαζομένῳ τὸ ἀγαθόν,
peace to everyone working the good,

Ἰουδαίῳ τε πρῶτον καὶ Ἕλληνι. **11** οὐ
both to Jew firstly and to Greek. not

γάρ ἐστιν προσωπολημψία παρὰ τῷ θεῷ.
For is respect of persons with - God.

12 Ὅσοι γὰρ ἀνόμως ἥμαρτον, ἀνόμως
For as many as without law sinned, without law

Chapter 2

God's Righteous Judgment

YOU, therefore, have no excuse, you who pass judgment on someone else, for at whatever point you judge the other, you are condemning yourself, because you who pass judgment do the same things. 2Now we know that God's judgment against those who do such things is based on truth. 3So when you, a mere man, pass judgment on them and yet do the same things, do you think you will escape God's judgment? 4Or do you show contempt for the riches of his kindness, tolerance and patience, not realizing that God's kindness leads you toward repentance?

5But because of your stubbornness and your unrepentant heart, you are storing up wrath against yourself for the day of God's wrath, when his righteous judgment will be revealed. 6God "will give to each person according to what he has done." *ᵉ* 7To those who by persistence in doing good seek glory, honor and immortality, he will give eternal life. 8But for those who are self-seeking and who reject the truth and follow evil, there will be wrath and anger. 9There will be trouble and distress for every human being who does evil: first for the Jew, then for the Gentile; 10but glory, honor and peace for everyone who does good: first for the Jew, then for the Gentile. 11For God does not show favoritism.

12All who sin apart from the law will also perish

ᵉ6 Psalm 62:12; Prov. 24:12

perish without the Law; and all who have sinned under the Law will be judged by the Law; [13]for not the hearers of the Law are just before God, but the doers of the Law will be justified. [14]For when Gentiles who do not have the Law do instinctively the things of the Law, these, not having the Law, are a law to themselves, [15]in that they show the work of the Law written in their hearts, their conscience bearing witness, and their thoughts alternately accusing or else defending them, [16]on the day when, according to my gospel, God will judge the secrets of men through Christ Jesus.

The Jew Is Condemned by the Law

[17]But if you bear the name "Jew," and rely upon the Law, and boast in God, [18]and know *His* will, and approve the things that are essential, being instructed out of the Law, [19]and are confident that you yourself are a guide to the blind, a light to those who are in darkness, [20]a corrector of the foolish, a teacher of the immature, having in the Law the embodiment of knowledge and of the truth, [21]you, therefore, who teach another, do you not teach yourself? You who preach that one should not steal, do you steal? [22]You who say that one should not commit adultery, do you commit adultery? You who abhor idols, do you rob temples? [23]You who boast in the Law, through your breaking the Law, do you dishonor God? [24]For "THE NAME OF GOD IS BLASPHEMED AMONG THE GENTILES BECAUSE OF YOU,"

καὶ ἀπολοῦνται· καὶ ὅσοι ἐν νόμῳ
also will perish; and as many as (under) in law

ἥμαρτον, διὰ νόμου κριθήσονται· **13** οὐ
sinned, through law will be judged; [1]not

γὰρ οἱ ἀκροαταὶ νόμου δίκαιοι παρὰ
[1]for the hearers of law [are] just with

[τῷ] θεῷ, ἀλλ' οἱ ποιηταὶ νόμου
[the] God, but the doers of law

δικαιωθήσονται. **14** ὅταν γὰρ ἔθνη τὰ
will be justified. For whenever nations —

μὴ νόμον ἔχοντα φύσει τὰ τοῦ νόμου
[1]not [3]law [2]having by nature the things of the law

ποιῶσιν, οὗτοι νόμον μὴ ἔχοντες ἑαυτοῖς
do, these [3]law [1]not [2]having to themselves

εἰσιν νόμος· **15** οἵτινες ἐνδείκνυνται τὸ
are a law; who show the

ἔργον τοῦ νόμου γραπτὸν ἐν ταῖς καρδίαις
work of the law written in the hearts

αὐτῶν, συμμαρτυρούσης αὐτῶν τῆς συνει-
of them, witnessing with of them the con-
= while their conscience witnesses with and their

δήσεως καὶ μεταξὺ ἀλλήλων τῶν λογισμῶν
science and between one another the thoughts
thoughts among themselves accuse or even excuse,

κατηγορούντων ἢ καὶ ἀπολογουμένων, **16** ἐν
accusing or even excusing,[a] in

ᾗ ἡμέρᾳ κρίνει ὁ θεὸς τὰ κρυπτὰ τῶν
what day judges — God the hidden things —

ἀνθρώπων κατὰ τὸ εὐαγγέλιόν μου διὰ
of men according to the gospel of me through

Χριστοῦ Ἰησοῦ. **17** Εἰ δὲ σὺ Ἰουδαῖος
Christ Jesus. But if thou [a]a Jew

ἐπονομάζῃ καὶ ἐπαναπαύῃ νόμῳ καὶ
[1]art named and restest on law and

καυχᾶσαι ἐν θεῷ **18** καὶ γινώσκεις τὸ
boastest in God and knowest the

θέλημα καὶ δοκιμάζεις τὰ διαφέροντα
will and approvest the things excelling

κατηχούμενος ἐκ τοῦ νόμου, **19** πέποιθάς τε
being instructed out of the law, and having persuaded

σεαυτὸν ὁδηγὸν εἶναι τυφλῶν, φῶς
thyself a guide to be of blind a light
[persons],

τῶν ἐν σκότει, **20** παιδευτὴν ἀφρόνων,
of the in darkness, an instructor of foolish
[ones] [persons],

διδάσκαλον νηπίων, ἔχοντα τὴν μόρφωσιν
a teacher of infants, having the form

τῆς γνώσεως καὶ τῆς ἀληθείας ἐν τῷ
— of knowledge and of the truth in the

νόμῳ· **21** ὁ οὖν διδάσκων ἕτερον σεαυτὸν
law: the there- teaching another thyself
[one] fore

οὐ διδάσκεις; ὁ κηρύσσων μὴ κλέπτειν
teachest thou not? the [one] proclaiming not to steal

κλέπτεις; **22** ὁ λέγων μὴ μοιχεύειν
stealest thou? the [one] saying not to commit adultery

μοιχεύεις; ὁ βδελυσσόμενος τὰ εἴδωλα
dost thou com- the detesting the idols
mit adultery? [one]

ἱεροσυλεῖς; **23** ὃς ἐν νόμῳ καυχᾶσαι, διὰ
dost thou rob who in law boastest, through
temples?

τῆς παραβάσεως τοῦ νόμου τὸν θεὸν
— transgression of the law — [a]God

ἀτιμάζεις; **24** τὸ γὰρ ὄνομα τοῦ θεοῦ
[1]dishonourest thou? for the name — of God

δι' ὑμᾶς βλασφημεῖται ἐν τοῖς ἔθνεσιν,
because you is blasphemed among the nations,
of

apart from the law, and all who sin under the law will be judged by the law. [13]For it is not those who hear the law who are righteous in God's sight, but it is those who obey the law who will be declared righteous. [14](Indeed, when Gentiles, who do not have the law, do by nature things required by the law, they are a law for themselves, even though they do not have the law, [15]since they show that the requirements of the law are written on their hearts, their consciences also bearing witness, and their thoughts now accusing, now even defending them.) [16]This will take place on the day when God will judge men's secrets through Jesus Christ, as my gospel declares.

The Jews and the Law

[17]Now you, if you call yourself a Jew; if you rely on the law and brag about your relationship to God; [18]if you know his will and approve of what is superior because you are instructed by the law; [19]if you are convinced that you are a guide for the blind, a light for those who are in the dark, [20]an instructor of the foolish, a teacher of infants, because you have in the law the embodiment of knowledge and truth— [21]you, then, who teach others, do you not teach yourself? You who preach against stealing, do you steal? [22]You who say that people should not commit adultery, do you commit adultery? You who abhor idols, do you rob temples? [23]You who brag about the law, do you dishonor God by breaking the law? [24]As it is written: "God's name is blasphemed among the Gentiles because of you." [f]

f 24 Isaiah 52:5; Ezek. 36:22

just as it is written.
25For indeed circumcision is of value, if you practice the Law; but if you are a transgressor of the Law, your circumcision has become uncircumcision.
26If therefore the uncircumcised man keeps the requirements of the Law, will not his uncircumcision be regarded as circumcision?
27And will not he who is physically uncircumcised, if he keeps the Law, while he not judge you who though having the letter of the Law and circumcision are a transgressor of the Law?
28For he is not a Jew who is one outwardly; neither is circumcision that which is outward in the flesh.
29But he is a Jew who is one inwardly; and circumcision is that which is of the heart, by the Spirit, not by the letter; and his praise is not from men, but from God.

καθὼς γέγραπται. 25 περιτομὴ μὲν γὰρ
as　　it has been written.　　circumcision indeed For

ὠφελεῖ ἐὰν νόμον πράσσῃς· ἐὰν δὲ
profits if law thou practisest; but if

παραβάτης νόμου ᾖς, ἡ περιτομή σου
a transgressor of law thou art, the circumcision of thee

ἀκροβυστία γέγονεν. 26 ἐὰν οὖν ἡ ἀκρο-
uncircumcision has become.　　If therefore the uncir-

βυστία τὰ δικαιώματα τοῦ νόμου φυλάσσῃ,
cumcision the ordinances of the law keeps,

οὐχ ἡ ἀκροβυστία αὐτοῦ εἰς περιτομὴν
not the uncircumcision of him for circumcision

λογισθήσεται; 27 καὶ κρινεῖ ἡ ἐκ φύσεως
will be reckoned? and *will judge ¹the ³by ⁴nature

ἀκροβυστία τὸν νόμον τελοῦσα σὲ τὸν
²uncircumcision ⁶the ⁷law ⁵keeping ⁹thee ¹⁰the

διὰ γράμματος καὶ περιτομῆς παραβάτην
¹³through ¹⁴letter ¹⁵and ¹⁶circumcision ¹¹transgressor

νόμου. 28 οὐ γὰρ ὁ ἐν τῷ φανερῷ
¹²of law.　For ²not ³the ⁵in ⁴the ⁷open

Ἰουδαῖός ἐστιν, οὐδὲ ἡ ἐν τῷ φανερῷ
⁸Jew ¹he is, nor ¹the ³in ⁴the ⁵open

ἐν σαρκὶ περιτομή· 29 ἀλλ' ὁ ἐν τῷ
⁶in ⁷flesh ²circumcision; but ¹the ³in ⁴the

κρυπτῷ Ἰουδαῖος, καὶ περιτομὴ καρδίας
⁵secret ²Jew [is], and circumcision [is] of heart

ἐν πνεύματι οὐ γράμματι, οὗ ὁ ἔπαινος
in spirit not letter, of the praise [is]
　　　　　　　　　　　　　　　whom

οὐκ ἐξ ἀνθρώπων ἀλλ' ἐκ τοῦ θεοῦ.
not from men but from - God.

25Circumcision has value if you observe the law, but if you break the law, you have become as though you had not been circumcised. 26If those who are not circumcised keep the law's requirements, will they not be regarded as though they were circumcised? 27The one who is not circumcised physically and yet obeys the law will condemn you who, even though you have the* written code and circumcision, are a lawbreaker.

28A man is not a Jew if he is only one outwardly, nor is circumcision merely outward and physical. 29No, a man is a Jew if he is one inwardly; and circumcision is circumcision of the heart, by the Spirit, not by the written code. Such a man's praise is not from men, but from God.

Chapter 3

All the World Guilty

THEN what advantage has the Jew? Or what is the benefit of circumcision?
2Great in every respect. First of all, that they were entrusted with the oracles of God.
3What then? If some did not believe, their unbelief will not nullify the faithfulness of God, will it?
4May it never be! Rather, let God be found true, though every man be found a liar, as it is written, "THAT THOU MIGHTEST BE JUSTIFIED IN THY WORDS, AND MIGHTEST PREVAIL WHEN THOU ART JUDGED."
5But if our unrighteousness demonstrates the righteousness of God, what shall we say? The God who inflicts wrath is not unrighteous, is He? (I am speaking in human terms.)
6May it never be! For otherwise how will God judge the world?
7But if through my lie the truth of God abounded to

---

3 Τί οὖν τὸ περισσὸν τοῦ Ἰουδαίου,
What therefore the advantage of the Jew,

ἢ τίς ἡ ὠφέλεια τῆς περιτομῆς; 2 πολὺ
or what the profit - of circumcision? Much

κατὰ πάντα τρόπον. πρῶτον μὲν [γὰρ]
by every way. ³Firstly ²indeed ¹for

ὅτι ἐπιστεύθησαν τὰ λόγια τοῦ θεοῦ.
because they were the oracles - of God.
　　entrusted [with]

3 τί γάρ; εἰ ἠπίστησάν τινες, μὴ ἡ
For what? If ²disbelieved ¹some, not the

ἀπιστία αὐτῶν τὴν πίστιν τοῦ θεοῦ
unbelief of them the faith - of God

καταργήσει; 4 μὴ γένοιτο· γινέσθω δὲ
will destroy? May it not be; but let be

ὁ θεὸς ἀληθής, πᾶς δὲ ἄνθρωπος ψεύστης,
- God true, and every man a liar,

καθάπερ γέγραπται· ὅπως ἂν δικαιωθῇς
as it has been So as - thou mayest
　　written: be justified

ἐν τοῖς λόγοις σου καὶ νικήσεις ἐν
in the sayings of thee and wilt overcome in

τῷ κρίνεσθαί σε. 5 εἰ δὲ ἡ ἀδικία
the to be judged thee.ᵇᵉ Now if the unright-
=when thou art judged.　　　　　　eousness

ἡμῶν θεοῦ δικαιοσύνην συνίστησιν, τί
of us ²of God ²a righteousness ¹commends, what

ἐροῦμεν; μὴ ἄδικος ὁ θεὸς ὁ ἐπιφέρων
shall we say? not unrighteous - God the [one] inflicting

τὴν ὀργήν; κατὰ ἄνθρωπον λέγω. 6 μὴ
- wrath? according to man I say. not

γένοιτο· ἐπεὶ πῶς κρινεῖ ὁ θεὸς τὸν
May it be; otherwise how will judge - God the

κόσμον; 7 εἰ δὲ ἡ ἀλήθεια τοῦ θεοῦ
world? But if the truth - of God

Chapter 3

God's Faithfulness

WHAT advantage, then, is there in being a Jew, or what value is there in circumcision? 2Much in every way! First of all, they have been entrusted with the very words of God.

3What if some did not have faith? Will their lack of faith nullify God's faithfulness? 4Not at all! Let God be true, and every man a liar. As it is written:

"So that you may be proved right when you speak and prevail when you judge."ʰ

5But if our unrighteousness brings out God's righteousness more clearly, what shall we say? That God is unjust in bringing his wrath on us? (I am using a human argument.) 6Certainly not! If that were so, how could God judge the world? 7Someone might argue, "If my falsehood en-

---

*27 Or who, by means of a
h4 Psalm 51:4

His glory, why am I also still being judged as a sinner?

8And why not *say* (as we are slanderously reported and as some affirm that we say), "Let us do evil that good may come"? Their condemnation is just.

9What then? Are we better than they? Not at all; for we have already charged that both Jews and Greeks are all under sin;

10as it is written,
"THERE IS NONE RIGHTEOUS, NOT EVEN ONE;
11 THERE IS NONE WHO UNDERSTANDS,
THERE IS NONE WHO SEEKS FOR GOD;
12 ALL HAVE TURNED ASIDE, TOGETHER THEY HAVE BECOME USELESS;
THERE IS NONE WHO DOES GOOD,
THERE IS NOT EVEN ONE."
13"THEIR THROAT IS AN OPEN GRAVE,
WITH THEIR TONGUES THEY KEEP DECEIVING,"
"THE POISON OF ASPS IS UNDER THEIR LIPS";
14"WHOSE MOUTH IS FULL OF CURSING AND BITTERNESS";
15"THEIR FEET ARE SWIFT TO SHED BLOOD,
16 DESTRUCTION AND MISERY ARE IN THEIR PATHS,
17 AND THE PATH OF PEACE HAVE THEY NOT KNOWN."
18"THERE IS NO FEAR OF GOD BEFORE THEIR EYES."

19Now we know that whatever the Law says, it speaks to those who are under the Law, that every mouth may be closed, and all the world may become accountable to God;
20because by the works of the Law no flesh will be justified in His sight; for through the Law *comes* the knowledge of sin.

Justification by Faith

21But now apart from the Law *the* righteousness of God has been manifested, being witnessed by the

ἐν τῷ ἐμῷ ψεύσματι ἐπερίσσευσεν εἰς
by - my lie abounded to
τὴν δόξαν αὐτοῦ, τί ἔτι κἀγὼ ὡς
the glory of him, why still I also as
ἁμαρτωλὸς κρίνομαι; 8 καὶ μὴ καθὼς
a sinner am judged? and not as
βλασφημούμεθα καὶ καθώς φασίν τινες
we are blasphemed and as ¹say ¹some
ἡμᾶς λέγειν ὅτι ποιήσωμεν τὰ κακὰ
us to say[,] - Let us do - evil things
= that we say,
ἵνα ἔλθη τὰ ἀγαθά; ὧν τὸ κρίμα
that may come - good things? of whom the judgment
ἔνδικόν ἐστιν. 9 Τί οὖν; προεχόμεθα;
just is. What therefore? Do we excel?
οὐ πάντως· προῃτιασάμεθα γὰρ ᾽Ιουδαίους
not at all; for we previously accused ²Jews
τε καὶ ῞Ελληνας πάντας ὑφ᾽ ἁμαρτίαν
¹both and Greeks all under sin
εἶναι, 10 καθὼς γέγραπται ὅτι οὐκ ἔστιν
to be, as it has been written[,] - There is not
δίκαιος οὐδὲ εἷς, οὐκ ἔστιν ὁ
a righteous man not one, there is not the [one]
συνίων, 11 οὐκ ἔστιν ὁ ἐκζητῶν τὸν θεόν·
under- there is not the seeking - God;
standing, [one]
12 πάντες ἐξέκλιναν, ἅμα ἠχρεώθησαν·
all turned away, together became unprofitable;
οὐκ ἔστιν ὁ ποιῶν χρηστότητα, οὐκ
there is not the [one] doing kindness, not
ἔστιν ἕως ἑνός. 13 τάφος ἀνεῳγμένος
there is so much as one. A grave *having been* opened
ὁ λάρυγξ αὐτῶν, ταῖς γλώσσαις αὐτῶν
the throat of them, with the tongues of them
ἐδολιοῦσαν, ἰὸς ἀσπίδων ὑπὸ τὰ χείλη
they acted poison of asps under the lips
deceitfully,
αὐτῶν· 14 ὧν τὸ στόμα ἀρᾶς καὶ πικρίας
of them; of whom the mouth ²of cursing ³and ⁴bitterness
γέμει· 15 ὀξεῖς οἱ πόδες αὐτῶν ἐκχέαι
¹is full; swift the feet of them to shed
αἷμα, 16 σύντριμμα καὶ ταλαιπωρία ἐν
blood, ruin and misery in
ταῖς ὁδοῖς αὐτῶν, 17 καὶ ὁδὸν εἰρήνης
the ways of them, and a way of peace
οὐκ ἔγνωσαν. 18 οὐκ ἔστιν φόβος θεοῦ
they knew not. There is not fear of God
ἀπέναντι τῶν ὀφθαλμῶν αὐτῶν. 19 οἴδαμεν
before the eyes of them. we know
δὲ ὅτι ὅσα ὁ νόμος λέγει τοῖς ἐν τῷ
But that whatever the law says to the in the
things [ones]
νόμῳ λαλεῖ, ἵνα πᾶν στόμα φραγῇ καὶ
law it speaks, in order that every mouth may be stopped and
ὑπόδικος γένηται πᾶς ὁ κόσμος τῷ
⁵under ⁴may become ¹all ²the ³world -
judgment
θεῷ· 20 διότι ἐξ ἔργων νόμου οὐ
to God; because by works of law not
δικαιωθήσεται πᾶσα σάρξ ἐνώπιον αὐτοῦ·
will be justified all flesh* before him;
διὰ γὰρ νόμου ἐπίγνωσις ἁμαρτίας.
for through law [is] full knowledge of sin.
21 Νυνὶ δὲ χωρὶς νόμου δικαιοσύνη
But now without law a righteousness
θεοῦ πεφανέρωται, μαρτυρουμένη ὑπὸ τοῦ
of God has been manifested, being witnessed by the

* That is, no flesh will be justified . . .

hances God's truthfulness and so increases his glory, why am I still condemned as a sinner?" 8Why not say —as we are being slanderously reported as saying and as some claim that we say—"Let us do evil that good may result"? Their condemnation is deserved.

No One Is Righteous

9What shall we conclude then? Are we any betterⁱ? Not at all! We have already made the charge that Jews and Gentiles alike are all under sin. 10As it is written:

"There is no one righteous, not even one;
11 there is no one who understands,
no one who seeks God.
12All have turned away,
they have together become worthless;
there is no one who does good,
not even one."ʲ
13"Their throats are open graves;
their tongues practice deceit."ᵏ
"The poison of vipers is on their lips."ˡ
14 "Their mouths are full of cursing and bitterness."ᵐ
15"Their feet are swift to shed blood;
16 ruin and misery mark their ways,
17and the way of peace they do not know."ⁿ
18 "There is no fear of God before their eyes."ᵒ

19Now we know that whatever the law says, it says to those who are under the law, so that every mouth may be silenced and the whole world held accountable to God. 20Therefore no one will be declared righteous in his sight by observing the law; rather, through the law we become conscious of sin.

Righteousness Through Faith

21But now a righteousness from God, apart from law, has been made known,

ⁱ9 Or *worse*
ʲ12 Psalms 14:1-3; 53:1-3; Eccles. 7:20
ᵏ13 Psalm 5:9
ˡ13 Psalm 140:3
ᵐ14 Psalm 10:7
ⁿ17 Isaiah 59:7,8
ᵒ18 Psalm 36:1

Law and the Prophets,
22even *the* righteousness of God through faith in Jesus Christ for all those who believe; for there is no distinction;
23for all have sinned and fall short of the glory of God,
24being justified as a gift by His grace through the redemption which is in Christ Jesus;
25whom God displayed publicly as a propitiation in His blood through faith. *This was* to demonstrate His righteousness, because in the forbearance of God He passed over the sins previously committed;
26for the demonstration, *I say,* of His righteousness at the present time, that He might be just and the justifier of the one who has faith in Jesus.
27Where then is boasting? It is excluded. By what kind of law? Of works? No, but by a law of faith.
28For we maintain that a man is justified by faith apart from works of the Law.
29Or is God *the God* of Jews only? Is He not *the God* of Gentiles also? Yes, of Gentiles also,
30since indeed God who will justify the circumcised by faith and the uncircumcised through faith is one.
31Do we then nullify the Law through faith? May it never be! On the contrary, we establish the Law.

Chapter 4

Justification by Faith Evidenced in Old Testament

WHAT then shall we say that Abraham, our forefather according to the flesh, has found?
2For if Abraham was justified by works, he has something to boast about; but not before God.
3For what does the Scripture say? "AND ABRAHAM BELIEVED GOD, AND IT WAS RECKONED TO HIM AS

νόμου   καὶ   τῶν   προφητῶν,   **22** δικαιοσύνη
law   and   the   prophets,   ²a righteousness

δὲ   θεοῦ   διὰ   πίστεως   ['Ιησοῦ]   Χριστοῦ,
¹and of God through   faith   of(in) Jesus   Christ,

εἰς   πάντας   τοὺς   πιστεύοντας·   οὐ   γὰρ
to   all   the [ones]   believing;   for not

ἐστιν   διαστολή·   **23** πάντες   γὰρ   ἥμαρτον
there is   difference;   for all   sinned

καὶ   ὑστεροῦνται   τῆς   δόξης   τοῦ   θεοῦ,
and   come short   of the   glory   -   of God,

24 δικαιούμενοι   δωρεὰν   τῇ   αὐτοῦ   χάριτι
being justified   freely   by the   of him   grace

διὰ   τῆς   ἀπολυτρώσεως   τῆς   ἐν   Χριστῷ
through the   redemption   -   in   Christ

'Ιησοῦ·   **25** ὃν   προέθετο   ὁ   θεὸς   ἱλαστήριον
Jesus;   whom   set forth   -   God   a propitiation

διὰ   πίστεως   ἐν   τῷ   αὐτοῦ   αἵματι,   εἰς
through   faith   by   the   of him   blood,   for

ἔνδειξιν   τῆς   δικαιοσύνης   αὐτοῦ   διὰ   τὴν
a showing   of the   righteousness   of him because of   the
forth

πάρεσιν   τῶν   προγεγονότων   ἁμαρτημάτων
passing by   of the   ²having previously   ¹sins
     occurred

26 ἐν   τῇ   ἀνοχῇ   τοῦ   θεοῦ,   πρὸς   τὴν
in   the   forbearance   -   of God,   for   the

ἔνδειξιν   τῆς   δικαιοσύνης   αὐτοῦ   ἐν   τῷ
showing   of the   righteousness   of him   in   the
forth

νῦν   καιρῷ,   εἰς   τὸ   εἶναι   αὐτὸν   δίκαιον
present time,   for   the   to be   him[b]   just
    =that he should be

καὶ   δικαιοῦντα   τὸν   ἐκ   πίστεως   'Ιησοῦ.
and   justifying   the [one]   of   faith   of(in) Jesus.

27 Ποῦ   οὖν   ἡ   καύχησις;   ἐξεκλείσθη.   διὰ
Where there- the   boasting?   It was shut out. Through
fore

ποίου   νόμου;   τῶν   ἔργων;   οὐχί,   ἀλλὰ
what   law?   -   of works?   no,   but

διὰ   νόμου   πίστεως.   **28** λογιζόμεθα   γὰρ
through a law   of faith.   For we reckon

δικαιοῦσθαι   πίστει   ἄνθρωπον   χωρὶς   ἔργων
²to be justified   ³by faith   ¹a man   without   works

νόμου.   **29** ἢ   'Ιουδαίων   ὁ   θεὸς   μόνον;
of law.   Or   of Jews [is he]   the   God   only?

οὐχὶ   καὶ   ἐθνῶν;   ναὶ   καὶ   ἐθνῶν,   **30** εἴπερ
not   also   of nations? Yes[,]   also of nations, since [there is]

εἷς   ὁ   θεὸς   ὃς   δικαιώσει   περιτομὴν   ἐκ
one   -   God   who   will justify   circumcision   by

πίστεως   καὶ   ἀκροβυστίαν   διὰ   τῆς   πίστεως.
faith   and   uncircumcision through the   faith.

31 νόμον   οὖν   καταργοῦμεν   διὰ   τῆς
³Law   ⁵therefore   ¹do we destroy   through   the

πίστεως;   μὴ   γένοιτο,   ἀλλὰ   νόμον   ἱστάνομεν.
faith?   May it not be,   but   ²law   ¹we establish.

4 Τί   οὖν   ἐροῦμεν   εὑρηκέναι   'Αβραὰμ
What therefore shall we say   to have found   Abraham

τὸν   προπάτορα   ἡμῶν   κατὰ   σάρκα;   **2** εἰ
the   forefather   of us according to flesh?   if

γὰρ   'Αβραὰμ   ἐξ   ἔργων   ἐδικαιώθη,   ἔχει
For   Abraham   by   works   was justified,   he has

καύχημα·   ἀλλ'   οὐ   πρὸς   θεόν.   **3** τί   γὰρ
a boast;   but   not   with   God.   For what

ἡ   γραφὴ   λέγει;   ἐπίστευσεν   δὲ   'Αβραὰμ
the scripture   says?   And ²believed   ¹Abraham

τῷ   θεῷ,   καὶ   ἐλογίσθη   αὐτῷ   εἰς
-   God,   and   it was reckoned   to him   for

---

to which the Law and the Prophets testify. 22This righteousness from God comes through faith in Jesus Christ to all who believe. There is no difference, 23for all have sinned and fall short of the glory of God, 24and are justified freely by his grace through the redemption that came by Christ Jesus. 25God presented him as a sacrifice of atonement,[p] through faith in his blood. He did this to demonstrate his justice, because in his forbearance he had left the sins committed beforehand unpunished— 26he did it to demonstrate his justice at the present time, so as to be just and the one who justifies those who have faith in Jesus.
27Where, then, is boasting? It is excluded. On what principle? On that of observing the law? No, but on that of faith. 28For we maintain that a man is justified by faith apart from observing the law. 29Is God the God of Jews only? Is he not the God of Gentiles too? Yes, of Gentiles too, 30since there is only one God, who will justify the circumcised by faith and the uncircumcised through that same faith. 31Do we, then, nullify the law by this faith? Not at all! Rather, we uphold the law.

Chapter 4

Abraham Justified by Faith

WHAT then shall we say that Abraham, our forefather, discovered in this matter? 2If, in fact, Abraham was justified by works, he had something to boast about—but not before God. 3What does the Scripture say? "Abraham believed God, and it was credited to him as righteousness."[q]

p25 Or as the one who would turn aside his wrath, taking away sin
q3 Gen. 15:6; also in verse 22

RIGHTEOUSNESS.''

4Now to the one who works, his wage is not reckoned as a favor, but as what is due.

5But to the one who does not work, but believes in Him who justifies the ungodly, his faith is reckoned as righteousness,

6just as David also speaks of the blessing upon the man to whom God reckons righteousness apart from works:

7"BLESSED ARE THOSE WHOSE LAWLESS DEEDS HAVE BEEN FORGIVEN, AND WHOSE SINS HAVE BEEN COVERED.

8"BLESSED IS THE MAN WHOSE SIN THE LORD WILL NOT TAKE INTO ACCOUNT.''

9Is this blessing then upon the circumcised, or upon the uncircumcised also? For we say, "FAITH WAS RECKONED TO ABRAHAM AS RIGHTEOUSNESS.''

10How then was it reckoned? While he was circumcised, or uncircumcised? Not while circumcised, but while uncircumcised;

11and he received the sign of circumcision, a seal of the righteousness of the faith which he had while uncircumcised, that he might be the father of all who believe without being circumcised, that righteousness might be reckoned to them,

12and the father of circumcision to those who not only are of the circumcision, but who also follow in the steps of the faith of our father Abraham which he had while uncircumcised.

13For the promise to Abraham or to his descendants that he would be heir of the world was not through the Law, but through the righteousness of faith.

14For if those who are of the Law are heirs, faith is

δικαιοσύνην. **4** τῷ δὲ ἐργαζομένῳ ὁ
righteousness.   Now to the [one] working   the

μισθὸς οὐ λογίζεται κατὰ χάριν ἀλλὰ
reward   is not reckoned according to grace   but

κατὰ ὀφείλημα· **5** τῷ δὲ μὴ ἐργαζομένῳ,
according to debt;   but to the [one] not working,

πιστεύοντι δὲ ἐπὶ τὸν δικαιοῦντα τὸν
but believing on the [one] justifying the

ἀσεβῆ, λογίζεται ἡ πίστις αὐτοῦ εἰς
impious man, is reckoned the faith of him for

δικαιοσύνην, **6** καθάπερ καὶ Δαυὶδ λέγει
righteousness,   even as also David says

τὸν μακαρισμὸν τοῦ ἀνθρώπου ᾧ ὁ
the blessedness of the man   to whom -

θεὸς λογίζεται δικαιοσύνην χωρὶς ἔργων·
God reckons righteousness without works :

7 μακάριοι ὧν ἀφέθησαν αἱ ἀνομίαι
Blessed [are they] of whom were forgiven the lawlessnesses

καὶ ὧν ἐπεκαλύφθησαν αἱ ἁμαρτίαι·
and of whom were covered over the sins;

8 μακάριος ἀνὴρ οὗ οὐ μὴ λογίσηται
blessed [is] a man of whom by no means ¹may reckon

κύριος ἁμαρτίαν **9** ὁ μακαρισμὸς οὖν
¹[the] Lord sin.   ¹blessedness ²then

οὗτος ἐπὶ τὴν περιτομὴν ἢ καὶ ἐπὶ
¹This on the circumcision or also on

τὴν ἀκροβυστίαν; λέγομεν γάρ· ἐλογίσθη
the uncircumcision? for we say : ²was reckoned

τῷ Ἀβραὰμ ἡ πίστις εἰς δικαιοσύνην.
- ⁴to Abraham ¹The(his) ²faith for ³righteousness.

10 πῶς οὖν ἐλογίσθη; ἐν περιτομῇ ὄντι
How then was it reckoned? in circumcision being

ἢ ἐν ἀκροβυστίᾳ; οὐκ ἐν περιτομῇ ἀλλ'
or in uncircumcision? not in circumcision but

ἐν ἀκροβυστίᾳ· **11** καὶ σημεῖον ἔλαβεν
in uncircumcision; and ¹a sign ¹he received

περιτομῆς σφραγῖδα τῆς δικαιοσύνης τῆς
of circumcision a seal of the righteousness of the

πίστεως τῆς ἐν τῇ ἀκροβυστίᾳ, εἰς
faith - [while] in uncircumcision, for
                                      =so

τὸ εἶναι αὐτὸν πατέρα πάντων τῶν
the to be him^b a father of all the
that he should be

πιστευόντων δι' ἀκροβυστίας, εἰς τὸ
[ones] believing through uncircumcision, for the
                                        =that right-

λογισθῆναι αὐτοῖς [τὴν] δικαιοσύνην, **12** καὶ
to be reckoned to them - righteousness,^b and
eousness should be reckoned to them,

πατέρα περιτομῆς τοῖς οὐκ ἐκ περιτομῆς
a father of circumcision to the not of circumcision
                        [ones]

μόνον ἀλλὰ καὶ τοῖς στοιχοῦσιν τοῖς
only but also to the [ones] walking the
                                      in the

ἴχνεσιν τῆς ἐν ἀκροβυστίᾳ πίστεως τοῦ
steps ¹of the ⁷in ⁸uncircumcision ²faith ³of the

πατρὸς ἡμῶν Ἀβραάμ. **13** Οὐ γὰρ διὰ
⁴father ⁵of us ⁶Abraham.   For not through

νόμου ἡ ἐπαγγελία τῷ Ἀβραὰμ ἢ τῷ
law the promise - to Abraham or to the

σπέρματι αὐτοῦ, τὸ κληρονόμον αὐτὸν
seed of him, the heir him
              =that he should be heir

εἶναι κόσμου, ἀλλὰ διὰ δικαιοσύνης πίστεως.
to be^b of [the] world, but through a righteousness of faith.

14 εἰ γὰρ οἱ ἐκ νόμου κληρονόμοι,
For if ¹the ²[are] ⁴of ⁵law ²heirs,

4Now when a man works, his wages are not credited to him as a gift, but as an obligation. 5However, to the man who does not work but trusts God who justifies the wicked, his faith is credited as righteousness. 6David says the same thing when he speaks of the blessedness of the man to whom God credits righteousness apart from works:

7"Blessed are they whose transgressions are forgiven, whose sins are covered.

8Blessed is the man whose sin the Lord will never count against him."

9Is this blessedness only for the circumcised, or also for the uncircumcised? We have been saying that Abraham's faith was credited to him as righteousness. 10Under what circumstances was it credited? Was it after he was circumcised, or before? It was not after, but before! 11And he received the sign of circumcision, a seal of the righteousness that he had by faith while he was still uncircumcised. So then, he is the father of all who believe but have not been circumcised, in order that righteousness might be credited to them. 12And he is also the father of the circumcised who not only are circumcised but who also walk in the footsteps of the faith that our father Abraham had before he was circumcised.

13It was not through law that Abraham and his offspring received the promise that he would be heir of the world, but through the righteousness that comes by faith. 14For if those who live by law are heirs, faith

8 Psalm 32:1,2

made void and the promise is nullified;

15for the Law brings about wrath, but where there is no law, neither is there violation.

16For this reason it is by faith, that it might be in accordance with grace, in order that the promise may be certain to all the descendants, not only to those who are of the Law, but also to those who are of the faith of Abraham, who is the father of us all,

17(as it is written, "A FATHER OF MANY NATIONS HAVE I MADE YOU") in the sight of Him whom he believed, even God, who gives life to the dead and calls into being that which does not exist.

18In hope against hope he believed, in order that he might become a father of many nations, according to that which had been spoken, "SO SHALL YOUR DESCENDANTS BE."

19And without becoming weak in faith he contemplated his own body, now as good as dead since he was about a hundred years old, and the deadness of Sarah's womb;

20yet, with respect to the promise of God, he did not waver in unbelief, but grew strong in faith, giving glory to God,

21and being fully assured that what He had promised, He was able also to perform.

22Therefore also IT WAS RECKONED TO HIM AS RIGHTEOUSNESS.

23Now not for his sake only was it written, that it was reckoned to him,

24but for our sake also, to whom it will be reckoned, as those who believe in Him who raised Jesus our Lord from the dead,

---

κεκένωται ἡ πίστις καὶ κατήργηται
has been emptied – faith and has been destroyed

ἡ ἐπαγγελία· 15 ὁ γὰρ νόμος ὀργὴν
the promise; for the law wrath

κατεργάζεται· οὗ δὲ οὐκ ἔστιν νόμος,
works; and where there is not law,

οὐδὲ παράβασις. 16 Διὰ τοῦτο ἐκ πίστεως,
neither [is there] transgression. Therefore [it is] of faith,

ἵνα κατὰ χάριν, εἰς τὸ εἶναι βεβαίαν
in [it may be] grace, for the to be firm
order according that to =so that the promise shall be firm

τὴν ἐπαγγελίαν παντὶ τῷ σπέρματι, οὐ
the promise to all the seed, not

τῷ ἐκ τοῦ νόμου μόνον ἀλλὰ καὶ τῷ
to the of the law only but also to the
[seed] [seed]

ἐκ πίστεως Ἀβραάμ, ὅς ἐστιν πατὴρ
of [the] faith of Abraham, who is father

πάντων ἡμῶν, 17 καθὼς γέγραπται ὅτι
of all us, as it has been written[,] –

πατέρα πολλῶν ἐθνῶν τέθεικά σε,
A father of many nations I have appointed thee,

κατέναντι οὗ ἐπίστευσεν θεοῦ τοῦ ζωο-
before whom he believed God the [one] quick-

ποιοῦντος τοὺς νεκροὺς καὶ καλοῦντος
ening the dead [ones] and calling

τὰ μὴ ὄντα ὡς ὄντα· 18 ὃς παρ' ἐλπίδα
the not being as being; who beyond hope
things

ἐπ' ἐλπίδι ἐπίστευσεν, εἰς τὸ γενέσθαι
on hope believed, for the to become
=so that he should become

αὐτὸν πατέρα πολλῶν ἐθνῶν κατὰ τὸ
him a father of many nations accord- the
ing to thing

εἰρημένον· οὕτως ἔσται τὸ σπέρμα σου·
having been said : So shall be the seed of thee;

19 καὶ μὴ ἀσθενήσας τῇ πίστει κατενόησεν
and not weakening in faith he considered

τὸ ἑαυτοῦ σῶμα νενεκρωμένον, ἑκατονταέτης
the of himself body to have died, a hundred years

που ὑπάρχων, καὶ τὴν νέκρωσιν τῆς
about being, and the death of the

μήτρας Σάρρας· 20 εἰς δὲ τὴν ἐπαγγελίαν
womb of Sarah; but against the promise

τοῦ θεοῦ οὐ διεκρίθη τῇ ἀπιστίᾳ, ἀλλὰ
– of God he did not decide – by unbelief, but

ἐνεδυναμώθη τῇ πίστει, δοὺς δόξαν τῷ
was empowered by faith, giving glory

θεῷ 21 καὶ πληροφορηθεὶς ὅτι ὃ ἐπήγγελται
to God and being fully that what he has
persuaded promised

δυνατός ἐστιν καὶ ποιῆσαι. 22 διὸ [καὶ]
able he is also to do. Wherefore also

ἐλογίσθη αὐτῷ εἰς δικαιοσύνην. 23 Οὐκ
it was to him for righteousness. not
reckoned

ἐγράφη δὲ δι' αὐτὸν μόνον ὅτι ἐλογίσθη
it was Now because him only that it was
written of reckoned

αὐτῷ, 24 ἀλλὰ καὶ δι' ἡμᾶς, οἷς μέλλει
to him, but also because us, to whom it is
of about

λογίζεσθαι, τοῖς πιστεύουσιν ἐπὶ τὸν
to be reckoned, to the [ones] believing on the [one]

ἐγείραντα Ἰησοῦν τὸν κύριον ἡμῶν ἐκ
having raised Jesus the Lord of us out of

---

has no value and the promise is worthless, 15because law brings wrath. And where there is no law there is no transgression.

16Therefore, the promise comes by faith, so that it may be by grace and may be guaranteed to all Abraham's offspring—not only to those who are of the law but also to those who are of the faith of Abraham. He is the father of us all. 17As it is written: "I have made you a father of many nations." *He is our father in the sight of God, in whom he believed—the God who gives life to the dead and calls things that are not as though they were.

18Against all hope, Abraham in hope believed and so became the father of many nations, just as it had been said to him, "So shall your offspring be."' 19Without weakening in his faith, he faced the fact that his body was as good as dead—since he was about a hundred years old—and that Sarah's womb was also dead. 20Yet he did not waver through unbelief regarding the promise of God, but was strengthened in his faith and gave glory to God, 21being fully persuaded that God had power to do what he had promised. 22This is why "it was credited to him as righteousness." 23The words "it was credited to him" were written not for him alone, 24but also for us, to whom God will credit righteousness—for us who believe in him who raised Jesus our Lord from the

s17 Gen. 17:5
t18 Gen. 15:5

25He who was delivered up because of our transgressions, and was raised because of our justification.

Chapter 5

Results of Justification

THEREFORE having been justified by faith, we have peace with God through our Lord Jesus Christ,

2through whom also we have obtained our introduction by faith into this grace in which we stand; and we exult in hope of the glory of God.

3And not only this, but we also exult in our tribulations, knowing that tribulation brings about perseverance;

4and perseverance, proven character; and proven character, hope;

5and hope does not disappoint, because the love of God has been poured out within our hearts through the Holy Spirit who was given to us.

6For while we were still helpless, at the right time Christ died for the ungodly.

7For one will hardly die for a righteous man; though perhaps for the good man someone would dare even to die.

8But God demonstrates His own love toward us, in that while we were yet sinners, Christ died for us.

9Much more then, having now been justified by His blood, we shall be saved from the wrath *of God* through Him.

10For if while we were enemies, we were reconciled to God through the death of His Son, much more, having been reconciled, we shall be saved by His life.

11And not only this, but

νεκρῶν,
[the] dead,

25 ὃς παρεδόθη διὰ τὰ παραπ-
who was delivered because of the of-

τώματα ἡμῶν καὶ ἠγέρθη διὰ τὴν
fences of us and was raised because of the

δικαίωσιν ἡμῶν.
justification of us.

5 Δικαιωθέντες οὖν ἐκ πίστεως εἰρήνην
Having been justified therefore by faith peace

ἔχομεν πρὸς τὸν θεὸν διὰ τοῦ κυρίου
we have with – God through the Lord

ἡμῶν Ἰησοῦ Χριστοῦ, **2** δι᾽ οὗ καὶ τὴν
of us Jesus Christ, through whom also the

προσαγωγὴν ἐσχήκαμεν [τῇ πίστει] εἰς
access we have had – by faith into

τὴν χάριν ταύτην ἐν ᾗ ἑστήκαμεν, καὶ
this grace in which we stand, and

καυχώμεθα ἐπ᾽ ἐλπίδι τῆς δόξης τοῦ
boast on hope of the glory of

θεοῦ. **3** οὐ μόνον δέ, ἀλλὰ καὶ καυχώμεθα
of God. And not only [so], but also we boast

ἐν ταῖς θλίψεσιν, εἰδότες ὅτι ἡ θλῖψις
in afflictions, knowing that – affliction

ὑπομονὴν κατεργάζεται, **4** ἡ δὲ ὑπομονὴ
patience works, – and patience

δοκιμήν, ἡ δὲ δοκιμὴ ἐλπίδα· **5** ἡ δὲ
proof, – and proof hope; – and

ἐλπὶς οὐ καταισχύνει, ὅτι ἡ ἀγάπη
hope does not put to shame, because the love

τοῦ θεοῦ ἐκκέχυται ἐν ταῖς καρδίαις
– of God has been poured out in the hearts

ἡμῶν διὰ πνεύματος ἁγίου τοῦ δοθέντος
of us through Spirit Holy – given

ἡμῖν· **6** εἴ γε Χριστὸς ὄντων ἡμῶν
to us; indeed 7Christ 2being 1us
= when we were weak

ἀσθενῶν ἔτι κατὰ καιρὸν ὑπὲρ ἀσεβῶν
4weaka 3yet baccord- 6time 8on 10impious
ing to behalf of ones

ἀπέθανεν. **7** μόλις γὰρ ὑπὲρ δικαίου
8died. For hardly on behalf of a just man

τις ἀποθανεῖται· ὑπὲρ γὰρ τοῦ ἀγαθοῦ
anyone will die; for on behalf of the good man

τάχα τις καὶ τολμᾷ ἀποθανεῖν· **8** συνίστησιν
perhaps some- even dares to die; 2commends
one

δὲ τὴν ἑαυτοῦ ἀγάπην εἰς ἡμᾶς ὁ θεὸς
but 3the 6of himself 4love 5to 7us – 1God

ὅτι ἔτι ἁμαρτωλῶν ὄντων ἡμῶν Χριστὸς
that yet sinners being usa Christ
= while we were yet sinners

ὑπὲρ ἡμῶν ἀπέθανεν. **9** πολλῷ οὖν μᾶλλον
on be- us died. By much there- rather
half of fore

δικαιωθέντες νῦν ἐν τῷ αἵματι αὐτοῦ
having been justified now by the blood of him

σωθησόμεθα δι᾽ αὐτοῦ ἀπὸ τῆς ὀργῆς.
we shall be saved through him from the wrath.

10 εἰ γὰρ ἐχθροὶ ὄντες κατηλλάγημεν
For if enemies being we were reconciled

τῷ θεῷ διὰ τοῦ θανάτου τοῦ υἱοῦ αὐτοῦ,
– to God through the death of the Son of him,

πολλῷ μᾶλλον καταλλαγέντες σωθησόμεθα
by much rather having been reconciled we shall be saved

ἐν τῇ ζωῇ αὐτοῦ· **11** οὐ μόνον δέ, ἀλλὰ
by the life of him; and not only [so], but

---

dead. 25He was delivered over to death for our sins and was raised to life for our justification.

Chapter 5

Peace and Joy

THEREFORE, since we have been justified through faith, weᵘ have peace with God through our Lord Jesus Christ, 2through whom we have gained access by faith into this grace in which we now stand. And weᵘ rejoice in the hope of the glory of God. 3Not only so, but weᵘ also rejoice in our sufferings, because we know that suffering produces perseverance; 4perseverance, character; and character, hope. 5And hope does not disappoint us, because God has poured out his love into our hearts by the Holy Spirit, whom he has given us.

6You see, at just the right time, when we were still powerless, Christ died for the ungodly. 7Very rarely will anyone die for a righteous man, though for a good man someone might possibly dare to die. 8But God demonstrates his own love for us in this: While we were still sinners, Christ died for us.

9Since we have now been justified by his blood, how much more shall we be saved from God's wrath through him! 10For if, when we were God's enemies, we were reconciled to him through the death of his Son, how much more, having been reconciled, shall we be saved through his life! 11Not only is this so, we also exult in God through our Lord Jesus Christ, through whom we have now received the reconciliation.

12Therefore, just as through one man sin entered into the world, and death through sin, and so death spread to all men, because all sinned—

13for until the Law sin was in the world; but sin is not imputed when there is no law.

14Nevertheless death reigned from Adam until Moses, even over those who had not sinned in the likeness of the offense of Adam, who is a ᵗtype of Him who was to come.

15But the free gift is not like the transgression. For if by the transgression of the one the many died, much more did the grace of God and the gift by the grace of the one Man, Jesus Christ, abound to the many.

16And the gift is not like *that which came* through the one who sinned; for on the one hand the judgment *arose* from one *transgression* resulting in condemnation, but on the other hand the free gift *arose* from many transgressions resulting in justification.

17For if by the transgression of the one, death reigned through the one, much more those who receive the abundance of grace and of the gift of righteousness will reign in life through the One, Jesus Christ.

18So then as through one transgression there resulted condemnation to all

---

καὶ καυχώμενοι ἐν τῷ θεῷ διὰ τοῦ
also boasting in - God through the
κυρίου ἡμῶν Ἰησοῦ [Χριστοῦ], δι’ οὗ
Lord of us Jesus Christ, through whom
νῦν τὴν καταλλαγὴν ἐλάβομεν.
now the reconciliation we received.

12 Διὰ τοῦτο ὥσπερ δι’ ἑνὸς ἀνθρώπου
Therefore as through one man
ἡ ἁμαρτία εἰς τὸν κόσμον εἰσῆλθεν,
- sin into the world entered,
καὶ διὰ τῆς ἁμαρτίας ὁ θάνατος, καὶ ²also
and through - sin - death, ²also
οὕτως εἰς πάντας ἀνθρώπους ὁ θάνατος
¹so to all men - death
διῆλθεν, ἐφ’ ᾧ πάντες ἥμαρτον· 13 ἄχρι
passed, inasmuch as all sinned; until
γὰρ νόμου ἁμαρτία ἦν ἐν κόσμῳ, ἁμαρτία
for law sin was in [the] world, sin
δὲ οὐκ ἐλλογεῖται μὴ ὄντος νόμου·
but is not reckoned not being lawᵃ;
=when there is no law;

14 ἀλλὰ ἐβασίλευσεν ὁ θάνατος ἀπὸ Ἀδὰμ
but ¹reigned - ¹death from Adam
μέχρι Μωϋσέως καὶ ἐπὶ τοὺς μὴ
until Moses even over the [ones] not
ἁμαρτήσαντας ἐπὶ τῷ ὁμοιώματι τῆς
sinning on the likeness of the
παραβάσεως Ἀδάμ, ὅς ἐστιν τύπος τοῦ
transgression of Adam, who is a type of the
μέλλοντος. 15 Ἀλλ’ οὐχ ὡς τὸ παράπτωμα,
[one] coming. But not as the offence,
οὕτως [καὶ] τὸ χάρισμα· εἰ γὰρ τῷ
so also the free gift; for if ¹by the
τοῦ ἑνὸς παραπτώματι οἱ πολλοὶ
³of the ⁴one [man] ²offence the many
ἀπέθανον, πολλῷ μᾶλλον ἡ χάρις τοῦ θεοῦ
died, by much rather the grace - of God
καὶ ἡ δωρεὰ ἐν χάριτι τῇ τοῦ ἑνὸς
and the gift in grace - of the one
ἀνθρώπου Ἰησοῦ Χριστοῦ εἰς τοὺς πολλοὺς
man Jesus Christ to the many
ἐπερίσσευσεν. 16 καὶ οὐχ ὡς δι’ ἑνὸς
abounded. And not as through one
[man]
ἁμαρτήσαντος τὸ δώρημα· τὸ μὲν γὰρ
sinning the gift; ³the ²on one hand ¹for
κρίμα ἐξ ἑνὸς εἰς κατάκριμα, τὸ δὲ
judgment [is] of one to condemna- on the other
[offence] tion, the
χάρισμα ἐκ πολλῶν παραπτωμάτων εἰς
free gift [is] of many offences to
δικαίωμα. 17 εἰ γὰρ τῷ τοῦ ἑνὸς
justification. For if ¹by the ³of the ⁴one [man]
παραπτώματι ὁ θάνατος ἐβασίλευσεν διὰ
²offence - death reigned through
τοῦ ἑνός, πολλῷ μᾶλλον οἱ τὴν περισσείαν
the one by much rather ¹the ³the ⁴abundance
[man], [ones]
τῆς χάριτος καὶ τῆς δωρεᾶς τῆς
⁵of the ⁶grace ⁷and ⁸of the ⁹gift -
δικαιοσύνης λαμβάνοντες ἐν ζωῇ βασιλεύ-
¹⁰of righteousness ²receiving ¹¹in ¹³life ¹¹will
σουσιν διὰ τοῦ ἑνὸς Ἰησοῦ Χριστοῦ.
reign through the one [man] Jesus Christ.
18 Ἄρα οὖν ὡς δι’ ἑνὸς παραπτώματος
So therefore as through one offence
εἰς πάντας ἀνθρώπους εἰς κατάκριμα,
to all men to condemnation,

---

but we also rejoice in God through our Lord Jesus Christ, through whom we have now received reconciliation.

Death Through Adam, Life Through Christ

12Therefore, just as sin entered the world through one man, and death through sin, and in this way death came to all men, because all sinned— 13for before the law was given, sin was in the world. But sin is not taken into account when there is no law. 14Nevertheless, death reigned from the time of Adam to the time of Moses, even over those who did not sin by breaking a command, as did Adam, who was a pattern of the one to come.

15But the gift is not like the trespass. For if the many died by the trespass of the one man, how much more did God's grace and the gift that came by the grace of the one man, Jesus Christ, overflow to the many! 16Again, the gift of God is not like the result of the one man's sin: The judgment followed one sin and brought condemnation, but the gift followed many trespasses and brought justification. 17For if, by the trespass of the one man, death reigned through that one man, how much more will those who receive God's abundant provision of grace and of the gift of righteousness reign in life through the one man, Jesus Christ.

18Consequently, just as the result of one trespass was condemnation for all men, so also the result of

---

ᵗ Or, *foreshadowing*

men, even so through one act of righteousness there resulted justification of life to all men.

19For as through the one man's disobedience the many were made sinners, even so through the obedience of the One the many will be made righteous.

20And the Law came in that the transgression might increase; but where sin increased, grace abounded all the more,

21that, as sin reigned in death, even so grace might reign through righteousness to eternal life through Jesus Christ our Lord.

οὕτως καὶ δι᾽ ἑνὸς δικαιώματος εἰς
so also through one righteous act to

πάντας ἀνθρώπους εἰς δικαίωσιν ζωῆς·
all men to justification of life;

19 ὥσπερ γὰρ διὰ τῆς παρακοῆς τοῦ
for as through the disobedience of the

ἑνὸς ἀνθρώπου ἁμαρτωλοὶ κατεστάθησαν
one man ⁴sinners ⁵were constituted

οἱ πολλοί, οὕτως καὶ διὰ τῆς ὑπακοῆς
¹the ²many, so also through the obedience

τοῦ ἑνὸς δίκαιοι κατασταθήσονται οἱ
of the one [man] ²righteous ⁵will be constituted ¹the

πολλοί. 20 νόμος δὲ παρεισῆλθεν ἵνα
²many. But law entered in order that

πλεονάσῃ τὸ παράπτωμα· οὗ δὲ ἐπλεόνασεν
might abound the offence; but where abounded

ἡ ἁμαρτία, ὑπερεπερίσσευσεν ἡ χάρις,
- sin, more abounded - grace,

21 ἵνα ὥσπερ ἐβασίλευσεν ἡ ἁμαρτία ἐν
in order that as reigned - sin by

τῷ θανάτῳ, οὕτως καὶ ἡ χάρις βασιλεύσῃ
- death, so also - grace might reign

διὰ δικαιοσύνης εἰς ζωὴν αἰώνιον διὰ
through righteousness to life eternal through

Ἰησοῦ Χριστοῦ τοῦ κυρίου ἡμῶν.
Jesus Christ the Lord of us.

---

one act of righteousness was justification that brings life for all men. 19For just as through the disobedience of the one man the many were made sinners, so also through the obedience of the one man the many will be made righteous.

20The law was added so that the trespass might increase. But where sin increased, grace increased all the more, 21so that, just as sin reigned in death, so also grace might reign through righteousness to bring eternal life through Jesus Christ our Lord.

Chapter 6

Believers Are Dead to Sin, Alive to God

WHAT shall we say then? Are we to continue in sin that grace might increase?

2May it never be! How shall we who died to sin still live in it?

3Or do you not know that all of us who have been baptized into Christ Jesus have been baptized into His death?

4Therefore we have been buried with Him through baptism into death, in order that as Christ was raised from the dead through the glory of the Father, so we too might walk in newness of life.

5For if we have become united with *Him* in the likeness of His death, certainly we shall be also *in the likeness* of His resurrection,

6knowing this, that our old self was crucified with *Him,* that our body of sin might be done away with, that we should no longer be slaves to sin;

7for he who has died is freed from sin.

---

6 Τί οὖν ἐροῦμεν; ἐπιμένωμεν τῇ
What therefore shall we say? May we continue

ἁμαρτίᾳ, ἵνα ἡ χάρις πλεονάσῃ; 2 μὴ
in sin, in order that - grace may abound? not

γένοιτο. οἵτινες ἀπεθάνομεν τῇ ἁμαρτίᾳ,
May it be. Who we died - to sin,

πῶς ἔτι ζήσομεν ἐν αὐτῇ; 3 ἢ ἀγνοεῖτε
how yet shall we live in it? or are ye ignorant

ὅτι ὅσοι ἐβαπτίσθημεν εἰς Χριστὸν
that as many as we were baptized into Christ

Ἰησοῦν, εἰς τὸν θάνατον αὐτοῦ ἐβαπτίσ-
Jesus, into the death of him we were

θημεν; 4 συνετάφημεν οὖν αὐτῷ διὰ τοῦ
baptized? ²We were ¹there him through -
buried with fore

βαπτίσματος εἰς τὸν θάνατον, ἵνα ὥσπερ
baptism into - death, in order as
that

ἠγέρθη Χριστὸς ἐκ νεκρῶν διὰ τῆς
was raised Christ from [the] dead through the

δόξης τοῦ πατρός, οὕτως καὶ ἡμεῖς ἐν
glory of the Father, so also we in

καινότητι ζωῆς περιπατήσωμεν. 5 εἰ γὰρ
newness of life might walk. For if

σύμφυτοι γεγόναμεν τῷ ὁμοιώματι τοῦ
united with we have become in the likeness of the

θανάτου αὐτοῦ, ἀλλὰ καὶ τῆς ἀναστάσεως
death of him, but(so) also of the(his) resurrection

ἐσόμεθα· 6 τοῦτο γινώσκοντες, ὅτι ὁ
we shall be; this knowing, that the

παλαιὸς ἡμῶν ἄνθρωπος συνεσταυρώθη, ἵνα
¹old ³of us ²man was crucified in or-
with [him], der that

καταργηθῇ τὸ σῶμα τῆς ἁμαρτίας, τοῦ
might be the body - of sin, -
destroyed

μηκέτι δουλεύειν ἡμᾶς τῇ ἁμαρτίᾳ· 7 ὁ
no longer to serve usbd - sin; ²the
=that we should no longer serve (one)

γὰρ ἀποθανὼν δεδικαίωται ἀπὸ τῆς
¹for having died has been justified from -

Chapter 6

Dead to Sin, Alive in Christ

WHAT shall we say, then? Shall we go on sinning so that grace may increase? 2By no means! We died to sin; how can we live in it any longer? 3Or don't you know that all of us who were baptized into Christ Jesus were baptized into his death? 4We were therefore buried with him through baptism into death in order that, just as Christ was raised from the dead through the glory of the Father, we too may live a new life.

5If we have been united with him like this in his death, we will certainly also be united with him in his resurrection. 6For we know that our old self was crucified with him so that the body of sin might be done away with,ᵛ that we should no longer be slaves to sin— 7because anyone who has died has been freed from sin.

ᵛ6 Or *be rendered powerless*

8Now if we have died with Christ, we believe that we shall also live with Him, 9knowing that Christ, having been raised from the dead, is never to die again; death no longer is master over Him. 10For the death that He died, He died to sin, once for all; but the life that He lives, He lives to God. 11Even so consider yourselves to be dead to sin, but alive to God in Christ Jesus. 12Therefore do not let sin reign in your mortal body that you should obey its lusts, 13and do not go on presenting the members of your body to sin as instruments of unrighteousness; but present yourselves to God as those alive from the dead, and your members as instruments of righteousness to God. 14For sin shall not be master over you, for you are not under law, but under grace. 15What then? Shall we sin because we are not under law but under grace? May it never be! 16Do you not know that when you present yourselves to someone as slaves for obedience, you are slaves of the one whom you obey, either of sin resulting in death, or of obedience resulting in righteousness? 17But thanks be to God that though you were slaves of sin, you became obedient from the heart to that form of teaching to which you were committed, 18and having been freed from sin, you became slaves of righteousness. 19I am speaking in human terms because of the weakness of your flesh. For just as you presented your members as slaves to impurity and to lawlessness,

---

ἁμαρτίας. 8 εἰ δὲ ἀπεθάνομεν σὺν Χριστῷ,
sin.　　　But if　we died　with　Christ

πιστεύομεν ὅτι καὶ συζήσομεν αὐτῷ,
we believe　that　also　we shall live with　him,

9 εἰδότες ὅτι Χριστὸς ἐγερθεὶς ἐκ νεκρῶν
knowing　that　Christ　having　from [the] dead
　　　　　　　　　　been raised

οὐκέτι ἀποθνήσκει, θάνατος αὐτοῦ οὐκέτι
no more　dies,　　death　³of him ¹no more

κυριεύει. 10 ὃ γὰρ ἀπέθανεν, τῇ ἁμαρτίᾳ
²lords it over.　For in that† he died,　　to sin

ἀπέθανεν ἐφάπαξ· ὃ δὲ ζῇ, ζῇ τῷ θεῷ.
he died　once;　but in that† he　he　to
　　　　　　　　　　lives, lives　God.

11 οὕτως καὶ ὑμεῖς λογίζεσθε ἑαυτοὺς
So　also　²ye　¹reckon　yourselves

εἶναι νεκροὺς μὲν τῇ ἁμαρτίᾳ ζῶντας
to be　dead　indeed　–　to sin　²living

δὲ τῷ θεῷ ἐν Χριστῷ Ἰησοῦ. 12 μὴ
¹but　–　to God in　Christ　Jesus.　　³not

οὖν βασιλευέτω ἡ ἁμαρτία ἐν τῷ θνητῷ
¹There-　²let ⁵reign　–　⁴sin　⁶in　⁷the　⁸mortal
fore

ὑμῶν σώματι εἰς τὸ ὑπακούειν ταῖς
¹⁰of you　⁹body　for　the　to obey　the
　　　　　　　= to obey its lusts,

ἐπιθυμίαις αὐτοῦ, 13 μηδὲ παριστάνετε τὰ
lusts　of it,　neither　present ye　the

μέλη ὑμῶν ὅπλα ἀδικίας τῇ ἁμαρτίᾳ,
members of you　weapons　of unright-　–　to sin,
　　　　　　　　eousness

ἀλλὰ παραστήσατε ἑαυτοὺς τῷ θεῷ ὡσεὶ
but　present ye　yourselves　–　to God　as

ἐκ νεκρῶν ζῶντας καὶ τὰ μέλη ὑμῶν
from [the] dead　living　and　the　members　of you

ὅπλα δικαιοσύνης τῷ θεῷ, 14 ἁμαρτία
weapons　of righteousness　–　to God,　²sin

γὰρ ὑμῶν οὐ κυριεύσει· οὐ γὰρ ἐστε
¹for　⁴of you　³shall not lord it over;　for ye are not

ὑπὸ νόμον ἀλλὰ ὑπὸ χάριν. 15 Τί οὖν;
under　law　but　under　grace.　What therefore?

ἁμαρτήσωμεν, ὅτι οὐκ ἐσμὲν ὑπὸ νόμον
may we sin,　because　we are not　under　law

ἀλλὰ ὑπὸ χάριν; μὴ γένοιτο. 16 οὐκ
but　under　grace?　May it not be.　　not

οἴδατε ὅτι ᾧ παριστάνετε ἑαυτοὺς δούλους
Know ye　that to　ye present　yourselves　slaves
whom

εἰς ὑπακοήν, δοῦλοί ἐστε ᾧ ὑπακούετε,
for　obedience,　slaves　ye are　whom　ye obey,

ἤτοι ἁμαρτίας εἰς θάνατον ἢ ὑπακοῆς
whether　of sin　to　death　or of obedience

εἰς δικαιοσύνην, 17 χάρις δὲ τῷ θεῷ
to　righteousness?　But thanks　–　to God

ὅτι ἦτε δοῦλοι τῆς ἁμαρτίας, ὑπηκούσατε
that ye were slaves　–　of sin,　²ye obeyed

δὲ ἐκ καρδίας εἰς ὃν παρεδόθητε τύπον
¹but　out of [the] heart　³to　⁴which ⁵ye were delivered ¹a form

διδαχῆς, 18 ἐλευθερωθέντες δὲ ἀπὸ τῆς
²of teaching,　and having been freed　from　the

ἁμαρτίας ἐδουλώθητε τῇ δικαιοσύνῃ.
sin　ye were enslaved　–　to righteousness.

19 ἀνθρώπινον λέγω διὰ τὴν ἀσθένειαν
Humanly　I say　because of the　weakness

τῆς σαρκὸς ὑμῶν. ὥσπερ γὰρ παρεστήσατε
of the　flesh　of you.　For as　ye presented

τὰ μέλη ὑμῶν δοῦλα τῇ ἀκαθαρσίᾳ καὶ
the members　of you　slaves　–　to uncleanness　and

8Now if we died with Christ, we believe that we will also live with him. 9For we know that since Christ was raised from the dead, he cannot die again; death no longer has mastery over him. 10The death he died, he died to sin once for all; but the life he lives, he lives to God. 11In the same way, count yourselves dead to sin but alive to God in Christ Jesus. 12Therefore do not let sin reign in your mortal body so that you obey its evil desires. 13Do not offer the parts of your body to sin, as instruments of wickedness, but rather offer yourselves to God, as those who have been brought from death to life; and offer the parts of your body to him as instruments of righteousness. 14For sin shall not be your master, because you are not under law, but under grace.

Slaves to Righteousness

15What then? Shall we sin because we are not under law but under grace? By no means! 16Don't you know that when you offer yourselves to someone to obey him as slaves, you are slaves to the one whom you obey—whether you are slaves to sin, which leads to death, or to obedience, which leads to righteousness? 17But thanks be to God that, though you used to be slaves to sin, you wholeheartedly obeyed the form of teaching to which you were entrusted. 18You have been set free from sin and have become slaves to righteousness. 19I put this in human terms because you are weak in your natural selves. Just as you used to offer the parts of your body in slavery to impurity and resulting in *further* lawlessness, so now present your members *as* slaves to righteousness, resulting in sanctification.

20For when you were slaves of sin, you were free in regard to righteousness.

21Therefore what benefit were you then deriving from the things of which you are now ashamed? For the outcome of those things is death.

22But now having been freed from sin and enslaved to God, you derive your benefit, resulting in sanctification, and the outcome, eternal life.

23For the wages of sin is death, but the free gift of God is eternal life in Christ Jesus our Lord.

Chapter 7

Believers United to Christ

OR do you not know, brethren (for I am speaking to those who know the law), that the law has jurisdiction over a person as long as he lives?

2For the married woman is bound by law to her husband while he is living; but if her husband dies, she is released from the law concerning the husband.

3So then if, while her husband is living, she is joined to another man, she shall be called an adulteress; but if her husband dies, she is free from the law, so that she is not an adulteress, though she is joined to another man.

4Therefore, my brethren, you also were made to die to the Law through the body of Christ, that you might be joined to another, to Him who was raised from the dead, that we might bear fruit for God.

5For while we were in the flesh, the sinful passions, which were *aroused*

τῇ ἀνομίᾳ εἰς τὴν ἀνομίαν, οὕτως νῦν
-    to iniquity unto -   iniquity,   so   now

παραστήσατε τὰ μέλη ὑμῶν δοῦλα τῇ
present ye   the members of you slaves the

δικαιοσύνῃ εἰς ἁγιασμόν. 20 ὅτε γὰρ
to righteousness unto sanctification. For when

δοῦλοι ἦτε τῆς ἁμαρτίας, ἐλεύθεροι ἦτε
slaves ye were of sin,   free   ye were

τῇ δικαιοσύνῃ. 21 τίνα οὖν καρπὸν εἴχετε
- to righteousness. What ²therefore ¹fruit had ye

τότε; ἐφ' οἷς νῦν ἐπαισχύνεσθε· τὸ γὰρ
then? Over which now ye are ashamed; for the

τέλος ἐκείνων θάνατος. 22 νυνὶ δὲ ἐλευ-
end of those things [is] death. But now having

θερωθέντες ἀπὸ τῆς ἁμαρτίας δουλωθέντες
been freed   from   -   sin   ²having been enslaved

δὲ τῷ θεῷ, ἔχετε τὸν καρπὸν ὑμῶν εἰς
¹and - to God, ye have the   fruit   of you to

ἁγιασμόν, τὸ δὲ τέλος ζωὴν αἰώνιον.
sanctification, and the end life   eternal.

23 τὰ γὰρ ὀψώνια τῆς ἁμαρτίας θάνατος,
For the wages   -   of sin   [is] death,

τὸ δὲ χάρισμα τοῦ θεοῦ ζωὴ αἰώνιος
but the free gift - of God life eternal

ἐν Χριστῷ Ἰησοῦ τῷ κυρίῳ ἡμῶν.
in Christ   Jesus the Lord   of us.

7 Ἢ ἀγνοεῖτε, ἀδελφοί, γινώσκουσιν γὰρ
Or are ye ignorant, brothers,   for to [ones] knowing

νόμον λαλῶ, ὅτι ὁ νόμος κυριεύει τοῦ
law   I speak, that the law lords it over the

ἀνθρώπου ἐφ' ὅσον χρόνον ζῇ; 2 ἡ γὰρ
man   over   such   time [as] he lives? For the

ὕπανδρος γυνὴ τῷ ζῶντι ἀνδρὶ δέδεται
²married ¹woman to the living husband has
                                          been bound

νόμῳ· ἐὰν δὲ ἀποθάνῃ ὁ ἀνήρ, κατήργηται
by law; but if   dies the husband, she has been
                                          discharged

ἀπὸ τοῦ νόμου τοῦ ἀνδρός. 3 ἄρα οὖν
from the law   of the husband.   Therefore

ζῶντος τοῦ ἀνδρὸς μοιχαλὶς χρηματίσει
living the husband[a] an adulteress she will be called
       = while the husband lives

ἐὰν γένηται ἀνδρὶ ἑτέρῳ· ἐὰν δὲ ἀποθάνῃ
if she ²husband ¹to a but if   dies
   becomes   different;

ὁ ἀνήρ, ἐλευθέρα ἐστὶν ἀπὸ τοῦ νόμου,
the husband, free she is from the law,

τοῦ μὴ εἶναι αὐτὴν μοιχαλίδα γενομένην
- not to be her[d] an adulteress having become
= so that she is not

ἀνδρὶ ἑτέρῳ. 4 ὥστε, ἀδελφοί μου, καὶ
²husband ¹to a   So,   brothers of me, also
       different.

ὑμεῖς ἐθανατώθητε τῷ νόμῳ διὰ τοῦ
ye   were put to death to the law through the

σώματος τοῦ Χριστοῦ, εἰς τὸ γενέσθαι
body   - of Christ, for *the* to become
                                   =that ye might belong

ὑμᾶς ἑτέρῳ, τῷ ἐκ νεκρῶν ἐγερθέντι,
you[b] . to a to the from dead having been
    different, [one] [the]   raised,

ἵνα καρποφορήσωμεν τῷ θεῷ. 5 ὅτε
in order we may bear fruit to God. when
that

γὰρ ἦμεν ἐν τῇ σαρκί, τὰ παθήματα
For we were in the flesh, the passions

---

to ever-increasing wickedness, so now offer them in slavery to righteousness leading to holiness. 20When you were slaves to sin, you were free from the control of righteousness. 21What benefit did you reap at that time from the things you are now ashamed of? Those things result in death! 22But now that you have been set free from sin and have become slaves to God, the benefit you reap leads to holiness, and the result is eternal life. 23For the wages of sin is death, but the gift of God is eternal life in[w] Christ Jesus our Lord.

Chapter 7

An Illustration From Marriage

DO you not know, brothers—for I am speaking to men who know the law—that the law has authority over a man only as long as he lives? 2For example, by law a married woman is bound to her husband as long as he is alive, but if her husband dies, she is released from the law of marriage. 3So then, if she marries another man while her husband is still alive, she is called an adulteress. But if her husband dies, she is released from that law and is not an adulteress, even though she marries another man.

4So, my brothers, you also died to the law through the body of Christ, that you might belong to another, to him who was raised from the dead, in order that we might bear fruit to God. 5For when we were controlled by the sinful nature,[x] the sinful passions

---

[w]23 Or *through*
[x]5 Or *the flesh*; also in verse 25

by the Law, were at work in the members of our body to bear fruit for death.

6But now we have been released from the Law, having died to that by which we were bound, so that we serve in newness of the ʲSpirit and not in oldness of the letter.

7What shall we say then? Is the Law sin? May it never be! On the contrary, I would not have come to know sin except through the Law; for I would not have known about coveting if the Law had not said, "YOU SHALL NOT COVET."

8But sin, taking opportunity through the commandment, produced in me coveting of every kind; for apart from the Law sin is dead.

9And I was once alive apart from the Law; but when the commandment came, sin became alive, and I died;

10and this commandment, which was to result in life, proved to result in death for me;

11for sin, taking opportunity through the commandment, deceived me, and through it killed me.

12So then, the Law is holy, and the commandment is holy and righteous and good.

13Therefore did that which is good become *a cause of* death for me? May it never be! Rather it was sin, in order that it might be shown to be sin by effecting my death through that which is good, that through the commandment sin might become utterly sinful.

The Conflict of Two Natures

14For we know that the Law is spiritual; but I am of flesh, sold into bondage to sin.

15For that which I am doing, I do not understand; for I am not practicing what

---

τῶν ἁμαρτιῶν τὰ διὰ τοῦ νόμου ἐνηργεῖτο
— of sins — through the law operated

ἐν τοῖς μέλεσιν ἡμῶν εἰς τὸ καρποφορῆσαι
in the members of us for the to bear fruit

τῷ θανάτῳ· 6 νυνὶ δὲ κατηργήθημεν ἀπὸ
— to death; but now we were discharged from

τοῦ νόμου, ἀποθανόντες ἐν ᾧ κατειχόμεθα,
the law, having died [to that] in which we were held fast,

ὥστε δουλεύειν [ἡμᾶς]ᵇ ἐν καινότητι
so as to serve usᵇ in newness

πνεύματος καὶ οὐ παλαιότητι γράμματος.
of spirit and not [in] oldness of letter.

7 Τί οὖν ἐροῦμεν; ὁ νόμος ἁμαρτία;
What therefore shall we say? the law sin?

μὴ γένοιτο· ἀλλὰ τὴν ἁμαρτίαν οὐκ
May it not be; yet — sin not

ἔγνων εἰ μὴ διὰ νόμου· τήν τε γὰρ
I knew except through law; — ²also ¹for

ἐπιθυμίαν οὐκ ᾔδειν εἰ μὴ ὁ νόμος
lust I knew not except the law

ἔλεγεν· οὐκ ἐπιθυμήσεις· 8 ἀφορμὴν δὲ
said : Thou shalt not lust; but ²occasion

λαβοῦσα ἡ ἁμαρτία διὰ τῆς ἐντολῆς
¹taking ¹sin through the commandment

κατειργάσατο ἐν ἐμοὶ πᾶσαν ἐπιθυμίαν·
wrought in me every lust;

χωρὶς γὰρ νόμου ἁμαρτία νεκρά. 9 ἐγὼ
for without law sin [is] dead. I

δὲ ἔζων χωρὶς νόμου ποτέ· ἐλθούσης δὲ
And was living without law then; but coming
=when the

τῆς ἐντολῆς ἡ ἁμαρτία ἀνέζησεν, 10 ἐγὼ
the commandmentᵃ — sin revived, ²I
commandment came

δὲ ἀπέθανον, καὶ εὑρέθη μοι ἡ ἐντολὴ
¹and died, and ¹was ²to me ¹the ³command-
found ment

ἡ εἰς ζωήν, αὕτη εἰς θάνατον· 11 ἡ γὰρ
— ²for ⁴life, ⁵this to death; — for

ἁμαρτία ἀφορμὴν λαβοῦσα διὰ τῆς
sin ²occasion ¹taking through the

ἐντολῆς ἐξηπάτησέν με καὶ δι' αὐτῆς
commandment deceived me and through it

ἀπέκτεινεν. 12 ὥστε ὁ μὲν νόμος ἅγιος,
killed [me]. So the — law [is] holy,

καὶ ἡ ἐντολὴ ἁγία καὶ δικαία καὶ ἀγαθή.
and the command- holy and just and good.
ment

13 Τὸ οὖν ἀγαθὸν ἐμοὶ ἐγένετο θάνατος;
²The ¹therefore good to me became death?

μὴ γένοιτο· ἀλλὰ ἡ ἁμαρτία, ἵνα φανῇ
May it not be; yet — sin, in or- it might
der that appear

ἁμαρτία, διὰ τοῦ ἀγαθοῦ μοι κατεργα-
sin, through the good ³to me ¹work-

ζομένη θάνατον, ἵνα γένηται καθ' ὑπερβολὴν
ing ²death, in or- ⁵might ⁶excessively†
der that become

ἁμαρτωλὸς ἡ ἁμαρτία διὰ τῆς ἐντολῆς.
⁷sinful — ¹sin ²through ³the ⁴commandment.

14 οἴδαμεν γὰρ ὅτι ὁ νόμος πνευματικός
For we know that the law spiritual

ἐστιν· ἐγὼ δὲ σάρκινός εἰμι, πεπραμένος
is; but I fleshy am, *having been sold*

ὑπὸ τὴν ἁμαρτίαν. 15 ὃ γὰρ κατεργάζομαι
under — sin. For what I work

οὐ γινώσκω· οὐ γὰρ ὃ θέλω τοῦτο
I know not; for not what I wish this

---

aroused by the law were at work in our bodies, so that we bore fruit for death.

6But now, by dying to what once bound us, we have been released from the law so that we serve in the new way of the Spirit, and not in the old way of the written code.

Struggling With Sin

7What shall we say, then? Is the law sin? Certainly not! Indeed I would not have known what sin was except through the law. For I would not have known what coveting really was if the law had not said, "Do not covet."ʸ 8But sin, seizing the opportunity afforded by the commandment, produced in me every kind of covetous desire. For apart from law, sin is dead. 9Once I was alive apart from law; but when the commandment came, sin sprang to life and I died. 10I found that the very commandment that was intended to bring life actually brought death. 11For sin, seizing the opportunity afforded by the commandment, deceived me, and through the commandment put me to death. 12So then, the law is holy, and the commandment is holy, righteous and good.

13Did that which is good, then, become death to me? By no means! But in order that sin might be recognized as sin, it produced death in me through what was good, so that through the commandment sin might become utterly sinful.

14We know that the law is spiritual; but I am unspiritual, sold as a slave to sin. 15I do not understand what I do. For what I want to do

ʸ7 Exodus 20:17; Deut. 5:21

I *would* like to do, but I am doing the very thing I hate.
16But if I do the very thing I do not wish *to do*, I agree with the Law, *confessing* that it is good.
17So now, no longer am I the one doing it, but sin which indwells me.
18For I know that nothing good dwells in me, that is, in my flesh; for the wishing is present in me, but the doing of the good *is* not.
19For the good that I wish; I do not do; but I practice the very evil that I do not wish.
20But if I am doing the very thing I do not wish, I am no longer the one doing it, but sin which dwells in me.
21I find then the principle that evil is present in me, the one who wishes to do good.
22For I joyfully concur with the law of God in the inner man,
23but I see a different law in the members of my body, waging war against the law of my mind, and making me a prisoner of the law of sin which is in my members.
24Wretched man that I am! Who will set me free from the body of this death?
25Thanks be to God through Jesus Christ our Lord! So then, on the one hand I myself with my mind am serving the law of God, but on the other, with my flesh the law of sin.

πράσσω, ἀλλ' ὃ μισῶ τοῦτο ποιῶ. 16 εἰ
I practise, but what I hate this I do. if

δὲ ὃ οὐ θέλω τοῦτο ποιῶ, σύμφημι
But what I wish not this I do, I agree with

τῷ νόμῳ ὅτι καλός. 17 νυνὶ δὲ οὐκέτι
the law that [it is] good. But now no longer

ἐγὼ κατεργάζομαι αὐτὸ ἀλλὰ ἡ ἐνοικοῦσα
I work it but 1the 2indwelling

ἐν ἐμοὶ ἁμαρτία. 18 οἶδα γὰρ ὅτι οὐκ
1in 2me 3sin. For I know that not

οἰκεῖ ἐν ἐμοί, τοῦτ' ἔστιν ἐν τῇ σαρκί
dwells in me, this is in the flesh

μου, ἀγαθόν· τὸ γὰρ θέλειν παράκειταί
of me, [that which is] – for to wish is present

μοι, τὸ δὲ κατεργάζεσθαι τὸ καλὸν
good;
to me, – but 2to work 3the 4good

οὔ· 19 οὐ γὰρ ὃ θέλω ποιῶ ἀγαθόν,
1not; for not what 2I wish 3I do 1good,

ἀλλὰ ὃ οὐ θέλω κακὸν τοῦτο πράσσω.
but what 2I wish not 1evil this I practise.

20 εἰ δὲ ὃ οὐ θέλω ἐγὼ τοῦτο ποιῶ,
But if what 2wish not 1I this I do,

οὐκέτι ἐγὼ κατεργάζομαι αὐτὸ ἀλλὰ ἡ
no longer I work it but 1the

οἰκοῦσα ἐν ἐμοὶ ἁμαρτία. 21 εὑρίσκω
2dwelling 3in 4me 2sin. I find

ἄρα τὸν νόμον τῷ θέλοντι ἐμοὶ ποιεῖν
then the law 2the [one] 3wishing 1to me to do

τὸ καλόν, ὅτι ἐμοὶ τὸ κακὸν παράκειται·
the good, that to me the evil is present;

22 συνήδομαι γὰρ τῷ νόμῳ τοῦ θεοῦ κατὰ
for I delight in the law – of God according to

τὸν ἔσω ἄνθρωπον, 23 βλέπω δὲ ἕτερον
the inner man, but I see a different

νόμον ἐν τοῖς μέλεσίν μου ἀντιστρατευόμενον
law in the members of me warring against

τῷ νόμῳ τοῦ νοός μου καὶ αἰχμαλωτίζοντά
the law of the mind of me and taking captive

με ἐν τῷ νόμῳ τῆς ἁμαρτίας τῷ ὄντι
me by the law – of sin the [one] being

ἐν τοῖς μέλεσίν μου. 24 Ταλαίπωρος
in the members of me. 1Wretched

ἐγὼ ἄνθρωπος· τίς με ῥύσεται ἐκ τοῦ
2I 3man; who me will deliver from the

σώματος τοῦ θανάτου τούτου; 25 χάρις
body of this death? Thanks

τῷ θεῷ διὰ Ἰησοῦ Χριστοῦ τοῦ κυρίου
– to God through Jesus Christ the Lord

ἡμῶν. Ἄρα οὖν αὐτὸς ἐγὼ τῷ μὲν
of us. So then 2[my]self 1I 4with 3on one
the hand

νοῒ δουλεύω νόμῳ θεοῦ, τῇ δὲ σαρκὶ
6mind serve [the] law of God, on the other flesh
with the

Chapter 8

Deliverance from Bondage

THERE is therefore now no condemnation for those who are in Christ Jesus.
2For the law of the Spirit of life in Christ Jesus has set *g*you free from the law

g Some ancient mss. read me

νόμῳ ἁμαρτίας. 8 οὐδὲν ἄρα νῦν κατάκριμα
[the] law of sin. 4No 1then 3now 5condemnation
3[there is]

τοῖς ἐν Χριστῷ Ἰησοῦ. 2 ὁ γὰρ νόμος τοῦ
to the in Christ Jesus. For the law of the
[ones]

πνεύματος τῆς ζωῆς ἐν Χριστῷ Ἰησοῦ
spirit – of life in Christ Jesus

ἠλευθέρωσέν σε ἀπὸ τοῦ νόμου τῆς
freed thee from the law –

I do not do, but what I hate I do.
16And if I do what I do not want to do, I agree that the law is good.
17As it is, it is no longer I myself who do it, but it is sin living in me.
18I know that nothing good lives in me, that is, in my sinful nature.*z* For I have the desire to do what is good, but I cannot carry it out.
19For what I do is not the good I want to do; no, the evil I do not want to do—this I keep on doing.
20Now if I do what I do not want to do, it is no longer I who do it, but it is sin living in me that does it.
21So I find this law at work: When I want to do good, evil is right there with me.
22For in my inner being I delight in God's law;
23but I see another law at work in the members of my body, waging war against the law of my mind and making me a prisoner of the law of sin at work within my members.
24What a wretched man I am! Who will rescue me from this body of death?
25Thanks be to God—through Jesus Christ our Lord!
So then, I myself in my mind am a slave to God's law, but in the sinful nature a slave to the law of sin.

Chapter 8

Life Through the Spirit

THEREFORE, there is now no condemnation for those who are in Christ Jesus,*a* 2because through Christ Jesus the law of the Spirit of life set me free

*z*18 Or *my flesh*
*a*1 Some later manuscripts *Jesus, who do not live according to the sinful nature but according to the Spirit.*

of sin and of death.

³For what the Law could not do, weak as it was through the flesh, God *did:* sending His own Son in the likeness of sinful flesh and *as an offering* for sin, He condemned sin in the flesh,

⁴in order that the requirement of the Law might be fulfilled in us, who do not walk according to the flesh, but according to the Spirit.

⁵For those who are according to the flesh set their minds on the things of the flesh, but those who are according to the Spirit, the things of the Spirit.

⁶For the mind set on the flesh is death, but the mind set on the Spirit is life and peace,

⁷because the mind set on the flesh is hostile toward God; for it does not subject itself to the law of God, for it is not even able *to do so;*

⁸and those who are in the flesh cannot please God.

⁹However, you are not in the flesh but in the Spirit, if indeed the Spirit of God dwells in you. But if anyone does not have the Spirit of Christ, he does not belong to Him.

¹⁰And if Christ is in you, though the body is dead because of sin, yet the spirit is alive because of righteousness.

¹¹But if the Spirit of Him who raised Jesus from the dead dwells in you, He who raised Christ Jesus from the dead will also give life to your mortal bodies ʰthrough His Spirit who indwells you.

¹²So then, brethren, we are under obligation, not to

ʰSome ancient mss. read *because of*

ἁμαρτίας καὶ τοῦ θανάτου. 3 τὸ γὰρ
of sin and - of death. For the

ἀδύνατον τοῦ νόμου, ἐν ᾧ ἠσθένει διὰ
impossible of the law, in which it was through
thing weak

τῆς σαρκός, ὁ θεὸς τὸν ἑαυτοῦ υἱὸν
the flesh, - ¹God ³the ⁵of himself ⁴Son

πέμψας ἐν ὁμοιώματι σαρκὸς ἁμαρτίας
²sending in likeness of flesh of sin

καὶ περὶ ἁμαρτίας κατέκρινεν τὴν ἁμαρτίαν
and concerning sin condemned - sin

ἐν τῇ σαρκί, 4 ἵνα τὸ δικαίωμα τοῦ
in the flesh, in order the ordinance of the
that

νόμου πληρωθῇ ἐν ἡμῖν τοῖς μὴ κατὰ
law may be in us the not accord-
fulfilled [ones] ing to

σάρκα περιπατοῦσιν ἀλλὰ κατὰ πνεῦμα.
flesh walking but according to spirit.

5 οἱ γὰρ κατὰ σάρκα ὄντες τὰ τῆς
For the [ones] accord- flesh being the of the
ing to things

σαρκὸς φρονοῦσιν, οἱ δὲ κατὰ πνεῦμα
flesh mind, but the accord- spirit
[ones] ing to

τὰ τοῦ πνεύματος. 6 τὸ γὰρ φρόνημα
the of the Spirit. For the mind
things

τῆς σαρκὸς θάνατος, τὸ δὲ φρόνημα
of the flesh [is] death, but the mind

τοῦ πνεύματος ζωὴ καὶ εἰρήνη. 7 διότι
of the Spirit life and peace. Wherefore

τὸ φρόνημα τῆς σαρκὸς ἔχθρα εἰς θεόν·
the mind of the flesh [is] enmity against God;

τῷ γὰρ νόμῳ τοῦ θεοῦ οὐχ ὑποτάσσεται,
for to the law - of God it is not subject,

οὐδὲ γὰρ δύναται· 8 οἱ δὲ ἐν σαρκὶ
neither indeed can it; and the [ones] ²in ³flesh

ὄντες θεῷ ἀρέσαι οὐ δύνανται. 9 ὑμεῖς
¹being ⁶God ⁵to please ⁴cannot. ye

δὲ οὐκ ἐστὲ ἐν σαρκὶ ἀλλὰ ἐν πνεύματι,
But are not in flesh but in Spirit,

εἴπερ πνεῦμα θεοῦ οἰκεῖ ἐν ὑμῖν. εἰ
since [the] Spirit of God dwells in you. if

δέ τις πνεῦμα Χριστοῦ οὐκ ἔχει, οὗτος
But anyone [the] Spirit of Christ has not, this one

οὐκ ἔστιν αὐτοῦ. 10 εἰ δὲ Χριστὸς
is not of him. But if Christ

ἐν ὑμῖν, τὸ μὲν σῶμα νεκρὸν διὰ
[is] in you, ²the ¹on one ³body [is] dead because
hand of

ἁμαρτίαν, τὸ δὲ πνεῦμα ζωὴ διὰ
sin, ²the ¹on the ³spirit [is] because
other life of

δικαιοσύνην. 11 εἰ δὲ τὸ πνεῦμα τοῦ
righteousness. But if the Spirit of the
[one]

ἐγείραντος τὸν Ἰησοῦν ἐκ νεκρῶν οἰκεῖ ἐν
having raised - Jesus from [the] dead dwells in

ὑμῖν, ὁ ἐγείρας ἐκ νεκρῶν Χριστὸν
you, the having from [the] dead Christ
[one] raised

Ἰησοῦν ζωοποιήσει καὶ τὰ θνητὰ σώματα
Jesus will quicken also the mortal bodies

ὑμῶν διὰ τοῦ ἐνοικοῦντος αὐτοῦ πνεύματος
of you through the ³indwelling ²of him ¹Spirit

ἐν ὑμῖν.
⁴in ⁵you.

12 Ἄρα οὖν, ἀδελφοί, ὀφειλέται ἐσμέν,
So then, brothers, debtors we are,

---

from the law of sin and death. ³For what the law was powerless to do in that it was weakened by the sinful nature,ᵇ God did by sending his own Son in the likeness of sinful man to be a sin offering.ᶜ And so he condemned sin in sinful man,ᵈ ⁴in order that the righteous requirements of the law might be fully met in us, who do not live according to the sinful nature but according to the Spirit.

⁵Those who live according to the sinful nature have their minds set on what that nature desires; but those who live in accordance with the Spirit have their minds set on what the Spirit desires. ⁶The mind of sinful manᵉ is death, but the mind controlled by the Spirit is life and peace; ⁷the sinful mindᶠ is hostile to God. It does not submit to God's law, nor can it do so. ⁸Those controlled by the sinful nature cannot please God.

⁹You, however, are controlled not by the sinful nature but by the Spirit, if the Spirit of God lives in you. And if anyone does not have the Spirit of Christ, he does not belong to Christ. ¹⁰But if Christ is in you, your body is dead because of sin, yet your spirit is alive because of righteousness. ¹¹And if the Spirit of him who raised Jesus from the dead is living in you, he who raised Christ from the dead will also give life to your mortal bodies through his Spirit, who lives in you.

¹²Therefore, brothers, we have an obligation—but it

ᵇ3 Or *the flesh;* also in verses 4, 5, 8, 9, 12 and 13
ᶜ3 Or *man, for sin*
ᵈ3 Or *in the flesh*
ᵉ6 Or *mind set on the flesh*
ᶠ7 Or *the mind set on the flesh*

the flesh, to live according to the flesh—

13for if you are living according to the flesh, you must die; but if by the Spirit you are putting to death the deeds of the body, you will live.

14For all who are being led by the Spirit of God, these are sons of God.

15For you have not received a spirit of slavery leading to fear again, but you have received a spirit of adoption as sons by which we cry out, "Abba! Father!"

16The Spirit Himself bears witness with our spirit that we are children of God,

17and if children, heirs also, heirs of God and fellow heirs with Christ, if indeed we suffer with *Him* in order that we may also be glorified with *Him*.

18For I consider that the sufferings of this present time are not worthy to be compared with the glory that is to be revealed to us.

19For the anxious longing of the creation waits eagerly for the revealing of the sons of God.

20For the creation was subjected to futility, not of its own will, but because of Him who subjected it, *i* in hope

21that the creation itself also will be set free from its slavery to corruption into the freedom of the glory of the children of God.

22For we know that the whole creation groans and suffers the pains of childbirth together until now.

23And not only this, but also we ourselves, having the first fruits of the Spirit, even we ourselves groan within ourselves, waiting eagerly for *our* adoption as sons, the redemption of our body.

24For in hope we have been saved, but hope that is

οὐ τῇ σαρκὶ τοῦ κατὰ σάρκα ζῆν. 13 εἰ
not to the flesh - accord- flesh to lived. if
ing to

γὰρ κατὰ σάρκα ζῆτε, μέλλετε ἀποθνῄσκειν·
For accord- flesh ye live, ye are to die:
ing to about

εἰ δὲ πνεύματι τὰς πράξεις τοῦ σώματος
but if by [the] Spirit the practices of the body

θανατοῦτε, ζήσεσθε. 14 ὅσοι γὰρ πνεύματι
ye put to death, ye will live. For as many as by [the] Spirit

θεοῦ ἄγονται, οὗτοι υἱοί εἰσιν θεοῦ.
of God are led, these sons are of God.

15 οὐ γὰρ ἐλάβετε πνεῦμα δουλείας πάλιν
For ye received not a spirit of slavery again

εἰς φόβον, ἀλλὰ ἐλάβετε πνεῦμα υἱοθεσίας,
for fear, but ye received a spirit of adoption,

ἐν ᾧ κράζομεν· ἀββὰ ὁ πατήρ. 16 αὐτὸ
by which we cry: Abba - Father. ³it(him)self

τὸ πνεῦμα συμμαρτυρεῖ τῷ πνεύματι ἡμῶν
¹The ²Spirit witnesses with the spirit of us

ὅτι. ἐσμὲν τέκνα θεοῦ. 17 εἰ δὲ τέκνα,
that. we are children of God. And if children,

καὶ κληρονόμοι· κληρονόμοι μὲν θεοῦ,
also heirs; heirs on one hand of God,

συγκληρονόμοι δὲ Χριστοῦ, εἴπερ συμπάσ-
joint heirs on the of Christ, since we suffer
other

χομεν ἵνα καὶ συνδοξασθῶμεν. 18 Λογίζομαι
with[him] in or- also we may be glorified I reckon
der that with [him].

γὰρ ὅτι οὐκ ἄξια τὰ παθήματα τοῦ
For that ⁶[are] ⁷not ⁸worthy ¹the ²sufferings ³of the

νῦν καιροῦ πρὸς τὴν μέλλουσαν δόξαν
⁴now ⁵time [to with the coming glory
(present) be compared]

ἀποκαλυφθῆναι εἰς ἡμᾶς. 19 ἡ γὰρ
to be revealed to us. For the

ἀποκαραδοκία τῆς κτίσεως τὴν ἀποκάλυψιν
anxious watching· of the creation ²the ³revelation

τῶν υἱῶν τοῦ θεοῦ ἀπεκδέχεται. 20 τῇ
⁴of the ⁵sons ⁶of God ¹is eagerly expecting. -

γὰρ ματαιότητι ἡ κτίσις ὑπετάγη, οὐχ
For to vanity the creation was subjected, not

ἑκοῦσα, ἀλλὰ διὰ τὸν ὑποτάξαντα, ἐφ'
willing[ly], but because of the [one] subjecting, in

ἐλπίδι 21 διότι καὶ αὐτὴ ἡ κτίσις
hope because even itself the creation

ἐλευθερωθήσεται ἀπὸ τῆς δουλείας τῆς
will be freed from the slavery -

φθορᾶς εἰς τὴν ἐλευθερίαν τῆς δόξης
of corruption to the freedom of the glory

τῶν τέκνων τοῦ θεοῦ. 22 οἴδαμεν γὰρ
of the children - of God. For we know

ὅτι πᾶσα ἡ κτίσις συστενάζει καὶ
that all the creation groans together and

συνωδίνει ἄχρι τοῦ νῦν· 23 οὐ μόνον δέ,
travails together until - now; and not only [so],

ἀλλὰ καὶ αὐτοὶ τὴν ἀπαρχὴν τοῦ πνεύματος
but also [our]selves ²the ³firstfruit ⁴of the ⁵Spirit

ἔχοντες [ἡμεῖς] καὶ αὐτοὶ ἐν ἑαυτοῖς
¹having we also [our]selves in ourselves

στενάζομεν υἱοθεσίαν ἀπεκδεχόμενοι, τὴν
groan adoption eagerly expecting, the

ἀπολύτρωσιν τοῦ σώματος ἡμῶν. 24 τῇ
redemption of the body of us. -

γὰρ ἐλπίδι ἐσώθημεν· ἐλπὶς δὲ βλεπομένη
For by hope we were saved; but hope being seen

---

is not to the sinful nature, to live according to it. 13For if you live according to the sinful nature, you will die; but if by the Spirit you put to death the misdeeds of the body, you will live, 14because those who are led by the Spirit of God are sons of God. 15For you did not receive a spirit that makes you a slave again to fear, but you received the Spirit of sonship. *g* And by him we cry, "Abba, *h* Father." 16The Spirit himself testifies with our spirit that we are God's children. 17Now if we are children, then we are heirs—heirs of God and co-heirs with Christ, if indeed we share in his sufferings in order that we may also share in his glory.

Future Glory

18I consider that our present sufferings are not worth comparing with the glory that will be revealed in us. 19The creation waits in eager expectation for the sons of God to be revealed. 20For the creation was subjected to frustration, not by its own choice, but by the will of the one who subjected it, in hope *i* that *i* the creation itself will be liberated from its bondage to decay and brought into the glorious freedom of the children of God.

22We know that the whole creation has been groaning as in the pains of childbirth right up to the present time. 23Not only so, but we ourselves, who have the firstfruits of the Spirit, groan inwardly as we wait eagerly for our adoption as sons, the redemption of our bodies. 24For in this hope we were saved. But hope that

---

i Some ancient mss. read *in hope; because the creation*

g 15 Or adoption
h 15 Aramaic for Father
i 20,21 Or subjected it in hope.
21For

seen is not hope; for ʲ why does one also hope for what he sees? 25But if we hope for what we do not see, with perseverance we wait eagerly for it.

Our Victory in Christ

26And in the same way the Spirit also helps our weakness; for we do not know how to pray as we should, but the Spirit Himself intercedes for *us* with groanings too deep for words;

27and He who searches the hearts knows what the mind of the Spirit is, because He intercedes for the saints according to *the will of* God.

28And we know that ᵏGod causes all things to work together for good to those who love God, to those who are called according to *His* purpose.

29For whom He foreknew, He also predestined *to become* conformed to the image of His Son, that He might be the first-born among many brethren;

30and whom He predestined, these He also called; and whom He called, these He also justified; and whom He justified, these He also glorified.

31What then shall we say to these things? If God *is* for us, who *is* against us?

32He who did not spare His own Son, but delivered Him up for us all, how will He not also with Him freely give us all things?

33Who will bring a charge against God's elect? God is the one who justifies;

34who is the one who condemns? Christ Jesus is He who died, yes, rather who was ˡraised, who is at the right hand of God, who also intercedes for us.

35Who shall separate us from the love of ᵐChrist? Shall tribulation, or distress, or persecution, or

 ʲ Some ancient mss. read who hopes for what he sees?
ᵏ Some ancient mss. read all things work together for good
ˡ Some ancient mss. read raised from the dead
ᵐ Some ancient mss. read God

οὐκ ἔστιν ἐλπίς· ὁ γὰρ βλέπει τις,
is not hope; for what sees anyone,

τί καὶ ἐλπίζει; 25 εἰ δὲ ὃ οὐ βλέπομεν
why also he hopes? but if what we do not see

ἐλπίζομεν, δι' ὑπομονῆς ἀπεκδεχόμεθα.
we hope [for], through patience we eagerly expect.

26 ὡσαύτως δὲ καὶ τὸ πνεῦμα συναντιλαμ-
And similarly also the Spirit takes

βάνεται τῇ ἀσθενείᾳ ἡμῶν· τὸ γὰρ τί
share in the weakness of us; – for what

προσευξώμεθα καθὸ δεῖ οὐκ οἴδαμεν, ἀλλὰ
we may pray as it behoves we know not, but

αὐτὸ τὸ πνεῦμα ὑπερεντυγχάνει στεναγμοῖς
it(him)self the Spirit supplicates on [our] behalf with groanings

ἀλαλήτοις· 27 ὁ δὲ ἐρευνῶν τὰς καρδίας
unutterable; and the [one] searching the hearts

οἶδεν τί τὸ φρόνημα τοῦ πνεύματος,
knows what [is] the mind of the Spirit,

ὅτι κατὰ θεὸν ἐντυγχάνει ὑπὲρ ἁγίων.
be-cause according to God he supplicates on behalf saints.

28 οἴδαμεν δὲ ὅτι τοῖς ἀγαπῶσιν τὸν
And we know that to the [ones] loving –

θεὸν πάντα συνεργεῖ [ὁ θεὸς] εἰς ἀγαθόν,
God ³all things ²works together – ¹God for good,

τοῖς κατὰ πρόθεσιν κλητοῖς οὖσιν. 29 ὅτι
to the [ones] ²according to ⁴purpose ³called ¹being. Because

οὓς προέγνω, καὶ προώρισεν συμμόρφους
whom he foreknew, also he foreordained conformed to

τῆς εἰκόνος τοῦ υἱοῦ αὐτοῦ, εἰς τὸ
of the image of the Son of him, for the =that he should be

εἶναι αὐτὸν πρωτότοκον ἐν πολλοῖς
to be himᵇ firstborn among many

ἀδελφοῖς· 30 οὓς δὲ προώρισεν, τούτους
brothers; but whom he foreordained, these

καὶ ἐκάλεσεν· καὶ οὓς ἐκάλεσεν, τούτους
also he called; and whom he called, these

καὶ ἐδικαίωσεν· οὓς δὲ ἐδικαίωσεν, τούτους
also he justified; but whom he justified, these

καὶ ἐδόξασεν. 31 Τί οὖν ἐροῦμεν πρὸς
also he glorified. What therefore shall we say to

ταῦτα; εἰ ὁ θεὸς ὑπὲρ ἡμῶν, τίς καθ'
these things? If – God on behalf of us, who against

ἡμῶν; ὅς γε τοῦ ἰδίου υἱοῦ οὐκ ἐφείσατο,
us? Who indeed the(his) own Son spared not,

32 ἀλλὰ ὑπὲρ ἡμῶν πάντων παρέδωκεν
but on behalf of us all delivered

αὐτόν, πῶς οὐχὶ καὶ σὺν αὐτῷ τὰ πάντα
him, how not also with him – all things

ἡμῖν χαρίσεται; 33 τίς ἐγκαλέσει κατὰ
to us will he freely give? Who will bring a charge against

ἐκλεκτῶν θεοῦ; θεὸς ὁ δικαιῶν· 34 τίς
chosen ones of God? God [is] the [one] justifying; who

ὁ κατακρινῶν; Χριστὸς Ἰησοῦς ὁ ἀποθανών,
the [one] condemning? Christ Jesus [is] the [one] having died,

μᾶλλον δὲ ἐγερθείς, ὅς ἐστιν ἐν δεξιᾷ
but rather having been raised, who is at [the] right [hand]

τοῦ θεοῦ, ὃς καὶ ἐντυγχάνει ὑπὲρ ἡμῶν.
– of God, who also supplicates on behalf of us.

35 τίς ἡμᾶς χωρίσει ἀπὸ τῆς ἀγάπης
Who us will separate from the love

τοῦ Χριστοῦ; θλῖψις ἢ στενοχωρία ἢ
– of Christ? affliction or distress or

---

is seen is no hope at all. Who hopes for what he already has? 25But if we hope for what we do not yet have, we wait for it patiently.

26In the same way, the Spirit helps us in our weakness. We do not know what we ought to pray for, but the Spirit himself intercedes for us with groans that words cannot express. 27And he who searches our hearts knows the mind of the Spirit, because the Spirit intercedes for the saints in accordance with God's will.

More Than Conquerors

28And we know that in all things God works for the good of those who love him,ʲ whoᵏ have been called according to his purpose. 29For those God foreknew he also predestined to be conformed to the likeness of his Son, that he might be the firstborn among many brothers. 30And those he predestined, he also called; those he called, he also justified; those he justified, he also glorified.

31What, then, shall we say in response to this? If God is for us, who can be against us? 32He who did not spare his own Son, but gave him up for us all—how will he not also, along with him, graciously give us all things? 33Who will bring any charge against those whom God has chosen? It is God who justifies. 34Who is he that condemns? Christ Jesus, who died—more than that, who was raised to life—is at the right hand of God and is also interceding for us. 35Who shall separate us from the love of Christ? Shall trouble or hardship or persecution or famine or

ʲ28 Some manuscripts And we know that all things work together for good to those who love God
ᵏ28 Or works together with those who love him to bring about what is good—with those who

famine, or nakedness, or peril, or sword?

36Just as it is written,
"FOR THY SAKE WE ARE BEING PUT TO DEATH ALL DAY LONG; WE WERE CONSIDERED AS SHEEP TO BE SLAUGHTERED."

37But in all these things we overwhelmingly conquer through Him who loved us. 38For I am convinced that neither death, nor life, nor angels, nor principalities, nor things present, nor things to come, nor powers,

39nor height, nor depth, nor any other created thing, shall be able to separate us from the love of God, which is in Christ Jesus our Lord.

Greek	English
διωγμὸς ἢ λιμὸς ἢ γυμνότης ἢ κίνδυνος	persecution or famine or nakedness or peril
ἢ μάχαιρα; 36 καθὼς γέγραπται ὅτι ἕνεκεν	or sword? As it has been written[,] – For the sake
σοῦ θανατούμεθα ὅλην τὴν ἡμέραν,	of thee we are being put to death all the day,
ἐλογίσθημεν ὡς πρόβατα σφαγῆς. 37 ἀλλ'	we were reckoned as sheep of(for) slaughter. But
ἐν τούτοις πᾶσιν ὑπερνικῶμεν διὰ τοῦ	in these things all we overconquer through the
ἀγαπήσαντος ἡμᾶς. 38 πέπεισμαι γὰρ	[one] having loved us. For I have been persuaded
ὅτι οὔτε θάνατος οὔτε ζωὴ οὔτε ἄγγελοι	that not death nor life nor angels
οὔτε ἀρχαὶ οὔτε ἐνεστῶτα οὔτε μέλλοντα	nor rulers nor things present nor things coming
οὔτε δυνάμεις 39 οὔτε ὕψωμα οὔτε βάθος	nor powers nor height nor depth
οὔτε τις κτίσις ἑτέρα δυνήσεται ἡμᾶς	nor any creature other will be able us
χωρίσαι ἀπὸ τῆς ἀγάπης τοῦ θεοῦ τῆς	to separate from the love – of God –
ἐν Χριστῷ Ἰησοῦ τῷ κυρίῳ ἡμῶν.	in Christ Jesus the Lord of us.

nakedness or danger or sword? 36As it is written:

"For your sake we face
    death all day long;
we are considered as
    sheep to be
    slaughtered."[l]

37No, in all these things we are more than conquerors through him who loved us. 38For I am convinced that neither death nor life, neither angels nor demons,[m] neither the present nor the future, nor any powers, 39neither height nor depth, nor anything else in all creation, will be able to separate us from the love of God that is in Christ Jesus our Lord.

Chapter 9

Solicitude for Israel

I am telling the truth in Christ, I am not lying, my conscience bearing me witness in the Holy Spirit, 2that I have great sorrow and unceasing grief in my heart.

3For I could wish that I myself were accursed, *separated* from Christ for the sake of my brethren, my kinsmen according to the flesh, 4who are Israelites, to whom belongs the adoption as sons and the glory and the covenants and the giving of the Law and the *temple* service and the promises, 5whose are the fathers, and from whom is the Christ according to the flesh, who is over all, God blessed forever. Amen.

6But *it is* not as though the word of God has failed. For they are not all Israel who are *descended* from Israel; 7neither are they all children because they are Abraham's descendants, but: "THROUGH ISAAC YOUR DESCENDANTS WILL BE NAMED."

8That is, it is not the children of the flesh who are

Greek	English
9 Ἀλήθειαν λέγω ἐν Χριστῷ, οὐ	Truth I say in Christ, not
ψεύδομαι, συμμαρτυρούσης μοι τῆς	I lie, witnessing with me the
συνειδήσεώς μου ἐν πνεύματι ἁγίῳ, 2 ὅτι	conscience[a] of me in [the] Spirit Holy, that
λύπη μοί ἐστιν μεγάλη καὶ ἀδιάλειπτος	grief to me is great and incessant = I have great grief and . . .
ὀδύνη τῇ καρδίᾳ μου. 3 ηὐχόμην γὰρ	pain[c] in the heart of me. For I was praying
ἀνάθεμα εἶναι αὐτὸς ἐγὼ ἀπὸ τοῦ Χριστοῦ	[a] a curse [b]to be [a][my]self [1]I from – Christ
ὑπὲρ τῶν ἀδελφῶν μου τῶν συγγενῶν	on behalf of the brothers of me the kinsmen
μου κατὰ σάρκα, 4 οἵτινές εἰσιν Ἰσραη-	of me according to flesh, who are Israel-
λῖται, ὧν ἡ υἱοθεσία καὶ ἡ δόξα καὶ	ites, of whom the adoption and the glory and
αἱ διαθῆκαι καὶ ἡ νομοθεσία καὶ ἡ	the covenants and the giving of [the] law and the
λατρεία καὶ αἱ ἐπαγγελίαι, 5 ὧν οἱ	service and the promises, of whom the
πατέρες, καὶ ἐξ ὧν ὁ Χριστὸς τὸ κατὰ	fathers, and from whom the Christ – according to
σάρκα· ὁ ὢν ἐπὶ πάντων θεὸς εὐλογητὸς	flesh; the [one] being over all God blessed
εἰς τοὺς αἰῶνας, ἀμήν. 6 Οὐχ οἷον δὲ	unto the ages, amen. Not of course
ὅτι ἐκπέπτωκεν ὁ λόγος τοῦ θεοῦ. οὐ	that has failed the word – of God. not
γὰρ πάντες οἱ ἐξ Ἰσραήλ, οὗτοι Ἰσραήλ·	For all the [ones] of Israel, these [are of] Israel;
7 οὐδ' ὅτι εἰσὶν σπέρμα Ἀβραάμ, πάντες	neither because they are seed of Abraham, all [are they]
τέκνα, ἀλλ'· ἐν Ἰσαὰκ κληθήσεταί σοι	children, but: In Isaac will be called to thee
σπέρμα. 8 τοῦτ' ἔστιν, οὐ τὰ τέκνα τῆς	seed.[c] This is, not the children of the = thy seed.

Chapter 9

God's Sovereign Choice

I SPEAK the truth in Christ—I am not lying, my conscience confirms it in the Holy Spirit— 2I have great sorrow and unceasing anguish in my heart. 3For I could wish that I myself were cursed and cut off from Christ for the sake of my brothers, those of my own race, 4the people of Israel. Theirs is the adoption as sons; theirs the divine glory, the covenants, the receiving of the law, the temple worship and the promises. 5Theirs are the patriarchs, and from them is traced the human ancestry of Christ, who is God over all, forever praised![n] Amen.

6It is not as though God's word had failed. For not all who are descended from Israel are Israel. 7Nor because they are his descendants are they all Abraham's children. On the contrary, "It is through Isaac that your offspring will be reckoned."[o] 8In other words, it is not the natural children

*l*36 Psalm 44:22
*m*38 Or *nor heavenly rulers*
*n*5 Or *Christ, who is over all. God be forever praised!* Or *Christ. God who is over all be forever praised!*
*o*7 Gen. 21:12

children of God, but the children of the promise are regarded as descendants.

9For this is a word of promise: "AT THIS TIME I WILL COME, AND SARAH SHALL HAVE A SON."

10And not only this, but there was Rebekah also, when she had conceived twins by one man, our father Isaac;

11for though the twins were not yet born, and had not done anything good or bad, in order that God's purpose according to His choice might stand, not because of works, but because of Him who calls,

12it was said to her, "THE OLDER WILL SERVE THE YOUNGER."

13Just as it is written, "JACOB I LOVED, BUT ESAU I HATED."

14What shall we say then? There is no injustice with God, is there? May it never be!

15For He says to Moses, "I WILL HAVE MERCY ON WHOM I HAVE MERCY, AND I WILL HAVE COMPASSION ON WHOM I HAVE COMPASSION."

16So then it does not depend on the man who wills or the man who runs, but on God who has mercy.

17For the Scripture says to Pharaoh, "FOR THIS VERY PURPOSE I RAISED YOU UP, TO DEMONSTRATE MY POWER IN YOU, AND THAT MY NAME MIGHT BE PROCLAIMED THROUGHOUT THE WHOLE EARTH."

18So then He has mercy on whom He desires, and He hardens whom He desires.

19You will say to me then, "Why does He still find fault? For who resists His will?"

20On the contrary, who are you, O man, who answers back to God? The thing molded will not say to the molder, "Why did you make me like this," will it?

σαρκὸς ταῦτα τέκνα τοῦ θεοῦ, ἀλλὰ
flesh these children of God, but

τὰ τέκνα τῆς ἐπαγγελίας λογίζεται εἰς
the children of the promise is(are) reckoned for

σπέρμα. 9 ἐπαγγελίας γὰρ ὁ λόγος οὗτος·
a seed. For ⁵of promise ³the ⁴word ¹this ²[is]:

κατὰ τὸν καιρὸν τοῦτον ἐλεύσομαι καὶ
According to this time I will come and

ἔσται τῇ Σάρρᾳ υἱός. 10 οὐ μόνον δέ,
will be - to Sara a son.ᶜ And not only [so],
=Sarah will have a son.

ἀλλὰ καὶ Ῥεβεκκὰ ἐξ ἑνὸς κοίτην ἔχουσα,
but also Rebecca ²from ³one ¹conceiving,†

Ἰσαὰκ τοῦ πατρὸς ἡμῶν· 11 μήπω γὰρ
Isaac the father of us; for not yet

γεννηθέντων μηδὲ πραξάντωνᵃ τι ἀγαθὸν
being bornᵃ nor practisingᵃ anything good

ἢ φαῦλον, ἵνα ἡ κατ' ἐκλογὴν πρόθεσις
or bad, in order ¹the ⁴accord- ⁵choice ²purpose
that ing to

τοῦ θεοῦ μένῃ, 12 οὐκ ἐξ ἔργων ἀλλ'
- ³of God might not of works but
remain,

ἐκ τοῦ καλοῦντος, ἐρρέθη αὐτῇ ὅτι ὁ
of the [one] calling, it was said to her[,] - The

μείζων δουλεύσει τῷ ἐλάσσονι· 13 καθάπερ
greater will serve the lesser; even as

γέγραπται· τὸν Ἰακὼβ ἠγάπησα, τὸν δὲ
it has been Jacob I loved, - but
written:

Ἡσαῦ ἐμίσησα.
Esau I hated.

14 Τί οὖν ἐροῦμεν; μὴ ἀδικία παρὰ
What therefore shall we say? not unrighteousness with

τῷ θεῷ; μὴ γένοιτο. 15 τῷ Μωϋσεῖ
- God? May it not be. - ²to Moses

γὰρ λέγει· ἐλεήσω ὃν ἂν ἐλεῶ, καὶ
¹For he says: I will whomever I have and
have mercy on mercy,

οἰκτιρήσω ὃν ἂν οἰκτίρω. 16 ἄρα οὖν
I will pity whomever I pity. So therefore
[it is]

οὐ τοῦ θέλοντος οὐδὲ τοῦ τρέχοντος,
not of the [one] wishing nor of the [one] running,

ἀλλὰ τοῦ ἐλεῶντος θεοῦ. 17 λέγει γὰρ
but of the [one] having mercy God. For says

ἡ γραφὴ τῷ Φαραὼ ὅτι εἰς αὐτὸ τοῦτο
the scripture - to Pharaoh[,] - For this very thing

ἐξήγειρά σε, ὅπως ἐνδείξωμαι ἐν σοὶ
I raised up thee, so as I may show forth in thee

τὴν δύναμίν μου, καὶ ὅπως διαγγελῇ τὸ
the power of me, and so as might be pub- the
lished abroad

ὄνομά μου ἐν πάσῃ τῇ γῇ. 18 ἄρα οὖν
name of me in all the earth. So therefore

ὃν θέλει ἐλεεῖ, ὃν δὲ θέλει σκληρύνει.
whom he he has but whom he wishes he hardens.
wishes mercy,

19 Ἐρεῖς μοι οὖν· τί ἔτι μέμφεται;
Thou wilt say to me therefore: Why still finds he fault?

τῷ γὰρ βουλήματι αὐτοῦ τίς ἀνθέστηκεν;
for ³the ⁴counsel ⁵of him ¹who ²resisted?

20 ὦ ἄνθρωπε, μενοῦν γε σὺ τίς εἶ ὁ
O man, nay rather ³thou ¹who ²art the

ἀνταποκρινόμενος τῷ θεῷ; μὴ ἐρεῖ τὸ
[one] replying against - God? not ³Will say ¹the

πλάσμα τῷ πλάσαντι· τί με ἐποίησας
²thing to the having formed: Why ²me ¹madest
formed [one] thou

---

who are God's children, but it is the children of the promise who are regarded as Abraham's offspring.

9For this was how the promise was stated: "At the appointed time I will return, and Sarah will have a son."ᵖ

10Not only that, but Rebekah's children had one and the same father, our father Isaac. 11Yet, before the twins were born or had done anything good or bad —in order that God's purpose in election might stand: 12not by works but by him who calls—she was told, "The older will serve the younger."�q 13Just as it is written: "Jacob I loved, but Esau I hated."ʳ

14What then shall we say? Is God unjust? Not at all! 15For he says to Moses,

"I will have mercy on
whom I have mercy,
and I will have
compassion on
whom I have
compassion."ˢ

16It does not, therefore, depend on man's desire or effort, but on God's mercy. 17For the Scripture says to Pharaoh: "I raised you up for this very purpose, that I might display my power in you and that my name might be proclaimed in all the earth."ᵗ 18Therefore God has mercy on whom he wants to have mercy, and he hardens whom he wants to harden.

19One of you will say to me: "Then why does God still blame us? For who resists his will?" 20But who are you, O man, to talk back to God? "Shall what is formed say to him who formed it, 'Why did you make me like this?' "ᵘ

ᵖ9 Gen. 18:10,14
�q12 Gen. 25:23
ʳ13 Mal. 1:2,3
ˢ15 Exodus 33:19
ᵗ17 Exodus 9:16
ᵘ20 Isaiah 29:16; 45:9

21Or does not the potter have a right over the clay, to make from the same lump one vessel for honorable use, and another for common use?

22What if God, although willing to demonstrate His wrath and to make His power known, endured with much patience vessels of wrath prepared for destruction?

23And *He did so* in order that He might make known the riches of His glory upon vessels of mercy, which He prepared beforehand for glory,

24*even* us, whom He also called, not from among Jews only, but also from among Gentiles?

25As He says also in Hosea,
"I WILL CALL THOSE WHO WERE NOT MY PEOPLE, 'MY PEOPLE,' AND HER WHO WAS NOT BELOVED, 'BELOVED.' "

26"AND IT SHALL BE THAT IN THE PLACE WHERE IT WAS SAID TO THEM, 'YOU ARE NOT MY PEOPLE,' THERE THEY SHALL BE CALLED SONS OF THE LIVING GOD."

27And Isaiah cries out concerning Israel, "THOUGH THE NUMBER OF THE SONS OF ISRAEL BE AS THE SAND OF THE SEA, IT IS THE REMNANT THAT WILL BE SAVED;

28FOR THE LORD WILL EXECUTE HIS WORD UPON THE EARTH, THOROUGHLY AND QUICKLY."

29And just as Isaiah foretold,
"EXCEPT THE LORD OF SABAOTH HAD LEFT TO US A POSTERITY, WE WOULD HAVE BECOME AS SODOM, AND WOULD HAVE RESEMBLED GOMORRAH."

30What shall we say then? That Gentiles, who did not pursue righteousness, attained righteousness, even the righteousness which is by faith;

31but Israel, pursuing a law of righteousness, did not arrive at *that* law.

32Why? Because *they did not pursue it* by faith, but as though *it were* by works. They stumbled over the stumbling stone,

---

οὕτως; **21** ἢ οὐκ ἔχει ἐξουσίαν ὁ κεραμεὺς
thus? or has not ²authority ¹the ²potter

τοῦ πηλοῦ ἐκ τοῦ αὐτοῦ φυράματος
of the clay out of the same lump

ποιῆσαι ὃ μὲν εἰς τιμὴν σκεῦος, ὃ δὲ
to make ¹this ³to ⁴honour ²vessel, that

εἰς ἀτιμίαν; **22** εἰ δὲ θέλων ὁ θεὸς
to dishonour? But if wishing – God

ἐνδείξασθαι τὴν ὀργὴν καὶ γνωρίσαι τὸ
to show forth the(his) wrath and to make known the

δυνατὸν αὐτοῦ ἤνεγκεν ἐν πολλῇ μακρο-
ability of him bore in much long-

θυμίᾳ σκεύη ὀργῆς κατηρτισμένα εἰς
suffering vessels of wrath *having been* fitted for

ἀπώλειαν, **23** καὶ ἵνα γνωρίσῃ τὸν πλοῦτον
destruction, and in or- he might make known the riches
                        der that

τῆς δόξης αὐτοῦ ἐπὶ σκεύη ἐλέους, ἃ
of the glory of him on vessels of mercy, which

προητοίμασεν εἰς δόξαν, **24** οὓς καὶ
he previously prepared for glory, whom also

ἐκάλεσεν ἡμᾶς οὐ μόνον ἐξ Ἰουδαίων
he called[,] us not only of Jews

ἀλλὰ καὶ ἐξ ἐθνῶν; **25** ὡς καὶ ἐν τῷ
but also of nations? As also in –

Ὡσηὲ λέγει· καλέσω τὸν οὐ λαόν μου
Osee he says: I will call the ²not ¹people of me

λαόν μου καὶ τὴν οὐκ ἠγαπημένην
a people of me and the not having been loved

ἠγαπημένην· **26** καὶ ἔσται ἐν τῷ τόπῳ
having been loved; and it shall be in the place

οὗ ἐρρέθη [αὐτοῖς]· οὐ λαός μου ὑμεῖς,
where it was said to them: not a people of me ye [are],

ἐκεῖ κληθήσονται υἱοὶ θεοῦ ζῶντος.
there they will be called sons ²God ¹of a living.

27 Ἠσαΐας δὲ κράζει ὑπὲρ τοῦ Ἰσραήλ·
But Esaias cries on behalf of – Israel:

ἐὰν ᾖ ὁ ἀριθμὸς τῶν υἱῶν Ἰσραὴλ
If be the number of the sons of Israel

ὡς ἡ ἄμμος τῆς θαλάσσης, τὸ ὑπόλειμμα
as the sand of the sea, the remnant

σωθήσεται· **28** λόγον γὰρ συντελῶν καὶ
will be saved; for ⁶an account ¹accomplishing ²and

συντέμνων ποιήσει κύριος ἐπὶ τῆς γῆς.
³cutting short ⁵will make ⁴[the] Lord on the earth.

29 καὶ καθὼς προείρηκεν Ἠσαΐας· εἰ μὴ
And as ²has previously said ¹Esaias: Except

κύριος σαβαὼθ ἐγκατέλιπεν ἡμῖν σπέρμα,
[the] Lord of hosts left to us a seed,

ὡς Σόδομα ἂν ἐγενήθημεν καὶ ὡς Γόμορρα
as Sodom we would have become and as Gomorra

ἂν ὡμοιώθημεν.
we would have been likened.

30 Τί οὖν ἐροῦμεν; ὅτι ἔθνη τὰ μὴ
What therefore shall we say? that nations – not

διώκοντα δικαιοσύνην κατέλαβεν δικαιοσύνην,
pursuing righteousness apprehended righteousness,

δικαιοσύνην δὲ τὴν ἐκ πίστεως· **31** Ἰσραὴλ
but a righteousness – of faith; ²Israel

δὲ διώκων νόμον δικαιοσύνης εἰς νόμον
¹but pursuing a law of righteousness ²to(at) ³a law

οὐκ ἔφθασεν. **32** διὰ τί; ὅτι οὐκ ἐκ
¹did not arrive. Why? Because not of

πίστεως ἀλλ' ὡς ἐξ ἔργων· προσέκοψαν
faith but as of works; they stumbled

τῷ λίθῳ τοῦ προσκόμματος, **33** καθὼς
at the stone – of stumbling, as

21Does not the potter have the right to make out of the same lump of clay some pottery for noble purposes and some for common use?

22What if God, choosing to show his wrath and make his power known, bore with great patience the objects of his wrath—prepared for destruction?

23What if he did this to make the riches of his glory known to the objects of his mercy, whom he prepared in advance for glory—

24even us, whom he also called, not only from the Jews but also from the Gentiles?

25As he says in Hosea:

"I will call them 'my people' who are not my people; and I will call her 'my loved one' who is not my loved one," [v]

26and,

"It will happen that in the very place where it was said to them, 'You are not my people,' they will be called 'sons of the living God.' " [w]

27Isaiah cries out concerning Israel:

"Though the number of the Israelites be like the sand by the sea, only the remnant will be saved.

28For the Lord will carry out his sentence on earth with speed and finality." [x]

29It is just as Isaiah said previously:

"Unless the Lord Almighty had left us descendants, we would have become like Sodom, we would have been like Gomorrah." [y]

Israel's Unbelief

30What then shall we say? That the Gentiles, who did not pursue righteousness, have obtained it, a righteousness that is by faith; 31but Israel, who pursued a law of righteousness, has not attained it. 32Why not? Because they pursued it not by faith but as if it were by works. They stumbled over the "stumbling

[v]25 Hosea 2:23
[w]26 Hosea 1:10
[x]28 Isaiah 10:22,23
[y]29 Isaiah 1:9

33just as it is written,
"BEHOLD, I LAY IN ZION
A STONE OF STUM-
BLING AND A ROCK OF
OFFENSE,
AND HE WHO BELIEVES
IN HIM WILL NOT BE
DISAPPOINTED."

Chapter 10

*The Word of Faith Brings
Salvation*

BRETHREN,   my
heart's desire and my
prayer to God for them is
for *their* salvation.
2For I bear them witness
that they have a zeal for
God, but not in accordance
with knowledge.
3For not knowing about
God's righteousness, and
seeking to establish their
own, they did not subject
themselves to the right-
eousness of God.
4For Christ is the end of
the law for righteousness to
everyone who believes.
5For Moses writes that
the man who practices the
righteousness which is
based on law shall live by
that righteousness.
6But the righteousness
based on faith speaks thus,
"DO NOT SAY IN YOUR
HEART, 'WHO WILL ASCEND
INTO HEAVEN?' (that is, to
bring Christ down),
7or 'WHO WILL DESCEND
INTO THE ABYSS?' (that is, to
bring Christ up from the
dead)."
8But what does it say?
"THE WORD IS NEAR YOU, IN
YOUR MOUTH AND IN YOUR
HEART"—that is, the word
of faith which we are
preaching,
9that if you confess with
your mouth Jesus *as* Lord,
and believe in your heart
that God raised Him from
the dead, you shall be
saved;
10for with the heart man
believes, resulting in righteousness, and with the
mouth he confesses, resulting in salvation.
11For the Scripture says,
"WHOEVER BELIEVES IN HIM

γέγραπται· ἰδοὺ τίθημι ἐν Σιὼν λίθον
it has been Behold I place in Sion a stone
written:

προσκόμματος καὶ πέτραν σκανδάλου, καὶ
of stumbling and a rock of offence, and

ὁ πιστεύων ἐπ' αὐτῷ οὐ καταισχυνθήσεται.
the [one] believing on him   will not be put to shame.

10 Ἀδελφοί, ἡ μὲν εὐδοκία τῆς ἐμῆς
Brothers, the - good pleasure of my

καρδίας καὶ ἡ δέησις πρὸς τὸν θεὸν
heart and the request to   -   God

ὑπὲρ αὐτῶν εἰς σωτηρίαν. **2** μαρτυρῶ
on behalf of them [is] for salvation.   I witness

γὰρ αὐτοῖς ὅτι ζῆλον θεοῦ ἔχουσιν, ἀλλ'
For to them that a zeal of God they have, but

οὐ κατ' ἐπίγνωσιν· **3** ἀγνοοῦντες γὰρ τὴν
not according to knowledge;   for not knowing the

τοῦ θεοῦ δικαιοσύνην, καὶ τὴν ἰδίαν
 - 3of God 1righteousness, and the(ir) own

ζητοῦντες στῆσαι, τῇ δικαιοσύνῃ τοῦ θεοῦ
seeking to establish, to the righteousness - of God

οὐχ ὑπετάγησαν. **4** τέλος γὰρ νόμου
they did not submit.   For end of law

Χριστὸς εἰς δικαιοσύνην παντὶ τῷ
Christ for righteousness to everyone

πιστεύοντι. **5** Μωϋσῆς γὰρ γράφει ὅτι
believing.   For Moses writes[,] -

τὴν δικαιοσύνην τὴν ἐκ νόμου ὁ ποιήσας
4the 1righteousness - 6of 7law 1The 3doing

ἄνθρωπος ζήσεται ἐν αὐτῇ. **6** ἡ δὲ
2man   will live by it.   But the

ἐκ πίστεως δικαιοσύνη οὕτως λέγει· μὴ
2of 3faith 1righteousness thus says: not

εἴπῃς ἐν τῇ καρδίᾳ σου· τίς ἀναβήσεται
Say in the heart of thee: Who will ascend

εἰς τὸν οὐρανόν; τοῦτ' ἔστιν Χριστὸν
into - heaven? this is Christ

καταγαγεῖν· **7** ἤ· τίς καταβήσεται εἰς
to bring down; or: Who will descend into

τὴν ἄβυσσον; τοῦτ' ἔστιν Χριστὸν ἐκ
the abyss? this is Christ from

νεκρῶν ἀναγαγεῖν. **8** ἀλλὰ τί λέγει;
[the] dead to bring up.   But what says it?

ἐγγύς σου τὸ ῥῆμά ἐστιν, ἐν τῷ στόματί
Near thee the word is, in the mouth

σου καὶ ἐν τῇ καρδίᾳ σου· τοῦτ' ἔστιν
of thee and in the heart of thee; this is

τὸ ῥῆμα τῆς πίστεως ὃ κηρύσσομεν.
the word - of faith which we proclaim.

9 ὅτι ἐὰν ὁμολογήσῃς ἐν τῷ στόματί
Because if thou confessest with the mouth

σου κύριον Ἰησοῦν, καὶ πιστεύσῃς ἐν
of thee Lord Jesus, and believest in

τῇ καρδίᾳ σου ὅτι ὁ θεὸς αὐτὸν ἤγειρεν
the heart of thee that - God him raised

ἐκ νεκρῶν, σωθήσῃ· **10** καρδίᾳ γὰρ
from [the] dead, thou wilt be saved; for with heart

πιστεύεται εἰς δικαιοσύνην, στόματι δὲ
[one] believes to righteousness, and with mouth

ὁμολογεῖται εἰς σωτηρίαν. **11** λέγει γὰρ
[one] confesses to salvation.   For says

ἡ γραφή· πᾶς ὁ πιστεύων ἐπ' αὐτῷ
the scripture: Everyone believing on him

---

stone." 33As it is written:

"See, I lay in Zion a
stone that causes
men to stumble
and a rock that makes
them fall,
and the one who trusts in
him will never be
put to shame." z

Chapter 10

BROTHERS,   my
heart's desire and
prayer to God for the Israelites is that they may be
saved. 2For I can testify
about them that they are
zealous for God, but their
zeal is not based on knowledge. 3Since they did not
know the righteousness
that comes from God and
sought to establish their
own, they did not submit to
God's righteousness.
4Christ is the end of the law
so that there may be righteousness for everyone who
believes.
5Moses describes in this
way the righteousness that
is by the law: "The man
who does these things will
live by them." a 6But the
righteousness that is by
faith says: "Do not say in
your heart, 'Who will as-
cend into heaven?' b" (that
is, to bring Christ down)
7"or 'Who will descend
into the deep?' c" (that is,
to bring Christ up from the
dead). 8But what does it
say? "The word is near
you; it is in your mouth and
in your heart," d that is, the
word of faith we are pro-
claiming. 9That if you confess with your mouth,
"Jesus is Lord," and be-
lieve in your heart that God
raised him from the dead,
you will be saved. 10For it
is with your heart that you
believe and are justified,
and it is with your mouth
that you confess and are
saved. 11As the Scripture
says, "Anyone who trusts

z33 Isaiah 8:14; 28:16
a5 Lev. 18:5
b6 Deut. 30:12
c7 Deut. 30:13
d8 Deut. 30:14

WILL NOT BE DISAPPOINTED."
12For there is no distinction between Jew and Greek; for the same *Lord* is Lord of all, abounding in riches for all who call upon Him;
13for "WHOEVER WILL CALL UPON THE NAME OF THE LORD WILL BE SAVED."
14How then shall they call upon Him in whom they have not believed? And how shall they believe in Him whom they have not heard? And how shall they hear without a preacher?
15And how shall they preach unless they are sent? Just as it is written, "HOW BEAUTIFUL ARE THE FEET OF THOSE WHO BRING GLAD TIDINGS OF GOOD THINGS!"
16However, they did not all heed the glad tidings; for Isaiah says, "LORD, WHO HAS BELIEVED OUR REPORT?"
17So faith *comes* from hearing, and hearing by the word of Christ.
18But I say, surely they have never heard, have they? Indeed they have;
"THEIR VOICE HAS GONE OUT INTO ALL THE EARTH,
AND THEIR WORDS TO THE ENDS OF THE WORLD."
19But I say, surely Israel did not know, did they? At the first Moses says,
"I WILL MAKE YOU JEALOUS BY THAT WHICH IS NOT A NATION,
BY A NATION WITHOUT UNDERSTANDING WILL I ANGER YOU."
20And Isaiah is very bold and says,
"I WAS FOUND BY THOSE WHO SOUGHT ME NOT,
I BECAME MANIFEST TO THOSE WHO DID NOT ASK FOR ME."
21But as for Israel He says, "ALL THE DAY LONG I HAVE STRETCHED OUT MY HANDS TO A DISOBEDIENT AND OBSTINATE PEOPLE."

οὐ   καταισχυνθήσεται.   **12** οὐ   γάρ   ἐστιν
will not be put to shame.   For there is no

διαστολὴ   Ἰουδαίου   τε   καὶ   Ἕλληνος.   ὁ
difference   ²of Jew   ¹both   ³and   ⁴of Greek.*   the

γὰρ   αὐτὸς   κύριος   πάντων,   πλουτῶν   εἰς
for   same   Lord   of all,   is rich   to

πάντας   τοὺς   ἐπικαλουμένους   αὐτόν·   **13** πᾶς
all   the [ones]   calling on   him;   ²everyone

γὰρ   ὃς   ἂν   ἐπικαλέσηται   τὸ   ὄνομα   κυρίου
¹for   whoever   calls on   the   name   of [the] Lord

σωθήσεται.   **14** Πῶς   οὖν   ἐπικαλέσωνται   εἰς
will be saved.   How therefore   may they call on   in [one]

ὃν   οὐκ   ἐπίστευσαν;   πῶς   δὲ   πιστεύσωσιν
whom they believed not?   And how   may they believe

οὗ   οὐκ   ἤκουσαν;   πῶς   δὲ   ἀκούσωσιν
of whom they heard not?   And how   may they hear

χωρὶς   κηρύσσοντος;   **15** πῶς   δὲ   κηρύξωσιν
without   [one] heralding?   And how   may they herald

ἐὰν   μὴ   ἀποσταλῶσιν;   καθάπερ   γέγραπται·
if   they are not sent?   As   it has been written:

ὡς   ὡραῖοι   οἱ   πόδες   τῶν   εὐαγγελιζομένων
How beautiful   the   feet   of the [ones] announcing *good*

ἀγαθά.   **16** ἀλλ'   οὐ   πάντες   ὑπήκουσαν   τῷ
good things.   But not   all   obeyed   the

εὐαγγελίῳ.   Ἠσαΐας   γὰρ   λέγει·   κύριε,
gospel.   For Esaias   says: Lord,

τίς   ἐπίστευσεν   τῇ   ἀκοῇ   ἡμῶν;   **17** ἄρα
who   believed   the   hearing   of us?   Then

ἡ   πίστις   ἐξ   ἀκοῆς,   ἡ   δὲ   ἀκοὴ   διὰ
-   faith [is] from   hearing,   and the   hearing through

ῥήματος   Χριστοῦ.   **18** ἀλλὰ   λέγω,   μὴ
a word   of Christ.   But   I say,   not

οὐκ   ἤκουσαν;   μενοῦν   γε·   εἰς   πᾶσαν
did they not hear?   Nay   rather: To   all

τὴν   γῆν   ἐξῆλθεν   ὁ   φθόγγος   αὐτῶν,
the   earth   went out   the   utterance   of them,

καὶ   εἰς   τὰ   πέρατα   τῆς   οἰκουμένης   τὰ
and   to   the   ends   of the   inhabited earth   the

ῥήματα   αὐτῶν.   **19** ἀλλὰ   λέγω,   μὴ   Ἰσραὴλ
words   of them.   But   I say,   not   Israel

οὐκ   ἔγνω;   πρῶτος   Μωϋσῆς   λέγει·   ἐγὼ
did not know?   First   Moses   says: I

παραζηλώσω   ὑμᾶς   ἐπ'   οὐκ   ἔθνει,   ἐπ'
will provoke to jealousy   you   on(by)   not   a nation,   on(by)

ἔθνει   ἀσυνέτῳ   παροργιῶ   ὑμᾶς.   **20** Ἠσαΐας
a nation unintelligent   I will anger   you.   Esaias

δὲ   ἀποτολμᾷ   καὶ   λέγει·   εὑρέθην   τοῖς
But   is quite bold   and   says: I was found   by the [ones]

ἐμὲ   μὴ   ζητοῦσιν,   ἐμφανὴς   ἐγενόμην   τοῖς
²me   ¹not   ²seeking,   manifest   I became   to the [ones]

ἐμὲ   μὴ   ἐπερωτῶσιν.   **21** πρὸς   δὲ   τὸν
²me   ¹not   ²inquiring [for].   But to   -

Ἰσραὴλ   λέγει·   ὅλην   τὴν   ἡμέραν   ἐξεπέτασα
Israel   he says: All   the   day   I stretched out

τὰς   χεῖράς   μου   πρὸς   λαὸν   ἀπειθοῦντα
the   hands   of me   to   a people   disobeying

καὶ   ἀντιλέγοντα.
and   contradicting.

---

in him will never be put to shame." *e* 12For there is no difference between Jew and Gentile—the same Lord is Lord of all and richly blesses all who call on him, 13for, "Everyone who calls on the name of the Lord will be saved." *f*
14How, then, can they call on the one they have not believed in? And how can they believe in the one of whom they have not heard? And how can they hear without someone preaching to them? 15And how can they preach unless they are sent? As it is written, "How beautiful are the feet of those who bring good news!" *g*
16But not all the Israelites accepted the good news. For Isaiah says, "Lord, who has believed our message?" *h* 17Consequently, faith comes from hearing the message, and the message is heard through the word of Christ. 18But I ask: Did they not hear? Of course they did:

"Their voice has gone out into all the earth,
their words to the ends of the world." *i*

19Again I ask: Did Israel not understand? First, Moses says,

"I will make you envious by those who are not a nation;
I will make you angry by a nation that has no understanding." *j*

20And Isaiah boldly says,

"I was found by those who did not seek me;
I revealed myself to those who did not ask for me." *k*

21But concerning Israel he says,

"All day long I have held out my hands to a disobedient and obstinate people." *l*

---

e11 Isaiah 28:16
f13 Joel 2:32
g15 Isaiah 52:7
h16 Isaiah 53:1
i18 Psalm 19:4
j19 Deut. 32:21
k20 Isaiah 65:1
l21 Isaiah 65:2

---

* That is, between these two classes.

Chapter 11

Israel Is Not Cast Away

I say then, God has not rejected His people, has He? May it never be! For I too am an Israelite, a descendant of Abraham, of the tribe of Benjamin.

2God has not rejected His people whom He foreknew. Or do you not know what the Scripture says in *the passage about* Elijah, how he pleads with God against Israel?

3"Lord, THEY HAVE KILLED THY PROPHETS, THEY HAVE TORN DOWN THINE ALTARS, AND I ALONE AM LEFT, AND THEY ARE SEEKING MY LIFE."

4But what is the divine response to him? "I HAVE KEPT for Myself SEVEN THOUSAND MEN WHO HAVE NOT BOWED THE KNEE TO BAAL."

5In the same way then, there has also come to be at the present time a remnant according to *God's* gracious choice.

6But if it is by grace, it is no longer on the basis of works, otherwise grace is no longer grace.

7What then? That which Israel is seeking for, it has not obtained, but those who were chosen obtained it, and the rest were hardened;

8just as it is written,
"GOD GAVE THEM A SPIRIT OF STUPOR,
EYES TO SEE NOT AND EARS TO HEAR NOT,
DOWN TO THIS VERY DAY."

9And David says,
"LET THEIR TABLE BECOME A SNARE AND A TRAP,
AND A STUMBLING BLOCK AND A RETRIBUTION TO THEM.

10"LET THEIR EYES BE DARKENED TO SEE NOT,
AND BEND THEIR BACKS FOREVER."

11I say then, they did not stumble so as to fall, did they? May it never be! But by their transgression salvation *has come* to the Gentiles, to make them jealous.

---

11 Λέγω οὖν, μὴ ἀπώσατο ὁ θεὸς
I say therefore, ²did *not* put away – ¹God

τὸν λαὸν αὐτοῦ; μὴ γένοιτο· καὶ γὰρ
the people of him? May it not be; for even

ἐγὼ Ἰσραηλίτης εἰμί, ἐκ σπέρματος
I an Israelite am, of [the] seed

Ἀβραάμ, φυλῆς Βενιαμίν. **2** οὐκ ἀπώσατο
of Abraham, of [the] of Benjamin. did not put away
    tribe

ὁ θεὸς τὸν λαὸν αὐτοῦ ὃν προέγνω.
– God the people of him whom he foreknew.

ἢ οὐκ οἴδατε ἐν Ἡλίᾳ τί λέγει ἡ
Or know ye not in Elias what says the

γραφή, ὡς ἐντυγχάνει τῷ θεῷ κατὰ τοῦ
scripture, how he supplicates – God against

Ἰσραήλ; **3** κύριε, τοὺς προφήτας σου
Israel? Lord, the prophets of thee

ἀπέκτειναν, τὰ θυσιαστήριά σου κατέσκαψαν,
they killed, the altars of thee they dug down,

κἀγὼ ὑπελείφθην μόνος καὶ ζητοῦσιν τὴν
and I was left behind alone and they seek the

ψυχήν μου. **4** ἀλλὰ τί λέγει αὐτῷ ὁ
life of me. But what says to him the

χρηματισμός; κατέλιπον ἐμαυτῷ ἑπτακισ-
[divine] response? I reserved to myself seven

χιλίους ἄνδρας, οἵτινες οὐκ ἔκαμψαν γόνυ
thousands men, who bowed not knee

τῇ Βάαλ. **5** οὕτως οὖν καὶ ἐν τῷ νῦν
– to Baal. So therefore also in the present

καιρῷ λεῖμμα κατ᾽ ἐκλογὴν χάριτος
time a remnant according to a choice of grace

γέγονεν· **6** εἰ δὲ χάριτι, οὐκέτι ἐξ ἔργων,
has become; and if by grace, no more of works,

ἐπεὶ ἡ χάρις οὐκέτι γίνεται χάρις. **7** Τί
since – grace no more becomes grace. What

οὖν; ὃ ἐπιζητεῖ Ἰσραήλ, τοῦτο οὐκ
there- What ²seeks after ¹Israel, this not
fore?

ἐπέτυχεν, ἡ δὲ ἐκλογὴ ἐπέτυχεν· οἱ δὲ
he obtained, but the choice obtained [it]; and the

λοιποὶ ἐπωρώθησαν, **8** καθάπερ γέγραπται·
rest were hardened, as it has been written:

ἔδωκεν αὐτοῖς ὁ θεὸς πνεῦμα κατανύξεως,
Gave to them – God a spirit of torpor,

ὀφθαλμοὺς τοῦ μὴ βλέπειν καὶ ὦτα
eyes – not to see[d] and ears

τοῦ μὴ ἀκούειν, ἕως τῆς σήμερον ἡμέρας.
– not to hear,[d] until the present† day.

9 καὶ Δαυὶδ λέγει· γενηθήτω ἡ τράπεζα
And David says: Let become the table

αὐτῶν εἰς παγίδα καὶ εἰς θήραν καὶ
of them for a snare and for a net and

εἰς σκάνδαλον καὶ εἰς ἀνταπόδομα αὐτοῖς,
for an offence and for a recompence to them,

10 σκοτισθήτωσαν οἱ ὀφθαλμοὶ αὐτῶν τοῦ
let be darkened the eyes of them –

μὴ βλέπειν, καὶ τὸν νῶτον αὐτῶν διὰ
not to see,[d] and the back of them al-

παντὸς σύγκαμψον.
ways bending.

11 Λέγω οὖν, μὴ ἔπταισαν ἵνα πέσωσιν;
I say therefore, did they *not* in order they might
       stumble that fall?

μὴ γένοιτο· ἀλλὰ τῷ αὐτῶν παραπτώματι
May it not be; but by the ²of them ¹trespass

ἡ σωτηρία τοῖς ἔθνεσιν, εἰς τὸ παραζηλῶσαι
– salvation to the nations, for the to provoke to
[came] jealousy

Chapter 11

The Remnant of Israel

I ASK then: Did God reject his people? By no means! I am an Israelite myself, a descendant of Abraham, from the tribe of Benjamin. 2God did not reject his people, whom he foreknew. Don't you know what the Scripture says in the passage about Elijah— how he appealed to God against Israel: 3"Lord, they have killed your prophets and torn down your altars; I am the only one left, and they are trying to kill me"[m]? 4And what was God's answer to him? "I have reserved for myself seven thousand who have not bowed the knee to Baal."[n] 5So too, at the present time there is a remnant chosen by grace. 6And if by grace, then it is no longer by works; if it were, grace would no longer be grace.[o]

7What then? What Israel sought so earnestly it did not obtain, but the elect did. The others were hardened, 8as it is written:

"God gave them a spirit
  of stupor,
eyes so that they could
  not see
and ears so that they
  could not hear,
to this very day."[p]

9And David says:

"May their table become
  a snare and a trap,
a stumbling block and a
  retribution for them.
10May their eyes be
  darkened so they
  cannot see,
and their backs be bent
  forever."[q]

Ingrafted Branches

11Again I ask: Did they stumble so as to fall beyond recovery? Not at all! Rather, because of their transgression, salvation has come to the Gentiles to make Israel envious. 12But

m3 1 Kings 19:10,14
n4 1 Kings 19:18
o6 Some manuscripts *by grace. Bu*
if by works, then it is no longer
grace; if it were, work would no
longer be work.
p8 Deut. 29:4; Isaiah 29:10
q10 Psalm 69:22,23

12Now if their transgression be riches for the world and their failure be riches for the Gentiles, how much more will their fulfillment be!

13But I am speaking to you who are Gentiles. Inasmuch then as I am an apostle of Gentiles, I magnify my ministry,

14if somehow I might move to jealousy my fellow countrymen and save some of them.

15For if their rejection be the reconciliation of the world, what will *their* acceptance be but life from the dead?

16And if the first piece *of dough* be holy, the lump is also; and if the root be holy, the branches are too.

17But if some of the branches were broken off, and you, being a wild olive, were grafted in among them and became partaker with them of the rich root of the olive tree,

18do not be arrogant toward the branches; but if you are arrogant, *remember that* it is not you who supports the root, but the root *supports* you.

19You will say then, "Branches were broken off so that I might be grafted in."

20Quite right, they were broken off for their unbelief, but you stand by your faith. Do not be conceited, but fear;

21for if God did not spare the natural branches, neither will He spare you.

22Behold then the kindness and severity of God; to those who fell, severity, but to you, God's kindness, if you continue in His kindness; otherwise you also will be cut off.

23And they also, if they do not continue in their unbelief, will be grafted in; for

---

αὐτούς. **12** εἰ δὲ τὸ παράπτωμα αὐτῶν
them. But if the trespass of them

πλοῦτος κόσμου καὶ τὸ ἥττημα αὐτῶν
[is] [the] of [the] and the defect of them
riches world

πλοῦτος ἐθνῶν, πόσῳ μᾶλλον τὸ πλήρωμα
[is] [the] of [the] by how more the fulness
riches nations, much

αὐτῶν. **13** Ὑμῖν δὲ λέγω τοῖς ἔθνεσιν.
of them. But to you ³I say[,] ¹the ²nations.

ἐφ᾽ ὅσον μὲν οὖν εἰμι ἐγὼ ἐθνῶν ἀπόστο-
Forasmuch in- there- ²am ¹I ⁴of ³an apos-
as deed fore nations

λος, τὴν διακονίαν μου δοξάζω, **14** εἴ πως
tle, the ministry of me I glorify, if somehow

παραζηλώσω μου τὴν σάρκα καὶ σώσω
I may provoke to of me the flesh and may save
jealousy

τινὰς ἐξ αὐτῶν. **15** εἰ γὰρ ἡ ἀποβολὴ
some of them. For if the casting away

αὐτῶν καταλλαγὴ κόσμου, τίς ἡ πρόσλημψις
of them [is] [the] of [the] what the reception
reconciliation world,

εἰ μὴ ζωὴ ἐκ νεκρῶν; **16** εἰ δὲ ἡ
if not life from [the] dead? And if the

ἀπαρχὴ ἁγία, καὶ τὸ φύραμα· καὶ εἰ
firstfruit [is] holy, also the lump; and if

ἡ ῥίζα ἁγία, καὶ οἱ κλάδοι. **17** Εἰ δέ
the root [is] holy, also the branches. But if

τινες τῶν κλάδων ἐξεκλάσθησαν, σὺ δὲ
some of the branches were broken off, and thou

ἀγριέλαιος ὢν ἐνεκεντρίσθης ἐν αὐτοῖς
²a wild olive ¹being wast grafted in among them

καὶ συγκοινωνὸς τῆς ῥίζης τῆς πιότητος
and a partaker of the ²root* ⁵of the ⁶fatness

τῆς ἐλαίας ἐγένου, **18** μὴ κατακαυχῶ
⁷of the ⁸olive-tree ¹didst become, boast not against

τῶν κλάδων· εἰ δὲ κατακαυχᾶσαι, οὐ
of the branches; but if thou boastest, not

σὺ τὴν ῥίζαν βαστάζεις ἀλλὰ ἡ ῥίζα σέ.
thou the root bearest but the root thee.

19 ἐρεῖς οὖν· ἐξεκλάσθησαν κλάδοι ἵνα
Thou wilt therefore: ²Were broken off ¹branches in order
say that

ἐγὼ ἐγκεντρισθῶ. **20** καλῶς· τῇ ἀπιστίᾳ
I might be grafted in. Well: – for unbelief

ἐξεκλάσθησαν, σὺ δὲ τῇ πίστει ἕστηκας.
they were broken off, and thou – by faith standest.

μὴ ὑψηλὰ φρόνει, ἀλλὰ φοβοῦ· **21** εἰ
²Not ³high things ¹mind, but fear; ²if

γὰρ ὁ θεὸς τῶν κατὰ φύσιν κλάδων
¹for – ³God ⁵the ⁷according to ⁸nature ⁶branches

οὐκ ἐφείσατο, οὐδὲ σοῦ φείσεται. **22** ἴδε
⁴spared not, neither thee will he spare. See

οὖν χρηστότητα καὶ ἀποτομίαν θεοῦ· ἐπὶ
therefore [the] kindness and [the] severity of God: ²on

μὲν τοὺς πεσόντας ἀποτομία, ἐπὶ δὲ
¹on one, the having fallen severity, ²on ¹on the
hand [ones] other

σὲ χρηστότης θεοῦ, ἐὰν ἐπιμένῃς τῇ
thee [the] kindness of God, if thou continuest in the
(his)

χρηστότητι, ἐπεὶ καὶ σὺ ἐκκοπήσῃ.
kindness, since also thou wilt be cut off.

23 κἀκεῖνοι δέ, ἐὰν μὴ ἐπιμένωσιν τῇ
And those also, if they continue not

ἀπιστίᾳ, ἐγκεντρισθήσονται· δυνατὸς γάρ
in unbelief, will be grafted in; for ²able

---

if their transgression means riches for the world, and their loss means riches for the Gentiles, how much greater riches will their fullness bring!

13I am talking to you Gentiles. Inasmuch as I am the apostle to the Gentiles, I make much of my ministry 14in the hope that I may somehow arouse my own people to envy and save some of them. 15For if their rejection is the reconciliation of the world, what will their acceptance be but life from the dead? 16If the part of the dough offered as firstfruits is holy, then the whole batch is holy; if the root is holy, so are the branches.

17If some of the branches have been broken off, and you, though a wild olive shoot, have been grafted in among the others and now share in the nourishing sap from the olive root, 18do not boast over those branches. If you do, consider this: You do not support the root, but the root supports you. 19You will say then, "Branches were broken off so that I could be grafted in." 20Granted. But they were broken off because of unbelief, and you stand by faith. Do not be arrogant, but be afraid. 21For if God did not spare the natural branches, he will not spare you either. 22Consider therefore the kindness and sternness of God: sternness to those who fell, but kindness to you, provided that you continue in his kindness. Otherwise, you also will be cut off. 23And if they do not persist in unbelief, they will

---

* Some MSS insert καί (and) here; as it is, the two nouns in the genitive must be in apposition; *cf.* Col. 1. 18, 2. 2; John 9. 44.

God is able to graft them in again.

24For if you were cut off from what is by nature a wild olive tree, and were grafted contrary to nature into a cultivated olive tree, how much more shall these who are the natural branches be grafted into their own olive tree?

25For I do not want you, brethren, to be uninformed of this mystery, lest you be wise in your own estimation, that a partial hardening has happened to Israel until the fulness of the Gentiles has come in;

26and thus all Israel will be saved; just as it is written,

"THE DELIVERER WILL
COME FROM ZION,
HE WILL REMOVE UN-
GODLINESS FROM
JACOB."

27"AND THIS IS MY COV-
ENANT WITH THEM,
WHEN I TAKE AWAY
THEIR SINS."

28From the standpoint of the gospel they are enemies for your sake, but from the standpoint of *God's* choice they are beloved for the sake of the fathers;

29for the gifts and the calling of God are irrevocable.

30For just as you once were disobedient to God, but now have been shown mercy because of their disobedience,

31so these also now have been disobedient, in order that because of the mercy shown to you they also may now be shown mercy.

32For God has shut up all in disobedience that He might show mercy to all.

33Oh, the depth of the riches both of the wisdom and knowledge of God! How unsearchable are His judgments and unfathomable His ways!

34For WHO HAS KNOWN THE MIND OF THE LORD, OR

ἐστιν ὁ θεὸς πάλιν ἐγκεντρίσαι αὐτούς.
²is – ¹God ⁷again ⁴to graft ⁵in ⁶them.

24 εἰ γὰρ σὺ ἐκ τῆς κατὰ φύσιν ἐξεκόπης
For if thou ²out ³the ⁵according ⁶nature ¹wast cut
of to out

ἀγριελαίου καὶ παρὰ φύσιν ἐνεκεντρίσθης
⁴wild olive and against nature wast grafted *in*

εἰς καλλιέλαιον, πόσῳ μᾶλλον οὗτοι οἱ
into a cultivated by how more these the
olive, much [ones]

κατὰ φύσιν ἐγκεντρισθήσονται τῇ ἰδίᾳ
according to nature will be grafted in the(ir) own

ἐλαίᾳ. 25 Οὐ γὰρ θέλω ὑμᾶς ἀγνοεῖν,
olive-tree. For I wish not you to be ignorant,

ἀδελφοί, τὸ μυστήριον τοῦτο, ἵνα μὴ
brothers, [of] this mystery, lest

ἦτε ἐν ἑαυτοῖς φρόνιμοι, ὅτι πώρωσις
ye be in yourselves wise, that hardness

ἀπὸ μέρους τῷ Ἰσραὴλ γέγονεν ἄχρι οὗ
from(in) part – to Israel has happened until

τὸ πλήρωμα τῶν ἐθνῶν εἰσέλθῃ, 26 καὶ
the fulness of the nations comes in, and

οὕτως πᾶς Ἰσραὴλ σωθήσεται, καθὼς
so all Israel will be saved, as

γέγραπται· ἥξει ἐκ Σιὼν ὁ ῥυόμενος,
it has been ³will ⁴out ⁵Sion ¹The ²delivering,
written: come of [one]

ἀποστρέψει ἀσεβείας ἀπὸ Ἰακώβ. 27 καὶ
he will turn away impiety from Jacob. And

αὕτη αὐτοῖς ἡ παρ' ἐμοῦ διαθήκη, ὅταν
this [is] with them ¹the ³from ⁴me ²covenant, when
of

ἀφέλωμαι τὰς ἁμαρτίας αὐτῶν. 28 κατὰ
I take away the sins of them. ¹According to

μὲν τὸ εὐαγγέλιον ἐχθροὶ δι' ὑμᾶς,
¹on one the gospel enemies because you,
hand of

κατὰ δὲ τὴν ἐκλογὴν ἀγαπητοὶ διὰ
²accord- ¹on the the choice beloved because
ing to other of

τοὺς πατέρας· 29 ἀμεταμέλητα γὰρ τὰ
the fathers; for unrepented the

χαρίσματα καὶ ἡ κλῆσις τοῦ θεοῦ.
free gifts and the calling – of God.

30 ὥσπερ γὰρ ὑμεῖς ποτε ἠπειθήσατε
For as ye then disobeyed

τῷ θεῷ, νῦν δὲ ἠλεήθητε τῇ τούτων
– God, but now ye obtained mercy ¹by the ²of these

ἀπειθείᾳ, 31 οὕτως καὶ οὗτοι νῦν ἠπείθησαν
²disobedience, so also these now disobeyed

τῷ ὑμετέρῳ ἐλέει ἵνα καὶ αὐτοὶ νῦν
– ²by your ³mercy ¹in order also they now
that

ἐλεηθῶσιν. 32 συνέκλεισεν γὰρ ὁ θεὸς
may obtain mercy. For ²shut up – ¹God

τοὺς πάντας εἰς ἀπείθειαν ἵνα τοὺς
– all in disobedience in order that –

πάντας ἐλεήσῃ.
to all he may show mercy.

33 Ὦ βάθος πλούτου καὶ σοφίας καὶ
O [the] depth of [the] riches and of [the] wisdom and

γνώσεως θεοῦ· ὡς ἀνεξερεύνητα τὰ κρίματα
of [the] of God; how inscrutable the judgments
knowledge

αὐτοῦ καὶ ἀνεξιχνίαστοι αἱ ὁδοὶ αὐτοῦ.
of him and unsearchable the ways of him.

34 τίς γὰρ ἔγνω νοῦν κυρίου; ἢ τίς
.For who knew [the] mind of [the] Lord? or who

---

be grafted in, for God is able to graft them in again.

24After all, if you were cut out of an olive tree that is wild by nature, and contrary to nature were grafted into a cultivated olive tree, how much more readily will these, the natural branches, be grafted into their own olive tree!

All Israel Will Be Saved

25I do not want you to be ignorant of this mystery, brothers, so that you may not be conceited: Israel has experienced a hardening in part until the full number of the Gentiles has come in.

26And so all Israel will be saved, as it is written:

"The deliverer will come
from Zion;
he will turn
godlessness away
from Jacob.

27And this is ʳ my
covenant with them
when I take away their
sins." ˢ

28As far as the gospel is concerned, they are enemies on your account; but as far as election is concerned, they are loved on account of the patriarchs, 29for God's gifts and his call are irrevocable. 30Just as you who were at one time disobedient to God have now received mercy as a result of their disobedience, 31so they too have now become disobedient in order that they too may nowʳ receive mercy as a result of God's mercy to you. 32For God has bound all men over to disobedience so that he may have mercy on them all.

Doxology

33Oh, the depth of the riches of the wisdom andᵘ knowledge of God!
How unsearchable his judgments,
and his paths beyond tracing out!
34"Who has known the mind of the Lord?
Or who has been his counselor?" ᵛ
35"Who has ever given to God.

ʳ27 Or *will be*
ˢ27 Isaiah 59:20,21; 27:9;
Jer. 31:33,34
ᵗ31 Some manuscripts do not have *now*.
ᵘ33 Or *riches and the wisdom and the*
ᵛ34 Isaiah 40:13

Left column (KJV)

WHO BECAME HIS COUNSEL-
OR?
35Or WHO HAS FIRST GIVEN
TO HIM THAT IT MIGHT BE
PAID BACK TO HIM AGAIN?
36For from Him and
through Him and to Him
are all things. To Him *be*
the glory forever. Amen.

Chapter 12

Dedicated Service

I urge you therefore,
brethren, by the mercies
of God, to present your
bodies a living and holy
sacrifice, acceptable to
God, *which is* your spiritual
service of worship.
2And do not be con-
formed to this world, but be
transformed by the renew-
ing of your mind, that you
may prove what the will of
God is, that which is good
and acceptable and perfect.
3For through the grace
given to me I say to every
man among you not to
think more highly of him-
self than he ought to think;
but to think so as to have
sound judgment, as God
has allotted to each a measure of faith.
4For just as we have
many members in one body
and all the members do not
have the same function,
5so we, who are many,
are one body in Christ, and
individually members one
of another.
6And since we have gifts
that differ according to the
grace given to us, *let each
exercise them accordingly:*
if prophecy, according to
the proportion of his faith;
7if service, in his serving;
or he who teaches, in his
teaching;
8or he who exhorts, in
his exhortation; he who
gives, with ⁿliberality; he
who leads, with diligence;

ⁿ Or, *simplicity*

Center column (interlinear Greek)

σύμβουλος αὐτοῦ ἐγένετο; 35 ἢ τίς
counsellor   of him   became?   or   who

προέδωκεν αὐτῷ, καὶ ἀνταποδοθήσεται
previously gave to him, and   it will be repaid

αὐτῷ; 36 ὅτι ἐξ αὐτοῦ καὶ δι' αὐτοῦ
to him? Because of   him and through him

καὶ εἰς αὐτὸν τὰ πάντα· αὐτῷ ἡ δόξα
and to   him   – all things; to him the glory

εἰς τοὺς αἰῶνας· ἀμήν.
unto the ages: Amen.

12 Παρακαλῶ οὖν ὑμᾶς, ἀδελφοί, διὰ
I beseech therefore you, brothers, through

τῶν οἰκτιρμῶν τοῦ θεοῦ, παραστῆσαι τὰ
the compassions   –   of God, to present the

σώματα ὑμῶν θυσίαν ζῶσαν ἁγίαν τῷ
bodies of you sacrifice a living holy   –

θεῷ εὐάρεστον, τὴν λογικὴν λατρείαν
²to God ¹well-pleasing, the reasonable service

ὑμῶν· **2** καὶ μὴ συσχηματίζεσθε τῷ αἰῶνι
of you; and not be ye not conformed – age

τούτῳ, ἀλλὰ μεταμορφοῦσθε τῇ ἀνακαινώσει
to this, but be ye transformed by the renewing

τοῦ νοός, εἰς τὸ δοκιμάζειν ὑμᾶς τί τὸ
of the mind, *for* the to prove youᵇ what the
=so that ye may prove

θέλημα τοῦ θεοῦ, τὸ ἀγαθὸν καὶ εὐάρεστον
will   – of God, the good   and well-pleasing

καὶ τέλειον.
and perfect.

3 Λέγω γὰρ διὰ τῆς χάριτος τῆς
For I say through the grace   –

δοθείσης μοι παντὶ τῷ ὄντι ἐν ὑμῖν,
given   to me to everyone being among you,

μὴ ὑπερφρονεῖν παρ' ὃ δεῖ φρονεῖν,
not to have high beyond what it to think,
      thoughts   behoves

ἀλλὰ φρονεῖν εἰς τὸ σωφρονεῖν, ἑκάστῳ
but to think *to* the to be sober-minded, ⁴to each

ὡς ὁ θεὸς ἐμέρισεν μέτρον πίστεως.
¹as – ²God ³divided a measure of faith.

4 καθάπερ γὰρ ἐν ἑνὶ σώματι πολλὰ
For as   in one body many

μέλη ἔχομεν, τὰ δὲ μέλη πάντα οὐ τὴν
members we have, but ²the ³members ¹all ¹not the

αὐτὴν ἔχει πρᾶξιν, **5** οὕτως οἱ πολλοὶ
⁷same ⁴has(ve) ⁸action, so   the many

ἓν σῶμά ἐσμεν ἐν Χριστῷ, τὸ δὲ καθ'
one body we are in Christ, – and each

εἰς ἀλλήλων μέλη. **6** ἔχοντες δὲ χαρίσματα
one ²of one ¹members. And having gifts
         another

κατὰ τὴν χάριν τὴν δοθεῖσαν ἡμῖν διάφορα,
²accord- ³the ⁴grace – ⁵given ⁶to us ¹differing.
ing to

εἴτε προφητείαν, κατὰ τὴν ἀναλογίαν τῆς
whether prophecy, according to the proportion of the

πίστεως· **7** εἴτε διακονίαν, ἐν τῇ διακονίᾳ·
faith;   or ministry, in the ministry;

εἴτε ὁ διδάσκων, ἐν τῇ διδασκαλίᾳ·
or the [one] teaching, in the teaching;

8 εἴτε ὁ παρακαλῶν, ἐν τῇ παρακλήσει·
or the [one] exhorting, in the exhortation;

ὁ μεταδιδοὺς ἐν ἁπλότητι, ὁ προϊστάμενος
the [one] sharing in simplicity, the [one] taking the lead

Right column (NIV)

that God should repay
him?" ʷ
36For from him and
through him and to
him are all things.
To him be the glory
forever! Amen.

Chapter 12

Living Sacrifices

THEREFORE, I urge
you, brothers, in view
of God's mercy, to offer
your bodies as living sacrifices, holy and pleasing to
God—this is your spiritu-
alˣ act of worship. 2Do not
conform any longer to the
pattern of this world, but be
transformed by the renew-
ing of your mind. Then you
will be able to test and approve what God's will is—
his good, pleasing and perfect will.
3For by the grace given
me I say to every one of
you: Do not think of yourself more highly than you
ought, but rather think of
yourself with sober judg-
ment, in accordance with
the measure of faith God
has given you. 4Just as each
of us has one body with
many members, and these
members do not all have
the same function, 5so in
Christ we who are many
form one body, and each
member belongs to all the
others. 6We have different
gifts, according to the grace
given us. If a man's gift is
prophesying, let him use it
in proportion to hisʸ faith.
7If it is serving, let him
serve; if it is teaching, let
him teach; 8if it is encouraging, let him encourage; if it
is contributing to the needs
of others, let him give generously; if it is leadership,
let him govern diligently; if

ʷ35 Job 41:11
ˣ1 Or *reasonable*
ʸ6 Or *in agreement with the*

he who shows mercy, with cheerfulness.

9Let love be without hypocrisy. Abhor what is evil; cling to what is good.

10Be devoted to one another in brotherly love; give preference to one another in honor;

11not lagging behind in diligence, fervent in spirit, serving the Lord;

12rejoicing in hope, persevering in tribulation, devoted to prayer,

13contributing to the needs of the saints, practicing hospitality.

14Bless those who persecute *you; bless and curse not.

15Rejoice with those who rejoice, and weep with those who weep.

16Be of the same mind toward one another; do not be haughty in mind, but associate with the lowly. Do not be wise in your own estimation.

17Never pay back evil for evil to anyone. Respect what is right in the sight of all men.

18If possible, so far as it depends on you, be at peace with all men.

19Never take your own revenge, beloved, but leave room for the wrath of God, for it is written, "VENGEANCE IS MINE, I WILL REPAY," says the Lord.

20"BUT IF YOUR ENEMY IS HUNGRY, FEED HIM, AND IF HE IS THIRSTY, GIVE HIM A DRINK; FOR IN SO DOING YOU WILL HEAP BURNING COALS UPON HIS HEAD."

21Do not be overcome by evil, but overcome evil with good.

Chapter 13

Be Subject to Government

LET every person be in subjection to the governing authorities. For there is no authority except from God, and those which

Some ancient mss. do not contain you

ἐν σπουδῇ, ὁ ἐλεῶν ἐν ἱλαρότητι. 9 ἡ
in diligence, the showing in cheerfulness. –
[one] mercy

ἀγάπη ἀνυπόκριτος. . ἀποστυγοῦντες τὸ
[Let] love [be] unassumed. Shrinking from the

πονηρόν, κολλώμενοι τῷ ἀγαθῷ· 10 τῇ
evil, cleaving to the good; –

φιλαδελφίᾳ εἰς ἀλλήλους φιλόστοργοι, τῇ
in brotherly love to one another loving warmly, –

τιμῇ ἀλλήλους προηγούμενοι, 11 τῇ σπουδῇ
in one another preferring, – in zeal
honour

μὴ ὀκνηροί, τῷ πνεύματι ζέοντες, τῷ
not slothful, – in spirit burning, the

κυρίῳ δουλεύοντες, 12 τῇ ἐλπίδι χαίροντες,
Lord serving, – in hope rejoicing,

τῇ θλίψει ὑπομένοντες, τῇ προσευχῇ
– in affliction showing endurance, – in prayer

προσκαρτεροῦντες, 13 ταῖς χρείαις τῶν
steadfastly continuing, to the needs of the

ἁγίων κοινωνοῦντες, τὴν φιλοξενίαν
saints imparting, – hospitality

διώκοντες. 14 εὐλογεῖτε τοὺς διώκοντας,
pursuing. Bless ye the [ones] 'persecuting,

εὐλογεῖτε καὶ μὴ καταρᾶσθε. 15 χαίρειν
bless and do not curse. To rejoice

μετὰ χαιρόντων, κλαίειν μετὰ κλαιόντων.
with rejoicing [ones], to weep with weeping [ones].

16 τὸ αὐτὸ εἰς ἀλλήλους φρονοῦντες· μὴ
The same thing toward one another minding; not

τὰ ὑψηλὰ φρονοῦντες ἀλλὰ τοῖς ταπεινοῖς
²the ³high things ¹minding but to the humble

συναπαγόμενοι. μὴ γίνεσθε φρόνιμοι παρ'
condescending. Become not wise with

ἑαυτοῖς. 17 μηδενὶ κακὸν ἀντὶ κακοῦ
yourselves. To no one evil instead of evil

ἀποδιδόντες· προνοούμενοι καλὰ ἐνώπιον
returning; providing for good things before

πάντων ἀνθρώπων· 18 εἰ δυνατόν, τὸ ἐξ
all men; if possible, as far as it

ὑμῶν, μετὰ πάντων ἀνθρώπων εἰρηνεύοντες·
rests with with all men seeking peace;
you,†

19 μὴ ἑαυτοὺς ἐκδικοῦντες, ἀγαπητοί, ἀλλὰ
not ²yourselves ¹avenging, beloved, but

δότε τόπον τῇ ὀργῇ· γέγραπται γάρ·
give place – to wrath; for it has been written:

ἐμοὶ ἐκδίκησις, ἐγὼ ἀνταποδώσω, λέγει
To me vengeance,ᶜ I will repay, says
=Vengeance is mine,

κύριος. 20 ἀλλὰ ἐὰν πεινᾷ ὁ ἐχθρός
[the] Lord. But if hungers the enemy

σου, ψώμιζε αὐτόν· ἐὰν διψᾷ, πότιζε
of thee, feed him; if he thirsts, give ²drink

αὐτόν· τοῦτο γὰρ ποιῶν ἄνθρακας πυρὸς
¹him; for this doing coals of fire

σωρεύσεις ἐπὶ τὴν κεφαλὴν αὐτοῦ. 21 μὴ
thou wilt heap on the head of him. not

νικῶ ὑπὸ τοῦ κακοῦ, ἀλλὰ νίκα
Be conquered by the evil, but conquer

ἐν τῷ ἀγαθῷ τὸ κακόν. 13 Πᾶσα
³by ⁴the ⁵good ¹the ²evil. ²Every

ψυχὴ ἐξουσίαις ὑπερεχούσαις ὑποτασσέσθω.
³soul ⁷authorities ⁶to superior ¹let ⁴be ⁵subject.

οὐ γὰρ ἔστιν ἐξουσία εἰ μὴ
For there is no authority except

ὑπὸ θεοῦ, αἱ δὲ οὖσαι ὑπὸ θεοῦ
by God, and the existing [ones] by God

---

it is showing mercy, let him do it cheerfully.

Love

9Love must be sincere. Hate what is evil; cling to what is good. 10Be devoted to one another in brotherly love. Honor one another above yourselves. 11Never be lacking in zeal, but keep your spiritual fervor, serving the Lord. 12Be joyful in hope, patient in affliction, faithful in prayer. 13Share with God's people who are in need. Practice hospitality.

14Bless those who persecute you; bless and do not curse. 15Rejoice with those who rejoice; mourn with those who mourn. 16Live in harmony with one another. Do not be proud, but be willing to associate with people of low position. ᶻ Do not be conceited.

17Do not repay anyone evil for evil. Be careful to do what is right in the eyes of everybody. 18If it is possible, as far as it depends on you, live at peace with everyone. 19Do not take revenge, my friends, but leave room for God's wrath, for it is written: "It is mine to avenge; I will repay,"ᵃ says the Lord. 20On the contrary:

"If your enemy is hungry, feed him;
if he is thirsty, give him something to drink.
In doing this, you will heap burning coals on his head."ᵇ

21Do not be overcome by evil, but overcome evil with good.

Chapter 13

Submission to the Authorities

EVERYONE must submit himself to the governing authorities, for there is no authority except that which God has established.

ᶻ16 Or *willing to do menial work*
ᵃ19 Deut. 32:35
ᵇ20 Prov. 25:21,22

exist are established by God.

²Therefore he who resists authority has opposed the ordinance of God; and they who have opposed will receive condemnation upon themselves.

³For rulers are not a cause of fear for good behavior, but for evil. Do you want to have no fear of authority? Do what is good, and you will have praise from the same;

⁴for it is a minister of God to you for good. But if you do what is evil, be afraid; for it does not bear the sword for nothing; for it is a minister of God, an avenger who brings wrath upon the one who practices evil.

⁵Wherefore it is necessary to be in subjection, not only because of wrath, but also for conscience' sake.

⁶For because of this you also pay taxes, for *rulers* are servants of God, devoting themselves to this very thing.

⁷Render to all what is due them: tax to whom tax *is due;* custom to whom custom; fear to whom fear; honor to whom honor.

⁸Owe nothing to anyone except to love one another; for he who loves his neighbor has fulfilled the law.

⁹For this, "YOU SHALL NOT COMMIT ADULTERY, YOU SHALL NOT MURDER, YOU SHALL NOT STEAL, YOU SHALL NOT COVET," and if there is any other commandment, it is summed up in this saying, "YOU SHALL LOVE YOUR NEIGHBOR AS YOURSELF."

¹⁰Love does no wrong to a neighbor; love therefore is the fulfillment of *the* law.

τεταγμέναι εἰσίν.   **2** ὥστε ὁ ἀντιτασσόμενος
having been   are.   So   the [one] resisting
ordained

τῇ ἐξουσίᾳ τῇ τοῦ θεοῦ διαταγῇ ἀνθέστη-
the   authority ²the   –   ⁴of God ³ordinance   ¹has op-

κεν· οἱ δὲ ἀνθεστηκότες ἑαυτοῖς κρίμα
posed; and the [ones]   having opposed   to themselves judgment

λήμψονται.   **3** οἱ γὰρ ἄρχοντες οὐκ εἰσὶν
will receive.   For the   rulers   are not

φόβος τῷ ἀγαθῷ ἔργῳ ἀλλὰ τῷ κακῷ.
a fear to the   good   work   but   to the   evil.

θέλεις δὲ μὴ φοβεῖσθαι τὴν ἐξουσίαν;
And wishest thou not   to fear   the   authority?

τὸ ἀγαθὸν ποίει, καὶ ἕξεις ἔπαινον ἐξ
²the   ³good   ¹do,   and   thou wilt   praise   from
                        have

αὐτῆς·   **4** θεοῦ γὰρ διάκονός ἐστιν σοὶ
it;   for of God   a minister   he is   to thee

εἰς τὸ ἀγαθόν. ἐὰν δὲ τὸ κακὸν ποιῇς,
for the   good.   But if   the   evil thou doest,

φοβοῦ· οὐ γὰρ εἰκῇ τὴν μάχαιραν φορεῖ·
fear;   for not in vain   the   sword   he bears;

θεοῦ γὰρ διάκονός ἐστιν ἔκδικος εἰς
for of God   a minister   he is   an avenger   for

ὀργὴν τῷ τὸ κακὸν πράσσοντι.   **5** διὸ
wrath to the [one] ²the   ³evil   ¹practising.   Wherefore

ἀνάγκη ὑποτάσσεσθαι, οὐ μόνον διὰ τὴν
it is necessary to be subject,   not   only because of –

ὀργὴν ἀλλὰ καὶ διὰ τὴν συνείδησιν.
wrath   but   also because of –   conscience.

6 διὰ τοῦτο γὰρ καὶ φόρους τελεῖτε·
For therefore   also   taxes   pay ye;

λειτουργοὶ γὰρ θεοῦ εἰσιν εἰς αὐτὸ τοῦτο
for ministers   of God they are for   this very thing

προσκαρτεροῦντες.   **7** ἀπόδοτε πᾶσιν τὰς
attending constantly.   Render   to all men   the

ὀφειλάς, τῷ τὸν φόρον τὸν φόρον,
dues,   to the [one] the   tax   the   tax,*

τῷ τὸ τέλος τὸ τέλος, τῷ τὸν φόβον
to the the   tribute   the   tribute, to the   the   fear
[one]   [one]

τὸν φόβον, τῷ τὴν τιμὴν τὴν τιμήν.
the   fear, to the [one] the   honour   the   honour.

8 Μηδενὶ μηδὲν ὀφείλετε, εἰ μὴ τὸ
To no one no(any)thing   owe ye,   except   –

ἀλλήλους ἀγαπᾶν· ὁ γὰρ ἀγαπῶν τὸν
one another   to love;   for the [one]   loving   the

ἕτερον νόμον πεπλήρωκεν.   **9** τὸ γὰρ
other   law   has fulfilled.   –   For

οὐ μοιχεύσεις, οὐ φονεύσεις, οὐ κλέψεις,
Thou shalt not   Thou shalt not kill,   Thou shalt not
commit adultery,   steal,

οὐκ ἐπιθυμήσεις, καὶ εἴ τις ἑτέρα ἐντολή,
Thou shalt not covet,   and   if   any   other command-
                          [there is]   ment,

ἐν τῷ λόγῳ τούτῳ ἀνακεφαλαιοῦται, [ἐν
²in   ³this ⁴word   ¹it is summed up,   in

τῷ]· ἀγαπήσεις τὸν πλησίον σου ὡς
– :   Thou shalt love   the   neighbour   of thee   as

σεαυτόν.   **10** ἡ ἀγάπη τῷ πλησίον κακὸν
thyself.   –   Love   ³to the ⁴neighbour   ²evil
                         (one's)

οὐκ ἐργάζεται· πλήρωμα οὖν νόμου ἡ
¹works not;   ²[is] ⁴fulfilment ¹therefore ⁵of law   –

The authorities that exist have been established by God. ²Consequently, he who rebels against the authority is rebelling against what God has instituted, and those who do so will bring judgment on themselves. ³For rulers hold no terror for those who do right, but for those who do wrong. Do you want to be free from fear of the one in authority? Then do what is right and he will commend you. ⁴For he is God's servant to do you good. But if you do wrong, be afraid, for he does not bear the sword for nothing. He is God's servant, an agent of wrath to bring punishment on the wrongdoer. ⁵Therefore, it is necessary to submit to the authorities, not only because of possible punishment but also because of conscience.

⁶This is also why you pay taxes, for the authorities are God's servants, who give their full time to governing. ⁷Give everyone what you owe him: If you owe taxes, pay taxes; if revenue, then revenue; if respect, then respect; if honor, then honor.

Love, for the Day Is Near

⁸Let no debt remain outstanding, except the continuing debt to love one another, for he who loves his fellowman has fulfilled the law. ⁹The commandments, "Do not commit adultery," "Do not murder," "Do not steal," "Do not covet," ᶜ and whatever other commandment there may be, are summed up in this one rule: "Love your neighbor as yourself." ᵈ ¹⁰Love does no harm to its neighbor. Therefore love is the fulfillment of the law.

---

* The phrase between the commas is elliptical; understand—to the [one] demanding] the tax [render] the tax. So of the following phrases.

ᶜ9 Exodus 20:13-15,17; Deut. 5:17-19,21
ᵈ9 Lev. 19:18

11And this *do,* knowing the time, that it is already the hour for you to awaken from sleep; for now ᵖ salvation is nearer to us than when we believed.

12The night is almost gone, and the day is at hand. Let us therefore lay aside the deeds of darkness and put on the armor of light.

13Let us behave properly as in the day, not in carousing and drunkenness, not in sexual promiscuity and sensuality, not in strife and jealousy.

14But put on the Lord Jesus Christ, and make no provision for the flesh in regard to *its* lusts.

ἀγάπη.   **11** Καὶ τοῦτο εἰδότες τὸν καιρόν,
²love.   And this[,] knowing the time,

ὅτι ὥρα ἤδη ὑμᾶς ἐξ ὕπνου ἐγερθῆναι·
that hour now you   out of sleep   to be raised;ᵇ
=it is now an hour for you to be raised out of sleep;

νῦν γὰρ ἐγγύτερον ἡμῶν ἡ σωτηρία
for now   nearer   [is] of us the salvation

ἢ ὅτε ἐπιστεύσαμεν.   **12** ἡ νὺξ προέκοψεν,
than when we believed.   The night advanced,

ἡ δὲ ἡμέρα ἤγγικεν.   ἀποθώμεθα οὖν
and the day has drawn near. Let us cast off therefore

τὰ ἔργα τοῦ σκότους, ἐνδυσώμεθα δὲ
the works of the darkness,   and let us put on

τὰ ὅπλα τοῦ φωτός.   **13** ὡς ἐν ἡμέρᾳ
the weapons of the light,   As in [the] day

εὐσχημόνως περιπατήσωμεν, μὴ κώμοις καὶ
becomingly   let us walk,   not in revellings and

μέθαις, μὴ κοίταις καὶ ἀσελγείαις, μὴ
in drunken not in beds* and   excesses,   not
bouts,

ἔριδι καὶ ζήλῳ·   **14** ἀλλὰ ἐνδύσασθε τὸν
in strife and in jealousy;   but   put ye on   the

κύριον Ἰησοῦν Χριστόν, καὶ τῆς σαρκὸς
Lord   Jesus   Christ,   and of the flesh

πρόνοιαν μὴ ποιεῖσθε εἰς ἐπιθυμίας.
forethought make not   for [its] lusts.

11And do this, understanding the present time. The hour has come for you to wake up from your slumber, because our salvation is nearer now than when we first believed. 12The night is nearly over; the day is almost here. So let us put aside the deeds of darkness and put on the armor of light. 13Let us behave decently, as in the daytime, not in orgies and drunkenness, not in sexual immorality and debauchery, not in dissension and jealousy. 14Rather, clothe yourselves with the Lord Jesus Christ, and do not think about how to gratify the desires of the sinful nature. ᵉ

Chapter 14

Principles of Conscience

NOW accept the one who is weak in faith, *but not for the purpose of* passing judgment on his opinions.

2One man has faith that he may eat all things, but he who is weak eats vegetables *only.*

3Let not him who eats regard with contempt him who does not eat, and let not him who does not eat judge him who eats, for God has accepted him.

4Who are you to judge the servant of another? To his own master he stands or falls; and stand he will, for the Lord is able to make him stand.

5One man regards one day above another, another regards every day *alike.* Let each man be fully convinced in his own mind.

6He who observes the day, observes it for the Lord, and he who eats, does so for the Lord, for he gives thanks to God; and he who eats not, for the Lord

---

14 Τὸν δὲ ἀσθενοῦντα τῇ πίστει
     Now the [one] being weak   in the faith

προσλαμβάνεσθε, μὴ εἰς διακρίσεις διαλογισ-
receive ye,   not to   judgments   of

μῶν.   **2** ὃς μὲν πιστεύει φαγεῖν πάντα,
thoughts.   One indeed believes to eat   all things,
             man†

ὁ δὲ ἀσθενῶν λάχανα ἐσθίει.   **3** ὁ ἐσθίων
but the being weak herbs   eats.   ³The ⁴eating
[one]   [one]

τὸν μὴ ἐσθίοντα μὴ ἐξουθενείτω, ὁ δὲ
³the ⁷not ⁸eating ²not ¹let ⁵despise, and ⁴the
[one]   [one]

μὴ ἐσθίων τὸν ἐσθίοντα μὴ κρινέτω,
⁴not ⁵eating ⁷the [one] ⁸eating ²not ¹let ³judge,

ὁ θεὸς· γὰρ αὐτὸν προσελάβετο.   **4** σὺ
-    for God   him   received.   ²Thou

τίς εἶ ὁ κρίνων ἀλλότριον οἰκέτην; τῷ
¹who ²art ⁴the ⁵judging ⁷belonging to ⁶a *household* to
         [one]   another   servant? the(his)

ἰδίῳ κυρίῳ στήκει ἢ πίπτει· σταθήσεται
own   lord he stands or falls; ³he will stand

δέ, δυνατεῖ γὰρ ὁ κύριος στῆσαι αὐτόν.
¹but,   for is able the Lord to stand him.

5 ὃς μὲν [γὰρ] κρίνει ἡμέραν παρ᾽
   one man† indeed   judges a day   above

ἡμέραν, ὃς δὲ κρίνει πᾶσαν ἡμέραν·
a day,   another†   judges every   day;

ἕκαστος ἐν τῷ ἰδίῳ νοῒ πληροφορείσθω.
each man in the(his) own mind let him be fully
                                    persuaded.

6 ὁ φρονῶν τὴν ἡμέραν κυρίῳ φρονεῖ.
   The minding the   day   to [the] he minds
   [one]   Lord   [it].

καὶ ὁ ἐσθίων κυρίῳ ἐσθίει, εὐχαριστεῖ γὰρ
And the eating to [the] he eats, for he gives thanks
    [one]   Lord

τῷ θεῷ· καὶ ὁ μὴ ἐσθίων κυρίῳ
-    to God; and the [one] not eating to [the] Lord

Chapter 14

The Weak and the Strong

ACCEPT him whose faith is weak, without passing judgment on disputable matters. 2One man's faith allows him to eat everything, but another man, whose faith is weak, eats only vegetables. 3The man who eats everything must not look down on him who does not, and the man who does not eat everything must not condemn the man who does, for God has accepted him. 4Who are you to judge someone else's servant? To his own master he stands or falls. And he will stand, for the Lord is able to make him stand.

5One man considers one day more sacred than another; another man considers every day alike. Each one should be fully convinced in his own mind. 6He who regards one day as special, does so to the Lord. He who eats meat, eats to the Lord, for he gives thanks to God; and he who abstains, does so to

---

he does not eat, and gives thanks to God.

7For not one of us lives for himself, and not one dies for himself;

8for if we live, we live for the Lord, or if we die, we die for the Lord; therefore whether we live or die, we are the Lord's.

9For to this end Christ died and lived *again,* that He might be Lord both of the dead and of the living.

10But you, why do you judge your brother? Or you again, why do you regard your brother with contempt? For we shall all stand before the judgment seat of God.

11For it is written,
"As I live, says the Lord, every knee shall bow to Me, And every tongue shall give praise to God."

12So then each one of us shall give account of himself to God.

13Therefore let us not judge one another anymore, but rather determine this—not to put an obstacle or a stumbling block in a brother's way.

14I know and am convinced in the Lord Jesus that nothing is unclean in itself; but to him who thinks anything to be unclean, to him it is unclean.

15For if because of food your brother is hurt, you are no longer walking according to love. Do not destroy with your food him for whom Christ died.

16Therefore do not let what is for you a good thing be spoken of as evil;

17for the kingdom of God is not eating and drinking, but righteousness and peace and joy in the Holy Spirit.

18For he who in this *way* serves Christ is acceptable

οὐκ ἐσθίει, καὶ εὐχαριστεῖ τῷ θεῷ.
he eats not, and gives thanks – to God.

7 οὐδεὶς γὰρ ἡμῶν ἑαυτῷ ζῇ, καὶ οὐδεὶς
For no one of us to himself lives, and no one

ἑαυτῷ ἀποθνῄσκει· 8 ἐάν τε γὰρ ζῶμεν,
to himself dies; for whether we live,

τῷ κυρίῳ ζῶμεν, ἐάν τε ἀποθνῄσκωμεν,
to the Lord we live, or if we die,

τῷ κυρίῳ ἀποθνῄσκομεν. ἐάν τε οὖν
to the Lord we die. Whether therefore

ζῶμεν ἐάν τε ἀποθνῄσκωμεν, τοῦ κυρίου
we live or if we die, of the Lord

ἐσμέν. 9 εἰς τοῦτο γὰρ Χριστὸς ἀπέθανεν
we are. for this For Christ died

καὶ ἔζησεν, ἵνα καὶ νεκρῶν καὶ ζώντων
and lived [again], in order both of dead and of living [ones]

κυριεύσῃ. 10 σὺ δὲ τί κρίνεις τὸν ἀδελφόν
he might be Lord. 3thou And 1why 2judgest the brother

σου; ἢ καὶ σὺ τί ἐξουθενεῖς τὸν ἀδελφόν
of thee? or 2indeed 4thou 1why 3despisest the brother

σου; πάντες γὰρ παραστησόμεθα τῷ
of thee? for all we shall stand before the

βήματι τοῦ θεοῦ. 11 γέγραπται γάρ·
tribunal – of God. For it has been written:

ζῶ ἐγώ, λέγει κύριος, ὅτι ἐμοὶ κάμψει
Live I, says [the] Lord, that to me will bend

πᾶν γόνυ, καὶ πᾶσα γλῶσσα ἐξομολογήσεται
every knee, and every tongue will confess

τῷ θεῷ. 12 ἄρα [οὖν] ἔκαστος ἡμῶν
– to God. So therefore each one of us

περὶ ἑαυτοῦ λόγον δώσει [τῷ θεῷ].
concerning himself account will give – to God.

13 Μηκέτι οὖν ἀλλήλους κρίνωμεν· ἀλλὰ
No longer therefore one another let us judge; but

τοῦτο κρίνατε μᾶλλον, τὸ μὴ τιθέναι
this judge ye rather, – not to put

πρόσκομμα τῷ ἀδελφῷ ἢ σκάνδαλον.
a stumbling-block to the brother or an offence.

14 οἶδα καὶ πέπεισμαι ἐν κυρίῳ Ἰησοῦ
I know and have been persuaded by [the] Lord Jesus

ὅτι οὐδὲν κοινὸν δι' ἑαυτοῦ· εἰ μὴ
that nothing [is] common through itself; except

τῷ λογιζομένῳ τι κοινὸν εἶναι, ἐκείνῳ
to the [one] reckoning anything common to be, to that man [it is]

κοινόν. 15 εἰ γὰρ διὰ βρῶμα ὁ ἀδελφός
common. For if because of food the brother

σου λυπεῖται, οὐκέτι κατὰ ἀγάπην
of thee is grieved, no longer according to love

περιπατεῖς. μὴ τῷ βρώματί σου ἐκεῖνον
thou walkest. 2Not 3by the 4food 5of thee 6that man

ἀπόλλυε, ὑπὲρ οὗ Χριστὸς ἀπέθανεν.
1destroy, on behalf of whom Christ died.

16 μὴ βλασφημείσθω οὖν ὑμῶν τὸ ἀγαθόν.
Let not be blasphemed therefore of you the good.

17 οὐ γάρ ἐστιν ἡ βασιλεία τοῦ θεοῦ
For not is the kingdom – of God

βρῶσις καὶ πόσις, ἀλλὰ δικαιοσύνη καὶ
eating and drinking, but righteousness and

εἰρήνη καὶ χαρὰ ἐν πνεύματι ἁγίῳ·
peace and joy in [the] Spirit Holy;

18 ὁ γὰρ ἐν τούτῳ δουλεύων τῷ Χριστῷ
for the [one] in this serving – Christ

the Lord and gives thanks to God. 7For none of us lives to himself alone and none of us dies to himself alone. 8If we live, we live to the Lord; and if we die, we die to the Lord. So, whether we live or die, we belong to the Lord.

9For this very reason, Christ died and returned to life so that he might be the Lord of both the dead and the living. 10You, then, why do you judge your brother? Or why do you look down on your brother? For we will all stand before God's judgment seat. 11It is written:

" 'As surely as I live,'
says the Lord,
'every knee will bow
before me;
every tongue will
confess to God.' "*f*

12So then, each of us will give an account of himself to God.

13Therefore let us stop passing judgment on one another. Instead, make up your mind not to put any stumbling block or obstacle in your brother's way. 14As one who is in the Lord Jesus, I am fully convinced that no food*g* is unclean in itself. But if anyone regards something as unclean, then for him it is unclean. 15If your brother is distressed because of what you eat, you are no longer acting in love. Do not by your eating destroy your brother for whom Christ died. 16Do not allow what you consider good to be spoken of as evil. 17For the kingdom of God is not a matter of eating and drinking, but of righteousness, peace and joy in the Holy Spirit, 18because anyone who serves

f 11 Isaiah 45:23
g 14 Or *that nothing*

to God and approved by men.

19So then *let us pursue the things which make for peace and the building up of one another.

20Do not tear down the work of God for the sake of food. All things indeed are clean, but they are evil for the man who eats and gives offense.

21It is good not to eat meat or to drink wine, or *to do anything* by which your brother stumbles.

22The faith which you have, have as your own conviction before God. Happy is he who does not condemn himself in what he approves.

23But he who doubts is condemned if he eats, because *his eating is* not from faith; and whatever is not from faith is sin.

Chapter 15

Self-denial on Behalf of Others

NOW we who are strong ought to bear the weaknesses of those without strength and not *just* please ourselves.

2Let each of us please his neighbor for his good, to his edification.

3For even Christ did not please Himself; but as it is written, "THE REPROACHES OF THOSE WHO REPROACHED THEE FELL UPON ME."

4For whatever was written in earlier times was written for our instruction, that through perseverance and the encouragement of the Scriptures we might have hope.

5Now may the God who gives perseverance and encouragement grant you to be of the same mind with one another according to Christ Jesus;

6that with one accord you may with one voice

εὐάρεστος   τῷ   θεῷ   καὶ   δόκιμος   τοῖς
[is] well-pleasing – to God and approved the

ἀνθρώποις.   **19** ἄρα   οὖν   τὰ   τῆς   εἰρήνης
by men.   So there- the   –   of peace
                     fore things

διώκωμεν   καὶ   τὰ   τῆς   οἰκοδομῆς   τῆς
let us pursue and the things – of building [up] –

εἰς   ἀλλήλους.   **20** μὴ   ἕνεκεν   βρώματος
for one another.   Not for the sake of food

κατάλυε   τὸ   ἔργον   τοῦ   θεοῦ.   πάντα
undo thou the work   –   of God.   All things

μὲν   καθαρά,   ἀλλὰ   κακὸν   τῷ   ἀνθρώπῳ
indeed [are] clean, but evil to the man

τῷ   διὰ   προσκόμματος   ἐσθίοντι.   **21** καλὸν
– ³through ³a stumbling-block ¹eating. Good [it is]

τὸ   μὴ   φαγεῖν   κρέα   μηδὲ   πιεῖν   οἶνον
– not to eat flesh nor to drink wine

μηδὲ   ἐν   ᾧ   ὁ   ἀδελφός   σου   προσκόπτει.
nor by which the brother of thee stumbles.
[anything]

22 σὺ   πίστιν   ἣν   ἔχεις   κατὰ   σεαυτὸν
³Thou ¹faith ²which ⁴hast ⁶by ⁷thyself

ἔχε   ἐνώπιον   τοῦ   θεοῦ.   μακάριος   ὁ
⁵have before – God. Blessed the
                              [one]

μὴ   κρίνων   ἑαυτὸν   ἐν   ᾧ   δοκιμάζει·
not judging himself in what he approves;

23 ὁ   δὲ   διακρινόμενος   ἐὰν   φάγῃ   κατα-
but the [one] doubting if he eats has been

κέκριται,   ὅτι   οὐκ   ἐκ   πίστεως·   πᾶν
condemned, because not of faith; ²all

δὲ   ὃ   οὐκ   ἐκ   πίστεως   ἁμαρτία   ἐστίν.
¹and which [is] not of faith sin is.

15 Ὀφείλομεν   δὲ   ἡμεῖς   οἱ   δυνατοὶ   τὰ
⁵Ought ¹so ²we ³the ⁴strong ⁷the

ἀσθενήματα   τῶν   ἀδυνάτων   βαστάζειν,   καὶ
⁸weaknesses ⁹of the ¹⁰not strong ⁶to bear, and

μὴ   ἑαυτοῖς   ἀρέσκειν.   **2** ἕκαστος   ἡμῶν
not [our]selves to please. Each one of us

τῷ   πλησίον   ἀρεσκέτω   εἰς   τὸ   ἀγαθὸν
the(his) neighbour let him please for – good

πρὸς   οἰκοδομήν·   **3** καὶ   γὰρ   ὁ   Χριστὸς
to building [up]; for even – Christ

οὐχ   ἑαυτῷ   ἤρεσεν·   ἀλλὰ   καθὼς   γέ-
²not ³himself ¹pleased; but as it has

γραπται·   οἱ   ὀνειδισμοὶ   τῶν   ὀνειδιζόντων
been written: The reproaches of the [ones] reproaching

σε   ἐπέπεσαν   ἐπ'   ἐμέ.   **4** ὅσα   γὰρ
thee fell *on* on me. For whatever things

προεγράφη,   εἰς   τὴν   ἡμετέραν   διδασκαλίαν
were previously for – our teaching
written,

ἐγράφη,   ἵνα   διὰ   τῆς   ὑπομονῆς   καὶ
were in order through – patience and
written, that

διὰ   τῆς   παρακλήσεως   τῶν   γραφῶν   τὴν
through the comfort of the writings –

ἐλπίδα   ἔχωμεν.   **5** ὁ   δὲ   θεὸς   τῆς   ὑπομονῆς
hope we may have. And the God – of patience

καὶ   τῆς   παρακλήσεως   δῴη   ὑμῖν   τὸ
and – of comfort give to you ²the

αὐτὸ   φρονεῖν   ἐν   ἀλλήλοις   κατὰ   Χριστὸν
³same ¹to mind among one another according to Christ
thing

Ἰησοῦν,   **6** ἵνα   ὁμοθυμαδὸν   ἐν   ἑνὶ   στόματι
Jesus, in order with one accord with one mouth
          that

Christ in this way is pleasing to God and approved by men.

19Let us therefore make every effort to do what leads to peace and to mutual edification. 20Do not destroy the work of God for the sake of food. All food is clean, but it is wrong for a man to eat anything that causes someone else to stumble. 21It is better not to eat meat or drink wine or to do anything else that will cause your brother to fall. 22So whatever you believe about these things keep between yourself and God. Blessed is the man who does not condemn himself by what he approves. 23But the man who has doubts is condemned if he eats, because his eating is not from faith; and everything that does not come from faith is sin.

Chapter 15

WE who are strong ought to bear with the failings of the weak and not to please ourselves. 2Each of us should please his neighbor for his good, to build him up. 3For even Christ did not please himself but, as it is written: "The insults of those who insult you have fallen on me." [h] 4For everything that was written in the past was written to teach us, so that through endurance and the encouragement of the Scriptures we might have hope.

5May the God who gives endurance and encouragement give you a spirit of unity among yourselves as you follow Christ Jesus, 6so that with one heart and mouth you may glorify the

---

a Many ancient mss. read *we pursue*   *h* 3 Psalm 69:9

glorify the God and Father of our Lord Jesus Christ. ⁷Wherefore, accept one another, just as Christ also accepted us to the glory of God.

⁸For I say that Christ has become a servant to the circumcision on behalf of the truth of God to confirm the promises given to the fathers,

⁹and for the Gentiles to glorify God for His mercy; as it is written,

"THEREFORE I WILL GIVE PRAISE TO THEE AMONG THE GENTILES, AND I WILL SING TO THY NAME."

¹⁰And again he says, "REJOICE, O GENTILES, WITH HIS PEOPLE."

¹¹And again, "PRAISE THE LORD ALL YOU GENTILES, AND LET ALL THE PEOPLES PRAISE HIM."

¹²And again Isaiah says, "THERE SHALL COME THE ROOT OF JESSE, AND HE WHO ARISES TO RULE OVER THE GENTILES, IN HIM SHALL THE GENTILES HOPE."

¹³Now may the God of hope fill you with all joy and peace in believing, that you may abound in hope by the power of the Holy Spirit.

¹⁴And concerning you, my brethren, I myself also am convinced that you yourselves are full of goodness, filled with all knowledge, and able also to admonish one another.

¹⁵But I have written very boldly to you on some points, so as to remind you again, because of the grace that was given me from God,

¹⁶to be a minister of

δοξάζητε τὸν θεὸν καὶ πατέρα τοῦ
ye may glorify the God and Father of the

κυρίου ἡμῶν Ἰησοῦ Χριστοῦ.
Lord of us Jesus Christ.

7 Διὸ προσλαμβάνεσθε ἀλλήλους, καθὼς
Wherefore receive ye one another, as

καὶ ὁ Χριστὸς προσελάβετο ἡμᾶς εἰς
also - Christ received us to

δόξαν τοῦ θεοῦ. 8 λέγω γὰρ Χριστὸν
[the] glory - of God. For I say Christ

διάκονον γεγενῆσθαι περιτομῆς ὑπὲρ
a minister to have become of [the] on be-
circumcision half of

ἀληθείας θεοῦ, εἰς τὸ βεβαιῶσαι τὰς
[the] truth of God, - - to confirm the

ἐπαγγελίας τῶν πατέρων, 9 τὰ δὲ ἔθνη
promises of the fathers, and ¹the ²nations

ὑπὲρ ἐλέους δοξάσαι τὸν θεόν, καθὼς
⁵on be- ⁴mercy ³to glorify - ⁴God, as
half of

γέγραπται· διὰ τοῦτο ἐξομολογήσομαί σοι
it has been written: Therefore I will confess to thee

ἐν ἔθνεσιν καὶ τῷ ὀνόματί σου ψαλῶ.
among nations and to the name of thee I will sing praise.

10 καὶ πάλιν λέγει· εὐφράνθητε, ἔθνη,
And again he says: Be glad, nations,

μετὰ τοῦ λαοῦ αὐτοῦ. 11 καὶ πάλιν·
with the people of him. And again:

αἰνεῖτε, πάντα τὰ ἔθνη, τὸν κύριον,
Praise, all the nations, the Lord,

καὶ ἐπαινεσάτωσαν αὐτὸν πάντες οἱ λαοί.
and let praise him all the peoples.

12 καὶ πάλιν Ἡσαΐας λέγει· ἔσται
And again Esaias says: There shall be

ἡ ῥίζα τοῦ Ἰεσσαί, καὶ ὁ ἀνιστάμενος
the root - of Jesse, and the [one] rising up

ἄρχειν ἐθνῶν· ἐπ’ αὐτῷ ἔθνη ἐλπιοῦσιν.
to rule nations; on him nations will hope.

13 Ὁ δὲ θεὸς τῆς ἐλπίδος πληρώσαι
Now the God - of hope fill

ὑμᾶς πάσης χαρᾶς καὶ εἰρήνης ἐν τῷ
you of(with) all joy and peace in -

πιστεύειν, εἰς τὸ περισσεύειν ὑμᾶς ἐν
to believe for - to abound you[b] in
(believing),

τῇ ἐλπίδι ἐν δυνάμει πνεύματος ἁγίου.
- hope by [the] power of [the] Spirit Holy.

14 Πέπεισμαι δέ, ἀδελφοί μου, καὶ
But I have been persuaded, brothers of me, even

αὐτὸς ἐγὼ περὶ ὑμῶν, ὅτι καὶ αὐτοί
²[my]self ¹I concerning you, that also [your]-
selves

μεστοί ἐστε ἀγαθωσύνης, πεπληρωμένοι
full ye are of goodness, having been filled

πάσης τῆς γνώσεως, δυνάμενοι καὶ
of(with) all - knowledge, being able also

ἀλλήλους νουθετεῖν. 15 τολμηροτέρως δὲ
one another to admonish. And more daringly

ἔγραψα ὑμῖν ἀπὸ μέρους, ὡς ἐπαναμιμνή-
I wrote to you in part, as remind-

σκων ὑμᾶς διὰ τὴν χάριν τὴν δοθεῖσάν
ing you by the grace - given

μοι ἀπὸ τοῦ θεοῦ 16 εἰς τὸ εἶναί με
to me from - God for the to be me[b]
= that I should be

God and Father of our Lord Jesus Christ. ⁷Accept one another, then, just as Christ accepted you, in order to bring praise to God. ⁸For I tell you that Christ has become a servant of the Jews[i] on behalf of God's truth, to confirm the promises made to the patriarchs ⁹so that the Gentiles may glorify God for his mercy, as it is written:

"Therefore I will praise you among the Gentiles; I will sing hymns to your name."[j]

¹⁰Again, it says,

"Rejoice, O Gentiles, with his people."[k]

¹¹And again,

"Praise the Lord, all you Gentiles, and sing praises to him, all you peoples."[l]

¹²And again, Isaiah says,

"The Root of Jesse will spring up, one who will arise to rule over the nations; the Gentiles will hope in him."[m]

¹³May the God of hope fill you with all joy and peace as you trust in him, so that you may overflow with hope by the power of the Holy Spirit.

Paul the Minister to the Gentiles

¹⁴I myself am convinced, my brothers, that you yourselves are full of goodness, complete in knowledge and competent to instruct one another. ¹⁵I have written you quite boldly on some points, as if to remind you of them again, because of the grace God gave me ¹⁶to be a minister of Christ

---

⁸ Greek *circumcision*
ʲ9 2 Samuel 22:50; Psalm 18:49
ᵏ10 Deut. 32:43
ˡ11 Psalm 117:1
ᵐ12 Isaiah 11:10

Christ Jesus to the Gentiles, ministering as a priest the gospel of God, that *my* offering of the Gentiles might become acceptable, sanctified by the Holy Spirit.
17Therefore in Christ Jesus I have found reason for boasting in things pertaining to God.
18For I will not presume to speak of anything except what Christ has accomplished through me, resulting in the obedience of the Gentiles by word and deed,
19in the power of signs and wonders, in the power of the Spirit; so that from Jerusalem and round about as far as Illyricum I have fully preached the gospel of Christ.
20And thus I aspired to preach the gospel, not where Christ was *already* named, that I might not build upon another man's foundation;
21but as it is written,
"THEY WHO HAD NO NEWS OF HIM SHALL SEE,
AND THEY WHO HAVE NOT HEARD SHALL UNDERSTAND."
22For this reason I have often been hindered from coming to you;
23but now, with no further place for me in these regions, and since I have had for many years a longing to come to you
24whenever I go to Spain—for I hope to see you in passing, and to be helped on my way there by you, when I have first enjoyed your company for a while—
25but now, I am going to Jerusalem serving the saints.
26For Macedonia and Achaia have been pleased to make a contribution for

λειτουργὸν Χριστοῦ ᾿Ιησοῦ εἰς τὰ ἔθνη,
a minister of Christ Jesus to the nations,

ἱερουργοῦντα τὸ εὐαγγέλιον τοῦ θεοῦ,
sacrificing the gospel - of God,

ἵνα γένηται ἡ προσφορὰ τῶν ἐθνῶν
in order ⁵may be ¹the ²offering ³of the ⁴nations
that

εὐπρόσδεκτος, ἡγιασμένη ἐν πνεύματι
acceptable, having been sanctified by [the] Spirit

ἁγίῳ. 17 ἔχω οὖν τὴν καύχησιν ἐν
Holy. I have therefore the boasting in

Χριστῷ ᾿Ιησοῦ τὰ πρὸς τὸν θεόν· 18 οὐ
Christ Jesus the things with* - God; ⁴not

γὰρ τολμήσω τι λαλεῖν ὧν οὐ
¹for ²I ³will ⁶dare ⁷any- ⁵to speak of [the] ³not
thing things which

κατειργάσατο Χριστὸς δι᾿ ἐμοῦ εἰς ὑπακοὴν
³did ⁴work ⁵out ¹Christ through me for obedience

ἐθνῶν, λόγῳ καὶ ἔργῳ, 19 ἐν δυνάμει
of [the] in word and work, by power
nations,

σημείων καὶ τεράτων, ἐν δυνάμει πνεύματος·
of signs and wonders, by power of [the] Spirit·

ὥστε με ἀπὸ ᾿Ιερουσαλὴμ καὶ κύκλῳ
so as me from Jerusalem and around
=I should fulfil the gospel . . . from . . . Illyricum.

μέχρι τοῦ ᾿Ιλλυρικοῦ πεπληρωκέναι τὸ
unto - Illyricum to have fulfilled[b] the

εὐαγγέλιον τοῦ Χριστοῦ. 20 οὕτως δὲ
gospel - of Christ. And so

φιλοτιμούμενον εὐαγγελίζεσθαι οὐχ ὅπου
eagerly striving to evangelize not where

ὠνομάσθη Χριστός, ἵνα μὴ ἐπ᾿ ἀλλότριον
²was named ¹Christ, in order not on ³belonging to
that another

θεμέλιον οἰκοδομῶ, 21 ἀλλὰ καθὼς
¹a foundation I should build, but as

γέγραπται· ὄψονται οἷς οὐκ ἀνηγγέλη
it has been They shall see to whom it was not announced
written:

περὶ αὐτοῦ, καὶ οἳ οὐκ ἀκηκόασιν
concerning him, and [those] who have not heard

συνήσουσιν. 22 διὸ καὶ ἐνεκοπτόμην τὰ
will understand. Wherefore also I was hindered -

πολλὰ τοῦ ἐλθεῖν πρὸς ὑμᾶς· 23 νυνὶ
many(much) - to come[d] to you; ²now

δὲ μηκέτι τόπον ἔχων ἐν τοῖς κλίμασι
¹but no longer ²place ¹having in - ²regions

τούτοις, ἐπιποθίαν δὲ ἔχων τοῦ ἐλθεῖν
¹these, and ²a desire ¹having - to come[d]

πρὸς ὑμᾶς ἀπὸ ἱκανῶν ἐτῶν, 24 ὡς ἂν
to you from several years, whenever

πορεύωμαι εἰς τὴν Σπανίαν· ἐλπίζω γὰρ
I journey to - Spain; for I hope

διαπορευόμενος θεάσασθαι ὑμᾶς καὶ ὑφ᾿
journeying through to behold you and by

ὑμῶν προπεμφθῆναι ἐκεῖ, ἐὰν ὑμῶν πρῶτον
you to be set forward there, if of(with) you firstly

ἀπὸ μέρους ἐμπλησθῶ, 25 — νυνὶ δὲ
in part I may be filled, — but now

πορεύομαι εἰς ᾿Ιερουσαλὴμ διακονῶν τοῖς
I am going to Jerusalem ministering to the

ἁγίοις. 26 ηὐδόκησαν γὰρ Μακεδονία καὶ
saints. For thought it good Macedonia and

᾿Αχαΐα κοινωνίαν τινὰ ποιήσασθαι εἰς
Achaia ²contribution ²some ¹to make for

Jesus to the Gentiles with the priestly duty of proclaiming the gospel of God, so that the Gentiles might become an offering acceptable to God, sanctified by the Holy Spirit.
17Therefore I glory in Christ Jesus in my service to God. 18I will not venture to speak of anything except what Christ has accomplished through me in leading the Gentiles to obey God by what I have said and done— 19by the power of signs and miracles, through the power of the Spirit. So from Jerusalem all the way around to Illyricum, I have fully proclaimed the gospel of Christ. 20It has always been my ambition to preach the gospel where Christ was not known, so that I would not be building on someone else's foundation. 21Rather, as it is written:

"Those who were not
told about him will
see,
and those who have
not heard will
understand." [n]

22This is why I have often been hindered from coming to you.

Paul's Plan to Visit Rome

23But now that there is no more place for me to work in these regions, and since I have been longing for many years to see you, 24I plan to do so when I go to Spain. I hope to visit you while passing through and to have you assist me on my journey there, after I have enjoyed your company for a while. 25Now, however, I am on my way to Jerusalem in the service of the saints there. 26For Macedonia and Achaia were pleased to make a contribution for the

* That is, the things that have to do with . . .   [n]21 Isaiah 52:15

the poor among the saints in Jerusalem.
27Yes, they were pleased *to do so,* and they are indebted to them. For if the Gentiles have shared in their spiritual things, they are indebted to minister to them also in material things.
28Therefore, when I have finished this, and have put my seal on this fruit of theirs, I will go on by way of you to Spain.
29And I know that when I come to you, I will come in the fulness of the blessing of Christ.
30Now I urge you, brethren, by our Lord Jesus Christ and by the love of the Spirit, to strive together with me in your prayers to God for me,
31that I may be delivered from those who are disobedient in Judea, and *that* my service for Jerusalem may prove acceptable to the saints;
32so that I may come to you in joy by the will of God and find *refreshing* rest in your company.
33Now the God of peace be with you all. Amen.

τοὺς πτωχοὺς τῶν ἁγίων τῶν ἐν Ἰερου-
the poor of the saints - in Jeru-
σαλήμ. 27 ηὐδόκησαν γάρ, καὶ ὀφειλέται
salem. For they thought it good, and debtors
εἰσὶν αὐτῶν· εἰ γὰρ τοῖς πνευματικοῖς
they are of them; for if in the spiritual things
αὐτῶν ἐκοινώνησαν τὰ ἔθνη, ὀφείλουσιν
of them ²shared ¹the ²nations, they ought
καὶ ἐν τοῖς σαρκικοῖς λειτουργῆσαι αὐτοῖς.
also in the fleshly things to minister to them.
28 τοῦτο οὖν ἐπιτελέσας, καὶ σφραγισάμενος
This therefore having completed, and having sealed
αὐτοῖς τὸν καρπὸν τοῦτον, 29 ἀπελεύσομαι
to them this fruit, I will go away
δι᾽ ὑμῶν εἰς Σπανίαν· οἶδα δὲ ὅτι
through you to Spain; and I know that
ἐρχόμενος πρὸς ὑμᾶς ἐν πληρώματι
coming to you in [the] fulness
εὐλογίας Χριστοῦ ἐλεύσομαι. 30 Παρακαλῶ
of [the] blessing of Christ I will come. I beseech
δὲ ὑμᾶς, [ἀδελφοί], διὰ τοῦ κυρίου
Now you, brothers, through the Lord
ἡμῶν Ἰησοῦ Χριστοῦ καὶ διὰ τῆς ἀγάπης
of us Jesus Christ and through the love
τοῦ πνεύματος, συναγωνίσασθαί μοι ἐν
of the Spirit, to strive with me in
ταῖς προσευχαῖς ὑπὲρ ἐμοῦ πρὸς τὸν
the prayers on behalf of me to -
θεόν, 31 ἵνα ῥυσθῶ ἀπὸ τῶν ἀπειθούντων
God, in order that I may be from the disobeying [ones]
delivered
ἐν τῇ Ἰουδαίᾳ καὶ ἡ διακονία μου
in - Judæa and the ministry of me
ἡ εἰς Ἰερουσαλὴμ εὐπρόσδεκτος τοῖς
- to Jerusalem ²acceptable ¹to the
ἁγίοις γένηται, 32 ἵνα ἐν χαρᾷ ἐλθὼν
²saints ¹may be, in order that in joy coming
πρὸς ὑμᾶς διὰ θελήματος θεοῦ συνανα-
to you through [the] will of God I may
παύσωμαι ὑμῖν. 33 ὁ δὲ θεὸς τῆς
rest with you. And the God -
εἰρήνης μετὰ πάντων ὑμῶν· ἀμήν.
of peace [be] with all you: Amen.

poor among the saints in Jerusalem. 27They were pleased to do it, and indeed they owe it to them. For if the Gentiles have shared in the Jews' spiritual blessings, they owe it to the Jews to share with them their material blessings. 28So after I have completed this task and have made sure that they have received this fruit, I will go to Spain and visit you on the way. 29I know that when I come to you, I will come in the full measure of the blessing of Christ.

30I urge you, brothers, by our Lord Jesus Christ and by the love of the Spirit, to join me in my struggle by praying to God for me. 31Pray that I may be rescued from the unbelievers in Judea and that my service in Jerusalem may be acceptable to the saints there, 32so that by God's will I may come to you with joy and together with you be refreshed. 33The God of peace be with you all. Amen.

Chapter 16

Greetings and Love Expressed

I commend to you our sister Phoebe, who is a servant of the church which is at Cenchrea;
2that you receive her in the Lord in a manner worthy of the saints, and that you help her in whatever matter she may have need of you; for she herself has also been a helper of many, and of myself as well.
3Greet Prisca and Aquila, my fellow workers in Christ Jesus,

16 Συνίστημι δὲ ὑμῖν Φοίβην τὴν
Now I commend to you Phœbe the
ἀδελφὴν ἡμῶν, οὖσαν [καὶ] διάκονον τῆς
sister of us, being also a minister of the
ἐκκλησίας τῆς ἐν Κεγχρεαῖς, 2 ἵνα
church - in Cenchrea, in order that
αὐτὴν προσδέξησθε ἐν κυρίῳ ἀξίως τῶν
²her ¹ye may receive in [the] Lord worthily of the
ἁγίων, καὶ παραστῆτε αὐτῇ ἐν ᾧ ἂν
saints, and may stand by her in ¹whatever
ὑμῶν χρήζῃ πράγματι· καὶ γὰρ αὐτὴ
²of you ²she may ²thing; for indeed she
have need
προστάτις πολλῶν ἐγενήθη καὶ ἐμοῦ αὐτοῦ.
a protectress of many became and of myself.
3 Ἀσπάσασθε Πρίσκαν καὶ Ἀκύλαν τοὺς
Greet ye Prisca and Aquila the
συνεργούς μου ἐν Χριστῷ Ἰησοῦ, 4 οἵτινες
fellow-workers of me in Christ Jesus, who

Chapter 16

Personal Greetings

I COMMEND to you our sister Phoebe, a servant*o* of the church in Cenchrea. 2I ask you to receive her in the Lord in a way worthy of the saints and to give her any help she may need from you, for she has been a great help to many people, including me.

3Greet Priscilla*p* and Aquila, my fellow workers in Christ Jesus. 4They

*o*1 Or *deaconess*
*p*3 Greek *Prisca,* a variant of *Priscilla*

478

4who for my life risked their own necks, to whom not only do I give thanks, but also all the churches of the Gentiles;

5also *greet* the church that is in their house. Greet Epaenetus, my beloved, who is the first convert to Christ from Asia.

6Greet Mary, who has worked hard for you.

7Greet Andronicus and Junias, my kinsmen, and my fellow prisoners, who are outstanding among the apostles, who also were in Christ before me.

8Greet Ampliatus, my beloved in the Lord.

9Greet Urbanus, our fellow worker in Christ, and Stachys my beloved.

10Greet Apelles, the approved in Christ. Greet those who are of the *household* of Aristobulus.

11Greet Herodion, my kinsman. Greet those of the *household* of Narcissus, who are in the Lord.

12Greet Tryphaena and Tryphosa, workers in the Lord. Greet Persis the beloved, who has worked hard in the Lord.

13Greet Rufus, a choice man in the Lord, also his mother and mine.

14Greet Asyncritus, Phlegon, Hermes, Patrobas, Hermas and the brethren with them.

15Greet Philologus and Julia, Nereus and his sister, and Olympas, and all the saints who are with them.

16Greet one another with a holy kiss. All the churches of Christ greet you.

ὑπὲρ τῆς ψυχῆς μου τὸν ἑαυτῶν τράχηλον
on be- the life of me ²the ⁴of ³neck
half of themselves

ὑπέθηκαν, οἷς οὐκ ἐγὼ μόνος εὐχαριστῶ
¹risked, to whom not I only give thanks

ἀλλὰ καὶ πᾶσαι αἱ ἐκκλησίαι τῶν ἐθνῶν,
but also all the churches of the nations,

5 καὶ τὴν κατ' οἶκον αὐτῶν ἐκκλησίαν.
and ¹the ³in ⁴house ⁵of them ²church.

ἀσπάσασθε Ἐπαίνετον τὸν ἀγαπητόν μου,
Greet Epænetus the beloved of me,

ὅς ἐστιν ἀπαρχὴ τῆς Ἀσίας εἰς Χριστόν.
who is firstfruit – of Asia for Christ.

6 ἀσπάσασθε Μαρίαν, ἥτις πολλὰ ἐκοπίασεν
Greet Mary, who many things laboured
(much)

εἰς ὑμᾶς. 7 ἀσπάσασθε Ἀνδρόνικον καὶ
for you. Greet Andronicus and

Ἰουνιᾶν τοὺς συγγενεῖς μου καὶ συναιχμα-
Junias the kinsmen of me and fellow-

λώτους μου, οἵτινές εἰσιν ἐπίσημοι ἐν
captives of me, who are notable among

τοῖς ἀποστόλοις, οἳ καὶ πρὸ ἐμοῦ γέγοναν
the apostles, who indeed before me have been

ἐν Χριστῷ. 8 ἀσπάσασθε Ἀμπλιᾶτον τὸν
in Christ. Greet Ampliatus the

ἀγαπητόν μου ἐν κυρίῳ. 9 ἀσπάσασθε
beloved of me in [the] Lord. Greet

Οὐρβανὸν τὸν συνεργὸν ἡμῶν ἐν Χριστῷ
Urbanus the fellow-worker of us in Christ

καὶ Στάχυν τὸν ἀγαπητόν μου. 10 ἀσπά-
and Stachys the beloved of me. Greet

ασθε Ἀπελλῆν τὸν δόκιμον ἐν Χριστῷ.
Apelles the approved in Christ.

ἀσπάσασθε τοὺς ἐκ τῶν Ἀριστοβούλου.
Greet the [ones] of the [family] of Aristobulus.

11 ἀσπάσασθε Ἡρῳδίωνα τὸν συγγενῆ μου.
Greet Herodion the kinsman of me.

ἀσπάσασθε τοὺς ἐκ τῶν Ναρκίσσου τοὺς
Greet the [ones] of the [family] of Narcissus –

ὄντας ἐν κυρίῳ. 12 ἀσπάσασθε Τρύφαιναν
being in [the] Lord. Greet Tryphæna

καὶ Τρυφῶσαν τὰς κοπιώσας ἐν κυρίῳ.
and Tryphosa the [ones] labouring in [the] Lord.

ἀσπάσασθε Περσίδα τὴν ἀγαπητήν, ἥτις
Greet Persis the beloved, who

πολλὰ ἐκοπίασεν ἐν κυρίῳ. 13 ἀσπάσασθε
many things laboured in [the] Lord. Greet
(much)

Ῥοῦφον τὸν ἐκλεκτὸν ἐν κυρίῳ καὶ
Rufus the chosen in [the] Lord and –

τὴν μητέρα αὐτοῦ καὶ ἐμοῦ. 14 ἀσπάσασθε
the mother of him and of me. Greet

Ἀσύγκριτον, Φλέγοντα, Ἑρμῆν, Πατροβᾶν,
Asyncritus, Phlegon, Hermes, Patrobas,

Ἑρμᾶν, καὶ τοὺς σὺν αὐτοῖς ἀδελφούς.
Hermas, and the ²with ³them ¹brothers.

15 ἀσπάσασθε Φιλόλογον καὶ Ἰουλίαν,
Greet Philologus and Julia,

Νηρέα καὶ τὴν ἀδελφὴν αὐτοῦ, καὶ
Nereus and the sister of him, and

Ὀλυμπᾶν, καὶ τοὺς σὺν αὐτοῖς πάντας
Olympas, and ²the ⁴with ⁵them ¹all

ἁγίους. 16 ἀσπάσασθε ἀλλήλους ἐν φιλήματι
³saints. Greet one another with kiss

ἁγίῳ. ἀσπάζονται ὑμᾶς αἱ ἐκκλησίαι
a holy. ⁵greet ⁴you ²the ³churches

---

risked their lives for me. Not only I but all the churches of the Gentiles are grateful to them.

5Greet also the church that meets at their house.

Greet my dear friend Epenetus, who was the first convert to Christ in the province of Asia.

6Greet Mary, who worked very hard for you.

7Greet Andronicus and Junias, my relatives who have been in prison with me. They are outstanding among the apostles, and they were in Christ before I was.

8Greet Ampliatus, whom I love in the Lord.

9Greet Urbanus, our fellow worker in Christ, and my dear friend Stachys.

10Greet Apelles, tested and approved in Christ. Greet those who belong to the household of Aristobulus.

11Greet Herodion, my relative.

Greet those in the household of Narcissus who are in the Lord.

12Greet Tryphena and Tryphosa, those women who work hard in the Lord.

Greet my dear friend Persis, another woman who has worked very hard in the Lord.

13Greet Rufus, chosen in the Lord, and his mother, who has been a mother to me, too.

14Greet Asyncritus, Phlegon, Hermes, Patrobas, Hermas and the brothers with them.

15Greet Philologus, Julia, Nereus and his sister, and Olympas and all the saints with them.

16Greet one another with a holy kiss.

All the churches of Christ send greetings.

17Now I urge you, brethren, keep your eye on those who cause dissensions and hindrances contrary to the teaching which you learned, and turn away from them.
18For such men are slaves, not of our Lord Christ but of their own appetites; and by their smooth and flattering speech they deceive the hearts of the unsuspecting.
19For the report of your obedience has reached to all; therefore I am rejoicing over you, but I want you to be wise in what is good, and innocent in what is evil.
20And the God of peace will soon crush Satan under your feet.
The grace of our Lord Jesus be with you.
21Timothy my fellow worker greets you, and so do Lucius and Jason and Sosipater, my kinsmen.
22I, Tertius, who write this letter, greet you in the Lord.
23Gaius, host to me and to the whole church, greets you. Erastus, the city treasurer greets you, and Quartus, the brother.
24[ʳThe grace of our Lord Jesus Christ be with you all. Amen.]
25Now to Him who is able to establish you according to my gospel and the preaching of Jesus Christ, according to the revelation of the mystery which has been kept secret for long ages past,
26but now is manifested, and by the Scriptures of the prophets, according to the

πᾶσαι τοῦ Χριστοῦ.
¹All – ⁴of Christ.

17 Παρακαλῶ δὲ ὑμᾶς, ἀδελφοί, σκοπεῖν
Now I beseech you, brothers, to watch

τοὺς τὰς διχοστασίας καὶ τὰ σκάνδαλα
¹the ³the ⁴divisions ⁵and ⁶the ⁷offences
[ones]

παρὰ τὴν διδαχὴν ἣν ὑμεῖς ἐμάθετε
⁸beside ⁹the ¹⁰teaching ¹¹which ¹²ye ¹³learned

ποιοῦντας, καὶ ἐκκλίνετε ἀπ' αὐτῶν· 18 οἱ
²making, and turn away from them; –

γὰρ τοιοῦτοι τῷ κυρίῳ ἡμῶν Χριστῷ
for such men ³the ⁴Lord ⁵of us ²Christ

οὐ δουλεύουσιν ἀλλὰ τῇ ἑαυτῶν κοιλίᾳ,
¹serve not but the of themselves belly,

καὶ διὰ τῆς χρηστολογίας καὶ εὐλογίας
and through – fair speech and flattering speech

ἐξαπατῶσιν τὰς καρδίας τῶν ἀκάκων.
deceive the hearts of the guileless.

19 ἡ γὰρ ὑμῶν ὑπακοὴ εἰς πάντας
²the ¹For ⁴of you ³obedience ⁶to ⁷all men

ἀφίκετο· ἐφ' ὑμῖν οὖν χαίρω, θέλω
⁵came; over you therefore I rejoice, ¹I wish

δὲ ὑμᾶς σοφοὺς εἶναι εἰς τὸ ἀγαθόν,
²and you wise to be to the good,

ἀκεραίους δὲ εἰς τὸ κακόν. 20 ὁ δὲ
but simple to the evil. And the

θεὸς τῆς εἰρήνης συντρίψει τὸν σατανᾶν
God – of peace will crush – Satan

ὑπὸ τοὺς πόδας ὑμῶν ἐν τάχει.
under the feet of you soon.

Ἡ χάρις τοῦ κυρίου ἡμῶν Ἰησοῦ
The grace of the Lord of us Jesus [be]

μεθ' ὑμῶν.
with you.

21 Ἀσπάζεται ὑμᾶς Τιμόθεος ὁ συνεργός
⁵greets ⁶you ¹Timothy ²the ³fellow-worker

μου, καὶ Λούκιος καὶ Ἰάσων καὶ
⁴of me, and Lucius and Jason and

Σωσίπατρος οἱ συγγενεῖς μου. 22 ἀσπάζ-
Sosipater the kinsmen of me. ⁷greet

ομαι ὑμᾶς ἐγὼ Τέρτιος ὁ γράψας τὴν
⁸you ¹I ²Tertius ³the [one] ⁴writing ⁵the

ἐπιστολὴν ἐν κυρίῳ. 23 ἀσπάζεται ὑμᾶς
⁶epistle in [the] Lord. ⁹greets ¹⁰you

Γάϊος ὁ ξένος μου καὶ ὅλης τῆς
¹Gaius ²the ³host ⁴of me ⁵and ⁶of all ⁷the

ἐκκλησίας. ἀσπάζεται ὑμᾶς Ἔραστος ὁ
⁸church. ⁶greets ⁷you ¹Erastus ²the

οἰκονόμος τῆς πόλεως καὶ Κούαρτος ὁ
³treasurer ⁴of the ⁵city and Quartus the
(?his)

ἀδελφός.‡
brother.

25 Τῷ δὲ δυναμένῳ ὑμᾶς στηρίξαι κατὰ
Now to the being able ²you ¹to establish according
[one] ing to

τὸ εὐαγγέλιόν μου καὶ τὸ κήρυγμα
the gospel of me and the proclamation

Ἰησοῦ Χριστοῦ, κατὰ ἀποκάλυψιν μυστηρίου
of Jesus Christ, according [the] revelation of [the]
to mystery

χρόνοις αἰωνίοις σεσιγημένου, 26 φανερω-
²in times ³eternal ¹having been kept silent, ²mani-

θέντος δὲ νῦν διά τε γραφῶν προφητικῶν
fested ¹but now and through writings prophetic

17I urge you, brothers, to watch out for those who cause divisions and put obstacles in your way that are contrary to the teaching you have learned. Keep away from them. 18For such people are not serving our Lord Christ, but their own appetites. By smooth talk and flattery they deceive the minds of naive people. 19Everyone has heard about your obedience, so I am full of joy over you; but I want you to be wise about what is good, and innocent about what is evil.
20The God of peace will soon crush Satan under your feet.
The grace of our Lord Jesus be with you.
21Timothy, my fellow worker, sends his greetings to you, as do Lucius, Jason and Sosipater, my relatives.
22I, Tertius, who wrote down this letter, greet you in the Lord.
23Gaius, whose hospitality I and the whole church here enjoy, sends you his greetings.
Erastus, who is the city's director of public works, and our brother Quartus send you their greetings.�q
25Now to him who is able to establish you by my gospel and the proclamation of Jesus Christ, according to the revelation of the mystery hidden for long ages past, 26but now revealed and made known through

ʳMany mss. do not contain this verse

‡ Verse 24 omitted by Nestle; cf. NIV footnote.

q23 Some manuscripts their greetings. 24May the grace of our Lord Jesus Christ be with all of you. Amen.

commandment of the eternal God, has been made known to all the nations, *leading* to obedience of faith;

27to the only wise God, through Jesus Christ, be the glory forever. Amen.

κατ᾽ ἐπιταγὴν τοῦ αἰωνίου θεοῦ εἰς
accord-   [the]   of the   eternal   God   ⁶for
ing to   command

ὑπακοὴν πίστεως εἰς πάντα τὰ ἔθνη
⁷obedience   ⁸of faith   ¹to   ²all   ⁴the   ⁵nations

γνωρισθέντος, 27 μόνῳ σοφῷ θεῷ, διὰ
¹made known,   ²only   ³wise   ¹to God, through

Ἰησοῦ Χριστοῦ, ᾧ ἡ δόξα εἰς τοὺς
Jesus   Christ,   to whom the   glory   unto   the
                     (him)ᵉ

αἰῶνας τῶν αἰώνων· ἀμήν.
ages   of the   ages: Amen.

the prophetic writings by the command of the eternal God, so that all nations might believe and obey him —27to the only wise God be glory forever through Jesus Christ! Amen.

Chapter 1

Appeal to Unity

PAUL, called *as* an apostle of Jesus Christ by the will of God, and Sosthenes our brother,

2to the church of God which is at Corinth, to those who have been sanctified in Christ Jesus, saints by calling, with all who in every place call upon the name of our Lord Jesus Christ, their *Lord* and ours:

3Grace to you and peace from God our Father and the Lord Jesus Christ.

4I thank *a*my God always concerning you, for the grace of God which was given you in Christ Jesus,

5that in everything you were enriched in Him, in all speech and all knowledge,

6even as the testimony concerning Christ was confirmed in you,

7so that you are not lacking in any gift, awaiting eagerly the revelation of our Lord Jesus Christ,

8who shall also confirm you to the end, blameless in the day of our Lord Jesus Christ.

9God is faithful, through whom you were called into fellowship with His Son, Jesus Christ our Lord.

10Now I exhort you, brethren, by the name of our Lord Jesus Christ, that you all agree, and there be no divisions among you, but you be made complete in the same mind and in the same judgment.

11For I have been in-

---

1 Παῦλος κλητὸς ἀπόστολος Χριστοῦ
Paul a called apostle of Christ

'Ιησοῦ διὰ θελήματος θεοῦ καὶ Σωσθένης
Jesus through [the] will of God and Sosthenes

ὁ ἀδελφὸς **2** τῇ ἐκκλησίᾳ τοῦ θεοῦ
the(?his) brother to the church – of God

τῇ οὔσῃ ἐν Κορίνθῳ, ἡγιασμένοις ἐν
– existing in Corinth, to [ones] in
having been sanctified

Χριστῷ 'Ιησοῦ, κλητοῖς ἁγίοις, σὺν πᾶσιν
Christ Jesus, called saints, with all

τοῖς ἐπικαλουμένοις τὸ ὄνομα τοῦ κυρίου
the [ones] calling on the name of the Lord

ἡμῶν 'Ιησοῦ Χριστοῦ ἐν παντὶ τόπῳ,
of us Jesus Christ in every place,

αὐτῶν καὶ ἡμῶν· **3** χάρις ὑμῖν καὶ
of them **and** of us: Grace to you and

εἰρήνη ἀπὸ θεοῦ πατρὸς ἡμῶν καὶ κυρίου
peace from God Father of us and Lord

'Ιησοῦ Χριστοῦ.
Jesus Christ.

4 Εὐχαριστῶ τῷ θεῷ πάντοτε περὶ
I gave thanks – to God always concerning

ὑμῶν ἐπὶ τῇ χάριτι τοῦ θεοῦ τῇ δοθείσῃ
you on the grace – of God – given

ὑμῖν ἐν Χριστῷ 'Ιησοῦ, **5** ὅτι ἐν παντὶ
to you in Christ Jesus, because in everything

ἐπλουτίσθητε ἐν αὐτῷ, ἐν παντὶ λόγῳ
ye were enriched in him, in all speech

καὶ πάσῃ γνώσει, **6** καθὼς τὸ μαρτύριον
and all knowledge, as the testimony

τοῦ Χριστοῦ ἐβεβαιώθη ἐν ὑμῖν, **7** ὥστε
– of Christ was confirmed in you, so as

ὑμᾶς μὴ ὑστερεῖσθαι ἐν μηδενὶ χαρίσματι,
you not to be wanting*b* in no(any) gift,

ἀπεκδεχομένους τὴν ἀποκάλυψιν τοῦ κυρίου
awaiting the revelation of the Lord

ἡμῶν 'Ιησοῦ Χριστοῦ· **8** ὃς καὶ βεβαιώσει
of us Jesus Christ; who also will confirm

ὑμᾶς ἕως τέλους ἀνεγκλήτους ἐν τῇ
you till [the] end blameless in the

ἡμέρα τοῦ κυρίου ἡμῶν 'Ιησοῦ [Χριστοῦ].
day of the Lord of us Jesus Christ.

9 πιστὸς ὁ θεός, δι' οὗ ἐκλήθητε εἰς
Faithful [is] – God, through whom ye were called to

κοινωνίαν τοῦ υἱοῦ αὐτοῦ 'Ιησοῦ Χριστοῦ
[the] fellowship of the Son of him Jesus Christ

τοῦ κυρίου ἡμῶν.
the Lord of us.

10 Παρακαλῶ δὲ ὑμᾶς, ἀδελφοί, διὰ
Now I beseech you, brothers, through

τοῦ ὀνόματος τοῦ κυρίου ἡμῶν 'Ιησοῦ
the name of the Lord of us Jesus

Χριστοῦ, ἵνα τὸ αὐτὸ λέγητε πάντες,
Christ, in order the same ye say all,
that thing

καὶ μὴ ᾖ ἐν ὑμῖν σχίσματα, ἦτε δὲ
and not be among you divisions, but ye may be

κατηρτισμένοι ἐν τῷ αὐτῷ νοῒ καὶ
having been joined in the same mind and
together

ἐν τῇ αὐτῇ γνώμῃ. **11** ἐδηλώθη γάρ μοι
in the same opinion. For it was shown to me

Chapter 1

PAUL, called to be an apostle of Christ Jesus by the will of God, and our brother Sosthenes,

2To the church of God in Corinth, to those sanctified in Christ Jesus and called to be holy, together with all those everywhere who call on the name of our Lord Jesus Christ—their Lord and ours:

3Grace and peace to you from God our Father and the Lord Jesus Christ.

Thanksgiving

4I always thank God for you because of his grace given you in Christ Jesus. 5For in him you have been enriched in every way—in all your speaking and in all your knowledge— 6because our testimony about Christ was confirmed in you. 7Therefore you do not lack any spiritual gift as you eagerly wait for our Lord Jesus Christ to be revealed. 8He will keep you strong to the end, so that you will be blameless on the day of our Lord Jesus Christ. 9God, who has called you into fellowship with his Son Jesus Christ our Lord, is faithful.

Divisions in the Church

10I appeal to you, brothers, in the name of our Lord Jesus Christ, that all of you agree with one another so that there may be no divisions among you and that you may be perfectly united in mind and thought. 11My brothers, some from

---

a Some ancient mss. do not contain *my*

formed concerning you, my brethren, by Chloe's *people*, that there are quarrels among you.

12Now I mean this, that each one of you is saying, "I am of Paul," and "I of Apollos," and "I of Cephas," and "I of Christ."

13Has Christ been divided? Paul was not crucified for you, was he? Or were you baptized in the name of Paul?

14*b*I thank God that I baptized none of you except Crispus and Gaius,

15that no man should say you were baptized in my name.

16Now I did baptize also the household of Stephanas; beyond that, I do not know whether I baptized any other.

17For Christ did not send me to baptize, but to preach the gospel, not in cleverness of speech, that the cross of Christ should not be made void.

The Wisdom of God

18For the word of the cross is to those who are perishing foolishness, but to us who are being saved it is the power of God.

19For it is written,
"I WILL DESTROY THE WISDOM OF THE WISE, AND THE CLEVERNESS OF THE CLEVER I WILL SET ASIDE."

20Where is the wise man? Where is the scribe? Where is the debater of this age? Has not God made foolish the wisdom of the world?

21For since in the wisdom of God the world through its wisdom did not *come to* know God, God was well-pleased through the foolishness of the message preached to save those who believe.

22For indeed Jews ask for signs, and Greeks search for wisdom;

23but we preach *c* Christ crucified, to Jews a stum-

περὶ ὑμῶν, ἀδελφοί μου, ὑπὸ τῶν
concerning you, brothers of me, by the [ones]

Χλόης, ὅτι ἔριδες ἐν ὑμῖν εἰσιν. 12 λέγω
of Chloe, that strifes among you there are. I say

δὲ τοῦτο, ὅτι ἕκαστος ὑμῶν λέγει· ἐγὼ
Now this, because each of you says: I

μέν εἰμι Παύλου, ἐγὼ δὲ Ἀπολλῶ,
indeed am of Paul, but I of Apollos,

ἐγὼ δὲ Κηφᾶ, ἐγὼ δὲ Χριστοῦ.
but I of Cephas, but I of Christ.

13 μεμέρισται ὁ Χριστός; μὴ Παῦλος
Has been divided - Christ? Not Paul

ἐσταυρώθη ὑπὲρ ὑμῶν, ἢ εἰς τὸ ὄνομα
was crucified on behalf of you, or in the name

Παύλου ἐβαπτίσθητε; **14** εὐχαριστῶ ὅτι
of Paul were ye baptized? I give thanks that

οὐδένα ὑμῶν ἐβάπτισα εἰ μὴ Κρίσπον
not one of you I baptized except Crispus

καὶ Γάϊον· **15** ἵνα μή τις εἴπῃ ὅτι
and Gaius; lest anyone should say that

εἰς τὸ ἐμὸν ὄνομα ἐβαπτίσθητε. **16** ἐβάπτισα δὲ
in - my name ye were baptized. But I baptized

καὶ τὸν Στεφανᾶ οἶκον· λοιπὸν οὐκ οἶδα
also the of Stephanas household; for the rest I know not

εἴ τινα ἄλλον ἐβάπτισα. **17** οὐ
if any other I baptized. ¹not

γὰρ ἀπέστειλέν με Χριστὸς βαπτίζειν
¹For ³sent ²me ⁴Christ to baptize

ἀλλὰ εὐαγγελίζεσθαι, οὐκ ἐν σοφίᾳ λόγου,
but to evangelize, not in wisdom of speech,

ἵνα μὴ κενωθῇ ὁ σταυρὸς τοῦ Χριστοῦ.
lest ⁴be made vain ¹the ²cross - ³of Christ.

18 Ὁ λόγος γὰρ ὁ τοῦ σταυροῦ τοῖς
For the word - of the cross ²to the [ones]

μὲν ἀπολλυμένοις μωρία ἐστίν, τοῖς
¹on one ³perishing ⁴folly ⁴is, ²to the hand [ones]

δὲ σῳζομένοις ἡμῖν δύναμις θεοῦ ἐστιν.
¹on the ⁴being saved ²to us ⁵[the] ⁷power ⁸of God ⁹it is. other

19 γέγραπται γάρ· ἀπολῶ τὴν σοφίαν
For it has been written: I will destroy the wisdom

τῶν σοφῶν, καὶ τὴν σύνεσιν τῶν συνετῶν
of the wise ones, and the understanding of the prudent

ἀθετήσω. **20** ποῦ σοφός; ποῦ γραμματεύς;
I will set Where [is the] where [is the] scribe? aside. wise man?

ποῦ συζητητὴς τοῦ αἰῶνος τούτου; οὐχὶ
where disputant of this age? ¹Not [is the]

ἐμώρανεν ὁ θεὸς τὴν σοφίαν τοῦ κόσμου;
¹made ²foolish - ³God ⁴the ⁵wisdom ⁶of the ⁷world?

21 ἐπειδὴ γὰρ ἐν τῇ σοφίᾳ τοῦ θεοῦ
for since in the wisdom - of God

οὐκ ἔγνω ὁ κόσμος διὰ τῆς σοφίας
⁶knew ⁷not ¹the ²world ³through ⁴the(its) ⁵wisdom

τὸν θεόν, εὐδόκησεν ὁ θεὸς διὰ τῆς
- ¹God, ²thought well - ¹God through the

μωρίας τοῦ κηρύγματος σῶσαι τοὺς
folly of the proclamation to save the

πιστεύοντας. **22** ἐπειδὴ καὶ Ἰουδαῖοι σημεῖα
[ones] believing. Seeing that both Jews ²signs

αἰτοῦσιν καὶ Ἕλληνες σοφίαν ζητοῦσιν,
¹ask and Greeks ⁴wisdom ³seek,

23 ἡμεῖς δὲ κηρύσσομεν Χριστὸν ἐσταυρωμένον,
²we ¹yet proclaim Christ having been crucified,

Chloe's household have informed me that there are quarrels among you.

12What I mean is this: One of you says, "I follow Paul"; another, "I follow Apollos"; another, "I follow Cephas *a*"; still another, "I follow Christ."

13Is Christ divided? Was Paul crucified for you? Were you baptized into *b* the name of Paul? 14I am thankful that I did not baptize any of you except Crispus and Gaius, 15so no one can say that you were baptized into my name. 16(Yes, I also baptized the household of Stephanas; beyond that, I don't remember if I baptized anyone else.) 17For Christ did not send me to baptize, but to preach the gospel—not with words of human wisdom, lest the cross of Christ be emptied of its power.

Christ the Wisdom and Power of God

18For the message of the cross is foolishness to those who are perishing, but to us who are being saved it is the power of God. 19For it is written:

"I will destroy the
    wisdom of the wise;
the intelligence of the
    intelligent I will
    frustrate." *c*

20Where is the wise man? Where is the scholar? Where is the philosopher of this age? Has not God made foolish the wisdom of the world? 21For since in the wisdom of God the world through its wisdom did not know him, God was pleased through the foolishness of what was preached to save those who believe. 22Jews demand miraculous signs and Greeks look for wisdom, 23but we preach Christ crucified: a stumbling block to Jews

---

b Some ancient mss. read *I give
thanks that*
c I.e., Messiah

a 12 That is, Peter
b 13 Or *in;* also in verse 15
c 19 Isaiah 29:14

bling block, and to Gentiles foolishness.

24but to those who are the called, both Jews and Greeks, Christ the power of God and the wisdom of God.

25Because the foolishness of God is wiser than men, and the weakness of God is stronger than men.

26For consider your calling, brethren, that there were not many wise according to the flesh, not many mighty, not many noble;

27but God has chosen the foolish things of the world to shame the wise, and God has chosen the weak things of the world to shame the things which are strong,

28and the base things of the world and the despised, God has chosen, the things that are not, that He might nullify the things that are,

29that no man should boast before God.

30But by His doing you are in Christ Jesus, who became to us wisdom from God, and righteousness and sanctification, and redemption,

31that, just as it is written, "LET HIM WHO BOASTS, BOAST IN THE LORD."

'Ιουδαίοις μὲν σκάνδαλον, ἔθνεσιν δὲ
to Jews on one hand an offence, to nations on the other

μωρίαν, 24 αὐτοῖς δὲ τοῖς κλητοῖς,
folly, but to them the called ones,

'Ιουδαίοις τε καὶ "Ελλησιν, Χριστὸν θεοῦ
²to Jews ¹both and to Greeks, Christ of God

δύναμιν καὶ θεοῦ σοφίαν. 25 ὅτι τὸ
power and of God wisdom. Because the

μωρὸν τοῦ θεοῦ σοφώτερον τῶν ἀνθρώπων
foolish - of God wiser [than] - men
thing

ἐστίν, καὶ τὸ ἀσθενὲς τοῦ θεοῦ ἰσχυρότερον
is, and the weak thing - of God stronger [than]

τῶν ἀνθρώπων. 26 Βλέπετε γὰρ τὴν
- men. For ye see the

κλῆσιν ὑμῶν, ἀδελφοί, ὅτι οὐ πολλοὶ
calling of you, brothers, that not many

σοφοὶ κατὰ σάρκα, οὐ πολλοὶ δυνατοί,
wise men according flesh, not many powerful,
to

οὐ πολλοὶ εὐγενεῖς· 27 ἀλλὰ τὰ μωρὰ
not many well born; but the foolish things

τοῦ κόσμου ἐξελέξατο ὁ θεὸς ἵνα καται-
of the world ²chose - ¹God in order he might
that

σχύνῃ τοὺς σοφούς, καὶ τὰ ἀσθενῆ τοῦ
shame the wise men, and the weak things of the

κόσμου ἐξελέξατο ὁ θεὸς ἵνα καταισχύνῃ
world ²chose - ¹God in order he might shame
that

τὰ ἰσχυρά, 28 καὶ τὰ ἀγενῆ τοῦ κόσμου
the strong things, and the base things of the world

καὶ τὰ ἐξουθενημένα ἐξελέξατο ὁ θεός,
and the things being despised ²chose - ¹God,

τὰ μὴ ὄντα, ἵνα τὰ ὄντα καταργήσῃ,
the not being, in order ²the ³being ¹he might
things that things abolish,

29 ὅπως μὴ καυχήσηται πᾶσα σάρξ*
so as not might boast all flesh*

ἐνώπιον τοῦ θεοῦ. 30 ἐξ αὐτοῦ δὲ ὑμεῖς
before - God. And of him ye

ἐστε ἐν Χριστῷ 'Ιησοῦ, ὃς ἐγενήθη
are in Christ Jesus, who became

σοφία ἡμῖν ἀπὸ θεοῦ, δικαιοσύνη τε
wisdom to us from God, ²righteousness ¹both

καὶ ἁγιασμὸς καὶ ἀπολύτρωσις, 31 ἵνα καθὼς
and sanctification and redemption, in order that as

γέγραπται· ὁ καυχώμενος ἐν κυρίῳ καυχάσθω.
it has been The [one] boasting ²in ³[the] ¹let him boast.
written: Lord

Chapter 2

Paul's Reliance upon the Spirit

AND when I came to you, brethren, I did not come with superiority of speech or of wisdom, proclaiming to you the ᵈtestimony of God.

2For I determined to know nothing among you except Jesus Christ, and Him crucified.

3And I was with you in weakness and in fear and in

---

2 Κἀγὼ ἐλθὼν πρὸς ὑμᾶς, ἀδελφοί,
And I coming to you, brothers,

ἦλθον οὐ καθ' ὑπεροχὴν λόγου ἢ σοφίας
came not accord- excellence of speech or of wisdom
ing to

καταγγέλλων ὑμῖν τὸ μαρτύριον τοῦ θεοῦ.
announcing to you the testimony - of God.

2 οὐ γὰρ ἔκρινά τι εἰδέναι ἐν ὑμῖν
For I decided not anything to know among you

εἰ μὴ 'Ιησοῦν Χριστὸν καὶ τοῦτον
except Jesus Christ and this one

ἐσταυρωμένον. 3 κἀγὼ ἐν ἀσθενείᾳ καὶ
having been crucified. And I in weakness and

---

and foolishness to Gentiles,

24but to those whom God has called, both Jews and Greeks, Christ the power of God and the wisdom of God. 25For the foolishness of God is wiser than man's wisdom, and the weakness of God is stronger than man's strength.

26Brothers, think of what you were when you were called. Not many of you were wise by human standards; not many were influential; not many were of noble birth. 27But God chose the foolish things of the world to shame the wise; God chose the weak things of the world to shame the strong. 28He chose the lowly things of this world and the despised things—and the things that are not—to nullify the things that are, 29so that no one may boast before him. 30It is because of him that you are in Christ Jesus, who has become for us wisdom from God—that is, our righteousness, holiness and redemption. 31Therefore, as it is written: "Let him who boasts boast in the Lord." ᵈ

Chapter 2

WHEN I came to you, brothers, I did not come with eloquence or superior wisdom as I proclaimed to you the testimony about God. ᵉ 2For I resolved to know nothing while I was with you except Jesus Christ and him crucified. 3I came to you in weakness and fear, and

---

ᵈSome ancient mss. read mystery

* That is, so that no flesh might boast. Cf. Mat. 24. 22.

ᵈ31 Jer. 9:24
ᵉ1 Some manuscripts as I proclaimed to you God's mystery

much trembling.

4And my message and my preaching were not in persuasive words of wisdom, but in demonstration of the Spirit and of power,

5that your faith should not rest on the wisdom of men, but on the power of God.

6Yet we do speak wisdom among those who are mature; a wisdom, however, not of this age, nor of the rulers of this age, who are passing away;

7but we speak God's wisdom in a mystery, the hidden *wisdom,* which God predestined before the ages to our glory;

8*the wisdom* which none of the rulers of this age has understood; for if they had understood it, they would not have crucified the Lord of glory;

9but just as it is written, "THINGS WHICH EYE HAS NOT SEEN AND EAR HAS NOT HEARD, AND *which* HAVE NOT ENTERED THE HEART OF MAN, ALL THAT GOD HAS PREPARED FOR THOSE WHO LOVE HIM."

10For to us God revealed *them* through the Spirit; for the Spirit searches all things, even the depths of God.

11For who among men knows the *thoughts* of a man except the spirit of the man, which is in him? Even so the *thoughts* of God no one knows except the Spirit of God.

12Now we have received, not the spirit of the world, but the Spirit who is from God, that we might know the things freely given to us by God,

13which things we also speak, not in words taught

ἐν φόβῳ καὶ ἐν τρόμῳ πολλῷ ἐγενόμην
in fear and in trembling much was

πρὸς ὑμᾶς, 4 καὶ ὁ λόγος μου καὶ τὸ
with you, and the speech of me and the

κήρυγμά μου οὐκ ἐν πειθοῖς σοφίας
proclamation of me not in ¹persuasive ²of wisdom

λόγοις, ἀλλ' ἐν ἀποδείξει πνεύματος καὶ
¹words, but in demonstration of spirit and

δυνάμεως, 5 ἵνα ἡ πίστις ὑμῶν μὴ ᾖ
of power, in order that the faith of you may not be

ἐν σοφίᾳ ἀνθρώπων ἀλλ' ἐν δυνάμει
in [the] wisdom of men but in [the] power

θεοῦ.
of God.

6 Σοφίαν δὲ λαλοῦμεν ἐν τοῖς τελείοις,
But ²wisdom ¹we speak among the perfect ones,

σοφίαν δὲ οὐ τοῦ αἰῶνος τούτου οὐδὲ
yet wisdom not of this age neither

τῶν ἀρχόντων τοῦ αἰῶνος τούτου τῶν
of the leaders of this age of the [ones]

καταργουμένων· 7 ἀλλὰ λαλοῦμεν θεοῦ
being brought to naught; but we speak ²of God

σοφίαν ἐν μυστηρίῳ, τὴν ἀποκεκρυμμένην,
¹a wisdom in mystery, - having been hidden,

ἣν προώρισεν ὁ θεὸς πρὸ τῶν αἰώνων
which ¹foreordained - ¹God before the ages

εἰς δόξαν ἡμῶν· 8 ἣν οὐδεὶς τῶν ἀρχόντων
for glory of us; which not one of the leaders

τοῦ αἰῶνος τούτου ἔγνωκεν· εἰ γὰρ
of this age has known; for if

ἔγνωσαν, οὐκ ἂν τὸν κύριον τῆς δόξης
they knew, not - the Lord - of glory

ἐσταύρωσαν· 9 ἀλλὰ καθὼς γέγραπται· ἃ
they would have but as it has been written: Things
crucified;* which

ὀφθαλμὸς οὐκ εἶδεν καὶ οὓς οὐκ ἤκουσεν
eye saw not and ear heard not

καὶ ἐπὶ καρδίαν ἀνθρώπου οὐκ ἀνέβη,
and on heart of man came not up,

ὅσα ἡτοίμασεν ὁ θεὸς τοῖς ἀγαπῶσιν
how many ¹prepared - ¹God for the [ones] loving

αὐτόν. 10 ἡμῖν γὰρ ἀπεκάλυψεν ὁ θεὸς
him. ¹For ⁴to us ²revealed - ³God

διὰ τοῦ πνεύματος· τὸ γὰρ πνεῦμα πάντα
through the Spirit; for the Spirit all things

ἐρευνᾷ, καὶ τὰ βάθη τοῦ θεοῦ. 11 τίς
searches, even the deep things - of God. ¹who

γὰρ οἶδεν ἀνθρώπων τὰ τοῦ ἀνθρώπου
¹For ⁴knows ⁵of men the things - of a man

εἰ μὴ τὸ πνεῦμα τοῦ ἀνθρώπου τὸ
except the spirit - of a man -

ἐν αὐτῷ; οὕτως καὶ τὰ τοῦ θεοῦ οὐδεὶς
in him? so also the things - of God no one

ἔγνωκεν εἰ μὴ τὸ πνεῦμα τοῦ θεοῦ.
has known except the Spirit - of God.

12 ἡμεῖς δὲ οὐ τὸ πνεῦμα τοῦ κόσμου
And we not the spirit of the world

ἐλάβομεν ἀλλὰ τὸ πνεῦμα τὸ ἐκ τοῦ θεοῦ,
received but the Spirit - from - God,

ἵνα εἰδῶμεν τὰ ὑπὸ τοῦ θεοῦ
in order we may the things by - God
that know

χαρισθέντα ἡμῖν· 13 ἃ καὶ λαλοῦμεν οὐκ
freely given to us; which things also we speak not

---

with much trembling. 4My message and my preaching were not with wise and persuasive words, but with a demonstration of the Spirit's power, 5so that your faith might not rest on men's wisdom, but on God's power.

Wisdom From the Spirit

6We do, however, speak a message of wisdom among the mature, but not the wisdom of this age or of the rulers of this age, who are coming to nothing. 7No, we speak of God's secret wisdom, a wisdom that has been hidden and that God destined for our glory before time began. 8None of the rulers of this age understood it, for if they had, they would not have crucified the Lord of glory. 9However, as it is written:

"No eye has seen, no ear has heard, no mind has conceived what God has prepared for those who love him"ᶠ—

10but God has revealed it to us by his Spirit.

The Spirit searches all things, even the deep things of God. 11For who among men knows the thoughts of a man except the man's spirit within him? In the same way no one knows the thoughts of God except the Spirit of God. 12We have not received the spirit of the world but the Spirit who is from God, that we may understand what God has freely given us. 13This is what we speak, not in words taught

---

ᵉ Some ancient mss. use *But*   * This rendering is demanded by the preceding ἄν.   ᶠ9 Isaiah 64:4

by human wisdom, but in those taught by the Spirit, combining spiritual *thoughts* with spiritual *words.*

14But a natural man does not accept the things of the Spirit of God; for they are foolishness to him, and he cannot understand them, because they are spiritually appraised.

15But he who is spiritual appraises all things, yet he himself is appraised by no man.

16For WHO HAS KNOWN THE MIND OF THE LORD, THAT HE SHOULD INSTRUCT HIM? But we have the mind of Christ.

ἐν   διδακτοῖς   ἀνθρωπίνης   σοφίας   λόγοις,
in   ¹taught   ²of human   ⁴wisdom   ¹words,

ἀλλ' ἐν   διδακτοῖς   πνεύματος,   πνευματικοῖς
but   in [words] taught   of [the] Spirit,   ⁸with spiritual things

πνευματικὰ   συγκρίνοντες.   14 ψυχικὸς   δὲ
⁵spiritual things   ¹comparing.   But a natural

ἄνθρωπος   οὐ   δέχεται   τὰ   τοῦ   πνεύματος
man   receives not   the things of the   Spirit

τοῦ   θεοῦ·   μωρία   γὰρ   αὐτῷ   ἐστιν,   καὶ
-    of God;   for folly   to him   they are,   and

οὐ   δύναται   γνῶναι,   ὅτι   πνευματικῶς
he cannot   to know,   because   ⁸spiritually

ἀνακρίνεται.   15 ὁ   δὲ   πνευματικὸς   ἀνακρίνει
¹they are ³discerned.   But the   spiritual man   ²discerns

μὲν   πάντα,   αὐτὸς   δὲ   ὑπ'   οὐδενὸς
¹on one   all things,   ³he   ¹on the   ⁴by   ⁵no one
hand   other

ἀνακρίνεται.   16 τίς   γὰρ   ἔγνω   νοῦν
⁸is discerned.   For who   knew   [the] mind

κυρίου,   ὃς   συμβιβάσει   αὐτόν;   ἡμεῖς   δὲ
of [the]   who   will instruct   him?   But we
Lord,

νοῦν   Χριστοῦ   ἔχομεν.
[the] mind of Christ   have.

---

us by human wisdom but in words taught by the Spirit, expressing spiritual truths in spiritual words. ᵍ 14The man without the Spirit does not accept the things that come from the Spirit of God, for they are foolishness to him, and he cannot understand them, because they are spiritually discerned. 15The spiritual man makes judgments about all things, but he himself is not subject to any man's judgment:

16"For who has known the
mind of the Lord
that he may instruct
him?" ʰ

But we have the mind of Christ.

Chapter 3

Foundations for Living

AND I, brethren, could not speak to you as to spiritual men, but as to men of flesh, as to babes in Christ.

2I gave you milk to drink, not solid food; for you were not yet able *to receive it.* Indeed, even now you are not yet able,

3for you are still fleshly. For since there is jealousy and strife among you, are you not fleshly, and are you not walking like mere men?

4For when one says, "I am of Paul," and another, "I am of Apollos," are you not *mere* men?

5What then is Apollos? And what is Paul? Servants through whom you believed, even as the Lord gave *opportunity* to each one.

6I planted, Apollos watered, but God was causing the growth.

7So then neither the one who plants nor the one who waters is anything, but God who causes the growth.

8Now he who plants and he who waters are one; but each will receive his own reward according to his own labor.

9For we are God's fellow workers; you are God's field, God's building.

10According to the grace

---

3 Κἀγώ,   ἀδελφοί,   οὐκ   ἠδυνήθην   λαλῆσαι
And I,   brothers,   was not able   to speak

ὑμῖν   ὡς   πνευματικοῖς   ἀλλ'   ὡς   σαρκίνοις,
to you   as   to spiritual men   but   as   to fleshy,

ὡς   νηπίοις   ἐν   Χριστῷ.   2 γάλα   ὑμᾶς
as   to infants   in   Christ.   ⁸Milk   ²you

ἐπότισα,   οὐ   βρῶμα·   οὔπω   γὰρ   ἐδύνασθε.
¹I gave   not   food;   for ye were not then able.
⁴to drink,

ἀλλ'   οὐδὲ   [ἔτι]   νῦν   δύνασθε,   3 ἔτι   γὰρ
But   neither   yet   now   are ye able,   for still

σαρκικοί   ἐστε.   ὅπου   γὰρ   ἐν   ὑμῖν   ζῆλος
fleshly   ye are.   For whereas   among   you   [there is]
jealousy

καὶ   ἔρις,   οὐχὶ   σαρκικοί   ἐστε   καὶ   κατὰ
and   strife,   ²not   ³fleshly   ¹are ye   ⁴and   ⁵according to

ἄνθρωπον   περιπατεῖτε;   4 ὅταν   γὰρ   λέγῃ
⁷man   ⁶walk?   For whenever   says

τις,   ἐγὼ   μέν   εἰμι   Παύλου,   ἕτερος   δέ·
anyone,   I   -   am   of Paul,   another:

ἐγὼ   Ἀπολλῶ,   οὐκ   ἄνθρωποί   ἐστε;   5 Τί
I   of Apollos,   ²not   ³men   ¹are ye?   What

οὖν   ἐστιν   Ἀπολλῶς;   τί   δέ   ἐστιν   Παῦλος;
there-   is   Apollos?   and what   is   Paul?
fore

διάκονοι   δι'   ὧν   ἐπιστεύσατε,   καὶ   ἑκάστῳ
Ministers through whom   ye believed,   even   ²to each one

ὡς   ὁ   κύριος   ἔδωκεν.   6 ἐγὼ   ἐφύτευσα,
¹as   the   Lord   gave.   I   planted,

Ἀπολλῶς   ἐπότισεν,   ἀλλὰ   ὁ   θεὸς   ηὔξανεν·
Apollos   watered,   but   -   God   made to
grow;

7 ὥστε   οὔτε   ὁ   φυτεύων   ἐστίν   τι   οὔτε
so as   neither   the [one] planting   is   anything   nor

ὁ   ποτίζων,   ἀλλ'   ὁ   αὐξάνων   θεός.   8 ὁ
the   watering,   but   ²the   ³making to   ¹God.   ²The
[one]   [one]   grow   [one]

φυτεύων   δὲ   καὶ   ὁ   ποτίζων   ἕν   εἰσιν,
³planting   ¹so   and the [one] watering   one*   are,

ἕκαστος   δὲ   τὸν   ἴδιον   μισθὸν   λήμψεται
and each one   the(his)   own   reward   will receive

Chapter 3

On Divisions in the Church

BROTHERS, I could not address you as spiritual but as worldly— mere infants in Christ. 2I gave you milk, not solid food, for you were not yet ready for it. Indeed, you are still not ready. 3You are still worldly. For since there is jealousy and quarreling among you, are you not worldly? Are you not acting like mere men? 4For when one says, "I follow Paul," and another, "I follow Apollos," are you not mere men?

5What, after all, is Apollos? And what is Paul? Only servants, through whom you came to believe—as the Lord has assigned to each his task. 6I planted the seed, Apollos watered it, but God made it grow. 7So neither he who plants nor he who waters is anything, but only God, who makes things grow. 8The man who plants and the man who waters have one purpose, and each will be rewarded according to his own labor. 9For we are God's fellow workers; you are God's field, God's building.

10By the grace God has

---

* Notice the neuter gender, though " thing " cannot very well be expressed; *cf.* John 10. 30.

ᵍ13 Or *Spirit, interpreting spiritual truths to spiritual men*
ʰ16 Isaiah 40:13

of God which was given to me, as a wise master builder I laid a foundation, and another is building upon it. But let each man be careful how he builds upon it.

11For no man can lay a foundation other than the one which is laid, which is Jesus Christ.

12Now if any man builds upon the foundation with gold, silver, precious stones, wood, hay, straw,

13each man's work will become evident; for the day will show it, because it is *to be* revealed with fire; and the fire itself will test the quality of each man's work.

14If any man's work which he has built upon it remains, he shall receive a reward.

15If any man's work is burned up, he shall suffer loss; but he himself shall be saved, yet so as through fire.

16Do you not know that you are a temple of God, and *that* the Spirit of God dwells in you?

17If any man destroys the temple of God, God will destroy him, for the temple of God is holy, and that is what you are.

18Let no man deceive himself. If any man among you thinks that he is wise in this age, let him become foolish that he may become wise.

19For the wisdom of this world is foolishness before God. For it is written, "*He is* THE ONE WHO CATCHES THE WISE IN THEIR CRAFTINESS'';

20and again, "THE LORD KNOWS THE REASONINGS of the wise, THAT THEY ARE USELESS.''

21So then let no one boast

κατὰ τὸν ἴδιον κόπον. 9 θεοῦ γὰρ ἐσμεν
accord- his own labour. For of God we are
ing to

συνεργοί· θεοῦ γεώργιον, θεοῦ οἰκοδομή
fellow-workers; ²of God ²a tillage, ³of God ⁴a building

ἐστε. 10 Κατὰ τὴν χάριν τοῦ θεοῦ τὴν
¹ye are. According to the grace - of God -

δοθεῖσάν μοι ὡς σοφὸς ἀρχιτέκτων
given to me as a wise master builder

θεμέλιον ἔθηκα, ἄλλος δὲ ἐποικοδομεῖ.
a foundation I laid, but another builds on [it].

ἕκαστος δὲ βλεπέτω πῶς ἐποικοδομεῖ.
But each one let him look how he builds on [it].

11 θεμέλιον γὰρ ἄλλον οὐδεὶς δύναται θεῖναι
For foundation other no one is able to lay

παρὰ τὸν κείμενον, ὅς ἐστιν Ἰησοῦς
beside the [one] being laid, who is Jesus

Χριστός. 12 εἰ δέ τις ἐποικοδομεῖ ἐπὶ
Christ. Now if anyone builds on on

τὸν θεμέλιον χρυσίον, ἀργύριον, λίθους
the foundation gold, silver, stones

τιμίους, ξύλα, χόρτον, καλάμην, 13 ἑκάστου
precious, woods, hay, stubble, of each one

τὸ ἔργον φανερὸν γενήσεται· ἡ γὰρ ἡμέρα
the work manifest will become; for the day

δηλώσει, ὅτι ἐν πυρὶ ἀποκαλύπτεται,
will declare because by fire it is revealed,
[it],

καὶ ἑκάστου τὸ ἔργον ὁποῖόν ἐστιν
and ²of each one ¹the ²work ³of what sort ⁴it is

τὸ πῦρ αὐτὸ δοκιμάσει. 14 εἴ τινος
⁴the ⁵fire ⁷it ⁶will prove. If of anyone

τὸ ἔργον μενεῖ ὃ ἐποικοδόμησεν, μισθὸν
the work remains which he built on, a reward

λήμψεται· 15 εἴ τινος τὸ ἔργον κατακαήσ-
he will receive; if of anyone the work will be con-

εται, ζημιωθήσεται, αὐτὸς δὲ σωθήσεται,
sumed, he will suffer loss, but he will be saved,

οὕτως δὲ ὡς διὰ πυρός. 16 Οὐκ οἴδατε
yet so as through fire. Know ye not

ὅτι ναὸς θεοῦ ἐστε καὶ τὸ πνεῦμα τοῦ
that a shrine of God ye are and the Spirit

θεοῦ ἐν ὑμῖν οἰκεῖ; 17 εἴ τις τὸν ναὸν
of God in you dwells? If anyone the shrine

τοῦ θεοῦ φθείρει, φθερεῖ τοῦτον ὁ θεός·
- of God defiles, ²will defile ³this man - ¹God;

ὁ γὰρ ναὸς τοῦ θεοῦ ἅγιός ἐστιν, οἵτινές
for the shrine - of God holy is, who(which)

ἐστε ὑμεῖς.
are ye.

18 Μηδεὶς ἑαυτὸν ἐξαπατάτω· εἴ τις
No one himself let deceive; if anyone

δοκεῖ σοφὸς εἶναι ἐν ὑμῖν ἐν τῷ αἰῶνι
thinks wise to be among you in - age

τούτῳ, μωρὸς γενέσθω, ἵνα γένηται
this, foolish let him in order he may
become, that become

σοφός. 19 ἡ γὰρ σοφία τοῦ κόσμοι
wise. For the wisdom - world

τούτου μωρία παρὰ τῷ θεῷ ἐστιν.
of this folly with - God is.

γέγραπται γάρ· ὁ δρασσόμενος τοὺς σοφοὺς
For it has been written: The [one] grasping the wise

ἐν τῇ πανουργίᾳ αὐτῶν· 20 καὶ πάλιν·
in the craftiness of them; and again :

κύριος γινώσκει τοὺς διαλογισμοὺς τῶν
[The] Lord knows the reasonings of the

σοφῶν, ὅτι εἰσὶν μάταιοι. 21 ὥστε μηδεὶς
wise, that they are vain. So as no one

---

given me, I laid a foundation as an expert builder, and someone else is building on it. But each one should be careful how he builds. 11For no one can lay any foundation other than the one already laid, which is Jesus Christ. 12If any man builds on this foundation using gold, silver, costly stones, wood, hay or straw, 13his work will be shown for what it is, because the Day will bring it to light. It will be revealed with fire, and the fire will test the quality of each man's work. 14If what he has built survives, he will receive his reward. 15If it is burned up, he will suffer loss; he himself will be saved, but only as one escaping through the flames.

16Don't you know that you yourselves are God's temple and that God's Spirit lives in you? 17If anyone destroys God's temple, God will destroy him; for God's temple is sacred, and you are that temple.

18Do not deceive yourselves. If any one of you thinks he is wise by the standards of this age, he should become a ''fool'' so that he may become wise. 19For the wisdom of this world is foolishness in God's sight. As it is written: ''He catches the wise in their craftiness''*i*; 20and again, ''The Lord knows that the thoughts of the wise are futile.''*j* 21So then, no more boasting

in men. For all things belong to you,
22whether Paul or Apollos or Cephas or the world or life or death or things present or things to come; all things belong to you,
23and you belong to Christ; and Christ belongs to God.

Chapter 4

Servants of Christ

LET a man regard us in this manner, as servants of Christ, and stewards of the mysteries of God.
2In this case, moreover, it is required of stewards that one be found trustworthy.
3But to me it is a very small thing that I should be examined by you, or by *any* human court; in fact, I do not even examine myself.
4For I am conscious of nothing against myself, yet I am not by this acquitted; but the one who examines me is the Lord.
5Therefore do not go on passing judgment before /the time, *but wait* until the Lord comes who will both bring to light the things hidden in the darkness and disclose the motives of *men's* hearts; and then each man's praise will come to him from God.
6Now these things, brethren, I have figuratively applied to myself and Apollos for your sakes, that in us you might learn not to exceed what is written, in order that no one of you might become arrogant in behalf of one against the other.
7For who regards you as superior? And what do you have that you did not receive? But if you did receive it, why do you boast as if you had not received it?
8You are already filled, you have already become rich, you have become kings without us; and *I* would indeed that you had become kings so that we also might reign with you.

κανχάσθω   ἐν   ἀνθρώποις·   πάντα   γὰρ   ὑμῶν
let boast   in   men;   for all things   of you

ἐστιν,   22 εἴτε   Παῦλος   εἴτε   'Απολλῶς
is(are),   whether   Paul   or   Apollos

εἴτε   Κηφᾶς,   εἴτε   κόσμος   εἴτε   ζωὴ   εἴτε
or   Cephas,   or   [the] world   or   life   or

θάνατος,   εἴτε   ἐνεστῶτα   εἴτε   μέλλοντα,
death,   or   things present   or   things coming,

πάντα   ὑμῶν,   23 ὑμεῖς   δὲ   Χριστοῦ,   Χριστὸς   δὲ
all things of you,   and ye   of Christ,   and Christ

θεοῦ.   4 Οὕτως   ἡμᾶς   λογιζέσθω   ἄνθρωπος   ὡς
of God.   So   ⁴us   ¹let ³reckon   ²a man   as

ὑπηρέτας   Χριστοῦ   καὶ   οἰκονόμους   μυστηρίων
attendants   of Christ   and   stewards   of mysteries

θεοῦ.   2 ὧδε   λοιπὸν   ζητεῖται   ἐν   τοῖς
of God.   Here   for the rest   is it sought   in   the

οἰκονόμοις   ἵνα   πιστός   τις   εὑρεθῇ.   3 ἐμοὶ
stewards   in order ²faithful ¹anyone   ²be found.   to me
                that

δὲ   εἰς   ἐλάχιστόν   ἐστιν   ἵνα   ὑφ'   ὑμῶν
And   for   a very little thing   it is   in order that   by   you

ἀνακριθῶ   ἢ   ὑπὸ   ἀνθρωπίνης   ἡμέρας·   ἀλλ'
I am judged   or   by   a human   day;*   but

οὐδὲ   ἐμαυτὸν   ἀνακρίνω·   4 οὐδὲν   γὰρ
not   myself   I judge;   for nothing

ἐμαυτῷ   σύνοιδα,   ἀλλ'   οὐκ   ἐν   τούτῳ
against myself I know,   but   not   by   this

δεδικαίωμαι·   ὁ   δὲ   ἀνακρίνων   με   κύριός
have I been   but the [one]   judging   me   [the] Lord
justified;

ἐστιν.   5 ὥστε   μὴ   πρὸ   καιροῦ   τι   κρίνετε,
is.   So as   not   before   time   anything   judge ye,

ἕως   ἂν   ἔλθῃ   ὁ   κύριος,   ὃς   καὶ   φωτίσει
until   comes the   Lord,   who   both   will shed
                        light on

τὰ   κρυπτὰ   τοῦ   σκότους   καὶ   φανερώσει
the hidden things of the   darkness   and   will manifest

τὰς   βουλὰς   τῶν   καρδιῶν·   καὶ   τότε   ὁ
the   counsels   of the   hearts;   and   then   the

ἔπαινος   γενήσεται   ἑκάστῳ   ἀπὸ   τοῦ   θεοῦ.
praise   will be   to each oneᶜ   from   -   God.

6 Ταῦτα   δέ,   ἀδελφοί,   μετεσχημάτισα   εἰς
Now these things,   brothers,   I adapted   to

ἐμαυτὸν   καὶ   'Απολλῶν   δι'   ὑμᾶς,   ἵνα
myself   and   Apollos   because   you,   in order
                of   that

ἐν   ἡμῖν   μάθητε   τὸ   μὴ   ὑπὲρ   ἃ
among   us   ye may learn   -   not [to think] above   what
                            things

γέγραπται,   ἵνα   μὴ   εἷς   ὑπὲρ   τοῦ   ἑνὸς
has(ve) been written,   lest   ³one on behalf of ⁴the   ¹one

φυσιοῦσθε   κατὰ   τοῦ   ἑτέρου.   7 τίς   γὰρ   σε
²ye are puffed up against   the   other.   For who   thee

διακρίνει;   τί   δὲ   ἔχεις   ὃ   οὐκ   ἔλαβες;
distinguishes?   and what   hast thou   which thou didst not receive?

εἰ   δὲ   καὶ   ἔλαβες,   τί   καυχᾶσαι   ὡς   μὴ
and if   indeed   thou didst   why   boastest thou   as   not
                receive,

λαβών;   8 ἤδη   κεκορεσμένοι   ἐστέ·   ἤδη
receiving?   Now   *having been* glutted   ye are;   now

ἐπλουτήσατε·   χωρὶς   ἡμῶν   ἐβασιλεύσατε·   καὶ
ye became rich;   without   us   ye reigned;·   and

ὄφελόν   γε   ἐβασιλεύσατε,   ἵνα
²an advantage   ³really   ¹[it is]   [that] ye reigned,   in order that

καὶ   ἡμεῖς   ὑμῖν   συμβασιλεύσωμεν.   9 δοκῶ
also   we   ²you   ¹might reign with.   I think

about men! All things are yours, 22whether Paul or Apollos or Cephasᵏ or the world or life or death or the present or the future—all are yours, 23and you are of Christ, and Christ is of God.

Chapter 4

Apostles of Christ

SO then, men ought to regard us as servants of Christ and as those entrusted with the secret things of God. 2Now it is required that those who have been given a trust must prove faithful. 3I care very little if I am judged by you or by any human court; indeed, I do not even judge myself. 4My conscience is clear, but that does not make me innocent. It is the Lord who judges me. 5Therefore judge nothing before the appointed time; wait till the Lord comes. He will bring to light what is hidden in darkness and will expose the motives of men's hearts. At that time each will receive his praise from God.
6Now, brothers, I have applied these things to myself and Apollos for your benefit, so that you may learn from us the meaning of the saying, "Do not go beyond what is written." Then you will not take pride in one man over against another. 7For who makes you different from anyone else? What do you have that you did not receive? And if you did receive it, why do you boast as though you did not?
8Already you have all you want! Already you have become rich! You have become kings—and that without us! How I wish that you really had become kings so that we might be kings with you! 9For it

/I.e., the appointed time of judgment

* ? of judgment.

9For, I think, God has exhibited us apostles last of all, as men condemned to death; because we have become a spectacle to the world, both to angels and to men.

10We are fools for Christ's sake, but you are prudent in Christ; we are weak, but you are strong; you are distinguished, but we are without honor.

11To this present hour we are both hungry and thirsty, and are poorly clothed, and are roughly treated, and are homeless;

12and we toil, working with our own hands; when we are reviled, we bless; when we are persecuted, we endure;

13when we are slandered, we try to conciliate; we have become as the scum of the world, the dregs of all things, even until now.

14I do not write these things to shame you, but to admonish you as my beloved children.

15For if you were to have countless tutors in Christ, yet you would not have many fathers; for in Christ Jesus I became your father through the gospel.

16I exhort you therefore, be imitators of me.

17For this reason I have sent to you Timothy, who is my beloved and faithful child in the Lord, and he will remind you of my ways which are in Christ, just as I teach everywhere in every church.

18Now some have become arrogant, as though I were not coming to you.

19But I will come to you soon, if the Lord wills, and I shall find out, not the words of those who are arrogant, but their power.

20For the kingdom of God

γάρ, ὁ θεὸς ἡμᾶς τοὺς ἀποστόλους
For, – God us the apostles

ἐσχάτους ἀπέδειξεν ὡς ἐπιθανατίους, ὅτι
last showed forth as doomed to death, because

θέατρον ἐγενήθημεν τῷ κόσμῳ καὶ ἀγγέλοις
a spectacle we became to the world both to angels

καὶ ἀνθρώποις. 10 ἡμεῖς μωροὶ διὰ
and to men. We [are] fools because of

Χριστόν, ὑμεῖς δὲ φρόνιμοι ἐν Χριστῷ·
Christ, but ye [are] prudent in Christ;

ἡμεῖς ἀσθενεῖς, ὑμεῖς δὲ ἰσχυροί· ὑμεῖς
we [are] weak, but ye [are] strong; ye [are]

ἔνδοξοι, ἡμεῖς δὲ ἄτιμοι. 11 ἄχρι τῆς
held in honour, but we [are] unhonoured. Until the

ἄρτι ὥρας καὶ πεινῶμεν καὶ διψῶμεν
present hour ²both ¹we ¹hunger and thirst

καὶ γυμνιτεύομεν καὶ κολαφιζόμεθα καὶ
and are naked and are buffeted and

ἀστατοῦμεν 12 καὶ κοπιῶμεν ἐργαζόμενοι
are unsettled and labour working

ταῖς ἰδίαις χερσίν· λοιδορούμενοι εὐλο-
with the(our) own hands; being reviled we

γοῦμεν, διωκόμενοι ἀνεχόμεθα, 13 δυσφημού-
bless, being persecuted we endure, being de-

μενοι παρακαλοῦμεν· ὡς περικαθάρματα τοῦ
famed we beseech; as refuse of the

κόσμου ἐγενήθημεν, πάντων περίψημα ἕως
world we became, ²of all things ¹offscouring until

ἄρτι.
now.

14 Οὐκ ἐντρέπων ὑμᾶς γράφω ταῦτα,
Not shaming you I write these things,

ἀλλ' ὡς τέκνα μου ἀγαπητὰ νουθετῶν.
but as children of me beloved admonishing.

15 ἐὰν γὰρ μυρίους παιδαγωγοὺς ἔχητε
For if ten thousand trainers ye have

ἐν Χριστῷ, ἀλλ' οὐ πολλοὺς πατέρας·
in Christ, yet not many fathers;

ἐν γὰρ Χριστῷ Ἰησοῦ διὰ τοῦ εὐαγγελίου
for in Christ Jesus through the gospel

ἐγὼ ὑμᾶς ἐγέννησα. 16 παρακαλῶ οὖν
I ²you ¹begat. I beseech therefore

ὑμᾶς, μιμηταί μου γίνεσθε. 17 Διὰ τοῦτο
you, imitators of me become ye. Because of this

αὐτὸ ἔπεμψα ὑμῖν Τιμόθεον, ὅς ἐστίν
very thing I sent to you Timothy, who is

μου τέκνον ἀγαπητὸν καὶ πιστὸν ἐν
of me a child beloved and faithful in

κυρίῳ, ὃς ὑμᾶς ἀναμνήσει τὰς ὁδούς
[the] Lord, who ²you ¹will remind [of] the ways

μου τὰς· ἐν Χριστῷ [Ἰησοῦ], καθὼς
of me – in Christ Jesus, as

πανταχοῦ ἐν πάσῃ ἐκκλησίᾳ διδάσκω.
everywhere in every church I teach.

18 ὡς μὴ ἐρχομένου δέ μου πρὸς ὑμᾶς
When not coming now meᵃ to you
= Now when I did not come

ἐφυσιώθησάν τινες· 19 ἐλεύσομαι δὲ ταχέως
¹were puffed up ²some; but I will come shortly

πρὸς ὑμᾶς, ἐὰν ὁ κύριος θελήσῃ, καὶ
to you, if the Lord wills, and

γνώσομαι οὐ τὸν λόγον τῶν πεφυσιωμένων
I will know not the speech of the having been
[ones] puffed up

ἀλλὰ τὴν δύναμιν· 20 οὐ γὰρ ἐν λόγῳ
but the power; for ⁴[is] ²not ³in ⁵speech

---

seems to me that God has put us apostles on display at the end of the procession, like men condemned to die in the arena. We have been made a spectacle to the whole universe, to angels as well as to men. 10We are fools for Christ, but you are so wise in Christ! We are weak, but you are strong! You are honored, we are dishonored! 11To this very hour we go hungry and thirsty, we are in rags, we are brutally treated, we are homeless. 12We work hard with our own hands. When we are cursed, we bless; when we are persecuted, we endure it; 13when we are slandered, we answer kindly. Up to this moment we have become the scum of the earth, the refuse of the world.

14I am not writing this to shame you, but to warn you, as my dear children. 15Even though you have ten thousand guardians in Christ, you do not have many fathers, for in Christ Jesus I became your father through the gospel. 16Therefore I urge you to imitate me. 17For this reason I am sending to you Timothy, my son whom I love, who is faithful in the Lord. He will remind you of my way of life in Christ Jesus, which agrees with what I teach everywhere in every church.

18Some of you have become arrogant, as if I were not coming to you. 19But I will come to you very soon, if the Lord is willing, and then I will find out not only how these arrogant people are talking, but what power they have. 20For the kingdom of God is not a matter

does not consist in words, but in power.
21What do you desire? Shall I come to you with a rod or with love and a spirit of gentleness?

Chapter 5

Immorality Rebuked

IT is actually reported that there is immorality among you, and immorality of such a kind as does not exist even among the Gentiles, that someone has his father's wife.
2And you have become arrogant, and have not mourned instead, in order that the one who had done this deed might be removed from your midst.
3For I, on my part, though absent in body but present in spirit, have already judged him who has so committed this, as though I were present.
4In the name of our Lord Jesus, when you are assembled, and I with you in spirit, with the power of our Lord Jesus,
5I have decided to deliver such a one to Satan for the destruction of his flesh, that his spirit may be saved in the day of the Lord *g*Jesus.
6Your boasting is not good. Do you not know that a little leaven leavens the whole lump *of dough*?
7Clean out the old leaven, that you may be a new lump, just as you are *in fact* unleavened. For Christ our Passover also has been sacrificed.
8Let us therefore celebrate the feast, not with old leaven, nor with the leaven of malice and wickedness, but with the unleavened bread of sincerity and truth.
9I wrote you in my letter not to associate with immoral people;
10I *did* not at all *mean* with the immoral people of this world, or with the covetous and swindlers, or

g Some ancient mss. do not contain *Jesus*

ἡ   βασιλεία   τοῦ   θεοῦ,   ἀλλ'   ἐν   δυνάμει.
¹the   ²kingdom   –   ³of God,   but   in   power.

21 τί   θέλετε;   ἐν   ῥάβδῳ   ἔλθω   πρὸς   ὑμᾶς,
What   will ye?   with   a rod   I come   to   you,

ἢ   ἐν   ἀγάπῃ   πνεύματί   τε   πραΰτητος;
or   in   love   and a spirit   of meekness?

5 Ὅλως   ἀκούεται   ἐν   ὑμῖν   πορνεία,
Actually   is heard   among   you   fornication,

καὶ   τοιαύτη   πορνεία   ἥτις   οὐδὲ   ἐν   τοῖς
and   such   fornication   which [is]   not   among   the

ἔθνεσιν,   ὥστε   γυναῖκά   τινα   τοῦ   πατρὸς
nations,   so as   ³wife   ¹one   ⁴of the   ⁵father

ἔχειν.   2 καὶ   ὑμεῖς   πεφυσιωμένοι   ἐστέ,
²to have.*b*   And   ye   having been puffed up   are,

καὶ   οὐχὶ   μᾶλλον   ἐπενθήσατε,   ἵνα   ἀρθῇ
and   not   rather   mourned,   *in order*   ²might be
                                        that   removed

ἐκ   μέσου   ὑμῶν   ὁ   τὸ   ἔργον   τοῦτο   πράξας,
⁴from   ⁵midst   ⁶of you   ¹the   ⁵this   ⁴deed   ³having done?
                        [one]

3 ἐγὼ   μὲν   γάρ,   ἀπὼν   τῷ   σώματι,
For I indeed,   being absent in the   body,

παρὼν   δὲ   τῷ   πνεύματι,   ἤδη   κέκρικα
but being present   in the   spirit,   already   have judged

ὡς   παρὼν   τὸν   οὕτως   τοῦτο   κατεργα-
as   being present   ¹the [one]   ²thus   ⁴this thing   ³having

σάμενον   4 ἐν   τῷ   ὀνόματι   τοῦ   κυρίου
wrought   in   the   name   of the   Lord

Ἰησοῦ   συναχθέντων   ὑμῶν   καὶ   τοῦ   ἐμοῦ
Jesus   being assembled   you   and   –   my
       =when you are assembled ...

πνεύματος   σὺν   τῇ   δυνάμει   τοῦ   κυρίου
spirit*a*   with   the   power   of the   Lord

ἡμῶν   Ἰησοῦ   5 παραδοῦναι   τὸν   τοιοῦτον
of us   Jesus   to deliver   such a person

τῷ   σατανᾷ   εἰς   ὄλεθρον   τῆς   σαρκός,
–   to Satan   for   destruction   of the   flesh,

ἵνα   τὸ   πνεῦμα   σωθῇ   ἐν   τῇ   ἡμέρᾳ   τοῦ
in order the   spirit   may be   in   the   day   of the
that   saved

κυρίου.   6 Οὐ   καλὸν   τὸ   καύχημα   ὑμῶν.
Lord.   Not   good [is]   the   boast   of you.

οὐκ   οἴδατε   ὅτι   μικρὰ   ζύμη   ὅλον   τὸ
Know ye not   that   a little   leaven   all   the

φύραμα   ζυμοῖ;   7 ἐκκαθάρατε   τὴν   παλαιὰν
lump   leavens?   Purge out   the   old

ζύμην,   ἵνα   ἦτε   νέον   φύραμα,   καθὼς
leaven,   in order   ye   a new   lump,   as
         that   may be

ἐστε   ἄζυμοι.   καὶ   γὰρ   τὸ   πάσχα   ἡμῶν
ye are   unleavened.   For indeed   the   passover   of us

ἐτύθη   Χριστός.   8 ὥστε   ἑορτάζωμεν   μὴ
was   Christ.   So as   let us keep feast   not
sacrificed[,]

ἐν   ζύμῃ   παλαιᾷ   μηδὲ   ἐν   ζύμῃ   κακίας
with   leaven   old   nor   with   leaven   of malice

καὶ   πονηρίας,   ἀλλ'   ἐν   ἀζύμοις   εἰλικρινείας
and   of evil,   but   with   unleavened   of sincerity
                              [loaves]

καὶ   ἀληθείας.   9 Ἔγραψα   ὑμῖν   ἐν   τῇ
and   of truth.   I wrote   to you   in   the

ἐπιστολῇ   μὴ   συναναμίγνυσθαι   πόρνοις,
epistle   not   to associate   with
              intimately *with*   fornicators,

10 οὐ   πάντως   τοῖς   πόρνοις   τοῦ   κόσμου
not   altogether   with the fornicators   –   world

τούτου   ἢ   τοῖς   πλεονέκταις   καὶ   ἅρπαξιν
of this   or   with the   covetous   and   rapacious

of talk but of power.
21What do you prefer? Shall I come to you with a whip, or in love and with a gentle spirit?

Chapter 5

Expel the Immoral Brother!

IT is actually reported that there is sexual immorality among you, and of a kind that does not occur even among pagans: A man has his father's wife. 2And you are proud! Shouldn't you rather have been filled with grief and have put out of your fellowship the man who did this? 3Even though I am not physically present, I am with you in spirit. And I have already passed judgment on the one who did this, just as if I were present. 4When you are assembled in the name of our Lord Jesus and I am with you in spirit, and the power of our Lord Jesus is present, 5hand this man over to Satan, so that the sinful nature*i* may be destroyed and his spirit saved on the day of the Lord.
6Your boasting is not good. Don't you know that a little yeast works through the whole batch of dough? 7Get rid of the old yeast that you may be a new batch without yeast—as you really are. For Christ, our Passover lamb, has been sacrificed. 8Therefore let us keep the Festival, not with the old yeast, the yeast of malice and wickedness, but with bread without yeast, the bread of sincerity and truth.
9I have written you in my letter not to associate with sexually immoral people—10not at all meaning the people of this world who are immoral or the greedy and swindlers, or idolaters.

i 5 Or *that his body*; or *that the flesh*

with idolaters; for then you would have to go out of the world. 11But actually, I wrote to you not to associate with any so-called brother if he should be an immoral person, or covetous, or an idolater, or a reviler, or a drunkard, or a swindler—not even to eat with such a one. 12For what have I to do with judging outsiders? Do you not judge those who are within *the church?* 13But those who are outside, God judges. REMOVE THE WICKED MAN FROM AMONG YOURSELVES.

Greek	Gloss
ἢ εἰδωλολάτραις, ἐπεὶ ὠφείλετε ἄρα ἐκ	or idolaters, since ye ought then out of
τοῦ κόσμου ἐξελθεῖν. 11 νῦν δὲ ἔγραψα	the world to go out. But now I wrote
ὑμῖν μὴ συναναμίγνυσθαι ἐάν τις ἀδελφὸς	to you not to associate intimately with if anyone a brother
ὀνομαζόμενος ᾖ πόρνος ἢ πλεονέκτης ἢ	being named is a fornicator or a covetous man or
εἰδωλολάτρης ἢ λοίδορος ἢ μέθυσος ἢ	an idolater or a railer or a drunkard or
ἅρπαξ, τῷ τοιούτῳ μηδὲ συνεσθίειν. 12 τί	a rapacious man, with such a man not to eat with. what
γάρ μοι τοὺς ἔξω κρίνειν; οὐχὶ τοὺς	For [is it] to me 2the ones 1without 1to judge? 2Not 4the ones
ἔσω ὑμεῖς κρίνετε; 13 τοὺς δὲ ἔξω	3within 1ye 3judge? But the ones without
ὁ θεὸς κρινεῖ. ἐξάρατε τὸν πονηρὸν ἐξ	- God will judge. Remove the evil man out of
ὑμῶν αὐτῶν.	yourselves.

In that case you would have to leave this world. 11But now I am writing you that you must not associate with anyone who calls himself a brother but is sexually immoral or greedy, an idolater or a slanderer, a drunkard or a swindler. With such a man do not even eat. 12What business is it of mine to judge those outside the church? Are you not to judge those inside? 13God will judge those outside. "Expel the wicked man from among you." m

Chapter 6

Lawsuits Discouraged

DOES any one of you, when he has a case against his neighbor, dare to go to law before the unrighteous, and not before the saints? 2Or do you not know that the saints will judge the world? And if the world is judged by you, are you not competent *to constitute* the smallest law courts? 3Do you not know that we shall judge angels? How much more, matters of this life? 4If then you have law courts dealing with matters of this life, do you appoint them as judges who are of no account in the church? 5I say *this* to your shame. *Is it* so, *that* there is not among you one wise man who will be able to decide between his brethren? 6but brother goes to law with brother, and that before unbelievers? 7Actually, then, it is already a defeat for you, that you have lawsuits with one another. Why not rather be wronged? Why not rather be defrauded? 8On the contrary, you yourselves wrong and defraud, and that *your* brethren. 9Or do you not know that the unrighteous shall not inherit the kingdom of God? Do not be deceived;

Greek	Gloss
6 Τολμᾷ τις ὑμῶν πρᾶγμα ἔχων πρὸς	Dares anyone of you 2a matter 1having against
τὸν ἕτερον κρίνεσθαι ἐπὶ τῶν ἀδίκων,	the(an) other to be judged before the unjust,
καὶ οὐχὶ ἐπὶ τῶν ἁγίων; 2 ἢ οὐκ οἴδατε	and not before the saints? or know ye not
ὅτι οἱ ἅγιοι τὸν κόσμον κρινοῦσιν; καὶ	that the saints the world will judge? and
εἰ ἐν ὑμῖν κρίνεται ὁ κόσμος, ἀνάξιοί	if 4by 5you 3is judged 1the 2world, 1unworthy
ἐστε κριτηρίων ἐλαχίστων; 3 οὐκ οἴδατε	2are ye 4judgments? 3of very little? Know ye not
ὅτι ἀγγέλους κρινοῦμεν, μήτι γε βιωτικά;	that angels we will judge, not to speak of things of this life?
4 βιωτικὰ μὲν οὖν κριτήρια ἐὰν ἔχητε,	4Of this life 1indeed 2therefore 3judgments 1if 2ye have,
τοὺς ἐξουθενημένους ἐν τῇ ἐκκλησίᾳ,	the ones being despised in the church,
τούτους καθίζετε; 5 πρὸς ἐντροπὴν ὑμῖν	these sit ye? For shame to you
λέγω. οὕτως οὐκ ἔνι ἐν ὑμῖν οὐδεὶς	I say. Thus there is no room among you [for] no one
σοφός, ὃς δυνήσεται διακρῖναι ἀνὰ μέσον	wise man, who will be able to discern in your midst
τοῦ ἀδελφοῦ αὐτοῦ; 6 ἀλλὰ ἀδελφὸς μετὰ	the brother of him? But brother with
ἀδελφοῦ κρίνεται, καὶ τοῦτο ἐπὶ ἀπίστων;	brother is judged, and this before unbelievers?
7 ἤδη μὲν οὖν ὅλως ἥττημα ὑμῖν ἐστιν	Now indeed there-fore altogether 1a failure 4with 1there is you
ὅτι κρίματα ἔχετε μεθ' ἑαυτῶν. διὰ τί	1that 2lawsuits 3ye have with yourselves. Why
οὐχὶ μᾶλλον ἀδικεῖσθε; διὰ τί οὐχὶ	not rather be wronged? Why not
μᾶλλον ἀποστερεῖσθε; 8 ἀλλὰ ὑμεῖς ἀδικεῖτε	rather be deprived? But ye do wrong
καὶ ἀποστερεῖτε, καὶ τοῦτο ἀδελφούς.	and deprive, and this brothers.
9 ἢ οὐκ οἴδατε ὅτι ἄδικοι θεοῦ βασιλείαν	Or know ye not that unrighteous 2of God 3[the] men 1kingdom
οὐ κληρονομήσουσιν; μὴ πλανᾶσθε· οὔτε	1will not inherit? Be not led astray; not

Chapter 6

Lawsuits Among Believers

IF any of you has a dispute with another, dare he take it before the ungodly for judgment instead of before the saints? 2Do you not know that the saints will judge the world? And if you are to judge the world, are you not competent to judge trivial cases? 3Do you not know that we will judge angels? How much more the things of this life! 4Therefore, if you have disputes about such matters, appoint as judges even men of little account in the church!n 5I say this to shame you. Is it possible that there is nobody among you wise enough to judge a dispute between believers? 6But instead, one brother goes to law against another—and this in front of unbelievers! 7The very fact that you have lawsuits among you means you have been completely defeated already. Why not rather be wronged? Why not rather be cheated? 8Instead, you yourselves cheat and do wrong, and you do this to your brothers. 9Do you not know that the wicked will not inherit the kingdom of God? Do

m13 Deut. 17:7; 19:19; 21:21; 22:21,24; 24:7
n4 Or matters, do you appoint as judges men of little account in the church?

neither fornicators, nor idolaters, nor adulterers, nor [h]effeminate, nor homosexuals,
10nor thieves, nor *the* covetous, nor drunkards, nor revilers, nor swindlers, shall inherit the kingdom of God.
11And such were some of you; but you were washed, but you were sanctified, but you were justified in the name of the Lord Jesus Christ, and in the Spirit of our God.

The Body Is the Lord's

12All things are lawful for me, but not all things are profitable. All things are lawful for me, but I will not be mastered by anything.
13Food is for the stomach, and the stomach is for food; but God will do away with both of them. Yet the body is not for immorality, but for the Lord; and the Lord is for the body.
14Now God has not only raised the Lord, but will also raise us up through His power.
15Do you not know that your bodies are members of Christ? Shall I then take away the members of Christ and make them members of a harlot? May it never be!
16Or do you not know that the one who joins himself to a harlot is one body *with her*? For He says, "THE TWO WILL BECOME ONE FLESH."
17But the one who joins himself to the Lord is one spirit *with Him.*
18Flee immorality. Every *other* sin that a man commits is outside the body, but the immoral man sins against his own body.
19Or do you not know that your body is a temple of the Holy Spirit who is in you,

πόρνοι οὔτε εἰδωλολάτραι οὔτε μοιχοὶ
fornicators nor idolaters nor adulterers

οὔτε μαλακοὶ οὔτε ἀρσενοκοῖται 10 οὔτε
nor voluptuous nor sodomites nor
persons

κλέπται οὔτε πλεονέκται, οὐ μέθυσοι,
thieves nor covetous persons, not drunkards,

οὐ λοίδοροι, οὐχ ἅρπαγες βασιλείαν θεοῦ
not revilers, not rapacious ²[the] kingdom ²of
persons God

κληρονομήσουσιν. 11 καὶ ταῦτά τινες ἦτε·
¹will inherit. And these ²some ¹ye were;
things [of you]

ἀλλὰ ἀπελούσασθε, ἀλλὰ ἡγιάσθητε, ἀλλὰ
but ye were washed, but ye were sanctified, but

ἐδικαιώθητε ἐν τῷ ὀνόματι τοῦ κυρίου
ye were justified in the name of the Lord

Ἰησοῦ Χριστοῦ καὶ ἐν τῷ πνεύματι
Jesus Christ and by the Spirit

τοῦ θεοῦ ἡμῶν.
of the God of us.

12 Πάντα μοι ἔξεστιν, ἀλλ' οὐ πάντα
All things to me [are] lawful, but not all things

συμφέρει. πάντα μοι ἔξεστιν, ἀλλ' οὐκ
expedient. All things to me [are] lawful, but not

ἐγὼ ἐξουσιασθήσομαι ὑπό τινος. 13 τὰ
I will be ruled by anyone. -

βρώματα τῇ κοιλίᾳ, καὶ ἡ κοιλία τοῖς
Foods for the belly, and the belly

βρώμασιν· ὁ δὲ θεὸς καὶ ταύτην καὶ
for foods; - but God both this and

ταῦτα καταργήσει. τὸ δὲ σῶμα οὐ τῇ
these will destroy. But the body [is] not

πορνείᾳ ἀλλὰ τῷ κυρίῳ, καὶ ὁ κύριος
for fornication but for the Lord, and the Lord

τῷ σώματι· 14 ὁ δὲ θεὸς καὶ τὸν κύριον
for the body; - and God both the Lord

ἤγειρεν καὶ ἡμᾶς ἐξεγερεῖ διὰ τῆς
raised and us will raise up through the

δυνάμεως αὐτοῦ. 15 οὐκ οἴδατε ὅτι τὰ
power of him. Know ye not that the

σώματα ὑμῶν μέλη Χριστοῦ ἐστιν; ἄρας
bodies of you members of Christ (is)are? Taking

οὖν τὰ μέλη τοῦ Χριστοῦ ποιήσω πόρνης
there- the members - of Christ shall I make ²of a
fore [them] harlot

μέλη; μὴ γένοιτο. 16 ἢ οὐκ οἴδατε ὅτι
¹members? May it not be. Or know ye not that

ὁ κολλώμενος τῇ πόρνῃ ἓν σῶμά ἐστιν;
the *being* joined - to a harlot one body is?
[one]

ἔσονται γάρ, φησίν, οἱ δύο εἰς σάρκα
For ⁴will be, ³he says, ¹the ²two ⁵into ⁶flesh

μίαν. 17 ὁ δὲ κολλώμενος τῷ κυρίῳ
⁶one. But the [one] *being* joined to the Lord

ἓν πνεῦμά ἐστιν. 18 φεύγετε τὴν πορνείαν.
one spirit is. Flee ye - fornication.

πᾶν ἁμάρτημα ὃ ἐὰν ποιήσῃ ἄνθρωπος
Every sin whichever ¹may do ¹a man

ἐκτὸς τοῦ σώματός ἐστιν· ὁ δὲ πορνεύων
outside the body is; but the committing
[one] fornication

εἰς τὸ ἴδιον σῶμα ἁμαρτάνει. 19
against the(his) own body sins. Or

οὐκ οἴδατε ὅτι τὸ σῶμα ὑμῶν ναὸς
know ye not that the body of you ²a shrine

τοῦ ἐν ὑμῖν ἁγίου πνεύματός ἐστιν,
³of the ⁶in ⁷you ⁴Holy ⁵Spirit ¹is,

not be deceived: Neither the sexually immoral nor idolaters nor adulterers nor male prostitutes nor homosexual offenders 10nor thieves nor the greedy nor drunkards nor slanderers nor swindlers will inherit the kingdom of God. 11And that is what some of you were. But you were washed, you were sanctified, you were justified in the name of the Lord Jesus Christ and by the Spirit of our God.

Sexual Immorality

12"Everything is permissible for me"—but not everything is beneficial. "Everything is permissible for me"—but I will not be mastered by anything. 13"Food for the stomach and the stomach for food"—but God will destroy them both. The body is not meant for sexual immorality, but for the Lord, and the Lord for the body. 14By his power God raised the Lord from the dead, and he will raise us also. 15Do you not know that your bodies are members of Christ himself? Shall I then take the members of Christ and unite them with a prostitute? Never! 16Do you not know that he who unites himself with a prostitute is one with her in body? For it is said, "The two will become one flesh."[o] 17But he who unites himself with the Lord is one with him in spirit.

18Flee from sexual immorality. All other sins a man commits are outside his body, but he who sins sexually sins against his own body. 19Do you not know that your body is a temple of the Holy Spirit, who is in

[h]I.e., effeminate by perversion

[o]16 Gen. 2:24

whom you have from God, and that you are not your own?

²⁰For you have been bought with a price: therefore glorify God in your body.

Chapter 7

Advice on Marriage

NOW concerning the things about which you wrote, it is good for a man not to touch a woman. ²But because of immoralities, let each man have his own wife, and let each woman have her own husband. ³Let the husband fulfill his duty to his wife, and likewise also the wife to her husband. ⁴The wife does not have authority over her own body, but the husband *does*; and likewise also the husband does not have authority over his own body, but the wife *does*. ⁵Stop depriving one another, except by agreement for a time that you may devote yourselves to prayer, and come together again lest Satan tempt you because of your lack of self-control. ⁶But this I say by way of concession, not of command. ⁷Yet I wish that all men were even as I myself am. However, each man has his own gift from God, one in this manner, and another in that. ⁸But I say to the unmarried and to widows that it is good for them if they remain even as I. ⁹But if they do not have self-control, let them marry; for it is better to marry than to burn. ¹⁰But to the married I give instructions, not I, but the Lord, that the wife should not leave her husband ¹¹(but if she does leave,

οὗ ἔχετε ἀπὸ θεοῦ, καὶ οὐκ ἐστὲ ἑαυτῶν;
which ye from God, and ye are not of
have yourselves?

20 ἠγοράσθητε γὰρ τιμῆς· δοξάσατε δὴ
For ye were bought of(with) a price; glorify ye then

τὸν θεὸν ἐν τῷ σώματι ὑμῶν.
- God in the body of you.

7 Περὶ δὲ ὧν ἐγράψατε, καλὸν ἀνθρώπῳ
Now about things ye wrote, [it is] good for a man
of which

γυναικὸς μὴ ἅπτεσθαι· **2** διὰ δὲ τὰς
ᵃa woman* ¹not ²to touch; but because of the

πορνείας ἕκαστος τὴν ἑαυτοῦ γυναῖκα
fornications each man ᵃthe ⁴of himself ²wife

ἐχέτω, καὶ ἑκάστη τὸν ἴδιον ἄνδρα
¹let him have, and each woman the(her) own husband

ἐχέτω. **3** τῇ γυναικὶ ὁ ἀνὴρ τὴν ὀφειλὴν
let her have. To the wife ²the ³husband ⁴the ⁵debt

ἀποδιδότω, ὁμοίως δὲ καὶ ἡ γυνὴ τῷ
¹let *him* pay, and likewise also the wife to the

ἀνδρί. **4** ἡ γυνὴ τοῦ ἰδίου σώματος
husband. The wife of the(her) own body

οὐκ ἐξουσιάζει ἀλλὰ ὁ ἀνήρ· ὁμοίως
has not authority but the husband; ³likewise

δὲ καὶ ὁ ἀνὴρ τοῦ ἰδίου σώματος οὐκ
¹and also the husband of the(his) own body not

ἐξουσιάζει ἀλλὰ ἡ γυνή. **5** μὴ ἀποστερεῖτε
has authority but the wife. Deprive not ye

ἀλλήλους, εἰ μήτι ἂν ἐκ συμφώνου πρὸς
each other, unless by agreement for

καιρὸν ἵνα σχολάσητε τῇ προσευχῇ καὶ
a time in order ye may have - for prayer and
that leisure

πάλιν ἐπὶ τὸ αὐτὸ ἦτε, ἵνα μὴ πειράζῃ
²again ¹together ¹ye may be, lest ²tempt

ὑμᾶς ὁ σατανᾶς διὰ τὴν ἀκρασίαν [ὑμῶν].
²you - ¹Satan because the want of of you.
of self-control

6 τοῦτο δὲ λέγω κατὰ συγγνώμην, οὐ
Now this I say by allowance, not

κατ᾽ ἐπιταγήν. **7** θέλω δὲ πάντας
by command. And I wish all

ἀνθρώπους εἶναι ὡς καὶ ἐμαυτόν· ἀλλὰ
men to be as even myself; but

ἕκαστος ἴδιον ἔχει χάρισμα ἐκ θεοῦ,
each man ²[his] own ¹has gift of God,

ὁ μὲν οὕτως, ὁ δὲ οὕτως.
one thus, another thus.

8 Λέγω δὲ τοῖς ἀγάμοις καὶ ταῖς χήραις,
Now I say to the unmarried men and to the widows,

καλὸν αὐτοῖς ἐὰν μείνωσιν ὡς κἀγώ· **9** εἰ δὲ
[it is] good for them if they remain as I also; but if

οὐκ ἐγκρατεύονται, γαμησάτωσαν· κρεῖττον
they do not exercise self-control, let them marry; better

γάρ ἐστιν γαμεῖν ἢ πυροῦσθαι. **10** τοῖς
for it is to marry than to burn. to the [ones]

δὲ γεγαμηκόσιν παραγγέλλω, οὐκ ἐγὼ
But having married I enjoin, not I

ἀλλὰ ὁ κύριος, γυναῖκα ἀπὸ ἀνδρὸς μὴ
but the Lord, a woman from [her] husband not

χωρισθῆναι, **11** — ἐὰν δὲ καὶ χωρισθῇ,
to be separated,ᵇ but if indeed she is
separated,

you, whom you have received from God? You are not your own; ²⁰you were bought at a price. Therefore honor God with your body.

Chapter 7

Marriage

NOW for the matters you wrote about: It is good for a man not to marry.ᵖ ²But since there is so much immorality, each man should have his own wife, and each woman her own husband. ³The husband should fulfill his marital duty to his wife, and likewise the wife to her husband. ⁴The wife's body does not belong to her alone but also to her husband. In the same way, the husband's body does not belong to him alone but also to his wife. ⁵Do not deprive each other except by mutual consent and for a time, so that you may devote yourselves to prayer. Then come together again so that Satan will not tempt you because of your lack of self-control. ⁶I say this as a concession, not as a command. ⁷I wish that all men were as I am. But each man has his own gift from God; one has this gift, another has that.

⁸Now to the unmarried and the widows I say: It is good for them to stay unmarried, as I am. ⁹But if they cannot control themselves, they should marry, for it is better to marry than to burn with passion. ¹⁰To the married I give this command (not I, but the Lord): A wife must not separate from her husband. ¹¹But if she does, she must

***

ᵗSome ancient mss. read *For*

* As the same Greek word γυνή means "wife" or "(?married) woman" it is not always easy to differentiate in translating. So also the one Greek word ἀνήρ means "man" or "husband"

ᵖ¹ Or "*It is good for a man not to have sexual relations with a woman.*"

let her remain unmarried, or else be reconciled to her husband), and that the husband should not send his wife away.

12But to the rest I say, not the Lord, that if any brother has a wife who is an unbeliever, and she consents to live with him, let him not send her away.

13And a woman who has an unbelieving husband, and he consents to live with her, let her not send her husband away.

14For the unbelieving husband is sanctified through his wife, and the unbelieving wife is sanctified through her believing husband; for otherwise your children are unclean, but now they are holy.

15Yet if the unbelieving one leaves, let him leave; the brother or the sister is not under bondage in such cases, but God has called /us to peace.

16For how do you know, O wife, whether you will save your husband? Or how do you know, O husband, whether you will save your wife?

17Only, as the Lord has assigned to each one, as God has called each, in this manner let him walk. And thus I direct in all the churches.

18Was any man called already circumcised? Let him not become uncircumcised. Has anyone been called in uncircumcision? Let him not be circumcised.

19Circumcision is nothing, and uncircumcision is nothing, but what matters is the keeping of the commandments of God.

20Let each man remain in that condition in which he was called.

21Were you called while a slave? Do not worry about it; but if you are able also to become free, rather do that.

μενέτω ἄγαμος ἢ τῷ ἀνδρὶ καταλλαγήτω,
let her remain unmarried or to husband be reconciled, the(her)

— καὶ ἄνδρα γυναῖκα μὴ ἀφιέναι. 12 Τοῖς
and a husband [his] wife not to leave.[b] to the

δὲ λοιποῖς λέγω ἐγώ, οὐχ ὁ κύριος·
And rest say I, not the Lord:

εἴ τις ἀδελφὸς γυναῖκα ἔχει ἄπιστον, καὶ
If any brother ²a wife ¹has unbelieving, and

αὕτη συνευδοκεῖ οἰκεῖν μετ' αὐτοῦ, μὴ
this one consents to dwell with him, not

ἀφιέτω αὐτήν· 13 καὶ γυνὴ ἥτις ἔχει
let him leave her; and a woman who has

ἄνδρα ἄπιστον, καὶ οὗτος συνευδοκεῖ οἰκεῖν
a husband unbelieving, and this one consents to dwell

μετ' αὐτῆς, μὴ ἀφιέτω τὸν ἄνδρα.
with her, let her not leave the(her) husband.

14 ἡγίασται γὰρ ὁ ἀνὴρ ὁ ἄπιστος ἐν
For ²has been sanctified ¹the ²husband – ³unbelieving by

τῇ γυναικί, καὶ ἡγίασται ἡ γυνὴ ἡ
the wife, and ²has been ¹the ²wife –
sanctified

ἄπιστος ἐν τῷ ἀδελφῷ· ἐπεὶ ἄρα τὰ
²unbelieving by the brother; since then the

τέκνα ὑμῶν ἀκάθαρτά ἐστιν, νῦν δὲ
children of you ²unclean ¹is(are), but now

ἅγιά ἐστιν. 15 εἰ δὲ ὁ ἄπιστος χωρίζ-
²holy ¹they are. But if the unbelieving separates
one

εται, χωριζέσθω· οὐ δεδούλωται ὁ
him/herself, let him/her be ²has not been enslaved ¹the
separated;

ἀδελφὸς ἢ ἡ ἀδελφὴ ἐν τοῖς τοιούτοις·
²brother ³or ⁴the ⁵sister in such matters;

ἐν δὲ εἰρήνῃ κέκληκεν ὑμᾶς ὁ θεός.
but ³in ²peace ²has called ⁴you – ¹God.

16 τί γὰρ οἶδας, γύναι, εἰ τὸν ἄνδρα
For what knowest thou, wife, if the(thy) husband

σώσεις; ἢ τί οἶδας, ἄνερ, εἰ τὴν
thou wilt or what knowest husband, if the(thy)
save? thou,

γυναῖκα σώσεις; 17 Εἰ μὴ ἑκάστῳ ὡς
wife thou wilt save? Only ²to each ¹as

μεμέρικεν ὁ κύριος, ἕκαστον ὡς κέκληκεν
⁴has divided ³the ²Lord, ⁴each ¹as ²has called

ὁ θεός, οὕτως περιπατείτω. καὶ οὕτως
– ¹God, so let him walk. And so

ἐν ταῖς ἐκκλησίαις πάσαις διατάσσομαι.
³in ⁴the ⁵churches ²all ¹I command.

18 περιτετμημένος τις ἐκλήθη; μὴ
⁴Having been circumcised ²anyone ¹was ³called? not

ἐπισπάσθω· ἐν ἀκροβυστίᾳ κέκληταί τις;
let him be un- in uncircumcision has been anyone?
circumcised; called

μὴ περιτεμνέσθω. 19 ἡ περιτομὴ οὐδέν
let him not be circumcised. – Circumcision nothing

ἐστιν, καὶ ἡ ἀκροβυστία οὐδέν ἐστιν,
is, and – uncircumcision nothing is,

ἀλλὰ τήρησις ἐντολῶν θεοῦ. 20 ἕκαστος
but [the] of command- of Each one
keeping ments God.

ἐν τῇ κλήσει ᾗ ἐκλήθη, ἐν ταύτῃ
in the calling in which he was called, in this

μενέτω. 21 δοῦλος ἐκλήθης; μή σοι
let him remain. A slave wast thou called? not to thee

μελέτω· ἀλλ' εἰ καὶ δύνασαι ἐλεύθερος
let it matter; but if indeed thou art able ²free

γενέσθαι, μᾶλλον χρῆσαι. 22 ὁ γὰρ ἐν
¹to become, ²rather ¹use [it]. For ¹the [one] ⁴in

---

remain unmarried or else be reconciled to her husband. And a husband must not divorce his wife.

12To the rest I say this (I, not the Lord): If any brother has a wife who is not a believer and she is willing to live with him, he must not divorce her. 13And if a woman has a husband who is not a believer and he is willing to live with her, she must not divorce him. 14For the unbelieving husband has been sanctified through his wife, and the unbelieving wife has been sanctified through her believing husband. Otherwise your children would be unclean, but as it is, they are holy.

15But if the unbeliever leaves, let him do so. A believing man or woman is not bound in such circumstances; God has called us to live in peace. 16How do you know, wife, whether you will save your husband? Or, how do you know, husband, whether you will save your wife?

17Nevertheless, each one should retain the place in life that the Lord assigned to him and to which God has called him. This is the rule I lay down in all the churches. 18Was a man already circumcised when he was called? He should not become uncircumcised. Was a man uncircumcised when he was called? He should not be circumcised. 19Circumcision is nothing and uncircumcision is nothing. Keeping God's commands is what counts. 20Each one should remain in the situation which he was in when God called him. 21Were you a slave when you were called? Don't let it trouble you— although if you can gain your freedom, do so. 22For

---

22For he who was called in the Lord while a slave, is the Lord's freedman; likewise he who was called while free, is Christ's slave.

23You were bought with a price; do not become slaves of men.

24Brethren, let each man remain with God in that *condition* in which he was called.

25Now concerning virgins I have no command of the Lord, but I give an opinion as one who by the mercy of the Lord is trustworthy.

26I think then that this is good in view of the present distress, that it is good for a man to remain as he is.

27Are you bound to a wife? Do not seek to be released. Are you released from a wife? Do not seek a wife.

28But if you should marry, you have not sinned; and if a virgin should marry, she has not sinned. Yet such will have trouble in this life, and I am trying to spare you.

29But this I say, brethren, the time has been shortened, so that from now on those who have wives should be as though they had none;

30and those who weep, as though they did not weep; and those who rejoice, as though they did not rejoice; and those who buy, as though they did not possess;

31and those who use the world, as though they did not make full use of it; for the form of this world is passing away.

32But I want you to be free from concern. One who is unmarried is concerned about the things of the Lord, how he may please the Lord;

33but one who is married is concerned about the

κυρίῳ κληθεὶς δοῦλος ἀπελεύθερος κυρίου
⁵[the] ²called ³a slave ⁷a freed man ⁶of [the]
Lord Lord

ἐστίν· ὁμοίως ὁ ἐλεύθερος κληθεὶς δοῦλός
⁴is; likewise ¹the ²a free man ²called ³a slave
[one]

ἐστιν Χριστοῦ. 23 τιμῆς ἠγοράσθητε· μὴ
⁴is ⁵of Christ. Of(with) a price ye were bought; not

γίνεσθε δοῦλοι ἀνθρώπων. 24 ἕκαστος ἐν
become slaves of men. Each one in

ᾧ ἐκλήθη, ἀδελφοί, ἐν τούτῳ μενέτω
what he was brothers, in this let him
[state] called, remain

παρὰ θεῷ.
with God.

25 Περὶ δὲ τῶν παρθένων ἐπιταγὴν
Now about the virgins a command

κυρίου οὐκ ἔχω, γνώμην δὲ δίδωμι ὡς
of [the] Lord I have not, but an opinion I give as

ἠλεημένος ὑπὸ κυρίου πιστὸς εἶναι.
having had mercy by [the] Lord faithful to be.

26 Νομίζω οὖν τοῦτο καλὸν ὑπάρχειν
I suppose therefore this good to be

διὰ τὴν ἐνεστῶσαν ἀνάγκην, ὅτι καλὸν
because of the present necessity, that [it is] good

ἀνθρώπῳ τὸ οὕτως εἶναι. 27 δέδεσαι
for a man - so to be. Hast thou
been bound

γυναικί; μὴ ζήτει λύσιν· λέλυσαι ἀπὸ
to a woman? do not seek release; hast thou been from
released

γυναικός; μὴ ζήτει γυναῖκα. 28 ἐὰν
a woman? do not seek a woman. if

δὲ καὶ γαμήσῃς, οὐχ ἥμαρτες, καὶ ἐὰν
But indeed thou marriest, thou sinnedst not, and if

γήμῃ ἡ παρθένος, οὐχ ἥμαρτεν· θλῖψιν
³marries ¹the ²virgin, she sinned not; ³affliction

δὲ τῇ σαρκὶ ἕξουσιν οἱ τοιοῦτοι, ἐγὼ
but ⁴in the ⁵flesh ²will have - ¹such, ²I

δὲ ὑμῶν φείδομαι. 29 Τοῦτο δέ φημι,
¹and ⁴you ³am sparing. But this I say,

ἀδελφοί, ὁ καιρὸς συνεσταλμένος ἐστίν·
brothers, the time *having been* shortened is;

τὸ λοιπὸν ἵνα καὶ οἱ ἔχοντες γυναῖκας
for the rest in order both the [ones] having wives
that

ὡς μὴ ἔχοντες ὦσιν, 30 καὶ οἱ κλαίοντες
as not having may be, and the [ones] weeping

ὡς μὴ κλαίοντες, καὶ οἱ χαίροντες ὡς
as not weeping, and the [ones] rejoicing as

μὴ χαίροντες, καὶ οἱ ἀγοράζοντες ὡς
not rejoicing, and the [ones] buying as

μὴ κατέχοντες, 31 καὶ οἱ χρώμενοι τὸν
not holding, and the [ones] using the

κόσμον ὡς μὴ καταχρώμενοι· παράγει
world as not abusing [it]; ⁴is passing
away

γὰρ τὸ σχῆμα τοῦ κόσμου τούτου.
for ¹the ²fashion ³of this world.

32 Θέλω δὲ ὑμᾶς ἀμερίμνους εἶναι. ὁ
But I wish you without care to be. The

ἄγαμος μεριμνᾷ τὰ τοῦ κυρίου, 33 πῶς
unmarried cares for the of the Lord, how
man things

ἀρέσῃ τῷ κυρίῳ· ὁ δὲ γαμήσας μεριμνᾷ
he may the Lord; but the having married cares for
please [one]

he who was a slave when he was called by the Lord is the Lord's freedman; similarly, he who was a free man when he was called is Christ's slave. 23You were bought at a price; do not become slaves of men. 24Brothers, each man, as responsible to God, should remain in the situation God called him to.

25Now about virgins: I have no command from the Lord, but I give a judgment as one who by the Lord's mercy is trustworthy. 26Because of the present crisis, I think that it is good for you to remain as you are. 27Are you married? Do not seek a divorce. Are you unmarried? Do not look for a wife. 28But if you do marry, you have not sinned; and if a virgin marries, she has not sinned. But those who marry will face many troubles in this life, and I want to spare you this.

29What I mean, brothers, is that the time is short. From now on those who have wives should live as if they had none; 30those who mourn, as if they did not; those who are happy, as if they were not; those who buy something, as if it were not theirs to keep; 31those who use the things of the world, as if not engrossed in them. For this world in its present form is passing away.

32I would like you to be free from concern. An unmarried man is concerned about the Lord's affairs—how he can please the Lord. 33But a married man is concerned about the afthings of the world, how he may please his k wife, 34and *his interests* are divided. And the woman who is unmarried, and the virgin, is concerned about the things of the Lord, that she may be holy both in body and spirit; but one who is married is concerned about the things of the world, how she may please her husband. 35And this I say for your own benefit; not to put a restraint upon you, but to promote what is seemly, and *to secure* undistracted devotion to the Lord. 36But if any man thinks that he is acting unbecomingly toward his virgin *daughter*, if she should be of full age, and if it must be so, let him do what he wishes, he does not sin; let her marry. 37But he who stands firm in his heart, being under no constraint, but has authority over his own will, and has decided this in his own heart, to keep his own virgin *daughter*, he will do well. 38So then both he who gives his own virgin *daughter* in marriage does well, and he who does not give her in marriage will do better. 39A wife is bound as long as her husband lives; but if her husband is dead, she is free to be married to whom she wishes, only in the Lord. 40But in my opinion she is happier if she remains as she is; and I think that I also have the Spirit of God.

Chapter 8

Take Care with Your Liberty

NOW concerning things sacrificed to idols, we

τὰ   τοῦ   κόσμου,   πῶς   ἀρέσῃ   τῇ   γυναικί,
the   of the   world,   how   he may   the(his)   wife,
things   please

34 καὶ   μεμέρισται.   καὶ   ἡ   γυνὴ   ἡ   ἄγαμος
and   has been divided.   And the ²woman –   ¹unmarried

καὶ   ἡ   παρθένος   μεριμνᾷ   τὰ   τοῦ   κυρίου,
and   the   virgin   cares for   the things of the   Lord,

ἵνα   ᾖ   ἁγία   καὶ   τῷ   σώματι   καὶ   τῷ
in   she   holy   both   in the   body   and   in
order   may   the
that   be

πνεύματι·   ἡ   δὲ   γαμήσασα   μεριμνᾷ   τὰ
spirit;   but the [one] having married   cares for   the
                                                      things

τοῦ   κόσμου,   πῶς   ἀρέσῃ   τῷ   ἀνδρί.
of the   world,   how she may please   the(her)   husband.

35 τοῦτο   δὲ   πρὸς   τὸ   ὑμῶν   αὐτῶν   σύμφορον
And ²this   ³for   ⁴the   ⁶of yourselves   ⁵advantage

λέγω,   οὐχ   ἵνα   βρόχον   ὑμῖν   ἐπιβάλω,
¹I say,   not   in order   ²a restraint   ³you   ¹I may put on,
                 that

ἀλλὰ   πρὸς   τὸ   εὔσχημον   καὶ   εὐπάρεδρον
but   for   the thing   comely   and   waiting on

τῷ   κυρίῳ   ἀπερισπάστως.   **36** Εἰ   δέ   τις
the   Lord   undistractedly.   But if   anyone

ἀσχημονεῖν   ἐπὶ   τὴν   παρθένον   αὐτοῦ
²to behave   ³toward   ⁴the   ⁵virgin   ⁶of him
dishonourably

νομίζει,   ἐὰν   ᾖ   ὑπέρακμος,   καὶ   οὕτως
¹thinks,   if   he/she is past the bloom   and   so
                 of youth,

ὀφείλει   γίνεσθαι,   ὃ   θέλει   ποιείτω·   οὐχ
ought   to be,   what he wishes   let him do;   not

ἁμαρτάνει·   γαμείτωσαν.   **37** ὃς   δὲ   ἕστηκεν
he sins;   let them marry.   But [he] who   stands

ἐν   τῇ   καρδίᾳ   αὐτοῦ   ἑδραῖος,   μὴ
in   the   heart   of him   firm,   not

ἔχων   ἀνάγκην,   ἐξουσίαν   δὲ   ἔχει   περὶ
having   necessity,   but authority   has concerning

τοῦ   ἰδίου   θελήματος,   καὶ   τοῦτο   κέκρικεν
the(his)   own   will,   and   this   has decided

ἐν   τῇ   ἰδίᾳ   καρδίᾳ,   τηρεῖν   τὴν   ἑαυτοῦ
in the(his)   own   heart,   to keep   the   of himself

παρθένον,   καλῶς   ποιήσει.   **38** ὥστε   καὶ
virgin,   ²well   ¹he will do.   So as   both

ὁ   γαμίζων   τὴν   ἑαυτοῦ   παρθένον   καλῶς
the   marrying   the   of himself   virgin   ²well
[one]

ποιεῖ,   καὶ   ὁ   μὴ   γαμίζων   κρεῖσσον   ποιήσει.
¹does,   and   the   not   marrying   ²better   ¹will do.
           [one]

39 Γυνὴ   δέδεται   ἐφ'   ὅσον   χρόνον   ζῇ
A wife   has been bound   for   so long a time as   lives

ὁ   ἀνὴρ   αὐτῆς·   ἐὰν   δὲ   κοιμηθῇ   ὁ   ἀνήρ,
the   husband   of her;   but if   sleeps   the   husband,

ἐλευθέρα   ἐστὶν   ᾧ   θέλει   γαμηθῆναι,   μόνον
²free   ¹she is   ⁴to   ⁵she   ³to be married,   only
           whom   wishes

ἐν   κυρίῳ.   **40** μακαριωτέρα   δέ   ἐστιν
in   [the] Lord.   But happier   she is

ἐὰν   οὕτως   μείνῃ,   κατὰ   τὴν   ἐμὴν   γνώμην·
if   so   she   according   –   my   opinion;
         remains,   to

δοκῶ   δὲ   κἀγὼ   πνεῦμα   θεοῦ   ἔχειν.
and I think   I also   [the] Spirit   of God   *to* have.

8 Περὶ   δὲ   τῶν   εἰδωλοθύτων,   οἴδαμεν
Now about   the   idolatrous sacrifices,   we know

---

fairs of this world—how he can please his wife— 34and his interests are divided. An unmarried woman or virgin is concerned about the Lord's affairs: Her aim is to be devoted to the Lord in both body and spirit. But a married woman is concerned about the affairs of this world—how she can please her husband. 35I am saying this for your own good, not to restrict you, but that you may live in a right way in undivided devotion to the Lord.

36If anyone thinks he is acting improperly toward the virgin he is engaged to, and if she is getting along in years and he feels he ought to marry, he should do as he wants. He is not sinning. They should get married. 37But the man who has settled the matter in his own mind, who is under no compulsion but has control over his own will, and who has made up his mind not to marry the virgin—this man also does the right thing. 38So then, he who marries the virgin does right, but he who does not marry her does even better. q

39A woman is bound to her husband as long as he lives. But if her husband dies, she is free to marry anyone she wishes, but he must belong to the Lord. 40In my judgment, she is happier if she stays as she is—and I think that I too have the Spirit of God.

Chapter 8

Food Sacrificed to Idols

NOW about food sacrificed to idols: We

know that we all have
knowledge. Knowledge
makes arrogant, but love
edifies.

2If anyone supposes that
he knows anything, he has
not yet known as he ought
to know;

3but if anyone loves
God, he is known by Him.

4Therefore concerning
the eating of things sacrificed to idols, we know that
[there is no such thing as
an idol in the world, and
that there is no God but
one.

5For even if there are so-
called gods whether in
heaven or on earth, as indeed there are many gods
and many lords,

6yet for us there is *but*
one God, the Father, from
whom are all things, and we
exist for Him; and one
Lord, Jesus Christ, by
whom are all things, and we
exist through Him.

7However not all men
have this knowledge; but
some, being accustomed to
the idol until now, eat *food*
as if it were sacrificed to an
idol; and their conscience
being weak is defiled.

8But food will not com-
mend us to God; we are
neither the worse if we do
not eat, nor the better if we
do eat.

9But take care lest this
liberty of yours somehow
become a stumbling block
to the weak.

10For if someone sees
you, who have knowledge,
dining in an idol's temple,
will not his conscience, if
he is weak, be strengthened
to eat things sacrificed to
idols?

11For through your
knowledge he who is weak
is ruined, the brother for
whose sake Christ died.

12And thus, by sinning
against the brethren and
wounding their conscience
when it is weak, you sin

ὅτι   πάντες   γνῶσιν   ἔχομεν.   ἡ   γνῶσις
that   ²all   ⁴knowledge   ¹we ³have.   -   Knowledge

φυσιοῖ,   ἡ   δὲ   ἀγάπη   οἰκοδομεῖ·   εἴ   τις
puffs up,   -   but   love   builds up;   if   anyone

δοκεῖ   ἐγνωκέναι   τι,   2 οὔπω   ἔγνω   καθὼς
thinks   to have known   anything,   not yet   he knew   as

δεῖ   γνῶναι·   3 εἰ   δέ   τις   ἀγαπᾷ   τὸν
it be-   to know;   but if   anyone   loves   -
hoves [him]

θεόν,   οὗτος   ἔγνωσται   ὑπ'   αὐτοῦ.   4 Περὶ
God,   this one   has been known   by   him.   About

τῆς   βρώσεως   οὖν   τῶν   εἰδωλοθύτων
the   eating   therefore   -   of idolatrous sacrifices

οἴδαμεν   ὅτι   οὐδὲν   εἴδωλον   ἐν   κόσμῳ,
we know   that   [there is] no   idol   in   [the] world,

καὶ   ὅτι   οὐδεὶς   θεὸς   εἰ   μὴ   εἷς.   5 καὶ
and   that [there is] no   God   except   one.   even

γὰρ   εἴπερ   εἰσὶν   λεγόμενοι   θεοὶ   εἴτε   ἐν
For   if   there are   *being* called   gods   either   in

οὐρανῷ   εἴτε   ἐπὶ   γῆς,   ὥσπερ   εἰσὶν   θεοὶ
heaven   or   on   earth,   even as   there are   gods

πολλοὶ   καὶ   κύριοι   πολλοί,   6 ἀλλ'   ἡμῖν
many   and   lords   many,   yet   to us

εἷς   θεὸς   ὁ   πατήρ,   ἐξ   οὗ   τὰ   πάντα   καὶ
[there God the   Father,   of whom   -   [are] all   and
is] one

ἡμεῖς   εἰς   αὐτόν,   καὶ   εἷς   κύριος   Ἰησοῦς
we   in   him,   and   one   Lord   Jesus

Χριστός,   δι'   οὗ   τὰ   πάντα   καὶ   ἡμεῖς
Christ,   through whom   -   [are] all   and   we
things

δι'   αὐτοῦ.   7 Ἀλλ'   οὐκ   ἐν   πᾶσιν   ἡ
through him.   But [there is] not   in   all men   the
(this)

γνῶσις·   τινὲς   δὲ   τῇ   συνηθείᾳ   ἕως   ἄρτι
knowledge;   and some   by the   habit   until   now

τοῦ   εἰδώλου   ὡς   εἰδωλόθυτον   ἐσθίουσιν,
³of the   ²idol   ⁴as   ⁵an idolatrous sacrifice   ¹eat,

καὶ   ἡ   συνείδησις   αὐτῶν   ἀσθενὴς   οὖσα
and   the   conscience   of them   ³weak   ¹being

μολύνεται.   8 βρῶμα   δὲ   ἡμᾶς   οὐ   παραστήσει
is defiled.   But food   -   us   ¹will not commend

τῷ   θεῷ·   οὔτε   ἐὰν   μὴ   φάγωμεν   ὑστερούμεθα,
-    to God;   neither   if   we eat not   are we behind,

οὔτε   ἐὰν   φάγωμεν   περισσεύομεν.   9 βλέπετε
nor   if   we eat   do we excel.   look ye

δὲ   μή   πως   ἡ   ἐξουσία   ὑμῶν   αὕτη
But   lest   somehow   *the*   ²authority   ³of you   ¹this

πρόσκομμα   γένηται   τοῖς   ἀσθενέσιν.   10 ἐὰν
a stumbling-block   becomes   to the   weak ones.   if

γάρ   τις   ἴδῃ   σὲ   τὸν   ἔχοντα   γνῶσιν   ἐν
For   anyone   sees   thee the [one] having   knowledge   ²in

εἰδωλείῳ   κατακείμενον,   οὐχὶ   ἡ   συνείδησις
³an idol's temple   ¹sitting,   ²not   ³the   ⁴conscience

αὐτοῦ   ἀσθενοῦς   ὄντος   οἰκοδομηθήσεται   εἰς
⁵of him   ⁷weak   ⁶[he]being⁸   ¹will ²be emboldened   -

τὸ   τὰ   εἰδωλόθυτα   ἐσθίειν;   11 ἀπόλλυται
-    ¹⁰the   ¹¹idolatrous sacrifices   ²to eat?   ³is destroyed

γὰρ   ὁ   ἀσθενῶν   ἐν   τῇ   σῇ   γνώσει,   ὁ
For   ¹the [one]   ²being weak   by   -   thy   knowledge, the

ἀδελφὸς   δι'   ὃν   Χριστὸς   ἀπέθανεν.   12 οὕτως
brother   because whom   Christ   died.   so
of

δὲ   ἁμαρτάνοντες   εἰς   τοὺς   ἀδελφοὺς   καὶ
And   sinning   against   the   brothers   and

τύπτοντες   αὐτῶν   τὴν   συνείδησιν   ἀσθενοῦσαν
wounding   of them   the   conscience   being weak

---

know that we all possess
knowledge.' Knowledge
puffs up, but love builds
up. 2The man who thinks
he knows something does
not yet know as he ought to
know. 3But the man who
loves God is known by
God.

4So then, about eating
food sacrificed to idols: We
know that an idol is nothing
at all in the world and that
there is no God but one.
5For even if there are so-
called gods, whether in
heaven or on earth (as indeed there are many
"gods" and many
"lords"), 6yet for us there
is but one God, the Father,
from whom all things came
and for whom we live; and
there is but one Lord, Jesus
Christ, through whom all
things came and through
whom we live.

7But not everyone knows
this. Some people are still
so accustomed to idols that
when they eat such food
they think of it as having
been sacrificed to an idol,
and since their conscience
is weak, it is defiled. 8But
food does not bring us near
to God; we are no worse if
we do not eat, and no better
if we do.

9Be careful, however,
that the exercise of your
freedom does not become a
stumbling block to the
weak. 10For if anyone with
a weak conscience sees
you who have this knowl-
edge eating in an idol's temple, won't he be embold-
ened to eat what has been
sacrificed to idols? 11So this
weak brother, for whom
Christ died, is destroyed by
your knowledge. 12When
you sin against your brothers in this way and wound
their weak conscience, you
sin against Christ. 13There-

/I.e., has no real existence

r/ Or "We all possess knowledge,"
as you say

against Christ.
13Therefore, if food causes my brother to stumble, I will never eat meat again, that I might not cause my brother to stumble.

Chapter 9

Paul's Use of Liberty

AM I not free? Am I not an apostle? Have I not seen Jesus our Lord? Are you not my work in the Lord?

2If to others I am not an apostle, at least I am to you; for you are the seal of my apostleship in the Lord.

3My defense to those who examine me is this: 4Do we not have a right to eat and drink?

5Do we not have a right to take along a believing wife, even as the rest of the apostles, and the brothers of the Lord, and Cephas?

6Or do only Barnabas and I not have a right to refrain from working?

7Who at any time serves as a soldier at his own expense? Who plants a vineyard, and does not eat the fruit of it? Or who tends a flock and does not use the milk of the flock?

8I am not speaking these things according to human judgment, am I? Or does not the Law also say these things?

9For it is written in the Law of Moses, "YOU SHALL NOT MUZZLE THE OX WHILE HE IS THRESHING." God is not concerned about oxen, is He?

10Or is He speaking altogether for our sake? Yes, for our sake it was written, because the plowman ought to plow in hope, and the thresher *to thresh* in hope of sharing *the crops.*

11If we sowed spiritual things in you, is it too much if we should reap material

εἰς Χριστὸν ἁμαρτάνετε. 13 διόπερ εἰ
*against ²Christ   ¹ye sin.   Wherefore   if

βρῶμα σκανδαλίζει τὸν ἀδελφόν μου, οὐ
food   offends   the   brother of me, by no

μὴ φάγω κρέα εἰς τὸν αἰῶνα, ἵνα μὴ
means I eat flesh unto the   age,   lest

τὸν ἀδελφόν μου σκανδαλίσω.
²the ³brother ⁴of me ¹I offend.

9 Οὐκ εἰμὶ ἐλεύθερος; οὐκ εἰμὶ ἀπόστολος;
  Am I not   free?   am I not   an apostle?

οὐχὶ Ἰησοῦν τὸν κύριον ἡμῶν ἑόρακα;
not   Jesus   the   Lord of us I have seen?

οὐ τὸ ἔργον μου ὑμεῖς ἐστε ἐν κυρίῳ;
not the work of me ye   are in [the] Lord?

2 εἰ ἄλλοις οὐκ εἰμὶ ἀπόστολος, ἀλλά
  If to others I am not an apostle,   yet

γε ὑμῖν εἰμι· ἡ γὰρ σφραγίς μου τῆς
indeed to you I am;   for the seal of me ¹of the

ἀποστολῆς ὑμεῖς ἐστε ἐν κυρίῳ. 3 Ἡ
²apostleship ye   are in [the] Lord.

ἐμὴ ἀπολογία τοῖς ἐμὲ ἀνακρίνουσίν ἐστιν
My defence   to the ²me ¹examining   is
              [ones]

αὕτη. 4 μὴ οὐκ ἔχομεν ἐξουσίαν φαγεῖν
this.   not Have we not authority to eat

καὶ πεῖν; 5 μὴ οὐκ ἔχομεν ἐξουσίαν
and to drink? not have we not authority

ἀδελφὴν γυναῖκα περιάγειν, ὡς καὶ οἱ
a sister a wife to lead about, as   also the

λοιποὶ ἀπόστολοι καὶ οἱ ἀδελφοὶ τοῦ
remaining apostles and the brothers of the

κυρίου καὶ Κηφᾶς; 6 ἢ μόνος ἐγὼ καὶ
Lord   and Cephas?   or only   I   and

Βαρναβᾶς οὐκ ἔχομεν ἐξουσίαν μὴ
Barnabas   have we not authority not

ἐργάζεσθαι; 7 Τίς στρατεύεται ἰδίοις
to work?   Who soldiers   at [his] own

ὀψωνίοις ποτέ; τίς φυτεύει ἀμπελῶνα καὶ
wages   at any time? who plants a vineyard and

τὸν καρπὸν αὐτοῦ οὐκ ἐσθίει; ἢ τίς
the fruit   of it eats not? or who

ποιμαίνει ποίμνην καὶ ἐκ τοῦ γάλακτος
shepherds a flock and of the   milk

τῆς ποίμνης οὐκ ἐσθίει; 8 μὴ κατὰ
of the flock   eats not? Not according to

ἄνθρωπον ταῦτα λαλῶ, ἢ καὶ ὁ νόμος
man   these things I speak, or also the   law

ταῦτα οὐ λέγει; 9 ἐν γὰρ τῷ Μωϋσέως
these things says not? for in the   of Moses

νόμῳ γέγραπται· οὐ κημώσεις βοῦν
law   it has been written: Thou shalt not muzzle an ox

ἀλοῶντα. μὴ τῶν βοῶν μέλει τῷ θεῷ;
threshing. not of oxen matters it - to God?

10 ἢ δι' ἡμᾶς πάντως λέγει; δι' ἡμᾶς
   or because of us altogether he says? because of us

γὰρ ἐγράφη, ὅτι ὀφείλει ἐπ' ἐλπίδι
for it was written, because ⁵ought ⁶on(in) ⁴hope

ὁ ἀροτριῶν ἀροτριᾶν, καὶ ὁ ἀλοῶν ἐπ'
¹the ²ploughing ⁴to plough, and the threshing on(in)
[one]   [one]

ἐλπίδι τοῦ μετέχειν. 11 εἰ ἡμεῖς ὑμῖν
hope of the to partake.   If   we   to you
              =of partaking.

τὰ πνευματικὰ ἐσπείραμεν, μέγα εἰ ἡμεῖς
-   spiritual things sowed, [is it] a great thing if we

fore, if what I eat causes my brother to fall into sin, I will never eat meat again, so that I will not cause him to fall.

Chapter 9

The Rights of an Apostle

AM I not free? Am I not an apostle? Have I not seen Jesus our Lord? Are you not the result of my work in the Lord? 2Even though I may not be an apostle to others, surely I am to you! For you are the seal of my apostleship in the Lord.

3This is my defense to those who sit in judgment on me. 4Don't we have the right to food and drink? 5Don't we have the right to take a believing wife along with us, as do the other apostles and the Lord's brothers and Cephas⁵? 6Or is it only I and Barnabas who must work for a living?

7Who serves as a soldier at his own expense? Who plants a vineyard and does not eat of its grapes? Who tends a flock and does not drink of the milk? 8Do I say this merely from a human point of view? Doesn't the Law say the same thing? 9For it is written in the Law of Moses: "Do not muzzle an ox while it is treading out the grain."' Is it about oxen that God is concerned? 10Surely he says this for us, doesn't he? Yes, this was written for us, because when the plowman plows and the thresher threshes, they ought to do so in the hope of sharing in the harvest. 11If we have sown spiritual seed among

⁵5 That is, Peter
'9 Deut. 25:4

things from you?
12If others share the right over you, do we not more? Nevertheless, we did not use this right, but we endure all things, that we may cause no hindrance to the gospel of Christ.
13Do you not know that those who perform sacred services eat the *food* of the temple, *and* those who attend regularly to the altar have their share with the altar?
14So also the Lord directed those who proclaim the gospel to get their living from the gospel.
15But I have used none of these things. And I am not writing these things that it may be done so in my case; for it would be better for me to die than have any man make my boast an empty one.
16For if I preach the gospel, I have nothing to boast of, for I am under compulsion; for woe is me if I do not preach the gospel.
17For if I do this voluntarily, I have a reward; but if against my will, I have a stewardship entrusted to me.
18What then is my reward? That, when I preach the gospel, I may offer the gospel without charge, so as not to make full use of my right in the gospel.
19For though I am free from all *men*, I have made myself a slave to all, that I might win the more.
20And to the Jews I became as a Jew, that I might win Jews; to those who are under the Law, as under the Law, though not being myself under the Law, that I might win those who are under the Law;

ὑμῶν   τὰ   σαρκικὰ   θερίσομεν;   12 εἰ   ἄλλοι
of you   -   fleshly things   shall reap?   If   others
τῆς   ὑμῶν   ἐξουσίας   μετέχουσιν,   οὐ
²of the   ⁴of you   ³authority   ¹have a share *of*,   not
μᾶλλον   ἡμεῖς;   ἀλλ'   οὐκ   ἐχρησάμεθα
rather   we?   But   we did not use
τῇ   ἐξουσίᾳ   ταύτῃ,   ἀλλὰ   πάντα   στέγομεν
this authority,   but   ²all things ¹we put up with
ἵνα   μή   τινα   ἐγκοπὴν   δῶμεν   τῷ   εὐαγγελίῳ
lest   ²anyone ²an obstacle ¹we should to the   gospel
                                        give
τοῦ   Χριστοῦ.   13 Οὐκ   οἴδατε   ὅτι   οἱ
 -      of Christ.   Know ye not   that   the
                                                      [ones]
τὰ   ἱερὰ   ἐργαζόμενοι   τὰ   ἐκ   τοῦ   ἱεροῦ
 - ²sacred things ¹working [at] ⁴the things ⁵of ⁶the   ⁷temple
ἐσθίουσιν,   οἱ   τῷ   θυσιαστηρίῳ   παρεδρεύοντες
³eat,   the   ²the   ³altar   ¹attending [on]
                 [ones]
τῷ   θυσιαστηρίῳ   συμμερίζονται;   14 οὕτως
²the   ³altar   ¹partake with?   So
καὶ   ὁ   κύριος   διέταξεν   τοῖς   τὸ   εὐαγγέλιον
also   the   Lord   ordained   the [ones] ²the   ³gospel
καταγγέλλουσιν   ἐκ   τοῦ   εὐαγγελίου   ζῆν.
¹announcing   ⁵of   ⁶the   ⁷gospel   ⁴to live.
15 ἐγὼ   δὲ   οὐ   κέχρημαι   οὐδενὶ   τούτων.
But I   have not used   *not* one   of these
                                                     things.
Οὐκ   ἔγραψα   δὲ   ταῦτα   ἵνα   οὕτως   γένηται
And I did not write   these   in order   so   it might be
                               things that
ἐν   ἐμοί·   καλὸν   γάρ   μοι   μᾶλλον   ἀποθανεῖν
in   me;   for good [it is] to me   rather   to die
ἢ   —   τὸ   καύχημά   μου   οὐδεὶς   κενώσει.
than —   the   boast   of me   no man   shall empty.
16 ἐὰν   γὰρ   εὐαγγελίζωμαι,   οὐκ   ἔστιν
For if   I preach good news,   there is not
                                          — I have no boast;
μοι   καύχημα·   ἀνάγκη   γάρ   μοι   ἐπίκειται·
to me   boast;ᵉ   for necessity   ²me   ¹is laid on;
οὐαὶ   γάρ   μοί   ἐστιν   ἐὰν   μὴ   εὐαγγελίσωμαι.
for woe   ²to me   ¹is   if   I do not preach good tidings.
17 εἰ   γὰρ   ἑκὼν   τοῦτο   πράσσω,   μισθὸν
For if   willingly   ²this   ¹I do,   ²a reward
ἔχω·   εἰ   δὲ   ἄκων,   οἰκονομίαν   πεπίστευμαι.
¹I have;   but if   unwillingly, ²a stewardship ¹I have been
                                             entrusted [with].
18 τίς   οὖν   μού   ἐστιν   ὁ   μισθός;   ἵνα
What therefore ⁴of me   ¹is   ²the   ³reward?   *in order
                                                     that*
εὐαγγελιζόμενος   ἀδάπανον   θήσω   τὸ
preaching good tidings   ⁴without charge ¹I may place ²the
εὐαγγέλιον,   εἰς   τὸ   μὴ   καταχρήσασθαι
³good tidings,   so as†   not   to use to the full
τῇ   ἐξουσίᾳ   μου   ἐν   τῷ   εὐαγγελίῳ.
the   authority   of me   in   the   good tidings.
19 Ἐλεύθερος   γὰρ   ὢν   ἐκ   πάντων   πᾶσιν
For ²free   ¹being of   all men   ²to all men
ἐμαυτὸν   ἐδούλωσα,   ἵνα   τοὺς   πλείονας
¹myself   ¹I enslaved, in order that the   more
κερδήσω·   20 καὶ   ἐγενόμην   τοῖς   Ἰουδαίοις
I might gain;   and   I became   to the   Jews
ὡς   Ἰουδαῖος,   ἵνα   Ἰουδαίους   κερδήσω·
as   a Jew,   in order that Jews   I might gain;
τοῖς   ὑπὸ   νόμον   ὡς   ὑπὸ   νόμον,   μὴ   ὢν
to the   under   law   as   under   law,   not being
ones
αὐτὸς   ὑπὸ   νόμον,   ἵνα   τοὺς   ὑπὸ   νόμον
[my]self   under   law,   in order   the   under   law
                          that   ones

you, is it too much if we reap a material harvest from you? 12If others have this right of support from you, shouldn't we have it all the more?
But we did not use this right. On the contrary, we put up with anything rather than hinder the gospel of Christ. 13Don't you know that those who work in the temple get their food from the temple, and those who serve at the altar share in what is offered on the altar? 14In the same way, the Lord has commanded that those who preach the gospel should receive their living from the gospel.
15But I have not used any of these rights. And I am not writing this in the hope that you will do such things for me. I would rather die than have anyone deprive me of this boast. 16Yet when I preach the gospel, I cannot boast, for I am compelled to preach. Woe to me if I do not preach the gospel! 17If I preach voluntarily, I have a reward; if not voluntarily, I am simply discharging the trust committed to me. 18What then is my reward? Just this: that in preaching the gospel I may offer it free of charge, and so not make use of my rights in preaching it.
19Though I am free and belong to no man, I make myself a slave to everyone, to win as many as possible. 20To the Jews I became like a Jew, to win the Jews. To those under the law I became like one under the law (though I myself am not under the law), so as to win those under the law. 21To

21to those who are without law, as without law, though not being without the law of God but under the law of Christ, that I might win those who are without law.

22To the weak I became weak, that I might win the weak; I have become all things to all men, that I may by all means save some.

23And I do all things for the sake of the gospel, that I may become a fellow partaker of it.

24Do you not know that those who run in a race all run, but *only* one receives the prize? Run in such a way that you may win.

25And everyone who competes in the games exercises self-control in all things. They then *do it* to receive a perishable wreath, but we an imperishable.

26Therefore I run in such a way, as not without aim; I box in such a way, as not beating the air;

27but I buffet my body and make it my slave, lest possibly, after I have preached to others, I myself should be disqualified.

κερδήσω· **21** τοῖς ἀνόμοις ὡς ἄνομος,
I might gain; to the ones without law as without law,

μὴ ὢν ἄνομος θεοῦ ἀλλ' ἔννομος Χριστοῦ,
not being without of God but under of Christ,
[the] law [the] law

ἵνα κερδάνω τοὺς ἀνόμους· **22** ἐγενόμην
in order I may gain the ones without law; I became
that

τοῖς ἀσθενέσιν ἀσθενής, ἵνα τοὺς ἀσθενεῖς
²to the ²weak ¹weak, in order the weak
that

κερδήσω· τοῖς πᾶσιν γέγονα πάντα, ἵνα
I might gain; - to all men I have all in order
become things, that

πάντως τινὰς σώσω. **23** πάντα δὲ ποιῶ
in any case ²some ¹I might save. But all things I do

διὰ τὸ εὐαγγέλιον, ἵνα συγκοινωνὸς αὐτοῦ
because the good tidings, in order ²a joint partaker ³of it
of that

γένωμαι. **24** Οὐκ οἴδατε ὅτι οἱ ἐν
¹I may become. Know ye not that the [ones] ²in

σταδίῳ τρέχοντες πάντες μὲν τρέχουσιν,
²a racecourse ¹running all indeed run,

εἷς δὲ λαμβάνει τὸ βραβεῖον; οὕτως
but one receives the prize? So

τρέχετε ἵνα καταλάβητε. **25** πᾶς δὲ ὁ
run in order that ye may obtain. And everyone

ἀγωνιζόμενος πάντα ἐγκρατεύεται, ἐκεῖνοι
struggling [in] all things exercises self-control, those

μὲν οὖν ἵνα φθαρτὸν στέφανον λάβωσιν,
indeed there- in order ²a corruptible ³crown ¹they may
fore that receive,

ἡμεῖς δὲ ἄφθαρτον. **26** ἐγὼ τοίνυν οὕτως
but we an incorruptible. I accordingly so

τρέχω ὡς οὐκ ἀδήλως, οὕτως πυκτεύω
run as not unclearly, so I box

ὡς οὐκ ἀέρα δέρων· **27** ἀλλὰ ὑπωπιάζω
as not ²air ¹beating; but I treat severely

μου τὸ σῶμα καὶ δουλαγωγῶ, μή πως
of me the body and lead [it] as a slave, lest

ἄλλοις κηρύξας αὐτὸς ἀδόκιμος γένωμαι.
to others having pro- ²[my]self ³disapproved ¹I ³may
claimed ⁴become.

those not having the law I became like one not having the law (though I am not free from God's law but am under Christ's law), so as to win those not having the law. 22To the weak I became weak, to win the weak. I have become all things to all men so that by all possible means I might save some. 23I do all this for the sake of the gospel, that I may share in its blessings.

24Do you not know that in a race all the runners run, but only one gets the prize? Run in such a way as to get the prize. 25Everyone who competes in the games goes into strict training. They do it to get a crown that will not last; but we do it to get a crown that will last forever. 26Therefore I do not run like a man running aimlessly; I do not fight like a man beating the air. 27No, I beat my body and make it my slave so that after I have preached to others, I myself will not be disqualified for the prize.

Chapter 10

Avoid Israel's Mistakes

FOR I do not want you to be unaware, brethren, that our fathers were all under the cloud, and all passed through the sea;

2and all ᵐwere baptized into Moses in the cloud and in the sea;

3and all ate the same spiritual food;

4and all drank the same spiritual drink, for they were drinking from a spiritual rock which followed them; and the rock was Christ.

5Nevertheless, with most of them God was not well-pleased; for they were laid low in the wilderness.

10 Οὐ θέλω γὰρ ὑμᾶς ἀγνοεῖν, ἀδελφοί,
For I wish not you to be ignorant, brothers,

ὅτι οἱ πατέρες ἡμῶν πάντες ὑπὸ τὴν
that the fathers of us all under the

νεφέλην ἦσαν καὶ πάντες διὰ τῆς θαλάσσης
cloud were and all through the sea

διῆλθον, **2** καὶ πάντες εἰς τὸν Μωϋσῆν
passed through, and all to - ²Moses

ἐβαπτίσαντο ἐν τῇ νεφέλῃ καὶ ἐν τῇ
¹were baptized in the cloud and in the

θαλάσσῃ, **3** καὶ πάντες τὸ αὐτὸ πνευματικὸν
sea, and all ¹the ²same ⁴spiritual

βρῶμα ἔφαγον, **4** καὶ πάντες τὸ αὐτὸ
⁵food ¹ate, and all ²the ³same

πνευματικὸν ἔπιον πόμα· ἔπινον γὰρ ἐκ
⁴spiritual ¹drank ²drink; for they drank of

πνευματικῆς ἀκολουθούσης πέτρας, ἡ πέτρα
a spiritual ²following ¹rock, ²the ³rock

δὲ ἦν ὁ Χριστός. **5** Ἀλλ' οὐκ ἐν τοῖς
¹and was *the* Christ. But ⁷not ¹in(with) ²the

πλείοσιν αὐτῶν εὐδόκησεν ὁ θεός·
³majority ⁴of them ⁶was ⁵well pleased - ⁵God;

κατεστρώθησαν γὰρ ἐν τῇ ἐρήμῳ.
for they were scattered in the desert.

Warnings From Israel's History

FOR I do not want you to be ignorant of the fact, brothers, that our forefathers were all under the cloud and that they all passed through the sea. 2They were all baptized into Moses in the cloud and in the sea. 3They all ate the same spiritual food 4and drank the same spiritual drink; for they drank from the spiritual rock that accompanied them, and that rock was Christ. 5Nevertheless, God was not pleased with most of them; their bodies were scattered over the desert.

ᵐ Some ancient mss. read *received baptism*

Chapter 10

6Now these things happened as examples for us, that we should not crave evil things, as they also craved.

7And do not be idolaters, as some of them were; as it is written, "THE PEOPLE SAT DOWN TO EAT AND DRINK, AND STOOD UP TO PLAY."

8Nor let us act immorally, as some of them did, and twenty-three thousand fell in one day.

9Nor let us try the Lord, as some of them did, and were destroyed by the serpents.

10Nor grumble, as some of them did, and were destroyed by the destroyer.

11Now these things happened to them as an example, and they were written for our instruction, upon whom the ends of the ages have come.

12Therefore let him who thinks he stands take heed lest he fall.

13No temptation has overtaken you but such as is common to man; and God is faithful, who will not allow you to be tempted beyond what you are able, but with the temptation will provide the way of escape also, that you may be able to endure it.

14Therefore, my beloved, flee from idolatry.

15I speak as to wise men; you judge what I say.

16Is not the cup of blessing which we bless a sharing in the blood of Christ? Is not the bread which we break a sharing in the body of Christ?

17Since there is one bread, we who are many

---

6 ταῦτα δὲ τύποι ἡμῶν ἐγενήθησαν, εἰς
Now these things types of us were, for

τὸ μὴ εἶναι ἡμᾶς ἐπιθυμητὰς κακῶν,
the not to be us[b] longers after evil things,
=so that we should not be . . .

καθὼς κἀκεῖνοι ἐπεθύμησαν. **7** μηδὲ
as those indeed longed. Neither

εἰδωλολάτραι γίνεσθε, καθώς τινες αὐτῶν·
idolaters be ye, as some of them;

ὥσπερ γέγραπται· ἐκάθισεν ὁ λαὸς φαγεῖν
as it has been written: Sat the people to eat

καὶ πεῖν, καὶ ἀνέστησαν παίζειν. **8** μηδὲ
and to drink, and stood up to play. Neither

πορνεύωμεν, καθώς τινες αὐτῶν ἐπόρνευσαν
let us commit as some of them committed
fornication, fornication

καὶ ἔπεσαν μιᾷ ἡμέρᾳ εἴκοσι τρεῖς
and fell in one day twenty-three

χιλιάδες. **9** μηδὲ ἐκπειράζωμεν τὸν κύριον,
thousands. Neither let us overtempt the Lord,

καθώς τινες αὐτῶν ἐπείρασαν καὶ ὑπὸ
as some of them tempted and by

τῶν ὄφεων ἀπώλλυντο. **10** μηδὲ γογγύζετε,
the serpents were destroyed. Neither murmur ye,

καθάπερ τινὲς αὐτῶν ἐγόγγυσαν, καὶ
even as some of them murmured, and

ἀπώλοντο ὑπὸ τοῦ ὀλεθρευτοῦ. **11** ταῦτα
were destroyed by the destroyer. Now these things

τυπικῶς συνέβαινεν ἐκείνοις, ἐγράφη δὲ
³typically ¹happened ²to those men, and was(were)
written

πρὸς νουθεσίαν ἡμῶν, εἰς οὓς τὰ
for admonition of us, to whom the

τέλη τῶν αἰώνων κατήντηκεν. **12** Ὥστε
ends of the ages has(ve) arrived. So as

ὁ δοκῶν ἑστάναι βλεπέτω μὴ πέσῃ.
the thinking to stand let him look lest he falls.
[one]

13 πειρασμὸς ὑμᾶς οὐκ εἴληφεν εἰ μὴ
Temptation you has not taken except

ἀνθρώπινος· πιστὸς δὲ ὁ θεός, ὃς οὐκ
[what is] human; but faithful [is] – God, who not

ἐάσει ὑμᾶς πειρασθῆναι ὑπὲρ ὃ δύνασθε,
will allow you to be tempted beyond what you are able
[to bear],

ἀλλὰ ποιήσει σὺν τῷ πειρασμῷ καὶ τὴν
but will make with the temptation also the

ἔκβασιν τοῦ δύνασθαι ὑπενεγκεῖν.
way out to be able to endure.[d]
=so that ye may be able . . .

14 Διόπερ, ἀγαπητοί μου, φεύγετε ἀπὸ
Wherefore, beloved of me, flee ye from

τῆς εἰδωλολατρίας. **15** ὡς φρονίμοις λέγω·
– idolatry. ²As ³to prudent men ¹I say;

κρίνατε ὑμεῖς ὃ φημι. **16** Τὸ ποτήριον
judge ye what I say. The cup

τῆς εὐλογίας ὃ εὐλογοῦμεν, οὐχὶ κοινωνία
– of blessing which we bless, ²not ³a communion

ἐστὶν τοῦ αἵματος τοῦ Χριστοῦ; τὸν
¹is it of the blood – of Christ? the

ἄρτον ὃν κλῶμεν, οὐχὶ κοινωνία τοῦ
bread which we break, ²not ³a communion ⁴of the

σώματος τοῦ Χριστοῦ ἐστιν; **17** ὅτι εἷς
⁵body – ⁶of Christ ¹is it? Because ⁴one

ἄρτος, ἓν σῶμα οἱ πολλοί ἐσμεν· οἱ γὰρ
⁵bread, ⁶one ⁷body ²the ³many ¹we are; – for

6Now these things occurred as examples[u] to keep us from setting our hearts on evil things as they did. 7Do not be idolaters, as some of them were; as it is written: "The people sat down to eat and drink and got up to indulge in pagan revelry."[v] 8We should not commit sexual immorality, as some of them did—and in one day twenty-three thousand of them died. 9We should not test the Lord, as some of them did —and were killed by snakes. 10And do not grumble, as some of them did— and were killed by the destroying angel.

11These things happened to them as examples and were written down as warnings for us, on whom the fulfillment of the ages has come. 12So, if you think you are standing firm, be careful that you don't fall! 13No temptation has seized you except what is common to man. And God is faithful; he will not let you be tempted beyond what you can bear. But when you are tempted, he will also provide a way out so that you can stand up under it.

Idol Feasts and the Lord's Supper

14Therefore, my dear friends, flee from idolatry. 15I speak to sensible people; judge for yourselves what I say. 16Is not the cup of thanksgiving for which we give thanks a participation in the blood of Christ? And is not the bread that we break a participation in the body of Christ? 17Because there is one loaf, we, who are many, are one

---

[u]6 Or *types*; also in verse 11
[v]7 Exodus 32:6

are one body; for we all partake of the one bread.

18Look at the nation Israel; are not those who eat the sacrifices sharers in the altar?

19What do I mean then? That a thing sacrificed to idols is anything, or that an idol is anything?

20No, but I say that the things which the Gentiles sacrifice, they sacrifice to demons, and not to God; and I do not want you to become sharers in demons.

21You cannot drink the cup of the Lord and the cup of demons; you cannot partake of the table of the Lord and the table of demons.

22Or do we provoke the Lord to jealousy? We are not stronger than He, are we?

23All things are lawful, but not all things are profitable. All things are lawful, but not all things edify.

24Let no one seek his own good, but that of his neighbor.

25Eat anything that is sold in the meat market, without asking questions for conscience' sake;

26FOR THE EARTH IS THE LORD'S, AND ALL IT CONTAINS.

27If one of the unbelievers invites you, and you wish to go, eat anything that is set before you, without asking questions for conscience' sake.

28But if anyone should say to you, "This is meat sacrificed to idols," do not eat it, for the sake of the one who informed you, and for conscience' sake;

29I mean not your own conscience, but the other man's; for why is my freedom judged by another's conscience?

30If I partake with thank-

πάντες ἐκ τοῦ ἑνὸς ἄρτου μετέχομεν.
all of the one bread we partake.

18 βλέπετε τὸν Ἰσραὴλ κατὰ σάρκα·
See ye - Israel according to [the] flesh;

οὐχ οἱ ἐσθίοντες τὰς θυσίας κοινωνοὶ
²not ³the [ones] ⁴eating ⁵the ⁶sacrifices ⁷sharers

τοῦ θυσιαστηρίου εἰσίν; 19 τί οὖν φημι;
⁸of the ⁹altar ¹are? What therefore do I say?

ὅτι εἰδωλόθυτόν τί ἐστιν; ἢ ὅτι εἰδωλόν
that an idolatrous ²anything ¹is? or that an idol
sacrifice

τί ἐστιν; 20 ἀλλ' ὅτι ἃ θύουσιν,
²anything ¹is? but that [the] things which sacrifice,

δαιμονίοις καὶ οὐ θεῷ θύουσιν· οὐ θέλω
to demons and not to God they sacrifice; ²not ¹I wish

δὲ ὑμᾶς κοινωνοὺς τῶν δαιμονίων γίνεσθαι.
¹and you sharers of the demons to become.

21 οὐ δύνασθε ποτήριον κυρίου πίνειν
Ye cannot ²a cup ³of [the] Lord ¹to drink

καὶ ποτήριον δαιμονίων· οὐ δύνασθε
and a cup of demons; ye cannot

τραπέζης κυρίου μετέχειν καὶ τραπέζης
²of a table ³of [the] Lord ¹to partake and of a table

δαιμονίων. 22 ἢ παραζηλοῦμεν τὸν κύριον;
of demons. Or do we make jealous the Lord?

μὴ ἰσχυρότεροι αὐτοῦ ἐσμεν;
Not ²stronger [than] ³he ¹are we?

23 Πάντα ἔξεστιν, ἀλλ' οὐ πάντα
All things [are] lawful, but not all things

συμφέρει· πάντα ἔξεστιν, ἀλλ' οὐ πάντα
are] expedient; all things lawful, but not all things
[are]

οἰκοδομεῖ. 24 μηδεὶς τὸ ἑαυτοῦ ζητείτω
edifies(fy). No one the thing of himself let him seek

ἀλλὰ τὸ τοῦ ἑτέρου. 25 Πᾶν τὸ ἐν
but the thing of the other. Everything ²in

μακέλλῳ πωλούμενον ἐσθίετε μηδὲν
³a meat market ¹being sold eat ye ²nothing

ἀνακρίνοντες διὰ τὴν συνείδησιν· 26 τοῦ
¹examining because of - conscience; ²of the

κυρίου γὰρ ἡ γῆ καὶ τὸ πλήρωμα
³Lord ¹for the earth and the fulness

αὐτῆς. 27 εἴ τις καλεῖ ὑμᾶς τῶν ἀπίστων
of it. If anyone invites you of the unbelievers

καὶ θέλετε πορεύεσθαι, πᾶν τὸ παρατι-
and ye wish to go, ²everything ³being set

θέμενον ὑμῖν ἐσθίετε μηδὲν ἀνακρίνοντες
before ⁴you ¹eat ⁵nothing ⁶examining

διὰ τὴν συνείδησιν. 28 ἐὰν δέ τις ὑμῖν
because - conscience. But if anyone ²to you
of

εἴπῃ· τοῦτο ἱερόθυτόν ἐστιν, μὴ ἐσθίετε
¹says: This ²slain in sacrifice ¹is, do not eat

δι' ἐκεῖνον τὸν μηνύσαντα καὶ τὴν
because that the pointing out and -
of man [one]

συνείδησιν· 29 συνείδησιν δὲ λέγω οὐχὶ
conscience: ³conscience ¹but ²I say not

τὴν ἑαυτοῦ ἀλλὰ τὴν τοῦ ἑτέρου. ἱνατί
the one of himself but the one of the other.* why

γὰρ ἡ ἐλευθερία μου κρίνεται ὑπὸ ἄλλης
For the freedom of me is judged by ²of another

συνειδήσεως; 30 εἰ ἐγὼ χάριτι μετέχω,
¹conscience? If I by grace partake,

---

body, for we all partake of the one loaf.

18Consider the people of Israel: Do not those who eat the sacrifices participate in the altar? 19Do I mean then that a sacrifice offered to an idol is anything, or that an idol is anything? 20No, but the sacrifices of pagans are offered to demons, not to God, and I do not want you to be participants with demons. 21You cannot drink the cup of the Lord and the cup of demons too; you cannot have a part in both the Lord's table and the table of demons. 22Are we trying to arouse the Lord's jealousy? Are we stronger than he?

The Believer's Freedom

23"Everything is permissible"—but not everything is beneficial. "Everything is permissible"—but not everything is constructive. 24Nobody should seek his own good, but the good of others.

25Eat anything sold in the meat market without raising questions of conscience, 26for, "The earth is the Lord's, and everything in it." ʷ

27If some unbeliever invites you to a meal and you want to go, eat whatever is put before you without raising questions of conscience. 28But if anyone says to you, "This has been offered in sacrifice," then do not eat it, both for the sake of the man who told you and for conscience' sake ˣ—29the other man's conscience, I mean, not yours. For why should my freedom be judged by another's conscience? 30If I take part in the meal with

---

* That is, not the conscience of the person invited, to whom the apostle's words are addressed, but the conscience of the person "pointing out."

ʷ26 Psalm 24:1
ˣ28 Some manuscripts *conscience' sake, for "the earth is the Lord's and everything in it"*

fulness, why am I slandered concerning that for which I give thanks? 31Whether, then, you eat or drink or whatever you do, do all to the glory of God. 32Give no offense either to Jews or to Greeks or to the church of God; 33just as I also please all men in all things, not seeking my own profit, but the *profit* of the many, that they may be saved.

τί βλασφημοῦμαι ὑπὲρ οὗ ἐγὼ εὐχαριστῶ;
why   am I evil   because   what   I   give thanks
  spoken of   of   [for]?

31 Εἴτε οὖν ἐσθίετε εἴτε πίνετε εἴτε
  Whether therefore   ye eat   or   ye drink   or

τι ποιεῖτε, πάντα εἰς δόξαν θεοῦ ποιεῖτε.
what   ye do,   all things   to   [the] glory   of God   do ye.
[ever]

32 ἀπρόσκοποι καὶ Ἰουδαίοις γίνεσθε καὶ
  ²Without offence   ³both   ⁴to Jews   ¹be ye   ⁵and

Ἕλλησιν καὶ τῇ ἐκκλησίᾳ τοῦ θεοῦ,
⁶to Greeks   and   to the   church   -   of God,

33 καθὼς κἀγὼ πάντα πᾶσιν ἀρέσκω,
  as   I also   [in] all things   all men   please,

μὴ ζητῶν τὸ ἐμαυτοῦ σύμφορον ἀλλὰ
not   seeking   the   of myself   advantage   but

thankfulness, why am I denounced because of something I thank God for? 31So whether you eat or drink or whatever you do, do it all for the glory of God. 32Do not cause anyone to stumble, whether Jews, Greeks or the church of God— 33even as I try to please everybody in every way. For I am not seeking my own good but the good of many, so that they may be saved. 1Follow my example, as I follow the example of Christ.

Chapter 11

Christian Order

BE imitators of me, just as I also am of Christ. 2Now I praise you because you remember me in everything, and hold firmly to the traditions, just as I delivered them to you. 3But I want you to understand that Christ is the head of every man, and the man is the head of a woman, and God is the head of Christ. 4Every man who has *something* on his head while praying or prophesying, disgraces his head. 5But every woman who has her head uncovered while praying or prophesying, disgraces her head; for she is one and the same with her whose head is shaved. 6For if a woman does not cover her head, let her also have her hair cut off; but if it is disgraceful for a woman to have her hair cut off or her head shaved, let her cover her head. 7For a man ought not to have his head covered, since he is the image and glory of God; but the woman is the glory of man. 8For man does not originate from woman, but woman from man; 9for indeed man was not

τὸ τῶν πολλῶν, ἵνα σωθῶσιν. 11 μιμηταί
the   of the   many,   in order   they may   Imitators
(that)   that   be saved.

μου γίνεσθε, καθὼς κἀγὼ Χριστοῦ.
of me   be ye,   as   I also [am]   of Christ.

2 Ἐπαινῶ δὲ ὑμᾶς ὅτι πάντα μου
  But I praise   you   because   ²all things   ³of me

μέμνησθε καὶ καθὼς παρέδωκα ὑμῖν τὰς
¹ye have   and   ⁴as   ⁵I delivered   ⁴to you   ²the
remembered

παραδόσεις κατέχετε. 3 Θέλω δὲ ὑμᾶς
³traditions   ¹ye hold fast.   But I wish   you

εἰδέναι ὅτι παντὸς ἀνδρὸς ἡ κεφαλὴ ὁ
to know   that   ⁵of every   ⁶man   ³the   ⁴head   -

Χριστός ἐστιν, κεφαλὴ δὲ γυναικὸς ὁ
¹Christ   ²is,   and [the] head   of a woman   the

ἀνήρ, κεφαλὴ δὲ τοῦ Χριστοῦ ὁ θεός.
man,   and [the] head   of Christ   -   God.

4 πᾶς ἀνὴρ προσευχόμενος ἢ προφητεύων
  Every   man   praying   or   prophesying

κατὰ κεφαλῆς ἔχων καταισχύνει τὴν
³down over   ⁴[his] head   ¹having   shames   the
      ²[anything]

κεφαλὴν αὐτοῦ. 5 πᾶσα δὲ γυνὴ προσ-
head   of him.   But every   woman   pray-

ευχομένη ἢ προφητεύουσα ἀκατακαλύπτῳ
ing   or   prophesying   unveiled

τῇ κεφαλῇ καταισχύνει τὴν κεφαλὴν αὐτῆς·
¹with   ²head   shames   the   head   of her;
the(her)

ἓν γάρ ἐστιν καὶ τὸ αὐτὸ τῇ ἐξυρημένῃ.
for   ²one   ¹it is   and   the   same with   the having been
           thing   woman   shaved.

6 εἰ γὰρ οὐ κατακαλύπτεται γυνή, καὶ
  For if   ²is not veiled   ¹a woman,   also

κειράσθω· εἰ δὲ αἰσχρὸν γυναικὶ τὸ
let her be shorn;   but if   shameful   for a woman   -

κείρασθαι ἢ ξυρᾶσθαι, κατακαλυπτέσθω.
to be shorn   or   *to be* shaved,   let her be veiled.

7 ἀνὴρ μὲν γὰρ οὐκ ὀφείλει κατα-
  For a man indeed   ought not   to be

καλύπτεσθαι τὴν κεφαλήν, εἰκὼν καὶ δόξα
veiled   the   head,ᵇ   ²[the] image   ³and   ⁴glory

θεοῦ ὑπάρχων· ἡ γυνὴ δὲ δόξα ἀνδρός
⁵of God   ¹being;   but the woman   ²[the] glory   ³of a man

ἐστιν. 8 οὐ γάρ ἐστιν ἀνὴρ ἐκ γυναικός,
¹is.   For ³not   ²is   ¹man   of   woman,

ἀλλὰ γυνὴ ἐξ ἀνδρός· 9 καὶ γὰρ οὐκ
but   woman   of   man;   for indeed   ³not

man. 8For man did not come from woman, but woman from man; 9neither was man created for wom-

thankfulness, why am I denounced because of something I thank God for? 31So whether you eat or drink or whatever you do, do it all for the glory of God. 32Do not cause anyone to stumble, whether Jews, Greeks or the church of God— 33even as I try to please everybody in every way. For I am not seeking my own good but the good of many, so that they may be saved. 1Follow my example, as I follow the example of Christ.

Propriety in Worship

2I praise you for remembering me in everything and for holding to the teachings,ʸ just as I passed them on to you. 3Now I want you to realize that the head of every man is Christ, and the head of the woman is man, and the head of Christ is God. 4Every man who prays or prophesies with his head covered dishonors his head. 5And every woman who prays or prophesies with her head uncovered dishonors her head—it is just as though her head were shaved. 6If a woman does not cover her head, she should have her hair cut off; and if it is a disgrace for a woman to have her hair cut or shaved off, she should cover her head. 7A man ought not to cover his head,ᶻ since he is the image and glory of God; but the woman is the glory of man. 8For man did not come from woman, but woman from man; 9neither was man created for wom-

ʸ2 Or *traditions*
ᶻ4-7 Or *4Every man who prays or prophesies with long hair dishonors his head. 5And every woman who prays or prophesies with no covering of hair on her head dishonors her head—she is just like one of the "shorn women." 6If a woman has no covering, let her be for now with short hair, but since it is a disgrace for a woman to have her hair shorn or shaved, she should grow it again. 7A man ought not to have long hair*

created for the woman's sake, but woman for the man's sake.

10Therefore the woman ought to have *a symbol of* authority on her head, because of the angels.

11However, in the Lord, neither is woman independent of man, nor is man independent of woman.

12For as the woman originates from the man, so also the man *has his birth* through the woman; and all things originate from God.

13Judge for yourselves: is it proper for a woman to pray to God *with head* uncovered?

14Does not even nature itself teach you that if a man has long hair, it is a dishonor to him,

15but if a woman has long hair, it is a glory to her? For her hair is given to her for a covering.

16But if one is inclined to be contentious, we have no other practice, nor have the churches of God.

17But in giving this instruction, I do not praise you, because you come together not for the better but for the worse.

18For, in the first place, when you come together as a church, I hear that divisions exist among you; and in part, I believe it.

19For there must also be factions among you, in order that those who are approved may have become evident among you.

20Therefore when you meet together, it is not to eat the Lord's Supper,

21for in your eating each one takes his own supper first; and one is hungry and

---

ἐκτίσθη ἀνὴρ διὰ τὴν γυναῖκα, ἀλλὰ
²was ⁴created ¹man because of the woman, but

γυνὴ διὰ τὸν ἄνδρα. 10 διὰ τοῦτο
woman because of the man. Therefore

ὀφείλει ἡ γυνὴ ἐξουσίαν ἔχειν ἐπὶ τῆς
ought the woman authority to have on the

κεφαλῆς διὰ τοὺς ἀγγέλους. 11 πλὴν
head because of the angels. Nevertheless

οὔτε γυνὴ χωρὶς ἀνδρὸς οὔτε ἀνὴρ χωρὶς
neither woman without man nor man without

γυναικὸς ἐν κυρίῳ· 12 ὥσπερ γὰρ ἡ
woman in [the] Lord; for as the

γυνὴ ἐκ τοῦ ἀνδρός, οὕτως καὶ ὁ ἀνὴρ
woman of the man, so also the man

διὰ τῆς γυναικός· τὰ δὲ πάντα ἐκ τοῦ
through the woman; - but all things of -

θεοῦ. 13 Ἐν ὑμῖν αὐτοῖς κρίνατε· πρέπον
God. Among you [your]selves judge: ²fitting

ἐστὶν γυναῖκα ἀκατακάλυπτον τῷ θεῷ
¹is it ³[for] ⁴a woman unveiled - ⁵to God

προσεύχεσθαι; 14 οὐδὲ ἡ φύσις αὐτὴ
⁵to pray? Not - nature [her]self

διδάσκει ὑμᾶς ὅτι ἀνὴρ μὲν ἐὰν κομᾷ,
teaches you that a man indeed if he wears his hair long,

ἀτιμία αὐτῷ ἐστιν, 15 γυνὴ δὲ ἐὰν
²a dishonour ³to him ¹it is, but a woman if

κομᾷ, δόξα αὐτῇ ἐστιν; ὅτι ἡ κόμη
she wears ²a glory ³to her ¹it is? because the long hair
her hair long,

ἀντὶ περιβολαίου δέδοται αὐτῇ. 16 Εἰ
instead of a veil has been given to her. if

δέ τις δοκεῖ φιλόνεικος εἶναι, ἡμεῖς
But anyone thinks ²contentious ¹to be, we

τοιαύτην συνήθειαν οὐκ ἔχομεν, οὐδὲ αἱ
²such ³a custom ¹have not, neither the

ἐκκλησίαι τοῦ θεοῦ.
churches - of God.

17 Τοῦτο δὲ παραγγέλλων οὐκ ἐπαινῶ
But this charging I do not praise

ὅτι οὐκ εἰς τὸ κρεῖσσον ἀλλὰ εἰς τὸ
because not for the better but for the

ἧσσον συνέρχεσθε. 18 πρῶτον μὲν γὰρ
worse ye come together. For firstly indeed

συνερχομένων ὑμῶν ἐν ἐκκλησίᾳ ἀκούω
coming together youᵃ in church I hear
=when ye come together

σχίσματα ἐν ὑμῖν ὑπάρχειν, καὶ μέρος
divisions among you to be, and ¹part

τι πιστεύω. 19 δεῖ γὰρ καὶ αἱρέσεις
²some I believe. For it behoves indeed sects

ἐν ὑμῖν εἶναι, ἵνα [καὶ] οἱ δόκιμοι
among you to be, in order also the approved
that ones

φανεροὶ γένωνται ἐν ὑμῖν. 20 Συν-
manifest may become among you. Coming

ερχομένων οὖν ὑμῶν ἐπὶ τὸ αὐτὸ οὐκ
together therefore youᵃ together not
=When therefore ye come

ἔστιν κυριακὸν δεῖπνον φαγεῖν· 21 ἕκαστος
it is of the Lord* a supper to eat; ²each one

γὰρ τὸ ἴδιον δεῖπνον προλαμβάνει ἐν
¹for the(his) own supper takes before in

τῷ φαγεῖν, καὶ ὃς μὲν πεινᾷ, ὃς δὲ
- to eat(eating), and one† hungers, another†

---

an, but woman for man.

10For this reason, and because of the angels, the woman ought to have a sign of authority on her head.

11In the Lord, however, woman is not independent of man, nor is man independent of woman. 12For as woman came from man, so also man is born of woman. But everything comes from God. 13Judge for yourselves: Is it proper for a woman to pray to God with her head uncovered? 14Does not the very nature of things teach you that if a man has long hair, it is a disgrace to him, 15but that if a woman has long hair, it is her glory? For long hair is given to her as a covering. 16If anyone wants to be contentious about this, we have no other practice—nor do the churches of God.

The Lord's Supper

17In the following directives I have no praise for you, for your meetings do more harm than good. 18In the first place, I hear that when you come together as a church, there are divisions among you, and to some extent I believe it. 19No doubt there have to be differences among you to show which of you have God's approval. 20When you come together, it is not the Lord's Supper you eat, 21for as you eat, each of you goes ahead without waiting for anybody else. One remains hungry, an-

---

* Note that κυριακός is an adjective, for which no exact English equivalent is available. Only other occurrence in N.T., Rev. 1. 10.

another is drunk.

22What! Do you not have houses in which to eat and drink? Or do you despise the church of God, and shame those who have nothing? What shall I say to you? Shall I praise you? In this I will not praise you.

The Lord's Supper

23For I received from the Lord that which I also delivered to you, that the Lord Jesus in the night in which He was betrayed took bread;

24and when He had given thanks, He broke it, and said, "This is My body, which *n*is for you; do this in remembrance of Me."

25In the same way *He took* the cup also, after supper, saying, "This cup is the new covenant in My blood; do this, as often as you drink *it*, in remembrance of Me."

26For as often as you eat this bread and drink the cup, you proclaim the Lord's death until He comes.

27Therefore whoever eats the bread or drinks the cup of the Lord in an unworthy manner, shall be guilty of the body and the blood of the Lord.

28But let a man examine himself, and so let him eat of the bread and drink of the cup.

29For he who eats and drinks, eats and drinks judgment to himself, if he does not judge the body rightly.

30For this reason many among you are weak and sick, and a number sleep.

31But if we judged ourselves rightly, we should not be judged.

32But when we are judged by the Lord, we are disciplined in order that we may not be condemned

---

μεθύει. **22** μὴ γὰρ οἰκίας οὐκ ἔχετε
is drunken. *Not* indeed ²houses ¹have ye not

εἰς τὸ ἐσθίειν καὶ πίνειν; ἢ τῆς ἐκκλησίας
\- - to eat and to drink? or the church

τοῦ θεοῦ καταφρονεῖτε, καὶ καταισχύνετε
\- of God despise ye, and shame

τοὺς μὴ ἔχοντας; τί εἴπω ὑμῖν; ἐπαινέσω
the not having? What may I say to you? shall I praise
[ones]

ὑμᾶς; ἐν τούτῳ οὐκ ἐπαινῶ. **23** Ἐγὼ
you? In this I praise not. I

γὰρ παρέλαβον ἀπὸ τοῦ κυρίου, ὃ καὶ
For received from the Lord, what also

παρέδωκα ὑμῖν, ὅτι ὁ κύριος Ἰησοῦς
I delivered to you, that the Lord Jesus

ἐν τῇ νυκτὶ ᾗ παρεδίδοτο ἔλαβεν ἄρτον
in the night in which he was took bread
betrayed

24 καὶ εὐχαριστήσας ἔκλασεν καὶ εἶπεν·
and having given thanks broke and said:

τοῦτό μού ἐστιν τὸ σῶμα τὸ ὑπὲρ
This of me is the body - on behalf of

ὑμῶν· τοῦτο ποιεῖτε εἰς τὴν ἐμὴν
you; this do ye for - my

ἀνάμνησιν. **25** ὡσαύτως καὶ τὸ ποτήριον
remembrance. Similarly also the cup

μετὰ τὸ δειπνῆσαι, λέγων· τοῦτο τὸ
after the to sup, saying: This -

ποτήριον ἡ καινὴ διαθήκη ἐστὶν ἐν τῷ
cup ²the ³new ⁴covenant ¹is in -

ἐμῷ αἵματι· τοῦτο ποιεῖτε, ὁσάκις ἐὰν
my blood; this do ye, as often as

πίνητε, εἰς τὴν ἐμὴν ἀνάμνησιν. **26** ὁσάκις
ye drink, for - my remembrance. as often

γὰρ ἐὰν ἐσθίητε τὸν ἄρτον τοῦτον καὶ
For as ye eat this bread and

τὸ ποτήριον πίνητε, τὸν θάνατον τοῦ
²the ³cup ¹drink, the death of the

κυρίου καταγγέλλετε, ἄχρι οὗ ἔλθη.
Lord ye declare, until he comes.

27 Ὥστε ὃς ἂν ἐσθίῃ τὸν ἄρτον ἢ
So as whoever eats the bread or

πίνῃ τὸ ποτήριον τοῦ κυρίου ἀναξίως,
drinks the cup of the Lord unworthily,

ἔνοχος ἔσται τοῦ σώματος καὶ τοῦ
guilty will be of the body and of the

αἵματος τοῦ κυρίου. **28** δοκιμαζέτω δὲ
blood of the Lord. But ¹let ³prove

ἄνθρωπος ἑαυτόν, καὶ οὕτως ἐκ τοῦ
²a man ⁴himself, and so of the

ἄρτου ἐσθιέτω καὶ ἐκ τοῦ ποτηρίου
bread let him eat and of the cup

πινέτω· **29** ὁ γὰρ ἐσθίων καὶ πίνων
let him drink; for the [one] eating and drinking

κρίμα ἑαυτῷ ἐσθίει καὶ πίνει μὴ διακρίνων
⁴judgment ⁵to ¹eats ²and ³drinks not discerning
himself

τὸ σῶμα. **30** διὰ τοῦτο ἐν ὑμῖν πολλοὶ
the body. Therefore among you many

ἀσθενεῖς καὶ ἄρρωστοι καὶ κοιμῶνται
[are] weak and feeble and ²sleep

ἱκανοί. **31** εἰ δὲ ἑαυτοὺς διεκρίνομεν,
¹a number. But if ourselves we discerned,

οὐκ ἂν ἐκρινόμεθα· **32** κρινόμενοι δὲ ὑπὸ
we should not be judged; but being judged by

τοῦ κυρίου παιδευόμεθα, ἵνα μὴ σὺν
the Lord we are chastened, lest with

---

other gets drunk. 22Don't you have homes to eat and drink in? Or do you despise the church of God and humiliate those who have nothing? What shall I say to you? Shall I praise you for this? Certainly not!

23For I received from the Lord what I also passed on to you: The Lord Jesus, on the night he was betrayed, took bread, 24and when he had given thanks, he broke it and said, "This is my body, which is for you; do this in remembrance of me." 25In the same way, after supper he took the cup, saying, "This cup is the new covenant in my blood; do this, whenever you drink it, in remembrance of me." 26For whenever you eat this bread and drink this cup, you proclaim the Lord's death until he comes.

27Therefore, whoever eats the bread or drinks the cup of the Lord in an unworthy manner will be guilty of sinning against the body and blood of the Lord. 28A man ought to examine himself before he eats of the bread and drinks of the cup. 29For anyone who eats and drinks without recognizing the body of the Lord eats and drinks judgment on himself. 30That is why many among you are weak and sick, and a number of you have fallen asleep. 31But if we judged ourselves, we would not come under judgment. 32When we are judged by the Lord, we are being disciplined so that we will not

---

n Some ancient mss. read *is broken*

along with the world.
33So then, my brethren, when you come together to eat, wait for one another.
34If anyone is hungry, let him eat at home, so that you may not come together for judgment. And the remaining matters I shall arrange when I come.

Chapter 12

The Use of Spiritual Gifts

NOW concerning spiritual *gifts*, brethren, I do not want you to be unaware.
2You know that when you were pagans, *you were* led astray to the dumb idols, however you were led.
3Therefore I make known to you, that no one speaking by the Spirit of God says, "Jesus is accursed"; and no one can say, "Jesus is Lord," except by the Holy Spirit.
4Now there are varieties of gifts, but the same Spirit.
5And there are varieties of ministries, and the same Lord.
6And there are varieties of effects, but the same God who works all things in all *persons*.
7But to each one is given the manifestation of the Spirit for the common good.
8For to one is given the word of wisdom through the Spirit, and to another the word of knowledge according to the same Spirit;
9to another faith by the same Spirit, and to another gifts of healing by the one Spirit,
10and to another the effecting of miracles, and to another prophecy, and to another the distinguishing of spirits, to another *various* kinds of tongues, and to another the interpretation of tongues.
11But one and the same Spirit works all these things, distributing to each

τῷ κόσμῳ κατακριθῶμεν. 33 Ὥστε,
the world we are condemned. So as,
ἀδελφοί μου, συνερχόμενοι εἰς τὸ φαγεῖν
brothers of me, coming together for the to eat
ἀλλήλους ἐκδέχεσθε. 34 εἴ τις πεινᾷ,
one another await ye. If anyone hungers,
ἐν οἴκῳ ἐσθιέτω, ἵνα μὴ εἰς κρίμα
at home let him eat, lest to judgment
συνέρχησθε. τὰ δὲ λοιπὰ ὡς ἂν ἔλθω
ye come together. And the remaining matters whenever I come
διατάξομαι.
I will arrange.

12 Περὶ δὲ τῶν πνευματικῶν, ἀδελφοί,
Now about the spiritual matters, brothers,
οὐ θέλω ὑμᾶς ἀγνοεῖν. 2 Οἴδατε ὅτι
I do not wish you to be ignorant. Ye know that
ὅτε ἔθνη ἦτε πρὸς τὰ εἴδωλα τὰ ἄφωνα
when ⁵nations ¹ye were ²to ⁴the ⁷idols - ⁶voiceless
ὡς ἂν ἤγεσθε ἀπαγόμενοι. 3 διὸ γνωρίζω
⁸however ⁹ye were led ¹⁰being led away.⁸ Where- I make fore known
ὑμῖν ὅτι οὐδεὶς ἐν πνεύματι θεοῦ λαλῶν
to you that no one ²by ³[the] Spirit ⁴of God ¹speaking
λέγει· ΑΝΑΘΕΜΑ ΙΗΣΟΥΣ, καὶ οὐδεὶς
says: A CURSE [IS] JESUS, and no one
δύναται εἰπεῖν· ΚΥΡΙΟΣ ΙΗΣΟΥΣ, εἰ μὴ
can to say: LORD JESUS, except
ἐν πνεύματι ἁγίῳ.
by [the] ¹Spirit ¹Holy.
4 Διαιρέσεις δὲ χαρισμάτων εἰσίν, τὸ δὲ αὐτὸ
Now differences of gifts there are, but the same
πνεῦμα· 5 καὶ διαιρέσεις διακονιῶν εἰσιν, καὶ
Spirit; and differences of ministries there are, and
ὁ αὐτὸς κύριος· 6 καὶ διαιρέσεις ἐνεργημάτων
the same Lord; and differences of operations
εἰσίν, ὁ δὲ αὐτὸς θεὸς ὁ ἐνεργῶν τὰ
there are, but the same God - operating -
πάντα ἐν πᾶσιν. 7 ἑκάστῳ δὲ δίδοται
all things in all. But to each one is given
ἡ φανέρωσις τοῦ πνεύματος πρὸς τὸ
the manifestation of the Spirit to the
συμφέρον. 8 ᾧ μὲν γὰρ διὰ τοῦ πνεύματος
profiting. For to one through the Spirit
δίδοται λόγος σοφίας, ἄλλῳ δὲ λόγος
is given a word of wisdom, and to another a word
γνώσεως κατὰ τὸ αὐτὸ πνεῦμα, 9 ἑτέρῳ
of accord- the same Spirit, to knowledge ing to another
πίστις ἐν τῷ αὐτῷ πνεύματι, ἄλλῳ δὲ
faith by the same Spirit, and to another
χαρίσματα ἰαμάτων ἐν τῷ ἑνὶ πνεύματι,
gifts of cures by the one Spirit,
10 ἄλλῳ δὲ ἐνεργήματα δυνάμεων, ἄλλῳ
and to another operations of powers, to another
[δὲ] προφητεία, ἄλλῳ δὲ διακρίσεις πνευ-
and prophecy, and to another discernings of
μάτων, ἑτέρῳ γένη γλωσσῶν, ἄλλῳ δὲ
spirits, to another kinds of tongues, and to another
ἑρμηνεία γλωσσῶν· 11 πάντα δὲ ταῦτα
interpretation of tongues: and ²all ³these things
ἐνεργεῖ τὸ ἓν καὶ τὸ αὐτὸ πνεῦμα,
⁷operates ¹the ²one ³and ⁴the ⁵same ⁶Spirit,

Chapter 12

Spiritual Gifts

NOW about spiritual gifts, brothers, I do not want you to be ignorant. 2You know that when you were pagans, somehow or other you were influenced and led astray to mute idols. 3Therefore I tell you that no one who is speaking by the Spirit of God says, "Jesus be cursed," and no one can say, "Jesus is Lord," except by the Holy Spirit.
4There are different kinds of gifts, but the same Spirit. 5There are different kinds of service, but the same Lord. 6There are different kinds of working, but the same God works all of them in all men.
7Now to each one the manifestation of the Spirit is given for the common good. 8To one there is given through the Spirit the message of wisdom, to another the message of knowledge by means of the same Spirit, 9to another faith by the same Spirit, to another gifts of healing by that one Spirit, 10to another miraculous powers, to another prophecy, to another distinguishing between spirits, to another speaking in different kinds of tongues,ᵃ and to still another the interpretation of tongues.ᵃ 11All these are the work of one and the same Spirit, and he gives

be condemned with the world.
33So then, my brothers, when you come together to eat, wait for each other. 34If anyone is hungry, he should eat at home, so that when you meet together it may not result in judgment.
And when I come I will give further directions.

---

* It is thought that there is a scribal error in this verse; see commentaries on the Greek text. We have been guided by G. G. Findlay, *The Expositor's Greek Testament.*

ᵃ10 Or *languages*; also in verse 28

one individually just as He wills.

12For even as the body is one and *yet* has many members, and all the members of the body, though they are many, are one body, so also is Christ.

13For by one Spirit we were all baptized into one body, whether Jews or Greeks, whether slaves or free, and we were all made to drink of one Spirit.

14For the body is not one member, but many.

15If the foot should say, "Because I am not a hand, I am not *a part* of the body," it is not for this reason any the less *a part* of the body.

16And if the ear should say, "Because I am not an eye, I am not *a part* of the body," it is not for this reason any the less *a part* of the body.

17If the whole body were an eye, where would the hearing be? If the whole were hearing, where would the sense of smell be?

18But now God has placed the members, each one of them, in the body, just as He desired.

19And if they were all one member, where would the body be?

20But now there are many members, but one body.

21And the eye cannot say to the hand, "I have no need of you"; or again the head to the feet, "I have no need of you."

22On the contrary, it is much truer that the members of the body which seem to be weaker are necessary;

23and those *members* of the body, which we deem less honorable, on these we bestow more abundant honor, and our unseemly *members come to* have more abundant seemliness,

διαιροῦν ἰδίᾳ ἑκάστῳ καθὼς βούλεται.
distributing ²separately† ¹to each one as he purposes.

12 Καθάπερ γὰρ τὸ σῶμα ἕν ἐστιν
For as the body ²one ¹is

καὶ μέλη πολλὰ ἔχει, πάντα δὲ τὰ
and ²members ¹many ¹has, but all the

μέλη τοῦ σώματος πολλὰ ὄντα ἕν ἐστιν
members of the body ²many ¹being ⁴one ³is(are)

σῶμα, οὕτως καὶ ὁ Χριστός· **13** καὶ γὰρ
body, so also the Christ; for indeed

ἐν ἑνὶ πνεύματι ἡμεῖς πάντες εἰς ἓν
⁴by ⁵one ⁶Spirit ¹we ²all ⁷into ⁸one

σῶμα ἐβαπτίσθημεν, εἴτε Ἰουδαῖοι εἴτε
⁹body ³were baptized, whether Jews or

Ἕλληνες, εἴτε δοῦλοι εἴτε ἐλεύθεροι, καὶ
Greeks, whether slaves or free, and

πάντες ἓν πνεῦμα ἐποτίσθημεν. **14** καὶ
all one Spirit *we* were given to drink. indeed

γὰρ τὸ σῶμα οὐκ ἔστιν ἓν μέλος ἀλλὰ
For the body is not one member but

πολλά. **15** ἐὰν εἴπῃ ὁ πούς· ὅτι οὐκ
many. If ²says ¹the ²foot: Because not

εἰμὶ χείρ, οὐκ εἰμὶ ἐκ τοῦ σώματος,
I am a hand, I am not of the body,

οὐ παρὰ τοῦτο οὐκ ἔστιν ἐκ τοῦ σώματος.
not for this it is not of the body.

16 καὶ ἐὰν εἴπῃ τὸ οὖς· ὅτι οὐκ εἰμὶ
And if says the ear: Because I am not

ὀφθαλμός, οὐκ εἰμὶ ἐκ τοῦ σώματος,
an eye, I am not of the body,

οὐ παρὰ τοῦτο οὐκ ἔστιν ἐκ τοῦ σώματος.
not for this it is not of the body.

17 εἰ ὅλον τὸ σῶμα ὀφθαλμός, ποῦ
If all the body [was] an eye, where

ἡ ἀκοή; εἰ ὅλον ἀκοή, ποῦ ἡ ὄσφρησις;
[would be] if all ·hearing, where the smelling?
the hearing?

18 νῦν δὲ ὁ θεὸς ἔθετο τὰ μέλη, ἓν
But now - God set the members, ²one

ἕκαστον αὐτῶν ἐν τῷ σώματι καθὼς
¹each of them in the body as

ἠθέλησεν. **19** εἰ δὲ ἦν τὰ πάντα ἓν
he wished. And if ¹was - ¹all one

μέλος, ποῦ τὸ σῶμα; **20** νῦν δὲ πολλὰ
member, where the body? But now many

μὲν μέλη, ἓν δὲ σῶμα. **21** οὐ δύναται
¹indeed ¹members, but one body. ¹cannot

δὲ ὁ ὀφθαλμὸς εἰπεῖν τῇ χειρί· χρείαν
And ¹the² ²eye to say to the hand: Need

σου οὐκ ἔχω, ἢ πάλιν ἡ κεφαλὴ τοῖς
of thee I have not, or again the head to the

ποσίν· χρείαν ὑμῶν οὐκ ἔχω· **22** ἀλλὰ
feet: Need of you I have not; but

πολλῷ μᾶλλον τὰ δοκοῦντα μέλη τοῦ
by much more ¹the ²seeming ³members ⁴of the

σώματος ἀσθενέστερα ὑπάρχειν ἀναγκαῖά ἐστιν,
⁵body ⁷weaker ⁶to be ⁸necessary ⁸is(are),

23 καὶ ἃ δοκοῦμεν ἀτιμότερα εἶναι
and ¹[members] ²we think ⁷less honourable ⁶to be
²which

τοῦ σώματος, τούτοις τιμὴν περισσοτέραν
³of the ⁵body, to these honour more abundant

περιτίθεμεν, καὶ τὰ ἀσχήμονα ἡμῶν
we put round, and the uncomely [members] of us

εὐσχημοσύνην περισσοτέραν ἔχει, **24** τὰ δὲ
⁵comeliness ⁴more abundant ¹has(ve), but th·

them to each one, just as he determines.

One Body, Many Parts

12The body is a unit, though it is made up of many parts; and though all its parts are many, they form one body. So it is with Christ. 13For we were all baptized by[b] one Spirit into one body—whether Jews or Greeks, slave or free—and we were all given the one Spirit to drink.

14Now the body is not made up of one part but of many. 15If the foot should say, "Because I am not a hand, I do not belong to the body," it would not for that reason cease to be part of the body. 16And if the ear should say, "Because I am not an eye, I do not belong to the body," it would not for that reason cease to be part of the body. 17If the whole body were an eye, where would the sense of hearing be? If the whole body were an ear, where would the sense of smell be? 18But in fact God has arranged the parts in the body, every one of them, just as he wanted them to be. 19If they were all one part, where would the body be? 20As it is, there are many parts, but one body. 21The eye cannot say to the hand, "I don't need you!" And the head cannot say to the feet, "I don't need you!" 22On the contrary, those parts of the body that seem to be weaker are indispensable, 23and the parts that we think are less honorable we treat with special honor. And the parts that are unpresentable are treated with special modesty, 24while our

b13 Or *with*; or *in*

24whereas our seemly *members* have no need *of it.* But God has so composed the body, giving more abundant honor to that *member* which lacked, 25that there should be no division in the body, but *that* the members should have the same care for one another. 26And if one member suffers, all the members suffer with it; if *one* member is honored, all the members rejoice with it.

27Now you are Christ's body, and individually members of it. 28And God has appointed in the church, first apostles, second prophets, third teachers, then miracles, then gifts of healings, helps, administrations, *various* kinds of tongues.

29All are not apostles, are they? All are not prophets, are they? All are not teachers, are they? All are not *workers of* miracles, are they?

30All do not have gifts of healings, do they? All do not speak with tongues, do they? All do not interpret, do they?

31But earnestly desire the greater gifts.

And I show you a still more excellent way.

Chapter 13

The Excellence of Love

IF I speak with the tongues of men and of angels, but do not have love, I have become a noisy gong or a clanging cymbal.

2And if I have *the gift of* prophecy, and know all mysteries and all knowledge; and if I have all faith, so as to remove mountains, but do not have love, I am nothing.

3And if I give all my possessions to feed *the poor,* and if I deliver my body *o*to be burned, but do not have love, it profits me nothing.

---

o Some ancient mss. read *that I may boast*

εὐσχήμονα ἡμῶν οὐ χρείαν ἔχει. ἀλλὰ ὁ
comely [members] of us ²no ³need ¹have(ve). But –

θεὸς συνεκέρασεν τὸ σῶμα, τῷ ὑστερουμένῳ
God blended together the body, ⁴to the [member] ⁵lacking

περισσοτέραν δοὺς τιμήν, 25 ἵνα μὴ ᾖ
¹more abundant ¹giving ²honour, lest there be

σχίσμα ἐν τῷ σώματι, ἀλλὰ τὸ αὐτὸ
division in the body, but ⁴the ⁵same

ὑπὲρ ἀλλήλων μεριμνῶσιν τὰ μέλη.
⁶on be-half of ⁷one another ³should care ¹the ²members.

26 καὶ εἴτε πάσχει ἓν μέλος, συμπάσχει
And whether ²suffers ¹one ³member, ⁴suffers with [it]

πάντα τὰ μέλη· εἴτε δοξάζεται μέλος,
⁴all ⁵the ⁶members; or ²is glorified ¹a member,

συγχαίρει πάντα τὰ μέλη. 27 ὑμεῖς
⁵rejoices with [it] ²all ⁴the ³members. ye

δὲ ἐστε σῶμα Χριστοῦ καὶ μέλη ἐκ
And are a body of Christ and members in

μέρους. 28 Καὶ οὓς μὲν ἔθετο ὁ θεὸς
part. And ²some† ²placed – ¹God

ἐν τῇ ἐκκλησίᾳ πρῶτον ἀποστόλους, δεύτε-
in the church firstly apostles, second-

ρον προφήτας, τρίτον διδασκάλους, ἔπειτα
ly prophets, thirdly teachers, then

δυνάμεις, ἔπειτα χαρίσματα ἰαμάτων,
powers, then gifts of cures,

ἀντιλήμψεις, κυβερνήσεις, γένη γλωσσῶν.
helps, governings, kinds of tongues.

29 μὴ πάντες ἀπόστολοι; μὴ πάντες
Not all [are] apostles? not all

προφῆται; μὴ πάντες διδάσκαλοι; μὴ
prophets; not all teachers? not

πάντες δυνάμεις; 30 μὴ πάντες χαρίσματα
all powers? not all ¹gifts

ἔχουσιν ἰαμάτων; μὴ πάντες γλώσσαις
¹have of cures? not all ¹with tongues

λαλοῦσιν; μὴ πάντες διερμηνεύουσιν;
¹speak? not all interpret?

31 ζηλοῦτε δὲ τὰ χαρίσματα τὰ μείζονα.
but desire ye eagerly the ²gifts – ¹greater.

Καὶ ἔτι καθ' ὑπερβολὴν ὁδὸν ὑμῖν
And yet ²according to ³excellence ¹a way ¹to you

δείκνυμι. 13 Ἐὰν ταῖς γλώσσαις τῶν ἀνθρώπων
¹I show. If in the tongues – of men

λαλῶ καὶ τῶν ἀγγέλων, ἀγάπην δὲ
I speak and – of angels, but love

μὴ ἔχω, γέγονα χαλκὸς ἠχῶν ἢ
I have not, I have become ²brass ¹sounding or

κύμβαλον ἀλαλάζον. 2 καὶ ἐὰν ἔχω
cymbal a tinkling. And if I have

προφητείαν καὶ εἰδῶ τὰ μυστήρια πάντα
prophecy and know ²the ¹mysteries ¹all

καὶ πᾶσαν τὴν γνῶσιν, κἂν ἔχω πᾶσαν
and all – knowledge, and if I have all

τὴν πίστιν ὥστε ὄρη μεθιστάναι, ἀγάπην
– faith so as mountains to remove, ¹love

δὲ μὴ ἔχω, οὐθέν εἰμι. 3 κἂν ψωμίσω
¹but I have not, nothing I am. And if I dole out

πάντα τὰ ὑπάρχοντά μου, καὶ ἐὰν παραδῶ
all the goods of me, and if I deliver

τὸ σῶμά μου ἵνα καυθήσομαι, ἀγάπην
the body of me in order that I shall be ¹love
that burned,

δὲ μὴ ἔχω, οὐδέν ὠφελοῦμαι. 4 Ἡ
¹but I have not, nothing I am profited. –

---

presentable parts need no special treatment. But God has combined the members of the body and has given greater honor to the parts that lacked it, 25so that there should be no division in the body, but that its parts should have equal concern for each other. 26If one part suffers, every part suffers with it; if one part is honored, every part rejoices with it.

27Now you are the body of Christ, and each one of you is a part of it. 28And in the church God has appointed first of all apostles, second prophets, third teachers, then workers of miracles, also those having gifts of healing, those able to help others, those with gifts of administration, and those speaking in different kinds of tongues. 29Are all apostles? Are all prophets? Are all teachers? Do all work miracles? 30Do all have gifts of healing? Do all speak in tongues*c*? Do all interpret? 31But eagerly desire*d* the greater gifts.

Love

And now I will show you the most excellent way.

Chapter 13

IF I speak in the tongues*e* of men and of angels, but have not love, I am only a resounding gong or a clanging cymbal. 2If I have the gift of prophecy and can fathom all mysteries and all knowledge, and if I have a faith that can move mountains, but have not love, I am nothing. 3If I give all I possess to the poor and surrender my body to the flames,*f* but have not love, I gain nothing.

---

*c*30 Or *other languages*
*d*31 Or *But you are eagerly desiring*
*e*1 Or *languages*
*f*3 Some early manuscripts *body that I may boast*

⁴Love is patient, love is kind, *and* is not jealous; love does not brag *and* is not arrogant,

⁵does not act unbecomingly; it does not seek its own, is not provoked, does not take into account a wrong *suffered,*

⁶does not rejoice in unrighteousness, but rejoices with the truth;

⁷bears all things, believes all things, hopes all things, endures all things.

⁸Love never fails; but if *there are gifts of* prophecy, they will be done away; if *there are* tongues, they will cease; if *there is* knowledge, it will be done away.

⁹For we know in part, and we prophesy in part;

¹⁰but when the perfect comes, the partial will be done away.

¹¹When I was a child, I used to speak as a child, think as a child, reason as a child; when I became a man, I did away with childish things.

¹²For now we see in a mirror dimly, but then face to face; now I know in part, but then I shall know fully just as I also have been fully known.

¹³But now abide faith, hope, love, these three; but the greatest of these is love.

ἀγάπη μακροθυμεῖ, χρηστεύεται ἡ ἀγάπη,
Love suffers long, is kind - love,

οὐ ζηλοῖ, ἡ ἀγάπη οὐ περπερεύεται,
is not jealous, - love does not vaunt itself,

οὐ φυσιοῦται, 5 οὐκ ἀσχημονεῖ, οὐ ζητεῖ
is not puffed up, does not act unbecomingly, does not seek

τὰ ἑαυτῆς, οὐ παροξύνεται, οὐ λογίζεται
the of is not provoked, does not reckon
things her(it)self,

τὸ κακόν, 6 οὐ χαίρει ἐπὶ τῇ ἀδικίᾳ,
the evil, rejoices not over the wrong,

συγχαίρει δὲ τῇ ἀληθείᾳ· 7 πάντα στέγει,
but rejoices with the truth; all things covers,

πάντα πιστεύει, πάντα ἐλπίζει, πάντα
all things believes, all things hopes, all things

ὑπομένει. 8 Ἡ ἀγάπη οὐδέποτε πίπτει·
endures. - Love never falls;

εἴτε δὲ προφητεῖαι, καταργηθήσονται· εἴτε
but whether prophecies, they will be abolished; or

γλῶσσαι, παύσονται· εἴτε γνῶσις, κατ-
tongues, they will cease; or knowledge, it will

αργηθήσεται. 9 ἐκ μέρους γὰρ γινώσκομεν
be abolished. For in part we know

καὶ ἐκ μέρους προφητεύομεν· 10 ὅταν
and in part we prophesy; ⁵when

δὲ ἔλθῃ τὸ τέλειον, τὸ ἐκ μέρους
¹but ⁵comes ³the ⁴perfect thing, the thing in part

καταργηθήσεται. 11 ὅτε ἤμην νήπιος,
will be abolished. When I was an infant,

ἐλάλουν ὡς νήπιος, ἐφρόνουν ὡς νήπιος,
I spoke as an infant, I thought as an infant,

ἐλογιζόμην ὡς νήπιος· ὅτε γέγονα ἀνήρ,
I reckoned as an infant; when I have become a man,

κατήργηκα τὰ τοῦ νηπίου. 12 βλέπομεν
I have the of the infant. we see
abolished things

γὰρ ἄρτι δι’ ἐσόπτρου ἐν αἰνίγματι,
For yet through a mirror in a riddle,

τότε δὲ πρόσωπον πρὸς πρόσωπον· ἄρτι
but then face to face; yet

γινώσκω ἐκ μέρους, τότε δὲ ἐπιγνώσομαι
I know in part, but then I shall fully know

καθὼς καὶ ἐπεγνώσθην. 13 νυνὶ δὲ μένει
as also I was fully known. But now remains

πίστις, ἐλπίς, ἀγάπη, τὰ τρία ταῦτα·
faith, hope, love, these three;

μείζων δὲ τούτων ἡ ἀγάπη.
and [the] greater of these [is] - love.

Chapter 14

Prophecy a Superior Gift

PURSUE love, yet desire earnestly spiritual *gifts,* but especially that you may prophesy.

²For one who speaks in a tongue does not speak to men, but to God; for no one understands, but in *his* spirit he speaks mysteries.

³But one who prophesies speaks to men for edification and exhortation and consolation.

⁴One who speaks in a tongue edifies himself; but one who prophesies edifies

---

Chapter 14

14 Διώκετε τὴν ἀγάπην, ζηλοῦτε δὲ
Pursue ye - love, but desire eagerly

τὰ πνευματικά, μᾶλλον δὲ ἵνα προφητεύητε.
the spiritual [gifts], and rather in order ye may prophesy.
that

2 ὁ γὰρ λαλῶν γλώσσῃ οὐκ ἀνθρώποις
For the [one] speaking in a tongue ⁵not to men

λαλεῖ ἀλλὰ θεῷ· οὐδεὶς γὰρ ἀκούει,
¹speaks but to God; for no one hears,

πνεύματι δὲ λαλεῖ μυστήρια· 3 ὁ δὲ
but in spirit he speaks mysteries; but the [one]

προφητεύων ἀνθρώποις λαλεῖ οἰκοδομὴν καὶ
prophesying to men speaks edification and

παράκλησιν καὶ παραμυθίαν. 4 ὁ λαλῶν
encouragement and consolation. The [one] speaking

γλώσσῃ ἑαυτὸν οἰκοδομεῖ· ὁ δὲ προφητεύων
in a tongue himself edifies; but the [one] prophesying

---

⁴Love is patient, love is kind. It does not envy, it does not boast, it is not proud. ⁵It is not rude, it is not self-seeking, it is not easily angered, it keeps no record of wrongs. ⁶Love does not delight in evil but rejoices with the truth. ⁷It always protects, always trusts, always hopes, always perseveres.

⁸Love never fails. But where there are prophecies, they will cease; where there are tongues, they will be stilled; where there is knowledge, it will pass away. ⁹For we know in part and we prophesy in part, ¹⁰but when perfection comes, the imperfect disappears. ¹¹When I was a child, I talked like a child, I thought like a child, I reasoned like a child. When I became a man, I put childish ways behind me. ¹²Now we see but a poor reflection as in a mirror; then we shall see face to face. Now I know in part; then I shall know fully, even as I am fully known.

¹³And now these three remain: faith, hope and love. But the greatest of these is love.

Chapter 14

Gifts of Prophecy and Tongues

FOLLOW the way of love and eagerly desire spiritual gifts, especially the gift of prophecy. ²For anyone who speaks in a tongue[g] does not speak to men but to God. Indeed, no one understands him; he utters mysteries with his spirit.[h] ³But everyone who prophesies speaks to men for their strengthening, encouragement and comfort. ⁴He who speaks in a tongue edifies himself, but he who prophesies edifies the

---

g 2 Or *another language;* also in verses 4, 13, 14, 19, 26 and 27
h 2 Or *by the Spirit*

the church.

5Now I wish that you all spoke in tongues, but *even* more that you would prophesy; and greater is one who prophesies than one who speaks in tongues, unless he interprets, so that the church may receive edifying.

6But now, brethren, if I come to you speaking in tongues, what shall I profit you, unless I speak to you either by way of revelation or of knowledge or of prophecy or of teaching?

7Yet *even* lifeless things, either flute or harp, in producing a sound, if they do not produce a distinction in the tones, how will it be known what is played on the flute or on the harp?

8For if the bugle produces an indistinct sound, who will prepare himself for battle?

9So also you, unless you utter by the tongue speech that is clear, how will it be known what is spoken? For you will be speaking into the air.

10There are, perhaps, a great many kinds of languages in the world, and no *kind* is without meaning.

11If then I do not know the meaning of the language, I shall be to the one who speaks a barbarian, and the one who speaks will be a barbarian to me.

12So also you, since you are zealous of spiritual *gifts*, seek to abound for the edification of the church.

13Therefore let one who speaks in a tongue pray that he may interpret.

14For if I pray in a tongue, my spirit prays, but my mind is without meaning.

15What is *the outcome* then? I shall pray with the

ἐκκλησίαν οἰκοδομεῖ. **5** θέλω δὲ πάντας
a church   edifies.   Now I wish   all

ὑμᾶς λαλεῖν γλώσσαις, μᾶλλον δὲ ἵνα
you to speak in tongues,   but rather   *in order that*

προφητεύητε· μείζων δὲ ὁ προφητεύων ἢ
ye may prophesy;   and greater the [one] prophesying than

ὁ λαλῶν γλώσσαις, ἐκτὸς εἰ μὴ διερμηνεύῃ,
the speaking in tongues, *except* unless he interprets,
[one]

ἵνα ἡ ἐκκλησία οἰκοδομὴν λάβῃ. **6** νῦν δέ,
in or- the church edification may receive. But now,
der that

ἀδελφοί, ἐὰν ἔλθω πρὸς ὑμᾶς γλώσσαις
brothers, if I come to you in tongues

λαλῶν, τί ὑμᾶς ὠφελήσω, ἐὰν μὴ ὑμῖν
speaking, what ²you ¹shall I profit, except ¹to you

λαλήσω ἢ ἐν ἀποκαλύψει ἢ ἐν γνώσει
¹I speak either in a revelation or in knowledge

ἢ ἐν προφητείᾳ ἢ διδαχῇ; **7** ὅμως τὰ
or in prophecy or *in* teaching? Yet –

ἄψυχα φωνὴν διδόντα, εἴτε αὐλὸς εἴτε
lifeless things ²a sound ¹giving, whether pipe or

κιθάρα, ἐὰν διαστολὴν τοῖς φθόγγοις μὴ
harp, if ²a distinction ¹in the ³sounds ⁴not

δῶ, πῶς γνωσθήσεται τὸ αὐλούμενον ἢ
¹they how will it be known the being piped or
give, thing

τὸ κιθαριζόμενον; **8** καὶ γὰρ ἐὰν ἄδηλον
the being harped? For indeed if ²an
thing uncertain

σάλπιγξ φωνὴν δῷ, τίς παρασκευάσεται
¹a trumpet ⁴sound ³gives, who will prepare himself

εἰς πόλεμον; **9** οὕτως καὶ ὑμεῖς διὰ
for war? so also ²ye ¹through

τῆς γλώσσης ἐὰν μὴ εὔσημον λόγον
²the ¹tongue unless a clear word

δῶτε, πῶς γνωσθήσεται τὸ λαλούμενον;
²give, how will it be known the thing being said?

ἔσεσθε γὰρ εἰς ἀέρα λαλοῦντες. **10** τοσαῦτα
for ¹ye will be ³into ⁴air ²speaking. ³So many

εἰ τύχοι γένη φωνῶν εἰσιν ἐν κόσμῳ,
¹it may be† ⁴kinds ⁵of sounds ²there are in [the] world,

καὶ οὐδὲν ἄφωνον· **11** ἐὰν οὖν μὴ εἰδῶ
and not one [is] voiceless; if therefore I know not

τὴν δύναμιν τῆς φωνῆς, ἔσομαι τῷ
the power of the sound, I shall be to the

λαλοῦντι βάρβαρος καὶ ὁ λαλῶν ἐν ἐμοὶ
[one] speaking a foreigner and the speaking in(to) me
[one]

βάρβαρος. **12** οὕτως καὶ ὑμεῖς. ἐπεὶ
a foreigner. So also ye, since

ζηλωταί ἐστε πνευμάτων, πρὸς τὴν
zealots ye are of spirit[ual thing]s, ²to ³the

οἰκοδομὴν τῆς ἐκκλησίας ζητεῖτε ἵνα περισ-
⁴edification ⁵of the ⁶church ¹seek ye in order ye may
that

σεύητε. **13** Διὸ ὁ λαλῶν γλώσσῃ προσευχ-
abound. Wherefore the speaking in a tongue let him
[one]

ἔσθω ἵνα διερμηνεύῃ. **14** ἐὰν γὰρ προσεύχωμαι
pray in order he may For if I pray
that interpret.

γλώσσῃ, τὸ πνεῦμά μου προσεύχεται,
in a tongue, the spirit of me prays,

ὁ δὲ νοῦς μου ἄκαρπός ἐστιν. **15** τί
but the mind of me unfruitful is. What

οὖν ἐστιν; προσεύξομαι τῷ πνεύματι,
therefore is it? I will pray with the spirit,

---

church. 5I would like every one of you to speak in tongues,[i] but I would rather have you prophesy. He who prophesies is greater than one who speaks in tongues,[i] unless he interprets, so that the church may be edified.

6Now, brothers, if I come to you and speak in tongues, what good will I be to you, unless I bring you some revelation or knowledge or prophecy or word of instruction? 7Even in the case of lifeless things that make sounds, such as the flute or harp, how will anyone know what tune is being played unless there is a distinction in the notes? 8Again, if the trumpet does not sound a clear call, who will get ready for battle? 9So it is with you. Unless you speak intelligible words with your tongue, how will anyone know what you are saying? You will just be speaking into the air. 10Undoubtedly there are all sorts of languages in the world, yet none of them is without meaning. 11If then I do not grasp the meaning of what someone is saying, I am a foreigner to the speaker, and he is a foreigner to me. 12So it is with you. Since you are eager to have spiritual gifts, try to excel in gifts that build up the church.

13For this reason anyone who speaks in a tongue should pray that he may interpret what he says. 14For if I pray in a tongue, my spirit prays, but my mind is unfruitful. 15So what shall I do? I will pray with my spir-

5 Or other languages; also in verses 6, 18, 22, 23 and 39

spirit and I shall pray with the mind also; I shall sing with the spirit and I shall sing with the mind also.

16Otherwise if you bless in the spirit only, how will the one who fills the place of the ungifted say the "Amen" at your giving of thanks, since he does not know what you are saying?

17For you are giving thanks well enough, but the other man is not edified.

18I thank God, I speak in tongues more than you all;

19however, in the church I desire to speak five words with my mind, that I may instruct others also, rather than ten thousand words in a tongue.

Instruction for the Church

20Brethren, do not be children in your thinking; yet in evil be babes, but in your thinking be mature.

21In the Law it is written, "BY MEN OF STRANGE TONGUES AND BY THE LIPS OF STRANGERS I WILL SPEAK TO THIS PEOPLE, AND EVEN SO THEY WILL NOT LISTEN TO ME," says the Lord.

22So then tongues are for a sign, not to those who believe, but to unbelievers; but prophecy *is for a sign*, not to unbelievers, but to those who believe.

23If therefore the whole church should assemble together and all speak in tongues, and ungifted men or unbelievers enter, will they not say that you are mad?

24But if all prophesy, and an unbeliever or an ungifted man enters, he is convicted by all, he is called to account by all;

25the secrets of his heart are disclosed; and so he will fall on his face and worship God, declaring that God is certainly among you.

26What is *the outcome*

προσεύξομαι δὲ καὶ τῷ νοΐ· ψαλῶ τῷ
⁹I will pray ¹and ²also with mind; I will with
the sing the

πνεύματι, ψαλῶ δὲ καὶ τῷ νοΐ. 16 ἐπεὶ
spirit, . ⁹I will sing ¹and ²also with the mind. Otherwise

ἐὰν εὐλογῇς [ἐν] πνεύματι, ὁ ἀναπληρῶν
if thou blessest in spirit, the [one] occupying

τὸν τόπον τοῦ ἰδιώτου πῶς ἐρεῖ τὸ
the place of the uninstructed how will he say the

ἀμὴν ἐπὶ τῇ σῇ εὐχαριστίᾳ; ἐπειδὴ τί
"amen" at thy giving thanks? Since what

λέγεις οὐκ οἶδεν· 17 σὺ μὲν γὰρ καλῶς
thou sayest he knows not; ⁴thou ²indeed ¹for ⁵well

εὐχαριστεῖς, ἀλλ' ὁ ἕτερος οὐκ οἰκοδομεῖται.
⁶givest thanks, but the other is not edified.

18 εὐχαριστῶ τῷ θεῷ, πάντων ὑμῶν μᾶλ-
I give thanks - to God, ⁵all ⁴you ³more

λον γλώσσαις λαλῶ· 19 ἀλλὰ ἐν ἐκκλησίᾳ
than ²in tongues ¹I speak; but in a church

θέλω πέντε λόγους τῷ νοΐ μου λαλῆσαι,
¹I wish ²five ⁵words ⁶with the ⁷mind ⁸of me ⁴to speak,

ἵνα καὶ ἄλλους κατηχήσω, ἢ μυρίους
in or- also others I may instruct, than ten
der that thousands

λόγους ἐν γλώσσῃ. 20 Ἀδελφοί, μὴ
words in a tongue. Brothers, ²not

παιδία γίνεσθε ταῖς φρεσίν, ἀλλὰ τῇ
²children ¹be ye in the(your) minds, but -

κακίᾳ νηπιάζετε, ταῖς δὲ φρεσὶν τέλειοι
in malice be ye infantlike, and in the(your) minds mature

γίνεσθε. 21 ἐν τῷ νόμῳ γέγραπται ὅτι
be ye. In the law it has been written that

ἐν ἑτερογλώσσοις καὶ ἐν χείλεσιν ἑτέρων
in other tongues and in lips of others

λαλήσω τῷ λαῷ τούτῳ, καὶ οὐδ' οὕτως
I will speak to this people, and not so

εἰσακούσονταί μου, λέγει κύριος. 22 ὥστε
will they hear me, says [the] Lord. So as

αἱ γλῶσσαι εἰς σημεῖόν εἰσιν οὐ τοῖς
the tongues ²for ¹a sign ³are not to the

πιστεύουσιν ἀλλὰ τοῖς ἀπίστοις, ἡ δὲ
[ones] believing but to the unbelievers, and the

προφητεία οὐ τοῖς ἀπίστοις ἀλλὰ τοῖς
prophecy [is] not to the unbelievers but to the

πιστεύουσιν. 23 Ἐὰν οὖν συνέλθῃ ἡ
[ones] believing. If therefore ⁴comes ¹the
together

ἐκκλησία ὅλη ἐπὶ τὸ αὐτὸ καὶ πάντες
²church ³whole together and all

λαλῶσιν γλώσσαις, εἰσέλθωσιν δὲ ἰδιῶται
speak in tongues, and ²enter ¹uninstructed

ἢ ἄπιστοι, οὐκ ἐροῦσιν ὅτι μαίνεσθε;
²or ⁴unbelievers, will they not say that ye rave?

24 ἐὰν δὲ πάντες προφητεύωσιν, εἰσέλθῃ δέ
but if all prophesy, and ²enters

τις ἄπιστος ἢ ἰδιώτης, ἐλέγχεται ὑπὸ
¹some ²unbeliever ³or ⁴uninstructed, he is convicted by

πάντων, ἀνακρίνεται ὑπὸ πάντων, 25 τὰ
all, he is judged by all, the

κρυπτὰ τῆς καρδίας αὐτοῦ φανερὰ γίνεται,
hidden of the heart of him ²manifest ¹becomes,
things

καὶ οὕτως πεσὼν ἐπὶ πρόσωπον προσκυνή-
and so falling on [his] face he will wor-

σει τῷ θεῷ, ἀπαγγέλλων ὅτι ὄντως
ship - God, declaring that really

ὁ θεὸς ἐν ὑμῖν ἐστιν. 26 Τί οὖν ἐστιν,
- God ²among ³you ¹is. What therefore is it,

---

it, but I will also pray with my mind; I will sing with my spirit, but I will also sing with my mind. 16If you are praising God with your spirit, how can one who finds himself among those who do not understand[j] say "Amen" to your thanksgiving, since he does not know what you are saying? 17You may be giving thanks well enough, but the other man is not edified. 18I thank God that I speak in tongues more than all of you. 19But in the church I would rather speak five intelligible words to instruct others than ten thousand words in a tongue.

20Brothers, stop thinking like children. In regard to evil be infants, but in your thinking be adults. 21In the Law it is written:

"Through men of
strange tongues
and through the lips of
foreigners
I will speak to this
people,
but even then they will
not listen to me,"[k]

says the Lord.

22Tongues, then, are a sign, not for believers but for unbelievers; prophecy, however, is for believers, not for unbelievers. 23So if the whole church comes together and everyone speaks in tongues, and some who do not understand[l] or some unbelievers come in, will they not say that you are out of your mind? 24But if an unbeliever or someone who does not understand[m] comes in while everybody is prophesying, he will be convinced by all that he is a sinner and will be judged by all, 25and the secrets of his heart will be laid bare. So he will fall down and worship God, exclaiming, "God is really among you!"

Orderly Worship

26What then shall we say,

---

j16 Or among the inquirers
k21 Isaiah 28:11,12
l23 Or some inquirers
m24 Or or some inquirer

then, brethren? When you assemble, each one has a psalm, has a teaching, has a revelation, has a tongue, has an interpretation. Let all things be done for edification.

27If anyone speaks in a tongue, *it should be* by two or at the most three, and *each* in turn, and let one interpret;

28but if there is no interpreter, let him keep silent in the church; and let him speak to himself and to God.

29And let two or three prophets speak, and let the others pass judgment.

30But if a revelation is made to another who is seated, let the first keep silent.

31For you can all prophesy one by one, so that all may learn and all may be exhorted;

32and the spirits of prophets are subject to prophets;

33for God is not *a God of* confusion but of peace, as in all the churches of the saints.

34Let the women keep silent in the churches; for they are not permitted to speak, but let them subject themselves, just as the Law also says.

35And if they desire to learn anything, let them ask their own husbands at home; for it is improper for a woman to speak in church.

36Was it from you that the word of God *first* went forth? Or has it come to you only?

37If anyone thinks he is a prophet or spiritual, let him recognize that the things which I write to you are the Lord's commandment.

38But if anyone *p*does not recognize *this*, he is not recognized.

39Therefore, my brethren, desire earnestly to prophesy, and do not forbid to speak in tongues.

40But let all things be done properly and in an orderly manner.

p Some ancient mss. read *is ignorant, let him be ignorant*

ἀδελφοί; ὅταν συνέρχησθε, ἕκαστος ψαλμὸν
brothers? whenever ye come together, each one a psalm
ἔχει, διδαχὴν ἔχει, ἀποκάλυψιν ἔχει, γλῶσ-
has, a teaching he has, a revelation he has, a
σαν ἔχει, ἑρμηνείαν ἔχει· πάντα πρὸς
tongue he has, an interpretation he has; ²all things ⁴for
οἰκοδομὴν γινέσθω. 27 εἴτε γλώσσῃ τις
⁵edification ¹let ³be. If in a tongue anyone
λαλεῖ, κατὰ δύο ἢ τὸ πλεῖστον τρεῖς,
speaks, by two or the most three,
καὶ ἀνὰ μέρος, 28 καὶ εἷς διερμηνευέτω·
and in turn,† and ²one ¹let ³interpret;
ἐὰν δὲ μὴ ᾖ διερμηνευτής, σιγάτω ἐν
but if there is not an interpreter, let him be silent in
ἐκκλησίᾳ, ἑαυτῷ δὲ λαλείτω καὶ τῷ
church, and to himself let him speak and -
θεῷ. 29 προφῆται δὲ δύο ἢ τρεῖς λαλεί-
to God. And prophets two or three let them
τωσαν, καὶ οἱ ἄλλοι διακρινέτωσαν·
speak, and the others let discern;
30 ἐὰν δὲ ἄλλῳ ἀποκαλυφθῇ καθημένῳ, ὁ
but if ¹to another ³[something] ²sitting, the
πρῶτος σιγάτω. 31 δύνασθε γὰρ καθ᾽
first let be silent. For ye can ³sin-
ἕνα πάντες προφητεύειν, ἵνα πάντες
gly† ¹all ²to prophesy, in order that all
μανθάνωσιν καὶ πάντες παρακαλῶνται.
may learn and all may be encouraged.
32 καὶ πνεύματα προφητῶν προφήταις
And [the] spirits of prophets to prophets
ὑποτάσσεται· 33 οὐ γάρ ἐστιν ἀκαταστασίας
is(are) subject; for²not ¹is ⁴of tumult
ὁ θεὸς ἀλλὰ εἰρήνης. Ὡς ἐν πάσαις
- ¹God but of peace. As in all
ταῖς ἐκκλησίαις τῶν ἁγίων, 34 ²the ³women
the churches of the saints, ²the ³women
ἐν ταῖς ἐκκλησίαις σιγάτωσαν· οὐ γὰρ
⁵in ⁶the ⁷churches ¹let ⁴be silent; ³not ¹for
ἐπιτρέπεται αὐταῖς λαλεῖν, ἀλλὰ ὑποτασ-
²it is ⁴permitted to them to speak, but let them
σέσθωσαν, καθὼς καὶ ὁ νόμος λέγει.
be subject, as also the law says.
35 εἰ δέ τι μαθεῖν θέλουσιν, ἐν οἴκῳ
But if ¹anything ²to learn ³they wish, ⁴at home
τοὺς ἰδίους ἄνδρας ἐπερωτάτωσαν· αἰσχρὸν
⁵the(ir) ⁶own ⁴husbands ¹let them question; ²a shame
γάρ ἐστιν γυναικὶ λαλεῖν ἐν ἐκκλησίᾳ.
¹for ²it is for a woman to speak in a church.
36 ἢ ἀφ᾽ ὑμῶν ὁ λόγος τοῦ θεοῦ ἐξῆλθεν,
Or from you the ³word ⁴of God ¹went forth,
ἢ εἰς ὑμᾶς μόνους κατήντησεν; 37 Εἴ
or to you only did it reach? If
τις δοκεῖ προφήτης εἶναι ἢ πνευματικός,
any- thinks ²a prophet ¹to be or a spiritual man,
one
ἐπιγινωσκέτω ἃ γράφω ὑμῖν ὅτι
let him clearly [the] things I write to you that
know which
κυρίου ἐστὶν ἐντολή· 38 εἰ δέ τις
of [the] Lord they are a commandment; but if anyone
ἀγνοεῖ, ἀγνοεῖται. 39 Ὥστε, ἀδελφοί
is ignorant, let him be ignorant. So as, brothers
μου, ζηλοῦτε τὸ προφητεύειν, καὶ τὸ
of me, be ye eager - to prophesy, and -
λαλεῖν μὴ κωλύετε γλώσσαις· 40 πάντα
²to speak ¹forbid not in tongues; ²all things
δὲ εὐσχημόνως καὶ κατὰ τάξιν γινέσθω.
and ⁴becomingly ⁵and ⁶according to ⁷order ¹let ³be done.

brothers? When you come together, everyone has a hymn, or a word of instruction, a revelation, a tongue or an interpretation. All of these must be done for the strengthening of the church. 27If anyone speaks in a tongue, two—or at the most three—should speak, one at a time, and someone must interpret. 28If there is no interpreter, the speaker should keep quiet in the church and speak to himself and God.

29Two or three prophets should speak, and the others should weigh carefully what is said. 30And if a revelation comes to someone who is sitting down, the first speaker should stop. 31For you can all prophesy in turn so that everyone may be instructed and encouraged. 32The spirits of prophets are subject to the control of prophets. 33For God is not a God of disorder but of peace.

As in all the congregations of the saints, 34women should remain silent in the churches. They are not allowed to speak, but must be in submission, as the Law says. 35If they want to inquire about something, they should ask their own husbands at home; for it is disgraceful for a woman to speak in the church.

36Did the word of God originate with you? Or are you the only people it has reached? 37If anybody thinks he is a prophet or spiritually gifted, let him acknowledge that what I am writing to you is the Lord's command. 38If he ignores this, he himself will be ignored. *n*

39Therefore, my brothers, be eager to prophesy, and do not forbid speaking in tongues. 40But everything should be done in a fitting and orderly way.

*n*38 Some manuscripts *If he is ignorant of this, let him be ignorant*

Chapter 15

The Fact of Christ's Resurrection

NOW I make known to you, brethren, the gospel which I preached to you, which also you received, in which also you stand,

²by which also you are saved, if you hold fast the word which I preached to you, unless you believed in vain.

³For I delivered to you as of first importance what I also received, that Christ died for our sins according to the Scriptures,

⁴and that He was buried, and that He was raised on the third day according to the Scriptures,

⁵and that He appeared to Cephas, then to the twelve;

⁶After that He appeared to more than five hundred brethren at one time, most of whom remain until now, but some have fallen asleep;

⁷then He appeared to James, then to all the apostles;

⁸and last of all, as it were to one untimely born, He appeared to me also.

⁹For I am the least of the apostles, who am not fit to be called an apostle, because I persecuted the church of God.

¹⁰But by the grace of God I am what I am, and His grace toward me did not prove vain; but I labored even more than all of them, yet not I, but the grace of God with me.

¹¹Whether then *it was* I or they, so we preach and so you believed.

¹²Now if Christ is preached, that He has been raised from the dead, how do some among you say that there is no resurrection of the dead?

¹³But if there is no resurrection of the dead, not even Christ has been raised;

¹⁴and if Christ has not

---

15 Γνωρίζω δὲ ὑμῖν, ἀδελφοί, τὸ
Now I make known to you, brothers, the

εὐαγγέλιον ὃ εὐηγγελισάμην ὑμῖν, ὃ καὶ
good tidings which I preached to you, which also

παρελάβετε, ἐν ᾧ καὶ ἑστήκατε, 2 δι'
ye received, in which also ye stand, through

οὗ καὶ σῴζεσθε, τίνι λόγῳ εὐηγγελισάμην
which also ye are saved, ²to what ⁴word ¹I preached

ὑμῖν εἰ κατέχετε, ἐκτὸς εἰ μὴ εἰκῇ
⁵to you ¹if ²ye hold fast, except unless in vain

ἐπιστεύσατε. 3 παρέδωκα γὰρ ὑμῖν ἐν
ye believed. For I delivered to you among

πρώτοις, ὃ καὶ παρέλαβον, ὅτι Χριστὸς
[the] first what also I received, that Christ
things,

ἀπέθανεν ὑπὲρ τῶν ἁμαρτιῶν ἡμῶν κατὰ
died on be- the sins of us accord-
half of ing to

τὰς γραφάς, 4 καὶ ὅτι ἐτάφη, καὶ ὅτι
the scriptures, and that he was buried, and that

ἐγήγερται τῇ ἡμέρᾳ τῇ τρίτῃ κατὰ
he has on the ²day – ¹third accord-
been raised ing to

τὰς γραφάς, 5 καὶ ὅτι ὤφθη Κηφᾷ,
the scriptures, and that he was seen by Cephas,

εἶτα τοῖς δώδεκα· 6 ἔπειτα ὤφθη ἐπάνω
then by the twelve; afterward he was seen ²over

πεντακοσίοις ἀδελφοῖς ἐφάπαξ, ἐξ ὧν οἱ
¹by ²five hundreds brothers at one time, of whom the

πλείονες μένουσιν ἕως ἄρτι, τινὲς δὲ
majority remain until now, though some

ἐκοιμήθησαν· 7 ἔπειτα ὤφθη Ἰακώβῳ, εἶτα
fell asleep; afterward he was seen by James, then

τοῖς ἀποστόλοις πᾶσιν· 8 ἔσχατον δὲ
by the apostles all; and lastly

πάντων ὡσπερεὶ τῷ ἐκτρώματι ὤφθη
of all even as if to the(an) abortion he was seen

κἀμοί. 9 Ἐγὼ γάρ εἰμι ὁ ἐλάχιστος
by me also. For I am the least

τῶν ἀποστόλων, ὃς οὐκ εἰμὶ ἱκανὸς
of the apostles, who am not sufficient

καλεῖσθαι ἀπόστολος, διότι ἐδίωξα τὴν
to be called an apostle, because I persecuted the

ἐκκλησίαν τοῦ θεοῦ· 10 χάριτι δὲ θεοῦ
church – of God; but by [the] grace of God

εἰμι ὅ εἰμι, καὶ ἡ χάρις αὐτοῦ ἡ εἰς
I am what I am, and the grace of him – to

ἐμὲ οὐ κενὴ ἐγενήθη, ἀλλὰ περισσότερον
me not empty was, but ²more abundantly
[than]

αὐτῶν πάντων ἐκοπίασα, οὐκ ἐγὼ δὲ
³them ⁴all ¹I laboured, ²not ⁵I ¹yet

ἀλλὰ ἡ χάρις τοῦ θεοῦ σὺν ἐμοί. 11 εἴτε
but the grace of God with me. Whether

οὖν ἐγὼ εἴτε ἐκεῖνοι, οὕτως κηρύσσομεν
therefore I or those, so we proclaim

καὶ οὕτως ἐπιστεύσατε.
and so ye believed.

12 Εἰ δὲ Χριστὸς κηρύσσεται ὅτι ἐκ
But if Christ is proclaimed that from

νεκρῶν ἐγήγερται, πῶς λέγουσιν ἐν ὑμῖν
[the] dead he has been raised, how say ²among ¹you

τινες ὅτι ἀνάστασις νεκρῶν οὐκ ἔστιν;
¹some that a resurrection of dead persons there is not?

13 εἰ δὲ ἀνάστασις νεκρῶν οὐκ ἔστιν,
Now if a resurrection of dead persons there is not,

οὐδὲ Χριστὸς ἐγήγερται· 14 εἰ δὲ Χριστὸς
neither Christ has been raised; and if Christ

Chapter 15

The Resurrection of Christ

NOW, brothers, I want to remind you of the gospel I preached to you, which you received and on which you have taken your stand. ²By this gospel you are saved, if you hold firmly to the word I preached to you. Otherwise, you have believed in vain.

³For what I received I passed on to you as of first importance*ᵒ*: that Christ died for our sins according to the Scriptures, ⁴that he was buried, that he was raised on the third day according to the Scriptures, ⁵and that he appeared to Peter,*ᵖ* and then to the Twelve. ⁶After that, he appeared to more than five hundred of the brothers at the same time, most of whom are still living, though some have fallen asleep. ⁷Then he appeared to James, then to all the apostles, ⁸and last of all he appeared to me also, as to one abnormally born.

⁹For I am the least of the apostles and do not even deserve to be called an apostle, because I persecuted the church of God. ¹⁰But by the grace of God I am what I am, and his grace to me was not without effect. No, I worked harder than all of them—yet not I, but the grace of God that was with me. ¹¹Whether, then, it was I or they, this is what we preach, and this is what you believed.

The Resurrection of the Dead

¹²But if it is preached that Christ has been raised from the dead, how can some of you say that there is no resurrection of the dead? ¹³If there is no resurrection of the dead, then not even Christ has been raised. ¹⁴And if Christ has not

---

ᵒ3 Or you at the first
ᵖ5 Greek Cephas

been raised, then our preaching is vain, your faith also is vain.

15Moreover we are even found to be false witnesses of God, because we witnessed against God that He raised *Christ, whom He did not raise, if in fact the dead are not raised.

16For if the dead are not raised, not even Christ has been raised;

17and if Christ has not been raised, your faith is worthless; you are still in your sins.

18Then those also who have fallen asleep in Christ have perished.

19If we have hoped in Christ in this life only, we are of all men most to be pitied.

The Order of Resurrection

20But now Christ has been raised from the dead, the first fruits of those who are asleep.

21For since by a man *came* death, by a man also *came* the resurrection of the dead.

22For as in Adam all die, so also in Christ all shall be made alive.

23But each in his own order: Christ the first fruits, after that those who are Christ's at His coming,

24then *comes* the end, when He delivers up the kingdom to the God and Father, when He has abolished all rule and all authority and power.

25For He must reign until He has put all His enemies under His feet.

26The last enemy that will be abolished is death.

27For HE HAS PUT ALL THINGS IN SUBJECTION UNDER HIS FEET. But when He says, "All things are put in subjection," it is evident

---

οὐκ   ἐγήγερται,   κενὸν   ἄρα   τὸ   κήρυγμα
has not been raised,   empty   then   the   proclamation

ἡμῶν,   κενὴ   καὶ   ἡ   πίστις   ὑμῶν·   15 εὑρισκ-
of us,   empty   also   the   faith   of you;   ¹we are

όμεθα   δὲ   καὶ   ψευδομάρτυρες   τοῦ   θεοῦ,
found   ¹and   also   false witnesses   -   of God,

ὅτι   ἐμαρτυρήσαμεν   κατὰ   τοῦ   θεοῦ   ὅτι
because   we witnessed   as to   -   God   that

ἤγειρεν   τὸν   Χριστόν,   ὃν   οὐκ   ἤγειρεν
he raised   -   Christ,   whom   he raised not

εἴπερ   ἄρα   νεκροὶ   οὐκ   ἐγείρονται.   16 εἰ
if   then   dead persons   are not raised.   if

γὰρ   νεκροὶ   οὐκ   ἐγείρονται,   οὐδὲ   Χριστὸς
For   dead persons   are not raised,   neither   Christ

ἐγήγερται·   17 εἰ   δὲ   Χριστὸς   οὐκ   ἐγήγερται,
has been raised;   and if   Christ   has not been raised,

ματαία   ἡ   πίστις   ὑμῶν   [ἐστιν],   ἔτι   ἐστὲ
⁵useless   ¹the   ²faith   ³of you   ⁴is,   ⁵still   ¹ye are

ἐν   ταῖς   ἁμαρτίαις   ὑμῶν.   18 ἄρα   καὶ   οἱ
in   the   sins   of you.   Then also the [ones]

κοιμηθέντες   ἐν   Χριστῷ   ἀπώλοντο.   19 εἰ
having fallen asleep in   Christ   perished.   If

ἐν   τῇ   ζωῇ   ταύτῃ   ἐν   Χριστῷ   ἠλπικότες
in   this life   ²in   ⁴Christ   ¹having hoped

ἐσμὲν   μόνον,   ἐλεεινότεροι   πάντων   ἀνθρώπων
¹we are   ⁵only,   more pitiful [than]   all   men

ἐσμέν.   20 Νυνὶ   δὲ   Χριστὸς   ἐγήγερται
we are.   But now   Christ   has been raised

ἐκ   νεκρῶν,   ἀπαρχὴ   τῶν   κεκοιμημένων.
from [the] dead,   firstfruit of the [ones] having fallen asleep.

21 ἐπειδὴ   γὰρ   δι'   ἀνθρώπου   θάνατος,   καὶ
For since   through   a man   death [came],   also

δι'   ἀνθρώπου   ἀνάστασις   νεκρῶν.   22 ὥσπερ
through   a man   a resurrection of dead persons   as
                                      [came].

γὰρ   ἐν   τῷ   Ἀδὰμ   πάντες   ἀποθνῄσκουσιν,
For   in   -   Adam   all   die,

οὕτως   καὶ   ἐν   τῷ   Χριστῷ   πάντες   ζωοποιη-
so   also   in   -   Christ   all   will be

θήσονται.   23 Ἕκαστος   δὲ   ἐν   τῷ   ἰδίῳ
made alive.   But each one   in the(his)   own

τάγματι·   ἀπαρχὴ   Χριστός,   ἔπειτα   οἱ   τοῦ
order: [the]   Christ,   afterward   the   -
        firstfruit   [ones]

Χριστοῦ   ἐν   τῇ   παρουσίᾳ   αὐτοῦ,   24 εἶτα
of Christ   in   the   presence   of him,   then

τὸ   τέλος,   ὅταν   παραδιδοῖ   τὴν   βασιλείαν
the   end,   whenever   he delivers   the   kingdom

τῷ   θεῷ   καὶ   πατρί,   ὅταν   καταργήσῃ
-   to God   even   [the] Father,   whenever   he abolishes

πᾶσαν   ἀρχὴν   καὶ   πᾶσαν   ἐξουσίαν   καὶ
all   rule   and   all   authority   and

δύναμιν.   25 δεῖ   γὰρ   αὐτὸν   βασιλεύειν
power.   For it behoves   him   to reign

ἄχρι   οὗ   θῇ   πάντας   τοὺς   ἐχθροὺς   ὑπὸ
until   he puts   all   the(his)   enemies   under

τοὺς   πόδας   αὐτοῦ.   26 ἔσχατος   ἐχθρὸς
the   feet   of him.   [The] last   enemy

καταργεῖται   ὁ   θάνατος·   πάντα   γὰρ   ὑπέταξεν
is abolished   -   death;   for all things   he subjected

ὑπὸ   τοὺς   πόδας   αὐτοῦ.   27 ὅταν   δὲ
under   the   feet   of him.   But whenever

εἴπῃ   ὅτι   πάντα   ὑποτέτακται,   δῆλον   ὅτι
he says   that   all things have been subjected,   [it is] clear   that

---

raised, our preaching is useless and so is your faith.

15More than that, we are then found to be false witnesses about God, for we have testified about God that he raised Christ from the dead. But he did not raise him if in fact the dead are not raised. 16For if the dead are not raised, then Christ has not been raised either. 17And if Christ has not been raised, your faith is futile; you are still in your sins. 18Then those also who have fallen asleep in Christ are lost. 19If only for this life we have hope in Christ, we are to be pitied more than all men.

20But Christ has indeed been raised from the dead, the firstfruits of those who have fallen asleep. 21For since death came through a man, the resurrection of the dead comes also through a man. 22For as in Adam all die, so in Christ all will be made alive. 23But each in his own turn: Christ, the firstfruits; then, when he comes, those who belong to him. 24Then the end will come, when he hands over the kingdom to God the Father after he has destroyed all dominion, authority and power. 25For he must reign until he has put all his enemies under his feet. 26The last enemy to be destroyed is death. 27For he "has put everything under his feet." ⁹ Now when it says that "everything" has been put under him, it is clear that this does not

---

a I.e., the Messiah

that He is excepted who put all things in subjection to Him. 28And when all things are subjected to Him, then the Son Himself also will be subjected to the One who subjected all things to Him, that God may be all in all. 29Otherwise, what will those do who are baptized for the dead? If the dead are not raised at all, why then are they baptized for them? 30Why are we also in danger every hour? 31I protest, brethren, by the boasting in you, which I have in Christ Jesus our Lord, I die daily. 32If from human motives I fought with wild beasts at Ephesus, what does it profit me? If the dead are not raised, LET US EAT AND DRINK, FOR TOMORROW WE DIE. 33Do not be deceived: "Bad company corrupts good morals." 34Become sober-minded as you ought, and stop sinning; for some have no knowledge of God. I speak *this* to your shame. 35But someone will say, "How are the dead raised? And with what kind of body do they come?" 36You fool! That which you sow does not come to life unless it dies; 37and that which you sow, you do not sow the body which is to be, but a bare grain, perhaps of wheat or of something else. 38But God gives it a body just as He wished, and to each of the seeds a body of its own. 39All flesh is not the same flesh, but there is one *flesh* of men, and another flesh of beasts, and another flesh of birds, and another of fish.

ἐκτὸς τοῦ ὑποτάξαντος αὐτῷ τὰ πάντα.
[it is] the having subjected to him - all
apart from [one] things.

28 ὅταν δὲ ὑποταγῇ αὐτῷ τὰ πάντα,
But whenever is(are) subjected to him - all things,

τότε καὶ αὐτὸς ὁ υἱὸς ὑποταγήσεται
then also ²[him]self ¹the ²Son will be subjected

τῷ ὑποτάξαντι αὐτῷ τὰ πάντα, ἵνα
to the having to him - all in order
[one] subjected things, that

ᾖ ὁ θεὸς πάντα ἐν πᾶσιν. 29 Ἐπεὶ
¹may- ¹God all in all. Other-
be things wise

τί ποιήσουσιν οἱ βαπτιζόμενοι ὑπὲρ τῶν
what will they do the [ones] being baptized on behalf of the

νεκρῶν; εἰ ὅλως νεκροὶ οὐκ ἐγείρονται,
dead? if actually dead persons are not raised,

τί καὶ βαπτίζονται ὑπὲρ αὐτῶν; 30 τί
why indeed are they baptized on behalf of them? why

καὶ ἡμεῖς κινδυνεύομεν πᾶσαν ὥραν;
also ²we ¹are ³in danger every hour?

31 καθ' ἡμέραν ἀποθνῄσκω, νὴ τὴν
Daily I die, by -

ὑμετέραν καύχησιν, ἀδελφοί, ἣν ἔχω ἐν
your boasting, brothers, which I have in

Χριστῷ Ἰησοῦ τῷ κυρίῳ ἡμῶν. 32 εἰ
Christ Jesus the Lord of us. If

κατὰ ἄνθρωπον ἐθηριομάχησα ἐν Ἐφέσῳ,
according man I fought with wild in Ephesus,
to beasts

τί μοι τὸ ὄφελος; εἰ νεκροὶ οὐκ ἐγείρονται,
what to me the profit?ᶜ If dead persons are not raised,
=what profit have I?

φάγωμεν καὶ πίωμεν, αὔριον γὰρ ἀποθνή-
let us eat and *let us* drink, for to-morrow we

σκομεν. 33 μὴ πλανᾶσθε· φθείρουσιν ἤθη
die. Be ye not led astray: ²Corrupt ⁵customs

χρηστὰ ὁμιλίαι κακαί. 34 ἐκνήψατε δικαίως
⁴good ²associations ¹bad. Become ye sober righteously

καὶ μὴ ἁμαρτάνετε· ἀγνωσίαν γὰρ θεοῦ
and do not sin; for ³ignorance ⁴of God

τινες ἔχουσιν· πρὸς ἐντροπὴν ὑμῖν λαλῶ.
¹some ²have· ³for ⁴shame ¹to you ¹¹I speak.

35 Ἀλλὰ ἐρεῖ τις· πῶς ἐγείρονται οἱ
But ²will say ¹someone: How are raised the

νεκροί; ποίῳ δὲ σώματι ἔρχονται; 36 ἄφρων,
dead? and with what body do they Foolish
sort [of] come? man,

σὺ ὃ σπείρεις, οὐ ζῳοποιεῖται ἐὰν μὴ
¹thou ¹what sowest, is not made alive unless

ἀποθάνῃ 37 καὶ ὃ σπείρεις, οὐ τὸ σῶμα
it dies; and what thou sowest, not the body

τὸ γενησόμενον σπείρεις, ἀλλὰ γυμνὸν
- going to become thou sowest, but a naked

κόκκον εἰ τύχοι σίτου ἤ τινος τῶν
grain it may be† of wheat or some one of the

λοιπῶν· 38 ὁ δὲ θεὸς δίδωσιν αὐτῷ
rest; - but God gives to it

σῶμα καθὼς ἠθέλησεν, καὶ ἑκάστῳ τῶν
a body as he wished, and to each of the

σπερμάτων ἴδιον σῶμα. 39 οὐ πᾶσα
seeds [its] own body. ³[is] not ¹All

σὰρξ ἡ αὐτὴ σάρξ, ἀλλὰ ἄλλη μὲν
²flesh the same flesh, but other(one) indeed

ἀνθρώπων, ἄλλη δὲ σὰρξ κτηνῶν, ἄλλη δὲ
of men, and another flesh of animals, and another

σὰρξ πτηνῶν, ἄλλη δὲ ἰχθύων. 40 καὶ
flesh of birds, and another of fishes. And [there

include God himself, who put everything under Christ. 28When he has done this, then the Son himself will be made subject to him who put everything under him, so that God may be all in all. 29Now if there is no resurrection, what will those do who are baptized for the dead? If the dead are not raised at all, why are people baptized for them? 30And as for us, why do we endanger ourselves every hour? 31I die every day—I mean that, brothers—just as surely as I glory over you in Christ Jesus our Lord. 32If I fought wild beasts in Ephesus for merely human reasons, what have I gained? If the dead are not raised,

"Let us eat and drink, for tomorrow we die."ʳ

33Do not be misled: "Bad company corrupts good character." 34Come back to your senses as you ought, and stop sinning; for there are some who are ignorant of God—I say this to your shame.

The Resurrection Body

35But someone may ask, "How are the dead raised? With what kind of body will they come?" 36How foolish! What you sow does not come to life unless it dies. 37When you sow, you do not plant the body that will be, but just a seed, perhaps of wheat or of something else. 38But God gives it a body as he has determined, and to each kind of seed he gives its own body. 39All flesh is not the same: Men have one kind of flesh, animals have another, birds another and fish another.

40There are also heavenly bodies and earthly bodies, but the glory of the heavenly is one, and the *glory* of the earthly is another. 41There is one glory of the sun, and another glory of the moon, and another glory of the stars; for star differs from star in glory. 42So also is the resurrection of the dead. It is sown a perishable *body*, it is raised an imperishable *body*; 43it is sown in dishonor, it is raised in glory; it is sown in weakness, it is raised in power; 44it is sown a natural body, it is raised a spiritual body. If there is a natural body, there is also a spiritual *body*. 45So also it is written, "The first MAN, Adam, BECAME A LIVING SOUL." The last Adam *became* a life-giving spirit. 46However, the spiritual is not first, but the natural; then the spiritual. 47The first man is from the earth, earthy; the second man is from heaven. 48As is the earthy, so also are those who are earthy; and as is the heavenly, so also are those who are heavenly. 49And just as we have borne the image of the earthy, ʳwe shall also bear the image of the heavenly.

The Mystery of Resurrection

50Now I say this, brethren, that flesh and blood cannot inherit the kingdom of God; nor does the perishable inherit the imperishable. 51Behold, I tell you a mystery; we shall not all sleep, but we shall all be changed, 52in a moment, in the twinkling of an eye, at the last trumpet; for the trumpet will sound, and the dead will be raised imper-

σώματα ἐπουράνια, καὶ σώματα ἐπίγεια·
are] bodies heavenly, and bodies earthly;
ἀλλὰ ἑτέρα μὲν ἡ τῶν ἐπουρανίων δόξα,
but ⁷other ⁶[is] ¹the ⁵of the ⁴heavenly ²glory,
(one) ⁸indeed [bodies]
ἑτέρα δὲ ἡ τῶν ἐπιγείων. **41** ἄλλη
and other the [glory] of the earthly [bodies]. Other(one)
δόξα ἡλίου, καὶ ἄλλη δόξα σελήνης,
glory of [the] sun, and another glory of [the] moon,
καὶ ἄλλη δόξα ἀστέρων· ἀστὴρ γὰρ
and another glory of [the] stars; for star
ἀστέρος διαφέρει ἐν δόξῃ. **42** οὕτως καὶ
from star differs in glory. So also
ἡ ἀνάστασις τῶν νεκρῶν. σπείρεται ἐν
the resurrection of the dead. It is sown in
φθορᾷ, ἐγείρεται ἐν ἀφθαρσίᾳ· **43** σπείρεται
corruption, it is raised in incorruption; it is sown
ἐν ἀτιμίᾳ, ἐγείρεται ἐν δόξῃ· σπείρεται
in dishonour, it is raised in glory; it is sown
ἐν ἀσθενείᾳ, ἐγείρεται ἐν δυνάμει· **44** σπείρ-
in weakness, it is raised in power; it is
εται σῶμα ψυχικόν, ἐγείρεται σῶμα
sown body a natural, it is raised body
πνευματικόν. Εἰ ἔστιν σῶμα ψυχικόν,
a spiritual. If there is body a natural,
ἔστιν καὶ πνευματικόν. **45** οὕτως καὶ
there is also a spiritual [body]. So also
γέγραπται· ἐγένετο ὁ πρῶτος ἄνθρωπος
it has been written: ⁵became ¹The ²first ³man
᾿Αδὰμ εἰς ψυχὴν ζῶσαν· ὁ ἔσχατος
⁴Adam – soul a living; the last
᾿Αδὰμ εἰς πνεῦμα ζωοποιοῦν. **46** ἀλλ'
Adam – spirit a life-giving. But
οὐ πρῶτον τὸ πνευματικόν ἀλλὰ τὸ
not firstly the spiritual [body] but the
ψυχικόν, ἔπειτα τὸ πνευματικόν. **47** ὁ
natural, afterward the spiritual. The
πρῶτος ἄνθρωπος ἐκ γῆς χοϊκός, ὁ
first man [was] out of earth earthy, the
δεύτερος ἄνθρωπος ἐξ οὐρανοῦ. **48** οἷος ὁ
second man [is] out of heaven. Such the
χοϊκός, τοιοῦτοι καὶ οἱ χοϊκοί, καὶ οἷος
earthy man, such also the earthy ones, and such
ὁ ἐπουράνιος, τοιοῦτοι καὶ οἱ ἐπουράνιοι·
the heavenly man, such also the heavenly ones;
49 καὶ καθὼς ἐφορέσαμεν τὴν εἰκόνα τοῦ
and as we bore the image of the
χοϊκοῦ, φορέσομεν καὶ τὴν εἰκόνα τοῦ
earthy man, we shall bear also the image of the
ἐπουρανίου. **50** Τοῦτο δέ φημι, ἀδελφοί,
heavenly man. And this I say, brothers,
ὅτι σὰρξ καὶ αἷμα βασιλείαν θεοῦ κληρο-
that flesh and blood ²[the] kingdom ⁴of God ¹to
νομῆσαι οὐ δύναται, οὐδὲ ἡ φθορὰ τὴν
inherit ¹cannot, neither – ¹corruption –
ἀφθαρσίαν κληρονομεῖ. **51** ἰδοὺ μυστήριον
²incorruption ²inherits. Behold[,] a mystery
ὑμῖν λέγω· πάντες οὐ κοιμηθησόμεθα,
to you I tell: all We shall not fall asleep,
πάντες δὲ ἀλλαγησόμεθα, **52** ἐν ἀτόμῳ,
but all . we shall be changed, in a moment,
ἐν ῥιπῇ ὀφθαλμοῦ, ἐν τῇ ἐσχάτῃ σάλπιγγι·
in a glance of an eye, at the last trumpet;
σαλπίσει γάρ, καὶ οἱ νεκροὶ ἐγερθήσονται
for a trumpet will and the dead will be raised
sound,

40There are also heavenly bodies and there are earthly bodies; but the splendor of the heavenly bodies is one kind, and the splendor of the earthly bodies is another. 41The sun has one kind of splendor, the moon another and the stars another; and star differs from star in splendor. 42So will it be with the resurrection of the dead. The body that is sown is perishable, it is raised imperishable; 43it is sown in dishonor, it is raised in glory; it is sown in weakness, it is raised in power; 44it is sown a natural body, it is raised a spiritual body.

If there is a natural body, there is also a spiritual body. 45So it is written: "The first man Adam became a living being"ˢ; the last Adam, a life-giving spirit. 46The spiritual did not come first, but the natural, and after that the spiritual. 47The first man was of the dust of the earth, the second man from heaven. 48As was the earthly man, so are those who are of the earth; and as is the man from heaven, so also are those who are of heaven. 49And just as we have borne the likeness of the earthly man, so shall weʳ bear the likeness of the man from heaven.

50I declare to you, brothers, that flesh and blood cannot inherit the kingdom of God, nor does the perishable inherit the imperishable. 51Listen, I tell you a mystery: We will not all sleep, but we will all be changed—52in a flash, in the twinkling of an eye, at the last trumpet. For the trumpet will sound, the dead will be raised imper-

ʳSome ancient mss. read *let us also*

ˢ45 Gen. 2:7
ʳ49 Some early manuscripts *so let us*

ishable, and we shall be changed.

53For this perishable must put on the imperishable, and this mortal must put on immortality.

54But when this perishable will have put on the imperishable, and this mortal will have put on immortality, then will come about the saying that is written, "DEATH IS SWALLOWED UP in victory.

55"O DEATH, WHERE IS YOUR VICTORY? O DEATH, WHERE IS YOUR STING?"

56The sting of death is sin, and the power of sin is the law;

57but thanks be to God, who gives us the victory through our Lord Jesus Christ.

58Therefore, my beloved brethren, be steadfast, immovable, always abounding in the work of the Lord, knowing that your toil is not *in* vain in the Lord.

ἄφθαρτοι, καὶ ἡμεῖς ἀλλαγησόμεθα. **53** Δεῖ
incorruptible, and we shall be changed. it behoves

γὰρ τὸ φθαρτὸν τοῦτο ἐνδύσασθαι
For - corruptible this to put on

ἀφθαρσίαν καὶ τὸ θνητὸν τοῦτο ἐνδύσασθαι
incorruption and - mortal this to put on

ἀθανασίαν. **54** ὅταν δὲ τὸ φθαρτὸν τοῦτο
immortality. And whenever this [that is] corruptible

ἐνδύσηται ἀφθαρσίαν καὶ τὸ θνητὸν τοῦτο
shall put on incorruption and this [that is] mortal

ἐνδύσηται ἀθανασίαν, τότε γενήσεται ὁ
shall put on immortality, then will be the

λόγος ὁ γεγραμμένος· κατεπόθη ὁ θάνατος
word - having been ¹was - ¹Death
             written: swallowed up

εἰς νῖκος. **55** ποῦ σου, θάνατε, τὸ νῖκος;
in victory. Where of thee, [O] death, the victory?

ποῦ σου, θάνατε, τὸ κέντρον; **56** τὸ δὲ
where of thee, [O] death, the sting? Now the

κέντρον τοῦ θανάτου ἡ ἁμαρτία, ἡ δὲ
sting - of death - [is] sin, and the

δύναμις τῆς ἁμαρτίας ὁ νόμος· **57** τῷ
power - of sin [is] the law; -

δὲ θεῷ χάρις τῷ διδόντι ἡμῖν τὸ νῖκος
but to God thanks the [one] giving to us the victory

διὰ τοῦ κυρίου ἡμῶν Ἰησοῦ Χριστοῦ.
through the Lord of us Jesus Christ.

58 Ὥστε, ἀδελφοί μου ἀγαπητοί, ἑδραῖοι
So as, brothers of me beloved, firm

γίνεσθε, ἀμετακίνητοι, περισσεύοντες ἐν τῷ
be ye, unmovable, abounding in the

ἔργῳ τοῦ κυρίου πάντοτε, εἰδότες ὅτι
work of the Lord always, knowing that

ὁ κόπος ὑμῶν οὐκ ἔστιν κενὸς ἐν κυρίῳ.
the labour of you is not empty in [the] Lord.

Chapter 16

Instructions and Greetings

16 Περὶ δὲ τῆς λογείας τῆς εἰς τοὺς
Now about the collection - for the

ἁγίους, ὥσπερ διέταξα ταῖς ἐκκλησίαις
saints, as I charged the churches

τῆς Γαλατίας, οὕτως καὶ ὑμεῖς ποιήσατε.
 - of Galatia, so also ¹ye ¹do.

2 κατὰ μίαν σαββάτου ἕκαστος ὑμῶν
Every one of a week each of you
=On the first day of every week

παρ᾽ ἑαυτῷ τιθέτω θησαυρίζων ὅ τι ἐὰν
by himself let him put storing up whatever

εὐοδῶται, ἵνα μὴ ὅταν ἔλθω τότε λογεῖαι
he is prospered, lest whenever I come then ²collections

γίνωνται. **3** ὅταν δὲ παραγένωμαι, οὓς
¹there are. And whenever I arrive, whom-

ἐὰν δοκιμάσητε, δι᾽ ἐπιστολῶν τούτους
ever ye approve, through epistles these

πέμψω ἀπενεγκεῖν τὴν χάριν ὑμῶν εἰς
I will send to carry the grace(gift) of you to

Ἰερουσαλήμ· **4** ἐὰν δὲ ἄξιον ᾖ τοῦ κἀμὲ
Jerusalem; and if ²fitting ¹it is - me also

πορεύεσθαι, σὺν ἐμοὶ πορεύσονται.
to go,ᵈ with me they shall go.

5 Ἐλεύσομαι δὲ πρὸς ὑμᾶς ὅταν Μακε-
And I will come to you whenever ²Mace-

δονίαν διέλθω· Μακεδονίαν γὰρ διέρχομαι,
donia ¹I pass for ²Macedonia ¹I am passing
      through;   through,*

* " Futuristic present "; *cf.* John 14. 3 and ch. 15. 32.

---

ishable, and we will be changed. 53For the perishable must clothe itself with the imperishable, and the mortal with immortality. 54When the perishable has been clothed with the imperishable, and the mortal with immortality, then the saying that is written will come true: "Death has been swallowed up in victory."ᵘ

55"Where, O death, is your victory? Where, O death, is your sting?"ᵛ

56The sting of death is sin, and the power of sin is the law. 57But thanks be to God! He gives us the victory through our Lord Jesus Christ.

58Therefore, my dear brothers, stand firm. Let nothing move you. Always give yourselves fully to the work of the Lord, because you know that your labor in the Lord is not in vain.

The Collection for God's People

NOW about the collection for God's people: Do what I told the Galatian churches to do. 2On the first day of every week, each one of you should set aside a sum of money in keeping with his income, saving it up, so that when I come no collections will have to be made. 3Then, when I arrive, I will give letters of introduction to the men you approve and send them with your gift to Jerusalem. 4If it seems advisable for me to go also, they will accompany me.

Personal Requests

5After I go through Macedonia, I will come to you— for I will be going through

ᵘ*54* Isaiah 25:8
ᵛ*55* Hosea 13:14

6and perhaps I shall stay with you, or even spend the winter, that you may send me on my way wherever I may go.

7For I do not wish to see you now *just* in passing; for I hope to remain with you for some time, if the Lord permits.

8But I shall remain in Ephesus until Pentecost;

9for a wide door for effective *service* has opened to me, and there are many adversaries.

10Now if Timothy comes, see that he is with you without cause to be afraid; for he is doing the Lord's work, as I also am.

11Let no one therefore despise him. But send him on his way in peace, so that he may come to me; for I expect him with the brethren.

12But concerning Apollos our brother, I encouraged him greatly to come to you with the brethren; and it was not at all *his* desire to come now, but he will come when he has opportunity.

13Be on the alert, stand firm in the faith, act like men, be strong.

14Let all that you do be done in love.

15Now I urge you, brethren (you know the household of Stephanas, that they were the first fruits of Achaia, and that they have devoted themselves for ministry to the saints),

16that you also be in subjection to such men and to everyone who helps in the work and labors.

17And I rejoice over the coming of Stephanas and Fortunatus and Achaicus; because they have supplied what was lacking on your part.

18For they have refreshed

6 πρὸς	ὑμᾶς	δὲ	τυχὸν	καταμενῶ ἢ
⁷with	⁸you	¹and	²possibly	³I will remain ⁴or

καὶ παραχειμάσω, ἵνα ὑμεῖς με προπέμ-
⁵even ⁶spend the winter, in order ⁷ye ⁸me ¹may set
that

ψητε οὗ ἐὰν πορεύωμαι. 7 οὐ θέλω γὰρ
forward wherever I may go. For I do not wish

ὑμᾶς ἄρτι ἐν παρόδῳ ἰδεῖν· ἐλπίζω γὰρ
¹you ⁴yet ⁴in ⁵passage ²to see; for I am hoping

χρόνον τινὰ ἐπιμεῖναι πρὸς ὑμᾶς, ἐὰν
³time ²some ¹to remain with you, if

ὁ κύριος ἐπιτρέψῃ. 8 ἐπιμενῶ δὲ ἐν
the Lord permits. But I will remain in

Ἐφέσῳ ἕως τῆς πεντηκοστῆς· 9 θύρα
Ephesus until - Pentecost; ⁵door

γάρ μοι ἀνέῳγεν μεγάλη καὶ ἐνεργής,
¹for ⁴to me ⁶opened ²a great ³and ⁴effective,

καὶ ἀντικείμενοι πολλοί. 10 Ἐὰν δὲ
and ²opposing ¹many. Now if
[there are]

ἔλθῃ Τιμόθεος, βλέπετε ἵνα ἀφόβως
²comes ¹Timothy, see in order that fearlessly

γένηται πρὸς ὑμᾶς· τὸ γὰρ ἔργον κυρίου
he is with you; for the work of [the] Lord

ἐργάζεται ὡς κἀγώ· 11 μή τις οὖν αὐτὸν
he works as I also; ²not ¹any- ¹there- ²him
one fore

ἐξουθενήσῃ. προπέμψατε δὲ αὐτὸν ἐν
¹despise. But set ye forward him in

εἰρήνῃ, ἵνα ἔλθῃ πρός με· ἐκδέχομαι γὰρ
peace, in order he may to me; for I am awaiting
that come

αὐτὸν μετὰ τῶν ἀδελφῶν. 12 Περὶ δὲ
him with the brothers. Now about

Ἀπολλῶ τοῦ ἀδελφοῦ, πολλὰ παρεκάλεσα
²Apollos the ¹brother, ²much ¹I besought

αὐτὸν ἵνα ἔλθῃ πρὸς ὑμᾶς μετὰ τῶν
²him in order he would to you with the
that come

ἀδελφῶν· καὶ πάντως οὐκ ἦν θέλημα
brothers; and altogether it was not [his] will

ἵνα νῦν ἔλθῃ, ἐλεύσεται δὲ ὅταν εὐκαιρήσῃ.
in ²now ¹he but he will come whenever he has
order should opportunity.
that come,

13 Γρηγορεῖτε, στήκετε ἐν τῇ πίστει,
Watch ye, stand in the faith,

ἀνδρίζεσθε, κραταιοῦσθε. 14 πάντα ὑμῶν
play the man, be strong. ¹All things ²of you

ἐν ἀγάπῃ γινέσθω.
⁴in ⁵love ¹let be.

15 Παρακαλῶ δὲ ὑμᾶς, ἀδελφοί· οἴδατε
Now I beseech you, brothers: Know ye

τὴν οἰκίαν Στεφανᾶ, ὅτι ἐστὶν ἀπαρχὴ
the household of Stephanas, that it is firstfruit

τῆς Ἀχαίας καὶ εἰς διακονίαν τοῖς
- of Achaia and to ministry to the

ἁγίοις ἔταξαν ἑαυτούς· 16 ἵνα καὶ ὑμεῖς
saints they appointed themselves; in order also ye
that

ὑποτάσσησθε τοῖς τοιούτοις καὶ παντὶ τῷ
may submit - to such ones and to everyone

συνεργοῦντι καὶ κοπιῶντι. 17 χαίρω δὲ
working with [?me] and labouring. Now I rejoice

ἐπὶ τῇ παρουσίᾳ Στεφανᾶ καὶ Φορτουνάτου
at the presence of Stephanas and of Fortunatus

καὶ Ἀχαϊκοῦ, ὅτι τὸ ὑμέτερον ὑστέρημα
and of Achaicus, that - ³your ⁴lack

οὗτοι ἀνεπλήρωσαν· 18 ἀνέπαυσαν γὰρ τὸ
¹these ²supplied; for they refreshed -

Macedonia. 6Perhaps I will stay with you awhile, or even spend the winter, so that you can help me on my journey, wherever I go. 7I do not want to see you now and make only a passing visit; I hope to spend some time with you, if the Lord permits. 8But I will stay on at Ephesus until Pentecost, 9because a great door for effective work has opened to me, and there are many who oppose me.

10If Timothy comes, see to it that he has nothing to fear while he is with you, for he is carrying on the work of the Lord, just as I am. 11No one, then, should refuse to accept him. Send him on his way in peace so that he may return to me. I am expecting him along with the brothers.

12Now about our brother Apollos: I strongly urged him to go to you with the brothers. He was quite unwilling to go now, but he will go when he has the opportunity.

13Be on your guard; stand firm in the faith; be men of courage; be strong. 14Do everything in love.

15You know that the household of Stephanas were the first converts in Achaia, and they have devoted themselves to the service of the saints. I urge you, brothers, 16to submit to such as these and to everyone who joins in the work, and labors at it. 17I was glad when Stephanas, Fortunatus and Achaicus arrived, because they have supplied what was lacking from you. 18For they re-my spirit and yours. Therefore acknowledge such men.

19The churches of Asia greet you. Aquila and Prisca greet you heartily in the Lord, with the church that is in their house.

20All the brethren greet you. Greet one another with a holy kiss.

21The greeting is in my own hand—Paul.

22If anyone does not love the Lord, let him be accursed. Maranatha.

23The grace of the Lord Jesus be with you.

24My love be with you all in Christ Jesus. Amen.

ἐμὸν πνεῦμα καὶ τὸ ὑμῶν. ἐπιγινώσκετε
my spirit and - of you(yours). Recognize ye

οὖν τοὺς τοιούτους.
therefore - such ones.

19 Ἀσπάζονται ὑμᾶς αἱ ἐκκλησίαι τῆς
⁴Greet ⁵you ¹the ²churches -

Ἀσίας. ἀσπάζεται ὑμᾶς ἐν κυρίῳ πολλὰ
³of Asia. ⁴Greets ⁵you ⁷in ⁸[the] Lord ⁶much

Ἀκύλας καὶ Πρίσκα σὺν τῇ κατ᾽ οἶκον
¹Aquila ²and ³Prisca ⁸with ¹⁰the ¹¹in [the] house

αὐτῶν ἐκκλησίᾳ. 20 ἀσπάζονται ὑμᾶς οἱ
¹²of them ¹¹church. ⁴Greet ⁵you ²the

ἀδελφοὶ πάντες. Ἀσπάσασθε ἀλλήλους ἐν
³brothers ¹all. Greet ye one another with

φιλήματι ἁγίῳ. 21 Ὁ ἀσπασμὸς τῇ
kiss a holy. ¹The ²greeting -

ἐμῇ χειρὶ Παύλου. 22 εἴ τις οὐ φιλεῖ
⁴with my ³hand ⁵of Paul. If anyone loves not

τὸν κύριον, ἤτω ἀνάθεμα. μαράνα θά.
the Lord, let him be a curse. Marana tha.

23 ἡ χάρις τοῦ κυρίου Ἰησοῦ μεθ᾽ ὑμῶν.
The grace of the Lord Jesus [be] with you.

24 ἡ ἀγάπη μου μετὰ πάντων ὑμῶν ἐν
The love of me [be] with ²all ¹you in

Χριστῷ Ἰησοῦ.
Christ Jesus.

---

freshed my spirit and yours also. Such men deserve recognition.

Final Greetings

19The churches in the province of Asia send you greetings. Aquila and Priscilla[w] greet you warmly in the Lord, and so does the church that meets at their house. 20All the brothers here send you greetings. Greet one another with a holy kiss.

21I, Paul, write this greeting in my own hand.

22If anyone does not love the Lord—a curse be on him. Come, O Lord[x]!

23The grace of the Lord Jesus be with you.

24My love to all of you in Christ Jesus. Amen.[y]

[w]19 Greek *Prisca*, a variant of *Priscilla*

[x]22 In Aramaic the expression *Come, O Lord* is *Marana tha*.

[y]24 Some manuscripts do not have *Amen*.

Chapter 1

Introduction

PAUL, an apostle of Christ Jesus by the will of God, and Timothy *our* brother, to the church of God which is at Corinth with all the saints who are throughout Achaia. [2]Grace to you and peace from God our Father and the Lord Jesus Christ.

[3]Blessed *be* the God and Father of our Lord Jesus Christ, the Father of mercies and God of all comfort; [4]who comforts us in all our affliction so that we may be able to comfort those who are in any affliction with the comfort with which we ourselves are comforted by God.

[5]For just as the sufferings of Christ are ours in abundance, so also our comfort is abundant through Christ.

[6]But if we are afflicted, it is for your comfort and salvation; or if we are comforted, it is for your comfort, which is effective in the patient enduring of the same sufferings which we also suffer;

[7]and our hope for you is firmly grounded, knowing that as you are sharers of our sufferings, so also you are *sharers* of our comfort.

[8]For we do not want you to be unaware, brethren, of our affliction which came *to us* in Asia, that we were burdened excessively, beyond our strength, so that we despaired even of life;

[9]indeed, we had the sentence of death within our-

---

1 Παῦλος ἀπόστολος Χριστοῦ Ἰησοῦ
Paul an apostle of Christ Jesus

διὰ θελήματος θεοῦ καὶ Τιμόθεος ὁ
through [the] will of God and Timothy the

ἀδελφὸς τῇ ἐκκλησίᾳ τοῦ θεοῦ τῇ οὔσῃ
brother to the church – of God – being

ἐν Κορίνθῳ σὺν τοῖς ἁγίοις πᾶσιν τοῖς
in Corinth with 'the 'saints 'all –

οὖσιν ἐν ὅλῃ τῇ Ἀχαΐᾳ· **2** χάρις ὑμῖν καὶ
being in all – Achaia: Grace to you and

εἰρήνη ἀπὸ θεοῦ πατρὸς ἡμῶν καὶ κυρίου
peace from God [the] Father of us and [the] Lord

Ἰησοῦ Χριστοῦ.
Jesus Christ.

3 Εὐλογητὸς ὁ θεὸς καὶ πατὴρ τοῦ
Blessed [be] the God and Father of the

κυρίου ἡμῶν Ἰησοῦ Χριστοῦ, ὁ πατὴρ
Lord of us Jesus Christ, the Father

τῶν οἰκτιρμῶν καὶ θεὸς πάσης παρακλήσ-
– of compassions and God of all com-

εως, **4** ὁ παρακαλῶν ἡμᾶς ἐπὶ πάσῃ
fort, the [one] comforting us on(in) all

τῇ θλίψει ἡμῶν, εἰς τὸ δύνασθαι ἡμᾶς
the affliction of us, [with a – to be able us[b]

view] to =our being able

παρακαλεῖν τοὺς ἐν πάσῃ θλίψει διὰ
to comfort the ones in every affliction through

τῆς παρακλήσεως ἧς παρακαλούμεθα αὐτοὶ
the comfort of(with) we are comforted [our-]

which selves

ὑπὸ τοῦ θεοῦ. **5** ὅτι καθὼς περισσεύει τὰ
by – God. Because as abounds the

παθήματα τοῦ Χριστοῦ εἰς ἡμᾶς, οὕτως
sufferings – of Christ in us, so

διὰ τοῦ Χριστοῦ περισσεύει καὶ ἡ παρά-
through – Christ abounds also the com-

κλησις ἡμῶν. **6** εἴτε δὲ θλιβόμεθα, ὑπὲρ
fort of us. Now whether we are on be-

afflicted, half of

τῆς ὑμῶν παρακλήσεως καὶ σωτηρίας· εἴτε
the 'of you 'comfort 'and 'salvation; whether

παρακαλούμεθα, ὑπὲρ τῆς ὑμῶν παρακλή-
we are comforted, on behalf of the 'of you 'com-

σεως τῆς ἐνεργουμένης ἐν ὑπομονῇ τῶν
fort – operating in endurance of the

αὐτῶν παθημάτων ὧν καὶ ἡμεῖς πάσχομεν,
same sufferings which also we suffer,

7 καὶ ἡ ἐλπὶς ἡμῶν βεβαία ὑπὲρ ὑμῶν
and the hope of us [is] firm on behalf of you

εἰδότες ὅτι ὡς κοινωνοί ἐστε τῶν παθημά-
knowing that as partakers ye are of the suffer-

των, οὕτως καὶ τῆς παρακλήσεως. **8** Οὐ
ings, so also of the comfort. not

γὰρ θέλομεν ὑμᾶς ἀγνοεῖν, ἀδελφοί, ὑπὲρ
For we wish you to be ignorant, brothers, as to

τῆς θλίψεως ἡμῶν τῆς γενομένης ἐν
the affliction of us – having been in

τῇ Ἀσίᾳ, ὅτι καθ᾽ ὑπερβολὴν ὑπὲρ
– Asia, that excessively† beyond

δύναμιν ἐβαρήθημεν, ὥστε ἐξαπορηθῆναι
power we were burdened, so as to despair

=so that we despaired even

ἡμᾶς καὶ τοῦ ζῆν· **9** ἀλλὰ αὐτοὶ ἐν
us[b] even – to live; but [our]selves in

of life;

ἑαυτοῖς τὸ ἀπόκριμα τοῦ θανάτου ἐσχήκα-
ourselves the sentence – of death we have

Chapter 1

PAUL, an apostle of Christ Jesus by the will of God, and Timothy our brother,

To the church of God in Corinth, together with all the saints throughout Achaia:

[2]Grace and peace to you from God our Father and the Lord Jesus Christ.

The God of All Comfort

[3]Praise be to the God and Father of our Lord Jesus Christ, the Father of compassion and the God of all comfort, [4]who comforts us in all our troubles, so that we can comfort those in any trouble with the comfort we ourselves have received from God. [5]For just as the sufferings of Christ flow over into our lives, so also through Christ our comfort overflows. [6]If we are distressed, it is for your comfort and salvation; if we are comforted, it is for your comfort, which produces in you patient endurance of the same sufferings we suffer. [7]And our hope for you is firm, because we know that just as you share in our sufferings, so also you share in our comfort.

[8]We do not want you to be uninformed, brothers, about the hardships we suffered in the province of Asia. We were under great pressure, far beyond our ability to endure, so that we despaired even of life. [9]Indeed, in our hearts we felt

selves in order that we should not trust in ourselves, but in God who raises the dead;

10who delivered us from so great a *peril of* death, and will deliver *us*, He on whom we have set our hope. And He will yet deliver us,

11you also joining in helping us through your prayers, that thanks may be given by many persons on our behalf for the favor bestowed upon us through *the prayers of* many.

Paul's Integrity

12For our proud confidence is this, the testimony of our conscience, that in holiness and godly sincerity, not in fleshly wisdom but in the grace of God, we have conducted ourselves in the world, and especially toward you.

13For we write nothing else to you than what you read and understand, and I hope you will understand until the end;

14just as you also partially did understand us, that we are your reason to be proud as you also are ours, in the day of our Lord Jesus.

15And in this confidence I intended at first to come to you, that you might twice receive a blessing;

16that is, to pass your way into Macedonia, and again from Macedonia to come to you, and by you to be helped on my journey to Judea.

17Therefore, I was not vacillating when I intended to do this, was I? Or that which I purpose, do I purpose according to the flesh, that with me there should

---

μεν, ἵνα μὴ πεποιθότες ὦμεν ἐφ' ἑαυτοῖς
had, in order ²not ³having ¹we on ourselves
　　　　that　　 trusted might be

ἀλλ' ἐπὶ τῷ θεῷ τῷ ἐγείροντι τοὺς
but on - God the [one] raising the

νεκρούς· 10 ὃς ἐκ τηλικούτου θανάτου
dead; who out of so great a death

ἐρρύσατο ἡμᾶς καὶ ῥύσεται, εἰς ὃν
delivered us and will deliver, in whom

ἠλπίκαμεν [ὅτι] καὶ ἔτι ῥύσεται, 11 συν-
we have hoped that indeed yet he will deliver, co-

υπουργούντων καὶ ὑμῶν ὑπὲρ ἡμῶν τῇ
operating also you² on behalf of us -
=while ye also coöperate

δεήσει, ἵνα ἐκ πολλῶν προσώπων τὸ
in petition, in order ⁴by ⁵many ⁶persons ⁷[for]
　　　　that　　　　　　　　　　　　　⁸the

εἰς ἡμᾶς χάρισμα διὰ πολλῶν εὐχαριστηθῇ
¹⁰to ¹¹us ⁹gift ¹²through ¹³many ¹thanks may
　　　　　　　　　　　　　　　be given

ὑπὲρ ἡμῶν.
²on behalf of ³us.

12 Ἡ γὰρ καύχησις ἡμῶν αὕτη ἐστίν,
For the boasting of us ¹this ¹is,

τὸ μαρτύριον τῆς συνειδήσεως ἡμῶν, ὅτι
the testimony of the conscience of us, because

ἐν ἁγιότητι καὶ εἰλικρινείᾳ τοῦ θεοῦ,
in sanctity and sincerity - of God,

οὐκ ἐν σοφίᾳ σαρκικῇ ἀλλ' ἐν χάριτι
not in wisdom fleshly but in [the] grace

θεοῦ, ἀνεστράφημεν ἐν τῷ κόσμῳ, περισ-
of God, we behaved in the world, ²more

σοτέρως δὲ πρὸς ὑμᾶς. 13 οὐ γὰρ ἄλλα
²especially ¹and with you. ²Not ¹for ⁴other
　　　　　　　　　　　　　　　　　 things

γράφομεν ὑμῖν ἀλλ' ἢ ἃ ἀναγινώσκετε
³we write to you *other* than what ye read

ἢ καὶ ἐπιγινώσκετε, ἐλπίζω δὲ ὅτι
or even perceive, and I hope that

ἕως τέλους ἐπιγνώσεσθε, 14 καθὼς καὶ
to [the] end ye will perceive, as also

ἐπέγνωτε ἡμᾶς ἀπὸ μέρους, ὅτι καύχημα
ye perceived us from(in) part, because ²boast

ὑμῶν ἐσμεν καθάπερ καὶ ὑμεῖς ἡμῶν
³of you ¹we are even as also ye of us

ἐν τῇ ἡμέρᾳ τοῦ κυρίου ἡμῶν Ἰησοῦ.
in the day of the Lord of us Jesus.

15 Καὶ ταύτῃ τῇ πεποιθήσει ἐβουλόμην
And in this - persuasion I determined

πρότερον πρὸς ὑμᾶς ἐλθεῖν ἵνα δευτέραν
formerly to you to come in order a second
　　　　　　　　　　　　　　　that

χάριν σχῆτε, 16 καὶ δι' ὑμῶν διελθεῖν
grace ye might have, and through you to pass *through*

εἰς Μακεδονίαν, καὶ πάλιν ἀπὸ Μακεδονίας
into Macedonia, and again from Macedonia

ἐλθεῖν πρὸς ὑμᾶς καὶ ὑφ' ὑμῶν
to come to you and by you

προπεμφθῆναι εἰς τὴν Ἰουδαίαν. 17 τοῦτο
to be set forward to - Judæa. This

οὖν βουλόμενος μήτι ἄρα τῇ ἐλαφρίᾳ
therefore determining *not* ²then - ¹fickleness

ἐχρησάμην; ἢ ἃ βουλεύομαι κατὰ σάρκα
¹did I use? or [the] I determine according [the]
　　　　　　 things which　　　　　　 to　 flesh

βουλεύομαι, ἵνα ᾖ παρ' ἐμοὶ τὸ ναί
do I determine, in order there with me the Yes
　　　　　　　 that may be

---

the sentence of death. But this happened that we might not rely on ourselves but on God, who raises the dead. 10He has delivered us from such a deadly peril, and he will deliver us. On him we have set our hope that he will continue to deliver us, 11as you help us by your prayers. Then many will give thanks on our*a* behalf for the gracious favor granted us in answer to the prayers of many.

Paul's Change of Plans

12Now this is our boast: Our conscience testifies that we have conducted ourselves in the world, and especially in our relations with you, in the holiness and sincerity that are from God. We have done so not according to worldly wisdom but according to God's grace. 13For we do not write you anything you cannot read or understand. And I hope that, 14as you have understood us in part, you will come to understand fully that you can boast of us just as we will boast of you in the day of the Lord Jesus.

15Because I was confident of this, I planned to visit you first so that you might benefit twice. 16I planned to visit you on my way to Macedonia and to come back to you from Macedonia, and then to have you send me on my way to Judea. 17When I planned this, did I do it lightly? Or do I make my plans in a worldly manner so that in the same breath I

a11 Many manuscripts *your*

be yes, yes and no, no *at the same time?*

18But as God is faithful, our word to you is not yes and no.

19For the Son of God, Christ Jesus, who was preached among you by us—by me and Silvanus and Timothy—was not yes and no, but is yes in Him.

20For as many as may be the promises of God, in Him they are yes; wherefore also by Him is our Amen to the glory of God through us.

21Now He who establishes us with you in Christ and anointed us is God,

22who also sealed us and gave *us* the Spirit in our hearts as a pledge.

23But I call God as witness to my soul, that to spare you I came no more to Corinth.

24Not that we lord it over your faith, but are workers with you for your joy; for in your faith you are standing firm.

Chapter 2

Reaffirm Your Love

BUT I determined this for my own sake, that I would not come to you in sorrow again.

2For if I cause you sorrow, who then makes me glad but the one whom I made sorrowful?

3And this is the very thing I wrote you, lest, when I came, I should have sorrow from those who ought to make me rejoice; having confidence in you all, that my joy would be *the joy* of you all.

4For out of much affliction and anguish of heart I wrote to you with many tears; not that you should be made sorrowful, but that you might know the love which I have especially for

---

ναὶ καὶ τὸ οὔ οὔ; **18** πιστὸς δὲ ὁ
yes and the No no? But faithful [is] –

θεὸς ὅτι ὁ λόγος ἡμῶν ὁ πρὸς ὑμᾶς
God that the word of us – to you

οὐκ ἔστιν ναὶ καὶ οὔ. **19** ὁ τοῦ θεοῦ
is not yes and no. ²the – ⁴of God

γὰρ υἱὸς Χριστὸς Ἰησοῦς ὁ ἐν ὑμῖν
¹For ³Son Christ Jesus ¹the ²among ⁴you [one]

δι᾽ ἡμῶν κηρυχθείς, δι᾽ ἐμοῦ καὶ Σιλουανοῦ
⁵through ⁶us ⁷proclaimed, through me and Silvanus

καὶ Τιμοθέου, οὐκ ἐγένετο ναὶ καὶ οὔ,
and Timothy, was not yes and no,

ἀλλὰ ναὶ ἐν αὐτῷ γέγονεν. **20** ὅσαι γὰρ
but ²Yes ³in ⁴him ¹has been. For as many

ἐπαγγελίαι θεοῦ, ἐν αὐτῷ τὸ ναί· διὸ
[as are] of God, in him [is] the Yes; wherefore
promises

καὶ δι᾽ αὐτοῦ τὸ ἀμὴν τῷ θεῷ πρὸς
also through him the Amen – ²to God ¹unto

δόξαν δι᾽ ἡμῶν. **21** ὁ δὲ βεβαιῶν ἡμᾶς
²glory through us. But the [one] making firm us

σὺν ὑμῖν εἰς Χριστὸν καὶ χρίσας ἡμᾶς
with you in Christ and having anointed us [is]

θεός, **22** ὁ καὶ σφραγισάμενος ἡμᾶς καὶ
God, the [one] both having sealed us and

δοὺς τὸν ἀρραβῶνα τοῦ πνεύματος ἐν
having the earnest of the Spirit in
given

ταῖς καρδίαις ἡμῶν.
the hearts of us.

23 Ἐγὼ δὲ μάρτυρα τὸν θεὸν ἐπικαλοῦμαι
Now ⁴I ⁷[as] witness – ⁶God ⁵invoke

ἐπὶ τὴν ἐμὴν ψυχήν, ὅτι φειδόμενος
¹on – ²my ³life, that sparing

ὑμῶν οὐκέτι ἦλθον εἰς Κόρινθον. **24** οὐχ ὅτι
you ²no more ¹I came to Corinth. Not that

κυριεύομεν ὑμῶν τῆς πίστεως, ἀλλὰ συνεργοί
we rule over ²of you ¹the ²faith, but ²fellow-
workers

ἐσμεν τῆς χαρᾶς ὑμῶν· τῇ γὰρ πίστει
¹we are of the joy of you; – for by faith

ἑστήκατε. **2** ἔκρινα δὲ ἐμαυτῷ τοῦτο, τὸ μὴ
ye stand. But I decided in myself this, – not

πάλιν ἐν λύπῃ πρὸς ὑμᾶς ἐλθεῖν. **2** εἰ
again ⁴in ³grief ²to ³you ¹to come. if

γὰρ ἐγὼ λυπῶ ὑμᾶς, καὶ τίς ὁ εὐφραίνων
For I grieve you, then who the making glad
[one]

με εἰ μὴ ὁ λυπούμενος ἐξ ἐμοῦ; **3** καὶ
me except the [one] being grieved by me? And

ἔγραψα τοῦτο αὐτὸ ἵνα μὴ ἐλθὼν λύπην
I wrote this very thing lest coming grief

σχῶ ἀφ᾽ ὧν ἔδει με χαίρειν, πεποιθὼς
I should from [those] it me to rejoice, having
have whom beloved confidence

ἐπὶ πάντας ὑμᾶς ὅτι ἡ ἐμὴ χαρὰ πάντων
in ²all ¹you that – my joy ²all

ὑμῶν ἐστιν. **4** ἐκ γὰρ πολλῆς θλίψεως
⁹of you ¹is. For out of much affliction

καὶ συνοχῆς καρδίας ἔγραψα ὑμῖν διὰ
and anxiety of heart I wrote to you through

πολλῶν δακρύων, οὐχ ἵνα λυπηθῆτε, ἀλλὰ
many tears, not in order ye should be but
that grieved,

τὴν ἀγάπην ἵνα γνῶτε ἣν ἔχω περισ-
²the ⁴love ¹in order ²ye should ⁵which I have more
that know

---

say, "Yes, yes" and "No, no"?

18But as surely as God is faithful, our message to you is not "Yes" and "No." 19For the Son of God, Jesus Christ, who was preached among you by me and Silas *b* and Timothy, was not "Yes" and "No," but in him it has always been "Yes." 20For no matter how many promises God has made, they are "Yes" in Christ. And so through him the "Amen" is spoken by us to the glory of God. 21Now it is God who makes both us and you stand firm in Christ. He anointed us, 22set his seal of ownership on us, and put his Spirit in our hearts as a deposit, guaranteeing what is to come.

23I call God as my witness that it was in order to spare you that I did not return to Corinth. 24Not that we lord it over your faith, but we work with you for your joy, because it is by faith you stand firm.

1So I made up my mind that I would not make another painful visit to you. 2For if I grieve you, who is left to make me glad but you whom I have grieved? 3I wrote as I did so that when I came I should not be distressed by those who ought to make me rejoice. I had confidence in all of you, that you would all share my joy. 4For I wrote you out of great distress and anguish of heart and with many tears, not to

---

b19 Greek Silvanus, a variant of Silas

Left column (English):

you.

5But if any has caused sorrow, he has caused sorrow not to me, but in some degree—in order not to say too much—to all of you.

6Sufficient for such a one is this punishment which was *inflicted by* the majority,

7so that on the contrary you should rather forgive and comfort *him*, lest somehow such a one be overwhelmed by excessive sorrow.

8Wherefore I urge you to reaffirm *your* love for him.

9For to this end also I wrote that I might put you to the test, whether you are obedient in all things.

10But whom you forgive anything, I *forgive* also; for indeed what I have forgiven, if I have forgiven anything, I *did it* for your sakes in the presence of Christ,

11in order that no advantage be taken of us by Satan; for we are not ignorant of his schemes.

12Now when I came to Troas for the gospel of Christ and when a door was opened for me in the Lord,

13I had no rest for my spirit, not finding Titus my brother; but taking my leave of them, I went on to Macedonia.

14But thanks be to God, who always leads us in His triumph in Christ, and manifests through us the sweet aroma of the knowledge of Him in every place.

15For we are a fragrance of Christ to God among those who are being saved and among those who are perishing;

16to the one an aroma from death to death, to the other an aroma from life to life. And who is adequate for these things?

17For we are not like many, *a*peddling the word

a Or, *corrupting*

Center column (Greek interlinear):

σοτέρως εἰς ὑμᾶς. 5 Εἰ δέ τις λελύπηκεν,
abundantly to you. But if anyone has grieved,

οὐκ ἐμὲ λελύπηκεν, ἀλλὰ ἀπὸ μέρους,
not me he has grieved, but from(in) part,

ἵνα μὴ ἐπιβαρῶ, πάντας ὑμᾶς. 6 ἱκανὸν
lest I am burdensome, ²all ¹you. Enough

τῷ τοιούτῳ ἡ ἐπιτιμία αὕτη ἡ ὑπὸ
for such a one this punishment - by

τῶν -πλειόνων, 7 ὥστε τοὐναντίον μᾶλλον
the majority, so as on the contrary rather

ὑμᾶς χαρίσασθαι καὶ παρακαλέσαι, μή πως
you to forgive and to comfort,*b* lest
=ye should rather forgive and comfort,

τῇ περισσοτέρᾳ λύπῃ καταποθῇ ὁ τοιοῦτος.
²by ⁴more abundant ⁵grief ³should be ¹such a one.
the swallowed up

8 διὸ παρακαλῶ ὑμᾶς κυρῶσαι εἰς αὐτὸν
Wherefore I beseech you to confirm to him

ἀγάπην· 9 εἰς τοῦτο γὰρ καὶ ἔγραψα,
[your] love; ²to ³this [end] ¹for indeed I wrote,

ἵνα γνῶ τὴν δοκιμὴν ὑμῶν, εἰ εἰς πάντα
in or- I might the proof of you, if in all things
der that know

ὑπήκοοί ἐστε. 10 ᾧ δέ τι χαρίζεσθε,
obedient ye are. Now *to* whom anything ye forgive,

κἀγώ· καὶ γὰρ ἐγὼ ὃ κεχάρισμαι, εἰ
I also; for indeed ²I ¹what ²have forgiven, if

τι κεχάρισμαι, δι' ὑμᾶς ἐν προσώπῳ
²any- ¹I have [it is] on you in [the] person
thing forgiven, account of

Χριστοῦ, 11 ἵνα μὴ πλεονεκτηθῶμεν ὑπὸ
of Christ, lest we are taken advantage of by

τοῦ σατανᾶ· οὐ γὰρ αὐτοῦ τὰ νοήματα
- Satan; for ²not ²of him ¹the ⁶designs

ἀγνοοῦμεν. 12 Ἐλθὼν δὲ εἰς τὴν Τρῳάδα εἰς
¹we ²are ⁴ignorant [of]. But coming to - Troas in

τὸ εὐαγγέλιον τοῦ Χριστοῦ, καὶ θύρας
the gospel of Christ, and a door

μοι ἀνεῳγμένης ἐν κυρίῳ, 13 οὐκ ἔσχηκα
to me having been by [the] Lord, I *have* had no
opened*a*

ἄνεσιν τῷ πνεύματί μου τῷ μὴ εὑρεῖν
rest to the spirit of me in the not to find
=when I did not find ...

με Τίτον τὸν ἀδελφόν μου, ἀλλὰ ἀποτα-
me*b* Titus the brother of me, but saying

ξάμενος αὐτοῖς ἐξῆλθον εἰς Μακεδονίαν.
farewell to them I went forth into Macedonia.

14 Τῷ δὲ θεῷ χάρις τῷ πάντοτε
But ²to God ¹thanks the [one] always

θριαμβεύοντι ἡμᾶς ἐν τῷ Χριστῷ καὶ
leading in triumph us in - Christ and

τὴν ὀσμὴν τῆς γνώσεως αὐτοῦ φανεροῦντι
⁴the ⁵odour ⁶of the ⁷knowledge ⁸of him ¹manifesting

δι' ἡμῶν ἐν παντὶ τόπῳ· 15 ὅτι Χριστοῦ
²through ³us in every place; because of Christ

εὐωδία ἐσμὲν τῷ θεῷ ἐν τοῖς σῳζομένοις
a sweet we are - to God in the [ones] being saved
smell

καὶ ἐν τοῖς ἀπολλυμένοις, 16 οἷς μὲν
and in the [ones] perishing, to the [latter]†

ὀσμὴ ἐκ θανάτου εἰς θάνατον, οἷς δὲ
an odour out of death unto death, to the [former]†

ὀσμὴ ἐκ ζωῆς εἰς ζωήν. καὶ πρὸς
an odour out of life unto life. And for

ταῦτα τίς ἱκανός; 17 οὐ γάρ ἐσμεν
these things who [is] competent? For we are not

ὡς οἱ πολλοὶ καπηλεύοντες τὸν λόγον
as the many hawking the word

Right column (English):

grieve you but to let you know the depth of my love for you.

Forgiveness for the Sinner

5If anyone has caused grief, he has not so much grieved me as he has grieved all of you, to some extent—not to put it too severely. 6The punishment inflicted on him by the majority is sufficient for him. 7Now instead, you ought to forgive and comfort him, so that he will not be overwhelmed by excessive sorrow. 8I urge you, therefore, to reaffirm your love for him. 9The reason I wrote you was to see if you would stand the test and be obedient in everything. 10If you forgive anyone, I also forgive him. And what I have forgiven—if there was anything to forgive—I have forgiven in the sight of Christ for your sake, 11in order that Satan might not outwit us. For we are not unaware of his schemes.

Ministers of the New Covenant

12Now when I went to Troas to preach the gospel of Christ and found that the Lord had opened a door for me, 13I still had no peace of mind, because I did not find my brother Titus there. So I said good-by to them and went on to Macedonia.

14But thanks be to God, who always leads us in triumphal procession in Christ and through us spreads everywhere the fragrance of the knowledge of him. 15For we are to God the aroma of Christ among those who are being saved and those who are perishing. 16To the one we are the smell of death; to the other, the fragrance of life. And who is equal to such a task? 17Unlike so many, we do not peddle the word of God of God, but as from sincerity, but as from God, we speak in Christ in the sight of God.

Chapter 3

Ministers of a New Covenant

ARE we beginning to commend ourselves again? Or do we need, as some, letters of commendation to you or from you?

2You are our letter, written in our hearts, known and read by all men;

3being manifested that you are a letter of Christ, cared for by us, written not with ink, but with the Spirit of the living God, not on tablets of stone, but on tablets of human hearts.

4And such confidence we have through Christ toward God.

5Not that we are adequate in ourselves to consider anything as *coming* from ourselves, but our adequacy is from God,

6who also made us adequate *as* servants of a new covenant, not of the letter, but of the Spirit; for the letter kills, but the Spirit gives life.

7But if the ministry of death, in letters engraved on stones, came with glory, so that the sons of Israel could not look intently at the face of Moses because of the glory of his face, fading *as* it was,

8how shall the ministry of the Spirit fail to be even more with glory?

9For if the ministry of condemnation has glory, much more does the ministry of righteousness abound in glory.

10For indeed what had

τοῦ θεοῦ, ἀλλ' ὡς ἐξ εἰλικρινείας, ἀλλ'
- of God, but as of sincerity, but

ὡς ἐκ θεοῦ κατέναντι θεοῦ ἐν Χριστῷ
as of God before God in Christ

λαλοῦμεν.
we speak.

3 Ἀρχόμεθα πάλιν ἑαυτοὺς συνιστάνειν;
Do we begin again ourselves to commend?

ἢ μὴ χρῄζομεν ὡς τινες συστατικῶν
or not need we as some commendatory

ἐπιστολῶν πρὸς ὑμᾶς ἢ ἐξ ὑμῶν; **2** ἡ
epistles to you or from you? The

ἐπιστολὴ ἡμῶν ὑμεῖς ἐστε, ἐγγεγραμμένη
epistle of us ye are, having been inscribed

ἐν ταῖς καρδίαις ἡμῶν, γινωσκομένη καὶ
in the hearts of us, being known and

ἀναγινωσκομένη ὑπὸ πάντων ἀνθρώπων,
being read by all men,

3 φανερούμενοι ὅτι ἐστὲ ἐπιστολὴ Χριστοῦ
being manifested that ye are an epistle of Christ

διακονηθεῖσα ὑφ' ἡμῶν, ἐγγεγραμμένη οὐ
ministered by us, having been inscribed not

μέλανι ἀλλὰ πνεύματι θεοῦ ζῶντος, οὐκ
by ink but by [the] Spirit of [2]God [1]a living, not

ἐν πλαξὶν λιθίναις ἀλλ' ἐν πλαξὶν καρδίαις
in [2]tablets [1]stony but in tablets [which are]

σαρκίναις.
[1]fleshy.   [2]hearts

4 Πεποίθησιν δὲ τοιαύτην ἔχομεν διὰ
[3]confidence [1]And [2]such we have through

τοῦ Χριστοῦ πρὸς τὸν θεόν. **5** οὐχ
- Christ toward - God. Not

ὅτι ἀφ' ἑαυτῶν ἱκανοί ἐσμεν λογίσασθαί
that [2]from [4]ourselves [3]competent [1]we are to reckon

τι ὡς ἐξ ἑαυτῶν, ἀλλ' ἡ ἱκανότης
any-thing as of ourselves, but the competence

ἡμῶν ἐκ τοῦ θεοῦ, **6** ὃς καὶ ἱκάνωσεν
of us [is] of - God, who also made competent

ἡμᾶς διακόνους καινῆς διαθήκης, οὐ
us [as] ministers of a new covenant, not

γράμματος ἀλλὰ πνεύματος· τὸ γὰρ γράμμα
of letter but of spirit; for the letter

ἀποκτείνει, τὸ δὲ πνεῦμα ζωοποιεῖ. **7** Εἰ
kills, but the spirit makes alive. if

δὲ ἡ διακονία τοῦ θανάτου ἐν γράμμασιν
Now the ministry - of death in letters

ἐντετυπωμένη λίθοις ἐγενήθη ἐν δόξῃ,
having been engraved in stones was in glory,

ὥστε μὴ δύνασθαι ἀτενίσαι τοὺς υἱοὺς
so as not to be able to gaze the sons
=so that the sons of Israel were not able to gaze

Ἰσραὴλ εἰς τὸ πρόσωπον Μωϋσέως διὰ
of Israel[b] at the face of Moses on account of

τὴν δόξαν τοῦ προσώπου αὐτοῦ τὴν
the glory of the face of him the

καταργουμένην, **8** πῶς οὐχὶ μᾶλλον ἡ
being done away, how [2]not [3]rather [4]the

διακονία τοῦ πνεύματος ἔσται ἐν δόξῃ;
[5]ministry [6]of the [7]Spirit [1]will [8]be in glory?

9 εἰ γὰρ ἡ διακονία τῆς κατακρίσεως
For if the ministry - of condemnation

δόξα, πολλῷ μᾶλλον περισσεύει ἡ διακονία
[was] by much rather [4]abounds [1]the [2]ministry
glory,

τῆς δικαιοσύνης δόξῃ. **10** καὶ γὰρ οὐ
- [3]of righteousness in glory. For indeed [2]not

---

for profit. On the contrary, in Christ we speak before God with sincerity, like men sent from God.

Chapter 3

ARE we beginning to commend ourselves again? Or do we need, like some people, letters of recommendation to you or from you? 2You yourselves are our letter, written on our hearts, known and read by everybody. 3You show that you are a letter from Christ, the result of our ministry, written not with ink but with the Spirit of the living God, not on tablets of stone but on tablets of human hearts.

4Such confidence as this is ours through Christ before God. 5Not that we are competent in ourselves to claim anything for ourselves, but our competence comes from God. 6He has made us competent as ministers of a new covenant—not of the letter but of the Spirit; for the letter kills, but the Spirit gives life.

The Glory of the New Covenant

7Now if the ministry that brought death, which was engraved in letters on stone, came with glory, so that the Israelites could not look steadily at the face of Moses because of its glory, fading though it was, 8will not the ministry of the Spirit be even more glorious? 9If the ministry that condemns men is glorious, how much more glorious is the ministry that brings righteousness! 10For what was glorious has no glory

glory in this case has no glory on account of the glory that surpasses *it*.

¹¹For if that which fades away *was* with glory, much more that which remains *is* in glory.

¹²Having therefore such a hope, we use great boldness in *our* speech,

¹³and *are* not as Moses, *who* used to put a veil over his face that the sons of Israel might not look intently at the end of what was fading away.

¹⁴But their minds were hardened; for until this very day at the reading of the old covenant the same veil remains unlifted, because it is removed in Christ.

¹⁵But to this day whenever Moses is read, a veil lies over their heart;

¹⁶but whenever a man turns to the Lord, the veil is taken away.

¹⁷Now the Lord is the Spirit; and where the Spirit of the Lord is, *there* is liberty.

¹⁸But we all, with unveiled face beholding as in a mirror the glory of the Lord, are being transformed into the same image from glory to glory, just as from the Lord, the Spirit.

δεδόξασται   τὸ   δεδοξασμένον   ἐν   τούτῳ
¹has been   ¹the   ²having been   in   this
glorified   [thing]   glorified

τῷ   μέρει   εἵνεκεν   τῆς   ὑπερβαλλούσης   δόξης.
-   respect   for the   the   excelling   glory.
sake of

11 εἰ   γὰρ   τὸ   καταργούμενον   διὰ   δόξης,
For if   the   being done away   [was]   glory,
[thing]   through

πολλῷ   μᾶλλον   τὸ   μένον   ἐν   δόξῃ.
by much   more   the [thing] remaining   [is] in   glory.

12 Ἔχοντες   οὖν   τοιαύτην   ἐλπίδα   πολλῇ
Having   therefore   such   hope   ¹much

παρρησίᾳ   χρώμεθα,   13 καὶ   οὐ   καθάπερ
²boldness   ¹we use,   and   not   as

Μωϋσῆς   ἐτίθει   κάλυμμα   ἐπὶ   τὸ   πρόσωπον
Moses   put   a veil   on   the   face

αὐτοῦ,   πρὸς   τὸ   μὴ   ἀτενίσαι   τοὺς   υἱοὺς
of him,   for   the   ²not   ¹to gaze   ¹the   ²sons

Ἰσραὴλ   εἰς   τὸ   τέλος   τοῦ   καταργουμένου.
³of Israelᵇ   at   the   end   of the [thing] being done away.

14 ἀλλὰ   ἐπωρώθη   τὰ   νοήματα   αὐτῶν.
But   were hardened   the   thoughts   of them.

ἄχρι   γὰρ   τῆς   σήμερον   ἡμέρας   τὸ   αὐτὸ
For until   the   present   day   the   same

κάλυμμα   ἐπὶ   τῇ   ἀναγνώσει   τῆς   παλαιᾶς
veil   ²on(at)   ¹the   ²reading   ³of the   ²old

διαθήκης   μένει,   μὴ   ἀνακαλυπτόμενον   ὅτι
¹covenant   ¹remains,   not   being unveiled*   that

ἐν   Χριστῷ   καταργεῖται.   15 ἀλλ'   ἕως
in   Christ   it is being done away.   But   until

σήμερον   ἡνίκα   ἂν   ἀναγινώσκηται   Μωϋσῆς
to-day   whenever   ¹is being read   ¹Moses

κάλυμμα   ἐπὶ   τὴν   καρδίαν   αὐτῶν   κεῖται·
a veil   ²on   ³the   ⁴heart   ⁵of them   ¹lies;

16 ἡνίκα   δὲ   ἐὰν   ἐπιστρέψῃ   πρὸς   κύριον,
but whenever   it§ turns   to   [the] Lord,

περιαιρεῖται   τὸ   κάλυμμα.   17 ὁ   δὲ   κύριος
²is taken away   ¹the   ²veil.   Now the   Lord

τὸ   πνεῦμά   ἐστιν·   οὗ   δὲ   τὸ   πνεῦμα
²the   ³Spirit   ¹is;   and where   the   Spirit

κυρίου,   ἐλευθερία.   18 ἡμεῖς   δὲ   πάντες
of [the]   [there is] freedom.   But we   all
Lord [is],

ἀνακεκαλυμμένῳ   προσώπῳ   τὴν   δόξαν
¹having been unveiled   ¹with face   ²the   ²glory

κυρίου   κατοπτριζόμενοι   τὴν   αὐτὴν   εἰκόνα
⁴of [the]   ¹beholding in   ⁶the   ⁷same   ⁸image
Lord   a mirror

μεταμορφούμεθα   ἀπὸ   δόξης   εἰς   δόξαν,
⁵are being changed [into]   from   glory   to   glory,

καθάπερ   ἀπὸ   κυρίου   πνεύματος.
even as   from [the] Lord   Spirit.

---

now in comparison with the surpassing glory. ¹¹And if what was fading away came with glory, how much greater is the glory of that which lasts!

¹²Therefore, since we have such a hope, we are very bold. ¹³We are not like Moses, who would put a veil over his face to keep the Israelites from gazing at it while the radiance was fading away. ¹⁴But their minds were made dull, for to this day the same veil remains when the old covenant is read. It has not been removed, because only in Christ is it taken away. ¹⁵Even to this day when Moses is read, a veil covers their hearts. ¹⁶But whenever anyone turns to the Lord, the veil is taken away. ¹⁷Now the Lord is the Spirit, and where the Spirit of the Lord is, there is freedom. ¹⁸And we, who with unveiled faces all reflectᶜ the Lord's glory, are being transformed into his likeness with ever-increasing glory, which comes from the Lord, who is the Spirit.

Chapter 4

Paul's Apostolic Ministry

THEREFORE, since we have this ministry, as we received mercy, we do not lose heart,

²but we have renounced the things hidden because of shame, not walking in craftiness or adulterating the word of God, but by the manifestation of truth com-

---

4 Διὰ   τοῦτο,   ἔχοντες   τὴν   διακονίαν
Therefore,   having   -   ministry

ταύτην,   καθὼς   ἠλεήθημεν,   οὐκ   ἐγκακοῦμεν,
this,   as   we obtained mercy,   we faint not,

2 ἀλλὰ   ἀπειπάμεθα   τὰ   κρυπτὰ   τῆς   αἰσχύνης,
but   we have renounced the hidden things   of shame,

μὴ   περιπατοῦντες   ἐν   πανουργίᾳ   μηδὲ
not   walking   in   craftiness   nor

δολοῦντες   τὸν   λόγον   τοῦ   θεοῦ,   ἀλλὰ
adulterating   the   word   -   of God,   but

τῇ   φανερώσει   τῆς   ἀληθείας   συνιστάνοντες
by the manifestation   of the   truth   commending

Chapter 4

Treasures in Jars of Clay

THEREFORE, since through God's mercy we have this ministry, we do not lose heart. ²Rather, we have renounced secret and shameful ways; we do not use deception, nor do we distort the word of God. On the contrary, by setting forth the truth plainly we

---

* That is, revealed (Conybeare and Howson).   § ? their heart.   ᶜ18 Or *contemplate*

mending ourselves to every man's conscience in the sight of God.

3And even if our gospel is veiled, it is veiled to those who are perishing,

4in whose case the god of this world has blinded the minds of the unbelieving, that they might not see the light of the gospel of the glory of Christ, who is the image of God.

5For we do not preach ourselves but Christ Jesus as Lord, and ourselves as your bond-servants for Jesus' sake.

6For God, who said, "Light shall shine out of darkness," is the One who has shone in our hearts to give the light of the knowledge of the glory of God in the face of Christ.

7But we have this treasure in earthen vessels, that the surpassing greatness of the power may be of God and not from ourselves;

8we are afflicted in every way, but not crushed; perplexed, but not despairing;

9persecuted, but not forsaken; struck down, but not destroyed;

10always carrying about in the body the dying of Jesus, that the life of Jesus also may be manifested in our body.

11For we who live are constantly being delivered over to death for Jesus' sake, that the life of Jesus also may be manifested in our mortal flesh.

12So death works in us, but life in you.

13But having the same

ἑαυτοὺς πρὸς πᾶσαν συνείδησιν ἀνθρώπων
ourselves to every conscience of men

ἐνώπιον τοῦ θεοῦ. 3 εἰ δὲ καὶ ἔστιν
before – God. But if indeed 4is

κεκαλυμμένον τὸ εὐαγγέλιον ἡμῶν, ἐν
5having been hidden 1the 2gospel 3of us, in

τοῖς ἀπολλυμένοις ἐστὶν κεκαλυμμένον, 4 ἐν
the [ones] perishing it is having been hidden, in

οἷς ὁ θεὸς τοῦ αἰῶνος τούτου ἐτύφλωσεν
whom the god of this age blinded

τὰ νοήματα τῶν ἀπίστων εἰς τὸ μὴ
the thoughts of the unbelieving [with a the not
[ones] view] to
=so that the enlightenment ... should not shine forth,

αὐγάσαι τὸν φωτισμὸν τοῦ εὐαγγελίου
to shine forth the enlightenment of the gospel

τῆς δόξης τοῦ Χριστοῦ, ὅς ἐστιν εἰκὼν
of the glory – of Christ, who is [the] image

τοῦ . θεοῦ. 5 οὐ γὰρ ἑαυτοὺς κηρύσσομεν
– of God. For 2not 3ourselves 1we proclaim

ἀλλὰ Χριστὸν Ἰησοῦν κύριον, ἑαυτοὺς δὲ
but Christ Jesus [as] Lord, and ourselves

δούλους ὑμῶν διὰ Ἰησοῦν. 6 ὅτι ὁ
slaves of you on account of Jesus. Because –

θεὸς ὁ εἰπών· ἐκ σκότους φῶς λάμψει,
God the [one] saying: Out of darkness light shall shine,

ὃς ἔλαμψεν ἐν ταῖς καρδίαις ἡμῶν πρὸς
[is] [he] shone in the hearts of us for
who

φωτισμὸν τῆς γνώσεως τῆς δόξης τοῦ
enlightenment of the knowledge of the glory –

θεοῦ ἐν προσώπῳ Χριστοῦ.
of God in [the] face of Christ.

7 Ἔχομεν δὲ τὸν θησαυρὸν τοῦτον ἐν
And we have this treasure in

ὀστρακίνοις σκεύεσιν, ἵνα ἡ ὑπερβολὴ
earthenware vessels, in order that the excellence

τῆς δυνάμεως ᾖ τοῦ θεοῦ καὶ μὴ ἐξ
of the power may be – of God and not of

ἡμῶν· 8 ἐν παντὶ θλιβόμενοι ἀλλ' οὐ
us; in every [way] being afflicted but not

στενοχωρούμενοι, ἀπορούμενοι ἀλλ' οὐκ
being restrained, being in difficulties but not

ἐξαπορούμενοι, 9 διωκόμενοι ἀλλ' οὐκ
despairing, being persecuted but not

ἐγκαταλειπόμενοι, καταβαλλόμενοι ἀλλ' οὐκ
being deserted, being cast down but not

ἀπολλύμενοι, 10 πάντοτε τὴν νέκρωσιν τοῦ
perishing, always 3the 4dying –

Ἰησοῦ ἐν τῷ σώματι περιφέροντες, ἵνα
2of Jesus 5in 6the 7body 1bearing about, in order
that

καὶ ἡ ζωὴ τοῦ Ἰησοῦ ἐν τῷ σώματι
also the life – of Jesus in the body

ἡμῶν φανερωθῇ. 11 ἀεὶ γὰρ ἡμεῖς οἱ
of us might be manifested. For always we the

ζῶντες εἰς θάνατον παραδιδόμεθα διὰ
[ones] living to death are being on ac-
delivered count of

Ἰησοῦν, ἵνα καὶ ἡ ζωὴ τοῦ Ἰησοῦ
Jesus, in order that also the life – of Jesus

φανερωθῇ ἐν τῇ θνητῇ σαρκὶ ἡμῶν.
might be in the mortal flesh of us.
manifested

12 ὥστε ὁ θάνατος ἐν ἡμῖν ἐνεργεῖται,
So as – death in us operates,

ἡ δὲ ζωὴ ἐν ὑμῖν. 13 ἔχοντες δὲ τὸ
– but life in you. And having the

---

commend ourselves to every man's conscience in the sight of God. 3And even if our gospel is veiled, it is veiled to those who are perishing. 4The god of this age has blinded the minds of unbelievers, so that they cannot see the light of the gospel of the glory of Christ, who is the image of God. 5For we do not preach ourselves, but Jesus Christ as Lord, and ourselves as your servants for Jesus' sake. 6For God, who said, "Let light shine out of darkness," d made his light shine in our hearts to give us the light of the knowledge of the glory of God in the face of Christ.

7But we have this treasure in jars of clay to show that this all-surpassing power is from God and not from us. 8We are hard pressed on every side, but not crushed; perplexed, but not in despair; 9persecuted, but not abandoned; struck down, but not destroyed. 10We always carry around in our body the death of Jesus, so that the life of Jesus may also be revealed in our body. 11For we who are alive are always being given over to death for Jesus' sake, so that his life may be revealed in our mortal body. 12So then, death is at work in us, but life is at work in you.

13It is written: "I be-spirit of faith, according to what is written, "I BE-LIEVED, THEREFORE I SPOKE," we also believe, therefore also we speak;

14knowing that He who raised the Lord Jesus will raise us also with Jesus and will present us with you.

15For all things *are* for your sakes, that the grace which is spreading to more and more people may cause the giving of thanks to abound to the glory of God.

16Therefore we do not lose heart, but though our outer man is decaying, yet our inner man is being renewed day by day.

17For momentary, light affliction is producing for us an eternal weight of glory far beyond all comparison,

18while we look not at the things which are seen, but at the things which are not seen; for the things which are seen are temporal, but the things which are not seen are eternal.

αὐτὸ πνεῦμα τῆς πίστεως, κατὰ τὸ
same spirit – of faith, according to the thing

γεγραμμένον· ἐπίστευσα, διὸ ἐλάλησα, καὶ
having been written: I believed, therefore I spoke, both

ἡμεῖς πιστεύομεν, διὸ καὶ λαλοῦμεν, **14** εἰδότες
we believe, and therefore we speak, knowing

ὅτι ὁ ἐγείρας τὸν κύριον Ἰησοῦν καὶ
that the having the Lord Jesus ²also
[one] raised

ἡμᾶς σὺν Ἰησοῦ ἐγερεῖ καὶ παραστήσει
²us ¹with ³Jesus ¹will raise and will present [us]

σὺν ὑμῖν. **15** τὰ γὰρ πάντα δι᾽ ὑμᾶς,
with you. – For all things [are] on ac- you,
count of

ἵνα ἡ χάρις πλεονάσασα διὰ τῶν πλειόνων
in or- – grace increased through the majority
der that

τὴν εὐχαριστίαν περισσεύσῃ εἰς τὴν δόξαν
¹the ²thanksgiving ¹may cause to abound to the glory

τοῦ θεοῦ. **16** Διὸ οὐκ ἐγκακοῦμεν, ἀλλ᾽
– of God. Wherefore we faint not, but

εἰ καὶ ὁ ἔξω ἡμῶν ἄνθρωπος διαφθείρεται,
if indeed the outward ²of us ¹man is being disabled,

ἀλλ᾽ ὁ ἔσω ἡμῶν ἀνακαινοῦται ἡμέρᾳ
yet the inward [man] of us is being renewed day

καὶ ἡμέρᾳ. **17** τὸ γὰρ παραυτίκα ἐλαφρὸν
and(by) day. For the present lightness

τῆς θλίψεως καθ᾽ ὑπερβολὴν εἰς ὑπερβολὴν
of the affliction ³excessively ⁴to ⁵excess

αἰώνιον βάρος δόξης κατεργάζεται ἡμῖν,
⁶an eternal ⁷weight ⁸of glory ¹works ²for us,

18 μὴ σκοπούντων ἡμῶν τὰ βλεπόμενα
not considering us° the things *being* seen
=while we do not consider

ἀλλὰ τὰ μὴ βλεπόμενα· τὰ γὰρ βλεπόμενα
but the not *being* seen; for the things *being* seen
things

πρόσκαιρα, τὰ δὲ μὴ βλεπόμενα αἰώνια.
[are] temporary, but the things not *being* seen [are] eternal.

5 Οἴδαμεν γὰρ ὅτι ἐὰν ἡ ἐπίγειος
For we know that if the earthly

ἡμῶν οἰκία τοῦ σκήνους καταλυθῇ,
²of us ¹house ²of the ³tabernacle is destroyed,

οἰκοδομὴν ἐκ θεοῦ ἔχομεν, οἰκίαν ἀχειρο-
a building of God we have, a house not made

ποίητον αἰώνιον ἐν τοῖς οὐρανοῖς. **2** καὶ
by hands eternal in the heavens. indeed

γὰρ ἐν τούτῳ στενάζομεν, τὸ οἰκητήριον
For in this° we groan, ³the ⁴dwelling-place

ἡμῶν τὸ ἐξ οὐρανοῦ ἐπενδύσασθαι ἐπιπο-
²of us – ⁵out of ⁷heaven ²to put on ¹greatly

θοῦντες, **3** εἴ γε καὶ ἐνδυσάμενοι οὐ
desiring, if indeed being clothed not

γυμνοὶ εὑρεθησόμεθα. **4** καὶ γὰρ οἱ
naked we shall be found. For indeed ²the
[ones]

ὄντες ἐν τῷ σκήνει στενάζομεν βαρούμενοι,
³being ⁴in ⁵the ⁶tabernacle ¹we groan being burdened,

ἐφ᾽ ᾧ οὐ θέλομεν ἐκδύσασθαι ἀλλ᾽
inasmuch as we do not wish to put off but

ἐπενδύσασθαι, ἵνα καταποθῇ τὸ θνητὸν
to put on, in order ²may be ¹the ²mortal
that swallowed up

ὑπὸ τῆς ζωῆς. **5** ὁ δὲ κατεργασάμενος
by the life. Now the [one] having wrought

* Neuter, going back to σκῆνος in the preceding verse.

---

lieved; therefore I have spoken." [e] With that same spirit of faith we also believe and therefore speak, 14because we know that the one who raised the Lord Jesus from the dead will also raise us with Jesus and present us with you in his presence. 15All this is for your benefit, so that the grace that is reaching more and more people may cause thanksgiving to overflow to the glory of God.

16Therefore we do not lose heart. Though outwardly we are wasting away, yet inwardly we are being renewed day by day. 17For our light and momentary troubles are achieving for us an eternal glory that far outweighs them all. 18So we fix our eyes not on what is seen, but on what is unseen. For what is seen is temporary, but what is unseen is eternal.

Chapter 5

Our Heavenly Dwelling

NOW we know that if the earthly tent we live in is destroyed, we have a building from God, an eternal house in heaven, not built by human hands. 2Meanwhile we groan, longing to be clothed with our heavenly dwelling, 3because when we are clothed, we will not be found naked. 4For while we are in this tent, we groan and are burdened, because we do not wish to be unclothed but to be clothed with our heavenly dwelling, so that what is mortal may be swallowed up by life. 5Now it is God

---

Chapter 5

The Temporal and Eternal

FOR we know that if the earthly tent which is our house is torn down, we have a building from God, a house not made with hands, eternal in the heavens.

2For indeed in this *house* we groan, longing to be clothed with our dwelling from heaven;

3inasmuch as we, having put it on, shall not be found naked.

4For indeed while we are in this tent, we groan, being burdened, because we do not want to be unclothed, but to be clothed, in order that what is mortal may be swallowed up by life.

5Now He who prepared

us for this very purpose is God, who gave to us the Spirit as a pledge.

6Therefore, being always of good courage, and knowing that while we are at home in the body we are absent from the Lord—

7for we walk by faith, not by sight—

8we are of good courage, I say, and prefer rather to be absent from the body and to be at home with the Lord.

9Therefore also we have as our ambition, whether at home or absent, to be pleasing to Him.

10For we must all appear before the judgment seat of Christ, that each one may be recompensed for his deeds in the body, according to what he has done, whether good or bad.

11Therefore knowing the fear of the Lord, we persuade men, but we are made manifest to God; and I hope that we are made manifest also in your consciences.

12We are not again commending ourselves to you but *are* giving you an occasion to be proud of us, that you may have *an answer* for those who take pride in appearance, and not in heart.

13For if we are beside ourselves, it is for God; if we are of sound mind, it is for you.

14For the love of Christ controls us, having concluded this, that one died for all, therefore all died;

15and He died for all, that they who live should no

Greek	English
ἡμᾶς	us
εἰς	for
αὐτὸ τοῦτο	this very thing
θεός, ὁ	God, [one] the
δοὺς	having [one] given

ἡμῖν	to us
τὸν ἀρραβῶνα	the earnest
τοῦ πνεύματος.	of the Spirit.
6 Θαρροῦντες	Being of good cheer
οὖν	therefore
πάντοτε	always
καὶ	and
εἰδότες	knowing
ὅτι	that

ἐνδημοῦντες ἐν τῷ σώματι ἐκδημοῦμεν
being at home in the body we are away from home

ἀπὸ τοῦ κυρίου· 7 διὰ πίστεως γὰρ
from the Lord; ²through ³faith ¹for

περιπατοῦμεν, οὐ διὰ εἴδους· 8 θαρροῦμεν
we walk, not through appearance; we are of good cheer

δὲ καὶ εὐδοκοῦμεν μᾶλλον ἐκδημῆσαι ἐκ
then and think it good rather to go away from home out of

τοῦ σώματος καὶ ἐνδημῆσαι πρὸς τὸν
the body and to come home to the

κύριον. 9 διὸ καὶ φιλοτιμούμεθα, εἴτε
Lord. Wherefore also we are ambitious, whether

ἐνδημοῦντες εἴτε ἐκδημοῦντες, εὐάρεστοι
being at home or being away from home, wellpleasing

αὐτῷ εἶναι. 10 τοὺς γὰρ πάντας ἡμᾶς
to him to be. For ²all ¹us

φανερωθῆναι δεῖ ἔμπροσθεν τοῦ βήματος
⁴to be manifested ¹it behoves before the tribunal

τοῦ Χριστοῦ, ἵνα κομίσηται ἕκαστος τὰ
of Christ, in order that ²may receive ¹each one the things

διὰ τοῦ σώματος πρὸς ἃ ἔπραξεν, εἴτε
through the body according to things he practised, either

ἀγαθὸν εἴτε φαῦλον.
good or worthless.

11 Εἰδότες οὖν τὸν φόβον τοῦ κυρίου
Knowing therefore the fear of the Lord

ἀνθρώπους πείθομεν, θεῷ δὲ πεφανερώμεθα·
²men ¹we persuade, and to God we have been made manifest;

ἐλπίζω δὲ καὶ ἐν ταῖς συνειδήσεσιν
and I hope also in the consciences

ὑμῶν πεφανερῶσθαι. 12 οὐ πάλιν ἑαυτοὺς
of you to have been made manifest. Not again ²ourselves

συνιστάνομεν ὑμῖν, ἀλλὰ ἀφορμὴν διδόντες
¹we commend to you, but ²an occasion ¹giving

ὑμῖν καυχήματος ὑπὲρ ἡμῶν, ἵνα ἔχητε
²to you of a boast on behalf of us, in order that ye may have [it]

πρὸς τοὺς ἐν προσώπῳ καυχωμένους καὶ
in reference to the ²in ³face ¹boasting and [ones]

μὴ ἐν καρδίᾳ. 13 εἴτε γὰρ ἐξέστημεν,
not in heart. For whether we are mad,

θεῷ· εἴτε σωφρονοῦμεν. ὑμῖν. 14 ἡ γὰρ
[it is] to God; or we are in our senses, [it is] for you. For the

ἀγάπη τοῦ Χριστοῦ συνέχει ἡμᾶς, κρίναντας
love – of Christ constrains us, judging

τοῦτο, ὅτι εἰς ὑπὲρ πάντων ἀπέθανεν·
this, that one on behalf of all men died;

ἄρα οἱ πάντες ἀπέθανον· 15 καὶ ὑπὲρ
then the all died; and ²on behalf of

πάντων ἀπέθανεν ἵνα οἱ ζῶντες μηκέτι
²all ¹he died in order that the living no more [ones]

who has made us for this very purpose and has given us the Spirit as a deposit, guaranteeing what is to come.

6Therefore we are always confident and know that as long as we are at home in the body we are away from the Lord. 7We live by faith, not by sight. 8We are confident, I say, and would prefer to be away from the body and at home with the Lord. 9So we make it our goal to please him, whether we are at home in the body or away from it. 10For we must all appear before the judgment seat of Christ, that each one may receive what is due him for the things done while in the body, whether good or bad.

The Ministry of Reconciliation

11Since, then, we know what it is to fear the Lord, we try to persuade men. What we are is plain to God, and I hope it is also plain to your conscience. 12We are not trying to commend ourselves to you again, but are giving you an opportunity to take pride in us, so that you can answer those who take pride in what is seen rather than in what is in the heart. 13If we are out of our mind, it is for the sake of God; if we are in our right mind, it is for you. 14For Christ's love compels us, because we are convinced that one died for all, and therefore all died. 15And he died for all, that those who live should no longer live for themselves, but for Him who died and rose again on their behalf.

16Therefore from now on we recognize no man according to the flesh; even though we have known Christ according to the flesh, yet now we know *Him thus* no longer.

17Therefore if any man is in Christ, *he is* a new creature; the old things passed away; behold, new things have come.

18Now all *these* things are from God, who reconciled us to Himself through Christ, and gave us the ministry of reconciliation,

19namely, that God was in Christ reconciling the world to Himself, not counting their trespasses against them, and He has committed to us the word of reconciliation.

20Therefore, we are ambassadors for Christ, as though God were entreating through us; we beg you on behalf of Christ, be reconciled to God.

21He made Him who knew no sin *to be* sin on our behalf, that we might become the righteousness of God in Him.

ἑαυτοῖς	ζῶσιν	ἀλλὰ	τῷ	ὑπὲρ	αὐτῶν
to themselves	may live	but	to the [one]	on behalf of	them

ἀποθανόντι	καὶ	ἐγερθέντι.	16 Ὥστε	ἡμεῖς
having died	and	having been raised.	So as	⁶we

ἀπὸ	τοῦ	νῦν	οὐδένα	οἴδαμεν	κατὰ	σάρκα·
¹from	-	²now	⁵no man	⁴know	according to	flesh;

εἰ	καὶ	ἐγνώκαμεν	κατὰ	σάρκα	Χριστόν,
if	indeed	¹we have known	³according to	⁴flesh	²Christ,

ἀλλὰ	νῦν	οὐκέτι	γινώσκομεν.	17 ὥστε
yet	now	no more	we know [him].	So as

εἴ	τις	ἐν	Χριστῷ,	καινὴ	κτίσις·	τὰ
if	anyone [is] in	Christ,	[he is] a new	creation;	the

ἀρχαῖα	παρῆλθεν,	ἰδοὺ	γέγονεν	καινά.
old things	passed away,	behold	they have become	new.

18 τὰ	δὲ	πάντα	ἐκ	τοῦ	θεοῦ	τοῦ	καταλ-
-	And	all things [are] of	-	God	the [one]	having

λάξαντος	ἡμᾶς	ἑαυτῷ	διὰ	Χριστοῦ	καὶ
reconciled	us	to himself	through	Christ	and

δόντος	ἡμῖν	τὴν	διακονίαν	τῆς	καταλλαγῆς,
having given to us	the	ministry	-	of reconciliation,

19 ὡς	ὅτι	θεὸς	ἦν	ἐν	Χριστῷ	κόσμον
as	that	God	was in	Christ	³[the] world

καταλλάσσων	ἑαυτῷ,	μὴ	λογιζόμενος	αὐτοῖς
¹reconciling	to himself,	not	reckoning	to them

τὰ	παραπτώματα	αὐτῶν,	καὶ	θέμενος
the	trespasses	of them,	and	placing

ἐν	ἡμῖν	τὸν	λόγον	τῆς	καταλλαγῆς.
in	us	the	word	-	of reconciliation.

20 Ὑπὲρ	Χριστοῦ	οὖν	πρεσβεύομεν	ὡς
On behalf of	Christ	therefore	we are ambassadors	as

τοῦ	θεοῦ	παρακαλοῦντος	δι᾽	ἡμῶν·	δεόμεθα
-	God	beseeching[a]	through	us;	we beg

ὑπὲρ	Χριστοῦ,	καταλλάγητε	τῷ	θεῷ.
on behalf of	Christ,	Be ye reconciled	-	to God.

21 τὸν	μὴ	γνόντα	ἁμαρτίαν	ὑπὲρ	ἡμῶν
³The [one]	²not	⁴knowing	⁵sin	⁷on behalf of	⁸us

ἁμαρτίαν	ἐποίησεν,	ἵνα	ἡμεῖς	γενώμεθα
⁶sin	¹he made,	in order that	we	might become

δικαιοσύνη	θεοῦ	ἐν	αὐτῷ.
[the] righteousness of	God	in	him.

---

longer live for themselves but for him who died for them and was raised again.

16So from now on we regard no one from a worldly point of view. Though we once regarded Christ in this way, we do so no longer. 17Therefore, if anyone is in Christ, he is a new creation; the old has gone, the new has come! 18All this is from God, who reconciled us to himself through Christ and gave us the ministry of reconciliation: 19that God was reconciling the world to himself in Christ, not counting men's sins against them. And he has committed to us the message of reconciliation. 20We are therefore Christ's ambassadors, as though God were making his appeal through us. We implore you on Christ's behalf: Be reconciled to God. 21God made him who had no sin to be sin[f] for us, so that in him we might become the righteousness of God.

Chapter 6

Their Ministry Commended

AND working together *with Him*, we also urge you not to receive the grace of God in vain—

2for He says,
> "AT THE ACCEPTABLE TIME I LISTENED TO YOU,
> AND ON THE DAY OF SALVATION I HELPED YOU";

behold, now is "THE ACCEPTABLE TIME," behold, now is "THE DAY OF SALVATION"—

3giving no cause for offense in anything, in order that the ministry be not discredited,

4but in everything commending ourselves as servants of God, in much endurance, in afflictions, in hardships, in distresses,

---

6 Συνεργοῦντες	δὲ	καὶ	παρακαλοῦμεν	μὴ
And working together	also		we beseech	²not

εἰς	κενὸν	τὴν	χάριν	τοῦ	θεοῦ	δέξασθαι
¹to no purpose	⁴the	²grace	-	of God	³to receive

ὑμᾶς·	2 λέγει	γάρ·	καιρῷ	δεκτῷ	ἐπήκουσά
¹you;	for he says:	In a time	acceptable	I heard

σου	καὶ	ἐν	ἡμέρᾳ	σωτηρίας	ἐβοήθησά
thee	and	in	a day	of salvation	I helped

σοι·	ἰδοὺ	νῦν	καιρὸς	εὐπρόσδεκτος,	ἰδοὺ
thee;	behold	now	a time	acceptable,	behold

νῦν	ἡμέρα	σωτηρίας·	3 —	μηδεμίαν	ἐν
now	a day	of salvation;	³no	⁴in

μηδενὶ	διδόντες	προσκοπήν,	ἵνα	μὴ
²no(any)thing	¹giving	⁵cause of stumbling,	lest

μωμηθῇ	ἡ	διακονία,	4 ἀλλ'	ἐν	παντὶ
⁶be blamed	¹the	²ministry,	but	in	everything

συνιστάνοντες	ἑαυτοὺς	ὡς	θεοῦ	διάκονοι,
commending	ourselves	as	²of God	¹ministers,

ἐν	ὑπομονῇ	πολλῇ,	ἐν	θλίψεσιν,	ἐν
in	²endurance	¹much,	in	afflictions,	in

ἀνάγκαις,	ἐν	στενοχωρίαις,	ἐν	πληγαῖς,
necessities,	in	straits,	in	stripes,

Chapter 6

AS God's fellow workers we urge you not to receive God's grace in vain. 2For he says,

> "In the time of my favor I heard you,
> and in the day of salvation I helped you."[g]

I tell you, now is the time of God's favor, now is the day of salvation.

Paul's Hardships

3We put no stumbling block in anyone's path, so that our ministry will not be discredited. 4Rather, as servants of God we commend ourselves in every way: in great endurance; in troubles, hardships and dis-

f21 Or be a sin offering
g2 Isaiah 49:8

5in beatings, in imprisonments, in tumults, in labors, in sleeplessness, in hunger,

6in purity, in knowledge, in patience, in kindness, in the Holy Spirit, in genuine love,

7in the word of truth, in the power of God; by the weapons of righteousness for the right hand and the left,

8by glory and dishonor, by evil report and good report; *regarded* as deceivers and yet true;

9as unknown yet well-known, as dying yet behold, we live; as punished yet not put to death,

10as sorrowful yet always rejoicing, as poor yet making many rich, as having nothing yet possessing all things.

11Our mouth has spoken freely to you, O Corinthians, our heart is opened wide.

12You are not restrained by us, but you are restrained in your own affections.

13Now in a like exchange—I speak as to children—open wide *to us* also.

14Do not be bound together with unbelievers; for what partnership have righteousness and lawlessness, or what fellowship has light with darkness?

15Or what harmony has Christ with Belial, or what has a believer in common with an unbeliever?

16Or what agreement has the temple of God with idols? For we are the temple of the living God; just as God said,

"I WILL DWELL IN THEM AND WALK AMONG THEM;
AND I WILL BE THEIR GOD, AND THEY SHALL BE MY PEOPLE.

---

5 ἐν φυλακαῖς, ἐν ἀκαταστασίαις, ἐν κόποις,
in prisons, in commotions, in labours,

ἐν ἀγρυπνίαις, ἐν νηστείαις, **6** ἐν ἁγνότητι,
in watchings, in fastings, in purity,

ἐν γνώσει, ἐν μακροθυμίᾳ, ἐν χρηστότητι,
in knowledge, in long-suffering, in kindness,

ἐν πνεύματι ἁγίῳ, ἐν ἀγάπῃ ἀνυποκρίτῳ,
in spirit a holy, in love unfeigned,

7 ἐν λόγῳ ἀληθείας, ἐν δυνάμει θεοῦ·
in a word of truth, in power of God;

διὰ τῶν ὅπλων τῆς δικαιοσύνης τῶν
through the weapons - of righteousness of the

δεξιῶν καὶ ἀριστερῶν, **8** διὰ δόξης καὶ
right [hand] and of left, through glory and

ἀτιμίας, διὰ δυσφημίας καὶ εὐφημίας·
dishonour, through ill report and good report;

ὡς πλάνοι καὶ ἀληθεῖς, **9** ὡς ἀγνοούμενοι
as deceivers and* true men, as being unknown

καὶ ἐπιγινωσκόμενοι, ὡς ἀποθνῄσκοντες καὶ
and* being well known, as dying and

ἰδοὺ ζῶμεν, ὡς παιδευόμενοι καὶ μὴ
behold we live, as being chastened and not

θανατούμενοι, **10** ὡς λυπούμενοι ἀεὶ δὲ
being put to death, as being grieved ²always ¹but

χαίροντες, ὡς πτωχοὶ πολλοὺς δὲ πλουτίζ-
rejoicing, as poor ²many ¹but ²en-

οντες, ὡς μηδὲν ἔχοντες καὶ πάντα
riching, as ²nothing ¹having ²and* ²all things

κατέχοντες.
¹possessing.

11 Τὸ στόμα ἡμῶν ἀνέῳγεν πρὸς ὑμᾶς,
The mouth of us has opened to you,

Κορίνθιοι, ἡ καρδία ἡμῶν πεπλάτυνται·
Corinthians, the heart of us has been enlarged;

12 οὐ στενοχωρεῖσθε ἐν ἡμῖν, στενοχωρεῖσθε
ye are not restrained in us, ²ye are restrained

δὲ ἐν τοῖς σπλάγχνοις ὑμῶν· **13** τὴν δὲ
¹but in the bowels of you; but [for] the

αὐτὴν ἀντιμισθίαν, ὡς τέκνοις λέγω,
same recompence, as to children I say,

πλατύνθητε καὶ ὑμεῖς.
be enlarged also ye.

14 Μὴ γίνεσθε ἑτεροζυγοῦντες ἀπίστοις·
Do not ye become unequally yoked [with] unbelievers;

τίς γὰρ μετοχὴ δικαιοσύνῃ καὶ ἀνομίᾳ,
for what share righteousness° and lawlessness,°
= have righteousness and lawlessness,

ἢ τίς κοινωνία φωτὶ πρὸς σκότος; **15** τίς
or what fellowship light° with darkness? what
= has light

δὲ συμφώνησις Χριστοῦ πρὸς Βελιάρ,
and agreement of Christ with Beliar,

ἢ τίς μερὶς πιστῷ μετὰ ἀπίστου; **16** τίς
or what part a believer° with an unbeliever? what
= has a believer

δὲ συγκατάθεσις ναῷ θεοῦ μετὰ εἰδώλων;
and union a shrine° of God with idols?
= has a shrine

ἡμεῖς γὰρ ναὸς θεοῦ ἐσμεν ζῶντος·
For ¹we ²a shrine ³God ²are ⁴of a living;

καθὼς εἶπεν ὁ θεὸς ὅτι ἐνοικήσω ἐν
as said - God[,] I will dwell among

αὐτοῖς καὶ ἐμπεριπατήσω, καὶ ἔσομαι
them and I will walk among [them], and I will be

αὐτῶν θεός, καὶ αὐτοὶ ἔσονταί μου λαός.
of them God, and they shall be of me a people.

* Evidently = and yet, as in some other places; *cf.* John 20. 29.

---

tresses; 5in beatings, imprisonments and riots; in hard work, sleepless nights and hunger; 6in purity, understanding, patience and kindness; in the Holy Spirit and in sincere love; 7in truthful speech and in the power of God; with weapons of righteousness in the right hand and in the left; 8through glory and dishonor, bad report and good report; genuine, yet regarded as impostors; 9known, yet regarded as unknown; dying, and yet we live on; beaten, and yet not killed; 10sorrowful, yet always rejoicing; poor, yet making many rich; having nothing, and yet possessing everything.

11We have spoken freely to you, Corinthians, and opened wide our hearts to you. 12We are not withholding our affection from you, but you are withholding yours from us. 13As a fair exchange—I speak as to my children—open wide your hearts also.

Do Not Be Yoked With Unbelievers

14Do not be yoked together with unbelievers. For what do righteousness and wickedness have in common? Or what fellowship can light have with darkness? 15What harmony is there between Christ and Belial[h]? What does a believer have in common with an unbeliever? 16What agreement is there between the temple of God and idols? For we are the temple of the living God. As God has said: "I will live with them and walk among them, and I will be their God, and they will be my people."[i]

---

h15 Greek *Beliar,* a variant of *Belial*
i16 Lev. 26:12; Jer. 32:38; Ezek. 37:27

17"Therefore, COME OUT FROM THEIR MIDST AND BE SEPARATE," says the Lord.
"AND DO NOT TOUCH WHAT IS UNCLEAN; And I will welcome you.
18"And I will be a father to you,
And you shall be sons and daughters to Me,"
Says the Lord Almighty.

Chapter 7

Paul Reveals His Heart

THEREFORE, having these promises, beloved, let us cleanse ourselves from all defilement of flesh and spirit, perfecting holiness in the fear of God.
2Make room for us in your hearts; we wronged no one, we corrupted no one, we took advantage of no one.
3I do not speak to condemn you; for I have said before that you are in our hearts to die together and to live together.
4Great is my confidence in you, great is my boasting on your behalf; I am filled with comfort. I am overflowing with joy in all our affliction.
5For even when we came into Macedonia our flesh had no rest, but we were afflicted on every side: conflicts without, fears within.
6But God, who comforts the depressed, comforted us by the coming of Titus;
7and not only by his coming, but also by the comfort with which he was comforted in you, as he reported to us your longing, your mourning, your zeal for me; so that I rejoiced even more.
8For though I caused you sorrow by my letter, I do not regret it; though I did regret it—for I see that that

---

17 διὸ ἐξέλθατε ἐκ μέσου αὐτῶν καὶ
Wherefore come ye out from [the] midst of them and
ἀφορίσθητε, λέγει κύριος, καὶ ἀκαθάρτου
be ye separated, says [the] Lord, and an unclean thing
μὴ ἅπτεσθε· 18 κἀγὼ εἰσδέξομαι ὑμᾶς, καὶ
do not touch; and I will welcome in you, and
ἔσομαι ὑμῖν εἰς πατέρα, καὶ ὑμεῖς ἔσεσθέ
I will be to you for a father, and ye shall be
μοι εἰς υἱοὺς καὶ θυγατέρας, λέγει κύριος
to me for sons and daughters, says [the] Lord
παντοκράτωρ. 7 ταύτας οὖν ἔχοντες τὰς ἐπ-
[the] Almighty. ³These ²therefore ¹having - ⁴pro-
αγγελίας, ἀγαπητοί, καθαρίσωμεν ἑαυτοὺς ἀπὸ
mises, beloved, let us cleanse ourselves from
παντὸς μολυσμοῦ σαρκὸς καὶ πνεύματος,
all pollution of flesh and of spirit,
ἐπιτελοῦντες ἁγιωσύνην ἐν φόβῳ θεοῦ.
perfecting holiness in [the] fear of God.
2 Χωρήσατε ἡμᾶς· οὐδένα ἠδικήσαμεν,
Make room for us; no one we wronged,
οὐδένα ἐφθείραμεν, οὐδένα ἐπλεονεκτήσαμεν.
no one we injured, no one we defrauded.
3 πρὸς κατάκρισιν οὐ λέγω· προείρηκα
For condemnation I say not; ¹I have previously said
γὰρ ὅτι ἐν ταῖς καρδίαις ἡμῶν ἐστε
¹for that in the hearts of us ye are
εἰς τὸ συναποθανεῖν καὶ συζῆν. 4 πολλή
for - to die with [you] and to live with [you]. Much
μοι παρρησία πρὸς ὑμᾶς, πολλή μοι
to meᵉ boldness toward you, much to meᵉ
=I have much   =I have much
καύχησις ὑπὲρ ὑμῶν· πεπλήρωμαι τῇ
boasting on behalf of you; I have been filled -
παρακλήσει, ὑπερπερισσεύομαι τῇ χαρᾷ ἐπὶ
with comfort, I overflow - with joy on(in)
πάσῃ τῇ θλίψει ἡμῶν. 5 Καὶ γὰρ
all the affliction of us. For indeed
ἐλθόντων ἡμῶν εἰς Μακεδονίαν οὐδεμίαν
coming usᵃ into Macedonia ⁵no
=when we came
ἔσχηκεν ἄνεσιν ἡ σὰρξ ἡμῶν, ἀλλ' ἐν
⁴has had ⁶rest ¹the ²flesh ³of us, but in
παντὶ θλιβόμενοι· ἔξωθεν μάχαι, ἔσωθεν
every way being afflicted; without [were] fightings, within
φόβοι. 6 ἀλλ' ὁ παρακαλῶν τοὺς ταπεινοὺς
[were] fears. But ¹the [one] ²comforting ⁴the ⁵humble
παρεκάλεσεν ἡμᾶς ὁ θεὸς ἐν τῇ παρουσίᾳ
⁶comforted ⁷us ¹God by the presence
Τίτου· 7 οὐ μόνον δὲ ἐν τῇ παρουσίᾳ
of Titus; and not only by the presence
αὐτοῦ, ἀλλὰ καὶ ἐν τῇ παρακλήσει ᾗ
of him, but also by the comfort with which
παρεκλήθη ἐφ' ὑμῖν, ἀναγγέλλων ἡμῖν
he was comforted over you, reporting to us
τὴν ὑμῶν ἐπιπόθησιν, τὸν ὑμῶν ὀδυρμόν,
¹the ²of you ³eager longing, ¹the ²of you ³mourning,
τὸν ὑμῶν ζῆλον ὑπὲρ ἐμοῦ, ὥστε με
¹the ²of you ²zeal on behalf of me, so as me
μᾶλλον χαρῆναι. 8 Ὅτι εἰ καὶ ἐλύπησα
more to rejoice.ᵇ Because if indeed I grieved
=so that I rejoiced more.
ὑμᾶς ἐν τῇ ἐπιστολῇ, οὐ μεταμέλομαι·
you by the epistle, I do not regret;
εἰ καὶ μετεμελόμην, βλέπω ὅτι ἡ ἐπιστολὴ
if indeed I regretted, I see that - epistle

17"Therefore come out from them and be separate, says the Lord. Touch no unclean thing, and I will receive you."ʲ
18"I will be a Father to you, and you will be my sons and daughters, says the Lord Almighty."ᵏ

Chapter 7

SINCE we have these promises, dear friends, let us purify ourselves from everything that contaminates body and spirit, perfecting holiness out of reverence for God.

Paul's Joy

2Make room for us in your hearts. We have wronged no one, we have corrupted no one, we have exploited no one. 3I do not say this to condemn you; I have said before that you have such a place in our hearts that we would live or die with you. 4I have great confidence in you; I take great pride in you. I am greatly encouraged; in all our troubles my joy knows no bounds.
5For when we came into Macedonia, this body of ours had no rest, but we were harassed at every turn —conflicts on the outside, fears within. 6But God, who comforts the downcast, comforted us by the coming of Titus, 7and not only by his coming but also by the comfort you had given him. He told us about your longing for me, your deep sorrow, your ardent concern for me, so that my joy was greater than ever.
8Even if I caused you sorrow by my letter, I do not regret it. Though I did re-

ʲ17 Isaiah 52:11; Ezek. 20:34,41
ᵏ18 2 Samuel 7:14; 7:8

letter caused you sorrow, though only for a while—

9I now rejoice, not that you were made sorrowful, but that you were made sorrowful to *the point of* repentance; for you were made sorrowful according to *the will of* God, in order that you might not suffer loss in anything through us.

10For the sorrow that is according to *the will of* God produces a repentance without regret, *leading* to salvation; but the sorrow of the world produces death.

11For behold what earnestness this very thing, this godly sorrow, has produced in you: what vindication of yourselves, what indignation, what fear, what longing, what zeal, what avenging of wrong! In everything you demonstrated yourselves to be innocent in the matter.

12So although I wrote to you *it was* not for the sake of the offender, nor for the sake of the one offended, but that your earnestness on our behalf might be made known to you in the sight of God.

13For this reason we have been comforted.

And besides our comfort, we rejoiced even much more for the joy of Titus, because his spirit has been refreshed by you all.

14For if in anything I have boasted to him about you, I was not put to shame; but as we spoke all things to you in truth, so also our boasting before Titus proved to be *the* truth.

15And his affection abounds all the more toward you, as he remembers the obedience of you all, how you received him with fear and trembling.

16I rejoice that in everything I have confidence in you.

ἐκείνη   εἰ   καὶ   πρὸς   ὥραν   ἐλύπησεν   ὑμᾶς,
that   if   indeed for   an hour it grieved   you,

9 νῦν   χαίρω,   οὐχ   ὅτι   ἐλυπήθητε,   ἀλλ'
  now   I rejoice, not   that   ye were grieved, but

ὅτι   ἐλυπήθητε   εἰς   μετάνοιαν·   ἐλυπήθητε
that   ye were grieved to   repentance;   ¹ye were grieved

γὰρ   κατὰ   θεόν,   ἵνα   ἐν   μηδενὶ   ζημιωθῆτε
¹for   according God,   in order in   nothing   ye might suffer
       to   that   loss

ἐξ   ἡμῶν.   10 ἡ   γὰρ   κατὰ   θεὸν   λύπη
by   us.   For ¹the ²according to ⁴God   ³grief

μετάνοιαν   εἰς   σωτηρίαν   ἀμεταμέλητον
⁷repentance   ⁸to   ⁶salvation   ⁹unregrettable

ἐργάζεται·   ἡ   δὲ   τοῦ   κόσμου   λύπη   θάνατον
⁵works;   ¹the ²of the ³world   ²grief   ⁵death

κατεργάζεται.   11 ἰδοὺ   γὰρ   αὐτὸ   τοῦτο
⁴works out.   For behold   this very thing[,]

τὸ   κατὰ   θεὸν   λυπηθῆναι   πόσην   κατειργά-
  ²according to ³God   ¹to be grieved[,]   ¹what   ³it worked

σατο   ὑμῖν   σπουδήν,   ἀλλὰ   ἀπολογίαν,   ἀλλὰ
out   ⁴in you   ⁴earnestness,   but [what] defence,   but

ἀγανάκτησιν,   ἀλλὰ   φόβον,   ἀλλὰ   ἐπιπόθησιν,
vexation,   but   fear,   but   eager desire,

ἀλλὰ   ζῆλον,   ἀλλὰ   ἐκδίκησιν.   ἐν   παντὶ
but   zeal,   but   vengeance.   In everything

συνεστήσατε   ἑαυτοὺς   ἁγνοὺς   εἶναι   τῷ
ye commended   yourselves   pure   to be   in the

πράγματι.   12 ἄρα   εἰ   καὶ   ἔγραψα   ὑμῖν,
affair.   Then   if   indeed I wrote   to you,

οὐχ   ἕνεκεν   τοῦ   ἀδικήσαντος   οὐδὲ   ἕνεκεν
not   for the   the [one] having done   nor   for the
       sake of   wrong   sake of

τοῦ   ἀδικηθέντος,   ἀλλ'   ἕνεκεν   τοῦ   φανερω-
the   having been   but   for the   the   - to be mani-
[one]   wronged,   sake of

θῆναι   τὴν   σπουδὴν   ὑμῶν   τὴν   ὑπὲρ   ἡμῶν
fested   the   earnestnessᵇᵈ of you   - on behalf of us

πρὸς   ὑμᾶς   ἐνώπιον   τοῦ   θεοῦ.   13 διὰ
toward   you   before   -   God.   There-

τοῦτο   παρακεκλήμεθα.   Ἐπὶ   δὲ   τῇ
fore   we have been comforted. But as to   the

παρακλήσει   ἡμῶν   περισσοτέρως   μᾶλλον
comfort   of us   abundantly   more

ἐχάρημεν   ἐπὶ   τῇ   χαρᾷ   Τίτου,   ὅτι   ἀναπέ-
we rejoiced   over   the   joy   of Titus, because has been

παυται   τὸ   πνεῦμα   αὐτοῦ   ἀπὸ   πάντων
rested   the   spirit   of him   from(by)   all

ὑμῶν·   14 ὅτι   εἴ   τι   αὐτῷ   ὑπὲρ   ὑμῶν
you;   because if ²anything ³to him ⁴on behalf of ⁵you

κεκαύχημαι,   οὐ   κατῃσχύνθην,   ἀλλ'   ὡς
¹I have boasted, I was not shamed,   but   as

πάντα   ἐν   ἀληθείᾳ   ἐλαλήσαμεν   ὑμῖν,   οὕτως
²all things ³in   ⁴truth   ¹we spoke   ⁵to you,   so

καὶ   ἡ   καύχησις   ἡμῶν   ἐπὶ   Τίτου   ἀλήθεια
also   the   boasting   of us   over   Titus   ⁵truth

ἐγενήθη.   15 καὶ   τὰ   σπλάγχνα   αὐτοῦ
¹became.   And   the   bowels   of him

περισσοτέρως   εἰς   ὑμᾶς   ἐστιν   ἀναμιμνησκομέ-
²abundantly   ³toward ⁴you   ¹is(are)   [he]   remember-

νου   τὴν   πάντων   ὑμῶν   ὑπακοήν,   ὡς   μετὰ
ingᵃ   ¹the   ²of all   ⁴you   ³obedience,   as   with

φόβου   καὶ   τρόμου   ἐδέξασθε   αὐτόν.
fear   and   trembling   ye received   him.

16 χαίρω   ὅτι   ἐν   παντὶ   θαρρῶ   ἐν   ὑμῖν.
  I rejoice   that   in everything I am confident in   you.

---

gret it—I see that my letter hurt you, but only for a little while— 9yet now I am happy, not because you were made sorry, but because your sorrow led you to repentance. For you became sorrowful as God intended and so were not harmed in any way by us. 10Godly sorrow brings repentance that leads to salvation and leaves no regret, but worldly sorrow brings death. 11See what this godly sorrow has produced in you: what earnestness, what eagerness to clear yourselves, what indignation, what alarm, what longing, what concern, what readiness to see justice done. At every point you have proved yourselves to be innocent in this matter. 12So even though I wrote to you, it was not on account of the one who did the wrong or of the injured party, but rather that before God you could see for yourselves how devoted to us you are. 13By all this we are encouraged.

In addition to our own encouragement, we were especially delighted to see how happy Titus was, because his spirit has been refreshed by all of you. 14I had boasted to him about you, and you have not embarrassed me. But just as everything we said to you was true, so our boasting about you to Titus has proved to be true as well. 15And his affection for you is all the greater when he remembers that you were all obedient, receiving him with fear and trembling. 16I am glad I can have complete confidence in you.

Chapter 8

Great Generosity

NOW, brethren, we *wish to* make known to you the grace of God which has been given in the churches of Macedonia,

2that in a great ordeal of affliction their abundance of joy and their deep poverty overflowed in the wealth of their liberality.

3For I testify that according to their ability, and beyond their ability *they gave* of their own accord,

4begging us with much entreaty for the favor of participation in the support of the saints,

5and *this,* not as we had expected, but they first gave themselves to the Lord and to us by the will of God.

6Consequently we urged Titus that as he had previously made a beginning, so he would also complete in you this gracious work as well.

7But just as you abound in everything, in faith and utterance and knowledge and in all earnestness and in the *b*love we inspired in you, *see* that you abound in this gracious work also.

8I am not speaking *this* as a command, but as proving through the earnestness of others the sincerity of your love also.

9For you know the grace of our Lord Jesus Christ, that though He was rich, yet for your sake He became poor, that you through His poverty might become rich.

10And I give *my* opinion in this matter, for this is to your advantage, who were the first to begin a year ago not only to do *this,* but also to desire *to do* it.

11But now finish doing it

---

8 Γνωρίζομεν δὲ ὑμῖν, ἀδελφοί, τὴν
Now we make known　to you,　brothers,　the

χάριν τοῦ θεοῦ τὴν δεδομένην ἐν ταῖς
grace　－ of God　－ *having been* given among the

ἐκκλησίαις τῆς Μακεδονίας, 2 ὅτι ἐν πολλῇ
churches　－ of Macedonia,　that in　much

δοκιμῇ θλίψεως ἡ περισσεία τῆς χαρᾶς
proving of affliction the abundance of the　joy

αὐτῶν καὶ ἡ κατὰ βάθους πτωχεία
of them　and　¹the ²according to ⁴depth　³poverty
　　　　　　=their extreme poverty

αὐτῶν ἐπερίσσευσεν εἰς τὸ πλοῦτος τῆς
of them　abounded　　to　the　riches　of the

ἁπλότητος αὐτῶν· 3 ὅτι κατὰ δύναμιν,
liberality　of them;　　that according [their]
　　　　　　　　　　　　to　power,

μαρτυρῶ, καὶ παρὰ δύναμιν, αὐθαίρετοι
I witness,　and　beyond [their] power,　of their own
　　　　　　　　　　　　　　　　　accord

4 μετὰ πολλῆς παρακλήσεως δεόμενοι ἡμῶν
with　much　beseeching　requesting　of us

τὴν χάριν καὶ τὴν κοινωνίαν τῆς διακονίας
the　grace　and　the　fellowship　of the ministry

τῆς εἰς τοὺς ἁγίους, 5 καὶ οὐ καθὼς
－ to　the　saints,　and not　as

ἠλπίσαμεν, ἀλλὰ ἑαυτοὺς ἔδωκαν πρῶτον
we hoped,　but　themselves　gave　first*ly*

τῷ κυρίῳ καὶ ἡμῖν διὰ θελήματος θεοῦ,
to the Lord　and　to us through [the] will　of God,

6 εἰς τὸ παρακαλέσαι ἡμᾶς Τίτον, ἵνα
for　－　to beseech　us*b*　Titus, in order
=that we should beseech　　　　　　that

καθὼς προενήρξατο οὕτως καὶ ἐπιτελέσῃ
as　previously he began　so　also　he should
　　　　　　　　　　　　　　　　complete

εἰς ὑμᾶς καὶ τὴν χάριν ταύτην. 7 ἀλλ’
in　you　also　this grace.　　But

ὥσπερ ἐν παντὶ περισσεύετε, πίστει καὶ
as　in everything　ye abound,　in faith　and

λόγῳ καὶ γνώσει καὶ πάσῃ σπουδῇ
in word　and　in knowledge and　in all　diligence

κα ὶ τῇ ἐξ ἡμῶν ἐν ὑμῖν ἀγάπῃ, ἵνα
and　－　²from ³us　⁴in(to)　⁵you　¹in love, [see] that

καὶ ἐν ταύτῃ τῇ χάριτι περισσεύητε.
²also　³in　⁴this　－　⁵grace　¹ye may abound.

8 Οὐ κατ’ ἐπιταγὴν λέγω, ἀλλὰ διὰ
¹Not ²by way of　⁴command　¹I say,*　but through

τῆς ἑτέρων σπουδῆς καὶ τὸ τῆς ὑμετέρας
¹the ²of others ³diligence also　⁵the　－　⁴of your

ἀγάπης γνήσιον δοκιμάζων· 9 γινώσκετε
⁶love　⁷reality　¹proving;　²ye know

γὰρ τὴν χάριν τοῦ κυρίου ἡμῶν Ἰησοῦ
¹for　the　grace　of the Lord　of us　Jesus

[Χριστοῦ], ὅτι δι’ ὑμᾶς ἐπτώχευσεν
Christ,　that on account you　⁴he impoverished
　　　　　　　　of　　　　　　[himself]

πλούσιος ὤν, ἵνα ὑμεῖς τῇ ἐκείνου πτωχείᾳ
¹rich　²being, in or-　ye　¹by ²of that　³poverty
　　　　　　der that　　the　one

πλουτήσητε. 10 καὶ γνώμην ἐν τούτῳ
might become rich.　And　⁴an opinion ¹in　²this

δίδωμι· τοῦτο γὰρ ὑμῖν συμφέρει, οἵτινες
³I give;　for this　²for you ¹is expedient,　who

οὐ μόνον τὸ ποιῆσαι ἀλλὰ καὶ τὸ θέλειν
not　only　the　to do　but　also　the　to will

προενήρξασθε ἀπὸ πέρυσι· 11 νυνὶ δὲ καὶ
previously *ye* began from　last year;　but now　also
　　　　　　　　　　=a year ago;

Chapter 8

Generosity Encouraged

AND now, brothers, we want you to know about the grace that God has given the Macedonian churches. 2Out of the most severe trial, their overflowing joy and their extreme poverty welled up in rich generosity. 3For I testify that they gave as much as they were able, and even beyond their ability. Entirely on their own, 4they urgently .pleaded with us for the privilege of sharing in this service to the saints. 5And they did not do as we expected, but they gave themselves first to the Lord and then to us in keeping with God's will. 6So we urged Titus, since he had earlier made a beginning, to bring also to completion this act of grace on your part. 7But just as you excel in everything—in faith, in speech, in knowledge, in complete earnestness and in your love for us*¹* —see that you also excel in this grace of giving.

8I am not commanding you, but I want to test the sincerity of your love by comparing it with the earnestness of others. 9For you know the grace of our Lord Jesus Christ, that though he was rich, yet for your sakes he became poor, so that you through his poverty might become rich.

10And here is my advice about what is best for you in this matter: Last year you were the first not only to give but also to have the desire to do so. 11Now fin-

---

b Lit., *love from us in you; some ancient mss. read your love for us*

* That is, Paul is not issuing a command. *Cf.* I. Cor. 7. 6.

¹7 Some manuscripts in our love for you

also; that just as *there was* the readiness to desire it, so *there may be* also the completion of it by your ability.

12For if the readiness is present, it is acceptable according to what *a man* has, not according to what he does not have.

13For *this* is not for the ease of others *and* for your affliction, but by way of equality—

14at this present time your abundance *being a supply* for their want, that their abundance also may become *a supply* for your want, that there may be equality;

15as it is written, "He who *gathered* MUCH DID NOT HAVE TOO MUCH, AND HE WHO *gathered* LITTLE HAD NO LACK."

16But thanks be to God, who puts the same earnestness on your behalf in the heart of Titus.

17For he not only accepted our appeal, but being himself very earnest, he has gone to you of his own accord.

18And we have sent along with him the brother whose fame in *the things of the* gospel *has spread* through all the churches;

19and not only *this*, but he has also been appointed by the churches to travel with us in this gracious work, which is being administered by us for the glory of the Lord Himself, and *to show* our readiness,

20taking precaution that no one should discredit us in our administration of this generous gift;

21for we have regard for what is honorable, not only in the sight of the Lord, but also in the sight of men.

22And we have sent with

τὸ ποιῆσαι ἐπιτελέσατε, ὅπως καθάπερ ἡ
¹the ²to do ¹complete ye, so as as the

προθυμία τοῦ θέλειν, οὕτως καὶ τὸ
eagerness of the to will, so also the

ἐπιτελέσαι ἐκ τοῦ ἔχειν. 12 εἰ γὰρ ἡ
to complete out of the to have. For if the
= what ye have.

προθυμία πρόκειται, καθὸ ἐὰν ἔχῃ
eagerness is already there, according to whatever one has

εὐπρόσδεκτος, οὐ καθὸ οὐκ ἔχει. 13 οὐ
it is acceptable, not according [what] one not
to has not.

γὰρ ἵνα ἄλλοις ἄνεσις, ὑμῖν θλῖψις,
For in order to others relief, to you distress,
that [there may be]

ἀλλ' ἐξ ἰσότητος 14 ἐν τῷ νῦν καιρῷ
but by equality at the present time

τὸ ὑμῶν περίσσευμα εἰς τὸ ἐκείνων
the ²of you ¹abundance [may be] for the ²of those

ὑστέρημα, ἵνα καὶ τὸ ἐκείνων περίσσευμα
¹lack, in order also the ²of those ¹abundance
that

γένηται εἰς τὸ ὑμῶν ὑστέρημα, ὅπως
may be for the ²of you ¹lack, so as

γένηται ἰσότης, 15 καθὼς γέγραπται· ὁ
there may be equality, as it has been He
written:

τὸ πολὺ οὐκ ἐπλεόνασεν, καὶ ὁ τὸ
the much did not abound, and he the

ὀλίγον οὐκ ἠλαττόνησεν. 16 Χάρις δὲ
little had not less. But thanks [be]

τῷ θεῷ τῷ διδόντι τὴν αὐτὴν σπουδὴν
- to God - giving the same diligence

ὑπὲρ ὑμῶν ἐν τῇ καρδίᾳ Τίτου, 17 ὅτι
on be- you in the heart of Titus, because
half of

τὴν μὲν παράκλησιν ἐδέξατο, σπουδαιότερος
²the ¹indeed ³exhortation ¹he received, ³more diligent

δὲ ὑπάρχων αὐθαίρετος ἐξῆλθεν πρὸς ὑμᾶς.
¹and ²being of his own he went to you.
accord forth

18 συνεπέμψαμεν δὲ μετ' αὐτοῦ τὸν
And we sent with with him the

ἀδελφὸν οὗ ὁ ἔπαινος ἐν τῷ εὐαγγελίῳ
brother of whom the praise in the gospel

διὰ πασῶν τῶν ἐκκλησιῶν, 19 οὐ μόνον δὲ
[is] all the churches, and not only [this]
through[out]

ἀλλὰ καὶ χειροτονηθεὶς ὑπὸ τῶν ἐκκλησιῶν
but also ³having been elected ⁴by ⁵the ⁶churches

συνέκδημος ἡμῶν ἐν τῇ χάριτι ταύτῃ
¹a travelling ²of us in this grace
companion

τῇ διακονουμένῃ ὑφ' ἡμῶν πρὸς τὴν
- being ministered by us to ¹the

αὐτοῦ τοῦ κυρίου δόξαν καὶ προθυμίαν
²[him]self ³of the ⁴Lord ¹glory and eagerness

ἡμῶν, 20 στελλόμενοι τοῦτο, μή τις ἡμᾶς
of us, avoiding this, lest anyone ²us

μωμήσηται ἐν τῇ ἁδρότητι ταύτῃ τῇ
¹should blame in this bounty -

διακονουμένῃ ὑφ' ἡμῶν· 21 προνοοῦμεν γὰρ
being ministered by us; for we provide

καλὰ οὐ μόνον ἐνώπιον κυρίου ἀλλὰ καὶ
good not only before [the] Lord but also
things

ἐνώπιον ἀνθρώπων. 22 συνεπέμψαμεν δὲ
before men. And we sent with

---

ish the work, so that your eager willingness to do it may be matched by your completion of it, according to your means. 12For if the willingness is there, the gift is acceptable according to what one has, not according to what he does not have.

13Our desire is not that others might be relieved while you are hard pressed, but that there might be equality. 14At the present time your plenty will supply what they need, so that in turn their plenty will supply what you need. Then there will be equality, 15as it is written: "He who gathered much did not have too much, and he who gathered little did not have too little." [m]

Titus Sent to Corinth

16I thank God, who put into the heart of Titus the same concern I have for you. 17For Titus not only welcomed our appeal, but he is coming to you with much enthusiasm and on his own initiative. 18And we are sending along with him the brother who is praised by all the churches for his service to the gospel. 19What is more, he was chosen by the churches to accompany us as we carry the offering, which we administer in order to honor the Lord himself and to show our eagerness to help. 20We want to avoid any criticism of the way we administer this liberal gift. 21For we are taking pains to do what is right, not only in the eyes of the Lord but also in the eyes of men.

22In addition, we are

m 15 Exodus 16:18

them our brother, whom we have often tested and found diligent in many things, but now even more diligent, because of *his* great confidence in you.

23As for Titus, *he is* my partner and fellow worker among you; as for our brethren, *they are* messengers of the churches, a glory to Christ.

24Therefore openly before the churches show them the proof of your love and of our reason for boasting about you.

αὐτοῖς τὸν ἀδελφὸν ἡμῶν, ὃν ἐδοκιμάσαμεν
them the brother of us, whom ¹we proved

ἐν πολλοῖς πολλάκις σπουδαῖον ὄντα, νυνὶ
¹in ²many things ⁴many times ³diligent ⁵being, ⁶now

δὲ πολὺ σπουδαιότερον πεποιθήσει πολλῇ
¹and much more diligent ¹in ²confidence ²much

τῇ εἰς ὑμᾶς. 23 εἴτε ὑπὲρ Τίτου, κοινωνὸς
– toward you. Whether as to Titus, ⁸partner

ἐμὸς καὶ εἰς ὑμᾶς συνεργός· εἴτε ἀδελφοὶ
¹my ²and ²for ¹you ⁴fellow-worker; or brothers

ἡμῶν, ἀπόστολοι ἐκκλησιῶν, δόξα Χριστοῦ.
of us, apostles of churches, [the] of Christ.
                                     glory

24 τὴν οὖν ἔνδειξιν τῆς ἀγάπης ὑμῶν
⁷The ¹therefore ⁸demonstration ⁹of the ¹⁰love ¹¹of you

καὶ ἡμῶν καυχήσεως ὑπὲρ ὑμῶν εἰς
¹²and ¹⁴of us ¹³boasting ¹⁵on behalf of ¹⁶you ¹⁷to

αὐτοὺς ἐνδεικνύμενοι εἰς πρόσωπον τῶν
¹⁸them ¹showing forth ²in ⁴[the] presence ⁵of the

ἐκκλησιῶν.
⁶churches.

Chapter 9

God Gives Most

FOR it is superfluous for me to write to you about this ministry to the saints;

2for I know your readiness, of which I boast about you to the Macedonians, *namely,* that Achaia has been prepared since last year, and your zeal has stirred up most of them.

3But I have sent the brethren, that our boasting about you may not be made empty in this case, that, as I was saying, you may be prepared;

4lest if any Macedonians come with me and find you unprepared, we (not to speak of you) should be put to shame by this confidence.

5So I thought it necessary to urge the brethren that they would go on ahead to you and arrange beforehand your previously promised bountiful gift, that the same might be ready as a bountiful gift, and not affected by covetousness.

6Now this *I say,* he who sows sparingly shall also

9 Περὶ μὲν γὰρ τῆς διακονίας τῆς
²Concerning ⁵indeed ¹for the ministry the

εἰς τοὺς ἁγίους περισσόν μοί ἐστιν τὸ
to the saints ³superfluous ⁴for me ¹it is –

γράφειν ὑμῖν· 2 οἶδα γὰρ τὴν προθυμίαν
to write to you; for I know the eagerness

ὑμῶν ἣν ὑπὲρ ὑμῶν καυχῶμαι Μακε-
of you which on behalf of you I boast to Mace-

δόσιν ὅτι Ἀχαΐα παρεσκεύασται ἀπὸ
donians that Achaia has made preparations from

πέρυσι, καὶ τὸ ὑμῶν ζῆλος ἠρέθισεν
last year, and the ²of you ¹zeal stirred up
= a year ago,

τοὺς πλείονας. 3 ἔπεμψα δὲ τοὺς ἀδελφούς,
the greater number. And I sent the brothers,

ἵνα μὴ τὸ καύχημα ἡμῶν τὸ ὑπὲρ
lest the boast, of us – on behalf

ὑμῶν κενωθῇ ἐν τῷ μέρει τούτῳ, ἵνα
of you should be in this respect, in order
        emptied   that

καθὼς ἔλεγον παρεσκευασμένοι ἦτε, 4 μή
as I said having been prepared ye were,

πως ἐὰν ἔλθωσιν σὺν ἐμοὶ Μακεδόνες
lest if ²come ³with ⁴me ¹Macedonians

καὶ εὕρωσιν ὑμᾶς ἀπαρασκευάστους
and find you unprepared

καταισχυνθῶμεν ἡμεῖς, ἵνα μὴ λέγωμεν
²should be shamed ¹we, in order we say not
                                 that

ὑμεῖς, ἐν τῇ ὑποστάσει ταύτῃ. 5 ἀναγκαῖον
ye, in this confidence. ³Necessary

οὖν ἡγησάμην παρακαλέσαι τοὺς ἀδελφοὺς
²there- ¹I thought [it] to beseech the brothers
fore

ἵνα προέλθωσιν εἰς ὑμᾶς καὶ προκαταρτί-
in order they go to you and arrange before-
that   forward

σωσιν τὴν προεπηγγελμένην εὐλογίαν ὑμῶν,
hand ¹the ⁴having been promised ²blessing ³of you,

ταύτην ἑτοίμην εἶναι οὕτως ὡς εὐλογίαν
this ready to be thus as a blessing

καὶ μὴ ὡς πλεονεξίαν. 6 Τοῦτο δέ,
and not as greediness. And this,

ὁ σπείρων φειδομένως φειδομένως καὶ
the [one] sowing sparingly ²sparingly ²also

Chapter 9

THERE is no need for me to write to you about this service to the saints. 2For I know your eagerness to help, and I have been boasting about it to the Macedonians, telling them that since last year you in Achaia were ready to give; and your enthusiasm has stirred most of them to action. 3But I am sending the brothers in order that our boasting about you in this matter should not prove hollow, but that you may be ready, as I said you would be. 4For if any Macedonians come with me and find you unprepared, we—not to say anything about you—would be ashamed of having been so confident. 5So I thought it necessary to urge the brothers to visit you in advance and finish the arrangements for the generous gift you had promised. Then it will be ready as a generous gift, not as one grudgingly given.

Sowing Generously

6Remember this: Whoever sows sparingly will also

reap sparingly; and he who sows bountifully shall also reap bountifully.

7Let each one *do* just as he has purposed in his heart; not grudgingly or under compulsion; for God loves a cheerful giver.

8And God is able to make all grace abound to you, that always having all sufficiency in everything, you may have an abundance for every good deed; 9as it is written,

"HE SCATTERED ABROAD, HE GAVE TO THE POOR,
HIS RIGHTEOUSNESS ABIDES FOREVER."

10Now He who supplies seed to the sower and bread for food, will supply and multiply your seed for sowing and increase the harvest of your righteousness; 11you will be enriched in everything for all liberality, which through us is producing thanksgiving to God.

12For the ministry of this service is not only fully supplying the needs of the saints, but is also overflowing through many thanksgivings to God.

13Because of the proof given by this ministry they will glorify God for *your* obedience to your confession of the gospel of Christ, and for the liberality of your contribution to them and to all,

14while you also, by prayer on your behalf, yearn for you because of the surpassing grace of God in you.

15Thanks be to God for His indescribable gift!

θερίσει, καὶ ὁ σπείρων ἐπ᾽ εὐλογίαις ἐπ᾽
[1]will reap, and the [one] sowing on(for) blessings [3]on(for)

εὐλογίαις καὶ θερίσει. 7 ἕκαστος καθὼς
[4]blessings [2]also [1]will reap.   Each one   as

προήρηται τῇ καρδίᾳ, μὴ ἐκ λύπης ἢ
he chose in the(his) heart, not of grief or

ἐξ ἀνάγκης· ἱλαρὸν γὰρ δότην ἀγαπᾷ ὁ
of necessity; for [a cheerful] [4]giver [3]loves [1]

θεός. 8 δυνατεῖ δὲ ὁ θεὸς πᾶσαν χάριν
[1]God. And [2]is able - [1]God [4]all [5]grace

περισσεῦσαι εἰς ὑμᾶς, ἵνα ἐν παντὶ
[3]to cause to abound toward you, in order that [5]in [6]everything

πάντοτε πᾶσαν αὐτάρκειαν ἔχοντες περισ-
[1]always [2]all [4]self-sufficiency [3]having ye may

σεύητε εἰς πᾶν ἔργον ἀγαθόν, 9 καθὼς
abound to every work good,   as

γέγραπται· ἐσκόρπισεν, ἔδωκεν τοῖς πένησιν,
it has been written: He scattered, he gave to the poor,

ἡ δικαιοσύνη αὐτοῦ μένει εἰς τὸν αἰῶνα.
the righteousness of him remains unto the age.

10 ὁ δὲ ἐπιχορηγῶν σπέρμα τῷ σπείροντι
Now the [one] providing seed for the [one] sowing

καὶ ἄρτον εἰς βρῶσιν χορηγήσει καὶ
[1]both [2]bread [4]for [5]food [3]will supply and

πληθυνεῖ τὸν σπόρον ὑμῶν καὶ αὐξήσει
will multiply the seed of you and will increase

τὰ γενήματα τῆς δικαιοσύνης ὑμῶν· 11 ἐν
the fruits of the righteousness of you; in

παντὶ πλουτιζόμενοι εἰς πᾶσαν ἁπλότητα,
everything being enriched to all liberality,

ἥτις κατεργάζεται δι᾽ ἡμῶν εὐχαριστίαν
which works out through us thanksgiving

τῷ θεῷ· 12 ὅτι ἡ διακονία τῆς λειτουργίας
- to God; because the ministry - service

ταύτης οὐ μόνον ἐστὶν προσαναπληροῦσα
of this not only is making up

τὰ ὑστερήματα τῶν ἁγίων, ἀλλὰ καὶ
the things lacking of the saints, but [is] also

περισσεύουσα διὰ πολλῶν εὐχαριστιῶν τῷ
abounding through many thanksgivings -

θεῷ· 13 διὰ τῆς δοκιμῆς τῆς διακονίας
to God; through the proof - ministry

ταύτης δοξάζοντες τὸν θεὸν ἐπὶ τῇ
of this glorifying - God on the

ὑποταγῇ τῆς ὁμολογίας ὑμῶν εἰς τὸ
submission of the confession of you to the

εὐαγγέλιον τοῦ Χριστοῦ καὶ ἁπλότητι
gospel - of Christ and [on the] liberality

τῆς κοινωνίας εἰς αὐτοὺς καὶ εἰς πάντας,
of the fellowship toward them and toward all men,

14 καὶ αὐτῶν δεήσει ὑπὲρ ὑμῶν ἐπιποθούν-
and [1]them [4]with [5]on be- [6]you [3]longing
                     request   half of

των ὑμᾶς διὰ τὴν ὑπερβάλλουσαν χάριν
after[2] [3]you on account of the excelling grace
                    of

τοῦ θεοῦ ἐφ᾽ ὑμῖν. 15 Χάρις τῷ θεῷ
- of God upon you.   Thanks - to God

ἐπὶ τῇ ἀνεκδιηγήτῳ αὐτοῦ δωρεᾷ.
for the indescribable of him gift.

---

reap sparingly, and whoever sows generously will also reap generously. 7Each man should give what he has decided in his heart to give, not reluctantly or under compulsion, for God loves a cheerful giver. 8And God is able to make all grace abound to you, so that in all things at all times, having all that you need, you will abound in every good work. 9As it is written:

"He has scattered
    abroad his gifts to
    the poor;
his righteousness
    endures forever." [n]

10Now he who supplies seed to the sower and bread for food will also supply and increase your store of seed and will enlarge the harvest of your righteousness. 11You will be made rich in every way so that you can be generous on every occasion, and through us your generosity will result in thanksgiving to God. 12This service that you perform is not only supplying the needs of God's people but is also overflowing in many expressions of thanks to God. 13Because of the service by which you have proved yourselves, men will praise God for the obedience that accompanies your confession of the gospel of Christ, and for your generosity in sharing with them and with everyone else. 14And in their prayers for you their hearts will go out to you, because of the surpassing grace God has given you. 15Thanks be to God for his indescribable gift!

Paul Describes Himself

NOW I, Paul, myself urge you by the meekness and gentleness of Christ—I who am meek when face to face with you,

---

10 Αὐτὸς δὲ ἐγὼ Παῦλος παρακαλῶ
[my]self Now I   Paul   beseech

ὑμᾶς διὰ τῆς πραΰτητος καὶ ἐπιεικείας
you through the meekness and forbearance

τοῦ Χριστοῦ, ὃς κατὰ πρόσωπον μὲν
- of Christ, who according to face indeed

Paul's Defense of His Ministry

BY the meekness and gentleness of Christ, I appeal to you—I, Paul, who am "timid" when face to face with you, but

n9 Psalm 112:9

but bold toward you when absent!

2I ask that when I am present I may not be bold with the confidence with which I propose to be courageous against some, who regard us as if we walked according to the flesh.

3For though we walk in the flesh, we do not war according to the flesh,

4for the weapons of our warfare are not of the flesh, but divinely powerful for the destruction of fortresses.

5We are destroying speculations and every lofty thing raised up against the knowledge of God, and we are taking every thought captive to the obedience of Christ,

6and we are ready to punish all disobedience, whenever your obedience is complete.

7You are looking at things as they are outwardly. If anyone is confident in himself that he is Christ's, let him consider this again within himself, that just as he is Christ's, so also are we.

8For even if I should boast somewhat further about our authority, which the Lord gave for building you up and not for destroying you, I shall not be put to shame,

9for I do not wish to seem as if I would terrify you by my letters.

10For they say, "His letters are weighty and strong, but his personal presence is unimpressive, and his speech contemptible."

11Let such a person consider this, that what we are in word by letters when absent, such persons we are also in deed when present.

12For we are not bold to class or compare ourselves with some of those who commend themselves; but

---

ταπεινὸς ἐν ὑμῖν, ἀπὼν δὲ θαρρῶ εἰς
[am] humble among you, but being absent am bold toward

ὑμᾶς· 2 δέομαι δὲ τὸ μὴ παρὼν θαρρῆσαι
you: now I request – not being present to be bold

τῇ πεποιθήσει ᾗ λογίζομαι τολμῆσαι ἐπί
in the confidence which I reckon to be daring toward

τινας τοὺς λογιζομένους ἡμᾶς ὡς κατὰ
some the [ones] reckoning us as ³according to

σάρκα περιπατοῦντας. 3 Ἐν σαρκὶ γὰρ
¹flesh ¹walking. in flesh For

περιπατοῦντες οὐ κατὰ σάρκα στρατενόμεθα,
walking not according to flesh we war,

4 τὰ γὰρ ὅπλα τῆς στρατείας ἡμῶν
for the weapons of the warfare of us [are]

οὐ σαρκικὰ ἀλλὰ δυνατὰ τῷ θεῷ πρὸς
not fleshly but powerful – to God to

καθαίρεσιν ὀχυρωμάτων, λογισμοὺς καθαιροῦν-
overthrow of strongholds, ¹reasonings ¹overthrow-

τες 5 καὶ πᾶν ὕψωμα ἐπαιρόμενον κατὰ
ing and every high thing rising up against

τῆς γνώσεως τοῦ θεοῦ, καὶ αἰχμαλωτίζοντες
the knowledge – of God, and taking captive

πᾶν νόημα εἰς τὴν ὑπακοὴν τοῦ Χριστοῦ,
every design to the obedience – of Christ,

6 καὶ ἐν ἑτοίμῳ ἔχοντες ἐκδικῆσαι πᾶσαν
and in readiness having to avenge all
=being ready

παρακοήν, ὅταν πληρωθῇ ὑμῶν ἡ ὑπακοή.
disobedience, whenever ⁴is fulfilled ²of you ¹the ²obedience.

7 Τὰ κατὰ πρόσωπον βλέπετε. εἴ τις
²The ³according ⁴face ¹ye look [at]. If any-
things to (appearance) one

πέποιθεν ἑαυτῷ Χριστοῦ εἶναι, τοῦτο
has persuaded himself ²of Christ ¹to be, this

λογιζέσθω πάλιν ἐφ' ἑαυτοῦ, ὅτι καθὼς
let him reckon again as to himself, that as

αὐτὸς Χριστοῦ, οὕτως καὶ ἡμεῖς. 8 ἐάν
he [is] of Christ, so also [are] we. ²if

τε γὰρ περισσότερόν τι καυχήσωμαι περὶ
²even ¹For ²more abundantly ²some- ⁴I should boast concern-
what ing

τῆς ἐξουσίας ἡμῶν, ἧς ἔδωκεν ὁ κύριος
the authority of us, which ²gave ¹the ¹Lord

εἰς οἰκοδομὴν καὶ οὐκ εἰς καθαίρεσιν
for edification and not for overthrow

ὑμῶν, οὐκ αἰσχυνθήσομαι, 9 ἵνα μὴ δόξω
of you, I shall not be shamed, in order that I may not seem

ὡσὰν ἐκφοβεῖν ὑμᾶς διὰ τῶν ἐπιστολῶν.
as though to frighten you through the epistles.

10 ὅτι αἱ ἐπιστολαὶ μέν, φησίν, βαρεῖαι
Because the(his) epistles indeed, he says, [are] weighty

καὶ ἰσχυραί, ἡ δὲ παρουσία τοῦ σώματος
and strong, but the presence of the(his) body [is]

ἀσθενὴς καὶ ὁ λόγος ἐξουθενημένος.
weak and the(his) speech being despised.

11 τοῦτο λογιζέσθω ὁ τοιοῦτος, ὅτι οἷοί
This let reckon such a one, that such as

ἐσμεν τῷ λόγῳ δι' ἐπιστολῶν ἀπόντες,
we are – in word through epistles being absent,

τοιοῦτοι καὶ παρόντες τῷ ἔργῳ. 12 Οὐ
such also being present – in work. ²not

γὰρ τολμῶμεν ἐγκρῖναι ἢ συγκρῖναι
¹For ²we dare to class with or to compare

ἑαυτούς τισιν τῶν ἑαυτοὺς συνιστανόντων·
ourselves with some of the ²themselves ¹commending;
[ones]

"bold" when away! 2I beg you that when I come I may not have to be as bold as I expect to be toward some people who think that we live by the standards of this world. 3For though we live in the world, we do not wage war as the world does. 4The weapons we fight with are not the weapons of the world. On the contrary, they have divine power to demolish strongholds. 5We demolish arguments and every pretension that sets itself up against the knowledge of God, and we take captive every thought to make it obedient to Christ. 6And we will be ready to punish every act of disobedience, once your obedience is complete.

7You are looking only on the surface of things.ᵒ If anyone is confident that he belongs to Christ, he should consider again that we belong to Christ just as much as he. 8For even if I boast somewhat freely about the authority the Lord gave us for building you up rather than pulling you down, I will not be ashamed of it. 9I do not want to seem to be trying to frighten you with my letters. 10For some say, "His letters are weighty and forceful, but in person he is unimpressive and his speaking amounts to nothing." 11Such people should realize that what we are in our letters when we are absent, we will be in our actions when we are present.

12We do not dare to classify or compare ourselves with some who commend themselves. When they

ᵒ7 Or Look at the obvious facts

when they measure themselves by themselves, and compare themselves with themselves, they are without understanding.

13But we will not boast beyond *our* measure, but within the measure of the sphere which God apportioned to us as a measure, to reach even as far as you.

14For we are not over-extending ourselves, as if we did not reach to you, for we were the first to come even as far as you in the gospel of Christ;

15not boasting beyond *our* measure, *that is,* in other men's labors, but with the hope that as your faith grows, we shall be, within our sphere, enlarged even more by you,

16so as to preach the gospel even to the regions beyond you, *and* not to boast in what has been accomplished in the sphere of another.

17But HE WHO BOASTS, LET HIM BOAST IN THE LORD.

18For not he who commends himself is approved, but whom the Lord commends.

ἀλλὰ αὐτοὶ ἐν ἑαυτοῖς ἑαυτοὺς μετροῦντες
but they ²among ⁴them-selves ³them-selves ¹measuring

καὶ συγκρίνοντες ἑαυτοὺς ἑαυτοῖς οὐ
and comparing themselves with themselves not

συνιᾶσιν. 13 ἡμεῖς δὲ οὐκ εἰς τὰ ἄμετρα
do understand. But we ⁴not ⁴immeasurably†

καυχησόμεθα, ἀλλὰ κατὰ τὸ μέτρον τοῦ
¹will ³boast, but according to the measure of the

κανόνος οὗ ἐμέρισεν ἡμῖν ὁ θεὸς μέτρου,
rule which ²divided ³to us – ¹God of(in) measure,

ἐφικέσθαι ἄχρι καὶ ὑμῶν. 14 οὐ γὰρ
to reach as far as even you. For not

ὡς μὴ ἐφικνούμενοι εἰς ὑμᾶς ὑπερεκτείνομεν
as not reaching to you do we overstretch

ἑαυτούς, ἄχρι γὰρ καὶ ὑμῶν ἐφθάσαμεν
ourselves, for as far as even you we came

ἐν τῷ εὐαγγελίῳ τοῦ Χριστοῦ, 15 οὐκ
in the gospel – of Christ, not

εἰς τὰ ἄμετρα καυχώμενοι ἐν ἀλλοτρίοις
immeasurably† boasting in others't

κόποις, ἐλπίδα δὲ ἔχοντες αὐξανομένης
labours, but ²hope ¹having =as your faith grows growing

τῆς πίστεως ὑμῶν ἐν ὑμῖν μεγαλυνθῆναι
the faith of you² among ³you ¹to be magnified

κατὰ τὸν κανόνα ἡμῶν εἰς περισσείαν,
according to the rule of us in abundance,

16 εἰς τὰ ὑπερέκεινα ὑμῶν εὐαγγελίσασθαι,
in the [parts] beyond you to preach good tidings,

οὐκ ἐν ἀλλοτρίῳ κανόνι εἰς τὰ ἕτοιμα
not ²in ³another's† ⁴rule ⁵in – ⁶things ready

καυχήσασθαι. 17 Ὁ δὲ καυχώμενος ἐν
¹to boast. But the [one] boasting ²in

κυρίῳ καυχάσθω· 18 οὐ γὰρ ὁ ἑαυτὸν
¹[the] Lord ¹let him boast; for not the [one] himself

συνιστάνων, ἐκεῖνός ἐστιν δόκιμος, ἀλλὰ
commending, that one is approved, but

ὃν ὁ κύριος συνίστησιν.
whom the Lord commends.

Chapter 11

Paul Defends His Apostleship

I wish that you would bear with me in a little foolishness; but indeed you are bearing with me.

2For I am jealous for you with a godly jealousy; for I betrothed you to one husband, that to Christ I might present you *as* a pure virgin.

3But I am afraid, lest as the serpent deceived Eve by his craftiness, your minds should be led astray from the simplicity and purity *of devotion* to Christ.

4For if one comes and preaches another Jesus whom we have not preached, or you receive a different spirit which you

---

11 Ὄφελον ἀνείχεσθέ μου μικρόν τι
I would that ye endured me a little [bit]

ἀφροσύνης· ἀλλὰ καὶ ἀνέχεσθέ μου.
of foolishness; but indeed ye do endure me.

2 ζηλῶ γὰρ ὑμᾶς θεοῦ ζήλῳ, ἡρμοσάμην
For I am jealous [of] you ²of God ¹with a jealousy, ²I betrothed

γὰρ ὑμᾶς ἑνὶ ἀνδρὶ παρθένον ἁγνὴν
¹for you to one husband ³virgin ²a pure

παραστῆσαι τῷ Χριστῷ· 3 φοβοῦμαι δὲ
¹to present – to Christ; and I fear

μή πως, ὡς ὁ ὄφις ἐξηπάτησεν Εὕαν
lest somehow, as the serpent deceived Eve

ἐν τῇ πανουργίᾳ αὐτοῦ, φθαρῇ τὰ νοήματα
by the cleverness of him, ³should ¹the ²thoughts be seduced

ὑμῶν ἀπὸ τῆς ἁπλότητος [καὶ τῆς
of you from the simplicity and the

ἁγνότητος] τῆς εἰς Χριστόν. 4 εἰ μὲν
purity – in Christ. ²if ³indeed

γὰρ ὁ ἐρχόμενος ἄλλον Ἰησοῦν κηρύσσει
¹For the [one] coming ²another ¹Jesus ¹proclaims

ὃν οὐκ ἐκηρύξαμεν, ἢ πνεῦμα ἕτερον
whom we did not proclaim, or ²spirit ¹a different

---

measure themselves by themselves and compare themselves with themselves, they are not wise.

13We, however, will not boast beyond proper limits, but will confine our boasting to the field God has assigned to us, a field that reaches even to you. 14We are not going too far in our boasting, as would be the case if we had not come to you, for we did get as far as you with the gospel of Christ. 15Neither do we go beyond our limits by boasting of work done by others.*p* Our hope is that, as your faith continues to grow, our area of activity among you will greatly expand, 16so that we can preach the gospel in the regions beyond you. For we do not want to boast about work already done in another man's territory. 17But, "Let him who boasts boast in the Lord."*q* 18For it is not the one who commends himself who is approved, but the one whom the Lord commends.

Chapter 11

Paul and the False Apostles

I HOPE you will put up with a little of my foolishness; but you are already doing that. 2I am jealous for you with a godly jealousy. I promised you to one husband, to Christ, so that I might present you as a pure virgin to him. 3But I am afraid that just as Eve was deceived by the serpent's cunning, your minds may somehow be led astray from your sincere and pure devotion to Christ. 4For if someone comes to you and preaches a Jesus other than the Jesus we preached, or if you receive a different spir-

p 13-15 Or *13*We, however, will not boast about things that cannot be measured, but we will boast according to the standard of measurement that the God of measure has assigned us—a measurement that relates even to you. *14* . . . . *15*Neither do we boast about things that cannot be measured in regard to the work done by others.
q17 Jer. 9:24

have not received, or a different gospel which you have not accepted, you bear *this* beautifully.

5For I consider myself not in the least inferior to the most eminent apostles.

6But even if I am unskilled in speech, yet I am not *so* in knowledge; in fact, in every way we have made *this* evident to you in all things.

7Or did I commit a sin in humbling myself that you might be exalted, because I preached the gospel of God to you without charge?

8I robbed other churches, taking wages *from them* to serve you;

9and when I was present with you and was in need, I was not a burden to anyone; for when the brethren came from Macedonia, they fully supplied my need, and in everything I kept myself from being a burden to you, and will continue to do so.

10As the truth of Christ is in me, this boasting of mine will not be stopped in the regions of Achaia.

11Why? Because I do not love you? God knows *I do!*

12But what I am doing, I will continue to do, that I may cut off opportunity from those who desire an opportunity to be regarded just as we are in the matter about which they are boasting.

13For such men are false apostles, deceitful workers, disguising themselves as apostles of Christ.

14And no wonder, for even Satan disguises himself as an angel of light.

15Therefore it is not surprising if his servants also disguise themselves as servants of righteousness; whose end shall be according to their deeds.

λαμβάνετε ὃ οὐκ ἐλάβετε, ἢ εὐαγγέλιον
1ye receive which ye did not receive, or 2gospel

ἕτερον ὃ οὐκ ἐδέξασθε, καλῶς ἀνέχεσθε.
1a different which ye did not receive, 2[him] 3well 1ye endure.

5 λογίζομαι γὰρ μηδὲν ὑστερηκέναι τῶν
For I reckon nothing to have come behind of the

ὑπερλίαν ἀποστόλων. 6 εἰ δὲ καὶ ἰδιώτης
super- apostles. But if indeed unskilled
[I am]

τῷ λόγῳ, ἀλλ' οὐ τῇ γνώσει, ἀλλ' ἐν
- in speech, yet not - in knowledge, but in

παντὶ φανερώσαντες ἐν πᾶσιν εἰς ὑμᾶς.
every having manifested in all things to you.
[way] [ourselves]

7 Ἢ ἁμαρτίαν ἐποίησα ἐμαυτὸν ταπεινῶν
Or 3sin 1did I commit 4myself 5humbling

ἵνα ὑμεῖς ὑψωθῆτε, ὅτι δωρεὰν τὸ τοῦ
in order ye might be because 2freely 1the -
that exalted,

θεοῦ εὐαγγέλιον εὐηγγελισάμην ὑμῖν;
4of God 3gospel 1I preached good tidings to you?

8 ἄλλας ἐκκλησίας ἐσύλησα λαβὼν ὀψώνιον
Other churches I robbed taking wages

πρὸς τὴν ὑμῶν διακονίαν, 9 καὶ παρὼν
for 1the 2of you 3ministry, and being present

πρὸς ὑμᾶς καὶ ὑστερηθεὶς οὐ κατενάρκησα
with you and lacking I was not an encumbrance

οὐθενός· τὸ γὰρ ὑστέρημά μου προσανε-
of no man; for the lack of me 4made

πλήρωσαν οἱ ἀδελφοὶ ἐλθόντες ἀπὸ Μακε-
up 1the 2brothers 3coming 4from 5Mace-

δονίας· καὶ ἐν παντὶ ἀβαρῆ ἐμαυτὸν
donia; and in every [way] unburdensome 1myself

ὑμῖν ἐτήρησα καὶ τηρήσω. 10 ἔστιν
2to you 3I kept and I will keep. 2is

ἀλήθεια Χριστοῦ ἐν ἐμοί, ὅτι ἡ καύχησις
1[The] truth 2of Christ in me, that - boasting

αὕτη οὐ φραγήσεται εἰς ἐμὲ ἐν τοῖς
this shall not be stopped in me in the

κλίμασιν τῆς Ἀχαΐας. 11 διὰ τί; ὅτι
regions - of Achaia. Why? because

οὐκ ἀγαπῶ ὑμᾶς; ὁ θεὸς οἶδεν. 12 Ὃ
I love not you? - God knows. what

δὲ ποιῶ, καὶ ποιήσω, ἵνα ἐκκόψω τὴν
But I do, also I will do, in order I may cut the
that off

ἀφορμὴν τῶν θελόντων ἀφορμήν, ἵνα ἐν
occasion of the desiring an occasion, in or- where-
[ones] der that

ᾧ καυχῶνται εὑρεθῶσιν καθὼς καὶ ἡμεῖς.
in they boast they may be found as also we.

13 οἱ γὰρ τοιοῦτοι ψευδαπόστολοι, ἐργάται
- For such [are] false apostles, 1workmen

δόλιοι, μετασχηματιζόμενοι εἰς ἀποστόλους
1deceitful, transforming themselves into apostles

Χριστοῦ. 14 καὶ οὐ θαῦμα· αὐτὸς γὰρ
of Christ. And no wonder; 2[him]self 1for

ὁ σατανᾶς μετασχηματίζεται εἰς ἄγγελον
- 2Satan transforms himself into an angel

φωτός. 15 οὐ μέγα οὖν εἰ καὶ οἱ
of light. No great thing therefore if also the

διάκονοι αὐτοῦ μετασχηματίζονται ὡς
ministers of him transform themselves as

διάκονοι δικαιοσύνης· ὧν τὸ τέλος ἔσται
ministers of righteousness; of whom the end will be

κατὰ τὰ ἔργα αὐτῶν.
according to the works of them.

it from the one you received, or a different gospel from the one you accepted, you put up with it easily enough. 5But I do not think I am in the least inferior to those "super-apostles." 6I may not be a trained speaker, but I do have knowledge. We have made this perfectly clear to you in every way.

7Was it a sin for me to lower myself in order to elevate you by preaching the gospel of God to you free of charge? 8I robbed other churches by receiving support from them so as to serve you. 9And when I was with you and needed something, I was not a burden to anyone; for the brothers who came from Macedonia supplied what I needed. I have kept myself from being a burden to you in any way, and will continue to do so. 10As surely as the truth of Christ is in me, nobody in the regions of Achaia will stop this boasting of mine. 11Why? Because I do not love you? God knows I do! 12And I will keep on doing what I am doing in order to cut the ground from under those who want an opportunity to be considered equal with us in the things they boast about.

13For such men are false apostles, deceitful workmen, masquerading as apostles of Christ. 14And no wonder, for Satan himself masquerades as an angel of light. 15It is not surprising, then, if his servants masquerade as servants of righteousness. Their end will be what their actions deserve.

16Again I say, let no one think me foolish; but if *you do,* receive me even as foolish, that I also may boast a little.

17That which I am speaking, I am not speaking as the Lord would, but as in foolishness, in this confidence of boasting.

18Since many boast according to the flesh, I will boast also.

19For you, being *so* wise, bear with the foolish gladly.

20For you bear with anyone if he enslaves you, if he devours you, if he takes advantage of you, if he exalts himself, if he hits you in the face.

21To *my* shame I *must* say that we have been weak *by comparison.* But in whatever respect anyone *else* is bold (I speak in foolishness), I am just as bold myself.

22Are they Hebrews? So am I. Are they Israelites? So am I. Are they descendants of Abraham? So am I.

23Are they servants of Christ? (I speak as if insane) I more so; in far more labors, in far more imprisonments, beaten times without number, often in danger of death.

24Five times I received from the Jews thirty-nine *lashes.*

25Three times I was beaten with rods, once I was stoned, three times I was shipwrecked, a night and a day I have spent in the deep.

26I *have been* on frequent journeys, in dangers from rivers, dangers from robbers, dangers from *my* countrymen, dangers from the Gentiles, dangers in the city, dangers in the wilderness, dangers on the sea, dangers among false brethren;

27I *have been* in labor and hardship, through many sleepless nights, in hunger and thirst, often without

---

16 Πάλιν λέγω, μή τίς με δόξῃ ἄφρονα
Again   I say,   ¹not ²anyone ⁴me ¹think ⁵foolish

εἶναι· εἰ δὲ μή γε, κἂν ὡς ἄφρονα
⁴to be;   otherwise,   even if   as   foolish

δέξασθέ με, ἵνα κἀγὼ μικρόν τι καυχήσ-
receive ye   me, in order   I also   a little [bit]   may
          that

ωμαι. **17** ὃ λαλῶ, οὐ κατὰ κύριον λαλῶ,
boast.   What I speak,   not according to [the] Lord I speak,
                  to

ἀλλ' ὡς ἐν ἀφροσύνῃ, ἐν ταύτῃ τῇ
but as in folly,   in   this   -

ὑποστάσει τῆς καυχήσεως. **18** ἐπεὶ πολλοὶ
confidence   -   of boasting.   Since   many

καυχῶνται κατὰ [τὴν] σάρκα, κἀγὼ
boast   according to the   flesh,   I also

καυχήσομαι. **19** ἡδέως γὰρ ἀνέχεσθε τῶν
will boast.   For gladly   ye endure   the

ἀφρόνων φρόνιμοι ὄντες· **20** ἀνέχεσθε γὰρ
fools   ²prudent ¹being;   for ye endure

εἴ τις ὑμᾶς καταδουλοῖ, εἴ τις κατεσθίει,
if anyone ²you ¹enslaves,   if anyone devours [you],

εἴ τις λαμβάνει, εἴ τις ἐπαίρεται, εἴ
if   anyone receives [you],*   if anyone lifts himself up,   if

τις εἰς πρόσωπον ὑμᾶς δέρει. **21** κατὰ
anyone ³in ⁴[the] face   ²you ¹beats(hits). According to

ἀτιμίαν λέγω, ὡς ὅτι ἡμεῖς ἠσθενήκαμεν·
dishonour I say,   as   that   we   have been weak;

ἐν ᾧ δ' ἄν τις τολμᾷ, ἐν ἀφροσύνῃ
but in whatever [respect] anyone dares,   in   folly

λέγω, τολμῶ κἀγώ. **22** Ἑβραῖοί εἰσιν;
I say,   ²dare ¹I ³also.   Hebrews   are they?

κἀγώ. Ἰσραηλῖταί εἰσιν; κἀγώ. σπέρμα
I also.   Israelites   are they?   I also.   Seed

Ἀβραάμ εἰσιν; κἀγώ. **23** διάκονοι Χριστοῦ
of Abraham are they? I also.   Ministers   of Christ

εἰσιν; παραφρονῶν λαλῶ, ὑπὲρ ἐγώ· ἐν
are they? being out of   I speak,   ²beyond ¹I: in
    my mind   (more)

κόποις περισσοτέρως, ἐν φυλακαῖς περισ-
labours   more abundantly,   in   prisons   more

σοτέρως, ἐν πληγαῖς ὑπερβαλλόντως, ἐν
abundantly,   in   stripes   excessively,   in

θανάτοις πολλάκις. **24** ὑπὸ Ἰουδαίων
deaths   many times.   By   Jews

πεντάκις τεσσεράκοντα παρὰ μίαν ἔλαβον,
five times   forty [stripes]   less   one   I received,

25 τρὶς ἐρραβδίσθην, ἅπαξ ἐλιθάσθην, τρὶς
thrice I was beaten with rods, once   I was stoned,   thrice

ἐναυάγησα, **26** νυχθήμερον ἐν τῷ βυθῷ
I was shipwrecked,   a night and a day   in   the   deep

πεποίηκα· ὁδοιπορίαις πολλάκις, κινδύνοις
I have done(been);   in travels   many times,   in perils

ποταμῶν, κινδύνοις λῃστῶν, κινδύνοις ἐκ
of rivers,   in perils   of robbers,   in perils   of

γένους, κινδύνοις ἐξ ἐθνῶν, κινδύνοις ἐν
[my] kind,   in perils   of   nations,   in perils   in

πόλει, κινδύνοις ἐν ἐρημίᾳ, κινδύνοις ἐν
a city,   in perils   in   a desert,   in perils   in(at)

θαλάσσῃ, κινδύνοις ἐν ψευδαδέλφοις, **27** κόπῳ
sea,   in perils   among   false brothers,   in labour

καὶ μόχθῳ, ἐν ἀγρυπνίαις πολλάκις, ἐν
and   hardship,   in   watchings   many times,   in

λιμῷ καὶ δίψει, ἐν νηστείαις πολλάκις,
famine   and   thirst,   in   fastings   many times,

Paul Boasts About His Sufferings

16I repeat: Let no one take me for a fool. But if you do, then receive me just as you would a fool, so that I may do a little boasting. **17**In this self-confident boasting I am not talking as the Lord would, but as a fool. **18**Since many are boasting in the way the world does, I too will boast. **19**You gladly put up with anyone who enslaves you or exploits you or takes advantage of you or pushes himself forward or slaps you in the face. **21**To my shame I admit that we were too weak for that!

What anyone else dares to boast about—I am speaking as a fool—I also dare to boast about. **22**Are they Hebrews? So am I. Are they Israelites? So am I. Are they Abraham's descendants? So am I. **23**Are they servants of Christ? (I am out of my mind to talk like this.) I am more. I have worked much harder, been in prison more frequently, been flogged more severely, and been exposed to death again and again. **24**Five times I received from the Jews the forty lashes minus one. **25**Three times I was beaten with rods, once I was stoned, three times I was shipwrecked, I spent a night and a day in the open sea, **26**I have been constantly on the move. I have been in danger from rivers, in danger from bandits, in danger from my own countrymen, in danger from Gentiles; in danger in the city, in danger in the country, in danger at sea; and in danger from false brothers. **27**I have labored and toiled and have often gone without sleep; I have known hunger and thirst and have often gone

---

* ? takes [you in].

food, in cold and exposure. 28Apart from *such* external things, there is the daily pressure upon me *of* concern for all the churches. 29Who is weak without my being weak? Who is led into sin without my intense concern? 30If I have to boast, I will boast of what pertains to my weakness. 31The God and Father of the Lord Jesus, He who is blessed forever, knows that I am not lying. 32In Damascus the ethnarch under Aretas the king was guarding the city of the Damascenes in order to seize me, 33and I was let down in a basket through a window in the wall, and *so* escaped his hands.

ἐν ψύχει καὶ γυμνότητι· 28 χωρὶς τῶν
in cold and nakedness; apart from the things

παρεκτὸς ἡ ἐπίστασίς μοι ἡ καθ' ἡμέραν,
without[,] the conspiring me - daily,
  against

ἡ μέριμνα πασῶν τῶν ἐκκλησιῶν. 29 τίς
the care of all the churches. Who

ἀσθενεῖ, καὶ οὐκ ἀσθενῶ; τίς σκανδαλίζεται,
is weak, and I am not weak? who is offended,

καὶ οὐκ ἐγὼ πυροῦμαι; 30 εἰ καυχᾶσθαι
and ²not ¹I ¹burn? If to boast

δεῖ, τὰ τῆς ἀσθενείας μου καυχήσομαι.
it be- the of the weakness of me I will boast.
hoves things
[me],

31 ὁ θεὸς καὶ πατὴρ τοῦ κυρίου Ἰησοῦ
The God and Father of the Lord Jesus

οἶδεν, ὁ ὢν εὐλογητὸς εἰς τοὺς αἰῶνας,
knows, the being blessed unto the ages,
  [one]

ὅτι οὐ ψεύδομαι. 32 ἐν Δαμασκῷ ὁ
that I am not lying. In Damascus the

ἐθνάρχης Ἀρέτα τοῦ βασιλέως ἐφρούρει
ethnarch of Aretas *of* the king guarded

τὴν πόλιν Δαμασκηνῶν πιάσαι με, 33 καὶ
the city of [the] Damascenes to seize me, and

διὰ θυρίδος ἐν σαργάνῃ ἐχαλάσθην διὰ
through a window in a basket I was lowered through

τοῦ τείχους καὶ ἐξέφυγον τὰς χεῖρας αὐτοῦ.
the wall and escaped the hands of him.

Chapter 12

Paul's Vision

BOASTING is necessary, though it is not profitable; but I will go on to visions and revelations of the Lord.

2I know a man in Christ who fourteen years ago—whether in the body I do not know, or out of the body I do not know, God knows—such a man was caught up to the third heaven. 3And I know how such a man—whether in the body or apart from the body I do not know, God knows— 4was caught up into Paradise, and heard inexpressible words, which a man is not permitted to speak. 5On behalf of such a man will I boast; but on my own behalf I will not boast, except in regard to *my* weaknesses. 6For if I do wish to boast I shall not be foolish, for I shall be speaking the truth; but I refrain *from this*, so that no one may credit me with more than he sees *in* me or hears from me.

12 Καυχᾶσθαι δεῖ, οὐ συμφέρον μέν,
To boast it behoves not expedient indeed,
  [me],

ἐλεύσομαι δὲ εἰς ὀπτασίας καὶ ἀποκαλύψεις
so I will come to visions and revelations

κυρίου. 2 οἶδα ἄνθρωπον ἐν Χριστῷ
of [the] Lord. I know a man in Christ

πρὸ ἐτῶν δεκατεσσάρων, — εἴτε ἐν
before years fourteen, (whether in

σώματι οὐκ οἶδα, εἴτε ἐκτὸς τοῦ σώματος
[the] body I know not, or outside the body

οὐκ οἶδα, ὁ θεὸς οἶδεν,) — ἁρπαγέντα
I know not, - God knows,) ¹caught

τὸν τοιοῦτον ἕως τρίτου οὐρανοῦ. 3 καὶ
- ¹such a one to [the] third heaven. And

οἶδα τὸν τοιοῦτον ἄνθρωπον — εἴτε
I know - such a man (whether

ἐν σώματι εἴτε χωρὶς τοῦ σώματος
in [the] body or apart from the body

[οὐκ οἶδα], ὁ θεὸς οἶδεν, — 4 ὅτι
I know not, - God knows,) that

ἡρπάγη εἰς τὸν παράδεισον καὶ ἤκουσεν
he was caught into the paradise and heard

ἄρρητα ῥήματα, ἃ οὐκ ἐξὸν ἀνθρώπῳ
unspeakable words, which it is not for a man
  permissible

λαλῆσαι. 5 ὑπὲρ τοῦ τοιούτου καυχήσομαι,
to speak. On behalf of - such a one I will boast,

ὑπὲρ δὲ ἐμαυτοῦ οὐ καυχήσομαι εἰ
but on behalf of myself I will not boast ex-

μὴ ἐν ταῖς ἀσθενείαις. 6 ἐὰν γὰρ θελήσω
cept in the(my) weaknesses. For if I shall wish

καυχήσασθαι, οὐκ ἔσομαι ἄφρων, ἀλήθειαν
to boast, I shall not be foolish, ²truth

γὰρ ἐρῶ· φείδομαι δέ, μή τις εἰς ἐμὲ
¹for ¹I will speak; but I spare, lest anyone to me

λογίσηται ὑπὲρ ὃ βλέπει με ἢ ἀκούει
reckons beyond what he sees me or hears

without food; I have been cold and naked. 28Besides everything else, I face daily the pressure of my concern for all the churches. 29Who is weak, and I do not feel weak? Who is led into sin, and I do not inwardly burn? 30If I must boast, I will boast of the things that show my weakness. 31The God and Father of the Lord Jesus, who is to be praised forever, knows that I am not lying. 32In Damascus the governor under King Aretas had the city of the Damascenes guarded in order to arrest me. 33But I was lowered in a basket from a window in the wall and slipped through his hands.

Chapter 12

Paul's Vision and His Thorn

I MUST go on boasting. Although there is nothing to be gained, I will go on to visions and revelations from the Lord. 2I know a man in Christ who fourteen years ago was caught up to the third heaven. Whether it was in the body or out of the body I do not know—God knows. 3And I know that this man—whether in the body or apart from the body I do not know, but God knows— 4was caught up to paradise. He heard inexpressible things, things that man is not permitted to tell. 5I will boast about a man like that, but I will not boast about myself, except about my weaknesses. 6Even if I should choose to boast, I would not be a fool, because I would be speaking the truth. But I refrain, so no one will think more of me than is warranted by what I do or say.

A Thorn in the Flesh

7And because of the surpassing greatness of the revelations, for this reason, to keep me from exalting myself, there was given me a thorn in the flesh, a messenger of Satan to buffet me—to keep me from exalting myself!

8Concerning this I entreated the Lord three times that it might depart from me.

9And He has said to me, "My grace is sufficient for you, for ᶜpower is perfected in weakness." Most gladly, therefore, I will rather boast about my weaknesses, that the power of Christ may dwell in me.

10Therefore I am well content with weaknesses, with insults, with distresses, with persecutions, with difficulties, for Christ's sake; for when I am weak, then I am strong.

11I have become foolish; you yourselves compelled me. Actually I should have been commended by you, for in no respect was I inferior to the most eminent apostles, even though I am a nobody.

12The signs of a true apostle were performed among you with all perseverance, by signs and wonders and miracles.

13For in what respect were you treated as inferior to the rest of the churches, except that I myself did not become a burden to you? Forgive me this wrong!

14Here for this third time I am ready to come to you, and I will not be a burden to you; for I do not seek what is yours, but you; for children are not responsible to save up for *their* parents, but parents for *their* children.

15And I will most gladly spend and be expended for

ἐξ ἐμοῦ **7** καὶ τῇ ὑπερβολῇ τῶν ἀποκα-
of me and by the excess of the revela-

λύψεων. διὸ ἵνα μὴ ὑπεραίρωμαι, ἐδόθη
tions. Where- lest I should be there was
fore exceedingly uplifted, given

μοι σκόλοψ τῇ σαρκί, ἄγγελος σατανᾶ,
to me a thorn in the flesh, a messenger of Satan,

ἵνα με κολαφίζῃ, ἵνα μὴ ὑπεραίρωμαι.
in order ²me ¹he might buffet, lest I should be
that exceedingly uplifted.

8 ὑπὲρ τούτου τρὶς τὸν κύριον παρεκάλεσα,
As to this thrice the Lord I besought,

ἵνα ἀποστῇ ἀπ' ἐμοῦ. **9** καὶ εἴρηκέν
in or- it might from me. And he *has* said
der that depart

μοι· ἀρκεῖ σοι ἡ χάρις μου· ἡ γὰρ
to me: ⁴Suffices ⁵thee ¹the ²grace ³of me; for the(my)

δύναμις ἐν ἀσθενείᾳ τελεῖται. Ἥδιστα
power in weakness is perfected. Most gladly

οὖν μᾶλλον καυχήσομαι ἐν ταῖς ἀσθενείαις,
therefore rather I will boast in the(my) weaknesses,

ἵνα ἐπισκηνώσῃ ἐπ' ἐμὲ ἡ δύναμις τοῦ
in order ⁴might over ⁵me ¹the ²power –
that overshadow

Χριστοῦ. **10** διὸ εὐδοκῶ ἐν ἀσθενείαις,
³of Christ. Wherefore I am well in weaknesses,
pleased

ἐν ὕβρεσιν, ἐν ἀνάγκαις, ἐν διωγμοῖς
in insults, in necessities, in persecutions

καὶ στενοχωρίαις, ὑπὲρ Χριστοῦ· ὅταν
and difficulties, on behalf of Christ; ¹whenever

γὰρ ἀσθενῶ, τότε δυνατός εἰμι.
¹for I am weak, then ²powerful ¹I am.

11 Γέγονα ἄφρων· ὑμεῖς με ἠναγκάσατε.
I have become foolish; ye me compelled.

ἐγὼ γὰρ ὤφειλον ὑφ' ὑμῶν συνίστασθαι.
For I ought by you to be commended.

οὐδὲν γὰρ ὑστέρησα τῶν ὑπερλίαν
For nothing I lacked of the super-

ἀποστόλων, εἰ καὶ οὐδέν εἰμι. **12** τὰ
apostles, ²if ¹even ¹nothing ²I am. ¹The

μὲν σημεῖα τοῦ ἀποστόλου κατειργάσθη
¹indeed signs of the apostle were wrought

ἐν ὑμῖν ἐν πάσῃ ὑπομονῇ, σημείοις τε
among you in all endurance, ²by signs ¹both

καὶ τέρασιν καὶ δυνάμεσιν. **13** τί γάρ
and by wonders and by powerful deeds. For what

ἐστιν ὃ ἡσσώθητε ὑπὲρ τὰς λοιπὰς
is it which ye were less than the remaining

ἐκκλησίας, εἰ μὴ ὅτι αὐτὸς ἐγὼ οὐ
churches, except that ²[my]self ¹I ¹not

κατενάρκησα ὑμῶν; χαρίσασθέ μοι τὴν
³encumbered ⁴of you? Forgive ye me –

ἀδικίαν ταύτην. **14** Ἰδοὺ τρίτον τοῦτο
wrong this. Behold ²[the] ¹this
third [time] ¹[is]

ἑτοίμως ἔχω ἐλθεῖν πρὸς ὑμᾶς, καὶ
I am ready† to come to you, and

οὐ καταναρκήσω· οὐ γὰρ ζητῶ τὰ ὑμῶν
I will not encumber [you]; ²not ¹for ²I seek τὰ of
the things you

ἀλλὰ ὑμᾶς. οὐ γὰρ ὀφείλει τὰ τέκνα
but you. For ⁴not ³ought ¹the ²children

τοῖς γονεῦσιν θησαυρίζειν, ἀλλὰ οἱ γονεῖς
for the parents to lay up treasure, but the parents

τοῖς τέκνοις. **15** ἐγὼ δὲ ἥδιστα δαπανήσω
for the children. But I most gladly will spend

καὶ ἐκδαπανηθήσομαι ὑπὲρ τῶν ψυχῶν
and will be spent out on behalf of the souls

7To keep me from becoming conceited because of these surpassingly great revelations, there was given me a thorn in my flesh, a messenger of Satan, to torment me. 8Three times I pleaded with the Lord to take it away from me. 9But he said to me, "My grace is sufficient for you, for my power is made perfect in weakness." Therefore I will boast all the more gladly about my weaknesses, so that Christ's power may rest on me. 10That is why, for Christ's sake, I delight in weaknesses, in insults, in hardships, in persecutions, in difficulties. For when I am weak, then I am strong.

Paul's Concern for the Corinthians

11I have made a fool of myself, but you drove me to it. I ought to have been commended by you, for I am not in the least inferior to the "super-apostles," even though I am nothing. 12The things that mark an apostle—signs, wonders and miracles—were done among you with great perseverance. 13How were you inferior to the other churches, except that I was never a burden to you? Forgive me this wrong!

14Now I am ready to visit you for the third time, and I will not be a burden to you, because what I want is not your possessions but you. After all, children should not have to save up for their parents, but parents for their children. 15So I will very gladly spend for you

---

ᶜ Later mss. read *My power*

your souls. If I love you the more, am I to be loved the less?

16But be that as it may, I did not burden you myself; nevertheless, crafty fellow that I am, I took you in by deceit. 17Certainly I have not taken advantage of you through any of those whom I have sent to you, have I? 18I urged Titus *to go*, and sent the brother with him. Titus did not take any advantage of you, did he? Did we not conduct ourselves in the same spirit *and walk* in the same steps?

19All this time you have been thinking that we are defending ourselves to you. *Actually*, it is in the sight of God that we have been speaking in Christ; and all for your upbuilding, beloved.

20For I am afraid that perhaps when I come I may find you to be not what I wish and may be found by you to be not what you wish; that perhaps *there may be* strife, jealousy, angry tempers, disputes, slanders, gossip, arrogance, disturbances; 21I am afraid that when I come again my God may humiliate me before you, and I may mourn over many of those who have sinned in the past and not repented of the impurity, immorality and sensuality which they have practiced.

ὑμῶν. εἰ περισσοτέρως ὑμᾶς ἀγαπῶ,
of you. If more abundantly ²you ¹I love,

ἧσσον ἀγαπῶμαι; 16 Ἔστω δέ, ἐγὼ οὐ
[the] less am I loved? But let it be, I not

κατεβάρησα ὑμᾶς· ἀλλὰ ὑπάρχων πανοῦργος
burdened you; but being crafty

δόλῳ ὑμᾶς ἔλαβον. 17 μή τινα ὧν
²with guile ²you ¹I took. Not anyone of whom

ἀπέσταλκα πρὸς ὑμᾶς, 18 δι᾽ αὐτοῦ
I have sent to you, through him

ἐπλεονέκτησα ὑμᾶς; παρεκάλεσα Τίτον καὶ
did I defraud you? I besought Titus and

συναπέστειλα τὸν ἀδελφόν· μήτι ἐπλεο-
sent with [him] the brother; not ²de-

νέκτησεν ὑμᾶς Τίτος; οὐ τῷ αὐτῷ
frauded ³you ¹Titus? ²not ³by the ⁴same

πνεύματι περιεπατήσαμεν; οὐ τοῖς αὐτοῖς
⁵spirit ¹walked we? not in the same

ἴχνεσιν;
steps?

19 Πάλαι δοκεῖτε ὅτι ὑμῖν ἀπολογούμεθα.
Already ye think that to you we are making a defence.

κατέναντι θεοῦ ἐν Χριστῷ λαλοῦμεν· τὰ
Before God in Christ we speak; –

δὲ πάντα, ἀγαπητοί, ὑπὲρ τῆς ὑμῶν
but all things, beloved, [are] on behalf of ¹the ²of you

οἰκοδομῆς. 20 φοβοῦμαι γὰρ μή πως ἐλθὼν
²edification. For I fear lest coming

οὐχ οἵους θέλω εὕρω ὑμᾶς, κἀγὼ εὑρεθῶ
²not ⁴such as ⁵I wish ¹I may find ³you, and I am found

ὑμῖν οἷον οὐ θέλετε, μή πως ἔρις,
by you such as ye wish not, lest strife,

ζῆλος, θυμοί, ἐριθεῖαι, καταλαλιαί, ψιθυρισ-
jealousy, angers, rivalries, detractions, whisper-

μοί, φυσιώσεις, ἀκαταστασίαι· 21 μὴ πάλιν
ings, puffings up, disturbances; lest again

ἐλθόντος μου ταπεινώσῃ με ὁ θεός μου
coming me° ⁴may humble ⁵me ¹the ²God ³of me
=when I come

πρὸς ὑμᾶς, καὶ πενθήσω πολλοὺς τῶν
with you, and I shall mourn many of the [ones]

προημαρτηκότων καὶ μὴ μετανοησάντων
having previously sinned and not repenting

ἐπὶ τῇ ἀκαθαρσίᾳ καὶ πορνείᾳ καὶ
over the uncleanness and fornication and

ἀσελγείᾳ ᾗ ἔπραξαν. 13 Τρίτον τοῦτο
lewdness which they practised. ²[The] third ¹this
[time] [is]

ἔρχομαι πρὸς ὑμᾶς· ἐπὶ στόματος
I am coming to you; at [the] mouth

δύο μαρτύρων καὶ τριῶν σταθήσεται
of two witnesses and of three shall be established

πᾶν ῥῆμα. 2 προείρηκα καὶ προλέγω,
every word. I have previously said and I say beforehand,

ὡς παρὼν τὸ δεύτερον καὶ ἀπὼν
as being present the second [time] and being absent

νῦν, τοῖς προημαρτηκόσιν καὶ τοῖς
now, to the [ones] having previously sinned and ¹to ²the

λοιποῖς πᾶσιν, ὅτι ἐὰν ἔλθω εἰς τὸ
⁴remaining ³all, that if I come in the [ones]

πάλιν οὐ φείσομαι, 3 ἐπεὶ δοκιμὴν ζητεῖτε
again I will not spare, since ²a proof ¹ye seek

---

everything I have and expend myself as well. If I love you more, will you love me less? 16Be that as it may, I have not been a burden to you. Yet, crafty fellow that I am, I caught you by trickery! 17Did I exploit you through any of the men I sent you? 18I urged Titus to go to you and I sent our brother with him. Titus did not exploit you, did he? Did we not act in the same spirit and follow the same course?

19Have you been thinking all along that we have been defending ourselves to you? We have been speaking in the sight of God as those in Christ; and everything we do, dear friends, is for your strengthening. 20For I am afraid that when I come I may not find you as I want you to be, and you may not find me as you want me to be. I fear that there may be quarreling, jealousy, outbursts of anger, factions, slander, gossip, arrogance and disorder. 21I am afraid that when I come again my God will humble me before you, and I will be grieved over many who have sinned earlier and have not repented of the impurity, sexual sin and debauchery in which they have indulged.

Chapter 13

Examine Yourselves

THIS is the third time I am coming to you. EVERY FACT IS TO BE CONFIRMED BY THE TESTIMONY OF TWO OR THREE WITNESSES. 2I have previously said when present the second time, and though now absent I say in advance to those who have sinned in the past and to all the rest as well, that if I come again, I will not spare *anyone*, 3since you are seeking

Chapter 13

Final Warnings

THIS will be my third visit to you. "Every matter must be established by the testimony of two or three witnesses."*ʳ* 2I already gave you a warning when I was with you the second time. I now repeat it while absent: On my return I will not spare those who sinned earlier or any of the others, 3since you are demanding proof that Christ

ʳ Deut. 19:15

for proof of the Christ who speaks in me, and who is not weak toward you, but mighty in you.

⁴For indeed He was crucified because of weakness, yet He lives because of the power of God. For we also are weak ᵈin Him, yet we shall live with Him because of the power of God *directed* toward you.

⁵Test yourselves *to see* if you are in the faith; examine yourselves! Or do you not recognize this about yourselves, that Jesus Christ is in you—unless indeed you fail the test?

⁶But I trust that you will realize that we ourselves do not fail the test.

⁷Now we pray to God that you do no wrong; not that we ourselves may appear approved, but that you may do what is right, even though we should appear unapproved.

⁸For we can do nothing against the truth, but *only* for the truth.

⁹For we rejoice when we ourselves are weak but you are strong; this we also pray for, that you be made complete.

¹⁰For this reason I am writing these things while absent, in order that when present I may not use severity, in accordance with the authority which the Lord gave me, for building up and not for tearing down.

¹¹Finally, brethren, rejoice, be made complete, be comforted, be likeminded, live in peace; and the God of love and peace shall be with you.

¹²Greet one another with a holy kiss.

¹³All the saints greet you.

¹⁴The grace of the Lord

τοῦ ἐν ἐμοὶ λαλοῦντος Χριστοῦ, ὃς εἰς
\- ³in ⁶me ⁵speaking ²of Christ, who toward

ὑμᾶς οὐκ ἀσθενεῖ ἀλλὰ δυνατεῖ ἐν ὑμῖν.
you is not weak but is powerful in you.

4 καὶ γὰρ ἐσταυρώθη ἐξ ἀσθενείας, ἀλλὰ
For indeed he was crucified out of weakness, but

ζῇ ἐκ δυνάμεως θεοῦ. καὶ γὰρ ἡμεῖς
he lives by [the] power of God. For indeed we

ἀσθενοῦμεν ἐν αὐτῷ, ἀλλὰ ζήσομεν σὺν
are weak in him, but we shall live with

αὐτῷ ἐκ δυνάμεως θεοῦ εἰς ὑμᾶς.
him by [the] power of God toward you.

5 Ἑαυτοὺς πειράζετε εἰ ἐστὲ ἐν τῇ
²Yourselves ¹test if ye are in the

πίστει, ἑαυτοὺς δοκιμάζετε· ἢ οὐκ
faith, ²yourselves ¹prove; or not

ἐπιγινώσκετε ἑαυτοὺς ὅτι Ἰησοῦς Χριστὸς
perceive ye yourselves that Jesus Christ [is]

ἐν ὑμῖν, εἰ μήτι ἀδόκιμοί ἐστε. 6 ἐλπίζω
in you, unless ²counterfeits ¹ye are. I hope

δὲ ὅτι γνώσεσθε ὅτι ἡμεῖς οὐκ ἐσμὲν
But that ye will know that we are not

ἀδόκιμοι. 7 εὐχόμεθα δὲ πρὸς τὸν θεὸν
counterfeits. Now we pray to \- God

μὴ ποιῆσαι ὑμᾶς κακὸν μηδέν, οὐχ
not to do youᵖ evil none, not
=that ye do no . . .

ἵνα ἡμεῖς δόκιμοι φανῶμεν, ἀλλ' ἵνα
in order we ²approved ¹may appear, but in order
that that

ὑμεῖς τὸ καλὸν ποιῆτε, ἡμεῖς δὲ ὡς
ye ³the ²good ¹may do, and we ¹as

ἀδόκιμοι ὦμεν. 8 οὐ γὰρ δυνάμεθά
²counterfeits ¹may be. For we cannot [do]

τι κατὰ τῆς ἀληθείας, ἀλλὰ ὑπὲρ τῆς
any- against the truth, but on behalf of the
thing

ἀληθείας. 9 χαίρομεν γὰρ ὅταν ἡμεῖς
truth. For we rejoice whenever we

ἀσθενῶμεν, ὑμεῖς δὲ δυνατοὶ ἦτε· τοῦτο
are weak, and ye powerful are; this

καὶ εὐχόμεθα, τὴν ὑμῶν κατάρτισιν. 10 Διὰ
also we pray, the ²of you ¹restoration. There-

τοῦτο ταῦτα ἀπὼν γράφω, ἵνα παρὼν
fore ²these things ³being ¹I write, in order being
absent that present

μὴ ἀποτόμως χρήσωμαι κατὰ τὴν ἐξουσίαν
²not ³sharply ¹I may deal according to the authority

ἣν ὁ κύριος ἔδωκέν μοι εἰς οἰκοδομὴν
which the Lord gave me for edification

καὶ οὐκ εἰς καθαίρεσιν.
and not for overthrow.

11 Λοιπόν, ἀδελφοί, χαίρετε, καταρτίζεσθε,
For the rest,† brothers, rejoice, restore yourselves,

παρακαλεῖσθε, τὸ αὐτὸ φρονεῖτε, εἰρηνεύετε,
admonish yourselves, the same thing think, be at peace,

καὶ ὁ θεὸς τῆς ἀγάπης καὶ εἰρήνης
and the God \- of love and of peace

ἔσται μεθ' ὑμῶν. 12 Ἀσπάσασθε ἀλλήλους
will be with you. Greet ye one another

ἐν ἁγίῳ φιλήματι. Ἀσπάζονται ὑμᾶς οἱ
with a holy kiss. ⁴greet ³you ¹the

ἅγιοι πάντες.
²saints ¹All.

13 Ἡ χάρις τοῦ κυρίου Ἰησοῦ Χριστοῦ
The grace of the Lord Jesus Christ

is speaking through me. He is not weak in dealing with you, but is powerful among you. ⁴For to be sure, he was crucified in weakness, yet he lives by God's power. Likewise, we are weak in him, yet by God's power we will live with him to serve you.

⁵Examine yourselves to see whether you are in the faith; test yourselves. Do you not realize that Christ Jesus is in you—unless, of course, you fail the test? ⁶And I trust that you will discover that we have not failed the test. ⁷Now we pray to God that you will not do anything wrong. Not that people will see that we have stood the test but that you will do what is right even though we may seem to have failed. ⁸For we cannot do anything against the truth, but only for the truth. ⁹We are glad whenever we are weak but you are strong; and our prayer is for your perfection. ¹⁰This is why I write these things when I am absent, that when I come I may not have to be harsh in my use of authority—the authority the Lord gave me for building you up, not for tearing you down.

Final Greetings

¹¹Finally, brothers, goodby. Aim for perfection, listen to my appeal, be of one mind, live in peace. And the God of love and peace will be with you.

¹²Greet one another with a holy kiss. ¹³All the saints send their greetings.

¹⁴May the grace of the

ᵈSome early mss. read *with Him*

Jesus Christ, and the love of God, and the fellowship of the Holy Spirit, be with you all.

καὶ   ἡ   ἀγάπη   τοῦ   θεοῦ   καὶ   ἡ   κοινωνία
and   the   love   -   of God   and   the   fellowship
τοῦ   ἁγίου   πνεύματος   μετὰ   πάντων   ὑμῶν.
of the   Holy   Spirit   [be] with   *all   ¹you.

Lord Jesus Christ, and the love of God, and the fellowship of the Holy Spirit be with you all.

Galatians

Chapter 1

Introduction

PAUL, an apostle (not *sent* from men, nor through the agency of man, but through Jesus Christ, and God the Father, who raised Him from the dead), ²and all the brethren who are with me, to the churches of Galatia: ³Grace to you and peace from God our Father, and the Lord Jesus Christ, ⁴who gave Himself for our sins, that He might deliver us out of this present evil age, according to the will of our God and Father, ⁵to whom *be* the glory forevermore. Amen.

Perversion of the Gospel

⁶I am amazed that you are so quickly deserting Him who called you by the grace of Christ, for a different gospel; ⁷which is *really* not another; only there are some who are disturbing you, and want to distort the gospel of Christ. ⁸But even though we, or an angel from heaven, should preach to you a gospel contrary to that which we have preached to you, let him be accursed. ⁹As we have said before, so I say again now, if any man is preaching to you a gospel contrary to that which you received, let him be accursed.

ΠΡΟΣ ΓΑΛΑΤΑΣ
To Galatians

1 Παῦλος   ἀπόστολος,   οὐκ   ἀπ'   ἀνθρώπων
Paul   an apostle,   not   from   men
οὐδὲ   δι'   ἀνθρώπου   ἀλλὰ   διὰ   Ἰησοῦ
nor   through   man   but   through   Jesus
Χριστοῦ   καὶ   θεοῦ   πατρὸς   τοῦ   ἐγείραντος
Christ   and   God   [the] Father   the [one]   having raised
αὐτὸν   ἐκ   νεκρῶν,   **2** καὶ   οἱ   σὺν   ἐμοὶ
him   out of   [the] dead,   and   ¹the   ⁴with   ⁵me
πάντες   ἀδελφοί,   ταῖς   ἐκκλησίαις   τῆς
¹all   ³brothers,   to the   churches
Γαλατίας·   **3** χάρις   ὑμῖν   καὶ   εἰρήνη   ἀπὸ
of Galatia: Grace   to you   and   peace   from
θεοῦ   πατρὸς   ἡμῶν   καὶ   κυρίου   Ἰησοῦ
God   Father   of us   and   Lord   Jesus
Χριστοῦ,   **4** τοῦ   δόντος   ἑαυτὸν   ὑπὲρ   τῶν
Christ,   the [one] having given   himself   on behalf of   the
ἁμαρτιῶν   ἡμῶν,   ὅπως   ἐξέληται   ἡμᾶς   ἐκ
sins   of us,   so as   he might deliver   us   out of
τοῦ   αἰῶνος   τοῦ   ἐνεστῶτος   πονηροῦ   κατὰ
the   ²age   the   ¹present   ²evil   according to
τὸ   θέλημα   τοῦ   θεοῦ   καὶ   πατρὸς   ἡμῶν,
the   will   of the   God   and   Father   of us,
5 ᾧ   ἡ   δόξα   εἰς   τοὺς   αἰῶνας   τῶν
to whom the   glory   unto   the   ages   of the
[be]
αἰώνων·   ἀμήν.
ages: Amen.

6 Θαυμάζω   ὅτι   οὕτως   ταχέως   μετατίθεσθε
I wonder   that   thus   quickly   ye are removing
ἀπὸ   τοῦ   καλέσαντος   ὑμᾶς   ἐν   χάριτι
from   the [one]   having called   you   by   [the] grace
Χριστοῦ   εἰς   ἕτερον   εὐαγγέλιον,   **7** ὃ   οὐκ
of Christ   to   another   gospel,   which   not
ἔστιν   ἄλλο·   εἰ   μὴ   τινές   εἰσιν   οἱ   ταράσ-
is   another;   only   ²some   ¹there are   -   troubl-
σοντες   ὑμᾶς   καὶ   θέλοντες   μεταστρέψαι
ing   you   and   wishing   to pervert
τὸ   εὐαγγέλιον   τοῦ   Χριστοῦ.   **8** ἀλλὰ
the   gospel   -   of Christ.   But
καὶ   ἐὰν   ἡμεῖς   ἢ   ἄγγελος   ἐξ   οὐρανοῦ
even   if   we   or   an angel   out of   heaven
εὐαγγελίσηται   [ὑμῖν]   παρ'   ὃ   εὐηγγελισάμεθα
should preach   to you   beside   what   we preached
a gospel
ὑμῖν,   ἀνάθεμα   ἔστω.   **9** ὡς   προειρήκαμεν,
to you,   ²a curse   ¹let him be.   As we have previously said,
καὶ   ἄρτι   πάλιν   λέγω,   εἴ   τις   ὑμᾶς   εὐαγ-
also   now   again   I say,   if anyone   ³you   ¹preaches
γελίζεται   παρ'   ὃ   παρελάβετε,   ἀνάθεμα
²a gospel   beside   what   ye received,   ²a curse
ἔστω.
¹let him be.

Galatians

Chapter 1

PAUL, an apostle—sent not from men nor by man, but by Jesus Christ and God the Father, who raised him from the dead—²and all the brothers with me,

To the churches in Galatia:

³Grace and peace to you from God our Father and the Lord Jesus Christ, ⁴who gave himself for our sins to rescue us from the present evil age, according to the will of our God and Father, ⁵to whom be glory for ever and ever. Amen.

No Other Gospel

⁶I am astonished that you are so quickly deserting the one who called you by the grace of Christ and are turning to a different gospel—⁷which is really no gospel at all. Evidently some people are throwing you into confusion and are trying to pervert the gospel of Christ. ⁸But even if we or an angel from heaven should preach a gospel other than the one we preached to you, let him be eternally condemned! ⁹As we have already said, so now I say again: If anybody is preaching to you a gospel other than what you accepted, let him be eternally condemned!

10For am I now seeking the favor of men, or of God? Or am I striving to please men? If I were still trying to please men, I would not be a bond-servant of Christ.

Paul Defends His Ministry

11For I would have you know, brethren, that the gospel which was preached by me is not according to man.

12For I neither received it from man, nor was I taught it, but I received it through a revelation of Jesus Christ.

13For you have heard of my former manner of life in Judaism, how I used to persecute the church of God beyond measure, and tried to destroy it;

14and I was advancing in Judaism beyond many of my contemporaries among my countrymen, being more extremely zealous for my ancestral traditions.

15But when He who had set me apart, even from my mother's womb, and called me through His grace, was pleased

16to reveal His Son in me, that I might preach Him among the Gentiles, I did not immediately consult with flesh and blood,

17nor did I go up to Jerusalem to those who were apostles before me; but I went away to Arabia, and returned once more to Damascus.

18Then three years later I went up to Jerusalem to become acquainted with Cephas, and stayed with him fifteen days.

19But I did not see any other of the apostles except James, the Lord's brother.

20(Now in what I am writing to you, I assure you before God that I am not lying.)

21Then I went into the re-

---

10 Ἄρτι γὰρ ἀνθρώπους πείθω ἢ τὸν
For now   men   do I persuade or   -

θεόν; ἢ ζητῶ ἀνθρώποις ἀρέσκειν; εἰ
God? or do I seek men to please? If

ἔτι ἀνθρώποις ἤρεσκον, Χριστοῦ δοῦλος
still men I pleased, ²of Christ ³a slave

οὐκ ἂν ἤμην. 11 γνωρίζω γὰρ ὑμῖν,
¹I would not have been. For I make known to you,

ἀδελφοί, τὸ εὐαγγέλιον τὸ εὐαγγελισθὲν
brothers, the gospel   -   preached

ὑπ' ἐμοῦ ὅτι οὐκ ἔστιν κατὰ ἄνθρωπον
by me that it is not according to man;

12 οὐδὲ γὰρ ἐγὼ παρὰ ἀνθρώπου παρέλαβον
for ⁴not ¹I ⁵from ⁶man ²received

αὐτὸ οὔτε ἐδιδάχθην, ἀλλὰ δι' ἀποκαλύψεως
³it nor was I taught but through a revelation
                [by man],

Ἰησοῦ Χριστοῦ. 13 Ἠκούσατε γὰρ τὴν
of Jesus Christ.   For ye heard

ἐμὴν ἀναστροφήν ποτε ἐν τῷ Ἰουδαϊσμῷ,
my conduct then in - Judaism,

ὅτι καθ' ὑπερβολὴν ἐδίωκον τὴν ἐκκλησίαν
that excessively† I persecuted the church

τοῦ θεοῦ καὶ ἐπόρθουν αὐτήν, 14 καὶ
- of God and wasted it,   and

προέκοπτον ἐν τῷ Ἰουδαϊσμῷ ὑπὲρ πολλοὺς
progressed in - Judaism beyond many

συνηλικιώτας ἐν τῷ γένει μου, περισ-
contemporaries in the race of me, ²abun-

σοτέρως ζηλωτὴς ὑπάρχων τῶν πατρικῶν
dantly ⁴a zealot ¹being ⁵of the ³ancestral

μου παραδόσεων. 15 Ὅτε δὲ εὐδόκησεν
⁷of me ⁶traditions. But when ¹⁴was pleased

ὁ ἀφορίσας με ἐκ κοιλίας μητρός μου
¹the ²having ³me ⁴from ⁵[the] womb ⁶of mother ⁷of me
[one] separated

καὶ καλέσας διὰ τῆς χάριτος αὐτοῦ
⁸and ⁹having called ¹⁰through ¹¹the ¹²grace ¹³of him

16 ἀποκαλύψαι τὸν υἱὸν αὐτοῦ ἐν ἐμοί,
to reveal the Son of him in me,

ἵνα εὐαγγελίζωμαι αὐτὸν ἐν τοῖς ἔθνεσιν,
in order I might preach him among the nations,
that

εὐθέως οὐ προσανεθέμην σαρκὶ καὶ αἵματι,
immediately I conferred not with flesh and blood,

17 οὐδὲ ἀνῆλθον εἰς Ἱεροσόλυμα πρὸς
neither did I go up to Jerusalem to

τοὺς πρὸ ἐμοῦ ἀποστόλους, ἀλλὰ ἀπῆλθον
¹the ²before ³me ²apostles, but I went away

εἰς Ἀραβίαν, καὶ πάλιν ὑπέστρεψα εἰς
into Arabia, and again returned to

Δαμασκόν. 18 Ἔπειτα μετὰ τρία ἔτη
Damascus. Then after three years

ἀνῆλθον εἰς Ἱεροσόλυμα ἱστορῆσαι Κηφᾶν,
I went up to Jerusalem to visit Cephas,

καὶ ἐπέμεινα πρὸς αὐτὸν ἡμέρας δεκαπέντε·
and remained with him days fifteen;

19 ἕτερον δὲ τῶν ἀποστόλων οὐκ εἶδον,
but other of the apostles I saw not,

εἰ μὴ Ἰάκωβον τὸν ἀδελφὸν τοῦ κυρίου.
except James the brother of the Lord.

20 ἃ δὲ γράφω ὑμῖν, ἰδοὺ ἐνώπιον τοῦ
Now what I write to you, behold before
things

θεοῦ ὅτι οὐ ψεύδομαι. 21 ἔπειτα ἦλθον
God - I lie not.   Then I went

10Am I now trying to win the approval of men, or of God? Or am I trying to please men? If I were still trying to please men, I would not be a servant of Christ.

Paul Called by God

11I want you to know, brothers, that the gospel I preached is not something that man made up. 12I did not receive it from any man, nor was I taught it; rather, I received it by revelation from Jesus Christ.

13For you have heard of my previous way of life in Judaism, how intensely I persecuted the church of God and tried to destroy it. 14I was advancing in Judaism beyond many Jews of my own age and was extremely zealous for the traditions of my fathers. 15But when God, who set me apart from birth[a] and called me by his grace, was pleased 16to reveal his Son in me so that I might preach him among the Gentiles, I did not consult any man, 17nor did I go up to Jerusalem to see those who were apostles before I was, but I went immediately into Arabia and later returned to Damascus.

18Then after three years, I went up to Jerusalem to get acquainted with Peter[b] and stayed with him fifteen days. 19I saw none of the other apostles—only James, the Lord's brother. 20I assure you before God that what I am writing you is no lie. 21Later I went to Syria and Cilicia. 22I was personally unknown to the

a15 Or from my mother's womb
b18 Greek Cephas

gions of Syria and Cilicia.
22And I was *still* unknown by sight to the churches of Judea which were in Christ;
23but only, they kept hearing, "He who once persecuted us is now preaching the faith which he once tried to destroy."
24And they were glorifying God because of me.

Chapter 2

The Council at Jerusalem

THEN after an interval of fourteen years I went up again to Jerusalem with Barnabas, taking Titus along also.
2And it was because of a revelation that I went up; and I submitted to them the gospel which I preach among the Gentiles, but *I did so* in private to those who were of reputation, for fear that I might be running, or had run, in vain.
3But not even Titus who was with me, though he was a Greek, was compelled to be circumcised.
4But *it was* because of the false brethren who had sneaked in to spy out our liberty which we have in Christ Jesus, in order to bring us into bondage.
5But we did not yield in subjection to them for even an hour, so that the truth of the gospel might remain with you.
6But from those who were of high reputation (what they were makes no difference to me; God shows no partiality)—well, those who were of reputation contributed nothing to me.
7But on the contrary, seeing that I had been entrusted with the gospel to the uncircumcised, just as Peter *had been* to the circumcised
8(for He who effectually worked for Peter in *his* apostleship to the circumcised effectually worked for me also to the Gentiles),

εἰς τὰ κλίματα τῆς Συρίας καὶ τῆς
into the regions - of Syria and -

Κιλικίας. 22 ἤμην δὲ ἀγνοούμενος τῷ
of Cilicia. And I was being unknown -

προσώπῳ ταῖς ἐκκλησίαις τῆς Ἰουδαίας
by face to the churches - of Judæa

ταῖς ἐν Χριστῷ. 23 μόνον δὲ ἀκούοντες
- in Christ. But only hearing

ἦσαν ὅτι ὁ διώκων ἡμᾶς ποτε νῦν
they were that the [one] ²persecuting ³us ¹then now

εὐαγγελίζεται τὴν πίστιν ἥν ποτε ἐπόρθει,
preaches the faith which then he was destroying,

24 καὶ ἐδόξαζον ἐν ἐμοὶ τὸν θεόν.
and they glorified ²in ³me - ¹God.

2 Ἔπειτα διὰ δεκατεσσάρων ἐτῶν πάλιν
Then through fourteen years again

ἀνέβην εἰς Ἱεροσόλυμα μετὰ Βαρναβᾶ,
I went up to Jerusalem with Barnabas,

συμπαραλαβὼν καὶ Τίτον· 2 ἀνέβην δὲ
taking with [me] also Titus; and I went up

κατὰ ἀποκάλυψιν· καὶ ἀνεθέμην αὐτοῖς
according to a revelation; and I put before them

τὸ εὐαγγέλιον ὃ κηρύσσω ἐν τοῖς ἔθνεσιν,
the gospel which I proclaim among the nations,

κατ' ἰδίαν δὲ τοῖς δοκοῦσιν, μή πως
²privately ¹but to the [ones] seeming,* lest

εἰς κενὸν τρέχω ἢ ἔδραμον. 3 ἀλλ'
in vain I run or I ran. But

οὐδὲ Τίτος ὁ σὺν ἐμοί, Ἕλλην ὤν,
not Titus the [one] with me, a Greek being,

ἠναγκάσθη περιτμηθῆναι· 4 διὰ δὲ τοὺς
was compelled to be circumcised; but on account of ¹the

παρεισάκτους ψευδαδέλφους, οἵτινες παρεισ-
²brought in secretly ³false brothers, who stole

ἦλθον κατασκοπῆσαι τὴν ἐλευθερίαν ἡμῶν
in to spy on the freedom of us

ἣν ἔχομεν ἐν Χριστῷ Ἰησοῦ, ἵνα ἡμᾶς
which we have in Christ Jesus, in order that ²us

καταδουλώσουσιν· 5 οἷς οὐδὲ πρὸς ὥραν
¹they will (might) enslave; to whom not for an hour

εἴξαμεν τῇ ὑποταγῇ, ἵνα ἡ ἀλήθεια
yielded we - in subjection, in order that the truth

τοῦ εὐαγγελίου διαμείνῃ πρὸς ὑμᾶς. 6 ἀπὸ
of the gospel might continue with you. from

δὲ τῶν δοκούντων εἶναί τι, — ὁποῖοί
But the [ones] seeming to be something, (of what kind

ποτε ἦσαν οὐδέν μοι διαφέρει· πρόσωπον
²then ¹they were 'nothing to me ³matters: ⁴[the] face

[ὁ] θεὸς ἀνθρώπου οὐ λαμβάνει — ἐμοὶ
- ⁵God ⁶of a man ⁷receives not,) ²to me

γὰρ οἱ δοκοῦντες οὐδὲν προσανέθεντο,
¹for the [ones] seeming* nothing added,

7 ἀλλὰ τοὐναντίον ἰδόντες ὅτι πεπίστευμαι
but on the contrary seeing that I have been entrusted [with]

τὸ εὐαγγέλιον τῆς ἀκροβυστίας καθὼς
the gospel of the uncircumcision as

Πέτρος τῆς περιτομῆς, 8 ὁ γὰρ ἐνεργήσας
Peter [that] of the circumcision, for the [one] operating

Πέτρῳ εἰς ἀποστολὴν τῆς περιτομῆς
in Peter to an apostleship of the circumcision

ἐνήργησεν καὶ ἐμοὶ εἰς τὰ ἔθνη, 9 καὶ
operated also in me to the nations, and

* Cf. the full expressions in vers. 6 (earlier) and 9.

churches of Judea that are in Christ. 23They only heard the report: "The man who formerly persecuted us is now preaching the faith he once tried to destroy." 24And they praised God because of me.

Chapter 2

Paul Accepted by the Apostles

FOURTEEN years later I went up again to Jerusalem, this time with Barnabas. I took Titus along also. 2I went in response to a revelation and set before them the gospel that I preach among the Gentiles. But I did this privately to those who seemed to be leaders, for fear that I was running or had run my race in vain. 3Yet not even Titus, who was with me, was compelled to be circumcised, even though he was a Greek. 4This matter arose, because some false brothers had infiltrated our ranks to spy on the freedom we have in Christ Jesus and to make us slaves. 5We did not give in to them for a moment, so that the truth of the gospel might remain with you.

6As for those who seemed to be important—whatever they were makes no difference to me; God does not judge by external appearance—those men added nothing to my message. 7On the contrary, they saw that I had been entrusted with the task of preaching the gospel to the Gentiles, c just as Peter had been to the Jews. d 8For God, who was at work in the ministry of Peter as an apostle to the Jews, was also at work in my ministry as an apostle to the Gentiles. 9James, Pe-

c7 Greek *uncircumcised*
d7 Greek *circumcised*; also in verses 8 and 9

9and recognizing the grace that had been given to me, James and Cephas and John, who were reputed to be pillars, gave to me and Barnabas the right hand of fellowship, that we *might go* to the Gentiles, and they to the circumcised.

10*They* only *asked* us to remember the poor—the very thing I also was eager to do.

Peter (Cephas) Opposed by Paul

11But when Cephas came to Antioch, I opposed him to his face, because he stood condemned.

12For prior to the coming of certain men from James, he used to eat with the Gentiles; but when they came, he *began* to withdraw and hold himself aloof, fearing the party of the circumcision.

13And the rest of the Jews joined him in hypocrisy, with the result that even Barnabas was carried away by their hypocrisy.

14But when I saw that they were not straightforward about the truth of the gospel, I said to Cephas in the presence of all, "If you, being a Jew, live like the Gentiles and not like the Jews, how *is it that* you compel the Gentiles to live like Jews?

15"We *are* Jews by nature, and not sinners from among the Gentiles;

16nevertheless knowing that a man is not justified by the works of the Law but through faith in Christ Jesus, even we have believed in Christ Jesus, that we may be justified by faith in Christ, and not by the works of the Law; since by the works of the Law shall no flesh be justified.

17"But if, while seeking to be justified in Christ, we

γνόντες τὴν χάριν τὴν δοθεῖσάν μοι,
knowing the grace - given to me,

'Ιάκωβος καὶ Κηφᾶς καὶ 'Ιωάννης, οἱ
James and Cephas and John, the

δοκοῦντες στῦλοι εἶναι, δεξιὰς ἔδωκαν
[ones] seeming ²pillars ¹to be, ²right [hands] ¹gave

ἐμοὶ καὶ Βαρναβᾷ κοινωνίας, ἵνα ἡμεῖς
²to me ³and ⁴to Barnabas ⁵of fellowship, in order we
that [should

εἰς τὰ ἔθνη, αὐτοὶ δὲ εἰς τὴν περιτομήν·
go] to the nations, but they to the circumcision;

10 μόνον τῶν πτωχῶν ἵνα μνημονεύωμεν,
only ²the ⁶poor *in order* ¹that ²we might remember,

ὃ καὶ ἐσπούδασα αὐτὸ τοῦτο ποιῆσαι.
which indeed ⁹I was eager ¹this very thing to do.

11 "Οτε δὲ ἦλθεν Κηφᾶς εἰς 'Αντιόχειαν,
But when ²came ¹Cephas to Antioch,

κατὰ πρόσωπον αὐτῷ ἀντέστην, ὅτι
against [his] face to him I opposed, because

κατεγνωσμένος ἦν. 12 πρὸ τοῦ γὰρ
²having been condemned ¹he was. Before the for
= For before some came ...

ἐλθεῖν τινας ἀπὸ 'Ιακώβου μετὰ τῶν
to come someᵇ from James ²with ³the

ἐθνῶν συνήσθιεν· ὅτε δὲ ἦλθον, ὑπέστελλεν
⁴nations ¹he ate *with*; but when they came, he withdrew

καὶ ἀφώριζεν ἑαυτόν, φοβούμενος τοὺς
and separated himself, fearing the [ones]

ἐκ περιτομῆς· 13 καὶ συνυπεκρίθησαν αὐτῷ
of [the] circumcision; and dissembled along with him

[καὶ] οἱ λοιποὶ 'Ιουδαῖοι, ὥστε καὶ
also the remaining Jews, so as even

Βαρναβᾶς συναπήχθη αὐτῶν τῇ ὑποκρίσει.
Barnabas was led away with ²of them ¹the ²dissembling.

14 ἀλλ' ὅτε εἶδον ὅτι οὐκ ὀρθοποδοῦσιν
But when I saw that they walk[ed] not straight

πρὸς τὴν ἀλήθειαν τοῦ εὐαγγελίου, εἶπον
with the truth of the gospel, I said

τῷ Κηφᾷ ἔμπροσθεν πάντων· εἰ σὺ
- to Cephas in front of all: If thou

'Ιουδαῖος ὑπάρχων ἐθνικῶς καὶ οὐκ
²a Jew ¹being as a Gentile and not

'Ιουδαϊκῶς ζῇς, πῶς τὰ ἔθνη ἀναγκάζεις
as a Jew livest, how ¹the ²nations ¹compellest thou

ἰουδαΐζειν; 15 'Ημεῖς φύσει 'Ιουδαῖοι καὶ
to judaize? We by nature Jews and

οὐκ ἐξ ἐθνῶν ἁμαρτωλοί, 16 εἰδότες δὲ
not ³of ²nations ¹sinners, and knowing

ὅτι οὐ δικαιοῦται ἄνθρωπος ἐξ ἔργων
that ²is not justified ¹a man by works

νόμου, ἐὰν μὴ διὰ πίστεως Χριστοῦ
of law, except(but) through faith of(in) Christ

'Ιησοῦ, καὶ ἡμεῖς εἰς Χριστὸν 'Ιησοῦν
Jesus,* even we ²in ³Christ ⁴Jesus

ἐπιστεύσαμεν, ἵνα δικαιωθῶμεν ἐκ πίστεως
¹believed, in order that we might be by faith
justified

Χριστοῦ καὶ οὐκ ἐξ ἔργων νόμου, ὅτι
of(in) Christ* and not by works of law, because

ἐξ ἔργων νόμου οὐ δικαιωθήσεται πᾶσα
by works of law not will be justified all
= no flesh will be justified.

σάρξ. 17 εἰ δὲ ζητοῦντες δικαιωθῆναι
flesh. But if seeking to be justified

---

terᵉ and John, those reputed to be pillars, gave me and Barnabas the right hand of fellowship when they recognized the grace given to me. They agreed that we should go to the Gentiles, and they to the Jews. 10All they asked was that we should continue to remember the poor, the very thing I was eager to do.

Paul Opposes Peter

11When Peter came to Antioch, I opposed him to his face, because he was clearly in the wrong. 12Before certain men came from James, he used to eat with the Gentiles. But when they arrived, he began to draw back and separate himself from the Gentiles because he was afraid of those who belonged to the circumcision group. 13The other Jews joined him in his hypocrisy, so that by their hypocrisy even Barnabas was led astray.

14When I saw that they were not acting in line with the truth of the gospel, I said to Peter in front of them all, "You are a Jew, yet you live like a Gentile and not like a Jew. How is it, then, that you force Gentiles to follow Jewish customs?

15"We who are Jews by birth and not 'Gentile sinners' 16know that a man is not justified by observing the law, but by faith in Jesus Christ. So we, too, have put our faith in Christ Jesus that we may be justified by faith in Christ and not by observing the law, because by observing the law no one will be justified.

17"If, while we seek to be justified in Christ, it be-

---

* Objective genitive, as is shown by the intervening sentence see also 3. 22, 26). Cf. " fear of God".

ourselves have also been found sinners, is Christ then a minister of sin? May it never be!

18"For if I rebuild what I have once destroyed, I prove myself to be a transgressor.

19"For through the Law I died to the Law, that I might live to God.

20"I have been crucified with Christ; and it is no longer I who live, but Christ lives in me; and the *life* which I now live in the flesh I live by faith in the Son of God, who loved me, and delivered Himself up for me.

21"I do not nullify the grace of God; for if righteousness *comes* through the Law, then Christ died needlessly."

Chapter 3

Faith Brings Righteousness

YOU foolish Galatians, who has bewitched you, before whose eyes Jesus Christ was publicly portrayed *as* crucified?

2This is the only thing I want to find out from you: did you receive the Spirit by the works of the Law, or by hearing with faith?

3Are you so foolish? Having begun by the Spirit, are you now being perfected by the flesh?

4Did you suffer so many things in vain—if indeed it was in vain?

5Does He then, who provides you with the Spirit and works miracles among you, do it by the works of the Law, or by hearing with faith?

6Even so Abraham BELIEVED GOD, AND IT WAS RECKONED TO HIM AS RIGHTEOUSNESS.

7Therefore, be sure that it is those who are of faith who are sons of Abraham.

8And the Scripture, foreseeing that God would justify the Gentiles by faith, preached the gospel beforehand to Abraham, *saying*, "ALL THE NATIONS SHALL BE

ἐν Χριστῷ εὑρέθημεν καὶ αὐτοὶ ἁμαρτωλοί,
in Christ we were found also [our]selves sinners,

ἆρα Χριστὸς ἁμαρτίας διάκονος; μὴ
then [is] Christ ²of sin ¹a minister? not

γένοιτο. 18 εἰ γὰρ ἃ κατέλυσα ταῦτα
May it be. For if what things I destroyed these things

πάλιν οἰκοδομῶ, παραβάτην ἐμαυτὸν συνισ-
again I build, ²a transgressor ³myself ¹I con-

τάνω. 19 ἐγὼ γὰρ διὰ νόμου νόμῳ
stitute. For I through law to law

ἀπέθανον ἵνα θεῷ ζήσω. 20 Χριστῷ συνεσ-
¹died in order to God I might live. With Christ I have that

ταύρωμαι· ζῶ δὲ οὐκέτι ἐγώ, ζῇ δὲ
been co-crucified; and ²live ³no more ¹I, but ²lives

ἐν ἐμοὶ Χριστός· ὃ δὲ νῦν ζῶ ἐν σαρκί,
³in ⁴me ¹Christ; and what now I live in [the] flesh,

ἐν πίστει ζῶ τῇ τοῦ υἱοῦ τοῦ θεοῦ
³by ²faith ¹I live - of(in) the Son - of God

τοῦ ἀγαπήσαντός με καὶ παραδόντος ἑαυτὸν
- loving me and giving up himself

ὑπὲρ ἐμοῦ. 21 Οὐκ ἀθετῶ τὴν χάριν
on behalf of me. I do not set aside the grace

τοῦ θεοῦ· εἰ γὰρ διὰ νόμου δικαιοσύνη,
- of God; for if through law righteousness [comes],

ἄρα Χριστὸς δωρεὰν ἀπέθανεν.
then Christ without cause died.

3 Ὦ ἀνόητοι Γαλάται, τίς ὑμᾶς
O foolish Galatians, who you

ἐβάσκανεν, οἷς κατ' ὀφθαλμοὺς Ἰησοῦς
bewitched, to before eyes Jesus
whom [the]

Χριστὸς προεγράφη ἐσταυρωμένος; 2 τοῦτο
Christ was portrayed having been crucified? This

μόνον θέλω μαθεῖν ἀφ' ὑμῶν, ἐξ ἔργων
only I wish to learn from you, by works

νόμου τὸ πνεῦμα ἐλάβετε ἢ ἐξ ἀκοῆς
of law the Spirit received ye or by hearing

πίστεως; 3 οὕτως ἀνόητοί ἐστε; ἐναρξάμενοι
of faith? thus foolish are ye? having begun

πνεύματι νῦν σαρκὶ ἐπιτελεῖσθε; 4 τοσαῦτα
in [the] Spirit now in [the] flesh are ye being so many things
perfected?

ἐπάθετε εἰκῆ; 5 εἴ γε καὶ εἰκῆ. ὁ
suffered ye in vain? if indeed in vain. The [one]

οὖν ἐπιχορηγῶν ὑμῖν τὸ πνεῦμα καὶ
therefore supplying to you the Spirit and

ἐνεργῶν δυνάμεις ἐν ὑμῖν ἐξ ἔργων
working powerful deeds among you [is it] by works

νόμου ἢ ἐξ ἀκοῆς πίστεως; 6 Καθὼς
of law or by hearing of faith? As

Ἀβραὰμ ἐπίστευσεν τῷ θεῷ, καὶ ἐλογίσθη
Abraham believed - God, and it was reckoned

αὐτῷ εἰς δικαιοσύνην. 7 γινώσκετε ἄρα
to him for righteousness. Know ye then

ὅτι οἱ ἐκ πίστεως, οὗτοι υἱοί εἰσιν
that the [ones] of faith, ¹these ²sons ³are

Ἀβραάμ. 8 προϊδοῦσα δὲ ἡ γραφὴ ὅτι
⁴of Abraham. And ²foreseeing ¹the ³scripture ⁴that

ἐκ πίστεως δικαιοῖ τὰ ἔθνη ὁ θεός,
⁹by ¹⁰faith ⁸would justify ⁷the ⁸nations - ⁵God,

προευηγγελίσατο τῷ Ἀβραὰμ ὅτι ἐνευλογη-
preached good tidings - to Abraham that ⁶will be
before

---

comes evident that we ourselves are sinners, does that mean that Christ promotes sin? Absolutely not! 18If I rebuild what I destroyed, I prove that I am a lawbreaker. 19For through the law I died to the law so that I might live for God. 20I have been crucified with Christ and I no longer live, but Christ lives in me. The life I live in the body, I live by faith in the Son of God, who loved me and gave himself for me. 21I do not set aside the grace of God, for if righteousness could be gained through the law, Christ died for nothing!"*f*

Chapter 3

Faith or Observance of the Law

YOU foolish Galatians! Who has bewitched you? Before your very eyes Jesus Christ was clearly portrayed as crucified. 2I would like to learn just one thing from you: Did you receive the Spirit by observing the law, or by believing what you heard? 3Are you so foolish? After beginning with the Spirit, are you now trying to attain your goal by human effort? 4Have you suffered so much for nothing—if it really was for nothing? 5Does God give you his Spirit and work miracles among you because you observe the law, or because you believe what you heard? 6Consider Abraham: "He believed God, and it was credited to him as righteousness."*g* 7Understand, then, that those who believe are children of Abraham. 8The Scripture foresaw that God would justify the Gentiles by faith, and announced the gospel in advance to Abraham: "All nations will be blessed

*f*21 Some interpreters end the quotation after verse 14.
*g*6 Gen. 15:6

BLESSED IN YOU.''
9So then those who are of faith are blessed with Abraham, the believer.

10For as many as are of the works of the Law are under a curse; for it is written, ''CURSED IS EVERYONE WHO DOES NOT ABIDE BY ALL THINGS WRITTEN IN THE BOOK OF THE LAW, TO PERFORM THEM.''

11Now that no one is justified by the Law before God is evident; for, ''THE RIGHTEOUS MAN SHALL LIVE BY FAITH.''

12However, the Law is not of faith; on the contrary, ''HE WHO PRACTICES THEM SHALL LIVE BY THEM.''

13Christ redeemed us from the curse of the Law, having become a curse for us—for it is written, ''CURSED IS EVERYONE WHO HANGS ON A TREE''—

14in order that in Christ Jesus the blessing of Abraham might come to the Gentiles, so that we might receive the promise of the Spirit through faith.

Intent of the Law

15Brethren, I speak in terms of human relations: even though it is *only* a man's covenant, yet when it has been ratified, no one sets it aside or adds conditions to it.

16Now the promises were spoken to Abraham and to his seed. He does not say, ''And to seeds,'' as *referring* to many, but *rather* to one, ''And to your seed,'' that is, Christ.

17What I am saying is this: the Law, which came four hundred and thirty years later, does not invalidate a covenant previously ratified by God, so as to nullify the promise.

18For if the inheritance is based on law, it is no longer based on a promise; but God has granted it to Abra-

---

θήσονται ἐν σοὶ πάντα τὰ ἔθνη. 9 ὥστε
blessed ¹in ²thee ³all ⁴the ⁵nations.   So as

οἱ ἐκ πίστεως εὐλογοῦνται σὺν τῷ πιστῷ
the[ones]of faith are blessed with the believing

᾿Αβραάμ. 10 ῞Οσοι γὰρ ἐξ ἔργων νόμου
Abraham.   For as many as ²of ³works ⁴of law

εἰσίν, ὑπὸ κατάραν εἰσίν· γέγραπται γὰρ
¹are, ⁴under ²a curse ⁵are; for it has been written[,]

ὅτι ἐπικατάρατος πᾶς ὃς οὐκ ἐμμένει
–   Accursed   everyone who   continues not

πᾶσιν τοῖς γεγραμμένοις ἐν τῷ βιβλίῳ
in all the things having been written in   the   roll

τοῦ νόμου τοῦ ποιῆσαι αὐτά. 11 ὅτι
of the law   –   to do⁴   them.   that

δὲ ἐν νόμῳ οὐδεὶς δικαιοῦται παρὰ τῷ
Now by law   no man   is justified   before   –

θεῷ δῆλον, ὅτι ὁ δίκαιος ἐκ πίστεως
God [is] clear, because the just man by   faith

ζήσεται· 12 ὁ δὲ νόμος οὐκ ἔστιν ἐκ
will live;   and the   law   is not   of

πίστεως, ἀλλ᾿ ὁ ποιήσας αὐτὰ ζήσεται
faith,   but   the [one] doing   them   will live

ἐν αὐτοῖς. 13 Χριστὸς ἡμᾶς ἐξηγόρασεν
by them.   Christ   ²us   ¹redeemed

ἐκ τῆς κατάρας τοῦ νόμου γενόμενος
out of the   curse   of the   law   becoming

ὑπὲρ ἡμῶν κατάρα, ὅτι γέγραπται·
²on behalf of ³us   ¹a curse,   because   it has been written:

ἐπικατάρατος πᾶς ὁ κρεμάμενος ἐπὶ
Accursed   everyone   who   hanging   on

ξύλου, 14 ἵνα εἰς τὰ ἔθνη ἡ εὐλογία
a tree,   in order that ⁵to ⁶the ⁷nations ¹the ²blessing

τοῦ ᾿Αβραὰμ γένηται ἐν ᾿Ιησοῦ Χριστῷ,
– ³of Abraham ⁴might be in   Jesus   Christ,

ἵνα τὴν ἐπαγγελίαν τοῦ πνεύματος λάβωμεν
in order ²the   ³promise   ⁴of the ⁵Spirit ¹we might
that   receive

διὰ τῆς πίστεως. 15 ᾿Αδελφοί, κατὰ
through the   faith.   Brothers, according to

ἄνθρωπον λέγω. ὅμως ἀνθρώπου κεκυρω-
man   I say.   Nevertheless ⁶of man   ⁷having been

μένην διαθήκην οὐδεὶς ἀθετεῖ ἢ ἐπιδια-
ratified   ⁵a covenant ¹no one ²sets aside ³or ⁴makes

τάσσεται. 16 τῷ δὲ ᾿Αβραὰμ ἐρρέθησαν
additions [to].   – Now to Abraham   were said

αἱ ἐπαγγελίαι καὶ τῷ σπέρματι αὐτοῦ.
the   promises   and to the   seed   of him.

οὐ λέγει· καὶ τοῖς σπέρμασιν, ὡς ἐπὶ
It says not: And to the   seeds,   as concerning

πολλῶν, ἀλλ᾿ ὡς ἐφ᾿ ἑνός· καὶ τῷ
many,   but   as concerning one: And to the

σπέρματί σου, ὅς ἐστιν Χριστός. 17 τοῦτο δὲ
seed   of thee, who   is   Christ.   And this

λέγω· διαθήκην προκεκυρωμένην ὑπὸ
I say: ¹⁰A covenant ¹¹having been previously ratified ¹²by

τοῦ θεοῦ ὁ μετὰ τετρακόσια καὶ τριάκοντα
– ¹³God ¹the ⁴after ⁵four hundred ⁶and ⁷thirty

ἔτη γεγονὼς νόμος οὐκ ἀκυροῖ, εἰς τὸ
⁸years ²having come ³law ⁸does not annul,   so as†
     into being

καταργῆσαι τὴν ἐπαγγελίαν. 18 εἰ γὰρ
to abolish   the   promise.   For if

ἐκ νόμου ἡ κληρονομία, οὐκέτι ἐξ
⁴of ⁵law ¹the ²inheritance ³[is],   no more [is it] of

ἐπαγγελίας· τῷ δὲ ᾿Αβραὰμ δι᾿ ἐπαγγελίας
promise;   – but   ²to Abraham ³through   ⁴promise

---

through you.''[h] 9So those who have faith are blessed along with Abraham, the man of faith.

10All who rely on observing the law are under a curse, for it is written: ''Cursed is everyone who does not continue to do everything written in the Book of the Law.''[i] 11Clearly no one is justified before God by the law, because, ''The righteous will live by faith.''[j] 12The law is not based on faith; on the contrary, ''The man who does these things will live by them.''[k] 13Christ redeemed us from the curse of the law by becoming a curse for us, for it is written: ''Cursed is everyone who is hung on a tree.''[l] 14He redeemed us in order that the blessing given to Abraham might come to the Gentiles through Christ Jesus, so that by faith we might receive the promise of the Spirit.

The Law and the Promise

15Brothers, let me take an example from everyday life. Just as no one can set aside or add to a human covenant that has been duly established, so it is in this case. 16The promises were spoken to Abraham and to his seed. The Scripture does not say ''and to seeds,'' meaning many people, but ''and to your seed,''[m] meaning one person, who is Christ. 17What I mean is this: The law, introduced 430 years later, does not set aside the covenant previously established by God and thus do away with the promise. 18For if the inheritance depends on the law, then it no longer depends on a promise; but God in his grace gave it to

*h*8 Gen. 12:3; 18:18; 22:18
*i*10 Deut. 27:26
*j*11 Hab. 2:4
*k*12 Lev. 18:5
*l*13 Deut. 21:23
*m*16 Gen. 12:7; 13:15; 24:7

ham by means of a promise.

19Why the Law then? It was added because of transgressions, having been ordained through angels by the agency of a mediator, until the seed should come to whom the promise had been made. 20Now a mediator is not for one *party only*; whereas God is *only* one. 21Is the Law then contrary to the promises of God? May it never be! For if a law had been given which was able to impart life, then righteousness would indeed have been based on law. 22But the Scripture has shut up all men under sin, that the promise by faith in Jesus Christ might be given to those who believe. 23But before faith came, we were kept in custody under the law, being shut up to the faith which was later to be revealed. 24Therefore the Law has become our tutor *to lead us* to Christ, that we may be justified by faith. 25But now that faith has come, we are no longer under a tutor. 26For you are all sons of God through faith in Christ Jesus. 27For all of you who have been baptized into Christ have clothed yourselves with Christ. 28There is neither Jew nor Greek, there is neither slave nor free man, there is neither male nor female; for you are all one in Christ Jesus. 29And if you belong to Christ, then you are Abraham's offspring, heirs according to promise.

Chapter 4

Sonship in Christ

NOW I say, as long as the heir is a child, he does not differ at all from a slave although he is owner of everything, 2but he is under guardians and managers until the

---

κεχάρισται ὁ θεός. 19 Τί οὖν ὁ νόμος;
¹has given ²[it] – ¹God. Why therefore the law?

τῶν παραβάσεων χάριν προσετέθη, ἄχρις
²the ⁴transgressions ³by reason of ¹it was added, until

ἂν ἔλθῃ τὸ σπέρμα ᾧ ἐπήγγελται,
³should come ¹the ²seed to whom it has been promised,

διαταγεὶς δι' ἀγγέλων, ἐν χειρὶ μεσίτου.
being ordained through angels, by [the] hand of a mediator.

20 ὁ δὲ μεσίτης ἑνὸς οὐκ ἔστιν, ὁ
Now the mediator ²of one ¹is not, –

δὲ θεὸς εἷς ἐστιν. 21 ὁ οὖν νόμος κατὰ
but God ²one ¹is. [Is] the ²therefore ¹law against

τῶν ἐπαγγελιῶν [τοῦ θεοῦ]; μὴ γένοιτο.
the promises – of God? May it not be.

εἰ γὰρ ἐδόθη νόμος ὁ δυνάμενος ζωοποι-
For if ²was given ¹a law – being able to make

ῆσαι, ὄντως ἐκ νόμου ἂν ἦν ἡ δικαιοσύνη·
alive, really ²by ⁴law ¹would – ³righteousness;
have been

22 ἀλλὰ συνέκλεισεν ἡ γραφὴ τὰ πάντα
but ²shut up ¹the ²scripture all mankind†

ὑπὸ ἁμαρτίαν ἵνα ἡ ἐπαγγελία ἐκ πίστεως
under sin in or- the promise by faith
der that

Ἰησοῦ Χριστοῦ δοθῇ τοῖς πιστεύουσιν.
of(in) Jesus Christ might be given to the [ones] believing.

23 Πρὸ τοῦ δὲ ἐλθεῖν τὴν πίστιν ὑπὸ
before the But to come the faithᵇ under
=But before faith came

νόμον ἐφρουρούμεθα συγκλειόμενοι εἰς τὴν
law we were guarded being shut up to the

μέλλουσαν πίστιν ἀποκαλυφθῆναι. 24 ὥστε
²being about ¹faith to be revealed. So as

ὁ νόμος παιδαγωγὸς ἡμῶν γέγονεν εἰς
the law ²a trainer ³of us ¹has become [up] to

Χριστόν, ἵνα ἐκ πίστεως δικαιωθῶμεν·
Christ, in order that by faith we might be justified;

25 ἐλθούσης δὲ τῆς πίστεως οὐκέτι ὑπὸ
but ²having come ¹the ²faithᵃ ¹no more ³under

παιδαγωγόν ἐσμεν. 26 Πάντες γὰρ υἱοὶ
²a trainer ⁴we are. For all sons

θεοῦ ἐστε διὰ τῆς πίστεως ἐν Χριστῷ
of God ye are through the faith in Christ

Ἰησοῦ· 27 ὅσοι γὰρ εἰς Χριστὸν ἐβαπτίσ-
Jesus; for as many as ²into ³Christ ¹ye were

θητε, Χριστὸν ἐνεδύσασθε. 28 οὐκ ἔνι
baptized, ¹Christ ¹ye put on. There cannot be

Ἰουδαῖος οὐδὲ Ἕλλην, οὐκ ἔνι δοῦλος
Jew nor Greek, there cannot be slave

οὐδὲ ἐλεύθερος, οὐκ ἔνι ἄρσεν καὶ θῆλυ·
nor freeman, there cannot be male and female;

πάντες γὰρ ὑμεῖς εἷς ἐστε ἐν Χριστῷ
for ²all ¹ye ⁴one ²are in Christ

Ἰησοῦ. 29 εἰ δὲ ὑμεῖς Χριστοῦ, ἄρα
Jesus. But if ye [are] of Christ, then

τοῦ Ἀβραὰμ σπέρμα ἐστέ, κατ' ἐπαγγελίαν
– ³of Abraham ¹a seed ²are ye, according to promise

κληρονόμοι. 4 Λέγω δέ, ἐφ' ὅσον χρόνον ὁ
heirs. But I say, over so long a time as the

κληρονόμος νήπιός ἐστιν, οὐδὲν διαφέρει
heir ²an infant ¹is, ¹nothing ¹he differs
³[from]

δούλου κύριος πάντων ὤν, 2 ἀλλὰ ὑπὸ
²a slave ⁵lord ⁷of all ⁴being, but ²under

ἐπιτρόπους ἐστὶν καὶ οἰκονόμους ἄχρι τῆς
³guardians ¹is and stewards until the

Abraham through a promise.

19What, then, was the purpose of the law? It was added because of transgressions until the Seed to whom the promise referred had come. The law was put into effect through angels by a mediator. 20A mediator, however, does not represent just one party; but God is one.

21Is the law, therefore, opposed to the promises of God? Absolutely not! For if a law had been given that could impart life, then righteousness would certainly have come by the law. 22But the Scripture declares that the whole world is a prisoner of sin, so that what was promised, being given through faith in Jesus Christ, might be given to those who believe.

23Before this faith came, we were held prisoners by the law, locked up until faith should be revealed. 24So the law was put in charge to lead us to Christ ⁿ that we might be justified by faith. 25Now that faith has come, we are no longer under the supervision of the law.

Sons of God

26You are all sons of God through faith in Christ Jesus, 27for all of you who were baptized into Christ have clothed yourselves with Christ. 28There is neither Jew nor Greek, slave nor free, male nor female, for you are all one in Christ Jesus. 29If you belong to Christ, then you are Abraham's seed, and heirs according to the promise.

Chapter 4

WHAT I am saying is that as long as the heir is a child, he is no different from a slave, although he owns the whole estate. 2He is subject to guardians and trustees until the time set by his father. 3So also, when we were

ⁿ24 Or *charge until Christ came*

date set by the father.
³So also we, while we were children, were held in bondage under the elemental things of the world.

⁴But when the fulness of the time came, God sent forth His Son, born of a woman, born under the Law,

⁵in order that He might redeem those who were under the Law, that we might receive the adoption as sons.

⁶And because you are sons, God has sent forth the Spirit of His Son into our hearts, crying, "Abba! Father!"

⁷Therefore you are no longer a slave, but a son; and if a son, then an heir through God.

⁸However at that time, when you did not know God, you were slaves to those which by nature are no gods.

⁹But now that you have come to know God, or rather to be known by God, how is it that you turn back again to the weak and worthless elemental things, to which you desire to be enslaved all over again?

¹⁰You observe days and months and seasons and years.

¹¹I fear for you, that perhaps I have labored over you in vain.

¹²I beg of you, brethren, become as I am, for I also have become as you are. You have done me no wrong;

¹³but you know that it was because of a bodily illness that I preached the gospel to you the first time;

¹⁴and that which was a trial to you in my bodily condition you did not despise or loathe, but you received me as an angel of God, as Christ Jesus Himself.

¹⁵Where then is that sense of blessing you had? For I bear you witness, that if possible, you would have plucked out your eyes and

---

προθεσμίας   τοῦ   πατρός.   3 οὕτως   καὶ
term previously   of the   father.   So   also
appointed

ἡμεῖς,   ὅτε   ἦμεν   νήπιοι,   ὑπὸ   τὰ   στοιχεῖα
we,   when   we were   infants,   under   the   elements

τοῦ   κόσμου   ἤμεθα   δεδουλωμένοι·   4 ὅτε
of the   world   we were   having been enslaved;   when

δὲ   ἦλθεν   τὸ   πλήρωμα   τοῦ   χρόνου,
but   came   the   fulness   of the   time,

ἐξαπέστειλεν   ὁ   θεὸς   τὸν   υἱὸν   αὐτοῦ,
sent forth   -   God   the   Son   of him,

γενόμενον   ἐκ   γυναικός,   γενόμενον   ὑπὸ
becoming   of   a woman,   becoming   under

νόμον,   5 ἵνα   τοὺς   ὑπὸ   νόμον   ἐξαγοράσῃ,
law,   in order that ¹the ones ²under ³law ¹he might redeem,

ἵνα   τὴν   υἱοθεσίαν   ἀπολάβωμεν.   6 Ὅτι   δὲ
in order ¹the ²adoption of sons ¹we might receive.   And because that

ἐστε   υἱοί,   ἐξαπέστειλεν   ὁ   θεὸς   τὸ
ye are   sons,   ²sent forth   -   ¹God   the

πνεῦμα   τοῦ   υἱοῦ   αὐτοῦ   εἰς   τὰς   καρδίας
Spirit   of the   Son   of him   into   the   hearts

ἡμῶν,   κρᾶζον·   ἀββᾶ   ὁ   πατήρ.   7 ὥστε
of us,   crying·   Abba   -   Father.   So as

οὐκέτι   εἶ   δοῦλος   ἀλλὰ   υἱός·   εἰ   δὲ   υἱός,
no more art thou a slave   but   a son;   and if   a son,

καὶ   κληρονόμος   διὰ   θεοῦ.
also   an heir   through   God.

8 Ἀλλὰ   τότε   μὲν   οὐκ   εἰδότες   θεὸν
But   then   indeed   not   knowing   God

ἐδουλεύσατε   τοῖς   φύσει   μὴ   οὖσιν   θεοῖς·
ye served as slaves ¹the ³by nature ⁴not   ²being   ⁵gods;

9 νῦν   δὲ   γνόντες   θεόν,   μᾶλλον   δὲ
but now   knowing   God,   but rather

γνωσθέντες   ὑπὸ   θεοῦ,   πῶς   ἐπιστρέφετε
being known   by   God,   how   turn ye

πάλιν   ἐπὶ   τὰ   ἀσθενῆ   καὶ   πτωχὰ   στοιχεῖα,
again   to the   weak   and   poor   elements,

οἷς   πάλιν   ἄνωθεν   δουλεῦσαι   θέλετε;
to which again   ²anew   ¹to serve   ¹ye wish?

10 ἡμέρας   παρατηρεῖσθε   καὶ   μῆνας   καὶ
²days   ¹Ye observe   and   months   and

καιροὺς   καὶ   ἐνιαυτούς.   11 φοβοῦμαι   ὑμᾶς
seasons   and   years.   I fear [for]   you

μή   πως   εἰκῆ   κεκοπίακα   εἰς   ὑμᾶς.
lest   in vain   I have laboured among   you.

12 Γίνεσθε   ὡς   ἐγώ,   ὅτι   κἀγὼ   ὡς
Be ye   as   I [am],   because   I also [am]   as

ὑμεῖς,   ἀδελφοί,   δέομαι   ὑμῶν.   οὐδέν   με
ye [are],   brothers,   I beg   of you.   Nothing   me

ἠδικήσατε·   13 οἴδατε   δὲ   ὅτι   δι'   ἀσθένειαν
ye wronged·   and ye know   that on account of weakness

τῆς   σαρκὸς   εὐηγγελισάμην   ὑμῖν   τὸ
of the   flesh   I preached good tidings   to you   -

πρότερον,   14 καὶ   τὸν   πειρασμὸν   ὑμῶν
formerly,   and   the   trial   of you

ἐν   τῇ   σαρκί   μου   οὐκ   ἐξουθενήσατε   οὐδὲ
in   the   flesh   of me   ye despised not   nor

ἐξεπτύσατε,   ἀλλὰ   ὡς   ἄγγελον   θεοῦ   ἐδέξασθέ
disdained ye,   but   as   a messenger of God   ye received

με,   ὡς   Χριστὸν   Ἰησοῦν.   15 ποῦ   οὖν
me,   as   Christ   Jesus.   Where therefore

ὁ   μακαρισμὸς   ὑμῶν;   μαρτυρῶ   γὰρ   ὑμῖν
the   felicitation   of you?*   for I witness   to you

ὅτι   εἰ   δυνατὸν   τοὺς   ὀφθαλμοὺς   ὑμῶν
that   if   possible   ²the   ³eyes   ⁴of you

---

children, we were in slavery under the basic principles of the world. ⁴But when the time had fully come, God sent his Son, born of a woman, born under law, ⁵to redeem those under law, that we might receive the full rights of sons. ⁶Because you are sons, God sent the Spirit of his Son into our hearts, the Spirit who calls out, "Abba,ᵒ Father." ⁷So you are no longer a slave, but a son; and since you are a son, God has made you also an heir.

Paul's Concern for the Galatians

⁸Formerly, when you did not know God, you were slaves to those who by nature are not gods. ⁹But now that you know God—or rather are known by God—how is it that you are turning back to those weak and miserable principles? Do you wish to be enslaved by them all over again? ¹⁰You are observing special days and months and seasons and years! ¹¹I fear for you, that somehow I have wasted my efforts on you.

¹²I plead with you, brothers, become like me, for I became like you. You have done me no wrong. ¹³As you know, it was because of an illness that I first preached the gospel to you. ¹⁴Even though my illness was a trial to you, you did not treat me with contempt or scorn. Instead, you welcomed me as if I were an angel of God, as if I were Christ Jesus himself. ¹⁵What has happened to all your joy? I can testify that, if you could have done so, you would have torn out your eyes and given them

---

* That is, "your felicitation [of me]".   ᵒ6 Aramaic for *Father*

given them to me.
16Have I therefore become your enemy by telling you the truth?
17They eagerly seek you, not commendably, but they wish to shut you out, in order that you may seek them.
18But it is good always to be eagerly sought in a commendable manner, and not only when I am present with you.
19My children, with whom I am again in labor until Christ is formed in you—
20but I could wish to be present with you now and to change my tone, for I am perplexed about you.

Bond and Free

21Tell me, you who want to be under law, do you not listen to the law?
22For it is written that Abraham had two sons, one by the bondwoman and one by the free woman.
23But the son by the bondwoman was born according to the flesh, and the son by the free woman through the promise.
24This is allegorically speaking: for these *women* are two covenants, one *proceeding* from Mount Sinai bearing children who are to be slaves; she is Hagar.
25Now this Hagar is Mount Sinai in Arabia, and corresponds to the present Jerusalem, for she is in slavery with her children.
26But the Jerusalem above is free; she is our mother.
27For it is written,
"REJOICE, BARREN WOMAN WHO DOES NOT BEAR;
BREAK FORTH AND SHOUT, YOU WHO ARE NOT IN LABOR;
FOR MORE ARE THE CHILDREN OF THE DESOLATE
THAN OF THE ONE WHO HAS A HUSBAND."
28And you brethren, like Isaac, are children of promise.
29But as at that time he who was born according to

ἐξορύξαντες ἐδώκατέ μοι. **16** ὥστε ἐχθρὸς
¹gouging out   ye gave [them] to me.   So that ²an enemy

ὑμῶν γέγονα ἀληθεύων ὑμῖν; **17** ζηλοῦσιν
³of you ¹have I become speaking truth to you?   They are zealous of

ὑμᾶς οὐ καλῶς, ἀλλὰ ἐκκλεῖσαι ὑμᾶς
you   not   well,   but   ²to exclude   ³you

θέλουσιν, **18** ἵνα αὐτοὺς ζηλοῦτε. καλὸν δὲ
¹wish,   in order them   ye may be   But [it is] good
    that   zealous of.

ζηλοῦσθαι ἐν καλῷ πάντοτε, καὶ μὴ
to be zealous   in   a good thing   always,   and   not

μόνον ἐν τῷ παρεῖναί με πρὸς ὑμᾶς,
only   in   the   to be present   me be   with   you,
        =when I am present

19 τέκνα μου, οὓς πάλιν ὠδίνω μέχρις οὗ
children of me,[for] whom again   I travail   until
                 in birth

μορφωθῇ Χριστὸς ἐν ὑμῖν· **20** ἤθελον δὲ
²is formed   ¹Christ   in   you;   and I wished

παρεῖναι πρὸς ὑμᾶς ἄρτι καὶ ἀλλάξαι
to be present   with   you   just now   and   to change

τὴν φωνήν μου, ὅτι ἀπορούμαι ἐν ὑμῖν.
the   voice   of me, because I am perplexed in(about) you.

21 Λέγετέ μοι, οἱ ὑπὸ νόμον θέλοντες
    Tell   me, the [ones] ²under   ³law   ¹wishing

εἶναι, τὸν νόμον οὐκ ἀκούετε; **22** γέγραπται
²to be,   ²the   ³law   ¹hear ye not?   ²it has been written

γὰρ ὅτι Ἀβραὰμ δύο υἱοὺς ἔσχεν, ἕνα
¹for   that   Abraham   two   sons   had,   one

ἐκ τῆς παιδίσκης καὶ ἕνα ἐκ τῆς ἐλευ-
of   the   maidservant   and   one   of   the   free

θέρας. **23** ἀλλ' ὁ [μὲν] ἐκ τῆς παιδίσκης
woman.   But   the [one] indeed   of   the   maidservant

κατὰ σάρκα γεγέννηται, ὁ δὲ ἐκ τῆς
according to flesh   has been born, and the [one] of   the

ἐλευθέρας διὰ τῆς ἐπαγγελίας. **24** ἅτινά
free woman   through   the   promise.   Which things

ἐστιν ἀλληγορούμενα· αὗται γάρ εἰσιν
is(are)   being allegorized;   for these   are

δύο διαθῆκαι, μία μὲν ἀπὸ ὄρους Σινά,
two   covenants, one indeed from   mount   Sina,

εἰς δουλείαν γεννῶσα, ἥτις ἐστὶν Ἁγάρ.
to   slavery   bringing forth, which   is   Hagar.

25 τὸ δὲ Ἁγὰρ Σινὰ ὄρος ἐστὶν ἐν
    ⁴The ¹now ²Hagar   ⁵Sina   ⁶mount   ³is   in

τῇ Ἀραβίᾳ· συστοιχεῖ δὲ τῇ νῦν
-   Arabia;   and corresponds   to the   now

Ἰερουσαλήμ, δουλεύει γὰρ μετὰ τῶν
Jerusalem,   for she serves as a slave   with   the

τέκνων αὐτῆς. **26** ἡ δὲ ἄνω Ἰερουσαλὴμ
children   of her.   But the   above   Jerusalem

ἐλευθέρα ἐστίν, ἥτις ἐστὶν μήτηρ ἡμῶν·
free   is,   who   is   mother   of us;

27 γέγραπται γάρ· εὐφράνθητι, στεῖρα ἡ
    for it has been written: Be thou glad,   barren[,]   the
                                [one]

οὐ τίκτουσα, ῥῆξον καὶ βόησον, ἡ οὐκ
not   bearing,   break forth and   shout, the [one] not

ὠδίνουσα· ὅτι πολλὰ τὰ τέκνα τῆς ἐρήμου
travailing; because many [are] the children of the   desolate

μᾶλλον ἢ τῆς ἐχούσης τὸν ἄνδρα. **28** ὑμεῖς
rather   than of the   having   the   husband.   ye
                 [one]

δέ, ἀδελφοί, κατὰ Ἰσαὰκ ἐπαγγελίας τέκνα
But,   brothers, ⁴according to ¹Isaac   ²of promise ³children

ἐστέ. **29** ἀλλ' ὥσπερ τότε ὁ κατὰ σάρκα
¹are.   But   even as   then the [one] according to flesh

---

to me. 16Have I now become your enemy by telling you the truth?
17Those people are zealous to win you over, but for no good. What they want is to alienate you from us,, so that you may be zealous for them. 18It is fine to be zealous, provided the purpose is good, and to be so always and not just when I am with you. 19My dear children, for whom I am again in the pains of childbirth until Christ is formed in you, 20how I wish I could be with you now and change my tone, because I am perplexed about you!

Hagar and Sarah

21Tell me, you who want to be under the law, are you not aware of what the law says? 22For it is written that Abraham had two sons, one by the slave woman and the other by the free woman. 23His son by the slave woman was born in the ordinary way; but his son by the free woman was born as the result of a promise.

24These things may be taken figuratively, for the women represent two covenants. One covenant is from Mount Sinai and bears children who are to be slaves: This is Hagar. 25Now Hagar stands for Mount Sinai in Arabia and corresponds to the present city of Jerusalem, because she is in slavery with her children. 26But the Jerusalem that is above is free, and she is our mother. 27For it is written:

"Be glad, O barren woman,
   who bears no children;
break forth and cry aloud,
   you who have no labor pains;
because more are the children of the desolate woman
than of her who has a husband."ᵖ

28Now you, brothers, like Isaac, are children of promise. 29At that time the son born in the ordinary way

ᵖ27 Isaiah 54:1

the flesh persecuted him *who was born* according to the Spirit, so it is now also. 30But what does the Scripture say? "CAST OUT THE BOND-WOMAN AND HER SON, FOR THE SON OF THE BONDWOMAN SHALL NOT BE AN HEIR WITH THE SON OF THE FREE WOMAN." 31So then, brethren, we are not children of a bond-woman, but of the free woman.

Chapter 5

Walk by the Spirit

IT was for freedom that Christ set us free; therefore keep standing firm and do not be subject again to a yoke of slavery. 2Behold I, Paul, say to you that if you receive cir-cumcision, Christ will be of no benefit to you. 3And I testify again to every man who receives circumcision, that he is un-der obligation to keep the whole Law. 4You have been severed from Christ, you who are seeking to be justified by law; you have fallen from grace. 5For we through the Spirit, by faith, are waiting for the hope of righteous-ness. 6For in Christ Jesus neither circumcision nor uncircumcision means any-thing, but faith working through love. 7You were running well; who hindered you from obeying the truth? 8This persuasion *did* not *come* from Him who calls you. 9A little leaven leavens the whole lump *of dough.* 10I have confidence in you in the Lord, that you will adopt no other view; but the one who is disturb-ing you shall bear his judg-ment, whoever he is. 11But I, brethren, if I still preach circumcision, why am I still persecuted? Then the stumbling block of the cross has been abolished. 12Would that those who are troubling you would even mutilate themselves.

γεννηθεὶς ἐδίωκεν τὸν κατὰ πνεῦμα, οὕτως
born persecuted the [one] according spirit, so
          [born]   to

καὶ νῦν. 30 ἀλλὰ τί λέγει ἡ γραφή;
also now. But what says the scripture?

ἔκβαλε τὴν παιδίσκην καὶ τὸν υἱὸν αὐτῆς·
Cast out the maidservant and the son of her;

οὐ γὰρ μὴ κληρονομήσει ὁ υἱὸς τῆς
for by no means ³shall inherit ¹the ²son ²of the

παιδίσκης μετὰ τοῦ υἱοῦ τῆς ἐλευθέρας.
⁴maidservant with the son of the free woman.

31 διό, ἀδελφοί, οὐκ ἐσμὲν παιδίσκης
Wherefore, brothers, we are not ²of a maidservant

τέκνα ἀλλὰ τῆς ἐλευθέρας.
¹children but of the free woman.

5 Τῇ ἐλευθερίᾳ ἡμᾶς Χριστὸς ἠλευθέρωσεν·
For *the* freedom ³us ¹Christ ²freed;

στήκετε οὖν καὶ μὴ πάλιν ζυγῷ δουλείας
stand firm therefore and not again with a yoke of slavery

ἐνέχεσθε.
be entangled.

2 Ἴδε ἐγὼ Παῦλος λέγω ὑμῖν ὅτι
Behold[,] I Paul te¹l you that

ἐὰν περιτέμνησθε Χριστὸς ὑμᾶς οὐδὲν
if ye are circumcised Christ ²you ¹nothing

ὠφελήσει. 3 μαρτύρομαι δὲ πάλιν παντὶ
¹will profit. And I testify again to every

ἀνθρώπῳ περιτεμνομένῳ ὅτι ὀφειλέτης ἐστὶν
man being circumcised that ²a debtor ¹he is

ὅλον τὸν νόμον ποιῆσαι. 4 κατηργήθητε
⁴all ²the ³law ¹to do. Ye were discharged

ἀπὸ Χριστοῦ οἵτινες ἐν νόμῳ δικαιοῦσθε,
from Christ who by law are justified,

τῆς χάριτος ἐξεπέσατε. 5 ἡμεῖς γὰρ
the ²grace ¹ye fell from. For we

πνεύματι ἐκ πίστεως ἐλπίδα δικαιοσύνης
in spirit by faith [the] hope of righteousness

ἀπεκδεχόμεθα. 6 ἐν γὰρ Χριστῷ Ἰησοῦ
eagerly expect. For in Christ Jesus

οὔτε περιτομή τι ἰσχύει οὔτε ἀκροβυστία,
neither circumcision ²anything ¹avails nor uncircumcision,

ἀλλὰ πίστις δι’ ἀγάπης ἐνεργουμένη.
but faith ²through ³love ¹operating.

7 Ἐτρέχετε καλῶς· τίς ὑμᾶς ἐνέκοψεν
Ye were running well; who ²you ¹hindered

ἀληθείᾳ μὴ πείθεσθαι; 8 ἡ πεισμονὴ οὐκ
⁵by truth ²not ⁴to be persuaded? the(this) persuasion not

ἐκ τοῦ καλοῦντος ὑμᾶς. 9 μικρὰ ζύμη
of the [one] calling you. A little leaven

ὅλον τὸ φύραμα ζυμοῖ. 10 ἐγὼ πέποιθα
all the lump leavens. I trust

εἰς ὑμᾶς ἐν κυρίῳ ὅτι οὐδὲν ἄλλο φρο-
as to† you in [the] Lord that ²nothing ¹other ¹ye

νήσετε· ὁ δὲ ταράσσων ὑμᾶς βαστάσει
will think; but the [one] troubling you shall bear

τὸ κρίμα, ὅστις ἐὰν ᾖ. 11 Ἐγὼ δέ,
the judgment, whoever he may be. ¹But ⁴I,

ἀδελφοί, εἰ περιτομὴν ἔτι κηρύσσω, τί
²brothers, ³if ⁷circumcision ⁵still ⁶proclaim, why

ἔτι διώκομαι; ἄρα κατήργηται τὸ
still am I being persecuted? then has been annulled the

σκάνδαλον τοῦ σταυροῦ. 12 Ὄφελον καὶ
offence of the cross. I would that indeed

ἀποκόψονται οἱ ἀναστατοῦντες ὑμᾶς.
⁴will(might) cut ¹the [ones] ²unsetting ³you.
themselves off

---

persecuted the son born by the power of the Spirit. It is the same now. 30But what does the Scripture say? "Get rid of the slave wom-an and her son, for the slave woman's son will never share in the inheri-tance with the free wom-an's son."*q* 31Therefore, brothers, we are not chil-dren of the slave woman, but of the free woman.

Chapter 5

Freedom in Christ

IT is for freedom that Christ has set us free. Stand firm, then, and do not let yourselves be bur-dened again by a yoke of slavery. 2Mark my words! I, Paul, tell you that if you let your-selves be circumcised, Christ will be of no value to you at all. 3Again I declare to every man who lets him-self be circumcised that he is obligated to obey the whole law. 4You who are trying to be justified by law have been alienated from Christ; you have fallen away from grace. 5But by faith we eagerly await through the Spirit the right-eousness for which we hope. 6For in Christ Jesus neither circumcision nor uncircumcision has any value. The only thing that counts is faith expressing itself through love. 7You were running a good race. Who cut in on you and kept you from obeying the truth? 8That kind of per-suasion does not come from the one who calls you. 9"A little yeast works through the whole batch of dough." 10I am confident in the Lord that you will take no other view. The one who is throwing you into confusion will pay the pen-alty, whoever he may be. 11Brothers, if I am still preaching circumcision, why am I still being perse-cuted? In that case the of-fense of the cross has been abolished. 12As for those agitators, I wish they would go the whole way and emasculate them-selves!

13For you were called to freedom, brethren; only do not *turn* your freedom into an opportunity for the flesh, but through love serve one another.

14For the whole Law is fulfilled in one word, in the *statement*, "YOU SHALL LOVE YOUR NEIGHBOR AS YOURSELF."

15But if you bite and devour one another, take care lest you are consumed by one another.

16But I say, walk by the Spirit, and you will not carry out the desire of the flesh.

17For the flesh sets its desire against the Spirit, and the Spirit against the flesh; for these are in opposition to one another, so that you may not do the things that you please.

18But if you are led by the Spirit, you are not under the Law.

19Now the deeds of the flesh are evident, which are: immorality, impurity, sensuality,

20idolatry, sorcery, enmities, strife, jealousy, outbursts of anger, disputes, dissensions, factions,

21envying, drunkenness, carousing, and things like these, of which I forewarn you just as I have forewarned you that those who practice such things shall not inherit the kingdom of God.

22But the fruit of the Spirit is love, joy, peace, patience, kindness, goodness, faithfulness,

23gentleness, self-control; against such things there is no law.

24Now those who belong to Christ Jesus have crucified the flesh with its passions and desires.

25If we live by the Spirit, let us also walk by the Spirit.

26Let us not become boastful, challenging one another, envying one another.

---

13 Ὑμεῖς γὰρ ἐπ᾿ ἐλευθερίᾳ ἐκλήθητε,
For ye for freedom were called,

ἀδελφοί· μόνον μὴ τὴν ἐλευθερίαν εἰς
brothers; only [use] not the freedom for

ἀφορμὴν τῇ σαρκί, ἀλλὰ διὰ τῆς ἀγάπης
advantage to the flesh, but through - love

δουλεύετε ἀλλήλοις. 14 ὁ γὰρ πᾶς νόμος
serve ye as slaves one another. For the whole law

ἐν ἑνὶ λόγῳ πεπλήρωται, ἐν τῷ· ἀγα-
in one word has been summed up, in the [word]: Thou

πήσεις τὸν πλησίον σου ὡς σεαυτόν.
shalt love the neighbour of thee as thyself.

15 εἰ δὲ ἀλλήλους δάκνετε καὶ κατεσθίετε,
But if ¹one another ¹ye bite ²and ³ye devour,

βλέπετε μὴ ὑπ᾿ ἀλλήλων ἀναλωθῆτε.
see lest by one another ye are destroyed.

16 Λέγω δέ, πνεύματι περιπατεῖτε καὶ
Now I say, in spirit walk ye and

ἐπιθυμίαν σαρκὸς οὐ μὴ τελέσητε. 17 ἡ
[the] lust of [the] flesh by no means ye will perform. the

γὰρ σὰρξ ἐπιθυμεῖ κατὰ τοῦ πνεύματος,
For flesh lusts against the spirit,

τὸ δὲ πνεῦμα κατὰ τῆς σαρκός, ταῦτα
and the spirit against the flesh, ²these

γὰρ ἀλλήλοις ἀντίκειται, ἵνα μὴ ἃ ἐὰν
¹for ⁴each other ³opposes, lest whatever things

θέλητε ταῦτα ποιῆτε. 18 εἰ δὲ πνεύματι
ye wish these ye do. But if by [the] Spirit

ἄγεσθε, οὐκ ἐστὲ ὑπὸ νόμον. 19 φανερὰ δέ
ye are led, ye are not under law. Now ⁶manifest

ἐστιν τὰ ἔργα τῆς σαρκός, ἅτινά ἐστιν
¹is(are) ¹the ²works of the ⁴flesh, which is(are)

πορνεία, ἀκαθαρσία, ἀσέλγεια, 20 εἰδωλο-
fornication, uncleanness, lewdness, idola-

λατρία, φαρμακεία, ἔχθραι, ἔρις, ζῆλος,
try, sorcery, enmities, strife, jealousy,

θυμοί, ἐριθεῖαι, διχοστασίαι, αἱρέσεις,
angers, rivalries, divisions, sects,

21 φθόνοι, μέθαι, κῶμοι, καὶ τὰ ὅμοια
envyings, drunken- revellings, and - like
nesses,

τούτοις, ἃ προλέγω ὑμῖν καθὼς προεῖπον,
to these, which I tell ²beforehand ¹you as I previously
said,

ὅτι οἱ τὰ τοιαῦτα πράσσοντες βασιλείαν
that the [ones] - ²such things ¹practising ⁴[the] kingdom

θεοῦ οὐ κληρονομήσουσιν. 22 ὁ δὲ καρπὸς
³of God ²will not inherit. But the fruit

τοῦ πνεύματός ἐστιν ἀγάπη, χαρά, εἰρήνη,
of the Spirit is love, joy, peace,

μακροθυμία, χρηστότης, ἀγαθωσύνη, πίστις,
longsuffering, kindness, goodness, faithfulness,

23 πραΰτης, ἐγκράτεια· κατὰ τῶν τοιούτων
meekness, self-control; against - such things

οὐκ ἔστιν νόμος. 24 οἱ δὲ τοῦ Χριστοῦ
there is no law. Now the ones - of Christ

Ἰησοῦ τὴν σάρκα ἐσταύρωσαν σὺν τοῖς
Jesus ²the ²flesh ¹crucified with the(its)

παθήμασιν καὶ ταῖς ἐπιθυμίαις. 25 Εἰ
passions and the(its) lusts. If

ζῶμεν πνεύματι, πνεύματι καὶ στοιχῶμεν.
we live in [the] Spirit, in [the] Spirit also let us walk.

26 μὴ γινώμεθα κενόδοξοι, ἀλλήλους
Let us not become vainglorious, one another

προκαλούμενοι, ἀλλήλοις φθονοῦντες.
provoking, one another envying.

13You, my brothers, were called to be free. But do not use your freedom to indulge the sinful nature*ʳ*; rather, serve one another in love. 14The entire law is summed up in a single command: "Love your neighbor as yourself."*ˢ* 15If you keep on biting and devouring each other, watch out or you will be destroyed by each other.

Life by the Spirit

16So I say, live by the Spirit, and you will not gratify the desires of the sinful nature. 17For the sinful nature desires what is contrary to the Spirit, and the Spirit what is contrary to the sinful nature. They are in conflict with each other, so that you do not do what you want. 18But if you are led by the Spirit, you are not under law.

19The acts of the sinful nature are obvious: sexual immorality, impurity and debauchery; 20idolatry and witchcraft; hatred, discord, jealousy, fits of rage, selfish ambition, dissensions, factions 21and envy; drunkenness, orgies, and the like. I warn you, as I did before, that those who live like this will not inherit the kingdom of God.

22But the fruit of the Spirit is love, joy, peace, patience, kindness, goodness, faithfulness, 23gentleness and self-control. Against such things there is no law. 24Those who belong to Christ Jesus have crucified the sinful nature with its passions and desires. 25Since we live by the Spirit, let us keep in step with the Spirit. 26Let us not become conceited, provoking and envying each other.

ʳ13 Or the flesh; also in verses 16, 17, 19 and 24
ˢ14 Lev. 19:18

Chapter 6

Bear One Another's Burdens

BRETHREN, even if a man is caught in any trespass, you who are spiritual, restore such a one in a spirit of gentleness; *each one* looking to yourself, lest you too be tempted.

2Bear one another's burdens, and thus fulfill the law of Christ.

3For if anyone thinks he is something when he is nothing, he deceives himself.

4But let each one examine his own work, and then he will have *reason for* boasting in regard to himself alone, and not in regard to another.

5For each one shall bear his own load.

6And let the one who is taught the word share all good things with him who teaches.

7Do not be deceived, God is not mocked; for whatever a man sows, this he will also reap.

8For the one who sows to his own flesh shall from the flesh reap corruption, but the one who sows to the Spirit shall from the Spirit reap eternal life.

9And let us not lose heart in doing good, for in due time we shall reap if we do not grow weary.

10So then, while we have opportunity, let us do good to all men, and especially to those who are of the household of the faith.

11See with what large letters I am writing to you with my own hand.

12Those who desire to make a good showing in the flesh try to compel you to be circumcised, simply that they may not be persecuted for the cross of Christ.

13For those who *a*are circumcised do not even keep the Law themselves, but

---

6 Ἀδελφοί, ἐὰν καὶ προλημφθῇ ἄνθρω-
Brothers, if indeed ²is overtaken ¹a

πος ἐν τινι παραπτώματι, ὑμεῖς οἱ
man in some trespass, ye the

πνευματικοὶ καταρτίζετε τὸν τοιοῦτον ἐν
spiritual [ones] restore – such a one in

πνεύματι πραΰτητος, σκοπῶν σεαυτόν, μὴ
a spirit of meekness, considering thyself, lest

καὶ σὺ πειρασθῇς. 2 Ἀλλήλων τὰ βάρη
also thou art tempted. Of one another the loads

βαστάζετε, καὶ οὕτως ἀναπληρώσετε τὸν
bear ye, and so ye will fulfil the

νόμον τοῦ Χριστοῦ. 3 εἰ γὰρ δοκεῖ
law of Christ. For if ³thinks

τις εἶναί τι μηδὲν ὤν, φρεναπατᾷ ἑαυτόν.
¹anyone ²to be ⁴some- ⁵no- ⁶being, he deceives himself.
thing thing

4 τὸ δὲ ἔργον ἑαυτοῦ δοκιμαζέτω ἕκαστος,
But the work of himself ¹let ²prove ³each man,

καὶ τότε εἰς ἑαυτὸν μόνον τὸ καύχημα
and then in himself alone the boast

ἕξει καὶ οὐκ εἰς τὸν ἕτερον· 5 ἕκαστος
he will and not in the other man; ¹each man
have

γὰρ τὸ ἴδιον φορτίον βαστάσει. 6 Κοινωνείτω δὲ
¹for the(his) own burden will bear. And ²let him share

ὁ κατηχούμενος τὸν λόγον τῷ κατη-
¹the ²being instructed [in] ³the ⁴word ⁵with the [one] in-
[one]

χοῦντι ἐν πᾶσιν ἀγαθοῖς. 7 Μὴ πλανᾶσθε,
structing in all good things. Be ye not led astray,

θεὸς οὐ μυκτηρίζεται. ὃ γὰρ ἐὰν σπείρῃ
God is not mocked. For whatever ¹may sow

ἄνθρωπος, τοῦτο καὶ θερίσει· 8 ὅτι ὁ
¹a man, this also he will reap; because the

σπείρων εἰς τὴν σάρκα ἑαυτοῦ ἐκ τῆς
[one] sowing to the flesh of himself from the

σαρκὸς θερίσει φθοράν, ὁ δὲ σπείρων
flesh will reap corruption, but the [one] sowing

εἰς τὸ πνεῦμα ἐκ τοῦ πνεύματος θερίσει
to the Spirit from the Spirit will reap

ζωὴν αἰώνιον. 9 τὸ δὲ καλὸν ποιοῦντες
life eternal. And ²the ³good ¹doing

μὴ ἐγκακῶμεν· καιρῷ γὰρ ἰδίῳ
let us not lose heart; for in its own time

θερίσομεν μὴ ἐκλυόμενοι. 10 Ἄρα οὖν
we shall reap not failing. Then therefore

ὡς καιρὸν ἔχομεν, ἐργαζώμεθα τὸ ἀγαθὸν
as ²time ¹we have, let us do the good

πρὸς πάντας, μάλιστα δὲ πρὸς τοὺς
to all men, and most of all to the

οἰκείους τῆς πίστεως.
members of of the faith.
the family

11 Ἴδετε πηλίκοις ὑμῖν γράμμασιν
Ye see in how large ²to you ¹letters

ἔγραψα τῇ ἐμῇ χειρί. 12 Ὅσοι θέλουσιν
²I wrote – with my hand. As many as wish

εὐπροσωπῆσαι ἐν σαρκί, οὗτοι ἀναγκάζουσιν
to look well in [the] flesh, these compel

ὑμᾶς περιτέμνεσθαι, μόνον ἵνα τῷ
you to be circumcised, only in order that ²for the

σταυρῷ τοῦ Χριστοῦ [Ἰησοῦ] μὴ
⁴cross – ³of Christ ⁵Jesus ¹not

διώκωνται. 13 οὐδὲ γὰρ οἱ περιτεμνόμενοι
²they are persecuted. For ¹not ¹the [ones] ²being circumcised

αὐτοὶ νόμον φυλάσσουσιν, ἀλλὰ θέλουσιν
²themselves ³law ⁴keep, but they wish

Chapter 6

Doing Good to All

BROTHERS, if someone is caught in a sin, you who are spiritual should restore him gently. But watch yourself, or you also may be tempted. 2Carry each other's burdens, and in this way you will fulfill the law of Christ. 3If anyone thinks he is something when he is nothing, he deceives himself. 4Each one should test his own actions. Then he can take pride in himself, without comparing himself to somebody else, 5for each one should carry his own load.

6Anyone who receives instruction in the word must share all good things with his instructor.

7Do not be deceived: God cannot be mocked. A man reaps what he sows. 8The one who sows to please his sinful nature, from that nature' will reap destruction; the one who sows to please the Spirit, from the Spirit will reap eternal life. 9Let us not become weary in doing good, for at the proper time we will reap a harvest if we do not give up. 10Therefore, as we have opportunity, let us do good to all people, especially to those who belong to the family of believers.

Not Circumcision but a New Creation

11See what large letters I use as I write to you with my own hand!

12Those who want to make a good impression outwardly are trying to compel you to be circumcised. The only reason they do this is to avoid being persecuted for the cross of Christ. 13Not even those who are circumcised obey the law, yet they want you

---

*a*Some ancient mss. read *have been*

¹8 Or *his flesh, from the flesh*

they desire to have you circumcised, that they may boast in your flesh. 14But may it never be that I should boast, except in the cross of our Lord Jesus Christ, through which the world has been crucified to me, and I to the world. 15For neither is circumcision anything, nor uncircumcision, but a new creation. 16And those who will walk by this rule, peace and mercy *be* upon them, and upon the Israel of God. 17From now on let no one cause trouble for me, for I bear on my body the brand-marks of Jesus. 18The grace of our Lord Jesus Christ be with your spirit, brethren. Amen.

ὑμᾶς περιτέμνεσθαι ἵνα ἐν τῇ ὑμετέρᾳ
you to be circumcised in order that ³in - ⁴your
σαρκὶ καυχήσωνται. 14 ἐμοὶ δὲ μὴ γένοιτο
⁴flesh ¹they may boast. But to me may it not be
καυχᾶσθαι εἰ μὴ ἐν τῷ σταυρῷ τοῦ
to boast except in the cross of the
κυρίου ἡμῶν Ἰησοῦ Χριστοῦ, δι' οὗ
Lord of us Jesus Christ, through whom
ἐμοὶ κόσμος ἐσταύρωται κἀγὼ κόσμῳ.
to me [the] world has been crucified and I to [the] world.
15 οὔτε γὰρ περιτομή τί ἐστιν οὔτε
For neither circumcision ²anything ¹is nor
ἀκροβυστία, ἀλλὰ καινὴ κτίσις. 16 καὶ
uncircumcision, but a new creation. And
ὅσοι τῷ κανόνι τούτῳ στοιχήσουσιν,
as many as by this rule will walk,
εἰρήνη ἐπ' αὐτοὺς καὶ ἔλεος, καὶ ἐπὶ τὸν
peace on them and mercy, and on the
Ἰσραὴλ τοῦ θεοῦ.
Israel - of God.
17 Τοῦ λοιποῦ κόπους μοι μηδεὶς
For the rest ²troubles ⁴me ¹no one
παρεχέτω· ἐγὼ γὰρ τὰ στίγματα τοῦ
¹let ²cause; for ³I ⁵the ⁴brands -
Ἰησοῦ ἐν τῷ σώματί μου βαστάζω.
⁶of Jesus ⁸in ⁷the ⁸body ⁹of me ²bear.
18 Ἡ χάρις τοῦ κυρίου ἡμῶν Ἰησοῦ
The grace of the Lord of us Jesus
Χριστοῦ μετὰ τοῦ πνεύματος ὑμῶν,
Christ with the spirit of you,
ἀδελφοί· ἀμήν.
brothers : Amen.

---

to be circumcised that they may boast about your flesh. 14May I never boast except in the cross of our Lord Jesus Christ, through which *a* the world has been crucified to me, and I to the world. 15Neither circumcision nor uncircumcision means anything; what counts is a new creation. 16Peace and mercy to all who follow this rule, even to the Israel of God.

17Finally, let no one cause me trouble, for I bear on my body the marks of Jesus.

18The grace of our Lord Jesus Christ be with your spirit, brothers. Amen.

Ephesians

Chapter 1

The Blessings of Redemption

PAUL, an apostle of Christ Jesus by the will of God, to the saints who are *a*at Ephesus, and *who are* faithful in Christ Jesus: 2Grace to you and peace from God our Father and the Lord Jesus Christ.

3Blessed *be* the God and Father of our Lord Jesus Christ, who has blessed us with every spiritual blessing in the heavenly *places* in Christ, 4just as He chose us in Him before the foundation of the world, that we should be holy and blameless before *b*Him. In love 5He predestined us to

---

ΠΡΟΣ ΕΦΕΣΙΟΥΣ
To Ephesians

1 Παῦλος ἀπόστολος Χριστοῦ Ἰησοῦ διὰ
Paul an apostle of Christ Jesus through
θελήματος θεοῦ τοῖς ἁγίοις τοῖς οὖσιν
[the] will of God to the saints -
[ἐν Ἐφέσῳ] καὶ πιστοῖς ἐν Χριστῷ
in Ephesus and faithful in Christ
Ἰησοῦ· 2 χάρις ὑμῖν καὶ εἰρήνη ἀπὸ
Jesus: Grace to you and peace from
θεοῦ πατρὸς ἡμῶν καὶ κυρίου Ἰησοῦ
God Father of us and Lord Jesus
Χριστοῦ.
Christ.
3 Εὐλογητὸς ὁ θεὸς καὶ πατὴρ τοῦ
Blessed the God and Father of the
κυρίου ἡμῶν Ἰησοῦ Χριστοῦ, ὁ εὐλογήσας
Lord of us Jesus Christ, the having
[one] blessed
ἡμᾶς ἐν πάσῃ εὐλογίᾳ πνευματικῇ ἐν
us with every blessing spiritual in
τοῖς ἐπουρανίοις ἐν Χριστῷ, 4 καθὼς
the heavenlies in Christ, as
ἐξελέξατο ἡμᾶς ἐν αὐτῷ πρὸ καταβολῆς
he chose us in him before [the] foundation
κόσμου, εἶναι ἡμᾶς ἁγίους καὶ ἀμώμους
of [the] world, to be us holy and unblemished*b*
= that we should be ...
κατενώπιον αὐτοῦ, ἐν ἀγάπη 5 προορίσας
before him, in love predestinating

Ephesians

Chapter 1

PAUL, an apostle of Christ Jesus by the will of God,

To the saints in Ephesus, *a* the faithful *b* in Christ Jesus:

2Grace and peace to you from God our Father and the Lord Jesus Christ.

Spiritual Blessings in Christ

3Praise be to the God and Father of our Lord Jesus Christ, who has blessed us in the heavenly realms with every spiritual blessing in Christ. 4For he chose us in him before the creation of the world to be holy and blameless in his sight. In love 5he *c* predestined us to

---

a Some ancient mss. do not contain *at Ephesus*
b Or, *Him, in love.*

---

u 14 Or *whom*

a 1 Some early manuscripts do not have *in Ephesus*.
b 1 Or *believers who are*
c 4,5 Or *sight in love.* 5He

adoption as sons through Jesus Christ to Himself, according to the kind intention of His will,

6to the praise of the glory of His grace, which He freely bestowed on us in the Beloved.

7In Him we have redemption through His blood, the forgiveness of our trespasses, according to the riches of His grace,

8which He lavished upon us. In all wisdom and insight

9He made known to us the mystery of His will, according to His kind intention which He purposed in Him

10with a view to an administration suitable to the fulness of the times, *that is,* the summing up of all things in Christ, things in the heavens and things upon the earth. In Him

11also we have obtained an inheritance, having been predestined according to His purpose who works all things after the counsel of His will,

12to the end that we who were the first to hope in cChrist should be to the praise of His glory.

13In Him, you also, after listening to the message of truth, the gospel of your salvation—having also believed, you were sealed in Him with the Holy Spirit of promise,

14who is given as a pledge of our inheritance, with a view to the redemption of *God's own* possession, to the praise of His glory.

15For this reason I too, having heard of the faith in the Lord Jesus which *exists* among you, and dyour love for all the saints,

---

ἡμᾶς εἰς υἱοθεσίαν διὰ Ἰησοῦ Χριστοῦ
us to adoption of sons through Jesus Christ

εἰς αὐτόν, κατὰ τὴν εὐδοκίαν τοῦ
to him[self], according to the good pleasure of the

θελήματος αὐτοῦ, 6 εἰς ἔπαινον δόξης
will of him, to [the] praise of [the] glory

τῆς χάριτος αὐτοῦ, ἧς ἐχαρίτωσεν ἡμᾶς
of the grace of him, of(with) he favoured us
which

ἐν τῷ ἠγαπημένῳ, 7 ἐν ᾧ ἔχομεν τὴν
in the [one] *having been* loved, in whom we have the

ἀπολύτρωσιν διὰ τοῦ αἵματος αὐτοῦ, τὴν
redemption through the blood of him, the

ἄφεσιν τῶν παραπτωμάτων, κατὰ τὸ
forgiveness – of trespasses, according to the

πλοῦτος τῆς χάριτος αὐτοῦ, 8 ἧς ἐπερίσ-
riches of the grace of him, which he made to

σευσεν εἰς ἡμᾶς ἐν πάσῃ σοφίᾳ καὶ
abound to us in all wisdom and

φρονήσει 9 γνωρίσας ἡμῖν τὸ μυστήριον
intelligence making known to us the mystery

τοῦ θελήματος αὐτοῦ, κατὰ τὴν εὐδοκίαν
of the will of him, according to the good pleasure

αὐτοῦ, ἣν προέθετο ἐν αὐτῷ 10 εἰς
of him, which he purposed in him[self] for

οἰκονομίαν τοῦ πληρώματος τῶν καιρῶν,
a stewardship of the fulness of the times,

ἀνακεφαλαιώσασθαι τὰ πάντα ἐν τῷ
to head up – all things in –

Χριστῷ, τὰ ἐπὶ τοῖς οὐρανοῖς καὶ τὰ
Christ, the things on(in) the heavens and the
things

ἐπὶ τῆς γῆς· ἐν αὐτῷ, 11 ἐν ᾧ καὶ
on the earth; in him, in whom also

ἐκληρώθημεν προορισθέντες κατὰ πρόθεσιν
we were chosen as being predestinated according to [the] purpose
[his] inheritance

τοῦ τὰ πάντα ἐνεργοῦντος κατὰ τὴν
of the – aall things 1operating according to the
[one]

βουλὴν τοῦ θελήματος αὐτοῦ, 12 εἰς τὸ
counsel of the will of him, for *the*

εἶναι ἡμᾶς εἰς ἔπαινον δόξης αὐτοῦ
to be usb to [the] praise of [the] glory of him
=that we should be

τοὺς προηλπικότας ἐν τῷ Χριστῷ· 13 ἐν
the having previously in – Christ; in
[ones] hoped

ᾧ καὶ ὑμεῖς, ἀκούσαντες τὸν λόγον
whom also ye, hearing the word

τῆς ἀληθείας, τὸ εὐαγγέλιον τῆς σωτηρίας
– of truth, the gospel of the salvation

ὑμῶν, ἐν ᾧ καὶ πιστεύσαντες ἐσφραγίσθητε
of you, in whom also believing ye were sealed

τῷ πνεύματι τῆς ἐπαγγελίας τῷ ἁγίῳ,
with 1the 3Spirit – 4of promise – 2holy,

14 ὅς ἐστιν ἀρραβὼν τῆς κληρονομίας
who is an earnest of the inheritance

ἡμῶν, εἰς ἀπολύτρωσιν τῆς περιποιήσεως,
of us, till [the] redemption of the possession,

εἰς ἔπαινον τῆς δόξης αὐτοῦ.
to [the] praise of the glory of him.

15 Διὰ τοῦτο κἀγώ, ἀκούσας τὴν καθ᾽
Therefore I also, hearing the aamong

ὑμᾶς πίστιν ἐν τῷ κυρίῳ Ἰησοῦ καὶ
ayou 1faith in the Lord Jesus and

τὴν ἀγάπην τὴν εἰς πάντας τοὺς ἁγίους,
the love – to all the saints,

---

be adopted as his sons through Jesus Christ, in accordance with his pleasure and will— 6to the praise of his glorious grace, which he has freely given us in the One he loves. 7In him we have redemption through his blood, the forgiveness of sins, in accordance with the riches of God's grace 8that he lavished on us with all wisdom and understanding. 9And hed made known to us the mystery of his will according to his good pleasure, which he purposed in Christ, 10to be put into effect when the times have reached their fulfillment—to bring all things in heaven and on earth together under one head, even Christ.

11In him we were also chosen,e having been predestined according to the plan of him who works out everything in conformity with the purpose of his will, 12in order that we, who were the first to hope in Christ, might be for the praise of his glory. 13And you also were included in Christ when you heard the word of truth, the gospel of your salvation. Having believed, you were marked in him with a seal, the promised Holy Spirit, 14who is a deposit guaranteeing our inheritance until the redemption of those who are God's possession—to the praise of his glory.

Thanksgiving and Prayer

15For this reason, ever since I heard about your faith in the Lord Jesus and your love for all the saints,

---

c I.e., the Messiah
d Many ancient mss. do not contain *your love*

d 8,9 Or *us. With all wisdom and understanding.* 9*he*
e 11 Or *were made heirs*

16do not cease giving thanks for you, while making mention *of you* in my prayers;

17that the God of our Lord Jesus Christ, the Father of glory, may give to you a spirit of wisdom and of revelation in the knowledge of Him.

18*I pray that* the eyes of your heart may be enlightened, so that you may know what is the hope of His calling, what are the riches of the glory of His inheritance in the saints,

19and what is the surpassing greatness of His power toward us who believe. *These are* in accordance with the working of the strength of His might

20which He brought about in Christ, when He raised Him from the dead, and seated Him at His right hand in the heavenly *places*,

21far above all rule and authority and power and dominion, and every name that is named, not only in this age, but also in the one to come.

22And He put all things in subjection under His feet, and gave Him as head over all things to the church,

23which is His body, the fulness of Him who fills all in all.

---

16 οὐ παύομαι εὐχαριστῶν ὑπὲρ ὑμῶν
do not cease giving thanks on behalf of you

μνείαν ποιούμενος ἐπὶ τῶν προσευχῶν
mention making on(in) the prayers

μου, 17 ἵνα ὁ θεὸς τοῦ κυρίου ἡμῶν
of me, in order that the God of the Lord of us

Ἰησοῦ Χριστοῦ, ὁ πατὴρ τῆς δόξης,
Jesus Christ, the Father - of glory,

δῴη ὑμῖν πνεῦμα σοφίας καὶ ἀποκαλύψεως
may give to you a spirit of wisdom and of revelation

ἐν ἐπιγνώσει αὐτοῦ, 18 πεφωτισμένους τοὺς
in a full knowledge of him, having been enlightened the

ὀφθαλμοὺς τῆς καρδίας [ὑμῶν,] εἰς τὸ
eyes of the heart of you, for the

εἰδέναι ὑμᾶς τίς ἐστιν ἡ ἐλπὶς τῆς
to know youᵇ what is the hope of the
=that ye should know

κλήσεως αὐτοῦ, τίς ὁ πλοῦτος τῆς δόξης
calling of him, what the riches of the glory

τῆς κληρονομίας αὐτοῦ ἐν τοῖς ἁγίοις,
of the inheritance of him in the saints,

19 καὶ τί τὸ ὑπερβάλλον μέγεθος τῆς
and what the excelling greatness of the

δυνάμεως αὐτοῦ εἰς ἡμᾶς τοὺς πιστεύοντας
power of him toward us· the [ones] believing

κατὰ τὴν ἐνέργειαν τοῦ κράτους τῆς
according to the operation of the might of the

ἰσχύος αὐτοῦ, 20 ἣν ἐνήργηκεν ἐν τῷ
strength of him, which he has operated in -

Χριστῷ ἐγείρας αὐτὸν ἐκ νεκρῶν, καὶ
Christ raising him from [the] dead, and

καθίσας ἐν δεξιᾷ αὐτοῦ ἐν τοῖς ἐπου-
seating [him] at [the] right [hand] of him in the heaven-

ρανίοις 21 ὑπεράνω πάσης ἀρχῆς καὶ
lies far above all rule and

ἐξουσίας καὶ δυνάμεως καὶ κυριότητος
authority and power and lordship

καὶ παντὸς ὀνόματος ὀνομαζομένου οὐ
and every name being named not

μόνον ἐν τῷ αἰῶνι τούτῳ ἀλλὰ καὶ
only in this age but also

ἐν τῷ μέλλοντι· 22 καὶ πάντα ὑπέταξεν
in the coming; and all things subjected

ὑπὸ τοὺς πόδας αὐτοῦ, καὶ αὐτὸν ἔδωκεν
under the feet of him, and ˢhim ¹gave

κεφαλὴν ὑπὲρ πάντα τῇ ἐκκλησίᾳ, 23 ἥτις
[to be] head over all things to the church, which

ἐστὶν τὸ σῶμα αὐτοῦ, τὸ πλήρωμα
is the body of him, the fulness

τοῦ τὰ πάντα ἐν πᾶσιν πληρουμένου.
of the - ²all things ³with ⁴all things ¹filling.
[one]

16I have not stopped giving thanks for you, remembering you in my prayers. 17I keep asking that the God of our Lord Jesus Christ, the glorious Father, may give you the Spirit/ of wisdom and revelation, so that you may know him better. 18I pray also that the eyes of your heart may be enlightened in order that you may know the hope to which he has called you, the riches of his glorious inheritance in the saints, 19and his incomparably great power for us who believe. That power is like the working of his mighty strength, 20which he exerted in Christ when he raised him from the dead and seated him at his right hand in the heavenly realms, 21far above all rule and authority, power and dominion, and every title that can be given, not only in the present age but also in the one to come. 22And God placed all things under his feet and appointed him to be head over everything for the church, 23which is his body, the fullness of him who fills everything in every way.

Chapter 2

Made Alive in Christ

AND you were dead in your trespasses and sins,

2in which you formerly walked according to the course of this world, according to the prince of the power of the air, of the spirit that is now working in the sons of disobedience.

3Among them we too all

Chapter 2

2 Καὶ ὑμᾶς ὄντας νεκροὺς τοῖς παραπτώ-
And you being dead in the tres-

μασιν καὶ ταῖς ἁμαρτίαις ὑμῶν, 2 ἐν
passes and in the sins of you, in

αἷς ποτε περιεπατήσατε κατὰ τὸν αἰῶνα
which then ye walked according to the age

τοῦ κόσμου τούτου, κατὰ τὸν ἄρχοντα
of this world, according to the ruler

τῆς ἐξουσίας τοῦ ἀέρος, τοῦ πνεύματος
of the authority of the air, of the spirit

τοῦ νῦν ἐνεργοῦντος ἐν τοῖς υἱοῖς τῆς
- now operating in the sons -

ἀπειθείας· 3 ἐν οἷς καὶ ἡμεῖς πάντες
of disobedience; among whom also we all

Chapter 2

Made Alive in Christ

AS for you, you were dead in your transgressions and sins, 2in which you used to live when you followed the ways of this world and of the ruler of the kingdom of the air, the spirit who is now at work in those who are disobedient. 3All of us

/17 Or a spirit

formerly lived in the lusts of our flesh, indulging the desires of the flesh and of the mind, and were by nature children of wrath, even as the rest.

4But God, being rich in mercy, because of His great love with which He loved us,

5even when we were dead in our transgressions, made us alive together *with Christ (by grace you have been saved),

6and raised us up with Him, and seated us with Him in the heavenly *places*, in Christ Jesus,

7in order that in the ages to come He might show the surpassing riches of His grace in kindness toward us in Christ Jesus.

8For by grace you have been saved through faith; and that not of yourselves, *it is* the gift of God;

9not as a result of works, that no one should boast.

10For we are His workmanship, created in Christ Jesus for good works, which God prepared beforehand, that we should walk in them.

11Therefore remember, that formerly you, the Gentiles in the flesh, who are called "Uncircumcision" by the so-called "Circumcision," *which is* performed in the flesh by human hands—

12*remember* that you were at that time separate from Christ, excluded from the commonwealth of Israel, and strangers to the covenants of promise, having no hope and without God in the world.

13But now in Christ Jesus you who formerly were far off have been brought near

---

ἀνεστράφημέν ποτε ἐν ταῖς ἐπιθυμίαις
conducted ourselves then in the lusts

τῆς σαρκὸς ἡμῶν, ποιοῦντες τὰ θελήματα
of the flesh of us, doing the wishes

τῆς σαρκὸς καὶ τῶν διανοιῶν, καὶ
of the flesh and of the understandings, and

ἤμεθα τέκνα φύσει ὀργῆς ὡς καὶ οἱ
were ²children ¹by nature of wrath as also the

λοιποί· 4 ὁ δὲ θεὸς πλούσιος ὢν ἐν
rest; - but God ¹rich ¹being in

ἐλέει, διὰ τὴν πολλὴν ἀγάπην αὐτοῦ
mercy, because of the much love of his

ἣν ἠγάπησεν ἡμᾶς, 5 καὶ ὄντας ἡμᾶς
[with] he loved us, even being us
which   =when we were

νεκροὺς τοῖς παραπτώμασιν συνεζωοποίησεν
dead - in trespasses quickened [us] with

τῷ Χριστῷ, — χάριτί ἐστε σεσωσμένοι,
- Christ, (by grace ye are *having been* saved,)

— 6 καὶ συνήγειρεν καὶ συνεκάθισεν ἐν
and raised [us] with and seated [us] with in

τοῖς ἐπουρανίοις ἐν Χριστῷ Ἰησοῦ, 7 ἵνα
the heavenlies in Christ Jesus, in order that

ἐνδείξηται ἐν τοῖς αἰῶσιν τοῖς ἐπερχομένοις
he might show in the ages - coming on
   forth

τὸ ὑπερβάλλον πλοῦτος τῆς χάριτος αὐτοῦ
the excelling riches of the grace of him

ἐν χρηστότητι ἐφ᾽ ἡμᾶς ἐν Χριστῷ
in kindness toward us in Christ

Ἰησοῦ. 8 τῇ γὰρ χάριτί ἐστε σεσωσμένοι
Jesus. - For by grace ye are *having been* saved

διὰ πίστεως· καὶ τοῦτο οὐκ ἐξ ὑμῶν,
through faith; and this not of you,

θεοῦ τὸ δῶρον· 9 οὐκ ἐξ ἔργων, ἵνα μή
of [is] the gift; not of works, lest
God

τις καυχήσηται. 10 αὐτοῦ γάρ ἐσμεν
anyone should boast. For of him we are

ποίημα, κτισθέντες ἐν Χριστῷ Ἰησοῦ
a product, created in Christ Jesus

ἐπὶ ἔργοις ἀγαθοῖς, οἷς προητοίμασεν
unto works good, which ¹previously prepared

ὁ θεὸς ἵνα ἐν αὐτοῖς περιπατήσωμεν.
- ¹God in order that in them we might walk.

11 Διὸ μνημονεύετε ὅτι ποτὲ ὑμεῖς τὰ
Wherefore remember ye that when ye the

ἔθνη ἐν σαρκί, οἱ λεγόμενοι ἀκροβυστία
nations in [the] flesh, the [ones] *being* called uncircumcision

ὑπὸ τῆς λεγομένης περιτομῆς ἐν σαρκὶ
by the *being* called circumcision in [the] flesh

χειροποιήτου, 12 ὅτι ἦτε τῷ καιρῷ ἐκείνῳ
made by hand, that ye were at that time

χωρὶς Χριστοῦ, ἀπηλλοτριωμένοι τῆς
without Christ, having been alienated from the

πολιτείας τοῦ Ἰσραὴλ καὶ ξένοι τῶν
commonwealth - of Israel and strangers of(from)
   the

διαθηκῶν τῆς ἐπαγγελίας, ἐλπίδα μὴ
covenants - of promise, hope not

ἔχοντες καὶ ἄθεοι ἐν τῷ κόσμῳ. 13 νυνὶ
having and godless in the world. now

δὲ ἐν Χριστῷ Ἰησοῦ ὑμεῖς οἵ ποτε
But in Christ Jesus ye the [ones] then

ὄντες μακρὰν ἐγενήθητε ἐγγὺς ἐν τῷ
being afar became near by the

---

also lived among them at one time, gratifying the cravings of our sinful nature*g* and following its desires and thoughts. Like the rest, we were by nature objects of wrath. 4But because of his great love for us, God, who is rich in mercy, 5made us alive with Christ even when we were dead in transgressions—it is by grace you have been saved. 6And God raised us up with Christ and seated us with him in the heavenly realms in Christ Jesus, 7in order that in the coming ages he might show the incomparable riches of his grace, expressed in his kindness to us in Christ Jesus. 8For it is by grace you have been saved, through faith—and this not from yourselves, it is the gift of God— 9not by works, so that no one can boast. 10For we are God's workmanship, created in Christ Jesus to do good works, which God prepared in advance for us to do.

One in Christ

11Therefore, remember that formerly you who are Gentiles by birth and called "uncircumcised" by those who call themselves "the circumcision" (that done in the body by the hands of men)— 12remember that at that time you were separate from Christ, excluded from citizenship in Israel and foreigners to the covenants of the promise, without hope and without God in the world. 13But now in Christ Jesus you who once were far away have been

---

by the blood of Christ.

14For He Himself is our peace, who made both *groups into* one, and broke down the barrier of the dividing wall,

15by abolishing in His flesh the enmity, *which is* the Law of commandments *contained* in ordinances, that in Himself He might make the two into one new man, *thus* establishing peace,

16and might reconcile them both in one body to God through the cross, by it having put to death the enmity.

17AND HE CAME AND PREACHED PEACE TO YOU WHO WERE FAR AWAY, AND PEACE TO THOSE WHO WERE NEAR;

18for through Him we both have our access in one Spirit to the Father.

19So then you are no longer strangers and aliens, but you are fellow citizens with the saints, and are of God's household,

20having been built upon the foundation of the apostles and prophets, Christ Jesus Himself being the corner *stone*,

21in whom the whole building, being fitted together is growing into a holy temple in the Lord;

22in whom you also are being built together into a dwelling of God in the Spirit.

Chapter 3

Paul's Stewardship

FOR this reason I, Paul, the prisoner of Christ Jesus for the sake of you Gentiles—

2if indeed you have heard of the stewardship of God's grace which was given to me for you;

3that by revelation there was made known to me the mystery, as I wrote before in brief.

4And by referring to this, when you read you can understand my insight into the mystery of Christ,

Middle column (Greek interlinear)

αἵματι τοῦ Χριστοῦ. 14 Αὐτὸς γάρ
blood   of Christ.   For he

ἐστιν ἡ εἰρήνη ἡμῶν, ὁ ποιήσας τὰ
is   the peace of us, the [one] having made -

ἀμφότερα ἓν καὶ τὸ μεσότοιχον τοῦ
both   one and ¹the ³middle wall   -

φραγμοῦ λύσας, τὴν ἔχθραν, ἐν τῇ σαρκὶ
⁴of partition ¹having the enmity, ²in ³the ⁴flesh
       broken,

αὐτοῦ 15 τὸν νόμον τῶν ἐντολῶν ἐν
⁵of him   ⁶the ⁷law ⁸of the ⁹commandments ¹⁰in

δόγμασιν καταργήσας, ἵνα τοὺς δύο κτίσῃ
¹¹decrees ¹having abolished, in order ⁴the ⁵two ⁶he might
              that   create

ἐν αὐτῷ εἰς ἕνα καινὸν ἄνθρωπον ποιῶν
⁸in ⁷him[self] ⁸into ⁹one ¹⁰new ¹¹man ¹making

εἰρήνην, 16 καὶ ἀποκαταλλάξῃ τοὺς
²peace,   and   might reconcile

ἀμφοτέρους ἐν ἑνὶ σώματι τῷ θεῷ διὰ
both   in one body - to God through

τοῦ σταυροῦ, ἀποκτείνας τὴν ἔχθραν ἐν
the cross,   killing   the enmity in

αὐτῷ· 17 καὶ ἐλθὼν εὐηγγελίσατο εἰρήνην
him[self]; and coming   preached   peace

ὑμῖν τοῖς μακρὰν καὶ εἰρήνην τοῖς ἐγγύς·
to you the ones afar and peace to the ones near;

18 ὅτι δι' αὐτοῦ ἔχομεν τὴν προσαγωγὴν
because through him ¹we ²have   ⁴access

οἱ ἀμφότεροι ἐν ἑνὶ πνεύματι πρὸς τὸν
- ³both   by one   Spirit   unto the

πατέρα. 19 ἄρα οὖν οὐκέτι ἐστὲ ξένοι
Father.   Then therefore no more are ye strangers

καὶ πάροικοι, ἀλλὰ ἐστὲ συμπολῖται τῶν
and sojourners, but ye are fellow-citizens of the

ἁγίων καὶ οἰκεῖοι τοῦ θεοῦ, 20 ἐποικοδομη-
saints and members of - of God,   having been
       the family

θέντες ἐπὶ τῷ θεμελίῳ τῶν ἀποστόλων
built *on* on the foundation of the apostles

καὶ προφητῶν, ὄντος ἀκρογωνιαίου αὐτοῦ
and prophets, ⁴being ⁵cornerstone ²[him]self

Χριστοῦ Ἰησοῦ, 21 ἐν ᾧ πᾶσα οἰκοδομὴ
¹Christ ²Jesus,ᵃ   in whom all [the] building

συναρμολογουμένη αὔξει εἰς ναὸν ἅγιον
being fitted together grows into shrine a holy

ἐν κυρίῳ, 22 ἐν ᾧ καὶ ὑμεῖς συνοικοδομεῖσθε
in [the] Lord, in whom also ye are being built together

εἰς κατοικητήριον τοῦ θεοῦ ἐν πνεύματι.
into a dwelling-place - of God in spirit.

3 Τούτου χάριν ἐγὼ Παῦλος ὁ δέσμιος
²of this ¹By reason of I   Paul   the prisoner

τοῦ Χριστοῦ Ἰησοῦ ὑπὲρ ὑμῶν τῶν
- of Christ Jesus on behalf of you the

ἐθνῶν 2 — εἴ γε ἠκούσατε τὴν οἰκονομίαν
nations — if indeed ye heard the stewardship

τῆς χάριτος τοῦ θεοῦ τῆς δοθείσης μοι
of the grace   - of God - given to me

εἰς ὑμᾶς, 3 ὅτι κατὰ ἀποκάλυψιν ἐγνωρίσθη
for you,   that by way of revelation was made known

μοι τὸ μυστήριον, καθὼς προέγραψα ἐν
to me the mystery, as I previously wrote in

ὀλίγῳ, 4 πρὸς ὃ δύνασθε ἀναγινώσκοντες
brief,   as to which ³ye can   ¹reading

νοῆσαι τὴν σύνεσίν μου ἐν τῷ μυστηρίῳ
to realize the understanding of me in the mystery

brought near through the blood of Christ.

14For he himself is our peace, who has made the two one and has destroyed the barrier, the dividing wall of hostility, 15by abolishing in his flesh the law with its commandments and regulations. His purpose was to create in himself one new man out of the two, thus making peace, 16and in this one body to reconcile both of them to God through the cross, by which he put to death their hostility. 17He came and preached peace to you who were far away and peace to those who were near. 18For through him we both have access to the Father by one Spirit.

19Consequently, you are no longer foreigners and aliens, but fellow citizens with God's people and members of God's household, 20built on the foundation of the apostles and prophets, with Christ Jesus himself as the chief cornerstone. 21In him the whole building is joined together and rises to become a holy temple in the Lord. 22And in him you too are being built together to become a dwelling in which God lives by his Spirit.

Chapter 3

Paul the Preacher to the Gentiles

FOR this reason I, Paul, the prisoner of Christ Jesus for the sake of you Gentiles—

2Surely you have heard about the administration of God's grace that was given to me for you, 3that is, the mystery made known to me by revelation, as I have already written briefly. 4In reading this, then, you will be able to understand my insight into the mystery of

5which in other generations was not made known to the sons of men, as it has now been revealed to His holy apostles and prophets in the Spirit;

6to be specific, that the Gentiles are fellow heirs and fellow members of the body, and fellow partakers of the promise in Christ Jesus through the gospel,

7of which I was made a minister, according to the gift of God's grace which was given to me according to the working of His power.

8To me, the very least of all saints, this grace was given, to preach to the Gentiles the unfathomable riches of Christ,

9and to bring to light what is the administration of the mystery which for ages has been hidden in God, who created all things,

10in order that the manifold wisdom of God might now be made known through the church to the rulers and the authorities in the heavenly places.

11This was in accordance with the eternal purpose which He carried out in Christ Jesus our Lord,

12in whom we have boldness and confident access through faith in Him.

13Therefore I ask you not to lose heart at my tribulations on your behalf, for they are your glory.

14For this reason, I bow my knees before the Father,

15from whom every family in heaven and on earth derives its name,

16that He would grant you, according to the riches of His glory, to be strengthened with power

---

τοῦ Χριστοῦ, **5** ὃ ἑτέραις γενεαῖς οὐκ
- of Christ, which in other generations not

ἐγνωρίσθη τοῖς υἱοῖς τῶν ἀνθρώπων ὡς
was made known to the sons - of men as

νῦν ἀπεκαλύφθη τοῖς ἁγίοις ἀποστόλοις
now it was revealed to the holy apostles

αὐτοῦ καὶ προφήταις ἐν πνεύματι, **6** εἶναι
of him and prophets in spirit, ³to be

τὰ ἔθνη συγκληρονόμα καὶ σύσσωμα καὶ
¹the ²nations joint-heirs and a joint-body and

συμμέτοχα τῆς ἐπαγγελίας ἐν Χριστῷ
joint-sharers of the promise in Christ

Ἰησοῦ διὰ τοῦ εὐαγγελίου, **7** οὗ ἐγενήθην
Jesus through the gospel, of which I became

διάκονος κατὰ τὴν δωρεὰν τῆς χάριτος
a minister according to the gift of the grace

τοῦ θεοῦ τῆς δοθείσης μοι κατὰ τὴν
- of God - given to me according to the

ἐνέργειαν τῆς δυνάμεως αὐτοῦ. **8** ἐμοὶ
operation of the power of him. To me

τῷ ἐλαχιστοτέρῳ πάντων ἁγίων ἐδόθη
the leaster* of all saints was given

ἡ χάρις αὕτη, τοῖς ἔθνεσιν εὐαγγελίσασθαι
this grace, to the nations to preach

τὸ ἀνεξιχνίαστον πλοῦτος τοῦ Χριστοῦ,
the unsearchable riches - of Christ,

9 καὶ φωτίσαι τίς ἡ οἰκονομία τοῦ
and to bring to light what [is] the stewardship of the

μυστηρίου τοῦ ἀποκεκρυμμένου ἀπὸ τῶν
mystery - having been hidden from the

αἰώνων ἐν τῷ θεῷ τῷ τὰ πάντα κτίσαντι,
ages in - God ¹the ²all things ²having created,
[one]

10 ἵνα γνωρισθῇ νῦν ταῖς ἀρχαῖς καὶ
in order might be made now to the rulers and
that known

ταῖς ἐξουσίαις ἐν τοῖς ἐπουρανίοις διὰ
to the authorities in the heavenlies through

τῆς ἐκκλησίας ἡ πολυποίκιλος σοφία τοῦ
the church the manifold wisdom of

θεοῦ, **11** κατὰ πρόθεσιν τῶν αἰώνων ἣν
of God, according to [the] purpose of the ages which

ἐποίησεν ἐν τῷ Χριστῷ Ἰησοῦ τῷ κυρίῳ
he made in - Christ Jesus the Lord

ἡμῶν, **12** ἐν ᾧ ἔχομεν τὴν παρρησίαν
of us, in whom we have boldness

καὶ προσαγωγὴν ἐν πεποιθήσει διὰ τῆς
and ·access in confidence through the

πίστεως αὐτοῦ. **13** διὸ αἰτοῦμαι μὴ
faith of(in) him.* Wherefore I ask [you] not

ἐγκακεῖν ἐν ταῖς θλίψεσίν μου ὑπὲρ
to faint in the afflictions of me on behalf

ὑμῶν, ἥτις ἐστὶν δόξα ὑμῶν. **14** Τούτου
of you, which is glory of you. ²of this

χάριν κάμπτω τὰ γόνατά μου πρὸς
¹By reason of I bend the knees of me unto

τὸν πατέρα, **15** ἐξ οὗ πᾶσα πατριὰ
the Father, of whom every fatherhood

ἐν οὐρανοῖς καὶ ἐπὶ γῆς ὀνομάζεται,
in heavens and on earth is named,

16 ἵνα δῷ ὑμῖν κατὰ τὸ πλοῦτος τῆς
in order he may you according to the riches of the
that give

δόξης αὐτοῦ δυνάμει κραταιωθῆναι διὰ
glory of him by power to become mighty through

* This is quite literal!—the apostle coins a word.

* See Gal. 2. 16.

Christ, 5which was not made known to men in other generations as it has now been revealed by the Spirit to God's holy apostles and prophets. 6This mystery is that through the gospel the Gentiles are heirs together with Israel, members together of one body, and sharers together in the promise in Christ Jesus.

7I became a servant of this gospel by the gift of God's grace given me through the working of his power. 8Although I am less than the least of all God's people, this grace was given me: to preach to the Gentiles the unsearchable riches of Christ, 9and to make plain to everyone the administration of this mystery, which for ages past was kept hidden in God, who created all things. 10His intent was that now, through the church, the manifold wisdom of God should be made known to the rulers and authorities in the heavenly realms, 11according to his eternal purpose which he accomplished in Christ Jesus our Lord. 12In him and through faith in him we may approach God with freedom and confidence. 13I ask you, therefore, not to be discouraged because of my sufferings for you, which are your glory.

A Prayer for the Ephesians

14For this reason I kneel before the Father, 15from whom his whole family ʰ in heaven and on earth derives its name. 16I pray that out of his glorious riches he may strengthen you with

ʰ15 Or *whom all fatherhood*

through His Spirit in the inner man;

17so that Christ may dwell in your hearts through faith; *and* that you, being rooted and grounded in love,

18may be able to comprehend with all the saints what is the breadth and length and height and depth,

19and to know the love of Christ which surpasses knowledge, that you may be filled up to all the fulness of God.

20Now to Him who is able to do exceeding abundantly beyond all that we ask or think, according to the power that works within us,

21to Him *be* the glory in the church and in Christ Jesus to all generations forever and ever. Amen.

τοῦ πνεύματος αὐτοῦ εἰς τὸν ἔσω ἄνθρω-
the   Spirit   of him   in   the   inward   man,

πον, 17 κατοικῆσαι τὸν Χριστὸν διὰ τῆς
to dwell - Christ[b] through -
=that Christ may dwell

πίστεως ἐν ταῖς καρδίαις ὑμῶν, ἐν
faith   in   the   hearts   of you,   in

ἀγάπῃ ἐρριζωμένοι καὶ τεθεμελιωμένοι,
love   *having been* rooted   and   *having been* founded,

18 ἵνα ἐξισχύσητε καταλαβέσθαι σὺν πᾶσιν
in order ye may have strength to apprehend   with   all
that

τοῖς ἁγίοις τί τὸ πλάτος καὶ μῆκος
the   saints   what [is] the   breadth   and   length

καὶ ὕψος καὶ βάθος, 19 γνῶναί τε τὴν
and   height   and   depth,   and to know   [1]the

ὑπερβάλλουσαν τῆς γνώσεως ἀγάπην τοῦ
[2]excelling   [3]knowledge   [2]love   -

Χριστοῦ, ἵνα πληρωθῆτε εἰς πᾶν τὸ
[3]of Christ, *in order* that ye may be filled   to   all   the

πλήρωμα τοῦ θεοῦ.
fulness   -   of God.

20 Τῷ δὲ δυναμένῳ ὑπὲρ πάντα ποιῆσαι
Now to the [one] being able   beyond   all things   to do

ὑπερεκπερισσοῦ ὧν αἰτούμεθα ἢ νοοῦμεν
superabundantly   *of* which   we ask   or   we think

κατὰ τὴν δύναμιν τὴν ἐνεργουμένην ἐν
according to the   power   -   operating   in

ἡμῖν, 21 αὐτῷ ἡ δόξα ἐν τῇ ἐκκλησίᾳ
us,   to him [be] the   glory   in   the   church

καὶ ἐν Χριστῷ Ἰησοῦ εἰς πάσας τὰς
and   in   Christ   Jesus   unto   all   the

γενεὰς τοῦ αἰῶνος τῶν αἰώνων· ἀμήν.
generations of the   age   of the   ages: Amen.

4 Παρακαλῶ οὖν ὑμᾶς ἐγὼ ὁ δέσμιος
[1]beseech [4]therefore [3]you [2]I [5]the [6]prisoner

ἐν κυρίῳ ἀξίως περιπατῆσαι τῆς κλήσεως
[8]in [9][the] Lord [10]worthily [7]to walk   of the   calling

ἧς ἐκλήθητε, 2 μετὰ πάσης ταπεινοφροσύνης
of(with) ye were   with   all   humility
which   called,

καὶ πραΰτητος, μετὰ μακροθυμίας,
and   meekness,   with   longsuffering,

ἀνεχόμενοι ἀλλήλων ἐν ἀγάπῃ, 3 σπου-
forbearing   one another   in   love,   being

δάζοντες τηρεῖν τὴν ἑνότητα τοῦ πνεύματος
eager   to keep   the   unity   of the   Spirit

ἐν τῷ συνδέσμῳ τῆς εἰρήνης· ἓν σῶμα
in   the   bond   of peace; [there is] one body

καὶ ἓν πνεῦμα, 4 καθὼς καὶ ἐκλήθητε
and   one   Spirit,   as   also   ye were called

ἐν μιᾷ ἐλπίδι τῆς κλήσεως ὑμῶν· 5 εἷς
in   one   hope   of the   calling   of you;   one

κύριος, μία πίστις, ἓν βάπτισμα, 6 εἷς
Lord,   one   faith,   one   baptism;   one

θεὸς καὶ πατὴρ πάντων, ὁ ἐπὶ πάντων
God   and   Father   of all,   the [one] over   all

καὶ διὰ πάντων καὶ ἐν πᾶσιν. 7 Ἑνὶ
and   through   all   and   in   all.   [2]to [4]one

δὲ ἑκάστῳ ἡμῶν ἐδόθη ἡ χάρις κατὰ
[1]But [3]each   of us   was given   -   grace according to

τὸ μέτρον τῆς δωρεᾶς τοῦ Χριστοῦ.
the   measure   of the   gift   -   of Christ.

8 διὸ λέγει· ἀναβὰς εἰς ὕψος ᾐχμαλώτευσεν
Where- he says: Having   to   height   he led captive
fore   ascended

---

power through his Spirit in your inner being, 17so that Christ may dwell in your hearts through faith. And I pray that you, being rooted and established in love, 18may have power, together with all the saints, to grasp how wide and long and high and deep is the love of Christ, 19and to know this love that surpasses knowledge—that you may be filled to the measure of all the fullness of God.

20Now to him who is able to do immeasurably more than all we ask or imagine, according to his power that is at work within us, 21to him be glory in the church and in Christ Jesus throughout all generations, for ever and ever! Amen.

Chapter 4

Unity of the Spirit

I, THEREFORE, the prisoner of the Lord, entreat you to walk in a manner worthy of the calling with which you have been called,

2with all humility and gentleness, with patience, showing forbearance to one another in love,

3being diligent to preserve the unity of the Spirit in the bond of peace.

4*There is* one body and one Spirit, just as also you were called in one hope of your calling;

5one Lord, one faith, one baptism,

6one God and Father of all who is over all and through all and in all.

7But to each one of us grace was given according to the measure of Christ's gift.

8 Therefore it says,
"WHEN HE ASCENDED
ON HIGH,
HE LED CAPTIVE A HOST

Chapter 4

Unity in the Body of Christ

AS a prisoner for the Lord, then, I urge you to live a life worthy of the calling you have received. 2Be completely humble and gentle; be patient, bearing with one another in love. 3Make every effort to keep the unity of the Spirit through the bond of peace. 4There is one body and one Spirit—just as you were called to one hope when you were called— 5one Lord, one faith, one baptism; 6one God and Father of all, who is over all and through all and in all.

7But to each one of us grace has been given as Christ apportioned it. 8This is why it[^i] says:

"When he ascended on high,
he led captives in his

[^i]8 Or *God*

OF CAPTIVES,
AND HE GAVE GIFTS TO
MEN.''

9(Now this *expression,* ''He ascended,'' what does it mean except that He also had descended into the lower parts of the earth?

10He who descended is Himself also He who ascended far above all the heavens, that He might fill all things.)

11And He gave some *as* apostles, and some *as* prophets, and some *as* evangelists, and some *as* pastors and teachers,

12for the equipping of the saints for the work of service, to the building up of the body of Christ;

13until we all attain to the unity of the faith, and of the knowledge of the Son of God, to a mature man, to the measure of the stature which belongs to the fulness of Christ.

14As a result, we are no longer to be children, tossed here and there by waves, and carried about by every wind of doctrine, by the trickery of men, by craftiness in deceitful scheming;

15but speaking the truth in love, we are to grow up in all *aspects* into Him, who is the head, *even* Christ,

16from whom the whole body, being fitted and held together by that which every joint supplies, according to the proper working of each individual part, causes the growth of the body for the building up of itself in love.

The Christian's Walk

17This I say therefore, and affirm together with the Lord, that you walk no longer just as the Gentiles also walk, in the futility of their mind,

18being darkened in their

αἰχμαλωσίαν, ἔδωκεν δόματα τοῖς ἀνθρώποις.
captivity,　he gave　gifts　-　to men.

9 τὸ δὲ ἀνέβη τί ἐστιν εἰ μὴ ὅτι καὶ
Now the　"he　what　is it　except　that also
ascended"

κατέβη εἰς τὰ κατώτερα μέρη τῆς γῆς;
he descended into the　lower　parts of the earth?

10 ὁ καταβὰς αὐτός ἐστιν καὶ ὁ ἀναβὰς
The descending himself　is　also the ascending
[one]　　　　　　　　　　　　　　　　[one]

ὑπεράνω πάντων τῶν οὐρανῶν, ἵνα
far above　all　the　heavens, in order that

πληρώσῃ τὰ πάντα. **11** καὶ αὐτὸς ἔδωκεν
he might fill -　all things.　And　he　gave

τοὺς μὲν ἀποστόλους, τοὺς δὲ προφήτας,
some†　apostles,　some†　prophets,

τοὺς δὲ εὐαγγελιστάς, τοὺς δὲ ποιμένας
some†　evangelists,　some†　shepherds

καὶ διδασκάλους, **12** πρὸς τὸν καταρτισμὸν
and　teachers,　for　the　perfecting

τῶν ἁγίων εἰς ἔργον διακονίας, εἰς
of the saints to [the] work of ministry,　to

οἰκοδομὴν τοῦ σώματος τοῦ Χριστοῦ,
building　of the　body　-　of Christ,

13 μέχρι καταντήσωμεν οἱ πάντες εἰς
until　¹we ²arrive　-　²all　at

τὴν ἑνότητα τῆς πίστεως καὶ τῆς ἐπιγνώ-
the　unity of the　faith　and of the full know-

σεως τοῦ υἱοῦ τοῦ θεοῦ, εἰς ἄνδρα τέλειον,
ledge of the Son　-　of God, at ¹man ¹a complete,

εἰς μέτρον ἡλικίας τοῦ πληρώματος τοῦ
at [the] measure of [the] of the　fulness　-
stature

Χριστοῦ, **14** ἵνα μηκέτι ὦμεν νήπιοι,
of Christ,　in order that no more　we may be　infants,

κλυδωνιζόμενοι καὶ περιφερόμενοι παντὶ ἀνέμῳ
being blown　and *being* carried round by every　wind

τῆς διδασκαλίας ἐν τῇ κυβείᾳ τῶν ἀνθρώ-
-　of teaching　in the　sleight　-　of

πων, ἐν πανουργίᾳ πρὸς τὴν μεθοδείαν
men,　in　cleverness　unto　the　craftiness

τῆς πλάνης, **15** ἀληθεύοντες δὲ ἐν ἀγάπῃ
-　of error,　but speaking truth　in　love

αὐξήσωμεν εἰς αὐτὸν τὰ πάντα, ὅς ἐστιν
we may grow　into　him　in all respects,†　who　is

ἡ κεφαλή, Χριστός, **16** ἐξ οὗ πᾶν τὸ
the　head,　Christ,　of whom all　the

σῶμα συναρμολογούμενον καὶ συμβιβαζόμενον
body　being fitted together　and *being* brought together

διὰ πάσης ἁφῆς τῆς ἐπιχορηγίας κατ'
through every　band　-　of supply　according
to

ἐνέργειαν ἐν μέτρῳ ἑνὸς ἑκάστου μέρους
[the] operation in　measure of ²one ¹each　part

τὴν αὔξησιν τοῦ σώματος ποιεῖται εἰς
³the　²growth　⁴of the　⁵body　¹makes　for

οἰκοδομὴν ἑαυτοῦ ἐν ἀγάπῃ.
building　of itself　in　love.

17 Τοῦτο οὖν λέγω καὶ μαρτύρομαι ἐν
This therefore I say　and　witness　in

κυρίῳ, μηκέτι ὑμᾶς περιπατεῖν καθὼς
[the] Lord,　no more　you　to walk　as

καὶ τὰ ἔθνη περιπατεῖ ἐν ματαιότητι
also　the　nations　walks　in　vanity

τοῦ νοὸς αὐτῶν, **18** ἐσκοτωμένοι τῇ
of the mind　of them,　⁴*having been* darkened ⁵in the
(their)

---

train
and gave gifts to
men.''ʲ

9(What does ''he ascended'' mean except that he also descended to the lower, earthly regionsᵏ? 10He who descended is the very one who ascended higher than all the heavens, in order to fill the whole universe.) 11It was he who gave some to be apostles, some to be prophets, some to be evangelists, and some to be pastors and teachers, 12to prepare God's people for works of service, so that the body of Christ may be built up 13until we all reach unity in the faith and in the knowledge of the Son of God and become mature, attaining to the whole measure of the fullness of Christ.

14Then we will no longer be infants, tossed back and forth by the waves, and blown here and there by every wind of teaching and by the cunning and craftiness of men in their deceitful scheming. 15Instead, speaking the truth in love, we will in all things grow up into him who is the Head, that is, Christ. 16From him the whole body, joined and held together by every supporting ligament, grows and builds itself up in love, as each part does its work.

Living as Children of Light

17So I tell you this, and insist on it in the Lord, that you must no longer live as the Gentiles do, in the futility of their thinking. 18They are darkened in their un-

---

understanding, excluded from the life of God, because of the ignorance that is in them, because of the hardness of their heart;
19and they, having become callous, have given themselves over to sensuality, for the practice of every kind of impurity with greediness.
20But you did not learn Christ this way,
21if indeed you have heard Him and have been taught in Him, just as truth is in Jesus,
22that, in reference to your former manner of life, you lay aside the old self, which is being corrupted in accordance with the lusts of deceit,
23and that you be renewed in the spirit of your mind,
24and put on the new self, which in *the likeness of God* has been created in righteousness and holiness of the truth.
25Therefore, laying aside falsehood, SPEAK TRUTH, EACH ONE *of you,* WITH HIS NEIGHBOR, for we are members of one another.
26BE ANGRY, AND *yet DO NOT SIN;* do not let the sun go down on your anger,
27and do not give the devil an opportunity.
28Let him who steals steal no longer; but rather let him labor, performing with his own hands what is good, in order that he may have *something* to share with him who has need.
29Let no unwholesome word proceed from your mouth, but only such *a word* as is good for edification according to the need *of the moment,* that it may give grace to those who hear.
30And do not grieve the Holy Spirit of God, by whom you were sealed for

διανοίᾳ ὄντες, ἀπηλλοτριωμένοι τῆς ζωῆς
1intellect 1being, having been alienated [from] the life
τοῦ θεοῦ, διὰ τὴν ἄγνοιαν τὴν οὖσαν
- of God, through the ignorance - being
ἐν αὐτοῖς, διὰ τὴν πώρωσιν τῆς καρδίας
in them, on account of the hardness of the heart
αὐτῶν, 19 οἵτινες ἀπηλγηκότες ἑαυτοὺς
of them, who having ceased to care 2themselves
παρέδωκαν τῇ ἀσελγείᾳ εἰς ἐργασίαν
1gave up - to lewdness for work
ἀκαθαρσίας πάσης ἐν πλεονεξίᾳ. 20 ὑμεῖς
2uncleanness 1of all in greediness. ye
δὲ οὐχ οὕτως ἐμάθετε τὸν Χριστόν,
But not so learned - Christ,
21 εἴ γε αὐτὸν ἠκούσατε καὶ ἐν αὐτῷ
if indeed 2him 1ye heard and 2by 3him
ἐδιδάχθητε καθώς ἐστιν ἀλήθεια ἐν τῷ
1were taught as 2is 1truth in -
Ἰησοῦ, 22 ἀποθέσθαι ὑμᾶς κατὰ τὴν
Jesus, to put off youb as regards the(your)
=that ye put off
προτέραν ἀναστροφὴν τὸν παλαιὸν ἄνθρωπον
former conduct the old man
τὸν φθειρόμενον κατὰ τὰς ἐπιθυμίας τῆς
- being corrupted according to the lusts -
ἀπάτης, 23 ἀνανεοῦσθαι δὲ τῷ πνεύματι
of deceit, and *to* be renewed in the spirit
τοῦ νοὸς ὑμῶν 24 καὶ ἐνδύσασθαι τὸν
of the mind of you and *to* put on the
καινὸν ἄνθρωπον τὸν κατὰ θεὸν κτισθέντα
new man - 2according to 3God 1created
ἐν δικαιοσύνῃ καὶ ὁσιότητι τῆς ἀληθείας.
in righteousness and holiness of the truth.
25 Διὸ ἀποθέμενοι τὸ ψεῦδος λαλεῖτε
Wherefore putting off the lie speak ye
ἀλήθειαν ἕκαστος μετὰ τοῦ πλησίον αὐτοῦ,
truth each man with the neighbour of him,
ὅτι ἐσμὲν ἀλλήλων μέλη. 26 ὀργίζεσθε
because we are of one another members. Be ye wrathful
καὶ μὴ ἁμαρτάνετε· ὁ ἥλιος μὴ
and do not sin; 2the 1sun 2not
ἐπιδυέτω ἐπὶ παροργισμῷ ὑμῶν, 27 μηδὲ
1let 2set *on* on provocation of you, nor
δίδοτε τόπον τῷ διαβόλῳ. 28 ὁ κλέπτων
give ye place to the devil. The [one] stealing
μηκέτι κλεπτέτω, μᾶλλον δὲ κοπιάτω
no more let him steal, but rather let him labour
ἐργαζόμενος ταῖς ἰδίαις χερσὶν τὸ ἀγαθόν,
working with the(his) own hands the good thing,
ἵνα ἔχῃ μεταδιδόναι τῷ χρείαν ἔχοντι.
in order he may to share [with] the [one] 2need 1having
that have
29 πᾶς λόγος σαπρὸς ἐκ τοῦ στόματος
Every 2word 1corrupt out of the mouth
ὑμῶν μὴ ἐκπορευέσθω, ἀλλὰ εἴ τις
of you let not proceed*, but if any
ἀγαθὸς πρὸς οἰκοδομὴν τῆς χρείας, ἵνα
[is] good to improvement of the need, in order that
δῷ χάριν τοῖς ἀκούουσιν. 30 καὶ μὴ λυπεῖτε
it may grace to the [ones] hearing. And do not grieve
give
τὸ πνεῦμα τὸ ἅγιον τοῦ θεοῦ, ἐν ᾧ
the Spirit - Holy - of God, by whom
ἐσφραγίσθητε εἰς ἡμέραν ἀπολυτρώσεως.
ye were sealed for a day of redemption.

derstanding and separated from the life of God because of the ignorance that is in them due to the hardening of their hearts.
19Having lost all sensitivity, they have given themselves over to sensuality so as to indulge in every kind of impurity, with a continual lust for more.
20You, however, did not come to know Christ that way. 21Surely you heard of him and were taught in him in accordance with the truth that is in Jesus. 22You were taught, with regard to your former way of life, to put off your old self, which is being corrupted by its deceitful desires; 23to be made new in the attitude of your minds; 24and to put on the new self, created to be like God in true righteousness and holiness.
25Therefore each of you must put off falsehood and speak truthfully to his neighbor, for we are all members of one body. 26"In your anger do not sin"¹: Do not let the sun go down while you are still angry, 27and do not give the devil a foothold. 28He who has been stealing must steal no longer, but must work, doing something useful with his own hands, that he may have something to share with those in need.
29Do not let any unwholesome talk come out of your mouths, but only what is helpful for building others up according to their needs, that it may benefit those who listen. 30And do not grieve the Holy Spirit of God, with whom you were sealed for the day of

* That is, " let no corrupt word proceed . . ."

¹26 Psalm 4:4

the day of redemption.
31Let all bitterness and
wrath and anger and clam-
or and slander be put away
from you, along with all
malice.
32And be kind to one an-
other, tender-hearted, forgiving each other, just as
God in Christ also has forgiven *f* you.

Chapter 5

Be Imitators of God

THEREFORE be imita-
tors of God, as be-
loved children;
2and walk in love, just as
Christ also loved *f*you, and
gave Himself up for us, an
offering and a sacrifice to
God as a fragrant aroma.
3But do not let immoral-
ity or any impurity or greed
even be named among you,
as is proper among saints;
4and *there must be no*
filthiness and silly talk, or
coarse jesting, which are
not fitting, but rather giving
of thanks.
5For this you know with
certainty, that no immoral
or impure person or covetous man, who is an idola-
ter, has an inheritance in
the kingdom of Christ and
God.
6Let no one deceive you
with empty words, for be-
cause of these things the
wrath of God comes upon
the sons of disobedience.
7Therefore do not be
partakers with them;
8for you were formerly
darkness, but now you are
light in the Lord; walk as
children of light
9(for the fruit of the light
consists in all goodness and
righteousness and truth),
10trying to learn what is
pleasing to the Lord.
11And do not participate
in the unfruitful deeds of
darkness, but instead even
expose them;
12for it is disgraceful even
to speak of the things which
are done by them in secret.
13But all things become

31 πᾶσα πικρία καὶ θυμὸς καὶ
All bitterness and anger and
ὀργὴ καὶ κραυγὴ καὶ βλασφημία ἀρθήτω
wrath and clamour and blasphemy let it be removed
ἀφ' ὑμῶν σὺν πάσῃ κακίᾳ. 32 γίνεσθε
from you with all evil. be ye
δὲ εἰς ἀλλήλους χρηστοί, εὔσπλαγχνοι,
And to one another kind, tenderhearted,
χαριζόμενοι ἑαυτοῖς καθὼς καὶ ὁ θεὸς
forgiving yourselves as also - God
ἐν Χριστῷ ἐχαρίσατο ὑμῖν. 5 Γίνεσθε
in Christ forgave you. Be ye
οὖν μιμηταὶ τοῦ θεοῦ, ὡς τέκνα
therefore imitators - of God, as children
ἀγαπητά, 2 καὶ περιπατεῖτε ἐν ἀγάπῃ,
beloved, and walk ye in love,
καθὼς καὶ ὁ Χριστὸς ἠγάπησεν ὑμᾶς
as also - Christ loved you
καὶ παρέδωκεν ἑαυτὸν ὑπὲρ ἡμῶν
and gave up himself on behalf of us
προσφορὰν καὶ θυσίαν τῷ θεῷ εἰς ὀσμὴν
an offering and a sacrifice - to God for an odour
εὐωδίας. 3 Πορνεία δὲ καὶ ἀκαθαρσία
of sweet smell. But fornication and ²uncleanness
πᾶσα ἢ πλεονεξία μηδὲ ὀνομαζέσθω ἐν
¹all or greediness not let it be named in
ὑμῖν, καθὼς πρέπει ἁγίοις, 4 καὶ αἰσχρότης
you, as is fitting for saints, and baseness
καὶ μωρολογία ἢ εὐτραπελία, ἃ οὐκ
and foolish talking or raillery, which things not
ἀνῆκεν, ἀλλὰ μᾶλλον εὐχαριστία. 5 τοῦτο
are becoming, but rather thanksgiving. this
γὰρ ἴστε γινώσκοντες, ὅτι πᾶς πόρνος
For be ye knowing, that every fornicator
ἢ ἀκάθαρτος ἢ πλεονέκτης, ὅ ἐστιν
or unclean man or greedy, who is
εἰδωλολάτρης, οὐκ ἔχει κληρονομίαν ἐν τῇ
an idolater, not has inheritance in the
βασιλείᾳ τοῦ Χριστοῦ καὶ θεοῦ. 6 Μηδεὶς
kingdom - of Christ and of God. ¹No man
ὑμᾶς ἀπατάτω κενοῖς λόγοις· διὰ ταῦτα
²you ¹let ²deceive with empty words; because of these things
γὰρ ἔρχεται ἡ ὀργὴ τοῦ θεοῦ ἐπὶ τοὺς
for is coming the wrath - of God on the
υἱοὺς τῆς ἀπειθείας. 7 μὴ οὖν γίνεσθε
sons - of disobedience. Not therefore be ye
συμμέτοχοι αὐτῶν· 8 ἦτε γάρ ποτε σκότος,
partakers of them; for ye were then darkness,
νῦν δὲ φῶς ἐν κυρίῳ· ὡς τέκνα φωτὸς
but now light in [the] Lord; as children of light
περιπατεῖτε, 9 — ὁ γὰρ καρπὸς τοῦ
walk ye, (for the fruit of the
φωτὸς ἐν πάσῃ ἀγαθωσύνῃ καὶ δικαιοσύνῃ
light [is] in all goodness and righteousness
καὶ ἀληθείᾳ, — 10 δοκιμάζοντες τί ἐστιν
and truth,) proving what is
εὐάρεστον τῷ κυρίῳ, 11 καὶ μὴ συγκοι-
well-pleasing to the Lord, and do not have fellow-
νωνεῖτε τοῖς ἔργοις τοῖς ἀκάρποις τοῦ
ship with the ²works - ¹unfruitful -
σκότους, μᾶλλον δὲ καὶ ἐλέγχετε, 12 τὰ
of darkness, but rather even reprove [them], ⁴the
γὰρ κρυφῇ γινόμενα ὑπ' αὐτῶν αἰσχρόν
for ⁶hidden things ⁷being done ⁸by ⁹them ²shameful
ἐστιν καὶ λέγειν· 13 τὰ δὲ πάντα ἐλεγχόμενα
¹it is ³even ⁴to speak [of]; - but all things being reproved

redemption. 31Get rid of all
bitterness, rage and anger,
brawling and slander, along
with every form of malice.
32Be kind and compassion-
ate to one another, forgiving each other, just as in
Christ God forgave you.

Chapter 5

BE imitators of God,
therefore, as dearly
loved children 2and live a
life of love, just as Christ
loved us and gave himself
up for us as a fragrant offering and sacrifice to God.
3But among you there
must not be even a hint of
sexual immorality, or of
any kind of impurity, or of
greed, because these are
improper for God's holy
people. 4Nor should there
be obscenity, foolish talk
or coarse joking, which are
out of place, but rather
thanksgiving. 5For of this
you can be sure: No immoral, impure or greedy person
—such a man is an idola-
ter—has any inheritance in
the kingdom of Christ and
of God. *m* 6Let no one deceive you with empty
words, for because of such
things God's wrath comes
on those who are disobedient. 7Therefore do not be
partners with them.
8For you were once dark-
ness, but now you are light
in the Lord. Live as children of light 9(for the fruit
of the light consists in all
goodness, righteousness
and truth) 10and find out
what pleases the Lord.
11Have nothing to do with
the fruitless deeds of darkness, but rather expose
them. 12For it is shameful
even to mention what the
disobedient do in secret.
13But everything exposed

f Some ancient mss. read *us*

m 5 Or *kingdom of the Christ and
God*

visible when they are exposed by the light, for everything that becomes visible is light.

14For this reason it says,
"Awake, sleeper,
And arise from the dead,
And Christ will shine on you."

15Therefore be careful how you walk, not as unwise men, but as wise,

16making the most of your time, because the days are evil.

17So then do not be foolish, but understand what the will of the Lord is.

18And do not get drunk with wine, for that is dissipation, but be filled with the Spirit,

19speaking to one another in psalms and hymns and spiritual songs, singing and making melody with your heart to the Lord;

20always giving thanks for all things in the name of our Lord Jesus Christ to God, even the Father;

21and be subject to one another in the fear of Christ.

Marriage Like Christ and the Church

22Wives, *be subject* to your own husbands, as to the Lord.

23For the husband is the head of the wife, as Christ also is the head of the church, He Himself *being* the Savior of the body.

24But as the church is subject to Christ, so also the wives *ought to be* to their husbands in everything.

25Husbands, love your wives, just as Christ also loved the church and gave Himself up for her;

26that He might sanctify her, having cleansed her by the washing of water with the word,

27that He might present to Himself the church in all her glory, having no spot or wrinkle or any such thing;

ὑπὸ τοῦ φωτὸς φανεροῦται· 14 πᾶν γὰρ
by the light is(are) manifested; for everything

τὸ φανερούμενον φῶς ἐστιν. διὸ λέγει·
- being manifested ²light ¹is. Wherefore he says:

ἔγειρε, ὁ καθεύδων, καὶ ἀνάστα ἐκ τῶν
Rise, the sleeping [one], and stand up out of the

νεκρῶν, καὶ ἐπιφαύσει σοι ὁ Χριστός.
dead [ones], and will shine on thee - Christ.

15 Βλέπετε οὖν ἀκριβῶς πῶς περιπατεῖτε,
See ye therefore carefully how ye walk,

μὴ ὡς ἄσοφοι ἀλλ' ὡς σοφοί, 16 ἐξαγοραζ-
not as unwise but as wise, redeem-

όμενοι τὸν καιρόν, ὅτι αἱ ἡμέραι πονηραί
ing the time, because the days evil

εἰσιν. 17 διὰ τοῦτο μὴ γίνεσθε ἄφρονες,
are. Therefore be ye not foolish,

ἀλλὰ συνίετε τί τὸ θέλημα τοῦ κυρίου.
but understand what the will of the Lord [is].

18 καὶ μὴ μεθύσκεσθε οἴνῳ, ἐν ᾧ ἐστιν
And be ye not drunk with wine, in which is

ἀσωτία, ἀλλὰ πληροῦσθε ἐν πνεύματι,
wantonness, but be filled by [the] Spirit,

19 λαλοῦντες ἑαυτοῖς ψαλμοῖς καὶ ὕμνοις
speaking to yourselves in psalms and hymns

καὶ ᾠδαῖς πνευματικαῖς, ᾄδοντες καὶ
and songs spiritual, singing and

ψάλλοντες τῇ καρδίᾳ ὑμῶν τῷ κυρίῳ,
psalming with the heart of you to the Lord,

20 εὐχαριστοῦντες πάντοτε ὑπὲρ πάντων
giving thanks always for all things

ἐν ὀνόματι τοῦ κυρίου ἡμῶν Ἰησοῦ
in [the] name of the Lord of us Jesus

Χριστοῦ τῷ θεῷ καὶ πατρί, 21 ὑποτασ-
Christ - to God even [the] Father, being

σόμενοι ἀλλήλοις ἐν φόβῳ Χριστοῦ. 22 Αἱ
subject to one another in [the] fear of Christ. The

γυναῖκες τοῖς ἰδίοις ἀνδράσιν ὡς τῷ
wives to the(ir) own husbands as to the

κυρίῳ, 23 ὅτι ἀνήρ ἐστιν κεφαλὴ τῆς
Lord, because a man is head of the

γυναικὸς ὡς καὶ ὁ Χριστὸς κεφαλὴ
woman as also - Christ [is] head

τῆς ἐκκλησίας, αὐτὸς σωτὴρ τοῦ σώματος.
of the church, [him]self Saviour of the body.

24 ἀλλὰ ὡς ἡ ἐκκλησία ὑποτάσσεται τῷ
But as the church is subject to the

Χριστῷ, οὕτως καὶ αἱ γυναῖκες τοῖς
to Christ, so also the wives to the(ir)

ἀνδράσιν ἐν παντί. 25 Οἱ ἄνδρες, ἀγαπᾶτε
husbands in everything. The husbands, love ye

τὰς γυναῖκας, καθὼς καὶ ὁ Χριστὸς
the(your) wives, as also - Christ

ἠγάπησεν τὴν ἐκκλησίαν καὶ ἑαυτὸν
loved the church and himself

παρέδωκεν ὑπὲρ αὐτῆς, 26 ἵνα αὐτὴν
gave up on behalf of it, in order that it

ἁγιάσῃ καθαρίσας τῷ λουτρῷ τοῦ
he might sanctify cleansing by the washing of the

ὕδατος ἐν ῥήματι, 27 ἵνα παραστήσῃ αὐτὸς
water by word, in order ²might present ¹he
that

ἑαυτῷ ἔνδοξον τὴν ἐκκλησίαν, μὴ ἔχουσαν
⁵to himself ⁶glorious ³the ⁴church, not having

σπίλον ἢ ῥυτίδα ἤ τι τῶν τοιούτων,
spot or wrinkle or any of the such things,

---

by the light becomes visible, 14for it is light that makes everything visible. This is why it is said:

"Wake up, O sleeper,
rise from the dead,
and Christ will shine on you."

15Be very careful, then, how you live—not as unwise but as wise, 16making the most of every opportunity, because the days are evil. 17Therefore do not be foolish, but understand what the Lord's will is. 18Do not get drunk on wine, which leads to debauchery. Instead, be filled with the Spirit. 19Speak to one another with psalms, hymns and spiritual songs. Sing and make music in your heart to the Lord, 20always giving thanks to God the Father for everything, in the name of our Lord Jesus Christ.

21Submit to one another out of reverence for Christ.

Wives and Husbands

22Wives, submit to your husbands as to the Lord. 23For the husband is the head of the wife as Christ is the head of the church, his body, of which he is the Savior. 24Now as the church submits to Christ, so also wives should submit to their husbands in everything.

25Husbands, love your wives, just as Christ loved the church and gave himself up for her 26to make her holy, cleansing n her by the washing with water through the word, 27and to present her to himself as a radiant church, without stain or wrinkle or any oth-

ⁿ26 Or *having cleansed*

but that she should be holy and blameless. 28So husbands ought also to love their own wives as their own bodies. He who loves his own wife loves himself; 29for no one ever hated his own flesh, but nourishes and cherishes, just as Christ also *does the* church, 30because we are members of His body. 31FOR THIS CAUSE A MAN SHALL LEAVE HIS FATHER AND MOTHER, AND SHALL CLEAVE TO HIS WIFE; AND THE TWO SHALL BECOME ONE FLESH. 32This mystery is great; but I am speaking with reference to Christ and the church. 33Nevertheless let each individual among you also love his own wife even as himself; and *let* the wife *see to it* that she respect her husband.

Chapter 6

Family Relationships

CHILDREN, obey your parents in the Lord, for this is right. 2HONOR YOUR FATHER AND MOTHER (which is the first commandment with a promise), 3THAT IT MAY BE WELL WITH YOU, AND THAT YOU MAY LIVE LONG ON THE EARTH. 4And, fathers, do not provoke your children to anger; but bring them up in the discipline and instruction of the Lord. 5Slaves, be obedient to those who are your masters according to the flesh, with fear and trembling, in the sincerity of your heart, as to Christ; 6not by way of eyeservice, as men-pleasers, but as slaves of Christ, doing the will of God from the heart.

ἀλλ' ἵνα ᾖ ἁγία καὶ ἄμωμος. **28** οὕτως
but *in order* it might holy and unblemished. So
that be

ὀφείλουσιν [καὶ] οἱ ἄνδρες ἀγαπᾶν τὰς
ought also the husbands to love the

ἑαυτῶν γυναῖκας ὡς τὰ ἑαυτῶν σώματα.
of themselves wives as the of themselves bodies.

ὁ ἀγαπῶν τὴν ἑαυτοῦ γυναῖκα ἑαυτὸν
The [one] loving the of himself wife himself

ἀγαπᾷ· **29** οὐδεὶς γάρ ποτε τὴν ἑαυτοῦ
loves; for no man ever the of himself

σάρκα ἐμίσησεν, ἀλλὰ ἐκτρέφει καὶ θάλπει
flesh hated, but nourishes and cherishes

αὐτήν, καθὼς καὶ ὁ Χριστὸς τὴν ἐκ-
it, as also – Christ the

κλησίαν, **30** ὅτι μέλη ἐσμὲν τοῦ σώματος
church, because members we are of the body

αὐτοῦ. **31** ἀντὶ τούτου καταλείψει ἄνθρωπος
of him. For this ²shall leave ¹a man

[τὸν] πατέρα καὶ [τὴν] μητέρα καὶ
the(his) father and the(his) mother and

προσκολληθήσεται πρὸς τὴν γυναῖκα αὐτοῦ,
shall cleave to the wife of him,

καὶ ἔσονται οἱ δύο εἰς σάρκα μίαν.
and ³shall be ¹the ²two ⁴for ⁵flesh ⁶one.

32 τὸ μυστήριον τοῦτο μέγα ἐστίν, ἐγὼ
This mystery great is, ²I

δὲ λέγω εἰς Χριστὸν καὶ [εἰς] τὴν
¹but say as to Christ and as to the

ἐκκλησίαν. **33** πλὴν καὶ ὑμεῖς οἱ
church. Nevertheless also ye *the*

καθ' ἕνα ἕκαστος τὴν ἑαυτοῦ γυναῖκα
one by one† each ¹the ²of himself ³wife

οὕτως ἀγαπάτω ὡς ἑαυτόν, ἡ δὲ
so let him love as himself, and the

γυνὴ ἵνα φοβῆται τὸν ἄνδρα. **6** Τὰ
wife *in order* that she fears the(her) husband. The

τέκνα, ὑπακούετε τοῖς γονεῦσιν ὑμῶν
children, obey ye the parents of you

ἐν κυρίῳ· τοῦτο γάρ ἐστιν δικαίον.
in [the] Lord; for this is right.

2 τίμα τὸν πατέρα σου καὶ τὴν μητέρα,
Honour the father of thee and the mother,

ἥτις ἐστὶν ἐντολὴ πρώτη ἐν ἐπαγγελίᾳ,
which is ²commandment ¹[the] first with a promise,

3 ἵνα εὖ σοι γένηται καὶ ἔσῃ μακρο-
in order well with thee it may be and thou may- long-
that est be

χρόνιος ἐπὶ τῆς γῆς. **4** Καὶ οἱ πατέρες,
timed(lived) on the earth. And the fathers,

μὴ παροργίζετε τὰ τέκνα ὑμῶν, ἀλλὰ
do not ye provoke to wrath the children of you, but

ἐκτρέφετε αὐτὰ ἐν παιδείᾳ καὶ νουθεσίᾳ
nurture them in [the] discipline and admonition

κυρίου. **5** Οἱ δοῦλοι, ὑπακούετε τοῖς
of [the] Lord. The slaves, obey ye ¹the(your)

κατὰ σάρκα κυρίοις μετὰ φόβου καὶ
²according to ⁴flesh ³lords with fear and

τρόμου ἐν ἁπλότητι τῆς καρδίας ὑμῶν
trembling in singleness of the heart of you

ὡς τῷ Χριστῷ, **6** μὴ κατ' ὀφθαλμοδουλίαν
as – to Christ, not by way of eye-service

ὡς ἀνθρωπάρεσκοι, ἀλλ' ὡς δοῦλοι Χριστοῦ
as men-pleasers, but as slaves of Christ

ποιοῦντες τὸ θέλημα τοῦ θεοῦ ἐκ ψυχῆς,
doing the will – of God from [the] soul,

---

er blemish, but holy and blameless. 28In this same way, husbands ought to love their wives as their own bodies. He who loves his wife loves himself. 29After all, no one ever hated his own body, but he feeds and cares for it, just as Christ does the church— 30for we are members of his body. 31"For this reason a man will leave his father and mother and be united to his wife, and the two will become one flesh."*o* 32This is a profound mystery—but I am talking about Christ and the church. 33However, each one of you also must love his wife as he loves himself, and the wife must respect her husband.

Chapter 6

Children and Parents

CHILDREN, obey your parents in the Lord, for this is right. 2"Honor your father and mother"— which is the first commandment with a promise— 3"that it may go well with you and that you may enjoy long life on the earth."*p* 4Fathers, do not exasperate your children; instead, bring them up in the training and instruction of the Lord.

Slaves and Masters

5Slaves, obey your earthly masters with respect and fear, and with sincerity of heart, just as you would obey Christ. 6Obey them not only to win their favor when their eye is on you, but like slaves of Christ, doing the will of God from

o31 Gen. 2:24
p3 Deut. 5:16

7With good will render service, as to the Lord, and not to men,

8knowing that whatever good thing each one does, this he will receive back from the Lord, whether slave or free.

9And, masters, do the same things to them, and give up threatening, knowing that both their Master and yours is in heaven, and there is no partiality with Him.

The Armor of God

10Finally, be strong in the Lord, and in the strength of His might.

11Put on the full armor of God, that you may be able to stand firm against the schemes of the devil.

12For our struggle is not against flesh and blood, but against the rulers, against the powers, against the world forces of this darkness, against the spiritual *forces* of wickedness in the heavenly *places*.

13Therefore, take up the full armor of God, that you may be able to resist in the evil day, and having done everything, to stand firm.

14Stand firm therefore, HAVING GIRDED YOUR LOINS WITH TRUTH, and HAVING PUT ON THE BREASTPLATE OF RIGHTEOUSNESS,

15and having shod YOUR FEET WITH THE PREPARATION OF THE GOSPEL OF PEACE;

16in addition to all, taking up the shield of faith with which you will be able to extinguish all the flaming missiles of the evil *one*.

17And take THE HELMET OF SALVATION, and the sword

---

7 μετ' εὐνοίας δουλεύοντες ὡς τῷ κυρίῳ
with goodwill serving as slaves as to the Lord

καὶ οὐκ ἀνθρώποις, **8** εἰδότες ὅτι ἕκαστος
and not to men, knowing that each man

ἐάν τι ποιήσῃ ἀγαθόν, τοῦτο κομίσεται
whatever ²he does ¹good thing, this he will get

παρὰ κυρίου, εἴτε δοῦλος εἴτε ἐλεύθερος.
from [the] Lord, whether a slave or a freeman.

9 Καὶ οἱ κύριοι, τὰ αὐτὰ ποιεῖτε πρὸς
And the lords, the same things do ye toward

αὐτούς, ἀνιέντες τὴν ἀπειλήν, εἰδότες ὅτι
them, forbearing the threatening, knowing that

καὶ αὐτῶν καὶ ὑμῶν ὁ κύριός ἐστιν
both of them and of you the Lord is

ἐν οὐρανοῖς, καὶ προσωπολημψία οὐκ
in heavens, and respect of persons not

ἔστιν παρ' αὐτῷ.
is with him.

10 Τοῦ λοιποῦ, ἐνδυναμοῦσθε ἐν κυρίῳ
For the rest,† be ye empowered in [the] Lord

καὶ ἐν τῷ κράτει τῆς ἰσχύος αὐτοῦ.
and in the might of the strength of him.

11 ἐνδύσασθε τὴν πανοπλίαν τοῦ θεοῦ
Put ye on the whole armour - of God

πρὸς τὸ δύνασθαι ὑμᾶς στῆναι πρὸς
for the to be able youᵇ to stand against
=so that ye are able . . .

τὰς μεθοδείας τοῦ διαβόλου· **12** ὅτι οὐκ
the craftinesses of the devil; because not

ἔστιν ἡμῖν ἡ πάλη πρὸς αἷμα καὶ σάρκα,
is to us the conflictᵉ against blood and flesh,
=our conflict is not

ἀλλὰ πρὸς τὰς ἀρχάς, πρὸς τὰς ἐξουσίας,
but against the rulers, against the authorities,

πρὸς τοὺς κοσμοκράτορας τοῦ σκότους
against the world rulers - darkness

τούτου, πρὸς τὰ πνευματικὰ τῆς πονηρίας
of this, against the spiritual [hosts] - of evil

ἐν τοῖς ἐπουρανίοις. **13** διὰ τοῦτο
in the heavenlies. Therefore

ἀναλάβετε τὴν πανοπλίαν τοῦ θεοῦ, ἵνα
take ye up the whole armour - of God, in order
that

δυνηθῆτε ἀντιστῆναι ἐν τῇ ἡμέρᾳ τῇ
ye may be able to resist in the day the

πονηρᾷ καὶ ἅπαντα κατεργασάμενοι στῆναι.
evil and all things having wrought to stand.

14 στῆτε οὖν περιζωσάμενοι τὴν ὀσφὺν
Stand ye therefore girding round the loin[s]

ὑμῶν ἐν ἀληθείᾳ, καὶ ἐνδυσάμενοι τὸν
of you with truth, and putting on the

θώρακα τῆς δικαιοσύνης, **15** καὶ ὑπο-
breastplate - of righteousness, and shoe-

δησάμενοι τοὺς πόδας ἐν ἑτοιμασίᾳ τοῦ
ing the feet with readiness of the

εὐαγγελίου τῆς εἰρήνης, **16** ἐν πᾶσιν
gospel - of peace, in all

ἀναλαβόντες τὸν θυρεὸν τῆς πίστεως, ἐν
taking up the shield - of faith, by

ᾧ δυνήσεσθε πάντα τὰ βέλη τοῦ πονηροῦ
which ye will be able ²all ³the ⁴darts ⁵of the ⁶evil one

τὰ πεπυρωμένα σβέσαι· **17** καὶ τὴν
- ⁵having been equipped ¹to quench; and the
with fire

περικεφαλαίαν τοῦ σωτηρίου δέξασθε, καὶ
helmet - of salvation take ye, and

---

your heart. 7Serve wholeheartedly, as if you were serving the Lord, not men, 8because you know that the Lord will reward everyone for whatever good he does, whether he is slave or free.

9And masters, treat your slaves in the same way. Do not threaten them, since you know that he who is both their Master and yours is in heaven, and there is no favoritism with him.

The Armor of God

10Finally, be strong in the Lord and in his mighty power. 11Put on the full armor of God so that you can take your stand against the devil's schemes. 12For our struggle is not against flesh and blood, but against the rulers, against the authorities, against the powers of this dark world and against the spiritual forces of evil in the heavenly realms. 13Therefore put on the full armor of God, so that when the day of evil comes, you may be able to stand your ground, and after you have done everything, to stand. 14Stand firm then, with the belt of truth buckled around your waist, with the breastplate of righteousness in place, 15and with your feet fitted with the readiness that comes from the gospel of peace. 16In addition to all this, take up the shield of faith, with which you can extinguish all the flaming arrows of the evil one. 17Take the helmet of salvation and the sword of the Spirit, which is the word of God.

18With all prayer and petition pray at all times in the Spirit, and with this in view, be on the alert with all perseverance and petition for all the saints,

19and *pray* on my behalf, that utterance may be given to me in the opening of my mouth, to make known with boldness the mystery of the gospel,

20for which I am an ambassador in chains; that *g in proclaiming* it I may speak boldly, as I ought to speak.

21But that you also may know about my circumstances, how I am doing, Tychicus, the beloved brother and faithful minister in the Lord, will make everything known to you.

22And I have sent him to you for this very purpose, so that you may know about us, and that he may comfort your hearts.

23Peace to the brethren, and love with faith, from God the Father and the Lord Jesus Christ.

24Grace be with all those who love our Lord Jesus Christ with *a love* incorruptible.

τὴν μάχαιραν τοῦ πνεύματος, ὅ ἐστιν
the sword of the Spirit, which• is

ῥῆμα θεοῦ, 18 διὰ πάσης προσευχῆς καὶ
[the] word of God, by means of all prayer and

δεήσεως, προσευχόμενοι ἐν παντὶ καιρῷ
petition, praying at every time

ἐν πνεύματι, καὶ εἰς αὐτὸ ἀγρυπνοῦντες
in spirit, and ²to ²it ¹watching

ἐν πάσῃ προσκαρτερήσει καὶ δεήσει περὶ
in all perseverance and petition concerning

πάντων τῶν ἁγίων, 19 καὶ ὑπὲρ ἐμοῦ,
all the saints, and on behalf of me,

ἵνα μοι δοθῇ λόγος ἐν ἀνοίξει τοῦ
in order to me may be given speech in opening of the
that

στόματός μου, ἐν παρρησίᾳ γνωρίσαι τὸ
mouth of me, in boldness to make known the

μυστήριον τοῦ εὐαγγελίου, 20 ὑπὲρ οὗ
mystery of the gospel, on behalf of which

πρεσβεύω ἐν ἁλύσει, ἵνα ἐν αὐτῷ παρ-
I am an in a chain, in order in it I may
ambassador that

ρησιάσωμαι ὡς δεῖ με λαλῆσαι.
speak boldly as it behoves me to speak.

21 Ἵνα δὲ εἰδῆτε καὶ ὑμεῖς τὰ κατ'
Now in order that ²may know ¹also ¹ye the things about

ἐμέ, τί πράσσω, πάντα γνωρίσει ὑμῖν
me, what I am doing, all things ¹⁰will make ¹¹to you
known

Τύχικος ὁ ἀγαπητὸς ἀδελφὸς καὶ πιστὸς
¹Tychicus ²the ³beloved ⁴brother ⁵and ⁶faithful

διάκονος ἐν κυρίῳ, 22 ὃν ἔπεμψα πρὸς
⁷minister ⁸in ⁹[the] Lord, whom I sent to

ὑμᾶς εἰς αὐτὸ τοῦτο, ἵνα γνῶτε τὰ
you for this very thing, in order ye may the
that know things

περὶ ἡμῶν καὶ παρακαλέσῃ τὰς καρδίας
concerning us and may comfort the hearts

ὑμῶν.
of you.

23 Εἰρήνη τοῖς ἀδελφοῖς καὶ ἀγάπη
Peace to the brothers and love

μετὰ πίστεως ἀπὸ θεοῦ πατρὸς καὶ
with faith from God [the] Father and

κυρίου Ἰησοῦ Χριστοῦ. 24 ἡ χάρις μετὰ
[the] Lord Jesus Christ. - Grace [be] with

πάντων τῶν ἀγαπώντων τὸν κύριον ἡμῶν
all the [ones] loving the Lord of us

Ἰησοῦν Χριστὸν ἐν ἀφθαρσίᾳ.
Jesus Christ in incorruptibility.

---

of the Spirit, which is the word of God. 18And pray in the Spirit on all occasions with all kinds of prayers and requests. With this in mind, be alert and always keep on praying for all the saints.

19Pray also for me, that whenever I open my mouth, words may be given me so that I will fearlessly make known the mystery of the gospel, 20for which I am an ambassador in chains. Pray that I may declare it fearlessly, as I should.

Final Greetings

21Tychicus, the dear brother and faithful servant in the Lord, will tell you everything, so that you also may know how I am and what I am doing. 22I am sending him to you for this very purpose, that you may know how we are, and that he may encourage you.

23Peace to the brothers, and love with faith from God the Father and the Lord Jesus Christ. 24Grace to all who love our Lord Jesus Christ with an undying love.

Philippians

Chapter 1

Thanksgiving

PAUL and Timothy, bond-servants of Christ Jesus, to all the saints in Christ Jesus who are in Philippi, including

g Some ancient mss. read *I may speak it boldly*

ΠΡΟΣ ΦΙΛΙΠΠΗΣΙΟΥΣ
To Philippians

1 Παῦλος καὶ Τιμόθεος δοῦλοι Χριστοῦ
Paul and Timothy slaves of Christ

Ἰησοῦ πᾶσιν τοῖς ἁγίοις ἐν Χριστῷ
Jesus to all the saints in Christ

Ἰησοῦ τοῖς οὖσιν ἐν Φιλίπποις σὺν
Jesus - being in Philippi with

* Neuter, agreeing with πνεῦμα, not feminine to agree with μάχαιρα.

Philippians

Chapter 1

PAUL and Timothy, servants of Christ Jesus,

To all the saints in Christ Jesus at Philippi, together

the overseers and deacons:
²Grace to you and peace from God our Father and the Lord Jesus Christ.
³I thank my God in all my remembrance of you,
⁴always offering prayer with joy in my every prayer for you all,
⁵in view of your participation in the gospel from the first day until now.
⁶For I am confident of this very thing, that He who began a good work in you will perfect it until the day of Christ Jesus.
⁷For it is only right for me to feel this way about you all, because I have you in my heart, since both in my imprisonment and in the defense and confirmation of the gospel, you all are partakers of grace with me.
⁸For God is my witness, how I long for you all with the affection of Christ Jesus.
⁹And this I pray, that your love may abound still more and more in real knowledge and all discernment,
¹⁰so that you may approve the things that are excellent, in order to be sincere and blameless until the day of Christ;
¹¹having been filled with the fruit of righteousness which *comes* through Jesus Christ, to the glory and praise of God.

The Gospel Is Preached

¹²Now I want you to know, brethren, that my circumstances have turned out for the greater progress of the gospel,
¹³so that my imprison-

ἐπισκόποις καὶ διακόνοις· **2** χάρις ὑμῖν
bishops and ministers: Grace to you

καὶ εἰρήνη ἀπὸ θεοῦ πατρὸς ἡμῶν καὶ
and peace from God Father of us and

κυρίου Ἰησοῦ Χριστοῦ.
[the] Lord Jesus Christ.

3 Εὐχαριστῶ τῷ θεῷ μου ἐπὶ πάσῃ
I thank the God of me at all

τῇ μνείᾳ ὑμῶν, **4** πάντοτε ἐν πάσῃ
the remembrance of you, always in every

δεήσει μου ὑπὲρ πάντων ὑμῶν μετὰ
petition of me on behalf of all you with

χαρᾶς τὴν δέησιν ποιούμενος, **5** ἐπὶ τῇ
joy the petition making, over the

κοινωνίᾳ ὑμῶν εἰς τὸ εὐαγγέλιον ἀπὸ
fellowship of you in the gospel from

τῆς πρώτης ἡμέρας ἄχρι τοῦ νῦν,
the first day until *the* now,

6 πεποιθὼς αὐτὸ τοῦτο, ὅτι ὁ ἐναρξάμενος
being confident this very thing, that the having begun
[of] [one]

ἐν ὑμῖν ἔργον ἀγαθὸν ἐπιτελέσει ἄχρι
in you work a good will complete [it] until

ἡμέρας Χριστοῦ Ἰησοῦ· **7** καθώς ἐστιν
[the] day of Christ Jesus; as it is

δίκαιον ἐμοὶ τοῦτο φρονεῖν ὑπὲρ πάντων
right for me this to think *on behalf of* all

ὑμῶν, διὰ τὸ ἔχειν με ἐν τῇ καρδίᾳ
you, because of the to have me[b] in the heart
= because I have you in the(my) heart,

ὑμᾶς, ἔν τε τοῖς δεσμοῖς μου καὶ ἐν
you, both in the bonds of me and in

τῇ ἀπολογίᾳ καὶ βεβαιώσει τοῦ εὐαγγελίου
the defence and confirmation of the gospel

συγκοινωνούς μου τῆς χάριτος πάντας
⁴partakers ²of me ⁵of the ³grace ¹all

ὑμᾶς ὄντας. **8** μάρτυς γάρ μου ὁ θεός,
¹you ²being. ⁴witness ¹For ⁵of me - ²God
³[is],

ὡς ἐπιποθῶ πάντας ὑμᾶς ἐν σπλάγχνοις
how I long after all you in [the] bowels

Χριστοῦ Ἰησοῦ. **9** Καὶ τοῦτο προσεύχομαι,
of Christ Jesus. And this I pray,

ἵνα ἡ ἀγάπη ὑμῶν ἔτι μᾶλλον καὶ
in order the love of you yet more and
that

μᾶλλον περισσεύῃ ἐν ἐπιγνώσει καὶ πάσῃ
more may abound in full knowledge and all

αἰσθήσει, **10** εἰς τὸ δοκιμάζειν ὑμᾶς τὰ
perception, for the to prove you[b] the
= that ye may prove things

διαφέροντα, ἵνα ἦτε εἰλικρινεῖς καὶ
differing, in order ye may sincere and
that be

ἀπρόσκοποι εἰς ἡμέραν Χριστοῦ, **11** πεπληρω-
unoffending in [the] day of Christ, having been

μένοι καρπὸν δικαιοσύνης τὸν διὰ Ἰησοῦ
filled [with] [the] fruit of righteousness - through Jesus

Χριστοῦ, εἰς δόξαν καὶ ἔπαινον θεοῦ.
Christ, to [the] glory and praise of God.

12 Γινώσκειν δὲ ὑμᾶς βούλομαι, ἀδελφοί,
Now ⁵to know ²you ¹I wish, brothers,

ὅτι τὰ κατ' ἐμὲ μᾶλλον εἰς προκοπὴν
that the about me⁰ ¹rather ³to ⁴[the] advance
things
= my affairs

τοῦ εὐαγγελίου ἐλήλυθεν, **13** ὥστε τοὺς
⁵of the ⁶gospel ¹has(ve) come, so as the

---

with the overseers[a] and deacons:
²Grace and peace to you from God our Father and the Lord Jesus Christ.

Thanksgiving and Prayer

³I thank my God every time I remember you. ⁴In all my prayers for all of you, I always pray with joy ⁵because of your partnership in the gospel from the first day until now, ⁶being confident of this, that he who began a good work in you will carry it on to completion until the day of Christ Jesus.
⁷It is right for me to feel this way about all of you, since I have you in my heart; for whether I am in chains or defending and confirming the gospel, all of you share in God's grace with me. ⁸God can testify how I long for all of you with the affection of Christ Jesus.
⁹And this is my prayer: that your love may abound more and more in knowledge and depth of insight, ¹⁰so that you may be able to discern what is best and may be pure and blameless until the day of Christ, ¹¹filled with the fruit of righteousness that comes through Jesus Christ—to the glory and praise of God.

Paul's Chains Advance the Gospel

¹²Now I want you to know, brothers, that what has happened to me has really served to advance the gospel. ¹³As a result, it has

---

⁰ *Cf.* ver. 27; ch. 2. 19, 20, 23; Eph. 6. 21, 22; Col. 4. 7, 8.

a1 Traditionally *bishops*

ment in *the cause of* Christ has become well known throughout the whole *a*praetorian guard and to everyone else,

14and that most of the brethren, trusting in the Lord because of my imprisonment, have far more courage to speak the word of God without fear.

15Some, to be sure, are preaching Christ even from envy and strife, but some also from good will;

16*b*the latter *do it* out of love, knowing that I am appointed for the defense of the gospel;

17the former proclaim Christ out of selfish ambition, rather than from pure motives, thinking to cause me distress in my imprisonment.

18What then? Only that in every way, whether in pretense or in truth, Christ is proclaimed; and in this I rejoice, yes, and I will rejoice.

19For I know that this shall turn out for my deliverance through your prayers and the provision of the Spirit of Jesus Christ,

20according to my earnest expectation and hope, that I shall not be put to shame in anything, but *that* with all boldness, Christ shall even now, as always, be exalted in my body, whether by life or by death.

To Live Is Christ

21For to me, to live is Christ, and to die is gain.

22But if *I am* to live on in the flesh, this *will mean* fruitful labor for me; and I do not know which to choose.

23But I am hard-pressed from both *directions*, having the desire to depart and be with Christ, for *that* is very much better;

24yet to remain on in the flesh is more necessary for your sake.

25And convinced of this, I

δεσμούς μου φανερούς ἐν Χριστῷ γενέσθαι
bonds of me ²manifest ³in ⁴Christ ¹to become

ἐν ὅλῳ τῷ πραιτωρίῳ καὶ τοῖς λοιποῖς
in all the prætorium and to ⁵the ⁶rest

πᾶσιν, 14 καὶ τοὺς πλείονας τῶν ἀδελφῶν
¹all, and the majority of the brothers

ἐν κυρίῳ πεποιθότας τοῖς δεσμοῖς μου
in [the] Lord being confident in the bonds of me

περισσοτέρως τολμᾶν ἀφόβως τὸν λόγον
²more exceedingly ¹to dare ³fearlessly ⁵the ⁴word

τοῦ θεοῦ λαλεῖν. 15 τινὲς μὲν καὶ διὰ
- ⁷of God ⁶to speak. Some indeed even be-cause of

φθόνον καὶ ἔριν, τινὲς δὲ καὶ δι᾽ εὐδοκίαν
envy and strife, but some also because good-will of

τὸν Χριστὸν κηρύσσουσιν· 16 οἱ μὲν ἐξ
- Christ proclaim, these† from

ἀγάπης, εἰδότες ὅτι εἰς ἀπολογίαν τοῦ
love, knowing that for defence of the

εὐαγγελίου κεῖμαι, 17 οἱ δὲ ἐξ ἐριθείας
gospel I am set, those† from rivalry

τὸν Χριστὸν καταγγέλλουσιν, οὐχ ἁγνῶς,
- ¹Christ ²announce, not purely,

οἰόμενοι θλῖψιν ἐγείρειν τοῖς δεσμοῖς μου.
thinking ²affliction ¹to raise to the bonds of me.

18 Τί γάρ; πλὴν ὅτι παντὶ τρόπῳ,
What then? nevertheless that in every way,

εἴτε προφάσει εἴτε ἀληθείᾳ, Χριστὸς
whether in pretence or in truth, Christ

καταγγέλλεται, καὶ ἐν τούτῳ χαίρω· ἀλλὰ
is announced, and in this I rejoice; yet

καὶ χαρήσομαι· 19 οἶδα γὰρ ὅτι τοῦτό
also I will rejoice; for I know that this

μοι ἀποβήσεται εἰς σωτηρίαν διὰ τῆς
to me will result in salvation through the

ὑμῶν δεήσεως καὶ ἐπιχορηγίας τοῦ
²of you ¹petition and supply of the

πνεύματος Ἰησοῦ Χριστοῦ, 20 κατὰ τὴν
spirit of Jesus Christ, according to the

ἀποκαραδοκίαν καὶ ἐλπίδα μου ὅτι ἐν
eager expectation and hope of me that in

οὐδενὶ αἰσχυνθήσομαι, ἀλλ᾽ ἐν πάσῃ παρ-
nothing I shall be shamed, but with all bold-

ρησίᾳ ὡς πάντοτε καὶ νῦν μεγαλυνθήσεται
ness as always also now shall be magnified

Χριστὸς ἐν τῷ σώματί μου, εἴτε διὰ
Christ in the body of me, whether through

ζωῆς εἴτε διὰ θανάτου. 21 ἐμοὶ γὰρ
life or through death. For to me

τὸ ζῆν Χριστὸς καὶ τὸ ἀποθανεῖν κέρδος.
- to live [is] Christ and to die [is] gain.

22 εἰ δὲ τὸ ζῆν ἐν σαρκί, τοῦτό μοι
But if - to live in [the] flesh, this to me

καρπὸς ἔργου, καὶ τί αἱρήσομαι οὐ
[is] fruit of [?my] work, and what I shall choose not

γνωρίζω. 23 συνέχομαι δὲ ἐκ τῶν δύο,
I perceive. But I am constrained by the two,

τὴν ἐπιθυμίαν ἔχων εἰς τὸ ἀναλῦσαι καὶ
²the ³desire ¹having for the to depart and

σὺν Χριστῷ εἶναι, πολλῷ γὰρ μᾶλλον
⁵with ⁴Christ ¹to be, for by much [this is] rather

κρεῖσσον· 24 τὸ δὲ ἐπιμένειν τῇ σαρκὶ
better; - but to remain in the flesh [is]

ἀναγκαιότερον δι᾽ ὑμᾶς. 25 καὶ τοῦτο
more necessary on account of you. And this

---

become clear throughout the whole palace guard*b* and to everyone else that I am in chains for Christ.

14Because of my chains, most of the brothers in the Lord have been encouraged to speak the word of God more courageously and fearlessly.

15It is true that some preach Christ out of envy and rivalry, but others out of goodwill. 16The latter do so in love, knowing that I am put here for the defense of the gospel. 17The former preach Christ out of selfish ambition, not sincerely, supposing that they can stir up trouble for me while I am in chains.*c* 18But what does it matter? The important thing is that in every way, whether from false motives or true, Christ is preached. And because of this I rejoice.

Yes, and I will continue to rejoice, 19for I know that through your prayers and the help given by the Spirit of Jesus Christ, what has happened to me will turn out for my deliverance.*d* 20I eagerly expect and hope that I will in no way be ashamed, but will have sufficient courage so that now as always Christ will be exalted in my body, whether by life or by death. 21For to me, to live is Christ and to die is gain. 22If I am to go on living in the body, this will mean fruitful labor for me. Yet what shall I choose? I do not know! 23I am torn between the two: I desire to depart and be with Christ, which is better by far; 24but it is more necessary for you that I remain in the body. 25Convinced of this, I know

---

a Or, *governor's palace*
b Some later mss. reverse the order of vv. 16 and 17

*b*13 Or *whole palace*
*c*16,17 Some late manuscripts have verses 16 and 17 in reverse order.
*d*19 Or *salvation*

572

PHILIPPIANS 1, 2

know that I shall remain and continue with you all for your progress and joy in the faith, 26so that your proud confidence in me may abound in Christ Jesus through my coming to you again.

27Only conduct yourselves in a manner worthy of the gospel of Christ; so that whether I come and see you or remain absent, I may hear of you that you are standing firm in one spirit, with one mind striving together for the faith of the gospel;

28in no way alarmed by *your* opponents—which is a sign of destruction for them, but of salvation for you, and that *too*, from God.

29For to you it has been granted for Christ's sake, not only to believe in Him, but also to suffer for His sake,

30experiencing the same conflict which you saw in me, and now hear *to be in* me.

Chapter 2

Be Like Christ

IF therefore there is any encouragement in Christ, if there is any consolation of love, if there is any fellowship of the Spirit, if any affection and compassion, 2make my joy complete by being of the same mind, maintaining the same love, united in spirit, intent on one purpose.

3Do nothing from selfishness or empty conceit, but with humility of mind let each of you regard one another as more important than himself;

4do not *merely* look out for your own personal interests, but also for the interests of others.

πεποιθὼς οἶδα, ὅτι μενῶ καὶ παραμενῶ
being confident / I know, / that / I shall remain / and / continue

πᾶσιν ὑμῖν εἰς τὴν ὑμῶν προκοπὴν καὶ
with all / you / for / the / 'of you / 'advance / 'and

χαρὰν τῆς πίστεως, 26 ἵνα τὸ καύχημα
'joy / 'of the / 'faith, / in order the / boast / that

ὑμῶν περισσεύῃ ἐν Χριστῷ Ἰησοῦ ἐν
of you / may abound / in / Christ / Jesus / in

ἐμοὶ διὰ τῆς ἐμῆς παρουσίας πάλιν
me / through / – / my / presence / again

πρὸς ὑμᾶς.
with / you.

27 Μόνον ἀξίως τοῦ εὐαγγελίου τοῦ
Only / 'worthily / 'of the / 'gospel / –

Χριστοῦ πολιτεύεσθε, ἵνα εἴτε ἐλθὼν καὶ
'of Christ / 'conduct yourselves, / in order whether / coming / and / that

ἰδὼν ὑμᾶς εἴτε ἀπὼν ἀκούω τὰ περὶ
seeing / you / or / being absent / I hear / the / things cerning / con-

ὑμῶν, ὅτι στήκετε ἐν ἑνὶ πνεύματι,
you, / that / ye stand / in / one / spirit,

μιᾷ ψυχῇ συναθλοῦντες τῇ πίστει τοῦ
with one soul / striving together / in the / faith / of the

εὐαγγελίου, 28 καὶ μὴ πτυρόμενοι ἐν
gospel, / and / not / being terrified / in

μηδενὶ ὑπὸ τῶν ἀντικειμένων, ἥτις ἐστὶν
no(any) thing / by / the [ones] / opposing, / which / is

αὐτοῖς ἔνδειξις ἀπωλείας, ὑμῶν δὲ
to them / a proof / of destruction, / but of you

σωτηρίας, καὶ τοῦτο ἀπὸ θεοῦ· 29 ὅτι
of salvation, / and / this / from / God; / because

ὑμῖν ἐχαρίσθη τὸ ὑπὲρ Χριστοῦ, οὐ
to you / it was given / – / on behalf of / Christ, / not

μόνον τὸ εἰς αὐτὸν πιστεύειν ἀλλὰ καὶ
only / – / in / him / to believe / but / also

τὸ ὑπὲρ αὐτοῦ πάσχειν, 30 τὸν αὐτὸν
– / on behalf of / him / to suffer, / the / same

ἀγῶνα ἔχοντες οἷον εἴδετε ἐν ἐμοὶ
struggle / having / which / ye saw / in / me

καὶ νῦν ἀκούετε ἐν ἐμοί. 2 Εἴ τις
and / now / hear / in / me. / 'If [there is] / 'any

οὖν παράκλησις ἐν Χριστῷ, εἴ τι
'therefore / comfort / in / Christ, / if / any

παραμύθιον ἀγάπης, εἴ τις κοινωνία
consolation / of love, / if / any / fellowship

πνεύματος, εἴ τις σπλάγχνα καὶ οἰκτιρμοί,
of spirit, / if / any / compassions / and / pities,

2 πληρώσατέ μου τὴν χαρὰν ἵνα τὸ
fulfil ye / of me / the / joy / in order that the

αὐτὸ φρονῆτε, τὴν αὐτὴν ἀγάπην ἔχοντες,
same thing ye think, / the / same / love / having,

σύμψυχοι, τὸ ἓν φρονοῦντες, 3 μηδὲν κατ᾽
one in soul, / the / one thing / thinking, / [doing] nothing / by way of

ἐριθείαν μηδὲ κατὰ κενοδοξίαν, ἀλλὰ τῇ
rivalry / nor / by way of / vainglory, / but / –

ταπεινοφροσύνῃ ἀλλήλους ἡγούμενοι ὑπερ-
in humility / 'one another / 'deeming / sur-

ἔχοντας ἑαυτῶν, 4 μὴ τὰ ἑαυτῶν ἕκαστοι
passing / themselves, / not / 'the things / 'of themselves / 'each ones

σκοποῦντες, ἀλλὰ καὶ τὰ ἑτέρων ἕκαστοι.
'looking at, / but / 'also / 'the things / 'of others / 'each ones.

---

that I will remain, and I will continue with all of you for your progress and joy in the faith, 26so that through my being with you again your joy in Christ Jesus will overflow on account of me.

27Whatever happens, conduct yourselves in a manner worthy of the gospel of Christ. Then, whether I come and see you or only hear about you in my absence, I will know that you stand firm in one spirit, contending as one man for the faith of the gospel 28without being frightened in any way by those who oppose you. This is a sign to them that they will be destroyed, but that you will be saved—and that by God. 29For it has been granted to you on behalf of Christ not only to believe on him, but also to suffer for him, 30since you are going through the same struggle you saw I had, and now hear that I still have.

Chapter 2

Imitating Christ's Humility

IF you have any encouragement from being united with Christ, if any comfort from his love, if any fellowship with the Spirit, if any tenderness and compassion, 2then make my joy complete by being like-minded, having the same love, being one in spirit and purpose. 3Do nothing out of selfish ambition or vain conceit, but in humility consider others better than yourselves. 4Each of you should look not only to your own interests, but also to the interests of others.

⁵Have this attitude in yourselves which was also in Christ Jesus,

⁶who, although He existed in the form of God, did not regard equality with God a thing to be grasped,

⁷but ᶜemptied Himself, taking the form of a bond-servant, *and* being made in the likeness of men.

⁸And being found in appearance as a man, He humbled Himself by becoming obedient to the point of death, even death on a cross.

⁹Therefore also God highly exalted Him, and bestowed on Him the name which is above every name,

¹⁰that at the name of Jesus EVERY KNEE SHOULD BOW, of those who are in heaven, and on earth, and under the earth,

¹¹and that every tongue should confess that Jesus Christ is Lord, to the glory of God the Father.

¹²So then, my beloved, just as you have always obeyed, not as in my presence only, but now much more in my absence, work out your salvation with fear and trembling;

¹³for it is God who is at work in you, both to will and to work for *His* good pleasure.

¹⁴Do all things without grumbling or disputing;

¹⁵that you may prove yourselves to be blameless and innocent, children of God above reproach in the midst of a crooked and perverse generation, among whom you appear as lights in the world,

¹⁶holding fast the word of life, so that in the day of Christ I may have cause to glory because I did not run in vain nor toil in vain.

¹⁷But even if I am being poured out as a drink offering upon the sacrifice and service of your faith, I re-

---

5 τοῦτο φρονεῖτε ἐν ὑμῖν ὃ καὶ ἐν
This think ye among you which also [was] in

Χριστῷ Ἰησοῦ, **6** ὃς ἐν μορφῇ θεοῦ
Christ Jesus, who in [the] form of God

ὑπάρχων οὐχ ἁρπαγμὸν ἡγήσατο τὸ εἶναι
subsisting ²not ³robbery ¹deemed [it] the to be

ἴσα θεῷ, **7** ἀλλὰ ἑαυτὸν ἐκένωσεν ²[the] form
equal with God, but himself emptied ²[the] form
things

δούλου λαβών, ἐν ὁμοιώματι ἀνθρώπων
¹of a slave ¹taking, ²in ¹likeness ¹of men

γενόμενος· καὶ σχήματι εὑρεθεὶς ὡς
¹becoming; and ²in fashion ¹being found as

ἄνθρωπος **8** ἐταπείνωσεν ἑαυτὸν γενόμενος
a man he humbled himself becoming

ὑπήκοος μέχρι θανάτου, θανάτου δὲ σταυροῦ.
obedient until death, and death of a cross.

9 διὸ καὶ ὁ θεὸς αὐτὸν ὑπερύψωσεν
Wherefore also - God ²him ¹highly exalted

καὶ ἐχαρίσατο αὐτῷ τὸ ὄνομα τὸ ὑπὲρ
and gave to him the name - above

πᾶν ὄνομα, **10** ἵνα ἐν τῷ ὀνόματι Ἰησοῦ
every name, in order in the name of Jesus
that

πᾶν γόνυ κάμψῃ ἐπουρανίων καὶ ἐπιγείων
every knee should of heavenly and earthly
bend [beings] [beings]

καὶ καταχθονίων, **11** καὶ πᾶσα γλῶσσα
and [beings] under the earth, and every tongue

ἐξομολογήσηται ὅτι κύριος Ἰησοῦς
should acknowledge that ²Lord ¹Jesus

Χριστὸς εἰς δόξαν θεοῦ πατρός.
²Christ [is] to [the] glory of God [the] Father.

12 Ὥστε, ἀγαπητοί μου, καθὼς πάντοτε
So as, beloved of me, as always

ὑπηκούσατε, μὴ ὡς ἐν τῇ παρουσίᾳ
ye obeyed, not as in the presence

μου μόνον ἀλλὰ νῦν πολλῷ μᾶλλον ἐν
of me only but now by more rather in

τῇ ἀπουσίᾳ μου, μετὰ φόβου καὶ τρόμου
the absence of me, with fear and trembling

τὴν ἑαυτῶν σωτηρίαν κατεργάζεσθε· **13** θεὸς
¹the ²of yourselves ²salvation work out; ¹God

γάρ ἐστιν ὁ ἐνεργῶν ἐν ὑμῖν καὶ τὸ
²for is the [one] operating in you both the

θέλειν καὶ τὸ ἐνεργεῖν ὑπὲρ τῆς εὐδοκίας.
to will and the to operate on behalf of the(his) goodwill.

14 πάντα ποιεῖτε χωρὶς γογγυσμῶν καὶ
All things do ye without murmurings and

διαλογισμῶν, **15** ἵνα γένησθε ἄμεμπτοι καὶ
disputings, in order that ye may be blameless and

ἀκέραιοι, τέκνα θεοῦ ἄμωμα μέσον
harmless, children of God faultless in the
midst of

γενεᾶς σκολιᾶς καὶ διεστραμμένης, ἐν
a generation crooked and *having been* perverted, among

οἷς φαίνεσθε ὡς φωστῆρες ἐν κόσμῳ,
whom ye shine as luminaries in [the] world,

16 λόγον ζωῆς ἐπέχοντες, εἰς καύχημα
a word of life holding up, for a boast

ἐμοὶ εἰς ἡμέραν Χριστοῦ, ὅτι οὐκ εἰς
to meᵉ in [the] day of Christ, that not in

κενὸν ἔδραμον οὐδὲ εἰς κενὸν ἐκοπίασα.
vain I ran nor in vain laboured.

17 Ἀλλὰ εἰ καὶ σπένδομαι ἐπὶ τῇ θυσίᾳ
But if indeed I am poured out on the sacrifice

καὶ λειτουργίᾳ τῆς πίστεως ὑμῶν, χαίρω
and service of the faith of you, I rejoice

---

⁵Your attitude should be the same as that of Christ Jesus:

⁶Who, being in very natureᵉ God, did not consider equality with God something to be grasped,

⁷but made himself nothing, taking the very natureᶠ of a servant, being made in human likeness.

⁸And being found in appearance as a man, he humbled himself and became obedient to death— even death on a cross!

⁹Therefore God exalted him to the highest place and gave him the name that is above every name,

¹⁰that at the name of Jesus every knee should bow, in heaven and on earth and under the earth,

¹¹and every tongue confess that Jesus Christ is Lord, to the glory of God the Father.

Shining as Stars

¹²Therefore, my dear friends, as you have always obeyed—not only in my presence, but now much more in my absence—continue to work out your salvation with fear and trembling, ¹³for it is God who works in you to will and to act according to his good purpose.

¹⁴Do everything without complaining or arguing, ¹⁵so that you may become blameless and pure, children of God without fault in a crooked and depraved generation, in which you shine like stars in the universe ¹⁶as you hold outᵍ the word of life—in order that I may boast on the day of Christ that I did not run or labor for nothing. ¹⁷But even if I am being poured out like a drink offering on the sacrifice and service coming from your faith, I

ᶜ I.e., laid aside His privileges

ᵉ6 Or *in the form of*
ᶠ7 Or *the form*
ᵍ16 Or *hold on to*

joice and share my joy with you all.
18And you too, *I urge you,* rejoice in the same way and share your joy with me.

Timothy and Epaphroditus

19But I hope in the Lord Jesus to send Timothy to you shortly, so that I also may be encouraged when I learn of your condition.
20For I have no one *else* of kindred spirit who will genuinely be concerned for your welfare.
21For they all seek after their own interests, not those of Christ Jesus.
22But you know of his proven worth that he served with me in the furtherance of the gospel like a child *serving* his father.
23Therefore I hope to send him immediately, as soon as I see how things *go* with me;
24and I trust in the Lord that I myself also shall be coming shortly.
25But I thought it necessary to send to you Epaphroditus, my brother, and fellow worker and fellow soldier, who is also your messenger and minister to my need;
26because he was longing *d*for you all and was distressed because you had heard that he was sick.
27For indeed he was sick to the point of death, but God had mercy on him, and not on him only but also on me, lest I should have sorrow upon sorrow.
28Therefore I have sent him all the more eagerly in order that when you see him again you may rejoice and I may be less concerned *about* you.
29Therefore receive him in the Lord with all joy, and hold men like him in high regard;
30because he came close to death for the work of Christ, risking his life to

d Some ancient mss. read *to see you all*

Middle column (interlinear)

καὶ συγχαίρω πᾶσιν ὑμῖν· 18 τὸ δὲ αὐτὸ
and rejoice with ²all ¹you; and the same
καὶ ὑμεῖς χαίρετε καὶ συγχαίρετέ μοι.
also ye rejoice and rejoice with me.
19 Ἐλπίζω δὲ ἐν κυρίῳ Ἰησοῦ Τιμόθεον
But I hope in [the] Lord Jesus ²Timothy
ταχέως πέμψαι ὑμῖν, ἵνα κἀγὼ εὐψυχῶ
⁴shortly ¹to send ³to you, in order I also may be of
that good cheer
γνοὺς τὰ περὶ ὑμῶν. 20 οὐδένα γὰρ
knowing the con- you. For no one
things cerning
ἔχω ἰσόψυχον, ὅστις γνησίως τὰ περὶ
I have likeminded, who genuinely ²the ³con-
things cerning
ὑμῶν μεριμνήσει· 21 οἱ πάντες γὰρ τὰ
⁴you ¹will care for; *the* for all ³the
things
ἑαυτῶν ζητοῦσιν, οὐ τὰ Χριστοῦ Ἰησοῦ.
²of them- ¹seek, not the of Christ Jesus.
selves things
22 τὴν δὲ δοκιμὴν αὐτοῦ γινώσκετε, ὅτι
But the character of him ye know, that
ὡς πατρὶ τέκνον σὺν ἐμοὶ ἐδούλευσεν
as ³a father ¹a child²[serves] ⁵with ⁴me ⁶he served
εἰς τὸ εὐαγγέλιον. 23 τοῦτον μὲν οὖν
in the gospel. This one – therefore
ἐλπίζω πέμψαι ὡς ἂν ἀφίδω τὰ περὶ
I hope to send ²whenever ¹I see ³the ⁴con-
things cerning
ἐμὲ ἐξαυτῆς· 24 πέποιθα δὲ ἐν κυρίῳ
⁶me ¹immediately; but I trust in [the] Lord
ὅτι καὶ αὐτὸς ταχέως ἐλεύσομαι. 25 Ἀναγ-
that ²also ³[my]self ⁴shortly ¹I will come. ¹neces-
καῖον δὲ ἡγησάμην Ἐπαφρόδιτον τὸν
sary But ¹I deemed [it] ⁶Epaphroditus ⁷the
ἀδελφὸν καὶ συνεργὸν καὶ συστρατιώτην
⁸brother ⁹and ¹⁰fellow-worker ¹¹and ¹²fellow-soldier
μου, ὑμῶν δὲ ἀπόστολον καὶ λειτουργὸν
¹³of me, ¹⁴and ¹⁵of you ¹⁶apostle ¹⁷and ¹⁸minister
τῆς χρείας μου, πέμψαι πρὸς ὑμᾶς,
¹⁹of the ²⁰need ²¹of me, ²to send ³to ¹you,
26 ἐπειδὴ ἐπιποθῶν ἦν πάντας ὑμᾶς, καὶ
since ²longing after ¹he was ⁴all ³you, and
ἀδημονῶν, διότι ἠκούσατε ὅτι ἠσθένησεν.
[was] being because ye heard that he ailed.
troubled,
27 καὶ γὰρ ἠσθένησεν παραπλήσιον θανάτῳ·
For indeed he ailed coming near to death;
ἀλλὰ ὁ θεὸς ἠλέησεν αὐτόν, οὐκ αὐτὸν
but – God had mercy on him, ²not ³him
δὲ μόνον ἀλλὰ καὶ ἐμέ, ἵνα μὴ λύπην
¹and only but also me, lest grief
ἐπὶ λύπην σχῶ. 28 σπουδαιοτέρως οὖν
on grief I should have. More eagerly therefore
ἔπεμψα αὐτόν, ἵνα ἰδόντες αὐτὸν πάλιν
I sent him, in order that seeing him again
χαρῆτε κἀγὼ ἀλυπότερος ὦ. 29 προσδέχεσθε
ye may ²and ¹I ³less grieved ⁴may be. Receive ye
rejoice
οὖν αὐτὸν ἐν κυρίῳ μετὰ πάσης χαρᾶς,
therefore him in [the] Lord with all joy,
καὶ τοὺς τοιούτους ἐντίμους ἔχετε, 30 ὅτι
and – ²such ones ¹honoured ³hold ye, because
διὰ τὸ ἔργον Χριστοῦ μέχρι θανάτου
on ac- the work of Christ ²as far as ³death
count of
ἤγγισεν παραβολευσάμενος τῇ ψυχῇ, ἵνα
¹he drew exposing the(his) life, in or-
near der that

am glad and rejoice with all of you. 18So you too should be glad and rejoice with me.

Timothy and Epaphroditus

19I hope in the Lord Jesus to send Timothy to you soon, that I also may be cheered when I receive news about you. 20I have no one else like him, who takes a genuine interest in your welfare. 21For everyone looks out for his own interests, not those of Jesus Christ. 22But you know that Timothy has proved himself, because as a son with his father he has served with me in the work of the gospel. 23I hope, therefore, to send him as soon as I see how things go with me. 24And I am confident in the Lord that I myself will come soon.
25But I think it is necessary to send back to you Epaphroditus, my brother, fellow worker and fellow soldier, who is also your messenger, whom you sent to take care of my needs. 26For he longs for all of you and is distressed because you heard he was ill. 27Indeed he was ill, and almost died. But God had mercy on him, and not on him only but also on me, to spare me sorrow upon sorrow. 28Therefore I am all the more eager to send him, so that when you see him again you may be glad and I may have less anxiety. 29Welcome him in the Lord with great joy, and honor men like him, 30because he almost died for the work of

complete what was deficient in your service to me.

Chapter 3

The Goal of Life

FINALLY, my brethren, rejoice in the Lord. To write the same things *again* is no trouble to me, and it is a safeguard for you.

²Beware of the dogs, beware of the evil workers, beware of the false circumcision;

³for we are the *true* circumcision, who worship in the Spirit of God and glory in Christ Jesus and put no confidence in the flesh,

⁴although I myself might have confidence even in the flesh. If anyone else has a mind to put confidence in the flesh, I far more:

⁵circumcised the eighth day, of the nation of Israel, of the tribe of Benjamin, a Hebrew of Hebrews; as to the Law, a Pharisee;

⁶as to zeal, a persecutor of the church; as to the righteousness which is in the Law, found blameless.

⁷But whatever things were gain to me, those things I have counted as loss for the sake of Christ.

⁸More than that, I count all things to be loss in view of the surpassing value of knowing Christ Jesus my Lord, for whom I have suffered the loss of all things, and count them but rubbish in order that I may gain Christ,

⁹and may be found in Him, not having a righteousness of my own derived from *the* Law, but that which is through faith in Christ, the righteousness

---

ἀναπληρώσῃ τὸ ὑμῶν ὑστέρημα τῆς πρός
he might fill up ¹the ²of you ⁴lack – ⁵toward

με λειτουργίας.
⁶me ⁴of service.

3 Τὸ λοιπόν, ἀδελφοί μου, χαίρετε ἐν
For the rest, brothers of me, rejoice ye in

κυρίῳ. τὰ αὐτὰ γράφειν ὑμῖν ἐμοὶ μὲν
[the] Lord. ¹The ²same things ³to write to you for me indeed

οὐκ ὀκνηρόν, ὑμῖν δὲ ἀσφαλές.
[is] not irksome, but for you safe.

2 Βλέπετε τοὺς κύνας, βλέπετε τοὺς
Look [to] the dogs, look [to] the

κακοὺς ἐργάτας, βλέπετε τὴν κατατομήν.•
evil workmen, look [to] the concision.•

3 ἡμεῖς γάρ ἐσμεν ἡ περιτομή, οἱ
For we are the circumcision, the [ones]

πνεύματι θεοῦ λατρεύοντες καὶ καυχώμενοι
¹by [the] Spirit ²of God ¹worshipping and boasting

ἐν Χριστῷ Ἰησοῦ καὶ οὐκ ἐν σαρκὶ
in Christ Jesus and ²not ³in [the] ⁴flesh

πεποιθότες, **4** καίπερ ἐγὼ ἔχων πεποίθησιν
¹trusting, even though I having trust

καὶ ἐν σαρκί. Εἴ τις δοκεῖ ἄλλος
also in [the] flesh. If any ¹thinks ²other man

πεποιθέναι ἐν σαρκί, ἐγὼ μᾶλλον·
to trust in [the] flesh, I more:

5 περιτομῇ ὀκταήμερος, ἐκ γένους Ἰσραήλ,
in circumcision eighth day, of [the] race of Israel,

φυλῆς Βενιαμίν, Ἑβραῖος ἐξ Ἑβραίων,
[the] tribe of Benjamin, a Hebrew of Hebrew [parents],

κατὰ νόμον Φαρισαῖος, **6** κατὰ ζῆλος
according [the] law a Pharisee, by way of zeal
to

διώκων τὴν ἐκκλησίαν, κατὰ δικαιοσύνην
persecuting the church, according [the]
to righteousness

τὴν ἐν νόμῳ γενόμενος ἄμεμπτος. **7** ἀλλὰ
– in [the] law being blameless. But

ἅτινα ἦν μοι κέρδη, ταῦτα ἥγημαι διὰ
what were to me gain, these I have ²on ac-
things deemed count of

τὸν Χριστὸν ζημίαν. **8** ἀλλὰ μενοῦν γε
– ²Christ ¹loss. But nay rather

καὶ ἡγοῦμαι πάντα ζημίαν εἶναι διὰ
²also ¹I deem ²all things ³loss ⁴to be on account of

τὸ ὑπερέχον τῆς γνώσεως Χριστοῦ Ἰησοῦ
the excellency of the knowledge of Christ Jesus

τοῦ κυρίου μου, δι' ὃν τὰ πάντα
the Lord of me, on ac- whom – all things
count of

ἐζημιώθην, καὶ ἡγοῦμαι σκύβαλα ἵνα
I suffered loss, and deem [them] refuse in order
that

Χριστὸν κερδήσω **9** καὶ εὑρεθῶ ἐν αὐτῷ,
Christ I might gain and be found in him,

μὴ ἔχων ἐμὴν δικαιοσύνην τὴν ἐκ νόμου,
not having my righteousness the [one] of law,

ἀλλὰ τὴν διὰ πίστεως Χριστοῦ, τὴν
but the [one] through faith of(in) Christ,• ¹the

Christ, risking his life to make up for the help you could not give me.

Chapter 3

No Confidence in the Flesh

FINALLY, my brothers, rejoice in the Lord! It is no trouble for me to write the same things to you again, and it is a safeguard for you.

²Watch out for those dogs, those men who do evil, those mutilators of the flesh. ³For it is we who are the circumcision, we who worship by the Spirit of God, who glory in Christ Jesus, and who put no confidence in the flesh—⁴though I myself have reasons for such confidence.

If anyone else thinks he has reasons to put confidence in the flesh, I have more: ⁵circumcised on the eighth day, of the people of Israel, of the tribe of Benjamin, a Hebrew of Hebrews; in regard to the law, a Pharisee; ⁶as for zeal, persecuting the church; as for legalistic righteousness, faultless.

⁷But whatever was to my profit I now consider loss for the sake of Christ. ⁸What is more, I consider everything a loss compared to the surpassing greatness of knowing Christ Jesus my Lord, for whose sake I have lost all things. I consider them rubbish, that I may gain Christ ⁹and be found in him, not having a righteousness of my own that comes from the law, but that which is through faith in Christ—the right-

---

• The apostle uses a "studiously contemptuous paronomasia" (Ellicott). He does not use περιτομή, the proper word for "circumcision", as this, though now abrogated in Christ, had still its spiritual aspects."

• See Gal. 2. 20.

which *comes* from God on the basis of faith, [10]that I may know Him, and the power of His resurrection and the fellowship of His sufferings, being conformed to His death; [11]in order that I may attain to the resurrection from the dead. [12]Not that I have already obtained *it*, or have already become perfect, but I press on in order that I may lay hold of that for which also I was laid hold of by Christ Jesus. [13]Brethren, I do not regard myself as having laid hold of *it* yet; but one thing *I do*: forgetting what *lies* behind and reaching forward to what *lies* ahead, [14]I press on toward the goal for the prize of the upward call of God in Christ Jesus. [15]Let us therefore, as many as are perfect, have this attitude; and if in anything you have a different attitude, God will reveal that also to you; [16]however, let us keep living by that same *standard* to which we have attained. [17]Brethren, join in following my example, and observe those who walk according to the pattern you have in us. [18]For many walk, of whom I often told you, and now tell you even weeping, *that they are* enemies of the cross of Christ, [19]whose end is destruction, whose god is *their* appetite, and *whose glory* is in their shame, who set their minds on earthly things. [20]For our citizenship is in heaven, from which also we eagerly wait for a Savior, the Lord Jesus Christ; [21]who will transform the body of our humble state into conformity with the body of His glory, by the

ἐκ θεοῦ δικαιοσύνην ἐπὶ τῇ πίστει,
[9]of ⁴God ²righteousness [based] on – faith,

10 τοῦ γνῶναι αὐτὸν καὶ τὴν δύναμιν
– to know[d] him and the power

τῆς ἀναστάσεως αὐτοῦ καὶ κοινωνίαν
of the resurrection of him and [the] fellowship

παθημάτων αὐτοῦ, συμμορφιζόμενος τῷ
of sufferings of him, being conformed to the

θανάτῳ αὐτοῦ, 11 εἴ πως καταντήσω εἰς
death of him, if [some]how I may attain *to* to

τὴν ἐξανάστασιν τὴν ἐκ νεκρῶν. 12 Οὐχ
the out-resurrection – from [the] dead. Not

ὅτι ἤδη ἔλαβον ἢ ἤδη τετελείωμαι,
that already I received or already have been perfected,

διώκω δὲ εἰ καὶ καταλάβω, ἐφ᾽ ᾧ
but I follow if indeed I may lay hold, inasmuch as

καὶ κατελήμφθην ὑπὸ Χριστοῦ Ἰησοῦ.
also I was laid hold of by Christ Jesus.

13 ἀδελφοί, ἐγὼ ἐμαυτὸν οὔπω λογίζομαι
Brothers, ²I ⁴myself ¹not yet ³reckon

κατειληφέναι· ἐν δέ, τὰ μὲν ὀπίσω
to have but one thing ³the ²on one ⁴behind
laid hold; [I do], things hand

ἐπιλανθανόμενος τοῖς δὲ ἔμπροσθεν ἐπεκ-
¹forgetting ³the ¹on the ⁴before ²stretching
things other

τεινόμενος, 14 κατὰ σκοπὸν διώκω εἰς
forward to, according to a mark I follow for

τὸ βραβεῖον τῆς ἄνω κλήσεως τοῦ θεοῦ
the prize of the above calling – of God

ἐν Χριστῷ Ἰησοῦ. 15 Ὅσοι οὖν τέλειοι,
in Christ Jesus. ²As many ¹there- [are]
as fore perfect,

τοῦτο φρονῶμεν· καὶ εἴ τι ἑτέρως
³this ¹let us think; and if anything otherwise

φρονεῖτε, καὶ τοῦτο ὁ θεὸς ὑμῖν ἀποκα-
ye think, even this – God to you will

λύψει· 16 πλὴν εἰς ὃ ἐφθάσαμεν, τῷ
reveal; nevertheless to what we arrived, by the

αὐτῷ στοιχεῖν. 17 Συμμιμηταί μου
same to walk. Fellow-imitators of me

γίνεσθε, ἀδελφοί, καὶ σκοπεῖτε τοὺς οὕτω
be ye, brothers, and mark the [ones] thus

περιπατοῦντας καθὼς ἔχετε τύπον ἡμᾶς.
walking as ye have ²an example ¹us.

18 πολλοὶ γὰρ περιπατοῦσιν οὓς πολλάκις
For many walk [of] whom often

ἔλεγον ὑμῖν, νῦν δὲ καὶ κλαίων λέγω,
I said to you, and now also weeping I say,

τοὺς ἐχθροὺς τοῦ σταυροῦ τοῦ Χριστοῦ,
the enemies of the cross – of Christ,

19 ὧν τὸ τέλος ἀπώλεια, ὧν ὁ θεὸς
of whom the end [is] destruction, of whom the god [is]

ἡ κοιλία καὶ ἡ δόξα ἐν τῇ αἰσχύνῃ
the belly and the glory in the shame

αὐτῶν, οἱ τὰ ἐπίγεια φρονοῦντες. 20 ἡμῶν
of them, the the earthly things thinking. of us
[ones]

γὰρ τὸ πολίτευμα ἐν οὐρανοῖς ὑπάρχει,
For the citizenship in heavens is,

ἐξ οὗ καὶ σωτῆρα ἀπεκδεχόμεθα κύριον
from where also ²a Saviour ¹we await Lord

Ἰησοῦν Χριστόν, 21 ὃς μετασχηματίσει τὸ
Jesus Christ, who will change the

σῶμα τῆς ταπεινώσεως ἡμῶν σύμμορφον
body of the humiliation of us [making it] conformed

τῷ σώματι τῆς δόξης αὐτοῦ, κατὰ τὴν
to the body of the glory of him, according to the

eousness that comes from God and is by faith. [10]I want to know Christ and the power of his resurrection and the fellowship of sharing in his sufferings, becoming like him in his death, [11]and so, somehow, to attain to the resurrection from the dead.

Pressing on Toward the Goal

[12]Not that I have already obtained all this, or have already been made perfect, but I press on to take hold of that for which Christ Jesus took hold of me. [13]Brothers, I do not consider myself yet to have taken hold of it. But one thing I do: Forgetting what is behind and straining toward what is ahead, [14]I press on toward the goal to win the prize for which God has called me heavenward in Christ Jesus. [15]All of us who are mature should take such a view of things. And if on some point you think differently, that too God will make clear to you. [16]Only let us live up to what we have already attained.

[17]Join with others in following my example, brothers, and take note of those who live according to the pattern we gave you. [18]For, as I have often told you before and now say again even with tears, many live as enemies of the cross of Christ. [19]Their destiny is destruction, their god is their stomach, and their glory is in their shame. Their mind is on earthly things. [20]But our citizenship is in heaven. And we eagerly await a Savior from there, the Lord Jesus Christ, [21]who, by the power that enables him to bring everything under his control, will transform our

exertion of the power that He has even to subject all things to Himself.

Chapter 4

Think of Excellence

THEREFORE, my beloved brethren whom I long *to see*, my joy and crown, so stand firm in the Lord, my beloved.

²I urge Euodia and I urge Syntyche to live in harmony in the Lord.

³Indeed, true comrade, I ask you also to help these women who have shared my struggle in *the cause of* the gospel, together with Clement also, and the rest of my fellow workers, whose names are in the book of life.

⁴Rejoice in the Lord always; again I will say, rejoice!

⁵Let your forbearing *spirit* be known to all men. The Lord is near.

⁶Be anxious for nothing, but in everything by prayer and supplication with thanksgiving let your requests be made known to God.

⁷And the peace of God, which surpasses all comprehension, shall guard your hearts and your minds in Christ Jesus.

⁸Finally, brethren, whatever is true, whatever is honorable, whatever is right, whatever is pure, whatever is lovely, whatever is of good repute, if there is any excellence and if anything worthy of praise, let your mind dwell on these things.

⁹The things you have learned and received and heard and seen in me, practice these things; and the God of peace shall be with you.

God's Provisions

¹⁰But I rejoiced in the Lord greatly, that now at last you have revived your concern for me; indeed,

---

ἐνέργειαν τοῦ δύνασθαι αὐτὸν καὶ ὑποτάξαι
operation of the to be able him^b even to subject
=of his ability

αὐτῷ τὰ πάντα. **4** Ὥστε, ἀδελφοί μου
to him[self] – all things. So as, brothers of me

ἀγαπητοὶ καὶ ἐπιπόθητοι, χαρὰ καὶ
beloved and longed for, joy and

στέφανός μου, οὕτως στήκετε ἐν κυρίῳ, ἀγαπητοί.
crown of me, so stand in [the] Lord, beloved.

2 Εὐοδίαν παρακαλῶ καὶ Συντύχην
¹Euodia ¹I beseech and ¹Syntyche

παρακαλῶ τὸ αὐτὸ φρονεῖν ἐν κυρίῳ.
¹I beseech ⁴the ⁵same thing ³to think in [the] Lord.

3 ναὶ ἐρωτῶ καὶ σέ, γνήσιε σύζυγε,
Yes[,] I ask also thee, genuine yoke-fellow,

συλλαμβάνου αὐταῖς, αἵτινες ἐν τῷ εὐαγ-
help them, who ²in ⁴the ⁵gos-

γελίῳ συνήθλησάν μοι μετὰ καὶ Κλήμεντος
pel ¹struggled with ²me with both Clement

καὶ τῶν λοιπῶν συνεργῶν μου, ὧν
and the remaining fellow-workers of me, of whom

τὰ ὀνόματα ἐν βίβλῳ ζωῆς. **4** Χαίρετε
the names [are] in [the] book of life. Rejoice ye

ἐν κυρίῳ πάντοτε· πάλιν ἐρῶ, χαίρετε.
in [the] Lord always; again I will say, rejoice.

5 τὸ ἐπιεικὲς ὑμῶν γνωσθήτω πᾶσιν
The forbearance of you let it be known to all

ἀνθρώποις. ὁ κύριος ἐγγύς. **6** μηδὲν
men. The Lord [is] near. ²Nothing

μεριμνᾶτε, ἀλλ' ἐν παντὶ τῇ προσευχῇ
¹be ye anxious but in everything – by prayer
about,

καὶ τῇ δεήσει μετὰ εὐχαριστίας τὰ
and – by petition with thanksgivings the

αἰτήματα ὑμῶν γνωριζέσθω πρὸς τὸν
requests of you let be made known to –

θεόν. **7** καὶ ἡ εἰρήνη τοῦ θεοῦ ἡ
God. And the peace – of God –

ὑπερέχουσα πάντα νοῦν φρουρήσει τὰς
surpassing all understanding will guard the

καρδίας ὑμῶν καὶ τὰ νοήματα ὑμῶν
hearts of you and the thoughts of you

ἐν Χριστῷ Ἰησοῦ. **8** Τὸ λοιπόν, ἀδελφοί,
in Christ Jesus. For the rest, brothers,

ὅσα ἐστὶν ἀληθῆ, ὅσα σεμνά, ὅσα δίκαια,
whatever are true, whatever grave, whatever just,
things things things

ὅσα ἁγνά, ὅσα προσφιλῆ, ὅσα εὔφημα,
whatever pure, whatever lovable, • whatever well-spoken
things things things of

εἴ τις ἀρετὴ καὶ εἴ τις ἔπαινος, **9** ταῦτα
if any virtue and if any praise, these things

λογίζεσθε· ἃ καὶ ἐμάθετε καὶ παρελάβετε
consider ye; which ²both ¹ye ³learned and ye received
things

καὶ ἠκούσατε καὶ εἴδετε ἐν ἐμοί, ταῦτα
and ye heard and ye saw in me, these

πράσσετε· καὶ ὁ θεὸς τῆς εἰρήνης ἔσται
practise; and the God – of peace will be

μεθ' ὑμῶν.
with you.

10 Ἐχάρην δὲ ἐν κυρίῳ μεγάλως ὅτι
Now I rejoiced in [the] Lord greatly that

ἤδη ποτὲ ἀνεθάλετε τὸ ὑπὲρ ἐμοῦ φρονεῖν·
al- at one ye revived the on behalf me to think;
ready time of
=now at length =your thought for me;

---

lowly bodies so that they will be like his glorious body.

Chapter 4

THEREFORE, my brothers, you whom I love and long for, my joy and crown, that is how you should stand firm in the Lord, dear friends!

Exhortations

²I plead with Euodia and I plead with Syntyche to agree with each other in the Lord. ³Yes, and I ask you, loyal yokefellow,^h help these women who have contended at my side in the cause of the gospel, along with Clement and the rest of my fellow workers, whose names are in the book of life.

⁴Rejoice in the Lord always. I will say it again: Rejoice! ⁵Let your gentleness be evident to all. The Lord is near. ⁶Do not be anxious about anything, but in everything, by prayer and petition, with thanksgiving, present your requests to God. ⁷And the peace of God, which transcends all understanding, will guard your hearts and your minds in Christ Jesus.

⁸Finally, brothers, whatever is true, whatever is noble, whatever is right, whatever is pure, whatever is lovely, whatever is admirable—if anything is excellent or praiseworthy—think about such things. ⁹Whatever you have learned or received or heard from me, or seen in me—put it into practice. And the God of peace will be with you.

Thanks for Their Gifts

¹⁰I rejoice greatly in the Lord that at last you have renewed your concern for me. Indeed, you have been

you were concerned *before*, but you lacked opportunity.

11Not that I speak from want; for I have learned to be content in whatever circumstances I am.

12I know how to get along with humble means, and I also know how to live in prosperity; in any and every circumstance I have learned the secret of being filled and going hungry, both of having abundance and suffering need.

13I can do all things through Him who strengthens me.

14Nevertheless, you have done well to share *with me* in my affliction.

15And you yourselves also know, Philippians, that at the first preaching of the gospel, after I departed from Macedonia, no church shared with me in the matter of giving and receiving but you alone;

16for even in Thessalonica you sent *a gift* more than once for my needs.

17Not that I seek the gift itself, but I seek for the profit which increases to your account.

18But I have received everything in full, and have an abundance; I am amply supplied, having received from Epaphroditus what you have sent, a fragrant aroma, an acceptable sacrifice, well-pleasing to God.

19And my God shall supply all your needs according to His riches in glory in Christ Jesus.

20Now to our God and Father *be* the glory forever and ever. Amen.

21Greet every saint in Christ Jesus. The brethren who are with me greet you.

22All the saints greet you, especially those of Caesar's household.

ἐφ᾽ ᾧ καὶ ἐφρονεῖτε, ἠκαιρεῖσθε δέ.
as to which indeed ye thought, but ye had no opportunity.

11 οὐχ ὅτι καθ᾽ ὑστέρησιν λέγω· ἐγὼ
Not that ³by way of ²lack ¹I say; ¹I

γὰρ ἔμαθον ἐν οἷς εἰμι αὐτάρκης εἶναι.
¹for learned in what I am ²self- ¹to be.
                      conditions   sufficient

12 οἶδα καὶ ταπεινοῦσθαι, οἶδα καὶ περισ-
I know both to be humbled, and I know to

σεύειν· ἐν παντὶ καὶ ἐν πᾶσιν μεμύημαι,
abound; in everything and in all things I have been
                                 initiated,

καὶ χορτάζεσθαι καὶ πεινᾶν, καὶ περισ-
both to be filled and to hunger, both to

σεύειν καὶ ὑστερεῖσθαι. 13 πάντα ἰσχύω
abound and to lack. ²All things ¹I can do

ἐν τῷ ἐνδυναμοῦντί με. 14 πλὴν καλῶς
in the [one] empowering me. Nevertheless ³well

ἐποιήσατε συγκοινωνήσαντές μου τῇ θλίψει.
¹ye did having partnership in ²of me ¹the ²affliction.

15 οἴδατε δὲ καὶ ὑμεῖς, Φιλιππήσιοι, ὅτι
And ²know ²also ¹ye, Philippians, that

ἐν ἀρχῇ τοῦ εὐαγγελίου, ὅτε ἐξῆλθον
in [the] of the gospel, when I went out

ἀπὸ Μακεδονίας, οὐδεμία μοι ἐκκλησία
from Macedonia, not one ²me ¹church

ἐκοινώνησεν εἰς λόγον δόσεως καὶ λήμψεως
¹shared with in matter of giving and receiving

εἰ μὴ ὑμεῖς μόνοι, 16 ὅτι καὶ ἐν
except ye only, because indeed in

Θεσσαλονίκῃ καὶ ἅπαξ καὶ δὶς εἰς τὴν
Thessalonica both once and twice to the
                                 = to my need

χρείαν μοι ἐπέμψατε. 17 οὐχ ὅτι ἐπιζητῶ
need to meᵒ ye sent. Not that I seek

τὸ δόμα, ἀλλὰ ἐπιζητῶ τὸν καρπὸν
the gift, but I seek the fruit

τὸν πλεονάζοντα εἰς λόγον ὑμῶν. 18 ἀπέχω
- increasing to account of you. I have

δὲ πάντα καὶ περισσεύω· πεπλήρωμαι
But all things and abound; I have been filled

δεξάμενος παρὰ Ἐπαφροδίτου τὰ παρ᾽
receiving from Epaphroditus the things from

ὑμῶν, ὀσμὴν εὐωδίας, θυσίαν δεκτήν,
you, an odour of sweet smell, a sacrifice acceptable,

εὐάρεστον τῷ θεῷ. 19 ὁ δὲ θεός μου
well-pleasing - to God. And the God of me

πληρώσει πᾶσαν χρείαν ὑμῶν κατὰ τὸ
will fill every need of you according to the

πλοῦτος αὐτοῦ ἐν δόξῃ ἐν Χριστῷ Ἰησοῦ.
riches of him in glory in Christ Jesus.

20 τῷ δὲ θεῷ καὶ πατρὶ ἡμῶν ἡ δόξα
to the Now God and Father of us [be] the glory

εἰς τοὺς αἰῶνας τῶν αἰώνων· ἀμήν.
unto the ages of the ages: Amen.

21 Ἀσπάσασθε πάντα ἅγιον ἐν Χριστῷ
Greet ye every saint in Christ

Ἰησοῦ. ἀσπάζονται ὑμᾶς οἱ σὺν ἐμοὶ
Jesus. ²greet ²you ¹The ³with ⁴me

ἀδελφοί. 22 ἀσπάζονται ὑμᾶς πάντες οἱ
²brothers. ⁴greet ³you ¹All ²the

ἅγιοι, μάλιστα δὲ οἱ ἐκ τῆς Καίσαρος
²saints, but most of all the ones of ¹the ²of Cæsar

οἰκίας.
²household.

---

concerned, but you had no opportunity to show it. 11I am not saying this because I am in need, for I have learned to be content whatever the circumstances. 12I know what it is to be in need, and I know what it is to have plenty. I have learned the secret of being content in any and every situation, whether well fed or hungry, whether living in plenty or in want. 13I can do everything through him who gives me strength.

14Yet it was good of you to share in my troubles. 15Moreover, as you Philippians know, in the early days of your acquaintance with the gospel, when I set out from Macedonia, not one church shared with me in the matter of giving and receiving, except you only; 16for even when I was in Thessalonica, you sent me aid again and again when I was in need. 17Not that I am looking for a gift, but I am looking for what may be credited to your account. 18I have received full payment and even more; I am amply supplied, now that I have received from Epaphroditus the gifts you sent. They are a fragrant offering, an acceptable sacrifice, pleasing to God. 19And my God will meet all your needs according to his glorious riches in Christ Jesus.

20To our God and Father be glory for ever and ever. Amen.

Final Greetings

21Greet all the saints in Christ Jesus. The brothers who are with me send greetings. 22All the saints send you greetings, especially those who belong to Caesar's household.

23The grace of the Lord Jesus Christ be with your spirit.

23 Ἡ χάρις τοῦ κυρίου Ἰησοῦ Χριστοῦ
The grace of the Lord Jesus Christ

μετὰ τοῦ πνεύματος ὑμῶν.
[be] with the spirit of you.

23The grace of the Lord Jesus Christ be with your spirit. Amen. i

Colossians

ΠΡΟΣ ΚΟΛΟΣΣΑΕΙΣ
To Colossians

Colossians

Chapter 1

Thankfulness for Spiritual Attainments

PAUL, an apostle of Jesus Christ by the will of God, and Timothy our brother,

2to the saints and faithful brethren in Christ *who are* at Colossae: Grace to you and peace from God our Father.

3We give thanks to God, the Father of our Lord Jesus Christ, praying always for you,

4since we heard of your faith in Christ Jesus and the love which you have for all the saints;

5because of the hope laid up for you in heaven, of which you previously heard in the word of truth, the gospel,

6which has come to you, just as in all the world also it is constantly bearing fruit and increasing, even as *it has been doing* in you also, since the day you heard *of it* and understood the grace of God in truth;

7just as you learned *it* from Epaphras, our beloved fellow bond-servant, who is a faithful servant of Christ on *a*our behalf,

8and he also informed us of your love in the Spirit.

9For this reason also, since the day we heard *of it,* we have not ceased to pray

1 Παῦλος ἀπόστολος Χριστοῦ Ἰησοῦ διὰ
Paul an apostle of Christ Jesus through

θελήματος θεοῦ καὶ Τιμόθεος ὁ ἀδελφὸς
[the] will of God and Timothy the brother

2 τοῖς ἐν Κολοσσαῖς ἁγίοις καὶ πιστοῖς
to the in Colossae saints and faithful

ἀδελφοῖς ἐν Χριστῷ· χάρις ὑμῖν καὶ
brothers in Christ: Grace to you and

εἰρήνη ἀπὸ θεοῦ πατρὸς ἡμῶν.
peace from God Father of us.

3 Εὐχαριστοῦμεν τῷ θεῷ πατρὶ τοῦ
We give thanks - to God Father of the

κυρίου ἡμῶν Ἰησοῦ [Χριστοῦ] πάντοτε
Lord of us Jesus Christ always

περὶ ὑμῶν προσευχόμενοι, **4** ἀκούσαντες
¹concerning ²you ³praying, having heard

τὴν πίστιν ὑμῶν ἐν Χριστῷ Ἰησοῦ
the faith of you in Christ Jesus

καὶ τὴν ἀγάπην ἣν ἔχετε εἰς πάντας
and the love which ye have toward all

τοὺς ἁγίους **5** διὰ τὴν ἐλπίδα τὴν
the saints because of the hope -

ἀποκειμένην ὑμῖν ἐν τοῖς οὐρανοῖς, ἣν
being laid up for you in *the* heavens, which

προηκούσατε ἐν τῷ λόγῳ τῆς ἀληθείας
ye previously heard in the word of the truth

τοῦ εὐαγγελίου **6** τοῦ παρόντος εἰς ὑμᾶς,
of the gospel - coming to you,

καθὼς καὶ ἐν παντὶ τῷ κόσμῳ ἐστὶν
as also in all the world it is

καρποφορούμενον καὶ αὐξανόμενον καθὼς
bearing fruit and growing as

καὶ ἐν ὑμῖν, ἀφ' ἧς ἡμέρας ἠκούσατε
also in you, from which day ye heard
    = the day on which

καὶ ἐπέγνωτε τὴν χάριν τοῦ θεοῦ ἐν
and fully knew the grace - of God in

ἀληθείᾳ· **7** καθὼς ἐμάθετε ἀπὸ Ἐπαφρᾶ
truth; as ye learned from Epaphras

τοῦ ἀγαπητοῦ συνδούλου ἡμῶν, ὅς ἐστιν
the beloved fellow-slave of us, who is

πιστὸς ὑπὲρ ὑμῶν διάκονος τοῦ Χριστοῦ,
¹ᵃfaithful ⁴on behalf ³you ²minister - ⁵of Christ,

8 ὁ καὶ δηλώσας ἡμῖν τὴν ὑμῶν ἀγάπην
the also having shown to us ¹the ²of you ³love
[one]

ἐν πνεύματι.
in spirit.

9 Διὰ τοῦτο καὶ ἡμεῖς, ἀφ' ἧς ἡμέρας
Therefore also we, from which day
    = the day on which

ἠκούσαμεν, οὐ παυόμεθα ὑπὲρ ὑμῶν
we heard, do not cease on behalf of you

PAUL, an apostle of Christ Jesus by the will of God, and Timothy our brother,

2To the holy and faithful *a* brothers in Christ at Colosse:

Grace and peace to you from God our Father. *b*

Thanksgiving and Prayer

3We always thank God, the Father of our Lord Jesus Christ, when we pray for you, 4because we have heard of your faith in Christ Jesus and of the love you have for all the saints—5the faith and love that spring from the hope that is stored up for you in heaven and that you have already heard about in the word of truth, the gospel that has come to you. All over the world this gospel is bearing fruit and growing, just as it has been doing among you since the day you heard it and understood God's grace in all its truth. 7You learned it from Epaphras, our dear fellow servant, who is a faithful minister of Christ on our *c* behalf, 8and who also told us of your love in the Spirit.

9For this reason, since the day we heard about you, we have not stopped

---

i23 Some manuscripts do not have *Amen.*
a2 Or *believing*
b2 Some manuscripts *Father and the Lord Jesus Christ*
c7 Some manuscripts *your*

for you and to ask that you may be filled with the knowledge of His will in all spiritual wisdom and understanding,

10so that you may walk in a manner worthy of the Lord, to please *Him* in all respects, bearing fruit in every good work and increasing in the knowledge of God;

11strengthened with all power, according to His glorious might, for the attaining of all steadfastness and patience; joyously

12giving thanks to the Father, who has qualified us to share in the inheritance of the saints in light.

The Incomparable Christ

13For He delivered us from the domain of darkness, and transferred us to the kingdom of His beloved Son,

14in whom we have redemption, the forgiveness of sins.

15And He is the image of the invisible God, the first-born of all creation.

16For by Him all things were created, *both* in the heavens and on earth, visible and invisible, whether thrones or dominions or rulers or authorities—all things have been created by Him and for Him.

17And He is before all things, and in Him all things hold together.

18He is also head of the body, the church; and He is the beginning, the first-born from the dead; so that He Himself might come to have first place in everything.

19For it was the *Father's* good pleasure for all the fulness to dwell in Him,

20and through Him to reconcile all things to Himself,

προσευχόμενοι καὶ αἰτούμενοι ἵνα πληρω-
praying   and   asking   in order ye may be
                                   that

θῆτε τὴν ἐπίγνωσιν τοῦ θελήματος αὐτοῦ
filled the full knowledge of the   will   of him
[with]

ἐν πάσῃ σοφίᾳ καὶ συνέσει πνευματικῇ,
in all   wisdom and understanding spiritual,

10 περιπατῆσαι ἀξίως τοῦ κυρίου εἰς
       to walk   worthily of the Lord   to

πᾶσαν ἀρεσκείαν, ἐν παντὶ ἔργῳ ἀγαθῷ
all   pleasing, in every work good

καρποφοροῦντες καὶ αὐξανόμενοι τῇ
bearing fruit   and growing   in the

ἐπιγνώσει τοῦ θεοῦ, **11** ἐν πάσῃ δυνάμει
full knowledge – of God,   with all   power

δυναμούμενοι κατὰ τὸ κράτος τῆς δόξης
being empowered according to the might of the glory

αὐτοῦ εἰς πᾶσαν ὑπομονὴν καὶ μακρο-
of him to all   endurance and long-

θυμίαν, μετὰ χαρᾶς **12** εὐχαριστοῦντες τῷ
suffering, with joy   giving thanks   to the

πατρὶ τῷ ἱκανώσαντι ὑμᾶς εἰς τὴν μερίδα
Father – having made ²fit ¹you for the   part

τοῦ κλήρου τῶν ἁγίων ἐν τῷ φωτί·
of the lot of the saints in the light;

13 ὃς ἐρρύσατο ἡμᾶς ἐκ τῆς ἐξουσίας
       who delivered us out of the authority

τοῦ σκότους καὶ μετέστησεν εἰς τὴν
of the darkness and transferred into the

βασιλείαν τοῦ υἱοῦ τῆς ἀγάπης αὐτοῦ,
kingdom   of the Son of the love   of him,

14 ἐν ᾧ ἔχομεν τὴν ἀπολύτρωσιν, τὴν
       in whom we have the redemption,   the

ἄφεσιν τῶν ἁμαρτιῶν· **15** ὅς ἐστιν εἰκὼν
forgiveness of the sins;   who is   an image
(our)

τοῦ θεοῦ τοῦ ἀοράτου, πρωτότοκος πάσης
of the God   – invisible,   firstborn   of all

κτίσεως, **16** ὅτι ἐν αὐτῷ ἐκτίσθη τὰ
creation,   because in him   were created –

πάντα ἐν τοῖς οὐρανοῖς καὶ ἐπὶ τῆς
all things in the heavens   and on the

γῆς, τὰ ὁρατὰ καὶ τὰ ἀόρατα, εἴτε
earth, the visible and the invisible, whether

θρόνοι εἴτε κυριότητες εἴτε ἀρχαὶ εἴτε
thrones or lordships   or rulers or

ἐξουσίαι· τὰ πάντα δι' αὐτοῦ καὶ εἰς
authorities; – all things through him   and for

αὐτὸν ἔκτισται· **17** καὶ αὐτός ἐστιν πρὸ
him have been created; and he   is   before

πάντων καὶ τὰ πάντα ἐν αὐτῷ συνέστηκεν,
all things and – all things in him   consisted,

18 καὶ αὐτός ἐστιν ἡ κεφαλὴ τοῦ σώματος,
       and he   is   the head   of the body,

τῆς ἐκκλησίας· ὅς ἐστιν ἀρχή, πρωτότοκος
of the church; who is [the]   firstborn
                        beginning,

ἐκ τῶν νεκρῶν, ἵνα γένηται ἐν πᾶσιν
from the dead,   in order ⁴may be ²in ³all
                  that   things

αὐτὸς πρωτεύων, **19** ὅτι ἐν αὐτῷ εὐδόκησεν
¹he   ⁵holding the   because in him   ⁴was well
      first place,   pleased

πᾶν τὸ πλήρωμα κατοικῆσαι **20** καὶ δι'
¹all ²the ³fulness to dwell   and through

αὐτοῦ ἀποκαταλλάξαι τὰ πάντα εἰς αὐτόν,
him   to reconcile   – all things to him[?self],

---

praying for you and asking God to fill you with the knowledge of his will through all spiritual wisdom and understanding.

10And we pray this in order that you may live a life worthy of the Lord and may please him in every way: bearing fruit in every good work, growing in the knowledge of God, 11being strengthened with all power according to his glorious might so that you may have great endurance and patience, and joyfully 12giving thanks to the Father, who has qualified you*d* to share in the inheritance of the saints in the kingdom of light. 13For he has rescued us from the dominion of darkness and brought us into the kingdom of the Son he loves, 14in whom we have redemption,*e* the forgiveness of sins.

The Supremacy of Christ

15He is the image of the invisible God, the firstborn over all creation. 16For by him all things were created: things in heaven and on earth, visible and invisible, whether thrones or powers or rulers or authorities; all things were created by him and for him. 17He is before all things, and in him all things hold together. 18And he is the head of the body, the church; he is the beginning and the firstborn from among the dead, so that in everything he might have the supremacy. 19For God was pleased to have all his fullness dwell in him, 20and through him to reconcile to himself all things, whether

---

*d*12 Some manuscripts *us*
*e*14 A few late manuscripts
redemption through his blood

having made peace through the blood of His cross; through Him, *I say,* whether things on earth or things in heaven.

21And although you were formerly alienated and hostile in mind, *engaged* in evil deeds,

22yet He has now reconciled you in His fleshly body through death, in order to present you before Him holy and blameless and beyond reproach—

23if indeed you continue in the faith firmly established and steadfast, and not moved away from the hope of the gospel that you have heard, which was proclaimed in all creation under heaven, and of which I, Paul, was made a minister.

24Now I rejoice in my sufferings for your sake, and in my flesh I do my share on behalf of His body (which is the church) in filling up that which is lacking in Christ's afflictions.

25Of *this church* I was made a minister according to the stewardship from God bestowed on me for your benefit, that I might fully carry out the *preaching of* the word of God,

26*that is,* the mystery which has been hidden from the *past* ages and generations; but has now been manifested to His saints,

27to whom God willed to make known what is the riches of the glory of this mystery among the Gentiles, which is Christ in you, the hope of glory.

28And we proclaim Him, admonishing every man and teaching every man

---

εἰρηνοποιήσας διὰ τοῦ αἵματος τοῦ σταυροῦ
making peace through the blood of the cross

αὐτοῦ, δι᾿ αὐτοῦ εἴτε τὰ ἐπὶ τῆς γῆς
of him, through him whether the things on the earth

εἴτε τὰ ἐν τοῖς οὐρανοῖς. 21 Καὶ ὑμᾶς
or the things in the heavens. And you

ποτε ὄντας ἀπηλλοτριωμένους καὶ ἐχθροὺς
then being *having been* alienated and enemies

τῇ διανοίᾳ ἐν τοῖς ἔργοις τοῖς πονηροῖς,
in *the* mind by the(your) works - evil,

22 νυνὶ δὲ ἀποκατήλλαξεν ἐν τῷ σώματι
but now he reconciled in the body

τῆς σαρκὸς αὐτοῦ διὰ τοῦ θανάτου,
of the flesh of him through the(his) death,

παραστῆσαι ὑμᾶς ἁγίους καὶ ἀμώμους
to present you holy and blameless

καὶ ἀνεγκλήτους κατενώπιον αὐτοῦ, 23 εἴ
and irreproachable before him, if

γε ἐπιμένετε τῇ πίστει τεθεμελιωμένοι
indeed ye continue in the faith having been founded

καὶ ἑδραῖοι καὶ μὴ μετακινούμενοι ἀπὸ
and steadfast and not being moved away from

τῆς ἐλπίδος τοῦ εὐαγγελίου οὗ ἠκούσατε,
the hope of the gospel which ye heard,

τοῦ κηρυχθέντος ἐν πάσῃ κτίσει τῇ
- proclaimed in all creation the

ὑπὸ τὸν οὐρανόν, οὗ ἐγενόμην ἐγὼ
under the heaven, of which ¹became ¹I

Παῦλος διάκονος.
¹Paul a minister.

24 Νῦν χαίρω ἐν τοῖς παθήμασιν ὑπὲρ
Now I rejoice in the(my) sufferings on behalf of

ὑμῶν, καὶ ἀνταναπληρῶ τὰ ὑστερήματα
you, and fill up the things lacking

τῶν θλίψεων τοῦ Χριστοῦ ἐν τῇ σαρκί
of the afflictions - of Christ in the flesh

μου ὑπὲρ τοῦ σώματος αὐτοῦ, ὅ ἐστιν
of me on behalf of the body of him, which is

ἡ ἐκκλησία, 25 ἧς ἐγενόμην ἐγὼ διάκονος
the church, of which became I a minister

κατὰ τὴν οἰκονομίαν τοῦ θεοῦ τὴν
according to the stewardship - of God -

δοθεῖσάν μοι εἰς ὑμᾶς πληρῶσαι τὸν
given to me for you to fulfil the

λόγον τοῦ θεοῦ, 26 τὸ μυστήριον τὸ
word - of God, the mystery -

ἀποκεκρυμμένον ἀπὸ τῶν αἰώνων καὶ
having been hidden from the ages and

ἀπὸ τῶν γενεῶν — νῦν δὲ ἐφανερώθη
from the generations — but now was manifested

τοῖς ἁγίοις αὐτοῦ, 27 οἷς ἠθέλησεν ὁ
to the saints of him, to whom ²wished -

θεὸς γνωρίσαι τί τὸ πλοῦτος τῆς δόξης
¹God to make known what [is] the riches of the glory

τοῦ μυστηρίου τούτου ἐν τοῖς ἔθνεσιν,
- mystery of this among the nations,

ὅς ἐστιν Χριστὸς ἐν ὑμῖν, ἡ ἐλπὶς τῆς
who is Christ in you, the hope of the

δόξης· 28 ὃν ἡμεῖς καταγγέλλομεν νου-
glory; whom we announce warn-

θετοῦντες πάντα ἄνθρωπον καὶ διδάσκοντες
ing every man and teaching

---

things on earth or things in heaven, by making peace through his blood, shed on the cross.

21Once you were alienated from God and were enemies in your minds because of* your evil behavior. 22But now he has reconciled you by Christ's physical body through death to present you holy in his sight, without blemish and free from accusation— 23if you continue in your faith, established and firm, not moved from the hope held out in the gospel. This is the gospel that you heard and that has been proclaimed to every creature under heaven, and of which I, Paul, have become a servant.

Paul's Labor for the Church

24Now I rejoice in what was suffered for you, and I fill up in my flesh what is still lacking in regard to Christ's afflictions, for the sake of his body, which is the church. 25I have become its servant by the commission God gave me to present to you the word of God in its fullness— 26the mystery that has been kept hidden for ages and generations, but is now disclosed to the saints. 27To them God has chosen to make known among the Gentiles the glorious riches of this mystery, which is Christ in you, the hope of glory.

28We proclaim him, admonishing and teaching everyone with all wisdom, so

---

21 Or minds, as shown by

with all wisdom, that we may present every man complete in Christ. 29And for this purpose also I labor, striving according to His power, which mightily works within me.

Chapter 2

You Are Built Up in Christ

FOR I want you to know how great a struggle I have on your behalf, and for those who are at Laodicea, and for all those who have not personally seen my face,

2that their hearts may be encouraged, having been knit together in love, and attaining to all the wealth that comes from the full assurance of understanding, resulting in a true knowledge of God's mystery, that is, Christ Himself,

3in whom are hidden all the treasures of wisdom and knowledge.

4I say this in order that no one may delude you with persuasive argument.

5For even though I am absent in body, nevertheless I am with you in spirit, rejoicing to see your good discipline and the stability of your faith in Christ.

6As you therefore have received Christ Jesus the Lord, so walk in Him,

7having been firmly rooted and now being built up in Him and established b in your faith, just as you were instructed, and overflowing with gratitude.

8See to it that no one takes you captive through philosophy and empty deception, according to the tradition of men, according to the elementary principles of the world, rather than according to Christ.

9For in Him all the ful-

πάντα ἄνθρωπον ἐν πάσῃ σοφίᾳ,
every man in all wisdom,
ἵνα παραστήσωμεν πάντα ἄνθρωπον
in or-der that we may present every man
τέλειον ἐν Χριστῷ· 29 εἰς ὃ καὶ κοπιῶ
mature in Christ; for which also I labour
ἀγωνιζόμενος κατὰ τὴν ἐνέργειαν αὐτοῦ
struggling accord-ing to the operation of him
τὴν ἐνεργουμένην ἐν ἐμοὶ ἐν δυνάμει.
- operating in me in power.
2 Θέλω γὰρ ὑμᾶς εἰδέναι ἡλίκον ἀγῶνα
For I wish you to know how great a struggle
ἔχω ὑπὲρ ὑμῶν καὶ τῶν ἐν Λαοδικείᾳ
I have on behalf of you and the [ones] in Laodicea
καὶ ὅσοι οὐχ ἑόρακαν τὸ πρόσωπόν μου
and as many as have not seen the face of me
ἐν σαρκί, 2 ἵνα παρακληθῶσιν αἱ καρδίαι
in flesh, in order that ⁴may be ¹the ²hearts
αὐτῶν, συμβιβασθέντες ἐν ἀγάπῃ καὶ εἰς
³of them, being joined together in love and for
πᾶν πλοῦτος τῆς πληροφορίας τῆς
all riches of the full assurance -
συνέσεως, εἰς ἐπίγνωσιν τοῦ μυστηρίου
of under-standing, for full knowledge of the mystery
τοῦ θεοῦ, Χριστοῦ, 3 ἐν ᾧ εἰσιν πάντες
- of God, of Christ, in whom ¹are ²all
οἱ θησαυροὶ τῆς σοφίας καὶ γνώσεως
³the ⁵treasures ⁴of wisdom ⁷and ⁶of knowledge
ἀπόκρυφοι. 4 Τοῦτο λέγω ἵνα μηδεὶς
¹hidden. This I say in order no one that
ὑμᾶς παραλογίζηται ἐν πιθανολογίᾳ. 5 εἰ
²you ¹may beguile with persuasive speech. if
γὰρ καὶ τῇ σαρκὶ ἄπειμι, ἀλλὰ τῷ
For indeed in the flesh I am absent, yet in the
πνεύματι σὺν ὑμῖν εἰμι, χαίρων καὶ
spirit ²with ³you ¹I am, rejoicing and
βλέπων ὑμῶν τὴν τάξιν καὶ τὸ στερέωμα
seeing ²of you ¹the ³order and the firmness
τῆς εἰς Χριστὸν πίστεως ὑμῶν.
of the ³in ⁴Christ ¹faith ²of you.
6 Ὡς οὖν παρελάβετε τὸν Χριστὸν
As therefore ye received - Christ
Ἰησοῦν τὸν κύριον, ἐν αὐτῷ περιπατεῖτε,
Jesus the Lord, in him walk ye,
7 ἐρριζωμένοι καὶ ἐποικοδομούμενοι ἐν αὐτῷ
having been rooted and being built up in him
καὶ βεβαιούμενοι τῇ πίστει καθὼς ἐδιδάχ-
and being confirmed in the faith as ye were
θητε, περισσεύοντες ἐν εὐχαριστίᾳ.
taught, abounding in thanksgiving.
8 Βλέπετε μή τις ὑμᾶς ἔσται ὁ συλαγωγῶν
Look ye lest ²anyone ⁴you ¹there - ⁵robbing shall be
διὰ τῆς φιλοσοφίας καὶ κενῆς ἀπάτης
through - philosophy and empty deceit
κατὰ τὴν παράδοσιν τῶν ἀνθρώπων, κατὰ
accord-ing to the tradition - of men, accord-ing to
τὰ στοιχεῖα τοῦ κόσμου καὶ οὐ κατὰ
the elements of the world and not accord-ing to
Χριστόν· 9 ὅτι ἐν αὐτῷ κατοικεῖ πᾶν
Christ; because in him dwells all

---

that we may present everyone perfect in Christ. 29To this end I labor, struggling with all his energy, which so powerfully works in me.

Chapter 2

I WANT you to know how much I am struggling for you and for those at Laodicea, and for all who have not met me personally. 2My purpose is that they may be encouraged in heart and united in love, so that they may have the full riches of complete understanding, in order that they may know the mystery of God, namely, Christ, 3in whom are hidden all the treasures of wisdom and knowledge. 4I tell you this so that no one may deceive you by fine-sounding arguments. 5For though I am absent from you in body, I am present with you in spirit and delight to see how orderly you are and how firm your faith in Christ is.

Freedom From Human Regulations Through Life With Christ

6So then, just as you received Christ Jesus as Lord, continue to live in him, 7rooted and built up in him, strengthened in the faith as you were taught, and overflowing with thankfulness.

8See to it that no one takes you captive through hollow and deceptive philosophy, which depends on human tradition and the basic principles of this world rather than on Christ.

9For in Christ all the full-

---

b Or, by

ness of Deity dwells in bodily form,

¹⁰and in Him you have been made complete, and He is the head over all rule and authority;

¹¹and in Him you were also circumcised with a circumcision made without hands, in the removal of the body of the flesh by the circumcision of Christ;

¹²having been buried with Him in baptism, in which you were also raised up with Him through faith in the working of God, who raised Him from the dead.

¹³And when you were dead in your transgressions and the uncircumcision of your flesh, He made you alive together with Him, having forgiven us all our transgressions,

¹⁴having canceled out the certificate of debt consisting of decrees against us *and* which was hostile to us; and He has taken it out of the way, having nailed it to the cross.

¹⁵When He had disarmed the rulers and authorities, He made a public display of them, having triumphed over them through Him.

¹⁶Therefore let no one act as your judge in regard to food or drink or in respect to a festival or a new moon or a Sabbath day—

¹⁷things which are a *mere* shadow of what is to come; but the substance belongs to Christ.

¹⁸Let no one keep defrauding you of your prize by delighting in self-abasement and the worship of the angels, taking his stand on *visions* he has seen, inflated without cause by his fleshly mind,

¹⁹and not holding fast to the head, from whom the entire body, being supplied and held together by the

---

τὸ πλήρωμα τῆς θεότητος σωματικῶς,
the fulness of the Godhead bodily,

10 καὶ ἐστὲ ἐν αὐτῷ πεπληρωμένοι, ὅς
and ye are in him having been filled, who

ἐστιν ἡ κεφαλὴ πάσης ἀρχῆς καὶ ἐξουσίας,
is the head of all rule and authority,

11 ἐν ᾧ καὶ περιετμήθητε περιτομῇ
in whom also ye were circumcised with a circumcision

ἀχειροποιήτῳ ἐν τῇ ἀπεκδύσει τοῦ σώματος
not handwrought by the putting off of the body

τῆς σαρκός, ἐν τῇ περιτομῇ τοῦ Χριστοῦ,
of the flesh, by the circumcision - of Christ,

12 συνταφέντες αὐτῷ ἐν τῷ βαπτίσματι,
co-buried with him in the baptism,

ἐν ᾧ καὶ συνηγέρθητε διὰ τῆς πίστεως
in whom also ye were co-raised through the faith

τῆς ἐνεργείας τοῦ θεοῦ τοῦ ἐγείραντος
of(in) the operation - of God - raising

αὐτὸν ἐκ νεκρῶν· **13** καὶ ὑμᾶς νεκροὺς
him from [the] dead; and you dead

ὄντας τοῖς παραπτώμασιν καὶ τῇ ἀκρο-
being in the trespasses and in the uncir-

βυστίᾳ τῆς σαρκὸς ὑμῶν, συνεζωοποίησεν
cumcision of the flesh of you, he co-quickened

ὑμᾶς σὺν αὐτῷ, χαρισάμενος ἡμῖν πάντα
you with him, forgiving us all

τὰ παραπτώματα· **14** ἐξαλείψας τὸ καθ᾽
the trespasses; wiping out ¹the ²against

ἡμῶν χειρόγραφον τοῖς δόγμασιν ὃ ἦν
¹us ²handwriting - in ordinances which was

ὑπεναντίον ἡμῖν, καὶ αὐτὸ ἦρκεν ἐκ
contrary to us, and ²it ¹has taken out of

τοῦ μέσου, προσηλώσας αὐτὸ τῷ σταυρῷ·
the midst(way), nailing it to the cross;

15 ἀπεκδυσάμενος τὰς ἀρχὰς καὶ τὰς
putting off the rulers and the

ἐξουσίας ἐδειγμάτισεν ἐν παρρησίᾳ,
authorities he exposed [them] with openness,

θριαμβεύσας αὐτοὺς ἐν αὐτῷ.
triumphing [over] them in it.

16 Μὴ οὖν τις ὑμᾶς κρινέτω ἐν βρώσει
²Not ³there-fore ⁴any-one ⁵you ¹let ⁶judge in eating

καὶ ἐν πόσει ἢ ἐν μέρει ἑορτῆς ἢ
and in drinking or in respect of a feast or

νεομηνίας ἢ σαββάτων, **17** ἅ ἐστιν σκιὰ
of a new moon or of sabbaths, which is(are) a shadow things

τῶν μελλόντων, τὸ δὲ σῶμα τοῦ Χριστοῦ.
of things coming, but the body [is] - of Christ.

18 μηδεὶς ὑμᾶς καταβραβευέτω θέλων ἐν
²No one ⁴you ¹let ³give judgment wishing in
against [to do so]

ταπεινοφροσύνῃ καὶ θρησκείᾳ τῶν ἀγγέλων,
humility* and worship of the angels,

ἃ ἑόρακεν ἐμβατεύων, εἰκῇ φυσιούμενος
¹things ³he has ¹intruding into, in vain being puffed up
which ²seen

ὑπὸ τοῦ νοὸς τῆς σαρκὸς αὐτοῦ, **19** καὶ
by the mind of the flesh of him, and

οὐ κρατῶν τὴν κεφαλήν, ἐξ οὗ πᾶν
not holding the head, from whom all

τὸ σῶμα διὰ τῶν ἁφῶν καὶ συνδέσμων
the body ⁴by means ⁵the ⁶joints ⁷and ⁸bands
of (its)

* Ellicott supplies " false ". Cf. ver. 22.

---

ness of the Deity lives in bodily form, ¹⁰and you have been given fullness in Christ, who is the head over every power and authority. ¹¹In him you were also circumcised, in the putting off of the sinful nature,[g] not with a circumcision done by the hands of men but with the circumcision done by Christ, ¹²having been buried with him in baptism and raised with him through your faith in the power of God, who raised him from the dead. ¹³When you were dead in your sins and in the uncircumcision of your sinful nature,[h] God made you[i] alive with Christ. He forgave us all our sins, ¹⁴having canceled the written code, with its regulations, that was against us and that stood opposed to us; he took it away, nailing it to the cross. ¹⁵And having disarmed the powers and authorities, he made a public spectacle of them, triumphing over them by the cross.[j]

¹⁶Therefore do not let anyone judge you by what you eat or drink, or with regard to a religious festival, a New Moon celebration or a Sabbath day. ¹⁷These are a shadow of the things that were to come; the reality, however, is found in Christ. ¹⁸Do not let anyone who delights in false humility and the worship of angels disqualify you for the prize. Such a person goes into great detail about what he has seen, and his unspiritual mind puffs him up with idle notions. ¹⁹He has lost connection with the Head, from whom the whole body, supported and held together by

[g]11 Or *the flesh*
[h]13 Or *your flesh*
[i]13 Some manuscripts *us*
[j]15 Or *them in him*

joints and ligaments, grows with a growth which is from God. 20If you have died with Christ to the elementary principles of the world, why, as if you were living in the world, do you submit yourself to decrees, such as, 21"Do not handle, do not taste, do not touch!" 22(which all *refer to* things destined to perish with the using)—in accordance with the commandments and teachings of men? 23These are matters which have, to be sure, the appearance of wisdom in self-made religion and self-abasement and severe treatment of the body, *but are* of no value against fleshly indulgence.

Chapter 3

Put On the New Self

IF then you have been raised up with Christ, keep seeking the things above, where Christ is, seated at the right hand of God. 2Set your mind on the things above, not on the things that are on earth. 3For you have died and your life is hidden with Christ in God. 4When Christ, who is our life, is revealed, then you also will be revealed with Him in glory. 5Therefore consider the members of your earthly body as dead to immorality, impurity, passion, evil desire, and greed, which amounts to idolatry. 6For it is on account of these things that the wrath of God will come c, 7and in them you also once walked, when you were living in them. 8But now you also, put them all aside: anger, wrath, malice, slander, *and* abusive speech from your mouth. 9Do not lie to one another, since you laid aside the old self with its *evil* practices,

c Some early mss. add *upon the sons of disobedience*

ἐπιχορηγούμενον καὶ συμβιβαζόμενον αὔξει
¹being supplied ²and ³being joined together will grow

τὴν αὔξησιν τοῦ θεοῦ.
[with] the growth – of God.

20 Εἰ ἀπεθάνετε σὺν Χριστῷ ἀπὸ τῶν στοι-
If ye died with Christ from the ele-

χείων τοῦ κόσμου, τί ὡς ζῶντες ἐν κόσμῳ
ments of the world, why as living in [the] world

δογματίζεσθε· **21** μὴ ἅψῃ μηδὲ γεύσῃ μηδὲ
are ye subject to Do not touch nor taste nor
[its] decrees:

θίγῃς, **22** ἅ ἐστιν πάντα εἰς φθορὰν
handle, which is(are) all for corruption
things

τῇ ἀποχρήσει, κατὰ τὰ ἐντάλματα καὶ
in the using, according to the injunctions and

διδασκαλίας τῶν ἀνθρώπων; **23** ἅτινά ἐστιν
teachings – of men? ¹which ²is(are)
things

λόγον μὲν ἔχοντα σοφίας ἐν ἐθελοθρησκίᾳ
²a repute ³indeed ⁴having of wisdom in self-imposed
worship

καὶ ταπεινοφροσύνῃ καὶ ἀφειδίᾳ σώματος, οὐκ
and humility and severity of [the] body, not

ἐν τιμῇ τινι πρὸς πλησμονὴν τῆς σαρκός.
in ²honour ¹any for satisfaction of the flesh.

3 Εἰ οὖν συνηγέρθητε τῷ Χριστῷ, τὰ
If therefore ye were co-raised – with Christ, the
things

ἄνω ζητεῖτε, οὗ ὁ Χριστός ἐστιν ἐν
above seek, where – Christ ¹is ²at

δεξιᾷ τοῦ θεοῦ καθήμενος· **2** τὰ ἄνω
⁴[the] right – ⁵of God ³sitting; the above
[hand] things

φρονεῖτε, μὴ τὰ ἐπὶ τῆς γῆς. **3** ἀπεθάνετε
mind ye, not the on the earth. ye died
things

γάρ, καὶ ἡ ζωὴ ὑμῶν κέκρυπται σὺν
For, and the life of you has been hidden with

τῷ Χριστῷ ἐν τῷ θεῷ· **4** ὅταν ὁ Χριστὸς
– Christ in – God; whenever – Christ

φανερωθῇ, ἡ ζωὴ ἡμῶν, τότε καὶ ὑμεῖς
is manifested, the life of us, then also ye

σὺν αὐτῷ φανερωθήσεσθε ἐν δόξῃ.
with him will be manifested in glory.

5 Νεκρώσατε οὖν τὰ μέλη τὰ ἐπὶ
Put ye to death therefore the members – on
(your)

τῆς γῆς, πορνείαν, ἀκαθαρσίαν, πάθος,
the earth, fornication, uncleanness, passion,

ἐπιθυμίαν κακήν, καὶ τὴν πλεονεξίαν ἥτις
desire bad, and – covetousness which

ἐστὶν εἰδωλολατρία, **6** δι' ἃ ἔρχεται ἡ
is idolatry, because which is coming the
of things

ὀργὴ τοῦ θεοῦ· **7** ἐν οἷς καὶ ὑμεῖς
wrath – of God; in which indeed ye

περιεπατήσατέ ποτε, ὅτε ἐζῆτε ἐν τούτοις·
walked then, when ye lived in these things;

8 νυνὶ δὲ ἀπόθεσθε καὶ ὑμεῖς τὰ πάντα,
but now ¹put ²away ⁴also ³ye – all things,

ὀργήν, θυμόν, κακίαν, βλασφημίαν, αἰσχρο-
wrath, anger, malice, blasphemy, a-

λογίαν ἐκ τοῦ στόματος ὑμῶν· **9** μὴ
buse out of the mouth of you; not

ψεύδεσθε εἰς ἀλλήλους, ἀπεκδυσάμενοι τὸν
lie ye to one another, having put off the

παλαιὸν ἄνθρωπον σὺν ταῖς πράξεσιν
old man with the practices

---

its ligaments and sinews, grows as God causes it to grow. 20Since you died with Christ to the basic principles of this world, why, as though you still belonged to it, do you submit to its rules: 21"Do not handle! Do not taste! Do not touch!"? 22These are all destined to perish with use, because they are based on human commands and teachings. 23Such regulations indeed have an appearance of wisdom, with their self-imposed worship, their false humility and their harsh treatment of the body, but they lack any value in restraining sensual indulgence.

Chapter 3

Rules for Holy Living

SINCE, then, you have been raised with Christ, set your hearts on things above, where Christ is seated at the right hand of God. 2Set your minds on things above, not on earthly things. 3For you died, and your life is now hidden with Christ in God. 4When Christ, who is your k life, appears, then you also will appear with him in glory. 5Put to death, therefore, whatever belongs to your earthly nature: sexual immorality, impurity, lust, evil desires and greed, which is idolatry. 6Because of these, the wrath of God is coming.ⁱ 7You used to walk in these ways, in the life you once lived. 8But now you must rid yourselves of all such things as these: anger, rage, malice, slander, and filthy language from your lips. 9Do not lie to each other, since you have taken off your old self with its practices 10and

4 Some manuscripts our
i6 Some early manuscripts coming on those who are disobedient

10and have put on the new self who is being renewed to a true knowledge according to the image of the One who created him

11—a *renewal* in which there is no *distinction between* Greek and Jew, circumcised and uncircumcised, barbarian, Scythian, slave and freeman, but Christ is all, and in all.

12And so, as those who have been chosen of God, holy and beloved, put on a heart of compassion, kindness, humility, gentleness and patience;

13bearing with one another, and forgiving each other, whoever has a complaint against anyone; just as the Lord forgave you, so also should you.

14And beyond all these things *put on* love, which is the perfect bond of unity.

15And let the peace of Christ rule in your hearts, to which indeed you were called in one body; and be thankful.

16Let the word of *d*Christ richly dwell within you, with all wisdom teaching and admonishing one another with psalms *and* hymns *and* spiritual songs, singing with thankfulness in your hearts to God.

17And whatever you do in word or deed, *do* all in the name of the Lord Jesus, giving thanks through Him to God the Father.

Family Relations

18Wives, be subject to your husbands, as is fitting in the Lord.

19Husbands, love your wives, and do not be embittered against them.

20Children, be obedient to your parents in all things,

αὐτοῦ, **10** καὶ ἐνδυσάμενοι τὸν νέον τὸν
of him,　　and　　having put on　the　new man　-

ἀνακαινούμενον εἰς ἐπίγνωσιν κατ' εἰκόνα
being renewed　in　full knowledge according [the]
　　　　　　　　　　　　　　　　　　　to　image

τοῦ κτίσαντος αὐτόν, **11** ὅπου οὐκ ἔνι
of the [one] creating　him,　　where　⁴have no place

Ἕλλην καὶ Ἰουδαῖος, περιτομὴ καὶ
¹Greek　¹and　　²Jew,　　circumcision　and

ἀκροβυστία, βάρβαρος, Σκύθης, δοῦλος,
uncircumcision,　barbarian,　Scythian,　slave,

ἐλεύθερος, ἀλλὰ πάντα καὶ ἐν πᾶσιν
freeman,　　but　²all things　⁴and　³in　¹all

Χριστός. **12** Ἐνδύσασθε οὖν, ὡς ἐκλεκτοὶ
¹Christ ²[is].　　Put ye on　therefore, as　chosen ones

τοῦ θεοῦ ἅγιοι καὶ ἠγαπημένοι, σπλάγχνα
-　of God　holy　and　having been loved,　bowels

οἰκτιρμοῦ, χρηστότητα, ταπεινοφροσύνην,
of compassion,　kindness,　　humility,

πραΰτητα, μακροθυμίαν, **13** ἀνεχόμενοι ἀλ-
meekness,　long-suffering,　　forbearing　one

λήλων καὶ χαριζόμενοι ἑαυτοῖς, ἐάν τις
another　and　forgiving　yourselves,　if　anyone

πρός τινα ἔχῃ μομφήν· καθὼς καὶ ὁ
²against ⁴anyone ¹has　²a complaint;　as　indeed the

κύριος ἐχαρίσατο ὑμῖν οὕτως καὶ ὑμεῖς·
Lord　forgave　you　so　also　ye;

14 ἐπὶ πᾶσιν δὲ τούτοις τὴν ἀγάπην,
³over　²all　¹and　these things　-　　love,

ὃ ἐστιν σύνδεσμος τῆς τελειότητος. **15** καὶ
which is　[the] bond　-　of completeness.　And

ἡ εἰρήνη τοῦ Χριστοῦ βραβευέτω ἐν ταῖς
²the ³peace　-　⁴of Christ　¹let ⁵rule　in　the

καρδίαις ὑμῶν, εἰς ἣν καὶ ἐκλήθητε
hearts　of you,　to　which indeed ye were called

ἐν ἑνὶ σώματι· καὶ εὐχάριστοι γίνεσθε.
in　one　body;　and　thankful　be ye.

16 ὁ λόγος τοῦ Χριστοῦ ἐνοικείτω ἐν
²The ³word　-　⁴of Christ　¹let ⁵indwell　in

ὑμῖν πλουσίως, ἐν πάσῃ σοφίᾳ διδάσκοντες
you　richly,　in　all　wisdom　teaching

καὶ νουθετοῦντες ἑαυτούς, ψαλμοῖς ὕμνοις
and　admonishing　yourselves,　in psalms[,]　hymns[,]

ὠδαῖς πνευματικαῖς ἐν τῇ χάριτι ἄδοντες
[and] ²songs ¹spiritual　with　-　grace　singing

ἐν ταῖς καρδίαις ὑμῶν τῷ θεῷ· **17** καὶ
in　the　hearts　of you　-　to God;　and

πᾶν ὅ τι ἐὰν ποιῆτε ἐν λόγῳ ἢ ἐν
every-　whatever　ye do　in　word　or　in
thing

ἔργῳ, πάντα ἐν ὀνόματι κυρίου Ἰησοῦ,
work,　all things [do] in　[the] name of [the] Lord　Jesus,

εὐχαριστοῦντες τῷ θεῷ πατρὶ δι' αὐτοῦ.
giving thanks　-　to God [the]　through　him.
　　　　　　　　　Father

18 Αἱ γυναῖκες, ὑποτάσσεσθε τοῖς
The　wives,　be ye subject to the(your)

ἀνδράσιν, ὡς ἀνῆκεν ἐν κυρίῳ. **19** Οἱ
husbands,　as　is befitting　in　[the] Lord.　The

ἄνδρες, ἀγαπᾶτε τὰς γυναῖκας καὶ μὴ
husbands,　love ye　the(your)　wives　and　not

πικραίνεσθε πρὸς αὐτάς. **20** Τὰ τέκνα,
be bitter　toward　them.　The　children,

ὑπακούετε τοῖς γονεῦσιν κατὰ πάντα,
obey ye　the(your)　parents　in all respects,

---

have put on the new self, which is being renewed in knowledge in the image of its Creator. 11Here there is no Greek or Jew, circumcised or uncircumcised, barbarian, Scythian, slave or free, but Christ is all, and is in all.

12Therefore, as God's chosen people, holy and dearly loved, clothe yourselves with compassion, kindness, humility, gentleness and patience. 13Bear with each other and forgive whatever grievances you may have against one another. Forgive as the Lord forgave you. 14And over all these virtues put on love, which binds them all together in perfect unity.

15Let the peace of Christ rule in your hearts, since as members of one body you were called to peace. And be thankful. 16Let the word of Christ dwell in you richly as you teach and admonish one another with all wisdom, and as you sing psalms, hymns and spiritual songs with gratitude in your hearts to God. 17And whatever you do, whether in word or deed, do it all in the name of the Lord Jesus, giving thanks to God the Father through him.

Rules for Christian Households

18Wives, submit to your husbands, as is fitting in the Lord.

19Husbands, love your wives and do not be harsh with them.

20Children, obey your parents in everything, for

---

for this is well-pleasing to the Lord.
21Fathers, do not ᵉexasperate your children, that they may not lose heart.
22Slaves, in all things obey those who are your masters on earth, not with external service, as those who merely please men, but with sincerity of heart, fearing the Lord.
23Whatever you do, do your work heartily, as for the Lord rather than for men;
24knowing that from the Lord you will receive the reward of the inheritance. It is the Lord Christ whom you serve.
25For he who does wrong will receive the consequences of the wrong which he has done, and that without partiality.

Chapter 4

Fellow Workers

MASTERS, grant to your slaves justice and fairness, knowing that you too have a Master in heaven.
2Devote yourselves to prayer, keeping alert in it with an attitude of thanksgiving;
3praying at the same time for us as well, that God may open up to us a door for the word, so that we may speak forth the mystery of Christ, for which I have also been imprisoned;
4in order that I may make it clear in the way I ought to speak.
5Conduct yourselves with wisdom toward outsiders, making the most of the opportunity.
6Let your speech always be with grace, seasoned, as it were, with salt, so that you may know how you should respond to each person.
7As to all my affairs, Tychicus, our beloved brother and faithful servant

---

τοῦτο γὰρ εὐάρεστόν ἐστιν ἐν κυρίῳ.
for this   well-pleasing   is   in   [the] Lord.

21 Οἱ πατέρες, μὴ ἐρεθίζετε τὰ τέκνα
The   fathers,   do not ye provoke   the   children

ὑμῶν, ἵνα μὴ ἀθυμῶσιν. 22 Οἱ δοῦλοι,
of you,   lest   they be disheartened.   The   slaves,

ὑπακούετε κατὰ πάντα τοῖς κατὰ σάρκα
obey ye   in all respects   ¹the   ²accord-   ⁴[the]
          (your)   ing to   flesh

κυρίοις, μὴ ἐν ὀφθαλμοδουλίαις ὡς
¹lords,   not   with   eyeservice   as

ἀνθρωπάρεσκοι, ἀλλ' ἐν ἁπλότητι καρδίας
men-pleasers,   but   in   singleness   of heart

φοβούμενοι τὸν κύριον. 23 ὃ ἐὰν ποιῆτε,
fearing   the   Lord.   Whatever   ye do,

ἐκ ψυχῆς ἐργάζεσθε ὡς τῷ κυρίῳ καὶ
from [the] soul   work ye   as   to the   Lord   and

οὐκ ἀνθρώποις, 24 εἰδότες ὅτι ἀπὸ κυρίου
not   to men,   knowing   that ₐ from [the] Lord

ἀπολήμψεσθε τὴν ἀνταπόδοσιν τῆς κλη-
ye will receive   the   reward   of the   in-

ρονομίας. τῷ κυρίῳ Χριστῷ δουλεύετε·
heritance.   The   Lord   Christ   ye serve;

25 ὃ γὰρ ἀδικῶν κομίσεται ὃ ἠδίκησεν,
for the [one]   doing wrong   will receive   what he did wrong,

καὶ οὐκ ἔστιν προσωπολημψία. 4 Οἱ κύριοι,
and   there is no   respect of persons.   The   lords,

τὸ δίκαιον καὶ τὴν ἰσότητα τοῖς δούλοις
¹the   ²just thing   ⁴and   ⁴the   ⁵equality   ⁷to the(your)   ⁸slaves

παρέχεσθε, εἰδότες ὅτι καὶ ὑμεῖς ἔχετε
¹supply ye,   knowing   that   also   ye   have

κύριον ἐν οὐρανῷ.
a Lord   in   heaven.

2 Τῇ προσευχῇ προσκαρτερεῖτε, γρηγο-
In the   prayer   continue ye,   watch-

ροῦντες ἐν αὐτῇ ἐν εὐχαριστίᾳ, 3 προσευ-
ing   in   it   with   thanksgiving,   pray-

χόμενοι ἅμα καὶ περὶ ἡμῶν, ἵνα ὁ
ing   together   also   concerning   us,   in order   –
                                              that

θεὸς ἀνοίξῃ ἡμῖν θύραν τοῦ λόγου,
God   may open   to us   a door   of the   word,

λαλῆσαι τὸ μυστήριον τοῦ Χριστοῦ, δι'
to speak   the   mystery   –   of   because
                                  Christ,   of

ὃ καὶ δέδεμαι, 4 ἵνα φανερώσω αὐτὸ
which indeed I have been   in order   I may manifest   it
          bound,   that

ὡς δεῖ με λαλῆσαι. 5 Ἐν σοφίᾳ
as   it behoves   me   to speak.   In   wisdom

περιπατεῖτε πρὸς τοὺς ἔξω, τὸν καιρὸν
walk ye   toward   the ones outside,   ¹the   ²time

ἐξαγοραζόμενοι. 6 ὁ λόγος ὑμῶν πάντοτε
¹redeeming.   The   speech   of you   always
                                [let it be]

ἐν χάριτι, ἅλατι ἠρτυμένος, εἰδέναι πῶς
in   grace,   with salt   having been   to know   how
                        seasoned,

δεῖ ὑμᾶς ἑνὶ ἑκάστῳ ἀποκρίνεσθαι.
it be-   you   ²one   ²each   ¹to answer.
hoves

7 Τὰ κατ' ἐμὲ πάντα γνωρίσει ὑμῖν Τύχικος
²The ³about ⁴me ¹all ⁵will make ⁷to you ¹Tychicus
things   known

ὁ ἀγαπητὸς ἀδελφὸς καὶ πιστὸς διάκονος
the   beloved   brother   and   faithful   minister

---

this pleases the Lord.
21Fathers, do not embitter your children, or they will become discouraged.
22Slaves, obey your earthly masters in everything; and do it, not only when their eye is on you and to win their favor, but with sincerity of heart and reverence for the Lord.
23Whatever you do, work at it with all your heart, as working for the Lord, not for men, 24since you know that you will receive an inheritance from the Lord as a reward. It is the Lord Christ you are serving.
25Anyone who does wrong will be repaid for his wrong, and there is no favoritism.

Chapter 4

MASTERS, provide your slaves with what is right and fair, because you know that you also have a Master in heaven.

Further Instructions

2Devote yourselves to prayer, being watchful and thankful. 3And pray for us, too, that God may open a door for our message, so that we may proclaim the mystery of Christ, for which I am in chains. 4Pray that I may proclaim it clearly, as I should. 5Be wise in the way you act toward outsiders; make the most of every opportunity. 6Let your conversation be always full of grace, seasoned with salt, so that you may know how to answer everyone.

Final Greetings

7Tychicus will tell you all the news about me. He is a dear brother, a faithful min-

---

ᵉ Some early mss. read provoke to anger

and fellow bond-servant in the Lord, will bring you information.
8For I have sent him to you for this very purpose, that you may know *about* our circumstances and that he may encourage your hearts;
9and with him Onesimus, *our* faithful and beloved brother, who is one of your *number.* They will inform you about the whole situation here.
10Aristarchus, my fellow prisoner, sends you his greetings; and *also* Barnabas' cousin Mark (about whom you received instructions: if he comes to you, welcome him);
11and *also* Jesus who is called Justus; these are the only fellow workers for the kingdom of God who are from the circumcision; and they have proved to be an encouragement to me.
12Epaphras, who is one of your number, a bondslave of Jesus Christ, sends you his greetings, always laboring earnestly for you in his prayers, that you may stand perfect and fully assured in all the will of God.
13For I bear him witness that he has a deep concern for you and for those who are in Laodicea and Hierapolis.
14Luke, the beloved physician, sends you his greetings, and *also* Demas.
15Greet the brethren who are in Laodicea and also ⸆Nympha and the church that is in her house.
16And when this letter is read among you, have it also read in the church of the Laodiceans; and you, for your part read my letter *that is coming* from Laodicea.
17And say to Archippus, "Take heed to the ministry

ⁱOr, *Nymphas* (masc.)

καὶ	σύνδουλος	ἐν	κυρίῳ,	**8** ὃν	ἔπεμψα
and	fellow-slave	in	[the] Lord,	whom	I sent

πρὸς	ὑμᾶς	εἰς	αὐτὸ	τοῦτο,	ἵνα	γνῶτε
to	you	for	this	very thing,	in order that	ye might know

τὰ	περὶ	ἡμῶν	καὶ	παρακαλέσῃ	τὰς
the things	concerning	us	and	he might comfort	the

καρδίας	ὑμῶν,	**9** σὺν	Ὀνησίμῳ	τῷ	πιστῷ
hearts	of you,	with	Onesimus	the	faithful

καὶ	ἀγαπητῷ	ἀδελφῷ,	ὅς	ἐστιν	ἐξ	ὑμῶν·
and	beloved	brother,	who	is	of	you;

πάντα	ὑμῖν	γνωρίσουσιν	τὰ	ὧδε.
¹all	²to you	⁴they will make known	³the	⁵here. things

10 Ἀσπάζεται	ὑμᾶς	Ἀρίσταρχος	ὁ
²greets	³you	¹Aristarchus	⁴the

συναιχμάλωτός	μου,	καὶ	Μάρκος	ὁ	ἀνεψιὸς
⁵fellow-captive	⁶of me,	and	Mark	the	cousin

Βαρναβᾶ,	(περὶ	οὗ	ἐλάβετε	ἐντολάς,	ἐὰν
of Barnabas,	(concerning	whom	ye received	commandments,	if

ἔλθῃ	πρὸς	ὑμᾶς,	δέξασθε	αὐτόν,)	**11** καὶ
he comes	to	you,	receive ye	him,)	and

Ἰησοῦς	ὁ	λεγόμενος	Ἰοῦστος,	οἱ	ὄντες
Jesus	the [one]	*being* named	Justus,	the [ones]	being

ἐκ . περιτομῆς	οὗτοι	μόνοι	συνεργοὶ	εἰς
of [the] circumcision	these	only	fellow-workers	for

τὴν	βασιλείαν	τοῦ	θεοῦ,	οἵτινες	ἐγενή-
the	kingdom	–	of God,	who	be-

θησάν	μοι	παρηγορία.	**12** ἀσπάζεται	ὑμᾶς
came	to me	a comfort.	²greets	³you

Ἐπαφρᾶς	ὁ	ἐξ	ὑμῶν,	δοῦλος	Χριστοῦ
¹Epaphras	the [one] of		you,	a slave	of Christ

Ἰησοῦ,	πάντοτε	ἀγωνιζόμενος	ὑπὲρ	ὑμῶν
Jesus,	always	struggling	on behalf of	you

ἐν	ταῖς	προσευχαῖς,	ἵνα	σταθῆτε	τέλειοι
in	the	prayers,	in order that	ye may stand	complete

καὶ	πεπληροφορημένοι	ἐν	παντὶ	θελήματι
and	having been fully assured	in	all	[the] will

τοῦ	Θεοῦ.	**13** μαρτυρῶ	γὰρ	αὐτῷ	ὅτι
–	of God.	For I bear witness		to him	that

ἔχει	πολὺν	πόνον	ὑπὲρ	ὑμῶν	καὶ	τῶν
he has	much	distress	on behalf of	you	and	the ones

ἐν	Λαοδικείᾳ	καὶ	τῶν	ἐν	Ἱεραπόλει.
in	Laodicea	and	the ones	in	Hierapolis.

14 ἀσπάζεται	ὑμᾶς	Λουκᾶς	ὁ	ἰατρὸς	ὁ
⁷greets	⁸you	¹Luke	²the	³physician	–

ἀγαπητὸς	καὶ	Δημᾶς.	**15** Ἀσπάσασθε
⁵beloved	⁶and	⁴Demas.	Greet ye

τοὺς	ἐν	Λαοδικείᾳ	ἀδελφοὺς	καὶ	Νύμφαν
¹the	³in	⁴Laodicea	²brothers	and	Nymphas

καὶ	τὴν	κατ᾽	οἶκον	αὐτῆς	ἐκκλησίαν.
and	¹the	²at	⁴[the] house	⁵of her	³church.

16 καὶ	ὅταν	ἀναγνωσθῇ	παρ᾽	ὑμῖν	ἡ
And	whenever	is read	before	you	the(this)

ἐπιστολή,	ποιήσατε	ἵνα	καὶ	ἐν	τῇ
epistle,	cause	*in order* that	²also	³in	⁴the

Λαοδικέων	ἐκκλησίᾳ	ἀναγνωσθῇ,	καὶ	τὴν
⁶of [the] Laodiceans	⁵church	¹it is read,	and	the [one]

ἐκ	Λαοδικείας	ἵνα	καὶ	ὑμεῖς	ἀναγνῶτε.
⁶of	⁷Laodicea	¹*in order* that	²also	³ye	⁴read.

17 καὶ	εἴπατε	Ἀρχίππῳ·	βλέπε	τὴν
And	tell	Archippus:	Look [to]	the

ister and fellow servant in the Lord. 8I am sending him to you for the express purpose that you may know about our circumstances and that he may encourage your hearts. 9He is coming with Onesimus, our faithful and dear brother, who is one of you. They will tell you everything that is happening here.
10My fellow prisoner Aristarchus sends you his greetings, as does Mark, the cousin of Barnabas. (You have received instructions about him; if he comes to you, welcome him.) 11Jesus, who is called Justus, also sends greetings. These are the only Jews among my fellow workers for the kingdom of God, and they have proved a comfort to me. 12Epaphras, who is one of you and a servant of Christ Jesus, sends greetings. He is always wrestling in prayer for you, that you may stand firm in all the will of God, mature and fully assured. 13I vouch for him that he is working hard for you and for those at Laodicea and Hierapolis. 14Our dear friend Luke, the doctor, and Demas send greetings. 15Give my greetings to the brothers at Laodicea, and to Nympha and the church in her house.
16After this letter has been read to you, see that it is also read in the church of the Laodiceans and that you in turn read the letter from Laodicea.
17Tell Archippus: "See to it that you complete the

ᵐ8 Some manuscripts *that he may know about your*

which you have received in the Lord, that you may fulfill it."

18I, Paul, write this greeting with my own hand. Remember my imprisonment. Grace be with you.

διακονίαν ἣν παρέλαβες ἐν κυρίῳ, ἵνα
ministry   which thou receivedst in [the] Lord, in order that

αὐτὴν πληροῖς.
²it   ¹thou mayest fulfil.

18 Ὁ ἀσπασμὸς τῇ ἐμῇ χειρὶ Παύλου.
The   greeting   -   by my hand[,] of Paul.

μνημονεύετέ μου τῶν δεσμῶν. ἡ χάρις
Remember ye of me the bonds.   - Grace [be]

μεθ' ὑμῶν.
with you.

---

work you have received in the Lord."

18I, Paul, write this greeting in my own hand. Remember my chains. Grace be with you.

---

1 Thessalonians

Chapter 1

Thanksgiving for These Believers

PAUL and Silvanus and Timothy to the church of the Thessalonians in God the Father and the Lord Jesus Christ: Grace to you and peace.

2We give thanks to God always for all of you, making mention *of you* in our prayers;

3constantly bearing in mind your work of faith and labor of love and steadfastness of hope in our Lord Jesus Christ in the presence of our God and Father,

4knowing, brethren beloved by God, *His* choice of you;

5for our gospel did not come to you in word only, but also in power and in the Holy Spirit and with full conviction; just as you know what kind of men we proved to be among you for your sake.

6You also became imitators of us and of the Lord, having received the word in much tribulation with the joy of the Holy Spirit,

7so that you became an example to all the believers in Macedonia and in Achaia.

ΠΡΟΣ ΘΕΣΣΑΛΟΝΙΚΕΙΣ Α
To Thessalonians 1

1 Παῦλος καὶ Σιλουανὸς καὶ Τιμόθεος
Paul   and Silvanus   and Timothy

τῇ ἐκκλησίᾳ Θεσσαλονικέων ἐν θεῷ πατρὶ
to the church of [the] Thessalonians in God [the] Father

καὶ κυρίῳ Ἰησοῦ Χριστῷ· χάρις ὑμῖν
and [the] Lord Jesus Christ: Grace [be] to you

καὶ εἰρήνη.
and peace.

2 Εὐχαριστοῦμεν τῷ θεῷ πάντοτε περὶ
We give thanks   -   to God always   con-

πάντων ὑμῶν, μνείαν ποιούμενοι ἐπὶ τῶν
²all   ¹you, mention making   on(in) the

προσευχῶν ἡμῶν, ἀδιαλείπτως **3** μνημο-
prayers   of us, unceasingly   remember-

νεύοντες ὑμῶν τοῦ ἔργου τῆς πίστεως
ing   of you the work of faith

καὶ τοῦ κόπου τῆς ἀγάπης καὶ τῆς
and the labour   -   of love and the

ὑπομονῆς τῆς ἐλπίδος τοῦ κυρίου ἡμῶν
endurance   -   of hope of(in) the Lord of us

Ἰησοῦ Χριστοῦ ἔμπροσθεν τοῦ θεοῦ καὶ
Jesus Christ   before   the God and

πατρὸς ἡμῶν, **4** εἰδότες, ἀδελφοὶ ἠγαπημένοι
Father of us,   knowing,   brothers having been loved

ὑπὸ [τοῦ] θεοῦ, τὴν ἐκλογὴν ὑμῶν,
by   -   God,   the choice   of you,

5 ὅτι τὸ εὐαγγέλιον ἡμῶν οὐκ ἐγενήθη
because the gospel   of us became not

εἰς ὑμᾶς ἐν λόγῳ μόνον, ἀλλὰ καὶ ἐν
to   you in word only,   but also in

δυνάμει καὶ ἐν πνεύματι ἁγίῳ καὶ
power   and in Spirit   Holy   and

πληροφορίᾳ πολλῇ, καθὼς οἴδατε οἷοι
²assurance ¹much,   as   ye know what sort

ἐγενήθημεν ἐν ὑμῖν δι' ὑμᾶς. **6** καὶ
we were   among you because of you.   And

ὑμεῖς μιμηταὶ ἡμῶν ἐγενήθητε καὶ τοῦ
¹ye   ³imitators ⁴of us ²became   and of the

κυρίου, δεξάμενοι τὸν λόγον ἐν θλίψει
Lord,   welcoming the word in ²affliction

πολλῇ μετὰ χαρᾶς πνεύματος ἁγίου, **7** ὥστε
¹much   with joy of ²Spirit ¹[the] Holy, so as

γενέσθαι ὑμᾶς τύπον πᾶσιν τοῖς πιστεύουσιν
to become you^b a pattern to all the [ones] believing
=so that ye became

ἐν τῇ Μακεδονίᾳ καὶ ἐν τῇ Ἀχαΐᾳ.
in   -   Macedonia and in   -   Achaia.

---

1 Thessalonians

Chapter 1

PAUL, Silas^a and Timothy,

To the church of the Thessalonians in God the Father and the Lord Jesus Christ:

Grace and peace to you. ^b

Thanksgiving for the Thessalonians' Faith

2We always thank God for all of you, mentioning you in our prayers. 3We continually remember before our God and Father your work produced by faith, your labor prompted by love, and your endurance inspired by hope in our Lord Jesus Christ.

4For we know, brothers loved by God, that he has chosen you, 5because our gospel came to you not simply with words, but also with power, with the Holy Spirit and with deep conviction. You know how we lived among you for your sake. 6You became imitators of us and of the Lord; in spite of severe suffering, you welcomed the message with the joy given by the Holy Spirit. 7And so you became a model to all the believers in Macedonia and

---

^a1 Greek *Silvanus*, a variant of *Silas*
^b1 Some early manuscripts *you from God our Father and the Lord Jesus Christ*

8For the word of the Lord has sounded forth from you, not only in Macedonia and Achaia, but also in every place your faith toward God has gone forth, so that we have no need to say anything.

9For they themselves report about us what kind of a reception we had with you, and how you turned to God from idols to serve a living and true God,

10and to wait for His Son from heaven, whom He raised from the dead, that is Jesus, who delivers us from the wrath to come.

---

8 ἀφ' ὑμῶν γὰρ ἐξήχηται ὁ λόγος τοῦ
⁸from ⁹you ¹For sounded the word of the

κυρίου οὐ μόνον ἐν τῇ Μακεδονίᾳ καὶ
Lord not only in - Macedonia and

'Ἀχαΐᾳ, ἀλλ' ἐν παντὶ τόπῳ ἡ πίστις
Achaia, but in every place the faith

ὑμῶν ἡ πρὸς τὸν θεὸν ἐξελήλυθεν, ὥστε
of you - toward - God has gone out, so as

μὴ χρείαν ἔχειν ἡμᾶς λαλεῖν τι· 9 αὐτοὶ
not need to have usᵇ to speak anything; ⁹[them]-
➔so that we have no need   selves

γὰρ περὶ ἡμῶν ἀπαγγέλλουσιν ὁποίαν
¹for ⁴concerning ⁵us ³they relate what sort of

εἴσοδον ἔσχομεν πρὸς ὑμᾶς, καὶ πῶς
entrance we had to you, and how

ἐπεστρέψατε πρὸς τὸν θεὸν ἀπὸ τῶν
ye turned to - God from the

εἰδώλων δουλεύειν θεῷ ζῶντι καὶ ἀληθινῷ,
idols to serve a God living and true,

10 καὶ ἀναμένειν τὸν υἱὸν αὐτοῦ ἐκ
and to await the Son of him from

τῶν οὐρανῶν, ὃν ἤγειρεν ἐκ τῶν νεκρῶν,
the heavens, whom he raised from the dead,

'Ἰησοῦν τὸν ῥυόμενον ἡμᾶς ἐκ τῆς ὀργῆς
Jesus the [one] delivering us from the wrath

τῆς ἐρχομένης.
- coming.

Achaia. 8The Lord's message rang out from you not only in Macedonia and Achaia—your faith in God has become known everywhere. Therefore we do not need to say anything about it, 9for they themselves report what kind of reception you gave us. They tell how you turned to God from idols to serve the living and true God, 10and to wait for his Son from heaven, whom he raised from the dead—Jesus, who rescues us from the coming wrath.

Chapter 2

Paul's Ministry

FOR you yourselves know, brethren, that our coming to you was not in vain,

2but after we had already suffered and been mistreated in Philippi, as you know, we had the boldness in our God to speak to you the gospel of God amid much opposition.

3For our exhortation does not *come* from error or impurity or by way of deceit;

4but just as we have been approved by God to be entrusted with the gospel, so we speak, not as pleasing men but God, who examines our hearts.

5For we never came with flattering speech, as you know, nor with a pretext for greed—God is witness—

6nor did we seek glory from men, either from you or from others, even

---

2 Αὐτοὶ γὰρ οἴδατε, ἀδελφοί, τὴν
For [your]selves ye know, brothers, the

εἴσοδον ἡμῶν τὴν πρὸς ὑμᾶς, ὅτι οὐ
entrance of us - to you, that not

κενὴ γέγονεν, 2 ἀλλὰ προπαθόντες καὶ
in vain it has been, but having previously and
                                        suffered

ὑβρισθέντες καθὼς οἴδατε ἐν Φιλίπποις
having been as ye know in Philippi
insulted

ἐπαρρησιασάμεθα ἐν τῷ θεῷ ἡμῶν λαλῆσαι
we were bold in the God of us to speak

πρὸς ὑμᾶς τὸ εὐαγγέλιον τοῦ θεοῦ ἐν
to you the gospel - of God in

πολλῷ ἀγῶνι. 3 ἡ γὰρ · παράκλησις
much struggle. For the exhortation

ἡμῶν οὐκ ἐκ πλάνης οὐδὲ ἐξ ἀκαθαρσίας
of us not of error nor of uncleanness

οὐδὲ ἐν δόλῳ, 4 ἀλλὰ καθὼς δεδοκιμάσμεθα
nor in guile, but as we have been
                                        approved

ὑπὸ τοῦ θεοῦ πιστευθῆναι τὸ εὐαγγέλιον
by - God to be entrusted [with] the gospel

οὕτως λαλοῦμεν, οὐχ ὡς ἀνθρώποις ἀρέ-
so we speak, not as ²men ¹pleas-

σκοντες, ἀλλὰ θεῷ τῷ δοκιμάζοντι τὰς
ing, but God the [one] proving the

καρδίας ἡμῶν. 5 οὔτε γάρ ποτε ἐν
hearts of us. For neither then with

λόγῳ κολακείας ἐγενήθημεν, καθὼς οἴδατε,
word of flattery were we, as ye know,

οὔτε ἐν προφάσει πλεονεξίας, θεὸς μάρτυς,
nor with pretext of covetousness, God [is] witness,

6 οὔτε ζητοῦντες ἐξ ἀνθρώπων δόξαν,
nor seeking from men glory,

οὔτε ἀφ' ὑμῶν οὔτε ἀπ' ἄλλων, 7 δυνάμε-
neither from you nor from others, being

Chapter 2

Paul's Ministry in Thessalonica

YOU know, brothers, that our visit to you was not a failure. 2We had previously suffered and been insulted in Philippi, as you know, but with the help of our God we dared to tell you his gospel in spite of strong opposition. 3For the appeal we make does not spring from error or impure motives, nor are we trying to trick you. 4On the contrary, we speak as men approved by God to be entrusted with the gospel. We are not trying to please men but God, who tests our hearts. 5You know we never used flattery, nor did we put on a mask to cover up greed—God is our witness. 6We were not looking for praise from men, not from you or anyone else.

though as apostles of Christ we might have asserted our authority.

7But we proved to be *a*gentle among you, as a nursing *mother* tenderly cares for her own children.

8Having thus a fond affection for you, we were well-pleased to impart to you not only the gospel of God but also our own lives, because you had become very dear to us.

9For you recall, brethren, our labor and hardship, how working night and day so as not to be a burden to any of you, we proclaimed to you the gospel of God.

10You are witnesses, and *so is* God, how devoutly and uprightly and blamelessly we behaved toward you believers;

11just as you know how we *were* exhorting and encouraging and imploring each one of you as a father *would* his own children,

12so that you may walk in a manner worthy of the God who calls you into His own kingdom and glory.

13And for this reason we also constantly thank God that when you received from us the word of God's message, you accepted *it* not *as* the word of men, but *for* what it really is, the word of God, which also performs its work in you who believe.

14For you, brethren, became imitators of the churches of God in Christ Jesus that are in Judea, for you also endured the same

---

νοι ἐν βάρει εἶναι ὡς Χριστοῦ ἀπόστολοι·
able ²with ³weight⁎ ¹to be as ²of Christ ¹apostles;

ἀλλὰ ἐγενήθημεν ἤπιοι ἐν μέσῳ ὑμῶν,
but we were gentle in [the] midst of you,

ὡς ἐὰν τροφὸς θάλπῃ τὰ ἑαυτῆς τέκνα·
as if a nurse should ¹the ²of herself ³children;
         cherish

8 οὕτως ὁμειρόμενοι ὑμῶν ηὐδοκοῦμεν
so longing for you we were well
                    pleased

μεταδοῦναι ὑμῖν οὐ μόνον τὸ εὐαγγέλιον
to impart to you not only the gospel

τοῦ θεοῦ ἀλλὰ καὶ τὰς ἑαυτῶν ψυχάς,
- of God but also ¹the ²of ourselves ³souls,

διότι ἀγαπητοὶ ἡμῖν ἐγενήθητε. 9 μνημο-
because ²beloved ³to us ¹ye became. ye re-

νεύετε γάρ, ἀδελφοί, τὸν κόπον ἡμῶν
member For, brothers, the labour of us

καὶ τὸν μόχθον· νυκτὸς καὶ ἡμέρας
and the toil; night and day

ἐργαζόμενοι πρὸς τὸ μὴ ἐπιβαρῆσαί τινα
working for *the* not to put a burden any-
                        on one

ὑμῶν ἐκηρύξαμεν εἰς ὑμᾶς τὸ εὐαγγέλιον
of you we proclaimed to you the gospel

τοῦ θεοῦ. 10 ὑμεῖς μάρτυρες καὶ ὁ
- of God. Ye [are] witnesses and -

θεός, ὡς ὁσίως καὶ δικαίως καὶ ἀμέμπτως
God, how holily and righteously and blamelessly

ὑμῖν τοῖς πιστεύουσιν ἐγενήθημεν, 11 καθά-
¹to you ²the [ones] ³believing ¹we were, even

περ οἴδατε ὡς ἕνα ἕκαστον ὑμῶν ὡς
as ye know how ²one ¹each of you as

πατὴρ τέκνα ἑαυτοῦ παρακαλοῦντες ὑμᾶς
a father children of himself exhorting you

καὶ παραμυθούμενοι 12 καὶ μαρτυρόμενοι εἰς
and consoling and witnessing for

τὸ περιπατεῖν ὑμᾶς ἀξίως τοῦ θεοῦ
the to walk you^b worthily - of God
=that ye should walk

τοῦ καλοῦντος ὑμᾶς εἰς τὴν ἑαυτοῦ
the [one] calling you to ¹the ²of himself

βασιλείαν καὶ δόξαν.
²kingdom ³and ⁴glory.

13 Καὶ διὰ τοῦτο καὶ ἡμεῖς εὐχαρισ-
And therefore also we give

τοῦμεν τῷ θεῷ ἀδιαλείπτως, ὅτι παρα-
thanks - to God unceasingly, that having

λαβόντες λόγον ἀκοῆς παρ' ἡμῶν τοῦ
received ¹[the] word ³of hearing ⁴from ⁵us -

θεοῦ ἐδέξασθε οὐ λόγον ἀνθρώπων ἀλλὰ
²of God ye welcomed not [as] a of men but
            [it] word

καθὼς ἀληθῶς ἐστιν λόγον θεοῦ, ὃς
as truly it is a word of God, which

καὶ ἐνεργεῖται ἐν ὑμῖν τοῖς πιστεύουσιν.
also operates in you the [ones] believing.

14 ὑμεῖς γὰρ μιμηταὶ ἐγενήθητε, ἀδελφοί,
For ye ²imitators ¹became, brothers,

τῶν ἐκκλησιῶν τοῦ θεοῦ τῶν οὐσῶν ἐν
of the churches - of God - being in

τῇ Ἰουδαίᾳ ἐν Χριστῷ Ἰησοῦ, ὅτι τὰ
- Judæa in Christ Jesus, because ⁴the

As apostles of Christ we could have been a burden to you, 7but we were gentle among you, like a mother caring for her little children. 8We loved you so much that we were delighted to share with you not only the gospel of God but our lives as well, because you had become so dear to us. 9Surely you remember, brothers, our toil and hardship; we worked night and day in order not to be a burden to anyone while we preached the gospel of God to you.

10You are witnesses, and so is God, of how holy, righteous and blameless we were among you who believed. 11For you know that we dealt with each of you as a father deals with his own children, 12encouraging, comforting and urging you to live lives worthy of God, who calls you into his kingdom and glory.

13And we also thank God continually because, when you received the word of God, which you heard from us, you accepted it not as the word of men, but as it actually is, the word of God, which is at work in you who believe. 14For you, brothers, became imitators of God's churches in Judea, which are in Christ Jesus: You suffered from

---

a Some ancient mss. read *babes*   ⁎ ? dignity, authority.

suffstartings at the hands of your own countrymen, even as they *did* from the Jews,

15who both killed the Lord Jesus and the prophets, and drove us out. They are not pleasing to God, but hostile to all men,

16hindering us from speaking to the Gentiles that they might be saved; with the result that they always fill up the measure of their sins. But wrath has come upon them *b*to the utmost.

17But we, brethren, having been bereft of you for a short while—in person, not in spirit—were all the more eager with great desire to see your face.

18For we wanted to come to you—I, Paul, more than once—and *yet* Satan thwarted us.

19For who is our hope or joy or crown of exultation? Is it not even you, in the presence of our Lord Jesus at His coming?

20For you are our glory and joy.

αὐτὰ   ἐπάθετε   καὶ   ὑμεῖς   ὑπὸ   τῶν   ἰδίων
²same   ³suffered   ²also   ¹ye   by   the(your) own
things

συμφυλετῶν,   καθὼς   καὶ   αὐτοὶ   ὑπὸ   τῶν
fellow-tribesmen,   as   also   they   by   the

Ἰουδαίων,   15 τῶν   καὶ   τὸν   κύριον
Jews,   the [ones]   ¹both   ³the   ⁴Lord

ἀποκτεινάντων   Ἰησοῦν   καὶ   τοὺς   προφήτας,
²killing   ⁵Jesus   and   the   prophets,

καὶ   ἡμᾶς   ἐκδιωξάντων,   καὶ   θεῷ   μὴ
and   ²us   ¹chasing ³out,   and   ²God   ¹not

ἀρεσκόντων,   καὶ   πᾶσιν   ἀνθρώποις   ἐναντίων,
²pleasing,   and   to all   men   contrary,

16 κωλυόντων   ἡμᾶς   τοῖς   ἔθνεσιν   λαλῆσαι
hindering   us   ²to the   ³nations   ¹to speak
=from speaking . . .

ἵνα   σωθῶσιν,   εἰς   τὸ   ἀναπληρῶσαι   αὐτῶν
in order they may   for   the   to fill up   ²of them
that   be saved,

τὰς   ἁμαρτίας   πάντοτε.   ἔφθασεν   δὲ   ἐπ᾽
¹the   ²sins   always.   But ²came   ⁴on

αὐτοὺς   ἡ   ὀργὴ   εἰς   τέλος.
⁵them   ¹the   ³wrath   to [the] end.

17 Ἡμεῖς   δέ,   ἀδελφοί,   ἀπορφανισθέντες
But we   brothers,   being bereaved

ἀφ᾽   ὑμῶν   πρὸς   καιρὸν   ὥρας   προσώπῳ
from   you   for   time   of an hour   in face
(presence)

οὐ   καρδίᾳ,   περισσοτέρως   ἐσπουδάσαμεν   τὸ
not   in heart,   more abundantly   were eager   ³the

πρόσωπον   ὑμῶν   ἰδεῖν   ἐν   πολλῇ   ἐπιθυμίᾳ.
²face   ⁴of you   ¹to see   with   much   desire.

18 διότι   ἠθελήσαμεν   ἐλθεῖν   πρὸς   ὑμᾶς,
Wherefore   we wished   to come   to   you,

ἐγὼ   μὲν   Παῦλος   καὶ   ἅπαξ   καὶ   δίς,
I   ²indeed   ¹Paul   both   once   and   twice
(again),

καὶ   ἐνέκοψεν   ἡμᾶς   ὁ   σατανᾶς.   19 τίς
and   ²hindered   ³us   -   ¹Satan.   what

γὰρ   ἡμῶν   ἐλπὶς   ἢ   χαρὰ   ἢ   στέφανος
For [is]   ²of us   ¹hope   or   joy   or   crown

καυχήσεως   —   ἢ   οὐχὶ   καὶ   ὑμεῖς   —
of boasting   —   -   not   even   ye   —

ἔμπροσθεν   τοῦ   κυρίου   ἡμῶν   Ἰησοῦ
before   the   Lord   of us   Jesus

ἐν   τῇ   αὐτοῦ   παρουσίᾳ;   20 ὑμεῖς   γὰρ
in(at) the   ²of him   ¹presence?   for ye

ἐστε   ἡ   δόξα   ἡμῶν   καὶ   ἡ   χαρά.
are   ¹the   ²glory   ³of us   ¹and   ⁴the   ⁵joy.

3 Διὸ   μηκέτι   στέγοντες   ηὐδοκήσαμεν
Wherefore   no longer   bearing up   we were well pleased

καταλειφθῆναι   ἐν   Ἀθήναις   μόνοι,   2 καὶ
to be left   in   Athens   alone,   and

ἐπέμψαμεν   Τιμόθεον,   τὸν   ἀδελφὸν   ἡμῶν
we sent   Timothy,   the   brother   of us

καὶ   συνεργὸν   τοῦ   θεοῦ   ἐν   τῷ   εὐαγγελίῳ
and   fellow-worker   -   of God   in   the   gospel

τοῦ   Χριστοῦ,   εἰς   τὸ   στηρίξαι   ὑμᾶς   καὶ
-   of Christ,   for   the   to establish   you   and

παρακαλέσαι   ὑπὲρ   τῆς   πίστεως   ὑμῶν   3 τὸ
to exhort   on behalf of the   faith   of you   -

μηδένα   σαίνεσθαι   ἐν   ταῖς   θλίψεσιν   ταύταις.
no one   to be drawn   by   these afflictions.
aside*b*

αὐτοὶ   γὰρ   οἴδατε   ὅτι   εἰς   τοῦτο   κείμεθα·
For [your]selves   ye know   that   to   this   we are
appointed;

---

your own countrymen the same things those churches suffered from the Jews, 15who killed the Lord Jesus and the prophets and also drove us out. They displease God and are hostile to all men 16in their effort to keep us from speaking to the Gentiles so that they may be saved. In this way they always heap up their sins to the limit. The wrath of God has come upon them at last. *c*

Paul's Longing to See the Thessalonians

17But, brothers, when we were torn away from you for a short time (in person, not in thought), out of our intense longing we made every effort to see you. 18For we wanted to come to you—certainly I, Paul, did, again and again—but Satan stopped us. 19For what is our hope, our joy, or the crown in which we will glory in the presence of our Lord Jesus when he comes? Is it not you? 20Indeed, you are our glory and joy.

Chapter 3

SO when we could stand it no longer, we thought it best to be left by ourselves in Athens. 2We sent Timothy, who is our brother and God's fellow worker*d* in spreading the gospel of Christ, to strengthen and encourage you in your faith, 3so that no one would be unsettled by these trials. You know quite well that we were destined for them. 4In fact,

---

Chapter 3

Encouragement of Timothy's Visit

THEREFORE when we could not endure *it* no longer, we thought it best to be left behind at Athens alone;

2and we sent Timothy, our brother and God's fellow worker in the gospel of Christ, to strengthen and encourage you as to your faith,

3so that no man may be disturbed by these afflictions; for you yourselves know that we have been destined for this.

---

b Or, *forever;* or, *altogether*

*c*16 Or *them fully*
*d*2 Some manuscripts *brother and fellow worker;* other manuscripts *brother and God's servant*

4For indeed when we were with you, we *kept* telling you in advance that we were going to suffer affliction; and so it came to pass, as you know.

5For this reason, when I could endure *it* no longer, I also sent to find out about your faith, for fear that the tempter might have tempted you, and our labor should be in vain.

6But now that Timothy has come to us from you, and has brought us good news of your faith and love, and that you always think kindly of us, longing to see us just as we also long to see you,

7for this reason, brethren, in all our distress and affliction we were comforted about you through your faith;

8for now we *really* live, if you stand firm in the Lord.

9For what thanks can we render to God for you in return for all the joy with which we rejoice before our God on your account,

10as we night and day keep praying most earnestly that we may see your face, and may complete what is lacking in your faith?

11Now may our God and Father Himself and Jesus our Lord direct our way to you;

12and may the Lord cause you to increase and abound in love for one another, and for all men, just as we also *do* for you;

13so that He may establish your hearts unblamable in holiness before our God and Father at the coming of

---

4 καὶ γὰρ ὅτε πρὸς ὑμᾶς ἦμεν,
for even when with you we were,

προελέγομεν ὑμῖν ὅτι μέλλομεν θλίβεσθαι,
we said before to you that we are about to be afflicted,

καθὼς καὶ ἐγένετο καὶ οἴδατε. **5** διὰ
as indeed it happened and ye know. There-

τοῦτο κἀγὼ μηκέτι στέγων ἔπεμψα εἰς
fore I also no longer bearing up sent for

τὸ γνῶναι τὴν πίστιν ὑμῶν, μή πως
the to know the faith of you, lest [some]how

ἐπείρασεν ὑμᾶς ὁ πειράζων καὶ εἰς
3tempted 4you 1the [one] 2tempting and in
= the tempter

κενὸν γένηται ὁ κόπος ἡμῶν. **6** Ἄρτι
vain became the labour of us. now

δὲ ἐλθόντος Τιμοθέου πρὸς ἡμᾶς ἀφ᾽
But coming Timothy* to us from
= when Timothy came

ὑμῶν καὶ εὐαγγελισαμένου ἡμῖν τὴν πίστιν
you and announcing good news* to us [of] the faith

καὶ τὴν ἀγάπην ὑμῶν, καὶ ὅτι ἔχετε
and the love of you, and that ye have

μνείαν ἡμῶν ἀγαθὴν πάντοτε, ἐπιποθοῦντες
2remem- 3of us 1good always, longing
brance

ἡμᾶς ἰδεῖν καθάπερ καὶ ἡμεῖς ὑμᾶς,
1us 2to see even as also we you,

7 διὰ τοῦτο παρεκλήθημεν, ἀδελφοί, ἐφ᾽
therefore we were comforted, brothers, over

ὑμῖν ἐπὶ πάσῃ τῇ ἀνάγκῃ καὶ θλίψει
you on all the distress and affliction

ἡμῶν διὰ τῆς ὑμῶν πίστεως, **8** ὅτι
of us through the 2of you 1faith, because

νῦν ζῶμεν ἐὰν ὑμεῖς στήκετε ἐν κυρίῳ.
now we live if ye stand in [the] Lord.

9 τίνα γὰρ εὐχαριστίαν δυνάμεθα τῷ θεῷ
For what thanks are we able – to God

ἀνταποδοῦναι περὶ ὑμῶν ἐπὶ πάσῃ τῇ
to return concerning you over all the

χαρᾷ ᾗ χαίρομεν δι᾽ ὑμᾶς ἔμπροσθεν
joy [with] we rejoice because you before
which of

τοῦ θεοῦ ἡμῶν, **10** νυκτὸς καὶ ἡμέρας
the God of us, night and day

ὑπερεκπερισσοῦ δεόμενοι εἰς τὸ ἰδεῖν ὑμῶν
exceedingly petitioning for the to see of you

τὸ πρόσωπον καὶ καταρτίσαι τὰ ὑστερήματα
the face and to adjust the shortcomings

τῆς πίστεως ὑμῶν; **11** Αὐτὸς δὲ ὁ θεὸς
of the faith of you? Now [him]self the God

καὶ πατὴρ ἡμῶν καὶ ὁ κύριος ἡμῶν
and Father of us and the Lord of us

Ἰησοῦς κατευθύναι τὴν ὁδὸν ἡμῶν πρὸς
Jesus may he direct the way of us to

ὑμᾶς· **12** ὑμᾶς δὲ ὁ κύριος πλεονάσαι
you; and 4you 1the 2Lord 3make 5to abound

καὶ περισσεύσαι τῇ ἀγάπῃ εἰς ἀλλήλους
and to exceed – in love to one another

καὶ εἰς πάντας, καθάπερ καὶ ἡμεῖς
and to all men, even as also we

εἰς ὑμᾶς, **13** εἰς τὸ στηρίξαι ὑμῶν τὰς
to you, for the to establish of you the

καρδίας ἀμέμπτους ἐν ἁγιωσύνῃ ἔμπροσθεν
hearts blameless in holiness before

τοῦ θεοῦ καὶ πατρὸς ἡμῶν ἐν τῇ παρουσίᾳ
the God and Father of us in(at) the presence

---

when we were with you, we kept telling you that we would be persecuted. And it turned out that way, as you well know. 5For this reason, when I could stand it no longer, I sent to find out about your faith. I was afraid that in some way the tempter might have tempted you and our efforts might have been useless.

Timothy's Encouraging Report

6But Timothy has just now come to us from you and has brought us good news about your faith and love. He has told us that you always have pleasant memories of us and that you long to see us, just as we also long to see you. 7Therefore, brothers, in all our distress and persecution we were encouraged about you because of your faith. 8For now we really live, since you are standing firm in the Lord. 9How can we thank God enough for you in return for all the joy we have in the presence of our God because of you? 10Night and day we pray most earnestly that we may see you again and supply what is lacking in your faith. 11Now may our God and Father himself and our Lord Jesus clear the way for us to come to you. 12May the Lord make your love increase and overflow for each other and for everyone else, just as ours does for you. 13May he strengthen your hearts so that you will be blameless and holy in the presence of our God and Father when

our Lord Jesus with all His saints.

Chapter 4

Sanctification and Love

FINALLY then, brethren, we request and exhort you in the Lord Jesus, that, as you received from us *instruction* as to how you ought to walk and please God (just as you actually do ᶜwalk), that you may excel still more.
2For you know what commandments we gave you ᵈby *the authority of* the Lord Jesus.
3For this is the will of God, your sanctification; *that is*, that you abstain from sexual immorality;
4that each of you know how to possess his own ᵉvessel in sanctification and honor,
5not in lustful passion, like the Gentiles who do not know God;
6and that no man transgress and defraud his brother in the matter because the Lord is *the* avenger in all these things, just as we also told you before and solemnly warned *you.*
7For God has not called us for the purpose of impurity, but in sanctification.
8Consequently, he who rejects *this* is not rejecting man but the God who gives His Holy Spirit to you.
9Now as to the love of the brethren, you have no need for *anyone* to write to you, for you yourselves are taught by God to love one another;
10for indeed you do practice it toward all the brethren who are in all Mace-

Middle column (Greek interlinear):

τοῦ κυρίου ἡμῶν Ἰησοῦ μετὰ πάντων
of the Lord of us Jesus with all

τῶν ἁγίων αὐτοῦ.
the saints of him.

4 Λοιπὸν οὖν, ἀδελφοί, ἐρωτῶμεν ὑμᾶς
For the rest therefore, brothers, we ask you

καὶ παρακαλοῦμεν ἐν κυρίῳ Ἰησοῦ, ἵνα
and we beseech in [the] Lord Jesus, in order that

καθὼς παρελάβετε παρ' ἡμῶν τὸ πῶς
as ye received from us the how

δεῖ ὑμᾶς περιπατεῖν καὶ ἀρέσκειν θεῷ,
it you to walk and to please God,
behoves

καθὼς καὶ περιπατεῖτε, ἵνα περισσεύητε
as indeed ye do walk, in order that ye abound

μᾶλλον. 2 οἴδατε γὰρ τίνας παραγγελίας
more. For ye know what injunctions

ἐδώκαμεν ὑμῖν διὰ τοῦ κυρίου Ἰησοῦ.
we gave you through the Lord Jesus.

3 Τοῦτο γάρ ἐστιν θέλημα τοῦ θεοῦ,
For this is [the] will — of God,

ὁ ἁγιασμὸς ὑμῶν, ἀπέχεσθαι ὑμᾶς ἀπὸ
the sanctification of you, to abstain youᵇ from

τῆς πορνείας, 4 εἰδέναι ἕκαστον ὑμῶν
— fornication, ³to know* ¹each oneᵇ ²of you

τὸ ἑαυτοῦ σκεῦος κτᾶσθαι ἐν ἁγιασμῷ
⁵the ⁷of himself ⁶vessel ⁴to possess in sanctification

καὶ τιμῇ, 5 μὴ ἐν πάθει ἐπιθυμίας
and honour, not in passion of lust

καθάπερ καὶ τὰ ἔθνη τὰ μὴ εἰδότα
even as indeed the nations — not knowing

τὸν θεόν, 6 τὸ μὴ ὑπερβαίνειν καὶ
God, — not to go beyond and

πλεονεκτεῖν ἐν τῷ πράγματι τὸν ἀδελφὸν
to defraud in the matter the brother

αὐτοῦ, διότι ἔκδικος κύριος περὶ πάντων
of him, be- ²[the] ¹[the] Lord con- all
cause avenger [is] cerning

τούτων, καθὼς καὶ προείπαμεν ὑμῖν καὶ
these, as in- we previously you and
deed told

διεμαρτυράμεθα. 7 οὐ γὰρ ἐκάλεσεν ἡμᾶς
solemnly witnessed. For ⁴not ²called ¹us

ὁ θεὸς ἐπὶ ἀκαθαρσίᾳ ἀλλ' ἐν ἁγιασμῷ.
— ¹God to uncleanness but in sanctification.

8 τοιγαροῦν ὁ ἀθετῶν οὐκ ἄνθρωπον
Wherefore the [one] rejecting ²not ³man

ἀθετεῖ ἀλλὰ τὸν θεὸν τὸν καὶ διδόντα
¹rejects but — God the in- giving
[one] deed

τὸ πνεῦμα αὐτοῦ τὸ ἅγιον εἰς ὑμᾶς.
the ²Spirit ³of him — ¹Holy to you.

9 Περὶ δὲ τῆς φιλαδελφίας οὐ χρείαν
Now concerning — brotherly love not need

ἔχετε γράφειν ὑμῖν· αὐτοὶ γὰρ ὑμεῖς
ye have to write to you; for ²[your]selves ¹ye
[for me]

θεοδίδακτοί ἐστε εἰς τὸ ἀγαπᾶν ἀλλήλους·
⁴taught by God ³are for the to love one another;

10 καὶ γὰρ ποιεῖτε αὐτὸ εἰς πάντας
for indeed ye do it toward all

τοὺς ἀδελφοὺς [τοὺς] ἐν ὅλῃ τῇ Μακεδο-
the brothers — in all — Macedo-

our Lord Jesus comes with all his holy ones.

Chapter 4

Living to Please God

FINALLY, brothers, we instructed you how to live in order to please God, as in fact you are living. Now we ask you and urge you in the Lord Jesus to do this more and more. 2For you know what instructions we gave you by the authority of the Lord Jesus.
3It is God's will that you should be sanctified: that you should avoid sexual immorality; 4that each of you should learn to control his own bodyᵉ in a way that is holy and honorable, 5not in passionate lust like the heathen, who do not know God; 6and that in this matter no one should wrong his brother or take advantage of him. The Lord will punish men for all such sins, as we have already told you and warned you. 7For God did not call us to be impure, but to live a holy life. 8Therefore, he who rejects this instruction does not reject man but God, who gives you his Holy Spirit.
9Now about brotherly love we do not need to write to you, for you yourselves have been taught by God to love each other. 10And in fact, you do love all the brothers throughout

---

ᶜ Or, *conduct yourselves*
ᵈ Lit., *through the Lord*
ᵉ I.e., body; or possibly, *wife*

* That is, " to be able "; see note on page xviii.

ᵉ4 Or *learn to live with his own wife; or learn to acquire a wife* donia. But we urge you, brethren, to excel still more,

11and to make it your ambition to lead a quiet life and attend to your own business and work with your hands, just as we commanded you;

12so that you may behave properly toward outsiders and not be in any need.

Those Who Died in Christ

13But we do not want you to be uninformed, brethren, about those who are asleep, that you may not grieve, as do the rest who have no hope.

14For if we believe that Jesus died and rose again, even so God will bring with Him those who have fallen asleep in Jesus.

15For this we say to you by the word of the Lord, that we who are alive, and remain until the coming of the Lord, shall not precede those who have fallen asleep.

16For the Lord Himself will descend from heaven with a shout, with the voice of *the* archangel, and with the trumpet of God; and the dead in Christ shall rise first.

17Then we who are alive and remain shall be caught up together with them in the clouds to meet the Lord in the air, and thus we shall always be with the Lord.

18Therefore comfort one another with these words.

νία.　Παρακαλοῦμεν　δὲ　ὑμᾶς,　ἀδελφοί,
nia.　But we exhort　　　　you,　brothers,

περισσεύειν　μᾶλλον,　11 καὶ　φιλοτιμεῖσθαι
to abound　　more,　　and　to strive eagerly

ἡσυχάζειν　καὶ　πράσσειν　τὰ　ἴδια　καὶ
to be quiet　and　to practise　the　own　and
　　　　　　　　　　　　(your)　things

ἐργάζεσθαι　ταῖς　χερσὶν　ὑμῶν,　καθὼς　ὑμῖν
to work　with the　hands　of you,　as　¹you

παρηγγείλαμεν,　12 ἵνα　περιπατῆτε　εὐσχη-
¹we enjoined,　　in or-　ye may walk　becom-
　　　　　　　der that

μόνως　πρὸς　τοὺς　ἔξω　καὶ　μηδενὸς
ingly　toward　the [ones]　outside　and　²of nothing

χρείαν　ἔχητε.
²need　¹ye may have.

13 Οὐ　θέλομεν　δὲ　ὑμᾶς　ἀγνοεῖν,　ἀδελφοί,
Now we do not wish　you　to be　brothers,
　　　　　　　　　ignorant,

περὶ　τῶν　κοιμωμένων,　ἵνα　μὴ　λυπῆσθε
con-　the　sleeping,　lest　ye grieve
cerning　[ones]

καθὼς　καὶ　οἱ　λοιποὶ　οἱ　μὴ　ἔχοντες
as　indeed　the　rest　the　-　not　having

ἐλπίδα.　14 εἰ　γὰρ　πιστεύομεν　ὅτι　Ἰησοῦς
hope.　　For if　we believe　that　Jesus

ἀπέθανεν　καὶ　ἀνέστη,　οὕτως　καὶ　ὁ　θεὸς
died　and　rose again,　so　also　-　⁴God

τοὺς　κοιμηθέντας　διὰ　τοῦ　Ἰησοῦ　ἄξει
¹the　²having slept　³through　-　⁴Jesus　will
[ones]　　　　　　　　　　　bring

σὺν　αὐτῷ.　15 Τοῦτο　γὰρ　ὑμῖν　λέγομεν
with　him.　For this　to you　we say

ἐν　λόγῳ　κυρίου,　ὅτι　ἡμεῖς　οἱ　ζῶντες
by　a word　of [the]　that　we　the　living
　　Lord,　　　　[ones]

οἱ　περιλειπόμενοι　εἰς　τὴν　παρουσίαν　τοῦ
-　remaining　to　the　presence　of the

κυρίου　οὐ　μὴ　φθάσωμεν　τοὺς　κοιμηθέντας·
Lord　by no　may precede　the　having slept;
　　means　　　　[ones]

16 ὅτι　αὐτὸς　ὁ　κύριος　ἐν　κελεύσματι,
be-　²[him]-　¹the　²Lord　with　a word of
cause　self　　　　　　　command,

ἐν　φωνῇ　ἀρχαγγέλου　καὶ　ἐν　σάλπιγγι
with　a voice　of an archangel　and　with　a trumpet

θεοῦ,　καταβήσεται　ἀπ'　οὐρανοῦ,　καὶ　οἱ
of God,　will descend　from　heaven,　and　the

νεκροὶ　ἐν　Χριστῷ　ἀναστήσονται　πρῶτον,
dead　in　Christ　will rise again　first*ly*,

17 ἔπειτα　ἡμεῖς　οἱ　ζῶντες　οἱ　περιλειπόμενοι
then　we　the　living　-　remaining
　　　　[ones]

ἅμα　σὺν　αὐτοῖς　ἁρπαγησόμεθα　ἐν　νεφέλαις
to-　with　them　shall be seized　in　clouds
gether

εἰς　ἀπάντησιν　τοῦ　κυρίου　εἰς　ἀέρα·
to　a meeting　of the　Lord　in　air;

καὶ　οὕτως　πάντοτε　σὺν　κυρίῳ　ἐσόμεθα.
and　so　always　with [the] Lord　we shall be.

18 Ὥστε　παρακαλεῖτε　ἀλλήλους　ἐν　τοῖς　λόγοις
Therefore　comfort ye　one　with　-　words
　　　　　　　another

τούτοις.
these.

Macedonia. Yet we urge you, brothers, to do so more and more.

11Make it your ambition to lead a quiet life, to mind your own business and to work with your hands, just as we told you, 12so that your daily life may win the respect of outsiders and so that you will not be dependent on anybody.

The Coming of the Lord

13Brothers, we do not want you to be ignorant about those who fall asleep, or to grieve like the rest of men, who have no hope. 14We believe that Jesus died and rose again and so we believe that God will bring with Jesus those who have fallen asleep in him. 15According to the Lord's own word, we tell you that we who are still alive, who are left till the coming of the Lord, will certainly not precede those who have fallen asleep. 16For the Lord himself will come down from heaven, with a loud command, with the voice of the archangel and with the trumpet call of God, and the dead in Christ will rise first. 17After that, we who are still alive and are left will be caught up together with them in the clouds to meet the Lord in the air. And so we will be with the Lord forever. 18Therefore encourage each other with these words.

Chapter 5

The Day of the Lord

NOW as to the times and the epochs, brethren, you have no need of anything to be written to you. 2For you yourselves know full well that the day of the Lord will come just like a thief in the night. 3While they are saying, "Peace and safety!" then destruction will come upon them suddenly like birth pangs upon a woman with child; and they shall not escape. 4But you, brethren, are not in darkness, that the day should overtake you like a thief; 5for you are all sons of light and sons of day. We are not of night nor of darkness; 6so then let us not sleep as others do, but let us be alert and *sober. 7For those who sleep do their sleeping at night, and those who get drunk get drunk at night. 8But since we are of *the day, let us be *sober, having put on the breastplate of faith and love, and as a helmet, the hope of salvation. 9For God has not destined us for wrath, but for obtaining salvation through our Lord Jesus Christ, 10who died for us, that whether we are awake or asleep, we may live together with Him. 11Therefore encourage one another, and build up one another, just as you also are doing.

Christian Conduct

12But we request of you, brethren, that you appreciate those who diligently labor among you, and have charge over you in the Lord and give you instruction, 13and that you esteem them very highly in love be-

*Or, self-controlled

---

5 Περὶ δὲ τῶν χρόνων καὶ τῶν καιρῶν,
But concerning the times and the seasons,

ἀδελφοί, οὐ χρείαν ἔχετε ὑμῖν γράφεσθαι·
brothers, ²not ³need ¹ye have ⁵to you ⁴to be written;

2 αὐτοὶ γὰρ ἀκριβῶς οἴδατε ὅτι ἡμέρα
for ²[your]selves ³accurately ¹ye know that [the] day

κυρίου ὡς κλέπτης ἐν νυκτὶ οὕτως
of [the] Lord as a thief at night so

ἔρχεται. **3** ὅταν λέγωσιν· εἰρήνη καὶ
it comes. Whenever they say: Peace and

ἀσφάλεια, τότε αἰφνίδιος αὐτοῖς ἐφίσταται
safety, then ¹sudden ⁴them ²comes on

ὄλεθρος ὥσπερ ἡ ὠδὶν τῇ ἐν γαστρὶ
³destruction as the birth pang to the pregnant

ἐχούσῃ, καὶ οὐ μὴ ἐκφύγωσιν. **4** ὑμεῖς
woman,† and by no may they ye
means escape.

δέ, ἀδελφοί, οὐκ ἐστὲ ἐν σκότει, ἵνα
But, brothers, are not in dark- *in or-
ness, der that

ἡ ἡμέρα ὑμᾶς ὡς κλέπτης καταλάβῃ·
the day you as a thief should overtake;

5 πάντες γὰρ ὑμεῖς υἱοὶ φωτός ἐστε
for all ye ²sons ³of light ¹are

καὶ υἱοὶ ἡμέρας. Οὐκ ἐσμὲν νυκτὸς
and sons of [the] day. We are not of [the]
night

οὐδὲ σκότους· **6** ἄρα οὖν μὴ καθεύδωμεν
nor of darkness; therefore let us not sleep

ὡς οἱ λοιποί, ἀλλὰ γρηγορῶμεν καὶ
as the rest, but let us watch and

νήφωμεν. **7** οἱ γὰρ καθεύδοντες νυκτὸς
be sober. For the [ones] sleeping by night

καθεύδουσιν, καὶ οἱ μεθυσκόμενοι νυκτὸς
sleep, and the [ones] being drunk by night

μεθύουσιν· **8** ἡμεῖς δὲ ἡμέρας ὄντες
are drunk; but we of [the] day being

νήφωμεν, ἐνδυσάμενοι θώρακα πίστεως καὶ
let us be sober, putting on a breastplate of faith and

ἀγάπης καὶ περικεφαλαίαν ἐλπίδα σωτηρίας·
of love and a helmet hope of salvation;

9 ὅτι οὐκ ἔθετο ἡμᾶς ὁ θεὸς εἰς ὀργὴν
because ²did not appoint ³us ¹God to wrath

ἀλλὰ εἰς περιποίησιν σωτηρίας διὰ τοῦ
but to obtainment of salvation through the

κυρίου ἡμῶν Ἰησοῦ Χριστοῦ, **10** τοῦ
Lord of us Jesus Christ, the

ἀποθανόντος περὶ ἡμῶν, ἵνα εἴτε γρηγορ-
[one] having died concern- us, in or- whether we
ing der that

ὦμεν εἴτε καθεύδωμεν ἅμα σὺν αὐτῷ
watch or we sleep ¹together ²with ³him

ζήσωμεν. **11** Διὸ παρακαλεῖτε ἀλλήλους
¹we may live. There- comfort ye one another
fore

καὶ οἰκοδομεῖτε εἰς τὸν ἕνα, καθὼς καὶ
and edify ye one the one(other), as indeed

ποιεῖτε.
ye do.

12 Ἐρωτῶμεν δὲ ὑμᾶς, ἀδελφοί, εἰδέναι
Now we ask you, brothers, to know

τοὺς κοπιῶντας ἐν ὑμῖν καὶ προϊσταμένους
the [ones] labouring among you and taking the lead

ὑμῶν ἐν κυρίῳ καὶ νουθετοῦντας ὑμᾶς,
of you in [the] Lord and admonishing you,

13 καὶ ἡγεῖσθαι αὐτοὺς ὑπερεκπερισσῶς
and consider them most exceedingly

Chapter 5

NOW, brothers, about times and dates we do not need to write to you, 2for you know very well that the day of the Lord will come like a thief in the night. 3While people are saying, "Peace and safety," destruction will come on them suddenly, as labor pains on a pregnant woman, and they will not escape.

4But you, brothers, are not in darkness so that this day should surprise you like a thief. 5You are all sons of the light and sons of the day. We do not belong to the night or to the darkness. 6So then, let us not be like others, who are asleep, but let us be alert and self-controlled. 7For those who sleep, sleep at night, and those who get drunk, get drunk at night. 8But since we belong to the day, let us be self-controlled, putting on faith and love as a breastplate, and the hope of salvation as a helmet. 9For God did not appoint us to suffer wrath but to receive salvation through our Lord Jesus Christ. 10He died for us so that, whether we are awake or asleep, we may live together with him. 11Therefore encourage one another and build each other up, just as in fact you are doing.

Final Instructions

12Now we ask you, brothers, to respect those who work hard among you, who are over you in the Lord and who admonish you. 13Hold them in the highest regard in love because of cause of their work. Live in peace with one another.

14And we urge you, brethren, admonish the unruly, encourage the fainthearted, help the weak, be patient with all men.

15See that no one repays another with evil for evil, but always seek after that which is good for one another and for all men.

16Rejoice always;

17pray without ceasing;

18in everything give thanks; for this is God's will for you in Christ Jesus.

19Do not quench the Spirit;

20do not despise prophetic *g* utterances.

21But examine everything *carefully*; hold fast to that which is good;

22abstain from every *h*form of evil.

23Now may the God of peace Himself sanctify you entirely; and may your spirit and soul and body be preserved complete, without blame at the coming of our Lord Jesus Christ.

24Faithful is He who calls you, and He also will bring it to pass.

25Brethren, pray for us *i*.

26Greet all the brethren with a holy kiss.

27I adjure you by the Lord to have this letter read to all the brethren.

28The grace of our Lord Jesus Christ be with you.

ἐν ἀγάπῃ διὰ τὸ ἔργον αὐτῶν. εἰρηνεύετε
in love be- the work of them. Be at peace
cause of

ἐν ἑαυτοῖς. 14 Παρακαλοῦμεν δὲ ὑμᾶς,
among yourselves. And we exhort you,

ἀδελφοί, νουθετεῖτε τοὺς ἀτάκτους, παρα-
brothers, admonish the idle, con-

μυθεῖσθε τοὺς ὀλιγοψύχους, ἀντέχεσθε τῶν
sole the faint-hearted, hold on to the
[ones]

ἀσθενῶν, μακροθυμεῖτε πρὸς πάντας.
being weak, be longsuffering with all men.

15 ὁρᾶτε μή τις κακὸν ἀντὶ κακοῦ τινι
See lest anyone ²evil ⁴instead ⁵evil ³to
of anyone

ἀποδῷ, ἀλλὰ πάντοτε τὸ ἀγαθὸν διώκετε
¹returns, but always ²the ³good ¹follow ye

εἰς ἀλλήλους καὶ εἰς πάντας. 16 Πάντοτε
in re- one another and in re- all men. Always
gard to gard to

χαίρετε, 17 ἀδιαλείπτως προσεύχεσθε, 18 ἐν
rejoice ye, unceasingly pray, in

παντὶ εὐχαριστεῖτε· τοῦτο γὰρ θέλημα
everything give thanks; for this [is] [the] will

θεοῦ ἐν Χριστῷ Ἰησοῦ εἰς ὑμᾶς. 19 τὸ
of God in Christ Jesus in regard to you. The

πνεῦμα μὴ σβέννυτε, 20 προφητείας μὴ
Spirit do not quench, prophecies not

ἐξουθενεῖτε· 21 πάντα δὲ δοκιμάζετε, τὸ
despise; and ²all things ¹prove, the

καλὸν κατέχετε· 22 ἀπὸ παντὸς εἴδους
good hold fast; from every form

πονηροῦ ἀπέχεσθε. 23 Αὐτὸς δὲ ὁ θεὸς
of evil abstain. And ⁴[him]self ¹the ²God

τῆς εἰρήνης ἁγιάσαι ὑμᾶς ὁλοτελεῖς, καὶ
– ³of peace may he sanctify you complete, and

ὁλόκληρον ὑμῶν τὸ πνεῦμα καὶ ἡ ψυχὴ
entire of you the spirit and the soul

καὶ τὸ σῶμα ἀμέμπτως ἐν τῇ παρουσίᾳ
and the body blamelessly in(at) the presence

τοῦ κυρίου ἡμῶν Ἰησοῦ Χριστοῦ τηρηθείη.
of the Lord of us Jesus Christ may be kept.

24 πιστὸς ὁ καλῶν ὑμᾶς, ὃς καὶ ποιήσει.
Faithful [is] the [one] calling you, who indeed will do [it].

25 Ἀδελφοί, προσεύχεσθε [καὶ] περὶ
Brothers, pray ye also concerning

ἡμῶν.
us.

26 Ἀσπάσασθε τοὺς ἀδελφοὺς πάντας
Greet ye ²the ³brothers ¹all

ἐν φιλήματι ἁγίῳ. 27 Ἐνορκίζω ὑμᾶς τὸν
with kiss a holy. I adjure you [by] the

κύριον ἀναγνωσθῆναι τὴν ἐπιστολὴν πᾶσιν
Lord ²to be read ¹the(this) ²epistle to all

τοῖς ἀδελφοῖς.
the brothers.

28 Ἡ χάρις τοῦ κυρίου ἡμῶν Ἰησοῦ
The grace of the Lord of us Jesus

Χριστοῦ μεθ' ὑμῶν.
Christ [be] with you.

---

their work. Live in peace with each other. 14And we urge you, brothers, warn those who are idle, encourage the timid, help the weak, be patient with everyone. 15Make sure that nobody pays back wrong for wrong, but always try to be kind to each other and to everyone else.

16Be joyful always; 17pray continually; 18give thanks in all circumstances, for this is God's will for you in Christ Jesus.

19Do not put out the Spirit's fire; 20do not treat prophecies with contempt. 21Test everything. Hold on to the good. 22Avoid every kind of evil.

23May God himself, the God of peace, sanctify you through and through. May your whole spirit, soul and body be kept blameless at the coming of our Lord Jesus Christ. 24The one who calls you is faithful and he will do it.

25Brothers, pray for us. 26Greet all the brothers with a holy kiss. 27I charge you before the Lord to have this letter read to all the brothers.

28The grace of our Lord Jesus Christ be with you.

g Or, *gifts*
h Or, *appearance*
i Some mss. add *also*

Chapter 1

Thanksgiving for Faith and Perseverance

PAUL and Silvanus and Timothy to the church of the Thessalonians in God our Father and the Lord Jesus Christ:

²Grace to you and peace from God the Father and the Lord Jesus Christ.

³We ought always to give thanks to God for you, brethren, as is *only* fitting, because your faith is greatly enlarged, and the love of each one of you toward one another grows *ever* greater;

⁴therefore, we ourselves speak proudly of you among the churches of God for your perseverance and faith in the midst of all your persecutions and afflictions which you endure.

⁵*This is* a plain indication of God's righteous judgment so that you may be considered worthy of the kingdom of God, for which indeed you are suffering.

⁶For after all it is *only* just for God to repay with affliction those who afflict you,

⁷and *to give* relief to you who are afflicted and to us as well when the Lord Jesus shall be revealed from heaven with His mighty angels in flaming fire,

⁸dealing out retribution to those who do not know God and to those who do not obey the gospel of our Lord Jesus.

⁹And these will pay the penalty of eternal destruction, away from the presence of the Lord and from the glory of His power,

¹⁰when He comes to be

---

1 Παῦλος καὶ Σιλουανὸς καὶ Τιμόθεος
Paul and Silvanus and Timothy

τῇ ἐκκλησίᾳ Θεσσαλονικέων ἐν θεῷ πατρὶ
to the church of [the] Thessalonians in God Father

ἡμῶν καὶ κυρίῳ Ἰησοῦ Χριστῷ· **2** χάρις
of us and [the] Lord Jesus Christ: Grace [be]

ὑμῖν καὶ εἰρήνη ἀπὸ θεοῦ πατρὸς καὶ
to you and peace from God [the] Father and

κυρίου Ἰησοῦ Χριστοῦ.
[the] Lord Jesus Christ.

3 Εὐχαριστεῖν ὀφείλομεν τῷ θεῷ πάντοτε
To give thanks we ought – to God always

περὶ ὑμῶν, ἀδελφοί, καθὼς ἄξιόν ἐστιν,
con- you, brothers, as ²meet ¹it is,
cerning

ὅτι ὑπεραυξάνει ἡ πίστις ὑμῶν καὶ
because ⁴grows ¹the ²faith ³of you and
exceedingly

πλεονάζει ἡ ἀγάπη ἑνὸς ἑκάστου πάντων
²increases ¹the ³love ⁴one ⁵of each ⁶all

ὑμῶν εἰς ἀλλήλους, **4** ὥστε αὐτοὺς ἡμᾶς
⁸of you ⁷to ⁹one another, so as [our]selves us
=so that we ourselves boast

ἐν ὑμῖν ἐγκαυχᾶσθαι ἐν ταῖς ἐκκλησίαις
in you to boast[b] in the churches
in you

τοῦ θεοῦ ὑπὲρ τῆς ὑπομονῆς ὑμῶν καὶ
– of God for the ¹endurance ⁴of you ³and

πίστεως ἐν πᾶσιν τοῖς διωγμοῖς ὑμῶν
²faith in all the persecutions of you

καὶ ταῖς θλίψεσιν αἷς ἀνέχεσθε, **5** ἔνδειγμα
and the afflictions which ye endure, a plain token

τῆς δικαίας κρίσεως τοῦ θεοῦ, εἰς τὸ
of the just judgment – of God, for the

καταξιωθῆναι ὑμᾶς τῆς βασιλείας τοῦ
to be accounted you[b] of the kingdom –
worthy
=so that ye may be accounted worthy

θεοῦ, ὑπὲρ ἧς καὶ πάσχετε, **6** εἴπερ
of God, on behalf which indeed ye suffer, since
of

δίκαιον παρὰ θεῷ ἀνταποδοῦναι τοῖς
[it is] a just with God to repay ²to the
thing [ones]

θλίβουσιν ὑμᾶς θλῖψιν **7** καὶ ὑμῖν τοῖς
²afflicting ⁴you ¹affliction and ⁴to you ³the
[ones]

θλιβομένοις ἄνεσιν μεθ' ἡμῶν, ἐν τῇ
⁵being afflicted ¹rest ²with ³us, at the

ἀποκαλύψει τοῦ κυρίου Ἰησοῦ ἀπ'
revelation of the Lord Jesus from

οὐρανοῦ μετ' ἀγγέλων δυνάμεως αὐτοῦ
heaven with angels of power of him

8 ἐν πυρὶ φλογός, διδόντος ἐκδίκησιν τοῖς
in fire of flame, giving full vengeance to the
[ones]

μὴ εἰδόσιν θεὸν καὶ τοῖς μὴ ὑπακούουσιν
not knowing God and to the not obeying
[ones]

τῷ εὐαγγελίῳ τοῦ κυρίου ἡμῶν Ἰησοῦ,
the gospel of the Lord of us Jesus,

9 οἵτινες δίκην τίσουσιν ὄλεθρον αἰώνιον
who ²[the] penalty ¹will pay ⁴destruction ³eternal

ἀπὸ προσώπου τοῦ κυρίου καὶ ἀπὸ
from [the] face of the Lord and from

τῆς δόξης τῆς ἰσχύος αὐτοῦ, **10** ὅταν
the glory of the strength of him, whenever

Chapter 1

PAUL, Silas[a] and Timothy,

To the church of the Thessalonians in God our Father and the Lord Jesus Christ:

²Grace and peace to you from God the Father and the Lord Jesus Christ.

Thanksgiving and Prayer

³We ought always to thank God for you, brothers, and rightly so, because your faith is growing more and more, and the love every one of you has for each other is increasing. ⁴Therefore, among God's churches we boast about your perseverance and faith in all the persecutions and trials you are enduring.

⁵All this is evidence that God's judgment is right, and as a result you will be counted worthy of the kingdom of God, for which you are suffering. ⁶God is just: He will pay back trouble to those who trouble you ⁷and give relief to you who are troubled, and to us as well. This will happen when the Lord Jesus is revealed from heaven in blazing fire with his powerful angels. ⁸He will punish those who do not know God and do not obey the gospel of our Lord Jesus. ⁹They will be punished with everlasting destruction and shut out from the presence of the Lord and from the majesty of his power ¹⁰on the day he

---

glorified in His saints on that day, and to be marveled at among all who have believed—for our testimony to you was believed.

11To this end also we pray for you always that our God may count you worthy of your calling, and fulfill every desire for goodness and the work of faith with power;

12in order that the name of our Lord Jesus may be glorified in you, and you in Him, according to the grace of our God and the Lord Jesus Christ.

ἔλθῃ ἐνδοξασθῆναι ἐν τοῖς ἁγίοις αὐτοῦ
he comes to be glorified in the saints of him
καὶ θαυμασθῆναι ἐν πᾶσιν τοῖς πιστεύσασιν,
and to be admired in all the [ones] having believed,
ὅτι ἐπιστεύθη τὸ μαρτύριον ἡμῶν ἐφ᾽
be- ⁵was believed ¹the ²testimony ³of us ⁴to
cause
ὑμᾶς, ἐν τῇ ἡμέρᾳ ἐκείνῃ. 11 Εἰς ὃ
⁵you, in that day. For which
καὶ προσευχόμεθα πάντοτε περὶ ὑμῶν,
indeed we pray always concerning you,
ἵνα ὑμᾶς ἀξιώσῃ τῆς κλήσεως ὁ θεὸς
in or- ⁴you ⁵may ⁶deem ⁶of the ³calling ¹the ²God
der that ⁷worthy
ἡμῶν καὶ πληρώσῃ πᾶσαν εὐδοκίαν
³of us and may fulfil every good pleasure
ἀγαθωσύνης καὶ ἔργον πίστεως ἐν δυνάμει,
of goodness and work of faith in power,
12 ὅπως ἐνδοξασθῇ τὸ ὄνομα τοῦ κυρίου
so as ⁷may be glorified ¹the ²name ³of the ⁴Lord
ἡμῶν Ἰησοῦ ἐν ὑμῖν, καὶ ὑμεῖς ἐν
⁵of us ⁶Jesus in you, and ye in
αὐτῷ, κατὰ τὴν χάριν τοῦ θεοῦ ἡμῶν
him, according to the grace of the ¹God ⁴of us
καὶ κυρίου Ἰησοῦ Χριστοῦ.
²and ³Lord Jesus Christ.

comes to be glorified in his holy people and to be marveled at among all those who have believed. This includes you, because you believed our testimony to you.

11With this in mind, we constantly pray for you, that our God may count you worthy of his calling, and that by his power he may fulfill every good purpose of yours and every act prompted by your faith. 12We pray this so that the name of our Lord Jesus may be glorified in you, and you in him, according to the grace of our God and the Lord Jesus Christ. [b]

Chapter 2

Man of Lawlessness

NOW we request you, brethren, with regard to the coming of our Lord Jesus Christ, and our gathering together to Him,

2that you may not be quickly shaken from your composure or be disturbed either by a spirit or a message or a letter as if from us, to the effect that the day of the Lord has come.

3Let no one in any way deceive you, for it will not come unless the [a]apostasy comes first, and the man of lawlessness is revealed, the son of destruction,

4who opposes and exalts himself above every so-called god or object of worship, so that he takes his seat in the temple of God, displaying himself as being God.

5Do you not remember that while I was still with you, I was telling you these things?

6And you know what restrains him now, so that in

2 Ἐρωτῶμεν δὲ ὑμᾶς, ἀδελφοί, ὑπὲρ
Now we request you, brothers, by
τῆς παρουσίας τοῦ κυρίου [ἡμῶν] Ἰησοῦ
the presence of the Lord of us Jesus
Χριστοῦ καὶ ἡμῶν ἐπισυναγωγῆς ἐπ᾽ αὐτόν,
Christ and ²of us ¹gathering together to him,
2 εἰς τὸ μὴ ταχέως σαλευθῆναι ὑμᾶς
- - not quickly to be shaken you[b]
ἀπὸ τοῦ νοὸς μηδὲ θροεῖσθαι, μήτε
from the(your) mind nor to be disturbed, neither
διὰ πνεύματος μήτε διὰ λόγου μήτε
through a spirit nor through speech nor
δι᾽ ἐπιστολῆς ὡς δι᾽ ἡμῶν, ὡς ὅτι
through an epistle as through us, as that
ἐνέστηκεν ἡ ἡμέρα τοῦ κυρίου. 3 μή
⁵is come ¹the ²day ³of the ⁴Lord. Not
τις ὑμᾶς ἐξαπατήσῃ κατὰ μηδένα τρόπον·
anyone ²you ¹may deceive by(in) no(any) way;
ὅτι ἐὰν μὴ ἔλθῃ ἡ ἀποστασία πρῶτον
because unless ⁴comes ¹the ²apostasy ⁴first/y
καὶ ἀποκαλυφθῇ ὁ ἄνθρωπος τῆς ἀνομίας,
and ⁵is revealed ¹the ²man - ³of lawlessness,
ὁ υἱὸς τῆς ἀπωλείας, 4 ὁ ἀντικείμενος
the son of perdition, the [one] setting against
καὶ ὑπεραιρόμενος ἐπὶ πάντα λεγόμενον
and exalting himself over everything being called
θεὸν ἢ σέβασμα, ὥστε αὐτὸν εἰς τὸν
God or object of worship, so as him in the
ναὸν τοῦ θεοῦ καθίσαι, ἀποδεικνύντα ἑαυ-
shrine - of God to sit,[b] showing him-
τὸν ὅτι ἐστὶν θεός. 5 Οὐ μνημονεύετε
self that he is a god. Do ye not remember
ὅτι ἔτι ὢν πρὸς ὑμᾶς ταῦτα ἔλεγον
that yet being with you ²these ¹I used
things to tell
ὑμῖν; 6 καὶ νῦν τὸ κατέχον οἴδατε,
³you? and now the restraining ye know,
[thing]

Chapter 2

The Man of Lawlessness

CONCERNING the coming of our Lord Jesus Christ and our being gathered to him, we ask you, brothers, 2not to become easily unsettled or alarmed by some prophecy, report or letter supposed to have come from us, saying that the day of the Lord has already come. 3Don't let anyone deceive you in any way, for that day will not come, until the rebellion occurs and the man of lawlessness[c] is revealed, the man doomed to destruction. 4He will oppose and will exalt himself over everything that is called God or is worshiped, so that he sets himself up in God's temple, proclaiming himself to be God. 5Don't you remember that when I was with you I used to tell you these things? 6And now you know what is holding him

[b]12 Or God and Lord, Jesus Christ
[c]3 Some manuscripts sin

his time he may be revealed.

7For the mystery of lawlessness is already at work; only he who now restrains *will do so* until he is taken out of the way.

8And then that lawless one will be revealed whom the Lord will slay with the breath of His mouth and bring to an end by the appearance of His coming;

9*that is*, the one whose coming is in accord with the activity of Satan, with all power and signs and false wonders,

10and with all the deception of wickedness for those who perish, because they did not receive the love of the truth so as to be saved.

11And for this reason God will send upon them a deluding influence so that they might believe what is false,

12in order that they all may be judged who did not believe the truth, but took pleasure in wickedness.

13But we should always give thanks to God for you, brethren beloved by the Lord, because God has chosen you *b*from the beginning for salvation through sanctification by the Spirit and faith in the truth.

14And it was for this He called you through our gospel, that you may gain the glory of our Lord Jesus Christ.

15So then, brethren, stand firm and hold to the traditions which you were taught, whether by word *of mouth* or by letter from us.

16Now may our Lord Jesus Christ Himself and God our Father, who has loved us and given us eter-

---

εἰς τὸ ἀποκαλυφθῆναι αὐτὸν ἐν τῷ
for the ⁸to be revealed ¹him*b* in the

αὐτοῦ καιρῷ. 7 τὸ γὰρ μυστήριον ἤδη
⁹of him ¹time. For the mystery ²already

ἐνεργεῖται τῆς ἀνομίας· μόνον ὁ κατέχων
³operates - ¹of lawless- only the restraining
ness; [there is] [one]

ἄρτι ἕως ἐκ μέσου γένηται. 8 καὶ τότε
just now until ²out of ¹[the] midst ¹it comes. And then

ἀποκαλυφθήσεται ὁ ἄνομος, ὃν ὁ κύριος
will be revealed the lawless whom the Lord
one,

[Ἰησοῦς] ἀνελεῖ τῷ πνεύματι τοῦ στό-
Jesus will destroy by the spirit of the mouth

ματος αὐτοῦ καὶ καταργήσει τῇ ἐπιφανείᾳ
of him and bring to nothing by the outshining

τῆς παρουσίας αὐτοῦ, 9 οὗ ἐστιν ἡ
of the presence of him, of whom ²is ¹the

παρουσία κατ' ἐνέργειαν τοῦ σατανᾶ ἐν
²presence according operation - of Satan with
to [the]

πάσῃ δυνάμει καὶ σημείοις καὶ τέρασιν
all power and signs and wonders

ψεύδους 10 καὶ ἐν πάσῃ ἀπάτῃ ἀδικίας
of a lie and with all deceit of unrighteousness

τοῖς ἀπολλυμένοις, ἀνθ' ὧν τὴν ἀγάπην
in the [ones] perishing, because the love

τῆς ἀληθείας οὐκ ἐδέξαντο εἰς τὸ σωθῆναι
of the truth they received not for the ²to be saved

αὐτούς. 11 καὶ διὰ τοῦτο πέμπει αὐτοῖς
¹them.*b* And therefore ²sends ³to them

ὁ θεὸς ἐνέργειαν πλάνης εἰς τὸ πιστεῦσαι
- ¹God an operation of error for the ¹to believe

αὐτοὺς τῷ ψεύδει, 12 ἵνα κριθῶσιν πάντες
¹them*b* the lie, in or- ¹⁰may be ¹all
der that judged

οἱ μὴ πιστεύσαντες τῇ ἀληθείᾳ ἀλλὰ
²the ³not ⁴having believed ⁵the ⁶truth ⁷but
[ones]

εὐδοκήσαντες τῇ ἀδικίᾳ.
⁸having had pleasure - ⁹in unrighteousness.

13 Ἡμεῖς δὲ ὀφείλομεν εὐχαριστεῖν τῷ
But we ought to thank -

θεῷ πάντοτε περὶ ὑμῶν, ἀδελφοὶ ἠγαπη-
God always concerning you, brothers having been

μένοι ὑπὸ κυρίου, ὅτι εἵλατο ὑμᾶς ὁ
loved by [the] Lord, because ²chose ³you -

θεὸς ἀπαρχὴν εἰς σωτηρίαν ἐν ἁγιασμῷ
¹God firstfruit to salvation by sanctification

πνεύματος καὶ πίστει ἀληθείας, 14 εἰς
of spirit ┘ and faith of(in) [the] truth, to

ὃ καὶ ἐκάλεσεν ὑμᾶς διὰ τοῦ εὐαγγελίου
which also he called you through the gospel

ἡμῶν, εἰς περιποίησιν δόξης τοῦ κυρίου
of us, to obtainment of [the] glory of the Lord

ἡμῶν Ἰησοῦ Χριστοῦ. 15 Ἄρα οὖν,
of us Jesus Christ. So then,

ἀδελφοί, στήκετε, καὶ κρατεῖτε τὰς
brothers, stand, and hold the

παραδόσεις ἃς ἐδιδάχθητε εἴτε διὰ λόγου
traditions which ye were taught either through speech

εἴτε δι' ἐπιστολῆς ἡμῶν. 16 Αὐτὸς δὲ
or through an epistle of us. And ⁶[him]self

ὁ κύριος ἡμῶν Ἰησοῦς Χριστὸς καὶ
¹the ²Lord ³of us ⁴Jesus ⁵Christ and

ὁ θεὸς ὁ πατὴρ ἡμῶν, ὁ ἀγαπήσας
the God the Father of us, the [one] having loved

---

back, so that he may be revealed at the proper time.

7For the secret power of lawlessness is already at work; but the one who now holds it back will continue to do so till he is taken out of the way. 8And then the lawless one will be revealed, whom the Lord Jesus will overthrow with the breath of his mouth and destroy by the splendor of his coming. 9The coming of the lawless one will be in accordance with the work of Satan displayed in all kinds of counterfeit miracles, signs and wonders, 10and in every sort of evil that deceives those who are perishing. They perish because they refused to love the truth and so be saved. 11For this reason God sends them a powerful delusion so that they will believe the lie 12and so that all will be condemned who have not believed the truth but have delighted in wickedness.

Stand Firm

13But we ought always to thank God for you, brothers loved by the Lord, because from the beginning God chose you*d* to be saved through the sanctifying work of the Spirit and through belief in the truth. 14He called you to this through our gospel, that you might share in the glory of our Lord Jesus Christ. 15So then, brothers, stand firm and hold to the teachings*e* we passed on to you, whether by word of mouth or by letter.

16May our Lord Jesus Christ himself and God our Father, who loved us and by his grace gave us eternal

---

b Some ancient mss. read *first fruits*

d13 Some manuscripts *because God chose you as his firstfruits*

e15 Or *traditions*

nal comfort and good hope by grace, 17comfort and strengthen your hearts in every good work and word.

Chapter 3

Exhortation

FINALLY, brethren, pray for us that the word of the Lord may spread rapidly and be glorified, just as *it did* also with you;

2and that we may be delivered from perverse and evil men; for not all have faith.

3But the Lord is faithful, and He will strengthen and protect you from the evil one.

4And we have confidence in the Lord concerning you, that you are doing and will *continue to* do what we command.

5And may the Lord direct your hearts into the love of God and into the steadfastness of Christ.

6Now we command you, brethren, in the name of our Lord Jesus Christ, that you keep aloof from every brother who leads an unruly life and not according to the tradition which you received from us.

7For you yourselves know how you ought to follow our example, because we did not act in an undisciplined manner among you,

8nor did we eat anyone's bread without paying for it, but with labor and hardship we *kept* working night and day so that we might not be a burden to any of you;

9not because we do not have the right *to this,* but in order to offer ourselves as a model for you, that you

Center column (interlinear)

ἡμᾶς καὶ δοὺς παράκλησιν αἰωνίαν καὶ
us and having given ²comfort ¹eternal ²and

ἐλπίδα ἀγαθὴν ἐν χάριτι, 17 παρακαλέσαι
³hope ⁴a good by grace, may he comfort

ὑμῶν τὰς καρδίας καὶ στηρίξαι ἐν παντὶ
of you the hearts and *may he* in every
　　　　　　　　　　　　　confirm

ἔργῳ καὶ λόγῳ ἀγαθῷ.
²work ³and ⁴word ¹good.

3 Τὸ λοιπὸν προσεύχεσθε, ἀδελφοί, περὶ
For the rest pray ye, brothers, concerning

ἡμῶν, ἵνα ὁ λόγος τοῦ κυρίου τρέχῃ
us, in order the word of the Lord may run
　　that

καὶ δοξάζηται καθὼς καὶ πρὸς ὑμᾶς,
and be glorified as indeed with you,

2 καὶ ἵνα ῥυσθῶμεν ἀπὸ τῶν ἀτόπων
and in order we may be from – perverse
　　that delivered

καὶ πονηρῶν ἀνθρώπων· οὐ γὰρ πάντων
and evil men; for ²[is] not ⁴of all men

ἡ πίστις. **3** Πιστὸς δέ ἐστιν ὁ κύριος,
¹the ³faith. But faithful is the Lord,

ὃς στηρίξει ὑμᾶς καὶ φυλάξει ἀπὸ τοῦ
who will confirm you and will guard from the

πονηροῦ. **4** πεποίθαμεν δὲ ἐν κυρίῳ
evil [?one]. And we are persuaded in [the] Lord

ἐφ’ ὑμᾶς, ὅτι ἃ παραγγέλλομεν [καὶ]
as to you, that what we charge both
　　　　　　　　　　　　things

ποιεῖτε καὶ ποιήσετε. **5** Ὁ δὲ κύριος
ye do and will do. And ²the ¹Lord

κατευθύναι ὑμῶν τὰς καρδίας εἰς τὴν
¹may direct ²of you ⁴the ³hearts into the

ἀγάπην τοῦ θεοῦ καὶ εἰς τὴν ὑπομονὴν
love – of God and into the patience

τοῦ Χριστοῦ.
– of Christ.

6 Παραγγέλλομεν δὲ ὑμῖν, ἀδελφοί, ἐν
Now we charge you, brothers, in

ὀνόματι τοῦ κυρίου Ἰησοῦ Χριστοῦ,
[the] name of the Lord Jesus Christ,

στέλλεσθαι ὑμᾶς ἀπὸ παντὸς ἀδελφοῦ
to draw back youᵇ from every brother

ἀτάκτως περιπατοῦντος καὶ μὴ κατὰ τὴν
²idly ¹walking and not according to the

παράδοσιν ἣν παρελάβετε παρ’ ἡμῶν.
tradition which ye received from us.

7 αὐτοὶ γὰρ οἴδατε πῶς δεῖ μιμεῖσθαι
For [your]selves ye know how it behoves to imitate

ἡμᾶς, ὅτι οὐκ ἠτακτήσαμεν ἐν ὑμῖν,
us, because we were not idle among you,

8 οὐδὲ δωρεὰν ἄρτον ἐφάγομεν παρά τινος,
nor ⁵[as] a gift ²bread ¹ate ³from ⁴anyone,

ἀλλ’ ἐν κόπῳ καὶ μόχθῳ νυκτὸς καὶ
but by labour and struggle by night and

ἡμέρας ἐργαζόμενοι πρὸς τὸ μὴ ἐπιβαρῆσαί
by day working for *the* not to emburden

τινα ὑμῶν· **9** οὐχ ὅτι οὐκ ἔχομεν
anyone of you; not that we have not

ἐξουσίαν, ἀλλ’ ἵνα ἑαυτοὺς τύπον δῶμεν
authority, but in or- ²our- ³an ¹we might
　　　　　　　der that selves example give

encouragement and good hope, 17encourage your hearts and strengthen you in every good deed and word.

Chapter 3

Request for Prayer

FINALLY, brothers, pray for us that the message of the Lord may spread rapidly and be honored, just as it was with you. 2And pray that we may be delivered from wicked and evil men, for not everyone has faith. 3But the Lord is faithful, and he will strengthen and protect you from the evil one. 4We have confidence in the Lord that you are doing and will continue to do the things we command. 5May the Lord direct your hearts into God's love and Christ's perseverance.

Warning Against Idleness

6In the name of the Lord Jesus Christ, we command you, brothers, to keep away from every brother who is idle and does not live according to the teachingᶠ you received from us. 7For you yourselves know how you ought to follow our example. We were not idle when we were with you, 8nor did we eat anyone's food without paying for it. On the contrary, we worked night and day, laboring and toiling so that we would not be a burden to any of you. 9We did this, not because we do not have the right to such help, but in order to make ourselves a

f 6 Or *tradition*

might follow our example. 10For even when we were with you, we used to give you this order: if anyone will not work, neither let him eat.

11For we hear that some among you are leading an undisciplined life, doing no work at all, but acting like busybodies.

12Now such persons we command and exhort in the Lord Jesus Christ to work in quiet fashion and eat their own bread.

13But as for you, brethren, do not grow weary of doing good.

14And if anyone does not obey our instruction in this letter, take special note of that man and do not associate with him, so that he may be put to shame.

15And yet do not regard him as an enemy, but admonish him as a brother.

16Now may the Lord of peace Himself continually grant you peace in every circumstance. The Lord be with you all!

17I, Paul, write this greeting with my own hand, and this is a distinguishing mark in every letter; this is the way I write.

18The grace of our Lord Jesus Christ be with you all.

ὑμῖν εἰς τὸ μιμεῖσθαι ἡμᾶς. 10 καὶ
to you for the to imitate us. even

γὰρ ὅτε ἦμεν πρὸς ὑμᾶς, τοῦτο παρηγ-
For when we were with you, this

γέλλομεν ὑμῖν, ὅτι εἴ τις οὐ θέλει
charged you, that if anyone does not wish

ἐργάζεσθαι, μηδὲ ἐσθιέτω. 11 ἀκούομεν
to work, to such let him eat. we hear [of]

γάρ τινας περιπατοῦντας ἐν ὑμῖν ἀτάκτως,
For some walking among you idly,

μηδὲν ἐργαζομένους ἀλλὰ περιεργαζομένους·
nothing working but working round;

12 τοῖς δὲ τοιούτοις παραγγέλλομεν καὶ
- and to such we charge and

παρακαλοῦμεν ἐν κυρίῳ Ἰησοῦ Χριστῷ
exhort in [the] Lord Jesus Christ

ἵνα μετὰ ἡσυχίας ἐργαζόμενοι τὸν
in or-der that ¹with ²quietness ¹working ²the

ἑαυτῶν ἄρτον ἐσθίωσιν. 13 Ὑμεῖς δέ,
³of them-selves ⁴bread ⁵they may eat. And ye,

ἀδελφοί, μὴ ἐγκακήσητε καλοποιοῦντες
brothers, do not lose heart doing good.

14 εἰ δέ τις οὐχ ὑπακούει τῷ λόγῳ
And if anyone obeys not the word

ἡμῶν διὰ τῆς ἐπιστολῆς, τοῦτον σημειοῦσθε,
of us through the epistle, this man mark,

μὴ συναναμίγνυσθαι αὐτῷ, ἵνα ἐντραπῇ·
not to mix with* him, in or-der that he may be put to shame;

15 καὶ μὴ ὡς ἐχθρὸν ἡγεῖσθε, ἀλλὰ
and yet not as an enemy deem ye [him], but

νουθετεῖτε ὡς ἀδελφόν. 16 Αὐτὸς δὲ
admonish as a brother. And ¹[him]self

ὁ κύριος τῆς εἰρήνης δῴη ὑμῖν τὴν
¹the ¹Lord - ²of peace may he give to you the (?his)

εἰρήνην διὰ παντὸς ἐν παντὶ τρόπῳ.
peace always in every way.

ὁ κύριος μετὰ πάντων ὑμῶν.
The Lord [be] with ²all ¹you.

17 Ὁ ἀσπασμὸς τῇ ἐμῇ χειρὶ Παύλου,
The greeting - by my hand[,] of Paul,

ὅ ἐστιν σημεῖον ἐν πάσῃ ἐπιστολῇ·
which is a sign in every epistle:

οὕτως γράφω. 18 ἡ χάρις τοῦ κυρίου
thus I write. The grace of the Lord

ἡμῶν Ἰησοῦ Χριστοῦ μετὰ πάντων ὑμῶν.
of us Jesus Christ [be] with ²all ¹you.

model for you to follow. 10For even when we were with you, we gave you this rule: "If a man will not work, he shall not eat."

11We hear that some among you are idle. They are not busy; they are busybodies. 12Such people we command and urge in the Lord Jesus Christ to settle down and earn the bread they eat. 13And as for you, brothers, never tire of doing what is right.

14If anyone does not obey our instruction in this letter, take special note of him. Do not associate with him, in order that he may feel ashamed. 15Yet do not regard him as an enemy, but warn him as a brother.

Final Greetings

16Now may the Lord of peace himself give you peace at all times and in every way. The Lord be with all of you.

17I, Paul, write this greeting in my own hand, which is the distinguishing mark in all my letters. This is how I write.

18The grace of our Lord Jesus Christ be with you all.

1 Timothy

Chapter 1

Misleadings in Doctrine and Living

PAUL, an apostle of Christ Jesus according to the commandment of God our Savior, and of Christ Jesus, who is our hope;

2to Timothy, my true child in the faith: Grace,

ΠΡΟΣ ΤΙΜΟΘΕΟΝ Α
To Timothy 1

1 Παῦλος ἀπόστολος Χριστοῦ Ἰησοῦ κατ'
Paul an apostle of Christ Jesus accord-ing to

ἐπιταγὴν θεοῦ σωτῆρος ἡμῶν καὶ Χριστοῦ
a command of God Saviour of us and of Christ

Ἰησοῦ τῆς ἐλπίδος ἡμῶν 2 Τιμοθέῳ
Jesus the hope of us to Timothy

γνησίῳ τέκνῳ ἐν πίστει· χάρις, ἔλεος,
a true child in [the] faith: Grace, mercy,

* Imperative infinitive, as elsewhere (Phil. 3. 16, etc.).

1 Timothy

Chapter 1

PAUL, an apostle of Christ Jesus by the command of God our Savior and of Christ Jesus our hope,

2To Timothy my true son in the faith:

mercy *and* peace from God the Father and Christ Jesus our Lord.

3As I urged you upon my departure for Macedonia, remain on at Ephesus, in order that you may instruct certain men not to teach strange doctrines,

4nor to pay attention to myths and endless genealogies, which give rise to mere speculation rather than *furthering* the administration of God which is by faith.

5But the goal of our instruction is love from a pure heart and a good conscience and a sincere faith.

6For some men, straying from these things, have turned aside to fruitless discussion,

7wanting to be teachers of the Law, even though they do not understand either what they are saying or the matters about which they make confident assertions.

8But we know that the Law is good, if one uses it lawfully,

9realizing the fact that law is not made for a righteous man, but for those who are lawless and rebellious, for the ungodly and sinners, for the unholy and profane, for those who kill their fathers or mothers, for murderers

10and immoral men and homosexuals and kidnappers and liars and perjurers, and whatever else is contrary to sound teaching,

11according to the glorious gospel of the blessed God, with which I have been entrusted.

12I thank Christ Jesus our Lord, who has strengthened me, because He considered me faithful, putting me into service;

13even though I was formerly a blasphemer and a persecutor and a violent aggressor. And yet I was shown mercy, because I acted ignorantly in unbelief;

εἰρήνη   ἀπὸ   θεοῦ   πατρὸς   καὶ   Χριστοῦ
peace   from   God   [the] Father   and   Christ

Ἰησοῦ   τοῦ   κυρίου   ἡμῶν.
Jesus   the   Lord   of us.

3 Καθὼς   παρεκάλεσά   σε   προσμεῖναι   ἐν
   As   I besought   thee   to remain   in

Ἐφέσῳ,   πορευόμενος   εἰς   Μακεδονίαν,   ἵνα
Ephesus,   [I] going   into   Macedonia,   in order that

παραγγείλῃς   τισὶν   μὴ   ἑτεροδιδασκαλεῖν
thou mightest charge   certain persons   not   to teach differently

4 μηδὲ   προσέχειν   μύθοις   καὶ   γενεαλογίαις
nor   to pay attention   to tales   and   to ²genealogies

ἀπεράντοις,   αἵτινες   ἐκζητήσεις   παρέχουσιν
¹unending,   which   ³questionings   ¹provide

μᾶλλον   ἢ   οἰκονομίαν   θεοῦ   τὴν   ἐν   πίστει·
rather   than   a stewardship   of God   -   in   faith:

5 τὸ   δὲ   τέλος   τῆς   παραγγελίας   ἐστὶν
now the   end   of the   charge   is

ἀγάπη   ἐκ   καθαρᾶς   καρδίας   καὶ   συνειδήσεως
love   out of   a clean   heart   and   conscience

ἀγαθῆς   καὶ   πίστεως   ἀνυποκρίτου,   6 ὧν
a good   and   faith   unfeigned,   from which things

τινες   ἀστοχήσαντες   ἐξετράπησαν   εἰς
some   missing aim   turned aside   to

ματαιολογίαν,   7 θέλοντες   εἶναι   νομοδιδάσ-
vain talking,   wishing   to be   law-

καλοι,   μὴ   νοοῦντες   μήτε   ἃ   λέγουσιν
teachers,   not   understanding   either   what things   they say

μήτε   περὶ   τίνων   διαβεβαιοῦνται.   8 οἴδαμεν
nor concerning what things   they emphatically assert.   we know

δὲ   ὅτι   καλὸς   ὁ   νόμος,   ἐάν   τις   αὐτῷ
Now that   ²[is] ⁴good   ¹the   ³law,   if   anyone   ³it

νομίμως   χρῆται,   9 εἰδὼς   τοῦτο,   ὅτι
²lawfully   ¹uses,   knowing   this,   that

δικαίῳ   νόμος   οὐ   κεῖται,   ἀνόμοις   δὲ
³for a just man   ¹law   ²is not laid down,   but for lawless men

καὶ   ἀνυποτάκτοις,   ἀσεβέσι   καὶ   ἁμαρτωλοῖς,
and   for unruly,   for impious   and   for sinners,

ἀνοσίοις   καὶ   βεβήλοις,   πατρολῴαις   καὶ
for unholy   and   for profane,   for parricides   and

μητρολῴαις,   ἀνδροφόνοις,   10 πόρνοις,   ἀρ-
for matricides,   for menkillers,   for fornicators,   for

σενοκοίταις,   ἀνδραποδισταῖς,   ψεύσταις,   ἐπιόρ-
paederasts,   for menstealers,   for liars,   for per-

κοις,   καὶ   εἴ   τι   ἕτερον   τῇ   ὑγιαινούσῃ
jurers,   and   if   any other thing   ²to the   ³being healthful

διδασκαλίᾳ   ἀντίκειται,   11 κατὰ   τὸ   εὐαγ-
⁴teaching   ¹opposes,   according to the   gos-

γέλιον   τῆς   δόξης   τοῦ   μακαρίου   θεοῦ,
pel   of the   glory   of the   blessed   God,

ὃ   ἐπιστεύθην   ἐγώ.   12 Χάριν   ἔχω   τῷ
which ²was entrusted   ¹I.   Thanks   I have   to the
   [with]

ἐνδυναμώσαντί . με   Χριστῷ   Ἰησοῦ   τῷ   κυρίῳ
[one] empowering   me   Christ   Jesus   the   Lord

ἡμῶν,   ὅτι   πιστόν   με   ἡγήσατο   θέμενος
of us,   because   ²faithful   ³me   ¹he deemed   putting [me]

εἰς   διακονίαν,   13 τὸ   πρότερον   ὄντα
into   [the] ministry,   formerly   being

βλάσφημον   καὶ   διώκτην   καὶ   ὑβριστήν·
a blasphemer   and   a persecutor   and   insolent;

ἀλλὰ   ἠλεήθην,   ὅτι   ἀγνοῶν   ἐποίησα   ἐν
but   I obtained mercy,   because   being ignorant   I acted   in

---

Grace, mercy and peace from God the Father and Chrst Jesus our Lord.

Warning Against False Teachers of the Law

3As I urged you when I went into Macedonia, stay there in Ephesus so that you may command certain men not to teach false doctrines any longer 4nor to devote themselves to myths and endless genealogies. These promote controversies rather than God's work —which is by faith. 5The goal of this command is love, which comes from a pure heart and a good conscience and a sincere faith. 6Some have wandered away from these and turned to meaningless talk. 7They want to be teachers of the law, but they do not know what they are talking about or what they so confidently affirm.

8We know that the law is good if one uses it properly. 9We also know that law *a* is made not for the righteous but for lawbreakers and rebels, the ungodly and sinful, the unholy and irreligious; for those who kill their fathers or mothers, for murderers, 10for adulterers and perverts, for slave traders and liars and perjurers—and for whatever else is contrary to the sound doctrine 11that conforms to the glorious gospel of the blessed God, which he entrusted to me.

The Lord's Grace to Paul

12I thank Christ Jesus our Lord, who has given me strength, that he considered me faithful, appointing me to his service. 13Even though I was once a blasphemer and a persecutor and a violent man, I was shown mercy because I acted in ignorance and un-

a9 Or that the law

14and the grace of our Lord was more than abundant, with the faith and love which are *found in* Christ Jesus.

15It is a trustworthy statement, deserving full acceptance, that Christ Jesus came into the world to save sinners, among whom I am foremost *of all*.

16And yet for this reason I found mercy, in order that in me as the foremost, Jesus Christ might demonstrate His perfect patience, as an example for those who would believe in Him for eternal life.

17Now to the King eternal, immortal, invisible, the only God, *be* honor and glory forever and ever. Amen.

18This command I entrust to you, Timothy, my son, in accordance with the prophecies previously made concerning you, that by them you may fight the good fight,

19keeping faith and a good conscience, which some have rejected and suffered shipwreck in regard to their faith.

20Among these are Hymenaeus and Alexander, whom I have delivered over to Satan, so that they may be taught not to blaspheme.

ἀπιστίᾳ, **14** ὑπερεπλεόνασεν δὲ ἡ χάρις
unbelief,　　　and superabounded　　the　grace

τοῦ κυρίου ἡμῶν μετὰ πίστεως καὶ
of the　Lord　of us　with　faith　and

ἀγάπης τῆς ἐν Χριστῷ Ἰησοῦ. **15** πιστὸς
love　　–　in　Christ　Jesus.　Faithful [is]

ὁ λόγος καὶ πάσης ἀποδοχῆς ἄξιος,
the　word　and　²of all　²acceptance　¹worthy,

ὅτι Χριστὸς Ἰησοῦς ἦλθεν εἰς τὸν κόσμον
that　Christ　Jesus　came　into　the　world

ἁμαρτωλοὺς σῶσαι· ὧν πρῶτός εἰμι ἐγώ·
sinners　to save;　of whom first(chief)　am　I;

16 ἀλλὰ διὰ τοῦτο ἠλεήθην, ἵνα ἐν
but　because of　this　I obtained　in or-　in
　　　　　　　　　　mercy,　der that

ἐμοὶ πρώτῳ ἐνδείξηται Ἰησοῦς Χριστὸς
me　first　might show forth　Jesus　Christ

τὴν ἅπασαν μακροθυμίαν, πρὸς ὑποτύπωσιν
–　all　longsuffering,　for　a pattern

τῶν μελλόντων πιστεύειν ἐπ' αὐτῷ εἰς
of the [ones] coming　to believe　on　him　to

ζωὴν αἰώνιον. **17** Τῷ δὲ βασιλεῖ τῶν
life　eternal.　Now to the　King　of the

αἰώνων, ἀφθάρτῳ ἀοράτῳ μόνῳ θεῷ, τιμὴ
ages,　incorruptible invisible　only　God,　[be]
　　　　　　　　　　　　　honour

καὶ δόξα εἰς τοὺς αἰῶνας τῶν αἰώνων·
and　glory unto　the　ages　of the　ages:

ἀμήν. **18** Ταύτην τὴν παραγγελίαν παρα-
Amen.　This　　the　charge　I com-

τίθεμαί σοι, τέκνον Τιμόθεε, κατὰ τὰς
mit　to thee,　child　Timothy,　according to　the

προαγούσας ἐπὶ σὲ προφητείας, ἵνα
preceding　²respecting ³thee　¹prophecies,　in order
　　　　　　　　　　　　　that

στρατεύῃ ἐν αὐταῖς τὴν καλὴν στρατείαν,
thou　by　them　the　good　warfare,
mightest war

19 ἔχων πίστιν καὶ ἀγαθὴν συνείδησιν,
having　faith　and　a good　conscience,

ἥν τινες ἀπωσάμενοι περὶ τὴν πίστιν
which some　thrusting away　²concerning ³the　⁴faith

ἐναυάγησαν· **20** ὧν ἐστιν Ὑμέναιος καὶ
¹made ship-　of whom　is　Hymenæus　and
wreck;

Ἀλέξανδρος, οὓς παρέδωκα τῷ σατανᾷ,
Alexander,　whom　I delivered　–　to Satan,

ἵνα παιδευθῶσιν μὴ βλασφημεῖν.
in or-　they may be taught　not　to blaspheme.
der that

---

belief. 14The grace of our Lord was poured out on me abundantly, along with the faith and love that are in Christ Jesus.

15Here is a trustworthy saying that deserves full acceptance: Christ Jesus came into the world to save sinners—of whom I am the worst. 16But for that very reason I was shown mercy so that in me, the worst of sinners, Christ Jesus might display his unlimited patience as an example for those who would believe on him and receive eternal life. 17Now to the King eternal, immortal, invisible, the only God, be honor and glory for ever and ever. Amen.

18Timothy, my son, I give you this instruction in keeping with the prophecies once made about you, so that by following them you may fight the good fight, 19holding on to faith and a good conscience. Some have rejected these and so have shipwrecked their faith. 20Among them are Hymenaeus and Alexander, whom I have handed over to Satan to be taught not to blaspheme.

Chapter 2

A Call to Prayer

FIRST of all, then, I urge that entreaties *and* prayers, petitions *and* thanksgivings, be made on behalf of all men,

2for kings and all who are in authority, in order that we may lead a tranquil and quiet life in all godliness and dignity.

3This is good and accept-

---

2 Παρακαλῶ οὖν πρῶτον πάντων
I exhort　therefore　first*ly*　of all

ποιεῖσθαι δεήσεις, προσευχάς, ἐντεύξεις,
to be made　petitions,　prayers,　intercessions,

εὐχαριστίας, ὑπὲρ πάντων ἀνθρώπων,
thanksgivings,　on behalf of　all　men,

2 ὑπὲρ βασιλέων καὶ πάντων τῶν ἐν
on behalf of　kings　and　all　the [ones] ³in

ὑπεροχῇ ὄντων, ἵνα ἤρεμον καὶ ἡσύχιον
²eminence ¹being,　in or-　²a tranquil ³and ⁴quiet
　　　　　　der that

βίον διάγωμεν ἐν πάσῃ εὐσεβείᾳ καὶ
⁵life ¹we may lead　in　all　piety　and

σεμνότητι. **3** τοῦτο καλὸν καὶ ἀπόδεκτον
gravity.　This [is]　good　and　acceptable

Chapter 2

Instructions on Worship

I URGE, then, first of all, that requests, prayers, intercession and thanksgiving be made for everyone —2for kings and all those in authority, that we may live peaceful and quiet lives in all godliness and holiness. 3This is good, and pleases able in the sight of God our Savior,

4who desires all men to be saved and to come to the knowledge of the truth.

5For there is one God, *and* one mediator also between God and men, *the* man Christ Jesus,

6who gave Himself as a ransom for all, the testimony *borne* at the proper time.

7And for this I was appointed a preacher and an apostle (I am telling the truth, I am not lying) as a teacher of the Gentiles in faith and truth.

8Therefore I want the men in every place to pray, lifting up holy hands, without wrath and dissension.

Women Instructed

9Likewise, *I want* women to adorn themselves with proper clothing, modestly and discreetly, not with braided hair and gold or pearls or costly garments;

10but rather by means of good works, as befits women making a claim to godliness.

11Let a woman quietly receive instruction with entire submissiveness.

12But I do not allow a woman to teach or exercise authority over a man, but to remain quiet.

13For it was Adam who was first created, *and* then Eve.

14And *it was* not Adam who was deceived, but the woman being quite deceived, fell into transgression.

15But *women* shall be preserved through the bearing of children if they continue in faith and love and sanctity with self-restraint.

Chapter 3

Overseers and Deacons

IT is a trustworthy statement: if any man aspires to the office of overseer, it is a fine work he desires *to do.*

2An overseer, then, must be above reproach, the

ἐνώπιον τοῦ σωτῆρος ἡμῶν θεοῦ, 4 ὃς
before the Saviour of us God, who

πάντας ἀνθρώπους θέλει σωθῆναι καὶ εἰς
³all ²men ¹wishes to be saved and ²to

ἐπίγνωσιν ἀληθείας ἐλθεῖν. 5 εἷς γὰρ
¹a full ⁴of truth ³to come. For ¹one
knowledge

θεός, εἷς καὶ μεσίτης θεοῦ καὶ ἀνθρώπων,
¹[there one also mediator of God and of men,
is] ²God,

ἄνθρωπος Χριστὸς Ἰησοῦς, 6 ὁ δοὺς
a man Christ Jesus, the [one] having
given

ἑαυτὸν ἀντίλυτρον ὑπὲρ πάντων, τὸ
himself a ransom on behalf of all, the

μαρτύριον καιροῖς ἰδίοις· 7 εἰς ὃ ἐτέθην
testimony in its own times; for which ¹was
appointed

ἐγὼ κῆρυξ καὶ ἀπόστολος, ἀλήθειαν λέγω,
¹I a herald and an apostle, ²truth ¹I say,

οὐ ψεύδομαι, διδάσκαλος ἐθνῶν ἐν πίστει
I do not lie, a teacher of nations in faith

καὶ ἀληθείᾳ. 8 Βούλομαι οὖν προσεύχεσθαι
and truth. I desire therefore ²to pray

τοὺς ἄνδρας ἐν παντὶ τόπῳ ἐπαίροντας
¹the ²men in every place lifting up

ὁσίους χεῖρας χωρὶς ὀργῆς καὶ διαλογισμοῦ.
holy hands without wrath and doubting.

9 Ὡσαύτως γυναῖκας ἐν καταστολῇ κοσμίῳ,
Similarly women in clothing orderly,

μετὰ αἰδοῦς καὶ σωφροσύνης κοσμεῖν
³with ⁴modesty ⁵and ⁶sobriety ¹to adorn

ἑαυτάς, μὴ ἐν πλέγμασιν καὶ χρυσίῳ
²themselves, not with plaiting and gold

ἢ μαργαρίταις ἢ ἱματισμῷ πολυτελεῖ,
or pearls or raiment costly,

10 ἀλλ' ὃ πρέπει γυναιξὶν ἐπαγγελλομέναις
but what suits women professing

θεοσέβειαν, δι' ἔργων ἀγαθῶν. 11 γυνὴ
reverence, by ²works ¹good. A woman
means of

ἐν ἡσυχίᾳ μανθανέτω ἐν πάσῃ ὑποταγῇ·
in silence let learn in all subjection;

12 διδάσκειν δὲ γυναικὶ οὐκ ἐπιτρέπω,
but ²to teach ¹a woman ¹I do not permit,

οὐδὲ αὐθεντεῖν ἀνδρός, ἀλλ' εἶναι ἐν
nor to exercise of(over) a man, but to be in
authority

ἡσυχίᾳ. 13 Ἀδὰμ γὰρ πρῶτος ἐπλάσθη,
silence. For Adam first was formed,

εἶτα Εὗα. 14 καὶ Ἀδὰμ οὐκ ἠπατήθη,
then Eve. And Adam was not deceived,

ἡ δὲ γυνὴ ἐξαπατηθεῖσα ἐν παραβάσει
but the woman being deceived ²in ¹transgression

γέγονεν· 15 σωθήσεται δὲ διὰ τῆς
¹has become; but she will be saved through the(her)

τεκνογονίας, ἐὰν μείνωσιν ἐν πίστει καὶ
childbearing, if they remain in faith and

ἀγάπῃ καὶ ἁγιασμῷ μετὰ σωφροσύνης.
love and sanctification with sobriety.

3 Πιστὸς ὁ λόγος· εἴ τις ἐπισκοπῆς
Faithful [is] the word: If anyone ²oversight

ὀρέγεται, καλοῦ ἔργου ἐπιθυμεῖ. 2 δεῖ
¹aspires to, ²a good ³work ¹he desires. It behoves

οὖν τὸν ἐπίσκοπον ἀνεπίλημπτον εἶναι,
there- the bishop without reproach to be,
fore

God our Savior, 4who wants all men to be saved and to come to a knowledge of the truth. 5For there is one God and one mediator between God and men, the man Christ Jesus, 6who gave himself as a ransom for all men—the testimony given in its proper time. 7And for this purpose I was appointed a herald and an apostle—I am telling the truth, I am not lying—and a teacher of the true faith to the Gentiles.

8I want men everywhere to lift up holy hands in prayer, without anger or disputing.

9I also want women to dress modestly, with decency and propriety, not with braided hair or gold or pearls or expensive clothes, 10but with good deeds, appropriate for women who profess to worship God.

11A woman should learn in quietness and full submission. 12I do not permit a woman to teach or to have authority over a man; she must be silent. 13For Adam was formed first, then Eve. 14And Adam was not the one deceived; it was the woman who was deceived and became a sinner. 15But women[b] will be saved[c] through childbearing—if they continue in faith, love and holiness with propriety.

Chapter 3

Overseers and Deacons

HERE is a trustworthy saying: If anyone sets his heart on being an overseer,[d] he desires a noble task. 2Now the overseer must be above reproach,

---

b15 Greek *she*
c15 Or *restored*
d1 Traditionally *bishop*; also in verse 2

husband of one wife, temperate, prudent, respectable, hospitable, able to teach,

3not addicted to wine or pugnacious, but gentle, uncontentious, free from the love of money.

4He must be one who manages his own household well, keeping his children under control with all dignity

5(but if a man does not know how to manage his own household, how will he take care of the church of God?);

6and not a new convert, lest he become conceited and fall into the condemnation incurred by the devil.

7And he must have a good reputation with those outside the church, so that he may not fall into reproach and the snare of the devil.

8Deacons likewise must be men of dignity, not double-tongued, or addicted to much wine or fond of sordid gain,

9but holding to the mystery of the faith with a clear conscience.

10And let these also first be tested; then let them serve as deacons if they are beyond reproach.

11Women must likewise be dignified, not malicious gossips, but temperate, faithful in all things.

12Let deacons be husbands of only one wife, and good managers of their children and their own households.

13For those who have served well as deacons obtain for themselves a high standing and great confidence in the faith that is in Christ Jesus.

14I am writing these things to you, hoping to come to you before long;

15but in case I am delayed, I write so that you may know how one ought to conduct himself in the household of God, which is

---

μιᾶς γυναικὸς ἄνδρα, νηφάλιον, σώφρονα,
of one wife husband, temperate, sensible,

κόσμιον, φιλόξενον, διδακτικόν, 3 μὴ
orderly, hospitable, apt at teaching, not

πάροινον, μὴ πλήκτην, ἀλλὰ ἐπιεικῆ,
an excessive not a striker, but forbearing,
drinker,

ἄμαχον, ἀφιλάργυρον, 4 τοῦ ἰδίου οἴκου
uncontentious, not avaricious, ²the(his) ⁴own ⁵household

καλῶς προϊστάμενον, τέκνα ἔχοντα ἐν
¹well ³ruling, children having in

ὑποταγῇ μετὰ πάσης σεμνότητος, 5 (εἰ
subjection with all gravity, ²(if

δέ τις τοῦ ἰδίου οἴκου προστῆναι οὐκ
¹but ³anyone ⁷the(his) ⁵own ⁶household ⁴to rule ⁸not*

οἶδεν, πῶς ἐκκλησίας θεοῦ ἐπιμελήσεται;)
⁴knows, how ²a church ³of God ¹will he care for ?)

6 μὴ νεόφυτον, ἵνα μὴ τυφωθεὶς εἰς
not a neophyte(recent lest being puffed up ²into
convert),

κρίμα ἐμπέσῃ τοῦ διαβόλου. 7 δεῖ δὲ
³judgment ¹he fall in of the devil. And it behoves

καὶ μαρτυρίαν καλὴν ἔχειν ἀπὸ τῶν
also ²witness ³a good ¹to have from the [ones]

ἔξωθεν, 7 ἵνα μὴ εἰς ὀνειδισμὸν ἐμπέσῃ
outside, lest ²into ³reproach ¹he fall in

καὶ παγίδα τοῦ διαβόλου. 8 Διακόνους
and a snare of the devil. [It behoves] deacons

ὡσαύτως σεμνούς, μὴ διλόγους, μὴ οἴνῳ
similarly [to be] grave, not double-tongued, not ²wine

πολλῷ προσέχοντας, μὴ αἰσχροκερδεῖς,
¹to much ¹being addicted, not fond of base gain,

9 ἔχοντας τὸ μυστήριον τῆς πίστεως ἐν
having the mystery of the faith with

καθαρᾷ συνειδήσει. 10 καὶ οὗτοι δὲ
a clean conscience. ⁴Also ²these ¹and

δοκιμαζέσθωσαν πρῶτον, εἶτα διακονείτωσαν
³let ⁶be proved firstly, then let them minister

ἀνέγκλητοι ὄντες. 11 γυναῖκας ὡσαύτως
²irreproachable ¹being. [It behoves]* wives similarly

σεμνάς, μὴ διαβόλους, νηφαλίους, πιστὰς
[to be] grave, not slanderers, sober, faithful

ἐν πᾶσιν. 12 διάκονοι ἔστωσαν μιᾶς
in all things. ²Deacons ¹let ³be ⁴of one

γυναικὸς ἄνδρες, τέκνα καλῶς προϊστάμενοι
⁶wife ⁵husbands, ²children ⁷well ¹ruling

καὶ τῶν ἰδίων οἴκων. 13 οἱ γὰρ καλῶς
³and ⁴the(ir) ⁵own ⁶households. For the [ones] ²well

διακονήσαντες βαθμὸν ἑαυτοῖς καλὸν
¹having ministered ⁶position ⁴for themselves ⁵a good

περιποιοῦνται καὶ πολλὴν παρρησίαν ἐν
³acquire and much boldness in

πίστει τῇ ἐν Χριστῷ Ἰησοῦ. 14 Ταῦτά
faith the [one] in Christ Jesus. These things

σοι γράφω ἐλπίζων ἐλθεῖν πρὸς σὲ
to thee I write hoping to come to thee

τάχιον· 15 ἐὰν δὲ βραδύνω, ἵνα εἰδῇς
shortly; but if I delay, in order thou
that mayest
know

πῶς δεῖ ἐν οἴκῳ θεοῦ ἀναστρέφεσθαι,
how it behoves in [the] of God to behave,
household

---

the husband of but one wife, temperate, self-controlled, respectable, hospitable, able to teach, 3not given to drunkenness, not violent but gentle, not quarrelsome, not a lover of money. 4He must manage his own family well and see that his children obey him with proper respect. 5(If anyone does not know how to manage his own family, how can he take care of God's church?) 6He must not be a recent convert, or he may become conceited and fall under the same judgment as the devil. 7He must also have a good reputation with outsiders, so that he will not fall into disgrace and into the devil's trap.

8Deacons, likewise, are to be men worthy of respect, sincere, not indulging in much wine, and not pursuing dishonest gain. 9They must keep hold of the deep truths of the faith with a clear conscience. 10They must first be tested; and then if there is nothing against them, let them serve as deacons.

11In the same way, their wivesᵉ are to be women worthy of respect, not malicious talkers but temperate and trustworthy in everything.

12A deacon must be the husband of but one wife and must manage his children and his household well. 13Those who have served well gain an excellent standing and great assurance in their faith in Christ Jesus.

14Although I hope to come to you soon, I am writing you these instructions so that, 15if I am delayed, you will know how people ought to conduct themselves in God's house-

---

* That is, " cannot "; see note on page xviii.

* See verses 7 and 8.

ᵉ11 Or way, deaconesses

the church of the living God, the pillar and support of the truth.

16And by common confession great is the mystery of godliness:

*a*He who was revealed in the flesh,
Was vindicated in the Spirit,
Beheld by angels,
Proclaimed among the nations,
Believed on in the world,
Taken up in glory.

Chapter 4

Apostasy

BUT the Spirit explicitly says that in later times some will fall away from the faith, paying attention to deceitful spirits and doctrines of demons,

2by means of the hypocrisy of liars seared in their own conscience as with a branding iron,

3*men* who forbid marriage *and advocate* abstaining from foods, which God has created to be gratefully shared in by those who believe and know the truth.

4For everything created by God is good, and nothing is to be rejected, if it is received with gratitude;

5for it is sanctified by means of the word of God and prayer.

A Good Minister's Discipline

6In pointing out these things to the brethren, you will be a good servant of Christ Jesus, *constantly* nourished on the words of the faith and of the sound doctrine which you have been following.

7But have nothing to do with worldly fables fit only for old women. On the other hand, discipline yourself for the purpose of godliness;

8for bodily discipline is only of little profit, but godliness is profitable for all things, since it holds promise for the present life and *also* for the *life* to come.

9It is a trustworthy

ἥτις ἐστὶν ἐκκλησία θεοῦ ζῶντος, στῦλος
vhich is [the] church ²God ¹of [the] living, pillar

καὶ ἑδραίωμα τῆς ἀληθείας. 16 καὶ
and bulwark of the truth. And

ὁμολογουμένως μέγα ἐστὶν τὸ τῆς εὐσεβείας
confessedly great is the – ²of piety

μυστήριον· ὃς ἐφανερώθη ἐν σαρκί,
¹mystery: Who was manifested in flesh,

ἐδικαιώθη ἐν πνεύματι, ὤφθη ἀγγέλοις,
was justified in spirit, *was seen* by angels,

ἐκηρύχθη ἐν ἔθνεσιν, ἐπιστεύθη ἐν κόσμῳ,
was pro- among nations, *was* believed in [the] world,
claimed

ἀνελήμφθη ἐν δόξῃ.
was taken up in glory.

4 Τὸ δὲ πνεῦμα ῥητῶς λέγει ὅτι
Now the Spirit ²in words† ¹says that

ἐν ὑστέροις καιροῖς ἀποστήσονταί τινες
in later times ²will depart from ¹some

τῆς πίστεως, προσέχοντες πνεύμασιν
the faith, attending to ²spirits

πλάνοις καὶ διδασκαλίαις δαιμονίων, 2 ἐν
¹misleading and teachings of demons, ²in

ὑποκρίσει ψευδολόγων, κεκαυστηριασμένων
³hypocrisy ¹of men who speak lies, having been branded on

τὴν ἰδίαν συνείδησιν, 3 κωλυόντων γαμεῖν,
the(ir) own conscience, forbidding to marry,

ἀπέχεσθαι βρωμάτων, ἃ ὁ θεὸς ἔκτισεν
[bidding] to foods, which – God created
abstain from

εἰς μετάλημψιν μετὰ εὐχαριστίας τοῖς
for partaking with thanksgiving by the

πιστοῖς καὶ ἐπεγνωκόσι τὴν ἀλήθειαν.
believers and [those] having fully the truth.
known

4 ὅτι πᾶν κτίσμα θεοῦ καλόν, καὶ
Because every creature of God [is] good, and

οὐδὲν ἀπόβλητον μετὰ εὐχαριστίας λαμβαν-
nothing to be put away ²with ³thanksgiving ¹being
[is]

όμενον· 5 ἁγιάζεται γὰρ διὰ λόγου θεοῦ
received; for it is *being* sanctified through a word of God

καὶ ἐντεύξεως. 6 Ταῦτα ὑποτιθέμενος
and petition. ²These things ¹suggesting

τοῖς ἀδελφοῖς καλὸς ἔσῃ διάκονος Χριστοῦ
³to the ⁴brothers ⁵a good ⁶thou ⁷minister of Christ
wilt be

Ἰησοῦ, ἐντρεφόμενος τοῖς λόγοις τῆς
Jesus, being nourished by the words of the

πίστεως καὶ τῆς καλῆς διδασκαλίας ᾗ
faith and of the good teaching which

παρηκολούθηκας· 7 τοὺς δὲ βεβήλους καὶ
thou hast followed; but the profane and

γραώδεις μύθους παραιτοῦ. γύμναζε δὲ
old-womanish tales refuse. And exercise

σεαυτὸν πρὸς εὐσέβειαν. 8 ἡ γὰρ σωματικὴ
thyself to piety. – For bodily

γυμνασία πρὸς ὀλίγον ἐστὶν ὠφέλιμος·
exercise ²for ³a little ¹is ¹profitable;

ἡ δὲ εὐσέβεια πρὸς πάντα ὠφέλιμός
– but piety ³for ⁴all things ¹profitable

ἐστιν, ἐπαγγελίαν ἔχουσα ζωῆς τῆς νῦν
¹is, promise having ²life ¹of the ¹now
(present)

καὶ τῆς μελλούσης. 9 πιστὸς ὁ λόγος
and of the coming. Faithful [is] the word

---

hold, which is the church of the living God, the pillar and foundation of the truth.

16Beyond all question, the mystery of godliness is great:

He*f* appeared in a body,*g*
was vindicated by the Spirit,
was seen by angels,
was preached among the nations,
was believed on in the world,
was taken up in glory.

Chapter 4

Instructions to Timothy

THE Spirit clearly says that in later times some will abandon the faith and follow deceiving spirits and things taught by demons. 2Such teachings come through hypocritical liars, whose consciences have been seared as with a hot iron. 3They forbid people to marry and order them to abstain from certain foods, which God created to be received with thanksgiving by those who believe and who know the truth. 4For everything God created is good, and nothing is to be rejected if it is received with thanksgiving, 5because it is consecrated by the word of God and prayer.

6If you point these things out to the brothers, you will be a good minister of Christ Jesus, brought up in the truths of the faith and of the good teaching that you have followed. 7Have nothing to do with godless myths and old wives' tales; rather, train yourself to be godly. 8For physical training is of some value, but godliness has value for all things, holding promise for both the present life and the life to come. 9This is a trustworthy statement deserving full acceptance.

10For it is for this we labor and strive, because we have fixed our hope on the living God, who is the Savior of all men, especially of believers.

11Prescribe and teach these things.

12Let no one look down on your youthfulness, but *rather* in speech, conduct, love, faith *and* purity, show yourself an example of those who believe.

13Until I come, give attention to the *public* reading *of Scripture,* to exhortation and teaching.

14Do not neglect the spiritual gift within you, which was *absorbed* upon you through prophetic utterance with the laying on of hands by the presbytery.

15Take pains with these things; be *absorbed* in them, so that your progress may be evident to all.

16Pay close attention to yourself and to your teaching; persevere in these things; for as you do this you will insure salvation both for yourself and for those who hear you.

καὶ	πάσης	ἀποδοχῆς	ἄξιος·	10 εἰς	τοῦτο
and	¹of all	²acceptance	¹worthy;	²to	³this
γὰρ	κοπιῶμεν	καὶ	ἀγωνιζόμεθα,		ὅτι
¹for	we labour	and	struggle,		because
ἠλπίκαμεν	ἐπὶ	θεῷ	ζῶντι,	ὅς	ἐστιν
we have set	on	³God	¹a living,	who	is
[our] hope					
σωτὴρ	πάντων	ἀνθρώπων,	μάλιστα	πιστῶν.	
[the]	of all	men,	especially	of believers.	
Saviour					

11 Παράγγελλε ταῦτα καὶ δίδασκε.
Charge thou these things and teach.

12 μηδείς σου τῆς νεότητος καταφρονείτω·
¹No one ²of thee ³the ⁴youth ¹let despise,

ἀλλὰ τύπος γίνου τῶν πιστῶν ἐν λόγῳ,
but ²a pattern ¹become of the believers in speech,
thou

ἐν ἀναστροφῇ, ἐν ἀγάπῃ, ἐν πίστει,
in behaviour, in love, in faith,

ἐν ἁγνείᾳ. 13 ἕως ἔρχομαι πρόσεχε
in purity. Until I come attend

τῇ ἀναγνώσει,* τῇ παρακλήσει, τῇ διδασ-
to the reading,* to the exhortation, to the teach-

καλίᾳ. 14 μὴ ἀμέλει τοῦ ἐν σοὶ
ing. Do not be neglectful ¹of the ²in ⁴thee

χαρίσματος, ὃ ἐδόθη σοι διὰ προφητείας
³gift, which was to thee by means of prophecy
given

μετὰ ἐπιθέσεως τῶν χειρῶν τοῦ πρε-
with laying on of the hands of the body

σβυτερίου. 15 ταῦτα μελέτα, ἐν τούτοις
of elders. ²These things ¹attend to, ²in ³these things

ἴσθι, ἵνα σου ἡ προκοπὴ φανερὰ ᾖ
¹be in order of thee the advance clear may
thou, that be

πᾶσιν. 16 ἔπεχε σεαυτῷ καὶ τῇ διδασκαλίᾳ,
to all men. Take heed to thyself and to the teaching,

ἐπίμενε αὐτοῖς· τοῦτο γὰρ ποιῶν καὶ
continue in them; for this doing both

σεαυτὸν σώσεις καὶ τοὺς ἀκούοντάς σου.
thyself thou wilt save and the [ones] hearing thee.

Chapter 5

Honor Widows

DO not sharply rebuke an older man, but *rather* appeal to *him* as a father, *to* the younger men as brothers,

2the older women as mothers, *and* the younger women as sisters, in all purity.

3Honor widows who are widows indeed;

4but if any widow has children or grandchildren, let them first learn to practice piety in regard to their own family, and to make some return to their parents; for this is acceptable in the sight of God.

5Now she who is a widow indeed, and who has been left alone has fixed

5 Πρεσβυτέρῳ μὴ ἐπιπλήξῃς, ἀλλὰ
An older man do not rebuke, but

παρακάλει ὡς πατέρα, νεωτέρους ὡς
exhort as a father, younger men as

ἀδελφούς, 2 πρεσβυτέρας ὡς μητέρας,
brothers, older women as mothers,

νεωτέρας ὡς ἀδελφὰς ἐν πάσῃ ἁγνείᾳ.
younger women as sisters with all purity.

3 Χήρας τίμα τὰς ὄντως χήρας. 4 εἰ δέ
¹Widows ¹honour ²the ⁴really ³widows. But if

τις χήρα τέκνα ἢ ἔκγονα ἔχει, μαν-
any widow ²children ³or ⁴grandchildren ¹has, let

θανέτωσαν πρῶτον τὸν ἴδιον οἶκον εὐσεβεῖν
them learn firstly ²the(ir) ¹own ⁴household ¹to show
piety to

καὶ ἀμοιβὰς ἀποδιδόναι τοῖς προγόνοις·
and ²requitals ¹to return to the(ir) forebears;

τοῦτο γάρ ἐστιν ἀπόδεκτον ἐνώπιον τοῦ
for this is acceptable before

θεοῦ. 5 ἡ δὲ ὄντως χήρα καὶ μεμονωμένη
God. But the really widow and *having been* left
alone

Chapter 5

Advice About Widows, Elders and Slaves

DO not rebuke an older man harshly, but exhort him as if he were your father. Treat younger men as brothers, 2older women as mothers, and younger women as sisters, with absolute purity.

3Give proper recognition to those widows who are really in need. 4But if a widow has children or grandchildren, these should learn first of all to put their religion into practice by caring for their own family and so repaying their parents and grandparents, for this is pleasing to God. 5The widow who is really in need and left all alone puts her

saying that deserves full acceptance 10(and for this we labor and strive), that we have put our hope in the living God, who is the Savior of all men, and especially of those who believe.

11Command and teach these things. 12Don't let anyone look down on you because you are young, but set an example for the believers in speech, in life, in love, in faith and in purity. 13Until I come, devote yourself to the public reading of Scripture, to preaching and to teaching. 14Do not neglect your gift, which was given you through a prophetic message when the body of elders laid their hands on you.

15Be diligent in these matters; give yourself wholly to them, so that everyone may see your progress. 16Watch your life and doctrine closely. Persevere in them, because if you do, you will save both yourself and your hearers.

* That is, the reading aloud in public worship of the Scriptures (as nearly always in the N.T.).

her hope on God, and continues in entreaties and prayers night and day. 6But she who gives herself to wanton pleasure is dead even while she lives. 7Prescribe these things as well, so that they may be above reproach. 8But if anyone does not provide for his own, and especially for those of his household, he has denied the faith, and is worse than an unbeliever. 9Let a widow be put on the list only if she is not less than sixty years old, *having been* the wife of one man, 10having a reputation for good works; *and* if she has brought up children, if she has shown hospitality to strangers, if she has washed the saints' feet, if she has assisted those in distress, *and* if she has devoted herself to every good work. 11But refuse *to put* younger widows *on the list*, for when they feel sensual desires in disregard of Christ, they want to get married, 12*thus* incurring condemnation, because they have set aside their previous pledge. 13And at the same time they also learn *to be* idle, as they go around from house to house; and not merely idle, but also gossips and busybodies, talking about things not proper *to mention*. 14Therefore, I want younger *widows* to get married, bear children, keep house, *and* give the enemy no occasion for reproach; 15for some have already turned aside to follow Satan. 16If any woman who is a believer has *dependent* widows, let her assist them, and let not the church be burdened, so that it may assist those who are widows indeed.

Concerning Elders

17Let the elders who rule well be considered worthy of double honor, especially

ἤλπικεν	ἐπὶ	θεὸν	καὶ	προσμένει	ταῖς
has set [her] hope	on	God	and	continues	in the
δεήσεσιν	καὶ	ταῖς	προσευχαῖς	νυκτὸς	καὶ
petitions	and	the	prayers	night	and
ἡμέρας·	6 ἡ	δὲ	σπαταλῶσα	ζῶσα	τέθνηκεν.
day;	but the [one]		living wantonly	²living	¹has died.

7 καὶ ταῦτα παράγγελλε, ἵνα ἀνεπίλημπτοι
And these things charge thou, in order that ²without reproach
ὦσιν. 8 εἰ δέ τις τῶν ἰδίων καὶ μάλιστα
¹they may be. But if anyone ²the(his) ³own ⁴and ⁵especially
οἰκείων οὐ προνοεῖ, τὴν πίστιν ἤρνηται
⁶[his] family ¹provides not [for], ²the ³faith ¹he has denied
καὶ ἔστιν ἀπίστου χείρων. 9 χήρα
and is ²an unbeliever ¹worse [than]. A widow
καταλεγέσθω μὴ ἔλαττον ἐτῶν ἑξήκοντα
let be enrolled ²not ³less [than] ⁵of years ⁴sixty
γεγονυῖα, ἑνὸς ἀνδρὸς γυνή, 10 ἐν ἔργοις
¹having become, of one man wife, ²by ⁴works
καλοῖς μαρτυρουμένη, εἰ ἐτεκνοτρόφησεν,
³good ¹being witnessed, if she brought up children,
εἰ ἐξενοδόχησεν, εἰ ἁγίων πόδας ἔνιψεν,
if she entertained strangers, if ³of saints ²feet ¹she washed,
εἰ θλιβομένοις ἐπήρκεσεν, εἰ παντὶ ἔργῳ
if ²being afflicted ¹she relieved, [ones], if ²every ⁴work
ἀγαθῷ ἐπηκολούθησεν. 11 νεωτέρας δὲ
³good ¹she followed after. But younger
χήρας παραιτοῦ· ὅταν γὰρ καταστρηνιάσωσιν
widows refuse; for whenever they grow wanton against
τοῦ Χριστοῦ, γαμεῖν θέλουσιν, 12 ἔχουσαι
- Christ, ²to marry ¹they wish, having
κρίμα ὅτι τὴν πρώτην πίστιν ἠθέτησαν·
judgment because ²the(ir) ³first ⁴faith ¹they set aside;
13 ἅμα δὲ καὶ ἀργαὶ μανθάνουσιν
and at the same time also ²idle ¹they learn [to be]
περιερχόμεναι τὰς οἰκίας, οὐ μόνον δὲ
going round the houses, ²not ³only ¹and
ἀργαὶ ἀλλὰ καὶ φλύαροι καὶ περίεργοι,
idle but also gossips and busybodies,
λαλοῦσαι τὰ μὴ δέοντα. 14 βούλομαι
speaking the things not proper. I will
οὖν νεωτέρας γαμεῖν, τεκνογονεῖν,
therefore younger women to marry, to bear children,
οἰκοδεσποτεῖν, μηδεμίαν ἀφορμὴν διδόναι
to be mistress of a house, ²no ³occasion ¹to give
τῷ ἀντικειμένῳ λοιδορίας χάριν· 15 ἤδη
to the [one] opposing ²reproach ¹on account of; ²already
γάρ τινες ἐξετράπησαν ὀπίσω τοῦ σατανᾶ.
¹for some turned aside behind - Satan.
16 εἴ τις πιστὴ ἔχει χήρας, ἐπαρκείτω
If any believing woman has widows, let her relieve
αὐταῖς, καὶ μὴ βαρείσθω ἡ ἐκκλησία,
them, and not let be burdened the church,
ἵνα ταῖς ὄντως χήραις ἐπαρκέσῃ. 17 Οἱ
in order that ²the ²really ¹widows ¹it may relieve. ²The
καλῶς προεστῶτες πρεσβύτεροι διπλῆς
⁵well ⁴ruling ³elders ⁶of double

hope in God and continues night and day to pray and to ask God for help. 6But the widow who lives for pleasure is dead even while she lives. 7Give the people these instructions, too, so that no one may be open to blame. 8If anyone does not provide for his relatives, and especially for his immediate family, he has denied the faith and is worse than an unbeliever.
9No widow may be put on the list of widows unless she is over sixty, has been faithful to her husband,[h] 10and is well known for her good deeds, such as bringing up children, showing hospitality, washing the feet of the saints, helping those in trouble and devoting herself to all kinds of good deeds.
11As for younger widows, do not put them on such a list. For when their sensual desires overcome their dedication to Christ, they want to marry. 12Thus they bring judgment on themselves, because they have broken their first pledge. 13Besides, they get into the habit of being idle and going about from house to house. And not only do they become idlers, but also gossips and busybodies, saying things they ought not to. 14So I counsel younger widows to marry, to have children, to manage their homes and to give the enemy no opportunity for slander. 15Some have in fact already turned away to follow Satan.
16If any woman who is a believer has widows in her family, she should help them and not let the church be burdened with them, so that the church can help those widows who are really in need.
17The elders who direct the affairs of the church well are worthy of double honor, especially those

---

h9 Or has had but one husband

those who work hard at preaching and teaching.

18For the Scripture says, "YOU SHALL NOT MUZZLE THE OX WHILE HE IS THRESHING," and "The laborer is worthy of his wages."

19Do not receive an accusation against an elder except on the basis of two or three witnesses.

20Those who continue in sin, rebuke in the presence of all, so that the rest also may be fearful of sinning.

21I solemnly charge you in the presence of God and of Christ Jesus and of His chosen angels, to maintain these principles without bias, doing nothing in a spirit of partiality.

22Do not lay hands upon anyone too hastily and thus share responsibility for the sins of others; keep yourself free from sin.

23No longer drink water exclusively, but use a little wine for the sake of your stomach and your frequent ailments.

24The sins of some men are quite evident, going before them to judgment; for others, their sins follow after.

25Likewise also, deeds that are good are quite evident, and those which are otherwise cannot be concealed.

τιμῆς ἀξιούσθωσαν, μάλιστα οἱ κοπιῶντες
19honour 1let 6be 7deemed especially the labouring
                 8worthy,   [ones]

ἐν λόγῳ καὶ διδασκαλίᾳ. 18 λέγει γὰρ
in speech and teaching.   For says

ἡ γραφή· βοῦν ἀλοῶντα οὐ φιμώσεις,
the scripture: An ox threshing thou shalt not muzzle,

καὶ· ἄξιος ὁ ἐργάτης τοῦ μισθοῦ αὐτοῦ.
and: Worthy [is] the workman of the pay of him.

19 κατὰ πρεσβυτέρου κατηγορίαν μὴ παρα-
Against an elder accusation do not re-

δέχου, ἐκτὸς εἰ μὴ ἐπὶ δύο ἢ τριῶν
ceive, except unless on [the two or three
                            word of]

μαρτύρων. 20 Τοὺς ἁμαρτάνοντας ἐνώπιον
witnesses. The [ones] sinning 5before

πάντων ἔλεγχε, ἵνα καὶ οἱ λοιποὶ φόβον
3all 1reprove in 4also 1the 2rest 2fear
thou, order that

ἔχωσιν. 21 Διαμαρτύρομαι ἐνώπιον τοῦ
4may have. I solemnly witness before –

θεοῦ καὶ Χριστοῦ Ἰησοῦ καὶ τῶν
God and Christ Jesus and the

ἐκλεκτῶν ἀγγέλων ἵνα ταῦτα φυλάξῃς
chosen angels in order these things thou guard
                    that

χωρὶς προκρίματος, μηδὲν ποιῶν κατὰ
without prejudgment, 1nothing 1doing by way of

πρόσκλισιν. 22 χεῖρας ταχέως μηδενὶ
inclination. 2Hands 4quickly 4no man

ἐπιτίθει, μηδὲ κοινώνει ἁμαρτίαις ἀλ-
1lay 3on, nor share 2sins 5in

λοτρίαις· σεαυτὸν ἁγνὸν τήρει. 23 Μηκέτι
others't; 2thyself 3pure 1keep. No longer

ὑδροπότει, ἀλλὰ οἴνῳ ὀλίγῳ χρῶ διὰ
drink water, but 3wine 2a little 1use on ac-
                                          count of

τὸν στόμαχον καὶ τὰς πυκνάς σου
the(thy) stomach and the frequent 2of thee

ἀσθενείας. 24 Τινῶν ἀνθρώπων αἱ ἁμαρτίαι
1weaknesses. 2of some 3men 1The 2sins

πρόδηλοί εἰσιν προάγουσαι εἰς κρίσιν,
6clear 5are going before to judgment,
beforehand

τισὶν δὲ καὶ ἐπακολουθοῦσιν· 25 ὡσαύτως
but some indeed they follow on; similarly

καὶ τὰ ἔργα τὰ καλὰ πρόδηλα, καὶ
also the 3works – 1good [are] clear and
                                beforehand,

τὰ ἄλλως ἔχοντα κρυβῆναι οὐ δύνανται.
the 3otherwise 1having 4to be hidden 2cannot.
[ones]   (being)

6 Ὅσοι εἰσὶν ὑπὸ ζυγὸν δοῦλοι, τοὺς
As many as are under a yoke slaves, 2the(ir)
                        [being]

ἰδίους δεσπότας πάσης τιμῆς ἀξίους ἡγείσ-
3own 4masters 6of all 7honour 5worthy 1let them

θωσαν, ἵνα μὴ τὸ ὄνομα τοῦ θεοῦ καὶ
deem, lest the name – of God and

ἡ διδασκαλία βλασφημῆται. 2 οἱ δὲ
the teaching be blasphemed. And 1the [ones]

πιστοὺς ἔχοντες δεσπότας μὴ καταφρο-
2believing 3having 4masters not let them

νείτωσαν, ὅτι ἀδελφοί εἰσιν, ἀλλὰ μᾶλλον
despise [them], because brothers they are, but rather

δουλευέτωσαν, ὅτι πιστοί εἰσιν καὶ
let them serve as slaves, because 6believing 5are 7and

ἀγαπητοὶ οἱ τῆς εὐεργεσίας ἀντιλαμ-
8beloved 1the [ones] 3of the 4good service 2receiving in

βανόμενοι.
return.

Chapter 6

Instructions to Those Who Minister

LET all who are under the yoke as slaves regard their own masters as worthy of all honor so that the name of God and our doctrine may not be spoken against.

2And let those who have believers as their masters not be disrespectful to them because they are brethren, but let them serve them all the more, because those who partake of the benefit are believers and beloved. Teach and

---

whose work is preaching and teaching. 18For the Scripture says, "Do not muzzle the ox while it is treading out the grain,"i and "The worker deserves his wages."j 19Do not entertain an accusation against an elder unless it is brought by two or three witnesses. 20Those who sin are to be rebuked publicly, so that the others may take warning.

21I charge you, in the sight of God and Christ Jesus and the elect angels, to keep these instructions without partiality, and to do nothing out of favoritism.

22Do not be hasty in the laying on of hands, and do not share in the sins of others. Keep yourself pure.

23Stop drinking only water, and use a little wine because of your stomach and your frequent illnesses.

24The sins of some men are obvious, reaching the place of judgment ahead of them; the sins of others trail behind them. 25In the same way, good deeds are obvious, and even those that are not cannot be hidden.

Chapter 6

ALL who are under the yoke of slavery should consider their masters worthy of full respect, so that God's name and our teaching may not be slandered. 2Those who have believing masters are not to show less respect for them because they are brothers. Instead, they are to serve them even better, because those who benefit from their service are believers, and dear to them. These are the things you are to teach and urge on them.

---

i18 Deut. 25:4
j18 Luke 10:7

preach these *principles*.

3If anyone advocates a different doctrine, and does not agree with sound words, those of our Lord Jesus Christ, and with the doctrine conforming to godliness,

4he is conceited *and* understands nothing; but he has a morbid interest in controversial questions and disputes about words, out of which arise envy, strife, abusive language, evil suspicions,

5and constant friction between men of depraved mind and deprived of the truth, who suppose that godliness is a means of gain.

6But godliness *actually* is a means of great gain, when accompanied by contentment.

7For we have brought nothing into the world, *b* so we cannot take anything out of it either.

8And if we have food and covering, with these we shall be content.

9But those who want to get rich fall into temptation and a snare and many foolish and harmful desires which plunge men into ruin and destruction.

10For the love of money is a root of all sorts of evil, and some by longing for it have wandered away from the faith, and pierced themselves with many a pang.

11But flee from these things, you man of God; and pursue righteousness, godliness, faith, love, perseverance *and* gentleness.

12Fight the good fight of faith; take hold of the eternal life to which you were called, and you made the good confession in the

---

Ταῦτα δίδασκε καὶ παρακάλει. 3 εἰ
These things teach thou and exhort. If

τις ἑτεροδιδασκαλεῖ καὶ μὴ προσέρχεται
anyone teaches differently and consents not

ὑγιαίνουσιν λόγοις τοῖς τοῦ κυρίου ἡμῶν
to *being* healthy words the of the Lord of us
[words]

'Ιησοῦ Χριστοῦ, καὶ τῇ κατ' εὐσέβειαν
Jesus Christ, and ¹to the ²accord- ⁴piety
ing to

διδασκαλίᾳ, 4 τετύφωται, μηδὲν ἐπιστά-
²teaching, he has been puffed up, ²nothing ¹under-

μενος, ἀλλὰ νοσῶν περὶ ζητήσεις καὶ
standing, but being diseased about questionings and

λογομαχίας, ἐξ ὧν γίνεται φθόνος, ἔρις,
battles of words, out of which comes envy, strife,

βλασφημίαι, ὑπόνοιαι πονηραί, 5 διαπαρα-
blasphemies, ²suspicions ¹evil, perpetual

τριβαὶ διεφθαρμένων ἀνθρώπων τὸν νοῦν
wranglings ²having been corrupted ¹of men the mind
=of men with corrupted mind

καὶ ἀπεστερημένων τῆς ἀληθείας, νομιζ-
and *having been* deprived of the truth, sup-

όντων πορισμὸν εἶναι τὴν εὐσέβειαν.
posing ³gain ²to be *the* ¹piety.*

6 ἔστιν δὲ πορισμὸς μέγας ἡ εὐσέβεια
But ¹is ²gain ²great *the* ¹piety

μετὰ αὐταρκείας· 7 οὐδὲν γὰρ εἰσηνέγκαμεν
²with ²self-sufficiency;* for nothing we have brought *in*

εἰς τὸν κόσμον, ὅτι οὐδὲ ἐξενεγκεῖν
into the world, because neither ¹to carry out

τι δυνάμεθα· 8 ἔχοντες δὲ διατροφὰς καὶ
³any- ¹can we; but having foods and
thing

σκεπάσματα, τούτοις ἀρκεσθησόμεθα. 9 οἱ
clothings, with these things we will be satisfied. the

δὲ βουλόμενοι πλουτεῖν ἐμπίπτουσιν εἰς
But [ones] resolving to be rich fall *in* into

πειρασμὸν καὶ παγίδα καὶ ἐπιθυμίας πολλὰς
temptation and a snare and ²lusts ¹many

ἀνοήτους καὶ βλαβεράς, αἵτινες βυθίζουσιν
²foolish ²and ²injurious, which ¹cause ²to sink

τοὺς ἀνθρώπους εἰς ὄλεθρον καὶ ἀπώλειαν.
¹men into ruin and destruction.

10 ῥίζα γὰρ πάντων τῶν κακῶν ἐστιν
For ⁴a root ⁵of all – ⁶evils ³is

ἡ φιλαργυρία, ἧς τινες ὀρεγόμενοι
¹the ²love of money,* of which some hankering after

ἀπεπλανήθησαν ἀπὸ τῆς πίστεως καὶ
wandered away from the faith and

ἑαυτοὺς περιέπειραν ὀδύναις πολλαῖς. 11 Σὺ
themselves ²pierced round ²pains ¹by many. thou

δέ, ὦ ἄνθρωπε θεοῦ, ταῦτα φεῦγε· δίωκε
But, O man of God, these things flee; ²pursue

δὲ δικαιοσύνην, εὐσέβειαν, πίστιν, ἀγάπην,
¹and righteousness, piety, faith, love,

ὑπομονήν, πραϋπαθίαν. 12 ἀγωνίζου τὸν
endurance, meekness. Struggle the

καλὸν ἀγῶνα τῆς πίστεως, ἐπιλαβοῦ τῆς
good struggle of the faith, lay hold on *the*

αἰωνίου ζωῆς, εἰς ἣν ἐκλήθης καὶ ὡμολό-
eternal life, to which thou wast and didst con-
called

γησας τὴν καλὴν ὁμολογίαν ἐνώπιον
fess the good confession before

Love of Money

3If anyone teaches false doctrines and does not agree to the sound instruction of our Lord Jesus Christ and to godly teaching, 4he is conceited and understands nothing. He has an unhealthy interest in controversies and quarrels about words that result in envy, strife, malicious talk, evil suspicions 5and constant friction between men of corrupt mind, who have been robbed of the truth and who think that godliness is a means to financial gain.

6But godliness with contentment is great gain. 7For we brought nothing into the world, and we can take nothing out of it. 8But if we have food and clothing, we will be content with that. 9People who want to get rich fall into temptation and a trap and into many foolish and harmful desires that plunge men into ruin and destruction. 10For the love of money is a root of all kinds of evil. Some people, eager for money, have wandered from the faith and pierced themselves with many griefs.

Paul's Charge to Timothy

11But you, man of God, flee from all this, and pursue righteousness, godliness, faith, love, endurance and gentleness. 12Fight the good fight of the faith. Take hold of the eternal life to which you were called when you made your good

---

b Later mss. read *it is clear that*

* For order of words see note on John 1. 1.

* For order of words see note on John 1. 1.

presence of many wit-
nesses.

13I charge you in the presence of God, who gives life
to all things, and of Christ
Jesus, who testified the
good confession before
Pontius Pilate,

14that you keep the com-
mandment without stain or
reproach until the appearing of our Lord Jesus
Christ,

15which He will bring
about at the proper time—
He who is the blessed and
only Sovereign, the King of
kings and Lord of lords;

16who alone possesses
immortality and dwells
in unapproachable light;
whom no man has seen or
can see. To Him be honor
and eternal dominion!
Amen.

17Instruct those who are
rich in this present world
not to be conceited or to fix
their hope on the uncer-
tainty of riches, but on
God, who richly supplies
us with all things to enjoy.

18Instruct them to do
good, to be rich in good
works, to be generous and
ready to share,

19storing up for them-
selves the treasure of a
good foundation for the future, so that they may take
hold of that which is life indeed.

20O Timothy, guard what
has been entrusted to you,
avoiding worldly and emp-
ty chatter and the opposing
arguments of what is falsely called "knowledge"—

21which some have pro-
fessed and thus gone astray
from the faith.
Grace be with you.

πολλῶν μαρτύρων. 13 παραγγέλλω ἐνώπιον
many witnesses.   I charge   before

τοῦ θεοῦ τοῦ ζωογονοῦντος τὰ πάντα
-   God the [one] quickening   - all things

καὶ Χριστοῦ Ἰησοῦ τοῦ μαρτυρήσαντος
and Christ   Jesus   the [one] having witnessed

ἐπὶ Ποντίου Πιλάτου τὴν καλὴν ὁμολογίαν,
in the Pontius Pilate   the   good   confession,
time of

14 τηρῆσαί σε τὴν ἐντολὴν ἄσπιλον
   1to keep 1thee* the(this) commandment unspotted

ἀνεπίλημπτον μέχρι τῆς ἐπιφανείας τοῦ
without reproach until the appearance of the

κυρίου ἡμῶν Ἰησοῦ Χριστοῦ, 15 ἣν
Lord of us   Jesus   Christ,   which§

καιροῖς ἰδίοις δείξει ὁ μακάριος καὶ
7in its/his own times 4will show 1the 5blessed 2and

μόνος δυνάστης, ὁ βασιλεὺς τῶν βασιλευ-
6only 7Potentate, the   King   of the [ones] reign-

όντων καὶ κύριος τῶν κυριευόντων, 16 ὁ
ing   and Lord of the [ones] ruling,   the

μόνος ἔχων ἀθανασίαν, φῶς οἰκῶν
only [one] having immortality,   5light 1inhabiting

ἀπρόσιτον, ὃν εἶδεν οὐδεὶς ἀνθρώπων οὐδὲ
unapproach- whom 2saw 1no one 3of men   nor
able,

ἰδεῖν δύναται· ᾧ τιμὴ καὶ κράτος αἰώνιον·
2to see 1can; to [be] and might eternal:
            whom honour

ἀμήν. 17 Τοῖς πλουσίοις ἐν τῷ νῦν
Amen.   2the   3rich   4in 5the 6now
                                      (present)

αἰῶνι παράγγελλε μὴ ὑψηλοφρονεῖν, μηδὲ
7age 1Charge thou not to be highminded,   nor

ἠλπικέναι ἐπὶ πλούτου ἀδηλότητι, ἀλλ'
to have set on 2of riches 1[the] uncertainty, but
[their] hope

ἐπὶ θεῷ τῷ παρέχοντι ἡμῖν πάντα
on God the [one] offering   to us all things

πλουσίως εἰς ἀπόλαυσιν, 18 ἀγαθοεργεῖν,
richly   for   enjoyment,   to work good,

πλουτεῖν ἐν ἔργοις καλοῖς, εὐμεταδότους
to be rich in 2works 1good,   2ready to impart

εἶναι, κοινωνικούς, 19 ἀποθησαυρίζοντας
1to be, generous,   treasuring away

ἑαυτοῖς θεμέλιον καλὸν εἰς τὸ μέλλον,
for   2foundation 1a good for the future,
themselves

ἵνα ἐπιλάβωνται τῆς ὄντως ζωῆς. 20 Ω
in or- they may lay the really life.   O
der that hold on

Τιμόθεε, τὴν παραθήκην φύλαξον, ἐκτρεπ-
Timothy, 2the   3deposit   1guard,   turning

όμενος τὰς βεβήλους κενοφωνίας καὶ
aside from the   profane empty utterances and

ἀντιθέσεις τῆς ψευδωνύμου γνώσεως, 21 ἣν
opposing of the falsely named knowledge,   which
tenets

τινες ἐπαγγελλόμενοι περὶ τὴν πίστιν
some   promising   concerning the faith

ἠστόχησαν.
missed aim.

Ἡ χάρις μεθ' ὑμῶν.
- Grace [be] with you.

---

confession in the presence
of many witnesses. 13In the
sight of God, who gives life
to everything, and of Christ
Jesus, who while testifying
before Pontius Pilate made
the good confession, I
charge you 14to keep this
command without spot or
blame until the appearing
of our Lord Jesus Christ,
15which God will bring
about in his own time—
God, the blessed and only
Ruler, the King of kings
and Lord of lords, 16who
alone is immortal and who
lives in unapproachable
light, whom no one has
seen or can see. To him be
honor and might forever.
Amen.

17Command those who
are rich in this present
world not to be arrogant
nor to put their hope in
wealth, which is so uncertain, but to put their hope in
God, who richly provides
us with everything for our
enjoyment. 18Command
them to do good, to be rich
in good deeds, and to be
generous and willing to
share. 19In this way they
will lay up treasure for
themselves as a firm foundation for the coming age,
so that they may take hold
of the life that is truly life.

20Timothy, guard what
has been entrusted to your
care. Turn away from god-
less chatter and the opposing ideas of what is falsely
called knowledge, 21which
some have professed and in
so doing have wandered
from the faith.

Grace be with you.

---

* "thee" is the direct object of the verb "charge" in ver. 13:
"I charge . . . thee to keep . . ."
§ The antecedent to this relative pronoun is "appearance",
not "Jesus Christ".

Chapter 1

Timothy Charged to Guard His Trust

PAUL, an apostle of Christ Jesus by the will of God, according to the promise of life in Christ Jesus,

2to Timothy, my beloved son: Grace, mercy *and* peace from God the Father and Christ Jesus our Lord.

3I thank God, whom I serve with a clear conscience the way my forefathers did, as I constantly remember you in my prayers night and day,

4longing to see you, even as I recall your tears, so that I may be filled with joy.

5For I am mindful of the sincere faith within you, which first dwelt in your grandmother Lois, and your mother Eunice, and I am sure that *it is* in you as well.

6And for this reason I remind you to kindle afresh the gift of God which is in you through the laying on of my hands.

7For God has not given us a spirit of timidity, but of power and love and discipline.

8Therefore do not be ashamed of the testimony of our Lord, or of me His prisoner; but join with *me* in suffering for the gospel according to the power of God,

9who has saved us, and called us with a holy calling, not according to our works, but according to His own purpose and grace which was granted us in Christ Jesus from all eternity,

10but now has been re-

---

1 Παῦλος ἀπόστολος Χριστοῦ Ἰησοῦ διὰ
Paul   an apostle   of Christ   Jesus through

θελήματος θεοῦ κατ' ἐπαγγελίαν ζωῆς
[the] will   of God by way of   a promise   of life

τῆς ἐν Χριστῷ Ἰησοῦ **2** Τιμοθέῳ ἀγαπητῷ
–   in   Christ   Jesus   to Timothy   beloved

τέκνῳ· χάρις, ἔλεος, εἰρήνη ἀπὸ θεοῦ
child: Grace,   mercy,   peace   from   God

πατρὸς καὶ Χριστοῦ Ἰησοῦ τοῦ κυρίου
[our] Father and   Christ   Jesus   the   Lord

ἡμῶν.
of us.

3 Χάριν ἔχω τῷ θεῷ, ᾧ λατρεύω
Thanks   I have   –   to God, whom   I worship

ἀπὸ προγόνων ἐν καθαρᾷ συνειδήσει, ὡς
from [my] forebears in   a clean   conscience,   as

ἀδιάλειπτον ἔχω τὴν περὶ σοῦ μνείαν
unceasingly   I have   ¹the ²concerning ⁴thee ²remembrance

ἐν ταῖς δεήσεσίν μου νυκτὸς καὶ ἡμέρας,
in   the   petitions   of me   night   and   day,

4 ἐπιποθῶν σε ἰδεῖν, μεμνημένος σου
longing   ²thee ¹to see,   having been   ²of thee
                 reminded

τῶν δακρύων, ἵνα χαρᾶς πληρωθῶ,
¹of the   ²tears,   in order of(with) joy I may be filled,
           that

5 ὑπόμνησιν λαβὼν τῆς ἐν σοὶ ἀνυποκρίτου
²recollection ¹taking ²of the ⁵in ⁷thee ⁴unfeigned

πίστεως, ἥτις ἐνῴκησεν πρῶτον ἐν τῇ
⁶faith,   which   indwelt   firstly   in   the

μάμμῃ σου Λωΐδι καὶ τῇ μητρί σου
grand-   of thee   Lois   and [in] the mother of thee
mother

Εὐνίκῃ, πέπεισμαι δὲ ὅτι καὶ ἐν σοί.
Eunice,   and I have been   that [it dwells] in   thee.
      persuaded   also

6 Δι' ἣν αἰτίαν ἀναμιμνήσκω σε ἀνα-
For   which   cause   I remind   thee   to fan

ζωπυρεῖν τὸ χάρισμα τοῦ θεοῦ, ὅ ἐστιν
the flame [of] the   gift   –   of God, which is

ἐν σοὶ διὰ τῆς ἐπιθέσεως τῶν χειρῶν
in   thee   through the   laying on   of the   hands

μου. **7** οὐ γὰρ ἔδωκεν ἡμῖν ὁ θεὸς
of me.   ²not For   ³gave   ⁴to us   –   ¹God

πνεῦμα δειλίας, ἀλλὰ δυνάμεως καὶ ἀγάπης
a spirit of cowardice, but   of power   and   of love

καὶ σωφρονισμοῦ. **8** μὴ οὖν ἐπαισχυνθῇς
and   of self-control.   ³not ¹Therefore   ²be ²thou
                           ashamed [of]

τὸ μαρτύριον τοῦ κυρίου ἡμῶν μηδὲ
the   testimony   of the   Lord   of us   nor

ἐμὲ τὸν δέσμιον αὐτοῦ, ἀλλὰ συγ-
[of] me the   prisoner   of him,   but   suffer

κακοπάθησον τῷ εὐαγγελίῳ κατὰ δύναμιν
ill with   the   gospel   according to [the] power

θεοῦ, **9** τοῦ σώσαντος ἡμᾶς καὶ καλέσαντος
of God,   of the having saved   us   and   having called
       [one]

κλήσει ἁγίᾳ, οὐ κατὰ τὰ ἔργα ἡμῶν
²calling ¹with a holy, not according to the   works   of us

ἀλλὰ κατὰ ἰδίαν πρόθεσιν καὶ χάριν,
but   according to [his] own   purpose   and   grace,

τὴν δοθεῖσαν ἡμῖν ἐν Χριστῷ Ἰησοῦ
–   given   to us   in   Christ   Jesus

πρὸ χρόνων αἰωνίων, **10** φανερωθεῖσαν δὲ
before   times   eternal,   but manifested

Chapter 1

PAUL, an apostle of Christ Jesus by the will of God, according to the promise of life that is in Christ Jesus,

2To Timothy, my dear son:

Grace, mercy and peace from God the Father and Christ Jesus our Lord.

Encouragement to Be Faithful

3I thank God, whom I serve, as my forefathers did, with a clear conscience, as night and day I constantly remember you in my prayers. 4Recalling your tears, I long to see you, so that I may be filled with joy. 5I have been reminded of your sincere faith, which first lived in your grandmother Lois and in your mother Eunice and, I am persuaded, now lives in you also. 6For this reason I remind you to fan into flame the gift of God, which is in you through the laying on of my hands. 7For God did not give us a spirit of timidity, but a spirit of power, of love and of self-discipline.

8So do not be ashamed to testify about our Lord, or ashamed of me his prisoner. But join with me in suffering for the gospel, by the power of God, 9who has saved us and called us to a holy life—not because of anything we have done but because of his own purpose and grace. This grace was given us in Christ Jesus before the beginning of time, 10but it has now been revealed by the appearing of our Savior Christ Jesus, who abolished death, and brought life and immortality to light through the gospel,

11for which I was appointed a preacher and an apostle and a teacher.

12For this reason I also suffer these things, but I am not ashamed; for I know whom I have believed and I am convinced that He is able to guard what I have entrusted to Him until that day.

13Retain the standard of sound words which you have heard from me, in the faith and love which are in Christ Jesus.

14Guard, through the Holy Spirit who dwells in us, the treasure which has been entrusted to you.

15You are aware of the fact that all who are in Asia turned away from me, among whom are Phygelus and Hermogenes.

16The Lord grant mercy to the house of Onesiphorus for he often refreshed me, and was not ashamed of my chains;

17but when he was in Rome, he eagerly searched for me, and found me—

18the Lord grant to him to find mercy from the Lord on that day—and you know very well what services he rendered at Ephesus.

νῦν διὰ τῆς ἐπιφανείας τοῦ σωτῆρος
now through the appearance of the Saviour

ἡμῶν Χριστοῦ Ἰησοῦ, καταργήσαντος μὲν
of us Christ Jesus, ²abrogating ¹on one hand

τὸν θάνατον φωτίσαντος δὲ ζωὴν καὶ
- death ³bringing to ²on the life and
light other

ἀφθαρσίαν διὰ τοῦ εὐαγγελίου, 11 εἰς ὃ
incorruption through the gospel, for which

ἐτέθην ἐγὼ κῆρυξ καὶ ἀπόστολος καὶ
²was ¹I a herald and an apostle and
appointed

διδάσκαλος· 12 δι' ἥν αἰτίαν καὶ ταῦτα
a teacher; for which cause also these things

πάσχω, ἀλλ' οὐκ ἐπαισχύνομαι, οἶδα γὰρ
I suffer, but I am not ashamed, for I know

ᾧ πεπίστευκα, καὶ πέπεισμαι ὅτι δυνατός
whom I have and I have been that ²able
believed, persuaded

ἐστιν τὴν παραθήκην μου φυλάξαι εἰς
¹he is ⁴the ⁵deposit ⁶of me ³to guard to

ἐκείνην τὴν ἡμέραν. 13 ὑποτύπωσιν ἔχε
that - day. ²a pattern ¹Have
thou

ὑγιαινόντων λόγων ὧν παρ' ἐμοῦ ἤκουσας
of being healthy words which ²from ³me ¹thou
heardest

ἐν πίστει καὶ ἀγάπῃ τῇ ἐν Χριστῷ
in faith and love - in Christ

Ἰησοῦ· 14 τὴν καλὴν παραθήκην φύλαξον
Jesus; the good deposit guard

διὰ πνεύματος ἁγίου τοῦ ἐνοικοῦντος ἐν
through Spirit [the] Holy - indwelling in

ἡμῖν. 15 Οἶδας τοῦτο, ὅτι ἀπεστράφησάν
us. Thou knowest this, that turned away from

με πάντες οἱ ἐν τῇ Ἀσίᾳ, ὧν ἐστιν
me all the ones in - Asia, of whom is

Φύγελος καὶ Ἑρμογένης. 16 δῴη ἔλεος
Phygelus and Hermogenes. ¹May ⁴give ⁶mercy

ὁ κύριος τῷ Ὀνησιφόρου οἴκῳ, ὅτι
²the ³Lord ⁵to the ⁸of Onesiphorus ⁷house- because
hold,

πολλάκις με ἀνέψυξεν καὶ τὴν ἅλυσίν
often me he refreshed and the chain

μου οὐκ ἐπαισχύνθη, 17 ἀλλὰ γενόμενος
of me was not ashamed [of], but coming to be

ἐν Ῥώμῃ σπουδαίως ἐζήτησέν με καὶ
in Rome ²diligently ¹he ³sought ⁴me ⁴and

εὗρεν· — 18 δῴη αὐτῷ ὁ κύριος εὑρεῖν
⁵found; (¹May ⁴give ⁵to him ²the ³Lord to find

ἔλεος παρὰ κυρίου ἐν ἐκείνῃ τῇ ἡμέρᾳ·
mercy from [the] Lord in that - day;)

— καὶ ὅσα ἐν Ἐφέσῳ διηκόνησεν,
and what things in Ephesus he served,

βέλτιον σὺ γινώσκεις.
very well thou knowest.

---

vealed through the appearing of our Savior, Christ Jesus, who has destroyed death and has brought life and immortality to light through the gospel. 11And of this gospel I was appointed a herald and an apostle and a teacher. 12That is why I am suffering as I am. Yet I am not ashamed, because I know whom I have believed, and am convinced that he is able to guard what I have entrusted to him for that day.

13What you heard from me, keep as the pattern of sound teaching, with faith and love in Christ Jesus. 14Guard the good deposit that was entrusted to you —guard it with the help of the Holy Spirit who lives in us.

15You know that everyone in the province of Asia has deserted me, including Phygelus and Hermogenes. 16May the Lord show mercy to the household of Onesiphorus, because he often refreshed me and was not ashamed of my chains. 17On the contrary, when he was in Rome, he searched hard for me until he found me. 18May the Lord grant that he will find mercy from the Lord on that day! You know very well in how many ways he helped me in Ephesus.

Chapter 2

Be Strong

YOU therefore, my son, be strong in the grace that is in Christ Jesus.

2And the things which you have heard from me in the presence of many witnesses, these entrust to faithful men, who will be

---

2 Σὺ οὖν, τέκνον μου, ἐνδυναμοῦ ἐν
Thou therefore, child of me, be empowered by

τῇ χάριτι τῇ ἐν Χριστῷ Ἰησοῦ, 2 καὶ
the grace - in Christ Jesus, and

ἃ ἤκουσας παρ' ἐμοῦ διὰ πολλῶν
what thou from me through many
things heardest

μαρτύρων, ταῦτα παράθου πιστοῖς ἀνθρώ-
witnesses, these commit to faithful men,

Chapter 2

YOU then, my son, be strong in the grace that is in Christ Jesus. 2And the things you have heard me say in the presence of many witnesses entrust to reliable men who will also

able to teach others also.
3Suffer hardship with *me*, as a good soldier of Christ Jesus.

4No soldier in active service entangles himself in the affairs of everyday life, so that he may please the one who enlisted him as a soldier.

5And also if anyone competes as an athlete, he does not win the prize unless he competes according to the rules.

6The hard-working farmer ought to be the first to receive his share of the crops.

7Consider what I say, for the Lord will give you understanding in everything.

8Remember Jesus Christ, risen from the dead, descendant of David, according to my gospel,

9for which I suffer hardship even to imprisonment as a criminal; but the word of God is not imprisoned.

10For this reason I endure all things for the sake of those who are chosen, that they may obtain the salvation which is in Christ Jesus *and* with *it* eternal glory.

11It is a trustworthy statement:
  For if we died with Him, we shall also live with Him;
12 If we endure, we shall also reign with Him; If we deny Him, He also will deny us;
13 If we are faithless, He remains faithful; for He cannot deny Himself.

An Unashamed Workman

14Remind *them* of these things, and solemnly charge *them* in the presence of God not to wrangle about words, which is useless, *and leads* to the ruin of the hearers.

15Be diligent to present yourself approved to God as a workman who does not need to be ashamed, handling accurately the word of truth.

ποις,	οἵτινες	ἱκανοὶ	ἔσονται	καὶ	ἑτέρους
who	²competent	¹will be		³also	⁴others

διδάξαι.	**3** Συγκακοπάθησον	ὡς	καλὸς	
⁵to teach.	Suffer ill with*	as	a good	

στρατιώτης	Χριστοῦ	Ἰησοῦ.	**4** οὐδεὶς	
soldier	of Christ	Jesus.	No one	

στρατευόμενος	ἐμπλέκεται	ταῖς	τοῦ βίου	
soldiering	is involved	¹with the	— ²of life	

πραγματείαις,	ἵνα τῷ	στρατολογήσαντι	
³affairs,	in order ⁴the that [one]	⁵having enlisted [him]	

ἀρέσῃ.	**5** ἐὰν	δὲ καὶ	ἀθλῇ	τις,	οὐ	
¹he may please.	And if	also	²wrestles	¹any-one,	not	

στεφανοῦται	ἐὰν μὴ	νομίμως	ἀθλήσῃ.	
he is crowned	unless	¹lawfully	¹he wrestles.	

6 τὸν	κοπιῶντα	γεωργὸν	δεῖ	πρῶτον	τῶν
²the	³labouring	¹husbandman	⁴It be-hoves	⁶firstly	⁷of the

καρπῶν	μεταλαμβάνειν.	**7** νόει	ὁ	λέγω·	
⁸fruits	⁵to partake.	Consider	what	I say;	

δώσει	γὰρ σοι	ὁ κύριος	σύνεσιν	ἐν	
for ²will give	⁴thee	¹the ³Lord	understanding	in	

πᾶσιν.	**8** μνημόνευε	Ἰησοῦν	Χριστὸν	
all things.	Remember	Jesus	Christ	

ἐγηγερμένον	ἐκ νεκρῶν,	ἐκ	σπέρματος	
having been raised	from [the] dead,	of	[the] seed	

Δαυίδ,	κατὰ τὸ	εὐαγγέλιόν	μου·	**9** ἐν	
of David,	according to the	gospel	of me;	in	

ᾧ	κακοπαθῶ	μέχρι	δεσμῶν	ὡς	κακοῦργος,
which	I suffer ill	unto	bonds	as	an evildoer,

ἀλλὰ	ὁ λόγος	τοῦ θεοῦ	οὐ	δέδεται.	
but	the word	— of God	has not	been bound.	

10 διὰ	τοῦτο	πάντα	ὑπομένω	διὰ	τοὺς
Therefore		all things	I endure	on ac-count of	the

ἐκλεκτούς,	ἵνα καὶ	αὐτοὶ	σωτηρίας	τύχωσιν	
chosen ones,	in or-der that ²also	¹they	⁴salvation	³may obtain	

τῆς	ἐν	Χριστῷ	Ἰησοῦ	μετὰ	δόξης
—	in	Christ	Jesus	with	glory

αἰωνίου.	**11** πιστὸς	ὁ	λόγος·	εἰ	γὰρ
eternal.	Faithful [is]	the	word:	for if	

συναπεθάνομεν,	καὶ	συζήσομεν·	**12** εἰ		
we died with [him],	also	we shall live with [him];	if		

ὑπομένομεν,	καὶ	συμβασιλεύσομεν·	εἰ	
we endure,	also	we shall reign with [him];	if	

ἀρνησόμεθα,	κἀκεῖνος	ἀρνήσεται	ἡμᾶς·	**13** εἰ	
we shall deny,	that one also	will deny	us;	if	

ἀπιστοῦμεν,	ἐκεῖνος	πιστὸς	μένει,	ἀρνή-	
we disbelieve,	that one	²faithful	¹remains,	²to	

σασθαι	γὰρ	ἑαυτὸν	οὐ	δύναται.	**14** Ταῦτα
deny	¹for	⁴himself	³he cannot.		These things

ὑπομίμνησκε,	διαμαρτυρόμενος	ἐνώπιον	τοῦ	
remind thou [them] [of],	solemnly witnessing	before	—	

θεοῦ	μὴ λογομαχεῖν,	ἐπ᾽ οὐδὲν	χρήσιμον,	
God	not to fight with words,	²for ³nothing	¹useful,	

ἐπὶ	καταστροφῇ	τῶν ἀκουόντων.	**15** σπού-
for	overthrowing	of the [ones] hearing.	¹Be

δασον	σεαυτὸν	δόκιμον	παραστῆσαι	τῷ
eager	²thyself	⁴approved	³to present	—

θεῷ,	ἐργάτην	ἀνεπαίσχυντον,	ὀρθοτομοῦντα
to God,	a workman	unashamed,	cutting straight

τὸν	λόγον	τῆς	ἀληθείας.	**16** τὰς	δὲ
the	word	—	of truth.	—	But

---

be qualified to teach others. 3Endure hardship with us like a good soldier of Christ Jesus. 4No one serving as a soldier gets involved in civilian affairs—he wants to please his commanding officer. 5Similarly, if anyone competes as an athlete, he does not receive the victor's crown unless he competes according to the rules. 6The hardworking farmer should be the first to receive a share of the crops. 7Reflect on what I am saying, for the Lord will give you insight into all this.

8Remember Jesus Christ, raised from the dead, descended from David. This is my gospel, 9for which I am suffering even to the point of being chained like a criminal. But God's word is not chained. 10Therefore I endure everything for the sake of the elect, that they too may obtain the salvation that is in Christ Jesus, with eternal glory.

11Here is a trustworthy saying:
  If we died with him, we will also live with him;
12if we endure, we will also reign with him.
If we disown him, he will also disown us;
13if we are faithless, he will remain faithful, for he cannot disown himself.

A Workman Approved by God

14Keep reminding them of these things. Warn them before God against quarreling about words; it is of no value, and only ruins those who listen. 15Do your best to present yourself to God as one approved, a workman who does not need to be ashamed and who correctly handles the word of truth. 16Avoid godless

---

* See 1. 8.

16But avoid worldly *and* empty chatter, for it will lead to further ungodliness, 17and their talk will spread like *a* gangrene. Among them are Hymenaeus and Philetus, 18*men* who have gone astray from the truth saying that the resurrection has already taken place, and thus they upset the faith of some. 19Nevertheless, the firm foundation of God stands, having this seal, "The Lord knows those who are His," and, "Let everyone who names the name of the Lord abstain from wickedness." 20Now in a large house there are not only gold and silver vessels, but also vessels of wood and of earthenware, and some to honor and some to dishonor. 21Therefore, if a man cleanses himself from these *things*, he will be a vessel for honor, sanctified, useful to the Master, prepared for every good work. 22Now flee from youthful lusts, and pursue righteousness, faith, love *and* peace, with those who call on the Lord from a pure heart. 23But refuse foolish and ignorant speculations, knowing that they produce quarrels. 24And the Lord's bondservant must not be quarrelsome, but be kind to all, able to teach, patient when wronged, 25with gentleness correcting those who are in opposition, if perhaps God may grant them repentance leading to the knowledge of the truth, 26and they may come to their senses *and escape* from the snare of the devil,

βεβήλους κενοφωνίας περιΐστασο· ἐπὶ πλεῖον
profane empty shun; ²to ⁴more
　　　utterances
γὰρ προκόψουσιν ἀσεβείας, 17 καὶ ὁ λόγος
¹for ²they will advance of impiety, and the word
αὐτῶν ὡς γάγγραινα νομὴν ἕξει· ὧν
of them as a canker feeding will have; of
　　　　　　　　　　　　　　whom
ἐστιν Ὑμέναιος καὶ Φίλητος, 18 οἵτινες
is(are) Hymenæus and Philetus, who
περὶ τὴν ἀλήθειαν ἠστόχησαν, λέγοντες
con- the truth missed aim, saying
cerning
ἀνάστασιν ἤδη γεγονέναι, καὶ ἀνατρέπουσιν
[the] already to have and overturn
resurrection become,
τὴν τινων πίστιν. 19 ὁ μέντοι στερεὸς
the ²of some ¹faith. ²the ¹However firm
θεμέλιος τοῦ θεοῦ ἕστηκεν, ἔχων τὴν
foundation - of God stands, having -
σφραγῖδα ταύτην· ἔγνω κύριος τοὺς ὄντας
seal this: ²knew ¹[The] the being
　　　　　　　　　　　Lord [ones]
αὐτοῦ, καὶ· ἀποστήτω ἀπὸ ἀδικίας πᾶς
of him, and: Let stand away from iniquity every-
ὁ ὀνομάζων τὸ ὄνομα κυρίου. 20 ἐν
one naming the name of [the] Lord. ¹in
μεγάλῃ δὲ οἰκίᾳ οὐκ ἔστιν μόνον σκεύη
²a great ¹Now ⁴house there is(are) not only vessels
χρυσᾶ καὶ ἀργυρᾶ, ἀλλὰ καὶ ξύλινα
golden and silvern, but also wooden
καὶ ὀστράκινα, καὶ ἃ μὲν εἰς τιμὴν ἃ δὲ
and earthen, and some to honour others
εἰς ἀτιμίαν· 21 ἐὰν οὖν τις ἐκκαθάρῃ
to dishonour; if therefore anyone cleanses
ἑαυτὸν ἀπὸ τούτων, ἔσται σκεῦος εἰς
himself from these [latter], he will be a vessel to
τιμήν, ἡγιασμένον, εὔχρηστον τῷ δεσπότῃ,
honour, *having been* suitable for the master,
　　　sanctified;
εἰς πᾶν ἔργον ἀγαθὸν ἡτοιμασμένον.
to every work good *having been* prepared.
22 τὰς δὲ νεωτερικὰς ἐπιθυμίας φεῦγε,
Now the ²youthful ³lusts ¹flee,
δίωκε δὲ δικαιοσύνην, πίστιν, ἀγάπην,
but pursue righteousness, faith, love,
εἰρήνην μετὰ τῶν ἐπικαλουμένων τὸν
peace with the [ones] calling on the
κύριον ἐκ καθαρᾶς καρδίας. 23 τὰς δὲ
Lord out of a clean heart. - But
μωρὰς καὶ ἀπαιδεύτους ζητήσεις παραιτοῦ,
foolish and uninstructed questionings refuse,
εἰδὼς ὅτι γεννῶσιν μάχας· 24 δοῦλον δὲ
knowing that they beget fights; and ²a slave
κυρίου οὐ δεῖ μάχεσθαι ἀλλὰ ἤπιον
³of [the] ¹it behoves not to fight but gentle
Lord
εἶναι πρὸς πάντας, διδακτικόν, ἀνεξίκακον,
to be toward all men, apt to teach, forbearing,
25 ἐν πραΰτητι παιδεύοντα τοὺς ἀντιδιατι-
in meekness instructing the [ones] oppos-
θεμένους, μήποτε δώῃ αὐτοῖς ὁ θεὸς
ing, [if] perhaps ¹may ³them - ¹God
　　　　　　give
μετάνοιαν εἰς ἐπίγνωσιν ἀληθείας, 26 καὶ
repentance for a full knowledge of truth, and
ἀνανήψωσιν ἐκ τῆς τοῦ διαβόλου παγίδος,
they may return out of ¹the ²of the ⁴devil ³snare,
to soberness

chatter, because those who indulge in it will become more and more ungodly. 17Their teaching will spread like gangrene. Among them are Hymenaeus and Philetus, 18who have wandered away from the truth. They say that the resurrection has already taken place, and they destroy the faith of some. 19Nevertheless, God's solid foundation stands firm, sealed with this inscription: "The Lord knows those who are his,"[a] and, "Everyone who confesses the name of the Lord must turn away from wickedness." 20In a large house there are articles not only of gold and silver, but also of wood and clay; some are for noble purposes and some for ignoble. 21If a man cleanses himself from the latter, he will be an instrument for noble purposes, made holy, useful to the Master and prepared to do any good work. 22Flee the evil desires of youth, and pursue righteousness, faith, love and peace, along with those who call on the Lord out of a pure heart. 23Don't have anything to do with foolish and stupid arguments, because you know they produce quarrels. 24And the Lord's servant must not quarrel; instead, he must be kind to everyone, able to teach, not resentful. 25Those who oppose him he must gently instruct, in the hope that God will grant them repentance leading them to a knowledge of the truth, 26and that they will come to their senses and escape from the trap of the

a Or, cancer

a19 Num. 16:5 (see Septuagint)

having been held captive by him to do his will.

Chapter 3

"Difficult Times Will Come"

BUT realize this, that in the last days difficult times will come.

2For men will be lovers of self, lovers of money, boastful, arrogant, revilers, disobedient to parents, ungrateful, unholy,

3unloving, irreconcilable, malicious gossips, without self-control, brutal, haters of good,

4treacherous, reckless, conceited, lovers of pleasure rather than lovers of God;

5holding to a form of godliness, although they have denied its power; and avoid such men as these.

6For among them are those who enter into households and captivate weak women weighed down with sins, led on by various impulses,

7always learning and never able to come to the knowledge of the truth.

8And just as Jannes and Jambres opposed Moses, so these men also oppose the truth, men of depraved mind, rejected as regards the faith.

9But they will not make further progress; for their folly will be obvious to all, as also that of those *two* came to be.

10But you followed my teaching, conduct, purpose, faith, patience, love, perseverance,

11persecutions, *and* sufferings, such as happened

ἐζωγρημένοι ὑπ' αὐτοῦ εἰς τὸ ἐκείνου θέλημα.
having been   by   him[,]   to ¹the ²of that   ²will.
caught   one*

3 Τοῦτο   δὲ   γίνωσκε,   ὅτι   ἐν   ἐσχάταις
And this   know thou, that   in   [the] last

ἡμέραις   ἐνστήσονται   καιροὶ   χαλεποί·
days   ²will be at hand   ³times   ¹grievous;

2 ἔσονται   γὰρ   οἱ   ἄνθρωποι   φίλαυτοι,
for ²will be   -   ¹men   self-lovers,

φιλάργυροι,   ἀλαζόνες,   ὑπερήφανοι,   βλάσφημοι,
money-lovers,   boasters,   arrogant,   blasphemers,

γονεῦσιν   ἀπειθεῖς,   ἀχάριστοι,   ἀνόσιοι,
²to parents ¹disobedient,   unthankful,   unholy,

3 ἄστοργοι,   ἄσπονδοι,   διάβολοι,   ἀκρατεῖς,
without natural implacable,   slanderers,   incontinent,
affection,

ἀνήμεροι,   ἀφιλάγαθοι,   4 προδόται,   προπετεῖς,
untamed,   haters of good   betrayers,   reckless,
[things/men],

τετυφωμένοι,   φιλήδονοι   μᾶλλον   ἢ   φιλόθεοι,
having been   pleasure-lovers   rather   than   God-lovers,
puffed up,

5 ἔχοντες   μόρφωσιν   εὐσεβείας   τὴν   δὲ
having   a form   of piety   but the

δύναμιν   αὐτῆς   ἠρνημένοι·   καὶ   τούτους
power   of it   having denied: and   ³these

ἀποτρέπου.   6 ἐκ   τούτων   γὰρ   εἰσιν   οἱ
²turn away ¹from.   ²of   ³these   ¹For   are   the

ἐνδύνοντες   εἰς   τὰς   οἰκίας   καὶ   αἰχμαλωτίζ-
[ones] creeping into   -   houses   and   captur-

οντες   γυναικάρια   σεσωρευμένα   ἁμαρτίαις,
ing   silly women   having been heaped*   with sins,

ἀγόμενα   ἐπιθυμίαις   ποικίλαις,   7 πάντοτε
being led*   lusts   by various,   always

μανθάνοντα   καὶ   μηδέποτε   εἰς   ἐπίγνωσιν
learning*   and   never   ²to ⁴a full knowledge

ἀληθείας   ἐλθεῖν   δυνάμενα.   8 ὃν   τρόπον
³of truth   ³to come   ¹being able.*   by what way

δὲ   Ἰάννης   καὶ   Ἰαμβρῆς   ἀντέστησαν
Now   Jannes   and   Jambres   opposed

Μωϋσεῖ,   οὕτως   καὶ   οὗτοι   ἀνθίστανται   τῇ
Moses,   so   ⁴ also   these   oppose   the

ἀληθείᾳ,   ἄνθρωποι   κατεφθαρμένοι   τὸν   νοῦν,
truth,   men   having been corrupted   the   mind,
=with corrupted mind,

ἀδόκιμοι   περὶ   τὴν   πίστιν.   9 ἀλλ'   οὐ
reprobate   as to   the   faith.   But   not

προκόψουσιν   ἐπὶ   πλεῖον·   ἡ   γὰρ   ἄνοια
they will advance   to   more;   for the   folly
=farther;

αὐτῶν   ἔκδηλος   ἔσται   πᾶσιν,   ὡς   καὶ
of them   very clear   will be   to all men,   as   also

ἡ   ἐκείνων   ἐγένετο.   10 Σὺ   δὲ   παρηκολού-
the   of those   became.   But thou   hast closely
[folly]

θησάς   μου   τῇ   διδασκαλίᾳ,   τῇ   ἀγωγῇ,
followed of me the   teaching,   the   conduct,

τῇ   προθέσει,   τῇ   πίστει,   τῇ   μακροθυμίᾳ,
the   purpose,   the   faith,   the   longsuffering,

τῇ   ἀγάπῃ,   τῇ   ὑπομονῇ,   11 τοῖς   διωγμοῖς,
the   love,   the   endurance,   the   persecutions,

τοῖς   παθήμασιν,   οἷά   μοι   ἐγένετο   ἐν
the   sufferings.   which   ²to me   ¹happened   in

---

devil, who has taken them captive to do his will.

Chapter 3

Godlessness in the Last Days

BUT mark this: There will be terrible times in the last days. 2People will be lovers of themselves, lovers of money, boastful, proud, abusive, disobedient to their parents, ungrateful, unholy, 3without love, unforgiving, slanderous, without self-control, brutal, not lovers of the good, 4treacherous, rash, conceited, lovers of pleasure rather than lovers of God— 5having a form of godliness but denying its power. Have nothing to do with them.

6They are the kind who worm their way into homes and gain control over weak-willed women, who are loaded down with sins and are swayed by all kinds of evil desires, 7always learning but never able to acknowledge the truth. 8Just as Jannes and Jambres opposed Moses, so also these men oppose the truth—men of depraved minds, who, as far as the faith is concerned, are rejected. 9But they will not get very far because, as in the case of those men, their folly will be clear to everyone.

Paul's Charge to Timothy

10You, however, know all about my teaching, my way of life, my purpose, faith, patience, love, endurance, 11persecutions, sufferings —what kinds of things hap-

---

* That is, of God (the remoter antecedent).

* Agreeing with "silly women" (neut. pl.).

to me at Antioch, at Iconium *and* at Lystra; what persecutions I endured, and out of them all the Lord delivered me!

12And indeed, all who desire to live godly in Christ Jesus will be persecuted.

13But evil men and impostors will proceed *from bad* to worse, deceiving and being deceived.

14You, however, continue in the things you have learned and become convinced of, knowing from whom you have learned *them;*

15and that from childhood you have known the sacred writings which are able to give you the wisdom that leads to salvation through faith which is in Christ Jesus.

16bAll Scripture is inspired by God and profitable for teaching, for reproof, for correction, for training in righteousness;

17that the man of God may be adequate, equipped for every good work.

Chapter 4

"Preach the Word"

I solemnly charge *you* in the presence of God and of Christ Jesus, who is to judge the living and the dead, and by His appearing and His kingdom:

2preach the word; be ready in season *and* out of season; reprove, rebuke, exhort, with great patience and instruction.

3For the time will come when they will not endure sound doctrine; but *wanting* to have their ears tickled, they will accumulate for themselves teachers in accordance to their own desires;

4and will turn away their ears from the truth, and will turn aside to myths.

'Αντιοχεία, ἐν 'Ικονίῳ, ἐν Λύστροις· οἷους
Antioch, in Iconium, in Lystra: what

διωγμοὺς ὑπήνεγκα, καὶ ἐκ πάντων με
persecutions I bore, and out of all ⁴me

ἐρρύσατο ὁ κύριος. 12 καὶ πάντες δὲ
³delivered ¹the ²Lord. ²indeed ³all ¹And

οἱ θέλοντες ζῆν εὐσεβῶς ἐν Χριστῷ
the [ones] wishing to live piously in Christ

'Ιησοῦ διωχθήσονται. 13 πονηροὶ δὲ ἄν-
Jesus will be persecuted. But evil men

θρωποι καὶ γόητες προκόψουσιν ἐπὶ τὸ
and impostors will advance to the

χεῖρον, πλανῶντες καὶ πλανώμενοι. 14 σὺ
worse, deceiving and being deceived. ²thou

δὲ μένε ἐν οἷς ἔμαθες καὶ ἐπιστώθης,
But ¹continue in what thou didst and wast assured of,
things learn

εἰδὼς παρὰ τίνων ἔμαθες, 15 καὶ ὅτι
knowing from whom* thou didst learn, and that

ἀπὸ βρέφους ἱερὰ γράμματα οἶδας, τὰ
from a babe ²sacred ²letters ¹thou know- the
est, [ones]

δυνάμενά σε σοφίσαι εἰς σωτηρίαν διὰ
being able thee to make wise to salvation through

πίστεως τῆς ἐν Χριστῷ 'Ιησοῦ. 16 πᾶσα
faith – in Christ Jesus. Every

γραφὴ θεόπνευστος καὶ ὠφέλιμος πρὸς
scripture [is] God-breathed and profitable for

διδασκαλίαν, πρὸς ἐλεγμόν, πρὸς ἐπανόρ-
teaching, for reproof, for cor-

θωσιν, πρὸς παιδείαν τὴν ἐν δικαιοσύνῃ,
rection, for instruction – in righteousness,

17 ἵνα ἄρτιος ᾖ ὁ τοῦ θεοῦ ἄνθρωπος,
in order ⁵fitted ⁴may ¹the – ³of God ²man,
that be

πρὸς πᾶν ἔργον ἀγαθὸν ἐξηρτισμένος.
for every work good *having been* furnished.

4 Διαμαρτύρομαι ἐνώπιον τοῦ θεοῦ καὶ
I solemnly witness before – God and

Χριστοῦ 'Ιησοῦ, τοῦ μέλλοντος κρίνειν
Christ Jesus, the [one] being about to judge

ζῶντας καὶ νεκρούς, καὶ τὴν ἐπιφάνειαν
living [ones] and dead, both [by] the appearance

αὐτοῦ καὶ τὴν βασιλείαν αὐτοῦ· 2 κήρυξον
of him and [by] the kingdom of him: proclaim

τὸν λόγον, ἐπίστηθι εὐκαίρως ἀκαίρως,
the word, be attentive seasonably[,] unseasonably,

ἔλεγξον, ἐπιτίμησον, παρακάλεσον, ἐν πάσῃ
reprove, admonish, exhort, with all

μακροθυμίᾳ καὶ διδαχῇ. 3 ἔσται γὰρ
longsuffering and teaching. For there will be

καιρὸς ὅτε τῆς ὑγιαινούσης διδασκαλίας
a time when ²the ³*being* healthy ⁴teaching

οὐκ ἀνέξονται, ἀλλὰ κατὰ τὰς ἰδίας
¹they will not bear with, but according to the(ir) own

ἐπιθυμίας ἑαυτοῖς ἐπισωρεύσουσιν διδασ-
lusts ²to themselves ¹they will heap up ²teach-

κάλους κνηθόμενοι τὴν ἀκοήν, 4 καὶ ἀπὸ
ers tickling the ear, and ⁵from

μὲν τῆς ἀληθείας τὴν ἀκοὴν ἀποστρέψουσιν,
¹on ⁴the ³truth ²the ⁴ear ¹will turn away,
one hand

ἐπὶ δὲ τοὺς μύθους ἐκτραπήσονται. 5 σὺ
²to ¹on the *the* ⁴tales ³will be turned aside. ¹thou
other

---

pened to me in Antioch, Iconium and Lystra, the persecutions I endured. Yet the Lord rescued me from all of them. 12In fact, everyone who wants to live a godly life in Christ Jesus will be persecuted, 13while evil men and impostors will go from bad to worse, deceiving and being deceived. 14But as for you, continue in what you have learned and have become convinced of, because you know those from whom you learned it, 15and how from infancy you have known the holy Scriptures, which are able to make you wise for salvation through faith in Christ Jesus. 16All Scripture is God-breathed and is useful for teaching, rebuking, correcting and training in righteousness, 17so that the man of God may be thoroughly equipped for every good work.

Chapter 4

IN the presence of God and of Christ Jesus, who will judge the living and the dead, and in view of his appearing and his kingdom, I give you this charge: 2Preach the Word; be prepared in season and out of season; correct, rebuke and encourage—with great patience and careful instruction. 3For the time will come when men will not put up with sound doctrine. Instead, to suit their own desires, they will gather around them a great number of teachers to say what their itching ears want to hear. 4They will turn their ears away from the truth and turn aside to myths.

---

bOr possibly, *Every Scripture inspired by God is also profitable*

* Plural.

5But you, be sober in all things, endure hardship, do the work of an evangelist, fulfill your ministry.

6For I am already being poured out as a drink offering, and the time of my departure has come.

7I have fought the good fight, I have finished the course, I have kept the faith;

8in the future there is laid up for me the crown of righteousness, which the Lord, the righteous Judge, will award to me on that day; and not only to me, but also to all who have loved His appearing.

Personal Concerns

9Make every effort to come to me soon;

10for Demas, having loved this present world, has deserted me and gone to Thessalonica; Crescens *has gone* to Galatia, Titus to Dalmatia.

11Only Luke is with me. Pick up Mark and bring him with you, for he is useful to me for service.

12But Tychicus I have sent to Ephesus.

13When you come bring the cloak that I left at Troas with Carpus, and the books, especially the parchments.

14Alexander the coppersmith did me much harm; the Lord will repay him according to his deeds.

15Be on guard against him yourself, for he vigorously opposed our teaching.

16At my first defense no one supported me, but all deserted me; may it not be counted against them.

17But the Lord stood with me, and strengthened me, in order that through me the proclamation might be fully accomplished, and

δὲ νῆφε ἐν πᾶσιν, κακοπάθησον, ἔργον
But ¹be in all things, suffer evil, ²[the] work
sober

ποίησον εὐαγγελιστοῦ, τὴν διακονίαν σου
¹do of an evangelist, ²the ³ministry ⁴of thee

πληροφόρησον. 6 Ἐγὼ γὰρ ἤδη σπένδομαι,
¹fulfill. For I already am being
poured out,

καὶ ὁ καιρὸς τῆς ἀναλύσεώς μου ἐφέστη-
and the time of the departure of me has

κεν. 7 τὸν καλὸν ἀγῶνα ἠγώνισμαι,
arrived. The good struggle I have struggled,

τὸν δρόμον τετέλεκα, τὴν πίστιν τετήρηκα·
the course I have finished, the faith I have kept:

8 λοιπὸν ἀπόκειταί μοι ὁ τῆς δικαιοσύνης
for the rest there is laid up for me ¹the – ²of righteousness

στέφανος, ὃν ἀποδώσει μοι ὁ κύριος
²crown, which ⁴will render ³to me ¹the ²Lord

ἐν ἐκείνῃ τῇ ἡμέρᾳ, ὁ δίκαιος κριτής,
²in ³that – ¹⁰day, ¹the ⁴righteous ²judge,

οὐ μόνον δὲ ἐμοὶ ἀλλὰ καὶ πᾶσι τοῖς
¹not ²only ¹and to me but also to all the [ones]

ἠγαπηκόσι τὴν ἐπιφάνειαν αὐτοῦ.
having loved the appearance of him.

9 Σπούδασον ἐλθεῖν πρός με ταχέως·
Hasten to come to me shortly;

10 Δημᾶς γάρ με ἐγκατέλιπεν ἀγαπήσας
²Demas ¹For ⁴me ³forsook loving

τὸν νῦν αἰῶνα, καὶ ἐπορεύθη εἰς Θεσσαλο-
the now age, and went to Thessalo-
(present)

νίκην, Κρήσκης εἰς Γαλατίαν, Τίτος εἰς
nica, Crescens to Galatia, Titus to

Δαλματίαν· 11 Λουκᾶς ἐστιν μόνος μετ᾽
Dalmatia; Luke is alone with

ἐμοῦ. Μάρκον ἀναλαβὼν ἄγε μετὰ σεαυτοῦ·
me. Mark taking bring with thyself;

ἔστιν γάρ μοι εὔχρηστος εἰς διακονίαν.
¹he is ¹for ⁴to me ²useful for ministry.

12 Τύχικον δὲ ἀπέστειλα εἰς Ἔφεσον.
And Tychicus I sent to Ephesus.

13 τὸν φαιλόνην, ὃν ἀπέλιπον ἐν Τρωάδι
The cloak, which I left in Troas

παρὰ Κάρπῳ, ἐρχόμενος φέρε, καὶ τὰ
with Carpus, coming bring thou, and the

βιβλία, μάλιστα τὰς μεμβράνας. 14 Ἀλέξ-
scrolls, especially the parchments. Alex-

ανδρος ὁ χαλκεὺς πολλά μοι κακὰ
ander the coppersmith ²many ³to me ⁴evils

ἐνεδείξατο· ἀποδώσει αὐτῷ ὁ κύριος κατὰ
¹showed; ²will render ⁴to him ¹the ²Lord according to

τὰ ἔργα αὐτοῦ· 15 ὃν καὶ σὺ φυλάσσου·
the works of him; whom also ²thou ¹guard
²[against];

λίαν γὰρ ἀντέστη τοῖς ἡμετέροις λόγοις.
for greatly he opposed – our words.

16 Ἐν τῇ πρώτῃ μου ἀπολογίᾳ οὐδείς
At the first ²of me ¹defence no one

μοι παρεγένετο, ἀλλὰ πάντες με ἐγκατέ-
²me ¹was beside, but all men ²me ¹for-

λιπον· μὴ αὐτοῖς λογισθείη· 17 ὁ δὲ
sook; not to them may it be reckoned; but the

κύριός μοι παρέστη καὶ ἐνεδυνάμωσέν με,
Lord ²me ¹stood with and empowered me,

ἵνα δι᾽ ἐμοῦ τὸ κήρυγμα πληροφορηθῇ
in or- through me the proclamation might be
der that accomplished

5But you, keep your head in all situations, endure hardship, do the work of an evangelist, discharge all the duties of your ministry.

6For I am already being poured out like a drink offering, and the time has come for my departure. 7I have fought the good fight, I have finished the race, I have kept the faith. 8Now there is in store for me the crown of righteousness, which the Lord, the righteous Judge, will award to me on that day—and not only to me, but also to all who have longed for his appearing.

Personal Remarks

9Do your best to come to me quickly, 10for Demas, because he loved this world, has deserted me and has gone to Thessalonica. Crescens has gone to Galatia, and Titus to Dalmatia. 11Only Luke is with me. Get Mark and bring him with you, because he is helpful to me in my ministry. 12I sent Tychicus to Ephesus. 13When you come, bring the cloak that I left with Carpus at Troas, and my scrolls, especially the parchments.

14Alexander the metalworker did me a great deal of harm. The Lord will repay him for what he has done. 15You too should be on your guard against him, because he strongly opposed our message.

16At my first defense, no one came to my support, but everyone deserted me. May it not be held against them. 17But the Lord stood at my side and gave me strength, so that through me the message might be fully proclaimed and all the that all the Gentiles might hear; and I was delivered out of the lion's mouth. 18The Lord will deliver me from every evil deed, and will bring me safely to His heavenly kingdom; to Him be the glory forever and ever. Amen.

19Greet Prisca and Aquila, and the household of Onesiphorus. 20Erastus remained at Corinth, but Trophimus I left sick at Miletus. 21Make every effort to come before winter. Eubulus greets you, also Pudens and Linus and Claudia and all the brethren. 22The Lord be with your spirit. Grace be with you.

καὶ ἀκούσωσιν πάντα τὰ ἔθνη, καὶ
and 'might hear 'all 'the 'nations, and

ἐρρύσθην ἐκ στόματος λέοντος. 18 ῥύσεταί
I was out of [the] mouth of [the] lion. 'will deliver
delivered

με ὁ κύριος ἀπὸ παντὸς ἔργου πονηροῦ
'me 'The 'Lord from every work wicked

καὶ σώσει εἰς τὴν βασιλείαν αὐτοῦ τὴν
and will save to the 'kingdom 'of him –

ἐπουράνιον· ᾧ ἡ δόξα εἰς τοὺς αἰῶνας
'heavenly: to [be] glory unto the ages
whom the

τῶν αἰώνων, ἀμήν.
of the ages, Amen.

19 Ἄσπασαι Πρίσκαν καὶ Ἀκύλαν καὶ
Greet Prisca and Aquila and

τὸν Ὀνησιφόρου οἶκον. 20 Ἔραστος
the 'of Onesiphorus 'household. Erastus

ἔμεινεν ἐν Κορίνθῳ, Τρόφιμον δὲ ἀπέλιπον
remained in Corinth, but Trophimus I left

ἐν Μιλήτῳ ἀσθενοῦντα. 21 Σπούδασον
in Miletus ailing. Hasten

πρὸ χειμῶνος ἐλθεῖν. Ἀσπάζεταί σε
before winter to come. Greets thee

Εὔβουλος καὶ Πούδης καὶ Λίνος καὶ
Eubulus and Pudens and Linus and

Κλαυδία καὶ οἱ ἀδελφοὶ πάντες.
Claudia and 'the 'brothers 'all.

22 Ὁ κύριος μετὰ τοῦ πνεύματός σου.
The Lord [be] with the spirit of thee.

ἡ χάρις μεθ' ὑμῶν.
– Grace [be] with you.

Gentiles might hear it. And I was delivered from the lion's mouth. 18The Lord will rescue me from every evil attack and will bring me safely to his heavenly kingdom. To him be glory for ever and ever. Amen.

Final Greetings

19Greet Priscilla[b] and Aquila and the household of Onesiphorus. 20Erastus stayed in Corinth, and I left Trophimus sick in Miletus. 21Do your best to get here before winter. Eubulus greets you, and so do Pudens, Linus, Claudia and all the brothers. 22The Lord be with your spirit. Grace be with you.

Titus

Chapter 1

Salutation

PAUL, a bond-servant of God, and an apostle of Jesus Christ, for the faith of those chosen of God and the knowledge of the truth which is according to godliness,

2in the hope of eternal life, which God, who cannot lie, promised long ages ago,

3but at the proper time manifested, *even* His word, in the proclamation with which I was entrusted according to the commandment of God our Savior;

4to Titus, my true child in a common faith: Grace and peace from God the Father and Christ Jesus our Savior.

ΠΡΟΣ ΤΙΤΟΝ
To Titus

1 Παῦλος δοῦλος θεοῦ, ἀπόστολος δὲ
Paul a slave of God, and an apostle

Ἰησοῦ Χριστοῦ κατὰ πίστιν ἐκλεκτῶν
of Jesus Christ according to [the] faith of chosen ones

θεοῦ καὶ ἐπίγνωσιν ἀληθείας τῆς κατ'
of God and full know- of [the] – accord-
ledge truth ing to

εὐσέβειαν 2 ἐπ' ἐλπίδι ζωῆς αἰωνίου,
piety on(in) hope life of eternal,

ἣν ἐπηγγείλατο ὁ ἀψευδὴς θεὸς πρὸ
which 'promised 'the 'unlying 'God before

χρόνων αἰωνίων, 3 ἐφανέρωσεν δὲ καιροῖς
times eternal, but 'manifested 'times

ἰδίοις τὸν λόγον αὐτοῦ ἐν κηρύγματι
'in [its] own the word of him in a proclamation

ὃ ἐπιστεύθην ἐγὼ κατ' ἐπιταγὴν τοῦ
which 'was entrust- 'I accord- [the] of the
ed [with] ing to command

σωτῆρος ἡμῶν θεοῦ, 4 Τίτῳ γνησίῳ τέκνῳ
Saviour of us God, to Titus a true child

κατὰ κοινὴν πίστιν· χάρις καὶ εἰρήνη
accord- a common faith: Grace and peace
ing to

ἀπὸ θεοῦ πατρὸς καὶ Χριστοῦ Ἰησοῦ
from God [the] Father and Christ Jesus

τοῦ σωτῆρος ἡμῶν.
the Saviour of us.

Titus

Chapter 1

PAUL, a servant of God and an apostle of Jesus Christ for the faith of God's elect and the knowledge of the truth that leads to godliness—2a faith and knowledge resting on the hope of eternal life, which God, who does not lie, promised before the beginning of time, 3and at his appointed season he brought his word to light through the preaching entrusted to me by the command of God our Savior,

4To Titus, my true son in our common faith:

Grace and peace from God the Father and Christ Jesus our Savior.

Qualifications of Elders

5For this reason I left you in Crete, that you might set in order what remains, and appoint elders in every city as I directed you,

6namely, if any man be above reproach, the husband of one wife, having children who believe, not accused of dissipation or rebellion.

7For the overseer must be above reproach as God's steward, not self-willed, not quick-tempered, not addicted to wine, not pugnacious, not fond of sordid gain,

8but hospitable, loving what is good, sensible, just, devout, self-controlled,

9holding fast the faithful word which is in accordance with the teaching, that he may be able both to exhort in sound doctrine and to refute those who contradict.

10For there are many rebellious men, empty talkers and deceivers, especially those of the circumcision,

11who must be silenced because they are upsetting whole families, teaching things they should not *teach*, for the sake of sordid gain.

12One of themselves, a prophet of their own, said, "Cretans are always liars, evil beasts, lazy gluttons."

13This testimony is true. For this cause reprove them severely that they may be sound in the faith,

14not paying attention to Jewish myths and commandments of men who turn away from the truth.

15To the pure, all things are pure; but to those who are defiled and unbelieving,

---

5 Τούτου χάριν ἀπέλιπόν σε ἐν Κρήτῃ,
For this reason†   I left   thee   in   Crete,

ἵνα τὰ λείποντα ἐπιδιορθώσῃ, καὶ
in or-   the   wanting   thou shouldest   and
der that   things   set in order,

καταστήσῃς κατὰ πόλιν πρεσβυτέρους, ὡς ἐγώ
shouldest appoint   in each city   elders,   as   I

σοι διεταξάμην, **6** εἰ τίς ἐστιν ἀνέγκλητος,
²thee   ¹charged,   if   anyone is   unreprovable,

μιᾶς γυναικὸς ἀνήρ, τέκνα ἔχων πιστά,
²of one   ²wife   ¹husband, ²children ¹having ²believing,

μὴ ἐν κατηγορίᾳ ἀσωτίας ἢ ἀνυπότακτα.
not in   accusation   of profligacy or   unruly.*

7 δεῖ γὰρ τὸν ἐπίσκοπον ἀνέγκλητον εἶναι
For it behoves the   bishop   ²unreprovable ¹to be

ὡς θεοῦ οἰκονόμον, μὴ αὐθάδη, μὴ
as   of God   a steward,   not   self-pleasing,   not

ὀργίλον, μὴ πάροινον, μὴ πλήκτην, μὴ
passionate, not   given to wine, not   a striker,   not

αἰσχροκερδῆ, **8** ἀλλὰ φιλόξενον, φιλάγαθον,
greedy of   but   hospitable,   a lover of good
base gain,   [men/things],

σώφρονα, δίκαιον, ὅσιον, ἐγκρατῆ, **9** ἀντεχ-
sensible,   just,   holy, self-controlled,   holding

όμενον τοῦ κατὰ τὴν διδαχὴν πιστοῦ
to   ¹the ²according to ³the   ⁴teaching   ⁵faithful

λόγου, ἵνα δυνατὸς ᾖ καὶ παρακαλεῖν
²word, in order ²able ¹he may both   to exhort
    that   be

ἐν τῇ διδασκαλίᾳ τῇ ὑγιαινούσῃ καὶ
by   the   ²teaching   the   ¹being healthy   and

τοὺς ἀντιλέγοντας ἐλέγχειν. **10** Εἰσὶν γὰρ
²the [ones] ²contradicting   ¹to convince.   For there are

πολλοὶ ἀνυπότακτοι, ματαιολόγοι καὶ
many   unruly men,   vain talkers   and

φρεναπάται, μάλιστα οἱ ἐκ τῆς περιτομῆς,
deceivers,   specially the ones of the   circumcision,

11 οὓς δεῖ ἐπιστομίζειν, οἵτινες ὅλους
whom it   to stop the   who   ²whole
    behoves   mouth,

οἴκους ἀνατρέπουσιν διδάσκοντες ἃ μὴ
²households ¹overturn   teaching   things ²not
    which

δεῖ αἰσχροῦ κέρδους χάριν. **12** εἶπέν
¹it be-   ⁴base   ³gain   ²for the   ⁷Said
hoves   sake of.

τις ἐξ αὐτῶν ἴδιος αὐτῶν προφήτης·
¹a cer- ²of   ³them   ⁴an own ⁵of them   ⁶prophet:
tain one

Κρῆτες ἀεὶ ψεῦσται, κακὰ θηρία, γαστέρες
Cretans always   liars,   evil   beasts,   ²gluttons
[are]

ἀργαί. **13** ἡ μαρτυρία αὕτη ἐστὶν ἀληθής.
¹idle.   This witness   is   true.

δι' ἣν αἰτίαν ἔλεγχε αὐτοὺς ἀποτόμως,
For which cause   reprove   them   severely,

ἵνα ὑγιαίνωσιν ἐν τῇ πίστει, **14** μὴ
in or-   they may   in   the   faith,   not
der that be healthy

προσέχοντες Ἰουδαϊκοῖς μύθοις καὶ
giving heed   to Jewish   tales   and

ἐντολαῖς ἀνθρώπων ἀποστρεφομένων τὴν
commandments of men   perverting   the

ἀλήθειαν. **15** πάντα καθαρὰ τοῖς καθαροῖς·
truth.   All things [are] clean   to the   clean;

τοῖς δὲ μεμιαμμένοις καὶ ἀπίστοις οὐδὲν
but to   *having been*   and   unfaithful nothing
the [ones]   defiled

Titus' Task on Crete

5The reason I left you in Crete was that you might straighten out what was left unfinished and appoint*a* elders in every town, as I directed you. 6An elder must be blameless, the husband of but one wife, a man whose children believe and are not open to the charge of being wild and disobedient. 7Since an overseer*b* is entrusted with God's work, he must be blameless—not overbearing, not quick-tempered, not given to drunkenness, not violent, not pursuing dishonest gain. 8Rather he must be hospitable, one who loves what is good, who is self-controlled, upright, holy and disciplined. 9He must hold firmly to the trustworthy message as it has been taught, so that he can encourage others by sound doctrine and refute those who oppose it.

10For there are many rebellious people, mere talkers and deceivers, especially those of the circumcision group. 11They must be silenced, because they are ruining whole households by teaching things they ought not to teach—and that for the sake of dishonest gain. 12Even one of their own prophets has said, "Cretans are always liars, evil brutes, lazy gluttons." 13This testimony is true. Therefore, rebuke them sharply, so that they will be sound in the faith 14and will pay no attention to Jewish myths or to the commands of those who reject the truth. 15To the pure, all things are pure, but to those who are corrupted and do not believe,

---

* In agreement with "children" (neut. pl.).

*a*5 Or ordain
*b*7 Traditionally *bishop*

nothing is pure, but both their mind and their conscience are defiled. 16They profess to know God, but by *their* deeds they deny *Him*, being detestable and disobedient, and worthless for any good deed.

καθαρόν, ἀλλὰ μεμίανται αὐτῶν καὶ ὁ
[is] clean, but ⁵has(ve) been defiled ⁷of them ¹both ⁸the

νοῦς καὶ ἡ συνείδησις. 16 θεὸν ὁμολο-
²mind ⁴and ³the ⁶conscience. ²God ¹they pro-

γοῦσιν εἰδέναι, τοῖς δὲ ἔργοις ἀρνοῦνται,
fess ²to know, but by the(ir) works they deny [him],

βδελυκτοὶ ὄντες καὶ ἀπειθεῖς καὶ πρὸς
¹abominable ²being and disobedient and to

πᾶν ἔργον ἀγαθὸν ἀδόκιμοι.
every ²work ¹good reprobate.

---

nothing is pure. In fact, both their minds and consciences are corrupted. 16They claim to know God, but by their actions they deny him. They are detestable, disobedient and unfit for doing anything good.

Chapter 2

Duties of the Older and Younger

BUT as for you, speak the things which are fitting for sound doctrine. 2Older men are to be temperate, dignified, sensible, sound in faith, in love, in perseverance. 3Older women likewise are to be reverent in their behavior, not malicious gossips, nor enslaved to much wine, teaching what is good, 4that they may encourage the young women to love their husbands, to love their children, 5to be sensible, pure, workers at home, kind, being subject to their own husbands, that the word of God may not be dishonored. 6Likewise urge the young men to be sensible; 7in all things show yourself to be an example of good deeds, *with* purity in doctrine, dignified, 8sound *in* speech which is beyond reproach, in order that the opponent may be put to shame, having nothing bad to say about us. 9Urge bondslaves to be subject to their own masters in everything, to be well-pleasing, not argumentative, 10not pilfering, but showing all good faith that they may adorn the doctrine of God our Savior in every respect. 11For the grace of God has appeared, bringing salvation to all men,

---

Chapter 2

What Must Be Taught to Various Groups

YOU must teach what is in accord with sound doctrine. 2Teach the older men to be temperate, worthy of respect, self-controlled, and sound in faith, in love and in endurance.

3Likewise, teach the older women to be reverent in the way they live, not to be slanderers or addicted to much wine, but to teach what is good. 4Then they can train the younger women to love their husbands and children, 5to be self-controlled and pure, to be busy at home, to be kind, and to be subject to their husbands, so that no one will malign the word of God.

6Similarly, encourage the young men to be self-controlled. 7In everything set them an example by doing what is good. In your teaching show integrity, seriousness 8and soundness of speech that cannot be condemned, so that those who oppose you may be ashamed because they have nothing bad to say about us.

9Teach slaves to be subject to their masters in everything, to try to please them, not to talk back to them, 10and not to steal from them, but to show that they can be fully trusted, so that in every way they will make the teaching about God our Savior attractive.

11For the grace of God that brings salvation has appeared to all men. 12It

---

2 Σὺ δὲ λάλει ἃ πρέπει τῇ ὑγιαινούσῃ
But ²thou ¹speak things becomes the being
which healthy

διδασκαλίᾳ. 2 Πρεσβύτας νηφαλίους εἶναι,
teaching. Aged men ²sober ¹to be,

σεμνούς, σώφρονας, ὑγιαίνοντας τῇ πίστει,
grave, sensible, being healthy in the faith,

τῇ ἀγάπῃ, τῇ ὑπομονῇ· 3 πρεσβύτιδας
— in love, — in endurance; aged women

ὡσαύτως ἐν καταστήματι ἱεροπρεπεῖς, μὴ
similarly in demeanour reverent, not

διαβόλους, μηδὲ οἴνῳ πολλῷ δεδουλωμένας,
slanderers, nor ²wine ²by much ¹having been
enslaved,

καλοδιδασκάλους, 4 ἵνα σωφρονίζωσιν τὰς
teachers of what is good, in or- they may train the
der that

νέας φιλάνδρους εἶναι, φιλοτέκνους,
young ²lovers of ¹to be, child-lovers,
women [their] husbands

5 σώφρονας, ἁγνάς, οἰκουργούς, ἀγαθάς,
sensible, pure, home-workers, good,

ὑποτασσομένας τοῖς ἰδίοις ἀνδράσιν,
being subject to the(ir) own husbands,

ἵνα μὴ ὁ λόγος τοῦ θεοῦ βλασφημῆται.
lest the word — of God be blasphemed.

6 Τοὺς νεωτέρους ὡσαύτως παρακάλει
The younger men similarly exhort

σωφρονεῖν 7 περὶ πάντα, σεαυτὸν παρ-
to be sensible about all things, ²thyself ¹show-

εχόμενος τύπον καλῶν ἔργων, ἐν τῇ
ing a pattern of good works, in the

διδασκαλίᾳ ἀφθορίαν, σεμνότητα, 8 λόγον
teaching, uncorruptness, gravity, ²speech

ὑγιῆ ἀκατάγνωστον, ἵνα ὁ ἐξ ἐναντίας
¹healthy ²irreprehensible, in or- the of contrary
der that man [the] [side]

ἐντραπῇ μηδὲν ἔχων λέγειν περὶ ἡμῶν
may be put ²nothing ¹having ⁴to say ⁵about ⁶us
to shame

φαῦλον. 9 Δούλους ἰδίοις δεσπόταις
³bad. Slaves to [their] own masters

ὑποτάσσεσθαι ἐν πᾶσιν, εὐαρέστους εἶναι,
to be subject in all things, well-pleasing to be,

μὴ ἀντιλέγοντας, 10 μὴ νοσφιζομένους, ἀλλὰ
not contradicting, not peculating, but

πᾶσαν πίστιν ἐνδεικνυμένους ἀγαθήν, ἵνα
²all ⁴faith ¹showing ³good, in order that

τὴν διδασκαλίαν τὴν τοῦ σωτῆρος ἡμῶν
²the ³teaching — ⁴of the ⁵Saviour ⁶of us

θεοῦ κοσμῶσιν ἐν πᾶσιν. 11 Ἐπεφάνη
⁷God ¹they may adorn in all things. ²appeared

γὰρ ἡ χάρις τοῦ θεοῦ σωτήριος πᾶσιν
For ¹the ²grace — ³of God ⁴saving to all

12instructing us to deny ungodliness and worldly desires and to live sensibly, righteously and godly in the present age,

13looking for the blessed hope and the appearing of the glory of our great God and Savior, Christ Jesus;

14who gave Himself for us, that He might redeem us from every lawless deed and purify for Himself a people for His own possession, zealous for good deeds.

15These things speak and exhort and reprove with all authority. Let no one disregard you.

Chapter 3

Godly Living

REMIND them to be subject to rulers, to authorities, to be obedient, to be ready for every good deed,

2to malign no one, to be uncontentious, gentle, showing every consideration for all men.

3For we also once were foolish ourselves, disobedient, deceived, enslaved to various lusts and pleasures, spending our life in malice and envy, hateful, hating one another.

4But when the kindness of God our Savior and *His* love for mankind appeared,

5He saved us, not on the basis of deeds which we have done in righteousness, but according to His mercy, by the washing of regeneration and renewing by the Holy Spirit,

6whom He poured out upon us richly through Jesus Christ our Savior,

7that being justified by His grace we might be made heirs according to *the* hope of eternal life.

ἀνθρώποις, **12** παιδεύουσα ἡμᾶς, ἵνα
men,   instructing   us,   in order that

ἀρνησάμενοι τὴν ἀσέβειαν καὶ τὰς κοσμικὰς
denying   -   impiety   and   -   worldly

ἐπιθυμίας σωφρόνως καὶ δικαίως καὶ
lusts   ³sensibly ²and ⁴righteously ⁵and

εὐσεβῶς ζήσωμεν ἐν τῷ νῦν αἰῶνι,
⁶piously ¹we might live in the now(present) age,

13 προσδεχόμενοι τὴν μακαρίαν ἐλπίδα καὶ
expecting   the   blessed   hope   and

ἐπιφάνειαν τῆς δόξης τοῦ μεγάλου θεοῦ
appearance of the glory of the great   God

καὶ σωτῆρος ἡμῶν Χριστοῦ Ἰησοῦ, **14** ὃς
and Saviour of us Christ   Jesus,   who

ἔδωκεν ἑαυτὸν ὑπὲρ ἡμῶν ἵνα λυτρώσηται
gave   himself on behalf us in or- he might
                of   der that ransom

ἡμᾶς ἀπὸ πάσης ἀνομίας καὶ καθαρίσῃ
us   from all   iniquity and *might* cleanse

ἑαυτῷ λαὸν περιούσιον, ζηλωτὴν καλῶν ἔργων.
for   a people [his] own zealous of good works.
himself   possession,

15 Ταῦτα λάλει καὶ παρακάλει καὶ ἔλεγχε
These things speak thou and exhort   and reprove

μετὰ πάσης ἐπιταγῆς· μηδείς σου περιφρονείτω.
with all   command; ²no one ³of thee ¹let ⁴despise.

3 Ὑπομίμνησκε αὐτοὺς ἀρχαῖς ἐξουσίαις
Remind thou   them   ²to rulers ³[and] ⁴authorities

ὑποτάσσεσθαι, πειθαρχεῖν, πρὸς πᾶν ἔργον
¹to be subject, to be obedient, ²to ³every ⁴work

ἀγαθὸν ἑτοίμους εἶναι, **2** μηδένα βλασ-
⁵good   ²ready ¹to be,   no one   to

φημεῖν, ἀμάχους εἶναι, ἐπιεικεῖς, πᾶσαν
rail at, uncontentious to be, forbearing, ²all

ἐνδεικνυμένους πραΰτητα πρὸς πάντας
¹showing forth   meekness to   all

ἀνθρώπους. **3** Ἦμεν γάρ ποτε καὶ ἡμεῖς
men.   For ³were ⁴then ⁵also ¹we

ἀνόητοι, ἀπειθεῖς, πλανώμενοι, δουλεύοντες
senseless, disobedient, being deceived, serving [as slaves]

ἐπιθυμίαις καὶ ἡδοναῖς ποικίλαις, ἐν κακίᾳ
²lusts   ³and ⁴pleasures ¹various,   ²in ³evil

καὶ φθόνῳ διάγοντες, στυγητοί, μισοῦντες
⁴and ⁵envy ¹living,   hateful,   hating

ἀλλήλους. **4** ὅτε δὲ ἡ χρηστότης καὶ
one another.   But when the kindness   and

ἡ φιλανθρωπία ἐπεφάνη τοῦ σωτῆρος ἡμῶν
the love to man ⁴appeared ¹of the ²Saviour ³of us

θεοῦ, **5** οὐκ ἐξ ἔργων τῶν ἐν δικαιοσύνῃ
⁴God,   not by works   -   ²in ³righteousness

ἃ ἐποιήσαμεν ἡμεῖς, ἀλλὰ κατὰ τὸ
¹which ⁵did   ⁴we,   but according to the

αὐτοῦ ἔλεος ἔσωσεν ἡμᾶς διὰ λουτροῦ
of him mercy he saved us through [the] washing

παλιγγενεσίας καὶ ἀνακαινώσεως πνεύματος
of regeneration and   renewal   ²Spirit

ἁγίου, **6** οὗ ἐξέχεεν ἐφ᾽ ἡμᾶς πλουσίως
¹of [the] which he shed on   us   richly
Holy,

διὰ Ἰησοῦ Χριστοῦ τοῦ σωτῆρος ἡμῶν,
through Jesus Christ the Saviour   of us,

7 ἵνα δικαιωθέντες τῇ ἐκείνου χάριτι
in or- being justified ¹by the ²of that one ³grace
der that

κληρονόμοι γενηθῶμεν κατ᾽ ἐλπίδα ζωῆς
heirs   we might   accord- a hope of life
             become   ing to

---

teaches us to say "No" to ungodliness and worldly passions, and to live self-controlled, upright and godly lives in this present age, 13while we wait for the blessed hope—the glorious appearing of our great God and Savior, Jesus Christ, 14who gave himself for us to redeem us from all wickedness and to purify for himself a people that are his very own, eager to do what is good.

15These, then, are the things you should teach. Encourage and rebuke with all authority. Do not let anyone despise you.

Chapter 3

Doing What Is Good

REMIND the people to be subject to rulers and authorities, to be obedient, to be ready to do whatever is good, 2to slander no one, to be peaceable and considerate, and to show true humility toward all men.

3At one time we too were foolish, disobedient, deceived and enslaved by all kinds of passions and pleasures. We lived in malice and envy, being hated and hating one another. 4But when the kindness and love of God our Savior appeared, 5he saved us, not because of righteous things we had done, but because of his mercy. He saved us through the washing of rebirth and renewal by the Holy Spirit, 6whom he poured out on us generously through Jesus Christ our Savior, 7so that, having been justified by his grace, we might become heirs having the hope of eternal

8This is a trustworthy statement; and concerning these things I want you to speak confidently, so that those who have believed God may be careful to engage in good deeds. These things are good and profitable for men.

9But shun foolish controversies and genealogies and strife and disputes about the Law; for they are unprofitable and worthless.

10Reject a factious man after a first and second warning,

11knowing that such a man is perverted and is sinning, being self-condemned.

Personal Concerns

12When I send Artemas or Tychicus to you, make every effort to come to me at Nicopolis, for I have decided to spend the winter there.

13Diligently help Zenas the lawyer and Apollos on their way so that nothing is lacking for them.

14And let our *people* also learn to engage in good deeds to meet pressing needs, that they may not be unfruitful.

15All who are with me greet you. Greet those who love us in *the* faith.

Grace be with you all.

αἰωνίου. **8** Πιστὸς ὁ λόγος, καὶ περὶ
eternal.   Faithful [is] the   word,   and   as to

τούτων βούλομαί σε διαβεβαιοῦσθαι, ἵνα
these   I wish   thee to affirm   in or-
things   confidently,   der that

φροντίζωσιν καλῶν ἔργων προΐστασθαι οἱ
⁴may take   ⁵of good ⁶works ⁷to maintain ¹the
thought   [ones]

πεπιστευκότες θεῷ. ταῦτά ἐστιν καλὰ
²having believed ³God. These things is(are) good

καὶ ὠφέλιμα τοῖς ἀνθρώποις· **9** μωρὰς
and profitable   -   to men;   ²foolish

δὲ ζητήσεις καὶ γενεαλογίας καὶ ἔριν
¹but questionings and genealogies and strife

καὶ μάχας νομικὰς περιΐστασο· εἰσὶν γὰρ
and ⁴fights ³legal shun thou;   for they are

ἀνωφελεῖς καὶ μάταιοι. **10** αἱρετικὸν
unprofitable and vain.   A factious

ἄνθρωπον μετὰ μίαν καὶ δευτέραν
man   after one and a second

νουθεσίαν παραιτοῦ, **11** εἰδὼς ὅτι ἐξέστραπ-
admonition avoid,   knowing that ⁵has been per-

ται ὁ τοιοῦτος καὶ ἁμαρτάνει ὢν αὐτο-
verted ¹such a man and   sins   being self-

κατάκριτος.
condemned.

12 Ὅταν πέμψω Ἀρτεμᾶν πρὸς σὲ
    Whenever I send   Artemas   to   thee

ἢ Τύχικον, σπούδασον ἐλθεῖν πρός με
or Tychicus, hasten   to come   to   me

εἰς Νικόπολιν· ἐκεῖ γὰρ κέκρικα παραχειμά-
in Nicopolis; for there I have decided to spend [the]

σαι. **13** Ζηνᾶν τὸν νομικὸν καὶ Ἀπολλὼν
winter.   Zenas the lawyer   and Apollos

σπουδαίως πρόπεμψον, ἵνα μηδὲν αὐτοῖς
urgently   send forward, in or- nothing to them
                           der that

λείπῃ. **14** μανθανέτωσαν δὲ καὶ οἱ ἡμέτεροι
may be lacking. And ¹let ⁴learn ²also - ³our [people]

καλῶν ἔργων προΐστασθαι εἰς τὰς ἀναγ-
⁶of good ⁷works ⁵to maintain for the neces-

καίας χρείας, ἵνα μὴ ὦσιν ἄκαρποι.
sary wants, lest   they be unfruitful.

15 Ἀσπάζονταί σε οἱ μετ᾽ ἐμοῦ πάντες.
   ²greet   ⁶thee ³the ⁵with ⁴me   ¹All.
             [ones]

ἄσπασαι τοὺς φιλοῦντας ἡμᾶς ἐν πίστει.
Greet thou the [ones] loving   us   in [the] faith.

Ἡ χάρις μετὰ πάντων ὑμῶν.
- Grace [be] with   ²all   ¹you.

---

life. 8This is a trustworthy saying. And I want you to stress these things, so that those who have trusted in God may be careful to devote themselves to doing what is good. These things are excellent and profitable for everyone.

9But avoid foolish controversies and genealogies and arguments and quarrels about the law, because these are unprofitable and useless. 10Warn a divisive person once, and then warn him a second time. After that, have nothing to do with him. 11You may be sure that such a man is warped and sinful; he is self-condemned.

Final Remarks

12As soon as I send Artemas or Tychicus to you, do your best to come to me at Nicopolis, because I have decided to winter there. 13Do everything you can to help Zenas the lawyer and Apollos on their way and see that they have everything they need. 14Our people must learn to devote themselves to doing what is good, in order that they may provide for daily necessities and not live unproductive lives.

15Everyone with me sends you greetings. Greet those who love us in the faith.

Grace be with you all.

Philemon

Chapter 1

Salutation

PAUL, a prisoner of Christ Jesus, and Timothy our brother, to Philemon our beloved *brother* and fellow worker,

2and to Apphia our sister, and to Archippus our

ΠΡΟΣ ΦΙΛΗΜΟΝΑ
To Philemon

1 Παῦλος δέσμιος Χριστοῦ Ἰησοῦ καὶ
   Paul   a prisoner of Christ Jesus and

Τιμόθεος ὁ ἀδελφὸς Φιλήμονι τῷ ἀγαπητῷ
Timothy the brother to Philemon the beloved

καὶ συνεργῷ ἡμῶν **2** καὶ Ἀπφίᾳ τῇ
and a fellow-worker of us and to Apphia the

ἀδελφῇ καὶ Ἀρχίππῳ τῷ συστρατιώτῃ
sister and to Archippus the fellow-soldier

Philemon

PAUL, a prisoner of Christ Jesus, and Timothy our brother,

To Philemon our dear friend and fellow worker, 2to Apphia our sister, to Archippus our fellow solfellow soldier, and to the church in your house:

³Grace to you and peace from God our Father and the Lord Jesus Christ.

Philemon's Love and Faith

⁴I thank my God always, making mention of you in my prayers,

⁵because I hear of your love, and of the faith which you have toward the Lord Jesus, and toward all the saints;

⁶and I pray that the fellowship of your faith may become effective *a*through the knowledge of every good thing which is in *b* you for Christ's sake.

⁷For I have come to have much joy and comfort in your love, because the hearts of the saints have been refreshed through you, brother.

⁸Therefore, though I have enough confidence in Christ to order you *to do* that which is proper,

⁹yet for love's sake I rather appeal *to you*—since I am such a person as Paul, the aged, and now also a prisoner of Christ Jesus—

Plea for Onesimus, a Free Man

¹⁰I appeal to you for my child, whom I have begotten in my imprisonment, *c*Onesimus,

¹¹who formerly was useless to you, but now is useful both to me and to me.

¹²And I have sent him back to you in person, that is, *sending* my very heart,

¹³whom I wished to keep with me, that in your behalf he might minister to me in my imprisonment for the gospel;

¹⁴but without your consent I did not want to do anything, that your goodness should not be as it were by compulsion, but of

---

ἡμῶν καὶ τῇ κατ' οἶκόν σου ἐκκλησίᾳ·
of us and ¹to the ²at ⁴house ⁵of thee ³church:

3 χάρις ὑμῖν καὶ εἰρήνη ἀπὸ θεοῦ πατρὸς
Grace to you and peace from God Father

ἡμῶν καὶ κυρίου Ἰησοῦ Χριστοῦ.
of us and Lord Jesus Christ.

4 Εὐχαριστῶ τῷ θεῷ μου πάντοτε μνείαν
I give thanks to the God of me always ²mention

σου ποιούμενος ἐπὶ τῶν προσευχῶν μου,
³of thee ¹making at the prayers of me,

5 ἀκούων σου τὴν ἀγάπην καὶ τὴν
hearing of thee the love and the

πίστιν ἣν ἔχεις πρὸς τὸν κύριον Ἰησοῦν
faith which thou hast toward the Lord Jesus

καὶ εἰς πάντας τοὺς ἁγίους, 6 ὅπως
and to all the saints, so as

ἡ κοινωνία τῆς πίστεώς σου ἐνεργὴς
the fellowship of the faith of thee ¹operative

γένηται ἐν ἐπιγνώσει παντὸς ἀγαθοῦ τοῦ
¹may in a full of every good thing –
become knowledge

ἐν ἡμῖν εἰς Χριστόν. 7 χαρὰν γὰρ
in us for Christ. ²joy ¹For

πολλὴν ἔσχον καὶ παράκλησιν ἐπὶ τῇ
²much ¹I had and consolation over the

ἀγάπῃ σου, ὅτι τὰ σπλάγχνα τῶν ἁγίων
love of because the bowels of the saints
thee,

ἀναπέπαυται διὰ σοῦ, ἀδελφέ. 8 Διό,
has(ve) been through thee, brother. Wherefore,
refreshed

πολλὴν ἐν Χριστῷ παρρησίαν ἔχων ἐπιτάσ-
²much ⁴in ⁵Christ ³boldness ¹having to

σειν σοι τὸ ἀνῆκον, 9 διὰ τὴν ἀγάπην
charge thee the befitting, because – love
thing of

μᾶλλον παρακαλῶ· τοιοῦτος ὢν ὡς Παῦλος
rather I beseech; such a one being as Paul

πρεσβύτης, νυνὶ δὲ καὶ δέσμιος Χριστοῦ
an old man, and now also a prisoner of Christ

Ἰησοῦ, 10 παρακαλῶ σε περὶ τοῦ ἐμοῦ
Jesus, I beseech thee con- – my
cerning

τέκνου, ὃν ἐγέννησα ἐν τοῖς δεσμοῖς,
child, whom I begat in the(my) bonds,

Ὀνήσιμον, 11 τόν ποτέ σοι ἄχρηστον
Onesimus, the [one] then ²to thee ¹useless
(formerly)

νυνὶ δὲ καὶ σοὶ καὶ ἐμοὶ εὔχρηστον,
but now ²both ³to thee ⁴and ⁵to me ¹useful,

12 ὃν ἀνέπεμψά σοι, αὐτόν, τοῦτ' ἔστιν
whom I sent back to thee, him, this is

τὰ ἐμὰ σπλάγχνα· 13 ὃν ἐγὼ ἐβουλόμην
– my bowels; whom I resolved

πρὸς ἐμαυτὸν κατέχειν, ἵνα ὑπὲρ σοῦ
with myself to retain, in order on thee
that behalf of

μοι διακονῇ ἐν τοῖς δεσμοῖς τοῦ εὐαγ-
to me he might in the bonds of the gos-
minister

γελίου, 14 χωρὶς δὲ τῆς σῆς γνώμης
pel, but without – thy opinion

οὐδὲν ἠθέλησα ποιῆσαι, ἵνα μὴ ὡς κατὰ
¹nothing ¹I was ²to do, in order that not ⁴as ⁵by way
willing of

ἀνάγκην τὸ ἀγαθόν σου ᾖ ἀλλὰ κατὰ
⁷necessity ¹the ⁶good ²of ⁵might but by way
thee be of

---

dier and to the church that meets in your home:

³Grace to you and peace from God our Father and the Lord Jesus Christ.

Thanksgiving and Prayer

⁴I always thank my God as I remember you in my prayers, ⁵because I hear about your faith in the Lord Jesus and your love for all the saints. ⁶I pray that you may be active in sharing your faith, so that you will have a full understanding of every good thing we have in Christ. ⁷Your love has given me great joy and encouragement, because you, brother, have refreshed the hearts of the saints.

Paul's Plea for Onesimus

⁸Therefore, although in Christ I could be bold and order you to do what you ought to do, ⁹yet I appeal to you on the basis of love. I then, as Paul—an old man and now also a prisoner of Christ Jesus— ¹⁰I appeal to you for my son Onesimus, *a* who became my son while I was in chains. ¹¹Formerly he was useless to you, but now he has become useful both to you and to me.

¹²I am sending him—who is my very heart—back to you. ¹³I would have liked to keep him with me so that he could take your place in helping me while I am in chains for the gospel. ¹⁴But I did not want to do anything without your consent, so that any favor you do will be spontaneous and

---

a Or, *in*
b Some ancient mss. read *us*
c I.e., *useful*

a 10 Onesimus means *useful*.

your own free will.

15For perhaps he was for this reason parted *from you* for a while, that you should have him back forever,

16no longer as a slave, but more than a slave, a beloved brother, especially to me, but how much more to you, both in the flesh and in the Lord.

17If then you regard me a partner, accept him as *you would* me.

18But if he has wronged you in any way, or owes you anything, charge that to my account;

19I, Paul, am writing this with my own hand, I will repay it (lest I should mention to you that you owe to me even your own self as well).

20Yes, brother, let me benefit from you in the Lord; refresh my heart in Christ.

21Having confidence in your obedience, I write to you, since I know that you will do even more than what I say.

22And at the same time also prepare me a lodging; for I hope that through your prayers I shall be given to you.

23Epaphras, my fellow prisoner in Christ Jesus, greets you,

24*as do* Mark, Aristarchus, Demas, Luke, my fellow workers.

25The grace of the Lord Jesus Christ be with your spirit. d

ἑκούσιον. 15 τάχα γὰρ διὰ τοῦτο ἐχωρίσθη
[being] For perhaps therefore he departed
voluntary.

πρὸς ὥραν, ἵνα αἰώνιον αὐτὸν ἀπέχῃς,
for an hour, in order ²eternally ³him ¹thou mightest
that receive,

16 οὐκέτι ὡς δοῦλον ἀλλὰ ὑπὲρ δοῦλον,
no longer as a slave but beyond a slave,

ἀδελφὸν ἀγαπητόν, μάλιστα ἐμοί, πόσῳ
a brother beloved, specially to me, ²by how
much

δὲ μᾶλλον σοὶ καὶ ἐν σαρκὶ καὶ ἐν
¹and more to thee both in [the] flesh and in

κυρίῳ. 17 εἰ οὖν με ἔχεις κοινωνόν,
[the] Lord If therefore me thou hast [as] a partner,

προσλαβοῦ αὐτὸν ὡς ἐμέ. 18 εἰ δέ
receive him as me. And if

τι ἠδίκησέν σε ἢ ὀφείλει, τοῦτο ἐμοὶ
any- he wronged thee or owes, ²this ³to me
thing

ἐλλόγα· 19 ἐγὼ Παῦλος ἔγραψα τῇ ἐμῇ
¹reckon: I Paul wrote – with my

χειρί, ἐγὼ ἀποτίσω· ἵνα μὴ λέγω σοι
hand, I will repay; lest I say to thee

ὅτι καὶ σεαυτόν μοι προσοφείλεις. 20 ναί,
that indeed ²thyself ³to me ¹thou owest besides. Yes,

ἀδελφέ, ἐγὼ σου ὀναίμην ἐν κυρίῳ·
brother, ²I ⁵of thee ¹may ³have ⁴help in [the] Lord;

ἀνάπαυσόν μου τὰ σπλάγχνα ἐν Χριστῷ.
refresh of me the bowels in Christ.

21 Πεποιθὼς τῇ ὑπακοῇ σου ἔγραψά
Having trusted to the obedience of thee I wrote

σοι, εἰδὼς ὅτι καὶ ὑπὲρ ἃ λέγω ποιήσεις.
to knowing that indeed beyond what I say thou wilt
thee, things do.

22 ἅμα δὲ καὶ ἑτοίμαζέ μοι ξενίαν·
And at the also prepare for me lodging;
same time

ἐλπίζω γὰρ ὅτι διὰ τῶν προσευχῶν
for I hope that through the prayers

ὑμῶν χαρισθήσομαι ὑμῖν.
of you I shall be given to you.

23 Ἀσπάζεταί σε Ἐπαφρᾶς ὁ συναιχμά-
²greets ³thee ¹Epaphras ⁴the ⁵fellow-

λωτός μου ἐν Χριστῷ Ἰησοῦ, 24 Μᾶρκος,
captive ⁶of me ⁵in ⁶Christ ⁷Jesus, [also] Mark,

Ἀρίσταρχος, Δημᾶς, Λουκᾶς, οἱ συνεργοί
Aristarchus, Demas, Luke, the fellow-
workers

μου.
of me.

25 Ἡ χάρις τοῦ κυρίου Ἰησοῦ Χριστοῦ
The grace of the Lord Jesus Christ

μετὰ τοῦ πνεύματος ὑμῶν.
[be] with the spirit of you.

---

not forced. 15Perhaps the reason he was separated from you for a little while was that you might have him back for good— 16no longer as a slave, but better than a slave, as a dear brother. He is very dear to me but even dearer to you, both as a man and as a brother in the Lord.

17So if you consider me a partner, welcome him as you would welcome me. 18If he has done you any wrong or owes you anything, charge it to me. 19I, Paul, am writing this with my own hand. I will pay it back—not to mention that you owe me your very self. 20I do wish, brother, that I may have some benefit from you in the Lord; refresh my heart in Christ. 21Confident of your obedience, I write to you, knowing that you will do even more than I ask. 22And one thing more: Prepare a guest room for me, because I hope to be restored to you in answer to your prayers.

23Epaphras, my fellow prisoner in Christ Jesus, sends you greetings. 24And so do Mark, Aristarchus, Demas and Luke, my fellow workers. 25The grace of the Lord Jesus Christ be with your spirit.

---

d Some ancient mss. add *Amen*

Hebrews

Chapter 1

God's Final Word in His Son

GOD, after He spoke long ago to the fathers in the prophets in many portions and in many ways,

---

ΠΡΟΣ ΕΒΡΑΙΟΥΣ
To Hebrews

1 Πολυμερῶς καὶ πολυτρόπως πάλαι ὁ
¹In many ⁴and ⁷in many ways ⁸of old –
portions

θεὸς λαλήσας τοῖς πατράσιν ἐν τοῖς
¹God ²having spoken ³to the ⁴fathers by the

Hebrews

Chapter 1

The Son Superior to Angels

IN the past God spoke to our forefathers through the prophets at many times and in various ways, 2but in

2in these last days has spoken to us in *His* Son, whom He appointed heir of all things, through whom also He made the world.

3And He is the radiance of His glory and the exact representation of His nature, and upholds all things by the word of His power. When He had made purification of sins, He sat down at the right hand of the Majesty on high;

4having become as much better than the angels, as He has inherited a more excellent name than they.

5For to which of the angels did He ever say,

"THOU ART MY SON,
TODAY I HAVE BEGOT-
TEN THEE"?

And again,

"I WILL BE A FATHER TO
HIM,
AND HE SHALL BE A
SON TO ME"?

6And when He again brings the first-born into the world, He says,

"AND LET ALL THE AN-
GELS OF GOD WORSHIP
HIM."

7And of the angels He says,

"WHO MAKES HIS AN-
GELS WINDS,
AND HIS MINISTERS A
FLAME OF FIRE."

8But of the Son *He says,*

"THY THRONE, O GOD,
IS FOREVER AND EVER,
AND THE RIGHTEOUS
SCEPTER IS THE SCEP-
TER OF *a*HIS KING-
DOM.

9"THOU HAST LOVED
RIGHTEOUSNESS AND
HATED LAWLESSNESS;
THEREFORE GOD, THY
GOD, HATH ANOINTED
THEE
WITH THE OIL OF GLAD-
NESS ABOVE THY COM-
PANIONS."

10And,

"THOU, LORD, IN THE
BEGINNING DIDST LAY
THE FOUNDATION OF
THE EARTH,

προφήταις **2** ἐπ’ ἐσχάτου τῶν ἡμερῶν
prophets   in   [the] last   –   days

τούτων ἐλάλησεν ἡμῖν ἐν υἱῷ, ὃν ἔθηκεν
of these   spoke   to us   in a Son, whom he appointed

κληρονόμον πάντων, δι’ οὗ καὶ ἐποίησεν
heir   of all, through whom indeed he made things,

τοὺς αἰῶνας· **3** ὃς ὢν ἀπαύγασμα τῆς
the   ages;   who being [the] radiance of the (his)

δόξης καὶ χαρακτὴρ τῆς ὑποστάσεως αὐτοῦ,
glory and [the]   of the   reality   of him, representation

φέρων τε τὰ πάντα τῷ ῥήματι τῆς
and bearing   –   all things by the   word   of the

δυνάμεως αὐτοῦ, καθαρισμὸν τῶν ἁμαρτιῶν
power   of him, ²cleansing   –   ³of sins

ποιησάμενος ἐκάθισεν ἐν δεξιᾷ τῆς
¹having made   sat   on [the] right [hand] of the

μεγαλωσύνης ἐν ὑψηλοῖς, **4** τοσούτῳ
greatness   in   high places,   ³by so much

κρείττων γενόμενος τῶν ἀγγέλων ὅσῳ
²better ¹becoming ⁴[than] the   angels   as

διαφορώτερον παρ’ αὐτοὺς κεκληρονόμηκεν
²a more excellent ⁴than ⁵them ¹he has inherited

ὄνομα. **5** Τίνι γὰρ εἶπέν ποτε τῶν
³name.   For to which ²said he ⁴ever ¹of the

ἀγγέλων· υἱός μου εἶ σύ, ἐγὼ σήμερον
²angels: Son   of me art thou,   I   to-day

γεγέννηκά σε; καὶ πάλιν· ἐγὼ ἔσομαι
have begotten thee? and   again: I   will be

αὐτῷ εἰς πατέρα, καὶ αὐτὸς ἔσται μοι
to him for a father,   and   he   shall be to me

εἰς υἱόν; **6** ὅταν δὲ πάλιν εἰσαγάγῃ
for a son?   and whenever again   he brings *in*

τὸν πρωτότοκον εἰς τὴν οἰκουμένην, λέγει·
the   firstborn   into   the inhabited [earth], he says:

καὶ προσκυνησάτωσαν αὐτῷ πάντες ἄγγελοι
And   let worship   him   all   angels

θεοῦ. **7** καὶ πρὸς μὲν τοὺς ἀγγέλους
of God.   And with re-   –   the   angels gard to

λέγει· ὁ ποιῶν τοὺς ἀγγέλους αὐτοῦ
he says: The making   the   angels   of him [one]

πνεύματα, καὶ τοὺς λειτουργοὺς αὐτοῦ
spirits,   and   the   ministers   of him

πυρὸς φλόγα· **8** πρὸς δὲ τὸν υἱόν· ὁ
²of fire ¹a flame;   but with regard to the Son: The

θρόνος σου ὁ θεὸς εἰς τὸν αἰῶνα τοῦ
throne of thee[,] – God[,]*[is] unto the   age   of the

αἰῶνος, καὶ ἡ ῥάβδος τῆς εὐθύτητος
age,   and the   rod   – of uprightness [is]

ῥάβδος τῆς βασιλείας αὐτοῦ. **9** ἠγάπησας
[the] rod of the   kingdom   of him.   Thou lovedst

δικαιοσύνην καὶ ἐμίσησας ἀνομίαν· διὰ
righteousness and   hatedst lawlessness;   there-

τοῦτο ἔχρισέν σε, ὁ θεός, ὁ θεός σου
fore ⁴anointed ⁵thee, – ²God,* ¹the ³God ⁶of thee

ἔλαιον ἀγαλλιάσεως παρὰ τοὺς μετόχους
[with] oil   of gladness   above   the   partners

σου. **10** καὶ· σὺ κατ’ ἀρχάς, κύριε,
of thee.   And: Thou at [the] beginnings, Lord,

τὴν γῆν ἐθεμελίωσας, καὶ ἔργα τῶν
²the ³earth ¹didst found,   and   ⁴works ⁵of the

---

these last days he has spoken to us by his Son, whom he appointed heir of all things, and through whom he made the universe. 3The Son is the radiance of God's glory and the exact representation of his being, sustaining all things by his powerful word. After he had provided purification for sins, he sat down at the right hand of the Majesty in heaven. 4So he became as much superior to the angels as the name he has inherited is superior to theirs.

5For to which of the angels did God ever say,

"You are my Son;
today I have become
your Father*a*"*b*?

Or again,

"I will be his Father,
and he will be my
Son"*c*?

6And again, when God brings his firstborn into the world, he says,

"Let all God's angels
worship him."*d*

7In speaking of the angels he says,

"He makes his angels
winds,
his servants flames of
fire."*e*

8But about the Son he says,

"Your throne, O God,
will last for ever and
ever,
and righteousness will
be the scepter of
your kingdom.
9You have loved
righteousness and
hated wickedness;
therefore God, your
God, has set you
above your
companions
by anointing you with
the oil of joy."*f*

10He also says,

"In the beginning, O
Lord, you laid the
foundations of the
earth,

---

a Some mss. read *Thy*   * Articular vocative; see ver. 10.

*a*5 Or *have begotten you*
*b*5 Psalm 2:7
*c*5 2 Samuel 7:14; 1 Chron. 17:13
*d*6 Deut. 32:43 (see Dead Sea Scrolls and Septuagint)
*e*7 Psalm 104:4
*f*9 Psalm 45:6,7

AND THE HEAVENS ARE THE WORKS OF THY HANDS;

11 THEY WILL PERISH, BUT THOU REMAINEST;
AND THEY ALL WILL BECOME OLD AS A GARMENT,

12 AND AS A MANTLE THOU WILT ROLL THEM UP;
AS A GARMENT THEY WILL ALSO BE CHANGED.
BUT THOU ART THE SAME,
AND THY YEARS WILL NOT COME TO AN END."

13 But to which of the angels has He ever said,
"SIT AT MY RIGHT HAND,
UNTIL I MAKE THINE ENEMIES A FOOTSTOOL FOR THY FEET"?

14 Are they not all ministering spirits, sent out to render service for the sake of those who will inherit salvation?

Chapter 2

Give Heed

FOR this reason we must pay much closer attention to what we have heard, lest we drift away *from it.*

2 For if the word spoken through angels proved unalterable, and every transgression and disobedience received a just recompense,

3 how shall we escape if we neglect so great a salvation? After it was at the first spoken through the Lord, it was confirmed to us by those who heard,

4 God also bearing witness with them, both by signs and wonders and by various miracles and by gifts of the Holy Spirit according to His own will.

Earth Subject to Man

5 For He did not subject to angels the world to come, concerning which we are speaking.

6 But one has testified somewhere, saying,
"WHAT IS MAN, THAT THOU REMEMBEREST HIM?
OR THE SON OF MAN, THAT THOU ART CONCERNED ABOUT HIM?

7 "THOU HAST MADE HIM FOR A LITTLE WHILE LOWER THAN THE ANGELS;

χειρῶν σού εἰσιν οἱ οὐρανοί· 11 αὐτοὶ
⁶hands ⁷of thee ²are ¹the ³heavens; they

ἀπολοῦνται, σὺ δὲ διαμένεις· καὶ πάντες
will perish, but thou remainest; and all

ὡς ἱμάτιον παλαιωθήσονται, 12 καὶ ὡσεὶ
as a garment will become old, and as

περιβόλαιον ἑλίξεις αὐτούς, ὡς ἱμάτιον
a mantle thou wilt roll up them, as a garment

καὶ ἀλλαγήσονται· σὺ δὲ ὁ αὐτὸς εἶ
also they will be changed; but thou the same art

καὶ τὰ ἔτη σου οὐκ ἐκλείψουσιν. 13 πρὸς
and the years of thee will not fail. ²to

τίνα δὲ τῶν ἀγγέλων εἴρηκέν ποτε·
²which ¹But of the angels has he said at any time:

κάθου ἐκ δεξιῶν μου ἕως ἂν θῶ τοὺς
Sit at [the] right of me until I put the

ἐχθρούς σου ὑποπόδιον τῶν ποδῶν σου;
enemies of thee a footstool of the feet of thee?

14 οὐχὶ πάντες εἰσὶν λειτουργικὰ πνεύματα
²not ³all ¹are they ⁴ministering ⁵spirits

εἰς διακονίαν ἀποστελλόμενα διὰ τοὺς
⁷for ⁸service ⁶being sent forth because of the [ones]

μέλλοντας κληρονομεῖν σωτηρίαν; 2 Διὰ
being about to inherit salvation? There-

τοῦτο δεῖ περισσοτέρως προσέχειν ἡμᾶς
fore ¹it behoves ²more abundantly ³to give heed ⁴us

τοῖς ἀκουσθεῖσιν, μήποτε παραρυῶμεν.
to the things heard, lest we drift away.

2 εἰ γὰρ ὁ δι’ ἀγγέλων λαληθεὶς λόγος
For if ¹the ⁴through ³angels ²spoken ¹word

ἐγένετο βέβαιος, καὶ πᾶσα παράβασις
was firm, and every transgression

καὶ παρακοὴ ἔλαβεν ἔνδικον μισθαποδοσίαν,
and disobedience received a just recompence,

3 πῶς ἡμεῖς ἐκφευξόμεθα τηλικαύτης
how ²we ¹shall ²escape ²so great

ἀμελήσαντες σωτηρίας; ἥτις ἀρχὴν λαβοῦσα
⁴neglecting ⁵a salvation? which ³a beginning ¹having received

λαλεῖσθαι διὰ τοῦ κυρίου, ὑπὸ τῶν
to be spoken through the Lord, by the

ἀκουσάντων εἰς ἡμᾶς ἐβεβαιώθη, 4 συνεπι-
[ones] hearing to us was confirmed, ²bearing

μαρτυροῦντος τοῦ θεοῦ σημείοις τε καὶ
witness with - ¹Godª ⁴by signs ³both and

τέρασιν καὶ ποικίλαις δυνάμεσιν καὶ
by wonders and by various powerful deeds and

πνεύματος ἁγίου μερισμοῖς κατὰ τὴν αὐτοῦ
³Spirit ²of [the] ¹by distribu- according the ²of him
Holy tions to

θέλησιν.
¹will.

5 Οὐ γὰρ ἀγγέλοις ὑπέταξεν τὴν
For not to angels subjected he the

οἰκουμένην τὴν μέλλουσαν, περὶ ἧς
²inhabited [earth] – ¹coming, about which

λαλοῦμεν. 6 διεμαρτύρατο δέ πού τις
we speak. But ¹solemnly witnessed ²some- ¹one
where

λέγων· τί ἐστιν ἄνθρωπος ὅτι μιμνήσκῃ
saying: What is man that thou rememberest

αὐτοῦ; ἢ υἱὸς ἀνθρώπου ὅτι ἐπισκέπτῃ
him? or a son of man that thou observest

αὐτόν; 7 ἠλάττωσας αὐτὸν βραχύ τι παρ’
him? Thou madest ³less ¹him ²a little than

---

and the heavens are the work of your hands;

11 They will perish, but you remain;
they will all wear out like a garment.

12 You will roll them up like a robe;
like a garment they will be changed.
But you remain the same,
and your years will never end." ᵍ

13 To which of the angels did God ever say,
"Sit at my right hand
until I make your enemies
a footstool for your feet" ʰ?

14 Are not all angels ministering spirits sent to serve those who will inherit salvation?

Chapter 2

Warning to Pay Attention

WE must pay more careful attention, therefore, to what we have heard, so that we do not drift away. 2 For if the message spoken by angels was binding, and every violation and disobedience received its just punishment, 3 how shall we escape if we ignore such a great salvation? This salvation, which was first announced by the Lord, was confirmed to us by those who heard him. 4 God also testified to it by signs, wonders and various miracles, and gifts of the Holy Spirit distributed according to his will.

Jesus Made Like His Brothers

5 It is not to angels that he has subjected the world to come, about which we are speaking. 6 But there is a place where someone has testified:

"What is man that you are mindful of him,
the son of man that you care for him?

7 You made him a little ⁱ lower than the angels;

ᵍ12 Psalm 102:25-27
ʰ13 Psalm 110:1
ⁱ7 Or *him for a little while*; also in verse 9

THOU HAST CROWNED HIM WITH GLORY AND HONOR,
ᵇAND HAST APPOINTED HIM OVER THE WORKS OF THY HANDS;
8 THOU HAST PUT ALL THINGS IN SUBJECTION UNDER HIS FEET."
For in subjecting all things to him, He left nothing that is not subject to him. But now we do not yet see all things subjected to him.

Jesus Briefly Humbled

9But we do see Him who has been made for a little while lower than the angels, *namely,* Jesus, because of the suffering of death crowned with glory and honor, that by the grace of God He might taste death for everyone.
10For it was fitting for Him, for whom are all things, and through whom are all things, in bringing many sons to glory, to perfect the author of their salvation through sufferings.
11For both He who sanctifies and those who are sanctified are all from one *Father*; for which reason He is not ashamed to call them brethren,
12saying,
"I WILL PROCLAIM THY NAME TO MY BRETHREN,
IN THE MIDST OF THE CONGREGATION I WILL SING THY PRAISE."
13And again,
"I WILL PUT MY TRUST IN HIM."
And again,
"BEHOLD, I AND THE CHILDREN WHOM GOD HAS GIVEN ME."
14Since then the children share in flesh and blood, He Himself likewise also partook of the same, that through death He might render powerless him who had the power of death, that is, the devil;
15and might deliver those who through fear of death were subject to slavery all their lives.

ἀγγέλους, δόξῃ καὶ τιμῇ ἐστεφάνωσας
angels, with glory and *with* honour thou crownedst

αὐτόν, 8 πάντα ὑπέταξας ὑποκάτω τῶν
him, all things thou subjectedst underneath the

ποδῶν αὐτοῦ. ἐν τῷ γὰρ ὑποτάξαι
feet of him. ¹in the For ²to subject[ing]

[αὐτῷ] τὰ πάντα οὐδὲν ἀφῆκεν αὐτῷ
²to him - ³all things ⁴nothing ⁵he left ⁶to him

ἀνυπότακτον. Νῦν δὲ οὔπω ὁρῶμεν
⁷unsubjected. But now not yet we see

αὐτῷ τὰ πάντα ὑποτεταγμένα· 9 τὸν δὲ
²to him - ¹all things ³having been subjected; ³the ¹but [one]

βραχύ τι παρ' ἀγγέλους ἠλαττωμένον
²a little ⁶than ⁷angels ⁴having been made less

βλέπομεν Ἰησοῦν διὰ τὸ πάθημα τοῦ
³we see ⁸Jesus because of the suffering -

θανάτου δόξῃ καὶ τιμῇ ἐστεφανωμένον,
of death with glory and *with* honour having been crowned,

ὅπως χάριτι θεοῦ ὑπὲρ παντὸς γεύσηται
so as by [the] grace of God ²on behalf of ⁴every man ¹he might taste

θανάτου. 10 ἔπρεπεν γὰρ αὐτῷ, δι'
of ²death. For it was fitting for him, because of

ὃν τὰ πάντα καὶ δι' οὗ τὰ πάντα,
whom - all things and through whom - all things,

πολλοὺς υἱοὺς εἰς δόξαν ἀγαγόντα τὸν
¹⁰many ¹¹sons ¹²to ¹³glory ⁹leading ⁴the

ἀρχηγὸν τῆς σωτηρίας αὐτῶν διὰ
⁵author ⁶of the ⁷salvation ⁸of them ⁹through

παθημάτων τελειῶσαι. 11 ὅ τε γὰρ
³sufferings ¹to perfect. ⁴the [one] ⁵both ¹For

ἁγιάζων καὶ οἱ ἁγιαζόμενοι ἐξ ἑνὸς
sanctifying and the [ones] being sanctified [are] ⁶of ⁵one

πάντες· δι' ἣν αἰτίαν οὐκ ἐπαισχύνεται
¹all; for which cause he is not ashamed

ἀδελφοὺς αὐτοὺς καλεῖν, 12 λέγων· ἀπαγ-
²brothers ³them ¹to call, saying: I will

γελῶ τὸ ὄνομά σου τοῖς ἀδελφοῖς μου,
announce the name of thee to the brothers of me,

ἐν μέσῳ ἐκκλησίας ὑμνήσω σε· 13 καὶ
in [the] midst of [the] church I will hymn thee; and

πάλιν· ἐγὼ ἔσομαι πεποιθὼς ἐπ' αὐτῷ·
again: I will be having trusted on(in) him;

καὶ πάλιν· ἰδοὺ ἐγὼ καὶ τὰ παιδία
and again: Behold[,] I and the children

ἃ μοι ἔδωκεν ὁ θεός. 14 Ἐπεὶ οὖν
whom ²to me ¹gave - ¹God. Since therefore

τὰ παιδία κεκοινώνηκεν αἵματος καὶ
the children has(ve) partaken of blood and

σαρκός, καὶ αὐτὸς παραπλησίως μετέσχεν
of flesh, ²also ²[him]self ⁴in like manner ¹he shared

τῶν αὐτῶν, ἵνα διὰ τοῦ θανάτου
the same things, in order that through the(?his) death

καταργήσῃ τὸν τὸ κράτος ἔχοντα τοῦ
he might destroy ¹the [one] ²the ³might ²having -

θανάτου, τοῦτ' ἔστιν τὸν διάβολον, 15 καὶ
of death, this is the devil, and

ἀπαλλάξῃ τούτους, ὅσοι φόβῳ θανάτου
release these, as many as by fear of death

διὰ παντὸς τοῦ ζῆν ἔνοχοι ἦσαν δουλείας.
through all the(ir) to ²involved ¹were slavery.
[time] live in

ᵇSome ancient mss. do not contain *And . . . hands*

you crowned him with glory and honor
8 and put everything under his feet."ʲ
In putting everything under him, God left nothing that is not subject to him. Yet at present we do not see everything subject to him. 9But we see Jesus, who was made a little lower than the angels, now crowned with glory and honor because he suffered death, so that by the grace of God he might taste death for everyone.
10In bringing many sons to glory, it was fitting that God, for whom and through whom everything exists, should make the author of their salvation perfect through suffering. 11Both the one who makes men holy and those who are made holy are of the same family. So Jesus is not ashamed to call them brothers. 12He says,
"I will declare your name to my brothers; in the presence of the congregation I will sing your praises."ᵏ
13And again,
"I will put my trust in him."ˡ
And again he says,
"Here am I, and the children God has given me."ᵐ
14Since the children have flesh and blood, he too shared in their humanity so that by his death he might destroy him who holds the power of death—that is, the devil—15and free those who all their lives were held in slavery by their fear

ʲ8 Psalm 8:4-6
ᵏ12 Psalm 22:22
ˡ13 Isaiah 8:17
ᵐ13 Isaiah 8:18

16For assuredly He does not give help to angels, but He gives help to the descendant of Abraham.

17Therefore, He had to be made like His brethren in all things, that He might become a merciful and faithful high priest in things pertaining to God, to make propitiation for the sins of the people.

18For since He Himself was tempted in that which He has suffered, He is able to come to the aid of those who are tempted.

16	οὐ	γὰρ	δήπου	ἀγγέλων	ἐπιλαμβάνεται,
	⁴not.	¹For	²of course	³of angels	⁵he takes hold,

ἀλλὰ	σπέρματος	Ἀβραὰμ	ἐπιλαμβάνεται.
but	of [the] seed	of Abraham	he takes hold.

17	ὅθεν	ὤφειλεν	κατὰ	πάντα	τοῖς	ἀδελφοῖς
	Whence	he owed (ought)	by all means†		¹to the (his)	²brothers

ὁμοιωθῆναι,	ἵνα	ἐλεήμων	γένηται	καὶ
¹to become like,	in order that	²a merciful	¹he might become	and

πιστὸς	ἀρχιερεὺς	τὰ	πρὸς	τὸν	θεόν,
faithful	high priest	[in] the things	in regard to	–	God,

εἰς	τὸ	ἱλάσκεσθαι	τὰς	ἁμαρτίας	τοῦ
for	the	to make propitiation for	the	sins	of the

λαοῦ.	18	ἐν	ᾧ	γὰρ	πέπονθεν	αὐτὸς
people.		²in	³what [way]	¹For	⁵has suffered	⁴he

πειρασθείς,	δύναται	τοῖς	πειραζομένοις
being tempted,	he is able	²the [ones]	³being tempted

βοηθῆσαι.
¹to help.

of death. 16For surely it is not angels he helps, but Abraham's descendants. 17For this reason he had to be made like his brothers in every way, in order that he might become a merciful and faithful high priest in service to God, and that he might make atonement for[n] the sins of the people. 18Because he himself suffered when he was tempted, he is able to help those who are being tempted.

Chapter 3

Jesus Our High Priest

THEREFORE, holy brethren, partakers of a heavenly calling, consider Jesus, the Apostle and High Priest of our confession.

2He was faithful to Him who appointed Him, as Moses also was in all His house.

3For He has been counted worthy of more glory than Moses, by just so much as the builder of the house has more honor than the house.

4For every house is built by someone, but the builder of all things is God.

5Now Moses was faithful in all His house as a servant, for a testimony of those things which were to be spoken later;

6but Christ *was faithful* as a Son over His house whose house we are, if we hold fast our confidence and the boast of our hope firm until the end.

7Therefore, just as the Holy Spirit says,
　"TODAY IF YOU HEAR HIS VOICE,
8　DO NOT HARDEN YOUR HEARTS AS WHEN THEY PROVOKED ME,

3	Ὅθεν,	ἀδελφοὶ	ἅγιοι,	κλήσεως
	Whence,	brothers	holy,	²calling

ἐπουρανίου	μέτοχοι,	κατανοήσατε	τὸν
¹of a heavenly	³sharers,	consider	the

ἀπόστολον	καὶ	ἀρχιερέα	τῆς	ὁμολογίας
apostle	and	high priest	of the	confession

ἡμῶν	Ἰησοῦν,	2	πιστὸν	ὄντα	τῷ	ποιήσαντι
of us[,]	Jesus,		faithful	being	to the [one]	making

αὐτόν,	ὡς	καὶ	Μωϋσῆς	ἐν	[ὅλῳ]	τῷ
him,	as	also	Moses	in	all	the

οἴκῳ	αὐτοῦ.	3	πλείονος	γὰρ	οὗτος	δόξης
household of him.			For ²of more		¹this one	⁴glory

παρὰ	Μωϋσῆν	ἠξίωται	καθ᾽	ὅσον	πλείονα
⁵than	⁶Moses	³has been counted worthy	by so much as		⁸more

τιμὴν	ἔχει	τοῦ	οἴκου	ὁ	κατασκευάσας
⁶honour	⁴has	⁵the	⁹house	¹the [one]	²having prepared

αὐτόν.	4	πᾶς	γὰρ	οἶκος	κατασκευάζεται
³it.		For every		house	is prepared

ὑπό	τινος,	ὁ	δὲ	πάντα	κατασκευάσας
by	someone,	but	¹the [one]	³all things	²having prepared

θεός.	5	καὶ	Μωϋσῆς	μὲν	πιστὸς	ἐν
[is] God.		And	Moses	on one hand	faithful	in

ὅλῳ	τῷ	οἴκῳ	αὐτοῦ	ὡς	θεράπων	εἰς
all	the	household	of him	as	a servant	for

μαρτύριον	τῶν	λαληθησομένων,	6	Χριστὸς
a testimony	of the things	being spoken [in the future],		Christ

δὲ	ὡς	υἱὸς	ἐπὶ	τὸν	οἶκον	αὐτοῦ·	οὗ
on the other	as	a Son	over	the	household	of him;	of whom

οἶκός	ἐσμεν	ἡμεῖς,	ἐὰν	τὴν	παρρησίαν
a household are		we,	if	²the	³confidence

καὶ	τὸ	καύχημα	τῆς	ἐλπίδος	[μέχρι
⁴and	⁵the	⁶boast	⁷of the	⁸hope	¹⁰until

τέλους	βεβαίαν]	κατάσχωμεν.	7	Διό,
¹¹[the] end	⁹firm	¹we hold fast.		Wherefore,

καθὼς	λέγει	τὸ	πνεῦμα	τὸ	ἅγιον·	σήμερον
as	says	the	Spirit	–	Holy:	To-day

ἐὰν	τῆς	φωνῆς	αὐτοῦ	ἀκούσητε,	8	μὴ
if	the	voice	of him	ye hear,		not

σκληρύνητε	τὰς	καρδίας	ὑμῶν	ὡς	ἐν
harden ye	the	hearts	of you	as	in

Chapter 3

Jesus Greater Than Moses

THEREFORE, holy brothers, who share in the heavenly calling, fix your thoughts on Jesus, the apostle and high priest whom we confess. 2He was faithful to the one who appointed him, just as Moses was faithful in all God's house. 3Jesus has been found worthy of greater honor than Moses, just as the builder of a house has greater honor than the house itself. 4For every house is built by someone, but God is the builder of everything. 5Moses was faithful as a servant in all God's house, testifying to what would be said in the future. 6But Christ is faithful as a son over God's house. And we are his house, if we hold on to our courage and the hope of which we boast.

Warning Against Unbelief

7So, as the Holy Spirit says:

　"Today, if you hear his voice,
8　do not harden your hearts
　as you did in the rebellion,

n17 Or and that he might turn aside God's wrath, taking away

AS IN THE DAY OF TRIAL
IN THE WILDERNESS,
9 WHERE YOUR FATHERS
TRIED *Me* BY TESTING
Me,
AND SAW MY WORKS
FOR FORTY YEARS.
10 "THEREFORE I WAS AN-
GRY WITH THIS GEN-
ERATION,
AND SAID, 'THEY AL-
WAYS GO ASTRAY IN
THEIR HEART;
AND THEY DID NOT
KNOW MY WAYS';
11 AS I SWORE IN MY
WRATH,
'THEY SHALL NOT ENTER
MY REST.' "

The Peril of Unbelief

12Take care, brethren,
lest there should be in any
one of you an evil, un-
believing heart, in falling
away from the living God.
13But encourage one an-
other day after day, as long
as it is *still* called "Today,"
lest any one of you be hardened by the deceitfulness
of sin.
14For we have become
partakers of Christ, if we
hold fast the beginning of
our assurance firm until the
end;
15while it is said,
"TODAY IF YOU HEAR HIS
VOICE,
DO NOT HARDEN YOUR
HEARTS, AS WHEN
THEY PROVOKED ME."
16For who provoked *Him*
when they had heard? In-
deed, did not all those who
came out of Egypt led by
Moses?
17And with whom was He
angry for forty years? Was
it not with those who
sinned, whose bodies fell in
the wilderness?
18And to whom did He
swear that they should not
enter His rest, but to those
who were disobedient?
19And *so* we see that they
were not able to enter because of unbelief.

τῷ παραπικρασμῷ κατὰ τὴν ἡμέραν τοῦ
the provocation in the day of the

πειρασμοῦ ἐν τῇ ἐρήμῳ, 9 οὗ ἐπείρασαν
temptation in the desert, when ᵗtempted

οἱ πατέρες ὑμῶν ἐν δοκιμασίᾳ καὶ εἶδον
¹the ²fathers ³of you in proving and saw

τὰ ἔργα μου τεσσεράκοντα ἔτη· 10 διὸ
the works of me forty years; wherefore

προσώχθισα τῇ γενεᾷ ταύτῃ καὶ εἶπον·
I was angry with this generation and I said:

ἀεὶ πλανῶνται τῇ καρδίᾳ· αὐτοὶ δὲ
Always they err in the heart; and they

οὐκ ἔγνωσαν τὰς ὁδούς μου, 11 ὡς
knew not the ways of me, as

ὤμοσα ἐν τῇ ὀργῇ μου· εἰ εἰσελεύσονται
I swore in the wrath of me: If they shall enter

εἰς τὴν κατάπαυσίν μου. 12 Βλέπετε,
into the rest of me. Look ye,

ἀδελφοί, μήποτε ἔσται ἔν τινι ὑμῶν
brothers, lest there shall be in anyone ⁴of you

καρδία πονηρὰ ἀπιστίας ἐν τῷ ἀποστῆναι
⁵heart ¹an evil of unbelief in *the* to depart[ing]

ἀπὸ θεοῦ ζῶντος, 13 ἀλλὰ παρακαλεῖτε
from God a living, but exhort

ἑαυτοὺς καθ' ἑκάστην ἡμέραν, ἄχρις οὗ
yourselves – each day, while

τὸ σήμερον καλεῖται, ἵνα μὴ σκληρυνθῇ
the to-day it is being called, lest ⁴be hardened

τις ἐξ ὑμῶν ἀπάτη τῆς ἁμαρτίας· 14 μέτ-
¹any- ²of ³you by [the] – of sin; ⁵shar-
one deceit

οχοι γὰρ τοῦ Χριστοῦ γεγόναμεν, ἐάνπερ
ers ¹for ⁴of ⁵Christ ³we have if indeed
the become,

τὴν ἀρχὴν τῆς ὑποστάσεως μέχρι τέλους
³the ⁵beginning ⁶of the ⁴assurance ⁷until ⁸[the] end

βεβαίαν κατάσχωμεν. 15 ἐν τῷ λέγεσθαι·
⁶firm ¹we hold fast. In the to be said⁰:
=While it is said:

σήμερον ἐὰν τῆς φωνῆς αὐτοῦ ἀκούσητε,
To-day if the voice of him ye hear,

μὴ σκληρύνητε τὰς καρδίας ὑμῶν ὡς
do not harden the hearts of you as

ἐν τῷ παραπικρασμῷ. 16 τίνες γὰρ
in the provocation. For some

ἀκούσαντες παρεπίκραναν; ἀλλ' οὐ πάντες
hearing provoked? yet not all

οἱ ἐξελθόντες ἐξ Αἰγύπτου διὰ
the [ones] coming out out of Egypt through

Μωϋσέως; 17 τίσιν δὲ προσώχθισεν τεσ-
Moses? but with whom was he angry for-

σεράκοντα ἔτη; οὐχὶ τοῖς ἁμαρτήσασιν,
ty years? [was it] with the [ones] sinning,
not

ὧν τὰ κῶλα ἔπεσεν ἐν τῇ ἐρήμῳ;
of the corpses fell in the desert?
whom

18 τίσιν δὲ ὤμοσεν μὴ εἰσελεύσεσθαι εἰς
and to whom swore he not to enter into

τὴν κατάπαυσιν αὐτοῦ εἰ μὴ τοῖς
the rest of him except to the

ἀπειθήσασιν; 19 καὶ βλέπομεν ὅτι οὐκ
[ones] disobeying? and we see that not

ἠδυνήθησαν εἰσελθεῖν δι' ἀπιστίαν.
they were able to enter because of disbelief.

---

during the time of
testing in the desert,
9where your fathers
tested and tried me
and for forty years saw
what I did.
10That is why I was angry
with that generation,
and I said, 'Their
hearts are always
going astray,
and they have not
known my ways.'
11So I declared on oath in
my anger,
'They shall never enter
my rest.' "ᵒ

12See to it, brothers, that
none of you has a sinful,
unbelieving heart that turns
away from the living God.
13But encourage one another daily, as long as it is
called Today, so that none
of you may be hardened by
sin's deceitfulness. 14We
have come to share in
Christ if we hold firmly till
the end the confidence we
had at first. 15As has just
been said:

"Today, if you hear his
voice,
do not harden your
hearts
as you did in the
rebellion."ᵖ

16Who were they who
heard and rebelled? Were
they not all those Moses led
out of Egypt? 17And with
whom was he angry for forty years? Was it not with
those who sinned, whose
bodies fell in the desert?
18And to whom did God
swear that they would never enter his rest if not to
those who disobeyed�q?
19So we see that they were
not able to enter, because
of their unbelief.

ᵒ11 Psalm 95:7-11
ᵖ15,7 Psalm 95:7,8
q18 Or *disbelieved*

Chapter 4

The Believer's Rest

THEREFORE, let us fear lest, while a promise remains of entering His rest, any one of you should seems to have come short of it.

2For indeed we have had good news preached to us, just as they also; but the word they heard did not profit them, because it was not united by faith in those who heard.

3cFor we who have believed enter that rest, just as He has said,

"As I swore in My wrath,
They shall not enter My rest,"

although His works were finished from the foundation of the world.

4For He has thus said somewhere concerning the seventh *day*, "And God rested on the seventh day from all His works";

5and again in this *passage*, "They shall not enter My rest."

6Since therefore it remains for some to enter it, and those who formerly had good news preached to them failed to enter because of disobedience,

7He again fixes a certain day, "Today," saying through David after so long a time just as has been said before,

"Today if you hear His voice,
Do not harden your hearts."

8For if Joshua had given them rest, He would not have spoken of another day after that.

9There remains therefore a Sabbath rest for the people of God.

10For the one who has entered His rest has himself also rested from his works, as God did from His.

---

4 Φοβηθῶμεν οὖν μήποτε καταλειπομένης
Let us fear therefore lest ²being left

ἐπαγγελίας εἰσελθεῖν εἰς τὴν κατάπαυσιν
¹a promise² to enter into the rest

αὐτοῦ δοκῇ τις ἐξ ὑμῶν ὑστερηκέναι.
of him ⁴seems ¹anyone ²of ³you to have come short.

2 καὶ γάρ ἐσμεν εὐηγγελισμένοι καθάπερ
For indeed we are having had good news even as
preached [to us]

κἀκεῖνοι· ἀλλ' οὐκ ὠφέλησεν ὁ λόγος
those also; but ⁴did not profit ¹the ²word

τῆς ἀκοῆς ἐκείνους μὴ συγκεκερασμένος
- ²of hearing those not having been mixed
together

τῇ πίστει τοῖς ἀκούσασιν. **3** Εἰσερχόμεθα
- with faith in the [ones] hearing. we enter

γὰρ εἰς [τὴν] κατάπαυσιν οἱ πιστεύσαντες,
For into the rest the [ones] believing,

καθὼς εἴρηκεν· ὡς ὤμοσα ἐν τῇ ὀργῇ
as he has said: As I swore in the wrath

μου· εἰ εἰσελεύσονται εἰς τὴν κατάπαυσίν
of me: If they shall enter into the rest

μου, καίτοι τῶν ἔργων ἀπὸ καταβολῆς
of me, though the works ²from ³[the] foundation

κόσμου γενηθέντων. **4** εἴρηκεν γάρ που
⁴of [the] ¹having come into For he has said some-
world being.ª where

περὶ τῆς ἑβδόμης οὕτως· καὶ κατέπαυσεν
con- the seventh [day] thus: And ²rested
cerning

ὁ θεὸς ἐν τῇ ἡμέρᾳ τῇ ἑβδόμῃ ἀπὸ
- ¹God in the ²day - ¹seventh from

πάντων τῶν ἔργων αὐτοῦ· **5** καὶ ἐν
all the works of him; and in

τούτῳ πάλιν· εἰ εἰσελεύσονται εἰς τὴν
this [place] again: If they shall enter into the

κατάπαυσίν μου. **6** ἐπεὶ οὖν ἀπολείπεται
rest of me. Since therefore it remains

τινὰς εἰσελθεῖν εἰς αὐτήν, καὶ οἱ πρότερον
[for] to enter into it, and the formerly
some [ones]

εὐαγγελισθέντες οὐκ εἰσῆλθον δι' ἀπείθειαν,
having good news did not enter because disobedience,
preached [to them] of

7 πάλιν τινὰ ὁρίζει ἡμέραν, σήμερον, ἐν
again ²a certain ¹he de- day, to-day, ²in
fines

Δαυὶδ λέγων μετὰ τοσοῦτον χρόνον, καθὼς
¹David ¹saying after such a time, as

προείρηται· σήμερον ἐὰν τῆς φωνῆς αὐτοῦ
he has To-day if the voice of him
previously said:

ἀκούσητε, μὴ σκληρύνητε τὰς καρδίας
ye hear, do not harden the hearts

ὑμῶν. **8** εἰ γὰρ αὐτοὺς Ἰησοῦς κατέπαυσεν,
of you. For if ³them ¹Jesus(Joshua) ²rested,

οὐκ ἂν περὶ ἄλλης ἐλάλει μετὰ ταῦτα
³not - ²concerning ⁴another ¹he ²would ⁴after ⁵these
⁴have spoken things

ἡμέρας. **9** ἄρα ἀπολείπεται σαββατισμὸς
¹day. Then ²remains ¹a sabbath rest

τῷ λαῷ τοῦ θεοῦ. **10** ὁ γὰρ εἰσελθὼν
to the people - of God. For the [one] having
entered

εἰς τὴν κατάπαυσιν αὐτοῦ καὶ αὐτὸς
into the rest of him also [him]self

κατέπαυσεν ἀπὸ τῶν ἔργων αὐτοῦ,
rested from the works of him,

ὥσπερ ἀπὸ τῶν ἰδίων ὁ θεός. **11** Σπου-
as from the(his) own - God [did]. Let us

Chapter 4

A Sabbath-Rest for the People of God

THEREFORE, since the promise of entering his rest still stands, let us be careful that none of you be found to have fallen short of it. 2For we also have had the gospel preached to us, just as they did; but the message they heard was of no value to them, because those who heard did not combine it with faith.ʳ 3Now we who have believed enter that rest, just as God has said,

"So I declared on oath in my anger,
'They shall never enter my rest.' "ˢ

And yet his work has been finished since the creation of the world. 4For somewhere he has spoken about the seventh day in these words: "And on the seventh day God rested from all his work."ᵗ 5And again in the passage above he says, "They shall never enter my rest."

6It still remains that some will enter that rest, and those who formerly had the gospel preached to them did not go in, because of their disobedience. 7Therefore God again set a certain day, calling it Today, when a long time later he spoke through David, as was said before:

"Today, if you hear his voice,
do not harden your hearts."ᵖ

8For if Joshua had given them rest, God would not have spoken later about another day. 9There remains, then, a Sabbath-rest for the people of God; 10for anyone who enters God's rest also rests from his own work, just as God did from his.

---

c Some ancient mss. read *Therefore*

ʳ2 Many manuscripts *because they did not share in the faith of those who obeyed*
ˢ3 Psalm 95:11; also in verse 5
ᵗ4 Gen. 2:2

11Let us therefore be diligent to enter that rest, lest anyone fall through *following* the same example of disobedience.

12For the word of God is living and active and sharper than any two-edged sword, and piercing as far as the division of soul and spirit, of both joints and marrow, and able to judge the thoughts and intentions of the heart.

13And there is no creature hidden from His sight, but all things are open and laid bare to the eyes of Him with whom we have to do.

14Since then we have a great high priest who has passed through the heavens, Jesus the Son of God, let us hold fast our confession.

15For we do not have a high priest who cannot sympathize with our weaknesses, but one who has been tempted in all things as *we are,* yet without sin.

16Let us therefore draw near with confidence to the throne of grace, that we may receive mercy and may find grace to help in time of need.

δάσωμεν οὖν εἰσελθεῖν εἰς ἐκείνην τὴν
be eager therefore to enter into that –

κατάπαυσιν, ἵνα μὴ ἐν τῷ αὐτῷ τις
rest, lest ³in ⁴the ⁵same ¹anyone

ὑποδείγματι πέσῃ τῆς ἀπειθείας. 12 Ζῶν
⁶example ²falls – of dis- [⁴is] ⁵living
obedience.

γὰρ ὁ λόγος τοῦ θεοῦ καὶ ἐνεργὴς
For ¹the ²word – ³of God and operative

καὶ τομώτερος ὑπὲρ πᾶσαν μάχαιραν
and sharper beyond every ⁶sword

δίστομον καὶ διϊκνούμενος ἄχρι μερισμοῦ
¹:two-mouthed and passing through as far as division
(edged)

ψυχῆς καὶ πνεύματος, ἁρμῶν τε καὶ
of soul and of spirit, ²of joints ¹both and

μυελῶν, καὶ κριτικὸς ἐνθυμήσεων καὶ
of marrows, and able to judge of thoughts and

ἐννοιῶν καρδίας· 13 καὶ οὐκ ἔστιν κτίσις
intentions of a heart; and there is no creature

ἀφανὴς ἐνώπιον αὐτοῦ, πάντα δὲ γυμνὰ
unmanifest before him, but all things [are] naked

καὶ τετραχηλισμένα τοῖς ὀφθαλμοῖς αὐτοῦ,
and *having been* laid open to the eyes of him,

πρὸς ὃν ἡμῖν ὁ λόγος.
with whom to us [is] the word(account).ᵒ
=is our account.

14 Ἔχοντες οὖν ἀρχιερέα μέγαν διεληλυ-
Having there- high priest a great having gone
fore

θότα τοὺς οὐρανούς, Ἰησοῦν τὸν υἱὸν
through the heavens, Jesus the Son

τοῦ θεοῦ, κρατῶμεν τῆς ὁμολογίας. 15 οὐ
– of God, let us hold the confession. ³not

γὰρ ἔχομεν ἀρχιερέα μὴ δυνάμενον
¹For ²we have a high priest not being able

συμπαθῆσαι ταῖς ἀσθενείαις ἡμῶν, πεπει-
to suffer with the weaknesses of us, ²having

ρασμένον δὲ κατὰ πάντα καθ᾽ ὁμοιότητα
been tempted ¹but in all respects† accord- [our] likeness
ing to

χωρὶς ἁμαρτίας. 16 προσερχώμεθα οὖν
apart from sin. Let us approach therefore

μετὰ παρρησίας τῷ θρόνῳ τῆς χάριτος,
with confidence *to* the throne of grace,

ἵνα λάβωμεν ἔλεος καὶ χάριν εὕρωμεν
in or- we may mercy and ²grace we ¹may
der that receive find

εἰς εὔκαιρον βοήθειαν.
for timely help.

11Let us, therefore, make every effort to enter that rest, so that no one will fall by following their example of disobedience.

12For the word of God is living and active. Sharper than any double-edged sword, it penetrates even to dividing soul and spirit, joints and marrow; it judges the thoughts and attitudes of the heart. 13Nothing in all creation is hidden from God's sight. Everything is uncovered and laid bare before the eyes of him to whom we must give account.

Jesus the Great High Priest

14Therefore, since we have a great high priest who has gone through the heavens, ᵘ Jesus the Son of God, let us hold firmly to the faith we profess. 15For we do not have a high priest who is unable to sympathize with our weaknesses, but we have one who has been tempted in every way, just as we are—yet was without sin. 16Let us then approach the throne of grace with confidence, so that we may receive mercy and find grace to help us in our time of need.

Chapter 5

The Perfect High Priest

FOR every high priest taken from among men is appointed on behalf of men in things pertaining to God, in order to offer both gifts and sacrifices for sins;

2he can deal gently with the ignorant and misguided, since he himself also is beset with weakness;

---

5 Πᾶς γὰρ ἀρχιερεὺς ἐξ ἀνθρώπων
For every high priest ¹out of ²men

λαμβανόμενος ὑπὲρ ἀνθρώπων καθίσταται
¹being taken on behalf of men is appointed [in]

τὰ πρὸς τὸν θεόν, ἵνα προσφέρῃ δῶρά
the in re- God, in order he may offer ²gifts
things gard to that

τε καὶ θυσίας ὑπὲρ ἁμαρτιῶν, 2 μετριο-
¹both and sacrifices on behalf of sins, ²to feel in

παθεῖν δυνάμενος τοῖς ἀγνοοῦσιν καὶ
due measure ¹being able for the [ones] not knowing and

πλανωμένοις, ἐπεὶ καὶ αὐτὸς περίκειται
being led astray, since also he is set round
[with]

Chapter 5

EVERY high priest is selected from among men and is appointed to represent them in matters related to God, to offer gifts and sacrifices for sins. 2He is able to deal gently with those who are ignorant and are going astray, since he himself is subject to weak-

ᵘ14 Or *gone into heaven*

3and because of it he is obligated to offer *sacrifices* for sins, as for the people, so also for himself.

4And no one takes the honor to himself, but *receives it* when he is called by God, even as Aaron was.

5So also Christ did not glorify Himself so as to become a high priest, but He who said to Him,

"THOU ART MY SON,
TODAY I HAVE BEGOTTEN THEE";

6just as He says also in another *passage*,

"THOU ART A PRIEST FOREVER
ACCORDING TO THE ORDER OF MELCHIZEDEK."

7In the days of His flesh, He offered up both prayers and supplications with loud crying and tears to the One able to save Him from death, and He was heard because of His piety.

8Although He was a Son, He learned obedience from the things which He suffered.

9And having been made perfect, He became to all those who obey Him the source of eternal salvation, 10being designated by God as a high priest according to the order of Melchizedek.

11Concerning *d*him we have much to say, and *it is* hard to explain, since you have become dull of hearing.

12For though by this time you ought to be teachers, you have need again for someone to teach you the elementary principles of the oracles of God, and you have come to need milk and not solid food.

ἀσθένειαν, 3 καὶ δι' αὐτὴν ὀφείλει, καθὼς
weakness, and because it he ought, as
of

περὶ τοῦ λαοῦ, οὕτως καὶ περὶ ἑαυτοῦ
concern- the people, so also concerning himself
ing

προσφέρειν περὶ ἁμαρτιῶν. 4 καὶ οὐχ
to offer concerning sins. And ²not

ἑαυτῷ τις λαμβάνει τὴν τιμήν, ἀλλὰ
⁴to him- ¹anyone ³takes the honour, but
self

καλούμενος ὑπὸ τοῦ θεοῦ, καθώσπερ καὶ
being called by - God, even as indeed

'Ααρών. 5 Οὕτως καὶ ὁ Χριστὸς οὐχ
Aaron. So also Christ ³not

ἑαυτὸν ἐδόξασεν γενηθῆναι ἀρχιερέα, ἀλλ'
²himself ¹glorified to become a high priest, but

ὁ λαλήσας πρὸς αὐτόν· υἱός μου εἶ
the [one] speaking to him: Son of me art

σύ, ἐγὼ σήμερον γεγέννηκά σε· 6 καθὼς
thou, I to-day have begotten thee; as

καὶ ἐν ἑτέρῳ λέγει· σὺ ἱερεὺς εἰς τὸν
also in another he says: Thou a priest unto the
[psalm] [art]

αἰῶνα κατὰ τὴν τάξιν Μελχισέδεκ. 7 ὃς
age according the order of Melchisedec. Who
to

ἐν ταῖς ἡμέραις τῆς σαρκὸς αὐτοῦ δεήσεις
in the days of the flesh of him ²petitions

τε καὶ ἱκετηρίας πρὸς τὸν δυνάμενον
³both ⁴and ¹entreaties ¹¹to ¹³the [one] ¹⁰being able

σῴζειν αὐτὸν ἐκ θανάτου μετὰ κραυγῆς
¹⁴to save ¹⁵him ¹⁶out of ¹⁷death ⁸with ⁹crying

ἰσχυρᾶς καὶ δακρύων προσενέγκας καὶ
⁷strong ⁸and ¹⁰tears ¹offering and

εἰσακουσθεὶς ἀπὸ τῆς εὐλαβείας, 8 καίπερ
being heard from(for) the(his) devoutness, though

ὢν υἱός, ἔμαθεν ἀφ' ὧν ἔπαθεν τὴν
being a Son, he ²from ³[the] ⁴he suffered -
learned things which

ὑπακοήν, 9 καὶ τελειωθεὶς ἐγένετο πᾶσιν
¹obedience, and being perfected he became to all

τοῖς ὑπακούουσιν αὐτῷ αἴτιος σωτηρίας
the [ones] obeying him [the] cause ²salvation

αἰωνίου, 10 προσαγορευθεὶς ὑπὸ τοῦ θεοῦ
¹of eternal, being designated by - God

ἀρχιερεὺς κατὰ τὴν τάξιν Μελχισέδεκ.
a high priest accord- the order of Melchisedec.
ing to

11 Περὶ οὗ πολὺς ἡμῖν ὁ λόγος καὶ
Concern- whom much to us the ¹word² ²and
ing
= we have much to say and hard . . .

δυσερμήνευτος λέγειν, ἐπεὶ νωθροὶ γεγόνατε
⁴hard to interpret ⁵to say, since du¹¹ ye have
become

ταῖς ἀκοαῖς. 12 καὶ γὰρ ὀφείλοντες
in *the* hearings. For indeed owing*

εἶναι διδάσκαλοι διὰ τὸν χρόνον, πάλιν
to be teachers because of the time, ³again

χρείαν ἔχετε τοῦ διδάσκειν ὑμᾶς τινα
²need ¹ye have - ⁵to teach*d* ⁴you ⁶someone

τὰ στοιχεῖα τῆς ἀρχῆς τῶν λογίων
the rudiments of the beginning of the oracles

τοῦ θεοῦ, καὶ γεγόνατε χρείαν ἔχοντες
- of God, and ye have become ²need ¹having

γάλακτος, οὐ στερεᾶς τροφῆς. 13 πᾶς
of milk, not of solid food. every

3This is why he has to offer sacrifices for his own sins, as well as for the sins of the people. 4No one takes this honor upon himself; he must be called by God, just as Aaron was. 5So Christ also did not take upon himself the glory of becoming a high priest. But God said to him,

"You are my Son;
today I have become your Father. *v*" *w*

6And he says in another place,

"You are a priest forever,
in the order of Melchizedek." *x*

7During the days of Jesus' life on earth, he offered up prayers and petitions with loud cries and tears to the one who could save him from death, and he was heard because of his reverent submission. 8Although he was a son, he learned obedience from what he suffered 9and, once made perfect, he became the source of eternal salvation for all who obey him 10and was designated by God to be high priest in the order of Melchizedek.

Warning Against Falling Away

11We have much to say about this, but it is hard to explain because you are slow to learn. 12In fact, though by this time you ought to be teachers, you need someone to teach you the elementary truths of God's word all over again. You need milk, not solid food!

---

*d*Or, *Him;* or, *this*

* That is, " ye ought . . . "

*v*5 Or *have begotten you*
*w*5 Psalm 2:7
*x*6 Psalm 110:4

13For everyone who partakes *only* of milk is not accustomed to the word of righteousness, for he is a babe.

14But solid food is for the mature, who because of practice have their senses trained to discern good and evil.

Chapter 6

The Peril of Falling Away

THEREFORE leaving the elementary teaching about the Christ, let us press on to maturity, not laying again a foundation of repentance from dead works and of faith toward God,

2of instruction about washings, and laying on of hands, and the resurrection of the dead, and eternal judgment.

3And this we shall do, if God permits.

4For in the case of those who have once been enlightened and have tasted of the heavenly gift and have been made partakers of the Holy Spirit,

5and have tasted the good word of God and the powers of the age to come,

6and *then* have fallen away, it is impossible to renew them again to repentance, since they again crucify to themselves the Son of God, and put Him to open shame.

7For ground that drinks the rain which often falls upon it and brings forth vegetation useful to those for whose sake it is also tilled, receives a blessing from God;

8but if it yields thorns and thistles, it is worthless and close to being cursed, and it ends up being burned.

Better Things for You

9But, beloved, we are convinced of better things concerning you, and things that accompany salvation, though we are speaking in this way.

10For God is not unjust so

γὰρ ὁ μετέχων γάλακτος ἄπειρος λόγου
For one partaking of milk [is] without of [the]
experience word

δικαιοσύνης, νήπιος γάρ ἐστιν· 14 τελείων δὲ
of righteousness, for ²an infant ¹he is; but ⁴of mature
men

ἐστιν ἡ στερεὰ τροφή, τῶν διὰ τὴν
²is the ¹solid ²food, of the because the(ir)
[ones] of

ἕξιν τὰ αἰσθητήρια γεγυμνασμένα ἐχόντων
con- ²the(ir) ³faculties *having been* ⁴exercised ¹having
dition

πρὸς διάκρισιν καλοῦ τε καὶ κακοῦ.
for distinction ²of good ¹both and of bad.

6 Διὸ ἀφέντες τὸν τῆς ἀρχῆς τοῦ Χριστοῦ
Wherefore leaving ¹the ²of the ⁴beginning - ³of Christ

λόγον ἐπὶ τὴν τελειότητα φερώμεθα, μὴ
²word ¹on to - ³maturity ⁵let us be borne, not

πάλιν θεμέλιον καταβαλλόμενοι μετανοίας
again ²a foundation ¹laying down of repentance

ἀπὸ νεκρῶν ἔργων, καὶ πίστεως ἐπὶ
from dead works, and of faith toward

θεόν, 2 βαπτισμῶν διδαχῆς, ἐπιθέσεώς τε
God, ²of baptisms ¹of teaching, and of laying on

χειρῶν, ἀναστάσεως νεκρῶν, καὶ κρίματος
of hands, of resurrection of dead persons, and ²judgment

αἰωνίου. 3 καὶ τοῦτο ποιήσομεν, ἐάνπερ
¹of eternal. And this will we do, if indeed

ἐπιτρέπῃ ὁ θεός. 4 Ἀδύνατον γὰρ τοὺς
²permits - ¹God. For [it is] impossible the
[for] [ones]

ἅπαξ φωτισθέντας γευσαμένους τε τῆς
once being enlightened and tasting of the

δωρεᾶς τῆς ἐπουρανίου καὶ μετόχους
²gift - ¹heavenly and sharers

γενηθέντας πνεύματος ἁγίου 5 καὶ καλὸν
becoming Spirit of [the] Holy and ²[the] good

γευσαμένους θεοῦ ῥῆμα δυνάμεις τε
¹tasting ⁴of God ³word and powerful deeds

μέλλοντος αἰῶνος, 6 καὶ παραπεσόντας, πάλιν
of a coming age, and falling away, again

ἀνακαινίζειν εἰς μετάνοιαν, ἀνασταυροῦντας again
to renew to repentance, crucifying again

ἑαυτοῖς τὸν υἱὸν τοῦ θεοῦ καὶ παρα-
for them- the Son - of God and putting
selves

δειγματίζοντας. 7 γῆ γὰρ ἡ πιοῦσα
[him] to open shame. For earth - drinking

τὸν ἐπ’ αὐτῆς ἐρχόμενον πολλάκις ὑετὸν
¹the ⁵upon ⁶it ²coming ³often ⁴rain

καὶ τίκτουσα βοτάνην εὔθετον ἐκείνοις
and bearing fodder suitable for those

δι’ οὓς καὶ γεωργεῖται, μεταλαμβάνει
on ac- whom indeed it is farmed, receives
count of

εὐλογίας ἀπὸ τοῦ θεοῦ· 8 ἐκφέρουσα δὲ
blessing from - God; but bringing forth

ἀκάνθας καὶ τριβόλους ἀδόκιμος καὶ
thorns and thistles [it is] disapproved and

κατάρας ἐγγύς, ἧς τὸ τέλος εἰς καῦσιν.
²a curse ¹near, of which the end [is] for burning.

9 Πεπείσμεθα δὲ περὶ ὑμῶν, ἀγαπητοί,
But we have been concerning you, beloved,
persuaded

τὰ κρείσσονα καὶ ἐχόμενα σωτηρίας, εἰ
the better things and having salvation, if

καὶ οὕτως λαλοῦμεν. 10 οὐ γὰρ ἄδικος
indeed ²so ¹we speak. For ²not ³unjust

---

food! 13Anyone who lives on milk, being still an infant, is not acquainted with the teaching about righteousness. 14But solid food is for the mature, who by constant use have trained themselves to distinguish good from evil.

Chapter 6

THEREFORE let us leave the elementary teachings about Christ and go on to maturity, not laying again the foundation of repentance from acts that lead to death,ʸ and of faith in God, 2instruction about baptisms, the laying on of hands, the resurrection of the dead, and eternal judgment. 3And God permitting, we will do so.

4It is impossible for those who have once been enlightened, who have tasted the heavenly gift, who have shared in the Holy Spirit, 5who have tasted the goodness of the word of God and the powers of the coming age, 6if they fall away, to be brought back to repentance, becauseᶻ to their loss they are crucifying the Son of God all over again and subjecting him to public disgrace.

7Land that drinks in the rain often falling on it and that produces a crop useful to those for whom it is farmed receives the blessing of God. 8But land that produces thorns and thistles is worthless and is in danger of being cursed. In the end it will be burned.

9Even though we speak like this, dear friends, we are confident of better things in your case—things that accompany salvation. 10God is not unjust; he will as to forget your work and the love which you have shown toward His name, in having ministered and in still ministering to the saints.

11And we desire that each one of you show the same diligence so as to realize the full assurance of hope until the end,

12that you may not be sluggish, but imitators of those who through faith and patience inherit the promises.

13For when God made the promise to Abraham, since He could swear by no one greater, He swore by Himself,

14saying, "I WILL SURELY BLESS YOU, AND I WILL SURELY MULTIPLY YOU."

15And thus, having patiently waited, he obtained the promise.

16For men swear by one greater *than themselves*, and with them an oath *given* as confirmation is an end of every dispute.

17In the same way God, desiring even more to show to the heirs of the promise the unchangeableness of His purpose, interposed with an oath,

18in order that by two unchangeable things, in which it is impossible for God to lie, we may have strong encouragement, we who have fled for refuge in laying hold of the hope set before us.

19This hope we have as an anchor of the soul, *a hope* both sure and steadfast and one which enters within the veil,

20where Jesus has entered as a forerunner for us, having become a high priest forever according to the order of Melchizedek.

ὁ θεὸς ἐπιλαθέσθαι τοῦ ἔργου ὑμῶν
- ¹God [is] to be forgetful of the work of you

καὶ τῆς ἀγάπης ἧς ἐνεδείξασθε εἰς τὸ
and of the love which ye showed to the

ὄνομα αὐτοῦ, διακονήσαντες τοῖς ἁγίοις
name of him, having ministered to the saints

καὶ διακονοῦντες. 11 ἐπιθυμοῦμεν δὲ
and ministering. But we desire

ἕκαστον ὑμῶν τὴν αὐτὴν ἐνδείκνυσθαι
each one of you the ³same ¹to show

σπουδὴν πρὸς τὴν πληροφορίαν τῆς ἐλπίδος
eagerness to the full assurance of *the* hope

ἄχρι τέλους, 12 ἵνα μὴ νωθροὶ γένησθε,
unto [the] end, lest dull ye become,

μιμηταὶ δὲ τῶν διὰ πίστεως καὶ μακρο-
but imitators of the through faith and long-
[ones]

θυμίας κληρονομούντων τὰς ἐπαγγελίας.
suffering inheriting the promises.

13 Τῷ γὰρ Ἀβραὰμ ἐπαγγειλάμενος ὁ
For ³to Abraham ¹making promise the

θεός, ἐπεὶ κατ' οὐδενὸς εἶχεν μείζονος
¹God, since ³by ²no one ¹he had ⁴greater

ὀμόσαι, ὤμοσεν καθ' ἑαυτοῦ, 14 λέγων·
to swear, swore by himself, saying:

εἰ μὴν εὐλογῶν εὐλογήσω σε καὶ πληθύνων
If surely blessing I will bless thee and multiplying

πληθυνῶ σε· 15 καὶ οὕτως μακροθυμήσας
I will multiply thee; and so being longsuffering

ἐπέτυχεν τῆς ἐπαγγελίας. 16 ἄνθρωποι γὰρ
he obtained the promise. For men

κατὰ τοῦ μείζονος ὀμνύουσιν, καὶ πάσης
by the greater swear, and ⁹of all

αὐτοῖς ἀντιλογίας πέρας εἰς βεβαίωσιν ὁ
²[is] ⁴to ⁷contradiction ⁵an end ⁶for ⁹confirmation ¹the
them

ὅρκος· 17 ἐν ᾧ περισσότερον βουλόμενος
²oath; wherein ³more abundantly ¹resolving

ὁ θεὸς ἐπιδεῖξαι τοῖς κληρονόμοις τῆς
- ¹God to show to the heirs of the

ἐπαγγελίας τὸ ἀμετάθετον τῆς βουλῆς
promise the unchangeableness of the resolve

αὐτοῦ ἐμεσίτευσεν ὅρκῳ, 18 ἵνα διὰ
of him interposed by an in or- through
oath, der that

δύο πραγμάτων ἀμεταθέτων, ἐν οἷς ἀδύνατον
two ²things ¹unchangeable, in which impossible
[it was]

ψεύσασθαι θεόν, ἰσχυρὰν παράκλησιν ἔχωμεν
²to lie ¹God,ᵇ ²a strong ³consolation ¹we may
have[,]

οἱ καταφυγόντες κρατῆσαι τῆς προκειμένης
the [ones] having fled to lay hold of the ²set before [us]

ἐλπίδος· 19 ἣν ὡς ἄγκυραν ἔχομεν τῆς
¹hope; which as an anchor we have of the

ψυχῆς ἀσφαλῆ τε καὶ βεβαίαν καὶ
soul ²safe ¹both and firm and

εἰσερχομένην εἰς τὸ ἐσώτερον τοῦ κατα-
entering into the inner [side] of the veil,

πετάσματος, 20 ὅπου πρόδρομος ὑπὲρ ἡμῶν
where a forerunner on us
behalf of

εἰσῆλθεν Ἰησοῦς, κατὰ τὴν τάξιν Μελχισέ-
entered[,] Jesus, ⁶according ⁷the ⁸order ⁹of Melchise-
to

δεκ ἀρχιερεὺς γενόμενος εἰς τὸν αἰῶνα.
dec ⁵a high priest ¹becoming ²unto ³the ⁴age.

---

not forget your work and the love you have shown him as you have helped his people and continue to help them. 11We want each of you to show this same diligence to the very end, in order to make your hope sure. 12We do not want you to become lazy, but to imitate those who through faith and patience inherit what has been promised.

The Certainty of God's Promise

13When God made his promise to Abraham, since there was no one greater for him to swear by, he swore by himself, 14saying, "I will surely bless you and give you many descendants."ᵃ 15And so after waiting patiently, Abraham received what was promised.

16Men swear by someone greater than themselves, and the oath confirms what is said and puts an end to all argument. 17Because God wanted to make the unchanging nature of his purpose very clear to the heirs of what was promised, he confirmed it with an oath. 18God did this so that, by two unchangeable things in which it is impossible for God to lie, we who have fled to take hold of the hope offered to us may be greatly encouraged. 19We have this hope as an anchor for the soul, firm and secure. It enters the inner sanctuary behind the curtain, 20where Jesus, who went before us, has entered on our behalf. He has become a high priest forever, in the order of Melchizedek.

ᵃ14 Gen. 22:17

Chapter 7

Melchizedek's Priesthood Like Christ's

FOR this Melchizedek, king of Salem, priest of the Most High God, who met Abraham as he was returning from the slaughter of the kings and blessed him,

2to whom also Abraham apportioned a tenth part of all *the spoils*, was first of all, by the translation *of his name*, king of righteousness, and then also king of Salem, which is king of peace.

3Without father, without mother, without genealogy, having neither beginning of days nor end of life, but made like the Son of God, he abides a priest perpetually.

4Now observe how great this man was to whom Abraham, the patriarch, gave a tenth of the choicest spoils.

5And those indeed of the sons of Levi who receive the priest's office have commandment in the Law to collect a tenth from the people, that is, from their brethren, although these are descended from Abraham.

6But the one whose genealogy is not traced from them collected a tenth from Abraham, and blessed the one who had the promises.

7But without any dispute the lesser is blessed by the greater.

8And in this case mortal men receive tithes, but in that case one *receives them*, of whom it is witnessed that he lives on.

9And, so to speak, through Abraham even Levi, who received tithes, paid tithes,

10for he was still in the loins of his father when

---

7 Οὗτος γὰρ ὁ Μελχισέδεκ, βασιλεὺς
For this   -   Melchisedec,   king

Σαλήμ, ἱερεὺς τοῦ θεοῦ τοῦ ὑψίστου,
of Salem,   priest   -   ⁸God   ¹of the   ²most high,

ὁ συναντήσας 'Αβραὰμ ὑποστρέφοντι ἀπὸ
the [one] meeting   Abraham   returning   from

τῆς κοπῆς τῶν βασιλέων καὶ εὐλογήσας
the slaughter   of the   kings   and   blessing

αὐτόν, **2** ᾧ καὶ δεκάτην ἀπὸ πάντων
him,   to whom indeed   ²a tenth   ⁴from   ³all

ἐμέρισεν 'Αβραάμ, πρῶτον μὲν ἑρμηνευ-
¹divided   ¹Abraham,   firstly   on one   being inter-
                                hand

όμενος βασιλεὺς δικαιοσύνης, ἔπειτα δὲ καὶ
preted   King   of righteousness,   then   on the also
                                      other

βασιλεὺς Σαλήμ, ὅ ἐστιν βασιλεὺς εἰρήνης,
King   of Salem, which is   King   of peace,

3 ἀπάτωρ, ἀμήτωρ, ἀγενεαλόγητος, μήτε
without father, without mother,   without pedigree,   ²neither

ἀρχὴν ἡμερῶν μήτε ζωῆς τέλος ἔχων,
³beginning ⁴of days   ⁵nor   ⁷of life   ⁶end   ¹having,

ἀφωμοιωμένος δὲ τῷ υἱῷ τοῦ θεοῦ, μένει
but *having been* made   *to* the Son   -   of God, remains
   like

ἱερεὺς εἰς τὸ διηνεκές. **4** Θεωρεῖτε δὲ
a priest   in   the   perpetuity.   Now behold ye

πηλίκος οὗτος, ᾧ δεκάτην 'Αβραὰμ
how great   this man   to   ⁸a tenth   ²Abraham
              [was],   whom

ἔδωκεν ἐκ τῶν ἀκροθινίων ὁ πατριάρχης.
⁴gave   ⁶of   ⁷the   ⁸spoils   ¹the   ³patriarch.

5 καὶ οἱ μὲν ἐκ τῶν υἱῶν Λευὶ τὴν
And   ³the ¹on one   ⁵of   ⁴the   ⁵sons   ⁶of Levi   ⁸the
      [ones] hand

ἱερατείαν λαμβάνοντες ἐντολὴν ἔχουσιν
⁹priesthood   ⁷receiving   ¹¹a commandment   ¹⁰have

ἀποδεκατοῦν τὸν λαὸν κατὰ τὸν νόμον,
to take tithes   the   people   accord-   the   law,
from   ing to

τοῦτ' ἔστιν τοὺς ἀδελφοὺς αὐτῶν, καίπερ
this   is   the   brothers   of them,   though

ἐξεληλυθότας ἐκ τῆς ὀσφύος 'Αβραάμ·
having come forth   out of   the   loin[s]   of Abraham;

6 ὁ δὲ μὴ γενεαλογούμενος ἐξ αὐτῶν
¹the ¹on the not   counting [his] pedigree   from   them
[one]   other

δεδεκάτωκεν 'Αβραάμ, καὶ τὸν ἔχοντα
has tithed   Abraham,   and   ³the [one] ¹having

τὰς ἐπαγγελίας εὐλόγηκεν. **7** χωρὶς δὲ
⁴the   ⁵promises   ¹has blessed.   And without

πάσης ἀντιλογίας τὸ ἔλαττον ὑπὸ τοῦ
all(any)   contradiction   the   less   ²by   ³the

κρείττονος εὐλογεῖται. **8** καὶ ὧδε μὲν
⁴better   ¹is blessed.   And   here   on one
                                   hand

δεκάτας ἀποθνήσκοντες ἄνθρωποι λαμβά-
⁴tithes   ¹dying   ²men   ³re-

νουσιν, ἐκεῖ δὲ μαρτυρούμενος ὅτι ζῆ.
ceive,   there   on the   being witnessed   that   he
          other   lives.

9 καὶ ὡς ἔπος εἰπεῖν, δι' 'Αβραὰμ
And   as   a word   to say,   through   Abraham
     =so to speak,

καὶ Λευὶς ὁ δεκάτας λαμβάνων δεδε-
indeed   Levi   ¹the [one] ²tithes   ³receiving   has

κάτωται· **10** ἔτι γὰρ ἐν τῇ ὀσφύϊ τοῦ
been tithed;   for   ²yet   ³in   ⁴the   ⁵loin[s]   ⁶of
                                       the(his)

Chapter 7

Melchizedek the Priest

THIS Melchizedek was king of Salem and priest of God Most High. He met Abraham returning from the defeat of the kings and blessed him, 2and Abraham gave him a tenth of everything. First, his name means "king of righteousness"; then also, "king of Salem" means "king of peace." 3Without father or mother, without genealogy, without beginning of days or end of life, like the Son of God he remains a priest forever.

4Just think how great he was: Even the patriarch Abraham gave him a tenth of the plunder! 5Now the law requires the descendants of Levi who become priests to collect a tenth from the people—that is, their brothers—even though their brothers are descended from Abraham. 6This man, however, did not trace his descent from Levi, yet he collected a tenth from Abraham and blessed him who had the promises. 7And without doubt the lesser person is blessed by the greater. 8In the one case, the tenth is collected by men who die; but in the other case, by him who is declared to be living. 9One might even say that Levi, who collects the tenth, paid the tenth through Abraham, 10because when Melchizedek

Melchizedek met him.

11Now if perfection was through the Levitical priesthood (for on the basis of it the people received the Law), what further need *was there* for another priest to arise according to the order of Melchizedek, and not be designated according to the order of Aaron? 12For when the priesthood is changed, of necessity there takes place a change of law also. 13For the one concerning whom these things are spoken belongs to another tribe, from which no one has officiated at the altar. 14For it is evident that our Lord was descended from Judah, a tribe with reference to which Moses spoke nothing concerning priests. 15And this is clearer still, if another priest arises according to the likeness of Melchizedek, 16who has become *such* not on the basis of a law of physical requirement, but according to the power of an indestructible life. 17For it is witnessed *of Him*,

"THOU ART A PRIEST FOREVER
ACCORDING TO THE ORDER OF MELCHIZEDEK."

18For, on the one hand, there is a setting aside of a former commandment because of its weakness and uselessness 19(for the Law made nothing perfect), and on the other hand there is a bringing in of a better hope, through which we draw near to God. 20And inasmuch as *it was* not without an oath 21(for they indeed became priests without an oath, but

---

πατρὸς ἦν ὅτε συνήντησεν αὐτῷ Μελχισέ-
[father] [he was] [when] [met] [him] [Melchise-

δεκ. 11 Εἰ μὲν οὖν τελείωσις διὰ τῆς
dec.] If - therefore perfection [through] [the

Λευιτικῆς ἱερωσύνης ἦν, ὁ λαὸς γὰρ
[Levitical] [priestly office] [was], [the] [people] [for

ἐπ᾽ αὐτῆς νενομοθέτηται, τίς ἔτι χρεία
[under] [it] has been furnished why yet need
with law,

κατὰ τὴν τάξιν Μελχισέδεκ ἕτερον
[was there] [the] [order] [of Melchisedec] [another
for] [accord-
ing to

ἀνίστασθαι ἱερέα καὶ οὐ κατὰ τὴν τάξιν
[to arise] [priest] and not [accord- [the] [order
ing to

Ἀαρὼν λέγεσθαι; 12 μετατιθεμένης γὰρ
[of Aaron] [to be said(named)? for [being changed

τῆς ἱερωσύνης ἐξ ἀνάγκης καὶ νόμου
[the] [priestly office] [of] [necessity and [of law

μετάθεσις γίνεται. 13 ἐφ᾽ ὃν γὰρ λέγεται
[a change] [there [[he] [with] [whom] [For [is(are) said
occurs. respect to

ταῦτα, φυλῆς ἑτέρας μετέσχηκεν, ἀφ᾽
[these things, [tribe] [of another] [has partaken, from

ἧς οὐδεὶς προσέσχηκεν τῷ θυσιαστηρίῳ·
which no one has devoted himself to the altar.

14 πρόδηλον γὰρ ὅτι ἐξ Ἰούδα ἀνατέταλκεν
for it is perfectly clear that out of Juda has risen

ὁ κύριος ἡμῶν, εἰς ἣν φυλὴν περὶ ἱερέων
the Lord of us, as to which tribe concerning priests

οὐδὲν Μωϋσῆς ἐλάλησεν. 15 καὶ περισ-
[nothing] [Moses] [spoke. And more

σότερον ἔτι κατάδηλόν ἐστιν, εἰ κατὰ
abundantly still quite clear is it, if according to

τὴν ὁμοιότητα Μελχισέδεκ ἀνίσταται ἱερεὺς
the likeness of Melchisedec arises priest

ἕτερος, 16 ὃς οὐ κατὰ νόμον ἐντολῆς
another, who not accord- [the] law [command-
ing to ment

σαρκίνης γέγονεν ἀλλὰ κατὰ δύναμιν ζωῆς
[of a fleshy has become but accord- [the] power life
ing to

ἀκαταλύτου. 17 μαρτυρεῖται γὰρ ὅτι σὺ
of an indissoluble. For it is witnessed that Thou

ἱερεὺς εἰς τὸν αἰῶνα κατὰ τὴν τάξιν
a priest unto the age according to the order

Μελχισέδεκ. 18 ἀθέτησις μὲν γὰρ γίνεται
of Melchisedec. [an annul- [on one [For [there
ment hand comes about

προαγούσης ἐντολῆς διὰ τὸ αὐτῆς ἀσθενὲς
of [the] command- because [the] [of it [weak[ness]
preceding ment of

καὶ ἀνωφελές, 19 οὐδὲν γὰρ ἐτελείωσεν
[and] [unprofitable[ness], for [nothing] [perfected

ὁ νόμος, ἐπεισαγωγὴ δὲ κρείττονος ἐλπίδος,
[the] [law, [a bringing in [on the of a better hope,
other

δι᾽ ἧς ἐγγίζομεν τῷ θεῷ. 20 καὶ καθ᾽
through we draw near - to God. And in pro-
which

ὅσον οὐ χωρὶς ὁρκωμοσίας, — οἱ μὲν
portion not without oath-taking, [the [on one
as (they) hand

γὰρ χωρὶς ὁρκωμοσίας εἰσὶν ἱερεῖς
[for [without [oath-taking [are [priests

---

met Abraham, Levi was still in the body of his ancestor.

Jesus Like Melchizedek

11If perfection could have been attained through the Levitical priesthood (for on the basis of it the law was given to the people), why was there still need for another priest to come—one in the order of Melchizedek, not in the order of Aaron? 12For when there is a change of the priesthood, there must also be a change of the law. 13He of whom these things are said belonged to a different tribe, and no one from that tribe has ever served at the altar. 14For it is clear that our Lord descended from Judah, and in regard to that tribe Moses said nothing about priests. 15And what we have said is even more clear if another priest like Melchizedek appears, 16one who has become a priest not on the basis of a regulation as to his ancestry but on the basis of the power of an indestructible life. 17For it is declared:

"You are a priest forever,
in the order of Melchizedek."[b]

18The former regulation is set aside because it was weak and useless 19(for the law made nothing perfect), and a better hope is introduced, by which we draw near to God.
20And it was not without an oath! Others became priests without any oath,

---

He with an oath through the One who said to Him,
"THE LORD HAS SWORN AND WILL NOT CHANGE HIS MIND,
'THOU ART A PRIEST FOREVER' ");
22so much the more also Jesus has become the guarantee of a better covenant.
23And the *former* priests, on the one hand, existed in greater numbers, because they were prevented by death from continuing,
24but He, on the other hand, because He abides forever, holds His priesthood permanently.
25Hence, also, He is able to save forever those who draw near to God through Him, since He always lives to make intercession for them.
26For it was fitting that we should have such a high priest, holy, innocent, undefiled, separated from sinners and exalted above the heavens;
27who does not need daily, like those high priests, to offer up sacrifices, first for His own sins, and then for the *sins* of the people, because this He did once for all when He offered up Himself.
28For the Law appoints men as high priests who are weak, but the word of the oath, which came after the Law, *appoints* a Son, made perfect forever.

γεγονότες, **21** ὁ δὲ μετὰ ὁρκωμοσίας διὰ
⁵having become, the the on the with oath-taking through
(he) other

τοῦ λέγοντος πρὸς αὐτόν· ὤμοσεν κύριος,
the (one) saying to him: swore [The] Lord,

καὶ οὐ μεταμεληθήσεται· σὺ ἱερεὺς εἰς
and will not change [his] mind: Thou [art] a priest unto

τὸν αἰῶνα· — **22** κατὰ τοσοῦτο καὶ
the age;) by so much indeed

κρείττονος διαθήκης γέγονεν ἔγγυος Ἰησοῦς.
⁴of a better ⁵covenant ²has become ³surety ¹Jesus.

23 καὶ οἱ μὲν πλείονές εἰσιν γεγονότες
And the on one ²many ¹are ³having become
(they) hand

ἱερεῖς διὰ τὸ θανάτῳ κωλύεσθαι παραμέ-
⁴priests because the ⁵by death ¹to be prevented ²to con-
of =being prevented by death from continuing;

νειν· **24** ὁ δὲ διὰ τὸ μένειν αὐτὸν εἰς
tinue; the on the because the to remain him unto
(he) other of
=because he remains

τὸν αἰῶνα ἀπαράβατον ἔχει τὴν ἱερωσύνην·
the age ²intransmissible ¹has ⁴the ³priestly office;

25 ὅθεν καὶ σώζειν εἰς τὸ παντελὲς
whence indeed ¹to save ²to ⁴the ⁵entire
= entirely

δύναται τοὺς προσερχομένους δι' αὐτοῦ
¹he is able the [ones] ¹approaching ²through ⁴him

τῷ θεῷ, πάντοτε ζῶν εἰς τὸ ἐντυγχάνειν
– ²to God, always living *for* the to intercede

ὑπὲρ αὐτῶν. **26** τοιοῦτος γὰρ ἡμῖν καὶ
on be- them. For ²such ⁴to us ³indeed
half of

ἔπρεπεν ἀρχιερεύς, ὅσιος, ἄκακος, ἀμίαντος,
⁴was ²a high priest, holy, harmless, undefiled,
suitable

κεχωρισμένος ἀπὸ τῶν ἁμαρτωλῶν, καὶ
having been from – sinners, and
separated

ὑψηλότερος τῶν οὐρανῶν γενόμενος· **27** ὃς
higher [than] the heavens becoming; who

οὐκ ἔχει καθ' ἡμέραν ἀνάγκην, ὥσπερ
has not ²daily ¹necessity, as

οἱ ἀρχιερεῖς, πρότερον ὑπὲρ τῶν ἰδίων
the high priests, firstly on behalf of the(his) own

ἁμαρτιῶν θυσίας ἀναφέρειν, ἔπειτα τῶν
sins sacrifices to offer up, then the [sins]

τοῦ λαοῦ· τοῦτο γὰρ ἐποίησεν ἐφάπαξ
of the people; for this he did once for all

ἑαυτὸν ἀνενέγκας. **28** ὁ νόμος γὰρ
himself offering up. For the law

ἀνθρώπους καθίστησιν ἀρχιερεῖς ἔχοντας
²men ¹appoints ⁵high priests ³having

ἀσθένειαν, ὁ λόγος δὲ τῆς ὁρκωμοσίας
⁴weakness, but the word of the oath-taking

τῆς μετὰ τὸν νόμον υἱὸν εἰς τὸν αἰῶνα
– after the law a Son ²unto ³the ⁴age
[appoints]

τετελειωμένον.
¹having been perfected.

Chapter 8

A Better Ministry

NOW the main point in what has been said *is this*: we have such a high priest, who has taken His seat at the right hand of the throne of the Majesty in the

8 Κεφάλαιον δὲ ἐπὶ τοῖς λεγομένοις,
Now a summary over(of) the things being said,

τοιοῦτον ἔχομεν ἀρχιερέα, ὃς ἐκάθισεν
²such ¹we have a high priest, who sat

ἐν δεξιᾷ τοῦ θρόνου τῆς μεγαλωσύνης
at [the] right of the throne of the greatness

21but he became a priest with an oath when God said to him:

"The Lord has sworn and will not change his mind:
'You are a priest forever.' "[b]

22Because of this oath, Jesus has become the guarantee of a better covenant.
23Now there have been many of those priests, since death prevented them from continuing in office;
24but because Jesus lives forever, he has a permanent priesthood.
25Therefore he is able to save completely[c] those who come to God through him, because he always lives to intercede for them.
26Such a high priest meets our need—one who is holy, blameless, pure, set apart from sinners, exalted above the heavens.
27Unlike the other high priests, he does not need to offer sacrifices day after day, first for his own sins, and then for the sins of the people. He sacrificed for their sins once for all when he offered himself.
28For the law appoints as high priests men who are weak; but the oath, which came after the law, appointed the Son, who has been made perfect forever.

Chapter 8

The High Priest of a New Covenant

THE point of what we are saying is this: We do have such a high priest, who sat down at the right hand of the throne of the Majesty in heaven, 2and

c25 Or forever

heavens,
2a minister in the sanctuary, and in the true tabernacle, which the Lord
pitched, not man.
3For every high priest is
appointed to offer both
gifts and sacrifices; hence it
is necessary that this *high
priest* also have something
to offer.
4Now if He were on
earth, He would not be a
priest at all, since there are
those who offer the gifts according to the Law;
5who serve a copy and
shadow of the heavenly
things, just as Moses was
warned *by God* when he
was about to erect the tabernacle; for, "SEE," He
says, "THAT YOU MAKE all
things ACCORDING TO THE
PATTERN WHICH WAS SHOWN
YOU ON THE MOUNTAIN."
6But now He has ob-
tained a more excellent
ministry, by as much as He
is also the mediator of a
better covenant, which has
been enacted on better
promises.

A New Covenant
7For if that first *cov-
enant* had been faultless,
there would have been no
occasion sought for a sec-
ond.
8For finding fault with
them, He says,
"BEHOLD, DAYS ARE
COMING, SAYS THE
LORD,
WHEN I WILL EFFECT A
NEW COVENANT
WITH THE HOUSE OF IS-
RAEL AND WITH THE
HOUSE OF JUDAH;
9 NOT LIKE THE COV-
ENANT WHICH I MADE
WITH THEIR FATHERS
ON THE DAY WHEN I
TOOK THEM BY THE
HAND
TO LEAD THEM OUT OF
THE LAND OF EGYPT;
FOR THEY DID NOT CON-
TINUE IN MY COV-
ENANT,
AND I DID NOT CARE
FOR THEM, SAYS THE
LORD.

ἐν τοῖς οὐρανοῖς, 2 τῶν ἁγίων λειτουργὸς
in the heavens, ³of the ²holy things ¹a minister

καὶ τῆς σκηνῆς τῆς ἀληθινῆς, ἣν ἔπηξεν
and of the ²tabernacle ¹true, which ³erected

ὁ κύριος, οὐκ ἄνθρωπος. 3 Πᾶς γὰρ
¹the ²Lord, not man. For every

ἀρχιερεὺς εἰς τὸ προσφέρειν δῶρά τε
high priest for the ⁵to offer ⁴gifts ⁵both

καὶ θυσίας καθίσταται· ὅθεν ἀναγκαῖον
⁶and ⁶sacrifices ¹is appointed; whence [it is] necessary

ἔχειν τι καὶ τοῦτον ὃ προσενέγκῃ. 4 εἰ
²to have ⁴some- ³also ¹this which he may offer. If
thing [priest]

μὲν οὖν ἦν ἐπὶ γῆς, οὐδ' ἂν ἦν ἱερεύς,
– there- he on earth, he would not be a priest,
fore were

ὄντων τῶν προσφερόντων κατὰ νόμον
[there] the [ones] offering³ ³according to ⁴law
being

τὰ δῶρα· 5 οἵτινες ὑποδείγματι καὶ σκιᾷ
¹the ²gifts; who ²an example ²and ⁴a
shadow

λατρεύουσιν τῶν ἐπουρανίων, καθὼς
¹serve of the heavenly things, as

κεχρημάτισται Μωϋσῆς μέλλων ἐπιτελεῖν
³has been warned ¹Moses being about to complete

τὴν σκηνήν· ὅρα γάρ φησιν, ποιήσεις
the tabernacle; for See[,] he says, thou shalt
make

πάντα κατὰ τὸν τύπον τὸν δειχθέντα
all according to the pattern – shown
things

σοι ἐν τῷ ὄρει· 6 νῦν δὲ διαφορωτέρας
to thee in the mount; but now ²a more excellent

τέτυχεν λειτουργίας, ὅσῳ καὶ κρείττονός
¹he has ministry, by so indeed ⁴of a better
obtained much

ἐστιν διαθήκης μεσίτης, ἥτις ἐπὶ κρείττοσιν
¹[as] ⁵covenant ³mediator, which ⁵on ⁶better
³he is

ἐπαγγελίαις νενομοθέτηται. 7 εἰ γὰρ ἡ
⁴promises ¹has been enacted. For if –

πρώτη ἐκείνη ἦν ἄμεμπτος, οὐκ ἂν
²first [covenant] ¹that was faultless, ³would not

δευτέρας ἐζητεῖτο τόπος. 8 μεμφόμενος
⁶of(for) a ²have been ¹place. finding fault [with]
second sought

γὰρ αὐτοὺς λέγει· ἰδοὺ ἡμέραι ἔρχονται,
For them he says: Behold[,] days are coming,

λέγει κύριος, καὶ συντελέσω ἐπὶ τὸν
says [the] Lord, and I will effect over the

οἶκον Ἰσραὴλ καὶ ἐπὶ τὸν οἶκον Ἰούδα
household of Israel and over the household of Juda

διαθήκην καινήν, 9 οὐ κατὰ τὴν διαθήκην
covenant a new, not accord- the covenant
ing to

ἣν ἐποίησα τοῖς πατράσιν αὐτῶν ἐν
which I made with the fathers of them in

ἡμέρα ἐπιλαβομένου μου τῆς χειρὸς αὐτῶν
[the] day taking me³ the hand of them
=when I took

ἐξαγαγεῖν αὐτοὺς ἐκ γῆς Αἰγύπτου, ὅτι
to lead forth them out [the] of Egypt, because
of land

αὐτοὶ οὐκ ἐνέμειναν ἐν τῇ διαθήκῃ μου,
they continued not in in the covenant of me,

κἀγὼ ἠμέλησα αὐτῶν, λέγει κύριος. 10 ὅτι
and I disregarded them, says [the] Lord. Because

who serves in the sanctu-
ary, the true tabernacle set
up by the Lord, not by
man.
3Every high priest is ap-
pointed to offer both gifts
and sacrifices, and so it was
necessary for this one also
to have something to offer.
4If he were on earth, he
would not be a priest, for
there are already men who
offer the gifts prescribed by
the law. 5They serve at a
sanctuary that is a copy and
shadow of what is in heav-
en. This is why Moses was
warned when he was about
to build the tabernacle:
"See to it that you make
everything according to the
pattern shown you on the
mountain." *d* 6But the ministry Jesus has received is
as superior to theirs as the
covenant of which he is mediator is superior to the old
one, and it is founded on
better promises.
7For if there had been
nothing wrong with that
first covenant, no place
would have been sought for
another. 8But God found
fault with the people and
said *e*:

"The time is coming,
declares the Lord,
when I will make a new
covenant
with the house of Israel
and with the house of
Judah.
9It will not be like the
covenant
I made with their
forefathers
when I took them by the
hand
to lead them out of
Egypt,
because they did not
remain faithful to
my covenant,
and I turned away from
them,
declares the Lord.

*d*5 Exodus 25:40
*e*8 Some manuscripts may be
translated *fault and said to the
people.*

10"FOR THIS IS THE COV-
ENANT THAT I WILL
MAKE WITH THE
HOUSE OF ISRAEL
AFTER THOSE DAYS,
SAYS THE LORD:
I WILL PUT MY LAWS
INTO THEIR MINDS,
AND I WILL WRITE
THEM UPON THEIR
HEARTS.
AND I WILL BE THEIR
GOD,
AND THEY SHALL BE
MY PEOPLE.
11"AND THEY SHALL NOT
TEACH EVERYONE HIS
FELLOW CITIZEN,
AND EVERYONE HIS
BROTHER, SAYING,
'KNOW THE LORD,'
FOR ALL SHALL KNOW
ME,
FROM THE LEAST TO
THE GREATEST OF
THEM.
12"FOR I WILL BE MERCI-
FUL TO THEIR INIQUI-
TIES,
AND I WILL REMEMBER
THEIR SINS NO MORE."
13When He said, "A new
covenant," He has made
the first obsolete. But
whatever is becoming ob-
solete and growing old is
ready to disappear.

αὕτη ἡ διαθήκη ἣν διαθήσομαι τῷ οἴκῳ
this [is] the covenant which I will with house-
covenant the hold

'Ισραήλ μετὰ τὰς ἡμέρας ἐκείνας, λέγει
of Israel after those days, says

κύριος, διδοὺς νόμους μου εἰς τὴν διάνοιαν
[the] Lord, giving laws of me into the mind

αὐτῶν, καὶ ἐπὶ καρδίας αὐτῶν ἐπιγράψω
of them, and on hearts of them I will inscribe

αὐτούς, καὶ ἔσομαι αὐτοῖς εἰς θεὸν
them, and I will be to them for God

καὶ αὐτοὶ ἔσονταί μοι εἰς λαόν. 11 καὶ
and they shall be to me for a people. And

οὐ μὴ διδάξωσιν ἕκαστος τὸν πολίτην
by no means may they teach each man the citizen

αὐτοῦ καὶ ἕκαστος τὸν ἀδελφὸν αὐτοῦ,
of him and each man the brother of him,

λέγων· γνῶθι τὸν κύριον, ὅτι πάντες
saying: Know thou the Lord, because all

εἰδήσουσίν με ἀπὸ μικροῦ ἕως μεγάλου
will know me from little to great

αὐτῶν. 12 ὅτι ἵλεως ἔσομαι ταῖς ἀδικίαις
of them. Because merciful I will be to the unrighteous-
nesses

αὐτῶν, καὶ τῶν ἁμαρτιῶν αὐτῶν οὐ μὴ
of them, and the sins of them by no means

μνησθῶ ἔτι. 13 ἐν τῷ λέγειν καινὴν
I may remember more. In the to say⁰ 'new'
=When he says

πεπαλαίωκεν τὴν πρώτην· τὸ δὲ παλαι-
he has made old the first; and the thing being

ούμενον καὶ γηράσκον ἐγγὺς ἀφανισμοῦ.
made old and growing aged [is] near vanishing.

10This is the covenant I
will make with the
house of Israel
after that time,
declares the Lord.
I will put my laws in
their minds
and write them on their
hearts.
I will be their God,
and they will be my
people.
11No longer will a man
teach his neighbor,
or a man his brother,
saying, 'Know the
Lord,'
because they will all
know me,
from the least of them
to the greatest.
12For I will forgive their
wickedness
and will remember
their sins no
more."ᶠ

13By calling this covenant
"new," he has made the
first one obsolete; and what
is obsolete and aging will
soon disappear.

Chapter 9

The Old and the New

NOW even the first *cov-
enant* had regulations
of divine worship and the
earthly sanctuary.
²For there was a taber-
nacle prepared, the outer
one, in which *were* the
lampstand and the table
and the sacred bread; this is
called the holy place.
³And behind the second
veil, there was a tabernacle
which is called the Holy of
Holies,
⁴having a golden altar of
incense and the ark of the
covenant covered on all
sides with gold, in which
was a golden jar holding the
manna, and Aaron's rod
which budded, and the ta-
bles of the covenant.
⁵And above it *were* the
cherubim of glory over-
shadowing the mercy seat;
but of these things we can-

Chapter 9

9 Εἶχε μὲν οὖν καὶ ἡ πρώτη δικαι-
⁵had ¹So then ²both ³the ⁴first ordin-
⁴[covenant]

ώματα λατρείας τό τε ἅγιον κοσμικόν.
ances of service ³the ¹and ⁴holy place ²worldly.

2 σκηνὴ γὰρ κατεσκευάσθη ἡ πρώτη,
For a tabernacle was prepared[,] the first,

ἐν ᾗ ἥ τε λυχνία καὶ ἡ τράπεζα καὶ
in which ³the ¹both lampstand and the table and
[were]

ἡ πρόθεσις τῶν ἄρτων, ἥτις λέγεται
the setting forth of the loaves, which is called

Ἅγια· 3 μετὰ δὲ τὸ δεύτερον καταπέτασμα
Holy; and after the second veil

σκηνὴ ἡ λεγομένη Ἅγια Ἁγίων, 4 χρυσοῦν
a taber- the *being* called Holy of Holies, ²a golden
nacle [one]

ἔχουσα θυμιατήριον καὶ τὴν κιβωτὸν τῆς
¹having altar and the ark of the

διαθήκης περικεκαλυμμένην πάντοθεν χρυσίῳ,
covenant *having been* covered round on all sides with gold,

ἐν ᾗ στάμνος χρυσῆ ἔχουσα τὸ μάννα
in which pot a golden having the manna
[were]

καὶ ἡ ῥάβδος 'Ααρὼν ἡ βλαστήσασα
and the rod of Aaron – budded

καὶ αἱ πλάκες τῆς διαθήκης, 5 ὑπεράνω
and the tablets of the covenant, ²above

δὲ αὐτῆς Χερουβὶν δόξης κατασκιάζοντα
¹and it cherubim of glory overshadowing

τὸ ἱλαστήριον· περὶ ὧν οὐκ ἔστιν νῦν
the mercy-seat; concern- which there is not now
ing things [?time]

Worship in the Earthly
Tabernacle

NOW the first covenant
had regulations for
worship and also an earthly
sanctuary. ²A tabernacle
was set up. In its first room
were the lampstand, the table and the consecrated
bread; this was called the
Holy Place. ³Behind the
second curtain was a room
called the Most Holy Place,
⁴which had the golden altar
of incense and the gold-
covered ark of the cove-
nant. This ark contained
the gold jar of manna, Aaron's staff that had budded,
and the stone tablets of the
covenant. ⁵Above the ark
were the cherubim of the
Glory, overshadowing the
atonement cover.ᵍ But we

ᶠ*12* Jer. 31:31-34
ᵍ*5* Traditionally *the mercy seat*

not now speak in detail.

6Now when these things have been thus prepared, the priests are continually entering the outer tabernacle, performing the divine worship,

7but into the second only the high priest *enters*, once a year, not without *taking* blood, which he offers for himself and for the sins of the people committed in ignorance.

8The Holy Spirit *is* signifying this, that the way into the holy place has not yet been disclosed, while the outer tabernacle is still standing,

9which *is* a symbol for the present time. Accordingly both gifts and sacrifices are offered which cannot make the worshiper perfect in conscience,

10since they *relate* only to food and drink and various washings, regulations imposed until a time of reformation.

11But when Christ appeared *as* a high priest of the good things ᶠto come, He entered through the greater and more perfect tabernacle, not made with hands, that is to say, not of this creation;

12and not through the blood of goats and calves, but through His own blood, He entered the holy place once for all, having obtained eternal redemption.

13For if the blood of goats and bulls and the ashes of a heifer sprinkling those who have been defiled, sanctify for the cleansing of the flesh,

14how much more will the blood of Christ, who through the eternal Spirit

---

λέγειν κατὰ μέρος. 6 τούτων δὲ οὕτως
to speak in detail. These things now thus
=Now when these things had

κατεσκευασμένων εἰς μὲν τὴν πρώτην
having been prepared° ⁸into ¹on one ⁷the ⁸first
been thus prepared hand

σκηνὴν διὰ παντὸς εἰσίασιν οἱ ἱερεῖς
⁸tabernacle ⁴at all times ⁵go in ⁵the ⁵priests

τὰς λατρείας ἐπιτελοῦντες, 7 εἰς δὲ τὴν
¹¹the ¹²services ¹⁰accomplishing, ⁵into ¹on the ⁸the
other

δευτέραν ἅπαξ τοῦ ἐνιαυτοῦ μόνος ὁ
⁵second ⁸once ⁹of(in) the ¹⁰year [goes] ⁴the
⁷alone

ἀρχιερεύς, οὐ χωρὶς αἵματος ὃ προσφέρει
⁵high priest, not without blood which he offers

ὑπὲρ ἑαυτοῦ καὶ τῶν τοῦ λαοῦ ἀγνοημά-
on be- himself and ¹the ⁵of the ⁴people ⁸ignor-
half of

των, 8 τοῦτο δηλοῦντος τοῦ πνεύματος
ances, ⁵this ⁴showing ¹the ⁵Spirit

τοῦ ἁγίου, μήπω πεφανερῶσθαι τὴν τῶν
- ¹Holy,ᵃ ⁵not yet ⁴to have been ¹the ⁸of the
manifested

ἁγίων ὁδὸν ἔτι τῆς πρώτης σκηνῆς
⁴holies ⁸way ¹⁰still ⁷the ⁸first ⁹tabernacle

ἐχούσης στάσιν, 9 ἥτις παραβολὴ εἰς τὸν
¹¹havingᵃ ¹²standing, which [was] a parable for the

καιρὸν τὸν ἐνεστηκότα, καθ' ἣν δῶρά
time - present, accord- which ¹gifts
ing to

τε καὶ θυσίαι προσφέρονται μὴ δυνάμεναι
¹both and sacrifices are being offered not being able

κατὰ συνείδησιν τελειῶσαι τὸν λατρεύοντα,
in respect conscience to perfect the [one] serving,
of

10 μόνον ἐπὶ βρώμασιν καὶ πόμασιν καὶ
only on foods and drinks and

διαφόροις βαπτισμοῖς, δικαιώματα σαρκὸς
various washings, ordinances of flesh

μέχρι καιροῦ διορθώσεως ἐπικείμενα.
¹until ³a time ⁴of amendment ¹being imposed.

11 Χριστὸς δὲ παραγενόμενος ἀρχιερεὺς
But Christ having appeared a high priest

τῶν γενομένων ἀγαθῶν, διὰ τῆς μείζονος
¹of the ³having come ²good things, through the greater
about

καὶ τελειοτέρας σκηνῆς οὐ χειροποιήτου,
and more perfect tabernacle not made by hand,

τοῦτ' ἔστιν οὐ ταύτης τῆς κτίσεως,
this is not of this - creation,

12 οὐδὲ δι' αἵματος τράγων καὶ μόσχων,
nor through blood of goats and of calves,

διὰ δὲ τοῦ ἰδίου αἵματος εἰσῆλθεν ἐφάπαξ
but the own blood entered once for
through (his) all

εἰς τὰ ἅγια, αἰωνίαν λύτρωσιν εὑράμενος.
into the holies, eternal redemption having found.

13 εἰ γὰρ τὸ αἷμα τράγων καὶ ταύρων
For if the blood of goats and of bulls

καὶ σποδὸς δαμάλεως ῥαντίζουσα τοὺς
and ashes of a heifer sprinkling the [ones]

κεκοινωμένους ἁγιάζει πρὸς τὴν τῆς
having been polluted sanctifies to ¹the ³of the

σαρκὸς καθαρότητα, 14 πόσῳ μᾶλλον τὸ
⁴flesh ²cleanness, by how much more the

αἷμα τοῦ Χριστοῦ, ὃς διὰ πνεύματος
blood - of Christ, who through ¹Spirit

---

cannot discuss these things in detail now.

6When everything had been arranged like this, the priests entered regularly into the outer room to carry on their ministry. 7But only the high priest entered the inner room, and that only once a year, and never without blood, which he offered for himself and for the sins the people had committed in ignorance. 8The Holy Spirit was showing by this that the way into the Most Holy Place had not yet been disclosed as long as the first tabernacle was still standing. 9This is an illustration for the present time, indicating that the gifts and sacrifices being offered were not able to clear the conscience of the worshiper. 10They are only a matter of food and drink and various ceremonial washings—external regulations applying until the time of the new order.

The Blood of Christ

11When Christ came as high priest of the good things that are already here, ʰ he went through the greater and more perfect tabernacle that is not manmade, that is to say, not a part of this creation. 12He did not enter by means of the blood of goats and calves; but he entered the Most Holy Place once for all by his own blood, having obtained eternal redemption. 13The blood of goats and bulls and the ashes of a heifer sprinkled on those who are ceremonially unclean sanctify them so that they are outwardly clean. 14How much more, then, will the blood of Christ, who through the eternal Spirit offered him-

---

ᶠSome ancient mss. read *that have come*

ʰ11 Some early manuscripts *are to come*

offered Himself without blemish to God, cleanse your conscience from dead works to serve the living God?

15And for this reason He is the mediator of a new covenant, in order that since a death has taken place for the redemption of the transgressions that were *committed* under the first covenant, those who have been called may receive the promise of the eternal inheritance.

16For where a covenant is, there must of necessity be the death of the one who made it.

17For a covenant is valid *only* when men are dead, /for it is never in force while the one who made it lives.

18Therefore even the first *covenant* was not inaugurated without blood.

19For when every commandment had been spoken by Moses to all the people according to the Law, he took the blood of the calves and the goats, with water and scarlet wool and hyssop, and sprinkled both the book itself and all the people,

20saying, "THIS IS THE BLOOD OF THE COVENANT WHICH GOD COMMANDED YOU."

21And in the same way he sprinkled both the tabernacle and all the vessels of the ministry with the blood.

22And according to the Law, *one may* almost *say*, all things are cleansed with blood, and without shedding of blood there is no forgiveness.

23Therefore it was necessary for the copies of the things in the heavens to be cleansed with these, but

---

αἰωνίου ἑαυτὸν προσήνεγκεν ἄμωμον τῷ
1[the] eternal 4himself 3offered unblemished -

θεῷ, καθαριεῖ τὴν συνείδησιν ἡμῶν ἀπὸ
to God, will cleanse the conscience of us from

νεκρῶν ἔργων εἰς τὸ λατρεύειν θεῷ
dead works for the to serve 1God

ζῶντι. 15 καὶ διὰ τοῦτο διαθήκης καινῆς
1[the] living. And therefore 4covenant 5of a new

μεσίτης ἐστίν, ὅπως θανάτου γενομένου⁴
1mediator 1he is, so as death having occurred⁴

εἰς ἀπολύτρωσιν τῶν ἐπὶ τῇ πρώτῃ
for redemption 1of the 2under * 4the 5first

διαθήκῃ παραβάσεων τὴν ἐπαγγελίαν
6covenant 1transgressions 10the 11promise

λάβωσιν οἱ κεκλημένοι τῆς αἰωνίου
9may receive 7the 8having been 12of the 13eternal
[ones] called

κληρονομίας. 16 Ὅπου γὰρ διαθήκη,
14inheritance. For where [there is] a
covenant,

θάνατον ἀνάγκη φέρεσθαι τοῦ διαθεμένου·
3[the] death 1[there is] 2to be offered 4of the 5making
necessity [one] covenant;

17 διαθήκη γὰρ ἐπὶ νεκροῖς βεβαία, ἐπεὶ
for a covenant over dead [? bodies] [is] firm, since

μήποτε ἰσχύει ὅτε ζῇ ὁ διαθέμενος.
never has it when 3lives 1the 2making
strength [one] covenant.

18 ὅθεν οὐδὲ ἡ πρώτη χωρὶς αἵματος
Whence neither the first [covenant] 2without 3blood

ἐγκεκαίνισται. 19 λαληθείσης γὰρ πάσης
1has been dedicated. For 2having been spoken 1every

ἐντολῆς κατὰ τὸν νόμον ὑπὸ Μωϋσέως
2command- 1accord- 10the 11law 4by 5Moses
ment⁴ ing to

παντὶ τῷ λαῷ, λαβὼν τὸ αἷμα τῶν
6to all 7the 8people, taking the blood of the

μόσχων καὶ τῶν τράγων μετὰ ὕδατος
calves and of the goats with water

καὶ ἐρίου κοκκίνου καὶ ὑσσώπου, αὐτό
and 2wool 1scarlet and hyssop, 2it[self]

τε τὸ βιβλίον καὶ πάντα τὸν λαὸν
3both 1the 4scroll 5and 7all 8the 9people

ἐρράντισεν, 20 λέγων· τοῦτο τὸ αἷμα τῆς
1he sprinkled, saying: This [is] the blood of the

διαθήκης ἧς ἐνετείλατο πρὸς ὑμᾶς ὁ
covenant which 2enjoined 3to 4you 1

θεός. 21 καὶ τὴν σκηνὴν δὲ καὶ πάντα
1God. 2both 3the 4tabernacle 1And and all

τὰ σκεύη τῆς λειτουργίας τῷ αἵματι
the vessels of the service with the blood

ὁμοίως ἐρράντισεν. 22 καὶ σχεδὸν ἐν
likewise he sprinkled. And 4almost 7by

αἵματι πάντα καθαρίζεται κατὰ τὸν νόμον,
8blood 5all things 6is(are) cleansed 1accord- 2the 3law,
ing to

καὶ χωρὶς αἱματεκχυσίας οὐ γίνεται
and without bloodshedding there becomes no

ἄφεσις. 23 ἀνάγκη οὖν τὰ μὲν ὑπο-
remission. [There was] therefore ²[for] ¹on one 4ex-
necessity 3the hand

δείγματα τῶν ἐν τοῖς οὐρανοῖς τούτοις
amples of the in the heavens 2by these
things

---

self unblemished to God, cleanse our consciences from acts that lead to death,/ so that we may serve the living God!

15For this reason Christ is the mediator of a new covenant, that those who are called may receive the promised eternal inheritance—now that he has died as a ransom to set them free from the sins committed under the first covenant.

16In the case of a will,/ it is necessary to prove the death of the one who made it, 17because a will is in force only when somebody has died; it never takes effect while the one who made it is living. 18This is why even the first covenant was not put into effect without blood. 19When Moses had proclaimed every commandment of the law to all the people, he took the blood of calves, together with water, scarlet wool and branches of hyssop, and sprinkled the scroll and all the people. 20He said, "This is the blood of the covenant, which God has commanded you to keep."k 21In the same way, he sprinkled with the blood both the tabernacle and everything used in its ceremonies. 22In fact, the law requires that nearly everything be cleansed with blood, and without the shedding of blood there is no forgiveness.

23It was necessary, then, for the copies of the heavenly things to be purified with these sacrifices, but

---

/Some ancient mss. read *for is it then . . . lives?*

* It may seem strange to translate a preposition which means "on" or "over" by "under"; but ἐπί has the meaning of "during the time of" (see Mark 2. 26; I. Tim. 6. 13).

*i*14 Or *from useless rituals*
*j*16 Same Greek word as *covenant*; also in verse 17
*k*20 Exodus 24:8

the heavenly things themselves with better sacrifices than these. 24For Christ did not enter a holy place made with hands, a *mere* copy of the true one, but into heaven itself, now to appear in the presence of God for us;

25nor was it that He should offer Himself often, as the high priest enters the holy place year by year with blood not his own. 26Otherwise, He would have needed to suffer often since the foundation of the world; but now once at the consummation of the ages He has been manifested to put away sin by the sacrifice of Himself.

27And inasmuch as it is appointed for men to die once and after this *comes* judgment,

28so Christ also, having been offered once to bear the sins of many, shall appear a second time for salvation without *reference to* sin, to those who eagerly await Him.

καθαρίζεσθαι,	αὐτὰ	δὲ	τὰ	ἐπουράνια
¹to be cleansed,	⁵[them]-selves	³on the	²[for]	⁴heavenly things

other ³the

κρείττοσιν	θυσίαις	παρὰ	ταύτας.	24 οὐ
by better	sacrifices	than	these.	not

γὰρ	εἰς	χειροποίητα	εἰσῆλθεν	ἅγια	Χριστός,
For	into	²made by hand	⁴entered	¹holies	³Christ,

ἀντίτυπα	τῶν	ἀληθινῶν,	ἀλλ᾽	εἰς	αὐτὸν
figures	of the	true things,	but	into	³[it]self

τὸν	οὐρανόν,	νῦν	ἐμφανισθῆναι	τῷ	προσώπῳ
¹the	²heaven,	now	to appear in	the	presence

τοῦ	θεοῦ	ὑπὲρ	ἡμῶν·	25 οὐδ᾽	ἵνα	πολ-
-	of God	on behalf of	us;	nor	*in order* that	often

λάκις	προσφέρῃ	ἑαυτόν,	ὥσπερ	ὁ	ἀρχιερεὺς
	he should offer	himself,	even as	the	high priest

εἰσέρχεται	εἰς	τὰ	ἅγια	κατ᾽	ἐνιαυτὸν
enters	into	the	holies		year by year†

ἐν	αἵματι	ἀλλοτρίῳ,	26 ἐπεὶ	ἔδει	αὐτὸν
with	blood	belonging to others,	since	it behoved	him

πολλάκις	παθεῖν	ἀπὸ	καταβολῆς	κόσμου·
often	to suffer	from	[the] foundation	of [the] world;

νυνὶ	δὲ	ἅπαξ	ἐπὶ	συντελείᾳ	τῶν	αἰώνων
but now		once	at	[the] completion of	the	ages

εἰς	ἀθέτησιν	τῆς	ἁμαρτίας	διὰ	τῆς	θυσίας
for	annulment	-	of sin	through	the	sacrifice

αὐτοῦ	πεφανέρωται.	27 καὶ	καθ᾽	ὅσον
of him	he has been manifested.	And		as

ἀπόκειται	τοῖς	ἀνθρώποις	ἅπαξ	ἀποθανεῖν,
it is reserved	-	to men	once	to die,

μετὰ	δὲ	τοῦτο	κρίσις,	28 οὕτως	καὶ
and after		this	judgment,	so	also

ὁ	Χριστός,	ἅπαξ	προσενεχθεὶς	εἰς	τὸ
-	Christ,	once	having been offered	*for*	*the*

πολλῶν	ἀνενεγκεῖν	ἁμαρτίας,	ἐκ	δευτέρου
³of many	¹to bear	²sins,	⁴a second [time]

χωρὶς	ἁμαρτίας	ὀφθήσεται	τοῖς	αὐτὸν
³without	⁴sin	¹will appear	⁵to the [ones]	⁷him

ἀπεκδεχομένοις	εἰς	σωτηρίαν.
⁶expecting	for	salvation.

the heavenly things themselves with better sacrifices than these. 24For Christ did not enter a man-made sanctuary that was only a copy of the true one; he entered heaven itself, now to appear for us in God's presence. 25Nor did he enter heaven to offer himself again and again, the way the high priest enters the Most Holy Place every year with blood that is not his own. 26Then Christ would have had to suffer many times since the creation of the world. But now he has appeared once for all at the end of the ages to do away with sin by the sacrifice of himself. 27Just as man is destined to die once, and after that to face judgment, 28so Christ was sacrificed once to take away the sins of many people; and he will appear a second time, not to bear sin, but to bring salvation to those who are waiting for him.

Chapter 10

One Sacrifice of Christ Is Sufficient

FOR the Law, since it has *only* a shadow of the good things to come *and* not the very form of things, *g*can never by the same sacrifices year by year, which they offer continually, make perfect those who draw near.

2Otherwise, would they not have ceased to be offered, because the worshipers, having once been cleansed, would no longer have had consciousness of sins?

3But in those *sacrifices* there is a reminder of sins year by year.

4For it is impossible for the blood of bulls and goats to take away sins.

5Therefore, when He comes into the world, He

10 Σκιὰν	γὰρ	ἔχων	ὁ	νόμος	τῶν
For ⁴a shadow	³having	¹the	²law	of the

μελλόντων	ἀγαθῶν,	οὐκ	αὐτὴν	τὴν	εἰκόνα
coming	good things,	not	³[it]self	¹the	²image

τῶν	πραγμάτων,	κατ᾽	ἐνιαυτὸν	ταῖς	αὐταῖς
of the	matters,	⁸every	⁹year†	³by the	⁴same

θυσίαις	ἃς	προσφέρουσιν	εἰς	τὸ	διηνεκὲς
⁵sacrifices	⁶which	⁷they offer		¹⁰continually†

οὐδέποτε	δύναται	τοὺς	προσερχομένους
²never	¹can	¹²the [ones]	¹³approaching

τελειῶσαι·	2 ἐπεὶ	οὐκ	ἂν	ἐπαύσαντο
¹¹to perfect;	since		would not they have ceased

προσφερόμεναι,	διὰ	τὸ	μηδεμίαν	ἔχειν
being offered,	because of	*the*	⁴no	⁵to have

ἔτι	συνείδησιν	ἁμαρτιῶν	τοὺς	λατρεύοντας
⁶still	⁸conscience	⁹of sins	¹the [ones]	²serving

ἅπαξ	κεκαθαρισμένους;	3 ἀλλ᾽	ἐν	αὐταῖς
³once	⁷having been cleansed?	But	in	them [there

ἀνάμνησις	ἁμαρτιῶν	κατ᾽	ἐνιαυτόν·
is] a remembrance	of sins		yearly†

4 ἀδύνατον	γὰρ	αἷμα	ταύρων	καὶ	τράγων
for [it is] impossible		blood	of bulls	and	*of* goats

ἀφαιρεῖν	ἁμαρτίας.	5 Διὸ	εἰσερχόμενος	εἰς
to take away	sins.	Wherefore	entering	into

Chapter 10

Christ's Sacrifice Once for All

THE law is only a shadow of the good things that are coming—not the realities themselves. For this reason it can never, by the same sacrifices repeated endlessly year after year, make perfect those who draw near to worship.

2If it could, would they not have stopped being offered? For the worshipers would have been cleansed once for all, and would no longer have felt guilty for their sins.

3But those sacrifices are an annual reminder of sins, 4because it is impossible for the blood of bulls and goats to take away sins.

5Therefore, when Christ came into the world, he

---

g Some ancient mss. read *they can*

says,

"SACRIFICE AND OFFER-
ING THOU HAST NOT
DESIRED,
BUT A BODY THOU
HAST PREPARED FOR
ME;
6 IN WHOLE BURNT OF-
FERINGS AND *sacri-
fices* FOR SIN THOU
HAST TAKEN NO PLEA-
SURE.
7"THEN I SAID, 'BEHOLD,
I HAVE COME
(IN THE ROLL OF THE
BOOK IT IS WRITTEN OF
ME)
TO DO THY WILL, O
GOD.' "
8After saying above,
"SACRIFICES AND OFFERINGS
AND WHOLE BURNT OFFER-
INGS AND *sacrifices* FOR SIN
THOU HAST NOT DESIRED,
NOR HAST THOU TAKEN PLEA-
SURE *in them*" (which are
offered according to the
Law),
9then He said, "BEHOLD,
I HAVE COME TO DO THY
WILL." He takes away the
first in order to establish
the second.
10By this will we have
been sanctified through the
offering of the body of
Jesus Christ once for all.
11And every priest stands
daily ministering and offering time after time the same
sacrifices, which can never
take away sins;
12but He, having offered
one sacrifice for sins for all
time, SAT DOWN AT THE
RIGHT HAND OF GOD,
13waiting from that time
onward UNTIL HIS ENEMIES
BE MADE A FOOTSTOOL FOR
HIS FEET.
14For by one offering He
has perfected for all time
those who are sanctified.
15And the Holy Spirit also
bears witness to us; for after saying,
16"THIS IS THE COVENANT
THAT I WILL MAKE

τὸν κόσμον λέγει· θυσίαν καὶ προσφορὰν
the world he says: Sacrifice and offering

οὐκ ἠθέλησας, σῶμα δὲ κατηρτίσω μοι·
thou didst not wish, but a body thou didst prepare for me;

6 ὁλοκαυτώματα καὶ περὶ ἁμαρτίας οὐκ
burnt offerings and concerning sins not
[sacrifices]

εὐδόκησας. 7 τότε εἶπον· ἰδοὺ ἥκω,
thou wast well Then I said: Behold I have
pleased [with]. come,

ἐν κεφαλίδι βιβλίου γέγραπται περὶ ἐμοῦ,
in a heading of a scroll it has been concerning me,
written

τοῦ ποιῆσαι ὁ θεὸς τὸ θέλημά σου.
- to do[,]d - God[,]* the will of thee.

8 ἀνώτερον λέγων ὅτι θυσίας καὶ προσ-
Above saying that sacrifices and offer·

φορὰς καὶ ὁλοκαυτώματα καὶ περὶ ἁμαρτίας
ings and burnt offerings and [sacrifices] sins
concerning

οὐκ ἠθέλησας οὐδὲ εὐδόκησας, αἵτινες
thou didst not wish nor *thou* wast well which
pleased [with],

κατὰ νόμον προσφέρονται, 9 τότε εἴρηκεν·
accord- law are offered, then he *has* said:
ing to

ἰδοὺ ἥκω τοῦ ποιῆσαι τὸ θέλημά σου.
Behold I have - to dod the will of thee.
come

ἀναιρεῖ τὸ πρῶτον ἵνα τὸ δεύτερον
He takes the first in order the second
away that

στήσῃ· 10 ἐν ᾧ θελήματι ἡγιασμένοι ἐσμὲν
he may by which will ¹having been ¹we are
set up; sanctified

διὰ τῆς προσφορᾶς τοῦ σώματος Ἰησοῦ
through the offering of the body of Jesus

Χριστοῦ ἐφάπαξ. 11 Καὶ πᾶς μὲν ἱερεὺς
Christ once for all. And ²every ¹on one ³priest
hand

ἕστηκεν καθ᾽ ἡμέραν λειτουργῶν καὶ τὰς
stands daily† ministering and ³the

αὐτὰς πολλάκις προσφέρων θυσίας, αἵτινες
⁴same ²often ⁵offering ⁴sacrifices, which

οὐδέποτε δύνανται περιελεῖν ἁμαρτίας· 12 οὗτος
never can *to* take away sins; ¹this
[priest]

δὲ μίαν ὑπὲρ ἁμαρτιῶν προσενέγκας
¹on the ⁴one ⁶on behalf of ⁷sins ³having offered
other

θυσίαν εἰς τὸ διηνεκὲς ἐκάθισεν ἐν δεξιᾷ
⁸sacrifice ⁹in - ¹⁰perpetuity ⁸sat at [the] right
[hand]

τοῦ θεοῦ, 13 τὸ λοιπὸν ἐκδεχόμενος ἕως
- of God, henceforth expecting till

τεθῶσιν οἱ ἐχθροὶ αὐτοῦ ὑποπόδιον τῶν
⁴are put ¹the ²enemies ³of him a footstool of the

ποδῶν αὐτοῦ. 14 μιᾷ γὰρ προσφορᾷ
feet of him. For by one offering

τετελείωκεν εἰς τὸ διηνεκὲς τοὺς ἁγιαζ-
he has perfected in - perpetuity the [ones] being

ομένους. 15 Μαρτυρεῖ δὲ ἡμῖν καὶ
sanctified. And ⁶witnesses ⁴to us ⁵indeed

τὸ πνεῦμα τὸ ἅγιον· μετὰ γὰρ τὸ
¹the ²Spirit - ³Holy; for after *the*

εἰρηκέναι· 16 αὕτη ἡ διαθήκη ἣν δια-
to have said: This [is] the covenant which I will
=having said:

said:

"Sacrifice and offering
you did not desire,
but a body you
prepared for me;
6with burnt offerings and
sin offerings
you were not pleased.
7Then I said, 'Here I
am—it is written
about me in the
scroll—
I have come to do your
will, O God.' "*

8First he said, "Sacrifices
and offerings, burnt offerings and sin offerings you
did not desire, nor were
you pleased with them"
(although the law required
them to be made). 9Then he
said, "Here I am, I have
come to do your will." He
sets aside the first to establish the second. 10And by
that will, we have been
made holy through the sacrifice of the body of Jesus
Christ once for all.
11Day after day every
priest stands and performs
his religious duties; again
and again he offers the
same sacrifices, which can
never take away sins. 12But
when this priest had of-
fered for all time one sacrifice for sins, he sat down at
the right hand of God.
13Since that time he waits
for his enemies to be made
his footstool, 14because by
one sacrifice he has made
perfect forever those who
are being made holy.
15The Holy Spirit also
testifies to us about this.
First he says:

16"This is the covenant I
will make with them

---

* The "articular vocative"; *cf.* 1. 8, 9.

*l*7 Psalm 40:6-8 (see Septuagint)

WITH THEM
AFTER THOSE DAYS,
SAYS THE LORD:
I WILL PUT MY LAWS
UPON THEIR HEART,
AND UPON THEIR MIND
I WILL WRITE THEM,"
He then says,
17"AND THEIR SINS AND
THEIR LAWLESS DEEDS
I WILL REMEMBER NO
MORE."
18Now where there is for-
giveness of these things,
there is no longer *any* offer-
ing for sin.

A New and Living Way

19Since therefore, breth-
ren, we have confidence to
enter the holy place by the
blood of Jesus,
20by a new and living way
which He inaugurated for
us through the veil, that is,
His flesh,
21and since *we have a*
great priest over the house
of God,
22let us draw near with a
sincere heart in full assurance of faith, having our
hearts sprinkled *clean* from
an evil conscience and our
bodies washed with pure
water.
23Let us hold fast the
confession of our hope
without wavering, for He
who promised is faithful;
24and let us consider how
to stimulate one another to
love and good deeds,
25not forsaking our own
assembling together, as is
the habit of some, but encouraging *one another*; and
all the more, as you see the
day drawing near.

Christ or Judgment

26For if we go on sinning
willfully after receiving the
knowledge of the truth,
there no longer remains a
sacrifice for sins,
27but a certain terrifying
expectation of judgment,
and THE FURY OF A FIRE
WHICH WILL CONSUME THE
ADVERSARIES.

θήσομαι πρὸς αὐτοὺς μετὰ τὰς ἡμέρας
covenant to them after - days
ἐκείνας, λέγει κύριος· διδοὺς νόμους μου
those, says [the] Lord: Giving laws of me
ἐπὶ καρδίας αὐτῶν, καὶ ἐπὶ τὴν διάνοιαν
on hearts of them, also on the mind
αὐτῶν ἐπιγράψω αὐτούς, 17 καὶ τῶν
of them I will inscribe them, and the
ἁμαρτιῶν αὐτῶν καὶ τῶν ἀνομιῶν αὐτῶν
sins of them and the iniquities of them
οὐ μὴ μνησθήσομαι ἔτι. 18 ὅπου δὲ
by no means I will remember still. Now where
ἄφεσις τούτων, οὐκέτι προσφορὰ περὶ
forgiveness of these [is], no longer offering concerning
[there is]
ἁμαρτίας.
sins.

19 Ἔχοντες οὖν, ἀδελφοί, παρρησίαν εἰς
Having therefore, brothers, confidence for
τὴν εἴσοδον τῶν ἁγίων ἐν τῷ αἵματι
the entering of the holies by the blood
Ἰησοῦ, 20 ἣν ἐνεκαίνισεν ἡμῖν ὁδὸν
of Jesus, which he dedicated for us[,] a way
πρόσφατον καὶ ζῶσαν διὰ τοῦ κατα-
fresh and living through the veil,
πετάσματος, τοῦτ' ἔστιν τῆς σαρκὸς αὐτοῦ,
this is the flesh of him,
21 καὶ ἱερέα μέγαν ἐπὶ τὸν οἶκον τοῦ
and priest a great over the household
θεοῦ, 22 προσερχώμεθα μετὰ ἀληθινῆς
of God, let us approach with a true
καρδίας ἐν πληροφορίᾳ πίστεως, ῥεραν-
heart in full assurance of faith, having been
τισμένοι τὰς καρδίας ἀπὸ συνειδήσεως
sprinkled [as to] the hearts from [1]conscience
πονηρᾶς καὶ λελουσμένοι τὸ σῶμα ὕδατι
[1]an evil and having been [as to] body [2]water
bathed the
καθαρῷ· 23 κατέχωμεν τὴν ὁμολογίαν τῆς
[1]in clean; let us hold fast the confession the
(our)
ἐλπίδος ἀκλινῆ, πιστὸς γὰρ ὁ ἐπαγ-
hope unyieldingly, for faithful [is] the [one] pro-
γειλάμενος, 24 καὶ κατανοῶμεν ἀλλήλους
mising, and let us consider one another
εἰς παροξυσμὸν ἀγάπης καὶ καλῶν ἔργων,
to incitement of love and of good works,
25 μὴ ἐγκαταλείποντες τὴν ἐπισυναγωγὴν
not forsaking the coming together
ἑαυτῶν, καθὼς ἔθος τισίν, ἀλλὰ παρα-
of [our]selves, as custom with some [is], but ex-
καλοῦντες, καὶ τοσούτῳ μᾶλλον ὅσῳ
horting, and by so much more as
βλέπετε ἐγγίζουσαν τὴν ἡμέραν. 26 Ἑκουσίως
ye see [3]drawing near [1]the [2]day. wilfully
γὰρ ἁμαρτανόντων ἡμῶν μετὰ τὸ λαβεῖν
For sinning us[a] after the to receive
=when we sin wilfully =receiving
τὴν ἐπίγνωσιν τῆς ἀληθείας, οὐκέτι περὶ
the full knowledge of the truth, [5]no more [1]con-
cerning
ἁμαρτιῶν ἀπολείπεται θυσία, 27 φοβερὰ
[2]sins [4]remains [1]a sacrifice, [3]fearful
δέ τις ἐκδοχὴ κρίσεως καὶ πυρὸς ζῆλος
[1]but [2]some expectation of judgment and [2]of fire [1]zeal
ἐσθίειν μέλλοντος τοὺς ὑπεναντίους.
[4]to consume [3]being about the adversaries.

after that time, says the
Lord.
I will put my laws in
their hearts,
and I will write them
on their minds." [m]

17Then he adds:

"Their sins and lawless
acts
I will remember no
more." [n]

18And where these have
been forgiven, there is no
longer any sacrifice for sin.

A Call to Persevere

19Therefore, brothers,
since we have confidence
to enter the Most Holy
Place by the blood of Jesus,
20by a new and living way
opened for us through the
curtain, that is, his body,
21and since we have a great
priest over the house of
God, 22let us draw near to
God with a sincere heart in
full assurance of faith, having our hearts sprinkled to
cleanse us from a guilty
conscience and having our
bodies washed with pure
water. 23Let us hold un-
swervingly to the hope we
profess, for he who prom-
ised is faithful. 24And let us
consider how we may spur
one another on toward love
and good deeds. 25Let us
not give up meeting together, as some are in the habit
of doing, but let us encourage one another—and all
the more as you see the
Day approaching.

26If we deliberately keep
on sinning after we have received the knowledge of
the truth, no sacrifice for
sins is left, 27but only a
fearful expectation of judgment and of raging fire that
will consume the enemies

m16 Jer. 31:33
n17 Jer. 31:34

28Anyone who has set aside the Law of Moses dies without mercy on *the testimony* of two or three witnesses.

29How much severer punishment do you think he will deserve who has trampled under foot the Son of God, and has regarded as unclean the blood of the covenant by which he was sanctified, and has insulted the Spirit of grace?

30For we know Him who said, "VENGEANCE IS MINE, I WILL REPAY." And again, "THE LORD WILL JUDGE HIS PEOPLE."

31It is a terrifying thing to fall into the hands of the living God.

32But remember the former days, when, after being enlightened, you endured a great conflict of sufferings,

33partly, by being made a public spectacle through reproaches and tribulations, and partly by becoming sharers with those who were so treated.

34For you showed sympathy to the prisoners, and accepted joyfully the seizure of your property, knowing that you have for yourselves a better possession and an abiding one.

35Therefore, do not throw away your confidence, which has a great reward.

36For you have need of endurance, so that when you have done the will of God, you may receive what was promised.

37 FOR YET IN A VERY LITTLE WHILE,
HE WHO IS COMING WILL COME, AND WILL NOT DELAY.
38 BUT MY RIGHTEOUS ONE SHALL LIVE BY FAITH;
AND IF HE SHRINKS

---

28 ἀθετήσας τις νόμον Μωϋσέως χωρὶς
¹Disregarding ¹anyone ²law ⁴of Moses ⁴without

οἰκτιρμῶν ἐπὶ δυσὶν ἢ τρισὶν μάρτυσιν
⁷compassions ⁸on [the ⁹two ¹⁰or ¹¹three ¹¹witnesses
word of]

ἀποθνήσκει· **29** πόσῳ δοκεῖτε χείρονος
¹dies; by how much think ye ²of worse

ἀξιωθήσεται τιμωρίας ὁ τὸν υἱὸν τοῦ
¹will be thought ³punishment ⁴the ⁶the ⁷Son -
worthy [one]

θεοῦ καταπατήσας καὶ τὸ αἷμα τῆς
⁵of God ⁸having trampled and ⁸the ⁴blood ⁵of the
[on]

διαθήκης κοινὸν ἡγησάμενος, ἐν ᾧ ἡγιάσθη,
⁶covenant ⁸common ¹having by which he was
deemed, sanctified,

καὶ τὸ πνεῦμα τῆς χάριτος ἐνυβρίσας.
and ⁸the ²Spirit - ⁴of grace ¹having insulted.

30 οἴδαμεν γὰρ τὸν εἰπόντα· ἐμοὶ
For we know the [one] having said: To me
=Vengeance

ἐκδίκησις, ἐγὼ ἀνταποδώσω· καὶ πάλιν·
vengeance,ᵒ I will repay; and again:
is mine,

κρινεῖ κύριος τὸν λαὸν αὐτοῦ. **31** φοβερὸν
²will judge [¹The] the people of him. A fearful
Lord thing [it is]

τὸ ἐμπεσεῖν εἰς χεῖρας θεοῦ ζῶντος.
the to fall *in* into [the] hands ²God ¹of a living.

32 Ἀναμιμνήσκεσθε δὲ τὰς πρότερον ἡμέρας,
But remember ye the ²formerly ¹days,

ἐν αἷς φωτισθέντες πολλὴν ἄθλησιν
in which being enlightened ²a much(great) ³struggle

ὑπεμείνατε παθημάτων, **33** τοῦτο μὲν
¹ye endured ⁴of sufferings, *this* on one hand

ὀνειδισμοῖς τε καὶ θλίψεσιν θεατριζόμενοι,
²to reproaches ³both ⁴and ⁵to afflictions ¹being exposed,

τοῦτο δὲ κοινωνοὶ τῶν οὕτως ἀναστρεφ-
this on the ⁶sharers ⁵of the ⁸thus ⁴liv-
other [ones]

ομένων γενηθέντες. **34** καὶ γὰρ τοῖς
ing ¹having become. For indeed in *the*

δεσμίοις συνεπαθήσατε, καὶ τὴν ἁρπαγὴν
bonds ye suffered together, and ⁴the ⁵seizure

τῶν ὑπαρχόντων ὑμῶν μετὰ χαρᾶς
⁶of the ⁷possessions ⁸of you ³with ⁴joy

προσεδέξασθε, γινώσκοντες ἔχειν ἑαυτοὺς
¹ye accepted, knowing ²to have ¹[your]selves

κρείσσονα ὕπαρξιν καὶ μένουσαν. **35** Μὴ
²a better ³possession ⁴and ⁵remaining. not

ἀποβάλητε οὖν τὴν παρρησίαν ὑμῶν, ἥτις
Cast ye away therefore the confidence of you, which

ἔχει μεγάλην μισθαποδοσίαν. **36** ὑπομονῆς
has a great recompence. ²of endurance

γὰρ ἔχετε χρείαν ἵνα τὸ θέλημα τοῦ
For ¹ye have ¹need in order ²the ¹will -
that

θεοῦ ποιήσαντες κομίσησθε τὴν ἐπαγγελίαν.
⁴of God ¹having ye may obtain the promise.
done

37 ἔτι γὰρ μικρὸν ὅσον ὅσον, ὁ ἐρχόμενος
For yet ⁴little ¹a very,* the coming [one]

ἥξει καὶ οὐ χρονίσει· **38** ὁ δὲ δίκαιός
will come and will not delay; but the just man

μου ἐκ πίστεως ζήσεται, καὶ ἐὰν ὑπο-
of me by faith will live, and if he

---

of God. 28Anyone who rejected the law of Moses died without mercy on the testimony of two or three witnesses. 29How much more severely do you think a man deserves to be punished who has trampled the Son of God under foot, who has treated as an unholy thing the blood of the covenant that sanctified him, and who has insulted the Spirit of grace? 30For we know him who said, "It is mine to avenge; I will repay,"ᵒ and again, "The Lord will judge his people."ᵖ 31It is a dreadful thing to fall into the hands of the living God.

32Remember those earlier days after you had received the light, when you stood your ground in a great contest in the face of suffering. 33Sometimes you were publicly exposed to insult and persecution; at other times you stood side by side with those who were so treated. 34You sympathized with those in prison and joyfully accepted the confiscation of your property, because you knew that you yourselves had better and lasting possessions.

35So do not throw away your confidence; it will be richly rewarded. 36You need to persevere so that when you have done the will of God, you will receive what he has promised. 37For in just a very little while,

"He who is coming will
   come and will not
   delay.
38 But my righteous oneᑫ
   will live by faith.
And if he shrinks back,

ᵒ30 Deut. 32:35
ᵖ30 Deut. 32:36; Psalm 135:14
ᑫ38 One early manuscript *But the righteous*

* *Cf.* our "so so".

BACK, MY SOUL HAS
NO PLEASURE IN HIM.
³⁹But we are not of those
who shrink back to de-
struction, but of those who
have faith to the preserving
of the soul.

στείληται,   οὐκ   εὐδοκεῖ   ἡ   ψυχή   μου
withdraws,   'is not well pleased   'the   'soul   'of me

ἐν αὐτῷ.   39 ἡμεῖς   δὲ   οὐκ   ἐσμὲν   ὑποστολῆς
in him.   But we   are not   of withdrawal

εἰς   ἀπώλειαν,   ἀλλὰ   πίστεως   εἰς   περιποίησιν
to   destruction,   but   of faith   to   possession

ψυχῆς.
of soul.

I will not be pleased
with him.''ʳ

³⁹But we are not of those
who shrink back and are
destroyed, but of those
who believe and are saved.

Chapter 11

The Triumphs of Faith

NOW faith is the assur-
ance of *things* hoped
for, the conviction of things
not seen.
   ²For by it the men of old
gained approval.
   ³By faith we understand
that the worlds were pre-
pared by the word of God,
so that what is seen was not
made out of things which
are visible.
   ⁴By faith Abel offered to
God a better sacrifice than
Cain, through which he obtained the testimony that
he was righteous, God testifying about his gifts, and
through faith, though he is
dead, he still speaks.
   ⁵By faith Enoch was tak-
en up so that he should not
see death; AND HE WAS NOT
FOUND BECAUSE GOD TOOK
HIM UP; for he obtained the
witness that before his being taken up he was pleasing to God.
   ⁶And without faith it is
impossible to please *Him*,
for he who comes to God
must believe that He is, and
that He is a rewarder of
those who seek Him.
   ⁷By faith Noah, being
warned *by God* about
things not yet seen, in reverence prepared an ark for
the salvation of his household, by which he con-
demned the world, and
became an heir of the righteousness which is accord-
ing to faith.

11 "Εστιν   δὲ   πίστις   ἐλπιζομένων   ὑπό-
   Now 'is   'faith   'of things being hoped   '[the]

στασις,   πραγμάτων   ἔλεγχος   οὐ   βλεπομένων.
reality,   'of things   '[the] proof   not   being seen.

2 ἐν   ταύτῃ   γὰρ   ἐμαρτυρήθησαν   οἱ
   by   this   For   'obtained witness   'the

πρεσβύτεροι.   3 Πίστει   νοοῦμεν   κατηρτίσθαι
'elders.   By faith we understand   'to have been
                                                       adjusted

τοὺς   αἰῶνας   ῥήματι   θεοῦ,   εἰς   τὸ   μὴ
'the   'ages   by a word   of God,   so as†   'not

ἐκ   φαινομένων   τὸ   βλεπόμενον   γεγονέναι.
'out   'things   'the   'being seen   'to have
of   appearing   thing   become.

4 Πίστει   πλείονα   θυσίαν   "Αβελ   παρὰ
   By faith   'a greater(? better)   'sacrifice   'Abel   'than

Κάϊν   προσήνεγκεν   τῷ   θεῷ,   δι'   ἧς
'Cain   'offered   τῷ   'to God, through which

ἐμαρτυρήθη   εἶναι   δίκαιος,   μαρτυροῦντος   ἐπὶ
he obtained   to be   just,   'witnessing   'over
witness

τοῖς   δώροις   αὐτοῦ   τοῦ   θεοῦ,   καὶ   δι'
'the   'gifts   'of him   -   'God,•   and through

αὐτῆς   ἀποθανὼν   ἔτι   λαλεῖ.   5 Πίστει
it   having died   still   he speaks.   By faith

'Ενὼχ   μετετέθη   τοῦ   μὴ   ἰδεῖν   θάνατον,
Enoch   was removed   τοῦ   not   to see   death,

καὶ   οὐχ   ηὑρίσκετο   διότι   μετέθηκεν   αὐτὸν
and   was not found   because   'removed   'him

ὁ   θεός.   6 πρὸ   γὰρ   τῆς   μεταθέσεως
-    'God.   For before   the(his)   removal

μεμαρτύρηται   εὐαρεστηκέναι   τῷ   θεῷ· χωρὶς
he has obtained   to have been well-   -   to God; 'without
witness   pleasing

δὲ   πίστεως   ἀδύνατον   εὐαρεστῆσαι· πιστεῦσαι
'but faith [it is] impossible to be well-pleasing [to God]; 'to believe

γὰρ   δεῖ   τὸν   προσερχόμενον   [τῷ]   θεῷ,
'for   'it   'the [one]   'approaching   'to God,
behoves

ὅτι   ἔστιν   καὶ   τοῖς   ἐκζητοῦσιν   αὐτὸν
that   he is   and   'to the [ones]   'seeking 'out   'him

μισθαποδότης   γίνεται.   7 Πίστει   χρηματισ-
'a rewarder   'becomes.   By faith   'having been
                                                   warned [by

θεὶς   Νῶε   περὶ   τῶν   μηδέπω   βλεπομένων,
God*]   'Noah concerning the things not yet   being seen,

εὐλαβηθεὶς   κατεσκεύασεν   κιβωτὸν   εἰς
being devout   prepared   an ark   for

σωτηρίαν   τοῦ   οἴκου   αὐτοῦ,   δι'   ἧς
[the] salvation of the   household   of him,   through which

κατέκρινεν   τὸν   κόσμον,   καὶ   τῆς   κατὰ
he condemned   the   world,   and   'of the   'accord-
                                                          ing to

πίστιν   δικαιοσύνης   ἐγένετο   κληρονόμος.
'faith   'righteousness   'became   'heir.

Chapter 11

By Faith

NOW faith is being sure
of what we hope for
and certain of what we do
not see. ²This is what the
ancients were commended
for.
   ³By faith we understand
that the universe was
formed at God's command,
so that what is seen was not
made out of what was visible.
   ⁴By faith Abel offered
God a better sacrifice than
Cain did. By faith he was
commended as a righteous
man, when God spoke well
of his offerings. And by
faith he still speaks, even
though he is dead.
   ⁵By faith Enoch was tak-
en from this life, so that he
did not experience death;
he could not be found, because God had taken him
away. For before he was
taken up, he was commended
as one who pleased God.
⁶And without faith it is im-
possible to please God, be-
cause anyone who comes
to him must believe that he
exists and that he rewards
those who earnestly seek
him.
   ⁷By faith Noah, when
warned about things not
yet seen, in holy fear built
an ark to save his family.
By his faith he condemned
the world and became heir
of the righteousness that
comes by faith.

• This must be understood, as the word always (or at
least generally) has reference to a divine communication.

8By faith Abraham, when he was called, obeyed by going out to a place which he was to receive for an inheritance; and he went out, not knowing where he was going.

9By faith he lived as an alien in the land of promise, as in a foreign *land*, dwelling in tents with Isaac and Jacob, fellow heirs of the same promise;

10for he was looking for the city which has foundations, whose architect and builder is God.

11By faith even Sarah herself received ability to conceive, even beyond the proper time of life, since she considered Him faithful who had promised;

12therefore, also, there was born of one man, and him as good as dead at that, *as many descendants* AS THE STARS OF HEAVEN IN NUMBER, AND INNUMERABLE AS THE SAND WHICH IS BY THE SEASHORE.

13All these died in faith, without receiving the promises, but having seen them and having welcomed them from a distance, and having confessed that they were strangers and exiles on the earth.

14For those who say such things make it clear that they are seeking a country of their own.

15And indeed if they had been thinking of that *country* from which they went out, they would have had opportunity to return.

16But as it is, they desire a better *country*, that is a heavenly one. Therefore God is not ashamed to be called their God; for He has prepared a city for them.

17By faith Abraham, when he was tested, offered up Isaac; and he who

---

8 Πίστει καλούμενος Ἀβραὰμ ὑπήκουσεν
By faith ¹being called ¹Abraham ¹¹obeyed

ἐξελθεῖν εἰς τόπον ὃν ἤμελλεν λαμβάνειν
²to go forth ⁴to ⁵a place ⁶which ⁷he was about ⁸to receive

εἰς κληρονομίαν, καὶ ἐξῆλθεν μὴ ἐπιστάμε-
⁹for ¹⁰an inheritance, and went forth not understand-

νος ποῦ ἔρχεται. **9** Πίστει παρῴκησεν
ing where he goes(went). By faith he sojourned

εἰς γῆν τῆς ἐπαγγελίας ὡς ἀλλοτρίαν,
in a land - of promise as a foreigner,

ἐν σκηναῖς κατοικήσας, μετὰ Ἰσαὰκ καὶ
in tents dwelling, with Isaac and

Ἰακὼβ τῶν συγκληρονόμων τῆς ἐπαγ-
Jacob the co-heirs of the ¹pro-

γελίας τῆς αὐτῆς· **10** ἐξεδέχετο γὰρ τὴν
mise - ¹same; for he expected the

τοὺς θεμελίους ἔχουσαν πόλιν, ἧς τεχνίτης
²the ³foundations ²having ¹city, of which ²artificer

καὶ δημιουργὸς ὁ θεός. **11** Πίστει καὶ
⁴and ⁵maker - ¹God ²[is]. By faith also

αὐτὴ Σάρρα δύναμιν εἰς καταβολὴν
²[her]self ¹Sara ⁴power ⁵for ⁶conception

σπέρματος ἔλαβεν καὶ παρὰ καιρὸν ἡλικίας,
⁷of seed ³received even beyond time of age,

ἐπεὶ πιστὸν ἡγήσατο τὸν ἐπαγγειλάμενον.
since ²faithful ¹she deemed the [one] having promised.

12 διὸ καὶ ἀφ᾽ ἑνὸς ἐγενήθησαν, καὶ
Wherefore indeed from one there became, and

ταῦτα νενεκρωμένου, καθὼς τὰ ἄστρα
that too† [he] having died,ª as the stars

τοῦ οὐρανοῦ τῷ πλήθει καὶ ὡς ἡ ἄμμος
of *the* heaven - in multitude and as the ³sand

ἡ παρὰ τὸ χεῖλος τῆς θαλάσσης ἡ
- ²by ⁴the ⁵lip ⁶of the ⁷sea -

ἀναρίθμητος. **13** Κατὰ πίστιν ἀπέθανον
¹innumerable. ⁴By way of ⁵faith ³died

οὗτοι πάντες, μὴ κομισάμενοι τὰς ἐπαγ-
¹these ²all, not having obtained the pro-

γελίας, ἀλλὰ πόρρωθεν αὐτὰς ἰδόντες καὶ
mises, but ⁶from afar ⁵them ¹seeing ²and

ἀσπασάμενοι, καὶ ὁμολογήσαντες ὅτι ξένοι
³greeting, and confessing that ²strangers

καὶ παρεπίδημοί εἰσιν ἐπὶ τῆς γῆς.
²and ⁴sojourners ¹they are on the earth
                                (? land).

14 οἱ γὰρ τοιαῦτα λέγοντες ἐμφανίζουσιν
For the [ones] ²such things ¹saying make manifest

ὅτι πατρίδα ἐπιζητοῦσιν. **15** καὶ εἰ μὲν
that ²a fatherland ¹they seek. And if on one hand

ἐκείνης ἐμνημόνευον ἀφ᾽ ἧς ἐξέβησαν,
²that ¹they remembered from which they came out,

εἶχον ἂν καιρὸν ἀνακάμψαι· **16** νῦν
they might time(opportunity) to return; now have had

δὲ κρείττονος ὀρέγονται, τοῦτ᾽ ἔστιν
on the other a better ¹they aspire to, this is

ἐπουρανίου. διὸ οὐκ ἐπαισχύνεται αὐτοὺς
a heavenly. Wherefore ²is not ashamed [of] ³them

ὁ θεὸς θεὸς ἐπικαλεῖσθαι αὐτῶν· ἡτοίμασεν
- ¹God ⁵God ⁴to be called ⁶of them; ²he prepared

γὰρ αὐτοῖς πόλιν. **17** Πίστει προσενήνοχεν
¹for for them a city. By faith ³has offered up

Ἀβραὰμ τὸν Ἰσαὰκ πειραζόμενος, καὶ
¹Abraham - ⁴Isaac ²being tested, and

8By faith Abraham, when called to go to a place he would later receive as his inheritance, obeyed and went, even though he did not know where he was going. **9**By faith he made his home in the promised land like a stranger in a foreign country; he lived in tents, as did Isaac and Jacob, who were heirs with him of the same promise. **10**For he was looking forward to the city with foundations, whose architect and builder is God.

11By faith Abraham, even though he was past age— and Sarah herself was barren—was enabled to become a father because heª considered him faithful who had made the promise. **12**And so from this one man, and he as good as dead, came descendants as numerous as the stars in the sky and as countless as the sand on the seashore.

13All these people were still living by faith when they died. They did not receive the things promised; they only saw them and welcomed them from a distance. And they admitted that they were aliens and strangers on earth. **14**People who say such things show that they are looking for a country of their own. **15**If they had been thinking of the country they had left, they would have had opportunity to return. **16**Instead, they were longing for a better country—a heavenly one. Therefore God is not ashamed to be called their God, for he has prepared a city for them.

17By faith Abraham, when God tested him, offered Isaac as a sacrifice.

ª*11 Or By faith even Sarah, who was past age, was enabled to bear children because she* had received the promises was offering up his only begotten *son;*

18*it was he* to whom it was said, "IN ISAAC YOUR DESCENDANTS SHALL BE CALLED."

19He considered that God is able to raise *men* even from the dead; from which he also received him back as a type.

20By faith Isaac blessed Jacob and Esau, even regarding things to come.

21By faith Jacob, as he was dying, blessed each of the sons of Joseph, and worshiped, *leaning* on the top of his staff.

22By faith Joseph, when he was dying, made mention of the exodus of the sons of Israel, and gave orders concerning his bones.

23By faith Moses, when he was born, was hidden for three months by his parents, because they saw he was a beautiful child; and they were not afraid of the king's edict.

24By faith Moses, when he had grown up, refused to be called the son of Pharoah's daughter;

25choosing rather to endure ill-treatment with the people of God, than to enjoy the passing pleasures of sin;

26considering the reproach of Christ greater riches than the treasures of Egypt; for he was looking to the reward.

27By faith he left Egypt, not fearing the wrath of the king; for he endured, as seeing Him who is unseen.

28By faith he kept the Passover and the sprinkling of the blood, so that he who

---

τὸν μονογενῆ προσέφερεν ὁ τὰς ἐπαγγελίας
*the ⁷only begotten (his) ⁵was offering up ¹the ²the ⁴promises [one]

ἀναδεξάμενος, 18 πρὸς ὃν ἐλαλήθη ὅτι
³having undertaken, as to whom it was spoken[,] –

ἐν Ἰσαὰκ κληθήσεταί σοι σπέρμα,
In Isaac shall be called to thee a seed,° = thy seed,

19 λογισάμενος ὅτι καὶ ἐκ νεκρῶν ἐγείρειν
reckoning that ⁴even ⁵from ⁶dead ¹to raise

δυνατὸς ὁ θεός· ὅθεν αὐτὸν καὶ ἐν
²[was] ³able – ¹God; whence ⁵him ¹indeed ²in

παραβολῇ ἐκομίσατο. 20 Πίστει καὶ περὶ
³a parable ⁴he obtained. By faith also ²concerning

μελλόντων εὐλόγησεν Ἰσαὰκ τὸν Ἰακὼβ
⁷coming things ³blessed ¹Isaac – ²Jacob

καὶ τὸν Ἠσαῦ. 21 Πίστει Ἰακὼβ
⁴and – ⁵Esau. By faith Jacob

ἀποθνῄσκων ἕκαστον τῶν υἱῶν Ἰωσὴφ
dying ²each ³of the ⁴sons ⁵of Joseph

εὐλόγησεν, καὶ προσεκύνησεν ἐπὶ τὸ ἄκρον
¹blessed, and worshipped on the tip

τῆς ῥάβδου αὐτοῦ. 22 Πίστει Ἰωσὴφ
of the rod of him. By faith Joseph

τελευτῶν περὶ τῆς ἐξόδου τῶν υἱῶν
dying ²concerning ³the ⁴exodus ⁵of the ⁶sons

Ἰσραὴλ ἐμνημόνευσεν καὶ περὶ τῶν
⁷of Israel ¹remembered and ²concerning ³the

ὀστέων αὐτοῦ ἐνετείλατο. 23 Πίστει
⁴bones ⁵of him ¹gave orders. By faith

Μωϋσῆς γεννηθεὶς ἐκρύβη τρίμηνον ὑπὸ
Moses having been born was hidden three months by

τῶν πατέρων αὐτοῦ, διότι εἶδον ἀστεῖον
the parents of him, because they saw ²[to be] fine

τὸ παιδίον, καὶ οὐκ ἐφοβήθησαν τὸ
¹the ²child, and they did not fear the

διάταγμα τοῦ βασιλέως. 24 Πίστει Μωϋσῆς
decree of the king. By faith Moses

μέγας γενόμενος ἠρνήσατο λέγεσθαι υἱὸς
²great ¹having become denied to be said(called) son

θυγατρὸς Φαραώ, 25 μᾶλλον ἑλόμενος
of [the] daughter of Pharaoh, rather choosing

συγκακουχεῖσθαι τῷ λαῷ τοῦ θεοῦ ἢ
to be ill treated with the people – of God than

πρόσκαιρον ἔχειν ἁμαρτίας ἀπόλαυσιν,
for a time to have ²of sin ¹enjoyment,

26 μείζονα πλοῦτον ἡγησάμενος τῶν
⁵greater ⁶riches ¹deeming ⁷[than] ⁸the

Αἰγύπτου θησαυρῶν τὸν ὀνειδισμὸν τοῦ
¹⁰of Egypt ⁹treasures ³the ²reproach –

Χριστοῦ· ἀπέβλεπεν γὰρ εἰς τὴν μισθ-
⁴of Christ; for he was looking away to the recom-

αποδοσίαν. 27 Πίστει κατέλιπεν Αἴγυπτον,
pence. By faith he left Egypt,

μὴ φοβηθεὶς τὸν θυμὸν τοῦ βασιλέως·
not fearing the anger of the king;

τὸν γὰρ ἀόρατον ὡς ὁρῶν ἐκαρτέρησεν.
for ²the ⁴unseen [one] ³as ⁵seeing ¹he endured.

28 Πίστει πεποίηκεν τὸ πάσχα καὶ τὴν
By faith he *has* made the passover and the

πρόσχυσιν τοῦ αἵματος, ἵνα μὴ ὁ
affusion of the blood, lest the

ὀλεθρεύων τὰ πρωτότοκα θίγῃ αὐτῶν.
[one] destroying ²the ³firstborns ¹should touch ⁴of them.

He who had received the promises was about to sacrifice his one and only son, 18even though God had said to him, "It is through Isaac that your offspring' will be reckoned." *ᵘ* 19Abraham reasoned that God could raise the dead, and figuratively speaking, he did receive Isaac back from death.

20By faith Isaac blessed Jacob and Esau in regard to their future.

21By faith Jacob, when he was dying, blessed each of Joseph's sons, and worshiped as he leaned on the top of his staff.

22By faith Joseph, when his end was near, spoke about the exodus of the Israelites from Egypt and gave instructions about his bones.

23By faith Moses' parents hid him for three months after he was born, because they saw he was no ordinary child, and thev were not afraid of the king's edict.

24By faith Moses, when he had grown up, refused to be known as the son of Pharaoh's daughter. 25He chose to be mistreated along with the people of God rather than to enjoy the pleasures of sin for a short time. 26He regarded disgrace for the sake of Christ as of greater value than the treasures of Egypt, because he was looking ahead to his reward. 27By faith he left Egypt, not fearing the king's anger; he persevered because he saw him who is invisible. 28By faith he kept the Passover and the sprinkling of blood, so that the

---

ʳ18 Greek *seed*
ᵘ18 Gen. 21:12

destroyed the first-born might not touch them.

29By faith they passed through the Red Sea as though *they were passing* through dry land; and the Egyptians, when they attempted it, were drowned.

30By faith the walls of Jericho fell down, after they had been encircled for seven days.

31By faith Rahab the harlot did not perish along with those who were disobedient, after she had welcomed the spies in peace.

32And what more shall I say? For time will fail me if I tell of Gideon, Barak, Samson, Jephthah, of David and Samuel and the prophets,

33who by faith conquered kingdoms, performed *acts of* righteousness, obtained promises, shut the mouths of lions,

34quenched the power of fire, escaped the edge of the sword, from weakness were made strong, became mighty in war, put foreign armies to flight.

35Women received *back* their dead by resurrection; and others were tortured, not accepting their release, in order that they might obtain a better resurrection;

36and others experienced mockings and scourgings, yes, also chains and imprisonment.

37They were stoned, they were sawn in two, [h]they were tempted, they were put to death with the sword; they went about in sheepskins, in goatskins, being destitute, afflicted, ill-treated

38(*men* of whom the world was not worthy), wandering in deserts and mountains and caves and holes in the ground.

39And all these, having gained approval through

---

29 Πίστει διέβησαν τὴν ἐρυθρὰν θάλασσαν
By faith they went the Red Sea
through

ὡς διὰ ξηρᾶς γῆς, ἧς πεῖραν λαβόντες
as through dry land, which 4trial 3taking

οἱ Αἰγύπτιοι κατεπόθησαν. 30 Πίστει
1the 2Egyptians were swallowed up. By faith

τὰ τείχη Ἰεριχὼ ἔπεσαν κυκλωθέντα ἐπὶ
the walls of Jericho fell having been during
encircled

ἑπτὰ ἡμέρας. 31 Πίστει Ῥαὰβ ἡ πόρνη
seven days. By faith Rahab the prostitute

οὐ συναπώλετο τοῖς ἀπειθήσασιν, δεξαμένη
did not perish with the [ones] disobeying, having received

τοὺς κατασκόπους μετ᾽ εἰρήνης. 32 Καὶ
the spies with peace. And

τί ἔτι λέγω; ἐπιλείψει με γὰρ διηγούμενον
what more may ⁴will fail ²me ¹for ⁴recounting
I say?

ὁ χρόνος περὶ Γεδεών, Βαράκ, Σαμψών,
³the ³time concerning Gedeon, Barak, Samson,

Ἰεφθάε, Δαυίδ τε καὶ Σαμουὴλ καὶ
Jephthae, ⁴David ¹both and Samuel and

τῶν προφητῶν, 33 οἱ διὰ πίστεως
the prophets, who through faith

κατηγωνίσαντο βασιλείας, ἠργάσαντο δι-
overcame kingdoms, wrought

καιοσύνην, ἐπέτυχον ἐπαγγελιῶν, ἔφραξαν
eousness, obtained promises, stopped

στόματα λεόντων, 34 ἔσβεσαν δύναμιν
mouths of lions, quenched [the] power

πυρός, ἔφυγον στόματα μαχαίρης, ἐδυναμώ-
of fire, escaped mouths(edges) of [the] sword, were en-

θησαν ἀπὸ ἀσθενείας, ἐγενήθησαν ἰσχυροὶ
powered from weakness, became strong

ἐν πολέμῳ, παρεμβολὰς ἔκλιναν ἀλλοτρίων.
in battle, ¹armies ²made to yield ²of foreigners.

35 ἔλαβον γυναῖκες ἐξ ἀναστάσεως τοὺς
²received ¹women ⁶by ⁷resurrection ³the

νεκροὺς αὐτῶν· ἄλλοι δὲ ἐτυμπανίσθησαν,
⁴dead ⁵of them; but others were beaten to death,

οὐ προσδεξάμενοι τὴν ἀπολύτρωσιν, ἵνα
not accepting – deliverance, in order that

κρείττονος ἀναστάσεως τύχωσιν· 36 ἕτεροι
²a better ²resurrection ¹they might others
obtain;

δὲ ἐμπαιγμῶν καὶ μαστίγων πεῖραν ἔλαβον,
and ²of mockings ⁴and ⁵of scourgings ³trial ¹took,

ἔτι δὲ δεσμῶν καὶ φυλακῆς· 37 ἐλιθάσ-
and more of bonds and of prison; they were

θησαν, ἐπειράσθησαν, ἐπρίσθησαν, ἐν φόνῳ
stoned, they were tried, they were ⁵by ⁴murder
sawn asunder,

μαχαίρης ἀπέθανον, περιῆλθον ἐν μηλωταῖς,
⁶of sword ¹they died, they went about in sheepskins,

ἐν αἰγείοις δέρμασιν, ὑστερούμενοι,
in goatskins, being in want,

θλιβόμενοι, κακουχούμενοι, 38 ὧν οὐκ ἦν
being afflicted, being ill treated, of whom was not

ἄξιος ὁ κόσμος, ἐπὶ ἐρημίαις πλανώμενοι
worthy the world, ²over ³deserts ¹wandering

καὶ ὄρεσιν καὶ σπηλαίοις καὶ ταῖς ὀπαῖς
and mountains and caves and the holes

τῆς γῆς. 39 Καὶ οὗτοι πάντες μαρτυρη-
of the earth. And these all having obtained

---

destroyer of the firstborn would not touch the firstborn of Israel.

29By faith the people passed through the Red Sea[v] as on dry land; but when the Egyptians tried to do so, they were drowned.

30By faith the walls of Jericho fell, after the people had marched around them for seven days.

31By faith the prostitute Rahab, because she welcomed the spies, was not killed with those who were disobedient.[w]

32And what more shall I say? I do not have time to tell about Gideon, Barak, Samson, Jephthah, David, Samuel and the prophets, 33who through faith conquered kingdoms, administered justice, and gained what was promised; who shut the mouths of lions, 34quenched the fury of the flames, and escaped the edge of the sword; whose weakness was turned to strength; and who became powerful in battle and routed foreign armies. 35Women received back their dead, raised to life again. Others were tortured and refused to be released, so that they might gain a better resurrection. 36Some faced jeers and flogging, while still others were chained and put in prison. 37They were stoned[x]; they were sawed in two; they were put to death by the sword. They went about in sheepskins and goatskins, destitute, persecuted and mistreated—38the world was not worthy of them. They wandered in deserts and mountains, and in caves and holes in the ground.

39These were all commended for their faith, yet

[v]29 That is, Sea of Reeds
[w]31 Or *unbelieving*
[x]37 Some early manuscripts *stoned; they were put to the test;*

their faith, did not receive what was promised, [40]because God had provided something better for us, so that apart from us they should not be made perfect.

θέντες   διὰ   τῆς   πίστεως   οὐκ   ἐκομίσαντο
witness   through   the(ir)   faith   obtained not
τὴν   ἐπαγγελίαν,   40 τοῦ   θεοῦ   περὶ   ἡμῶν
the   promise,   –   God   concerning   [2]us
κρεῖττόν   τι   προβλεψαμένου,   ἵνα   μὴ   χωρὶς
[3]better   [2]some-   [1]having foreseen,   in or-   not   without
                thing   der that
ἡμῶν   τελειωθῶσιν.
us   they should be perfected.

---

none of them received what had been promised. [40]God had planned something better for us so that only together with us would they be made perfect.

Chapter 12

Jesus, the Example

THEREFORE, since we have so great a cloud of witnesses surrounding us, let us also lay aside every encumbrance, and the sin which so easily entangles us, and let us run with endurance the race that is set before us,

[2]fixing our eyes on Jesus, the author and perfecter of faith, who for the joy set before Him endured the cross, despising the shame, and has sat down at the right hand of the throne of God.

[3]For consider Him who has endured such hostility by sinners against Himself, so that you may not grow weary and lose heart.

A Father's Discipline

[4]You have not yet resisted to the point of shedding blood in your striving against sin;

[5]and you have forgotten the exhortation which is addressed to you as sons,
"MY SON, DO NOT RE-
GARD LIGHTLY THE
DISCIPLINE OF THE
LORD,
NOR FAINT WHEN YOU
ARE REPROVED BY
HIM;
[6] FOR THOSE WHOM THE
LORD LOVES HE DISCI-
PLINES,
AND HE SCOURGES
EVERY SON WHOM HE
RECEIVES.''

[7]It is for discipline that you endure; God deals with you as with sons; for what son is there whom his father does not discipline?

[8]But if you are without discipline, of which all have become partakers, then you are illegitimate children and not sons.

[9]Furthermore, we had

Chapter 12

12 Τοιγαροῦν   καὶ   ἡμεῖς,   τοσοῦτον   ἔχοντες
So therefore   [2]also   [1]we,   [3]such   [1]having
περικείμενον   ἡμῖν   νέφος   μαρτύρων,   ὄγκον
[2]lying around   [3]us   [4]a cloud   [5]of witnesses,   [5]encum-
                                                    brance
ἀποθέμενοι   πάντα   καὶ   τὴν   εὐπερίστατον
[1]putting away   [2]every   [3]and   [4]the   [5]most besetting
ἁμαρτίαν,   δι'   ὑπομονῆς   τρέχωμεν   τὸν
[6]sin,   through   endurance   let us run   [1]the
προκείμενον   ἡμῖν   ἀγῶνα,   2 ἀφορῶντες   εἰς
[2]set before   [4]us   [3]contest(race),   looking away   to
τὸν   τῆς   πίστεως   ἀρχηγὸν   καὶ   τελειωτὴν
[1]the   [2]of the   [3]faith   [3]author   [3]and   [3]finisher
᾽Ιησοῦν,   ὃς   ἀντὶ   τῆς   προκειμένης   αὐτῷ
Jesus,   who   against   [1]the   [2]set before   [4]him
χαρᾶς   ὑπέμεινεν   σταυρὸν   αἰσχύνης   κατα-
[3]joy   endured   a cross   [2]shame   [1]de-
φρονήσας,   ἐν   δεξιᾷ   τε   τοῦ   θρόνου   τοῦ
spising,   [3]at   [4][the]   [1]and   [5]of the   [6]throne   [6]
                right [hand]
θεοῦ   κεκάθικεν.   3 ἀναλογίσασθε   γὰρ   τὸν
[7]of   [2]has taken   For consider ye   [1]the
God   [his] seat.   [one]
τοιαύτην   ὑπομεμενηκότα   ὑπὸ   τῶν   ἁμαρτω-
[3]such   [2]having endured   [4]by   –   [6]of sin-
λῶν   εἰς   ἑαυτὸν   ἀντιλογίαν,   ἵνα   μὴ   κάμητε
ners   [5]against   [7]himself   [6]contradiction,   lest   ye grow
                                                    weary
ταῖς   ψυχαῖς   ὑμῶν   ἐκλυόμενοι.   4 Οὔπω
[2]in the   [3]souls   [4]of you   [1]fainting.   Not yet
μέχρις   αἵματος   ἀντικατέστητε   πρὸς   τὴν
[1]until   [2]blood   [3]ye resisted   [4]against   –
ἁμαρτίαν   ἀνταγωνιζόμενοι,   5 καὶ   ἐκλέλησθε
[5]sin   [4]struggling against,   and   ye have
                                            forgotten
τῆς   παρακλήσεως,   ἥτις   ὑμῖν   ὡς   υἱοῖς
the   exhortation,   which   [1]with you   [3]as   [4]with sons
διαλέγεται·   υἱέ   μου,   μὴ   ὀλιγώρει   παιδείας
[1]discourses: Son   of me,   do not make   [the]
                                    light of   discipline
κυρίου,   μηδὲ   ἐκλύου   ὑπ'   αὐτοῦ   ἐλεγχόμενος·
of [the]   nor   faint   [2]by   [3]him   [1]being reproved;
Lord,
6 ὃν   γὰρ   ἀγαπᾷ   κύριος   παιδεύει,   μαστιγοῖ
for whom   [2]loves   [1][the] Lord   he disciplines,   [4]scourges
δὲ   πάντα   υἱὸν   ὃν   παραδέχεται.   7 εἰς
[3]and   every   son   whom   he receives.   For
παιδείαν   ὑπομένετε·   ὡς   υἱοῖς   ὑμῖν
discipline   endure ye;   [4]as   [5]with sons   [3]with you
προσφέρεται   ὁ   θεός·   τίς   γὰρ   υἱὸς   ὃν
[2]is dealing   –   [1]God;   for what   son whom
                                            [is there]
οὐ   παιδεύει   πατήρ;   8 εἰ   δὲ   χωρίς   ἐστε
[2]disciplines not   [1]a father?   But if   [2]without   [1]ye are
παιδείας,   ἧς   μέτοχοι   γεγόνασιν   πάντες,
discipline,   of which   [3]sharers   [2]have become   [1]all,
ἄρα   νόθοι   καὶ   οὐχ   υἱοί   ἐστε.   9 εἶτα
then   bastards   and   not   sons   ye are.   Furthermore

God Disciplines His Sons

THEREFORE, since we are surrounded by such a great cloud of witnesses, let us throw off everything that hinders and the sin that so easily entangles, and let us run with perseverance the race marked out for us. [2]Let us fix our eyes on Jesus, the author and perfecter of our faith, who for the joy set before him endured the cross, scorning its shame, and sat down at the right hand of the throne of God. [3]Consider him who endured such opposition from sinful men, so that you will not grow weary and lose heart.

[4]In your struggle against sin, you have not yet resisted to the point of shedding your blood. [5]And you have forgotten that word of encouragement that addresses you as sons:

"My son, do not make
    light of the Lord's
    discipline,
and do not lose heart
    when he rebukes
    you,
[6]because the Lord
    disciplines those he
    loves,
and he punishes
    everyone he accepts
    as a son."[y]

[7]Endure hardship as discipline; God is treating you as sons. For what son is not disciplined by his father? [8]If you are not disciplined (and everyone undergoes discipline), then you are illegitimate children and not true sons. [9]Moreover, we

earthly fathers to discipline us, and we respected them; shall we not much rather be subject to the Father of spirits, and live?

10For they disciplined us for a short time as seemed best to them, but He *disciplines us* for *our* good, that we may share His holiness.

11All discipline for the moment seems not to be joyful, but sorrowful; yet to those who have been trained by it, afterwards it yields the peaceful fruit of righteousness.

12Therefore, strengthen the hands that are weak and the knees that are feeble, 13and make straight paths for your feet, so that *the limb* which is lame may not be put out of joint, but rather be healed.

14Pursue peace with all men, and the sanctification without which no one will see the Lord.

15See to it that no one comes short of the grace of God; that no root of bitterness springing up causes trouble, and by it many be defiled;

16that *there be* no immoral or godless person like Esau, who sold his own birthright for a *single* meal.

17For you know that even afterwards, when he desired to inherit the blessing, he was rejected, for he found no place for repentance, though he sought it with tears.

Contrast of Sinai and Zion

18For you have not come to *a mountain* that may be touched and to a blazing fire, and to darkness and gloom and whirlwind,

---

τοὺς   μὲν   τῆς   σαρκὸς   ἡμῶν   πατέρας
the   -   ᵃof the ⁴flesh   ᵃof us   ²fathers

εἴχομεν   παιδευτὰς   καὶ   ἐνετρεπόμεθα·   οὐ
¹we had   ⁶correctors   and   we respected [them]:   ¹not

πολὺ   μᾶλλον   ὑποταγησόμεθα   τῷ   πατρὶ
⁸much   ⁷more   ¹shall ²we ⁴be ⁵subject   to the   Father

τῶν   πνευμάτων   καὶ   ζήσομεν;   10 οἱ   μὲν
 -     of spirits   and   and we shall live ?   ²they ¹indeed

γὰρ   πρὸς   ὀλίγας   ἡμέρας   κατὰ   τὸ   δοκοῦν
¹for   for   a few   days   accord-   the   seeming
                                  ing to   thing   [good]

αὐτοῖς   ἐπαίδευον,   ὁ   δὲ   ἐπὶ   τὸ   συμφέρον
to them   disciplined [us],   but he   for   the(our)   profit

εἰς   τὸ   μεταλαβεῖν   τῆς   ἁγιότητος   αὐτοῦ.
for   the   to partake   of the   sanctity   of him.

11 πᾶσα   μὲν   παιδεία   πρὸς   μὲν   τὸ   παρὸν
²All   ¹on   ³discipline   ⁴for   ¹in-   ⁵the   ⁶present
       one hand   deed

οὐ   δοκεῖ   χαρᾶς   εἶναι   ἀλλὰ   λύπης,   ὕστερον
seems not   ²of joy   ¹to be   but   of grief,   ²later

δὲ   καρπὸν   εἰρηνικὸν   τοῖς   δι'   αὐτῆς
¹on the   ⁵fruit   ⁶peaceable   ⁷to the   ⁸through   ¹⁰it
other   [ones]

γεγυμνασμένοις   ἀποδίδωσιν   δικαιοσύνης.
⁹having been exercised   ³it gives back   ⁴of righteousness.

12 Διὸ   τὰς   παρειμένας   χεῖρας   καὶ   τὰ
Where-   ²the   ³having been   ⁴hands   ⁵and   ⁶the
fore   wearied

παραλελυμένα   γόνατα   ἀνορθώσατε,   13 καὶ
⁷having been paralysed   ⁸knees   ¹straighten ye,   and

τροχιὰς   ὀρθὰς   ποιεῖτε   τοῖς   ποσὶν   ὑμῶν,
tracks   straight   make   for the   feet   of you,

ἵνα   μὴ   τὸ   χωλὸν   ἐκτραπῇ,   ἰαθῇ   δὲ
lest   the   lame   be turned   ¹may   ¹but
                       aside,   be cured

μᾶλλον.   14 Εἰρήνην   διώκετε   μετὰ   πάντων,
²rather.   Peace   follow   with   all men,

καὶ   τὸν   ἁγιασμόν,   οὗ   χωρὶς   οὐδεὶς
and   the   sanctification,   ²which   ¹without   no one·

ὄψεται   τὸν   κύριον,   15 ἐπισκοποῦντες   μὴ
will see   the   Lord,   observing   not(lest)

τις   ὑστερῶν   ἀπὸ   τῆς   χάριτος   τοῦ   θεοῦ,
anyone failing   from   the   grace   -   of God,

μή   τις   ῥίζα   πικρίας   ἄνω   φύουσα   ἐνοχλῇ
not   any   root   of bitterness   ²up   ¹growing   disturb
(lest)

καὶ   διὰ   ταύτης   μιανθῶσιν   οἱ   πολλοί,
and   through   this   ²be defiled   the   ¹many,

16 μή   τις   πόρνος   ἢ   βέβηλος   ὡς   Ἠσαῦ,
not(lest) any   fornicator   or   profane man   as   Esau,

ὃς   ἀντὶ   βρώσεως   μιᾶς   ἀπέδοτο   τὰ
who   against   ²eating   ¹one   gave up   the

πρωτοτόκια   ἑαυτοῦ.   17 ἴστε   γὰρ   ὅτι
rights of   of himself.   For ye know   that
the firstborn

καὶ   μετέπειτα   θέλων   κληρονομῆσαι   τὴν
indeed   afterwards   wishing   to inherit   the

εὐλογίαν   ἀπεδοκιμάσθη,   μετανοίας   γὰρ
blessing   he was rejected,   for ⁴of repentance

τόπον   οὐχ   εὗρεν,   καίπερ   μετὰ   δακρύων
²place   ¹not   ¹he found,   though   with   tears

ἐκζητήσας   αὐτήν.   18 Οὐ   γὰρ   προσεληλύθατε
seeking out   it.   For ¹not   ¹ye ²have ⁴approached

ψηλαφωμένῳ   καὶ   κεκαυμένῳ   πυρὶ   καὶ
to [a mountain]   and   having been   with   and
being felt   ignited   fire

γνόφῳ   καὶ   ζόφῳ   καὶ   θυέλλῃ   19 καὶ
to darkness   and   to deep gloom   and   to whirlwind   and

---

have all had human fathers who disciplined us and we respected them for it. How much more should we submit to the Father of our spirits and live! 10Our fathers disciplined us for a little while as they thought best; but God disciplines us for our good, that we may share in his holiness. 11No discipline seems pleasant at the time, but painful. Later on, however, it produces a harvest of righteousness and peace for those who have been trained by it. 12Therefore, strengthen your feeble arms and weak knees. 13"Make level paths for your feet," *z* so that the lame may not be disabled, but rather healed.

Warning Against Refusing God

14Make every effort to live in peace with all men and to be holy; without holiness no one will see the Lord. 15See to it that no one misses the grace of God and that no bitter root grows up to cause trouble and defile many. 16See that no one is sexually immoral, or is godless like Esau, who for a single meal sold his inheritance rights as the oldest son. 17Afterward, as you know, when he wanted to inherit this blessing, he was rejected. He could bring about no change of mind, though he sought the blessing with tears.

18You have not come to a mountain that can be touched and that is burning with fire; to darkness, gloom and storm; 19to a

z13 Prov. 4:26

19and to the blast of a trumpet and the sound of words which *sound was such that* those who heard begged that no further word should be spoken to them.

20For they could not bear the command, "IF EVEN A BEAST TOUCHES THE MOUNTAIN, IT WILL BE STONED."

21And so terrible was the sight, *that* Moses said, "I AM FULL OF FEAR and trembling."

22But you have come to Mount Zion and to the city of the living God, the heavenly Jerusalem, and to myriads of angels,

23to the general assembly and church of the first-born who are enrolled in heaven, and to God, the Judge of all, and to the spirits of righteous men made perfect,

24and to Jesus, the mediator of a new covenant, and to the sprinkled blood, which speaks better than *the blood of* Abel.

The Unshaken Kingdom

25See to it that you do not refuse Him who is speaking. For if those did not escape when they refused him who warned them on earth, much less *shall* we *escape* who turn away from Him who *warns* from heaven.

26And His voice shook the earth then, but now He has promised, saying, "YET ONCE MORE I WILL SHAKE NOT ONLY THE EARTH, BUT ALSO THE HEAVEN."

27And this *expression*, "Yet once more," denotes the removing of those things which can be shaken, as of created things, in order that those things which cannot be shaken may remain.

28Therefore, since we receive a kingdom which cannot be shaken, let us show gratitude, by which we may offer to God an acceptable service with reverence and awe;

29for our God is a consuming fire.

σάλπιγγος ἤχῳ καὶ φωνῇ ῥημάτων, ἧς
²of trumpet ¹to a sound and to a voice of words, which

οἱ ἀκούσαντες παρῃτήσαντο μὴ προστεθῆναι
the [ones] hearing entreated not to be added

αὐτοῖς λόγον· 20 οὐκ ἔφερον γὰρ τὸ
to them a word; ²not ¹they bore ¹for the thing

διαστελλόμενον· κἂν θηρίον θίγῃ τοῦ ὄρους,
being charged: If even a beast touches the mountain,

λιθοβοληθήσεται· 21 καὶ, οὕτω φοβερὸν ἦν
it shall be stoned; and, so fearful was

τὸ φανταζόμενον, Μωϋσῆς εἶπεν· ἔκφοβός
the thing appearing, Moses said: ¹Terrified

εἰμι καὶ ἔντρομος· 22 ἀλλὰ προσεληλύθατε
¹I am and trembling; but ye have approached

Σιὼν ὄρει καὶ πόλει θεοῦ ζῶντος,
²Zion ¹to mount and to a city ²God ¹of [the] living,

Ἰερουσαλὴμ ἐπουρανίῳ, καὶ μυριάσιν
²Jerusalem ¹to a heavenly, and to myriads

ἀγγέλων, 23 πανηγύρει καὶ ἐκκλησίᾳ
of angels, to an assembly and a church

πρωτοτόκων ἀπογεγραμμένων ἐν οὐρανοῖς,
of firstborn [ones] having been enrolled in heavens,

καὶ κριτῇ θεῷ πάντων, καὶ πνεύμασι
and ²judge ¹to God of all men, and to spirits

δικαίων τετελειωμένων, 24 καὶ διαθήκης
of just men having been made and ⁴covenant perfect,

νέας μεσίτῃ Ἰησοῦ, καὶ αἵματι ῥαντισμοῦ
²of a ²mediator ¹to Jesus, and to blood of sprinkling new

κρεῖττον λαλοῦντι παρὰ τὸν Ἄβελ.
²a better thing ¹speaking than – Abel.

25 Βλέπετε μὴ παραιτήσησθε τὸν λαλοῦντα·
Look ye [that] ²not ¹ye refuse the [one] speaking;

εἰ γὰρ ἐκεῖνοι οὐκ ἐξέφυγον ἐπὶ γῆς
for if those escaped not ⁴on ⁵earth

παραιτησάμενοι τὸν χρηματίζοντα, πολὺ
¹refusing ²the [one] ³warning, much

μᾶλλον ἡμεῖς οἱ τὸν ἀπ' οὐρανῶν
more we* ¹the ³the [one] ⁵from ⁶heavens [ones] ⁴[warning]

ἀποστρεφόμενοι· 26 οὗ ἡ φωνὴ τὴν γῆν
²turning from; of whom the voice ³the ⁴earth

ἐσάλευσεν τότε, νῦν δὲ ἐπήγγελται λέγων·
²shook ¹then, but now he has promised saying:

ἔτι ἅπαξ ἐγὼ σείσω οὐ μόνον τὴν
Yet once I will shake not only the

γῆν ἀλλὰ καὶ τὸν οὐρανόν. 27 τὸ δὲ
earth but also *the* heaven. Now the [phrase]

ἔτι ἅπαξ δηλοῖ τὴν τῶν σαλευομένων
'Yet once' declares ¹the ³of the things ⁴being shaken

μετάθεσιν ὡς πεποιημένων, ἵνα μείνῃ τὰ
²removal as of things having been made, der that remain things ⁴may ¹the

μὴ σαλευόμενα. 28 Διὸ βασιλείαν ἀσάλευτος
²not ¹being shaken. Wherefore ³kingdom ²an unshakable

παραλαμβάνοντες ἔχωμεν χάριν, δι' ἧς
¹receiving let us have grace, through which

λατρεύωμεν εὐαρέστως τῷ θεῷ, μετὰ
we may serve ²well-pleasingly – ¹God, with

εὐλαβείας καὶ δέους· 29 καὶ γὰρ ὁ θεὸς
devoutness and awe; for indeed the God

ἡμῶν πῦρ καταναλίσκον.
of us [is] fire a consuming.

* That is, "much more [shall] we [not escape]"; or, putting it in another way, "much less shall we escape."

---

trumpet blast or to such a voice speaking words that those who heard it begged that no further word be spoken to them, 20because they could not bear what was commanded: "If even an animal touches the mountain, it must be stoned." *a* 21The sight was so terrifying that Moses said, "I am trembling with fear." *b*

22But you have come to Mount Zion, to the heavenly Jerusalem, the city of the living God. You have come to thousands upon thousands of angels in joyful assembly, 23to the church of the firstborn, whose names are written in heaven. You have come to God, the judge of all men, to the spirits of righteous men made perfect, 24to Jesus the mediator of a new covenant, and to the sprinkled blood that speaks a better word than the blood of Abel.

25See to it that you do not refuse him who speaks. If they did not escape when they refused him who warned them on earth, how much less will we, if we turn away from him who warns us from heaven? 26At that time his voice shook the earth, but now he has promised, "Once more I will shake not only the earth but also the heavens." *c* 27The words "once more" indicate the removing of what can be shaken—that is, created things—so that what cannot be shaken may remain.

28Therefore, since we are receiving a kingdom that cannot be shaken, let us be thankful, and so worship God acceptably with reverence and awe, 29for our "God is a consuming fire." *d*

Chapter 13

The Changeless Christ

LET love of the brethren continue.

2Do not neglect to show hospitality to strangers, for by this some have entertained angels without knowing it.

3Remember the prisoners, as though in prison with them, and those who are ill-treated, since you yourselves also are in the body.

4Let marriage be held in honor among all, and let the marriage bed be undefiled; for fornicators and adulterers God will judge.

5Let your character be free from the love of money, being content with what you have; for He Himself has said, "I WILL NEVER DESERT YOU, NOR WILL I EVER FORSAKE YOU,"

6so that we confidently say,

"THE LORD IS MY HELPER, I WILL NOT BE AFRAID.
WHAT SHALL MAN DO TO ME?"

7Remember those who led you, who spoke the word of God to you; and considering the result of their conduct, imitate their faith.

8Jesus Christ is the same yesterday and today, yes and forever.

9Do not be carried away by varied and strange teachings; for it is good for the heart to be strengthened by grace, not by foods, through which those who were thus occupied were not benefited.

10We have an altar, from which those who serve the tabernacle have no right to eat.

11For the bodies of those animals whose blood is brought into the holy place by the high priest as an offering for sin, are burned outside the camp.

12Therefore Jesus also, that He might sanctify the

---

13 Ἡ   φιλαδελφία   μενέτω.   **2** τῆς
\-   ²brotherly love   ¹Let it remain.   -

φιλοξενίας   μὴ   ἐπιλανθάνεσθε·   διὰ   ταύτης
of hospitality   Be ye not forgetful;   ²through   ³this

γὰρ   ἔλαθόν   τινες   ξενίσαντες   ἀγγέλους.
¹for   ⁵unconsciously†   ⁴some   ⁶entertaining(ed)   ⁷angels.

3 μιμνήσκεσθε   τῶν   δεσμίων   ὡς   συνδεδεμένοι,
Be ye mindful   of the   prisoners   as   having been bound with [them],

τῶν   κακουχουμένων   ὡς   καὶ   αὐτοὶ   ὄντες
of the   being ill treated [ones]   as   also   [your]selves   being

ἐν   σώματι.   **4** Τίμιος   ὁ   γάμος   ἐν   πᾶσιν
in [the] body.   ⁴honourable   -   ²marriage   in   all
   ¹[Let]   ³[be]

καὶ   ἡ   κοίτη   ἀμίαντος·   πόρνους   γὰρ
and   the   bed   undefiled;   for fornicators

καὶ   μοιχοὺς   κρινεῖ   ὁ   θεός.   **5** Ἀφιλάργυρος
and   adulterers   ²will judge   -   ¹God.   ⁵without love of money

ὁ   τρόπος,   ἀρκούμενοι   τοῖς   παροῦσιν·
¹[Let]   ²way of   being satisfied   the things   present;
  ³the   life ⁴[be],   with
(your)

αὐτὸς   γὰρ   εἴρηκεν·   οὐ   μή   σε   ἀνῶ   οὐδ'
for he   has said: By no means thee   will I leave   nor

οὐ   μή   σε   ἐγκαταλίπω·   **6** ὥστε   θαρροῦντας
by no(any) thee   I forsake;   so as   being of good cheer
means

ἡμᾶς   λέγειν·   κύριος   ἐμοὶ   βοηθός,   οὐ
us   to say[b]:   [The] Lord   to me° [is] a helper,   not

φοβηθήσομαι·   τί   ποιήσει   μοι   ἄνθρωπος;
I will fear;   what   ¹will ³do   ⁴to me   ²man ?

7 Μνημονεύετε   τῶν   ἡγουμένων   ὑμῶν,
Remember   the [ones]   leading   of you,

οἵτινες   ἐλάλησαν   ὑμῖν   τὸν   λόγον   τοῦ
who   spoke   to you   the   word   -

θεοῦ,   ὧν   ἀναθεωροῦντες   τὴν   ἔκβασιν   τῆς
of God,   ¹of whom   ⁵looking at   ²the   ³result   ⁴of the

ἀναστροφῆς   μιμεῖσθε   τὴν   πίστιν.   **8** Ἰησοῦς
⁶conduct   imitate ye   the(ir)   faith.   Jesus

Χριστὸς   ἐχθὲς   καὶ   σήμερον   ὁ   αὐτός·
Christ   ⁴yesterday   ⁵and   ⁶to-day   ¹[is] ²the   ³same

καὶ   εἰς   τοὺς   αἰῶνας.   **9** Διδαχαῖς   ποικίλαις
and   unto   the   ages.   ¹teachings   ²by various

καὶ   ξέναις   μὴ   παραφέρεσθε·   καλὸν   γὰρ
³and   ⁴strange   ¹Do not be carried away;   for [it is] good

χάριτι   βεβαιοῦσθαι   τὴν   καρδίαν,   οὐ
⁴by grace   ³to be confirmed   ¹the   ²heart,[b]   not

βρώμασιν,   ἐν   οἷς   οὐκ   ὠφελήθησαν   οἱ
by foods,   by   which   ²were not profited   ¹the

περιπατοῦντες.   **10** ἔχομεν   θυσιαστήριον   ἐξ
²[ones] walking.   We have   an altar   of

οὗ   φαγεῖν   οὐκ   ἔχουσιν   ἐξουσίαν   οἱ   τῇ
which   ⁷to eat   ⁵have not   ⁶authority   ¹the   ³the
   [ones]

σκηνῇ   λατρεύοντες.   **11** ὧν   γὰρ   εἰσφέρεται
⁴tabernacle   ²serving.   For ³of what   ¹is brought in

ζῴων   τὸ   αἷμα   περὶ   ἁμαρτίας   εἰς   τὰ
⁴animals   ¹the   ²blood   ⁵concerning   ⁶sins   into   the

ἅγια   διὰ   τοῦ   ἀρχιερέως,   τούτων   τὰ
holies   through   the   high priest,   of these   the

σώματα   κατακαίεται   ἔξω   τῆς   παρεμβολῆς.
bodies   is(are) burned   outside   the   camp.

12 διὸ   καὶ   Ἰησοῦς,   ἵνα   ἁγιάσῃ   διὰ
Where-   in-   Jesus,   in order   he might ²through
fore   deed   that   sanctify

Chapter 13

Concluding Exhortations

KEEP on loving each other as brothers.

2Do not forget to entertain strangers, for by so doing some people have entertained angels without knowing it. 3Remember those in prison as if you were their fellow prisoners, and those who are mistreated as if you yourselves were suffering.

4Marriage should be honored by all, and the marriage bed kept pure, for God will judge the adulterer and all the sexually immoral. 5Keep your lives free from the love of money and be content with what you have, because God has said,

"Never will I leave you; never will I forsake you."[e]

6So we say with confidence,

"The Lord is my helper; I will not be afraid. What can man do to me?"[f]

7Remember your leaders, who spoke the word of God to you. Consider the outcome of their way of life and imitate their faith. 8Jesus Christ is the same yesterday and today and forever.

9Do not be carried away by all kinds of strange teachings. It is good for our hearts to be strengthened by grace, not by ceremonial foods, which are of no value to those who eat them. 10We have an altar from which those who minister at the tabernacle have no right to eat.

11The high priest carries the blood of animals into the Most Holy Place as a sin offering, but the bodies are burned outside the camp. 12And so Jesus also suffered outside the city

[e]5 Deut. 31:6
[f]6 Psalm 118:6,7

people through His own
blood, suffered outside the
gate.
13Hence, let us go out to
Him outside the camp,
bearing His reproach.
14For here we do not have
a lasting city, but we are
seeking *the city* which is to
come.

God-pleasing Sacrifices

15Through Him then, let
us continually offer up a
sacrifice of praise to God,
that is, the fruit of lips that
give thanks to His name.
16And do not neglect do-
ing good and sharing; for
with such sacrifices God is
pleased.
17Obey your leaders, and
submit *to them*; for they
keep watch over your
souls, as those who will
give an account. Let them
do this with joy and not
with grief, for this would be
unprofitable for you.
18Pray for us, for we are
sure that we have a good
conscience, desiring to
conduct ourselves honor-
ably in all things.
19And I urge *you* all the
more to do this, that I may
be restored to you the
sooner.

Benediction

20Now the God of peace,
who brought up from the
dead the great Shepherd of
the sheep through the
blood of the eternal cov-
enant, *even* Jesus our
Lord,
21equip you in every good
thing to do His will, working in us that which is pleasing in His sight, through
Jesus Christ, to whom *be*
the glory forever and ever.

τοῦ ἰδίου αἵματος τὸν λαόν, ἔξω τῆς
⁴the(his) ⁵own ⁶blood ¹the ²people, outside the
πύλης ἔπαθεν. 13 τοίνυν ἐξερχώμεθα πρὸς
gate suffered. So let us go forth to
αὐτὸν ἔξω τῆς παρεμβολῆς τὸν ὀνειδισμὸν
him outside the camp the reproach
αὐτοῦ φέροντες· 14 οὐ γὰρ ἔχομεν ὧδε
of him bearing; for ²not ¹we have here
μένουσαν πόλιν, ἀλλὰ τὴν μέλλουσαν
a continuing city, but the [one] coming
ἐπιζητοῦμεν. 15 Δι' αὐτοῦ οὖν ἀναφέρωμεν
we seek. Through him therefore let us offer up
θυσίαν αἰνέσεως διὰ παντὸς τῷ θεῷ,
a sacrifice of praise always - to God,
τοῦτ' ἔστιν καρπὸν χειλέων ὁμολογούντων
this is fruit of lips confessing
τῷ ὀνόματι αὐτοῦ. 16 τῆς δὲ εὐποιΐας
to the name of him. But of the doing good
καὶ κοινωνίας μὴ ἐπιλανθάνεσθε· τοιαύταις
and sharing be ye not forgetful; ²with such
γὰρ θυσίαις εὐαρεστεῖται ὁ θεός. 17 Πεί-
¹for sacrifices ²is well pleased - ¹God. Obey
θεσθε τοῖς ἡγουμένοις ὑμῶν καὶ ὑπείκετε·
ye the [ones] leading of you and submit to
[them];
αὐτοὶ γὰρ ἀγρυπνοῦσιν ὑπὲρ τῶν ψυχῶν
for they watch on behalf of the souls
ὑμῶν ὡς λόγον ἀποδώσοντες· ἵνα μετὰ
of you as ²account ¹rendering*; in or- with
der that
χαρᾶς τοῦτο ποιῶσιν καὶ μὴ στενάζ-
joy ²this ¹they may do and not groan-
οντες· ἀλυσιτελὲς γὰρ ὑμῖν τοῦτο.
ing; for profitless to you this
[would be].
18 Προσεύχεσθε περὶ ἡμῶν· πειθόμεθα
Pray ye concerning us; ²we are persuaded
γὰρ ὅτι καλὴν συνείδησιν ἔχομεν, ἐν
¹for that a good conscience we have, ⁴in
πᾶσιν καλῶς θέλοντες ἀναστρέφεσθαι.
⁵all [respects] ²well ¹wishing ³to behave.
19 περισσοτέρως δὲ παρακαλῶ τοῦτο
And more abundantly I beseech [you] this
ποιῆσαι, ἵνα τάχιον ἀποκατασταθῶ ὑμῖν.
to do, in or- sooner I may be restored to you.
der that
20 Ὁ δὲ θεὸς τῆς εἰρήνης, ὁ ἀναγαγὼν
Now the God - of peace, the having led up
[one]
ἐκ νεκρῶν τὸν ποιμένα τῶν προβάτων
out [the] dead the ²shepherd ³of the ⁴sheep
of
τὸν μέγαν ἐν αἵματι διαθήκης αἰωνίου,
the ¹great in (? with) blood ²covenant ¹of an eternal,
τὸν κύριον ἡμῶν Ἰησοῦν, 21 καταρτίσαι
the Lord of us Jesus, may he adjust
ὑμᾶς ἐν παντὶ ἀγαθῷ εἰς τὸ ποιῆσαι
you in every good thing for the to do
τὸ θέλημα αὐτοῦ, ποιῶν ἐν ἡμῖν· τὸ
the will of him, doing in us the
[thing]
εὐάρεστον ἐνώπιον αὐτοῦ διὰ Ἰησοῦ
wellpleasing before him through Jesus
Χριστοῦ, ᾧ ἡ δόξα εἰς τοὺς αἰῶνας
Christ, to [be] glory unto the ages
whom the

gate to make the people
holy through his own
blood. Then, let us, go to
him outside the camp,
bearing the disgrace he
bore. 14For here we do not
have an enduring city, but
we are looking for the city
that is to come.
15Through Jesus, there-
fore, let us continually offer to God a sacrifice of
praise—the fruit of lips that
confess his name. 16And do
not forget to do good and to
share with others, for with
such sacrifices God is
pleased.
17Obey your leaders and
submit to their authority.
They keep watch over you
as men who must give an
account. Obey them so that
their work will be a joy, not
a burden, for that would be
of no advantage to you.
18Pray for us. We are sure
that we have a clear con-
science and desire to live
honorably in every way. 19I
particularly urge you to
pray so that I may be re-
stored to you soon.
20May the God of peace,
who brought the blood of
the eternal covenant
brought back from the dead
our Lord Jesus, that great
Shepherd of the sheep,
21equip you with every-
thing good for doing his
will, and may he work in us
what is pleasing to him,
through Jesus Christ, to
whom be glory for ever and

* In the future.

Amen.
22But I urge you, brethren, bear with this word of exhortation, for I have written to you briefly.
23Take notice that our brother Timothy has been released, with whom, if he comes soon, I shall see you.
24Greet all of your leaders and all the saints. Those from Italy greet you.
25Grace be with you all.

τῶν   αἰώνων·   ἀμήν.   **22** Παρακαλῶ   δὲ
of the   ages: Amen.   And I beseech

ὑμᾶς,   ἀδελφοί,   ἀνέχεσθε   τοῦ   λόγου   τῆς
you,   brothers,   endure   the   word   -

παρακλήσεως·   καὶ   γὰρ   διὰ   βραχέων
of beseeching;   for indeed   through   few [words]

ἐπέστειλα   ὑμῖν.   **23** Γινώσκετε   τὸν   ἀδελφὸν
I wrote   to you.   Know ye   the   brother

ἡμῶν   Τιμόθεον   ἀπολελυμένον,   μεθ'   οὗ
of us   Timothy   having been released,   with   whom

ἐὰν   τάχιον   ἔρχηται   ὄψομαι   ὑμᾶς.
if   sooner   I come   I will see   you.

24 Ἀσπάσασθε   πάντας   τοὺς   ἡγουμένους
Greet ye   all   the [ones]   leading

ὑμῶν   καὶ   πάντας   τοὺς   ἁγίους.   Ἀσπάζονται
of you   and   all   the   saints.   ⁴greet

ὑμᾶς   οἱ   ἀπὸ   τῆς   Ἰταλίας.
¹you   ¹The [ones]   ²from   -   ³Italy.

25 Ἡ   χάρις   μετὰ   πάντων   ὑμῶν.
-    Grace [be]   with   all   you.

ever. Amen.
22Brothers, I urge you to bear with my word of exhortation, for I have written you only a short letter.
23I want you to know that our brother Timothy has been released. If he arrives soon, I will come with him to see you.
24Greet all your leaders and all God's people. Those from Italy send you their greetings.
25Grace be with you all.

James

Chapter 1

Testing Your Faith

JAMES, a bond-servant of God and of the Lord Jesus Christ, to the twelve tribes who are dispersed abroad, greetings.
2Consider it all joy, my brethren, when you encounter various trials,
3knowing that the testing of your faith produces endurance.
4And let endurance have its perfect result, that you may be perfect and complete, lacking in nothing.
5But if any of you lacks wisdom, let him ask of God, who gives to all men generously and without reproach, and it will be given to him.
6But let him ask in faith without any doubting, for the one who doubts is like the surf of the sea driven and tossed by the wind.
7For let not that man expect that he will receive anything from the Lord,

ΙΑΚΩΒΟΥ ΕΠΙΣΤΟΛΗ
²Of James ¹Epistle

1 Ἰάκωβος   θεοῦ   καὶ   κυρίου   Ἰησοῦ
James   ²of God   ³and   ⁴of [the] Lord   ⁵Jesus

Χριστοῦ   δοῦλος   ταῖς   δώδεκα   φυλαῖς   ταῖς
⁶Christ   ¹a slave   to the   twelve   tribes   -

ἐν   τῇ   διασπορᾷ   χαίρειν.*
in   the   dispersion   greeting.*

2 Πᾶσαν   χαρὰν   ἡγήσασθε,   ἀδελφοί   μου,
All   joy   deem [it],   brothers   of me,

ὅταν   πειρασμοῖς   περιπέσητε   ποικίλοις,
whenever   ²trials   ¹ye fall   ²into various,

3 γινώσκοντες   ὅτι   τὸ   δοκίμιον   ὑμῶν   τῆς
knowing   that   the   approved part   ³of you   ¹of the
= that which is approved in your faith

πίστεως   κατεργάζεται   ὑπομονήν.   **4** ἡ   δὲ
²faith   works   endurance.   - And

ὑπομονὴ   ἔργον   τέλειον   ἐχέτω,   ἵνα   ἦτε
endurance   ³work   ²perfect   ¹let it   in or-   ye may
have,   der that   be

τέλειοι   καὶ   ὁλόκληροι,   ἐν   μηδενὶ   λειπόμενοι.
perfect   and   entire,   in   nothing   wanting.

5 Εἰ   δέ   τις   ὑμῶν   λείπεται   σοφίας,   αἰτείτω
if   But   any-   of you   wants   wisdom,   let him
one   ask

παρὰ   τοῦ   διδόντος   θεοῦ   πᾶσιν   ἁπλῶς
from   ²the   ²giving   ¹God   to all   unre-
[one]   men   servedly

καὶ   μὴ   ὀνειδίζοντος,   καὶ   δοθήσεται   αὐτῷ.
and   not   reproaching,   and   it will be given   to him.

6 αἰτείτω   δὲ   ἐν   πίστει,   μηδὲν   διακριν-
But let him ask   in   faith,   nothing   doubt-

όμενος·   ὁ   γὰρ   διακρινόμενος   ἔοικεν   κλύδωνι
ing;   for the [one] doubting   is like   a wave

θαλάσσης   ἀνεμιζομένῳ   καὶ   ῥιπιζομένῳ.
of [the] sea   being driven by wind   and   being tossed.

7 μὴ   γὰρ   οἰέσθω   ὁ   ἄνθρωπος   ἐκεῖνος
For let not ³suppose   ¹that   ²man

ὅτι   λήμψεταί   τι   παρὰ   τοῦ   κυρίου,   **8** ἀνὴρ
that   he will   any-   from   the   Lord,   a man
receive   thing

James

Chapter 1

JAMES, a servant of God and of the Lord Jesus Christ,

To the twelve tribes scattered among the nations:

Greetings.

Trials and Temptations

2Consider it pure joy, my brothers, whenever you face trials of many kinds, 3because you know that the testing of your faith develops perseverance. 4Perseverance must finish its work so that you may be mature and complete, not lacking anything. 5If any of you lacks wisdom, he should ask God, who gives generously to all without finding fault, and it will be given to him. 6But when he asks, he must believe and not doubt, because he who doubts is like a wave of the sea, blown and tossed by the wind. 7That man should not think he will receive anything from the Lord;

* See note on Phil. 3.16 in Introduction.

8being a double-minded man, unstable in all his ways. 9But let the brother of humble circumstances glory in his high position; 10and *let* the rich man *glory* in his humiliation, because like flowering grass he will pass away. 11For the sun rises with a scorching wind, and withers the grass; and its flower falls off, and the beauty of its appearance is destroyed; so too the rich man in the midst of his pursuits will fade away. 12Blessed is a man who perseveres under trial; for once he has been approved, he will receive the crown of life, which *the Lord* has promised to those who love Him. 13Let no one say when he is tempted, "I am being tempted by God"; for God cannot be tempted by evil, and He Himself does not tempt anyone. 14But each one is tempted when he is carried away and enticed by his own lust. 15Then when lust has conceived, it gives birth to sin; and when sin is accomplished, it brings forth death. 16Do not be deceived, my beloved brethren. 17Every good thing bestowed and every perfect gift is from above, coming down from the Father of lights, with whom there is no variation, or shifting shadow. 18In the exercise of His will He brought us forth by the word of truth, so that we might be, as it were, the first fruits among His creatures. 19*a*This you know, my beloved brethren. But let

δίψυχος,   ἀκατάστατος   ἐν   πάσαις   ταῖς
two-souled,   unsettled   in   all   the

ὁδοῖς   αὐτοῦ.   9 Καυχάσθω   δὲ   ὁ   ἀδελφὸς
ways   of him.   But let ⁴boast   ¹the   ³brother

ὁ   ταπεινὸς   ἐν   τῷ   ὕψει   αὐτοῦ,   10 ὁ   δὲ
–   ²humble   in   the   height   of him,   the   and

πλούσιος   ἐν   τῇ   ταπεινώσει   αὐτοῦ,   ὅτι
rich one   in   the   humiliation   of him,   because

ὡς   ἄνθος   χόρτου   παρελεύσεται.   11 ἀνέτειλεν
as   a flower   of grass   he will pass away.   ⁴rose

γὰρ   ὁ   ἥλιος   σὺν   τῷ   καύσωνι   καὶ   ἐξήρανεν
¹For   ²the   ³sun   with   the   hot wind   and   dried

τὸν   χόρτον,   καὶ   τὸ   ἄνθος   αὐτοῦ   ἐξέπεσεν
the   grass,   and   the   flower   of it   fell out

καὶ   ἡ   εὐπρέπεια   τοῦ   προσώπου   αὐτοῦ
and   the   comeliness   of the   appearance   of it

ἀπώλετο·   οὕτως   καὶ   ὁ   πλούσιος   ἐν   ταῖς
perished;   thus   also   the   rich man   in   the

πορείαις   αὐτοῦ   μαρανθήσεται.   12 Μακάριος
goings   of him   will fade away.   Blessed

ἀνὴρ   ὃς   ὑπομένει   πειρασμόν,   ὅτι   δόκιμος
[the]   who   endures   trial,   because ²approved
man

γενόμενος   λήμψεται   τὸν   στέφανον   τῆς
¹having become he will receive the   crown   –

ζωῆς,   ὃν   ἐπηγγείλατο   τοῖς   ἀγαπῶσιν   αὐτόν.
of life,   which he promised   to the [ones] loving   him.

13 Μηδεὶς   πειραζόμενος   λεγέτω   ὅτι   ἀπὸ
¹no man   ³being tempted   ²Let ⁴say[,]   –   From

θεοῦ   πειράζομαι·   –   γὰρ   θεὸς   ἀπείραστός
God   I am tempted;   –   for   God   ³untempted

ἐστιν   κακῶν,   πειράζει   δὲ   αὐτὸς   οὐδένα.
¹is   of(with)   and ²tempts   ¹he   no man.
         evil things,

14 ἕκαστος   δὲ   πειράζεται   ὑπὸ   τῆς   ἰδίας
But each man   is tempted   by   the(his)   own

ἐπιθυμίας   ἐξελκόμενος   καὶ   δελεαζόμενος·
lusts   being drawn out   and   *being* enticed;

15 εἶτα   ἡ   ἐπιθυμία   συλλαβοῦσα   τίκτει
then   –   lust   having conceived   bears

ἁμαρτίαν,   ἡ   δὲ   ἁμαρτία   ἀποτελεσθεῖσα
sin,   the   and   sin   having been
                                              fully formed

ἀποκύει   θάνατον.   16 Μὴ   πλανᾶσθε,   ἀδελφοί
brings forth death.   Do not err,   ²brothers

μου   ἀγαπητοί.
³of me   ¹beloved.

17 Πᾶσα΄   δόσις   ἀγαθὴ   καὶ   πᾶν   δώρημα
Every   ²giving   ¹good   and   every   ¹gift

τέλειον   ἄνωθέν   ἐστιν   καταβαῖνον   ἀπὸ   τοῦ
¹perfect   ⁴from above ²is   coming down   from   the

πατρὸς   τῶν   φώτων,   παρ᾽   ᾧ   οὐκ   ἔνι
Father   of the   lights,   with   whom   ⁵has no place

παραλλαγὴ   ἢ   τροπῆς   ἀποσκίασμα.   18 βου-
¹change   ²or   ⁴of turning ³shadow.   Having

ληθεὶς   ἀπεκύησεν   ἡμᾶς   λόγῳ   ἀληθείας,
purposed   he brought forth us   by a word   of truth,

εἰς   τὸ   εἶναι   ἡμᾶς   ἀπαρχήν   τινα   τῶν
for   the   to be   us*b*   ²firstfruit   ¹a certain ³of
=that we should be   the

αὐτοῦ   κτισμάτων.
⁵of him   ⁴creatures.

19 Ἴστε,   ἀδελφοί   μου   ἀγαπητοί.   ἔστω
Know ye,   ²brothers   ³of me   ¹beloved.   ²let be

8he is a double-minded man, unstable in all he does. 9The brother in humble circumstances ought to take pride in his high position. 10But the one who is rich should take pride in his low position, because he will pass away like a wild flower. 11For the sun rises with scorching heat and withers the plant; its blossom falls and its beauty is destroyed. In the same way, the rich man will fade away even while he goes about his business. 12Blessed is the man who perseveres under trial, because when he has stood the test, he will receive the crown of life that God has promised to those who love him. 13When tempted, no one should say, "God is tempting me." For God cannot be tempted by evil, nor does he tempt anyone; 14but each one is tempted when, by his own evil desire, he is dragged away and enticed. 15Then, after desire has conceived, it gives birth to sin; and sin, when it is full-grown, gives birth to death. 16Don't be deceived, my dear brothers. 17Every good and perfect gift is from above, coming down from the Father of the heavenly lights, who does not change like shifting shadows. 18He chose to give us birth through the word of truth, that we might be a kind of firstfruits of all he created.

Listening and Doing

19My dear brothers, take note of this: Everyone

everyone be quick to hear, slow to speak *and* slow to anger;
20for the anger of man does not achieve the righteousness of God.
21Therefore putting aside all filthiness and *all* that remains of wickedness, in humility receive the word implanted, which is able to save your souls.
22But prove yourselves doers of the word, and not merely hearers who delude themselves.
23For if anyone is a hearer of the word and not a doer, he is like a man who looks at his natural face in a mirror;
24for once he has looked at himself and gone away, he has immediately forgotten what kind of person he was.
25But one who looks intently at the perfect law, the *law* of liberty, and abides by it, not having become a forgetful hearer but an effectual doer, this man shall be blessed in what he does.
26If anyone thinks himself to be religious, and yet does not bridle his tongue but deceives his *own* heart, this man's religion is worthless.
27This is pure and undefiled religion in the sight of *our* God and Father, to visit orphans and widows in their distress, *and* to keep oneself unstained by the world.

Chapter 2

The Sin of Partiality

MY brethren, do not hold your faith in our glorious Lord Jesus Christ with *an attitude of* personal favoritism.
2For if a man comes into your assembly with a gold

b Or, there is one God

δὲ πᾶς ἄνθρωπος ταχὺς εἰς τὸ ἀκοῦσαι,
1But every man swift for the to hear,

βραδὺς εἰς τὸ λαλῆσαι, βραδὺς εἰς ὀργήν·
slow for the to speak, slow to wrath;

20 ὀργὴ γὰρ ἀνδρὸς δικαιοσύνην θεοῦ
for [the] wrath of a man 1[the] righteousness 2of God

οὐκ ἐργάζεται. 21 διὸ ἀποθέμενοι πᾶσαν
1works not. Wherefore putting away all

ῥυπαρίαν καὶ περισσείαν κακίας ἐν πραΰ-
filthiness and superfluity of evil in meek-

τητι δέξασθε τὸν ἔμφυτον λόγον τὸν
ness receive ye the implanted word –

δυνάμενον σῶσαι τὰς ψυχὰς ὑμῶν. 22 γίν-
being able to save the souls of you. be-

εσθε δὲ ποιηταὶ λόγου, καὶ μὴ ἀκροαταὶ
come ye And doers of [the] word, and not hearers

μόνον παραλογιζόμενοι ἑαυτούς. 23 ὅτι
only misleading yourselves. Because

εἴ τις ἀκροατὴς λόγου ἐστὶν καὶ οὐ
if anyone 2a hearer 3of [the] word 1is and not

ποιητής, οὗτος ἔοικεν ἀνδρὶ κατανοοῦντι
a doer, this one is like a man perceiving

τὸ πρόσωπον τῆς γενέσεως αὐτοῦ ἐν
the face of the birth of him in

ἐσόπτρῳ· 24 κατενόησεν γὰρ ἑαυτὸν καὶ
a mirror; for he perceived himself and

ἀπελήλυθεν, καὶ εὐθέως ἐπελάθετο ὁποῖος
has gone away, and straightway forgot what sort

ἦν. 25 ὁ δὲ παρακύψας εἰς νόμον
he was. But the [one] having looked *into* into 2law

τέλειον τὸν τῆς ἐλευθερίας καὶ παραμείνας,
2perfect 1the – of freedom and remaining,

οὐκ ἀκροατὴς ἐπιλησμονῆς γενόμενος ἀλλὰ
not 2a hearer 3of forgetfulness* 1becoming but

ποιητὴς ἔργου, οὗτος μακάριος ἐν τῇ
a doer of [the] work, this one 2blessed 3in 4the

ποιήσει αὐτοῦ ἔσται. 26 Εἴ τις δοκεῖ
5doing 6of him 1will be. If anyone thinks

θρησκὸς εἶναι, μὴ χαλιναγωγῶν γλῶσσαν
2religious 1to be, not bridling tongue

ἑαυτοῦ ἀλλὰ ἀπατῶν καρδίαν ἑαυτοῦ,
of himself but deceiving heart of himself,

τούτου μάταιος ἡ θρησκεία. 27 θρησκεία
of this one vain the religion. Religion

καθαρὰ καὶ ἀμίαντος παρὰ τῷ θεῷ
clean and undefiled before the God

καὶ πατρὶ αὕτη ἐστίν, ἐπισκέπτεσθαι
and Father 2this 1is, to visit

ὀρφανοὺς καὶ χήρας ἐν τῇ θλίψει αὐτῶν,
orphans and widows in the affliction of them,

ἄσπιλον ἑαυτὸν τηρεῖν ἀπὸ τοῦ κόσμου.
unspotted himself to keep from the world.

2 Ἀδελφοί μου, μὴ ἐν προσωπολημψίαις
Brothers of me, not in respects of persons

ἔχετε τὴν πίστιν τοῦ κυρίου ἡμῶν Ἰησοῦ
have ye the faith of the Lord of us Jesus

Χριστοῦ τῆς δόξης.* 2 ἐὰν γὰρ εἰσέλθῃ
Christ[,] of the glory.* For if [there] enters

εἰς συναγωγὴν ὑμῶν ἀνὴρ χρυσοδακτύλιος
into a synagogue of you a man gold-fingered

* Genitive of quality: " a forgetful hearer."

* That is, taking "the glory" as in apposition to "Jesus Christ"; see Luke 2. 32b.

---

should be quick to listen, slow to speak and slow to become angry, 20for man's anger does not bring about the righteous life that God desires. 21Therefore, get rid of all moral filth and the evil that is so prevalent and humbly accept the word planted in you, which can save you.
22Do not merely listen to the word, and so deceive yourselves. Do what it says. 23Anyone who listens to the word but does not do what it says is like a man who looks at his face in a mirror 24and, after looking at himself, goes away and immediately forgets what he looks like. 25But the man who looks intently into the perfect law that gives freedom, and continues to do this, not forgetting what he has heard, but doing it—he will be blessed in what he does.
26If anyone considers himself religious and yet does not keep a tight rein on his tongue, he deceives himself and his religion is worthless. 27Religion that God our Father accepts as pure and faultless is this: to look after orphans and widows in their distress and to keep oneself from being polluted by the world.

Chapter 2

Favoritism Forbidden

MY brothers, as believers in our glorious Lord Jesus Christ, don't show favoritism. 2Suppose a man comes into your meeting wearing a gold ring

ring and dressed in fine clothes, and there also comes in a poor man in dirty clothes, ³and you pay special attention to the one who is wearing the fine clothes, and say, "You sit here in a good place," and you say to the poor man, "You stand over there, or sit down by my footstool," ⁴have you not made distinctions among yourselves, and become judges with evil motives? ⁵Listen, my beloved brethren: did not God choose the poor of this world *to be* rich in faith and heirs of the kingdom which He promised to those who love Him? ⁶But you have dishonored the poor man. Is it not the rich who oppress you and personally drag you into court? ⁷Do they not blaspheme the fair name by which you have been called? ⁸If, however, you are fulfilling the royal law, according to the Scripture, "YOU SHALL LOVE YOUR NEIGHBOR AS YOURSELF," you are doing well. ⁹But if you show partiality, you are committing sin *and* are convicted by the law as transgressors. ¹⁰For whoever keeps the whole law and yet stumbles in one *point*, he has become guilty of all. ¹¹For He who said, "Do NOT COMMIT ADULTERY," also said, "Do NOT COMMIT MURDER." Now if you do not commit adultery, but do commit murder, you have become a transgressor of the law. ¹²So speak and so act, as those who are to be judged by *the* law of liberty. ¹³For judgment *will be* merciless to one who has shown no mercy; mercy triumphs over judgment.

Faith and Works

¹⁴What use is it, my

ἐν ἐσθῆτι λαμπρᾷ, εἰσέλθῃ δὲ καὶ πτωχὸς
in ²clothing ¹splendid, and [there] enters also a poor man
ἐν ῥυπαρᾷ ἐσθῆτι, 3 ἐπιβλέψητε δὲ ἐπὶ
in shabby clothing, and ye look *on* on
τὸν φοροῦντα τὴν ἐσθῆτα τὴν λαμπρὰν
the [one] wearing the clothing – splendid
καὶ εἴπητε· σὺ κάθου ὧδε καλῶς, καὶ
and say: ¹Sit here well, and
τῷ πτωχῷ εἴπητε· σὺ στῆθι ἐκεῖ ἢ
to the poor man ye say: ²thou ¹Stand there or
κάθου ὑπὸ τὸ ὑποπόδιόν μου, 4 οὐ
sit under the footstool of me, not
διεκρίθητε ἐν ἑαυτοῖς καὶ ἐγένεσθε κριταὶ
did ye dis- among yourselves and became judges
criminate
διαλογισμῶν πονηρῶν; 5 Ἀκούσατε, ἀδελφοί
²thoughts ¹of evil ?§ Hear ye, brothers
μου ἀγαπητοί. οὐχ ὁ θεὸς ἐξελέξατο
of me beloved. ²not – ³God ¹Chose
τοὺς πτωχοὺς τῷ κόσμῳ πλουσίους ἐν
the poor in the world rich in
πίστει καὶ κληρονόμους τῆς βασιλείας
faith and heirs of the kingdom
ἧς ἐπηγγείλατο τοῖς ἀγαπῶσιν αὐτόν;
which he promised to the [ones] loving him?
6 ὑμεῖς δὲ ἠτιμάσατε τὸν πτωχόν. οὐχ
But ye dishonoured the poor man. [Do] not
οἱ πλούσιοι καταδυναστεύουσιν ὑμῶν, καὶ
the rich men oppress you, and
αὐτοὶ ἕλκουσιν ὑμᾶς εἰς κριτήρια; 7 οὐκ
they drag you to tribunals ? [Do] not
αὐτοὶ βλασφημοῦσιν τὸ καλὸν ὄνομα τὸ
they blaspheme the good name –
ἐπικληθὲν ἐφ᾽ ὑμᾶς; 8 εἰ μέντοι νόμον
called *on* on you ? If indeed ³law
τελεῖτε βασιλικὸν κατὰ τὴν γραφήν·
¹ye fulfil ²a royal according to the scripture:
ἀγαπήσεις τὸν πλησίον σου ὡς σεαυτόν,
Thou shalt love the neighbour of thee as thyself,
καλῶς ποιεῖτε· 9 εἰ δὲ προσωπολημπτεῖτε,
²well ¹ye do; but if ye respect persons,
ἁμαρτίαν ἐργάζεσθε, ἐλεγχόμενοι ὑπὸ τοῦ
²sin ¹ye work, being reproved by the
νόμου ὡς παραβάται. 10 ὅστις γὰρ
law as transgressors. For ¹[he] who
ὅλον τὸν νόμον τηρήσῃ, πταίσῃ δὲ ἐν
³all ⁴the ⁵law ²keeps, yet stumbles in
ἑνί, γέγονεν πάντων ἔνοχος. 11 ὁ γὰρ
one he has ²of all ¹guilty. For the
thing, become [one]
εἰπών· μὴ μοιχεύσῃς, εἶπεν καὶ· μὴ
saying: Do not commit adultery, said also: not
φονεύσῃς· εἰ δὲ οὐ μοιχεύεις, φονεύεις
Do murder; now if thou dost not ²murderest
commit adultery,
δέ, γέγονας παραβάτης νόμου. 12 οὕτως
¹but, thou hast a transgressor of [the] So
become law.
λαλεῖτε καὶ οὕτως ποιεῖτε ὡς διὰ νόμου
speak ye and so do ye as ³through ⁴a law
ἐλευθερίας μέλλοντες κρίνεσθαι. 13 ἡ γὰρ
⁵of freedom ¹being about ²to be judged. For the
κρίσις ἀνέλεος τῷ μὴ ποιήσαντι ἔλεος·
judg- [will be] unmerci- to the not do(show)ing mercy;
ment be] ful [one]
κατακαυχᾶται ἔλεος κρίσεως. 14 Τί τὸ
²exults over ¹mercy *of* judgment. What [is] the
§ Genitive of quality: " evil-thinking judges."

---

and fine clothes, and a poor man in shabby clothes also comes in. ³If you show special attention to the man wearing fine clothes and say, "Here's a good seat for you," but say to the poor man, "You stand there" or "Sit on the floor by my feet," ⁴have you not discriminated among yourselves and become judges with evil thoughts?

⁵Listen, my dear brothers: Has not God chosen those who are poor in the eyes of the world to be rich in faith and to inherit the kingdom he promised those who love him? ⁶But you have insulted the poor. Is it not the rich who are exploiting you? Are they not the ones who are dragging you into court? ⁷Are they not the ones who are slandering the noble name of him to whom you belong?

⁸If you really keep the royal law found in Scripture, "Love your neighbor as yourself,"ᵃ you are doing right. ⁹But if you show favoritism, you sin and are convicted by the law as lawbreakers. ¹⁰For whoever keeps the whole law and yet stumbles at just one point is guilty of breaking all of it. ¹¹For he who said, "Do not commit adultery,"ᵇ also said, "Do not murder."ᶜ If you do not commit adultery but do commit murder, you have become a lawbreaker.

¹²Speak and act as those who are going to be judged by the law that gives freedom, ¹³because judgment without mercy will be shown to anyone who has not been merciful. Mercy triumphs over judgment!

Faith and Deeds

¹⁴What good is it, my

ᵃ8 Lev. 19:18
ᵇ11 Exodus 20:14; Deut. 5:18
ᶜ11 Exodus 20:13; Deut. 5:17

brethren, if a man says he has faith, but he has no works? Can that faith save him?

15If a brother or sister is without clothing and in need of daily food,

16and one of you says to them, "Go in peace, be warmed and be filled," and yet you do not give them what is necessary for *their* body, what use is that?

17Even so faith, if it has no works, is dead, *being* by itself.

18But someone may *well* say, "You have faith, and I have works; show me your faith without your works, and I will show you my faith by my works."

19You believe that ᵇGod is one. You do well; the demons also believe, and shudder.

20But are you willing to recognize, you foolish fellow, that faith without works is useless?

21Was not Abraham our father justified by works, when he offered up Isaac his son on the altar?

22You see that faith was working with his works, and as a result of the works, faith was perfected;

23and the Scripture was fulfilled which says, "AND ABRAHAM BELIEVED GOD, AND IT WAS RECKONED TO HIM AS RIGHTEOUSNESS," and he was called the friend of God.

24You see that a man is justified by works, and not by faith alone.

25And in the same way was not Rahab the harlot also justified by works, when she received the messengers and sent them out

---

ὄφελος, ἀδελφοί μου, ἐὰν πίστιν λέγῃ
profit, brothers of me, if ⁴faith ⁵says

τις ἔχειν ἔργα δὲ μὴ ἔχῃ· μὴ δύναται
¹any-one ²to have ⁶works ³but ⁷not ⁸has? not can

ἡ πίστις σῶσαι αὐτόν; 15 ἐὰν ἀδελφὸς
the faith to save him? If a brother

ἢ ἀδελφὴ γυμνοὶ ὑπάρχωσιν καὶ λειπόμενοι
or a sister ²naked ¹are and lacking

τῆς ἐφημέρου τροφῆς, 16 εἴπῃ δέ τις
of the daily food, and ⁴says ¹any-one

αὐτοῖς ἐξ ὑμῶν· ὑπάγετε ἐν εἰρήνῃ,
⁶to them ²of ³you: Go ye in peace,

θερμαίνεσθε καὶ χορτάζεσθε, μὴ δῶτε
be warmed and filled, ⁴not ⁵ye give

δὲ αὐτοῖς τὰ ἐπιτήδεια τοῦ σώματος,
¹but ²them the necessaries of the body,

τί τὸ ὄφελος; 17 οὕτως καὶ ἡ πίστις,
what [is] the profit? So indeed - faith,

ἐὰν μὴ ἔχῃ ἔργα, νεκρά ἐστιν καθ'
if it has not works, ²dead ¹is by

ἑαυτήν. 18 ἀλλ' ἐρεῖ τις· σὺ πίστιν
itself. But ²will say ¹someone: Thou ²faith

ἔχεις, κἀγὼ ἔργα ἔχω· δεῖξόν μοι τὴν
¹hast, and I ²works ¹have; show me the

πίστιν σου χωρὶς τῶν ἔργων, κἀγώ
faith of thee without the works, and I

σοι δείξω ἐκ τῶν ἔργων μου τὴν πίστιν.
thee will show ⁴by ⁵the ⁶works ¹of me ²the ³faith.

19 σὺ πιστεύεις ὅτι εἷς ἐστιν ὁ θεός;
Thou believest that ²one ¹is - ¹God?

καλῶς ποιεῖς· καὶ τὰ δαιμόνια πιστεύουσιν
²well ¹thou doest; also the demons believe

καὶ φρίσσουσιν. 20 θέλεις δὲ γνῶναι,
and shudder. But art thou willing to know,

ὦ ἄνθρωπε κενέ, ὅτι ἡ πίστις χωρὶς
O ²man ¹vain, that - faith without

τῶν ἔργων ἀργή ἐστιν; 21 Ἀβραὰμ ὁ
- works barren is? Abraham the

πατὴρ ἡμῶν οὐκ ἐξ ἔργων ἐδικαιώθη,
father of us not by works was justified,

ἀνενέγκας Ἰσαὰκ τὸν υἱὸν αὐτοῦ ἐπὶ
offering up Isaac the son of him on

τὸ θυσιαστήριον; 22 βλέπεις ὅτι ἡ πίστις
the altar? Thou seest that - faith

συνήργει τοῖς ἔργοις αὐτοῦ, καὶ ἐκ
worked with the works of him, and by

τῶν ἔργων ἡ πίστις ἐτελειώθη, 23 καὶ
the works the faith was perfected, and

ἐπληρώθη ἡ γραφὴ ἡ λέγουσα· ἐπίστευσεν
was fulfilled the scripture - saying: believed

δὲ Ἀβραὰμ τῷ θεῷ, καὶ ἐλογίσθη αὐτῷ
And Abraham - God, and it was reckoned to him

εἰς δικαιοσύνην, καὶ φίλος θεοῦ ἐκλήθη.
for righteousness, and ²friend ³of God ¹he was called.

24 ὁρᾶτε ὅτι ἐξ ἔργων δικαιοῦται ἄνθρωπος
Ye see that by works ²is justified ¹a man

καὶ οὐκ ἐκ πίστεως μόνον. 25 ὁμοίως
and not by faith only. likewise

δὲ καὶ Ῥαὰβ ἡ πόρνη οὐκ ἐξ ἔργων
And also Rahab the prostitute not by works

ἐδικαιώθη, ὑποδεξαμένη τοὺς ἀγγέλους καὶ
was justified, entertaining the messengers and

---

brothers, if a man claims to have faith but has no deeds? Can such faith save him? 15Suppose a brother or sister is without clothes and daily food. 16If one of you says to him, "Go, I wish you well; keep warm and well fed," but does nothing about his physical needs, what good is it? 17In the same way, faith by itself, if it is not accompanied by action, is dead.

18But someone will say, "You have faith; I have deeds."

Show me your faith without deeds, and I will show you my faith by what I do. 19You believe that there is one God. Good! Even the demons believe that—and shudder.

20You foolish man, do you want evidence that faith without deeds is useless ᵈ? 21Was not our ancestor Abraham considered righteous for what he did when he offered his son Isaac on the altar? 22You see that his faith and his actions were working together, and his faith was made complete by what he did. 23And the scripture was fulfilled that says, "Abraham believed God, and it was credited to him as righteousness," ᵉ and he was called God's friend. 24You see that a person is justified by what he does and not by faith alone.

25In the same way, was not even Rahab the prostitute considered righteous for what she did when she gave lodging to the spies and sent them off in a dif-

---

ᵈ20 Some early manuscripts *dead*
ᵉ23 Gen. 15:6

by another way?
²⁶For just as the body without *the* spirit is dead, so also faith without works is dead.

Chapter 3

The Tongue Is a Fire

LET not many *of you* become teachers, my brethren, knowing that as such we shall incur a stricter judgment.

²For we all stumble in many *ways*. If anyone does not stumble in what he says, he is a perfect man, able to bridle the whole body as well.

³Now if we put the bits into the horses' mouths so that they may obey us, we direct their entire body as well.

⁴Behold, the ships also, though they are so great and are driven by strong winds, are still directed by a very small rudder, wherever the inclination of the pilot desires.

⁵So also the tongue is a small part of the body, and *yet* it boasts of great things. Behold, how great a forest is set aflame by such a small fire!

⁶And the tongue is a fire, the very world of iniquity; the tongue is set among our members as that which defiles the entire body, and sets on fire the course of *our* life, and is set on fire by hell.

⁷For every species of beasts and birds, of reptiles and creatures of the sea, is tamed, and has been tamed by the human race.

⁸But no one can tame the tongue; *it is* a restless evil *and* full of deadly poison.

⁹With it we bless *our* Lord and Father; and with it we curse men, who have been made in the likeness of God;

ἑτέρᾳ ὁδῷ ἐκβαλοῦσα; 26 ὥσπερ γὰρ τὸ
by a   way   sending [them]   For as   the
different   forth ?

σῶμα χωρὶς πνεύματος νεκρόν ἐστιν, οὕτως
body   without   spirit   ²dead   ¹is,   so

καὶ ἡ πίστις χωρὶς ἔργων νεκρά ἐστιν.
also -   faith   without   works   ²dead   ¹is.

3 Μὴ πολλοὶ διδάσκαλοι γίνεσθε, ἀδελφοί
      ³not   ³many   ⁴teachers   ¹Become ye,   brothers

μου, εἰδότες ὅτι μεῖζον κρίμα λημψόμεθα.
of me, knowing   that   greater   judgment   we shall receive.

2 πολλὰ γὰρ πταίομεν ἅπαντες· εἴ τις
For [in] many [respects] we stumble   all;   if   anyone

ἐν λόγῳ οὐ πταίει, οὗτος τέλειος ἀνήρ,
²in ³word ¹stumbles not,   this [is] a perfect   man,

δυνατὸς χαλιναγωγῆσαι καὶ ὅλον τὸ σῶμα.
able   to bridle   ²indeed all the   body.

3 εἰ δὲ τῶν ἵππων τοὺς χαλινοὺς εἰς
Now if -   ²of horses   -   ³bridles   ²into

τὰ στόματα βάλλομεν εἰς τὸ πείθεσθαι
¹the ⁴mouths   ¹we put   for   the   to obey
                                          =to make them obey us,

ὑτοὺς ἡμῖν, καὶ ὅλον τὸ σῶμα αὐτῶν
them^b   *to* us,   and   ²all   ²the ⁴body ⁵of them

ὑετάγομεν. **4** ἰδοὺ καὶ τὰ πλοῖα, τηλικαῦτα
¹we direct.   Behold also the   ships,   ¹so great

ὄντα καὶ ὑπὸ ἀνέμων σκληρῶν ἐλαυνόμενα,
being ³and ⁵by   ⁷winds   ⁸hard(strong)   ⁶being driven,

μετάγεται ὑπὸ ἐλαχίστου πηδαλίου ὅπου
is(are) directed   by   a very little   helm   where

ἡ ὁρμὴ τοῦ εὐθύνοντος βούλεται· **5** οὕτως
the impulse of the [one] steering   resolves;   so

καὶ ἡ γλῶσσα μικρὸν μέλος ἐστὶν καὶ
also the   tongue   ²a little   ³member   ¹is   and

μεγάλα αὐχεῖ. ἰδοὺ ἡλίκον πῦρ ἡλίκον
great things boasts.   Behold   how little a fire ¹how great

ὕλην ἀνάπτει· **6** καὶ ἡ γλῶσσα πῦρ,
²wood   ¹kindles;   and   the   tongue   [is] a fire,

ὁ κόσμος τῆς ἀδικίας, ἡ γλῶσσα καθίστα-
the world   -   of iniquity, the   tongue   is

ται ἐν τοῖς μέλεσιν ἡμῶν, ἡ σπιλοῦσα
set among the   members   of us,   the   spotting

ὅλον τὸ σῶμα καὶ φλογίζουσα τὸν
all   the   body   and   inflaming   the

τροχὸν τῆς γενέσεως καὶ φλογιζομένη
course   -   of nature   and   being inflamed

ὑπὸ τῆς γεέννης. **7** πᾶσα γὰρ φύσις
by   -   gehenna.   For every   nature

θηρίων τε καὶ πετεινῶν, ἑρπετῶν τε
²of beasts ¹both and   of birds,   ²of reptiles ¹both

καὶ ἐναλίων δαμάζεται καὶ δεδάμασται
and   of marine   is tamed   and   has been tamed
        creatures

τῇ φύσει τῇ ἀνθρωπίνῃ, **8** τὴν δὲ
by the ²nature -   ¹human,   the   but

γλῶσσαν οὐδεὶς δαμάσαι δύναται ἀνθρώπων·
tongue   ¹no one   ⁴to tame   ²is able   ²of men;

ἀκατάστατον κακόν, μεστὴ ἰοῦ θανατηφόρου.
an unruly   evil,   full   ²poison ¹of death-dealing.

9 ἐν αὐτῇ εὐλογοῦμεν τὸν κύριον καὶ
By   this   we bless   the   Lord   and

πατέρα, καὶ ἐν αὐτῇ καταρώμεθα τοὺς
Father,   and   by   this   we curse   -

ἀνθρώπους τοὺς καθ' ὁμοίωσιν θεοῦ
men   -   ²according to ³likeness   ⁴of God

---

ferent direction? ²⁶As the body without the spirit is dead, so faith without deeds is dead.

Chapter 3

Taming the Tongue

NOT many of you should presume to be teachers, my brothers, because you know that we who teach will be judged more strictly. ²We all stumble in many ways. If anyone is never at fault in what he says, he is a perfect man, able to keep his whole body in check.

³When we put bits into the mouths of horses to make them obey us, we can turn the whole animal. ⁴Or take ships as an example. Although they are so large and are driven by strong winds, they are steered by a very small rudder wherever the pilot wants to go. ⁵Likewise the tongue is a small part of the body, but it makes great boasts. Consider what a great forest is set on fire by a small spark. ⁶The tongue also is a fire, a world of evil among the parts of the body. It corrupts the whole person, sets the whole course of his life on fire, and is itself set on fire by hell.

⁷All kinds of animals, birds, reptiles and creatures of the sea are being tamed and have been tamed by man, ⁸but no man can tame the tongue. It is a restless evil, full of deadly poison.

⁹With the tongue we praise our Lord and Father, and with it we curse men, who have been made

10from the same mouth come *both* blessing and cursing. My brethren, these things ought not to be this way.

11Does a fountain send out from the same opening *both* fresh and bitter *water?*

12Can a fig tree, my brethren, produce olives, or a vine produce figs? Neither *can* salt water produce fresh.

Wisdom from Above

13Who among you is wise and understanding? Let him show by his good behavior his deeds in the gentleness of wisdom.

14But if you have bitter jealousy and selfish ambition in your heart, do not be arrogant and *so* lie against the truth.

15This wisdom is not that which comes down from above, but is earthly, natural, demonic.

16For where jealousy and selfish ambition exist, there is disorder and every evil thing.

17But the wisdom from above is first pure, then peaceable, gentle, reasonable, full of mercy and good fruits, unwavering, without hypocrisy.

18And the seed whose fruit is righteousness is sown in peace by those who make peace.

γεγονότας· 10 ἐκ τοῦ αὐτοῦ στόματος ἐξέρχεται
¹having become; out of the same mouth comes forth

εὐλογία καὶ κατάρα. οὐ χρή, ἀδελφοί
blessing and cursing. It is not fitting, brothers

μου, ταῦτα οὕτως γίνεσθαι. 11 μήτι
of me, these things so to be. Not

ἡ πηγὴ ἐκ τῆς αὐτῆς ὀπῆς βρύει τὸ
the fountain out of the same hole sends forth the

γλυκὺ καὶ τὸ πικρόν; 12 μὴ δύναται,
sweet and the bitter? Not can,

ἀδελφοί μου, συκῆ ἐλαίας ποιῆσαι ἢ
brothers of me, a fig-tree ²olives ¹to produce or

ἄμπελος σῦκα; οὔτε ἁλυκὸν γλυκὺ
a vine figs? neither ¹salt ⁴sweet

ποιῆσαι ὕδωρ. 13 Τίς σοφὸς καὶ ἐπιστήμων
³to make ²water. Who [is] wise and knowing

ἐν ὑμῖν; δειξάτω ἐκ τῆς καλῆς ἀναστροφῆς
among you? let him show by the(his) good conduct

τὰ ἔργα αὐτοῦ ἐν πραΰτητι σοφίας.
the works of him in meekness of wisdom.*

14 εἰ δὲ ζῆλον πικρὸν ἔχετε καὶ ἐριθείαν
But if ²jealousy ²bitter ¹ye have and rivalry

ἐν τῇ καρδίᾳ ὑμῶν, μὴ κατακαυχᾶσθε
in the heart of you, do not exult over

καὶ ψεύδεσθε κατὰ τῆς ἀληθείας. 15 οὐκ
and lie against the truth. ⁴not

ἔστιν αὕτη ἡ σοφία ἄνωθεν κατερχομένη,
²is ¹This - ²wisdom ⁵from above ⁵coming down,

ἀλλὰ ἐπίγειος, ψυχική, δαιμονιώδης· 16 ὅπου
but [is] earthly, natural, demon-like; ²where

γὰρ ζῆλος καὶ ἐριθεία, ἐκεῖ ἀκαταστασία
¹for jealousy and rivalry [are], there [is] tumult

καὶ πᾶν φαῦλον πρᾶγμα. 17 ἡ δὲ ἄνωθεν
and every worthless practice. But ¹the ³from above

σοφία πρῶτον μὲν ἁγνή ἐστιν, ἔπειτα
²wisdom ⁵firstly - ⁴pure ⁴is, then

εἰρηνική, ἐπιεικής, εὐπειθής, μεστὴ ἐλέους
peaceable, forbearing, compliant, full of mercy

καὶ καρπῶν ἀγαθῶν, ἀδιάκριτος, ἀνυπό-
and ¹fruits ¹of good, without uncertainty, un-

κριτος. 18 καρπὸς δὲ δικαιοσύνης ἐν
feigned. And [the] fruit of righteousness ²in

εἰρήνῃ σπείρεται τοῖς ποιοῦσιν εἰρήνην.
²peace ¹is sown for the [ones] making peace.

---

in God's likeness. 10Out of the same mouth come praise and cursing. My brothers, this should not be. 11Can both fresh water and salt*ᶠ* water flow from the same spring? 12My brothers, can a fig tree bear olives, or a grapevine bear figs? Neither can a salt spring produce fresh water.

Two Kinds of Wisdom

13Who is wise and understanding among you? Let him show it by his good life, by deeds done in the humility that comes from wisdom. 14But if you harbor bitter envy and selfish ambition in your hearts, do not boast about it or deny the truth. 15Such "wisdom" does not come down from heaven but is earthly, unspiritual, of the devil. 16For where you have envy and selfish ambition, there you find disorder and every evil practice.

17But the wisdom that comes from heaven is first of all pure; then peace-loving, considerate, submissive, full of mercy and good fruit, impartial and sincere. 18Peacemakers who sow in peace raise a harvest of righteousness.

Chapter 4

Things to Avoid

WHAT is the source of quarrels and conflicts among you? Is not the source your pleasures that wage war in your members?

2You lust and do not have; *so* you commit murder. And you are envious and cannot obtain; *so* you fight and quarrel. You do not have because you do not ask.

3You ask and do not receive, because you ask with wrong motives, so

---

4 Πόθεν πόλεμοι καὶ πόθεν μάχαι ἐν
Whence wars and whence fights among

ὑμῖν; οὐκ ἐντεῦθεν, ἐκ τῶν ἡδονῶν
you? not thence, out of the pleasures

ὑμῶν τῶν στρατευομένων ἐν τοῖς μέλεσιν
of you - soldiering in the members

ὑμῶν; 2 ἐπιθυμεῖτε, καὶ οὐκ ἔχετε·
of you? Ye desire, and have not;

φονεύετε καὶ ζηλοῦτε, καὶ οὐ δύνασθε
ye murder and are jealous, and are not able

ἐπιτυχεῖν· μάχεσθε καὶ πολεμεῖτε. οὐκ
to obtain; ye fight and ye war. not

ἔχετε διὰ τὸ μὴ αἰτεῖσθαι ὑμᾶς· 3 αἰτεῖτε
Ye have be- *the* not to ask you*ᵇ*; ye ask
cause of
= because ye ask not;

καὶ οὐ λαμβάνετε, διότι κακῶς αἰτεῖσθε,
and receive not, because ²ill ¹ye ask,

Chapter 4

Submit Yourselves to God

WHAT causes fights and quarrels among you? Don't they come from your desires that battle within you? 2You want something but don't get it. You kill and covet, but you cannot have what you want. You quarrel and fight. You do not have, because you do not ask God. 3When you ask, you do not receive, because you ask with wrong motives, that

---

* Genitive of quality : " a wise meekness."

ᶠ11 Greek *bitter* (see also verse 14)

that you may spend *it* on your pleasures.
⁴You adulteresses, do you not know that friendship with the world is hostility toward God? Therefore whoever wishes to be a friend of the world makes himself an enemy of God.
⁵Or do you think that the Scripture speaks to no purpose: "ᶜHe jealously desires the Spirit which He has made to dwell in us"?
⁶But He gives a greater grace. Therefore *it* says, "GOD IS OPPOSED TO THE PROUD, BUT GIVES GRACE TO THE HUMBLE."
⁷Submit therefore to God. Resist the devil and he will flee from you.
⁸Draw near to God and He will draw near to you. Cleanse your hands, you sinners; and purify your hearts, you double-minded.
⁹Be miserable and mourn and weep; let your laughter be turned into mourning, and your joy to gloom.
¹⁰Humble yourselves in the presence of the Lord, and He will exalt you.
¹¹Do not speak against one another, brethren. He who speaks against a brother, or judges his brother, speaks against the law, and judges the law; but if you judge the law, you are not a doer of the law, but a judge of it.
¹²There is *only* one Lawgiver and Judge, the One who is able to save and to destroy; but who are you who judge your neighbor?
¹³Come now, you who say, "Today or tomorrow, we shall go to such and such a city, and spend a year there and engage in business and make a profit."
¹⁴Yet you do not know

ἵνα ἐν ταῖς ἡδοναῖς ὑμῶν δαπανήσητε.
in or-der that / in / the / pleasures / of you / ye may spend.

4 μοιχαλίδες, οὐκ οἴδατε ὅτι ἡ φιλία
Adulteresses, / know ye not / that / the / friendship

τοῦ κόσμου ἔχθρα τοῦ θεοῦ ἐστιν; ὃς
of the / world / ²enmity - / ³of God / ¹is ? / Who-

ἐὰν οὖν βουληθῇ φίλος εἶναι τοῦ κόσμου,
ever therefore / ¹resolves / ²a friend / ³to be / of the / world,

ἐχθρὸς τοῦ θεοῦ καθίσταται. 5 ἢ δοκεῖτε
²an enemy - / ³of God / ¹is constituted. / Or / think ye

ὅτι κενῶς ἡ γραφὴ λέγει· πρὸς φθόνον
that / vainly / the / scripture / says: / ²to / ¹envy

ἐπιποθεῖ τὸ πνεῦμα ὃ κατῴκισεν ἐν
²yearns / ¹The / ¹Spirit / ¹which / ⁴dwelt / ³in

ἡμῖν; 6 μείζονα δὲ δίδωσιν χάριν· διὸ
⁴you? / But / ²greater / ¹he gives / ³grace; / where-fore

λέγει· ὁ θεὸς ὑπερηφάνοις ἀντιτάσσεται,
it* says: / - God / ²arrogant men / ¹resists,

ταπεινοῖς δὲ δίδωσιν χάριν. 7 ὑποτάγητε
but to humble men / he gives / grace. / Be ye subject

οὖν τῷ θεῷ· ἀντίστητε δὲ τῷ διαβόλῳ,
there-fore - / to God; / but oppose / the / devil,

καὶ φεύξεται ἀφ' ὑμῶν· 8 ἐγγίσατε τῷ
and / he will flee / from / you; / draw near -

θεῷ, καὶ ἐγγίσει ὑμῖν. καθαρίσατε
to God, / and / he will draw near / to you. / Cleanse

χεῖρας, ἁμαρτωλοί, καὶ ἁγνίσατε καρδίας,
hands, / sinners, / and / purify / hearts,

δίψυχοι. 9 ταλαιπωρήσατε καὶ πενθήσατε
two-souled / Be ye distressed / and / mourn
(double-minded).

καὶ κλαύσατε· ὁ γέλως ὑμῶν εἰς πένθος
and / weep; / the / laughter / of you / to / mourning

μετατραπήτω καὶ ἡ χαρὰ εἰς κατήφειαν.
let it be turned / and / the / joy / to / dejection.

10 ταπεινώθητε ἐνώπιον κυρίου, καὶ ὑψώσει
Be ye humbled / before / [the] Lord, / and / he will exalt

ὑμᾶς. 11 Μὴ καταλαλεῖτε ἀλλήλων, ἀδελφοί.
you. / Speak not against / one another, / brothers.

ὁ καταλαλῶν ἀδελφοῦ ἢ κρίνων τὸν
The [one] / speaking against / a brother / or / judging / the

ἀδελφὸν αὐτοῦ καταλαλεῖ νόμου καὶ κρίνει
brother / of him / speaks against / law / and / judges

νόμον· εἰ δὲ νόμον κρίνεις, οὐκ εἶ
law; / and if· / law / thou judgest, / thou art not

ποιητὴς νόμου ἀλλὰ κριτής. 12 εἷς ἐστιν
a doer / of law / but / a judge. / One / is

ⁱομοθέτης καὶ κριτής, ὁ δυνάμενος
lawgiver / and / judge, / the [one] / being able

σῶσαι καὶ ἀπολέσαι· σὺ δὲ τίς εἶ, ὁ
to save / and / to destroy; / ⁴thou / ¹and / ²who / ³art, the

κρίνων τὸν πλησίον;
[one] judging / the(thy) / neighbour?

13 Ἄγε νῦν οἱ λέγοντες· σήμερον ἢ
Come / now / the [ones] / saying: / To-day / or

αὔριον πορευσόμεθα εἰς τήνδε τὴν πόλιν
to-morrow / we will go / into / this / - / city

καὶ ποιήσομεν ἐκεῖ ἐνιαυτὸν καὶ ἐμπορευ-
and / we will do / there / a year / and / we will

σόμεθα καὶ κερδήσομεν· 14 οἵτινες οὐκ
trade / and / we will make a profit; / who / not

you may spend what you get on your pleasures.
⁴You adulterous people, don't you know that friendship with the world is hatred toward God? Anyone who chooses to be a friend of the world becomes an enemy of God. ⁵Or do you think Scripture says without reason that the spirit he caused to live in us envies intensely?[g] ⁶But he gives us more grace. That is why Scripture says:

"God opposes the proud but gives grace to the humble."[h]

⁷Submit yourselves, then, to God. Resist the devil, and he will flee from you. ⁸Come near to God and he will come near to you. Wash your hands, you sinners, and purify your hearts, you double-minded. ⁹Grieve, mourn and wail. Change your laughter to mourning and your joy to gloom. ¹⁰Humble yourselves before the Lord, and he will lift you up.
¹¹Brothers, do not slander one another. Anyone who speaks against his brother or judges him speaks against the law and judges it. When you judge the law, you are not keeping it, but sitting in judgment on it. ¹²There is only one Lawgiver and Judge, the one who is able to save and destroy. But you—who are you to judge your neighbor?

Boasting About Tomorrow
¹³Now listen, you who say, "Today or tomorrow we will go to this or that city, spend a year there, carry on business and make money." ¹⁴Why, you do

---

ᶜOr, *The Spirit which He has made to dwell in us jealously desires us*

* That is, " the scripture " (as ver. 5).

[g]5 Or *that God jealously longs for the spirit that he made to live in us; or that the Spirit he caused to live in us longs jealously*
[h]6 Prov. 3:34

what your life will be like tomorrow. You are *just* a vapor that appears for a little while and then vanishes away.

15Instead, *you ought to* say, "If the Lord wills, we shall live and also do this or that."

16But as it is, you boast in your arrogance; all such boasting is evil.

17Therefore, to one who knows *the* right thing to do, and does not do it, to him it is sin.

Chapter 5

Misuse of Riches

COME now, you rich, weep and howl for your miseries which are coming upon you.

2Your riches have rotted and your garments have become moth-eaten.

3Your gold and your silver have rusted; and their rust will be a witness against you and will consume your flesh like fire. It is in the last days that you have stored up your treasure!

4Behold, the pay of the laborers who mowed your fields, *and* which has been withheld by you, cries out *against you;* and the outcry of those who did the harvesting has reached the ears of the Lord of Sabaoth.

5You have lived luxuriously on the earth and led a life of wanton pleasure; you have fattened your hearts in a day of slaughter.

6You have condemned and put to death the righteous *man;* he does not resist you.

Exhortation

7Be patient, therefore, brethren, until the coming of the Lord. Behold, the farmer waits for the precious produce of the soil, being patient about it, until it gets the early and late

ἐπίστασθε τῆς αὔριον ποία ἡ ζωὴ ὑμῶν.
ye know *of the* morrow what the life of you
[will be].

ἀτμὶς γάρ ἐστε ἡ πρὸς ὀλίγον φαινομένη,
For a vapour ye are – for a little while appearing,

ἔπειτα καὶ ἀφανιζομένη· 15 ἀντὶ τοῦ
thereafter indeed disappearing; instead of the

λέγειν ὑμᾶς· ἐὰν ὁ κύριος θελήσῃ, καὶ
to say you: If the Lord wills, both
=your saying:

ζήσομεν καὶ ποιήσομεν τοῦτο ἢ ἐκεῖνο.
we will live and we will do this or that.

16 νῦν δὲ καυχᾶσθε ἐν ταῖς ἀλαζονείαις
But now ye boast in the vauntings

ὑμῶν· πᾶσα καύχησις τοιαύτη πονηρά
of you; all boasting such evil

ἐστιν. 17 εἰδότι οὖν καλὸν ποιεῖν καὶ
is. to [one] There- good to do and
knowing* fore

μὴ ποιοῦντι, ἁμαρτία αὐτῷ ἐστιν.
not doing, sin to him it is.

5 Ἄγε νῦν οἱ πλούσιοι, κλαύσατε
Come now the rich men, weep ye

ὀλολύζοντες ἐπὶ ταῖς ταλαιπωρίαις ὑμῶν
crying aloud over the hardships of you

ταῖς ἐπερχομέναις. 2 ὁ πλοῦτος ὑμῶν
– coming upon. The riches of you

σέσηπεν, καὶ τὰ ἱμάτια ὑμῶν σητόβρωτα
have become and the garments of you moth-eaten
corrupted,

γέγονεν, 3 ὁ χρυσὸς ὑμῶν καὶ ὁ ἄργυρος
have become, the gold of you and the silver

κατίωται, καὶ ὁ ἰὸς αὐτῶν εἰς μαρτύριον
has become and the poison of them for a testimony
rusted over,

ὑμῖν ἔσται καὶ φάγεται τὰς σάρκας
to(against) will and will eat the fleshes
you be

ὑμῶν ὡς πῦρ. ἐθησαυρίσατε ἐν ἐσχάταις
of you as fire. Ye treasured in [the] last

ἡμέραις. 4 ἰδοὺ ὁ μισθὸς τῶν ἐργατῶν
days. Behold[,] the wages of the workmen

τῶν ἀμησάντων τὰς χώρας ὑμῶν ὁ
– having reaped the lands of you –

ἀφυστερημένος ἀφ' ὑμῶν κράζει, καὶ αἱ
being kept back from(by) you cries, and the

βοαὶ τῶν θερισάντων εἰς τὰ ὦτα κυρίου
cries of the having reaped into the ears of [the]
[ones] Lord

σαβαὼθ εἰσελήλυθαν. 5 ἐτρυφήσατε ἐπὶ
of hosts have entered. Ye lived daintily on

τῆς γῆς καὶ ἐσπαταλήσατε, ἐθρέψατε τὰς
the earth and lived riotously, ye nourished the

καρδίας ὑμῶν ἐν ἡμέρᾳ σφαγῆς. 6 κατε-
hearts of you in a day of slaughter. Ye

δικάσατε, ἐφονεύσατε τὸν δίκαιον· οὐκ
condemned, ye murdered the righteous man; not

ἀντιτάσσεται ὑμῖν.
he resists you.

7 Μακροθυμήσατε οὖν, ἀδελφοί, ἕως τῆς
Be ye longsuffering therefore, brothers, until the

παρουσίας τοῦ κυρίου. ἰδοὺ ὁ γεωργὸς
presence of the Lord. Behold[,] the farmer

ἐκδέχεται τὸν τίμιον καρπὸν τῆς γῆς,
awaits the precious fruit of the earth,

μακροθυμῶν ἐπ' αὐτῷ ἕως λάβῃ πρόιμον
being over it until he receives early
longsuffering

* See note on page xviii.

not even know what will happen tomorrow. What is your life? You are a mist that appears for a little while and then vanishes.

15Instead, you ought to say, "If it is the Lord's will, we will live and do this or that." 16As it is, you boast and brag. All such boasting is evil. 17Anyone, then, who knows the good he ought to do and doesn't do it, sins.

Chapter 5

Warning to Rich Oppressors

NOW listen, you rich people, weep and wail because of the misery that is coming upon you. 2Your wealth has rotted, and moths have eaten your clothes. 3Your gold and silver are corroded. Their corrosion will testify against you and eat your flesh like fire. You have hoarded wealth in the last days. 4Look! The wages you failed to pay the workmen who mowed your fields are crying out against you. The cries of the harvesters have reached the ears of the Lord Almighty. 5You have lived on earth in luxury and self-indulgence. You have fattened yourselves in the day of slaughter.[i] 6You have condemned and murdered innocent men, who were not opposing you.

Patience in Suffering

7Be patient, then, brothers, until the Lord's coming. See how the farmer waits for the land to yield its valuable crop and how patient he is for the autumn

i5 Or *yourselves as in a day of feasting*

rains.

8You too be patient; strengthen your hearts, for the coming of the Lord is at hand.

9Do not complain, brethren, against one another, that you yourselves may not be judged; behold, the Judge is standing right at the door.

10As an example, brethren, of suffering and patience, take the prophets who spoke in the name of the Lord.

11Behold, we count those blessed who endured. You have heard of the endurance of Job and have seen the outcome of the Lord's dealings, that the Lord is full of compassion and is merciful.

12But above all, my brethren, do not swear, either by heaven or by earth or with any other oath; but let your yes be yes, and your no, no; so that you may not fall under judgment.

13Is anyone among you suffering? Let him pray. Is anyone cheerful? Let him sing praises.

14Is anyone among you sick? Let him call for the elders of the church, and let them pray over him, anointing him with oil in the name of the Lord;

15and the prayer offered in faith will drestore the one who is sick, and the Lord will raise him up, and if he has committed sins, they will be forgiven him.

16Therefore, confess your sins to one another, and pray for one another, so that you may be healed. The effective prayer of a righteous man can accomplish much.

17Elijah was a man with a nature like ours, and he prayed earnestly that it might not rain; and it did

dOr, save

καὶ ὄψιμον. 8 μακροθυμήσατε καὶ ὑμεῖς,
and latter [rain]. Be ³longsuffering ²also ¹ye,

στηρίξατε τὰς καρδίας ὑμῶν, ὅτι ἡ
establish the hearts of you, because the

παρουσία τοῦ κυρίου ἤγγικεν. 9 μὴ
presence of the Lord has drawn near. not

στενάζετε, ἀδελφοί, κατ' ἀλλήλων ἵνα μὴ
Murmur ye, brothers, against one another lest

κριθῆτε· ἰδοὺ ὁ κριτὴς πρὸ τῶν θυρῶν
ye be behold[,] the judge ²before ³the ⁴doors
judged;

ἕστηκεν. 10 ὑπόδειγμα λάβετε, ἀδελφοί,
¹stands. ²an example ¹Take ye, ²brothers,

τῆς κακοπαθίας καὶ τῆς μακροθυμίας
- ²of suffering ill ³and - ⁴of longsuffering

τοὺς προφήτας, οἳ ἐλάλησαν ἐν τῷ
¹the ²prophets, who spoke in the

ὀνόματι κυρίου. 11 ἰδοὺ μακαρίζομεν τοὺς
name of [the] Lord. Behold we count blessed the

ὑπομείναντας· τὴν ὑπομονὴν Ἰὼβ ἠκούσατε,
[ones] enduring; ²the ²endurance ⁴of Job ¹ye heard [of],

καὶ τὸ τέλος κυρίου εἴδετε, ὅτι πολύ-
and ²the ⁴end ⁴of [the] Lord ¹ye saw, that ⁴very

σπλαγχνός ἐστιν ὁ κύριος καὶ οἰκτίρμων.
compassionate ³is ¹the ²Lord and pitiful.

12 Πρὸ πάντων δέ, ἀδελφοί μου, μὴ
²before ³all things ¹But, brothers of me, not

ὀμνύετε, μήτε τὸν οὐρανὸν μήτε τὴν
swear ye, neither by the heaven nor by the

γῆν μήτε ἄλλον τινὰ ὅρκον· ἤτω δὲ
earth nor ²other ¹any oath; but let be

ὑμῶν τὸ ναὶ ναί, καὶ τὸ οὒ οὔ, ἵνα μὴ
of you the Yes yes, and the No no, lest

ὑπὸ κρίσιν πέσητε. 13 Κακοπαθεῖ τις
¹under ²judgment ¹ye fall. Suffers ill anyone

ἐν ὑμῖν; προσευχέσθω· εὐθυμεῖ τις;
among you? let him pray; is cheerful anyone?

ψαλλέτω. 14 ἀσθενεῖ τις ἐν ὑμῖν;
let him sing a psalm. Is weak anyone among you?

προσκαλεσάσθω τοὺς πρεσβυτέρους τῆς
let him summon the elders of the

ἐκκλησίας, καὶ προσευξάσθωσαν ἐπ' αὐτὸν
church, and let them pray over him

ἀλείψαντες ἐλαίῳ ἐν τῷ ὀνόματι τοῦ
having anointed with oil ın the name of the
[him]

κυρίου. ¹5 καὶ ἡ εὐχὴ τῆς πίστεως
Lord. And the prayer - of faith

σώσει τὸν κάμνοντα, καὶ ἐγερεῖ αὐτὸν
will heal the [one] being sick, and ³will raise ⁴him

ὁ κύριος· κἂν ἁμαρτίας ᾖ πεποιηκώς,
¹the ²Lord; and if ²sins ¹he ²having done,
may be

ἀφεθήσεται αὐτῷ. 16 ἐξομολογεῖσθε οὖν
it will be forgiven him. Confess ye therefore

ἀλλήλοις τὰς ἁμαρτίας, καὶ προσεύχεσθε
to one the(your) sins, and pray ye
another

ὑπὲρ ἀλλήλων, ὅπως ἰαθῆτε. πολὺ
on be- one another, so as ye may ⁶much(very)
half of be cured.

ἰσχύει δέησις δικαίου ἐνεργουμένη.
⁴is ⁶strong ¹a petition ²of a ³being made effective.
righteous man

17 Ἠλίας ἄνθρωπος ἦν ὁμοιοπαθὴς ἡμῖν,
Elias ²a man ¹was of like feeling to us,

---

and spring rains. 8You too, be patient and stand firm, because the Lord's coming is near. 9Don't grumble against each other, brothers, or you will be judged. The Judge is standing at the door!

10Brothers, as an example of patience in the face of suffering, take the prophets who spoke in the name of the Lord. 11As you know, we consider blessed those who have persevered. You have heard of Job's perseverance and have seen what the Lord finally brought about. The Lord is full of compassion and mercy.

12Above all, my brothers, do not swear—not by heaven or by earth or by anything else. Let your "Yes" be yes, and your "No," no, or you will be condemned.

The Prayer of Faith

13Is any one of you in trouble? He should pray. Is anyone happy? Let him sing songs of praise. 14Is any one of you sick? He should call the elders of the church to pray over him and anoint him with oil in the name of the Lord. 15And the prayer offered in faith will make the sick person well; the Lord will raise him up. If he has sinned, he will be forgiven. 16Therefore confess your sins to each other and pray for each other so that you may be healed. The prayer of a righteous man is powerful and effective.

17Elijah was a man just like us. He prayed earnestly that it would not rain, not rain on the earth for three years and six months. 18And he prayed again, and the sky poured rain, and the earth produced its fruit. 19My brethren, if any among you strays from the truth, and one turns him back, 20let him know that he who turns a sinner from the error of his way will save his soul from death, and will cover a multitude of sins.

καὶ　προσευχῇ　προσηύξατο　τοῦ　μὴ　βρέξαι,
and　²in prayer　¹he prayed　　not　to rain,⁴
= that it should not rain,

καὶ　οὐκ　ἔβρεξεν　ἐπὶ　τῆς　γῆς　ἐνιαυτοὺς
and　it rained not　on　the　earth　²years

τρεῖς　καὶ　μῆνας　ἕξ·　18　καὶ　πάλιν　προσ-
¹three　and　¹months　¹six;　　and　again　he

ηύξατο,　καὶ　ὁ　οὐρανὸς　ὑετὸν　ἔδωκεν　καὶ
prayed,　and　the　heaven　²rain　¹gave　and

ἡ　γῆ　ἐβλάστησεν　τὸν　καρπὸν　αὐτῆς.
the earth　brought forth　the　fruit　of it.

19　Ἀδελφοί　μου,　ἐάν　τις　ἐν　ὑμῖν　πλανηθῇ
Brothers　of me,　if　anyone　among you　errs

ἀπὸ　τῆς　ἀληθείας　καὶ　ἐπιστρέψῃ　τις
from　the　truth　and　²turns　¹anyone

αὐτόν,　20　γινώσκετε　ὅτι　ὁ　ἐπιστρέψας
him,　　know ye　that　the [one]　turning

ἁμαρτωλὸν　ἐκ　πλάνης　ὁδοῦ　ᵃαὐτοῦ　σώσει
a sinner　out of [the] error　of way　of him　will save

ψυχὴν　αὐτοῦ　ἐκ　θανάτου　καὶ　καλύψει
soul　of him　out of　death　and　will hide

πλῆθος　ἁμαρτιῶν.
a multitude　of sins.

and it did not rain on the land for three and a half years. 18Again he prayed, and the heavens gave rain, and the earth produced its crops. 19My brothers, if one of you should wander from the truth and someone should bring him back, 20remember this: Whoever turns a sinner from the error of his way will save him from death and cover over a multitude of sins.

---

1 Peter

Chapter 1

A Living Hope, and a Sure Salvation

PETER, an apostle of Jesus Christ, to those who reside as aliens, scattered throughout Pontus, Galatia, Cappadocia, Asia, and Bithynia, who are chosen 2according to the foreknowledge of God the Father, by the sanctifying work of the Spirit, that you may obey Jesus Christ and be sprinkled with His blood: May grace and peace be yours in fullest measure. 3Blessed be the God and Father of our Lord Jesus Christ, who according to His great mercy has caused us to be born again to a living hope through the resurrection of Jesus Christ from the dead, 4to obtain an inheritance which is imperishable and undefiled and will not fade away, reserved in heaven for you, 5who are protected by the power of God through faith for a salvation ready to be revealed in the last

ΠΕΤΡΟΥ Α
Of Peter 1

1　Πέτρος　ἀπόστολος　Ἰησοῦ　Χριστοῦ
Peter　an apostle　of Jesus　Christ

ἐκλεκτοῖς　παρεπιδήμοις　διασπορᾶς　Πόντου,
to [the] chosen　sojourners　of [the] dispersion　of Pontus,

Γαλατίας,　Καππαδοκίας,　Ἀσίας　καὶ
of Galatia,　of Cappadocia,　of Asia　and

Βιθυνίας,　2　κατὰ　πρόγνωσιν　θεοῦ　πατρός,
of Bithynia,　according to　[the] foreknowledge　of God　Father,

ἐν　ἁγιασμῷ　πνεύματος,　εἰς　ὑπακοὴν　καὶ
in　sanctification　of spirit,　to　obedience　and

ῥαντισμὸν　αἵματος　Ἰησοῦ　Χριστοῦ·　χάρις
sprinkling　of [the] blood　of Jesus　Christ;　Grace

ὑμῖν　καὶ　εἰρήνη　πληθυνθείη.
to you　and　peace　may it be multiplied.

3　Εὐλογητὸς　ὁ　θεὸς　καὶ　πατὴρ　τοῦ
Blessed [be]　the　God　and　Father　of the

κυρίου　ἡμῶν　Ἰησοῦ　Χριστοῦ,　ὁ　κατὰ　τὸ
Lord　of us　Jesus　Christ,　the accord-[one]　ing to　the

πολὺ　αὐτοῦ　ἔλεος　ἀναγεννήσας　ἡμᾶς　εἰς
much　of him　mercy　having regenerated　us　to
(great)

ἐλπίδα　ζῶσαν　δι᾽　ἀναστάσεως　Ἰησοῦ
²hope　¹a living　through　[the] resurrection　of Jesus

Χριστοῦ　ἐκ　νεκρῶν,　4　εἰς　κληρονομίαν
Christ　from　[the] dead,　to　an inheritance

ἄφθαρτον　καὶ　ἀμίαντον　καὶ　ἀμάραντον,
incorruptible　and　undefiled　and　unfading,

τετηρημένην　ἐν　οὐρανοῖς　εἰς　ὑμᾶς　5　τοὺς
having been kept　in　heavens　for　you　the [ones]

ἐν　δυνάμει　θεοῦ　φρουρουμένους　διὰ　πίστεως
²by　³[the] power　⁴of God　¹being guarded　through　faith

εἰς　σωτηρίαν　ἑτοίμην　ἀποκαλυφθῆναι　ἐν
to　a salvation　ready　to be revealed　at

1 Peter

Chapter 1

PETER, an apostle of Jesus Christ,

To God's elect, strangers in the world, scattered throughout Pontus, Galatia, Cappadocia, Asia and Bithynia, 2who have been chosen according to the foreknowledge of God the Father, through the sanctifying work of the Spirit, for obedience to Jesus Christ and sprinkling by his blood:

Grace and peace be yours in abundance.

Praise to God for a Living Hope

3Praise be to the God and Father of our Lord Jesus Christ! In his great mercy he has given us new birth into a living hope through the resurrection of Jesus Christ from the dead, 4and into an inheritance that can never perish, spoil or fade —kept in heaven for you, 5who through faith are shielded by God's power until the coming of the salvation that is ready to be revealed in the last time.

time.
6In this you greatly re-joice, even though now for a little while, if necessary, you have been distressed by various trials,
7that the proof of your faith, *being* more precious than gold which is perish-able, even though tested by fire, may be found to result in praise and glory and hon-or at the revelation of Jesus Christ;
8and though you have not seen Him, you love Him, and though you do not see Him now, but be-lieve in Him, you greatly rejoice with joy inexpressi-ble and full of glory,
9obtaining as the out-come of your faith the sal-vation of *a*your souls.
10As to this salvation, the prophets who prophesied of the grace that *would come* to you made careful search and inquiry,
11seeking to know what person or time the Spirit of Christ within them was in-dicating as He predicted the sufferings of Christ and the glories to follow.
12It was revealed to them that they were not serving themselves, but you, in these things which now have been announced to you through those who preached the gospel to you by the Holy Spirit sent from heaven—things into which angels long to look.
13Therefore, gird your minds for action, keep so-ber *in spirit,* fix your hope completely on the grace to be brought to you at the revelation of Jesus Christ.
14As obedient children, do not be conformed to the former lusts *which were yours* in your ignorance,
15but like the Holy One who called you, be holy

καιρῷ   ἐσχάτῳ.   6 ἐν   ᾧ   ἀγαλλιᾶσθε,
²time   ¹[the] last.   In   which   ye exult,
ὀλίγον   ἄρτι   εἰ   δέον   λυπηθέντες   ἐν
a little [while]   yet   if   necessary   grieving   by
ποικίλοις   πειρασμοῖς,   7 ἵνα   τὸ   δοκίμιον
manifold   trials,   in order that   the   proving
ὑμῶν   τῆς   πίστεως   πολυτιμότερον   χρυσίου
²of you   ¹of the   ³faith[,]   much more precious [than]   ²gold
τοῦ   ἀπολλυμένου,   διὰ   πυρὸς   δὲ   δοκιμαζ-
-     ¹of perishing,   ³through   ⁴fire   ¹yet   ⁵being
ομένου,   εὑρεθῇ   εἰς   ἔπαινον   καὶ   δόξαν
proved,   may be found   to   praise   and   glory
καὶ   τιμὴν   ἐν   ἀποκαλύψει   Ἰησοῦ   Χριστοῦ·
and   honour   at   [the] revelation   of Jesus   Christ;
8 ὃν   οὐκ   ἰδόντες   ἀγαπᾶτε,   εἰς   ὃν   ἄρτι
whom   not   having seen   ye love,   in   whom   yet
μὴ   ὁρῶντες   πιστεύοντες   δὲ   ἀγαλλιᾶσθε
not   seeing   ³believing   ¹but   ye exult
χαρᾷ   ἀνεκλαλήτῳ   καὶ   δεδοξασμένῃ,
with joy   unspeakable   and   *having been* glorified,
9 κομιζόμενοι   τὸ   τέλος   τῆς   πίστεως
obtaining   the   end   of the(your)   faith
σωτηρίαν   ψυχῶν.   10 περὶ   ἧς   σωτηρίας
[the] salvation   of [your] souls.   Concerning   which   salvation
ἐξεζήτησαν   καὶ   ἐξηρεύνησαν   προφῆται   οἱ
²sought out   ¹⁰and   ¹¹searched out   ¹prophets   ²the
περὶ   τῆς   εἰς   ὑμᾶς   χάριτος   προφητεύσαντες,
³con-   ⁵the   ⁶for   ⁷you   ⁴grace   ³[ones] prophesying,
cerning
11 ἐρευνῶντες   εἰς   τίνα   ἢ   ποῖον   καιρὸν
searching   for   what   or what sort of   time
ἐδήλου   τὸ   ἐν   αὐτοῖς   πνεῦμα   Χριστοῦ
⁴made clear   ²the   ³in   ⁴them   ¹Spirit   ⁵of Christ
προμαρτυρόμενον   τὰ   εἰς   Χριστὸν   παθήματα
⁷forewitnessing   ⁸the   ¹⁰for   ¹¹Christ   ⁹sufferings
καὶ   τὰς   μετὰ   ταῦτα   δόξας.   12 οἷς
¹²and   ¹³the   ¹⁵after   ¹⁶these   ¹⁴glories.   To whom
ἀπεκαλύφθη   ὅτι   οὐχ   ἑαυτοῖς   ὑμῖν   δὲ
it was revealed   that   not   to themselves   ²to you   ¹but
διηκόνουν   αὐτά,   ἃ   νῦν   ἀνηγγέλη   ὑμῖν
they   the same   which   now   were   to you
ministered   things,   announced
διὰ   τῶν   εὐαγγελισαμένων   ὑμᾶς   ἐν
through   the [ones]   having evangelized   you   by
πνεύματι   ἁγίῳ   ἀποσταλέντι   ἀπ᾽   οὐρανοῦ,
²Spirit   ¹[the] Holy   sent forth   from   heaven,
εἰς   ἃ   ἐπιθυμοῦσιν   ἄγγελοι   παρακύψαι.
into   ¹which   ³long   ²angels   ⁴to look into.
things
13 Διὸ   ἀναζωσάμενοι   τὰς   ὀσφύας   τῆς
Wherefore   girding up   the   loins   of the
διανοίας   ὑμῶν,   νήφοντες,   τελείως   ἐλπίσατε
mind   of you,   being sober,   perfectly   hope
ἐπὶ   τὴν   φερομένην   ὑμῖν   χάριν   ἐν
on   ¹the   ²being brought   ⁴to you   ³grace   at
ἀποκαλύψει   Ἰησοῦ   Χριστοῦ.   14 ὡς   τέκνα
[the] revelation   of Jesus   Christ.   As   children
ὑπακοῆς,   μὴ   συσχηματιζόμενοι   ταῖς   πρότε-
of obedience,*   not   fashioning yourselves   to the   ⁶form-
ρον   ἐν   τῇ   ἀγνοίᾳ   ὑμῶν   ἐπιθυμίαις,   15 ἀλλὰ
erly   ³in   ¹the   ⁴ignorance   ⁵of you   ¹longings,   but
κατὰ   τὸν   καλέσαντα   ὑμᾶς   ἅγιον   καὶ
accord-   ¹the   ²having called   ⁴you   ³holy [one]   ⁷also
ing to

6In this you greatly rejoice, though now for a little while you may have had to suffer grief in all kinds of trials. 7These have come so that your faith—of greater worth than gold, which per-ishes even though refined by fire—may be proved genuine and may result in praise, glory and honor when Jesus Christ is re-vealed. 8Though you have not seen him, you love him; and even though you do not see him now, you believe in him and are filled with an inexpressible and glorious joy, 9for you are receiving the goal of your faith, the salvation of your souls.
10Concerning this salva-tion, the prophets, who spoke of the grace that was to come to you, searched intently and with the great-est care, 11trying to find out the time and circumstances to which the Spirit of Christ in them was pointing when he predicted the sufferings of Christ and the glories that would follow. 12It was revealed to them that they were not serving them-selves but you, when they spoke of the things that have now been told you by those who have preached the gospel to you by the Holy Spirit sent from heav-en. Even angels long to look into these things.

Be Holy

13Therefore, prepare your minds for action; be self-controlled; set your hope fully on the grace to be given you when Jesus Christ is revealed. 14As obedient children, do not conform to the evil desires you had when you lived in ignorance. 15But just as he who called you is holy, so

---

a Some ancient mss. do not contain *your*

* Genitive of quality: " obedient children."

yourselves also in all *your* behavior;

16because it is written, "YOU SHALL BE HOLY, FOR I AM HOLY."

17And if you address as Father the One who impartially judges according to each man's work, conduct yourselves in fear during the time of your stay *upon earth*;

18knowing that you were not redeemed with perishable things like silver or gold from your futile way of life inherited from your forefathers,

19but with precious blood, as of a lamb unblemished and spotless, *the blood* of Christ.

20For He was foreknown before the foundation of the world, but has appeared in these last times for the sake of you

21who through Him are believers in God, who raised Him from the dead and gave Him glory, so that your faith and hope are in God.

22Since you have in obedience to the truth purified your souls for a sincere love of the brethren, fervently love one another from [b]the heart,

23for you have been born again not of seed which is perishable but imperishable, *that is*, through the living and abiding word of God.

24For,
"ALL FLESH IS LIKE GRASS,
AND ALL ITS GLORY LIKE THE FLOWER OF GRASS.
THE GRASS WITHERS,
AND THE FLOWER FALLS OFF,
25 BUT THE WORD OF THE LORD ABIDES FOREVER."
And this is the word which was preached to you.

Chapter 2

As Newborn Babes

THEREFORE, putting aside all malice and all guile and hypocrisy and envy and all slander,

2like newborn babes, long for the pure milk of the

b Some mss. read a clean heart

αὐτοὶ ἅγιοι ἐν πάσῃ ἀναστροφῇ γενήθητε,
[your]- *holy* *in* *all* *conduct* *become ye,*
selves

16 διότι γέγραπται· [ὅτι] ἅγιοι ἔσεσθε,
because it has been written: - Holy ye shall be,

ὅτι ἐγὼ ἅγιος. 17 καὶ εἰ πατέρα
because I [am] holy. And if *Father*

ἐπικαλεῖσθε τὸν ἀπροσωπολήμπτως κρίνοντα
ye invoke [as] the [one] without respect to persons judging

κατὰ τὸ ἑκάστου ἔργον, ἐν φόβῳ τὸν
accord- the of each man work, in fear the
ing to

τῆς παροικίας ὑμῶν χρόνον ἀναστράφητε,
of the sojourning of you time pass,

18 εἰδότες ὅτι οὐ φθαρτοῖς, ἀργυρίῳ ἢ
knowing that not with corruptible silver or
things,

χρυσίῳ, ἐλυτρώθητε ἐκ τῆς ματαίας ὑμῶν
gold, ye were redeemed from the vain of you

ἀναστροφῆς πατροπαραδότου, 19 ἀλλὰ τιμίῳ
conduct delivered from but with
[your] fathers, precious

αἵματι ὡς ἀμνοῦ ἀμώμου καὶ ἀσπίλου
blood[,] as of a lamb unblemished and unspotted[,]

Χριστοῦ, 20 προεγνωσμένου μὲν πρὸ κατα-
of Christ, *having been* foreknown on one from [the]
hand

βολῆς κόσμου, φανερωθέντος δὲ ἐπ' ἐσχάτου
founda- of [the] manifested on the in [the] last
tion world, other

τῶν χρόνων δι' ὑμᾶς 21 τοὺς δι' αὐτοῦ
of the times because of you the ones through him

πιστοὺς εἰς θεὸν τὸν ἐγείραντα αὐτὸν
believing in God the [one] having raised him

ἐκ νεκρῶν καὶ δόξαν αὐτῷ δόντα, ὥστε
from [the] dead and glory to him having given, so as

τὴν πίστιν ὑμῶν καὶ ἐλπίδα εἶναι εἰς
the faith of you and hope to be in

θεόν. 22 Τὰς ψυχὰς ὑμῶν ἡγνικότες
God. The souls of you having purified

ἐν τῇ ὑπακοῇ τῆς ἀληθείας εἰς φιλαδελφίαν
by - obedience of(to) the truth to brotherly love

ἀνυπόκριτον, ἐκ καρδίας ἀλλήλους ἀγαπήσατε
unfeigned, from [the] heart one another love ye

ἐκτενῶς, 23 ἀναγεγεννημένοι οὐκ ἐκ σπορᾶς
earnestly, having been regenerated not by seed

φθαρτῆς ἀλλὰ ἀφθάρτου, διὰ λόγου ζῶντος
corruptible but incorruptible, through word [the] living

θεοῦ καὶ μένοντος. 24 διότι πᾶσα σὰρξ
of God and remaining. Because all flesh [is]

ὡς χόρτος, καὶ πᾶσα δόξα αὐτῆς ὡς
as grass, and all [the] glory of it as

ἄνθος χόρτου· ἐξηράνθη ὁ χόρτος, καὶ
a flower of grass; was dried the grass, and

τὸ ἄνθος ἐξέπεσεν· 25 τὸ δὲ ῥῆμα κυρίου
the flower fell out; but the word of [the] Lord

μένει εἰς τὸν αἰῶνα. τοῦτο δέ ἐστιν
remains unto the age. And this is

τὸ ῥῆμα τὸ εὐαγγελισθὲν εἰς ὑμᾶς.
the word - preached [as good news] to you.

2 Ἀποθέμενοι οὖν πᾶσαν κακίαν καὶ
Putting away therefore all malice and

πάντα δόλον καὶ ὑποκρίσεις καὶ φθόνους
all guile and hypocrisies and envies

καὶ πάσας καταλαλιάς, 2 ὡς ἀρτιγέννητα
and all detractions, as new born

βρέφη τὸ λογικὸν ἄδολον γάλα ἐπιποθήσατε,
babes the spiritual pure milk desire ye,

---

be holy in all you do; 16for it is written: "Be holy, because I am holy." [a]

17Since you call on a Father who judges each man's work impartially, live your lives as strangers here in reverent fear. 18For you know that it was not with perishable things such as silver or gold that you were redeemed from the empty way of life handed down to you from your forefathers, 19but with the precious blood of Christ, a lamb without blemish or defect. 20He was chosen before the creation of the world, but was revealed in these last times for your sake. 21Through him you believe in God, who raised him from the dead and glorified him, and so your faith and hope are in God.

22Now that you have purified yourselves by obeying the truth so that you have sincere love for your brothers, love one another deeply, from the heart. [b] 23For you have been born again, not of perishable seed, but of imperishable, through the living and enduring word of God. 24For,

"All men are like grass, and all their glory is like the flowers of the field;
the grass withers and the flowers fall,
25 but the word of the Lord stands forever." [c]

And this is the word that was preached to you.

Chapter 2

THEREFORE, rid yourselves of all malice and all deceit, hypocrisy, envy, and slander of every kind. 2Like newborn babies, crave pure spiritual milk,

a16 Lev. 11:44,45; 19:2; 20:7
b22 Some early manuscripts from a pure heart
c25 Isaiah 40:6-8

word, that by it you may grow in respect to salvation,
3if you have tasted the kindness of the Lord.

As Living Stones

4And coming to Him as to a living stone, rejected by men, but choice and precious in the sight of God, 5you also, as living stones, are being built up as a spiritual house for a holy priesthood, to offer up spiritual sacrifices acceptable to God through Jesus Christ. 6For *this* is contained in Scripture:
"BEHOLD I LAY IN ZION
A CHOICE STONE, A
PRECIOUS CORNER
stone,
AND HE WHO BELIEVES
IN HIM SHALL NOT BE
DISAPPOINTED."
7This precious value, then, is for you who believe. But for those who disbelieve,
"THE STONE WHICH THE
BUILDERS REJECTED,
THIS BECAME THE VERY
CORNER *stone*,"
8and,
"A STONE OF STUMBLING
AND A ROCK OF OF-
FENSE";
for they stumble because they are disobedient to the word, and to this *doom* they were also appointed.
9But you are A CHOSEN RACE, A royal PRIESTHOOD, A HOLY NATION, A PEOPLE FOR God's OWN POSSESSION, that you may proclaim the excellencies of Him who has called you out of darkness into His marvelous light; 10for you once were NOT A PEOPLE, but now you are THE PEOPLE OF GOD; you had NOT RECEIVED MERCY, but now you have RECEIVED MERCY.
11Beloved, I urge you as aliens and strangers to abstain from fleshly lusts, which wage war against the soul.
12Keep your behavior excellent among the Gentiles, so that in the thing in which

---

ἵνα   ἐν   αὐτῷ   αὐξηθῆτε   εἰς   σωτηρίαν,
in or- by   it   ye may grow to   salvation,
der that

3 εἰ   ἐγεύσασθε   ὅτι   χρηστὸς   ὁ   κύριος.
  if   ye tasted   that   ³good   ¹the ²Lord [is].

4 πρὸς   ὃν   προσερχόμενοι,   λίθον   ζῶντα,
  to   whom   approaching,   ²stone   ¹a living,

ὑπὸ   ἀνθρώπων   μὲν   ἀποδεδοκιμασμένον   παρὰ
by   men   on one   *having been* rejected   ³by
                    hand

δὲ   θεῷ   ἐκλεκτὸν   ἔντιμον,   5 καὶ
¹on the ⁴God ²chosen[,]   precious,   ²also
other

αὐτοὶ   ὡς   λίθοι   ζῶντες   οἰκοδομεῖσθε   οἶκος
¹[your]- ²as   ³stones   ⁴living   are being built ²house
selves

πνευματικὸς   εἰς   ἱεράτευμα   ἅγιον,   ἀνενέγκαι
¹a spiritual   for   ²priesthood   ¹a holy,   to offer

πνευματικὰς   θυσίας   εὐπροσδέκτους   θεῷ   διὰ
spiritual   sacrifices acceptable   to   through
                                               God

Ἰησοῦ   Χριστοῦ·   6 διότι   περιέχει   ἐν   γραφῇ·
Jesus   Christ;   because   it is   in   scripture:
                                  contained

ἰδοὺ   τίθημι   ἐν   Σιὼν   λίθον   ἐκλεκτὸν
Behold   I lay   in   Sion   ²stone   ¹a chosen

ἀκρογωνιαῖον   ἔντιμον,   καὶ   ὁ   πιστεύων
²corner foundation ¹precious,   and the [one] believing

ἐπ'   αὐτῷ   οὐ   μὴ   καταισχυνθῇ.   7 ὑμῖν
on   it(him) by no means will be shamed.   To you
                                                 =Yours

οὖν   ἡ   τιμὴ   τοῖς   πιστεύουσιν·   ἀπιστοῦσιν
there- ³[is] ⁶honour ¹the [ones] ²believingᶜ;   ²to unbelieving
fore   ⁴the   [ones]
⁵who believe is the honour;

δὲ   λίθος   ὃν   ἀπεδοκίμασαν   οἱ   οἰκοδομοῦντες,
¹but a stone which   ²rejected   ¹the [ones] ²building,

οὗτος   ἐγενήθη   εἰς   κεφαλὴν   γωνίας   8 καὶ
this   came to be for   head   of [the] corner   and

λίθος   προσκόμματος   καὶ   πέτρα   σκανδάλου·
a stone   of stumbling   and   a rock   of offence·

οἳ   προσκόπτουσιν   τῷ   λόγῳ   ἀπειθοῦντες,
who   stumble   at the word   disobeying,

9 εἰς   ὃ   καὶ   ἐτέθησαν·   ὑμεῖς   δὲ   γένος
  to   which indeed they were   but ye   [are] ²race
                       appointed;

ἐκλεκτόν,   βασίλειον   ἱεράτευμα,   ἔθνος   ἅγιον,
¹a chosen,   a royal   priesthood,   nation   a holy,

λαὸς   εἰς   περιποίησιν,   ὅπως   τὰς   ἀρετὰς
a people for   possession,   so as   ²the   ³virtues

ἐξαγγείλητε   τοῦ   ἐκ   σκότους   ὑμᾶς   καλέ-
¹ye may tell out ⁴of the ²out   ⁵darkness   ⁶you   ⁸having
               [one] of

σαντος   εἰς   τὸ   θαυμαστὸν   αὐτοῦ   φῶς·
called   into   the   marvellous   ²of him   ¹light;

10 οἳ   ποτε   οὐ   λαός,   νῦν   δὲ   λαὸς   θεοῦ,
   who   then   not   a   but [are] now   a people of
           [were]   people,   now   God,

οἱ   οὐκ   ἠλεημένοι,   νῦν   δὲ   ἐλεηθέντες.
the   not   having been pitied, but now   pitied.
[ones]

11 Ἀγαπητοί,   παρακαλῶ   ὡς   παροίκους
   Beloved,   I exhort [you] as   sojourners

καὶ   παρεπιδήμους   ἀπέχεσθαι   τῶν   σαρκικῶν
and   aliens   to abstain from –   fleshly

ἐπιθυμιῶν,   αἵτινες   στρατεύονται   κατὰ   τῆς
lusts,   which   war   against the

ψυχῆς·   12 τὴν   ἀναστροφὴν   ὑμῶν   ἐν   τοῖς
soul;   ²the   ³conduct   ¹of you   ²among ¹the

ἔθνεσιν   ἔχοντες   καλήν,   ἵνα   ἐν   ᾧ   κατα-
⁷nations   ¹having   ⁸good,   in order while they
                                   that

---

so that by it you may grow up in your salvation, 3now that you have tasted that the Lord is good.

The Living Stone and a Chosen People

4As you come to him, the living Stone—rejected by men but chosen by God and precious to him— 5you also, like living stones, are being built into a spiritual house to be a holy priesthood, offering spiritual sacrifices acceptable to God through Jesus Christ. 6For in Scripture it says:
"See, I lay a stone in
Zion,
a chosen and precious
cornerstone,
and the one who trusts in
him
will never be put to
shame." ᵈ
7Now to you who believe, this stone is precious. But to those who do not believe,
"The stone the builders
rejected
has become the
capstone," ᵉ ⸍ ᶠ
8and,
"A stone that causes
men to stumble
and a rock that makes
them fall." ᵍ

They stumble because they disobey the message—which is also what they were destined for.
9But you are a chosen people, a royal priesthood, a holy nation, a people belonging to God, that you may declare the praises of him who called you out of darkness into his wonderful light. 10Once you were not a people, but now you are the people of God; once you had not received mercy, but now you have received mercy.
11Dear friends, I urge you, as aliens and strangers in the world, to abstain from sinful desires, which war against your soul. 12Live such good lives among the pagans that, though they accuse you of

---

ᵈ6 Isaiah 28:16
ᵉ7 Or cornerstone
ᶠ7 Psalm 118:22
ᵍ8 Isaiah 8:14

they slander you as evildoers, they may on account of your good deeds, as they observe *them,* glorify God in the day of *c* visitation.

Honor Authority

13Submit yourselves for the Lord's sake to every human institution, whether to a king as the one in authority,

14or to governors as sent by him for the punishment of evildoers and the praise of those who do right.

15For such is the will of God that by doing right you may silence the ignorance of foolish men.

16Act as free men, and do not use your freedom as a covering for evil, but *use it* as bondslaves of God.

17Honor all men; love the brotherhood, fear God, honor the king.

18Servants, be submissive to your masters with all respect, not only to those who are good and gentle, but also to those who are unreasonable.

19For this *finds* favor, if for the sake of conscience toward God a man bears up under sorrows when suffering unjustly.

20For what credit is there if, when you sin and are harshly treated, you endure it with patience? But if when you do what is right and suffer *for it* you patiently endure it, this *finds* favor with God.

Christ Is Our Example

21For you have been called for this purpose, since Christ also suffered for you, leaving you an example for you to follow in His steps,

22WHO COMMITTED NO SIN, NOR WAS ANY DECEIT FOUND IN HIS MOUTH;

23and while being reviled, He did not revile in return; while suffering, He uttered no threats, but kept entrusting *Himself* to Him who judges righteously;

λαλοῦσιν ὑμῶν ὡς κακοποιῶν, ἐκ τῶν
speak against you as evildoers, by the (your)

καλῶν ἔργων ἐποπτεύοντες δοξάσωσιν τὸν
good works observing they may glorify –

θεὸν ἐν ἡμέρᾳ ἐπισκοπῆς.
God in a day of visitation.

13 Ὑποτάγητε πάσῃ ἀνθρωπίνῃ κτίσει
Submit to every human ordinance

διὰ τὸν κύριον· εἴτε βασιλεῖ ὡς ὑπερέχοντι,
be- the Lord: whether to a king as being supreme,
cause of

14 εἴτε ἡγεμόσιν ὡς δι᾽ αὐτοῦ πεμπομένοις
or to governors as through him being sent

εἰς ἐκδίκησιν κακοποιῶν ἔπαινον δὲ
for vengeance of(on) evildoers ²praise ¹but

ἀγαθοποιῶν· 15 ὅτι οὕτως ἐστὶν τὸ
of welldoers; because so is the

θέλημα τοῦ θεοῦ, ἀγαθοποιοῦντας φιμοῦν
will – of God, doing good to silence

τὴν τῶν ἀφρόνων ἀνθρώπων ἀγνωσίαν·
¹the – ²of foolish ⁴men ³ignorance;

16 ὡς ἐλεύθεροι, καὶ μὴ ὡς ἐπικάλυμμα
as free, and not ³as ⁴a cloak

ἔχοντες τῆς κακίας τὴν ἐλευθερίαν, ἀλλ᾽
¹having the ⁵of evil the ²freedom, but

ὡς θεοῦ δοῦλοι. 17 πάντας τιμήσατε,
as of God slaves. ²All men ¹honour ye,

τὴν ἀδελφότητα ἀγαπᾶτε, τὸν θεὸν
²the ³brotherhood ¹love, – ²God

φοβεῖσθε, τὸν βασιλέα τιμᾶτε. 18 Οἱ
¹fear, ²the ³king ¹honour. –

οἰκέται, ὑποτασσόμενοι ἐν παντὶ φόβῳ
House submitting yourselves in all fear
servants,

τοῖς δεσπόταις, οὐ μόνον τοῖς ἀγαθοῖς
to the(your) masters, not only to the good

καὶ ἐπιεικέσιν ἀλλὰ καὶ τοῖς σκολιοῖς.
and forbearing but also to the perverse.

19 τοῦτο γὰρ χάρις εἰ διὰ συνείδησιν
For this [is] a favour if because of conscience

θεοῦ ὑποφέρει τις λύπας πάσχων ἀδίκως.
of God ²bears ¹anyone griefs suffering unjustly.

20 ποῖον γὰρ κλέος εἰ ἁμαρτάνοντες καὶ
For what glory [is it] if sinning and

κολαφιζόμενοι ὑπομενεῖτε; ἀλλ᾽ εἰ ἀγαθο-
being buffeted ye endure? but if doing

ποιοῦντες καὶ πάσχοντες ὑπομενεῖτε, τοῦτο
good and suffering ye endure, this [is]

χάρις παρὰ θεῷ. 21 εἰς τοῦτο γὰρ
a favour with God. ²to ³this ¹For

ἐκλήθητε, ὅτι καὶ Χριστὸς ἔπαθεν ὑπὲρ
ye were because indeed Christ suffered on be-
called, half of

ὑμῶν, ὑμῖν ὑπολιμπάνων ὑπογραμμὸν ἵνα
you, ²to you ¹leaving behind an example in order that

ἐπακολουθήσητε τοῖς ἴχνεσιν αὐτοῦ· 22 ὃς
ye should follow the steps of him; who

ἁμαρτίαν οὐκ ἐποίησεν οὐδὲ εὑρέθη δόλος
³sin ²not ¹did nor was ²found ¹guile

ἐν τῷ στόματι αὐτοῦ· 23 ὃς λοιδορούμενος
in the mouth of him; who being reviled

οὐκ ἀντελοιδόρει, πάσχων οὐκ ἠπείλει,
reviled not in return, suffering he threatened not,

παρεδίδου δὲ τῷ κρίνοντι δικαίως· 24 ὃς
but delivered to the judging righteously; who
[himself] [one]

---

doing wrong, they may see your good deeds and glorify God on the day he visits us.

Submission to Rulers and Masters

13Submit yourselves for the Lord's sake to every authority instituted among men: whether to the king, as the supreme authority,

14or to governors, who are sent by him to punish those who do wrong and to commend those who do right.

15For it is God's will that by doing good you should silence the ignorant talk of foolish men. 16Live as free men, but do not use your freedom as a cover-up for evil; live as servants of God. 17Show proper respect to everyone: Love the brotherhood of believers, fear God, honor the king.

18Slaves, submit yourselves to your masters with all respect, not only to those who are good and considerate, but also to those who are harsh. 19For it is commendable if a man bears up under the pain of unjust suffering because he is conscious of God. 20But how is it to your credit if you receive a beating for doing wrong and endure it? But if you suffer for doing good and you endure it, this is commendable before God. 21To this you were called, because Christ suffered for you, leaving you an example, that you should follow in his steps.

22"He committed no sin, and no deceit was found in his mouth." *h*

23When they hurled their insults at him, he did not retaliate; when he suffered, he made no threats. Instead, he entrusted himself to him who judges justly.

---

c I.e., Christ's coming again in judgment

*h*22 Isaiah 53:9

24and He Himself bore our sins in His body on the cross, that we might die to sin and live to righteousness; for by His wounds you were healed.

25For you were continually straying like sheep, but now you have returned to the Shepherd and Guardian of your souls.

Chapter 3

Godly Living

1IN the same way, you wives, be submissive to your own husbands so that even if any *of them* are disobedient to the word, they may be won without a word by the behavior of their wives,

2as they observe your chaste and respectful behavior.

3And let not your adornment be *merely* external— braiding the hair, and wearing gold jewelry, or putting on dresses;

4but *let it be* the hidden person of the heart, with the imperishable quality of a gentle and quiet spirit, which is precious in the sight of God.

5For in this way in former times the holy women also, who hoped in God, used to adorn themselves, being submissive to their own husbands;

6Thus Sarah obeyed Abraham, calling him lord, and you have become her children if you do what is right without being frightened by any fear.

7You husbands likewise, live with *your wives* in an understanding way, as with a weaker vessel, since she is a woman; and grant her honor as a fellow heir of the grace of life, so that your prayers may not be hindered.

8To sum up, let all be harmonious, sympathetic,

τὰς ἁμαρτίας ἡμῶν αὐτὸς ἀνήνεγκεν ἐν
³the ⁴sins ⁵of us ¹[him]self ²carried up in

τῷ σώματι αὐτοῦ ἐπὶ τὸ ξύλον, ἵνα
the body of him onto the tree, in order that

ταῖς ἁμαρτίαις ἀπογενόμενοι τῇ δικαιοσύνῃ
- ²to sins ¹dying - ⁴to righteousness

ζήσωμεν· οὗ τῷ μώλωπι ἰάθητε.
³we might live; ⁴of ¹by the ²bruise ye were cured.
whom

25 ἦτε γὰρ ὡς πρόβατα πλανώμενοι,
²ye were ¹For ⁴as ⁵sheep ³wandering,

ἀλλὰ ἐπεστράφητε νῦν ἐπὶ τὸν ποιμένα
but ye turned now to the shepherd

καὶ ἐπίσκοπον τῶν ψυχῶν ὑμῶν.
and bishop of the souls of you.

3 Ὁμοίως γυναῖκες, ὑποτασσόμεναι τοῖς
Likewise wives, submitting yourselves to the (your)

ἰδίοις ἀνδράσιν, ἵνα καὶ εἴ τινες ἀπειθοῦσιν
own husbands, in order even if any disobey
that

τῷ λόγῳ, διὰ τῆς τῶν γυναικῶν ἀναστροφῆς
the word, through ¹the ²of the ⁴wives ⁵conduct
the(ir)

ἄνευ λόγου κερδηθήσονται, **2** ἐποπτεύσαντες
without a word they will(may) be gained, observing

τὴν ἐν φόβῳ ἁγνὴν ἀναστροφὴν ὑμῶν.
¹the ²in ³fear ⁴pure ²conduct ¹of you.

3 ὧν ἔστω οὐχ ὁ ἔξωθεν ἐμπλοκῆς
Of whom let it be not ¹the ²outward ⁵of plaiting

τριχῶν καὶ περιθέσεως χρυσίων ἢ ἐνδύσεως
⁶of hairs ⁴and ⁷of putting ⁸of gold ⁹or ¹⁰of clothing
round(on) [ornaments]

ἱματίων κόσμος, **4** ἀλλ' ὁ κρυπτὸς τῆς
¹¹of(with) ³adorning, but ¹the ²hidden ⁴of the
garments

καρδίας ἄνθρωπος ἐν τῷ ἀφθάρτῳ τοῦ
⁵heart ³man in(?by) the incorruptible of the
[adorning]

πραέος καὶ ἡσυχίου πνεύματος, ὅ ἐστιν
meek and quiet spirit, which is

ἐνώπιον τοῦ θεοῦ πολυτελές. **5** οὕτως
before - God of great value. so

γάρ ποτε καὶ αἱ ἅγιαι γυναῖκες αἱ
For then indeed the holy women -

ἐλπίζουσαι εἰς θεὸν ἐκόσμουν ἑαυτάς,
hoping in God adorned themselves,

ὑποτασσόμεναι τοῖς ἰδίοις ἀνδράσιν, **6** ὡς
submitting themselves to the(ir) own husbands, as

Σάρρα ὑπήκουσεν τῷ Ἀβραάμ, κύριον
Sara obeyed - Abraham, ³lord

αὐτὸν καλοῦσα· ἧς ἐγενήθητε τέκνα
²him ¹calling; of whom ye became children

ἀγαθοποιοῦσαι καὶ μὴ φοβούμεναι μηδεμίαν
doing good and not fearing no(any)

πτόησιν. **7** Οἱ ἄνδρες ὁμοίως, συνοικοῦντες
terror. - Husbands likewise, dwelling together

κατὰ γνῶσιν ὡς ἀσθενεστέρῳ σκεύει τῷ
accord- knowledge as with a weaker vessel the
ing to

γυναικείῳ, ἀπονέμοντες τιμὴν ὡς καὶ
female, assigning honour as indeed

συγκληρονόμοις χάριτος ζωῆς, εἰς τὸ μὴ
co-heirs of [the] grace of life, for the not

ἐγκόπτεσθαι τὰς προσευχὰς ὑμῶν. **8** Τὸ δὲ
to be hindered the prayers of you.ᵇ Now the

τέλος πάντες ὁμόφρονες, συμπαθεῖς,
end[,] [be ye] all of one mind, sympathetic,

Chapter 3

Wives and Husbands

1WIVES, in the same way be submissive to your husbands so that, if any of them do not believe the word, they may be won over without words by the behavior of their wives, **2**when they see the purity and reverence of your lives. **3**Your beauty should not come from outward adornment, such as braided hair and the wearing of gold jewelry and fine clothes. **4**Instead, it should be that of your inner self, the unfading beauty of a gentle and quiet spirit, which is of great worth in God's sight. **5**For this is the way the holy women of the past who put their hope in God used to make themselves beautiful. They were submissive to their own husbands, **6**like Sarah, who obeyed Abraham and called him her master. You are her daughters if you do what is right and do not give way to fear.

7Husbands, in the same way be considerate as you live with your wives, and treat them with respect as the weaker partner and as heirs with you of the gracious gift of life, so that nothing will hinder your prayers.

Suffering for Doing Good

8Finally, all of you, live in harmony with one another; be sympathetic, love as brotherly, kindhearted, and humble in spirit;

9not returning evil for evil, or insult for insult, but giving a blessing instead; for you were called for the very purpose that you might inherit a blessing.

10For,

"LET HIM WHO MEANS TO LOVE LIFE AND SEE GOOD DAYS REFRAIN HIS TONGUE FROM EVIL AND HIS LIPS FROM SPEAKING GUILE.

11"AND LET HIM TURN AWAY FROM EVIL AND DO GOOD; LET HIM SEEK PEACE AND PURSUE IT.

12"FOR THE EYES OF THE LORD ARE UPON THE RIGHTEOUS, AND HIS EARS ATTEND TO THEIR PRAYER, BUT THE FACE OF THE LORD IS AGAINST THOSE WHO DO EVIL."

13And who is there to harm you if you prove zealous for what is good?

14But even if you should suffer for the sake of righteousness, *you are* blessed. AND DO NOT FEAR THEIR INTIMIDATION, AND DO NOT BE TROUBLED,

15but *d*sanctify Christ as Lord in your hearts, always *being* ready to make a defense to everyone who asks you to give an account for the hope that is in you, yet with gentleness and reverence;

16and keep a good conscience so that in the thing in which you are slandered, those who revile your good behavior in Christ may be put to shame.

17For it is better, if God should will it so, that you suffer for doing what is right rather than for doing what is wrong.

18For Christ also died for sins once for all, *the* just for *the* unjust, in order that He might bring us to God, hav-

---

φιλάδελφοι, εὔσπλαγχνοι, ταπεινόφρονες,
loving [the] brothers, compassionate, humble-minded,

9 μὴ ἀποδιδόντες κακὸν ἀντὶ κακοῦ ἢ
not giving back evil instead of evil or

λοιδορίαν ἀντὶ λοιδορίας, τοὐναντίον δὲ
reviling instead of reviling, but on the contrary

εὐλογοῦντες, ὅτι εἰς τοῦτο ἐκλήθητε ἵνα
blessing, because to this ye were called in order that

εὐλογίαν κληρονομήσητε. 10 ὁ γὰρ θέλων
blessing ye might inherit. For the [one] wishing

ζωὴν ἀγαπᾶν καὶ ἰδεῖν ἡμέρας ἀγαθάς,
²life ¹to love and to see ²days ¹good,

παυσάτω τὴν γλῶσσαν ἀπὸ κακοῦ καὶ
let him the(his) tongue from evil and
restrain

χείλη τοῦ μὴ λαλῆσαι δόλον, 11 ἐκκλινάτω
[his] lips - not to speak[d] guile, ²let him turn aside

δὲ ἀπὸ κακοῦ καὶ ποιησάτω ἀγαθόν,
¹and from evil and let him do good,

ζητησάτω εἰρήνην καὶ διωξάτω αὐτήν·
let him seek peace and pursue it;

12 ὅτι ὀφθαλμοὶ κυρίου ἐπὶ δικαίους καὶ
because [the] eyes of [the] [of] [are] on [the] righteous and
Lord

ὦτα αὐτοῦ εἰς δέησιν αὐτῶν, πρόσωπον
[the] of him [open] to [the] of them, ²[the] face
ears petition

δὲ κυρίου ἐπὶ ποιοῦντας κακά.
¹but of [the] [is] [ones] doing evil things.
Lord against

13 Καὶ τίς ὁ κακώσων ὑμᾶς ἐὰν τοῦ
And who the harming you if ²of the
[is] [one]

ἀγαθοῦ ζηλωταὶ γένησθε; 14 ἀλλ' εἰ καὶ
⁴good ²zealots ¹ye become? but if indeed

πάσχοιτε διὰ δικαιοσύνην, μακάριοι. τὸν
ye suffer because of righteousness, blessed [are ye]. ²the

δὲ φόβον αὐτῶν μὴ φοβηθῆτε μηδὲ
¹But ⁴fear ⁵of them ³fear ye not nor

ταραχθῆτε, 15 κύριον δὲ τὸν Χριστὸν
be ye troubled, ¹but ⁴[as] ⁵Lord - ²Christ

ἁγιάσατε ἐν ταῖς καρδίαις ὑμῶν, ἕτοιμοι
²sanctify in the hearts of you, ready

ἀεὶ πρὸς ἀπολογίαν παντὶ τῷ αἰτοῦντι
always for defence to every one asking

ὑμᾶς λόγον περὶ τῆς ἐν ὑμῖν ἐλπίδος,
you a word concerning ¹the ³in ⁴you ²hope,

16 ἀλλὰ μετὰ πραΰτητος καὶ φόβου,
but with meekness and fear,

συνείδησιν ἔχοντες ἀγαθήν, ἵνα ἐν ᾧ
²conscience ¹having ²a good, in order that while

καταλαλεῖσθε καταισχυνθῶσιν οἱ ἐπηρεάζον-
ye are spoken against ²may be shamed [by] ¹the [ones] ²abusing

τες ὑμῶν τὴν ἀγαθὴν ἐν Χριστῷ
[you] ¹of you ⁴the ³good ³in ⁶Christ

ἀναστροφήν. 17 κρεῖττον γὰρ ἀγαθοποι-
⁵conduct. For [it is] better doing

οῦντας, εἰ θέλοι τὸ θέλημα τοῦ θεοῦ,
good, if ⁴wills ¹the ²will - ³of God,

πάσχειν ἢ κακοποιοῦντας. 18 ὅτι καὶ
to suffer than doing evil. Because indeed

Χριστὸς ἅπαξ περὶ ἁμαρτιῶν ἀπέθανεν,
Christ once ²concerning ³sins ¹died,

δίκαιος ὑπὲρ ἀδίκων, ἵνα ὑμᾶς προσαγάγῃ
a righteous on be- unrighteous in or- ²you ¹he might
man half of ones, der that bring

---

brothers, be compassionate and humble. 9Do not repay evil with evil or insult with insult, but with blessing, because to this you were called so that you may inherit a blessing. 10For,

"Whoever would love life
  and see good days
must keep his tongue
  from evil
and his lips from
  deceitful speech.
11He must turn from evil
  and do good;
he must seek peace and
  pursue it.
12For the eyes of the Lord
  are on the righteous
and his ears are
  attentive to their
  prayer,
but the face of the Lord
  is against those who
  do evil."[i]

13Who is going to harm you if you are eager to do good? 14But even if you should suffer for what is right, you are blessed. "Do not fear what they fear[j]; do not be frightened."[k] 15But in your hearts set apart Christ as Lord. Always be prepared to give an answer to everyone who asks you to give the reason for the hope that you have. But do this with gentleness and respect, 16keeping a clear conscience, so that those who speak maliciously against your good behavior in Christ may be ashamed of their slander. 17It is better, if it is God's will, to suffer for doing good than for doing evil. 18For Christ died for sins once for all, the righteous for the unrighteous, to bring you to

---

[d]I.e., set apart

[i]12 Psalm 34:12-16
[j]14 Or *not fear their threats*
[k]14 Isaiah 8:12

ing been put to death in the flesh, but made alive in the spirit;

19in which also He went and made proclamation to the spirits *now* in prison,

20who once were disobedient, when the patience of God kept waiting in the days of Noah, during the construction of the ark, in which a few, that is, eight persons, were brought safely through *the* water.

21And corresponding to that, baptism now saves you—not the removal of dirt from the flesh, but an appeal to God for a good conscience—through the resurrection of Jesus Christ,

22who is at the right hand of God, having gone into heaven, after angels and authorities and powers had been subjected to Him.

τῷ θεῷ, θανατωθεὶς μὲν σαρκὶ ζωοποιηθεὶς
— to being put to on one in [the] quickened
God, death hand flesh[,]

δὲ πνεύματι 19 ἐν ᾧ καὶ τοῖς ἐν
on the in [the] in which indeed ²to the ⁴in
other spirit;

φυλακῇ πνεύμασιν πορευθεὶς ἐκήρυξεν,
³prison ⁵spirits ¹going ⁶he proclaimed,

20 ἀπειθήσασίν ποτε ὅτε ἀπεξεδέχετο ἡ
to disobeying ones then when ⁴waited ¹the

τοῦ θεοῦ μακροθυμία ἐν ἡμέραις Νῶε
— ³of God ²longsuffering in [the] days of Noe

κατασκευαζομένης κιβωτοῦ, εἰς ἣν ὀλίγοι,
²being prepared ¹an ark,ᵃ in which a few,

τοῦτ' ἔστιν ὀκτὼ ψυχαί, διεσώθησαν δι'
this is eight souls, were through
quite saved

ὕδατος. 21 ὃ καὶ ὑμᾶς ἀντίτυπον νῦν
water. ¹Which ³also ⁴us ²figure ⁴now

σῴζει βάπτισμα, οὐ σαρκὸς ἀπόθεσις
⁵saves [even] baptism, not ³of [the] ¹a putting
flesh away

ῥύπου ἀλλὰ συνειδήσεως ἀγαθῆς ἐπερώτημα
⁵of [the] but ²conscience ³of a good ¹an answer
filth

εἰς θεόν, δι' ἀναστάσεως Ἰησοῦ Χριστοῦ,
toward God, through [the] resurrection of Jesus Christ,

22 ὅς ἐστιν ἐν δεξιᾷ θεοῦ, πορευθεὶς
who is at [the] right of God, having gone
[hand]

εἰς οὐρανόν, ὑποταγέντων αὐτῷ ἀγγέλων
into heaven, ⁶being subjected ⁷to him ¹angels

καὶ ἐξουσιῶν καὶ δυνάμεων.
²and ³authorities ⁴and ⁵powersᵃ.

4 Χριστοῦ οὖν παθόντος σαρκὶ καὶ ὑμεῖς
¹Christ ¹there- having in [the] ²also ¹ye
fore sufferedᵃ flesh

τὴν αὐτὴν ἔννοιαν ὁπλίσασθε, ὅτι ὁ
⁴the ⁵same ³mind ²arm your- because the
selves [with], [one]

παθὼν σαρκὶ πέπαυται ἁμαρτίας, 2 εἰς
having in [the] flesh has ceased from sin, for
suffered

τὸ μηκέτι ἀνθρώπων ἐπιθυμίαις ἀλλὰ
the ¹no longer ⁸of men ⁸in [the] lusts ¹⁰but

θελήματι θεοῦ τὸν ἐπίλοιπον ἐν σαρκὶ
¹¹in [the] will ¹²of God ³the ⁴remaining ⁵in ⁷[the] flesh

βιῶσαι χρόνον. 3 ἀρκετὸς γὰρ ὁ παρεληλυ-
⁶to live ²time. For ⁶sufficient ¹the ³having passed

θὼς χρόνος τὸ βούλημα τῶν ἐθνῶν
away ²time ⁴[is] ⁷the ⁸purpose ⁹of the ¹⁰nations

κατειργάσθαι, πεπορευμένους ἐν ἀσελγείαις,
⁵to have worked out, having gone [on] in licentiousnesses,

ἐπιθυμίαις, οἰνοφλυγίαις, κώμοις, πότοις
lusts, debaucheries, carousals, drinking
bouts

καὶ ἀθεμίτοις εἰδωλολατρίαις. 4 ἐν ᾧ
and unlawful idolatries. While

ξενίζονται μὴ συντρεχόντων ὑμῶν εἰς
they are surprised ²not ³running with ¹youᵃ to

τὴν αὐτὴν τῆς ἀσωτίας ἀνάχυσιν, βλασ-
the same ²of profligacy ¹excess, blas-

φημοῦντες· 5 οἳ ἀποδώσουσιν λόγον τῷ
pheming; who will render account to the
[one]

ἑτοίμως ἔχοντι κρῖναι ζῶντας καὶ νεκρούς.
readily having to judge living and dead.
= who is ready

6 εἰς τοῦτο γὰρ καὶ νεκροῖς εὐηγγελίσθη,
²for ³this ¹For indeed ²to ¹good news
dead men was preached,

God. He was put to death in the body but made alive by the Spirit, 19through whom/ also he went and preached to the spirits in prison 20who disobeyed patiently in the days of Noah while the ark was being built. In it only a few people, eight in all, were saved through water, 21and this water symbolizes baptism that now saves you also—not the removal of dirt from the body but the pledgeᵐ of a good conscience toward God. It saves you by the resurrection of Jesus Christ, 22who has gone into heaven and is at God's right hand—with angels, authorities and powers in submission to him.

Chapter 4

Keep Fervent in Your Love

THEREFORE, since Christ has ᵉsuffered in the flesh, arm yourselves also with the same purpose, because he who has suffered in the flesh has ceased from sin,

2so as to live the rest of the time in the flesh no longer for the lusts of men, but for the will of God.

3For the time already past is sufficient *for you* to have carried out the desire of the Gentiles, having pursued a course of sensuality, lusts, drunkenness, carousals, drinking parties and abominable idolatries.

4And in *all* this, they are surprised that you do not run with *them* into the same excess of dissipation, and they malign *you*;

5but they shall give account to Him who is ready to judge the living and the dead.

6For the gospel has for this purpose been preached even to those who are dead, that though they are

Chapter 4

Living for God

THEREFORE, since Christ suffered in his body, arm yourselves also with the same attitude, because he who has suffered in his body is done with sin. 2As a result, he does not live the rest of his earthly life for evil human desires, but rather for the will of God. 3For you have spent enough time in the past doing what pagans choose to do—living in debauchery, lust, drunkenness, orgies, carousing and detestable idolatry. 4They think it strange that you do not plunge with them into the same flood of dissipation, and they heap abuse on you. 5But they will have to give account to him who is ready to judge the living and the dead. 6For this is the reason the gospel was preached even to those who are now dead, so that

---

ᵉ I.e., suffered death

l18,19 Or *alive in the spirit,*
19through which
m21 Or *response*

judged in the flesh as men, they may live in the spirit according to *the will of* God.

7The end of all things is at hand; therefore, be of sound judgment and sober *spirit* for the purpose of prayer.

8Above all, keep fervent in your love for one another, because love covers a multitude of sins.

9Be hospitable to one another without complaint.

10As each one has received a *special* gift, employ it in serving one another, as good stewards of the manifold grace of God.

11Whoever speaks, *let him speak*, as it were, the utterances of God; whoever serves, *let him do so* as by the strength which God supplies; so that in all things God may be glorified through Jesus Christ, to whom belongs the glory and dominion forever and ever. Amen.

Share the Sufferings of Christ

12Beloved, do not be surprised at the fiery ordeal among you, which comes upon you for your testing, as though some strange thing were happening to you;

13but to the degree that you share the sufferings of Christ, keep on rejoicing; so that also at the revelation of His glory, you may rejoice with exultation.

14If you are reviled for the name of Christ, you are blessed, because the Spirit of glory and of God rests upon you.

15By no means let any of you suffer as a murderer, or thief, or evildoer, or a troublesome meddler;

16but if *anyone suffers* as a Christian, let him not feel ashamed, but in that name let him glorify God.

Greek	English
ἵνα	in order
κριθῶσι	²they might be judged
μὲν	that
κατὰ	¹on one
ἀνθρώπους	according to men
σαρκί,	in [the] flesh,
ζῶσι	²might live
δὲ	other
κατὰ	¹on the according to
θεὸν	God
πνεύματι.	in [the] spirit.

7 Πάντων δὲ τὸ τέλος ἤγγικεν.
Now of all things the end has drawn near.

σωφρονήσατε οὖν καὶ νήψατε εἰς
Be ye soberminded therefore and be ye sober unto

προσευχάς· 8 πρὸ πάντων τὴν εἰς ἑαυτοὺς
prayers; before all things – ⁴to ⁵yourselves

ἀγάπην ἐκτενῆ ἔχοντες, ὅτι ἀγάπη
³love ²fervent ¹having, because love

καλύπτει πλῆθος ἁμαρτιῶν· 9 φιλόξενοι εἰς
covers a multitude of sins; [be] hospitable to

ἀλλήλους ἄνευ γογγυσμοῦ· 10 ἕκαστος καθὼς
one another without murmuring; each one as

ἔλαβεν χάρισμα, εἰς ἑαυτοὺς αὐτὸ διακον-
he received a gift, ³to ⁴yourselves ²it ¹minister-

οῦντες ὡς καλοὶ οἰκονόμοι ποικίλης χάριτος
ing as good stewards of [the] manifold grace

θεοῦ· 11 εἴ τις λαλεῖ, ὡς λόγια θεοῦ·
of God; if anyone speaks, as [the] of God; oracles

εἴ τις διακονεῖ, ὡς ἐξ ἰσχύος ἧς χορηγεῖ
if anyone ministers, as by strength which ²supplies

ὁ θεός· ἵνα ἐν πᾶσιν δοξάζηται ὁ θεὸς
– ¹God; in or- in all things ²may be glorified – ¹God
der that

διὰ Ἰησοῦ Χριστοῦ, ᾧ ἐστιν ἡ δόξα
through Jesus Christ, to whom isᶜ the glory
=whose is

καὶ τὸ κράτος εἰς τοὺς αἰῶνας τῶν
and the might unto the ages of the

αἰώνων· ἀμήν.
ages : Amen.

12 Ἀγαπητοί, μὴ ξενίζεσθε τῇ ἐν ὑμῖν
Beloved, be not surprised [at] ¹the ⁴among ⁵you

πυρώσει πρὸς πειρασμὸν ὑμῖν γινομένῃ,
²fiery trial ⁶for ⁷trial ⁸to you ³happening,

ὡς ξένου ὑμῖν συμβαίνοντος, 13 ἀλλὰ
as a surprising ²to you ¹occurringᵃ, but
thing

καθὸ κοινωνεῖτε τοῖς τοῦ Χριστοῦ
²as ³ye share ⁴the – ⁶of Christ

παθήμασιν χαίρετε, ἵνα καὶ ἐν τῇ ἀπο-
⁵sufferings ¹rejoice, in order also at the reve-
that

καλύψει τῆς δόξης αὐτοῦ χαρῆτε ἀγαλ-
lation of the glory of him ye may exult-
rejoice

λιώμενοι. 14 εἰ ὀνειδίζεσθε ἐν ὀνόματι
ing. If ye are reproached in [the] name

Χριστοῦ, μακάριοι, ὅτι τὸ τῆς δόξης
of Christ, blessed [are ye], because ¹the – ²of glory

καὶ τὸ τοῦ θεοῦ πνεῦμα ἐφ᾽ ὑμᾶς
⁴and ⁵the(?that) – ⁶of God ³spirit ⁸on ⁹you

ἀναπαύεται. 15 μὴ γάρ τις ὑμῶν πασχέτω
⁷rests. ³Not ¹for ⁴anyone ⁵of you ²let ⁶suffer

ὡς φονεὺς ἢ κλέπτης ἢ κακοποιὸς ἢ
as a murderer or a thief or an evildoer or

ὡς ἀλλοτριεπίσκοπος· 16 εἰ δὲ ὡς
as a pryer into other men's affairs; but if as

Χριστιανός, μὴ αἰσχυνέσθω, δοξαζέτω δὲ
a Christian, let him not be shamed, but let him glorify

τὸν θεὸν ἐν τῷ ὀνόματι τούτῳ. 17 ὅτι
– God by this name. Because

they might be judged according to men in regard to the body, but live according to God in regard to the spirit.

7The end of all things is near. Therefore be clear minded and self-controlled so that you can pray. 8Above all, love each other deeply, because love covers over a multitude of sins. 9Offer hospitality to one another without grumbling. 10Each one should use whatever gift he has received to serve others, faithfully administering God's grace in its various forms. 11If anyone speaks, he should do it as one speaking the very words of God. If anyone serves, he should do it with the strength God provides, so that in all things God may be praised through Jesus Christ. To him be the glory and the power for ever and ever. Amen.

Suffering for Being a Christian

12Dear friends, do not be surprised at the painful trial you are suffering, as though something strange were happening to you. 13But rejoice that you participate in the sufferings of Christ, so that you may be overjoyed when his glory is revealed. 14If you are insulted because of the name of Christ, you are blessed, for the Spirit of glory and of God rests on you. 15If you suffer, it should not be as a murderer or thief or any other kind of criminal, or even as a meddler. 16However, if you suffer as a Christian, do not be ashamed, but praise God that you bear that name.

17For *it is* time for judgment to begin with the household of God; and if *it begins* with us first, what *will be* the outcome for those who do not obey the gospel of God?

18AND IF IT IS WITH DIFFICULTY THAT THE RIGHTEOUS IS SAVED, WHAT WILL BECOME OF THE GODLESS MAN AND THE SINNER?

19Therefore, let those also who suffer according to the will of God entrust their souls to a faithful Creator in doing what is right.

[ὁ] καιρὸς τοῦ ἄρξασθαι τὸ κρίμα ἀπὸ
the time - to begin[d] the judgment from
[?has come]

τοῦ οἴκου τοῦ θεοῦ· εἰ δὲ πρῶτον ἀφ'
the household - of God; and if firstly from

ἡμῶν, τί τὸ τέλος τῶν ἀπειθούντων
us, what [will be] the end of the [ones] disobeying

τῷ τοῦ θεοῦ εὐαγγελίῳ; 18 καὶ εἰ ὁ
the - ²of God ¹gospel? and if the

δίκαιος μόλις σώζεται, ὁ [δὲ] ἀσεβὴς
righteous man scarcely is saved, ³the - ⁴impious

καὶ ἁμαρτωλὸς ποῦ φανεῖται; 19 ὥστε
⁵and ⁶sinner ¹where ²will ⁷appear? so as

καὶ οἱ πάσχοντες κατὰ τὸ θέλημα τοῦ
indeed the suffering accord- the will -
[ones] ing to

θεοῦ πιστῷ κτίστῃ παρατιθέσθωσαν τὰς
of God ⁵to a ⁶Creator ¹let them commit ²the
faithful

ψυχὰς αὐτῶν ἐν ἀγαθοποιΐᾳ.
³souls ⁴of them in welldoing.

17For it is time for judgment to begin with the family of God; and if it begins with us, what will the outcome be for those who do not obey the gospel of God? 18And,

"If it is hard for the righteous to be saved,
what will become of the ungodly and the sinner?" [n]

19So then, those who suffer according to God's will should commit themselves to their faithful Creator and continue to do good.

Chapter 5

Serve God Willingly

THEREFORE, I exhort the elders among you, as *your* fellow elder and witness of the sufferings of Christ, and a partaker also of the glory that is to be revealed,

2shepherd the flock of God among you, exercising oversight not under compulsion, but voluntarily, according to *the will of* God; and not for sordid gain, but with eagerness;

3nor yet as lording it over those allotted to your charge, but proving to be examples to the flock.

4And when the Chief Shepherd appears, you will receive the unfading crown of glory.

5You younger men, likewise, be subject to your elders; and all of you, clothe yourselves with humility toward one another, for GOD IS OPPOSED TO THE PROUD, BUT GIVES GRACE TO THE HUMBLE.

6Humble yourselves, therefore, under the mighty hand of God, that He may exalt you at the proper time,

7casting all your anxiety upon Him, because He

5 Πρεσβυτέρους οὖν ἐν ὑμῖν παρακαλῶ
Elders there- among you I exhort
fore

ὁ συμπρεσβύτερος καὶ μάρτυς τῶν τοῦ
the co-elder and witness of the

Χριστοῦ παθημάτων, ὁ καὶ τῆς μελλούσης
²of Christ ³sufferings, ¹the ³also ⁴of the ⁵being about

ἀποκαλύπτεσθαι δόξης κοινωνός· 2 ποιμάνατε
⁷to be revealed ⁶glory ²sharer: shepherd

τὸ ἐν ὑμῖν ποίμνιον τοῦ θεοῦ, μὴ
¹the ⁴among ⁵you ²flock - ³of God, not

ἀναγκαστῶς ἀλλὰ ἑκουσίως κατὰ θεόν,
by way of but willingly accord- God,
compulsion ing to

μηδὲ αἰσχροκερδῶς ἀλλὰ προθύμως, 3 μηδ'
nor from eagerness for but eagerly, nor
base gain

ὡς κατακυριεύοντες τῶν κλήρων* ἀλλὰ
as exercising lordship over the lots* but

τύποι γινόμενοι τοῦ ποιμνίου· 4 καὶ
²examples ¹becoming of the flock; and

φανερωθέντος τοῦ ἀρχιποίμενος κομιεῖσθε
appearing the chief shepherd[a] ye will receive
=when the chief shepherd appears

τὸν ἀμαράντινον τῆς δόξης στέφανον.
the unfading ²of glory ¹crown.

5 Ὁμοίως, νεώτεροι, ὑποτάγητε πρεσβυτέ-
Likewise, younger men, submit yourselves to older

ροις· πάντες δὲ ἀλλήλοις τὴν ταπεινοφρο-
men; and all ²to one another - ¹humil-

σύνην ἐγκομβώσασθε, ὅτι ὁ θεὸς ὑπερηφάνοις
ity ¹gird ye on, because - God ¹arrogant men

ἀντιτάσσεται, ταπεινοῖς δὲ δίδωσιν χάριν.
¹resists, but to humble men he gives grace.

6 Ταπεινώθητε οὖν ὑπὸ τὴν κραταιὰν
Be ye humbled therefore under the mighty

χεῖρα τοῦ θεοῦ, ἵνα ὑμᾶς ὑψώσῃ ἐν
hand - of God, in order ²you ¹he may exalt in
that

καιρῷ, 7 πᾶσαν τὴν μέριμναν ὑμῶν
time, ²all ³the ¹anxiety ⁴of you

ἐπιρίψαντες ἐπ' αὐτόν, ὅτι αὐτῷ μέλει
¹casting on him, because ²to him ¹it matters

Chapter 5

To Elders and Young Men

TO the elders among you, I appeal as a fellow elder, a witness of Christ's sufferings and one who also will share in the glory to be revealed: 2Be shepherds of God's flock that is under your care, serving as overseers—not because you must, but because you are willing, as God wants you to be; not greedy for money, but eager to serve; 3not lording it over those entrusted to you, but being examples to the flock. 4And when the Chief Shepherd appears, you will receive the crown of glory that will never fade away.

5Young men, in the same way be submissive to those who are older. All of you, clothe yourselves with humility toward one another, because,

"God opposes the proud but gives grace to the humble." [o]

6Humble yourselves, therefore, under God's mighty hand, that he may lift you up in due time. 7Cast all your anxiety on him because he cares for you.

---

* That is, the various spheres assigned to the elders.

[n]18 Prov. 11:31
[o]5 Prov. 3:34

cares for you.
[8]Be of sober *spirit*, be on the alert. Your adversary, the devil, prowls about like a roaring lion, seeking someone to devour.

[9]But resist him, firm in *your* faith, knowing that the same experiences of suffering are being accomplished by your brethren who are in the world.

[10]And after you have suffered for a little while, the God of all grace, who called you to His eternal glory in Christ, will Himself perfect, confirm, strengthen *and* establish you.

[11]To Him *be* dominion forever and ever. Amen

[12]Through Silvanus, our faithful brother (for so I regard *him*), I have written to you briefly, exhorting and testifying that this is the true grace of God. Stand firm in it!

[13]/She who is in Babylon, chosen together with you, sends you greetings, and *so does* my son, Mark.

[14]Greet one another with a kiss of love.

Peace be to you all who are in Christ.

περὶ   ὑμῶν.   **8** Νήψατε,   γρηγορήσατε.   ὁ
concerning you.   Be ye sober,   watch ye.   The

ἀντίδικος   ὑμῶν   διάβολος   ὡς   λέων   ὠρυόμενος
adversary   of you   [the] devil   as   a lion   roaring

περιπατεῖ   ζητῶν   τινα   καταπιεῖν·   **9** ᾧ
walks about   seeking   whom   to devour;   whom

ἀντίστητε   στερεοὶ   τῇ   πίστει,   εἰδότες   τὰ
oppose   firm   in the   faith,   knowing   the

αὐτὰ   τῶν   παθημάτων   τῇ   ἐν   τῷ   κόσμῳ
same   *of the* sufferings   [2]in   [3]in   [4]the   [7]world
things

ὑμῶν   ἀδελφότητι   ἐπιτελεῖσθαι.   **10** Ὁ   δὲ
[6]of you   [3]brotherhood   [1]to be accomplished.   [5]the   [1]Now

θεὸς   πάσης   χάριτος,   ὁ   καλέσας   ὑμᾶς
God   of all   grace,   the [one] having called   you

εἰς   τὴν   αἰώνιον   αὐτοῦ   δόξαν   ἐν   Χριστῷ,
to   the   [1]eternal   [3]of him   [2]glory   in   Christ,

ὀλίγον   παθόντας   αὐτὸς   καταρτίσει,   στηρίξει,
[1][you]   [2]having   [him]self   will adjust,   confirm,
[3]a little   suffered

σθενώσει,   θεμελιώσει.   **11** αὐτῷ   τὸ   κράτος
strengthen,   found.   To him [is][c] the   might
   = His is*

εἰς   τοὺς   αἰῶνας   τῶν   αἰώνων·   ἀμήν.
unto   the   ages   of the   ages: Amen.

12 Διὰ   Σιλουανοῦ   ὑμῖν   τοῦ   πιστοῦ
Through   Silvanus   to you the   faithful

ἀδελφοῦ,   ὡς   λογίζομαι,   δι'   ὀλίγων   ἔγραψα,
brother,   as   I reckon,   by   a few   I wrote,
   means of [words]

παρακαλῶν   καὶ   ἐπιμαρτυρῶν   ταύτην   εἶναι
exhorting   and   witnessing   this   to be

ἀληθῆ   χάριν   τοῦ   θεοῦ,   εἰς   ἣν   στῆτε.
[the] true   grace   –   of God,   in   which   ye stand.

13 Ἀσπάζεται   ὑμᾶς   ἡ   ἐν   Βαβυλῶνι
[10]greets   [11]you   [1]The   [3]in   [4]Babylon

συνεκλεκτὴ   καὶ   Μάρκος   ὁ   υἱός   μου.
[2]co-chosen   [5]and   [6]Mark   [7]the   [8]son   [9]of me.
[? church]

14 ἀσπάσασθε   ἀλλήλους   ἐν   φιλήματι   ἀγάπης.
Greet ye   one another   with   a kiss   of love.

Εἰρήνη   ὑμῖν   πᾶσιν   τοῖς   ἐν   Χριστῷ.
Peace   to you   all   the ones   in   Christ.

---

[8]Be self-controlled and alert. Your enemy the devil prowls around like a roaring lion looking for someone to devour. [9]Resist him, standing firm in the faith, because you know that your brothers throughout the world are undergoing the same kind of sufferings.

[10]And the God of all grace, who called you to his eternal glory in Christ, after you have suffered a little while, will himself restore you and make you strong, firm and steadfast. [11]To him be the power for ever and ever. Amen.

Final Greetings

[12]With the help of Silas,[p] whom I regard as a faithful brother, I have written to you briefly, encouraging you and testifying that this is the true grace of God. Stand fast in it.

[13]She who is in Babylon, chosen together with you, sends you her greetings, and so does my son Mark. [14]Greet one another with a kiss of love.

Peace to all of you who are in Christ.

---

2 Peter

Chapter 1

Growth in Christian Virtue

[a][S]IMON Peter, a bond-servant and apostle of Jesus Christ, to those who have received a faith of the same kind as ours, by the righteousness of our God and Savior, Jesus Christ;

[2]Grace and peace be multiplied to you in the knowledge of God and of Jesus our Lord;

[3]seeing that His divine power has granted to us

ΠΕΤΡΟΥ   Β
Of Peter 2

1 Συμεὼν   Πέτρος   δοῦλος   καὶ   ἀπόστολος
Symeon   Peter   a slave   and   an apostle

Ἰησοῦ   Χριστοῦ   τοῖς   ἰσότιμον   ἡμῖν
of Jesus   Christ   [1]to the   [2]equally   [3]with
   [ones]   precious   us

λαχοῦσιν   πίστιν   ἐν   δικαιοσύνῃ   τοῦ   θεοῦ
[3]having   [4]faith   in   righteousness   of the   God
obtained   [the]

ἡμῶν   καὶ   σωτῆρος   Ἰησοῦ   Χριστοῦ·
of us   and   Saviour   Jesus   Christ :

2 χάρις   ὑμῖν   καὶ   εἰρήνη   πληθυνθείη   ἐν
Grace   to you   and   peace   *may it* be multiplied   by

ἐπιγνώσει   τοῦ   θεοῦ   καὶ   Ἰησοῦ   τοῦ
a full knowledge   –   of God   and   of Jesus   the

κυρίου   ἡμῶν.
Lord   of us.

3 Ὡς   τὰ   πάντα   ἡμῖν   τῆς   θείας   δυνάμεως
As   –   all things   to us   the   divine   power
   =his divine power has given us all things . . .

* Cf. 4. 11 (a statement of fact, not a wish).

---

2 Peter

Chapter 1

[S]IMON Peter, a servant and apostle of Jesus Christ,

To those who through the righteousness of our God and Savior Jesus Christ have received a faith as precious as ours:

[2]Grace and peace be yours in abundance through the knowledge of God and of Jesus our Lord.

Making One's Calling and Election Sure

[3]His divine power has given us everything we

---

[f]Some mss. read *The church which*
[a]Most early mss. read *Simeon*

[p]12 Greek *Silvanus*, a variant of *Silas*

everything pertaining to life and godliness, through the true knowledge of Him who called us by His own glory and excellence. 4For by these He has granted to us His precious and magnificent promises, in order that by them you might become partakers of *the* divine nature, having escaped the corruption that is in the world by lust.

5Now for this very reason also, applying all diligence, in your faith supply moral excellence, and in *your* moral excellence, knowledge; 6and in *your* knowledge, self-control, and in *your* self-control, perseverance, and in *your* perseverance, godliness; 7and in *your* godliness, brotherly kindness, and in *your* brotherly kindness, love. 8For if these *qualities* are yours and are increasing, they render you neither useless nor unfruitful in the true knowledge of our Lord Jesus Christ. 9For he who lacks these *qualities* is blind *or* shortsighted, having forgotten *his* purification from his former sins.

10Therefore, brethren, be all the more diligent to make certain about His calling and choosing you; for as long as you practice these things, you will never stumble;

11for in this way the entrance into the eternal kingdom of our Lord and Savior Jesus Christ will be abundantly supplied to you.

12Therefore, I shall always be ready to remind you of these things, even though you *already* know *them*, and have been established in the truth which is present with *you.*

αὐτοῦ τὰ πρὸς ζωὴν καὶ εὐσέβειαν δεδωρημένης
of him - [belong- life and piety having given[a]
          ing] to

διὰ τῆς ἐπιγνώσεως τοῦ καλέσαντος ἡμᾶς
through the full knowledge of the [one] having called us

ἰδίᾳ δόξῃ καὶ ἀρετῇ, 4 δι' ὧν τὰ τίμια
to [his] glory and virtue, through which the [2]precious
own   things

καὶ μέγιστα ἡμῖν ἐπαγγέλματα δεδώρηται,
[4]and [5]very great [3]to us [2]promises [1]he has given,

ἵνα διὰ τούτων γένησθε θείας κοινωνοὶ
in or- through these ye might [2]of a divine [1]sharers
der that become

φύσεως, ἀποφυγόντες τῆς ἐν τῷ κόσμῳ
[3]nature, escaping from [1]the [2]in [4]the [5]world

ἐν ἐπιθυμίᾳ φθορᾶς. 5 καὶ αὐτὸ τοῦτο
[8]by [7]lust [6]corruption. [3]also [2]for this very thing
                                              (reason)

δὲ σπουδὴν πᾶσαν παρεισενέγκαντες
[1]But [5]diligence [4]all [6]bringing in

ἐπιχορηγήσατε ἐν τῇ πίστει ὑμῶν τὴν
supply in the faith of you the

ἀρετήν, ἐν δὲ τῇ ἀρετῇ τὴν γνῶσιν,
virtue, and in - virtue - knowledge,

6 ἐν δὲ τῇ γνώσει τὴν ἐγκράτειαν,
and in - knowledge - self-control,

ἐν δὲ τῇ ἐγκρατείᾳ τὴν ὑπομονήν, ἐν
and in - self-control - endurance, [2]in

δὲ τῇ ὑπομονῇ τὴν εὐσέβειαν, 7 ἐν δὲ
[1]and - endurance - piety, and in

τῇ εὐσεβείᾳ τὴν φιλαδελφίαν, ἐν δὲ
- piety - brotherly friendship, and in

τῇ φιλαδελφίᾳ τὴν ἀγάπην. 8 ταῦτα
- brotherly friendship - love. these things

γὰρ ὑμῖν ὑπάρχοντα καὶ πλεονάζοντα
For [2]in you [1]being and abounding

οὐκ ἀργοὺς οὐδὲ ἀκάρπους καθίστησιν
[3]not [4]barren [5]nor [6]unfruitful [1]makes [2][you]

εἰς τὴν τοῦ κυρίου ἡμῶν Ἰησοῦ Χριστοῦ
in [1]the [3]of the [4]Lord [5]of us [6]Jesus [7]Christ

ἐπίγνωσιν· 9 ᾧ γὰρ μὴ πάρεστιν ταῦτα,
[2]full knowledge; for [he] [3]not [2]is(are) [1]these
                      in whom   [4]present things,

τυφλός ἐστιν μυωπάζων, λήθην λαβὼν
[2]blind [1]is being short-sighted, forgetfulness taking
                                    = being forgetful

τοῦ καθαρισμοῦ τῶν πάλαι αὐτοῦ ἁμαρτιῶν.
of the cleansing of the [2]in time [3]of him [1]sins.
                            past

10 διὸ μᾶλλον, ἀδελφοί, σπουδάσατε
Wherefore rather, brothers, be ye diligent

βεβαίαν ὑμῶν τὴν κλῆσιν καὶ ἐκλογὴν
[2]firm [7]of you [3]the [4]calling [5]and [6]choice

ποιεῖσθαι· ταῦτα γὰρ ποιοῦντες οὐ μὴ
[1]to make; for these things doing by no means

πταίσητέ ποτε. 11 οὕτως γὰρ πλουσίως
ye will fail ever. For so [2]richly

ἐπιχορηγηθήσεται ὑμῖν ἡ εἴσοδος εἰς τὴν
[1]will be supplied [2]to you the entrance into the

αἰώνιον βασιλείαν τοῦ κυρίου ἡμῶν καὶ
eternal kingdom of the Lord of us and

σωτῆρος Ἰησοῦ Χριστοῦ.
Saviour Jesus Christ.

12 Διὸ μελλήσω ἀεὶ ὑμᾶς ὑπομιμνήσκειν
Wherefore I *will* intend always you to remind

περὶ τούτων, καίπερ εἰδότας καὶ
concerning these things, though knowing and

ἐστηριγμένους ἐν τῇ παρούσῃ ἀληθείᾳ.
having been confirmed in the present truth.

---

need for life and godliness through our knowledge of him who called us by his own glory and goodness. 4Through these he has given us his very great and precious promises, so that through them you may participate in the divine nature and escape the corruption in the world caused by evil desires.

5For this very reason, make every effort to add to your faith goodness; and to goodness, knowledge; 6and to knowledge, self-control; and to self-control, perseverance; and to perseverance, godliness; 7and to godliness, brotherly kindness; and to brotherly kindness, love. 8For if you possess these qualities in increasing measure, they will keep you from being ineffective and unproductive in your knowledge of our Lord Jesus Christ. 9But if anyone does not have them, he is nearsighted and blind, and has forgotten that he has been cleansed from his past sins.

10Therefore, my brothers, be all the more eager to make your calling and election sure. For if you do these things, you will never fall, 11and you will receive a rich welcome into the eternal kingdom of our Lord and Savior Jesus Christ.

Prophecy of Scripture

12So I will always remind you of these things, even though you know them and are firmly established in the truth you now have. 13I

13And I consider it right, as long as I am in this *earthly* dwelling, to stir you up by way of reminder,

14knowing that the laying aside of my *earthly* dwelling is imminent, as also our Lord Jesus Christ has made clear to me.

15And I will also be diligent that at any time after my departure you may be able to call these things to mind.

Eyewitnesses

16For we did not follow cleverly devised tales when we made known to you the power and coming of our Lord Jesus Christ, but we were eyewitnesses of His majesty.

17For when He received honor and glory from God the Father, such an utterance as this was made to Him by the Majestic Glory, "This is My beloved Son with whom I am well-pleased"—

18and we ourselves heard this utterance made from heaven when we were with Him on the holy mountain.

19And *so* we have the prophetic word *made* more sure, to which you do well to pay attention as to a lamp shining in a dark place, until the day dawns and the morning star arises in your hearts.

20But knows this first of all, that no prophecy of Scripture is *a matter* of one's own interpretation,

21for no prophecy was ever made by an act of human will, but men moved by the Holy Spirit spoke from God.

---

13 δίκαιον δὲ ἡγοῦμαι, ἐφ' ὅσον εἰμὶ
And ²right ¹I deem [it], so long as† I am

ἐν τούτῳ τῷ σκηνώματι, διεγείρειν ὑμᾶς
in this – tabernacle, to rouse you

ἐν ὑπομνήσει, **14** εἰδὼς ὅτι ταχινή ἐστιν
by a reminder, knowing that soon is

ἡ ἀπόθεσις τοῦ σκηνώματός μου, καθὼς
the putting off of the tabernacle of me, as

καὶ ὁ κύριος ἡμῶν Ἰησοῦς Χριστὸς
indeed the Lord of us Jesus Christ

ἐδήλωσέν μοι· **15** σπουδάσω δὲ καὶ
made clear to me; and I will be diligent also

ἑκάστοτε ἔχειν ὑμᾶς μετὰ τὴν ἐμὴν
always ¹to have ²you ³after – ⁴my

ἔξοδον τὴν τούτων μνήμην ποιεῖσθαι.
⁵exodus ⁸the ¹⁰of these things ⁹memory ¹to cause.

16 οὐ γὰρ σεσοφισμένοις μύθοις ἐξακολου-
For not ³having been ²fables ¹follow-
cleverly devised

θήσαντες ἐγνωρίσαμεν ὑμῖν τὴν τοῦ κυρίου
ing we made known to you ¹the ⁵of the ⁴Lord

ἡμῶν Ἰησοῦ Χριστοῦ δύναμιν καὶ
⁶of us ⁷Jesus ⁸Christ ²power ³and

παρουσίαν, ἀλλ' ἐπόπται γενηθέντες τῆς
⁴presence, but ²eyewitnesses ¹having become ³of the

ἐκείνου μεγαλειότητος. **17** λαβὼν γὰρ
⁴of that one ⁴majesty. For receiving

παρὰ θεοῦ πατρὸς τιμὴν καὶ δόξαν
from God [the] Father honour and glory

φωνῆς ἐνεχθείσης αὐτῷ τοιᾶσδε ὑπὸ τῆς
²a voice ³being borne² ⁴to him ¹such by the

μεγαλοπρεποῦς δόξης· ὁ υἱός μου ὁ
magnificent glory: The Son of me the

ἀγαπητός μου οὗτός ἐστιν, εἰς ὃν ἐγὼ
beloved of me this is, in whom I

εὐδόκησα, — **18** καὶ ταύτην τὴν φωνὴν
was wellpleased,— and this – voice

ἡμεῖς ἠκούσαμεν ἐξ οὐρανοῦ ἐνεχθεῖσαν
we heard ²out of ²heaven ¹being borne

σὺν αὐτῷ ὄντες ἐν τῷ ἁγίῳ ὄρει. **19** καὶ
⁵with ⁶him ⁴being in the holy mountain. And

ἔχομεν βεβαιότερον τὸν προφητικὸν λόγον,
we have more firm the prophetic word,

ᾧ καλῶς ποιεῖτε προσέχοντες ὡς λύχνῳ
to ²well ¹ye do taking heed as to a lamp
which

φαίνοντι ἐν αὐχμηρῷ τόπῳ, ἕως οὗ
shining in a murky place, until

ἡμέρα διαυγάσῃ καὶ φωσφόρος ἀνατείλῃ
day dawns and [the] daystar rises

ἐν ταῖς καρδίαις ὑμῶν· **20** τοῦτο πρῶτον
in the hearts of you; ²this ³firstly

γινώσκοντες, ὅτι πᾶσα προφητεία γραφῆς
¹knowing, that every prophecy of scripture
=no . . . is . . .

ἰδίας ἐπιλύσεως οὐ γίνεται· **21** οὐ γὰρ
of [its] own solution not becomes; for not

θελήματι ἀνθρώπου ἠνέχθη προφητεία
by will of man ²was borne ¹prophecy

ποτέ, ἀλλὰ ὑπὸ πνεύματος ἁγίου φερόμενοι
at any but ⁶by ⁸Spirit ⁷[the] ⁵being borne
time, Holy

ἐλάλησαν ἀπὸ θεοῦ ἄνθρωποι.
²spoke ³from· ⁴God ¹men.

---

think it is right to refresh your memory as long as I live in the tent of this body, 14because I know that I will soon put it aside, as our Lord Jesus Christ has made clear to me. 15And I will make every effort to see that after my departure you will always be able to remember these things.

16We did not follow cleverly invented stories when we told you about the power and coming of our Lord Jesus Christ, but we were eyewitnesses of his majesty. 17For he received honor and glory from God the Father when the voice came to him from the Majestic Glory, saying, "This is my Son, whom I love; with him I am well pleased." *a* 18We ourselves heard this voice that came from heaven when we were with him on the sacred mountain.

19And we have the word of the prophets made more certain, and you will do well to pay attention to it, as to a light shining in a dark place, until the day dawns and the morning star rises in your hearts. 20Above all, you must understand that no prophecy of Scripture came about by the prophet's own interpretation. 21For prophecy never had its origin in the will of man, but men spoke from God as they were carried along by the Holy Spirit.

---

a 17 Matt. 17:5; Mark 9:7; Luke 9:35

Chapter 2

The Rise of False Prophets

BUT false prophets also arose among the people, just as there will also be false teachers among you, who will secretly introduce destructive heresies, even denying the Master who bought them, bringing swift destruction upon themselves. ²And many will follow their sensuality, and because of them the way of the truth will be maligned; ³and in *their* greed they will exploit you with false words; their judgment from long ago is not idle, and their destruction is not asleep.

⁴For if God did not spare angels when they sinned, but cast them into hell and committed them to pits of darkness, reserved for judgment;

⁵and did not spare the ancient world, but preserved Noah, a preacher of righteousness, with seven others, when He brought a flood upon the world of the ungodly;

⁶and *if* He condemned the cities of Sodom and Gomorrah to destruction by reducing *them* to ashes, having made them an example to those who would live ungodly thereafter;

⁷and *if* He rescued righteous Lot, oppressed by the sensual conduct of unprincipled men

⁸(for by what he saw and heard *that* righteous man, while living among them, felt *his* righteous soul tormented day after day with *their* lawless deeds),

⁹then the Lord knows how to rescue the godly from temptation, and to keep the unrighteous under punishment for the day of judgment,

¹⁰and especially those

---

2 Ἐγένοντο δὲ καὶ ψευδοπροφῆται ἐν
But there were also false prophets among

τῷ λαῷ, ὡς καὶ ἐν ὑμῖν ἔσονται
the people, as indeed among you there will be

ψευδοδιδάσκαλοι, οἵτινες παρεισάξουσιν
false teachers, who will secretly bring in

αἱρέσεις ἀπωλείας, καὶ τὸν ἀγοράσαντα
opinions of destruction,* and ⁴the ⁵having bought

αὐτοὺς δεσπότην ἀρνούμενοι, ἐπάγοντες
⁶them ⁵Master ¹denying, bringing on

ἑαυτοῖς ταχινὴν ἀπώλειαν· **2** καὶ πολλοὶ
themselves swift destruction; and many

ἐξακολουθήσουσιν αὐτῶν ταῖς ἀσελγείαις,
will follow ³of them ²the ¹licentiousnesses,

δι᾽ οὓς ἡ ὁδὸς τῆς ἀληθείας βλασφημη-
be- whom the way of the truth will be
cause of

θήσεται· **3** καὶ ἐν πλεονεξίᾳ πλαστοῖς
blasphemed; and by covetousness with fabricated

λόγοις ὑμᾶς ἐμπορεύσονται· οἷς τὸ κρίμα
words ²you ¹they will make for the judg-
merchandise of; whom ment

ἔκπαλαι οὐκ ἀργεῖ, καὶ ἡ ἀπώλεια
of old lingers not, and the destruction

αὐτῶν οὐ νυστάζει. **4** εἰ γὰρ ὁ θεὸς
of them slumbers not. For if - God

ἀγγέλων ἁμαρτησάντων οὐκ ἐφείσατο, ἀλλὰ
²angels ³sinning ¹spared not, but

σιροῖς ζόφου ταρταρώσας παρέδωκεν
²in pits ³of gloom ¹consigning to Tartarus ⁴delivered [them]

εἰς κρίσιν τηρουμένους, **5** καὶ ἀρχαίου
⁵to ⁶judgment ⁷being kept, and ²[the] ancient

κόσμου οὐκ ἐφείσατο, ἀλλὰ ὄγδοον Νῶε
³world ¹spared not, but ²[the] ³Noe
eighth man

δικαιοσύνης κήρυκα ἐφύλαξεν, κατακλυσμὸν
⁶of righteousness ⁴a herald ⁵guarded, ²a flood

κόσμῳ ἀσεβῶν ἐπάξας, **6** καὶ πόλεις
⁴a world ⁵of impious men ¹bringing ³on, and ²[the] cities

Σοδόμων καὶ Γομόρρας τεφρώσας
⁴of Sodom ⁵and ⁶Gomorra ¹covering [them]
with ashes

καταστροφῇ κατέκρινεν, ὑπόδειγμα μελ-
⁷by an overthrow ²condemned, ³an example ⁸of men

λόντων ἀσεβεῖν τεθεικώς, **7** καὶ δίκαιον
intending ⁴to live ¹having set(made), and ²righteous
impiously

Λὼτ καταπονούμενον ὑπὸ τῆς τῶν ἀθέσμων
³Lot ⁴being oppressed ⁵by ⁶the ⁷of the ⁹lawless

ἐν ἀσελγείᾳ ἀναστροφῆς ἐρρύσατο· **8** βλέμ-
⁸in ⁹licentiousness ⁷conduct ¹delivered; ²in

ματι γὰρ καὶ ἀκοῇ ὁ δίκαιος ἐγκατοικῶν
seeing ¹for and in hear- the righteous dwelling
ing (that) man

ἐν αὐτοῖς ἡμέραν ἐξ ἡμέρας ψυχὴν
among them day after† day ²[his] ⁴soul

δικαίαν ἀνόμοις ἔργοις ἐβασάνιζεν·
³righteous ⁴with [their] lawless ⁵works ¹tormented;

9 οἶδεν κύριος εὐσεβεῖς ἐκ πειρασμοῦ
³knows* ¹[the] Lord ⁴pious men ⁵out of ⁶trial

ῥύεσθαι, ἀδίκους δὲ εἰς ἡμέραν κρίσεως
²to deliver, ⁵unjust men ¹but ⁶for ⁷a day ⁸of judgment

κολαζομένους τηρεῖν, **10** μάλιστα δὲ τοὺς
⁴being punished ³to keep, and most of all ¹the

Chapter 2

False Teachers and Their Destruction

BUT there were also false prophets among the people, just as there will be false teachers among you. They will secretly introduce destructive heresies, even denying the sovereign Lord who bought them—bringing swift destruction on themselves. ²Many will follow their shameful ways and will bring the way of truth into disrepute. ³In their greed these teachers will exploit you with stories they have made up. Their condemnation has long been hanging over them, and their destruction has not been sleeping.

⁴For if God did not spare angels when they sinned, but sent them to hell,[b] putting them into gloomy dungeons[c] to be held for judgment; ⁵if he did not spare the ancient world when he brought the flood on its ungodly people, but protected Noah, a preacher of righteousness, and seven others; ⁶if he condemned the cities of Sodom and Gomorrah by burning them to ashes, and made them an example of what is going to happen to the ungodly; ⁷and if he rescued Lot, a righteous man, who was distressed by the filthy lives of lawless men ⁸(for that righteous man, living among them day after day, was tormented in his righteous soul by the lawless deeds he saw and heard)— ⁹if this is so, then the Lord knows how to rescue godly men from trials and to hold the unrighteous for the day of judgment, while continuing their punishment.[d] ¹⁰This is especially true of

---

*b*4 Greek *Tartarus*
*c*4 Some manuscripts *into chains of darkness*
*d*9 Or *unrighteous for punishment until the day of judgment*

---

* Genitive of quality : "destructive opinions."

* That is, "the Lord can deliver"; see note on page xviii.

who indulge the flesh in *its* corrupt desires and despise authority. Daring, self-willed, they do not tremble when they revile angelic majesties,
11whereas angels who are greater in might and power do not bring a reviling judgment against them before the Lord.
12But these, like unreasoning animals, born as creatures of instinct to be captured and killed, reviling where they have no knowledge, will in the destruction of those creatures also be destroyed,
13suffering wrong as the wages of doing wrong. They count it a pleasure to revel in the daytime. They are stains and blemishes, reveling in their *b* deceptions, as they carouse with you,
14having eyes full of adultery and that never cease from sin, enticing unstable souls, having a heart trained in greed, accursed children;
15forsaking the right way they have gone astray, having followed the way of Balaam, the *son* of Beor, who loved the wages of unrighteousness,
16but he received a rebuke for his own transgression; *for* a dumb donkey, speaking with a voice of a man, restrained the madness of the prophet.
17These are springs without water, and mists driven by a storm, for whom the black darkness has been reserved.
18For speaking out arrogant *words* of vanity they entice by fleshly desires, by sensuality, those who barely escape from the ones who live in error,
19promising them free-

ὀπίσω σαρκὸς ἐν ἐπιθυμίᾳ μιασμοῦ
²after ⁴flesh ⁵in ⁶lust ⁷of defilement*
πορευομένους καὶ κυριότητος καταφρονοῦντας.
¹[ones] going ⁸and ¹⁰dominion ⁹despising.
τολμηταὶ αὐθάδεις, δόξας οὐ τρέμουσιν
¹darers ¹Self-satisfied, glories they do not tremble [at]
βλασφημοῦντες, 11 ὅπου ἄγγελοι ἰσχύϊ καὶ
blaspheming, where angels ⁵in strength ⁶and
δυνάμει μείζονες ὄντες οὐ φέρουσιν κατ'
⁷in power ²greater ¹being do not bring against
αὐτῶν παρὰ κυρίῳ βλάσφημον κρίσιν.
them before [the] Lord railing judgment.
12 οὗτοι δέ, ὡς ἄλογα ζῷα γεγεννημένα
But these ¹as ⁴without ²animals ⁵having been
men, reason born
φυσικὰ εἰς ἅλωσιν καὶ φθοράν, ἐν οἷς
²natural for capture and corruption, ⁹In ³things
which
ἀγνοοῦσιν βλασφημοῦντες, ἐν τῇ φθορᾷ
⁴they are ¹railing, in the corruption
ignorant [of]
αὐτῶν καὶ φθαρήσονται, 13 ἀδικούμενοι
of them indeed they will be corrupted, suffering wrong
μισθὸν ἀδικίας· ἡδονὴν ἡγούμενοι τὴν
[as] wages of wrong; ³[to be] pleasure ¹deeming –
ἐν ἡμέρᾳ τρυφήν, σπίλοι καὶ μῶμοι
⁴in ⁴[the] day ²luxury, spots and blemishes
ἐντρυφῶντες ἐν ταῖς ἀπάταις αὐτῶν
revelling in the deceits of them
συνευωχούμενοι ὑμῖν, 14 ὀφθαλμοὺς ἔχοντες
feasting along with you, ²eyes ¹having
μεστοὺς μοιχαλίδος καὶ ἀκαταπαύστους
full of an adulteress and not ceasing from
ἁμαρτίας, δελεάζοντες ψυχὰς ἀστηρίκτους,
sin, alluring ²souls ¹unsteady,
καρδίαν γεγυμνασμένην πλεονεξίας ἔχοντες,
²a heart ¹having been exercised ⁴of(in) covetousness ¹having,
κατάρας τέκνα· 15 καταλείποντες εὐθεῖαν
²of curse ¹children; forsaking a straight
ὁδὸν ἐπλανήθησαν, ἐξακολουθήσαντες τῇ
way they erred, following the
ὁδῷ τοῦ Βαλαὰμ τοῦ Βεώρ, ὃς μισθὸν
way – of Balaam the [son] of who ²[the]
Beor, wages
ἀδικίας ἠγάπησεν, 16 ἔλεγξιν δὲ ἔσχεν
³of wrong ¹loved, and ²reproof ¹had
ἰδίας παρανομίας· ὑποζύγιον ἄφωνον ἐν
of [his] own transgression; ²ass ¹a dumb ⁴with
ἀνθρώπου φωνῇ φθεγξάμενον ἐκώλυσεν
³of a man ⁴voice ³speaking restrained
τὴν τοῦ προφήτου παραφρονίαν. 17 οὗτοί
¹the ²of the ⁴prophet ³madness. These men
εἰσιν πηγαὶ ἄνυδροι καὶ ὁμίχλαι ὑπὸ
are ²springs ¹waterless and mists ²by
λαίλαπος ἐλαυνόμεναι, οἷς ὁ ζόφος τοῦ
³storm ¹being driven, for whom the gloom of the
σκότους τετήρηται. 18 ὑπέρογκα γὰρ
darkness has been kept. For ²immoderate [words]
ματαιότητος φθεγγόμενοι δελεάζουσιν ἐν
³of vanity ¹speaking they allure by
ἐπιθυμίαις σαρκὸς ἀσελγείαις τοὺς ὀλίγως
[the] lusts of [the] flesh in excesses the [ones] almost
ἀποφεύγοντας τοὺς ἐν πλάνῃ ἀναστρε-
escaping ¹the [ones] ³in ⁴error ²liv-
φομένους, 19 ἐλευθερίαν αὐτοῖς ἐπαγγελ-
ing, ²freedom ³to them ¹promis-

those who follow the corrupt desire of the sinful nature*e* and despise authority.
Bold and arrogant, these men are not afraid to slander celestial beings; 11yet even angels, although they are stronger and more powerful, do not bring slanderous accusations against such beings in the presence of the Lord. 12But these men blaspheme in matters they do not understand. They are like brute beasts, creatures of instinct, born only to be caught and destroyed, and like beasts they too will perish.
13They will be paid back with harm for the harm they have done. Their idea of pleasure is to carouse in broad daylight. They are blots and blemishes, reveling in their pleasures while they feast with you.*f*
14With eyes full of adultery, they never stop sinning; they seduce the unstable; they are experts in greed—an accursed brood! 15They have left the straight way and wandered off to follow the way of Balaam son of Beor, who loved the wages of wickedness. 16But he was rebuked for his wrongdoing by a donkey—a beast without speech—who spoke with a man's voice and restrained the prophet's madness.
17These men are springs without water and mists driven by a storm. Blackest darkness is reserved for them. 18For they mouth empty, boastful words and, by appealing to the lustful desires of sinful human nature, they entice people who are just escaping from those who live in error. 19They promise them free-

---

b Some ancient mss. read *love feasts,* (cf. Jude 12)
* Genitive of quality: "defiling lust."

e 10 Or *the flesh*
f 13 Some manuscripts *in their love feasts*

dom while they themselves are slaves of corruption; for by what a man is overcome, by this he is enslaved.

20For if after they have escaped the defilements of the world by the knowledge of the Lord and Savior Jesus Christ, they are again entangled in them and are overcome, the last state has become worse for them than the first.

21For it would be better for them not to have known the way of righteousness, than having known it, to turn away from the holy commandment delivered to them.

22It has happened to them according to the true proverb, "A DOG RETURNS TO ITS OWN VOMIT," and, "A sow, after washing, *returns* to wallowing in the mire."

λόμενοι, αὐτοὶ δοῦλοι ὑπάρχοντες τῆς
ing, [them]selves ²slaves ¹being -

φθορᾶς· ᾧ γάρ τις ἥττηται, τούτῳ
of corrup- for by whom anyone has been to this
tion; defeated, man

δεδούλωται. 20 εἰ γὰρ ἀποφυγόντες τὰ
he has been enslaved. For if having escaped the

μιάσματα τοῦ κόσμου ἐν ἐπιγνώσει τοῦ
defilements of the world by a full knowledge of the

κυρίου καὶ σωτῆρος Ἰησοῦ Χριστοῦ,
Lord and Saviour Jesus Christ,

τούτοις δὲ πάλιν ἐμπλακέντες ἡττῶνται,
yet by these again having been have been
entangled defeated,

γέγονεν αὐτοῖς τὰ ἔσχατα χείρονα τῶν
²have become ⁴to them ¹the ³last things worse [than] the

πρώτων. 21 κρεῖττον γὰρ ἦν αὐτοῖς
first. For better it was for them

μὴ ἐπεγνωκέναι τὴν ὁδὸν τῆς δικαιοσύνης,
not to have fully known the way - of righteousness,

ἢ ἐπιγνοῦσιν ὑποστρέψαι ἐκ τῆς παρα-
than fully knowing to turn from ¹the ⁴de-

δοθείσης αὐτοῖς ἁγίας ἐντολῆς. 22 συμβέ-
livered ⁵to them ²holy ³commandment. ¹has

βηκεν αὐτοῖς τὸ τῆς ἀληθοῦς παροιμίας·
happened ²to them ¹The ²of the ³true ⁴proverb:
thing

κύων ἐπιστρέψας ἐπὶ τὸ ἴδιον ἐξέραμα,
[The] dog turning upon the(its) own vomit,

καὶ· ὗς λουσαμένη εἰς κυλισμὸν βορβόρου.
and: [The] washed to wallowing of mud.
sow

Chapter 3

3 Ταύτην ἤδη, ἀγαπητοί, δευτέραν ὑμῖν
¹This ⁵now, ⁶beloved, ²second ³to you

γράφω ἐπιστολήν, ἐν αἷς διεγείρω ὑμῶν
⁴I write ³epistle, in [both] which I rouse ⁴of you

ἐν ὑπομνήσει τὴν εἰλικρινῆ διάνοιαν,
⁵by ⁶reminder ¹the ³sincere ²mind,

2 μνησθῆναι τῶν προειρημένων ῥημάτων
to remember the ²having been ¹words
previously spoken

ὑπὸ τῶν ἁγίων προφητῶν καὶ τῆς τῶν
by the holy prophets and ¹the ⁵of the

ἀποστόλων ὑμῶν ἐντολῆς τοῦ κυρίου καὶ
⁴apostles ⁵of you ²commandment of the Lord and

σωτῆρος, 3 τοῦτο πρῶτον γινώσκοντες, ὅτι
Saviour, ²this ³firstly ¹knowing, that

ἐλεύσονται ἐπ᾽ ἐσχάτων τῶν ἡμερῶν ἐν
there will come during [the] last of the days ³in

ἐμπαιγμονῇ ἐμπαῖκται κατὰ τὰς ἰδίας
⁴mocking ¹mockers ⁵according to ⁶the(ir) ⁷own

ἐπιθυμίας αὐτῶν πορευόμενοι 4 καὶ λέγοντες·
⁸lusts of them ²going and saying:

ποῦ ἐστιν ἡ ἐπαγγελία τῆς παρουσίας
Where is the promise of the presence

αὐτοῦ; ἀφ᾽ ἧς γὰρ οἱ πατέρες ἐκοι-
of him? ²from ³which [day]¹for the fathers fell
= for from the day when . . .

μήθησαν, πάντα οὕτως διαμένει ἀπ᾽
asleep, all things so remains from

ἀρχῆς κτίσεως. 5 λανθάνει γὰρ αὐτοὺς
[the] of creation. For ¹is concealed ²them
beginning [from]

τοῦτο θέλοντας ὅτι οὐρανοὶ ἦσαν ἔκπαλαι
¹this wishing* that heavens were of old

* That is, they wish it to be so.

Chapter 3

Purpose of This Letter

THIS is now, beloved, the second letter I am writing to you in which I am stirring up your sincere mind by way of reminder, 2that you should remember the words spoken beforehand by the holy prophets and the commandment of the Lord and Savior *spoken* by your apostles.

The Coming Day of the Lord

3Know this first of all, that in the last days mockers will come with *their* mocking, following after their own lusts, 4and saying, "Where is the promise of His coming? For *ever* since the fathers fell asleep, all continues just as it was from the beginning of creation." 5For when they maintain this, it escapes their notice that by the word of God *the* heavens existed long ago

---

Chapter 3

The Day of the Lord

DEAR friends, this is now my second letter to you. I have written both of them as reminders to stimulate you to wholesome thinking. 2I want you to recall the words spoken in the past by the holy prophets and the command given by our Lord and Savior through your apostles.

3First of all, you must understand that in the last days scoffers will come, scoffing and following their own desires. 4They will say, "Where is this 'coming' he promised? Ever since our fathers died, everything goes on as it has since the beginning of creation." 5But they deliberately forget that long ago by God's word the heavens existed and the earth was

---

dom, while they themselves are slaves of depravity—for a man is a slave to whatever has mastered him. 20If they have escaped the corruption of the world by knowing our Lord and Savior Jesus Christ and are again entangled in it and overcome, they are worse off at the end than they were at the beginning. 21It would have been better for them not to have known the way of righteousness, than to have known it and then to turn their backs on the sacred command that was passed on to them. 22Of them the proverbs are true: "A dog returns to its vomit,"[g] and, "A sow that is washed goes back to her wallowing in the mud."

g22 Prov. 26:11

and *the* earth was formed out of water and by water, 6through which the world at that time was destroyed, being flooded with water.

7But the present heavens and earth by His word are being reserved for fire, kept for the day of judgment and destruction of ungodly men.

8But do not let this one *fact* escape your notice, beloved, that with the Lord one day is as a thousand years, and a thousand years as one day.

9The Lord is not slow about His promise, as some count slowness, but is patient toward you, not wishing for any to perish but for all to come to repentance.

A New Heaven and Earth

10But the day of the Lord will come like a thief, in which the heavens will pass away with a roar and the elements will be destroyed with intense heat, and the earth and its works will be *c*burned up.

11Since all these things are to be destroyed in this way, what sort of people ought you to be in holy conduct and godliness,

12looking for and hastening the coming of the day of God, on account of which the heavens will be destroyed by burning, and the elements will melt with intense heat!

13But according to His promise we are looking for new heavens and a new earth, in which righteousness dwells.

14Therefore, beloved, since you look for these

καὶ   γῆ   ἐξ   ὕδατος   καὶ   δι᾽   ὕδατος
and   earth   by   water   and   through   water

συνεστῶσα   τῷ   τοῦ   θεοῦ   λόγῳ,   6 δι᾽
¹having been   ²by   -   ⁴of God   ³word,   through
held together   the

ὧν   ὁ   τότε   κόσμος   ὕδατι   κατακλυσθεὶς
which the   then§   world   ²by water   ¹being inundated
things

ἀπώλετο·   7 οἱ   δὲ   νῦν   οὐρανοὶ   καὶ   ἡ
perished;   but the   now   heavens   and   the

γῆ   τῷ   αὐτῷ   λόγῳ   τεθησαυρισμένοι   εἰσὶν
earth by   the   same   word   ²having been stored up   ¹are

πυρὶ   τηρούμενοι   εἰς   ἡμέραν   κρίσεως   καὶ
³for fire   ¹being kept   in   a day   of judgment   and

ἀπωλείας   τῶν   ἀσεβῶν   ἀνθρώπων.   8 ªἘν
destruction   of *the*   impious   men.   ²one

δὲ   τοῦτο   μὴ   λανθανέτω   ὑμᾶς,   ἀγαπητοί,
But   ¹this   let not be concealed   you,   beloved,
²thing   [from]

ὅτι   μία   ἡμέρα   παρὰ   κυρίῳ   ὡς   χίλια
that   one   day   with [the] Lord [is]   as a thousand

ἔτη   καὶ   χίλια   ἔτη   ὡς᾽   ἡμέρα   μία.   9 οὐ
years   and a thousand years   as   ³day   ¹one.   ²not

βραδύνει   κύριος   τῆς   ἐπαγγελίας,   ὥς   τινες
²is ⁴slow   ¹[The]   of the   promise,   as   some
     Lord   (his)

βραδύτητα   ἡγοῦνται,   ἀλλὰ   μακροθυμεῖ   εἰς
²slowness   ¹deem,   but   is longsuffering toward

ὑμᾶς,   μὴ   βουλόμενός   τινας   ἀπολέσθαι
you,   not   purposing   any   to perish

ἀλλὰ   πάντας   εἰς   μετάνοιαν   χωρῆσαι.
but   all men   ³to   ²repentance   ¹to come.

10 Ἥξει   δὲ   ἡμέρα   κυρίου   ὡς   κλέπτης,
But will come   [the] day   of [the] Lord as   a thief,

ἐν   ᾗ   οἱ   οὐρανοὶ   ῥοιζηδὸν   παρελεύσονται,
in   which   the   heavens   ²with rushing   ¹will pass away,
     sound

στοιχεῖα   δὲ   καυσούμενα   λυθήσεται,   καὶ
and [the] elements   burning   will be dissolved,   and

γῆ   καὶ   τὰ   ἐν   αὐτῇ   ἔργα   εὑρεθήσεται.
[the]   and   ¹the   ²in   ⁴it   ²works   will be
earth   discovered.

11 Τούτων   οὕτως   πάντων   λυομένων
²these things   ²thus   ¹All   ⁴being dissolvedª

ποταποὺς   δεῖ   ὑπάρχειν   [ὑμᾶς]   ἐν   ἁγίαις
what sort   it be-   ²to be   ¹you   in   holy
of men   hoves

ἀναστροφαῖς   καὶ   εὐσεβείαις,   12 προσδοκῶντας
conduct*   and   piety,*   awaiting

καὶ   σπεύδοντας   τὴν   παρουσίαν   τῆς   τοῦ
and   hastening   the   presence   ¹of the   -

θεοῦ   ἡμέρας,   δι᾽   ἣν   οὐρανοὶ   πυρούμενοι
²of God   ¹day,   on ac- which   [the]   being set on fire
     count of   heavens

λυθήσονται   καὶ   στοιχεῖα   καυσούμενα
will be dissolved   and   [the] elements   burning

τήκεται.   13 καινοὺς   δὲ   οὐρανοὺς   καὶ
melts.   But new   heavens   and

γῆν   καινὴν   κατὰ   τὸ   ἐπάγγελμα   αὐτοῦ
²earth   ¹a new   accord- the   promise   of him
     ing to

προσδοκῶμεν,   ἐν   οἷς   δικαιοσύνη   κατοικεῖ.
we await,   in   which   righteousness   dwells.

14 Διό,   ἀγαπητοί,   ταῦτα   προσδοκῶντες
Wherefore,   beloved,   ²these things   ¹awaiting

---

formed out of water and by water. 6By these waters also the world of that time was deluged and destroyed. 7By the same word the present heavens and earth are reserved for fire, being kept for the day of judgment and destruction of ungodly men.

8But do not forget this one thing, dear friends: With the Lord a day is like a thousand years, and a thousand years are like a day. 9The Lord is not slow in keeping his promise, as some understand slowness. He is patient with you, not wanting anyone to perish, but everyone to come to repentance.

10But the day of the Lord will come like a thief. The heavens will disappear with a roar; the elements will be destroyed by fire, and the earth and everything in it will be laid bare.ʰ

11Since everything will be destroyed in this way, what kind of people ought you to be? You ought to live holy and godly lives 12as you look forward to the day of God and speed its coming.ⁱ That day will bring about the destruction of the heavens by fire, and the elements will melt in the heat. 13But in keeping with his promise we are looking forward to a new heaven and a new earth, the home of righteousness.

14So then, dear friends, since you are looking for-

---

*c*Some ancient mss. read *discovered*

§ This is allowable English : *cf.* " the then Prime Minister."

* The Greek plurals cannot be literally reproduced in English.

ʰ10 Some manuscripts *be burned up*
ⁱ12 Or *as you wait eagerly for the day of God to come*

things, be diligent to be found by Him in peace, spotless and blameless,

15and regard the patience of our Lord *to be* salvation; just as also our beloved brother Paul, according to the wisdom given to him, wrote to you,

16as also in all *his* letters, speaking in them of these things, in which are some things hard to understand, which the untaught and unstable distort, as *they do* also the rest of the Scriptures, to their own destruction.

17You therefore, beloved, knowing this beforehand, be on your guard lest, being carried away by the error of unprincipled men, you fall from your own steadfastness,

18but grow in the grace and knowledge of our Lord and Savior Jesus Christ. To Him *be* the glory, both now and to the day of eternity. Amen.

σπουδάσατε ἄσπιλοι καὶ ἀμώμητοι αὐτῷ
be diligent   ⁵spotless   ⁶and   ⁷unblemished   ⁸by him

εὑρεθῆναι ἐν εἰρήνῃ, 15 καὶ τὴν τοῦ
¹to be found   ²in   ⁴peace,   and   ³the   ⁴of the

κυρίου ἡμῶν μακροθυμίαν σωτηρίαν ἡγεῖσθε,
⁵Lord   ⁶of us   ³longsuffering   ⁷salvation   ¹deem,

καθὼς καὶ ὁ ἀγαπητὸς ἡμῶν ἀδελφὸς
as   indeed   the   beloved   ²of us   ¹brother

Παῦλος κατὰ τὴν δοθεῖσαν αὐτῷ σοφίαν
Paul   accord-ing to   ¹the   ²given   ⁴to him   ³wisdom

ἔγραψεν ὑμῖν, 16 ὡς καὶ ἐν πάσαις
wrote   to you,   as   also   in   all [his]

ἐπιστολαῖς λαλῶν ἐν αὐταῖς περὶ τούτων,
epistles   speaking   in   them   concerning   these things,

ἐν αἷς ἐστιν δυσνόητά τινα, ἃ οἱ
in   which   is(are)   ³hard to understand   ¹some things,   which   the

ἀμαθεῖς καὶ ἀστήρικτοι στρεβλοῦσιν ὡς
unlearned   and   unsteady   twist   as

καὶ τὰς λοιπὰς γραφὰς πρὸς τὴν ἰδίαν
also   the   remaining   scriptures   to   the(ir) own

αὐτῶν ἀπώλειαν. 17 Ὑμεῖς οὖν, ἀγαπητοί,
of them   destruction.   Ye   therefore,   beloved,

προγινώσκοντες φυλάσσεσθε ἵνα μὴ τῇ
knowing before   guard   lest   ²by the

τῶν ἀθέσμων πλάνῃ συναπαχθέντες ἐκπέ-
⁴of the   ⁵lawless   ⁶error   ¹being led away *with*   ye fall

σητε τοῦ ἰδίου στηριγμοῦ, 18 αὐξάνετε
from   the(your) own   stability,   ²grow ye

δὲ ἐν χάριτι καὶ γνώσει τοῦ κυρίου
¹but   in   grace   and   knowledge   of the   Lord

ἡμῶν καὶ σωτῆρος Ἰησοῦ Χριστοῦ.
of us   and   Saviour   Jesus   Christ.

αὐτῷ ἡ δόξα καὶ νῦν καὶ εἰς
To him° [is] the   glory   both   now   and   unto
= His is*   = for ever.

ἡμέραν αἰῶνος. §
a day   of age. §

---

ward to this, make every effort to be found spotless, blameless and at peace with him. 15Bear in mind that our Lord's patience means salvation, just as our dear brother Paul also wrote you with the wisdom that God gave him. 16He writes the same way in all his letters, speaking in them of these matters. His letters contain some things that are hard to understand, which ignorant and unstable people distort, as they do the other Scriptures, to their own destruction.

17Therefore, dear friends, since you already know this, be on your guard so that you may not be carried away by the error of lawless men and fall from your secure position. 18But grow in the grace and knowledge of our Lord and Savior Jesus Christ. To him be glory both now and forever! Amen.

---

1 John

Chapter 1

Introduction
The Incarnate Word

WHAT was from the beginning, what we have heard, what we have seen with our eyes, what we beheld and our hands handled, concerning the Word of Life—

2and the life was manifested, and we have seen and bear witness and proclaim to you the eternal life, which was with the Father and was manifested to us—

3what we have seen and heard we proclaim to you

ΙΩΑΝΝΟΥ Α
Of John 1

1 Ὃ ἦν ἀπ' ἀρχῆς, ὃ ἀκηκόαμεν,
What   was   from   [the] beginning,   what   we have heard,

ὃ ἑωράκαμεν τοῖς ὀφθαλμοῖς ἡμῶν, ὃ
what   we have seen   with the   eyes   of us,   what

ἐθεασάμεθα καὶ αἱ χεῖρες ἡμῶν ἐψηλάφησαν,
we beheld   and   the   hands   of us   touched,

περὶ τοῦ λόγου τῆς ζωῆς, — 2 καὶ
concern-ing   the   word   –   of life,   —   and

ἡ ζωὴ ἐφανερώθη, καὶ ἑωράκαμεν καὶ
the   life   was manifested,   and   we have seen   and

μαρτυροῦμεν καὶ ἀπαγγέλλομεν ὑμῖν τὴν
we bear witness   and   *we* announce   to you   the

ζωὴν τὴν αἰώνιον, ἥτις ἦν πρὸς τὸν
life   –   eternal,   which   was   with   the

πατέρα καὶ ἐφανερώθη ἡμῖν, — 3 ὃ
Father   and   was manifested   to us,   —   what

ἑωράκαμεν καὶ ἀκηκόαμεν, ἀπαγγέλλομεν
we have seen   and   *we* have heard,   we announce

---

1 John

Chapter 1

The Word of Life

THAT which was from the beginning, which we have heard, which we have seen with our eyes, which we have looked at and our hands have touched—this we proclaim concerning the Word of life. 2The life appeared; we have seen it and testify to it, and we proclaim to you the eternal life, which was with the Father and has appeared to us. 3We proclaim to you what we have seen

---

* See note on I. Pet. 5. 11.   § ? "An age-lasting (*i.e.* eternal) day."

also, that you also may have fellowship with us; and indeed our fellowship is with the Father, and with His Son Jesus Christ. 4And these things we write, so that our joy may be made complete.

God Is Light

5And this is the message we have heard from Him and announce to you, that God is light, and in Him there is no darkness at all. 6If we say that we have fellowship with Him and yet walk in the darkness, we lie and do not practice the truth; 7but if we walk in the light as He Himself is in the light, we have fellowship with one another, and the blood of Jesus His Son cleanses us from all sin. 8If we say that we have no sin, we are deceiving ourselves, and the truth is not in us. 9If we confess our sins, He is faithful and righteous to forgive us our sins and to cleanse us from all unrighteousness. 10If we say that we have not sinned, we make Him a liar, and His word is not in us.

Chapter 2

Christ Is Our Advocate

MY little children, I am writing these things to you that you may not sin. And if anyone sins, we have an *a*Advocate with the Father, Jesus Christ the righteous; 2and He Himself is the propitiation for our sins; and not for ours only, but

---

*a*Gr., *Paracletos*, one called alongside to help

καὶ ὑμῖν, ἵνα καὶ ὑμεῖς κοινωνίαν ἔχητε
also to you, in order *also* *ye* *fellowship* *may*
　　　　　that　　　　　　　　　　　　have

μεθ’ ἡμῶν. καὶ ἡ κοινωνία δὲ ἡ ἡμετέρα
with us. *indeed the* *fellowship* *And* – *our*

μετὰ τοῦ πατρὸς καὶ μετὰ τοῦ υἱοῦ
[is] with the Father and with the Son

αὐτοῦ Ἰησοῦ Χριστοῦ. 4 καὶ ταῦτα
of him Jesus Christ. And these things

γράφομεν ἡμεῖς ἵνα ἡ χαρὰ ἡμῶν ᾖ
write we in order the joy of us may
　　　　　　　that　　　　　　　　　be

πεπληρωμένη.
having been fulfilled.

5 Καὶ ἔστιν αὕτη ἡ ἀγγελία ἣν
And *is* *this* the message which

ἀκηκόαμεν ἀπ’ αὐτοῦ καὶ ἀναγγέλλομεν
we have heard from him and *we announce*

ὑμῖν, ὅτι ὁ θεὸς φῶς ἐστιν καὶ σκοτία
to you, that – God *light* *is* and *darkness*

ἐν αὐτῷ οὐκ ἔστιν οὐδεμία. 6 Ἐὰν
in *him* *not* *is* none. If

εἴπωμεν ὅτι κοινωνίαν ἔχομεν μετ’ αὐτοῦ
we say that *fellowship* *we have* with him

καὶ ἐν τῷ σκότει περιπατῶμεν, ψευδόμεθα
and *in* *the* *darkness* *we walk*, we lie

καὶ οὐ ποιοῦμεν τὴν ἀλήθειαν· 7 ἐὰν
and are not doing the truth; *if*

δὲ ἐν τῷ φωτὶ περιπατῶμεν ὡς αὐτός
but *in* *the* *light* *we walk* as he

ἔστιν ἐν τῷ φωτί, κοινωνίαν ἔχομεν
is in the light, *fellowship* *we have*

μετ’ ἀλλήλων καὶ τὸ αἷμα Ἰησοῦ τοῦ
with each other and the blood of Jesus the

υἱοῦ αὐτοῦ καθαρίζει ἡμᾶς ἀπὸ πάσης
Son of him cleanses us from all

ἁμαρτίας. 8 ἐὰν εἴπωμεν ὅτι ἁμαρτίαν
sin. If we say that sin

οὐκ ἔχομεν, ἑαυτοὺς πλανῶμεν καὶ ἡ
we have not, *ourselves* *we deceive* and the

ἀλήθεια οὐκ ἔστιν ἐν ἡμῖν. 9 ἐὰν
truth is not in us. If

ὁμολογῶμεν τὰς ἁμαρτίας ἡμῶν, πιστός
we confess the sins of us, faithful

ἔστιν καὶ δίκαιος, ἵνα ἀφῇ ἡμῖν τὰς
he is and righteous, in order he may us the
　　　　　　　　　　　that forgive

ἁμαρτίας καὶ καθαρίσῃ ἡμᾶς ἀπὸ πάσης
sins and *he* may cleanse us from all

ἀδικίας. 10 ἐὰν εἴπωμεν ὅτι οὐχ
iniquity. If we say that not

ἡμαρτήκαμεν, ψεύστην ποιοῦμεν αὐτὸν
we have sinned, a liar we make him

καὶ ὁ λόγος αὐτοῦ οὐκ ἔστιν ἐν ἡμῖν.
and the word of him is not in us.

2 Τεκνία μου, ταῦτα γράφω ὑμῖν ἵνα
Little children of me, these things I write to you in order
　　　　　　　　　　　　　　　　　　　　that

μὴ ἁμάρτητε. καὶ ἐάν τις ἁμάρτῃ,
ye sin not. And if anyone sins,

παράκλητον ἔχομεν πρὸς τὸν πατέρα,
an advocate we have with the Father,

Ἰησοῦν Χριστὸν δίκαιον· 2 καὶ αὐτὸς
Jesus Christ [the] righteous; and he

ἱλασμός ἐστιν περὶ τῶν ἁμαρτιῶν ἡμῶν,
a propitiation *is* concerning the sins of us,

οὐ περὶ τῶν ἡμετέρων δὲ μόνον ἀλλὰ
not *concerning* – *ours* *but* only but

---

and heard, so that you also may have fellowship with us. And our fellowship is with the Father and with his Son, Jesus Christ. 4We write this to make our*a* joy complete.

Walking in the Light

5This is the message we have heard from him and declare to you: God is light; in him there is no darkness at all. 6If we claim to have fellowship with him yet walk in the darkness, we lie and do not live by the truth. 7But if we walk in the light, as he is in the light, we have fellowship with one another, and the blood of Jesus, his Son, purifies us from all*b* sin.

8If we claim to be without sin, we deceive ourselves and the truth is not in us. 9If we confess our sins, he is faithful and just and will forgive us our sins and purify us from all unrighteousness. 10If we claim we have not sinned, we make him out to be a liar and his word has no place in our lives.

Chapter 2

MY dear children, I write this to you so that you will not sin. But if anybody does sin, we have one who speaks to the Father in our defense—Jesus Christ, the Righteous One. 2He is the atoning sacrifice for our sins, and not only for ours but also for*c* the

---

*a*4 Some manuscripts *your*
*b*7 Or *every*
*c*2 Or *He is the one who turns aside God's wrath, taking away our sins, and not only ours but also*

also for *those of* the whole world.

3And by this we know that we have come to know Him, if we keep His commandments.

4The one who says, "I have come to know Him," and does not keep His commandments, is a liar, and the truth is not in him;

5but whoever keeps His word, in him the love of God has truly been perfected. By this we know that we are in Him:

6the one who says he abides in Him ought himself to walk in the same manner as He walked.

7Beloved, I am not writing a new commandment to you, but an old commandment which you have had from the beginning; the old commandment is the word which you have heard.

8On the other hand, I am writing a new commandment to you, which is true in Him and in you, because the darkness is passing away, and the true light is already shining.

9The one who says he is in the light and *yet* hates his brother is in the darkness until now.

10The one who loves his brother abides in the light and there is no cause for stumbling in him.

11But the one who hates his brother is in the darkness and walks in the darkness, and does not know where he is going because the darkness has blinded his eyes.

12I am writing to you, little children, because your sins are forgiven you for

---

καὶ περὶ ὅλου τοῦ κόσμου. 3 καὶ ἐν
also concerning all the world. And by

τούτῳ γινώσκομεν ὅτι ἐγνώκαμεν αὐτόν,
this we know that we have known him,

ἐὰν τὰς ἐντολὰς αὐτοῦ τηρῶμεν. 4 ὁ
if ²the ³command- ⁴of him ¹we keep. The
ments [one]

λέγων ὅτι ἔγνωκα αὐτόν, καὶ τὰς ἐντολὰς
saying[,] – I have known him, and ²the ⁴command-
ments

αὐτοῦ μὴ τηρῶν, ψεύστης ἐστίν, καὶ
⁵of him ¹not ³keeping, ²a liar ¹is, and

ἐν τούτῳ ἡ ἀλήθεια οὐκ ἔστιν· 5 ὃς δ'
in this man the truth is not; but who-

ἂν τηρῇ αὐτοῦ τὸν λόγον, ἀληθῶς ἐν
ever keeps ²of him ¹the ²word, truly in

τούτῳ ἡ ἀγάπη τοῦ θεοῦ τετελείωται.
this man the love – of God has been perfected.

ἐν τούτῳ γινώσκομεν ὅτι ἐν αὐτῷ ἐσμεν.
By this we know that ¹in ²him ¹we are.

6 ὁ λέγων ἐν αὐτῷ μένειν ὀφείλει καθὼς
The [one] saying in him to remain ought as

ἐκεῖνος περιεπάτησεν καὶ αὐτὸς οὕτως
that [one]* walked also [him]self so

περιπατεῖν.
to walk.

7 Ἀγαπητοί, οὐκ ἐντολὴν καινὴν γράφω
Beloved, ²not ⁴commandment ³a new ¹I write

ὑμῖν, ἀλλ' ἐντολὴν παλαιὰν ἣν εἴχετε
to you, but ²commandment ¹an old which ye had

ἀπ' ἀρχῆς· ἡ ἐντολὴ ἡ παλαιά ἐστιν
from [the] the ²command- – ¹old is
beginning; ment

ὁ λόγος ὃν ἠκούσατε. 8 πάλιν ἐντολὴν
the word which ye heard. Again ²commandment

καινὴν γράφω ὑμῖν, ὃ ἐστιν ἀληθὲς
¹a new I write to you, what is true

ἐν αὐτῷ καὶ ἐν ὑμῖν, ὅτι ἡ σκοτία
in him and in you, because the darkness

παράγεται καὶ τὸ φῶς τὸ ἀληθινὸν
is passing and the ²light ¹true

ἤδη φαίνει. 9 ὁ λέγων ἐν τῷ φωτὶ
already shines. The [one] saying in the light

εἶναι καὶ τὸν ἀδελφὸν αὐτοῦ μισῶν
to be and the brother of him hating

ἐν τῇ σκοτίᾳ ἐστὶν ἕως ἄρτι. 10 ὁ
in the darkness is until now. The

ἀγαπῶν τὸν ἀδελφὸν αὐτοῦ ἐν τῷ φωτὶ
[one] loving the brother of him in the light

μένει, καὶ σκάνδαλον ἐν αὐτῷ οὐκ ἔστιν·
remains, and offence in him is not;

11 ὁ δὲ μισῶν τὸν ἀδελφὸν αὐτοῦ ἐν
but the [one] hating the brother of him in

τῇ σκοτίᾳ ἐστὶν καὶ ἐν τῇ σκοτίᾳ
the darkness is and in the darkness

περιπατεῖ, καὶ οὐκ οἶδεν ποῦ ὑπάγει,
walks, and knows not where he is going,

ὅτι ἡ σκοτία ἐτύφλωσεν τοὺς ὀφθαλμοὺς
be- the darkness blinded the eyes
cause

αὐτοῦ. 12 Γράφω ὑμῖν, τεκνία, ὅτι
of him. I write to you, little because
children,

ἀφέωνται ὑμῖν αἱ ἁμαρτίαι διὰ τὸ ὄνομα
have been *to* you the sins on ac- the name
forgiven (your) count of

* In a number of places John uses this demonstrative adjective as a substitute for " Christ " : " the remoter antecedent." See also John 2. 21.

---

sins of the whole world.

3We know that we have come to know him if we obey his commands. 4The man who says, "I know him," but does not do what he commands is a liar, and the truth is not in him. 5But if anyone obeys his word, God's love*d* is truly made complete in him. This is how we know we are in him: 6Whoever claims to live in him must walk as Jesus did.

7Dear friends, I am not writing you a new command but an old one, which you have had since the beginning. This old command is the message you have heard. 8Yet I am writing you a new command; its truth is seen in him and you, because the darkness is passing and the true light is already shining.

9Anyone who claims to be in the light but hates his brother is still in the darkness. 10Whoever loves his brother lives in the light, and there is nothing in him*e* to make him stumble. 11But whoever hates his brother is in the darkness and walks around in the darkness; he does not know where he is going, because the darkness has blinded him.

12I write to you, dear children, because your sins have been forgiven on

---

*d*5 Or *word, love for God*
*e*10 Or *it*

His name's sake.
13I am writing to you, fathers, because you know Him who has been from the beginning. I am writing to you, young men, because you have overcome the evil one. I have written to you, children, because you know the Father.
14I have written to you, fathers, because you know Him who has been from the beginning. I have written to you, young men, because you are strong, and the word of God abides in you, and you have overcome the evil one.

Do Not Love the World

15Do not love the world, nor the things in the world. If anyone loves the world, the love of the Father is not in him.
16For all that is in the world, the lust of the flesh and the lust of the eyes and the boastful pride of life, is not from the Father, but is from the world.
17And the world is passing away, and *also* its lusts; but the one who does the will of God abides forever.
18Children, it is the last hour; and just as you heard that antichrist is coming, even now many antichrists have arisen; from this we know that it is the last hour.
19They went out from us, but they were not *really* of us; for if they had been of us, they would have remained with us; but *they went out,* in order that it might be shown that they all are not of us.
20But you have an anointing from the Holy One, and you all know.
21I have not written to you because you do not know the truth, but because you do know it, and because no lie is of the

αὐτοῦ.	**13** γράφω	ὑμῖν,	πατέρες,	ὅτι
of him.	I write	to you,	fathers,	because

ἐγνώκατε	τὸν	ἀπ'	ἀρχῆς.	γράφω ὑμῖν,
ye have known	the [one]	from	[the] beginning.	I write to you,

νεανίσκοι,	ὅτι	νενικήκατε τὸν	πονηρόν.
young men,	because	ye have overcome the	evil one.

14 ἔγραψα ὑμῖν, παιδία, ὅτι ἐγνώκατε
I wrote to you, young children, because ye have known

τὸν πατέρα. ἔγραψα ὑμῖν, πατέρες,
the Father. I wrote to you, fathers,

ὅτι ἐγνώκατε τὸν ἀπ' ἀρχῆς. ἔγραψα
because ye have known the from [one] [the] beginning. I wrote

ὑμῖν, νεανίσκοι, ὅτι ἰσχυροί ἐστε καὶ
to you, young men, because strong ye are and

ὁ λόγος τοῦ θεοῦ ἐν ὑμῖν μένει καὶ
the word - of God in you remains and

νενικήκατε τὸν πονηρόν. **15** Μὴ ἀγαπᾶτε
ye have overcome the evil one. Love ye not

τὸν κόσμον μηδὲ τὰ ἐν τῷ κόσμῳ.
the world nor the things in the world.

ἐάν τις ἀγαπᾷ τὸν κόσμον, οὐκ ἔστιν
If anyone loves the world, ⁸not ⁵is

ἡ ἀγάπη τοῦ πατρὸς ἐν αὐτῷ· **16** ὅτι
¹the ⁴love ³of the ²Father in him; because

πᾶν τὸ ἐν τῷ κόσμῳ, ἡ ἐπιθυμία τῆς
all that in the world, the lust of the
whicht [is]

σαρκὸς καὶ ἡ ἐπιθυμία τῶν ὀφθαλμῶν
flesh and the lust of the eyes

καὶ ἡ ἀλαζονεία τοῦ βίου, οὐκ ἔστιν
and the vainglory - of life, is not

ἐκ τοῦ πατρός, ἀλλὰ ἐκ τοῦ κόσμου
of the Father, but of the world

ἐστίν. **17** καὶ ὁ κόσμος παράγεται καὶ
is. And the world is passing away and

ἡ ἐπιθυμία αὐτοῦ· ὁ δὲ ποιῶν τὸ θέλημα
the lust of it; but the [one] doing the will

τοῦ θεοῦ μένει εἰς τὸν αἰῶνα.
- of God remains unto the age.

18 Παιδία, ἐσχάτη ὥρα ἐστίν, καὶ
Young children, a last hour it is, and

καθὼς ἠκούσατε ὅτι ἀντίχριστος ἔρχεται,
as ye heard that antichrist is coming,

καὶ νῦν ἀντίχριστοι πολλοὶ γεγόνασιν·
even now ²antichrists ¹many have arisen;

ὅθεν γινώσκομεν ὅτι ἐσχάτη ὥρα ἐστίν.
whence we know that a last hour it is.

19 ἐξ ἡμῶν ἐξῆλθαν, ἀλλ' οὐκ ἦσαν
From us they went out, but they were not

ἐξ ἡμῶν· εἰ γὰρ ἐξ ἡμῶν ἦσαν, μεμενή-
of us; for if of us they were, they would

κεισαν ἂν μεθ' ἡμῶν· ἀλλ' ἵνα φανερω-
have remained with us; but in order it might be
that

θῶσιν ὅτι οὐκ εἰσὶν πάντες ἐξ ἡμῶν.
manifested that they are not all of us.

20 καὶ ὑμεῖς χρῖσμα ἔχετε ἀπὸ τοῦ
And ye an anointing have from the

ἁγίου, καὶ οἴδατε πάντες. **21** οὐκ ἔγραψα
Holy One, and ¹ye ²know ³all. I wrote not

ὑμῖν ὅτι οὐκ οἴδατε τὴν ἀλήθειαν, ἀλλ'
to you because ye know not the truth, but

ὅτι οἴδατε αὐτήν, καὶ ὅτι πᾶν ψεῦδος
because ye know it, and because every lie
=no lie is . . .

account of his name.
13I write to you, fathers, because you have known him who is from the beginning. I write to you, young men, because you have overcome the evil one. I write to you, dear children, because you have known the Father.
14I write to you, fathers, because you have known him who is from the beginning. I write to you, young men, because you are strong, and the word of God lives in you, and you have overcome the evil one.

Do Not Love the World

15Do not love the world or anything in the world. If anyone loves the world, the love of the Father is not in him. 16For everything in the world—the cravings of sinful man, the lust of his eyes and the boasting of what he has and does—comes not from the Father but from the world. 17The world and its desires pass away, but the man who does the will of God lives forever.

Warning Against Antichrists

18Dear children, this is the last hour; and as you have heard that the antichrist is coming, even now many antichrists have come. This is how we know it is the last hour. 19They went out from us, but they did not really belong to us. For if they had belonged to us, they would have remained with us; but their going showed that none of them belonged to us. 20But you have an anointing from the Holy One, and all of you know the truth.ᶠ 21I do not write to you because you do not know the truth, but because you know it and because no lie comes from the truth.

ᶠ20 Some manuscripts *and you know all things*

truth.

22Who is the liar but the one who denies that Jesus is the Christ? This is the antichrist, the one who denies the Father and the Son.

23Whoever denies the Son does not have the Father; the one who confesses the Son has the Father also.

24As for you, let that abide in you which you heard from the beginning. If what you heard from the beginning abides in you, you also will abide in the Son and in the Father.

The Promise Is Eternal Life

25And this is the promise which He Himself made to us: eternal life.

26These things I have written to you concerning those who are trying to deceive you.

27And as for you, the anointing which you received from Him abides in you, and you have no need for anyone to teach you; but as His anointing teaches you about all things, and is true and is not a lie, and just as it has taught you, you abide in Him.

28And now, little children, abide in Him, so that when He appears, we may have confidence and not shrink away from Him in shame at His coming.

29If you know that He is righteous, you know that everyone also who practices righteousness is born of Him.

Chapter 3

Children of God Love One Another

SEE how great a love the Father has bestowed upon us, that we should be called children of God; and *such* we are. For this reason the world does not

---

ἐκ τῆς ἀληθείας οὐκ ἔστιν. 22 Τίς
of the truth is not. Who

ἐστιν ὁ ψεύστης εἰ μὴ ὁ ἀρνούμενος
is the liar except the [one] denying

ὅτι Ἰησοῦς οὐκ ἔστιν ὁ χριστός; οὗτός
that Jesus not is the Christ? this

ἐστιν ὁ ἀντίχριστος, ὁ ἀρνούμενος τὸν
is the antichrist, the [one] denying the

πατέρα καὶ τὸν υἱόν. 23 πᾶς ὁ ἀρνούμενος
Father and the Son. Everyone denying

τὸν υἱὸν οὐδὲ τὸν πατέρα ἔχει· ὁ
the Son ²neither ³the ⁴Father ¹has; the

ὁμολογῶν τὸν υἱὸν καὶ τὸν πατέρα ἔχει.
[one] confessing the Son ²also ³the ⁴Father ¹has.

24 ὑμεῖς ὃ ἠκούσατε ἀπ' ἀρχῆς, ἐν
²Ye ¹what heard from [the] beginning, in

ὑμῖν μενέτω. ἐὰν ἐν ὑμῖν μείνῃ ὃ ἀπ'
you let it remain. If ¹in ²you ²remains ¹what ³from

ἀρχῆς ἠκούσατε, καὶ ὑμεῖς ἐν τῷ υἱῷ
⁴[the] ²ye heard, ⁶both ¹ye ⁴in ⁵the ⁶Son
beginning

καὶ [ἐν] τῷ πατρὶ μενεῖτε. 25 καὶ
⁷and ⁸in ⁹the ¹⁰Father ⁵will remain. And

αὕτη ἐστὶν ἡ ἐπαγγελία ἣν αὐτὸς ἐπηγ-
this is the promise which he pro-

γείλατο ἡμῖν, τὴν ζωὴν τὴν αἰώνιον.
mised us, the life — eternal.

26 Ταῦτα ἔγραψα ὑμῖν περὶ τῶν πλανών-
These I wrote to you concern- the leading
things ing [ones]

των ὑμᾶς. 27 καὶ ὑμεῖς τὸ χρῖσμα
²astray ¹you. And ⁴ye ¹the ²anointing

ὃ ἐλάβετε ἀπ' αὐτοῦ μένει ἐν ὑμῖν,
³which received from him remains in you,

καὶ οὐ χρείαν ἔχετε ἵνα τις διδάσκῃ
and ²no ¹need ¹ye have *in order* anyone should
that teach

ὑμᾶς· ἀλλ' ὡς τὸ αὐτοῦ χρῖσμα διδάσκει
you; but as the ²of him ¹anointing teaches

ὑμᾶς περὶ πάντων, καὶ ἀληθές ἐστιν
you concerning all things, and ²true ¹is

καὶ οὐκ ἔστιν ψεῦδος, καὶ καθὼς ἐδίδαξεν
and is not a lie, and as he/it taught

ὑμᾶς, μένετε ἐν αὐτῷ.
you, remain ye in him.

28 Καὶ νῦν, τεκνία, μένετε ἐν αὐτῷ,
And now, little children, remain ye in him,

ἵνα ἐὰν φανερωθῇ σχῶμεν παρρησίαν καὶ
in or- if he is manifested we may confidence and
der that have

μὴ αἰσχυνθῶμεν ἀπ' αὐτοῦ ἐν τῇ παρουσίᾳ
not be shamed from him in the presence

αὐτοῦ. 29 ἐὰν εἰδῆτε ὅτι δίκαιός ἐστιν,
of him. If ye know that ²righteous ¹he is,

γινώσκετε ὅτι καὶ πᾶς ὁ ποιῶν τὴν
know ye that also every one doing the

δικαιοσύνην ἐξ αὐτοῦ γεγέννηται.
righteousness ²of ³him ¹has been born.

3 Ἴδετε ποταπὴν ἀγάπην δέδωκεν ἡμῖν
See ye what manner of love ²has given ¹to us

ὁ πατὴρ ἵνα τέκνα θεοῦ κληθῶμεν,
¹the ²Father *in order* ³children ⁴of God ¹we may be
that called,

καὶ ἐσμέν. διὰ τοῦτο ὁ κόσμος οὐ
and we are. Therefore the world ²not

22Who is the liar? It is the man who denies that Jesus is the Christ. Such a man is the antichrist—he denies the Father and the Son. 23No one who denies the Son has the Father; whoever acknowledges the Son has the Father also. 24See that what you have heard from the beginning remains in you. If it does, you also will remain in the Son and in the Father. 25And this is what he promised us—even eternal life.

26I am writing these things to you about those who are trying to lead you astray. 27As for you, the anointing you received from him remains in you, and you do not need anyone to teach you. But as his anointing teaches you about all things and as that anointing is real, not counterfeit—just as it has taught you, remain in him.

Children of God

28And now, dear children, continue in him, so that when he appears we may be confident and unashamed before him at his coming.

29If you know that he is righteous, you know that everyone who does what is right has been born of him.

Chapter 3

HOW great is the love the Father has lavished on us, that we should be called children of God! And that is what we are! The reason the world does know us, because it did not know Him.

²Beloved, now we are children of God, and it has not appeared as yet what we shall be. We know that, when He appears, we shall be like Him, because we shall see Him just as He is.

³And everyone who has this hope *fixed* on Him purifies himself, just as He is pure.

⁴Everyone who practices sin also practices lawlessness; and sin is lawlessness.

⁵And you know that He appeared in order to take away sins; and in Him there is no sin.

⁶No one who abides in Him sins; no one who sins has seen Him or knows Him.

⁷Little children, let no one deceive you; the one who practices righteousness is righteous, just as He is righteous;

⁸the one who practices sin is of the devil; for the devil has sinned from the beginning. The Son of God appeared for this purpose, that He might destroy the works of the devil.

⁹No one who is born of God practices sin, because His seed abides in him; and he cannot sin, because he is born of God.

¹⁰By this the children of God and the children of the devil are obvious: anyone who does not practice righteousness is not of God, nor the one who does not love his brother.

¹¹For this is the message

γινώσκει ἡμᾶς, ὅτι οὐκ ἔγνω αὐτόν.
¹knows ²us, because it knew not him.

2 ἀγαπητοί, νῦν τέκνα θεοῦ ἐσμεν, καὶ
Beloved, ¹now ²children ⁴of God ¹we are, and

οὔπω ἐφανερώθη τί ἐσόμεθα. οἴδαμεν
not yet was it manifested what we shall be. We know

ὅτι ἐὰν φανερωθῇ ὅμοιοι αὐτῷ ἐσόμεθα,
that if he(?it) is manifested like him we shall be,

ὅτι ὀψόμεθα αὐτὸν καθώς ἐστιν. 3 καὶ
be- we shall see him as he is. And
cause

πᾶς ὁ ἔχων τὴν ἐλπίδα ταύτην ἐπ'
everyone having this hope on

αὐτῷ ἁγνίζει ἑαυτὸν καθὼς ἐκεῖνος ἁγνός
him purifies himself as that one* ¹pure

ἐστιν. 4 πᾶς ὁ ποιῶν τὴν ἁμαρτίαν
¹is. Everyone doing – sin

καὶ τὴν ἀνομίαν ποιεῖ, καὶ ἡ ἁμαρτία
²also – ³lawlessness ¹does, and – sin

ἐστὶν ἡ ἀνομία. 5 καὶ οἴδατε ὅτι ἐκεῖνος
is – lawlessness. And ye know that that one*

ἐφανερώθη ἵνα τὰς ἁμαρτίας ἄρῃ, καὶ
was manifested in order – sins he might and
that bear,

ἁμαρτία ἐν αὐτῷ οὐκ ἔστιν. 6 πᾶς ὁ
sin ²in ³him ¹is not. Everyone

ἐν αὐτῷ μένων οὐχ ἁμαρτάνει· πᾶς ὁ
²in ³him ¹remaining sins not; everyone

ἁμαρτάνων οὐχ ἑώρακεν αὐτὸν οὐδὲ
sinning has not seen him nor

ἔγνωκεν αὐτόν. 7 Τεκνία, μηδεὶς πλανάτω
has known him. Little ²no man ¹let ³lead
children, ⁴astray

ὑμᾶς· ὁ ποιῶν τὴν δικαιοσύνην δίκαιός
⁴you; the [one] doing righteousness ⁵righteous

ἐστιν, καθὼς ἐκεῖνος δίκαιός ἐστιν· 8 ὁ
¹is, as that one* ²righteous ¹is; the

ποιῶν τὴν ἁμαρτίαν ἐκ τοῦ διαβόλου
[one] doing – sin ²of ³the ⁴devil

ἐστίν, ὅτι ἀπ' ἀρχῆς ὁ διάβολος ἁμαρτάνει.
¹is, because ⁴from ⁵[the] ¹the ²devil ³sins.
beginning

εἰς τοῦτο ἐφανερώθη ὁ υἱὸς τοῦ θεοῦ,
For this was manifested the Son – of God,

ἵνα λύσῃ τὰ ἔργα τοῦ διαβόλου.
in or- he might the works of the devil.
der that undo

9 Πᾶς ὁ γεγεννημένος ἐκ τοῦ θεοῦ
Everyone having been begotten of – God

ἁμαρτίαν οὐ ποιεῖ, ὅτι σπέρμα αὐτοῦ
²sin ²not ¹does, because seed of him

ἐν αὐτῷ μένει· καὶ οὐ δύναται ἁμαρτάνειν,
in him remains; and he cannot to sin,

ὅτι ἐκ τοῦ θεοῦ γεγέννηται. 10 ἐν
because of – God he has been begotten. By

τούτῳ φανερά ἐστιν τὰ τέκνα τοῦ θεοῦ
this ²manifest ¹is(are) the children – of God

καὶ τὰ τέκνα τοῦ διαβόλου· πᾶς ὁ
and the children of the devil; everyone

μὴ ποιῶν δικαιοσύνην οὐκ ἔστιν ἐκ
not doing righteousness is not of

τοῦ θεοῦ, καὶ ὁ μὴ ἀγαπῶν τὸν ἀδελφὸν
– God, and the not loving the brother
[one]

αὐτοῦ. 11 ὅτι αὕτη ἐστὶν ἡ ἀγγελία
of him. Because this is the message

---

not know us is that it did not know him. ²Dear friends, now we are children of God, and what we will be has not yet been made known. But we know that when he appears, ᵍ we shall be like him, for we shall see him as he is. ³Everyone who has this hope in him purifies himself, just as he is pure.

⁴Everyone who sins breaks the law; in fact, sin is lawlessness. ⁵But you know that he appeared so that he might take away our sins. And in him is no sin. ⁶No one who lives in him keeps on sinning. No one who continues to sin has either seen him or known him.

⁷Dear children, do not let anyone lead you astray. He who does what is right is righteous, just as he is righteous. ⁸He who does what is sinful is of the devil, because the devil has been sinning from the beginning. The reason the Son of God appeared was to destroy the devil's work. ⁹No one who is born of God will continue to sin, because God's seed remains in him; he cannot go on sinning, because he has been born of God. ¹⁰This is how we know who the children of God are and who the children of the devil are: Anyone who does not do what is right is not a child of God; nor is anyone who does not love his brother.

Love One Another
¹¹This is the message you

---

* See ch. 2. 6.

ᵍ2 Or *when it is made known*

which you have heard from the beginning, that we should love one another; 12not as Cain, who was of the evil one, and slew his brother. And for what reason did he slay him? Because his deeds were evil, and his brother's were righteous. 13Do not marvel, brethren, if the world hates you. 14We know that we have passed out of death into life, because we love the brethren. He who does not love abides in death. 15Everyone who hates his brother is a murderer; and you know that no murderer has eternal life abiding in him. 16We know love by this, that He laid down His life for us; and we ought to lay down our lives for the brethren. 17But whoever has the world's goods, and beholds his brother in need and closes his heart against him, how does the love of God abide in him? 18Little children, let us not love with word or with tongue, but in deed and truth. 19We shall know by this that we are of the truth, and shall assure our heart before Him, 20in whatever our heart condemns us; for God is greater than our heart, and knows all things. 21Beloved, if our heart

---

ἣν ἠκούσατε ἀπ' ἀρχῆς, ἵνα ἀγαπῶμεν
which ye heard from [the] in order we should love
    beginning, that

ἀλλήλους· 12 οὐ καθὼς Κάϊν ἐκ τοῦ
one another; not as Cain ⁵of ⁶the

πονηροῦ ἦν καὶ ἔσφαξεν τὸν ἀδελφὸν
⁴evil one ¹was and slew the brother

αὐτοῦ· καὶ χάριν τίνος ἔσφαξεν αὐτόν;
of him; and for the what slew he him?
    sake of

ὅτι τὰ ἔργα αὐτοῦ πονηρὰ ἦν, τὰ δὲ
be- the works of him ²evil ¹was(were), the
cause   [works]

τοῦ ἀδελφοῦ αὐτοῦ δίκαια. 13 μὴ
of the brother of him righteous. not

θαυμάζετε, ἀδελφοί, εἰ μισεῖ ὑμᾶς ὁ
Marvel ye, brothers, if ³hates ⁴you ¹the

κόσμος. 14 ἡμεῖς οἴδαμεν ὅτι μεταβεβή-
²world. We know that we have re-

καμεν ἐκ τοῦ θανάτου εἰς τὴν ζωήν,
moved out of the death into the life,

ὅτι ἀγαπῶμεν τοὺς ἀδελφούς· ὁ μὴ
because we love the brothers; the [one] not

ἀγαπῶν μένει ἐν τῷ θανάτῳ. 15 πᾶς
loving remains in - death. Every-

ὁ μισῶν τὸν ἀδελφὸν αὐτοῦ ἀνθρωποκτόνος
one hating the brother of him ²a murderer

ἐστίν, καὶ οἴδατε ὅτι πᾶς ἀνθρωποκτόνος
¹is, and ye know that every murderer
       =no murderer has . . .

οὐκ ἔχει ζωὴν αἰώνιον ἐν αὐτῷ μένουσαν.
has not life eternal in him remaining.

16 ἐν τούτῳ ἐγνώκαμεν τὴν ἀγάπην, ὅτι
By this we have known - love, because

ἐκεῖνος ὑπὲρ ἡμῶν τὴν ψυχὴν αὐτοῦ
that one* on behalf of us the life of him

ἔθηκεν· καὶ ἡμεῖς ὀφείλομεν ὑπὲρ τῶν
laid down; and we ought on behalf of the

ἀδελφῶν τὰς ψυχὰς θεῖναι. 17 ὃς δ'
brothers the(our) lives to lay down. Who-

ἂν ἔχῃ τὸν βίον τοῦ κόσμου καὶ θεωρῇ
ever has the means of the world and beholds
   of life

τὸν ἀδελφὸν αὐτοῦ χρείαν ἔχοντα καὶ
the brother of him ²need ¹having and

κλείσῃ τὰ σπλάγχνα αὐτοῦ ἀπ' αὐτοῦ,
shuts the bowels of him from him,

πῶς ἡ ἀγάπη τοῦ θεοῦ μένει ἐν αὐτῷ;
how ²the ³love - ⁴of God ¹remains in him?

18 Τεκνία, μὴ ἀγαπῶμεν λόγῳ μηδὲ τῇ
Little children, let us not love in word nor in the

γλώσσῃ, ἀλλὰ ἐν ἔργῳ καὶ ἀληθείᾳ.
tongue, but in work and truth.

19 ἐν τούτῳ γνωσόμεθα ὅτι ἐκ τῆς ἀληθείας
By this we shall know that ²of ³the ⁴truth

ἐσμέν, καὶ ἔμπροσθεν αὐτοῦ πείσομεν
¹we are, and before him shall persuade

τὴν καρδίαν ἡμῶν 20 ὅτι ἐὰν καταγινώσκῃ
the heart of us that if ⁴blames [us]

ἡμῶν ἡ καρδία, ὅτι μείζων ἐστὶν ὁ
³of us ¹the ²heart, that greater is -

θεὸς τῆς καρδίας ἡμῶν καὶ γινώσκει
God [than] the heart of us and knows

πάντα. 21 Ἀγαπητοί, ἐὰν ἡ καρδία
all things. Beloved, if the(our) heart

* See ch. 2. 6, 3. 3, 5, 7.

---

heard from the beginning: We should love one another. 12Do not be like Cain, who belonged to the evil one and murdered his brother. And why did he murder him? Because his own actions were evil and his brother's were righteous. 13Do not be surprised, my brothers, if the world hates you. 14We know that we have passed from death to life, because we love our brothers. Anyone who does not love remains in death. 15Anyone who hates his brother is a murderer, and you know that no murderer has eternal life in him. 16This is how we know what love is: Jesus Christ laid down his life for us. And we ought to lay down our lives for our brothers. 17If anyone has material possessions and sees his brother in need but has no pity on him, how can the love of God be in him? 18Dear children, let us not love with words or tongue but with actions and in truth. 19This then is how we know that we belong to the truth, and how we set our hearts at rest in his presence 20whenever our hearts condemn us. For God is greater than our hearts, and he knows everything. 21Dear friends, if our does not condemn us, we have confidence before God;

22and whatever we ask we receive from Him, because we keep His commandments and do the things that are pleasing in His sight.

23And this is His commandment, that we believe in the name of His Son Jesus Christ, and love one another, just as He commanded us.

24And the one who keeps His commandments abides in Him, and He in him. And we know by this that He abides in us, by the Spirit whom He has given us.

μὴ καταγινώσκῃ, παρρησίαν ἔχομεν πρὸς
does not blame [us], confidence we have with

τὸν θεόν, **22** καὶ ὃ ἐὰν αἰτῶμεν λαμβάν-
- God, and whatever we ask we re-

ομεν ἀπ' αὐτοῦ, ὅτι τὰς ἐντολὰς αὐτοῦ
ceive from him, because ²the ³command- ⁴of him
                                           ments

τηροῦμεν καὶ τὰ ἀρεστὰ ἐνώπιον αὐτοῦ
¹we keep and ²the ³pleasing ⁴before ⁵him
                things

ποιοῦμεν. **23** καὶ αὕτη ἐστὶν ἡ ἐντολὴ
¹we do. And this is the command-
                               ment

αὐτοῦ, ἵνα πιστεύσωμεν τῷ ὀνόματι τοῦ
of him, in order we should believe the name of the
     that

υἱοῦ αὐτοῦ Ἰησοῦ Χριστοῦ καὶ ἀγαπῶμεν
Son of him Jesus Christ and love

ἀλλήλους καθὼς ἔδωκεν ἐντολὴν ἡμῖν.
one another as he gave commandment to us.

24 καὶ ὁ τηρῶν τὰς ἐντολὰς αὐτοῦ ἐν
And the keeping the command- of him in
    [one]   ments

αὐτῷ μένει καὶ αὐτὸς ἐν αὐτῷ· καὶ
him remains and he in him; and

ἐν τούτῳ γινώσκομεν ὅτι μένει ἐν ἡμῖν,
by this we know that he remains in us,

ἐκ τοῦ πνεύματος οὗ ἡμῖν ἔδωκεν.
by the Spirit whom to us he gave.

---

hearts do not condemn us, we have confidence before God 22and receive from him anything we ask, because we obey his commands and do what pleases him. 23And this is his command: to believe in the name of his Son, Jesus Christ, and to love one another as he commanded us. 24Those who obey his commands live in him, and he in them. And this is how we know that he lives in us: We know it by the Spirit he gave us.

Chapter 4

Testing the Spirits

BELOVED, do not believe every spirit, but test the spirits to see whether they are from God; because many false prophets have gone out into the world.

2By this you know the Spirit of God: every spirit that confesses that Jesus Christ has come in the flesh is from God;

3and every spirit that does not confess Jesus is not from God; and this is the *spirit* of the antichrist, of which you have heard that it is coming, and now it is already in the world.

4You are from God, little children, and have overcome them; because greater is He who is in you than he who is in the world.

5They are from the world; therefore they speak *as* from the world, and the world listens to them.

---

4 Ἀγαπητοί, μὴ παντὶ πνεύματι
   Beloved, ¹not ²every ³spirit

πιστεύετε, ἀλλὰ δοκιμάζετε τὰ πνεύματα
¹believe ye, but prove the spirits

εἰ ἐκ τοῦ θεοῦ ἐστιν, ὅτι πολλοὶ
if of - God they are, because many

ψευδοπροφῆται ἐξεληλύθασιν εἰς τὸν
false prophets have gone forth into the

κόσμον. **2** ἐν τούτῳ γινώσκετε τὸ πνεῦμα
world. By this know ye the Spirit

τοῦ θεοῦ· πᾶν πνεῦμα ὃ ὁμολογεῖ Ἰησοῦν
- of God: every spirit which confesses Jesus

Χριστὸν ἐν σαρκὶ ἐληλυθότα ἐκ τοῦ
Christ ²in ³[the] flesh ¹having come ⁵of -

θεοῦ ἐστιν, **3** καὶ πᾶν πνεῦμα ὃ μὴ
⁴God ⁶is, and every spirit which not

ὁμολογεῖ τὸν Ἰησοῦν ἐκ τοῦ θεοῦ οὐκ
confesses - Jesus ²of - ⁴God ¹not

ἔστιν· καὶ τοῦτό ἐστιν τὸ τοῦ ἀντιχρίστου,
¹is; and this is the of the antichrist,
                                [spirit]

ὃ ἀκηκόατε ὅτι ἔρχεται, καὶ νῦν ἐν
which ye have that it is coming, and ²now ¹in
   heard

τῷ κόσμῳ ἐστὶν ἤδη. **4** ὑμεῖς ἐκ τοῦ
²the ³world ¹is ⁴already. Ye of -

θεοῦ ἐστε, τεκνία, καὶ νενικήκατε αὐτούς,
God are, little and have overcome them,
           children,

ὅτι μείζων ἐστὶν ὁ ἐν ὑμῖν ἢ ὁ ἐν
because greater is the in you than the in
                [one]   [one]

τῷ κόσμῳ. **5** αὐτοὶ ἐκ τοῦ κόσμου
the world. ¹They ²of ⁴the ⁵world

εἰσίν· διὰ τοῦτο ἐκ τοῦ κόσμου λαλοῦσιν
²are; therefore ²of ³the ⁴world ¹they speak

καὶ ὁ κόσμος αὐτῶν ἀκούει. **6** ἡμεῖς
and the world them hears. ¹We

Chapter 4

Test the Spirits

DEAR friends, do not believe every spirit, but test the spirits to see whether they are from God, because many false prophets have gone out into the world. 2This is how you can recognize the Spirit of God: Every spirit that acknowledges that Jesus Christ has come in the flesh is from God, 3but every spirit that does not acknowledge Jesus is not from God. This is the spirit of the antichrist, which you have heard is coming and even now is already in the world.

4You, dear children, are from God and have overcome them, because the one who is in you is greater than the one who is in the world. 5They are from the world and therefore speak from the viewpoint of the world, and the world listens to them. 6We are from

6We are from God; he who knows God listens to us; he who is not from God does not listen to us. By this we know the spirit of truth and the spirit of error.

God Is Love

7Beloved, let us love one another, for love is from God; and everyone who loves is born of God and knows God. 8The one who does not love does not know God, for God is love. 9By this the love of God was manifested in us, that God has sent His only begotten Son into the world so that we might live through Him. 10In this is love, not that we loved God, but that He loved us and sent His Son to be the propitiation for our sins. 11Beloved, if God so loved us, we also ought to love one another. 12No one has beheld God at any time; if we love one another, God abides in us, and His love is perfected in us. 13By this we know that we abide in Him and He in us, because He has given us of His Spirit. 14And we have beheld and bear witness that the Father has sent the Son to be the Savior of the world. 15Whoever confesses that Jesus is the Son of God, God abides in him, and he in God. 16And we have come to know and have believed the love which God has for

---

ἐκ τοῦ θεοῦ ἐσμεν· ὁ γινώσκων τὸν
of - God are; the [one] knowing -

θεὸν ἀκούει ἡμῶν, ὃς οὐκ ἔστιν ἐκ
God hears us, [he] who is not of

τοῦ θεοῦ οὐκ ἀκούει ἡμῶν. ἐκ τούτου
- God hears not us. From this

γινώσκομεν τὸ πνεῦμα τῆς ἀληθείας καὶ
we know the spirit - of truth and

τὸ πνεῦμα τῆς πλάνης.
the spirit - of error.

7 Ἀγαπητοί, ἀγαπῶμεν ἀλλήλους, ὅτι
Beloved, let us love one another, because

ἡ ἀγάπη ἐκ τοῦ θεοῦ ἐστιν, καὶ πᾶς ὁ
- love of - God is, and everyone

ἀγαπῶν ἐκ τοῦ θεοῦ γεγέννηται καὶ
loving of - God has been begotten and

γινώσκει τὸν θεόν. 8 ὁ μὴ ἀγαπῶν
knows - God. The [one] not loving

οὐκ ἔγνω τὸν θεόν, ὅτι ὁ θεὸς ἀγάπη
knew not - God, because - God love

ἐστίν. 9 ἐν τούτῳ ἐφανερώθη ἡ ἀγάπη
is. By this was manifested the love

τοῦ θεοῦ ἐν ἡμῖν, ὅτι τὸν υἱὸν αὐτοῦ
- of God in(to) us, because the Son of him

τὸν μονογενῆ ἀπέσταλκεν ὁ θεὸς εἰς
- only begotten has sent - God into

τὸν κόσμον ἵνα ζήσωμεν δι' αὐτοῦ.
the world in order that we might live through him.

10 ἐν τούτῳ ἐστὶν ἡ ἀγάπη, οὐχ ὅτι
In this is love, not that

ἡμεῖς ἠγαπήκαμεν τὸν θεόν, ἀλλ' ὅτι
we have loved - God, but that

αὐτὸς ἠγάπησεν ἡμᾶς καὶ ἀπέστειλεν τὸν
he loved us and sent the

υἱὸν αὐτοῦ ἱλασμὸν περὶ τῶν ἁμαρτιῶν
Son of him a propitiation concerning the sins

ἡμῶν. 11 ἀγαπητοί, εἰ οὕτως ὁ θεὸς
of us. Beloved, if so - God

ἠγάπησεν ἡμᾶς, καὶ ἡμεῖς ὀφείλομεν
loved us, also we ought

ἀλλήλους ἀγαπᾶν. 12 θεὸν οὐδεὶς πώποτε
one another to love. God no man ever

τεθέαται· ἐὰν ἀγαπῶμεν ἀλλήλους, ὁ θεὸς
has beheld; if we love one another, - God

ἐν ἡμῖν μένει καὶ ἡ ἀγάπη αὐτοῦ
in us remains and the love of him

τετελειωμένη ἐν ἡμῖν ἐστιν. 13 Ἐν
having been perfected in us is. By

τούτῳ γινώσκομεν ὅτι ἐν αὐτῷ μένομεν
this we know that in him we remain

καὶ αὐτὸς ἐν ἡμῖν, ὅτι ἐκ τοῦ πνεύματος
and he in us, because of the Spirit

αὐτοῦ δέδωκεν ἡμῖν. 14 καὶ ἡμεῖς
of him he has given us. And we

τεθεάμεθα καὶ μαρτυροῦμεν ὅτι ὁ πατὴρ
have beheld and bear witness that the Father

ἀπέσταλκεν τὸν υἱὸν σωτῆρα τοῦ κόσμου.
has sent the Son [as] Saviour of the world.

15 ὃς ἐὰν ὁμολογήσῃ ὅτι Ἰησοῦς ἐστιν
Whoever confesses that Jesus is

ὁ υἱὸς τοῦ θεοῦ, ὁ θεὸς ἐν αὐτῷ μένει
the Son - of God, - God in him remains

καὶ αὐτὸς ἐν τῷ θεῷ. 16 καὶ ἡμεῖς
and he in - God. And we

ἐγνώκαμεν καὶ πεπιστεύκαμεν τὴν ἀγάπην
have known and have believed the love

God, and whoever knows God listens to us; whoever is not from God does not listen to us. This is how we recognize the Spirit[h] of truth and the spirit of falsehood.

God's Love and Ours

7Dear friends, let us love one another, for love comes from God. Everyone who loves has been born of God and knows God. 8Whoever does not love does not know God, because God is love. 9This is how God showed his love among us: He sent his one and only Son[i] into the world that we might live through him. 10This is love: not that we loved God, but that he loved us and sent his Son as an atoning sacrifice for[j] our sins. 11Dear friends, since God so loved us, we also ought to love one another. 12No one has ever seen God; but if we love one another, God lives in us and his love is made complete in us. 13We know that we live in him and he in us, because he has given us of his Spirit. 14And we have seen and testify that the Father has sent his Son to be the Savior of the world. 15If anyone acknowledges that Jesus is the Son of God, God lives in him and he in God. 16And so we know and rely on the love God has for us.

h6 Or spirit
i9 Or his only begotten Son
j10 Or as the one who would turn aside his wrath, taking away

us. God is love, and the one who abides in love abides in God, and God abides in him.

17By this, love is perfected with us, that we may have confidence in the day of judgment; because as He is, so also are we in this world.

18There is no fear in love; but perfect love casts out fear, because fear involves punishment, and the one who fears is not perfected in love.

19We love, because He first loved us.

20If someone says, "I love God," and hates his brother, he is a liar; for the one who does not love his brother whom he has seen, cannot love God whom he has not seen.

21And this commandment we have from Him, that the one who loves God should love his brother also.

ἦν ἔχει ὁ θεὸς ἐν ἡμῖν. Ὁ θεὸς ἀγάπη
which ²has – ¹God in(to) us. – God ³love

ἐστίν, καὶ ὁ μένων ἐν τῇ ἀγάπῃ ἐν
¹is, and the remaining in – love ²in
[one]

τῷ θεῷ μένει καὶ ὁ θεὸς ἐν αὐτῷ
– God ¹remains and – God ²in ³him

μένει. 17 Ἐν τούτῳ τετελείωται ἡ ἀγάπη
¹remains. By this ²has been perfected – ¹love

μεθ' ἡμῶν, ἵνα παρρησίαν ἔχωμεν ἐν
with us, in order that ²confidence ¹we may have in

τῇ ἡμέρᾳ τῆς κρίσεως, ὅτι καθὼς ἐκεῖνός
the day – of judgment, because as that one•

ἐστιν καὶ ἡμεῖς ἐσμεν ἐν τῷ κόσμῳ
is ²also ¹we ²are in – world

τούτῳ. 18 φόβος οὐκ ἔστιν ἐν τῇ ἀγάπῃ,
this. Fear is not in – love,

ἀλλ' ἡ τελεία ἀγάπη ἔξω βάλλει τὸν
but – perfect love ²out ¹casts the

φόβον, ὅτι ὁ φόβος κόλασιν ἔχει, ὁ δὲ
fear, because – fear ²punishment ¹has, and the

φοβούμενος οὐ τετελείωται ἐν τῇ ἀγάπῃ.
[one] fearing has not been perfected in – love.

19 ἡμεῖς ἀγαπῶμεν, ὅτι αὐτὸς πρῶτος
We love, because he first

ἠγάπησεν ἡμᾶς. 20 ἐάν τις εἴπῃ ὅτι
loved us. If anyone says[,]

ἀγαπῶ τὸν θεόν, καὶ τὸν ἀδελφὸν αὐτοῦ
I love – God, and ²the ³brother ⁴of him

μισῇ, ψεύστης ἐστίν· ὁ γὰρ μὴ ἀγαπῶν
¹hates, ²a liar ¹he is; for the [one] not loving

τὸν ἀδελφὸν αὐτοῦ ὃν ἑώρακεν, τὸν
the brother of him whom he has seen,

θεὸν ὃν οὐχ ἑώρακεν οὐ δύναται ἀγαπᾶν.
²God ⁴whom ³he has not seen ¹he cannot ⁵to love.

21 καὶ ταύτην τὴν ἐντολὴν ἔχομεν ἀπ'
And this – commandment we have from

αὐτοῦ, ἵνα ὁ ἀγαπῶν τὸν θεὸν ἀγαπᾷ
him, in order the loving – God loves
that [one]

καὶ τὸν ἀδελφὸν αὐτοῦ.
also the brother of him.

God is love. Whoever lives in love lives in God, and God in him. 17In this way, love is made complete among us so that we will have confidence on the day of judgment, because in this world we are like him. 18There is no fear in love. But perfect love drives out fear, because fear has to do with punishment. The one who fears is not made perfect in love.

19We love because he first loved us. 20If anyone says, "I love God," yet hates his brother, he is a liar. For anyone who does not love his brother, whom he has seen, cannot love God, whom he has not seen. 21And he has given us this command: Whoever loves God must also love his brother.

Chapter 5

Overcoming the World

WHOEVER believes that Jesus is the *b*Christ is born of God; and whoever loves the Father loves the *child* born of Him.

2By this we know that we love the children of God, when we love God and observe His commandments.

3For this is the love of God, that we keep His commandments; and His commandments are not

Chapter 5

5 Πᾶς ὁ πιστεύων ὅτι Ἰησοῦς ἐστιν
Everyone believing that Jesus is

ὁ χριστὸς ἐκ τοῦ θεοῦ γεγέννηται, καὶ
the Christ ²of – ³God ¹has been begotten, and

πᾶς ὁ ἀγαπῶν τὸν γεννήσαντα ἀγαπᾷ
everyone loving the [one] begetting loves

τὸν γεγεννημένον ἐξ αὐτοῦ. 2 ἐν τούτῳ
the having been begotten of him. By this
[one]

γινώσκομεν ὅτι ἀγαπῶμεν τὰ τέκνα τοῦ
we know that we love the children –

θεοῦ, ὅταν τὸν θεὸν ἀγαπῶμεν καὶ τὰς
of God, whenever – ²God ¹we love and ²the

ἐντολὰς αὐτοῦ ποιῶμεν. 3 αὕτη γάρ
²command- ⁴of him ¹we do. For this
ments

ἐστιν ἡ ἀγάπη τοῦ θεοῦ, ἵνα τὰς ἐντολὰς
is the love – of God, in order ²the ³command-
that ments

αὐτοῦ τηρῶμεν· καὶ αἱ ἐντολαὶ αὐτοῦ
⁴of him ¹we keep; and the commandments of him

Faith in the Son of God

EVERYONE who believes that Jesus is the Christ is born of God, and everyone who loves the father loves his child as well. 2This is how we know that we love the children of God: by loving God and carrying out his commands. 3This is love for God: to obey his commands. And his commands

---

b I.e., Messiah   • See ch. 2. 6, 3. 3, 5, 7, 16.

burdensome.

4For whatever is born of God overcomes the world; and this is the victory that has overcome the world—our faith.

5And who is the one who overcomes the world, but he who believes that Jesus is the Son of God?

6This is the one who came by water and blood, Jesus Christ; not with the water only, but with the water and with the blood.

7And it is the Spirit who bears witness, because the Spirit is the truth.

8For there are three that bear witness, ᶜthe Spirit and the water and the blood; and the three are in agreement.

9If we receive the witness of men, the witness of God is greater; for the witness of God is this, that He has borne witness concerning His Son.

10The one who believes in the Son of God has the witness in himself; the one who does not believe God has made Him a liar, because he has not believed in the witness that God has borne concerning His Son.

11And the witness is this, that God has given us eternal life, and this life is in His Son.

12He who has the Son has the life; he who does not have the Son of God does not have the life.

This Is Written That You May Know

13These things I have written to you who believe

βαρεῖαι οὐκ εἰσίν, 4 ὅτι πᾶν τὸ γεγεν-
heavy are not, because everything having

νημένον ἐκ τοῦ θεοῦ νικᾷ τὸν κόσμον·
been begotten of - God overcomes the world;

καὶ αὕτη ἐστὶν ἡ νίκη ἡ νικήσασα τὸν
and this is the victory - overcoming the

κόσμον, ἡ πίστις ἡμῶν. 5 Τίς ἐστιν
world, the faith of us. ³Who ²is

[δὲ] ὁ νικῶν τὸν κόσμον εἰ μὴ ὁ
¹and the overcoming the world except the
[one]

πιστεύων ὅτι Ἰησοῦς ἐστιν ὁ υἱὸς τοῦ
[one] believing that Jesus is the Son -

θεοῦ; 6 οὗτός ἐστιν ὁ ἐλθὼν δι᾽ ὕδατος
of God? This is the coming through water
[one]

καὶ αἵματος, Ἰησοῦς Χριστός· οὐκ ἐν
and blood, Jesus Christ; not by

τῷ ὕδατι μόνον, ἀλλ᾽ ἐν τῷ ὕδατι καὶ
the water only, but by the water and

ἐν τῷ αἵματι· καὶ τὸ πνεῦμά ἐστιν τὸ
by the blood; and the Spirit is the

μαρτυροῦν, ὅτι τὸ πνεῦμά ἐστιν ἡ ἀλήθεια.
[one] bearing be- the Spirit is the truth.
witness, cause

7 ὅτι τρεῖς εἰσιν οἱ μαρτυροῦντες, 8 τὸ
Because three there are the bearing witness, the
[ones]

πνεῦμα καὶ τὸ ὕδωρ καὶ τὸ αἷμα, καὶ
Spirit and the water and the blood, and

οἱ τρεῖς εἰς τὸ ἕν εἰσιν. 9 εἰ τὴν
the three ²in the ³one ¹are. If ²the

μαρτυρίαν τῶν ἀνθρώπων λαμβάνομεν, ἡ
³witness - ⁴of men ¹we receive, the

μαρτυρία τοῦ θεοῦ μείζων ἐστίν, ὅτι
witness - of God ²greater ¹is, because

αὕτη ἐστὶν ἡ μαρτυρία τοῦ θεοῦ, ὅτι
this is the witness - of God, because

μεμαρτύρηκεν περὶ τοῦ υἱοῦ αὐτοῦ. 10 ὁ
he has borne concern- the Son of him. The
witness ing

πιστεύων εἰς τὸν υἱὸν τοῦ θεοῦ ἔχει
[one] believing in the Son - of God has

τὴν μαρτυρίαν ἐν αὐτῷ. ὁ μὴ πιστεύων
the witness in him. The not believing
[one]

τῷ θεῷ ψεύστην πεποίηκεν αὐτόν, ὅτι
- God ²a liar ¹has made ²him, because

οὐ πεπίστευκεν εἰς τὴν μαρτυρίαν ἣν
he has not believed in the witness which

μεμαρτύρηκεν ὁ θεὸς περὶ τοῦ υἱοῦ
¹has borne witness - ¹God concerning the Son

αὐτοῦ. 11 καὶ αὕτη ἐστὶν ἡ μαρτυρία,
of him. And this is the witness,

ὅτι ζωὴν αἰώνιον ἔδωκεν ὁ θεὸς ἡμῖν,
that ³life ⁴eternal ²gave - ¹God ³to us,

καὶ αὕτη ἡ ζωὴ ἐν τῷ υἱῷ αὐτοῦ
and this - life ²in ³the ⁴Son ⁵of him

ἐστιν. 12 ὁ ἔχων τὸν υἱὸν ἔχει τὴν
¹is. The [one] having the Son has the

ζωήν· ὁ μὴ ἔχων τὸν υἱὸν τοῦ θεοῦ
life; the not having the Son - of God
[one]

τὴν ζωὴν οὐκ ἔχει.
the life has not.

13 Ταῦτα ἔγραψα ὑμῖν ἵνα εἰδῆτε ὅτι
These I wrote to you in order ye may that
things that know

---

are not burdensome, 4for everyone born of God overcomes the world. This is the victory that has overcome the world, even our faith. 5Who is it that overcomes the world? Only he who believes that Jesus is the Son of God.

6This is the one who came by water and blood—Jesus Christ. He did not come by water only, but by water and blood. And it is the Spirit who testifies, because the Spirit is the truth. 7For there are three that testify: 8theᵏ Spirit, the water and the blood; and the three are in agreement. 9We accept man's testimony, but God's testimony is greater because it is the testimony of God, which he has given about his Son. 10Anyone who believes in the Son of God has this testimony in his heart. Anyone who does not believe God has made him out to be a liar, because he has not believed the testimony God has given about his Son. 11And this is the testimony: God has given us eternal life, and this life is in his Son. 12He who has the Son has life; he who does not have the Son of God does not have life.

Concluding Remarks

13I write these things to you who believe in the

ᶜ A few late mss. read in heaven, the Father, the Word, and the Holy Spirit, and these three are one. And there are three that bear witness on earth, the Spirit

ᵏ7,8 Late manuscripts of the Vulgate *testify in heaven: the Father, the Word and the Holy Spirit, and these three are one.* 8*And there are three that testify on earth: the* (not found in any Greek manuscript before the sixteenth century) in the name of the Son of God, in order that you may know that you have eternal life.

14And this is the confidence which we have before Him, that, if we ask anything according to His will, He hears us.

15And if we know that He hears us *in* whatever we ask, we know that we have the requests which we have asked from Him.

16If anyone sees his brother committing a sin not *leading* to death, he shall ask and *God* will for him give life to those who commit sin not *leading* to death. There is a sin *leading* to death; I do not say that he should make request for this.

17All unrighteousness is sin, and there is a sin not *leading* to death.

18We know that no one who is born of God sins; but He who was born of God keeps him and the evil one does not touch him.

19We know that we are of God, and the whole world lies in *the power of* the evil one.

20And we know that the Son of God has come, and has given us understanding, in order that we might know Him who is true, and we are in Him who is true, in His Son Jesus Christ. This is the true God and eternal life.

21Little children, guard yourselves from idols.

ζωὴν ἔχετε αἰώνιον, τοῖς πιστεύουσιν
²life ¹ye have ²eternal, to the [ones] believing

εἰς τὸ ὄνομα τοῦ υἱοῦ τοῦ θεοῦ. 14 Καὶ
in the name of the Son - of God. And

αὕτη ἐστὶν ἡ παρρησία ἣν ἔχομεν πρὸς
this is the confidence which we have toward

αὐτόν, ὅτι ἐάν τι αἰτώμεθα κατὰ τὸ
him, that if ²anything ¹we ask according to the

θέλημα αὐτοῦ ἀκούει ἡμῶν. 15 καὶ
will of him he hears us. And

ἐὰν οἴδαμεν ὅτι ἀκούει ἡμῶν ὃ ἐὰν
if we know that he hears us whatever

αἰτώμεθα, οἴδαμεν ὅτι ἔχομεν τὰ αἰτήματα
we ask, we know that we have the requests

ἃ ἠτήκαμεν ἀπ' αὐτοῦ. 16 Ἐάν τις
which we have from him. If anyone
asked

ἴδῃ τὸν ἀδελφὸν αὐτοῦ ἁμαρτάνοντα
sees the brother of him sinning

ἁμαρτίαν μὴ πρὸς θάνατον, αἰτήσει, καὶ
a sin not unto death, he shall ask, and

δώσει αὐτῷ ζωήν, τοῖς ἁμαρτάνουσιν
he will give to him life, to the [ones] sinning

μὴ πρὸς θάνατον. ἔστιν ἁμαρτία πρὸς
not unto death. There is a sin unto

θάνατον· οὐ περὶ ἐκείνης λέγω ἵνα
death; not concerning that do I say *in order
that*

ἐρωτήσῃ. 17 πᾶσα ἀδικία ἁμαρτία ἐστίν,
he should inquire. All iniquity ¹sin ¹is,

καὶ ἔστιν ἁμαρτία οὐ πρὸς θάνατον.
and there is a sin not unto death.

18 Οἴδαμεν ὅτι πᾶς ὁ γεγεννημένος ἐκ
We know that everyone having been begotten of

τοῦ θεοῦ οὐχ ἁμαρτάνει, ἀλλ' ὁ γεννηθεὶς
- God sins not, but the [one] begotten

ἐκ τοῦ θεοῦ τηρεῖ αὐτόν, καὶ ὁ πονηρὸς
of - God keeps him, and the evil one

οὐχ ἅπτεται αὐτοῦ. 19 οἴδαμεν ὅτι ἐκ
does not touch him. We know that of

τοῦ θεοῦ ἐσμεν, καὶ ὁ κόσμος ὅλος ἐν
- God we are, and the ²world ¹whole in

τῷ πονηρῷ κεῖται. 20 οἴδαμεν δὲ ὅτι
the evil one lies. ²we know ¹And that

ὁ υἱὸς τοῦ θεοῦ ἥκει, καὶ δέδωκεν
the Son - of God is come, and has given

ἡμῖν διάνοιαν ἵνα γινώσκωμεν τὸν
to us an understanding in order we might know the
that

ἀληθινόν· καὶ ἐσμὲν ἐν τῷ ἀληθινῷ,
true [one]; and we are in the true [one],

ἐν τῷ υἱῷ αὐτοῦ Ἰησοῦ Χριστῷ. οὗτός
in the Son of him Jesus Christ. This

ἐστιν ὁ ἀληθινὸς θεὸς καὶ ζωὴ αἰώνιος.
is the true God and life eternal.

21 Τεκνία, φυλάξατε ἑαυτὰ ἀπὸ τῶν
Little children, guard yourselves from *the*

εἰδώλων.
idols.

---

name of the Son of God so that you may know that you have eternal life. 14This is the confidence we have in approaching God: that if we ask anything according to his will, he hears us. 15And if we know that he hears us—whatever we ask—we know that we have what we asked of him.

16If anyone sees his brother commit a sin that does not lead to death, he should pray and God will give him life. I refer to those whose sin does not lead to death. There is a sin that leads to death. I am not saying that he should pray about that. 17All wrongdoing is sin, and there is sin that does not lead to death.

18We know that anyone born of God does not continue to sin; the one who was born of God keeps him safe, and the evil one cannot harm him. 19We know that we are children of God, and that the whole world is under the control of the evil one. 20We know also that the Son of God has come and has given us understanding, so that we may know him who is true. And we are in him who is true—even in his Son Jesus Christ. He is the true God and eternal life.

21Dear children, keep yourselves from idols.

Chapter 1

Walk According to His Commandments

THE elder to the chosen lady and her children, whom I love in truth; and not only I, but also all who know the truth,

2for the sake of the truth which abides in us and will be with us forever:

3Grace, mercy *and* peace will be with us, from God the Father and from Jesus Christ, the Son of the Father, in truth and love.

4I was very glad to find *some* of your children walking in truth, just as we have received commandment *to do* from the Father.

5And now I ask you, lady, not as writing to you a new commandment, but the one which we have had from the beginning, that we love one another.

6And this is love, that we walk according to His commandments. This is the commandment, just as you have heard from the beginning, that you should walk in it.

7For many deceivers have gone out into the world, those who do not acknowledge Jesus Christ *as* coming in the flesh. This is the deceiver and the antichrist.

8Watch yourselves, that you might not lose what we have accomplished, but that you may receive a full reward.

9Anyone who goes too far and does not abide in the teaching of Christ, does not have God; the one who abides in the teaching, he

---

1 Ὁ   πρεσβύτερος   ἐκλεκτῇ   κυρίᾳ   καὶ
  The   elder   to [the] chosen lady   and
τοῖς   τέκνοις   αὐτῆς,   οὓς   ἐγὼ   ἀγαπῶ   ἐν
to the children of her, whom   I   love   in
ἀληθείᾳ,   καὶ   οὐκ   ἐγὼ   μόνος   ἀλλὰ   καὶ
truth,   and   not   I   alone   but   also
πάντες   οἱ   ἐγνωκότες   τὴν   ἀλήθειαν,   2 διὰ
 all   the having known the   truth,   because of
        [ones]
τὴν   ἀλήθειαν   τὴν   μένουσαν   ἐν   ἡμῖν,
the   truth   -   remaining   among   us,
καὶ   μεθ᾽   ἡμῶν   ἔσται   εἰς   τὸν   αἰῶνα.
and   with   us   will be unto   the   age.
3 ἔσται   μεθ᾽   ἡμῶν   χάρις   ἔλεος   εἰρήνη
 ⁴will be ⁵with   ⁶us   ¹Grace[,] ²mercy[,] ³peace
παρὰ   θεοῦ   πατρός,   καὶ   παρὰ   Ἰησοῦ
from   God   [the] Father, and   from   Jesus
Χριστοῦ   τοῦ   υἱοῦ   τοῦ   πατρός,   ἐν   ἀληθείᾳ
 Christ   the   Son   of the Father,   in   truth
καὶ   ἀγάπῃ.
and   love.

4 Ἐχάρην   λίαν   ὅτι   εὕρηκα   ἐκ   τῶν
  I rejoiced greatly because I have   of   the
                              found [some]
τέκνων   σου   περιπατοῦντας   ἐν   ἀληθείᾳ,
children of thee   walking   in   truth,
καθὼς   ἐντολὴν   ἐλάβομεν   παρὰ   τοῦ   πατρός.
 as   command- we received   from   the   Father.
        ment
5 καὶ   νῦν   ἐρωτῶ   σε,   κυρία,   οὐχ   ὡς
  And   now I request thee,   lady,   not   as
ἐντολὴν   γράφων   σοι   καινήν,   ἀλλὰ   ἣν
²command- ¹writing ⁴to thee ³a new,   but   which
ment
εἴχομεν   ἀπ᾽   ἀρχῆς,   ἵνα   ἀγαπῶμεν
we had   from   [the]   in order we should
               beginning,   that   love
ἀλλήλους.   6 καὶ   αὕτη   ἐστὶν   ἡ   ἀγάπη,
one another.   And   this   is   -   love,
ἵνα   περιπατῶμεν   κατὰ   τὰς   ἐντολὰς
in order we should walk accord-   the   command-
that   ing to   ments
αὐτοῦ·   αὕτη   ἡ   ἐντολή   ἐστιν,   καθὼς
of him;   this   the ²commandment ¹is,   as
ἠκούσατε   ἀπ᾽   ἀρχῆς,   ἵνα   ἐν   αὐτῇ
ye heard   from   [the]   in order ²in   ³it
               beginning,   that
περιπατῆτε.   7 ὅτι   πολλοὶ   πλάνοι   ἐξῆλθον
¹ye should walk.   Because many   deceivers went forth
εἰς   τὸν   κόσμον,   οἱ   μὴ   ὁμολογοῦντες
into   the   world,   the   not   confessing
                      [ones]
Ἰησοῦν   Χριστὸν   ἐρχόμενον   ἐν   σαρκί·
 Jesus   Christ   coming   in [the] flesh;
οὗτός   ἐστιν   ὁ   πλάνος   καὶ   ὁ   ἀντίχριστος.
 this   is   the deceiver   and   the   antichrist.
8 βλέπετε   ἑαυτούς,   ἵνα   μὴ   ἀπολέσητε
  See   yourselves, lest   ye lose
ἃ   ἠργασάμεθα,   ἀλλὰ   μισθὸν   πλήρη
[the] we wrought,   but   ²reward   ¹a full
things which
ἀπολάβητε.   9 πᾶς   ὁ   προάγων   καὶ   μὴ
¹ye may receive. Everyone going forward   and   not
μένων   ἐν   τῇ   διδαχῇ   τοῦ   Χριστοῦ   θεὸν
remaining in   the teaching   -   of Christ   ²God
οὐκ   ἔχει·   ὁ   μένων   ἐν   τῇ   διδαχῇ,   οὗτος
¹not   ¹has; the remaining in   the teaching, this one
               [one]

THE elder,
  To the chosen lady and her children, whom I love in the truth—and not I only, but also all who know the truth— 2because of the truth, which lives in us and will be with us forever:

3Grace, mercy and peace from God the Father and from Jesus Christ, the Father's Son, will be with us in truth and love.

4It has given me great joy to find some of your children walking in the truth, just as the Father commanded us. 5And now, dear lady, I am not writing you a new command but one we have had from the beginning. I ask that we love one another. 6And this is love: that we walk in obedience to his commands. As you have heard from the beginning, his command is that you walk in love.

7Many deceivers, who do not acknowledge Jesus Christ as coming in the flesh, have gone out into the world. Any such person is the deceiver and the antichrist. 8Watch out that you do not lose what you have worked for, but that you may be rewarded fully. 9Anyone who runs ahead and does not continue in the teaching of Christ does not have God; whoever continues in the teaching has both the Father and the Son.

10If anyone comes to you and does not bring this teaching, do not receive him into *your* house, and do not give him a greeting;

11for the one who gives him a greeting participates in his evil deeds.

12Having many things to write to you, I do not want to *do so* with paper and ink; but I hope to come to you and speak face to face, that your joy may be made full.

13The children of your chosen sister greet you.

καὶ   τὸν   πατέρα   καὶ   τὸν   υἱὸν   ἔχει.
²both   ³the   ⁴Father   ⁵and   ⁶the   ⁷Son   ¹has.

10 εἴ   τις   ἔρχεται   πρὸς   ὑμᾶς   καὶ   ταύτην
If anyone comes   to   you   and   this

τὴν   διδαχὴν   οὐ   φέρει,   μὴ   λαμβάνετε
-   teaching   brings not,   do not ye receive

αὐτὸν   εἰς   οἰκίαν,   καὶ   χαίρειν   αὐτῷ   μὴ
him   into   [your]   and   ⁴to rejoice   ⁵him   ²not
house,

λέγετε·   11 ὁ   λέγων   γὰρ   αὐτῷ   χαίρειν
¹tell ye*;   ⁴the   ⁵telling   ¹for   him   to rejoice
[one]

κοινωνεῖ   τοῖς   ἔργοις   αὐτοῦ   τοῖς   πονηροῖς.
shares   in the   ⁴works   ²of him   -   ¹evil.

12 Πολλὰ   ἔχων   ὑμῖν   γράφειν   οὐκ
¹Many things   ²having   ⁴to you   ³to write   ⁶not

ἐβουλήθην   διὰ   χάρτου   καὶ   μέλανος,   ἀλλὰ
⁵I purpose   by means   paper   and   ink,   but
   of

ἐλπίζω   γενέσθαι   πρὸς   ὑμᾶς   καὶ   στόμα
I am hoping   to be   with   you   and   ²mouth

πρὸς   στόμα   λαλῆσαι,   ἵνα   ἡ   χαρὰ   ἡμῶν
³to   ⁴mouth   ¹to speak,   in or-   the   joy   of us
               der that

πεπληρωμένη   ᾖ.   13 Ἀσπάζεταί   σε   τὰ
having been   may be.   ⁷greets   ⁶thee   ¹The
fulfilled

τέκνα   τῆς   ἀδελφῆς   σου   τῆς   ἐκλεκτῆς.
²children   ³of the   ⁵sister   ⁶of thee   -   ⁴chosen.

has both the Father and the Son. 10If anyone comes to you and does not bring this teaching, do not take him into your house or welcome him. 11Anyone who welcomes him shares in his wicked work.

12I have much to write to you, but I do not want to use paper and ink. Instead, I hope to visit you and talk with you face to face, so that our joy may be complete.

13The children of your chosen sister send their greetings.

---

3 John

Chapter 1

You Walk in the Truth

THE elder to the beloved Gaius, whom I love in truth.

2Beloved, I pray that in all respects you may prosper and be in good health, just as your soul prospers.

3For I was very glad when brethren came and bore witness to your truth, *that is,* how you are walking in truth.

4I have no greater joy than this, to hear of my children walking in the truth.

5Beloved, you are acting faithfully in whatever you accomplish for the brethren, and especially when *they are* strangers;

6and they bear witness to

ΙΩΑΝΝΟΥ Γ
Of John 3

1 Ὁ   πρεσβύτερος   Γαΐῳ   τῷ   ἀγαπητῷ,
The   elder   to Gaius   the   beloved,

ὃν   ἐγὼ   ἀγαπῶ   ἐν   ἀληθείᾳ.
whom   I   love   in   truth.

2 Ἀγαπητέ,   περὶ   πάντων   εὔχομαί   σε
Beloved,   concerning   all things   I pray   thee

εὐοδοῦσθαι   καὶ   ὑγιαίνειν,   καθὼς   εὐοδοῦταί
to prosper   and   to be in health,   as   ⁴prospers
thou mayest prosper . . .

σου   ἡ   ψυχή.   3 ἐχάρην   γὰρ   λίαν   ἐρχομένων
²of   ¹the   ³soul.   For I rejoiced   greatly   coming
thee   =when [some]

ἀδελφῶν   καὶ   μαρτυρούντων   σου   τῇ
brothers   and   bearing witness⁶   of thee   in the
brothers came and bore witness

ἀληθείᾳ,   καθὼς   σὺ   ἐν   ἀληθείᾳ   περιπατεῖς.
truth,   as   thou   in   truth   walkest.

4 μειζοτέραν   τούτων   οὐκ   ἔχω   χαράν,   ἵνα
⁶greater   ⁴[than]   ⁵these   ¹I have no   ³joy,   ²in or-
            things   der that

ἀκούω   τὰ   ἐμὰ   τέκνα   ἐν   τῇ   ἀληθείᾳ
I hear   -   my   children   ³in   ²the   ⁴truth

περιπατοῦντα.   5 Ἀγαπητέ,   πιστὸν   ποιεῖς
¹walking.   Beloved,   faithfully   thou
                                          doest

ὃ   ἐὰν   ἐργάσῃ   εἰς   τοὺς   ἀδελφοὺς   καὶ
whatever   thou workest   for   the   brothers   and

τοῦτο   ξένους,   6 οἳ   ἐμαρτύρησάν   σου   τῇ
this   strangers,   who   bore witness   of thee   -

* That is, "do not greet him."

3 John

THE elder,

To my dear friend Gaius, whom I love in the truth.

2Dear friend, I pray that you may enjoy good health and that all may go well with you, even as your soul is getting along well. 3It gave me great joy to have some brothers come and tell about your faithfulness to the truth and how you continue to walk in the truth. 4I have no greater joy than to hear that my children are walking in the truth.

5Dear friend, you are faithful in what you are doing for the brothers, even though they are strangers to you. 6They have told the your love before the church; and you will do well to send them on their way in a manner worthy of God. 7For they went out for the sake of the Name, accepting nothing from the Gentiles. 8Therefore we ought to support such men, that we may be fellow workers with the truth. 9I wrote something to the church; but Diotrephes, who loves to be first among them, does not accept what we say. 10For this reason, if I come, I will call attention to his deeds which he does, unjustly accusing us with wicked words; and not satisfied with this, neither does he himself receive the brethren, and he forbids those who desire *to do so,* and puts *them* out of the church. 11Beloved, do not imitate what is evil, but what is good. The one who does good is of God; the one who does evil has not seen God. 12Demetrius has received a *good* testimony from everyone, and from the truth itself; and we also bear witness, and you know that our witness is true. 13I had many things to write to you, but I am not willing to write *them* to you with pen and ink; 14but I hope to see you shortly, and we shall speak face to face. Peace *be* to you. The friends greet you. Greet the friends by name.

ἀγάπη ἐνώπιον ἐκκλησίας, οὓς καλῶς
in love before [the] church, whom well
ποιήσεις προπέμψας ἀξίως τοῦ θεοῦ·
thou wilt do sending forward worthily - of God;
7 ὑπὲρ γὰρ τοῦ ὀνόματος ἐξῆλθαν μηδὲν
for on behalf of the name they went forth ²nothing
λαμβάνοντες ἀπὸ τῶν ἐθνικῶν. 8 ἡμεῖς
¹taking from the Gentiles. We
οὖν ὀφείλομεν ὑπολαμβάνειν τοὺς τοιούτους,
there- ought to entertain - such men,
fore
ἵνα συνεργοὶ γινώμεθα τῇ ἀληθείᾳ.
in or- ²co-workers ¹we may become in the truth.
der that
9 Ἔγραψά τι τῇ ἐκκλησίᾳ· ἀλλ' ὁ
I wrote some- to the church; but the
thing [one]
φιλοπρωτεύων αὐτῶν Διοτρέφης οὐκ
loving to be first of them Diotrephes not
ἐπιδέχεται ἡμᾶς. 10 διὰ τοῦτο, ἐὰν
receives us. Therefore, if
ἔλθω, ὑπομνήσω αὐτοῦ τὰ ἔργα ἃ ποιεῖ
I come, I will remember ²of him ¹the ³works which he does
λόγοις πονηροῖς φλυαρῶν ἡμᾶς, καὶ μὴ
⁴words ³with evil ¹prating against ²us, and not
ἀρκούμενος ἐπὶ τούτοις οὔτε αὐτὸς
being satisfied on(with) these ²neither ¹he
ἐπιδέχεται τοὺς ἀδελφοὺς καὶ τοὺς
²receives the brothers and the
βουλομένους κωλύει καὶ ἐκ τῆς ἐκκλησίας
[ones] purposing he prevents and ²out of ¹the ⁴church
ἐκβάλλει.
¹puts out.
11 Ἀγαπητέ, μὴ μιμοῦ τὸ κακὸν ἀλλὰ
Beloved, imitate not the bad but
τὸ ἀγαθόν. ὁ ἀγαθοποιῶν ἐκ τοῦ θεοῦ
the good. The doing good ²of - ¹God
[one]
ἐστιν· ὁ κακοποιῶν οὐχ ἑώρακεν τὸν
¹is; the [one] doing ill has not seen -
θεόν. 12 Δημητρίῳ μεμαρτύρηται ὑπὸ
God. To Demetrius witness has been borne by
πάντων καὶ ὑπὸ αὐτῆς τῆς ἀληθείας·
all and by ²[it]self ¹the ²truth;
καὶ ἡμεῖς δὲ μαρτυροῦμεν, καὶ οἶδας
²also ¹we ¹and bear witness, and thou
knowest
ὅτι ἡ μαρτυρία ἡμῶν ἀληθής ἐστιν.
that the witness of us ²true ¹is.
13 Πολλὰ εἶχον γράψαι σοι, ἀλλ' οὐ
²Many things ¹I had to write to thee, but not
θέλω διὰ μέλανος καὶ καλάμου σοι
I wish ²by means of ⁴ink ³and ⁵pen ¹to thee
γράφειν· 14 ἐλπίζω δὲ εὐθέως σε ἰδεῖν,
¹to write; but I am hoping ²immediately ³thee ¹to see,
καὶ στόμα πρὸς στόμα λαλήσομεν.
and ²mouth ³to ⁴mouth ¹we will speak.
15 Εἰρήνη σοι. ἀσπάζονταί σε οἱ φίλοι.
Peace to thee. ²greet ⁴thee ¹The ³friends.
ἀσπάζου τοὺς φίλους κατ' ὄνομα.
Greet thou the friends by name.

church about your love. You will do well to send them on their way in a manner worthy of God. 7It was for the sake of the Name that they went out, receiving no help from the pagans. 8We ought therefore to show hospitality to such men so that we may work together for the truth. 9I wrote to the church, but Diotrephes, who loves to be first, will have nothing to do with us. 10So if I come, I will call attention to what he is doing, gossiping maliciously about us. Not satisfied with that, he refuses to welcome the brothers. He also stops those who want to do so and puts them out of the church. 11Dear friend, do not imitate what is evil but what is good. Anyone who does what is good is from God. Anyone who does what is evil has not seen God. 12Demetrius is well spoken of by everyone—and even by the truth itself. We also speak well of him, and you know that our testimony is true. 13I have much to write you, but I do not want to do so with pen and ink. 14I hope to see you soon, and we will talk face to face.

Peace to you. The friends here send their greetings. Greet the friends there by name.

Chapter 1

*The Warnings of History
to the Ungodly*

JUDE, a bond-servant of Jesus Christ, and brother of James, to those who are the called, beloved in God the Father, and kept for Jesus Christ:

2May mercy and peace and love be multiplied to you.

3Beloved, while I was making every effort to write you about our common salvation, I felt the necessity to write to you appealing that you contend earnestly for the faith which was once for all delivered to the saints.

4For certain persons have crept in unnoticed, those who were long beforehand marked out of this condemnation, ungodly persons who turn the grace of our God into licentiousness and deny our only Master and Lord, Jesus Christ.

5Now I desire to remind you, though you know all things once for all, that *a*the Lord, after saving a people out of the land of Egypt, subsequently destroyed those who did not believe.

6And angels who did not keep their own domain, but abandoned their proper abode, He has kept in eternal bonds under darkness for the judgment of the great day.

7Just as Sodom and Gomorrah and the cities around them, since they in the same way as these indulged in gross immorality and went after strange flesh, are exhibited as an example, in undergoing the punishment of eternal fire.

8Yet in the same manner these men, also by dreaming, defile the flesh, and reject authority, and revile angelic majesties.

---

1 Ἰούδας   Ἰησοῦ   Χριστοῦ   δοῦλος,   ἀδελφὸς
   Jude   of Jesus   Christ   a slave,   ²brother

δὲ   Ἰακώβου,   τοῖς   ἐν   θεῷ   πατρὶ
¹and   of James,   ¹to the   ⁴by   ⁵God   ⁶[the]
          [ones]   Father

ἠγαπημένοις   καὶ   Ἰησοῦ   Χριστῷ
³having been loved   ⁷and   ⁹for Jesus   ¹⁰Christ

τετηρημένοις   κλητοῖς.   2 ἔλεος   ὑμῖν   καὶ
⁸having been kept   ²called.   Mercy   to you   and

εἰρήνη   καὶ   ἀγάπη   πληθυνθείη.
peace   and   love   may *it* be multiplied.

3 Ἀγαπητοί,   πᾶσαν   σπουδὴν   ποιούμενος
   Beloved,   ²all   ³haste   ¹making

γράφειν   ὑμῖν   περὶ   τῆς   κοινῆς   ἡμῶν
to write   to you   concerning   the   common   ⁵of us

σωτηρίας,   ἀνάγκην   ἔσχον   γράψαι   ὑμῖν
¹salvation,   necessity   I had   to write   to you

παρακαλῶν   ἐπαγωνίζεσθαι   τῇ   ἅπαξ
exhorting   to contend for   ¹the   ²once

παραδοθείσῃ   τοῖς   ἁγίοις   πίστει.   4 παρεισε-
⁴delivered   ³to the   ⁴saints   ³faith.   ⁵crept

δύησαν   γάρ   τινες   ἄνθρωποι,   οἱ   πάλαι
in   For   ²certain   ¹men,   the [ones]   of old

προγεγραμμένοι   εἰς   τοῦτο   τὸ   κρίμα,
having been   for   this   -   judgment,
previously written

ἀσεβεῖς,   τὴν   τοῦ   θεοῦ   ἡμῶν   χάριτα
impious men,   ³the   ⁴of the   ⁵God   ⁶of us   ²grace

μετατιθέντες   εἰς   ἀσέλγειαν   καὶ   τὸν   μόνον
¹making   ²a pretext   for   wantonness   and   ²the   ¹only

δεσπότην   καὶ   κύριον   ἡμῶν   Ἰησοῦν   Χριστὸν
³Master   ⁴and   ⁵Lord   ⁶of us   ⁷Jesus   ⁸Christ

ἀρνούμενοι.   5 Ὑπομνῆσαι   δὲ   ὑμᾶς   βούλομαι,
¹denying.   But   ²to remind   ³you   ¹I purpose,

εἰδότας   ἅπαξ   πάντα,   ὅτι   κύριος   λαὸν
³knowing   ¹once   all   that   [the]   ¹[the]
             things,   Lord   people

ἐκ   γῆς   Αἰγύπτου   σώσας   τὸ   δεύτερον
²out   ⁴[the]   ⁵of Egypt   ¹having   in the second place
of   land   saved

τοὺς   μὴ   πιστεύσαντας   ἀπώλεσεν,   6 ἀγγέλους
²the   ²not   ⁴believing   ¹destroyed,   ²angels
[ones]

τε   τοὺς   μὴ   τηρήσαντας   τὴν   ἑαυτῶν
¹and   -   not   having kept   the   ²of themselves

ἀρχὴν   ἀλλὰ   ἀπολιπόντας   τὸ   ἴδιον
¹rule   but   having deserted   the(ir)   own

οἰκητήριον   εἰς   κρίσιν   μεγάλης   ἡμέρας
habitation   ⁶for ⁷[the] judgment   ⁸of [the] great   ⁹day

δεσμοῖς   ἀϊδίοις   ὑπὸ   ζόφον   τετήρηκεν·
³bonds   ²in everlasting   ⁴under   ⁵gloom   ¹he has kept;

7 ὡς   Σόδομα   καὶ   Γόμορρα   καὶ   αἱ   περὶ
  as   Sodom   and   Gomorra   and   ¹the   ²round

αὐτὰς   πόλεις,   τὸν   ὅμοιον   τρόπον   τούτοις
⁴them   ²cities,   in the   like   manner   to these

ἐκπορνεύσασαι   καὶ   ἀπελθοῦσαι   ὀπίσω   σαρκὸς
committing   and   going away   after   ²flesh
fornication

ἑτέρας,   πρόκεινται   δεῖγμα   πυρὸς   αἰωνίου
¹different,   are set forth   an example   ⁴fire   ³of eternal

δίκην   ὑπέχουσαι.   8 Ὁμοίως   μέντοι   καὶ
²ven-   ¹undergoing.   Likewise   indeed   also
geance

οὗτοι   ἐνυπνιαζόμενοι   σάρκα   μὲν   μιαίνουσιν,
these   dreaming [ones]   ²flesh   ¹on one   ³defile,
                             hand

κυριότητα   δὲ   ἀθετοῦσιν,   δόξας   δὲ
³lordship   ¹on the other   ²despise,   and ²glories

JUDE, a servant of Jesus Christ and a brother of James,

To those who have been called, who are loved by God the Father and kept by *a* Jesus Christ:

2Mercy, peace and love be yours in abundance.

*The Sin and Doom of
Godless Men*

3Dear friends, although I was very eager to write to you about the salvation we share, I felt I had to write and urge you to contend for the faith that was once for all entrusted to the saints. 4For certain men whose condemnation was written about *b* long ago have secretly slipped in among you. They are godless men, who change the grace of our God into a license for immorality and deny Jesus Christ our only Sovereign and Lord. 5Though you already know all this, I want to remind you that the Lord *c* delivered his people out of Egypt, but later destroyed those who did not believe. 6And the angels who did not keep their positions of authority but abandoned their own home—these he has kept in darkness, bound with everlasting chains for judgment on the great Day. 7In a similar way, Sodom and Gomorrah and the surrounding towns gave themselves up to sexual immorality and perversion. They serve as an example of those who suffer the punishment of eternal fire.

8In the very same way, these dreamers pollute their own bodies, reject authority and slander celestial

a1 Or *for;* or *in*
b4 Or *men who were marked out
for condemnation*
c5 Some early manuscripts *Jesus*

9But Michael the archangel, when he disputed with the devil and argued about the body of Moses, did not dare pronounce against him a railing judgment, but said, "The Lord rebuke you."

10But these men revile the things which they do not understand; and the things which they know by instinct, like unreasoning animals, by these things they are destroyed.

11Woe to them! For they have gone the way of Cain, and for pay they have rushed headlong into the error of Balaam, and perished in the rebellion of Korah.

12These men are those who are hidden reefs in your love feasts when they feast with you without fear, caring for themselves; clouds without water, carried along by winds; autumn trees without fruit, doubly dead, uprooted;

13wild waves of the sea, casting up their own shame like foam; wandering stars, for whom the black darkness has been reserved forever.

14And about these also Enoch, *in* the seventh *generation* from Adam, prophesied, saying, "Behold, the Lord came with many thousands of His holy ones,

15to execute judgment upon all, and to convict all the ungodly of all their ungodly deeds which they have done in an ungodly way, and of all the harsh things which ungodly sinners have spoken against Him."

16These are grumblers, finding fault, following after their *own* lusts; they speak arrogantly, flattering people for the sake of *gain*-

βλασφημοῦσιν. 9 Ὁ δὲ Μιχαὴλ ὁ ἀρχάγ-
¹rail at.　　　　– But　Michael　the　arch-

γελος, ὅτε τῷ διαβόλῳ διακρινόμενος
angel,　when　²with the　³devil　¹contending

διελέγετο περὶ τοῦ Μωϋσέως σώματος,
he argued　about　¹the　²of Moses　³body,

οὐκ ἐτόλμησεν κρίσιν ἐπενεγκεῖν βλασφημίας,
durst not　　²a judgment ¹to bring on　　of railing,

ἀλλὰ εἶπεν· ἐπιτιμήσαι σοι κύριος. 10 οὗτοι
but　said :　　¹rebuke　³thee ¹[The] Lord.　these men

δὲ ὅσα μὲν οὐκ οἴδασιν βλασφημοῦσιν,
But　what on one　they know not　　　they rail at,
things hand

ὅσα δὲ φυσικῶς ὡς τὰ ἄλογα ζῷα
what on　other　²naturally　²as　⁴the　²without ²animals
things　　　　　　　　　　　　　　reason

ἐπίστανται, ἐν τούτοις φθείρονται. 11 οὐαὶ
¹they understand,　by　these　they are corrupted.　Woe

αὐτοῖς, ὅτι τῇ ὁδῷ τοῦ Κάϊν ἐπορεύθησαν,
to them, because in the way　–　of Cain　they went,

καὶ τῇ πλάνῃ τοῦ Βαλαὰμ μισθοῦ
and　²to the　²error　　²of Balaam　⁴of(for) reward

ἐξεχύθησαν, καὶ τῇ ἀντιλογίᾳ τοῦ Κόρε
¹gave themselves　and　²in the　³dispute　–　²of Korah
up,

ἀπώλοντο. 12 Οὗτοί εἰσιν οἱ ἐν ταῖς
¹perished.　　These men　are　¹the　²in　³the

ἀγάπαις ὑμῶν σπιλάδες συνευωχούμενοι
¹love feasts　²of you　³rocks　　feasting together

ἀφόβως, ἑαυτοὺς ποιμαίνοντες, νεφέλαι
without fear,　²themselves　¹feeding,　　²clouds

ἄνυδροι ὑπὸ ἀνέμων παραφερόμεναι, δένδρα
¹waterless　²by　³winds　⁴being carried away,　²trees

φθινοπωρινὰ ἄκαρπα δὶς ἀποθανόντα
¹autumn　without fruit　twice　dying

ἐκριζωθέντα, 13 κύματα ἄγρια θαλάσσης
having been uprooted,　²waves　¹fierce　²of [the] sea

ἐπαφρίζοντα τὰς ἑαυτῶν αἰσχύνας, ἀστέρες
¹foaming up　²the ¹of themselves　³shames,　²stars

πλανῆται, οἷς ὁ ζόφος τοῦ σκότους
¹wandering,　for whom the　gloom　–　of darkness

εἰς αἰῶνα τετήρηται. 14 Ἐπροφήτευσεν
unto　[the] age　has been kept.　　¹prophesied

δὲ καὶ τούτοις ἕβδομος ἀπὸ Ἀδὰμ
¹And　²also　²to these men　⁴[the] seventh　²from　⁴Adam

Ἐνὼχ λέγων· ἰδοὺ ἦλθεν κύριος ἐν
²Enoch　saying :　Behold　came　[the] Lord　with

ἁγίαις μυριάσιν αὐτοῦ, 15 ποιῆσαι κρίσιν
saints　ten thousands　of him,　　to do　judgment

κατὰ πάντων καὶ ἐλέγξαι πάντας τοὺς
against　all men　and　to rebuke　all　the

ἀσεβεῖς περὶ πάντων τῶν ἔργων ἀσεβείας
impious concerning　all　the　works　of impiety

αὐτῶν ὧν ἠσέβησαν καὶ περὶ πάντων
of them which they impiously did and concerning　all

τῶν σκληρῶν ὧν ἐλάλησαν κατ' αὐτοῦ
the　hard things　which　²spoke　³against　⁴him

ἁμαρτωλοὶ ἀσεβεῖς. 16 Οὗτοί εἰσιν γογ-
²sinners　¹impious.　　These men　are　¹mur-

γυσταὶ μεμψίμοιροι, κατὰ τὰς ἐπιθυμίας
murers　¹querulous,　²according to ³the　⁴lusts

αὐτῶν πορευόμενοι, καὶ τὸ στόμα αὐτῶν
²of them　¹going,　　and　the　mouth　of them

λαλεῖ ὑπέρογκα, θαυμάζοντες πρόσωπα
speaks　arrogant things,　admiring　　faces

beings. 9But even the archangel Michael, when he was disputing with the devil about the body of Moses, did not dare to bring a slanderous accusation against him, but said, "The Lord rebuke you!" 10Yet these men speak abusively against whatever they do not understand; and what things they do understand by instinct, like unreasoning animals—these are the very things that destroy them.

11Woe to them! They have taken the way of Cain; they have rushed for profit into Balaam's error; they have been destroyed in Korah's rebellion.

12These men are blemishes at your love feasts, eating with you without the slightest qualm—shepherds who feed only themselves. They are clouds without rain, blown along by the wind; autumn trees, without fruit and uprooted—twice dead. 13They are wild waves of the sea, foaming up their shame; wandering stars, for whom blackest darkness has been reserved forever.

14Enoch, the seventh from Adam, prophesied about these men: "See, the Lord is coming with thousands upon thousands of his holy ones, to judge everyone, and to convict all the ungodly of all the ungodly acts they have done in the ungodly way, and of all the harsh words ungodly sinners have spoken against him." 16These men are grumblers and faultfinders; they follow their own evil desires; they boast about themselves and flat-

ing an advantage.

Keep Yourselves in the Love of God

17But you, beloved, ought to remember the words that were spoken beforehand by the apostles of our Lord Jesus Christ,

18that they were saying to you, "In the last time there shall be mockers, following after their own ungodly lusts."

19These are the ones who cause divisions, worldly-minded, devoid of the Spirit.

20But you, beloved, building yourselves up on your most holy faith; praying in the Holy Spirit;

21keep yourselves in the love of God, waiting anxiously for the mercy of our Lord Jesus Christ to eternal life.

22And have mercy on some, who are doubting;

23save others, snatching them out of the fire; and on some have mercy with fear, hating even the garment polluted by the flesh.

24Now to Him who is able to keep you from stumbling, and to make you stand in the presence of His glory blameless with great joy,

25to the only God our Savior, through Jesus Christ our Lord, *be* glory, majesty, dominion and authority, before all time and now and forever. Amen.

ὠφελείας   χάριν.
²advantage ¹for the sake of.

17 Ὑμεῖς   δέ,   ἀγαπητοί,   μνήσθητε   τῶν
But ye,   beloved, be mindful of the

ῥημάτων   τῶν   προειρημένων   ὑπὸ   τῶν
words   previously spoken   by   the

ἀποστόλων   τοῦ   κυρίου   ἡμῶν   Ἰησοῦ
apostles   of the   Lord   of us   Jesus

Χριστοῦ,   **18** ὅτι   ἔλεγον   ὑμῖν·   ἐπ᾽   ἐσχάτου
Christ,   because they told you: At   [the] last

τοῦ   χρόνου   ἔσονται   ἐμπαῖκται   κατὰ   τὰς
of the time   will be   mockers   ²according to ³the

ἑαυτῶν   ἐπιθυμίας   πορευόμενοι   τῶν   ἀσεβειῶν.
⁵of them-   ⁴lusts   ¹going   –   ⁶of impious
selves   things.

19 Οὗτοί   εἰσιν   οἱ   ἀποδιορίζοντες,   ψυχικοί,
These men are the [ones] making separations, natural,

πνεῦμα   μὴ   ἔχοντες.   **20** ὑμεῖς   δέ,   ἀγαπητοί,
³spirit   ¹not ²having.   But ye,   beloved,

ἐποικοδομοῦντες   ἑαυτοὺς   τῇ   ἁγιωτάτῃ   ὑμῶν
building up   yourselves in the most holy · ²of you

πίστει,   ἐν   πνεύματι   ἁγίῳ   προσευχόμενοι,
¹faith,   ³in   ⁵Spirit   ⁴[the] Holy ¹praying.

21 ἑαυτοὺς   ἐν   ἀγάπῃ   θεοῦ   τηρήσατε,
²yourselves ³in   ⁴[the] love ⁵of God   ¹keep,

προσδεχόμενοι   τὸ   ἔλεος   τοῦ   κυρίου   ἡμῶν
awaiting   the   mercy   of the Lord   of us

Ἰησοῦ   Χριστοῦ   εἰς   ζωὴν   αἰώνιον.   **22** καὶ
Jesus   Christ   to   life   eternal.   And

οὓς   μὲν   ἐλεᾶτε   διακρινομένους   **23** σώζετε
some   ²pity ye ¹[who are] wavering   ²save

ἐκ   πυρὸς   ἁρπάζοντες,   οὓς   δὲ   ἐλεᾶτε
³out of ¹fire   ¹seizing,   others   pity

ἐν   φόβῳ,   μισοῦντες   καὶ   τὸν   ἀπὸ   τῆς
with fear,   hating   even   ¹the   ⁴from ⁵the

σαρκὸς   ἐσπιλωμένον   χιτῶνα.
⁶flesh   ³having been spotted ²tunic.

24 Τῷ   δὲ   δυναμένῳ   φυλάξαι   ὑμᾶς
Now to the [one] *being* able to guard   you

ἀπταίστους   καὶ   στῆσαι   κατενώπιον   τῆς
without   and   to set   [you] before   the
stumbling

δόξης   αὐτοῦ   ἀμώμους   ἐν   ἀγαλλιάσει,
glory   of him   unblemished with   exultation,

25 μόνῳ   θεῷ   σωτῆρι   ἡμῶν   διὰ   Ἰησοῦ
to [the] only God   Saviour   of us   through Jesus

Χριστοῦ   τοῦ   κυρίου   ἡμῶν   δόξα   μεγαλωσύνη
Christ   the   Lord   of us [be] glory[,] greatness[,]

κράτος   καὶ   ἐξουσία   πρὸ   παντὸς   τοῦ
might[,]   and   authority before   all   the

αἰῶνος   καὶ   νῦν   καὶ   εἰς   πάντας   τοὺς
age   and   now   and   unto   all   the

αἰῶνας·   ἀμήν.
ages: Amen.

---

ter others for their own advantage.

A Call to Persevere

17But, dear friends, remember what the apostles of our Lord Jesus Christ foretold. 18They said to you, "In the last times there will be scoffers who will follow their own ungodly desires." 19These are the men who divide you, who follow mere natural instincts and do not have the Spirit.

20But you, dear friends, build yourselves up in your most holy faith and pray in the Holy Spirit. 21Keep yourselves in God's love as you wait for the mercy of our Lord Jesus Christ to bring you to eternal life.

22Be merciful to those who doubt; 23snatch others from the fire and save them; to others show mercy, mixed with fear—hating even the clothing stained by corrupted flesh.

Doxology

24To him who is able to keep you from falling and to present you before his glorious presence without fault and with great joy—25to the only God our Savior be glory, majesty, power and authority, through Jesus Christ our Lord, before all ages, now and forevermore! Amen.

ΑΠΟΚΑΛΥΨΙΣ ΙΩΑΝΝΟΥ
A Revelation of John

Chapter 1

The Revelation of Jesus Christ

THE Revelation of Jesus Christ, which God gave Him to show to His bond-servants, the things which must shortly take place; and He sent and communicated *it* by His angel to His bond-servant John,

2who bore witness to the word of God and to the testimony of Jesus Christ, *even* to all that he saw.

3Blessed is he who reads and those who hear the words of the prophecy, and heed the things which are written in it; for the time is near.

Message to the Seven Churches

4John to the seven churches that are in Asia: Grace to you and peace, from Him who is and who was and who is to come; and from the seven Spirits who are before His throne;

5and from Jesus Christ, the faithful witness, the first-born of the dead, and the ruler of the kings of the earth. To Him who loves us, and released us from our sins by His blood,

6and He has made us *to be* a kingdom, priests to His God and Father; to Him *be* the glory and the dominion forever and ever. Amen.

7Behold, He is coming with the clouds, and every eye will see Him, even those who pierced Him; and all the tribes of the earth will mourn over Him. Even so. Amen.

8"I am the Alpha and the Omega," says the Lord

Chapter 1

Prologue

THE revelation of Jesus Christ, which God gave him to show his servants what must soon take place. He made it known by sending his angel to his servant John, 2who testifies to everything he saw—that is, the word of God and the testimony of Jesus Christ. 3Blessed is the one who reads the words of this prophecy, and blessed are those who hear it and take to heart what is written in it, because the time is near.

Greetings and Doxology

4John,

To the seven churches in the province of Asia:

Grace and peace to you from him who is, and who was, and who is to come, and from the seven spirits[a] before his throne, 5and from Jesus Christ, who is the faithful witness, the firstborn from the dead, and the ruler of the kings of the earth.

To him who loves us and has freed us from our sins by his blood, 6and has made us to be a kingdom and priests to serve his God and Father—to him be glory and power for ever and ever! Amen.

7Look, he is coming with the clouds,
    and every eye will see him,
even those who pierced him;
    and all the peoples of
    the earth will mourn
    because of him.
            So shall it be!
                Amen.

8"I am the Alpha and the Omega," says the Lord

---

1 Ἀποκάλυψις Ἰησοῦ Χριστοῦ, ἣν
A revelation   of Jesus   Christ,   which

ἔδωκεν αὐτῷ ὁ θεός, δεῖξαι τοῖς δούλοις
²gave ³to him - ¹God, to show to the slaves

αὐτοῦ ἃ δεῖ γενέσθαι ἐν τάχει, καὶ
of him things it be- to occur with speed, and
    which hoves

ἐσήμανεν ἀποστείλας διὰ τοῦ ἀγγέλου
he signified sending through the angel

αὐτοῦ τῷ δούλῳ αὐτοῦ Ἰωάννῃ, **2** ὃς
of him to the slave of him   John, who

ἐμαρτύρησεν τὸν λόγον τοῦ θεοῦ καὶ
bore witness [of] the word   - of God and

τὴν μαρτυρίαν Ἰησοῦ Χριστοῦ, ὅσα εἶδεν.
the witness of Jesus Christ, as many as he saw.
                            things as

3 Μακάριος ὁ ἀναγινώσκων καὶ οἱ
Blessed [is] the [one] reading   and   the

ἀκούοντες τοὺς λόγους τῆς προφητείας
[ones] hearing the words of the prophecy

καὶ τηροῦντες τὰ ἐν αὐτῇ γεγραμμένα·
and keeping the things ²in ³it ¹having been written;

ὁ γὰρ καιρὸς ἐγγύς.
²the ¹for time [is] near.

4 Ἰωάννης ταῖς ἑπτὰ ἐκκλησίαις ταῖς
John to the seven churches -

ἐν τῇ Ἀσίᾳ· χάρις ὑμῖν καὶ εἰρήνη
in the Asia: Grace to you and peace

ἀπὸ ὁ ὢν καὶ ὁ ἦν καὶ ὁ ἐρχόμενος,
from the being and the was and the [one] coming,
    [one]   [one who]
= the one who is

καὶ ἀπὸ τῶν ἑπτὰ πνευμάτων ἃ ἐνώπιον
and from the seven spirits which before
                            [are]

τοῦ θρόνου αὐτοῦ, **5** καὶ ἀπὸ Ἰησοῦ
the throne of him,   and from Jesus

Χριστοῦ, ὁ μάρτυς ὁ πιστός, ὁ πρωτότοκος
Christ, the ²witness - ¹faithful, the firstborn

τῶν νεκρῶν καὶ ὁ ἄρχων τῶν βασιλέων
of the dead and the ruler of the kings

τῆς γῆς. Τῷ ἀγαπῶντι ἡμᾶς καὶ λύσαντι
of the earth. To loving us   and having
         the [one]   loosed

ἡμᾶς ἐκ τῶν ἁμαρτιῶν ἡμῶν ἐν τῷ
us out of the sins of us by the

αἵματι αὐτοῦ, **6** καὶ ἐποίησεν ἡμᾶς
blood of him,   and made   us

βασιλείαν, ἱερεῖς τῷ θεῷ καὶ πατρὶ
a kingdom, priests to the God and Father

αὐτοῦ, αὐτῷ ἡ δόξα καὶ τὸ κράτος
of him, to him[e] [is] the glory and the might
= his is

εἰς τοὺς αἰῶνας τῶν αἰώνων· ἀμήν.
unto the ages of the ages: Amen.

7 Ἰδοὺ ἔρχεται μετὰ τῶν νεφελῶν,
Behold he comes with the clouds,

καὶ ὄψεται αὐτὸν πᾶς ὀφθαλμὸς καὶ
and ³will see ⁴him ¹every ²eye and

οἵτινες αὐτὸν ἐξεκέντησαν, καὶ κόψονται
[those] who ²him ¹pierced, and ⁶will wail

ἐπ᾽ αὐτὸν πᾶσαι αἱ φυλαὶ τῆς γῆς.
⁷over ⁸him ¹all ³the ²tribes ⁴of the ⁵land.

ναί, ἀμήν.
Yes, amen.

8 Ἐγώ εἰμι τὸ ἄλφα καὶ τὸ ὦ, λέγει
I am the alpha and the omega, says

God, "who is and who was and who is to come, the Almighty."

The Patmos Vision

9I, John, your brother and fellow partaker in the tribulation and kingdom and perseverance *which are* in Jesus, was on the island called Patmos, because of the word of God and the testimony of Jesus.

10I was *a*in the Spirit on the Lord's day, and I heard behind me a loud voice like *the sound* of a trumpet, 11saying, "Write in a book what you see, and send *it* to the seven churches: to Ephesus and to Smyrna and to Pergamum and to Thyatira and to Sardis and to Philadelphia and to Laodicea."

12And I turned to see the voice that was speaking with me. And having turned I saw seven golden lampstands;

13and in the middle of the lampstands one like *b*a son of man, clothed in a robe reaching to the feet, and girded across His breast with a golden girdle.

14And His head and His hair were like white wool, like snow; and His eyes were like a flame of fire;

15and His feet *were* like burnished bronze, when it has been caused to glow in a furnace, and His voice *was* like the sound of many waters.

16And in His right hand He held seven stars; and out of His mouth came a sharp two-edged sword; and His face was like the

κύριος ὁ θεός, ὁ ὢν καὶ ὁ ἦν
[the] - God, the [one] being and the was
Lord =the one who is [one who]

καὶ ὁ ἐρχόμενος, ὁ παντοκράτωρ.
and the [one] coming, the Almighty.

9 Ἐγὼ Ἰωάννης, ὁ ἀδελφὸς ὑμῶν καὶ
I John, the brother of you and

συγκοινωνὸς ἐν τῇ θλίψει καὶ βασιλείᾳ
co-sharer in the affliction and kingdom

καὶ ὑπομονῇ ἐν Ἰησοῦ, ἐγενόμην ἐν
and endurance in Jesus, came to be in

τῇ νήσῳ τῇ καλουμένῃ Πάτμῳ διὰ
the island - being called Patmos on account of

τὸν λόγον τοῦ θεοῦ καὶ τὴν μαρτυρίαν
the word - of God and the witness

Ἰησοῦ. 10 ἐγενόμην ἐν πνεύματι ἐν
of Jesus. I came to be in [the] spirit on

τῇ κυριακῇ ἡμέρᾳ, καὶ ἤκουσα ὀπίσω
the imperial* day, and heard behind

μου φωνὴν μεγάλην ὡς σάλπιγγος
me ¹voice ¹a great(loud) as of a trumpet

11 λεγούσης· ὃ βλέπεις γράψον εἰς βιβλίον
saying: What thou seest write in a scroll

καὶ πέμψον ταῖς ἑπτὰ ἐκκλησίαις, εἰς
and send to the seven churches, to

Ἔφεσον καὶ εἰς Σμύρναν καὶ εἰς Πέργαμον
Ephesus and to Smyrna and to Pergamum

καὶ εἰς Θυάτιρα καὶ εἰς Σάρδεις καὶ
and to Thyatira and to Sardis and

εἰς Φιλαδέλφειαν καὶ εἰς Λαοδίκειαν.
to Philadelphia and to Laodicea.

12 Καὶ ἐπέστρεψα βλέπειν τὴν φωνὴν
And I turned to see the voice

ἥτις ἐλάλει μετ᾽ ἐμοῦ· καὶ ἐπιστρέψας
which spoke with me; and having turned

εἶδον ἑπτὰ λυχνίας χρυσᾶς, 13 καὶ ἐν
I saw seven ²lampstands ¹golden, and in

μέσῳ τῶν λυχνιῶν ὅμοιον υἱὸν ἀνθρώπου,
[the] of the lampstands [one] like a son of man,*
midst

ἐνδεδυμένον ποδήρη καὶ περιεζωσμένον
having been clothed to the feet and having been girdled round

πρὸς τοῖς μαστοῖς ζώνην χρυσᾶν· 14 ἡ
at the breasts ²girdle ¹[with] a golden; *the

δὲ κεφαλὴ αὐτοῦ καὶ αἱ τρίχες λευκαὶ
¹and head of him and the hairs white

ὡς ἔριον λευκὸν ὡς χιών, καὶ οἱ ὀφθαλμοὶ
as wool white as snow, and the eyes

αὐτοῦ ὡς φλὸξ πυρός, 15 καὶ οἱ πόδες
of him as a flame of fire, and the feet

αὐτοῦ ὅμοιοι χαλκολιβάνῳ ὡς ἐν καμίνῳ
of him like to burnished brass as ²in ¹a furnace

πεπυρωμένης, καὶ ἡ φωνὴ αὐτοῦ ὡς
¹having been fired, and the voice of him as

φωνὴ ὑδάτων πολλῶν, 16 καὶ ἔχων ἐν
a sound waters of many, and having in

τῇ δεξιᾷ χειρὶ αὐτοῦ ἀστέρας ἑπτά,
the right hand of him ²stars ¹seven,

καὶ ἐκ τοῦ στόματος αὐτοῦ ῥομφαία
and out of the mouth of him ⁴sword

δίστομος ὀξεῖα ἐκπορευομένη, καὶ ἡ ὄψις
³two- ²a sharp ¹proceeding, and the face
mouthed(edged)

God, "who is, and who was, and who is to come, the Almighty."

One Like a Son of Man

9I, John, your brother and companion in the suffering and kingdom and patient endurance that are ours in Jesus, was on the island of Patmos because of the word of God and the testimony of Jesus. 10On the Lord's Day I was in the Spirit, and I heard behind me a loud voice like a trumpet, 11which said: "Write on a scroll what you see and send it to the seven churches: to Ephesus, Smyrna, Pergamum, Thyatira, Sardis, Philadelphia and Laodicea."

12I turned around to see the voice that was speaking to me. And when I turned I saw seven golden lampstands, 13and among the lampstands was someone "like a son of man," *b* dressed in a robe reaching down to his feet and with a golden sash around his chest. 14His head and hair were white like wool, as white as snow, and his eyes were like blazing fire. 15His feet were like bronze glowing in a furnace, and his voice was like the sound of rushing waters. 16In his right hand he held seven stars, and out of his mouth came a sharp double-edged sword. His face was like

---

*a*Or, in spirit
*b*Or, the Son of Man

* See I. Cor. 11. 20.

* Anarthrous; see also ch. 14. 14 and John 5. 27, and *cf.* Heb. 2. 6.   *b*13 Daniel 7:13

sun shining in its strength.
17And when I saw Him, I fell at His feet as a dead man. And He laid His right hand upon me, saying, "Do not be afraid; I am the first and the last,
18and the living One; and I was dead, and behold, I am alive forevermore, and I have the keys of death and of Hades.
19"Write therefore the things which you have seen, and the things which are, and the things which shall take place after these things.
20"As for the mystery of the seven stars which you saw in My right hand, and the seven golden lampstands: the seven stars are the angels of the seven churches, and the seven lampstands are the seven churches.

αὐτοῦ ὡς ὁ ἥλιος φαίνει ἐν τῇ δυνάμει
of him as the sun shines in the power

αὐτοῦ. 17 Καὶ ὅτε εἶδον αὐτόν, ἔπεσα
of it. And when I saw him, I fell

πρὸς τοὺς πόδας αὐτοῦ ὡς νεκρός· καὶ
at the feet of him as dead; and

ἔθηκεν τὴν δεξιὰν αὐτοῦ ἐπ᾿ ἐμὲ λέγων·
he placed the right [hand] of him on me saying:

μὴ φοβοῦ· ἐγώ εἰμι ὁ πρῶτος καὶ
Fear not: I am the first and

ὁ ἔσχατος 18 καὶ ὁ ζῶν, καὶ ἐγενόμην
the last and the living [one], and I became

νεκρὸς καὶ ἰδοὺ ζῶν εἰμι εἰς τοὺς
dead and behold ³living ¹I am unto the

αἰῶνας τῶν αἰώνων, καὶ ἔχω τὰς κλεῖς
ages of the ages, and I have the keys

τοῦ θανάτου καὶ τοῦ ᾅδου. 19 γράψον
– of death and – of hades. Write thou

οὖν ἃ εἶδες καὶ ἃ εἰσὶν καὶ ἃ
there- [the] thou and [the] are and [the]
fore things sawest things things
which which which

μέλλει γενέσθαι μετὰ ταῦτα. 20 τὸ
(is)are about to occur after these things. The

μυστήριον τῶν ἑπτὰ ἀστέρων οὓς εἶδες
mystery of the seven stars which thou sawest

ἐπὶ τῆς· δεξιᾶς μου, καὶ τὰς ἑπτὰ
on the right [hand] of me, and the seven

λυχνίας τὰς χρυσᾶς· οἱ ἑπτὰ ἀστέρες
¹lampstands – ¹golden: the seven stars

ἄγγελοι τῶν ἑπτὰ ἐκκλησιῶν εἰσιν, καὶ
messengers* of the seven churches are, and

αἱ λυχνίαι αἱ ἑπτὰ ἑπτὰ ἐκκλησίαι εἰσίν.
the ²lampstands – ¹seven ⁴seven ⁵churches ³are.

---

the sun shining in all its brilliance.
17When I saw him, I fell at his feet as though dead. Then he placed his right hand on me and said: "Do not be afraid. I am the First and the Last. 18I am the Living One; I was dead, and behold I am alive for ever and ever! And I hold the keys of death and Hades.
19"Write, therefore, what you have seen, what is now and what will take place later. 20The mystery of the seven stars that you saw in my right hand and the seven golden lampstands is this: The seven stars are the angels[c] of the seven churches, and the seven lampstands are the seven churches.

Chapter 2

Message to Ephesus

"TO the angel of the church in Ephesus write:
The One who holds the seven stars in His right hand, the One who walks among the seven golden lampstands, says this: 2'I know your deeds and your toil and perseverance, and that you cannot endure evil men, and you put to the test those who call themselves apostles, and they are not, and you found them to be false;
3and you have perseverance and have endured for My name's sake, and have not grown weary.
4'But I have this against you, that you have left your

---

2 Τῷ ἀγγέλῳ τῆς ἐν Ἐφέσῳ ἐκκλησίας
To the messenger ¹of the ²in ⁴Ephesus ²church

γράψον·
write thou:

Τάδε λέγει ὁ κρατῶν τοὺς ἑπτὰ
These things says the [one] holding the seven

ἀστέρας ἐν τῇ δεξιᾷ αὐτοῦ, ὁ περιπατῶν
stars in the right [hand] of him, the [one] walking

ἐν μέσῳ τῶν ἑπτὰ λυχνιῶν τῶν
in [the] midst of the seven ²lampstands –

χρυσῶν· 2 οἶδα τὰ ἔργα σου καὶ τὸν
¹golden: I know the works of thee and the

κόπον καὶ τὴν ὑπομονήν σου, καὶ ὅτι
labour and the endurance of thee, and that

οὐ δύνῃ βαστάσαι κακούς, καὶ ἐπείρασας
thou canst not to bear bad men, and didst try

τοὺς λέγοντας ἑαυτοὺς ἀποστόλους καὶ
the [ones] say(call)ing themselves apostles and

οὐκ εἰσίν, καὶ εὗρες αὐτοὺς ψευδεῖς·
are not, and didst find them liars;

3 καὶ ὑπομονὴν ἔχεις, καὶ ἐβάστασας
and ²endurance ¹thou hast, and didst bear

διὰ τὸ ὄνομά μου, καὶ οὐ κεκοπίακας.
be- the name of me, and hast not grown weary.
cause of

4 ἀλλὰ ἔχω κατὰ σοῦ ὅτι τὴν ἀγάπην
But I have against thee that ³the ⁴love

Chapter 2

To the Church in Ephesus

"TO the angel[d] of the church in Ephesus write:

These are the words of him who holds the seven stars in his right hand and walks among the seven golden lampstands: 2I know your deeds, your hard work and your perseverance. I know that you cannot tolerate wicked men, that you have tested those who claim to be apostles but are not, and have found them false. 3You have persevered and have endured hardships for my name, and have not grown weary.
4Yet I hold this against you: You have

---

* This, of course, is the prime meaning of the word: whether these beings were " messengers " from the churches, or supernatural beings, " angels " as usually understood, is a matter of exegesis.

c20 Or messengers
d1 Or messenger; also in verses 8, 12 and 18

first love.
5'Remember therefore from where you have fallen, and repent and do the deeds you did at first; or else I am coming to you, and will remove your lampstand out of its place—unless you repent.
6'Yet this you do have, that you hate the deeds of the Nicolaitans, which I also hate.
7'He who has an ear, let him hear what the Spirit says to the churches. To him who overcomes, I will grant to eat of the tree of life, which is in the Paradise of God.'

Message to Smyrna
8''And to the angel of the church in Smyrna write: The first and the last, who was dead, and has come to life, says this:
9'I know your tribulation and your poverty (but you are rich), and the blasphemy by those who say they are Jews and are not, but are a synagogue of Satan.
10'Do not fear what you are about to suffer. Behold, the devil is about to cast some of you into prison, that you may be tested, and you will have tribulation ten days. Be faithful until death, and I will give you the crown of life.
11'He who has an ear, let him hear what the Spirit says to the churches. He who overcomes shall not be hurt by the second death.'

Message to Pergamum
12''And to the angel of the church in Pergamum write:

σου   τὴν   πρώτην   ἀφῆκας.   **5** μνημόνευε
5'of thee -   2first   1thou didst leave.   Remember

οὖν   πόθεν   πέπτωκας,   καὶ   μετανόησον
therefore whence thou hast fallen, and   repent

καὶ   τὰ   πρῶτα   ἔργα   ποίησον·   εἰ   δὲ
and   2the   3first   4works   1do;   and if

μή,   ἔρχομαί   σοι   καὶ   κινήσω   τὴν   λυχνίαν
not, I am coming to thee   and   will move   the   lampstand

σου   ἐκ   τοῦ   τόπου   αὐτῆς,   ἐὰν   μὴ
of thee out of   the   place   of it,   unless

μετανοήσῃς.   **6** ἀλλὰ   τοῦτο   ἔχεις,   ὅτι
thou repentest.   But   this   thou hast,   that

μισεῖς   τὰ   ἔργα   τῶν   Νικολαϊτῶν,   ἃ
thou hatest the   works of the   Nicolaitans,   which

κἀγὼ   μισῶ.   **7** Ὁ   ἔχων   οὓς   ἀκουσάτω
I also   hate.   The [one] having an ear   let him hear

τί   τὸ   πνεῦμα   λέγει   ταῖς   ἐκκλησίαις.
what   the   Spirit   says   to the   churches.

Τῷ   νικῶντι   δώσω   αὐτῷ   φαγεῖν   ἐκ
To the   overcoming   I will give to him   to eat   of
[one]

τοῦ   ξύλου   τῆς   ζωῆς,   ὅ   ἐστιν   ἐν   τῷ
the   tree   -   of life,   which   is   in   the

παραδείσῳ   τοῦ   θεοῦ.
paradise   of God.

8 Καὶ   τῷ   ἀγγέλῳ   τῆς   ἐν   Σμύρνῃ
And   to the   messenger   1of the   2in   4Smyrna

ἐκκλησίας   γράψον·
3church   write thou:

Τάδε   λέγει   ὁ   πρῶτος   καὶ   ὁ   ἔσχατος,
These things says   the   first   and   the   last,

ὃς   ἐγένετο   νεκρὸς   καὶ   ἔζησεν·   **9** οἶδά
who   became   dead   and   lived [again]:   I know

σου   τὴν   θλῖψιν   καὶ   τὴν   πτωχείαν,   ἀλλὰ
4of thee 1the   2affliction 3and   4the   3poverty,   but

πλούσιος   εἶ,   καὶ   τὴν   βλασφημίαν   ἐκ
rich   thou art,   and   the   railing   of

τῶν   λεγόντων   Ἰουδαίους   εἶναι   ἑαυτούς,
the [ones] say(call)ing   3Jews   2to be   1themselves,

καὶ   οὐκ   εἰσὶν   ἀλλὰ   συναγωγὴ   τοῦ   σατανᾶ.
and   they are not   but   a synagogue   -   of Satan.

10 μὴ   φοβοῦ   ἃ   μέλλεις   πάσχειν.   ἰδοὺ
Do not fear [the]   thou art   to suffer.   Behold[,]
          things which about

μέλλει   βάλλειν   ὁ   διάβολος   ἐξ   ὑμῶν
3is about   4to cast   1the   2devil   [some] of   you

εἰς   φυλακὴν   ἵνα   πειρασθῆτε,   καὶ   ἕξετε
into   prison   in order that ye may be tried, and ye will have

θλῖψιν   ἡμερῶν   δέκα.   γίνου   πιστὸς   ἄχρι
affliction   2days   1ten.   Be thou   faithful   until

θανάτου,   καὶ   δώσω   σοι   τὸν   στέφανον
death,   and   I will give thee   the   crown

τῆς   ζωῆς.   **11** Ὁ   ἔχων   οὓς   ἀκουσάτω
-    of life.   The [one] having an ear   let him hear

τί   τὸ   πνεῦμα   λέγει   ταῖς   ἐκκλησίαις.
what   the   Spirit   says   to the   churches.

Ὁ   νικῶν   οὐ   μὴ   ἀδικηθῇ   ἐκ   τοῦ   θανάτου
The   over-   by no   will be   by   the   2death
[one] coming means   hurt

τοῦ   δευτέρου.
-    1second.

12 Καὶ   τῷ   ἀγγέλῳ   τῆς   ἐν   Περγάμῳ
And   to the   messenger   1of the   2in   4Pergamum

ἐκκλησίας   γράψον·
3church   write thou:

forsaken your first love.
5Remember the height from which you have fallen! Repent and do the things you did at first. If you do not repent, I will come to you and remove your lampstand from its place.
6But you have this in your favor: You hate the practices of the Nicolaitans, which I also hate.
7He who has an ear, let him hear what the Spirit says to the churches. To him who overcomes, I will give the right to eat from the tree of life, which is in the paradise of God.

To the Church in Smyrna
8''To the angel of the church in Smyrna write:

These are the words of him who is the First and the Last, who died and came to life again.
9I know your afflictions and your poverty—yet you are rich! I know the slander of those who say they are Jews and are not, but are a synagogue of Satan. 10Do not be afraid of what you are about to suffer. I tell you, the devil will put some of you in prison to test you, and you will suffer persecution for ten days. Be faithful, even to the point of death, and I will give you the crown of life.
11He who has an ear, let him hear what the Spirit says to the churches. He who overcomes will not be hurt at all by the second death.

To the Church in Pergamum
12''To the angel of the church in Pergamum write:

The One who has the sharp two-edged sword says this:

13'I know where you dwell, where Satan's throne is; and you hold fast My name, and did not deny My faith, even in the days of Antipas, My witness, My faithful one, who was killed among you, where Satan dwells.

14'But I have a few things against you, because you have there some who hold the teaching of Balaam, who kept teaching Balak to put a stumbling block before the sons of Israel, to eat things sacrificed to idols, and to commit *acts of immorality.*

15'Thus you also have some who in the same way hold the teaching of the Nicolaitans.

16'Repent therefore; or else I am coming to you quickly, and I will make war against them with the sword of My mouth.

17'He who has an ear, let him hear what the Spirit says to the churches. To him who overcomes, to him I will give *some* of the hidden manna, and I will give him a white stone, and a new name written on the stone which no one knows but he who receives it.'

Message to Thyatira

18"And to the angel of the church in Thyatira write:
The Son of God, who has eyes like a flame of fire, and His feet are like burnished bronze, says this:

19'I know your deeds, and your love and faith and service and perseverance, and that your deeds of late are greater than at first.

Τάδε λέγει ὁ ἔχων τὴν ῥομφαίαν τὴν
These things says the having the ²sword –
    [one]

δίστομον τὴν ὀξεῖαν· 13 *οἶδα ποῦ κατοικεῖς·*
¹two-mouthed – ²sharp: I know where thou
(edged)   dwellest;

ὅπου ὁ θρόνος τοῦ σατανᾶ· καὶ κρατεῖς
where the throne – of Satan [is]; and thou holdest

τὸ ὄνομά μου, καὶ οὐκ ἠρνήσω τὴν
the name of me, and didst not deny the

πίστιν μου καὶ ἐν ταῖς ἡμέραις Ἀντιπᾶς
faith of me even in the days of Antipas

ὁ μάρτυς μου ὁ πιστός μου, ὃς
¹the ²witness ⁴of me the ³faithful *of me,* who

ἀπεκτάνθη παρ᾽ ὑμῖν, ὅπου ὁ σατανᾶς
was killed among you, where – Satan

κατοικεῖ. 14 *ἀλλ᾽ ἔχω κατὰ σοῦ ὀλίγα,*
dwells. But I have against thee a few
    things,

ὅτι ἔχεις ἐκεῖ κρατοῦντας τὴν διδαχὴν
be- thou there [ones] holding the teaching
cause hast

Βαλαάμ, ὃς ἐδίδασκεν τῷ Βαλὰκ βαλεῖν
of Balaam, who taught – Balak to cast

σκάνδαλον ἐνώπιον τῶν υἱῶν Ἰσραήλ,
a stumbling-block before the sons of Israel,

φαγεῖν εἰδωλόθυτα καὶ πορνεῦσαι. 15 *οὕτως*
to eat idol sacrifices and to commit fornication. So

ἔχεις καὶ σὺ κρατοῦντας τὴν διδαχὴν
²hast ³also ¹thou [ones] holding the teaching

τῶν Νικολαϊτῶν ὁμοίως. 16 *μετανόησον*
of the Nicolaitans likewise. Repent thou

οὖν· εἰ δὲ μή, ἔρχομαί σοι ταχὺ καὶ
therefore; otherwise, I am coming to thee quickly and

πολεμήσω μετ᾽ αὐτῶν ἐν τῇ ῥομφαίᾳ
will fight with them with the sword

τοῦ στόματός μου. 17 *Ὁ ἔχων οὖς*
of the mouth of me. The [one] having an ear

ἀκουσάτω τί τὸ πνεῦμα λέγει ταῖς
let him hear what the Spirit says to the

ἐκκλησίαις. Τῷ νικῶντι δώσω αὐτῷ
churches. To the [one] overcoming I will give *to him*

τοῦ μάννα τοῦ κεκρυμμένου, καὶ δώσω
of the ²manna – ¹having been hidden, and I will give

αὐτῷ ψῆφον λευκήν, καὶ ἐπὶ τὴν ψῆφον
him ²stone ¹a white, and on the stone

ὄνομα καινὸν γεγραμμένον, ὃ οὐδεὶς οἶδεν
²name ¹a new *having been* written, which no man knows

εἰ μὴ ὁ λαμβάνων.
except the [one] receiving [it].

18 *Καὶ τῷ ἀγγέλῳ τῆς ἐν Θυατίροις*
And to the messenger ¹of the ²in ⁴Thyatira

ἐκκλησίας γράψον·
³church write thou:

Τάδε λέγει ὁ υἱὸς τοῦ θεοῦ, ὁ ἔχων
These things says the Son – of God, the having
    [one]

τοὺς ὀφθαλμοὺς [αὐτοῦ] ὡς φλόγα πυρός,
the eyes of him as a flame of fire,

καὶ οἱ πόδες αὐτοῦ ὅμοιοι χαλκολιβάνῳ·
and the feet of him like *to* burnished brass:

19 *οἶδά σου τὰ ἔργα καὶ τὴν ἀγάπην*
I know of thee the works and the love

καὶ τὴν πίστιν καὶ τὴν διακονίαν καὶ
and the faith and the ministry and

τὴν ὑπομονήν σου, καὶ τὰ ἔργα σου
the endurance *of thee,* and the ²works ³of thee

τὰ ἔσχατα πλείονα τῶν πρώτων. 20 *ἀλλὰ*
the ¹last more [than] the first. But

These are the words of him who has the sharp, double-edged sword. 13I know where you live—where Satan has his throne. Yet you remain true to my name. You did not renounce your faith in me, even in the days of Antipas, my faithful witness, who was put to death in your city—where Satan lives.

14Nevertheless, I have a few things against you: You have people there who hold to the teaching of Balaam, who taught Balak to entice the Israelites to sin by eating food sacrificed to idols and by committing sexual immorality. 15Likewise you also have those who hold to the teaching of the Nicolaitans. 16Repent therefore! Otherwise, I will soon come to you and will fight against them with the sword of my mouth.

17He who has an ear, let him hear what the Spirit says to the churches. To him who overcomes, I will give some of the hidden manna. I will also give him a white stone with a new name written on it, known only to him who receives it.

To the Church in Thyatira

18"To the angel of the church in Thyatira write:

These are the words of the Son of God, whose eyes are like blazing fire and whose feet are like burnished bronze. 19I know your deeds, your love and faith, your service and perseverance, and that you are now doing more than you did at first.

20'But I have *this* against you, that you tolerate the woman Jezebel, who calls herself a prophetess, and she teaches and leads My bond-servants astray, so that they commit *acts of* immorality and eat things sacrificed to idols. 21'And I gave her time to repent; and she does not want to repent of her immorality. 22'Behold, I will cast her upon a bed *of sickness*, and those who commit adultery with her into great tribulation, unless they repent of her deeds. 23'And I will kill her children with pestilence; and all the churches will know that I am He who searches the minds and hearts; and I will give to each one of you according to your deeds. 24'But I say to you, the rest who are in Thyatira, who do not hold this teaching, who have not known the deep things of Satan, as they call them—I place no other burden on you. 25'Nevertheless what you have, hold fast until I come. 26'And he who overcomes, and he who keeps My deeds until the end, TO HIM I WILL GIVE AUTHORITY OVER THE NATIONS; 27'AND HE SHALL RULE THEM WITH A ROD OF IRON, AS THE VESSELS OF THE POTTER ARE BROKEN TO PIECES, as I also have received *authority* from My Father; 28and I will give him the morning star. 29'He who has an ear, let him hear what the Spirit says to the churches.'

ἔχω κατὰ σοῦ ὅτι ἀφεῖς τὴν γυναῖκα
I have against thee that thou permittest the woman
'Ιεζάβελ, ἡ λέγουσα ἑαυτὴν προφῆτιν,
Jezabel, the [one] say(call)ing herself a prophetess,
καὶ διδάσκει καὶ πλανᾷ τοὺς ἐμοὺς
and she teaches and deceives – my
δούλους πορνεῦσαι καὶ φαγεῖν εἰδωλόθυτα·
slaves to commit fornication and to eat idol sacrifices;
21 καὶ ἔδωκα αὐτῇ χρόνον ἵνα μετανοήσῃ,
and I gave her time in order that she might repent,
καὶ οὐ θέλει μετανοῆσαι ἐκ τῆς πορνείας
and she wishes not to repent of the fornication
αὐτῆς. 22 ἰδοὺ βάλλω αὐτὴν εἰς κλίνην,
of her. Behold[,] I am casting her into a bed,
καὶ τοὺς μοιχεύοντας μετ' αὐτῆς εἰς
and the [ones] committing adultery with her into
θλῖψιν μεγάλην, ἐὰν μὴ μετανοήσωσιν
¹affliction ¹great, unless they shall repent
ἐκ τῶν ἔργων αὐτῆς· 23 καὶ τὰ τέκνα
of the works of her; and the children
αὐτῆς ἀποκτενῶ ἐν θανάτῳ· καὶ γνώσονται
of her I will kill with death; and ⁴will know
πᾶσαι αἱ ἐκκλησίαι ὅτι ἐγώ εἰμι ὁ
¹all ²the ³churches that I am the [one]
ἐρευνῶν νεφροὺς καὶ καρδίας, καὶ δώσω
searching kidneys and hearts, and I will give
ὑμῖν ἑκάστῳ κατὰ τὰ ἔργα ὑμῶν.
to you each one according to the works of you.
24 ὑμῖν δὲ λέγω τοῖς λοιποῖς τοῖς ἐν
But to you I say to the rest – in
Θυατίροις, ὅσοι οὐκ ἔχουσιν τὴν διδαχὴν
Thyatira, as many as have not – teaching
ταύτην, οἵτινες οὐκ ἔγνωσαν τὰ βαθέα
this, who knew not the deep things
τοῦ σατανᾶ, ὡς λέγουσιν· οὐ βάλλω
of Satan, as they say: I am not casting
ἐφ' ὑμᾶς ἄλλο βάρος· 25 πλὴν ὃ ἔχετε
on you another burden; nevertheless what ye have
κρατήσατε ἄχρι οὗ ἂν ἥξω. 26 Καὶ
hold until I shall come. And
ὁ νικῶν καὶ ὁ τηρῶν ἄχρι τέλους τὰ
the over- and the keeping until [the] the [one] coming [one] end
ἔργα μου, δώσω αὐτῷ ἐξουσίαν ἐπὶ
works of me, I will give him authority over
τῶν ἐθνῶν, 27 καὶ ποιμανεῖ αὐτοὺς ἐν
the nations, and he will shepherd them with
ῥάβδῳ σιδηρᾷ, ὡς τὰ σκεύη τὰ κεραμικὰ
²staff ¹an iron, as *the* ²vessels ¹clay
συντρίβεται, ὡς κἀγὼ εἴληφα παρὰ
is(are) broken, as I also have received from
τοῦ πατρός μου, 28 καὶ δώσω αὐτῷ τὸν
the Father of me, and I will give him the
ἀστέρα τὸν πρωϊνόν. 29 Ὁ ἔχων οὖς
²star – ¹morning. The [one] having an ear
ἀκουσάτω τί τὸ πνεῦμα λέγει ταῖς
let him hear what the Spirit says to the
ἐκκλησίαις.
churches.

20Nevertheless, I have this against you: You tolerate that woman Jezebel, who calls herself a prophetess. By her teaching she misleads my servants into sexual immorality and the eating of food sacrificed to idols. 21I have given her time to repent of her immorality, but she is unwilling. 22So I will cast her on a bed of suffering, and I will make those who commit adultery with her suffer intensely, unless they repent of her ways. 23I will strike her children dead. Then all the churches will know that I am he who searches hearts and minds, and I will repay each of you according to your deeds. 24Now I say to the rest of you in Thyatira, to you who do not hold to her teaching and have not learned Satan's so-called deep secrets (I will not impose any other burden on you): 25Only hold on to what you have until I come. 26To him who overcomes and does my will to the end, I will give authority over the nations— 27'He will rule them with an iron scepter; he will dash them to pieces like pottery' ᵉ— just as I have received authority from my Father. 28I will also give him the morning star. 29He who has an ear, let him hear what the Spirit says to the churches.

<hr>
ᶜ Some mss. read *their*   ᵉ27 Psalm 2:9

Chapter 3

Message to Sardis

" AND to the angel of the church in Sardis write:

He who has the seven Spirits of God, and the seven stars, says this: 'I know your deeds, that you have a name that you are alive, but you are dead. 2'Wake up, and strengthen the things that remain, which were about to die; for I have not found your deeds completed in the sight of My God. 3'Remember therefore what you have received and heard; and keep *it*, and repent. If therefore you will not wake up, I will come like a thief, and you will not know at what hour I will come upon you. 4'But you have a few people in Sardis who have not soiled their garments; and they will walk with Me in white; for they are worthy. 5'He who overcomes shall thus be clothed in white garments; and I will not erase his name from the book of life, and I will confess his name before My Father, and before His angels. 6'He who has an ear, let him hear what the Spirit says to the churches.'

Message to Philadelphia

7'And to the angel of the church in Philadelphia write:

He who is holy, who is true, who has the key of David, who opens and no one will shut, and who shuts and no one opens, says this: 8'I know your ᵈdeeds. Behold, I have put before you an open door which no one can shut, because you have a little power, and have kept My word, and have not denied My name. 9'Behold, I will cause *those* of the synagogue of

---

3

Καὶ τῷ ἀγγέλῳ τῆς ἐν Σάρδεσιν
And to the messenger ¹of the ²in ⁴Sardis
ἐκκλησίας γράψον·
³church write thou:
Τάδε λέγει ὁ ἔχων τὰ ἑπτὰ πνεύματα
These things says the having the seven Spirits
[one]
τοῦ θεοῦ καὶ τοὺς ἑπτὰ ἀστέρας· οἶδά
- of God and the seven stars: I know
σου τὰ ἔργα, ὅτι ὄνομα ἔχεις ὅτι ζῇς,
³of ¹the ²works, that a name thou that thou
thee hast livest,
καὶ νεκρὸς εἶ. 2 γίνου γρηγορῶν, καὶ
and [yet] ³dead ¹thou art. Be thou watching, and
στήρισον τὰ λοιπὰ ἃ ἔμελλον ἀποθανεῖν·
establish the remain- which were to die;
ing about
οὐ γὰρ εὕρηκά σου ἔργα πεπληρωμένα
for I have not found of thee works *having been* fulfilled
ἐνώπιον τοῦ θεοῦ μου· 3 μνημόνευε οὖν
before the God of me; remember therefore
πῶς εἴληφας καὶ ἤκουσας, καὶ τήρει
how thou hast received and didst hear, and keep
καὶ μετανόησον. ἐὰν οὖν μὴ γρηγορήσῃς,
and repent. If therefore thou dost not watch,
ἥξω ὡς κλέπτης, καὶ οὐ μὴ γνῷς ποίαν
I will as a thief, and by no thou at what
come means knowest
ὥραν ἥξω ἐπὶ σέ. 4 ἀλλὰ ἔχεις ὀλίγα
hour I will come on thee. But thou hast a few
ὀνόματα ἐν Σάρδεσιν ἃ οὐκ ἐμόλυναν τὰ
names in Sardis which did not defile the
ἱμάτια αὐτῶν, καὶ περιπατήσουσιν μετ'
garments of them, and they shall walk with
ἐμοῦ ἐν λευκοῖς, ὅτι ἄξιοί εἰσιν. 5 Ὁ
me in white because ³worthy ¹they are. The
[garments], [one]
νικῶν οὕτως περιβαλεῖται ἐν ἱματίοις
overcoming ²thus ¹shall be clothed in ²garments
λευκοῖς, καὶ οὐ μὴ ἐξαλείψω τὸ ὄνομα
¹white, and by no means will I blot *out* the name
αὐτοῦ ἐκ τῆς βίβλου τῆς ζωῆς, καὶ
of him out of the scroll - of life, and
ὁμολογήσω τὸ ὄνομα αὐτοῦ ἐνώπιον τοῦ
I will confess the name of him before the
πατρός μου καὶ ἐνώπιον τῶν ἀγγέλων
Father of me and before the angels
αὐτοῦ. 6 Ὁ ἔχων οὖς ἀκουσάτω τί τὸ
of him. The [one] having an ear let him hear what the
πνεῦμα λέγει ταῖς ἐκκλησίαις.
Spirit says to the churches.

7

Καὶ τῷ ἀγγέλῳ τῆς ἐν Φιλαδελφείᾳ
And to the messenger ¹of the ²in ⁴Philadelphia
ἐκκλησίας γράψον·
³church write thou:
Τάδε λέγει ὁ ἅγιος, ὁ ἀληθινός, ὁ
These says the holy, the true, the
things [one], [one], [one]
ἔχων τὴν κλεῖν Δαυίδ, ὁ ἀνοίγων καὶ
having the key of David, the [one] opening and
οὐδεὶς κλείσει, καὶ κλείων καὶ οὐδεὶς
no one shall shut, and shutting and no one
ἀνοίγει· 8 οἶδά σου τὰ ἔργα· ἰδοὺ
opens: I know of thee the works; behold[,]
δέδωκα ἐνώπιόν σου θύραν ἠνεωγμένην,
I have given before thee a door *having been* opened,

Chapter 3

To the Church in Sardis

" TO the angelᶠ of the church in Sardis write:

These are the words of him who holds the seven spiritsᵍ of God and the seven stars. I know your deeds; you have a reputation of being alive, but you are dead. 2Wake up! Strengthen what remains and is about to die, for I have not found your deeds complete in the sight of my God. 3Remember, therefore, what you have received and heard; obey it, and repent. But if you do not wake up, I will come like a thief, and you will not know at what time I will come to you.

4Yet you have a few people in Sardis who have not soiled their clothes. They will walk with me, dressed in white, for they are worthy. 5He who overcomes will, like them, be dressed in white. I will never blot out his name from the book of life, but will acknowledge his name before my Father and his angels. 6He who has an ear, let him hear what the Spirit says to the churches.

To the Church in Philadelphia

7'To the angel of the church in Philadelphia write:

These are the words of him who is holy and true, who holds the key of David. What he opens no one can shut, and what he shuts no one can open. 8I know your deeds. See, I have placed before you an open door that no one can shut. I know that you have little strength, yet you have kept my word and have not denied my name. 9I will make those who are of the synagogue of Satan,

---

ᵈOr, deeds (behold . . . shut), that you

ᶠ1 Or messenger; also in verses 7 and 14
ᵍ1 Or the sevenfold Spirit

Satan, who say that they are Jews, and are not, but lie—behold, I will make them to come and bow down at your feet, and to know that I have loved you.

10‘Because you have kept the word of My perseverance, I also will keep you from the hour of testing, that *hour* which is about to come upon the whole world, to test those who dwell upon the earth.

11‘I am coming quickly; hold fast what you have, in order that no one take your crown.

12‘He who overcomes, I will make him a pillar in the temple of My God, and he will not go out from it anymore; and I will write upon him the name of My God, and the name of the city of My God, the new Jerusalem, which comes down out of heaven from My God, and My new name.

13‘He who has an ear, let him hear what the Spirit says to the churches.’

Message to Laodicea

14“And to the angel of the church in Laodicea write: The Amen, the faithful and true Witness, the ᵉBeginning of the creation of God, says this:

15‘I know your deeds,

ἦν οὐδεὶς δύναται κλεῖσαι αὐτήν· ὅτι
which no one can *to* shut it; because

μικρὰν ἔχεις δύναμιν, καὶ ἐτήρησάς μου
²a little ¹thou hast power, and didst keep of me

τὸν λόγον καὶ οὐκ ἠρνήσω τὸ ὄνομά
the word and didst not deny the name

μου. 9 ἰδοὺ διδῶ ἐκ τῆς συναγωγῆς
of me. Behold[,] I may [some] the synagogue
(will) give of

τοῦ σατανᾶ, τῶν λεγόντων ἑαυτοὺς
- of Satan, the [ones] say(call)ing themselves

Ἰουδαίους εἶναι, καὶ οὐκ εἰσὶν ἀλλὰ
Jews to be, and they are not but

ψεύδονται· ἰδοὺ ποιήσω αὐτοὺς ἵνα
they lie; behold[,] I will make them in order
that

ἥξουσιν καὶ προσκυνήσουσιν ἐνώπιον τῶν
they shall and they shall worship before the
come

ποδῶν σου, καὶ γνῶσιν ὅτι ἐγὼ ἠγάπησά
feet of thee, and they that I loved
shall know

σε. 10 ὅτι ἐτήρησας τὸν λόγον τῆς
thee. Because thou didst keep the word of the

ὑπομονῆς μου, κἀγώ σε τηρήσω ἐκ
endurance of me, I also ²thee ¹will keep out of

τῆς ὥρας τοῦ πειρασμοῦ τῆς μελλούσης
the hour - of trial - being about

ἔρχεσθαι ἐπὶ τῆς οἰκουμένης ὅλης, πειράσαι
to come on ²the ³inhabited [earth] ¹all, to try

τοὺς κατοικοῦντας ἐπὶ τῆς γῆς. 11 ἔρχομαι
the [ones] dwelling on the earth. I am coming

ταχύ· κράτει ὃ ἔχεις, ἵνα μηδεὶς λάβῃ
quickly; hold what thou in order no one takes
hast,

τὸν στέφανόν σου. 12 Ὁ νικῶν, ποιήσω
the crown of thee. The [one] overcoming, I will make

αὐτὸν στῦλον ἐν τῷ ναῷ τοῦ θεοῦ
him a pillar in the shrine of the God

μου, καὶ ἔξω οὐ μὴ ἐξέλθῃ ἔτι, καὶ
of me, and out by no he will [any] and
means go forth longer,

γράψω ἐπ’ αὐτὸν τὸ ὄνομα τοῦ θεοῦ
I will write on him the name of the God

μου καὶ τὸ ὄνομα τῆς πόλεως τοῦ
of me and the name of the city of the

θεοῦ μου, τῆς καινῆς Ἰερουσαλὴμ ἡ
God of me, of the new Jerusalem -

καταβαίνουσα ἐκ τοῦ οὐρανοῦ ἀπὸ τοῦ
descending out of - heaven from the

θεοῦ μου, καὶ τὸ ὄνομά μου τὸ καινόν.
God of me, and ¹the ²name ⁴of me - ³new.

13 Ὁ ἔχων οὖς ἀκουσάτω τί τὸ πνεῦμα
The [one] having an ear let him hear what the Spirit

λέγει ταῖς ἐκκλησίαις.
says to the churches.

14 Καὶ τῷ ἀγγέλῳ τῆς ἐν Λαοδικείᾳ
And to the messenger ¹of the ²in ⁴Laodicea

ἐκκλησίας γράψον·
³church write thou:

Τάδε λέγει ὁ ἀμήν, ὁ μάρτυς ὁ
These things says the Amen, the ⁴witness ο

πιστὸς καὶ ἀληθινός, ἡ ἀρχὴ τῆς κτίσεως
¹faithful ²and ³true, the chief of the creation

τοῦ θεοῦ. 15 οἶδά σου τὰ ἔργα, ὅτι
- of God: I know of thee the works, that

---

who claim to be Jews though they are not, but are liars—I will make them come and fall down at your feet and acknowledge that I have loved you. 10Since you have kept my command to endure patiently, I will also keep you from the hour of trial that is going to come upon the whole world to test those who live on the earth.

11I am coming soon. Hold on to what you have, so that no one will take your crown. 12Him who overcomes I will make a pillar in the temple of my God. Never again will he leave it. I will write on him the name of my God and the name of the city of my God, the new Jerusalem, which is coming down out of heaven from my God; and I will also write on him my new name. 13He who has an ear, let him hear what the Spirit says to the churches.

To the Church in Laodicea

14“To the angel of the church in Laodicea write:

These are the words of the Amen, the faithful and true witness, the ruler of God's creation. 15I know your deeds,

---

ᵉI.e., origin or source

that you are neither cold nor hot; I would that you were cold or hot.

16‘So because you are lukewarm, and neither hot nor cold, I will spit you out of My mouth.

17‘Because you say, "I am rich, and have become wealthy, and have need of nothing," and you do not know that you are wretched and miserable and poor and blind and naked,

18I advise you to buy from Me gold refined by fire, that you may become rich, and white garments, that you may clothe yourself, and *that* the shame of your nakedness may not be revealed; and eye salve to anoint your eyes, that you may see.

19‘Those whom I love, I reprove and discipline; be zealous therefore, and repent.

20‘Behold, I stand at the door and knock; if anyone hears My voice and opens the door, I will come in to him, and will dine with him, and he with Me.

21‘He who overcomes, I will grant to him to sit down with Me on My throne, as I also overcame and sat down with My Father on His throne.

22‘He who has an ear, let him hear what the Spirit says to the churches.' "

οὔτε ψυχρὸς εἶ οὔτε ζεστός. ὄφελον
neither cold art thou nor hot. I would that†

ψυχρὸς ἦς ἢ ζεστός. 16 οὕτως ὅτι
cold thou wast or hot. So because

χλιαρὸς εἶ, καὶ οὔτε ζεστὸς οὔτε ψυχρός,
lukewarm thou art, and neither hot nor cold,

μέλλω σε ἐμέσαι ἐκ τοῦ στόματός μου.
I am ²thee ¹to vomit out of the mouth of me.
about*

17 ὅτι λέγεις ὅτι πλούσιός εἰμι καὶ
Because thou sayest[,] – ²rich ¹I am and

πεπλούτηκα καὶ οὐδὲν χρείαν ἔχω, καὶ
I have become rich and ²no ³need ¹I have, and

οὐκ οἶδας ὅτι σὺ εἶ ὁ ταλαίπωρος
knowest not that thou art the [one] wretched

καὶ ἐλεεινὸς καὶ πτωχὸς καὶ τυφλὸς
and pitiable and poor and blind

καὶ γυμνός, 18 συμβουλεύω σοι ἀγοράσαι
and naked, I counsel thee to buy

παρ’ ἐμοῦ χρυσίον πεπυρωμένον ἐκ πυρὸς
from me gold *having been* refined by fire
by fire

ἵνα πλουτήσῃς, καὶ ἱμάτια λευκὰ ἵνα
in or- thou mayest and ²garments ¹white in order
der that be rich, that

περιβάλῃ καὶ μὴ φανερωθῇ ἡ αἰσχύνη
thou mayest and *may not be* ¹the ²shame
be clothed manifested

τῆς γυμνότητός σου, καὶ κολλύριον
²of the ²nakedness ¹of thee, and eyesalve

ἐγχρῖσαι τοὺς ὀφθαλμούς σου ἵνα βλέπῃς.
to anoint the eyes of in order thou
thee that mayest see.

19 ἐγὼ ὅσους ἐὰν φιλῶ ἐλέγχω καὶ
¹I ¹as many as love I rebuke and

παιδεύω· ζήλευε οὖν καὶ μετανόησον.
I chasten; be hot therefore and repent thou.

20 Ἰδοὺ ἔστηκα ἐπὶ τὴν θύραν καὶ
Behold[,] I stand at the door and

κρούω· ἐάν τις ἀκούσῃ τῆς φωνῆς μου
I knock; if anyone hears the voice of me

καὶ ἀνοίξῃ τὴν θύραν, εἰσελεύσομαι πρὸς
and opens the door, I will enter to

αὐτὸν καὶ δειπνήσω μετ’ αὐτοῦ καὶ
him and I will dine with him and

αὐτὸς μετ’ ἐμοῦ. 21 Ὁ νικῶν, δώσω
he with me. The overcoming, I will
[one] give

αὐτῷ καθίσαι μετ’ ἐμοῦ ἐν τῷ θρόνῳ
him to sit with me in the throne

μου, ὡς κἀγὼ ἐνίκησα καὶ ἐκάθισα
of me, as I also overcame and sat

μετὰ τοῦ πατρός μου ἐν τῷ θρόνῳ
with the Father of me in the throne

αὐτοῦ. 22 Ὁ ἔχων οὖς ἀκουσάτω τί
of him. The [one] having an ear let him hear what

τὸ πνεῦμα λέγει ταῖς ἐκκλησίαις.
the Spirit says to the churches.

---

that you are neither cold nor hot. I wish you were either one or the other! 16So, because you are lukewarm— neither hot nor cold—I am about to spit you out of my mouth. 17You say, 'I am rich; I have acquired wealth and do not need a thing.' But you do not realize that you are wretched, pitiful, poor, blind and naked. 18I counsel you to buy from me gold refined in the fire, so you can become rich; and white clothes to wear, so you can cover your shameful nakedness; and salve to put on your eyes, so you can see.

19Those whom I love I rebuke and discipline. So be earnest, and repent. 20Here I am! I stand at the door and knock. If anyone hears my voice and opens the door, I will come in and eat with him, and he with me.

21To him who overcomes, I will give the right to sit with me on my throne, just as I overcame and sat down with my Father on his throne. 22He who has an ear, let him hear what the Spirit says to the churches.''

Chapter 4

Scene in Heaven

AFTER these things I looked, and behold, a door *standing* open in heaven, and the first voice which I had heard, like *the sound* of a trumpet speak-

---

4 Μετὰ ταῦτα εἶδον, καὶ ἰδοὺ θύρα
After these things I saw, and behold[,] a door

ἠνεῳγμένη ἐν τῷ οὐρανῷ, καὶ ἡ φωνὴ
having been in – heaven, and the ²voice
opened

ἡ πρώτη ἣν ἤκουσα ὡς σάλπιγγος
¹first which I heard as of a trumpet

Chapter 4

The Throne in Heaven

AFTER this I looked, and there before me was a door standing open in heaven. And the voice I had first heard speaking to me like a

---

* As so often (see also ch. 1, 19, 2, 10), this verb does not necessarily connote imminence, but only simple futurity.

ing with me, said, "Come up here, and I will show you what must take place after these things."

²Immediately I was [f] in the Spirit; and behold, a throne was standing in heaven, and One sitting on the throne.

³And He who was sitting *was* like a jasper stone and a sardius in appearance; and *there was* a rainbow around the throne, like an emerald in appearance.

⁴And around the throne *were* twenty-four thrones; and upon the thrones *I saw* twenty-four elders sitting, clothed in white garments, and golden crowns on their heads.

The Throne and Worship of the Creator

⁵And from the throne proceed flashes of lightning and sounds and peals of thunder. And *there were* seven lamps of fire burning before the throne, which are the seven Spirits of God;

⁶and before the throne *there was*, as it were, a sea of glass like crystal; and in the center and around the throne, four living creatures full of eyes in front and behind.

⁷And the first creature *was* like a lion, and the second creature like a calf, and the third creature had a face like that of a man, and the fourth creature *was* like a flying eagle.

⁸And the four living creatures, each one of them having six wings, are full of eyes around and within; and day and night they do not cease to say,

---

λαλούσης   μετ'   ἐμοῦ,   λέγων·   ἀνάβα   ὧδε,
speaking   with   me,   saying: Come up   here,

καὶ   δείξω   σοι   ἃ   δεῖ   γενέσθαι   μετὰ
and   I will   thee   things   it be-   to occur   after
       show   which   hoves

ταῦτα.   εὐθέως   ἐγενόμην   ἐν   πνεύματι·
these things.   Immediately   I became   in   spirit;

2 καὶ   ἰδοὺ   θρόνος   ἔκειτο   ἐν   τῷ   οὐρανῷ,
and   behold[,]   a throne   was set   in   –   heaven,

καὶ   ἐπὶ   τὸν   θρόνον   καθήμενος,   3 καὶ
and   on   the   throne   a sitting [one],   and

ὁ   καθήμενος   ὅμοιος   ὁράσει   λίθῳ   ἰάσπιδι
the [one] sitting [was]   like   in appearance   ¹stone   ¹to a jasper

καὶ   σαρδίῳ,   καὶ   ἶρις   κυκλόθεν   τοῦ
²and   ³a sardius,   and   a rain-   round   the
                              [there was] bow

θρόνου   ὅμοιος   ὁράσει   σμαραγδίνῳ.   4 καὶ
throne   like   in appearance   *to* an emerald.   And

κυκλόθεν   τοῦ   θρόνου   θρόνους   εἴκοσι
round   the   throne [I saw]   ²thrones   ¹twenty-

τέσσαρας,   καὶ   ἐπὶ   τοὺς   θρόνους   εἴκοσι
four,   and   on   the   thrones   twenty-

τέσσαρας   πρεσβυτέρους   καθημένους   περι-
four   elders   sitting   *having been*

βεβλημένους   ἐν   ἱματίοις   λευκοῖς,   καὶ   ἐπὶ
clothed   in   garments   white,   and   on

τὰς   κεφαλὰς   αὐτῶν   στεφάνους   χρυσοῦς.
the   heads   of them   ²crowns   ¹golden.

5 καὶ   ἐκ   τοῦ   θρόνου   ἐκπορεύονται   ἀστραπαὶ
And   out of the   throne   come forth   lightnings

καὶ   φωναὶ   καὶ   βρονταί·   καὶ   ἑπτὰ   λαμπάδες
and   voices*   and   thunders;   and   seven   lamps

πυρὸς   καιόμεναι   ἐνώπιον   τοῦ   θρόνου,   ἅ
of fire [are] burning   before   the   throne, which

εἰσιν   τὰ   ἑπτὰ   πνεύματα   τοῦ   θεοῦ·   6 καὶ
are   the   seven   Spirits   –   of God;   and

ἐνώπιον   τοῦ   θρόνου   ὡς   θάλασσα   ὑαλίνη
before   the   throne   as   ²sea   ¹a glassy

ὁμοία   κρυστάλλῳ·   καὶ   ἐν   μέσῳ   τοῦ
like   *to* crystal;   and   in   [the] midst   of the

θρόνου   καὶ   κύκλῳ   τοῦ   θρόνου   τέσσερα
throne   and   round   the   throne   four

ζῷα   γέμοντα   ὀφθαλμῶν   ἔμπροσθεν   καὶ
living   filling(full)   of eyes   before   and
creatures

ὄπισθεν.   7 καὶ   τὸ   ζῷον   τὸ   πρῶτον
behind.   And   the   ²living   –   ¹first
                              creature

ὅμοιον   λέοντι,   καὶ   τὸ   δεύτερον   ζῷον
[was]   *to* a lion,   and   the   second   living
like   creature

ὅμοιον   μόσχῳ,   καὶ   τὸ   τρίτον   ζῷον   ἔχων
like   *to* a calf,   and   the   third   living   having
                                              creature

τὸ   πρόσωπον   ὡς   ἀνθρώπου,   καὶ   τὸ
the(its)   face   as   of a man,   and   the

τέταρτον   ζῷον   ὅμοιον   ἀετῷ   πετομένῳ.
fourth   living creature   like   eagle   *to* a flying.

8 καὶ   τὰ   τέσσερα   ζῷα,   ἓν   καθ'   ἓν
And   the   four   living   one   by   one
                        creatures,

αὐτῶν   ἔχων   ἀνὰ   πτέρυγας   ἕξ,   κυκλόθεν
of them   having   each   ²wings   ¹six,   around

καὶ   ἔσωθεν   γέμουσιν   ὀφθαλμῶν·   καὶ
and   within   are full   of eyes;   and

ἀνάπαυσιν   οὐκ   ἔχουσιν   ἡμέρας   καὶ   νυκτὸς
respite   they have not   day   and   night

---

trumpet said, "Come up here, and I will show you what must take place after this." ²At once I was in the Spirit, and there before me was a throne in heaven with someone sitting on it. ³And the one who sat there had the appearance of jasper and carnelian. A rainbow, resembling an emerald, encircled the throne. ⁴Surrounding the throne were twenty-four other thrones, and seated on them were twenty-four elders. They were dressed in white and had crowns of gold on their heads. ⁵From the throne came flashes of lightning, rumblings and peals of thunder. Before the throne, seven lamps were blazing. These are the seven spirits [h] of God. ⁶Also before the throne there was what looked like a sea of glass, clear as crystal.

In the center, around the throne, were four living creatures, and they were covered with eyes, in front and in back. ⁷The first living creature was like a lion, the second was like an ox, the third had a face like a man, the fourth was like a flying eagle. ⁸Each of the four living creatures had six wings and was covered with eyes all around, even under his wings. Day and night they never stop saying:

"HOLY, HOLY, HOLY, *is* THE LORD GOD, THE ALMIGHTY, who was and who is and who is to come."
9And when the living creatures give glory and honor and thanks to Him who sits on the throne, to Him who lives forever and ever,
10the twenty-four elders will fall down before Him who sits on the throne, and will worship Him who lives forever and ever, and will cast their crowns before the throne, saying,
11"Worthy art Thou, our Lord and our God, to receive glory and honor and power; for Thou didst create all things, and because of Thy will they existed, and were created."

Chapter 5

The Book with Seven Seals

AND I saw in the right hand of Him who sat on the throne a book written inside and on the back, sealed up with seven seals.
2And I saw a strong angel proclaiming with a loud voice, "Who is worthy to open the book and to break its seals?"
3And no one in heaven, or on the earth, or under the earth, was able to open the book, or to look into it.
4And I *began* to weep greatly, because no one was found worthy to open the book, or to look into it;
5and one of the elders *said to me, "Stop weeping; behold, the Lion that is

λέγοντες·   ἄγιος   ἄγιος   ἄγιος   κύριος   ὁ
saying: Holy[,] holy[,] holy[,] Lord   _

θεὸς   ὁ   παντοκράτωρ,   ὁ   ἦν   καὶ   ὁ   ὢν
God   the   Almighty,   [one who] the was and the being
                                                = the one who is

καὶ   ὁ   ἐρχόμενος.   9 Καὶ   ὅταν   δώσουσιν
and   the   coming [one].   And whenever ²shall give

τὰ   ζῷα   δόξαν   καὶ   τιμὴν   καὶ   εὐχαριστίαν
¹the ²living glory   and   honour   and   thanks
     creatures

τῷ   καθημένῳ   ἐπὶ   τῷ   θρόνῳ   τῷ   ζῶντι
to the sitting   on   the throne[,] to the living
[one]   [one]

εἰς   τοὺς   αἰῶνας   τῶν   αἰώνων,   10 πεσοῦνται
unto   the   ages   of the ages,   ⁴will fall

οἱ   εἴκοσι   τέσσαρες   πρεσβύτεροι   ἐνώπιον
¹the ²twenty-four   ³elders   before

τοῦ   καθημένου   ἐπὶ   τοῦ   θρόνου,   καὶ
the [one] sitting on   the   throne,   and

προσκυνήσουσιν   τῷ   ζῶντι   εἰς   τοὺς   αἰῶνας
they will worship the [one] living unto the   ages

τῶν   αἰώνων,   καὶ   βαλοῦσιν   τοὺς   στεφάνους
of the ages,   and   will cast   the   crowns

αὐτῶν   ἐνώπιον   τοῦ   θρόνου,   λέγοντες·
of them before   the   throne,   saying:

11 ἄξιος   εἶ,   ὁ   κύριος   καὶ   ὁ   θεὸς   ἡμῶν,
Worthy art thou, the Lord   and   the God   of us,

λαβεῖν   τὴν   δόξαν   καὶ   τὴν   τιμὴν   καὶ
to receive the   glory   and   the   honour   and

τὴν   δύναμιν,   ὅτι   σὺ   ἔκτισας   τὰ   πάντα,*
the   power,   because thou createdst   - all things,*

καὶ   διὰ   τὸ   θέλημά   σου   ἦσαν   καὶ
and   on ac- the   will   of thee they were   and
      count of

ἐκτίσθησαν.
they were created.

5 Καὶ   εἶδον   ἐπὶ   τὴν   δεξιὰν   τοῦ
And   I saw   on   the   right   of the
                                 [hand]   [one]

καθημένου   ἐπὶ   τοῦ   θρόνου   βιβλίον
sitting   on   the   throne   a scroll

γεγραμμένον   ἔσωθεν   καὶ   ὄπισθεν,
having been written within and on the reverse side,

κατεσφραγισμένον   σφραγῖσιν   ἑπτά.   2 καὶ
having been sealed with ²seals   ¹seven.   And

εἶδον   ἄγγελον   ἰσχυρὸν   κηρύσσοντα   ἐν
I saw   angel   a strong   proclaiming   in

φωνῇ   μεγάλῃ·   τίς   ἄξιος   ἀνοῖξαι   τὸ
²voice ¹a great(loud): Who [is] worthy to open the

βιβλίον   καὶ   λῦσαι   τὰς   σφραγῖδας   αὐτοῦ;
scroll   and   to loosen the   seals   of it?

3 καὶ   οὐδεὶς   ἐδύνατο   ἐν   τῷ   οὐρανῷ
And   no one   was able   in   -   heaven

οὐδὲ   ἐπὶ   τῆς   γῆς   οὐδὲ   ὑποκάτω   τῆς
nor   on   the   earth   nor   underneath the

γῆς   ἀνοῖξαι   τὸ   βιβλίον   οὔτε   βλέπειν
earth to open   the   scroll   nor to see(look at)

αὐτό.   4 καὶ   ἔκλαιον   πολύ,   ὅτι   οὐδεὶς
it.   And   I wept   much, because no one

ἄξιος   εὑρέθη   ἀνοῖξαι   τὸ   βιβλίον   οὔτε
worthy was found to open   the   scroll   nor

βλέπειν   αὐτό.   5 καὶ   εἷς   ἐκ   τῶν   πρεσ-
to look at it.   And   one   of   the   el-

βυτέρων   λέγει   μοι·   μὴ   κλαῖε·   ἰδοὺ
ders   says   to me: Weep not;   behold[,]

* τὰ πάντα = the universe.

"Holy, holy, holy is the Lord God Almighty, who was, and is, and is to come."
9Whenever the living creatures give glory, honor and thanks to him who sits on the throne and who lives for ever and ever, 10the twenty-four elders fall down before him who sits on the throne, and worship him who lives for ever and ever. They lay their crowns before the throne and say:

11"You are worthy, our Lord and God, to receive glory and honor and power, for you created all things, and by your will they were created and have their being."

Chapter 5

The Scroll and the Lamb

THEN I saw in the right hand of him who sat on the throne a scroll with writing on both sides and sealed with seven seals. 2And I saw a mighty angel proclaiming in a loud voice, "Who is worthy to break the seals and open the scroll?" 3But no one in heaven or on earth or under the earth could open the scroll or even look inside it. 4I wept and wept because no one was found who was worthy to open the scroll or look inside. 5Then one of the elders said to me, "Do not weep! See, the Lion of from the tribe of Judah, the Root of David, has overcome so as to open the book and its seven seals."

6And I saw gbetween the throne (with the four living creatures) and the elders a Lamb standing, as if slain, having seven horns and seven eyes, which are the seven Spirits of God, sent out into all the earth.

7And He came, and He took it out of the right hand of Him who sat on the throne.

8And when He had taken the book, the four living creatures and the twenty-four elders fell down before the Lamb, having each one a harp, and golden bowls full of incense, which are the prayers of the saints.

9And they *sang a new song, saying,
"Worthy art Thou to take the book, and to break its seals; for Thou wast slain, and didst purchase for God with Thy blood men from every tribe and tongue and people and nation.

10"And Thou hast made them to be a kingdom and priests to our God; and they will reign upon the earth."

Angels Exalt the Lamb

11And I looked, and I heard the voice of many angels around the throne and the living creatures and the elders; and the number of them was myriads of myriads, and thousands of thousands,

12saying with a loud voice,
"Worthy is the Lamb that was slain to receive power and

ἐνίκησεν ὁ λέων ὁ ἐκ τῆς φυλῆς Ἰούδα,
1⁰overcame ¹the ²Lion – ³of ⁴the ⁵tribe ⁶Juda,

ἡ ῥίζα Δαυίδ, ἀνοῖξαι τὸ βιβλίον καὶ
⁷the ⁸root ⁹of David, to open the scroll and

τὰς ἑπτὰ σφραγῖδας αὐτοῦ. 6 Καὶ εἶδον
the seven seals of it. And I saw

ἐν μέσῳ τοῦ θρόνου καὶ τῶν τεσσάρων
in [the] midst of the throne and of the four

ζῴων καὶ ἐν μέσῳ τῶν πρεσβυτέρων
living creatures and in [the] midst of the elders

ἀρνίον ἑστηκὸς ὡς ἐσφαγμένον, ἔχων
a Lamb standing as having been slain, having

κέρατα ἑπτὰ καὶ ὀφθαλμοὺς ἑπτά, οἵ
²horns ¹seven and ²eyes ¹seven, which

εἰσιν τὰ ἑπτὰ πνεύματα τοῦ θεοῦ
are the seven Spirits – of God

ἀπεσταλμένοι εἰς πᾶσαν τὴν γῆν. 7 καὶ
having been sent forth into all the earth. And

ἦλθεν καὶ εἴληφεν ἐκ τῆς δεξιᾶς τοῦ
he came and has taken out of the right [hand] of the

καθημένου ἐπὶ τοῦ θρόνου. 8 Καὶ ὅτε
[one] sitting on the throne. And when

ἔλαβεν τὸ βιβλίον, τὰ τέσσερα ζῷα
he took the scroll, the four living creatures

καὶ οἱ εἴκοσι τέσσαρες πρεσβύτεροι ἔπεσαν
and the twenty-four elders fell

ἐνώπιον τοῦ ἀρνίου, ἔχοντες ἕκαστος
before the Lamb, having each one

κιθάραν καὶ φιάλας χρυσᾶς γεμούσας
a harp and ²bowls ¹golden being full

θυμιαμάτων, αἵ εἰσιν αἱ προσευχαὶ τῶν
of incenses, which are the prayers of the

ἁγίων. 9 καὶ ᾄδουσιν ᾠδὴν καινὴν
saints. And they sing ²song ¹a new

λέγοντες· ἄξιος εἶ λαβεῖν τὸ βιβλίον
saying: Worthy art thou to receive the scroll

καὶ ἀνοῖξαι τὰς σφραγῖδας αὐτοῦ, ὅτι
and to open the seals of it, because

ἐσφάγης καὶ ἠγόρασας τῷ θεῷ ἐν τῷ
thou wast slain and didst purchase – to God by the

αἵματί σου ἐκ πάσης φυλῆς καὶ γλώσσης
blood of thee out of every tribe and tongue

καὶ λαοῦ καὶ ἔθνους, 10 καὶ ἐποίησας
and people and nation, and didst make

αὐτοὺς τῷ θεῷ ἡμῶν βασιλείαν καὶ
them to the God of us a kingdom and

ἱερεῖς, καὶ βασιλεύσουσιν ἐπὶ τῆς γῆς.
priests, and they will reign on(? over) the earth.

11 καὶ εἶδον, καὶ ἤκουσα φωνὴν ἀγγέλων
And I saw, and I heard a sound ²angels

πολλῶν κύκλῳ τοῦ θρόνου καὶ τῶν
¹of many round the throne and the

ζῴων καὶ τῶν πρεσβυτέρων, καὶ ἦν
living creatures and the elders, and ⁴was

ὁ ἀριθμὸς αὐτῶν μυριάδες μυριάδων καὶ
¹the ²number ³of them myriads of myriads and

χιλιάδες χιλιάδων, 12 λέγοντες φωνῇ
thousands of thousands, saying ²voice

μεγάλῃ· ἄξιός ἐστιν τὸ ἀρνίον τὸ
¹with a great Worthy is the Lamb –
(loud):

ἐσφαγμένον λαβεῖν τὴν δύναμιν καὶ πλοῦτον
having been slain to receive the power and riches

---

the tribe of Judah, the Root of David, has triumphed. He is able to open the scroll and its seven seals."

6Then I saw a Lamb, looking as if it had been slain, standing in the center of the throne, encircled by the four living creatures and the elders. He had seven horns and seven eyes, which are the seven spiritsⁱ of God sent out into all the earth. 7He came and took the scroll from the right hand of him who sat on the throne. 8And when he had taken it, the four living creatures and the twenty-four elders fell down before the Lamb. Each one had a harp and they were holding golden bowls full of incense, which are the prayers of the saints. 9And they sang a new song:

"You are worthy to take the scroll
and to open its seals,
because you were slain,
and with your blood
you purchased men for God
from every tribe and language and people and nation.
10You have made them to be a kingdom and priests to serve our God,
and they will reign on the earth."

11Then I looked and heard the voice of many angels, numbering thousands upon thousands, and ten thousand times ten thousand. They encircled the throne and the living creatures and the elders. 12In a loud voice they sang:

"Worthy is the Lamb, who was slain,
to receive power and

---

g Lit., *in the middle of the throne and of the four living creatures, and in the middle of the elders*

i 6 Or *the sevenfold Spirit*

riches and wisdom and might and honor and glory and blessing."

13And every created thing which is in heaven and on the earth and under the earth and on the sea, and all things in them, I heard saying,

"To Him who sits on the throne, and to the Lamb, *be* blessing and honor and glory and dominion forever and ever."

14And the four living creatures kept saying, "Amen." And the elders fell down and worshiped.

καὶ σοφίαν καὶ ἰσχὺν καὶ τιμὴν καὶ
and wisdom and strength and honour and

δόξαν καὶ εὐλογίαν. 13 καὶ πᾶν κτίσμα
glory and blessing. And every creature

ὃ ἐν τῷ οὐρανῷ καὶ ἐπὶ τῆς γῆς καὶ
which ³in - ³heaven ⁴and ⁵on ⁶the ⁷earth ⁸and

ὑποκάτω τῆς γῆς καὶ ἐπὶ τῆς θαλάσσης
⁹underneath ¹⁰the ¹¹earth ¹²and ¹³on ¹⁴the ¹⁵sea

[ἐστίν], καὶ τὰ ἐν αὐτοῖς πάντα, ἤκουσα
¹is, and - ²in ³them ¹all things, I heard

λέγοντας· τῷ καθημένῳ ἐπὶ τῷ θρόνῳ
saying: To the [one] sitting on the throne

καὶ τῷ ἀρνίῳ ἡ εὐλογία καὶ ἡ τιμὴ
and to the Lamb the blessing and the honour

καὶ ἡ δόξα καὶ τὸ κράτος εἰς τοὺς
and the glory and the might unto the

αἰῶνας τῶν αἰώνων. 14 καὶ τὰ τέσσαρα
ages of the ages. And the four

ζῷα ἔλεγον· ἀμήν, καὶ οἱ πρεσβύτεροι
living said: Amen, and the elders
creatures

ἔπεσαν καὶ προσεκύνησαν.
fell and worshipped.

---

wealth and wisdom and strength and honor and glory and praise!"

13Then I heard every creature in heaven and on earth and under the earth and on the sea, and all that is in them, singing:

"To him who sits on the throne and to the Lamb be praise and honor and glory and power, for ever and ever!"

14The four living creatures said, "Amen," and the elders fell down and worshiped.

Chapter 6

The Book Opened
The First Seal—False Christ

AND I saw when the Lamb broke one of the seven seals, and I heard one of the four living creatures saying as with a voice of thunder, "Come."

2And I looked, and behold, a white horse, and he who sat on it had a bow; and a crown was given to him; and he went out conquering, and to conquer.

The Second Seal—War

3And when He broke the second seal, I heard the second living creature saying, "Come."

4And another, a red horse, went out; and to him who sat on it, it was granted to take peace from the earth, and that *men* should slay one another; and a great sword was given to him.

The Third Seal—Famine

5And when He broke the third seal, I heard the third living creature saying, "Come." And I looked, and behold, a black horse; and he who sat on it had a

---

6 Καὶ εἶδον ὅτε ἤνοιξεν τὸ ἀρνίον
And I saw when ²opened ¹the ¹Lamb

μίαν ἐκ τῶν ἑπτὰ σφραγίδων, καὶ ἤκουσα
one of the seven seals, and I heard

ἑνὸς ἐκ τῶν τεσσάρων ζῴων λέγοντος
one of the four living creatures saying

ὡς φωνῇ βροντῆς· ἔρχου. 2 καὶ εἶδον,
as with a sound of thunder: Come. And I saw,

καὶ ἰδοὺ ἵππος λευκός, καὶ ὁ καθήμενος
and behold[,] ²horse ¹a white, and the [one] sitting

ἐπ᾽ αὐτὸν ἔχων τόξον, καὶ ἐδόθη αὐτῷ
on it having a bow, and ²was given ³to him

στέφανος, καὶ ἐξῆλθεν νικῶν καὶ ἵνα
¹a crown, and he went forth overcoming and in order that

νικήσῃ. 3 Καὶ ὅτε ἤνοιξεν τὴν σφραγῖδα
he might And when he opened the ²seal
overcome.

τὴν δευτέραν, ἤκουσα τοῦ δευτέρου ζῴου
- ¹second, I heard the second living
creature

λέγοντος· ἔρχου. 4 καὶ ἐξῆλθεν ἄλλος
saying: Come. And ⁴went forth ¹another

ἵππος πυρρός, καὶ τῷ καθημένῳ ἐπ᾽
²horse[,] ³red, and to the [one] sitting on

αὐτὸν ἐδόθη αὐτῷ λαβεῖν τὴν εἰρήνην
it was given to him to take - peace

ἐκ τῆς γῆς καὶ ἵνα ἀλλήλους σφάξουσιν,
out the earth and in order ²one ¹they
of that another shall slay,

καὶ ἐδόθη αὐτῷ μάχαιρα μεγάλη. 5 Καὶ
and ²was given ⁴to him ³sword ¹a great. And

ὅτε ἤνοιξεν τὴν σφραγῖδα τὴν τρίτην,
when he opened the ²seal - ¹third,

ἤκουσα τοῦ τρίτου ζῴου λέγοντος· ἔρχου.
I heard the third living saying: Come.
creature

καὶ εἶδον, καὶ ἰδοὺ ἵππος μέλας, καὶ
And I saw, and behold[,] ²horse ¹a black, and

ὁ καθήμενος ἐπ᾽ αὐτὸν ἔχων ζυγὸν
the [one] sitting on it having a balance

Chapter 6

The Seals

I WATCHED as the Lamb opened the first of the seven seals. Then I heard one of the four living creatures say in a voice like thunder, "Come!" 2I looked, and there before me was a white horse! Its rider held a bow, and he was given a crown, and he rode out as a conqueror bent on conquest.

3When the Lamb opened the second seal, I heard the second living creature say, "Come!" 4Then another horse came out, a fiery red one. Its rider was given power to take peace from the earth and to make men slay each other. To him was given a large sword.

5When the Lamb opened the third seal, I heard the third living creature say, "Come!" I looked, and there before me was a black horse! Its rider was holding pair of scales in his hand.

6And I heard as it were a voice in the center of the four living creatures saying, "A ^hquart of wheat for a ⁱdenarius, and three quarts of barley for a denarius; and do not harm the oil and the wine."

The Fourth Seal—Death

7And when He broke the fourth seal, I heard the voice of the fourth living creature saying, "Come."

8And I looked, and behold, an ashen horse; and he who sat on it had the name Death; and Hades was following with him. And authority was given to them over a fourth of the earth, to kill with sword and with famine and with pestilence and by the wild beasts of the earth.

The Fifth Seal—Martyrs

9And when He broke the fifth seal, I saw underneath the altar the souls of those who had been slain because of the word of God, and because of the testimony which they had maintained;

10and they cried out with a loud voice, saying, "How long, O Lord, holy and true, wilt Thou refrain from judging and avenging our blood on those who dwell on the earth?"

11And there was given to each of them a white robe; and they were told that they should rest for a little while longer, until the number of their fellow servants and their brethren who were to be killed even as they had been, should be completed also.

The Sixth Seal—Terror

12And I looked when He broke the sixth seal, and there was a great earth-

---

ἐν τῇ χειρὶ αὐτοῦ. 6 καὶ ἤκουσα ὡς
in the hand of him. And I heard as

φωνὴν ἐν μέσῳ τῶν τεσσάρων ζῴων
a voice in [the] of the four living
midst creatures

λέγουσαν· χοῖνιξ σίτου δηναρίου, καὶ τρεῖς
saying: A of of(for) and three
choenix wheat a denarius,

χοίνικες κριθῶν δηναρίου· καὶ τὸ ἔλαιον
choenixes of barley of(for) and ²the ³oil
a denarius;

καὶ τὸν οἶνον μὴ ἀδικήσῃς. 7 Καὶ
⁴and ⁵the ⁶wine ¹do not harm. And

ὅτε ἤνοιξεν τὴν σφραγῖδα τὴν τετάρτην,
when he opened the seal the ¹fourth,

ἤκουσα φωνὴν τοῦ τετάρτου ζῴου λέγοντος·
I heard [the] voice of the fourth living creature saying:

ἔρχου. 8 καὶ εἶδον, καὶ ἰδοὺ ἵππος
Come. And I saw, and behold[,] ¹horse

χλωρός, καὶ ὁ καθήμενος ἐπάνω αὐτοῦ,
¹a pale green, and the [one] sitting upon it,

ὄνομα αὐτῷ [ὁ] θάνατος, καὶ ὁ ἅδης
name to him^e - death, and - hades

ἠκολούθει μετ' αὐτοῦ, καὶ ἐδόθη αὐτοῖς
followed with him, and ¹was ²to them
given

ἐξουσία ἐπὶ τὸ τέταρτον τῆς γῆς,
¹authority over the fourth [part] of the earth,

ἀποκτεῖναι ἐν ρομφαίᾳ καὶ ἐν λιμῷ
to kill with sword and with famine

καὶ ἐν θανάτῳ καὶ ὑπὸ τῶν θηρίων
and with death and by the wild beasts

τῆς γῆς. 9 Καὶ ὅτε ἤνοιξεν τὴν πέμπτην
of the earth. And when he opened the fifth

σφραγῖδα, εἶδον ὑποκάτω τοῦ θυσιαστηρίου
seal, I saw underneath the altar

τὰς ψυχὰς τῶν ἐσφαγμένων διὰ τὸν
the souls of the having been on account the
[ones] slain of

λόγον τοῦ θεοῦ καὶ διὰ τὴν μαρτυρίαν
word - of God and on the witness
account of

ἣν εἶχον. 10 καὶ ἔκραξαν φωνῇ μεγάλῃ
which they had. And they cried ²voice ¹with a
great(loud)

λέγοντες· ἕως πότε, ὁ δεσπότης ὁ ἅγιος
saying: Until when, the Master - holy

καὶ ἀληθινός, οὐ κρίνεις καὶ ἐκδικεῖς
and true, judgest thou not and avengest

τὸ αἷμα ἡμῶν ἐκ τῶν κατοικούντων
the blood of us of the [ones] dwelling

ἐπὶ τῆς γῆς; 11 καὶ ἐδόθη αὐτοῖς ἑκάστῳ
on the earth? And ³was ⁴to them ⁵each one
given

στολὴ λευκή, καὶ ἐρρέθη αὐτοῖς ἵνα
²robe ¹a white, and it was said to them in order
that

ἀναπαύσωνται ἔτι χρόνον μικρόν, ἕως
they should rest yet ²time ¹a little, until

πληρωθῶσιν καὶ οἱ σύνδουλοι αὐτῶν καὶ
should be fulfilled also the fellow-slaves of them and

οἱ ἀδελφοὶ αὐτῶν οἱ μέλλοντες ἀποκτέν-
the brothers of them the [ones] being about to be

νεσθαι ὡς καὶ αὐτοί. 12 Καὶ εἶδον
killed as also they. And I saw

ὅτε ἤνοιξεν τὴν σφραγῖδα τὴν ἕκτην,
when he opened the ²seal - ¹sixth,

καὶ σεισμὸς μέγας ἐγένετο, καὶ ὁ ἥλιος
and ²earthquake ¹a great occurred, and the sun

---

a pair of scales in his hand.

6Then I heard what sounded like a voice among the four living creatures, saying, "A quart^j of wheat for a day's wages,^k and three quarts of barley for a day's wages,^l and do not damage the oil and the wine!"

7When the Lamb opened the fourth seal, I heard the voice of the fourth living creature say, "Come!" 8I looked, and there before me was a pale horse! Its rider was named Death, and Hades was following close behind him. They were given power over a fourth of the earth to kill by sword, famine and plague, and by the wild beasts of the earth.

9When he opened the fifth seal, I saw under the altar the souls of those who had been slain because of the word of God and the testimony they had maintained. 10They called out in a loud voice, "How long, Sovereign Lord, holy and true, until you judge the inhabitants of the earth and avenge our blood?" 11Then each of them was given a white robe, and they were told to wait a little longer, until the number of their fellow servants and brothers who were to be killed as they had been was completed.

12I watched as he opened the sixth seal. There was a great earthquake. The sun

---

^hGr., *choenix*; i.e., a dry measure almost equal to a quart
ⁱThe denarius was equivalent to one day's wage

^j6 Greek *a choinix* (probably about a liter)
^k6 Greek *a denarius*
^l6 Greek *a denarius*

quake; and the sun became black as sackcloth *made* of hair, and the whole moon became like blood;

13and the stars of the sky fell to the earth, as a fig tree casts its unripe figs when shaken by a great wind.

14And the sky was split apart like a scroll when it is rolled up; and every mountain and island were moved out of their places.

15And the kings of the earth and the great men and the *j*commanders and the rich and the strong and every slave and free man, hid themselves in the caves and among the rocks of the mountains;

16and they *said to the mountains and to the rocks, "Fall on us and hide us from the presence of Him who sits on the throne, and from the wrath of the Lamb;

17for the great day of their wrath has come; and who is able to stand?''

ἐγένετο μέλας ὡς σάκκος τρίχινος, καὶ
became　 black 　as　 sackcloth　 made of hair, 　and

ἡ σελήνη ὅλη ἐγένετο ὡς αἷμα, 13 καὶ
the ⁵moon ¹whole became 　as 　blood, 　　　　and

οἱ ἀστέρες τοῦ οὐρανοῦ ἔπεσαν εἰς τὴν
the 　stars 　 of heaven 　 — 　 fell 　to 　the

γῆν, ὡς συκῆ βάλλει τοὺς ὀλύνθους
earth, 　as 　a fig-tree 　casts 　the 　unripe figs

αὐτῆς ὑπὸ ἀνέμου μεγάλου σειομένη,
of it 　ᵇby 　⁴wind 　ᵃa great(strong) 　ᵇbeing shaken,

14 καὶ ὁ οὐρανὸς ἀπεχωρίσθη ὡς βιβλίον
and the 　heaven 　 departed 　as 　a scroll

ἐλισσόμενον, καὶ πᾶν ὄρος καὶ νῆσος
being rolled up, 　and 　every 　mountain and 　island

ἐκ τῶν τόπων αὐτῶν ἐκινήθησαν. 15 καὶ
out of the 　places 　of them 　were moved. 　　　And

οἱ βασιλεῖς τῆς γῆς καὶ οἱ μεγιστᾶνες
the 　kings 　of the 　earth 　and 　the 　great men

καὶ οἱ χιλίαρχοι καὶ οἱ πλούσιοι καὶ
and 　the 　 chiliarchs 　and 　the 　rich men 　and

οἱ ἰσχυροὶ καὶ πᾶς δοῦλος καὶ ἐλεύθερος
the strong men and 　every 　slave 　and 　free man

ἔκρυψαν ἑαυτοὺς εἰς τὰ σπήλαια καὶ
hid 　 themselves 　 in 　the 　 caves 　 and

εἰς τὰς πέτρας τῶν ὀρέων, 16 καὶ
in 　the 　 rocks 　 of the 　mountains, 　　　and

λέγουσιν τοῖς ὄρεσιν καὶ ταῖς πέτραις·
they say 　 to the 　mountains and 　to the 　 rocks:

πέσετε ἐφ' ἡμᾶς καὶ κρύψατε ἡμᾶς
Fall ye 　 on 　 us 　 and 　 hide 　 us

ἀπὸ προσώπου τοῦ καθημένου ἐπὶ τοῦ
from 　[the] face 　of the [one] 　 sitting 　on 　the

θρόνου καὶ ἀπὸ τῆς ὀργῆς τοῦ ἀρνίου,
throne 　and 　from 　the 　wrath 　of the 　Lamb,

17 ὅτι ἦλθεν ἡ ἡμέρα ἡ μεγάλη τῆς
because ⁷came ¹the ⁵day 　 — 　²great 　⁴of the

ὀργῆς αὐτῶν, καὶ τίς δύναται σταθῆναι;
⁵wrath 　⁶of them, 　and 　who 　can 　 *to* stand ?

---

turned black like sackcloth made of goat hair, the whole moon turned blood red, 13and the stars in the sky fell to earth, as late figs drop from a fig tree when shaken by a strong wind. 14The sky receded like a scroll, rolling up, and every mountain and island was removed from its place.

15Then the kings of the earth, the princes, the generals, the rich, the mighty, and every slave and every free man hid in caves and among the rocks of the mountains. 16They called to the mountains and the rocks, ''Fall on us and hide us from the face of him who sits on the throne and from the wrath of the Lamb! 17For the great day of their wrath has come, and who can stand?''

Chapter 7

An Interlude

AFTER this I saw four angels standing at the four corners of the earth, holding back the four winds of the earth, so that no wind should blow on the earth or on the sea or on any tree.

2And I saw another angel ascending from the rising of the sun, having the seal of the living God; and he cried out with a loud voice to the four angels to whom it was granted to harm the earth and the sea,

3saying, "Do not harm the earth or the sea or the

---

7 Μετὰ τοῦτο εἶδον τέσσαρας ἀγγέλους
After 　this 　I saw 　four 　angels

ἑστῶτας ἐπὶ τὰς τέσσαρας γωνίας τῆς
standing 　on 　the 　four 　corners 　of the

γῆς, κρατοῦντας τοὺς τέσσαρας ἀνέμους
earth, 　holding 　the 　four 　winds

τῆς γῆς, ἵνα μὴ πνέη ἄνεμος ἐπὶ τῆς
of the earth, in order ³not ⁵should ¹wind 　on 　the
　　　　　　　that 　　⁴blow

γῆς μήτε ἐπὶ τῆς θαλάσσης μήτε ἐπὶ
earth 　nor 　on 　the 　 sea 　 nor 　on

πᾶν δένδρον. 2 καὶ εἶδον ἄλλον ἄγγελον
every(any) tree. 　　　And 　I saw 　another 　angel

ἀναβαίνοντα ἀπὸ ἀνατολῆς ἡλίου, ἔχοντα
coming up 　from 　[the] rising 　of [the] sun, 　having

σφραγῖδα θεοῦ ζῶντος, καὶ ἔκραξεν φωνῇ
a seal 　God of [the] living, and 　he cried 　²voice

μεγάλη τοῖς τέσσαρσιν ἀγγέλοις οἷς
¹with a 　to the 　 four 　 angels 　 to whom
great(loud)

ἐδόθη αὐτοῖς ἀδικῆσαι τὴν γῆν καὶ
it was given *to* them 　to harm 　the 　earth 　and

τὴν θάλασσαν, 3 λέγων· μὴ ἀδικήσητε
the 　 sea, 　　　 saying: 　Do not harm

τὴν γῆν μήτε τὴν θάλασσαν μήτε τὰ
the 　earth 　nor 　the 　 sea 　 nor 　the

Chapter 7

144,000 Sealed

AFTER this I saw four angels standing at the four corners of the earth, holding back the four winds of the earth to prevent any wind from blowing on the land or on the sea or on any tree. 2Then I saw another angel coming up from the east, having the seal of the living God. He called out in a loud voice to the four angels who had been given power to harm the land and the sea: 3''Do not harm the land or the sea or the trees

---

*ʲ*I.e., chiliarchs, in command of one thousand troops

trees, until we have sealed the bond-servants of our God on their foreheads.''

A Remnant of Israel—144,000

4And I heard the number of those who were sealed, one hundred and forty-four thousand sealed from every tribe of the sons of Israel:

5from the tribe of Judah, twelve thousand *were* sealed, from the tribe of Reuben twelve thousand, from the tribe of Gad twelve thousand,

6from the tribe of Asher twelve thousand, from the tribe of Naphtali twelve thousand, from the tribe of Manasseh twelve thousand,

7from the tribe of Simeon twelve thousand, from the tribe of Levi twelve thousand, from the tribe of Issachar twelve thousand,

8from the tribe of Zebulun twelve thousand, from the tribe of Joseph twelve thousand, from the tribe of Benjamin, twelve thousand *were* sealed.

A Multitude from the Tribulation

9After these things I looked, and behold, a great multitude, which no one could count, from every nation and *all* tribes and peoples and tongues, standing before the throne and before the Lamb, clothed in white robes, and palm branches *were* in their hands;

10and they cry out with a loud voice, saying, ''Salvation to our God who sits on the throne, and to the Lamb.''

11And all the angels were standing around the throne and *around* the elders and the four living creatures; and they fell on their faces before the throne and worshiped God,

12saying, ''Amen, blessing and glo-

δένδρα, ἄχρι σφραγίσωμεν τοὺς δούλους
trees, until we *may* seal the slaves

τοῦ θεοῦ ἡμῶν ἐπὶ τῶν μετώπων αὐτῶν.
of the God of us on the foreheads of them.

4 Καὶ ἤκουσα τὸν ἀριθμὸν τῶν ἐσφραγισ-
And I heard the number of the [ones] *having been*

μένων, ἑκατὸν τεσσεράκοντα τέσσαρες
sealed, a hundred [and] forty-four

χιλιάδες ἐσφραγισμένοι ἐκ πάσης φυλῆς
thousands *having been* sealed out of every tribe

υἱῶν Ἰσραήλ· 5 ἐκ φυλῆς Ἰούδα δώδεκα
of sons of Israel: of [the] tribe Juda twelve

χιλιάδες ἐσφραγισμένοι, ἐκ φυλῆς Ῥουβὴν
thousands *having been* sealed, of [the] tribe Reuben

δώδεκα χιλιάδες, ἐκ φυλῆς Γὰδ δώδεκα
twelve thousands, of [the] tribe Gad twelve

χιλιάδες, 6 ἐκ φυλῆς Ἀσὴρ δώδεκα
thousands, of [the] tribe Aser twelve

χιλιάδες, ἐκ φυλῆς Νεφθαλὶμ δώδεκα
thousands, of [the] tribe Nephthalim twelve

χιλιάδες, ἐκ φυλῆς Μανασσῆ δώδεκα
thousands, of [the] tribe Manasse twelve

χιλιάδες, 7 ἐκ φυλῆς Συμεὼν δώδεκα
thousands, of [the] tribe Symeon twelve

χιλιάδες, ἐκ φυλῆς Λευὶ δώδεκα χιλιάδες,
thousands, of [the] tribe Levi twelve thousands,

ἐκ φυλῆς Ἰσσαχὰρ δώδεκα χιλιάδες,
of [the] tribe Issachar twelve thousands,

8 ἐκ φυλῆς Ζαβουλὼν δώδεκα χιλιάδες,
of [the] tribe Zabulon twelve thousands,

ἐκ φυλῆς Ἰωσὴφ δώδεκα χιλιάδες, ἐκ
of [the] tribe Joseph twelve thousands, of

φυλῆς Βενιαμὶν δώδεκα χιλιάδες ἐσφραγισ-
[the] tribe Benjamin twelve thousands *having been*

μένοι. 9 Μετὰ ταῦτα εἶδον, καὶ ἰδοὺ ὄχλος
sealed. After these things I saw, and behold[,] ²crowd

πολύς, ὃν ἀριθμῆσαι αὐτὸν οὐδεὶς ἐδύνατο,
¹a much which ³to number it ¹no one ⁴was able,
(great),

ἐκ παντὸς ἔθνους καὶ φυλῶν καὶ λαῶν
out of every nation and tribes and peoples

καὶ γλωσσῶν, ἑστῶτες ἐνώπιον τοῦ θρόνου
and tongues, standing before the throne

καὶ ἐνώπιον τοῦ ἀρνίου, περιβεβλημένους
and before the Lamb, *having been* clothed [with]

στολὰς λευκάς, καὶ φοίνικες ἐν ταῖς
²robes ¹white, and palms in the

χερσὶν αὐτῶν· 10 καὶ κράζουσιν φωνῇ
hands of them; and they cry ²voice

μεγάλη λέγοντες· ἡ σωτηρία τῷ θεῷ
¹with a great(loud) saying: – Salvation to the Godᵉ

ἡμῶν τῷ καθημένῳ ἐπὶ τῷ θρόνῳ καὶ
of us – sitting on the throne and

τῷ ἀρνίῳ. 11 καὶ πάντες οἱ ἄγγελοι
to the Lamb.ᶜ And all the angels

εἱστήκεισαν κύκλῳ τοῦ θρόνου καὶ τῶν
stood round the throne and the

πρεσβυτέρων καὶ τῶν τεσσάρων ζῴων,
elders and the four living creatures,

καὶ ἔπεσαν ἐνώπιον τοῦ θρόνου ἐπὶ
and fell before the throne on

τὰ πρόσωπα αὐτῶν καὶ προσεκύνησαν
the faces of them and worshipped

τῷ θεῷ, 12 λέγοντες· ἀμήν, ἡ εὐλογία
– God, saying: Amen, – blessing

---

until we put a seal on the foreheads of the servants of our God.'' 4Then I heard the number of those who were sealed: 144,000 from all the tribes of Israel.

5From the tribe of Judah 12,000 were sealed,
from the tribe of Reuben 12,000,
from the tribe of Gad 12,000,
6from the tribe of Asher 12,000,
from the tribe of Naphtali 12,000,
from the tribe of Manasseh 12,000,
7from the tribe of Simeon 12,000,
from the tribe of Levi 12,000,
from the tribe of Issachar 12,000,
8from the tribe of Zebulun 12,000,
from the tribe of Joseph 12,000,
from the tribe of Benjamin 12,000.

The Great Multitude in White Robes

9After this I looked and there before me was a great multitude that no one could count, from every nation, tribe, people and language, standing before the throne and in front of the Lamb. They were wearing white robes and were holding palm branches in their hands. 10And they cried out in a loud voice:

''Salvation belongs to our God,
who sits on the throne,
and to the Lamb.''

11All the angels were standing around the throne and around the elders and the four living creatures. They fell down on their faces before the throne and worshiped God, 12saying:

''Amen!
Praise and glory

ry and wisdom and thanksgiving and honor and power and might, *be* to our God forever and ever. Amen."

13And one of the elders answered, saying to me, "These who are clothed in the white robes, who are they, and from where have they come?"

14And I said to him, "My lord, you know." And he said to me, "These are the ones who come out of the great tribulation, and they have washed their robes and made them white in the blood of the Lamb.

15"For this reason, they are before the throne of God; and they serve Him day and night in His temple; and He who sits on the throne shall spread His tabernacle over them.

16"They shall hunger no more, neither thirst anymore; neither shall the sun beat down on them, nor any heat;

17for the Lamb in the center of the throne shall be their shepherd, and shall guide them to springs of the water of life; and God shall wipe every tear from their eyes."

καὶ ἡ δόξα καὶ ἡ σοφία καὶ ἡ εὐχαριστία
and – glory and – wisdom and – thanks

καὶ ἡ τιμὴ καὶ ἡ δύναμις καὶ ἡ ἰσχὺς
and – honour and – power and – strength

τῷ θεῷ ἡμῶν εἰς τοὺς αἰῶνας τῶν
to the God° of us unto the ages of the

αἰώνων· ἀμήν. 13 Καὶ ἀπεκρίθη εἷς
ages: Amen. And ²answered ¹one

ἐκ τῶν πρεσβυτέρων λέγων μοι· οὗτοι
²of ³the ⁴elders saying to me: These

οἱ περιβεβλημένοι τὰς στολὰς τὰς
the having been clothed the ²robes –
[ones] [with]

λευκὰς τίνες εἰσὶν καὶ πόθεν ἦλθον;
¹white who are they and whence came they?

14 καὶ εἴρηκα αὐτῷ· κύριέ μου, σὺ
And I *have* said to him: Lord of me, thou

οἶδας. καὶ εἶπέν μοι· οὗτοί εἰσιν οἱ
knowest. And he told me: These are the

ἐρχόμενοι ἐκ τῆς θλίψεως τῆς μεγάλης
[ones] coming out of the ²affliction – ¹great

καὶ ἔπλυναν τὰς στολὰς αὐτῶν καὶ
and washed the robes of them and

ἐλεύκαναν αὐτὰς ἐν τῷ αἵματι τοῦ
whitened them in the blood of the

ἀρνίου. 15 διὰ τοῦτό εἰσιν ἐνώπιον τοῦ
Lamb. Therefore are they before the

θρόνου τοῦ θεοῦ, καὶ λατρεύουσιν αὐτῷ
throne – of God, and serve him

ἡμέρας καὶ νυκτὸς ἐν τῷ ναῷ αὐτοῦ,
day and night in the shrine of him,

καὶ ὁ καθήμενος ἐπὶ τοῦ θρόνου σκηνώσει
and the [one] sitting on the throne will spread [his] tent

ἐπ᾽ αὐτούς. 16 οὐ πεινάσουσιν ἔτι οὐδὲ
over them. They will not hunger longer nor

διψήσουσιν ἔτι, οὐδὲ μὴ πέσῃ ἐπ᾽ αὐτοὺς
will they thirst longer, neither *not* fall on them

ὁ ἥλιος οὐδὲ πᾶν καῦμα, 17 ὅτι τὸ
the sun nor every(any) heat, because the

ἀρνίον τὸ ἀνὰ μέσον τοῦ θρόνου ποιμανεῖ
Lamb – in the midst of the throne will shepherd

αὐτοὺς καὶ ὁδηγήσει αὐτοὺς ἐπὶ ζωῆς
them and will lead them upon ³of life

πηγὰς ὑδάτων· καὶ ἐξαλείψει ὁ θεὸς
¹fountains ²of waters; and ²will wipe off – ¹God

πᾶν δάκρυον ἐκ τῶν ὀφθαλμῶν αὐτῶν.
every tear out of the eyes of them.

---

and wisdom and thanks and honor and power and strength be to our God for ever and ever. Amen!"

13Then one of the elders asked me, "These in white robes—who are they, and where did they come from?"

14I answered, "Sir, you know."

And he said, "These are they who have come out of the great tribulation; they have washed their robes and made them white in the blood of the Lamb.

15Therefore,

"they are before the throne of God
and serve him day and night in his temple;
and he who sits on the throne will spread his tent over them.
16Never again will they hunger;
never again will they thirst.
The sun will not beat upon them,
nor any scorching heat.
17For the Lamb at the center of the throne will be their shepherd;
he will lead them to springs of living water.
And God will wipe away every tear from their eyes."

Chapter 8

The Seventh Seal—the Trumpets

AND when He broke the seventh seal, there was silence in heaven for about half an hour.

2And I saw the seven angels who stand before God; and seven trumpets were given to them.

3And another angel came and stood at the altar, holding a golden censer; and much incense was given to

---

8 Καὶ ὅταν ἤνοιξεν τὴν σφραγῖδα τὴν
And whenever he opened the ²seal

ἑβδόμην, ἐγένετο σιγὴ ἐν τῷ οὐρανῷ
¹seventh, occurred a silence in the heaven

ὡς ἡμίωρον. 2 Καὶ εἶδον τοὺς ἑπτὰ
about a half-hour. And I saw the seven

ἀγγέλους οἳ ἐνώπιον τοῦ θεοῦ ἑστήκασιν,
angels who before – God stood,

καὶ ἐδόθησαν αὐτοῖς ἑπτὰ σάλπιγγες.
and there were given to them seven trumpets.

3 Καὶ ἄλλος ἄγγελος ἦλθεν καὶ ἐστάθη
And another angel came and stood

ἐπὶ τοῦ θυσιαστηρίου ἔχων λιβανωτὸν
on the altar having ²censer

χρυσοῦν, καὶ ἐδόθη αὐτῷ θυμιάματα πολλά,
¹a golden, and there was to him incenses many
          given   (much),

Chapter 8

The Seventh Seal and the Golden Censer

WHEN he opened the seventh seal, there was silence in heaven for about half an hour.

2And I saw the seven angels who stand before God, and to them were given seven trumpets.

3Another angel, who had a golden censer, came and stood at the altar. He was given much incense to of-him, that he might add it to the prayers of all the saints upon the golden altar which was before the throne. 4And the smoke of the incense, with the prayers of the saints, went up before God out of the angel's hand.

5And the angel took the censer; and he filled it with the fire of the altar and threw it to the earth; and there followed peals of thunder and sounds and flashes of lightning and an earthquake.

6And the seven angels who had the seven trumpets prepared themselves to sound them.

7And the first sounded, and there came hail and fire, mixed with blood, and they were thrown to the earth; and a third of the earth was burned up, and a third of the trees were burned up, and all the green grass was burned up.

8And the second angel sounded, and *something* like a great mountain burning with fire was thrown into the sea; and a third of the sea became blood;

9and a third of the creatures, which were in the sea and had life, died; and a third of the ships were destroyed.

10And the third angel sounded, and a great star fell from heaven, burning like a torch, and it fell on a third of the rivers and on the springs of waters;

11and the name of the star

ἵνα   δώσει   ταῖς   προσευχαῖς   τῶν   ἁγίων
in order he will with the   prayers   of ²the ³saints
that   give [it]

πάντων   ἐπὶ   τὸ   θυσιαστήριον   τὸ   χρυσοῦν
¹all   on   the   ²altar   -   ¹golden

τὸ   ἐνώπιον   τοῦ   θρόνου.   4 καὶ   ἀνέβη
-      before   the   throne.   And   went up

ὁ καπνὸς   τῶν   θυμιαμάτων   ταῖς   προσευχαῖς
the smoke   of the   incenses   with the   prayers

τῶν   ἁγίων   ἐκ   χειρὸς   τοῦ   ἀγγέλου   ἐνώπιον
of the saints   out of [the] hand of the   angel   before

τοῦ   θεοῦ.   5 καὶ   εἴληφεν   ὁ   ἄγγελος
-       God.   And   ³has taken   ¹the   ²angel

τὸν   λιβανωτόν,   καὶ   ἐγέμισεν   αὐτὸν   ἐκ
the   censer,   and   filled   it   from

τοῦ   πυρὸς   τοῦ   θυσιαστηρίου   καὶ   ἔβαλεν
the   fire   of the   altar   and   cast

εἰς   τὴν   γῆν·   καὶ   ἐγένοντο   βρονταὶ   καὶ
into   the   earth;   and   there occurred thunders   and

φωναὶ   καὶ   ἀστραπαὶ   καὶ   σεισμός.
sounds   and   lightnings   and   an earthquake.

6 Καὶ   οἱ   ἑπτὰ   ἄγγελοι   οἱ   ἔχοντες
And   the   seven   angels   -   having

τὰς   ἑπτὰ   σάλπιγγας   ἡτοίμασαν   αὐτοὺς
the   seven   trumpets   prepared   themselves

ἵνα   σαλπίσωσιν.   7 Καὶ   ὁ   πρῶτος
in order they might   And   the   first
that   trumpet.

ἐσάλπισεν·   καὶ   ἐγένετο   χάλαζα   καὶ   πῦρ
trumpeted;   and   there occurred hail   and   fire

μεμιγμένα   ἐν   αἵματι   καὶ   ἐβλήθη   εἰς
having been in   blood   and   it was cast to
mixed   (with)

τὴν   γῆν·   καὶ   τὸ   τρίτον   τῆς   γῆς
the   earth;   and   the   third [part] of the   earth

κατεκάη,   καὶ   τὸ   τρίτον   τῶν   δένδρων
was burnt   and   the   third [part] of the   trees
down(up),

κατεκάη,   καὶ   πᾶς   χόρτος   χλωρὸς   κατεκάη.
was burnt   and   all   ²grass   ¹green   was burnt
down(up),   down(up).

8 Καὶ   ὁ   δεύτερος   ἄγγελος   ἐσάλπισεν·
And   the   second   angel   trumpeted;

καὶ   ὡς   ὄρος   μέγα   πυρὶ   καιόμενον   ἐβλήθη
and   as   ²mountain ¹a great ⁴with fire ³burning   was cast

εἰς   τὴν   θάλασσαν·   καὶ   ἐγένετο   τὸ   τρίτον
into   the   sea;   and   ²became   ¹the   ³third
                                                             [part]

τῆς   θαλάσσης   αἷμα,   9 καὶ   ἀπέθανεν   τὸ
⁴of the ⁵sea   ⁶blood,   and   ¹⁰died   ¹the

τρίτον   τῶν   κτισμάτων   τῶν   ἐν   τῇ   θαλάσσῃ,
²third   ³of the ⁴creatures   -   ⁵in   ⁶the   ⁷sea,
[part]

τὰ   ἔχοντα   ψυχάς,   καὶ   τὸ   τρίτον   τῶν
-      ⁸having   ⁹souls,   and   the   third [part] of the

πλοίων   διεφθάρησαν.   10 Καὶ   ὁ   τρίτος
ships   were destroyed.   And   the   third

ἄγγελος   ἐσάλπισεν·   καὶ   ἔπεσεν   ἐκ   τοῦ
angel   trumpeted;   and   fell   out of -

οὐρανοῦ   ἀστὴρ   μέγας   καιόμενος   ὡς
heaven   star   a great   burning   as

λαμπάς,   καὶ   ἔπεσεν   ἐπὶ   τὸ   τρίτον   τῶν
a lamp,   and   it fell   onto   the   third [part] of the

ποταμῶν   καὶ   ἐπὶ   τὰς   πηγὰς   τῶν   ὑδάτων.
rivers   and   onto   the   fountains of the   waters.

11 καὶ   τὸ   ὄνομα   τοῦ   ἀστέρος   λέγεται
And   the   name   of the   star   is said(called)

---

fer, with the prayers of all the saints, on the golden altar before the throne. 4The smoke of the incense, together with the prayers of the saints, went up before God from the angel's hand. 5Then the angel took the censer, filled it with fire from the altar, and hurled it on the earth; and there came peals of thunder, rumblings, flashes of lightning and an earthquake.

The Trumpets

6Then the seven angels who had the seven trumpets prepared to sound them.

7The first angel sounded his trumpet, and there came hail and fire mixed with blood, and it was hurled down upon the earth. A third of the earth was burned up, a third of the trees were burned up, and all the green grass was burned up.

8The second angel sounded his trumpet, and something like a huge mountain, all ablaze, was thrown into the sea. A third of the sea turned into blood, 9a third of the living creatures in the sea died, and a third of the ships were destroyed.

10The third angel sounded his trumpet, and a great star, blazing like a torch, fell from the sky on a third of the rivers and on the springs of water— 11the name of the star is Worm-is called Wormwood; and a third of the waters became wormwood; and many men died from the waters, because they were made bitter.

12And the fourth angel sounded, and a third of the sun and a third of the moon and a third of the stars were smitten, so that a third of them might be darkened and the day might not shine for a third of it, and the night in the same way.

13And I looked, and I heard an eagle flying in midheaven, saying with a loud voice, "Woe, woe, woe, to those who dwell on the earth, because of the remaining blasts of the trumpet of the three angels who are about to sound!"

ὁ Ἄψινθος. καὶ ἐγένετο τὸ τρίτον τῶν
Wormwood. And became the third of
[part] the

ὑδάτων εἰς ἄψινθον, καὶ πολλοὶ τῶν
waters into wormwood, and many of the

ἀνθρώπων ἀπέθανον ἐκ τῶν ὑδάτων ὅτι
men died from the waters because

ἐπικράνθησαν. 12 Καὶ ὁ τέταρτος ἄγγελος
they were made bitter. And the fourth angel

ἐσάλπισεν· καὶ ἐπλήγη τὸ τρίτον τοῦ
trumpeted; and was struck the third [part] of the

ἡλίου καὶ τὸ τρίτον τῆς σελήνης καὶ
sun and the third [part] of the moon and

τὸ τρίτον τῶν ἀστέρων, ἵνα σκοτισθῇ
the third of the stars, in order might be
[part] that darkened

τὸ τρίτον αὐτῶν καὶ ἡ ἡμέρα μὴ φάνῃ
the third [part] of them and the day might not appear

τὸ τρίτον αὐτῆς, καὶ ἡ νὺξ ὁμοίως.
the third [part] of it, and the night likewise.

13 Καὶ εἶδον, καὶ ἤκουσα ἑνὸς ἀετοῦ
And I saw, and I heard one eagle

πετομένου ἐν μεσουρανήματι λέγοντος φωνῇ
flying in mid-heaven saying voice

μεγάλῃ· οὐαὶ οὐαὶ οὐαὶ τοὺς κατοικοῦν-
with a Woe[,] woe[,] woe to the [ones] dwell-
great(loud):

τας ἐπὶ τῆς γῆς ἐκ τῶν λοιπῶν φωνῶν
ing on the earth from the remaining voices

τῆς σάλπιγγος τῶν τριῶν ἀγγέλων τῶν
of the trumpet of the three angels –

μελλόντων σαλπίζειν.
being about to trumpet.

Chapter 9

The Fifth Trumpet—the Bottomless Pit

AND the fifth angel sounded, and I saw a star from heaven which had fallen to the earth; and the key of the bottomless pit was given to him.

2And he opened the bottomless pit; and smoke went up out of the pit, like the smoke of a great furnace; and the sun and the air were darkened by the smoke of the pit.

3And out of the smoke came forth locusts upon the earth; and power was given them, as the scorpions of the earth have power.

4And they were told not that they should not hurt the grass of the earth, nor any green thing, nor any tree, but only the men who do

---

9 Καὶ ὁ πέμπτος ἄγγελος ἐσάλπισεν·
And the fifth angel trumpeted;

καὶ εἶδον ἀστέρα ἐκ τοῦ οὐρανοῦ πεπτω-
and I saw a star out of – heaven having

κότα εἰς τὴν γῆν, καὶ ἐδόθη αὐτῷ
fallen onto the earth, and was given to it

ἡ κλεὶς τοῦ φρέατος τῆς ἀβύσσου. 2 καὶ
the key of the shaft of the abyss. And

ἤνοιξεν τὸ φρέαρ τῆς ἀβύσσου· καὶ
he opened the shaft of the abyss; and

ἀνέβη καπνὸς ἐκ τοῦ φρέατος ὡς
went up a smoke out of the shaft as

καπνὸς καμίνου μεγάλης, καὶ ἐσκοτώθη
smoke furnace of a great, and was darkened

ὁ ἥλιος καὶ ὁ ἀὴρ ἐκ τοῦ καπνοῦ
the sun and the air by the smoke

τοῦ φρέατος. 3 καὶ ἐκ τοῦ καπνοῦ
of the shaft. And out of the smoke

ἐξῆλθον ἀκρίδες εἰς τὴν γῆν, καὶ ἐδόθη
came forth locusts to the earth, and was given

αὐτοῖς ἐξουσία ὡς ἔχουσιν ἐξουσίαν οἱ
to them authority as have authority the

σκορπίοι τῆς γῆς. 4 καὶ ἐρρέθη αὐτοῖς
scorpions of the earth. And it was said to them

ἵνα μὴ ἀδικήσουσιν τὸν χόρτον τῆς
in order they shall not harm the grass of the
that

γῆς οὐδὲ πᾶν χλωρὸν οὐδὲ πᾶν δένδρον,
earth nor every greenstuff nor every tree,
(any) (any)

εἰ μὴ τοὺς ἀνθρώπους οἵτινες οὐκ ἔχουσιν
except the men who have not

---

wood.*m* A third of the waters turned bitter, and many people died from the waters that had become bitter.

12The fourth angel sounded his trumpet, and a third of the sun was struck, a third of the moon, and a third of the stars, so that a third of them turned dark. A third of the day was without light, and also a third of the night.

13As I watched, I heard an eagle that was flying in midair call out in a loud voice: "Woe! Woe! Woe to the inhabitants of the earth, because of the trumpet blasts about to be sounded by the other three angels!"

Chapter 9

THE fifth angel sounded his trumpet, and I saw a star that had fallen from the sky to the earth. The star was given the key to the shaft of the Abyss. 2When he opened the Abyss, smoke rose from it like the smoke from a gigantic furnace. The sun and sky were darkened by the smoke from the Abyss. 3And out of the smoke locusts came down upon the earth and were given power like that of scorpions of the earth. 4They were told not to harm the grass of the earth or any plant or tree, but only those people who

---

m 11 That is, Bitterness

not have the seal of God on their foreheads.

5And they were not permitted to kill anyone, but to torment for five months; and their torment was like the torment of a scorpion when it stings a man.

6And in those days men will seek death and will not find it; and they will long to die and death flees from them.

7And the appearance of the locusts was like horses prepared for battle; and on their heads, as it were, crowns like gold, and their faces were like the faces of men.

8And they had hair like the hair of women, and their teeth were like *the teeth* of lions.

9And they had breastplates like breastplates of iron; and the sound of their wings was like the sound of chariots, of many horses rushing to battle.

10And they have tails like scorpions, and stings; and in their tails is their power to hurt men for five months.

11They have as king over them, the angel of the abyss; his name in Hebrew is [k]Abaddon, and in the Greek he has the name Apollyon.

12The first woe is past; behold, two woes are still coming after these things.

The Sixth Trumpet—Army from the East

13And the sixth angel sounded, and I heard a voice from the [l]four horns of the golden altar which is before God,

14one saying to the sixth

τὴν σφραγῖδα τοῦ θεοῦ ἐπὶ τῶν μετώπων.
the   seal   -   of God on   the(ir) foreheads.

5 καὶ ἐδόθη αὐτοῖς ἵνα μὴ ἀποκτείνωσιν
And it was to them in order they should not kill
    given   that

αὐτούς, ἀλλ' ἵνα βασανισθήσονται μῆνας
them,   but in order they shall be tormented ²months
            that

πέντε· καὶ ὁ βασανισμὸς αὐτῶν ὡς
¹five; and the torment   of them [is] as

βασανισμὸς σκορπίου, ὅταν παίσῃ ἄνθρωπον.
[the] torment of a scorpion, whenever it stings a man.

6 καὶ ἐν ταῖς ἡμέραις ἐκείναις ζητήσουσιν
And in   those   days   ¹will seek

οἱ ἄνθρωποι τὸν θάνατον καὶ οὐ μὴ
- ¹men   -   death   and by no means

εὑρήσουσιν αὐτόν, καὶ ἐπιθυμήσουσιν
will they find it, and   they will long

ἀποθανεῖν καὶ φεύγει ὁ θάνατος ἀπ'
to die   and ¹flees   - ¹death   from

αὐτῶν. 7 καὶ τὰ ὁμοιώματα τῶν ἀκρίδων
them.   And the likenesses of the locusts

ὅμοιοι ἵπποις ἡτοιμασμένοις εἰς πόλεμον,
like   to horses having been prepared for war,

καὶ ἐπὶ τὰς κεφαλὰς αὐτῶν ὡς στέφανοι
and on the heads   of them as crowns

ὅμοιοι χρυσῷ, καὶ τὰ πρόσωπα αὐτῶν
like   to gold, and the faces   of them

ὡς πρόσωπα ἀνθρώπων, 8 καὶ εἶχον
as faces   of men,   and they had

τρίχας ὡς τρίχας γυναικῶν, καὶ οἱ
hairs as hairs of women, and the

ὀδόντες αὐτῶν ὡς λεόντων ἦσαν, 9 καὶ
teeth   of them ²as ³of lions ¹were, and

εἶχον θώρακας ὡς θώρακας σιδηροῦς,
they had breastplates as ²breastplates ¹iron,

καὶ ἡ φωνὴ τῶν πτερύγων αὐτῶν ὡς
and the sound of the wings   of them as

φωνὴ ἁρμάτων ἵππων πολλῶν τρεχόντων
sound ²chariots ³of horses ¹of many running

εἰς πόλεμον. 10 καὶ ἔχουσιν οὐρὰς ὁμοίας
to war.   And they have tails   like

σκορπίοις καὶ κέντρα, καὶ ἐν ταῖς οὐραῖς
to scorpions and stings, and ⁶with ⁷the ⁸tails

αὐτῶν ἡ ἐξουσία αὐτῶν ἀδικῆσαι τοὺς
⁹of them ¹the ²authority ³of them ⁴[is] to harm -

ἀνθρώπους μῆνας πέντε. 11 ἔχουσιν ἐπ'
⁵men   ¹¹months ¹⁰five.   They have over

αὐτῶν βασιλέα τὸν ἄγγελον τῆς ἀβύσσου,
them   a king   the angel   of the abyss,

ὄνομα αὐτῷ Ἑβραϊστὶ Ἀβαδδών, καὶ
name   to him in Hebrew Abaddon,   and

ἐν τῇ Ἑλληνικῇ ὄνομα ἔχει Ἀπολλύων.
in the Greek   ²[the] name ¹he has Apollyon.

12 Ἡ οὐαὶ ἡ μία ἀπῆλθεν· ἰδοὺ ἔρχεται
The ¹woe - ¹one(first) passed away; behold ⁴comes

ἔτι δύο οὐαὶ μετὰ ταῦτα.
¹yet ²two ³woes after these things.

13 Καὶ ὁ ἕκτος ἄγγελος ἐσάλπισεν·
And the sixth angel   trumpeted;

καὶ ἤκουσα φωνὴν μίαν ἐκ τῶν τεσσάρων
and I heard ¹voice ¹one out of the four

κεράτων τοῦ θυσιαστηρίου τοῦ χρυσοῦ
horns   of the ²altar   -   ¹golden

τοῦ ἐνώπιον τοῦ θεοῦ, 14 λέγοντα τῷ
-   before   -   God,   saying   to the

---

did not have the seal of God on their foreheads. 5They were not given power to kill them, but only to torture them for five months. And the agony they suffered was like that of the sting of a scorpion when it strikes a man. 6During those days men will seek death, but will not find it; they will long to die, but death will elude them.

7The locusts looked like horses prepared for battle. On their heads they wore something like crowns of gold, and their faces resembled human faces. 8Their hair was like women's hair, and their teeth were like lions' teeth. 9They had breastplates like breastplates of iron, and the sound of their wings was like the thundering of many horses and chariots rushing into battle. 10They had tails and stings like scorpions, and in their tails they had power to torment people for five months. 11They had as king over them the angel of the Abyss, whose name in Hebrew is Abaddon, and in Greek, Apollyon.[n]

12The first woe is past; two other woes are yet to come.

13The sixth angel sounded his trumpet, and I heard a voice coming from the horns[o] of the golden altar that is before God. 14It said to the sixth angel who had

---

[k] I.e., destruction
[l] Some ancient mss. do not contain four

[n] 11 *Abaddon* and *Apollyon* mean *Destroyer*.
[o] 13 That is, projections

angel who had the trumpet, "Release the four angels who are bound at the great river Euphrates."

15And the four angels, who had been prepared for the hour and day and month and year, were released, so that they might kill a third of mankind.

16And the number of the armies of the horsemen was two hundred million; I heard the number of them.

17And this is how I saw in the vision those horses and those who sat on them: *the riders had breastplates the color* of fire and of hyacinth and of brimstone; and the heads of the horses are like the heads of lions; and out of their mouths proceed fire and smoke and brimstone.

18A third of mankind was killed by these three plagues, by the fire and the smoke and the brimstone, which proceeded out of their mouths.

19For the power of the horses is in their mouths and in their tails; for their tails are like serpents and have heads; and with them they do harm.

20And the rest of mankind, who were not killed by these plagues, did not repent of the works of their hands, so as not to worship demons, and the idols of gold and of silver and of brass and of stone and of wood, which can neither see nor hear nor walk;

ἕκτῳ ἀγγέλῳ, ὁ ἔχων τὴν σάλπιγγα·
sixth   angel,   –   having   the   trumpet:

λῦσον τοὺς τέσσαρας ἀγγέλους τοὺς
Loose   the   four   angels   –

δεδεμένους ἐπὶ τῷ ποταμῷ τῷ μεγάλῳ
having been bound at   the   ²river   –   ¹great

Εὐφράτῃ. **15** καὶ ἐλύθησαν οἱ τέσσαρες
Euphrates.   And   were loosed   the   four

ἄγγελοι οἱ ἡτοιμασμένοι εἰς τὴν ὥραν
angels   –   *having been* prepared for   the   hour

καὶ ἡμέραν καὶ μῆνα καὶ ἐνιαυτόν,
and   day   and   month   and   year,

ἵνα ἀποκτείνωσιν τὸ τρίτον τῶν ἀνθρώπων.
in or- they should kill   the   third   –   of men.
der that   [part]

16 καὶ ὁ ἀριθμὸς τῶν στρατευμάτων τοῦ
   And   the   number   of the   bodies of soldiers   of the

ἱππικοῦ δισμυριάδες μυριάδων· ἤκουσα τὸν
cavalry [was] two myriads of myriads;   I heard   the

ἀριθμὸν αὐτῶν. **17** καὶ οὕτως εἶδον
number   of them.   And   thus   I saw

τοὺς ἵππους ἐν τῇ ὁράσει καὶ τοὺς
the   horses   in   the   vision   and   the

καθημένους ἐπ' αὐτῶν, ἔχοντας θώρακας
[ones] sitting   on   them,   having   breastplates

πυρίνους καὶ ὑακινθίνους καὶ θειώδεις·
fire-coloured and   dusky red   and   sulphurous;

καὶ αἱ κεφαλαὶ τῶν ἵππων ὡς κεφαλαὶ
and   the   heads   of the   horses   as   heads

λεόντων, καὶ ἐκ τῶν στομάτων αὐτῶν
of lions,   and   out of   the   mouths   of them

ἐκπορεύεται πῦρ καὶ καπνὸς καὶ θεῖον.
proceeds   fire   and   smoke   and   sulphur.

18 ἀπὸ τῶν τριῶν πληγῶν τούτων ἀπεκτάν-
   From   *the*   ¹three   ²plagues   ¹these   were

θησαν τὸ τρίτον τῶν ἀνθρώπων, ἐκ
killed   the   third [part]   –   of men,   by

τοῦ πυρὸς καὶ τοῦ καπνοῦ καὶ τοῦ
the   fire   and   the   smoke   and   the

θείου τοῦ ἐκπορευομένου ἐκ τῶν στομάτων
sulphur   –   proceeding   out of   the   mouths

αὐτῶν. **19** ἡ γὰρ ἐξουσία τῶν ἵππων
of them.   For the   authority   of the   horses

ἐν τῷ στόματι αὐτῶν ἐστιν καὶ ἐν
²in   ³the   ⁴mouth   ⁵of them   ¹is   and   in

ταῖς οὐραῖς αὐτῶν· αἱ γὰρ οὐραὶ αὐτῶν
the   tails   of them;   for the   tails   of them

ὅμοιαι ὄφεσιν, ἔχουσαι κεφαλάς, καὶ ἐν
[are] like *to* serpents,   having   heads,   and with

αὐταῖς ἀδικοῦσιν. **20** καὶ οἱ λοιποὶ τῶν
them   they do harm.   And   the   rest   –

ἀνθρώπων, οἳ οὐκ ἀπεκτάνθησαν ἐν ταῖς
of men,   who   were not killed   by   –

πληγαῖς ταύταις, οὐδὲ μετενόησαν ἐκ
plagues   these,   not even   repented   of

τῶν ἔργων τῶν χειρῶν αὐτῶν, ἵνα μὴ
the   works   of the   hands   of them, in order not
                                      that

προσκυνήσουσιν τὰ δαιμόνια καὶ τὰ εἴδωλα
they will worship   –   demons   and   –   idols

τὰ χρυσᾶ καὶ τὰ ἀργυρᾶ καὶ τὰ χαλκᾶ
–   golden   and   –   silver   and   –   bronze

καὶ τὰ λίθινα καὶ τὰ ξύλινα, ἃ οὔτε
and   –   stone   and   –   wooden, which ²neither

βλέπειν δύνανται οὔτε ἀκούειν οὔτε
²to see   ¹can   nor   *to* hear   nor

---

the trumpet, "Release the four angels who are bound at the great river Euphrates." 15And the four angels who had been kept ready for this very hour and day and month and year were released to kill a third of mankind. 16The number of the mounted troops was two hundred million. I heard their number.

17The horses and riders I saw in my vision looked like this: Their breastplates were fiery red, dark blue, and yellow as sulfur. The heads of the horses resembled the heads of lions, and out of their mouths came fire, smoke and sulfur. 18A third of mankind was killed by the three plagues of fire, smoke and sulfur that came out of their mouths. 19The power of the horses was in their mouths and in their tails; for their tails were like snakes, having heads with which they inflict injury.

20The rest of mankind that were not killed by these plagues still did not repent of the work of their hands; they did not stop worshiping demons, and idols of gold, silver, bronze, stone and wood—idols that cannot see or

21and they did not repent of their murders nor of their sorceries nor of their immorality nor of their thefts.

Chapter 10

The Angel and the Little Book

AND I saw another strong angel coming down out of heaven, clothed with a cloud; and the rainbow was upon his head, and his face was like the sun, and his feet like pillars of fire;

2and he had in his hand a little book which was open. And he placed his right foot on the sea and his left on the land;

3and he cried out with a loud voice, as when a lion roars; and when he had cried out, the seven peals of thunder uttered their voices.

4And when the seven peals of thunder had spoken, I was about to write; and I heard a voice from heaven saying, "Seal up the things which the seven peals of thunder have spoken, and do not write them."

5And the angel whom I saw standing on the sea and on the land lifted up his right hand to heaven,

6and swore by Him who lives forever and ever, WHO CREATED HEAVEN AND THE THINGS IN IT, AND THE EARTH AND THE THINGS IN IT, AND THE SEA AND THE THINGS IN IT, that there shall be delay no longer,

7but in the days of the voice of the seventh angel, when he is about to sound, then the mystery of God is

περιπατεῖν, 21 καὶ οὐ μετενόησαν ἐκ τῶν
to walk,   and they repented not of the

φόνων αὐτῶν οὔτε ἐκ τῶν φαρμακειῶν
murders of them nor of the sorceries

αὐτῶν οὔτε ἐκ τῆς πορνείας αὐτῶν
of them nor of the fornication of them

οὔτε ἐκ τῶν κλεμμάτων αὐτῶν.
nor of the thefts of them.

10 Καὶ εἶδον ἄλλον ἄγγελον ἰσχυρὸν
And I saw another ²angel ¹strong

καταβαίνοντα ἐκ τοῦ οὐρανοῦ, περιβεβλημέ-
coming down out of -   heaven, having been clothed

νον νεφέλην, καὶ ἡ ἶρις ἐπὶ τὴν κεφαλὴν
[with] a cloud, and the rainbow on the head

αὐτοῦ, καὶ τὸ πρόσωπον αὐτοῦ ὡς ὁ
of him, and the face of him as the

ἥλιος, καὶ οἱ πόδες αὐτοῦ ὡς στῦλοι
sun, and the feet of him as pillars

πυρός, 2 καὶ ἔχων ἐν τῇ χειρὶ αὐτοῦ
of fire, and having in the hand of him

βιβλαρίδιον ἠνεῳγμένον. καὶ ἔθηκεν τὸν
a little scroll having been opened. and he placed ¹the

πόδα αὐτοῦ τὸν δεξιὸν ἐπὶ τῆς θαλάσσης,
²foot ⁴of him - ³right on the sea,

τὸν δὲ εὐώνυμον ἐπὶ τῆς γῆς, 3 καὶ
and the left on the land, and

ἔκραξεν φωνῇ μεγάλῃ ὥσπερ λέων μυκᾶται.
cried ¹voice great(loud) as a lion roars.

καὶ ὅτε ἔκραξεν, ἐλάλησαν αἱ ἑπτὰ
And when he cried, ¹spoke(uttered) ¹the ²seven

βρονταὶ τὰς ἑαυτῶν φωνάς. 4 Καὶ ὅτε
³thunders ⁵the ⁷of themselves ⁶voices. And when

ἐλάλησαν αἱ ἑπτὰ βρονταί, ἤμελλον
spoke the seven thunders, I was about

γράφειν· καὶ ἤκουσα φωνὴν ἐκ τοῦ
to write; and I heard a voice out of -

οὐρανοῦ λέγουσαν· σφράγισον ἃ ἐλάλησαν
heaven saying: Seal thou [the] ⁴spoke
                                    things which

αἱ ἑπτὰ βρονταί, καὶ μὴ αὐτὰ γράψῃς.
¹the ²seven ³thunders, and ⁵not ³them thou mayest
                                         ¹write.

5 Καὶ ὁ ἄγγελος, ὃν εἶδον ἑστῶτα
And the angel, whom I saw standing

ἐπὶ τῆς θαλάσσης καὶ ἐπὶ τῆς γῆς,
on the sea and on the land,

ἦρεν τὴν χεῖρα αὐτοῦ τὴν δεξιὰν εἰς
lifted ¹the ³hand ⁴of him - ²right to

τὸν οὐρανόν, 6 καὶ ὤμοσεν ἐν τῷ ζῶντι
- heaven, and swore by the [one] living

εἰς τοὺς αἰῶνας τῶν αἰώνων, ὃς ἔκτισεν
unto the ages of the ages, who created

τὸν οὐρανὸν καὶ τὰ ἐν αὐτῷ καὶ τὴν
the heaven and the things in it and the

γῆν καὶ τὰ ἐν αὐτῇ καὶ τὴν θάλασσαν
earth and the in it and the sea
          things

καὶ τὰ ἐν αὐτῇ, ὅτι χρόνος οὐκέτι
and the things in it, that time ¹no longer

ἔσται, 7 ἀλλ' ἐν ταῖς ἡμέραις τῆς
¹shall be, but in the days of the

φωνῆς τοῦ ἑβδόμου ἀγγέλου, ὅταν μέλλῃ
voice of the seventh angel, whenever he is about

σαλπίζειν, καὶ ἐτελέσθη τὸ μυστήριον
to trumpet, even was finished the mystery

Chapter 10

The Angel and the Little Scroll

THEN I saw another mighty angel coming down from heaven. He was robed in a cloud, with a rainbow above his head; his face was like the sun, and his legs were like fiery pillars. 2He was holding a little scroll, which lay open in his hand. He planted his right foot on the sea and his left foot on the land, 3and he gave a loud shout like the roar of a lion. When he shouted, the voices of the seven thunders spoke. 4And when the seven thunders spoke, I was about to write; but I heard a voice from heaven say, "Seal up what the seven thunders have said and do not write it down."

5Then the angel I had seen standing on the sea and on the land raised his right hand to heaven. 6And he swore by him who lives for ever and ever, who created the heavens and all that is in them, the earth and all that is in it, and the sea and all that is in it, and said, "There will be no more delay! 7But in the days when the seventh angel is about to sound his trumpet, the mystery of

hear or walk. 21Nor did they repent of their murders, their magic arts, their sexual immorality or their thefts.

finished, as He preached to His servants the prophets.

8And the voice which I heard from heaven, *I heard* again speaking with me, and saying, "Go, take the book which is open in the hand of the angel who stands on the sea and on the land."

9And I went to the angel, telling him to give me the little book. And he *said to me, "Take it, and eat it; and it will make your stomach bitter, but in your mouth it will be sweet as honey."

10And I took the little book out of the angel's hand and ate it, and it was in my mouth sweet as honey; and when I had eaten it, my stomach was made bitter.

11And they *said to me, "You must prophesy again concerning many peoples and nations and tongues and kings."

τοῦ   θεοῦ,   ὡς   εὐηγγέλισεν   τοὺς   ἑαυτοῦ
-    of God,   as   he preached [to]   the   ²of him*self*

δούλους   τοὺς   προφήτας.   8 Καὶ   ἡ   φωνὴ
¹slaves   the   prophets.   And   the   voice

ἦν   ἤκουσα   ἐκ   τοῦ   οὐρανοῦ,   πάλιν
which   I heard   out of   -   heaven,   again

λαλοῦσαν   μετ᾽   ἐμοῦ   καὶ   λέγουσαν·   ὕπαγε
speaking   with   me   and   saying: Go thou

λάβε   τὸ   βιβλίον   τὸ   ἠνεῳγμένον   ἐν   τῇ
take   the   scroll   -   *having been* opened   in   the

χειρὶ   τοῦ   ἀγγέλου   τοῦ   ἑστῶτος   ἐπὶ
hand   of the   angel   the   -   standing   on

τῆς   θαλάσσης   καὶ   ἐπὶ   τῆς   γῆς.   9 καὶ
the   sea   and   on   the   land.   And

ἀπῆλθα   πρὸς   τὸν   ἄγγελον,   λέγων   αὐτῷ
I went away   toward   the   angel,   telling   him

δοῦναί   μοι   τὸ   βιβλαρίδιον.   καὶ   λέγει
to give   me   the   little scroll.   And   he says

μοι·   λάβε   καὶ   κατάφαγε   αὐτό,   καὶ
to me: Take   and   devour   it,   and

πικρανεῖ   σου   τὴν   κοιλίαν,   ἀλλ᾽   ἐν   τῷ
it will embitter   ²of thee   ¹the   ²stomach,   but   in   the

στόματί   σου   ἔσται   γλυκὺ   ὡς   μέλι.
mouth   of thee   it will be   sweet   as   honey.

10 καὶ   ἔλαβον   τὸ   βιβλαρίδιον   ἐκ   τῆς
And   I took   the   little scroll   out of   the

χειρὸς   τοῦ   ἀγγέλου   καὶ   κατέφαγον   αὐτό,
hand   of the   angel   and   devoured   it,

καὶ   ἦν   ἐν   τῷ   στόματί   μου   ὡς   μέλι
and   it was   in   the   mouth   of me   as   ²honey

γλυκύ·   καὶ   ὅτε   ἔφαγον   αὐτό,   ἐπικράνθη
¹sweet;   and   when   I ate   it,   ⁴was made bitter

ἡ   κοιλία   μου.   11 καὶ   λέγουσίν   μοι·
¹the   ²stomach   ³of me.   And   they say   to me:

δεῖ   σε   πάλιν   προφητεῦσαι   ἐπὶ   λαοῖς
It behoves thee   again   to prophesy   before   peoples

καὶ   ἔθνεσιν   καὶ   γλώσσαις   καὶ   βασιλεῦσιν
and   nations   and   tongues   and   ¹kings

πολλοῖς.   11 Καὶ   ἐδόθη   μοι   κάλαμος   ὅμοιος
¹many.   And   was given to me   a reed   like

ῥάβδῳ,   λέγων·   ἔγειρε   καὶ   μέτρησον   τὸν   ναὸν
to a staff,   saying: Rise   and   measure   the   shrine

τοῦ   θεοῦ   καὶ   τὸ   θυσιαστήριον   καὶ   τοὺς
of God   and   the   altar   and   the

προσκυνοῦντας   ἐν   αὐτῷ.   2 καὶ   τὴν
[ones] worshipping   in   it.   And   the

αὐλὴν   τὴν   ἔξωθεν   τοῦ   ναοῦ   ἔκβαλε
²court   -   ¹outside   of the   shrine   cast *out*

ἔξωθεν   καὶ   μὴ   αὐτὴν   μετρήσῃς,   ὅτι
outside   and   ²not   ²it   thou mayest   because   ¹measure,

ἐδόθη   τοῖς   ἔθνεσιν,   καὶ   τὴν   πόλιν   τὴν
it was given to the   nations,   and   the   ²city   -

ἁγίαν   πατήσουσιν   μῆνας   τεσσεράκοντα
¹holy   they will trample   ²months   ¹forty-

[καὶ]   δύο.   3 καὶ   δώσω   τοῖς   δυσὶν
and   ²two.   And   I will give   to the   two

μάρτυσίν   μου,   καὶ   προφητεύσουσιν   ἡμέρας
witnesses   of me,   and   they will prophesy   ⁵days

χιλίας   διακοσίας   ἑξήκοντα   περιβεβλημένοι
¹a thousand   ²two hundred   ³[and] ⁴sixty   *having been* clothed

σάκκους.   4 οὗτοί   εἰσιν   αἱ   δύο   ἐλαῖαι
[in] sackclothes.   These   are   the   two   olive-trees

καὶ   αἱ   δύο   λυχνίαι   αἱ   ἐνώπιον   τοῦ
and   the   two   lampstands   -   ²before   ⁴the

God will be accomplished, just as he announced to his servants the prophets."

8Then the voice that I had heard from heaven spoke to me once more: "Go, take the scroll that lies open in the hand of the angel who is standing on the sea and on the land."

9So I went to the angel and asked him to give me the little scroll. He said to me, "Take it and eat it. It will turn your stomach sour, but in your mouth it will be as sweet as honey."

10I took the little scroll from the angel's hand and ate it. It tasted as sweet as honey in my mouth, but when I had eaten it, my stomach turned sour. 11Then I was told, "You must prophesy again about many peoples, nations, languages and kings."

Chapter 11

The Two Witnesses

AND there was given me a measuring rod like a staff; and someone said, "Rise and measure the temple of God, and the altar, and those who worship in it.

2"And leave out the court which is outside the temple, and do not measure it, for it has been given to the nations; and they will tread under foot the holy city for forty-two months.

3"And I will grant authority to my two witnesses, and they will prophesy for twelve hundred and sixty days, clothed in sackcloth."

4These are the two olive trees and the two lampstands that stand before the

---

Chapter 11

The Two Witnesses

I WAS given a reed like a measuring rod and was told, "Go and measure the temple of God and the altar, and count the worshipers there. 2But exclude the outer court; do not measure it, because it has been given to the Gentiles. They will trample on the holy city for 42 months. 3And I will give power to my two witnesses, and they will prophesy for 1,260 days, clothed in sackcloth." 4These are the two olive trees and the two lampstands that stand before the

Lord of the earth.

5And if anyone desires to harm them, fire proceeds out of their mouth and devours their enemies; and if anyone would desire to harm them, in this manner he must be killed.

6These have the power to shut up the sky, in order that rain may not fall during the days of their prophesying; and they have power over the waters to turn them into blood, and to smite the earth with every plague, as often as they desire.

7And when they have finished their testimony, the beast that comes up out of the abyss will make war with them, and overcome them and kill them.

8And their dead *m*bodies *will lie* in the street of the great city which *n*mystically is called Sodom and Egypt, where also their Lord was crucified.

9And those from the peoples and tribes and tongues and nations *m*will look at their dead *m*bodies for three and a half days, and will not permit their dead bodies to be laid in a tomb.

10And those who dwell on the earth *will* rejoice over them and make merry; and they will send gifts to one another, because these two prophets tormented those who dwell on the earth.

11And after the three and a half days the breath of life from God came into them, and they stood on their feet; and great fear fell

---

κυρίου τῆς γῆς ἑστῶτες. 5 καὶ εἴ τις
4Lord 5of the 6earth 1standing.   And if anyone

αὐτοὺς θέλει ἀδικῆσαι, πῦρ ἐκπορεύεται
3them 1wishes 2to harm, fire proceeds

ἐκ τοῦ στόματος αὐτῶν καὶ κατεσθίει
out of the mouth of them and devours

τοὺς ἐχθροὺς αὐτῶν· καὶ εἴ τις θελήσῃ
the enemies of them; and if anyone should wish

αὐτοὺς ἀδικῆσαι, οὕτως δεῖ αὐτὸν
3them 1to harm, thus it behoves him

ἀποκτανθῆναι. 6 οὗτοι ἔχουσιν τὴν ἐξουσίαν
to be killed.   These have the authority

κλεῖσαι τὸν οὐρανόν, ἵνα μὴ ὑετὸς
to shut - heaven, in order that 2not 1rain

βρέχῃ τὰς ἡμέρας τῆς προφητείας αὐτῶν,
3may the days of the prophecy of them,
4rain(fall)

καὶ ἐξουσίαν ἔχουσιν ἐπὶ τῶν ὑδάτων
and authority they have over the waters

στρέφειν αὐτὰ εἰς αἷμα καὶ πατάξαι
to turn them into blood and to strike

τὴν γῆν ἐν πάσῃ πληγῇ ὁσάκις ἐὰν
the earth with every [kind of] plague as often as

θελήσωσιν. 7 Καὶ ὅταν τελέσωσιν τὴν
they may wish.   And whenever they finish the

μαρτυρίαν αὐτῶν, τὸ θηρίον τὸ ἀναβαῖνον
witness of them, the beast the - coming up

ἐκ τῆς ἀβύσσου ποιήσει μετ' αὐτῶν
out of the abyss 1will make 3with 4them

πόλεμον καὶ νικήσει αὐτοὺς καὶ ἀποκτενεῖ
2war and will overcome them and will kill

αὐτούς. 8 καὶ τὸ πτῶμα αὐτῶν ἐπὶ
them.   And the corpse of them on

τῆς πλατείας τῆς πόλεως τῆς μεγάλης,
the open street of the 2city 1great,

ἥτις καλεῖται πνευματικῶς Σόδομα καὶ
which is called spiritually Sodom and

Αἴγυπτος, ὅπου καὶ ὁ κύριος αὐτῶν
Egypt, where indeed the Lord of them

ἐσταυρώθη. 9 καὶ βλέπουσιν ἐκ τῶν
was crucified.   And 10see 1[some] of 2the

λαῶν καὶ φυλῶν καὶ γλωσσῶν καὶ
3peoples 4and 5tribes 6and 7tongues 8and

ἐθνῶν τὸ πτῶμα αὐτῶν ἡμέρας τρεῖς
9nations the corpse of them 4days 3three

καὶ ἥμισυ, καὶ τὰ πτώματα αὐτῶν
1and 2a half, and 2the 3corpses 4of them

οὐκ ἀφίουσιν τεθῆναι εἰς μνῆμα. 10 καὶ
1they do not allow to be placed in a tomb.   And

οἱ κατοικοῦντες ἐπὶ τῆς γῆς χαίρουσιν
the [ones] dwelling on the earth rejoice

ἐπ' αὐτοῖς καὶ εὐφραίνονται, καὶ δῶρα
over them and are glad, and 2gifts

πέμψουσιν ἀλλήλοις, ὅτι οὗτοι οἱ δύο
1they will send to one another, because these the two

προφῆται ἐβασάνισαν τοὺς κατοικοῦντας
prophets tormented the [ones] dwelling

ἐπὶ τῆς γῆς. 11 Καὶ μετὰ [τὰς] τρεῖς
on the earth.   And after the 1three

ἡμέρας καὶ ἥμισυ πνεῦμα ζωῆς ἐκ τοῦ
4days 2and 3a half a spirit of life out of -

θεοῦ εἰσῆλθεν ἐν αὐτοῖς, καὶ ἔστησαν
God entered in[to] them, and they stood

ἐπὶ τοὺς πόδας αὐτῶν, καὶ φόβος μέγας
on the feet of them, and 2fear 1great

Lord of the earth. 5If anyone tries to harm them, fire comes from their mouths and devours their enemies. This is how anyone who wants to harm them must die. 6These men have power to shut up the sky so that it will not rain during the time they are prophesying; and they have power to turn the waters into blood and to strike the earth with every kind of plague as often as they want.

7Now when they have finished their testimony, the beast that comes up from the Abyss will attack them, and overpower and kill them. 8Their bodies will lie in the street of the great city, which is figuratively called Sodom and Egypt, where also their Lord was crucified. 9For three and a half days men from every people, tribe, language and nation will gaze on their bodies and refuse them burial. 10The inhabitants of the earth will gloat over them and will celebrate by sending each other gifts, because these two prophets had tormented those who live on the earth.

11But after the three and a half days a breath of life from God entered them, and they stood on their feet, and terror struck

---

m Some ancient mss. read *body*
n Lit., *spiritually*

upon those who were beholding them.
¹²And they heard a loud voice from heaven saying to them, "Come up here." And they went up into heaven in the cloud, and their enemies beheld them.
¹³And in that hour there was a great earthquake, and a tenth of the city fell; and seven thousand people were killed in the earthquake, and the rest were terrified and gave glory to the God of heaven.
¹⁴The second woe is past; behold, the third woe is coming quickly.

The Seventh Trumpet—Christ's Reign Foreseen

¹⁵And the seventh angel sounded; and there arose loud voices in heaven, saying,
"The kingdom of the world has become *the kingdom* of our Lord, and of His ⁰Christ; and He will reign forever and ever."
¹⁶And the twenty-four elders, who sit on their thrones before God, fell on their faces and worshiped God,
¹⁷saying,
"We give Thee thanks, O Lord God, the Almighty, who art and who wast, because Thou hast taken Thy great power and hast begun to reign.
¹⁸And the nations were enraged, and Thy wrath came, and the time *came* for the dead to be judged, and *the time* to give their reward to Thy bond-servants the prophets and to the saints and to those who fear Thy name, the small and

⁰ I.e., Messiah

ἐπέπεσεν ἐπὶ τοὺς θεωροῦντας αὐτούς.
fell on   on   the [ones] beholding   them.
12 καὶ ἤκουσαν φωνῆς μεγάλης ἐκ τοῦ
And they heard ¹voice ¹a great(loud) out of
οὐρανοῦ λεγούσης αὐτοῖς· ἀνάβατε ὧδε·
heaven   saying   to them: Come ye up here;
καὶ ἀνέβησαν εἰς τὸν οὐρανὸν ἐν τῇ
and they went up to   –   heaven   in the
νεφέλῃ, καὶ ἐθεώρησαν αὐτοὺς οἱ ἐχθροὶ
cloud, and ⁴beheld   ⁵them the ⁶enemies
αὐτῶν. **13** Καὶ ἐν ἐκείνῃ τῇ ὥρᾳ ἐγένετο
⁷of them. And in that   the hour ⁸occurred
σεισμὸς μέγας, καὶ τὸ δέκατον τῆς
⁹earthquake ¹a great, and the tenth [part] of the
πόλεως ἔπεσεν, καὶ ἀπεκτάνθησαν ἐν τῷ
city   fell, and ⁴were killed   ⁶in ⁷the
σεισμῷ ὀνόματα ἀνθρώπων χιλιάδες ἑπτά,
⁸earthquake ¹names ⁴of men ³thousands ²seven,
καὶ οἱ λοιποὶ ἔμφοβοι ἐγένοντο καὶ
and the rest ¹terrified ²became   and
ἔδωκαν δόξαν τῷ θεῷ τοῦ οὐρανοῦ.
gave   glory to the God – of heaven.
14 Ἡ οὐαὶ ἡ δευτέρα ἀπῆλθεν· ἰδοὺ
The ²woe – ¹second passed away; behold[,]
ἡ οὐαὶ ἡ τρίτη ἔρχεται ταχύ.
the ²woe – ¹third is coming quickly.
15 Καὶ ὁ ἕβδομος ἄγγελος ἐσάλπισεν·
And the seventh angel   trumpeted;
καὶ ἐγένοντο φωναὶ μεγάλαι ἐν τῷ
and there were voices great(loud) in –
οὐρανῷ, λέγοντες· ἐγένετο ἡ βασιλεία
heaven, saying: ²became ¹The ¹kingdom
τοῦ κόσμου τοῦ κυρίου ἡμῶν καὶ τοῦ
²of the ⁴world of the Lord of us and of the
⁵[the kingdom]
χριστοῦ αὐτοῦ, καὶ βασιλεύσει εἰς τοὺς
Christ of him, and he shall reign unto the
αἰῶνας τῶν αἰώνων. **16** καὶ οἱ εἴκοσι
ages   of the ages.   And the twenty-
τέσσαρες πρεσβύτεροι, οἱ ἐνώπιον τοῦ
four   elders,   –   ²before   –
θεοῦ καθήμενοι ἐπὶ τοὺς θρόνους αὐτῶν,
³God ¹sitting on   the thrones   of them,
ἔπεσαν ἐπὶ τὰ πρόσωπα αὐτῶν καὶ
fell   on the faces   of them and
προσεκύνησαν τῷ θεῷ, **17** λέγοντες·
worshiped   – God,   saying:
εὐχαριστοῦμέν σοι, κύριε ὁ θεὸς ὁ
We thank   thee, [O] Lord – God the
παντοκράτωρ, ὁ ὢν καὶ ὁ ἦν, ὅτι
Almighty,   the [one] being and the was, because
= the one who is [one who]
εἴληφας τὴν δύναμίν σου τὴν μεγάλην
thou hast taken ¹the ³power ⁴of thee – ²great
καὶ ἐβασίλευσας· **18** καὶ τὰ ἔθνη ὠργίσ-
and didst reign;   and the nations were
θησαν, καὶ ἦλθεν ἡ ὀργή σου καὶ ὁ
wrathful, and ⁴came ¹the ²wrath ³of thee and the
καιρὸς τῶν νεκρῶν κριθῆναι καὶ δοῦναι
time   of the dead to be judged and to give
τὸν μισθὸν τοῖς δούλοις σου τοῖς προφήταις
the reward to the slaves of thee to the prophets
καὶ τοῖς ἁγίοις καὶ τοῖς φοβουμένοις
and to the saints and to the [ones] fearing
τὸ ὄνομά σου, τοῖς μικροῖς καὶ τοῖς
the name of thee, to the small and to the

---

those who saw them.
¹²Then they heard a loud voice from heaven saying to them, "Come up here." And they went up to heaven in a cloud, while their enemies looked on.
¹³At that very hour there was a severe earthquake and a tenth of the city collapsed. Seven thousand people were killed in the earthquake, and the survivors were terrified and gave glory to the God of heaven.
¹⁴The second woe has passed; the third woe is coming soon.

The Seventh Trumpet

¹⁵The seventh angel sounded his trumpet, and there were loud voices in heaven, which said:

"The kingdom of the
  world has become
  the kingdom of our
  Lord and of his
  Christ,
and he will reign for
  ever and ever."

¹⁶And the twenty-four elders, who were seated on their thrones before God, fell on their faces and worshiped God, ¹⁷saying:

"We give thanks to you,
  Lord God Almighty,
the One who is and
  who was,
because you have taken
  your great power
  and have begun to
  reign.
¹⁸The nations were angry;
  and your wrath has
  come.
The time has come for
  judging the dead,
  and for rewarding your
    servants the
    prophets
  and your saints and
    those who reverence
    your name,

the great, and to destroy those who destroy the earth.''

19And the temple of God which is in heaven was opened; and the ark of His covenant appeared in His temple, and there were flashes of lightning and sounds and peals of thunder and an earthquake and a great hailstorm.

μεγάλοις, καὶ διαφθεῖραι τοὺς διαφθείροντας
great, and to destroy the [ones] destroying

τὴν γῆν. 19 καὶ ἠνοίγη ὁ ναὸς τοῦ
the earth. And was opened the shrine

θεοῦ ὁ ἐν τῷ οὐρανῷ, καὶ ὤφθη ἡ
of God - in - heaven, and was seen the

κιβωτὸς τῆς διαθήκης αὐτοῦ ἐν τῷ
ark of the covenant of him in the

ναῷ αὐτοῦ, καὶ ἐγένοντο ἀστραπαὶ καὶ
shrine of him, and occurred lightnings and

φωναὶ καὶ βρονταὶ καὶ σεισμὸς καὶ
voices and thunders and an earthquake and

χάλαζα μεγάλη.
³hail ¹a great.

---

both small and great—and for destroying those who destroy the earth.''

19Then God's temple in heaven was opened, and within his temple was seen the ark of his covenant. And there came flashes of lightning, rumblings, peals of thunder, an earthquake and a great hailstorm.

Chapter 12

The Woman, Israel

AND a great sign appeared in heaven: a woman clothed with the sun, and the moon under her feet, and on her head a crown of twelve stars;

2and she was with child; and she *cried out, being in labor and in pain to give birth.

The Red Dragon, Satan

3And another sign appeared in heaven: and behold, a great red dragon having seven heads and ten horns, and on his heads *were seven diadems.

4And his tail *swept away a third of the stars of heaven, and threw them to the earth. And the dragon stood before the woman who was about to give birth, so that when she gave birth he might devour her child.

The Male Child, Christ

5And she gave birth to a son, a male *child, who is to rule all the nations with a rod of iron; and her child was caught up to God and to His throne.

6And the woman fled into the wilderness where she *had a place prepared by God, so that there she might be nourished for one thousand two hundred and sixty days.

---

12 Καὶ σημεῖον μέγα ὤφθη ἐν τῷ
And ¹sign ¹a great was seen in -

οὐρανῷ, γυνὴ περιβεβλημένη τὸν ἥλιον,
heaven, a woman *having been* clothed [with] the sun,

καὶ ἡ σελήνη ὑποκάτω τῶν ποδῶν αὐτῆς,
and the moon underneath the feet of her,

καὶ ἐπὶ τῆς κεφαλῆς αὐτῆς στέφανος
and on the head of her a crown

ἀστέρων δώδεκα, 2 καὶ ἐν γαστρὶ ἔχουσα,
²stars ¹of twelve, and in womb having,
= being pregnant,

καὶ κράζει ὠδίνουσα καὶ βασανιζομένη
and she cries suffering birth-pains and being distressed

τεκεῖν. 3 καὶ ὤφθη ἄλλο σημεῖον
to bear. And was seen another sign

ἐν τῷ οὐρανῷ, καὶ ἰδοὺ δράκων μέγας
in - heaven, and behold[,] ³dragon ¹a great

πυρρός, ἔχων κεφαλὰς ἑπτὰ καὶ κέρατα
²red, having ²heads ¹seven and ¹horns

δέκα καὶ ἐπὶ τὰς κεφαλὰς αὐτοῦ ἑπτὰ
¹ten and on the heads of him seven

διαδήματα, 4 καὶ ἡ οὐρὰ αὐτοῦ σύρει
diadems, and the tail of him draws

τὸ τρίτον τῶν ἀστέρων τοῦ οὐρανοῦ,
the third [part] of the stars - of heaven,

καὶ ἔβαλεν αὐτοὺς εἰς τὴν γῆν. Καὶ
and cast them to the earth. And

ὁ δράκων ἔστηκεν ἐνώπιον τῆς γυναικὸς
the dragon stood before the woman

τῆς μελλούσης τεκεῖν, ἵνα ὅταν τέκῃ
- *being* about to bear, in order whenever she
that bears

τὸ τέκνον αὐτῆς καταφάγῃ. 5 καὶ
³the ²child ⁴of her ¹he might devour. And

ἔτεκεν υἱὸν ἄρσεν, ὃς μέλλει ποιμαίνειν
she bore a son[,] a male, who is about to shepherd

πάντα τὰ ἔθνη ἐν ῥάβδῳ σιδηρᾷ· καὶ
all the nations with ²staff ¹an iron; and

ἡρπάσθη τὸ τέκνον αὐτῆς πρὸς τὸν
⁴was seized ¹the ²child ³of her to -

θεὸν καὶ πρὸς τὸν θρόνον αὐτοῦ. 6 καὶ
God and to the throne of him. And

ἡ γυνὴ ἔφυγεν εἰς τὴν ἔρημον, ὅπου
the woman fled into the desert, where

ἔχει ἐκεῖ τόπον ἡτοιμασμένον ἀπὸ
she has *there* a place *having been* prepared from

τοῦ θεοῦ, ἵνα ἐκεῖ τρέφωσιν αὐτὴν
- God, in order that there they might nourish her

ἡμέρας χιλίας διακοσίας ἑξήκοντα.
⁵days ¹a thousand ²two hundred ³[and] ⁴sixty.

Chapter 12

The Woman and the Dragon

A GREAT and wondrous sign appeared in heaven: a woman clothed with the sun, with the moon under her feet and a crown of twelve stars on her head. 2She was pregnant and cried out in pain as she was about to give birth. 3Then another sign appeared in heaven: an enormous red dragon with seven heads and ten horns and seven crowns on his heads. 4His tail swept a third of the stars out of the sky and flung them to the earth. The dragon stood in front of the woman who was about to give birth, so that he might devour her child the moment it was born. 5She gave birth to a son, a male child, who will rule all the nations with an iron scepter. And her child was snatched up to God and to his throne. 6The woman fled into the desert to a place prepared for her by God, where she might be taken care of for 1,260 days.

The Angel, Michael

7And there was war in heaven, Michael and his angels waging war with the dragon. And the dragon and his angels waged war,

8and they were not strong enough, and there was no longer a place found for them in heaven.

9And the great dragon was thrown down, the serpent of old who is called the devil and Satan, who deceives the whole world; he was thrown down to the earth, and his angels were thrown down with him.

10And I heard a loud voice in heaven, saying,

"Now the salvation, and the power, and the kingdom of our God and the authority of His Christ have come, for the accuser of our brethren has been thrown down, who accuses them before our God day and night.

11"And they overcame him because of the blood of the Lamb and because of the word of their testimony, and they did not love their life even to death.

12"For this reason, rejoice, O heavens and you who dwell in them. Woe to the earth and the sea, because the devil has come down to you, having great wrath, knowing that he has *only* a short time."

13And when the dragon saw that he was thrown down to the earth, he persecuted the woman who gave birth to the male *child*.

14And the two wings of the great eagle were given to the woman, in order that she might fly into the wil-

---

7 Καὶ ἐγένετο πόλεμος ἐν τῷ οὐρανῷ,
And occurred war in – heaven,

ὁ Μιχαὴλ καὶ οἱ ἄγγελοι αὐτοῦ τοῦ
– Michael and the angels of him –

πολεμῆσαι μετὰ τοῦ δράκοντος. καὶ ὁ
to make war[d] with the dragon. And the

δράκων ἐπολέμησεν καὶ οἱ ἄγγελοι αὐτοῦ,
dragon warred and the angels of him,

8 καὶ οὐκ ἴσχυσεν, οὐδὲ τόπος εὑρέθη
and prevailed not, not even place was found

αὐτῶν ἔτι ἐν τῷ οὐρανῷ. **9** καὶ ἐβλήθη
of them still in – heaven. And was cast

ὁ δράκων ὁ μέγας, ὁ ὄφις ὁ ἀρχαῖος,
[1]the [2]dragon – [2]great, [4]the [6]serpent – [6]old,

ὁ καλούμενος Διάβολος καὶ ὁ Σατανᾶς,
– being called Devil and the Satan,

ὁ πλανῶν τὴν οἰκουμένην ὅλην, ἐβλήθη
the deceiving the [2]inhabited [1]whole, was cast
[one] [earth]

εἰς τὴν γῆν, καὶ οἱ ἄγγελοι αὐτοῦ μετ᾽
to the earth, and the angels of him with

αὐτοῦ ἐβλήθησαν. **10** καὶ ἤκουσα φωνὴν
him were cast. And I heard [2]voice

μεγάλην ἐν τῷ οὐρανῷ λέγουσαν ἄρτι
[1]a great(loud) in – heaven saying: Now

ἐγένετο ἡ σωτηρία καὶ ἡ δύναμις καὶ
became the salvation and the power and

ἡ βασιλεία τοῦ θεοῦ ἡμῶν καὶ ἡ ἐξουσία
the kingdom of the God of us and the authority

τοῦ χριστοῦ αὐτοῦ, ὅτι ἐβλήθη ὁ κατήγωρ
of the Christ of him, because [6]was cast [1]the [2]accuser

τῶν ἀδελφῶν ἡμῶν, ὁ κατηγορῶν αὐτοὺς
[3]of the [4]brothers [5]of us, the [one] accusing them

ἐνώπιον τοῦ θεοῦ ἡμῶν ἡμέρας καὶ
before the God of us day and

νυκτός. **11** καὶ αὐτοὶ ἐνίκησαν αὐτὸν
night. And they overcame him

διὰ τὸ αἷμα τοῦ ἀρνίου καὶ διὰ τὸν
be- the blood of the Lamb and because the
cause of of

λόγον τῆς μαρτυρίας αὐτῶν, καὶ οὐκ
word of the witness of them, and not

ἠγάπησαν τὴν ψυχὴν αὐτῶν ἄχρι θανάτου.
they loved the life of them until death.

12 διὰ τοῦτο εὐφραίνεσθε, οὐρανοὶ καὶ
Therefore be ye glad, heavens and

οἱ ἐν αὐτοῖς σκηνοῦντες· οὐαὶ τὴν
the [2]in [3]them [1]tabernacling; woe [to] the
[ones]

γῆν καὶ τὴν θάλασσαν, ὅτι κατέβη ὁ
earth and the sea, because [2]came down [1]the

διάβολος πρὸς ὑμᾶς ἔχων θυμὸν μέγαν,
[2]devil to you having [2]anger [1]great,

εἰδὼς ὅτι ὀλίγον καιρὸν ἔχει. **13** Καὶ
knowing that [2]few(short) [3]time [1]he has. And

ὅτε εἶδεν ὁ δράκων ὅτι ἐβλήθη εἰς
when [2]saw [1]the [2]dragon that he was cast to

τὴν γῆν, ἐδίωξεν τὴν γυναῖκα ἥτις
the earth, he pursued the woman who

ἔτεκεν τὸν ἄρσενα. **14** καὶ ἐδόθησαν
bore the male. And were given

τῇ γυναικὶ αἱ δύο πτέρυγες τοῦ ἀετοῦ
to the woman the two wings of the [2]eagle

τοῦ μεγάλου, ἵνα πέτηται εἰς τὴν ἔρημον
– [1]great, that she might to the desert
[in order fly
that]

7And there was war in heaven. Michael and his angels fought against the dragon, and the dragon and his angels fought back.
8But he was not strong enough, and they lost their place in heaven. 9The great dragon was hurled down—that ancient serpent called the devil, or Satan, who leads the whole world astray. He was hurled to the earth, and his angels with him.
10Then I heard a loud voice in heaven say:

"Now have come the salvation and the power and the kingdom of our God,
and the authority of his Christ.
For the accuser of our brothers,
who accuses them before our God day and night,
has been hurled down.
11They overcame him by the blood of the Lamb
and by the word of their testimony;
they did not love their lives so much as to shrink from death.
12Therefore rejoice, you heavens and you who dwell in them!
But woe to the earth and the sea,
because the devil has gone down to you!
He is filled with fury,
because he knows that his time is short."

13When the dragon saw that he had been hurled to the earth, he pursued the woman who had given birth to the male child. 14The woman was given the two wings of a great eagle, so that she might fly to the derness to her place, where she *was nourished for a time and times and half a time, from the presence of the serpent.

15And the serpent poured water like a river out of his mouth after the woman, so that he might cause her to be swept away with the flood.

16And the earth helped the woman, and the earth opened its mouth and drank up the river which the dragon poured out of his mouth.

17And the dragon was enraged with the woman, and went off to make war with the rest of her offspring, who keep the commandments of God and hold to the testimony of Jesus.

Chapter 13

The Beast from the Sea

AND he stood on the sand of the seashore. And I saw a beast coming up out of the sea, having ten horns and seven heads, and on his horns *were* ten diadems, and on his heads *were* blasphemous names.

2And the beast which I saw was like a leopard, and his feet were *like those of* a bear, and his mouth like the mouth of a lion. And the dragon gave him his power and his throne and great authority.

3And *I* saw one of his heads as if it had been slain, and his fatal wound was healed. And the whole

---

εἰς τὸν τόπον αὐτῆς, ὅπου τρέφεται
to the place of her, where she is nourished

ἐκεῖ καιρὸν καὶ καιροὺς καὶ ἥμισυ καιροῦ
there a time and times and half of a time

ἀπὸ προσώπου τοῦ ὄφεως. 15 καὶ ἔβαλεν
from [the] face of the serpent. And ³cast

ὁ ὄφις ἐκ τοῦ στόματος αὐτοῦ ὀπίσω
¹the ²serpent out of the mouth of him behind

τῆς γυναικὸς ὕδωρ ὡς ποταμόν, ἵνα
the woman water as a river, in order that

αὐτὴν ποταμοφόρητον ποιήσῃ. 16 καὶ
²her ³carried off by [the] river ¹he might make. And

ἐβοήθησεν ἡ γῆ τῇ γυναικί, καὶ ἤνοιξεν
³helped ¹the ²earth the woman, and ²opened

ἡ γῆ τὸ στόμα αὐτῆς καὶ κατέπιεν
¹the ²earth the mouth of it and swallowed

τὸν ποταμὸν ὃν ἔβαλεν ὁ δράκων ἐκ
the river which ²cast ¹the ²dragon out of

τοῦ στόματος αὐτοῦ. 17 καὶ ὠργίσθη
the mouth of him. And ³was enraged

ὁ δράκων ἐπὶ τῇ γυναικί, καὶ ἀπῆλθεν
¹the ²dragon over the woman, and went away

ποιῆσαι πόλεμον μετὰ τῶν λοιπῶν τοῦ
to make war with the rest of the

σπέρματος αὐτῆς, τῶν τηρούντων τὰς
seed of her, the [ones] keeping the

ἐντολὰς τοῦ θεοῦ καὶ ἐχόντων τὴν
commandments - of God and having the

μαρτυρίαν Ἰησοῦ· (18) καὶ ἐστάθη ἐπὶ τὴν
witness of Jesus; and he stood on the

ἄμμον τῆς θαλάσσης.
sand of the sea.

13 Καὶ εἶδον ἐκ τῆς θαλάσσης θηρίον
And I saw ²out of ⁴the ⁵sea ¹a beast

ἀναβαῖνον, ἔχον κέρατα δέκα καὶ κεφαλὰς
²coming up, having ²horns ¹ten and ²heads

ἑπτά, καὶ ἐπὶ τῶν κεράτων αὐτοῦ δέκα
¹seven, and on the horns of it* ten

διαδήματα, καὶ ἐπὶ τὰς κεφαλὰς αὐτοῦ
diadems, and on the heads of it

ὀνόματα βλασφημίας. 2 καὶ τὸ θηρίον
names of blasphemy. And the beast

ὃ εἶδον ἦν ὅμοιον παρδάλει, καὶ οἱ
which I saw was like to a leopard, and the

πόδες αὐτοῦ ὡς ἄρκου, καὶ τὸ στόμα
feet of it as of a bear, and the mouth

αὐτοῦ ὡς στόμα λέοντος. καὶ ἔδωκεν
of it as [the] mouth of a lion. And ³gave

αὐτῷ ὁ δράκων τὴν δύναμιν αὐτοῦ καὶ
⁴to it ¹the ²dragon the power of it and

τὸν θρόνον αὐτοῦ καὶ ἐξουσίαν μεγάλην.
the throne of it and ²authority ¹great.

3 καὶ μίαν ἐκ τῶν κεφαλῶν αὐτοῦ ὡς
And one of the heads of it as

ἐσφαγμένην εἰς θάνατον, καὶ ἡ πληγὴ
having been slain to death, and the stroke

τοῦ θανάτου αὐτοῦ ἐθεραπεύθη. καὶ
of the death of it was healed. And

---

place prepared for her in the desert, where she would be taken care of for a time, times and half a time, out of the serpent's reach. 15Then from his mouth the serpent spewed water like a river, to overtake the woman and sweep her away with the torrent. 16But the earth helped the woman by opening its mouth and swallowing the river that the dragon had spewed out of his mouth. 17Then the dragon was enraged at the woman and went off to make war against the rest of her offspring—those who obey God's commandments and hold to the testimony of Jesus.

1And the dragonᵖ stood on the shore of the sea.

The Beast out of the Sea

And I saw a beast coming out of the sea. He had ten horns and seven heads, with ten crowns on his horns, and on each head a blasphemous name. 2The beast I saw resembled a leopard, but had feet like those of a bear and a mouth like that of a lion. The dragon gave the beast his power and his throne and great authority. 3One of the heads of the beast seemed to have had a fatal wound, but the fatal wound had been healed. The whole world

---

* αὐτοῦ, of course, may be neuter or masculine—" of it " or " of him". δράκων being masculine (=Satan), we have kept to the masculine. But θηρίον is neuter. Yet if it stands for a person, as ἀρνίον certainly does, it too should be treated, as to the pronoun, as a masculine. However, not to enter the province of interpretation, we have rendered αὐτοῦ by " of it", though it will be seen that αὐτόν (him) is used in ver. 8, τίς (who?) in ver. 4, and ὅς (who) in ver. 14. See also ch. 17. 11.

earth was amazed *and followed* after the beast;

⁴and they worshiped the dragon, because he gave his authority to the beast; and they worshiped the beast, saying, "Who is like the beast, and who is able to wage war with him?"

⁵And there was given to him a mouth speaking arrogant words and blasphemies; and authority to act for forty-two months was given to him.

⁶And he opened his mouth in blasphemies against God, to blaspheme His name and His tabernacle, *that is*, those who dwell in heaven.

⁷And it was given to him to make war with the saints and to overcome them; and authority over every tribe and people and tongue and nation was given to him.

⁸And all who dwell on the earth will worship him, *everyone* whose name has not been *p*written from the foundation of the world in the book of life of the Lamb who has been slain.

⁹If anyone has an ear, let him hear.

¹⁰If anyone *q is destined* for captivity, to captivity he goes; if anyone kills with the sword, with the sword he must be killed. Here is the perseverance and the faith of the saints.

The Beast from the Earth

¹¹And I saw another beast coming up out of the earth; and he had two horns like a lamb, and he spoke as a dragon.

¹²And he exercises all the authority of the first beast in his presence. And he

---

ἐθαυμάσθη ὅλη ἡ γῆ ὀπίσω τοῦ θηρίου,
⁴wondered ¹all ²the ³earth after the beast,

4 καὶ προσεκύνησαν τῷ δράκοντι, ὅτι
and they worshipped the dragon, because

ἔδωκεν τὴν ἐξουσίαν τῷ θηρίῳ, καὶ
he gave the authority to the beast, and

προσεκύνησαν τῷ θηρίῳ λέγοντες· τίς
they worshipped the beast saying: Who

ὅμοιος τῷ θηρίῳ, καὶ τίς δύναται
[is] like to the beast, and who can

πολεμῆσαι μετ' αὐτοῦ; 5 καὶ ἐδόθη αὐτῷ
to make war with it? And was given to it

στόμα λαλοῦν μεγάλα καὶ βλασφημίας,
a mouth speaking great things and blasphemies,

καὶ ἐδόθη αὐτῷ ἐξουσία ποιῆσαι μῆνας
and was given to it authority to act ²months

τεσσεράκοντα [καὶ] δύο. 6 καὶ ἤνοιξεν
¹forty-two. And it opened

τὸ στόμα αὐτοῦ εἰς βλασφημίας πρὸς
the mouth of it in blasphemies against

τὸν θεόν, βλασφημῆσαι τὸ ὄνομα αὐτοῦ
- God, to blaspheme the name of him

καὶ τὴν σκηνὴν αὐτοῦ, τοὺς ἐν τῷ
and the tabernacle of him, ¹the [ones] ²in -

οὐρανῷ σκηνοῦντας. 7 καὶ ἐδόθη αὐτῷ
⁴heaven ³tabernacling. And it was given to it

ποιῆσαι πόλεμον μετὰ τῶν ἁγίων καὶ
to make war with the saints and

νικῆσαι αὐτούς, καὶ ἐδόθη αὐτῷ ἐξουσία
to overcome them, and ²was given ³to it ¹authority

ἐπὶ πᾶσαν φυλὴν καὶ λαὸν καὶ γλῶσσαν
over every tribe and people and tongue

καὶ ἔθνος. 8 καὶ προσκυνήσουσιν αὐτὸν
and nation. And ⁷will worship ⁸him

πάντες οἱ κατοικοῦντες ἐπὶ τῆς γῆς,
¹all ²the [ones] ³dwelling ⁵on ⁶the ⁴earth,

οὗ οὐ γέγραπται τὸ ὄνομα αὐτοῦ ἐν
⁹of ⁷has not been written ¹the ²name *of him* in
whom

τῷ βιβλίῳ τῆς ζωῆς τοῦ ἀρνίου τοῦ
the scroll - of life of the Lamb -

ἐσφαγμένου ἀπὸ καταβολῆς κόσμου.
having been slain from [the] foundation of [the] world.

9 Εἴ τις ἔχει οὖς ἀκουσάτω. 10 εἴ
If anyone has an ear let him hear. If

τις εἰς αἰχμαλωσίαν, εἰς αἰχμαλωσίαν
anyone [is] for captivity, to captivity

ὑπάγει· εἴ τις ἐν μαχαίρῃ ἀποκτενεῖ,
he goes; if anyone by a sword will kill,

δεῖ αὐτὸν ἐν μαχαίρῃ ἀποκτανθῆναι.
it behoves him by a sword to be killed.

Ὧδέ ἐστιν ἡ ὑπομονὴ καὶ ἡ πίστις
Here is the endurance and the faith

τῶν ἁγίων.
of the saints.

11 Καὶ εἶδον ἄλλο θηρίον ἀναβαῖνον
And I saw another beast coming up

ἐκ τῆς γῆς, καὶ εἶχεν κέρατα δύο
out of the earth, and it had ²horns ¹two

ὅμοια ἀρνίῳ, καὶ ἐλάλει ὡς δράκων.
like to a lamb, and spoke as a dragon.

12 καὶ τὴν ἐξουσίαν τοῦ πρώτου θηρίου
And ³the ⁴authority ⁵of the ⁶first ⁷beast

πᾶσαν ποιεῖ ἐνώπιον αὐτοῦ. καὶ ποιεῖ
²all ¹it does(exercises) before it. And it makes

---

was astonished and followed the beast. ⁴Men worshiped the dragon because he had given authority to the beast, and they also worshiped the beast and asked, "Who is like the beast? Who can make war against him?"

⁵The beast was given a mouth to utter proud words and blasphemies and to exercise his authority for forty-two months. ⁶He opened his mouth to blaspheme God, and to slander his name and his dwelling place and those who live in heaven. ⁷He was given power to make war against the saints and to conquer them. And he was given authority over every tribe, people, language and nation. ⁸All inhabitants of the earth will worship the beast —all whose names have not been written in the book of life belonging to the Lamb that was slain from the creation of the world. *q*

⁹He who has an ear, let him hear.

¹⁰If anyone is to go into captivity,
    into captivity he will
    go.
If anyone is to be killed*r*
    with the sword,
    with the sword he will
    be killed.

This calls for patient endurance and faithfulness on the part of the saints.

The Beast out of the Earth

¹¹Then I saw another beast, coming out of the earth. He had two horns like a lamb, but he spoke like a dragon. ¹²He exercised all the authority of the first beast on his behalf,

---

p Or, *written in the book . . . slain from the foundation of the world*
q Or, *leads into captivity*

a 8 Or *written from the creation of the world in the book of life belonging to the Lamb that was slain*
r 10 Some manuscripts *anyone kills*

makes the earth and those who dwell in it to worship the first beast, whose fatal wound was healed.

13And he performs great signs, so that he even makes fire come down out of heaven to the earth in the presence of men.

14And he deceives those who dwell on the earth because of the signs which it was given him to perform in the presence of the beast, telling those who dwell on the earth to make an image to the beast who *had the wound of the sword and has come to life.

15And there was given to him to give breath to the image of the beast, that the image of the beast might even ʳspeak and cause as many as do not worship the image of the beast to be killed.

16And he causes all, the small and the great, and the rich and the poor, and the free men and the slaves, to be given a mark on their right hand, or on their forehead,

17and he provides that no one should be able to buy or to sell, except the one who has the mark, either the name of the beast or the number of his name.

18Here is wisdom. Let him who has understanding calculate the number of the beast, for the number is that of a man; and his number is ˢsix hundred and sixty-six.

τὴν γῆν καὶ τοὺς ἐν αὐτῇ κατοικοῦντας
the earth and ¹the [ones] ²in ⁴it ³dwelling

ἵνα προσκυνήσουσιν τὸ θηρίον τὸ πρῶτον,
in or- they shall worship the ²beast - ¹first,
der that

οὗ ἐθεραπεύθη ἡ πληγὴ τοῦ θανάτου
of which ⁴was healed · ¹the ²stroke ³of death

αὐτοῦ. 13 καὶ ποιεῖ σημεῖα μεγάλα,
of it. And it does ²signs ¹great,

ἵνα καὶ πῦρ ποιῇ ἐκ τοῦ οὐρανοῦ
in or- ²even ⁴fire ¹it ³makes ⁶out of - ⁷heaven
der that

καταβαίνειν εἰς τὴν γῆν ἐνώπιον τῶν
⁵to come down onto the earth beforᵉ -

ἀνθρώπων. 14 καὶ πλανᾷ τοὺς κατοι-
men. And it deceives the [ones] dwell-

κοῦντας ἐπὶ τῆς γῆς διὰ τὰ σημεῖα
ing on the earth because of the signs

ἃ ἐδόθη αὐτῷ ποιῆσαι ἐνώπιον τοῦ
which it was given to it to do before the

θηρίου, λέγων τοῖς κατοικοῦσιν ἐπὶ τῆς
beast, telling to the [ones] dwelling on the

γῆς ποιῆσαι εἰκόνα τῷ θηρίῳ, ὃς ἔχει
earth to make an image to the beast, who has

τὴν πληγὴν τῆς μαχαίρης καὶ ἔζησεν.
the stroke of the sword and lived [again].

15 καὶ ἐδόθη αὐτῷ δοῦναι πνεῦμα τῇ
And it was given to it to give spirit to the

εἰκόνι τοῦ θηρίου, ἵνα καὶ λαλήσῃ ἡ
image of the beast, in order ⁶even ⁵might ¹the
that ⁷speak

εἰκὼν τοῦ θηρίου, καὶ ποιήσῃ [ἵνα]
¹image ²of the ⁴beast, and might make in order
that

ὅσοι ἐὰν μὴ προσκυνήσωσιν τῇ εἰκόνι
as many as might not worship the image

τοῦ θηρίου ἀποκτανθῶσιν. 16 καὶ ποιεῖ
of the beast should be killed. And it makes

πάντας, τοὺς μικροὺς καὶ τοὺς μεγάλους,
all men, the small and the great,

καὶ τοὺς πλουσίους καὶ τοὺς πτωχούς,
both the rich and the poor,

καὶ τοὺς ἐλευθέρους καὶ τοὺς δούλους,
both the free men and the slaves,

ἵνα δῶσιν αὐτοῖς χάραγμα ἐπὶ τῆς
in order they to them a mark on the
that should give

χειρὸς αὐτῶν τῆς δεξιᾶς ἢ ἐπὶ τὸ
²hand ³of them - ¹right or on the

μέτωπον αὐτῶν, 17 [καὶ] ἵνα μή τις
forehead of them, and lest anyone

δύνηται ἀγοράσαι ἢ πωλῆσαι εἰ μὴ
could to buy or to sell except

ὁ ἔχων τὸ χάραγμα τὸ ὄνομα τοῦ
the having the mark[,] the name of the
[one]

θηρίου ἢ τὸν ἀριθμὸν τοῦ ὀνόματος
beast or the number of the name

αὐτοῦ. 18 Ὧδε ἡ σοφία ἐστίν. ὁ ἔχων
of it. Here - ²wisdom ¹is. The having
[one]

νοῦν ψηφισάτω τὸν ἀριθμὸν τοῦ θηρίου·
reason let him count the number of the beast;

ἀριθμὸς γὰρ ἀνθρώπου ἐστίν. καὶ ὁ
for ²[the] ³number ¹it is. ⁴of a man And the

ἀριθμὸς αὐτοῦ ἑξακόσιοι ἑξήκοντα ἕξ.
number of it [is] six hundredˢ [and] sixty-six.

---

and made the earth and its inhabitants worship the first beast, whose fatal wound had been healed. 13And he performed great and miraculous signs, even causing fire to come down from heaven to earth in full view of men. 14Because of the signs he was given power to do on behalf of the first beast, he deceived the inhabitants of the earth. He ordered them to set up an image in honor of the beast who was wounded by the sword and yet lived. 15He was given power to give breath to the image of the first beast, so that it could speak and cause all who refused to worship the image to be killed. 16He also forced everyone, small and great, rich and poor, free and slave, to receive a mark on his right hand or on his forehead, 17so that no one could buy or sell unless he had the mark, which is the name of the beast or the number of his name.

18This calls for wisdom. If anyone has insight, let him calculate the number of the beast, for it is man's number. His number is 666.

ʳSome ancient mss. read *speak, and he will cause*

ˢSome mss. read 616

Chapter 14

The Lamb and the 144,000 on Mount Zion

AND I looked, and behold, the Lamb *was* standing on Mount Zion, and with Him one hundred and forty-four thousand, having His name and the name of His Father written on their foreheads.

2And I heard a voice from heaven, like the sound of many waters and like the sound of loud thunder, and the voice which I heard *was* like *the sound* of harpists playing on their harps.

3And they *sang a new song before the throne and before the four living creatures and the elders; and no one could learn the song except the one hundred and forty-four thousand who had been purchased from the earth.

4These are the ones who have not been defiled with women, for they ' have kept themselves chaste. These *are* the ones who follow the Lamb wherever He goes. These have been purchased from among men as first fruits to God and to the Lamb.

5And no lie was found in their mouth; they are blameless.

Vision of the Angel with the Gospel

6And I saw another angel flying in midheaven, having an eternal gospel to preach to those who live on the earth, and to every nation and tribe and tongue and people;

7and he said with a loud voice, "Fear God, and give Him glory, because the hour of His judgment has come; and worship Him who made the heaven and the earth and sea and springs of waters."

---

14 Καὶ εἶδον, καὶ ἰδοὺ τὸ ἀρνίον
And I saw, and behold[,] the Lamb

ἑστὸς ἐπὶ τὸ ὄρος Σιών, καὶ μετ᾽ αὐτοῦ
standing on the mount Sion, and with him

ἑκατὸν τεσσεράκοντα τέσσαρες χιλιάδες
a hundred [and] forty-four thousands

ἔχουσαι τὸ ὄνομα αὐτοῦ καὶ τὸ ὄνομα
having the name of him and the name

τοῦ πατρὸς αὐτοῦ γεγραμμένον ἐπὶ τῶν
of the Father of him *having been* written on the

μετώπων αὐτῶν. **2** καὶ ἤκουσα φωνὴν
foreheads of them. And I heard a sound

ἐκ τοῦ οὐρανοῦ ὡς φωνὴν ὑδάτων πολλῶν
out of — heaven as a sound ²waters ¹of many

καὶ ὡς φωνὴν βροντῆς μεγάλης, καὶ
and as a sound ²thunder ¹of great(loud), and

ἡ φωνὴ ἣν ἤκουσα ὡς κιθαρῳδῶν
the sound which I heard [was] as of harpers

κιθαριζόντων ἐν ταῖς κιθάραις αὐτῶν.
harping with the harps of them.

3 καὶ ᾄδουσιν ᾠδὴν καινὴν ἐνώπιον τοῦ
And they sing ²song ¹a new before the

θρόνου καὶ ἐνώπιον τῶν τεσσάρων ζῴων
throne and before the four living creatures

καὶ τῶν πρεσβυτέρων· καὶ οὐδεὶς ἐδύνατο
and the elders; and no man could

μαθεῖν τὴν ᾠδὴν εἰ μὴ αἱ ἑκατὸν
to learn the song except the hundred

τεσσεράκοντα τέσσαρες χιλιάδες, οἱ
[and] forty-four thousands, the

ἠγορασμένοι ἀπὸ τῆς γῆς. **4** οὗτοί εἰσιν
[ones] *having been* purchased from the earth. These are

οἳ μετὰ γυναικῶν οὐκ ἐμολύνθησαν·
[those] ²with ³women ¹were not defiled;
who

παρθένοι γάρ εἰσιν. οὗτοι οἱ ἀκολουθοῦντες
for ²celibates ¹they are. These the [ones] following
[are]

τῷ ἀρνίῳ ὅπου ἂν ὑπάγῃ. οὗτοι ἠγοράσ-
the Lamb wherever he may go. These were

θησαν ἀπὸ τῶν ἀνθρώπων ἀπαρχὴ τῷ
purchased from — men firstfruit

θεῷ καὶ τῷ ἀρνίῳ, **5** καὶ ἐν τῷ στόματι
to God and to the Lamb, and in the mouth

αὐτῶν οὐχ εὑρέθη ψεῦδος· ἄμωμοί εἰσιν.
of them was not found a lie; ²unblemished ¹they are.

6 Καὶ εἶδον ἄλλον ἄγγελον πετόμενον
And I saw another angel flying

ἐν μεσουρανήματι, ἔχοντα εὐαγγέλιον
in mid-heaven, having ²gospel

αἰώνιον εὐαγγελίσαι ἐπὶ τοὺς καθημένους
¹an eternal to preach over the [ones] sitting

ἐπὶ τῆς γῆς καὶ ἐπὶ πᾶν ἔθνος καὶ
on the earth and over every nation and

φυλὴν καὶ γλῶσσαν καὶ λαόν, **7** λέγων
tribe and tongue and people, saying

ἐν φωνῇ μεγάλῃ· φοβήθητε τὸν θεὸν
in ²voice ¹a great(loud): Fear ye — God

καὶ δότε αὐτῷ δόξαν, ὅτι ἦλθεν ἡ ὥρα
and give ²to him ¹glory, because came the hour

τῆς κρίσεως αὐτοῦ, καὶ προσκυνήσατε
of the judgment of him, and worship

τῷ ποιήσαντι τὸν οὐρανὸν καὶ τὴν γῆν
the [one] having made the heaven and the earth

καὶ θάλασσαν καὶ πηγὰς ὑδάτων. **8** Καὶ
and sea and fountains of waters. And

Chapter 14

The Lamb and the 144,000

THEN I looked, and there before me was the Lamb, standing on Mount Zion, and with him 144,000 who had his name and his Father's name written on their foreheads. 2And I heard a sound from heaven like the roar of rushing waters and like a loud peal of thunder. The sound I heard was like that of harpists playing their harps. 3And they sang a new song before the throne and before the four living creatures and the elders. No one could learn the song except the 144,000 who had been redeemed from the earth. 4These are those who did not defile themselves with women, for they kept themselves pure. They follow the Lamb wherever he goes. They were purchased from among men and offered as firstfruits to God and the Lamb. 5No lie was found in their mouths; they are blameless.

The Three Angels

6Then I saw another angel flying in midair, and he had the eternal gospel to proclaim to those who live on the earth—to every nation, tribe, language and people. 7He said in a loud voice, "Fear God and give him glory, because the hour of his judgment has come. Worship him who made the heavens, the earth, the sea and the springs of water."

---

¹Lit., *are chaste men*

8And another angel, a second one, followed, saying, "Fallen, fallen is Babylon the great, she who has made all the nations drink of the wine of the passion of her immorality."

Doom for Worshipers of the Beast

9And another angel, a third one, followed them, saying with a loud voice, "If anyone worships the beast and his image, and receives a mark on his forehead or upon his hand,

10he also will drink of the wine of the wrath of God, which is mixed in full strength in the cup of His anger, and he will be tormented with fire and brimstone in the presence of the holy angels and in the presence of the Lamb.

11"And the smoke of their torment goes up forever and ever; and they have no rest day and night, those who worship the beast and his image, and whoever receives the mark of his name."

12Here is the perseverance of the saints who keep the commandments of God and their faith in Jesus.

13And I heard a voice from heaven, saying, "Write, 'Blessed are the dead who die in the Lord from now on!'" "Yes," says the Spirit, "that they may rest from their labors, for their deeds follow with them."

The Reapers

14And I looked, and behold, a white cloud, and sitting on the cloud was one like ªa son of man, having a golden crown on His head,

---

ἄλλος ἄγγελος δεύτερος ἠκολούθησεν λέγων·
another angel a second followed saying:

ἔπεσεν ἔπεσεν Βαβυλὼν ἡ μεγάλη, ἣ
Fell[,] fell Babylon the great, which

ἐκ τοῦ οἴνου τοῦ θυμοῦ τῆς πορνείας
of the wine of the anger of the fornication

αὐτῆς πεπότικεν πάντα τὰ ἔθνη. 9 Καὶ
of her has made to drink all the nations. And

ἄλλος ἄγγελος τρίτος ἠκολούθησεν αὐτοῖς
another angel a third followed them

λέγων ἐν φωνῇ μεγάλῃ· εἴ τις προσκυνεῖ
saying in ²voice ¹a great(loud): If anyone worships

τὸ θηρίον καὶ τὴν εἰκόνα αὐτοῦ, καὶ
the beast and the image of it, and

λαμβάνει χάραγμα ἐπὶ τοῦ μετώπου αὐτοῦ
receives a mark on the forehead of him

ἢ ἐπὶ τὴν χεῖρα αὐτοῦ, 10 καὶ αὐτὸς
or on the hand of him, even he

πίεται ἐκ τοῦ οἴνου τοῦ θυμοῦ τοῦ
shall drink of the wine of the anger

θεοῦ τοῦ κεκερασμένου ἀκράτου ἐν τῷ
of God - having been mixed undiluted in the

ποτηρίῳ τῆς ὀργῆς αὐτοῦ, καὶ βασανισθήσε-
cup of the wrath of him, and will be torment-

ται ἐν πυρὶ καὶ θείῳ ἐνώπιον ἀγγέλων
ed by fire and sulphur before ¹angels

ἁγίων καὶ ἐνώπιον τοῦ ἀρνίου. 11 καὶ
¹holy and before the Lamb. And

ὁ καπνὸς τοῦ βασανισμοῦ αὐτῶν εἰς
the smoke of the torment of them unto

αἰῶνας αἰώνων ἀναβαίνει, καὶ οὐκ ἔχουσιν
ages of ages goes up, and they have not

ἀνάπαυσιν ἡμέρας καὶ νυκτὸς οἱ προσκυ-
rest day and night the [ones] wor-

νοῦντες τὸ θηρίον καὶ τὴν εἰκόνα αὐτοῦ,
shipping the beast and the image of it,

καὶ εἴ τις λαμβάνει τὸ χάραγμα τοῦ
and if anyone receives the mark of the

ὀνόματος αὐτοῦ. 12 Ὧδε ἡ ὑπομονὴ
name of it. ¹Here ²the ⁴endurance

τῶν ἁγίων ἐστίν, οἱ τηροῦντες τὰς
³of the ³saints ²is, the [ones] keeping the

ἐντολὰς τοῦ θεοῦ καὶ τὴν πίστιν Ἰησοῦ.
command-ments - of God and the faith of Jesus.

13 Καὶ ἤκουσα φωνῆς ἐκ τοῦ οὐρανοῦ
And I heard a voice out of - heaven

λεγούσης· γράψον· μακάριοι οἱ νεκροὶ
saying: Write thou: Blessed [are] the dead

οἱ ἐν κυρίῳ ἀποθνῄσκοντες ἀπ' ἄρτι.
¹the ²in ⁴[the] Lord ³dying from now.
[ones]

ναί, λέγει τὸ πνεῦμα, ἵνα ἀναπαήσονται
Yes, says the Spirit, in order they shall rest
that

ἐκ τῶν κόπων αὐτῶν· τὰ γὰρ ἔργα
from the labours of them; for the work·

αὐτῶν ἀκολουθεῖ μετ' αὐτῶν.
of them follows with them.

14 Καὶ εἶδον, καὶ ἰδοὺ νεφέλη λευκή,
And I saw, and behold[,] ²cloud ¹a white,

καὶ ἐπὶ τὴν νεφέλην καθήμενον ὅμοιον
and on the cloud [one] sitting like

υἱὸν ἀνθρώπου, ἔχων ἐπὶ τῆς κεφαλῆς
a son of man,* having on the head

8A second angel followed and said, "Fallen! Fallen is Babylon the Great, which made all the nations drink the maddening wine of her adulteries."

9A third angel followed them and said in a loud voice: "If anyone worships the beast and his image and receives his mark on the forehead or on the hand,

10he, too, will drink of the wine of God's fury, which has been poured full strength into the cup of his wrath. He will be tormented with burning sulfur in the presence of the holy angels and of the Lamb.

11And the smoke of their torment rises for ever and ever. There is no rest day or night for those who worship the beast and his image, or for anyone who receives the mark of his name." 12This calls for patient endurance on the part of the saints who obey God's commandments and remain faithful to Jesus.

13Then I heard a voice from heaven say, "Write: Blessed are the dead who die in the Lord from now on."

"Yes," says the Spirit, "they will rest from their labor, for their deeds will follow them."

The Harvest of the Earth

14I looked, and there before me was a white cloud, and seated on the cloud was one "like a son of man"ˢ with a crown of gold on his head and a

---

and a sharp sickle in His hand.

15And another angel came out of the temple, crying out with a loud voice to Him who sat on the cloud, "Put in your sickle and reap, because the hour to reap has come, because the harvest of the earth is ripe."

16And He who sat on the cloud swung His sickle over the earth; and the earth was reaped.

17And another angel came out of the temple which is in heaven, and he also had a sharp sickle.

18And another angel, the one who has power over fire, came out from the altar; and he called with a loud voice to him who had the sharp sickle, saying, "Put in your sharp sickle, and gather the clusters from the vine of the earth, because her grapes are ripe."

19And the angel swung his sickle to the earth, and gathered *the clusters from* the vine of the earth, and threw them into the great wine press of the wrath of God.

20And the wine press was trodden outside the city, and blood came out from the wine press, up to the horses' bridles, for a distance of ᵛtwo hundred miles.

αὐτοῦ στέφανον χρυσοῦν καὶ ἐν τῇ χειρὶ
of him crown   a golden   and in the hand

αὐτοῦ δρέπανον ὀξύ. 15 καὶ ἄλλος ἄγγελος
of him sickle   a sharp.   And another   angel

ἐξῆλθεν ἐκ τοῦ ναοῦ, κράζων ἐν φωνῇ
went forth out of the shrine, crying in ²voice

μεγάλη τῷ καθημένῳ ἐπὶ τῆς νεφέλης·
¹a great to the sitting   on   the   cloud:
(loud) [one]

πέμψον τὸ δρέπανόν σου καὶ θέρισον,
Send(Thrust) the sickle of thee and reap thou,

ὅτι ἦλθεν ἡ ὥρα θερίσαι, ὅτι ἐξηράνθη
because came the hour to reap, because was dried

ὁ θερισμὸς τῆς γῆς. 16 καὶ ἔβαλεν
the harvest of the earth.   And   ²thrust

ὁ καθήμενος ἐπὶ τῆς νεφέλης τὸ δρέπανον
¹the ²sitting   ³on ⁴the ⁵cloud   the sickle
[one]

αὐτοῦ ἐπὶ τὴν γῆν, καὶ ἐθερίσθη ἡ
of him over the earth, and ²was reaped ¹the

γῆ. 17 Καὶ ἄλλος ἄγγελος ἐξῆλθεν ἐκ
²earth. And another angel   went forth out of

τοῦ ναοῦ τοῦ ἐν τῷ οὐρανῷ, ἔχων καὶ
the shrine - in - heaven, ²having ²also

αὐτὸς δρέπανον ὀξύ. 18 καὶ ἄλλος ἄγγελος
¹he   ²sickle ⁴a sharp.   And another angel

ἐξῆλθεν ἐκ τοῦ θυσιαστηρίου, [ὁ] ἔχων
went forth out of the altar,   the [one] having

ἐξουσίαν ἐπὶ τοῦ πυρός, καὶ ἐφώνησεν
authority over the fire,   and he spoke

φωνῇ μεγάλη τῷ ἔχοντι τὸ δρέπανον
²voice ¹in a great to the having the ²sickle
(loud)   [one]

τὸ ὀξὺ λέγων· πέμψον σου τὸ δρέπανον
- ¹sharp saying: Send(Thrust) ⁴of thee ¹the ²sickle

τὸ ὀξὺ καὶ τρύγησον τοὺς βότρυας τῆς
- ²sharp and gather the clusters of the

ἀμπέλου τῆς γῆς, ὅτι ἤκμασαν αἱ
vine   of the earth, because ⁴ripened ¹the

σταφυλαὶ αὐτῆς. 19 καὶ ἔβαλεν ὁ ἄγγελος
²grapes   ³of it.   And ²thrust ¹the ³angel

τὸ δρέπανον αὐτοῦ εἰς τὴν γῆν, καὶ
the sickle   of him into the earth,   and

ἐτρύγησεν τὴν ἄμπελον τῆς γῆς καὶ
gathered   the vine   of the earth and

ἔβαλεν εἰς τὴν ληνὸν τοῦ θυμοῦ τοῦ
cast   into the ²winepress ³of the ⁴anger

θεοῦ τὸν μέγαν. 20 καὶ ἐπατήθη ἡ
⁵of God - ¹great.   And ³was trodden ¹the

ληνὸς ἔξωθεν τῆς πόλεως, καὶ ἐξῆλθεν
winepress outside the city,   and ⁴went out

αἷμα ἐκ τῆς ληνοῦ ἄχρι τῶν χαλινῶν
¹blood out of the winepress as far as the bridles

τῶν ἵππων, ἀπὸ σταδίων χιλίων ἑξακοσίων.
of the horses, from ²furlongs ¹a thousand ³six hundred.

---

sharp sickle in his hand.

15Then another angel came out of the temple and called in a loud voice to him who was sitting on the cloud, "Take your sickle and reap, because the time to reap has come, for the harvest of the earth is ripe."

16So he who was seated on the cloud swung his sickle over the earth, and the earth was harvested.

17Another angel came out of the temple in heaven, and he too had a sharp sickle. 18Still another angel, who had charge of the fire, came from the altar and called in a loud voice to him who had the sharp sickle, "Take your sharp sickle and gather the clusters of grapes from the earth's vine, because its grapes are ripe." 19The angel swung his sickle on the earth, gathered its grapes and threw them into the great winepress of God's wrath. 20They were trampled in the winepress outside the city, and blood flowed out of the press, rising as high as the horses' bridles for a distance of 1,600 stadia.ᶠ

Chapter 15

A Scene of Heaven

AND I saw another sign in heaven, great and marvelous, seven angels who had seven plagues, *which are* the last, because in them the wrath of God is finished.

2And I saw, as it were, a sea of glass mixed with fire.

---

15 Καὶ εἶδον ἄλλο σημεῖον ἐν τῷ
And I saw another sign   in   -

οὐρανῷ μέγα καὶ θαυμαστόν, ἀγγέλους
heaven[,] great and wonderful,   ¹angels

ἑπτὰ ἔχοντας πληγὰς ἑπτὰ τὰς ἐσχάτας,
²seven having ³plagues ¹seven the   last,

ὅτι ἐν αὐταῖς ἐτελέσθη ὁ θυμὸς τοῦ
because in them ⁴was finished ¹the ²anger

θεοῦ. 2 Καὶ εἶδον ὡς θάλασσαν ὑαλίνην
³of God.   And I saw as ²sea   ¹a glassy

Chapter 15

Seven Angels With Seven Plagues

I SAW in heaven another great and marvelous sign: seven angels with the seven last plagues—last, because with them God's wrath is completed. 2And I saw what looked like a sea of glass mixed with fire

---

ᵛLit., *sixteen hundred stadia.* A stadion was about six hundred feet.

ᶠ20 That is, about 180 miles (about 300 kilometers)

and those who had come off victorious from the beast and from his image and from the number of his name, standing on the sea of glass, holding harps of God.

3And they *sang the song of Moses the bond-servant of God and the song of the Lamb, saying,
"Great and marvelous are Thy works,
O Lord God, the Almighty;
Righteous and true are Thy ways,
Thou King of the ʷnations.
4"Who will not fear, O Lord, and glorify Thy name?
For Thou alone art holy;
For ALL THE NATIONS WILL COME AND WORSHIP BEFORE THEE,
For Thy righteous acts have been revealed."

5After these things I looked, and the temple of the tabernacle of testimony in heaven was opened,
6and the seven angels who had the seven plagues came out of the temple, clothed in ˣlinen, clean and bright, and girded around their breasts with golden girdles.
7And one of the four living creatures gave to the seven angels seven golden bowls full of the wrath of God, who lives forever and ever.
8And the temple was filled with smoke from the glory of God and from His power; and no one was able to enter the temple until the seven plagues of the seven angels were finished.

Chapter 16

Six Bowls of Wrath

AND I heard a loud voice from the temple, saying to the seven angels, "Go and pour out the seven

ʷ Some ancient mss. read ages
ˣ Some mss. read stone

μεμιγμένην πυρί, καὶ τοὺς νικῶντας
having been mixed with fire, and the [ones] overcoming
ἐκ τοῦ θηρίου καὶ ἐκ τῆς εἰκόνος αὐτοῦ
of the beast and of the image of it
καὶ ἐκ τοῦ ἀριθμοῦ τοῦ ὀνόματος αὐτοῦ
and of the number of the name of it
ἑστῶτας ἐπὶ τὴν θάλασσαν τὴν ὑαλίνην,
standing on the ²sea - ¹glassy,
ἔχοντας κιθάρας τοῦ θεοῦ. 3 καὶ ᾄδουσιν
having harps - of God. And they sing
τὴν ᾠδὴν Μωϋσέως τοῦ δούλου τοῦ
the song of Moses the slave -
θεοῦ καὶ τὴν ᾠδὴν τοῦ ἀρνίου, λέγοντες·
of God and the song of the Lamb, saying:
μεγάλα καὶ θαυμαστὰ τὰ ἔργα σου,
Great and wonderful the works of thee,
κύριε ὁ θεὸς ὁ παντοκράτωρ· δίκαιαι
[O] Lord - God the Almighty; righteous
καὶ ἀληθιναὶ αἱ ὁδοί σου, ὁ βασιλεὺς
and true the ways of thee, the king
τῶν ἐθνῶν· 4 τίς οὐ μὴ φοβηθῇ, κύριε,
of the nations; who will not fear, [O] Lord,
καὶ δοξάσει τὸ ὄνομά σου; ὅτι μόνος
and will glorify the name of thee? because [thou]
only
ὅσιος, ὅτι πάντα τὰ ἔθνη ἥξουσιν καὶ
[art] holy, because all the nations will come and
προσκυνήσουσιν ἐνώπιόν σου, ὅτι τὰ
will worship before thee, because the
δικαιώματά σου ἐφανερώθησαν. 5 Καὶ
ordinances of thee were made manifest. And
μετὰ ταῦτα εἶδον, καὶ ἠνοίγη ὁ ναὸς
after these things I saw, and was opened the shrine
τῆς σκηνῆς τοῦ μαρτυρίου ἐν τῷ οὐρανῷ,
of the tabernacle of the testimony in - heaven,
6 καὶ ἐξῆλθον οἱ ἑπτὰ ἄγγελοι οἱ ἔχοντες
and ⁵came forth ¹the ²seven ³angels - ⁴having
τὰς ἑπτὰ πληγὰς ἐκ τοῦ ναοῦ, ἐνδεδυμένοι
⁵the ⁶seven ⁷plagues out of the shrine, having been
clothed [in]
λίνον καθαρὸν λαμπρὸν καὶ περιεζωσμένοι
²linen ¹clean ³bright and having been girdled
περὶ τὰ στήθη ζώνας χρυσᾶς. 7 καὶ
round the breasts [with] ²girdles ¹golden. And
ἓν ἐκ τῶν τεσσάρων ζῴων ἔδωκεν τοῖς
one of the four living gave to the
creatures
ἑπτὰ ἀγγέλοις ἑπτὰ φιάλας χρυσᾶς
seven angels seven ²bowls ¹golden
γεμούσας τοῦ θυμοῦ τοῦ θεοῦ τοῦ ζῶντος
being filled of(with) anger of God - living
the -
εἰς τοὺς αἰῶνας τῶν αἰώνων. 8 καὶ
unto the ages of the ages. And
ἐγεμίσθη ὁ ναὸς καπνοῦ ἐκ τῆς δόξης
was filled the shrine of(with) smoke of the glory
τοῦ θεοῦ καὶ ἐκ τῆς δυνάμεως αὐτοῦ,
— of God and of the power of him,
καὶ οὐδεὶς ἐδύνατο εἰσελθεῖν εἰς τὸν
and no one could to enter into the
ναὸν ἄχρι τελεσθῶσιν αἱ ἑπτὰ πληγαὶ
shrine until should be finished the seven plagues
τῶν ἑπτὰ ἀγγέλων. 16 Καὶ ἤκουσα
of the seven angels. And I heard
μεγάλης φωνῆς ἐκ τοῦ ναοῦ λεγούσης τοῖς
a great(loud) voice out of the shrine saying to the
ἑπτὰ ἀγγέλοις· ὑπάγετε καὶ ἐκχέετε τὰς ἑπτὰ
seven angels: Go ye and pour out the seven

---

and, standing beside the sea, those who had been victorious over the beast and his image and over the number of his name. They held harps given them by God 3and sang the song of Moses the servant of God and the song of the Lamb:

"Great and marvelous are your deeds,
Lord God Almighty.
Just and true are your ways,
King of the ages.
4Who will not fear you, O Lord,
and bring glory to your name?
For you alone are holy.
All nations will come and worship before you,
for your righteous acts have been revealed."

5After this I looked and in heaven the temple, that is, the tabernacle of the Testimony, was opened.
6Out of the temple came the seven angels with the seven plagues. They were dressed in clean, shining linen and wore golden sashes around their chests.
7Then one of the four living creatures gave to the seven angels seven golden bowls filled with the wrath of God, who lives for ever and ever. 8And the temple was filled with smoke from the glory of God and from his power, and no one could enter the temple until the seven plagues of the seven angels were completed.

Chapter 16

The Seven Bowls of God's Wrath

THEN I heard a loud voice from the temple saying to the seven angels, "Go, pour out the seven bowls of the wrath of God into the earth.''

2And the first *angel* went and poured out his bowl into the earth; and it became a loathsome and malignant sore upon the men who had the mark of the beast and who worshiped his image.

3And the second *angel* poured out his bowl into the sea, and it became blood like *that* of a dead man; and every living ʸthing in the sea died.

4And the third *angel* poured out his bowl into the rivers and the springs of waters; and ᶻthey became blood.

5And I heard the angel of the waters saying, ''Righteous art Thou, who art and who wast, O Holy One, because Thou didst judge these things;

6for they poured out the blood of saints and prophets, and Thou hast given them blood to drink. They deserve it.''

7And I heard the altar saying, ''Yes, O Lord God, the Almighty, true and righteous are Thy judgments.''

8And the fourth *angel* poured out his bowl upon the sun; and it was given to it to scorch men with fire.

9And men were scorched with fierce heat; and they blasphemed the name of God who has the power over these plagues; and they did not repent, so as to give Him glory.

10And the fifth *angel* poured out his bowl upon the throne of the beast; and his kingdom became dark-

---

φιάλας τοῦ θυμοῦ τοῦ θεοῦ εἰς τὴν γῆν.
bowls of the anger - of God onto the earth.

2 Καὶ ἀπῆλθεν ὁ πρῶτος καὶ ἐξέχεεν τὴν
And ²went away ¹the ²first and poured out the

φιάλην αὐτοῦ εἰς τὴν γῆν· καὶ ἐγένετο
bowl of him onto the earth; and ⁵came

ἕλκος κακὸν καὶ πονηρὸν ἐπὶ τοὺς ἀνθρώπους
⁵sore ¹a bad ²and ³evil on the men

τοὺς ἔχοντας τὸ χάραγμα τοῦ θηρίου καὶ
- having the mark of the beast and

τοὺς προσκυνοῦντας τῇ εἰκόνι αὐτοῦ. 3 Καὶ
- worshipping the image of it. And

ὁ δεύτερος ἐξέχεεν τὴν φιάλην αὐτοῦ
the second poured out the bowl of him

εἰς τὴν θάλασσαν· καὶ ἐγένετο αἷμα
onto the sea; and it became blood

ὡς νεκροῦ, καὶ πᾶσα ψυχὴ ζωῆς ἀπέθανεν,
as of a dead and every soul of life died,
man,

τὰ ἐν τῇ θαλάσσῃ. 4 Καὶ ὁ τρίτος
the in the sea. And the third
things

ἐξέχεεν τὴν φιάλην αὐτοῦ εἰς τοὺς
poured out the bowl of him onto the

ποταμοὺς καὶ τὰς πηγὰς τῶν ὑδάτων·
rivers and the fountains of the waters;

καὶ ἐγένετο αἷμα. 5 Καὶ ἤκουσα τοῦ
and it became blood. And I heard the

ἀγγέλου τῶν ὑδάτων λέγοντος· δίκαιος
angel of the waters saying· Righteous

εἶ, ὁ ὢν καὶ ὁ ἦν, ὁ ὅσιος, ὅτι
art the being and the was, the holy because
thou, [one] [one who] [one],
=the one who is

ταῦτα ἔκρινας, 6 ὅτι αἷμα ἁγίων
²these ¹thou judgedst, because ²[the] blood ³of saints
things

καὶ προφητῶν ἐξέχεαν, καὶ αἷμα αὐτοῖς
⁴and ⁵of prophets ¹they shed, and blood to them

δέδωκας πεῖν· ἄξιοί εἰσιν. 7 Καὶ ἤκουσα
thou hast to drink; ²worthy ¹they are. And I heard
given

τοῦ θυσιαστηρίου λέγοντος· ναί, κύριε
the altar saying· Yes, [O] Lord

ὁ θεὸς ὁ παντοκράτωρ, ἀληθιναὶ καὶ
- God the Almighty, true and

δίκαιαι αἱ κρίσεις σου. 8 Καὶ ὁ τέταρτος
righteous the judgments of thee. And the fourth

ἐξέχεεν τὴν φιάλην αὐτοῦ ἐπὶ τὸν ἥλιον·
poured out the bowl of him onto the sun;

καὶ ἐδόθη αὐτῷ καυματίσαι τοὺς
and it was given to him to burn -

ἀνθρώπους ἐν πυρί. 9 καὶ ἐκαυματίσθησαν
men with fire. And ²were burnt [with]

οἱ ἄνθρωποι καῦμα μέγα, καὶ ἐβλασ-
- ¹men ⁴heat ³great, and they blas-

φήμησαν τὸ ὄνομα τοῦ θεοῦ τοῦ ἔχοντος
phemed the name - of God the [one] having

τὴν ἐξουσίαν ἐπὶ τὰς πληγὰς ταύτας,
the authority over these plagues,

καὶ οὐ μετενόησαν δοῦναι αὐτῷ δόξαν.
and they repented not to give ²to him ¹glory.

10 Καὶ ὁ πέμπτος ἐξέχεεν τὴν φιάλην
And the fifth poured out the bowl

αὐτοῦ ἐπὶ τὸν θρόνον τοῦ θηρίου· καὶ
of him onto the throne of the beast; and

ἐγένετο ἡ βασιλεία αὐτοῦ ἐσκοτωμένη,
⁴became ¹the ²kingdom ³of it having been darkened,

---

bowls of God's wrath on the earth.''

2The first angel went and poured out his bowl on the land, and ugly and painful sores broke out on the people who had the mark of the beast and worshiped his image.

3The second angel poured out his bowl on the sea, and it turned into blood like that of a dead man, and every living thing in the sea died.

4The third angel poured out his bowl on the rivers and springs of water, and they became blood. 5Then I heard the angel in charge of the waters say:

''You are just in these judgments,
  you who are and who were, the Holy One,
  because you have so judged;
6for they have shed the blood of your saints and prophets,
  and you have given them blood to drink as they deserve.''

7And I heard the altar respond:

''Yes, Lord God Almighty,
true and just are your judgments.''

8The fourth angel poured out his bowl on the sun, and the sun was given power to scorch people with fire. 9They were seared by the intense heat and they cursed the name of God, who had control over these plagues, but they refused to repent and glorify him.

10The fifth angel poured out his bowl on the throne of the beast, and his kingdom was plunged into dark-

---

ʸ Lit., *soul*. Some ancient mss. read *thing, the things in the sea.*
ᶻ Some ancient mss. read *it became*

ened; and they gnawed their tongues because of pain,

11and they blasphemed the God of heaven because of their pains and their sores; and they did not repent of their deeds.

12And the sixth *angel* poured out his bowl upon the great river, the Euphrates; and its water was dried up, that the way might be prepared for the kings from the east.

Armageddon

13And I saw *coming* out of the mouth of the dragon and out of the mouth of the beast and out of the mouth of the false prophet, three unclean spirits like frogs;

14for they are spirits of demons, performing signs, which go out to the kings of the whole world, to gather them together for the war of the great day of God, the Almighty.

15("Behold, I am coming like a thief. Blessed is the one who stays awake and keeps his garments, lest he walk about naked and men see his shame.")

16And they gathered them together to the place which in Hebrew is called *a* Har-Magedon.

Seventh Bowl of Wrath

17And the seventh *angel* poured out his bowl upon the air; and a loud voice came out of the temple from the throne, saying, "It is done."

18And there were flashes of lightning and sounds and peals of thunder; and there was a great earthquake, such as there had not been since man came to be upon the earth, so great an earthquake *was it, and* so mighty.

19And the great city was split into three parts, and

καὶ ἐμασῶντο τὰς γλώσσας αὐτῶν ἐκ
and they(men) gnawed the tongues of them from

τοῦ πόνου, 11 καὶ ἐβλασφήμησαν τὸν θεὸν
the pain, and *they* blasphemed the God

τοῦ οὐρανοῦ ἐκ τῶν πόνων αὐτῶν καὶ
- of heaven from the pains of them and

ἐκ τῶν ἑλκῶν αὐτῶν, καὶ οὐ μετενόησαν
from the sores of them, and they repented not

ἐκ τῶν ἔργων αὐτῶν. 12 Καὶ ὁ ἕκτος
of the works of them. And the sixth

ἐξέχεεν τὴν φιάλην αὐτοῦ ἐπὶ τὸν ποταμὸν
poured out the bowl of him onto the ²river

τὸν μέγαν Εὐφράτην· καὶ ἐξηράνθη τὸ
- ¹great Euphrates; and ⁴was dried ¹the

ὕδωρ αὐτοῦ, ἵνα ἑτοιμασθῇ ἡ ὁδὸς τῶν
²water ³of it, in order might be ¹the ³way ²of the
         that prepared

βασιλέων τῶν ἀπὸ ἀνατολῆς ἡλίου. 13 Καὶ
⁴kings - ⁵from ⁶[the] rising ⁷of [the] sun. And

εἶδον ἐκ τοῦ στόματος τοῦ δράκοντος
I saw out of the mouth of the dragon

καὶ ἐκ τοῦ στόματος τοῦ θηρίου καὶ
and out of the mouth of the beast and

ἐκ τοῦ στόματος τοῦ ψευδοπροφήτου
out of the mouth of the false prophet

πνεύματα τρία ἀκάθαρτα ὡς βάτραχοι·
³spirits ¹three ²unclean [coming] as frogs;

14 εἰσὶν γὰρ πνεύματα δαιμονίων ποιοῦντα
for they are spirits of demons doing

σημεῖα, ἃ ἐκπορεύεται ἐπὶ τοὺς βασιλεῖς
signs, which goes forth unto the kings

τῆς οἰκουμένης ὅλης, συναγαγεῖν αὐτοὺς
of the ²inhabited [earth] ¹whole, to assemble them

εἰς τὸν πόλεμον τῆς ἡμέρας τῆς μεγάλης
to the war of the ²day - ¹great

τοῦ θεοῦ τοῦ παντοκράτορος. 15 Ἰδοὺ
- of God *of the* Almighty. Behold

ἔρχομαι ὡς κλέπτης· μακάριος ὁ γρηγορῶν
I am coming as a thief; blessed [is] the [one] watching

καὶ τηρῶν τὰ ἱμάτια αὐτοῦ, ἵνα μὴ
and keeping the garments of him, lest

γυμνὸς περιπατῇ καὶ βλέπωσιν τὴν
naked he walk and they(men) see the

ἀσχημοσύνην αὐτοῦ. 16 Καὶ συνήγαγεν
shame of him. And [t]he[y] assembled

αὐτοὺς εἰς τὸν τόπον τὸν καλούμενον
them in the place - being called

Ἑβραϊστὶ Ἁρμαγεδών. 17 Καὶ ὁ ἕβδομος
in Hebrew Harmagedon. And the seventh

ἐξέχεεν τὴν φιάλην αὐτοῦ ἐπὶ τὸν ἀέρα·
poured out the bowl of him on the air;

καὶ ἐξῆλθεν φωνὴ μεγάλη ἐκ τοῦ ναοῦ
and ²came out ¹voice ¹a great(loud) out of the shrine

ἀπὸ τοῦ θρόνου λέγουσα· γέγονεν. 18 καὶ
from the throne saying: It has occurred. And

ἐγένοντο ἀστραπαὶ καὶ φωναὶ καὶ βρονταί,
there were lightnings and voices and thunders,

καὶ σεισμὸς ἐγένετο μέγας, οἷος οὐκ
and ²earthquake ³occurred ¹a great, such as not

ἐγένετο ἀφ᾽ οὗ ἄνθρωπος ἐγένετο ἐπὶ
did occur from when↑ man was on

τῆς γῆς, τηλικοῦτος σεισμὸς οὕτω μέγας.
the earth, such an earthquake so great.

19 καὶ ἐγένετο ἡ πόλις ἡ μεγάλη εἰς
And ⁴became ¹the ²city - ³great into

---

ness. Men gnawed their tongues in agony 11and cursed the God of heaven because of their pains and their sores, but they refused to repent of what they had done.

12The sixth angel poured out his bowl on the great river Euphrates, and its water was dried up to prepare the way for the kings from the East. 13Then I saw three evil*u* spirits that looked like frogs; they came out of the mouth of the dragon, out of the mouth of the beast and out of the mouth of the false prophet. 14They are spirits of demons performing miraculous signs, and they go out to the kings of the whole world, to gather them for the battle on the great day of God Almighty.

15"Behold, I come like a thief! Blessed is he who stays awake and keeps his clothes with him, so that he may not go naked and be shamefully exposed."

16Then they gathered the kings together to the place that in Hebrew is called Armageddon.

17The seventh angel poured out his bowl into the air, and out of the temple came a loud voice from the throne, saying, "It is done!" 18Then there came flashes of lightning, rumblings, peals of thunder and a severe earthquake. No earthquake like it has ever occurred since man has been on earth, so tremendous was the quake. 19The great city split into three

---

the cities of the nations fell. And Babylon the great was remembered before God, to give her the cup of wine of His fierce wrath.

20And every island fled away, and the mountains were not found.

21And huge hailstones, about [b]one hundred pounds each, *came down from heaven upon men; and men blasphemed God because of the plague of the hail, because its plague *was extremely severe.

τρία μέρη, καὶ αἱ πόλεις τῶν ἐθνῶν
three parts, and the cities of the nations

ἔπεσαν. καὶ Βαβυλὼν ἡ μεγάλη ἐμνήσθη
fell. And Babylon the great was remembered

ἐνώπιον τοῦ θεοῦ δοῦναι αὐτῇ τὸ ποτήριον
before God to give to her/it* the cup

τοῦ οἴνου τοῦ θυμοῦ τῆς ὀργῆς αὐτοῦ.
of the wine of the anger of the wrath of him.

20 καὶ πᾶσα νῆσος ἔφυγεν, καὶ ὄρη
And every island fled, and mountains

οὐχ εὑρέθησαν. 21 καὶ χάλαζα μεγάλη
were not found. And [1]hail [1]a great

ὡς ταλαντιαία καταβαίνει ἐκ τοῦ οὐρανοῦ
as a talent in size comes down out of – heaven

ἐπὶ τοὺς ἀνθρώπους· καὶ ἐβλασφήμησαν
on – men; and [2]blasphemed

οἱ ἄνθρωποι τὸν θεὸν ἐκ τῆς πληγῆς
– [1]men – God from the plague

τῆς χαλάζης, ὅτι μεγάλη ἐστὶν ἡ πληγὴ
of the hail, because [2]great [4]is [1]the [3]plague

αὐτῆς σφόδρα.
[5]of it [6]exceeding.

parts, and the cities of the nations collapsed. God remembered Babylon the Great and gave her the cup filled with the wine of the fury of his wrath. 20Every island fled away and the mountains could not be found. 21From the sky huge hailstones of about a hundred pounds each fell upon men. And they cursed God on account of the plague of hail, because the plague was so terrible.

Chapter 17

The Doom of Babylon

AND one of the seven angels who had the seven bowls came and spoke with me, saying, "Come here, I shall show you the judgment of the great harlot who sits on many waters,

2with whom the kings of the earth committed *acts of immorality*, and those who dwell on the earth were made drunk with the wine of her immorality."

3And he carried me away [c]in the Spirit into a wilderness; and I saw a woman sitting on a scarlet beast, full of blasphemous names, having seven heads and ten horns.

4And the woman was clothed in purple and scarlet, and adorned with gold and precious stones and pearls, having in her hand a gold cup full of abominations and of the unclean things of her immorality,

5and upon her forehead a name *was* written, a mys-

17 Καὶ ἦλθεν εἷς ἐκ τῶν ἑπτὰ ἀγγέλων
And came one of the seven angels

τῶν ἐχόντων τὰς ἑπτὰ φιάλας, καὶ
– having the seven bowls, and

ἐλάλησεν μετ᾽ ἐμοῦ λέγων· δεῦρο, δείξω
spoke with me saying: Come, I will show

σοι τὸ κρίμα τῆς πόρνης τῆς μεγάλης
thee the judgment of the [3]harlot – [1]great

τῆς καθημένης ἐπὶ ὑδάτων πολλῶν, 2 μεθ᾽
– sitting on [2]waters [1]many, with

ἧς ἐπόρνευσαν οἱ βασιλεῖς τῆς γῆς,
whom [5]practised [1]the [2]kings [3]of the [4]earth,
fornication

καὶ ἐμεθύσθησαν οἱ κατοικοῦντες τὴν γῆν
and [5]became drunk [1]the [2]dwelling [on] [3]the [4]earth
[ones]

ἐκ τοῦ οἴνου τῆς πορνείας αὐτῆς. 3 καὶ
from the wine of the fornication of her. And

ἀπήνεγκέν με εἰς ἔρημον ἐν πνεύματι.
he carried away me into a desert in spirit.

καὶ εἶδον γυναῖκα καθημένην ἐπὶ θηρίον
And I saw a woman sitting on [2]beast

κόκκινον, γέμοντα ὀνόματα βλασφημίας,
[1]a scarlet, being filled [with] names of blasphemy,

ἔχοντα κεφαλὰς ἑπτὰ καὶ κέρατα δέκα.
having [2]heads [1]seven and [2]horns [1]ten.

4 καὶ ἡ γυνὴ ἦν περιβεβλημένη πορφυροῦν
And the woman was *having been* clothed [in] purple

καὶ κόκκινον, καὶ κεχρυσωμένη χρυσίῳ
and scarlet, and *having been* gilded with gold

καὶ λίθῳ τιμίῳ καὶ μαργαρίταις, ἔχουσα
and [2]stone [1]precious and pearls, having

ποτήριον χρυσοῦν ἐν τῇ χειρὶ αὐτῆς
[2]cup [1]a golden in the hand of her

γέμον βδελυγμάτων καὶ τὰ ἀκάθαρτα
being filled of(with) and the unclean things
abominations

τῆς πορνείας αὐτῆς, 5 καὶ ἐπὶ τὸ
of the fornication of her, and on the

μέτωπον αὐτῆς ὄνομα γεγραμμένον,
forehead of her a name *having been* written,

Chapter 17

The Woman on the Beast

ONE of the seven angels who had the seven bowls came and said to me, "Come, I will show you the punishment of the great prostitute, who sits on many waters. 2With her the kings of the earth committed adultery and the inhabitants of the earth were intoxicated with the wine of her adulteries."

3Then the angel carried me away in the Spirit into a desert. There I saw a woman sitting on a scarlet beast that was covered with blasphemous names and had seven heads and ten horns. 4The woman was dressed in purple and scarlet, and was glittering with gold, precious stones and pearls. She held a golden cup in her hand, filled with abominable things and the filth of her adulteries. 5This title was written on her forehead:

[b] Lit., *the weight of a talent*
[c] Or, *in spirit*

* Even in English a city is often personified as feminine.

tery, "BABYLON THE GREAT, THE MOTHER OF HARLOTS AND OF THE ABOMINATIONS OF THE EARTH."

6And I saw the woman drunk with the blood of the saints, and with the blood of the witnesses of Jesus. And when I saw her, I wondered greatly.

7And the angel said to me, "Why do you wonder? I shall tell you the mystery of the woman and of the beast that carries her, which has the seven heads and the ten horns.

8"The beast that you saw was and is not, and is about to come up out of the abyss and dto go to destruction. And those who dwell on the earth will wonder, whose name has not been written in the book of life from the foundation of the world, when they see the beast, that he was and is not and will come.

9"Here is the mind which has wisdom. The seven heads are seven mountains on which the woman sits,

10and they are seven kings; five have fallen, one is, the other has not yet come; and when he comes, he must remain a little while.

11"And the beast which was and is not, is himself also an eighth, and is one of the seven, and he goes to destruction.

12"And the ten horns which you saw are ten kings, who have not yet received a kingdom, but they receive authority as kings with the beast for one hour.

μυστήριον, ΒΑΒΥΛΩΝ Η ΜΕΓΑΛΗ,
a mystery, BABYLON THE GREAT,

Η ΜΗΤΗΡ ΤΩΝ ΠΟΡΝΩΝ ΚΑΙ
The Mother of the Harlots and

ΤΩΝ ΒΔΕΛΥΓΜΑΤΩΝ ΤΗΣ ΓΗΣ.
of the Abominations of the Earth.

6 καὶ εἶδον τὴν γυναῖκα μεθύουσαν ἐκ
And I saw the woman being drunk from

τοῦ αἵματος τῶν ἁγίων καὶ ἐκ τοῦ
the blood of the saints and from the

αἵματος τῶν μαρτύρων Ἰησοῦ. Καὶ
blood of the witnesses of Jesus. And

ἐθαύμασα ἰδὼν αὐτὴν θαῦμα μέγα. 7 καὶ
³I wondered ¹seeing ²her ⁵[with] ⁶wonder ⁴a great. And

εἶπέν μοι ὁ ἄγγελος· διὰ τί ἐθαύμασας;
³said ²to me ¹the ⁴angel: Why didst thou wonder?

ἐγὼ ἐρῶ σοι τὸ μυστήριον τῆς γυναικὸς
I will tell thee the mystery of the woman

καὶ τοῦ θηρίου τοῦ βαστάζοντος αὐτὴν
and of the beast - carrying her

τοῦ ἔχοντος τὰς ἑπτὰ κεφαλὰς καὶ τὰ
- having the seven heads and the

δέκα κέρατα. 8 Τὸ θηρίον ὃ εἶδες ἦν
ten horns. The beast which thou was sawest

καὶ οὐκ ἔστιν, καὶ μέλλει ἀναβαίνειν
and is not, and is about to come up

ἐκ τῆς ἀβύσσου καὶ εἰς ἀπώλειαν ὑπάγει·
out of the abyss and ²to ³destruction ¹goes;

καὶ θαυμασθήσονται οἱ κατοικοῦντες ἐπὶ
and ⁴will wonder ²the [ones] ³dwelling ⁵on

τῆς γῆς, ὧν οὐ γέγραπται τὸ ὄνομα
⁶the ⁷earth, of whom ²has not been written ¹the ¹name

ἐπὶ τὸ βιβλίον τῆς ζωῆς ἀπὸ καταβολῆς
on the scroll - of life from [the] foundation

κόσμου, βλεπόντων τὸ θηρίον ὅτι ἦν
of [the] world, seeing the beast that it was

καὶ οὐκ ἔστιν καὶ παρέσται. 9 ὧδε
and is not and is present. Here [is]

ὁ νοῦς ὁ ἔχων σοφίαν. αἱ ἑπτὰ
the mind - having wisdom. The seven

κεφαλαὶ ἑπτὰ ὄρη εἰσίν, ὅπου ἡ γυνὴ
heads ²seven ³mountains ¹are, where the woman

κάθηται ἐπ' αὐτῶν, καὶ βασιλεῖς ἑπτά
sits on them, and ²kings ¹seven

εἰσιν· 10 οἱ πέντε ἔπεσαν, ὁ εἷς ἔστιν,
¹are: the five fell, the one is,

ὁ ἄλλος οὔπω ἦλθεν, καὶ ὅταν ἔλθῃ
the other not yet came, and whenever he comes

ὀλίγον αὐτὸν δεῖ μεῖναι. 11 καὶ τὸ
²a little ³him ¹it behoves ²to And the
[while] remain.

θηρίον ὃ ἦν καὶ οὐκ ἔστιν, καὶ αὐτὸς
beast which was and is not, even he

ὄγδοός ἔστιν, καὶ ἐκ τῶν ἑπτά ἔστιν,
²an eighth ¹is, and ²of ³the ⁴seven ¹is,

καὶ εἰς ἀπώλειαν ὑπάγει. 12 καὶ τὰ
and to destruction goes. And the

δέκα κέρατα ἃ εἶδες δέκα βασιλεῖς
ten horns which thou ²ten ³kings
sawest

εἰσιν, οἵτινες βασιλείαν οὔπω ἔλαβον,
¹are, who a kingdom not yet received,

ἀλλὰ ἐξουσίαν ὡς βασιλεῖς μίαν ὥραν
but ²authority ¹as ⁴kings ⁶one ⁵hour

λαμβάνουσιν μετὰ τοῦ θηρίου. 13 οὗτοι
¹receive with the beast. These

6I saw that the woman was drunk with the blood of the saints, the blood of those who bore testimony to Jesus.

When I saw her, I was greatly astonished. 7Then the angel said to me: "Why are you astonished? I will explain to you the mystery of the woman and of the beast she rides, which has the seven heads and ten horns. 8The beast, which you saw, once was, now is not, and will come up out of the Abyss and go to his destruction. The inhabitants of the earth whose names have not been written in the book of life from the creation of the world will be astonished when they see the beast, because he once was, now is not, and yet will come.

9"This calls for a mind with wisdom. The seven heads are seven hills on which the woman sits. 10They are also seven kings. Five have fallen, one is, the other has not yet come; but when he does come, he must remain for a little while. 11The beast who once was, and now is not, is an eighth king. He belongs to the seven and is going to his destruction.

12"The ten horns you saw are ten kings who have not yet received a kingdom, but who for one hour receive authority as kings along with the beast.

---

dSome ancient mss. read he goes

13"These have one purpose and they give their power and authority to the beast.

Victory for the Lamb

14"These will wage war against the Lamb, and the Lamb will overcome them, because He is Lord of lords and King of kings, and those who are with Him *are the* called and chosen and faithful."

15And he *said to me, "The waters which you saw where the harlot sits, are peoples and multitudes and nations and tongues.

16"And the ten horns which you saw, and the beast, these will hate the harlot and will make her desolate and naked, and will eat her flesh and will burn her up with fire.

17"For God has put it in their hearts to execute His purpose by having a common purpose, and by giving their kingdom to the beast, until the words of God should be fulfilled.

18"And the woman whom you saw is the great city, which reigns over the kings of the earth."

μίαν γνώμην ἔχουσιν, καὶ τὴν δύναμιν
one mind have, and the power

καὶ ἐξουσίαν αὐτῶν τῷ θηρίῳ διδόασιν.
and authority of them to the beast they give.

14 οὗτοι μετὰ τοῦ ἀρνίου πολεμήσουσιν
These ⁴with ³the ⁴Lamb ¹will make war

καὶ τὸ ἀρνίον νικήσει αὐτούς, ὅτι κύριος
and the Lamb will overcome them, because ²Lord

κυρίων ἐστὶν καὶ βασιλεὺς βασιλέων, καὶ
¹of lords ³he is and King of kings, and

οἱ μετ᾽ αὐτοῦ κλητοὶ καὶ ἐκλεκτοὶ καὶ
the with him [are] called and chosen and
[ones]

πιστοί. **15** Καὶ λέγει μοι· τὰ ὕδατα
faithful. And he says to me: The waters

ἃ εἶδες, οὗ ἡ πόρνη κάθηται, λαοὶ
which thou where the harlot sits, peoples
sawest,

καὶ ὄχλοι εἰσὶν καὶ ἔθνη καὶ γλῶσσαι.
and crowds are and nations and tongues.

16 καὶ τὰ δέκα κέρατα ἃ εἶδες καὶ
And the ten horns which thou sawest and

τὸ θηρίον, οὗτοι μισήσουσιν τὴν πόρνην,
the beast, these will hate the harlot,

καὶ ἠρημωμένην ποιήσουσιν αὐτὴν καὶ
and ²having been desolated ¹will make ³her and

γυμνήν, καὶ τὰς σάρκας αὐτῆς φάγονται,
naked, and ²the ³fleshes ⁴of her ¹will eat,

καὶ αὐτὴν κατακαύσουσιν [ἐν] πυρί· **17** ὁ
and ²her ¹will consume with fire;

γὰρ θεὸς ἔδωκεν εἰς τὰς καρδίας αὐτῶν
for God gave into the hearts of them

ποιῆσαι τὴν γνώμην αὐτοῦ, καὶ ποιῆσαι
to do the mind of him, and to make

μίαν γνώμην καὶ δοῦναι τὴν βασιλείαν
one mind and to give the kingdom

αὐτῶν τῷ θηρίῳ, ἄχρι τελεσθήσονται οἱ
of them to the beast, until ⁴shall be accomplished ¹the

λόγοι τοῦ θεοῦ. **18** καὶ ἡ γυνὴ ἣν
²words – ³of God. And the woman whom

εἶδες ἔστιν ἡ πόλις ἡ μεγάλη ἡ ἔχουσα
thou is the ²city – ¹great – having
sawest

βασιλείαν ἐπὶ τῶν βασιλέων τῆς γῆς.
a kingdom over the kings of the earth.

13They have one purpose and will give their power and authority to the beast. 14They will make war against the Lamb, but the Lamb will overcome them because he is Lord of lords and King of kings—and with him will be his called, chosen and faithful followers."

15Then the angel said to me, "The waters you saw, where the prostitute sits, are peoples, multitudes, nations and languages. 16The beast and the ten horns you saw will hate the prostitute. They will bring her to ruin and leave her naked; they will eat her flesh and burn her with fire. 17For God has put it into their hearts to accomplish his purpose by agreeing to give the beast their power to rule, until God's words are fulfilled. 18The woman you saw is the great city that rules over the kings of the earth."

Chapter 18

Babylon Is Fallen

AFTER these things I saw another angel coming down from heaven, having great authority, and the earth was illumined with his glory.

2And he cried out with a mighty voice, saying, "Fallen, fallen is Babylon the great! And she has become a dwelling place of demons and a prison of every unclean spirit, and a prison of every unclean and hateful bird.

3"For all the nations ᶜhave drunk of the wine of the passion of her immoral-

---

18 Μετὰ ταῦτα εἶδον ἄλλον ἄγγελον
After these things I saw another angel

καταβαίνοντα ἐκ τοῦ οὐρανοῦ, ἔχοντα
coming down out of – heaven, having

ἐξουσίαν μεγάλην, καὶ ἡ γῆ ἐφωτίσθη
¹authority ²great, and the earth was enlightened

ἐκ τῆς δόξης αὐτοῦ. **2** καὶ ἔκραξεν
from the glory of him. And he cried

ἐν ἰσχυρᾷ φωνῇ λέγων· ἔπεσεν ἔπεσεν
in a strong voice saying: Fell[,] fell

Βαβυλὼν ἡ μεγάλη, καὶ ἐγένετο κατοικητή-
Babylon the great, and became a dwelling-

ριον δαιμονίων καὶ φυλακὴ παντὸς
place of demons and a prison of every

πνεύματος ἀκαθάρτου καὶ φυλακὴ παντὸς
²spirit ¹unclean and a prison of every

ὀρνέου ἀκαθάρτου καὶ μεμισημένου, **3** ὅτι
⁴bird ¹unclean ²and ³having been hated, because

ἐκ τοῦ οἴνου τοῦ θυμοῦ τῆς πορνείας
⁶of ⁵the ⁷wine ¹of the ²anger ¹⁰of the ¹¹fornication

Chapter 18

The Fall of Babylon

AFTER this I saw another angel coming down from heaven. He had great authority, and the earth was illuminated by his splendor. 2With a mighty voice he shouted:

"Fallen! Fallen is Babylon the Great! She has become a home for demons and a haunt for every evilᵛ spirit, a haunt for every unclean and detestable bird. 3For all the nations have drunk the maddening wine of her adulteries.

ᶜMany ancient mss. read *have fallen by*

ᵛ2 Greek *unclean*

ity, and the kings of the earth have committed *acts of* immorality with her, and the merchants of the earth have become rich by the wealth of her sensuality.''

4And I heard another voice from heaven, saying, "Come out of her, my people, that you may not participate in her sins and that you may not receive of her plagues;

5for her sins have piled up as high as heaven, and God has remembered her iniquities.

6"Pay her back even as she has paid, and give back *to her* double according to her deeds; in the cup which she has mixed, mix twice as much for her.

7"To the degree that she glorified herself and lived sensuously, to the same degree give her torment and mourning; for she says in her heart, 'I SIT *as* A QUEEN AND I AM NOT A WIDOW, and will never see mourning.'

8"For this reason in one day her plagues will come, pestilence and mourning and famine, and she will be burned up with fire; for the Lord God who judges her is strong.

Lament for Babylon

9"And the kings of the earth, who committed *acts of* immorality and lived sensuously with her, will weep and lament over her when they see the smoke of her burning,

10standing at a distance because of the fear of her torment, saying, 'Woe, woe, the great city, Babylon, the strong city! For in

αὐτῆς πέπωκαν πάντα τὰ ἔθνη, καὶ
¹²of her ⁴have drunk ¹all ³the ²nations, and

οἱ βασιλεῖς τῆς γῆς μετ' αὐτῆς ἐπόρνευσαν,
the kings of the earth with her practised fornication,

καὶ οἱ ἔμποροι τῆς γῆς ἐκ τῆς δυνάμεως
and the merchants of the earth ¹from ²the ²power

τοῦ στρήνους αὐτῆς ἐπλούτησαν. 4 Καὶ
³of the ⁴luxury ⁵of her ¹became rich. And

ἤκουσα ἄλλην φωνὴν ἐκ τοῦ οὐρανοῦ
I heard another voice out of – heaven

λέγουσαν· ἐξέλθατε ὁ λαός μου ἐξ αὐτῆς,
saying: Come ye out[,] the people of me[,] out of her,

ἵνα μὴ συγκοινωνήσητε ταῖς ἁμαρτίαις
lest ye share in the sins

αὐτῆς, καὶ ἐκ τῶν πληγῶν αὐτῆς ἵνα
of her, and ³of ⁴the ⁵plagues ⁶of her ¹lest

μὴ λάβητε· 5 ὅτι ἐκολλήθησαν αὐτῆς αἱ
²ye receive; because ⁴joined together ³of her ¹the

ἁμαρτίαι ἄχρι τοῦ οὐρανοῦ, καὶ ἐμνημό-
²sins up to – heaven, and ²remem-

νευσεν ὁ θεὸς τὰ ἀδικήματα αὐτῆς.
bered ¹God the misdeeds of her.

6 ἀπόδοτε αὐτῇ ὡς καὶ αὐτὴ ἀπέδωκεν,
Give ye back to her as indeed she gave back,

καὶ διπλώσατε τὰ διπλᾶ κατὰ τὰ ἔργα
and double ye the double according to the works

αὐτῆς· ἐν τῷ ποτηρίῳ ᾧ ἐκέρασεν
of her; in the cup in which she mixed

κεράσατε αὐτῇ διπλοῦν· 7 ὅσα ἐδόξασεν
mix ye to her double; by what she glorified things

αὐτὴν καὶ ἐστρηνίασεν, τοσοῦτον δότε
her[self] and luxuriated, by so much give ye

αὐτῇ βασανισμὸν καὶ πένθος. ὅτι ἐν
to her torment and sorrow. Because in

τῇ καρδίᾳ αὐτῆς λέγει ὅτι κάθημαι
the heart of her she says[,] – I sit

βασίλισσα καὶ χήρα οὐκ εἰμὶ καὶ πένθος
a queen and a widow I am not and sorrow

οὐ μὴ ἴδω· 8 διὰ τοῦτο ἐν μιᾷ ἡμέρᾳ
by no means I see; therefore in one day

ἥξουσιν αἱ πληγαὶ αὐτῆς, θάνατος καὶ
will come the plagues of her, death and

πένθος καὶ λιμός, καὶ ἐν πυρὶ κατακαυ-
sorrow and famine, and with fire she will be

θήσεται· ὅτι ἰσχυρὸς κύριος ὁ θεὸς ὁ
consumed; because strong [is] [the] Lord – God the

κρίνας αὐτήν. 9 καὶ κλαύσουσιν καὶ
[one] judging her. And ¹will weep ⁴and

κόψονται ἐπ' αὐτὴν οἱ βασιλεῖς τῆς
⁵wail ⁶over ⁷her ¹the ²kings ³of the

γῆς οἱ μετ' αὐτῆς πορνεύσαντες καὶ
⁴earth ¹⁰the ¹¹with ¹²her ¹³having practised and
[ones] fornication

στρηνιάσαντες, ὅταν βλέπωσιν τὸν καπνὸν
having luxuriated, whenever they see the smoke

τῆς πυρώσεως αὐτῆς, 10 ἀπὸ μακρόθεν
of the burning of her, ¹from ²afar

ἑστηκότες διὰ τὸν φόβον τοῦ βασανισμοῦ
¹standing because of the fear of the torment

αὐτῆς, λέγοντες· οὐαὶ οὐαί, ἡ πόλις
of her, saying: Woe[,] woe, the ²city

ἡ μεγάλη, Βαβυλὼν ἡ πόλις ἡ ἰσχυρά,
– ¹great, Babylon the ²city – ¹strong,

The kings of the earth committed adultery with her,
and the merchants of the earth grew rich from her excessive luxuries.''

4Then I heard another voice from heaven say:

"Come out of her, my people,
so that you will not share in her sins,
so that you will not receive any of her plagues;

5for her sins are piled up to heaven,
and God has remembered her crimes.

6Give back to her as she has given;
pay her back double for what she has done.
Mix her a double portion from her own cup.

7Give her as much torture and grief
as the glory and luxury she gave herself.
In her heart she boasts,
'I sit as queen; I am not a widow,
and I will never mourn.'

8Therefore in one day her plagues will overtake her:
death, mourning and famine.
She will be consumed by fire,
for mighty is the Lord God who judges her.

9"When the kings of the earth who committed adultery with her and shared her luxury see the smoke of her burning, they will weep and mourn over her. 10Terrified at her torment, they will stand far off and cry:

" 'Woe! Woe, O great city,
O Babylon, city of power!

one hour your judgment has come.'

11"And the merchants of the earth weep and mourn over her, because no one buys their cargoes any more;

12cargoes of gold and silver and precious stones and pearls and fine linen and purple and silk and scarlet, and every *kind of* citron wood and every article of ivory and every article *made* from very costly wood and bronze and iron and marble,

13and cinnamon and spice and incense and perfume and frankincense and wine and olive oil and fine flour and wheat and cattle and sheep, and *cargoes of* horses and chariots and slaves and human lives.

14"And the fruit you long for has gone from you, and all things that were luxurious and splendid have passed away from you and *men* will no longer find them.

15"The merchants of these things, who became rich from her, will stand at a distance because of the fear of her torment, weeping and mourning,

16saying, 'Woe, woe, the great city, she who was clothed in fine linen and purple and scarlet, and adorned with gold and precious stones and pearls;

17for in one hour such great wealth has been laid waste!' And every shipmaster and every passenger and sailor, and as many as

---

ὅτι μιᾷ ὥρᾳ ἦλθεν ἡ κρίσις σου. 11 καὶ
be-cause one in Hour came the judgment of thee. And

οἱ ἔμποροι τῆς γῆς κλαίουσιν καὶ
the merchants of the earth weep and

πενθοῦσιν ἐπ᾽ αὐτήν, ὅτι τὸν γόμον
sorrow over her, because 'the 'cargo

αὐτῶν οὐδεὶς ἀγοράζει οὐκέτι, 12 γόμον
'of them 'no one 'buys 'any more, cargo

χρυσοῦ καὶ ἀργύρου καὶ λίθου τιμίου
of gold and of silver and 'stone 'of valuable

καὶ μαργαριτῶν καὶ βυσσίνου καὶ πορφύρας
and of pearls and of fine linen and of purple

καὶ σηρικοῦ καὶ κοκκίνου, καὶ πᾶν
and of silk and of scarlet, and all

ξύλον θύϊνον καὶ πᾶν σκεῦος ἐλεφάντινον
'wood 'thyine and every 'vessel 'ivory

καὶ πᾶν σκεῦος ἐκ ξύλου τιμιωτάτου
and every vessel of 'wood 'very valuable

καὶ χαλκοῦ καὶ σιδήρου καὶ μαρμάρου,
and of bronze and of iron and of marble,

13 καὶ κιννάμωμον καὶ ἄμωμον καὶ
and cinnamon and spice and

θυμιάματα καὶ μύρον καὶ λίβανον καὶ
incenses and ointment and frankincense and

οἶνον καὶ ἔλαιον καὶ σεμίδαλιν καὶ σῖτον
wine and oil and fine meal and corn

καὶ κτήνη καὶ πρόβατα, καὶ ἵππων
and beasts of burden and sheep, and of horses

καὶ ῥεδῶν καὶ σωμάτων, καὶ ψυχὰς
and of carriages and of bodies, and souls

ἀνθρώπων. 14 καὶ ἡ ὀπώρα σου τῆς
of men. And the fruit 'of thee 'of the

ἐπιθυμίας τῆς ψυχῆς ἀπῆλθεν ἀπὸ σοῦ,
'lust 'of the 'soul went away from thee,

καὶ πάντα τὰ λιπαρὰ καὶ τὰ λαμπρὰ
and all the sumptuous things and the bright things

ἀπώλετο ἀπὸ σοῦ, καὶ οὐκέτι οὐ μὴ
perished from thee, and no more by no(any) means

αὐτὰ εὑρήσουσιν. 15 οἱ ἔμποροι τούτων,
'them 'shall they find. The merchants of these things,

οἱ πλουτήσαντες ἀπ᾽ αὐτῆς, ἀπὸ μακρόθεν
the having been rich from her, 'from 'afar
[ones]

στήσονται διὰ τὸν φόβον τοῦ βασανισμοῦ
'will stand because of the fear of the torment

αὐτῆς κλαίοντες καὶ πενθοῦντες, 16 λέγοντες·
of her weeping and sorrowing, saying:

οὐαὶ οὐαί, ἡ πόλις ἡ μεγάλη, ἡ περι-
Woe[,] woe, the 'city - 'great, the - having

βεβλημένη βύσσινον καὶ πορφυροῦν καὶ
been clothed [with] fine linen and purple and

κόκκινον, καὶ κεχρυσωμένη ἐν χρυσίῳ
scarlet, and having been gilded with gold

καὶ λίθῳ τιμίῳ καὶ μαργαρίτῃ, 17 ὅτι
and 'stone 'valuable and pearl, because

μιᾷ ὥρᾳ ἠρημώθη ὁ τοσοῦτος πλοῦτος.
in one hour 'was made 'such great 'wealth.
desolate

καὶ πᾶς κυβερνήτης καὶ πᾶς ὁ ἐπὶ
And every steersman and 'every 'one 'to

τόπον πλέων καὶ ναῦται καὶ ὅσοι τὴν
'a place 'sailing and sailors and as many as 'the

In one hour your doom has come!'

11"The merchants of the earth will weep and mourn over her because no one buys their cargoes any more—12cargoes of gold, silver, precious stones and pearls; fine linen, purple, silk and scarlet cloth; every sort of citron wood, and articles of every kind made of ivory, costly wood, bronze, iron and marble; 13cargoes of cinnamon and spice, of incense, myrrh and frankincense, of wine and olive oil, of fine flour and wheat; cattle and sheep; horses and carriages; and bodies and souls of men.

14"They will say, 'The fruit you longed for is gone from you. All your riches and splendor have vanished, never to be recovered.' 15The merchants who sold these things and gained their wealth from her will stand far off, terrified at her torment. They will weep and mourn 16and cry out:

"'Woe! Woe, O great city,
dressed in fine linen,
purple and scarlet,
and glittering with gold, precious stones and pearls!
17In one hour such great wealth has been brought to ruin!'

"Every sea captain, and all who travel by ship, the sailors, and all who earn as make their living by the sea, stood at a distance, 18and were crying out as they saw the smoke of her burning, saying, 'What *city* is like the great city?'

19"And they threw dust on their heads and were crying out, weeping and mourning, saying, 'Woe, woe, the great city, in which all who had ships at sea became 'rich by her wealth, for in one hour she has been laid waste!'

20"Rejoice over her, O heaven, and you saints and apostles and prophets, because God has pronounced judgment for you against her."

21And a strong angel took up a stone like a great millstone and threw it into the sea, saying, "Thus will Babylon, the great city, be thrown down with violence, and will not be found any longer.

22And the sound of harpists and musicians and flute-players and trumpeters will not be heard in you any longer; and no craftsman of any craft will be found in you any longer; and the sound of a mill will not be heard in you any longer;

23and the light of a lamp will not shine in you any longer; and the voice of the bridegroom and bride will not be heard in you any longer; for your merchants were the great men of the earth, because all the nations were deceived by your sorcery.

24"And in her was found the blood of prophets and of saints and of all who have been slain on the earth."

θάλασσαν ἐργάζονται, ἀπὸ μακρόθεν ἔστησαν
²sea ¹work, ²from ³afar ¹stood

18 καὶ ἔκραζον βλέποντες τὸν καπνὸν
and cried out seeing the smoke

τῆς πυρώσεως αὐτῆς λέγοντες· τίς ὁμοία
of the burning of her saying: Who(What) [is] like

τῇ πόλει τῇ μεγάλῃ; 19 καὶ ἔβαλον
to the ²city - ¹great? And they cast

χοῦν ἐπὶ τὰς κεφαλὰς αὐτῶν καὶ ἔκραζον
dust on the heads of them and cried out

κλαίοντες καὶ πενθοῦντες, λέγοντες· οὐαὶ
weeping and sorrowing, saying: Woe[,]

οὐαί, ἡ πόλις ἡ μεγάλη, ἐν ᾗ ἐπλούτησαν
woe, the ²city - ¹great, by which ⁴were rich

πάντες οἱ ἔχοντες τὰ πλοῖα ἐν τῇ
¹all ²the [ones] ³having ⁴the ⁵ships ⁶in ⁷the

θαλάσσῃ ἐκ τῆς τιμιότητος αὐτῆς, ὅτι
⁸sea from the worth of her, because

μιᾷ ὥρᾳ ἠρημώθη. 20 Εὐφραίνου ἐπ'
in one hour she was made desolate. Be thou glad over

αὐτῇ, οὐρανὲ καὶ οἱ ἅγιοι καὶ οἱ ἀπό-
her, heaven and the saints and the apost-

στολοι καὶ οἱ προφῆται, ὅτι ἔκρινεν ὁ
les and the prophets, because ²judged ¹

θεὸς τὸ κρίμα ὑμῶν ἐξ αὐτῆς. 21 Καὶ
¹God the judgment of you by her. And

ἦρεν εἷς ἄγγελος ἰσχυρὸς λίθον ὡς
⁴lifted ¹one ²angel ³strong a stone as

μύλινον μέγαν, καὶ ἔβαλεν εἰς τὴν θά-
²millstone ¹a great, and threw into the sea

λασσαν λέγων· οὕτως ὁρμήματι βληθήσεται
saying: Thus with a rush ⁵shall be thrown

Βαβυλὼν ἡ μεγάλη πόλις, καὶ οὐ μὴ
¹Babylon ²the ³great ⁴city, and by no means

εὑρεθῇ ἔτι. 22 καὶ φωνὴ κιθαρῳδῶν
[shall] be longer. And sound of harpers
found

καὶ μουσικῶν καὶ αὐλητῶν καὶ σαλπιστῶν
and of musicians and of flutists and of trumpeters

οὐ μὴ ἀκουσθῇ ἐν σοὶ ἔτι, καὶ πᾶς
by no means [shall] be heard in thee longer, and every

τεχνίτης πάσης τέχνης οὐ μὴ εὑρεθῇ
craftsman of every craft by no means [shall] be found

ἐν σοὶ ἔτι, καὶ φωνὴ μύλου οὐ μὴ
in thee longer, and sound of a mill by no means

ἀκουσθῇ ἐν σοὶ ἔτι, 23 καὶ φῶς
[shall] be heard in thee longer, and light

λύχνου οὐ μὴ φάνῃ ἐν σοὶ ἔτι, καὶ
of a by no means [shall] in thee longer, and
lamp shine

φωνὴ νυμφίου καὶ νύμφης οὐ μὴ
voice of bridegroom and of bride by no means

ἀκουσθῇ ἐν σοὶ ἔτι· ὅτι [οἱ] ἔμποροί
[shall] be heard in thee longer; because the merchants

σου ἦσαν οἱ μεγιστᾶνες τῆς γῆς, ὅτι
of thee were the great ones of the earth, because

ἐν τῇ φαρμακείᾳ σου ἐπλανήθησαν πάντα
by the sorcery of thee ⁴were deceived ¹all

τὰ ἔθνη, 24 καὶ ἐν αὐτῇ αἷμα προφητῶν
²the ³nations, and in her ²blood ³of prophets

καὶ ἁγίων εὑρέθη καὶ πάντων τῶν
⁴and ⁵of saints ¹was found and of all the [ones]

ἐσφαγμένων ἐπὶ τῆς γῆς.
having been slain on the earth.

---

their living from the sea, will stand far off. 18When they see the smoke of her burning, they will exclaim, 'Was there ever a city like this great city?' 19They will throw dust on their heads, and with weeping and mourning cry out:

" 'Woe! Woe, O great city,
where all who had
ships on the sea
became rich through
her wealth!
In one hour she has been
brought to ruin!
⁰Rejoice over her, O
heaven!
Rejoice, saints and
apostles and
prophets!
God has judged her for
the way she treated
you.' "

21Then a mighty angel picked up a boulder the size of a large millstone and threw it into the sea, and said:

"With such violence
the great city of
Babylon will be
thrown down,
never to be found
again.
22The music of harpists
and musicians, flute
players and
trumpeters,
will never be heard in
you again.
No workman of any
trade
will ever be found in
you again.
The sound of a millstone
will never be heard in
you again.
23The light of a lamp
will never shine in you
again.
The voice of bridegroom
and bride
will never be heard in
you again.
Your merchants were
the world's great
men.
By your magic spell all
the nations were led
astray.
24In her was found the
blood of prophets
and of the saints,
and of all who have
been killed on the
earth."

Chapter 19

The Fourfold Hallelujah

AFTER these things I heard, as it were, a loud voice of a great multitude in heaven, saying,
"Hallelujah! Salvation and glory and power belong to our God;
[2]BECAUSE HIS JUDGMENTS ARE TRUE AND RIGHTEOUS; for He has judged the great harlot who was corrupting the earth with her immorality, and HE HAS AVENGED THE BLOOD OF HIS BOND-SERVANTS ON HER."
[3]And a second time they said, "Hallelujah! HER SMOKE RISES UP FOREVER AND EVER."
[4]And the twenty-four elders and the four living creatures fell down and worshiped God who sits on the throne saying, "Amen. Hallelujah!"
[5]And a voice came from the throne, saying,
"Give praise to our God, all you His bond-servants, you who fear Him, the small and the great."
[6]And I heard, as it were, the voice of a great multitude and as the sound of many waters and as the sound of mighty peals of thunder, saying,
"Hallelujah! For the Lord our God, the Almighty, reigns.

Marriage of the Lamb

[7]"Let us rejoice and be glad and give the glory to Him, for the marriage of the Lamb has come and His bride has made herself ready."
[8]And it was given to her to clothe herself in fine linen, bright and clean; for the fine linen is the righteous acts of the saints.
[9]And he *said to me, "Write, 'Blessed are those

---

19 Μετὰ ταῦτα ἤκουσα ὡς φωνὴν
After these things I heard as 'voice
μεγάλην ὄχλου πολλοῦ ἐν τῷ οὐρανῷ
'a great 'crowd 'of a much in – heaven
(loud) (great)
λεγόντων· ἀλληλουϊά· ἡ σωτηρία καὶ ἡ
saying: Halleluia: The salvation and the
δόξα καὶ ἡ δύναμις τοῦ θεοῦ ἡμῶν,
glory and the power of the God of us,
2 ὅτι ἀληθιναὶ καὶ δίκαιαι αἱ κρίσεις
because true and righteous the judgments
αὐτοῦ· ὅτι ἔκρινεν τὴν πόρνην τὴν
of him; because he judged the 'harlot
μεγάλην ἥτις ἔφθειρεν τὴν γῆν ἐν τῇ
'great who defiled the earth with the
πορνείᾳ αὐτῆς, καὶ ἐξεδίκησεν τὸ αἷμα
fornication of her, and he avenged the blood
τῶν δούλων αὐτοῦ ἐκ χειρὸς αὐτῆς.
of the slaves of him out of [the] hand of her.
3 καὶ δεύτερον εἴρηκαν· ἀλληλουϊά· καὶ
And secondly they have said: Halleluia; and
ὁ καπνὸς αὐτῆς ἀναβαίνει εἰς τοὺς
the smoke of her goes up unto the
αἰῶνας τῶν αἰώνων. **4** καὶ ἔπεσαν οἱ
ages of the ages. And 'fell 'the
πρεσβύτεροι οἱ εἴκοσι τέσσαρες καὶ τὰ
'elders – 'twenty-four 'and 'the
τέσσερα ζῷα, καὶ προσεκύνησαν τῷ θεῷ
'four 'living and worshipped – God
creatures,
τῷ καθημένῳ ἐπὶ τῷ θρόνῳ λέγοντες·
– sitting on the throne saying:
ἀμὴν ἀλληλουϊά. **5** καὶ φωνὴ ἀπὸ τοῦ
Amen[,] halleluia. And a voice 'from 'the
θρόνου ἐξῆλθεν λέγουσα· αἰνεῖτε τῷ θεῷ
'throne 'came out saying: Praise ye the God
ἡμῶν, πάντες οἱ δοῦλοι αὐτοῦ, οἱ
of us, all the slaves of him, the
φοβούμενοι αὐτόν, οἱ μικροὶ καὶ οἱ
[ones] fearing him, the small and the
μεγάλοι. **6** Καὶ ἤκουσα ὡς φωνὴν ὄχλου
great. And I heard as a sound 'crowd
πολλοῦ καὶ ὡς φωνὴν ὑδάτων πολλῶν
'of a and as a sound 'waters 'of many
much(great)
καὶ ὡς φωνὴν βροντῶν ἰσχυρῶν, λεγόντων·
and as a sound 'thunders 'of strong saying:
(loud),
ἀλληλουϊά, ὅτι ἐβασίλευσεν κύριος ὁ θεὸς
Halleluia, because 'reigned '[the] Lord 'the 'God
ἡμῶν ὁ παντοκράτωρ. **7** χαίρωμεν καὶ
'of us 'the 'Almighty. Let us rejoice and
ἀγαλλιῶμεν, καὶ δώσομεν τὴν δόξαν αὐτῷ,
let us exult, and we will give the glory to him,
ὅτι ἦλθεν ὁ γάμος τοῦ ἀρνίου, καὶ
because 'came 'the 'marriage 'of the 'Lamb, and
ἡ γυνὴ αὐτοῦ ἡτοίμασεν ἑαυτήν, **8** καὶ
the wife of him prepared herself, and
ἐδόθη αὐτῇ ἵνα περιβάληται βύσσινον
it was to her in order she might be 'fine linen
given that clothed [with]
λαμπρὸν καθαρόν· τὸ γὰρ βύσσινον τὰ
'bright 'clean; for the fine linen 'the
δικαιώματα τῶν ἁγίων ἐστίν. **9** Καὶ
'righteous deeds 'of the 'saints 'is. And
λέγει μοι· γράψον· μακάριοι οἱ εἰς τὸ
he tells me: Write thou; blessed 'the [ones] 'to 'the

Chapter 19

Hallelujah!

AFTER this I heard what sounded like the roar of a great multitude in heaven shouting:
"Hallelujah!
Salvation and glory and power belong to our God,
[2] for true and just are his judgments.
He has condemned the great prostitute who corrupted the earth by her adulteries.
He has avenged on her the blood of his servants."
[3]And again they shouted:
"Hallelujah!
The smoke from her goes up for ever and ever."
[4]The twenty-four elders and the four living creatures fell down and worshiped God, who was seated on the throne. And they cried:
"Amen, Hallelujah!"
[5]Then a voice came from the throne, saying:
"Praise our God,
all you his servants,
you who fear him,
both small and great!"
[6]Then I heard what sounded like a great multitude, like the roar of rushing waters and like loud peals of thunder, shouting:
"Hallelujah!
For our Lord God Almighty reigns.
[7]Let us rejoice and be glad
and give him glory!
For the wedding of the Lamb has come,
and his bride has made herself ready.
[8]Fine linen, bright and clean,
was given her to wear."

(Fine linen stands for the righteous acts of the saints.)

[9]Then the angel said to me, "Write: 'Blessed are

who are invited to the marriage supper of the Lamb.' '' And he *said to me, ''These are true words of God.''

10And I fell at his feet to worship him. And he *said to me, ''Do not do that; I am a fellow servant of yours and your brethren who hold the testimony of Jesus; worship God. For the testimony of Jesus is the spirit of prophecy.''

The Coming of Christ

11And I saw heaven opened; and behold, a white horse, and He who sat upon it *is* called Faithful and True; and in righteousness He judges and wages war.

12And His eyes *are* a flame of fire, and upon His head are many diadems; and He has a name written *upon Him* which no one knows except Himself.

13And *He is* clothed with a robe dipped in blood; and His name is called The Word of God.

14And the armies which are in heaven, clothed in fine linen, white *and* clean, were following Him on white horses.

15And from His mouth comes a sharp sword, so that with it He may smite the nations; and He will rule them with a rod of iron; and He treads the wine press of the fierce wrath of God, the Almighty.

16And on His robe and on His thigh He has a name written, ''KING OF KINGS, AND LORD OF LORDS.''

δεῖπνον τοῦ γάμου τοῦ ἀρνίου κεκλημένοι.
⁵supper ⁶of ⁷marriage ⁸of ⁹Lamb ¹having been
    the   the   called.

καὶ λέγει μοι· οὗτοι οἱ λόγοι ἀληθινοὶ
And he says to me: ¹These - ²words ³true

τοῦ θεοῦ εἰσιν. 10 καὶ ἔπεσα ἔμπροσθεν
- ²of God ¹are.   And I fell before

τῶν ποδῶν αὐτοῦ προσκυνῆσαι αὐτῷ.
the feet of him to worship him.

καὶ λέγει μοι· ὅρα μή· σύνδουλός σού
And he says to me: See thou not; ¹a fellow- ³of
                    [do it]   ²slave thee

εἰμι καὶ τῶν ἀδελφῶν σου τῶν ἐχόντων
¹I am and of the brothers of thee - having

τὴν μαρτυρίαν Ἰησοῦ· τῷ θεῷ προσκύνησον.
the witness of Jesus; - ²God ¹worship thou.

ἡ γὰρ μαρτυρία Ἰησοῦ ἐστιν τὸ πνεῦμα
For the witness of Jesus is the spirit

τῆς προφητείας.
- of prophecy.

11 Καὶ εἶδον τὸν οὐρανὸν ἠνεῳγμένον,
And I saw - heaven having been opened,

καὶ ἰδοὺ ἵππος λευκός, καὶ ὁ καθήμενος
and behold[,] ²horse ¹a white, and the [one] sitting

ἐπ' αὐτὸν πιστὸς καλούμενος καὶ ἀληθινός,
on it ²faithful ¹being called and true,

καὶ ἐν δικαιοσύνῃ κρίνει καὶ πολεμεῖ.
and in righteousness he judges and makes war.

12 οἱ δὲ ὀφθαλμοὶ αὐτοῦ φλὸξ πυρός,
And the eyes of him [are as] a flame of fire,

καὶ ἐπὶ τὴν κεφαλὴν αὐτοῦ διαδήματα
and on the head of him ²diadems

πολλά, ἔχων ὄνομα γεγραμμένον ὃ οὐδεὶς
¹many, having a name having been written which no one

οἶδεν εἰ μὴ αὐτός, 13 καὶ περιβεβλημένος
knows except [him]self, and having been
                                   clothed [with]

ἱμάτιον βεβαμμένον αἵματι, καὶ κέκληται
a garment having been in blood, and ⁴has been
         dipped   called

τὸ ὄνομα αὐτοῦ ὁ λόγος τοῦ θεοῦ.
¹the ²name ³of him The Word - of God.

14 καὶ τὰ στρατεύματα τὰ ἐν τῷ οὐρανῷ
And the armies - in - heaven

ἠκολούθει αὐτῷ ἐφ' ἵπποις λευκοῖς, ἐνδεδυμένοι
followed him on ²horses ¹white, having been
                                    dressed [in]

βύσσινον λευκὸν καθαρόν. 15 καὶ ἐκ
²fine linen ¹white ³clean.   And out of

τοῦ στόματος αὐτοῦ ἐκπορεύεται ῥομφαία
the mouth of him proceeds ²sword

ὀξεῖα, ἵνα ἐν αὐτῇ πατάξῃ τὰ ἔθνη·
¹a sharp, in order with it he may the nations;
          that   smite

καὶ αὐτὸς ποιμανεῖ αὐτοὺς ἐν ῥάβδῳ
and he will shepherd them with ²staff

σιδηρᾷ· καὶ αὐτὸς πατεῖ τὴν ληνὸν
¹an iron; and he treads the winepress

τοῦ οἴνου τοῦ θυμοῦ τῆς ὀργῆς τοῦ
of the wine of the anger[,] of the wrath -

θεοῦ τοῦ παντοκράτορος. 16 καὶ ἔχει
of God of the Almighty.   And he has

ἐπὶ τὸ ἱμάτιον καὶ ἐπὶ τὸν μηρὸν
on the garment and on the thigh

αὐτοῦ ὄνομα γεγραμμένον· ΒΑΣΙΛΕΥΣ
of him a name having been written: KING

ΒΑΣΙΛΕΩΝ ΚΑΙ ΚΥΡΙΟΣ ΚΥΡΙΩΝ.
OF KINGS AND LORD OF LORDS.

---

those who are invited to the wedding supper of the Lamb!'' '' And he added, ''These are the true words of God.''

10At this I fell at his feet to worship him. But he said to me, ''Do not do it! I am a fellow servant with you and with your brothers who hold to the testimony of Jesus. Worship God! For the testimony of Jesus is the spirit of prophecy.''

The Rider on the White Horse

11I saw heaven standing open and there before me was a white horse, whose rider is called Faithful and True. With justice he judges and makes war. 12His eyes are like blazing fire, and on his head are many crowns. He has a name written on him that no one knows but he himself. 13He is dressed in a robe dipped in blood, and his name is the Word of God. 14The armies of heaven were following him, riding on white horses and dressed in fine linen, white and clean. 15Out of his mouth comes a sharp sword with which to strike down the nations. ''He will rule them with an iron scepter.'' ʷ He treads the winepress of the fury of the wrath of God Almighty. 16On his robe and on his thigh he has this name written:

KING OF KINGS AND LORD OF LORDS.

ʷ15 Psalm 2:9

17And I saw an angel standing in the sun; and he cried out with a loud voice, saying to all the birds which fly in midheaven, "Come, assemble for the great supper of God;

18in order that you may eat the flesh of kings and the flesh of /commanders and the flesh of mighty men and the flesh of horses and of those who sit on them and the flesh of all men, both free men and slaves, and small and great."

19And I saw the beast and the kings of the earth and their armies, assembled to make war against Him who sat upon the horse, and against His army.

Doom of the Beast and False Prophet

20And the beast was seized, and with him the false prophet who performed the signs in his presence, by which he deceived those who had received the mark of the beast and those who worshiped his image; these two were thrown alive into the lake of fire which burns with brimstone.

21And the rest were killed with the sword which came from the mouth of Him who sat upon the horse, and all the birds were filled with their flesh.

---

17 Καὶ εἶδον ἕνα ἄγγελον ἑστῶτα ἐν
And I saw one angel standing in

τῷ ἡλίῳ, καὶ ἔκραξεν ἐν φωνῇ μεγάλῃ
the sun, and he cried out in ⁹voice ¹a great (loud)

λέγων πᾶσιν τοῖς ὀρνέοις τοῖς πετομένοις
saying to all the birds flying

ἐν μεσουρανήματι· δεῦτε συνάχθητε εἰς
in mid-heaven: Come ye[,] assemble ye to

τὸ δεῖπνον τὸ μέγα τοῦ θεοῦ, **18** ἵνα
the ⁹supper – ¹great – of God, in order that

φάγητε σάρκας βασιλέων καὶ σάρκας
ye may eat flesh*es* of kings and flesh*es*

χιλιάρχων καὶ σάρκας ἰσχυρῶν καὶ σάρκας
of chiliarchs and flesh*es* of strong men and flesh*es*

ἵππων καὶ τῶν καθημένων ἐπ' αὐτῶν,
of horses and of the [ones] sitting on them,

καὶ σάρκας πάντων ἐλευθέρων τε καὶ
and flesh*es* of all ¹free men ¹both and

δούλων καὶ μικρῶν καὶ μεγάλων. **19** Καὶ
slaves both small and great. And

εἶδον τὸ θηρίον καὶ τοὺς βασιλεῖς τῆς
I saw the beast and the kings of the

γῆς καὶ τὰ στρατεύματα αὐτῶν συνηγμένα
earth and the armies of them *having been assembled*

ποιῆσαι τὸν πόλεμον μετὰ τοῦ καθημένου
to make the war with the [one] sitting

ἐπὶ τοῦ ἵππου καὶ μετὰ τοῦ στρατεύματος
on the horse and with the army

αὐτοῦ. **20** καὶ ἐπιάσθη τὸ θηρίον καὶ
of him. And ⁹was seized ¹the ⁹beast and

μετ' αὐτοῦ ὁ ψευδοπροφήτης ὁ ποιήσας
with it the false prophet the [one] having done

τὰ σημεῖα ἐνώπιον αὐτοῦ, ἐν οἷς ἐπλάνη-
the signs before it, by which he de-

σεν τοὺς λαβόντας τὸ χάραγμα τοῦ
ceived the [ones] having received the mark of the

θηρίου καὶ τοὺς προσκυνοῦντας τῇ εἰκόνι
beast and the [ones] worshipping the image

αὐτοῦ· ζῶντες ἐβλήθησαν οἱ δύο εἰς
of it; ⁴living ⁹were cast ¹the ⁹two into

τὴν λίμνην τοῦ πυρὸς τῆς καιομένης*
the lake – of fire – burning*

ἐν θείῳ. **21** καὶ οἱ λοιποὶ ἀπεκτάνθησαν
with sulphur. And the rest were killed

ἐν τῇ ῥομφαίᾳ τοῦ καθημένου ἐπὶ τοῦ
with the sword of the [one] sitting on the

ἵππου τῇ ἐξελθούσῃ ἐκ τοῦ στόματος
horse – proceeding§ out of the mouth

αὐτοῦ, καὶ πάντα τὰ ὄρνεα ἐχορτάσθησα·
of him, and all the birds were filled

ἐκ τῶν σαρκῶν αὐτῶν.
by the flesh*es* of them.

17And I saw an angel standing in the sun, who cried in a loud voice to all the birds flying in midair, "Come, gather together for the great supper of God, 18so that you may eat the flesh of kings, generals, and mighty men, of horses and their riders, and the flesh of all people, free and slave, small and great."

19Then I saw the beast and the kings of the earth and their armies gathered together to make war against the rider on the horse and his army. 20But the beast was captured, and with him the false prophet who had performed the miraculous signs on his behalf. With these signs he had deluded those who had received the mark of the beast and worshiped his image. The two of them were thrown alive into the fiery lake of burning sulfur. 21The rest of them were killed with the sword that came out of the mouth of the rider on the horse, and all the birds gorged themselves on their flesh.

Chapter 20

Satan Bound

AND I saw an angel coming down from heaven, having the key of the abyss and a great chain in his hand.

---

20 Καὶ εἶδον ἄγγελον καταβαίνοντα ἐκ
And I saw an angel coming down out of

τοῦ οὐρανοῦ, ἔχοντα τὴν κλεῖν τῆς
– heaven, having the key of the

ἀβύσσου καὶ ἅλυσιν μεγάλην ἐπὶ τὴν χεῖρα
abyss and ⁹chain ¹a great on the hand

Chapter 20

The Thousand Years

AND I saw an angel coming down out of heaven, having the key to the Abyss and holding in his hand a great chain. 2He

---

/I.e., chiliarchs, in command of one thousand troops

* Feminine, agreeing with λίμνη, not with the neuter πῦρ.

§ Agreeing, of course, with ῥομφαίᾳ.

²And he laid hold of the dragon, the serpent of old, who is the devil and Satan, and bound him for a thousand years,

³and threw him into the abyss, and shut *it* and sealed *it* over him, so that he should not deceive the nations any longer, until the thousand years were completed; after these things he must be released for a short time.

⁴And I saw thrones, and they sat upon them, and judgment was given to them. And I *saw* the souls of those who had been beheaded because of the testimony of Jesus and because of the word of God, and those who had not worshiped the beast or his image, and had not received the mark upon their forehead and upon their hand; and they came to life and reigned with Christ for a thousand years.

⁵The rest of the dead did not come to life until the thousand years were completed. This is the first resurrection.

⁶Blessed and holy is the one who has a part in the first resurrection; over these the second death has no power, but they will be priests of God and of Christ and will reign with Him for a thousand years.

Satan Freed, Doomed

⁷And when the thousand years are completed, Satan will be released from his prison,

⁸and will come out to deceive the nations which are in the four corners of the earth, Gog and Magog, to gather them together for the war; the number of

---

αὐτοῦ. 2 καὶ ἐκράτησεν τὸν δράκοντα,
of him. And he laid hold [of] the dragon,

ὁ ὄφις ὁ ἀρχαῖος, ὅς ἐστιν Διάβολος
the ²serpent - ¹old, who is Devil

καὶ ὁ Σατανᾶς, καὶ ἔδησεν αὐτὸν χίλια
and - Satan, and bound him a thousand

ἔτη, 3 καὶ ἔβαλεν αὐτὸν εἰς τὴν ἄβυσσον,
years, and cast him into the abyss,

καὶ ἔκλεισεν καὶ ἐσφράγισεν ἐπάνω αὐτοῦ,
and shut and sealed over him,

ἵνα μὴ πλανήσῃ ἔτι τὰ ἔθνη, ἄχρι
in or-der that he should· not deceive longer the nations, until

τελεσθῇ τὰ χίλια ἔτη· μετὰ ταῦτα
⁴are finished ¹the ²thousand ³years; after these things

δεῖ λυθῆναι αὐτὸν μικρὸν χρόνον.
it behoves ²to be loosed ¹him a little time.

4 Καὶ εἶδον θρόνους, καὶ ἐκάθισαν ἐπ᾽
And I saw thrones, and they sat on

αὐτούς, καὶ κρίμα ἐδόθη αὐτοῖς, καὶ
them, and judgment was given to them, and

τὰς ψυχὰς τῶν πεπελεκισμένων διὰ τὴν
the souls of the [ones] having been beheaded because the of

μαρτυρίαν Ἰησοῦ καὶ διὰ τὸν λόγον
witness of Jesus and because of the word

τοῦ θεοῦ, καὶ οἵτινες οὐ προσεκύνησαν
- of God, and who did not worship

τὸ θηρίον οὐδὲ τὴν εἰκόνα αὐτοῦ καὶ
the beast nor the image of it and

οὐκ ἔλαβον τὸ χάραγμα ἐπὶ τὸ μέτωπον
did not receive the mark on the forehead

καὶ ἐπὶ τὴν χεῖρα αὐτῶν· καὶ ἔζησαν
and on the hand of them; and they lived [again]

καὶ ἐβασίλευσαν μετὰ τοῦ Χριστοῦ χίλια
and reigned with - Christ a thousand

ἔτη. 5 οἱ λοιποὶ τῶν νεκρῶν οὐκ ἔζησαν
years. The rest of the dead did not live [again]

ἄχρι τελεσθῇ τὰ χίλια ἔτη. Αὕτη ἡ
until were finished the thousand years. This [is] the

ἀνάστασις ἡ πρώτη. 6 μακάριος καὶ
²resurrection - ¹first. Blessed and

ἅγιος ὁ ἔχων μέρος ἐν τῇ ἀναστάσει
holy [is] the [one] having part in the ²resurrection

τῇ πρώτῃ· ἐπὶ τούτων ὁ δεύτερος θάνατος
- ¹first; over these the second death

οὐκ ἔχει ἐξουσίαν, ἀλλ᾽ ἔσονται ἱερεῖς
has not authority, but they will be priests

τοῦ θεοῦ καὶ τοῦ Χριστοῦ, καὶ βασιλεύ-
- of God and - of Christ, and will

σουσιν μετ᾽ αὐτοῦ [τὰ] χίλια ἔτη.
reign with him the thousand years.

7 Καὶ ὅταν τελεσθῇ τὰ χίλια ἔτη,
And whenever are finished the thousand years,

λυθήσεται ὁ σατανᾶς ἐκ τῆς φυλακῆς
²will be loosed - ¹Satan out of the prison

αὐτοῦ, 8 καὶ ἐξελεύσεται πλανῆσαι τὰ
of him, and will go forth to deceive the

ἔθνη τὰ ἐν ταῖς τέσσαρσιν γωνίαις τῆς
nations - in the four corners of the

γῆς, τὸν Γὼγ καὶ Μαγώγ, συναγαγεῖν
earth, - Gog and Magog, to assemble

αὐτοὺς εἰς τὸν πόλεμον, ὧν ὁ ἀριθμὸς
them to the war, of whom the number

---

seized the dragon, that ancient serpent, who is the devil, or Satan, and bound him for a thousand years. ³He threw him into the Abyss, and locked and sealed it over him, to keep him from deceiving the nations anymore until the thousand years were ended. After that, he must be set free for a short time.

⁴I saw thrones on which were seated those who had been given authority to judge. And I saw the souls of those who had been beheaded because of their testimony for Jesus and because of the word of God. They had not worshiped the beast or his image and had not received his mark on their foreheads or their hands. They came to life and reigned with Christ a thousand years. ⁵(The rest of the dead did not come to life until the thousand years were ended.) This is the first resurrection. ⁶Blessed and holy are those who have part in the first resurrection. The second death has no power over them, but they will be priests of God and of Christ and will reign with him for a thousand years.

Satan's Doom

⁷When the thousand years are over, Satan will be released from his prison ⁸and will go out to deceive the nations in the four corners of the earth—Gog and Magog—to gather them for battle. In number they are

them is like the sand of the seashore.

9And they came up on the broad plain of the earth and surrounded the camp of the saints and the beloved city, and fire came down from heaven and devoured them.

10And the devil who deceived them, was thrown into the lake of fire and brimstone, where the beast and the false prophet are also; and they will be tormented day and night forever and ever.

Judgment at the Throne of God

11And I saw a great white throne and Him who sat upon it, from whose presence earth and heaven fled away, and no place was found for them.

12And I saw the dead, the great and the small, standing before the throne, and books were opened; and another book was opened, which is *the book* of life; and the dead were judged from the things which were written in the books, according to their deeds.

13And the sea gave up the dead which were in it, and death and Hades gave up the dead which were in them; and they were judged, every one *of them* according to their deeds.

14And death and Hades were thrown into the lake of fire. This is the second death, the lake of fire.

15And if anyone's name was not found written in the book of life, he was thrown into the lake of fire.

αὐτῶν ὡς ἡ ἄμμος τῆς θαλάσσης. 9 καὶ
of them as the sand of the sea. And
[is]

ἀνέβησαν ἐπὶ τὸ πλάτος τῆς γῆς, καὶ
they went up over the breadth of the land, and

ἐκύκλευσαν τὴν παρεμβολὴν τῶν ἁγίων
encircled the camp of the saints

καὶ τὴν πόλιν τὴν ἠγαπημένην· καὶ
and the ⁵city - having been ¹loved; and

κατέβη πῦρ ἐκ τοῦ οὐρανοῦ καὶ κατέφαγεν
⁵came ¹fire out - heaven and devoured
down of

αὐτούς· 10 καὶ ὁ διάβολος ὁ πλανῶν αὐτοὺς
them; and the Devil - deceiving them

ἐβλήθη εἰς τὴν λίμνην τοῦ πυρὸς καὶ
was cast into the lake - of fire and

θείου, ὅπου καὶ τὸ θηρίον καὶ ὁ
sulphur, where [were] also the beast and the

ψευδοπροφήτης, καὶ βασανισθήσονται ἡμέρας
false prophet, and they will be tormented day

καὶ νυκτὸς εἰς τοὺς αἰῶνας τῶν αἰώνων.
and night unto the ages of the ages.

11 Καὶ εἶδον θρόνον μέγαν λευκὸν καὶ
And I saw ³throne ¹a great ²white and

τὸν καθήμενον ἐπ' αὐτὸν οὗ ἀπὸ τοῦ
the sitting on it ⁵of ¹from ²the
[one] whom

προσώπου ἔφυγεν ἡ γῆ καὶ ὁ οὐρανός,
⁵face ⁴fled ¹the ²earth ³and ⁴the ⁵heaven,

καὶ τόπος οὐχ εὑρέθη αὐτοῖς. 12 καὶ
and a place was not found for them. And

εἶδον τοὺς νεκρούς, τοὺς μεγάλους καὶ
I saw the dead, the great and

τοὺς μικρούς, ἑστῶτας ἐνώπιον τοῦ θρόνου,
the small, standing before the throne,

καὶ βιβλία ἠνοίχθησαν· καὶ ἄλλο βιβλίον
and scrolls were opened; and another scroll

ἠνοίχθη, ὅ ἐστιν τῆς ζωῆς· καὶ ἐκρίθησαν
was which is [the - of life; and ⁴were judged
opened, scroll]

οἱ νεκροὶ ἐκ τῶν γεγραμμένων ἐν τοῖς
¹the ²dead by the having been in the
things written
written

βιβλίοις κατὰ τὰ ἔργα αὐτῶν. 13 καὶ
scrolls accord- the works of them. And
ing to

ἔδωκεν ἡ θάλασσα τοὺς νεκροὺς τοὺς
²gave ¹the ²sea the dead -

ἐν αὐτῇ, καὶ ὁ θάνατος καὶ ὁ ᾅδης
in it, and - death and - hades

ἔδωκαν τοὺς νεκροὺς τοὺς ἐν αὐτοῖς,
gave the dead - in them,

καὶ ἐκρίθησαν ἕκαστος κατὰ τὰ ἔργα
and they were judged each one according to the works

αὐτῶν. 14 καὶ ὁ θάνατος καὶ ὁ ᾅδης
of them. And - death and - hades

ἐβλήθησαν εἰς τὴν λίμνην τοῦ πυρός.
were cast into the lake - of fire.

οὗτος ὁ θάνατος ὁ δεύτερός ἐστιν, ἡ
This ²the, ⁴death - ³second ¹is, the

λίμνη τοῦ πυρός. 15 καὶ εἴ τις οὐχ
lake - of fire. And if anyone not

εὑρέθη ἐν τῇ βίβλῳ τῆς ζωῆς γεγραμ-
was found ²in ³the ⁴scroll - ⁵of life ¹having been

μένος, ἐβλήθη εἰς τὴν λίμνην τοῦ πυρός.
written, he was cast into the lake - of fire.

like the sand on the seashore. 9They marched across the breadth of the earth and surrounded the camp of God's people, the city he loves. But fire came down from heaven and devoured them. 10And the devil, who deceived them, was thrown into the lake of burning sulfur, where the beast and the false prophet had been thrown. They will be tormented day and night for ever and ever.

The Dead Are Judged

11Then I saw a great white throne and him who was seated on it. Earth and sky fled from his presence, and there was no place for them. 12And I saw the dead, great and small, standing before the throne, and books were opened. Another book was opened, which is the book of life. The dead were judged according to what they had done as recorded in the books. 13The sea gave up the dead that were in it, and death and Hades gave up the dead that were in them, and each person was judged according to what he had done. 14Then death and Hades were thrown into the lake of fire. The lake of fire is the second death. 15If anyone's name was not found written in the book of life, he was thrown into the lake of fire.

Chapter 21

The New Heaven and Earth

AND I saw a new heaven and a new earth; for the first heaven and the first earth passed away, and there is no longer *any* sea.

2And I saw the holy city, new Jerusalem, coming down out of heaven from God, made ready as a bride adorned for her husband.

3And I heard a loud voice from the throne, saying, "Behold, the tabernacle of God is among men, and He shall dwell among them, and they shall be His people, and God Himself shall be among them,g

4and He shall wipe away every tear from their eyes; and there shall no longer be *any* death; there shall no longer be *any* mourning, or crying, or pain; the first things have passed away."

5And He who sits on the throne said, "Behold, I am making all things new." And He *said, "Write, for these words are faithful and true."

6And He said to me, "It is done. I am the Alpha and the Omega, the beginning and the end. I will give to the one who thirsts from the spring of the water of life without cost.

7"He who overcomes shall inherit these things, and I will be his God and he will be My son.

8"But for the cowardly and unbelieving and abominable and murderers and immoral persons and sorcerers and idolaters and all liars, their part *will be* in the lake that burns with fire and brimstone, which is the second death."

---

21 Καὶ εἶδον οὐρανὸν καινὸν καὶ γῆν
And I saw ²heaven ¹a new and ²oearth

καινήν· ὁ γὰρ πρῶτος οὐρανὸς · καὶ ἡ
¹a new; for the first heaven and the

πρώτη γῆ ἀπῆλθαν, καὶ ἡ θάλασσα
first earth passed away, and the sea

οὐκ ἔστιν ἔτι. **2** καὶ τὴν πόλιν τὴν
is not longer. And ²the ⁴city –

ἁγίαν Ἰερουσαλὴμ καινὴν εἶδον κατα-
⁵holy ²Jerusalem ³new ¹I saw coming

βαίνουσαν ἐκ τοῦ οὐρανοῦ ἀπὸ τοῦ θεοῦ,
down out of – heaven from – God,

ἡτοιμασμένην ὡς νύμφην κεκοσμημένην
having been prepared as a bride *having been adorned*

τῷ ἀνδρὶ αὐτῆς. **3** καὶ ἤκουσα φωνῆς
for the husband of her. And I heard ²voice

μεγάλης ἐκ τοῦ θρόνου λεγούσης· ἰδοὺ
¹a great(loud) out of the throne saying: Behold[,]

ἡ σκηνὴ τοῦ θεοῦ μετὰ τῶν ἀνθρώπων,
the tabernacle – of God [is] with – men,

καὶ σκηνώσει μετ᾽ αὐτῶν, καὶ αὐτοὶ
and he will tabernacle with them, and they

λαοὶ αὐτοῦ ἔσονται, καὶ αὐτὸς ὁ θεὸς
²peoples ³of him ¹will be, and ²[him]self – ¹God

μετ᾽ αὐτῶν ἔσται, **4** καὶ ἐξαλείψει πᾶν
with them will be, and will wipe off every

δάκρυον ἐκ τῶν ὀφθαλμῶν αὐτῶν, καὶ
tear out of the eyes of them, and

ὁ θάνατος οὐκ ἔσται ἔτι, οὔτε πένθος
– death will not be longer, nor sorrow

οὔτε κραυγὴ οὔτε πόνος οὐκ ἔσται ἔτι·
nor clamour nor pain will *not* be longer;

ὅτι τὰ πρῶτα ἀπῆλθαν. **5** καὶ εἶπεν
because the first things passed away. And ²said

ὁ καθήμενος ἐπὶ τῷ θρόνῳ· ἰδοὺ καινὰ
¹the [one] ³sitting ⁴on ⁵the ⁶throne: Behold ⁷new

ποιῶ πάντα. καὶ λέγει· γράψον, ὅτι
³I make ⁸all things. And he says: Write thou, because

οὗτοι οἱ λόγοι πιστοὶ καὶ ἀληθινοί εἰσιν.
these – words faithful and true are.

6 καὶ εἶπέν μοι· γέγοναν. ἐγὼ τὸ ἄλφα
And he said to me: It has occurred.• I [am] the alpha

καὶ τὸ ὦ, ἡ ἀρχὴ καὶ τὸ τέλος. ἐγὼ
and the omega, the beginning and the end. ²I

τῷ διψῶντι δώσω ἐκ τῆς πηγῆς
³to the [one] ⁴thirsting ¹will give out of the fountain

τοῦ ὕδατος τῆς ζωῆς δωρεάν. **7** ὁ νικῶν
of the water of life freely. The over-
[one] coming

κληρονομήσει ταῦτα, καὶ ἔσομαι αὐτῷ
shall inherit these things, and I will be to him

θεὸς καὶ αὐτὸς ἔσται μοι υἱός. **8** τοῖς δὲ
God and he shall be to me a son. But for the

δειλοῖς καὶ ἀπίστοις καὶ ἐβδελυγμένοις
cowardly and unbelieving and *having become* foul

καὶ φονεῦσιν καὶ πόρνοις καὶ φαρμακοῖς
and murderers and fornicators and sorcerers

καὶ εἰδωλολάτραις καὶ πᾶσιν τοῖς ψευδέσιν
and idolaters and all the false [ones]

τὸ μέρος αὐτῶν ἐν τῇ λίμνῃ τῇ καιομένῃ
the part of them in the lake – burning

πυρὶ καὶ θείῳ, ὅ ἐστιν ὁ θάνατος ὁ
with fire and *with* which is the ²death

δεύτερος. sulphur,
¹second [, shall be].

Chapter 21

The New Jerusalem

THEN I saw a new heaven and a new earth, for the first heaven and the first earth had passed away, and there was no longer any sea. 2I saw the Holy City, the new Jerusalem, coming down out of heaven from God, prepared as a bride beautifully dressed for her husband. 3And I heard a loud voice from the throne saying, "Now the dwelling of God is with men, and he will live with them. They will be his people, and God himself will be with them and be their God. 4He will wipe every tear from their eyes. There will be no more death or mourning or crying or pain, for the old order of things has passed away."

5He who was seated on the throne said, "I am making everything new!" Then he said, "Write this down, for these words are trustworthy and true."

6He said to me: "It is done. I am the Alpha and the Omega, the Beginning and the End. To him who is thirsty I will give to drink without cost from the spring of the water of life. 7He who overcomes will inherit all this, and I will be his God and he will be my son. 8But the cowardly, the unbelieving, the vile, the murderers, the sexually immoral, those who practice magic arts, the idolaters and all liars—their place will be in the fiery lake of burning sulfur. This is the second death."

---

g Some ancient mss. add, *and be their God*

• Collective neuter plural; *cf.* ch. 16. 17.

9And one of the seven angels who had the seven bowls full of the seven last plagues, came and spoke with me, saying, "Come here, I shall show you the bride, the wife of the Lamb."

The New Jerusalem

10And he carried me away *h*in the Spirit to a great and high mountain, and showed me the holy city, Jerusalem, coming down out of heaven from God,

11having the glory of God. Her brilliance was like a very costly stone, as a stone of crystal-clear jasper.

12It had a great and high wall, with twelve gates, and at the gates twelve angels; and names *were* written on them, which are *those* of the twelve tribes of the sons of Israel.

13*There* were three gates on the east and three gates on the north and three gates on the south and three gates on the west.

14And the wall of the city had twelve foundation stones, and on them *were* the twelve names of the twelve apostles of the Lamb.

15And the one who spoke with me had a gold measuring rod to measure the city, and its gates and its wall.

16And the city is laid out as a square, and its length is as great as the width; and he measured the city with the rod, *f*fifteen hundred miles; its length and width and height are equal.

17And he measured its

---

9 Καὶ ἦλθεν εἷς ἐκ τῶν ἑπτὰ ἀγγέλων
And came one of the seven angels

τῶν ἐχόντων τὰς ἑπτὰ φιάλας, τῶν
– having the seven bowls, –

γεμόντων τῶν ἑπτὰ πληγῶν τῶν ἐσχάτων,
being filled of(with) seven ²plagues – ¹last,
the

καὶ ἐλάλησεν μετ' ἐμοῦ λέγων· δεῦρο,
and spoke with me saying: Come,

δείξω σοι τὴν νύμφην τὴν γυναῖκα
I will show thee the bride[,] the wife

τοῦ ἀρνίου. **10** καὶ ἀπήνεγκέν με ἐν
of the Lamb. And he bore away me in

πνεύματι ἐπὶ ὄρος μέγα καὶ ὑψηλόν,
spirit onto ²mountain ¹a great ¹and ²high,

καὶ ἔδειξέν μοι τὴν πόλιν τὴν ἁγίαν
and showed me the ²city – ¹holy

Ἰερουσαλὴμ καταβαίνουσαν ἐκ τοῦ οὐρανοῦ
Jerusalem coming down out of – heaven

ἀπὸ τοῦ θεοῦ, **11** ἔχουσαν τὴν δόξαν
from – God, having the glory

τοῦ θεοῦ· ὁ φωστὴρ αὐτῆς ὅμοιος λίθῳ
– of God; the light of it [was] like *to a* stone

τιμιωτάτῳ, ὡς λίθῳ ἰάσπιδι κρυσταλλίζοντι·
very valuable, as ²stone ¹to a jasper *being* clear as crystal;

12 ἔχουσα τεῖχος μέγα καὶ ὑψηλόν,
having ⁴wall ¹a great ²and ³high,

ἔχουσα πυλῶνας δώδεκα, καὶ ἐπὶ τοῖς
having ²gates ¹twelve, and at the

πυλῶσιν ἀγγέλους δώδεκα, καὶ ὀνόματα
gates ²angels ¹twelve, and names

ἐπιγεγραμμένα, ἃ ἐστιν τῶν δώδεκα
having been inscribed, which is(are) of the twelve

φυλῶν υἱῶν Ἰσραήλ. **13** ἀπὸ ἀνατολῆς
tribes of sons of Israel. From east

πυλῶνες τρεῖς, καὶ ἀπὸ βορρᾶ πυλῶνες
²gates ¹three, and from north ²gates

τρεῖς, καὶ ἀπὸ νότου πυλῶνες τρεῖς,
¹three, and from south ²gates ¹three,

καὶ ἀπὸ δυσμῶν πυλῶνες τρεῖς. **14** καὶ
and from west ²gates ¹three. And

τὸ τεῖχος τῆς πόλεως ἔχων θεμελίους
the wall of the city having ²foundations

δώδεκα, καὶ ἐπ' αὐτῶν δώδεκα ὀνόματα
¹twelve, and on them twelve names

τῶν δώδεκα ἀποστόλων τοῦ ἀρνίου. **15** Καὶ
of the twelve apostles of the Lamb. And

ὁ λαλῶν μετ' ἐμοῦ εἶχεν μέτρον κάλαμον
the speak- with me had ²measure ³reed
[one] ing

χρυσοῦν, ἵνα μετρήσῃ τὴν πόλιν καὶ
¹a golden, in order he might the city and
that measure

τοὺς πυλῶνας αὐτῆς καὶ τὸ τεῖχος αὐτῆς.
the gates of it and the wall of it.

16 καὶ ἡ πόλις τετράγωνος κεῖται, καὶ
And the city ²square ¹lies, and

τὸ μῆκος αὐτῆς ὅσον τὸ πλάτος. καὶ
the length of it [is] as much as the breadth. And

ἐμέτρησεν τὴν πόλιν τῷ καλάμῳ ἐπὶ
he measured the city with the reed at

σταδίων δώδεκα χιλιάδων· τὸ μῆκος καὶ
²furlongs ¹twelve ⁴thousands; the length and

τὸ πλάτος καὶ τὸ ὕψος αὐτῆς ἴσα ἐστίν.
the breadth and the height of it ²equal ¹is(are).

17 καὶ ἐμέτρησεν τὸ τεῖχος αὐτῆς ἑκατὸν
And he measured the wall of it *of* a hundred

9One of the seven angels who had the seven bowls full of the seven last plagues came and said to me, "Come, I will show you the bride, the wife of the Lamb." 10And he carried me away in the Spirit to a mountain great and high, and showed me the Holy City, Jerusalem, coming down out of heaven from God. 11It shone with the glory of God, and its brilliance was like that of a very precious jewel, like a jasper, clear as crystal. 12It had a great, high wall with twelve gates, and with twelve angels at the gates. On the gates were written the names of the twelve tribes of Israel. 13There were three gates on the east, three on the north, three on the south and three on the west. 14The wall of the city had twelve foundations, and on them were the names of the twelve apostles of the Lamb.

15The angel who talked with me had a measuring rod of gold to measure the city, its gates and its walls. 16The city was laid out like a square, as long as it was wide. He measured the city with the rod and found it to be 12,000 stadia*x* in length, and as wide and high as it is long. 17He measured its

---

h Or, *in spirit*

i Lit., *twelve thousand stadia; a stadion was about 600 ft.*

x16 That is, about 1,400 miles (about 2,200 kilometers)

wall, *j*seventy-two yards, *according to* human measurements, which are *also* angelic *measurements.*

18And the material of the wall was jasper; and the city was pure gold, like clear glass.

19The foundation stones of the city wall were adorned with every kind of precious stone. The first foundation stone was jasper; the second, sapphire; the third, chalcedony; the fourth, emerald;

20the fifth, sardonyx; the sixth, sardius; the seventh, chrysolite; the eighth, beryl; the ninth, topaz; the tenth, chrysoprase; the eleventh, jacinth; the twelfth, amethyst.

21And the twelve gates were twelve pearls; each one of the gates was a single pearl. And the street of the city was pure gold, like transparent glass.

22And I saw no temple in it, for the Lord God, the Almighty, and the Lamb, are its temple.

23And the city has no need of the sun or of the moon to shine upon it, for the glory of God has illumined it, and its lamp *is* the Lamb.

24And the nations shall walk by its light, and the kings of the earth shall bring their glory into it.

25And in the daytime (for there shall be no night there) its gates shall never be closed;

26and they shall bring the glory and the honor of the nations into it;

27and nothing unclean

τεσσεράκοντα τεσσάρων πηχῶν, μέτρον
[and] forty-four cubits, a measure

ἀνθρώπου, ὅ ἐστιν ἀγγέλου. 18 καὶ
of a man, which is of an angel. And

ἡ ἐνδώμησις τοῦ τείχους αὐτῆς ἴασπις,
the coping of the wall of it [was] jasper,

καὶ ἡ πόλις χρυσίον καθαρὸν ὅμοιον
and the city [was] ²gold ¹clean(pure) like

ὑάλῳ καθαρῷ. 19 οἱ θεμέλιοι τοῦ τείχους
²glass ¹to clean(pure). The foundations of the wall

τῆς πόλεως παντὶ λίθῳ τιμίῳ κεκοσμημένοι·
of the city ³with ²stone ²precious ¹having been adorned;
every

ὁ θεμέλιος ὁ πρῶτος ἴασπις, ὁ δεύτερος
the foundation first jasper, the second

σάπφιρος, ὁ τρίτος χαλκηδών, ὁ τέταρτος
sapphire, the third chalcedony, the fourth

σμάραγδος, 20 ὁ πέμπτος σαρδόνυξ, ὁ
emerald, the fifth sardonyx, the

ἕκτος σάρδιον, ὁ ἕβδομος χρυσόλιθος,
sixth sardius, the seventh chrysolite,

ὁ ὄγδοος βήρυλλος, ὁ ἔνατος τοπάζιον,
the eighth beryl, the ninth topaz,

ὁ δέκατος χρυσόπρασος, ὁ ἑνδέκατος
the tenth chrysoprasus, the eleventh

ὑάκινθος, ὁ δωδέκατος ἀμέθυστος. 21 καὶ
hyacinth, the twelfth amethyst. And

οἱ δώδεκα πυλῶνες δώδεκα μαργαρῖται·
the twelve gates [were] twelve pearls;

ἀνὰ εἷς ἕκαστος τῶν πυλώνων ἦν ἐξ
respec-²one ¹each of the gates was of
tively†

ἑνὸς μαργαρίτου. καὶ ἡ πλατεῖα τῆς
one pearl. And the street of the

πόλεως χρυσίον καθαρὸν ὡς ὕαλος διαυγής.
city [was] ²gold ¹clean(pure) as ²glass ¹transparent.

22 Καὶ ναὸν οὐκ εἶδον ἐν αὐτῇ· ὁ γὰρ
And a shrine I saw not in it; for the

κύριος ὁ θεὸς ὁ παντοκράτωρ ναὸς αὐτῆς
Lord - God the Almighty shrine of it

ἐστιν, καὶ τὸ ἀρνίον. 23 καὶ ἡ πόλις
is, and the Lamb. And the city

οὐ χρείαν ἔχει τοῦ ἡλίου οὐδὲ τῆς
not need has of the sun nor of the

σελήνης, ἵνα φαίνωσιν αὐτῇ· ἡ γὰρ
moon, in order they might in it; for the
that shine

δόξα τοῦ θεοῦ ἐφώτισεν αὐτήν, καὶ
glory - of God enlightened it, and

ὁ λύχνος αὐτῆς τὸ ἀρνίον. 24 καὶ
the lamp of it [is] the Lamb. And

περιπατήσουσιν τὰ ἔθνη διὰ τοῦ φωτὸς
²shall walk about ¹the ²nations through the light

αὐτῆς, καὶ οἱ βασιλεῖς τῆς γῆς φέρουσιν
of it, and the kings of the earth bring

τὴν δόξαν αὐτῶν εἰς αὐτήν· 25 καὶ οἱ
the glory of them into it; and the

πυλῶνες αὐτῆς οὐ μὴ κλεισθῶσιν ἡμέρας,
gates of it by no means may be shut by day,

νὺξ γὰρ οὐκ ἔσται ἐκεῖ· 26 καὶ οἴσουσιν
for night shall not be there; and they will
bring

τὴν δόξαν καὶ τὴν τιμὴν τῶν ἐθνῶν
the glory and the honour of the nations

εἰς αὐτήν. 27 καὶ οὐ μὴ εἰσέλθῃ εἰς
into it. And by no means may enter into

wall and it was 144 cubits *y* thick, *z* by man's measurement, which the angel was using. 18The wall was made of jasper, and the city of pure gold, as pure as glass. 19The foundations of the city walls were decorated with every kind of precious stone. The first foundation was jasper, the second sapphire, the third chalcedony, the fourth emerald, 20the fifth sardonyx, the sixth carnelian, the seventh chrysolite, the eighth beryl, the ninth topaz, the tenth chrysoprase, the eleventh jacinth, and the twelfth amethyst. *a* 21The twelve gates were twelve pearls, each gate made of a single pearl. The great street of the city was of pure gold, like transparent glass.

22I did not see a temple in the city, because the Lord God Almighty and the Lamb are its temple. 23The city does not need the sun or the moon to shine on it, for the glory of God gives it light, and the Lamb is its lamp. 24The nations will walk by its light, and the kings of the earth will bring their splendor into it. 25On no day will its gates ever be shut, for there will be no night there. 26The glory and honor of the nations will be brought into it. 27Nothing impure will ever enter it,

---

j Lit., *one hundred forty-four cubits*

y 17 That is, about 200 feet (about 65 meters)
z 17 Or *high*
a 20 The precise identification of some of these precious stones is uncertain.

and no one who practices abomination and lying, shall ever come into it, but only those whose names are written in the Lamb's book of life.

Chapter 22

The River and the Tree of Life

AND he showed me a river of the water of life, clear as crystal, coming from the throne of God and of *k*the Lamb, 2in the middle of its street. And on either side of the river was the tree of life, bearing twelve *l kinds of* fruit, yielding its fruit every month; and the leaves of the tree were for the healing of the nations. 3And there shall no longer be any curse; and the throne of God and of the Lamb shall be in it, and His bond-servants shall serve Him; 4and they shall see His face, and His name *shall be* on their foreheads. 5And there shall no longer be *any* night; and they shall not have need of the light of a lamp nor the light of the sun, because the Lord God shall illumine them; and they shall reign forever and ever. 6And he said to me, "These words are faithful and true"; and the Lord, the God of the spirits of the prophets, sent His angel to show to his bond-servants the things which must shortly take place. 7"And behold, I am coming quickly. Blessed is he who heeds the words of the prophecy of this book." 8And I, John, am the one who heard and saw these

*k*Or, *the Lamb. In the middle of its street, and on either side of the river, was*
*l*Or, *crops of fruit*

αὐτὴν πᾶν κοινὸν καὶ [ὁ] ποιῶν
it every(any) profane thing and the [one] making

βδέλυγμα καὶ ψεῦδος, εἰ μὴ οἱ γεγραμ-
an and a lie, except the having been
abomination [ones]

μένοι ἐν τῷ βιβλίῳ τῆς ζωῆς τοῦ ἀρνίου.
written in the scroll - of life of the Lamb.

22 Καὶ ἔδειξέν μοι ποταμὸν ὕδατος
And he showed me a river of water

ζωῆς λαμπρὸν ὡς κρύσταλλον, ἐκπορευόμε-
of life bright as crystal, proceed-

νον ἐκ τοῦ θρόνου τοῦ θεοῦ καὶ τοῦ
ing out of the throne - of God and of the

ἀρνίου. 2 ἐν μέσῳ τῆς πλατείας αὐτῆς
Lamb. In [the] midst of the street of it

καὶ τοῦ ποταμοῦ ἐντεῦθεν καὶ ἐκεῖθεν
and of the river hence and thence

ξύλον ζωῆς ποιοῦν καρποὺς δώδεκα,
a tree of life producing fruits twelve,

κατὰ μῆνα ἕκαστον ἀποδιδοῦν τὸν καρπὸν
accord- ²month ¹each rendering the fruit
ing to

αὐτοῦ, καὶ τὰ φύλλα τοῦ ξύλου εἰς
of it, and the leaves of the tree [will be] for

τεραπείαν τῶν ἐθνῶν. 3 καὶ πᾶν κατάθεμα
healing of the nations. And every curse
= no curse will be any

οὐκ ἔσται ἔτι. καὶ ὁ θρόνος τοῦ θεοῦ
will not be longer. And the throne - of God
longer.

καὶ τοῦ ἀρνίου ἐν αὐτῇ ἔσται, καὶ οἱ
and of the Lamb ³in ²it ¹will be, and the

δοῦλοι αὐτοῦ λατρεύσουσιν αὐτῷ, 4 καὶ
slaves of him will do service to him, and

ὄψονται τὸ πρόσωπον αὐτοῦ, καὶ τὸ
they will see the face of him, and the

ὄνομα αὐτοῦ ἐπὶ τῶν μετώπων αὐτῶν.
name of him [will be] on the foreheads of them.

5 καὶ νὺξ οὐκ ἔσται ἔτι, καὶ οὐκ
And night will not be longer, and not

ἔχουσιν χρείαν φωτὸς λύχνου καὶ φωτὸς
they have need of light of lamp and of light

ἡλίου, ὅτι κύριος ὁ θεὸς φωτίσει ἐπ᾽
of sun, because [the] Lord - God will shed light on

αὐτούς, καὶ βασιλεύσουσιν εἰς τοὺς
them, and they will reign unto the

αἰῶνας τῶν αἰώνων.
ages of the ages.

6 Καὶ εἶπέν μοι· οὗτοι οἱ λόγοι πιστοὶ
And he said to me: These - words [are] faithful

καὶ ἀληθινοί, καὶ ὁ κύριος ὁ θεὸς τῶν
and true, and the Lord the God of the

πνευμάτων τῶν προφητῶν ἀπέστειλεν τὸν
spirits of the prophets sent the

ἄγγελον αὐτοῦ δεῖξαι τοῖς δούλοις αὐτοῦ
angel of him to show to the slaves of him

ἃ δεῖ γενέσθαι ἐν τάχει. 7 καὶ ἰδοὺ
things it be- to occur quickly. And behold
which hoves

ἔρχομαι ταχύ. μακάριος ὁ τηρῶν τοὺς
I am coming quickly. Blessed [is] the [one] keeping the

λόγους τῆς προφητείας τοῦ βιβλίου τούτου.
words of the prophecy of this scroll.

8 Κἀγὼ Ἰωάννης ὁ ἀκούων καὶ βλέπων
And I John [am] the [one] hearing and seeing

ταῦτα. καὶ ὅτε ἤκουσα καὶ ἔβλεψα,
these things. And when I heard and I saw,

nor will anyone who does what is shameful or deceitful, but only those whose names are written in the Lamb's book of life.

Chapter 22

The River of Life

THEN the angel showed me the river of the water of life, as clear as crystal, flowing from the throne of God and of the Lamb 2down the middle of the great street of the city. On each side of the river stood the tree of life, bearing twelve crops of fruit, yielding its fruit every month. And the leaves of the tree are for the healing of the nations. 3No longer will there be any curse. The throne of God and of the Lamb will be in the city, and his servants will serve him. 4They will see his face, and his name will be on their foreheads. 5There will be no more night. They will not need the light of a lamp or the light of the sun, for the Lord God will give them light. And they will reign for ever and ever. 6The angel said to me, "These words are trustworthy and true. The Lord, the God of the spirits of the prophets, sent his angel to show his servants the things that must soon take place."

Jesus Is Coming

7"Behold, I am coming soon! Blessed is he who keeps the words of the prophecy in this book."

8I, John, am the one who heard and saw these things.

things. And when I heard and saw, I fell down to worship at the feet of the angel who showed me these things.

9And he *said to me, "Do not do that; I am a fellow servant of yours and of your brethren the prophets and of those who heed the words of this book; worship God."

The Final Message

10And he *said to me, "Do not seal up the words of the prophecy of this book, for the time is near.

11"Let the one who does wrong, still do wrong; and let the one who is filthy, still be filthy; and let the one who is righteous, still practice righteousness; and let the one who is holy, still keep himself holy."

12"Behold, I am coming quickly, and My reward is with Me, to render to every man according to what he has done.

13"I am the Alpha and the Omega, the first and the last, the beginning and the end."

14Blessed are those who wash their robes, that they may have the right to the tree of life, and may enter by the gates into the city.

15Outside are the dogs and the sorcerers and the immoral persons and the murderers and the idolaters, and everyone who loves and practices lying.

16"I, Jesus, have sent My angel to testify to you these things for the churches. I am the root and the offspring of David, the bright morning star."

17And the Spirit and the bride say, "Come." And let the one who hears say, "Come." And let the one

ἔπεσα προσκυνῆσαι ἔμπροσθεν τῶν ποδῶν
I fell to worship before the feet

τοῦ ἀγγέλου τοῦ δεικνύοντός μοι ταῦτα.
of the angel the showing me these things.

9 καὶ λέγει μοι· ὅρα μή· σύνδουλός
And he tells me: See thou [do] not; ²a fellow-slave

σού εἰμι καὶ τῶν ἀδελφῶν σου τῶν
²of thee ¹I am and of the brothers of thee the

προφητῶν καὶ τῶν τηρούντων τοὺς λόγους
prophets and of the [ones] keeping the words

τοῦ βιβλίου τούτου· τῷ θεῷ προσκύνησον.
of this scroll: – ²God ¹worship thou.

10 Καὶ λέγει μοι· μὴ σφραγίσῃς τοὺς
And he tells me: Seal not the

λόγους τῆς προφητείας τοῦ βιβλίου τούτου·
words of the prophecy of this scroll;

ὁ καιρὸς γὰρ ἐγγύς ἐστιν 11 ὁ ἀδικῶν
²the ³time ¹for ⁴near ⁵is. The acting
[one] unjustly

ἀδικησάτω ἔτι, καὶ ὁ ῥυπαρὸς ῥυπανθήτω
let him act still, and the filthy [one] let him act
unjustly filthily

ἔτι, καὶ ὁ δίκαιος δικαιοσύνην ποιησάτω
still, and the righteous [one] ²righteousness ¹let him do

ἔτι, καὶ ὁ ἅγιος ἁγιασθήτω ἔτι.
still, and the holy [one] let him be hallowed still.

12 Ἰδοὺ ἔρχομαι ταχύ, καὶ ὁ μισθός
Behold I am coming quickly, and the reward

μου μετ' ἐμοῦ, ἀποδοῦναι ἑκάστῳ ὡς
of me [is] with me, to render to each man as

τὸ ἔργον ἐστὶν αὐτοῦ. 13 ἐγὼ τὸ ἄλφα
the work ¹is ²of him. I [am] the alpha

καὶ τὸ ὦ, ὁ πρῶτος καὶ ὁ ἔσχατος,
and the omega, the first and the last,

ἡ ἀρχὴ καὶ τὸ τέλος. 14 μακάριοι οἱ
the begin- and the end. Blessed the
ning [are] [ones]

πλύνοντες τὰς στολὰς αὐτῶν, ἵνα ἔσται
washing the robes of them, in or- ⁴will be
der that

ἡ ἐξουσία αὐτῶν ἐπὶ τὸ ξύλον τῆς
¹the ²authority ³of them over the tree –

ζωῆς καὶ τοῖς πυλῶσιν εἰσέλθωσιν εἰς
of life and ²by the ³gates ¹they may enter into

τὴν πόλιν. 15 ἔξω οἱ κύνες καὶ οἱ φαρμακοὶ
the city. Outside the dogs and the sorcerers
[are]

καὶ οἱ πόρνοι καὶ οἱ φονεῖς καὶ οἱ
and the fornicators and the murderers and the

εἰδωλολάτραι καὶ πᾶς φιλῶν καὶ ποιῶν
idolaters and everyone loving and making

ψεῦδος.
a lie.

16 Ἐγὼ Ἰησοῦς ἔπεμψα τὸν ἄγγελόν
I Jesus sent the angel

μου μαρτυρῆσαι ὑμῖν ταῦτα ἐπὶ ταῖς
of me to witness to you these things over(in) the

ἐκκλησίαις. ἐγώ εἰμι ἡ ῥίζα καὶ τὸ
churches. I am the root and the

γένος Δαυίδ, ὁ ἀστὴρ ὁ λαμπρὸς ὁ
offspring of David, the ²star – ¹bright –

πρωϊνός.
¹morning.

17 Καὶ τὸ πνεῦμα καὶ ἡ νύμφη λέγουσιν·
And the Spirit and the bride say:

ἔρχου. καὶ ὁ ἀκούων εἰπάτω· ἔρχου.
Come. And the [one] hearing let him say: Come.

And when I had heard and seen them, I fell down to worship at the feet of the angel who had been showing them to me. 9But he said to me, "Do not do it! I am a fellow servant with you and with your brothers the prophets and of all who keep the words of this book. Worship God!"

10Then he told me, "Do not seal up the words of the prophecy of this book, because the time is near. 11Let him who does wrong continue to do wrong; let him who is vile continue to be vile; let him who does right continue to do right; and let him who is holy continue to be holy."

12"Behold, I am coming soon! My reward is with me, and I will give to everyone according to what he has done. 13I am the Alpha and the Omega, the First and the Last, the Beginning and the End.

14"Blessed are those who wash their robes, that they may have the right to the tree of life and may go through the gates into the city. 15Outside are the dogs, those who practice magic arts, the sexually immoral, the murderers, the idolaters and everyone who loves and practices falsehood.

16"I, Jesus, have sent my angel to give youb this testimony for the churches. I am the Root and the Offspring of David, and the bright Morning Star."

17The Spirit and the bride say, "Come!" And let him who hears say, "Come!"

b16 The Greek is plural.

who is thirsty come; let the one who wishes take the water of life without cost.

18I testify to everyone who hears the words of the prophecy of this book: if anyone adds to them, God shall add to him the plagues which are written in this book;

19and if anyone takes away from the words of the book of this prophecy, God shall take away his part from the tree of life and from the holy city, which are written in this book.

20He who testifies to these things says, "Yes, I am coming quickly." Amen. Come, Lord Jesus.

21The grace of the Lord Jesus be with *all. Amen.

καὶ ὁ διψῶν ἐρχέσθω, ὁ θέλων λαβέτω
And　the thirsting　let him　the　wishing　let him
　　　　[one]　　　come,　[one]　　　take

ὕδωρ ζωῆς δωρεάν.
[the]　of life　freely.
water

18 Μαρτυρῶ ἐγὼ παντὶ τῷ ἀκούοντι
　　¹witness　¹I　to everyone　　hearing

τοὺς λόγους τῆς προφητείας τοῦ βιβλίου
the　words　of the　prophecy　-　¹scroll

τούτου· ἐάν τις ἐπιθῇ ἐπ' αὐτά, ἐπιθήσει
¹of this:　If anyone adds upon(to) them,*　¹will add

ὁ θεὸς ἐπ' αὐτὸν τὰς πληγὰς τὰς
-　¹God　upon　him　the　plagues　-

γεγραμμένας ἐν τῷ βιβλίῳ τούτῳ· 19 καὶ
having been written in　　this scroll;　　and

ἐάν τις ἀφέλη ἀπὸ τῶν λόγων τοῦ
if　anyone takes away　from　the　words　of the

βιβλίου τῆς προφητείας ταύτης, ἀφελεῖ
scroll　of this prophecy,　　　　¹will take
　　　　　　　　　　　　　　　　　　away

ὁ θεὸς τὸ μέρος αὐτοῦ ἀπὸ τοῦ ξύλου
-　¹God　the　part　of him　from　the　tree

τῆς ζωῆς καὶ ἐκ τῆς πόλεως τῆς ἁγίας,
-　of life　and out of the　²city　-　¹holy,

τῶν γεγραμμένων ἐν τῷ βιβλίῳ τούτῳ.
of the　having been　in　　this scroll.
things　written

20 Λέγει ὁ μαρτυρῶν ταῦτα· ναί, ἔρχομαι
Says the　witnessing　these　Yes,　I am
　[one]　　　　　　　things:　　　coming

ταχύ. Ἀμήν, ἔρχου κύριε Ἰησοῦ.
quickly.　Amen,　come[,]　Lord　Jesus.

21 Ἡ χάρις τοῦ κυρίου Ἰησοῦ μετὰ
The　grace　of the　Lord　Jesus [be]　with

πάντων.
all.

Whoever is thirsty, let him come; and whoever wishes, let him take the free gift of the water of life.

18I warn everyone who hears the words of the prophecy of this book: If anyone adds anything to them, God will add to him the plagues described in this book. 19And if anyone takes words away from this book of prophecy, God will take away from him his share in the tree of life and in the holy city, which are described in this book.

20He who testifies to these things says, "Yes, I am coming soon."
Amen. Come, Lord Jesus.

21The grace of the Lord Jesus be with God's people. Amen.